May 6–11, 2017
Denver, CO, USA

I0882089

Association for Computing Machinery

Advancing Computing as a Science & Profession

CHI'17

Proceedings of the 2017 ACM SIGCHI Conference on Human Factors in Computing Systems

Sponsored by:

ACM SIGCHI

Supported by:

Bloomberg, Facebook, Google, IBM Research, Microsoft, & NSF

Association for
Computing Machinery

Advancing Computing as a Science & Profession

The Association for Computing Machinery
2 Penn Plaza, Suite 701
New York, New York 10121-0701

Copyright © 2017 by the Association for Computing Machinery, Inc. (ACM). Permission to make digital or hard copies of portions of this work for personal or classroom use is granted without fee provided that copies are not made or distributed for profit or commercial advantage and that copies bear this notice and the full citation on the first page. Copyright for components of this work owned by others than ACM must be honored. Abstracting with credit is permitted. To copy otherwise, to republish, to post on servers or to redistribute to lists, requires prior specific permission and/or a fee. Request permission to republish from: permissions@acm.org or Fax +1 (212) 869-0481.

For other copying of articles that carry a code at the bottom of the first or last page, copying is permitted provided that the per-copy fee indicated in the code is paid through www.copyright.com.

Notice to Past Authors of ACM-Published Articles
ACM intends to create a complete electronic archive of all articles and/or other material previously published by ACM. If you have written a work that has been previously published by ACM in any journal or conference proceedings prior to 1978, or any SIG Newsletter at any time, and you do NOT want this work to appear in the ACM Digital Library, please inform permissions@acm.org, stating the title of the work, the author(s), and where and when published.

ISBN: 978-1-4503-4655-9 (Digital)

ISBN: 978-1-4503-5464-6 (Print)

Additional copies may be ordered prepaid from:

ACM Order Department
PO Box 30777
New York, NY 10087-0777, USA

Phone: 1-800-342-6626 (USA and Canada)
+1-212-626-0500 (Global)
Fax: +1-212-944-1318
E-mail: acmhelp@acm.org
Hours of Operation: 8:30 am – 4:30 pm ET

Printed in the USA

CHI 2017 is the premier international conference for the field of Human-Computer Interaction (HCI). This year it was held in Denver, bordering the beautiful Rocky Mountain region in the U.S., and reflected in our logo. The CHI 2017 conference began with two days of workshops and symposia, followed by four days of a technical program with 17 parallel sessions of provocative papers, panels, case studies, SIGs (Special Interest Groups), courses, and the popular student research, design, and game competitions. The growing alt.chi forum, now in its twelfth year, presented stimulating new ideas in HCI. The Interactivity forum showcased cutting-edge technology. For its second year, the CHI Art Exhibit merged art and technology in fascinating ways.

This innovative work can be found in the Proceedings and Extended Abstracts, archived in the ACM Digital Library. For papers, the conference received 2400 submissions which were rigorously reviewed, resulting in 600 accepted papers. To ensure a better fit with reviewers, new subcommittees were created. Across all tracks, CHI received nearly 5000 submissions and accepted over 1000.

Our conference theme this year, *Explore, Innovate, Inspire*, informed our planning process. A new venue held this year was CHI Stories. We generally know little of the personalities that drive the research presented at CHI. CHI Stories is a chance for CHI community members to share personal stories of inspiration, challenge, successes and failures, and grit. We also focused on inclusion this year. Hundreds of CHI attendees volunteered their skills in a Day of Service partnering with non-profit organizations. Inclusion was also manifest throughout the conference, for example, in the Diversity and Inclusion Lunch and by using telepresence robots to enable people with disabilities to participate remotely in the conference. Our keynote speakers were chosen to reflect our conference theme. The speakers were Neri Oxman, who combines computational design, digital fabrication, materials science and synthetic biology; Ben Shneiderman a founder of the CHI conference who, along with some key CHI personalities, gave a perspective on CHI's history and future; Wael Ghonim, credited with starting the Arab Spring and nominated for the Nobel Peace Prize; and best-selling author Nicholas Carr who challenges us to examine the unforeseen impacts of technology, particularly with automation.

The world has experienced a dramatic change this past year. We live in extraordinary times and this calls for extraordinary thinking, something that the CHI community excels at. One of the challenges the community faced this year was responding to a U.S. executive order to ban citizens of certain countries from entering the country to attend CHI. As CHI is committed to inclusion, we decided to hold events at the conference to discuss and plan how we can continue our commitment to inclusion. The conference held a panel to discuss impacts of current political events on science, and hastily organized a panel to promote a conversation of civil liberties in science and a SIG on how the CHI community can participate in change. We are proud to have expanded telepresence options through the use of robots to enable people to participate in the conference remotely if they were physically unable to enter the country. We had a keynote speaker who inspired us on the topic of Internet activism. Our art exhibit, *I'll Be Watching You,* examined the contemporary issue of surveillance.

We are extremely grateful to a legion of volunteers who made CHI 2017 possible, including over 7000 reviewers across all areas of the technical program, 254 senior members of the papers program committee, over 100 members of the CHI 2017 conference organization committee and importantly, the more than 175 student volunteers. We also thank SIGCHI (the Special Interest Group on Computer-Human Interaction of ACM) as well as the ACM itself for its continued support.

Gloria Mark, University of California Irvine, CHI 2017 General Conference Co-Chair

Susan Fussell, Cornell University, CHI 2017 General Conference Co-Chair

Cliff Lampe, University of Michigan, CHI 2017 Technical Program Chair

m.c. schraefel, University of Southampton, CHI 2017 Technical Program Chair

Juan Pablo Hourcade, University of Iowa, CHI 2017 Papers Co-Chair

Caroline Appert, Université Paris-Sud, CHI 2017 Papers Co-Chair

Daniel Wigdor, University of Toronto, CHI 2017 Papers Co-Chair

Loren Terveen, University of Minnesota, President, ACM SIGCHI Executive Committee

Scooter Morris, University of San Francisco, ACM SIGCHI Liaison

Table of Contents

Table of Contents

Table of Contents

Table of Contents

Table of Contents

Table of Contents

Table of Contents

Table of Contents

Table of Contents

Table of Contents

Table of Contents

Table of Contents

Table of Contents

Table of Contents

Table of Contents

Table of Contents

Table of Contents

Table of Contents

Table of Contents

Table of Contents

Table of Contents

Table of Contents

Table of Contents

Table of Contents

Table of Contents

Table of Contents

Table of Contents

Table of Contents

Table of Contents

Table of Contents

Table of Contents

Table of Contents

Table of Contents

CHI 2017 Organization

Conference Chairs
Gloria Mark, University of California, Irvine
Susan Fussell, Cornell University

Assistants to General Chairs
Yiran Wang, University of California, Irvine
Ge Gao, Cornell University

Senior Technical Program Chair
Cliff Lampe, University of Michigan

Technical Program Chair
m.c. schraefel, University of Southampton

Assistant to the Technical Program Chairs
Lindsay Blackwell, University of Michigan

Papers Chairs
Caroline Appert, Univ. Paris-Sud & CNRS
Juan Pablo Hourcade, University of Iowa
Daniel Wigdor, University of Toronto

Assistant to Papers Chairs
Michael Glueck, University of Toronto

alt.chi Chairs
Karrie Karahalios, University of Illinois at Urbana – Champaign
Jessa Lingel, University of Pennsylvania
Janet Vertesi, Princeton University

Case Studies Chairs
Stephen Snow, University of Southampton
Jessica Tsimeris, Google

Courses Chairs
Erik Andersen, Cornell University
Hilary Hutchinson, Google
Max Wilson, University of Nottingham

Demos Chairs
Ido Guy, Yahoo
Stephen Voida, University of Colorado Boulder

Doctoral Consortium Chairs
Anna Cox, University College London
Jeff Bigham, Carnegie Mellon University
Kenton O'Hara, Microsoft Research, UK

Interactive Installations Chairs
Adrian Friday, Lancaster University
Shengdong Zhao, National University of Singapore

Late Breaking Work Chairs
Sharon Ding, Fudan University
Ingrid Erikson, Rutgers University
Bryan Semaan, Syracuse University
Fanis Tsandilas, INRIA

Panels Chairs
Sarita Schoenebeck, University of Michigan
Jude Yew, National University of Singapore

Student Design Competition Chairs
Joonhwan Lee, Seoul National University
Scott Minneman, California College of Arts

Student Game Competition Chairs
Floyd Mueller, RMIT University
Josh Tanenbaum, University of California, Irvine

Student Research Competition Chairs
Jeremy Birnholtz, Northwestern University
Jenn Thom, Spotify

Special Interest Groups Chairs
Lindsay Reynolds, Facebook
Bert Scerbo, Disney

Systems Chairs
Michael Stewart, Virginia Tech
Dorota Filipczuk, University of Southampton

Symposia Chair
Lana Yarosh, University of Minnesota

Video Showcase Chairs
Danyel Fisher, Microsoft Research
Catherine Letondal, ENAC

Workshops Chairs
Duncan Brumby, University College London
Christopher Frauenberger, Vienna University of Technology, Austria
Shamsi Iqbal, Microsoft Research

Art Chairs
Jiffer Harriman, University of Colorado
Andruid Kerne, Texas A&M University
HyunJoo Oh, University of Colorado Boulder
Thecla Schiphorst, Simon Fraser University

CHI Stories Chairs
Nazanin Andalibi, Drexel University
Nick Diakopoulos, University of Maryland, College Park
Andrea Forte, Drexel University
Misa Maruyama, University of Hawaii at Manoa
Scott Robertson, University of Hawaii at Manoa

Career Development Workshop Chairs
Luigina Ciolfi, Sheffield Hallam University
Michael Muller, IBM Research

Journals Chair
Hrvoje Benko, Microsoft Research

Remix Chairs
Susan Dray, Dray & Associates
Amy Voida, University of Colorado Boulder

Student Volunteer Chairs
Patrick Carrington, University of Maryland, Baltimore County (UMBC)
Anna Kötteritzsch, Universität der Bundeswehr München

Video Previews Chair
Carla Griggio, Inria

Awards Chair
Steven Drucker, Microsoft

Accessibility Chairs
Erin Brady, Indiana University – Purdue University Indianapolis
Sean Goggins, Missouri University
Shaun Kane, University of Colorado Boulder

Data Chair
Boyu Gao, Konkuk University
Toni-Jan Keith Monserrat, University of the Philippines Los Baños

Diversity and Inclusivity Lunch Chairs
Anke Brock, Inria Bordeaux
Allison Druin, University of Maryland
Gopinaath Kannabiran, Indiana University, Bloomington

Language Inclusion Chair
Tilman Dingler, University of Stuttgart

Local Arrangements Chairs
Jed Brubaker, University of Colorado Boulder
Tom Yeh, University of Colorado Boulder

Social Impact Chairs
Kathy Baxter, Salesforce
Elizabeth Gerber, Northwestern University
Jill Woelfer, Google

Social Media Chairs
Dan Afergan, Google
Bart Knijnenburg, Clemson University
Vicky McArthur, University of Toronto Mississauga

Telepresence Chairs
Min Kyung Lee, Carnegie Mellon University
Carman Neustaedter, Simon Fraser University

Translations Chairs
Hao-Chuan Wang, National Tsing Hua University
Naomi Yamashita, Nippon Telegraph and Telephone

Design Director
Donghee Yvette Wohn, New Jersey Institute of Technology

Logo Design/Artwork
Jia Zhang, MIT Media Lab

Web Designer
Xiying Wang, Cornell University

Webmaster
Xiying Wang, Cornell University

ACM Liaison
Farrah Khan, ACM

SIGCHI Liaison
Scooter Morris, University of California, San Francisco

Conference Management
Paul Henning, Conference & Logistics Consultants, Inc.
Stacey Ogren, Conference & Logistics Consultants, Inc.
Lois Sarfo-Mensah, Conference & Logistics Consultants, Inc.
Michael O'Connell, Conference & Logistics Consultants, Inc.

Registration
Taylor Vick, Executive Events, Inc.

Sponsorship and Exhibits
Carol Klyver, Foundations of Excellence

Technical Liaison
Sara Drenner, BI WORLDWIDE

Uncovering the Values and Constraints of Real-time Ridesharing for Low-resource Populations

Tawanna R. Dillahunt, Vaishnav Kameswaran, Linfeng Li, Tanya Rosenblat
School of Information
University of Michigan
{tdillahu,vaikam,llinfeng,trosenbl}@umich.edu

ABSTRACT
Real-time ridesharing services (e.g., Uber and Lyft) are often touted as sharing-economy leaders and dramatically lower the cost of transportation. However, how to make these services work better among low-income and transportation-scarce households, how these individuals experience these services, and whether they encounter barriers in enlisting these services is unknown. To address these questions, we onboarded 13 low-income individuals living in transportation-scarce environments to Uber as passengers. Our participants found these services to be reliable and benefited from rich social interactions with drivers; however, barriers such as cost, limited payment methods, and low digital literacy can make such services infeasible. We contribute platform designs that could lead to increased digital literacy and application transparency. To be more inclusive and to reach critical mass, we suggest that these companies foster belief in commons and community trust by coordinating with local businesses in low-resource areas with lower digital literacy.

ACM Classification Keywords
H.5.m. Information Interfaces and Presentation: Misc.

Author Keywords
sharing economy; mobility; low-income populations; transportation scarcity; real-time ridesharing services; Uber

INTRODUCTION
Research has found that improved transportation mobility is a key predictor for upward social mobility in the United States [11, 15, 16]. In fact, the relationship between social mobility and transportation is stronger than that between social mobility and factors like crime, percentage of two-parent families in a community, and elementary-school test scores [11, 15]. Further, car ownership is associated with an increased likelihood of higher incomes and employment [43], though vehicle ownership can be more onerous for low-income individuals because of costs of acquisition, gas, and maintenance. In transportation-scarce environments, inadequate means of public transportation can hinder access to job opportunities [33] and healthy food [53], can lead to social exclusion [14, 50], and can negatively impact people's health and well-being [54]. This is particularly true for low-income households.

Permission to make digital or hard copies of all or part of this work for personal or classroom use is granted without fee provided that copies are not made or distributed for profit or commercial advantage and that copies bear this notice and the full citation on the first page. Copyrights for components of this work owned by others than the author(s) must be honored. Abstracting with credit is permitted. To copy otherwise, or republish, to post on servers or to redistribute to lists, requires prior specific permission and/or a fee. Request permissions from Permissions@acm.org.
CHI'17, May 06–May 11, 2017, Denver, CO, USA.
Copyright is held by the owner/author(s). Publication rights licensed to ACM.
ACM 978-1-4503-4655-9/17/05...$15.00.
DOI: http://dx.doi.org/10.1145/3025453.3025470

Real-time ridesharing services such as Uber and Lyft can lower the cost of transportation by making use of under-used private cars. These services provide riders with flexibility in schedule and destination. Despite the lower cost, these services might still be out of reach for low-income households because of the payment mechanisms required to use these services and the need for mobile Internet access. It is possible that the biggest gain for using these services is for middle and high-income households [48] who use these services rather than taxis. Furthermore, research suggests that low-income individuals do not benefit in the same way as higher-income individuals because some drivers are reluctant to serve poorer areas as a result of perceived safety issues and distance [32, 37]. Drivers have also been known to discriminate against passengers based on race and gender [24, 45].

We conducted an exploratory study to understand how real-time ridesharing services might benefit low-income individuals living in transportation-scarce areas. We address the following research questions:

- RQ1: What are the digital sharing economy's feasibility requirements for low-income individuals living in transportation-scarce environments?
- RQ2: How do these individuals describe their experience using the service as passengers?
- RQ3: What barriers do these groups of individuals face in the onboarding process to use real-time ridesharing services?

While typical users of these services are relatively homogeneous groups consisting of younger demographics [13], those with higher income levels [13], and those who are highly proficient technology users [52], our target riders are atypical. The riders/passengers in this study are also stakeholders but have not been studied in this context. Therefore, we contribute results from atypical users that include riders across a wide range of age groups who are low-income and live in transportation-scarce environments and who are less proficient with technology.

Our findings demonstrate the types of benefits that riders receive such as reliable transport and rich social interactions with drivers. While these outcomes are beneficial, our findings suggest that these services are infeasible for our riders because of cost, limited access to credit cards, and low digital literacy. Addressing these issues could help to reduce social isolation [14, 50] and support upward mobility [11, 15, 16] among atypical users. We contribute design recommendations and suggestions for how these services could reach critical mass among our target users by alleviating such issues. We frame these suggestions around regulation and trust, and inclusive infrastructures and explain how these results generalize to broader populations and to the broader sharing economy.

RELATED WORK

The sharing economy involves the sharing of under-utilized assets and services among people [10], and there is an increasing amount of research around the sharing economy in the areas of economics, business, law, public policy and more recently HCI and CSCW [4, 9, 18, 19, 25, 30, 31, 32, 47]. In this section, we discuss the potential for real-time ridesharing services to address inequities in transportation in low-income areas. We discuss the sharing economy's principles and requirements and the contextual factors contributing to these requirements. Finally, we summarize sharing economy research in HCI and CSCW and how we extend this work.

Real-time Ridesharing Services

Access to travel options for socially disadvantaged groups is a major rationale for providing public transportation. For example, access to transportation enables low-income populations to have better health care [5, 7] and job opportunities. In fact, improved transportation mobility is a key predictor for upward social mobility [12, 16]. But even though services such as Uber and Lyft offer an alternative to car ownership and can dramatically lower transportation costs by making private cars more productive, researchers have found that low-income households are much less likely than high-income households to use and benefit from these services [32, 47]. There are several possible explanations. Some drivers are reluctant to serve poorer areas because of the perceived safety issues and drivers' distance from low socioeconomic neighborhoods [32, 37]. In addition, ridesharing services may still be too expensive for low-income people [32]. Finally, many low-income people do not have the payment mechanisms or the Internet access required to use these services.

Research suggests that Uber is "faster and cheaper" than taxis in low-income areas of Los Angeles [44]. Smart et al. hired 18 riders from a temporary staffing agency who were ethnically diverse to use UberX and taxi services in low-income communities. While the study found that Uber was faster and cheaper than taxis, the study did not fully engage riders from low-income areas as participants, nor did it provide a first-hand account of the experiences of low-income individuals with limited access to transportation or to mobile Internet access [44]. In addition, past HCI researchers have identified the potential for real-time ridesharing services such as Uber to support the mobility of groups with limited access to public transportation [25], which we investigate in detail.

Sharing Economy Principles and Requirements

Researchers of the sharing economy and its applications have identified several factors needed for the sharing economy to work. For example, some form of regulation [46] to create trust [49] is a key requirement. Other requirements include belief in the commons (i.e., belief that the system adds value to the community as a whole) [10], economic benefits [49] (e.g., consumers of the sharing economy must see the cost and value, or the economic benefits of the service such as saving money), efficacy [49] (e.g., enough individuals participating so that there is a choice, or critical mass [10] and social proof so participants have enough information about how services work), ease of use [49], and idling capacity (underused resources) [10]. Understanding whether and how these principles vary across applications is limited in HCI and CSCW work.

Dillahunt and Malone conducted a set of participatory-design-inspired workshops to understand whether applications of the sharing economy (e.g., Lyft, Airbnb, TaskRabbit, NeighborGoods) were feasible among populations who were un(der)employed, financially constrained, and from low-socioeconomic status neighborhoods [19]. In this study, participants raised critical mass as a concern for applications such as NeighborGoods and TaskRabbit but not for Airbnb and Lyft [19]. Trust was found to be a key requirement for the sharing economy to be successful, and distrust in technology was problematic among their target users to mediate safety [19]. The participants were not comfortable providing systems with their credit card information [19] and mistrusted user ratings of providers for Lyft. Trust spans privacy protection [31], safety [19, 49], trust between strangers [10, 19, 28, 49], monetary transactions managed by the platform [19, 28, 49], and upfront social commitment and time investment to build trusted relationships [31]. While applications like NeighborGoods do not require credit cards or have user ratings, all applications require trust, especially those technologies that *do* rely on monetary and social transactions [29].

As Dillahunt and Malone's results suggest, requirements of the sharing economy likely vary across application type and even socioeconomic contexts; however, very limited research analyzes which principles are most critical to which applications and why. For example, while the car sharing service Zipcar was founded on the principle of community, or belief in the commons, in an in-depth interview with 40 Zipcar drivers in Boston, researchers found that drivers were very individualistic and utilitarian, suggesting that self-interest is why Zipcar works [8]. Lampinen et al. suggest that a general understanding of how the sharing economy's benefits and risks vary among socioeconomic contexts is limited in HCI and CSCW work as well [31]. This is exacerbated because the users of these services tend to be relatively homogeneous groups consisting of younger demographics (32% Gen X and 24% Millennials, in contrast to 15% Baby Boomers) [13], those with higher income levels [13], highly proficient technology users [52], and more innovative users [49]. Our research helps to fill these gaps. In addition, the results may help to uncover which sharing economy principles are more relevant to real-time ridesharing among limited-resource populations.

Sharing Economy Research in CSCW and HCI

When taken holistically, HCI and CSCW research has described the motivations for using sharing-economy services, the requirements for the sharing economy to work (as previously discussed), and the opportunities for new research around labor, technology, and the design of these systems.

Motivations for using these services include community and sustainability (by providers) [9] and value and convenience (for users) [9]. Additional motivations include the benefits of social interactions and social connections [9, 25], benefits to the community [19], economic benefits [9, 19, 49], and enjoyment [49]. A deeper understanding is needed regarding sharing-economy outcomes such as value and convenience, sustainability, and any concrete benefits from social interactions and social connections.

Individuals living in contexts such as low-income or low-socioeconomic status environments, for example, may not benefit in the same way as others using these systems as suggested in past CSCW and HCI work [18, 19, 26, 32, 47]. These individuals may be at a disadvantage for two reasons: 1) drivers may choose to serve only wealthier populations [32, 44, 47], and 2) these riders pay higher premiums because of low critical mass [47]. Research has found that physical appearance factors such as race, gender, and age have led to price discrimination for people using Airbnb [21].

From the perspective of real-time ridesharing services like Uber, researchers from HCI and CSCW have empirically evaluated the impact of algorithmic management on Uber drivers [32] and contributed opportunities for new research in understanding labor, technology, and design [25, 39]. This work tends to focus on drivers and not passengers, and additional work is needed to understand how these insights translate into useful information for drivers *and* passengers, as well as regulators and decision-makers at these companies [39].

We contribute to the existing work by documenting the experiences of riders rather than drivers, and riders who are low-income individuals who live in transportation-scarce environments in the United States. By studying the use of real-time ridesharing services within this understudied group, we create an opportunity to investigate other factors that remain unexplored, such as trust, sharing-economy principles most relevant to these groups, potential discrimination-related issues, digital literacy, and social-interaction benefits.

STUDY METHODS

Our goal was to reach a diverse population of low-income participants who live in a transportation-scarce area of the U.S. with nearby Uber availability. To meet our objectives, all authors first discussed site-selection and our study methods, which included participant recruitment, observations made during the recruitment process, and incentives. In our observations, we documented why some individuals were ineligible for or did not wish to participate in our study. We obtained consent from our participants per institutional review board requirements to complete all aspects of this study.

Site Selection

To meet the transportation requirement for our first research question, we selected Detroit, MI, a U.S. city where transportation is a scarce resource. The city has reduced and eliminated much of its bus service [35], and according to a recent Public Health and Policy article, 40% of the citizens do not own cars [23]. Among lower-earning Detroit residents with limited transportation services, more than 10,000 travel each day to low-paying jobs in suburban communities that do not offer public transit [17, 34]. We also studied people in Detroit because Uber offers services here; at the time of our study UberX, UberXL, UberBLACK, UberSELECT, and UberSUV were available while Uber's POOL and Go services were unavailable. Uber for Business (U4B) was also available and allows employers to add their employees to their accounts. U4B allows employees to charge their rides to their employers, which worked well for our study; it provided us with a way to monitor ride-sharing usage among study participants by giving us ride details like source and destination addresses, cost, duration of rides, and driver names. Note that drivers in our study were unaware that participants were on U4B accounts.

Recruiting, Observations, and Incentive Process

Recruitment played an important role in helping us to identify the feasibility requirements for our target participants (RQ1) and to understand the barriers participants and potential participants faced in the onboarding process (RQ3). As such, we documented field notes during our recruitment process to capture these barriers. To ensure that we reached a wide range of participants from low-income areas of Detroit with limited access to transportation, we turned to a census-based website to identify low-income areas [1] and used walkscore.com to identify areas with low walkability scores as an indicator of limited mobility. We accepted participants from ZIP codes with scores of 50-59, or somewhat walkable, to 25-49, or car dependent, according to [3]. We initially identified 10 ZIP codes to target our recruitment and expanded these areas because of recruitment difficulties. We recruited both online via Craigslist and Facebook, and offline using snowball and reputational case sampling to reach participants regardless of their level of digital literacy and Internet access [42]. We posted flyers in public locations such as bus stops, barbershops, and hair salons. Additionally, we used snowball sampling and sent flyers to two community organizations that support economic and social mobility. One center specifically provides job-training services and serves clients with intellectual and developmental disabilities. Flyers contained our contact phone number and email address. We pre-screened participants for the following criteria: 1) They resided in our pre-determined ZIP codes (i.e., low-income and transportation-scarce areas), 2) they had access to an Internet and data-enabled smartphone and 3) they had limited access to reliable transportation (e.g., personal car, taxi, public bus).

We gave these individuals first priority to participate in our study. While some individuals who did not meet our pre-screening requirements were not given first-priority, we did contact those who lived in ZIP codes with slightly higher walkability scores (e.g., car-dependent to somewhat walkable, versus car-dependent), yet were still lower income, at a later time. We also report data about participants who chose not to participate in our study or were ineligible.

To mitigate potential barriers for participation, we provided participants with $75 worth of Uber rides. U4B allowed us to onboard our participants as employees. Their rides were automatically billed to us as employers; however, this reduced our ability to investigate issues around monetary transactions and to experiment with pricing. Despite this, we gained some insights from interviews and the onboarding process.

To understand whether participants experienced difficulties being picked up from certain locations, we did not set trip guidelines in U4B. This allowed participants to take trips at any time and to any place. To mitigate issues of technology literacy, we helped to onboard participants by walking them through the Uber installation process onto their smartphones either in person, or via phone. We recorded these service access barriers in our field notes (RQ1, RQ3); we also documented information from third-party organizations and people who did not wish to take part in our study (RQ1), who were ineligible, or who were unable to participate (RQ3).

Diary and Semi-structured Interviews

To understand our participants' experiences using Uber (RQ2), we asked them to either complete a small journal, which we provided, or send us a text message describing their experiences. Participants also had the option of texting us a picture of their written entries. For consistency, we asked all participants to address these minimum tasks and questions to help document their experiences: 1) Briefly describe the reason for your trip; 2) What was the name of your Uber driver? (Participants saw driver names via the Uber application; this allowed us to match records and trips); 3) Did you have a discussion with the Uber driver?; 4) Provide us with a summary of your conversation (e.g., What led to the conversation? Did you learn anything new?); 5) On a scale of 1-5 how did you rate your driver and why? Other details like cost, duration, start and end destinations were available through the U4B account.

All members of the research team received email notifications when each participant took a ride. The business account also provided us with details of the trip taken. For example, we had access to our participants' starting location and destination, trip distance, and trip time to help us with labeling our data. We developed a python script to automatically detect each participants' remaining balance and used Twilio to send a text notification with this information. We removed participants from our account before they exceeded their $75 allocation. If they had money left over, we gave it to them after the interview. If they exceeded their allocation, we deducted it from their interview compensation.

Finally, to gain a detailed understanding of their experience using the site and to address questions related to their diary entries, we paid participants $25 to take part in a semi-structured interview. Semi-structured interviews provide richly detailed data and allow for exploring nuances of individual experiences [51]. These interviews helped us to understand how participants managed their Uber rides, details about their interactions with the drivers, and their overall impressions of the service, and the interviews enabled us to probe more deeply into our participants' journal entries. All interviews were digitally recorded and transcribed. Participants provided us with their demographic details, a preferred alias, and information about their familiarity with technology in a short survey at the end of the interview. Shortly after each interview, researchers wrote summaries highlighting key insights. We contacted participants after interviews for any necessary clarification and to see whether they continued or planned to continue using the service.

Analysis

Data points included researcher notes and observations made during recruitment (RQ1 and RQ3), diary entries about ride experiences (RQ2), data obtained from the Uber business account (e.g., points of origin and destination, timing and duration of rides, decisions to accept surge pricing and the surge price multiplier while available; RQ1), and interview and survey data (RQ1, RQ2, RQ3). The first two authors supported analysis activities and held regular meetings to discuss and contextualize the results.

We analyzed journal entries by categorizing participant responses (e.g., trip purposes, conversation starters, learned something new). We summarized data obtained from the Uber business account such as number of trips taken, number of surges, the surge price multiplier, and duration of rides (see Table 1). We analyzed interview transcripts using a hybrid approach - we created codes using both a pre-set and an open coding process. We started with a priori codes that addressed our first research question. We used codes as outlined in the "Sharing Economy Principles.." subsection of our related work [10, 19, 28, 31, 49]. Code examples included *safety, economic benefits, critical mass and trust.* We followed a similar approach to address our third research question and used our requirements as a priori codes.

To address our second research question, we pre-coded interview transcripts by highlighting and underlining significant participant quotes and interview text that stood out as noteworthy [40]. We did this after receiving transcripts for each interview and added these codes to a shared codebook. Based on these emergent codes, we generated additional questions as we coded and continued coding with these questions in mind: Why are participants using Uber? Under what conditions do they use Uber over other transportation means? How do participants describe their drivers, the cars, and their overall experience? Then, we refined our codes and broke some of our emergent codes into sub-codes to better organize our data.

Finally, we analyzed our non-participant data. These included pre-screening surveys (access to smart phone and a data plan or Wi-Fi) and recruitment observation field notes. We discussed the challenges encountered while recruiting offline and broadly coded them as barriers to using ride-sharing services. Understanding data from participants who opted out of our study or who were ineligible for our study helps to mitigate our use of non-random sampling methods, which are inherently biased.

Alias Demographics	No of rides	Average distance per ride (miles)	Average duration per ride (min)	Average cost per ride ($)	Number of surge rides	Avg surge value	Avg waiting time (min)
Ace, M, 20, HS, Office Assistant	6	5.35	13.83	14.38	5	2.00	7.17
Rosalyn, F, 22, SC, Student	6	6.58	13.83	12.48	2	2.10	10.67
Melan, F, 20-25, NA, NA	5	7.85	36.20	23.10	5	1.60	12.00
Acorn, F, 52, MS, Self-employed	9	3.35	9.78	8.46	5	1.52	9.56
Mostavo, M, 30-40, NA, Unemployed	6	7.46	16	11.91	0	0	9.33
Frog, F, 50, SC, Unemployed	9	4.62	10.11	7.86	1	1.30	10.33
Vette, F, 53, SC, Unemployed	3	6.04	11.67	23.29	0	0	11.00
TCash, M, 26, SC, Dry Cleaning	8	4.26	12.38	9.77	4	1.65	9.38
Jeff, M, 30, SC, Medical Assistant	8	5.84	10.25	9.31	3	1.60	10.13
Dae Dae, M, 37, Job corps, Automotive	5	4.98	12	20.86	0	0	10.60
Dale, M, 39, HS Not Completed, Unemployed	11	3.45	8.55	7.41	2	1.50	13.09
Bobby, M, 21, HS, Unemployed Unable to Work	6	4.08	11.67	17.73	0	0	15.50
*Que, M, 25-30, NA, NA	-	-	-	-	-	-	-

Table 1. Uber Ride Summary (HS=High school, SC=Some college, MS=Master's Degree, *Unable to participate due to personal reasons)

RESULTS

In summary, we successfully onboarded 13 participants (Table 1); however, soon after we onboarded Que, he had to withdraw from the study for personal reasons. Although no new patterns or themes arose from our data (e.g., we reached thematic/data saturation [36]) after conducting eight interviews, we continued to interview and recruit participants for rigor. Our interviews lasted 30-60 minutes. Overall, we had 160 codes total; 31 were a priori and 129 were new codes that emerged. After using a priori codes to address RQ1, we then used an open-coding process to address RQ2 and RQ3.

We received 25 online responses (e.g., from online advertisements to Craigslist and Facebook), four organizational referrals, and five participants from snowball sampling. Only four of the 25 online participant responses satisfied our requirements. We approached approximately 30 individuals in our offline recruiting efforts. While two individuals expressed interest, neither of them contacted us. We documented and analyzed our recruiting observations, and report these results in this section as well. The mean income for all distinct ZIP codes (N=9) was $33,327 (standard deviation [SD]=$7,670.91); the mean walk score was 53.1 (SD=5.95). We also investigated transit and bike scores though this information was unavailable for three ZIP codes. These results were 37 (SD=2.51) and 56 (SD=5.35), respectively, which translated to "some transit" and "bikeable," though three of our participants were unable to bike because of accessibility issues.

Participants' incomes were in the $0-$19,999 USD range and all participants lacked access to reliable public transportation. Rosalyn and Dae Dae each owned a car, though both were inoperable and in need of maintenance. Three participants (Rosalyn, Acorn and Frog) had used Uber previously; Rosalyn was currently a student, Acorn was our most educated participant and Frog our most technically proficient. Our participants took a total of 82 trips lasting 1,062 minutes and spanning 413.62 miles. Based on survey results, our participants generally expressed comfort with using computers or smart phones for basic tasks like searching for information online and checking email. In the next subsections, we present the results for each research question.

Requirements of the Sharing Economy

We specified the necessary sharing-economy requirements for our target population based on a priori codes and new requirements that surfaced in our open coding. Requirements such as idling capacity [10], upfront social commitment and time, and privacy protection as mentioned by Lampinen et al. [31] did not surface in our results–perhaps because Uber is not a new system. Drivers picked up all of our participants upon request. As a result, there were no issues of idling capacity or any obvious signs of discrimination. Although we saw some aspects of belief in the commons, efficacy, ease of use, social proof, and critical mass in our results, these were not as salient as regulation and trust, and economic benefits.

Regulation and Trust

Aspects of trust arising in our results included the lack of transparency around the regulatory platform (e.g., monetary transactions, surge-pricing decisions, decision-makers) and in two cases, trust between strangers.

To recruit, we visited several public offline sites in our targeted ZIP codes such as barbershops, hair salons, and wig shops because these businesses tend to reach a diverse clientele. While posting flyers on the public bulletin boards and as a result of leaving flyers with owners, individuals began to inquire about the study. We noted the perceptions and concerns regarding ridesharing systems, specifically Uber. For example, improper monetary transactions led some individuals to distrust the platform. In one case, three women at a hair salon stated that they had encountered invalid charges on their credit card from Uber. One of these women stated that she was charged by Uber but had never used the service and wondered how to get her money back; she was not able to find a number to call Uber. In this case, the fact that there was not a physical entity (i.e. no place to inquire about the charge), might have led to distrust. Another woman, not hearing the full conversation but familiar with Uber, asked, "Where's Uber located?"

A lack of transparency in the way surge pricing works also contributed to one of our participants questioning Uber. Surge pricing occurs when fare prices are multiplied because of high demand. However, one participant, Acorn, during the interview showed us a price surge that had happened when rides were apparently available: *Yeah, it could be higher or it could be lower or it could have ended. Yeah, now you see what I'm talking about and there's two cars together so I don't understand why it's surging. - Acorn (Interview)*

Acorn described how in one case, the surge price went away as a result of her closing and reopening the application. In fact, the majority of our participants took rides during a surge. This type of misunderstanding could lead to distrust in the platform. There were also misunderstandings about the differences in the types of Uber vehicles available. While UberX vehicles are "everyday" four-door vehicles that are 2001 or newer, UberSELECT vehicles are "a step above everyday" (e.g., 2008 or newer luxury vehicles), and UberSUV vehicles must be 2007 or newer, black and have leather interior. Dae Dae selected Uber SUV on a couple of occasions. He was surprised after we contacted him about approaching his $75 allocation. He was unaware of the price differences between Uber SUV and UberX and stated that this should be clearer in the application. Vette chose UberSELECT and when asked in the interview why, she responded, *I figured maybe that would be cheaper. - Vette (Interview)*

Three study participants (Rosalyn, Acorn, and Frog) who had previously used Uber were asked whether they had faced issues when using the service previously. One participant reported issues linking her debit card to her Uber account to pay for rides. This resulted in creative workarounds. For example, she tried using a friend's credit card (which she saw as ineffective and burdensome), and she tried syncing her debit card through her PayPal account (which did not work). She found another way, but it was also inconvenient: *Then we got my sister-in-law, we used her credit card for a while, and just paid her back; and that works fine. It was still an inconvenience, doing that, using her credit card, and calling her and saying, 'Hey, can we use ... Is it okay, it's going to be about this cost. Do you mind?' - Frog (Interview)*

When using her sister-in-law's credit card, she had to first seek permission to use the credit card and then arrange for re-payment. On the other hand, when she was unable to sync her debit card through a PayPal account to link to Uber, she attempted to contact both parties (Uber and PayPal) to resolve the issue. This was unsuccessful and ultimately she was not able to continue using the Uber service. *It [Uber application] won't do the credit card thing, because of the debit card with the PayPal... tried linking my debit card through PayPal, so you sign in with PayPal and then request Uber; and it'll say 'Credit Card Not Valid.'... I tried to contact Uber; contacted PayPal, and one blames the other, and the other blames the oth- You know, one says it's the other one's fault; the other one says it's the other one's fault. - Frog (Interview)*

With regard to trust, while all participants said they felt safe taking Uber, Vette and TCash took some precautions just in case. Vette, for example, sent screen shots of her trip details: *To my family members so if something were to happen, then they would know a pers- Put a face to the person, and a license plate, and a description of the car. That's why I like the app...We live in different days and times now, so you never know; but I never had a bad experience. I felt safe, but I'd rather always be safe than sorry. (Interview).* TCash stated in an interview that *I don't trust nobody, but I was comfortable with every Uber driver.* In this case, TCash was comfortable with every driver he "selected,", which we discuss later.

Economic Benefits

At least three participants (Acorn, Jeff, Frog) said that Uber in some cases cost 50% less than taxis. While participants said that Uber cost about the same as jitneys, they said they felt safer with Uber. For example, Frog described how she divided her trips to Walmart into monthly or bi-monthly trips to save money. Taking Uber was much cheaper than taking a cab: *That's only like once or twice a month, like a long distance, like to Walmart, because of the cost difference. I would definitely use Uber because it's so much cheaper. - Frog(Interview)*

Although these participants indicated they found economic benefits in using Uber, we paid for their use of the service and it was unclear from their comments whether the participants would benefit financially in the long term from using Uber. Therefore, we followed up with participants after 3 weeks to see whether they had continued to use the service. We were able to reach seven of our participants, and of these only one person, Rosalyn, had continued to use the service. Ace, for example, said that he managed to get a car and no longer needed to use Uber; Acorn, who had used Uber before our study, moved to an area where Uber was no longer available.

Belief in the Commons

Per our field notes, community organizations and participants who referred other individuals to our study showed a belief in the commons. A representative from one community organization that helped in our recruiting efforts described how the lack of transportation is a barrier for employment. In other words, when its clients do get an interview or find job fairs to attend, many struggle to find transportation. The representative said the organization was happy to help us in our recruitment because of the value the services brought to the community. Similarly, Vette stated in an interview, *I have known people to have actually lost their jobs due to the public transportation failure.* She referred at least three people to our study who were having issues getting to work. Dae Dae provided us with the name of a single mother because he felt that these services were most beneficial for mothers who had no transportation and had to transport their kids.

Efficacy, Social Proof and Critical Mass

Our results suggest that efficacy is a requirement that may need to be broken down further given the socioeconomic context of our target population. This was especially true among individuals who we were unable to recruit because they felt uncomfortable using their smart phones in this way. This was also true among those we aimed to recruit who were not able to access Uber on the phone or in person. In other words, if something went wrong, the perception was that they could not reach Uber to address the issue; in one case we as researchers had to serve as a bridge to contact Uber when one of our participants was double-charged for a ride. This suggests a lack of social proof or connections to those who feel comfortable reaching out to these companies. As a result of the interviews, diary entries, and our recruiting observations, we found several requirements for improving access to ridesharing services.

To summarize, our results identified regulation and trust issues resulting from the lack of platform visibility (no physical location, no friends who knew how to use it) and charge discrepancies. This service did not appear to be economically beneficial in the long term based on those participants we were able to reach in our follow-up. However, participants felt safe, trusted their drivers, and described several benefits from using the service. Finally, we identified: opportunities to increase support for belief in commons, limited efficacy resulting from low digital literacy, and a lack of critical mass and social proof, as suggested in our offline recruitment efforts.

Uber Experiences

To understand how individuals described their experience using the service (RQ2), we generated emergent codes and refined our codes into sub-codes to better organize our data. We also generated extra questions such as "How do participants describe their drivers, the cars, and their overall experience?", "Why are participants using Uber?", and "Under what conditions do they use Uber over other transportation means?"

Based on participant diaries, interviews, and U4B data, participants took rides to get to work, to run personal errands like grocery shopping and pharmacy pickups, to get to medical appointments and job interviews, to visit family, and for one participant, to go to restaurants and movies. Our participants described meeting retired school principals, former police officers, and aspiring entrepreneurs. Participants described rich social interactions when using the real-time ridesharing service and used the service primarily because of its reliability.

Rich Social Interactions and Common Courtesy

All participants noted in their journal entries the drivers' courtesy, friendliness, or helpful nature. Two participants also noted sensory aspects of the drivers such as the smell of the vehicle or driver, the cleanliness of the vehicle, and the feeling of comfort from accommodations such as being offered water, having the car door opened, or receiving help with groceries. Given that at least five participants knew less than 5% of their neighbors, these conversations appeared to be beneficial: *People are not as friendly as they used to be. I wave at people on my block. They wave, I wave back; but as far as conversing with them, no. - Vette (Interview)*

Our findings also show that rides allowed for rich social interactions between the riders and drivers. Our interviews and participant journal entries revealed conversations about the city and other exchanges such as job leads, which we labeled as business/networking. For the most part, drivers were eager to share their experiences as Uber drivers in the city and often told their passengers about the city's history. For example, Ace, Rosalyn, and Melan had drivers who held conversations about local sites; Frog learned about historical landmarks during at least one of her rides.

We were talking about the growth in the city, like how the youth are, and how things change...when I was riding with Sam. He was telling me what certain businesses used to be that I didn't even know about. Riding down the Midtown area, down West Grand Boulevard. We were riding down there, he was telling me what certain businesses used to be - Ace (Interview)

There were at least two instances of riders (Ace, TCash) and drivers using car rides to network and form business relationships. This is an indication of the potential of such ridesharing services to enhance weak ties and contribute to the formation of connecting ties to new people and perhaps to the building of social capital [19]. *It was right after I finished, it was my ride after that. And she was also a young entrepreneur trying to start up her own business and everything. We got contact information, exchanged contact information and everything. So I had a pretty good experience using Uber. Met nice good people. - Ace (Interview)*

Dale was unemployed and receiving disability payments from a serious injury. When asked in the interview about whether a driver stood out to him, he said, Mr. Wayne: *He asked me when he took me to Target did I work there and I told him that I was trying to get a job there, and he said if I have my license that Wayne County downtown was doing hiring for part[-time] cleanup janitorial stuff.* Dale was most grateful for Mr. Wayne's encouragement. He said, *Most of them [the drivers] were nice but he [Mr.Wayne] made me feel comfortable, and talked to me, and gave me encouragement not to stop looking.*

Not all participants chatted or networked with their drivers during each ride. Bobby, Mostavo, Melan and Vette each reported one case in which they did not engage in conversations with their driver. These participants described texting during the ride, wearing headphones, and simply having "quiet but polite" (Vette) drivers.

Perceptions of Discrimination

No participants described explicit forms of being discriminated against at pickups, perhaps because it was unclear to them whether any drivers had canceled rides for this reason. However, when asked whether he learned about his drivers, Dae Dae commented in the interview that all of his drivers except one were foreigners, and he said this might be why they didn't see him as different: *By them having different nationalities, they didn't discriminate, they didn't see me being a black guy, they just saw me being a person who needed some help. That's beautiful. They felt comfortable to talk to me. They was dressed very professional and I was dressed [in] urban wear, but they never judged me by how I was dressed.*

On the other hand, there were some indications of discrimination on the part of our passengers. For example, TCash selected Uber drivers he felt comfortable with based on profile pictures. He said in the interview that he had canceled three rides with drivers he thought he would feel uncomfortable with: *I try to stay away from any type of situation to where I feel like I would be uncomfortable or anything, so when I look for Uber, I look for a person that's going to make me feel comfortable. You could say in a way, I kind of stereotype, so not necessarily with the race, but I stereotype age-wise. I want an older person picking me up.*

Bobby made a similar comment in the interview. When asked whether he had ever canceled a ride, he said yes. *Today before, I pressed the thing and requested a car and the picture and this is going to sound racist but I'm not racist at all, it popped up with a Muslim with the whole towel thing on and it just creeped me out a little bit so I canceled it and requested a different driver.*

Accurate estimates of arrival times

By far, the primary reason participants used Uber was for reliability. At least six participants (Ace, Jeff, Dale, Rosalyn, Vette, TCash) noted that the application provided accurate estimates of arrival times, which allowed them to make better use of their waiting time and to prepare for the ride. This stood in stark contrast to experiences with existing transportation infrastructures like buses and cabs, which were often delayed by many hours. Participants spoke on the convenience of real-time ridesharing: *Buses are not on time. They don't have as many buses on the routes like they used to. They have shut down routes at a certain time, where they had routes that would run all night,* said Vette. TCash agreed: *You have to wait too long [for buses]. Sometimes the bus don't come. Sometimes it come longer than expected. I prefer Uber, because you can actually see when they're coming, can see where they're at. I prefer Uber over bus transportation. I do a lot of cab also...the only difference from a cab and an Uber, if you ask me, I would say the conversation. Sometimes, you get better conversation from Uber drivers...Cab drivers, it's just more like get you to your destination and that's it...There's really no trust, also.*

The majority of Dale's rides were to job interviews, so timing was especially important. He compared taxis versus Uber based on time and the cleanliness of the vehicle: *Uber got me to the interviews that I had and I got there safely, and on time, and the transportation was a lot cleaner.* When asked to specify what he meant by "cleaner," he said: *Some cabs, they don't take the time to detail their vehicle. Uber, it was fresh, no cigarette smoke smell and the people were nice.*

Knowing the car's arrival time was an important benefit to participants for other reasons, as well. *That's what I like, because you can see them coming to you. We live in an apartment building, so no- If it's under 15 minutes, if it's a nice day, I'll go downstairs and wait; but if it's crappy weather, I'll stay upstairs until, like, two or three minutes, and then go downstairs. I don't want to make them wait any extra time, because I know their time is money - Frog (Interview)*

Participants used the service if they knew they were running late and would miss their bus or if they had no bus fare. Missing a bus in some cases was a significant loss of time. For example, Jeff only used Uber to get to and from work; he typically took two buses to get to work, so he used Uber as a backup plan. *It was a time where I got to the bus stop and I had just missed the bus, and the next bus was in 45 minutes. I was like, I got a little bit on my Uber...I can get home quicker... -Jeff (Interview).*

Barriers

Finally, we provide the results of our third research question, *What barriers do these groups of individuals face in using ridesharing services?* An analysis of interested participants who we could not recruit revealed three impediments to using Uber: low digital literacy or access (e.g., a lack of access to smartphones, the Internet, or Wi-Fi), limited access to credit cards, and accessibility and mobility issues. Interview results also revealed barriers.

Low Digital Literacy

Three of the 25 people who expressed interest online in the study used a basic mobile phone with no Internet capabilities. These participants, like 32% of the U.S. population who do not own a smart phone [6], could not access the Uber application and consequently the service. One potential participant had a smart phone with no regular access to a data plan. While she knew that she could access Wi-Fi near her home, she feared being unable to hail a ride for her return trip.

Another challenge was adding participants onto the business account. This was a multi-stage process, which uncovered ease of use as a sharing-economy barrier that was left unaddressed. Adding participants to the account required that participants download the Uber application, create an Uber account for first-time users (N=11), accept an email invitation from the business (e.g., requires logging into an email account) and re-start the application. We guided participants through this process either face-to-face or step-by-step via phone. In four cases this proved insufficient; we saw that participants also requested assistance from family members and friends.

This proved to be too daunting for at least one potential participant. An older man, perhaps in his early 60s and walking with a cane, was very interested in joining our study; however, he talked about his discomfort with his smart phone and felt he needed assistance initiating rides via the phone application. The barber in the shop where we met the man asked whether his grandson could assist the man. The older gentleman took a flyer and stated that he would contact us later in the day, but he never did. Additionally, throughout the study we made contact with participants via email, although in multiple cases participants expressed discomfort in accessing and sending emails. In those cases, we resorted to text messaging.

Lack of Credit Access

At least six participants (Mostavo, Frog, Que, Vette, Dae Dae, Bobby) in the study did not have a credit card, another prerequisite for using Uber. In the beginning of our study, this was a necessity even if participants were added to the business account and were not expected to pay for Uber rides. The company changed this policy at some point during our study. We circumvented the rule by onboarding participants using a prepaid credit card that we purchased.

Accessibility and Mobility

Three of our participants (Acorn, Frog, Bobby) had mobility issues that required special accommodations. Acorn and Frog sought information to better prepare for the ride ahead, and this information was not available in the application at the time of our study. Frog, who had a shoulder injury, worried about whether the driver would provide assistance with her shopping bags and desired a way to find out beforehand: *I'm limited on how much I can carry with my shoulder, so I always say, 'Well, I can't carry much' and they notice that, and they notice ... I don't always use this arm, like when I'm closing doors and that, because it's sore and hurts. It's getting better, so ... And they're willing to help you. That's what I like...*

Bobby spoke very highly of the drivers who aided him in getting into the car and said one driver helped him to his apartment door. However, there were still other accessibility concerns. Acorn, for example, had a sense of social anxiety around not knowing whether her walker would fit in the vehicle. She wanted to be able to see the size of the vehicle before initiating a ride: *Sometimes I think, 'God, can that walker fit in that vehicle?' but we've gone into every vehicle, even if it has to [go] across the seat, the rear seat...That way, when a similar vehicle is showing up, I know how to do it...*

DISCUSSION

It takes time to instill a culture of sharing in communities, which requires a regular progression from initial trust between strangers, to a more pervasive belief in the commons, to critical mass [10]. Our results show that uptake of the real-time ridesharing system led to positive experiences such as rich social interactions and common courtesy, and reliable transportation to work, interviews, and other appointments among those who chose to participate in our study. To the best of our knowledge, these social benefits from real-time ridesharing services have not been observed in prior studies.

At least two of our participants held a belief in the commons and all of our participants felt comfortable with their drivers. Our results suggest that *potential* participants in the sharing economy required additional regulation and trust, efficacy, social proof, ease of use, and open forms of payment. These barriers stemmed primarily from financial limitations–as suggested in prior work [32]–as well as low digital literacy, and limited Internet access. We generalize what prevented *potential*, or non-participants from receiving the same value that our participants received into two categories: regulation and trust, and (inclusive) infrastructures [46]. We provide design implications for real-time ride sharing services and general sharing-economy applications for low-resource populations.

Regulation and Trust

Trust in the platform [28] and in the brand [28, 46], ease of use, and social proof/critical mass were the sharing-economy requirements that generated the most controversy in our study. Sundararajan defines two similar dimensions of trust as brand certification, and cultural dialog (familiarity) [46], and we believe these to be associated with social proof. Our study results revealed that some non-participants distrusted Uber because it had no physical presence in their community. In fact, though we successfully recruited some individuals from the web, where users are more likely to be technology-savvy, and more than half through referrals, as suggested by [19], we were unable to recruit from popular community locations. As Botsman alludes [10], initial trust (between strangers) leads to a more pervasive belief in the commons and eventually to critical mass. Our findings suggest that initial trust in the platform and in the company along with a perceived value to the community would eventually lead to critical mass among our targeted populations. Although in a slightly different context, Karlan et al. also suggested that hiring workers through referrals, or existing network connections, could create trust through familiarity [27]. While sharing-economy systems support electronic referrals in this way, this sense of familiarity is lost among people with low digital literacy.

Lack of Familiarity and Trust

Our results suggest that for sharing-economy applications to effectively work within low-resource communities, companies must build and certify their brand to facilitate familiarity, or cultural dialog within a community in order to build trust. Demonstrating the value that these services offer to communities such as reliable transportation to work, reduced social isolation, common courtesy, and affordable rates could also be beneficial. Facilitating services, like UberPOOL–which provides lower rates as a result of split passenger fares with third-party organizations like job-training centers–could be successful as well. However, in a community where individuals are less likely to be online because of issues of digital literacy and access, brand certification for and adoption of online companies is difficult. In addition, if few people are online, within a community, there is little opportunity to obtain social proof and build critical mass, requirements for the sharing economy to work [10]. For example, we were unable to recruit participants when visiting barbershops and hair salons, primarily because of monetary exchange issues and the absence of face-to-face interactions with the company, which fostered mistrust. This innate feature would lead to issues across other sharing-economy applications.

Designing for Platform Trust

To address the aforementioned trust issues, we suggest platform designs that could lead to increased digital literacy, brand identity, visibility, and application transparency. For example, installing public kiosks in intermediate locations such as third-party organizations, barbershops, and community businesses through which people could call real-time ridesharing services would eliminate the need for smartphones while accommodating multiple forms of payment including cash, gift vouchers, and credit/debit cards. An open system such as this could also increase transparency [41] in terms of how to operate these systems because there would be others who had used the system and could support those who were less comfortable using the technology. This could be beneficial to the community (adds belief in the commons), and could help to build trust within low-resource communities. A public kiosk approach would present an opportunity to train local shop owners or employees how to handle transaction-related issues. While community engagement might be difficult, an alternative would be to establish signs, like at bus stops, near public Wi-Fi hot spots to increase visibility and also enable access for users without reliable data plans to initiate rides.

This type of system is crucial to building trust. Keymolen argues this: "[T]he development of trust online is not just about you and me, but about you, me and the system that brings us together. Only when users are aware of the workings of technology and the mutual shaping effects technology-in-use has, can trust thrive online" [28, p.147]. Similarly, designers must reduce uncertainty and perceived risks in order to engineer trustworthiness [38]. Several participants expressed not knowing that certain services cost more than others (e.g., UberSUV, UberSELECT). In addition, Acorn expressed uncertainty about why prices were surging. To further increase transparency, applications should make the price structure clear to users without compromising system simplicity. For example, while the Uber application indicates how many cars are nearby, the application could also provide information about the nearby demand (e.g., how many riders are waiting). As suggested by Frog, allowing riders who need assistance to indicate that they need assistance would enable riders to be transparent about their needs, which could lessen anxiety about using the service. For example, UberACCESS allows those needing extra assistance or access to wheelchair-accessible vehicles to request safe and reliable rides [20]. This design suggestion is one that could be generalized to other areas of transport. For example, current bus systems do not communicate their capacity (e.g., how many seats are available, how many spaces for bicycles are available) in real time.

Inclusive Infrastructures

While sharing-economy application infrastructures do allow for financial exchanges, they do so in a context that is not inclusive. Understanding the contextual differences among system users and designing for these differences is not a simple task [4], yet many of the barriers we encountered in our recruiting were consistent with prior literature on low-resourced U.S populations. For example, the dependence on credit cards for payments excludes close to 7% of the U.S. population [22], who do not have bank accounts. Of this 7%, 4.9% have low income [22]. Requiring a credit card for payment excludes people without a bank account [25]; at least half of our study participants did not have a credit card. We agree with Glöss et al. [25] that gift cards could address this issue as well as the cash payments supported by Uber's cash payment integration, which is currently operational in various parts of the world. Both options could go a long way in making Uber more inclusive in that they would allow people without bank accounts or debit/credit cards to sign up and use the service [2].

In fact, seamless integration into Uber's current payment system is simple. The use of coupon codes is already supported and has been used via business promotions. To account for context, these coupon codes should be sold in familiar places (e.g., local businesses, grocery stores) and accept cash or debit and credit card payments. Local business owners could receive a transaction fee from the company for selling the coupon codes, thereby contributing to the commons.

LIMITATIONS AND CONCLUSION

Our study was limited to a specific context (e.g., people with low-income and few transportation options) and to one U.S. city. Additionally, while we were able to monitor rides taken with the business account, we were unable to effect pricing to identify price points. More than 30% of the rides were surge rides, which seems high, though it is unclear how this percentage compares to that in other areas. If this share is above average then at least one of the following could be true: our sample is less price-sensitive, though unlikely; the ride times were during peak times only; or perhaps most interestingly, surge pricing could reflect that few drivers go to these areas and our population paid more for the services because of driver unavailability, which is similar to findings in [47]. We would like to better understand aspects of pricing and affordability, perhaps in a more controlled environment. While our results suggest that participants did not encounter discrimination as it relates to perceived issues of safety, distance, or race, we were unable to determine whether Uber drivers during this study rejected pick-up requests from our participants and confirm Lee et al.'s results [32]. We would like to investigate this further. Finally, Uber application features are ever-changing (e.g., participants mistakenly selected options such as UberSELECT and UberXL at the time of our study; however, at the time of publication, Uber options included prices). Nevertheless, our underlying contributions hold true.

Our work extends the HCI and CSCW sharing economy research by presenting results of the use of a sharing-economy application among passengers from a low-resource city, a relatively unexplored population in this area of study. Our participants had positive interactions with drivers that led to new information about the city, job leads, and encouragement. Our findings contribute the importance of regulation and trust for inclusivity, particularly among populations did not participate in the study because of non-familiarity with the service, limited social proof, and platform distrust. We also confirm requirements of sharing-economy applications in other contexts. This suggests that our results are likely to be applicable to a wider user base including those who are disabled or in environments with developing infrastructure (e.g., limited Internet access and connectivity or credit card availability) where Uber and similar services operate. Broadly, our results contribute to a growing knowledge around how digital divides exist in society and present a call to the HCI community for greater understanding of the design of systems to consider all aspects of society. Our contributions could inform HCI researchers, designers, policy makers, and private companies in their development of future real-time ridesharing services and sharing-economy systems.

REFERENCES

1. 2012. Detroit, MI. City-Data.com. http://www.city-data.com/city/Detroit-Michigan.html. (2012). Accessed: May 16, 2016.
2. 2015. Help Us Test Cash Payments. (2015). https://newsroom.uber.com/?s=cash+payment/
3. 2016. How Walk Score Works. (2016). https://www.redfin.com/how-walk-score-works
4. Syed Ishtiaque Ahmed, Nicola J Bidwell, Himanshu Zade, Srihari H Muralidhar, Anupama Dhareshwar, Baneen Karachiwala, Tandong Neba Cedrick, and Jacki O'Neill. 2016. Peer-to-peer in the workplace: A view from the road. In *Proceedings of the 34th Annual ACM Conference on Human Factors in Computing Systems, CHI 2016, San Jose, U.S.* ACM Association for Computing Machinery. DOI: http://dx.doi.org/10.1145/2858036.2858393
5. Syed M Ahmed, Jeanne P Lemkau, Nichol Nealeigh, and Barbara Mann. 2001. Barriers to healthcare access in a non-elderly urban poor American population. *Health & Social Care in the Community* 9, 6 (2001), 445–453.
6. Monica Anderson. 2015. Technology Device Ownership. (2015). http://www.pewinternet.org/2015/10/29/technology-device-ownership-2015/
7. Thomas A Arcury, John S Preisser, Wilbert M Gesler, and James M Powers. 2005. Access to transportation and health care utilization in a rural region. *The Journal of Rural Health* 21, 1 (2005), 31–38.
8. Fleura Bardhi and Giana M. Eckhardt. 2012. Access-Based Consumption: The Case of Car Sharing. *Journal of Consumer Research* 39, 4 (2012), 881–898. DOI:http://dx.doi.org/10.1086/666376
9. Victoria Bellotti, Alexander Ambard, Daniel Turner, Christina Gossmann, Kamila Demkova, and John M. Carroll. 2015. A Muddle of Models of Motivation for Using Peer-to-Peer Economy Systems. In *Proceedings of the 33rd Annual ACM Conference on Human Factors in Computing Systems (CHI '15)*. ACM, New York, NY, USA, 1085–1094. DOI: http://dx.doi.org/10.1145/2702123.2702272
10. Rachel Botsman and Ro Rogers. 2010. *What's mine is yours: the rise of collaborative consumption.* HarperCollins Publisher. http://www.harpercollins.com/book/index.aspx?isbn=9780061963544
11. Mikayla Bouchard. 2015a. Transportation Emerges as Crucial to Escaping Poverty. http://www.nytimes.com/2015/05/07/upshot/transportation-emerges-as-crucial-to-escaping-poverty.html. (7 May 2015). Accessed:2016-04-23.
12. Mikayla Bouchard. 2015b. Transportation Emerges as Crucial to Escaping Poverty. *The New York Times (May 7)* (2015).
13. Campbell Mithun. 2012. National Study quantifies the "Sharing Economy" movement. (2012). http://www.prnewswire.com/news-releases/national-study-//quantifies-the-sharing-economy-movement-138949069.html
14. Noel Cass, Elizabeth Shove, and John Urry. 2005. Social exclusion, mobility and access1. *The Sociological Review* 53, 3 (2005), 539–555. DOI: http://dx.doi.org/10.1111/j.1467-954X.2005.00565.x
15. Raj Chetty, Nathaniel Hendren, and Lawrence F Katz. 2015. The Effects of Exposure to Better Neighborhoods on Children: New Evidence from the Moving to Opportunity Experiment. *American Economic Review* 106, August (2015), 90. DOI: http://dx.doi.org/10.3386/w21156
16. Raj Chetty, Nathaniel. Hendren, Patrick Kline, and Emmanuel Saez. 2014. Where is the land of Opportunity? The Geography of Intergenerational Mobility in the United States. *The Quarterly Journal of Economics* 129, 4 (September 2014), 1553–1623. DOI: http://dx.doi.org/10.1093/qje/qju022
17. Data Driven Detroit. 2015. Uphill Both Ways: Where are the Jobs in Metro Detroit? (March 2015). http://blog.datadrivendetroit.org/2015/03/04/uphill-both-ways-where-are-the-jobs-in-metro-detroit Retrieved 12/16/2015.
18. Tawanna Dillahunt, Airi Lampinen, Jacki O'Neill, Loren Terveen, and Cory Kendrick. 2016. Does the Sharing Economy Do Any Good?. In *Proceedings of the 19th ACM Conference on Computer Supported Cooperative Work and Social Computing Companion (CSCW '16 Companion)*. ACM, New York, NY, USA, 197–200. DOI: http://dx.doi.org/10.1145/2818052.2893362
19. Tawanna R. Dillahunt and Amelia R. Malone. 2015. The Promise of the Sharing Economy Among Disadvantaged Communities. In *Proceedings of the 33rd Annual ACM Conference on Human Factors in Computing Systems (CHI '15)*. ACM, New York, NY, USA, 2285–2294. DOI: http://dx.doi.org/10.1145/2702123.2702189
20. Kate Donahue. 2014. UberACCESS: Expanding Transportation Options. (2014). https://newsroom.uber.com/us-california/uberaccess-sd/
21. Benjamin G. Edelman and Michael Luca. 2014. Digital Discrimination: The Case of Airbnb.com. *SSRN Electronic Journal* (jan 2014). DOI: http://dx.doi.org/10.2139/ssrn.2377353
22. FDIC. 2013. *FDIC National Survey of Unbanked and Underbanked Households*. Technical Report.
23. Shannon Firth. 2016. Q&A With Detroit's New Director of Public Health | Medpage Today. (27 January 2016). http://www.medpagetoday.com/PublicHealthPolicy/PublicHealth/55883
24. Yanbo Ge, Christopher R. Knittel, Don MacKenzie, and Stephen Zoepf. 2016. Racial and gender discrimination in

transportation network companies. (2016). DOI: http://dx.doi.org/10.3386/w22776

25. Mareike Glöss, Moira McGregor, and Barry Brown. 2016. Designing for Labour: Uber and the On-Demand Mobile Workforce. In *Proceedings of the 2016 CHI Conference on Human Factors in Computing Systems (CHI '16)*. ACM, New York, NY, USA, 1632–1643. DOI: http://dx.doi.org/10.1145/2858036.2858476
26. Tapio Ikkala and Airi Lampinen. 2014. Defining the Price of Hospitality: Networked Hospitality Exchange via Airbnb. In *Proceedings of the 17th ACM Conference on Computer Supported Cooperative Work & Social Computing*. ACM Association for Computing Machinery, 173–176. DOI:http://dx.doi.org/10.1145/2556420.2556506
27. Dean Karlan, Markus Mobius, Tanya Rosenblat, and Adam Szeidl. 2009. Trust and Social Collateral. *The Quarterly Journal of Economics* 124, 3 (2009), 1307–1361. DOI: http://dx.doi.org/10.1162/qjec.2009.124.3.1307
28. Esther Keymolen. 2013. Trust and technology in collaborative consumption. Why it is not just about you and me. *Bridging distances in technology and regulation* (2013), 135–150. https://pure.uvt.nl/portal/files/1519132/TP2013
29. Airi Lampinen, Victoria Bellotti, Coye Cheshire, and Mary L. Gray. 2015a. Studying the "Sharing Economy": Perspectives to peer-to-peer exchange. *CSCW'15 Companion* (2015), 117–121. DOI: http://dx.doi.org/10.1145/2685553.2699339
30. Airi Lampinen, Victoria Bellotti, Andrés Monroy-Hernández, Coye Cheshire, and Alexandra Samuel. 2015b. Studying the "Sharing Economy": Perspectives to peer-to-peer exchange. *CSCW'15 Companion* (2015), 117–121. DOI: http://dx.doi.org/10.1145/2685553.2699339
31. Airi Lampinen, Kai Huotari, and Coye Cheshire. 2015c. Challenges to Participation in the Sharing Economy : The Case of Local Online Peer- to-Peer Exchange in a Single Parents' Network. *Interaction Design and Architecture(s) Journal* 24 (2015), 16–32.
32. Min Kyung Lee, Daniel Kusbit, Evan Metsky, and Laura Dabbish. 2015. Working with Machines: The Impact of Algorithmic and Data-Driven Management on Human Workers. In *Proceedings of the 33rd Annual ACM Conference on Human Factors in Computing Systems (CHI '15)*. ACM, New York, NY, USA, 1603–1612. DOI: http://dx.doi.org/10.1145/2702123.2702548
33. Sara Lichtenwalter, Gary Koeske, and Esther Sales. 2006. Examining Transportation and Employment Outcomes: Evidence for Moving Beyond The Bus Pass. *Journal of Poverty* 10, 1 (2006), 93–115. DOI: http://dx.doi.org/10.1300/J134v10n01_05
34. Rick Mathews. 2013. Detroit bankrupt: To see Detroit's decline, look at 40 years of federal policy. *Policy.Mic* 27 (2013). http://goo.gl/WXAQ1o Retrieved May 12, 2016.
35. Kelly McLaughlin. 2015. Detroit has become such an 'economic desert' that residents now commute up to four-hours each day just to find work. (March 2015). http://www.dailymail.co.uk/news/article-2975237/Dearth-jobs-barrier-post-bankruptcy-Detroits-growth.html Retrieved 12/16/2015.
36. Michelle O'Reilly and Nicola Parker. 2012. 'Unsatisfactory Saturation': a critical exploration of the notion of saturated sample sizes in qualitative research. *Qualitative Research* (2012), 1468794112446106.
37. Lisa Rayle, Danielle Dai, Nelson Chan, Robert Cervero, and Susan Shaheen. 2016. Just a better taxi? A survey-based comparison of taxis, transit, and ridesourcing services in San Francisco. *Transport Policy* 45 (2016), 168–178.
38. Jens Riegelsberger, M. Angela Sasse, and John D. McCarthy. 2005. The mechanics of trust: A framework for research and design. *International Journal of Human-Computer Studies* 62, 3 (2005), 381 – 422. DOI: http://dx.doi.org/10.1016/j.ijhcs.2005.01.001
39. Alex Rosenblat and Luke Stark. 2015. Uber's Drivers: Information Asymmetries and Control in Dynamic Work. (2015), 1–17. DOI: http://dx.doi.org/10.2139/ssrn.2686227
40. Johnny Saldaña. 2012. *The Coding Manual for Qualitative Researchers* (2 ed.). Thousand Oaks, CA: Sage.
41. Nithya Sambasivan, Ed Cutrell, Kentaro Toyama, and Bonnie Nardi. 2010. Intermediated Technology Use in Developing Communities. In *Proceedings of the SIGCHI Conference on Human Factors in Computing Systems (CHI '10)*. ACM, New York, NY, USA, 2583–2592. DOI: http://dx.doi.org/10.1145/1753326.1753718
42. Jean J Schensul and Margaret D LeCompte. 1999. *Essential Ethnographic Methods: A Mixed Methods Approach*. AltaMira Press. 386 pages.
43. Michael J Smart and Nicholas J Klein. 2015. A Longitudinal Analysis of Cars, Transit, and Employment Outcomes. *Publication MNTRC Report 12-49* (2015).
44. Rosanna Smart, Brad Rowe, Angela Hawken, Mark Kleiman, Nate Mladenovic, Peter Gehred, and Clarissa Manning. 2015. Faster and Cheaper: How Ride-Sourcing Fills a Gap in Low-Income Los Angeles Neighborhoods. *BOTEC Analysis Corporation* (July 2015).
45. Jennifer Stark and Nicholas Diakopoulos. 2016. Uber seems to offer better service in areas with more white people. That raises some tough questions. (2016). https://www.washingtonpost.com/news/wonk/wp/2016/03/10/uber-seems-to-offer-better-service-in-areas-with-more-white-people-that-raises-some-tough-questions/?utm
46. Arun Sundararajan. 2016. *The Sharing Economy: The End of Employment and the Rise of Crowd-Based Capitalism*. MIT Press.

47. Jacob Thebault-Spieker, Loren G. Terveen, and Brent Hecht. 2015. Avoiding the South Side and the Suburbs: The Geography of Mobile Crowdsourcing Markets. In *Proceedings of the 18th ACM Conference on Computer Supported Cooperative Work & Social Computing (CSCW '15)*. ACM, New York, NY, USA, 265–275. DOI: http://dx.doi.org/10.1145/2675133.2675278

48. Kentaro Toyama. 2015. Geek Heresy: Rescuing Social Change from the Cult of Technology. (2015). http://www.amazon.com/Geek-Heresy-Rescuing-Social-Technology/dp/161039528X

49. Iis P. Tussyadiah and Juho Pesonen. 2016. Drivers and barriers of peer-to-peer accommodation stay: An exploratory study with American and Finnish travellers. *Current Issues in Tourism* 3500, April (2016), 1–18. DOI: http://dx.doi.org/10.1080/13683500.2016.1141180

50. John Urry. 2012. Social networks, mobile lives and social inequalities. *Journal of Transport Geography* 21 (2012), 24 – 30. DOI: http://dx.doi.org/10.1016/j.jtrangeo.2011.10.003 Social Impacts and Equity Issues in Transport.

51. Gill Valentine. 1997. *'"Tell Me About..." Using Interviews as a Research Methodology'* (second ed.). Routledge, New York, NY, USA. 110–126 pages.

52. P.B. van de Glind. 2013. The consumer potential of Collaborative Consumption: Identifying the motives of Dutch Collaborative Consumers & Measuring the consumer potential of Collaborative Consumption within the municipality of Amsterdam. (aug 2013). http://dspace.library.uu.nl/handle/1874/280661

53. Renee E. Walker, Christopher R. Keane, and Jessica G. Burke. 2010. Disparities and access to healthy food in the United States: A review of food deserts literature. *Health & Place* 16, 5 (2010), 876 – 884. DOI: http://dx.doi.org/10.1016/j.healthplace.2010.04.013

54. Gillian B. White. 2015. Stranded: How America's Failing Public Transportation Increases Inequality. The Atlantic. (May 2015).

Supporting Community Health Workers in India through Voice- and Web-Based Feedback

Brian DeRenzi[†] **Nicola Dell**[‡] **Jeremy Wacksman**[ϕ] **Scott Lee**[Ψ] **Neal Lesh**[ϕ]

†University of Cape Town
bderenzi@cs.uct.ac.za

‡Cornell Tech
nixdell@cornell.edu

ϕDimagi, Inc.
jwacksman,nlesh@dimagi.com

ΨHarvard University
slee@hbs.edu

ABSTRACT

Our research aims to support community health workers (CHWs) in low-resource settings by providing them with personalized information regarding their work. This information is delivered through a combination of voice- and web-based feedback that is derived from data already collected by CHWs. We describe the in situ participatory design approach used to create usable and appropriate feedback for low-literate CHWs and present usage data from a 12-month study with 71 CHWs in India. We show how the system supported and motivated CHWs, and how they used *both* the web- and voice-based systems, and each of the visualizations, for different reasons. We also show that the comparative feedback provided by the system introduced elements of competition that discouraged some CHWs while motivating others. Taken together, our findings suggest that providing personalized voice- and web-based feedback could be an effective way to support and motivate CHWs in low-resource settings.

Author Keywords

ICTD; HCI4D; CHW; ASHA; community health; mHealth.

INTRODUCTION

The critical lack of trained medical professionals in many low-income countries has resulted in the establishment of community health programs that aim to provide vulnerable populations with access to essential health services. The success of community health programs hinges on the work of lightly-trained community health workers (CHWs), who are members of local communities that receive basic medical training and who then assess, treat, and refer patients according to established health protocols. For many community members, CHWs are the primary link to the broader public health infrastructure. However, CHWs operating in low-resource contexts face a diverse set of challenges as they work to deliver health care to their communities, including poor infrastructure, low levels of education and literacy, limited training and supervision, isolation, lack of support, and the need to balance CHW work with other duties such as agriculture, child care, and family responsibilities.

In an effort to ameliorate some of these challenges, researchers in the fields of HCI for Development (HCI4D) and Information and Communication Technologies for Development (ICTD) have been exploring ways in which mobile devices could support and strengthen CHW programs. Examples include providing CHWs with decision support [11], job aids [15], health information [21, 27], and reminder messages [10, 22]. However, the majority of these systems deliver generic messages or videos that are not personalized to the CHW's individual context. A range of data collection systems also allow CHWs to collect and submit data to a central database [4, 5, 16, 18]. However, although the collected data is usually made available to supervisors and decision-makers, it has thus far not been made available to the CHWs themselves. As a result, CHWs often receive little to no feedback regarding their own work unless facilitated by a supervisor.

Our research addresses this gap by providing CHWs with personalized, on-demand feedback about their own work that is derived from the data that they have collected. Specifically, we worked with Accredited Social Health Activists (ASHAs), the largest cohort of CHWs in India, to create and deploy the ASHA Self-Tracking Application (ASTA). ASTA provides ASHAs with personalized information about their work through two interfaces that run in parallel: a web-based and a voice-based interface. The web-based interface consists of three visualizations: (1) a *comparison graph* that shows how many clients an ASHA has visited that month compared to a subset of her peers, providing an indication of progress towards the monthly goal of visiting all clients; (2) a *calendar graph* that shows the number of visits the ASHA made each day of the current month; and (3) a *historical graph* that shows the total number of clients visited each month for the past five months. The parallel voice-based system provides the same information as the comparison graph over a phone line, telling an ASHA how many clients she has visited out of the total number she has registered, and her current rank relative to a subset of her peers.

A prior paper [13] analyzed the impact of the system on ASHA performance, finding that ASHAs with access to the system made an average of 21.5% more client visits than ASHAs with access to a control system. However, the prior paper did not describe in detail or analyze the participatory design process used to create the system. It also did not ex-

Permission to make digital or hard copies of all or part of this work for personal or classroom use is granted without fee provided that copies are not made or distributed for profit or commercial advantage and that copies bear this notice and the full citation on the first page. Copyrights for components of this work owned by others than ACM must be honored. Abstracting with credit is permitted. To copy otherwise, or republish, to post on servers or to redistribute to lists, requires prior specific permission and/or a fee. Request permissions from permissions@acm.org.

CHI 2017, May 06-11, 2017, Denver, CO, USA

© 2017 ACM. ISBN 978-1-4503-4655-9/17/05...$15.00

DOI: http://dx.doi.org/10.1145/3025453.3025514

amine system usage behavior or discuss the ways in which each of the web- and voice-based systems, and the individual visualizations, may have motivated, supported, or discouraged ASHAs. To fill these gaps, this paper completely avoids discussing how the system affected ASHA performance and makes an entirely new set of research contributions.

First, we describe the in situ participatory design approach used to create the visualizations and interfaces that constitute the ASTA system. We highlight the complexities of designing graph-based feedback that can be understood by low-literate ASHAs who do not have high levels of education or experience with technology. Our experiences yield valuable insights and lessons learned that will be useful for others interested in designing interactive systems for low-literate populations in resource-constrained settings. **Second**, we present usage data from a 12-month deployment with 71 ASHAs in Uttar Pradesh, India. We show that ASHAs used *both* the web- and voice-based systems and reveal the benefits of providing more than one interaction modality. We also show that ASHAs used each of the three web-based visualizations for a variety of different reasons. Finally, we show how the comparative feedback provided by the system introduced elements of competition among ASHAs, which further motivated some ASHAs while leaving others feeling discouraged. Taken together, our findings suggest that giving ASHAs personalized feedback regarding their own work could be an effective way to motivate and support ASHA work processes.

BACKGROUND AND RELATED WORK

Our research contributes to a growing body of literature in HCI4D and ICTD that seeks to understand how computing technologies can be used to aid underserved populations around the world [7, 8, 30]. Focusing specifically on CHW programs, early work by DeRenzi et al. [11] showed that decision-support systems running on mobile PDA devices could help CHWs adhere to established medical protocols, while Florez at al. studied how mobile devices could be used to provide CHWs with digital job aids [15]. Ramachandran et al. [28] aimed to use mobile messaging and videos to improve health worker efficacy, noting the political, social, and cultural challenges associated with technology interventions that promote behavior change [27]. More recently, Kumar et al. [21] have explored equipping CHWs in India with community-led videos that they can use to promote behavior change. Their work stresses the importance of paying attention to local contexts and societal norms [20]. Learning from this prior work, our research takes an in situ, participatory design approach to try and ensure that the systems we create are usable and appropriate for the context.

Another set of relevant projects focus on sending reminder messages to CHWs or patients [6, 10, 22]. One particularly relevant project examined the role of supervisors in supporting CHW work [10]. The paper showed that informing a CHW's supervisor if she did not complete her work was an effective way to maintain CHW performance. However, when the communication to the supervisor was removed, the amount of work done by CHWs decreased. Our work takes a different approach in that, rather than involving the CHWs supervisor, the system attempts to motivate CHWs by providing them with useful information regarding the amount of work accomplished and the amount remaining.

All of the prior work described so far has enabled the one-way transfer of information (e.g., messages, videos) from a server or database to a CHW. Another set of projects enables the collection and one-way transfer of data in the opposite direction: from CHWs to a central database [4, 5, 16, 18]. The collected data is usually made available to supervisors and decision-makers, including partner, donor, and government organizations. However, to date, the data collected by CHWs has not been made available to the CHWs themselves. As a result, CHWs usually receive little to no feedback regarding their own work unless facilitated by a supervisor. They have no way to analyze their past work or plan for future work. Our work addresses this gap by providing CHWs with on-demand information about their own work. This information is delivered to CHWs through a combination of voice-based feedback and web-based visualizations derived from the data the CHW herself has collected and submitted. To the best of our knowledge, we are the first to provide CHWs with personalized, on-demand feedback about their own work.

Finally, since many of the CHWs in our research had low levels of literacy, our design work draws heavily on research that examines how to create technologies for low-literate populations, including research that focuses on understanding the challenges faced by novice and low-literate technology users [23, 25], designing interfaces that have minimal text or are entirely text-free [24], combining audio and text interaction for semi-literate users [14], and creating voice-based systems that provide information to low-literate populations [26, 31]. Our designs incorporate many of the design recommendations provided by this body of work. Moreover, rather than choosing a single interaction modality, we chose to provide *both* voice- and web-based systems that operate in parallel.

Background and Research Context

This section provides background information regarding the ASHAs involved in our work and the context in which our research took place. We conducted our work within an existing mobile health program, the Reducing Maternal and Newborn Deaths (ReMiND) program [3] in Uttar Pradesh, India. The ReMiND program is being implemented by Catholic Relief Services (CRS) [29] in conjunction with Vatsalya [32], with the goal of improving maternal health and reducing neonatal mortality in Uttar Pradesh, which currently suffers critical shortages of health centers and health workers [2], and experiences high rates of maternal and infant mortality [1].

The ASHAs who participated in our research were already enrolled in the ReMiND program and had been trained to provide members of their communities with basic health services, counseling, and referrals. In keeping with the goals of the ReMiND program, the ASHAs that we worked with were particularly focused on maternal and newborn health. All ASHAs in the ReMiND program had previously been given Nokia C-2 feature phones running a CommCare application [12] that was designed to guide their work and aid data collection. Feature phones were chosen because they were locally available, affordable, familiar to many ASHAs, physically rugged, and had a long battery life. The CommCare application was in Hindi and contained localized images and audio prompts that helped ASHAs to register and monitor pregnant women. Supervisory staff then used the CommCare data submitted by ASHAs to monitor ASHA activity and make supportive visits based on performance. However, the CommCare application did not provide the ASHAs themselves with any information or feedback about their work. The visualizations that we designed and deployed in our research therefore represent the first time that ASHAs received information back from the system regarding their own work.

Prior Work

This is the second paper to be published on this research. The first paper [13] focused exclusively on analyzing the impact that the feedback and visualizations had on ASHA *performance*, measured as the number of client visits made by ASHAs. Findings from the paper showed that ASHAs with access to the system made an average of 21.5% more client visits than ASHAs with access to a control system. It also showed a correlation between system usage and performance.

However, although the prior paper briefly describes the design of the system, it does not analyze the diverse infrastructural, informational, and human challenges associated with designing usable and appropriate feedback mechanisms for ASHAs. It also does not provide lessons learned through the in-situ, participatory design approach that will be useful for other HCI4D researchers. Moreover, unlike the prior paper, this paper provides a detailed breakdown and analysis of system usage over a 12-month deployment, highlighting the benefits and limitations of each of the voice- and web-based systems. It also provides a rich, qualitative analysis of the ways in which each of the feedback systems and individual visualizations supported and motivated ASHA work processes. This detailed analysis of system usage, combined with qualitative data that reveals ASHA opinions, feelings, and reactions to the feedback, yields important new insights that will be valuable for the HCI4D and ICTD communities.

SYSTEM DESIGN

Design Challenges

In addition to the diverse environmental, infrastructural, and human challenges that result from working with low-literate ASHAs in rural India, our feedback mechanisms were built on top of an existing mobile health project and we needed to work within the constraints imposed by this project, including the devices already provided and information being collected.

Device Constraints

The feature phones provided to ASHAs presented substantial design constraints. For example, the devices had relatively small screen sizes (two inches) and low resolution (240 x 320 pixels). This gave us a very small physical and virtual area in which to design visualizations that provided useful information to ASHAs. We were also constrained by the limited functionality of the feature phone platform. Had we been able to design for a smartphone platform, it would have been straightforward to create a standalone application for the visualizations. Instead, we needed to create a web-based application that ran inside the browser (opera mini) and displayed high-quality PNG versions of the visualizations. It was also challenging to find an easy way for ASHAs to access their personalized website. Eventually we added a shortcut key to the home screen that opened the application, which paralleled a shortcut key that the ASHAs used to open CommCare.

Information Constraints

One decision that we needed to make early on was to define how the system would compute performance. We initially explored using a measure of visit quality, but quickly discovered that we were constrained by a need to use the data and metadata already being collected by the existing CommCare application. In light of this constraint, and to remain consistent with other aspects of the ASHAs supervision model, the key metric of visiting every pregnant client once per month became the focus. In addition to simplicity and ease of computation, this metric encourages ASHAs to register more clients and make more visits, both of which are desirable outcomes.

Infrastructural and Environmental Challenges

Most ASHAs worked in areas with relatively poor connectivity, so our intervention needed to work over a 2G network connection. It was also important that the visualizations not incur large data charges that would exceed the amount already provided to ASHAs through the ReMiND program. The physical working environment also presented a challenge since ASHAs frequently work outside in bright sunlight, which made it difficult to read detailed graphics or text.

Human Challenges

Perhaps the most important and complex set of challenges that we needed to coordinate were the needs of the ASHAs themselves. Most of these challenges stemmed from the fact that the ASHAs had variable–but generally low–education and literacy levels. The ASHAs had also had diverse levels of comprehension of graphs, written Hindi text, and more abstract visual metaphors. The main challenge was therefore to design visualizations that were intuitive for ASHAs and easily understandable with minimal training.

Design Methodology

Our design work involved a diverse range of literate and non-literate ASHAs and took place in two roughly sequential phases. In the first phase, we worked with ASHAs at multiple project sites, repeating the same process with each ASHA. At each site, we would begin by introducing (on paper) the concept of graphs and visualizations to ensure the ASHA understood visual representation of quantitative information. After introducing bar graphs, line graphs, and pie charts, we showed the ASHAs initial mockups of our visualizations (see Figure 1). An important part of the first phase was to learn how to quickly train ASHAs to read graphs. One effective strategy that we eventually converged on was to start by using the child health card, a familiar reference point for most ASHAs that also includes a graph. We also provided a variety of simple analogies to familiar topics, such as food or farming, to introduce and discuss graph concepts. In the second phase of our design work, we worked closely with a set of

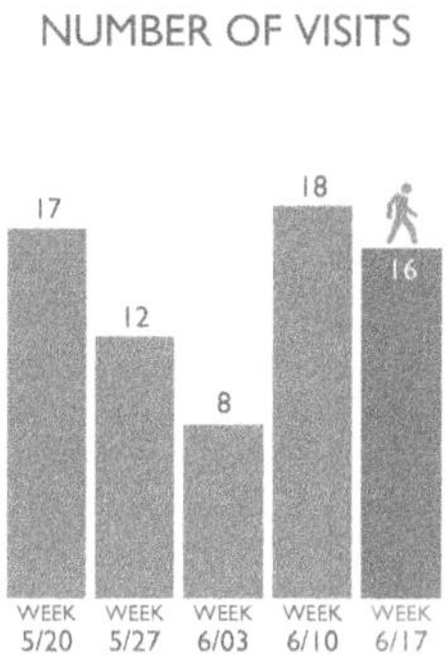

Figure 1. An early design used to elicit feedback during our iterative, participatory fieldwork.

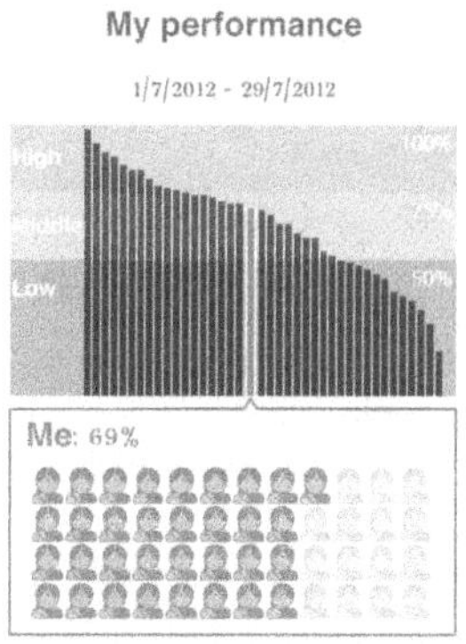

Figure 2. Intermediate design that incorporated colors from the child growth chart.

ASHAs in a neighboring block, following a rapid participatory design process to gather feedback on over 20 design iterations. During this iterative process we combined input from ASHAs, observations from field staff, and intuitions from the design team to create many new sets of visualizations before converging on the final set of visualizations that we deployed.

The voice-based system was created after the graphical system was complete. The design process for the voice system was short because we had already learned what information was understandable and appropriate for ASHAs. As a result, we were able to simply provide the information that was conveyed by the graphical system in spoken Hindi format. Before deployment, we pilot tested the voice system to ensure it was working properly and could be understood by ASHAs.

Findings and Lessons from Design Iterations

The initial designs we presented to the ASHAs in the first phase of our design process were simple and minimalist in an attempt to make them as understandable as possible. During the period of rapid iteration, we found that our designs increased in complexity as we tried to integrate different metaphors from ASHAs' day-to-day work. Our final set of visualizations then returned to a minimalist context-appropriate approach to communicating performance information.

Interpretation is context-dependent

We experienced numerous challenges creating visualizations that made sense to ASHAs. For example, our first set of visualizations used the color red to highlight the current day, but this led to confusion because, as we quickly discovered, red is used to highlight national holidays and weekends on Indian calendars. In an effort to match ASHAs existing work contexts, we also tried using the green, yellow, and red color coding from the child growth chart that they already use (see Figure 2). However, in some cases this backfired because ASHAs thought that the "you" label on the visualization was referring to a client and the colors showed the client's status. Another ASHA had a predetermined association with colors that came from a local rhyme. For example, to her green meant a beauty queen and yellow a "dirty fellow." Early iterations of the visualizations were developed with very rough approximations of workload, which resulted in challenges eliciting feedback from ASHAs because they became hyper-focused on the unrealistic workload. Finally, one iteration showed the percentage of clients visited, but one ASHA associated this with grades received in school, suggesting that the 71% in the example was just 4% less than a 'distinction'. All these findings highlight the importance of paying attention to the context and involving ASHAs in the design process.

Training is a critical part of the process

Training plays an enormous role in the success of technology interventions in low-resource contexts. In our case, it was necessary to train ASHAs not only on the technical components of accessing the visualizations, but also on the conceptual understanding of graphs. Our participatory design work made it clear that the concept of 'average' group performance was too abstract to be easily understood by the majority of the ASHAs without substantial training. It was much more clear to directly reference numbers. Similarly, there was confusion around labeling the ASHA's performance as 'me'. Instead, we discovered that it was better to use the terms 'you' and 'other ASHAs'. There are inherent tensions between making graphs immediately understandable and making graphs that contain rich information but that require training. Striking the correct balance so that all ASHAs can interpret a visualization with roughly one day of training takes iteration on both the graphs and the training methods.

Different stakeholders have different priorities

During our iterative design phase, ASHAs repeatedly asked us to create visualizations that included ASHA names so that they would know who was performing better than they were. This request revealed fundamental tensions between what the ASHAs wanted and what the implementing partner wanted (i.e., not shaming lower performing ASHAs). Balancing each stakeholder's priorities required compromise from all parties.

It is beneficial to build on familiar concepts

We found it beneficial to build on concepts that ASHAs were already familiar with. For example, during our fieldwork we noted that it was common for ASHAs to have calendars in their homes. Subsequently, the ASHAs responded favorably to our calendar visualizations, saying that they liked to be able to look back and see which days they had worked. In general, we tried to build on existing ASHA knowledge so that they would be comfortable with the resulting visualizations.

The final visualizations

The final set of visualizations are shown in Figure 3 (note that although the visualizations are shown in English for readability, the versions that we deployed with ASHAs were in Hindi). The *comparison graph* shows an ASHA's performance for that calendar month compared to a random subset of her peers. It consists of a basic histogram with qualitative labels on the y-axis. The visualization also contains repeated information. For example, the number of client visits an ASHA has made is conveyed by the histogram, the written text, and the pregnant women icons. The subset to which the ASHA was compared remained constant for the calendar month, but changed from month to month, which ensured that

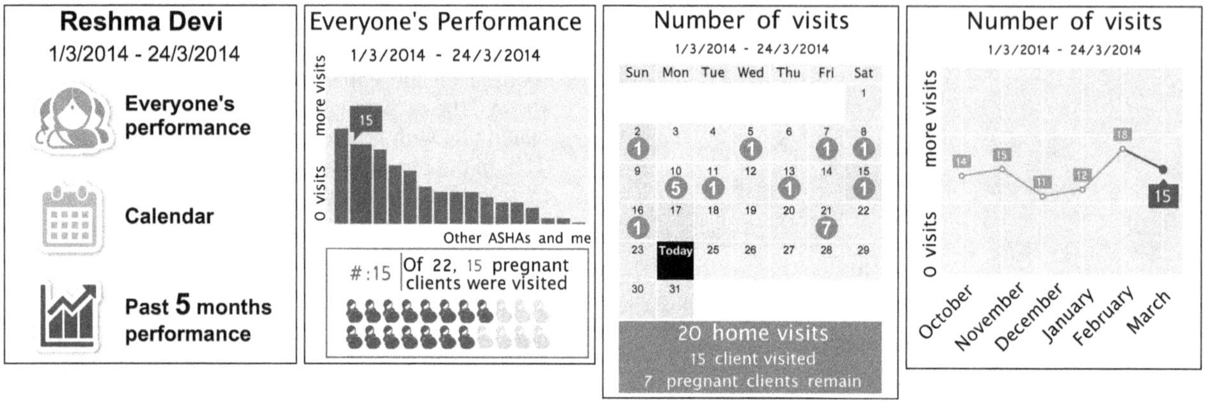

Figure 3. Screenshots from the final ASTA web system. Although we show the text in English here for readability the deployed application was in Hindi.

ASHAs did not get permanently stuck in either a high- or low-performing group. The *calendar graph* shows the number of client visits the ASHA made each day of the month. Finally, the *historical graph* gives a sense of continuity, showing the number of visits made each month for the past five months.

FIELD EVALUATION

To evaluate the impact of the system on ASHAs, we conducted a 12-month deployment with 71 ASHAs in Uttar Pradesh, India. This section describes the ASHAs who participated in our study and our research methodology. The study was IRB approved by Maulana Azad Medical College, Harvard University, and the University of Washington.

Participants

We invited all the ASHAs in the ReMiND project to take part in our study and recruited a total of 71 ASHAs who participated for a period of 12 months (note that the ASHAs involved in the design phase of our research were from a different block and, to avoid the potential for bias, they did not take part in the study). All participants were female and ranged in age from 21 to 55 years (M = 32). In addition to their ASHA work, most ASHAs were also involved with agriculture (69%; n = 49) or a non-agricultural family business (11%; n = 8). Household sizes ranged from two to 19, with a median size of six. The ASHAs came from a range of socioeconomic backgrounds, with self-reported individual monthly income ranging from 300 to 3000 INR (approx. US$5 to $50). Participants reported relatively low levels of education, with 39% having completed grade 10 and 7% having no formal schooling. Many of the ASHAs were also low-literate, with almost 31% (n = 22) unable to easily read a basic Hindi sentence. Almost all participants (96%; n = 68) had access to a mobile phone at home other than their work phone.

Procedure

We began by explaining the purpose of the study and answering any questions that ASHAs had. Then we interviewed participants to collect information regarding demographic characteristics, socioeconomic status, health knowledge, experience with technology, and prior work experience. All interviews were done in Hindi with data collected electronically before being translated into English and analyzed using Stata.

After completing the initial interview, ASHAs participated in a two-hour, in-person training session in which they were taught to use the system. The training session was designed to gradually introduce ASHAs to graph concepts. At the beginning of the session, the ASHAs were shown the growth charts that they used to monitor a child's growth as an example of how a graph can represent important information. Then, simple bar charts were introduced that compared the costs of different food items or the amount of milk sold by different individuals. As the concepts became clear, specific examples that were relevant to ASHA work were introduced. After practicing interpreting these graphs in a large paper format, the ASHAs were provided with access to our system on their phones and taught to interpret the visualizations. Finally, the ASHAs were trained to use the voice-based system.

After completing the training session, participants were free to interact with both the web- and voice-based systems as often as they chose. Participating ASHAs also received a weekly SMS reminder that encouraged them to check their information. Throughout the study a research assistant was available to assist ASHAs if they encountered technical issues or to resolve confusion. At the study midpoint (6 months), we interviewed all participants to understand their opinions and experiences using the system, check their devices were working, and provide supplementary training if necessary. At the end of the 12-month deployment we performed semi-structured qualitative interviews with 19 participants. We interviewed a diverse subset of participants, including ASHAs with varying literacy levels and system usage patterns to create a representative sample of all participants. ASHAs were asked about their opinions of and reactions to the system, their preferences between the voice- and web-based systems, any confusion that they felt when looking at the visualizations, how the system affected their work processes and motivations, and their general usage habits. We also observed the ASHAs using the system and asked them questions about their understanding of the visualizations. In all of the interviews, we attempted to reduce participant response bias [9] by telling participants that negative feedback would be particularly useful and help us to improve the system, and by reminding them that their responses would remain anonymous.

Data Collection and Analysis

We used a mixed methods approach in our study. Our quantitative data consists of system usage logs that recorded when and how often ASHAs accessed the system, which interaction modalities they used, how often they looked at each of the different visualizations, and so on. For the web-based system, we recorded a timestamp and the specific visualization(s) accessed. For the voice-based system, we recorded a timestamp, the length of the phone call, and how much of the recording the ASHA listened to before disconnecting. We also created the notion of an active "session", which we defined as a period of interaction with one of the systems that terminated after 10 minutes of inactivity. If an ASHA called into the voice-system multiple times within a 10-minute window, this was treated as one voice session. If, during that time, she also used the web system, it would be counted as one web session and one voice session. Our qualitative data consists of semi-structured interview data collected at the beginning, middle, and end of the study. All interviews were conducted in Hindi and translated into English for analysis. After translation, two of the authors independently performed open coding on the interview data to identify common patterns and recurring topics of interest. The authors then met and discussed the topics and codes that had emerged before further clustering the data into major themes. Following this, we conducted iterative analyses to further refine the themes and organize our prominent findings that we present below.

FINDINGS

The goal of our study was to analyze ASHA opinions, preferences, and system usage behaviors to understand the ways in which giving them access to feedback impacted their motivations and work processes. We structure our findings around four main questions that show (1) how the system supported ASHA work processes; (2) how ASHAs made use of *both* the web- and voice-based systems; (3) how ASHAs used each of the three web-based visualizations for different reasons; and (4) how ASHAs felt about the feedback they received.

How did the system support ASHA work processes?

The system usage logs show that ASHAs used the system throughout the study to obtain information about their work. Figure 4 depicts the total number of web- and voice-based sessions for each ASHA during the 12-month study. The horizontal lines on the graph show users who accessed the system at least weekly (n = 40 or 56%) or five times per week (n = 5 or 7%). Only three ASHAs accessed the system less than an average of once a month. Qualitative interview data suggests that the system supported ASHAs by providing them with useful information about their work and that the feedback motivated them to do more work. However, ASHAs were sometimes prevented from doing work by external factors beyond their control. In these cases, the feedback reminded them of their poor performance and made them feel bad. We now discuss these findings in detail.

ASHAs found it useful to have information about their work

Our analysis revealed that the system supported ASHA work processes by providing them with useful information and feedback regarding their work, and many ASHAs described how they used the information provided by the system to understand their own productivity:

"[The system] is very good. It gives information about our work. It motivates us to do work. It is like a helper. And it also tells about the weakness in my work." (P2)

The 'weakness' mentioned by this ASHA refers to the fact that, in showing ASHAs how many clients they had visited out of the total number that they had registered, the system implicitly highlights not only how much work they have done, but also how much work is still remaining for the month:

"The system tells us information about our work, like on which dates I made visits, my last 5 months performance, how many people I have met, how many are remaining - it gives me all the information." (P19)

Several ASHAs also mentioned that looking at the visualizations helped them to plan their time, and the system acted as a reminder that they needed to complete their ASHA duties:

"I feel good ... I can know how much work I did. Like on 17 November I delivered a newborn so I couldn't make visits. But seeing the graph I think it's time to give a visit." (P3)

Being able to use the information provided by the system to plan their work was seen as a big improvement by many ASHAs, who said that previously they would just visit clients *"according to our own motivation."*

The system motivated ASHAs to do more work

Many of the ASHAs we interviewed described how the information that they received from the system motivated them to do more work. In some cases, ASHAs were motivated to reach a good position within their comparison group:

"I liked seeing how much work I had completed and how far ahead I am. I felt motivated to move ahead to the next position and do more work." (P18)

In other cases, ASHAs explained that they were instead motivated to try and achieve the greatest number of client visits by registering as many pregnant women as possible:

"I felt motivated ... like I completed eight home visits so by seeing this it motivated me to do more work. It also motivated me to add new pregnant women in my lists because then I can do more home visits." (P4)

This finding validates our choice to use the total number of client visits as the primary metric rather than the percentage of clients visited, which could incentivize ASHAs to register fewer women to achieve a higher percentage. Overall, the fact that the system motivated ASHAs to register more pregnant women is encouraging and highlights the potential for the system to positively impact ASHA work processes.

External challenges prevented ASHAs from doing their work

Although many ASHAs said that the system motivated them to do more work, several told us they felt discouraged when they were prevented from doing work by external factors out of their control. For example, many ASHAs and clients were

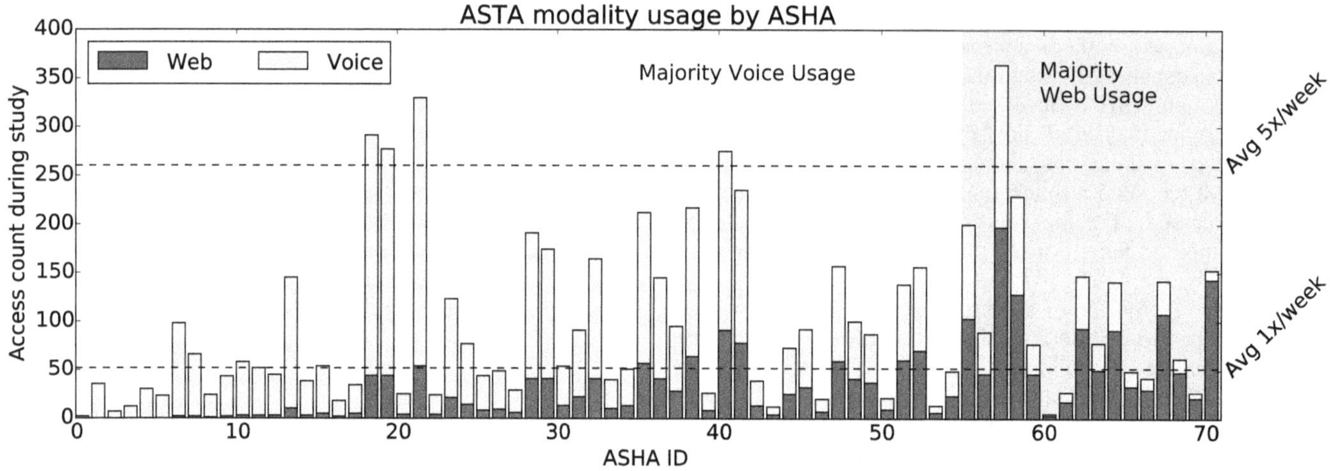

Figure 4. Individual ASHA usage of the voice and web systems during the study. The ASHAs are ordered from greater portion of voice-based use to greater portion of web-based use. The shaded region represents majority web use and the white region represents majority voice use. The two horizontal lines represent an average of weekly and daily (weekdays) system usage.

heavily involved in farming and these responsibilities sometimes prevented them from participating in ASHA visits:

"I feel bad when I cannot do much work. When I go to the home visits many people are not available because of harvesting which is why my work is less." (P5)

Several ASHAs also described how they often did not receive the money that was owed to them by the government and as a result they were not motivated to work. In these cases, the system continued to show the ASHA that she was performing poorly, which often made the ASHA feel bad despite her performance being justified by lack of compensation.

How did ASHAs use the web- and voice-based systems?

Figure 4 depicts the total number of usage sessions for each ASHA over the 12-month study. At a high level, the system usage data reveals that most ASHAs made use of *both* the web- and voice-based systems. The ASHAs in Figure 4 are ordered from greater portion of voice-based use to greater portion of web-based use. The shaded region on the right represents the tipping point where ASHAs used the web-based system for the majority of their sessions. Most ASHAs (n = 55, 77.5%) used the voice system more frequently than the web system. We now discuss the reasons ASHAs gave for preferring one system over another and why it was beneficial to provide more than one way to interact with the system.

Benefits and limitations of the web-based system

The main reason ASHAs gave for preferring the web system over the voice system was because the three visualizations provided a richer, more detailed description of their work:

"I like [the web-based system] more because there are three programs, like calendar, comparison, and previous five months, while the [voice-based] system only tells my position and the number of home visits." (P12)

In addition to providing a greater volume of information, ASHAs also appreciated that they were able to look at the visualizations for as long as they liked, which gave them time to interpret the graphs at their own pace. By contrast, the voice-based system delivered information at a constant pace and, if ASHAs missed some of the information, they would need to repeat the entire message. Some of the ASHAs also perceived that the voice-based system was provided primarily for illiterate ASHAs and that if they knew how to read they should rather use the web-based system:

"I like [the web system] because I have no difficulty reading. I think the [voice system] is for people who can't read." (P1)

Despite this perception, we found that the proportion of low-literate ASHAs in the majority web usage group and majority voice usage group was roughly equivalent (31.25% vs. 30.9% respectively), which suggests that literacy level did not play a significant role in determining system preference.

The main limitation of the web-based system that the ASHAs described was that the small size of the screen made it difficult to read and interpret the graphs. Moreover, when we asked the ASHAs to show us how they used the web-based system, we found that several of them were unable to read some of the numbers on the screen, which they explained was due to their poor eyesight and the *"very, very small"* size of the numbers.

Benefits and limitations of the voice-based system

The main reasons that ASHAs gave for preferring the voice-based system over the web-based system was that IVR was *"easier to use and takes less time."* ASHAs simply needed to leave a missed call and the system called them back:

"I like the [voice system]. You push the two button and you hear all of the information. I can use it as often as I want and it doesn't use my balance. And it is easy to use." (P14)

In addition to being easier to use, several ASHAs said that they liked the voice-based system because listening to information was more familiar for them than reading graphs. Several mentioned that they already used their phones for listening to songs, and so it made more sense to them to also listen to the information provided by the system. The voice-based system was also particularly useful for ASHAs who were illiterate, had poor eyesight, or who otherwise had difficulty interpreting the web-based visualizations.

The main limitations of the voice-based system were that it provided a relatively small amount of information compared to the web-based system and that, if ASHAs needed anything repeated, they had to listen to the entire message again. One ASHA also complained that she would have liked the automated voice-based system to respond and engage in conversation with her, telling us, *"She always just tells you things, but she never listens or talks with you." (P9)*

It was beneficial to provide multiple interaction modalities

The fact that most ASHAs used both the web-based and the voice-based systems suggests that it was beneficial for them to have more than one way of accessing information about their work. Many ASHAs explained that although they generally preferred to use the web-based system, they would use the voice-based system *"if I have less time or if the network is poor."* Others told us that they would use the voice-based system if their phone's battery was low or if they experienced technical difficulties accessing the web-based visualizations.

Several ASHAs pointed out that when a phone has zero balance, it is not possible to make a missed call to access the voice system. Similarly, when the data bundle expires, it is not possible to access the web system, though this was rare in practice. In either case, ASHAs would use their second choice system until the research assistant was able to address their barrier to access. These findings speak to the benefits of having more than one way to access information. Some ASHAs also liked to compare the information provided by the two systems to see if it matched, *"I like to cross check the visual and voice systems to see if they are consistent" (P5).* Finally, several ASHAs said that they used both systems because they wanted to try all of the options, while others felt obliged to use both simply because both had been provided.

How did ASHAs use the three web-based visualizations?

In addition to analyzing how ASHAs used the web- and voice-based interfaces, we were also interested to understand how they used the three different web-based visualizations. Figure 5 shows the proportion that each ASHA accessed each of the three visualizations as a percentage of the total number of times they used the web-based system. All but one of the ASHAs made use of all three visualizations during the study period, which is encouraging and suggests that each of the visualizations served a different purpose and provided ASHAs with different information. Overall, the comparison graph was used the most, followed by the calendar graph, with the historical graph used the least. In summary, 34 ASHAs accessed the comparison graph more than the other two visualizations, 23 accessed the calendar view the most, and 10 accessed the historical view the most, with four ASHAs accessing each of the visualizations equally. We now discuss the perceived value of the three web-based visualizations and the reasons that ASHAs gave for using each visualization.

Reasons for using the comparison graph

The main reasons that ASHAs gave for liking the comparison graph was that it showed them their position in the group, the amount of work they had done, and the amount of work remaining. Several ASHAs liked the visual depiction of the quantity of work completed, with one ASHA describing how the bar increased as she worked *"like a bucket filling with water until it is full and you are done."* Another ASHA explained how the visual appearance of the bar chart helped to make the information understandable even for illiterate ASHAs:

"Those ASHAs who cannot read, when they see the graph they can still know how much work they have completed and how much remains." (P10)

Reasons for using the calendar graph

Many of the ASHAs who liked the calendar view did so because they used calendars in their daily lives and were already familiar with the calendar-based information. The calendar view also clearly showed which days were holidays, and ASHAs expressed that they liked knowing when they were allowed to skip work. However, some ASHAs told us that they found the calendar view challenging to interpret and so they would ignore the calendar visualization:

"I used the calendar the least because I cannot easily understand it. So I do not spend much time on it. I just open it and then go on to the next page." (P15)

This finding highlights the benefits of providing a variety of different visualizations, since any one graph is unlikely to fit the needs and constraints of all ASHAs.

Reasons for using the historical graph

The historical graph showed the number of visits an ASHA made each month for the last five months, and many ASHAs liked that this graph provided a sense of prior work activities:

"I like the last five month performance because it is like a stair that my work is going up and down. I can see how many more [visits] I did and how many fewer." (P16)

ASHAs also described how this graph encouraged them to plan for the future, with several telling us how they would use information about their performance during the past month to plan their work for the next month. However, the ASHAs also told us that although they appreciated the historical information, they did not need to look at it as often as the other graphs since the information changed relatively infrequently:

"I don't look at the [historical graph] often because it doesn't change. You can look at it once and you don't need to look again. I look at the calendar and my performance more to see my information." (P10)

How did ASHAs feel about the feedback they received?

We chose to provide ASHAs with comparative feedback that shows their number of visits relative to a subset of their peers. This comparison introduced competitive elements among the ASHAs and different participants reacted to these elements in different ways. In addition to introducing competition, the feedback also prompted discussion among ASHAs and generally increased their awareness of each others' work.

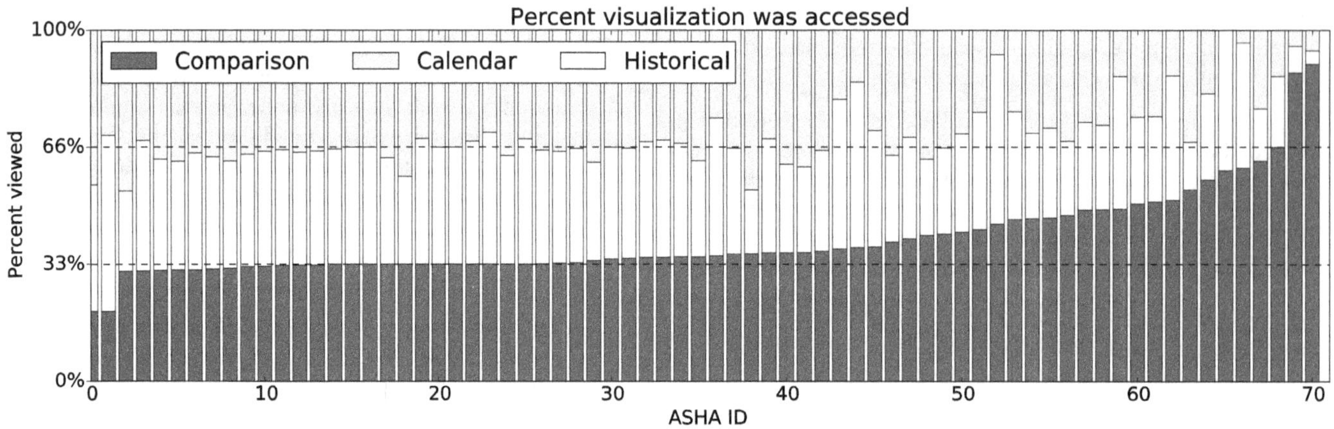

Figure 5. Individual ASHA usage of the three different web-based visualizations. The ASHAs are ordered by increasing use of the comparison graph.

Comparative feedback introduced competitive elements
Much of the data obtained from interviews with ASHAs suggested that the comparative feedback provided by the system introduced competitive elements to ASHA work. However, the effects that these competitive elements had on ASHAs differed between individuals. For example, some ASHAs told us that they were not affected by the competitive elements and that they simply focused on trying to do their work, claiming, *"I am only competing with myself"*. Other ASHAs were highly competitive and went so far as to blame the system or other external factors for even a small drop in their performance. For example, one competitive ASHA told us:

"I was always in the first place, except one time I was second, maybe because there was a problem with the network." (P1)

Many ASHAs explained that the competitive elements introduced by the system had a positive effect on their work by motivating them to visit more clients:

"I liked the [comparison graph] better because I could tell what my position was. I treated it as a competition which motivated me to do more work." (P4)

Unsurprisingly, ASHAs who achieved a high level of performance, and therefore a high overall position, said that the feedback provided by the system made them feel good about themselves. Many ASHAs also equated their position with the amount of work they had done, describing how if they were in first position, that meant that they had done 'enough' work, but if they were in last position it meant they should be working harder. However, the competitive elements introduced by our comparative feedback certainly did not work for all of the ASHAs, and in some cases had the adverse effect of making ASHAs feel bad about their work:

"It feels bad to see you are in the last position. After completing my work I was still in last position. I do not have very many pregnant women in my area." (P15)

As this ASHA points out, our choice to use the total number of visits made by an ASHA as the primary performance metric disadvantages ASHAs who work in areas with few pregnant clients. We chose this metric so that ASHAs would not be incentivized to register fewer clients but if an ASHA happens to not have many pregnant clients in her area, she will not be able to make many visits, and her overall performance will be low through no fault of her own. The fact that the feedback ended up discouraging some ASHAs is a negative consequence that we plan to address through future research (discussed in detail in our Discussion section).

The system prompted discussion among ASHAs
Many ASHAs described how the feedback provided by the system made them more aware of the other ASHAs operating in their area and prompted group discussions. Many ASHAs requested that we provide them with the names of the ASHAs in their comparison group so that they would know who they were being compared against. However, there was concern that publicly revealing the names of ASHAs who were performing poorly may further discourage them. Several ASHAs also described how they would get together as a group and discuss the information provided by the system. In addition to comparing their performance to each other by showing each other their personalized graphs, some ASHAs would use the group discussions to try and motivate low-performing ASHAs to do their work. For example, one of the high-performing ASHAs explained:

"Sometimes we discuss and I ask other ASHAs — who are these ASHAs in the bottom position? I explain to them — do your work so you are not in the bottom position." (P2)

Another example of ASHAs trying to help each other occurred when one ASHA used her device to play feedback for another ASHA who was experiencing technical difficulties:

"One time I played the IVR for another ASHA because hers was not working but mine was." (P12)

Unfortunately, since the voice-based feedback played by the system was personalized to the ASHA calling in, the information would only be relevant to that ASHA and would not have helped the ASHA experiencing technical difficulties. Nevertheless, it is encouraging that the system motivated ASHAs to help and support other ASHAs in their area.

DISCUSSION

Our analysis of how ASHAs used the system, combined with qualitative data that reveals ASHA opinions, feelings, and reactions to the feedback, demonstrates the value of providing ASHAs in low-resource environments with personalized, on-demand information that is derived from the data they have collected. Our findings and analysis also highlight rich opportunities for future research that focuses on designing and deploying new feedback mechanisms that may better support and motivate field workers in low-resource contexts. We now discuss some of the key takeaways from our work.

Designing feedback mechanisms and visualizations for low-literate ASHAs who do not have high levels of education or experience with technology required a large amount of patience, iteration, and in situ participatory design. Our experiences echo those described in a recent review of the HCI4D literature by Dell and Kumar [8], which points out, *"Just because the physical infrastructure has improved doesn't mean the human infrastructure has improved."* In our case, the technological infrastructure in India has improved to make it feasible to deploy two-way mobile communication systems in which ASHAs collect and submit data to the system, and the system in turn provides feedback to ASHAs. However, even though the technological infrastructure exists, a large amount of iterative design work was required to create a system that enables the humans in this ecosystem - the ASHAs - to understand and interpret the information provided. One key takeaway from our work is therefore that it demonstrates the importance of HCI4D researchers interested in designing for low-literate populations to spend time in the field ensuring that their system is delivering information that is relevant, understandable, and appropriate for the context.

Our work also highlights how new technologies should not be thought of in isolation, but rather in the context of a wide range of external factors that might impact ASHA work processes. For example, our findings show that ASHAs sometimes failed to receive the monetary compensation owed to them by the government and so were disincentivized from doing work. At other times, ASHAs and/or their clients needed to spend their time harvesting crops and so were unable to participate in home visits. All these factors make up the broad ecosystem in which the technology is being used and it is important to consider this larger context when designing, deploying, and evaluating new technology interventions.

Another key takeaway from our work centers on the nature of the comparative feedback provided by our system. Many of the ASHAs who participated in our study found it useful to receive feedback regarding their work and used the information provided to reflect on their own work practices, evaluate themselves, coordinate their activities, and plan for the future. However, in choosing to provide ASHAs with feedback that compared them to a subset of their peers, we also introduced competitive elements among the ASHAs, and our findings show that this competition affected ASHAs in different ways, motivating some participants while leaving others feeling discouraged. To overcome this limitation, we plan to conduct future research that explores a range of alternative feedback mechanisms that may appeal to ASHAs who are motivated in different ways. For example, we could explore more nuanced ways of measuring ASHA performance, such as by assigning different numbers of 'points' for different tasks. Using such a system, an ASHA who maybe has fewer clients registered, but whose clients engage in desired health behaviors, could still achieve high performance.

In addition, comparative feedback is certainly not the only kind of feedback that could be provided. For example, we plan to explore mechanisms that may encourage ASHAs by promoting teamwork [17], which may appeal to ASHAs who prefer collaboration over competition. Teams that achieve certain goals, or that are most improved, could then be publicly acknowledged by, for example, awarding a 'team of the month'. Moreover, we plan to explore how we might tailor the feedback provided to an individual ASHA based on personality types that could be identified through baseline surveys. For example, prior work suggests that personality traits may be tied to different motivational criteria for performance [19]. By identifying in advance whether or not an ASHA will be better motivated by, for example, competition or collaboration, we will be able to ensure that individual ASHAs receive feedback that is supportive and encouraging.

Finally, our work clearly highlights the benefits of providing participants with more than one way to interact with the system. The majority of ASHAs made use of both the web- and voice-based systems, with different ASHAs preferring each of the systems for different reasons. In addition, having multiple systems provided redundancy that enabled ASHAs to still access information even if one of the systems happened to be unavailable. We therefore recommend that other researchers working in low-resource contexts consider providing participants with multiple ways of interacting with the system.

CONCLUSION

This paper describes the design and deployment of mobile voice- and web-based systems that aim to support ASHAs by providing them with feedback regarding their work. We described the in-situ, participatory design approach that we used to create feedback systems that were appropriate and usable for low-literate ASHAs. We then described usage data from a 12-month deployment of the system with 71 ASHAs in India. We showed that the system supported ASHA work processes by providing motivation and information that helped their work. We also performed a detailed analysis of system usage and described ASHA opinions and feelings regarding the feedback that they received. Taken together, our findings yield valuable insights and lessons learned that will be useful to anyone interested in designing and deploying technologies with underserved populations in low-resource contexts.

ACKNOWLEDGMENTS

We thank all our ASHA participants for their time, feedback, and the important work they do; Vatsalya and CRS for being strong collaborators; and the research assistants for their hard work. This research was funded by the Massachusetts General Hospital Consortium for Affordable Medical Technologies (CAMTech) and NSF Grant No. IIS-1111433.

REFERENCES

1. 2011. Census of India. `http://censusindia.gov.in/2011-prov-results/paper2/data_files/UP/7-pop-12-22.pdf`. (2011).
2. 2012. Uttar Pradesh State Profile. `http://nrhm.gov.in/nrhm-in-state/state-wise-information/uttar-pradesh.html`. (2012).
3. 2013. *Baseline Study Summary: ReMiND*. Technical Report. Catholic Relief Services.
4. Matt Berg, James Wariero, and Vijay Modi. 2009. *Every child counts: The use of SMS in Kenya to support the community based management of acute malnutrition and malaria in children under five*. Columbia University.
5. Evan Borkum, Anitha Sivasankaran, Swetha Sridharan, Dana Rotz, Sukhmani Sethi, Mercy Manoranjini, Lakshmi Ramakrishnan, and Anu Rangarajan. 2015. *Evaluation of the Information and Communication Technology (ICT) Continuum of Care Services (CCS) Intervention in Bihar*. Technical Report. Mathematica Policy Research.
6. C Bourne, V Knight, R Guy, H Wand, H Lu, and A McNulty. 2011. Short message service reminder intervention doubles sexually transmitted infection/HIV retesting rates among men who have sex with men. *Sexually transmitted infections* 87, 3 (2011), 229–231.
7. Marshini Chetty and Rebecca E. Grinter. 2007. HCI4D: HCI Challenges in the Global South. In *CHI '07 Extended Abstracts on Human Factors in Computing Systems (CHI EA '07)*. 2327–2332.
8. Nicola Dell and Neha Kumar. 2016. The Ins and Outs of HCI for Development. In *Proceedings of the 2016 CHI Conference on Human Factors in Computing Systems (CHI '16)*. 2220–2232.
9. Nicola Dell, Vidya Vaidyanathan, Indrani Medhi, Edward Cutrell, and William Thies. 2012. "Yours is Better!": Participant Response Bias in HCI. In *Proceedings of the SIGCHI Conference on Human Factors in Computing Systems (CHI '12)*. ACM, New York, NY, USA, 1321–1330.
10. Brian DeRenzi, Leah Findlater, Jonathan Payne, Benjamin Birnbaum, Joachim Mangilima, Tapan Parikh, Gaetano Borriello, and Neal Lesh. 2012. Improving Community Health Worker Performance Through Automated SMS. In *International Conference on Information and Communication Technologies and Development (ICTD '12)*. 25–34.
11. Brian DeRenzi, Neal Lesh, Tapan Parikh, Clayton Sims, Werner Maokla, Mwajuma Chemba, Yuna Hamisi, Marc Mitchell, and Gaetano Borriello. 2008. e-IMCI: Improving pediatric health care in low-income countries. In *SIGCHI conference on human factors in computing systems*. ACM, 753–762.
12. Brian DeRenzi, Clayton Sims, Jonatham Jackson, Gaetano Borriello, and Neal Lesh. 2011. A framework for case-based community health information systems. In *Global Humanitarian Technology Conference (GHTC), 2011 IEEE*. IEEE, 377–382.
13. Brian DeRenzi, Jeremy Wacksman, Nicola Dell, Neal Lesh, Gaetano Borriello, and Scott Lee. 2016. Closing the Feedback Loop: A 12-month Evaluation of ASTA, a Self-Tracking Application for ASHAs. In *International Conference on Information and Communication Technologies and Development (ICTD '16)*.
14. Leah Findlater, Ravin Balakrishnan, and Kentaro Toyama. 2009. Comparing Semiliterate and Illiterate Users' Ability to Transition from Audio+Text to Text-only Interaction. In *SIGCHI Conference on Human Factors in Computing Systems (CHI '09)*. 1751–1760.
15. Jose F Florez-Arango, M Sriram Iyengar, Kim Dunn, and Jiajie Zhang. 2011. Performance factors of mobile rich media job aids for community health workers. *Journal of the American Medical Informatics Association* 18, 2 (2011), 131–137.
16. Carl Hartung, Yaw Anokwa, Waylon Brunette, Adam Lerer, Clint Tseng, and Gaetano Borriello. 2010. Open Data Kit: Building Information Services for Developing Regions. In *International Conference on Information and Communication Technologies and Development (ICTD)*. 10.
17. Guido Hertel, Udo Konradt, and Borris Orlikowski. 2004. Managing distance by interdependence: Goal setting, task interdependence, and team-based rewards in virtual teams. *European Journal of work and organizational psychology* 13, 1 (2004), 1–28.
18. M Sriram Iyengar, Jose F Florez-Arango, and Carlos A Garcia. 2009. GuideView: a system for developing structured, multimodal, multi-platform persuasive applications. In *International Conference on Persuasive Technology*. ACM, 31.
19. Timothy A Judge and Remus Ilies. 2002. Relationship of personality to performance motivation: a meta-analytic review. *Journal of applied psychology* 87, 4 (2002), 797.
20. Neha Kumar and Richard J. Anderson. 2015. Mobile Phones for Maternal Health in Rural India. In *Proceedings of the 33rd Annual ACM Conference on Human Factors in Computing Systems (CHI '15)*. ACM, New York, NY, USA, 427–436.
21. Neha Kumar, Trevor Perrier, Michelle Desmond, Kiersten Israel-Ballard, Vikrant Kumar, Sudip Mahapatra, Anil Mishra, Shreya Agarwal, Rikin Gandhi, Pallavi Lal, and Richard Anderson. 2015. Projecting Health: Community-led Video Education for Maternal Health. In *Proceedings of the Seventh International Conference on Information and Communication Technologies and Development (ICTD '15)*. ACM, New York, NY, USA, Article 17, 10 pages.

22. Walley J. Katabira E. Muchuro S. Balidawa H. Namagala E. Ikoona E. Kunutsor, S. 2010. Using mobile phones to improve clinic attendance amongst an antiretroviral treatment cohort in rural Uganda: a crosssectional and prospective study. *AIDS and behavior* 14, 6 (2010), 1347–1352.

23. Indrani Medhi, Somani Patnaik, Emma Brunskill, S.N. Nagasena Gautama, William Thies, and Kentaro Toyama. 2011. Designing Mobile Interfaces for Novice and Low-literacy Users. *ACM Trans. Comput.-Hum. Interact.* 18, 1 (May 2011).

24. Indrani Medhi, Aman Sagar, and Kentaro Toyama. 2006. Text-free user interfaces for illiterate and semi-literate users. In *Information and Communication Technologies and Development, 2006. ICTD'06. International Conference on*. IEEE, 72–82.

25. Maletsabisa Molapo and Gary Marsden. 2013. Software Support for Creating Digital Health Training Materials in the Field. In *International Conference on Information and Communication Technologies and Development: Full Papers - Volume 1 (ICTD '13)*. 205–214.

26. Neil Patel, Deepti Chittamuru, Anupam Jain, Paresh Dave, and Tapan S. Parikh. 2010. Avaaj Otalo: A Field Study of an Interactive Voice Forum for Small Farmers in Rural India. In *SIGCHI Conference on Human Factors in Computing Systems (CHI '10)*. 733–742.

27. Divya Ramachandran, John Canny, Prabhu Dutta Das, and Edward Cutrell. 2010a. Mobile-izing Health Workers in Rural India. In *SIGCHI Conference on Human Factors in Computing Systems (CHI '10)*. 1889–1898.

28. Divya Ramachandran, Vivek Goswami, and John Canny. 2010b. Research and Reality: Using Mobile Messages to Promote Maternal Health in Rural India. In *Proceedings of the 4th ACM/IEEE International Conference on Information and Communication Technologies and Development (ICTD '10)*. ACM, New York, NY, USA, 35:1–35:10.

29. Catholic Relief Services. 2016. www.crs.org. (2016).

30. Kentaro Toyama. 2010. Human-Computer Interaction and Global Development. *Foundations and Trends in Human-Computer Interaction* 4, 1 (2010), 1–79.

31. Aditya Vashistha, Edward Cutrell, Gaetano Borriello, and William Thies. 2015. Sangeet Swara: A Community-Moderated Voice Forum in Rural India. In *SIGCHI Conference on Human Factors in Computing Systems (CHI '15)*.

32. Vatsalya. 2016. www.vatsalya.org. (2016).

We Play We Learn: Exploring the Value of Digital Educational Games in Rural Egypt

Shaimaa Lazem, Hussein Aly Jad
City for Scientific Research and Technological Applications (SRTA-City)
New Borg El-Arab City, Alexandria, Egypt
{slazem@srtacity.sci.eg, hjad@srtacity.sci.eg}

ABSTRACT

The Egyptian education system faces urgent challenges. Proposed governmental reforms tend to focus on increasing access to physical and digital resources. There is insufficient understanding as to how the provided resources are currently used in rural areas. We explored the extent to which digital technology could motivate primary students to collaboratively learn a challenging topic in the National Mathematics Curriculum. We designed and researched a digital game to support memorizing multiplication facts. We used an incentive structure that encouraged individual learning with rewarding teamwork. The game was tested with mixed ability and gender groups of students using the Teams-Game-Tournament collaboration technique. A key outcome was that the students with educationally disadvantaged backgrounds benefited from using the game format. They devised their own play and study strategies. We discuss implications on future designs of the game, and considerations for its integration in Egyptian schools.

Author Keywords
Edutainment; Play; Game-Based Learning; Games; Collaborative Learning; ICTD; ICT4D; HCI4D; Egypt

ACM Classification Keywords
H.5.2 Information Interfaces and Presentation: User Interfaces—*input devices and strategies*, interaction styles; K.3.1 Computer And Education: Computer Uses in Education—*collaborative learning*

INTRODUCTION
The education system in Egypt faces urgent challenges. The curriculum focuses on learning for examination, and emphasizes memorizing rather than asking questions. There is little-to-no attention paid to lifelong and 21st century learning skills such as creativity, collaboration, and communication. Lack of teamwork skills is a frequent complaint from the labor market [13]. Lesson plans are centralized and rigid, which limits teachers' ability to try pedagogical approaches they see appropriate.

Warschauer [24] identified four categories all necessary to enable using Information and Communication Technologies (ICT) for development: Physical resources (i.e., computers and Internet), digital resources (i.e., software and digital material), human resources (i.e., trained teachers), and social resources, which refer to community, institutional, and societal structures that support access to ICT. Recent governmental implementations of reform strategies are centered on increasing access to physical and digital resources through equipping schools with computer labs and broadband connections, and producing digital versions of the National Curriculum. There is significantly less attention paid to human and social resources in rural schools. Further, there is insufficient understanding as to how the provided physical and digital resources are currently used. The literature shows that introducing technologies in developing countries is not sufficient in itself to produce positive educational outcomes [23].

The presented research explores using educational games, as a part of a socio-technical learning environment designed to provide an improved learning experience in a rural school. We designed and researched a digital game to support memorizing multiplication facts for primary students. Our contributions are 1) We demonstrate how the students with educationally disadvantaged backgrounds benefited from using the designed learning environment. 2) We show how the students achieved a balance between having fun and learning 3) We provide implications for future designs that could be deployed in similar contexts.

BASELINE RESEARCH: UNDERSTANDING THE NEEDS OF THE COMMUNITY
Borg El-Arab city, originally populated by Bedouin, is in the North-West coast of Egypt, about 40 KM west of the Alexandria metropolitan area. Borg El-Arab had major developments in the past couple of decades, with the establishment of an industrial zone, a science park, an airport, and a stadium. It then attracted immigrants from other country and urban areas in Egypt. Old Borg El-Arab is part of the city that is mainly populated by Bedouin, and the least receiving to governmental services.

Permission to make digital or hard copies of all or part of this work for personal or classroom use is granted without fee provided that copies are not made or distributed for profit or commercial advantage and that copies bear this notice and the full citation on the first page. Copyrights for components of this work owned by others than ACM must be honored. Abstracting with credit is permitted. To copy otherwise, or republish, to post on servers or to redistribute to lists, requires prior specific permission and/or a fee. Request permissions from Permissions@acm.org.
CHI 2017, May 06-11, 2017, Denver, CO, USA
© 2017 ACM.
ISBN 978-1-4503-4655-9/17/05...$15.00
DOI: http://dx.doi.org/10.1145/3025453.3025593

The researched primary school was in Old Borg El-Arab, where 60% of its students were city residents and 40% lived in villages far from the school. The school had a computer lab that accommodated up to 30 students and contained ten personal computers. Computer classes were optional for primary students. The computer activities included watching cartoons, children songs, and digital curriculum software. About 12 students visited the lab on regular basis.

Our interview with a schoolteacher revealed some stresses students and teachers experience in the school. The teachers, despite being specialized in one subject (e.g., math), had to teach other topics due to the lack of qualified teachers in that rural community. Moreover, teacher training opportunities were rare. On average, three students from each classroom were expected to leave the school after the primary stage (6 years) as their parents would not appreciate the value of further education. Sometimes parents would keep male students in the school if they get good grades.

In her class, about 50% of students found mathematics difficult. Multiplication facts were particularly challenging as the curriculum had one semester gap between teaching multiplication facts, and teaching division. The students struggled with the later if they were not fluent in memorizing the facts. Her teaching pedagogy focused on helping the students memorize the facts through hand counting, or incremental addition. She tried to engage them using activities such as signing and interactive plays. She posted the activities on the school Facebook group to involve their parents as well. She did some experiments with collaborative activities (e.g., team competitions) that appealed to her students. She did not continue her attempts because the physical set up of her classroom was not supportive for teamwork, and she had to rotate all the desks for each collaborative activity.

We conducted interviews with 13 students from the chosen school, eight of them were Bedouin. The students were from the third grade (eight and nine year olds). All of them, except three from Bedouin origins, had computers at home. They used them to play games that were not "educational". The students' favorite subjects were (some of them reported more than one subject): 8 Arabic (the mother tongue language), 4 mathematics, 3 English, 1 French, and 1 drawing. The students preferred school subjects that they thought easy, fun to study, and/or useful. For instance, they reported that studying Arabic helped them learn new words, and write letters to friends. The students did not receive detailed feedback on their homework or their exam sheets.

We further administrated an individual questionnaire about learning mathematics. The questionnaire was an appropriated, shortened, and translated version from the Motivated Strategies for Learning Questionnaire [17]. The adapted questionnaire included 13 questions with 5-point Likert scales. We used sad and happy smiley faces in the scale so the students could easily mark their preferences. A researcher was present to explain the questions to the students. The students' responses to the following question were considerably negative.

Q: Even when I do poorly on a test I try to learn from my mistakes ("Strongly disagree", reported 7 times)

The question was related to the intrinsic value of learning mathematics. The students' inability to learn from their mistakes, we argued, aligned with their complaints about not receiving feedback on their schoolwork. We did not feel the teacher would be comfortable discussing this issue with us.

SUPPORTING LEARNING USING TECHNOLOGY

Based on our understanding of the community needs, synthesizing the literature, and our observations during pilot studies, we developed the following design criteria.

Conceptualizing learning: The teacher spent most of her time assisting the students in rehearsing and memorizing the multiplication facts instead of explaining different representations and models for multiplication, and solving complex examples. Further, the students did not often receive sufficient feedback on their exam and school reports. The fact that the school served the Bedouin community, where many of the parents were illiterates, could explain the teacher's need to practice inside the classroom as the parents would not necessarily help the students at home.

The review by Kirkwood and Price [11] showed that in technology-enhanced learning, there are multiple reasons for designing technology interventions: replicating or supplementing existing teaching practices, or transforming students' experience through structural changes of learning activities. We argued that the learning experience for the students in the researched school could be enhanced by offloading the multiplication facts practice on the part of technology. We therefore conceptualized learning as memorizing the multiplication facts. Further, our view of enhancing learning included the quantitative improvements of memorization times and test scores, and the qualitative changes in learning (e.g., students' engagement with and attitudes towards technology).

Minimal Intervention: we proposed embedding the learning component in the technology intervention. Therefore, the learning environment could be administrated by a facilitator rather than a qualified teacher. The teacher's time could be then dedicated to helping the students understand the mathematical underpinnings of multiplication.

Digital Games: the students were lacking motivation in their current learning environment. We proposed a technology intervention in the format of a game as educational games were proved successful in engaging students with challenging topics [26].

Retrieval Practice: following our characterization of learning as memorizing, the game employed the retrieval practice learning strategy. That is, encouraging the students to get information "out" of their minds through practice [1].

Team Play: we proposed a collaborative game design to allow the students who lack educational support at home to benefit from interacting with more capable peers.

Visible Play: during the pilot studies, we tested multiple game prototypes with two input styles: an interactive floor, and a keyboard. The physical movement on the floor made the students' recall tactics and their effort to memorize visible to their peers thus encouraging them to help one another. Therefore, we used the interactive floor in our study.

RELATED WORK

Digital games have been explored to assist students develop conceptual understanding [4,8] and/ or achieve fluency in memorizing multiplication facts [18]. Plass et al., [20] compared individual, competitive, and collaborative play of a multiplication facts game. The competition and collaboration modes of play led to more enjoyment. Further, collaboration increased students' willingness to play the game again, while competition led to greater in-game learning. Bakker [2] compared three conditions for playing online multiplication games in a wide-scale longitudinal study. The treatment conditions were: playing at school, playing at home, and playing at home with debriefing at school. The last condition was found to be the most effective.

The previous studies took place in developed education systems, where students were likely to receive reasonable support from school and/or home. It was difficult to predict a similar impact or attitude towards technology in our rural school given that play is sometimes considered an unaffordable goal in developing countries [9]. We informed our design with literature that explored technology use in similar low-resource contexts.

Using low-cost interfaces for educational entertainment (edutainment) applications was introduced in [22], and [25]. An information kiosk was designed including a computer that was fully contained behind a shop window. Street kids accessed the computer by tracking their fingers on an inexpensive fabric externally mounted on the shop window.

Minimal invasive learning was introduced by Sugata Mitra after his famous Hole-in-the-Wall experiments [17]. Mitra left an unattended computer fixed to a slum wall in India. The slum children learned how to use the computer and the Internet on their own. When tested, they achieved comparable scores to students who studied school computing curriculum [10,14]. Dangwal and Thounaojam [7] showed that children at the Hole-in-the-wall learning stations adopted self-regulatory learning strategies. The strategies were correlated with self-motivation that derived the children to determine their learning goals, plan, observe, and evaluate their behavior. Dangwal and Kapur [6] further examined the social patterns used by children while working on those stations. They explored knowledge transmission and sharing along with self-learning strategies employed by the children, while they learned computer skills. They collected data from 250 children in 17 sites across India for nine months (average age 10-11 year olds). They identified individual learning strategies (e.g., trial and error, rehearsal, self-discovery, demonstration, verbal input, observation, practice and drill) that were used by the children. The group learning strategies included outsider help, input from peer leader, and practice and drill. The children learned in groups and kept working individually to consolidate what they learned and master the computer skills. Dangwal and Kapur [5] provided insights into group dynamics at the Hole-in-the-wall stations. The learning stations built on the children curiosity to learn so they became active learners who explored the world alone and with the help of their peers.

MULTIPLICATION FACTS GAME

This section describes the hardware and software components of the game.

Interactive Mat

The interactive mat (Figure 1) was introduced in [12] as a low-cost technology that could be used for edutainment applications. The technology consisted of a computer, a thick brown paper mat, and an inexpensive webcam. The floor mat was the game playground or its input physical space. It contained a nine-block grid (3× 3). In a standard set up, the computer running the game was connected to the camera for position tracking, and a data show to project the game on a wall. The camera was mounted on the ceiling, and the floor mat was encompassed in the camera's field of view. The movement on the mat was tracked by the camera and mapped into one of the nine blocks. The game interface had a nine-block grid matching the floor grid. Since almost every school in Borg El-Arab had a data show, and at least one computer in its lab, the proposed setup was affordable.

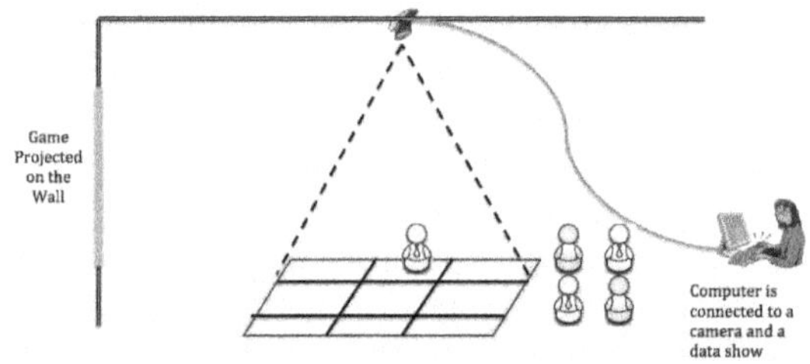

Figure 1: Interactive Mat, Figure replicated from [12].

Game Mechanics and Interface

The multiplication facts game was designed to help the students memorize facts using retrieval practice. The game had ten basic levels matching multiplication tables from one to ten. In a typical play scenario, a student started at the first basic level (multiplication table 1). After correctly solving a pre-defined number of questions, the student was qualified to play in the next level and so forth. Starting from the basic level 3, the game had revision levels following each basic level. Questions in a revision level were picked randomly from the previous basic levels. The purpose of including a revision level was to reward the student for successfully passing a basic level (i.e., memorizing a new table), by solving less challenging questions and gaining game points.

Figure 2 shows a snapshot from the game interface. The question on the screen had eight possible answers matching the eight blocks of the mat (game board). The block in the middle was used for camera calibration. The potential answers were randomly distributed on the game board, where one answer was correct. The incorrect answers were put according to a parameter called board_difficulty. The parameter took values between zero and seven, and hence each question had 8 possible boards. The board_difficulty represented the number of wrong answers that could be confused with the right answer (e.g., the digits were swapped, + or - one to the correct answer). For instance, a zero board_difficulty indicated that all the mistaken answers were 3-digit numbers and thus cannot be confused with a correct answer, which was often a 2-digit number.

When a student stood on a certain block, the block number was sent to the game. The text matching the block, on which the student stood, turned to red and a depleting progress bar appeared to signal the remaining time until submitting the answer. Based on our pilot studies, we used six seconds as the timeout value. If the student changed the block before the bar ends, the timeout value was reset to six seconds. Upon submitting the answer, a visual feedback appeared to the student denoting a right or a wrong solution. For each basic or revision level, the questions were chosen randomly from a question bank. The game adapted to the individual differences in learning by allowing students to advance at their own pace. The questions were selected from the same level until the student correctly answered a pre-defined number of questions to pass that level. Table 1 shows the game parameters that were refined in the pilot studies.

According to the framework introduced by Borkulo et al. [3] for multiplication facts games, the game design provided the following learning-supportive characteristics. *Challenge*: the game challenged students to answer as many questions as they could in their turns, and to correctly solve a certain number of questions to pass a basic or a revision level and enter the next level. Furthermore, we arranged team competitions. *Feedback*: the game showed whether a submitted answer was correct or wrong. The score was shown on the screen right top corner so students could check their progress with respect to the other players. *Reward*: students were rewarded by reaching the next game level when the challenge was fulfilled. There was a form of external recognition in our setup, when a winner team was announced. *Practice*: for each basic level x, the question bank included 12 possible questions ($x \times 1$ to $x \times 12$), where each question had 8 possible boards. That led to 96 possible practice options for table x. Since the questions were randomly selected, some of them were repeated to students with different board_difficulty, and thus the students had numerous opportunities to practice the same question. They had additional practice in revision levels. For the domain-specific supportive characteristics, the game provided practice of the commutative property ($a \times b = b \times a$).

Figure 2: A snapshot from the multiplication facts game.

Parameter	Value
Turn time	2 mins
Progress bar timeout	6 secs
# of questions per board_difficulty in basic levels	3
# of correct questions to pass a basic level	16
# of correct questions to pass a revision level	12
Maximum board_difficulty in a revision level	8

Table 1: Game parameters refined over multiple pilot studies.

APPROACH

Our research team included a former math teacher, who established a rapport with the school administration, teachers, and students. Over one year, the team conducted the baseline research and ran several pilot studies in the school's computer lab to refine the game parameters. We could not run the formal study as an after-school club since all the school activities had to end at 2 PM allowing students enough time to reach their homes in daylight. We ran the study in our lab during the winter break. The school arranged for picking up the participating students from their homes, and we picked them up from the school. Two staff members from the school were present with the students all the time.

Participants

Chosen students were recruited with the help of the teacher we interviewed, who provided the history of potential participants' grades. The students were selected to form a mixed ability and gender sample. The school communicated with their families, and helped us getting the parents' consents. The study was observed by two schoolteachers. The students were informed they could withdraw at any point. We selected ten students from the school, all in the third primary grade (ages between eight and nine year olds). Another three students, from higher grades (4th to 6th), joined the trial. Two students were added based on a request from our gatekeeper to the school, and the third was the son of a schoolteacher. It is worth noting that refusing to take the new students would have been interpreted as if we refuse to help community children. Further, it would have affected the trust we built with the school. We managed to enroll them in our setup by categorizing them based on their pre-test results as explained in the next section.

We started the trial with 13 students (8 males and 5 females). Only eight students (5 males and 3 females) continued until the last day as shown in Table 2. Four students dropped because the study coincided with emerged family plans for the winter break. One student was dismissed when he bullied another student. In the pilot studies, we observed that some students did not attend school regularly. We thus considered the commitment from the eight students as a positive sign, especially the trial took place during their school break.

Many of the students had their own mobile phones or tablets with them. We did not ban using the electronic devices during the trial. We asked them to stop using the devices when they were fully distracted from the study, often playing games. That happened once or twice in the whole trial.

Study Description

We administrated a pre-test in the first day of the trial that included questions covering the multiplication facts. The questions were similar to the practice problems in the school workbook. The students solved the test individually. The test was marked out of 20 points. Based on their scores, the students were divided into 4 categories ($A \geq 15$, $15 > B \geq 10$, $10 > C \geq 5$, and $5 > D \geq 0$), and assigned to three teams (T1, T2, and T3 as shown in Table 2).

We used the Teams-Games-Tournament (TGT) collaboration technique [21]. In a typical TGT, mixed ability and gender teams have the chance to revisit the material together as a team. Then, the teams play in a tournament, where team representatives (with the same ability), play against each other. The representatives' scores of each team are added together to form the team score.

In our TGT, each team was seated on a table, and given one revision sheet that had multiplication facts from table one to table ten. We did not provide review instructions to the teams. Instead, we suggested they ask one another questions from the sheet. Further, the students' roles in the teams were not assigned by the researchers. The review phase took ten to 15 minutes. The tournaments started after the students finished the review. The students took turns to play, each turn was timed to two minutes (Table 1). A and B students from the three teams played in one tournament, while C and D students played in a second tournament. Since the students could benefit from watching the game feedback before their turn, we randomized the students' order in every tournament to avoid such learning effect. We explained to the students that to excel in the game, they needed to correctly solve as many questions as they could in their turns.

A round was completed when all the students took turns in their tournaments. The students played four to five rounds. They had a lunch break after the second or the third round. We frequently checked whether the students experienced physical fatigue, and provided chairs so the spectators could sit and watch the play. The students' scores in the tournament were shown on the game interface. We recorded the tournaments' scores on a white board. At the end of each day, we gathered the students around the white board and announced the winner team of the day. A team score was calculated as the mathematical mean of its representatives' scores in all the rounds. We used the mean so the team would not be penalized when some team members did not show up. We explained the purpose of using the mean and the calculation method to the students. The scoring system rewarded individual learning and teamwork [21].

The schoolteachers observed the study, and we agreed that they would not interfere with the students' activities. The research team had three members. One focused on data collection instruments and registering the students to the game at the tournament time. Two researchers facilitated the sessions by guiding the students to their team tables, maintaining the scores on the white board, and randomizing the students' order in the tournaments.

We set a contract with the students before they join the trial. As they watch the game, they should not shout with the correct answer if a player does not know it. That was a behavior we observed in the pilot studies. We explained that getting scores by cheating would not help the player to learn multiplication facts. A couple of days after the trial started, we had to set another policy. Five points were deducted from the team score for each time a student misbehaved with her/his colleagues (e.g., light pushing). Such behaviors were considered typical in a Bedouin-dominant community, especially the trial was perceived as a play experiment more than a typical classroom. The schoolteachers thought the deduction policy was appropriate. We would advise the penalized student and her/his team several times, since it is a team punishment. We would then write a note about the deduction on the board. We removed the note if the students managed to apologize to each other. Otherwise, we implemented the deduction when the teams' scores were calculated, and the winner team was announced.

The trial lasted for eight days. On the ninth day, we invited the students to receive awards based on their collective team performances; nonetheless, we awarded all of them.

Research Questions

The research questions aimed at identifying quantitative and qualitative improvements, if any, to the students' learning experience as a direct result of the designed learning environment. We use the term environment because the design included social resources (peer students), and material resources (the paper-based revision sheet, the white board, and the digital game), all of which contributed to the students' learning experience. The first question explored quantitative improvements of students' performances in memorizing multiplication facts. The second and third questions focused on qualitative developments. The second question examined the students' use of self-regulation strategies to take control of their learning without the teacher's guidance. Such behavior was evidenced in the minimally invasive Hole-in-the-Wall experiments [7]. The third question examined the implications of designing the digital intervention in the format of a game.

RQ1: Did the students' performances improve in memorizing multiplication facts? to what extent?

RQ2: How, if any, did the students (individuals or teams) use self-regulation skills during the revision phase?

RQ3: What, if any, were the perspectives brought by the game play to the students' learning experience?

DATA COLLECTION

We recorded videos for each team at the review time, and for all the students at the tournament time, when they gathered around the mat to play. The game logged, for each student, the questions they answered correctly and the time they took to answer them. Further, semi-structured interviews were conducted with each team in the last day of the trial to reflect on their learning experience. The teams were told that reporting negative comments will help us with developing the next version of the game. Each student had a chance to answer. The questions included: Did you like the game? why/why not? What did you do to score in the game? What do you think about group play? Did you encounter any physical fatigue? What did you do when your group members did not get good scores or when they did not show up to the trial? Who is your favorite player/team?

An individual post-test, with difficulty comparable to the pre-test, was administrated after the last day of the trial. The students were not informed about the test in advance. We did not arrange a team review session before the post-test.

DATA ANALYSIS

We used a mixed-method analysis approach as follows. For RQ1, we compared the pre-test and post-test scores. We further used the game data to examine the improvements in "thinking time", or the time between the question's appearance on the screen and the student's standing on the answer block. As for RQ2 and RQ3, we transcribed the recorded videos of the review and play sessions. The transcription included the students' talk, their interaction and play techniques, and spectators' behavior. We further transcribed the interviews. We used the transcriptions to devise individual and team profiles. The team profile described the team members' review strategies with any other interesting observations from the videos. The individual profile described the student's background information, play technique, and views as expressed in the interview. We used the profiles to answer RQ2 and RQ3.

FINDINGS

RQ1: Improvements in Memorizing Multiplication Facts

A paired-samples t-test was conducted to compare the pre-test and the post-test results for the eight students who completed the trial. A significant difference was found between the scores of the pre-test (M= 10.25, SD= 5.31) and the post-test (M= 15.63, SD= 3.50), with p-value= $0.01 < 0.05^*$. Table 2 shows the tests' results.

The two A students remained in the same category. The two B students advanced to category A, while three C students progressed to category B. One student, Stu05, progressed from category C to category A. Stu05, though finishing the game at basic level six, achieved an A-level performance in the post-test. That, in turn, suggested she did not only learn from her play, but also from reviewing with her team, and/or watching other students' play in advanced levels.

Student	Gender	Team	Pre-test score – out of 20 - (category)	Post-test score – out of 20 - (category)	Last Basic Level
Stu01	M	T1	17 (A)	20 (A)	10
Stu02	F	T1	6 (C)	11 (B)	9
Stu03	M	T1	13 (B)	16 (A)	7
Stu04	M	T1	0 (D)	N/A	1
Stu05	F	T2	5 (C)	19 (A)	6
Stu06	F	T2	11 (B)	18 (A)	7
Stu07	M	T2	18 (A)	17 (A)	10
Stu08	M	T2	7 (C)	N/A	5
Stu09	F	T2	4 (D)	N/A	2
Stu10	M	T3	5 (C)	12 (B)	7
Stu11	M	T3	7 (C)	12 (B)	8
Stu12	M	T3	20 (A)	N/A	7
Stu13	F	T3	2 (D)	N/A	1

Table 2: The students' pre-test and post-test scores (N/A indicates dropping out from the trial). The right column presents the last basic level completed by the student.

Figure 3 shows the mean "thinking time" across the game levels, and its corresponding linear regression trends. The "thinking time" was calculated for the questions that were correctly answered. Therefore, the decrease in "thinking time" reflects an improvement in memorization skills.

The "thinking time" for all the students (except for Stu06) decreased as they progressed in the game levels. Stu06 thinking time increased as she progressed suggesting she found higher multiplication tables difficult to memorize. The A students, Stu01and Stu07, had the lowest "thinking time", aligning with them being the high achievers in the tests' scores. Their "thinking time" slightly reduced as they advanced in the game levels.

Stu05 showed the steepest curve aligning with the fact that she progressed from category C to category A.

Even though the "thinking time" of Stu02 showed an exemplary trend as she finished the basic level 9, her achievements were not mirrored in the post-test. She scored

11 out of 20 (borderline B). Reviewing her profile revealed that she preferred to do homework with her father because she often worried about making mistakes. We thus argued that teamwork provided her with the self-assurance she needed to progress in the game, the thing that she missed when she solved the post-test alone.

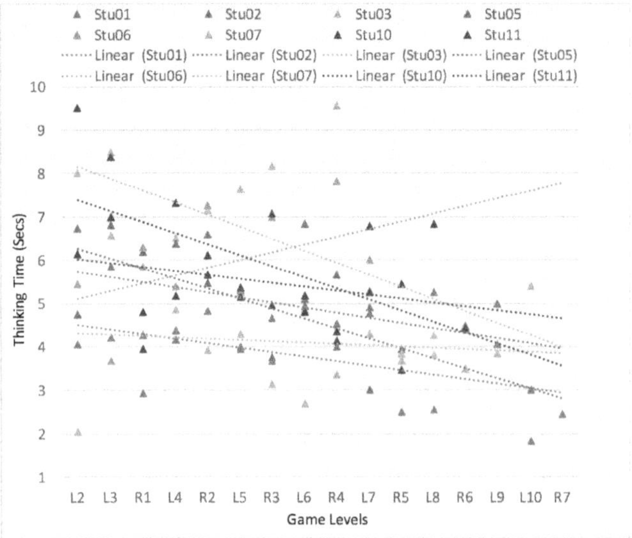

Figure 3: Mean thinking time in basic levels (Ls) and review levels (Rs) for all the students. We start by L2 since L1 (multiplication table 1) does not require memorization.

RQ2: Self-Regulatory Behavior

Self-regulatory behavior is an essential quality for students' learning and academic progress. It includes three components: actual cognitive strategies students use to learn (e.g., rehearsal), students' meta-cognitive strategies for planning, monitoring, and modifying their cognition; and students' management and control of their effort to maintain cognitive engagement [17].

Cognitive Strategies

On the first day, the students noticed that the revision sheet had the multiplication tables from one to ten, while the game included questions such as $x \times 11$ and $x \times 12$. That was an unintended mistake from the research team. The students completed the revision sheet with the missing facts. We believe the behavior started in one team, and replicated by the other two teams. When the students did not know the answers to the new questions (i.e., $x \times 12$), they asked the research team for assistance.

Some students started the rehearsal for the game at home, the night before, or in the morning while they were waiting for the bus. On the bus, the teacher accompanied them wrote the multiplication facts on small notes, and they used it to practice. The teams adopted various revision and rehearsal strategies as follows.

Team members took turns in holding the revision sheet and reading aloud, where each student read one multiplication table of her/his choice. Alternatively, they put the sheet on the table, where all of them could see the answers, and one student read aloud. A singing strategy is where the whole team repeated the multiplication facts. Moreover, they used review strategies that focused on questions and answers. For instance, one student asked questions from the sheet, and the rest took turns to answer. As another option, a student repeated a multiplication table from memory, a second student held the sheet and corrected any mistakes in the rehearsal. One team, T2, had trouble memorizing multiplication table seven. They divided the table into chunks, each included 3 questions (i.e., 7×1, 7×2, 7×3). They repeated each chunk ten times, asked one another questions about that chunk, and then moved to the next one.

Metacognitive strategies

The students identified gaps in their knowledge or multiplication tables they found difficult to memorize without help from the research team. Further, they put more effort in rehearsing those tables. Stu10 had difficult time memorizing table six. He asked one of his teammates to review the table with him (i.e., Stu10 rehearsed the table from memory, and his teammate corrected his mistakes). Further, Stu10 read the table loudly from the sheet, and then asked another teammate to review the table again with him. Another example is Stu06, who decided to review table seven although she was playing basic level four.

The team T1 agreed that each student should review the multiplication facts required for her/his next level in the game. Stu01, A-level student and the team leader, monitored the performance of the team. At revision time, he asked his teammates random questions from their assigned multiplication tables. If they made many mistakes, the team would review the tables together. Stu01 praised his team when they answered his revision questions, even if they did not do well later in the game. When he observed they were getting low scores, he suggested a punishment policy that his father used with him. They rehearsed the table and then took turns to ask and answer questions. If someone answered incorrectly, another teammate would hit her/him gently on the back of the hand several times (they agreed on the number of times). When we discussed their policy in the interview, they thought it was, at least partially, beneficial.

- *Stu01: Stu02 got 310 instead of 270.*
- *Stu02: yes, the punishment worked for me*
- *Stu03: It worked a bit for me, I did not care about it, the most important thing was to memorize.*

Management and Control of Effort

The students were not focused on watching the game all the time. We witnessed incidents such as a student was playing the game, and two male students were waiting for their turns and fully concentrating on the game questions. At the same time, two female students were playing a traditional girls' game. The other students were alternating between talking and watching the game. The students controlled their effort during the session. They would focus right before their turn "*When Stu07 played before me, I concentrated while he played.*". Some students used the game time, when they were not playing, for revision "*I reviewed with the person sitting next to me, we took turns to whisper the answer [...] sometimes, when no one was available to review, I did it by myself*".

The students' might have been previously aware of the cognition and metacognition strategies. Nonetheless, the literature suggests they must be motivated to use them [17]. The learning environment, we argue, provided sufficient motivation for the students to develop or use previously known self-regulation strategies.

RQ3: Examining the Students' Play

The students reported in the interview they liked the game because it taught them the multiplication facts through a novel playful experience. Our observations supported what the students said. Despite the competition, when a student played, spectators from all the teams cheered and supported her/him. They cheered "bravo" for the correct answer and "yeee" for the wrong one. When a student was close to score 100, for the first time in the game, everyone cheered "100..100". Some spectators, occasionally, hugged the player after finishing his turn on the mat. They praised play techniques who led to the highest individual scores.

Stu01, A-level student, once cried when his teammates got bad scores. After comforting him, we discretely discussed his emotional reaction. He felt he was putting extra effort to increase his scores but his team was letting him down. We explained to him that he was learning and progressing, which was valuable. We encouraged him to explore ways by which he could assist his teammates to get better scores.

The physical interaction on the mat made visible the play strategies adopted by the students during their "thinking time". We summarize them as follows.

Strategy a: a student moved directly to the correct answer if s/he knew it (mostly adopted by A-level students).

Strategy b: a student stepped away from the camera's field of view or kept rotating on the mat, while rehearsing the multiplication table from the beginning. When s/he identified the answer, s/he stood on the corresponding block.

Strategy c: a student stood on a random block, and rehearsed the table from the beginning, while monitoring the progress bar at the same time. When the progress bar was about to end, and the student did not figure out the answer, s/he moved to another block to reset the bar time. When s/he decided on answer, s/he stood on the matching block.

Strategy d: Stu05 adopted a shortcut strategy, when all the blocks had 3-digit numbers except for one block that included a 2-digit number, (i.e., *board_difficulty*=0), she would immediately stand on the 2-digit block. Her strategy was then adopted by the rest of the students. She monitored whether the strategy worked all the time or not. In the interview, she told us that once Stu01 stood on a block that was corresponding to a 3-digit answer and the game showed he was correct. She recalled the question, 10×11, and we told her that the correct answer was a 3-digit number.

Strategy e: another shortcut strategy, was initially suggested by us, when we observed that some students kept moving on the mat for a relatively long time without deciding on the answer. We suggested submitting a random answer so they use the remaining time to solve other game questions.

The students perceived the timeout (the duration of the red progress bar) according to their ability. High achievers (A students) thought it was very long to wait for six seconds after standing on the correct block, as they could use the time to solve more questions. Other students thought it was quite short, as they needed more time to recall the correct answer. Stu03 thought the progress bar was the best thing about the game. When he did not know the answer to a question and the bar ended, he was pleased that he did not need to think about the question.

Some students employed distinctive body postures during their play: jumping or walking to the answer block, putting the hands in pockets, or holding the hands in front of the body. We believe they did so, at least partly, to be accurately captured by the camera, based on some issues with the lighting in the pilot studies. The students did not try to mimic the play techniques or body postures of one another except for employing the shortcut *Strategies d* and *e*. They did not discuss their techniques during the revision time. We believe they were trying to develop personal play styles that were not necessarily relevant to memorizing multiplication facts.

DISCUSSION

We feel that our strongest contribution is evidencing the transformative effect for integrating ICT in educational settings, when technology responds to local challenges. In the studied community, the challenges were: the limited opportunities for the teacher to develop her practice, the lack of social support and academic feedback for the students, and the lack of motivation to study mathematics. The research showed the feasibility of shifting the rote learning to the game. The designed learning environment helped the students maintain or advance their academic achievements. The students developed mutual dependence in rehearsing the facts and used self-regulation strategies during the team phase, with minimal supervision from adults, supporting the findings from [7]. The teacher could improve her pedagogy through using the time spared by the game to focus on the conceptual understanding of multiplication, and integrate 21st century learning skills in her lessons. Incorporating visible play in the game mechanics made the students' thinking explicit, and allowed them to receive feedback on their strategies. The shortcut *Strategy e* encouraged the students not to spend too much time on a difficult question and attempt others. Practiced in the game, the strategy could potentially benefit medium and low achievers in exams.

The results have limitations stemming from the small sample of students and the fact that the experiment was conducted in a lab during the school break. The study period was short and the findings could have been influenced by the novelty of the technology. The positive results from our small study motivated the school to engage in future design-based research. We utilize our working relationship with the school to plan follow-up studies in school settings.

Our findings support the studies arguing that a successful integration of ICT in educational settings does not stop at introducing physical and digital resources [23]. In the researched school, the computer lab had ten underutilized computers. Our design required one computer and a bespoke game, combined with peer-learning as a social resource to positively affect the students' study skills and their academic accomplishments. Moreover, the students achieved a balance between fun and learning with almost no effort on our part to reinforce such balance. Therefore, the study contributes to the debate about the role of play in ICT for development [9] by demonstrating that a fun learning experience is a practical goal in developing countries.

Implications

Based on our findings and observations, we suggest the following design implications.

Accommodate high achievers adopting group assessment approach put the high achievers at a disadvantage. They had to help their less-capable peers and tolerate team loss when other teammates neglected to study. The game mechanics should accommodate high achievers by allowing them to solve more questions. For instance, the timeout for the progress bar could be shortened if the "thinking time" hit a low threshold. The game could additionally reward the helping behavior, which may require logging the students' activities during the revision phase.

Incorporate learning analytics the game analytics (Figure 3) provided insights into the students' performances such as Stu02 who performed well in the game despite her low results in paper-based exams. Future designs should examine using the game analytics to provide a personalized and improved learning experience [19,20] .

Enable emerged behavior our design was influenced by the individual assessment in the Egyptian system. The students solved the questions "alone", despite their collaboration during the revision. In the pilot studies, we observed a student who was physically moving his teammate to stand in the right block, when that teammate did not know the correct answer. Adopting the institution perspective, we interpreted the student's attempts as cheating and discouraged such behavior in the formal study. We observed another unusual, and relatively successful, form of interaction in the review phase of T1. The gentle pat on the back of the hand was against the institution view on physical punishment. Both observations raise questions about the extent to which educational games, when played inside the school, should adopt its institutional views. Moreover, how such adoption might preclude emergent and possibly effective forms of collaboration as defined by the children and influenced by their culture and play norms.

Play down the role of competition the competitive nature of the game engaged the children with memorizing the facts. In a rough community, the continuous competition could eventually create tensions among students. Thus, competition should not be the sole driver for learning. The game design should highlight the value of learned knowledge by linking the game to classroom discussions as suggested by [2]. The game could occasionally offer a non-competitive play mode, where the students' scores are not recorded.

CONCLUSIONS

The study demonstrated that digital games, as a component of the designed socio-technical learning ecology, motivated the students who did not receive proper support to thrive intellectually. The students, besides having fun, progressed academically using self-regulating strategies. The introduced learning environment, we argue, could be beneficial in similar challenging contexts such as poor neighborhoods, and refugee camps. We plan studies in school settings, where the game is re-designed per the proposed implications. We explore alternatives to provide consistent technical assistance for the school staff, including technical solutions to reduce game setup time and efforts. We plan to engage teachers in re-designing the game, and explore interaction between the game and classroom activities.

ACKNOWLEDGMENTS

We thank the school staff, the students, and their families for participating in the research.

REFERENCES

1. Pooja K. Agarwal, Patrice M. Bain, and Roger W. Chamberlain. 2012. The Value of Applied Research: Retrieval Practice Improves Classroom Learning and Recommendations from a Teacher, a Principal, and a Scientist. *Educational Psychology Review* 24, 3: 437–448. http://doi.org/10.1007/s10648-012-9210-2
2. M Bakker. 2014. Using mini-games for learning multiplication and division: A longitudinal effect study. Retrieved September 27, 2014 from http://repository.ubn.ru.nl/dspace31xmlui/handle/2066/127128
3. Sylvia van Borkulo, Marja van den Heuvel-Panhuizen, Marjoke Bakker, and Hanneke Loomans. 2012. One Mini-Game Is Not Like the Other: Different Opportunities to Learn Multiplication Tables. In *Serious Games: The Challenge. Communications in Computer and Information Science (vol 280)*, Stefan De Wannemacker, Sylke Vandercruysse and Geraldine Clarebout (eds.). Springer Berlin Heidelberg, Berlin, Heidelberg, 61–64. http://doi.org/10.1007/978-3-642-33814-4_9
4. Kuo En Chang, Yao Ting Sung, Yu Lung Chen, and Long Hua Huang. 2008. Learning multiplication through computer-assisted learning activities.

Computers in Human Behavior 24, 6: 2904–2916. http://doi.org/10.1016/j.chb.2008.04.015

5. Ritu Dangwal and Preeti Kapur. 2008. Children's learning processes using unsupervised "hole in the wall" computers in shared public spaces. *Australasian Journal of Educational Technology* 24, 3: 339–354.
6. Ritu Dangwal and Preeti Kapur. 2009. Learning through teaching: Peer-mediated instruction in minimally invasive education. *British Journal of Educational Technology* 40, 1: 5–22. http://doi.org/10.1111/j.1467-8535.2008.00863.x
7. Dangwal R and Thounaojam M. 2011. Self Regulatory Behaviour and Minimally Invasive (MIE) Education : A Case study in the Indian Context. *International Journal Of nal of Education and Development using ICT* 7, 1: 120–140.
8. André R. Denham. 2013. Strategy Instruction and Maintenance of Basic Multiplication Facts through Digital Game Play. *International Journal of Game-Based Learning* 3, 2: 36–54. http://doi.org/10.4018/ijgbl.2013040103
9. Pedro Ferreira. 2015. Why Play? Examining the Roles of Play in ICTD. *Aarhus Series on Human Centered Computing* 1, 1: 41–52. http://doi.org/10.7146/aahcc.v1i1.21264
10. Parimala Inamdar. 2004. Computer skills development by children using "hole in the wall" facilities in rural India. *Australasian Journal of Educational Technology* 20, 3: 1–13. Retrieved from http://www.ascilite.org.au/ajet/ajet20/inamdar.html
11. Adrian Kirkwood and Linda Price. 2014. Technology-enhanced learning and teaching in higher education: what is "enhanced" and how do we know? A critical literature review. *Learning, Media and Technology* 39, 1: 6–36. http://doi.org/10.1080/17439884.2013.770404
12. Shaimaa Lazem, Asmaa Shoa'la, Walaa M Sheta, and Marwa Elteir. 2014. Designing Low-Cost Technologies to Improve the Quality of Learning and Health Services in Future Egyptian Smart Cities - Three Case Studies. *Proceedings of the 1st Africa and Middle East Conference on Software Engineering*, http://2014.amecse-conferences.org/wp-content/uploads/2014/07/AMECSE2014-Proceedings.pdf, 41–51.
13. Louisa Loveluck. 2012. Education in Egypt: Key Challenges. *Report*. Retrieved January 6, 2017 from https://pdfs.semanticscholar.org/6748/1746ba3653f62228a230b44fb15512e6db40.pdf
14. Sugata Mitra. 2005. Self organising systems for mass computer literacy: Findings from the "hole in the wall" experiments. *International Journal of Development Issues* 4, 1: 71–81. http://doi.org/10.1108/eb045849
15. Sugata Mitra. 2014. The future of schooling: Children and learning at the edge of chaos. *Prospects* 44: 547–558. http://doi.org/10.1007/s11125-014-9327-9
16. Sugata Mitra and Ritu Dangwal. 2010. Limits to self-organising systems of learning - The Kalikuppam experiment. *British Journal of Educational Technology* 41, 5: 672–688. http://doi.org/10.1111/j.1467-8535.2010.01077.x
17. Paul R. Pintrich and Elisabeth V. de Groot. 1990. Motivational and self-regulated learning components of classroom academic performance. *Journal of Educational Psychology* 82, 1: 33–40. http://doi.org/10.1037//0022-0663.82.1.33
18. Jan L. Plass, Paul A. O'Keefe, Bruce D. Homer, et al. 2013. The impact of individual, competitive, and collaborative mathematics game play on learning, performance, and motivation. *Journal of Educational Psychology* 105, 4: 1050–1066. http://doi.org/10.1037/a0032688
19. Martin Schön, Martin Ebner, and Georg Kothmeier. 2012. It's just about learning the multiplication table. *Proceedings of the 2nd International Conference on Learning Analytics and Knowledge - LAK '12*, 73–81. http://doi.org/10.1145/2330601.2330624
20. Valerie J Shute. 2011. Stealth Assessment in Computer-Based Games To Support Learning. *Computer Games and Instruction* 55, 2: 503–524.
21. Robert E. Slavin. 1983. When does cooperative learning increase student achievement? *Psychological Bulletin* 94, 3: 429–445. http://doi.org/10.1037/0033-2909.94.3.429
22. Hannah Slay, Peter Wentworth, and Jonathon Locke. 2006. BingBee, an information kiosk for social enablement in marginalized communities. *Proceedings of the 2006 annual research conference of the South African institute of computer scientists and information technologists on IT research in developing countries - SAICSIT '06*, ACM Press, 107–116. http://doi.org/10.1145/1216262.1216274
23. Emeline Therias, Jon Bird, and Paul Marshall. 2015. Más Tecnologia, Más Cambio?: Investigating an Educational Technology Project in Rural Peru. *Proceedings of the 33rd Annual ACM Conference on Human Factors in Computing Systems*, ACM, 447–456. http://doi.org/10.1145/2702123.2702595
24. Mark Warschauer. 2003. Dissecting the "Digital Divide": A Case Study in Egypt. *The Information Society* 19, 4: 297–304. http://doi.org/10.1080/01972240309490
25. P Wentworth. 2010. BingBee @ RaglanRoad - A field trial with unattended educational kiosks. *IST-Africa, 2010*, 1–8.
26. Nicola Whitton. 2014. *Digital Games and Learning: Research and Theory*. Routledge, London.

Sidestepping the Elephant in the Classroom: Using Culturally Localized Technology to Teach Around Taboos

Piya Sorcar
Stanford University
Stanford, California
sorcar@stanford.edu

Benjamin Strauber
Stanford University
Stanford, California
strauber@stanford.edu

Prashant Loyalka
Stanford University
Stanford, California
loyalka@stanford.edu

Neha Kumar
Georgia Institute of Technology
Atlanta, Georgia
neha.kumar@gatech.edu

Shelley Goldman
Stanford University
Stanford, California
sgoldman@stanford.edu

ABSTRACT

Cultural taboos can restrict student learning on topics of critical importance. In India, such taboos have led multiple states to ban materials intended to educate youth about HIV, putting millions at risk. We present the design of TeachAIDS, a software application that leverages cultural insights, learning science, and affordances of technology to provide comprehensive HIV education while circumventing taboos. Using a mixed-methods evaluation, we demonstrate that this software leaves students with significantly increased knowledge about HIV and reduced stigma toward individuals infected with the virus. Validating the effectiveness of TeachAIDS in circumventing taboos, students report comfort in learning from the software, and it has since been deployed in tens of thousands of schools throughout India. The methodology presented here has broader implications for the design and implementation of interactive technologies for providing education on sensitive topics in health and other areas.

Author Keywords

Taboo Topics; Education; HIV; AIDS; India; HCI4D

ACM Classification Keywords

H.5.m. Information Interfaces and Presentation (e.g., HCI): Miscellaneous

INTRODUCTION

In every culture, there are taboo topics whose open discussion is considered inappropriate [57], especially within the classroom [18]. Depending on the culture, these topics can range from menstruation to racial inequality to homosexuality [13, 39, 18]. Inability or disinclination to foster open discussion leaves education on these topics incomplete or nonexistent.

When the topic in question involves significant threat to life or well-being, withholding education can be dangerous. Such is true with HIV, a virus that has claimed more than 35 million lives worldwide [71] and subjected millions more to social stigma and ostracism [37, 40, 72]. In India, which has the third-largest population of HIV-infected individuals in the world [68], taboos around the virus' modes of transmission have kept millions of youth from learning about it. State-sponsored adolescent education programs targeting HIV education have been banned across many states [9], leaving students uninformed about the virus. Even where HIV education is provided, it is often incomplete because of embarrassment, moral judgment, or lack of knowledge on the part of teachers [69, 14].

Culture and laws are slow and hard to change; we must find ways to circumvent taboos when they restrict education on critical topics. In India, working around taboos to provide HIV education can help curb the virus' spread by encouraging behavior change [32] and reduce stigma against infected individuals [66], impacting millions of lives. Any educational solution that addresses these goals must be *culturally acceptable* to ensure adoption and *complete* to ensure efficacy. Achieving this balance is challenging but possible by appropriately leveraging cultural insights, learning science principles, and the affordances of information and communications technology (ICT). Using cultural customizations to get around identified taboos and using techniques from learning science to fill identified gaps in knowledge can ensure acceptability without sacrificing completeness. Affordances of ICT, such as anonymity and uniformity, can enhance comfort and completeness by mitigating the impact of educators' embarrassment, moral judgment, or lack of knowledge.

We present TeachAIDS, an interactive educational software application that circumvents taboos to teach urban Indian youth about HIV. We describe the iterative design approach we used, which leveraged learning science, cultural insights, and the affordances of ICT. We also present a quantitative and qualitative evaluation of the design to highlight that it succeeded in increasing knowledge and reducing stigma around HIV. Finally, we discuss takeaways for the design of interventions for other cultures and topics and note that the software was deployed throughout India following the completion of this study.

Permission to make digital or hard copies of part or all of this work for personal or classroom use is granted without fee provided that copies are not made or distributed for profit or commercial advantage and that copies bear this notice and the full citation on the first page. Copyrights for third-party components of this work must be honored. For all other uses, contact the Owner/Author.
Copyright is held by the owner/author(s).
CHI 2017, May 06-11, 2017, Denver, CO, USA
ACM 978-1-4503-4655-9/17/05.
http://dx.doi.org/10.1145/3025453.3025958

BACKGROUND AND RELATED WORK

In this section, we first describe our motivation for focusing on HIV education in India. We next discuss how learning science, cultural insights, and affordances of ICT can be leveraged to provide education that is both complete and culturally acceptable. Finally, we discuss research in the area of Human-Computer Interaction (HCI) and global development that has addressed the needs of individuals with HIV and other health topics.

HIV Education in India

Although HIV is a problem throughout the world, we focus on India here. This is because of lack of knowledge and stigma around HIV and limits on HIV education in India. Studies of adolescents and adults in India have found that significant percentages of people believe HIV can be cured [41, 26], are uncertain whether a contraceptive pill can prevent HIV infection [41], cannot identify all modes of HIV transmission [42, 23], do not know that condoms can prevent HIV [42, 23], or have never heard of HIV [44, 23]. In one study, many people reported believing HIV-positive individuals should be quarantined, be kept out of classes, or commit suicide [1]. Children with HIV have been expelled from schools within the last few years just for being infected [60, 35], and individuals involuntarily tested for HIV have had surgeries canceled if seropositive [33]. Lack of knowledge about HIV is associated with increased stigma [38, 7].

HIV education in India has been limited by laws and social norms. Explicit discussion or depiction of topics relevant to HIV transmission is often considered highly inappropriate, especially in the classroom. These topics include sexual acts and organs, intravenous drug use, and breastfeeding [9, 14, 65]. Materials made by India's National AIDS Control Organisation (NACO) to teach about HIV have been banned in numerous states largely due to explicit discussion of such topics [9, 14].

To our knowledge, no standard curriculum has been approved for schools across all Indian states. Thus, where HIV is taught, it is frequently left to educators to create or adapt their own materials. Teachers often provide incomplete information due to embarrassment, moral judgment, or lack of knowledge, and students are uncomfortable learning [14, 69].

Mass media interventions intended to educate people about HIV have been created and deployed through television, posters, and other media. These include the BBC World Service Trust's Haath se Haath Milaa Media Project, The Heroes Project, ZMQ Software Systems, and the Buladi Campaign [22, 59, 63]. However, constraints of time and space make it difficult to transmit complete information using mass media.

This leaves a gap for a school-based intervention that circumvents taboos to deliver complete information about HIV while leaving learners comfortable. Because of dangers posed by lack of knowledge and stigma around HIV, it is important that an effective solution be made widely available.

Insights from the Learning Sciences

Providing complete information should involve helping students form a sufficiently accurate mental model of the target topic. A mental model is a representation of how the world works, a view of how concepts and facts are connected that allows learners to store and access information more readily and reason through new situations when they encounter them [29]. It is unlikely students will form a sufficient mental model when they merely memorize a set of unconnected facts, a common problem in HIV education that leaves students unprepared to face unfamiliar situations [4]. Given that students often come in with inaccurate mental models, it is important to build toward more accurate conceptions in driving conceptual change [70, 61]. Efforts must also be taken to help students connect scientific knowledge (e.g., biological processes) to real-world scenarios (e.g., situations where HIV might be transmitted) [43].

Through consultations with experts in the learning sciences, public health, and medicine, mental mapping components—the relationships among HIV/AIDS content and concepts—can be identified. Through interviews, surveys, and tests of a representative sample of students, we can determine what knowledge and common misconceptions students have about HIV/AIDS and design a curriculum accordingly. Once these parameters are understood, we can incorporate other common learning techniques such as interactivity, analogies, and mnemonic devices [58, 8].

Cultural Sensitivity

Making a curriculum culturally acceptable requires understanding the nature of local taboos and finding ways to teach while respecting them. Surveys of students and teachers can be used to determine how comfortable they are with images and discussions of different levels of explicitness, identifying a *taboo tipping point* that should not be crossed. Subsequently, common cultural euphemisms can be used to address taboo-violating topics like sex in a way that does not cross this line. Such euphemisms can be drawn, for example, from common cultural reference points like Bollywood.

Customizing features like language, accent, and appearance of characters can increase learner comfort and attention by making learning materials more relatable, trustworthy, and familiar. Past work, for example, has shown that people are more likely to trust and be influenced by characters who share their accent and appearance [15, 46, 47, 54, 6].

Unique Affordances of ICT

ICT has a number of unique affordances [28] that have contributed to its success in teaching about sensitive topics. First, ICT can be used anonymously and privately [2, 5]. This can relieve students and teachers of the discomfort and embarrassment inherent in discussing a conversational taboo with another human [17, 31], a problem that can lead to incomplete knowledge transmission [69, 14]. Second, past work suggests that parents, teachers, and administrators view ICT as a reliable and respectable means of engaging material [50], which may help support adoption of educational resources for sensitive topics. Third, ICT interventions can be transmitted with a high degree of fidelity [49] and uniformity. This ensures that sensitive topics will be taught in the same way every time, with no information lost because of embarrassment, moral judgment, or lack of knowledge on the part of teachers.

HCI and Global Development

A body of HCI research focuses on understanding and designing for underserved, under-represented, and under-resourced populations across the world [16]. Much HCI for Development (HCI4D) research examines interventions for global health, including HIV/AIDS, maternal health, and human milk banking, among others [48, 52, 11]. ICT-based HIV/AIDS interventions successfully increase antiretroviral therapy (ART) compliance [24], provide healthcare decision support and confidential delivery of test results [27], and address patients' privacy needs to protect them from high stigma [30]. HIV/AIDS education and awareness-based interventions that focus on information dissemination include Project Masiluleke in South Africa [53], Text to Change in Uganda [67], Freedom HIV in India [19], and Learning about Living in Nigeria [36]. They use text messages and mobile games as vehicles for providing education on HIV/AIDS and related topics such as stigma and privacy. By considering interventions that leverage digital storytelling and incorporating a learning sciences-based approach, we can create a carefully designed conceptual framework that prioritizes cultural acceptability [55, 20, 56, 10].

DESIGNING TEACHAIDS

TeachAIDS consists of a twenty-minute animated curriculum that uses a conceptual explanation of biological principles and culturally familiar euphemisms to teach students about HIV. The animation consists of a back-and-forth question-answer conversation between a male doctor and a young male student. The doctor teaches about critical concepts relevant to understanding HIV transmission and prevention. We describe the human-centered design process we used to create the animation, outlining the key insights we discovered through this process and how they contributed to the final design.[1] This process, as well as the following quantitative and qualitative evaluation, received IRB approval from Stanford University.

Design Process

The design process consisted of the two phases below.

Phase 1: Initial Interviews and Surveys

To gauge students' knowledge of HIV and comfort learning about it, we conducted interviews with young adults born and raised in India as well as Indian school teachers, administrators, and leaders managing local non-governmental organizations (NGOs). Using semi-structured interviews, we asked participants questions to determine what educational interventions students had been exposed to, how knowledgeable students were about HIV, and what topics around HIV made them uncomfortable. We also showed existing educational interventions to students and collected their reactions. Following these interviews, we conducted an in-depth anonymous survey of 200 Indian urban college students to understand gaps in their knowledge around major HIV concepts. We also tested images and language around transmission modes used in actual HIV materials to ascertain student comfort levels.

In parallel, we interviewed dozens of experts in public health and medicine to determine what concepts around HIV were essential for student knowledge. We also interviewed cultural experts[2] and anthropologists with expertise in India to identify the most taboo concepts related to HIV as well as effective alternative methods of communicating them.

Phase 2: Prototyping and Testing

We triangulated our understanding of student knowledge states with knowledge considered important by experts to build a map of essential concepts around HIV transmission and prevention. We made sure to address concepts that students did not fully understand and about which students were found to commonly have questions, as revealed by initial interviews and surveys. We next worked with educators and learning scientists, who helped us further simplify these concepts in order to build a comprehensive curriculum.

Having developed this curriculum, we began creating and testing prototypes with Indian young adults as the user group. We tested approximately 150 iterations of the design. We began with paper prototypes; we then moved to PowerPoint and ultimately animations. In testing, we asked users to go through a think-aloud exercise as they interacted with the tool and to provide overall feedback. After each test, we incorporated insights gained into the next iteration.

Design Insights and Outcomes

Conceptualizing a Complete Curriculum

We designed the curriculum based on the questions and misconceptions students had about HIV and the information public health and medical experts considered essential for them to have. We took the union of these two sets to ensure that the knowledge students received was complete and that no critical information was missing.

Biology-Based Mental Model: Consistent with previous research [41, 23], our initial interviews identified significant gaps in student knowledge around transmission modalities (e.g., can you get HIV from kissing or hugging?) and prevention methods (e.g., can a condom prevent HIV?). Health and education experts helped us determine that a biological framing would allow us to teach these and other necessary concepts relevant to HIV prevention. In addition to helping students develop a clear mental model, a biology-based approach proved beneficial because biology is a standard topic taught in schools with which students and teachers are familiar and comfortable.

Our interviews had revealed that many students thought of HIV as a frightening abstraction associated with moral impurity rather than a biological concept. To address this, we first described biological concepts relevant to HIV (e.g., viruses, the human body) and used this to explain features of its transmission and prevention (e.g., high concentrations of the virus only exist in certain bodily fluids, HIV can only enter the

[1]This software, current versions of which can be found at http://teachaids.org/software, was the basis for Dr. Sorcar's thesis at Stanford University. The thesis [64] and a related book chapter [65] explore in greater detail the theoretical framework and design considerations around developing technology-based interventions for taboo topics.

[2]These included scholars studying India and others deeply familiar with the culture.

Figure 1. Scenes from TeachAIDS software. Doctor character (left); Kissing euphemism from Bollywood (center); "Suhaag Raat" wedding night (right).

body through particular pathways). We then linked these concepts to real-world scenarios like sexual activity with the help of cultural euphemisms, as described below. This linkage allowed students to reason through whether any given scenario carried a risk of HIV infection. Because stigma against HIV-infected individuals is associated with lack of knowledge and moral judgment, we hypothesized that this biology-based approach could drive decreases in stigma by *(a)* helping students recognize that the ways HIV can be contracted from an HIV-positive individual are quite limited and *(b)* shifting focus from moral judgment to biological understanding.

Learning Science Techniques: Having decided to use a biological framing, we used learning science elements like analogies and mnemonic devices to further simplify complex concepts, making them easier to understand and retain. For example, we used an analogy relating the body to a country, immune cells to soldiers protecting the country, and HIV to a foreign invader that can only enter the country in certain ways. This allowed students to understand the mechanism of HIV infection more clearly by relating it to something with which they were familiar. We also developed localized mnemonic devices to help students remember especially important concepts and reason through risk of infection in situations they had not previously encountered. One of these is the *Three-Point Mantra*, which helps learners remember the three high-risk fluids through which HIV can spread. Another is *The Triangle Test*, which helps learners identify whether they are at risk of infection and when to seek support from a medical professional.

Culturally Customizing for Comfort

Interviews, surveys, and testing helped us identify that taboos surrounding the depiction and discussion of sex represented the greatest potential obstacle to providing complete HIV education, but it was important for us to use images and language depicting sex to relate the biology-driven understanding of HIV transmission to real-world situations. We discuss here examples of how we identified the nature of these taboos and then circumvented them. We also describe how we used other cultural customizations to make materials more familiar and relevant to learners.

Graphics: In interviews and surveys with students and administrators, we showed images of intimacy of varying levels of explicitness, discovering that even the least explicit images were deemed unacceptable (e.g., two people kissing, a black and white line drawing of a naked couple embracing). Relying on insights derived from the cultural experts, we instead used common depictions of intimacy from Bollywood that we knew would be both acceptable and commonly understood. To represent kissing, we panned from an image of a couple leaning in for a kiss to an image of two doves pecking, a common Bollywood trope. To represent sex, we showed an image of a newlywed woman sitting on a bed decorated with flowers on her wedding night (*suhaag raat*), another commonly used reference in Bollywood (see fig. 1).

We also used interviews and surveys to determine how much skin was acceptable to show for a variety of scenarios, such as a woman breastfeeding. For each scenario, we iteratively tested out a collection of images with different levels of skin exposure, getting feedback in some cases directly from students and in others from whether the version of the survey containing an image of a certain level of exposure was allowed to be deployed in schools. This helped us determine where the 'taboo tipping point' was for skin exposure for various scenes in the animation (see fig. 2).

In addition, we depicted many characters and objects using cultural elements specific to India. These include clothes (e.g., *salwar*, *dhoti*, *sari*, *bangles*, *bindi*), mannerisms (e.g., *namaskar*), food (e.g., *roti*, *sabji*), and animals (e.g., *brahman cow*, or a white cow with horns). We took steps to give the materials relevance to people across different demographic groups; these included using characters from across different geographies and religions of India.

Language: Our interviews revealed that certain sex-related language could be written but not spoken, and that some ways of discussing sex were completely unacceptable. We found that words like "semen" or "vaginal secretion" made learners uncomfortable when spoken but were acceptable in written form. Interviews also revealed that discussion of specific orifices (e.g., "vagina") combined with sexual actions (e.g., "penetration") was unacceptable. Instead, we clearly defined words such as "natural openings" and "direct transfer" individually earlier in the animation and then used them later, in combination, to discuss transmission.

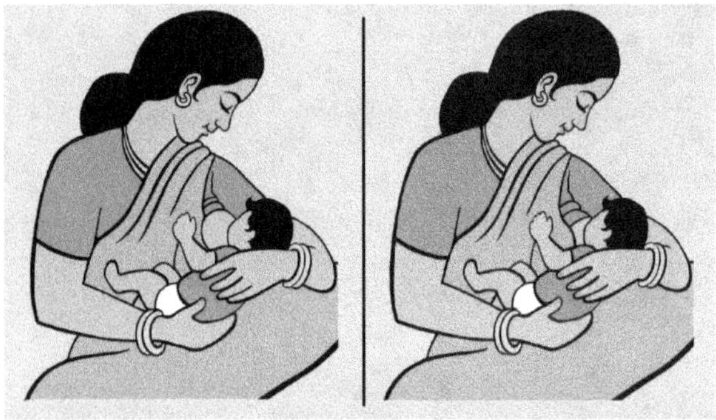

Figure 2. Example of the image testing process to identify a taboo tipping point. The exposure of skin (in picture on right) was the final version approved by learners and other stakeholders for the TeachAIDS software.

We also customized the sound and appearance of the animations by drawing on research that suggests that people find agents similar to them more trustworthy, motivating, and comfortable [15, 46, 47, 54, 6]. Characters all spoke with an Indian accent, and the voice for each character was chosen from a wider selection using feedback by learners. We ensured certain words and phrases whose usage varies across English dialects were properly represented in Indian English. These include "prevention is better than cure" ("an ounce of prevention is worth a pound of cure" in American English), "appearances can be deceptive" ("looks can be deceiving"), and "cold and cough" ("flu").

Drawing on Affordances of ICT

We designed and implemented TeachAIDS in ways that leveraged specific affordances of ICT for teaching around taboos. Interviews indicated that students were embarrassed to learn about topics related to HIV in group settings and hesitant to talk about them with peers. For anonymity and privacy, students can watch the animation individually on separate computers with their own set of headphones, and the entire curriculum can be presented without the teacher's involvement. We incorporated a student character so that learners can easily relate and a doctor character to lend increased credibility to the information presented; however, to strengthen the feeling of anonymity, we did not give names to the doctor or student avatars, a decision that also avoided the potential issue of students associating the student character with any peers who might share the same name. We also confirmed through our interviews that teachers are often embarrassed to teach about HIV or do not have full knowledge about it, leading important information to be omitted. The software that students interact with is an executable file that plays the entire set of animations. This can ensure that the same complete information about HIV is presented uniformly each time, regardless of teachers' embarrassment or lack of knowledge.

QUANTITATIVE RESEARCH FINDINGS

We now describe the data, analytical approach, and results from the quantitative side of the evaluation, which examined students' changes in knowledge, attitudes, and comfort as they engaged with TeachAIDS to learn about HIV.

Data Collection

The sample for the quantitative evaluation consisted of 295 students randomly selected from three high schools in New Delhi and Haryana in India. The number of students recruited at each institution was based on the number of functioning computers at each site. All students were recruited on a voluntary basis and assured that they could discontinue participation at any time if they experienced discomfort. No students refused to participate.

We asked the sampled students to take a 15-minute baseline survey (hereafter known as the "pretest" at T1), which measured students' pre-intervention knowledge and attitudes about HIV. The knowledge questions measured how educated each student was around HIV transmission and prevention issues. The attitudinal questions measured general acceptance and tolerance around HIV and HIV-positive individuals. Immediately after the pretest, students in the treatment group (n=198) were assigned to receive the TeachAIDS intervention (for more information, see the Assignment, Balance and Attrition subsection below), and students in the control group (n=97) silently read text unrelated to HIV or science for the same amount of time as the intervention group.

Immediately after the administration of the pretest and intervention, we measured students' post-treatment outcomes with a 20-minute survey (hereafter known as the "posttest" at T2). The posttest contained similar questions to the pretest but in an alternate order. The survey also consisted of questions about students' backgrounds and their subjective reactions to the intervention. The background-related questions were added to the end of the posttest instead of the pretest so as not to influence student performance on either. Furthermore, approximately one month after the posttest, all students were asked to take another 20-minute survey (hereafter known as the "retention test" at T3). The retention test again contained similar questions as the pretest and posttest but in random order. It also contained questions about subjective reactions to the intervention and interest in sharing information about HIV with others.

In each survey administration (pretest, posttest, and retention test) students were asked to fill out the survey forms individually. Each administration was closely proctored by our survey enumerators, who were local school administrators trained for this activity.

Variables

We measured student knowledge and attitudes by drawing on and adapting survey questions that are commonly used in the research literature. For example, we drew on questions from the Stereotypes About AIDS scale [62] and the Assessment of Knowledge and Beliefs About HIV/AIDS Among Adolescents scale [34], among other sources. Altogether, we analyzed responses to 40 questions about knowledge and 17 questions about attitudes. Knowledge measures included questions like "Can you get HIV from touching a public toilet seat?" and "Can you get HIV from a blood transfusion?" Attitude measures asked students to give affirmative or negative responses to statements like "I won't talk to or interact with anyone with HIV/AIDS" and "People with HIV/AIDS should not be allowed to handle food in restaurants."

To estimate the total knowledge and total attitude scores at T1, T2, and T3, we calculated the number of questions that were answered correctly in each category. Similar to other studies using the knowledge questions, each student selected an answer of *yes, no,* or *not sure*. A correct answer was assigned *1*, and *0* was given to any answers that were incorrect, "not sure", or had a missing value. For the attitude questions, the students could reply with *agree*, or *disagree*, or *not sure*. A value of *1* was assigned to the responses reflecting greater acceptance or positive attitudes towards HIV and AIDS related issues, and *0* was assigned for responses reflecting less acceptance or negative attitudes. After calculating the total correct scores (for knowledge and attitudes separately and in each survey administration separately), we transformed them into z-scores. We then constructed a binary indicator to distinguish between the treatment and control conditions. Specifically, the indicator *TeachAIDS* equaled 1 if the student received the TeachAIDS animated software and 0 if they were in the control condition. Finally, we constructed a set of control variables using background information collected during the posttest. In particular, we controlled for gender (female = 0, male = 1), age (calculated in years), mother's education level, and father's education level. The analyses also controlled for the standardized pretest knowledge and attitudinal measures.

Assignment, Balance, and Attrition

Two high schools (one in Delhi and one in Haryana) received the treatment condition, while one high school (in Delhi) received the control condition. The assignment was done at the school level in order to avoid contamination between the treatment conditions, as it was plausible that students would share knowledge or attitudes with their peers between the posttest and retention test. Because of this, we tested for balance across the treatment and control samples, adjusting standard errors to account for the fact that students were nested within schools. We found no statistical differences in student background characteristics across schools or between the control and treatment groups.

Students in the treatment condition received TeachAIDS while students in the control condition were asked to read silently from one of their existing non-science textbooks. In particular, the control condition was not given a comparable HIV program as no standard, nationally approved curriculum existed at the time. However, teachers informed us that the student participants had learned about HIV through exposure to larger HIV awareness campaigns in the mass media.

Statistical Approach

To determine the impact of TeachAIDS on student knowledge and attitudes, we ran the following adjusted regression model:

$$Y_{ij} = \beta_0 + \beta_1 TeachAIDS_j + Z_{ij}\beta + \epsilon_{ij}$$

Where Y_{ij} represents the outcome (knowledge or attitudes, posttest or retention test) of student i in institution j, $TeachAIDS_j$ represents the binary treatment indicator for

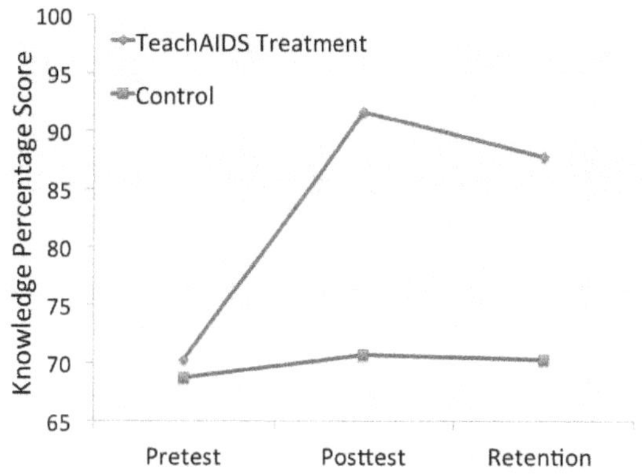

Figure 3. Knowledge percentage scores for TeachAIDS treatment and control groups at pretest, posttest, and retention test.

whether the student received TeachAIDS or not, and Z_{ij} represents a vector of baseline student characteristics (controls including pretest measures, gender, age, mother's education level, and father's education level). In the above equation, β_1 represents the impact of TeachAIDS on student outcomes. In all of the analyses, we use the vce(cluster) option in Stata 13.0 to adjust the standard errors. We make this adjustment because unlike the standard case in which unobservable values are independently and identically distributed, the unobservable values of students are likely more similar within schools than across schools [3]. Using the cluster adjustment results in larger standard error estimates and thus leads to a more conservative interpretation of the statistical results.

Results

Gains in Knowledge

In the model that fully adjusts for all covariates (including pretest measures and demographic features), students who had undergone the TeachAIDS intervention scored 1.44 standard deviations higher on knowledge measures at posttest than students who did not undergo the intervention, significant at the level of $p<0.01$ (t-value = 55.54). Importantly, at the retention test one month later, students who had undergone the TeachAIDS intervention still scored 1.14 standard deviations higher on knowledge measures than students who did not undergo the intervention, significant at the level of $p<0.01$ (t-value = 40.64). There was no significant difference between groups at pretest.

These results suggest that the TeachAIDS intervention drove significant increases in knowledge about HIV and that these increases largely persisted over time. Total scores on the knowledge measures at pretest, posttest, and retention test for the treatment and control groups are shown in Figure 1. Consistent with these improvements in knowledge, 96.5% of students said they learned more about prevention through the TeachAIDS tutorial than through any other prior communications channel, including television and school.

Changes in Attitudes

In the adjusted model, students who had undergone the TeachAIDS intervention scored 0.40 standard deviations

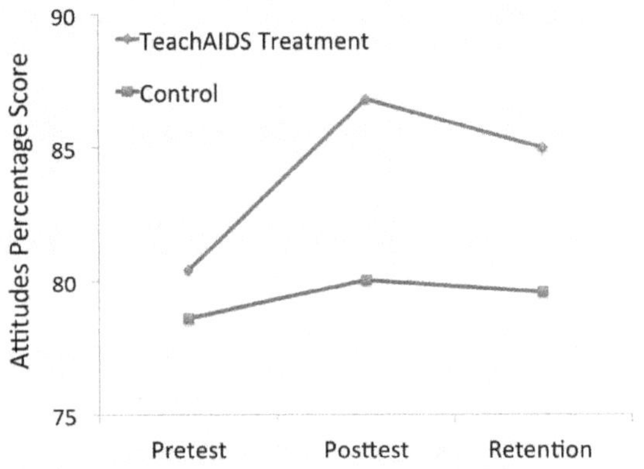

Figure 4. Attitude percentage scores for TeachAIDS treatment and control groups at pretest, posttest, and retention test.

higher on attitude measures at posttest than students who did not undergo the intervention, significant at the level of $p<0.01$ (t-value = 20.20). Importantly, in the retention test one month later, students who had undergone the TeachAIDS intervention still scored 0.24 standard deviations higher on attitude measures than students who did not undergo the intervention, significant at the level of $p<0.01$ (t-value = 58.75). There was no significant difference between groups at pretest. These results suggest that the TeachAIDS intervention drove decreases in negative attitudes about HIV and HIV-positive individuals, and that these decreases largely persisted over time. Total scores on the attitude measures at pretest, posttest, and retention test for the treatment and control groups are shown in Figure 2.

Results revealed that after watching the animated tutorial, a greater proportion of intervention students indicated they felt less afraid of interacting with HIV-infected people rather than feeling more afraid ($p<0.01$) and were less afraid of being infected with HIV rather than more afraid ($p<0.01$). One month later, 89% of students exposed to the intervention reported having shared information about HIV with others, and 75% reported having sought additional HIV-related information on their own.

Comfort levels

Though HIV and its modes of transmission are generally considered taboo to discuss in India, 99% of intervention students indicated they were comfortable learning from TeachAIDS. Additionally, 77% of students said they preferred learning about HIV from the TeachAIDS tutorial, while only 1% preferred learning about HIV from their teacher, with the remainder showing equal preference for either option. Also, 96% of students said they would be willing to forward the tutorial to others they cared about, and 78% said they would be willing to join our team to stop the spread of HIV. This further suggests that TeachAIDS successfully circumvents taboos, with students comfortable learning from it, sharing it with others, and being public messengers of HIV prevention.

QUALITATIVE RESEARCH FINDINGS

The original plan was to directly interview select students to understand their experience of engaging with TeachAIDS. This was met with strong disapproval from school administrators and teachers, yet they did allow us to design a survey that sought detailed, open-ended feedback anonymously. This survey included broader questions around students' comfort in watching and interacting with the animated curriculum and what they liked or did not like.

The responses were insightful and validating. We present results from an open-coding process and the identification of themes. We describe how the students perceived the learning content, including the elements of the design they found acceptable.

The Learning Experience

Students across the board responded with positive feedback on the learning experience. This included feedback on the curriculum and the information presented, the use of animation, and the intervention's potential to reach a wider audience across the country.

Complete, Clear, Concise Curriculum

Many students shared that the curriculum addressed all their questions and concerns and that the content was comprehensive and complete, leaving *"no doubts"* in their mind.[3] One student *(F, 17)* said and many agreed, *"all the necessary information was present."* Another *(M, 17)* shared that he had known much of the information previously, but that TeachAIDS explained concepts to him in more detail. To this point, another student added:

> *"the animated tutorial was beautifuuly designed, covering various areas related to HIV/AIDS . It answered all the quetions and cleared most of the doubts" [sic] (F, 16 yrs).*

In addition to completeness, students praised the curriculum for its clarity and ease of understanding. They mentioned the material had been presented *"nicely"* and *"systematically."* One student *(F, 16)* voiced that *"everything was to the point and easy to understand."* In general, students found the curriculum to be well organized and appreciated the *"step by step" (M, 16)* approach.

Although we went through multiple iterations with students and experts to ensure the materials included all relevant and necessary information, some students posed additional questions not explored directly in the materials. For example, one student *(F, 16)* asked, *"should a child blame his parents for hiv?" [sic].* She was skeptical about the ease of getting tested for HIV because it would involve asking parents' permission, which would be awkward. Students were also interested in learning more about treatment options for HIV, that is, whether it could be cured if detected early. One of them *(M, 16)* asked if yoga could prevent HIV.[4] Subsequent iterations of the software have addressed these questions.

[3] In India, the word "doubt" is common terminology for "question".

[4] Though the animation did not mention yoga, this question may have been raised because of the media attention to political leaders who have suggested replacing "sex education" with yoga [21].

Engaging and "Fun" Animation

Students found the process of interacting with the curriculum *"user friendly"* and *"fun."* One student shared: *"i want to tell that the animation was a very entertaining means of informing people... " [sic] (F, 18 yrs)*. Students liked the animation (particularly the doctor's animated mustache) and found that it made the material easier to learn and entertaining. One student *(M, 16)* mentioned, *"because the animated part is the best way to understand each and every thing about the hiv virus" [sic]*. Though students consistently appeared to identify several benefits to using an animated curriculum, there was one outlier student *(F, 16)* who thought it was *"very boring"*, but still *"learnt a few new facts about HIV" [sic]*.

Targeting a Broader Audience

The students' favorable response to the curriculum was further validated by their overwhelmingly strong sentiment that the curriculum need not be limited to eleventh graders alone—a far broader audience could engage with it. They suggested that this audience could include younger students (starting with seventh graders), as well as those in other schools, *"every school,"* across the country, and in *"every part of the world" (M, 16)*. Students also suggested that we create similar tutorials on other sensitive topics related to public health, requesting *"please do spread information and preventive measures about other diseases as well" (M, 16)*. Finally, they advised that the materials could cater just as well to those who lived in villages or were unable to read.

The Sociocultural Experience

The findings indicated that, in addition to having an effective learning experience, students found the curriculum to be culturally acceptable and relatable. One of the major design objectives was to ensure that the students felt comfortable learning from the curriculum. This also meant ensuring that the students did not feel threatened or embarrassed due to the presence of their teacher or peers. We now present findings that demonstrate the high comfort levels of the students as they engaged with the material.

Comfortable

Many students mentioned that they felt shy or embarrassed at the thought of discussing sensitive topics with their teachers and that the curriculum saved them from this discomfort:

> *"in this way u dont have to bother about what others are thinking" [sic] (F, 17 yrs).*

Learning through the curriculum made them feel at ease, as one student *(F, 16)* shared, *"It was more comfortable to have an interactive learning through an animation series rather than a live person even doctor" [sic]*. There were a few students who remarked that they were fine with a live person disseminating the same content as long as this content was accurate. Some pointed out that the animated curriculum was better for those from more conservative backgrounds. Indeed, the most common response from students was that this kind of material was not *"easy to discuss with anyone" (M, 16)*.

Although the respondents were all students, they also mentioned the teacher's perspective. For example, one student

Figure 5. School children in New Delhi, India, engaging with the TeachAIDS animated software.

said that the animation was more friendly than a teacher would have been. Feeling uncomfortable with the teacher appeared to be the norm, but some students also had concern for how their teachers would feel, sharing, *"well....i am comfortable with teachers.....i am just doubtfull of the teacher though...." [sic] (F, 16)*. Engaging with the curriculum thus also freed the students of this concern for their teachers.

The qualitative data provided further evidence for the quantitative findings that TeachAIDS left students feeling comfortable. Below we highlight two specific reasons shared—that their engagement with the curriculum was one-on-one and that there was complete anonymity in this exchange.

Learning One-on-One

Students had a strong positive response to the one-on-one nature of the learning experience. They mentioned this experience was preferable to having a teacher go through the curriculum with them as it saved them from *"embarrassment"*. A few students shared they were able to discuss this sensitive topic with friends, though this did not seem to be the norm:

> *"yes this is true because i dont have the guts to talk to my parents about aids , i just talk about it with my friends but i didnt know this much about it" [sic] (F, 16 yrs).*

The need for privacy was strong among students given the intense social stigma associated with HIV. They appreciated the opportunity to engage with the curriculum without anyone else being part of the learning experience. We also found that students were sensitive to the issue of gender. For example, one student shared her hesitation that stemmed from her teacher being male, making it harder for her to talk about HIV openly in the classroom:

> *"class teachers arent always the best peopletp talk to about sensitive issues ike these because one they are males which doesn not make us feel any comfprtable and a anonymous tutprial conveys the important message without making us feel uncomfortable which we would have felt sitting and learning in a group with all the classmates around" [sic] (F, 18 yrs).*

Although the students were learning in a group surrounded by their classmates, their engagement with the material took place one-on-one—that is, each student used one desktop (see fig. 5). Using headphones made them feel that they were watching *"alone.... and no one was standing on my shoulder or seeing what i was doing" [sic] (M, 16).*

Anonymity

In addition to learning one-on-one, even if in a full room of peers, students drew comfort from the fact that their participation was anonymous. That is, no one would know that (or how) they were engaging with the curriculum. Talking to teachers about topics such as these seemed quite challenging for the students. Thus, the ability to learn from an *"anonymous tutor [who didn't know] whom he was teaching to" (M, 17)* was received well. Our design decision to not use names in the animation but to instead refer to the characters as *"doctor"* and *"student"* further reinforced a sense of anonymity.

LIMITATIONS

The generalizability of these results may be limited because the students who participated in this study are not fully representative of the country's student population. Due to the taboo nature of the topic of HIV, we were only able to test the intervention in private schools. Additionally, the sample schools were in North India, used English as a medium of instruction, and were attended by students from middle-income backgrounds. For example, the participants may have started with higher knowledge and attitude levels and hence been differentially affected by the intervention compared to less-educated individuals. Students from different socioeconomic and geographic backgrounds may also show different levels of comfort with the topics covered in the animations. Future studies should involve participants from more diverse backgrounds to explore these issues.

DISCUSSION

We would first like to share parts of the design process that we learned from and found particularly challenging and insightful. We then share how the software could be improved and how our approach might translate to other cultures or sensitive topics.

Challenges in Designing for Sensitive Topics

The process of identifying the taboo tipping point in the context of schools was challenging, as it required great sensitivity in designing a survey that would itself not be rejected for being inappropriate. The survey went through seven iterations before it was finally approved. The first iteration included questions asking students to draw pictures about their understanding of HIV, which was outright rejected. In the sixth iteration, we were instructed to change the name of the survey from "HIV/AIDS Survey" to something more "scientific" or "general." This led us ultimately to use "General Health Survey", itself a euphemism. Because approval by gatekeepers was a key goal in designing TeachAIDS, we were able to glean insights from the survey rejections (if, for example, the survey was rejected for having an image with too much skin) to help identify the taboo tipping point.

Understanding and adjusting for the constraints imposed by gatekeepers was key in other parts of the design process as well, especially because of the sensitivity of this topic and perceptions of student knowledge. Multiple gatekeepers initially claimed that an intervention was unnecessary as students would have learned all relevant information from mass media, implying there would be a ceiling effect in pretest knowledge levels. This was in fact not the case, making the increase in knowledge driven by the software a surprise to them. We worked with private schools as we were not allowed to run the TeachAIDS intervention in public schools without formal approval of the curricula by NACO. However, private schools were also worried about the reactions of parents when they found out their children were learning about HIV in class. Since private schools are run by fees paid by the parents, their approvals and blessings matter. Showing the software to gatekeepers including the schools' administrators and owners allowed us to convince them that it was appropriate for students in the upper grades. It had the side benefit of providing education on this topic to these gatekeepers, a group whose knowledge and attitudes of HIV could have a real impact on students' lives. Once the software was developed, dozens of NGOs were interested in it but scared to use it. We learned that all HIV materials, including ours, needed to be approved by NACO in order to be used by any organizations across the country.

Improving the Approach

A number of considerations could lead to pedagogically beneficial improvements for future versions of the software.

Gender: For this study, the TeachAIDS materials were shown in mixed-gender classrooms. However, while teaching sensitive subjects, educators often divide the classroom by gender suggesting it may maximize comfort for all learners. In the interviews and surveys, a number of female students specifically noted discomfort learning about sensitive subjects from a male (human) instructor. Given these responses, female students may perhaps show greater comfort or changes in knowledge and attitudes while learning from a female (animated) instructor. It is possible for these differences to be greater in urban vs. rural settings, as gender dynamics vary. To address this, female and male student comfort and learning could be measured using gender-specific versions of the TeachAIDS software across various contexts.

Privacy: Students noted they were comfortable because they were watching materials "alone", but they were not alone. More investigation is needed to understand how technology can create a virtual private learning environment for the learners. This is especially important because a one-computer-per-child administration of the software with headphones is not feasible in many scholastic environments.

Rural vs. Urban: The ways in which knowledge gaps and social stigma differ between urban groups (who have received greater exposure to mass media) and rural populations should be explored further. Evidence suggests that rural populations may know less about HIV than urban ones [23], meaning TeachAIDS could be particularly useful in rural areas. However, rural schools are much less likely to have access to technological resources that would allow them to play the software. Additionally, compared to urban students, students in rural areas might not have the same background knowledge to help them understand the biological concepts explained in the animation. They also might have a different taboo tipping point around each image (e.g. less or more skin exposure) and sensitive term (e.g. less or more explicit language) used. Given this, would the learning effects of the software change in a rural setting? Aside from official central and state government approvals, are there other gatekeepers whose buy-in would be needed to share education on taboo topics in more rural communities?

Using this Approach with Other Cultures

The approach presented here may be used to create culturally acceptable materials for cultures beyond North India. Knowledge states and myths around HIV may vary significantly across cultures. Both the taboo tipping point and cultural euphemisms to address it will also vary significantly, as will particular accents, language, and cultural artifacts. Interviews and testing with users and conversations with cultural experts can help us identify these.

Differences across cultures in knowledge about HIV and myths surrounding HIV may necessitate differences in what information is presented. For example, in Zimbabwe, there is a myth that having a sexual encounter with a virgin may cure an HIV-positive person [45, 25]. In places like South Africa, the myth that AIDS is not caused by HIV has been promoted by influential leaders for many years [12, 51]. Changing such beliefs can only be accomplished by first fully understanding them and what has led people to hold them.

Elements of how information is presented must also differ across cultures. Language is key; even within India, linguistic and cultural diversity justify the creation of different versions for different languages and regions. Further, analogies like comparing the immune system to an army work well in India but may not work well where the military is not trusted, and the depiction of the body as a country may be sensitive for groups who have been displaced from their homeland or whose countries are not recognized formally by the United Nations. The doctor character as an authority is a natural choice in urban India, where interviews with students and cultural experts identified doctors as the most trusted source on this topic. However, in places where doctors are scarce and people are more accustomed to rural health care workers, such workers may be a better representative. In other places, the most authoritative and trusted sources may be village chiefs or religious leaders.

Using this Approach with Other Topics

Our design process could be used to create educational tools for other important topics like sexual assault and racism around which conversational taboos exist. To help designers of such tools, it may be valuable to generate a repository of images, words, and metaphors that are culturally appropriate within a given culture or across cultures. These could include, for example, images of the body that show a culturally appropriate amount of skin. It would also be important to identify necessary changes; for example, a doctor as the teacher and the comparison of the body to a country would be useful for some health topics but potentially not others.

POST-STUDY DEVELOPMENT

Since this study, the TeachAIDS software has been officially approved and distributed by the National AIDS Control Organisation in India. It has been approved for in-school use by the governments of states like Karnataka that had previously banned other forms of HIV education. States such as Andhra Pradesh, where HIV-positive children were expelled from schools, have also formally adopted and distributed locally customized versions of TeachAIDS. These examples provide further evidence that TeachAIDS successfully circumvents the local taboos that had prevented previous interventions from being adopted and scaled. The success of this model and approach has led to the development of further customized versions of TeachAIDS, which are being used as standard materials for HIV prevention education in every state across India, as well as other countries.[5] To date, NACO has distributed 100,000 physical copies of the software, which have been shown in more than 30,000 schools in India. TeachAIDS has also been adopted enthusiastically by other groups within India, such as hospital personnel, midwives, military doctors, and corporations.

CONCLUSION

To create TeachAIDS, we used a human-centered design approach relying on insights from learners and experts, incorporation of learning science techniques, attention to cultural acceptance, and utilization of the affordances of technology. Our process has led to the development of an intervention that effectively addresses the tension between complete knowledge and cultural sensitivity that often hinders education on taboo topics. This intervention drives increased knowledge and decreased attitudes of stigma, leaves learners comfortable, and has found widespread adoption across India, even in places where other HIV education materials had been banned. As described, we believe the process we detail in this paper can be used to develop teaching materials for sensitive topics in a wide variety of other fields and cultures. As with any intervention, good design is a necessary but not sufficient prerequisite of large-scale adoption. Other critical facets of the process of adoption, such as the challenges around managing politics and stakeholders, will be addressed in future papers.

ACKNOWLEDGEMENTS

We dedicate this paper to the amazing late Professor Clifford Nass, who was an ardent supporter and essential partner in the development of TeachAIDS. His incomparable mind established the foundation for the research in this paper and for TeachAIDS overall. This is work he wanted to bring to the CHI community. In addition, without exaggeration, there have been thousands of people who have made it possible for TeachAIDS to exist. To the dedicated students, teachers, and celebrities around the world, as well as professors, staff, and students at Stanford, we offer our deepest gratitude and thanks to each and every one of you.

[5]The cultural transferability of the design of TeachAIDS – within and across countries – will be the focus of future publications.

REFERENCES

1. BK Ambati, J Ambati, and AM Rao. 1997. Dynamics of knowledge and attitudes about AIDS among the educated in southern India. *AIDS Care* 9, 3 (1997), 319–330.
2. Nazanin Andalibi, Oliver L Haimson, Munmun De Choudhury, and Andrea Forte. 2016. Understanding social media disclosures of sexual abuse through the lenses of support seeking and anonymity. In *Proceedings of CHI 2016*. ACM, 3906–3918.
3. Joshua D Angrist and Jörn-Steffen Pischke. 2008. *Mostly harmless econometrics: An empiricist's companion*. Princeton University Press.
4. Terry Kit-fong Au and Laura F Romo. 1996. Building a coherent conception of HIV transmission: A new approach to AIDS education. In *The Psychology of Learning and Motivation: Advances in Research and Theory*, Douglas L Medin (Ed.). Vol. 35. Academic Press, 193–241.
5. John A Bargh, Katelyn YA McKenna, and Grainne M Fitzsimons. 2002. Can you see the real me? Activation and expression of the true self on the Internet. *Journal of Social Issues* 58, 1 (2002), 33–48.
6. Amy L Baylor. 2009. Promoting motivation with virtual agents and avatars: Role of visual presence and appearance. *Philosophical Transactions of the Royal Society of London B: Biological Sciences* 364, 1535 (2009), 3559–3565.
7. Mesfin Awoke Bekalu and Steven Eggermont. 2015. Socioeconomic and socioecological determinants of AIDS stigma and the mediating role of AIDS knowledge and media use. *Journal of Communication in Healthcare* 8, 4 (2015), 316–324.
8. Francis S Bellezza. 1981. Mnemonic devices: Classification, characteristics, and criteria. *Review of Educational Research* 51, 2 (1981), 247–275.
9. Tami Benzaken, Ashutosh H Palep, and Paramjit S Gill. 2011. Exposure to and opinions towards sex education among adolescent students in Mumbai: A cross-sectional survey. *BMC Public Health* 11, 1 (2011), 1.
10. Nicola J Bidwell, Thomas Reitmaier, Gary Marsden, and Susan Hansen. 2010. Designing with mobile digital storytelling in rural Africa. In *Proceedings of CHI 2010*. ACM, 1593–1602.
11. Rohit Chaudhri, Darivanh Vlachos, Gaetano Borriello, Kiersten Israel-Ballard, Anna Coutsoudis, Penny Reimers, and Noah Perin. 2013. Decentralized human milk banking with ODK sensors. In *Proceedings of the 3rd ACM Symposium on Computing for Development*. ACM, 4.
12. Pride Chigwedere, George R Seage III, Sofia Gruskin, Tun-Hou Lee, and Max Essex. 2008. Estimating the lost benefits of antiretroviral drug use in South Africa. *JAIDS Journal of Acquired Immune Deficiency Syndromes* 49, 4 (2008), 410–415.
13. Joan C Chrisler. 2013. Teaching taboo topics: Menstruation, menopause, and the psychology of women. *Psychology of Women Quarterly* 37, 1 (2013), 128–132.
14. David J Clarke. 2008. *Heroes and Villains: Teachers in the Education Response to HIV*. International Institute for Educational Planning.
15. Nils Dahlbäck, QianYing Wang, Clifford Nass, and Jenny Alwin. 2007. Similarity is more important than expertise: Accent effects in speech interfaces. In *Proceedings of CHI 2007*. ACM, 1553–1556.
16. Nicola Dell, Trevor Perrier, Neha Kumar, Mitchell Lee, Rachel Powers, and Gaetano Borriello. 2015. Paper-digital workflows in global development organizations. In *Proceedings of CSCW 2015*. ACM, 1659–1669.
17. Alexandra E Evans, Elizabeth W Edmundson-Drane, and Karol K Harris. 2000. Computer-assisted instruction: An effective instructional method for HIV prevention education? *Journal of Adolescent Health* 26, 4 (2000), 244–251.
18. Ronald W Evans, Patricia G Avery, and Patricia Velde Pederson. 1999. Taboo topics: Cultural restraint on teaching social issues. *The Social Studies* 90, 5 (1999), 218–224.
19. Freedom HIV/AIDS. 2016. `http://www.freedomhivaids.in/` Accessed September 20, 2016.
20. David M Frohlich, Dorothy Rachovides, Kiriaki Riga, Ramnath Bhat, Maxine Frank, Eran Edirisinghe, Dhammike Wickramanayaka, Matt Jones, and Will Harwood. 2009. StoryBank: Mobile digital storytelling in a development context. In *Proceedings of CHI 2009*. ACM, 1761–1770.
21. Amelia Gentleman. 2007. Sex education curriculum angers Indian conservatives. *The New York Times* (May 2007). `http://www.nytimes.com/2007/05/24/world/asia/24iht-letter.1.5851113.html`
22. Maitrayee Ghosh. 2007. ICT and AIDS literacy: A challenge for information professionals in India. *Program* 41, 2 (2007), 134–147.
23. Kapil Goel, Sartaj Ahmad, Rahul Bansal, Pawan Parashar, Gagan Garg, and Parul Goel. 2014. A community based study on awareness of HIV/AIDS among young males of Meerut, Uttar Pradesh. *International Journal of Contemporary Medicine* 2, 1 (2014), 85.
24. Robert M Grant, Javier R Lama, Peter L Anderson, Vanessa McMahan, Albert Y Liu, Lorena Vargas, Pedro Goicochea, Martín Casapía, Juan Vicente Guanira-Carranza, Maria E Ramirez-Cardich, and others. 2010. Preexposure chemoprophylaxis for HIV prevention in men who have sex with men. *New England Journal of Medicine* 363, 27 (2010), 2587–2599.

25. Nora Ellen Groce and Reshma Trasi. 2004. Rape of individuals with disability: AIDS and the folk belief of virgin cleansing. *The Lancet* 363, 9422 (2004), 1663–1664.
26. Pratibha Gupta, Fatima Anjum, Pankaj Bhardwaj, JP Srivastav, Zeashan Haider Zaidi, and others. 2013. Knowledge about HIV/AIDS among secondary school students. *North American Journal of Medical Sciences* 5, 2 (2013), 119–123.
27. Brandon L Guthrie, Robert Y Choi, Rose Bosire, James N Kiarie, Romel D Mackelprang, Anne Gatuguta, Grace C John-Stewart, and Carey Farquhar. 2010. Predicting pregnancy in HIV-1-discordant couples. *AIDS and Behavior* 14, 5 (2010), 1066–1071.
28. Michael Hammond. 2010. What is an affordance and can it help us understand the use of ICT in education? *Education and Information Technologies* 15, 3 (2010), 205–217.
29. Natalie Jones, Helen Ross, Timothy Lynam, Pascal Perez, and Anne Leitch. 2011. Mental models: An interdisciplinary synthesis of theory and methods. *Ecology and Society* 16, 1 (2011), 46.
30. Anirudha Joshi, Mandar Rane, Debjani Roy, Shweta Sali, Neha Bharshankar, N. Kumarasamy, Sanjay Pujari, Davidson Solomon, H. Diamond Sharma, D. G. Saple, and others. 2011. Design opportunities for supporting treatment of people living with HIV/AIDS in India. In *IFIP Conference on Human-Computer Interaction*. Springer, 315–332.
31. Susan M Kiene and William D Barta. 2006. A brief individualized computer-delivered sexual risk reduction intervention increases HIV/AIDS preventive behavior. *Journal of Adolescent Health* 39, 3 (2006), 404–410.
32. Douglas B Kirby, BA Laris, and Lori A Rolleri. 2007. Sex and HIV education programs: Their impact on sexual behaviors of young people throughout the world. *Journal of Adolescent Health* 40, 3 (2007), 206–217.
33. Keshavan Kodandapani and Patricia T Alpert. 2007. AIDS in India: When denial kills. *Home Health Care Management & Practice* 20, 1 (2007), 21–26.
34. Cheryl Koopman and Helen Reid. 1998. Assessment of knowledge and beliefs about HIV/AIDS among adolescents. In *Handbook of Sexuality-Related Measures: A Compendium*. Vol. 2. Sage Publications, 321–324.
35. Indrajit Kundu. 2015. West Bengal: School bars HIV positive child to attend classes. *India Today* (November 2015). `http://indiatoday.intoday.in/story/west-bengal-school-bars-hiv-positive-child-to-attend-classes/1/525750.html`
36. Learning About Living in Nigeria. 2016. `http://www.learningaboutliving.com/` Accessed September 20, 2016.
37. Pranee Liamputtong. 2015. *Stigma, Discrimination and Living with HIV/AIDS*. Springer.
38. Alan R Lifson, Workneh Demissie, Alemayehu Tadesse, Kassu Ketema, Randy May, Bereket Yakob, Meka Metekia, Lucy Slater, and Tibebe Shenie. 2012. HIV/AIDS stigma-associated attitudes in a rural Ethiopian community: Characteristics, correlation with HIV knowledge and other factors, and implications for community intervention. *BMC International Health and Human Rights* 12, 1 (2012), 1.
39. Katherine Cumings Mansfield and Gaëtane Jean-Marie. 2015. Courageous conversations about race, class, and gender: Voices and lessons from the field. *International Journal of Qualitative Studies in Education* 28, 7 (2015), 819–841.
40. Nita Mawar, Seema Sahay, Apoorvaa Pandit, and Uma Mahajan. 2005. The third phase of HIV pandemic: Social consequences of HIV/AIDS stigma & discrimination & future needs. *Indian Journal of Medical Research* 122, 6 (2005), 471.
41. Alexandra McManus and Lipi Dhar. 2008. Study of knowledge, perception and attitude of adolescent girls towards STIs/HIV, safer sex and sex education: A cross sectional survey of urban adolescent school girls in South Delhi, India. *BMC Women's Health* 8, 1 (2008), 1.
42. Anand D Meundi, Ambikadevi Amma, Aruna Rao, Sangeetha Shetty, and Avinash K Shetty. 2007. Cross-sectional population-based study of knowledge, attitudes, and practices regarding HIV/AIDS in Dakshina Kannada district of Karnataka, India. *Journal of the International Association of Physicians in AIDS Care* (2007).
43. M Mikkilä-Erdmann, M Penttinen, E Anto, and E Olkinuora. 2008. Constructing mental models during learning from science text. In *Understanding Models for Learning and Instruction*. Springer, 63–79.
44. Suchismita Mishra, Basanta Kumar Swain, and Bontha Veerraju Babu. 2008. Sexual risk behaviour, knowledge and attitude related to HIV transmission: A study among a migrant tribal group living in the slums of Bhubaneswar City, Orissa, India. *Journal of Public Health* 16, 5 (2008), 331–337.
45. Chika Moses. 2013. Virgin cleansing: HIV positive father rapes 2-year-old daughter in hopes for cure. *Pilot Africa* (April 2013). `http://www.pilotafrica.com/2013/04/26/virgin-cleansing-hiv-positive-father-rapes-2-year-old-daughter-in-hopes-for-cure/`
46. Clifford Nass and Scott Brave. 2005. *Wired for Speech: How Voice Activates and Advances the Human-Computer Relationship*. MIT Press Cambridge.
47. Clifford Nass, Katherine Isbister, and Eun-Ju Lee. 2000. Truth is beauty: Researching embodied conversational agents. In *Embodied Conversational Agents*. 374–402.

48. Meena Natarajan and Tapan Parikh. 2013. Understanding barriers to information access and disclosure for HIV+ women. In *Proceedings of the Sixth International Conference on Information and Communication Technologies and Development: Full Papers-Volume 1*. ACM, 143–152.
49. Seth M Noar, Larson B Pierce, and Hulda G Black. 2010. Can computer-mediated interventions change theoretical mediators of safer sex? A meta-analysis. *Human Communication Research* 36, 3 (2010), 261–297.
50. Joyojeet Pal, Meera Lakshmanan, and Kentaro Toyama. 2009. My child will be respected: Parental perspectives on computers and education in Rural India. *Information Systems Frontiers* 11, 2 (2009), 129–144.
51. Alice Park. 2012. Thabo Mbeki and AIDS Denialism. *Time* (August 2012). `http://healthland.time.com/2012/08/21/legitimate-rape-todd-akin-and-other-politicians-who-confuse-science/slide/questioning-the-origin-of-aids/`
52. Trevor Perrier, Nicola Dell, Brian DeRenzi, Richard Anderson, John Kinuthia, Jennifer Unger, and Grace John-Stewart. 2015. Engaging pregnant women in Kenya with a hybrid computer-human SMS communication system. In *Proceedings of CHI 2015*. ACM, 1429–1438.
53. PopTech: Project Masiluleke. 2016. `http://www.poptech.org/project_m` Accessed September 20, 2016.
54. Jean A Pratt, Karina Hauser, Zsolt Ugray, and Olga Patterson. 2007. Looking at human–computer interface design: Effects of ethnicity in computer agents. *Interacting with Computers* 19, 4 (2007), 512–523.
55. Divya Ramachandran, John Canny, Prabhu Dutta Das, and Edward Cutrell. 2010. Mobile-izing health workers in rural India. In *Proceedings of CHI 2010*. ACM, 1889–1898.
56. Thomas Reitmaier, Nicola J Bidwell, and Gary Marsden. 2010. Field testing mobile digital storytelling software in rural Kenya. In *Proceedings of the 12th International Conference on Human Computer Interaction with Mobile Devices and Services*. ACM, 283–286.
57. Ouidade Sabri, Delphine Manceau, and Bernard Pras. 2010. Taboo: An underexplored concept in marketing. *Recherche et Applications en Marketing (English Edition)* 25, 1 (2010), 59–85.
58. Daniel L Schwartz, Jessica M Tsiang, and Kristen P Blair. 2016. *The ABCs of How We Learn: 26 Scientifically Proven Approaches, How They Work, and When to Use Them*. W. W. Norton and Company.
59. Arna Seal, Paromita Goswami, and Mridula S Mishra. 2007. From recall to redressal: A deconstructional content analysis of the Buladi HIV/AIDS campaign in West Bengal. *SSRN* (2007).
60. Dipti Singh. 2014. Goa school expels 13 HIV+ orphans, some parents say expel 23 others too. *The Indian Express* (July 2014). `http://indianexpress.com/article/india/india-others/goa-school-expels-13-hiv-orphans-some-parents-say-expel-23-others-too/`
61. John P Smith III, Andrea A Disessa, and Jeremy Roschelle. 1994. Misconceptions reconceived: A constructivist analysis of knowledge in transition. *The Journal of the Learning Sciences* 3, 2 (1994), 115–163.
62. William E Snell, Phillip D Finney, and Lisa J Godwin. 1991. Stereotypes about AIDS. *Contemporary Social Psychology* (1991).
63. Suruchi Sood, Corinne L Shefner-Rogers, and Manisha Sengupta. 2006. The impact of a mass media campaign on HIV/AIDS knowledge and behavior change in North India: Results from a longitudinal study. *Asian Journal of Communication* 16, 3 (2006), 231–250.
64. Piya Sorcar. 2009. *Teaching taboo topics without talking about them: An epistemic study of a new approach to HIV/AIDS prevention education in India*. Ph.D. Dissertation.
65. Piya Sorcar and Clifford Nass. 2010. Teaching taboo topics through technology. In *Handbook of Research on Digital Media and Advertising: User Generated Content Consumption*. Information Science Reference, 393–435.
66. Anne L Stangl, Jennifer K Lloyd, Laura M Brady, Claire E Holland, and Stefan Baral. 2013. A systematic review of interventions to reduce HIV-related stigma and discrimination from 2002 to 2013: How far have we come? *Journal of the International AIDS Society* 16, 3 (2013).
67. Text to Change Mobile. 2016. `http://ttcmobile.com/` Accessed September 20, 2016.
68. UNICEF. 2016. *HIV/AIDS*. `http://www.unicef.in/Story/1123/HIV-AIDS` Accessed September 20, 2016.
69. Ravi K Verma, S Sureender, and M Guruswamy. 1997. What do school children and teachers in rural Maharashtra think of AIDS and sex? *Health Transition Review* (1997), 481–486.
70. Stella Vosniadou and Christos Ioannides. 1998. From conceptual development to science education: A psychological point of view. *International Journal of Science Education* 20, 10 (1998), 1213–1230.
71. World Health Organization. 2016. *HIV/AIDS*. `http://www.who.int/mediacentre/factsheets/fs360/en/` Accessed September 20, 2016.
72. Chen Zhang, Xiaoming Li, Yu Liu, Shan Qiao, Liying Zhang, Yuejiao Zhou, Zhiyong Shen, and Zhengzhu Tang. 2016. Emotional, Physical and Financial Burdens of Stigma against People Living with HIV/AIDS in China. *AIDS Care* 28, sup1 (2016), 124–131.

What Can Be Predicted from Six Seconds of Driver Glances?

Lex Fridman[1] Heishiro Toyoda[2] Sean Seaman[3] Bobbie Seppelt[3]
Linda Angell[3] Joonbum Lee[1] Bruce Mehler[1] Bryan Reimer[1]
[1] Massachusetts Institute of Technology
[2] Toyota Collaborative Safety Research Center
[3] Touchstone Evaluations

ABSTRACT

We consider a large dataset of real-world, on-road driving from a 100-car naturalistic study to explore the predictive power of driver glances and, specifically, to answer the following question: what can be predicted about the state of the driver and the state of the driving environment from a 6-second sequence of macro-glances? The context-based nature of such glances allows for application of supervised learning to the problem of vision-based gaze estimation, making it robust, accurate, and reliable in messy, real-world conditions. So, it's valuable to ask whether such macro-glances can be used to infer behavioral, environmental, and demographic variables? We analyze 27 binary classification problems based on these variables. The takeaway is that glance can be used as part of a multi-sensor real-time system to predict radio-tuning, fatigue state, failure to signal, talking, and several environment variables.

ACM Classification Keywords

I.5 Pattern Recognition.

Author Keywords

Gaze patterns; driver state prediction; naturalistic on-road study; hidden Markov models.

INTRODUCTION

As the level of vehicle automation continues to increase, the car is more and more becoming a multi-sensor computational system tasked with understanding (1) the state of the driver [37] and (2) the state of the driving environment [25]. From a computer vision perspective, both of these tasks have over a decade of active research that proposes various methods for robust, real-time processing of inward-facing and outward-facing video to extract actionable knowledge with which the car can assist the driver [33]. Driver gaze classification is one of the more successful recent outcomes of these computer vision efforts promising above 90% gaze region classification accuracy [11] in the wild when simplifying the general gaze estimation problem by considering broad segmentation of gaze base on attention allocation semantics: forward roadway, left mirror, right mirror, rearview mirror, instrument cluster, center stack, and other regions. The promise of accurate real-time gaze classification is what motivates the question posed in this work: once the system infers gaze region from video, what can we predict about the state of the driver and the state of the environment? Put another way, a gaze classification system can be seen as one of several sensors available in the vehicle, and so it is valuable to investigate what actionable information can be inferred from this sensor in order to design a better interface between human and machine in the driving context.

The driving task and the driving environment places the driver under a wide array of physical and cognitive demands. Intuitively, visual demand can be predicted from gaze [29]. However, glance allocation strategies provide a window through which we can predict the more general mental and physical state of the driver outside of just where they are looking (i.e., activity [23], inattention [7], fatigue [15]). The possibility of inference about aspects of the external driving environment based on macro-glances is an open question for which this paper provides promising results. In this paper, "macro-glances" refer to the discretization of driver gaze (see the "Macro-Glances and Micro-Glances" section).

The generalizability of our exploratory look at what can and cannot be predicted from driver macro-glances relies inextricably on the characteristics of the dataset. We use 4,816 annotated six-second epochs of baseline driving from the 100-Car Naturalistic Driving Study database [6]. This dataset includes approximately 2,000,000 vehicle miles, almost 43,000 hours of data, 241 primary and secondary drivers, 12 to 13 months of data collection for each vehicle, and data from a highly capable instrumentation system including five channels of video and vehicle kinematics. This data contains many extreme cases of driving behavior and performance, including severe fatigue, impairment, judgment error, risk taking, willingness to engage in secondary tasks, aggressive driving, and traffic violations. Therefore, we believe that conclusions derived from this data are applicable to general real-world driving.

The contribution, novelty, and validity of this work can be summarized most briefly as follows:

- **Contribution:** Show that just 6 seconds of coarse driver gaze regions can be used to predict a lot of things about the driver, the car, and the driving environment. This helps (1) provide a greater understanding of the "human" in human-to-vehicle interaction and (2) pave the way for a real-time HMI system in the car based on driver gaze that is robust

Permission to make digital or hard copies of all or part of this work for personal or classroom use is granted without fee provided that copies are not made or distributed for profit or commercial advantage and that copies bear this notice and the full citation on the first page. Copyrights for components of this work owned by others than the author(s) must be honored. Abstracting with credit is permitted. To copy otherwise, or republish, to post on servers or to redistribute to lists, requires prior specific permission and/or a fee. Request permissions from Permissions@acm.org. CHI 2017, May 06 - 11, 2017, Denver, CO, USA Copyright is held by the owner/author(s). Publication rights licensed to ACM. ACM 978-1-4503-4655-9/17/05$15.00 DOI: http://dx.doi.org/10.1145/3025453.3025929

to challenging real-world conditions. See the "Framework for Gaze-Based HMI in the Car" section below.

- **Novelty:** Drive gaze has been used to predict attention allocation, but not to predict everything else. We try to do just that for the first time and show when it works and when it doesn't.
- **Validity:** The results are based on a large naturalistic on-road study with little to no constraints on the participants, so the data is representative of the general population and is extensive enough to provide a high degree of generalizability.

RELATED WORK

The 100-Car Naturalistic Driving Study dataset has been extensively used to analyze various aspects of driver behavior in the wild [6]. Much of the focus has been on the crashes and near-crashes in the data, and describing the factors that lead to these crashes [22] especially with regard to the long glances away from the road [20]. We focus instead on the baseline driving epochs which are more representative of the variability of driver behavior and driving environment.

Macro-Glances and Micro-Glances

We define the terms "macro-glances" and "micro-glances" to help specify the distinction between context-dependent and context-independent allocations of gaze:

- **Micro-Glances:** Context-independent gaze allocation achieved by fixational eye movement (i.e., saccades) and changes in head orientation. The target "location" of micro-glances is defined by the exact 3D coordinates of the fixation point. Example: driver looking at a stop sign.
- **Macro-Glances:** Gaze allocation categorized into discrete regions that are defined by the context. The target "location" of macro-glances is one of these pre-defined regions and not the exact 3D coordinates of the fixation point. Example: driver looking at the forward roadway.

In this work, we analyze the sequence of driver macro-glances which contains both spatial and temporal information. In particular, the temporal characteristics of the transition between glance regions is the main feature being utilized. This is in contrast to the traditional method of measuring driver state, such as measuring the total time visual attention is directed away from the forward roadway [2] or to elements specific to the operation of the HMI [12]. While these measures are intuitive and have some demonstrated utility, a shortcoming common to both approaches is that they aggregate behavioral information over a given time span to a single number, disregarding temporal dynamics that has to be considered in making predictions about the driver's physical and mental state. A good example of where temporal information is very important but has not been investigated as much as the aggregate measure is in using blink for fatigue classification [24]. Furthermore, work studying a driver's situational awareness of the driving environment has shown the complexity and context-dependent nature of a driver's gaze dynamics [8, 4].

It is intuitive that high-resolution micro-glances such as blinks and individual saccades could be used to predict the behavioral and environmental variables in this work. For example, glances patterns have been correlated with lane change behavior [28]. The open question is whether short-windowed macro-glances can be used for these classification problems. This is an important question because detection and tracking of driver micro-glances in in-the-wild on-road data is much less accurate than detection of macro-glances. The ability to rely on macro-glances alone for predictive tasks allows for the design of robust, real-time driver assistance systems that modify the behavior of the vehicle based on the detected states.

Prediction from Driver Glances

Driver glances have been used to to predict several aspects of driver state including cognitive load [21], secondary activity [27], and drowsiness [35], as covered in this section. The key novel contribution of our work is that we are using glance patterns to predict aspects of driving that are not obviously related to gaze and thus have not been analyzed in prior literature. These aspects include demographics (e.g., age, gender), behavior (e.g., failure to signal, talking), and environment (intersection proximity, lighting conditions, road type). In other words, this work serves as a new and useful exploration of what broad macro eye-movement reveal about the state of the driver and the state of the driving environment.

Cognitive Load and Secondary Tasks

As reviewed in [3], some initial work has been conducted that may be useful in the development of algorithms for identifying periods of driving during which different types of task loading occur. Much of this work was initially focused on identifying visual demand, or periods of visual or visual-manual task loading (e.g., [34, 18, 16, 27]). Additional work been directed at developing algorithms to identify cognitive load using eye glance behavior and driving performance metrics as inputs. Using data collected in a driving simulator, Zhang et al. explored a decision tree approach in [40] to estimate drivers' cognitive workload. Also working with simulator based data, Liang et al. used similar measures in a support vector machine (SVM) approach using a 40-second window with 95% overlap between windows in [21] to detect cognitive distraction, and obtained 91.6% accuracy in the structured predictions to which the model was applied. In [19] Liang et al. worked with Bayesian network models and found that they could identify cognitive load reliably with an average accuracy of 80.1%. They also found that dynamic Bayesian networks (DBNs) gave a better performance than static Bayesian network models. Further, blink frequency and eye fixation measures were particularly indicative of cognitive task workload in structured experimental data. Building on the previous simulator based work, Liang used a hierarchical layered algorithm in [18], which incorporated both a DBN and a supervised clustering algorithm, to identify feature behaviors when drivers were in different cognitive states. Three groups of performance measures were used at the lowest level of this algorithm: (1) eye movement temporal measures (blink frequency, fixation duration, etc.), (2) eye movement spatial measures (spatial location of gaze in x, y, z), and (3) driving performance measures (steering error, steering wheel standard deviation, lane position standard deviation) that were summarized across 30-second time windows, with no overlap between windows. Liang interpreted a sequential analysis as indicating that from a risk state identification perspective, it is not necessary to detect cognitive distraction if visual distraction is present as the latter dominates. A recent work [39] compared alternate SVM based classification approaches in a simulation context with experimentally defined periods of visual-manual, cognitive, and combined distraction. A "two-stage" classifier first considered visual-manual distraction and then detecting dual or cognitive distraction states was evaluated against a "direct-mapping" classifier developed to identify all distraction states at the same time. Advantages and limitations to both approaches appeared. Liang's [18] work is also relevant to the current effort in that it considers issues related to applying detection algorithms to naturalistic data.

Drowsiness and Impairment

Detection of driver arousal from blink rates, eye movement, and gaze patterns has received considerable attention in the simulated context and on small on-road datasets over two decades. A 10 year old survey paper [35] on driver fatigue detection covers the features of eye and eyelid movement that have continued to be used in papers that followed it. To the best of our knowledge, these features have not yet been proven to be robust to the highly variable naturalistic driving conditions, perhaps due to the costs and challenges associated with evaluating algorithms that require the collection of large driver-facing video datasets. The drowsiness detectors that have been implemented in many commercial vehicles have relied instead on measures of vehicle dynamics and driving performance [9, 30].

GLANCE MODEL AND PREDICTION APPROACH

Each six-second driving epoch contains the gaze region and a timestamp at the beginning of the epoch. Following this tuple is an arbitrary number of similar tuples marking the macro-glance transitions and their associated timestamps. These "glance transitions" refer to the moments in time when, based on the frame-by-frame annotations, the driver's gaze changed from one region to another. "Glance transitions" are event-based (see discrete event simulation [10]) in that they do not contain any self-transitions and only include changes of state. The duration of a glance is encoded in the difference of the timestamps of adjacent transitions.

For the purpose of modeling both glance transitions and durations as a Hidden Markov Model (HMM), we discretize the sequence of "glance transitions" into 25 state samples (spaced 250 milliseconds apart). By definition, the resulting sequence of states allow for self-transitions. The probability of such self-transitions form a simple model of state duration that was evaluated to be sufficient in this context. Explicit modeling of state duration for HMMs is an active area of research [38] and would be an effective extension to the model used in this work if epochs of longer and non-uniform durations were considered. The sampling rate of 4 Hz for the 6-second epochs was determined to be the lowest-resolution sampling that had below 1% information loss over the original data. The result is that each six-second epoch of "glance transitions" is reduced to a sequence of 25 macro-glance states and induced state transitions.

For classification, a fixed-length sequence of discrete values can be viewed as a categorical feature vector input to a traditional classifier. We investigated this approach using parameter grid search of Random Forest and SVM classifiers, both of which resulted in worse performance than what is reported in the "Dataset and Results" section. The better performing approach was to model the temporal structure of the sequence using a classic hidden Markov model (HMM). Each of the gaze regions in the sequence are modeled as the discrete observation of the HMM. These observations can take on 8 values: (1) rearview mirror, (2) center stack, (3) eyes closed, (4) interior object, (5) right, (6) forward, (7) instrument cluster, and (8) left. An important point about this approach is that distinct macro-glance duration is not explicitly modeled. The explicit-duration hidden semi-Markov model (HSMM) [14] was evaluated for its ability to model the sticky dynamics of each state. However, this approach did not perform well. We believe that this is due to the limited and uniform length of each training sequence (see the "Conclusion" section for discussion of future work that proposes further investigation of this kind of explicit duration modeling).

As described in the "Dataset and Results" section, each prediction question is modeled a binary classification problem. One HMM is trained per class. The number of hidden states in the HMM is set to 8, which does not correspond to any directly identifiable states in the driving context. Instead, this parameter was programmatically determined to maximize classification performance. One HMM is constructed for each of the two classes in the binary classification problem. The HMM model parameters are learned using the GHMM implementation of the Baum-Welch algorithm [31]. This process uses 80% of the sequences from each of the two classes. As shown in Table 1, the classes are often unbalanced. In order to balance the training set, the minority class is over-sampled using the SMOTE algorithm [5].

The result of the training process are two HMM models. Each model can be use to provide a log-likelihood of an observed sequence. The HMM-based binary classifier then takes a 25-observation sequence, computes the log-likelihood from each of the two HMM models, and returns the class associated with the maximum log-likelihood.

DATASET AND RESULTS

The 100-Car Naturalistic Driving Study dataset includes approximately 2,000,000 vehicle miles, almost 43,000 hours of data, 241 primary and secondary drivers, 12 to 13 months of data collection for each vehicle, and data from a highly capable instrumentation system including five channels of video and vehicle kinematics [6]. Our work uses 4,816 six-second baseline driving epochs randomly selected from this dataset. Each epoch was manually annotated for macro-glances based on the video of the driver's face. This annotation serves as the

Binary Classification Problem	Type	Accuracy (Average)	Accuracy (St. Dev.)	Class 1 Size (Epochs)	Class 2 Size (Epochs)
Weather (Clear vs Raining)	Environment	51.6%	2.7%	4,261	345
Behavior (Speeding)	Behavior/State	52.3%	7.4%	3,497	101
Seatbelt (Yes vs No)	Environment	55.8%	2.4%	4,101	601
Traffic Density (Low vs Medium)	Environment	56.2%	0.4%	2,385	2,255
Traffic Divider (Present vs Not Present)	Environment	56.6%	1.8%	3,102	1,423
Travel Lanes (2 or Less vs 3 or More)	Environment	57.7%	1.2%	2,725	1,975
Alignment (Straight vs Curve)	Environment	57.7%	2.6%	4,186	519
Age (Young vs Mature)	Demographic	58.3%	1.9%	1,657	1,188
Traffic Density (Medium vs High)	Environment	58.6%	4.0%	2,255	176
Behavior (Following Too Closely)	Behavior/State	59.1%	2.3%	3,497	871
Lighting (Day vs Night with Light)	Environment	59.2%	1.7%	3,257	1,059
Gender (Male vs Female)	Demographic	59.7%	0.6%	2,514	1,773
Surface Condition (Wet vs Dry)	Environment	60.3%	1.9%	4,309	452
Age (Young vs Middle)	Demographic	60.7%	0.9%	1,657	1,442
Traffic Density (Low vs High)	Environment	61.2%	3.9%	2,385	176
Locality (Rural vs Interstate)	Environment	61.9%	0.8%	1,362	1,298
Locality (City vs Interstate)	Environment	62.6%	2.6%	1,555	1,298
Lighting (Night with vs without Light)	Environment	63.8%	2.2%	831	456
Age (Middle vs Mature)	Demographic	63.8%	1.5%	1,442	1,188
Locality (City vs Rural)	Environment	63.8%	0.9%	1,555	1,362
Traffic Light/Sign (Present vs Not Present)	Environment	64.0%	1.9%	4,252	377
Lighting (Day vs Night without Light)	Environment	66.6%	1.9%	3,257	456
Near an Intersection (Yes vs No)	Environment	70.9%	3.6%	4,025	764
Distraction (Talking)	Behavior/State	75.4%	2.0%	1,330	575
Behavior (Failed to Signal)	Behavior/State	75.5%	1.5%	3,497	247
Distraction (Fatigue)	Behavior/State	80.4%	3.1%	1,330	181
Distraction (Adjusting Radio)	Behavior/State	88.3%	2.1%	1,330	201

Table 1: This table answers the central question posed by this work: what aspects of the driver and driving environment can be predicted using a short sequence macro-glances? Each row specifies the binary classification problem, the variable type, accuracy mean and standard deviation, and the number of 6-second epochs associated with each glance. The rows are sorted according to average classification accuracy in ascending order.

training and evaluation variables for each of the binary classification tasks in the "Binary Classification Performance" section.

Baseline Epoch Dataset

The 100-car study was the first large-scale naturalistic driving study of its kind [6, 17] and the forerunner of the much larger and subsequent SHRP2 naturalistic study. As such, the 100-car study was intended to develop the instrumentation, methods, and procedures for the SHRP2 and to offer an opportunity to begin to learn about how crashes develop, arise, and culminate based on recording of the pre-crash period (which had not been possible prior to the development of methods used in the naturalistic 100-car study).

From the data that were acquired during the 100-car study, two databases were constructed: (1) an event database, and

(2) a baseline database. The event database was comprised of epochs of driving that ended with a conflict. Conflicts were classified at four levels of severity: crash, near-crash, crash-relevant, and proximity-type conflicts. These event epochs were each 6 seconds long âĂŞ (consisting of 5 seconds prior to a precipitating event and 1 second after). After data-acquisition, human analysts performed detailed extraction and coding of data that had been recorded during the study for each 6 s period (including frame-by-frame analysis of glance behavior). In addition, if a secondary task was underway by a driver during this period, analysts coded it, and information about it.

The baseline database was constructed of 20,000 epochs – also each 6 seconds long. These baseline epochs were ones in which the vehicle maintained a velocity over 5 mph âĂŞ and in which driving occurred without incident (without any conflict occurring). Eye glance analyses were conducted on 5,000 of these baseline epochs. Baseline epochs were selected at random from all recorded data (excluding event data) – and this selection did not make use of any kinematic triggers. The 6-second length of these epochs was chosen to match the length of event epochs. Event variables such as "precipitating factor" and "evasive maneuver" (which were coded for event epochs) were not coded for baseline epochs âĂŞ since no conflict occurred within them. While the baseline epochs are free from safety-critical events (i.e., do not contain crashes, near-crashes, or incidents), these epochs of "just driving" nevertheless are rich records of behaviors that are undertaken by ordinary drivers on real roads during everyday driving. This makes them an excellent source of data for the work reported here.

The number of baseline epochs selected from each vehicle for the baseline database was determined by each vehicle's involvement in crash, near-crash, and incident epochs in the event database. A stratified proportional sample of baseline epochs was constructed such that vehicles which were involved in more conflicts, also contributed more baseline epochs to the baseline database. This was done to create the required basis for a case-control design needed for odds-ratio calculations that were planned for subsequent analyses on the dataset.

From the 100-car study, a specific dataset was prepared and made accessible to the scientific community for analysis. It may be downloaded (along with documentation) from [1]. This database contains only de-identified data (i.e., no video data are available).

Binary Classification Performance

We evaluate the degree to which discriminative signal is present in 6-second bursts of macro-glances for the purpose of predicting the following variables. We provide a brief description of each variable and the number of categorical values considered.

- Driving Environment
  - **Proximity to an Intersection (2 values):** A vehicle is at or close to an intersection.
  - **Lighting (3 values):** Daylight or evening, with the latter case considering with and without light.
  - **Traffic Sign (2 values):** Presence of a traffic light or stop sign.
  - **Locality (3 values):** Rural, interstate, and city.
  - **Traffic Density (3 values):** Low, medium, or high. This level is based entirely on number of vehicles, and the ability of the driver to select the driving speed.
  - **Surface Condition (2 values):** Wet or dry.
  - **Weather (2 values):** Clear or rain.
  - **Alignment (2 values):** Geographic curvature of the road: straight or curved.
  - **Travel Lanes (2 values):** 2.5 is the threshold. The two categories are "≤ 2" and "≥ 3".
  - **Traffic Divider (2 values):** Presence or absence of a median divider.
  - **Seatbelt (2 values):** Wearing or not wearing a seatbelt.
- Driver Demographics
  - **Age (3 values):** Young, middle, or mature. 23.5 is the threshold between young and middle. 40.5 is the threshold between middle and mature. Selected for dataset balance not behavioral profile.
  - **Gender (2 values):** Female or male.
- Driver State and Behavior
  - **Behavior (4 values):** Following too closely, failed to signal, speeding, or none.
  - **Distraction (4 values):** Adjusting radio, fatigue, talking, or not distracted.

These variables took on more values than those listed above, but the values were pruned in two ways. First, values for distraction that were directly related to glance were removed. Obviously, 100% accuracy can be achieved in predicting glance region from glance region, so we are only interested in predicting driver state that does not directly relate to glance. Second, we only considered values that were well-represented in the data. The threshold was 100 epochs. In some cases, the categorical values were combined. For example, age was collapsed into three groups: young, middle, and mature. The partitioning was performed in a way that the numbers of epochs associated with each value was balanced.

For variables that take on more than 2 values, we reduce the problem to a binary classification one between all pairs of values. This allows us to explore the discriminating potential of macro-glances with regard to variables that take on 2, 3, or 4 values. For behavior and distraction variables, we only consider the pairing of values with the baseline state of "none" and "not distracted", respectively.

Table 1 shows the result of applying the HMM-based classification method in the "Glance Model and Prediction Approach" section to the binary classification problems associated with the variables listed above. This table contains

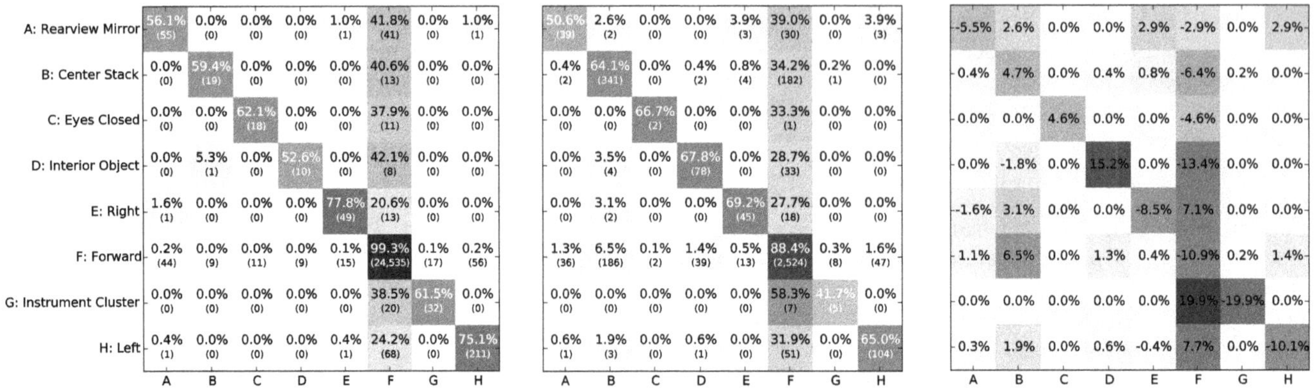

(a) Glance transition matrix for the first binary prediction class: "not distracted".

(b) Glance transition matrix for the first binary prediction class: "adjusting radio".

(c) The difference between the transition matrix for the two classes of "not distracted" and "adjusting radio".

Figure 1: An example of two glance transition matrices (first two subfigures) and their difference (third subfigure) that illustrates the discriminating characteristics of the glance dynamics based on which the two HMM models can make binary predictions. The y-axis is the "transition from" region and the x-axis is the "transition to" region. In the first two subfigures, the percentages designate the probability of transitions and the values in parentheses show the absolute number of times those transitions appear in the dataset. The third subfigure shows the difference in probabilities between the first two subfigures. Blue indicates a positive difference, red indicates a negative difference. The intensity of color fill in each matrix cell, across all three subfigures, indicates magnitude of the values associated with the transition in that cell. The transition matrices and their differences for each of the binary classification problems considered in this paper are provided in the appendix.

the answer to the question posed in the title of this paper. As expected, the problem of predicting anything about the driver or driving environment from just 6 seconds of macro-glances is very difficult, because both the duration of the sequence is too short and the resolution of the captured dynamics is too coarse. Nevertheless, accuracy of above 75% is achieved for the prediction of the following four driver behaviors and states: talking, fatigue, radio-tuning activity, and failure to signal. Also, 70.9% accuracy is achieved in predicting whether or not the vehicle is approaching an intersection. To provide intuition as to why this prediction works at all, Fig. 1 provides a visualization for the dynamics of the radio-tuning activity classification problem. The first two subfigures show the glance transition matrices for the "not distracted" and "adjusting radio" classes. The third subfigure shows the difference in transition probabilities between the first two subfigures. These matrices show that there are significant aggregate differences in macro-glance transitions for the two classes. The results in Table 1 show that these differences can be detected from six-second epochs for several variables critical for the design of intelligent driver assistance systems.

Framework for Gaze-Based HMI in the Car

The focus of this paper is to begin to answer the open question whether temporal patterns of macro-glances in the car contain sufficient discriminative signal to predict the state of the driver, the car, and the world. Our approach naturally leads to a real-time application of its various detectors in a vehicle. Fig. 2 shows an illustrative example of a driver approaching an intersection while operating a Tesla vehicle in Autopilot mode. Fig. 3 proposes how such a sequence of videos would be processing through time. In this proposed system, a sliding window of 6 seconds is used to make a series of binary predictions. Each of the predictions along with an estimated confidence are exposed through a CAN network API. HMI systems in the car are then able to alter their communication strategy with the driver and the external environment based on the predictions each system listens to for cases when the prediction confidence exceeds a minimum threshold.

In fact, an HMI system may utilize multiple sensor streams, only part of which would be the sensors derived from macro-glances. This is grounded in the design of joint cognitive systems envisioned and developed over the previous 3 decades [36, 13, 26]. For example, for the case in Fig. 2, the prediction may be that the driver's macro-glances are not indicative of proximity to an intersection even though based on the GPS coordinates reported on the CAN network, the car is in fact approaching intersection. This, in combination with the fact that the Tesla is operating under Autopilot and is thus driving itself, can be used by the car's external signaling system to infer that the driver is not paying attention and is unaware of the intersection. This information can then be conveyed to pedestrians and other vehicles, so that they make their movement decisions with a higher degree of caution.

CONCLUSION

This work asks what can and cannot be predicted from short bursts of driver macro-glances. We consider a representative sample of 4,816 annotated six-second epochs of driving from a 100-car naturalistic study. The variables under consideration fall into three categories: driving environment, driver behavior/state, and driver demographic characteristics. We form binary-classification problems from all the well-represented variables available in the dataset and model regularly-sampled macro-glances as a hidden Markov model

Figure 2: Illustrative sequence of snapshots collected in a Tesla vehicle of a driver's macro-glances. A time of $t = 0$ is marked as the point at which the driver can be annotated as being near an intersection.

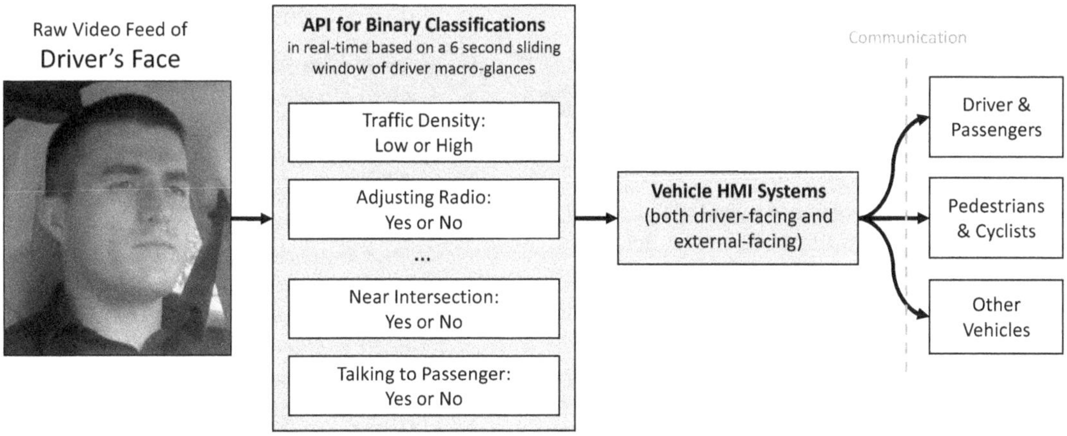

Figure 3: A framework for a system that processes (in real-time) the video of the driver's face and exposes an API to the HMI systems operating in the car that can appropriately alter their communication strategy with the driver, vehicle passengers, and the external driving environment based on the binary sensor signals.

for each class to make the binary prediction. The results show that radio-tuning activity, fatigue state, failure to signal, talking, and proximity to an intersection can be predicted with 70.9% to 88.3% accuracy. Based on these results, the general conclusion of this work is that macro-glances can be part of a multi-sensor system for predicting external environment factors, but on its own is only sufficient to predict a limited but important set of variables related to driver behavior and state. Nevertheless, significant improvements in accuracy may be achievable through further development of the underlying algorithmic approach. To this end, future work will investigate whether other approaches that capture temporal dynamics in the data, such as Hidden Semi-Markov Models (HSMM) [14] or Recurrent Neural Networks (RNN) [32], may perform better than HMMs, in which case macro-glances alone may be used as the basis for environment, behavior, state, and demographic prediction in future real-time driver assistance systems. Furthermore, using macro glance epochs of heterogeneous duration for training and evaluation may result in significant increases in prediction accuracy due to the fact that some environmental or behavioral factors may reveal themselves on different time-scales. For example, detection of talking may only need 1-2 seconds of macro-glances, while the detection of rural versus urban environmental conditions may requires an epoch of 10-20 seconds.

Acknowledgment
Support for this work was provided by the Santos Family Foundation, the New England University Transportation Center, and the Toyota Class Action Settlement Safety Research and Education Program. The views and conclusions being expressed are those of the authors, and have not been sponsored, approved, or endorsed by Toyota or plaintiffs' class counsel. Data was drawn from studies supported by the Insurance Institute for Highway Safety (IIHS).

REFERENCES
1. 2016. VTTI 100-Car Data. http://forums.vtti.vt.edu/. (2016).
2. National Highway Traffic Safety Administration and others. 2012. Visual-manual NHTSA driver distraction guidelines for in-vehicle electronic devices. *Washington, DC: National Highway Traffic Safety Administration (NHTSA), Department of Transportation (DOT)* (2012).
3. Linda Angell, Miguel A Perez, and Susan A Soccolich. 2015. Identification of Cognitive Load in Naturalistic Driving. *NSTSCE; 15-UT-037* (2015).
4. Cheryl A Bolstad, Haydee M Cuevas, Jingjing Wang-Costello, Mica R Endsley, and Linda S Angell. 2008. Measurement of situation awareness for automobile technologies of the future. (2008).
5. Nitesh V. Chawla, Kevin W. Bowyer, Lawrence O. Hall, and W. Philip Kegelmeyer. 2002. SMOTE: synthetic minority over-sampling technique. *Journal of artificial intelligence research* (2002), 321–357.
6. Thomas A Dingus, Sheila G Klauer, Vicki L Neale, A Petersen, SE Lee, JD Sudweeks, MA Perez, J Hankey, DJ Ramsey, S Gupta, and others. 2006. *The 100-car naturalistic driving study, Phase II-results of the 100-car field experiment.* Technical Report.
7. Tiziana D'Orazio, Marco Leo, Cataldo Guaragnella, and Arcangelo Distante. 2007. A visual approach for driver inattention detection. *Pattern Recognition* 40, 8 (2007), 2341–2355.
8. Mica R Endsley. 1995. Toward a theory of situation awareness in dynamic systems. *Human Factors: The Journal of the Human Factors and Ergonomics Society* 37, 1 (1995), 32–64.
9. Azim Eskandarian and Ali Mortazavi. 2007. Evaluation of a smart algorithm for commercial vehicle driver drowsiness detection. In *2007 IEEE intelligent vehicles symposium*. IEEE, 553–559.
10. George Fishman. 2013. *Discrete-event simulation: modeling, programming, and analysis*. Springer Science & Business Media.
11. Lex Fridman, Joonbum Lee, Bryan Reimer, and Trent Victor. 2016, In Print. Owl and Lizard: Patterns of Head Pose and Eye Pose in Driver Gaze Classification. *IET Computer Vision* (2016, In Print).
12. Driver Focus-Telematics Working Group and others. 2006. Statement of principles, criteria and verification procedures on driver interactions with advanced in-vehicle information and communication systems. *Alliance of Automotive Manufacturers* (2006).
13. Erik Hollnagel and David D Woods. 1983. Cognitive systems engineering: New wine in new bottles. *International Journal of Man-Machine Studies* 18, 6 (1983), 583–600.
14. Matthew J. Johnson and Alan S. Willsky. 2013. Bayesian Nonparametric Hidden Semi-Markov Models. *Journal of Machine Learning Research* 14 (February 2013), 673–701.
15. Rami N Khushaba, Sarath Kodagoda, Sara Lal, and Gamini Dissanayake. 2011. Driver drowsiness classification using fuzzy wavelet-packet-based feature-extraction algorithm. *Biomedical Engineering, IEEE Transactions on* 58, 1 (2011), 121–131.
16. Katja Kircher, Christer Ahlstrom, and Albert Kircher. 2009. Comparison of two eye-gaze based real-time driver distraction detection algorithms in a small-scale field operational test. In *Proc. 5th Int. Symposium on Human Factors in Driver Assessment, Training and Vehicle Design*. 16–23.
17. Sheila G Klauer, Thomas A Dingus, Vicki L Neale, Jeremy D Sudweeks, and David J Ramsey. 2006. *The impact of driver inattention on near-crash/crash risk: An analysis using the 100-car naturalistic driving study data.* Technical Report. National Highway Traffic Safety Administration.
18. Yulan Liang. 2009. Detecting driver distraction. (2009).

19. Yulan Liang, John Lee, and Michelle Reyes. 2007. Nonintrusive detection of driver cognitive distraction in real time using Bayesian networks. *Transportation Research Record: Journal of the Transportation Research Board* 2018 (2007), 1–8.

20. Yulan Liang, John D Lee, and Lora Yekhshatyan. 2012. How dangerous is looking away from the road? Algorithms predict crash risk from glance patterns in naturalistic driving. *Human Factors: The Journal of the Human Factors and Ergonomics Society* 54, 6 (2012), 1104–1116.

21. Yulan Liang, Michelle L Reyes, and John D Lee. 2007. Real-time detection of driver cognitive distraction using support vector machines. *IEEE transactions on intelligent transportation systems* 8, 2 (2007), 340–350.

22. Dominique Lord and Fred Mannering. 2010. The statistical analysis of crash-frequency data: a review and assessment of methodological alternatives. *Transportation Research Part A: Policy and Practice* 44, 5 (2010), 291–305.

23. Jannette Maciej and Mark Vollrath. 2009. Comparison of manual vs. speech-based interaction with in-vehicle information systems. *Accident Analysis & Prevention* 41, 5 (2009), 924–930.

24. R Martins and JM Carvalho. 2015. Eye blinking as an indicator of fatigue and mental load a systematic review. *Occupational Safety and Hygiene III* (2015), 231.

25. Joel C McCall and Mohan M Trivedi. 2006. Video-based lane estimation and tracking for driver assistance: survey, system, and evaluation. *Intelligent Transportation Systems, IEEE Transactions on* 7, 1 (2006), 20–37.

26. David Bryan Miller and Wendy Ju. 2015. Joint cognition in automated driving: Combining human and machine intelligence to address novel problems. In *2015 AAAI Spring Symposium Series*.

27. Mauricio Munoz, Bryan Reimer, Joonbum Lee, Bruce Mehler, and Lex Fridman. 2016. Distinguishing Patterns in Drivers' Visual Attention Allocation Using Hidden Markov Models. *Transportation Research Part F: Traffic Psychology and Behaviour* 43 (2016), 90–103. DOI:http://dx.doi.org/10.1016/j.trf.2016.09.015

28. Timo Pech, Philipp Lindner, and Gerd Wanielik. 2014. Head tracking based glance area estimation for driver behaviour modelling during lane change execution. In *Intelligent Transportation Systems (ITSC), 2014 IEEE 17th International Conference on*. IEEE, 655–660.

29. Bryan Reimer, Bruce Mehler, Ian Reagan, David Kidd, and Jonathan Dobres. 2016. Multi-modal demands of a smartphone used to place calls and enter addresses during highway driving relative to two embedded systems. *Ergonomics* 59, 12 (2016), 1565–1585.

30. David Sandberg, Torbjörn Akerstedt, Anna Anund, Göran Kecklund, and Mattias Wahde. 2011. Detecting driver sleepiness using optimized nonlinear combinations of sleepiness indicators. *IEEE Transactions on Intelligent Transportation Systems* 12, 1 (2011), 97–108.

31. Alexander Schliep, Benjamin Georgi, Wasinee Rungsarityotin, I Costa, and A Schonhuth. 2004. The general hidden markov model library: Analyzing systems with unobservable states. *Proceedings of the Heinz-Billing-Price* 2004 (2004), 121–135.

32. Jürgen Schmidhuber. 2015. Deep learning in neural networks: An overview. *Neural Networks* 61 (2015), 85–117.

33. Sayanan Sivaraman and Mohan Manubhai Trivedi. 2013. Looking at vehicles on the road: A survey of vision-based vehicle detection, tracking, and behavior analysis. *Intelligent Transportation Systems, IEEE Transactions on* 14, 4 (2013), 1773–1795.

34. Trent W Victor, Joanne L Harbluk, and Johan A Engström. 2005. Sensitivity of eye-movement measures to in-vehicle task difficulty. *Transportation Research Part F: Traffic Psychology and Behaviour* 8, 2 (2005), 167–190.

35. Qiong Wang, Jingyu Yang, Mingwu Ren, and Yujie Zheng. 2006. Driver fatigue detection: a survey. In *Intelligent Control and Automation, 2006. WCICA 2006. The Sixth World Congress on*, Vol. 2. IEEE, 8587–8591.

36. David D Woods. 1985. Cognitive technologies: The design of joint human-machine cognitive systems. *AI magazine* 6, 4 (1985), 86.

37. Guosheng Yang, Yingzi Lin, and Prabir Bhattacharya. 2010. A driver fatigue recognition model based on information fusion and dynamic Bayesian network. *Information Sciences* 180, 10 (2010), 1942–1954.

38. Shun-Zheng Yu. 2010. Hidden semi-Markov models. *Artificial Intelligence* 174, 2 (2010), 215–243.

39. Yu Zhang and David Kaber. 2016. Evaluation of strategies for integrated classification of visual-manual and cognitive distractions in driving. *Human Factors: The Journal of the Human Factors and Ergonomics Society* (2016), 0018720816647607.

40. Yilu Zhang, Yuri Owechko, and Jing Zhang. 2004. Driver cognitive workload estimation: A data-driven perspective. In *Intelligent Transportation Systems, 2004. Proceedings. The 7th International IEEE Conference on*. IEEE, 642–647.

Using Advisory 3D Sound Cues to Improve Drivers' Performance and Situation Awareness

Minjuan Wang[1], Sus Lundgren Lyckvi[1,3], Chenhui Hong[2], Palle Dahlstedt[1,3], Fang Chen[1]
[1]Interaction Design, Department of Applied IT,
[2] Systems, Control and Mechatronics, Department of Signals and Systems
Chalmers University of Technology, Gothenburg, Sweden
[3] University of Gothenburg, Gothenburg, Sweden
[minw; sus.lyckvi; palle; fang.chen]@chalmers.se, chenhui@student.chalmers.se

ABSTRACT

Within vehicle Human Machine Interface design, visual displays are predominant, taking up more and more of the visual channel for each new system added to the car, e.g. navigation systems, blind spot information and forward collision warnings. Sounds however, are mainly used to alert or warn drivers together with visual information. In this study we investigated the design of auditory displays for advisory information, by designing a 3D auditory advisory traffic information system (3DAATIS) which was evaluated in a drive simulator study with 30 participants. Our findings indicate that overall, drivers' performance and situation awareness improved when using this system. But, more importantly, the results also point towards the advantages and limitations of the use of advisory 3D-sounds in cars, e.g. attention capture vs. limited auditory resolution. These findings are discussed and expressed as design implications.

Author Keywords

3D Auditory Advisory Traffic Information System; auditory display; in-vehicle design; drive behavior

ACM Classification Keywords

H.5.2 [Information interfaces and presentation]: User Interfaces.

INTRODUCTION

In everyday life, we extract a wealth of information from sounds to obtain a continuous, holistic situation awareness of our surroundings. Humans are well adapted for listening to simultaneous sounds and also have the ability to focus on the more interesting information, filtering out the rest [30]. The capability to quickly and correctly judge the position of a threat has been of vital importance for our survival. Even though the accuracy in sound localization is comparatively poor, about 4-10 degrees [4], our ability to simultaneously interpret both the direction and content of a sound has been recognized and successfully applied in early interactive information systems [11]. In addition, the omni-directionality and attention capture aspects of sounds are important advantages of auditory displays. Hence, many computer applications utilize the advantages of sound, using it not only for warnings, but even more so for feedback or as a means to convey system state, games being the prime example of the latter.

Permission to make digital or hard copies of all or part of this work for personal or classroom use is granted without fee provided that copies are not made or distributed for profit or commercial advantage and that copies bear this notice and the full citation on the first page. Copyrights for components of this work owned by others than the author(s) must be honored. Abstracting with credit is permitted. To copy otherwise, or republish, to post on servers or to redistribute to lists, requires prior specific permission and/or a fee. Request permissions from Permissions@acm.org.
CHI 2017, May 06 - 11, 2017, Denver, CO, USA
Copyright is held by the owner/author(s). Publication rights licensed to ACM.
ACM 978-1-4503-4655-9/17/05...$15.00
DOI: http://dx.doi.org/10.1145/3025453.3025634

In cars however, sound is commonly thought of as a way to warn about critical situations, or to enhance the visual display by providing auditory feedback. There are however several concerns when using auditory displays [14,20]: Sounds can be annoying, and since they are good at attracting the users' attention, repeated or continuous sounds can cause fatigue and reduced attentiveness. Even some types of music can cause accidents, as shown by Brodsky [7]. In addition, there is the issue of privacy and disturbance, since sound is omnidirectional and cannot be directed at a single user. Lastly, other sounds may interfere with, or mask, the system sound. Despite these limitations, sound has a range of information capacities and advantages that makes it particularly useful to convey information in certain contexts. It can be used to provide an additional information channel for users whose eyes are busy attending to a different task, like for instance airplane pilots [3] and drivers [23]. And, since humans are very good at hearing patterns in sound [6], audio is a well-known approach for the monitoring of systems in visually intensive environments, since it can reduce the visual overload and can be heard over the background of other sounds, such as noise or music.

Currently, new Advanced Driver Assistance Systems (ADAS) are introduced into the car environment together with visual displays placed in the central console, the Digital Information Display (DIM) or the Head-up Display (HUD). This despite the fact that the main activities of driving implies that users must look at, and focus on, the road. As a result, drivers may miss important information because their visual system is overloaded – they simply have too much to look at. A way to avoid this overload could be to present some information in the form of sounds instead, in this sharing the information load between senses.

In this study, we explore *how driver performance and Situation Awareness can be increased by using a 3D Auditory Advisory Information System* (3DAATIS), in this investigating the benefits and drawbacks that come with the use of spatial sound cues. We will describe the study and the results of it, including the design implications we have found when it comes to using sound as information carrier in a normal driving situation.

RELATED WORK

Within HCI, three types of auditory signs can be used to translate symbolic visual artifacts into auditory artifacts: auditory icons, spearcons and earcons [14]. Auditory icons are based on a natural sound coupled to what they are supposed to represent. Spearcons consist of a spoken phrase, which has been speeded up until it is not recognized as speech. Earcons are symbolic sounds made up of rhythm, pitch, timbre, register (the relative high/low of the pitch) and the dynamics (the relative loudness) [5]. One example is a pinging sound to signal that a new email has arrived). McGookin and Brewster [21] have studied identification of concurrently presented earcons, testing up to 4 simultaneous earcons. Hardly surprising they found that it was easier to identify fewer icons than many, but when the earcons had different timbre, and were slightly offset in time, accuracy increased. Despite the fact that they are the hardest to learn and map, earcons are the most commonly used signs in cars as well as in everyday software, this due to the lack of natural sounds representing the activities they represent.

Auditory Displays Supporting Situation Awareness (SA)

Summala has stated that a driver's goal is to drive without discomfort and stay within his or her comfort zone [25]. Hence, drivers are required to have a good Situation Awareness (SA) in regards to the surrounding traffic environment, making it possible for them to foresee potential hazards in advance. According to Endsley [9], SA is the perception of elements in the environment within a volume of time and space, the comprehension of their meaning, and the projection of their status in the near future. Thus, a good strategy to enhance driver's SA is to present information regarding other road users' location and danger in relation to drivers and how the situation is evolving over time.

In one of the earlier studies regarding sound in cars, Tan and Lerner [1] did an extensive study of how subjects perceived warning sounds in a car environment. The main conclusions from this study were that albeit sound is promising for warnings in cars, even the better-performing combinations of sounds and speaker directions did not result in a great accuracy. Their experiment featured 16 speakers and six different sounds. Subjects observed a naturalistic video of driving and their task was to specify the direction of the sounds they heard, and their response times and accuracy were tested, among other things; 90% of the subjects responded within the right quadrant (i.e. within 45 degrees in either direction from the exact location), but there were always some cases of perceptual reversal, i.e. that subjects pointed 90 degrees or more off. It is notable that the study dealt only with immediate responses to warning sounds (as opposed to advisory sounds), and that there was no real driving task involved.

Recent studies have demonstrated that auditory information improves safety in driving, shortens response time, enhances accuracy and increases drivers' SA. For example, studies show that looming warning signals (i.e. sounds whose intensity increase as the distance between the driver's vehicle and the lead vehicle decreases) and its visual analogue provide very powerful signals to the human perceptual system and that they also capture attention [18]. Gray [13] performed a comparative study and found that looming auditory warnings produced the best combination of response speed and accuracy. In the study, participants experienced four non-looming auditory warnings (constant intensity, pulsed, ramped, and car horn), three looming auditory warnings (veridical, signals shorter than actual time to collision (TTC) time, signals longer than actual TTC time) under a no-warning condition. However, in their study, only a rear end collision scenario was studied, and it focused on warning the drivers – how looming auditory cues works in other types of non-critical traffic scenarios needs to be studied further.

Exploring auditory signs, Fagerlönn and Alm [12] conducted an experiment to examine the use of different types of auditory signs to support truck drivers' situation awareness. Their results showed that abstract (earcon-like) sounds required significantly longer learning times and longer response performances in comparison with to sounds that have a natural meaning in the driving context. In the study, the participants were asked to memorize different types of auditory signs and their corresponding road users. Then, their ability to map them correctly was tested, giving the sound as cue. However, this cognitive process is quite different from a real driving situation, since drivers who get a sound cue typically also visually assess the situation.

Liu and Jhuang [19] conducted a driving simulator study to evaluate the effects of five in-vehicle warning information displays (one visual; two auditory displays using static and spatialized sound respectively; and two audiovisual displays using static and spatialized sound respectively). The results showed that a spatialized auditory display significantly improved drivers' performance in reacting to the divided attention task and making accurate decisions. In a similar vein, Baillie et al [2] conducted a simulator study where five separate auditory feedback methods were compared during both autonomous and manual driving scenarios. Their results showed that the spatialized auditory presentation method was superior to the other methods, and in addition that drivers felt significantly more in control during scenarios containing sound vs. no sound. In both of these studies, the focus was to evaluate drivers' response to different types of displays. How they utilized the information for decision making when interacting with different road users was not studied.

Summary

Together, these studies indicate that the concept of giving *spatialized auditory advisory traffic information* is a promising approach to enhance driver's situation awareness. However, most of these studies were either focusing on the perception of the sounds per se [1,12] or how drivers respond to sounds in drive simulator drives lacking complex traffic situations [1,11]. Watson and Sanderson [29] have stated that an auditory display's effectiveness at communicating information should be evaluated according to its context of use; how drivers interact with auditory information may differ in a more realistic driving situation with different traffic scenarios. Since drivers typically visually confirm the sound information, the interaction with the auditory display, as well as the information needs may be very different. In this study we thus tested our system under as real as possible driving conditions, in which it differs from the others mentioned here.

BACKGROUND: OUR PREVIOUS WORK

This particular study is a part of a larger research project, which aims to explore the design of advisory traffic information systems in cars. The particular study described in this paper was thus preceded by two other studies upon which this one is being based.

The first study [26,27] was a focus group study which studied drivers' requirements on 3DAATIS, as well as their expressed information needs. The results showed that users were positive to the concept, and gave a quite detailed view on in which situations they felt that they needed auditory information. The result of the study was a list of design recommendations in regards to sound design, information prioritization, road user categorization, etc.

This was followed up by a second study, an expert focus group study with five sound experts: one in-vehicle acoustic researcher, two acoustic designers from Swedish automotive OEMs and two in-vehicle interaction designers. The purpose was to narrow down the design requirements collected from the first study. The framing was that it should be possible to use these recommendations for a sound system in vehicles being produced five years from when the workshop was held. The result from the workshop was a number of design decisions.

1. Sound cues should be presented on the *critical level* (warning sounds), and the *safety level* (advisory sounds which direct drivers attention to potential hazard).
2. Only *one type of sound* was to be used, since the intention of this system is to direct drivers attention to potential hazards, which they can then confirm visually.
3. *The sound was to convey urgency, direction and movement.* Direction and movement quite naturally go together, since the sounds are displaying moving objects after all. The urgency parameter distinguished whether a sound was advisory or warning.

The results from the focus group lay the foundation for the design of the system tested in this study.

Within the project, studies on visual advisory traffic information systems were carried out in parallel. In this study we reused the information presentation thresholds for advisory and warning levels. These thresholds were tested and adjusted iteratively according the characteristics of the drive simulator used in both studies [28].

RESEARCH AIM

In this particular study we set out to test our 3DAATIS focusing on the following questions:

How can a 3D Auditory Advisory Information System influence driver's situational awareness and driving performance?

From this, what can we learn about the design of 3DAATIS?

METHOD

The study utilized a within-subject design, treatment conditions (without 3DAATIS / with 3DAATIS), and five traffic incidents scenarios (see below) as independent variables. In this section we will describe participants, hardware, software, sound design, scenarios, procedure and data collection in detail, starting with a brief overview.

The Study in Short

For this study, we developed a prototype of a 3D sound system, which aims to provide relevant advisory information regarding road users in the vicinity of the own vehicle. This information includes in which direction the road users move and which risk level they are at (in terms of time/ distance to collision).

The study was a simulator study. Participants came in one by one, making two drives, one baseline, one with 3DAATIS, in random order. The drives featured the same eight scenarios, again in randomized order. Twice during each drive, the simulation was frozen and the participant's situation awareness was measured. In addition, driver performance data was collected. Finally, the participants' opinions on the system were collected in a post-interview.

Participants

In all, 30 participants took part in the study (18 men and 12 women; mean age 40 years, range 21-63 years), and their average driving experience was 18.3 years (ranging from 3 to 45 years). The participants were recruited around a science park in an urban area, this since highly educated, well-payed people can afford a car with different ADAS functions – thus they were in the right segment of buyers.

System Design

The aim of the 3DAATIS was that participants should be able to identify the *origin and moving location* of a sound cue. For example, when a car comes up from rear and takes over, participants should hear a sound "coming" from the back and "moving" closer, "passing" on the left side as the approaching car takes over. Moreover, they should be able to *map an increasing risk level with changes in the sound*. There were two levels: advisory and warning sounds.

At this point, we decided on using 3D-sound (i.e. surround sound), since we found it to be the best solution. The alternative would have been to use binaural sound. But, when using speakers with binaural sound, the complex acoustics of the car interior blurs directionality. If using head phones instead, absolute sound localization (relative to the outside world and not the listeners head) becomes confusing as soon as users move their head. Lastly there was also a pragmatic argument for using 3D-sound: we aimed to develop a solution feasible for cars in the close future, i.e. it should not rely on an expensive, hard-to-calibrate system, or on all drivers wearing head phones.

The sound design process for the 3DAATIS was based on the results from the expert focus group session described in "Background: Our Previous Work". Following Meera's recommendation, an earcon was designed by sound experts [5]. The sound sample was designed based on the OEM's sound attributes which had tested well in regards to user acceptance. The sound is somewhat similar to a plucked string, with a strong attack, followed by a decaying tail consisting primarily of the fundamental, with a few overtones. Overtones were added to decrease the risk of masking by other sounds, and a new exponentially decaying tail helped decrease annoyance. This is also what makes it somewhat similar to the plucking of a string, which is generally perceived as a pleasant sound. The sound sample was tested with several sound experts as well as within the research group, and several design iterations were done in order to make sure that the sound design was appropriate for the purpose of advisory signals. Figure 1 shows a sonogram of the used sound sample.

To allow for continuous localization, the sound is looped. As long as the other road user (i.e. the subject of the sound cues) is within the advisory level, the repetitive sound is projected from the accurate relative angle, continuously tracking the object as it moves. We used a form of "fake Doppler" effect to communicate a rapidly changing distance to other road users. Real Doppler effects are mostly detectable at quite high relative speeds and if the observer is somewhat distant from the sound source, which makes it less useful in traffic situations. However, as humans are very sensitive to pitch changes, we added a slight gradual increase in pitch with closing distance (from 268Hz to 288Hz), to call for increased attention, as well as an increase in the repetition rate (from 667ms to 620ms).

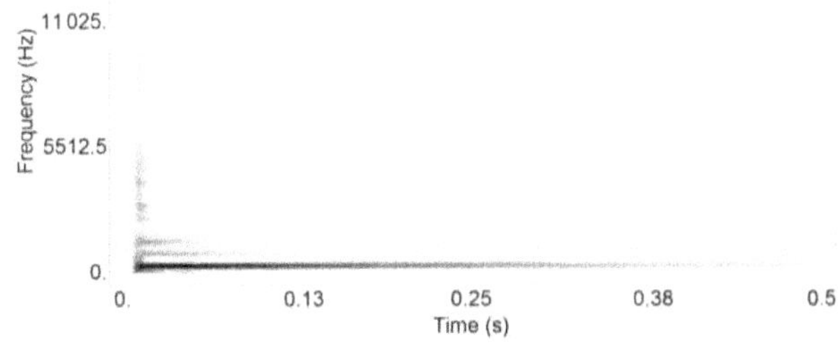

Figure 1: A sonogram of the sound used

When the situation gets critical, the system increases the pitch of the sound (up to 445Hz-469Hz, again varying with distance) while further shortening the loop (198ms-187ms), since this increases the perceived urgency while keeping continuity from the ongoing advisory sound. If the car is surrounded by more than one road user, several sounds are played, one per subject, from the accurate relative angle, with the correct urgency level. The different pitches and repetition rates help distinguish the sounds from each other.

The activation thresholds of *advisory* and *warning* information levels are based on two free parameters:

- *Time-to-collision* (TTC): The assumed reaction time of the driver of the following vehicle in seconds.
- *Safety margin* (SM): The distance of the closest point between the participant's vehicle and other approaching vehicles in meters when they are in parallel lanes.

The thresholds had been tested in our previous studies [28]; this was necessary since the perception of distance is different when driving in a real car vs in the simulator, and thus we adapted the thresholds accordingly; see Table 1.

Software

The prototype was developed using a combination of the dataflow programming environment Pure Data and Matlab. The latter was used to receive simulator data and send direction, distance, and time-to-collision data to the Pure Data patch, which in turn generated the relevant sounds (i.e. warning or advisory) and projected them in a 5.1-channel surround sound system. Sound directionality was achieved through equal energy-panning between speaker pairs. The 3DAATIS information was presented at 65 dB with a traffic ambient noise at 45 dB in the background.

Hardware

A PC running STISIM Drive® software was utilized as driver simulator. A HD projector was used to project the simulated drive scenarios on the front wall. Two webcams were installed to record what the drivers saw on the road, as

Information Level	Sound Effects	TTC	SM
Advisory	Original sound sample	3 to 6 s	< 3 m
Critical	Increased pitch and frequency of looping	< 3 s	< 2 m

Table 1. Thresholds for warnings in terms of Time to Collision (seconds) or Safety Margin (meters).

well as their reactions to the incidents, e.g. steering and braking. This video data was synchronized with drivers' simulation data to better allocate the starting point of drivers' reactions to the incidents. A Logitech G25 Racing Wheel, which included gas and brake pedals and a gearbox was installed in front of an actual car seat.

Another PC ran the 3DAATIS system as described in the previous section. In addition, a5.1-channel surround-sound system (Logitech Z-5500) was used for the auditory system. The arrangement of loudspeakers and seating position of participants were calibrated according to Dolby 5.1 home theatre speaker guidelines. However, the centre speaker was not used in this experiment (in a 5.1 setup it is primarily intended for dialogue sound in movies). Sound-absorbing curtains were installed on three sides of the test area to ensure a good surround sound effect.

The Traffic Incidents Scenarios Studied

In order to design test incident scenarios that represents real traffic situations, the research team had, in an earlier study [28] observed over 100 naturalistic driving videos. For this particular study, we chose scenarios that cover common critical situations found in the naturalistic drive videos.

To test the effects of the design, we chose three scenarios involving vehicles, and two involving pedestrians. The order of the scenarios and the physical environments, e.g. buildings, trees and the brands of the event cars were randomized for each new test drive. Below we will describe the five scenarios we actually studied. **The car (a) represents the driver's car in all scenarios**.

Cut In

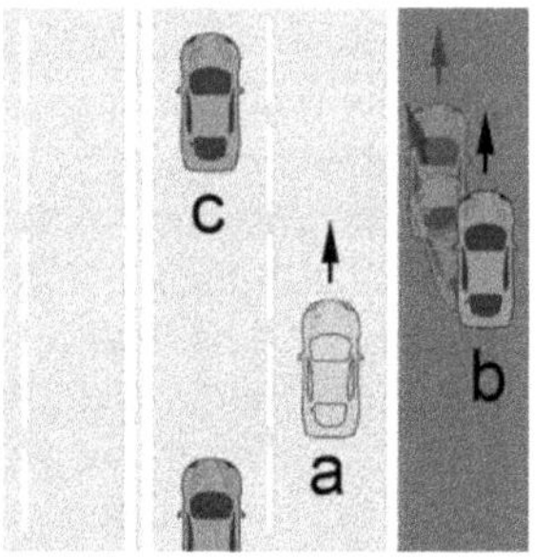

In this event, car b (parked on the sidewalk on the right) attempts to start up and cut into the driver's lane, then it sees the driver's car in the rear view mirror, so it steers back to the sidewalk. On the lane to the left of car a (the driver's car), there are another two cars; one is in the front and behind. Hence, changing lanes is not a good strategy. The considered safe approach in this scenario is to *brake or steer slightly to the left.*

Intersection

Here, the driver (in car a), has a green light. However, two pedestrians start crossing the street right in front of the driver anyway. One pedestrian is walking from right to left quite slowly, whereas the other is walking from left to right relatively fast. Of these two, the faster one starts walking first, and is partly hidden in the A pillar blind spot, whereas the slower one starts later. In this scenario, the considered safe behavior is to *brake and wait for the pedestrians to pass.*

Overtake

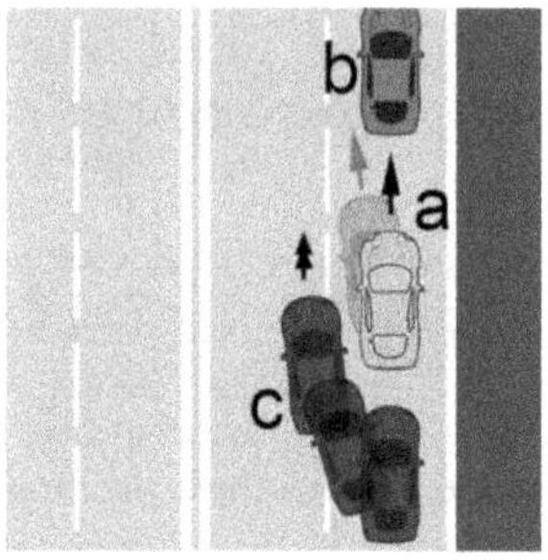

One car (b) drives in front of the driver's car (a) at a slower speed and force the drivers to change lane. Another vehicle (c) appears from behind, having a very high speed, overtaking both a and b at a close distance. Here, the safest possible way to avoid the accident is stop change lane and *keep one's position behind car b.*

Pedestrian

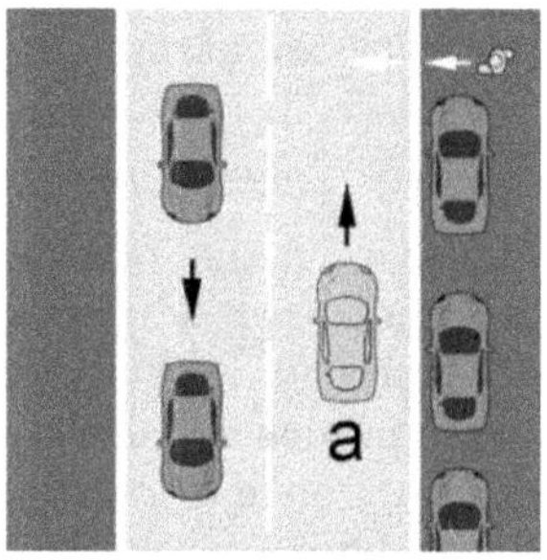

Here, a single lane in a residential area, a pedestrian suddenly walks out between the cars on the right side of the road. The driver (in car a) has a visual disadvantage in this scenario; visual contact with the pedestrian is made at a very short distance. Thus, the safest possible way to avoid the accident is *to brake and steer at the same time.*

Red Cab

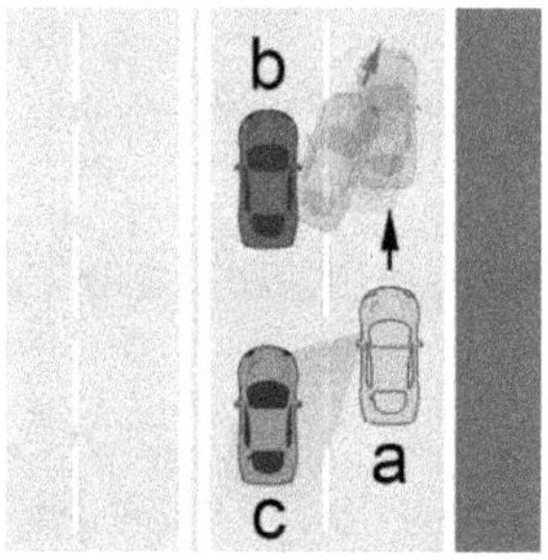

Here, two slow cars (b and c) drive in the left lane. Car b suddenly cuts into the driver's lane very fast directly in front of the driver's car (car a). At this moment, the other car (c) is in the blind spot of car a. In this scenario, the considered safe approach is to *slow down in order to avoid an accident.*

Overall Procedure

First, the participant was introduced to the study and filled out a demographic questionnaire on hearing capabilities, driving experience etc. Thereafter, the participant was given instructions regarding the test drives. The researchers explained the purpose and the procedure of the experiment in general, and instructed drivers to keep the speed at 60 km/h, follow traffic regulations, and stay in the right lane if possible. After getting some instructions on how to drive in the simulator and how the 3DAATIS works, each subject got to train until they fully understood the simulator and 3DAATIS features. Three questions were asked after training to make sure the participants understood the 3D localization sound. When participants were satisfied and fully understood the principles of sound system, the main test started.

Each subject drove twice, once with the 3DAATIS and once baseline. As mentioned, the 3DAATIS information was presented at 65 dB with a traffic ambient noise at 45 dB in the background, in the baseline only the latter. This as the focus of this study was to understand how drivers utilize 3DAATIS under different traffic scenarios. The drives featured eight scenarios of which five were tested; the remaining three were added in order to reduce learning effects between test drives under different conditions. Both the order of conditions and the order of the scenarios was randomized. At two points during each drive (at the same scenarios) the simulation was frozen and the screen turned off, and the participant had to fill out a SAGAT form on Situation Awareness. In addition to this data, the drivers' performance data was also logged during the drives. After the driving, a post interview was conducted with each participant, collecting their feedback regarding the system. Finally, the participants were rewarded with two movie tickets.

DATA COLLECTION

The study featured collection of both quantitative and qualitative data, since we not only measured participants' SA and performance, but also their attitude to the system and how they experienced it.

Measuring Situation Awareness

The drivers' situation awareness was measured using a query technique called Situation Awareness Global Assessment Technique (SAGAT) [10]. It is a freeze on-line probe technique, designed for real-time, human-in-the-loop simulations and provides diagnostic information regarding how well the system in question supports the operator's various SA requirements. The simulation is frozen and subjects are queried as to their perception of the situation at that instant. SAGAT queries cover data criteria corresponding to the three levels of SA: *perception, comprehension* and *projection.*

In our study, the drive simulation froze twice per condition (baseline vs. with 3DAATIS) directly after two randomly selected scenarios (*Cut In, Red Cab, Pedestrian* and/or *Overtake*). The *Intersection* scenario was not measured – in that scenario, participants are waiting for the traffic lights and can then already see the pedestrians at a distance.

During the freeze, the drive simulator displays were blanked while the participants were queried as to their perception of the traffic scenario at that instant. They were asked to draw the locations of other road users in relation to the own car, as well as their direction. This measured the first two levels of SA, *perception* and *comprehension*. Then, they were also asked to mark the road user they perceived to pose a potential danger to them in terms of causing an accident, measuring the *projection*-level of SA, i.e. how well they understood the situation and what was going to happen. A standard predesigned SAGAT questionnaire was used.

The subject's perceptions were then directly compared to the real situation from the frozen simulation scenarios. This was done by two researchers, who also scored the answers, giving 1 for a correct perception, and 0 for the wrong perception. Scores were given twice, once for *perception* and *comprehension* once for *projection.*

Measuring Driving Performance

To understand how the drivers responded to the events, participants' driving behavior was collected in terms of steering wheel angle, and the cars' acceleration and deceleration due to the gas and brake pedals respectively, all measured via sensors in the pedals and steering wheel (i.e. simulator log data), and double-checked with video observations. Collectively, these measures provide a clear description of how the 3DAATIS influenced drivers' response to events. The detailed measurements are as follows:

- **Video observations** of participants' simulator drive. One camera focused on the throttle and brake pedals, another on the driver's hand on the steering wheel. Camera video data were synchronized with simulator driving data.
- **Number of collisions**: Whether a participant manages a scenario with or without a collision.
- **Response time** (RT): The remaining time to a (potential) collision when drivers first react to the event (e.g. brake, release gas pedal or steer away). This measure reflects driver's safety awareness regarding the situations. (seconds)
- **Steering profile** reflects drivers' steering behaviors.
  - *Steering wheel angle (Mean):* How much the steering wheel is turned (degrees)
  - *Steering wheel angle (Range):* The difference between maximum and minimum steering angles when reacting to the event. (degrees)
- **Gas profile:** Longitudinal acceleration due to the throttle (ft/s^2); basically how much the drivers accelerate or decelerate when releasing or pressing the gas pedal
  - *Acceleration (Mean): The average acceleration of the vehicle from initial gas pedal depression until the driver either brakes, collides or passes the other road user.*
  - *Acceleration (Range): The difference between maximum and minimum acceleration during reaction period. It reflects the amplitude of gas pedal response.*
- **Brake profile:** The deceleration due to the brakes (ft/s^2)
  - *Deceleration (Mean): The average deceleration of the vehicle from initial brake depression until the car either stops, collides, or passes the other road user.*
  - *Deceleration (Range): The difference between maximum and minimum deceleration value during each reaction period. It reflects the amplitude of brake response.*

Measuring Usefulness and Experience

In order to understand how participants think about the 3DAATIS, a standard Van der Laan's System Acceptance Measurement was collected. This a 5 Likert scale, ranging from -2 to 2, including nine items. It measures two dimensions, *usefulness* and *satisfaction* [16]. In addition we also carried out semi-structured post-interviews after the participants had finished the driving task. Here, we aimed to investigate when the participants found the sounds to be helpful vs confusing, and what general feedback they had on the system and its sounds.

DATA ANALYSIS

For the SAGAT score, the number of collisions and the acceptance analysis, a Chi-square test was conducted to see whether there was a significant difference between conditions. The significance of such difference was corrected by the Fisher Exact test, when the expected frequency of an even spread of responses for each scale is less than 5 in some cases.

For driver performance data, a paired t-test was used to determine whether there was a statistically significant difference in drivers' performance between baseline and when using 3DAATIS. Only the measurements with significant effects were reported here.

As for the post-interviews section, its semi-structured interviews covered topics like, sound design, perceived useful sectors and information redundancy. Interviews were recorded and transcribed, using a thematic analysis method.

RESULTS

Drivers' Situation Awareness

No statistically significant differences were observed from the results of SAGAT. As seen in Figure 2, the results showed a tendency that participants increase both how well they could perceive the *position* of surrounding road users (SA P), as well as their ability to *understand* the situation, identifying road users with which they might have potential conflicts (SA U). This is especially evident in the two scenarios where the participants had a visual disadvantage (*Pedestrian* and *Overtake*). In the *Red Cab* scenario, however, the participants' SA accuracy rate was slightly decreased when using 3DAATIS in both regards to both perception and understanding of the situation.

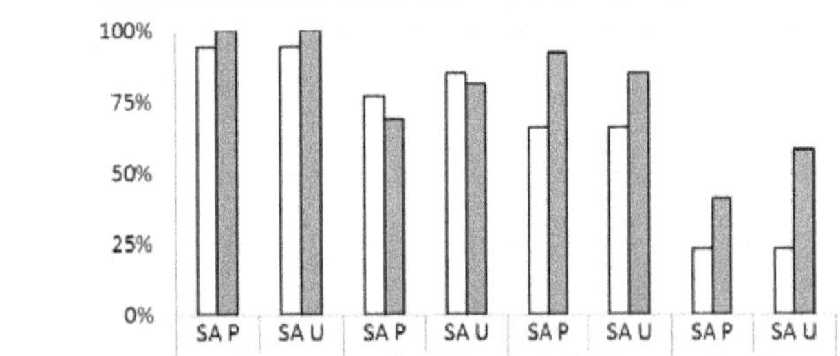

	Cut In		Red Cab		Pedestrian		Overtake	
	SA P	SA U	SA P	SA U	SA P	SA U	SA P	SA U
Baseline	94%	94%	77%	85%	66%	66%	23%	23%
With 3DAATIS	100%	100%	69%	81%	92%	85%	41%	58%

Figure 2: How respondents Situation Awareness changed between baseline and 3DAATIS.

Number of Collisions

The number of collisions is one of the most important indicators to assess driving performance. The results showed that when driving with the 3DAATIS, the number of collisions decreased significantly in *Cut In* and *Pedestrian* (P<0.05). However, in the *Intersection, Red cab* and *Overtake* scenario, the number of collisions did not change significantly between conditions, see detailed numbers in Figure 3.

Driving Performance

Table 3 shows the detailed numbers, but below we will discuss the significant findings for each scenario.

Cut-In. In the *Cut In*-scenario, the response time with 3DAATIS was 1.05 seconds earlier than the baseline and the mean and range of acceleration was significantly reduced, when driving with 3DAATIS. This means that the driver's gas pedal changes in a more deliberate manner, i.e. that the subject is prepared for the situation.

Red Cab. In the *Red Cab*-scenario, the response time was 1.07 seconds earlier than the baseline, however, the drivers performed less good with 3DAATIS than baseline, which is in line with our findings in regards to Situation Awareness and Collisions. When driving with the 3DAATIS, the mean and range of acceleration was significantly higher, which means that participants' response was rash. This may indicate that drivers were unprepared and perhaps startled or confused by the sound.

Intersection. Here, no significant differences were observed on any measurements, except for the response time which increased around 1.89 seconds with the 3DAATIS. One possible explanation is that the natural response when becoming aware of pedestrians in front is to break; under the 3DAATIS condition this simply happened sooner but did not change the drivers' behaviors otherwise.

Pedestrian. When driving with the 3DAATIS, participants responded 0.66 seconds in advance and were more accurate and efficient, in terms of greater changes in acceleration (i.e. a quick release of the gas pedal) and greater steering wheel angle. Video records showed that when participants drove without 3DAATIS, most of them hit the full brake when they saw the pedestrian walking out, but when they

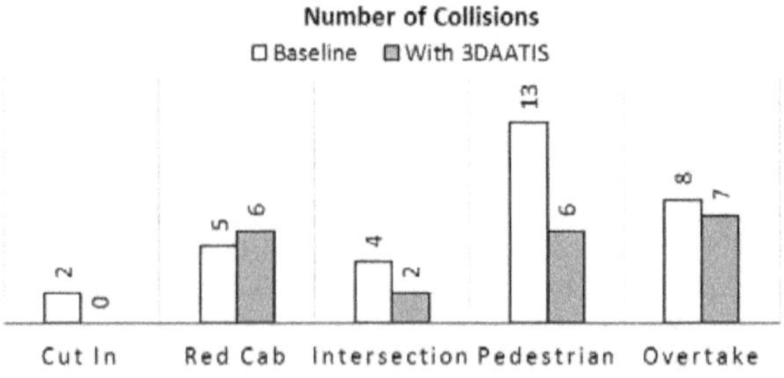

Figure 3: Number of Collisions

Scenarios No.	Measures	Baseline Mean (SD)	With 3DAATIS Mean (SD)	df	t
Cut In	Response time (s)	2.27 (0.74)	3.32 (1.75)	26	-3.01*
	Acceleration Range (ft/s^2)	8.53 (3.74)	5.59 (2.61)	17	2.67*
	Acceleration Mean (ft/s^2)	0.42 (0.15)	0.33 (0.11)	16	2.08*
Red Cab	Response time (s)	2.25 (0.71)	3.32 (1.77)	28	-2.92*
	Acceleration Range (ft/s^2)	5.14 (2.30)	7.02 (2.29)	19	-3.75**
	Acceleration Mean (ft/s^2)	0.34 (0.13)	0.48 (0.18)	19	-2.78*
Intersection	Response time (s)	3.84 (1.51)	5.73 (1.75)	22	-4.12**
Pedestrian	Response time (s)	1.24 (0.35)	1.9 (0.13)	26	-3.94**
	Acceleration Range (ft/s^2)	8.16 (5.94)	14.28 (12.53)	23	-2.08*
	Acceleration Mean (ft/s^2)	0.73 (0.50)	1.11 (0.57)	20	-2.36*
	MSteering wheel Range (degree)	17.61 (10.66)	31.70 (31.52)	20	-2.36*
Overtake	Response time (s)	0.57 (0.56)	2.80 (1.14)	24	-2.35*

*P<.05. ** P<.001

Table 2. Driving performance measurements during the response period.

drove with 3DAATIS, they were more prepared and decelerated in advance, leading to a smoother driving.

Overtake. This scenario was somewhat different from the others, since the overtaking vehicle moves so fast. Thus, when the 3DAATIS started to alert the driver, the sounds started directly at the warning level, giving participants only 2-3 seconds to react. No significant differences were observed in any of the performance measures, and from video observations, we also found that when the warning started, the subjects adjusted the steering wheel or gas pedal instantly but in a non-sufficient way. Therefore, even though the response time was 2.8 seconds ahead, the number of collisions still remained the same when driving with the 3DAATIS.

Drivers' Subjective Feedback to 3DAATIS

The results from the Van der Laan's system acceptance measurement were very positive for *usefulness.* It was measured on 5 scales, yielding mean results from 0.47 to 1.13, with a total mean value of 0.77 (SD: 0.77). Since the scale runs from -2 to 2, these are positive results.

As for *satisfaction*, mean results on four scales ranged between -0.4 and 0.23, with a total mean value of -0.18 (SD 0.91). This could have indicated that the sounds were disturbing or annoying, but the post-interviews disproved this; participants quite liked the sounds. Possibly the ratings are neutral simply because the system aims to be transparent and non-disturbing, it is not meant to evoke any feelings, positive or negative. A paired T-test shows that the usefulness rate was significantly higher than satisfaction (t_{29}= 8.42, p<0.001). It indicates that the participants thought the system is more useful that satisfying.

The post interviews started with the participants marking in which sectors around the car they found the sound information useful. Then, a follow-up discussion was carried out to collect their motivations. We also asked r their perceived pros and cons with the system and the sounds.

As is shown in Figure 4, most of the participants considered information from the rear blind spots sectors to be the most useful. Overall, they appreciated advisory information for any situation when they could not see for themselves. Cases they mentioned were quickly overtaking cars, other cars in lane change situations, playing children or other pedestrians in blind spots, or when the view was being blocked by something, as in the case of *Pedestrian.* One participant stated that "*I have too much to look for, sound will be good to make sure that I don't miss this information.*"

Even from the front zone, participants wanted information, if it was related an emergency or an unexpected event. In addition, participants wanted the system to be able to notify them under conditions when their visibility was otherwise reduced too, e.g. when driving in fog, heavy rain or during a snowfall. The latter implies some more intelligence from the system in adapting to these conditions.

Positive Aspects of the System

Some participants stated that the sounds made it easy to understand which urgency state they were currently in. Some mentioned that they like the auditory information, since it made them feel protected and taken care of.

Negative Aspects of the System

In some cases, participants found the sounds to be confusing or misleading. Several participants mentioned front-rear-confusion – a known problem in sound design; it

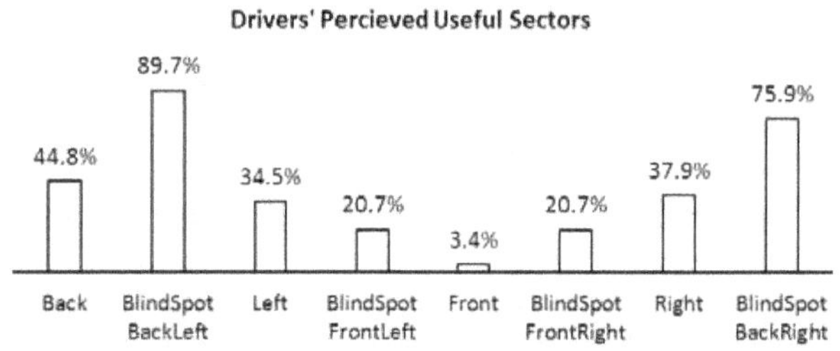

Figure 4. In which areas around the car the respondents found the information to be helpful.

is hard to distinguish the directions of sounds coming from one's exact front or back. For instance, some participants explained how they in the *Overtake*-scenario (with the fast car approaching from behind) didn't understand where the sound information came from. Therefore, they didn't know how to respond. Yet others had issues with the 3d-aspects, and suggested different sounds for right vs left side of the car, so that they'd know where to look.

Another source of confusion was when there were multiple road users in the same sector, then it was distracting and difficult to distinguish the exact location of each road user by sound. Some participants suggested that the system should only provide one sound cue from the same sector, just pointing drivers' towards the general direction of road users without communicating how many, leaving it to the driver to make a visual confirmation. Others instead wanted different sounds for different types of road users (which does not really solve the problem if there are two road users of the same kind). In contrast to this, and in line with the recommendations from the sound experts, other participants said that they felt distracted and stressed when hearing two sound cues at the same time.

DISCUSSION

In this experiment, we *studied whether spatialized sound cues can be used to present situational information in such a way that it supports situation awareness and driving performance in a real driving context*. In general, the results were promising. Participants perceived the system as being useful, response times were better, and in a majority of situations SA and driving performance increased. Interesting findings were obtained in those situations the system supported SA and performance, and those it did not, resulting in a number of design implications, as being discussed below.

As for acceptance, the 3DAATIS received notable positive scores on perceived usefulness, which means that **participants are open for spatialized sound cues.** Moreover, we used only one sound displaying three dimensions (direction, movements and urgency), and participants did not have any problem understanding this underlying concept, meaning that it was **easy to learn**. To some extent these findings go against the common car-industry notion that auditory displays should be avoided in the vehicle compartment, due to distraction and annoyance when the number of sound increases. However we did consider these negative effects in several ways. Firstly, our focus was on ***advisory*** sounds (being more pleasant and less urgent than warning sounds).Secondly we aimed to design the system as to only make sounds when really needed, as shown by our thresholds (table 1 and related text).The fact that the sound cues (65 dB) worked together with ambient traffic sounds (45 dB) is promising.

The most important finding is that **spatial sound cues work ideally in situations involving single road users in the front and side sectors**. In less complex situations, or when single road users occur in front or in the front side sectors, drivers can quickly perceive and associate the localized sound cues with what they see from the traffic situation outside of the car; feedback is instant. Therefore, even though sound localization resolution is quite low, drivers' performance and Situation Awareness in these situations was still increased, as exemplified in the scenarios *Cut In, Intersection* and *Pedestrian.*

The second was that **if the situation is complex, spatial sound cues can be confusing**. If, for instance, there are several road users around the car, and/or sound cues come from the back, the limited auditory localization resolution and/or front-back confusion makes the information ambiguous, confusing drivers. This was clearly shown in the scenarios *Red Cab* and *Overtake* in terms of number of collision, response time and driving performance. In the *Red Cab*-scenario neither the system nor the human capability to discern the exact direction of the sound could help the drivers to tell the two vehicles' sounds apart; the angle between them was too small. Others have made similar findings. Tan et al [1] carried out an extensive test on sounds and sound localization accuracy by placing participants in a car equipped with 16 speakers (as opposed to the 4 we used), concluding that localization in general is accurate enough to orient the listener towards the direction of sound source, but with mean errors about 10 to 20 degree. In addition, several cases of perceptual reversals (i.e. more than 90 degrees off) were observed. From this, we take that **in these situations, supporting sound cues with visual information to avoid confusion ought to be beneficial**.

Like other car-related studies [12,24], our study also concluded that it **is beneficial to support drivers with both advisory/situational information sound cues and warning sounds.** The results from the SAGAT enquiry showed increased understanding and projection of the future situation in three (*Cut In, Pedestrian* and *Overtake*) of the four scenarios tested for this. Again, *Red Cab* was the outlier. In addition, drivers' response time improved in all scenarios as compared to baseline. These results suggest that drivers, whose attention has already been directed towards a potential hazardous situation, either avoid it all together, or react faster to the warning sound. It is worth noting especially, that in the *Overtake*-scenario, the overtaking car came up so fast, that the system went directly into warning-mode, skipping over the advisory level, which also indicates that the advisory level really adds to SA and performance. For *Overtake*, drivers did react faster, but not necessarily in the right way; the front-rear confusion came into play as mentioned above.

We believe that the last finding is particularly interesting in the light of semi-automated driving. As more and more ADAS are introduced, bringing even more displays into the car and overloading the visual channel, we believe that an auditory display could be good candidate to offload the visual channel and highlight the most important situational information. Moreover, as drivers might switch between driving and other secondary tasks during semi-autonomous driving, jumping directly to the warning level might be too abrupt. Instead, **advisory level sound cues should be used to bring drivers back to into the loop with good situation awareness**. For instance, Lee et al [17] investigated how users, working with another task, responded to collision warnings, showing that graded alerts led to a greater safety margin and a lower rate of inappropriate responses to nuisance warnings. In addition, they found that graded alerts were more trusted than single stage alerts. (One could argue that if the car is truly self-driving it should not be necessary for drivers to take over, but until the car industry has solved the ethical dilemmas that may arise in acritical situation, there still needs to be a way for humans to quickly take back control.)

Here, we believe that the car industry has a lot to learn from the game industry, since it has long experimented with the use of ambient sounds as a means to provide players with a general sense of what is going on in the environment – this is especially relevant for any location based games where players move around in the real world [8,15,22].

Sound Design Implications

Our experiment was not specifically designed to give conclusions on the sound design, but from the post-interview and test results, we can still draw some conclusions.

The sound designed was based on an OEM car manufacturer's tested sound library. Keeping the aesthetics, we designed custom sounds devoid of the harsh and inharmonious qualities associated with warning sounds, which we assumed would work better for advisory purposes. Despite the fact that the sounds now were no longer typical, attention-grabbing, warning sounds, drivers still observed and responded to them. Thus, one conclusion is that **non-obtrusive, harmonious sounds work well for advisory driver information**.

Another implicit conclusion is that the setup of the speaker system is crucial, as is calibration of panning algorithms and acoustic preparation of the listening environment. Our rather basic setup was a simple proof of concept, and can naturally be much improved. In a real car, a larger number of speakers must probably be used for improved precision, but, resolution of directional localization will always be somewhat limited because of how human perception works. Similarly, it is worthwhile to investigate the use of different timbre as suggested by [21].

POTENTIAL LIMITATIONS AND FUTURE WORK

A potential limitation of this research is that the test only ran for an hour. The subjective feedback and driving performance could be different after a long period of use. A second limitation that is the current 3DAATIS only used time/distance to collision and trajectory as system parameters, which resulted in a number of false alarms. One last limitation is that our system was presented through a 5.1 surround sound system, ergo the resolution for sound localization was not optimized. It could have influenced the results in scenarios like *Overtake* and *Redcab* negatively.

In addition to addressing these limitations, there are many possible directions for future studies. The first would be to conduct the study in a higher fidelity drive environment and follow the drivers' behavior and acceptance changes over a period of time. The second would be to integrate other parameters into the system algorithm to enhance the information accuracy, i.e. current acceleration, drivers' attentional status etc. One other possibility is to increase the fidelity of the sound system. Further, toying with the sound attributes, like timbre, is also worthwhile. Lastly, it would be worth to explore how the 3DAATIS can work in tandem with other modalities for conveying information in complex situations.

CONCLUSION

This study is a proof of concept, showing that advisory, spatialized sound cues can be successfully used in a 3D Auditory Advisory Traffic Information System in order to improve drivers' situation awareness and performance. Unlike previous studies this one included a simulator drive under as natural conditions as possible, featuring other road users and complex situations.

The most important implications of this research are that:

- Spatial sound cues work ideally in situations involving single road users in the front and side sectors
- In complex situations, spatial sound cues can be confusing; in these cases, supporting them with visual information ought to be beneficial.
- It is beneficial to support drivers with both advisory information sound cues and warning sounds.
- Non-obtrusive, harmonious sounds work well for advisory driver information.

A lot of work remains before this can be implemented in real cars, but our results point in a positive direction and show that this will be a worthwhile addition for drivers, increasing driver safety and situation awareness.

ACKNOWLEDGEMENTS

This project is a part of Swedish FFI ADAS presentation project. We would like to thank Fredrik Hagman (Volvo Cars) who designed the sound samples, as well as Samuel Palm (Volvo Cars) who provided continuous support and design insights throughout the entire project. Last but not least, thanks also to all our study participants.

REFERENCES

1. Tan A.K. and Lerner Neil D. 1996. Acoustic localization of in-vehicle crash avoidance warnings as a cue to hazard direction. U.S. Department of Transportation National Highway Traffic Safety

Administration. Retrieved from http://trid.trb.org/view.aspx?id=474030
2. David Beattie, Lynne Baillie, Martin Halvey, and Rod Mccall. 2014. What's around the corner? Enhancing Driver Awareness in Autonomous Vehicles via In-Vehicle Spatial Auditory Displays. Proceedings of the 8th Nordic Conference on Human-Computer Interaction Fun, Fast, Foundational - NordiCHI '14: 189–198. http://doi.org/10.1145/2639189.2641206
3. Durand R Begault. 1993. Head-up auditory displays for traffic collision avoidance system advisories: A preliminary investigation. Human Factors: The Journal of the Human Factors and Ergonomics Society 35, 4: 707--717. http://doi.org/10.1177/001872089303500409
4. Durand R Begault. 1999. Auditory and non-auditory factors that potentially influence virtual acoustic imagery. Audio Engineering Society Conference: 16th International Conference: Spatial Sound Reproduction. Retrieved from http://www.aes.org/e-lib/browse.cfm?elib=8052
5. Meera M Blattner, Denise A Sumikawa, Robert M Greenberg, et al. 1989. Earcons and icons: Their structure and common design principles. Human--Computer Interaction 4, 1: 11--44.
6. Sara Bly. 1982. Presenting information in sound. Proceedings of the 1st Conference on Human Factors in Computing Systems (CHI '82), 371–375. http://doi.org/10.1145/800049.801814
7. Warren Brodsky. 2015. Driving with music: cognitive-behavioural implications. Ashgate Publishing, Ltd.
8. Inger Ekman, Laura Ermi, Jussi Lahti, Jani Nummela, Petri Lankoski, and Frans Mäyrä. 2005. Designing sound for a pervasive mobile game. Proceedings of the 2005 ACM SIGCHI International Conference on Advances in computer entertainment technology, 110–116.
9. Mica R Endsley. 1988. Design and evaluation for situation awareness enhancement. Proceedings of the Human Factors and Ergonomics Society Annual Meeting 32, 2: 97--101. http://doi.org/10.1177/154193128803200221
10. Mica R Endsley. 1988. Situation awareness global assessment technique (SAGAT). Aerospace and Electronics Conference, 1988. NAECON 1988., Proceedings of the IEEE 1988 National, 789--795. Retrieved November 6, 2014 from http://scholar.google.com/scholar?hl=en&btnG=Search&q=intitle:A+methodology+for+the+objective+measurement+of+pilot+situation+awareness#0
11. Mark A. Ericson and Richard L. McKinley. 2001. The intelligibility of multiple talkers spatially separated in noise(No. AFRL-HE-WP-SR-2001-0009).
12. Johan Fagerlonn and Alm Håkan. 2010. Auditory signs to support traffic awareness. IET Intelligent Transport Systems 4, 4: 262--269. http://doi.org/10.1049/iet-its.2009.0144
13. Rob Gray. 2011. Looming auditory collision warnings for driving. Human Factors: The Journal of the Human Factors and Ergonomics Society 53, 1: 63–74. http://doi.org/10.1177/0018720810397833
14. Philip Kortum. 2008. HCI beyond the GUI: Design for haptic, speech, olfactory, and other nontraditional interfaces. Morgan Kaufmann.
15. Jason Kurczak, T. C. Nicholas Graham, Claire Joly, and Regan L. Mandryk. 2011. Hearing is believing: evaluating ambient audio for location-based games. Proceedings of the 8th International Conference on Advances in Computer Entertainment Technology, 32. http://doi.org/10.1145/2071423.2071463
16. Van Der Laan, Jinke D, Adriaan Heino, and Dick De Waard. 1997. A simple procedure for the assessment of acceptance of advanced transport telematics. Transportation Research Part C: Emerging Technologies 5, 1: 1–10.
17. John D Lee, Joshua D Hoffman, and Elizabeth Hayes. 2004. Collision warning design to mitigate driver distraction. Proceedings of the SIGCHI Conference on Human factors in Computing Systems, 65–72. Retrieved March 24, 2012 from http://dl.acm.org/citation.cfm?id=985701
18. Fabrizio Leo, Vincenzo Romei, Elliot Freeman, Elisabetta Ladavas, and Jon Driver. 2011. Looming sounds enhance orientation sensitivity for visual stimuli on the same side as such sounds. Experimental brain research 213, 2–3: 193–201. http://doi.org/10.1007/s00221-011-2742-8
19. Yung-Ching Liu and Jing-Wun Jhuang. 2011. Effects of in-vehicle warning information displays with or without spatial compatibility on driving behaviors and response performance. Applied ergonomics: 1–8. http://doi.org/10.1016/j.apergo.2011.10.005
20. Tara Matthews, Tye Rattenbury, and Scott Carter. 2007. Defining, designing, and evaluating peripheral displays: An analysis using activity theory. Human–Computer Interaction 22, 1–2: 221–261. http://doi.org/10.1080/07370020701307997
21. David K McGookin and Stephen A Brewster. 2004. Understanding concurrent earcons: applying auditory scene analysis principles to concurrent earcon recognition. ACM Transactions on Applied Perception (TAP) 1, 2: 130–155. http://doi.org/10.1145/1024083.1024087
22. Natasa Paterson, Katsiaryna Naliuka, Soren Kristian Jensen, Tara Carrigy, Mads Haahr, and Fionnuala Conway. 2010. Design, implementation and evaluation of audio for a location aware augmented reality game. Proceedings of the 3rd International Conference on Fun and Games - Fun and Games '10, 149–156. http://doi.org/10.1145/1823818.1823835
23. Miguel a. Recarte and Luis M. Nunes. 2003. Mental workload while driving: Effects on visual search, discrimination, and decision making. Journal of Experimental Psychology: Applied 9, 2: 119–137. http://doi.org/10.1037/1076-898X.9.2.119

24. Nash Stanton, Roger Lew, Nolan Boyle, et al. 2011. An Implementation of a Graded Deceleration Display in Brake Light Warning Systems. Proceedings of the Human Factors and Ergonomics Society Annual Meeting 55, 1: 1573–1577. http://doi.org/10.1177/1071181311551328
25. Heikki Summala. 2007. Towards understanding motivational and emotional factors in driver behaviour: Comfort through satisficing. In Modelling driver behaviour in automotive environments. Springer London, 189–207. Retrieved November 17, 2014 from http://link.springer.com/chapter/10.1007/978-1-84628-618-6_11
26. MinJuan Wang, Yi Ci Li, and Fang Chen. 2012. How can we design 3D auditory interfaces which enhance traffic safety for Chinese drivers? Proceedings of the 4th International Conference on Automotive User Interfaces and Interactive Vehicular Applications, ACM Press, 77–83. http://doi.org/10.1145/2390256.2390268
27. Minjuan Wang, Sus Lundgren Lyckvi, and Fang Chen. 2016. Same , Same but Different : How Design Requirements for an Auditory Advisory Traffic Information System Differ Between Sweden and China. 8th International Conference on Automotive User Interfaces and Interactive Vehicular Applications.
28. Minjuan Wang, Sus Lundgren Lyckvi, and Fang Chen. 2016. Why and How Traffic Safety Cultures Matter when Designing Advisory Traffic Information Systems. Proceedings of the SIGCHI Conference on Human Factors in Computing Systems. http://doi.org/10.1145/2858036.2858467
29. Marcus O Watson and Penelope M Sanderson. 2007. Designing for attention with sound: challenges and extensions to ecological interface design. Human Factors: The Journal of the Human Factors and Ergonomics Society 49, 2: 331–346.
30. Deborah Withington. 2000. The Use of Directional Sound to Improve the Safety of Auditory Warnings. Proceedings of the Human Factors and Ergonomics Society Annual Meeting 44, 22: 726–729. http://doi.org/10.1177/154193120004402260

Designing Gamified Applications That Make Safe Driving More Engaging

Fabius Steinberger, Ronald Schroeter, Marcus Foth, Daniel Johnson
Queensland University of Technology (QUT)
Brisbane, Australia
{fabius.steinberger, r.schroeter, m.foth, dm.johnson}@qut.edu.au

ABSTRACT
Low levels of engagement while driving can pose road safety risks, e.g., inattention during low traffic or routine trips. Interactive technologies that increase task engagement could therefore offer safety benefits, e.g., through performance feedback, increased challenge, and incentives. As a means to build upon these notions, we chose to explore gamification of the driving task. The research aim was to study how to design gamified applications that make safe driving more engaging. We present six design lenses which bring into focus considerations most relevant to creating engaging car applications. A user study enhanced our understanding of design requirements and revealed user personas to support the development of such applications. These lenses and personas informed two prototypes, which we evaluated in driving simulator studies. Our results indicate that the gamified conditions increased driver engagement and reduced driving speeds. As such, our work contributes towards the design of engaging applications that are both appropriate to the safety-critical driving context and compelling to users.

Author Keywords
Road safety; task engagement; gamification.

ACM Classification Keywords
H.5.m. Information interfaces and presentation (e.g., HCI).

INTRODUCTION
More than one million people die in car accidents every year [81]. Road crash statistics such as these offer evidence of the severe consequences resulting from human error, especially among young drivers [81]. Recently, there has been an increase in people accessing social media and apps while driving, as reported in Australia [10], Germany [79], and the US [49]. These kinds of distractions are often sought when engagement in the driving task is low, which may occur on familiar routes, in low traffic, or on long distance drives [70]. Similarly, the mundane nature of low-engagement driving situations may trigger equally dangerous behaviours, such as speeding [39,41,63,70]. However, drivers perform best and safest when they are adequately engaged in the driving task [85]. New car features offering semi-automated driving amplify the significance of this issue. Relinquishing manual control further decreases engagement, yet requires drivers to remain vigilant and take over control at any time [9].

Permission to make digital or hard copies of all or part of this work for personal or classroom use is granted without fee provided that copies are not made or distributed for profit or commercial advantage and that copies bear this notice and the full citation on the first page. Copyrights for components of this work owned by others than the author(s) must be honored. Abstracting with credit is permitted. To copy otherwise, or republish, to post on servers or to redistribute to lists, requires prior specific permission and/or a fee. Request permissions from Permissions@acm.org.
CHI 2017, May 06 - 11, 2017, Denver, CO, USA
Copyright is held by the owner/author(s). Publication rights licensed to ACM.
ACM 978-1-4503-4655-9/17/05...$15.00
DOI: http://dx.doi.org/10.1145/3025453.3025511

Figure 1: Study participants discussing driving experiences.

To limit disengagement and safety risks, Heslop et al. [26] and Schroeter et al. [62] proposed to develop and test interventions that encourage engagement in the driving task. As such, increasing the stimulus of the driving task itself can address safety risks caused by driver disengagement [62]. Studies by Markey et al. [38] revealed four effective strategies associated with heightened task engagement: increase challenge, offer performance feedback, provide social approval, and give incentives such as money rewards. Gamification (commonly defined as 'the use of game design elements in non-game contexts' [14]) puts these strategies to advantage. It has been shown to increase engagement in various settings [22,23,66]. Therefore, gamification provides a useful perspective from which to create and analyse engaging driving experiences.

The *research aim* of this work is to explore how to design gamified applications that make safe driving more engaging. Such apps could be implemented for, e.g., mobile devices or windscreen displays. Either of these approaches requires similar conceptual design considerations. These considerations are the focus of our paper.

To address this research aim, we present a user study, our iterative design process, and two prototype evaluations. Our study data reflect the diversity of user preferences, in particular regarding the presentation style of driving applications, which we discuss by way of three design personas. Key findings from our prototype evaluations include an increase in self-reported task engagement and a decrease in speeding violations. We address usability and safety considerations such as visual distraction in our design recommendations.

The contribution of our work is threefold. First, we offer six lenses through which to view the design of gamified driving applications. Second, we present new empirical data from a user study and ten design recommendations derived from it. Finally, through two prototype evaluations, we show how these lenses and recommendations can help to implement concrete applications that successfully increase task engagement. These contributions are timely as there is an increased attention on the use of apps in the car [51] and on keeping drivers in the loop in semi-automated vehicles [9].

BACKGROUND AND RELATED WORK

Engagement has been described as the quantity and quality of mental resources directed at a task [19,40,47]. Previous work has identified the positive impact of engagement (e.g., improved task performance, flow) as well as the negative consequences associated with a lack of engagement (e.g., boredom, mental retirement) [11,38,58,83]. Kurzban et al. [30] put forward a comprehensive theory, which describes that states like flow, boredom, and fatigue promote the efficient use of mental resources. In this theory, called *opportunity-cost-model of subjective effort and task performance*, the authors argue that these states result from an evolutionary process. A cost-benefit analysis may promote re-allocation of resources from the task at hand to a more valuable task. This impairs the performance of the former task. Therefore, to sustain or increase task engagement in the driving context, it seems promising to enhance (or add value to) the primary driving task itself. To this end, we propose to tap into interactive technology.

In line with the opportunity-cost-model, Markey et al. [38] explored four determinants of value. As discussed, these are: increased challenge, performance feedback, social observation, and money rewards. All four strategies have been shown to relate to increased task engagement [38], feelings of competence [12], and a sense of progress [36]. Similarly, Orji and Moffatt [52] recently conducted a review of persuasive technology literature. It revealed that commonly used strategies for aiding users to adopt beneficial behaviours include tracking, monitoring, and performance feedback, as well as providing social support, rewards, and objectives. In terms of implementation, the authors identified mobile devices, social media, and games as most frequently used strategies.

Research on gamification has shown improvements in motivation and engagement [22,23,66]. Game elements such as progress and success feedback, goals, points, badges, levels, challenges, social feedback, leaderboards, avatars, and narrative, can all contribute to those engagement improvements, provided there is a good match between design and audience. We therefore propose to inform the design of engaging driving apps building upon gamification. However, in the safety-critical driving context, designing around game elements requires careful consideration, e.g., to avoid additional distractions [74].

Insurance companies and software developers have started to offer driving applications using gamification [14] and quantified-self [75] approaches. Gamified driving applications in particular have been explored as a means to influence eco-driving, driving safety, and navigation (see [15,78] for reviews). Such apps reward good driving with points and allow users to share their accomplishments with their social networks. Many apps offer insights after the drive and therefore do not influence driving behaviour in-situ. Other related applications provide feedback or stimuli during the drive, but without taking into account when it is safe to do so [e.g., 42,55]. As a consequence, they may become distractions themselves.

Irrespective of whether applications provide feedback in-situ or post-drive, gamified driving requires extensive user testing, as Diewald et al. [15] pointed out. However, there is a shortage of literature reporting both design recommendations and user studies. Steinberger et al. [74] proposed an approach for balancing safety and fun involving conceptual layers for designing driving gamification derived from game design cognition. Stevens et al. [3] established guidelines for in-vehicle information systems (IVIS), but little work has been done with regard to interactive applications. In terms of methodological approaches, Loehmann et al. [35] proposed storyboards and experience prototyping as tools to translate concepts into interactive products in the realm of automotive app design.

We build upon these related works and specifically explore the design of driving engagement through gamification. In particular, more work is needed to understand user requirements and contextual constraints in this safety-critical space – a gap this paper aims to address.

SIX DESIGN LENSES

To lay the basis for our work, we first present six lenses through which to view the design of gamified driving applications: *data, presentation, time, interface, social context,* and *road conditions*. Design lenses are analytical tools, which have been shown in HCI research to be useful for recognising design opportunities, formalising design criteria, and critiquing design work [48,87]. They therefore enhance the ways in which interactive technology can be developed and understood. Previous literature has shown the utility of design lenses, e.g., for informing sustainable HCI [54], crafting material interactions [82], evaluating player experience [60], and framing ludic engagement [48].

We identified the following six lenses *(L1 - L6)* from our own experience researching in-car user experiences. They do not represent a complete account, but rather a first articulation based on our engagement with the literature [e.g., 15,35,78] and our own research experience in the domain [e.g., 65,71,72]. They are a result of many cycles of concept development, design work, and user testing, and therefore the synthesis of an iterative process. The presented lenses were selected based on their relevance and usefulness in terms of balancing user experience design opportunities and road safety. Note that these lenses are not mutually exclusive, but rather complementary. Our study provides initial validation of a subset (four) of these design lenses as useful for our goal of engaging safe-driving. We believe that the lenses provide a structured foundation for designing gamified driving applications and offer practicable opportunities for researchers and practitioners who are interested in further exploring this space. Readers are invited to also consider the design lenses for a broader utility around user experience in the automotive domain.

L1: Data Lens – "What to Convey?"

There are three data streams relevant for providing feedback to drivers on their on-road behaviour [72].

Vehicle data includes location, direction, speed, acceleration, pedal pressure, fuel intake, etc. They can be gathered from smartphones, connected Bluetooth connectors for on-board diagnostics (OBD), or intelligent cars themselves [43]. The data can be exploited to facilitate feedback systems that go beyond the information displayed on the instrument cluster (speedometer, fuel gauge, etc.).

Road data includes specific traffic conditions, information such as following distance and road signs. These kind of data can be gathered through camera imagery, crowd-sourcing, map data, or smartphone sensors [1]. These data are required for context-awareness and can be used to gamify specific driving scenarios.

Driver data regarding the driver's mental and physiological conditions can be fed into applications. Biometrics, e.g., related to arousal, can contribute as an indicator for engagement in the driving task. For example, boredom while commuting would be reflected in low arousal levels and therefore suggest that adding gamification may be appropriate. Biometrics may furthermore feed into dynamic difficulty adjustment (DDA, [77]), e.g., to adapt gamified challenges to the current driver state so as to ensure optimal levels of engagement. Lastly, camera imagery and smartphone sensors can be used to detect facial expressions or characterise unsafe driving styles [86].

L2: Presentation Lens – "How to Convey?"

Generally, system output may, e.g., be visual, auditory, or tactile [53]. The following three parameters are an attempt at reflecting the variety of presentation styles, although they may not be applicable to every output modality.

Raw: A presentation of *raw* data is the most straightforward style, both to implement and for drivers to comprehend. For example, a digital speedometer displays numerical data as numbers. Graphs or sound may be used to convey raw data instantaneously or over time.

Abstract: Non-intrusive presentations could be achieved through *abstract* ambient visualisations that subtly convey information through colours, brightness, or sound. For example, ambient red colour may reflect speeding violations. This way, the level of granularity decreases for the benefit of reduced cognitive load.

Themed: Output on the other end of the presentation style spectrum can be playful, or *themed*. Themes and narratives can be added on top of gamification experiences or reward structures. They can amplify the intended effect of immersion and engagement if they resonate with users [74].

L3: Time Lens – "When to Convey?"

The activation and duration of applications may differ:

During – continuous: Applications displaying information *during* trips may offer them *continuously* throughout the entire drive. They could be switched on prior to commencing a trip and act as ambient feedback systems that continuously emit minimal audible cues or display data in real-time, similar to speedometers or fitness trackers.

During – event-triggered: Driving games can be activated by elements in the road environment. For example, a speed sign or a set of traffic lights could activate a gamified driving task. These interventions could add additional engagement on top of a continuous feedback loop, similar to mini games within a videogame.

Before/After: Driving challenges or feedback can furthermore be displayed *before* or *after* drives when the vehicle is not in motion. For example, a challenge might be suggested at the beginning of the drive ("try to use less than X amount of fuel while driving to work today") and take place mainly in the driver's head during the trip. Detailed feedback could be provided after a journey, e.g., performance indicators accumulated throughout the entire drive and information that cannot be displayed in a subtle, non-intrusive manner. As part of post-drive feedback, it is also possible to display leader boards or similar statistics.

L4: Interface Lens – "Where to Convey?"

Designing new interfaces to engage drivers poses the question of which technology platform to use. Relevant data streams and presentations may rely on different technologies for implementation, such as:

Car as a platform: Integrated dashboard or head-up display (HUD) applications, e.g., using Apple CarPlay and Android Auto, make smartphone applications accessible to drivers. Opportunities for novel in-vehicle applications are facilitated by recent automobile technology developments, including those with semi-automated driving features. The car and driving environment can be viewed as a development platform on which safety interventions can thrive (though within the context of due consideration of emerging ethical and safety issues [61,84]).

Consumer electronics: Smartphones, smart watches, physical activity trackers, and dashboard cameras have entered the driving space. These devices have essentially become automotive user interfaces, even though they were never designed as such [51]. Their increasingly sophisticated sensing, networking, and output capabilities provide an untapped opportunity to develop driving apps. We propose to leverage such devices available to drivers today for immediate safety and user experience benefits.

L5: Social Context Lens – "With Whom?"

Interactions with other road users and passengers present another lens through which to view the gamified driving.

Other road users include drivers of nearby vehicles as well as pedestrians and cyclists. Besides these co-located road users, one can also take into account drivers that have shared the same road at a different point in time, e.g., ten minutes earlier or every morning as part of commuting. Applications may target other road users to reward achievements [64], allow social expression [57], enable serendipitous encounters [76], or facilitate shared road trip experiences [29]. Users of driving games may compete with each other and compare their progress on leaderboards.

Passengers, on the other hand, can be a source of social entertainment themselves. Novel in-car interfaces can support such interactions. For example, they may allow for collaborative navigation input or information sharing among passengers [45].

L6: Road Conditions Lens – "When Is It Appropriate?"

Apps should be created with road conditions in mind, e.g.:

Highway and suburban driving are often associated with commuting, low traffic, or constant speeds. The latter are common antecedents of low levels of engagement [70] and should therefore be at the focus of gamified driving.

Inner-city driving is often related to congestion, low visibility, and fear of being caught speeding and, as such, often associated with high levels of vigilance and stress [70]. Added stimuli in these conditions may cause distractions or incentivise unsafe behaviour.

Currently, developers need to rely on drivers to activate applications within appropriate conditions. In the near future, the increased contextual awareness of connected and semi-automated cars will provide a more fine-grained evaluation of appropriateness and greater scope for exploring automated interventions.

USER STUDY

The presented lenses allow designers to understand opportunities for gamified driving more broadly. As a next step, we aimed to derive specific design recommendations and user preferences for future prototypes. To this end, we conducted a study involving potential users early on in the design process, inspired by human-centred design [27] as well as experience design [24]. We were then able to look at the study data through appropriate lenses.

Storyboards

In preparation for the user study, we created five storyboards to brainstorm initial gamified driving concepts and to solicit feedback from study participants, as suggested for early design exploration in general [8] and for designing car applications more specifically [35]. Our concepts were inspired by a review of driving-related video games [73], and we followed a design approach for balancing fun and safety in gamified driving [74]. Each storyboard was built around a typical driving situation (e.g., red light or new speed limit), rather than a specific technology.

BrakeMaster gamifies approaches to red lights. Ideally, the driver will slow down gradually instead of braking abruptly. When the car comes to a halt, the game will display a playful assessment of the braking performance.

CoastMaster encourages drivers to smoothly and timely slow down to a new speed limit. The goal is to pass a road sign at the speed it displays and awards extra points for coasting and avoiding harsh braking.

Mirror Music reminds drivers to periodically check their rear-view and side mirrors. If the driver neglects to check the mirrors, music played through the car stereo will decrease in volume to gently remind the driver to glance at the mirrors. Conceptually, this is about providing awareness and feedback on how often drivers check their mirrors.

Zombie Cloud is a concept to help drivers avoid tailgating. It signals a minimum safe distance to the frontward car by virtually augmenting the driving environment. Virtual toxic clouds surround nearby vehicles and signal that a safe distance should be maintained.

Coin Collector encourages drivers to keep to their lane. Virtually displayed coins, as known from games such as Super Mario, suggest an ideal driving path. They can only be collected if the vehicle stays within bounds. To prevent speeding or tailgating, coins will disappear as soon as the driver is going too fast or too close to the frontward vehicle.

Participants

Overall, 24 drivers participated in the study (age M=20.25, SD=1.82; driving experience M=2.88 years, SD=1.36; all male). We deliberately recruited young male adults, since research confirmed that they are particularly susceptible to crashing [81], risky driving [80], phone distractions [88], and feeling disengaged [16]. The pre-existing interest in digital games prevalent in this group [6] made exploring gamification particularly promising. We recruited participants on our university campus and at car meet-ups. Data saturation [5] determined our sample size, i.e., data collection concluded when minimal new information was obtained from further sessions.

Procedure

Each of the study sessions consisted of two participants who knew each other. The rationale was to provide a comfortable setting for participants in the two-part study.

The first part took place in a driving simulator, where a real car is positioned in front of a projection screen. We played back 20 minutes of real-world video footage of typical inner-city, highway, and suburban driving. This safe setup has been proven to be effective in immersing participants in the driving context [69]. Figure 1 shows two participants in the simulator vehicle, where we encouraged them to chat with each other while watching the video footage, borrowing from think-aloud techniques [50].

The second part of the study continued with interviews in a nearby room, which lasted approx. 30-40 minutes. There, we presented the storyboards to induce participant feedback (Figure 2), a technique proposed by Greenberg et al. [21] and previously used in designing in-car experiences [35].

Audio recordings were made of all sessions and later transcribed verbatim. The transcribed responses were analysed independently by two researchers based on thematic coding methods, as proposed by Miles et al. [46].

Figure 2: Study participants discussing storyboards.

RESULTS & DESIGN RECOMMENDATIONS

Our understanding of user requirements was enhanced by viewing the interview data through appropriate design lenses. This richer understanding allowed us to formulate ten design recommendations *(Recommendations 1 - 10)*.

Engaged Driving (Data Lens & Road Conditions Lens)

The interview data revealed participants' desire to alleviate boredom while driving as well as coping strategies to make driving more engaging. We found that engagement is particularly associated with economic and anticipatory driving. Participants said they would typically focus on fuel consumption if they had to pay for petrol themselves (rather than their company or parents) or if they were low on fuel (P17, P18, P15, P14). In these situations, they would be more aware of their driving style and attempt to *"get the max amount [of kilometres per litre] as possible"* (P14). Others would exploit gaps to go past other cars (P24) and try to get ahead of slow traffic (P17). Zipping in and out of lanes was described as *"a bit fun," "more entertaining,"* and *"making you feel you're achieving something"* (P21, P19, P24). P13 and P14 reported purposely driving over lane markers: *"my car is really stiff, I feel every bump so I just try and hit every cat eye."* Five participants praised anticipatory concepts such as *CoastMaster*, which requires drivers to look ahead and take road characteristics into account. Finally, it was pointed out that speeding itself *"is kind of a reward, it's more fun to drive faster"* (P8). These responses underpin a demand for engagement we aim to meet with gamifying simple driving tasks.

Recommendation 1 – Anticipatory Driving: Applications aimed at increased task engagement should build upon the notions of economic and anticipatory driving.

In-Car Setting (Social Context Lens)

Three participants indicated feeling engaged when they could interact with others (P8, P9, P14). For example, P8 reported enjoying talking to other passengers in the car or to someone on his phone. Three participants (P13, P14, P19) reported feeling more engaged when they could show off. P19, e.g., enjoys *"hearing the sound of your car when you accelerate"* and P14 reportedly tries to make his car *"sound louder than everyone else's."*

Recommendation 2 – Use Competition: Applications should build upon the notions of competition and social approval.

Reward Structure (Presentation Lens)

Strikingly, participants reported they would be inclined to aim for the lowest score rather than the encouraged safe performance. As claimed by P24 (also P23, P16), he would *"pride [himself] on being zero stars at all times."* Similarly, a participant addressed the choice of a zombie theme in the tailgating scenario: *"Zombies would encourage me to drive closer to the car in front of me"* (P8). As a design implication, we recommend displaying no rewards or feedback at all for selected relevant use cases. In *CoastMaster*, e.g., if users exceed the speed limit, we suggest displaying 'invalid user input.' This may reduce users' temptation to explore the game boundaries, and therefore keep them from undesired and unsafe behaviours.

Rewards may be perceived differently in another way. In the *Mirror Music* storyboard, for instance, the music playback would be kept at the same volume only if drivers checked their mirrors frequently. Two participants signalled they would not use an app that turns down their music as *"listening to music is the best part of driving"* (P4) and *"something like this would annoy me to tears"* (P9).

Recommendation 3 – Allow Customisation of System Feedback: Apps should be customisable by the driver (e.g., choosing whether the music in the car is affected by their performance). This helps to avoid that feedback is perceived as punishment.

Challenge and Progress (Data & Road Conditions Lens)

Participants expected an adequate level of challenge from driving for it to be regarded as fun. Participants suggested that *"a game should only challenge driving activities that you aren't good at already"* (P7, also P8, P21). P15 admitted being *"pretty horrible at braking,"* and said an app aimed at smooth braking would be a fun learning activity. Four participants likewise pointed out they liked the educational aspect of concepts that encourage smooth driving (P16, P24, P23, P22). Three participants revealed that apps might succumb to the novelty effect (P1, P7, P16). P16 proposed to offer various levels of difficulty in order to maintain a sense of challenge and progress.

Recommendation 4 – Improve Driving Skills: Exploiting people's interest in skill progression is a promising pathway to explore for gamified driving (studies on motivation, games, and gamification support this notion [2,13]). Maintaining a sense of challenge can be achieved by offering different gaming themes, various levels of difficulty, competing with other users, or new driving challenges. Driving challenges may be designed around smooth driving to maximise passenger comfort, around efficient driving to address range anxiety in electric vehicles, to increase situational awareness in semi-automated driving, or to keep skilling the driver as vehicle automation may have deskilling effects. Such challenges may be complemented by enticing new user interface technologies, e.g., augmented reality using 3D head-up displays or windscreen displays.

Themes (Presentation Lens)

Our analysis revealed that *presentation* was not only by far most discussed (119 of 227 interview statements), but also showed the greatest disagreement between positive (25) and negative statements (36). Regarding the negative statements (dislike, disagree, etc.), we must note that we had initially designed the storyboards in a playful way making use of rich themes such as zombies (see *Storyboards* section). Our original rationale behind this presentation style assumed that playful themes would be compelling to users, based on literature which suggested that themes and narratives increased the likelihood of engagement [66].

We found that there was no consensus about which presentation style was favoured most (*raw, abstract,* or *themed*). Furthermore, even within *themes*, participants' opinions strongly diverged. For example, P6 said, *"I'm a big zombie fan so I think that'd be good fun,"* while P23 revealed he was not a *"zombie person."* It is unlikely that any one theme will appeal to everyone.

Recommendation 5 – Provide Users with Choices: In terms of design, users need to be given driving application choices, just like on app stores, or in media consumption in general, because there are likely no 'one size fits all' solutions. (Note that within research projects of limited scope it may not be possible to provide a rich selection of different apps).

Recommendation 6 – Avoid Testing Themes Early: In terms of testing, we recommend to explore themes at late stages in the process. This is because themes can easily dilute the results if there is a mismatch between user preference and theme. Note that delaying theme considerations does not preclude identifying game mechanics early on.

Recommendation 7 – Know Preferences When Testing: When testing themes, we recommend to assess user preferences to establish potential matches and mismatches. A game mechanic can be applied in tandem with varying themes, so customising themes may be an option.

We further unpack the implications of highly varied user preferences by presenting different personas, for which we formulate specific design recommendations.

Design Personas

Viewing the interview data through a *presentation* lens revealed differences and patterns in user preferences. Design personas are useful to reflect such differences and patterns [56]. They are a common tool in interaction design to illustrate different user types that might use a product in a similar way, and serve as a tool to conceptualise and communicate design concepts [33].

We propose three design personas representing three different preference clusters concerning *presentation* styles, which we argue are most critical in designing compelling apps: *Motorhead Max*, *Imaginative Ian*, and *Competitive Cody*. These personas are not necessarily mutually exclusive, but serve to facilitate the design process.

Motorhead Max

Motorhead Max is someone who identifies as car-savvy. This persona typifies drivers who would prefer to receive as much data as possible about their vehicle and their driving. Their preferred presentation style is raw data such as numbers or simple graphs without elaborate styling. They feel competent in interpreting these raw data and draw pleasure from monitoring, optimising, and comparing data. *Motorhead Max* represents quantified-self enthusiasts who have an interest in personal informatics such as physical activity tracking. Providing real-time performance feedback is one promising strategy to increase task engagement [38]. *Motorhead Max* responds to this strategy.

Evidence: Four participants who identified as car enthusiasts (P11, P17, P18, P20) indicated they would prefer raw data and simple visual representations. For example, P17 said he was *"more looking for the raw data than anything."* Two participants pointed out their interest in technology and stated *"the more information about my car and my driving the better"* (P14, also P13). It appears that those drivers would prefer *"a more technical evaluation of your driving"* (P20) rather than playing a driving game. Other participants added that driving feedback needed to be performance-related (P15) and accurate (P22). This accuracy would allow users to improve over time. In order to maximise their fuel efficiency, they would *"check their gears and revs"* (P9) and avoid braking if not necessary (P21). One participant recollected *"making a bit of a gamble of trying to get to a petrol station"* (P24), which resulted in him feeling very attentive about his driving style. Another participant said that he would use instantaneous fuel economy displays *"as a bit of a game to see how high [he] could get it up, for no particular reason apart from self-satisfaction"* (P18). Lastly, a participant pointed out that, as an added benefit, being mindful about fuel consumption would *"also prevent [him] from speeding"* (P23).

Recommendation 8 for Motorhead Max – Provide Vehicle Data: A driving app would have to be able to gather real-time driving data and display them to cater to *Motorhead Max's* interest. Vehicle data is most important to this persona, as is data accuracy. Inspiration regarding the presentation of these data may be drawn from IVIS as well as quantified-self apps.

Imaginative Ian

Imaginative Ian is someone who is attentive about their driving style as well as their surroundings. This persona represents drivers who make use of their spatial and situational awareness not only to respond to their environment, but also to anticipate what may lie ahead. If conditions allow, they may use their awareness and imagination to come up with ways to make their driving more challenging or satisfying for themselves. For example, they try to optimise their smooth driving to maximise passenger comfort. In terms of preferred presentation style, they expect simple and abstract information where the level of detail from plain raw data has been reduced. Their main interest lies in receiving just enough input that would allow them to imagine their own safe-driving games. Otherwise, they would focus on their surroundings and prefer for the data to disappear. Making the task at hand more challenging is one promising strategy to increase task engagement [38]. *Imaginative Ian* responds to this strategy.

Evidence: These characteristics are informed by participants who said they had already created games in their everyday drives. For example, P9 would often coast down to red lights when he anticipated they were about to turn green. Participants reported they would read their speed or fuel economy, compare it to previous drives or other drivers, and try to improve. Continuous challenges or continuous feedback loops were favoured by three participants (P21, P9, P8) and described as *"more relevant and engaging for longer"* (P21). These participants responded well to anticipatory storyboard concepts such as *CoastMaster*, which require drivers to look ahead (P23, P14, P24, P13, P22). Three participants mentioned they would *"start experimenting with the app just to learn how it works and then stop"* (P4, also P9, P7). More *"subtle background information,"* however, was considered unlikely to become less interesting (P9, P10).

Recommendation 9 for Imaginative Ian – Design Non-Intrusive Apps: To increase user acceptance for *Imaginative Ian*, driving apps should be non-intrusive. User interfaces need to be carefully designed for this persona to avoid visual distractions, e.g., by making use of ambient design. Furthermore, applications may display nothing at all and just emit minimal audible cues. For example, a challenge might be suggested at the beginning of the drive ("try to use less than X amount of fuel to work today") and take place mainly in the driver's head during the trip.

Competitive Cody

Competitive Cody portraits users who enjoy games that incorporate rewards and competition among users. While they may not be enthusiastic about cars, they respond to the playful and social elements provided by games. They personify users who check their position on leaderboards and challenge their friends. As they draw pleasure from the game's artwork, which amplifies the desired effect on immersion and engagement, they prefer *themed* presentations. Providing rewards and social approval are promising strategies to increase task engagement [38]. *Competitive Cody* responds to these strategies.

Evidence: This persona has been drawn from interview data in which seven participants indicated they would be inclined to perform better if there was an opportunity to receive real-world rewards, e.g., discounts at service stations (P7, P8, P9, P10, P16, P14, P13). It also personifies participants who favoured playful themes over data, such as P6: *"I'm a big zombie fan so I think that'd be good fun."* Furthermore, P8 and P16 suggested to compare their own scores with other users in the area or compete with friends. Themed performance feedback was often desired *post-drive*. P11, e.g., suggested to derive scores and statistics such as an average performance for each trip.

Recommendation 10 for Competitive Cody – Consider Pre-Drive and Post-Drive Contents: Driving games may provide an engaging stimulus to otherwise boring drives, which gives *Competitive Cody* something to do and look forward to. Designers can avoid challenges related to visual distraction through pre-drive and post-drive app contents (when the vehicle is not in motion) while still addressing *Competitive Cody's* desires in terms of artwork and competition. If the game is activated and played *during* drives, designers could resort to immersive augmented reality technologies such as 3D head-up displays with world-fixed graphics [20].

PROTOTYPE EVALUATIONS

Equipped with these insights, we implemented two prototypes, *BrakeMaster* and *CoastMaster*. Considering the ubiquity of smartphones in everyday life, including the driving context [51], we presented the prototypes as smartphone apps to our participants. Note that, conceptually, nothing speaks against implementing them as dashboard or head-up display applications. We evaluated both applications with users to explore the feasibility and usability of gamified driving. We also collected data regarding task engagement. The results are promising.

BrakeMaster

We created a first prototype to learn and iterate quickly, as proposed by Buxton et al. [8]. We chose to first prototype *BrakeMaster*, which seemed easiest in terms of development scope. It does not require to display any visuals while the vehicle is in motion, and therefore we did not have to consider visual distraction in the design at this point. This prototype offers a technical representation of the driving performance rather than a playful theme. This change to the original storyboard addresses *Motorhead Max's* interest in accessing raw data *(Recommendation 8)* and avoids a potential mismatch of user preference and implemented theme *(Recommendation 6)*.

We implemented *BrakeMaster* as an Android application that connects to on-board diagnostics (OBD). It shows a black screen while driving. Upon approaching a red light, an audio instruction signals the beginning of a new challenge, inviting the driver to match a deceleration curve instead of braking abruptly. When the car has come to a halt, the app will display an assessment of the braking performance visually as a graph (Figure 3) and via audio feedback before the vehicle is set into motion again *(Recommendation 4)*. We suggest to base the exact nature of desired braking patterns on transportation literature and to be context-dependent. (More on gathering real-time driving data from mobile and wearable devices in [72].)

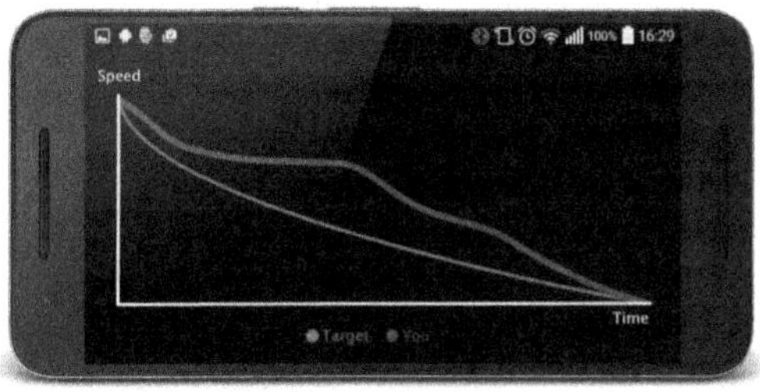

Figure 3. Prototype implementation of *BrakeMaster*.

Evaluation Study

We conducted a driving simulator study using the prototype to learn about its usability and user experience. Given the explorative nature of our rapid prototyping approach, the only participant selection criterion for this first evaluation was the possession of a valid driver's license. Overall, ten people (*M*=29, *SD*=4.42) participated in the study. We designed the evaluation as eight minutes of suburban driving. Participants encountered nine signalled intersections and five red lights, which triggered *Brake-Master* challenges. A smartphone running *BrakeMaster* was placed behind the steering wheel where dashboard displays are usually positioned. In terms of data collection, we administered the System Usability Scale (SUS), which provides a metric for overall product usability and can be used on small sample sizes with reliable results [7]. Semi-structured interviews were conducted with five participants.

Evaluation Results

The mean SUS score for *BrakeMaster* was *M*=78.5 (*SD*=16.55), on a scale from 0 (worst) 100 (best). According to literature [4,32], these data suggest good and above average usability and indicate that the game objective was well understood and desirable enough to be pursued. The interviews support these data. P1 felt *"happy to engage with the challenge and to get positive results,"* and he reported feeling *"a small sense of accomplishment"* when receiving positive feedback. P6 felt that *BrakeMaster* targets a familiar issue and said, *"highway driving or typically monotonous driving is just repetitive, but you have to focus on it."* Furthermore, P6, being *"fairly competitive,"* said, *"I like the idea of playing the game,"* although in the long run, the game should change from time to time to remain interesting. P7 said that the visual feedback helped him improve his driving performance. Considering the motivation behind the app, these results are promising. We therefore decided to continue our path with a second prototype iteration.

CoastMaster

Equipped with considerations from the first evaluation, we created a second prototype. This time, we explored a different scenario, i.e., approaching speed limits with *CoastMaster*. By gamifying a different driving situation, we address the participants' desire for more variation *(Recommendation 5)*. *CoastMaster* targets transitions to new speed limits. Since these transitions occur while the vehicle is in motion, and given driving is a highly visual task [67], complexity is added to the design. We therefore focussed on viewing this design iteration through the *presentation lens (L3)*, which included investigating usability and visual distraction.

Research suggests that eye glances greater than two seconds significantly increase crash risk and should therefore be minimised [28]. The literature around ambient interface design provided a useful perspective on this requirement. In applying ambient interface design, we also responded to *Imaginative Ian's* preference of simple, abstract visualisation *(Recommendations 6 and 9)*. This persona is important to consider when prototyping *CoastMaster*, which particularly targets anticipatory drivers *(Recommendation 1)*. Our designs were informed by heuristics for ambient displays [37] and IVIS design guidelines [3]. In the end, we independently arrived at a design similar to the digital speedometer proposed by Smith et al. [68], which may suggest a level of maturity in the design of this particular use case. (More information on the design process can be found in [71].)

CoastMaster serves as an ambient speedometer and gamifies transitions to new speed limits. Similar to related work by Ecker et al. [17], it encourages users to coast down to new speed limits without unnecessary pedal usage. The game objectives are: firstly, to stay within the speed limit, and, secondly, to do so with limited pedal usage even when the speed limit is changing. Upon approaching a lower speed limit, a visual icon and an audio cue signal the beginning of a challenge. For example, the goal of the challenge may be to coast down from 80 km/h to a new speed limit of 60 km/h. During the coast down phase, a vertical bar will move across the screen representing the remaining distance to the approaching speed sign (Figure

4). Along this vertical bar, a trace visualises pedal use, i.e., using no pedal (blue), using the accelerator pedal (yellow), and using the brake pedal (red). Once the car passes the speed sign, the app will display an assessment of the gameplay performance, which is also conveyed through an audio cue. Red background colour signifies exceeding the new speed limit (failed challenge), and a reference line allows users to assess their own smooth driving performance *(Recommendation 7)*. *CoastMaster* was implemented as a web app using HTML5 and JavaScript.

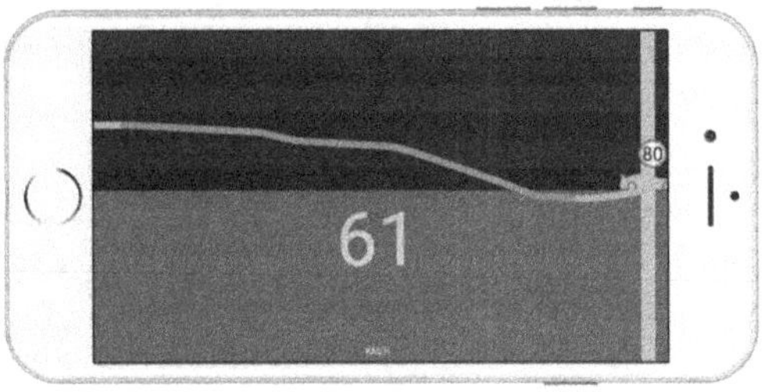

Figure 4. Prototype implementation of *CoastMaster*.

Evaluation Study

In a driving simulator study (*N*=24), we compared a gamified and a non-gamified interface with regards to user experience, driving performance, and visual distraction. 19 male drivers aged between 18 and 25 (*M*=22, *SD*=2.94) were recruited in line with our research program focus. The remaining five participants were road safety researchers (*M*=30.8, *SD*=4.76) who would provide feedback from their perspective. We designed the evaluation as a within-subjects, repeated measures experiment with two counterbalanced conditions across participants, *control* and *game*, and ten minutes of driving per condition. During each condition, participants would encounter 13 speed limit signs that resulted in eight slowdown transitions, i.e., eight *CoastMaster* challenges in the *game* condition, which each lasted approx. ten seconds. In terms of data collection, participants completed a disengagement questionnaire (subscale of MSBS [18]), which was previously used in task engagement studies [38]. Furthermore, the AttrakDiff 2 Questionnaire [25], a widely used instrument in HCI and AutoUI research to quantify hedonic and pragmatic qualities, was administered. To investigate visual distraction, we measured long (>2s) eye glances away from the driving environment with the ASL Mobile Eye-XG eye tracker. We also recorded driving speed. Lastly, we recorded driving speed and conducted semi-structured interviews with all 24 participants.

Evaluation Results

Disengagement is significantly higher in *control* (*M*=3.08, *SD*=0.14) compared to *game* (*M*=2.85, *SD*=0.07), as a paired t-test revealed ($t(24)$=-1.88, p<.05).

The AttrakDiff data suggest an increase in hedonic quality (HQ) through the gamified component (0.69 in *game* vs. -0.01 in *control*), on a scale from -3 (worst) to 3 (best). A closer look at HQ demonstrates a significantly higher value in HQ-*Stimulation* (*Z*=-2.9143, *p*=.004) in *game* (0.87) compared to *control* (-0.21). A Shapiro-Wilk normality test revealed that not all of the measurements are normally distributed. Therefore, a Wilcoxon signed-rank test was used to calculate significance. In the interviews, participants self-reported having more fun, feeling more challenged, and feeling less bored through the gamified component. Most participants agreed that the game component added *"that bit extra in it"* (P20) that made the drive more fun and challenging. P13 and P19 felt *"satisfied"* when their performance overlapped with the reference line illustrating the desired performance. Other participants felt *"frustrated and betrayed"* (P6) when they failed to achieve the desired performance.

The number of long (>2s) eye glances was significantly higher (*Z*=-2.87, *p*=.004) in the *game* condition (*M*=12.12, *SD*=9.31) compared to *control* (*M*=7.82, *SD*=8.40). The fact that participants glance at the screen more often in the *game* condition suggests visual distraction. The AttrakDiff data provides some insight into the cause of this: The pragmatic quality (PQ), i.e., the usability, is significantly (*Z*=-2.42, *p*=.016) lower in *game* (1.32) compared to *control* (1.46). This indicates that the ambient speedometer by itself was perceived and understood more easily than the version with the added game component. In the interviews, 22 participants pointed out they could see the speedometer information in their periphery.

We calculated the mean driving speed throughout the entire drive for each participant in both conditions (similar to Meschtscherjakov et. al [44] who studied an ambient LED system to support speed control). Our results show a significant (*Z*=-2.14, *p*=.032) mean speed drop of 0.79 km/h in *game* (*M*=62.1 km/h, *SD*=3.14) compared to *control* (speed *M*=62.89 km/h, *SD*=3.1). We then isolated the road segments that included coasting challenges, i.e., 250 meters before a speed limit sign. These segments reveal a significant (*Z*=-8.01, *p*<.001) lower mean driving speed in the *game* condition by 4.19 km/h (*M*=63.02 km/h, *SD*=4.89 in *game* vs. *M*=67.20 km/h, *SD*=4.22 in *control*). This result is due to earlier and smoother deceleration.

In summary, disengagement, driving speed, and interview data suggest increased task engagement through the gamified component.

DISCUSSION

We now discuss our work with respect to our research aim of exploring the design of gamified driving applications. Returning to the motivation of our work, we also discuss our results in light of task engagement and road safety.

Implications for Design

This paper presented six design lenses *(L1 - L6)* through which to view the design of gamified driving applications. We have shown, by applying four of them in our presented work, how they can be useful in various stages of the design process. As a result, we provided ten concrete design recommendations *(Recommendations 1 - 10)*, which researchers and practitioners can apply and extend in their own work. Similarly, our three presented user personas can serve as tools when designing driving related applications, and can be expanded accordingly.

Through the interviews, we identified that many drivers come up with their own gameful experiences. This relates to the concept of bottom-up gamification [31]. Rather than providing gamefulness from top-down, some users prefer the autonomy in imagining their own games around real-time performance feedback or other data. Lessel et al. [31] have shown that this approach is appealing for some user groups, and our data confirm this, which is also reflected in the *Imaginative Ian* persona.

Drawing attention to semi-automated driving, cars are gradually evolving through several levels of partial, conditional, and high automation [59]. One can expect some form of manual control in various geographies for at least the next two decades [34], which emphasises the ongoing need for task engagement and corroborates the relevance of this work. Our lenses, recommendations, and personas offer tools for exploring ways to keep drivers in the loop, e.g., to respond to handover requests.

Task Engagement and Road Safety

Our prototype evaluations have shown promising results in terms of increasing task engagement. These results upheld the predictions of the *opportunity-cost-model* by Kurzban et al. [30], which projects that, in general, attentional resources are allocated to compelling (or valuable) tasks. Our work indicates that this model holds true in the driving context. Our results also mirror findings by Markey et al. [38] whose experiments demonstrated that engagement can be increased through added challenge and providing real-time performance feedback. Our work suggests that these strategies can encourage engagement in the driving task as well. We acknowledge that our engagement data was self-reported by participants. More work is needed to collect objective data, e.g., through physiological and driving performance measures.

In terms of road safety, *CoastMaster* successfully encouraged safe driving as we have observed significantly lower driving speed as well as earlier and smoother deceleration. The mean driving speed reduction through the gamified component is comparable with related ambient display studies [44]. We have furthermore observed that visual distraction *during* challenges is too high. As pointed out [44], there is a trade-off between providing ambient information and driver distraction. This aspect needs to be addressed through further design iterations. A potential avenue to explore is ambient sound, which some participants said they might prefer, and how it might complement ambient visuals. Finally, our proposed personas and prototypes may be useful to more accurately model the impact on driving behaviour and, as such, better predict road safety benefits.

Limitations and Future Work

Although the study was carefully designed and carried out, we are aware of some limitations. We acknowledge that neither the list of design lenses nor the personas provided may be complete. Due to the composition of our initial user study, the findings reflect the views of young male adults. We cannot generalise our findings to drivers of all ages and genders. However, we believe young drivers to be a major potential user group of safe-driving apps. Furthermore, we expect to have identified the main design requirements, given we targeted the population most prone to feeling disengaged [16] and using phones in the car [88], but more research is needed in this regard. Lastly, we needed to remind participants to assume a safe implementation of the low-fidelity storyboards. We are aware this was a difficult task for participants and, more broadly, acknowledge this a common challenge in low-fidelity prototyping [21].

More work is needed to test applications like those proposed in this paper in order to evaluate safety-critical aspects such as lateral lane control, reaction times, distraction, and hazard perception. Future work should also investigate gamified driving with regards to flow [11] and boredom [30]. To this end, our proposed personas may be useful in recruiting the right study participants. In our future work we will sample participants that fit into the persona for whom future prototypes will be designed. Finally, more research is required to design not only for other demographics, but also for other safety-critical contexts, e.g., operating machinery in mining or manufacturing, air traffic control, or truck driving. To our knowledge and according to a recent literature review by Seaborn and Fels [66], gamification has not been studied in these domains.

CONCLUSION

Gamified driving offers an untapped opportunity to re-engage drivers in the safe-driving task and to create novel driving experiences. This paper presented empirical studies to investigate the design of gamified applications that make driving more engaging. We discussed how the six design lenses *data, presentation, time, interface, social context,* and *road conditions* are useful to bring into focus user needs and contextual requirements throughout the entire design process. Applying the lenses informed ten concrete design recommendations, e.g., around anticipatory driving and skill progression. Three presented user personas alleviate challenges faced by designers who develop driving applications for users with distinct preferences. As our prototype evaluations indicated, these tools can support the design of applications that make drivers feel more engaged in the driving task and be less tempted to take risks. As such, our contributions pave the way to developing new safety interventions for researchers and practitioners who aim to curb the road toll.

ACKNOWLEDGEMENTS

This work was supported under the Australian Research Council's Discovery Early Career Researcher Award (ARC DECRA) funding scheme (project number DE140101542).

REFERENCES

1. L. Andreone, A. Amditis, E. Deregibus, and S. Damiani. 2005. Beyond context-awareness: driver-vehicle-environment adaptivity. From the COMUNICAR Project to the AIDE concept. *16th IFAC WORLD.*
2. Andrés Francisco Aparicio, Francisco Luis Gutiérrez Vela, José Luis González Sánchez, and José Luis Isla Montes. 2012. Analysis and application of gamification. In *Proceedings of the 13th International Conference on Interacción Persona-Ordenador*, 17.
3. A Stevens, A Quimby, A Board, T Kersloot, P Burns. 2004. *Design Guidelines for Safety of In-Vehicle Information Systems*. TRL Limited.
4. Aaron Bangor, Philip T. Kortum, and James T. Miller. 2008. An Empirical Evaluation of the System Usability Scale. *International journal of human-computer interaction* 24, 6: 574–594.
5. Donna Bonde. 2013. *Qualitative Interviews: When enough is enough.* Research by Design. Retrieved from http://www.researchbydesign.com.au/media/RBD-WhitePaper-Margin-of-Error.pdf
6. Jeffrey E. Brand, Pascaline Lorentz, and Trishita Mathew. 2014. *Digital Australia 2014 (DA14).* Bond University for the Interactive Games & Entertainment Association.
7. John Brooke and Others. 1996. SUS-A quick and dirty usability scale. *Usability evaluation in industry* 189, 194: 4–7.
8. B. Buxton. 2010. *Sketching User Experiences: Getting the Design Right and the Right Design.* Elsevier Science.
9. Stephen M. Casner, Edwin L. Hutchins, and Don Norman. 2016. The Challenges of Partially Automated Driving. *Communications of the ACM* 59, 5: 70–77.
10. Neelima Chohan. 2015. Young drivers ignore dangerous phone warning. *HeraldSun*. Retrieved 9 September 2015 from http://www.heraldsun.com.au/news/victoria/young-drivers-ignore-dangerous-phone-warning/story-fni0fit3-1227339646687
11. M. Csikszentmihalyi. 1997. *Finding Flow: The Psychology of Engagement with Everyday Life.* BasicBooks.
12. Edward L. Deci, Robert J. Vallerand, Luc G. Pelletier, and Richard M. Ryan. 1991. Motivation and Education: The Self-Determination Perspective. *Educational psychologist* 26, 3-4: 325–346.
13. E. L. Deci and R. M. Ryan. 2012. Motivation, personality, and development within embedded social contexts: An overview of self-determination theory. *The Oxford handbook of human motivation.*
14. S. Deterding, D. Dixon, R. Khaled, and L. Nacke. 2011. From game design elements to gamefulness: defining gamification. In *MindTrek '11 Proceedings of the 15th International Academic MindTrek Conference: Envisioning Future Media Environments.*
15. Stefan Diewald, Andreas Möller, Luis Roalter, Tobias Stockinger, and Matthias Kranz. 2013. Gameful Design in the Automotive Domain: Review, Outlook and Challenges. In *Proceedings of the 5th International Conference on Automotive User Interfaces and Interactive Vehicular Applications*, 262–265.
16. Amos Drory. 1982. Individual differences in boredom proneness and task effectiveness at work. *Personnel psychology* 35, 1: 141–151.
17. Ronald Ecker, Philipp Holzer, Verena Broy, and Andreas Butz. 2011. EcoChallenge: a race for efficiency. In *Proceedings of the 13th International Conference on Human Computer Interaction with Mobile Devices and Services*, 91–94.
18. Shelley A. Fahlman, Kimberley B. Mercer-Lynn, David B. Flora, and John D. Eastwood. 2013. Development and validation of the multidimensional state boredom scale. *Assessment* 20, 1: 68–85.
19. Stephen H. Fairclough, Liverpool John Moores, Katie C. Ewing, Liverpool John Moores, Jenna Roberts, and Liverpool John Moores. 2009. Measuring task engagement as an input to physiological computing. In *Proc. of Int. Conf. on Affective Computing and Intelligent Interaction*, 1–9.
20. J. L. Gabbard, G. M. Fitch, and Hyungil Kim. 2014. Behind the Glass: Driver Challenges and Opportunities for AR Automotive Applications. *Proceedings of the IEEE* 102, 2: 124–136.
21. Saul Greenberg, Sheelagh Carpendale, Nicolai Marquardt, and Bill Buxton. 2011. *Sketching user experiences: The workbook.* Elsevier.
22. J. Hamari, J. Koivisto, and H. Sarsa. 2014. Does Gamification Work? -- A Literature Review of Empirical Studies on Gamification. In *2014 47th Hawaii International Conference on System Sciences*, 3025–3034.
23. Juho Hamari, Jonna Koivisto, and Tuomas Pakkanen. 2014. Do Persuasive Technologies Persuade? - A Review of Empirical Studies. In *Persuasive Technology* (Lecture Notes in Computer Science), 118–136.
24. Marc Hassenzahl. 2010. Experience Design: Technology for All the Right Reasons. *Synthesis Lectures on Human-Centered Informatics* 3, 1: 1–95.
25. Marc Hassenzahl, Annika Wiklund-Engblom, Anette Bengs, Susanne Hägglund, and Sarah Diefenbach. 2015. Experience-Oriented and Product-Oriented Evaluation: Psychological Need Fulfillment, Positive

Affect, and Product Perception. *International journal of human-computer interaction* 31, 8: 530–544.

26. Simon Heslop. 2014. Driver boredom: Its individual difference predictors and behavioural effects. *Transportation research. Part F, Traffic psychology and behaviour* 22: 159–169.
27. ISO. 2010. *ISO 9241-210:2010 - Ergonomics of human-system interaction -- Part 210: Human-centred design for interactive systems.*
28. Sheila G. Klauer, Thomas A. Dingus, Vicki L. Neale, Jeremy D. Sudweeks, David J. Ramsey, and Others. 2006. The impact of driver inattention on near-crash/crash risk: An analysis using the 100-car naturalistic driving study data. Retrieved from https://vtechworks.lib.vt.edu/handle/10919/55090
29. Martin Knobel, Marc Hassenzahl, Melanie Lamara, Tobias Sattler, Josef Schumann, Kai Eckoldt, and Andreas Butz. 2012. Clique Trip: Feeling Related in Different Cars. In *Proceedings of the Designing Interactive Systems Conference* (DIS '12), 29–37.
30. Robert Kurzban, Angela Duckworth, Joseph W. Kable, and Justus Myers. 2013. An opportunity cost model of subjective effort and task performance. *The Behavioral and brain sciences* 36, 6: 661–679.
31. P. Lessel, M. Altmeyer, M. Müller, and C. Wolff. 2016. Don't Whip Me With Your Games: Investigating Bottom-Up Gamification.
32. James R. Lewis and Jeff Sauro. 2009. The Factor Structure of the System Usability Scale. In *Human Centered Design* (Lecture Notes in Computer Science), 94–103.
33. W. Lidwell, K. Holden, and J. Butler. 2010. *Universal Principles of Design, Revised and Updated: 125 Ways to Enhance Usability, Influence Perception, Increase Appeal, Make Better Design Decisions, and Teach Through Design.* Rockport Publishers.
34. Todd Litman. 2015. Autonomous vehicle implementation predictions: Implications for transport planning. In *Transportation Research Board 94th Annual Meeting.*
35. Sebastian Loehmann. 2015. Experience Prototyping for Automotive Applications. University of Munich (LMU).
36. George F. Loewenstein and Dražen Prelec. 1993. Preferences for sequences of outcomes. *Psychological review* 100, 1: 91.
37. Jennifer Mankoff, Anind K. a. K. Dey, Gary Hsieh, Julie Kientz, Scott Lederer, and Morgan Ames. 2003. Heuristic Evaluation of Ambient Displays. *Proceedings of the SIGCHI conference on Human factors in computing systems*, 5: 169–176.
38. Amanda Rose Markey. 2014. Three Essays on Boredom. Carnegie Mellon University.
39. Aleksandar Matic, Martin Pielot, and Nuria Oliver. 2015. Boredom-computer Interaction: Boredom Proneness and the Use of Smartphone. In *Proceedings of the 2015 ACM International Joint Conference on Pervasive and Ubiquitous Computing* (UbiComp '15), 837–841.
40. Gerald Matthews, Sian E. Campbell, Shona Falconer, Lucy A. Joyner, Jane Huggins, Kirby Gilliland, Rebecca Grier, and Joel S. Warm. 2002. Fundamental dimensions of subjective state in performance settings: task engagement, distress, and worry. *Emotion* 2, 4: 315–340.
41. S. Matthies, A. Philipsen, and J. Svaldi. 2012. Risky decision making in adults with ADHD. *Journal of behavior therapy and experimental psychiatry* 43, 3: 938–946.
42. R. McCall and V. Koenig. 2012. Gaming concepts and incentives to change driver behaviour. In *Ad Hoc Networking Workshop (Med-Hoc-Net), 2012 The 11th Annual Mediterranean*, 146–151.
43. Rufeng Meng, Chengfeng Mao, and Romit Roy Choudhury. 2014. *Driving Analytics: Will it be OBDs or Smartphones?* Zendrive Inc. Retrieved from http://blog.zendrive.com/103460130120/
44. Alexander Meschtscherjakov, Christine Döttlinger, Christina Rödel, and Manfred Tscheligi. 2015. ChaseLight: ambient LED stripes to control driving speed. In *Proceedings of the 7th International Conference on Automotive User Interfaces and Interactive Vehicular Applications*, 212–219.
45. Alexander Meschtscherjakov, Alina Krischkowsky, Katja Neureiter, Alexander Mirnig, Axel Baumgartner, Verena Fuchsberger, and Manfred Tscheligi. 2016. Active Corners: Collaborative In-Car Interaction Design. In *Proceedings of the 2016 ACM Conference on Designing Interactive Systems* (DIS '16), 1136–1147.
46. Matthew B. Miles, A. Michael Huberman, and Johnny Saldaña. 2013. *Qualitative data analysis: A methods sourcebook.* SAGE Publications, Incorporated.
47. Brian W. Miller. 2015. Using Reading Times and Eye-Movements to Measure Cognitive Engagement. *Educational psychologist* 50, 1: 31–42.
48. Ann J. Morrison, Peta Mitchell, and Margot Brereton. 2007. The Lens of Ludic Engagement: Evaluating Participation in Interactive Art Installations. In *Proceedings of the 15th ACM International Conference on Multimedia* (MM '07), 509–512.
49. NHTSA. 2016. *Distracted Driving 2014.* Retrieved from

https://crashstats.nhtsa.dot.gov/Api/Public/ViewPublication/812260

50. Jakob Nielsen. 1994. *Usability engineering*. Elsevier.
51. Carl Jörgen Normark. 2015. Vehicle interaction tailored to you. *Interactions* 22, 1: 32–36.
52. ita Orji and Karyn Moffatt. 2016. Persuasive technology for health and wellness: State-of-the-art and emerging trends. *Health informatics journal*.
53. S. Oviatt. 2003. Multimodal interfaces. *The human-computer interaction handbook*
54. Sarah Pink, Pink Sarah, Kerstin Leder Mackley, Mitchell Val, Hanratty Marcus, Escobar-Tello Carolina, Bhamra Tracy, and Morosanu Roxana. 2008. Applying the lens of sensory ethnography to sustainable HCI. *ACM transactions on computer-human interaction: a publication of the Association for Computing Machinery* 20, 4: 1–18.
55. Danil V. Prokhorov, Steven F. Kalik, and Chenna K. R. Varri. 2011. System and method for reducing boredom while driving. *US Patent*. Retrieved from http://www.google.com/patents/US7982620
56. J. Pruitt and T. Adlin. 2010. *The Persona Lifecycle: Keeping People in Mind Throughout Product Design*. Elsevier Science.
57. Andry Rakotonirainy, Frank Feller, and Narelle L. Haworth. 2008. Using in-vehicle avatars to prevent road violence. *Pervasive and mobile computing*: 70–74.
58. Susann Rohwedder and Robert J. Willis. 2010. Mental Retirement. *The journal of economic perspectives: a journal of the American Economic Association* 24, 1: 119–138.
59. SAE International. 2014. *J3016: Taxonomy and Definitions for Terms Related to On-Road Motor Vehicle Automated Driving Systems*. Retrieved 4 July 2016 from http://standards.sae.org/j3016_201401/
60. N. Schaffer. 2008. Heuristic evaluation of games. *Game Usability: Advice from the Experts for Advancing*.
61. Erwin Schoitsch, Christoph Schmittner, Zhendong Ma, and Thomas Gruber. 2016. The Need for Safety and Cyber-Security Co-engineering and Standardization for Highly Automated Automotive Vehicles. In *Advanced Microsystems for Automotive Applications 2015*, Tim Schulze, Beate Müller and Gereon Meyer (eds.). Springer International Publishing, 251–261.
62. Ronald Schroeter, Jim Oxtoby, and Daniel Johnson. 2014. AR and Gamification Concepts to Reduce Driver Boredom and Risk Taking Behaviours. In *Proceedings of the 6th International Conference on Automotive User Interfaces and Interactive Vehicular Applications*, 1–8.
63. Ronald Schroeter, Jim Oxtoby, Daniel M. Johnson, and Fabius Steinberger. 2015. Exploring boredom proneness as a predictor of mobile phone use in the car. In *Proceedings of 27th Australian Conference on Human-Computer Interaction (OZCHI 2015)*.
64. Ronald Schroeter, Andry Rakotonirainy, and Marcus Foth. 2012. The social car: new interactive vehicular applications derived from social media and urban informatics. In *Proceedings of the 4th International Conference on Automotive User Interfaces and Interactive Vehicular Applications*, 107–110.
65. Ronald Schroeter and Fabius Steinberger. 2016. Pokémon DRIVE: Towards increased situational awareness in semi-automated driving. In *Proc. OzCHI 2016*.
66. Katie Seaborn and Deborah I. Fels. 2015/2. Gamification in theory and action: A survey. *International journal of human-computer studies* 74: 14–31.
67. M. Sivak. 1996. The information that drivers use: is it indeed 90% visual? *Perception* 25, 9: 1081–1089.
68. Tim Smith, Harsha Vardhan, Barnaby Malet, and David Mingay. 2014. *Are we there yet? Thoughts on in-car HMI*. ustwo. Retrieved from http://cdn.ustwo.com/automotive/AreWeThereYet_V1.0.pdf
69. Alessandro Soro, Andry Rakotonirainy, Ronald Schroeter, and Sabine Wollstädter. 2014. Using Augmented Video to Test In-Car User Experiences of Context Analog HUDs. In *Adjunct Proceedings of the 6th International Conference on Automotive User Interfaces and Interactive Vehicular Applications*, 1–6.
70. Fabius Steinberger, April Moeller, and Ronald Schroeter. 2016. The Antecedents, Experience, and Coping Strategies of Driver Boredom in Young Adult Males. *Journal of safety research*.
71. Fabius Steinberger, Patrick Proppe, Ronald Schroeter, and Florian Alt. 2016. CoastMaster – An Ambient Speedometer to Gamify Safe Driving. In *Proceedings of Automotive User Interfaces 2016*.
72. Fabius Steinberger, Ronald Schroeter, and Diana Babiac. 2017. Engaged Drivers – Safe Drivers: Gathering Real-Time Data from Mobile and Wearable Devices for Safe-Driving Apps. In *Automotive User Interfaces - Creating Interactive Experiences in the Car*, Gerrit Meixner and Christian Mueller (eds.). Springer.
73. Fabius Steinberger, Ronald Schroeter, and Verena Lindner. 2015. From gearstick to joystick – Challenges in designing new interventions for the safety-critical driving context. In *OzCHI 2015 Workshop on Ethical Encounters in HCI*.

74. Fabius Steinberger, Ronald Schroeter, Verena Lindner, Zachary Fitz-Walter, Joshua Hall, and Daniel Johnson. 2015. Zombies on the Road: A Holistic Design Approach to Balancing Gamification and Safe Driving. In *Proceedings of the 7th International Conference on Automotive User Interfaces and Interactive Vehicular Applications*, 320–327.

75. Melanie Swan. 2012. Sensor Mania! The Internet of Things, Wearable Computing, Objective Metrics, and the Quantified Self 2.0. *Journal of Sensor and Actuator Networks* 1, 3: 217–253.

76. Sarah-Kristin Thiel, Marcus Foth, and Ronald Schroeter. 2015. Ad Hoc Communities on the Road: Serendipitous Social Encounters to Enhance Tourist Experiences. In *Proceedings of the Annual Meeting of the Australian Special Interest Group for Computer Human Interaction* (OzCHI '15), 643–652.

77. Tim J. W. Tijs, Dirk Brokken, and Wijnand A. IJsselsteijn. 2008. Dynamic Game Balancing by Recognizing Affect. In *Fun and Games*, Panos Markopoulos, Boris de Ruyter, Wijnand IJsselsteijn and Duncan Rowland (eds.). Springer Berlin Heidelberg, 88–93.

78. Atiyeh Vaezipour, Andry Rakotonirainy, and Narelle Haworth. 2015. Reviewing In-vehicle Systems to Improve Fuel Efficiency and Road Safety. *Procedia Manufacturing* 3: 3192–3199.

79. Mark Vollrath, Anja Katharina Huemer, Carolin Teller, Anastasia Likhacheva, and Jana Fricke. 2016. Do German drivers use their smartphones safely?—Not really! *Accident; analysis and prevention* 96: 29–38.

80. Barry C. Watson, Angela Watson, Victor Siskind, and Judy J. Fleiter. 2009. Characteristics and predictors of high-range speeding offenders. *Proceedings of 2009 Australasian Road Safety Research, Policing and Education Conference.*

81. WHO. 2015. *Global status report on road safety 2015.* World Health Organization.

82. Mikael Wiberg. 2013. Methodology for materiality: interaction design research through a material lens. *Personal and Ubiquitous Computing* 18, 3: 625–636.

83. Timothy D. Wilson, David A. Reinhard, Erin C. Westgate, Daniel T. Gilbert, Nicole Ellerbeck, Cheryl Hahn, Casey L. Brown, and Adi Shaked. 2014. Social psychology. Just think: the challenges of the disengaged mind. *Science* 345, 6192: 75–77.

84. Eray Yağdereli, Cemal Gemci, and A. Ziya Aktaş. 2015. A study on cyber-security of autonomous and unmanned vehicles. *The Journal of Defense Modeling and Simulation: Applications, Methodology, Technology* 12, 4: 369–381.

85. R. M. Yerkes and J. D. Dodson. 1908. The relation of strength of stimulus to rapidity of habit-formation. *The Journal of comparative neurology.*

86. Chuang-Wen You, Martha Montes-de-Oca, Thomas J. Bao, Nicholas D. Lane, Hong Lu, Giuseppe Cardone, Lorenzo Torresani, and Andrew T. Campbell. 2012. CarSafe: A Driver Safety App That Detects Dangerous Driving Behavior Using Dual-cameras on Smartphones. In *Proceedings of the 2012 ACM Conference on Ubiquitous Computing* (UbiComp '12), 671–672.

87. John Zimmerman, Jodi Forlizzi, and Shelley Evenson. 2007. Research Through Design As a Method for Interaction Design Research in HCI. In *Proceedings of the SIGCHI Conference on Human Factors in Computing Systems* (CHI '07), 493–502.

88. 2012. *State of the road: Mobile phones and driving fact sheet.* CARRS-Q. Retrieved from https://www.police.qld.gov.au/EventsandAlerts/campaigns/Documents/mobile_phones_and_distraction_fs.pdf

Tunneled In: Drivers with Active Secondary Tasks Need More Time to Transition from Automation

Brian Mok*, Mishel Johns*, David Miller†, Wendy Ju*
Department of Mechanical Engineering* and Communication†
Stanford University, Stanford, CA, USA
{brianmok, mishel, davebmiller, wendyju}@stanford.edu

ABSTRACT
In partially automated driving, rapid transitions of control present a severe hazard. How long does it take a driver to take back control of the vehicle when engaged with other non-driving tasks? In this driving simulator study, we examined the performance of participants (N=30) after an abrupt loss of automated vehicle control. We tested three transition time conditions, with an unstructured transition of control occurring 2s, 5s, or 8s before entering a curve. As participants were occupied with an active secondary task (playing a game on a tablet) while the automated driving mode was enabled, they needed to disengage from the task and regain control of the car when the transition occurred. Few drivers in the 2 second condition were able to safely negotiate the road hazard situation, while the majority of drivers in the 5 or 8 second conditions were able to navigate the hazard situation safely.

Author Keywords
Car Simulator; Controlled Study; Autonomous Vehicles; Transition of Control; Human Machine Interaction.

ACM Classification Keywords
H.1.2. User/Machine Systems.

INTRODUCTION
With automated driving systems in the future, it is expected that drivers will not be required to maintain vigilance in monitoring the car's activity and will be given the freedom to perform other secondary tasks. However, there will still be scenarios where it will be necessary for the driver to take over control of the vehicle. Given the various states of distraction that drivers may be in when a transition of control is required, it is important to understand how they would react in these emergency situations. This insight would then allow us to better craft safety standards and augment existing policies for automated driving. For example, in the National Highway and Traffic Safety Administration's (NHTSA) levels of automation paradigm, it is stated that vehicles of Level 3 automation (Limited Self-Driving) should provide drivers with "sufficiently comfortable transition time" when taking back control [12]. This subsequently dictates how far in advance automated vehicles need to perceive events or hazards, an important design requirement for auto manufacturers. NHTSA has not defined how long this time should be and has indicated that further evaluation is need. So, a worst-case benchmark must be established to determine this minimum necessary time.

Permission to make digital or hard copies of all or part of this work for personal or classroom use is granted without fee provided that copies are not made or distributed for profit or commercial advantage and that copies bear this notice and the full citation on the first page. Copyrights for components of this work owned by others than ACM must be honored. Abstracting with credit is permitted. To copy otherwise, or republish, to post on servers or to redistribute to lists, requires prior specific permission and/or a fee. Request permissions from Permissions@acm.org.
CHI 2017, May 06-11, 2017, Denver, CO, USA
© 2017 ACM. ISBN 978-1-4503-4655-9/17/05$15.00
DOI: http://dx.doi.org/10.1145/3025453.3025713

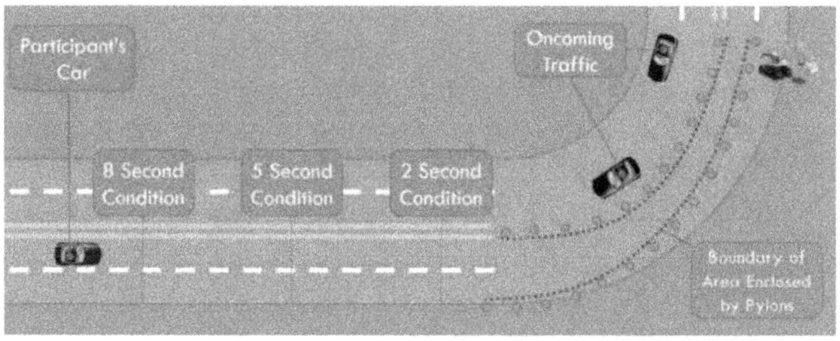

Figure 1: Diagram of the Critical Transition Event

This study (N=30) was conducted with a driving simulator, in which the human driver and an automated driving system could alternately control the vehicle. While the car's automated driving system was in control, the participants were asked to perform an active secondary task (i.e., playing a game on a tablet computer). As the car continued to drive autonomous in the freeway section of the simulation scenario, it would suddenly encounter a road hazard. After an emergency alert was issued from the vehicle, the driver needed to disengage from the secondary task to negotiate the hazard. An unstructured transition, in which control is immediately returned to the driver, was utilized. Three different transition conditions were tested, with the unstructured transition occurring 2 seconds, 5 seconds, or 8 seconds before the road hazard. The post-transition driving performance and post-drive attitudes of the participants toward the car were examined. These results help determine how much time is needed for drivers to assess the situation and successfully regain control.

BACKGROUND
This study seeks to understand how drivers react when control of the vehicle is suddenly relinquished back to them from the automated driving system. In the framework of automated vehicles, the takeover time for unstructured transitions of control have not been extensively examined. While there have been some studies that utilized

unstructured transitions, such as Louw et al. who observed performance differences between automation conditions [8], the experiment designs did not present a worst-case scenario as the participants were informed in advance to expect a transition. In our prior works [9] [10], the participants were only subjected to a single challenging critical event, which prevented any priming or learning effects. Subsequently in both studies, very significant differences in post-transition performance were observed between the different transition time conditions (2 seconds, 5 seconds, and 8 seconds) tested. The effects of secondary tasks were also examined. The participants were instructed to monitor the car in our first study [9] and watch a video in our second study [10]. However, there was no significant difference in performance with regards to the secondary task, possibly since these two tasks were less taxing. Thus, in this third study, it is vital to investigate the effects of a secondary task that requires much more active engagement—playing a game—to determine a minimum time required for transitions.

Structured transitions, in which drivers are given a period of time to get ready to resume control while automation continues to drive, do not present a worst-case scenario that can be used to determine a minimum time. However, there are many studies that use this paradigm to examine driver behavior. Damböck et al. tested several takeover times and determined that notifications greater than 8 seconds might not lead to greater post-transition driving performance [5]. Many studies also examined the effects of secondary tasks on drivers' performance [3] [7] [13] [15]. Gold et al. found that distracted drivers given shorter takeover request times tended to respond quicker but exhibited worse performance [6]. Beukel et al. found a similar result, with longer advanced warnings leading to more successfully avoided collisions by distracted drivers [1]. NHTSA also tried to determine "sufficiently comfortable" time in their on-road driving study [2]. However, only reaction time, not post-transition performance, was examined in this study.

METHODOLOGY

Simulator

The first component of our high-immersion fixed-base driving simulator is a modified Toyota Avalon, which provides an immersive full car interface. To increase the presence of the simulator [8], haptic feedback is incorporated into the steering wheel and pedals. The other component of the driving simulator is the audio/visual display. A 270-degree field of view cylindrical screen surrounds the car. The videos of five projectors blend together to create a seamless simulated driving environment. A sixth projector is used to display the rear view and LCD panels are installed in the side view mirrors. External speakers and a subwoofer simulate road noise, which varies from 40 to 55 dB (measured from driver's seat). Speakers inside the cabin provide audio alerts from the car to the participant at 50 dB. Several *GoPro* cameras are installed inside the car's cabin so that driver's behavior during the study can be monitored and recorded. *Realtime Technologies' SimCreator* software is used to create the audio and visual components of the simulation.

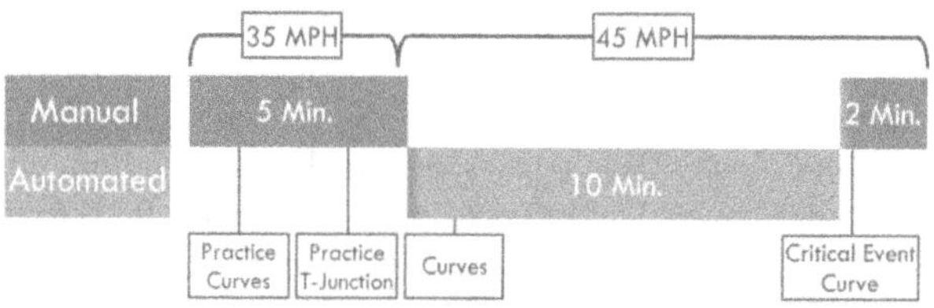

Figure 2: Diagram of the Simulated Driving Course

Course

During the duration of the course, the automated driving mode would perform the majority of the driving task. As Figure 2 shows, there are three different sections in the course. The first 5-minute section was designed to allow the participants to practice and become acclimated to driving in the simulator. At the end of this first section, participants were asked to enable the automated driving mode and the vehicle drove on for 10 minutes in the second section. This second section was mostly composed of a long segment of straight road, but also contained several curves at the beginning to demonstrate that the automated driving mode was normally capable of negotiating many road types. This was important due to the design of the critical event.

At the beginning of the last section, the car approached a curve which lacked lane markings. It was designed to appear as though construction was in progress (Figure 1). A set of pylons was placed to indicate where the center divider was located. Another set of pylons was used to close off the right lane (where an excavator was placed) and force the participants to stay in the left lane. This area provided a realistic scenario in which the car's automated driving system might have difficulty negotiating in real life. As this scenario required participants to both comprehend the situation and then react accordingly, it was an excellent indicator of participants' ability to regain control of the car.

Full control of the car was returned to participants a few seconds (i.e., 2, 5 or 8 seconds) before entering this critical event. An audible alert, "Emergency, Automation Off," and a visual alert on the instrument cluster indicated that the unstructured transition had occurred. The control of car was instantly given back to the participants in the drive mode, with the steering wheel centered, and with no additional input to the brake or throttle. Once the car entered the curve, traffic was spawned in the two oncoming lanes to encourage the participants to stay between the pylons and not take evasive actions in that direction. After the event, the participants drove manually until the end of the course.

Transition Time Manipulation

Based on prior research and related works, 2 seconds, 5 seconds, and 8 seconds were chosen to be the three transition time conditions for this study. The transition time was defined to be the amount of time it took for the car to reach the lane closure. For every condition, the car would travel at 45 mph (chosen based on the road type used) at the point of transition, and would always enter the critical event in the left lane. Given the speed and lane position when transition occurred, the transition point for each condition was placed at an appropriate distance from the pylons.

Secondary Task

Participants were instructed to do an activity while the car's automated driving mode was enabled. They were given an active secondary task in the form of playing a game on an iPad. The game selected was the popular iOS application: *Temple Run 2*. It was a good application for the study because it required the participants to be constantly engaged to play effectively. Unlike other games that allow for breaks during play, *Temple Run 2* is a perpetual experience where the players need to avoid obstacles that appear every few seconds. As the game became harder and faster over time, it could be very taxing on the participants and add an element of fatigue. To see how they would naturally disengage from this task, participants were not told what to do with the iPad in the advent of an emergency.

Procedure

The participants were first asked to sign a consent form and complete the pre-drive questionnaire. They were then led into the driving simulator room. To ensure that they would only be engaged with the given task, the participants were asked to relinquish their electronic devices during the study. They were briefed on the vehicle's automated driving system and how to enable it. They were instructed to play the game on the tablet when the automated driving mode was on; participants were encouraged to aim for the high score and to play again if they lost in the game. To establish a worst-case benchmark, participants were not informed of the transition in advance and were not additionally incentivized to perform well in the driving task. Overall, the simulated driving task took 15 to 20 minutes to complete. After finishing the driving task, participants were asked to complete the post-drive questionnaire.

Participants

A total of 30 participants were recruited for the study. The participant population had an age distribution that ranged from 17 to 59 years old (M = 32.3 years, SD = 10.8 years). Their reported years of driving experience ranged from 1 year to 44 years (M = 12.2 years, SD = 11.4 years). Genders of the participants were equally distributed across each condition, 50% male and 50% female.

ANALYSIS

Driving Behavior Data

The simulation driving data (position in the road, driver inputs, etc.) was collected at 60Hz. The driving metrics selected for analysis allowed for a better understanding of how participants performed on the curve. Given how the transition and critical event were designed, certain other traditional metrics for takeover, such as time to evasive action, were not appropriate for evaluating performance. For example, several participants in the 8 second condition did not instantly detect the road hazard as they were still far away from the critical event. This led to a slower reaction despite good performance. The data was analyzed using Python to extract measures of driving performance and *R* to perform the various statistical tests. The following measures were calculated over the duration of the curve.

Negotiating the Critical Event

From the road offset, it can be determined if the car stayed within the appropriate area that was enclosed by the pylons. By using position of the pylons, the boundaries for this area can be defined as a set of two equations with regards to road offset (see Figure 1). A binary measure of whether the curve was successfully negotiated without a collision into the pylons showed a significant difference between conditions on the Chi Squared test (χ^2=9.55, df=2, p<0.01). All participants in 8 second condition negotiated the curve successfully, while 8 of the 10 participants in 2 second condition and 4 of the 10 participants in 5 second condition failed. Video analysis also confirmed this finding.

Standard Deviation of Road Offset

The distance of the vehicle from the centerline of the road (variation in road offset) can be used as a measure of driving performance. [14] [4] This is similar to a measure defined by SAE J2944 [16]: the standard deviation in lane position. Control was returned to the participants with the steering wheel was centered. This initial steering wheel position should not cause any detrimental artifacts on the standard deviation of road offset post-transition. Performing ANOVA, the standard deviation of the road offset (in meters) in the curved section of the road showed significant differences between the conditions. However, as one of the groups was non-normal (Shapiro-Wilk Normality test p = 0.017 for the 5 second group), the non-parametric Kruskal-Wallis rank sum test was used to confirm the result. The test showed significant differences between the transition time conditions, χ^2=18.49, df=2, p=9.67e-5. Conducting the post-hoc pairwise analysis using the Wilcoxon rank sum test with Bonferroni correction showed differences between the 5 second (M=0.6, SD=0.46) and 2 second (M=1.88, SD=0.84) conditions (p<0.01) and significant differences between the 8 second (M=0.28, SD=0.12) and 2 second conditions (p<0.001) and moderately significant differences between the 8 second and 5 second conditions (p=0.10).

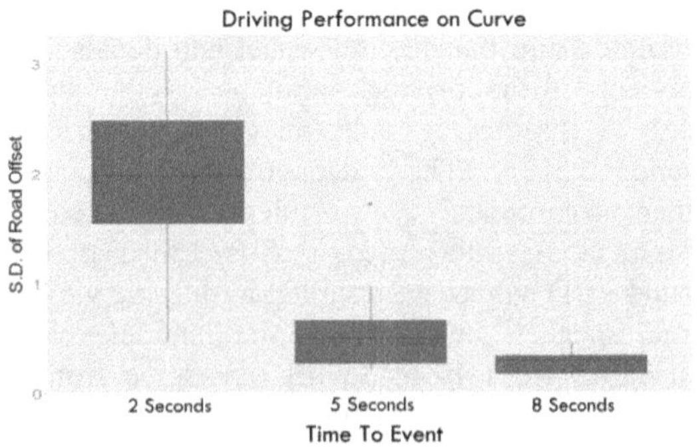

Figure 3: Road Offset Standard Deviation

Standard Deviation of Steering Wheel Position

Standard deviation of the steering wheel position (in radians) [4] is also used to measure driving performance. The measure passed the Shapiro-Wilk test of normality ($p > 0.1$) but failed the Levene's test for Homogeneity of Variance ($p < 0.05$), so the non-parametric Kruskal-Wallis rank sum test was again used. The test showed significant differences between transition time conditions, χ^2=12.68, df=2, p=1.7e-3. A post-hoc pairwise analysis using the Wilcoxon rank sum test with Bonferroni correction showed significant differences between the 5 second (M=0.48, SD=0.33) and 2 second (M=1.29, SD=0.85) conditions ($p<0.05$) and significant differences between the 8 second (M=0.19, SD=0.08) and 2 second conditions ($p<0.01$) and moderately significant differences between the 8 second and 5 second conditions (p=0.10).

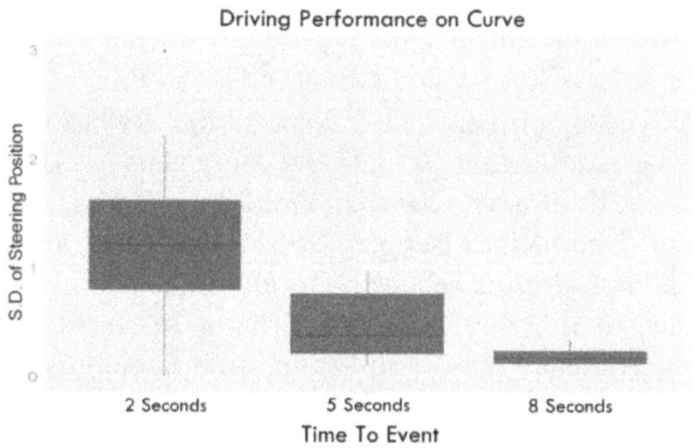

Figure 4: Steering Wheel Position Standard Deviation

Initial Evasion Strategy

To determine if the time conditions affected or limited participants' decision making, their initial evasion strategy (brake first vs. steer first) was examined. Of those participants who tried to brake first, there were 6 in the 2 second condition, 7 in the 5 second condition and 8 in the 8 second condition. Performing a Chi Squared test (χ^2=0.952, df=2, p=0.621), no significant differences were found.

Disengaging from the Task

Through video analysis, we examined how participants disengaged from playing the game when they were prompted to take over control. Most participants (28/30) dropped the tablet on the passenger seat or on their lap. There were 2 participants tried to hold on to the tablet while negotiating the critical event. Surprisingly, 5 participants tried to pause the game even after hearing the alert.

Attitudinal Data

In part of the post-drive questionnaire, participants were asked how well certain words described the automated driving system. A 7-point Likert Scale was used (1 = *describes poorly*; 7 = *describes well*). Performing ANOVA, no significant differences were found.

DISCUSSION AND RESULTS

It appears that the 2 second transition time condition does not provide sufficient time for the participants to regain control and negotiate the road hazard. Participants in this condition performed significantly worse than those in the other two conditions. The participants in the 2 second condition exhibited both a significantly greater road offset standard deviation and steering wheel standard deviation during the event. Also, a large majority of these participants hit the critical event's pylons. Eight participants were unable to stay in the lane and some participants even drove straight ahead into the grass, which was rarely observed in previous studies. So, any transition from automation should occur more than two seconds before the critical event.

Similarly, the 5 second condition also appears to be not sufficient, as a few lane deviations or collisions with pylons still occurred. Four of the participants were unsuccessful in negotiating the critical event. While the participants in the 5 second condition appeared to perform significantly better than those of the 2 second condition, they also did not perform as well as those in the 8 second condition.

The participants of the 8 second condition did not deviate from the critical event's left lane or hit any of the pylons. It is the shortest of the tested transition times that has yielded excellent driver performance. Hence, the minimum amount of time required for drivers to regain control should be between 5 and 8 seconds, which is a range that automotive manufacturers should consider when designing cars.

We also noted an interesting result in the analysis of the self-reported attitudinal data. In previous studies, there were significant differences in how trustworthy the car appeared to the participants and how much participants liked the car. However, we did not see any significant difference between conditions for this study. Interestingly, participants in the 2 second condition in this study had a much wider range of responses compared to those participants in prior studies.

CONCLUSION AND FUTURE WORK

This study has yielded significant results on how drivers performed post transition with automated driving systems. There appears to be a minimum amount of time needed for transition of control, between 5 seconds and 8 seconds. The results of this study (where the participants were given an active secondary task) are not similar to those of our prior studies (where the participants were given no task or a passive secondary task). In both previous studies, the 2 second condition is also not long enough, but the 5 second condition is adequate for transition of control.

In our future work, we want to test the effectiveness of different alert modalities. While it is established that having both audio and visual alerts are important [11], do drivers perform better when given other types of alerts, such as haptic or movement-based? Additionally, we also seek to validate these results by performing an on-road study.

ACKNOWLEDGMENT

The authors thank Jan Becker, Key Lee, Srinath Sibi, and Nikhil Gowda for their contributions to the study. The project is supported by Robert Bosch LLC.

REFERENCES

1. Arie P. van den Beukel and Mascha C. van der Voort. 2013. The influence of time-criticality on Situation Awareness when retrieving human control after automated driving. In 16th International IEEE Conference on Intelligent Transportation Systems (ITSC 2013), 2000–2005.
2. Myra Blanco, Jon Atwood, Holland M. Vasquez, Tammy E. Trimble, Vikki L. Fitchett, Josh Radlbeck, Gregory M. Fitch, Sheldon M. Russell, Charles A. Green, Brian Cullinane, and others. 2013. Human Factors Evaluation of Level 2 and Level 3 Automated Driving Concepts. Vergina Tech, Automated Vehicle Systems Group Research.
3. Avinoam Borowsky and Tal Oron-Gilad. 2016. The effects of automation failure and secondary task on drivers' ability to mitigate hazards in highly or semi-automated vehicles. *Advances in Transportation Studies*, 1.
4. Karel A. Brookhuis, Gerbrand de Vries, and Dick de Waard. 1991. The effects of mobile telephoning on driving performance. Accident Analysis & Prevention 23, 4: 309–316.
5. Daniel Damböck and Klaus Bengler. Übernahmezeiten beim hochautomatisierten Fahren.
6. Christian Gold, Daniel Dambock, Lutz Lorenz, and Klaus Bengler. 2013. "Take over!" How long does it take to get the driver back into the loop? Proceedings of the Human Factors and Ergonomics Society Annual Meeting 57, 1: 1938–1942.
7. Toshio Ito, Arata Takata, and Kenta Oosawa. 2016. Time Required for Take-over from Automated to Manual Driving.
8. Tyron Louw, Natasha Merat, and Andrew Hamish Jamson. 2015. Engaging With Highly Automated Driving: To Be Or Not To Be In The Loop? In 8th International Driving Symposium on Human Factors in Driver Assessment, Training and Vehicle Design, 189–195.
9. Brian Mok, Mishel Johns, Key Jung Lee, Hillary Ive, David Miller, and Wendy Ju. 2015. Timing of unstructured transitions of control in automated driving. In 2015 IEEE Intelligent Vehicles Symposium (IV), 1167–1172.
10. Brian Mok, Mishel Johns, Key Jung Lee, David Miller, David Sirkin, Hillary Ive, and Wendy Ju. 2015. Emergency, Automation Off: Unstructured Transition Timing for Distracted Drivers of Automated Vehicles. In Intelligent Transportation Systems (ITSC), 2015 IEEE 18th International Conference on, 2458–2464.
11. Frederik Naujoks, Christoph Mai, and Alexandra Neukum. 2014. The effect of urgency of take-over requests during highly automated driving under distraction conditions. *Advances in Human Aspects of Transportation*, Part I: 431.
12. NHTSA. 2013. U.S. Department of Transportation Releases Policy on Automated Vehicle Development | National Highway Traffic Safety Administration (NHTSA). Retrieved August 6, 2014 from http://www.nhtsa.gov/About+NHTSA/Press+Releases/U.S.+Department+of+Transportation+Releases+Policy+on+Automated+Vehicle+Development
13. Jonas Radlmayr, Christian Gold, Lutz Lorenz, Mehdi Farid, and Klaus Bengler. 2014. How traffic situations and non-driving related tasks affect the take-over quality in highly automated driving. In Proceedings of the Human Factors and Ergonomics Society Annual Meeting, 2063–2067.
14. Joris C Verster and Thomas Roth. 2011. Standard operation procedures for conducting the on-the-road driving test, and measurement of the standard deviation of lateral position (SDLP). International Journal of General Medicine 4: 359–371.
15. Kathrin Zeeb, Axel Buchner, and Michael Schrauf. 2015. What determines the take-over time? An integrated model approach of driver take-over after automated driving. In *Accident Analysis & Prevention* 78: 212–221.
16. J2944: Operational Definitions of Driving Performance Measures and Statistics - SAE International. Retrieved September 18, 2016 from http://standards.sae.org/j2944_201506/

An Evaluation of Input Controls for In-Car Interactions

Alexander Ng[1], Stephen A. Brewster[1]
Glasgow Interactive Systems Group
School of Computing Science
University of Glasgow, UK
[1]{first.last}@glasgow.ac.uk

Frank Beruscha[2], Wolfgang Krautter[2]
Corporate Sector Research and Advance Engineering
Robert Bosch GmbH
Renningen, Germany
[2]{first.last}@de.bosch.com

ABSTRACT
The way drivers operate in-car systems is rapidly changing as traditional physical controls, such as buttons and dials, are being replaced by touchscreens and touch-sensing surfaces. This has the potential to increase driver distraction and error as controls may be harder to find and use. This paper presents an in-car, on the road driving study which examined three key types of input controls to investigate their effects: a physical dial, pressure-based input on a touch surface and touch input on a touchscreen. The physical dial and pressure-based input were also evaluated with and without haptic feedback. The study was conducted with users performing a list-based targeting task using the different controls while driving on public roads. Eye-gaze was recorded to measure distraction from the primary task of driving. The results showed that target accuracy was high across all input methods (greater than 94%). Pressure-based targeting was the slowest while directly tapping on the targets was the faster selection method. Pressure-based input also caused the largest number of glances towards to the touchscreen but the duration of each glance was shorter than directly touching the screen. Our study will enable designers to make more appropriate design choices for future in-car interactions.

Author Keywords
Pressure-based input; Touch input; Touchscreens; In-car interactions; Haptic feedback.

ACM Classification Keywords
H.5.2. User Interfaces [Input devices and strategies]

INTRODUCTION
In-car controls on centre consoles are undergoing major changes as traditional buttons, dials and switchgear are replaced by touchscreens and touch-sensing surfaces. The replacement of these physical components allows more aesthetically pleasing in-car interiors and the design of more flexible and dynamic user interfaces. New methods such as force input (commonly known as pressure-based input in related literature) are now available on mobile devices such as Apple's iPhones and MacBook Pros and are likely to transfer to in-car centre consoles in the future. However, the tactile sensations from pressing on physical buttons and grasping rotary dials are lost when inputting on smooth touchscreens and many in-car touch surfaces lack any form of haptic feedback. This is a safety concern as drivers are likely to spend more time looking at and interacting with the touchscreen and new touch surfaces than at the road ahead [4,12].

This paper presents a real world, on the road driving study which compared the input performance and visual attention required of three main input controls that are currently found or likely to feature in cars in the future: (1) touch input in the form of direct target selection or onscreen buttons, (2) physical dial and (3) pressure-based buttons on a touch-surface. Furthermore, we evaluated the rotary dial and pressure-based buttons with haptic feedback to see if vibrotactile cues were still effective in driving situations to improve targeting performance and reduce visual attention on the screen. Doing the test with drivers when driving means that we can collect the most robust and reliable results about the performance of the controls in real world conditions.

BACKGROUND
Related work has examined drivers' ratings for physical switches in cars and reported the importance of touch over auditory and visual cues to judge the quality of buttons and dials [2]. As touchscreen infotainment systems became popular in cars, researchers investigated in-car touch-based interactions [3,6,9,11,20,24]. Kern and Schmidt [10] discussed the increased number of input devices (e.g. touchscreens, physical buttons and dials) and output modalities (e.g. analog, digital and virtual speedometers) found in cars and safety concerns regarding driver distraction due to complex interactions with in-car systems. Therefore, studies such as Pitts *et al.* [17] explored the effectiveness of haptic feedback for in-car touchscreens and found that a combination of visual, audible and haptic feedback was subjectively preferred over visual feedback only. Richter *et al.* [19] showed that haptic feedback reduced input error rate and improved overall task completion time on a force-sensitive touchscreen device in their simulated driving study.

Recent studies on pressure-based input on centre consoles have become more common. Huber *et al.* [8] conducted a preliminary elicitation study which explored the mappings of

Permission to make digital or hard copies of all or part of this work for personal or classroom use is granted without fee provided that copies are not made or distributed for profit or commercial advantage and that copies bear this notice and the full citation on the first page. Copyrights for components of this work owned by others than ACM must be honored. Abstracting with credit is permitted. To copy otherwise, or republish, to post on servers or to redistribute to lists, requires prior specific permission and/or a fee. Request permissions from Permissions@acm.org.
CHI 2017, May 06-11, 2017, Denver, CO, USA
© 2017 ACM. ISBN 978-1-4503-4655-9/17/05…$15.00.
DOI: http://dx.doi.org/10.1145/3025453.3025736

different force-based gestures on a touchpad to common in-car commands. The results from their driving simulator study found that participants used two levels of force to differentiate between a tap and a press to interact with in-car applications.

In our previous study [15], we conducted two experiments to compare different pressure-based input techniques with a standard physical dial. Pressure-based input with touchscreen mobile devices has been broadly studied (e.g. [1,13,14,22,23,25]) but little is known about the effectiveness of pressure for in-car interactions. In our first experiment, *positional* and *rate-based* controls [25], two common pressure input techniques, were investigated along with pressure-based buttons using a driving simulator. Results showed that *positional* input performed the poorest in terms accuracy and was the slowest input method. Furthermore, *positional* control caused more lane deviation than the other input methods. Input with *rated-based* pressure control and pressure-based buttons were comparable to the physical dial. Target selections with haptic feedback further improved accuracy and selection time.

In our second experiment [15], the input techniques were evaluated inside a moving vehicle where participants, who sat in the front passenger seat, experienced real world driving noises, vibrations and forces to see if haptic feedback was still perceivable and how the input techniques performed compared to the simulator study. Accuracy was high (> 98%) but selection times were slower when compared to the first experiment. One limitation of the second experiment was that users were not driving the vehicle so a true representation of how well the pressure input methods perform in actual driving situations cannot be clearly measured. Furthermore, it is unclear how visually distracting or how much attention is required to operate these input methods. Therefore, we extended our previous experiments by getting users to drive and interact with the input controls at the same time.

STUDY

A study was conducted to compare the input performance and visual distraction during driving of four interaction methods using a list-based targeting task on a touchscreen. There were two touchscreen input methods: selecting the targets in the list directly (*$Touch_{Direct}$*) and using onscreen buttons (*$Touch_{Buttons}$*), a standard physical dial (*Dial*) and pressure-based buttons (*$Pressure_{Buttons}$*) using force sensors mounted onto a case below the touchscreen. List-based target selection tasks are used to compare input techniques [13,25] and are commonly found in touchscreen applications, such as lists of songs, street names or points of interest.

Task

We used the same list-based targeting task as our previous study [15] to allow a comparison of the results. There were ten targets in the list numbered '1' to '10' from top to bottom. A standard start position labelled '.' was placed at the top so that some form of cursor movement had to be performed for all input controls, except for *$Touch_{Direct}$*. The current target to select was highlighted in red and a blue cursor marked the current position in the list, except for *$Touch_{Direct}$*. By default, the cursor was placed on the '.' labelled item at the start of each target selection. There was no looping when the cursor reached either end of the list. Each target in the list measured 133 x 16mm and the interface used for each input control is shown in Figure 1. A beep was played to indicate the start of each trial and the participants were asked to select the target as quickly and accurately as possible but it was emphasised that it was essential to drive the vehicle as safely as possible and keep within the speed limits. The task ran on a Microsoft Surface 2 which has a 10.6" (1920 x 1080 pixel, ~208 ppi) touchscreen. The tablet was positioned in portrait orientation to replicate large touchscreens found in cars, such as the 2016 Volvo XC90.

For *$Pressure_{Buttons}$*, two force sensors from Peratech (www.peratech.com) were mounted onto a 3D printed case, which was placed below the touchscreen to simulate an in-car touch-surface (see Figure 2). The two sensors allowed bi-directional movement and applying greater than 3N on the left or right sensors moved the cursor down and up the list respectively. Users had to lift off the sensor and apply pressure again for the cursor to move. The 3N cut-off meant that light touches caused by car movements did not trigger interaction. To select a target, users had to apply greater than 2N on both sensors at the same time. This method was deemed to be least difficult to perform after testing other common selection mechanisms such as Dwell and Quick Release [1,18,25].

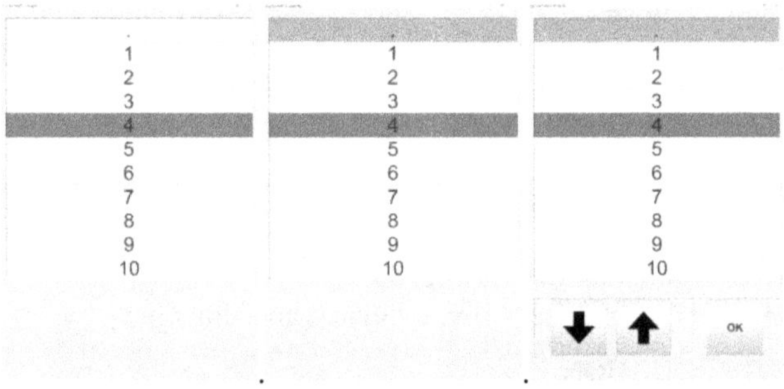

Figure 1. The list-based interface for *$Touch_{Direct}$* (left), *$Pressure_{Buttons}$* and *Dial* (middle) and *$Touch_{Buttons}$* (right).

A Griffin PowerMate controller (griffintechnology.com/us/powermate) was used for the *Dial* condition. The cursor moved down and up the list by turning the dial clockwise and anticlockwise respectively. The dial was pushed in to select targets. To select the targets with *$Touch_{Direct}$*, participants simply tapped on the highlighted target area on the touchscreen. For *$Touch_{Buttons}$*, onscreen buttons were placed below the list of targets. There were 'UP' and 'DOWN' buttons to move the cursor through the list and an 'OK' button to select the target. The 'OK' button was placed away from the arrow buttons to avoid accidental selection. Each button measured 25 x 25mm.

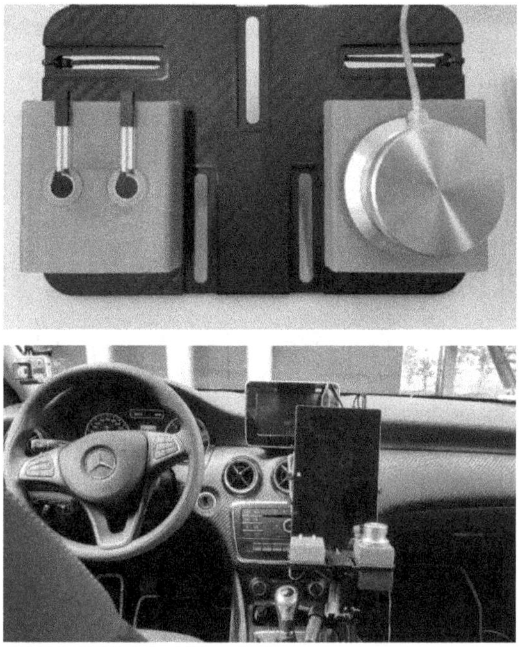

Figure 2. The force sensors and dial were placed on top of 3D printed cases (top). The touchscreen and hardware setup inside the car (bottom).

Haptic Feedback

In our previous lab study [15], we evaluated $Pressure_{Buttons}$ and *Dial* with and without haptic feedback and found that selection times were significantly quicker with tactile cues and were subjectively preferred. Furthermore, related work has reported the benefits of providing haptic feedback with in-car controls (e.g. [5,7,16,17,19,21]). We wanted to see if haptic feedback would still be effective for input in real world driving situations. One Adafruit medium surface transducer (www.adafruit.com/product/1785) was placed inside each printed case to give vibrotactile feedback on the movement of the cursor (50ms, 200hz sine wave) and the selection of a target (300ms, 300hz sine wave). The two touch input conditions were not evaluated with haptic feedback because finger contact on the touchscreen was so short, tactile feedback could not be felt.

Experimental Design

Twenty-six participants (15 males), aged between 26 – 58 (mean = 42.7, SD = 10.9) with a full driving license took part in the study. Twenty-two participants were right-handed, two left-handed and the remaining two were ambidextrous.

The participants drove a manual Mercedes-Benz GLA. The touchscreen tablet, sensors and components were securely mounted onto the centre console without obstructing the drivers' ability to change gear (see Figure 2 and 3). A GoPro Hero3 camera was mounted on the inside windscreen to record eye movements. The driving route consisted of town roads (50 km/h), dual carriageways (100 km/h) and highways (120 km/h). The distance of one loop of the route was approximately 56 km. The participants were given a training session to familiarise them with each input control before any driving started. An experimenter sat in the front passenger seat at all times to overview the experiment and ensure safety (see Figure 3).

Figure 3. A participant performing the list-based targeting task while driving. Visual attention is taken away from the roads during input. An experimenter sat beside the user to ensure safety.

A within-subjects design was used for the study. The Independent Variables were **Input Method** (four levels: $Pressure_{Buttons}$, *Dial*, $Touch_{Direct}$ and $Touch_{Buttons}$) and **Type of Feedback** (two levels: with and without haptic feedback for $Pressure_{Buttons}$ and *Dial* only). Hence, there was a total of six conditions as haptic feedback was not examined for the two touchscreen input methods. The Dependent Variables were target accuracy (%), selection time (ms), glance count towards the touchscreen (the number of times the participants looked at the touchscreen during input) and the duration per glance (the amount of time spent for each eye-gaze on the screen, ms). A trial was selected accurately if the highlighted target in the list was acquired. Selection time was the duration from the target being displayed onscreen until the selection of the target. The experimental hypotheses were based on the findings from our related lab study [15] (H1 and H2) and from observations from pilot tests (H3 and H4):

H1: Target selections with $Pressure_{Buttons}$ will take significantly longer than the other input methods;

H2: Haptic feedback will significantly improve accuracy and selection time for $Pressure_{Buttons}$ and *Dial*;

H3: $Touch_{Direct}$ will have significantly lower eye-gaze count than the other input methods;

H4: $Pressure_{Buttons}$ and $Touch_{Buttons}$ will have significantly longer duration per eye-gaze than *Dial* and $Touch_{Direct}$.

RESULTS

Each of the ten targets was selected twice, therefore a total of 3120 trials (*26 participants x 6 conditions x 20 selections*) was recorded for the targeting task. Two sets of video recordings (P1 and P2) were corrupted and therefore were removed from the final data analysis. The data for target accuracy, selection time, glance count and duration per glance were all not normally distributed. Because the design of the study was unbalanced, two separate non-parametric tests were conducted. Firstly, Friedman tests were conducted to compare the four input methods without haptic feedback. Secondly, Aligned Rank Transform [26] was applied before conducting a two-factor (Type of Feedback and Input Method) repeated-measures ANOVA to compare the effectiveness of haptic feedback between *Pressure*$_{Buttons}$ and *Dial*.

Target Accuracy

The mean accuracy for each condition is shown in Figure 4. The results from conducting the Freidman test showed a significant difference for Input Technique, $\chi2(3) = 12.64$, $p < 0.05$. However, *post hoc* Wilcoxon signed-rank tests showed no significant differences between any pairs.

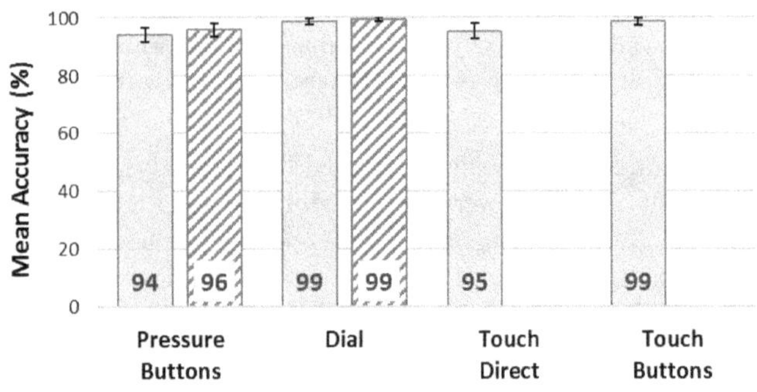

Figure 4. The mean target accuracy (%) for each condition. Solid and striped bars represent controls without and with haptic feedback respectively. Error bars denote CI (95%).

The ANOVA on *Pressure*$_{Buttons}$ and *Dial* showed a significant effect for Input Technique, $F(1, 75) = 25.14$, $p < 0.05$. *Dial* was more accurate than *Pressure*$_{Buttons}$. A significant main effect was found for Type of Feedback, $F(1, 75) = 5.66$, $p < 0.05$. Haptic feedback improved target accuracy, a mean difference of 4% over no tactile feedback. The interaction between the factors was not significant, $F(1, 25) = 3.2$, $p > 0.05$.

Selection Time

The mean selection time for each condition is shown in Figure 5. The Freidman test for selection time showed a significant difference for Input Technique, $\chi2(3) = 55.25$, $p < 0.05$. Wilcoxon signed-rank tests showed that *Touch*$_{Direct}$ was quicker than all the other input methods. The other pairwise comparisons were not significant.

The ANOVA on *Pressure*$_{Buttons}$ and *Dial* showed a significant main effect for Input Technique, $F(1, 75) = 41.27$, $p < 0.05$. Input using the dial was quicker than the pressure-based buttons. The main effect for Type of Feedback was not significant, $F(1, 75) = 2.96$, $p > 0.05$. The interaction between the factors was not significant, $F(1, 75) = 0.57$, $p > 0.05$.

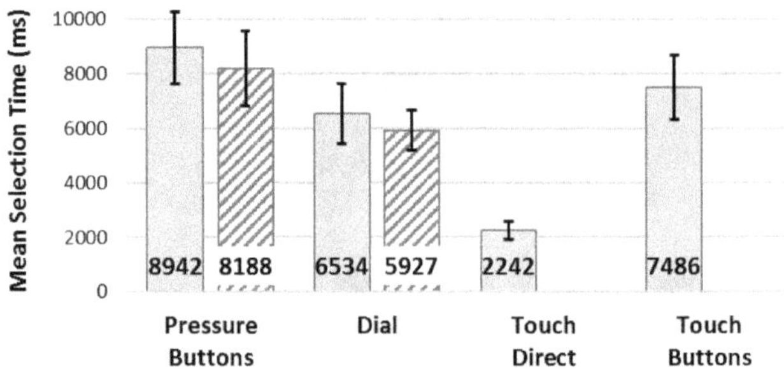

Figure 5. The mean selection time (ms) for each condition. Solid and striped bars represent controls without and with haptic feedback respectively. Error bars denote CI (95%).

Glance Count & Duration

The mean number of glances at the touchscreen and duration per glance for each condition are shown in Figure 6 and Figure 7 respectively. The Friedman test for glance count showed a significant difference for Input Technique, $\chi2(3) = 60.59$, $p < 0.05$. *Post hoc* Wilcoxon signed-rank tests showed that all pairwise comparisons were significant except between *Touch*$_{Buttons}$ and *Dial*.

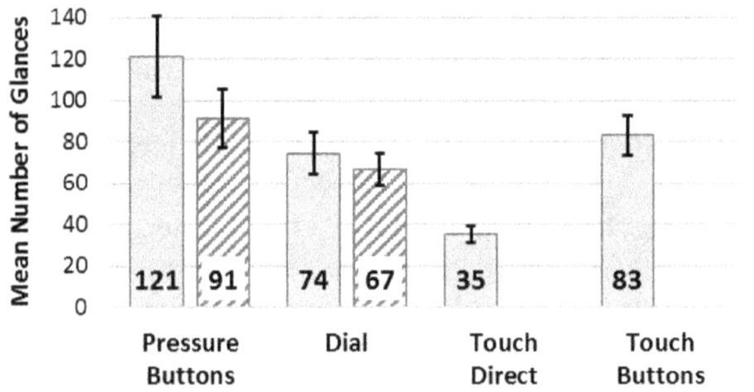

Figure 6. The mean number of glances at the touchscreen for each condition. Solid and striped bars represent controls without and with haptic feedback respectively. Error bars denote CI (95%).

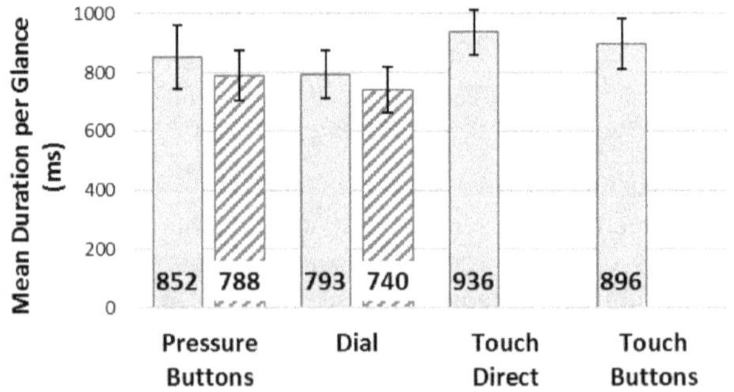

Figure 7. The mean duration (ms) per glance at the touchscreen for each condition. Solid and striped bars represent controls without and with haptic feedback respectively. Error bars denote CI (95%).

The ANOVA on $Pressure_{Buttons}$ and *Dial* for glance count showed a significant main effect for Input Technique, $F(1, 69) = 89.82$, $p < 0.05$. The number of glances at the touchscreen was lower for *Dial* than $Pressure_{Buttons}$. A significant main effect was observed for Type of Feedback, $F(1, 69) = 28.01$, $p < 0.05$. Input with vibrotactile feedback caused a lower number of glances than without. The interaction between the factors was significant, $F(1, 69) = 14.5$, $p < 0.05$, but not required to support or reject the hypotheses.

The Friedman test for duration per eye-gaze showed a significant difference for Input Technique, $\chi2(3) = 21.35$, $p < 0.05$. *Post hoc* Wilcoxon signed-rank tests showed that all pairwise comparisons were significant except between $Touch_{Buttons}$ and *Dial*.

The ANOVA on $Pressure_{Buttons}$ and *Dial* for eye-gaze duration showed a significant main effect for Input Technique, $F(1, 69) = 6.65$, $p < 0.05$. The duration per glance at the touchscreen was longer for $Pressure_{Buttons}$ than *Dial*. A significant main effect was observed for Type of Feedback, $F(1, 69) = 5.86$, $p < 0.05$. Input with haptic feedback reduce the duration per glance, a small mean difference of 58.5ms. The interaction between the factors was not significant, $F(1, 69) = 0.00$, $p > 0.05$.

DISCUSSION

The results for accuracy showed that input with the dial while driving was more accurate than using the pressure-based buttons. Accuracy for the dial was near identical to our in-car non-driving study [15], with a difference of 1%. However, driving had a bigger effect on the accuracy of pressure-based buttons, a decline of 6% when compared to just sitting inside a moving vehicle where users achieved 100% accuracy. Target accuracy with and without haptic feedback for the dial was the same while the number of correct selections improved by 2% for pressure-based buttons when vibrotactile cues were used.

It is worth noting that in general, accuracy across all input techniques was high (>90%) regardless of haptic feedback. We chose relatively large targets to utilise the available touchscreen which meant they were easier to hit. Furthermore, it allowed a direct comparison to our previous studies to observe changes in performance in different experimental driving setups. Real world list-based interfaces and applications are likely to require scrolling through a larger set of elements [11] which we plan to evaluate in the future.

Pressure-based buttons were slower than the dial and directly tapping on the targets in the list but not when using the onscreen buttons, therefore, hypothesis H1 cannot be fully supported. Our previous in-car study [15] found that the dial took approximately 3.4s (for both with and without haptic feedback) and pressure-based buttons took 5.2s (no feedback) and 4.9s (with haptic feedback). In comparison, the results from the driving study presented in this paper showed that driving increased selection time considerably. Pressure input without haptic feedback required almost 9s to select a target, compared to 2.2s for direct touch selection, both techniques having similar accuracy. The difference in selection times with and without haptic feedback for the dial and pressure-based buttons input were not statistically significant, therefore, hypothesis H2 cannot be fully supported.

We predicted that direct touch input would be the quickest technique and used it as the baseline measure to compare against the other input controls. Pressure-based buttons had a similar accuracy to direct touch input but selection time took almost four times longer and was the slowest method overall. Our implementation of pressure input to replicate physical buttons may benefit from further refinement to reduce incorrect selections and improve input speed. A continuous pressure input such as rate-based control (i.e. the user's finger does not need to lift off the sensor for the cursor to move) is likely to reduce selection time as shown in our previous study [15]. The mapping between the input pressure range and the speed of the cursor will need careful design to avoid constantly overshooting the target. Furthermore, our selection mechanism of having to use two fingers on both sensors might have been awkward to perform while driving and hence slowed down input. A more effective selection method is likely to improve targeting speed.

Pressure input caused the largest number of glances at the touchscreen of all the input methods, therefore, hypothesis H3 is supported. Tapping on the targets directly resulted in the fewest glances, perhaps due to the other three input techniques requiring multiple actions to select a target. In particular, pressure-based and onscreen buttons required more time to aim at the sensors and onscreen widgets, perhaps due to the smaller targeting area of the sensors and the onscreen buttons. Furthermore, the loss of mechanical feedback when finding the flat pressure sensors and onscreen buttons is likely to have caused the drivers to look for the controls more often. However, visual distraction can be reduced with haptic feedback as our results showed that glance count at the touchscreen declined when haptic feedback was present, illustrating the importance of providing tactile cues for in-car user interfaces.

While directly tapping on the targets required the smallest number of glances at the touchscreen, the duration per glance for direct touch was longer than the other three input methods. Therefore, hypothesis H4 is rejected. It is interesting that there was a trade-off between longer but less frequent glances for the touch conditions and shorter but more frequent glances for pressure input and the physical dial. Perhaps this was due to the lack of haptic feedback for the touch conditions and that the users spent more time looking to aim precisely at the touchscreen for direct touch since an inaccurate selection cannot be corrected. An input technique or in-car application that caused long fixations on the touchscreen or input surface is likely to be more problematic than one which requires shorter bursts of attention, which would allow the driver to switch focus between looking ahead on the road and input more often.

CONCLUSIONS

A study was conducted to evaluate three different input methods to interact with a centre console touchscreen in real world driving situations. The findings showed that directly selecting targets in an abstract list-based interface was the quickest technique. Input using a physical dial and onscreen buttons took longer than direct touch but resulted in near perfect accuracy. Designers will need to consider what is more important, target speed or accuracy, when mapping physical and touch-based input controls to infotainment applications and tasks.

Pressure-based buttons caused more glances at the touchscreen than touch input and the dial, therefore needs improvements before it can be recommended as a safe alternative to physical controls for in-car interfaces. A different implementation such as rate-based pressure control might be more useful to improve selection time in driving situations. Pressure input provides an extra input dimension and could supplement touch interactions if these problems can be overcome. In the future, we plan to integrate pressure input on touchscreens to design new interaction techniques that will hopefully improve input performance and require minimal visual attention while driving.

Driving studies on public roads provide designers and researchers with the most realistic setting to test the limitations of new input techniques and applications. It is difficult to simulate the noise, movements and vibrations of a moving vehicle, which could have a major impact on usability and driver distraction, with a cost-effective in-lab setup. In-car touchscreens and touch-surfaces are rapidly replacing physical controls, allowing the development of novel interaction techniques and applications with complex functions. Our results show that engineers will need to test the effectiveness and safety of their designs in real world driving scenarios to ensure they get a full picture of their usability.

ACKNOWLEDGEMENTS

This research is funded by the Horizon 2020 HAPPINESS project (Grant agreement no. 645145).

REFERENCES

1. Stephen Brewster and Michael Hughes. 2009. Pressure-Based Text Entry for Mobile Devices. In *Proceedings of the 11th International Conference on Human-Computer Interaction with Mobile Devices and Services - MobileHCI '09*. ACM Press, 1–4. DOI: http://doi.org/10.1145/1613858.1613870

2. Gary Burnett and Ainojie Irune. 2009. Drivers Quality Ratings for Switches in Cars : Assessing the Role of the Vision , Hearing and Touch Senses. In *Proceedings of the 1st International Conference on Automotive User Interfaces and Interactive Vehicular Applications - AutomotiveUI '09*. ACM Press, 107–114. DOI: http://doi.org/10.1145/1620509.1620530

3. Gary Burnett, Elizabeth Crundall, David Large, Glyn Lawson, and Lee Skrypchuk. 2013. A Study of Unidirectional Swipe Gestures on In-Vehicle Touch Screens. In *Proceedings of the 5th International Conference on Automotive User Interfaces and Interactive Vehicular Applications - AutomotiveUI '13*. ACM Press, 22–29. DOI: http://doi.org/10.1145/2516540.2516545

4. David Crundall, Peter Chapman, Steven Trawley, Lyn Collins, Editha van Loon, Ben Andrews and Geoffrey Underwood. 2012. Some Hazards are More Attractive Than Others: Drivers of Varying Experience Respond Differently to Different Types of Hazard. *Accident Analysis and Prevention* 45: 600–609. DOI: http://doi.org/10.1016/j.aap.2011.09.049

5. Lisa Diwischek and Jason Lisseman. 2015. Tactile Feedback for Virtual Automotive Steering Wheel Switches. In *Proceedings of the 7th International Conference on Automotive User Interfaces and Interactive Vehicular Applications - AutomotiveUI '15*. ACM Press, 31–38. DOI: http://doi.org/10.1145/2799250.2799271

6. Ronald Ecker, Verena Broy, Katja Hertzschuch, and Andreas Butz. 2010. Visual cues supporting direct touch gesture interaction with in-vehicle information systems. In *Proceedings of the 2nd International Conference on Automotive User Interfaces and Interactive Vehicular Applications - AutomotiveUI '10*. ACM Press, 80–87. DOI: http://doi.org/10.1145/1969773.1969788

7. John K. Holmen and Mehrdad Hosseini Zadeh. 2010. Effects of Varying Haptic Feedback on Driver Distraction during Vehicular Window Adjustment. In *Proceedings of the 2nd International Conference on Automotive User Interfaces and Interactive Vehicular Applications - AutomotiveUI '10*. ACM Press 88–91. DOI: http://doi.org/10.1145/1969773.1969789

8. Jochen Huber, Mohamed Sheik-Nainar, and Nada Matic. 2016. Towards an Interaction Language for Force-enabled Touchpads in Cars. In *Adjunct Proceedings of the 8th International Conference on Automotive User Interfaces and Interactive Vehicular Applications - AutomotiveUI '16*. ACM Press, 195–200.

9. Dagmar Kern, Angela Mahr, Sandro Castronovo, Albrecht Schmidt, and Christian Müller. 2010. Making Use of Drivers' Glances onto the Screen for Explicit Gaze-Based Interaction. In *Proceedings of the 2nd International Conference on Automotive User Interfaces and Interactive Vehicular Applications - AutomotiveUI '10*. ACM Press, 110–113. DOI: http://doi.org/10.1145/1969773.1969792

10. Dagmar Kern and Albrecht Schmidt. 2009. Design Space for Driver-based Automotive User Interfaces. In *Proceedings of the 1st International Conference on Automotive User Interfaces and Interactive Vehicular Applications - AutomotiveUI '09*. ACM Press, 3–10. DOI: http://doi.org/10.1145/1620509.1620511

11. Annegret Lasch and Tuomo Kujala. 2012. Designing Browsing for In-car Music Player: Effects of Touch Screen Scrolling Techniques, Items per Page and Screen

Orientation on Driver Distraction. In *Proceedings of the 4th International Conference on Automotive User Interfaces and Interactive Vehicular Applications - AutomotiveUI '12.* ACM Press, 41–48. DOI: http://doi.org/10.1145/2390256.2390262

12. Yulan Liang and John D. Lee. 2010. Combining Cognitive and Visual Distraction: Less than the sum of its parts. *Accident Analysis and Prevention* 42, 3, 881–890. DOI: http://doi.org/10.1016/j.aap.2009.05.001
13. Ross McLachlan, Daniel Boland, and Stephen Brewster. 2014. Transient and Transitional States: Pressure as an Auxiliary Input Modality for Bimanual Interaction. In *Proceedings of the 32nd annual ACM conference on Human factors in computing systems - CHI '14.* ACM Press, 401–410. DOI: http://doi.org/10.1145/2556288.2557260
14. Ross McLachlan and Stephen Brewster. 2015. Bimanual Input for Tablet Devices with Pressure and Multi-Touch Gestures. In *Proceedings of the 17th International Conference on Human-Computer Interaction with Mobile Devices and Services - MobileHCI '15.* ACM Press, 547–556. DOI: http://doi.org/10.1145/2785830.2785878
15. Alexander Ng and Stephen A. Brewster. 2016. Investigating Pressure Input and Haptic Feedback for In-Car Touchscreens and Touch Surfaces. In *Proceedings of the 8th International Conference on Automotive User Interfaces and Interactive Vehicular Applications, AutomotiveUI '16.* ACM Press, 121–128. DOI: http://doi.org/10.1145/3003715.3005417
16. Matthew J Pitts, Gary Burnett, Lee Skrypchuk, Tom Wellings, Alex Attridge, and Mark A Williams. 2012. Visual-Haptic Feedback Interaction in Automotive Touchscreens. *Displays* 33, 1: 7–16. DOI: http://doi.org/10.1016/j.displa.2011.09.002
17. Matthew J Pitts, Mark A Williams, and Alex Attridge. 2009. Assessing Subjective Response to Haptic Feedback in Automotive Touchscreens. In *Proceedings of the 1st International Conference on Automotive User Interfaces and Interactive Vehicular Applications - AutomotiveUI '09.* ACM Press, 11–18. DOI: http://doi.org/10.1145/1620509.1620512
18. Gonzalo Ramos, Matthew Boulos, and Ravin Balakrishnan. 2004. Pressure Widgets. In *Proceedings of the 2004 conference on Human factors in computing systems - CHI '04.* ACM Press, 487–494. DOI: http://doi.org/10.1145/985692.985754
19. Hendrik Richter, Ronald Ecker, Christopher Deisler, and Andreas Butz. 2010. HapTouch and the 2+1 State Model: Potentials of Haptic Feedback on Touch Based In-Vehicle Information Systems. In *Proceedings of the 2nd International Conference on Automotive User Interfaces and Interactive Vehicular Applications - - AutomotiveUI '09.* ACM Press, 72–79. DOI: http://doi.org/10.1145/1969773.1969787
20. Sonja Rümelin and Andreas Butz. 2013. How to Make Large Touch Screens Usable While Driving. In *Proceedings of the 5th International Conference on Automotive User Interfaces and Interactive Vehicular Applications - AutomotiveUI '13.* ACM Press, 48–55. DOI: http://doi.org/10.1145/2516540.2516557
21. Annie Rydström, Camilla Grane, and Peter Bengtsson. 2009. Driver Behaviour during Haptic and Visual Secondary Tasks. In *Proceedings of the 1st International Conference on Automotive User Interfaces and Interactive Vehicular Applications - AutomotiveUI '09.* ACM Press, 121–127. DOI: http://doi.org/10.1145/1620509.1620533
22. Daniel Spelmezan, Caroline Appert, Olivier Chapuis, and Emmanuel Pietriga. 2013. Side Pressure for Bidirectional Navigation on Small Devices. In *Proceedings of the 15th international conference on Human-computer interaction with mobile devices and services - MobileHCI '13.* ACM Press 11–20. DOI: http://doi.org/10.1145/2493190.2493199
23. Craig Stewart, Eve Hoggan, Laura Haverinen, Hugues Salamin, and Giulio Jacucci. 2012. An Exploration of Inadvertent Variations in Mobile Pressure Input. In *Proceedings of the 14th International Conference on Human Computer Interaction with Mobile Devices and Services - MobileHCI '12.* ACM Press, 35–38. DOI: http://doi.org/10.1145/2371574.2371581
24. Patrick Tchankue, Janet Wesson, and Dieter Vogts. 2011. The Impact of an Adaptive User Interface on Reducing Driver Distraction. In *Proceedings of the 3rd International Conference on Automotive User Interfaces and Interactive Vehicular Applications - AutomotiveUI '11.* ACM Press, 87–94. DOI: http://doi.org/10.1145/2381416.2381430
25. Graham Wilson, Stephen A Brewster, Martin Halvey, Andrew Crossan, and Craig Stewart. 2011. The Effects of Walking, Feedback and Control Method on Pressure-based Interaction. In *Proceedings of the 13th International Conference on Human Computer Interaction with Mobile Devices and Services - MobileHCI '11*, ACM Press, 147-156. DOI: http://doi.org/10.1145/2037373.2037397
26. Jacob O Wobbrock, Leah Findlater, Darren Gergle, and James J Higgins. 2011. The Aligned Rank Transform for Nonparametric Factorial Analyses Using Only Anova Procedures. In *Proceedings of the 2011 annual conference on Human factors in computing systems - CHI '11.* ACM Press, 143-146. DOI: http://doi.org/10.1145/1978942.1978963

When Empathy Is Not Enough: Assessing the Experiences of Autistic Children with Technologies

Katharina Spiel[1], **Christopher Frauenberger**[1], **Eva Hornecker**[2], **Geraldine Fitzpatrick**[1]
[1]TU Wien (Vienna University of Technology), Austria
[2] Bauhaus-Universitaet Weimar, Germany
katharina.spiel@tuwien.ac.at christopher.frauenberger@tuwien.ac.at
eva.hornecker@uni-weimar.de geraldine.fitzpatrick@tuwien.ac.at

ABSTRACT
Capturing and describing the multi-faceted experiences autistic children have with technologies provides a unique research challenge. Approaches based on pragmatist notions of experience, which mostly rely on empathy, are particularly limited if used alone. To address this we have developed an approach that combines Actor-Network Theory and Critical Discourse Analysis. Drawing on this approach, we discuss the experiences autistic children had with technologies resulting from the collaborative design process in the OutsideTheBox project. We construct a holistic picture of the experience by drawing on diverse data sources ranging from interviews to log-data, and most importantly, the first-hand perspective of autistic children. In four case studies, we demonstrate how this approach allowed us to develop unique individual and structural insights into the experiences of autistic children with technology.

ACM Classification Keywords
H.5.m. Information Interfaces and Presentation (e.g. HCI): Miscellaneous

Author Keywords
Experience; Co-Design Evaluation; Autism; Children

INTRODUCTION
When evaluating technologies for autistic children[1] researchers rarely take their experiences into account. The design and evaluation of such technologies typically focuses on the perceived deficits of individuals diagnosed with autism. Examples include diagnostic tools (e.g., [38]), or assistive technologies in the everyday life (e.g., a communication aid [35] or a visual schedule [18]). Others target specific intervention goals (e.g., [3] following SCERTS[2]), or investigate the potential therapeutic effects of playful technology (e.g., [12, 37] on Topobos and Reactable respectively). It is uncommon that technologies are designed for experiences that are meaningful for autistic children or that aim at fun and enjoyment (notable exceptions include [27] or [33]).

Often, these are then evaluated along extrinsically defined measures. For example, technologies for diagnostic procedures are assessed based on whether they correctly identify autism [38]. Those aimied at everyday life are assessed based on whether they provide the intended support and whether the children like it – as reported by parents, teachers and formal carers [35, 18]. Others, involved with intervention or therapy evaluations, ask whether a child can do a given task better than before [12, 37]. Such evaluations use extrinsic benchmarks of success of a technology, but ignore the multi-faceted experience of autistic children and most importantly the child's own perspective.

Within OutsideTheBox we take a different approach that is focused on positive experiences of autistic children. The technologies we develop are aimed to make sense in an autistic child's life without reducing them to psychosocial limitations. The only two pre-defined requirements are that the technology enables children to make positive experiences through them and that they scaffold the children in sharing those experiences with others. While we have reported on the participatory design process elsewhere [15], this paper reports on the evaluation of the resulting artifacts. When preparing the evaluation of these technologies, we faced the challenge of needing to assess or qualify the experience autistic children have with technologies. To address this, we use a novel approach, based on Actor-Network-Theory (ANT) and Critical Discourse Analysis (CDA), to understand and capture the experience of autistic children with technology [32]. The main contribution of this paper is to show how that approach to experience evaluation can be applied across a range of case studies and what insights can be yielded from this.

[1]While the discussion about advantages and disadvantages of person-first language is still ongoing, we opt for label-first in order to respect the predominant self-chosen form (cf., [20]).

[2]SC - Social Communication, ER - Emotional Regulation, TS - Transactional Support, see http://www.scerts.com

Permission to make digital or hard copies of all or part of this work for personal or classroom use is granted without fee provided that copies are not made or distributed for profit or commercial advantage and that copies bear this notice and the full citation on the first page. Copyrights for components of this work owned by others than the author(s) must be honored. Abstracting with credit is permitted. To copy otherwise, or republish, to post on servers or to redistribute to lists, requires prior specific permission and/or a fee. Request permissions from Permissions@acm.org.
CHI 2017, May 06 - 11, 2017, Denver, CO, USA
Copyright is held by the owner/author(s). Publication rights licensed to ACM.
ACM 978-1-4503-4655-9/17/05...$15.00
DOI: http://dx.doi.org/10.1145/3025453.3025785

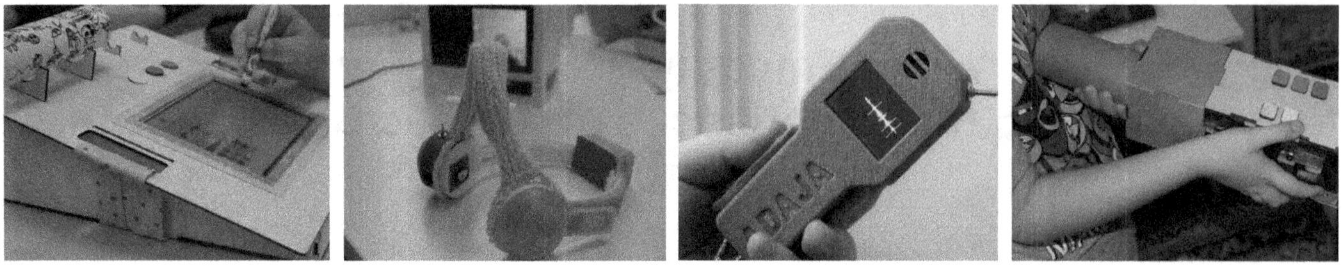

Figure 1. All Technologies developed during the first year of OutsideTheBox – from left to right: ProDraw, ThinkM, Adaja and DSmart

We start by providing background in autism before continuing with experience is currently used in Human-Computer Interaction (HCI). We then highlight the challenges in eliciting feedback from autistic children, which, we speculate, is one of the reasons that their perspective often remains excluded. We present four case-studies from OutsideTheBox, drawing out individual as well as structural insights and showing how we combined diverse data sources to paint a holistic and multi-faceted picture of the children's experience with the technology. We end by reflecting on the implications of our results on experience-centred design with autistic children.

BACKGROUND

To describe our research context better, we present related work in the areas of autism and sense making and discuss strategies to elicit first-hand perspectives from autistic children. We then review a prominent HCI experience concept and show the structural frame in which we embed our empathic research acknowledging, the unique situatedness of autistic children and including their direct opinions.

Autism & Sense Making

Current research suggests that autism is caused by a combination of environmental and genetic factors [11]. While symptoms differ greatly for each individual, differences of reciprocal socio-communicative interaction along with repetitive interests and behaviours are almost always present. It is estimated that about 1 in 68 children are autistic [29].

Ultimately, the symptoms are suspected to be rooted in an underlying perceptual difference. Through experiencing the world differently and, hence, making sense of it differently as well [5], communication between autistic and allistic[3] people can be difficult. Consequently, allistic researchers may have difficulties when trying to make sense of the reactions of autistic users appropriately. this is further complicated with non-verbal autistic children. Given this challenge, we deem it necessary to try and gather first-hand perspectives from autistic children via several elicitation strategies.

Eliciting Feedback from Autistic Children

Common strategies to gather data explaining the interaction between autistic children and technology are indirect measures such as observations or interaction logging. Since researchers can find it difficult to directly communicate with autistic children, qualitative feedback is often gathered from proxies such as parents or carers (see e.g., [27] or [1]). Doing so, however, partly ignores the limits of an outside perspective on felt experience. Egilson et al. showed recently, for example, that parents tend to report a lower quality of life for their autistic children than those children report for themselves [10]. Even though it might be challenging to consider direct input from autistic children [34], Kirby et al. provide an illustrative example of what a first-person perspective on the experiences of autistic children might offer [21]. In their research, children used normalising, storytelling and the description of responses as conversational strategies.

Little previous work is available that directly includes the perspective of autistic or non-verbal children in qualitative research. Dockett et al. successfully used video, photography and drawings to elicit feedback from very young allistic children who were non-verbal [7]. Other potential avenues to enable input from autistic children can be found in participatory design approaches. Qualitative interviews with autistic children with verbal skills, for example, should rely on contextual, closed questions [14]. Annotated screen-shots [2] or smileys [28] have also been used successfully.

Experience in HCI

Traditionally in HCI, quantitative methods such as questionnaires have often been used to evaluate user experiences (e.g., for games [19]). However, these often just address issues such as usefulness, usability, engagement etc. and are unable to access or capture the nuances or emergent aspects of many uniquely situated experiences. Exploring another perspective on experience, McCarthy and Wright conceptualised a pragmatist understanding of experience in HCI [25]. This established a notion of *felt* experience and aesthetic pleasure that puts the person in the centre .

McCarthy and Wright's concept relies heavily on the notion of researchers' empathy with users [39]. While they focus on the dialectical kind of empathy more than on the affective kind of 'being in another person's shoes', being empathic helps to inform design and evaluation with neurotypical users as long as they can draw from a similar set of lived experiences. It is limited, however, when daily life and experiences differ greatly between designers and the people they are designing with/for – as is the case with autistic children. There has been recent work into how potential tensions arising by the limits of empathy between researchers and autistic children can be addressed [17]. However, we deem the gap between the life worlds of allistic researchers and autistic children so

[3]Meaning non-autistic, as coined by [22]

fundamental, that we require an approach that does not solely rely on researchers' empathy, even though we are acutely aware of how necessary empathy is in our research context. By itself, it just is not enough.

Assessing Experience Beyond Empathy

In assessing the experiences autistic children have when interacting with technology we were driven by an understanding of disability that acknowledges the uniquely situated interplay between medically determined aspects and socially constructed conceptions that disabled people encounter (cf. [31, 13]). To meet this unique situatedness appropriately for every individual case, we require an approach that considers *multiple viewpoints*, is *flexible* in terms of data acquisition and *open* for contradicting statements, allows for constant *critical* reflection and, most importantly, goes beyond empathy.

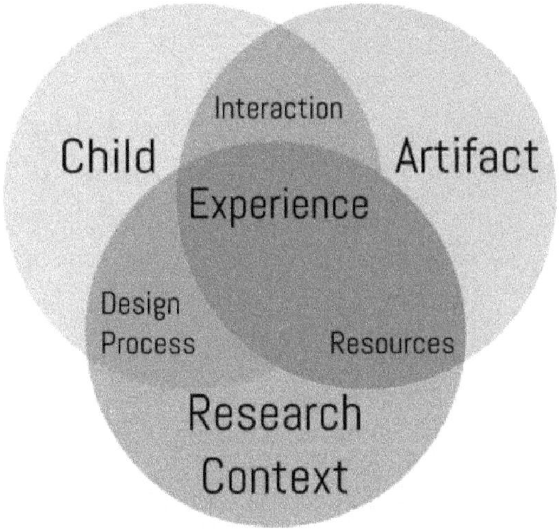

Figure 2. Core Actors Establishing the Experience an Autistic Child has with Technologies

Spiel et al. [32] offer such an approach using Actor-Network Theory and Critical Discourse analysis. ANT allows for the identification of human and non-human actors as well as the importance of actants, and then combined with CDA, the relationship between actors and actants can be critically qualified. The child is very prominent in our concept and their first-hand perspective is essential. Understanding the child as uniquely situated within their social context makes it important to directly elicit the first-hand perspectives of autistic children, while not solely relying on them because the perspectives of others are also included.

We identified three core actors contributing to the experiences an autistic child has with a technology in a research project: The child, the technology and the research context in which the experience is assessed. Further conceptual actors include the interaction between artifact and child, the researchers' resources, as well as the co-design process between researchers and children. Those address the mutual effects core actors have on each other (see also the nucleus of actors Figure 2).

Through an iteratively applied process, the structured approach allows for insights into the experiences autistic children have with technologies. The five steps of the process are

1. Define Context and Discourse
2. Gather Data
3. Analyse Data and Identify Statements
4. Contextualise Statements
5. Repeat previous steps until no new insights occur

These steps complement our empathic research in a flexible structure that can be adapted to unique research contexts as we show in our four case studies below.

CASE STUDIES

The goal of the OutsideTheBox is to develop individual smart objects with autistic children. We do this through a series of co-design sessions over the span of a school year, where we meet regularly with the children for several design sessions every other week. Table 1 shows the individual children of the first year who will be the basis of the case studies we present[4]. With each child we go through four phases:

- Contextual Explorations – to get to know each other
- Ideation and Conceptualisation – to find an idea of what we build
- Design and Prototyping – to establish how we are going to build the object
- Testing and Evaluation – to assess whether the object fulfils jointly defined research goals

The project consists of three core researchers, two of whom directly work with the children as either Play Partner or Active Observer. The Play Partner engages directly with the child, supports them and assists in solving tasks that the Active Observer poses. The Active Observer is gives out the tasks to the child and the Play Partner and structure the sessions as a whole. Both of the researchers played a consistent role during all of the collaborations with one child, but experienced both roles across children.

All four parts of the process with the first year co-operations presented here have been completed. We handed the final prototypes to the individual children, if wanted, and conducted a series of evaluation sessions with each of them. The finished objects are shown in Figure 1. We have described the design processes [15] as well as the final prototypes in more detail elsewhere [33], as well as the theoretical and conceptual foundation of our experience approach using ANT and CDA [32]. Here, we report on the final phase – testing and evaluation to illustrate how ANT and CDA were applied and what they can offer for design.

For each case study we performed the steps mentioned in the description of our methodological approach. Our data sources

[4] All of the children we worked with during the first year were male and will be identified with male pronouns. However, we recognise that autistic experiences differ for female individuals and that part of that experience is framed by the invisibility of the condition in women [4].

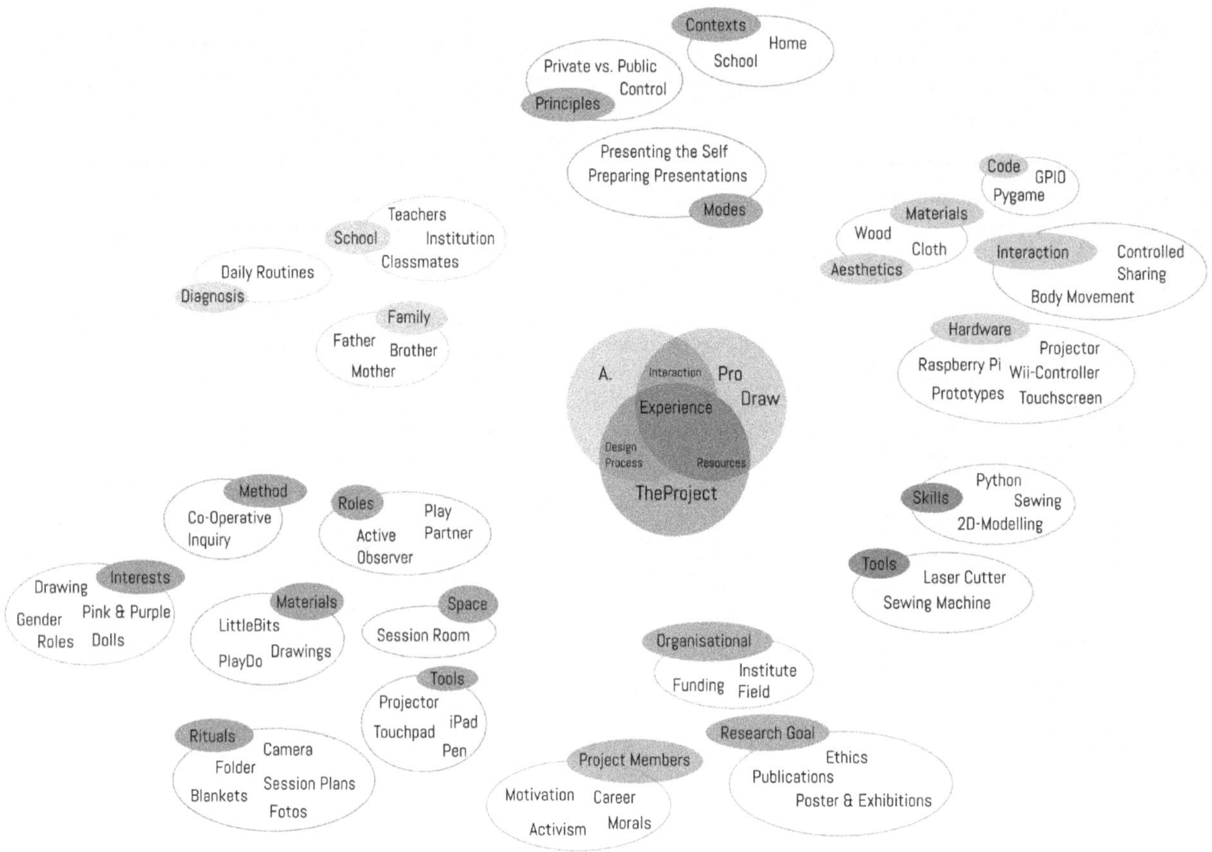

Figure 3. Evaluation Actor-Network for Andy

Name (Age)	Diagnosis	Method	Object name	#
Andy (8)	PDD-NOS	CI	ProDraw	10
Blaine (6)	HFA	CI	ThinkM	14
Claude (6)	HFA	FW	Adaja	13
Dean (8)	Autism	FW	DSmart	14

Table 1. Research Partners in the first year of OutsideTheBox together with age, diagnosis, design method used, name of the finished object and number of meetings; FW: Future Workshops, CI: Co-Operative Inquiry; HFA: High Functioning Autism, PDD-NOS: Pervasive Developmental Disorder - Not Otherwise Specified;

included contextual interviews with parents and teachers, research diaries from the researchers, protocols of meetings within OutsideTheBox, session plans, evaluation questionnaires , logs, protocols of team meetings, reflection on the prototypes, sketches, workshop materials, audio recordings of evaluation meetings within the university as well as video recordings and photos of the design and evaluation sessions.

Since neither the research institution nor the funding body requires a formal ethics procedure, we developed our own ethical framework inspired by the ethics procedures of the Economic and Social Research Council in the UK and an applied in-action reflective approach [16] – including a review board consisting of members of the same institution who were not part of the project.

In order to provide the necessary depth and breadth, we show only selected steps of the process for each case study. Andy's case illustrates the construction of actor-networks, Blaine's case shows how log data can be converted in statements, Claude's actor-network is presented in contrast to Andy's to extract more general knowledge and with Dean's case we emphasise the importance of diverse data gathering methods. To identify which of the concept step we performed, we use the icons assigned to each step above. Repetitions of steps are not explicitly detailed, but rather, all results identified in one step are discussed together. Each case study first describes the design context before the evaluation steps are presented. Furthermore, every case includes a paragraph about direct elicitation of first-hand perspectives of the autistic children and closes on a description of their experiences with their technologies. We argue that our systematic approach uncovered a richer and more detailed picture about these experiences than an evaluation solely relying on designers' empathetic assessment.

Andy and ProDraw

We always met Andy[5] in the same room directly next to his classroom. He used the German language on a very basic level and refused to speak in the language his family was mainly communicating in. However, he loved drawing and was quite good at it. He communicated his thoughts and

[5] All names have been changed to protect the children's identities.

ideas with sketches, which he was eager to share. Using Cooperative Inquiry [9] we explored several materials during the initial session. It soon became clear, that Andy's preferred pastime as well as mode of communication were expressed using pen and paper. As a result of the co-design process, Andy's final object, called ProDraw, facilitates the sharing of these drawings by allowing Andy to project them on a wall and animate them through body movements. Our main interest in the evaluation was whether Andy used ProDraw as an enjoyable communicative device.

Define Context and Discourse
Figure 3 shows the actor network as established by the final iteration of our methodological approach. Of Andy's social network, we have mostly interacted with his teacher who also joined us for the first session and was available in the adjacent room if needed for later ones. Andy's classmates played a role by continuously showing appreciation for what he did together with us. At early prototype stages they were impressed by what Andy might be building. When they investigated the final prototype, they expressed jealousy and admiration. As per feedback of the teacher, this was rarely the case before.

The interaction paradigm for ProDraw was based on both Andy's desire for drawing and controlling the process in sharing it with others, as well as the parents' and teachers' remarks that it was difficult to get Andy to exercise. So, for example, since Andy enthusiastically jumped up and down to animate the drawings, this aspect was implemented in the final object.

Resources available to the research team determine the material properties of any finalised object. We reflect on this by showing how access to certain tools and certain skills of the team members shaped ProDraw aesthetically and determined which hard- and software components were used.

All of the project members come with individual motivations and are at different stages of their career. Their morals influence their actions and decisions not only within OutsideTheBox, but also in their own everyday lives. We also identify as activists for disability rights to different degrees.

Each session was filled with little rituals between Andy and the research team. For example, Andy started out refusing to work with the research team every single time. He sat in a corner and tried to hide. One time, a researcher grabbed a nearby blanket and encouraged a hide and seek game. Andy took it and used it as a security blanket that encouraged him to interact with us. Without this ritual our cooperation could not have happened. It is crucial for the existence of ProDraw.

Gather Data
We gathered first-hand impressions of Andy on his experiences with ProDraw in several ways. In an evaluation session we asked him to freely draw on ProDraw and then draw the interaction scenario and how he felt about it on a piece of paper. We also recorded his interactions with ProDraw on video so that we could analyse utterances and behaviours during that interaction.

Analyse Data and Identify Statements
Table 2 shows selected statements for actors contributing to Andy's experience, together with the data sources they were extracted from. It shows that an actor can have multiple statements assigned to them to express different aspects. A statement can be a salient quote from the data (as might be the case with human actors) or a paraphrased sentences (as is the case for non-human actors). More details about this process can be found in Blaine's case study. For quite a while, we did not know anything about Andy's preferred placing for ProDraw or how the family integrated the object into their daily life. The process of identifying statements helped us uncover these missing perspectives and fill this gap in our knowledge.

Contextualise Statements
The actor-network, together with the statements, let us determine individual insights for Andy's experience with ProDraw. The object enabled Andy to express control and execute it (compare the first statement attributed to him in Table 2; this insight is established by *content* analysis of statements). Andy was proud about building the object together with us, especially because envy and admiration was expressed by classmates, teachers and his parent (this insight is established by a *contextual* analysis of statements). However, Andy did not want to use and share the object in the home environment – probably also because there was a bug that made it crash upon certain actions (this insight is established by *contextual* and *power* analysis). Hence, Andy wanted ProDraw to be placed within the school environment, where it could facilitate positive experiences.

Andy's experiences with ProDraw were deeply entangled with different use contexts and how other people reacted to him using it. To Andy it was a sharing device that could be used to communicate with all the positive and negative feedback that comes with communicating with others. While Andy's classmates and teachers gave positive and encouraging feedback, Andy's brother teased and made fun of the drawings. ProDraw, hence, mediated communicative experiences for Andy. It was only enjoyable as much as the communication was enjoyable.

Blaine and ThinkM

Blaine's interest in science and technology inspired us to follow a very technical approach with him. Using Future Workshops [36] to conceptually rid ourselves from current technological limitations, we developed ThinkM together. He expressed pride in what he co-created by presenting and explaining ThinkM happily to others, but refrained from using it much. During the last evaluation session he enquired about potential fixes we implemented, but was especially enthusiastic when allowed to use prototyping tools he knew already from the main design phase. We were interested in evaluating the effect ThinkM had on Blaine and whether it supported reflection on situations, actions and reactions.

Gather Data
With Blaine's case study we demonstrate how log data can be converted into a statement. ThinkM consists of two parts: a headband recording pictures and pulse data and a base station which allows for ret-

Actor	Statements	Source
Classmates	Wow, Andy, you've made this? I want to have what Andy has.	video recordings researchers' diaries
Parent	Andy preferred playing outside during summer. Andy did not interact with us through ProDraw.	interviews
Andy	Look, what I do. Don't look now! I don't want to take ProDraw home. It's ok, if ProDraw stays in school. Let me show you, what I've seen on TV.	session recordings researchers' diaries drawings
ProDraw	I couldn't function properly due to a bug.	logs
OutsideTheBox	ProDraw enables embodied sharing.	protocols of team discussions
Blankets	I provided Andy with security.	video recordings

Table 2. Selection of Statements Identified in Andy's Actor-Network

rospective analysis of those pictures together with the pulse data. The base station deletes pictures over time to emulate forgetfulness and counteract privacy concerns. ThinkM records pulse data alongside the pictures taken with the headband. The timestamps of the recordings give implicit information about when the headband was used and for how long. Additionally the base station recorded whenever it was switched on or off, when it acquired new pictures from the headband and whenever it would delete pictures. During evaluation, the pictures were only moved and not actually deleted to be available for later analysis.

While Blaine had high verbal skills, he preferred talking about concrete things that were to his core interest and remained largely silent when prompted about abstract qualifying judgements. We gathered first-hand data by asking closed contextual questions and observing situations in which Blaine explained ThinkM to other children during an exhibition.

Analyse Data and Identify Statements

The pulse data shows us that the headband was used two times during the time ThinkM was with Blaine for evaluation purposes. Since on both those occasions, the data was split into separate files (the headband had been put on and off again), we can see that the initial pulse was higher when the headband was put on the first time (mean: 108 and 99) compared to the second time (mean: 78 and 75). Two statements can be attributed to ThinkM from this data: "I'm barely used." and "It's exciting to use me, but the excitement doesn't seem to last long."

According to parents, the first set of pictures shows the inside of the home environment, when Blaine initially presented ThinkM to family members. The second set consists of only one picture in which Blaine's grandparent can be seen. This event was also tied to demonstrating the functionality of the object. The statement attributed to ThinkM from the picture data (contextually analysed) can then be: "If I'm used it's to explain to others how I work."

The base station repeats the pattern, but was used for a total of seven times during the evaluation phase. Pictures had been transferred at the beginning of two of those, which coincides with the data of the headband. The base station confirms the statement given by the headband: "I'm barely used."

Contextualise Statements

Both parts of ThinkM combined provided us with three statements. Critically analysing how they were constructed, though, we have to reject the statement "It's exciting to use me, but the excitement doesn't seem to last long.", because we did not have enough data to confirm this. The statement coming from the pictures relied heavily on the interpretation of the parents, which means, the statement should be attributed to them instead of the pictures. This leaves us with one statement for ThinkM: "I'm barely used." This does not describe all aspects of the experience, but the main perspective of the object on it.

Combining more statements and putting them in context to each other, we have several insights. During evaluation sessions and in the final phases of design, Blaine expressed a close connection to ThinkM and the way it was designed and built. Despite these findings, the object was barely used outside in the home environment. This might indicate, that Blaine considered ThinkM more as a tangible token of our cooperation than an object that can be used.

Hence, ThinkM facilitates an 'in-memento' experience for Blaine. Using the object evokes the experiences of the design process anew instead of creating newly situated ones. Blaine shares this experience with others, which could be interpreted as following the design brief of OutsideTheBox, even if in unexpected ways. While this does not answer the question we were initially set out to answer, the methodology allowed us to learn more about the failure of the device as intended next to the positive effects of the process of designing it.

Claude and Adaja

In Claude's school we were first located in a nurse's room that was equipped with only a table and three chairs. Our collaboration drew on Co-Operative Inquiry as design method. After a couple of sessions we met in a brighter and more engaging therapy room. Claude was verbal, but sometimes switched to his mother tongue, which was not spoken by any of the researchers. Claude's interests constantly changed, which made it hard for the researchers to extract a core interest. More consistently, though, Claude was fascinated by visual patterns that he could manipulate. Still, his smart object, Adaja, only temporarily caught Claude's attention. The evaluation was driven by the question of how and what Claude investigated.

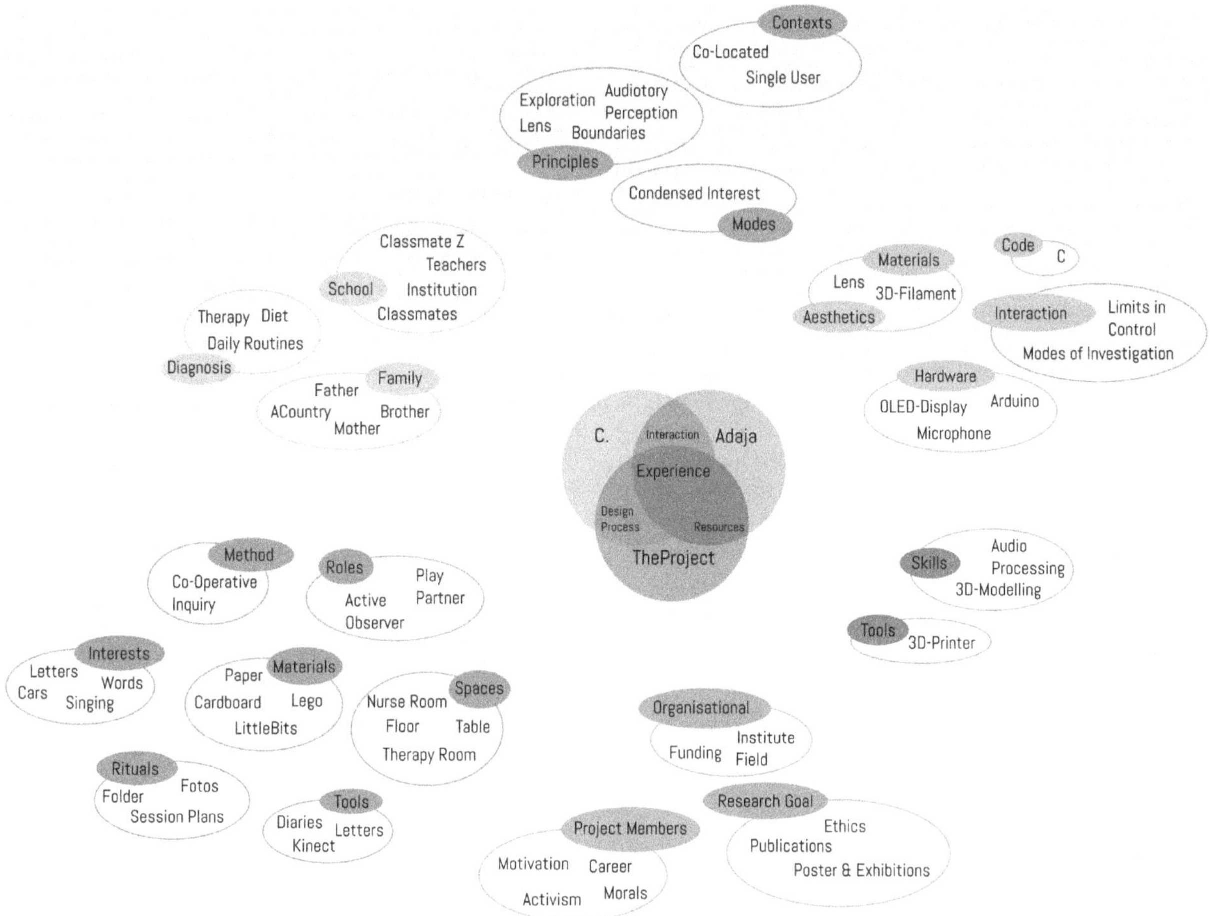

Figure 4. Evaluation Actor-Network for Claude

Define Context and Discourse
Figure 4 shows Claude's actor network, which we analyse in contrast to Andy's actor network (see Figure 3). Regarding his immediate environment, Claude had a close friend in class. Additionally, Claude's life was more impacted by the diagnosis. There were therapy sessions and dietary rules to consider. While both children's families came from foreign countries, for Claude this was much more part of his identity, which was expressed e.g., by singing in his mother tongue.

There was no overlap in interests between Andy and Claude that we could identify. Consequently, their objects follow different interaction paradigms, aesthetics and even hardware, which also required different resources from the researchers. Adaja has the form of a lens and displays the intensity of noise around it. If there is too much noise, it has a regulatory function in that it displays the words 'too loud'. Claude constructed the name Adaja through a play with letters and words which reflected interests in that area.

While OutsideTheBox and its sub-actors remained stable, the interaction in the design process was volatile, even though method and roles stayed the same. We used different materials and rituals played a less important role. Different tools addressed the different interests and needs of Claude. We can explore which actors remain stable and which are flexible by comparing two or more actor networks directly.

Gather Data
To account for Claude's perspective on the interaction, we developed a small game inspired by Theater Workshop methods [30]. Three large pieces of paper signified answers of 'yes', 'no' and 'don't know' at different spots on the floor in the room. One facilitator asked closed contextual questions while the other together with Claude each answered the question by moving to their answer spot in the room. He quickly picked up on the rules of the game and moved around consistently. We tested the validity of answers given with a couple of test questions about things we knew Claude liked or disliked. When directly interacting with the object, he referred to how it had been created together, but did not engage with it in a self-driven manner. He seemed to enjoy playing with Adaja during the evaluation sessions, but handed it back afterwards and was not interested in keeping it.

Contextualise Statements
As insights for Claude we determined that the experience with Adaja was tied to the design process. While he liked meeting and spending time with us, he had limited interest in taking the object with him

or using it outside of dedicated meetings. The researchers expressed frustration and a feeling of Adaja not being made from a co-design procedure as much as made for Claude out of time pressure and the need to create an object. However, the researchers gathered valuable insights about the design process, which helped them restructure future design co-operations. For Claude, the object in its actualisation was less important than the experiences made while designing it.

Dean and DSmart

Dean's main interest lies in movies and stories. Our sessions took place at a room in school as well as at his home as per request of his parents. Through Future Workshops in combination with Fictional Inquiry [6], we developed DSmart, a tool to support storytelling and show trailers of upcoming movies. When encouraged, he liked using it (according to the parents), but did not suggest doing so on his own. Dean also expressed a strong preference for the trailer function. The focus of our evaluation was on the feelings Dean had when interacting with DSmart.

Gather Data

At the time we conducted evaluations, Dean was quite friendly with the researchers. Even though he was shy about expressing his own opinion unfiltered. Because of that, we conducted a dedicated evaluation session with them that was based on a mix of Fictional Inquiry and Theater Methods. In a social outing Dean and one of the facilitators watched the movie *Inside Out* [8] in a cinema. Inspired by the five emotions in the movie (Joy, Sadness, Anger, Fear, Disgust) , we supplied five chairs with five coloured cloths as props. We also provided three different scenarios that were familiar to Dean. He could pick any emotion for each scenario and show us how he would interact with DSmart in that context. Through that we could identify core emotions affecting the experiences Dean had with DSmart.

Analyse Data and Identify Statements

In Table 3 we show selected statements for actors in Dean's actor network and the data sources we analysed to extract these statements. It shows how the silver carpet, a piece of cloth that spatially marked the area of future in form of 'the Year 3000', was relevant to the experience of designing DSmart, but not any more for the final physical realisation. Dean expressed a lot of frustration in cases where DSmart did not function properly or as quickly as expected. This explained why the buttons had been damaged.

Contextualise Statements

More generally: Dean had to be encouraged to make direct experiences with DSmart, but did express preferences in how to use it then. Positive experiences were also provided by the acknowledgement of what he achieved through our design work together in that others wanted to engage with him through it. While the storytelling function was tied to an audience, to Dean it was also related to the task of telling a story. The experience of watching trailers of upcoming movies together and deeply engaging with others in their topic of interest was more important to Dean. The feelings they had when interacting with the prototype were determined by the robustness with which it worked. While this overshadows the experiences they had with DSmart, it gave us the valuable insight on how important it is to create more robust research products [26] instead of research prototypes when designing for the lived experiences of autistic children.

DISCUSSION

Through the application of our approach on evaluating the experiences of autistic children with technology [32] on a range of case studies, we were able to gain methodological insights, especially into potential research settings in which the approach could be used. Additionally, we could extract implications for experience-centred design with autistic children. We did so by combining the children's first-hand perspective on their experience with the perspective of other important actors such as the technology, the social environment or the research team. Andy's case showed how an experience can be mediated by a technology, whereas Blaine re-appropriated the object into a memento of a school project. Claude refused to make experiences with Adaja and Dean created specific use cases for the interaction with DSmart.

Methodological Insights

Several insights help us understand the methodological approach better. We present these here, again tied graphically to the step within the process, if a clear one can be attributed.

Define Context and Discourse

We found a set of stable actors that played a role for all of the case studies (see Figure 5) within OutsideTheBox. This does not mean that they are the only actors or actor groups that are relevant to a single case study, but that they, in principle, span over all of ours. As can be seen by the comparative analysis of Andy's and Claude's actor networks, each child brings their own unique contexts. Due to the nature of research projects, the actors tied to the project are comparatively stable. The sub-actors for the nucleus are partly stable (such as family, diagnosis and school as sub-actors to the child) and the sub-sub-actors are even more volatile. The further an actor is away from their core actor, the more flexible it is. For future case studies, we can draw on this to set up initial actor networks faster.

The actor networks show us what kinds of information we can get from the child's environment and teach us about the involvement of the child. By adapting, for example, materials, methods and tools, we can see that our process addresses the skills and abilities for every single child and, hence, fulfils the part of the research goal where we desire to conduct research in which the child can express their own agency.

Contextualise Statements

Across all case studies, we could see that acceptance in the home setting was lacking. Parents reported in three of the four cases that their children rarely tell them anything about school. For Blaine, this was especially pronounced. All of our design sessions, however, were done within the school building of each child, although our goal was to design holistically for their lives. With a strict separation of these contexts, we worked in a limited space. Hence, for future case studies we will attempt to carefully

Actor	Statements	Source
Teacher	I'm very impressed by what Dean achieved with you.	interviews
Parent	Dean never uses DSmart on his own. Dean only uses DSmart with me. Dean is in an ABA therapy programme.	interviews
Dean	Let's look at trailers! I am frustrated by DSmart not working properly.	session recordings researchers' diaries
DSmart	My buttons have been pressed a lot and hard; some of them are damaged.	object appearance
OutsideTheBox	Within DSmart reactive embodiment emerges.	protocols of team discussions
Silver Carpet	With me, Dean travels into the year 3000.	video recordings

Table 3. Selection of Statements Identified in Dean's Actor-Network

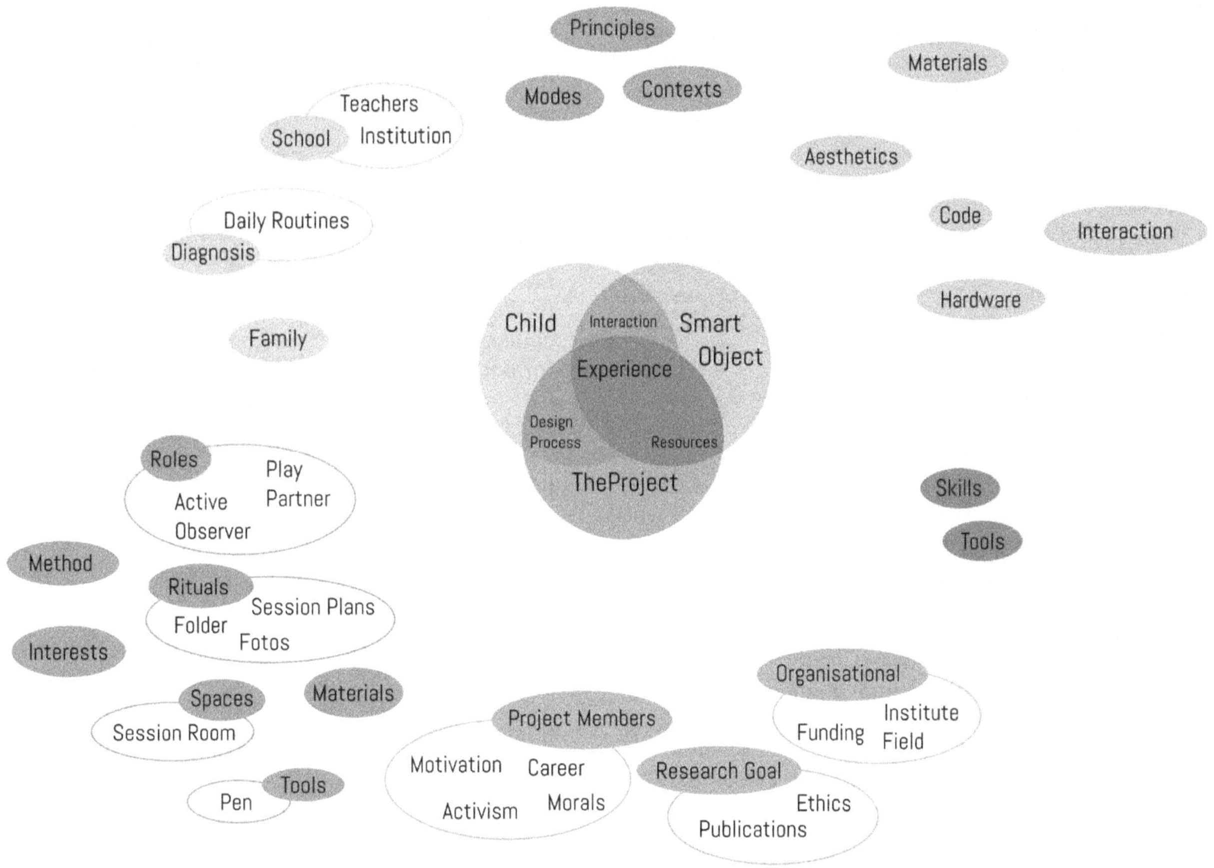

Figure 5. Stable Actors in an Actor Networks within the Context of OutsideTheBox

bridge into the everyday lives of the children by conducting dedicated sessions at other places such as the university and occasionally also visiting the home or meeting the parents together with their children. This way, the design activities might be associated less with the school environment.

Gather Data

In terms of data acquisition we found that dedicated evaluation meetings with parents and children yielded more than continuous little tasks. None of the children or parents filled in their evaluation diaries although the intervals were designed so that they required comparatively little time investment (about 10 min/week) – regardless of how involved the parents were within the project. It could be that keeping track of regularly answering diary questions requires more cognitive effort than dedicating time to an evaluation meeting. While we initially tried to tax the parents less in terms of time it appears to be more respectful of their time management and overall resources to schedule dedicated evaluation sessions and prepare these with specific questions and starting points for discussions.

During evaluation sessions with the children we found how closed contextually situated questions yielded results that require less interpretation (reproducing the findings in [14]). We also made good experiences with playing out different use contexts with the children. For the next evaluation we will involve the children directly in the definition of evaluation goals and data gathering methods. This should increase the acceptance for those methods and yield richer results.

Implications for Experience-Centred Co-Design

Our evaluation brought forward several implications for designing assistive technologies for autistic children that focus on their well-being and abilities. First of all, it is important to create a space that is individually tailored to the creative abilities of an autistic child. Freedoms and structures need to be carefully negotiated so that the design space does not become too arbitrary or too restricted [23]. Materials, methods, tools and some rituals provide conceptual flexibility to address unique preferences, whereas roles and other rituals should be pre-defined as a form of structuring the interaction.

We see another implication in the non-use we noticed among the children. The physical space in which co-design happens and the actual space for which we design should overlap – at least to some degree. Children in general view school and home environments as distinctly different spaces in which different rules are at play [24]. For some autistic children, this is even more pronounced. When designing for everyday life, designers tend to implicitly refer to the home environment (or away from school environment of a child). If a technology is supposed to be used outside of school, design sessions need to be conducted in that space as well, if not exclusively. Otherwise, the developed technologies will only be tokens of the design process, that are exhibited, but not used.

While we as researchers might be frustrated by the non-use especially because we hoped to have a tangible positive impact on an autistic child's life, we recognise there are also limits to participatory engagement. For one, autistic children are usually embedded in a rigorously planned environment with school, therapy and family events as structures and activities. Participatory design activities have to compete for attention in this space. Additionally, children's technological space is framed by parents' encouragements. We speculate that parents, who do not necessarily understand the technology and how it might be important to the child, might be less inclined to encourage its use. It appears crucial to ensure a mutual understanding of a resulting technology between a child and their social environment. Designers should make an effort to facilitate this understanding.

In the evaluation of the designs, researchers might have more success if they actively seek out interaction with the stakeholders they are interested in hearing from (be it e.g., the child themselves, their family or their teachers). Families with younger children are very busy. Regular questionnaires – even if the time used to fill them in is comparatively short – require constant reflection and mental effort to keep them in the routine. If there is no obvious intrinsic incentive for the families to provide the data, the acquisition will fail. It is easier for them to have dedicated evaluation sessions with interviews together with the child.

Ultimately, we could show how essential it is to include multiple perspectives when assessing user experiences of autistic children. Researchers' empathy is limited as it essentially assumes the researchers' perspective as privileged. We show how the children can be attributed with agency in an analytic framework that does not neglect associated difficulties.

CONCLUSION

We presented the practical application of a novel approach to assessing experience in the context of how autistic children experience their interaction with technologies. For each case we provided a detailed account about how the experiences of the children come together using Actor Network Theory combined with Critical Discourse Analysis. Through that, the assessment of experiences of autistic children does not solely rely on the empathy of researchers, instead it considers multiple viewpoints and makes sure that autistic children contribute to the construction of the experience as well.

While the case studies presented here are situated in a very specific context, we argue that our approach can initiate a wider discussion about the conception of experience in HCI. While the pragmatic perspective advocated by McCarthy and Wright [25] has meant a step forward in terms of a situated and nuanced understanding of experience, we argue that our approach can make a significant contribution towards a conceptualisation that is increasingly multi-faceted, multi-sourced and both extrinsic as well as intrinsic.

Future work includes more case studies so that we can report further on the structural aspects of the experiences autistic children have with technologies. We see additional potential for our approach to be applied in design, i.e., as a reflective tool that allows designers to reflect on their work. To this end, we have started to use ANT to document our current collaborations in OutsideTheBox and use the insights to plan participatory design activities. In order to increase the agency and discursive power the children have over the process, we intend to explore methods of participatory evaluation and how the actor-networks could be co-constructed.

With this paper we have reported on the first application of a novel concept of experience in the context of evaluating the interactions of autistic children with technology. We have demonstrated how our approach leads to unique insights, grounded in diverse data sources, most importantly including the perspective of children themselves.

ACKNOWLEDGEMENTS

This research is funded by the Austrian Science Fund (FWF): [P26281-N23] "OutsideTheBox - Rethinking Assistive Technologies with Children with Autism" project. Our deepest gratitude to Julia Makhaeva for being part of this research endeavour. Francisco Nunez, Petr Slovak and anonymous reviewers helped refine earlier versions of this paper. Kearsley Schieder-Wethy assisted in proof reading and grammatical corrections.

We would also like to thank our participating families, schools and the city of Vienna, in particular the department for inclusion in public education which facilitated access to our participants. Above all, we thank the children who continue to inspire our work.

REFERENCES

1. Andrea Alessandrini, Alessandro Cappelletti, and Massimo Zancanaro. 2013. Audio-augmented Paper for the Therapy of Low-functioning Autism Children. In *CHI*

'13 Extended Abstracts on Human Factors in Computing Systems (CHI EA '13). ACM, Paris, France, 505–510. DOI:http://dx.doi.org/10.1145/2468356.2468445

2. Laura Benton, Hilary Johnson, Emma Ashwin, Mark Brosnan, and Beate Grawemeyer. 2012. Developing IDEAS: Supporting Children with Autism Within a Participatory Design Team. In *Proceedings of the SIGCHI Conference on Human Factors in Computing Systems (CHI '12)*. ACM, New York, NY, USA, 2599–2608. DOI: http://dx.doi.org/10.1145/2207676.2208650
3. Sara Bernardini, Kaska Porayska-Pomsta, and Tim J. Smith. 2014. ECHOES: An intelligent serious game for fostering social communication in children with autism. *Information Sciences* 264, 0 (April 2014), 41–60. DOI: http://dx.doi.org/10.1016/j.ins.2013.10.027
4. Elizabeth K. Cridland, Sandra C. Jones, Peter Caputi, and Christopher A. Magee. 2014. Being a Girl in a Boys' World: Investigating the Experiences of Girls with Autism Spectrum Disorders During Adolescence. *Journal of Autism and Developmental Disorders* 44, 6 (2014), 1261–1274. DOI: http://dx.doi.org/10.1007/s10803-013-1985-6
5. Hanne De Jaegher. 2013. Embodiment and sense-making in autism. *Frontiers in Integrative Neuroscience* 7 (2013), 15. DOI:http://dx.doi.org/10.3389/fnint.2013.00015
6. Christian Dindler and Ole Sejer Iversen. 2007. Fictional Inquiry - design collaboration in a shared narrative space. *CoDesign* 3, 4 (Dec. 2007), 213–234.
7. Sue Dockett, Sarah Main, and Lynda Kelly. 2011. Consulting Young Children: Experiences from a Museum. *Visitor Studies* 14, 1 (April 2011), 13–33. DOI: http://dx.doi.org/10.1080/10645578.2011.557626
8. Pete Docter and Ronnie Del Carmen. 2015. Inside Out. (2015).
9. Allison Druin. 1999. Cooperative Inquiry: Developing New Technologies for Children with Children. In *Proceedings of the SIGCHI Conference on Human Factors in Computing Systems (CHI '99)*. ACM, New York, NY, USA, 592–599. DOI: http://dx.doi.org/10.1145/302979.303166
10. Snoefridur T. Egilson, Linda B. Olafsdottir, Thora Leosdottir, and Evald Saemundsen. 2016. Quality of life of high-functioning children and youth with autism spectrum disorder and typically developing peers: Self- and proxy-reports. *Autism* April, 2016 (2016), 1362361316630881. DOI: http://dx.doi.org/10.1177/1362361316630881
11. Marc Fakhoury. 2015. Autistic spectrum disorders: A review of clinical features, theories and diagnosis. *International Journal of Developmental Neuroscience* 43 (June 2015), 70–77. DOI: http://dx.doi.org/10.1016/j.ijdevneu.2015.04.003
12. William Farr, Nicola Yuill, and Hayes Raffle. 2010. Social benefits of a tangible user interface for children with Autistic Spectrum Conditions. *Autism* 14, 3 (2010), 237–252. DOI: http://dx.doi.org/10.1177/1362361310363280
13. Christopher Frauenberger. 2015. Disability and Technology - A Critical Realist Perspective. In *Proceedings of the 17th International ACM SIGACCESS Conference on Computers & Accessibility*. ACM Press, Lisbon, Portugal, 8. DOI: http://dx.doi.org/10.1145/2700648.2809851
14. Christopher Frauenberger, Judith Good, Alyssa Alcorn, and Helen Pain. 2012. Supporting the Design Contributions of Children with Autism Spectrum Conditions. In *Proceedings of the 11th International Conference on Interaction Design and Children (IDC '12)*. ACM, New York, NY, USA, 134–143. DOI: http://dx.doi.org/10.1145/2307096.2307112
15. Christopher Frauenberger, Julia Makhaeva, and Katharina Spiel. 2016a. Designing Smart Objects with Autistic Children: Four Design Exposès. In *Proceedings of the 2016 CHI Conference on Human Factors in Computing Systems (CHI '16)*. ACM, New York, NY, USA, 130–139. DOI:http://dx.doi.org/10.1145/2858036.2858050
16. Christopher Frauenberger, Marjo Rauhala, and Geraldine Fitzpatrick. 2016b. In-Action Ethics. *Interacting with Computers* 28 (2016), published online first. Issue 6. DOI: http://dx.doi.org/10.1093/iwc/iww024
17. Katie Gaudion, Ashley Hall, Jeremy Myerson, and Liz Pellicano. 2015. Design and wellbeing: Bridging the empathy gap between neurotypical designers and autistic adults. In *Design for Sustainable Well-being and Empowerment*. IISc Press and TU Delft, Delft, Netherlands, 61–77.
18. Sen H. Hirano, Michael T. Yeganyan, Gabriela Marcu, David H. Nguyen, Lou Anne Boyd, and Gillian R. Hayes. 2010. vSked: evaluation of a system to support classroom activities for children with autism. In *Proceedings of the 28th international conference on Human factors in computing systems (CHI '10)*. ACM, Atlanta, Georgia, USA, 1633–1642. DOI: http://dx.doi.org/10.1145/1753326.1753569
19. Wijnand IJsselsteijn, Karolien Poels, and Yvonne De Kort. 2008. The Game Experience Questionnaire: Development of a self-report measure to assess player experiences of digital games. (2008).
20. Lorcan Kenny, Caroline Hattersley, Bonnie Molins, Carole Buckley, Carol Povey, and Elizabeth Pellicano. 2015. Which terms should be used to describe autism? Perspectives from the UK autism community. *Autism* 20, 4 (July 2015), 442–462. DOI: http://dx.doi.org/10.1177/1362361315588200
21. Anne V. Kirby, Virginia A. Dickie, and Grace T. Baranek. 2015. Sensory experiences of children with autism spectrum disorder: In their own words. *Autism* 19, 3 (April 2015), 316–326. DOI: http://dx.doi.org/10.1177/1362361314520756

22. Andrew Main. 2003. allism: an introduction to a little-known condition. (2003). http://www.fysh.org/~zefram/allism/allism_intro.txt

23. Julia Makhaeva, Christopher Frauenberger, and Katharina Spiel. 2016. Creating Creative Spaces for Co-designing with Autistic Children: The Concept of a "Handlungsspielraum". In *Proceedings of the 14th Participatory Design Conference: Full Papers - Volume 1 (PDC '16)*. ACM, New York, NY, USA, 51–60. DOI: http://dx.doi.org/10.1145/2940299.2940306

24. Berry Mayall. 1994. Children in action at home and school. *ChildrenâĂŹs childhoods: Observed and experienced* (1994), 114–127.

25. John McCarthy and Peter Wright. 2007. *Technology as Experience*. MIT Press, Cambridge, USA.

26. William Odom, Ron Wakkary, Youn-kyung Lim, Audrey Desjardins, Bart Hengeveld, and Richard Banks. 2016. From Research Prototype to Research Product. In *Proceedings of the 2016 CHI Conference on Human Factors in Computing Systems (CHI '16)*. ACM, New York, NY, USA, 2549–2561. DOI: http://dx.doi.org/10.1145/2858036.2858447

27. Narcis Pares, Paul Masri, Gerard van Wolferen, and Chris Creed. 2005. Achieving dialogue with children with severe autism in an adaptive multisensory interaction: the "MEDIATE" project. *IEEE Transactions on Visualization and Computer Graphics* 11, 6 (Nov. 2005), 734–743. DOI:http://dx.doi.org/10.1109/TVCG.2005.88

28. Sarah Parsons and Sue Cobb. 2013. Who chooses what I need? Child voice and user-involvement in the development of learning technologies for children with autism. (July 2013). http://eprints.soton.ac.uk/356044/

29. Ginny Russell, Stephan Collishaw, Jean Golding, Susan E Kelly, and Tamsin Ford. 2015. Changes in diagnosis rates and behavioural traits of autism spectrum disorder over time. *British Journal of Psychiatry Open* 1, 2 (2015), 110–115. DOI: http://dx.doi.org/10.1192/bjpo.bp.115.000976

30. Steve Sato and Tony Salvador. 1999. Methods & Tools: Playacting and Focus Troupes:: Theater Techniques for Creating Quick, Intense, Immersive, and Engaging Focus Group Sessions. *interactions* 6, 5 (Sept. 1999), 35–41. DOI:http://dx.doi.org/10.1145/312683.312715

31. Tom Shakespeare. 2014. *Disability Rights and Wrongs Revisited* (second endition ed.). Routledge, Oxon ,UK.

32. Katharina Spiel, Christopher Frauenberger, and Geraldine Fitzpatrick. 2016a. Experiences of Autistic Children with Technologies. *International Journal of Child Computer Interaction* Under Review (2016).

33. Katharina Spiel, Julia Makhaeva, and Christopher Frauenberger. 2016b. Embodied Companion Technologies for Autistic Children. In *Proceedings of the TEI '16: Tenth International Conference on Tangible, Embedded, and Embodied Interaction (TEI '16)*. ACM, New York, NY, USA, 245–252. DOI: http://dx.doi.org/10.1145/2839462.2839495

34. Laura Sterponi, Kenton de Kirby, and Jennifer Shankey. 2015. Rethinking Language in Autism. *Autism* 19, 5 (July 2015), 517–526. DOI: http://dx.doi.org/10.1177/1362361314537125

35. Ippei Torii, Kaoruko Ohtani, Nahoko Shirahama, Takahito Niwa, and Naohiro Ishii. 2012. Voice output communication aid application for personal digital assistant for autistic children. In *2012 IEEE/ACIS 11th International Conference on Computer and Information Science (ICIS)*. IEEE, Orlando, FL, USA, 329–333. DOI: http://dx.doi.org/10.1109/ICIS.2012.117

36. Giasemi Vavoula and Mike Sharples. 2007. Future technology workshop: A collaborative method for the design of new learning technologies and activities. *International Journal of Computer-Supported Collaborative Learning* 2, 4 (2007), 393–419. DOI: http://dx.doi.org/10.1007/s11412-007-9026-0

37. Lilia Villafuerte, Milena Markova, and Sergi Jorda. 2012. Acquisition of Social Abilities Through Musical Tangible User Interface: Children with Autism Spectrum Condition and the Reactable. In *CHI '12 Extended Abstracts on Human Factors in Computing Systems (CHI EA '12)*. ACM, New York, NY, USA, 745–760. DOI: http://dx.doi.org/10.1145/2212776.2212847

38. Tracy L. Westeyn, Gregory D. Abowd, Thad E. Starner, Jeremy M. Johnson, Peter W. Presti, and Kimberly A. Weaver. 2012. Monitoring childrenâĂŹs developmental progress using augmented toys and activity recognition. *Personal and Ubiquitous Computing* 16, 2 (Feb. 2012), 169–191. DOI: http://dx.doi.org/10.1007/s00779-011-0386-0

39. Peter Wright and John McCarthy. 2008. Empathy and experience in HCI. In *Proceeding of the twenty-sixth annual SIGCHI conference on Human factors in computing systems (CHI '08)*. ACM, Florence, Italy, 637–646. DOI: http://dx.doi.org/10.1145/1357054.1357156

ProCom: Designing and Evaluating a Mobile and Wearable System to Support Proximity Awareness for People with Autism

LouAnne E. Boyd
UC Irvine
Irvine, USA
boydl@uci.edu

Xinlong Jiang
Institute of Computing Technology, CAS; University of Chinese Academy of Sciences, Beijing, China,
jiangxinlong@ict.ac.cn

Gillian R. Hayes
UC Irvine
Irvine, USA
gillianrh@ics.uci.edu

ABSTRACT
People with autism are at risk for social isolation due to differences in their perception and engagement with the social world. In this work, we aim to address one specific concern related to socialization—the understanding, awareness, and use of interpersonal space. Over the course of a year, we iteratively designed and tested a series of concepts for supporting children with autism in perceiving, understanding, and responding to physical proximity with other people. During this process, we developed ProCom, a prototype system for measuring proximity without requiring instrumentation of the environment or another person. We used a variety of low and high fidelity prototypes, culminating in ProCom, to assess the feasibility, utility, and challenges of this approach. The results of these iterative design engagements indicate that wearable assistive technologies can support people in developing awareness of physical proximity in social settings. However, challenges related to both personal and collective use remain.

Author Keywords
Autism, social skills, self-monitoring, proximity, wearable computing, children, parallel design

ACM Classification Keywords
K.4.2 [Computers and Society]: Social Issues- Assistive technologies for persons with disabilities

INTRODUCTION
People with autism often struggle with normative communication and socialization patterns [16,39]. These challenges in turn can lead to social isolation. However, people with autism are not anti-social, far from it. In fact, children with autism often report a desire for more peer social interaction, while experiencing poor social support and more loneliness than their typically developing peers [3]. Despite interest in socialization, children and adolescents with autism are at increased risk for peer rejection and social isolation when they are integrated into mainstream classrooms [8]. Finally, social skill difficulties may precede mood and anxiety problems later in life [17].

Although recent HCI research has focused on supporting socialization for people with autism in face-to-face contexts, these have largely focused on learning how to process emotions of the face (e.g., [1,32]). A wider variety of nonverbal social behaviors, however, are important to socialization, such as head nodding, making eye contact, gesturing, monitoring proximity, and touch [22]. These social behaviors tend to be underrepresented in the intervention literature, perhaps because they can be more difficult to quantify and are less well-understood neuro-biologically. In our work, we tackle one of these issues, proximity regulation, which is the ability to sense and respond to the physical distance between individuals [16,27,28]. Proximity regulation is critical for successful social interaction, as its disregulation can lead to personal space violations (and ensuing feelings of discomfort), as well as the inadvertent miscommunication of social intentions (e.g., aggression, defensiveness, social interest or disinterest, etc.) [20,21].

Estimating the appropriate proximity to stand from someone is a complex and dynamic social judgment [20,27,28,36]. This skill depends on many factors, such as age, gender, emotions, culture, and the relationship between the people in the interaction. Despite the complex reasoning required, most people naturally learn where to stand during social interactions [20,21,29,35,36] by the age of five [31]. However, for people with autism, this may not be automatic [27,39], leading them to act in ways that are unexpected by others [15]. These unexpected behaviors can make people feel uncomfortable, and result in limited opportunities to make and maintain relationships [18].

Certainly, one set of solutions to these challenges lies in making neurotypical people more aware of and sensitive to the challenges people with autism experience related to

Permission to make digital or hard copies of all or part of this work for personal or classroom use is granted without fee provided that copies are not made or distributed for profit or commercial advantage and that copies bear this notice and the full citation on the first page. Copyrights for components of this work owned by others than ACM must be honored. Abstracting with credit is permitted. To copy otherwise, or republish, to post on servers or to redistribute to lists, requires prior specific permission and/or a fee. Request permissions from Permissions@acm.org.
CHI 2017, May 06-11, 2017, Denver, CO, USA
© 2017 ACM. ISBN 978-1-4503-4655-9/17/05…$15.00
DOI: http://dx.doi.org/10.1145/3025453.3026014

social proximity. This approach would potentially reduce the discomfort felt by non-normative behaviors and should be explored in the interest of considerations for a neurodiverse world. In the short term, however, therapists, parents, and people with autism themselves have expressed concern about limitations in opportunities brought on by differential experiences with proximity. Thus, child development specialists have explored, with moderate success, teaching expected social distances through self-awareness training, which progresses through self-monitoring, self-regulation, and self-evaluation [4]. Standing too close or too far away, and turning one's body away from the speaker have been targets of therapy [6].

Current best practices in educational settings tend to use video modeling lessons in virtual scenes [10]. While these technologies can deliver essential guidance, they still cannot offer timely assistance *in situ*. Whereas video lessons and existing assistive applications are limited and fixed, real life has endless contexts and changes dynamically. Consequently, technology that provides real-time context awareness, such as proximity during social interaction, could help people with autism use proximity more successfully. In this work, we were interested in understanding how assistive technologies might augment face-to-face interactions, particularly related to proximity.

To address these questions, we conducted a series of iterative design explorations over the course of a year. We initially explored a variety of concepts and potential designs related to sensing and visualizing interpersonal space with both adult designers and children. We then iterated on these concepts, validating our designs with a cooperative design team member with autism. We then designed and developed ProCom, a single-user prototype system that combines wearable sensors with a mobile application. We used ProCom as a technological probe to evaluate how such a design might function in practice to help people with autism develop awareness of their real-time proximity. In particular, a key concept that emerged in our work and was tested with ProCom was the potential to do this kind of sensing while only instrumenting the user, not the environment or other social actors. We tested this approach and probed for further design insight through a laboratory study with children with autism combined with interviews with them and their parents.

This work contributes to the nascent but growing field of mobile and wearable assistive technology related to behavioral health. Specifically, we present analysis of visual metaphors appropriate for understanding and describing relative location and proximity sensing for a population that can struggle with these concepts and demonstrate how these metaphors might reasonably translate into usable designs. Additionally, we demonstrate how a combination wearable and mobile system for sensing and visualizing proximity information can be understood and acted upon by children with autism. HCI researchers—as well as therapists, clinicians, and people with autism—can build on this work to enable new kinds of measurements, interventions, and assistance for real-time face-to-face interactions in a self-contained mobile system.

BACKGROUND AND RELATED WORK

To understand the potential for novel technological interventions to support people with autism, we provide background on the concept of proximity in socialization. We then follow with a summary of the role proximity has played in technological systems to date, ways technologists have measured proximity, and HCI research focused on supporting face-to-face social interactions. Taken together, this related literature indicates that social proximity sensing is an interesting and challenging problem for the behavioral health informatics space that, when leveraged properly, has the potential to support people with autism to have more successful social interactions through self-regulation.

Proximity

Proximity is a basic spatial requirement of humans to mediate behavior, communication, and social interaction [39]. In general, proximity includes two concepts: personal proximity and social proximity. Personal proximity, often referenced as personal space, travels with each individual everywhere they go and may expand or contract depending on context. There are well established metrics regarding proximity, or "personal interaction bubbles," in which space is divided into four parts: intimate space, personal space, social space, and public space (see Figure 1) [19]. Most people value their personal space and feel discomfort, anger, or anxiety when others encroach on it [21].

In this model, intimate space is for embracing, touching or whispering; personal space is for interactions among good friends or family; social space is for interactions among acquaintances; and public distance is used for awareness of

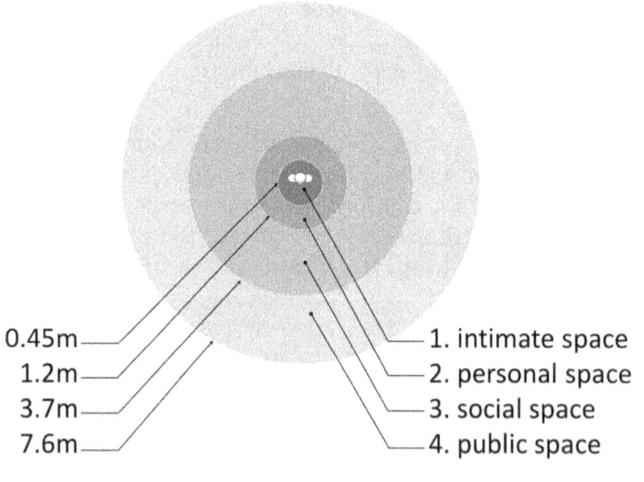

Figure 1: Interpersonal spaces showing radius in meters, including four parts: intimate space, personal space, social space, and public space.

one's surroundings. This concept has been adapted to teach social proximity to people with developmental disabilities [6,44].

Technology for proximity measurement

A variety of methods have been used to measure proximity, all of which are successful for a variety of applications but limited for social proximity usage. Indoor localization methods use radio waves, magnetic fields, acoustic signals, or other sensory information collected by mobile devices [46]. Outdoor-positioning, a much simpler proposition, typically uses GPS to measure each individual's position and then calculate proximity via position sharing. With the development of mobile phones, location-based methods can be easily deployed in wearable applications, but they can often only be used in calibrated environments. Additionally, these methods only perform well for large-scale localization when meter-level accuracy is sufficient.

Computer vision has been used in prior projects related to people with autism. For example, distance-based features measured by camera have been used to automatically detect and classify positive and negative robot interactions with children with autism [13,14]. There are two challenges with this approach, however. First, given what we know about people with autism experiencing proximity differently than their typically developing peers, this judgment may not accurately depict the quality of the interpersonal interaction. Second, a vision-based approach like this requires instrumenting the experimental space with an overhead camera to detect the positions of the participants and other objects in the room. This kind of heavy surveillance is expensive, difficult to install, and may cause discomfort or behavior change in the participants.

Other solutions provide mobile devices with an awareness of the presences of other devices with less instrumentation requirements than full overhead computer vision systems [2]. For example, Dearman, *et al.* determined the relative orientation of proximate devices using the backside camera [9]. This approach uses the camera to automatically take a picture of the ground while the user engages with the phone. By stitching together two pictures using features common in both images, the relative orientation can be determined. This approach requires no additional equipment but only works for orientation measurement when two people, with two devices, stand within 1.5 meters of each other. Several commercial products (e.g., Google's Project Tango or the Microsoft Kinect) use computer vision to give devices the ability to understand their position relative to the environment around them. Tango is designed to work best indoors at moderate distances between 0.5 to 4 meters, which cannot cover the intimate space desired in this work. Kinect cannot be applied in mobile applications.

Finally, portable sensors offer some hope for proximity measurement in behavioral health informatics systems. For example, Gessaroli *et al.* used a digital laser range finder to measure the distance between the confederate's toes and the participant's toes in research of personal space regulation in childhood autism [18]. This approach provides valuable clinically relevant data but would not be appropriate for an intervention given its placement of a laser site on the target. An alternative is acoustic ranging sensors [34], including ultrasound and audible acoustic, that are used for centimeter-level accurate proximity detection. When in use, the sensors emit a sound impulse and measure the elapsed time of the returned echo signal reflected off a detected object. However, they do not work well in measuring distance to a person due to the inherent sound absorption of clothing.

Technology for social interaction for autism

Recently, there have been considerable advances in the research on innovative technology for social interaction of people with autism [5]. Virtual Environments (VE) have been shown to be useful for social interventions for people with autism. Specifically, using VE, interventionists can mimic specific social situations in which the user can participate in role-playing. For example, proximity zones have been differentiated in virtual space as participants were observed to maintain different distances when approached by differing virtual objects: people and cylinders [23]. Likewise, youth with autism vary distance from others in virtual space to practice one's virtual presence, virtual co-presence, and virtual social presence [47]. There is utility in using VE to practice social interactions; but VE has not yet supported mastery in face-to-face interactions.

Shared physical environments, such as interactive computer games on tabletops and tablets, have been shown to support social interactions for collocated users. For example, MOSOCO [12] is a mobile augmented reality system that provided step-by-step guidance for face-to-face social skills, including proximity. This work demonstrated the importance of interaction immediacy [45], often prompted by physical nearness, in the dynamics of social interactions. Our work goes beyond MOSOCO's simulated system to detect proximity with a single user functional prototype.

Wearable devices can deliver information in real-time, face-to-face interactions—a best practice for learning social skills, which are best learned in real-world scenarios [48]. To support the generalization of skills, researchers paired a mobile computer with a wearable device (combined with camera and other sensors) to record and analyze facial expressions and head movements of the person with whom the wearer is interacting. This research indicates that these systems are successful in providing actionable information

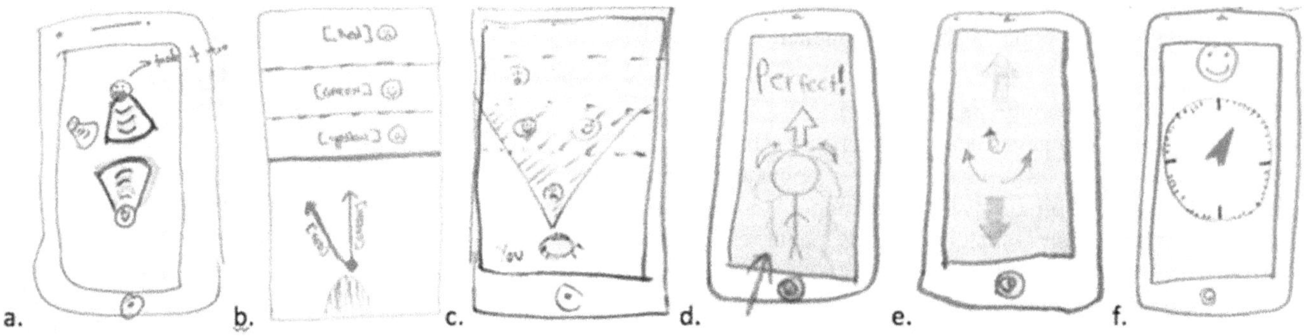

Figure 2: Interfaces designs from parallel design activity

to support understanding of emotions in others for children with autism [25,32]. More broadly, wearable technologies can assist the growing number of individuals diagnosed with autism in perceiving communication in a natural rather than a structured environment (e.g., [7]), bootstrapping their ability to learn and develop in social settings with privacy and autonomy. We extend these projects by providing single-user self-awareness of nonverbal communication through proximity.

DESIGNING FOR PROXIMITY

Social rules of interaction are dynamic, context-sensitive, and often hidden [37]. Usable technology to reveal this dynamic context must be designed with an understanding of norms for interpersonal space and precise measurement. Likewise, a comprehensible interface must provide information precise enough to avoid violations of interpersonal space. This requirement is complicated by the reality that even a slight change in body position or closeness can dramatically change the interpretation from friendly to dominating [16]. At the same time, these precise measurements must be representable, comprehensible, and actionable for a person with autism during a live interaction. We used parallel design [38] with children and adults to inform our designs. We then developed a functional prototype to test a subset of these design concepts, first with a design partner with autism and then through a larger feasibility and validation study as described in the next section.

Parallel Design

We conducted parallel design sessions with six adults and five typically developing children (ages 9-11). Participants were selected by accepting an invitation to volunteer to draw at a departmental graduate student social event at our university and in the first author's community-sporting event. The designer group was told to design a interface for a mobile phone that will communicate interpersonal space to be used for children with social skills challenges, then the six adults made drawings simultaneously but independently. The lead author privately asked for a quick explanation upon collecting each drawing. The typically developing children in the targeted age range were asked one by one to draw a screen to help other children with special needs understand "when they are not facing a person or standing too close or far."

We collected eleven sets of designs from participants, totaling 65 sub-components (e.g., widgets, screens, and so on). We analyzed designs with attention to the repeated components for insight into the group's thinking about interpersonal space. We evaluated each design component and the designs as a whole to identify central themes and outliers that make up metaphors [42] about interpersonal space. Two members of the research team analyzed each component separately in form and concept. They then met together to group common and diverse features from among these sets. From these groupings, the most common features were identified. The larger research group discussed and compiled a list of design concepts and then translated them into the interface design of a functional prototype.

Four primary themes related to face-to-face interactions emerged from the parallel design sessions: precise measurements, zones of proximity, direction and movement, and type of awareness feedback. Porting physical measurement tools into the virtual space was a common design choice for proximity. Regarding feedback, participants tended towards providing judgment or providing awareness, using colors or text. For example, some designs included text reading "Perfect," or green and red arrows indicating that the user should move or go in the green direction (see Figure 2d & 2e). Research on wearable systems indicates the importance of rapidly comprehensible information to support the ability of a single user to privately access a tool before, during, or after a face-to-face conversation [41]; therefore an emphasis on quick and accurate information became central to the development process. We combined the most salient design features with the technical requirements of a wearable system to develop a functional prototype.

Precise Measurements

Porting physical measurement tools into the virtual space was a common design choice for proximity, though less so for orientation. Visual references of common real world measurement tools can aid in the comprehensibility of a sensing system that is likely to be unfamiliar to its users.

Nearly all of the designs included a notion of "zones" indicating ranges of appropriate personal space and orientation. Specifically, nine elements illustrated distinct areas or zones to indicate multiple spaces between people, suggesting there is a range of spaces associated with proximity (see Figure 2a, 2b, 2c, & 2f).

Without discussing each other's designs, participants demonstrated consensus about the relative size and number of zones—personal space, a social space, or a space beyond an interaction. These zones are similar to but not the same as the four zones from the literature (see Figure 1). These components then became central to our final design.

Motion and Directionality

Designing for appropriate proxemics behavior requires a basic understanding of individual users' proximity and orientation. The social proxemics literature indicates that there are thresholds that when crossed convey a change in the interaction. For example, moving across the personal space threshold is detectable and becomes uncomfortable within 45 centimeters of a person [2]. Therefore, any assistive technologies in this space must be sensitive to changes as small as 10 centimeters at the personal and social boundary. This level of accuracy can be challenging for wearable systems. In particular, most that are that sensitive (e.g., [49]) cannot be mobile, and most that are mobile (e.g., [46]), are only accurate at 30 centimeters or greater.

Although we did not ask participants to explicitly consider motion in their designs, nearly all (9 of 11) explicitly addressed whether the user was observing or approaching others or others were approaching the user, such as the use of arrows or dials pointing towards or away from the user (see Figure 2b, 2d, & 2e). This result indicates that any sensing system we might employ to support social proxemics should update rapidly, at least as rapidly as most people walk when approaching someone in a social setting, and the visualization of those sensor readings must indicate directionality and support prediction of future proximity and orientation.

Feedback: Balancing Judgment with Awareness

We gave no explicit instructions to the design participants regarding how they might convey information regarding proximity and orientation. However, the methods exhibited by the participants tended towards either providing judgment or providing awareness, with some limited overlap between these categories. In terms of judgment, people used a variety of approaches to convey when the user is doing something "right" or "wrong." Even in the case in which the participant used a physical metaphor (the compass, as described above), this feedback also included emoticons as a means for providing additional feedback (See Figure 2f).

Holistic View vs. User Perspective

Given the prompt to design a tool to support individual awareness of proximity, it is perhaps surprising that the designs tended to use an overheard view of the scene (9 of the 11 designs) rather than a first person perspective (at ground level, 2 of the 11 designs). An overview perspective suggests an understanding of space that extends beyond the immediate interaction and could extend to other kinds of environments, such as a party or other larger group gathering. A "street level" approach would be closer to the user's actual experience and interpretation and may have its own benefits. However, this approach would likely limit understanding to that interaction. In discussions, participants in the design study described grappling to some degree with this decision and ultimately modeling it on an overhead view. This choice connects closely to the default design pattern for online mapping applications, which may have had some influence in professional designers' views. The children participants, however, did not have the same experience with these kinds of applications, suggesting that more investigation may be needed to unpack the differences in these views. Regardless of the specific view chosen, research indicates the importance of rapidly comprehensible information to support the ability of a single user to privately access a tool before, during, or after a face-to-face conversation [41].

Functional Prototype

To more deeply understand the four themes from our parallel design sessions and demonstrate the feasibility of this approach, we created ProCom, a prototype system that includes a wearable sensor module and connected mobile application[24]. In this section, we describe the technical implementation of this system and evaluation of the system demonstrating that it works as expected.

Determining Relative Distance

Building on the requirements uncovered in our design study, we narrowed the range of view on the interface to 90 degrees to capture the person directly in front of the wearer. This also limits the challenges imposed by other passersby to the system's interpretation.

We define directly forward as 0°. Center-left angle is represented by a negative number, and center-right angle is represented by a position number, so the IR sensors' view should be $\boldsymbol{\theta} = \{\theta_1, \dots, \theta_{91}\} = \{-45^\circ, \dots, 45^\circ\}$. When users turn on the system, IR sensors periodically sweep back and forth between -45° and 45°. In each step, the IR sensors rotate 1° and get a distance value. For every period, we obtain a data array s that contains 91 distance values $s = \{d_1, \dots, d_{91}\}$, which is the distance from the sensor to surrounding objects, and the global minimum value indicates the nearest object to user. Then, the system uses a Mean-Filter with a window length $L_{win} = 5$ to remove noise, getting $s' = \{d'_1, \dots, d'_{91}\}$.

The global minimum distance d_i' in s' indicates the distance to the interaction partner will be θ_i. This configuration allows for the measurement of relative distance without additional work or opting in on the part of a potential interaction partner for the purpose of a feasibility experiment. One limitation of this approach is that other people who are not the primary target of a social interaction but are between the user and the partner may disrupt the sensors. Similarly, a room crowded with furniture and unmapped by the system could pose challenges. These are both issues we leave open for future work.

Visualizating Data on the Move

The ProCom mobile interface includes an aerial view with the user depicted at the bottom and concentric slices of a wedge to represent proximity zones, which represent the normative distance for social interactions (see Figure 3).

Specifically, ProCom shows the change in proximity as two people get closer, in this case two acquaintances. The green zone is a good comfortable social space at a distance from the user of 120 to 370 cm. The yellow (45 to 120 cm) is getting too close, and the red zone is much too close for an acquaintance at 45 cm or less. These zones represent the space of a person in a vis-a-vis formation (90°), one of two most common formations for pairs of people in a social interaction [19,26,33]. The zones are customizable depending on the level of intimacy the user has with another person, but in this implementation we focused on stranger or new acquaintances to test the viability of the system.

Accuracy of Distance Measurement

To validate the accuracy with which ProCom measures distance, two research participants stood face-to-face in a 6 x 6.5 m^2 room, while one of them was wearing the ProCom box on his chest. We then changed their relative distance d by 5 cm at a time from 20 to 400 cm, $d = \{20, 25, \ldots, 400\}$. For each distance condition, we collected 20 results from our system, and then calculated the maximum, minimum, and mean value of 20 results. Our results indicate that ProCom can provide distance results with high accuracy. Bias values grew in our experiments as distance increased. However, even with these errors at larger distances, ProCom still maintained accuracy within 15 centimeters, an appropriate level of variation for therapeutic interventions. Moreover, when distance was less than 100 cm, ProCom performed more stably with bias less than 5 cm.

FEASIBILITY STUDY

In our final design exploration, we used ProCom in an experimental style feasibility test of our approach. To reduce the burden on children with autism and their families in participating in research, we had relied on our combined decades of experience with children with autism until this point in the research. At this point, however, we explicitly recruited children with autism to understand how they might interpret and act on the visualizations, to validate the technical validity of the system with this population, and to uncover design considerations we had not encountered previously. To scope our question about behavior change, we explicitly aimed to assess the association between using the intervention and the likelihood that participants position themselves a normative distance from the volunteer during the social interaction with a new acquaintance. Although we considered different contexts and designed the tool to be dynamic by creating different color schemes for each relationship type *(i.e.,* family, friend, acquaintance, and stranger,) we only tested the acquaintance relationship in the lab as this case is most commonly described as problematic by families and educators. To unpack specific design considerations, we observed children interacting with ProCom and discussed these interactions with them and their parents following the sessions.

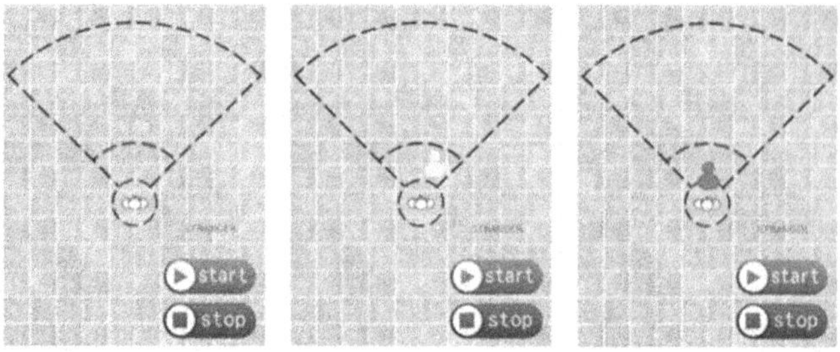

Figure 3: ProCom's three interfaces for green, yellow and red zones of social proximity. The outlined wedge shape provides boundaries for face-to-face body orientation.

Participants

Participants were recruited through fliers distributed to local services agencies and on Facebook. The fliers advertised a "study using wearable systems detecting interpersonal space." Parents contacted the first author to gather more information and set up a time to run the study. Mothers and occasionally siblings were present during the trials that took place in a large open indoor space. Ten children with autism (ages 7-14, 7 boys) participated in individual one-hour study sessions. The hour included the experiment as well as child and parent interviews. Participants demonstrated a wide range in verbal abilities during the sessions, with some participants not using verbal communication during the session (P4), to providing one or two word responses (P1, P2, P3, P5, P8) to highly verbal (P6, P7, P9, & P10).

Methods

After parent consent and child assent, each child was assigned to four control (no phone) and intervention (with phone) trials in randomized sets of two. Then, the first author, a Board Certified Behavior Analyst, delivered a brief social skills lesson focused on the zones of interpersonal space to introduce the purpose of the system and create a shared baseline. The first and second author showed the children how to use the system. After this brief introduction, the trials began, and we randomly alternated which condition came first for each block of "no phone" and "with phone" trials across four blocks.

During each trial, participants stood with the researcher at the start point (500 cm from a stationary volunteer). The trial would then begin when the participant was told they could start. During the control trials, the researcher touched the start button on the phone as the participant began to walk toward the volunteer. In the intervention trials, the participant started the app on the phone when they were ready and proceeded to walk.

The research volunteers were asked to remain in place without shifting their bodies and to wait to speak until the child initiated the interaction. The trials ended when the participant indicated they were done or at 30 seconds, whichever came first. Trials were video recorded for comparison to the log data.

After each trial, the mother and the volunteer independently completed a Likert scale to assess proximity in the context of each trial (-2 = "too close", -1 = "a bit close", 0 = "just right", 1 = "a bit far", 2 = "too far"). Parent and research volunteer ratings of proximity were compared to each other and to the data we collected from the sensor to determine the social validity of the system's proximity measure.

After all trials were completed, the child and mother were interviewed for up to 30 minutes. These semi-structured interviews consisted of asking the parent and child together what they thought of the study, and the system.

Findings

Overall, ProCom's measurements of proximity agreed with both parent and volunteer ratings, indicating that the system effectively measured proximity within the normative cultural context in which it was designed to work. However, the likelihood that participants would stand in the "acceptable" (green) zone varied across trials and participants. Four of the nine participants stood in the green zone in the "no phone" control condition; the 5 who stood outside the green zone in the control condition showed medium effects in terms of improvement as we discuss below. All parents but one reported that the system could have been helpful to teach interpersonal space to their children in their daily lives.

Effectiveness of the System to Change Behavior

We captured the proximity measurements from the sensors (1 event for ~1 second) for each of the 60 trials. To verify the measurements for reflecting the proximity between the child and the researcher, we hand coded the video and correspondence to the log data (Inter-Observer Agreement 96%). Approximately 20% of the proximity measurements within the "first stop" to "end" time intervals were marked as invalid due to the system malfunction or interference (*i.e.* the participant put his or her hand in front of the sensor). None of Participant 8's log data was captured due to a battery charging error.

Next, we viewed the video recording of each event to determine the first point at which the participant stopped as the starting point for the interaction. On average participants spent the first 10 seconds of the trial walking toward the volunteer. We concluded each trial at the end of 30 seconds or the child terminated the interaction by walking away, turning toward researcher or parent, or otherwise indicting they were done with the trial (e.g., for one trial P2 said "cut" to end). Then we compared log data to the video and removed events with interference. Despite limited lost data, we have adequate information to make our claims. Lost data occurred when the child stood sideways or held the phone in front of the sensor. Even with these

ID	Age	Gender	No Phone Mean in cm	Avg. Volunteers Rating (-2 to 2)	Avg. Caregiver Rating (-2 to 2)	With Phone Mean in cm	Diff in Means	% of green trials by condition
P1	7	M	130	--	--	110	-20	100/50
P2	11	M	62	--	--	67	5	0/0
P3	12	M	120	--	--	143	23	50/100
P4	14	M	125	-0.37	-0.62	164	39	25/50
P5	11	F	26	-2	-1.5	33	6	0/0
P6	8	F	94	1.5	0.68	132	38	25/50
P7	7	M	167	1.5	0.87	162	-6	100/100
P9	8	M	165	1.5	0.87	171	5	100/100
P10	8	M	242	1.42	1.42	259	16	100/100

Table 1: Participant demographics and results from log measurements and human raters.

occasion events, we were able to collect 15 measurements to average after the participant's first stop.

We calculated the average distance during each trial and compared no phone sessions. Four participants demonstrated proximity in the green zone during the no phone trials (P1, P7, P9, P10), and three maintained proximity the green zone during from trials (P7, P9, P10)—thus generally demonstrating that participated distance who are already exhibit expected proximity maintain this distance while using the ProCom system. The four participants that demonstrated proximity in the yellow zone (a bit too close) without the phone, moved into the green zone with the phone, doubling the number of sessions they averaged the green zone proximity. The one participant (P5) that was in the red zone without the phone remained fair with the phone although she did have an increase of 6 cm toward the green zone and treatment trials (see Table 1). In terms of changing zones, five participants remained in the same zone, one moved unexpectedly into the yellow zone from the green zone, and three performed better moving from the other zone into the green zone. From these data, we conclude that participants who stand in the yellow zone can be encourage to stand in the green zone as we see P3, P4, and P6 change their average distance by stepping back 23, 93 and 38 centimeters respectively.

Additionally, to explore the social validity of physical measurement of proximity *in situ,* we surveyed parents and volunteers after each trial. We averaged the parent and volunteer ratings per participant by condition (see Table 1). Parent and volunteer independent ratings were highly correlated, indicating they agreed with each other on the specific level of proximity ranging from too close to too far (r =.83, p < .01). This high correlation confirms there was a shared understanding of what a comfortable social distance should be for each interaction. These distances also corresponded to those ProCom was reporting, indicating shared understanding of these cultural norms with the system (r = .86, p < .01).

Actionable and Usable in Everyday Life

Given the cognitive and emotional differences many children with autism experience, we were particularly concerned in this work that the device be actionable and easy to comprehend. Six of the participants (P3, P6, P7, P8, P9, P10) were able to use the system immediately, glancing at the phone and stopping in the green zone (see Figure 4d). They also looked during the interaction and adjusted positions when they stepped into the yellow zone. When the trial ended, they glanced again. These behaviors support the design concept of providing dynamic visualizations and demonstrate ProCom's feasibility.

Some participants articulated their understanding of the interface (*i.e.,* P2 and P3 both mentioned that the colors changed as the person moves). P6 noted that the system "*tells you to stop, you can see,*" adding "*it started out a green and it stops being green and it went to red and I backed up.*" P10 said for him that ProCom "*answered questions about closeness and told him to back up a little bit.*"

Parents expressed understanding of and interest in the system. For the children who did not seem to demonstrate a need for the device in the lab (i.e., they were in the green zone in the control trials), all but one parent still expressed interest in using ProCom in day-to-day activities.

"*I want them to know not to stand too close because it's annoying the person in front of you and they're going to be like 'back up' but it's not something they are motivated to care about. They've never really been motivated to care, I care – but they don't. I don't want to have to constantly tell them, you know remind them. With (ProCom) they're still getting feedback – instead of having the person talking about it. Just them being able to learn it without me having always tell them.*" - mother of P6 & P7

Likewise, the mothers of those who did show a need also confirmed a desire to use such a system.

"*I feel he doesn't know how close to get or how to close not to get. Its like an abstract idea for him... walking between spaces or Disneyland or anywhere you're trying to walk through a group, it's like he's not even aware that he walked in through them, that's how low his proximity compass is.*" The mother of P1 expressed the relief such a system would have been when her son was first learning this skill: "*If we had a system like this, then maybe it would've been easier maybe, it would've been much more short-lived perhaps. Maybe we would be less stressed out because behaviors like that prevent us from going out to a lot of public places.*" – mother of P2

All the children stated that they liked the ProCom system, with a few caveats. For example, a 12-year-old boy (P3) said "*it was really cool but creepy how it knows where you are.*" P7, an 11 year-old girl, was concerned over the impression that others may have of the system being used for surveillance. She explained her concern about what others would think of her wearing a sensing system. She suggested "*If you made like a decorative belt and made little dots this size, it would actually look like a belt so it doesn't look like you're spying on everybody.*" These "creepiness" and "spying" concerns indicate that children with autism are concerned about the acceptability and impact of these devices on others and should be helped to explain why and how systems work in addition to supported in using them directly.

Challenges of Novel Technologies for Intervention

Novel technologies provide immense opportunities for interventions. They can, however be problematic, especially for vulnerable populations such as ours.

Three participants (P1, P4, & P5) started walking towards the conversation partner but then turned away to explore the system instead of interacting (see Figure 5b). During the time for conversation, these participants attended to the system only by touching the screen, watching or touching the sensors, swinging the sensors, or shaking the phone. This result implies, perhaps unsurprisingly, that some time may be required for children to adjust to a technology as novel as this one before an intervention may take effect.

Similarly, for four participants, the research team and parents needed to do additional work to ensure the child's comfort while using the system. For example for P8, the mother spent several minutes acclimating her daughter to wearing the system by describing its parts and actions and letting her observe her mother handling the system that makes a soft swishing noise when the sensors are turned on. P4 and P5 took off or turned off the system between trials. Another participant put his fingers in his ears during the trials with phone trials (see Figure 5a) after which his mother said *"I'm so proud of you because you tolerated that on your body. [then addressing researcher] Not too long ago he wouldn't have been able to do it." – Mother of a 7 year old boy (P1).*

These results indicate that wearables, while opening new possibilities, provide additional challenges to overcome for this population. In particular, researchers and designers must consider all of the potential additional sensory and attention challenges inherent to the device when creating it and when developing an intervention that uses it.

Enlisting Collaboration

As a social tool, we hoped that ProCom would support proximity awareness and improve social interactions. As a novel tool, however, some participants also made it collaborative or used it as a means for socializing further.

Two participants commented about ProCom to the conversation partner. A 12 year old boy (P2) gave ProCom a name and introduced it to his partner upon approaching by saying *"Hello, this is Otto."* Another 12 year-old boy stood side by side with the volunteer (see Figure 5c) and held the phone between them to share its interface.

In an alternate style of cooperative use, some mothers supported their children during the trials by intervening when their children became disengaged from the conversation or started playing with the system. When P1 disengaged with the conversation partner, his mother called to him after the trial with suggestions of what he could say by talking during the trial and saying, *"Ask him what his favorite dessert is."* These parent prompts were common for the few children who became distracted by the technology during the trials.

These results enforce the idea that even a system explicitly built for a single user can be co-opted to be cooperative. An open challenge then, in this particular case, is ensuring that the children feel autonomous and empowered enough to use the system alone while also comfortable enough to share it when they choose. Similarly, some parents wanted additional feedback about the child. As a different kind of collaboration, these shared data might enable collective reflection within families.

DISCUSSION

We explored three design activities to support a wearable system for social proximity: parallel design sessions; probed a functional prototype with an adult with autism; and feasibility study with children with autism to explore proximity during a real-time interaction. Testing the design choices to create a dynamic visualization shows us that children with autism respond to real time information during a conversation. Some participants explored the visualization dynamically to adjust their proximity while engaged in conversation and others explored the technology at the cost of the conversation. In the cases during which the child disengaged with the volunteer, parents intervened to prompt their children to stay engaged—leaving open questions for design. It may be unreasonable to expect every wearable system to be immediately usable by every person, especially within neurodiverse communities. However, the need for wearable systems to be useable for a range of abilities is emerging [11]. The popularity of wearables to support health goals is rising, bringing challenges in extending to designing for children.

One way to support the uptake of wearable assistive technology is to consider "step up" versions of systems to support learning. Prior literature in personal informatics indicates three phases of use: understanding the collected data, reflecting on it, and taking action [30]. This "stage-based" approach is complicated in wearable assistive technologies for children, because caregivers often initiate use of a system and are interested in behavior change. Meanwhile, the users may not be motivated to use the system or have an understanding of its purpose. Therefore designers could support an initial "ramp up" phase to assist parents in teaching their children to use the system.

Ramping Up through Collective Use

Learning to use wearable assistive technology could involve verbal, gestural, or physical prompting to teach a user how to check one's position in relation to others and reference the feedback from the system. Although children receive ongoing prompts from others in day-to-day life, the choice to respond or not to respond to the information on a dynamic screen is left up to the user. Users who depend on others, either conversation partners or parents are engaged in a collaborative experience. Dependent users gain support from those who understand the purpose of the technology is assistive (*i.e.,* parents, therapists, conversational partners) [40]. Therefore, designing for assistance suggests designing in a way to make the support needed visible enough to enlist others to collaborate in achieving the social task when needed.

A collaborative approach could reduce the work the parents do to prepare their children to use a system due to sensory sensitivities. A ramp up mode could be designed to support the systematic de-sensitization parents use to support a child in adopting a new tool. Once a system is comfortable and comprehensible, the motivation of the child to use the system becomes a primary issue. Supporting motivation of the primary user might involve building in extrinsic rewards (*i.e.,* point systems) thus supporting parent and child. Designers could add in a mode with extrinsic motivation to support independent use.

Lastly, consideration of the social context during the use of the system will impact the possible concerns associated with assistive devices. Once the system can be used independently, the invisibility may become preferred as the users may choose to explore less familiar settings. Once a user is independent, then the visibility of the system and co-users can be minimized. This reduction in visibility could reduce the self-consciousness (*i.e.,* not wanting to appear as if they are spying on others) the child may feel when use is obvious to others.

Limitations

As a functional prototype, ProCom was limited to a specific use. We created one context for students to approach an acquaintance and stop when they chose to engage in conversation as an ecologically valid interaction. We designed for a face-to face-interaction up to 90 degrees; yet we did see other formations and presented them in Figure 5. A future version of the system could capture 180 degrees or more to make use of these contexts as well as support for customization of the zones.

Customizing for individual needs and family preferences was mentioned frequently during test sessions. This request is consistent with literature regarding the potential for stigma associated with wearing assistive technologies [40,43]. Many of our interviews focused on how this system could be used outside the lab. Parents suggested making the sensor watch sized or in a hat to minimize its appearance. One parent added she wanted it to be fashionable for her daughter to wear it. This work is limited by not including children with autism in the design of the system; however future work will look at customization and supporting ways to express one's choices and preferences for interpersonal space.

CONCLUSION

For people with autism to use a system to develop proximity awareness, that system must be available anytime anywhere and in any environment, function without explicit participation from others (unless in a training phase), and be private and unobtrusive. No existing proximity detection systems met these requirements, leading to our iterative development of ProCom. However, this is just a first step toward developing a truly accessible and adaptable intervention for supporting proximity awareness.

Our work is built on clinical literature, our experience over many years of developing social skills interventions for people with autism, our parallel design study, an experiment with an effective functional prototype and parent interviews that show the potential utility of such a system. We have demonstrated that this system's design is usable, comprehensible, and effective in supporting awareness of interpersonal space for people with autism. Additionally, although our work demonstrates that an approach using mobile, sweeping, dual IR sensors is in fact technologically feasible and accurate in an experimental setting, more work is needed to ensure that this approach would be reasonable for long-term use in everyday life.

In this work, we explored the fundamental challenge of understanding and using interpersonal space for children with autism.

Our design explorations in interactive visualization allowed individual users to sense and reflect on their proximity. Some users could engage with the system seamlessly while maintaining a social interaction, others required assistance. This work contributes to design insights about wearable assistive technology by demonstrating that this approach is technically feasible, and immediately effective. By understanding the impact our design choices had on interactions, we open a new design space for single user proximity sensing.

Future directions for design could be to consider could consider the generalization of the procedural knowledge introduced here as well as adding features to enlist the support of one's immediate environment, shifting the burden or consequences of not following the norm to the group. This is particularity challenging as this requires not only revealing an atypicality in oneself to a conversational partner, or in the current interaction, but also lacks a way to share this confidential information, as well as determine strategies to address the problem, not any of these factors are well understood.

ACKNOWLEDGMENTS

This work was supported by Robert and Barbara Kleist. We would like to thank the families that participated in this work and our research assistants Annie Ling and Aminah Tamimi. We also thank professor Yiqiang Chen of Institute of Computing Technology, Chinese Academy of Sciences. We thank our volunteers: Jing Li, Zhihao Zhang, Yongzhi Li, and Amid Ayobi and STAR lab. This work was also supported in part by National Key Research and Development Plan under Grant No. 2016YFB1001200, Natural Science Foundation of China (NSFC) under Grant No.61572471. This work was approved by IRB HS2016-2631.

REFERENCES

1. Bretagne Abirached, Yan Zhang, and Ji Hyun Park. 2012. Understanding User Needs for Serious Games

for Teaching Children with Autism Spectrum Disorders Emotions. In EdMedia: World Conference on Educational Media and Technology, vol. 2012, no. 1, pp. 1054-1063.

2. Till Ballendat, Nicolai Marquardt, and Saul Greenberg. 2010. Proxemic Interaction: Designing for a Proximity and Orientation-aware Environment. In *ACM International Conference on Interactive Tabletops and Surfaces* (ITS '10), 121–130. DOI:http://dx.doi.org/10.1145/1936652.1936676
3. Nirit Bauminger and Connie Kasari. 2000. Loneliness and friendship in high-functioning children with autism. *Child development* 71, 2: 447–456.
4. Scott Bellini. 2007. *Building Social Relationships: A Systematic Approach to Teaching Social Interaction Skills to Children And Adolescents With Autism Spectrum Disorders and Other Social Difficulties*. AAPC Publishing.
5. Sofiane Boucenna, Antonio Narzisi, Elodie Tilmont, Filippo Muratori, Giovanni Pioggia, David Cohen, and Mohamed Chetouani. 2014. Interactive Technologies for Autistic Children: A Review. *Cognitive Computation* 6, 4: 722–740. DOI:http://dx.doi.org/10.1007/s12559-014-9276-x
6. LouAnne Boyd, Christina McReynolds, and Karen Chanin. 2013. *The Social Compass Curriculum: a story-based intervention package for students with autism spectrum disorders*. Brookes Publishing Co.
7. LouAnne Boyd, Alejandro Rangel, Helen Tomimbang, Andrea Toldeo-Conejo, Kanika Patel, Monica Tentori, and Gillian R. Hayes. 2016. SayWAT: Augmenting Face-to-Face Conversations for Adults with Autism. In *Proceedings of the ACM CHI conference on Human Factors in Computing Systems (CHI '16)*. ACM, New York, NY, USA. DOI:http://dx.doi.org/10.1145%2F2858036.2858215
8. Brandt Chamberlain, Connie Kasari, and Erin Rotheram-Fuller. 2007. Involvement or isolation? The social networks of children with autism in regular classrooms. *Journal of Autism and Developmental Disorders* 37, 2: 230–242. DOI:http://dx.doi.org/10.1007/s10803-006-0164-4
9. David Dearman, Richard Guy, and Khai Truong. 2012. Determining the Orientation of Proximate Mobile Devices Using Their Back Facing Camera. In *Proceedings of the SIGCHI Conference on Human Factors in Computing Systems* (CHI '12), 2231–2234. DOI:http://dx.doi.org/10.1145/2207676.2208377
10. Justin A. Ehrlich and James R. Miller. 2009. A Virtual Environment for Teaching Social Skills: AViSSS. *IEEE Computer Graphics and Applications* 29, 4: 10–16. DOI:http://dx.doi.org/10.1109/MCG.2009.57
11. Pier L. Emiliani and Constantine Stephanidis. 2005. Universal access to ambient intelligence environments: Opportunities and challenges for people with disabilities. *IBM Systems Journal* 44, 3: 605–619. DOI:http://dx.doi.org/10.1147/sj.443.0605
12. Lizbeth Escobedo, David H. Nguyen, LouAnne Boyd, Sen Hirano, Alejandro Rangel, Daniel Garcia-Rosas, Monica Tentori, and Gillian Hayes. 2012. MOSOCO: A Mobile Assistive Tool to Support Children with Autism Practicing Social Skills in Real-life Situations. In *Proceedings of the SIGCHI Conference on Human Factors in Computing Systems* (CHI '12), 2589–2598. DOI:http://dx.doi.org/10.1145/2207676.2208649
13. David Feil-Seifer and Maja Mataric. 2011. Automated Detection and Classification of Positive vs. Negative Robot Interactions with Children with Autism Using Distance-based Features. In *Proceedings of the 6th International Conference on Human-robot Interaction* (HRI '11), 323–330. DOI:http://dx.doi.org/10.1145/1957656.1957785
14. David Feil-Seifer and Maja Mataric. 2012. Distance-Based Computational Models for Facilitating Robot Interaction with Children. *Journal of Human-Robot Interaction* 1, 1.
15. Deborah G. Garfin and Catherine Lord. 1986. Communication as a Social Problem in Autism. In *Social Behavior in Autism*, Eric Schopler and Gary B. Mesibov (eds.). Springer US, 133–151.
16. Daniel Gatica-Perez. 2009. Automatic nonverbal analysis of social interaction in small groups: A review. *Image and Vision Computing* 27, 12: 1775–1787. DOi:http://dx.doi.org/10.1016/j.imavis.2009.01.004
17. Peter F. Gerhardt and Ilene Lainer. 2011. Addressing the Needs of Adolescents and Adults with Autism: A Crisis on the Horizon. *Journal of Contemporary Psychotherapy* 41, 1: 37–45. DOI:http://dx.doi.org/10.1007/s10879-010-9160-2
18. Erica Gessaroli, Erica Santelli, Giuseppe di Pellegrino, and Francesca Frassinetti. 2013. Personal Space Regulation in Childhood Autism Spectrum Disorders. *PLOS ONE* 8, 9: e74959. DOT:http://dx.doi.org/10.1371/journal.pone.0074959
19. Edward T. Hall. 1963. A System for the Notation of Proxemic Behavior1. *American Anthropologist* 65, 5: 1003–1026. DOI:http://dx.doi.org/10.1525/aa.1963.65.5.02a00020
20. Edward T. Hall, Ray L. Birdwhistell, Bernhard Bock, Paul Bohannan, A. Richard Diebold, Marshall Durbin, Munro S. Edmonson, J. L. Fischer, Dell Hymes, Solon T. Kimball, Weston La Barre, S. J. Frank Lynch, J. E. McClellan, Donald S. Marshall, G. B. Milner, Harvey B. Sarles, George L Trager, and Andrew P. Vayda. 1968. Proxemics [and Comments and Replies]. *Current Anthropology* 9, 2/3: 83–108.
21. Edward Twitchell Hall. 1966. *The hidden dimension (1st ed.)*. Doubleday & Co, New York, NY, US.

22. Owen Hargie, Christine Saunders, and David Dickson. 1994. *Social Skills in Interpersonal Communication.* Psychology Press.
23. Tina Iachini, Yann Coello, Francesca Frassinetti, and Gennaro Ruggiero. 2014. Body Space in Social Interactions: A Comparison of Reaching and Comfort Distance in Immersive Virtual Reality. *PLOS ONE* 9, 11: e111511. DOI:http://dx.doi.org/10.1371/journal.pone.0111511
24. Xinlong Jiang, LouAnne E. Boyd, Yiqiang Chen, and Gillian R. Hayes. 2016. ProCom: Designing a Mobile and Wearable System to Support Proximity Awareness for People with Autism. In *Proceedings of the 2016 ACM International Joint Conference on Pervasive and Ubiquitous Computing: Adjunct* (UbiComp '16), 93–96. DOI:http://dx.doi.org/10.1145/2968219.2971445
25. R. el Kaliouby, A. Teeters, and R. W. Picard. 2006. An exploratory social-emotional prosthetic for autism spectrum disorders. In *International Workshop on Wearable and Implantable Body Sensor Networks, 2006. BSN 2006*, 2 pp.–4. DOI:http://dx.doi.org/10.1109/BSN.2006.34
26. Adam Kendon. 1990. *Conducting interaction: Patterns of behavior in focused encounters.* CUP Archive.
27. Daniel P. Kennedy and Ralph Adolphs. 2014. Violations of Personal Space by Individuals with Autism Spectrum Disorder. *PLOS ONE* 9, 8: e103369. DOI:http://dx.doi.org/10.1371/journal.pone.0103369
28. D. P. Kennedy, J. N. Constantino, and R. Adolphs. 2010. Personal space and interpersonal distance in autism: insights from the SRS. In *International Meeting for Autism Research (IMFAR). Philadelphia.*
29. Sara Kiesler and Jonathon N. Cummings. 2002. What do we know about proximity and distance in work groups? : a legacy of research. *Distributed work 1 (2002) 57-80.*
30. Ian Li, Anind Dey, and Jodi Forlizzi. 2010. A stage-based model of personal informatics systems. In *Proceedings of the SIGCHI Conference on Human Factors in Computing Systems*, 557–566.
31. Jacob Lomranz, Ariela Shapira, Netta Choresh, and Yitzchak Gilat. 1975. Children's personal space as a function of age and sex. *Developmental Psychology* 11, 5: 541.
32. Miriam Madsen, Rana El Kaliouby, Matthew Goodwin, and Rosalind Picard. 2008. Technology for just-in-time in-situ learning of facial affect for persons diagnosed with an autism spectrum disorder. In *Proceedings of the 10th international ACM SIGACCESS conference on Computers and accessibility*, 19–26.
33. Ross Mead, Amin Atrash, and Maja J. Matarić. 2011. Proxemic Feature Recognition for Interactive Robots: Automating Metrics from the Social Sciences. In *Social Robotics*, Bilge Mutlu, Christoph Bartneck, Jaap Ham, Vanessa Evers and Takayuki Kanda (eds.). Springer Berlin Heidelberg, 52–61.
34. Prasant Misra, Salil S. Kanhere, Sanjat Jha, and Wen Hu. 2015. Sparse representation based acoustic rangefinders: from sensor platforms to mobile devices. *IEEE Communications Magazine* 53, 1: 249–257. DOI:http://dx.doi.org/10.1109/MCOM.2015.7010542
35. Peter R. Monge and Kenneth K. Kirste. 1980. Measuring Proximity in Human Organization. *Social Psychology Quarterly* 43, 1: 110–115. DOI:http://dx.doi.org/10.2307/3033753
36. Peter R. Monge, Lynda White Rothman, Eric M. Eisenberg, Katherine I. Miller, and Kenneth K. Kirste. 1985. The Dynamics of Organizational Proximity. *Management Science* 31, 9: 1129–1141. DOI:http://dx.doi.org/10.1287/mnsc.31.9.1129
37. Brenda Smith Myles, Melissa Trautman, and Ronda L Schelvan. 2004. *The hidden curriculum: practical solutions for understanding unstated rules in social situations.* Autism Asperger Pub. Co., Shawnee Mission, KS.
38. Jakob Nielsen and Jan M. Faber. 1996. Improving system usability through parallel design. *Computer* 29, 2: 29–35. DOI:http://dx.doi.org/10.1109/2.485844
39. Anat Perry, Nikolay Nichiporuk, and Robert T. Knight. 2015. Where does one stand: a biological account of preferred interpersonal distance. *Social Cognitive and Affective Neuroscience*: nsv115. DOI:http://dx.doi.org/10.1093/scan/nsv115
40. Halley Profita, Reem Albaghli, Leah Findlater, Paul Jaeger, and Shaun K. Kane. 2016. The AT Effect: How Disability Affects the Perceived Social Acceptability of Head-Mounted Display Use. In *Proceedings of the 2016 CHI Conference on Human Factors in Computing Systems* (CHI '16), 4884–4895. DOI:http://dx.doi.org/10.1145/2858036.2858130
41. Dan Saffer. 2013. *Microinteractions: Designing with Details.* O'Reilly Media, Inc.
42. Phoebe Sengers, Kirsten Boehner, Shay David, and Joseph "Jofish" Kaye. 2005. Reflective Design. In *Proceedings of the 4th Decennial Conference on Critical Computing: Between Sense and Sensibility* (CC '05), 49–58. DOI:http://dx.doi.org/10.1145/1094562.1094569
43. Kristen Shinohara and Jacob O. Wobbrock. 2011. In the shadow of misperception: assistive technology use and social interactions. In *Proceedings of the SIGCHI Conference on Human Factors in Computing Systems*, 705–714.
44. James Stanfield. Social Boundaries: *The Circles Curriculum.* Santa Barbara, CA 2017
45. Monica Tentori and Gillian R. Hayes. 2010. Designing for interaction immediacy to enhance social skills of children with autism. 51. DOI:http://dx.doi.org/10.1145/1864349.1864359

46. Jorge Torres-Solis, Tiago H. Falk, and Tom Chau. 2010. *A review of indoor localization technologies: towards navigational assistance for topographical disorientation*. INTECH Open Access Publisher.
47. Xianhui Wang, James Laffey, Wanli Xing, Yanfei Ma, and Janine Stichter. 2016. Exploring embodied social presence of youth with Autism in 3D collaborative virtual learning environment: A case study. *Computers in Human Behavior* 55, Part A: 310–321. DOI:http://dx.doi.org/10.1016/j.chb.2015.09.006
48. Susan Williams White, Kathleen Keonig, and Lawrence Scahill. 2006. Social Skills Development in Children with Autism Spectrum Disorders: A Review of the Intervention Research. *Journal of Autism and Developmental Disorders* 37, 10: 1858–1868. DOI:http://dx.doi.org/10.1007/s10803-006-0320-x
49. Zhengyou Zhang. 2012. Microsoft Kinect Sensor and Its Effect. *IEEE MultiMedia* 19, 2: 4–10. DOI:http://dx.doi.org/10.1109/MMUL.2012.24

Smartphone-Based Gaze Gesture Communication for People with Motor Disabilities

Xiaoyi Zhang
University of Washington
Seattle, WA, USA
xiaoyiz@cs.washington.edu

Harish Kulkarni
Microsoft Research
Redmond, WA, USA
harish.kulkarni@microsoft.com

Meredith Ringel Morris
Microsoft Research
Redmond, WA, USA
merrie@microsoft.com

ABSTRACT
Current eye-tracking input systems for people with ALS or other motor impairments are expensive, not robust under sunlight, and require frequent re-calibration and substantial, relatively immobile setups. Eye-gaze transfer (e-tran) boards, a low-tech alternative, are challenging to master and offer slow communication rates. To mitigate the drawbacks of these two status quo approaches, we created GazeSpeak, an eye gesture communication system that runs on a smartphone, and is designed to be low-cost, robust, portable, and easy-to-learn, with a higher communication bandwidth than an e-tran board. GazeSpeak can interpret eye gestures in real time, decode these gestures into predicted utterances, and facilitate communication, with different user interfaces for speakers and interpreters. Our evaluations demonstrate that GazeSpeak is robust, has good user satisfaction, and provides a speed improvement with respect to an e-tran board; we also identify avenues for further improvement to low-cost, low-effort gaze-based communication technologies.

Author Keywords
Eye gesture; accessibility; augmentative and alternative communication (AAC); Amyotrophic lateral sclerosis (ALS).

ACM Classification Keywords
H.5.m. Information Interfaces and Presentation (e.g., HCI); K.4.2. Assistive Technologies for Persons with Disabilities.

INTRODUCTION
Eye gaze keyboards [21,28] are a common communication solution for people with Amyotrophic Lateral Sclerosis (ALS) and other motor impairments. ALS is a neurodegenerative disease that leads to loss of muscle control, including the ability to speak or type; because eye muscle movement is typically retained, people with late-stage ALS usually rely on eye tracking input for communication. Unfortunately, the hardware for commercial gaze-operated keyboards is expensive. For example, the poplar Tobii Dyanvox [28] eye gaze hardware and software package costs between $5,000 and $10,000, depending on the specific model and configuration. Additionally, eye trackers do not work in certain conditions that interfere with infrared light (IR) (such as outdoors), and require a stand to keep the apparatus relatively static with respect to the user, which makes it difficult to use in certain situations such as in a car or in bed.

Permission to make digital or hard copies of all or part of this work for personal or classroom use is granted without fee provided that copies are not made or distributed for profit or commercial advantage and that copies bear this notice and the full citation on the first page. Copyrights for components of this work owned by others than the author(s) must be honored. Abstracting with credit is permitted. To copy otherwise, or republish, to post on servers or to redistribute to lists, requires prior specific permission and/or a fee. Request permissions from Permissions@acm.org.
CHI 2017, May 06 - 11, 2017, Denver, CO, USA
Copyright is held by the owner/author(s). Publication rights licensed to ACM.
ACM 978-1-4503-4655-9/17/05...$15.00
DOI: http://dx.doi.org/10.1145/3025453.3025790

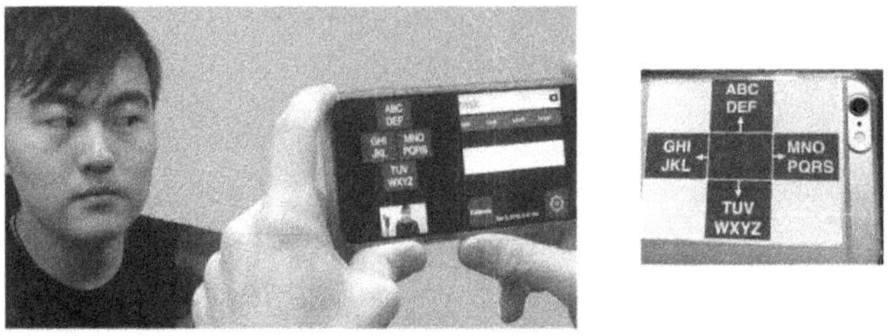

(a) (b)

Figure 1. The communication partner of a person with motor disabilities can use the GazeSpeak smartphone app to translate eye gestures into words. (a) The interpreter interface is displayed on the smartphone's screen. (b) The speaker sees a sticker depicting the four letter groupings affixed to the phone's case.

Eye-gaze transfer (e-tran) boards [3,17] are an alternative, low-tech communication solution, where clusters of letters are printed on a transparent plastic board. The communication partner holds the board, and observes the gaze pattern of the person with ALS (PALS), who selects a letter by making two coarse eye gestures: one to select which of several letter groupings contain the target letter, and a second to indicate the position within the group. Unfortunately, e-tran boards have several drawbacks: their cost is relatively low compared to gaze-tracking systems, but is not negligible (~$100); the large plastic board (e.g., one popular model [17] measures 14″ x 18″) is not easily portable; patients need to perform two eye gestures to enter one letter, which may take more than 8 seconds [25] including correcting mistakes; our survey of PALS' caregivers indicated they found e-tran to have a high learning curve, as they have to decode and remember entered characters and predict words.

In this work, we investigate how to provide low-cost, portable, robust gaze-based communication for PALS that is easy for patients and caregivers to use. Our solution uses a smartphone to capture eye gestures and interpret them using computer vision techniques. Our system, GazeSpeak, consists of computer-vision-based eye gaze recognition, a text prediction engine, and text entry interfaces that provide feedback to the speaker (PALS) and interpreter (caregiver or communication partner). GazeSpeak is as portable as a mobile phone, patients perform only one eye gesture per character, and the mobile phone records the entered characters and predicts words automatically. Further, GazeSpeak does not require re-calibration under similar lighting conditions, and it does not require a bulky stand, as caregivers can hold the phone. GazeSpeak has no additional cost other than a smartphone, which most people in the U.S. (68% in 2015) [2] already own.

We evaluate the error rate of our eye gesture recognition, as well as satisfaction and usability for both the speaker and interpreter. We also compare the communication speed of GazeSpeak to that of an e-tran board. We find GazeSpeak is robust, has good user satisfaction, and provides a speed improvement with respect to e-tran. GazeSpeak offers a viable low-cost, portable, lighting-robust alternative for situations in which eye-tracking systems are unaffordable or impractical.

The specific contributions of this work include:

- The GazeSpeak system, including algorithms to robustly recognize eye gestures in real time on a hand-held smartphone and decode these gestures into predicted utterances, and user interfaces to facilitate the speaker and interpreter communication roles.
- User study results demonstrating GazeSpeak's error rate and communication speed, as well as feedback from PALS and their communication partners on usability, utility, and directions for further work.

RELATED WORK

Low-Tech Gaze Input Solutions

As shown in Figure 2, an e-tran board [3,17] is a low-tech AAC (augmentative and alternative communication) solution that comprises a transparent board containing groups of symbols, such as letters. An interpreter holds the board and observes and decodes the eye gestures of the speaker; the speaker gazes in the direction of a group to select a cluster of symbols and then again to disambiguate the location of a specific symbol within the cluster. Another low-tech solution, EyeLink [25], is also a transparent board printed with letters. To use EyeLink, the speaker keeps staring at the desired letter, while the interpreter moves the board

(a) (b) (c)

Figure 2. Low-tech gaze input solutions: a) E-tran board; b) EyeLink; c) Laser pointer on communication board.

(a) (b)

Figure 3. High-tech gaze recognition solutions: (a) Tobii Dynavox eye-tracking computer [28]; **(b) EyeSpeak eye-tracking glasses** [18].

until she can "link" her own eye gaze with that of the speaker, and note the letter on the board where their eyes meet. Families and occupational/speech therapists may also develop myriad custom low-tech communication solutions, such as attaching a laser pointer to a patient's head (if they have head movement control) that can be used to point at letters printed out on a poster or board. While relatively cheap (costing tens or low hundreds of dollars for materials), low-tech solutions provide low communication bandwidth (entering a letter takes 8-12 seconds [25]) and place a high learning/cognitive burden on the interpreter. Low tech solutions, while not optimal, are nonetheless important in offering a communication option in situations where other options are unavailable.

High-Tech Gaze Recognition Solutions

As shown in Figure 3, commercial gaze-operated keyboards allow PALS to type characters to complete a sentence [21,29], or select symbols to build sentences word by word [30]. Typically, systems are dwell-based [15,20] (i.e., the user dwells their gaze on a key for a period, typically several hundred milliseconds, in order to select that key), though dwell-free gaze systems [13,37] are an emerging area of research and commercial development that may offer further speed improvements. Other, less common, gaze input interfaces may include techniques like scanning [4] or zooming [34].

Specialized hardware and setups are used in eye gaze tracking systems. Head-mounted eye trackers [1,18] keep the eyes and the camera close and relatively static during head movement. However, such systems are expensive, and their bulk/weight is not typically comfortable for constant use as required by someone with a motor disability; head-worn systems may also interfere with eye contact and the ability to observe the environment, making them even more impractical for constant use.

Other eye tracker solutions mount a camera on a computer monitor or table, and find pupil locations based on reflections. Because of the longer distance between eye and camera, commercial systems [27,28] often emit IR to increase light reflection from the eyes. IR makes eye movement more detectable, but limits outdoor usage due to interference from the strong IR in sunlight. Eye trackers range in price from hundreds to thousands of dollars depending on quality; some relatively low-cost commercial eye trackers are available (e.g., the Tobii EyeX costs around $150 USD); however, people who rely on eye gaze for

AAC must also purchase a computer to connect to the eye tracker and proprietary software that allows the eye gaze to control a keyboard and other computer programs; such bundles [28] typically cost between \$5,000 - \$10,000. In the United States, government health insurance (Medicare) has only just begun to help pay for AAC devices [32]; some insurers do not consider access to AAC as a medical necessity.

There are also attempts at using low-cost webcams or phone cameras to recognize eye gaze location, and use direct gaze pointing as an input method. WebGazer [24] uses a webcam to infer the gaze locations of web visitors on a page in real time, and self-calibrates while visitors interact with content on the screen with their mouse cursor. Any movement of the camera or head requires additional interactions to re-calibrate. However, PALS or other motor impairments cannot move the mouse to interact, which would break WebGazer's self-calibration algorithm. iTracker [12] uses an iPhone's front camera to estimate gaze location on the screen. Calibration can increase accuracy, but is not required, as it is pre-trained on a large-scale eye tracking database. However, extending this method to additional mobile devices may require collecting large eye tracking datasets for each device type. In addition, its prediction error on the iPhone 5 is almost 30% of the screen width.

Besides gaze location, eye-switches and eye gestures can also be used as an input method. Eye-switches [7] use voluntary eye blinks as binary signals, which helps in scanning input methods. In a 2D letter grid, the system moves the focus line by line, and the first eye-switch can select the line that contains the desired letter; then the system moves the focus letter by letter on that line, and the second eye-switch selects the desired letter. EyeWrite [37] is the first letter-like gestural text entry system for the eyes, and uses a Tobii IR eye tracker to capture gaze input. Its letter-drawing interface is a square with four corners. The user has to move gaze to the corners to map out a letter. EyeWrite does not require the dwell time to select a letter, except needing slight dwell time to signal character segmentation. Testing found EyeWrite's text entry speed was around 5 wpm. Vaitukaitis and Bulling [31] presented a prototype that could recognize different continuous eye gesture patterns on a laptop and mobile phone. For example, the user can move his gaze left, then up, then right, and finally down to draw a diamond pattern. However, their evaluation was conducted in an indoor setting with controlled lighting, requiring fixed device position and distance to participants. Even with these carefully controlled conditions, the performance of this prototype was less than 5 frames per second on the phone with only 60% accuracy. In our work, we do not use compound eye gestures to draw letters or shapes; rather, we use simple, single-direction gestures (e.g., look left) to select among groups of letters.

DESIGN GOALS

Before we started to build GazeSpeak, we conducted an online survey targeted at communication partners (spouses, caregivers, etc.) of PALS, and advertised our survey via an email list about ALS in the Seattle metropolitan area. We received 22 responses; this low number is not surprising given the low incidence rate of ALS, about 1 in 50,000 people [26].

All of the respondents indicated owning either an iPhone or Android phone. 36% of them said their companion with ALS did not own an eye-tracking system. For those whose companion did have an eye-tracker, 28% of them reported that the PALS was unable to use the eye-tracking system during more than half of the waking hours, due to issues such as system crashes, positioning at angles or locations where mounting the system is impractical (being in bed, inclined in a chair, or using the bathroom), being in situations with limited space (such as traveling in a car), or outdoors due to interference from sunlight. They also noted that when their companions with ALS only want to convey a quick communication, the start-up costs of such systems (which respondents indicated required frequent re-calibration in practice) seemed too long in proportion to the length of the communication.

64% of respondents indicated having used e-tran boards as an alternative when eye tracking was not available. Some who had not tried e-tran boards indicated they had not done so because their companion was in earlier stages of ALS's progression and still retained some speech capabilities. The self-reported learning curve for e-tran was varied; 36% of respondents reported it took a few hours to master, 14% spent a day, 29% spent a week, and 21% indicated it took more than a month. Respondents reported challenges in using e-tran boards: the interpreter may misread the eye gesture, forget the sequence of previously specified letters, and finds the board heavy/uncomfortable to hold; for the speaker, it is difficult to correct a mistake in gesture or interpretation. Respondents indicated that one or two words is the typical length of an utterance specified via e-tran board.

These survey responses added to our knowledge of the concerns facing end-users of gaze-based AAC; based on these responses and the other cost and practicality issues discussed in the *Introduction* and *Related Work* sections, we articulated several design goals for GazeSpeak:

1) *Create a low-cost/high-tech alternative in an eco-system that currently offers only high-cost/high-tech and low-cost/low-tech solutions*: GazeSpeak is meant to be affordable for people who may not be able to purchase an expensive, multi-thousand-dollar eye tracking solution. Since smartphone ownership is common in the U.S. [2] and was ubiquitous among our survey respondents, a smartphone app seems a reasonable way to reach a large audience at no additional cost to end-users. We do not expect that our smartphone app should exceed the

performance (in terms of text entry rates) of expensive, commercial eye tracker setups; however, we do expect that GazeSpeak will offer performance and usability enhancements as compared to the current low-cost alternative. In addition to supporting a low-cost solution, the mobile phone form-factor preserves (and even exceeds some of) the advantages of current low-tech solutions in being smaller, lighter, more portable, and more robust to varied lighting sources than high-cost commercial eye-tracking setups.

2) *Simplify the e-tran process through automation*: While cheap and flexible for many scenarios, e-tran still has several drawbacks that we aim to mitigate with GazeSpeak, particularly: (1) slow speed of text entry, (2) difficulty of error correction, and (3) high cognitive burden for the interpreter.

SYSTEM DESIGN AND IMPLEMENTATION

GazeSpeak application currently supports iOS devices released after 2012. It uses the phone's built-in camera, touch screen, and speaker, and does not require extra hardware. To improve learnability and usability, a simple guide representing the four keyboard groupings and associated gesture directions can be printed and taped to the back of the phone's case (Figure 1b). To use this system, the interpreter holds the phone and points the back camera toward the speaker (PALS) (Figure 1a and Figure 8).

The app consists of three major components: 1) eye gesture recognition, 2) a predictive text engine, and 3) a text entry interface.

Eye Gesture Recognition

GazeSpeak can robustly recognize six eye gestures for both eyes: look up, look down, look left, look right, look center, and close eyes. If the speaker can wink (closing only one eye at a time), it also recognizes winking the left eye and winking the right eye. The recognition code is written in C++ and depends on open-source libraries: Dlib [11] and OpenCV [5]. To save development time, we only implemented eye gesture recognition on iOS; however, GazeSpeak could be easily extended to other platforms that support these dependencies, such as Android, Windows, Mac and Linux.

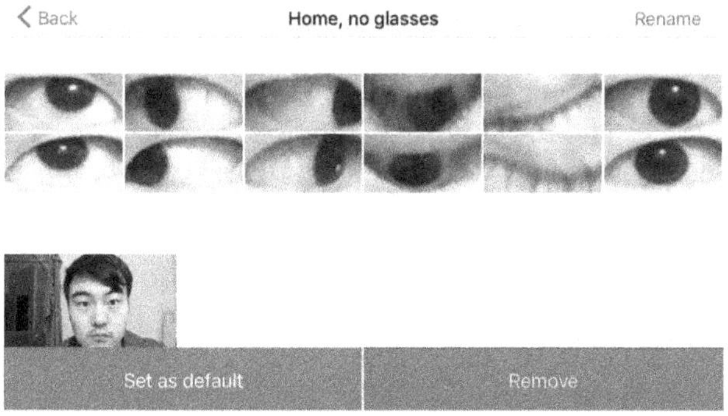

Figure 4. Calibration review screen. A photo at the bottom left serves as a reminder of context (e.g., indoors, glasses off) that can also be added to the calibration name (top). This screen also shows the calibration templates captured for the *up*, *left*, *right*, *down*, *closed* and *center* gestures for each eye.

Calibration

GazeSpeak collects a set of eye gestures from the speaker as calibration templates. When the interpreter holds the phone with the rear camera facing the speaker, they can press the "calibrate" button. The app then plays audio instructions that tell the speaker to prepare to calibrate, and then instructs him to look up, down, left, right, center, and to close both eyes. Template matching will be more robust if these six gestures are distinct from each other, so for best performance, the speaker should make eye gestures that are exaggerated (far up, to the rightmost, etc.) to the extent possible while not being uncomfortable (Figure 4). In addition, while looking down, eyelashes may cover eyes naturally, which makes it appear to be similar to closed eyes. Thus, for the *look down* gesture, we suggest speakers try to keep their eyes open as wide as they are able while looking down, to improve performance (Figure 4). This calibration sequence takes ten seconds. Calibration is only required for the first time using the app, or if lighting conditions vary drastically (having a separate outdoor and indoor calibration may improve performance). Calibrations taken under different circumstances can be stored, labeled, loaded as needed, and transferred between different iOS devices.

To obtain calibration templates for eye gaze recognition, GazeSpeak performs the following four steps:

1) *Detect face and align landmarks*: We use iOS's built-in face detector to obtain a rectangle containing the speaker's face. (OpenCV's face detector could be used when extending GazeSpeak to other platforms that do not have built-in face detection support.) Then, we use dlib's implementation of fast face alignment [10] to extract landmarks on the face.

2) *Extract an image of each eye*: Once we get face landmarks, we calculate the bounding rectangle of eye landmarks. Then we extract images of each eye and process them separately.

3) *Normalize eye images*: We resize each eye image to 80x40 pixels. Then we convert the image to the HSV color space and only keep its V channel (value, i.e., brightness).

4) *Store eye gesture template*: We save the normalized eye images on the phone, using the filenames to indicate the eye (left/right) and gesture (up/down/left/right/center/closed).

Recognition Algorithm

Once there is a new or existing calibration for the speaker, he may perform eye gestures to communicate while the interpreter aims the rear phone camera toward the speaker (Figure 1a). The interpreter can see the camera view on the screen and ensure the speaker's face is in the view (Figure 5x). For each camera frame, GazeSpeak performs the following steps as shown in Figure 5. It detects the face and

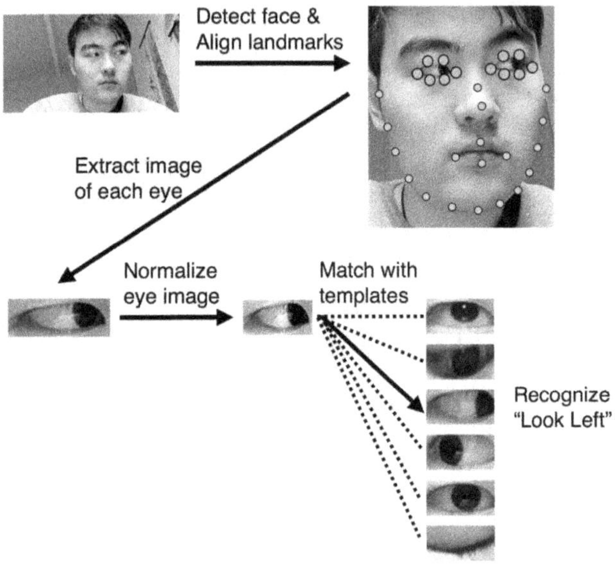

Figure 5. Flowchart of eye gesture recognition algorithm.

aligns landmarks, extracts an image of each eye, and normalizes the eye images (the same first three steps as during calibration). Then GazeSpeak classifies eye gestures by matching the normalized eye images extracted from the current video frame with the calibration templates.

Mean squared error (MSE) [16] measures the difference between two images. We use MSE to find the closest match for the normalized eye images among the six eye gesture templates obtained during calibration. Structural similarity [33] and the sum of absolute differences [35] are also candidates for measuring the difference between two images; however, MSE achieved the best recognition rate in our iterative testing and development of the system.

Performance

We tested our eye gesture recognition on recent models of the iPhone and iPad. For the iPhone, the recognition speed ranges from 27 frames per second (fps) (iPhone 6s Plus) to 17 fps (iPhone 5s). For the iPad, it ranges from 34 fps (iPad Pro 9.7) to 16 fps (iPad mini 2). The slowest device still processes enough frames to confirm gestures for text entry.

Robustness

Our algorithm works in a variety of lighting conditions, including indoors and outdoors. Since it uses an RGB rather than IR camera, its performance is unlikely to be degraded under sunlight. In low-light conditions, GazeSpeak can turn on the phone's flashlight to make the speaker's face visible. To avoid flash burn to the eyes, we need to apply a diffuser-like tape such as 3M tape (less than $1) over the flashlight. Our algorithm tolerates two major transformations: *Scaling* (e.g., if the interpreter moves the phone closer to the speaker), *Translation* (e.g., if the speaker moves his head a bit, or the interpreter slightly moves the phone while holding it), and *Scaling + Translation* (e.g., the interpreter puts down the phone, and later holds it in a slightly different position). *Rotation* of speaker's head or the phone significantly changes perceived face shape and thus reduces recognition accuracy. Our app shows the face image and recognition results to visually assist the interpreter in self-correcting the positioning.

Accuracy

To assess the accuracy of our gesture recognition system, we recruited 12 participants through email lists within our organization, and paid each participant $5 for a 30-minute session. They reported a mean of 29 years old (min 20, max 44); five were male and seven were female. Six had a normal (uncorrected) vision, one wore contact lenses, and five wore glasses. Participants had varied skin and eye colors. During the study, each participant performed each of up/down/left/right/closed eye gestures 30 times; after each gesture, the participant looked back to center. In total, we recorded 300 eye gestures for each participant (30 x 5 + an additional 150 gazes toward the center).

	Up	Down	Left	Right	Close	Center
Mean	88.6%	75.3%	87.8%	86.9%	77.5%	98.6%
Stdev	5.2%	17.5%	4.8%	7.4%	13.5%	1.8%

Table 1. GazeSpeak's recognition rate of each eye gesture.

For our 12 participants, the algorithm correctly recognized an average of 86% of all eye gestures (min = 68%, max = 92%, med = 89%, stdev = 6.9%). Table 1 reports the recognition accuracy for each of the six eye gestures. GazeSpeak's algorithm can recognize the center gesture with near perfect accuracy; looking up, left, or right also had good recognition rates. Looking down and closing the eyes are harder to recognize due to their sometimes-similar appearance, as explained in the *Calibration* section.

We did not see any effect from age, gender, eye color, or skin color on the accuracy. For participants without corrective lenses, our system achieved 89.7% accuracy. Wearing contact lenses (only one participant) did not have a noticeable effect on accuracy (89%). However, an independent-samples t-test indicates wearing glasses significantly lowers the recognition accuracy to 80.4% ($t(9) = 2.714$, $p = 0.024$). Although glasses do not the affect the face detector, we suspect they may interrupt facial landmark alignment, sometimes resulting in mislabeling the eye area. Because we analyzed the recorded gesture videos offline, when we record the video, we did not have the recognition results as feedback to warn us to move the phone when the facial landmark alignment went wrong; however, when using GazeSpeak in real time, the interpreter can adjust the phone angle until she hears the correct recognition audio feedback, thus mitigating error for users with glasses. In fact, during our *Usability Study* (next section), we encountered very few recognition errors, even for speakers with glasses, likely because interpreters were able to use GazeSpeak's video and audio feedback to mitigate error.

Predictive Text Engine

To avoid fatigue from making complex eye gestures, improve learnability, and improve recognition rates,

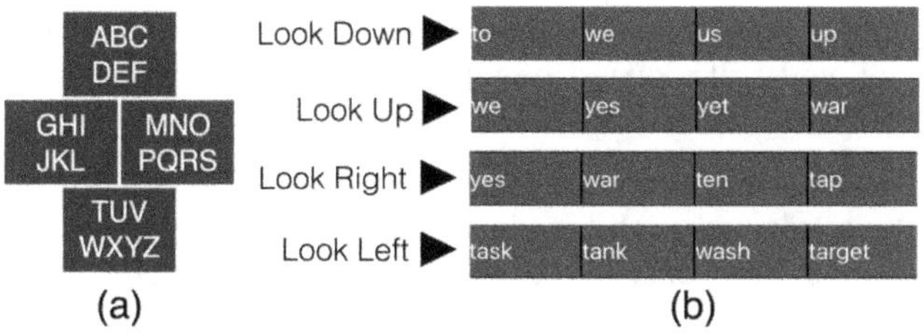

Figure 6. Word predictions update after each gesture in this example four-gesture sequence to spell the word "task".

GazeSpeak uses a small number of simple eye gestures (up/down/left/right) to refer to all 26 letters of the English alphabet, using only one gesture per character entered (to reduce fatigue and increase throughput). This design leads to an ambiguous keyboard (Figure 6a) in which the letters of the alphabet are clustered into four groups that can each be indicated with one of the up, down, left, or right gestures. GazeSpeak implements a predictive text engine [22,23] to find all possible words that could be created with the letters in the groups indicated by a gesture sequence. Our implementation uses a trie [14] data structure to store common words and their frequencies in oral English: we select the most common 5,000 words (frequency min=4,875, max=22,038,615, mean=12,125) from this wordlist [6]. This trie can also be extended by an interpreter, who can add the speaker's frequently-used words (including out-of-dictionary words, such as names). For a series of eye gestures with length *n*, our trie structure allows us to rapidly look up its matching words and word frequencies in O(n) time. GazeSpeak can also look up high-frequency words whose initial characters match the gesture sequence thus far.

We display a list of likely words based on the current gesture sequence on the phone's screen for the interpreter (Figure 6b); we currently show the top four predictions by default, though additional predictions can be cycled through by horizontal scrolling. The prediction and auto-complete features help the interpreter predict possible words while the speaker is still entering text, enabling guessing ahead to improve throughput, and easing the interpretation burden that is present in using a low-tech e-tran board.

For instance, in order to enter the word *TASK*, the speaker first looks down for T, then looks up for A, looks right for S, and looks left for K. The predictions after each eye gesture in this sequence are shown in Figure 6.

To make it easier for the speaker to learn the gesture direction associated with a given letter, our four groups are simply clusters in alphabetical order (Figure 6a). An alternative letter grouping may reduce the conflict rate for word prediction; however, learnability was a higher design priority for this audience, as learnability is one of the challenges of using e-tran boards that motivated GazeSpeak's creation. The word prediction conflict rate is reasonably low for this intuitive letter grouping. The 5,000 most common words in our dictionary can be represented by 3248 unique eye gesture sequences. 83.5% of sequences match a unique word, 92.6% match two or fewer words, 97.7% match four or fewer words, 99.2% match six or fewer words, and 99.6% match 8 or fewer words.

If a word is not in the trie, the speaker has to use a scan-based method to type the word letter by letter. To type a letter, he stares at the direction that contains that letter; GazeSpeak would read each letter in that key, and the speaker looks back to center once he hears the desired letter.

Text Entry Interface

The speaker and interpreter use different interfaces. The speaker sees the back of the phone, and thus the screen-less text entry interface consists of two major components: 1) a sticker displaying the four-key keyboard, and 2) audio feedback. The interpreter sees the phone screen, which shows four major components as in Figure 7: 1) the four-key keyboard, 2) the input box and word predictions, 3) the sentence box and 4) the camera preview.

Speaker Interface

On the back of the phone, a four-key sticker (figure 1b) reminds the speaker of the letter groupings associated with each of the four gesture directions. To enter one character, the speaker moves his eyes in the direction associated with that letter's group. Once GazeSpeak detects that the eyes have settled in one direction, it speaks aloud the direction it detected (e.g., "Up"). The speaker can then move his eyes to enter the next character. When the speaker mistypes or hears feedback indicating an incorrect gesture recognition, he can wink his left eye (if the speaker cannot wink, an alternative is to close both eyes for at least two seconds); this gesture removes the last character from the current sequence. When the speaker finishes a sequence for an entire word, he can wink his right eye (or alternatively look center for at least two seconds) to indicate the end of the word; then the system will speak aloud the first word prediction based on the entire series of eye gestures. The speaker can wink his right eye again to confirm this prediction, or perform a *look right* gesture to hear the next prediction. After a word has been confirmed, it is added to the sentence being constructed (Figure 7d). After the speaker confirms the last word of the sentence, he can wink his right eye again to confirm the end of the sentence, and the system will play the whole sentence aloud.

When a tripod or phone stand is available, speakers could also choose to use GazeSpeak in the front-facing mode with minimum help from the caregivers. The speaker sees the screen, and the interface is similar to the interpreter interface in Figure 7. The major difference happens when the speaker indicates the end of the word. In addition to speaking aloud the first word, the system turns the first prediction red in order to visually indicate the current focus. The speaker can still perform a *look right* gesture to hear the next prediction, and see the visual focus switch to that prediction.

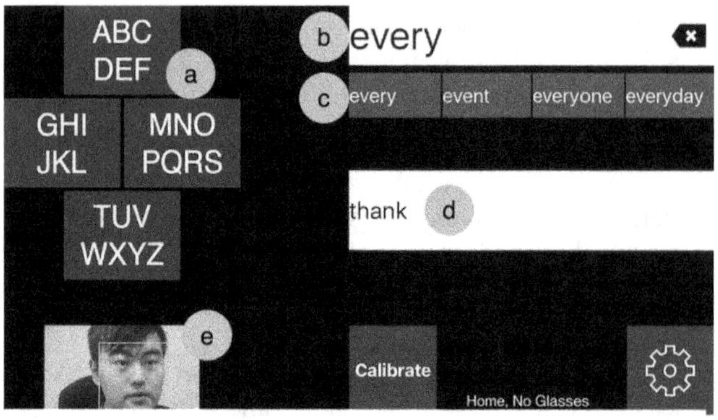

Figure 7. Interpreter interface: (a) four-key keyboard; (b) the word input box shows top prediction of characters entered in the current sequence; (c) top four word predictions; (d) the sentence box shows prior words in the communication; (e) camera preview with a green face detection box.

Interpreter Interface

With information displayed on the phone screen, the interpreter can speed up the communication process. The input box (Figure 7b) shows the most likely word based on the current gesture sequence, and its length also indicates the number of eye gestures performed so far in the current sequence. When using low-tech e-tran boards, the ability to make guesses about likely words based on partial information is an important part of speeding up communication throughput; we designed GazeSpeak to support this existing communication practice. Even before the speaker finishes a word, if the interpreter sees a likely word prediction based on her knowledge of context, she can either say the word aloud or tap the prediction box to let GazeSpeak play the word aloud. The speaker can confirm or reject the prediction, either using gestures recognized by GazeSpeak (right-winking to confirm or left-winking to reject) or using mutually-agreed upon conventions common in e-tran communication (e.g., using other motions depending on the speaker's range of mobility, such as nods, eyebrow raises, etc.). With a confirmation, the interpreter can then long-press the word to add it to the sentence box, and the speaker can proceed to begin a gesture sequence for the next word in the sentence. With a rejection of the prediction, the interpreter should let the speaker continue the eye gestures to complete the word. Once the speaker indicates the end of the sentence, the interpreter should confirm the sentence with the speaker by saying the sentence aloud or touching the sentence box to let GazeSpeak play it.

There is also a manual mode that can be used when GazeSpeak has a hard time recognizing the speaker's eyes; for example, if an oxygen mask or other medical equipment covers the speaker's face, when the eye movement capability is very limited, or when the speaker wears highly reflective glasses. In this case, the interpreter can note the eye gestures of the speaker, and touch the corresponding keys on the four-key keyboard. This manual mode still allows the interpreter to take advantage of GazeSpeak's predictive text engine to quickly decode what the speaker would like to say and to keep track of the words the speaker said, and still reduces the number of eye gestures required per character as compared to using an e-tran board.

USABILITY STUDY

We conducted a lab-based usability study to understand the relative performance, usability, and user preference for different modes of gesture decoding, comparing GazeSpeak to an e-tran board. Because ALS is a low-incidence disease (impacting 1 in 50,000 people [26]), recruiting a sufficient number of PALS to participate in a controlled study was impractical; additionally, the fatigue associated with ALS would make providing data for a controlled experiment such as this (which lasted nearly an hour in total) prohibitive for many potential participants. While we recognize that using able-bodied participants reduces the ecological validity of our study, it was a necessary tradeoff for being able to gather a sufficient amount of systematic data to evaluate GazeTalk's baseline performance characteristics. We also conducted shorter, less formal testing sessions of GazeTalk with PALS and their caregivers, which we discuss in the next section.

Participants

For this evaluation, we recruited pairs of able-bodied participants from our organization; participants did not have prior experience with e-tran boards. Performing a lab study with able-bodied users allowed us to supplement the data possible to obtain from PALS with a larger and more controlled experiment; further, these participants provide a realistic insight into the learnability and usability of the system to first-time, novice adopters of the technology in either the interpreter or speaker role. Partners in our study were not necessarily acquainted with each other prior to the study; a close relationship might facilitate better guessing and speed input. However, in some situations e-tran may be used by a visitor or other medical professional who would be less familiar with the speaker's context; our study better resembles that scenario.

We recruited participants through email lists within our organization, and paid each participant $15 for a one-hour session. Interested participants completed a brief questionnaire about basic demographics and screening for e-tran board experience (which would be a disqualifier). From the eligible pool, we randomly selected twenty-four participants for a total of twelve pairs; two pairs did not show up for their assigned timeslot. The remaining twenty participants completed the study and reported an average age of 32 years (min 20, max 52); fourteen were male and six were female. When pairs arrived at the study session, they were randomly assigned to either the speaker or interpreter role. Among the ten speakers, five had a normal (uncorrected) vision, two wore contact lenses, and three wore glasses.

Procedure

We employed a within-subjects design to examine the input speed, usability, and user preference among three input methods: an e-tran board, GazeSpeak's default operation style, and GazeSpeak's front-facing mode. We used a Latin Square design to counterbalance the ordering of the three input methods across participant pairs. For sentences to be entered during testing, we randomly picked a set of eighteen five-word-long sentences (29-31 characters each) from the Mackenzie and Sourkeroff phrase sets commonly used for evaluating text entry techniques [19] to use as our testing corpus.

Participation began with a brief introduction of the purpose of the study. We then randomly assigned the speaker and interpreter roles to the members of a pair (these roles were held constant for all three input methods). Participants sat face to face (in chairs set 18-inches apart).

For each of the three conditions, we presented a tutorial on how to use the communication method, and let the pair practice until they felt comfortable using the method to communicate a two-word example utterance (e.g., "hello world"). We then privately showed the speaker a sentence from the testing corpus, and instructed them to communicate that sentence as quickly and accurately as possible to their partner without speaking, using only the current communication method. We then started a timer and stopped the timer when the interpreter correctly decoded the sentence. This procedure continued until either six sentences had been successfully communicated or ten minutes had elapsed, at which point we stopped the session in order to avoid excessive fatigue. Participants then completed a short questionnaire providing feedback about their experience using that communication method, and took a short break if they felt fatigued. After repeating this procedure for all three communication methods, participants completed a final questionnaire ranking their preferences among all three methods.

Results

For each 10-minute session using a given interface, we prepared six sentences for the speaker to communicate to the interpreter. In the two GazeSpeak conditions, all pairs successfully communicated all six phrases. However, in the e-tran condition, pairs completed an average of 4 phrases.

	Mean	Median	Min	Max	Stdev
E-tran	143.4	122.5	72	298	57.4
GazeSpeak	80.9	77.5	51	132	18.8
GazeSpeak Front-Facing Mode	77.1	76	56	120	11.5

Table 2. The time (in seconds) spent to complete a sentence using each input method.

Participants, on average, spent 137.8 seconds to complete a sentence using the e-tran board, 80.9 seconds using GazeSpeak's default mode and 77.1 seconds using GazeSpeak's front-facing mode. A one-way repeated measures ANOVA indicates that mean input time differed significantly between input methods ($F(1.067, 9.602) = 21.032$, $p = 0.002$). Follow-up pairwise paired-samples t-tests show that both modes of GazeSpeak bring a statistically significant reduction in input time as compared to the e-tran board (default mode vs. e-tran: $t(9) = 4.136$, $p = 0.003$, and front-facing mode vs. e-tran: $t(9) = 3.983$, $p = 0.003$).

	E-tran		GazeSpeak		Front-Facing	
	S	I	S	I	S	I
It is unnecessarily complex	2.9	2.4	1.7	1.7	1.6	2.1
I feel confident to use it	3.0	3.3	4.3	4.3	4.3	3.8

Table 3. Speaker(S) and Interpreter(I)'s average agreement level (1=strongly disagree, 5=strongly agree) on each statement.

The questionnaires completed after each condition asked participants to indicate their level of agreement with several statements about that condition's input method on a 5-point Likert scale (Table 3). The Friedman test indicates there were statistically significant differences in perceived complexity between input methods ($\chi^2 = 8.5$, $p = 0.014$). A Wilcoxon signed-rank test shows that GazeSpeak's default mode has a statistically significant reduction in perceived complexity over the e-tran board ($Z = -2.834$, $p = 0.005$). There are no significant differences between GazeSpeak's default and front-facing mode ($Z = -0.612$, $p = 0.541$), or between e-tran board and GazeSpeak front-facing mode ($Z = -1.794$, $p = 0.073$). Part of the e-tran board's complexity may be due to its diagonal directions; for instance, P21 (speaker) and other speakers made comments such as "*looking diagonal was difficult.*" A Friedman test also indicates there were statistically significant differences in perceived confidence in correctly communicating using each input methods ($\chi^2 = 7.4$, $p = 0.024$). Participants reported feeling more confident using any mode of GazeSpeak than e-tran (default mode vs. e-tran: $Z = -2.871$, $p = 0.004$, and front-facing mode vs. e-tran: $Z = -1.970$, $p = 0.049$).

	E-tran		GazeSpeak		Front-Facing	
	S	I	S	I	S	I
Mentally Demanding	4.8	4.5	3.3	2.5	3.4	2.6
Task Difficulty	3.9	3.5	2.4	2.4	3.1	1.9
Feel Stressed/Discouraged	3.9	2.2	2.1	1.9	2.4	1.8

Table 4. Speakers' (S) and Interpreters' (I) average ratings (1=Very low, 7=Very high) for NASA TLX items.

Our study questionnaires also included items from the NASA TLX scale [8], reported on a 7-point scale (Table 4). Participants rated the e-tran board as more mentally demanding than both modes of GazeSpeak (Friedman test: $\chi^2 = 13.5$, $p = 0.001$, default mode vs. e-tran: $Z = -3.471$, $p = 0.001$, and front-facing mode vs. e-tran: $Z = -2.774$, $p = 0.006$). P12 (interpreter) described aspects of using the e-tran board that were challenging, such as "*to keep track of what had been spelled out so far, as well as which eye movements were to select a letter vs looking at the board.*" P5 (speaker) noted that using GazeSpeak makes it "*very simple to memorize the gestures, resulting in much less confusion and mistakes [than with e-tran].*" Compare to the e-tran board, both modes of GazeSpeak were considered less difficult to use (Friedman test: χ^2 = 7.0, p = 0.03, default mode vs. e-tran: Z = -2.560, p = 0.01, and front-facing mode vs. e-tran: Z = -1.930, p = 0.05). P18 (interpreter) explained this preference, "*I liked that the technology on the phone was doing the hard work whereas I was only responsible for keeping track of when the speaker was done with spelling a word. It was much easier for me as an interpreter with the technology than without the technology.*" Using GazeSpeak in front-facing mode made participants feel less stressed or discouraged than using the e-tran board (Z = -1.951, p = 0.05). For speakers, using GazeSpeak's default mode significantly reduced feelings of stress and discouragement compared to using the e-tran board (Z = -2.328, p = 0.02). As P13 (speaker) described, "*It [GazeSpeak] was way simpler than the first one [e-tran]. Only having to do one of four movements for a letter was much easier to indicate and I didn't feel like I had to emphasize the movements as much. The instant [audio] feedback on which direction I went was also helpful.*"

	E-tran		GazeSpeak		Front-Facing	
	S	I	S	I	S	I
Average Rank	2.9	2.8	1.6	2	1.5	1.2

Table 5. Speaker(S) and Interpreter(I)'s average rank (1=Best, 3=Worst) of each input method.

After completing all sessions, participants ranked all three input methods based on their experience (Table 5). Overall, participants preferred GazeSpeak to the e-tran board; the e-tran board was not selected by any participants as their favorite input method. A one-sample chi-square test showed a significant difference in the rankings of preferences for each system, with the e-tran board most likely to be ranked least favorite by all participants, regardless of role ($\chi^2(1, N = 20) = 9.80$, p = 0.002). P8 (interpreter) articulated the reasoning behind this preference: "*The smartphone app was better at interpreting the eye gestures and recounting the words.*"

Interpreters favored GazeSpeak's front-facing mode as their top-ranked interface (likely because this mode resulted in less active interpreter involvement), $\chi^2(1, N = 10) = 6.40$, p = 0.01, whereas participants in the speaker role were not significantly more likely to have a clear preference between front-facing or rear-facing GazeSpeak, $\chi^2(1, N = 10) = 0.40$, p = 0.53. However, preferences for front and rear-facing use will likely vary with in-context use from the target user groups, as issues such as communication urgency, speed, autonomy, context, and others are likely quite different for PALS and their caregivers than for able-bodied users testing GazeSpeak in a lab setting (for example, while interpreters in our lab study enjoyed their reduced responsibilities with the front-facing UI, real-world communication partners of PALS may prefer a more active role in helping their partner communicate more quickly).

The key learnings from this study are that GazeSpeak, in both configurations, was quick for participants to learn to use, and resulted in faster communication and greater user preference than an e-tran board.

FEEDBACK FROM PALS AND THEIR CAREGIVERS

We included PALS and their communication partners throughout our design process. Before we started the development, we did a formative survey to identify end-user needs. During different stages of app development, we invited PALS and partners to our lab and did iterative demos/informal testing. When the GazeSpeak prototype was mature, we visited seven PALS and their caregivers to demonstrate GazeSpeak and obtain their feedback. In addition to demonstrating the system and giving a tutorial, we let them try GazeSpeak. One of the PALS, using GazeSpeak's default mode with his caregiver, completed one of our 5-word (30-character) testing sentences in 62 seconds, after only a brief tutorial. He also believed that communicating with his caregiver in his real life will be even faster than typing testing sentences: "*I will say the same thing over and over, so my caregiver can predict the words really fast.*" Caregivers liked the general concept: "*I love the phone technology; I just think that would be so slick.*" Caregivers envisioned GazeSpeak could be useful outdoors because they would not have to use "*the big Tobii*"; they also noted it would be useful in the car, as Tobii and its mount are so bulky that one PALS's spouse noted she does not allow her husband to use it in the car due to concerns that it could be a safety hazard in the event of a crash.

These informal tests with PALS also identified important opportunities for improvement, revealing usability issues not uncovered in our lab study with able-bodied participants. Two of the seven PALS wore oxygen masks, which confused GazeSpeak's face detector, resulting in failed eye gesture recognition. The use of manual mode, mentioned in the end of *Interpreter Interface* section, is one possible solution that could be used in this circumstance; however, a

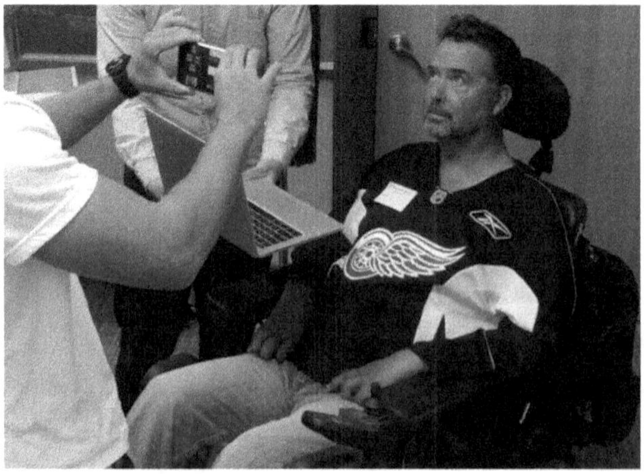

Figure 8. A PALS using GazeSpeak with his caregiver.

more desirable solution would be to train a detector for faces with an oxygen mask, or train a detector for eyes in the absence of other facial landmarks. Also, testing with PALS revealed variation in the speed with which they could move their eyes; four of the PALS with more advanced disease progression could not move their eyes as quickly as our automated calibration sequence demanded. Consequently, we improved GazeSpeak by (1) slowing down the calibration sequence to allow more time to perform each gesture and (2) adding a "manual calibration" option in which the caregiver can control the pacing of capturing each calibration image before moving on to the next one. Caregivers requested that the screen show more predictions if an eye gesture sequence represents more than four words, especially when the caregivers extend the dictionary to include names and other custom vocabulary. One PALS commented: "*Having more options could slow the caregiver down, but the fact that my caregiver and I work independently could mean it will be faster [overall].*" Automatic feedback on the quality of an acquired calibration would also give caregivers extra confidence in using the system.

DISCUSSION

We created GazeSpeak, a low-cost and high-tech AAC solution for people who rely on eye gaze communication, as an alternative to current high-cost/high-tech and low-cost/low-tech solutions. Compared to a low-tech e-tran board, GazeSpeak is smaller (a phone is about 6% of a typical board's size) and lighter (about 30% of a typical board's weight). Compared to a high-end IR-based eye-tracking system, GazeSpeak is also smaller and lighter, it does not require a fixed mounting and is therefore more portable, and it is more robust to varied lighting sources, since IR light such as bright sunlight does not interfere with a smartphone's camera. To reduce the difficulty of error correction, GazeSpeak does not only allow interpreters to manually recognize mutually-agreed upon conventions common in e-tran communication, but also allows the speaker to correct errors by recognizing a left wink or closing both eyes for a period of time; GazeSpeak also reduces the cognitive complexity of communication as compared to e-tran board use: for the speaker, letter entry is simplified from two gestures per character in e-tran to one in GazeSpeak, and for the interpreter, GazeSpeak improves upon e-tran by showing predictions of likely words and by keeping track of prior words spoken in the current utterance. Our usability study showed that GazeSpeak significantly improves communication speed compared to an e-tran board.

To make GazeSpeak even more robust and suitable to a wider range of end-user needs and abilities, we include a manual input mode for use when eye gestures cannot be recognized, and a front-facing mode that can be used when a phone stand is available. The front-facing mode allows GazeSpeak to be used without the help of an interpreter, offering the possibility of a lower-cost, but lower-fidelity and less general-purpose, alternative to commercial eye-tracking solutions if someone cannot afford one. In following principles of ability-based design [36], GazeSpeak gracefully adds/degrades functionality depending on a user's capabilities, such as allowing backspacing if left-winking is possible, offering dual-eye closing as an alternative to winking, and still functioning without the backspace capability at all if the speaker can perform neither of those gestures. We have also implemented a head-tracking mode that can be used as an alternative to eye gestures depending on the capabilities and preferences of the speaker.

Our feedback sessions with PALS and their communication partners found areas for further improvement of GazeSpeak. To improve eye gesture recognition availability, we can improve the face detection and eye detection algorithms to have robustness in cases of face-worn medical equipment. We can also further improve the word prediction by automatically updating the weight of prediction from daily usage, and making word prediction based on already-typed words and other contextual information (e.g., location information from the phone's GPS [9]), and offering a larger n-best list for interpreters to select from.

While our evaluations gave insight into usability and performance for novice users, additional types of evaluation can offer additional value. For example, longer-term studies of use would give insight into the relative learning curves of GazeSpeak versus other AAC methods, and would allow characterization of expert-level performance. More formal, long-term data collection from PALS and their communication partners, while logistically complex, is particularly important for understanding in situ use of this new type of AAC. GazeSpeak may also hold value for other audiences besides PALS (e.g. people with cerebral palsy, spinal cord injury, stroke, traumatic brain injury, etc.). Because PALS can have different eye movement pattern than other motor-impaired users, additional testing may be necessary to modify GazeSpeak to support such users.

CONCLUSION

In this paper, we introduce GazeSpeak, a smartphone app to facilitate communication for people with motor disabilities like ALS. In real time, GazeSpeak robustly recognizes eye gestures and decodes them to words. Our user studies show that GazeSpeak surpasses e-tran boards (a commonly-used low-tech solution) in both communication speed and usability, with a low rate of wrong recognition. Feedback from PALS and their communication partners affirmed the value of offering a portable, low-cost technology to supplement IR-based eye tracking systems in situations where they are impractical to use (or are unaffordable to purchase).

ACKNOWLEDGEMENTS

We thank the MSR Enable team for their support and insight and all of the PALS and their communication partners who participated in our survey and testing.

REFERENCES

1. Javier S. Agustin, Henrik Skovsgaard, John P. Hansen, and Dan W. Hansen. 2009. Low-cost Gaze Interaction: Ready to Deliver the Promises. In *Conference on Human Factors in Computing (CHI)*, 4453–4458. http://doi.org/10.1145/1520340.1520682
2. Monica Anderson. 2015. Technology Device Ownership: 2015. Retrieved September 15, 2016 from http://www.pewinternet.org/2015/10/29/technology-device-ownership-2015/
3. Gary Becker. 1996. Vocal Eyes Becker Communication System. Retrieved September 15, 2016 from http://jasonbecker.com/eye_communication.html
4. Pradipta Biswas and Pat Langdon. 2011. A new input system for disabled users involving eye gaze tracker and scanning interface. *Journal of Assistive Technologies* 5, 2: 58–66. http://doi.org/10.1108/17549451111149269
5. Gary Bradski. 2000. The OpenCV Library. *Doctor Dobbs Journal* 25: 120–126.
6. Mark Davies. 2008. The Corpus of Contemporary American English: 520 million words, 1990-present. Retrieved from http://corpus.byu.edu/coca/
7. Kristen Grauman, Margrit Betke, Jonathan Lombardi, James Gips, and Gary R. Bradski. 2003. Communication via eye blinks and eyebrow raises: Video-based human-computer interfaces. *Universal Access in the Information Society* 2, 4: 359–373. http://doi.org/10.1007/s10209-003-0062-x
8. Sandra G. Hart and Lowell E. Staveland. 1988. Development of NASA-TLX (Task Load Index): Results of Empirical and Theoretical Research. *Advances in Psychology* 52, C: 139–183. http://doi.org/10.1016/S0166-4115(08)62386-9
9. Shaun K. Kane, Barbara Linam-Church, Kyle Althoff, and Denise McCall. 2012. What We Talk About: Designing a Context-Aware Communication Tool for People with Aphasia. In *Proceedings of the 14th international ACM SIGACCESS conference on Computers and accessibility - ASSETS '12*, 49. http://doi.org/10.1145/2384916.2384926
10. Vahid Kazemi and Josephine Sullivan. 2014. One millisecond face alignment with an ensemble of regression trees. In *Proceedings of the IEEE Computer Society Conference on Computer Vision and Pattern Recognition*, 1867–1874. http://doi.org/10.1109/CVPR.2014.241
11. Davis E. King. 2009. Dlib-ml: A Machine Learning Toolkit. *Journal of Machine Learning Research* 10: 1755–1758.
12. Kyle Krafka, Aditya Khosla, Petr Kellnhofer, et al. 2016. Eye tracking for Everyone. In *IEEE Conference on Computer Vision and Pattern Recognition (CVPR).*
13. Per Ola Kristensson and Keith Vertanen. 2012. The potential of dwell-free eye-typing for fast assistive gaze communication. In *Proceedings of the Symposium on Eye Tracking Research and Applications*, 241–244. http://doi.org/10.1145/2168556.2168605
14. Rene De La Briandais. 1959. File searching using variable length keys. In *Papers presented at the western joint computer conference*, 295–298.
15. Chris Lankford. 2000. Effective eye-gaze input into windows. In *Proceedings of the 2000 Symposium on Eye Tracking Research & Applications*, 23–27. http://doi.org/10.1145/355017.355021
16. Erich Leo Lehmann and George Casella. 2006. *Theory of point estimation*. Springer Science & Business Media.
17. Low Tech Solutions. 2016. E-tran Board. Retrieved September 15, 2016 from http://store.lowtechsolutions.org/e-tran-board/
18. LusoVu. 2016. EyeSpeak. Retrieved September 15, 2016 from http://www.myeyespeak.com/eyespeak/
19. Scott MacKenzie and William Soukoreff. 2003. Phrase sets for evaluating text entry techniques. In *CHI '03 Extended Abstracts on Human Factors in Computing Systems*, 754–755. http://doi.org/10.1145/765968.765971
20. Päivi Majaranta, Ulla-Kaija Ahola, and Oleg Špakov. 2009. Fast gaze typing with an adjustable dwell time. In *Proceedings of the 27th international conference on Human factors in computing systems - CHI 09*, 357. http://doi.org/10.1145/1518701.1518758
21. Microsoft Research. 2016. Hands-Free Keyboard. Retrieved September 15, 2016 from https://www.microsoft.com/en-us/research/project/hands-free-keyboard/
22. Steven Nowlan, Ali Ebrahimi, David Richard Whaley, Pierre Demartines, Sreeram Balakrishnan, and Sheridan Rawlins. 2001. Data entry apparatus having a limited number of character keys and method. Retrieved from https://www.google.com/patents/US6204848
23. Nuance. 2016. T9 Text Input. Retrieved September 15, 2016 from http://www.nuance.com/for-business/by-product/t9/index.htm
24. Alexandra Papoutsaki, Patsorn Sangkloy, James Laskey, Nediyana Daskalova, Jeff Huang, and James Hays. 2016. WebGazer: Scalable Webcam Eye Tracking Using User Interactions. In *Proceedings of the 25th International Joint Conference on Artificial Intelligence*, 3839–3845.

25. Sarah Marie Swift. 2012. Low-Tech, Eye-Movement-Accessible AAC and Typical Adults.
26. The ALS Association. 2016. Facts You Should Know. Retrieved September 15, 2016 from http://www.alsa.org/about-als/facts-you-should-know.html
27. TheEyeTribe. 2016. The Eye Tribe. Retrieved September 15, 2016 from https://theeyetribe.com/
28. Tobii. 2016. Tobii Dynavox Webshop. Retrieved September 15, 2016 from https://www.tobiiati-webshop.com/
29. Tobii. 2016. Communicator 5 - Tobii Dynavox. Retrieved September 15, 2016 from http://www.tobiidynavox.com/communicator5/
30. Tobii. 2016. Sono Lexis - Tobii Dynavox. Retrieved September 15, 2016 from http://www.tobiidynavox.com/sono-lexis/
31. Vytautas Vaitukaitis and Andreas Bulling. 2012. Eye gesture recognition on portable devices. In *Proceedings of the 2012 ACM Conference on Ubiquitous Computing - UbiComp '12*, 711. http://doi.org/10.1145/2370216.2370370
32. David Vitter. 2015. S.768 - Steve Gleason Act of 2015. Retrieved September 15, 2016 from https://www.congress.gov/bill/114th-congress/senate-bill/768
33. Zhou Wang, Alan Conrad Bovik, Hamid Rahim Sheikh, and Eero P. Simoncelli. 2004. Image quality assessment: From error visibility to structural similarity. *IEEE Transactions on Image Processing* 13, 4: 600–612. http://doi.org/10.1109/TIP.2003.819861
34. David J. Ward, Alan F. Blackwell, and David J. C. MacKay. 2002. Dasher: A Gesture-Driven Data Entry Interface for Mobile Computing. *Human-Computer Interaction* 17, 2/3: 199–228.
35. Craig Watman, David Austin, Nick Barnes, Gary Overett, and Simon Thompson. 2004. Fast sum of absolute differences visual landmark detector. In *IEEE International Conference on Robotics and Automation, 2004. Proceedings. ICRA '04. 2004*, 4827–4832 Vol.5. http://doi.org/10.1109/ROBOT.2004.1302482
36. Jacob O. Wobbrock, Shaun K. Kane, Krzysztof Z. Gajos, Susumu Harada, and Jon Froehlich. 2011. Ability-Based Design: Concept, Principles and Examples. *ACM Transactions on Accessible Computing* 3, 3: 1–27. http://doi.org/10.1145/1952383.1952384
37. Jacob O. Wobbrock, James Rubinstein, Michael W. Sawyer, and Andrew T. Duchowski. 2008. Longitudinal evaluation of discrete consecutive gaze gestures for text entry. In *Proceedings of the 2008 symposium on Eye tracking research & applications*, 11. http://doi.org/10.1145/1344471.1344475

Exploring the Design Space of AAC Awareness Displays

Kiley Sobel[1,2], Alexander Fiannaca[1,2], Jon Campbell[2], Harish Kulkarni[2], Ann Paradiso[2], Edward Cutrell[2], Meredith Ringel Morris[2]
[1]University of Washington, Seattle, WA, USA; [2]Microsoft Research, Redmond, WA, USA
ksobel@uw.edu, {alfianna, jon.campbell, harish.kulkarni, annpar, cutrell, merrie}@microsoft.com

ABSTRACT
Augmentative and alternative communication (AAC) devices are a critical technology for people with disabilities that affect their speech. One challenge with AAC systems is their inability to portray aspects of nonverbal communication that typically accent, complement, regulate, or substitute for verbal speech. In this paper, we explore the design space of awareness displays that can supplement AAC devices, considering their output features and their effects on the perceptions of interlocutors. Through designing prototypes and getting feedback on our designs from people with ALS, their primary caregivers, and other communication partners, we consider (1) the consistent tensions that arose between abstractness and clarity in meaning for these designs and (2) the ways in which these designs can further mark users as "other." Overall, we contribute a generative understanding of designing AAC awareness displays to augment and contextualize communication.

Author Keywords
AAC; accessibility; ALS; awareness displays; conversational awareness; conversational flow; emotion expression; nonverbal communication; disability.

ACM Classification Keywords
K.4.2. Social issues: Assistive technologies.

INTRODUCTION
Amyotrophic Lateral Sclerosis (ALS) is a neurodegenerative disease that progressively weakens individuals' muscles to the point where they are unable to walk, speak, eat, or breathe without the help of assistive technology [31]. As people with ALS (PALS) lose their ability to speak, they can use augmentative and alternative communication (AAC) systems to communicate. PALS typically input text into AAC devices using eye gaze, which is generally not impaired during the disease progression [3], and the device speaks aloud the words they have typed in a synthetic voice using text-to-speech (TTS) technology.

Permission to make digital or hard copies of all or part of this work for personal or classroom use is granted without fee provided that copies are not made or distributed for profit or commercial advantage and that copies bear this notice and the full citation on the first page. Copyrights for components of this work owned by others than the author(s) must be honored. Abstracting with credit is permitted. To copy otherwise, or republish, to post on servers or to redistribute to lists, requires prior specific permission and/or a fee. Request permissions from Permissions@acm.org.
CHI 2017, May 06 - 11, 2017, Denver, CO, USA
Copyright is held by the owner/author(s). Publication rights licensed to ACM.
ACM 978-1-4503-4655-9/17/05…$15.00
DOI: http://dx.doi.org/10.1145/3025453.3025610

One challenge with AAC systems is their inability to portray aspects of nonverbal communication that typically accent, complement, regulate, or substitute for verbal speech. This is particularly salient for people with ALS, who are not able to nonverbally communicate through movements like gesturing or making facial expressions. This lack of nonlinguistic information affects aspects of communication such as conversational flow, emotion expressivity, and personality representation [19,33]. Conversational flow is not only affected because of the slow speed of eye gaze input, but also because little information is given to conversation partners about PALS' conversation "status" (e.g., listening, typing, or resting) or social cueing (i.e., indications for turn-taking) [19]. The devices also do not allow much emotional expressivity, mostly due to minimal paralinguistic changes in speech output [19]; and AAC systems are not considered fashionable or reflective of speakers' personalities [19]. Consequently, AAC devices, while improving communication and quality of life for PALS beyond simple communication boards [7], could still be significantly improved in supporting more effective and expressive participation in conversations [19].

In this paper, we explore the design space of awareness displays for AAC devices, considering their output features and their effects on the perceptions of both speakers and listeners. The term "awareness display" mainly stems from work by Tran et al. [56,57], who focus on the importance of interlocutors' awareness of the subtle, social, and contextual cues that are necessary for people to naturally communicate in person. In our case, we focus on designing awareness displays for conversational flow and emotional information to augment and contextualize communication for AAC users and their conversation partners.

Using an integrative research approach, we documented our process as we designed various displays. This design process began by creating a taxonomy of the dimensions that are significant to AAC awareness displays. We then iteratively designed six different displays that varied along two key dimensions of this taxonomy, *resolution* and *abstractness*. The six designs incorporated the following components: text, emoticons, emoji, an avatar, skins (i.e., thematic animations), and colored LED clusters. Based on feedback from people's initial understandings and perceptions of the designs, we built three (text, emoji, colored LED clusters) into an eye gaze controlled AAC device. We used this integrated system as the basis of an exploratory user study that allowed us to better understand 24 communication partners' perceptions of the three designs in the context of one-on-one small talk. Finally, we presented the designs to seven people with ALS and their communication partners.

By reflecting on this design process, the artifacts, and people's perceptions, we discuss (1) the tensions that arose between peoples' preferences toward clarity over abstractness in the designs; and (2) the ways in which these designs can further mark people with ALS (or AAC users) as "other" [34,49], play into currently normative patterns of communication, and/or create new communication paradigms that might better reflect speakers' personalities. Overall, we contribute a generative understanding of designing AAC awareness displays to augment and improve conversational cueing and emotional expressivity during communication.

RELATED WORK

AAC Devices for People with ALS

People with ALS rely on AAC devices to communicate [5]. They often start by controlling these systems with touch, and later transition to eye gaze input as they progressively lose motor control [15]. A main area of research in AAC has focused on improving the speed of eye gaze input (e.g. [21,22,28,38,58]). Another area of work is on advancing text-to-speech (TTS) technology to improve the quality of synthetic speech [63]. This has included creating customized system voices (i.e., *voice fonts*) so that the output speech matches the speaker's voice to a greater degree [59,68]. Others have explored using natural language generation to improve aspects of communication, like storytelling [46] and joking [61], by suggesting relevant messages.

While AAC technologies are used by many people with ALS [5] and have improved communication in many ways [7], research has not fully addressed the needs of PALS in regard to AAC [4,19,63]. In their interview study with seven PALS and their close companions, Kane et al. [19] studied how PALS deal with changes in their ability to communicate and how AAC device use has impacted their self-expression. Their findings illuminated PALS' challenges related to (1) conversation pacing and flow (i.e., turn-taking) due to the lack of 'feedthrough' [2] when they are using the device; (2) conveying emotions, mostly due to the lack of voice modulation; (3) their decreased ability to argue, be humorous and sarcastic, and sound warm and less stern; and (4) shifting roles in their lives; for instance, those who were once extroverted became more passive, and those who cared about fashion no longer felt stylish. Kane et al. [19] urge researchers to think beyond AAC performance metrics (like wpm) to matters like users' ability to be emotionally expressive and participate equally, take turns in, and direct conversations. In our work, we begin to address these issues, which we conceptualize through the design of awareness technology.

Awareness Technology

Awareness technology refers to systems that make onlookers or partners more aware of a user's identity, status in a conversation, or emotional state [56,57]. A good example of this is online messaging systems. Users of these systems may have a handle and icon that make other users aware of their identity. Typing indicators (e.g., "…"), away messages, and idle times make users more aware of conversational flow. Emoticons, emoji, GIFs, stickers, and other related ideograms plus stylized text (like ALL CAPS or *asterisks*) add emotional awareness to conversations.

Few AAC researchers have utilized the concept of awareness in their work. One example is Feuston [11], who developed *Expressiv*, a system that projects facial expressions onto a person with ALS to augment her ability to emote; this design, while provocative, was not validated with actual AAC users [11]. Directly building on this work, Vujic et al. [60] developed MoodLens, which shows emoticons in an 8x8 pixel display on a wearer's eyeglasses. Through evaluation with 20 participants who watched videos of someone using MoodLens, the authors found that the system improved expressivity and was considered socially acceptable to these viewers (who did not have or know anyone with ALS). We develop this work further by exploring multiple design options and by considering the perspectives of actual AAC users and interlocutors in a natural conversation.

Moreover, Toby Churchill Ltd. developed the Lightwriter®, a TTS device that has a text display facing conversation partners [8]; the display shows the letters as the speaker types or otherwise inputs them. Similarly, AACrobat connects AAC devices to a conversation partner's mobile phone app; the app displays text as it is typed or shows a status message ("typing…"), depending on the AAC user's privacy preferences [12]. Pullin [42] speculated how designers might design systems to present text being composed via AAC devices in unconventional, artistic forms.

Researchers have also investigated how technology can make individuals with certain disabilities more aware of their communication partners' nonverbal behaviors (e.g., [6,20,24,30,43,48,62]). For example, *EmoAssist* is a smartphone-based system for people with visual impairments, which translates nonverbal communicative behaviors like yawns and smiles to audio output [44].

In other areas of design research (not specific to disability), there has been more work done that has specifically addressed conversational, emotional, and identity awareness during communication. Schierer and Picard [47] developed a theory for building objects that communicate emotions and offer a framework to map affect to light, sound, color, and movement. Many researchers have used this theory to create wearables that make co-located and remote viewers more aware of the wearer's emotional state (e.g., [1,9,27,32,64,65]). Likewise, researchers have created shape-changing interfaces to communicate emotion during interpersonal remote communication (e.g., [37,53]). Researchers in remote communication have also designed and studied awareness for robotic telepresence [25,45,51], video chat [54], and text and online instant messaging [10,16]. Finally, Leung et al. [24] designed a system that projects a visualization of a person's real-time online social identity to the public, above a person onto the ceiling, connecting her virtual and physical selves. We drew on all of this research and design for our AAC awareness display work.

Social Acceptability & Identity in Accessibility Research

In his book *Design Meets Disability,* design researcher Graham Pullin [42] discusses the various tensions that arise when we "design for disability" (p. 2). These include conflicts between designing for people's diverse individual identities vs. their clinically shared abilities; for fashion (which usually has the purpose of standing out) vs. discretion; and for pure information exchange vs. aesthetic expression (particularly in the development of AAC).

Relatedly, Kane et al. [18] and Shinohara et al. [50] found that assistive technology (AT) being too conspicuous in public may cause some individuals to stop using the devices that would otherwise help them. Shinohara et al. [50] conceptualize an approach connected to these issues called design for *social acceptance*. Because AT often looks extremely different than mainstream devices and draws unwanted attention, these authors argue that we should not only consider functionality and usability when designing AT but also take into account (mis)perceptions and aesthetics that might stigmatize users or maximize socially acceptability [50]. However, Profita et al. [41] found that public observers may consider a conspicuous (or commonly negatively perceived) device as more socially acceptable if the device is AT. We draw on these tensions and the notion of *social acceptability* in our study of awareness displays.

DESIGN PROCESS

While there is often friction about whether accessibility research is a "problem solving" endeavor (from a medical or engineering perspective) or a more open-ended and/or creative effort (from a design perspective) [42], we agree with Pullin [42] that "design for disability would benefit from a better balance of these complementary approaches" (p. 45). Following other significant HCI work in accessibility that incorporates exploratory research methods and follows a holistic process that considers a person more fully, we took a more integrative exploratory approach to our research. We designed, considered the experiences of multiple actors, and engaged in constant reflection in this multi-faceted and complex communication situation. We began our research by iteratively designing while documenting and reflecting on the process. Later, we carried out lab studies with users with and without disabilities since our design must address the needs of both conversation partners (i.e., what Pullin [42] calls "resonant design"). Ultimately, using an integrative methodology prompted us to think beyond one perspective [13,42] and explore awareness displays from complementary angles.

Awareness Display Taxonomy

At the beginning of our design process, we created a taxonomy of the dimensions that one could explore when designing AAC awareness displays. We began by brainstorming as many factors as possible without judgment, based on the related literature and our expertise in design, HCI, accessibility, AAC devices, and doing research with people with ALS. We iterated on this list over three brainstorm sessions, continually expanding and narrowing down the factors until we reached consensus [36]. We then iteratively grouped the factors according to five broad themes (Table 1): *input features, output features, practicality, scenario,* and *user perception. Input features* denote ways in which the awareness display will be controlled, and *output features* include the ways it will be presented toward communication partners. *Practicality* includes engineering-focused considerations for the design. Within *scenario* are factors that relate to when, where, and why the display will be used. *User perception* refers to the ways the person controlling the awareness display or his communication partners perceive the experience with and qualities of the display.

While extensive, our taxonomy is not necessarily exhaustive, and the dimensions are not all mutually exclusive, nor are they completely orthogonal (i.e., many influence each other – e.g., resolution may influence cost). It is also important to note that the factors may differ depending on which "user" we are considering: the person speaking through the AAC device or her communication partner. This encapsulation of the design space works as an exploratory tool to think with, which we used to narrow down and examine our designs.

Initial Designs & Reflection

After developing our taxonomy, we decided to focus on two main dimensions of AAC awareness displays: *output features* and their effect on *user perception.* Within output features, we varied (1) the *display resolution* and (2) the *abstractness* of the display's meaning. *Display resolution* is interesting mainly due to issues of practicality (e.g., a lower resolution display could be less expensive, use less energy, and be smaller/less obtrusive). *Abstractness* of meaning is interesting because this has implications for user perception and usability. For instance, while less abstract designs may be easier to learn, more abstract designs may be subtler and provide ambiguity typical in communication.

We iteratively brainstormed and designed different types of outputs that varied along these two dimensions, as well as a variety of other output constraints. For instance, we began with prototypes for both audio and visual output, but later scoped to only visual designs. For the sake of space in this paper, we will present the six visual designs on which we most consistently iterated: **text** (low res, low abstractness); **emoticons** (low res, medium abstractness); **emoji** (high res, medium abstractness); **avatar** (high res, medium abstractness); **skins**, in our case, animated nature scenes (high res, high abstractness); and a **colored LED cluster** similar to the design concept proposed (but never evaluated) by Kane et al. [19] (low res, high abstractness).

For each of these six displays, we implemented a set of five conversational cues and six emotions. The five conversational cues were based on work by Kane et al. [19], describing important concepts that PALS often wish to express in conversation: *listening*, *talking*, *typing*, saying *"Hold on,"* and asking *"Pardon me?"* We choose the six emotions based on models of universal emotions [35,39,40] and Kane et al.'s work [19]: *happy*, *sad*, *angry*, *sarcastic*, *laughing*, and *caring*. Examples of each of the designs with detailed descriptions are in Table 2; please see the Appendix and Video Figure to view all of the designs' contents.

The process of designing the six types of displays along two awareness dimensions brought up two themes that consistently emerged throughout the study. The first theme was ***discomfort with abstractness in meaning***. For highly abstract designs and the cues and emotions that could be represented multiple ways, the choices that we made (although based on prior work and theory of affective objects [47]) sometimes felt too indiscriminate and too ambiguous, depending on the context. For example, for **skins**, choosing what nature scene would represent *listening* felt personal and at the same time disconnected from its meaning; could waves washing ashore perhaps associate with the movement of a slow head nod? Would a pink sunset feel *caring* to communication partners, or would it evoke calmness?

For the **colored LED cluster**, we had to make choices about whether we wanted to play into normative paradigms of representation that might be more familiar (e.g., animated audio signal processing waves to signify *listening*; a smiley-looking face for *happy*) or create more abstract color animations (e.g., slow blinking green lights as a sign of being engaged, nodding, and *listening*; fast moving, blinking bright yellow lights for *happy*). This idea leads to the second theme that arose throughout the design process: tensions between designing "socially acceptable" or normative displays (e.g., **emoticons** and **emoji** are already used in text and online messaging) vs. digital artifacts that might further ***mark speakers as "other"*** because they are uncommon in current forms of communication. For our initial designs, especially those that were more abstract, we positioned our designs as artifacts that indicate '*what might be*' as opposed to *'what is'* [14]. In this process, we realized that this decision might come into conflict with the experiences of PALS, their caregivers, and communication partners *now*, marking these abstract designs as "different," and the common designs as preferable, especially without long-term in situ use. However, in this exploration, we became interested in what types of feelings and perceptions the designs evoked in people, which served to create generative understandings of this design space.

Communication Partner Interpretation

The initial process of design and reflection led to our first mixed-methods exploration into how people with little or no experience communicating with AAC users with ALS might interpret and perceive the different types of displays. While such users are not representative of frequent communication

Category	Dimension
Input Features	Always on vs. sometimes on
	Amount of customizability vs. static input
	Amount of user input
	Continuous vs. discrete
	Explicit/manual vs. implicit/automatic
	Location (e.g., from body, in device)
	Prediction
	Scaffolding for user
	Sensing/aware of context
	Transformation of input
	Type (e.g. GSR, sentiment analysis, etc.)
Output Features	Abstract vs. clear (meaning)
	Always on vs. sometimes on
	Amount of output/time scale
	Augmentative vs. replacement vs. separate
	Continuous vs. discrete
	Dynamic vs. static
	Embodiment
	Form factor (virtual, physical, 2D, 3D, etc.)
	Location (on person, chair, etc.)
	Low vs. high tech
	Modality (audio, visual, multi, etc.)
	Recognizable features (e.g., street signs, symbols)
	Resolution
Practicality	Cost
	Battery life/power
	Efficacy
	Maintenance (setup, over time)
	Materials
	Noticeability/visibility
	Optimized for ability
	Portability/size
	Reliability
	Training
Scenario	Location (co-located vs. remote)
	Private vs. public communication
	Purpose (type of awareness)
	Scalability (dyads, small or large groups)
	Target audience demographic
	Target user demographic (age, ability)
	Type of design (universal, accessibility, etc.)
User Perceptions	Aesthetically pleasing/beauty
	Burden/complexity
	Comfort
	Disruptiveness
	Dys-appearance [23]
	Habituation
	Impact on autonomy
	Learnability (how to interpret meaning)
	Learnability (how to use)
	Privacy
	Related to personality/personal style
	Social acceptability [50]
	Subtlety

Table 1. Taxonomy of dimensions to consider when designing AAC awareness displays (in alphabetical order).

partners of PALS (e.g., spouses, friends, professional caregivers, etc.), they do provide a reasonable facsimile of the kinds of casual conversation partners PALS encounter (e.g., employees in a store, an infrequent visitor, etc.). These people would not have time to learn how to interpret an AAC awareness display and would have to quickly interpret its meaning.

We deployed two online questionnaires (one for conversational flow and one for emotion) that involved three parts each. The first part presented unlabeled non-text designs for each intended meaning (i.e., *talking*, *typing*, etc.) in random order. We asked an open-ended question about what participants thought each meant, in one word, regarding communication. We did not include **skins** in the conversational flow questionnaire because pilot-testing within our research team indicated they were largely uninterpretable. **Text** was not shown in this first part or the second because the **text** display already presents an unambiguous meaning. Second, after respondents indicated what they thought the designs meant, they ranked them according to how accurately they felt that the designs depicted our intended meaning (i.e., "depiction accuracy"). For example, in the emotion survey, participants were shown the **emoticon**, **emoji**, **avatar**, **skins**, and **colored LED cluster** designs for *happy*. Then, participants ranked them from most to least accurate in depicting *happiness*. In the third part of the questionnaire, we showed all of the displays, including **text**, and asked the participants to rank them from their most to least favorite designs overall. We also asked them to describe why they chose this ranking. The goal of the two questionnaires was to help us narrow down which design concepts to include in more thorough user testing, by eliminating designs that would be difficult for casual or new communication partners to interpret without training, and by including designs that would help us further unpack users' perceptions.

Participants

We recruited a total of 81 participants from a large technology company by randomly sampling employees in technical and non-technical positions. Forty participants completed the emotion questionnaire (*Q1-Q40*), and 41 (*Q41-Q81*) completed the conversational flow questionnaire. Ages ranged from 19 to 64 (mean = 37.9 years; SD = 11.2). Thirty-seven (45.7%) identified as female, and 44 as male. Only five participants (6.2%) did not use any form of pictures or symbols (e.g., emoji, emoticon, stickers) in online or text communication. Three participants (3.7%) reported having spoken with someone who uses an AAC device.

Analysis & Findings

Using a joint inductive-deductive approach to qualitative analysis [52], one researcher coded each one-word design interpretation response per its dictionary meaning. She then grouped the responses according to synonymous meanings. For example, "sad," "gloomy," "melancholy," "upset," and "somber" fit into a general theme of *sadness*. Two to three researchers met to review the codes and thematic groupings and to discuss and clarify disagreements. We then calculated the percentage of thematic responses that correctly corresponded to the intended meaning for each design. Table 3 shows these percentages aggregated for each design.

We also calculated aggregate weighted scores for each design in terms of (1) depiction accuracy and (2) preference by adding all participant rankings for a particular design for each of these measures (items ranked first have a higher value or "weight"). Table 4 shows the weights for depiction accuracy averaged across all content for each type of awareness display. For conversational flow, the designs from most to least favorite were **text** (weight of 190), **emoji** (160), **avatar** (105), and **emoticon**, tied with **colored LED clusters** (80). For emotion, the most to least favorite designs were **emoji** (218), **avatar**, tied with **text** (160), **emoticon** (154), **skins** (75), and **colored LED clusters** (73).

Conversational flow	*Emotion*	*Awareness display type*
		**Text (left: *listening*; right: *sarcastic*):** The exact meanings in plain text. For conversational flow, they are presented in sentences. The emotions are individual words.
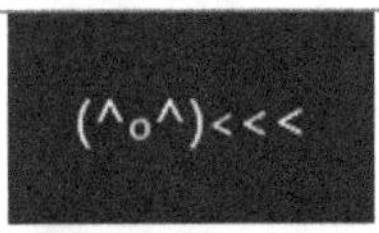		**Emoticon (left: *talking*; right: *happy*):** Pictorial representations using ASCII punctuation marks, numbers, and letters (i.e., emoticons). For emoticons that did not have Western style representations (e.g., *happy*), we used or created Japanese style emoticons (e.g., *talking*).
		**Emoji (left: *hold on*; right: *laughing*):** Static expressive symbols, currently popularly used in text and online communication. Here, the emoji are from Windows 10. The majority of emotions are face-based, while the conversational cues are other types of ideograms.
		**Avatar (left: *Pardon me?*; right: *angry*):** An animated Xbox Live Avatar, available through Windows. Animations last from anywhere between 1-15 seconds. The animations repeat until the corresponding key is released or the action (i.e., *typing*) stops.
		**Skins (left: *talking*; right: *sad*):** Animated thematic videos; in our case, nature scenes retrieved from Creative Commons. Animations lasted from between 1-12 seconds and repeated as necessary. (Left by Always Shooting / CC BY 2.0; right by Frank Vincentz / CC BY-SA 3.0.)
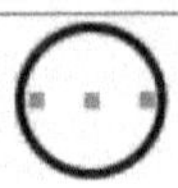		**Colored LED cluster (left: *typing*; right: *caring*):** Brightly colored LEDs animate within a circle, and repeat as necessary. Some emotions are modeled after faces/emoticons, while conversational cues are abstract symbols and movement.

Table 2. Examples of each type of awareness display for various conversational cues and emotions. Please see the Appendix and the Video Figure for all of the displays' contents.

Finally, following our prior qualitative analysis process [52], we open coded participants' qualitative explanations for their favorite ranking order, which resulted in six consistent themes: (1) **Text** is most precise, which is preferable for conversation flow. (2) The abstract displays (**colored LED cluster** and **skins**) are "too" individually interpretable. (3) Interpretation should be "direct" and "quick." (4) **Emoji** are common and "universal." (5) The **avatar** is more expressive and better for conveying affective information. (6) The **skins** are more beautiful and interesting.

To increase its interpretability, one participant (*Q70*) suggested combining **text** with the **avatar**. Similarly, another (*Q58*) indicated the **colored LED cluster** needs a key. Only one participant (*Q33*) noted how abstract and multiple interpretations might be more realistic to the communication of emotion: *"I like the abstraction of the [skins], how it leaves room for interpretation and doesn't attempt to oversimplify something as complex as emotion and feeling."*

Reflections & Implications for our Design Process

The quantitative answers and qualitative themes that emerged from this study paralleled some of the initial threads of our design process. The notion that communication should be straightforward, "leav[ing] no room for interpretation" (*Q56*), plays into the ***discomfort with abstract meanings*** we had while designing. From the perspective of potential casual interpreters of AAC awareness displays, less abstract designs were favored for both conversational flow and emotion awareness. This was despite the fact that, even without any contextual communication clues, participants guessed the meanings almost equally on average across all of the displays (with the exception of **emoji** and **skins** being on opposite extremes) (see Table 3).

Furthermore, the continual reference to **emoji** as common and universal relates to the concept that other types of displays might further ***mark AAC device users as "other."*** By choosing to incorporate currently conventional forms of communication into our designs, we may increase not only their understandability but also their social acceptability [50] and, in turn, decrease stigma. However, this comes into conflict with the idea of designing for *'what might be'* [14].

Using these results and reflections, we chose three designs to integrate into a working system for further evaluation: **text**, **emoji**, and the **colored LED cluster**. We chose **text** because of its straightforward nature; **emoji** because it is normative and performed well in terms of interpretability and preference in our questionnaire; and the **colored LED cluster** because, while some people were uncomfortable with it, its inclusion in the next step of our process allowed us to further investigate a design that landed on different parts of the *resolution* and *abstractness* spectra. Because lower resolution displays have some *practical* advantages, it was important to include this design in later evaluations.

	emoticon	*emoji*	*avatar*	*skins*	*LEDs*
convo	32%	72%	49%	N/A	45%
emotion	58%	76%	58%	30%	55%

Table 3. Percent of responses overall in which reported design meanings were similar to their intended meanings.

	emoticon	*emoji*	*avatar*	*skins*	*LEDs*
convo	89	144	90	N/A	87
emotion	122	179	144	64	91

Table 4. Average weight of depiction accuracy for each display design (higher numbers indicate better accuracy).

ONE-ON-ONE CONVERSATIONS

To extend our exploration, we wanted to see how these three display designs might affect conversation partners' perceptions during a one-on-one chat with a person using an AAC device. Supplementing the interpretation questionnaire, this lab study allowed us to probe more deeply into how conversation partners interpret and perceive the displays in a more realistic context that did not ignore the challenges of communicating when dialogue is mediated by an AAC system.

Participants

We recruited 24 participants (*S1-S24*) with a variety of job roles (e.g., human resources assistants, legal specialists, software engineers) from our organization. The participants were randomly assigned to one of the three display types such that there were eight participants per type. One participant identified as non-binary, 12 as female, and 11 as male. Three participants were in the 46-55 age range; 10 were 26-35; and 11 were 18-25. Only one reported not using any form of pictures or symbols (e.g., emoji, emoticons) in digital communication. All participants were fluent in English, although three were non-native English speakers. None of the participants had previously spoken to someone who uses an AAC device.

Materials

We integrated the awareness display into a fully operational eye gaze controlled AAC device, implemented in C# on a Microsoft Surface Pro 4. The display could be set to show **text**, **emoji**, or an animated image simulating a **colored LED cluster**. The content appeared on an Adafruit Qualia 9.7" DisplayPort Monitor (2048x1536) on a vertical desk stand, facing the conversation partner (Figure 1).

We modified the AAC device's keyboard by adding keys for all six emotions (*happy, sad, angry, sarcastic, laughing*, and *caring*) and for three conversational cues (*listening, hold on*, and *pardon me?*). The system could already detect when the

Figure 1. Lab study setup. Interlocutors sat on either side of AAC device and stand (left). The awareness display faced the conversation partner (right).

user was *typing* or playing text as speech (i.e., *talking*). Typing on the device, speaking through the device, or clicking the added keys (via mouse, touch, or eye gaze) showed the corresponding cue on the awareness display.

Setting & Procedure

We ran the sessions in a room with two ceiling-mounted cameras recording each interlocutor's face and the awareness display. The lead researcher acted as the study facilitator and AAC device user. Rather than controlling the system with her eye gaze, she used the trackpad while looking directly at the AAC keyboard to type on the device; however, she typed at a slow pace that was comparable to the speed of typing with eye gaze (~20 wpm [28]). This is because gaze typing is very fatiguing, so the researcher would have been unable to conduct several study sessions in succession if using gaze input. Gaze input is also extremely error prone, and we did not want errors in speech output to confound the already complex communication dynamics we were attempting to isolate in this study.

After a participant signed a consent form, the researcher explained to him what they would be doing during the session, including describing what an AAC device is, showing a video clip of a person with ALS using an eye gaze controlled AAC device, and making clear that AAC system typing is very slow. Then, the researcher (i.e., the AAC device user) and her conversation partner sat on opposite sides of a round table with the AAC device between them (Figure 1); from this point onward, the researcher did not speak verbally, and relied only on the AAC device to communicate. The researcher usually began the conversation by asking the participant where he was from originally. The rest of the conversation continued as it would naturally in any situation between two people meeting or getting to know each other. Occasionally, when the researcher seemed to be dominating the conversation, she reminded the participant that he could ask her questions so that the chat would be more balanced, as opposed to an interview.

For the first five minutes of talking, they spoke without the awareness display monitor connected to the AAC device. The purpose of this time was for the participant to get used to chatting with a device mediating the conversation. After these five minutes, the lead researcher told the participant that she would be connecting the display to give him more information about the conversation. They spoke with the awareness display connected for 15 minutes (a typical amount of time in AAC research [17]).

Afterward, the participant filled out a computer-based questionnaire about their time talking with the awareness display turned on. The questionnaire asked a set of Likert-scale questions based on scales in AAC research by Wisenburn and Higginbotham [66] and Todman [55]. It also asked 5-point Likert-scale questions specifically about the awareness display content as it related to our *user perception* taxonomy dimension (e.g., how *distracting, familiar, subtle, complex, understandable, helpful,* and *abstract* the display was, where 1 = not at all, and 5 = extremely). For participants who viewed the **emoji** and **colored LED cluster** displays, we asked them if they understood what the display's content related to conversation flow indicated and how well they thought it represented that meaning. Finally, we asked for open-ended comments about their experience and the awareness display. Participants received a US$10 Amazon gift card for their 30-minute participation.

Data Analysis

For the quantitative post-conversation questionnaire, we performed an Aligned Rank Transform [67] on the Likert-scale data to run multivariate analysis of variance tests; based on these results, we then performed pairwise comparison t-tests to check for individual significant differences between the three displays. For clarity, in the findings, we report untransformed means of Likert data. Using a grounded theory approach [52], the lead researcher open coded participants' comments and her own brief reflexive notes from the study sessions; she grouped the codes thematically and then iteratively refined them. Subsequently, two to three researchers met to review the codes and themes. They discussed disagreements, clarified misunderstandings, and refined the themes. For study sessions for which there were pertinent participant responses or notes, we reviewed the recordings to support overall data analysis. We did not code the conversations themselves because we were interested in participants' *perceptions*, as opposed to actual effects on the dialogue.

Findings

The conversation partners who viewed the **colored LED cluster** design had issues with its ambiguity. Some qualitative responses mentioned how the conversation flow animations were "confusing" and "too abstract." Participant *S19* even suggested using more concrete representations instead: *"Using icons such as an Ear [sic] for listening... may be clearer to understand what the other person was doing."* Quantitative differences in conversation partners' perceptions complemented these notions. Participants perceived the **colored LED cluster** to be significantly less helpful for conversational flow (M=2.8; SD=0.89) than both **text** (M=3.9; SD=1.3) and **emoji** (M=4.5; SD=0.76) (p<0.05, η^2=0.38, 1-β=0.86), and significantly less understandable (M=2.9; SD=1.1) than both **text** (M=4.5; SD=1.1) and **emoji** (M=4.5; SD=0.54) (p<0.05, η^2=0.43, 1-β=0.92). Moreover, the **colored LED cluster** was perceived as being significantly worse at depicting *listening* (η^2=0.68, 1-β=1.0), *typing* (η^2=0.42, 1-β=0.84), and *hold on* (η^2=0.32, 1-β=0.66) (all on average "neutral") compared to **emoji** (on average "very well") (all p<0.05).

Participants who only saw **text** made comments related to it being precise. One participant who saw **text** (*S5*) wanted there to be even more precision. She said, *"The information on the screen was helpful, but the emotions displayed could've been a little bit more nuanced ([e.g.,] annoyed/frustrated vs. angry)."* Because of how precise **text** is, there might need to be more distinct emotions displayed on the screen to match the granularity of expression that people know text can allow.

The **text** display also prompted two participants to make comments about wanting to see what the lead researcher was typing as she typed it, whereas no conversation partners who saw the **emoji** or **colored LED cluster** designs made such comments. *S3* said, *"[It would be] helpful if it showed some of the text being input, ahead of the text-to-speech, to help me understand what's coming, and potentially steer the conversation ahead of the other person completing a thought/sentence."*

In terms of emotions, the **emoji** design was perceived by many participants as being particularly expressive. *S14* who saw the **emoji** said, *"The emojis [sic] were very helpful, especially when I'd tell a joke in the middle of what I'm saying [and the researcher would respond with a laughing emoji]. The emojis [sic] allowed much more emotional and real time interaction with things like smiles and laughs or sympathy in real-time with what I'm saying..."* Moreover, two participants who saw the **emoji** display mentioned how the communication was "like texting," while no participants who saw the **text** and **colored LED cluster** displays mentioned something similar.

Finally, one issue around eye contact came up for participants in this user study. Because participants who saw the **text**, **emoji**, and **colored LED cluster** displays all brought up a challenge with eye contact, we believe that this has more to do with personality and the awareness display in general, rather than a particular design. During some conversations, the lead researcher noticed how conversation partners seemed to try very hard to keep eye contact with her while they were talking during the study, and this resulted in them not looking down at the awareness display. Although others seemed to glance up and down from her face to the screen, she also observed some participants staring at the screen instead of looking at her face. Pointedly, *S2* who saw the **text** design noted, *"I think the screen helped me understand what the other person was doing, but it felt like a tradeoff, of making eye contact vs. looking at the screen. It might make me less aware of the person's face, and lose a bit of the humanity of the dialog."*

PALS & THEIR CLOSE CONVERSATION PARTNERS

The last stage in our exploration involved getting direct feedback about the three types of awareness displays from seven people with ALS (*P1-P7*) and their close conversation partners (e.g., family members, significant others, and/or professional caregivers) (*C1-C10*). PALS' ages ranged from their 40's to 60's, and they had lived with ALS for three to five years. One of the seven was female (ALS is more common in men [29]). Four of the PALS use gaze- or head-mouse-based AAC for all communications, and three (*P1*, *P4*, and *P7*) retained some dysarthric speech ability, and did not yet use an AAC device regularly; however, they owned or planned to obtain AAC devices for anticipated future use.

To be sensitive of their limited availability and tendency to fatigue easily, and to ensure they focused on the *output* as opposed to the *input* mechanisms, we had the PALS and their conversation partners watch a five-minute video describing the awareness display. Similar to our Video Figure, this video showed the **text**, **emoji**, and the **colored LED cluster** designs and included recordings of two people using the three display types during short conversations. This allowed the PALS and their conversation partners to see how the displays work both in and out of context.

After watching the video, conversation partners filled out a questionnaire that asked them how much they liked each type of display (separately for conversational flow and emotions), and asked them to describe a situation (if any) in which they felt this type of display might be helpful and why. While the conversation partner(s) filled out the questionnaire, a researcher asked an equivalent set of quantitative questions to the PALS. Because communication for PALS can be slow and fatiguing, we focused mostly on multiple-choice questions rather than open-ended comments; the researcher would read the question and the set of possible answers, and then would say each answer aloud until the PAL gave an agreed-upon signal (e.g., blinking, grunting, typing via AAC) to indicate their answer choice. To those who were able to speak or type a longer response, the researcher also asked for any qualitative feedback on each of the displays, including suggestions or justifications for their multiple-choice responses. Again, we followed our prior qualitative analysis processes [52] of individual open coding and thematic grouping, and discussions with two to three researchers to discuss, clarify, and refine codes and themes.

Findings

On average, across all of the participants for both conversational flow and emotions, the **colored LED cluster** was rated the lowest in terms of how much they would want the display (i.e., all "neutral," rather than toward "very much") and was ranked on average as least favorite. For most of the PALS, **text** was ranked as most favorite for conversational flow and second favorite for emotions. On average, PALS ranked **emoji** as their second favorite for conversational flow and most favorite for emotions. These findings held overall for their close conversation partners too. Table 5 shows the average favorite rankings for the designs.

Qualitative feedback about the displays from PALS and their close conversation partners expanded on theses quantitative answer choices. Many conversation partners noted how the **colored LED cluster** is ambiguous and **text** is more straightforward. *P3*'s brother (*C6*) noted it would be necessary *"to train people as to what some of the different abstract lights [i.e., the **colored LED cluster**] represent - text is easier."* Similarly, *P7*'s wife (*C10*) said the **colored LED cluster** would *"not [be] easily understood by [casual] visitors, so I wouldn't want to have to explain what he is saying through the lights."* *P1* explained that if we could get the **colored LED cluster** to look more descriptive, he would like it more.

He then suggested putting a key next to the **colored LED cluster** to make the meanings clearer. Likewise, *P1*'s nephew and caregiver (*C2*) remarked for emotions, *"[**Text** is] to the point, but less fun than emoji."*

A few participants suggested combining **text** and **emoji** designs to make their meanings more obvious or more expressive. *P3*'s brother (*C6*) thought that **emoji** could be added to **text** to stress its meaning. *P1* requested the opposite so that if someone does not understand the **emoji**, it will be clearer: *"If it's not a big deal, make an **emoji** with a little **text** on them." P6*'s husband (*C9*) suggested combining all three designs to be more interesting, or stylizing the text to make it more expressive.

However, some recognized unique benefits of the **colored LED cluster** that the lab study participants, who were unfamiliar with AAC devices and people who use them, did not. Specifically, *P5*'s wife (*C8*) recognized, *"I could see the [**colored LED cluster**] **display** easily if I weren't in the immediate vicinity."* She also called it *"an attention grabber."* Likewise, *P1*'s nephew and caregiver (*C2*) called the **colored LED cluster** *"accessible"* and *"attention grabbing." P1* said the **colored LED cluster** was *"more fun."*

A few of the PALS' close conversation partners noted how **emoji** and **text** are normative, and, thus, more "normal." For instance, *P3*'s significant other (*C5*) said, *"[**Emoji**] are most similar to what others use (texting) so nice that it is more 'normal.'"* Correspondingly, *P2*'s wife (*C3*) explained that **text** and **emoji** for conversation flow are *"[m]ore like normal conversation."*

The conversation partner participants also liked how **emoji** are, as their name denotes, more emotional as well. *P2*'s wife (*C3*) specified that *"**emoji** communicate feelings better,"* while *P5*'s wife (*C8*) indicated, *"**Emojis** [sic] would provide immediate insight."*

In regard to issues of personality, a few PALS conveyed how they would want to be able to add other types of emotions and customize what is shown on the display. For instance, *P4*, who really liked the **emoji** design, mentioned that "shocked" is another emotion he would want for the awareness display. *P7* said he might also like to have "concerned," "frightened," and "upset." *P1* expressed how, when he was able to move more, he would smile and nod a lot when other people were talking to him. He lamented that now *"they [conversation partners] think I'm bored."* Therefore, he wanted to be able to better show "enthusiastic listening" on the awareness display. As a type of suggestion, he told us when he communicates online with a group currently, he likes to use a GIF of a bag of movie popcorn being eaten to indicate he is paying attention and to portray this "enthusiastic listening" feeling.

Finally, all of the PALS and their conversation partners were receptive to and liked the general idea of an awareness display. The PALS said things like the following: *"It's a great idea"* (*P1*); *"That would be useful"* (*P2*); *"I like the general concept"* (*P3*); and *"I think it's a good concept"* (*P7*). Their close conversation partners gave more detail for why this type of display might be important to them personally or for communication overall. *P3*'s significant other (*C5*) explained, *"I think it would be most helpful for people that aren't around very often. People that get uncomfortable waiting for a response from [him] (so 'typing' would help); or that don't get his sense of humor/way of speaking."* On a more personal note, *P2*'s wife (*C3*) said, *"I miss [my husband]'s voice, and our conversations. Anything that can help restore some of that would be so wonderful."*

		text	*emoji*	*LEDs*
PALS	*convo*	1 (0.5)	2 (0.7)	3 (0.5)
	emotion	2 (0.0)	1 (0.8)	3 (0.8)
CPs	*convo*	2 (0.7)	2 (0.7)	3 (0.5)
	emotion	2 (0.7)	1 (0.3)	3 (0.5)

Table 5. Average ranking, rounded to one significant digit, (with SD) for favorite displays of PALS and conversation partners (CPs) (1: most favorite; 3: least favorite).

DISCUSSION

From the beginning to the end of our study, matters related to ***abstractness in meaning*** and further ***marking AAC device users as "other"*** persisted in our reflections and findings. These issues were entangled with other dimensions of our taxonomy, as well (which we indicate with *italics*).

In both the questionnaire and lab studies, participants recognized the difficulty in interpreting more ambiguous awareness indicators. Thus, they perceived them to be *less learnable*. Despite it being more *practical*, especially in terms of *cost, power, maintenance*, and *reliability* due to it being a *low resolution* display, the **colored LED cluster** might not be appropriate for most forms of conversation. The PALS and their close conversation partners brought up similar concerns, but also identified situations in which such a *low resolution, highly abstract* display might be appropriate (i.e., to grab attention or flag an emergency).

At the same time, the least abstract of the displays, **text**, was favored by participants because of its precision, especially for conversation flow. Clarity seemed to be key in this context. However, this was at the expense of "fun" (*C2*), *beauty*, and ambiguity common in typical conversations. In addition, lab study participants who saw the **text** design brought up matters that could affect the display's *efficacy* or perceived *complexity* and challenge a speaker's *privacy*. Specifically, **text** for emotions may not be nuanced enough, causing more misinterpretations in conversations. Or, if we included more emotions (i.e., "frustrated" and "annoyed" instead of "angry," like *S5* wanted), we may increase the *burden* on the speaker to pick from more options. At the same time, the fact that only lab study participants who saw the **text** display commented on wanting to see the speaker's typed words as she typed them (like with [8,12,42]) points to possible issues with *privacy* that might arise with having such a display (if listeners assume the speaker can show their typed text). This is an important issue, as Fiannaca et al. [12] found that PALS are only willing to share text as it is being typed with very close conversation partners in certain scenarios; otherwise, they consider it rude or an invasion of *privacy*.

The **emoji** design seemed to be a nice middle ground, although the *highest resolution* of the displays, to be able to increase interpretability and be more emotional, yet capture and represent multiple feelings with one face. Subsequently, this was the design usually favored by the participants, particularly for emotion awareness. Following some of the PALS' and their close conversation partners' suggestions, combining **text** and **emoji** in one design might be most *effective* for conversations. Also, a *high resolution* display is flexible enough to show **text** for conversation flow and **emoji** for emotions, perhaps making it more *effective* too.

Next, as we experienced from the start, a continual conflict emerged between designing *socially acceptable,* normative display content as opposed to that which may further mark speakers as "other." While participants throughout our evaluations described the **emoji** displays as "universal" and even "normal," we argue that this is not a reason to choose such a display design for the long term. Designing for what is current and popular may not be *practical* or sustainable. However, using a *higher resolution* display that could show **emoji** now, and other types of designs now and later allows for both *customizability* and adaptability to changing *socially acceptable* trends. It is even more important to make the display flexible in this way, for people like *P4, P7,* and *P1* who wanted to add their own content, so that the designs can better *fit to the speaker's personality and style.* This makes any question or tension about if we are trying to model realistic conversation or designing for quickness and functionality at the expense of stylish designs more of a moot point. Again, *higher resolution* gives more flexibility to address both. The challenge is balancing this customization with *burden*. If this requires too much effort for *input* or caregiver support for *maintenance*, it might not be used. And, if a high-resolution display adds too much *cost*, *weight*, or *energy* use to a system, it may not be *practical*.

Finally, because it was most contextualized, one issue came up in the lab study that centered around eye contact. If we design an awareness display to be too *large*, *disruptive*, and *not subtle*, we may be taking away from, in the words of *S2,* "the humanity" of the communication. Removing "humanity" means further marking the speaker as "other," which is where more *abstract*, *subtle,* and *ambient* designs might be more appropriate. Rather than putting **text** or an **emoji** front and center, something more like the **colored LED cluster**, but less bright, *smaller*, and in a more *peripheral location* or closer to the eyes (like [60]) might better *augment* communication, keeping focus on the person, not on the device; however, displays near the eyes, while possibly drawing attention upward, risk interfering with gaze-operated AAC.

Limitations & Future Work

In this work, we took an integrative approach to evaluating our awareness display designs, as different methods offer different insights and help balance out each other's limitations. However, readers should bear in mind the limitations of each method when interpreting our findings. Participants in the questionnaire and in-lab conversation studies were not regular communication partners of people with ALS and cannot represent that perspective, but do give insight into the reactions of casual conversation partners and the walk-up-and-usability of a system. The purpose of the conversation study with the researcher simulating AAC use was to lend further realism and context to the interpretation of the awareness displays beyond what was possible in the online questionnaire; though, of course, this does not lend nearly as much realism as an organic conversation with an authentic AAC device user. Our evaluations with PALS and close conversation partners were, by necessity, shorter and less formal than the other studies, but add crucial perspectives of the most frequent, important stakeholders in such systems. Being aware of possible acquiescence bias for these evaluations with PALS is important; however, the fact that participants gave constructive criticisms to the colored LED cluster designs indicates that this bias was reduced.

An extremely important next step is a long-term deployment of awareness displays to true AAC device users. Future work should also be done to validate the number of cues and emotions needed for awareness displays and if this changes over time. Further exploration of resolution and abstractness, since our results may be tied to our representations and their fidelity, is necessary too. Finally, future work needs to unpack more factors within *output features, practicality, scenario,* and *user perceptions*, and the entirety of *input features*, which may have major implications that relate to *burden*, *comfort,* and *impact on autonomy*.

CONCLUSION

We explored the design space of awareness displays for augmentative and alternative communication. By reflecting on our design process and reporting on various interlocutors' perceptions of the display, we revealed key conflicts that arose in regard to (1) the designs being more abstract vs. straightforward and (2) the designs playing into normative paradigms of communication vs. further marking speakers as "other." As an important takeaway from our discussion, we considered how *higher resolution* displays give more flexibility to find the right mix of normativity, abstraction, ambience, and customizability. Our taxonomy provides more directions researchers can investigate in this space. Overall, we contribute a generative understanding of designing AAC awareness displays to augment and improve conversational cueing and emotional expressivity during communication. We hope researchers can use our work to better understand the tensions and potential effects of specific design choices on the perceptions of conversation partners and those who use eye-gaze controlled AAC devices.

ACKNOWLEDGMENTS

We thank our participants and the MSR Enable team.

REFERENCES

1. Sudhanshu S.D.P. Ayyagari, Kunal Gupta, Matt Tait, and Mark Billinghurst. 2015. CoSense: Creating Shared Emotional Experiences. In *Proceedings of the 33rd Annual ACM Conference Extended Abstracts on Human Factors in Computing Systems* (CHI EA '15). ACM, New York, NY, USA, 2007-2012. DOI: http://dx.doi.org/10.1145/2702613.2732839
2. Kevin Baker, Saul Greenberg, and Carl Gutwin. 2001. Heuristic Evaluation of Groupware Based on the Mechanics of Collaboration. In *Engineering for Human-Computer Interaction*, Murray Reed Little and Laurence Nigay (eds.). Springer Berlin Heidelberg, Berlin, Heidelberg, 123-139.
3. Laura J. Ball, Amy S. Nordness, Susan Fager, Katie Kersch, Brianae Mohr, Gary L. Pattee, and David Beukelman. 2010. Eye-gaze access of AAC technology for persons with amyotrophic lateral sclerosis. *Journal of Medical Speech-Language Pathology* 18, 3 (2010), 11-23.
4. Susan Baxter, Pam Enderby, Philippa Evans, and Simon Judge. 2012. Barriers and facilitators to the use of high-technology augmentative and alternative communication devices: a systematic review and qualitative synthesis. *International Journal of Language & Communication Disorders* 47, 2 (March 2012), 115-129. DOI: http://doi.org/10.1111/j.1460-6984.2011.00090.x
5. David Beukelman, Pat Mirenda, Kathryn Garrett, and Janice Light. 2012. *Augmentative and Alternative Communication: Supporting Children and Adults with Complex Communication Needs, Fourth Edition*. Paul H. Brookes Publishing Co, Baltimore.
6. LouAnne E. Boyd, Alejandro Rangel, Helen Tomimbang, Andrea Conejo-Toledo, Kanika Patel, Monica Tentori, and Gillian R. Hayes. 2016. SayWAT: Augmenting Face-to-Face Conversations for Adults with Autism. In *Proceedings of the 2016 CHI Conference on Human Factors in Computing Systems* (CHI '16). ACM, New York, NY, USA, 4872-4883. DOI: http://dx.doi.org/10.1145/2858036.2858215
7. Marco Caligari, Marco Godi, Simone Guglielmetti, Franco Franchignoni, and Antonio Nardone. 2013. Eye tracking communication devices in amyotrophic lateral sclerosis: Impact on disability and quality of life. *Amyotrophic Lateral Sclerosis and Frontotemporal Degeneration* 14, 7-8 (July 2013), 546–552. DOI: http://dx.doi.org/10.3109/21678421.2013.803576
8. Toby Churchill. Lightwriter® SL40. Retrieved September 10, 2016 from http://www.toby-churchill.com/products/lightwriter-sl40/.
9. Felecia Davis, Asta Roseway, Erin Carroll, and Mary Czerwinski. 2013. Actuating mood: design of the textile mirror. In *Proceedings of the 7th International Conference on Tangible, Embedded and Embodied Interaction* (TEI '13). ACM, New York, NY, USA, 99-106. DOI: http://dx.doi.org/10.1145/2460625.2460640
10. Shelly Farnham, Harry R. Chesley, Debbie E. McGhee, Reena Kawal, and Jennifer Landau. 2000. Structured online interactions: improving the decision-making of small discussion groups. In *Proceedings of the 2000 ACM Conference on Computer Supported Cooperative Work* (CSCW '00). ACM, New York, NY, USA, 299-308. DOI: http://dx.doi.org/10.1145/358916.359001
11. Jessica Feuston. 2015. *Expressiv: An Expressive System for Individuals with Facial Paralysis*. MS Thesis. Georgia Institute of Technology, Atlanta, GA.
12. Alexander Fiannaca, Ann Paradiso, Mira Shah, and Meredith Ringel Morris. 2017. AACrobat: Using mobile devices to lower communication barriers and provide autonomy with gaze-based AAC. To appear in *Proceedings of the 2017 ACM Conference on Computer Supported Cooperative Work.* DOI: http://dx.doi.org/10.1145/2998181.2998215
13. Christopher Frauenberger. 2015. Disability and Technology: A Critical Realist Perspective. In *Proceedings of the 17th International ACM SIGACCESS Conference on Computers & Accessibility* (ASSETS '15). ACM, New York, NY, USA, 89-96. DOI: http://dx.doi.org/10.1145/2700648.2809851
14. William Gaver. 2012. What should we expect from research through design? In *Proceedings of the SIGCHI Conference on Human Factors in Computing Systems* (CHI '12). ACM, New York, NY, USA, 937-946. DOI: http://dx.doi.org/10.1145/2207676.2208538
15. Katya Hill. 2010. Advances in augmentative and alternative communication as quality-of-life technology. *Physical Medicine and Rehabilitation Clinics of North America* 21, 1 (February 2010), 43-58. DOI: http://dx.doi.org/10.1016/j.pmr.2009.07.007
16. Ellen Isaacs, Alan Walendowski, and Dipti Ranganthan. 2002. Hubbub: a sound-enhanced mobile instant messenger that supports awareness and opportunistic interactions. In *Proceedings of the SIGCHI Conference on Human Factors in Computing Systems* (CHI '02). ACM, New York, NY, USA, 179-186. DOI: http://dx.doi.org/10.1145/503376.503409
17. Aura Kagan, Joanne Winckel, Sandra Black, Judith Felson Duchan, Nina Simmons-Mackie & Paula Square. 2004. A Set of Observational Measures for Rating Support and Participation in Conversation Between Adults with Aphasia and Their Conversation Partners. *Topics in Stroke Rehabilitation* 11, 1 (January 2004), 67-83, DOI: http://dx.doi.org/10.1310/CL3V-A94A-DE5C-CVBE
18. Shaun K. Kane, Chandrika Jayant, Jacob O. Wobbrock, and Richard E. Ladner. 2009. Freedom to roam: a study of mobile device adoption and accessibility for

people with visual and motor disabilities. In *Proceedings of the 11th international ACM SIGACCESS conference on Computers and accessibility* (Assets '09). ACM, New York, NY, USA, 115-122. DOI: http://dx.doi.org/10.1145/1639642.1639663

19. Shaun K. Kane, Meredith Ringel Morris, Ann Paradiso, and Jon Campbell. 2017. "At times avuncular and cantankerous, with the reflexes of a mongoose": Understanding self-expression through augmentative and alternative communication devices. To appear in *Proceedings of the 2017 ACM Conference on Computer Supported Cooperative Work.* DOI: http://dx.doi.org/10.1145/2998181.2998284
20. Sreekar Krishna and Sethuraman Panchanathan. 2010. Assistive technologies as effective mediators in interpersonal social interactions for persons with visual disability. In *International Conference on Computers for Handicapped Persons*, 316-323. DOI: http://dx.doi.org/10.1007/978-3-642-14100-3_47
21. Per Ola Kristensson and Keith Vertanen. 2012. The potential of dwell-free eye-typing for fast assistive gaze communication. In *Proceedings of the Symposium on Eye Tracking Research and Applications* (ETRA '12), Stephen N. Spencer (Ed.). ACM, New York, NY, USA, 241-244. DOI: http://dx.doi.org/10.1145/2168556.2168605
22. Andrew Kurauchi, Wenxin Feng, Ajjen Joshi, Carlos Morimoto, and Margrit Betke. 2016. EyeSwipe: Dwell-free text entry using gaze paths. In *Proceedings of the 2016 CHI Conference on Human Factors in Computing Systems* (CHI '16). ACM, New York, NY, USA, 1952-1956. DOI: http://dx.doi.org/10.1145/2858036.2858335
23. Drew Leder. 1990. *The Absent Body*. University of Chicago Press.
24. Daniel G. Lee, Deborah I. Fels, and John Patrick Udo. 2007. Emotive captioning. *Computers in Entertainment (CIE) - Interactive TV*. 5, 2 (August 2007), 1-15. DOI: http://dx.doi.org/10.1145/1279540.1279551
25. Min Kyung Lee and Leila Takayama. 2011. "Now, I have a body": Uses and social norms for mobile remote presence in the workplace. *In Proceedings of the SIGCHI Conference on Human Factors in Computing Systems* (CHI '11). ACM, New York, NY, USA, 33-42. DOI: http://dx.doi.org/10.1145/1978942.1978950
26. Mandy Leung, Martin Tomitsch, and Andrew Vande Moere. 2011. Designing a personal visualization projection of online social identity. In *CHI '11 Extended Abstracts on Human Factors in Computing Systems* (CHI EA '11). ACM, New York, NY, USA, 1843-1848. DOI: http://dx.doi.org/10.1145/1979742.1979882
27. Diana MacLean, Asta Roseway, and Mary Czerwinski. 2013. MoodWings: A wearable biofeedback device for real-time stress intervention. In *Proceedings of the 6th International Conference on Pervasive Technologies Related to Assistive Environments* (PETRA '13). ACM, New York, NY, USA. DOI: http://dx.doi.org/10.1145/2504335.2504406
28. Päivi Majaranta, Ulla-Kaija Ahola, and Oleg Špakov. 2009. Fast gaze typing with an adjustable dwell time. In *Proceedings of the SIGCHI Conference on Human Factors in Computing Systems* (CHI '09). ACM, New York, NY, USA, 357-360. DOI: http://dx.doi.org/10.1145/1518701.1518758
29. Pamela A. McCombe and Robert D. Henderson. 2010. Effects of gender in amyotrophic lateral sclerosis. *Gender Medicine* 7, 6 (December 2010), 557-570. DOI: http://dx.doi.org/10.1016/j.genm.2010.11.010
30. Troy McDaniel, Shantanu Bala, Jacob Rosenthal, Ramin Tadayon, Arash Tadayon, and Sethuraman Panchanathan. 2014. Affective haptics for enhancing access to social interactions for individuals who are blind. In *International Conference on Universal Access in Human-Computer Interaction*, 419-429. DOI: http://dx.doi.org/10.1007/978-3-319-07437-5_40
31. Hiroshi Mitsumoto. 2009. *Amyotrophic Lateral Sclerosis: A Guide for Patients and Families*. Demos Medical Publishing.
32. Gökhan Mura. 2008. Wearable Technologies for Emotion Communication. *Middle East Technical University (METU) Journal of the Faculty of Architecture*. 25, 1 (April 2008), 153-161.
33. Joan Murphy. 2004. "I Prefer Contact This Close": Perceptions of AAC by People with Motor Neurone Disease and their Communication Partners. *Augmentative and Alternative Communication* 20, 4 (January 2004), 259–271. DOI: http://doi.org/10.1080/07434610400005663
34. Michael Oliver. 2009. *Understanding Disability: From Theory to Practice*. London: Palgrave Macmillan.
35. Andrew Ortony and Terence J. Turner. 1990. What's basic about basic emotions? *Psychological Review* 97, 3 (July 1990), 315-331. DOI: http://dx.doi.org/10.1037/0033-295x.97.3.315
36. Alex F. Osborn. *Applied imagination: Principles and procedures of creative problem-solving*. Scribners.
37. Joohee Park, Young-Woo Park, and Tek-Jin Nam. 2014. Wrigglo: shape-changing peripheral for interpersonal mobile communication. In *Proceedings of the SIGCHI Conference on Human Factors in Computing Systems* (CHI '14). ACM, New York, NY, USA, 3973-3976. DOI: http://dx.doi.org/10.1145/2556288.2557166
38. Diogo Pedrosa, Maria da Graça Pimentel, and Khai N. Truong. 2015. Filteryedping: A dwell-free eye typing technique. In *Proceedings of the 33rd Annual ACM*

Conference Extended Abstracts on Human Factors in Computing Systems (CHI EA '15). ACM, New York, NY, USA, 303-306. DOI: http://dx.doi.org/10.1145/2702613.2725458

39. Robert Plutchik. 1980. *Emotion: A Psychoevolutionary Synthesis*. Harper & Row New York.
40. Jonathan Posner, James A. Russell, and Bradley S. Peterson. 2005. The circumplex model of affect: An integrative approach to affective neuroscience, cognitive development, and psychopathology. *Development and psychopathology* 17, 3 (September 2005), 715-734. DOI: http://dx.doi.org/10.1017/s0954579405050340
41. Halley Profita, Reem Albaghli, Leah Findlater, Paul Jaeger, and Shaun K. Kane. 2016. The AT Effect: How Disability Affects the Perceived Social Acceptability of Head-Mounted Display Use. In *Proceedings of the 2016 CHI Conference on Human Factors in Computing Systems* (CHI '16), 4884-4895. DOI: http://dx.doi.org/10.1145/2858036.2858130
42. Graham Pullin. 2009. *Design meets disability*. MIT press.
43. Joshua Rader, Troy McDaniel, Artemio Ramirez Jr, Shantanu Bala, and Sethuraman Panchanathan. 2014. A Wizard of Oz Study Exploring How Agreement/Disagreement Nonverbal Cues Enhance Social Interactions for Individuals Who Are Blind. In *HCI International 2014 – Posters' Extended Abstracts*, 243-248. DOI: http://dx.doi.org/10.1007/978-3-319-07854-0_43
44. A. K. M. Mahbubur Rahm, A. S. M. Iftekhar Anam, and Mohammed Yeasin. EmoAssist: emotion enabled assistive tool to enhance dyadic conversation for the blind. *Multimedia Tools and Applications*, 1-32. DOI: http://dx.doi.org/10.1007/s11042-016-3295-4
45. Irene Rae, Leila Takayama, and Bilge Mutlu. 2013. In-body experiences: embodiment, control, and trust in robot-mediated communication. In *Proceedings of the SIGCHI Conference on Human Factors in Computing Systems* (CHI '13). ACM, New York, NY, USA, 1921-1930. DOI: http://dx.doi.org/10.1145/2470654.2466253
46. Ehud Reiter, Ross Turner, Norman Alm, Rolf Black, Martin Dempster, and Annalu Waller. 2009. Using NLG to help language-impaired users tell stories and participate in social dialogues. In *Proceedings of the 12th European Workshop on Natural Language Generation* (ENLG'09). Association for Computational Linguistics, 1-8.
47. Jocelyn Scheirer and Rosalind Picard. 2000. Affective objects. *MIT Media Lab Technical Report 524*.
48. Jerry C. Schnepp, Rosalee J. Wolfe, John C. McDonald, and Jorge A. Toro. 2012. Combining emotion and facial nonmanual signals in synthesized American sign language. In *Proceedings of the 14th international ACM SIGACCESS conference on Computers and accessibility* (ASSETS '12). ACM, New York, NY, USA, 249-250. DOI: http://dx.doi.org/10.1145/2384916.2384977
49. Tom Shakespeare. 1994. Cultural representation of disabled people: Dustbins for disavowal? *Disability & Society* 9, 3 (January 1994), 283-299. DOI: http://dx.doi.org/10.1080/09687599466780341
50. Kristen Shinohara and Jacob O. Wobbrock. 2011. In the shadow of misperception: assistive technology use and social interactions. In *Proceedings of the SIGCHI Conference on Human Factors in Computing Systems* (CHI '11), 705-714. DOI: http://dx.doi.org/10.1145/1978942.1979044
51. David Sirkin, Gina Venolia, John Tang, George Robertson, Taemie Kim, Kori Inkpen, Mara Sedlins, Bongshin Lee, and Mike Sinclair. 2011. Motion and attention in a kinetic videoconferencing proxy. In *IFIP Conference on Human-Computer Interaction*. Springer Berlin Heidelberg, 162-180. DOI: http://dx.doi.org/10.1007/978-3-642-23774-4_16
52. Anselm Strauss and Juliet Corbin. 1998. *Basics of qualitative research: Techniques and procedures for developing grounded theory*. Sage Publications, Inc.
53. Haodan Tan, John Tiab, Selma Šabanović, and Kasper Hornbæk. 2016. Happy Moves, Sad Grooves: Using Theories of Biological Motion and Affect to Design Shape-Changing Interfaces. In *Proceedings of the 2016 ACM Conference on Designing Interactive Systems* (DIS '16). ACM, New York, NY, USA, 1282-1293. DOI: http://dx.doi.org/10.1145/2901790.2901845
54. John C. Tang. 2007. Approaching and leave-taking: Negotiating contact in computer-mediated communication. *ACM Transactions on Computer-Human Interaction* 14, 1 (May 2007), 1-26. DOI: http://dx.doi.org/10.1145/1229855.1229860
55. John Todman. 2000. Rate and quality of conversations using a text-storage AAC system: Single-case training study. *Augmentative and Alternative Communication* 16, 3 (January 2000), 164-179. DOI: http://dx.doi.org/10.1080/07434610012331279024
56. Minh Hong Tran, Yun Yang, and Gitesh K. Raikundalia. 2005. Supporting awareness in instant messaging: an empirical study and mechanism design. In *Proceedings of the 17th Australia conference on Computer-Human Interaction: Citizens Online: Considerations for Today and the Future* (OZCHI '05). Computer-Human Interaction Special Interest Group (CHISIG) of Australia, Narrabundah, Australia, Australia, 1-10.
57. Minh Hong Tran, Yun Yang, and Gitesh K. Raikundalia. 2009. Conversational Awareness in Text-

Based Computer Mediated Communication. In *Awareness Systems*, 313-333. Springer London. DOI: http://dx.doi.org/10.1007/978-1-84882-477-5_13

58. Outi Tuisku, Päivi Majaranta, Poika Isokoski, and Kari-Jouko Räihä. 2008. Now Dasher! Dash away!: Longitudinal study of fast text entry by eye gaze. In *Proceedings of the 2008 Symposium on Eye Tracking Research & Applications* (ETRA '08). ACM, New York, NY, SUA, 19–26. DOI: http://dx.doi.org/10.1145/1344471.1344476
59. Christophe Veaux, Junichi Yamagishi, and Simon King. 2013. Towards personalized synthesized voices for individuals with vocal disabilities: Voice banking and reconstruction. In *4th Workshop on Speech and Language Processing for Assistive Technologies* (SPLAT 2013). Association for Computational Linguistics, 107-111.
60. Angela Vujic, Thad Starner, and Melody Jackson. 2016. MoodLens: towards improving nonverbal emotional expression with an in-lens fiber optic display. In *Proceedings of the 2016 ACM International Symposium on Wearable Computers* (ISWC '16). ACM, New York, NY, USA, 36-39. DOI: http://dx.doi.org/10.1145/2971763.2971798
61. Annalu Waller, Rolf Black, David A. O'Mara, Helen Pain, Graeme Ritchie, and Ruli Manurung. 2009. Evaluating the STANDUP pun generating software with children with cerebral palsy. *ACM Transactions on Accessible Computing* (TACCESS) 1, 3 (February 2009), 1-27. DOI: http://dx.doi.org/10.1145/1497302.1497306
62. Peter Washington, Catalin Voss, Nick Haber, Serena Tanaka, Jena Daniels, Carl Feinstein, Terry Wino-grad, and Dennis Wall. 2016. A Wearable Social Interaction Aid for Children with Autism. In *Proceedings of the 2016 CHI Conference Extended Abstracts on Human Factors in Computing Systems* (CHI EA '16). ACM, New York, NY, USA, 2348-2354. DOI: http://dx.doi.org/10.1145/2851581.2892282
63. Mary Wickenden. 2011. Whose voice is that?: Issues of identity, voice and representation arising in an ethnographic study of the lives of disabled teenagers who use augmentative and alternative communication (AAC). *Disability Studies Quarterly* 31, 4 (October 2011). DOI: http://dx.doi.org/10.18061/dsq.v31i4.1724
64. Amanda Williams, Shelly Farnham, and Scott Counts. 2006. Exploring wearable ambient displays for social awareness. In *CHI '06 Extended Abstracts on Human Factors in Computing Systems* (CHI EA '06). ACM, New York, NY, USA, 1529-1534. DOI: http://dx.doi.org/10.1145/1125451.1125731
65. Michele A. Williams, Asta Roseway, Chris O'Dowd, Mary Czerwinski, and Meredith Ringel Morris. 2015. SWARM: An Actuated Wearable for Mediating Affect. In *Proceedings of the Ninth International Conference on Tangible, Embedded, and Embodied Interaction* (TEI '15). ACM, New York, NY, USA, 293-300. DOI: http://dx.doi.org/10.1145/2677199.2680565
66. Bruce Wisenburn and D. Jeffery Higginbotham. 2009. Participant evaluations of rate and communication efficacy of an AAC application using natural language processing. *Augmentative and Alternative Communication* 25, 2 (January 2009), 78-89. DOI: http://dx.doi.org/10.1080/07434610902739876
67. Jacob O. Wobbrock, Leah Findlater, Darren Gergle, and James J. Higgins. 2011. The aligned rank transform for nonparametric factorial analyses using only anova procedures. In *Proceedings of the SIGCHI Conference on Human Factors in Computing Systems* (CHI '11). ACM, New York, NY, USA, 143-146. DOI: http://dx.doi.org/10.1145/1978942.1978963
68. Junichi Yamagishi, Christophe Veaux, Simon King, and Steve Renals. 2012. Speech synthesis technologies for individuals with vocal disabilities: Voice banking and reconstruction. *Acoustical Science and Technology* 33, 1 (2012), 1-5. DOI: http://dx.doi.org/10.1250/ast.33.1

Trust, but Verify: Optimistic Visualizations of Approximate Queries for Exploring Big Data

Dominik Moritz
University of Washington
domoritz@cs.uw.edu

Danyel Fisher
Microsoft Research
danyelf@microsoft.com

Bolin Ding, Chi Wang
DMX, Microsoft Research
bolind@microsoft.com,
chiw@microsoft.com

ABSTRACT

Analysts need interactive speed for exploratory analysis, but big data systems are often slow. With sampling, data systems can produce approximate answers fast enough for exploratory visualization, at the cost of accuracy and trust. We propose *optimistic visualization*, which approaches these issues from a user experience perspective. This method lets analysts explore approximate results interactively, and provides a way to detect and recover from errors later. *Pangloss* implements these ideas. We discuss design issues raised by optimistic visualization systems. We test this concept with five expert visualizers in a laboratory study and three case studies at Microsoft. Analysts reported that they felt more confident in their results, and used optimistic visualization to check that their preliminary results were correct.

ACM Classification Keywords

H.5.2. Information Interfaces and Presentation: UI; H.2.4. Database Management: Systems

Author Keywords

Data visualization; exploratory analysis; optimistic visualization; approximation; uncertainty

INTRODUCTION

Data analysts want to be able to derive insights from increasingly large datasets. Exploratory visualization, however, runs into an obstacle where the scale of the data is sufficiently large that a screen cannot render each point, and where database queries would take a long time to return. By sampling the dataset, though, we can create a visualization with approximate values in interactive time. This is known as *Approximate Query Processing* (AQP).

There are several well-known challenges with approximations. The most critical of these is trust: approximate values can be, by their nature, possibly incorrect. In an exploratory visualization, an analyst might see dozens of visualizations that are accurate 95% of the time. Can an analyst trust an approximation with a business-critical decision?

Permission to make digital or hard copies of all or part of this work for personal or classroom use is granted without fee provided that copies are not made or distributed for profit or commercial advantage and that copies bear this notice and the full citation on the first page. Copyrights for components of this work owned by others than the author(s) must be honored. Abstracting with credit is permitted. To copy otherwise, or republish, to post on servers or to redistribute to lists, requires prior specific permission and/or a fee. Request permissions from permissions@acm.org.

CHI 2017, May 06 - 11, 2017, Denver, CO, USA

© 2017 Copyright held by the owner/author(s). Publication rights licensed to ACM.

ISBN 978-1-4503-4655-9/17/05...$15.00

DOI: http://dx.doi.org/10.1145/3025453.3025456

In this paper, rather than addressing the problems with AQP from an algorithmic or systems perspective, we formulate them as user experience problems. What user experience would enable analysts to gain the benefits of approximate queries, while still being able to trust the results?

We propose an approach which we call *optimistic visualization*. Optimistic visualization produces approximate results quickly, and computes precise results in the background. The analyst can make observations on the approximation, and later check them against the precise results.

We call this approach "optimistic" because the analyst expects the approximation to be very close to the precise value; in those rare cases when there is a significant difference between the approximate and precise results, the analyst can decide which parts of the exploration have to be redone. Optimism provides a way to detect and recover from errors, and so increases confidence in working with samples. The technique can be combined with other approximation techniques such as confidence intervals and online aggregation.

We present *Pangloss*, an optimistic visualization tool based on AQP. With it, analysts can rapidly explore very large multidimensional datasets by grouping, aggregating, and filtering. Working in a sample-based system affects the user experience of visual data exploration. We describe the design decisions that went into the system. We validated our decisions by running a user study with five participants exploring a 170 million row dataset about flight delays; we then deployed our prototype system to three data scientists using their own data.

BACKGROUND AND RELATED WORK

The concept of optimistic visualization builds on past research on data exploration, AQP, and uncertainty visualization. We first discuss the importance of rapid iteration in exploratory data analysis, and then the ways in which it changes when working with very large datasets. Last, we focus specifically on sample-based queries and visualization.

Exploratory Visualization

Exploratory data analysis (EDA), a term coined by Tukey [38], is broadly understood as a process of examining multidimensional data by looking at the distributions and correlations of fields. As Card et al. [5] note, this process prizes iteration and speed of exploration; an analyst might look at dozens or hundreds of graphs as they get to know the data.

The process of moving through these dimensions is iterative. An analyst begins with a broad question, and creates views that address some part of it. This view can inform a more-specific question, leading them to create another view to address that question [42, 35, 34]. These increasingly-specific questions require analysts to change representations, to filter the data by zooming or filtering views, and to choose new fields to explore. Some of these views will contain interesting insights; others will be dead ends with less value. When the analyst has sufficiently addressed the broad question and follow up questions, they often continue with a new broad question and chains of specific follow up questions.

Visualization tools—whether point-and-click, such as Tableau (an extension of Polaris [37]) and PowerBI, or programming, like Matplotlib—support this process with tools that allow users to rapidly specify and refine their visualizations.

Each step in this process involves generating *observations* of the data. Optimistic visualization helps analysts confirm (or challenge) their observations. An observation is a single fact about the data; it is the unit of knowledge that allows an analyst to move on to the next step of their analysis [43]. For example, when examining a dataset of flight data, an observation might be "Delta is the airline with the most flights in the dataset." It is a more modest unit than the insights that the research community has focused on as the outcome of the analysis process. An insight can bring in external context and the results of a number of queries; an example might be "the biggest airlines have trouble with congestion near the holidays, while smaller airlines do not" [43, 28].

The visualization system must be fast enough to enable iteration. Liu and Heer show that analysts lose effectiveness when a result takes more than 500 ms to return [24]; Norman argues that when a computer operation takes more than a second, users lose their flow of thought [27].

Big Data Visualization

These requirements for responsiveness become urgent when dealing with large datasets. As Fisher [12] and Godfrey et al. [14] outline, when dataset sizes exceed even a few million records, analysts run into two fundamental issues: visual scalability and data processing scalability.

It is impractical to display every element of a large dataset: the number of records may far exceed the available pixels. For example, drawing raw data in a scatterplot without aggregation leads to overplotting—drawing many points in the same place—and visual clutter. The data can be grouped by a dimension, however, and a single aggregate measure computed for each group. The simplest such aggregate visualization is a bar chart, in which each bar represents the aggregated value of a group. Elmqvist [9] outlines visualizations that work with aggregate data; Wickham proposes the bin-summarize-smooth framework [40] as a general strategy for visualizing big data.

Data retrieval and processing are the other major bottleneck. Handling very large datasets can be comparatively slow. Analysts sometimes resort to an offline process: formulating and submitting a query, waiting for a result, and then formulating a follow up question. This is not only frustrating but requires analysts to carefully design their queries to be worth the wait and the resources.

There are three major technologies to achieve more-responsive queries. Data cubes precompute and store partially-aggregated results; at query time, the system can assemble these partial answers quickly [23, 25, 15]. Unfortunately, these cubes require a designer to select the fields to optimize. Second, the query can be spread across many computers, which assemble an answer [4, 32]. In these distributed *Online Analytical Processing* (OLAP) systems [6], though, network latencies can last into the seconds. The third major approach is to sample the dataset.

Approximate Query Processing

Optimistic visualization is based on the technique of Approximate Query Processing (AQP). In AQP, the tool uses a representative subset, or sample, of the data; the goal is to look at less data more quickly. Tools can estimate the true value of an aggregation function based on that sample. As a simple example, we can approximate the sum of a set of values by computing the sum of 10% of the values and then estimating the true sum to be ten times the aggregate value of the sample. This value is an estimate, and carries some uncertainty, which can be expressed as error bounds. Those bounds widen with the variance of the data, and narrow with the square root of the size of the sample.

Some tools create a sample of the data before the user begins their analysis. In these systems, the precision of the approximation greatly diminishes as the analyst filters away more records. For example, every record in a census can help the approximation for "average age", but far fewer will be helpful for "average age of unemployed men living in Aspen, Colorado". Choosing a sample that is large enough to lead to statistically meaningful results while maintaining interactive response times is important.

Sampling can be integrated directly into databases [30]; other systems build on different sampling and estimation methods [2, 8, 22]. These systems pick a sample and compute a result along with estimated error bounds; the analyst may choose either a maximum amount of time that the query runs, or desired error bounds. Interactive systems tend to use time bounds to get a best-effort approximation within that time bound.

Progressive Visualization with Online Aggregation

Rather than forcing the user to settle for a fixed-size sample, or wait for the system to reach a fixed level of precision, Online Aggregation (OLA) picks ever-growing samples and displays results to the user; when the analyst determines the visualization has tight-enough bounds, they can end the process. OLA computes aggregations and confidence intervals and returns them to the user. Hellerstein et al. [19] first suggested the idea; it has been adopted by the visualization community as a "progressive analytics" approach [13, 10, 36, 33, 39].

Optimistic visualization can be seen as an asynchronous form of progressive sampling; it places the updates in the background, allowing the analyst to continue their analysis without watching for updates. The CONTROL project [18] noted that progressiveness adds costs; e.g. "ripple joins" [16] require multiple passes over the data, and so may take longer to reach a precise result. Pangloss can use existing, highly-optimized database systems for the precise results.

Visualizing Approximations

There are a number of techniques for communicating approximate query results [31]. Commonly used methods are confidence intervals [26], visualizing distributions [41], or visualizing possible instances of the underlying statistical model [20]. Researchers are less certain of ways to visualize uncertainty on some visualization types such as heatmaps.

Even with the help of visualization, users struggle to correctly interpret uncertainty and can draw incorrect conclusions [21, 7]. In a visual data exploration where an analyst creates tens or hundreds of visualizations, the "rare" cases when the true values are outside the estimated bounds become likely. Worse, many confidence estimates are inaccurate: Agarwal et al. examined logs of 70,000 approximate queries from Facebook and found a large fraction had error estimates that were too wide or too narrow [1].

Optimistic visualization ensures that precise results will eventually be available so that the analyst can discover places where estimates were unavailable, hard to understand, or far from the true value.

OPTIMISTIC DATA VISUALIZATION

We address the challenges of sample-based visualization with *optimistic visualization*. In an optimistic visualization system, an analyst begins by constructing a fast, approximate query and seeing results instantly. The analyst may choose to *remember* that query, in which case it will run in the background. While the query is running, the analyst continues their exploration. The system allows the analyst to know when the query is complete; at which point the analyst can verify their observations. The system shows the error between the approximate and precise views.

In most cases, the final result validates their earlier work. Should a past approximation turn out to be inaccurate, however, the analyst must then re-evaluate how much exploration must be redone. There are a number of edge cases for approximation: it is difficult to choose good confidence intervals on some functions, such as percentile measures; some datasets have high enough variances that confidence intervals are extremely wide; and some approximations turn out to be incorrect.

Even in these riskier scenarios, optimistic visualization allows the analyst to feel certain that their final results will confirm whether their assumptions were justified. Without optimism the analyst can only rely on the *uncertainty*—the estimated error of the approximation—to make a decision. The uncertainty should be a good predictor of the *approximation error*; the true error of the approximation. However, only the precise results can confirm this; analysts have to know when the approximation error was significantly larger than the uncertainty.

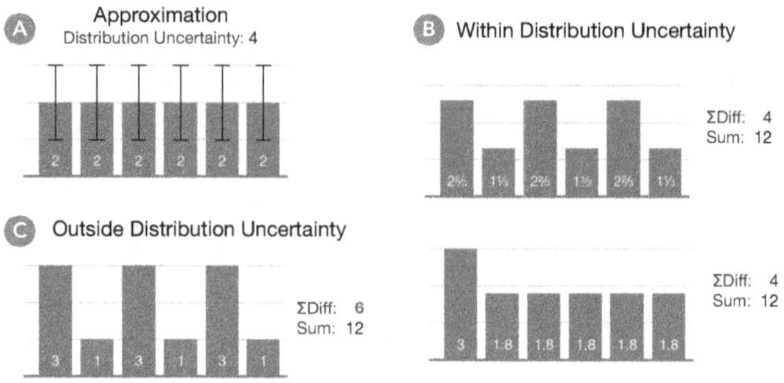

Figure 1. The uncertainty implied by the confidence intervals from (A) is larger than the distribution uncertainty of 4 (here for illustration defined as the sum of absolute, unnormalized differences). (B) are possible instances that stay within both the confidence intervals and the distribution uncertainty. The values for all groups in (C) are within the confidence intervals but the distribution is off by 6. The sum of the values is always 12.

In progressive visualization systems [13, 33, 39] analysts watch progressive updates as more data arrives. During the waiting period, though, values continuously change [11]. Analysts can be distracted by these *dancing bars*; they can also incorrectly assess trends as the confidence intervals converge. Progressive systems require accurate communication of uncertainties so analysts can decide when to stop. However, some forms of uncertainty are difficult to visualize, and true errors can be outside the estimated bounds. Optimistic visualization defers the confirmation and moves the computation of the precise result into the background; analyst can continue their exploration sooner.

An optimistic visualization is most effective when the complete query takes long enough to get in the way of interactivity, but shorter than an analysis session—it is highly effective when a query takes several minutes to return.

THE PANGLOSS SYSTEM

We implemented optimistic visualization in the Pangloss system. Pangloss is a web based UI that queries Sample+Seek [8], an AQP system. Because Sample+Seek has some unique features, we discuss it in some detail before presenting our interface.

Sample+Seek for Approximate Query Processing

Sample+Seek [8] is designed to be highly responsive for aggregate queries on a single table. It incrementally loads more records into the sample until either the uncertainty bound is lower than a predefined threshold or until a timeout. Instead of uniformly sampling records—as many other AQP system do—Sample+Seek uses *measure-biased* sampling, a method that biases sampling according to the aggregation measure. Measure-biased sampling has a tremendous advantage over uniform sampling: fewer samples are necessary for the same accuracy in a visualization. This sampling method has been developed to optimize the *distribution uncertainty*. It is a metric of the uncertainty across all groups in the result, and is defined as the expected distance (e.g., sum of distances, Euclidean, etc.) between the normalized distributions of the approximate answer and the precise one. For example, the

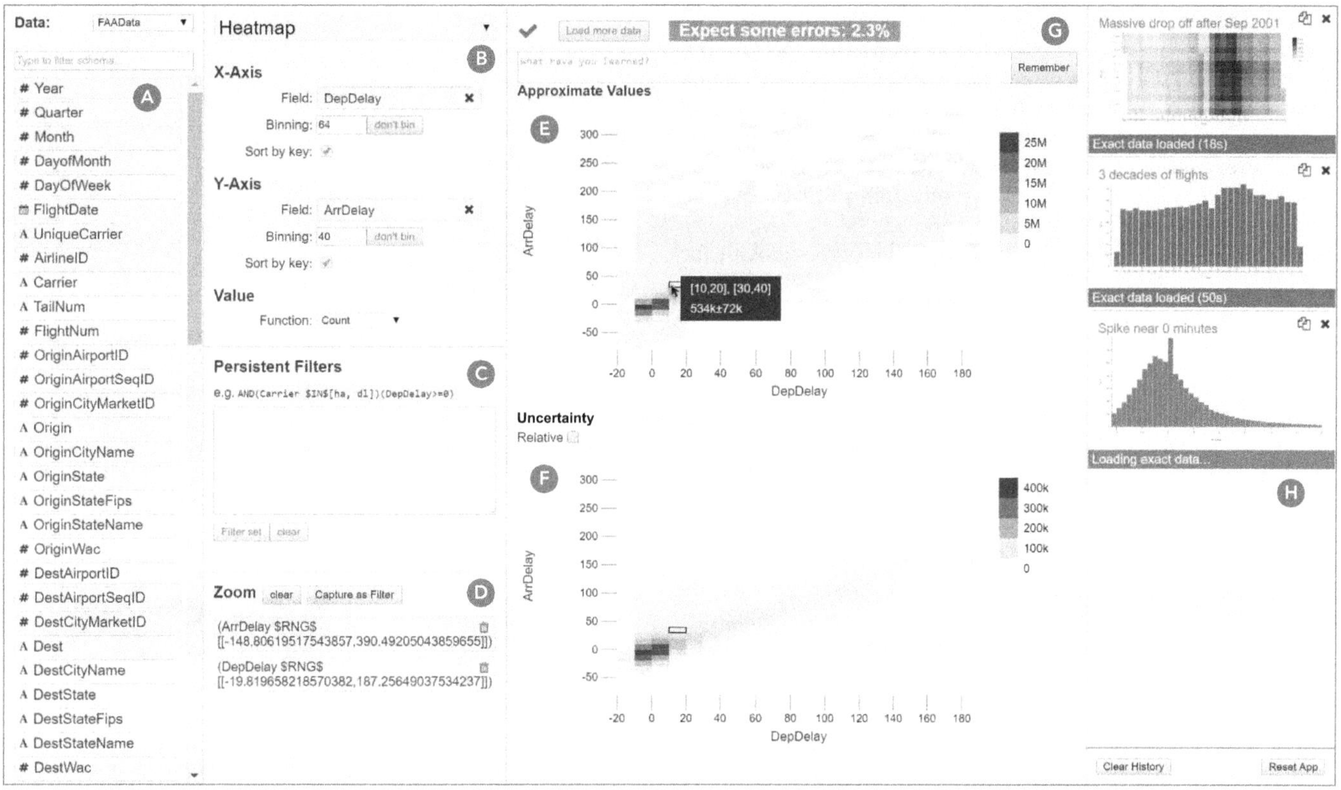

Figure 2. The Pangloss UI, exploring a flight delay dataset, with a list of fields (A), chart specification forms (B), a textfield for filters (C), zoom specification (D), approximate visualization (E), visualization of the uncertainty (F), field for annotations and "remember" button (G), and a list of views in the history (H). Two precise results are ready, while a third is loading.

Euclidean distance between the normalized distribution answer $x = \langle 0.39, 0.61\rangle$ and the approximation $\hat{x} = \langle 0.40, 0.60\rangle$ is $||x - \hat{x}||_2 = \sqrt{0.01^2 + 0.01^2} = 0.014$.

More general, the distribution uncertainty with Euclidean distance is [8]:

$$\sqrt{\sum_{\text{group } i} \left(\frac{\text{group } i\text{'s value}}{\text{total group value}} - \frac{\text{estimated group } i\text{'s value}}{\text{total estimated group value}} \right)^2}$$

Distribution uncertainty is different from familiar per-group confidence intervals [18, 13, 20]. Rather than seeing each group as having its own confidence interval, the distribution uncertainty is a total amount by which the whole visualization is likely to be imprecise. Distribution uncertainty recognizes that uncertainties are not independent. As Figure 1 illustrates, one group might be off by a lot, or many groups might be off by just a little.

Besides the distribution uncertainty, we also compute a confidence interval for each group. However, the sum of these per-group uncertainties are worst-case estimates, and can be significantly higher than the overall distribution uncertainty. When we visualize confidence intervals, the possible range of uncertainty they imply is far greater than the distribution uncertainty (Figure 1). For the analyst, knowing the overall distribution uncertainty means that they do not have to expect the worst case for all groups.

Sample+Seek supports aggregate measures such as count, sum, and average. Queries can have multiple group-by dimensions, of either categorical values or binned numerical values. Queries can also filter the data, based on boolean predicates. When predicates are selective, AQP systems need to look at many records before they find records that match the filters. Sample+Seek maintains indices that help rapidly identify matching records. Each query uses a different sample because we limit the time per query.

In the algorithm a sample is always a strict subset of all rows. Even if we scan all rows, we can only get within a fixed factor of the precise answer. This prevents us from providing users with progressively improving results.

In the original Sample+Seek [8], data samples were kept in memory; Pangloss uses a modified version that supports larger datasets and reduces the memory footprint by keeping the dataset as a randomly shuffled file on disk. Our version of Sample+Seek is able to respond within 100 ms with acceptable levels of approximation error.

Designing the Pangloss UI

Sample-based visualizations require a different user experience than more traditional visualization systems. In this section, we discuss the Pangloss user interface, highlighting design decisions that accommodate the unusual aspects of AQP and optimistic visualization. The interface is implemented as a web application, using the React framework and D3 [3].

The interface, shown in Figure 2, uses interaction paradigms well-known in visualization tools such as Tableau and PowerBI. On the left is a searchable schema (A) with fields that can be dropped to the chart specification (B). Below the chart specification form are fields for filtering (C) and showing the current zoom predicates (D). The largest area of the screen is taken up by the view (E) and its uncertainty (F). Above the view is a textbox for observations and a button to *remember* the current view (G), which computes the precise result for this view. Remembered views are listed in the history on the right; they are drawn as orange while they are still loading, and turn blue when precise result is available (H).

Approximate Visualizations

Pangloss supports two core visualization types: bar charts and heatmaps. The bar chart shows aggregated measures grouped by values; it can also be used as a histogram by binning numeric fields. The heatmap, a generalization of density plot, allows users to see the interaction between two dimensions; aggregate values are encoded using a color scale. Each dimension of the heatmap can be binned. Other visualizations can be implemented in this system; in theory, any aggregation-oriented visualization [9] can be accommodated.

Because many queries have long tails, Pangloss limits the number of bars or cells that can be shown to a top k and shows a warning if groups are hidden (Figure 3-A). When dealing with samples, the values further down the tail are based on fewer samples, and so are likely to be very uncertain; we chose not to add tools to scroll over to the tail of the distribution. Of course, an analyst can filter the highest values, working their way down the distribution.

The distribution uncertainty of the approximation is displayed above the main view (Figure 3-B). The system computes confidence intervals for each group; however, these per-group intervals are worst case estimates (Figure 1). For bar charts, Pangloss draws the confidence intervals directly on the bar chart. As there is no standard way to show confidence intervals for heatmaps, Pangloss instead displays a second parallel heatmap that shows uncertainty (Figure 7, right). In all visualizations, tooltips show the group name or bin bounds, the approximate value, and the uncertainty (Figure 4).

Zooming with Samples

Pangloss supports zooming and filtering, like most visualization systems. In in-memory visualization tools, zooming and focusing only change the domain of the dimensions and measures; the group categories stay constant. With samples, every zoom focus interaction changes the predicate, forcing a new query to run on the AQP system. Consequently, the aggregate value and the uncertainty can change.

As we noted above, the groups themselves can change as the user adds filters: collecting a new sample might mean that numerical ranges might expand and new groups might appear. The semantics of filtering, then, call for a design decision. An analyst cannot know whether there are more groups to be seen until they filter. If the analyst filters ten categories down to three, do we interpret that as a *negative* filter, removing seven,

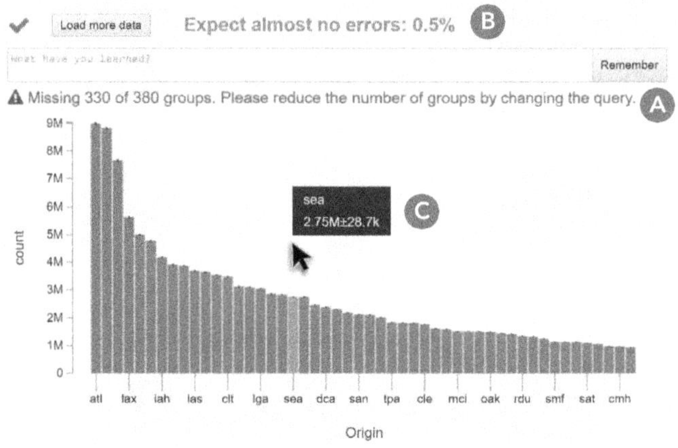

Figure 3. A bar chart for a result with a long tail. The view warns that it only shows the top groups (A). Above the chart is the distribution uncertainty (B). Tooltips in bar charts are shown for the area above the bar (C).

Figure 4. Left, tooltips for approximations show the group, the value, and the associated uncertainty. Right, tooltips for precise results show how much the estimate was off.

or a *positive* one, limiting to just those three? The difference is that "removing seven" might discover more groups (Figure 5).

To ensure that analysts never lose information, Pangloss treats categorical filters as negative by default; analysts can explicitly select positive filters if they need. Similarly, with numerical data, the domain can change (Figure 9); we add an inequality constraint (as opposed to a range predicate) when the user brushes all the way to the end of an axis.

Functions and Transformations with Samples

In most visualization systems, the user can carry out transformations and functions on the data. For example, it is easy to add a logarithmic transformation over a visualization, or to compute average by dividing sum by count. Distribution uncertainty, however, is a global measure across a view. As such, the distribution uncertainty for a value will be very different from the log of that same measure value; they will be based on different numbers of samples. Just as zooms must be computed as separate computed queries, so too must be transforms and functions.

Many existing visualization systems and techniques build on assumptions that are not true when samples are used to approximate results. With samples we cannot assume that the result of an aggregation query does not miss groups. Consequently, if we calculate the average of a measure as the ratio of the sum and the count, we can only do so for the common groups in the two samples. We cannot, however, compute the combined distribution uncertainty.

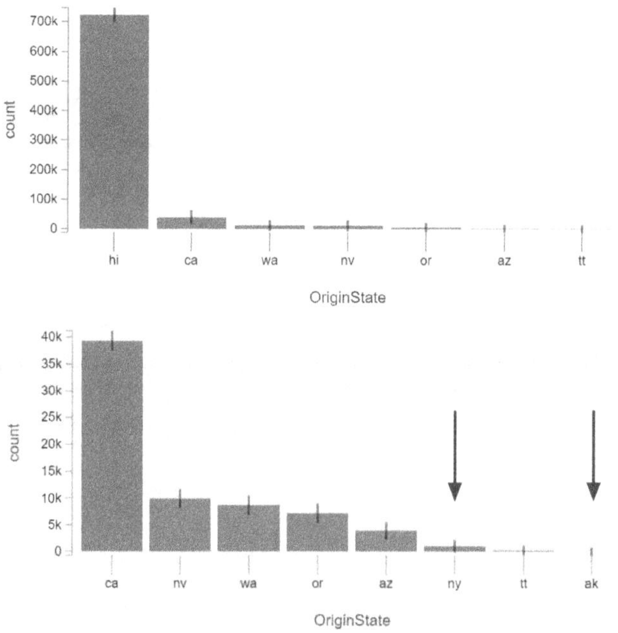

Figure 5. Above, an approximate histogram of origin states for Hawaiian Airlines flights. Below, if we filter out Hawaii, a new query runs on the AQP system and the approximation also shows that New York and Alaska (arrows) are also origin states. Because the new predicate is more selective, the uncertainty decreases for all groups.

Remembering Views and History

The heart of optimistic visualization is the process of selecting a view and re-running its query to get a precise result. In Pangloss, we call this *remembering* the view. We wish to support analysts being able to look back at a past view, and verify the observation they made with it.

One important design decision is which views should be remembered. We considered verifying every past view that Pangloss produces, modeled after Graphical Histories [17]. There are several disadvantages to keeping this complete history. First, we expect users to review the precise views; it would be overwhelming to review every view. Second, precise queries are computationally expensive; issuing hundreds of them can overwhelm back-end data systems. As such, we want to encourage users to remember only views that are relevant for observations.

In Pangloss, we decided to make this an explicit process. The "Remember" button (Figure 2-G) stores the view in the history and runs the precise query in the background. We would like to encourage analysts to track the observations; we support it by allowing them to add a small textual annotation describing the remembered view.

The entries in the history (Figure 2-H) change when a precise result is available: we render approximate views in orange shades, and precise views in blue. Views in the history are immutable, but users can revise their annotations to note new information. In addition, users can make a mutable (and approximate) copy of the view if they wish to modify it.

Queries for precise answers are sent to a commercial SQLServer database. On current hardware precise queries return within 30 seconds to a few minutes for datasets of around 50 GB to 1 TB.

Visualizing Approximation Error

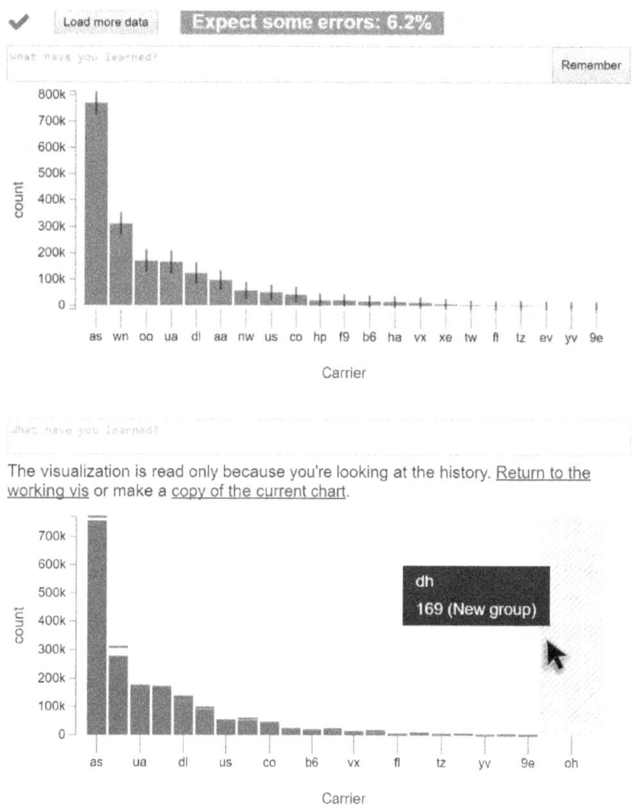

Figure 6. Above, approximate bar chart for count of flights out of Washington state, grouped by airline, with per-group confidence intervals and distribution uncertainty. Below, the precise result for the same chart shows the values as blue bars, the approximate result as orange lines, and highlights airlines that were missing from the approximation (e.g., Independence Air (dh) with 169 flights).

Once the precise query has completed, an analyst must be able to verify whether their observation during the exploration was justified. Several types of changes might occur between the approximate and the precise views. First, the values of some groups can change; if the chart is sorted, this also means that bars might be in a new order. Second, some groups that were not in the chart before might have been added. Last, binned data might change its range.

We wish to support the analyst in comparing the approximate and precise views.

What should happen when a bar is added, or the relative order of sorted bars changes? There are advantages to both maintaining *stability*, by keeping the layout of the approximate visualization with revised values, or *precision* by showing the precise view. We settled on the latter, because our major goal

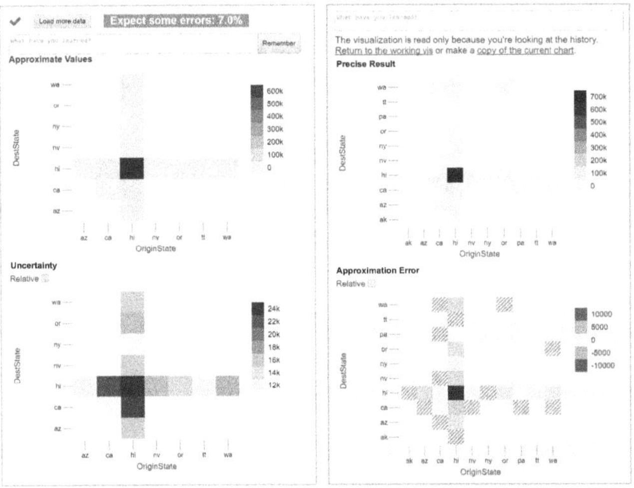

Figure 7. Approximate (left) and precise (right) heatmaps, examining origin and destination states for Hawaiian Airlines. (Left) The approximate view shows the estimated count above and the uncertainty below. (Right) The precise view shows the count above and the approximation error below. Both lower images toggle to show relative or absolute differences.

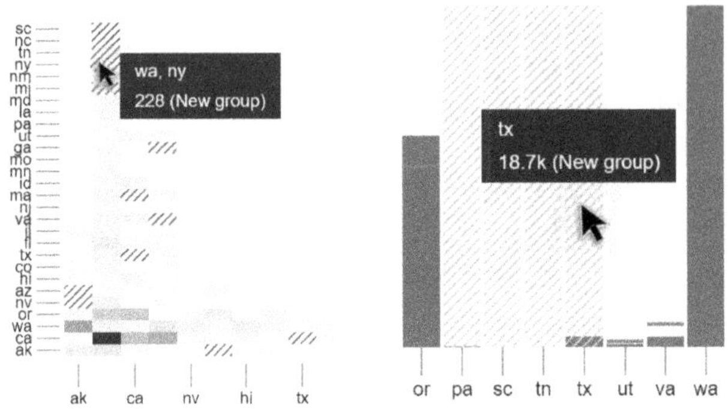

Figure 8. To draw attention to new groups, the corresponding cells in heatmaps (left) and bars (right) are highlighted with a stripe pattern.

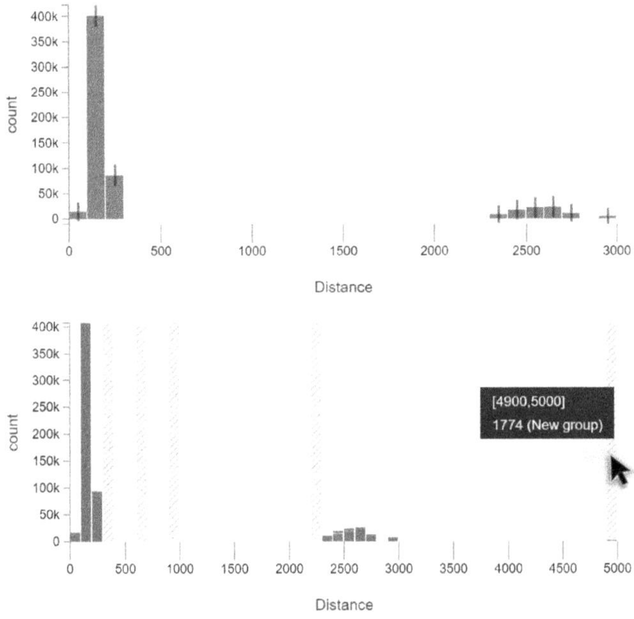

Figure 9. Approximate histogram at the top shows that Hawaiian Airlines has short range (inter state) and long range (island to mainland) flights. The precise histogram below shows additional flights around 5000 miles. The range has changed but bins are still aligned.

is encouraging users to interpret the view they see. The final visualization emphasizes the precise values.

Visualizing the difference along with the true values in the same chart poses challenges similar to uncertainty visualizations; we use similar methods. Pangloss superimposes the approximate value on the bars as orange lines, as in Figure 6. This makes changes in order very visible, as the orange lines no longer decrease monotonically. When a new group appears, we highlight it with a gray striped background (Figure 8, right). It is worth noting that a histogram's range might change between sample and final. Therefore, in the precise query, we fix the bin width and the offset so that the precise histogram always aligns with the approximate one (Figure 9).

For heatmaps, one chart shows the true value, while the approximation error is shown in a separate chart (Figure 7). The analyst can toggle between seeing absolute error, which shows the difference between the estimate and the actual value, and relative error, measured as a percentage. We found that each is useful for different circumstances: relative error is good when cells have similar values; on the other hand, a small amount of error can still be thousands of percentage points from a small cell value. Consistent with how new bars are highlighted, any new cells have a diagonally striped pattern (Figure 8, left).

USER STUDIES

There are several motivating concepts behind Pangloss that we wished to validate. First, are analysts comfortable with incomplete or inaccurate results, and are they willing to use them to explore approximate data? Progressive visualization systems [13, 33, 39] allow analysts to linger at one view until it reaches a level of accuracy; Pangloss does not. Second, optimistic visualization expects users to proceed with their exploration even without precise results; we wanted to know whether they would do so. Last, we wanted to know how users would interact with precise results, and whether checking those results would interfere with their flow.

We believed these questions would be best addressed by collecting rich stories of users interacting with the system; we modeled our user study after Fisher et al. [13]. We carried out two studies. We first wished to establish that Pangloss works as a data analytics toolkit that can enable users to come up with usable insights. We chose a single dataset and recruited data analysts from within Microsoft. We encouraged them to explore the data, providing them with guiding questions. The shared dataset allows us to factor out feedback specific to the data.

We wanted to also validate that this system works for real-world situations. We solicited data scientists from Microsoft, and asked them to share a current dataset with us; we loaded it into Pangloss. We then invited them to explore the system and interviewed them about their experience.

Flight Delay Study

Our first study used the "BTS Flight Delays dataset" [29]. The full dataset is 70 GB, and contains records on about 170 million commercial domestic flights from the last three decades within the United States. Each record represents one flight, with its arrival and departure time and location, as well any delays and reroutes in flight. There are a total of 109 fields in the raw data; for the user study, we removed some of the sparser fields, to result in 78 fields. Pangloss is able to maintain the 100 ms response time for histograms and bar charts at a 1%–2% uncertainty level; heatmaps had higher uncertainty of 2%–5%. Views with averages and highly selective predicates have much larger errors. In contrast, a full SQL query on the dataset runs in one minute.

We recruited five data scientists for the study. All participants were associated with a product or consulting team, including IT Support, software development, and post-deployment monitoring. Each of them was familiar with creating visualizations in R, PowerBI, Tableau, or Excel. We call them P1 through P5 below.

Three of the sessions were carried out in person; two others, with analysts located further away, were carried out by video-sharing session. At Microsoft, it is not unusual to meet via video-sharing; all users were familiar with the technology. Sessions lasted an hour. We started sessions with a tutorial, which guided subjects through a series of training questions to help them learn the system. We then invited them to explore the data using the tool; we gave some introductory questions but invited them to pursue questions that caught their curiosity for half an hour. At the end of the time, if the users had not reviewed precise results, we encouraged them to do so. Near the end of the hour, we asked our subjects to discuss advantages and tradeoffs of Pangloss.

We encouraged users to think aloud; all sessions were voice- and screen-recorded. Remote users used the tool in their web browser, so that they did not suffer from video-sharing lag.

Flight Delay Study Results

During the study, most users were resistant, at first, to explicitly recording their observations: we needed to remind almost all users to record observations they were making. After the first few, however, it became more habitual for them to record their observations over time. Only one user refused to use the "remember" function.

We had feared that some users would be unwilling to explore their data, knowing that their initial results were inaccurate; perhaps they would wait to ensure their earlier investigation was valid. We saw this only once; P2, mid-analysis, paused to wait for his remembered view to complete. A moment later, impatient, he resumed his flow, and continued to "remember" things. By the end of the study, four of our users were regularly "remembering" visualizations. Users "remembered" 4-7 views during their half hour.

Some users found opportunities to check in on their history during the study. P4 said, "I was thinking what to do next—and I saw that it had loaded, so I went back and checked it ... [the passive update is] very nice for not interrupting your workflow."

Interacting with Big Data: All users had dealt with slow queries in big data systems, and appreciated the speed of Pangloss. As P4 said, "[with a competitor] I was willing to wait 70-80 seconds. It wasn't ideally interactive, but it meant I was looking at all the data." All the users commented on the responsiveness of the system.

Our users were also familiar with sampling; for example, P4 had used sampling for other projects: "We can't look at all the sensor data at once—it wouldn't work. So we sample."

Waiting for Precise Results: We wondered whether analysts would find the precise version of the visualization useful: after all, they had already seen the approximate version. P1 said, "From my perspective, [uncertainty] almost passed me by. Nothing that I saw after-the-fact fundamentally changed any conclusions."

Despite that, this made Pangloss feel safer to him: P1 said he checked whether the precise results "are fundamentally different in a way that warrants my attention—if the top 5 are different, that's important." P5 used precise results to feel more confident in the approximations: "[The precise view] is an enabler. [Sometimes] you have a doubt whether sampling has made it better or worse, but seeing something right away at first glimpse is really great."

Our participants most often decided to remember very uncertain results: the large distribution uncertainty and wide confidence intervals cued them to "remember" their findings and request a more precise results. In contrast, they chose to trust more certain results.

The data scientists also talked about the importance of presenting precise data to their teams. While they might be able to use sample data with approximation, P3 said, "I know some information gets lost when I use samples ... If I want to give my boss specific numbers, I don't want to use samples." P2 said, "full and complete data always makes the most sense."

We wondered whether going back to check the results of queries would disrupt their workflow. P4 felt that the color change to cue the arrival of precise results was not disruptive, and "the ability to keep working ... and know that you will get a complete visualization is very handy."

Limitations: Users did bump into the limitations of Pangloss, which shows specific visualizations of aggregate data. P5 said "When I'm using R, it's like I'm on a mountaintop, I can go anywhere I want; when I'm using your system, there is a path that I need to follow." Similarly, P3 wanted to see lower-level data: "you want to go down to the sample level to see which samples are causing this pattern."

Case Studies

Our second study emphasized real-world use of datasets. We recruited data analysts from an internal list of data scientists. We looked specifically for users who had datasets over 10 gigabytes with structured tabular data, and selected three candidates. We ingested their data into Sample+Seek, and then scheduled meetings with the groups: we met with David in person, while we met remotely with Madhu and Faraz. [1]

We followed a similar protocol to the Flight Delay study: each session started off with a short demonstration and tutorial. When subjects made observations out loud, we encouraged them to "remember" the views. At the end of the experiment, if they had not reviewed some of the remembered values, we encouraged them to click through those observations, and to evaluate whether their observations had changed. These case study sessions ran between an hour and a half and two hours.

Case Study 1: David and Software Crashes
David works on the telemetry team for a family of software products. His team is responsible for helping developers identify which features are causing problems for their users. They do so by examining telemetry across multiple builds of their software, both beta and released, categorizing the circumstances under which software fails.

David's dataset consists of activities that users are carrying out in these products with error information. Their data collection gathers 100 TB/day of raw timestamped event data. This is too much for their system (or for Pangloss) to analyze; instead, his team pre-aggregates this data into summaries, which average around 200 MB/day. These summaries consist of activities, hierarchically categorized by product and feature; broken down by minute of the day; it stores the number of times that users attempted to use the feature, and how many of them succeeded.

His team's visualization technology cannot view more than a gigabyte of data, representing a week of data. This can miss out on deployment problems that emerge over longer ranges of time, and makes it hard to compare between builds of the software. Pangloss was able to load three months' data.

David is used to working with slow queries: as he began to navigate his data, he excitedly said that "instantaneous visualizations are great!" He freely jumped between different slices of the data, admiring "the power of being able to pivot so quickly." David applied multiple filters to the data, limiting it by date, code branch, and application.

At first, he did not see the utility in remembering his queries: "going back and looking at the more precise data would be valuable if I were drawing any real conclusions—if I was going to send an email to somebody. But in a lot of these cases, if I didn't see anything too exciting in the approximate number, I'd be OK with that." We insisted he remember his first few queries to get precise results; by partway through the session, he did so on his own. When we went back through his results at the end, he reflected "Now that I've been sitting here for an hour, after I go back, it makes a lot of sense [to have these annotations], but as I was doing it, I was thinking, 'I want to move on, I want to move on."

Like some of the users in the flight delay study, he began to think about the value of precise data: "A lot of what we do gets used in ship rooms and standups; ship decisions are made on those numbers. Those meetings cost thousands of dollars a minute. You need super-precise data for them."

During the study, David ran into a surprising result: one day had an aberrantly low value for a particular data series. He went off wanting to delve into it more: "I'm going to go over this with my team and send them some screenshots. I want to find out what happened on 8/8 with this stream."

David had been limited by the amount of data they collected; Pangloss allowed him and his team to broaden their view.

Case Study 2: Madhu and Search Terms
Madhu works on the advertising platform for a search engine. His team is responsible for trying to predict trends in searches and keywords. They analyze usage data from the search engine, looking for terms and concepts that are gaining in popularity. Madhu wanted to look at trends and changes in the popularity of these topics across different countries. His dataset consisted of topics, with categories, countries, and timestamps. As in David's case, the dataset he gave us was pre-aggregated: each of these categories was then labeled with the number of impressions—that is, the number of people who searched for terms that matched this category—and the number of people who clicked through on those searches. Madhu gave us 994 million rows of data, covering eight months of usage.

Madhu was excited that Pangloss could let him get to know the shape of his full dataset. In the past, he had not felt like he could explore his data: queries took too long, and so he would focus only on specific questions that he needed to answer.

Madhu searched carefully for patterns: he wanted to find ways that the data changed in regular and systematic ways. He spent most of his time in the heatmap, looking at a dozen or more keywords at a time. He did manage to find trends in the data, including a weekly pattern in one keyword, and another that spiked over a month. He found these results useful enough that he later asked whether he could send us a new, less aggregated dataset, and asked for a follow-up appointment with his team, in the hope that more of his colleagues had an opportunity to understand how the data they worked with operated.

Case Study 3: Faraz and Social Computing
Faraz is a data scientist who works with a Twitter "firehose" feed. One of his projects is to assess the credibility of Twitter users. His team expects that Twitter users can be distinguished by their followers lists, and by the keywords they use. His dataset looks at Twitter users, their hashtags, and the people who they follow; his statistical algorithms also label users who are likely to be spammers.

Faraz looked at the top k charts of the most commonly-used tags, finding terms like "brexit" and "rio2016" were popular; he contrasted this list to keywords tweeted by persons who were labeled as likely to be spammers. Looking at the precise view, he asked to look further down, at tail queries.

Faraz encountered some of the unintuitive aspects of dealing with sample-based analysis: for example, when seeing the top ten keywords, his first impulse was to "remember" just the top keywords. This would not have the desired effect: the full

[1] All names are anonymized.

query might discover new words, but his filtered list would not show them.

Faraz became accustomed to seeing very high uncertainty levels for his high cardinality data. He began to use the approximate query as a draft, less concerned about the answer it showed and more concerned about whether it showed that he had the right query. "I'm doing exploratory data analysis and I don't need full accuracy." When he accidentally formed a view with a bad filter, he quickly noticed the approximate view was incorrect and adjusted the query; after he felt sure he had the right query, he remembered the view.

Pangloss allowed Faraz to explore complex aspects of his data rapidly, and come back to check his results later.

Discussion of User Studies

We were gratified that users were able to use Pangloss to explore their large datasets, and take away actionable and novel conclusions. Users were willing to trust the approximation, and to generate precise results afterward.

Our user studies taught us more about how users see approximate data. Our users see precision broadly: they want both rapid interaction for exploratory phase, and to present precise results to decision makers. Precision is not just a way to verify the approximation, but is an end in itself. In small-data systems, the same tool can fulfill both these roles; here, Pangloss separated those goals.

The process of recording observations during exploratory visualization was unintuitive to all of our users. Most of our users were grateful to have been forced to record their observations, and later found it useful to reconstruct their path. This suggests that Pangloss does not have the right balance of encouraging users to record their observations. There is a broad spectrum of possible approaches–from notebook interfaces that require explicit queries, to systems that automatically recommend visualizations [42]; this design space would reward further exploration.

Users wanted more features from Pangloss: several wanted to be able to see the underlying data: although big data demands aggregations, analysts wanted to see individual records to spot-check their results, and to get a sense of what sat in a bucket. Other users asked for transformations, aggregations, and ways to project the data that Pangloss does not currently support.

CONCLUSIONS

In these conclusions, we note a number of implications of optimistic visualization that emerge from both the user study as well as from our design work.

The concept of optimistic visualization can help users adopt approximate and progressive systems. It is comparatively easy to implement, but the benefits for the users are large. For example, user David used optimism to build confidence in the approximate results after seeing the results of precise queries. Some of our users needed precise data. Under progressive visualization, that means waiting until computation finishes. In Pangloss they could run it in the background. Future work should combine progressive and optimistic, and explore the design space to understand what best benefits users: a system might improve the results for remembered views in the background, allowing the user to check on progress and how the approximation has changed.

Existing visualization tools and techniques make assumptions that do not hold for approximate results. In a sampling environment, more selective predicates can have surprising effects. Additional groups may appear, and both aggregate values and uncertainty levels might change. The same can happen in the transition from approximate to precise results. New visualization systems must be able to handle shifting axes and changing color scales. We will need to develop a vocabulary of visual cues to highlight order changes, new groups (Figure 8), and other qualitative changes.

There are many opportunities to refine the user experience of optimistic visualization for data exploration to address the issues raised during the user studies. One question is how to identify whether a precise view is meaningfully different from the approximation. In Pangloss every precise result is treated the same; it could be valuable to highlight views with significant differences. Whether a change is significant depends on the observation: the observation that A is higher than B is different than observing that $A > 50$; the precise results might invalidate one but not the other.

One interesting question is in deciding what to remember; our users found that the major challenge when using the system. In Pangloss, users must select views explicitly. Pangloss supports an exploratory process; there are cues in the sets of visualizations that the analyst creates to decide which views are worth remembering. With better provenance tracking, we might be able to better decide which observations should be remembered; we might also group visualizations in the history by their broad tasks.

Optimistic visualization comes from a close collaboration between database and visualization researchers. The ideas in this paper have emerged from understanding constraints and opportunities in both areas. We believe that building collaborations between these two fields is critical for improving data analysis going into the future.

This paper contributes the concept of optimistic visualization. We have showed a first implementation of optimism; and discussed ways in which the exploratory data analysis process is different under approximate data. We have shown ways to visualize the difference between the approximate and precise view. Last, we have presented the results of eight users working with an optimistic system, and showed that it can help meet their needs for both speed and precise results.

ACKNOWLEDGMENTS

We thank our participants for their time and the enthusiasm for our prototype. This paper has benefitted from the advice of Jessica Hullman, Arnd Christian König, Steven Drucker, and feedback from the VIBE group at Microsoft Research; and from the comments of the anonymous reviewers.

REFERENCES

1. Sameer Agarwal, Henry Milner, Ariel Kleiner, Ameet Talwalkar, Michael Jordan, Samuel Madden, Barzan Mozafari, and Ion Stoica. 2014. Knowing when You'Re Wrong: Building Fast and Reliable Approximate Query Processing Systems. In *Proceedings of the International Conference on Management of Data (SIGMOD '14)*. ACM. DOI:http://dx.doi.org/10/f3tvrz
2. Sameer Agarwal, Barzan Mozafari, Aurojit Panda, Henry Milner, Samuel Madden, and Ion Stoica. 2013. BlinkDB: Queries with Bounded Errors and Bounded Response Times on Very Large Data. In *Proceedings of the European Conference on Computer Systems (EuroSys '13)*. ACM. DOI:http://dx.doi.org/10/bwrd
3. Michael Bostock, Vadim Ogievetsky, and Jeffrey Heer. 2011. D3 Data-Driven Documents. In *IEEE Transactions on Visualization and Computer Graphics (INFOVIS '11)*. IEEE Educational Activities Department. DOI: http://dx.doi.org/10/b7bhhf
4. Mihai Budiu, Rebecca Isaacs, Derek Murray, Gordon Plotkin, Paul Barham, Samer Al-Kiswany, Yazan Boshmaf, Qingzhou Luo, and Alexandr Andoni. 2015. Interacting with large distributed datasets using Sketch. In *Eurographics Symposium on Parallel Graphics and Visualization*. University of Wisconsin-Madison. DOI: http://dx.doi.org/10/f3tvr9
5. Stuart K. Card, George G. Robertson, and Jock D. Mackinlay. 1991. The Information Visualizer, an Information Workspace. In *Proceedings of the Conference on Human Factors in Computing Systems (CHI '91)*. ACM. DOI:http://dx.doi.org/10/cvtdps
6. Surajit Chaudhuri and Umeshwar Dayal. 1997. An Overview of Data Warehousing and OLAP Technology. In *Proceedings of the International Conference on Management of Data (SIGMOD '97)*. ACM. DOI: http://dx.doi.org/10/bst468
7. Geoff Cumming and Sue Finch. 2005. Inference by eye: confidence intervals and how to read pictures of data. (2005). DOI:http://dx.doi.org/10/c4nsck
8. Bolin Ding, Silu Huang, Surajit Chaudhuri, Kaushik Chakrabarti, and Chi Wang. 2016. Sample + Seek: Approximating Aggregates with Distribution Precision Guarantee. In *Proceedings of the International Conference on Management of Data (SIGMOD '16)*. ACM. DOI:http://dx.doi.org/10/f3tvr2
9. Niklas Elmqvist and Jean-Daniel Fekete. 2010. Hierarchical Aggregation for Information Visualization: Overview, Techniques, and Design Guidelines. In *IEEE Transactions on Visualization and Computer Graphics (INFOVIS '10)*. DOI:http://dx.doi.org/10/db2gxw
10. Jean-Daniel Fekete and Romain Primet. 2016. Progressive Analytics: A Computation Paradigm for Exploratory Data Analysis. (2016). https://arxiv.org/abs/1607.05162
11. Nivan Ferreira, Danyel Fisher, and Arnd Christian König. 2014. Sample-oriented task-driven visualizations: allowing users to make better, more confident decisions. In *Proceedings of the Conference on Human Factors in Computing Systems (CHI '14)*. ACM. DOI: http://dx.doi.org/10/f3tvr6
12. Danyel Fisher. 2016. Big Data Exploration Requires Collaboration Between Visualization and Data Infrastructures. In *Proceedings of the Workshop on Human-In-the-Loop Data Analytics (HILDA '16)*. ACM. DOI:http://dx.doi.org/10/f3tvr7
13. Danyel Fisher, Igor O. Popov, Steven M. Drucker, and Monica M. C. Schraefel. 2012. Trust me, I'm partially right: incremental visualization lets analysts explore large datasets faster. In *Proceedings of the Conference on Human Factors in Computing Systems (CHI '12)*. ACM. DOI:http://dx.doi.org/10/f3tvr5
14. P. Godfrey, J. Gryz, and P. Lasek. 2016. Interactive Visualization of Large Data Sets. In *IEEE Transactions on Knowledge and Data Engineering*. DOI: http://dx.doi.org/10/f3tvr8
15. Jim Gray, Surajit Chaudhuri, Adam Bosworth, Andrew Layman, Don Reichart, Murali Venkatrao, Frank Pellow, and Hamid Pirahesh. 1997. Data Cube: A Relational Aggregation Operator Generalizing Group-By, Cross-Tab, and Sub-Totals. In *Data Mining Knowledge Discovery*. Kluwer Academic Publishers. DOI: http://dx.doi.org/10/brp273
16. Peter J. Haas and Joseph M. Hellerstein. 1999. Ripple Joins for Online Aggregation. In *Proceedings of the International Conference on Management of Data (SIGMOD '99)*. ACM. DOI:http://dx.doi.org/10/dqgn68
17. Jeffrey Heer, Jock Mackinlay, Chris Stolte, and Maneesh Agrawala. 2008. Graphical Histories for Visualization: Supporting Analysis, Communication, and Evaluation. In *IEEE Transactions on Visualization and Computer Graphics (INFOVIS '08)*. DOI: http://dx.doi.org/10/b5fvmx
18. Joseph M. Hellerstein, Ron Avnur, Andy Chou, Christian Hidber, Chris Olston, Vijayshankar Raman, Tali Roth, and Peter J. Haas. 1999. Interactive Data Analysis: The Control Project. (1999). DOI: http://dx.doi.org/10/bsjgrh
19. Joseph M. Hellerstein, Peter J. Haas, and Helen J. Wang. 1997. Online Aggregation. In *Proceedings of the International Conference on Management of Data (SIGMOD '97)*. ACM. DOI:http://dx.doi.org/10/bbk4fr
20. Jessica Hullman, Paul Resnick, and Eytan Adar. 2015. Hypothetical Outcome Plots Outperform Error Bars and Violin Plots for Inferences about Reliability of Variable Ordering *(PloS one)*. Public Library of Science. DOI: http://dx.doi.org/10/f3tvsd
21. Susan Joslyn and Jared LeClerc. 2013. Decisions with uncertainty: the glass half full. (2013). DOI: http://dx.doi.org/10/f3tvrx

22. Niranjan Kamat, Prasanth Jayachandran, Karthik Tunga, and Arnab Nandi. 2014. Distributed and interactive cube exploration. In *International Conference on Data Engineering*. IEEE. DOI:http://dx.doi.org/10/f3tvsb

23. Lauro Lins, James T Klosowski, and Carlos Scheidegger. 2013. Nanocubes for real-time exploration of spatiotemporal datasets. In *IEEE Transactions on Visualization and Computer Graphics (INFOVIS '13)*. DOI:http://dx.doi.org/10/bwrc http://nanocubes.net/.

24. Zhicheng Liu and Jeffrey Heer. 2014. The effects of interactive latency on exploratory visual analysis. In *IEEE transactions on visualization and computer graphics (INFOVIS '14)*. DOI:http://dx.doi.org/10/f3tvrw

25. Zhicheng Liu, Biye Jiang, and Jeffrey Heer. 2013. imMens: Real-time Visual Querying of Big Data. In *Proceedings of the Eurographics Conference on Visualization (EuroVis '13)*. DOI: http://dx.doi.org/10/f3tvr4

26. Jerzy Neyman. 1937. Outline of a theory of statistical estimation based on the classical theory of probability. (1937). DOI:http://dx.doi.org/10/b79jvq

27. Jakob Nielsen. 1993. Response times: The 3 important limits. (1993).

28. Chris North. 2006. Toward Measuring Visualization Insight. (2006). DOI:http://dx.doi.org/10/b2758v

29. Bureau of Transportation Statistics. 2016. Airline Delays, Cancellations and Tarmac Times. (2016). http://www.rita.dot.gov/bts/data_and_statistics/by_mode/airline_and_airports/airline_delay.html

30. Frank Olken and Doron Rotem. 1986. Simple Random Sampling from Relational Databases *(VLDB '86)*. http://dl.acm.org/citation.cfm?id=645913.671474

31. Chris Olston and Jock D. Mackinlay. 2002. Visualizing Data with Bounded Uncertainty. In *Proceedings of the IEEE Symposium on Information Visualization (INFOVIS '02)*. http://dl.acm.org/citation.cfm?id=857191.857754

32. Alexandre Perrot, Romain Bourqui, Nicolas Hanusse, Frédéric Lalanne, and David Auber. 2015. Large interactive visualization of density functions on big data infrastructure. In *Symposium on Large Data Analysis and Visualization (LDAV)*. IEEE. DOI: http://dx.doi.org/10/f3tvr3

33. Nicola Pezzotti, Boudewijn Lelieveldt, Laurens van der Maaten, Thomas Hollt, Elmar Eisemann, and Anna Vilanova. 2015. Approximated and User Steerable tSNE for Progressive Visual Analytics. In *IEEE Transactions on Visualization and Computer Graphics (INFOVIS '16)*. IEEE. DOI:http://dx.doi.org/10/f3tvrt

34. Peter Pirolli and Stuart Card. 2005. The sensemaking process and leverage points for analyst technology as identified through cognitive task analysis. In *Proceedings of international conference on intelligence analysis*.

35. John Stasko, Carsten Görg, and Zhicheng Liu. 2008. Jigsaw: Supporting Investigative Analysis Through Interactive Visualization. (2008).

36. Charles D Stolper, Adam Perer, and David Gotz. 2014. Progressive visual analytics: User-driven visual exploration of in-progress analytics. (2014). DOI: http://dx.doi.org/10/f3tvrv

37. Chris Stolte, Diane Tang, and Pat Hanrahan. 2002. Polaris: A system for query, analysis, and visualization of multidimensional relational databases. In *IEEE Transactions on Visualization and Computer Graphics (INFOVIS '02)*. IEEE. http://dl.acm.org/citation.cfm?id=857190.857686

38. John W Tukey. 1977. Exploratory data analysis. (1977).

39. Cagatay Turkay, Erdem Kaya, Selim Balcisoy, and Helwig Hauser. 2017. Designing Progressive and Interactive Analytics Processes for High-Dimensional Data Analysis. In *IEEE Transactions on Visualization and Computer Graphics (INFOVIS '16)*. IEEE. DOI: http://dx.doi.org/10/f3tvsc

40. Hadley Wickham. 2013. Bin-summarise-smooth: a framework for visualising large data. (2013).

41. Hadley Wickham and Lisa Stryjewski. 2011. 40 years of boxplots. (2011).

42. K. Wongsuphasawat, D. Moritz, A. Anand, J. Mackinlay, B. Howe, and J. Heer. 2016. Voyager: Exploratory Analysis via Faceted Browsing of Visualization Recommendations. In *IEEE Transactions on Visualization and Computer Graphics (INFOVIS '15)*. DOI:http://dx.doi.org/10/bdsz https://idl.cs.washington.edu/papers/voyager/.

43. Ji Soo Yi, Youn-ah Kang, John T. Stasko, and Julie A. Jacko. 2008. Understanding and Characterizing Insights: How Do People Gain Insights Using Information Visualization?. In *Proceedings of the Workshop on BEyond Time and Errors: Novel evaLuation Methods for Information Visualization (BELIV '08)*. ACM. DOI: http://dx.doi.org/10/c7m5hm

iSphere: Focus+Context Sphere Visualization for Interactive Large Graph Exploration

Fan Du
University of Maryland
fan@cs.umd.edu

Nan Cao
Tongji University
nan.cao@gmail.com

Yu-Ru Lin
University of Pittsburgh
yurulin@pitt.edu

Panpan Xu
Hong Kong University of Science and Technology
pxu@cse.ust.hk

Hanghang Tong
Arizona State University
hanghang.tong@asu.edu

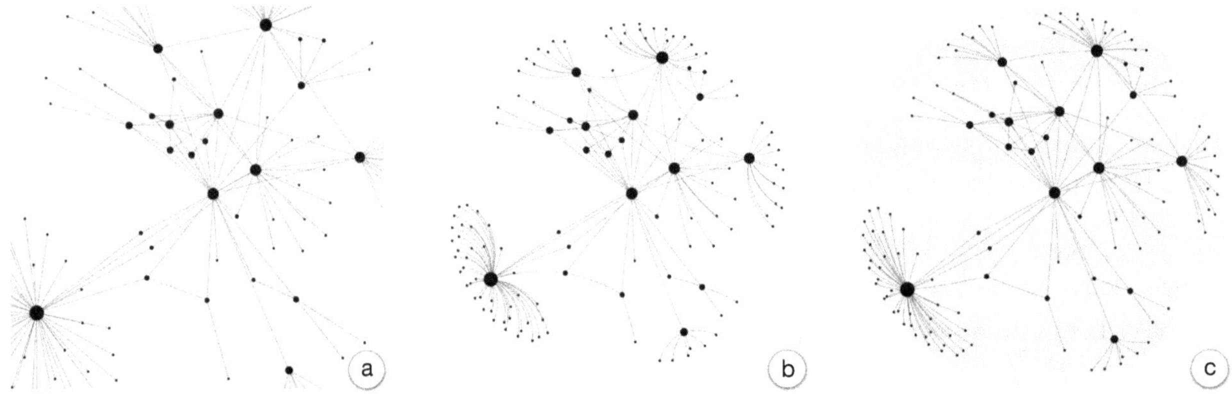

Figure 1. The node-link diagram shown in (a) the zoomable plane and the focus+context displays, (b) hyperbolic display and (c) iSphere display.

ABSTRACT
Interactive exploration plays a critical role in large graph visualization. Existing techniques, such as zoom-and-pan on a 2D plane and hyperbolic browser facilitate large graph exploration by showing both the details of a focal area and its surrounding context that guides the exploration process. However, existing techniques for large graph exploration are limited in either providing too little context or presenting graphs with too much distortion. In this paper, we propose a novel focus+context technique, iSphere, to address the limitation. iSphere maps a large graph onto a Riemann Sphere that better preserves graph structures and shows greater context information. We conduct extensive experiment studies on different graph exploration tasks under various conditions. The results show that iSphere performs the best in task completion time compared to the baseline techniques in link and path exploration tasks. This research also contributes to understanding large graph exploration on small screens.

Permission to make digital or hard copies of all or part of this work for personal or classroom use is granted without fee provided that copies are not made or distributed for profit or commercial advantage and that copies bear this notice and the full citation on the first page. Copyrights for components of this work owned by others than ACM must be honored. Abstracting with credit is permitted. To copy otherwise, or republish, to post on servers or to redistribute to lists, requires prior specific permission and/or a fee. Request permissions from permissions@acm.org.
CHI 2017, May 06–11, 2017, Denver, CO, USA
© 2017 ACM. ISBN 978-1-4503-4655-9/17/05...$15.00
DOI: http://dx.doi.org/10.1145/3025453.3025628

Author Keywords
Graph visualization; graph exploration; focus+context.

ACM Classification Keywords
H.5.2 User Interfaces: Graphical user interfaces (GUI)

INTRODUCTION
Interactive exploration is one of the major approaches for navigating through large graph data, which is widely adopted by many graph visualization systems [10, 12, 40, 42]. It has been used for, for example, navigating through a big road network on Google Maps or finding relational patterns such as communities or critical paths between communities in a large social network [10]. Various visualization and interaction techniques have been developed for supporting *large* graph exploration, that is, the exploration of a large graph on a relatively *small* screen. In particular, users can query to find and visualize the parts of interest of a large graph in a node-link diagram [10–12], explore an aggregated graph via semantic zooming [2, 6, 19, 39, 47, 50], use brushing on a graph overview to show the detailed structures in a separate view [2, 27], or directly perform zooming and panning on a graph in a focus+context display [42, 46].

However, most of the above techniques have limitations for exploring a large graph. For example, the query based approach is only useful when the properties of the desired structure are known, so that queries can be formulated. Semantic zoom is usually inefficient when the hierarchy of the aggregated graph is deep. Overview+detail based approaches break the spatial continuity of a graph representation, making it inefficient for, for example, tracing a long path in the graph. Focus+context displays circumscribe the aforementioned issues by showing both the focal details and overview context smoothly and continuously within the same view, and they have been the core of recent hybrid techniques that aim to use a small screen more efficiently [38, 56]. Two techniques in this category, plane (Fig. 1(a)) and hyperbolic [31,42] (Fig. 1(b)) displays, have been widely used for graph exploration, but also have limitations. The first technique often shows too little context to guide the exploration while the second one tends to introduce too much distortion when displaying the graph links, making path tracing difficult [31, 57].

To address the above issues, we introduce a novel focus+context display, iSphere (Fig. 1(c)), for supporting interactive large graph exploration. It maps a node-link diagram onto a Riemann Sphere [3] and orthogonally projects the sphere onto a 2D plane. The produced focus+context view, similar to the hyperbolic display, has a focal area in the middle surrounded by context suppressed at the periphery of the circular display. We compared iSphere with the plane and hyperbolic displays in two controlled user studies, based on three graph exploration tasks, which were designed for exploring three fundamental graph elements: nodes, links, and paths. In particular, *Study I* investigated iSphere's performance in a full-sized window on a regular laptop computer and *Study II* investigated iSphere's performance in smaller windows, mimicking the screen sizes of the mainstream personal-computing devices, i.e., tablets, mobile phones, and smart watches.

The study results showed iSphere had the best performance under several testing conditions. In particular, it significantly outperformed the hyperbolic display in path exploration tasks and significantly outperformed the plane display in both link and path exploration tasks in smaller windows. These results suggested the potential of using iSphere on mobile devices for exploring the routes inside a large graph. Overall, this paper has the following contributions:

- We propose a novel focus+context display for large graph exploration, which shows more context when compared to the plane display and better preserves graph structures when compared to the hyperbolic display.
- We report the first, to the best of our knowledge, comprehensive user studies, comparing two different focus+context techniques as well as the zoomable plane, while varying exploration tasks, screen sizes, and graph sizes.
- We provide extensive analysis and discussion of the study results that give insight to when, why, and how different graph displays are useful or have limitations. We further discuss the benefit of applying iSphere on smaller screens (tablets, mobile phones, smart watches) and how it helps users make sense of a large graph during the exploration, which provides insight into the trade-offs between the amount of distortion and contextual details on small displays.

GRAPH EXPLORATION TECHNIQUES

In this section, we review and compare interaction and visualization techniques developed for exploring large-scale graphs shown in node-link diagrams. We focus on the most generic and related techniques, including (1) query based approach, (2) semantic zoom in hierarchical graphs, (3) zooming and panning, (4) overview+detail, and (5) focus+context. More comprehensive and general surveys can be found in [40, 51].

Interaction Techniques

There are three generic interaction techniques that are developed for exploring a large graph, including (1) the query based approach, (2) semantic zoom in hierarchical graphs, and (3) zooming and panning.

Query Based Approach. Query (or search) is the simplest approach for exploring a large graph, which has been adopted by many graph visualization systems. Via this approach, users can query the labels of nodes or links to find and visualize a graph portion of their own interests. For example, FacetAtlas [11] was designed for exploring a word co-occurrence graph extracted from documents by querying on different topics. g-Miner [10] supports the exploration of large multivariate graphs via querying on both the graph structure and node attributes. However, query based graph exploration is only efficient when users' tasks are clear so that queries can be formulated. In many real world applications, users explore the graph without a specific goal, which cannot be accomplished with query based approaches.

Semantic Zoom in Hierarchical Graph. Semantic zoom is commonly used in hierarchical graph visualizations [2,6,19,39, 47, 50], in which the nodes in a large graph are hierarchically aggregated into so-called "meta-nodes" and the graph structure with respect to the meta-nodes is displayed. It reduces the total number of nodes and links to be visualized at a time [20]. Usually, the first level of the hierarchy is shown by default. When users zoom into the next level, the graph at the specified level is visualized. In contrast to the ordinary graphical zoom, semantic zoom not only changes the graphical representation, but also updates the data to be displayed [54].

When compared to the query based approach, hierarchical graph visualizations provide additional context to guide the data navigation procedure. The meta-nodes show potential options to be zoomed into. However, important information such as how a leaf connects to other leaves under different branches is still missing. Users have to zoom back and forth to navigate through different branches. When the hierarchy is deep or has a large fan-out, semantic zoom is inefficient.

Graphical Zooming and Panning. One solution to avoid the inefficient semantic zoom is to flatten or even remove the hierarchy. However, the *presentation problem*, i.e., the lack of space for showing a large dataset [18], makes node-link diagrams incapable of representing a large graph without any aggregation. Zooming and panning [44] are the most commonly used interactions that address this issue. They are often used together to help users control the exploration. Many zoomable user interfaces [9,44] have been developed, and they are also frequently used for exploring large graph data [48]. We adopted these interactions in iSphere to support a continuous exploration in a focus+context display.

Visualization Techniques

Two generic visualization design principles, overview+detail and focus+context, are also used for exploring large graphs.

Overview+Detail. An overview+detail user interface of a large graph consists of multiple views with an overview (overall view) illustrating the entire graph and other views showing the details of the graph from different perspectives. A typical implementation of this technique combines the two views together based on two different approaches: (1) the overview is displayed in a small inspection window that floats on top of another big window with a selected portion of the graph shown in detail (or in the opposite) [27], and (2) the details are visualized in a small inspection lens which floats on top of the overview window [30, 34]. The overview and the detail view are linked together by interactions. Users can choose to visualize the details of any part by brushing on the overview in the first design or moving the lens in the second design.

Although simple to implement and widely used, showing overview and details in two separated views breaks the spacial continuity of the visual representation, making this technique difficult for a user to, for example, trace or recall a long path in a large graph.

Focus+Context. Focus+context [7] is another generic visualization design principle that is commonly used for big data exploration. It enables viewers to see the objects of primary interest presented in full details while at the same time get an overview-impression of the surrounding context. A focus+context display guarantees the spacial continuity and enables a smooth data navigation via zooming and panning. Although many techniques have been developed [13], here, we only focus on those designs for representing graphs.

The simplest way for representing a large graph is to directly show the graph in a zoomable and pannable window, in which only a small portion of the data is shown in a focal viewport. Users can navigate through the entire data by zooming and panning the viewport. Distortion oriented techniques [37] have been developed to improve this design by magnifying the focal area while showing more surrounding context without increasing the display size or losing the spacial continuity. These techniques, such as the polyfocal projection [29], the Bifocal Display [5], and various types of graphical fisheye views [22, 37, 46] and topological fisheye views [1, 14, 25], produce similar results in which the context regions are suppressed, leaving space for showing more details in the focal area. However, given the limited distortion rate, these approaches are incapable of transforming the entire visualization plane into a focus+context display [41]. Besides, past user studies on distortion techniques indicate that introducing distortion will impair users' performance as they must remain aware about the distortions in shape and position and mentally undo them when needed [23]. Therefore, the distortion oriented techniques are often used as an interactive lens to magnify a small focal region inside a large display [49].

There have also been hybrid focus+context techniques that focused on how to use a small screen more efficiently. For example, to better allocate space to display details of a user's interest, Li and Takatsuka proposed a context-based filtering technique that combines the degree of interest of Logical Fisheye View and geometric distortion [38]. ViSizer [56] automatically resizes a visualization to fit any display by combining multi-focus+context and grid deformation to avoid feature congestion. Such hybrid techniques are complementary as they can be used to augment existing focus+context methods.

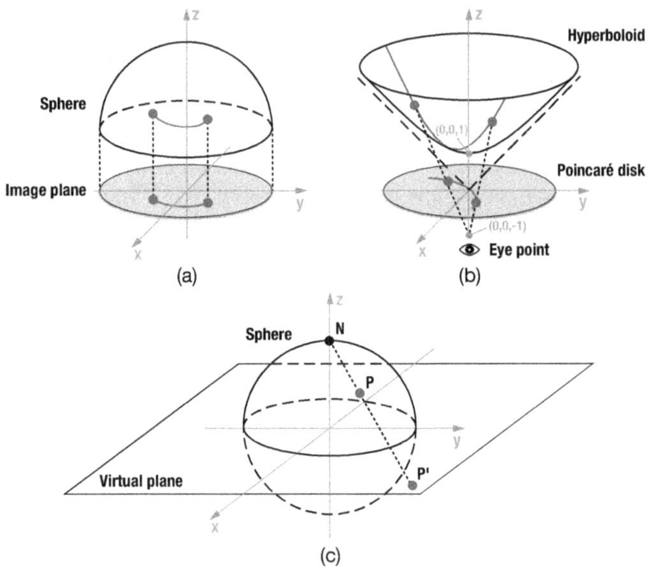

Figure 2. Illustrations of (a) the orthogonal projection from a sphere to a Euclidean plane, (b) the perspective projection from a hyperboloid surface to the Poincaré disk, and (c) the conformal mapping from the Riemann Sphere to a virtual plane.

Non-Euclidean geometry was used for producing a focus+context display with a much higher distortion rate. In three dimensions, there are two types of non-Euclidean geometries, namely, elliptic geometry and hyperbolic geometry [55]. Elliptic geometry can be visualized as the surface of a sphere in the three dimensional space on which "lines" on a Euclidean plane are shown as big circles. When the sphere is shown in a 2D display on the screen based on the orthogonal projection, it automatically generates a focus+context display (Fig. 2(a)). Using this technique, Kobourov and Wampler [31] extended the traditional force directed layout to directly lay out a graph on the surface of a sphere. Ito et al. [28] also proposed algorithms for visualizing a bipartite graph on a sphere. However, these techniques are limited by the "presentation problem" as the surface area of a sphere is limited. Recently, Kwon et al. [33] applied spherical graph layout in an immersion system, but its usage on a 2D plane remains unclear.

Hyperbolic geometry can be represented by the Poincaré disk model [21] in two dimensions. As shown in Fig. 2(b), this model compresses the infinite surface of the forward sheet (S^+) of a two-sheet hyperboloid into a circular disk based on a prospective projection at (0,0,-1). In this way, the point (0,0,1) on the hyperboloid surface is projected onto the center of the Poincaré disk. The points that are infinitely far away are projected onto the boundary of the Poincaré disk. This approach provides an extremely high distortion rate that suppresses the surface of S^+ into a unit disk which can be displayed in an arbitrary-sized window. In addition, when compared to other models [4], the Poincaré disk model, also known as the conformal disk model, preserves angles, which is an important property for representing structures and shapes. These nice properties attracted attention in the field of information visualization and the Poincaré disk model has been extensively used to produce a focus+context view for exploring large tree structures [35], graphs [31, 42] (in both 2D and 3D), and multidimensional data [16, 53]. Besides, Kreuseler et al. [32] extend this model by introducing additional degrees of freedom for exploring complex hierarchical graphs, which allows users to change the focal area by moving the center of the projection. These are the state-of-the-art focus+context techniques that are most related to iSphere. However, as discussed in [31], although the Poincaré disk model preserves angles, it distorts lines, which makes path tracing in a graph difficult [31, 57].

iSphere circumscribes the aforementioned issues by introducing a focus+context display with a moderate distortion rate that provides more context than the plane display and also reduces the distortion of links when compared to the hyperbolic display. Our user studies showed that iSphere was efficient for supporting graph exploration tasks and was significantly better than the hyperbolic display in many situations.

ISPHERE VISUALIZATION

In this section, we discuss the design philosophy and technical details about the implementation of iSphere.

Design Philosophy

iSphere was designed for visualizing and exploring large graphs. We attempted to develop a generic technique that can be used for all types of graphs (directed/undirected, unipartite/bipartite/multipartite, planar/non-planar) of different sizes that are visualized in a node-link diagram but is *independent* of any type of node-link graph layouts. To this end, we introduced a projection based approach that transforms the graph visualization into a focus+context display as a whole.

Specifically, we first visualize a graph on a virtual (or conceptual) plane ($\mathbb{P}$). It has an infinite size so that graphs in any scale can be clearly shown. We then map $\mathbb{P}$ onto a unit sphere $\mathbb{S}$ based on the inverse of the stereographic projection [15]. After that, $\mathbb{S}$ is scaled and rendered into a two-dimensional view port based on the orthogonal projection, which transforms $\mathbb{P}$ into a focus+context display. We describe the details of each step in the rest of this section.

Placing a Graph in a Virtual Plane

The vertices of a graph can be placed onto the virtual plane ($\mathbb{P}$) by using any of the existing graph layout algorithms. This procedure usually runs offline as most of the current layout algorithms are inefficient when the graph is large. In our implementation, stress majorization [24] is applied.

Mapping the Virtual Plane onto the Riemann Sphere

The virtual plane, with the graph visualized on it, is then mapped onto the surface of a unit sphere, also known as the Riemann Sphere ($\mathbb{S}$), based on the inverse of the stereographic projection. This projection was first introduced for producing a map, which projects the surface of a sphere (e.g., the Earth) onto a plane (e.g., a map). It is obtained by projecting a point $P(x,y,z)$ on sphere $\mathbb{S}$ from the sphere's north pole N to a point $P'(X,Y)$ that intersects sphere at the equator (Fig. 2(c)). The projection is given by the following formula:

$$(X,Y) = \left(\frac{x}{1-z}, \frac{y}{1-z}\right)$$

In iSphere, we perform the inverse of this projection to map the virtual plane onto the surface of $\mathbb{S}$, formally described as:

$$(x,y,z) = \left(\frac{2X}{X^2+Y^2+1}, \frac{2Y}{X^2+Y^2+1}, \frac{X^2+Y^2-1}{X^2+Y^2+1}\right)$$

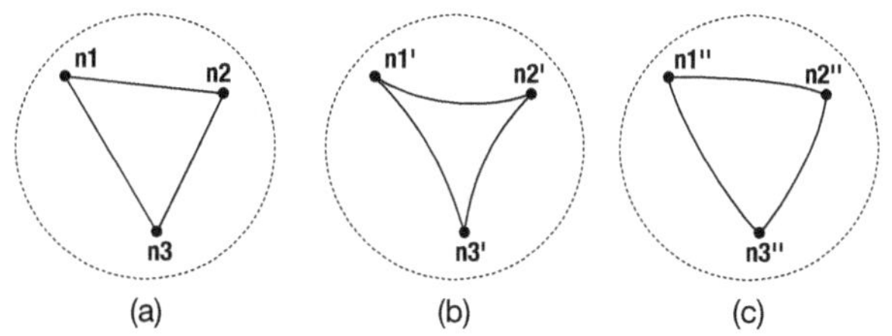

Figure 3. An illustration of a triangle displayed on (a) a Euclidean plane, (b) a Poincaré disk, and (c) a Riemann Sphere.

This is a *conformal* mapping, through which angles are preserved. As shown in Fig. 2(c), in this mapping, the plane region inside the sphere is mapped onto the surface of the south hemisphere, thus being magnified and becoming the focus of the view. The plane region outside the sphere is suppressed and mapped onto the north hemisphere as the context. Particularly, all the points infinitely far away from the plane center are compressed into the north pole.

Rendering

Usually, the south hemisphere of $\mathbb{S}$ is rendered in front of users based on orthogonal projection as it displays the focal area in the above mapping model. In our system, each node of the graph is mapped on the sphere. However, the mapping procedure can be parallelized at the pixel level while rendering on a GPU, making it efficient and general enough for representing any visualization shown on $\mathbb{P}$ beyond node-link diagrams.

When graph links are arbitrary curves (e.g., bundled arcs) on $\mathbb{P}$, they have to be rendered at the pixel level by mapping each pixel (or densely sampling some of the pixels) in the curve onto the sphere and connecting them by an interpolating spline as an approximation. This procedure can also be accelerated by a GPU. When graph links are displayed as straight line segments on $\mathbb{P}$, the rendering can be simplified based on a property of the stereographic projection, i.e., a straight line is mapped to a large circle on $\mathbb{S}$. Therefore, a link when visualized on $\mathbb{S}$ will be a circular arc segment, which can be determined by the mapping results of the link's endpoints and midpoint. We implemented the second approach assuming that all the links are straight lines on $\mathbb{P}$.

Interactions

Zooming and panning are also implemented in iSphere for navigating through the virtual plane. Users can zoom in or out by decreasing or increasing the radius of $\mathbb{S}$ to exclude or include the content inside the focal area (i.e., the south hemisphere). They can also pan the graph on $\mathbb{S}$ based on the Möbius transformation [17]. Another equivalent implementation of these interactions is to keep $\mathbb{S}$ unchanged and simply zooming and panning on the virtual plane. The mapping is refreshed in each mouse operation. Both methods provide a smooth and continuous transforming effect. Especially, the effect of panning on iSphere looks like the rotation of a sphere, which was preferred by most of the participants in our user studies.

Comparing to the Hyperbolic Display

A hyperbolic based focus+context display [31,35] shares many similar properties and functions with iSphere. First, both of them distort the original Euclidean plane into a circular focus+context display in which the center region is magnified for showing the focus and the surrounding region is suppressed for the context. Second, they both provide a conformal transformation, so that the graph structures are preserved on these displays. Third, they both map an infinite information space (i.e., S^+ on a Poincaré disk and $\mathbb{P}$ on a Riemann Sphere) into a unit display that can be visualized in windows of any size.

They also have many distinct properties. First, the hyperbolic display has a much higher distortion rate. Intuitively, it maps points infinitely far away in the information space onto the edge of a Poincaré disk, making the entire space visible to users. In this case, high-level topology tasks such as identifying clusters may be easier. However, the heavy distortion impacts user interaction as small movements can trigger big visual changes. In contrast, iSphere maps the information space onto a 3D Riemann Sphere, which is orthogonally projected onto a 2D display, thus only showing half of the sphere (i.e., information space) and hiding nodes that are far away from the focus. Second, on a Poincaré disk, a hyperbolic line is an arc of a Euclidean circle contained within the disk that is perpendicular to the boundary of the disk, which is different from the line shown on a Riemann sphere as discussed above. Third, hyperbolic geometry has a constant negative sectional curvature, whereas the Riemann Sphere's is always positive. These properties lead to different representations of a structure. As illustrated in Fig. 3, a triangle on a Euclidean plane is shown differently on a Poincaré disk (curving inward) or on a Riemann Sphere (curving outward).

In the following sections, we will investigate how these properties affect users' performance in graph exploration tasks.

EXPERIMENT DESIGN

In this section, we introduce the design of the user studies and provide rationales for the key design decisions based on our pilot studies and literature survey.

Baselines

In the studies, we compare the different displays introduced above (Fig. 1), including the plane display (D_p), the hyperbolic display (D_h), and the proposed iSphere display (D_s). All of them support zooming and panning (Fig. 4) and were implemented in Java. In particular, developing a two dimensional hyperbolic display for showing a generic graph visualization is non-trivial as the original system was introduced for representing and exploring a tree or a tree-like graph [35] based on a radial layout. To ensure a fair comparison, we kept the layout method (i.e., the stress majorization [24]) unchanged in all three displays. We implemented the projection techniques introduced in [31] and implemented zooming by adjusting distances between nodes based on the Poincaré metric [8] and panning based on the Möbius transformation [17].

Tasks

Following the task taxonomy of graph visualizations [36], we designed three graph exploration tasks in our studies that respectively focused on exploring nodes, links, and paths:

T1: *Finding target(s) in the neighbors of a given node (node exploration).* Given a node A, find a target node B with the highest degree in A's neighborhood.

T2: *Finding target(s) in the common neighbors of two given nodes (link exploration).* Given two nodes A and B, find a target node C with the highest degree among the common neighbors of A and B.

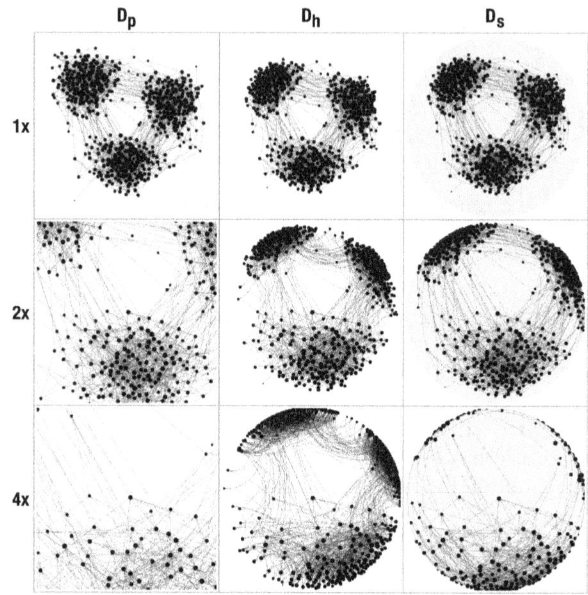

Figure 4. Illustrations of the zooming effect of D_p, D_h, and D_s. The graph contains 512 nodes and 4,096 links.

T3: *Finding target(s) on a given path (path exploration).* Given a path from node A to node B, find a target node C with the highest degree among the nodes on the path.

All these tasks were designed to investigate a wide-range exploration of the graph via zooming and panning in both the plane display and focus+context displays, so that the displays' pros and cons can be revealed. For example, to find the most connected neighbor of a given node A in a large graph, users must zoom into details and pan around to see and compare different neighbors of A. A distortion based focus+context display might be helpful as it shows more context that guides the navigation when compared to the plane display. Here, users were asked to select one single target instead of multiple targets (e.g., all the neighbors of a node) in order to minimize their operations. Fixing the target number also ensures a fair comparison of the task completion time in all cases, as selecting different amounts of targets will cost different length of time which could confound the study results. We did not include high-level topology tasks (e.g., identifying clusters) since our pilot users were able to complete them easily through zooming functions. When the zooming factor is small enough, all three techniques look quite similar, which makes such tasks not differentiable and less informative.

Variables

The primary variable to test in the user studies was the three different displays shown in Fig. 1. In addition, a display's capability of supporting the exploration of a large graph can be affected by the size and community structure of the graph, as well as the size of the display window—these are additional variables used for generating different testing conditions in our studies. In particular, we applied the graph data model introduced by Sah et al. [45] to produce undirected random graphs whose sizes and community structures were precisely controlled for different testing conditions. We also chose to use four different window sizes in the studies. In addition, a pilot study with 4 users was conducted to determine many other conditions that may affect users' performance.

We did not include distortion lens based techniques in the experiments because such techniques alone are often insufficient to cover a relatively large virtual plane. To make the study conditions comparable, we have to use the lens on top of a zooming and panning display, but this setting confounds with other factors—it is hard to tell if the changes in performance are caused by the distortion lens or the zooming and panning. Therefore, we focused on techniques that are able to display an infinitely large virtual plane directly. We believe a distortion lens is more like a widget instead of a display, which can be attached to all three types of displays described in this paper.

Graph Size. We controlled the graph size via two parameters: the number of nodes and the average degree of the graph. We tested a wide range of different choices in the pilot study and selected the parameters that best differentiated users' performance. In particular, we chose graphs with at most $2,048$ nodes to ensure that all the tasks can be completed by users in approximately 30 seconds. To the best of our knowledge, this is the largest graph scale that has ever been tested in a controlled user study. However, such graph size is still far from "big." To investigate the scalability of each display while keeping the tests to be completed within a bearable time for users, we proposed to conduct a scale-up experiment to illustrate the performance trends when the size of the graph is exponentially increased. Specifically we tested users' performance based on small graphs ($2^7 = 128$ nodes), medium graphs ($2^9 = 512$ nodes), and large graphs ($2^{11} = 2,048$ nodes) in a row. In addition, we chose 8 as the average degree as it produced the most feasible tasks according to our pilot users—neither too dense nor too sparse. Accordingly, the number of links of a small/medium/large graph was set to $1,024/4,096/16,384$.

Graph Structure. We controlled the community structure of a graph based on modularity [43], which is a measurement designed to estimate the strength of the division of a graph into clusters. Intuitively, a graph with a high modularity shows clear modular structures (i.e., clusters) (Fig. 5(a)), whereas, a graph with a low modularity shows no clear structures (Fig. 5(b)). We tested a wide range of modularity scores in the pilot study and selected 0.3 and 0.6 as low and high modularity scores, respectively. We also fixed the number of clusters to be three in the testing graphs to produce testing cases with a moderate difficulty.

Window Size. We displayed the generated graphs inside areas of four different sizes to mimic the screen sizes of the mainstream personal-computing devices, i.e., laptop computers, tablets, mobile phones, and smart watches. Particularly, we chose the window size for mimicking laptop computers to be $1,366 \times 768$ pixels (361×203 mm on a standard 96 dpi display), which is the most common screen size according to the latest display statistics [52]. We also chose to use iPad Air, iPhone 6, and iWatch to represent tablets, mobile phones, and smart watches, whose screens are 148×197 mm, 58×104 mm, and 36×42 mm in dimension, respectively.

In the pilot study, we also found that despite the graph size, graph modular structure, and window size, the difficulty of a task also heavily depends on the number of nodes needed to be explored and their distributions in the testing graph. To control the difficulty, we fixed these factors when producing the testing data. In particular, we selected a node A whose degree was 15 and neighbors were scattered inside different

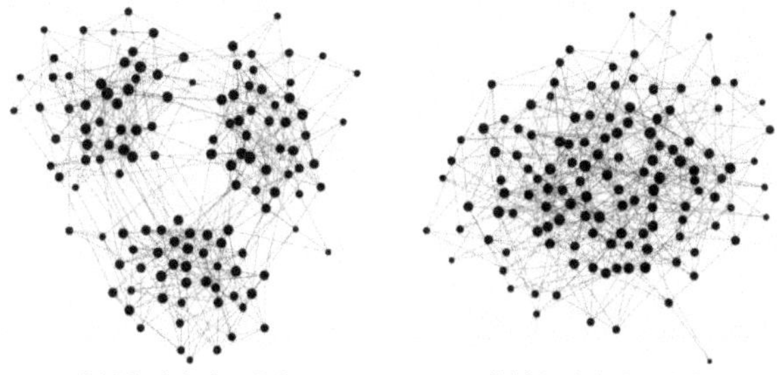

Figure 5. Examples of (a) a high-modularity graph and (b) a low-modularity graph, both of size 128 nodes and 1,024 links.

clusters for *T1*, selected two nodes A and B belonging to different clusters and sharing exactly three common neighbors for *T2*, and selected a path with the length of 5 and all its containing nodes scattered in three different clusters for *T3*. These parameters were determined in the pilot study to ensure a moderate difficulty of each task.

Study Conditions

A full investigation of the above independent variables and tasks leads to a total of 648 testing trials[1] for each participant, which takes about five hours to finish, thus making the study impossible to be conducted. To reduce the fatigue issue and ensure the quality of the results, instead of testing all the conditions at once, we designed two within-subject studies[2] in a row to cover different testing conditions.

Study I tests how different techniques (D_p, D_h, D_s), graph sizes (small, medium, large), and modularity settings (low, high) affect a user's performance on exploring a graph. We used a full-sized window on a regular laptop computer (i.e., $1,366 \times 768$ pixels). In this study, each participant needed to perform 54 study trials three times, once for each of the three tested graph exploration techniques, yielding a total of $2,916$ ($18 \times 3 \times 54$) trials as summarized in Table 1.

Study II tests how different window sizes (i.e., tablet, mobile phone, smart watch) affect a user's performance on exploring a large graph using D_s or D_p. Here, we chose to only use large graphs to increase the difficulty of the tasks. We also eliminated the cases of using D_h given its poor performance on small screens according to our pilot study (several users even failed to complete the tasks using D_h when the screen is of the size of a smart watch). In this way, as summarized in Table 1, each participant needed to perform 54 study trials twice, once for each tested graph exploration technique, yielding a total of $1,944$ ($18 \times 2 \times 54$) trials.

	Study I	*Study II*
Techniques	D_p, D_h, D_s	D_p, D_s
Tasks	T1, T2, T3	T1, T2, T3
Window Sizes	Laptop Computer	Tablet, Phone, Watch
Graph Sizes	Small, Medium, Large	Large
Graph Modularities	Low, High	Low, High
Repetitions	3	3
Participants	18	18
Total trials	2,916	1,944

Table 1. The design of the study trials.

[1] 3 (techniques) $\times$ 3 (tasks) $\times$ 4 (window sizes) $\times$ 3 (graph sizes) $\times$ 2 (modularities) $\times$ 3 (repetitions) = 648 trials.

[2] The two studies were designed and conducted separately. *Study II* was designed following the suggestions from *Study I*'s participants.

Hypotheses

In the studies, we were interested in comparing the effectiveness of the plane display and two different focus+context displays in supporting large graph exploration. We believed that when the graph is small or the window is large, they would make little difference. However, when the size of the graph increases or the size of the window decreases, preserving the graph context properly becomes critical as it can guide users' navigation and help them find the target more efficiently.

As discussed previously, the three tested displays preserve different amounts of context in the periphery of the view ports in different ways. D_h has the highest distortion rate, in which the entire graph is shown in the display with a part in the center as the focus surrounded by the remaining graph suppressed as the context. D_s has a lower distortion rate, in which only the related part is shown as the context, surrounding the focal area. D_p has no distortion, showing the least amount of context. On one hand, a higher distortion rate increases the amount of context that can guide the data exploration. On the other hand, it also leads to more curved graph links and distorted graph structures, and unfavorably impacts interaction by triggering big visual changes, which may affect users' performance. Therefore, an effective graph exploration lies in balancing these two factors. In the following, we hypothesize the impact of different techniques (D_p, D_h, D_s in *Study I* and D_p, D_s in *Study II*) on graph exploration with different graph conditions and window sizes.

Among the three displays, D_h and D_s provide more contextual information (D_h the most) than D_p, thus better facilitating the node exploration task. Hence, we hypothesize:

H1(a): D_h is more effective than D_s and D_p in performing *T1* when graph size increases in *Study I*.

H1(b): D_s is more effective than D_p in performing *T1* when window size decreases in *Study II*.

Meanwhile, D_s shows more context than D_p and its links are less distorted when compared to D_h. Hence, we hypothesize that for the link and path exploration tasks, it will perform better than the other two techniques:

H2(a): D_s is more effective than D_h and D_p for *T2* when graph size increases in *Study I*.

H2(b): D_s is more effective than D_p for *T2* when window size decreases in *Study II*.

H3(a): D_s is more effective than D_h and D_p for *T3* when graph size increases in *Study I*.

H3(b): D_s is more effective than D_p for *T3* when window size decreases in *Study II*.

Besides graph size, in *T3*, users' performance will also be affected by graph topological structure: when the modular structure in the testing graph is clear, D_p will perform the best as it best preserves the structure without any distortion. When the modular structure is unclear, users will benefit from the focus+context displays with distortion and we believe D_s will perform the best given its moderate distortion rate:

H4: D_p is more effective than D_h and D_s in performing *T3* when modularity is high.

H5: D_s is more effective than D_h and D_p in performing *T3* when modularity is low.

USER STUDY

We conducted the user studies designed above with a total of 36 participants. In this section, we will describe the study procedure and results, and discuss our findings.

Participants and Apparatus

We recruited two groups of 18 volunteers to participate in *Study I* (12 males, 6 females; aging from 23 to 34, $M = 26.55$, $SD = 3.03$), and *Study II* (11 males, 7 females; aging from 19 to 25, $M = 20.44$, $SD = 1.54$), respectively. All participants were students or researchers in computer science with normal or corrected-to-normal vision.

The experiments were conducted on a laptop computer equipped with a mouse, a keyboard, and a 15.4-inch display with $1,440 \times 900$ pixels and 60 Hz refreshing rate. Graph visualizations were displayed in a window with a white background. Graph nodes were black dots. The size of each node reflected its degree, formally defined as $radius = 2 \times \log_2(degree + 1)$ pixels. Graph links were black lines of one pixel in width. Our study system supports picking and selection mechanisms [26] to assist users' exploration. In particular, when the mouse hovers over a node in the graph, the node and its adjacent links are highlighted in blue. When the mouse clicks on the node, the highlighting will persist until the next click. As suggested in [26], these interactive enhancements can help users focus on graph elements and reduce the frustrations caused by getting lost in a graph.

Procedure

At the beginning of each study, we introduced the tested graph exploration techniques to the participants and showed them how the same graph is displayed differently using each technique (Fig. 1). This helped them get familiar with the visualizations and get some intuition about how the graph display is distorted in each technique. Then, we explained the three graph exploration tasks to the participants and showed them how to perform the tasks using our study system. In particular, users can zoom and pan the display to navigate through a graph and can select a node to highlight its adjacent links. In each task, we guided users' exploration by highlighting a node whose neighbors needed to be explored (*T1*), two nodes whose common neighbors needed to be explored (*T2*), or a path whose containing nodes needed to be explored (*T3*).

Before the formal study, the users needed to perform practice trials to ensure a full understanding of all the tasks. The trials covered the three tasks and the tested graph exploration techniques, using three small-size graphs (128 nodes, 1,024 links, 0.3 modularity). We encouraged the participants to ask questions and provided solutions of the practice trials.

After the training and practice, we conducted the formal study. We counterbalanced the order of the techniques using a 3×3 or 2×2 Latin Square in *Study I* and *Study II*, respectively. The order of the study trials for each technique was randomized. We reused the same set of graphs for all three techniques to ensure a fair comparison. We mirrored and rotated a graph before reusing it, which ensured that the participants were unable to memorize the correct answers. Each study trial had a 40-second limit and each formal study session took about 60 minutes. Participants can take a break after completing the trials for each technique. We conducted *Study I* and *Study II* separately at different times and *Study I* was conducted first.

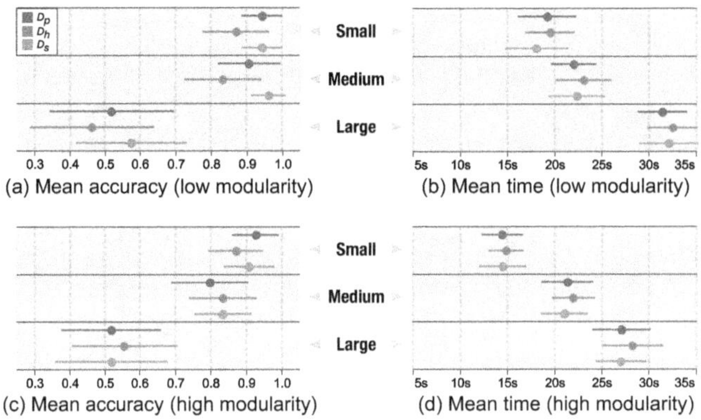

Figure 6. Node exploration task (T1) results of *Study I*. Error bars represent 95% confidence intervals (CIs).

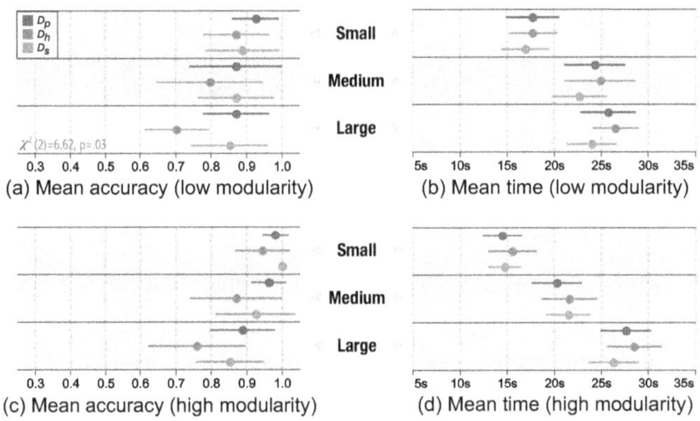

Figure 7. Link exploration task (T2) results of *Study I*. Error bars are 95% CIs. Rows with significant results are in a white background.

Collected Data and Statistical Analysis

We recorded the task completion time and accuracy (1 if the target node was found; otherwise, 0) to measure users' performance in each of the study tasks. We normalized the completion times with a log-transformation and applied the Repeated Measures ANOVA test to compare the means across multiple techniques, with paired t-test for pairwise comparisons. Since the accuracy results did not follow a normal distribution, we analyzed them using the Friedman test and pairwise Wilcoxon test. The normality of the data was determined by Shapiro-Wilk test. All tests used a significance level of .05.

Results of *Study I*

The study results were summarized in Fig. 6-8. We broke down the results by graph modularity (low = 0.3, high = 0.6) and graph size (small, medium, large).

T1: Node Exploration Task

Accuracy: There was no significant difference in accuracy among the displays in all the conditions (Fig. 6(a,c)).

Completion Time: We also did not find significant difference in task completion time among different techniques in all the testing conditions (Fig. 6(b,d)).

Overall, these results rejected **H1(a)**. The three displays had similar performances in *T1*.

T2: Link Exploration Task

Accuracy: In low-modularity condition (Fig. 7(a)), significant differences were detected when the graph size was large ($\chi^2(2) = 6.62$, $p = .03$). Post-hoc analysis showed that D_s ($M = .85$) and D_p ($M = .87$) were significantly more accurate than D_h ($M = .70$). In high-modularity condition (Fig. 7(c)), the three displays had similar accuracies.

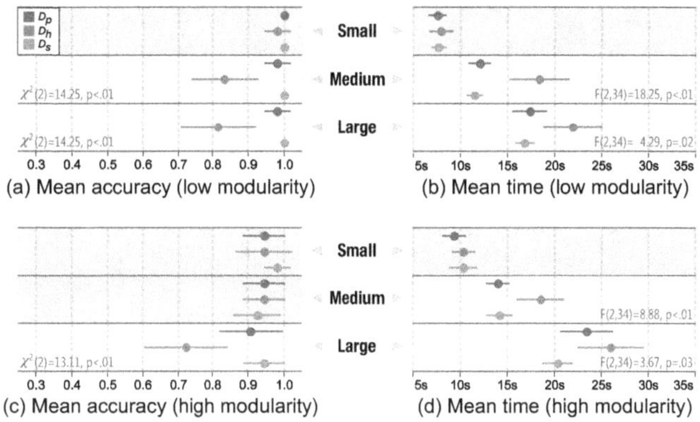

Figure 8. Path exploration task (T3) results of *Study I*. Error bars are 95% CIs. Significant rows are highlighted in a white background.

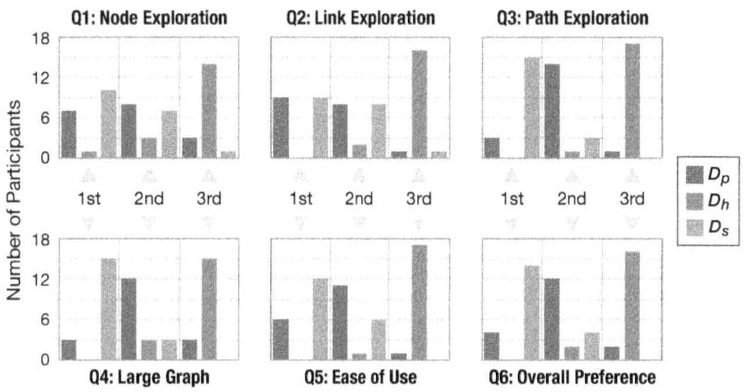

Figure 9. Ranking results for the three graph exploration techniques.

Completion Time: We did not find any significant difference in all the graph conditions in completion time.

Overall, D_s was more accurate than D_h in *T2* when the modularity was low and graph was large, partially supporting **H2(a)**. No significant differences were found between D_s and D_p.

T3: Path Exploration Task

Accuracy: As shown in Fig. 8(a,c), when the graphs were large, significant differences existed in both low ($M(D_p) = .98, M(D_h) = .81, M(D_s) = 1$; $\chi^2(2) = 14.25$, $p < .01$) and high ($M(D_p) = .90$, $M(D_h) = .72$, $M(D_s) = .94$; $\chi^2(2) = 13.11$, $p < .01$) modularity conditions. In the case of medium graphs, it only existed when the modular structure in the testing graphs was unclear with a low modularity ($M(D_p) = .98$, $M(D_h) = .83$, $M(D_s) = 1$; $\chi^2(2) = 14.25$, $p < .01$). No significance was found in all conditions with small graphs.

Completion Time: The completion time results were reported in Fig. 8(b,d). In the low-modularity condition, we found significant differences among the three displays when the graphs were medium ($M(D_p) = 12.03s$, $M(D_h) = 18.35s$, $M(D_s) = 11.49s$; $F_{2,34} = 18.25$, $p < .01$) or large ($M(D_p) = 17.35s$, $M(D_h) = 21.96s$, $M(D_s) = 16.81s$; $F_{2,34} = 4.29$, $p = .02$). In the high-modularity condition, significant differences also exist in graphs that were medium ($M(D_p) = 13.96s$,

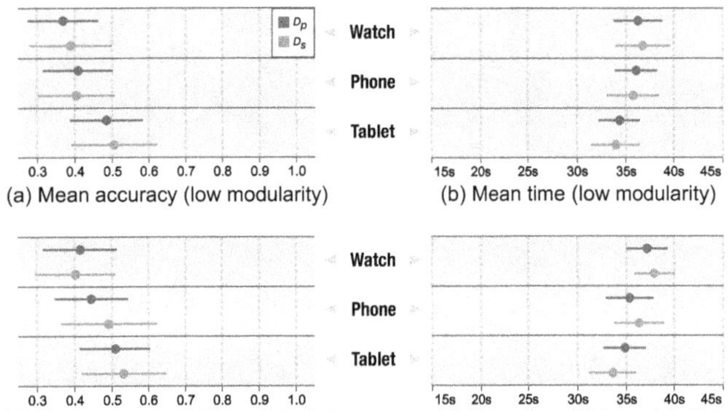

(a) Mean accuracy (low modularity) (b) Mean time (low modularity)

(c) Mean accuracy (high modularity) (d) Mean time (high modularity)

Figure 10. Node exploration task (T1) results of *Study II*. Error bars are 95% confidence intervals (CIs).

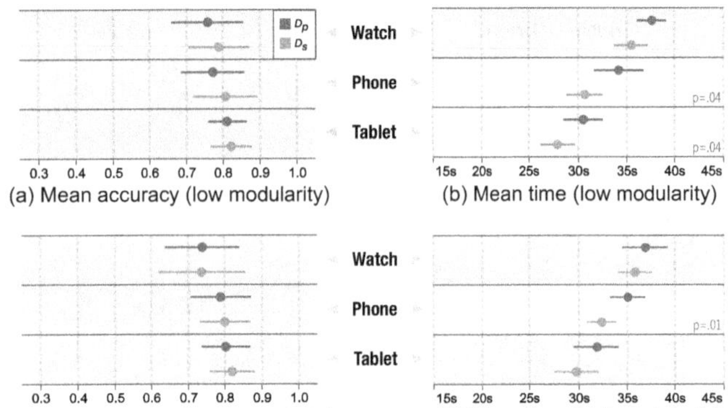

(a) Mean accuracy (low modularity) (b) Mean time (low modularity)

(c) Mean accuracy (high modularity) (d) Mean time (high modularity)

Figure 11. Link exploration task (T2) results of *Study II*. Error bars are 95% CIs. Rows with significant results are in a white background.

$M(D_h) = 18.51s$, $M(D_s) = 14.11s$; $F_{2,34} = 8.88$, $p < .01$) or large ($M(D_p) = 23.44s$, $M(D_h) = 26.03s$, $M(D_s) = 20.34s$; $F_{2,34} = 3.67$, $p = .03$). Post-hoc analysis showed that in both modularities D_s and D_p were significantly faster than D_h in medium graphs, and only D_s was significantly faster than D_h in large graphs.

Overall, D_s and D_p had better performances than D_h in *T3*, especially when the graph size increases. The above findings partially supported **H3(a)** and **H4-5**.

Post-Study Questionnaire

Users were asked to complete a questionnaire for ranking the three different displays according to their effectiveness in supporting (Q1) node exploration, (Q2) link exploration, (Q3) path exploration, and (Q4) large graph exploration as well as according to their (Q5) ease of use and (Q6) the users' overall preference, regarding the conditions tested in *Study I*. Overall, all the results ranked D_s as the best and D_h as the worst. The detailed results were summarized in Fig. 9.

Results of *Study II*

Fig. 10-12 summarized the results of *Study II*. We broke down the results by graph modularity (low = 0.3, high = 0.6) and window size (watch, phone, tablet), and controlled the graph size to be large (2,048 nodes, 16,384 links) in all study trials.

T1: Node Exploration Task

Accuracy: We found no significant difference in accuracy between D_p and D_s in all testing conditions (Fig. 10(a,c)).

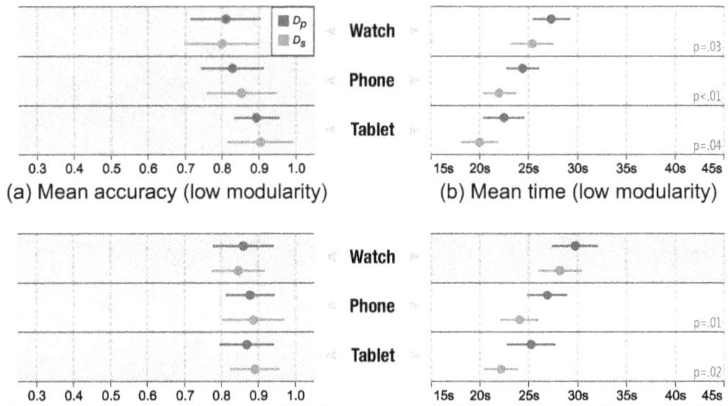

(a) Mean accuracy (low modularity) (b) Mean time (low modularity)

(c) Mean accuracy (high modularity) (d) Mean time (high modularity)

Figure 12. Path exploration task (T3) results of *Study II*. Error bars represent 95% CIs. Significant rows are highlighted in a white background.

Completion Time: No significant difference was found in task completion time in all testing conditions (Fig. 10(b,d)).

Overall, the results rejected **H1(b)** and showed D_p and D_s had similar performance in *T1* in windows of different sizes.

T2: Link Exploration Task

Accuracy: No significant difference in accuracy was observed between the two displays in all conditions (Fig. 11(a,c)).

Completion Time: When the graph modularity was low (Fig. 11(b)), the mean completion times of D_s were $30.71s$ and $27.99s$ when displayed in a window of phone size or tablet size, which was significantly faster than D_p whose mean times were $34.19s$ and $30.54s$, respectively. In the condition of high modularity and phone-size window (Fig. 11(d)), D_s ($M = 32.37s$) also significantly outperformed D_p ($M = 35.10s$).

Overall, D_s was faster than D_p in *T2*, especially when displayed in smaller windows, which supported **H2(b)**.

T3: Path Exploration Task

Accuracy: We did not observe significant differences in accuracy in the path exploration task (Fig. 12(a,c)).

Completion Time: As shown in Fig. 12(b,d), when the graph modularity was low, study trials using D_s cost significantly shorter time than D_p for all window sizes: watch ($M(D_s) = 25.36s$, $M(D_p) = 27.34s$), phone ($M(D_s) = 22.00s$, $M(D_p) = 24.39s$), and Tablet ($M(D_s) = 19.90s$, $M(D_p) = 22.44s$). When the modularity was high, D_s also performed significantly better than D_p when using windows of phone ($M(D_s) = 24.02s$, $M(D_p) = 26.88s$) and tablet sizes ($M(D_s) = 22.11s$, $M(D_p) = 25.19s$).

Overall, these results indicated that D_s was faster than D_p in *T3* under both modularity conditions, which partially supported **H3(b)** and **H5**, but contradicted **H4**.

Post-Study Questionnaire

A post-study questionnaire was also conducted after *Study II*, in which we asked the users to select the more effective technique between D_p and D_s when they were displayed in windows of different sizes. More users chose D_s to be more effective for windows of watch size (10 out of 18) and phone size (11 out of 18). However, for windows of tablet size, 12 out of 18 users thought D_p was more effective.

DISCUSSION

Our user study results provided valuable insights into when, why, and how different focus+context techniques and the zoomable display are useful or have limitations in different situations, which will be discussed in this section.

Why was D_h considered as the worst technique in Study I?

In the questionnaire, D_h was considered as the least effective tool in supporting large graph exploration (Q4). One user mentioned that *"it is very difficult to traverse all neighbor nodes in hyperbolic layout because the relative distance between the nodes keeps changing."* Another user said *"the shape of the graph changes greatly even [after] applying minor panning interaction."* Some other users also complained that *"the [distorted] links confused me; it is hard to predict the direction I am moving to."* All these complaints were due to the same issue—the severe distortion in D_h that brought too much visual clutter, especially during the graph navigation. Just like some users suggested: *"Hyperbolic is poor for interactions; it might be useful if the graph is static (not interactive)."*

Why was D_s only conditionally superior than D_p in Study I?

It was a surprising finding in *Study I* that D_s showed no significantly better performance when compared to D_p. To investigate the reasons, we informally interviewed the users who ranked D_p as the most effective in Q1-3. All of them felt that *"tracing on a straight line is more intuitive and effective than tracing on a curve."* It seems that this benefit made up D_p's limitation of showing too little context when the exploration tasks were simple (e.g., *T1* and *T2*). However, according to the study results, D_p was not scalable when users were required to trace a long path. As shown in Fig. 8, there was a clear trend of dropping performance when the graph size increased. This was also confirmed by users' comments: *"It seems I need to spend more time on tracing on a long path in a large graph [on D_p]; when the path is too long, I cannot remember the previous candidates, ..., showing more context helps me to memorize."* Therefore, we believe D_s will outperform D_p when exploring a large graph in real world situations.

Why was D_s the most popular among users in Study I?

In *Study I*, although D_s only performed slightly better than D_p, it was a technique that provided much better user experience and favored by most of our users (16 out of 18). One user said that *"sphere's magnification [of the focal area] helps me see details at current focus; for the plane display, I need to zoom in to achieve the same level of detail, ..., for large dataset, the sphere looks less dense than the other two [techniques], so it makes the exploration easier."* Some users also mentioned that *"sphere shows more things in the limited space."* One user said *"[when using iSphere] less interactions were needed especially for finding common neighbors and tracking paths."* In addition, many users particularly favored the effect of the panning operation on D_s, which looked like sphere rotation and was considered to be easier and more interesting to operate by our users. The users also believed it is more efficient: *"The center view of the sphere automatically expands the distances between nodes; I only have to rotate the sphere without zooming in [to see the details]."*

Why did D_s outperform D_p on smaller windows in Study II?

After *Study II*, we informally interviewed the users who considered D_s to be more effective than D_p in the questionnaire questions. One commonly reported reason was that *"sphere needs less drag and zoom operations,"* as a user explained *"you need to drag and zoom a lot if the screen cannot show many nodes at a time, ..., sphere can show more nodes on the screen, so it requires less operations."* Another potential reason was raised that *"sphere looks less crowded than plane."* One user mentioned *"the sphere is less distracting because it makes the screen seem larger,"* and another said that *"it was more efficient to use sphere for tracing paths because it can avoid being too crowded around the paths you are tracing."* Besides, a user was concerned about large screens and commented that *"if all nodes can be displayed clearly, follow links in a plane display is easier because the lines are straight."*

When should iSphere (D_s) be used?

We believe when producing a focus+context display for exploring graphs, choosing a technique with a proper distortion rate is important. A high distortion rate will capture more context information but will also severely distort the information space, which significantly harms users' perception. According to the above user study and questionnaire results, we believe iSphere is a proper solution, which assists in exploring graphs especially for performing path-tracing related tasks when the screen is small or the graph is large and has unclear modular structures (i.e., when there are more details to memorize). Our findings suggested that iSphere can be used as a better alternative to the traditional plane based graph visualization techniques (D_p) as it has a similar or better performance, provides better user experiences, and has a better scalability.

CONCLUSION

In this paper, we have presented a novel focus+context technique, iSphere, to facilitate large graph exploration. Specifically, iSphere maps a node-link diagram onto a Riemann Sphere and orthogonally projects the sphere into a 2D plane. The produced focus+context view, similar to the hyperbolic display, has a focal area in the middle surrounded by context suppressed at the periphery of the circular display. We conducted two comprehensive controlled user studies to compare iSphere with two state-of-the-art baseline techniques, plane display and hyperbolic display, based on three graph exploration tasks. The user study results showed that iSphere significantly outperformed the hyperbolic display in path exploration tasks and the plane display in link and path exploration tasks in smaller windows. Based on the results, we have discussed when, why, and how different focus+context techniques and the zoomable display are useful or have limitations.

Our study results revealed great potentials of using iSphere in mobile devices. Besides, many promising future directions worth pursing, including (1) comparison of iSphere with other focus+context techniques in a wider range of graph exploration tasks, (2) study of iSphere when its graph links are not distorted and drawn as straight lines, and (3) study of the generalizability of iSphere and applying it to improve visualizations beyond graph explorers.

ACKNOWLEDGMENTS

Nan Cao is the corresponding author. We thank all the study participants and reviewers for their comments. This work is a part of the research supported by NSFC grant No.61602306, NSF grant No.1637067, DTRA grant: HDTRA1-16-0017, ARO grant: W911NF-16-1-0168, and the IBM SUR Award.

REFERENCES

1. James Abello, Stephen G Kobourov, and Roman Yusufov. 2004. Visualizing large graphs with compound-fisheye views and treemaps. In *International Symposium on Graph Drawing*. 431–441.
2. James Abello, Frank Van Ham, and Neeraj Krishnan. 2006. ASK-graphview: A large scale graph visualization system. *IEEE Transactions on Visualization and Computer Graphics* 12, 5 (2006), 669–676.
3. Lars Valerian Ahlfors and Leo Sario. 2015. *Riemann Surfaces*. Princeton University Press.
4. James Anderson. 2006. *Hyperbolic Geometry*. Springer Science & Business Media.
5. Mark D Apperley, I Tzavaras, and Robert Spence. 1982. A bifocal display technique for data presentation. In *Proceedings of Eurographics*, Vol. 82. 27–43.
6. Michael Balzer and Oliver Deussen. 2007. Level-of-detail visualization of clustered graph layouts. In *6th International Asia-Pacific Symposium on Visualization*. 133–140.
7. Patrick Baudisch, Nathaniel Good, and Paul Stewart. 2001. Focus plus context screens: Combining display technology with visualization techniques. In *Proceedings of the 14th Annual ACM Symposium on User Interface Software and Technology*. 31–40.
8. Alan F Beardon and Ch Pommerenke. 1978. The Poincaré metric of plane domains. *Journal of the London Mathematical Society* 2, 3 (1978), 475–483.
9. Benjamin B Bederson, James D Hollan, Ken Perlin, Jonathan Meyer, David Bacon, and George Furnas. 1996. Pad++: A zoomable graphical sketchpad for exploring alternate interface physics. *Journal of Visual Languages & Computing* 7, 1 (1996), 3–32.
10. Nan Cao, Yu-Ru Lin, Liangyue Li, and HangHang Tong. 2015. g-Miner: Interactive visual group mining on multivariate graphs. In *Proceedings of the SIGCHI Conference on Human Factors in Computing Systems*. 279–288.
11. Nan Cao, Jimeng Sun, Yu-Ru Lin, David Gotz, Shixia Liu, and Huamin Qu. 2010. FacetAtlas: Multifaceted visualization for rich text corpora. *IEEE Transactions on Visualization and Computer Graphics* 16, 6 (2010), 1172–1181.
12. Duen Horng Chau, Aniket Kittur, Jason I Hong, and Christos Faloutsos. 2011. Apolo: Interactive large graph sensemaking by combining machine learning and visualization. In *Proceedings of the 17th ACM SIGKDD International Conference on Knowledge Discovery and Data Mining*. 739–742.
13. Andy Cockburn, Amy Karlson, and Benjamin B Bederson. 2009. A review of overview+detail, zooming, and focus+context interfaces. *Comput. Surveys* 41, 1 (2009), 2:1–2:31.
14. Aurélie Cohé, Bastien Liutkus, Gilles Bailly, James Eagan, and Eric Lecolinet. 2016. SchemeLens: A content-aware vector-based fisheye technique for navigating large systems diagrams. *IEEE Transactions on Visualization and Computer Graphics* 22, 1 (2016), 330–338.
15. Harold Scott Macdonald Coxeter. 1969. *Introduction to Geometry*. Wiley.
16. Andrej Cvetkovski and Mark Crovella. 2016. Multidimensional scaling in the Poincaré disk. *Applied Mathematics & Information Sciences* 10, 1 (2016), 125–133.
17. Arnold Douglas and Jonathan Rogness. 2009. Möbius transformations revealed. *Notices of American Mathematical Society* 55, 10 (2009), 1226–1231.
18. Juan C. Dürsteler. 2002. Focus+context. `www.infovis.net/printMag.php?num=85&lang=2`. (2002). [Online; accessed 1-Sept-2016].
19. Peter Eades and Qing-Wen Feng. 1997. Multilevel visualization of clustered graphs. In *Graph Drawing*. 101–112.
20. Niklas Elmqvist and Jean-Daniel Fekete. 2010. Hierarchical aggregation for information visualization: Overview, techniques, and design guidelines. *IEEE Transactions on Visualization and Computer Graphics* 16, 3 (2010), 439–454.
21. Werner Fenchel. 1989. *Elementary Geometry in Hyperbolic Space*. Walter de Gruyter.
22. G W Furnas. 1986. Generalized fisheye views. In *Proceedings of the SIGCHI Conference on Human Factors in Computing Systems*. 16–23.
23. George W Furnas. 2006. A fisheye follow-up: Further reflections on focus+context. In *Proceedings of the SIGCHI conference on Human Factors in computing systems*. 999–1008.
24. Emden R Gansner, Yehuda Koren, and Stephen North. 2005a. Graph drawing by stress majorization. In *Graph Drawing*. 239–250.
25. Emden R Gansner, Yehuda Koren, and Stephen C North. 2005b. Topological fisheye views for visualizing large graphs. *IEEE Transactions on Visualization and Computer Graphics* 11, 4 (2005), 457–468.
26. Mohammad Ghoniem, Jean-Daniel Fekete, and Philippe Castagliola. 2004. A comparison of the readability of graphs using node-link and matrix-based representations. In *IEEE Symposium on Information Visualization*. 17–24.
27. Kasper Hornbæk, Benjamin B. Bederson, and Catherine Plaisant. 2002. Navigation patterns and usability of zoomable user interfaces with and without an overview. *ACM Transactions on Computer-Human Interaction* 9, 4 (2002), 362–389.
28. Takao Ito, Kazuo Misue, and Jiro Tanaka. 2009. Sphere anchored map: A visualization technique for bipartite graphs in 3D. In *International Conference on Human-Computer Interaction*. 811–820.
29. Naftali Kadmon and Eli Shlomi. 1978. A polyfocal projection for statistical surfaces. *The Cartographic Journal* 15, 1 (1978), 36–41.

30. P. Karnick, D. Cline, S. Jeschke, A. Razdan, and P. Wonka. 2010. Route visualization using detail lenses. *IEEE Transactions on Visualization and Computer Graphics* 16, 2 (2010), 235–247.
31. Stephen G Kobourov and Kevin Wampler. 2005. Non-Euclidean spring embedders. *IEEE Transactions on Visualization and Computer Graphics* 11, 6 (2005), 757–767.
32. Matthias Kreuseler, Norma Lopez, and Heidrun Schumann. 2000. A scalable framework for information visualization. In *IEEE Symposium on Information Visualization*. 27–36.
33. Oh-Hyun Kwon, Chris Muelder, Kyungwon Lee, and Kwan-Liu Ma. 2015. Spherical layout and rendering methods for immersive graph visualization. In *IEEE Pacific Visualization Symposium*. 63–67.
34. Eric LaMar, Bernd Hamann, Kenneth Joy, and others. 2001. A magnification lens for interactive volume visualization. In *Proceedings of the 9th Pacific Conference on Computer Graphics and Applications*. 223–232.
35. John Lamping, Ramana Rao, and Peter Pirolli. 1995. A focus+context technique based on hyperbolic geometry for visualizing large hierarchies. In *Proceedings of the SIGCHI Conference on Human Factors in Computing Systems*. 401–408.
36. Bongshin Lee, Catherine Plaisant, Cynthia Sims Parr, Jean-Daniel Fekete, and Nathalie Henry. 2006. Task taxonomy for graph visualization. In *Proceedings of the AVI Workshop on BEyond Time and Errors: Novel Evaluation Methods for Information Visualization*. 1–5.
37. Ying K Leung and Mark D Apperley. 1994. A review and taxonomy of distortion-oriented presentation techniques. *ACM Transactions on Computer-Human Interaction* 1, 2 (1994), 126–160.
38. Wanchun Li and Masahiro Takatsuka. 2004. Adding filtering to geometric distortion to visualize a clustered graph on small screens. In *Proceedings of the Australasian Symposium on Information Visualisation*, Vol. 35. 71–79.
39. Zhiyuan Lin, Nan Cao, Hanghang Tong, Fei Wang, U Kang, and Duen Horng Polo Chau. 2013. Demonstrating interactive multi-resolution large graph exploration. In *IEEE 13th International Conference on Data Mining Workshops*. 1097–1100.
40. Kwan-Liu Ma and Chris W Muelder. 2013. Large-scale graph visualization and analytics. *Computer* 46, 7 (2013), 39–46.
41. Tomer Moscovich, Fanny Chevalier, Nathalie Henry, Emmanuel Pietriga, and Jean-Daniel Fekete. 2009. Topology-aware navigation in large networks. In *Proceedings of the SIGCHI Conference on Human Factors in Computing Systems*. 2319–2328.
42. Tamara Munzner. 1998. Exploring large graphs in 3D hyperbolic space. *IEEE Computer Graphics and Applications* 18, 4 (1998), 18–23.
43. M. E. J. Newman. 2006. Modularity and community structure in networks. *Proceedings of the National Academy of Sciences* 103, 23 (2006), 8577–8582.
44. Ken Perlin and David Fox. 1993. Pad: An alternative approach to the computer interface. In *Proceedings of the 20th Annual Conference on Computer Graphics and Interactive Techniques*. 57–64.
45. Pratha Sah, Lisa Singh, Aaron Clauset, and Shweta Bansal. 2014. Exploring community structure in biological networks with random graphs. *BMC Bioinformatics* 15, 1 (2014), 220.
46. Manojit Sarkar and Marc H. Brown. 1994. Graphical fisheye views. *Commun. ACM* 37, 12 (1994), 73–83.
47. Lei Shi, Nan Cao, Shixia Liu, Weihong Qian, Li Tan, Guodong Wang, Jimeng Sun, and Ching-Yung Lin. 2009. Himap: Adaptive visualization of large-scale online social networks. In *IEEE Pacific Visualization Symposium*. 41–48.
48. Christian Tominski, James Abello, and Heidrun Schumann. 2009. CGV—an interactive graph visualization system. *Computers & Graphics* 33, 6 (2009), 660–678.
49. C Tominski, S Gladisch, U Kister, R Dachselt, and H Schumann. 2016. Interactive lenses for visualization: An extended survey. *Computer Graphics Forum* (2016).
50. Frank Van Ham and Jarke J van Wijk. 2004. Interactive visualization of small world graphs. In *IEEE Symposium on Information Visualization*. 199–206.
51. Tatiana Von Landesberger, Arjan Kuijper, Tobias Schreck, Jörn Kohlhammer, Jarke J van Wijk, Jean-Daniel Fekete, and Dieter W Fellner. 2011. Visual analysis of large graphs: State-of-the-art and future research challenges. *Computer Graphics Forum* 30, 6 (2011), 1719–1749.
52. w3schools. 2015. Browser display statistics. `w3schools.com/browsers/browsers_display.asp`. (2015). [Online; accessed 1-Sept-2016].
53. Jörg A Walter. 2004. H-MDS: A new approach for interactive visualization with multidimensional scaling in the hyperbolic space. *Information Systems* 29, 4 (2004), 273–292.
54. InfoVis Wiki. 2014. Semantic zoom. `infovis-wiki.net/index.php/Semantic_Zoom`. (2014). [Online; accessed 1-Sept-2016].
55. Harold E Wolfe. 2012. *Introduction to Non-Euclidean Geometry*. Dover Publications.
56. Yingcai Wu, Xiaotong Liu, Shixia Liu, and Kwan-Liu Ma. 2013. ViSizer: A visualization resizing framework. *IEEE Transactions on Visualization and Computer Graphics* 19, 2 (2013), 278–290.
57. Kai Xu, Chris Rooney, Peter Passmore, Dong-Han Ham, and Phong H Nguyen. 2012. A user study on curved edges in graph visualization. *IEEE Transactions on Visualization and Computer Graphics* 18, 12 (2012), 2449–2456.

TagRefinery: A Visual Tool for Tag Wrangling

Christoph Kralj
University of Vienna
Vienna, Austria
christoph.kralj@gmail.com

Mohsen Kamalzadeh
Simon Fraser University
Burnaby, Canada
mkamalza@sfu.ca

Torsten Möller
University of Vienna
Vienna, Austria
torsten.moeller@univie.ac.at

ABSTRACT
We present TagRefinery, an interactive visual application aiding the cleaning and processing of open tag spaces, such as those in Last.fm or YouTube. Our pre-design analysis showed a need to support a spectrum of user expertise from novice to advanced, which resulted in two distinct interface modes. Summative evaluations of TagRefinery showed that it could effectively guide the novice users through the workflow by giving them brief but helpful explanations on why each step was required, and providing visual and statistical aids to help them in making important decisions. This is while our more expert users greatly appreciated the amount of control and granularity over the workflow that our more advanced interface mode offered. Both the underlying tag cleaning workflow and the interface were designed iteratively in a participatory design process in collaboration with research on a music recommendation interface based on Last.fm tags.

ACM Classification Keywords
H.3.3. Information Search and Retrieval: Selection process; H.5.2. User Interfaces: Graphical user interfaces (GUI), User-centered design; I.2.7. Natural Language Processing: Text analysis

Author Keywords
Data Wrangling; data cleaning; social tags; folksonomy; visual data analysis; user centred design; graphical interface

MOTIVATION
With the rapid rise of online content consumption and subscription services, the range of choices for the user has become massive and rather intimidating. This is true for almost any digital content, such as movies, music, academic papers, and books. One key ingredient of many such libraries is the tags or keywords made by users or experts. These tags can help us find both information that we are looking for, and new interesting content that we may not actively seek. Tag spaces, which are often called folksonomies, can be diverse and rich on information, and have been utilized in various areas such as information retrieval interfaces, recommendation algorithms, and music listening history analysis [2, 12, 13, 27, 28]. However, they can also suffer from various issues that are caused by their open and free-form nature. The greatest of these issues is noise, which includes spelling errors, subjective terms (such as "awesome" and "favourite"), and other tags which do not describe the content in a useful way (such as "seen live" in case of music). While a body of literature has previously concentrated on understanding the semantic structure of social tag spaces [16, 17], there is a lack of procedures and interfaces targeted at aiding researchers in cleaning such datasets. In this paper we present an interactive graphical user interface plus a novel tag processing workflow that aim to simplify the process of cleaning open tag spaces, while retaining as much information from the data as possible.

Depending on the intended use of the cleaned dataset, different researchers might have varying standards for the overall quality of the output. For instance, if tags are being cleaned for use in recommendation algorithms and interfaces, one would need a dataset devoid of subjective tags as they lack useful descriptive information. Meanwhile, such tags might be essential in behavioural research on why people identify items as their favourites. As such, a full automation of the process, while desirable, appears out of reach. In TagRefinery, the user plays a central role in cleaning the tag space by providing key inputs at various stages.

TagRefinery's workflow was born out of our need to clean the Last.fm folksonomy for our colleagues who worked on a music recommendation project [12]. As we continued revising our workflow, we saw the necessity of being able to quickly visualize aspects of the dataset in order to aid the process of choosing various important parameters in the workflow. This led to a participatory design practice, in which we solicited from them frequent feedback on both the underlying workflow and the graphical interface. In all stages, external users were also recruited for more impartial formative and summative evaluations.

As researchers with an interest in utilizing tags do not necessarily posses knowledge of text cleaning and natural language processing techniques, the application caters to a broad range of expertise by providing two different interface modes: *Guided* and *Advanced*, plus one overview and experimentation screen called the *Linked* view. The Guided mode, which targets novice users, walks the user through all steps of the workflow and provides short explanations of why each step is performed. Our Advanced mode presents a structural view, facilitating quick access to all parameters of the workflow

Permission to make digital or hard copies of all or part of this work for personal or classroom use is granted without fee provided that copies are not made or distributed for profit or commercial advantage and that copies bear this notice and the full citation on the first page. Copyrights for components of this work owned by others than the author(s) must be honored. Abstracting with credit is permitted. To copy otherwise, or republish, to post on servers or to redistribute to lists, requires prior specific permission and/or a fee. Request permissions from permissions@acm.org.
CHI'17, May 06 - 11, 2017, Denver, CO, USA
Copyright is held by the owner/author(s). Publication rights licensed to ACM.
ACM 978-1-4503-4655-9/17/05...$15.00
DOI: http://dx.doi.org/10.1145/3025453.3025868

and more detailed configurations. Finally, the Linked view presents an overview of the parameters of the most crucial steps of the workflow, enabling quick experimentation on these values and how their changes affect the output.

Summative evaluations were carried out from two points of view: (a) usability, and (b) usefulness. Our results indicated a high degree of usability (an average SUS [5] score of 80.83). All our participants felt the interface was intuitive and easy to follow. For the second study, we performed two case studies with participants whose work involved processing of various kinds of text data, which while similar to folksonomies, had key differences that could help us understand how well TagRefinery can adapt to use cases other than cleaning social tag spaces. These participants helped us identify a number of key functionalities for future improvement. In addition, all participants mentioned that they did not know of a tool that supported the same tasks and workflow as TagRefinery.

In summary, the contributions of this study are:

- We report on the iterative design process of a graphical interface for cleaning and filtering folksonomies, discuss the lessons we learned, and provide design considerations for future research on tag cleaning interfaces.
- We identify the distinct needs of our potential users based on their level of expertise in text processing techniques. We also discuss the different usage behaviours of novice vs. experienced users, and examine whether each interface mode of TagRefinery proved appropriate for its intended users.
- We introduce a novel workflow for cleaning tag spaces, upon which the above interface is built, and report on the outcomes of cleaning the Last.fm folksonomy in collaboration with research on a music recommendation interface.

RELATED WORK

Our contributions relate to several fields of research. In this section we discuss how our approaches differ from or build upon previous work in each of these fields.

Information Retrieval

Folksonomies are powerful sources of data in information retrieval. Contrary to fixed taxonomies, which might lack sufficient categories and terms to accommodate all items [10], social tag spaces lack a hierarchical structure, and thus give the users the freedom to fully express their needs and views [18]. Previous studies have confirmed the descriptive power of social tags in various domains with encouraging results [24]. In the music domain, Levy and Sandler [17] analysed user tags from Last.fm, and found that despite their noisy and subjective nature, the tags defined a low-dimensional semantic space that is highly effective in capturing music similarity. Despite these, as mentioned earlier, folksonomies suffer from several issues. Lamere [15] discusses some of these issues with regard to the Last.fm folksonomy. One of the most prominent problems is the immense amount of noise that open social tag spaces suffer from. Our approach focuses on cleaning noise from tag spaces, while saving as much information as possible on the annotated items. While the above mentioned studies and many more have focused on the semantic structure and descriptive power of tag spaces, few have contributed to ways of cleaning and filtering them. In the mentioned studies, tag datasets are typically only processed through a simple occurrence-based filter that removes tags which appear rarely; a method that leads to much loss of information in the removed tags.

Interfaces and Visualization

To the best of our knowledge there are no previous tools or techniques that target the tasks supported by TagRefinery. The most similar tools are Wrangler [14] and OpenRefine [1]. Wrangler facilitates easy and computer suggested data transformations (e.g. regular expressions) and utilizes semantic data types for validation and type conversion. From a workflow perspective, Wrangler is used right before TagRefinery to fix issues such as missing values and malformed cells, and to transform the data to the proper format for TagRefinery. However, it does not provide a step-by-step workflow for cleaning folksonomies. OpenRefine is an open source application for cleaning data which provides the classic spreadsheet view. While it has some features in common with our algorithms, such as clustering based on word similarity, it is not catered to any specific workflow and requires a high level of expertise from the user. Some more complex operations even need user created scripts necessitating an affinity for coding, which we did not want to require from users. In comparison, TagRefinery is carefully crafted for the specific purpose of folksonomy cleaning.

Natural Language Processing

Correcting spelling errors is one of the most critical parts of our workflow. Ringlstetter et al. [20] showed that web documents suffer from an impressive amount of spelling errors. Most studies in the spell checking literature apply the noisy channel model to fix errors. This model consists of two parts: a source (prior) and a channel (error) model to account for spelling transformations on letter sequences [4]. Different models are mostly distinguished by the error model. Examples include the use of pronunciation similarities [25] or generic string to string edits [4] to describe the error model. Another approach is to search for correct alternatives by semantic distance based on WordNet [11]. The noisy channel spell checkers and the WordNet method are not suitable for our purposes as they are based on dictionaries to be used as ground-truth. That would however limit our ability to detect meaningful but niche and completely new words. In addition, the fact that tags generally lack a grammatical structure [10] significantly reduces the effectiveness of more sophisticated approaches such as those based on Hidden Markov Models, like the one by Fossati and Di Eugenio [8]. Our approach is statistical and uses the available information on the popularity of tags in the dataset along with user input to decide which tags are likely to be correct. This makes our technique independent of language, which is crucial for open folksonomies.

[1] http://openrefine.org/

Tags often contain multiple words. These are called Multiword Expressions (MWEs) in the natural language processing community and detecting them plays a critical role in our workflow. MWEs are an important part of our languages and are difficult to tackle [21] in all NLP problems. Associative measures like co-occurrence patterns are a common way of identifying MWEs [6, 7]. There are a number of works that combine associative measures and semantic properties [7, 26] or statistical measures and alignment-based information [9, 19] with prediction models to identify MWEs. Supervised models have also been proposed recently for identifying MWEs [22], however, such approaches do not fit our case as we have no training data. We use co-occurrence and statistical measures [6], which are not dependent on language.

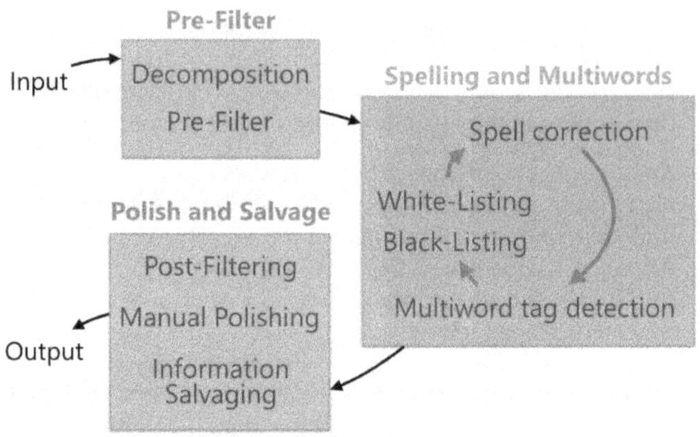

Figure 1. TagRefinery's workflow for cleaning social tags.

TAGREFINERY – DATA AND WORKFLOW

In this section we first discuss the Last.fm data, which was our main test dataset through-out the design of TagRefinery. We then describe our workflow and explain why each of its steps can be crucial to achieving a clean output and retaining as much information as possible from the noisy tags. In the next section, we dive into our discussion on TagRefinery's interaction design by reporting on our pre-design analysis, design requirements, and design choices.

Data

The Last.fm dataset, which we formed through mining tags for one million songs[2], was the main dataset based on which we developed our techniques[3]. Many social tag datasets come with meta-information on the tags and annotated items. For instance, the Last.fm API provides the percentage of taggers who applied a tag to a song, the number of listeners for each song, and the number of times a song has been played. If such meta-information exists, it can be used to generate a preliminary *quality* measure for each of the tags, which is then utilized in various stages of the pipeline. Computation of this *quality* measure should be done manually before importing the data into TagRefinery. As an example, the user could precompute TF-IDF values and use those as *quality* measure. If no such measure is imported, the tool uses the number of items each tag appears in as a replacement. The formula for the specific *quality* measure we used for the Last.fm dataset is described in Appendix A. To avoid confusion, we will always use italic type for referring to this measure.

Workflow

Figure 1 shows a diagram of the underlying tag cleaning workflow. There are three high-level phases: (a) Pre-Filter, (b) Spelling and Multiwords, and (c) Polish and Salvage. These span nine more granular steps that are discussed in detail in Appendix B. We settle with a brief explanation of the workflow here.

1. **Pre-Filter:** Since tags can contain numerous words, all tags are first decomposed into single words in order to perform spell correction later[4]. With larger datasets (hundreds of thousands of tags), the complete workflow can take hours to run. Hence, the Pre-Filter step can be used to temporarily limit the set of words to the ones with the highest number of occurrences, which will act as representatives of the dataset in achieving a clean set of tags. Once such a set is reached, tags removed as a result of this or future steps can be salvaged for any useful information that they might contain. Essentially, this step can be used to perform a type of smart sampling on the input dataset, with little possibility of losing important information.

2. **Spelling and Multiwords:** With the open nature of tag spaces, it is difficult to employ dictionaries as ground-truth in spelling correction, which is the common method in text cleaning tasks. Instead, our ground-truth includes the words with the highest *quality* (above a user-chosen threshold), along with any words or tags imported by the user (white-lists). Spell correction is achieved by replacing lower *quality* words that are found sufficiently similar to a ground-truth word with the latter. The threshold on similarity is also decided by the user. Besides fixing spelling errors like "roock" to "rock", this step also unifies different word-forms, such as "visualization" and "visualisation".

   Once spell correction is performed, we look back at the initial tags and re-construct those that contained multiple words. Two different techniques are used to this end; one looks for frequently appearing sequences regardless of the individual words (such as "hard rock") and one finds unique sequences whose individual words do not appear frequently (such as "Jon Bon Jovi"). We call these two types of tags *frequent* and *unique* multiword tags. This helps us cover a greater span of possible multiword expressions.

3. **Polish and Salvage** Once the multiword tags are reconstructed, the tag *quality* value is re-computed, as the dataset might have changed significantly. At this stage, the user can filter the output set of tags based on tag *quality*, manually remove individual tags (e.g. to remove subjective tags in recommendation use cases) or replace them with others (e.g.

[2]The Million Song Dataset [3]

[3]The data that is fed to TagRefinery is offline and no longer connected to the online source (in this case Last.fm) when processed. If the dataset is updated, our workflow needs to be run again.

[4]*Quality* of single words is the maximum *quality* among all tags that the word originates from.

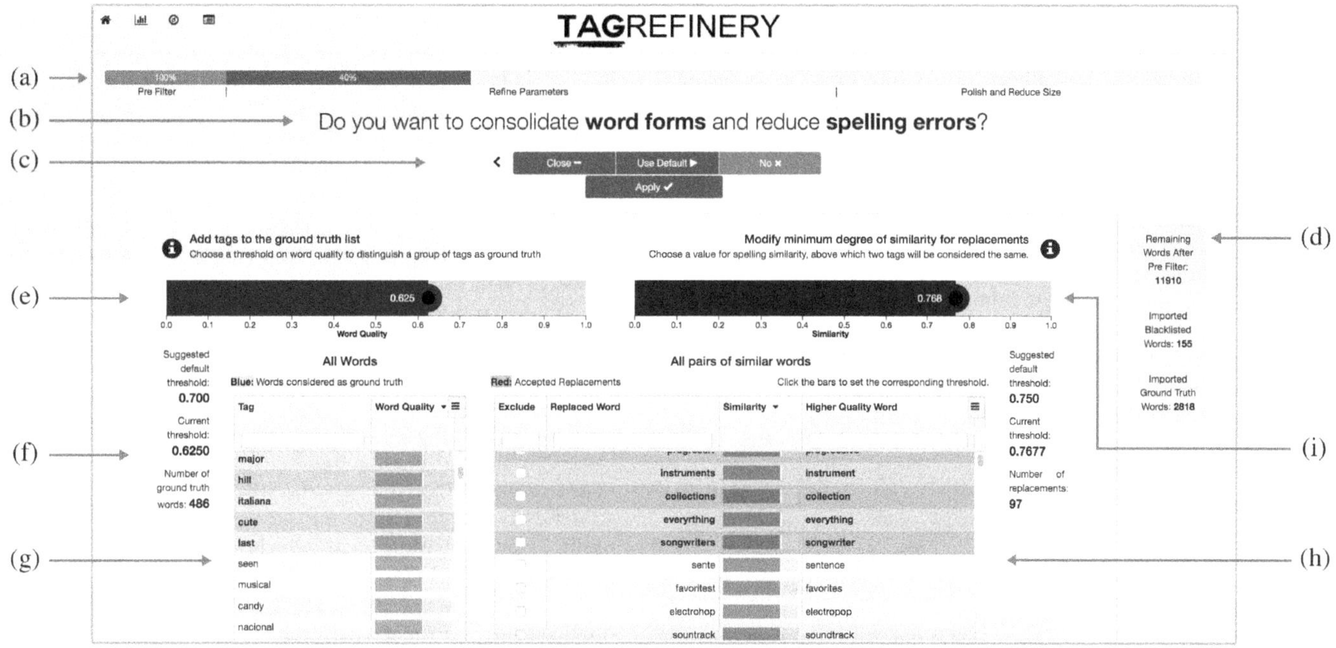

Figure 2. Spell correction screen from Guided mode. (a) Progress bar for whole workflow. (b) Question asking the user whether the current step should be performed. (c) User's options to skip step, use defaults, or customize parameters of step. (d) Status column showing outcome of each step. (e) Interactive bar for threshold on word *quality*. (f) Statistics on word *quality* threshold and accepted ground-truth words. (g) List of all words and their *quality*. Highlighted words are counted as ground-truth with current threshold on word *quality*. (h) List of all possible word pairs for replacement. Highlighted pairs are accepted with current threshold on word similarity. (i) Interactive bar for threshold on word similarity

to consolidate synonyms), and finally salvage useful information out of tags previously removed in any of the filtering steps. For instance, the term "hiphop" is salvaged from the tag "raphiphopsong" which is likely to be completely lost if no salvaging is performed. This process prioritizes tags with a larger number of words. As an example, if the final set of clean tags includes both "rock" and "hard-rock" and the tag "hardrockfestival" has previously been filtered out from the final set, the part "hard-rock" will be salvaged from it.

We first started by analysing the problems our colleagues had with the Last.fm folksonomy. Through mutliple iterations, the current steps were defined and the order was refined. The most prominent issue in the Last.fm folksonomy (and other social tag spaces) is noise. As such, spell correction is the main language related task performed in the workflow. To be able to fix spelling errors within multiword tags such as "hard roock", we first needed to decompose them into single words. The multiword expression detectors were then added to revive tags that are longer than one word. The earlier versions of the workflow did not include the salvaging step. After a closer look at the results, we observed that numerous meaningful tags could be found within those removed in either Pre or Post-Filtering. This led to the addition of the Information Salvaging step. Naturally, we also required the possibility of quick experimentation with the workflow and real-time interactions with the interface, which is difficult considering the often enormous sizes of folksonomies. This requirement led to the addition of the Pre-Filter step, which acts as a way of sampling the input and increasing performance.

Our envisioned usage of the workflow involves going through Pre-Filter once, then iterating and refining parameters in Spelling and Multiwords, and finally performing Polish and Salvage once to finalize the dataset. This is due to the fact that the middle part of the workflow has the highest impact on the quality of the output tags, and thus is most likely to require iteration and refinement. Figure 1 depicts these three phases and our expected iteration in the middle. A similar diagram [5] is also shown to the users when they open the tool for the first time, in order to help them form the correct mental model.

TAGREFINERY – INTERACTION DESIGN

Pre-design analysis

Users:

The common way of cleaning text data is with the use of various NLP tools that are accessible through command-line interfaces. While users with a background in computer programming may feel at home with such methods, the population of researchers in need of tag cleaning tools is much more diverse. Therefore, our initial goal was to create an easy to use application with no assumption of previous knowledge on NLP or data cleaning techniques.

However, given the range of expertise in our targeted audience, we quickly realized that while novice users may be satisfied with the specific sequence of tasks in our workflow, more advanced users might require to run the tasks out of order and with more granular control. Through several iterations, this requirement finally led to two interfaces modes targeting the two

[5]excluding the decomposition step which is always hidden from the user

ends of the spectrum of expertise: **(a) Guided** mode for the newcomers and novices in data cleaning, and **(b) Advanced** mode for users that are either experts in data processing or have ample prior experience with TagRefinery itself. This mode provides additional parameters which are not visible in the Guided mode.

The parameters from the Spelling and Multiwords steps are highly interconnected. Early experiments with the workflow indicated that often the user would need to access and study these parameters and their relation altogether in one large overview. Therefore, we added a screen called the **Linked** view which allows for quick iterations over different parameter combinations from these steps with immediate feedback from the interface. This mode is intended for all user types.

Effort vs. Quality of output:
Besides supporting different kinds of users, our two interface modes also cover a spectrum between effort put into the process and the quality of the output. The task of cleaning a folksonomy is itself an iterative process. Our colleagues from the music recommendation research [12] went through numerous versions of their tag set as they refined and finalized their requirements for the output. By providing the Guided mode and default parameters, which were empirically found through experimentation with different datasets, TagRefinery allows the user to quickly produce an output without much effort. As the user delves deeper into the parameters, the output can become more and more clean and polished.

Interface modes

The user is first presented with the Guided mode, which walks him/her through the workflow. Once the end is reached, the user is encouraged to try the Advanced mode and the Linked view through prominently placed buttons on the screen. As such, the Guided mode acts as an introduction to the workflow and helps the user understand each step.

Guided mode

In each step of the Guided mode, the user can either choose to skip the step completely, use our default parameters, or customize the parameters. Each step also provides a brief explanation of what it does and how the underlying technique operates. The default settings use our preset thresholds and parameters which have been chosen based on empirical observations. When the user chooses to customize parameters, the view is expanded to display the controls and visualizations for manipulating the parameters. To convey to the user our intended way of using the workflow and having them form the correct mental model, the Guided mode displays a simplified form of the diagram from Figure 1 in the very beginning. In addition, there is a progress bar at the top of the screen which is divided into the same major stages in Figure 1[6].

Figure 2 depicts a screen-shot of the spell correction step of the workflow in the Guided mode, expanded for parameter customization. The question (Figure 2(b)) below the progress bar asks the user whether (s)he wants to perform the step, and the user's options are displayed in the form of three buttons: "Yes", "No" and "Use Default". The "Yes" button also has a gear icon next to it which indicates that clicking on "Yes" would allow the user to customize the parameters of the current step (Figure 2 (e-i)). In the screenshot, the "Yes" option has been chosen, which turns its button into "Close" and adds an "Apply" option (Figure 2(c)). To increase the user's awareness of the current status of the dataset and workflow, throughout the Guided mode, a status column on the right side (Figure 2(d)) displays the outcome of every past step. For instance, it displays how many words remain in the dataset after Pre-Filtering and how many replacements have been made in the spell correction phase. The dark red bar at the top left (Figure 2(e)) can be used to set a threshold on word *quality*, to designate a group of words as ground-truth in spell correction. The statistics on the left (Figure 2(f)) indicate the number of currently selected ground-truth words and the current threshold. The list on the left (Figure 2(g)) shows all words in the dataset along with their *quality* (light grey bars) and the ones that qualify as ground-truth with the current threshold (with blue highlight). The list on the right (Figure 2(h)) shows all pairs of possible replacements between lower *quality* and higher *quality* words and their degree of similarity (light grey bars). Lastly, the dark grey bar at the top right (Figure 2(i)) can be used to specify the required minimum degree of similarity for a replacement to be accepted (red highlight). The thresholds set by the two sliders at the top are linked to the respective lists below. Manipulating each causes the small white vertical lines in the lists to move with the threshold and the lists to scroll with the current borderline word. Both lists can be sorted based on various attributes, and searching for specific words is possible as well.

Advanced mode

This mode provides a structural, and quick to navigate interface to all the steps of the workflow and includes access to some additional customizations. For instance, the user can specify a lower bound on word length in spell correction, in order to prevent small words from being replaced. This is supported because the similarity scores between small words can be much higher than between longer words, and this can cause undesirable replacements. Outside the added customizations, most controls and widgets resemble those shown in the Guided mode in order to retain visual consistency.

Linked view

Figure 3 shows the Linked view. The current status of the workflow is reported at the top right (Figure 3(a)). On the left, the histogram for setting the ground-truth threshold in spell correction (Figure 3(b)), the bar for setting the word similarity threshold in spell correction (Figure 3(c)), and histograms for frequent (Figure 3(d)) and unique (Figure 3(e)) multiword tag detection are displayed. The user can also choose to see the pre-filtering histogram by clicking the Pre-Filter button at the top right (Figure 3(f)). The list of all output tags after spell correction and multiword tag detection is also shown in the bottom right (Figure 3(g)). Changing any of the parameters elicits immediate feedback from the interface. The list on the

[6]The names of these high level phases were slightly different in the evaluated interface. They were: "Pre-Filter", "Refine Parameters" and "Polish and Reduce Size". After final evaluations, we learned that they needed to change in order to better reflect the workflow. The updated names are used in Figure 1.

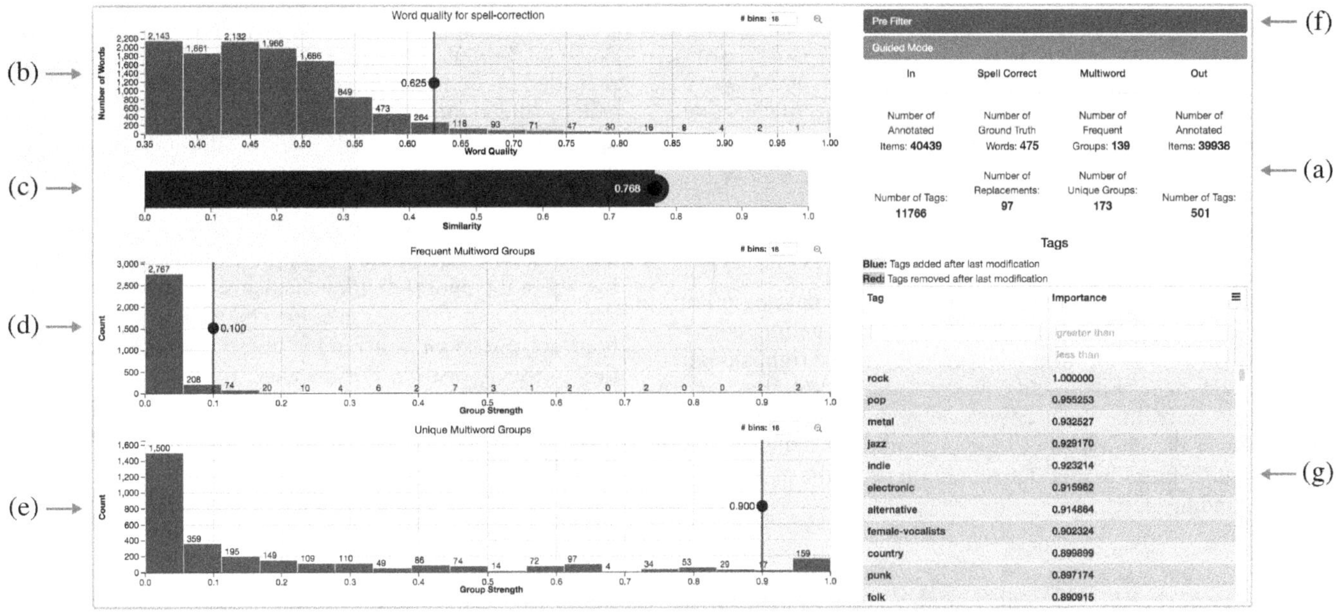

Figure 3. The Linked view of TagRefinery. (a) statistics (b) word *quality* threshold for spell correction. (c) similarity threshold for spell correction. (d) group strength for frequent multiword tags. (e) group strength for unique multiword tags. (f) show/hide pre-filtering step. (g) list of output tags highlighting changes made in this screen.

bottom right also demonstrates the effect of each change to the parameters by highlighting (in blue and red) tags which were added or removed due to the most recent change. Hence, this screen can be used to quickly study the interactions between parameters and how they affect the final set of tags.

Formative evaluations and design choices

TagRefinery went through major transformations in its course from paper prototypes to web application (Figure 2). Images of some of these old designs are provided in supplementary materials.

During the design process, 4 stages of formative evaluations were performed, each with 3 new users. Out of these 12 participants, one was an NLP professor and 4 others had a general computing science education. The rest came from non IT related backgrounds. Each user had 30 minutes to play around with the tool, and the main focus in these tests was the usability of the Guided mode. Some of the design choices we made through this process are discussed below.

Task flow:
The initial prototypes of the interface were similar to what is currently our Advanced mode. However, we found that due to the unfamiliarity of the workflow for our participants, they found it difficult to understand the logic behind the interface, and the order in which they were supposed to perform the tasks. This is in spite of the interface containing visual cues as to what the correct flow of tasks was. We decided that having a Guided mode that blocks access to later steps was critical in easing the users into the tool. This proved to be a successful strategy in later tests and turned the tool from something that was deemed unusable by most participants to a tool that was easy to understand and follow.

Visualizing the tags:
One of the common ways of visualizing tags is with tag-clouds, however, this technique was not suitable for our purposes as our datasets can contain thousands of tags and a tag-cloud can only provide a summary of the top tags with no real use in inspecting thresholds and outputs of the workflow. Scatter-plots are similarly unsuitable as the extreme long-tailed distribution of tag *quality* or occurrence makes it difficult to discern any meaningful clusters or patterns. Hence, we settled for simple colour-coded interactive lists accompanied by histograms.

Histograms vs. bars for parameter setting:
Initially, all thresholds were set through interacting with histograms (with user adjustable numbers of bins) that showed distributions of the value on which the threshold was being set. During our formative tests we observed that for some tasks the histograms could have adverse effects on the users' decision making. For instance, when selecting a group of words as ground-truth in spell correction (Figure 2), due to the extreme long-tail shape of the histogram of word *quality*, some users' first impression was that the dataset had very low overall quality. On the other hand, some users benefited from the added information and tried to set their threshold at the start of the long tail, which indicates a slow-down in changes to word *quality* beyond that point. This strategy can be sensible for choosing high *quality* words as ground-truth because it detects a major shift in word *quality* and removes words beneath it. It however does not lend well to choosing the threshold on similarity between pairs of words for a replacement to take place. That is because for similarity, one would generally look for higher values (75% or higher) to be conservative about losing information in the replaced words. However, the histogram for similarity had a shape that was analogous to that of the word *quality* histogram, and this could invoke similar visual

strategies in the user for the two tasks. In the current version, the spell correction step in the Guided mode does not show histograms (still shown in Linked view) to prevent the above issues, however, finding a visualization that helps in choosing the similarity threshold remains an open design question.

Awareness of dataset and workflow state:
Some of our formative testers tended to forget about the changes they had made to the dataset in earlier steps. For instance, a user had filtered all the words of the dataset in the Pre-Filter stage and was wondering why he was getting empty lists of words later on. The status column on the right side in the Guided mode (Figure 2(d)) was added to rectify this issue by always providing the user with contextual information on the state of the dataset up to the present step. Clicking on each of the blocks in this status column takes the user to the corresponding step.

Observing and interacting with lists of tags and words:
In our earlier designs we downplayed the task of inspecting the lists of words in all steps by making them only appear on-demand. The reasoning behind this decision was that we found the lists to add to the visual clutter of the tool. In our usability tests however we observed that most participants were interested in checking the lists, paid extra attention to how their interactions changed the outcome of each step, and tried to obtain this understanding through constantly switching between parameter setting and scrolling the lists. Therefore, we made the lists a prominent part of all screens and implemented links between them and parameter controls to give the user a constant feedback.

Refining interacting parameters:
Our spell correction algorithm (Figure 2) deals with two parameters that are closely intertwined: the threshold on word *quality* that decides what words should be treated as ground-truth, and the threshold on similarity between pairs of words to accept a replacement. Designing ways of changing the two parameters while staying aware of the changes happening to the dataset proved difficult. Early on, the presentation was different; the user had to click on each ground-truth word on the left side to view a cluster of similar words that would be replaced with it on the right side. We also allowed the user to set different thresholds on pairwise word similarity for each of these clusters of similar words, which gave the user much more control over the spell correction task. However, both of these proved too complex and often unnecessary. It was more important to show an overview of all the replacements than to provide granular control over each cluster. As such, the list on the right side was changed to the current list of pairs of words, and the threshold was limited to one global value. The possibility to reject or add individual pairs of words to replacement was added to rectify the loss of control that this new design caused. Earlier designs also showed numbers for word *quality* and similarity strength, instead of the light grey bars and visual thresholds, and this did not end up successful either. In the final version we visualized these values and made the lists interact with the threshold setting sliders at the top.

Details on demand:
As Shneiderman's mantra points out [23], details should be provided on demand. This was crucial in the design process of the Guided mode. Each step asks a question from the user and provides a brief high-level description of the underlying algorithm, but hides all other distracting elements in order to help the user focus on the question. All of our users liked the fact that they could choose the "Use Default" button for each step and get familiar with the workflow without worrying about the underlying mechanisms. An additional level of detail is shown when the user hovers the mouse pointer over a boldface phrase or word in the question or the brief description of the algorithm. For instance, the phrase "word forms" is written in boldface in the spell correction screen, hovering the mouse over which opens a tool-tip that says: "Like - favourite, favorite, favourites or favorites". A third level of detail is provided when the user clicks on the "i" icons on the screens (e.g. in Figure 2, above the interactive threshold bars). This brings up a text with additional information on what the corresponding widget does.

SUMMATIVE EVALUATIONS

Summative evaluations were done on both usability and usefulness of the final design. None of the users had previously seen the tool in a formative test.

Usability

This was tested with 6 participants (3 females, median age = 26). One was a data scientist and the rest had a general computer science background. Each session took 60 minutes, which was divided into 10 minutes for introduction to the interface and brief training, 30 minutes for the main task, and 20 minutes for an interview and the SUS questionnaire [5]. In the main task, users started with the Guided mode and were given a 3000-word subset of the Last.fm dataset (to have fast run-times). The task was to clean the dataset and output 200 tags for a recommendation service. Once the users reached the end in the Guided mode, they could progress to the Advanced mode or the Linked view. All sessions were screen captured and the users were encouraged to "think-aloud" while performing the task. It is worth noting that this was solely an attempt at testing the usability of the interface as a perfect output needs much more iteration and fine tuning than what a lab study allows. As such, we did not provide any specifications for the output and the users' results were not comparable to each other or any reference cleaned dataset.

All users finished the main task. The average SUS score was 80.83 with a standard deviation of 5.16. This is considered a strong score in the literature[7] [1] and indicates a positive response from the participants.

The interviews were manually coded to extract the most prominent concepts and concerns. All 6 users mentioned that they had never seen a tool with similar capabilities before. All participants also appreciated the sequential nature of the Guided mode and its ease of use, remarking that the possibility of choosing the "Use Default" option gave them peace of mind over their decisions if they were not sure of what values to set

[7] Literature average is said to be around 70 [1]

for the parameters. Four participants reported that they liked the various lists of tags and how they gave them feedback about the current state of the system. Another prominent concept (4 users) was the clean design which let the users focus on one problem at a time without confusing them with unnecessary clutter. Two users found the Linked view most interesting and liked its capabilities to "reason about the connection between the parameters and the output". On the negative side, 3 users reported that not all steps were completely clear for them, 2 said that the spell correction screen was difficult to understand at first use, and 1 user did not initially comprehend what was meant by a "multiword" tag.

Usefulness

Here, we first reflect on our results from the Last.fm dataset and the feedback we got from our collaboration with the music recommendation project [12]. We then report on our case studies with 2 expert participants who were given 1 hour to experiment on their own data using TagRefinery while giving qualitative feedback.

Case study 1: Song tags from Last.fm

With this dataset, the overarching goal was to reduce the size of the set of tags in a way that the outcome was both descriptive of the music collection (not losing important tags), and at the same time small enough so that a user of the music recommendation tool could look through all tags in a short time. Initially, the dataset contained 428,887 songs (with at least one tag), 250,898 tags, and 5,476,264 (song,tag) annotations. In the end, our colleagues settled with 358 final tags after manual polishing (422 before polishing). With these, the number of songs with at least one clean tag was reduced to 226,612, and the number of (song,tag) annotations was reduced to 2,299,154.

The value of the information salvaging step was clearly visible in the Last.fm dataset. Without salvaging, the final dataset with 358 tags contained 1,748,002 (song,tag) annotations. However, after salvaging useful information from removed tags, this number rose to 2,299,154. This translates to a significant increase of 31%.

As discussed earlier, it is difficult to conceive a holistic measure for the quality of the final tag set, however, a close inspection of the resulting tags revealed a desirable level of overall quality in them (before manual polishing). There were very few tags for which we could not find a meaning that was related to music description through searching the web. These were manually removed in the polishing step. Our music recommendation colleagues also required all subjective tags (like "awesome") to be removed, which was done manually.

In general, the feedback from both our colleagues and the users of their recommendation tool has been highly encouraging. There are however areas that could use improvement, such as handling synonyms and antonyms for item retrieval purposes.

Case study 2: Research paper keywords

One of our expert participants' research involved cleaning keywords from the visualization literature. He had a dataset of 5,369 keywords which were made up of 2,656 unique single words and 8,211 (paper, keyword) pairs. Like other users, he mentioned that he did not know of a tool with comparable capabilities and was intrigued by the overall idea. That said, he found some issues at first use for which the tool was not configured properly, and required some missing features.

For instance, the user was surprised to see some of the detected multiword tags that seemed inappropriate. One example was the multiword tag "h.5.2 information interfaces", which had the sixth highest occurrence frequency in his dataset. After some exploration, he realized that since a large number of keywords contained strings such as "h.5.2 [information interfaces and presentation]:", the initial parts of these keywords had been identified as one multiword tag. To fix this, we had to modify our workflow to look for sequences of tags longer than 3 words, which is our default when working with folksonomies. Furthermore, removing special characters like "]" and "[", which the tool performs by default, proved detrimental in the case of paper keyword data. However, since the tool gives the user control of what characters to keep or remove in the Black-Listing step (from the Spelling and Multiwords stage in Figure 1), this issue can easily be fixed.

This user also felt a need for specifying custom regular expressions that would allow him to remove certain types of undesirable tags instead of going through the lists manually. In addition, he expressed a need for more contextual information on demand, like being able to quickly observe the context (keyword) from which a word or multiword tag had been extracted, and having this integrated into the spell correction and multiword tag detection steps. Currently, this functionality is only available in the final screen.

Case study 3: Paper abstracts

The data and goals here were fairly different from our intended use cases of TagRefinery, however, we still found the results interesting. The user for this case study had full abstracts of academic papers, which he needed to clean before analysing for topic models. His dataset consisted of 4,037 abstracts, which contained 16,471 unique words. Each abstract was fed to TagRefinery as a single tag containing hundreds of words. The goal here was to consolidate different word-forms to one (such as "visualization" and "visualisation"), without applying incorrect replacements. As such, the approach here was more conservative than what we typically have with folksonomies.

This participant also found TagRefinery simple and straightforward to use on his data. While he explored his words, he realized that he needed to remove all words that contained no alphabetical characters, such as 0/, 017, 043, etc. Like the previous case study, this again calls for the ability to remove strings that match user provided regular expressions. This expert also needed to filter out words that appeared in all of the abstracts. He achieved this using the histogram in Pre-Filtering which shows the occurrence distribution of words. Another interesting phenomenon was that using our tool, the user realized that there were types of words that he needed to remove that he had not realized beforehand. As such, beside supporting his goals, the tool helped him refine his requirements for a clean dataset by exploring his data from a new point of view.

DISCUSSION

Our main goal in this project was to create both a workflow for cleaning social tag datasets, and a usable and intuitive interface that made it easy to interact with the workflow for users with no technical background in text processing or computer programming. Thus, we decided not to evaluate TagRefinery against command-line tools such as Python libraries, which are the usual method for processing text data. Nevertheless, even in the command-line space, no specific framework exists that caters to social tags. None of the 18 users that tested our tool in its various phases of design and development knew of any comparable software. It is evident that there is a gap in the literature when it comes to comprehensive workflows and interfaces for cleaning tag data, and TagRefinery is an important step toward filling this gap.

At its current form, TagRefinery is tailored to cleaning social tag spaces like that of Last.fm; a fact that is confirmed by the positive feedback from our colleagues who worked on a music recommendation tool. Nevertheless, we were also curious to know how well the tool could be expanded to other types of data, such as keywords of academic papers. When working with users who brought their own data, we were delighted to find that TagRefinery could help them explore their data effortlessly and reason about its characteristics. Using the tool gave these participants a level of insight into the distributions and patterns of their words and multiword tags that they did not possess previously, helping them form new requirements for their cleaned datasets.

The reaction to our interface modes was also encouraging. The participants who did not have much experience in text processing appreciated the Guided mode and the trust it induced. On the other hand, participants with more background knowledge tended to like the Advanced mode more, as it provided them with precise and quick control over all aspects of the workflow. Along with valuable feedback on our final design, our summative evaluations also helped us gain more insight into how these two types of users interacted with TagRefinery and how their needs could be better served. These matters are discussed below.

Design lessons and remaining questions

Guided mode as gateway:

As we had hoped, the Guided mode proved useful in conveying the correct mental model to the users. It rarely happened that a participant would choose to skip a step. The prominent choices were to either trust the system by choosing the default option, or expanding the task to observe it more closely. This indicates that the interface succeeded in making the users care about all the steps of the workflow. Even for our more advanced users, we found the Guided mode a necessary introduction and gateway to the workflow. There were however some interesting differences in how users interacted with the interface, which are discussed next.

Novice vs. expert/Quick vs. meticulous:

Using the application for the first time, participants with no data processing experience tended to start by quickly going through all the steps and pressing the "Use Default" button, in order to see what the results looked like. They then went back and closely inspected each step. This way, the Guided mode provided them with a clear starting point and helped them warm-up to the workflow. This is while users with prior experience in data cleaning meticulously went through each step by expanding its customization controls and trying to reason about what the algorithms did before progressing to the next step. This observation emphasizes the importance of strong default parameters, as these are the main points of entry for novice users and build their trust in the tool. These are currently chosen based on experimentation with a number of folksonomies, but there is much room for improvement. A worthwhile effort is to build algorithms that examine the dataset and the possible outputs for each threshold in order to achieve smart suggestions based on the data.

On the other hand, our expert users required some functionalities that were not included in TagRefinery, such as the regular expression feature discussed before. These users wanted to pick and choose tasks and possibly add their own algorithms in-between. Therefore, one important future improvement for our Advanced interface mode is to adopt a module-based paradigm, where the users can build their own widgets into the interface or export and import data between steps.

Refining interacting parameters:

Earlier we explained how we reached the current design for the spell correction screen which deals with two interacting parameters (Figure 2). This design made the task significantly more understandable to our final participants. The white vertical threshold line overlaying the lists made it clear as to how exactly the parameters were acting on the dataset, and the real-time highlighting of accepted and rejected replacements while changing the thresholds made the interactions between the parameters more transparent.

That said, the problem of interacting parameters is not limited to spell correction. The whole workflow can be seen as a system of interacting thresholds with one output. Continuing from the above point on smarter default parameters, coming up with a holistic quality measure for any given output can be another worthwhile addition. Based on such a measure, the output space can be sampled based on various values for the interacting parameters and this can greatly reduce the amount of time the user needs to dedicate to examining and refining them. A holistic quality value can be achieved through combining our current language independent techniques with domain specific dictionaries (music, paper keywords, etc.) and web mining approaches (for words that do not appear in any dictionary). As the quality of the output can be subjective and dependent on the specific use case, the user should be allowed to give weights to different quality factors in achieving the final measure.

Explanations, terms, and expressions:

In order to cater to all users and not just data cleaning or NLP experts, one critical factor in designing the interface was coming up with terms and phrases that would clearly describe what each step or widget performs. The names of steps and various parameters have gone through numerous iterations, and the current versions have proved relatively successful in usability tests. The short explanations provided in each step (before the view is expanded for parameter customization) were carefully worded to quickly give the user an understanding of the logic behind each step. In our final evaluations we saw that most novice users (who quickly went through the steps on first use) ignored these the first time they went through the workflow, but when they returned and studied each step, they found that the explanations helped them gain a better understanding of the algorithms.

Limitations and future work

We have achieved an initial understanding of how our tool might be used for various text processing tasks, however, our user base for summative evaluations was fairly small. The next step would be to make the tool publicly available in order to obtain more real world feedback. We have already started this phase and are in the process of collaborating with more researchers.

One shortcoming of the current approach is that new words cannot be quickly added to the final dataset as that would require running most of the workflow again. Considering the highly dynamic nature of social tag spaces, this is important to address for use cases that require up-to-date datasets. One way of alleviating this issue can be a supervised learning system which extracts the "rules" of a specific dataset, so that such rules can easily be applied to newly inserted tags in order to classify them as either truth or noise. Models that are widely used in speech recognition and spelling correction can be the place to start. Examples include Hidden Markov Models (HMM), Naive Bayes and Maximum Entropy classifiers.

Regarding the workflow, incorporating algorithms for removal of other types of noise would be an important next step. For instance, phenomenons such synonymy and polysemy[8] are not handled by TagRefinery and should be rectified in the Manual Polishing step by the user. Another area of improvement can be providing a choice between different tag *quality* formulas. For the Last.fm data, we use the available meta-data on popularity of songs and the weight of a (song,tag) annotation to compute tag *quality* prior to the workflow. Building visual tools for the user to help define this measure based on their dataset and its available meta-information is a worthwhile design space to explore.

Our case studies with expert users helped us better understand what functionalities are most important when it comes to adapting TagRefinery to data types other than social tags. One prominent requested feature was the ability to specify custom regular expressions at various stages of the workflow in order to remove certain types of tags. This functionality is critical when one deals with a tag space that is more structured than a typical folksonomy (such as paper keywords), as recurring patterns of characters and terms are more likely to occur in such cases. In addition, compared to cleaning folksonomies, some text processing tasks are more conservative about keeping the words and tags intact and making only the most trusted replacements in spell correction. To adapt to these requirements, the workflow would have to be able to switch to different sets of default parameters and blacklists (e.g. removing or keeping special characters in the beginning).

Moving beyond various bundles of default values, as discussed earlier, the tool can be transformed in more radical ways to accommodate different workflows. As it stands now, some of the steps in the workflow cater well to other text processing tasks (e.g. spell correction and multiword detection), but some might only be needed in a folksonomy cleaning scenario (e.g. information salvaging). Having a number of preset or modular workflows that target various tasks can be a step in the right direction here.

CONCLUSION

TagRefinery was built to give researchers who work with open tag spaces (folksonomies) an easy to use workflow and visual interface for cleaning tags and (item,tag) annotations. Both the workflow and interface were iteratively designed in collaboration with a music recommendation project based on Last.fm tags [12], and were refined through several formative usability tests.

TagRefinery targets a range of user expertise from novice to advanced and provides two different interface modes to accommodate this spectrum: Guided, and Advanced. The Guided mode moves the users through all the steps of the workflow one by one, giving them the ability to use default parameters, customize parameters, or completely skip the step. The Advanced mode provides a more complex interface with direct fine grained control over all parameters of the workflow. In addition, TagRefinery includes an overview screen called the Linked view, which provides a big-picture view of the most important parameters of the workflow along with immediate feedback. At all stages, the interface provides visual and statistical aids to the users to help them customize the parameters of each step according to their dataset and its intended use.

The principal stages of our workflow are (a) Pre-Filtering, (b) Spelling and Multiwords, and (c) Polish and Salvage. To remove language dependence and keep up with the dynamic nature of folksonomies, our algorithms are all based on statistical methods, with the possibility of adding user provided dictionaries for increased accuracy.

Our user evaluations showed a high level of usability, with even non-expert users easily understanding the logic and mental model of the workflow. Our expert users, on the other hand, were enthusiastic about the fact that they knew no other tool with similar functionalities. They found that TagRefinery gave them novel ways of exploring and inspecting their data, giving them unexpected and sometimes surprising insights.

ACKNOWLEDGEMENTS

We would like to sincerely thank Michael Sedlmair for his valuable input during various stages of this project. We would also like to thank the participants of our user studies for their constructive feedback, and the reviewers of this paper for their comprehensive comments during the revision cycle.

REFERENCES

1. Aaron Bangor, Philip Kortum, and James Miller. 2009. Determining What Individual SUS Scores Mean: Adding

[8] One word having different meanings, such as "Love" meaning both a user liking a song and a song being about love

an Adjective Rating Scale. *J. Usability Studies* 4, 3 (May 2009), 114–123. http://dl.acm.org/citation.cfm?id=2835587.2835589

2. Dominikus Baur, Jennifer Bttgen, and Andreas Butz. 2012. Listening Factors: A Large-Scale Principal Components Analysis of Long-Term Music Listening Histories. In *Proceedings of the SIGCHI Conference on Human Factors in Computing Systems (CHI'09)*. 1273–1276. http://dl.acm.org/citation.cfm?id=2208581

3. Thierry Bertin-Mahieux, Daniel P. W. Ellis, Brian Whitman, and Paul Lamere. 2011. The Million Song Dataset. In *Proceedings of the International Society for Music Information Retrieval Conference (ISMIR'11)*. International Society for Music Information Retrieval, Miami, Florida, USA, 591–596. http://ismir2011.ismir.net/papers/OS6-1.pdf

4. Eric Brill and Robert C. Moore. 2000. An Improved Error Model for Noisy Channel Spelling Correction. In *Proceedings of the Annual Meeting on Association for Computational Linguistics (ACL'00)*. Stroudsburg, PA, USA, 286–293. DOI: http://dx.doi.org/10.3115/1075218.1075255

5. John Brooke. 1996. SUS-A quick and dirty usability scale. *Usability evaluation in industry* 189, 194 (1996), 4–7. http://hell.meiert.org/core/pdf/sus.pdf

6. Stefan Evert and Brigitte Krenn. 2005. Using small random samples for the manual evaluation of statistical association measures. *Computer Speech and Language* 19, 4 (2005), 450–466. DOI: http://dx.doi.org/10.1016/j.csl.2005.02.005

7. Afsaneh Fazly, Paul Cook, and Suzanne Stevenson. 2009. Unsupervised Type and Token Identification of Idiomatic Expressions. *Computational Linguistics* 35, May 2008 (2009), 61–103. DOI: http://dx.doi.org/10.1162/coli.08-010-R1-07-048

8. Davide Fossati and Barbara Di Eugenio. 2008. I saw TREE trees in the park: How to Correct Real-Word Spelling Mistakes. In *Proceedings of the International Conference on Language Resources and Evaluation (LREC'08)* (28-30). Marrakech, Morocco, 896–901. http://www.lrec-conf.org/proceedings/lrec2008/

9. Spence Green, Marie-Catherine de Marneffe, and Christopher D. Manning. 2012. Parsing Models for Identifying Multiword Expressions. *Computational Linguistics* 39, 1 (Nov 2012), 195–227. DOI: http://dx.doi.org/10.1162/COLI_a_00139

10. Manish Gupta, Rui Li, Zhijun Yin, and Jiawei Han. 2010. Survey on social tagging techniques. *ACM SigKDD Explorations Newsletter* 12, 1 (2010), 58–72. DOI: http://dx.doi.org/10.1145/1882471.1882480

11. Graeme Hirst and Alexander Budanitsky. 2005. Correcting real-word spelling errors by restoring lexical cohesion. *Natural Language Engineering* 11, December 2003 (2005), 87–111. DOI: http://dx.doi.org/10.1017/S1351324904003560

12. Mohsen Kamalzadeh, Christoph Kralj, Torsten Möller, and Michael Sedlmair. 2016. TagFlip: Active Mobile Music Discovery with Social Tags. In *Proceedings of the ACM International Conference on Intelligent User Interfaces (IUI'16)*. ACM Press, 19–30. DOI: http://dx.doi.org/10.1145/2856767.2856780

13. Yvonne Kammerer, Rowan Nairn, Peter Pirolli, and Ed H. Chi. 2009. Signpost from the Masses: Learning Effects in an Exploratory Social Tag Search Browser. In *Proceedings of the SIGCHI Conference on Human Factors in Computing Systems (CHI'09)*. New York, NY, USA, 625–634. DOI: http://dx.doi.org/10.1145/1518701.1518797

14. Sean Kandel, Andreas Paepcke, Joseph Hellerstein, and Jeffrey Heer. 2011. Wrangler: Interactive Visual Specification of Data Transformation Scripts. In *Proceedings of the SIGCHI Conference on Human Factors in Computing Systems (CHI'011)*. ACM, New York, NY, USA, 3363–3372. DOI: http://dx.doi.org/10.1145/1978942.1979444

15. Paul Lamere. 2008. Social Tagging and Music Information Retrieval. *Journal of New Music Research* 37, 2 (2008), 101–114. http://www.tandfonline.com/doi/abs/10.1080/09298210802479284

16. C. Laurier, M. Sordo, Joan Serrà, and Perfecto Herrera. 2009. Music Mood Representations from Social Tags. In *Proceedings of the International Society of Music Information Retrieval Conference (ISMIR'09)*. Kobe, Japan, 381–386. http://mtg.upf.edu/node/1466

17. Mark Levy and Mark B. Sandler. 2007. A Semantic Space for Music Derived from Social Tags. In *Proceedings of the International Society of Music Information Retrieval Conference (ISMIR'07)*. Vienna, Austria, 411–416. http://ismir2007.ismir.net/proceedings/ISMIR2007_p411_levy.pdf

18. Emanuele Quintarelli. 2005. Folksonomies: Power to the People. (2005). http://www-dimat.unipv.it/biblio/isko/doc/folksonomies.htm

19. Carlos Ramisch, Helena De Medeiros Caseli, Aline Villavicencio, Andŕe Machado, and Maria José Finatto. 2010. A hybrid approach for multiword expression identification. *Lecture Notes in Computer Science (including subseries Lecture Notes in Artificial Intelligence and Lecture Notes in Bioinformatics)* 6001 LNAI (2010), 65–74. DOI: http://dx.doi.org/10.1007/978-3-642-12320-7_9

20. Christoph Ringlstetter, Klaus U. Schulz, and Stoyan Mihov. 2006. Orthographic Errors in Web Pages: Toward Cleaner Web Corpora. *Computational Linguistics* 3, December 2005 (2006), 295–340. DOI: http://dx.doi.org/10.1162/coli.2006.32.3.295

21. Ivan A. Sag, Timothy Baldwin, Francis Bond, Ann Copestake, and Dan Flickinger. 2002. *Multiword Expressions: A Pain in the Neck for NLP*. 1–15. DOI: http://dx.doi.org/10.1007/3-540-45715-1_1

22. Nathan Schneider, Emily Danchik, Chris Dyer, and Noah A. Smith. 2014. Discriminative lexical semantic segmentation with gaps: running the MWE gamut. *Transactions of the Association for Computational Linguistics* 2 (April 2014), 193–206. http://www.transacl.org/wp-content/uploads/2014/04/51.pdf

23. Ben Shneiderman. 1996. The Eyes Have It: A Task by Data Type Taxonomy for Information Visualizations. In *Proceedings of the IEEE Symposium on Visual Languages (VL'96)*. 336–343. http://dl.acm.org/citation.cfm?id=832277.834354

24. Louise F. Spiteri. 2007. The structure and form of folksonomy tags: The road to the public library catalog. *Information Technology and Libraries* 26, 3 (2007), 13. http://ejournals.bc.edu/ojs/index.php/ital/article/view/3272

25. Kristina Toutanova and Robert C. Moore. 2002. Pronunciation Modeling for Improved Spelling Correction. In *Proceedings of the Annual Meeting on Association for Computational Linguistics (ACL'02)*. Association for Computational Linguistics, Stroudsburg, PA, USA, 144–151. DOI: http://dx.doi.org/10.3115/1073083.1073109

26. Tim Van de Cruys and Begoña Villada Moirón. 2007. Semantics-based Multiword Expression Extraction. In *Proceedings of the Workshop on a Broader Perspective on Multiword Expressions (MWE'07)*. 25–32. http://dl.acm.org/citation.cfm?id=1613704.1613708

27. Jesse Vig, Shilad Sen, and John Riedl. 2011. Navigating the tag genome. In *Proceedings of the ACM International Conference on Intelligent User Interfaces (IUI'11)*. 93–102. http://doi.acm.org/10.1145/1502650.1502661

28. Ju-Chiang Wang, Yu-Chin Shih, Meng-Sung Wu, Hsin-Min Wang, and Shyh-Kang Jeng. 2011. Colorizing Tags in Tag Cloud: A Novel Query-by-Tag Music Search System. In *Proceedings of the ACM Conference on Multimedia (MM'11)*. DOI: http://dx.doi.org/10.1145/2072298.2072337

TopoGroups: Context-Preserving Visual Illustration of Multi-Scale Spatial Aggregates

Jiawei Zhang,[1] Abish Malik,[1] Benjamin Ahlbrand,[1]
Niklas Elmqvist,[2] Ross Maciejewski,[3] and David S. Ebert[1]

[1]Purdue University {zhan1486|amalik|bahlbran|ebertd}@purdue.edu
[2]University of Maryland elm@umd.edu
[3]Arizona State University rmacieje@asu.edu

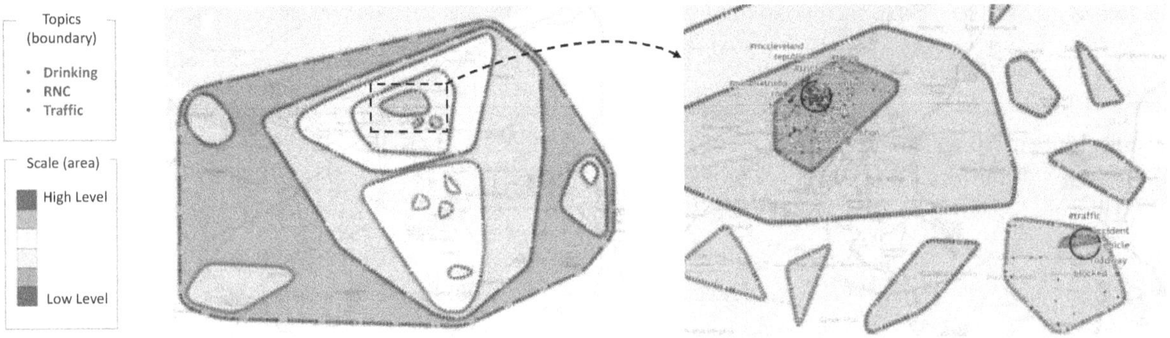

Figure 1. The TopoGroups technique showing multiple levels of spatial aggregation of social media posts around Cleveland, OH, during the 2016 Republican National Convention. TopoGroups supports effective comparison, correlation and analysis of multi-scale aggregates by combining them into the same display, thereby helping users to understand the spatial distribution as well as identify trends and anomalies at different granularity levels.

ABSTRACT

Spatial datasets, such as tweets in a geographic area, often exhibit different distribution patterns at multiple levels of scale, such as live updates about events occurring in very specific locations on the map. Navigating in such multi-scale data-rich spaces is often inefficient, requires users to choose between overview or detail information, and does not support identifying spatial patterns at varying scales. In this paper, we propose TopoGroups, a novel context-preserving technique that aggregates spatial data into hierarchical clusters to improve exploration and navigation at multiple spatial scales. The technique uses a boundary distortion algorithm to minimize the visual clutter caused by overlapping aggregates. Our user study explores multiple visual encoding strategies for TopoGroups including color, transparency, shading, and shapes in order to convey the hierarchical and statistical information of the geographical aggregates at different scales.

ACM Classification Keywords

H.5.m. Information Interfaces and Presentation (e.g. HCI): Miscellaneous

Permission to make digital or hard copies of all or part of this work for personal or classroom use is granted without fee provided that copies are not made or distributed for profit or commercial advantage and that copies bear this notice and the full citation on the first page. Copyrights for components of this work owned by others than ACM must be honored. Abstracting with credit is permitted. To copy otherwise, or republish, to post on servers or to redistribute to lists, requires prior specific permission and/or a fee. Request permissions from permissions@acm.org.
CHI 2017, May 06-11, 2017, Denver, CO, USA.
Copyright © 2017 ACM ISBN 978-1-4503-4655-9/17/05 ...$15.00.
http://dx.doi.org/10.1145/3025453.3025801

Author Keywords

Context preservation; social media; multi-scale analysis; geospatial visualization.

INTRODUCTION

In geography, Tobler [35] tells us that *"everything is related to everything else, but near things are more related than distant things."* Practically speaking, this means that spatial datasets—such as geotagged tweets in an area, weather station measurements across a region, or Yelp reviews for tourist spots in a city—often exhibit different patterns at multiple different levels of scale. For example, while tweets in a particular city may be dominated by the visit of a foreign dignitary (say, the Pope visiting Philadelphia in September 2015; `#popeinphilly`), there may be other, more local patterns in the same geographic region (such as a Black Lives Matter protest in the same city; `#BLM`). Using traditional visualization approaches to navigate such geospatial datasets often causes global patterns to overshadow local ones, can be tedious and inefficient [24], and does not provide an overview when focusing on specific details (and vice versa). What's more, choosing the proper scale and interpreting the results become non-trivial tasks [28].

We propose TopoGroups, a multi-scale visual analytics technique based on automatic hierarchical spatial clustering of data. TopoGroups models multi-scale spatial clusters as a hierarchical tree structure where each node in the tree represents a specific cluster, and each edge indicates a parent-child relationship of clusters at adjacent scales. The technique visualizes multiple levels of the hierarchy at the same time to provide information about patterns at multiple scales of aggregation (Figure 1). The boundary of each cluster is modeled using an implicit curve that is distorted to reduce overlap between clusters at adjacent scales. The TopoGroups technique also allows for coupling navigation to the visual representation; double-clicking on a specific cluster automatically zooms and pans the viewport to fit the entire viewport to its extents.

The design space of the TopoGroups technique includes multiple visual encoding choices using color, transparency, shading, and shape for representing aggregation level, cluster contents, and statistical aspects of the spatial data. To determine the strengths and weaknesses of each visual encoding strategy, we conducted several controlled laboratory experiments where participants are asked to perform spatial analysis tasks under different visual encodings. Our results yield guidelines on which visual encodings to use depending on the user, task, and application. We also discuss ideas for how TopoGroups can be extended with text visualization encoding to show terms, phrases, and topics for each cluster. The practical applications for TopoGroups include geographic information systems (GIS), geospatial visual analytics, and online geographic services such as Google Maps, Bing Maps, and OpenStreetMap.

BACKGROUND

To facilitate effective exploration of geospatial datasets at multiple spatial scales, researchers in the visual analysis field have proposed various visual and interaction methods. Below we discuss work related to multi-scale interactive navigation, multi-scale visual summary, and context-preserving design.

Multi-Scale Navigation

Interactive maps allow users to explore geospatial datasets at multiple scales by directly zooming in and out of a region of interest. Although this technique has been applied in various visual analytics frameworks [4, 29, 5], there exists several limitations: First, users need to switch between different spatial scales in order to observe the corresponding results, which adds heavy interaction overload. Moreover, since the map typically only visualizes the results at the current scale, users can easily lose the semantic context of the previous scales as they interact across multiple scales.

In order to reduce the interaction overload and maintain the semantic context, researchers have proposed several frameworks that juxtapose multiple maps at different scales, which allow users to visually compare the multi-scale analysis results without the need to perform numerous zooming operations. Ferreira et al. [14] develop an interactive system to visualize spatiotemporal distributions of birds. Their system provides multiple coordinated geographical map views to facilitate the effective visual comparison of different spatial regions across multiple scales. Javed et al. [23] propose a novel visual design named stack zooming. As users navigate on the map from higher to lower scales, the corresponding geographical views stack on each other in order to indicate the hierarchical relationships across multiple scales. Delort [9] establishes a hierarchical tree based on the spatial clustering results that enables users to interactively select different cluster nodes at different scales and visualizes the clusters using a Voronoi partition. Zhang et al. [42] propose a two-staged animated transition technique in order to provide a smooth visual transition as users navigate through multiple spatial scales.

Similarly to the juxtaposition approach, our method aims to summarize multi-scale visual results in a single, compact visualization to reduce the interaction overload and further facilitate effective correlation and analysis across different scales.

Multi-Scale Visual Summary

Besides the aforementioned interaction-based approaches, there also exist visual approaches that create summaries of the analysis results at multiple scales in a single visualization. This approach effectively maintains the context of exploration and reduces the overload caused by jumping across different views for visual comparison. Dykes and Brunsdon [11] use multiple line charts to encode the relationships between the statistical results and the geographical scales. Turkay et al. [37] propose *attribute signature*, which summarizes the multi-scale statistical results in a static visualization that avoids the tedious zooming operations and meanwhile maintains the context of different scales. Goodwin et al. [18] propose a novel glyph design named *Scale Mosaic*, in which they use a set of concentric rectangular rings to encode the correlations of the statistical variables from global to local scales.

Although these solutions manage to facilitate effective multi-scale analysis and context preservation, most of them are oriented toward statistical analysis (such as correlation analysis) of multivariate geographical data, where the analysis result at one scale can be represented as numeric values. In contrast, our work aim to provide a visual summary of multi-scale spatial clusters. To the best of our knowledge, little work has been done in the visual analytics field to focus on combining the multi-scale spatial aggregates in the same visual space.

Context-Preserving Visual Design

Overview+Detail and Focus+Context techniques [6] have been widely applied in the visualization field to provide efficient context preservation. Overview+detail separates the focus and context into separate views, while focus+context seamlessly integrates the focus within the context, often by applying distortion such as fisheye distortion [16, 17]. For overview+detail, the stack zooming technique [21] has been applied to both time-series exploration as well as geographical navigation [23]. In terms of focus+context, Gutwin [19] improves fisheye views by dynamically adjusting the distortion effect based on the movement of the cursor to allow users to more effectively target objects. Pietriga and Appert [30] explore several dimensions including transparency and time to control the transition between the context of focus. Variants of fisheye techniques have been applied to various usage scenarios, such as the system diagrams [7, 40], word cloud layout [8], and road visualization [33]. Other related examples can be found in the survey paper by Tominski et al. [36].

Similar to focus+context, our approach combines the visualization of different scales in the same display. We design an overlap minimization method that distorts the contour of spatial clusters to reduce visual clutter, making it easier for users to identify aggregates at different scales.

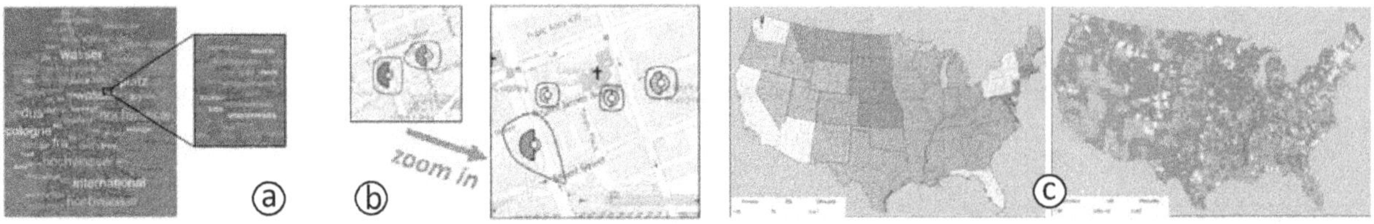

Figure 2. Examples of multi-scale clustering: (a) Keywords are aggregated and displayed on the map (Tag Map). Zooming into the map shows lower-level sub-events [34]; (b) Spatial clusters are visualized at consecutive zoom levels. Large clusters at a higher zoom level split into multiple small ones at a lower level [42]; (c) Clustering results of demographic statistics under different geographical resolutions (left: state level, right: county level) [43].

CHALLENGES AND TASK CHARACTERIZATION

Spatial clustering is an important component within spatial data mining [2], which generally refers to approaches that groups spatial data points into classes based on their spatial proximity. Spatial clustering provides valuable insights into the spatial data distribution, characteristics of the individual groups, as well as trends and anomalies within the dataset. Creating these clusters and exploring their characteristics across multiple spatial scales is an important but challenging task.

Varying scale is an inherent property in multi-scale data analysis and spatial clustering analysis (e.g., [3, 28, 22, 25]). Spatial datasets can be aggregated by varying granularity levels that are determined by a distance measure between pairwise data points in the clustering process. Accordingly, clustering results often vary significantly across different scales, as Figure 2 shows. Although the variation in scale provides a unique perspective to characterize the spatial data attributes [28], compared to a single scale, the size of analysis space in the multi-scale scenario exhibits an approximate quadratic growth. Moreover, navigating and correlating across scales remains a non-trivial task to domain experts in various fields where multi-scale analysis is critical in their domain-specific tasks. The challenges faced can be characterized into two major aspects, **interaction overload** and **cognitive overload**.

Spatial scales typically range from an overview (the global view) to low level details (individual data points). From the global perspective, the entire dataset is aggregated as a single object, which may provide overall summary information, but is too coarse-grained to reveal potential spatial patterns. From the detail perspective, each individual data point is regarded as one cluster, where no actual aggregation exists for analysis. Therefore, users have to identify the appropriate scales between these polar extremes that can best characterize the hidden spatial patterns. Conventional navigation paradigms such as the zooming operation require the users to switch to each individual scale in order to understand the analysis result at that scale, adding significant **interaction overload** to the analysis process. Moreover, in most multi-scale analysis scenarios, understanding how the spatial attributes and patterns evolve across scales is critical. For example, crime in certain regions may be unnaturally high; however, this may be explained if local geospatial patterns (e.g., petty thefts at the mall) are analyzed. Hence, users require the ability to effectively correlate analytical results between different scales. With conventional navigation paradigms, users have to remember the analysis result at different scales during the navigation and mentally correlating those results further increases their **cognitive overload** in the analysis process.

We characterize a set of representative analytical tasks that are involved in the navigation and exploration of multi-scale spatial aggregates [1, 27, 31, 32]. The task characterization guides the design of our context-preserving technique and provides motivation for research in similar areas.

- T1 Establish an overview of the geographical distribution of aggregates at multiple scales.
- T2 Distinguish different aggregates at the same and/or across different scales in the geographical space and identify their potential relationships.
- T3 Locate aggregates of interest at the same and/or across different scales. Determine the spatial extent of the aggregates.
- T4 Measure and compare the volume of domain-specific attributes for the aggregates at the same and/or across scales.
- T5 Access raw data items (e.g., geographical location, domain attributes) associated with a specific aggregate on demand.

TOPOGROUPS: MULTI-SCALE SPATIAL AGGREGATES

In order to tackle the aforementioned challenges, we propose TopoGroups, a visual analytics approach that enables effective context-preserving navigation and exploration of spatial clusters at multiple scales. Motivated by past work [18, 37, 39], TopoGroups aims to superimpose clusters of multiple scales into a single visual display (T1, T2, T3, T4). With such a design, the user can easily understand the structure of the space at several levels of scale, reducing **cognitive load**. Furthermore, this also minimizes the need for navigating across multiple scales, thus reducing **interaction overload** as well.

TopoGroups consists of two major steps, following the hierarchical aggregation model proposed by Elmqvist and Fekete [12]. First, we model the multi-scale spatial clusters as a hierarchical representation where each scale (zoom level) maps to a specific layer in the hierarchical structure. This step has been described as *data space aggregation* [12]. Second, we design our visual interface that allows users to explore the spatial clusters both hierarchically and spatially, while maintaining the context of navigation at different spatial scales. This step has been described as *simplified visual representations of the aggregates in visual space* [12].

Generating the Spatial Aggregate Hierarchy

Geospatial datasets are typically represented by latitude and longitude in a geographical coordinate system, and can be transformed into planar coordinates based on map projection

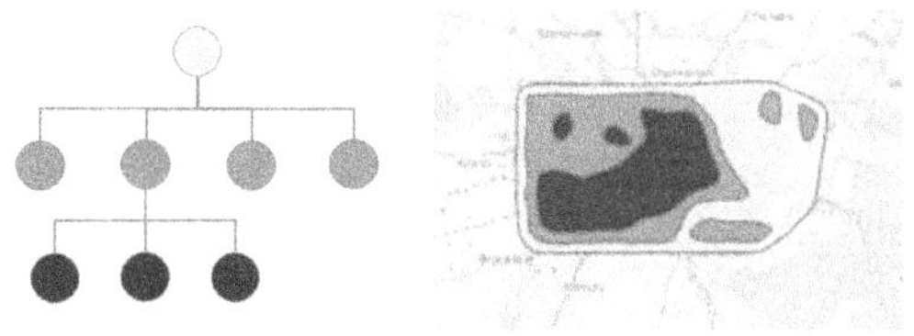

Figure 3. The hierarchical (left) and the corresponding geospatial (right) representations of the multi-scale aggregates

methods. In TopoGroups, the geo-spatial data points are projected into 2D screen space coordinates, where the clustering is performed. TopoGroups utilizes the common algorithm where each data point only belongs to one cluster at a single scale (e.g., the DBSCAN [13] algorithm). We also note that the clustering process maintains a consistent distance measure (Euclidean distance in screen space) across different spatial scales (zoom level). Under such conditions, geospatial data clustering highly depends on the spatial scales (zoom levels) of the geographical space. As the spatial scale varies from a higher (abstract) level to a lower (detailed) level, the screen space distance of any pair of geo-spatial points increases accordingly. Intuitively, the clusters at a higher level split into smaller ones at a lower level. Hence, the multi-scale nature of spatial clustering is consistent with a hierarchical representation that can be represented as a dendrogram (Figure 3).

We represent the multi-scale aggregates using a tree structure that naturally depicts the hierarchical relationships of the clusters at different scales. In this hierarchy, nodes represent individual spatial clusters, while the edges represent the parent-child relationships of clusters at adjacent spatial scales. The clusters that are formed at the same spatial scales correspond to the nodes that have the same depth in the tree.

Context-Preserving Visualization

In order to visualize the multi-scale hierarchy, TopoGroups creates a boundary-based visual representation using an implicit curve for each aggregate in the hierarchy (Figure 4(a)). The benefits of this particular representation lie in three aspects, referring to the six guidelines *G1* through *G6* by Elmqvist and Fekete [12]. First, the boundary within the context of a geographical space naturally depicts the spatial scope of the aggregate, which is intuitive and interpretable to the users (*G2, G6*). Second, while the data points are typically represented as small circles, the implicit curve is easily distinguishable from the data items (*G4*). Third, since the visual space inside the boundary of the higher level clusters can be utilized to visualize the lower level clusters, the boundary-based representation produces minimum visual clutter (*G3*).

We note that the overlapping of the boundaries at different scales may exist, as shown in Figure 4(b). To this end, we propose a bottom-up distortion algorithm (Figure 5) toward effective overlap minimization of the multi-scale spatial boundaries (*G3, G5*). This is inspired by the nested treemap design that adds padding to adjacent rectangles in order to highlight the parent nodes in the hierarchy more effectively [10]. Motivated by the force-directed drawing algorithm [15], our algorithm traverses the hierarchy from the bottom level and for each non-leaf node, the algorithm repositions the control points of the boundary that overlap with its children for the sake of both an aesthetic visual result and performance efficiency. The algorithm ensures an optimal amount of distance between adjacent boundaries to provide a visual budget for the boundary-based visual encodings and avoid visual clutter.

In order to facilitate effective visual perception of the hierarchical and statistical information of the geographical aggregates, TopoGroups provides a set of visual encoding strategies combining different perceptual dimensions including color, transparency, shading, and shapes. The strategies have been applied to the inner area of the aggregates as well as the boundary, which is inspired by Bristle Maps [20, 26] where map features (roads, subway line, city blocks, etc.) are associated with visual elements—bristles—in order to visually encode the multivariate information in the geographical region of interest. In TopoGroups, we aim to convey both univariate and multivariate attributes of the spatial aggregates through our visual encoding strategies. In the rest of this section, we illustrate our visual designs based on a practical usage scenario of multi-scale spatial aggregates generated from location-based social media data (Twitter) in Cleveland, OH during the 2016 Republican National Convention.

Univariate Attributes

Aggregates' univariate attributes typically include the volume of data points, size of the geographical area, scale of aggregation (zoom level), etc. This type of attributes can be encoded using either the color of the inner area of the cluster, or the width/color of the boundary. For example, the analyst is interested in investigating the scale of aggregation at which different clusters have formed in Cleveland during the RNC event, and learning the relationships of different clusters across scales. To this end, TopoGroups encodes the scale of the individual clusters by rendering the inner area using specific color schemes. Figure 6 illustrates the encoding strategy based on a blue-red color scheme where dark blue represents the abstract level while dark red represents the detailed level (T2, T3). Clusters of the same color indicate that they are generated at the same level. Different color schemes such as sequential or qualitative schemes can also be applied here. In order to evaluate whether color encoding can enhance the understanding of hierarchical relationships of multi-scale aggregates, and which color scheme achieves the best result, we conducted a user study (Details are discussed in the evaluation section).

In addition to filling the color, TopoGroups applies the halo effect on the boundary of the clusters (Figure 6(b)) in order to visually indicate the sidedness of the boundary [38]. The halo is only rendered at one side of the boundary (outer side of the cluster) in order to provide a visual cue in terms of which side of the boundary belongs to the cluster. The halo effect is especially helpful when the user zooms into a certain level where only the partial cluster is visualized in the viewport.

Multivariate Attributes

Aggregates' multivariate attributes are typically generated from classification or categorization of the data items, such as different topics extracted from social media message content. Assuming the analyst is curious about the major topics during

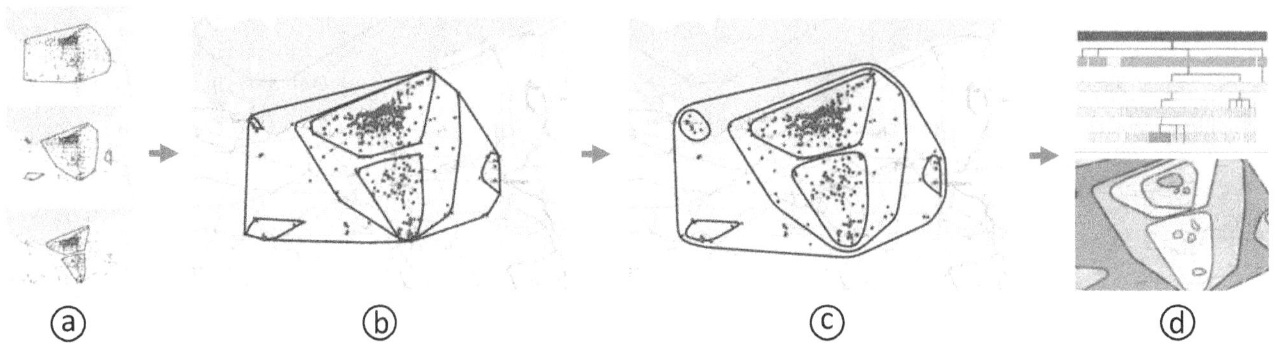

Figure 4. Spatial aggregates are generated (a) at multiple scales and coupled into one visual display using a boundary-based representation (b). The boundaries are properly distorted and smoothed to avoid visual clutter (c). Visual encodings and interactions are designed to facilitate effective exploration of multi-scale aggregates (d).

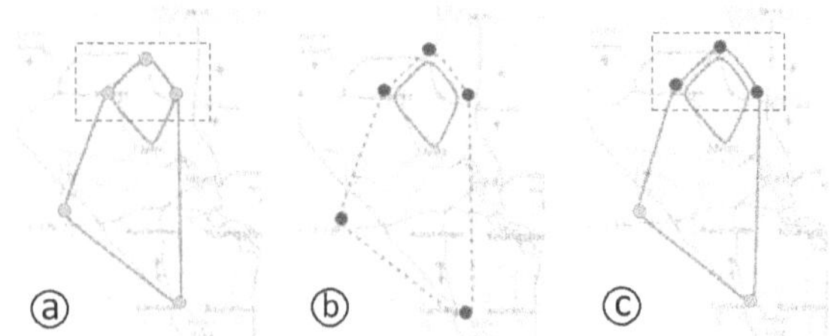

Figure 5. Boundary overlap minimization: (a) The boundaries of the parent and child overlap (highlighted in the dashed box); (b) The parent's boundary is inflated in order to avoid the overlap; (c) Part of the inflation result is used to form the new boundary of the parent.

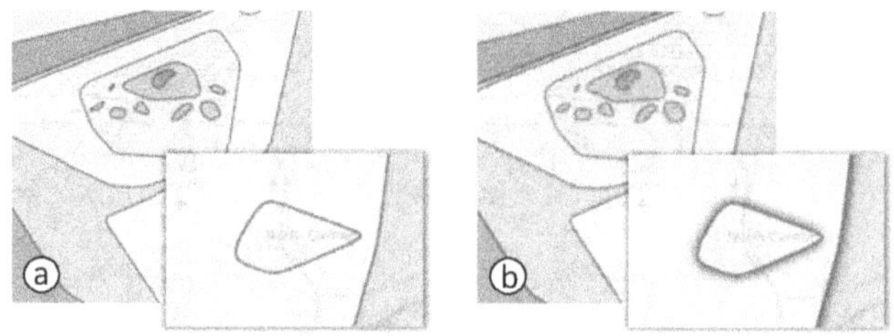

Figure 6. The area inside the multi-scale clusters is filled based on a blue-red color scheme from blue (abstract level) to red (detailed level) to indicate the aggregation level. The comparison of the visualization without halo (a) and with halo (b) is shown. With halo, it is easier for the user to determine which side of the boundary belongs to this cluster.

the RNC event, and wishes to further examine the prominent topics in different clusters at different scales, TopoGroups automatically extracts major topics (e.g., RNC-related, traffic and accident, drinking and entertainment) and provides several boundary-based encoding strategies to convey the quantitative information of different topics for the individual aggregates (T4) as Figure 7 shows. In all three designs, each color corresponds to a specific category:

- **Continuous colored segments**: Figure 7(a) shows line segments being used as the major visual element to convey the quantity of categories. The length of the colored segment is in proportion to the quantity of the corresponding category. Segments repeat to fill the entire boundary.
- **Discrete colored dashes**: Figure 7(b) shows a sequence of dashes being used to convey the quantity of categories. The number of colored dashes in each sequence is in proportion to the quantity of the corresponding category. Sequences repeat to fill the entire boundary. We choose the dash as the visual element in this design instead of circle or other similar shapes for the sake of visual discrimination between aggregates and data items (*G4*).
- **Stacked lines**: Figure 7(c) shows the entire boundary line of the cluster being used to convey the quantity of categories. The width of the boundary lines is in proportion to the quantity of the corresponding category. The lines for different categories are stacked next to each other.

We have conducted a user study to assess the efficacy of these techniques in conveying the categorical distribution, the details of which are discussed in the evaluation section. We also note that for both the continuous segments and discrete dashes, we fill the entire boundary of the clusters by concatenating the segments or dash sequences repetitively along the boundary. The rationale behind such a design is that the repetitive patterns avoid misleading the users in terms of interpreting the categorical information (Figure 8(b)). Without the repetitive patterns, the visualization can convey the wrong categorical information particularly when only a partial cluster is shown in the viewport (Figure 8(a)).

As Figure 1(left) shows, with the effective visual encodings provided in TopoGroups, the analyst clearly notices that while most of the tweets are related to RNC at an abstract scale (the major color in the outward cluster is red), as she investigates lower levels, the clusters within Cleveland are more related to RNC, while in the nearby cities more tweets relate to traffic (green) and drinking (blue). As she further zooms into the city of Cleveland, she identifies that drinking and traffic related tweets form several clusters around the suburban regions (Figure 1(right)). Therefore, TopoGroups provides a comprehensive picture in terms of how the different topics are correlated with the clusters at different spatial scales, and how they evolve from the overview level to the detailed level.

Interaction and Interface Design

TopoGroups consists of two visual and interactive dialogs: an interactive map view that visualizes the multi-scale aggregates within the same geographical display, and a tree view that

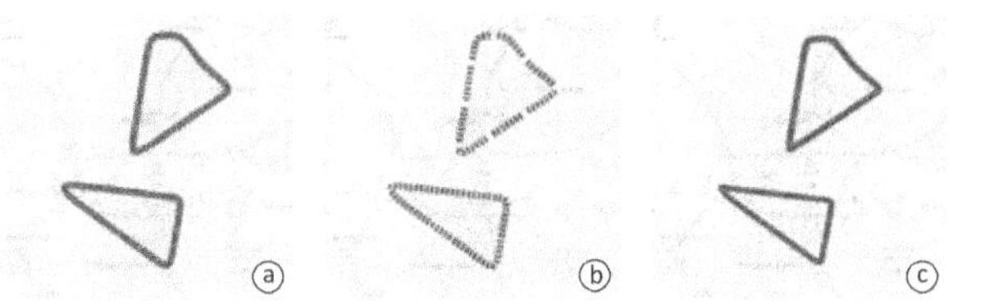

Figure 7. Design alternatives for encoding categorical information on the boundary: (a) Continuous colored segments; (b) Discrete colored dashes; (c) Stacked Lines.

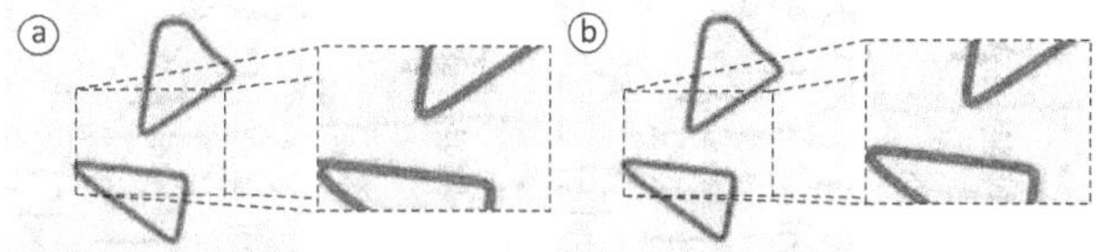

Figure 8. Without the repeating patterns (a), the visualization may convey the wrong categorical information when only the partial cluster is in the viewport. This visual confusion can be avoided by introducing the repeating patterns (b).

illustrates the hierarchical relationships of the multi-scale aggregates. These two dialogs are coordinated and seamlessly integrated when the users navigate across different scales.

General Navigation: The interactive map view allows the users to navigate across different spatial scales through common zooming operations (T2, T3). Each time the user zooms in or out, the map navigates to either the higher or lower adjacent level, respectively. TopoGroups visualizes the multi-scale spatial aggregates that are visible or partially visible in the map viewport. Aggregates that occupy too small screen space (i.e., less than 100 pixels) are not rendered (*G1*). TopoGroups also provides a configurable parameter S that restricts the number of adjacent scales to visualize (*G1*) in order to avoid computational performance issue and potential overload on the user. For example, if the user navigates to zoom level 10, with $S = 2$, then only the levels from 8 to 12 are visualized. After a visual inspection of the results, we found $S = 2$ to produce reasonable results with respect to performance and readability.

Muti-Scale Navigation through Selecting Targets: TopoGroups supports simple yet intuitive interactions that allow users to navigate across multiple levels. As the user double-clicks on a target aggregate, the map automatically pans to the target aggregate and zooms in to fit its extent (T3). With this design, the conventional navigation paradigm that requires multiple panning and zooming operations is simplified by a single and intuitive interaction that significantly alleviates the interaction overload. Furthermore, by double-clicking on the region outside the target aggregate, TopoGroups automatically resets the view back to the previous geographical space.

Exploring the Hierarchy — The Tree View: The tree view in TopoGroups illustrates the multi-scale hierarchy using both a dendrogram and a node-link diagram [41] (T1, T2). The dendrogram illustrates the scale of aggregation, as the nodes of the same scale are aligned based on the same vertical offset (Figure 4(d)). However, this may cause significant visual clutter when the number of nodes is large. Hence, TopoGroups provides a complementary node-link representation that fully utilizes the two dimensional space. The node-link diagram simply regards the hierarchical structure as a graph rendered using a force-directed layout. The user can toggle between the two views in the control panel.

The tree view is coordinated with the map view through the *brushing and linking* paradigm. As the user navigates on the map, the aggregates visible in the geographical space are highlighted in the tree view. With this design, while the user may focus on exploring the detailed levels on the map, the tree view provides a context of the entire structure to the user. When the user selects one or more nodes in the tree view, the corresponding aggregates on the map view highlight accordingly. The tree view supports filtering based on the domain-specific attributes of the aggregates such as geographical size, data volume and density. The user can also filter to show only a subtree by specifying a node as the root of that subtree. The view supports sorting the children (from left to right) of each tree node based on the aforementioned attributes.

Details-on-Demand: TopoGroups supports easy access to details-on-demand of the raw data items (T5). When the user right-clicks on the specific aggregate and selects the relevant option, the data items that belong to this aggregate are shown on the map as circles. Simultaneously, a separate message table shows the semantic content of those data items in a list and highlights the keywords relevant to different categories based on the same color scheme.

Implementation Details

TopoGroups consists of a multi-layered SVG canvas. The map layer stays at the bottom of the hierarchy and provides an interactive map visualization. On top of the map layer is the visualization layer, which is the primary workspace for rendering various visual elements including boundaries, halos, categorical encodings, etc. The toolbox layer stays on top of the hierarchy, showing interactive menus and the toolbar.

TopoGroups applies cardinal spline interpolation to smooth the boundary of the spatial aggregates. In order to fill color inside the boundary, the SVG `<mask>` command is used to create masks according to the boundary of the inner children aggregates, thus avoid rendering those areas. TopoGroups achieves the shadow (halo) effect by initiating an SVG filter (`<filter>`) and associates a Gaussian blur (`<feGaussianBlur>`) to the filter. The size of the shadow is controlled by the standard deviation (SD) of the Gaussian blur (`<stdDeviation>`). A higher SD value results in a larger shadow in screen space. The SD value in TopoGroups is set as 5, which achieves a satisfactory visual effect.

TopoGroups utilizes SVG dash styling to render colored line segments (each line segment is regarded as a long dash) and dash sequences along the boundary. Specifically, the `<stroke-dasharray>` attribute defines the patterns and gaps of the dash styling, and the `<stroke-dashoffset>` attribute controls the offset where the pattern begins. In order to visualize multiple categories, TopoGroups pre-calculates the dash patterns and offset for each category based on the categorical distribution, and then renders them iteratively.

EVALUATION

TopoGroups visualizes the hierarchical spatial aggregates and provides visual encoding strategies to indicate domain-specific attributes associated with individual aggregates. Our evaluation focuses on design alternatives for TopoGroups that convey hierarchical and categorical information, as we believe these low-level visual encodings are critical factors for multi-scale perception and context preservation. In order to focus on the task primitives, we break down the experiment into two aspects (Study 1: structural/hierarchical; Study 2: semantic/categorical) rather than introduce more complexity in the tasks, which may obfuscate the results.

Participants and Apparatus

We recruited 20 participants (age range of 19 to 28, 7 female, 13 male) for Study 1, and 20 participants (age range of 22 to 36, 6 female, 14 male) for Study 2. Most participants were students and staffs from our college of engineering, who have some basic understanding of the concepts being tested (e.g., spatial clustering, hierarchical structures). The participants were paid \$5 for participation in one study. The experiments were conducted on a windows-based computer with a 30-inch Dell monitor. The interface for the main visualization occupied an area of 1600x1600 pixels.

Procedure

The two studies were conducted independently and had similar procedures. At the start of the study, the investigator asked the participants to sign a consent form and introduced the research background and the different visualization designs. Then the investigator provided a training session and presented sample questions covering major visual designs and task types to familiarize the participants with the tasks. In order to ensure that they did not have any difficulty or misunderstanding, the participants were provided with the correct answer and were asked to raise any questions or concerns to the investigator during the training. The accuracy and the completion time for each trial were recorded. After each study, the participants were asked to complete an online demographic survey.

User Study 1: Encoding the Hierarchical Information

This experiment evaluated the efficacy of color and different color schemes in terms of conveying the hierarchical structure of the spatial aggregates within the geographical space.

Techniques and Task Design

In this experiment, we utilized four different visual encoding strategies (visualization technique V) in the experiment:

- NoC Only the boundaries of the clusters are visualized. No color is rendered inside the cluster.
- SEQ A sequential color scheme is used to indicate the scale of aggregates. In TopoGroups blue is used as the main hue. Lighter colors represent higher scales (abstract level), and darker colors represent lower scales (detailed level).
- B-R A blue-red color scheme is used to indicate the scale of aggregates, which starts from blue (higher scales), transitions to yellow (middle scales), and ends at red (lower scales).
- QT A qualitative color scheme is used to indicate the scale.

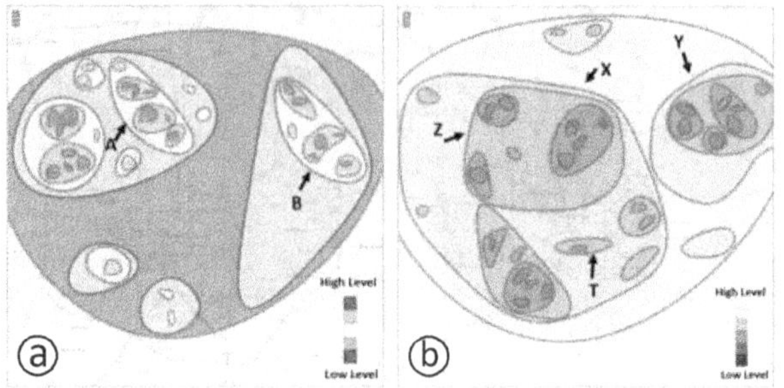

Figure 9. Task design in Study 1: (a) Comparing scales of aggregation (TSC); (b) Identifying parent-children relationships (TPC).

We developed two classes of typical tasks. The first class investigated the participants' performance in terms of visual comparison between scales of individual aggregates (TSC). A typical task of this class highlights two aggregates denoted as A and B, and the participants are asked to decide which one is at a higher (or lower) level (Figure 9(a)). The second class of tasks evaluated the participants' understanding in terms of parent-child relationships among aggregates at different scales (TPC). A typical task of this class specified a cluster denoted as T, and highlighted a set of clusters denoted as X, Y, Z. The participants were asked to decide which cluster among X, Y and Z contains T in the visualization (Figure 9(b)).

We controlled the difficulty level D of each trial based on the complexity of the cluster hierarchy. The hierarchy complexity is defined based on two parameters: the height (or depth) of the hierarchy (L), and the average number of children for each non-leaf node (C). Moreover, we define three difficulty levels: *easy* ($L \in \{3,4\}; C = 2$), *middle* ($L \in \{6,7\}; C = 4$), *hard* ($L \in \{9,10\}; C = 6$). Each trial consists of a multiple-choice question along with the visualization. The four techniques were presented in a counter-balanced order. The whole study consisted of 4 (technique) $\times$ 2 (task type) $\times$ 3 (complexity of hierarchy) $\times$ 2 (repetition) = 48 trials.

Results and Observations

The accuracy was quite high (average of 96.04%) across all visualization techniques for both tasks. Since there was no time limit for the tasks, the users were able to correctly identify the hierarchy of the spatial aggregates shown.

The completion time for the type 1 task (TSC) is shown in Figure 10(a). The results have been analyzed based on a repeated-measure analysis of variance (assumptions met). Visualization technique V had a significant main effect on completion time ($F(3, 57) = 27.12$, $p < .0001$). Pairwise comparison between visualization techniques using a Tukey HSD showed that all pairs have statistical significance ($p < .05$), except for the pair of no color (NoC) and sequential scheme (SEQ). As expected, the difficulty level D had a significant main effect on completion time as well ($F(2, 38) = 48.54$, $p < .0001$). Furthermore, there was a significant interaction effect between visualization technique V and difficulty level D on completion time ($F(6, 114) = 6.60$, $p < .0001$) As shown in Figure 10(a), the sequential scheme (SEQ) has the highest completion time (mean: 19.70 seconds), followed by no color (NoC) (mean: 18.14 seconds), then the qualitative scheme (QT) (mean: 14.49

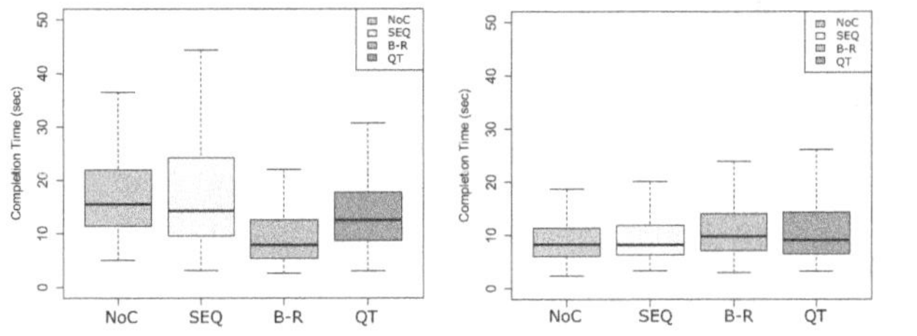

(a) Completion Time (TSC) (b) Completion Time (TPC)

Figure 10. Completion time for the two types of tasks in Study 1. As the result indicates, color encoding the areas helps identify the scale of aggregation (a), but not the parent-child relationships (b).

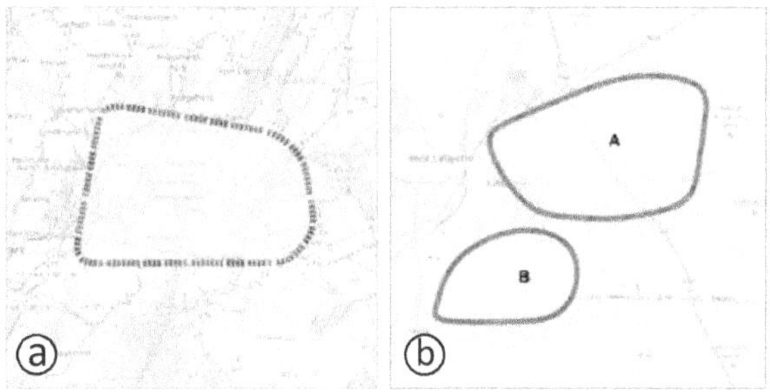

Figure 11. Task design in Study 2: Comparing categories within one aggregate (a) and across multiple aggregates (b).

seconds), and finally the blue-red scheme (B-R) (mean: 10.18 seconds). The blue-red color scheme had the lowest completion time, which can be explained by noting that this scheme consists of different hues diverging from the middle, making the encoding space a bit larger while retaining a step to step relationship between the shades at each level. The qualitative color scheme follows the blue-red scheme in completion time. This scheme facilitates the user tracing across multiple scales since equal levels are quickly identifiable by their color, and adjacent levels are also easily distinguishable. The sequential color scheme and no color scheme had the longest completion time. This can be explained by noting the sequential color scheme is based on a single hue, and requires a higher cognitive load for a user to identify the equal levels between very similar shades of the same color. Similarly, without rendering color in the aggregates, users have to identify the scales purely based on the nested boundaries, which adds to the cognitive overload. Based on the post-experiment survey, users seem to prefer the blue-red color scheme: one user commented: "I liked the contours with the blue-red color as it is the easiest to view and decreases my response time to answer."

The completion time for the type 2 task (TPC) is shown in Figure 10(b). Based on a repeated-measure analysis of variance, visualization type V had a significant main effect on completion time ($F(3, 57) = 2.87$, $p < .05$). However, for pairwise comparisons using a Tukey HSD, only no color (NoC) vs qualitative scheme (QT) and sequential scheme (SEQ) vs qualitative scheme (QT) were marginally significant ($p < .05$). The difference between the completion time for each technique (Figure 10(b)) was relatively small (QT: 11.92 seconds, B-R: 11.31 seconds, SEQ: 10.06 seconds and NoC: 10.04 seconds). This can be explained by the fact that although color changes across scale, there is little color diversity among different sub-groups of aggregates. As users are not able to intuitively identify these differences with the help of color, color may be of limited benefit in identifying the parent-child relationship.

Our guidelines for color encoding the multi-scale aggregates in order to convey hierarchical information are summarized in two aspects. First, color encoding the areas of multi-scale aggregates helps to identify the aggregation level. We found that a blue-red (or similar) color scheme is most effective toward this end. Second, while encoding the areas of multi-scale aggregates can assist identification of the aggregation level, it does not fully convey the parent-child relationships. Additional encoding or interaction designs are required, such as providing different sub-clusters with individualized color encoding or highlighting sub-clusters when a parent is selected.

User Study 2: Encoding Categories on the Boundary

This section describes the experiment that evaluates the design alternatives in TopoGroups that encodes categorical information at individual aggregates.

Techniques and Task Design

In this experiment, we evaluated three design choices (visualization technique V) (Figure 7) for encoding categorical information on the boundary of the spatial aggregates: continuous colored segments (CS), discrete colored dashes (DD) and stacked lines (SL). Two types of tasks were involved in the experiment. For the first type of task, the participants were shown a single aggregate on the map, with the boundary being visualized according to an underlying categorical distribution (category set denoted as $S = \{C1, C2, C3...\}$). The participants were asked to identify the category that has the highest/lowest volume within category set S in the visualization (Figure 11(a)). For the second type of task, the participants were shown two aggregates denoted as A and B on the map, with the boundaries being visualized according to two different categorical distribution of the same category set: with one category denoted as $C1$ highlighted, the participants were asked to determine in which cluster (A or B) the category $C1$ is more prominent (has a higher proportion among all categories) (Figure 11(b)). For each type of task, the same visual design was applied to all the aggregates. The different categories were visualized based on a qualitative color scheme, appropriately adjusted so that when concatenating segments of different colors or stacking lines of different colors, the adjacent colors were easily distinguishable. Although the proposed designs are applied to multi-scale aggregates, the scale itself has a minimum effect on the visual perception of categories. Hence, we limit this study to a single scale to emphasize the impact of comparing categories within and across different aggregates.

We controlled the difficulty level D of each trial based on the size of the category set (2 and 4). Each trial consisted of a multiple-choice question along with the visualization. The three techniques were presented in a counter-balanced order. The whole study consisted of 3 (technique) $\times$ 2 (task type) $\times$ 2 (difficulty level) $\times$ 3 (repetition) = 36 trials.

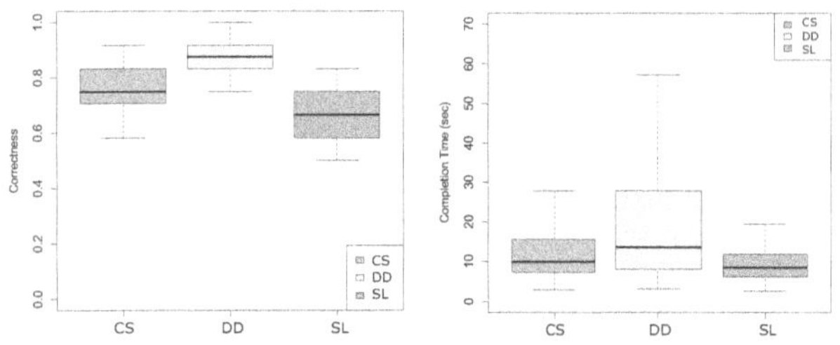

(a) Accuracy (b) Completion Time

Figure 12. Accuracy and completion time for Study 2. Among the three design alternatives, the discrete dash design achieves the highest accuracy (a) and meanwhile requires the longest time (b).

Results and Observations

The results of accuracy (Figure 12(a)) show that the discrete dashes (DD) had the highest accuracy (average: 85.42%), followed by continuous segments (CS) (average: 76.67%) and stacked lines (SL) (average: 67.50%). The results have been analyzed based on the linear regression (glimmix) with the assumptions satisfied. Visualization technique V had a significant main effect on completion time ($F(2, 38) = 10.76$, $p < .0001$). Pairwise comparison between visualization techniques using a Tukey HSD showed that all pairs had statistical significance ($p < .05$). As expected, difficulty level D had a significant main effect on completion time ($F(1, 19) = 45.11$, $p < .0001$). The results reflect that calculating the number of dashes is more accurate than visually comparing the length of different segments, especially when the difference between the values is small. Furthermore, stacked lines was the least effective as the visualization budget (the entire width of lines) is too limited to visually reflect the variation of different values.

In terms of the completion time, the participants spent a relatively long time on the discrete dashes (DD) (20.46 seconds), followed by continuous segments (CS) (12.57 seconds) and stacked lines (SL) (9.00 seconds). Visualization technique V had a significant main effect on completion time ($F(2, 38) = 47.08$, $p < .0001$). Pairwise comparison between visualization techniques using a Tukey HSD showed that all pairs have statistical significance ($p < .05$). As expected, difficulty level D had a significant main effect on completion time as well ($F(1, 19) = 45.88$, $p < .0001$). The results indicate that although DD achieves the highest accuracy, it requires a longer time for the users to count the number of dashes in each category for comparison. In terms of visual perception, the number of visual units in this design is the largest, requiring a longer time for the users to perceive. When the length of the boundary is large, or the size of the dash is small, this can potentially result in a larger number of dashes and overload the users.

Our guidelines for encoding categories on the boundary are summarized in the following two aspects. First, the discrete dash design is the most effective in terms of the accuracy. This is useful in analyses where comparison accuracy is critical, and the quantitative difference between categories are potentially not obvious. Second, the continuous segment design should be used for analyses where speed is favored over accuracy, as the discrete dash design may overload users in extreme cases.

Experimental Results in Practice

Analyzing criminal, traffic and civil (CTC) incident data collected in the cities of West Lafayette and Lafayette, Indiana (more than 170000 incidents from 2010 to 2016) illustrates the use and benefit of the TopoGroups technique. Assume a police officer is interested in several crime types in these regions, including *liquor law violation*, *robbery* and *theft*, he starts the analysis by visualizing the multi-scale clusters at an overview level (Figure 13(left)). The user observes that while a huge cluster is formed at an abstract scale (county level) that covers the two cities, as the officer investigates lower scales (city level), the cluster splits into two smaller ones that are located around the downtown area of the two cities, indicating a high frequency of incidents. Furthermore, the two clusters are visually separated by the Wabash River, which is consistent with the fact that the river is a natural boundary between the two cities. With the continuous segment design applied to show the distribution of different crimes, the user also notices that while most of the incidents are related to *theft* at a higher scale (the major color in the outward cluster is green), the cluster within downtown West Lafayette is more related to *liquor law violation* (blue), while most incidents related to *theft* come from Lafayette and suburban areas in West Lafayette. Since Purdue University is located in downtown West Lafayette, this indicates the campus is safer than other regions (little *robbery* or *theft*), although many *liquor law violations* occur.

The user further zooms in to lower scales (street level) to examine the different patterns in the two cities. Figure 13(middle) shows the downtown West Lafayette where the campus is located. Interestingly, the user identifies several clusters around the campus malls and student activity centers where the *liquor law violation* is prominent. The mall on the east side of the campus also has a considerable number of *robbery* and *theft* incidents. The officer then navigates to Lafayette where the visual result indicates active *robbery* and *theft* activities around major shopping malls and supermarkets. Therefore with TopoGroups, while the user navigates across different scales or targets a specific scale, the visualization effectively preserves the context at other adjacent scales, thus reducing interaction and cognitive overload during the analysis process.

DISCUSSION

TopoGroups distorts the boundary of aggregates and couples multi-scale results in a single display in order to preserve the context of multiple scales. Our distortion method (Fig 5) has a minimal effect in terms of lowering the fidelity (*G5*) and interpretability (*G6*) of the boundary representation, since the proposed distortion approach enlarges the parent boundary that overlaps with its children. Hence, the data points that belong to a specific aggregate are guaranteed to stay within the boundary of the same aggregate after the distortion is applied. However, we note that the boundary itself is an approximate representation for aggregates, since the boundary merely depicts the spatial coverage of the corresponding data items instead of their accurate spatial distribution, and the distortion may further exaggerate the boundary and provide misleading results to the users. Compared to TopoGroups, conventional techniques (e.g., [14, 23, 42]) typically visualize a single-scale result in one visualization. Although they need interaction and

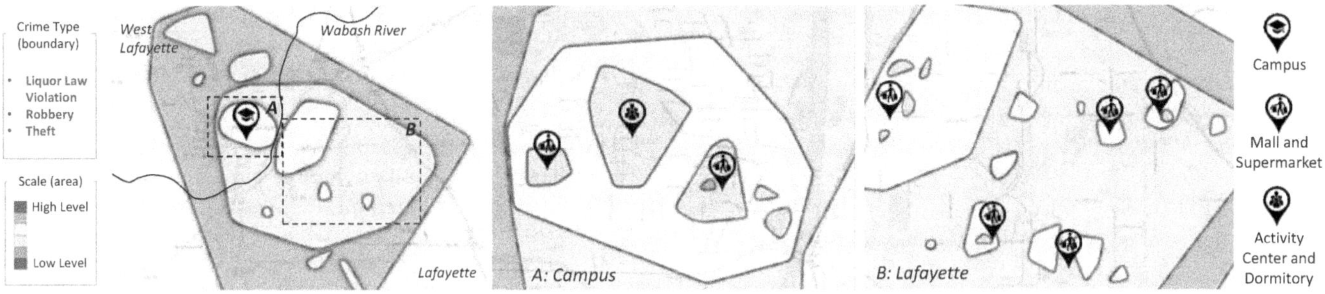

Figure 13. Multi-scale spatial aggregates of CTC incident data in West Lafayette and Lafayette, IN. Left: The campus has a high frequency of liquor violations while other regions show more incidents related to robbery and theft. Middle: Most incidents related to liquor violations occur around the campus malls and student activity centers. Right: Robbery and theft occur frequently around the shopping malls and supermarkets.

may create cognitive overload, these techniques present the original (accurate) analysis results that are intuitive for users to understand. Hence, conventional techniques are preferred in analysis tasks where geographical accuracy is required.

Although TopoGroups provides users with a configurable parameter S to restrict the number of adjacent scales visible from the current scale, further evaluations are required to explore the scalability of our approach. First, as the number of scales visible on the map increases, the amount of multi-scale information presented in the visual space increases accordingly, which can potentially burden or distract users especially when focusing on a specific level. Second, too many levels visible on the map may make it difficult for users to perceive the underlying map due to occlusion. Hence, TopoGroups is favored in analysis tasks that mainly require comparison or correlation of the analysis results across scales. In contrast, conventional techniques are more suitable for scenarios where users target several individual (discrete) scales of interest within the multi-scale analysis space.

Since TopoGroups summarizes the categorical information along the boundary within a geographical context, the users may associate the categorical information with the geographic information in the background. Unfortunately, the users may have the wrong interpretation that the visualization represents the local statistics near the boundary. We note that this is a limitation of this current design, and preventing this requires clear explanation or training to the users before they use the system. Future work could address this design limitation by encoding the locality of information into the boundary itself. For example, categorical data points could be projected to the nearest point on the cluster boundary, which would reduce potential errors over larger areas, and indicate the spatial distribution of the categorical information contained within.

Although TopoGroups visualizes multiple scales in the same display, the user may only focus on a specific scale (i.e., the current zoom level) while other scales are used to provide contextual information. A potential improvement might be to allocate more visualization budget (screen space) to the level on which one is focusing. This can be achieved by adding a weight parameter to the distortion algorithm so that boundaries of adjacent scales are shifted with larger offsets. This could provide an opportunity to encode more information within the chosen scale, perhaps layering different techniques on top of one another. For example, a semi-transparent sedimentation layer as a background would allow for users to quickly understand the categorical distribution while still being able to add other information relevant to the analysis space.

As a future extension, we would like to extend TopoGroups to visualize the semantic knowledge underlying the multi-scale aggregates. The prominent terms or phrases extracted from the content associated with the data items can be embedded within the aggregates, in order to maintain the semantic context across different scales. A potential issue associated with this text-based visualization is that some keywords that are of lower significance may have a longer length; thus, occupy more space and unduly draw the users' attention. A potential solution for this might be to dynamically adjust the font weight (thickness) in order to make the important words stand out.

CONCLUSION AND FUTURE WORK

Our primary contribution in this paper is a novel context-preserving visualization and navigation technique called TopoGroups for representing discrete spatial data as hierarchically clustered shapes. In terms of visual representation, we have explored the design space of different visual encodings for the boundaries and contents of each shape using color, transparency, and labels. In terms of interaction, we have described appropriate interactions for manipulating TopoGroups, including smoothly navigating in the cluster hierarchy. Results from a user study yielded guidelines on optimal visual encodings and interactions for the technique.

Spatially distributed data is ubiquitous, particularly in the domain of geolocated social media posts, so we see many potential future research directions in this area. Our future work includes integrating TopoGroups with text visualization, exploring the use of advanced text analytics techniques such as topic modeling, and applying the TopoGroups technique to full-fledged spatial visualization systems.

ACKNOWLEDGEMENTS

This work was funded by the U.S. Department of Homeland Security VACCINE Center under Award Number 2009-ST-061-CI0003.

REFERENCES

1. Robert Amar, James Eagan, and John Stasko. 2005. Low-level components of analytic activity in information

visualization. In *IEEE Symposium on Information Visualization*. 111–117.

2. Natalia Andrienko and Gennady Andrienko. 2006. *Exploratory analysis of spatial and temporal data: a systematic approach*. Springer Science & Business Media.
3. Caroline Appert and Jean-Daniel Fekete. 2006. OrthoZoom scroller: 1D multi-scale navigation. In *Proceedings of the SIGCHI conference on Human Factors in computing systems*. ACM, 21–30.
4. Harald Bosch, Dennis Thom, Florian Heimerl, Edwin Puttmann, Stephan Koch, Robert Kruger, Michael Worner, and Thomas Ertl. 2013. Scatterblogs2: Real-time monitoring of microblog messages through user-guided filtering. *IEEE Transactions on Visualization and Computer Graphics* 19, 12 (2013), 2022–2031.
5. Isaac Cho, Wewnen Dou, Derek Xiaoyu Wang, Eric Sauda, and William Ribarsky. 2016. VAiRoma: a visual analytics system for making sense of places, times, and events in Roman history. *IEEE Transactions on Visualization and Computer Graphics* 22, 1 (2016), 210–219.
6. Andy Cockburn, Amy Karlson, and Benjamin B Bederson. 2009. A review of overview+detail, zooming, and focus+context interfaces. *Comput. Surveys* 41, 1 (2009), 1–31.
7. Aurélie Cohé, Bastien Liutkus, Gilles Bailly, James Eagan, and Eric Lecolinet. 2016. SchemeLens: A content-aware vector-based fisheye technique for navigating large systems diagrams. *IEEE Transactions on Visualization and Computer Graphics* 22, 1 (2016), 330–338.
8. Weiwei Cui, Yingcai Wu, Shixia Liu, Furu Wei, Michelle X Zhou, and Huamin Qu. 2010. Context preserving dynamic word cloud visualization. In *Proceedings of the IEEE Pacific Symposium on Visualization*. 121–128.
9. Jean-Yves Delort. 2010. Vizualizing large spatial datasets in interactive maps. In *Proceedings of the International Conference on Advanced Geographic Information Systems, Applications, and Services*. IEEE, 33–38.
10. Peter Demian and Renate Fruchter. 2006. Finding and understanding reusable designs from large hierarchical repositories. *Information Visualization* 5, 1 (2006), 28–46.
11. Jason Dykes and Chris Brunsdon. 2007. Geographically weighted visualization: interactive graphics for scale-varying exploratory analysis. *IEEE Transactions on Visualization and Computer Graphics* 13, 6 (2007), 1161–1168.
12. Niklas Elmqvist and Jean-Daniel Fekete. 2010. Hierarchical aggregation for information visualization: Overview, techniques, and design guidelines. *IEEE Transactions on Visualization and Computer Graphics* 16, 3 (2010), 439–454.
13. Martin Ester, Hans-Peter Kriegel, Jörg Sander, Xiaowei Xu, and others. 1996. A density-based algorithm for discovering clusters in large spatial databases with noise.. In *KDD*, Vol. 96. 226–231.
14. Nivan Ferreira, Lauro Lins, Daniel Fink, Steve Kelling, Chris Wood, Juliana Freire, and Claudio Silva. 2011. Birdvis: Visualizing and understanding bird populations. *IEEE Transactions on Visualization and Computer Graphics* 17, 12 (2011), 2374–2383.
15. Thomas MJ Fruchterman and Edward M Reingold. 1991. Graph drawing by force-directed placement. *Software: Practice and Experience* 21, 11 (1991), 1129–1164.
16. George W. Furnas. 1986. Generalized fisheye views. In *Proceedings of the ACM Conference on Human Factors in Computing Systems*. 16–23.
17. George W. Furnas. 2006. A fisheye follow-up: further reflections on focus + context. In *Proceedings of the ACM Conference on Human Factors in Computing Systems*. 999–1008.
18. Sarah Goodwin, Jason Dykes, Aidan Slingsby, and Cagatay Turkay. 2016. Visualizing multiple variables across scale and geography. *IEEE Transactions on Visualization and Computer Graphics* 22, 1 (2016), 599–608.
19. Carl Gutwin. 2002. Improving focus targeting in interactive fisheye views. In *Proceedings of the ACM Conference on Human Factors in Computing Systems*. 267–274.
20. Tobias Isenberg. 2013. Visual abstraction and stylisation of maps. *The Cartographic Journal* 50, 1 (2013), 8–18.
21. Waqas Javed and Niklas Elmqvist. 2010. Stack zooming for multi-focus interaction in time-series data visualization. In *Proceedings of the IEEE Pacific Symposium on Visualization*. 33–40.
22. Waqas Javed, Sohaib Ghani, and Niklas Elmqvist. 2012a. GravNav: Using a gravity model for multi-scale navigation. In *Proceedings of the International Working Conference on Advanced Visual Interfaces*. ACM, 217–224.
23. Waqas Javed, Sohaib Ghani, and Niklas Elmqvist. 2012b. PolyZoom: multiscale and multifocus exploration in 2d visual spaces. In *Proceedings of the ACM Conference on Human Factors in Computing Systems*. 287–296.
24. Susanne Jul and George W. Furnas. 1998a. Critical zones in desert fog: aids to multiscale navigation. In *Proceedings of the ACM Symposium on User Interface Software and Technology*. 97–106.
25. Susanne Jul and George W. Furnas. 1998b. Critical Zones in Desert Fog: Aids to Multiscale Navigation. In *Proceedings of the ACM Symposium on User Interface Software and Technology*. 97–106.

26. SungYe Kim, Ross Maciejewski, Abish Malik, Yun Jang, David S Ebert, and Tobias Isenberg. 2013. Bristle Maps: A multivariate abstraction technique for geovisualization. *IEEE Transactions on Visualization and Computer Graphics* 19, 9 (2013), 1438–1454.

27. Etien L Koua, Alan MacEachren, and M-J Kraak. 2006. Evaluating the usability of visualization methods in an exploratory geovisualization environment. *International Journal of Geographical Information Science* 20, 4 (2006), 425–448.

28. Nina Siu-Ngan Lam and Dale A Quattrochi. 1992. On the issues of scale, resolution, and fractal analysis in the mapping sciences. *The Professional Geographer* 44, 1 (1992), 88–98.

29. Abish Malik, Ross Maciejewski, Sherry Towers, Sean McCullough, and David S Ebert. 2014. Proactive spatiotemporal resource allocation and predictive visual analytics for community policing and law enforcement. *IEEE Transactions on Visualization and Computer Graphics* 20, 12 (2014), 1863–1872.

30. Emmanuel Pietriga and Caroline Appert. 2008. Sigma lenses: focus-context transitions combining space, time and translucence. In *Proceedings of the ACM Conference on Human Factors in Computing Systems*. 1343–1352.

31. Victoria Rautenbach, Serena Coetzee, and Arzu Çöltekin. 2016. Development and evaluation of a specialized task taxonomy for spatial planning–A map literacy experiment with topographic maps. *ISPRS Journal of Photogrammetry and Remote Sensing* (2016).

32. Ben Shneiderman. 1996. The eyes have it: A task by data type taxonomy for information visualizations. In *Proceedings of the IEEE Symposium on Visual Languages*. 336–343.

33. Guodao Sun, Yang Liu, Wenbin Wu, Ronghua Liang, and Huamin Qu. 2014. Embedding temporal display into maps for occlusion-free visualization of spatio-temporal data. In *Proceedings of the IEEE Pacific Symposium on Visualization*. 185–192.

34. Dennis Thom, Robert Krüger, and Thomas Ertl. 2016. Can Twitter Save Lives? A Broad-scale Study on Visual Social Media Analytics for Public Safety. *IEEE Transactions on Visualization and Computer Graphics* 22, 7 (2016), 1816–1829.

35. Waldo Tobler. 1970. A computer movie simulating urban growth in the Detroit region. *Economic Geography* 46, 2 (1970), 234–240.

36. Christian Tominski, Stefan Gladisch, Ulrike Kister, Raimund Dachselt, and Heidrun Schumann. 2016. Interactive Lenses for Visualization: An Extended Survey. In *Computer Graphics Forum*. Wiley Online Library, 1–28.

37. Cagatay Turkay, Aidan Slingsby, Helwig Hauser, Jo Wood, and Jason Dykes. 2014. Attribute signatures: Dynamic visual summaries for analyzing multivariate geographical data. *IEEE Transactions on Visualization and Computer Graphics* 20, 12 (2014), 2033–2042.

38. Jarke J Van Wijk and Huub Van de Wetering. 1999. Cushion treemaps: Visualization of hierarchical information. In *Proceedings of the IEEE Symposium on Information Visualization*. 73–78.

39. Leland Wilkinson. 2006. *The Grammar of Graphics*. Springer Science & Business Media.

40. Insoo Woo, SungYe Kim, Ross Maciejewski, David S Ebert, Timothy D Ropp, and Krystal Thomas. 2009. SDViz: A context-preserving interactive visualization system for technical diagrams. In *Computer Graphics Forum*, Vol. 28. 943–950.

41. Jing Xia, Wei Chen, Yumeng Hou, Wanqi Hu, Xinxin Huang, and David S Ebert. 2016. DimScanner: A Relation-based Visual Exploration Approach Towards Data Dimension Inspection. In *Proceedings of the IEEE Conference on Visual Analytics Science and Technology*. 181–190.

42. Jiawei Zhang, Benjamin Ahlbrand, Abish Malik, Junghoon Chae, Zhiyu Min, Sungahn Ko, and David S Ebert. 2016a. A visual Analytics framework for microblog data analysis at multiple scales of aggregation. In *Computer Graphics Forum*, Vol. 35. 441–450.

43. Yifan Zhang, Wei Luo, Elizabeth A. Mack, and Ross Maciejewski. 2016b. Visualizing the impact of geographical vriations on multivariate clustering. In *Computer Graphics Forum*, Vol. 35. 101–110.

A Design Perspective on Data

Melanie Feinberg
School of Library and Information Science (SILS)
The University of North Carolina at Chapel Hill
mfeinber@unc.edu

ABSTRACT
Empirical studies invariably show that data generation is situationally contingent and interpretively flexible, even when data is collected automatically. This essay situates data generation within a design perspective, demonstrating how data creation can be understood as a multilayered set of interlocking design activities. By showing how data is infused with design, this paper argues that any "use" of data represents a continuation of its design. We are always designers of data, never its mere appropriators.

Author Keywords
Data; design; infrastructure; metadata; materiality

ACM Classification Keywords
H.5.m. Information interfaces and presentation (e.g., HCI): Miscellaneous

INTRODUCTION
It is well understood that data involves more than mere recording of facts. Researchers across disciplines have described the mixture of human motivations, historical traditions, environmental and technological affordances, and particular goals in which data is conceptualized, structured, captured, aggregated, and analyzed [see, for example, 3, 12, 17, 18, 25]. In HCI, user studies describe the richly situated environments in which data is constituted [as in 2, 16, 21, 26]. Most recently, studies of personal informatics detail how data collected by automated mechanisms (as with fitness trackers or household sensors) is dependent on context for its meaning, in accordance with user behavior that might be systematic and consistent, or that might equally be fluid and improvisational—or sometimes both [for example, see 5, 6, 8, 23, 27]. For instance, a step counter on a smartphone might be implemented by one person as a meticulous, comprehensive log, while another person uses it an opportunistic and haphazard recording of partial activity. Although the counter is just recording steps, its deployment is situational, creative, and flexible. Design of data doesn't stop with the design of a step-counting feature; it proceeds through the data collection patterns of smartphone users, and it continues as counts are generated and aggregated over time.

Permission to make digital or hard copies of all or part of this work for personal or classroom use is granted without fee provided that copies are not made or distributed for profit or commercial advantage and that copies bear this notice and the full citation on the first page. Copyrights for components of this work owned by others than ACM must be honored. Abstracting with credit is permitted. To copy otherwise, or republish, to post on servers or to redistribute to lists, requires prior specific permission and/or a fee. Request permissions from Permissions@acm.org.
CHI 2017, May 06-11, 2017, Denver, CO, USA
© 2017 ACM. ISBN 978-1-4503-4655-9/17/05…$15.00
DOI: http://dx.doi.org/10.1145/3025453.3025837

What does it mean, then, to "use" step count data as an element of some subsequent design, perhaps to visualize activity patterns in a neighborhood or to suggest health improvement goals? In this paper, I illustrate how all "use" of data involves its design: how data is never merely the input to design, but always its object. I show how data creation can be understood as a multilayered set of interlocking design activities, and how data use is the continuation of these activities.

While "data" may appear conceptually simple—a data point is just a value, often a number, like the number of steps taken each day—any data requires some kind of *conceptual infrastructure* to have meaning. The number of steps involves the designation of a form of measurement (steps) and a scale of measurement (positive integers of whole steps). Data also involves *collection processes* that individually implement the conceptual infrastructure (how each step is counted) and *aggregation processes* that integrate many acts of independent collection (the association of each step with a particular device across established time units). To make my argument, I trace the role of design in these areas: infrastructure development, collection, and aggregation. I demonstrate how design figures into these activities using a variety of examples. (Although some examples are drawn from a research study, this paper is not a report of findings. It's an essay in which research findings are deployed as one form of evidence.) To provide context for my discussion, the next section briefly reviews accounts of data collection as an interpretively flexible, locally contingent performance, as presented in HCI and aligned fields.

RELATED WORK
Data collection has become a pervasive, everyday activity. Applications routinely collect data to algorithmically shape interaction experience, and individuals increasingly elect to collect data on themselves to inform their own behavior. Accordingly, descriptive accounts of data creation and use have proliferated in the CHI community. Many studies focus on personal tracking data, and the moniker "human-data interaction" has been proposed to understand how people interact with their personal data [5]. When researchers look at practices of personal data collection and use, they observe a diverse set of creative, flexible approaches to data creation, tightly integrated within a local context [6, 8, 27]. Rooksby and colleagues, for example, describe how people employ fitness tracking devices to

collect data in highly individual ways, even though the actual data is collected automatically by sensors. Someone might choose to wear a fitness tracker only for certain activities or at all times, in effect creating different kinds of datasets to align with their own, dynamic needs, preferences, and understanding [23]. Similarly, Tolmie and colleagues describe the deployment of household sensors in three households and the variations in behavior that give rise to variations in data [27]. Leaving the garage door open, which makes the kitchen temperature drop: this is a data creation event, just like deciding when to wear a fitness tracker. Others have made similar observations in the context of government data [2, 21]. McMillan and colleagues, for example, interview stakeholders in northern European cities to understand how "the production and use of data is shaped by local contingencies of influence, power, money, and bureaucracy" [21].

The creative, situated, and interpretive nature of data collection is well established across disciplines. Goodwin describes how archeologists apply the Munsell color chart to earth samples [12]. Latour recounts how botanists distill the forest into a cabinet of specimens [18]. Bowker reveals differences in collection and testing of lake water samples over time [3]. Star and Griesemer note competing concerns of trappers and naturalists collecting biodiversity specimens in the Sierra Nevada [25]. All these studies and many others demonstrate how the practice of data collection—even in science—is informed by disciplinary convention, situational contingencies, and individual flair. Notably, interpretive flexibility in data creation occurs despite the use of standardized schemas, vocabularies, and protocols to enforce consistent, semantically interoperable data. With a professional tradition dating from the nineteenth century, libraries have developed an incredible array of guidelines, processes, and roles devoted to reliable data collection. Nonetheless, Carlyle notes how complex, dynamic realities constantly challenge catalogers to interpret rules anew—even for matters that seem banal and straightforward, like determining the author of a book [4]. Kansa, Kansa, and Arbuckle describe how zooarcheologists working in the same region in Turkey, using the same system to describe tooth wear on fossils, nonetheless structured tooth data so differently that skilled human editors could not easily aggregate it [17]. Jackson and Barbrow discuss the insufficiency of an extremely detailed collection protocol for a single ecology lab to enable frictionless data collection [16]. From a "big rock in the middle of the stream" to bears "disrupting the collection equipment" the world presents an unruly environment that cannot be circumscribed by standards but must be interpreted in light of them. Across such accounts, the same conclusion arises: although data collection might be mundane and tedious, it is also dynamic, creative, and unpredictably diverse, even when data is collected without apparent human intervention.

Given this interdisciplinary consensus, it is significant that work practice often contradicts it. For example, standard practices of information professionals (people who generate, curate, and aggregate data as a primary job responsibility, including librarians, archivists, and data managers) continue to approach interpretive flexibility in data creation as a problem to be solved. As noted in the preceding paragraph, scholars of information studies have long acknowledged the role of interpretive judgment in data creation. For example, in 1968, Wilson argued that a document's subject (its aboutness) could not be conclusively determined [30]. As Furner has observed, there is no scholarly opposition to Wilson's argument [9]. Nonetheless, professional practice continues to operate as if documents "have" subjects that can be accurately and consistently identified. What causes this conceptual dissonance? Professional goals and values align poorly with empirical realities of data variability and interpretive flexibility. In information professions, data utility is seen as dependent upon globally consistent meaning [13, 15, 32]. Accordingly, like Sisyphyus eternally pushing that rock up the hill, data professionals strive to approximate universality and objectivity in data collection, even if such goals can never be achieved. In this view, if creative interpretation can't be eliminated in data collection, practice rules and guidelines might at least minimize it.

This inconsistency—where one knows conceptually that data is interpretively fluid and yet acts as if it were, might be, or should be objective and universal—is not limited to information professionals. In the studies of archeologists, botanists, ecologists, and so on cited earlier in this section, scientists, also, cling to an ideal of globally reliable, semantically interoperable data collection. Why? Their professional goals and values, also, align poorly with empirical realities of interpretive flexibility in data creation. Just like information professionals, scientists attempt to account for and ameliorate situational conditions that complicate data interoperability. They make these efforts so that, after data is collected, they can aggregate and "use" (or reuse) it, without considering how the character of the data might continue to evolve through its aggregation and use.

This conceptual dissonance can also surface in HCI. Descriptive studies of data creation in HCI emphasize its creative situatedness, and design research has embraced interpretively flexible design outcomes [see, for example, 10, 24, 29]. But design projects in HCI can omit the work performed on data, making it seem as if data were a stable material to be "used." For example, Gaver and colleagues built beautiful, custom "datacatcher" devices to convey socioeconomic data about a user's location [11]. Their paper focuses on the effort to design and build the datacatchers, to distribute them, and to document their use. The team's activities with the data conveyed through the device are minimally documented. The project's data work is briefly described as pulling from "hundreds of data sets from 14 online sources," with "templates to transform numerical or category data into sentences." Torres, O'Leary, and Paulos created evocative art objects to display data sources, such as a set of fans whose speeds varied depending on Twitter mentions of candidates for president of the United States. Their paper also uses a minimal approach to describe their work with data. For example, the paper does not elaborate upon the design choice to employ "mentions" as the data element (and not, say, the content of the mention or the sentiment of the mention) [28]. Worthy, Matthews, and Viller deployed a technology probe to spark reflections on data gathering and the Internet of Things [31]. The probe collected sensor data from participant households, but the paper focuses on the general idea of data collection rather than what was actually collected.

In the following sections of this paper, I argue for a view of data as a multilayered design artifact, which implies that we can never incorporate data into a product without redesigning the data itself. To understand data from this perspective, I draw on ideas of thing-design, use-design, and design after design from Johan Redström [22]. Thing-design focuses design on an object: a chair. Use-design focuses design on an activity: sitting. Design after design involves the "user" of an artifact adapting it to a new purpose. By installing, configuring, and adapting software, the "user" of a computer is also a "designer" of her personal experience with it. Redström describes design after design as a series of processes in which the product of one design activity becomes the material for subsequent design activities: a textile is designed and then used as material for a dress, for instance [22]. The A. Telier group draws on these ideas to propose the idea of infrastructuring a goal of participatory design. Infrastructuring involves creating conditions under which dialogues to imagine new design possibilities are facilitated [1]. The A. Telier group focuses on infrastructuring as enabling dialogue between people, drawing on an older sense of the word *thing* as a meeting place to resolve disputes. But such conversations can occur between people and design materials as well. I use these concepts to present data as a dynamic cascade of design decisions, with each "product" serving as "material" for the next move in an ongoing design chain.

THE ROLE OF DESIGN IN DATA INFRASTRUCTURE

All data relies on decisions regarding what to record, how those values should be collected, and the form in which those values should be expressed. These decisions constitute the infrastructure under which data is initially created, subsequently aggregated, and ultimately used. For instance, weather is typically represented with temperature data. We all know that temperature is measured with a certain scale (usually Fahrenheit or Celsius). But the collection of temperature data relies on other decisions as well: the device used for measurement (such as a thermometer), the placement of that device (on the ground, in the air, in the sun, in the shade), the times at which measurements are taken. Moreover, the selection of temperature as a useful property to understand weather is itself part of the data infrastructure.

In the vocabulary of relational databases, data infrastructure involves the selection and definition of entities, attributes, and value parameters, plus the processes established to facilitate data creation. For the example of temperature, the entity might be weather, with an attribute of temperature, as expressed in degrees Celsius. Although a typical entity-relationship diagram wouldn't specify data collection procedures, such processes are often defined and documented as part of data generation protocols. For example, the protocol for ecological field data described by Jackson and Barbrow details not just what kinds of data to collect and the form in which observations should be collected but the processes for doing so [16].

Many elements of data infrastructure might also be described as "metadata." I've chosen not to use "metadata" because that term can be employed to indicate a wide range of data-related notions that are both more and less than the idea of data infrastructure defined here. One might refer to the date that a photo is taken as metadata in both a general sense (the date of capture as a kind of data to describe photos, just as the temperature is a kind of data to describe weather) and in a specific one (the actual date and time at which a specific photo is taken). "Date taken" is metadata about photos in general, and "July 10, 2016" is metadata about a specific photo. In the context of data infrastructure, I mean the general sense and not the specific one.

In HCI, the development of data infrastructure is not commonly considered as a design activity, perhaps because such decisions often seem banal and obvious, or because they seem more associated with subject-matter expertise and scientific methods than with a design perspective. The use of temperature to understand weather, and the means in which temperature is measured, seem a matter for meteorologists to specify, not for designers to interrogate or imagine differently. I'll use a set of examples of data infrastructure from a specific context—online dating services—to show how design is relevant to these kinds of decisions, no matter how mundane or scientific they appear.

Many online dating services support the creation of user profiles to facilitate both retrieval (finding a set of potential dates) and selection (determining the best option in the set of matches). Users are asked to describe themselves along a wide variety of attributes, many of which are similar across services. Two of these common attributes are body type and ethnicity, physical characteristics that might—naively—seem simple and straightforward, not a matter for design. These attributes are typically expressed via a set of controlled values, which vary across dating sites. Tables 1 and 2 show controlled values available for daters to describe themselves according to these attributes in five dating services. I've used these online dating examples many times to explore the space of data infrastructure in the classroom. Students' responses are always the same. When

Match	OK Cupid	Black Planet Love	JDate		Gluten-Free Singles
No answer	Rather not say	Athletic/muscular	Lean/slender	Proportional	Slim
Slender	Thin	Disabled	Average/medium build|	Ripped	About average
Athletic and toned	Overweight	Large frame	Athletic/fit	Rubenesque	Athletic
A few extra pounds	Average build	Medium	A few extra pounds	Small frame	Pumped up
About average	Fit	Toned	Large/broad build	Soft	Have some extra pounds
Heavyset	Jacked		Cuddly	Stocky	Big and lovely
Stocky	A little extra		Firm and toned	Voluptuous	
	Full figured		Husky	Zaftig	
	Curvy		Petite	Muscular	
	Used up		Portly	Modelesque	

Table 1. Body Type options in five online dating sites, as collected in July, 2016. Match and OK Cupid are large sites that serve a general population, while Black Planet Love, JDate, and Gluten-Free Singles target particular characteristics of race (Black people), religion (Jewish people), or lifestyle (people who follow a gluten-free diet).

Match	OK Cupid	Black Planet Love		JDate	Gluten-Free Singles	
Asian	Asian	Asian/Pacific Islander	*Note:* A separate item for Additional Ancestry lists about 15 cultural groups, primarily of African, Caribbean, and Latin American origins.	*none*	African	Indian
Black/African descent	Middle Eastern	Black/African American			African/American	Latino
East Indian	Black	Hispanic/Latino			Asian	Mediterranean
Latino/Hispanic	Native American	White			White/Caucasian	Middle Eastern
Middle Eastern	Hispanic/Latin	Other			East Indian	Mixed
Native American	Pacific Islander				Hispanic	
Pacific Islander	Indian					
White/Caucasian	White					
Other	Other					

Table 2. Ethnicity options in the five online dating sites, as collected in July, 2016 (Black Planet Love labels this as Race, not Ethnicity). These are implemented as checkboxes except for Gluten-Free Singles, which uses a menu.

I ask them to think about characteristics like body type and ethnicity in a general sense, these properties seem like relatively stable concepts that can be defined in a general, neutral, and objective way. The project of creating data infrastructure for these characteristics, such as lists of controlled values, seems like a scientific kind of project, not a design one, and it doesn't seem problematic to think about creating a universal set of such values that would work across, say, all online dating services. Then I distribute the controlled vocabularies that are actually used to describe body types in these dating services (see Table 1). After students stop laughing at values like Big and Lovely, Jacked, and Cuddly, I ask if the variation between dating services is problematic. Shouldn't there be a single authoritative means of capturing this information for all situations? After seeing these real implementations, students always respond that the variation is not problematic at all: this diversity represents different understandings of body types for the different communities represented by the different dating services. Moreover, the idea of body type itself is revealed, as implemented in dating sites, to be different than the students might have initially conceived. Body type is not neutral, objective, and general but personal, performative, and situational: it has to do with how you feel about your body and how you want others to perceive your attitude toward your physique, rather than your actual proportions. It is easy for students to imagine selecting different values for body type in different dating services—to be Slender in Match, Average in OK Cupid, and Proportional in JDate, for example—because the infrastructure is different, but also because the infrastructure indicates that the community and accompanying situation is different—and so daters, too, will have different identities in each.

To continue this discussion in the classroom, I observe that it is of course possible to represent the concept of body type in other ways, perhaps as a set of quantitative measurements for height, weight, and the circumference of various body parts. Wouldn't that have some advantages? The data would be less subjective and more interoperable [13, 32]. Invariably this is derided as a terrible idea. Someone often comments that people would lie. Imagine, I say, a system where your bathroom scale updates your profile automatically, along with sensors in your clothes to continually measure your waist, hips, and other body parts (not far-fetched with the Internet of Things). People look aghast. That would be even more terrible! That's weird, I observe. You mean you don't want accurate data? It's not that, the students say. What they mean is this: they've realized that the idea of body type as a performative, personal concept is more useful and illuminating in the dating context than body type as a set of quantitative measurements. Accuracy is both relative and insufficient.

The ultimate lesson from this example, though, is not that certain kinds of data infrastructure (the performative, situational idea of body type) are designed, while other implementations (the quantitative, universal idea of body type) are not designed, but that *all* data infrastructure is designed. As noted earlier, Redström uses the example of a chair to illustrate the distinctions between "thing-design" and "use-design" [22]. Although designing a chair involves specifying a thing, it also involves the suggestion of certain activities to be performed with that thing: ways of sitting. The process of design might emphasize characteristics of the artifact or its uses. Determining the infrastructure for quantitative data collection generated by conventional-seeming automatic means (like weight from a scale) might appear to involve few design decisions on the artifact axis, but such decisions of data infrastructure nonetheless specify quite distinct modes of use. Height and weight can be collected in a manner that is perhaps less subject to human interpretation than selecting from one of the Body Type vocabularies. But the *design choice* of using height and weight is not disinterested or neutral. Using height and weight to represent body type circumscribes a particular, situated idea of what "body type" means, and the activities that can be performed with height and weight data are different than the activities that can be performed with selections from the Body Type vocabularies. Deciding what data to collect, the form in which it is collected, and the means of collection—these are design decisions, in that they entail particular activities with the resulting artifact.

The data infrastructure for ethnicity in the five online dating services illustrates this further (see Table 2). Particularly in the United States, the primary market for these dating sites, ethnicity and race are politically and socially fraught concepts. The experience of race and ethnicity varies widely in the U.S. population. White people don't tend to notice social privileges accorded to their race, but people in historically oppressed groups are constantly reminded of racial disparities. To specify race/ethnicity categories in dating profiles and enable potential matches to be excluded or included based on these characteristics is to acknowledge these realities and to express a position on the social salience of particular group identities. The differences between the five dating services demonstrate this. Black Planet labels this category Race, and not Ethnicity, and the values used for the Race category position physical appearance as primarily determining the social experience of race. Cultural experience is secondary to perception of physical characteristics in Black Planet—it's how other people see you that is most important. In contrast, Match, OK Cupid, and Gluten-Free Singles distinguish groups according to cultural distinctions as well as physical appearance: Some East Indians (Indians, Pakistanis, Bangadeshis) might appear similar in physical appearance to some Middle Eastern people (Arabs, Egyptians, Iranians), but these groups are separated as culturally distinct. In this perspective it is not surprising that JDate, which targets a single cultural group—Jews—lacks a category for ethnicity or race, although there are non-white Jews of different national heritages. To include such a category would be to deny the primacy of Jewishness as a group differentiator. As with body types, to quantify such data is to miss the point: representing race by, say, DNA markers of ancestry would be to express *an entirely different concept,* one that facilitates quite different activities. Choosing to collect "data" in a particular form, with a particular process, expressed in a particular manner: these are design decisions, no matter how mundane and conventional such decisions might appear.

If we take the A. Telier's group's perspective of design as infrastructuring to facilitate dialogue-things, the conversations possible with race-as-DNA data are different than the conversations possible with data from ethnicity-as-user-selected-labels [1]. The conversations facilitated by data infrastructure are not limited to users of the data created with that infrastructure: to people trying to find matches on dating sites. Other conversations involve the use of data infrastructure to collect data (in this example, people filling out profiles) and to aggregate data (the construction of sets of profiles within and across dating sites.) Data infrastructure provides a set of conditions under which design after design can occur. The next sections look at collection and aggregation from this perspective.

THE ROLE OF DESIGN IN DATA COLLECTION

In this section, I describe a view of data collection as a form of design after design, where each act of data creation involves a dialogue with the data infrastructure [22]. Redström's concept of design after design aligns with empirical accounts of data collection. As discussed in the related work section, people collecting data interpret data infrastructure creatively, flexibly, and situationally. Data infrastructure does not *determine* data; it provides conditions under which people *create* data. In the context of data collection, data infrastructure is a design material.

As a material, data infrastructure is manipulated in diverse ways by different actors. An online dater might select a body type aspirationally, realistically, or pessimistically. Relative consistency of interpretation within a particular community can also change over time. Library catalogers today employ greater specificity and exhaustivity of indexing when applying subject headings to documents than in earlier eras; there are more headings, and headings are more specific, than in the past [7].

Nonetheless, it remains slightly strange to conceive of data collection as design, just as it remains non-obvious to think of customizing one's computer as design. One might recognize *in the abstract* that customizing one's computer is a form of design, but it doesn't much seem like it when you're installing a new application or changing settings. The same holds true for data collection. Although data collection does involve creative decision making, it is simultaneously banal and tedious. Think about your personal data collection: perhaps you track your menstrual cycle or take regular blood pressure readings. Without thinking much about them, you probably see these activities as rote and mechanistic. But if you stop and consider the details of your practice, you're also performing these tasks with a degree of creativity and flexibility. I, for one, know that I interpret the data labels in the Clue menstrual tracking app in a way that is unique to me. I *am* manipulating data infrastructure as a material in a form of design after design. And yet—I wouldn't call it design when I'm doing it.

A design perspective on data collection acknowledges empirical realities of practice and enables innovative reconceptualizations of data creation and use. To continue this argument, I use evidence from a dataset created as a semester project in two separate courses for graduate students in a master's program in information studies, conducted in spring and fall of 2015 (Course A and Course B). The dataset comprises records that describe a particularly complex information object: video games, which encompass tremendous diversity in form, structure, and content. The data infrastructure for the study included a schema, documentation, and vocabularies developed as a set of standards for video game description [19, 20]. Using these data standards, student participants each described 7 or 8 video games of their choice and 3 games common to all participants. After creating the data, students analyzed the data for their class and composed 3000-word essays that assessed interpretive flexibility in the aggregated data.

Combined, the dataset from the two courses includes 282 records, created by 26 student participants (15 in Course A and 11 in Course B). The schema used to describe the video games includes 45 elements for describing each game, including such disparate attributes as Mood, Platform, Price, Digital Rights Management, Visual Style, Networked Features, and Publisher. The dataset and its accompanying essays are useful evidence because the full provenance of each record is known: the data creator, the data infrastructure employed, and the immediate context (each course). Moreover, while some schema elements appear clearly interpretive (such as Mood or Visual Style), others appear much less so (such as Platform and Price). Like one's use of a menstrual tracking app or blood pressure monitor, recording a video game's price seems banal. Accordingly, Price is an illustrative example.

In the video game schema documentation, instructions for the Price element are:

Definition: The manufacturer's suggested retail price (MSRP) at time of initial release in the region where the game was released.

Instruction: Determine the Manufacturer's Suggested Retail Price (MSRP) from the CSI. Record the price with the currency, source, and the date when this information was acquired. If unknown, specify "Unknown".

Example: 59.99 (USD, Amazon.com, 2014-03-25)

"CSI" means "chief source of information." The schema documentation lists primary and secondary choices for the CSI, including the game box (for games sold in separate packaging), the site where a downloadable game was obtained, and secondary game sites (including professional media, fan sites, and Wikipedia).

For one of the 3 common games, Final Fantasy 7, the following was recorded for the Price element in Course A:

- Blank
- Unknown (2 times)
- 4.99
- 11.99 (3 times)
- 14.99 (6 times)
- 19.00
- 149.99

For the 12 entries that included price information, 7 followed the basic structure of the suggested price format. Of the 5 remaining entries, 2 omitted a source and date, one omitted a source, one omitted a date, and one used a full URL instead of the source name. Of the 10 entries that included a date, 8 indicated when the price information was acquired (in spring of 2015), as the schema documentation directs. One of the others was the release date. The final date was not in 2015, so it wasn't when the price information was acquired, but it wasn't the release date, either—its significance is unclear.

The following price information was recorded for Final Fantasy 7 in Course B:

- Blank (5 times)
- Unknown
- 11.99
- 14.42
- 14.99 (3 times)

Of the 6 entries that included price information, none of the entries used the recommended price format. Three used a full URL instead of the source name. Three didn't include a source. Five entries included a date; all of these indicated when the price information was acquired (in fall of 2015).

Where is the design in recording the price of Final Fantasy 7 as Unknown, 11.99, 14.99, blank, or something else? This seems like a fact that can only be accurate or inaccurate, but I suggest that it is something else: part of a dialogue with the data infrastructure regarding what games and prices are (thing-design) and what activities might be facilitated in describing price (use-design).

In the video game schema, a descriptive element like Price implies a certain level of abstraction in terms of documenting a game: an edition for a particular platform (such as Playstation 4 or iOS). The definition of Price in the schema documentation clarifies that price applies to a "release" in a "region" (the schema includes additional elements for Retail Release Date and Region Code). A release in a region suggests a level of abstraction similar to that of "manifestation" in the Functional Requirements for Bibliographic Records (FRBR) model [15, 19]. A FRBR manifestation is a set of objects that include the same intellectual content and physical characteristics, such as the set of original LPs for Marvin Gaye's *What's Going On?* on Tamia Records. For video games, it is reasonable to see a manifestation as something like Final Fantasy 7 for the Playstation 1 as released in the United States.

But the schema documentation doesn't *specify* a level of abstraction for creating data, and other elements seem to apply equally to all editions, or to all editions with the same "intellectual content" but perhaps different "physical characteristics" (the "work" or "expression" level in FRBR). Mood and Visual Style, for example, would presumably be the same for versions of Final Fantasy 7 on Playstation or PC, and also the same for versions in Japanese or English. There is room for a data creator to make different choices about level of abstraction.

Price intersects with level of abstraction more specifically as well. The schema directs creators to record the MSRP at the time of initial release. The first edition of Final Fantasy 7 for Playstation 1 was released in 1997, but other editions of Final Fantasy 7 were available in 2015, when the data was collected. In developing the schema, Lee and colleagues sought to facilitate the information-seeking needs of a wide variety of user types: serious and casual gamers, parents of young players, developers and other industry professionals, collectors, scholars and educators, and curators/librarians [19]. In evaluating the schema, Lee and colleagues surveyed over 1200 respondents about the usefulness of each element in the schema, and price information was determined to be useful by the largest percentage of people (82 percent) [20]. But which price is useful for whom? The price that a particular seller was asking to purchase a particular copy of the game when the data was created? The price that the manufacturer suggested for a particular version at the time of the game's release—which no one may have paid? Collectors and scholars are interested in games for different reasons than gamers and parents, and different kinds of prices may align better or worse with different uses of the data. More importantly, different data creators might come to different, equally defensible decisions based on the same goals and evidence.

The diversity of approaches that Course A and Course B data creators took to implement price information demonstrates this. Three creators described multiple editions in their records; these creators left Price blank or used Unknown, enabling them to avoid listing multiple prices. Creators that indicated a price of 14.99 documented the first U.S. release of the game, for Playstation 1. Creators that indicated a price of 11.99 documented a PC version of the game available for streaming in 2015, when data was collected. No one described the first release for PCs, from 1998 (with a price of 77.98). The strangely high price (149.99) is associated with the first U.S. release and is compatible with purchasing the original discs for that release in 2015.

Individual data creators tended to apply a reasonably consistent interpretation of price throughout their own records, which indicates that these decisions were principled, not accidental. For example, data creator A02 (from Course A) used the format "price-currency-release date" ("4.99 USD 1997-01-31") for all entries. This structure aligns with an interpretation that "MSRP" implies price information is necessarily associated with the release date, no matter when that information was recorded (in other words, the manufacturer sets the MSRP at time of release, and it doesn't change after that).

For apparently objective elements like Price, creators were unsettled by the diversity of approaches to implementing the data infrastructure of the schema, even if they were individually consistent and principled in their actions. In their essays, many suggested changes to the schema and its documentation to constrain the interpretive flexibility they observed. Creator A09 proposed that that "the more objective the element, the less semantic diversity [should be] allowed," and others made similar assessments. Many creators suggested that the schema documentation should clearly specify a level of abstraction for description.

Such proposals constitute a typical response to situations like the Price element: to build more data infrastructure to make the data collection task require less interpretation and restrict opportunities to adapt the intended thing-design of infrastructure developers [an approach advocated in 17]. Indeed, a subsequent version of the video game schema specifies a set of entities (such as series, franchise, and edition) to establish and relate video game versions. But increasing the complexity of data infrastructure makes it more difficult for creators to implement, thus displacing the locus of interpretive flexibility without diminishing it. It is also possible to constrain the intended use-design of the data: if we were only selling games, then the price is the seller's current offer, about which there is less variability. This limits the data's utility for aggregation and reuse in other contexts, however—one of our primary goals with data. Moreover, experience demonstrates that variability will never be entirely contained. Any position that data creation can be perfectly specified contradicts our vast, cross-disciplinary empirical evidence regarding data collection practices.

In contrast, understanding data creation as a process of design after design allows us to imagine working *with,* rather than against, inevitabilities of interpretive flexibility. For example, instead of designing data infrastructure that specifies a correct level of abstraction for a certain kind of data (to establish that prices *must* refer to individual copies of a game or that moods *must* refer to all versions of a game release), one could design data infrastructure that enables data creators to set the level of abstraction for any statement (so that a price *could* refer to a large set of versions and a mood *could* refer to one person's individual copy). In other words, we might purposefully design data infrastructure to function more directly as design material—to support a range of possibilities for data creation, just like we design computer interfaces to function as material for new ways of working and living with devices.

This kind of approach might seem strange in regards to data—isn't data useful when it is reliable and consistent, not when it is interpretively creative and potentially ambiguous or contradictory? If we aren't sure what data means, then how can we trust it, or even use it, when it's aggregated? The following section demonstrates how aggregated data can be interpretively creative and still useful, if we think about utility in a slightly different way.

THE ROLE OF DESIGN IN DATA AGGREGATION

The "data" we use is invariably the product of multiple acts of data creation. Just as all data requires infrastructure to be intelligible, it requires aggregation to be meaningful. Tracking the number of steps you take in a day is worthless unless you compare that number to a reference standard, and tracking the steps taken in one single day provides little information about overall activity or fitness. Although all data involves some type of aggregation, the digital environment increases the potential scale of aggregation tremendously. (A common assertion regarding "big data" is that this increase in scale is so vast as to be revolutionary.)

The standard approach to aggregation involves making each data source compatible in both syntax and semantics [13, 32]. One data source is then mapped to another, or multiple data sources are mapped to a common structure. Standardized data infrastructure and controlled implementation of data collection are often employed to facilitate aggregation. Especially in large-scale aggregation, datasets might be "cleaned" to transform inconsistencies or remove problematic variation. Cleaning can be automatic or manual. Kansa, Kansa, and Arbuckle describe the extensive work of human data editors, with the assistance of some automatic tools, to aggregate 17 zooarcheology datasets from central and western Neolithic Turkey [17]. Although data creators had employed similar data infrastructure, they had implemented it differently, and mapping from one dataset to another was not trivial.

The example of Final Fantasy 7's price from the previous section illustrates this well. Data creators made different decisions in implementing the data infrastructure that resulted in different understandings of price and the entity it refers to (a unique item; the game as released for the Playstation 1 in the U.S. in 1997; the game as released for the Playstation 1 in the U.S. 1997 as available in 2015 for streaming on a computer; and so on). Some data creators rejected the data infrastructure's conceptualization of price, leaving the information blank or using the value Unknown.

To clean this data, a typical approach would take the predominant level of abstraction for video games associated with price and map all the data to that level of abstraction: for example, to make price associated with a set of versions released on the same date in the same locality for the same platform (the version for Playstation 1 in the U.S. in 1997 or the streaming version for PCs in all localities in 2015). Records that included data for multiple such versions could be split apart. Records that included data for individual items could be mapped upwards to the appropriate level of abstraction. Such mapping operations enable data to be more reliably compared and are often described as reducing noise or errors. But these cleaning transformations necessarily involve simplifying assumptions. In this approach, some data would be thrown away, such as price information for individual items (the 149.00 price for a current set of individual Playstation 1 discs).

Understanding aggregation as yet another layer of design in data creation, I suggest, enables us to imagine alternate approaches to data integration and use. One kind of alternate approach might consider how to take advantage of variation in aggregated data, instead of suppressing variation. Although ambiguity in the level of abstraction associated with price makes it difficult to perform some kinds of operations on the video game data, such as tracking price changes over time, this same ambiguity provides useful, interesting evidence of another sort: it empirically shows how video games such as Final Fantasy 7 are complex digital entities with many versions that differ in complex, intersecting ways. The ways that data creators have implemented price provides evidence for understanding the kinds of characteristics (current availability, historical importance) that mark particularly salient version sets.

Another example from the video game data illustrates this differently. This example looks at the Mood element, which is described as follows in the schema documentation:

Definition: The pervading atmosphere or tone of the video game which evokes or recalls a certain emotion or state of mind.

Instruction: Identify the prevailing mood(s) of the game according to the CSI; for most games, the experience of playing the game or watching the gameplay video may be the most reliable source of this information. Select the most appropriate term(s) from the CV for this element. If no mood is applicable, write N/A.

"CV" indicates a controlled vocabulary, which was created as a part of the video game data infrastructure. Terms in this vocabulary included:

Adventurous	*Horror*	*Humorous*	*Sad*
Aggressive	*Humorous*	*Mysterious*	*Sarcastic*
Competitive	*Imaginative*	*Peaceful*	*Sensual*
Comradery	*Immersive*	*Quirky*	*Solitary*
Cute	*Intense*	*Romantic*	

Here is how data creators in Course A applied these terms to another of the 3 common games, Journey.

- Adventurous, Peaceful, Solitary
- Comradery, Immersive
- Comradery, Immersive, Peaceful, Solitary, Imaginative
- Immersive
- Immersive; Imaginative
- Peaceful
- Peaceful
- Peaceful
- Peaceful
- Peaceful
- Peaceful, Comradery
- Peaceful, Comradery, Imaginative, Sad
- Quirky, Peaceful
- Solitary, Adventurous, Immersive, Meditative, Mystery

What is most interesting here is not that a preponderance of creators (9 out of 14) described Journey's mood as solely or partially Peaceful. It is that 5 out of 15 creators also found Journey to be solely or partially Immersive, and that there is only one instance of overlap between these groups.

The data from Course B shows similar patterns:

- *Blank* (2 times)
- Adventurous, Immersive
- Adventurous, Immersive, Imaginative
- Adventurous, Peaceful, Comradery
- Adventurous, Peaceful, Imaginative
- Peaceful
- Peaceful
- Peaceful, Adventurous
- Peaceful, Quirky, Solitary
- Solitary

For data creators in Course B who implemented mood, a similar percentage (6 out of 9) found Journey to be solely or partially Peaceful. Fewer creators found Journey to be Immersive (2 out of 9) but there was no overlap between Immersive or Peaceful. In Course B, a larger group (5 out of 9) characterized Journey as Adventurous, and this description occurred whether Journey was also Immersive or Peaceful (as was true with Course A, where Adventurous was associated with both Immersive and Peaceful camps). A single creator in Course B, unique amongst all the suggestions of Journey's mood, found it to be just Solitary. Across Course A and Course B, there were alternate invocations of Solitary (5 uses) and Comradery (also 5 uses)—although one person did use these terms together.

These patterns show that, for this data element, merely combining assigned Mood values and taking the most popular ones is not sufficient to understand how data creators interpret Journey's mood. If you did that with this dataset, you'd describe Journey as Peaceful (15 uses), Adventurous (7 uses) and Immersive (7 uses). It's only when looking at how terms are used in combination that one sees Peaceful and Immersive as indicative of *distinct* interpretations of Journey's mood, and not partially constituative of a *single* interpretation of Journey's mood. We see this in alternate uses of Solitary and Comradery to a lesser degree. These patterns also demonstrate how some judgments appear across creation contexts (a number of creators across A and B describe Journey as only Peaceful) while others vary across them (Adventurous is more salient in Course B, as are blank values; creators that use 4 or more mood values are only associated with Course A).

These kinds of observations do not establish a definitive answer regarding the mood of Journey or any other game. Indeed, such observations suggest that no single interpretation will *ever* account for the diversity of approaches to data creation that appear even in this tiny video game dataset. Instead, these insights make use of data creators' different data implementation decisions—a form of design after design—which are made visible through the context provided by the experimental dataset. If we view data aggregation as part of an interlocking set of design layers, we can imagine approaches to aggregation that enact further possibilities for tracing the subtleties of data creation and learning from them, rather than minimizing or erasing those subtleties.

USING DATA, DESIGNING DATA: AN EXAMPLE

I have presented data as an evolving product of interlocking design decisions regarding infrastructure, collection, and aggregation. In this understanding, data takes on a new character with each use, as it is manipulated to fit its new context. This perspective prompts us to make use of data from a more active position: as always designers of data, never its mere appropriators.

By understanding devices and applications for data collection, access, display, and visualization as infrastructuring in an ongoing, dynamic process of data creation, designers can devise artifacts that negotiate and interrogate their relationships with data, acknowledging the artifact's role in shaping data itself. As one example, Houben and colleagues' Physikit is set of 4 cubes that express ambient data visualizations [14]. Each cube expresses data via a different physical modality: light, air flow, vibration, and rotation. Physikit includes a Web configuration tool for users to create rules that control each cube (so that air flow increases as data rises or that a light turns on when a certain threshold is reached). Physikit presents a clever approach to user-controlled, tangible visualization. But although the Physikit designers describe the project as human-data design, Physikit is conceived as a conduit for data, not enmeshed with it. Physikit was "designed to work with any data," and the data source used in the project field study—environmental data collected with the Smart Citizen sensor kit (SCK)—was presented as an external plug-in. In the field study, the designers' goal was to see how participant households would "use" Physikit cubes to understand SCK data.

In my reading of the findings, participants' activities with the cubes were directed toward understanding not just the data and the cubes, but the relationships between SCK, data, and cubes, as implemented in the household setting. Participants "became increasingly suspicious about the accuracy of the kit" and tried to understand "how the data worked." Such experiences reorient the object of design for projects like Physikit. A design-oriented perspective on data suggests that Physikit is not just the cubes and the configuration tool; it's the implementation of a specific dataset with the cubes and configuration tool, and the mechanisms for negotiating those relations. Physikit is infrastructure for making data, not just visualizing it.

Understanding Physikit and other projects in this way suggests a more active role for design in the data itself, as well as in its access and display. For example, Houben and colleagues describe how parents in one household that used the Physikit devised a visualization rule to turn on the light cube when the noise measured by the SCK reached a certain level, to demonstrate to their children how loud they could be. According to Houben and colleagues, the plan "backfired" when the cube lit up for the mother more than the children, showing that she was the noisy one.

Another interpretation of this situation, however, is that the noise data created by family members aligns differently with perceptions of loudness. The SCK sensors record noise levels in decibels, a measurement that describes a ratio, often of power, between two sounds. Decibels, however, are not the only factor in human perception of loudness. A high-pitched sound may be perceived as louder than a deeper sound. A loud high-pitched sound is also unpleasant, whereas a loud deep sound is often perceived as having greater sonority. But all of this is situational also: the pulsing bass in a neighbor's dance music is terrible when you're trying to sleep but invigorating when you're getting ready to go out for the evening.

In the Physikit, when the light cube turns on, the SCK sensor is always measuring higher decibels, but the loudness might vary—or some hearers might perceive the sound as louder than others. If the children's voices are at a higher frequency than the parents', for instance, the decibel level at which the parents become angry and frustrated is probably less than the decibel level at which the parents perceive themselves to be overly loud. As detected by the SCK sensor and visualized by Physikit, the noise data generated by parents and children may very well be different: that is, when the light goes on and the children are making the noise, they might *be* too loud, but when the light goes on and the parents are making the noise, they might *not* be too loud—according to their ears, anyway—even if the decibel levels are the same.

How might Physikit examine this relationship between data, data creator, and data interpreter? One way might be to position the signal (the light) as an implementation question, not as a statement. The light is a cue to ask: is it too loud now? What are the qualities of sound that make it too loud? For whom are these qualities of sound problematic? In the context of aggregation, the salient question is not "Are we louder than other families?" but "How do different households understand and implement loudness?" The visualization can be a reconfigured as a mechanism to understand, contextualize, and interrogate loudness for particular environments.

Of course, although there is an opportunity for projects such as Physikit to examine particularities of data integration, adopting a design perspective on data does not require such a focus. There is no "using" Physikit without a particular dataset, however, and that dataset will have a different character expressed through Physikit than it will through some other means. We can more explicitly acknowledge and describe this kind of relationship in our design projects. This paper contributes by promoting an understanding of this dual relationship: as data plays a role in the design of devices like Physikit, devices like Physikit play an equal role in the ongoing design of data.

Although we have long known that data is interpretively flexible and inherently situational, this knowing has been surprisingly difficult to reconcile with the doing of design, and with the ways that we explain and document design work. What are we doing *to* data when we are doing things *with* it? This paper provides a framework for describing our own roles in shaping data, even with mundane, innocuous-seeming actions such as selecting a form of quantitative measurement, establishing a protocol for automatic data generation, or implementing a mechanism for combining datasets. When we are defining, collecting, and aggregating data, how are we redesigning it? This paper begins a conversation on how to more clearly articulate this kind of design work.

REFERENCES

1. A. Telier. (Thomas Binder, Giorgio De Michelis, Pelle Ehn, Giulio Jacucci, Per Linde and Ina Wagner.) 2011. *Design Things*. Cambridge, MA: MIT Press.
2. Kirsten Boehner and Carl DiSalvo. 2016. Data, Design and civics: an exploratory study of civic tech. In *Proceedings of the 2016 CHI Conference on Human Factors in Computing Systems* (CHI '16)., 2970-2981. http://dx.doi.org/10.1145/2858036.2858326
3. Geoffrey Bowker. 2000. Biodiversity datadiversity. *Social Studies of Science* 30, 5: 643-683.
4. Allyson Carlyle. 2015. The policeman's beard was what? Representation and reality in knowledge organization and description. *Proceedings of the iConference 2015.* http://hdl.handle.net/2142/73642
5. Andy Crabtree and Richard Mortier. 2015. Human data interaction: historical lessons from social studies and CSCW In: P*roceedings of the 14th European Conference on Computer Supported Cooperative Work.* 1-20.
6. Chris Elsden, Bettina Nissen, Andrew Garbett, David Chatting, David Kirk, and John Vines. 2016. Metadating: exploring the romance and future of personal data. In *Proceedings of the 2016 CHI Conference on Human Factors in Computing Systems* (CHI '16), 685-698. http://dx.doi.org/10.1145/2858036.2858173
7. Melanie Feinberg. 2015. Genres without writers: information systems and distributed authorship. In *Genre Theory in Information Studies,* edited by J. Andersen. London: Emerald.
8. Joel E. Fischer, Andy Crabtree, Tom Rodden, James A. Colley, Enrico Costanza, Michael O. Jewell, and Sarvapali D. Ramchurn. 2016. "Just whack it on until it gets hot": working with IoT data in the home. In *Proceedings of the 2016 CHI Conference on Human Factors in Computing Systems* (CHI '16), 5933-5944. http://dx.doi.org/10.1145/2858036.2858518
9. Jonathan Furner. 2010. Philosophy and information studies. *Annual Review of Information Science and Technology,* 44: 161-200.
10. William Gaver, Jacob Beaver, and Steve Benford. 2003. Ambiguity as a resource for design. In *Proceedings of the SIGCHI Conference on Human Factors in Computing Systems (CHI '03),* 233-240. http://dx.doi.org/10.1145/642611.642653
11. William Gaver, Andy Boucher, Nadine Jarvis, David Cameron, Mark Hauenstein, Sarah Pennington, John Bowers, James Pike, Robin Beitra, and Liliana Ovalle. 2016. The Datacatcher: batch deployment and documentation of 130 location-aware, mobile devices that put sociopolitically-relevant big data in people's hands: polyphonic interpretation at scale. In *Proceedings of the 2016 CHI Conference on Human Factors in Computing Systems* (CHI '16), 1597-1607. http://dx.doi.org/10.1145/2858036.2858472
12. Charles Goodwin. 1994. Professional vision. *American Anthropologist* 96(3): 606-633.
13. Jane Greenberg. 2009. Metadata and digital information. In Bates, Marcia, and Mary Niles Maack (eds). *Encyclopedia of Library and Information Sciences.* 3rd ed. CRC Press.
14. Steven Houben, Connie Golsteijn, Sarah Gallacher, Rose Johnson, Saskia Bakker, Nicolai Marquardt, Licia Capra, and Yvonne Rogers. 2016. Physikit: data engagement through physical ambient visualizations in the home. In *Proceedings of the 2016 CHI Conference on Human Factors in Computing Systems* (CHI '16)., 1608-1619. http://dx.doi.org/10.1145/2858036.2858059
15. International Federation of Library Associations (IFLA). 1998. Functional requirements for bibliographic records (FRBR). http://www.ifla.org/files/assets/cataloguing/frbr/frbr_2008.pdf
16. Steven J. Jackson and Sarah Barbrow. 2015. Standards and/as innovation: protocols, creativity, and interactive systems development in ecology. In *Proceedings of the 33rd Annual ACM Conference on Human Factors in Computing Systems* (CHI '15), 1769-1778. http://dx.doi.org/10.1145/2702123.2702564
17. Eric Kansa, Sarah Kansa, and Benjamin Arbuckle. 2014. Publishing and pushing: mixing models for communicating research data in archeology. *International Journal of Digital Curation* 9,1: 57-70.
18. Bruno Latour. 1999. *Pandora's hope: essays on the reality of science studies.* Cambridge, MA: Harvard University Press.
19. Jin Ha Lee, Hyerim Cho, Violet Fox, and Andrew Perti. 2013. User-centered approach in creating a metadata schema for video games and interactive media. *Proceedings of the 13th ACM/IEEE-CS Joint Conference on Digital Libraries (JCDL),* 229-238.
20. Jin Ha Lee, Rachel Clarke, and Andrew Perti. 2015. Empirical evaluation of metadata for video games and interactive media. *Journal for the Association of Information Science and Technology (JASIST).*
21. Donald McMillan, Arvid Engström, Airi Lampinen, and Barry Brown. 2016. Data and the city. In *Proceedings of the 2016 CHI Conference on Human Factors in Computing Systems* (CHI '16), 2933-2944. http://dx.doi.org/10.1145/2858036.2858434
22. Johan Redström. 2008. RE: definitions of use. *Design Studies* 29:4, 410–23.
23. John Rooksby, Mattias Rost, Alistair Morrison, and Matthew Chalmers. 2014. Personal tracking as lived

informatics. In *Proceedings of the 32nd annual ACM conference on Human factors in computing systems* (CHI '14), 1163-1172. http://doi.acm.org/10.1145/2556288.2557039

24. Phoebe Sengers and Bill Gaver. 2006. Staying open to interpretation: engaging multiple meanings in design and evaluation. In P*roceedings of the 6th conference on Designing Interactive systems (DIS '06),* 99-108. http://dx.doi.org/10.1145/1142405.1142422

25. Susan Leigh Star and James Griesemer. 1989. Institutional ecology, "translations" and boundary objects: amateurs and professionals in Berkeley's Museum of Vertebrate Zoology, 1907-1939. *Social Studies of Science* 19, 3: 387-420.

26. Alex S. Taylor, Siân Lindley, Tim Regan, David Sweeney, Vasillis Vlachokyriakos, Lillie Grainger, and Jessica Lingel. 2015. Data-in-place: thinking through the relations between data and community. In *Proceedings of the 33rd Annual ACM Conference on Human Factors in Computing Systems* (CHI '15), 2863-2872. http://dx.doi.org/10.1145/2702123.2702558

27. Peter Tolmie, Andy Crabtree, Tom Rodden, James Colley, and Ewa Luger. 2016. "This has to be the cats": personal data legibility in networked sensing systems. In *Proceedings of the 19th ACM Conference on Computer-Supported Cooperative Work & Social Computing* (CSCW '16), 491-502. http://dx.doi.org/10.1145/2818048.2819992

28. Cesar Torres, Jasper O'Leary, and Eric Paulos. 2016. LiveObjects: leveraging theatricality for an expressive Internet of Things. In *Proceedings of the 2016 ACM Conference Companion Publication on Designing Interactive Systems* (DIS '16 Companion), 5-8. http://dx.doi.org/10.1145/2908805.2908807

29. Ron Wakkary, Audrey Desjardins, and Sabrina Hauser. 2016. Unselfconscious interaction: a conceptual construct. *Interacting With Computers* 28, 4: 501-520.

30. Patrick Wilson. 1968. *Two kinds of power: an essay on bibliographic control.* Berkeley and Los Angeles: University of California Press.

31. Peter Worthy, Ben Matthews, and Stephen Viller. 2016. Trust me: doubts and concerns living with the Internet of Things. In *Proceedings of the 2016 ACM Conference on Designing Interactive Systems* (DIS '16), 427-434. https://doi.org/10.1145/2901790.2901890

32. Marcia Zeng and Lois Mai Chan. 2009. Semantic interoperability. In Bates, Marcia, and Mary Niles Maack (eds). *Encyclopedia of Library and Information Sciences.* 3rd ed. CRC Press.

Bitbarista: Exploring Perceptions of Data Transactions in the Internet of Things

Larissa Pschetz
L.Pschetz@ed.ac.uk

Ella Tallyn
E.Tallyn@ed.ac.uk

Rory Gianni
rgianni@exseed.ed.ac.uk

Chris Speed
C.Speed@ed.ac.uk

Design Informatics
University of Edinburgh
78 West Port, Edinburgh, EH1 2LE

ABSTRACT
We are surrounded by a proliferation of connected devices performing increasingly complex data transactions. Traditional design methods tend to simplify or conceal this complexity to improve ease of use. However, the hidden nature of data is causing increasing discomfort. This paper presents BitBarista, a coffee machine designed to explore perceptions of data processes in the Internet of Things. BitBarista reveals social, environmental, qualitative and economic aspects of coffee supply chains. It allows people to choose a source of future coffee beans, situating their choices within the pool of decisions previously made. In doing so, it attempts to engage them in the transactions that are required to produce coffee. Initial studies of BitBarista with 42 participants reveal challenges of designing for connected systems, particularly in terms of perceptions of data gathering and sharing, as well as assumptions generated by current models of consumption. A discussion is followed by a series of suggestions for increasing positive attitudes towards data use in interactive systems.

ACM Classification Keywords
H.5.2 Information Interfaces and Presentation (e.g. HCI): User Interfaces

Author Keywords
Design; Internet of Things; Data Transactions; Privacy; Supply Chains

Figure 1. Bitbarista ready to serve a coffee

INTRODUCTION
Since modernists claimed that *less is more*, principles of minimalism and simplicity have become increasingly influential in design. In Interface Design, Norman [21] classically advocated for interfaces that are clear from clutter and distraction, allowing users to focus on the task at hand. Nielsen [20] defended the need for interfaces where dialogues do not contain information that is "rarely needed". Although much has happened in interface design since then, the drive for minimal information remains largely influential. Apple Inc. is praised for its user interfaces with fewer buttons, menus and dialogue boxes. Amazon Dash offers a simple one-button device as an interface for ordering goods. Behind the scenes, however, these devices are performing increasingly complex tasks. Smartphones are constantly exchanging data to offer users the right information at the right time, and connected devices such as the Amazon Dash conceal intricate exchanges with multiple stakeholders.

As reported by previous research, however, the accuracy with which technology infers users' activities can be disturbing [26]. Events such as the 2011 disclosure of GPS data storage by Apple Inc. without open consent create suspicion towards what happens behind the scenes. Discomfort levels increase as people acknowledge that data transactions may occur without explicit agreement. This is problematic, particularly as more everyday objects become enhanced with digital connectivity. This tension between interfaces that hide complexity of data transactions to increase ease of use, and the amount of

Permission to make digital or hard copies of all or part of this work for personal or classroom use is granted without fee provided that copies are not made or distributed for profit or commercial advantage and that copies bear this notice and the full citation on the first page. Copyrights for components of this work owned by others than ACM must be honored. Abstracting with credit is permitted. To copy otherwise, or republish, to post on servers or to redistribute to lists, requires prior specific permission and/or a fee. Request permissions from permissions@acm.org.
CHI 2017, May 6-11, 2017, Denver, CO, USA.
Copyright is held by the owner/author(s). Publication rights licensed to ACM.
ACM ISBN 978-1-4503-4655-9/17/05 ...$15.00.
http://dx.doi.org/10.1145/3025453.3025878

background transactions that are necessary to sustain seamless interactions, argues for revisiting arguments for more seamful design approaches [7], increasing visual complexity [18], as well as recent arguments for more transparency regarding data exchanges [15].

In this paper we present Bitbarista, an Internet connected coffee machine that attempts to communicate complex data processes involved in analysing price changes and selecting best choices for near-future coffee bean supplies. The machine envisions a scenario in which it would be able to gather consistent information on the state of coffee producing countries, revealing issues that affect end-prices. Nowadays, consumers are often unaware of these issues, which may include political, work and climatic changes. Instead of reducing information overload, the machine proposes to expose its analytics process, attempting to communicate the way data is narrowed down to a few options. The aim is to explore perceptions of transactions in the Internet of Things (IoT) by presenting a scenario in which exposing this complexity would have a positive effect on how users perceive the machine. Our initial study of Bitbarista identifies positive attitudes towards the displaying of data, as well as the challenges of adopting alternative approaches to data transactions.

RELATED WORK

Work within the design community has focused on raising awareness of data transactions taking place, by developing sophisticated sensory cues and exploring people's involvement and engagement with data and IoT devices. Houben et al. [15] developed Physikit, a tangible interface for users to engage with these transactions. Metha et al. [19] present a haptic system that creates an 'itch' to warn people of data sharing, enabling users to set their privacy preference using a 'scratch', finally suggesting that haptic systems, being nonvisual and silent, are ideal for communications regarding privacy issues. These are important proposals to make hidden data exchanges more detectable. However, previous work [1] has shown that simply providing more control and more transparency around data exchanges are not straightforward solutions to the problem of increasing levels of user comfort in this context.

The benefit to users of personalisation has been demonstrated in studies, which also acknowledge the need to protect privacy, thus highlighting the tension between the desire for personalised experiences and discomfort with sharing personal information [4, 9, 17]. Other studies have explored perceptions of data gathering and use practices [14, 6, 26, 12, 23, 30] as well as users' disclosure of personal data and perceptions of related security risks, for example on social media sites [31, 13, 8]. These studies reveal that designing for complex data transactions is an area in need of considerable attention.

Efforts to address the problems of security and privacy in this context have focussed on trust building [9], offering a balance of control over data [17], improving the efficacy of consent and permission processes [16, 28, 5, 2], and raising awareness of the security risks of disclosing personal information [3, 29]. Dupree et al. [11] developed personas representing different types of attitude towards privacy and security concerns and behaviour, in an attempt to clarify the range of attitudes and approaches to managing data.

In terms of understanding perceptions of data transaction in IoT, Worthy et al. [30] used a probe described as an ambiguous IoT device, installed in participants home for the period of a week, to explore concerns arising from its presence and activities. The study showed that the artefact faded into the background of participants' routines and trust was identified as a critical factor. With more ambient characteristics, Worthy et al.'s probe presents remarkably different affordances when compared to Bitbarista.

Approaches to date respond to current models of data access and gathering. They often treat these models as a given, rather than attempting to propose a different one. In contrast, Bitbarista proposes a system where choices offered are based not on users' previous choices and preferences, but on the broader contextual picture behind those choices, and how these affects others in the complex web of data transactions. We propose a system that increases the transparency of data used in the transaction taking place in an attempt to build trust.

There have been a few commercial systems that contribute to expand awareness of data, such as online tools that inform on background information of products (e.g. provenance.org and carbon footprint toolkits). Bitbarista is different from these tools in that it integrates different data sets into the design of a physical machine and displays it in the context of purchase, creating a direct link with users.

BitBarista can also be placed among movements that attempt to look beyond traditional principles of design. Slow Technology [22], Slow Design [27] and Temporal Design [24], for instance, attempt to look beyond dominant narratives of efficiency and time-saving. In line with these movements, Reflective Design [25] focuses on engaging people in critical reflection, as does Critical Design [10] from a different angle. Some proposals have also endeavoured to inform users about the complexity of factors that lead to critical events in the world, such as Wired's Cutthorat Capitalism (wired.com, 2009), a game that attempts to create empathy and communicate motivations for piracy in Somalia. Bitbarista aligns with these design movements in the sense that it proposes an alternative way of integrating data in the design of interactive systems, one that is not focused on efficiency but on information. It also attempts to create a more direct link between consumers and producers across the globe.

BITBARISTA

Bitbarista is a technology probe designed to explore perceptions of data processes in the Internet of Things. The coffee machine is connected to the internet and serves coffee in exchange of a bitcoin contribution towards its next coffee supply. It purportedly browses online data on the state of coffee-producing countries looking for information on climate, work conditions, political situation, infrastructure, price stability and demand, and selects top-ranked options in 4 categories: best quality, lowest price, lowest environmental impact and highest social responsibility. The machine offers users the opportunity to choose one of these options for its next supply,

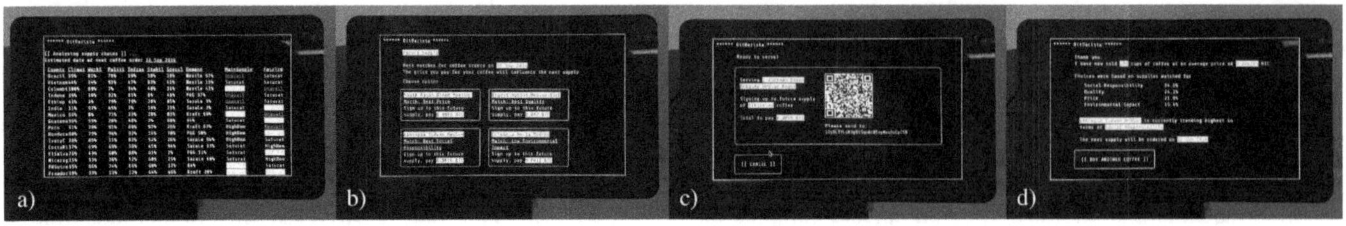

Figure 2. Bitbarista a) Analysing data on the state of coffee producing countries; b) Narrowing down results to 4 options; c) Selling coffee for bitcoin contribution towards next supply; d) Situating choice within the pool of choices previously made

paying for their coffee accordingly. After the purchase, a new screen situates the choice within the pool of choices previously made, all anonymised, displaying the supply most likely to be ordered next. The machine presents some autonomous features: it can administrate its revenues, order coffee, and rewards people for helping with its maintenance, e.g. by refilling coffee beans, filling its water tank, and cleaning it.

Bitbarista attempts to illustrate the complexity of factors involved in coffee supply chains, from production to distribution and purchase, in order to give users a stronger sense of participation in this process. It suggests that data could help to bring end consumers closer to the source of products, reducing intermediaries, and asking how users would receive this proximity. The autonomy of the machine to purchase coffee and set up prices are central in this context. The machine also indicates that choices are made collectively. It asks how people would react to making choices with this collectivity in mind, while placing choices in the future rather than the present. Although the machine only purports to browse data in real time, and the data that it claims to have found is not fully available at the moment, its categories were defined based on recent technical reports on coffee production[1], and the process that it illustrates is not far-fetched. Our motivation was to design a connected device that would provide a more positive attitude towards data display, usage and sharing.

Bitbarista is different from most IoT devices in the sense that **a)** it displays rather than conceals data processes; **b)** it connects data to the situation experienced, placing users within the forces that govern this data; and **c)** it offers options for users to choose how they would like to participate in this process.

Ultimately Bitbarista was designed to investigate **a)** if communicating the complexity of events that result in products being available for consumption would have a positive impact on users, and could therefore be seen as a feasible design approach, **b)** the overarching perceptions towards diverse sets of relatively unprocessed data, e.g. how participants relate, categorise and imagine data in the context of IoT. **c)** how comfortable people would feel interacting with an IoT system that uses data to illustrate this complexity.

[1]e.g. www.ico.org/news/icc-111-5-r1e-world-coffee-outlook.pdf, www.agra-net.com/agra/international-coffee-report/daily-market-report

BITBARISTA STUDY

In order to understand the effect of BitBarista, we carried out an initial study with 42 participants in total. In particular, the study aimed to understand:
a) how aware participants were of the complexity of issues involved in supply chains and in which extent connected devices could help increase this awareness.
b) what impact data presented by Bitbarista would have on participants. If, for instance, they would be more empathetic towards data that connects to positive principles of environmental and social responsibility. In particular, we wanted to find out if these principles would increase their level of trust in the machine, and if different kinds of data would lead to different levels of trust represented, for instance, by a willingness to share data with these systems. We also aimed to explore if people would be more naturally inclined to share principles with a system, for example if they thought this system could help promote these principles.
c) if different sorts of data would motivate different attitudes towards data use and sharing. If, for instance, sharing principles and ideas would be regarded more positively than sharing other kinds of data.

Questionnaire as a probe

The study was organised around a questionnaire that complemented Bitbarista as a probe. The questionnaire was lightweight and quick to complete. It was designed not to test the interaction or to validate design decisions, but to provoke discussion around the 3 points above. It differed from traditional questionnaires as some of its questions left space for interpretation. Central to the study was the interaction with the machine. The questionnaire followed up from this interaction, raising issues around data transactions more generally, e.g. by asking about ideas of autonomy, or diverse sorts of data that could be perceived as personal. After filling in the questionnaire participants were asked about motives behind each response in a semi-structured interview. The questionnaire had 5 questions in total and was divided in two sections:

Section I) Participant profile:
Q1) The only question of this section consisted of a series of 5-point Likert scales (1 = strongly disagree, 5 = strongly agree) which attempted to understand how participants saw the impact of their purchasing choices: if they considered that their choices affected what is available in shops, if they affected producers, suppliers, people across the globe, and if participants thought their purchasing choices would have an impact in the future. It also asked if participants felt their

purchasing choices were constantly tracked. The aim was to understand how much they felt part of the complexity of factors that Bitbarista attempted to illustrate.

Section II) Perceptions of data transactions around Bitbarista
This section consisted of 4 additional questions, answered via a series of checkboxes:
Q2) The second question presented 10 checkbox options to investigate how participants understood and perceived Bitbarista's features. These options were defined in 3 strands:
a) 4 options corresponded to features that accurately defined what was presented, and were introduced to test comprehension of the machine. These options were: "Connect to the web", "Gather information from producers", "Gather data on the state of producing countries", and "Buy coffee".
b) 3 options were inaccurate, and could be seen as potentially invasive. They were not presented as features of the machine, and were introduced to investigate issues of privacy. "Talk to banks", "Find out how many Bitcoin I have", and "Access data on my phone" were inaccurate features, as the machine uses bitcoin for transactions and therefore does not need to establish any direct connection with the phone, talk to banks, etc.
c) Finally, 3 options were open-ended: features that were not presented as characteristic of Bitbarista but which could be interpreted as such. These options were introduced to probe into ideas of autonomy. "Decide what kind of coffee I drink", "Change the price of my coffee", and "Talk to other coffee machines", were open-ended.

Q3) The next question concerned participants' perception of whom Bitbarista was working for: if it was working for themselves, for coffee growers, coffee distributors, a coffee machine manufacturer, a technology company, or simply for itself. The idea was that participant's perceptions of motives behind Bitbarista would be likely to influence how they perceived the system as a whole.
Q4) The fourth question asked whether participants perceived sharing different kinds of data (e.g. buying history, buying principles, personalisation settings, etc.) to have a positive, negative or no impact on Bitbarista.
Q5) The final question referred to what Bitbarista could do in the future, if it would help improve the quality of their coffee, help coffee growers, help to support a fairer production chain and if it would go about learning participants' preferences, access their data and give access to their bitcoin account.

Probing situations
The questionnaire attempted to invite reflection on particular issues around data awareness, access and sharing in the Internet of Things. It was implemented in two situations, firstly in an exhibition space, where participants interacted with the machine, filled the questionnaire, but were not interviewed, secondly in a more formal environment where participants were interviewed about their answers after using the machine and filling in the questionnaire.

I) Exhibition
Bitbarista was set up in an technology-related exhibition space within a larger festival in the UK. Participants were therefore members of the public who chose to visit this exhibition, and were not formally recruited or interviewed. A sign was attached to the machine explaining how it worked, and focusing on its ability to take bitcoin payment and to reward people for carrying out small maintenance services. Invigilators carried a smartphone with a bitcoin wallet, which was lent to visitors if they did not have their own. They also asked participants to fill the questionnaire after they had purchased a coffee. This interaction was sometimes followed by a conversation, which was not audio recorded. We gathered 28 questionnaire responses in two weeks of the exhibition, as reported in the next section.

Table 1. Q1: How participants perceived the influence of their buying choices (Average of Likert scale 1= strongly disagree, 5=strongly agree)

My buying choices	*Phase I*	*Phase II*	*Both*
Affect what is available in the shops	3.6	3.7	3.7
Affect producers and or suppliers	3.7	3.9	3.8
Affect people across the globe	4.0	3.8	3.9
Will have an impact in the future	3.8	3.6	3.7
Are constantly tracked	3.6	3.6	3.6

II) Interview Study
We subsequently organised a study in a more controlled environment. Feedback received in the exhibition did not affect the design of this study. We recruited 14 participants in total (6 females and 8 males). 11 in campus (6 support staff, 5 PhD students) and 3 externals. 6 aged 20-29, 4 30-39, 3 40-49 and 1 50-59. Participants presented diverse backgrounds, including security, technical staff, and researchers and students in informatics, arts and the humanities.

BitBarista was set up in a dedicated room, where the study took place. Participants were asked to consider a scenario in which the machine was installed in their work space. In case they did not own a bitcoin wallet, they were asked to use a mobile phone setup for the study, and to imagine that this was their own. Participants used the machine to purchase a coffee, were invited to fill the questionnaire and were asked about their answers in an interview. The questionnaire probe was used to guide and loosely structure the interview, while guaranteeing thematic consistency across participants. Interviews took 20-40 minutes, enabling us to delve into the thinking that drove responses to the questionnaire, and to reflect on motives behind responses given in the exhibition space.

Before interacting with the machine, participants were asked about their technology literacy, usage of portable devices, knowledge of IoT and bitcoin. 3 participants considered themselves novices (P2, P4, P12), 3 experts (P10, P11, P14), and 8 considered themselves dabblers in technology. 2 did not own a smartphone or tablet (P4, P12). 7 were confident about their knowledge of IoT, and 6 were confident about their knowledge of bitcoin. Only one participant owned a bitcoin wallet (P13).

RESPONSES TO QUESTIONNAIRE
Most answers to the questionnaire were relatively consistent in the exhibition and interview setup. Questions were not meant to assess participants' knowledge or the success of the machine, but to trigger conversation.Therefore what motivated responses became clearer after the interviews.

Table 2. Q2: Percentage of participants who perceived BitBarista as having the following features:

	Phase I	*Phase II*	*Both*
Accurate features (related to understanding of the machine)	Total aggregated 83%		
Connect to the web	93%	93%	93%
Gather information from producers	86%	86%	86%
Gather data on the state of producing countries	61%	86%	73%
Buy coffee	79%	79%	79%
Inaccurate features (related to issues of privacy)	Total aggregated 51%		
Talk to banks	29%	43%	36%
Find out how many bitcoin I have	68%	43%	55%
Access data on my phone	61%	64%	62%
Open-ended features (related to ideas of autonomy)	Total aggregated 44%		
Decide what kind of coffee I drink	36%	29%	32%
Change the price of my coffee	57%	50%	53%
Talk to other coffee machines	50%	43%	46%

Table 3. Q3: Participants who agreed Bitbarista is working for:

Bitbarista is working for	*Phase I*	*Phase II*	*Both*
Me	64%	79%	71%
Coffee growers	61%	64%	62%
Coffee distributor	36%	71%	54%
Coffee machine manufacturer	46%	57%	55%
Technology company	54%	79%	66%
Itself	54%	15%	34%

Table 4. Q4: Perceptions of the effect of sharing data with Bitbarista (positive=1, neutral =0, and negative effect =-1)

	Phase I	*Phase II*	*Both*
My coffee preferences	0.74	0.77	0.75
My buying principles	0.63	0.58	0.61
My thoughts on creating a better future	0.61	0.58	0.60
My buying history	0.67	0.23	0.45
My mobile phone number	-0.20	-0.31	-0.25
My facebook page	-0.17	-0.31	-0.24
My credit card details	-0.35	-0.23	-0.29

Participant profile: impact of consumption vs privacy

Responses to the participant-profile section of the questionnaire, which aimed to understand how participants considered purchasing choices, scored higher for socio economic impact (3.8 average across responses to the first 4 questions) than for perception of choices being constantly tracked (3.6 average) (see **Table 1**). This suggests slightly higher concern about the impact of consumption than about privacy.

Bitbarista features: conduit for human-decisions and data

In the second section of the questionnaire, Bitbarista features presented as accurate (its ability to connect to the web, buy coffee, gather information on producers and the state of producing countries) were acknowledged in 83% of the cases. Inaccurate features scored lower (51%) while open-ended features, introduced to investigate ideas of autonomy, (decide what kind of coffee I drink, change the price of my coffee, and talk to other coffee machines) scored the lowest (44%) (see **Table 2**). In the interviews, it became clear that the open-ended "decide what kind of coffee I drink" was not marked because participants understood the machine as a conduit for human-made decisions, while the option "change the price of my coffee" was not marked because they saw Bitbarista as a neutral conduit for data. Such responses indicate a lack of perceived autonomy of the machine, as discussed in the next section.

What lies behind Bitbarista: technology companies in line with coffee growers

Regarding whom Bitbarista is working for (**Table 3**), high scores were observed in "for me", for "coffee growers", and for a "technology company", which suggests that participants were able to reconcile the interests of possibly disparate entities. We observed a significant difference in results for "coffee distributor" and "itself" in responses given at the exhibition and in the interview study. "Coffee distributor" scored low in the exhibition and high in the interview study, and for "itself" scored high in the exhibition and low in the interview study. As discussed in "Limitations and Future Work" section, we assume that this difference refers to the way Bitbarista was introduced to participants, emphasising its autonomous features in the exhibition, and holding a neutral position in the interview study.

Overarching perception towards diverse data

Perceptions of kinds of data shared with Bitbarista (**Table 4**) were consistently positive in both phases for options "buying history", "buying principles", "thoughts on creating a better future", and "coffee preferences", and consistently negative for "mobile phone number", "facebook page" and "credit card details". As suggested by the interviews, this difference potentially relates to how participants understood the context in which data would be used, as some participants suggested that negative views are related to a lack of perceived connection between the kind of data and what Bitbarista does.

"My buying history" was seen more positively in the exhibition than in the interview study. As also suggested by the interviews, this may be due to participants being concerned that their buying history could be revealed to work colleagues, once they were asked to consider their work environment as a scenario of usage in the interview study. Sharing "my coffee preferences" was consistently regarded as positive, indicating the importance of differentiating between preferences (set by users) and history (recorded automatically).

Bitbarista in the future: supporting a fairer production chain while learning about users preferences

Perceptions of what Bitbarista could do in the future (**Table 5**) differed slightly in the exhibition and in the interview study, with all options scoring higher in the interview study, except "give access to my bitcoin wallet". Options that scored the

Table 5. Q5: Participants who thought that BitBarista could:

Bitbarista could:	*Phase I*	*Phase II*	*Both*
Help improve the quality of my coffee	61%	64%	62%
Help coffee growers	64%	93%	79%
Support a fairer production chain	61%	100%	80%
Learn about my preferences	78%	86%	82%
Access my personal data	50%	57%	54%
Give access to my bitcoin account	43%	36%	39%

highest were "help coffee growers", "support a fairer production chain" and "learn about my preferences", which indicates a positive attitude towards Bitbarista's use of data to support different consumption models.

INTERVIEW RESPONSES

Interviews with the 14 participants were audio-recorded, transcribed, and coded into 12 labels. The coding was carried out by two researchers individually, who cross-checked consistency and extended the number of labels to 18. These labels were grouped into the the main themes represented by the subsections below.

Extended Connectivity

In discussions triggered by Question 2 (see Table 2), it became clear that most participants believed that Bitbarista would carry out data transactions beyond the observed system. As indicated by questionnaire responses, participants understood that BitBarista was connected to the Internet and that it was able to gather data regarding coffee growers and their circumstances, but the interviews also revealed that participants assumed a direct connection between Bitbarista and the smartphone, after the latter was used to complete the purchase. This belief led the majority of participants to assume that BitBarista would connect to other systems and applications on the Internet, that it would be able to gather personal data, trace their coffee choices back to them, and exchange this information with third parties. While most were uncomfortable about this exchange, a few had a more positive perspective as they trusted that this exchange would be done for a good cause.

Assumption of data exchange with the smartphone.

Most participants (**P1, P2, P3, P4, P5, P8, P12, P14**) were convinced that BitBarista would gather data from the phone: *"my phone is connected to the network, and this is connected to the network [and] any time two devices talk to each other, there's potential for them to talk in more ways than you intend"* (**P2**). In two cases (**P1, P4**) this perception remained even after being told that no data was exchanged between the devices *"yeah, you tell me it's a one-way system, but it might be a two-way system [...] Like all these things develop over time. Turns out they should get updated, 'oh by the way, we've all thought of something where we're going to need your data'"* (**P1**). Other participants were uncertain about the nature of the connection between BitBarista and the phone (**P6, P7, P9, P10, P11**) *"I'm not even sure about how it could track, but I'm guessing it would"* (**P6**). Only **P13** trusted the system to ask for permission before accessing data on the phone: *"Usually they all ask for permission"*.

Assumption of personal identification.

Most participants took for granted that Bitbarista would be able to identify them. This assumption was largely drawn from previous experience with digital devices where preferences and behaviours were tracked (**P1, P2, P3, P4, P5, P6, P8, P9, P11, P13**). For example, **P6** noted *"I think just because it's digital it's already even causing traces, and possibly how I'm, um, kind of frequently buying coffee"*. In some cases they understood the data connection discussed above to have been made through the bitcoin wallet, but didn't understand how this worked: *"I assume it would remember me by the bitcoin wallet. Um, so yeah, it should know who I am"* **P13**. **P2** thought that smartphone payment would guarantee identification, while payment via a touchscreen on the machine would guarantee anonymity: *"If I was only touching the screen and it was in an office then it wouldn't be able to identify me"*.

Personal identification as expanding vs limiting experience

Participants also saw benefits in Bitbarista identifying them. **P2** considered this identification a reward for effort put into deliberately making ethical choices: *"do I care if it can be traced back to me? I'm actually quite happy to say I'd buy this kind of coffee, because I make, I try to make ethical choices when I buy my coffee and I'm, like, putting a lot of effort into that so then I don't mind"*. This identification was also seen as allowing for a more personalised coffee experience (**P1, P2, P3, P4, P11**). It would learn about personal preferences, logging and creating a data set of choices, together with time records of purchases, therefore creating a record of coffee drinking habits, while being able to respond to these records *"if it will analyse my buying history and it will adapt accordingly, that means that it will help improve the quality of my coffee, as in the coffee that I like, um, so that would be great"* (**P1**).

Conversely, **P6, P11, P13** thought that gathering data about their choices would reduce the possibility of expanding their experience. This data would constrain their future choices as participants would only be presented with choices recorded in their profile, rather than completely new ones: *"when everyone's getting similar messages, it's just very easy to fall into, kind of, a pattern that isn't really - your own traces."*, and **P11** says, *"If you constantly push the 'I want to save the environment', would it...yeah, offer more of that sort of thing?"*

Data gathered might misrepresent participants.

Among participants who did see positive aspects in being identified, 3 of them also reported mixed feelings about this identification, as the data gathered about coffee preferences was also regarded as sensitive (**P2, P3, P4**). **P4** described how she would not want her choices to be revealed in an office environment *"What if someone in the office has less money than another person [...] I'd feel embarrassed, I wouldn't want to use it if I was the person who couldn't afford the thing"*. This view takes into account, not just the interactions with the machine, but the broader context of the office space in which choices are made.

As expressed by **P4** above, there was a concern that data gathered about coffee choices could potentially misrepresent participants (**P3, P4, P5, P13**). *"I would maybe choose the cheapest option on a certain day, and then on another day I might want to be more environmentally friendly, so, you know, it's maybe not a true representation of me, it might be just that I don't have enough bitcoins this week so I'm going to pick the cheapest one"* (**P5**). **P13** expressed concern, less for what the machine recorded and more for how other people might interpret and judge what was recorded *"Cause people, people make judgments on things they see somewhere else, without context. It, it isn't so much that something knows about those things, it's that someone will make a decision about what they found out from that thing"*.

Data gathering accepted if relevant to what Bitbarista does

Participants **P2, P3, P7, P9, P10** were concerned about the system gathering information that they considered irrelevant to purchasing coffee, such as their phone number and bank account details: *"if Bitbarista got information, got personal data about me that was irrelevant to my coffee buying choices that I didn't want it to have then I don't think I'd be very happy about it"* (**P2**). This was compared to experiences with other systems *"I don't really understand why some things need to have access to your location, to your photos, or even things that, are things not related to what it does"* (**P9**). (**P4, P14**) conversely mentioned being comfortable about Bitbarista accessing data that is relevant *"if you are collecting data on the preferences of people, on coffee drinkers all the time, then that has the potential to improve the quality of the coffee you drink."* (**P14**).

Data transactions beyond Bitbarista

Negatively viewed in the context of marketing purposes

Most participants (**P1, P2, P4, P5, P6, P7, P9, P10, P13, P14**) assumed that data transactions would be carried out beyond the Bitbarista system *"every time you give information to your device you give it to a company of some kind"* (**P2**), *"it's technical, so somebody must be getting something from it"* (**P10**). This assumption was mostly accompanied by negative feelings *"actually, if it was able to access data on my phone then I probably wouldn't want to use it"* (**P10**). **P2, P4, P5, P7, P9, P11, P13** thought that their data could be used for other purposes, such as targeted marketing or assumed that it would be crossed with other personal data such as from their social media accounts *"from a kind of gut reaction [...] possibly it's connecting to other things like Facebook, or Amazon, and it may be looking at preferences and, you know, maybe soon I'm going to get a lot of coffee ads in my Facebook"* (**P5**).

P4, P6 and **P9** reported a sense of powerlessness stemming from the necessity to interact with devices and data gathering systems, while at the same time being unable to control access to their personal data from these devices: *"I'm always very reluctant to say yes to that, but then sometimes you can't get it if you don't say yes to it. Um, but it is a sort of 'hmm', just because otherwise you won't be able to use it at all, and I will say yes to it"* **P9**.

Positively viewed if within the Bitbarista system.

In contrast to the above, participants were generally neutral and even enthusiastic about the possibility of Bitbarista talking to other coffee machines (**P1, P2, P3, P9, P11, P13, P14**): *"so they all, you know, would they come to know what you wanted, then as you walked up to them, would it produce your coffee for you"* (**P11**), *"if there was like a whole network in the building, like, maybe they could borrow beans from each other. I could see that working"* (**P13**).

Positively viewed if for a good cause.

Participants **P5, P7, P10, P13** said that although uncomfortable with aspects of data sharing beyond the Bitbarista system, in particular if it was used for marketing purposes, they would be happy if their data was used for a good cause, in this case shared directly with coffee growers, who might be able to make positive use of the data to benefit their businesses. For example **P7** said *"there are problems with people who share their data and how marketers can use it, but then I feel like this is about how can you make the supply chain a bit more responsible, so, if, if it is used for a good cause, I think that it would have a positive impact"*, **P10** affirmed that *"if it was fair trade sort of stuff, then actually it was helping these people who were, who might need my information, my data would, would help them"* and **P13** noticed *"it's more focused and it's, you feel like that's going to help. Yeah, that feels okay, for it to understand my coffee preferences"*.

Bitbarista data: display, accuracy and neutrality

Data transparency.

All participants were positive about the idea of accessing more information on the state of coffee-producing countries, *"people might be more, um, might be more thoughtful of what coffee they're selecting"* (**P9**). Bitbarista presented data from these countries in a crude format, displaying raw figures rather than a simplified version designed for easy consumption. **P2, P7** and **P9** commented that this made them feel that the information presented was more objective and accountable *"the fact that it's looking through lots of different kinds of numbers and comparing them, and I can see it, I think that seeing it doing that makes me feel like I'm observing a decision-making process that somehow... it's totally, I realise it's totally subjective, but it feels more objective"* (**P2**). As discussed in the next section, most participants also commented on the positive effect of this information on their choices.

Questioning data accuracy and dependability of supply chains

It is however concerning that the great majority of participants (**all except P1**) did not question the origin of the data *"I think the biggest magic of all is that they get all this data about social responsibility and whatever it is, wherever this data is coming from"* **P7**. Only **P1** did so *"it's nice that it can analyse the different coffee supply options using data that it probably finds, but where does it actually get the data from?"*. **P1, P4, P6, P7, P11, P14** did however question the accuracy and dependability of data provided by humans to the machine *"I think the risk would be in people providing the data"* (**P1**), *"because it's very difficult to, you know, check the supply chains and if they actually are as responsible as they pretend to say"* (**P7**) *"I think that's hard to gauge [...] 'cause some parts of the process might be very corrupt and another part might treat people really well"* (**P6**). **P13** questioned the ethics behind those writing algorithms for the system *"if someone wrote an* *algorithm to like, make money off the coffee machines instead of like, help local producers"*. **P4** and **P6** finally questioned the possibility of reducing complex data on the state of producing countries to 4 simple choices, *"the problem is that it's, it's a summary of something that's really quite complex"* (**P6**).

BitBarista as passive conduit for data.
As mentioned, Bitbarista was designed with simple autonomous behaviours and we introduced a few options in the questionnaire to trigger conversation on this autonomy. As reflected by questionnaire responses, few participants thought that the machine would be able to decide what kind of coffee is served (32%), how much the contribution towards each coffee cup would be (53%) and if it communicated with other coffee machines (46%). In other words, participants perceived Bitbarista as largely passive, a device controlled by human-decisions or fluctuations in the accessed data. This was reflected in the interviews of participants **P1, P2, P7, P10, P13, P14** *"somebody's programmed it to work a certain way. And so it's actually that person's intention and also their action"* (**P2**), *"does the machine itself change the price of my coffee? Like that doesn't seem like it does, it's more that it accesses trends, accesses coffee but doesn't, doesn't change the price of my coffee"* (**P14**).

Reflections on the supply chain
As mentioned above, the data display provided participants with a sense of what happens within supply chains, and participants were positive about this experience. This positivity was mostly evident in the interviews of participants **P2, P3, P5, P6, P8, P9, P13, P14**, who commented on a number of ways in which they felt this would be beneficial to them and the wider supply chain.

Effect of data on choices within and beyond Bitbarista
Participants **P2, P3, P5, P6, P8, P9, P13** commented on how the data provided caused them to reflect on their coffee choices: *"it's allowing me to make more informed choices, and I could pick a more environmentally friendly grower, or I could pick one that's the cheapest"* (**P5**), *"if it's on a screen in front of you, you're doing it, and then you're more aware. And that will influence my choice"* (**P9**). **P2 and P9** described how the experience would also cause them to reflect more on their choices beyond Bitbarista, *"then I would probably change my choice from what was in supermarket"* (**P9**).

Reflections on the effect of Bitbarista on supply chains
P3, P5, P6, P14 stated in the interviews that choices made as a result of the information displayed could impact the supply chain, and possibly reduce some of the intermediaries that were perceived as benefitting unfairly for their role: *"Because I think, obviously, it gives people more choice and then it exponentially affects people down the line more"* (**P5**). **P14** went further to consider the a new model for supply chains *"because a coffee grower could sell directly to the machine, and this becomes their point of presence or whatever, that perhaps makes their relationship a lot more tangible, whereas before they were always behind a distributor, for instance"*.

Reflections on business models behind Bitbarista
Some participants (**P4, P5, P7, P8, P11, P13**) expressed uncertainty about the business model behind Bitbarista and the organisations and individuals involved in it, assuming that some sort of profit would be made by someone: *"I'm not exactly sure where the revenue is being directed and to whom. I just don't know who actually, um, makes money from this, whether it is somebody who sells it, or if it gives money back to the coffee producers, or...this is the one I'm not certain about"* (**P7**). **P5** reflected on how profit would be made through the commercialisation of data *"if there's somebody who was to buy the data from the company, or, you know, if the company was selling data or the manufacturers or the, the coffee growers were then selling the data or accessing the data"*. **P4** questioned if the model would work for other entities in the supply chain, *"I mean the whole bitcoin thing you are going for, in these developing countries, I don't know how that works for someone in Ethiopia who probably doesn't own a computer, I don't understand how this translates for everyone else"*.

DISCUSSION

Awareness of supply chains
The Bitbarista system presented people with a broader context of data transactions to support their choices. As revealed by questionnaire responses, participants in the initial study exhibited concern about the impact of their buying choices on people across the globe, producers, suppliers as well as shops. Indeed they were even slightly more concerned with the impact of their buying choices than with the possibility of these choices to be constantly tracked.

Given this background, most reported that Bitbarista had a positive impact on their awareness of the supply chain. In the interviews, 10 out of 14 participants declared that Bitbarista increased reflection regarding the context in which their choices were situated. They discussed the potential of Bitbarista to support more informed choices that would ultimately have an impact on coffee growers. 4 participants explicitly described its potential to reduce intermediaries and consequently increase the number of coffee options available. Despite largely tied to traditional models of consumption and profit, 6 reflected on business models behind Bitbarista, with one of them considering a more alternative approach.

This positive perspective also influenced participants willingness to share data. The majority believed that sharing certain types of data in the context of the Bitbarista system would be positive, provided it was for a good cause, either in providing an improved coffee experience, or by the data being used to help disadvantaged actors within the supply chain. Despite some suspicion about the reliability of the data used to illustrate what actually happens in coffee supply chains, the study suggests that displaying this complexity of data back to users can potentially increase accountability and trust in the system.

Impact of Bitbarista's data display
Despite the reservations expressed above, participants were on the whole positive about an apparent transparency of information provided by the Bitbarista data display. 3 even stressed

the relative rawness of the data as a positive aspect of the system, commenting that it seemed more objective, and therefore possibly more accurate, enabling them to make an informed decision rather than be persuaded by marketing forces.

There were nonetheless criticisms towards the way the system handled the data. Bitbarista displayed various sorts of data sets from coffee producing countries, and then offered 4 choices as a result of this analysis. Some participants viewed this as reductive. Somewhat surprisingly, despite some scepticism as to the accountability of data provided by humans to the system, only one participant questioned the origin of the datasets.

BitBarista was seen as a passive conduit for data and other people's decisions. This is apparent from the responses in question 2, in which participants were asked to judge whether BitBarista was capable of a number of autonomous behaviours, and most answered in the negative. BitBarista?s perceived passivity was also apparent in comments regarding its connection to the supply chain, the data it displays, and the choices it derives from this. Participants discussed who might be responsible for decisions regarding its behaviour and functions, and expressed uncertainty about who might be manipulating or using the system.

The idea of an autonomous object that can make decisions about, for example, the pricing of coffee, and present this information independently, is new, and does not accord with traditional assumptions about linear chains of value connected to monetary transactions. Creating awareness of these new models, and the positive potential of such unfamiliar systems presents a major challenge to designers.

Overarching perceptions towards diverse sorts of data

A number of participants commented that they felt positive about data that seemed relevant to the particular transaction taking place. This confirms results of previous studies (e.g. [17, 6]) that show that sharing data perceived as irrelevant to a transaction tends to be considered unacceptable. This is largely a question around user perceptions of what is relevant, and as suggested by Bitbarista, it is possible that this may be expanded by enabling people to see the broader picture of their transactions.

It suggests that people may benefit from being shown how their data might be shared beyond the immediate transaction, and used across the various entities involved in the supply chain. Ultimately this could enable people to make more informed decisions about whether data sharing is relevant and appropriate, and if it will have a positive benefit either to themselves or to others.

While participants were positive about identification with their choices, 4 of them expressed concern about being misrepresented by their data. Data drawn from a single anonymous choice may be acceptable. However when this forms part of a 'buying history' linked to them and in a way that may characterise them, participants were concerned that this could lead to profiling and inaccurate judgement. Others were concerned that it would lead to being offered reductive choices in the future based only on what they have chosen in the past, thus reducing the possibilities of new experiences.

Perception of data transactions and normalisation of data gathering

The study of Bitbarista shows that, although participants were presented with a system that gathers no data, almost all of them assumed that it did. 62% of all participants and 8 of 14 interview participants believed that Bitbarista would gather data from the mobile phone. 11 out of 14 participants also believed that Bitbarista would be able to identify them through their interactions with the system.

As the Internet of Things expands and data transactions increase, there is a rising need to rethink approaches to data. User discomfort and anxiety around data gathering has been documented in numerous studies. In a study published in 2014, Shklovski et al. [26] showed that users were not aware of the extent of data gathering practices of applications on mobile devices. Once they understood this, it caused them discomfort, even though they still continued to use them. In 2016, Phelan et al.[23] reported rapidly changeable attitudes of users towards privacy issues, and that although users may accept or reject privacy risks based on considered assessment, they are still uncomfortable about the potential results of decisions. In another study published in 2016, Bilogrevic & Ortlieb [6] found that users are also aware of the potential for data aggregation to de-anonymise their data, and showed that users perceive the aggregation of the least sensitive data sets to be less comfortable than the most sensitive data sets in isolation. It is predictable that the level of uncertainty and discomfort will escalate as consumers enter into more and more contracts with increasing numbers of services and smart objects.

This reveals a great challenge for designing for non-data gathering systems, because absence of data gathering and sharing counteracts people's previous experiences, and goes against their assumptions of what an IoT system does. So when a new IoT device is introduced, people will assume that data gathering is taking place unless they are informed explicitly that it is not. And even then this may not be enough to gain trust. We question if the practice of continual data gathering is always necessary or indeed useful, as in the absence of accurate knowledge, invasive practices are assumed. People do not feel that they can control this, and this may ultimately inhibit engagement.

LIMITATIONS OF THE STUDY AND FUTURE DIRECTIONS

The design of Bitbarista and the study reported in this paper have provided initial insights on the effect of using an IoT device to contextually display data related to coffee supply chains. There is potential to expand on the study presented here, addressing the limitations of the work, as well as expanding on the design of Bitbarista by considering its specifics.

The study explored insights derived from an initial interaction with BitBarista. Few variations in responses gathered in the exhibition space and in the interview study, as reported in section "Responses to questionnaire" suggest that these responses may have been affected by differences in the implementation of the study. In the first case, the study was carried out with ad-hoc visitors of a technology-related exhibition, while in the second participants from a range of demographics were recruited. In the exhibition space, the interaction was brief, while in the more controlled environment, participants had time to reflect on their choices and responses. The way Bitbarista was presented, reinforcing its autonomous features in the exhibition, but holding a more neutral position in the interview study, may have affected particular responses, such as to the question of whether Bitbarista was working for itself. However it did not affect responses to more nuanced questions regarding autonomous features of the machine, which scored low in both situations.

All in all, the study could be elaborated to include specifically consistent groups from different demographics, thus comparing and contrasting the perceptions of people with different interests, backgrounds and technical knowledge. It could also consider more naturalistic approaches where interaction time would be defined by users, would take place on a regular basis, and understanding of the machine would not be mediated by introductions but would grow over time instead.

A more naturalistic approach would not only allow us to understand how reactions develop over time, but also how the collectivity of participants may affect attitudes towards not just coffee, but to more general purchasing choices. Only a few participants in this initial study had their own bitcoin wallet, and therefore did not use their own mobile phones to carry out the purchase. A more naturalistic approach would involve setting up their phones with a digital wallet beforehand, or restricting participation to those who already have the system installed. The last however would conflict with the intention of involving groups with varied backgrounds.

Future design directions

We identify different ways in which the design of Bitbarista could be further explored, by considering, for instance:
a) the specifics of interface design and presentation of the data, in order to optimise organisation of the information, screen size, typography, and details of the interaction such as response time, etc.
b) a design exploration of autonomous machines that could offer alternatives to dominant models of profit, e.g. how the design of Bitbarista could be optimised to reinforce its autonomous characteristics, therefore affecting views of its position within the supply chain, and how it could act as a direct and neutral link to coffee growers.
c) the design of algorithms that return reliable options of coffee supplies back to users
d) the practicalities of involving producers in the commercialisation of coffee through Bitbarista.

CONCLUSION AND IMPLICATIONS FOR DESIGN

In this paper we present Bitbarista, a coffee machine that proposes a new approach to data access and usage for the design of IoT devices. Rather than focusing on ease-of-use, Bitbarista attempts to reveal data transactions, communicating and placing users within the complexity of factors involved in coffee production, distribution and purchase. In the paper, we present a study designed to gain initial insights into perceptions of data transactions, not only around the Bitbarista system but also around interactive systems more broadly. To do so, we designed a questionnaire that complements Bitbarista as a probe. The questionnaire subtly provokes discussion on issues around data access, sharing, and machine autonomy.

In line with previous studies, we found that participants were more comfortable about data transactions that were perceived as relevant for the interaction taking place. Bitbarista however expands the notion of what is relevant, by placing participants within a broader context of production and consumption. Responses to the study suggests that despite usually feeling uncomfortable about sharing data deemed as personal, they were happy to do so in this context, as this was perceived to be for a good cause. However, interview responses also showed that participants were weary of data gathering taking place in unclear or secretive ways, and that trust is not easy to gain. Increasing transparency of data transactions, as Bitbarista does, is therefore a good step forward. Based on these conclusions, we draw a few implications for design as reported below.

Implications for design

The main design implication of this study is to highlight how communicating the complexity of transactions and the reasons for these transactions to occur can have a positive impact on how users perceive an IoT system. This includes:
a) communicating what kind of data is gathered from users, and making it absolutely clear when no data is gathered. A non-data gathering convention or certificate would be something to consider in this case.
b) allowing people to understand the model of value creation behind the system. The Internet of Things opens space for new models to be created that do not necessarily fit usual assumptions of linear chains of value connected to monetary transactions. More effort could be invested in designing systems and interfaces that embody and communicate these new propositions.
c) allowing machine-made decisions to be questioned and personalisation to be constantly tailored by users. While automatisation and concealment of transactions may facilitate ease of use, inviting people to follow and go back in this process in order to tailor its parameters may increase trust. Perhaps it is time to make a case for interfaces that increase complexity and time of use, even displaying information that is "rarely needed".

ACKNOWLEDGMENTS

We would like to thank Mark Kobine for his help with the Bitbarista casing and participants for their time in contributing to this research. The work was supported by two UK research grants, the development of the technology through the Art & Humanities Research Council project: Design in Action (AHJ0051261), and the user study through the Engineering and Physical Sciences Research Council project: PETRAS (EPN02334X1).

REFERENCES

1. Alessandro Acquisti, Idris Adjerid, and Laura Brandimarte. 2013. Gone in 15 Seconds: The Limits of Privacy Transparency and Control. *IEEE Security and*

Privacy 11, 4 (July 2013), 72–74. DOI: http://dx.doi.org/10.1109/MSP.2013.86

2. Idris Adjerid, Alessandro Acquisti, Laura Brandimarte, and George Loewenstein. 2013. Sleights of Privacy: Framing, Disclosures, and the Limits of Transparency. In *Proceedings of the Ninth Symposium on Usable Privacy and Security (SOUPS '13)*. ACM, New York, NY, USA, Article 9, 11 pages. DOI: http://dx.doi.org/10.1145/2501604.2501613
3. Hazim Almuhimedi, Florian Schaub, Norman Sadeh, Idris Adjerid, Alessandro Acquisti, Joshua Gluck, Lorrie Faith Cranor, and Yuvraj Agarwal. 2015. Your Location Has Been Shared 5,398 Times!: A Field Study on Mobile App Privacy Nudging. In *Proceedings of the 33rd Annual ACM Conference on Human Factors in Computing Systems (CHI '15)*. ACM, New York, NY, USA, 787–796. DOI: http://dx.doi.org/10.1145/2702123.2702210
4. Naveen Farag Awad and M. S. Krishnan. 2006. The Personalization Privacy Paradox: An Empirical Evaluation of Information Transparency and the Willingness to Be Profiled Online for Personalization. *MIS Q.* 30, 1 (March 2006), 13–28. http://dl.acm.org/citation.cfm?id=2017284.2017287
5. Tim Baarslag, Alper T. Alan, Richard C. Gomer, Ilaria Liccardi, Helia Marreiros, Enrico H. Gerding, and m.c. schraefel. 2016. Negotiation As an Interaction Mechanism for Deciding App Permissions. In *Proceedings of the 2016 CHI Conference Extended Abstracts on Human Factors in Computing Systems (CHI EA '16)*. ACM, New York, NY, USA, 2012–2019. DOI: http://dx.doi.org/10.1145/2851581.2892340
6. Igor Bilogrevic and Martin Ortlieb. 2016. "If You Put All The Pieces Together...": Attitudes Towards Data Combination and Sharing Across Services and Companies. In *Proceedings of the 2016 CHI Conference on Human Factors in Computing Systems (CHI '16)*. ACM, New York, NY, USA, 5215–5227. http://doi.acm.org/10.1145/2858036.2858432
7. Matthew Chalmers and Areti Galani. 2004. Seamful Interweaving: Heterogeneity in the Theory and Design of Interactive Systems. In *Proceedings of the 5th Conference on Designing Interactive Systems: Processes, Practices, Methods, and Techniques (DIS '04)*. ACM, New York, NY, USA, 243–252. DOI: http://dx.doi.org/10.1145/1013115.1013149
8. Daphne Chang, Erin L. Krupka, Eytan Adar, and Alessandro Acquisti. 2016. Engineering Information Disclosure: Norm Shaping Designs. In *Proceedings of the 2016 CHI Conference on Human Factors in Computing Systems (CHI '16)*. ACM, New York, NY, USA, 587–597. DOI: http://dx.doi.org/10.1145/2858036.2858346
9. Ramnath K. Chellappa and Raymond G. Sin. 2005. Personalization Versus Privacy: An Empirical Examination of the Online Consumer's Dilemma. *Inf. Technol. and Management* 6, 2-3 (April 2005), 181–202. DOI: http://dx.doi.org/10.1007/s10799-005-5879-y
10. Anthony Dunne and Fiona Raby. 2001. *Design Noir: The Secret Life of Electronic Objects* (1 ed.). Birkhaeuser Basel. http://www.worldcat.org/isbn/3764365668
11. Janna Lynn Dupree, Richard Devries, Daniel M. Berry, and Edward Lank. 2016. Privacy Personas: Clustering Users via Attitudes and Behaviors Toward Security Practices. In *Proceedings of the 2016 CHI Conference on Human Factors in Computing Systems (CHI '16)*. ACM, New York, NY, USA, 5228–5239. DOI: http://dx.doi.org/10.1145/2858036.2858214
12. Adrienne Porter Felt, Serge Egelman, and David Wagner. 2012. I'Ve Got 99 Problems, but Vibration Ain'T One: A Survey of Smartphone Users' Concerns. In *Proceedings of the Second ACM Workshop on Security and Privacy in Smartphones and Mobile Devices (SPSM '12)*. ACM, New York, NY, USA, 33–44. DOI: http://dx.doi.org/10.1145/2381934.2381943
13. Andrew Gambino, Jinyoung Kim, S. Shyam Sundar, Jun Ge, and Mary Beth Rosson. 2016. User Disbelief in Privacy Paradox: Heuristics That Determine Disclosure. In *Proceedings of the 2016 CHI Conference Extended Abstracts on Human Factors in Computing Systems (CHI EA '16)*. ACM, New York, NY, USA, 2837–2843. DOI: http://dx.doi.org/10.1145/2851581.2892413
14. Liang Gou, Michelle X. Zhou, and Huahai Yang. 2014. KnowMe and ShareMe: Understanding Automatically Discovered Personality Traits from Social Media and User Sharing Preferences. In *Proceedings of the 32Nd Annual ACM Conference on Human Factors in Computing Systems (CHI '14)*. ACM, New York, NY, USA, 955–964. http://doi.acm.org/10.1145/2556288.2557398
15. Steven Houben, Connie Golsteijn, Sarah Gallacher, Rose Johnson, Saskia Bakker, Nicolai Marquardt, Licia Capra, and Yvonne Rogers. 2016. Physikit: Data Engagement Through Physical Ambient Visualizations in the Home. In *Proceedings of the 2016 CHI Conference on Human Factors in Computing Systems (CHI '16)*. ACM, New York, NY, USA, 1608–1619. DOI: http://dx.doi.org/10.1145/2858036.2858059
16. Carlos Jensen and Colin Potts. 2004. Privacy Policies As Decision-making Tools: An Evaluation of Online Privacy Notices. In *Proceedings of the SIGCHI Conference on Human Factors in Computing Systems (CHI '04)*. ACM, New York, NY, USA, 471–478. DOI: http://dx.doi.org/10.1145/985692.985752
17. Pedro Giovanni Leon, Blase Ur, Yang Wang, Manya Sleeper, Rebecca Balebako, Richard Shay, Lujo Bauer, Mihai Christodorescu, and Lorrie Faith Cranor. 2013. What Matters to Users?: Factors That Affect Users' Willingness to Share Information with Online Advertisers. In *Proceedings of the Ninth Symposium on Usable Privacy and Security (SOUPS '13)*. ACM, New York, NY, USA, Article 7, 12 pages. DOI: http://dx.doi.org/10.1145/2501604.2501611

18. M. Lima. 2013. *Visual Complexity: Mapping Patterns of Information*. Princeton Architectural Press. https://books.google.co.uk/books?id=59xlmQEACAAJ

19. Vikram Mehta, Arosha K. Bandara, Blaine A. Price, and Bashar Nuseibeh. 2016. Privacy Itch and Scratch: On Body Privacy Warnings and Controls. In *Proceedings of the 2016 CHI Conference Extended Abstracts on Human Factors in Computing Systems (CHI EA '16)*. ACM, New York, NY, USA, 2417–2424. http://doi.acm.org/10.1145/2851581.2892475

20. Jakob Nielsen. 1994. Enhancing the Explanatory Power of Usability Heuristics. In *Proceedings of the SIGCHI Conference on Human Factors in Computing Systems (CHI '94)*. ACM, New York, NY, USA, 152–158. DOI: http://dx.doi.org/10.1145/191666.191729

21. Donald A. Norman. 1998. *The Invisible Computer*. MIT Press, Cambridge, MA, USA.

22. William Odom, Richard Banks, Abigail Durrant, David Kirk, and James Pierce. 2012. Slow technology: critical reflection and future directions. In *Proceedings of the Designing Interactive Systems Conference (DIS '12)*. ACM, 816–817. DOI: http://dx.doi.org/10.1145/2317956.2318088

23. Chanda Phelan, Cliff Lampe, and Paul Resnick. 2016. It's Creepy, But It Doesn'T Bother Me. In *Proceedings of the 2016 CHI Conference on Human Factors in Computing Systems (CHI '16)*. ACM, New York, NY, USA, 5240–5251. DOI: http://dx.doi.org/10.1145/2858036.2858381

24. Larissa Pschetz, Michelle Bastian, and Chris Speed. 2016. Temporal Design: Looking at Time as Social Coordination. In *Proceedings of the Design Research Society Conference (RTD '16)*. http://www.drs2016.org/442

25. Phoebe Sengers, Kirsten Boehner, Shay David, and Joseph 'Jofish' Kaye. 2005. Reflective design. In *Proceedings of the 4th decennial conference on Critical computing: between sense and sensibility (CC '05)*. ACM, New York, NY, USA, 49–58. DOI: http://dx.doi.org/10.1145/1094562.1094569

26. Irina Shklovski, Scott D. Mainwaring, Halla Hrund Skúladóttir, and Höskuldur Borgthorsson. 2014. Leakiness and Creepiness in App Space: Perceptions of Privacy and Mobile App Use. In *Proceedings of the 32Nd Annual ACM Conference on Human Factors in Computing Systems (CHI '14)*. ACM, New York, NY, USA, 2347–2356. DOI: http://dx.doi.org/10.1145/2556288.2557421

27. Carolyn F. Strauss and Alastair Fuad-Luke. 2009. The Slow Design Principles. www.slowlab.net/CtC_SlowDesignPrinciples.pdf. (2009). Online, Last accessed: 19.01.2014.

28. Joshua Tan, Khanh Nguyen, Michael Theodorides, Heidi Negrón-Arroyo, Christopher Thompson, Serge Egelman, and David Wagner. 2014. The Effect of Developer-specified Explanations for Permission Requests on Smartphone User Behavior. In *Proceedings of the SIGCHI Conference on Human Factors in Computing Systems (CHI '14)*. ACM, New York, NY, USA, 91–100. DOI: http://dx.doi.org/10.1145/2556288.2557400

29. Yang Wang, Pedro Giovanni Leon, Alessandro Acquisti, Lorrie Faith Cranor, Alain Forget, and Norman Sadeh. 2014. A Field Trial of Privacy Nudges for Facebook. In *Proceedings of the SIGCHI Conference on Human Factors in Computing Systems (CHI '14)*. ACM, New York, NY, USA, 2367–2376. DOI: http://dx.doi.org/10.1145/2556288.2557413

30. Peter Worthy, Ben Matthews, and Stephen Viller. 2016. Trust Me: Doubts and Concerns Living with the Internet of Things. In *Proceedings of the 2016 ACM Conference on Designing Interactive Systems (DIS '16)*. ACM, New York, NY, USA, 427–434. DOI: http://dx.doi.org/10.1145/2901790.2901890

31. Bo Zhang, Mu Wu, Hyunjin Kang, Eun Go, and S. Shyam Sundar. 2014. Effects of Security Warnings and Instant Gratification Cues on Attitudes Toward Mobile Websites. In *Proceedings of the SIGCHI Conference on Human Factors in Computing Systems (CHI '14)*. ACM, New York, NY, USA, 111–114. DOI: http://dx.doi.org/10.1145/2556288.2557347

Centralized, Parallel, and Distributed Information Processing during Collective Sensemaking

Peter Krafft[*], **Kaitlyn Zhou**[†], **Isabelle Edwards**[†], **Kate Starbird**[†], **Emma S. Spiro**[†]
[*]Massachusettts Institute of Technology, [†]University of Washington
Cambridge, MA; Seattle, WA
pkrafft@mit.edu, [katezhou,iare,kstarbi,espiro]@uw.edu

ABSTRACT
Widespread rumoring can hinder attempts to make sense of what is going on during disaster scenarios. Understanding how and why rumors spread in these contexts could assist in the design of systems that facilitate timely and accurate sensemaking. We address a basic question in this line: To what extent does rumor evolution occur (1) through reliance on a centralized information source, (2) in parallel information silos, or (3) through a web of complex informational interactions? We develop a conceptual model and associated analysis algorithms that allow us to distinguish between these possibilities. We analyze a case of rumoring on Twitter during the Boston Marathon Bombing. We find that rumor spreading was predominantly a parallel process in this case, which is consistent with a hypothesis that information silos may underlie the persistence of false rumors. Special attention towards detecting and resolving parallel information threads during collective sensemaking may hence be warranted.

ACM Classification Keywords
H.5.3 Information Interfaces & Presentation: Groups & Organization Interfaces: Collaborative computing, Computer-supported cooperative work; K.4.2 Social Issues; J.4 Social and Behavioral Sciences: Sociology

Author Keywords
Collective sensemaking; rumoring; rumor spreading; rumor evolution; collective intelligence; computational social science; computational modeling; social media; sociotechnical systems; Twitter

INTRODUCTION
Collective sensemaking is a central component of response to disaster scenarios. In these situations, accurate and efficient collective sensemaking can lead to life-saving information revelation, impacting both decision making and actions of affected populations. Communicating and interacting with others are key elements in the sensemaking process, where individuals and groups must collectively come to understand what is going on around them [30]. Today, collective sensemaking increasingly occurs in online settings [15]; social media platforms help facilitate crisis communication, but are also rife with misinformation [25, 38]. Building tools to improve collective sensemaking, particularly on social media, could therefore have a meaningful impact on peoples' lives. To build functional tools, we must better understand how the complex process of collective sensemaking occurs in these settings.

Rumors can often align with attempts to understand unfolding events when information is scarce, and as such rumoring behavior is often considered a form of collective sensemaking [30]. Rumors—defined as unverified information—often arise in situations characterized by extreme uncertainty and a lack of official information sources, as is the case in crisis contexts. Rumors provide explanations arising from the "collective sensibilities of the ... public" [6], lessening anxiety and restoring a sense of control in ambiguous conditions. Rumors are emblematic of collective sensemaking because in situations in which this process occurs, people often cannot or do not distinguish facts from false rumors.

Studies of rumoring behavior have a long history in the social sciences; prior work has tended to focus on the process of rumor spreading and the subsequent changes in content that result from serial transmission [3]. Although scholars proposed specific mechanisms leading to this phenomena (e.g. the tendency for rumors to retain specific content *(sharpening)* and lose other details *(leveling)*), empirical analysis of the collective sensemaking processes is lacking. Mapping how variations and permutations of rumor stories unfold and change over time could improve our understanding of collective sensemaking and our ability to facilitate efficient and accurate information gathering and decision making.

In this study, we focus on rumoring behavior immediately following the 2013 Boston Marathon Bombing. We map the dynamics of collective sensemaking by exploring variations of a particular rumor story over time. Occurring simultaneously, as well as in sequence, distinct threads of communication composed into a complex and widespread false rumor about a young girl who died while running the marathon in support of the Sandy Hook school shooting victims.

Permission to make digital or hard copies of all or part of this work for personal or classroom use is granted without fee provided that copies are not made or distributed for profit or commercial advantage and that copies bear this notice and the full citation on the first page. Copyrights for components of this work owned by others than ACM must be honored. Abstracting with credit is permitted. To copy otherwise, or republish, to post on servers or to redistribute to lists, requires prior specific permission and/or a fee. Request permissions from permissions@acm.org.
CHI 2017, May 6-11, 2017, Denver, CO, USA.
Copyright is held by the owner/author(s). Publication rights licensed to ACM.
ACM ISBN 978-1-4503-4655-9/17/05 ...$15.00.
http://dx.doi.org/10.1145/3025453.3026012

Feature	Meaning	Example Tweet
boy	Child was a boy, not a girl	Everyone is posting the little girl running saying 8 year old killed in Boston marathon... It was an 8 year old boy that was killed guys..
charity	Child was running for charity	So sad, this precious 8 year old was running in the Boston Marathon for charity. #RIPBabyGirl http://t.co/yldeNmxKYA
father	Child was waiting for father at the finish line	I thought it was an eight year old boy that was waiting for his father to cross the line that died in Boston not a girl running herself
sandy	Child was running for Sandy Hook victims	R.I.P. to this 8yr old girl who died in Bostons explosions, while running for the Sandy Hook kids. RT for respect. http://t.co/ZBhI4on7tN
spectator	Child was a spectator, not running in the race	Im pretty sure this lil girl wasnt running the marathon & died. Her tag says 5k on it. Stop posting this picture. http://t.co/EoFmmnQHgG
young	Child died	One of the casualties was an 8 year old girl running the marathon. The theme was 26 miles for 26 victims. The things people do make me sick.

Table 1: Descriptions and examples of the features identified in our tagging procedure.

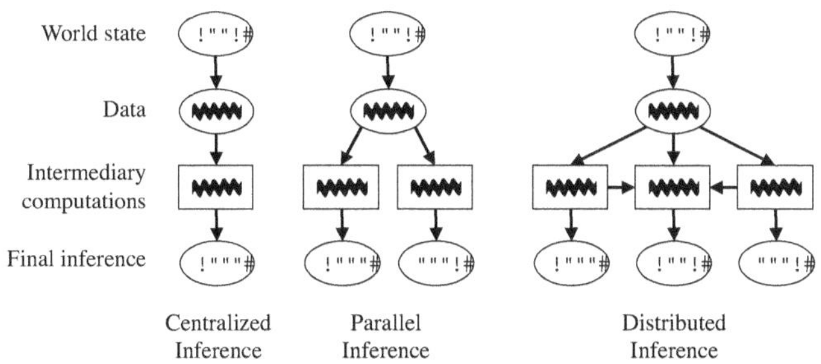

Figure 1: Inference algorithms take as input data that is assumed to be reflective of some underlying world state of interest. The algorithms then perform intermediary computations before arriving at final inferences.

Our approach is to map the information space of rumor-related discussion. From a computational point of view, it is natural to think of collective sensemaking as a form of inference from observations. Inference is the process of arriving at knowledge via the observation of data. For instance, one might wish to infer the parameters of a model, such as the value of the gravitational constant g in the Newtonian model of physics. In this illustrative hypothetical example we might attempt to find the gravitational constant that best explains trajectories of a set of falling objects we have observed. To find this best value of g, one common approach is to try a sequence of values and observe the explanatory power of each element in this sequence. However, such processes are often sensitive to the initial element of the sequence, or the sequence itself might involve random choices. Therefore running multiple sequences in parallel can improve the speed or accuracy of inference. In a more complex scenario, data may be distributed across different locations, and servers at each location must periodically communicate intermediate inferences with each other in a carefully designed distributed algorithm to ensure that final inferences are accurate. Figure 1 illustrates schematic diagrams of centralized, parallel, and distributed architectures for inference algorithms.

In the case of collective sensemaking, individuals are observing and participating in discussion about a rumor on social media; they are forming beliefs or opinions based on their observations and interactions. Given that this process frequently occurs across geographically distributed participants, it is natural to ask whether the collective sensemaking we observe in these situations is consistent with processes of parallel or distributed inference. Abstracting this process may then allow us to draw on a variety of inference procedures that have been studied in the vast literature on optimization and machine learning to develop more precise mathematical models of collective sensemaking (e.g., [5, 16, 21, 29]).

BACKGROUND

Rumoring Behavior on Social Media

Early work on rumors studied the motivation for rumors, when and how they propagate, and how representations of information mutate as a rumor evolves through a population [2, 7, 27]. Recent work extends theories of rumoring to online environments, categorizing prominent attributes of rumors in social media platforms [6, 22, 38]. The relationship between attributes of this sort and the propensity for a rumor to spread has also been studied [20, 33]. Other works have looked at how information propagates through social networks without attending to how the representations of information change [4, 8, 10, 12, 37].

In closely related recent work, researchers examined how memes evolved through news articles [31] and how rumors evolved through the network of Facebook posts [1, 11]. This prior work focused on understanding the details of how rumors mutate individually, as well as how those mutations and the attributes of the resulting rumors were related to their propagation rates, but this prior work also identified points when distinct rumors or rumor variants merged together. Ultimately our results are largely consistent with the related results of this prior research, but our focus is on the information processing implications rather than the implications for genetic models of memetics.

To the best of our knowledge, none of this prior empirical work has attempted to infer the dependencies between rumor or conversation threads in order to measure the extent of parallel and distributed information processing occurring during collective sensemaking. Our work also contrasts with the closely related prior work on rumor evolution on Facebook in the richness of the rumor we study. Prior work has focused on studying quoted text and edits between quotes. This choice allowed for large-scale data analysis but limited the types of rumors that could be studied and the contextual detail that could be brought to bear in understanding this phenomenon. Here we use a semi-automated coding system using regular expressions to tag conceptual content of tweets associated with the rumor we study, and hence we can study the process of collective sensemaking at a different level of analysis. Compared to using quotes, we are able to observe conceptual changes rather than just textual changes, and our methods are applicable to any social media rumor rather than just copy-and-paste reposts.

Social Computation

Our work also connects to a growing literature that attempts to conceptualize human groups and social systems as information processing systems [9, 13, 17, 18, 19]. While rumoring behavior and collective sensemaking have been discussed informally in computational terms previously (e.g., [37]), to the best of our knowledge, ours is the first work that leverages an explicit information processing model in order to better understand observed rumoring behavior, and among the first to do so for collective sensemaking behavior (cf. [32]). Of course, many formal models of rumor behavior exist, including large bodies of literature on cultural diffusion [14] and on gossip algorithms [28], but the formal models in this area that are connected with data tend to lack coherent interpretations as systems that actually perform information processing, and the models that do have interpretations as information processing systems tend to be divorced from empirical data. The present work marries a formal information processing view of social systems with the empirical study of rumoring behavior and collective sensemaking.

ARCHITECTURES OF SOCIAL COMPUTATION

In designing software systems, one of the basic architectural decisions to be made first is whether the system will be implemented in a centralized, parallel, or distributed manner. This choice involves deciding not only whether to use multiple processing units but also how and when multiple processing units would communicate with each other during computation (typically either not at all or through shared memory in the parallel case, or through message passing in a prespecified network structure in the distributed case).

When viewing social phenomena through the lens of computation, it is also natural to ask in which of these capacities a phenomenon is operating. In the social context, the question is fundamentally about the complexity of the patterns of information flow between people. However, it is difficult to disassociate the terms parallel and distributed information processing from the algorithmic techniques typically associated with those areas in computer science. Our first step is therefore to achieve a level of conceptual clarity around what it means for an arbitrary information processing system to be operating in a centralized, parallel, or distributed capacity. This characterization obviously must be general enough so that it can apply to systems of people, who are clearly not arranged according to the typical architectures of centralized, parallel, or distributed software.

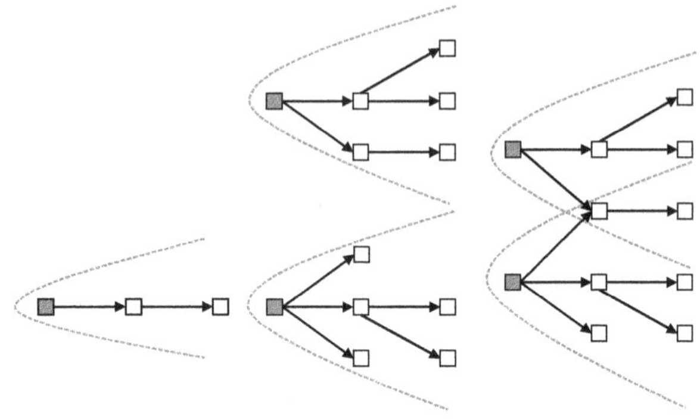

(a) Centralized (b) Parallel (c) Distributed

Figure 2: Informational dependency graphs associated with centralized, parallel, and distributed computation. The nodes represent computation blocks and the edges informational dependencies. The dotted lines show the downstream "influence cones" of the highlighted blue nodes—the set of nodes that their computation affects. Centralized computation is associated with sharp cones in an information pipeline. Parallel computation is associated with non-intersecting information silos. Distributed computation displays intersecting cones that form an information web.

Basic Framework

We first suppose that information processing, whether in software or in society, consists of compositions of "computation blocks". In the case of social computation, a block might be a single person thinking about a single fact. In the context of our work, each computation block will be associated with a new inference event. These computation blocks are composed via informational dependencies, in which the output of one computation block is communicated as input into another block. In the social case, an informational dependency could arise from one person communicating an inference to another person. An informational dependency could also occur between one person thinking about a fact at one point in time and the same person rethinking that fact at a later point in time with the benefit of the inferences gleaned on the first occasion. The distinction between centralized, parallel, and distributed processing can then be understood in terms of the structure of the network of informational dependencies between computation blocks. These graph structures are illustrated in Figure 2.

Before describing each of these structures in turn, it is worth noting that unlike in software systems, where all engaged processing units play a functional role in the computation, social systems may also have people that perform actions that are not functionally relevant to the computation effectively embodied by the system. For example, a person may participate in a system by passively consuming the news. These tangential actors are informationally passive, and while they enrich the system, they will not affect its computational architecture.

Centralized Processing

Centralized processing is characterized by chain-structured informational dependency graphs. Centralized algorithms for inference typically involve a single processor taking data observations and gradually updating inferences based on that data (in a series of computation blocks). In the social context, one example of a centralized collective sensemaking phenomenon would be a crowd of people passively consuming news from a single source, perhaps one that updates its stories over time. The computation blocks in this case are found within the news source, and the passive observers are excluded from the information architecture.

Parallel Processing

Parallel processing is characterized by tree-structured informational dependency graphs. Parallel algorithms for inference typically involve multiple processors running isolated instances of an identical algorithm. While atypical for parallel inference algorithms, we also treat spawning child processes, e.g. that run replicated computation starting at the last observed parent state, as included within the scope of parallel architectures. In the social context, parallel processing could occur through multiple people actively engaging with news from a single source by modifying that news according to their own experiences. Parallel processing could also occur through distinct groups of people passively consuming news from single distinct sources. Or parallel processing could occur through people interpreting a situation using their own experiences without reference to information from others.

As is evident in these examples, parallel processing can be associated with rigid "information silos". From a technical point of view, in a parallel process, the descendants of two computation blocks with no path between them form distinct information silos. No two downstream computation blocks from each of those parent blocks will share new information between them.

Distributed Processing

Distributed processing is characterized by trellis-structured informational dependency graphs, i.e., directed acyclic graphs. Distributed algorithms for inference mainly involve periodically reciprocally sharing intermediary processed data or inferences between processors. In the social context, distributed processing could occur if people integrate information from multiple news sources or synthesize ideas heard from multiple people.

MODELING COLLECTIVE SENSEMAKING

The goal of our work is to understand the extent to which observed processes of collective sensemaking on social media are centralized versus parallel or distributed. If people mainly draw upon a single global source for their information about a particular scenario, and only copy, embellish, or refine that information privately, collective sensemaking would appear essentially like a centralized process. If individuals or small groups mostly replicate or refine distinct non-interacting threads, the process would appear essentially parallel. If multiple threads exist and continuously interact with each other, the process would be truly distributed. Each of these potential conclusions suggests different classes of algorithms to look towards in further work developing models of collective sensemaking as inference.

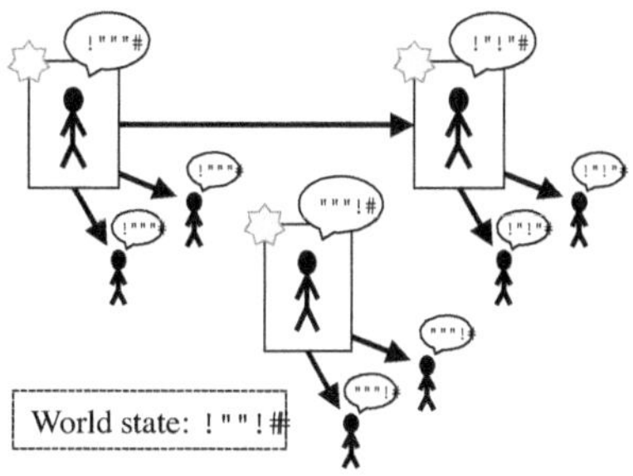

Figure 3: An illustration of our conceptual model of collective sensemaking/rumor spreading. Computation occurs at the boxed individuals who create new hypotheses. Each utterance shown in the figure would be an observation in our dataset.

To grapple with these questions, we suppose that the problem of collective sensemaking can be viewed as one of inferring an unknown present state of the world. We suppose that the state of the world can be represented by a binary vector of features. For example, in a disaster context, some features might be "there was a tornado", "there is a fire", "someone has died", et cetera. We also suppose that people communicate hypotheses about the world, again represented as binary vectors consisting of the features of the world state (e.g., using the features above, (1,1,0) indicates a hypothesis that there was a tornado and there is a fire, but nobody has died). Collective sensemaking involves the process of propagating, augmenting, refining, merging, supporting, and extinguishing these candidate hypotheses. We will define one thread in a process of collective sensemaking as the collected expressions of one candidate hypothesis (a particular combination of nonzero features).

To simplify the analysis, we assume that individual features or combinations of features are only discovered once, and all other occurrences of those features or combinations are copies or modifications of those first occurrences. While this simplifying assumption likely misses the complexity of real-world collective sensemaking, where truly independent sources could post essentially identical observations for example, the assumption allows us to begin to map a very complicated phenomena. Our conceptual model is illustrated in Figure 3.

DATA

The dataset we analyze consists of observations of collective sensemaking unfolding during the 2013 Boston Marathon Bombing. On April 15, 2013 two bombs were detonated near the finish line of the Boston Marathon. Hundreds of spectators and runners were injured by the blasts, and three individuals were killed. In the week that followed, police launched a significant manhunt for two suspects, during which time social media users collectively attempted to help apprehend the suspects. Several rumors propagated during this time, including the case study in this paper.

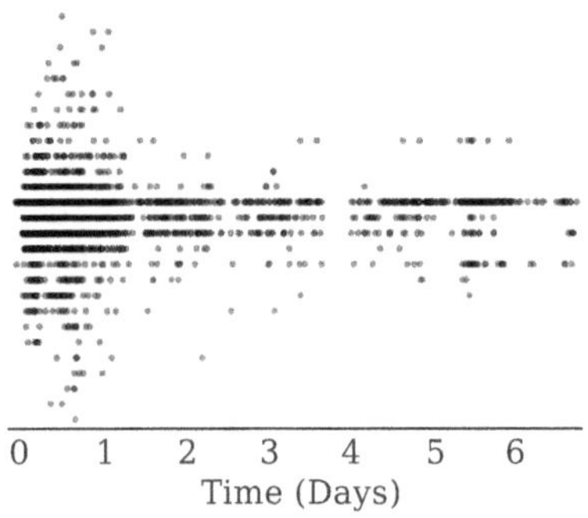

Figure 4: A plot of the temporal dynamics and frequency of the observed instances of each rumor thread. There is one row for each rumor thread, and one point for each tweet.

Collection

The data we analyze was collected in a prior study by using the Twitter Streaming API with the search terms "blast", "boston", "bomb", "explosion", and "marathon" [22]. Data collection began a few hours after the explosion of the first bomb and continued for seven days; some periods of observation have missing data due to rate limits of the Twitter API. Prior work has examined this data, identifying multiple rumor stories and qualitatively coding individual tweets based on their relevance to each rumor [22, 35, 38].

Tagging

Although the dataset we use was studied in prior work, we enrich the data by adding feature tags to 4,826 tweets associated with one larger rumor story. These tags correspond to "features" in our conceptual model. We focus on the "Girl Running" rumor, which contained claims and references to a young girl who was killed while running the marathon in honor of the victims of the 2012 shooting at the Sandy Hook elementary school in Newtown, CT. We focus on this rumor because it is well-defined while still containing interesting complexity in the number of distinct ideas present in the conversation. We use 4,826 distinct tweets identified as related to this rumor (via manual coding in prior work).

In an iterative and collaborative process, we compiled a list of distinct information features within the larger rumor story. Two authors of the present work took a random sample of 100 of these tweets, examining each tweet individually to identify and note new information that was being introduced into the rumor landscape. Using a list of keywords and phrases to identify each of these features, and after discussion among the research team, a consensus was reached about the set of appropriate features. Throughout this process, the level of detail of the features was refined. For example, two features that overlapped conceptually and empirically would likely be merged into a single feature; other cases were separated into multiple more specific features. For each feature, a regular expression-based query was developed to automatically retrieve and identify tweets from the dataset related to that particular rumor feature. Finally, some irrelevant and unreliable features were removed prior to analysis. The resulting set of

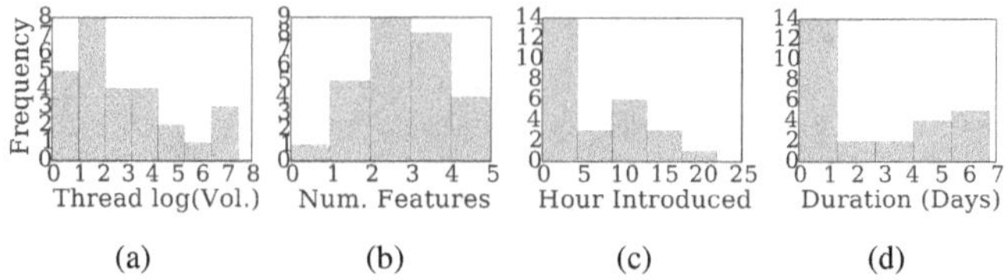

Figure 5: (a) Distribution of the logarithm of the volume (number of tweets) of each thread. (b) Distribution of the number of features associated with each thread. (c) Histogram of the times at which we first observe an instance of each thread. (d) Histogram of the duration of each thread.

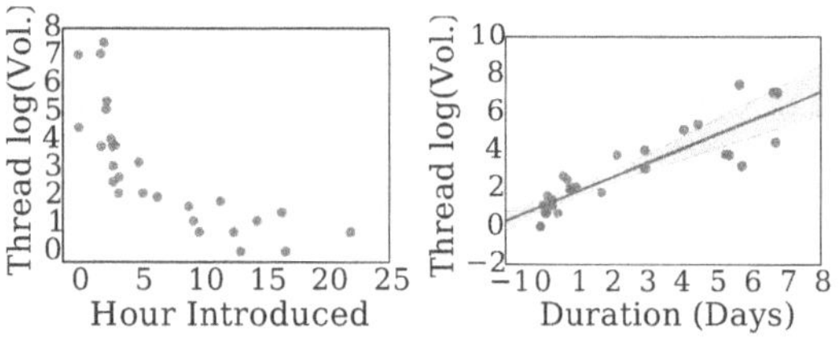

Figure 6: (Left) The time a thread first appeared versus its ultimate total tweet volume. (Right) The duration of time over which we observe a thread versus its total volume.

features identified in this process, along with basic descriptions and example tweets, is shown in Table 1. We consider a single thread of discussion to be the set of tweets associated with a particular combination of these features.

Descriptive Statistics

This dataset consists of 27 distinct rumor threads. In this section we present visualizations of basic descriptive statistics of these threads to provide context for our analysis. The time stamps of all tweets associated with the 27 threads are shown in Figure 4. Immediately this plot begins to hint at the structure of collective sensemaking in this case. We see that there are three threads that dominate in terms of the volume of tweets, and tweets associated with each of these three threads occur throughout our observation window. Figure 5 displays the distribution of tweet volume by thread as a histogram, again showing that most threads have low volume. We also observe that most threads have an intermediate number of features associated with them. Figure 5 also shows that most observed threads are created early, and last only a short time. Figure 6 shows that the most popular threads tend to be introduced earlier, and the length of time a thread exists appears to have an exponential relationship with the total volume of tweets associated with it. These results indicate the early-comers are likely to persist and enjoy widespread attention.

METHODS

Our main goal is to evaluate the degree to which rumoring behavior and by extension the collective sensemaking process observed in this case displays signatures consistent with centralized, parallel, or distributed information processing. We combine quantitative and qualitative assessment of the rumor threads in this analysis to give insight into how communication was unfolding over time. For the quantitative component of our analysis, we develop an automated method for classifying threads into different types of dependencies, associated with either centralized, parallel, or distributed computation.[1] For the qualitative component of our analysis, we look at example tweets from threads associated with different types of dependencies, drawing on expert knowledge of this particular case study. Our qualitative component adds richness and context for our observed results, increasing understanding as well as lending face validity to quantitative results.

Analysis Approach

To understand whether threads are formed in a centralized, parallel, or distributed manner we attempt to reconstruct the dependency structure between threads. Given our conceptual model we firstly suppose that any tweet that consists entirely of a previously observed combination of features belongs to the thread associated with that combination. When we see a tweet with a new combination of features, all of which are features that have been observed previously, we can deduce that this tweet must have been derived from some prior thread or threads. There are two possibilities in this case. If that specific combination of features has appeared as a subset of a combination of features that appeared in a single previous tweet, then the new thread could have been formed by a deletion event. If that specific combination of features has never appeared at all in any previous tweet, then the new thread must be from a merge of two prior threads. For example, if we observe the threads (1,1,0) and (1,0,1), and then later observe (1,1,1), this latter thread could have been due to a merge of these two earlier threads. Finally, when we find a new feature together with an otherwise old combination of features, we can think about this tweet as forming from a mutation event. Since all tweets we analyze were detected as associated with the Girl Running rumor, we treat threads that consist of completely novel features as mutations on the base thread $(0,0,\ldots,0)$.

Each of these types of dependencies are associated with centralized, parallel, or distributed processing. Centralized and parallel processing would consist only of mutations and deletions events since in these forms of computation there is either only a single thread or multiple non-interacting threads. Distributed processing would also include merge events between threads since it consists of multiple interacting threads of computation.

Even with the deductions just described, there is still ambiguity in the dependency structure between threads. This ambiguity arises from cases where a thread could have been formed either by a deletion event or a merge event. For example, if a tweet with features $(1,1,1,1)$ exists already, as well as tweets with features $(1,0,0,0)$ and $(0,1,0,0)$, then a new tweet with features $(1,1,0,0)$ could have been a refinement of the first thread, or a merge of the second and third threads. We resolve these ambiguities in three different ways, detailed below. We use three different methods in order to provide a more robust analysis.

[1]The code for our quantitative analysis is online at https://github.com/pkrafft/Centralized-Parallel-and-Distributed-Information-Processing-during-Collective-Sensemaking.

Algorithm 1 Merge Event Lower Bound (MELB)

```
for rumor thread r, sorted by first appearance time do
    s := r with newly observed features stripped
    if s has been observed previously then
        count r as a mutation
    else
        if the features in s are a subset of a prior thread's then
            count r as a deletion
        else
            count r as a merge
```

Algorithm 2 Merge Event Upper Bound (MEUB)

```
for rumor thread r, sorted by first appearance time do
    s := r with newly observed features stripped
    if prior threads not strict supersets of s could merge to s then
        count r as a merge
    else
        if s has been observed previously then
            count r as a mutation
        else
            count r as a deletion
```

Counting Thread Types

Our first two methods of resolving ambiguous dependencies establish lower and upper bounds on the number of merge events that could have occurred between threads. Establishing a merge event lower bound (MELB) provides the most severe test within the confines of our conceptual model of whether distributed processing is occurring at all in the collective sensemaking event we study. The purpose of the lower bound is to avoid overestimation and a false positive declaration of distributed information processing. To establish a lower bound on the number of merge events, we simply attribute thread creation to deletion events whenever there is a case where a thread could have formed from either a deletion or a merge event. Therefore, with this method, merge events are likely undercounted. Obtaining a merge event upper bound (MEUB) allows us to avoid a false negative declaration of distributed information processing. To establish an upper bound, we attribute any thread creation to merge events whenever there is a case where a thread could have formed either from a deletion or a merge event. Pseudocode for these two methods is shown in Algorithms 1 and 2.

Inferring Dependencies

Our third method resolves the same ambiguity in a different way. This method first defines a set of three atomic actions that can be composed to lead to new threads. The first action consists of merging all of the features of two threads, the second action consists of deleting one feature from one thread, and the third action consists of creating a new feature on one thread. These actions can be composed any number of times in the creation of a new thread, but this method assumes that newly observed threads were formed by the minimal number of actions upon previously existing threads. When this heuristic does not completely determine a single set of potential dependencies (for example, if a new thread could have been formed by a single deletion from an old thread, or a single merge of two old threads), then the dependency set with the highest mean tweet volume among the potential dependencies

Type	Dependencies	MELB Method	MEUB Method
None	Single	1	1
Mutation	Single	6	6
Deletion	Single	10	3
Merge	Multiple	10	17

Table 2: Counts of the different thread dependency types. One thread (with zero features) represents discussion detected as relating to the rumor not displaying distinctive features.

with minimal edit distance is chosen. The algorithm we wrote for identifying the set of simplest dependencies for each new thread is a complex recursive algorithm, and hence we omit a description of its details due to space limitations. This method not only allows us to count the number of times each type of dependency occurred, it also allows us to identify which specific prior threads likely contributed to a new thread. Thus we can directly reconstruct and examine a specific plausible dependency structure of threads using this method.

RESULTS

The descriptive statistics we examined of our dataset already indicated that multiple prominent threads of discussion were occurring simultaneously during the propagation of the Girl Running rumor. This finding suggests that collective sensemaking in this case was either primarily parallel or primarily distributed. Distinguishing between these two possibilities requires examining how the main threads of discussion might have arisen. Beyond the major two or three threads of discussion, there were also a substantial number of threads with a lower volume of tweets associated with them. We are also interested in examining the common dependency patterns among these lower volume threads. The results from counting the number of instances of each possible type of dependency are shown in Table 2. A visualization of specific inferred dependencies between threads is shown in Figure 8.

Parallel Information Processing

The results of the MELB method, shown in Table 2, indicate that most threads we observe could have been formed either by mutations or deletions from old threads. Both the mutation and deletion actions only operate on a single existing thread, and hence are associated with centralized or parallel processing. Furthermore, as shown in Figure 7, threads with single dependencies tend to have higher total volume than threads with multiple dependencies (a difference that is statistically significant $p = 0.0437$ under a two-sided t-test with the MELB method and at $p < 0.001$ with the MEUB method). In fact, threads with either no dependencies or only a single dependency account for about 97% of the tweets we observe (including retweets) under the MELB method and still about 96% under the MEUB method. We further observe that a large portion of this percentage is attributable just to three threads, all of which have either zero or one possible dependency. Hence from our quantitative analysis, the process of collective sensemaking in this case appears to be predominantly parallel as opposed to distributed. Figure 8 indicates

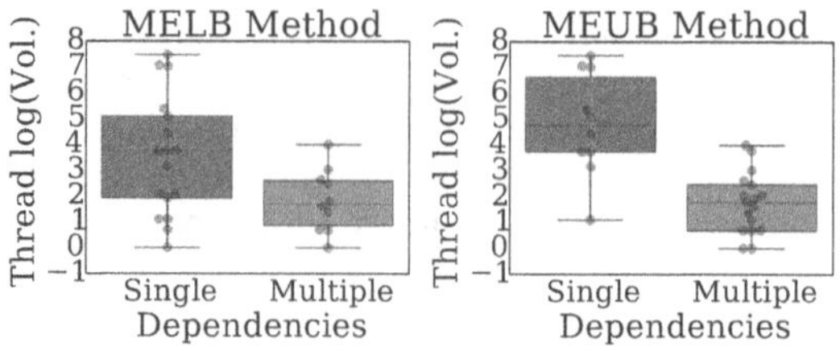

Figure 7: Threads with single dependencies tend to have higher log volume than threads with multiple dependencies. Each point in each plot is a single thread.

that our third method for inferring dependencies also supports this interpretation.

Examples

We look at three examples of threads with dependencies and dynamics that indicate parallel processing. As has been previously noted in investigations of the rumor studied here [22], and as confirmed by our quantitative analysis, this rumor consisted mainly of two threads. One thread involved reports that a young girl had died in the 2013 Boston Marathon Bombing, possibly while running in the marathon. In our data, this thread is associated with the "young" feature. Since this thread consists only of a single feature, the only possible ways in which it could have been created are through a deletion event of a more complicated thread, or through an innovation on top of the general discussion thread (that has no features). Our quantitative analysis reveals that "young" was indeed an innovation without prior dependencies beyond the general discussion around the event. Looking at the actual text of the tweets in our dataset, the first tweet we observe referencing this thread is the following: "RT @XXX: An eight year old girl who was doing an amazing thing running a marathon, was killed. I cant stand our world anymore".[2]

The main variant of this thread, which has been recognized in prior work [22], involved reports that the young girl who had died was running in memory of the victims of the Sandy Hook school shooting. In our data, this thread is associated with the "young,sandy" combination of features. Since this thread has two features, and since we can confirm that the "young" thread existed first within our tweets, the "young,sandy" thread could have been formed either by a merge of the "young" thread and a separate "sandy" thread, or it could have formed from a simplification of a more complex thread, or from a mutation of the "young" thread.

Our dependency inference method indicates that the "young,sandy" thread was in fact formed by a mutation of the "young" thread. That is, the first appearance of the "sandy" feature co-appeared with the "young" feature. The first tweet we observe with this combination was "RT @XXX: + Boston Marathon Bombing has me sobbing a fucking river. An 8 year old, a little girl who was running for Sandy Hooks,

[2]The first such tweet we observed was a retweet. This is either because the rumor was propagating earlier than the beginning of the data collection or because Twitter API rate limits led the data collection to miss the earliest tweet.

..." and we have no clear references to Sandy Hook before this tweet. However, we do observe earlier references to the little girl who died having been running for charity. The first such tweet we observe (classified as in the "young,charity" thread) was "So sad, this precious 8 year old was running in the Boston Marathon for charity. #RIPBabyGirl http://t.co/yldeNmxKYA". It could therefore be that "young,sandy" mutated from this thread rather than the "young" thread alone.

In either case, all of these threads have single dependencies among the existing threads of discussion, and hence are characteristic of parallel information processing. Participants in the online discussion appear to have seen prior reports in a single thread and introduced variants of the rumors that then propagated in parallel.

One final piece of evidence that supports the fact that these threads were indeed propagating in parallel highly isolated threads of discussion is that eventually (indeed actually rather early on) threads appeared that identified the rumor about the young girl as being false. For instance, this tweet appeared almost immediately after the first instance of the "young" thread that we observed, "Just wanna tell you that you have to qualify for the Boston Marathon so a 8 year old wouldnt be running!!!! that picture isnt of the girl!!!", and a number of similar subsequent tweets also appeared. Yet the main rumor threads persisted despite these denials.

Distributed Information Processing

While the few threads that include the vast majority of tweets we observe appear to be associated with parallel information processing, we also find signatures of distributed information processing in the tail of the discussion activity. As shown in Table 2 we identify at least ten threads, a substantial proportion of the total number of threads we observe, that cannot have been formed by deletions from or mutations of prior threads. This 40% or so of threads do not constitute a large volume of tweets, but they may shed light on how some people access the information available during collective sensemaking, and they highlight the complexity in the details of the collective sensemaking process.

Examples

We examine two examples of inferred merge events to check whether these cases appear to be legitimate rather than artifacts of the tagging procedure or of our inference procedure. The first example occurs between the threads "young,boy" and "young,sandy", which appear to merge into "young,sandy,boy". Here are the tweets associated with "boy" that appear before the first appearance of "young,sandy,boy":

- "Everyone is posting the little girl running saying 8 year old killed in Boston marathon... It was an 8 year old boy that was killed guys.."
- "RT @XXX: For those seeing photo of 8 yr old girl running with claims that she died: CNN has reported it was an 8 yr old BOY wh ..."

The next tweet with a "boy" feature is then in the "young,sandy,boy" thread: "HES A BOY @XXX: R.I.P. to the 8 year-old girl who died in Bostons explosions, while running for the Sandy Hook kids. #prayforb..."

Clearly this tweet has integrated information about the boy who died while spectating with an observation of the Sandy Hook thread. The "young,boy" thread also continues in parallel with tweets such as the following:

- "Just sayin it was an 8 year old boy that died, not a girl, for all those who posted a picture of a little girl running #GodBless #Boston"
- "RT @XXX: Is this true? CNN says it was a boy RT @XXX: Girl, 8, died in #Boston while running ..."

And eventually we see another "young,sandy,boy" instance: "An 8 year old girl died, and an 8 year old boy in Boston today. And they both were running in honor of sandy hook. Like really?"

Another merge event we observe occurs between the "young,boy" and "spectator" threads. Here we find a reference to the fact that the girl people had been talking about could not have been running in the marathon because of her age, as well as a reference to the report that a young boy had died, not a girl: "It was a boy that died not the 8 year old girl.. plus she wasnt running you need to be 18 to run the marathon. #prayforboston"

These threads, though comparatively low in volume, indicate that some people are paying attention to multiple parallel threads that are occurring, and integrating information from across them into new threads. Again, however, these merge events appear primarily to create new parallel threads rather than extinguishing old threads.

DISCUSSION

The results presented above explore collective sensemaking during the 2013 Boston Marathon Bombing. The evidence we examined suggested that collective sensemaking in this case contained both parallel and distributed information processing. These results have implications for understanding collective sensemaking in the context of crisis events.

Sources of Parallel and Distributed Processing

Given the observed high degree of parallelism in this case study of collective sensemaking, as well as some degree of distributed information processing, it is important to consider how these components (and their combination) may arise in social media systems; collective sensemaking in online environments may well be constrained by the features of the platforms used. In this case, the structure of collective sensemaking during extreme events is driven primarily by the affordances and limitations of the platform interface itself. Twitter, for example, allows users to search for distinct content of interest using keywords or hashtags. Search results then display tweets associated with distinct subsets of the larger discussion surrounding this rumor, and the event itself. Users can also receive content through pre-existing or newly formed social relationships (i.e. follower ties). Alternate mechanisms of exposure might be third-party platforms, or even word-of-mouth.

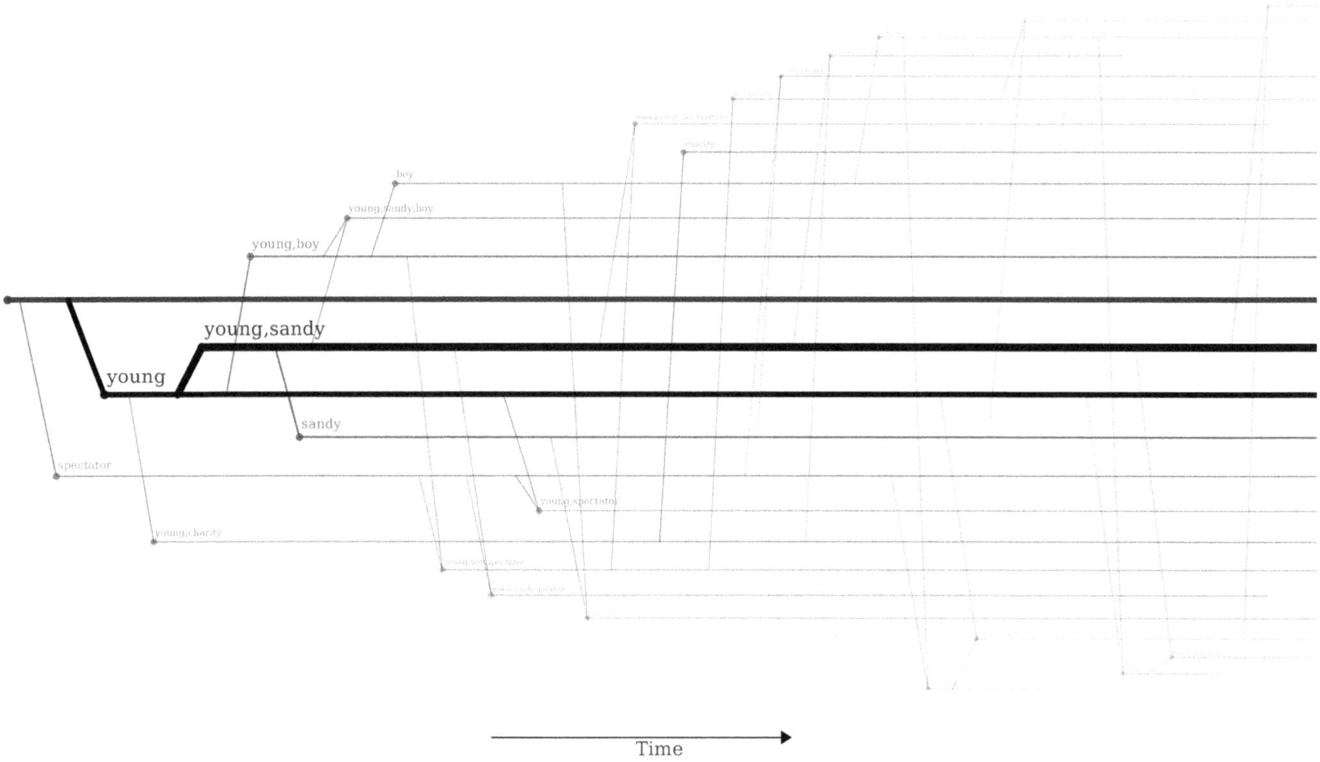

Figure 8: A reconstruction of the dependencies between threads of the rumor we study. Each horizontal line is a thread, with the thickness of the line being monotonically related to the volume of tweets associated with the thread.

Given the similarity between the language used in affirming and denying tweets (e.g. copy and pasting an affirming tweet and adding a denial of the content at the beginning or end), and given how persistent the dominant threads were even in the face of conflicting information, the limited display of information in the interface seems unlikely to represent the whole story. It is likely extremely difficult for users to have a complete and accurate picture of all rumor-related conversation in the total information space; users instead see a very specific, potentially biased, subset of crisis communication. It is unsurprising then, given these features of the communication channel, that multiple parallel discussions may exist.

Another source of parallelism is suggested when examining the text of the example tweets, as well as referencing prior work about rumoring during crisis events, specifically on social media platforms. Social media posts persist, though perhaps not visibly, and can be "re-discovered" at much later time points. Users who may have missed detailed rumor discussion, and even resolution of uncertainty within the rumor, can re-introduce rumors by re-posting outdated content. Indeed, prior work has observed cases of rumor resurgence [4, 22].

Moreover, rumor-related messages often contain references to external sources, such as mass media outlets. In the case reviewed here, for example, a large portion of the conversation surrounding denials of the Girl Running rumor explicitly referenced content from CNN which noted it was actually a young boy who was killed while spectating. Each individual thread of discussion we examined was centralized by definition since they consisted of the same information content. It is possible that distinct threads obtain their coherency from some centralized, external information source such as CNN. Some amount of parallelism could therefore be due to different people attending to difference news outlets.

Finally, there has been continued interest in the ability of the distributed crowd on social media platforms to engage in crisis response and recovery activities, coordinating aid activities, situational awareness, crisis mapping, donations, etc. [23, 24, 36, 34]. Distributed information processing could arise from the coordinated actions of populations that have prior experience with crowdwork and crisis participation, and who are tweeting about various different discussion threads.

Relation to Theories of Rumoring

It is also interesting to consider how our information processing perspective relates to traditional characterizations of rumoring processes such sharpening and leveling, as well as other social phenomena such as information silos and echo chambers. Deletion events can likely be viewed as sharpening or leveling. Merge events, mutations, and innovations are probably related to "assimilation". Echo chambers and the spread of false news could potentially be exacerbated by parallel rumoring while potentially being mitigated by centralized or distributed rumoring. Future work could study these connections in more depth.

Implications for Design

Research that improves our understanding of collective sensemaking, and the types of information processing that accompany it, has many implications for the design of systems to help facilitate these processes. For example, making observed parallel processing visible to users could help online crowds transition from parallel to centralized or distributed systems for collective sensmaking, perhaps increasing efficiency and allowing human resources to be directed at multiple tasks rather than multiple versions of the same task.

Prior work has often focused on building systems to detect rumors (e.g. [26]). Less attention has been paid to building systems that help facilitate collective sensemaking and rumoring behavior itself. Such work could aid in crisis response, allowing online crowds to reach consensus or at least collective understanding of appropriate response actions. These systems could also assist in decision making by directly facilitating communication and interaction that builds understanding and awareness of crisis situations and how events unfold. Our study represents just one step in this direction.

Methodological Limitations

One limitation of our study is in the raw data itself. The dataset was collected using Twitter's Streaming API, and using particular keyword searches. Hence, it is likely the case we only have a sample (albeit a large sample) of the full set of tweets discussing this rumor. If multiple threads were introduced close together in time, lacking comprehensive coverage of all tweets could disrupt the dependencies we infer.

Our tagging procedure also introduces a potential source of error. Features were manually curated through an extensive and resource intensive procedure, but ultimately the features associated with specific tweets were determined automatically via regular expressions and are therefore noisy. Tagging is susceptible to both false positives and false negatives; errors could disrupt our inferred dependencies for the same reason that missing tweets do.

We also need to consider possible error due to our modeling assumptions. The main modeling assumption we leverage is that features are only innovated once. This assumption is almost certainly not met, but it may be approximately satisfied if most people get their information from looking at what others say rather than investigating the event independently, or if each feature is innovated by a single source external to the platform (such as a news source). If this assumption is not satisfied, then we may inappropriately infer merge events when none have actually occurred. Without this assumption, then, apparent merge events between threads could also be attributable to a thread rediscovering a feature contained in a separate thread, rather than having an actual interaction with that thread.

While strong assumptions simplify models and limit their immediate application in real-world settings, they also provide necessary parsimony when exploring complex phenomena. Moreover, the qualitative analysis used to augment our quantitative findings helps to evaluate the impact of all of these limitations. By carefully checking the inferences from our quantitative analysis against prior work and against the text of the tweets in the raw data, we can gain confidence in our conclusions. Future work could examine probabilistic models that account for gaps in our data, for unreliable features, and for varying probabilities of different features being discovered independently in order to relax our modeling assumptions and assign probabilities to merge events.

Finally, we must be careful not to generalize too readily from the single Girl Running rumor that we study. The amount of parallel and distributed information processing that we observe could be tied to the type of rumor we chose to study (a clearly false rumor that was likely intentionally started by a person who knew it to be untrue). Further, many of the affirming permutations around this rumor were likely purposeful misinformation, so the sensemaking process was mostly around questioning/correcting the rumor. Future work could conduct the type of analysis we have performed here with a broader set of rumors.

CONCLUSIONS

In this work we present a new way to analyze and characterize individual rumoring scenarios. Our conceptual model opens the door to richer mathematical models of rumor spreading than currently exist. Our analysis methods and conceptual model also lead to inferential capabilities and attendant visualizations that could be leveraged immediately in a system for collective sensemaking.

We illustrate these techniques using data from a rumor that has been extensively analyzed previously using mixed-method, interpretivist research methods, including detailed qualitative analysis in conjunction with temporal signatures [22, 35, 38]. This prior work serves as a comparison for the current work, allowing us to demonstrate how our new methodological approach leads to additional insights about how the rumor changed over time, and providing insight into why it kept propagating (widely) after it had been corrected. This prior work also demonstrates that this rumor is similar in temporal signature shape to the majority of Twitter rumors, and highly representative of one of three Twitter rumor types.

Our substantive finding that rumoring in the case we studied was largely centralized and parallel may be central to explaining why rumors resurface even after they have been corrected, but is also interesting in its own right. Given that the rumoring process could easily have been highly distributed, some underlying forces must be favoring centralized and parallel rumor evolution. Future work could identify these underlying forces. Finally, future work could compare how the prominence of different dependency types and the underlying forces leading to them vary across different types of rumors or different social media and interaction contexts.

ACKNOWLEDGEMENTS

This work was supported in part by the NSF GRFP under grant #1122374, by NSF grants 1420255, 1541688, and 1640940 and by ARO W911NF-15-1-0270. Any opinions, findings, and conclusions or recommendations expressed in this material are those of the authors and do not necessarily reflect those of the sponsors.

REFERENCES

1. Lada A Adamic, Thomas M Lento, Eytan Adar, and Pauline C Ng. 2016. Information evolution in social networks. In *Proceedings of the Ninth ACM International Conference on Web Search and Data Mining*. ACM, 473–482.
2. Gordon W Allport and Leo Postman. 1946. An analysis of rumor. *Public Opinion Quarterly* 10, 4 (1946), 501–517.
3. Gordon W Allport and Leo Postman. 1947. *The Psychology of Rumor*. Henry Holt.
4. Ahmer Arif, Kelley Shanahan, Fang-Ju Chou, Yoanna Dosouto, Kate Starbird, and Emma S Spiro. 2016. How Information Snowballs: Exploring the Role of Exposure in Online Rumor Propagation. In *Proceedings of the 19th ACM Conference on Computer-Supported Cooperative Work & Social Computing*. ACM, 466–477.
5. Dimitri P Bertsekas and John N Tsitsiklis. 1989. *Parallel and Distributed Computation: Numerical Methods*. Prentice Hall.
6. Prashant Bordia and Nicholas DiFonzo. 2004. Problem solving in social interactions on the Internet: Rumor as social cognition. *Social Psychology Quarterly* 67, 1 (2004), 33–49.
7. Theodore Caplow. 1947. Rumors in war. *Social Forces* (1947), 298–302.
8. Justin Cheng, Lada A Adamic, Jon M Kleinberg, and Jure Leskovec. 2016. Do Cascades Recur?. In *Proceedings of the 25th International Conference on World Wide Web*. International World Wide Web Conferences Steering Committee, 671–681.
9. Simon DeDeo. 2014. Group Minds and the Case of Wikipedia. *Human Computation* (2014).
10. P Alex Dow, Lada A Adamic, and Adrien Friggeri. 2013. The Anatomy of Large Facebook Cascades. In *Seventh International AAAI Conference on Weblogs and Social Media*.
11. Adrien Friggeri, Lada Adamic, Dean Eckles, and Justin Cheng. 2014. Rumor cascades. In *Eighth International AAAI Conference on Weblogs and Social Media*.
12. Sharad Goel, Duncan J Watts, and Daniel G Goldstein. 2012. The structure of online diffusion networks. In *Proceedings of the 13th ACM Conference on Electronic Commerce*. ACM, 623–638.
13. Rob Goldstone and Georg Theiner. 2017. The Multiple, Interacting Levels of Cognitive Systems (MILCS) Perspective on Group Cognition. *Philosophical Psychology* (2017).
14. Adrien Guille, Hakim Hacid, Cecile Favre, and Djamel A Zighed. 2013. Information diffusion in online social networks: A survey. *ACM SIGMOD Record* 42, 2 (2013), 17–28.
15. Thomas Heverin and Lisl Zach. 2012. Use of microblogging for collective sense-making during violent crises: A study of three campus shootings. *Journal of the American Society for Information Science and Technology* 63, 1 (2012), 34–47.
16. Eshcar Hillel, Zohar S Karnin, Tomer Koren, Ronny Lempel, and Oren Somekh. 2013. Distributed exploration in multi-armed bandits. In *Advances in Neural Information Processing Systems*. 854–862.
17. Edwin Hutchins. 1995. *Cognition in the Wild*. MIT Press.
18. Michael Kearns, Siddharth Suri, and Nick Montfort. 2006. An experimental study of the coloring problem on human subject networks. *Science* 313, 5788 (2006), 824–827.
19. Peter M Krafft, Julia Zheng, Wei Pan, Nicolás Della Penna, Yaniv Altshuler, Erez Shmueli, Joshua B Tenenbaum, and Alex Pentland. 2016. Human collective intelligence as distributed Bayesian inference. *arXiv preprint arXiv:1608.01987* (2016).
20. Sejeong Kwon, Meeyoung Cha, Kyomin Jung, Wei Chen, and Yajun Wang. 2013. Prominent features of rumor propagation in online social media. In *2013 IEEE 13th International Conference on Data Mining*. IEEE, 1103–1108.
21. Nancy A Lynch. 1996. *Distributed Algorithms*. Morgan Kaufmann.
22. Jim Maddock, Kate Starbird, Haneen J Al-Hassani, Daniel E Sandoval, Mania Orand, and Robert M Mason. 2015. Characterizing online rumoring behavior using multi-dimensional signatures. In *Proceedings of the 18th ACM Conference on Computer Supported Cooperative Work & Social Computing*. ACM, 228–241.
23. Andrew Mao, Winter Mason, Siddharth Suri, and Duncan J Watts. 2016. An experimental study of team size and performance on a complex task. *PloS one* 11, 4 (2016), e0153048.
24. Patrick Meier. 2012. Crisis mapping in action: How open source software and global volunteer networks are changing the world, one map at a time. *Journal of Map & Geography Libraries* 8, 2 (2012), 89–100.
25. Vahed Qazvinian, Emily Rosengren, Dragomir R Radev, and Qiaozhu Mei. 2011. Rumor has it: Identifying misinformation in microblogs. In *Proceedings of the Conference on Empirical Methods in Natural Language Processing*. Association for Computational Linguistics, 1589–1599.
26. Paul Resnick, Samuel Carton, Souneil Park, Yuncheng Shen, and Nicole Zeffer. 2014. Rumorlens: A system for analyzing the impact of rumors and corrections in social media. In *Proc. Computational Journalism Conference*.
27. Stanley Schachter and Harvey Burdick. 1955. A field experiment on rumor transmission and distortion. *The Journal of Abnormal and Social Psychology* 50, 3 (1955), 363.

28. Devavrat Shah. 2009. *Gossip Algorithms*. Now Publishers Inc.
29. Ohad Shamir. 2014. Fundamental limits of online and distributed algorithms for statistical learning and estimation. In *Advances in Neural Information Processing Systems*. 163–171.
30. Tamotsu Shibutani. 1966. *Improvised News: A Sociological Study of Rumor*. Ardent Media.
31. Matthew P Simmons, Lada A Adamic, and Eytan Adar. 2011. Memes Online: Extracted, Subtracted, Injected, and Recollected. *International AAAI Conference on Weblogs and Social Media* 11 (2011), 17–21.
32. Paul R. Smart and Katia P. Sycara. 2013. Collective Sensemaking and Military Coalitions. *IEEE Intelligent Systems* 28 (2013), 50–56.
33. Emma S Spiro, Sean Fitzhugh, Jeannette Sutton, Nicole Pierski, Matt Greczek, and Carter T Butts. 2012. Rumoring during extreme events: A case study of Deepwater Horizon 2010. In *Proceedings of the 4th Annual ACM Web Science Conference*. ACM, 275–283.
34. Kate Starbird. 2013. Delivering patients to sacré coeur: Collective intelligence in digital volunteer communities. In *Proceedings of the SIGCHI Conference on Human Factors in Computing Systems*. ACM, 801–810.
35. Kate Starbird, Jim Maddock, Mania Orand, Peg Achterman, and Robert M Mason. 2014. Rumors, false flags, and digital vigilantes: Misinformation on twitter after the 2013 boston marathon bombing. *iConference 2014 Proceedings* (2014).
36. Kate Starbird, Grace Muzny, and Leysia Palen. 2012. Learning from the crowd: Collaborative filtering techniques for identifying on-the-ground Twitterers during mass disruptions. In *Proceedings of 9th International Conference on Information Systems for Crisis Response and Management, ISCRAM*.
37. Kate Starbird and Leysia Palen. 2012. (How) will the revolution be retweeted?: Information diffusion and the 2011 Egyptian uprising. In *Proceedings of the ACM 2012 Conference on Computer Supported Cooperative Work*. ACM, 7–16.
38. Kate Starbird, Emma Spiro, Isabelle Edwards, Kaitlyn Zhou, Jim Maddock, and Sindhuja Narasimhan. 2016. Could This Be True?: I Think So! Expressed Uncertainty in Online Rumoring. In *Proceedings of the 2016 CHI Conference on Human Factors in Computing Systems*. ACM, 360–371.

Quietto: An Interactive Timepiece Molded in Concrete and Milled Wood

Kyung-Ryong Lee, Geon-il Goh, Young-Woo Park
IPD Lab, Graduate School of Creative Design Engineering, UNIST
50, UNIST-gil, Ulsan 44919, Republic of Korea
{rgodragon, k2i0927, ywpark}@unist.ac.kr

ABSTRACT
We introduce Quietto: an interactive timepiece made of molded concrete and milled wood. It shows upcoming daily schedules and the time through the quiet, ambient motions of a clock hand and light through the concrete touch interface. The results of an in-field user observation of 10 participants over 3 days showed the possibilities of using concrete as a unique and attractive material for designing a tangible interface due to its unexpected haptic feeling. We also found that Quietto provides an intuitive and effective representation of its users' daily schedules and can be used as a private, personal device. Through its distinctive design, Quietto can provide a new way of understanding scheduling through its concrete texture and amusing interaction qualities.

Author Keywords
Concrete; Interactive Timepiece; Schedule; Ambient

ACM Classification Keywords
H.5.2 Information interfaces and presentation: User interfaces—Input devices and strategies, interaction styles.

INTRODUCTION
In the creation of interactive devices, the material and appearance are one of the significant factors [9], and their sensorial properties influence the product experience [1, 10, 6]. In particular, as recent smart devices require exquisite visual-tactile interaction with users, we can see that the unique texture and aesthetics quality represented by the materials have a significant relationship with the formation of constant value and attachment to the product [17]. Additionally, the fabrication of some products' forms was attempted with wood [15] or fabric [7]; thus, those seem to add new sensibility to the products through harmonizing naturally with the furniture in the house and providing the users with pleasant interactive experiences. Within this trend, concrete in particular is often used in designing everyday products, such as clocks [13] and lamps [4], due to its unique color and texture. Moreover, concrete has been applied in interaction with users with a feature that represents traces of moisture [16], however, in the field of HCI, making prototypes with concrete through a professional mold-making process has rarely been studied.

Furthermore, the need to increase crafting quality by applying new materials is very important because it is directly related to the investigation of creative interaction with materials and aesthetic taste through those materials [2]. In addition, the outer material sensibility of smart devices may add more value in terms of their user interaction when the shape of the device reflects conventional and familiar product forms [12]. This aids in providing digital information to promote harmony with a user's daily environment, rather than showing information on a digital display. One example is daily schedules, which are still mostly represented on a phone screen or monitor display. Thus, intuitively representing the remaining and blank time before upcoming appointments is limited. Previously, there were few studies on representing time and schedules through the conventional form of a clock; however, these cases were dependent on a light display [7] or a computer monitor [5]. Other cases have applied tangible interaction for snoozing time [18] with a form that can balance by itself or with LEGO blocks for schedule inputs [11]. Accordingly, there is still a need to design a tangible interaction with time and schedules with an engaging concrete material along with representing time in the form of a conventional timepiece.

We propose a novel interactive concrete timepiece called Quietto and discuss the new experiences it can create by representing time and schedules through tangible interaction.

Figure 1. Five Quiettos: representing current time

QUIETTO DESIGN
Quietto is an interactive desk-top timepiece molded in concrete and milled wood that represents users' daily schedules by the physical movement of a clock hand and

Permission to make digital or hard copies of all or part of this work for personal or classroom use is granted without fee provided that copies are not made or distributed for profit or commercial advantage and that copies bear this notice and the full citation on the first page. Copyrights for components of this work owned by others than ACM must be honored. Abstracting with credit is permitted. To copy otherwise, or republish, to post on servers or to redistribute to lists, requires prior specific permission and/or a fee. Request permissions from Permissions@acm.org.
CHI 2017, May 06-11, 2017, Denver, CO, USA
© 2017 ACM. ISBN 978-1-4503-4655-9/17/05...$15.00
DOI: http://dx.doi.org/10.1145/3025453.3025670

light using real-time data retrieved from Google Calendar. The main functions and features of Quietto are as follows:

- Tangible interaction with time and schedule: Quietto design began with understanding the purpose of watching clocks. We considered that the purpose is not only to know the current time, but also to make plans after that. Because of this, we represented the schedules through the interval between the current time and the upcoming schedule. In spite of showing the entire schedules, we focused on representing the intervals through a tangible interaction. Through this intentional restriction of a function, also called as counterfunctionality [14], we wanted to identify new ways of understanding schedule. Consequently, Quietto shows the time remaining from the current time to the upcoming events through physical movement of the hour hand and an LED light.
- Concrete and wood interface: Our major focus was to represent the movement through the material itself (not through a button), in order to provide a natural experience of controlling the physical movement of time. Thus, in the process of selecting the material, we chose a concrete material that has a soft feeling to the touch, creates a visual sense of stability, and of course, matches well with the wood. Therefore, the cast concrete manufactured through a mold and the natural wood made by CNC machining are used as a touch interface for interaction with users.
- Quiet & ambient interaction: Quietto brings an ambient interaction [8] with the user through the quiet movement of a stepping motor and a subtle LED light that glows from behind the wood. This works in harmony with a desk-top environment.

Interaction Technique

Quietto represents the current time through the hour hand on the iron rod in the middle of wood and the minute hand in a transmitted LED light displayed on the circular rim of the wood (Figure 2, a). If the user touches the top of the concrete, the hour and minute hands move to show the start time of upcoming appointment (Figure 2, b). If the user maintains the touch for more than two seconds, Quietto shows the entire schedule for the day through the green LED light (Figure 2, c). When the user releases his or her hand, the hour and minute hands move back to the current time (Figure 2, d). In addition, Quietto gives notifications through the LED light fifteen minutes before the start of the upcoming schedule. Quietto automatically receives information from Google Calendar every five minutes. If the user wants immediate updates, touching the inside of the circular wood (Figure 2, e) causes Quietto to receive real-time data from Google Calendar.

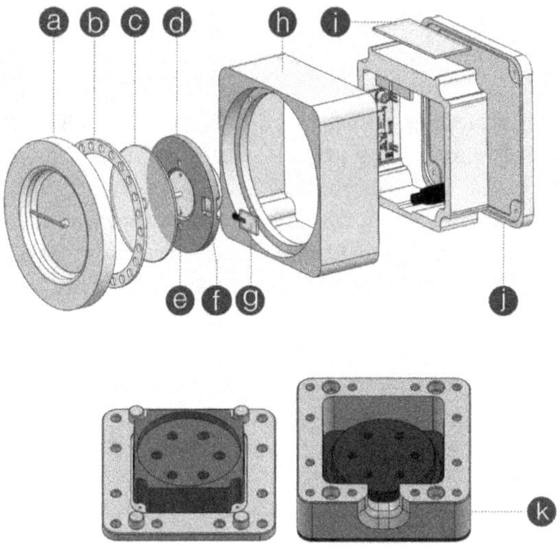

Figure 3. A detailed structure of Quietto (a) Milled wood, (b) Bracket for LED, (c) Copper plate, (d) Bracket for stepper motor, (e) Circular acrylic plate, (f) Stepper motor, (g) Hall sensor, (h) Concrete body, (i) Copper plate, (j) Backplate, (k) Plastic mold

Implementation

Hardware

We first made the concrete body from a mixture of water and ordinary Portland cement (OPC). The mixture was poured into the four-layer CNC-machined plastic mold (Figure 3, k) which was fabricated for making a 3-D structural concrete form. When designing the mold, we added a one-degree gradient to the assembly parts, and a lubricant was sprayed inside of the mold for easy removal of the solidified concrete form (Figure 3, h). At the center of the concrete body, we machined the natural wood into a circular shape (Figure 3, a). To place the LED stripe, grooves were carved into the back of the wood. A white 2T acrylic plate (Figure 3, b) was inserted between the wood and the LED stripe for uniform lighting. To implement the capacitive touch sensing on the concrete and wood, we cut out two copper plates (Figure 3,

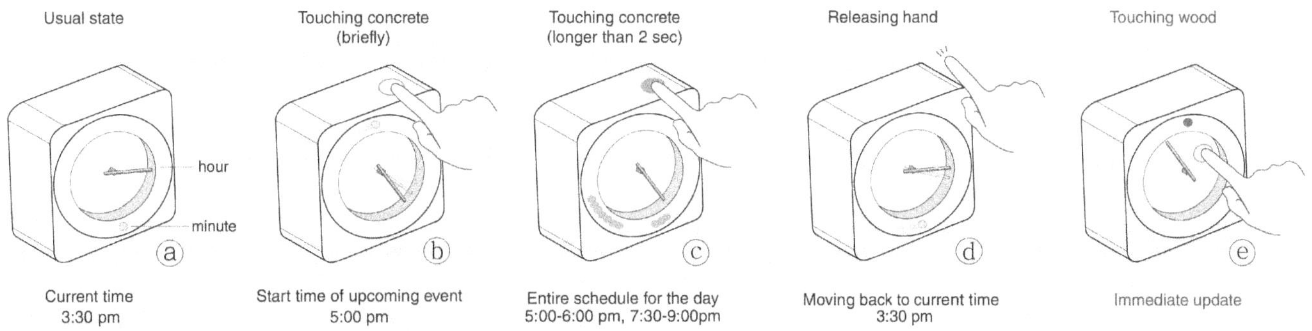

Figure 2. Interactions of Quietto

c, i) into proper shapes and placed them on each material. Then, 2.4-mega-ohm resistors were connected with the copper plates individually and calibrated for each Quietto. To hold a stepper motor (Figure 3, f), we made a circular bracket (Figure 3, d) with a 5T acrylic plate and drilled two screw holes into it. Because the hour hand has to be positioned correctly to display accurate time, we made a tiny circular acrylic plate (Figure 3, e) with two magnets and fixed it upon the axis of the stepper motor. Accordingly, when the stepper motor rotates, the magnets rotate together. As a result, the hall sensor (Figure 3, g) in the bracket detects the location of the magnets and recognizes the correct position of the hour hand. We used Arduino Yun, which is Wi-Fi ready, to obtain each user's Google Calendar data in real-time via the Internet. A stepper motor driver was placed on the inside of the concrete body. Lastly, the backplate (Figure 3, j) of the Quietto was finished with the CNC-machined wood.

Software

When Arduino Yun is booted up, it initializes its application processor (AP) and microcontroller unit (MCU). The AP, which is based on the Linux system, connects to the Internet via wireless connection, and it retrieves the current time and users' daily schedule information from the server. Meanwhile, the MCU detects the signal of the hall-effect sensor to calibrate the correct position of the stepper motor, which holds the hour hand. If the calibration has been conducted, the MCU is ready to obtain the current time and the user's daily schedule information. After that, it rotates the hour hand to the current hour and turns on the LED light to the current minute. Capacitive touch is implemented by the calculation of difference for a resistor-capacitor time constant. A send pin is connected with the 2.4MΩ resistor and goes into the two receive pins, which are attached to two copper plates individually. This causes a send-receive delay that the MCU detects; the MCU then recognizes the touching status of each copper plate. To reduce the interference between two copper plates, we calculated the average by finding the sum of samples in every 100 ms.

Data logger

When the user interacts with Quietto through touch, statistical data is created and sent via Arduino Yun to our database server. Each data record is composed of a timestamp, unique identifier, touch location and duration. If the duration is too long (>20000 ms) or short (<100 ms), we classify the record as invalid data and reject it from the statistics. The statistical data is collected in real time.

USER STUDY

We conducted an in-field study to explore the value of Quietto when used as a table clock. Through this experiment, we wanted to investigate the following: (1) how does the visual and tactile feel of concrete perform as a touch interface? (2) how does the tangible interaction between the current time and daily schedules affect a user's scheduling?

Ten people in their twenties (aged 22-26, 6 males and 4 females, P1-P10) participated. We recruited them because they used Google Calendar and worked in an office. Five identical Quiettos were built for the experiment over a period of 5 weeks. To extract the true user experience, we performed in-field user observation over 3 days rather than an in-lab study [3]. The day before the beginning of the experiment, we visited the participants' offices to install and test the Quiettos. Consequently, they were able to make full use of the Quiettos without failure during the experiment. The interview was conducted for 20 minutes every evening after the completion of more than 8 hours of the participants' daily schedules. The interview questions mainly focused on overall usability, feeling and the experience of interaction with the concrete and the advantages and disadvantages of the new representation of a digital schedule through Quietto. The data collected were in total 586 minutes, and all of the data were transcribed. They were analyzed using the affinity-diagramming method and through an iterative process of grouping by our research team. Some issues were culled according to the reports of the lead participant.

FINDINGS

The frequency of the participants' touch on the concrete body for checking schedules was a total of 607 times over 3 days, and on average, participants used the Quietto 20 times per day. In comparison with the number of touches in the first day (an average of 39 times), users touched the Quietto 16 times in the second day. These usage logging data were utilized to supplement the interview transcription.

Concrete as an Attractive and Unexpected Tangible Interface

We explored how participants used the concrete touch interface of Quietto, and we were able to find common points. Seven participants stated that the experience of touching concrete was unexpected and engaging. P9 said, *"When I saw the concrete with my eyes, it looked rough, but when I touched it, it was very soft such that I wanted to touch it again."* P3 mentioned, *"It (concrete) is somewhat contradictory when seen. It looks rough but is very soft. Also, it looks rather heavy, but it is not heavy."* In particular, P5 stated, *"It is the complete opposite of what I thought. What I thought was that it would feel like rough and cool, but it wasn't. It was soft and warm."*

We thus identified that the sensorial and interpretive properties of concrete material [6] can provide new touch experiences through its unexpected but positive texture. In accordance with this point, five participants mentioned that the touch experience of the concrete was notably different from the touch screens or plastic touches that were mainly used as materials for conventional digital interfaces. During the interview, P3 stated, *"The screen and body of a mobile phone is unnatural, and it feels like it will get dirty when I touch it frequently; however, concrete contains a natural sense of feeling so that it feels like it will not get dirty even when I keep touching it."* In addition, four participants mentioned the stable feeling with regard to the concrete's appearance of being heavy. P10 said, *"If the product is too lightweight, then it feels like it is plastic, but Quietto was different. It had a stable feeling by providing a courteous feeling."*

In line with a previous study [16], we identified the combination of concrete and digital technology has increased user's curiosity about the device, in particular it aroused participants' interest on touch interaction with the device. In addition, our findings have implications about the possibility of concrete could be utilized as new tangible interfaces through its positive visual and tactile quality.

Intuitive and Effective Representation of Daily Schedule

We heard from nine participants that it was a new experience when Quietto showed the digital schedules through the representation of physical time intervals in the form of an analog clock. Specifically, P8 mentioned, *"The way that Quietto informed me of my schedule was new because it was not a function that an original clock has. It was a calendar of a day. ...omit... Within a day, it was good to check the starting point of today's schedule from here."* She also stated that she could immediately notice that the (upcoming) appointment was far away if the clock hand rotated significantly and that there would be an appointment soon if it rotated a little. Additionally, P2 mentioned, *"Digital calendars feel like the time flow seems to be interrupted because the schedules are aligned in cells, but through Quietto, I could identify at a glance when my appointments were during the day and when the free time was because it is represented continuously."* This finding has a common point with a previous study [5] that the analog representation of schedules was helpful to recognize the schedules. In addition, participants gave their opinions about effective time management and checking schedules through Quietto. Particularly, seven participants answered that they managed time more effectively because they could finish their obligations on time. Also, five participants mentioned that Quietto helped them to remember forgotten obligations and perform them promptly.

Private and Ambient Personal Schedule Clock

We expected there could be privacy issues when personal schedule information was displayed at a public office (working) space, even though it was located on one's desk. On the contrary, all the participants stated that they did not feel that their privacy had been violated during the 3 days of use. Seven participants said this was because the details of their schedule were not shown on the device. P9 stated, *"The schedule can be seen, but I didn't care because it (Quietto) did not show the details."* We thus learned that Quietto could be a private device displaying information that only the user could recognize through the indirect representation of personal scheduling information.

DISCUSSION & IMPLICATIONS

Our findings from the field trial implied that Quietto's unique finishing and the experience it evokes gave a lifelike feeling to the clock when interacting with time and schedules, and this feeling was expanded due to the concrete's engaging texture when touching it. Along with this, easy and simple identification of the time of an upcoming schedule showed the possibility of providing a closer interaction between the product and user beyond the simple time-telling function of a clock. Based on the results, we propose the following implications for improving Quietto and opening a new design space using concrete. First, if the schedule is delayed or needs modification, without changing the schedule on Google Calendar and through the input of adjusting the schedule time by slightly moving the hour hand with a finger, Quietto could be an improved interactive scheduling timepiece. Second, the concrete used as the touch interface presents a new opportunity for various fields including architecture and design. For example, in a new building, concrete walls are used as an interior. They could display touch-type switches to turning light fixtures on or off; in this way, they could be designed or modified to be a new type of interior. Moreover, based on the nine participants' positive comments about the design that it combined concrete and wood, blending concrete and wood in pieces of furniture could also create a novel interface to control home appliances.

CONCLUSION

We introduced Quietto, an interactive desktop timepiece made of concrete and wood that represents users' daily schedules through the physical movement of a clock hand and light. Its appearance was completed through the combination of concrete body cast with a carefully designed mold and CNC-machined circular timber. The result of an in-field user observation of 10 participants over 3 days presented a new opportunity to use concrete as an attractive material for designing a tangible interface due to its unique tactile feeling. In addition, through the physical representation of a daily schedule and time, Quietto helped users comprehend their schedules more intuitively and manage them more efficiently. Simultaneously, it played a role as a private device. Through its distinctive appearance and interaction, Quietto could open a new design space and provide a new way of understanding time through its concrete texture and engaging interaction qualities.

ACKNOWLEDGEMENT

This work was supported by the 2016 Research Fund (1.160049.01) of UNIST (Ulsan National Institute of Science & Technology)

REFERENCES

1. Ashby, M. & Johnson, K. 2002. *Materials and design: The art and science of material selection in product design*. Oxford: Butterworth-Heinemann.
2. Bardzell, S., Rosner, D.K. and Bardzell, J. 2012. Crafting quality in design: integrity, creativity, and public sensibility. In *Proceedings of the Designing Interactive Systems Conference* (DIS'12), 11-20. http://doi.acm.org/10.1145/2317956.2317959

3. Brown, B., Reeves, S. and Sherwood, S. 2011. Into the wild: challenges and opportunities for field trial methods. In *Proceedings of the SIGCHI Conference on Human Factors in Computing Systems* (CHI '11), 1657-1666.
4. Concrete Brick Lamp, 2014 from Kickstarter
5. Dragicevic, P. and Huot, S. 2002. SpiraClock: a continuous and non-intrusive display for upcoming events. In *CHI'02 Ext. Abstracts on Human Factors in Computing Systems*, 604-605. http://doi.acm.org/10.1145/506443.506505
6. Giaccardi, E. and Karana, E. 2015. Foundations of Materials Experience: An Approach for HCI. In *Proceedings of the SIGCHI Conference on Human Factors in Computing Systems* (CHI '15), 2447-2456. http://doi.acm.org/10.1145/2702123.2702337
7. Glance Clock, 2015 from Indiegogo
8. Ishii, H., Wisneski, C., Brave, S., Dahley, A., Gorbet, M., Ullmer, B. and Yarin, P., 1998. ambientROOM: integrating ambient media with architectural space. In *Proceedings of the SIGCHI Conference on Human Factors in Computing Systems* (CHI '98), 173-174. http://doi.acm.org/10.1145/286498.286652
9. Jung, H. and Stolterman, E. 2011. Form and materiality in interaction design: a new approach to HCI. In *CHI'11 Ext. Abstracts on Human Factors in Computing Systems*, 399-408. http://doi.acm.org/10.1145/1979742.1979619
10. Kesteren, I. E. H., Stappers, P. J., Bruijn, J. C. M. 2007. Materials in products selection: tools for including user-interaction in materials selection, *International Journal of Design*, 1 (3).
11. LEGO wall planner, 2014 from http://www.bit-planner.com/
12. Norman, D.A. 1999. Affordance, conventions, and design. Interactions, 6(3), pp.38-43. http://doi.acm.org/10.1145/301153.301168
13. Para Clock, 2012 from Kickstarter
14. Pierce, J. and Paulos, E. 2015. Making Multiple Uses of the Obscura 1C Digital Camera: Reflecting on the Design, Production, Packaging and Distribution of a Counterfunctional Device. In *Proceedings of the SIGCHI Conference on Human Factors in Computing Systems* (CHI '15), 2103-2112. http://doi.acm.org/10.1145/2702123.2702405
15. Rhei, 2015 from http://hellorhei.com/
16. Wang, Y., Liu, S., Lu, Y., Duan, J., Yao, C. and Ying, F. 2016. Designing with Concrete For Enhancing Everyday Interactions. In *CHI'16 Ext. Abstracts on Human Factors in Computing Systems*, 1497-1502. http://doi.acm.org/10.1145/2851581.2892372
17. Wiberg, M. 2014. Methodology for Materiality: interaction design research through a material lens, *Personal and Ubiquitous Computing*, Springer-Verlag, UK, 18(3): 625-636.
18. Zekveld, J., Funk, M. and Bakker, S. 2016. The Tumble Clock: Bringing Users in Touch with their Snooze Time. In *Proceedings of the Designing Interactive Systems Conference* (DIS'16), 900-904. http://doi.acm.org/10.1145/2901790.2901857

Locked or Not? Mental Models of IoT Feature Interaction

Svetlana Yarosh
University of Minnesota
Computer Science & Engineering
lana@umn.edu

Pamela Zave
AT&T Labs Research
Bedminster, NJ, USA
pamela@research.att.com

ABSTRACT
Internet of Things (IoT) frequently involves conflicting interactions between devices and features that must be resolved to a single system state. The problem of feature interaction (FI) resolution has been investigated in Software Engineering through approaches that focus on verifiability but usually do not include the user in the evaluation. This paper bridges the gap between IoT approaches in HCI and Software Engineering by applying qualitative methods to understanding users' mental models of one representative FI resolution mechanism. Our contributions are in identifying common mental model errors and biases and how these may inform future IoT systems and research.

Author Keywords
IoT; home automation; feature interaction; mental models

ACM Classification Keywords
H.5.2. [Information Interfaces and Presentation]: User Interfaces: *User-Centered Design.*

INTRODUCTION
Edwards and Grinter's groundbreaking work on Ubiquitous Computing in the home articulated "impromptu interoperability" of devices in a smart home as a key challenge for home technologies [5]. Researchers in Software Engineering (SE) have been investigating a similar challenge in many other domains (e.g., telecommunications [20]) and typically address it through a feature-composition approach. To understand this issue, consider the following scenario:

> *Jill's new smart home door lock seemed like a good idea when all it did was provide convenient keypad access. But then, her husband installed a new feature to keep it automatically locked at night. Next, her daughter installed a new driveway sensor to unlock the door if the family car drove up. Now, as Jill is driving away from her house in the evening, she is confused. 'Is my door locked or unlocked?' she worries.*

The behavior of Jill's door lock and many other complex IoT systems can be described in terms of largely independent increments called *features*. A feature may have its own purpose, triggering situation, or intended beneficiary. In many IoT applications (as in Jill's scenario), multiple rules may attempt to influence the state of one actuator. A *feature interaction* (FI) is a logical conflict in determining the value of a particular actuator or system output. If FIs are not resolved before system implementation in a comprehensive analysis phase, then they must be resolved at runtime to produce well-defined system behavior. As long as FIs are resolved in a verifiable way, new features and devices can be added to such a system through integration with the central controller but without the need to modify or inform any existing features or devices of the upgrades.

Permission to make digital or hard copies of all or part of this work for personal or classroom use is granted without fee provided that copies are not made or distributed for profit or commercial advantage and that copies bear this notice and the full citation on the first page. Copyrights for components of this work owned by others than ACM must be honored. Abstracting with credit is permitted. To copy otherwise, or republish, to post on servers or to redistribute to lists, requires prior specific permission and/or a fee. Request permissions from Permissions@acm.org.
CHI 2017, May 06-11, 2017, Denver, CO, USA
© 2017 ACM. ISBN 978-1-4503-4655-9/17/05 $15.00
DOI: http://dx.doi.org/10.1145/3025453.3025617

Software Engineers have investigated FI resolution as a major challenge in creating secure and verifiable IoT systems. However, most SE investigations do not validate their proposed solutions with users. On the other hand, HCI takes a user-centered approach, but has not addressed issues of FI resolution. In this note, we seek to bridge the two communities. We apply HCI methods to understand user mental models of a FI resolution approach (one developed in industry and integrated into commercial home automation systems). Our investigation focuses on two questions:

R1: How well do participants understand the example FI resolution mechanism after an initial exposure?
R2: What common mental model errors do participants make when beginning to understand FI resolution?

In this note, we describe a mixed-methods lab-based investigation where we elicited user mental models of the resolution mechanism by asking users to respond to twenty IoT home automation scenarios. Our results focus on the mental model errors and biases common in the way users perceive FI resolution. In the discussion, we reflect on lessons for both HCI and SE researchers as we collectively advance IoT in the home.

RELATED WORK
Three bodies of related work inspired this study: home automation in HCI, qualitative methods for understanding users' mental models, and feature interaction in SE. Our first major influence is the significant body of HCI investigations on home automation. Some previous work in this domain has examined user perceptions and practices around existing systems, such as the Nest thermostat [19]. Others look more holistically at the role of home automation, such as how power users find satisfaction in their ability to automate various aspects of their daily life [17]. Most of these studies confirm that home automation is notoriously chal-

lenging for the user to set up, control, and secure [2]. In addition to studying existing systems, HCI researchers have designed new approaches to home automation. Most of these focus on novel interaction with a single home automation feature (e.g., [10]), on supporting user scripting of system events (e.g., [9], [13]), and on developing infrastructures of sensors and actuators (e.g., [1]). All of these systems are likely to face FI resolution issues [15], which have largely been left as an exercise to the user to resolve.

Second, we were inspired by methodological approaches for understanding users' mental models of complex systems. Rasmussen's work highlights that the user must represent the internal structure of a system with a "mental model" which may help drive goal-oriented action [12]. Our research questions in this work focus on eliciting the users' initial mental models of FI resolution mechanism infrastructure by understanding the errors they make in explaining the mechanism's functionality. This study was inspired by work on folk understanding of home control interfaces, namely Kempton's use of qualitative interview methods to identify two distinct mental models of home heating control [7]. Like Kempton, we turn to qualitative methods to reveal some of the assumptions inherent in the SE approach, by highlighting situations where the user's mental model is in conflict with the actual behavior of the system.

Finally, feature interaction (FI) is a subfield of SE, traditionally focused on addressing the multi-device and multi-feature needs of telecommunication technology (e.g., [20]). Most SE approaches have focused on detecting undesirable FI [8,16], assertion-based testing of behavior during FI [11], and runtime verifiability [18]. However, while these approaches present a number of sound and verifiable solutions, none of them have been validated in with user-centered methods.

RESOLUTION MECHANISM FOR FI

We chose one representative FI resolution mechanism to use in our study. The description of the resolution mechanism and features came from our previous work in SE, which established this as a verifiable and scalable approach to FI resolution [21,22]. It is the approach currently considered for real-world IoT systems, like AT&T's Digital Life [23]. We applied this resolution mechanism to a hypothetical smart lock with four features (in order of priority): (1) a lock/unlock function keypad (2) an intruder defense function that will attempt to lock the doors if sensors detect an intruder, (3) a hands-free operation function that will attempt to unlock the door if it senses the resident's car in the driveway, and (4) a night lock that will attempt to lock the door during hours specified as night.

These features were described to users in a manual (see supplementary materials), along with the three key aspects of the FI resolution mechanism: priority, duration, and "don't care means no change:"

Priority: in some situations one feature might want the door locked for security, while another feature wants the door unlocked for convenience. We manage these situations by allowing features to override lower-priority features. At any time, the actuator setting is determined by the preferences of the highest-priority feature.
Duration: To make the priorities work correctly, we need the concept that each operation has "duration." When the duration of an operation is over, the feature no longer affects whether the door is open or not.
"Don't care means no change:" After an operation's duration expires, the rule is "don't care means no change." For example, if the unlocking feature does not care anymore because the duration period is over, and if no other feature wants the door locked, then the door will stay unlocked until some feature does want the door locked.

METHODS

We conducted a mixed methods lab investigation of participant mental models of the FI resolution mechanism described above. Twenty adult participants (12 female, 8 male) with diverse technical skills and occupations (see supplementary materials) participated. We deemed that data saturation was reached before getting to 20 participants, as by participant 16 we began seeing the mental model errors repeating and no new ones introduced. After each participant expressed that he or she had a clear understanding of the resolution mechanism, we posed 20 scenarios (see supplementary materials), asking him or her to specify whether the door is locked or unlocked in the described situation and explain why they think so.

One example of a scenario is below:

According to your house schedule, it is night. You drive home and park and then walk quickly to the door. Is the door locked or unlocked? [Correct Answer: Unlocked]

Participants were not told the correct response during the scenario part of the study, but could ask how they did during the debriefing.

Qualitative data-driven analysis was carried out using Seidman's thematic analysis guidelines [14]. All study sessions were transcribed and open-coded by the lead author. The lead author and another research clustered codes through affinity mapping. Once the two researchers achieved consensus on the error codebook, the lead author coded all the transcripts using this guide. We triangulated quantitative data (e.g., questions gotten right) with the qualitative data from participant responses to understand the participants' mental models of the FI resolution mechanism.

RESULTS

R1: FI Resolution Mechanism Understanding

On average, participants got 88% of the questions right (17.5 questions, *SD*=1.4). This may seem fairly high, but needs to be considered in the context of two factors: (1) since the responses were binary, random guessing would have produced a 50% success rate, and (2) every participant got at least one question wrong. Clearly, understanding FI resolution is a fairly complex task.

Many participants made errors that could be classified as "careless:" misreading the manual or scenario, forgetting about a feature of the system, or confusing the order of the priorities. However, a greater number of participants made mistakes that pointed to persistent errors in their mental models of the FI resolution mechanism. Table 1 reports the frequency of all of these mistakes.

Many participants had trouble understanding or explaining the system, e.g.:

> *I'm not sure how I would be able to explain it ... Sometimes my door is locked or unlocked. I'm not sure when.* -P6

This is not how any person wants to feel about the front door of his or her house. There were also 31 separate cases (out of 400) in the study where a participant predicted that the door would be locked but it was actually unlocked based on the model. These are potential security hazards. It is clear from this investigation that a short written description of the basic interaction model and its features does not provide adequate exposure for all participants to be confident and correct in their understanding.

R2: Common Mental Model Errors & Biases

To understand the mental models of our participants, we holistically examined their responses to scenarios and the verbal explanations they gave for their answers. Two scenarios emerged as being particularly important to developing this understanding and we refer to them throughout:

> ***Grocery Scenario.*** *[During the day.] You drive home and park. Your car is full of groceries and other shopping, which take many trips to bring into the house. Five minutes after you drove in, you are still making trips to the car. Is the door locked or unlocked? [Correct Answer: Unlocked]*
>
> ***Weekend Scenario.*** *You have set the night period (for Night Lock) to begin at 11 p.m. and end at 7 a.m. On Saturday morning, you get up at 9 a.m. At that time, is the door locked or unlocked? [Correct Answer: Locked]*

On the surface, these two scenarios test very similar ideas: they both ask about a single feature and both require an understanding of the "don't care means no change" aspect of the resolution mechanism. However, only 3 out of the 20 participants answered the grocery scenario correctly. The weekend scenario was the second most incorrectly answered question, but 15 out of the 20 participants were able to get it correct. With in-depth analysis, we came to understand the mental model errors that led to this result.

Feature as Toggle

Some participants seemed to have trouble understanding the idea of "don't care means no change." Instead, these 20% of participants thought that after the duration for an operation expires, the system would toggle the state of the door. This mistake was most commonly articulated in talking about hands-free operation, leading to a wrong answer to the grocery scenario question, e.g.:

> *The door would be locked after that point because three minutes have gone by. It unlocks for three minutes and then locks afterwards.* -P9

Because these participants did not understand the "don't care means no change" mechanism, we would also expect them to get the weekend morning scenario wrong. That is in fact what we saw in the data—all of these participants expected the door to toggle to "unlocked" in the weekend morning scenario.

Sensor Events as Interrupts

Another common mistake was in considering sensor events (intruder alert, car driving up) as different from user-initiated or user-scheduled events (pushing the lock button, scheduling a night lock). Though the 35% of participants who made this error generally understood the idea of "don't care means no change," they thought that "no change" after a sensor event duration expired meant reverting to the previous state, e.g.:

> *I guess the answer depends on whether the door was locked to begin with. If it was locked right before the intruder was detected, it has no reason to automatically unlock the door, but if the door* ***was*** *unlocked then several minutes later, it should have returned it to the state where it was beforehand.* -P18

This was another common reason for a wrong answer to the grocery scenario since the participant thought of the door as being locked before the hands-free sensor event interrupted this state, e.g.:

> *I think based on the manual that it would lock after those 3 minutes because it was locked before.* -P12

Since the night lock feature was perceived as a user-scheduled event, we would expect these participants to give the correct answer to the weekend scenario. All of them did.

Invisible Default

Though the word "default" was never used in the manual or suggested by the researcher, 25% of the participants assumed that there must be a system default and answered the questions with this default in mind, e.g.:

> *It looks like it defaults to locked unless you do something else and it's only unlocked for a minute or two.* -P5

Participants who made the default error generally assumed a locked default and thus gave the wrong response to the grocery scenario. All of these participants gave the correct

	Type of Error Made	% People
General Task Complexity Issues	Careless error reading	10%
	Forgets a feature	25%
	Confuses priorities	25%
Mental Model Mistakes	Feature as toggle	20%
	Sensor events as interrupts	35%
	Invisible default	25%
	Articulated lock bias	50%

Table 1. User error types

answer to the weekend scenario, but the wrong reason, e.g.:

> *I think it's still locked, because the program ran out but the default is still locked.* -P15

They were not able to see that the door was locked not because of a lock default but simply because the night lock feature was no longer expressing a preference and no other feature had issued an unlock request.

Articulated Lock Bias

The most common source of errors made by participants was a bias against suggesting that the door state would be unlocked. Most frequently, it was expressed by making statements such as "*it should be locked because there's been nothing to indicate an unlock*" (P4). One participant got all questions right except the grocery scenario. She was surprised to learn that she got this question wrong and explicitly articulated this lock bias:

> *I guess it makes sense to me when the door would stay **locked** until something changes, but it seems weirder that the door would stay **unlocked**...* -P17

Unlike other mental model errors, where participants made the same mistake consistently, the lock bias merely stated that they were less sure of the answer when it was unlocked. Participants who expressed this bias correctly answered 94% of "locked" scenarios, they were only successful in 72% of the "unlocked" ones. They were more conservative with saying that the door was unlocked than saying that it was locked.

DISCUSSION

Mental Models and Biases in Specific Contexts

While HCI has not considered FI (beyond basic if-then triggers [6]), SE typically considers feature interaction resolution mechanisms independent of the domain and features involved (e.g., [3]). Feature interaction resolution mechanisms that work for telecommunications should apply to home automations or to enterprise warehouse management. However, while that is true for questions of verifiability, our study shows that the context and features involved *may* impact the users' understanding of the behavior of the resolution mechanism. We found three context-dependent biases to be particularly salient.

First, system states may have meanings. To users in this study, the binary states of the system—locked or unlocked—were not functionally equal or equally likely. The idea of an "unlocked door" carried inherent negative meaning for at least half of the participants in the study. Users may carry similar biases in approaching system states in other domains and these must be understood and addressed in order to create predictable systems that users can trust.

Second, user- and sensor-triggered events may carry different expectations. For example, more than a third of our participants expected the system to return to the last user-specified state after the duration of a sensor event expired, even though they otherwise understood the "don't care means no change" aspect of the resolution mechanism.

Third, powerful concepts like "system default" may be embedded in the particular domain. The idea of default was so strongly embedded in the participants' understanding of how IoT works, that some users were *sure* they had seen it *somewhere* in the manual. Just as an optical illusion may make people see motion or depth where there is none, a bias like the expectation of a default made participants remember seeing it even though it was not in the manual. "Default" is just one powerful example and one that was most salient in this study and context, however other feature interaction contexts may come with their own embedded biases. **Based on our findings, we recommend that researchers conduct evaluations of potential FI resolution mechanisms *in specific contexts of use* in order to respond to users' mental models in each domain.** This could help anticipate and account for specific errors due to inherent meanings of states, emphases on some types of triggers over others, and embedded biases like "default."

Lessons for HCI

IoT device scripting and home automation are notoriously challenging for most users [17], but FI resolution mechanisms may be able to provide a good metaphor for complex systems. While the HCI community has developed infrastructure for home automation [2], as well as a nuanced ways of discussing the challenges and opportunities of ubiquitous computing in the home [2,5], the resolution of interaction between features remains largely unexplored. A few HCI studies recognize the challenge and need for resolving the heterogeneity of devices and features [5] and the utility in encapsulating those features into independent functions [4], but we have not explicitly considered the resolution of conflicting functions and features in a complex system with multiple devices. The standard HCI approach of mostly "if-then" scripting (e.g., [6]) for interacting with IoT and home automation leaves the significant tasks of understanding and resolving the resulting feature interactions entirely to the end user. We show that even with a well-specified, verifiable FI resolution mechanism, reasoning about feature interaction is a challenge for most users. Connecting with Software Engineering research can help achieve IoT solutions that are verifiable and scalable [15,22], but achieving these goals in way that match users' mental models is a task that may be particularly well-suited to the skills of HCI researchers. **In this work, we position FI resolution mechanisms as an important area of for future research in IoT and home automation—one that may be particularly well suited to collaboration between SE and HCI investigators.**

ACKNOWLEDGMENTS

With grateful acknowledgement of Eric Cheung's resolution mechanism work, Tom Jenkins' analysis help, Alicia Abella's support, and our participants' time and effort.

REFERENCES

1. A. J. Bernheim Brush, Jaeyeon Jung, Ratul Mahajan, and James Scott. 2012. HomeLab: Shared Infrastructure for Home Technology Field Studies. In *Proc. of Ubicomp*, 1108–1113.
2. A J Bernheim Brush, Bongshin Lee, Ratul Mahajan, Sharad Agarwal, Stefan Saroiu, and Colin Dixon. 2011. Home Automation in the Wild: Challenges and Opportunities. In *Proc. of CHI*, 2115–2124.
3. Muffy Calder, Mario Kolberg, Evan H. Magill, and Stephan Reiff-Marganiec. 2003. Feature interaction: a critical review and considered forecast. *Computer Networks* 41, 1: 115–141.
4. Colin Dixon, Ratul Mahajan, Sharad Agarwal, A. J. Brush, Bongshin Lee, Stefan Saroiu, and Victor Bahl. 2010. The Home Needs an Operating System (and an App Store). In *Proc. of Workshop on Hot Topics in Networks*, 18:1–18:6.
5. W. Keith Edwards and Rebecca E. Grinter. 2001. At Home with Ubiquitous Computing: Seven Challenges. *UbiComp*: 256–272.
6. Justin Huang and Maya Cakmak. 2015. Supporting Mental Model Accuracy in Trigger-action Programming. In *Proceedings of the 2015 ACM International Joint Conference on Pervasive and Ubiquitous Computing* (UbiComp '15), 215–225. https://doi.org/10.1145/2750858.2805830
7. Willet Kempton. 1986. Two Theories of Home Heat Control. *Cognitive Science* 10: 75–90.
8. P. Leelaprute, T. Matsuo, T. Tsuchiya, and T. Kikuno. 2008. Detecting Feature Interactions in Home Appliance Networks. In *Proc. of Software Engineering, Artificial Intelligence, Networking, and Parallel/Distributed Computing*, 895–903. https://doi.org/10.1109/SNPD.2008.158
9. Sarah Mennicken, Jonas Hofer, Anind Dey, and Elaine M. Huang. 2014. Casalendar: A Temporal Interface for Automated Homes. In *Ext. Abst. of CHI*, 2161–2166.
10. Miji Park, Juhyun Eune, and Suzung Kim. 2010. Tangible User Interface Design for Home Automation Energy Management Appliances. In *Proc. of SIGRAPH Asia*.
11. Ajitha Rajan, Lydie du Bousquet, Yves Ledru, German Vega, and Jean-Luc Richier. 2010. Assertion-based Test Oracles for Home Automation Systems. In *Proc. of Workshop on Model-Based Methodologies for Pervasive and Embedded Software*, 45–52.
12. J. Rasmussen. 1983. Skills, rules, and knowledge; signals, signs, and symbols, and other distinctions in human performance models. *IEEE Transactions on Systems, Man and Cybernetics* SMC-13, 3: 257–266. https://doi.org/10.1109/TSMC.1983.6313160
13. Michael Rietzler, Julia Greim, Marcel Walch, Florian Schaub, Björn Wiedersheim, and Michael Weber. 2013. homeBLOX: Introducing Process-driven Home Automation. In *Proc. of Ubicomp 2013*, 801–808.
14. Irving Seidman. 1998. *Interviewing as Qualitative Research: A Guide for Researchers in Education And the Social Sciences*. Teachers College Press, New York.
15. C. Soares, R.S. Moreira, R. Morla, J. Torres, and P. Sobral. 2012. Prognostic of feature interactions between independently developed pervasive systems. In *Proc. of Conference on Prognostics and Health Management*. https://doi.org/10.1109/ICPHM.2012.6299523
16. C. Soares, R.S. Moreira, R. Morla, J. Torres, and P. Sobral. 2012. Graph-based approach for interference free integration of pervasive applications. In *Proc. of Symposium on Wireless and Pervasive Computing (ISWPC)*. https://doi.org/10.1109/ISWPC.2012.6263661
17. Leila Takayama, Caroline Pantofaru, David Robson, Bianca Soto, and Michael Barry. 2012. Making Technology Homey: Finding Sources of Satisfaction and Meaning in Home Automation. In *Proc. of Ubicomp*, 511–520.
18. Michael Wilson, Mario Kolberg, and Evan H. Magill. 2008. Considering Side Effects in Service Interactions in Home Automation – an Online Approach. In *Feature Interactions in Software and Communication Systems IX*. IOS Press, 172–187.
19. Rayoung Yang and Mark W. Newman. 2013. Learning from a Learning Thermostat: Lessons for Intelligent Systems for the Home. In *Proc. of Ubicomp*, 93–102.
20. Pamela Zave. 2011. Mid-call, Multi-party, and Multi-device Telecommunication Features and Their Interactions. In *Proc. of IPTcomm*, 17:1–17:12.
21. Pamela Zave and Eric Cheung. 2014. *A resolution mechanism for feature interactions in ubiquitous computing*. AT&T Research Labs.
22. Pamela Zave, Eric Cheung, and Svetlana Yarosh. 2015. Toward user-centric feature composition for the Internet of Things. *arXiv:1510.06714 [cs]*. Retrieved December 21, 2016 from http://arxiv.org/abs/1510.06714
23. AT&T Home Security and Automation. Retrieved December 21, 2016 from https://my-digitallife.att.com/learn/home-security-and-automation

Robust Gaze Features for Enabling Language Proficiency Awareness

Jakob Karolus
University of Stuttgart
Stuttgart, Germany
jakob.karolus@vis.uni-stuttgart.de

Paweł W. Woźniak
University of Stuttgart
Stuttgart, Germany
pawel.wozniak@vis.uni-stuttgart.de

Lewis L. Chuang
Max Planck Institute for Biological Cybernetics
Tübingen, Germany
lewis.chuang@tuebingen.mpg.de

Albrecht Schmidt
University of Stuttgart
Stuttgart, Germany
albrecht.schmidt@vis.uni-stuttgart.de

ABSTRACT
We are often confronted with information interfaces designed in an unfamiliar language, especially in an increasingly globalized world, where the language barrier inhibits interaction with the system. In our work, we explore the design space for building interfaces that can detect the user's language proficiency. Specifically, we look at how a user's gaze properties can be used to detect whether the interface is presented in a language they understand. We report a study (N=21) where participants were presented with questions in multiple languages, whilst being recorded for gaze behavior. We identified fixation and blink durations to be effective indicators of the participants' language proficiencies. Based on these findings, we propose a classification scheme and technical guidelines for enabling language proficiency awareness on information displays using gaze data.

ACM Classification Keywords
H.5.m Information interfaces and presentation (e.g., HCI): Miscellaneous.; H.1.2 Model and Principles: User/Machine Systems—Human information processing

Author Keywords
Eye-tracking; machine learning; language-aware interfaces; adaptive interfaces.

INTRODUCTION
In an increasingly globalized world, users are constantly exposed to unfamiliar cultures and languages. Concurrently, our lives are increasing reliant on digital technology as our environments - in public, at work or at home - are pervaded by digital artifacts such as public displays and shared mobile devices. When visiting foreign countries, especially those that are multilingual, users are often faced with the challenge of navigating an interface in an unfamiliar language. While alternative language versions are often available, accessing them (usually through a poorly visible button or a submenu) tend to be cumbersome. The problem is compounded by screen space limitations. In this paper, we present work that contributes towards a new generation of systems that will detect a user's language proficiencies and can subsequently adapt their interface language to their users' perceived proficiency, as depicted in Figure 1.

Permission to make digital or hard copies of all or part of this work for personal or classroom use is granted without fee provided that copies are not made or distributed for profit or commercial advantage and that copies bear this notice and the full citation on the first page. Copyrights for components of this work owned by others than the author(s) must be honored. Abstracting with credit is permitted. To copy otherwise, or republish, to post on servers or to redistribute to lists, requires prior specific permission and/or a fee. Request permissions from Permissions@acm.org.
CHI 2017, May 06 - May 11, 2017, Denver, CO, USA
Copyright is held by the owner/author(s). Publication rights licensed to ACM.
ACM 978-1-4503-4655-9/17/05...$15.00
DOI: http://dx.doi.org/10.1145/3025453.3025601

Figure 1. User interacting with a language-aware interface.

Our daily communications afford us interpersonal cues that allow us to moderate our language and responses to our conversation partners. Telltale facial expressions and body language can indicate the interest and engagement levels of our conversation partners. Gaze can readily indicate whether they are focused on the conversation or distracted by something else, such as looking at their phone or recognizing another person in the background [15, 19]. We are typically able to interpret these implicit signals and adapt our conversation strategy by changing the topic or requesting attention. Here, we explore how user interfaces can use information, such as its user's gaze, to recognize its user's state.

In this paper, we contribute to the understanding about human gaze properties to build interfaces that recognize the lack of understanding of the user. Specifically, we investigate whether we can effectively detect if the user is confused by the interface language. We examined users' gaze properties (gathered through an embedded eye tracker) when reading short sentences in multiple languages. Afterwards, we evaluated how gaze properties can be interpreted to detect if the interface is presented in a language that the user understands.

Eye tracking is widely used in the domain of reading analysis. However, existing approaches have usually focused on one specific language and are used for post-hoc analysis [31, 50]. We propose an approach that relies on characteristic gaze properties to infer a user's requirement for real-time assistance. The goal is to recognize a user's likelihood for comprehending displayed text, given limited gaze data that is based on reading a short sentence in a given language. We anticipate that users are unlikely to persist in using a system beyond a single sentence, in a language that they lack proficiency in. In this regard, the current work contrasts with eye movement research that is based on reading entire documents. When working with eye gaze interaction, prior calibration often is a hindrance for readily available interaction. We will discuss the aforementioned limitations and analyze their impact on user experience given our approach. To the best of our knowledge, this work represents the first approach to rapid detection of language comprehension for the design of information displays.

In our study with 21 participants we recorded their eye movements while presenting them simple questions in varying languages. The participants were tasked to answer the shown questions to the best of their abilities. Depending on their language proficiency, some questions could be answered easily while others were impossible.

We evaluate the feasibility of language-aware interfaces, based on our experimental results. First, we identified that users exhibited shorter average fixation duration as well as longer average and summed blink duration, when presented with languages that they were proficient in. Based on these results, we developed a classification strategy and provide some technical guidelines to facilitate real-time language proficiency detection on information displays.

This paper is organized as follows. First, we review past efforts in using eye-tracking for assessing language comprehension and data processing methods used to that end. Next, we provide the detail of the experiment we conducted. Following this, we present the analysis of our experimental results, which form the basis of building an automated classifier for rating our users' language comprehension. We discuss the details of the classifier and its alternative designs in the following sections. Finally, we provide technical guidelines and minimum requirements for implementing language comprehension detection using gaze properties on information displays.

RELATED WORK

A user's gaze can be used as an explicit input to computing interfaces, albeit to varying levels of effectiveness. Most prominently, gaze has been used as a substitute or supplement for manual cursor control [45, 40], e.g. in MAGIC-Pointing [51] and typing [29]. Interfaces have also been developed that respond to distinctive and contrived gaze gestures [11] as a form of explicit interaction.

Besides this, gaze can also serve as an implicit input for context-aware applications, such as activity recognition [6] while wearing custom made EOG[1]-glasses [5]. *iTourist* [36] successfully plans city trips based on recorded gaze patterns. Gaze contingent displays [12] use the gaze point of the user to define a region of interest. The information is used to highlight specific elements in the user's view [2] or to selectively render foveated regions at high resolution in order to save computing costs [17, 32].

Other work in the domain of implicit interaction focuses on human-like interaction in virtual environments, e.g. for conversational agents [47, 49]. It has been shown that gaze directional cues can serve as a predictor for conversational attention. Moreover, virtual agents that respond to users' gaze have been shown to increase their users' emotional response and allocated attention [30]. This suggests that gaze-responsive systems are perceived as being more human-like in their interactions and, hence, elicit more user-attention.

Computer systems can also rely on gaze inputs to assist users in accomplishing their task. In tutoring systems, the user's gaze information can be relied on by the system to determine when it is necessary to provide feedback and guidance to the user [10]. For example, patterns in gaze behavior could reveal that the user is confused by a given topic, which prompts the system to provide further guidance [34]. Learning new topics often involves reading provided material, such as a book, a document or even a simple time-table of a bus station. The connection between eye movements and reading has already been researched thoroughly [37, 38]. There exist psychologically plausible models that describe many phenomena in reading [24, 39].

In recent years, researchers built upon these findings to examine language proficiencies [31, 50], as well as develop systems that have educational purposes. These include e.g. real-time annotations [7, 3, 26] or translations during reading [48]. In this scenario the users' eye movements provide contextual information about what they are reading, how fast [28] or even how much they understand [21] and provide assistance accordingly [44, 22]. These systems showcase the capabilities of gaze-assisted language detection and/or translation. A vital part of real-time assistive systems is the exact point in time when to assist, e.g. by displaying a translation. Besides manual activation via gestures or being reliant on user profiles, we explore an implicit method that can be used for real-time interaction.

In our work, we adopt the paradigm of real-time gaze analysis to enable interactive systems that react upon the user's gaze as well as utilize the research findings on reading processes. We aim to combine the real-time properties of gaze-contingent displays with the inherently longer lasting process of recognizing the users understanding based on their reading patterns.

[1]Electrooculography

In contrast to past work on proficiency analysis, we propose a method than only relies on a short sentence in the respective language, hence enabling interactive interfaces. In our study, we evaluate the feasibility and accuracy of language proficiency detection on information displays.

METHOD

For our study design, we considered previous research findings on eye movements and reading to identify gaze characteristics that could be viable candidates for inferring language proficiency in our application context.

Research reports an average duration for fixations of about 200*ms* to 250*ms* and an average saccade length of 7 to 9 letters, but fixation durations can range from 50*ms* to 500*ms* depending on the context of the task and user state. Pertinently, the fixation durations increase with conceptually more difficult text, leading us to hypothesize that fixation durations should vary with a user's language proficiency. In addition, text difficulty is reported to correlate with saccade length as well as the frequency of saccade regressions[2] and refixations. Hence, "difficult" languages should exhibit lower saccade length and a higher frequency[3] of regressions and refixations. [37, 16]

Moreover, blink rate and pupil diameters have been reported to be associated with cognitive load and human information processing. For example, Siegle et al. [46] demonstrated a phasic increase of blinks prior and pursuant to the anticipation of an increase in the load of information processing, which was manipulated with basic psychological tests (i.e., Stroop task, digit-sorting task). Pupil dilation, on the other hand, reflected sustained information processing, over longer periods.

Based on these previous findings, we formulate our first research question:

RQ1: Can we determine whether a user is able to use the interface in a given language from gaze properties available by a gaze tracker?

To implement a real-time and language-aware user interface, it is vital that the system is able to tell a user's proficiency in the display language in a mere seconds. This implies that the users should only be presented with at most a few sentences of an unknown language before the system decides on the respective proficiency. This is the basis for the second research question:

RQ2: Can we determine whether a user understands the current interface language fast enough to build efficient language-aware interfaces? If so, what are the technical requirements?

Based on these questions, we investigate the following hypotheses in our study:

H1: Increased language proficiency level will result in a lower average gaze fixation duration.

H2: Increased language proficiency level will decrease the number of refixations in a given time period.

[2]Saccades opposite to the reading direction

[3]Standard frequency is about 10 to 15%.

Lower average gaze fixation duration as well as lower refixation ratio is connected to text difficulty when reading [37]. In our study we aim to vary text difficulty by changing the display language, hence creating several different text difficulty levels. Participants should therefore find it easier to answer questions in their proficient languages.

H3: Increased language proficiency level will increase the average blink duration.

H4: Increased language proficiency level will increase the total blink ratio.

Proficient users of a language should experience lower cognitive load during reading than non-proficient users. We assume that this increases blink duration and total blink ratio when presented with a language in which the user is proficient. During unknown languages cognitive load increases as the user is trying to figure out the question, hence blinks are less frequent.

If we reflect on one primary use case – public displays in commuting areas – the user usually looks for predefined information (e.g. bus departure, flight details). The method of presenting this information is often ordered and predictable, such as a time-table, and does not change across languages. Yet this is of no help for the user if he cannot locate the name of his destination or instructions for the payment process.

Information like this is expressed in simple sentences as well as simple language, to ensure readability. Hence, we chose our questions to be of "Basic User" ([8], p. 23) level with regard to the *Common European Framework of Reference for Languages* (CEFR) [8]. This framework defines six levels of foreign language proficiency: basic (A1, A2), independent (B1, B2) and proficient user (C1, C2) [8]. For our study we added an extra non-proficient level (X).

We collected questions in 13 different languages (15 questions each). By choosing to display simple questions to the participants, we provide an engaging task [20] as reading the text is required to answer correctly. The respective translations were provided by either native or highly proficient users of that language. Table 1 shows a few example questions. Most are part of the Indo-European language family [9], yet we included some outliers such as Finnish and Hungarian as well as languages not using the Latin alphabet (Greek, Arabic) to analyze their effect. See Table 2 for a complete overview on the used languages and the respective proficiency levels exhibited by our participants.

Participants

We recruited twenty-nine participants from the University of Stuttgart and the Stuttgart Media University via mailing lists. The data of 21 participants (12 females, age: 19-36 years) were used for further analysis. The eye-tracking data of three participants were removed because glasses and make-up interfered with the reliability of eye-movement recording. We excluded the data of five more participants, as the recording was not stable enough during the whole study[4]. Two participants had prior experience with eye-tracking studies. Out of the 21 participants, 17 were native German readers, two were native

[4]Participants started to move more towards the end of the study.

Language	Example questions	
English	How many days are within a week?	What is the first letter of your first name?
French	Combien de jours y a-t-il dans une semaine?	Quelle est la première lettre de votre prénom?
Danish	Hvor mange dage er der i en uge?	Hvad er det første bogstav i dit fornavn?
Finnish	Kuinka monta päivää on viikossa?	Mikä on etunimesi ensimmäinen kirjain?

Table 1. Example questions used in our study in four different languages.

Language	Proficiencies of participants
English	B2, C1, C2
German	X, B2, C1, C2
Danish	X
Dutch	X, A1
Finnish	X
French	X, A1, A2, B1, B2
Greek	X, A1, C1
Romanian	X
Spanish	X, A1, A2, B1, C2
Turkish	X
Slovenian	X
Arabic	X, A1
Hungarian	X

Table 2. Languages used in this study and respective proficiencies present in our participant base.

English readers as well as one native Spanish and Indonesian participant. All participants had normal or corrected-to-normal vision. Each participant was paid an allowance of 10 Euros.

Apparatus

Our setup consisted of a 22 inch LCD display (resolution: 1680x1050) and a remote eye tracker (SMI RED 250; 250Hz sampling frequency) that was positioned below the display. Our participants were seated at a distance that felt comfortable for them and well within the reliable tracking range of the system ($0.5\,m - 0.7\,m$) in an enclosed cubicle. Figure 2 shows a picture of the apparatus.

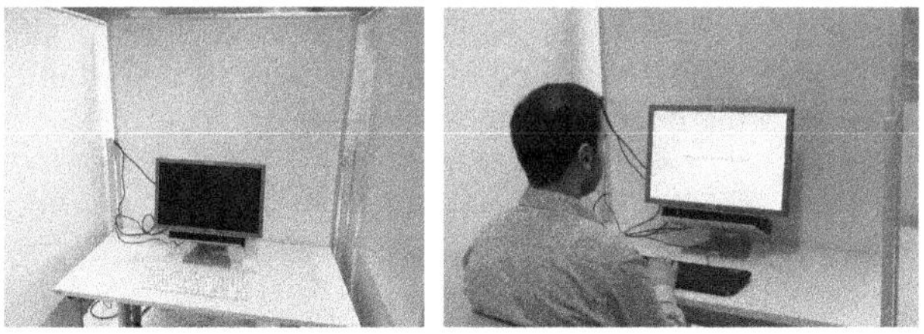

Figure 2. Apparatus showing LCD monitor with attached eye tracking device and participant during the study.

Procedure

After introducing the prospective participants to our study, we handed them a detailed study description. It stated to follow on-screen instructions worded as simple questions, that each require a single key-press to answer. The study description sheet additionally contained an example question. Prospective participants were made aware to expect these questions in different languages and to answer to the best of their knowledge, yet favoring correctness over speed. The respective answer could be given in any preferred language[5]. If a question was impossible to answer, prospective participants were made aware not to press anything and wait for the next question. Timings between each question (10 seconds) and the overall study time (two session of 12.5 minutes each) were provided on the information sheet. The available answer time of 10 seconds per question was conservatively chosen, preventing unnecessary pressure due to lack of time. After providing informed consent, the participants were asked to complete a demographic questionnaire, polling sex, age, work field, highest educational qualification, their native language and their eyesight. They also rated their reading level for specific languages based on the provided CEFR's self-assessment test[6] ([8], pp. 26-27). Additionally, the participants were asked to provide their proficiency level for languages that were not listed. The experimenter was present to answer any questions that might arise.

Before starting the experiment, the eye tracking device was calibrated using a five-point calibration. We only accepted calibration accuracy below one degree of visual angle. During the experiment, we sequentially displayed 150 questions to the participants, in random order. Each question was visible for exactly ten seconds and could be answered by a single key press, such as one letter or one number (see Table 1). Participant keystrokes were collected during this period. The experiment was conducted in two sessions of 12.5 minutes with an intervening rest period. It was possible to ask questions during the experiment, which occurred two times. The respective experiment question was hence marked for deletion. Before resuming with session two, another calibration analog to the start of the experiment was performed. Ethical approval for this study was obtained from the Ethics Committee at the University of Konstanz.

Post-processing

We applied the following post processing steps to the obtained eye-tracking data including event detection[7] using a velocity-based fixation algorithm [41] with a velocity threshold of 35 degrees of visual angle per second and blink detection based on pupil diameter change. Eye movement events were allocated to the respective question and any data after the point in time when the participants provided an answer for the respective question, as indicated by the recorded keystrokes, was discarded. Note that we did not distinguish between wrong

[5] E.g. answering in one's native language or in English.

[6] If needed. Most participants were familiar with the framework and provided information based on language tests.

[7] utilizing the SMI Event Detector

and correct answers, since language proficiency as stated by the participants was used as ground truth. We observed a mean answer time for all participants of 4.9 seconds with a standard deviation of 0.2 seconds. Thus, we conservatively limited the overall observation time for each question to a maximum of 4.5 seconds. Additionally, we discarded fixations with durations, less than $50ms$ and more than $600ms$, that were outside the range of reported values in reading research [37, 38, 43].

Measures

All measures were collected on a per question basis. We derived the following metrics from the eye tracking data. For fixations, we examined the average fixation duration. We also recorded refixations that occurred when the user's gaze revisited the location of a previous fixation. This area was bounded by a 30 pixel radius[8] around the previous fixation's location. The chosen radius is a conservative interpretation of the distance of consecutive fixations during reading [37]. The amount of refixations was normalized by the total fixation count for the respective question (refixation ratio).

For blinks, we calculated average duration as well. Total blink ratio relates the total blink duration to the respective answer time of each question.

All the measures were grouped by the reported language proficiency based on the CEFR [8]. Hence, we end up with seven groups: non-proficient (X), basic user (A1, A2), independent user (B1, B2) and proficient user (C1, C2).

Results

As mentioned before, we looked at data available after having interacted with the screen for a maximum of 4.5 seconds or the user's respective answer time, whichever was shorter. Sample size did vary for different metrics, e.g. if the user did not blink during one particular question.

Average Fixation Duration (AFD)

The grand mean of AFD was $239.86ms$ ($SD = 53.22ms$). Participants with C2 proficiency in the tested language exhibited the shortest average fixation durations ($M = 194.02ms$, $SD = 37.24ms$) while no knowledge of a given language produced the longest fixations ($M = 249.19ms$, $SD = 53.04ms$). As all metrics in our experiment are unevenly distributed in terms of proficiencies (participants have varying levels of proficiency in different languages), we decided to compute the slope coefficient for each of the participants using ordinal logistic regression. We then conducted a t-test comparing the obtained slope coefficients with a constant function. The test shows that language proficiency has a significant effect on AFD, $t(20) = -3.78$, $p < 0.01$.

Refixation Ratio (RFR)

The grand mean of RFR was 0.24 ($SD = 0.15$). Participants with C2 proficiency in the tested language exhibited the lowest refixation ratio ($M = 0.15$, $SD = 0.13$) while participants who did not know the given language had the highest ratio ($M = 0.26$, $SD = 0.15$). Analogously to AFD, slope coefficients

[8] Covers roughly 1-2 letters.

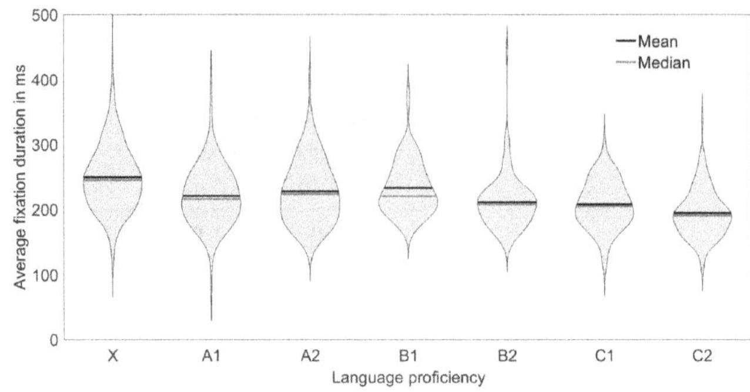

Figure 3. Violin plot showing the distribution of the average fixation duration (AFD) grouped by proficiency according to CEFR [8].

were computed and compared with $y = 0$ using a t-test. The test showed that language proficiency had a significant effect on RFR, $t(20) = -2.48$, $p < 0.05$.

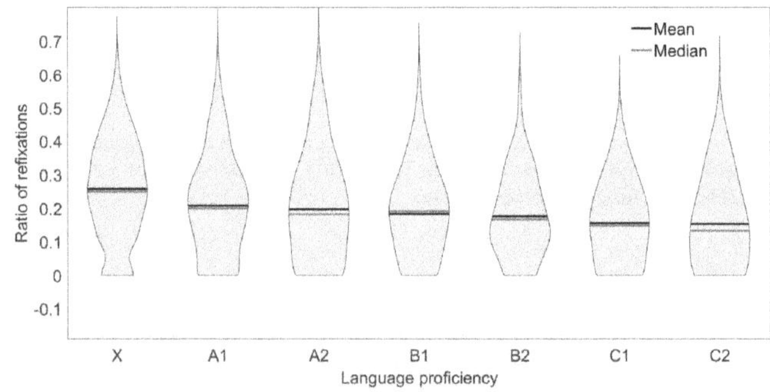

Figure 4. Violin plot showing the distribution of refixation count per overall fixation count (RFR) grouped by proficiency according to CEFR [8].

Average Blink Duration (ABD)

The grand mean of ABD was $413.47ms$ ($SD = 395.52ms$). Participants with C2 proficiency in the tested language exhibited the longest average blink time ($M = 752.05ms$, $SD = 391.00ms$) while participants who did not know the given language blinked the shortest ($M = 306.41ms$, $SD = 332.29ms$). Again, we calculated slope coefficients for each participant and used a t-test to compare with no slope yielding a result of $t(20) = 2.71$, $p < 0.05$. Figure 5 shows the distribution of average blink durations.

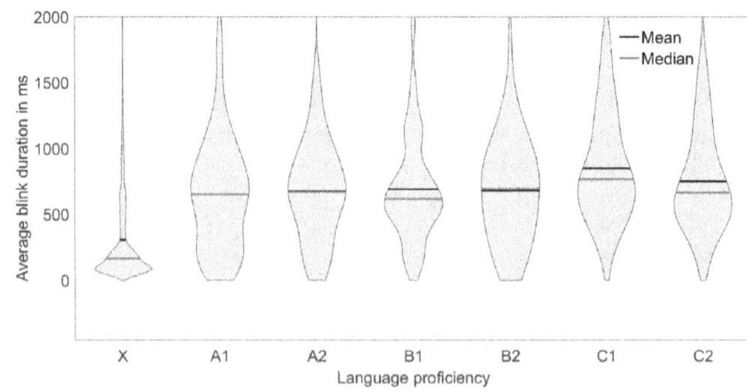

Figure 5. Violin plot showing the distribution of the average blink duration (ABD) grouped by proficiency according to CEFR [8].

Total Blink Ratio (TBR)

The grand mean of TBR was 0.15 ($SD = 0.14$). Participants with C2 proficiency in the tested language exhibited the highest total blink ratio ($M = 0.30$, $SD = 0.14$) while participants who did not know the given language had the lowest ratio ($M = 0.11$, $SD = 0.11$). Using a method analogous to the previous metrics, we obtained $t(20) = 2.75$, $p < 0.05$. Figure 6 shows the distribution of total blink ratio.

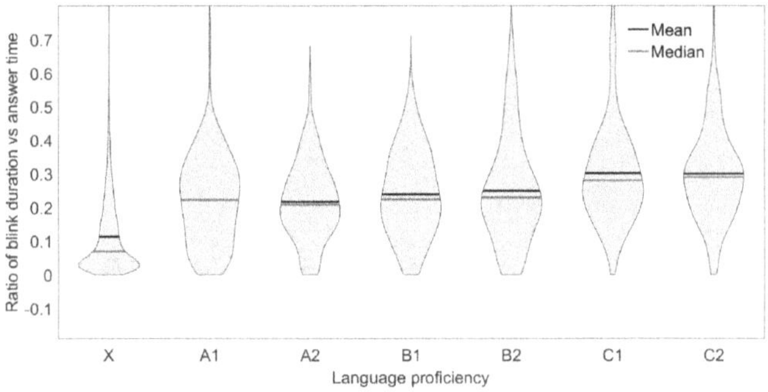

Figure 6. Violin plot showing the distribution of the ratio given total blink duration and answer time (TBR) grouped by proficiency according to CEFR [8].

Result Interpretation and Implications

Statistics on average fixation duration and refixation ratio showed a significant effect of language proficiency on all metrics. We conclude that increased language proficiency levels will result in a lower AFD and a lower RFR (as t-scores are negative). This confirms **H1** and **H2**.

Our results indicate that average blink duration and total blink ratio were significant metrics as well, confirming **H3** and **H4**. However, standard deviation was also quite high for these metrics, which might lead to unstable classification results. Especially for proficient levels (A to C), blink duration is quite high compared to values found in literature [20]. This could be due to participants "relaxing" during easy questions, which relates to longer blink durations [20]. Nevertheless, simple blink detection (e.g. via a RGB camera) could be an alternative for systems where eye tracking is not feasible.

Our statistical analysis indicates that we can provide a positive answer to **RQ1**. All metrics showed a significant difference for non-proficient vs proficient users (except the B1 level), indicating that our approach is feasible. In other words, pur experiment shows that the eye gaze metrics we chose do carry information about language comprehension.

The second research question (**RQ2**) concerned the technical requirements of applying such an approach to language-aware interfaces. In the next section, we pursue **RQ2** further by implementing classifiers for language proficiency detection.

BUILDING A LANGUAGE-AWARE SYSTEM

In the previous sections, we evaluated the statistic relevance of certain metrics extracted from our eye-tracking data. AFD, ABD, TBR and RFR showed promising results in discerning proficiency levels. Yet, to realize systems that support real-time detection of language proficiency it is necessary to find a discriminative feature set that defines certain proficiency levels. Ideally, we want the margin between neighboring levels as large as possible and choose these levels based on the application scenario. In this section, we provide answers to our second research question and evaluate the needed technical requirements for language-aware interfaces.

We highlight specific factors that need to be considered when implementing such an adaptive display. From an HCI perspective, we want to maximize the user experience when interacting with the system such as providing assistance when needed and only when needed. Furthermore, an interactive system should be able to provide feedback in a reasonable time span. Ideally, it should not take longer than a few seconds for the system to make a decision. From a technical standpoint, we might need to consider limitations that may arise with the application scenario, such as low-cost hardware that will result in noisy data. As such we tested our findings on an artificially downsampled dataset.

Baseline Classifier

Based on our previous results, we decided to train a binary classifier that predicts whether people are not proficient or proficient (levels A to C) in the displayed languages. This choice conforms with our aspired application scenario in two ways. Firstly, public displays such as timetables exhibits "predictable information" [8] that can be read by a basic language user (A level proficiency). Hence, the choice to include all proficiency levels into one class seems reasonable. Secondly, overeager assistance systems tend to be rejected by the users. To achieve a good user experience, minimizing false proficiency classification on proficient users should therefore be a primary goal.

We constructed a dataset containing the following features from our eye-tracking data as described in the previous sections: average fixation duration (AFD), refixation ratio (RFR), average blink duration (ABD) and total blink ratio (TBR). We used the same maximum observation time as before (4.5 seconds). After balancing the class distribution, we evaluated the dataset using 10-fold cross validation on four different common classifiers[9]. All classifiers were executed with standard parameters. An overview on achieved accuracy is given in Table 3.

	J48	SVM	NN	BayesNet
Accuracy	78.3%	64.9%	78.8%	77.6%
F-Measure	78.3%	64.3%	78.8%	77.6%

Table 3. Accuracies and F-Measures for selected classifiers.

While most classifiers exhibited a similar average accuracy, it is vital in our case to report the false positive rate (FPR) of each class. As mentioned before, our primary goal was to keep the ratio of falsely classifying proficient users (classified as non-proficient) to a minimum, while our secondary goal was

[9] J48: Java derivate of C4.5 [35]
SVM: LibLINEAR package. L2-loss (dual form) [13]
Neural network: MultiLayer Perceptron [18]
BayesNet: Bayesian network [18]

to maximize true positive rate (TPR) of either class. Table 4 shows more detailed descriptive statistics on the decision tree J48, including false and true positive rate for both classes. This allows us to spot irregularities that may arise between classification accuracy of the two classes.

Class	TPR	FPR	Precision	Recall
NP	75.4%	18.8%	80.0%	75.4%
P	81.2%	24.6%	76.8%	81.2%

Table 4. Classifier statistics on J48 given proficient users (class P) and non-proficient users (class NP).

True positive rate was higher for the class of proficient language users (class P), yet this came with a higher false positive rate as well. In other words, in 24.6% of cases we wrongly classify a non-proficient user (class NP) as being proficient. Of course this is inconvenient for the user as he will not be provided with the needed assistance. However, our primary goal was to keep the false positive rate of the class of non-proficient users to a minimum. In the standard configuration J48 misclassified 18.8% of all instances as non-proficient when they were in fact instances of proficient users. Hence, the system would attempt to provide assistance although the user would be able to read the given language, which is undesirable and has a negative impact on user experience.

Figure 7 illustrates the top three levels of the resulting tree model[10]. Average blink duration is used as a first separation step. After just two tests (on ABD and AFD) almost 32%[11] of instances are correctly assigned to the non-proficient class (3.6% are wrongly classified in this step). The built tree exhibits several of these "heavy" leaves that carry most of the instances. This indicates that pruning may be a meaningful strategy.

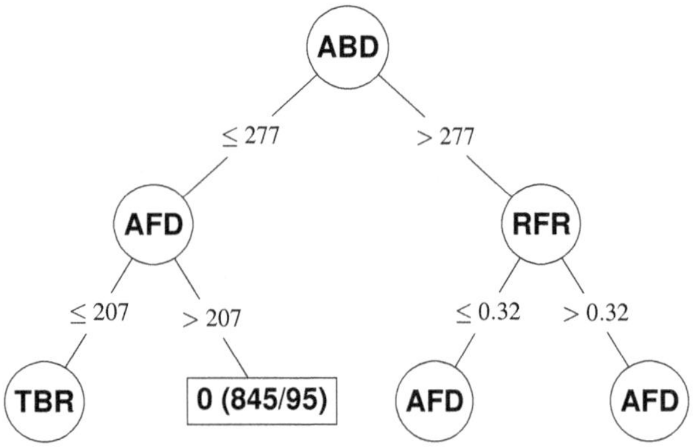

Figure 7. Top three levels of the built decision tree using J48 with standard parameters. ABD and AFD are given in milliseconds; TBR and RFR are given as ratios. Leaf nodes (rectangles) indicate predicted class (0 for NP; 1 for P) and show (correctly classified/misclassified) instances. Values are rounded for visual clarity.

A more heavily pruned tree is shown in Figure 8, basing its decision on only three remaining features (ABD, RFR and AFD), while still achieving 77.64% accuracy. Additionally, true and false positive rate of each class do not change by more than two percentage points, indicating that heavy pruning is indeed a valid option. This avoids overfitting to the training set and may generalize better for unseen data.

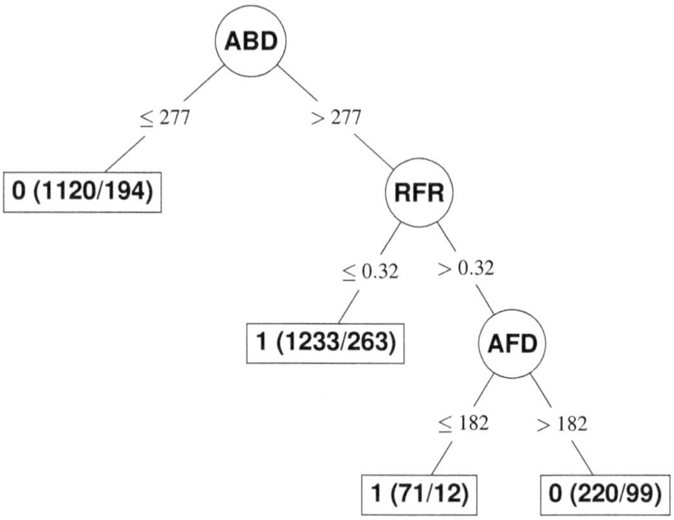

Figure 8. Complete decision tree using J48 and heavy pruning. ABD and AFD are given in milliseconds; RFR is given as ratio. Leaf nodes (rectangles) indicate predicted class (0 for NP; 1 for P) and show (correctly classified/misclassified) instances. Values are rounded for visual clarity.

Cost-Sensitive Classifier

To further reduce the false positive rate of the non-proficient class, we introduced a different cost function for the classifier. We penalized classifying proficient users as non-proficient more severely. This is a compromise between maximizing overall classification accuracy (results shown in Table 3 and Table 4) and minimizing the false positive rate of one class. We decided that not more than one out of ten users should be wrongly classified as non-proficient. To achieve this goal, misclassifying a proficient user had to be three times more expensive than misclassifying a non-proficient user. Table 5 shows the results after applying such a function.

Class	TPR	FPR	Precision	Recall
NP	58.9%	9.90%	85.6%	58.9%
P	90.1%	41.1%	77.1%	74.5%

Table 5. Classifier statistics on cost-sensitive J48 (standard parameters) given proficient users (class P) and non-proficient users (class NP).

Overall accuracy dropped only slightly to 74.5%, yet the gap between the true positive rate of both classes increased. While TPR of the proficient class increased[12], the TPR of the non-proficient class decreased to 58.9%. It was now more expensive to classify as non-proficient, hence it was safer to classify as proficient. The same applied for the false positive rates. We successfully pushed the FPR of the non-proficient class to below 10%, yet this also meant that the FPR of the proficient class increased and fewer users were to get the needed assistance.

[10]using J48 and standard parameters

[11]845 out of a total of 2643 instances

[12]It was more likely to classify an instance as proficient.

Class Distribution

Generally, it is important to adjust the cost function based on the scenario and think about how to penalize wrong classifications. Besides the cost function, the distribution of instances into respective classes is vital. In a different scenario, such as displaying advertisements on public displays, it is more favorable to emphasize highly proficient users. Since using puns in advertisements to spark the interest of potential customers is a common technique, aiming for a binary classifier that separates C-level language users from other users is more beneficial. If the users do not understand the display pun due to their proficiency level being too low, it seems reasonable to combine them with the non-proficient users. Table 6 shows classification results for a grouping into the classes highly-proficient HP (C1 and C2) and less-proficient LP (X, A1, A2, B1 and B2). Overall accuracy was 79.3%. The false positive rate for both classes was around 21%. Again, we can ask ourselves whether misclassifying one class is more severe than the other and adjust a cost function as we see fit.

Class	TPR	FPR	Precision	Recall
LP	79.2%	20.6%	79.3%	79.2%
HP	79.4%	20.8%	79.2%	79.4%

Table 6. Classifier statistics on J48 with different class distribution: highly-proficient (class HP: C1 and C2) and less-proficient (class LP: X, A1, A2, B1 and B2) users. Levels according to [8].

Recording Duration

As outlined previously, fast responsiveness and interactivity are vital for an adaptive information display. Hence, we evaluated a minimum recording duration that allowed for a sensible classification of non-proficient users. For this purpose, we limited the maximum observation time for our dataset in one second intervals from one to five seconds[13]. Figure 9 shows accuracy as well as true and false positive rate over time.

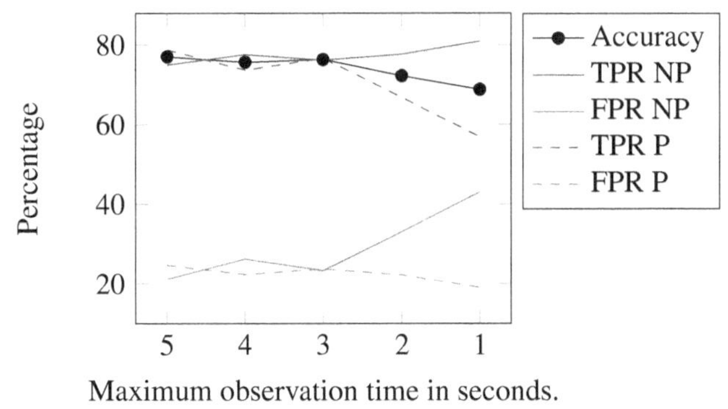

Figure 9. Accuracy, true and false positive rate of proficient (class P: A1 to C2) and non-proficient (class NP: X) class given different maximum observation times of recorded gaze data.

The classifier metrics did not change much when reducing the maximum observation time to only three seconds. After that, we saw a strong increase in the false positive rate of class NP. Further investigation revealed that the classes exhibit a strong overlap, thus making accurate classification difficult. We believe that this is due to the reduced sample size, hence allowing noise in the recording to have a larger influence.

Hardware Limitations

In this study, we used a high-quality eye-tracking device with a sampling rate of $250Hz$. However, eye-trackers for commercial product integration can be expected to have lower sampling rates. To evaluate the viability of our approach for its stated purpose, we downsampled[14] our recording data to the following sampling rates $125Hz$, $62.5Hz$ and $31.25Hz$, which approximated the sampling rates of low-cost eye-tracking devices.

Reducing sampling rate introduces noise in the event (e.g. fixation, saccades) detection of eye-movement behavior. Here, we showed the effects for the average fixation duration. A classification accuracy of 64.7% was achieved from the original sampled data (i.e., $250Hz$). Figure 10 illustrates how classification accuracy, as well as true and false positive rate for each class, varied when decreasing the sampling rate.

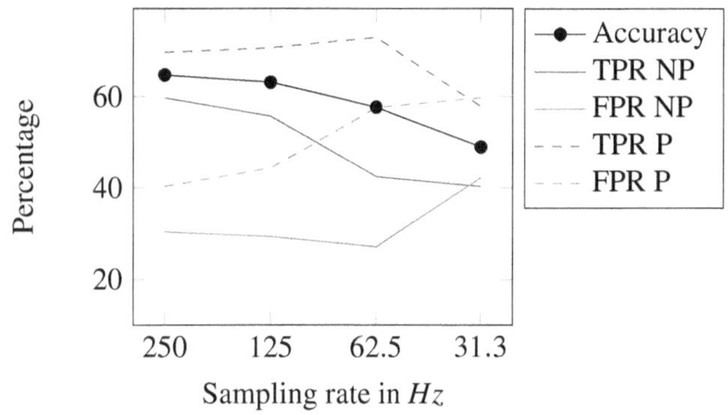

Figure 10. Accuracy, true and false positive rate of proficient (class P: A1 to C2) and non-proficient (class NP: X) class given different sampling rates of the underlying gaze dataset (logarithmic scale).

Sampling at a rate of $125Hz$ had only minor influence on the classification results. Further downsampling drastically reduced true positive rate of class NP (FPR of class P increases), yet the false positive rate of the non-proficient class stayed constant. Hence, at a sampling rate of $62.5Hz$ detecting a non-proficient speaker correctly was less likely. For the lowest sampling rate $31.25Hz$, FPR for the non-proficient class strongly increased. At this rate, a sample was obtained every 32ms, which was about the mean difference that we found between the two classes (NP and P) at high sampling rates. Thus, temporal downsampling rendered information between categories less discriminable and sensible classification was not possible at this resolution.

DISCUSSION

Through the initial statistical analysis and our investigation of how to build classifiers using our data set, we have shown that rapid automated detection of language comprehension is possible. The data we extracted from the user's gaze enables

[13]Before then our dataset used a maximum observation time of 4.5 seconds

[14]By omitting every n-th sample.

us to reliably predict their proficiency in a given language. It needs to be noted that our proposed classifiers operate on a coarse level. Their primary purpose is to determine whether the user is able to understand the interface presented in a given language. More sophisticated methods and larger gaze pattern samples are still required to estimate exact proficiency levels, as shown in previous work.

We can conclude that the answer to **RQ2** is positive — it is possible to build a reliable automated system that will promptly detect whether a user is able to comprehend the content presented in a given interface. An emergent question is how these systems can be used in practice and what technical prerequisites are needed for deployment. Below, we further elaborate on **RQ2** by providing a set of four technical guidelines for implementing language-aware systems that use gaze data.

Guidelines for Language-Aware Interfaces

Based on our classification analysis, we propose the following technical guidelines for interfaces that are to be designed to be aware of the user's language proficiencies.

Firstly, we recommend that designers of future systems **adapt the cost function of the classifier as well as the class distribution to their particular application**. The application scenario highly influences classification accuracy, as we have shown when grouping different proficiency levels for binary classification. Fine-grained detection down to the proficiency levels of the CEFR [8] did not deliver satisfying accuracy. Cost functions can be introduced to better fit the use case scenario. Here, a compromise has to be made between a more eager assistance system and a more rigorous one. Depending on the application scenario, one might opt for either direction. Besides adjusting the cost function, changing the class distribution is also a possibility, e.g. when considering advertisement banners instead of public displays in an airport. Hence, determining whether a user is able to use an interface in a given language from gaze properties is entirely possible. Achieved accuracy depends on the application scenario and the selected proficiency levels. If fine-grained detection and high accuracy is needed, e.g. in an language education software that observes the learning process of a student, other sources of context should be used in conjunction, while eye tracking can provide an auxiliary input.

Secondly, we suggest **a minimum interaction period of three seconds and a sampling rate not less than 100 Hz**, while lower rates might still be applicable for specific scenarios. In our study, we evaluated how long and how often a language-aware interface should record eye movements of interacting users. Higher resolution or longer recording duration only slightly improve classification results. These findings confirm the feasibility for language-aware interfaces in public displays, as "calibration time" is short enough for user interaction and sampling rate is not too high for low-cost eye-tracking devices.

Especially for public displays or similar interfaces, we recommend to **ensure that light sources do not interfere with the recording**. Locations of public displays are diverse in lighting and environmental conditions. Bad lighting can lead to artifacts during gaze recording and hinder classification. This hardly poses a problem in buildings or underground, yet displays positioned outside can be problematic due to the infrared radiation from the sun. Gaze recording that does not rely on infrared video-based eye trackers can solve this problem, if the technique is accurate enough. In combination with regression-based models [4], it is possible to explicitly learn for distinct gaze characteristics such as fixations, circumventing the need for accurate gaze data in the first place.

Finally, we remind designers to **guide the user into a suitable interaction range**. Reliable tracking is possible only within a rather limited sweet spot. Solutions to solve this problem have already been shown in *GazeHorizon* [52] and *GravitySpot* [1]. If eye-tracking is to be used in a public display scenario, additional challenges need to be considered [33].

Limitations

The scope of the current work addresses how gaze features are discriminable for language proficiency. An adaptive language-aware interface should consider additional probabilistic priors. In this regard, we feel that modifications to our current classification approach (e.g., by adding a "location prior"[15]) holds promise for subsequent work. However, we verified that proficiency in a given language could not generalize to proficiency in related languages[16]. Hence, further research has to be conducted to evaluate different language-switching mechanisms with regard to user experience and accuracy. Design guidelines can serve to constrain the diversity of interaction behavior, increase the predictability of desired behavior, which will render interactions more predictable. If gaze behavior is predictable based on screen content, e.g. predominantly horizontal saccades when reading text vs a search pattern when viewing pictures, the constraints on calibration accuracy are less severe and interaction might be possible without prior per-user calibration. Detecting blinks and fixations – as used in our metrics – is feasible using only relative gaze data.

In our study, we used a set of languages that reflected the possible linguistic abilities of our participant base. We mostly selected languages that are spoken in Europe. However, we believe that as long as reading direction and alphabet are kept the same, the results of our study are reproducible with other languages. Even reading direction might have only a minor influence [37]. Statistics on whether the alphabet was a confounding factor (e.g. Arabic, Greek) have shown that there was no significant difference on the four metrics discussed previously. Nevertheless, this was a subjective result based on the subset of our used languages.

Another limiting factor was the uneven distribution of proficiency levels. Naturally, we had a lot of data samples for non-proficient users, but missed out on proficient levels. B1-level proficiency was especially rare among the participants.

Based on the application scenario, participants might react differently. For example, when on a stressful trip figuring out

[15]E.g. emphasizing predominant languages at the system's deploy location.

[16]By comparing metrics for German C2 speakers between German and Dutch.

their next connection on an information display versus reading questions during a calm lab study. This will likely introduce another noise factor that influences the resulting data. The nature of this noise and its impact in an in-the-wild system is to be evaluated. Consequently, before deployment, extensive pre-testing needs to be conducted for a particular interface to determine what comprehension levels are required in a given interaction scenario.

CONCLUSION AND FUTURE WORK

In this paper, we examined the perception of different languages and their influence on a person's eye movements. Contrary to common approaches in reading comprehension, which focused on post-hoc evaluations, we evaluated the feasibility of real-time language proficiency detection suitable for language-aware interfaces.

In our study, we presented 150 questions in different languages to our participants and analyzed the effect of language proficiency on certain gaze characteristics. We found that proficiency had a significant effect on the average fixation duration and refixation ratio as well as average blink duration and total blink ratio measured over a maximum timespan of 4.5 seconds.

To effectively utilize these results in real-time adaptive information displays, we proposed a classification scheme that realizes language proficiency detection and recommended technical guidelines on recording duration and sampling rate of the eye-tracking device. Moreover, if gaze behavior is predictable based on screen content, constraints on calibration accuracy are less severe. Hence, it is well suited to be used in public displays where "walk-up" interaction is required [33]. Additionally, it enables the usage of less accurate and cheap eye tracking devices as exact gaze position is not necessary. We contributed a set of four technical guidelines for deploying gaze-based language-aware systems. We hope that these guidelines will help designers build real-life systems that detect when the user does not understand the interface language.

Further work that can benefit from our results includes techniques for language switching. New approaches can attempt providing a broader selection of initial languages, i.e. displaying multiple languages at once or traversing a language tree based on probabilistic "location priors" that allows fine-grained proficiency classification. The user's initial language choice – given by the first gaze position – and the reading direction enables alphabet detection. Yet, utilizing exact gaze position would require a per-user calibrated eye-tracking device. Here, new methods on implicit calibration relying on predicted gaze targets [25] or smooth pursuit as shown in *TextPursuits* [27] are applicable. If access to fully calibrated gaze data is available, more elaborate comparing methods are possible, such as directly comparing scanpaths [14, 23] or clustering approaches [42]. To foster research in this direction, the data set is available to the research community for further analysis and improvement on our institute's homepage[17].

[17]http://www.hcilab.org/publications/

We envision that our idea of real-time adaptive information displays is not only applicable to language awareness, but also holds true for higher level concepts, such as different forms of graph visualizations, schematics or maps. This does imply that such a system recognizes a user's level of understanding and it is able to switch to an appropriate visualization to assist the user. We hope that our work will inspire further developments that will yield more understanding on how gaze properties can be used to build more efficient adaptive interfaces.

ACKNOWLEDGEMENTS

We thank all colleagues and friends that provided us with the necessary language translations. This research is financially supported by the German Research Foundation (DFG) within the projects C02, C03 and task force TF3 of SFB/Transregio 161 and supported by the SimTech Cluster of Excellence. Part of this research was supported by the European Union's Horizon 2020 Programme under ERCEA grant no. 683008 AMPLIFY.

REFERENCES

1. Florian Alt, Andreas Bulling, Gino Gravanis, and Daniel Buschek. 2015. GravitySpot: Guiding Users in Front of Public Displays Using On-Screen Visual Cues. In *Proceedings of the 28th Annual ACM Symposium on User Interface Software & Technology (UIST '15)*. ACM, New York, NY, USA, 47–56. DOI: http://dx.doi.org/10.1145/2807442.2807490
2. Florian Alt, Alireza Sahami Shirazi, Albrecht Schmidt, and Julian Mennenöh. 2012. Increasing the User's Attention on the Web: Using Implicit Interaction Based on Gaze Behavior to Tailor Content. In *Proceedings of the 7th Nordic Conference on Human-Computer Interaction: Making Sense Through Design (NordiCHI '12)*. ACM, New York, NY, USA, 544–553. DOI: http://dx.doi.org/10.1145/2399016.2399099
3. Ralf Biedert, Georg Buscher, Sven Schwarz, Jörn Hees, and Andreas Dengel. 2010. Text 2.0. In *CHI '10 Extended Abstracts on Human Factors in Computing Systems (CHI EA '10)*. ACM, New York, NY, USA, 4003–4008. DOI: http://dx.doi.org/10.1145/1753846.1754093
4. Björn Browatzki, Heinrich H. Bülthoff, and Lewis L. Chuang. 2014. A Comparison of Geometric- and Regression-Based Mobile Gaze-Tracking. *Frontiers in Human Neuroscience* 8 (April 2014). DOI: http://dx.doi.org/10.3389/fnhum.2014.00200
5. Andreas Bulling, Daniel Roggen, and Gerhard Tröster. 2008. It's in Your Eyes: Towards Context-Awareness and Mobile HCI Using Wearable EOG Goggles. In *Proceedings of the 10th International Conference on Ubiquitous Computing (UbiComp '08)*. ACM, New York, NY, USA, 84–93. DOI: http://dx.doi.org/10.1145/1409635.1409647
6. Andreas Bulling, Jamie A. Ward, Hans Gellersen, and Gerhard Tröster. 2009. Eye Movement Analysis for Activity Recognition. In *Proceedings of the 11th International Conference on Ubiquitous Computing*

(UbiComp '09). ACM, New York, NY, USA, 41–50. DOI: http://dx.doi.org/10.1145/1620545.1620552

7. Shiwei Cheng, Zhiqiang Sun, Lingyun Sun, Kirsten Yee, and Anind K. Dey. 2015. Gaze-Based Annotations for Reading Comprehension. In *Proceedings of the 33rd Annual ACM Conference on Human Factors in Computing Systems (CHI '15)*. ACM, New York, NY, USA, 1569–1572. DOI: http://dx.doi.org/10.1145/2702123.2702271
8. Council of Europe. 2001. *Common European Framework of Reference for Languages: Learning, Teaching, Assessment*. Cambridge University Press.
9. Guy Deutscher. 2006. *The Unfolding of Language: An Evolutionary Tour of Mankind's Greatest Invention*. Henry Holt and Company.
10. Sidney D'Mello, Andrew Olney, Claire Williams, and Patrick Hays. 2012. Gaze Tutor: A Gaze-Reactive Intelligent Tutoring System. *International Journal of Human-Computer Studies* 70, 5 (May 2012), 377–398. DOI:http://dx.doi.org/10.1016/j.ijhcs.2012.01.004
11. Heiko Drewes and Albrecht Schmidt. 2007. Interacting with the Computer Using Gaze Gestures. In *Proceedings of the 11th IFIP TC 13 International Conference on Human-Computer Interaction - Volume Part II (INTERACT'07)*. Springer-Verlag, Berlin, Heidelberg, 475–488. DOI: http://dx.doi.org/10.1007/978-3-540-74800-7_43
12. Andrew T. Duchowski, Nathan Cournia, and Hunter Murphy. 2004. Gaze-Contingent Displays: A Review. *Cyberpsychology & Behavior: The Impact of the Internet, Multimedia and Virtual Reality on Behavior and Society* 7, 6 (Dec. 2004), 621–634. DOI: http://dx.doi.org/10.1089/cpb.2004.7.621
13. Rong-En Fan, Kai-Wei Chang, Cho-Jui Hsieh, Xiang-Rui Wang, and Chih-Jen Lin. 2008. LIBLINEAR - A Library for Large Linear Classification. (2008). http://www.csie.ntu.edu.tw/~cjlin/liblinear/ The Weka classifier works with version 1.33 of LIBLINEAR.
14. Matt Feusner and Brian Lukoff. 2008. Testing for Statistically Significant Differences Between Groups of Scan Patterns. In *Proceedings of the 2008 Symposium on Eye Tracking Research & Applications (ETRA '08)*. ACM, 43–46. DOI:http://dx.doi.org/10.1145/1344471.1344481
15. Tom Foulsham, Joey T. Cheng, Jessica L. Tracy, Joseph Henrich, and Alan Kingstone. 2010. Gaze Allocation in a Dynamic Situation: Effects of Social Status and Speaking. *Cognition* 117, 3 (Dec. 2010), 319–331. DOI: http://dx.doi.org/10.1016/j.cognition.2010.09.003
16. Joseph H Goldberg and Xerxes P Kotval. 1999. Computer Interface Evaluation Using Eye Movements: Methods and Constructs. *International Journal of Industrial Ergonomics* 24, 6 (Oct. 1999), 631–645. DOI: http://dx.doi.org/10.1016/S0169-8141(98)00068-7
17. Brian Guenter, Mark Finch, Steven Drucker, Desney Tan, and John Snyder. 2012. Foveated 3D Graphics. *ACM Trans. Graph.* 31, 6 (Nov. 2012), 164:1–164:10. DOI: http://dx.doi.org/10.1145/2366145.2366183
18. Mark Hall, Eibe Frank, Geoffrey Holmes, Bernhard Pfahringer, Peter Reutemann, and Ian H. Witten. 2009. The WEKA Data Mining Software: An Update. *SIGKDD Explor. Newsl.* 11, 1 (Nov. 2009), 10–18. DOI: http://dx.doi.org/10.1145/1656274.1656278
19. Lotta Hirvenkari, Johanna Ruusuvuori, Veli-Matti Saarinen, Maari Kivioja, Anssi Peräkylä, and Riitta Hari. 2013. Influence of Turn-Taking in a Two-Person Conversation on the Gaze of a Viewer. *PLoS ONE* 8, 8 (Aug. 2013). DOI: http://dx.doi.org/10.1371/journal.pone.0071569
20. Kenneth Holmqvist, Marcus Nyström, Richard Andersson, Richard Dewhurst, Halszka Jarodzka, and Joost van de Weijer. 2011. *Eye Tracking: A Comprehensive Guide to Methods and Measures*. OUP Oxford.
21. Aulikki Hyrskykari, Päivi Majaranta, Antti Aaltonen, and Kari-Jouko Räihä. 2000. Design Issues of iDICT: A Gaze-Assisted Translation Aid. In *Proceedings of the 2000 Symposium on Eye Tracking Research & Applications (ETRA '00)*. ACM, New York, NY, USA, 9–14. DOI:http://dx.doi.org/10.1145/355017.355019
22. Aulikki Hyrskykari, Päivi Majaranta, and Kari-Jouko Räihä. 2003. Proactive Response to Eye Movements. In *INTERACT*, Vol. 3. IOS press Amsterdam, 129–136.
23. Halszka Jarodzka, Kenneth Holmqvist, and Marcus Nyström. 2010. A Vector-based, Multidimensional Scanpath Similarity Measure. In *Proceedings of the 2010 Symposium on Eye-Tracking Research & Applications (ETRA '10)*. ACM, 211–218. DOI: http://dx.doi.org/10.1145/1743666.1743718
24. Marcel A. Just and Patricia A. Carpenter. 1980. A Theory of Reading: From Eye Fixations to Comprehension. *Psychological review* 87, 4 (1980), 329.
25. Pawel Kasprowski and Katarzyna Harezlak. 2016. Implicit Calibration Using Predicted Gaze Targets. In *Proceedings of the Ninth Biennial ACM Symposium on Eye Tracking Research & Applications (ETRA '16)*. ACM, 245–248. DOI: http://dx.doi.org/10.1145/2857491.2857511
26. Dagmar Kern, Paul Marshall, and Albrecht Schmidt. 2010. Gazemarks: Gaze-Based Visual Placeholders to Ease Attention Switching. In *Proceedings of the SIGCHI Conference on Human Factors in Computing Systems (CHI '10)*. ACM, New York, NY, USA, 2093–2102. DOI: http://dx.doi.org/10.1145/1753326.1753646
27. Mohamed Khamis, Ozan Saltuk, Alina Hang, Katharina Stolz, Andreas Bulling, and Florian Alt. 2016. TextPursuits: Using Text for Pursuits-Based Interaction and Calibration on Public Displays. In *Proceedings of the 2016 ACM International Joint Conference on Pervasive and Ubiquitous Computing (UbiComp '16)*. ACM, New York, NY, USA, 274–285. DOI: http://dx.doi.org/10.1145/2971648.2971679

28. Kai Kunze, Katsutoshi Masai, Masahiko Inami, Ömer Sacakli, Marcus Liwicki, Andreas Dengel, Shoya Ishimaru, and Koichi Kise. 2015. Quantifying Reading Habits: Counting How Many Words You Read. In *Proceedings of the 2015 ACM International Joint Conference on Pervasive and Ubiquitous Computing (UbiComp '15)*. ACM, New York, NY, USA, 87–96. DOI: http://dx.doi.org/10.1145/2750858.2804278

29. Päivi Majaranta and Kari-Jouko Räihä. 2002. Twenty Years of Eye Typing: Systems and Design Issues. In *Proceedings of the 2002 Symposium on Eye Tracking Research & Applications (ETRA '02)*. ACM, New York, NY, USA, 15–22. DOI: http://dx.doi.org/10.1145/507072.507076

30. Linda Marschner, Sebastian Pannasch, Johannes Schulz, and Sven-Thomas Graupner. 2015. Social Communication with Virtual Agents: The Effects of Body and Gaze Direction on Attention and Emotional Responding in Human Observers. *International Journal of Psychophysiology* 97, 2 (Aug. 2015), 85–92. DOI: http://dx.doi.org/10.1016/j.ijpsycho.2015.05.007

31. Pascual Martínez-Gómez and Akiko Aizawa. 2014. Recognition of Understanding Level and Language Skill Using Measurements of Reading Behavior. In *Proceedings of the 19th International Conference on Intelligent User Interfaces (IUI '14)*. ACM, New York, NY, USA, 95–104. DOI: http://dx.doi.org/10.1145/2557500.2557546

32. Michael Mauderer, David R. Flatla, and Miguel A. Nacenta. 2016. Gaze-Contingent Manipulation of Color Perception. In *Proceedings of the 2016 CHI Conference on Human Factors in Computing Systems (CHI '16)*. ACM, New York, NY, USA, 5191–5202. DOI: http://dx.doi.org/10.1145/2858036.2858320

33. Jörg Müller, Florian Alt, Daniel Michelis, and Albrecht Schmidt. 2010. Requirements and Design Space for Interactive Public Displays. In *Proceedings of the 18th ACM International Conference on Multimedia (MM '10)*. ACM, New York, NY, USA, 1285–1294. DOI: http://dx.doi.org/10.1145/1873951.1874203

34. Ayano Okoso, Takumi Toyama, Kai Kunze, Joachim Folz, Marcus Liwicki, and Koichi Kise. 2015. Towards Extraction of Subjective Reading Incomprehension: Analysis of Eye Gaze Features. In *Proceedings of the 33rd Annual ACM Conference Extended Abstracts on Human Factors in Computing Systems (CHI EA '15)*. ACM, New York, NY, USA, 1325–1330. DOI: http://dx.doi.org/10.1145/2702613.2732896

35. Ross Quinlan. 1993. *C4.5: Programs for Machine Learning*. Morgan Kaufmann Publishers, San Mateo, CA.

36. Pernilla Qvarfordt and Shumin Zhai. 2005. Conversing with the User Based on Eye-Gaze Patterns. In *Proceedings of the SIGCHI Conference on Human Factors in Computing Systems (CHI '05)*. ACM, New York, NY, USA, 221–230. DOI: http://dx.doi.org/10.1145/1054972.1055004

37. K. Rayner. 1998. Eye Movements in Reading and Information Processing: 20 Years of Research. *Psychological Bulletin* 124, 3 (Nov. 1998), 372–422.

38. Keith Rayner, Timothy J. Slattery, and Nathalie N. Bélanger. 2010. Eye Movements, the Perceptual Span, and Reading Speed. *Psychonomic bulletin & review* 17, 6 (2010), 834–839. DOI: http://dx.doi.org/10.3758/PBR.17.6.834

39. Erik D. Reichle, Alexander Pollatsek, Donald L. Fisher, and Keith Rayner. 1998. Toward a Model of Eye Movement Control in Reading. *Psychological Review* 105, 1 (1998), 125–157. DOI: http://dx.doi.org/10.1037/0033-295X.105.1.125

40. Dario D. Salvucci and John R. Anderson. 2000. Intelligent Gaze-Added Interfaces. In *Proceedings of the SIGCHI Conference on Human Factors in Computing Systems (CHI '00)*. ACM, New York, NY, USA, 273–280. DOI: http://dx.doi.org/10.1145/332040.332444

41. Dario D. Salvucci and Joseph H. Goldberg. 2000. Identifying Fixations and Saccades in Eye-Tracking Protocols. In *Proceedings of the 2000 Symposium on Eye Tracking Research & Applications*. ACM, 71–78. DOI: http://dx.doi.org/10.1145/355017.355028

42. Anthony Santella and Doug DeCarlo. 2004. Robust Clustering of Eye Movement Recordings for Quantification of Visual Interest. In *Proceedings of the 2004 Symposium on Eye Tracking Research & Applications (ETRA '04)*. ACM, 27–34. DOI: http://dx.doi.org/10.1145/968363.968368

43. Sara C. Sereno and Keith Rayner. 2003. Measuring Word Recognition in Reading: Eye Movements and Event-Related Potentials. *Trends in cognitive sciences* 7, 11 (2003), 489–493. DOI: http://dx.doi.org/10.1016/j.tics.2003.09.010

44. John L. Sibert, Mehmet Gokturk, and Robert A. Lavine. 2000. The Reading Assistant: Eye Gaze Triggered Auditory Prompting for Reading Remediation. In *Proceedings of the 13th Annual ACM Symposium on User Interface Software and Technology (UIST '00)*. ACM, New York, NY, USA, 101–107. DOI: http://dx.doi.org/10.1145/354401.354418

45. Linda E. Sibert and Robert J. K. Jacob. 2000. Evaluation of Eye Gaze Interaction. In *Proceedings of the SIGCHI Conference on Human Factors in Computing Systems (CHI '00)*. ACM, New York, NY, USA, 281–288. DOI: http://dx.doi.org/10.1145/332040.332445

46. Greg J. Siegle, Naho Ichikawa, and Stuart Steinhauer. 2008. Blink before and after You Think: Blinks Occur prior to and Following Cognitive Load Indexed by Pupillary Responses. *Psychophysiology* 45, 5 (Sept. 2008), 679–687. DOI: http://dx.doi.org/10.1111/j.1469-8986.2008.00681.x

47. William Steptoe, Robin Wolff, Alessio Murgia, Estefania Guimaraes, John Rae, Paul Sharkey, David Roberts, and Anthony Steed. 2008. Eye-Tracking for Avatar Eye-Gaze and Interactional Analysis in Immersive Collaborative Virtual Environments. In *Proceedings of the 2008 ACM Conference on Computer Supported Cooperative Work (CSCW '08)*. ACM, New York, NY, USA, 197–200. DOI: http://dx.doi.org/10.1145/1460563.1460593

48. Takumi Toyama, Daniel Sonntag, Andreas Dengel, Takahiro Matsuda, Masakazu Iwamura, and Koichi Kise. 2014. A Mixed Reality Head-Mounted Text Translation System Using Eye Gaze Input. In *Proceedings of the 19th International Conference on Intelligent User Interfaces (IUI '14)*. ACM, New York, NY, USA, 329–334. DOI: http://dx.doi.org/10.1145/2557500.2557528

49. Roel Vertegaal, Robert Slagter, Gerrit van der Veer, and Anton Nijholt. 2001. Eye Gaze Patterns in Conversations: There Is More to Conversational Agents Than Meets the Eyes. In *Proceedings of the SIGCHI Conference on Human Factors in Computing Systems (CHI '01)*. ACM, New York, NY, USA, 301–308. DOI: http://dx.doi.org/10.1145/365024.365119

50. Kazuyo Yoshimura, Koichi Kise, and Kai Kunze. 2015. The Eye as the Window of the Language Ability: Estimation of English Skills by Analyzing Eye Movement While Reading Documents. In *Document Analysis and Recognition (ICDAR), 2015 13th International Conference on*. IEEE, 251–255. DOI: http://dx.doi.org/10.1109/ICDAR.2015.7333762

51. Shumin Zhai, Carlos Morimoto, and Steven Ihde. 1999. Manual and Gaze Input Cascaded (MAGIC) Pointing. In *Proceedings of the SIGCHI Conference on Human Factors in Computing Systems (CHI '99)*. ACM, 246–253. DOI: http://dx.doi.org/10.1145/302979.303053

52. Yanxia Zhang, Ming Ki Chong, Jörg Müller, Andreas Bulling, and Hans Gellersen. 2015. Eye Tracking for Public Displays in the Wild. *Personal and Ubiquitous Computing* 19, 5-6 (Aug. 2015), 967–981. DOI: http://dx.doi.org/10.1007/s00779-015-0866-8

A Multifaceted Study on Eye Contact based Speaker Identification in Three-party Conversations

Yu Ding
University of Houston
Houston, TX, USA
yding7@uh.edu

Yuting Zhang
University of Houston
Houston, TX, USA
yzhang115@uh.edu

Meihua Xiao
East China Jiaotong University
Nanchang, Jiangxi, China
xiaomh@ecjtu.edu.cn

Zhigang Deng
University of Houston
Houston, TX, USA
zdeng4@uh.edu

ABSTRACT

To precisely understand human gaze behaviors in three-party conversations, this work is dedicated to look into whether the speaker can be reliably identified from the interlocutors in a three-party conversation on the basis of the interactive behaviors of eye contact, where speech signals are not provided. Derived from a pre-recorded, multimodal, and three-party conversational behavior dataset, a statistical framework is proposed to determine *who is the speaker* from the interactive behaviors of eye contact. Additionally, with the aid of virtual human technologies, a user study is conducted to study whether subjects are capable of distinguishing the speaker from the listeners according to the gaze behaviors of the interlocutors alone. Our results show that eye contact provides a reliable cue for the identification of the speaker in three-party conversations.

ACM Classification Keywords

H.1.2. User/Machine Systems: Human information processing

Author Keywords

eye gaze; eye contact; face-to-face communication; multiparty conversation; human-human interaction; head gestures; eye-head coordination; perception of gaze; nonverbal behaviors.

INTRODUCTION

Occurring in the visual channel, nonverbal behaviors contribute to the flow of conversation including gaze, facial expressions, head rotations, gestures, etc. These behaviors are of importance in technology-mediated communication, such as videoconferencing and interactions with embodied conversational agents (ECAs) in virtual worlds. Indeed, the rendition of natural nonverbal behaviors is essential to increase the appreciation and the effectiveness of mediated interactions [7, 39, 11, 6, 14].

Permission to make digital or hard copies of all or part of this work for personal or classroom use is granted without fee provided that copies are not made or distributed for profit or commercial advantage and that copies bear this notice and the full citation on the first page. Copyrights for components of this work owned by others than the author(s) must be honored. Abstracting with credit is permitted. To copy otherwise, or republish, to post on servers or to redistribute to lists, requires prior specific permission and/or a fee. Request permissions from Permissions@acm.org.
CHI 2017, May 06 - 11, 2017, Denver, CO, USA
Copyright is held by the owner/author(s). Publication rights licensed to ACM.
ACM 978-1-4503-4655-9/17/05 $15.00
DOI: http://dx.doi.org/10.1145/3025453.3025644

To improve the quality of mediated interaction, tremendous progresses have been made to synthesize nonverbal behaviors for virtual humans as the speaker or a listener in a conversation. Often, the synthesized speaker behaviors are assumed to be independent of listeners [5, 4, 15, 25, 24, 27, 9, 8, 10]. On the other hand, the behaviors of virtual listeners in some previous works [26, 30, 29] are typically driven by the detected motions of the user (i.e., the human speaker), which implicitly rely on an over-simplified hypothesis that the listener behaviors are submissive to those of the speaker.

It could be untrue that the behaviors of the speaker and listeners are independent of each other or that one is submissive to the other one. Indeed, the interactions between two interlocutors exhibit varying degrees and patterns of mutual influence along several aspects such as talking style/prosody, gestural behavior, engagement level, emotion, and many other types of user states [3], which implies that the speaker and listener behaviors interact with each other. In the works mentioned, such interactions have not yet been merged into the synthesized animations for virtual speakers and listeners. This could probably result from that it is also unclear whether merging such interactions can improve the quality of mediated interactions.

Additionally, the above works targeting two-party conversations on behavior synthesis could not be straightforwardly extended to multiparty conversations due to the obvious change of the spatial arrangement between the speaker and the listeners. Such a gap could probably result from that the occurrences of a specific interaction, namely eye contact in multiparty conversations, have been relatively understudied to date.

In light of the above gaps, an intriguing yet widely open research question is, whether the rendition of interactions of nonverbal behaviors can improve the quality of mediated interaction. As the first step, we focus on the specific interaction of eye contact and conduct a multifaceted study on whether the speaker can be effectively identified from the interlocutors in a three-party conversation based on eye contact, which could provide detailed and precise understanding of human-human interaction than the direct rendition of eye contact. This would also provide indisputable evidence that eye contact can offer informative feature to the synthesis of nonverbal behaviors.

Eye contact occurs when two interlocutors are looking at each other. It is determined by the gaze directions of the interlocutors. The gaze is manifested via the combination of head orientation and eye orientation [22, 23]. It can be determined by head orientation only if the eyes keep still at the center of the orbit. So, it is critical to investigate the difference between the contributions of head and of eyeball to the identification of the speaker from the interlocutors, which could facilitate researchers to work on the better synthesis of gaze, head and eyeball in various applications.

The seminal work by Rienks et al. [35] has reported that people can use knowledge of head motions in the azimuth plane to distinguish the speaker from the listeners but that head alone does not provide a sufficient cue for reliable identification of the speaker in a multiparty conversation. Their investigation is carried out through subjective judgments where human observers are invited to watch the video clips of four virtual humans in a meeting and to identify the speaking virtual human. The virtual humans are only rotating their heads in the azimuth plane by displaying pre-recorded human data; neither other nonverbal behaviors are rendered nor speech signals are provided. Moreover, in each video clip, only one speaker is speaking, without turn-taking, overlapping speech, and silence.

Our study relies on a collected three-party conversational behavior dataset. The simultaneously collected data include the azimuth angles of head and eyeball and speech signals. Such data enables us to get insights into eye contact occurrences in a conversation. The objective and subjective studies are both carried out to identify the speaker from the interlocutors in three-party conversations. In the objective study, a Markov process is trained to encode the differences of eye contact patterns according to the interlocutors' statuses (speaking or listening), and then it is used to distinguish the speaker from the listener(s) using eye contact information as the input. In the subjective study, participants are invited to judge who is speaking and who is/are listening by observing the gaze behaviors of virtual humans in a conversation without speech signals, where the virtual humans are animated by pre-recorded human movement data. Moreover, our work takes insight into the trend of the identification accuracy along with the increasing length of speaker turn in both objective and subjective studies.

To the best of our knowledge, the only previous work that is directly relevant to our work is the aforementioned work [35]. There are several major differences between our work and [35]:

1. Our study is exactly based on eye contact behavior, while technically speaking their work is not. Specifically, our study considers both the head orientation and eyeball behavior to estimate eye contact, but their work considered head orientation alone. Indeed, their work fundamentally relies on a key assumption that the participants' focus of attention can be well approximated by head orientation. However, our study proves this key assumption in a multiparty setting may not always be valid, and found the gaze behaviors estimated from the joint head orientation and eyeball movement data clearly outperform head orientations alone, in terms of speaker identification in a three-party setting.

2. The work [35] did not provide experimental evidence to support the trend of the identification accuracy along with the increasing length of speaker turn. By contrast, our objective analysis method concretely shows that the speaker identification accuracy of using eye contact as the cue is more than 70% when the length of speaker turn is longer than 2 seconds (see Figure 7). Also, our subjective study results (see Figure 11) show that the identification accuracy is more than 80% when the speaker turn is longer than 3 seconds; the accuracy can be lower only if the length of turn speaker is less than 1 second. This is a new finding that has never been reported previously.

3. The work [35] mainly used subjective studies for speaker identification. Statistical objective analysis on the recorded human motion data was not conducted. By contrast, our work performs both statistical objective analysis and subjective studies to look into this problem from a multifaceted perspective, which gives new insights on this research problem of speaker identification.

BACKGROUND

Speaker diarization is an emerging research topic for automatic conversation/meeting analysis. It aims at determining "who spoke when?" in audio or video recording, where turn-taking often occurs and multiple speakers could simultaneously speak (overlapping speech). To achieve the goal, besides speech features, visual features are often also used to improve the recognition accuracy [12, 16, 20, 32]. These visual features characterize only individual behaviors, while interactive functions of behaviors are neglected, e.g., eye contact.

None of the previous works on speaker diarization explicitly employs eye contact as a cue to improve the recognition accuracy. It probably attributes to the lacking of awareness of eye contact occurrence between the speaker and the listener(s). Comprehensively reviewing all the prior efforts on speaker diarization is beyond the scope of this paper. Readers of interest are referred to recent survey articles [1, 38].

Our work differs from speaker diarization. Our aim is to obtain insights on the precise understanding of human-human interaction by eye contact, according to the interlocutors' statuses (speaking or listening). Our work could offer researchers a new insight into the relation between interlocutor statuses and eye contact as well as provide a new useful clue to improve the state of the art in speaker diarization.

Predictions of turn-taking/keeping, the next speaker, and the lasting time between two speaker-turns can be carried out according to interactive gaze patterns, such as convergence, divergence, and eye contact (dyad-link), which was reported in some previous works [17, 18, 19, 21, 34]. Their positive results indicate that interactive gaze patterns are closely related to the occurrences of turn-taking and turn-keeping. Moreover, their works suggest that humans are very skilled at encoding and decoding interactive gaze patterns for smoothing the flow of conversation.

Although gaze patterns used in these works occur in the phase of turn-taking/keeping, i.e., the last 1000 ms of an utterance and the follow-up pause (200 ms), rather than during the whole utterance, the successful use of interactive gaze patterns for identifying turn-taking and turn-keeping inspires us how to design our analysis.

Identifications of interactive gaze patterns (mentioned above) and of conversation regime (such as monologue and discussion) can be conducted according to head orientations and who is speaking, which is reported in previous works [33, 13]. Their validated results suggest that gaze patterns are correlated with the interlocutors' statuses (speaking or listening).

CONTRIBUTIONS

Our work contributes to the understanding of eye contact patterns and of head and eyeball movements in three-party conversations. It provides an important clue to extend the existing works on head and eyeball animation generation to multi-party conversations, and to bridge the gap between listener and speaker animations. In addition, this work provides a new clue to an emerging research topic of speaker diarization and to automatic conversation/meeting analysis (video editing, navigation, retrieval, or higher-level inference).

DATA ACQUISITION AND PROCESSING

In this work, we collected a multimodal conversational behavior dataset for three-party conversations, using the acquisition setup described below. In total, 2 three-party conversation datasets were captured, which involved 6 different participants. Each three-party conversation dataset consists of 6 sessions, each of which lasted about ten minutes. The participants took a break of several minutes between two successive sessions. The participants of one three-party conversation dataset are 3 males and those of the other are 3 females. The participants (ages are from 19 to 25) did not know each other before the experiment. No instructions were made into their conversations; they freely talked with each other on the topics of self-introduction, life, hobbies, favorite restaurants and movies, traveling plan, career plan, etc.

Acquisition setup. The datasets of three-party conversation were recorded from three interlocutors standing at the three vertices of an equilateral triangle with a distance of about 1 meter to other interlocutors, which is designed to eliminate any potential bias from the sitting position and group formation. The interlocutors were instructed to stick to their original locations as much as possible, but they were allowed to naturally move their torsos and heads, and change facial expressions during the conversation. A snapshot and the layout of the three-party conversation capture are shown in Figure 1.

The collected conversational behavior data contain body movement, eyeball movement, eyelid movement, and acoustic speech, all of which were acquired simultaneously at 30 frames

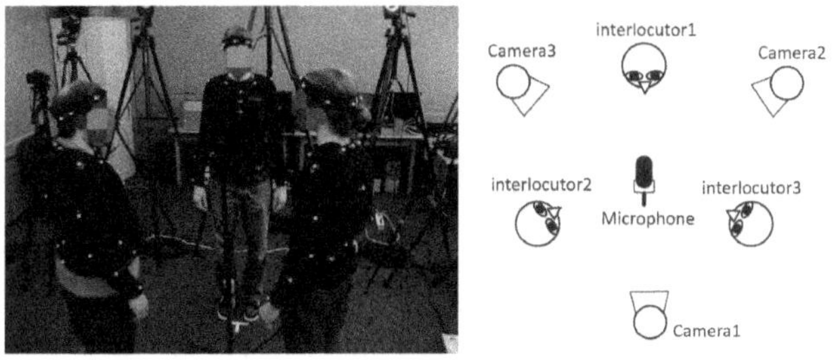

(a) (b)

Figure 1. The layout of the recorded three-party conversations. (a) A snapshot of the data acquisition process. (b) Illustration of the eye tracking data acquisition process.

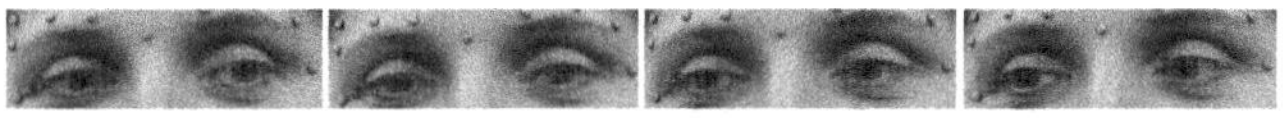

Figure 2. Detection of eyeballs movement. The detected eye and pupils are rendered respectively by the green dashed lines and the solid red circles. As can be seen, the solid red circles almost cover the human pupils. The images from left to right display a detected gaze aversion from left to right.

per second. The body movement includes hand gesture, torso movement, and head movement. The body movement was recorded by a ten-cameras VICON optical motion capture system, where each interlocutor wore a mocap suit attached with optical markers. We downsampled the mocap data from the originally captured 120 frames/second to 30 frames/second. The torso and head movements were recorded as the sequences of 3-dimensional skeleton rotation angles. Moreover, acoustic speech was recorded by a wireless microphone positioned in the center of the interlocutors (see Figure 1). The speech transcription and its time information were obtained manually by a language expert.

To acquire the accurate 3D movements of the eyeballs and the eyelids of all the interlocutors, we employed the proven, hybrid mocap and HD video capture scheme proposed by Binh et al. [24]: specifically, the movement of the front face of each interlocutor was recorded by a Cannon HD camera (Figure 1-(b)). Then, with the aid of accurate 3D head movement at each frame that can be accurately estimated from several mocap markers on the head, a specially-designed tracking algorithm was used to offline process the video to track the movements of the eyeballs and the eyelids frame by frame [24]. When the eyelids were detected as being closed, the eyeballs movement could not be detected and it was inferred by smoothing the movement trajectory with linear interpolation. Figure 2 shows a few images of the acquired eyeball movements.

Gaze is approximated by adding the azimuth angles of the eyeballs, the head, and the torso. In our work, the rotational angle of the torso is always merged into that of the head; it is viewed as a part of the head rotational angle. So the head rotational angle in the remaining writing represents the combination of the azimuth angles of the head and the torso.

Considering the locations of the interlocutors at the three vertices of an equilateral triangle, we assume that an interlocutor looks at none of the other interlocutors if his/her eye gaze ori-

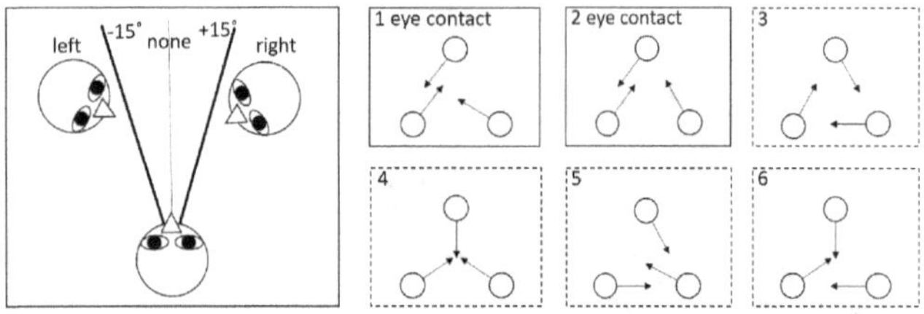

Figure 3. Illustrations of discrete gaze labels, of eye contact and of no eye contact. The left image shows that the gaze at each time frame, estimated from head and eyeball data or from only head data, is labeled by three discrete gaze labels: left, none and right. The gaze between 15° to the left and 15° to the right is labeled by *none*; the gaze beyond 15° to the left/right is labeled by *left* / *right*. In the right six images, the images with No.1 and No.2 show two cases of eye contact. The other images show four cases of none eye contact.

ents in the range between -15° (left) and +15° (right)[1]. Also we assume that he/she looks at another interlocutor to his/her left or right if his/her eye gaze orients beyond 15° to left/right. Based on these assumptions, the eye gaze of each interlocutor at each frame can be mapped to one of the three discrete labels: looking at none of the other interlocutors (*none*), looking at the right interlocutor (*right*), and looking at the left interlocutor ($left$), which is illustrated in the left panel of Figure 3.

Eye contact is detected at each time frame by judging whether any two of three interlocutors are looking at each other, which is determined from their gaze labels (*none*, *right* and $left$). The right panel of Figure 3 shows two cases with eye contact and four cased without eye contact. To describe the occurrence of eye contact between them at each time frame, a 3-dimensional feature vector, s^i, is defined and it has four possible values as follows.

1. $s^1 = [0,0,0]$: eye contact does not occur.
2. $s^2 = [1,1,0]$: eye contact occurs between the 1st and the 2nd interlocutors.
3. $s^3 = [0,1,1]$: eye contact occurs between the 2nd and the 3rd interlocutors.
4. $s^4 = [1,0,1]$: eye contact occurs between the 1st and the 3rd interlocutors.

s^i consists of three elements, which respectively represent whether the three interlocutors involve eye contact or not. The element can be 0 or 1. 0 stands for no involvement of eye contact; 1 stands for the involvement of eye contact. Furthermore, $S^k = [s_1,...,s_t,...,s_T]$, a sequence of s^i, is used to describe the occurrences of eye contact along with time frame. k in S^k stands for the index of motion episode with one specific speaker speaking, which is clipped from the whole recorded motion stream, according to speech information. The set of S^k is noted by $\{S^k\}$, $k = 1,2,...,K$, where K is the total number of motion episodes. In our dataset, 2486 motion episodes are collected (K=2486) with the duration ranging from 0.5 second to 20.3 seconds (averaged duration is 2.27 seconds and SD = 2.40). Note that those motion episodes with length less than 0.5 second are screened out as done in Rienks et al. [35].

Note that although the peripheral vision of an interlocutor may also include other interlocutor(s) besides the primary eye-contact target, at a particular time instance an interlocutor can at most gaze at one other interlocutor as the focus of his/her attention. Therefore, despite certain loss of information, our study treats eye contact as a binary variable. Ignoring the peripheral vision could still retain the most prominent information of the interlocutors' focus of attention for our study.

EXPERIMENT: IDENTIFYING THE SPEAKER

In our work, both subjective judgement and objective analysis are conducted. In the objective analysis, eye contact (a specific interactive behavior) rather than individual gaze (or head orientation) is taken into account as input features. It is based on the assumption that eye contact could provide more useful cues than individual gazes as it displays interactive behaviors between interlocutors. Moreover, in the subjective judgment, the gaze azimuth angles are used to animate virtual humans in a conversation, where whether eye contact occurs or not is not explicitly indicated.

Our first set of hypotheses are:

- **H1-obj**: objective eye contact data can be used to effectively identify the speaker from the interlocutors in three-party conversations (objective analysis).
- **H1-sub**: humans are capable of using knowledge of gaze patterns to distinguish the speaker from the listeners in three-party conversations (subjective judgment).

The investigation of H1-obj and H1-sub could offer new insight into the understanding of interactive gaze patterns among interlocutors in three-party conversations.

Furthermore, eye contact and gaze are estimated by combining the eyeball and head rotation angles. Such a combination could provide more precise information about the attention of interlocutors than head rotation angles alone. Our second set of hypotheses are:

- **H2-obj**: objective analysis can identify the speaker with a higher accuracy from the joint head and eyeball movement data than the head movement data alone.
- **H2-sub**: subjective judgment can identify the speaker with a higher accuracy from the joint head and eyeball movement data than the head movement data alone.

The investigation of H2-obj and H2-sub allows us to understand the contribution of eyeballs to face-to-face communication in three-party conversations.

The objective analysis and subjective judgment aim at determining who is speaking according to the head and eyeball azimuth angles in a speaker turn, which could last between 0.5 second and 20.3 seconds in our dataset. Considering that long speaker turns could provide more information for the speaker identification than short ones, we formulate our third set of hypotheses as follows:

[1] A common strategy employed in graphics literature is to define a cutoff displacement of 10°-15° above which targets are acquired by a gaze shift [36][28][31]. In our work, 15° is used to distinguish the gaze target.

- **H3-obj**: objective analysis can obtain a higher speaker identification accuracy from long speaker turns than from those short ones.
- **H3-sub**: subjective judgment can obtain a higher speaker identification accuracy from long speaker turns than from those short ones.

In the following writing, we will describe the conducted objective analysis and subjective judgment including methodology, results, and discussion.

Objective Analysis

To objectively identify the speaker, a Markov process can be built based on $\{S^k\}$. In each experiment, the used set of S^k is splitted into a training set and a test set. Two pre-processing steps are performed to the training set before a Markov process is trained. Note that such pre-processing steps are not applied to the test set.

Building Markov Process

Assuming S^k is one of the motion episodes in the training set, the first pre-processing is to make the first element of s_t, t=1,...,T, in S^k always correspond to the known speaker by switching the 1st interlocutor and the known index of the speaker in s_t. For example, if the 1st, the 2nd and the 3rd elements in s_t respectively correspond to one listener, the other listener, and the speaker, the 3rd and the 1st elements are switched. If the 1st element originally corresponds to the speaker, the order of the elements are kept without switching. After this manipulation, while the 1st element of s_t corresponds to the speaker, the 2nd and the 3rd elements correspond to the listeners.

Afterwards, the second pre-processing is to create a new set by switching the 2nd and the 3rd elements of all the $\{s_t\}$ in the original training set, which corresponds to two listeners (see the first pre-processing above). Then, we combine the new created set with the original training set to obtain the new training set that is used to build the Markov process. In our recorded data, two listeners stand symmetrically around the speaker. Therefore, this new training set is designed to eliminate any potential bias from the right or the left listener.

The built Markov process, λ, consists of four states, each of which corresponds to one feature vector, s^i, where $i = 1,2,3$ or 4. The transition probabilities are calculated from the training set, by counting and normalizing the number of transitions between the feature vectors.

The built Markov process is expected to capture the transition probabilities of four eye contact patterns (s^1, s^2, s^3, and s^4), viewing the speaker as the first interlocutor. How to use the Markov process to identify the speaker is described below.

Using Markov Process

The aim of speaker identification is to infer the speaker index from S^k in the test set, using λ. At the identification step, the speaker index is unknown in the test set; it can be the 1st, the 2nd, or the 3rd. Given S^k, a probability can be inferred from the transition probabilities at all the time steps, and it quantifies the probability of S^k from the Markov process. The probability calculation is detailed below.

Since the Markov process is trained on the set of $\{S^k\}$ with the speaker being the first interlocutor, we expect that a test speaker turn, $S^{k_1} = [s_1^{k_1}, ..., s_{T_{k1}}^{k_1}]$, results in a higher probability when the first interlocutor is the speaker than when he/she is a listener. Based on this hypothesis, we alter the interlocutors' indexes twice. The first is to switch the 1st and the 2nd elements of $\{s_t^{k_1}\}_{t=1}^{T_{k1}}$ and the altered speaker turn is denoted by $S^{k_2} = [s_1^{k_2}, ..., s_{T_{k1}}^{k_2}]$; the second is to switch the 1st and the 3rd elements of $\{s_t^{k_1}\}_{t=1}^{T_{k1}}$ and the altered speaker turn is denoted by $S^{k_3} = [s_1^{k_3}, ..., s_{T_{k1}}^{k_3}]$. We then applied λ to S^{k_1} as well as S^{k_2} and S^{k_3} respectively to obtain their probabilities. To this end, S^{k_i} with the maximum probability is selected, and the i is selected as the speaker index.

The probability of S^{k_i} is calculated as follows.

$$p(S^{k_i}|\lambda) = \prod_{t=1}^{T_{k1}-1} \frac{P(s_{t+1}^{k_i}|s_t^{k_i},\lambda)}{\sum_{1\le j\le 3} P(s_{t+1}^{k_j}|s_t^{k_j},\lambda)} \quad (1)$$

where $p(S^{k_i}|\lambda)$ stands for the probability of S^{k_i}, given the built Markov process; $P(s_{t+1}^{k_i}|s_t^{k_i},\lambda)$ is the transition probability of feature vectors from $s_t^{k_i}$ to $s_{t+1}^{k_i}$, which also applies to $P(s_{t+1}^{k_j}|s_t^{k_j},\lambda)$. To avoid the problem of numeric overflow, the operation of summation is to normalize the probabilities so that the probabilities of three variations are summed to be 1 at each time step, as follows.

$$\sum_{1\le i\le 3} \frac{P(s_{t+1}^{k_i}|s_t^{k_i},\lambda)}{\sum_{1\le j\le 3} P(s_{t+1}^{k_j}|s_t^{k_j},\lambda)} = 1 \quad (2)$$

The above objective analysis is applied to validate the hypotheses H1-obj, H2-obj, and H3-obj. According to the hypotheses, more details as well as the results will be described below.

Objective Analysis Results

Test of the hypotheses H1-obj and H2-obj. Two types of Markov processes are built based on $\{S^k\}$. The first one, denoted by $\{S^k\}_{he}$, is built from the eye contact data that is estimated from the joint azimuth angles of the head and the eyeballs; the second one, denoted by $\{S^k\}_h$, is done from the eye contact data that is estimated from the azimuth angles of the head alone. In each experiment, $\{s^k\}_{he}$ and $\{s^k\}_h$ are respectively randomly splitted into a training set (80%) and a test set (20%). The training sets from $\{s^k\}_{he}$ and $\{s^k\}_h$ are used to respectively build two Markov processes, noted by λ_{he} and λ_h. Then, the test sets from $\{s^k\}_{he}$ and $\{s^k\}_h$ are respectively applied to λ_{he} and λ_h. We ran the above *repeated random sub-sampling validation* experiments 20 times for $\{s^k\}_{he}$ and $\{s^k\}_h$, respectively. To this end, by comparing the recognition result with the ground-truth, we can obtain a recognition accuracy rate in each experiment. The averaged experiment results are reported in Figure 4 and Figure 7.

To test the hypothesis H1-obj, we compared our experiment results with the baseline (33.3%) that is obtained by random

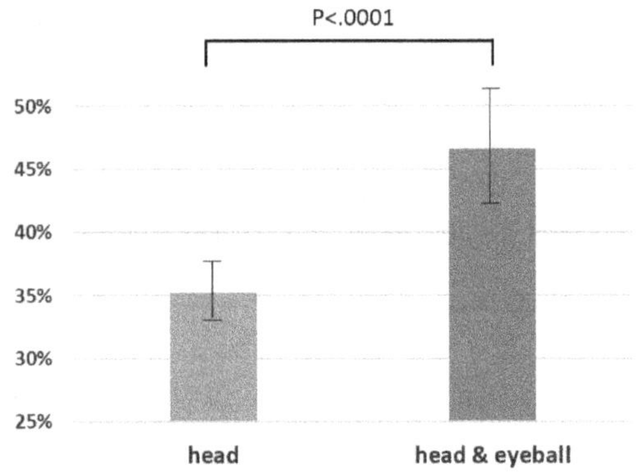

Figure 4. Average results of speaker identification in our objective analysis. The vertical bars visualize the standard deviations.

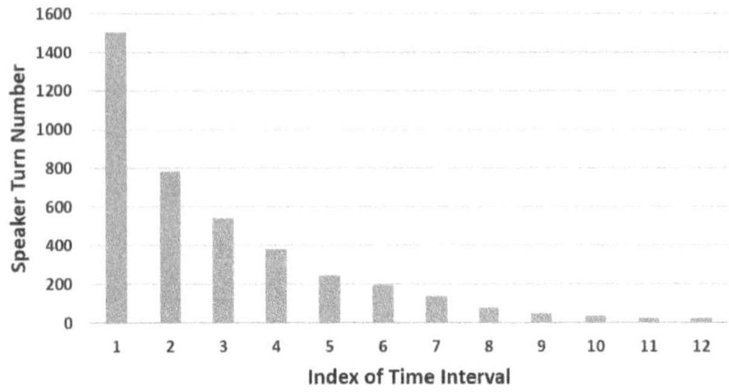

Figure 5. The number of speaker turns in each Interval. The intervals are defined by a 2-seconds moving window and a step size of 1 second. As the exceptions, the 1st and 12th intervals contain the speaker turns whose lengths are in the range of $[0.5,2]$ and $[11,20.3]$, respectively. Each speaker turn consists of many frames. The total frame number of all the speaker turns in each interval can be found in Figure 6.

selection (one out of three interlocutors). We conducted One-Sided t-Test on the results of 20 validation experiments. For $\{s^k\}_h$, the recognition accuracy (M=0.376, SD=0.009) is significantly greater than the baseline: t(19)=20.7967, p<0.0001. For $\{s^k\}_{he}$, the recognition accuracy (M=0.4664, SD=0.0165) is also significantly greater than the baseline: t(19)=35.2144, p<0.0001. Therefore, the hypothesis H1-obj is accepted (assuming the significance level = 0.05).

To test the hypothesis H2-obj, we conducted a Paired-Sample t-Test to compare the 20 validation experiment results between λ_{he} and λ_h. The comparison results indicate that the joint head and eyeball movement data (M=0.4664, SD=0.0165) result in a significantly greater recognition accuracy than the head movement data alone (M=0.376, SD=0.009): t(19)=22.8802,p<0.0001. The hypothesis H2-obj is accepted.

Test of the hypothesis H3-obj. To take into account the length of speaker turn, the length range is splitted into overlapping intervals with a 2-seconds moving window and a step size of 1 second. Each speaker turn is classified into two successive intervals. For example, one speaker turn with the length of 2.3 seconds is grouped into two successive intervals in the ranges of $[1,3]$ and $[2,4]$. The number of speaker turns in each

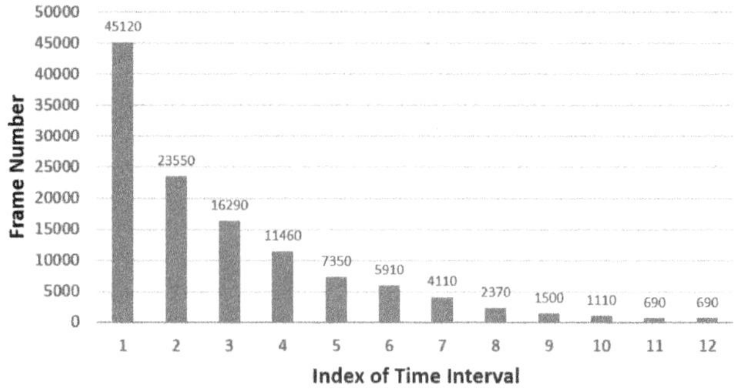

Figure 6. The frame number of all the speaker turns in each Interval. The intervals are defined by a 2-seconds moving window and a step size of 1 second. As the exceptions, the 1st and 12th intervals contain the speaker turns whose lengths are in the range of $[0.5,2]$ and $[11,20.3]$, respectively. The number of speaker turns in each interval can be found in Figure 5.

interval is illustrated in Figure 5. In fact, the 1st interval in the range of $(0,2]$ only contains those speaker turns whose lengths are in the range of $[0.5,2]$, since we discarded those speaker turns with the length less than 0.5 second in our dataset (refer to the aforementioned data acquisition and processing section). As can be seen from Figure 5, the number of speaker turns decreases with the increase of the length of speaker turn. As such, the $12th$ interval in the figure contains all the speaker turns with the length more than 11 seconds (i.e., in the range of $[11,20.3]$). Each speaker turn is characterized by a sequence of frames. The frame number of all the speaker turns in each time interval is shown in Figure 6.

The speaker turns from a specific interval are used to calculate the identification accuracy for this interval. That is, each interval is associated with an identification accuracy. To calculate the recognition accuracy for each interval, the used set of S^k only involves the speaker turns in a specific interval. In each experiment, 80% of the speaker turns are used as the training samples and 20% as the test samples. To this end, two estimates of $\{S^k\}$, $\{s^k\}_{he}$ from the joint head and eyeball movement data and $\{s^k\}_h$ from the head movement data alone are investigated. Figure 7 depicts the result of each time interval.

The red points in Figure 7 represent the recognition results from the joint head and eyeball movement data. As illustrated in this figure, it rapidly increases between the $1st$ and the $4th$ intervals; it stays steady between the $4th$ and the $7th$ intervals; and it increases with obvious fluctuations between the $7th$ and the $12th$ intervals. These observations suggest its overall increasing trend despite its fluctuations at some places. However, it does not monotonically increase. More investigations are needed to look into those fluctuations as the future work. Similar observations can also be seen from the blue curve representing the recognition results based on the head movement data alone, although the increasing trend of the blue curve is less obvious than that of the red one.

In addition, the red points in Figure 7 are consistently higher than the blue points. The joint head and eyeball movement data results in a higher recognition accuracy in every interval

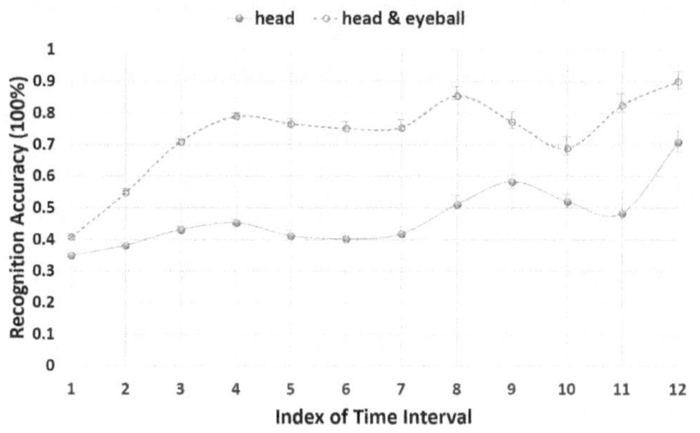

Figure 7. The objective speaker identification accuracy as a function of the length of speaker turn. The red dashed curve shows the results from the joint head and eyeball movement data while the blue solid curve shows the results from the head movement data alone. The plotted results are obtained by averaging the outcomes of 20 repeated random sub-sampling validation experiments. The standard deviations are plotted as vertical bars.

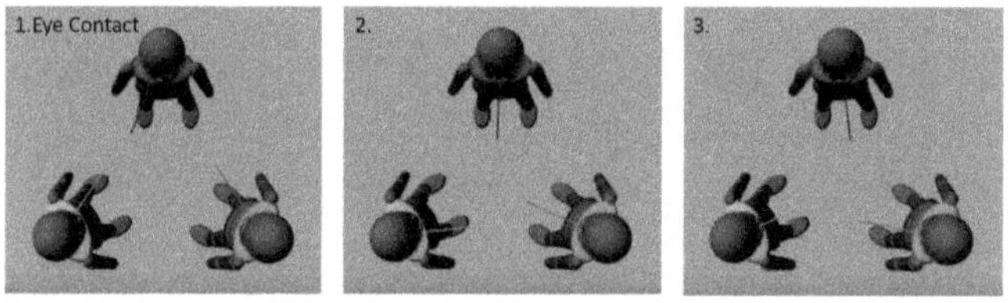

Figure 8. Several snapshots of rendered virtual character animation clips in our study. The colored lines represent the gaze orientations of the virtual characters. The 1st panel shows the occurrence of eye contact; the other two panels show two cases of no eye contact.

than the head movement data alone, which is in line with the validated hypothesis H2-obj. Moreover, we observe that, the speaker identification accuracy from the joint head and eyeball movement data or from the head movement data alone is clearly higher than the baseline (33.3%) in every interval, which is also in line with the validated hypothesis H1-obj.

In Figure 7, the accuracy from the joint head and eyeball data is about 40% in the $1st$ time interval, and the accuracies in other time intervals (i.e., since the 3rd interval) are more than 70%. However, as shown in Figure 5, the number of the speaker turns in the $1st$ time interval is much higher than those in the other time intervals. That is why the averaged accuracy (counting all the intervals) from the joint head and eyeball data in Figure 4 is about 46%.

Subjective Judgment

Subjective judgments are obtained through a user study, where participants are invited to watch episode animation clips displaying three rendered virtual characters (interlocutors) in a conversation. Each animation clip contains a single speaker turn where only a virtual character is speaking and the other two are listening without turn-taking and overlapping speech. The animations are rendered from the top view of the virtual characters (refer to Figure 8). The virtual characters are animated only by the gaze azimuth data and speech signals are not provided. Gaze orientation is represented by a solid line, which allows participants to clearly observe the gazes of the virtual characters at each time instant. In the animations, torsos and gaze lines of the three virtual characters are colored by red, green, and yellow, respectively. The occurrences of eye contact are not explicitly indicated in the animation clips. The animation clips are played at a speed of 30 frames per second, as the originally recorded human movement data.

To test the hypothesis H1-sub, gazes are estimated by the joint head and eyeball movement data. The hypothesis H1-sub is accepted if the subjective identification accuracy is statistically higher than the baseline (33.3%). To test the hypothesis H2-sub, gazes are estimated not only by the joint head and eyeball movement data but also by the head movement data alone. The hypothesis H2-sub is accepted if the subjective identification accuracy on the animations driven by the joint head and eyeball movement data is statistically higher than that by the head movement data alone. To test the hypothesis H3-sub, the duration of speaker turn need to be taken into account. The hypothesis H3-sub is accepted if the subjective recognition accuracy increases along with the length of speaker turn.

Protocol: Participants are asked to provide demographic information, including age, gender, education level, occupation, etc., before the experiment; then, they are invited to view animation clips of three virtual characters in a conversation. Their task is to choose the speaker in each clip. We describe the elements of the protocol in this user study as follows. (1) Participants: in total, there were 34 participants consisting of 22 males and 12 females with the age ranging from 21 to 70 (M=30.06 years, SD=9.9 years). (2) Stimuli: the range of speaker turn length was splitted into 5 non-overlapping intervals: 0.5 to 3 seconds, 3 to 6 seconds, 6 to 9 seconds, 9 to 12 seconds, and 12 to 20.3 seconds. 5 speaker turns were randomly selected from each interval. To this end, a total of 25 speaker turns were chosen (5 intervals x 5 samples per interval). The shortest selected sample lasts 1.1 seconds, and the longest one lasts 13.6 seconds. Furthermore, 2 different versions (conditions) of the virtual character animations were created for each speaker turn:

- **Condition 1**: gaze is estimated based on head orientation alone.
- **Condition 2**: gaze is estimated based on the joint head and eyeball orientations.

In total, 50 animation clips (without speech) were generated, which consists of 25 pair-wise animation clips with Conditions 1 and 2.

Procedure: The 50 animation clips are presented to each participant in a random order (refer to Figure 9). When participants watch the animation clips, they are explicitly informed that they can watch these animations as many times as they want; that only one interlocutor is speaking without turn-taking, and that the lines represent the gaze orientations of the virtual characters. Meanwhile, they are not explicitly informed whether the gaze orientation is estimated by the joint head and eyeball movement data or by the head movement data alone. After watching each animation clip, the participants are asked to select which character (red, green, or yellow) is the speaker in the animation, described below.

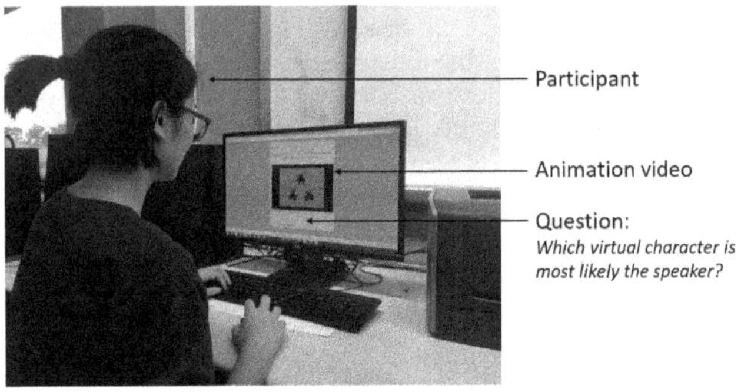

Figure 9. A user study snapshot of a participant

- Which virtual character is most likely the speaker?

Results: We report two types of recognition accuracies, whose difference is whether the length of speaker turn is viewed as a dependent variable. The length of speaker turn is not taken as a dependent variable in the first type while it is taken in the second type. The condition mentioned above is always taken as a dependent variable.

Considering the condition as a dependent variable, the first type contains two recognition accuracies: one is calculated based on the subjective judgment results from those 25 animation clips with Condition 1, and the other one is calculated based on the subjective judgement results from those 25 animation clips with Condition 2. The results are reported in Figure 10.

The second type is to calculate the recognition accuracy for each animation clip. The results are reported in Figure 11, where the blue and red points represent the results with Condition 1 and Condition 2, respectively. In this figure, the vertical axis represents the recognition accuracy, and the horizontal axis represents the index of an animation clip. Note that the animation clips in this figure are ordered by their lengths (i.e., the length of speaker turn) in an increasing order. The red and blue points positioned with the same values in the horizontal axis are associated with the two pair-wise animations (corresponding to Conditions 1 and 2, respectively).

Test of the hypotheses H1-sub and H2-sub. To test the hypothesis H1-sub, the first type of recognition accuracy is compared with the baseline (33.3%). The results are shown in Figure 10. One-sided t-Test is conducted on the subjective judgment results from the 25 animation clips with Condition 1 and the other 25 clips with Condition 2. According to the results with Condition 1, the recognition accuracy (M=67.7%, SD=0.25) is statistically higher than the baseline: $t(24)=6.92$, $p<.0001$. Also, according to the results with Condition 2, the recognition accuracy (M=81.4%, SD=0.21) is statistically higher than the baseline: $t(24)=11.75$, $p<.0001$. The hypothesis H1-sub is accepted not only for Condition 1 but also for Condition 2.

To test the hypothesis H2-sub, a paired-sample t-Test is conducted to compare the subjective judgment results with Conditions 1 and 2. The comparison results show that the results with Condition 2 (M=81.4%, SD=0.21) lead to statistically

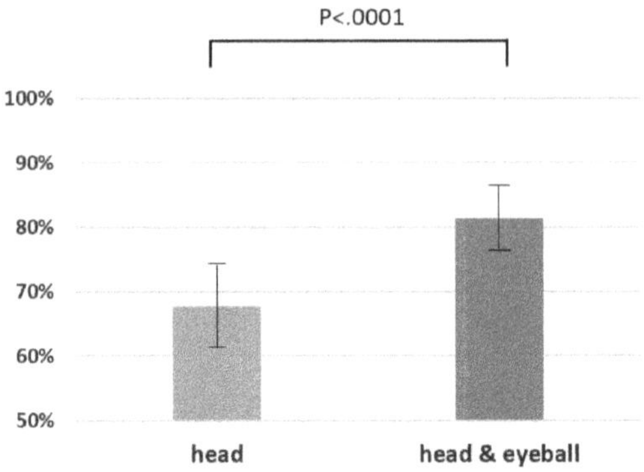

Figure 10. Overall subjective speaker identification accuracies (blue for condition 1 and red for condition 2). Standard deviations are plotted as the vertical bars.

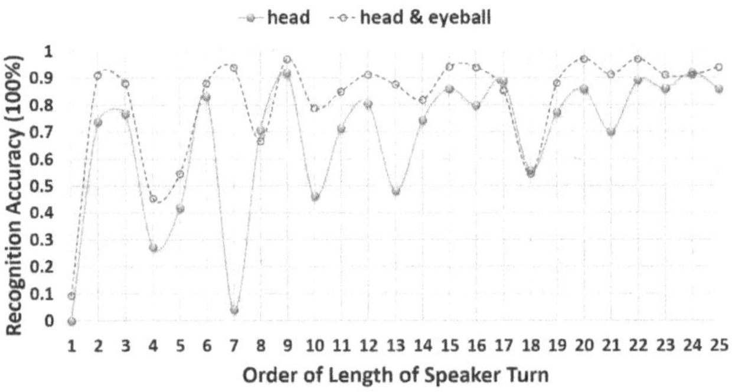

Figure 11. Subjective speaker identification accuracy as a function of speaker turn length. The red hollow circles show the results with Condition 2 (joint head and eyeball motion data) while the blue solid circles show the results with Condition 1 (only head motion data). In 21 out of 25 pairwise comparisons, Condition 2 outperforms Condition 1, while Condition 1 outperforms Condition 2 in 4 pairwise comparisons, whose indexes are 8, 17, 18 and 24.

higher recognition accuracies than those with Condition 1 (M=67.7%, SD=0.25): $t(24)=3.65$, $p<.01$. Therefore, the hypothesis H2-sub is accepted.

Test of the hypothesis H3-sub. To test the hypothesis H3-sub, the second type of recognition accuracy is taken into account, which is illustrated in Figure 11. As shown in this figure, the red and the blue curves do not show any obvious (increasing or decreasing) trend along with the length of speaker turn, which does not provide sufficient evidence to statistically test the hypothesis H3-sub.

Additionally, as observed in Figure 11, Condition 2 outperforms Condition 1 in 21 pair-wise comparisons while Condition 1 outperforms Condition 2 in 4 pair-wise comparisons ($8th$, $17th$, $18th$ and $24th$). In other words, Condition 1 outperforms Condition 2 with the probability of $16\%(=4/25)$. This implies that the hypothesis H3-sub cannot be rigorously validated for each pair-wise comparison, although in our experiments it holds true with the probability of $84\%(=21/25)$. On the other hand, the probability of the hypothesis H3-sub holding true, 84%, is substantially larger than the probability of the hypothesis H3-sub holding false, 16%, which is in line with the validated hypothesis H2-sub.

Furthermore, the recognition accuracies shown by the red points in Figure 11 are higher than the baseline (33.3%) except for the shortest (1st) speaker turn that lasts 1.1 seconds, while most of the blue points are higher than the baseline except for the shortest speaker turn (1.1 seconds) and the $7th$ one (6.2 seconds). These observations provide empirical evidence that in general the hypothesis H1-sub (either condition 1 or condition 2) holds true, in particular, when the length of speaker turn becomes large.

DISCUSSION

In this section, we discuss the experimental results from a multifaceted perspective, including both the objective analysis and the subjective judgment, along with the formulated hypotheses.

Discussion on the Hypotheses H1-obj and H1-sub

Both the hypotheses H1-obj and H1-sub are validated by the joint head and eyeball azimuth angles (Condition 2). This suggests that the joint head and eyeball movement data provides a reliable cue to identify the speaker from the interlocutors in a three-party conversation, which can be not only captured by the proposed objective analysis method but also perceived by human subjects.

The statistical validation of the hypothesis H1-obj suggests that the interactive behavior of eye contact plays an important role in speaker identification. This also serves an empirical foundation to properly merge eye contact into synthesized head and eyeball animations in order to build more socially engaging, realistic conversational characters in various applications.

Rienks et al. [35] reported that humans use the knowledge of gaze patterns to distinguish the speaker from listeners, which is in line with the successful validation of the hypothesis H1-sub in our work. Although eye contact is not explicitly indicated in the used animation clips, the validation of the hypothesis H1-sub suggests that human viewers could be intrinsically skilled at decoding the occurrences of eye contact or other interactive gaze patterns (e.g., convergence or divergence).

Additionally, Rienks et al. [35] reported that gaze estimated by the head azimuth angle alone does not provide a sufficient cue for reliable speaker identification, which is not supported by the validated hypothesis H1-sub in our work. This difference could result from three factors. First, the video clips used in [35] record virtual humans from the side view, which degrades the perceptual judgment on the gaze orientations for participants, while the animation clips in our work are created from the top view, which allows the participants to faithfully perceive and observe the gaze orientations. Second, from the participants' perspective, the subtle rotation angle of gaze could be easily overlooked. To overcome this problem, a gaze line is used in our work for highlighting the gaze orientation with even subtle angle change. Third, more importantly, the eyeball rotation angle is not considered in their work, while it is used in our work to estimate the gaze orientation. This factor is also supported by the statistically validated hypotheses H2-obj and H2-sub.

Discussion on the hypotheses H2-obj and H2-sub

The statistical validation of the hypotheses H2-obj and H2-sub suggests that the joint head and eyeball movement data provides a more reliable cue to identify the speaker from the interlocutors than the head movement data alone. In our study, the contribution of eyeball movement to the speaker identification can be well captured by our objective analysis method as well as subjective perception study experiment.

In the validation of the hypothesis H2-obj, a significant gap between Conditions 1 and 2 indicates that the eyeball movement is critical to improve the recognition accuracy in the objective analysis process. Not surprisingly, in the validation of the hypothesis H2-sub, a similar significant gap exists between Conditions 1 and 2. This suggests that the role of eyeball movement in three-party conversations can be directly perceived by human observers. With being said, we also observe that the head movement data alone can provide a reasonable cue for speaker identification. This observation suggests that human viewers are sensible to head movement for conversation coordination and are skilled in decoding information from the head movement.

The statistical valiation of the hypotheses H2-obj and H2-sub also provide convincing evidence that the eyeball movement is crucial to accurately estimate human gaze in a conversation, which contradicts to the previous finding that gaze can be well approximated by head orientations alone [37, 2].

Discussion on the hypotheses H3-obj and H3-sub

The hypothesis H3-obj is partially true in the range from 1 to 4 seconds; alternatively, fluctuations are observed in the range from 6 to 12 seconds. Moreover, the overall recognition accuracy in the range from 6 to 12 seconds is higher than that in the range from 1 to 4 seconds. Coincidentally, such observations were also reported in Rienks et al. [35]. On one hand, the observed overall increasing trend can be explained by more information provided in a longer speaker turn. On the other hand, the fluctuations observed in long intervals could be explained as follows: the information complexity increases with the increased length of speaker turn so that the proposed Markov process falls short of well capturing the increasing information complexity; therefore, its performance has fluctations in this range.

Although the hypothesis H3-sub is not statistically validated by the subjective judgments in our work, we observe that the averaged recognition accuracy (81%) is much higher than baseline (33.3%). This suggests that humans are intrinsically skilled at identifying the speaker so that the identification accuracy is independent of the length of speaker turn, to a certain extent.

CONCLUSIONS

In this work, we have conducted a multifaceted study to understand whether the speaker can be rigorously identified from the interlocutors involved in three-party conversations based on their gaze/head orientations. Based on recorded three-party conversational behavior datasets, a Markov process based statistical framework is proposed to model the sequence of eye contact between the human interlocutors, and further used to identify the speaker. Meanwhile, a user study is conducted to study this question using virtual characters in a conversation, animated by pre-recorded human movement data. Then, participants are invited to select the speaking virtual character by watching the animation clips of virtual three-party conversations.

Our results show that the proposed objective analysis method and humans are both capable of identifying the speaker and that interactive eye contact behaviors provide a rigorious cue for reliable speaker identification. Moreover, the gaze behaviors estimated from the joint head and eyeball movement data clearly outperforms those from head movement data alone. Additionally, the performance of the objective analysis depends on the length of speaker turn while human judgment is less dependent on it. Finally, our work indicates that the eyeball movement is essential to the accurate estimation of the gaze.

Some limitations exist in our current work:

1. This work relies on our definition of eye contact: eye contact is determined by the left-right angles of head and eyeball while the up-down angles are ignored. For some special cases such as interlocutors have very different heights, only the left-right angles could be insufficient to accurately estimate the occurrences of eye contact.

2. Eye contact used in the objective analysis is only one of the gaze interactive behaviors in multiparty conversations. The previous works [33, 13] have defined a few gaze interactive behaviors such as convergence and divergence. These interactive gaze behaviors are not considered in our current work.

3. The gaze lines used in the subjective judgment study play an important role in highlighting the gaze orientations. However, such visual representations may exaggerate the humans' perceptual capabilities on the conversational gaze.

4. The used datasets only contain three interlocutors standing at the three vertices of an equilateral triangle in a strict laboratory setting. It is still unclear whether our results can be rigorously generalized to other spatial arrangements of the interlocutors, to multiparty conversations with more than three interlocutors, or to coarse-grained gaze estimation. Furthermore, our work has not investigated the potential biases from individuals (e.g., gender, social status, emotion, etc.) and conversational topics.

5. Our work does not provide knowledge about what kind of gaze patterns are more reliable recognizer of speaker role and also overlooks the confidence of participants recognizing the speaker in the subjective experiments.

6. The participants in our subjective study acted as side observers instead of immersive interlocutors.

We will leave the tackling of the above limitations as the future work. Additionally, we will work on emerging the rendition of eye contact in the animation synthesis for virtual speaking and listening characters.

ACKNOWLEDGMENTS

This research is in part supported by NSF IIS-1524782 and National Natural Science Foundation of China Grant (No. 61328204). We would like to thank Binh Huy Le, Li Wei, Mingxuan Luo, Yaser Karbaschi, and Nafiseh Mehdipour for helping with the acquisition and processing of the used human motion dataset. We also wish to thank the anonymous CHI reviewers for their constructive comments.

REFERENCES

1. X. Anguera, S. Bozonnet, N. Evans, C. Fredouille, G. Friedland, and O. Vinyals. 2012. Speaker Diarization: A Review of Recent Research. *IEEE Transactions on Audio, Speech, and Language Processing* 20, 2 (2012), 356–370.

2. A. C. Beall, J. N. Bailenson, J. Loomis, J. Blascovich, and C. S. Rex. 2003. Non-Zero-Sum Gaze in Immersive Virtual Environments. In *International Conference on Human-Computer Interaction*. 1108–1112.

3. J. K Burgoon, L. A. Stern, and L. Dillman. 1995. *Interpersonal Adaptation: Dyadic Interaction Patterns*. Cambridge University Press.

4. C. Busso, Z. Deng, M. Grimm, U. Neumann, and S. Narayanan. 2007. Rigid Head Motion in Expressive Speech Animation: Analysis and Synthesis. *IEEE Trans. on Audio, Speech & Language Processing* 15, 3 (2007), 1075–1086.

5. C. Busso, Z. Deng, U. Neumann, and S. Narayanan. 2005. Natural head motion synthesis driven by acoustic prosodic features. *JVCA* 16, 3-4 (2005), 283–290.

6. J. Cassell and K. R. Thórisson. 1999. The Power of a Nod and a Glance: Envelope Vs. Emotional Feedback in Animated Conversational Agents. *Applied Artificial Intelligence* 13, 4 & 5 (1999), 519–538.

7. R. Alex Colburn, Michael F. Cohen, and Steven M. Drucker. 2000. *The Role of Eye Gaze in Avatar Mediated Conversational Interfaces*. Technical Report MSR-TR-2000-81. Microsoft Research. 9 pages.

8. Y. Ding, C. Pelachaud, and T. Artières. 2013. Modeling Multimodal Behaviors from Speech Prosody. In *International Conference on Intelligent Virtual Agents*. 217–228.

9. Y Ding, M Radenen, T Artières, and C Pelachaud. 2012. Eyebrow Motion Synthesis Driven by Speech. In *Workshop Affect, Compagnon Artificiel, Interaction (WACAI)*. 103–110.

10. Y. Ding, M. Radenen, T. Artières, and C. Pelachaud. 2013. Speech-driven Eyebrow Motion Synthesis With Contextual Markovian Models. In *ICASSP*. 3756–3760.

11. M. Garau, M. Slater, S. Bee, and M. A. Sasse. 2001. The impact of eye gaze on communication using humanoid avatars. In *Proceedings of the SIGCHI Conference on Human Factors in Computing Systems*. 309–316.

12. D. Gatica-Perez, G. Lathoud, J. Odobez, and I. McCowan. 2007. Audiovisual probabilistic tracking of multiple

speakers in meetings. *IEEE Transactions on Audio, Speech, and Language Processing* 15, 2 (2007), 601–616.

13. S. Gorga and K. Otsuka. 2010. Conversation scene analysis based on dynamic Bayesian network and image-based gaze detection. In *ICMI-MLMI*. 54.
14. D.K.J. Heylen, I. van Es, A. Nijholt, and Dr. E.M.A.G. van Dijk. 2002. Experimenting with the Gaze of a Conversational Agent. In *Proceedings International CLASS Workshop on Natural, Intelligent and Effective Interaction in Multimodal Dialogue Systems*. 93–100.
15. G. Hofer and H. Shimodaira. 2007. Automatic Head Motion Prediction from Speech Data. In *Proc. Interspeech*. 722–725.
16. H. Hung, Y. Huang, C. Yeo, and D. Gatica-Perez. 2008. Associating audio-visual activity cues in a dominance estimation framework. In *IEEE Computer Society Conference on Computer Vision and Pattern Recognition Workshops*. 1–6.
17. R. Ishii, S. Kumano, and K. Otsuka. 2015. Predicting next speaker based on head movement in multi-party meetings. In *ICASSP*. 2319–2323.
18. R. Ishii, K. Otsuka, S. Kumano, and J. Yamato. 2014. Analysis and modeling of next speaking start timing based on gaze behavior in multi-party meetings. In *ICASSP*. 694–698.
19. R. Ishii, K. Otsuka, S. Kumano, and J. Yamato. 2016. Prediction of Who Will Be the Next Speaker and When Using Gaze Behavior in Multiparty Meetings. *ACM Trans. Interact. Intell. Syst.* 6, 1 (2016), 4:1–4:31.
20. K. Ishizuka, S. Araki, K. Otsuka, T. Nakatani, and M. Fujimoto. 2009. A Speaker Diarization Method Based on the Probabilistic Fusion of Audio-visual Location Information. In *ICMI-MLMI*. 55–62.
21. T. Kawahara, T. Iwatate, and K. Takanashi. 2012. Prediction of Turn-Taking by Combining Prosodic and Eye-Gaze Information in Poster Conversations. In *INTERSPEECH*. 727–730.
22. C. L. Kleinke. 1986. Gaze and eye contact: A research review. *Psychological Bulletin* 100, 1 (1986), 78–100.
23. B. J. Lance and S. C. Marsella. 2008. A Model of Gaze for the Purpose of Emotional Expression in Virtual Embodied Agents. In *AAMAS*. 199–206.
24. B. H. Le, X. Ma, and Z. Deng. 2012. Live Speech Driven Head-and-Eye Motion Generators. *IEEE Transactions on Visualization and Computer Graphics* 18, 11 (2012), 1902–1914.
25. X. Ma and Z. Deng. 2009. Natural Eye Motion Synthesis by Modeling Gaze-Head Coupling. In *IEEE Virtual Reality Conference*. 143–150.
26. R. Maatman, J. Gratch, and S. Marsella. 2005. Natural behavior of a listening agent. In *International Workshop on IVA*. 25–36.
27. S. Mariooryad and C. Busso. 2012. Generating Human-Like Behaviors Using Joint, Speech-Driven Models for Conversational Agents. *IEEE Transactions on Audio, Speech, and Language Processing* 20, 8 (2012), 2329–2340.
28. S. Masuko and J. Hoshino. 2007. Head-eye Animation Corresponding to a Conversation for CG Characters. *Comput. Graph. Forum* 26 (2007), 303–312.
29. L. Morency, I. de Kok, and J. Gratch. 2008. Predicting Listener Backchannels: A Probabilistic Multimodal Approach. In *International Conference on Intelligent Virtual Agents*. 176–190.
30. L. Morency, I. de Kok, and J. Gratch. 2010. A probabilistic multimodal approach for predicting listener backchannels. *Autonomous Agents and Multi-Agent Systems* 20, 1 (2010), 70–84.
31. A. Normoyle, J. B. Badler, T. Fan, N. I. Badler, V. J. Cassol, and S. R. Musse. 2013. Evaluating Perceived Trust from Procedurally Animated Gaze. In *Motion in Games*. 141–148.
32. A. Noulas, G. Englebienne, and B. J. A. Krose. 2012. Multimodal Speaker Diarization. *IEEE Trans. Pattern Anal. Mach. Intell.* 34, 1 (2012), 79–93.
33. K. Otsuka. 2011. Multimodal Conversation Scene Analysis for Understanding People's Communicative Behaviors in Face-to-Face Meetings. In *Human Interface and the Management of Information*. 171–179.
34. K. Otsuka, H. Sawada, and J. Yamato. 2007. Automatic inference of cross-modal nonverbal interactions in multiparty conversations: "who responds to whom, when, and how?" from gaze, head gestures, and utterances. In *ICMI*. 255–262.
35. R. J. Rienks, R. Poppe, and D. Heylen. 2010. Differences in head orientation behavior for speakers and listeners: an experiment in a virtual environment. *ACM Transactions on Applied Perception* 7, 1 (2010), 2:1–2:13.
36. K. Ruhland, C. E Peters, S. Andrist, J. B Badler, N. I Badler, M. Gleicher, B. Mutlu, and R. McDonnell. 2015. A Review of Eye Gaze in Virtual Agents, Social Robotics and HCI: Behaviour Generation, User Interaction and Perception. *Computer Graphics Forum* 34, 6 (2015), 299–326.
37. R. Stiefelhagen. 2002. Tracking Focus of Attention in Meetings. In *ICMI*. 273–280.
38. S. E. Tranter and D. A. Reynolds. 2006. An overview of automatic speaker diarization systems. *IEEE Transactions on Audio, Speech, and Language Processing* 14, 5 (2006), 1557–1565.
39. R. Vertegaal, G. van der Veer, and H. Vons. 2000. Effects of Gaze on Multiparty Mediated Communication. In *Graphics Interface*. Morgan Kaufmann, 95–102.

Supporting Making Fixations and the Effect on Gaze Gesture Performance

Howell Istance
University of Tampere
Tampere, Finland
howell.istance@staff.uta.fi

Aulikki Hyrskykari
University of Tampere
Tampere, Finland
ah@staff.uta.fi

ABSTRACT
Gaze gestures are deliberate patterns of eye movements that can be used to invoke commands. These are less reliant on accurate measurement and calibration than other gaze-based interaction techniques. These may be used with wearable displays fitted with eye tracking capability, or as part of an assistive technology. The visual stimuli in the information on the display that can act as fixation targets may or may not be sparse and will vary over time. The paper describes an experiment to investigate how the amount of information provided on a display to assist making fixations affects gaze gesture performance. The impact of providing visualization guides and small fixation targets on the time to complete gestures and error rates is presented. The number and durations of fixations made during gesture completion is used to explain differences in performance as a result of practice and direction of eye movement.

Author Keywords
Gaze gestures; gaze gesture performance; fixation targets; fixation duration.

ACM Classification Keywords
H.5.2 User interfaces: Input devices and strategies.

INTRODUCTION
The use of eye tracking technology is becoming more widespread and can be integrated with mobile devices, public displays and wearable displays, as well as it's more established use with desktop computers. This provides both information about where a person is looking on a display or in the world, and opportunities to use gaze-based interaction techniques. These techniques divide into three groups: those based on extended fixations (or dwells); those based on patterns of saccadic eye movements, or gaze gestures; and those based on recognizing smooth pursuit patterns of motion. [18].

Permission to make digital or hard copies of all or part of this work for personal or classroom use is granted without fee provided that copies are not made or distributed for profit or commercial advantage and that copies bear this notice and the full citation on the first page. Copyrights for components of this work owned by others than ACM must be honored. Abstracting with credit is permitted. To copy otherwise, or republish, to post on servers or to redistribute to lists, requires prior specific permission and/or a fee. Request permissions from Permissions@acm.org.

CHI 2017, May 06-11, 2017, Denver, CO, USA
© 2017 ACM. ISBN 978-1-4503-4655-9/17/05...$15.00
DOI: http://dx.doi.org/10.1145/3025453.3025920

Wearable near eye displays are becoming increasingly popular as consumer electronic devices. The VR headset (of type HTC Vive) can be fitted with relatively high quality eye tracking capability [27]. It will also be possible to fit gaze tracking capability to see-through 'smartglasses' (of type Epson Moverio), which can project information onto the user's view of the world. It is likely that the position of these glasses with the respect to the head will be less stable than the VR headset. It is also likely that less processing power will be available to smartglasses leading to lower sample rates of gaze position.

Saccadic gaze gestures are deliberate patterns of eye movements that can be identified and used to give a particular command [15], for example, to zoom into the display, to show the next email, or to switch off the augmented information. They offer a hands-free interaction technique that is less reliant on accurate measurement of gaze position, and less reliant on maintaining good calibration. Dwell-based interaction requires both of these features.

There are several use cases for saccadic gaze gestures that suggest themselves. One is using smartglasses, say at a workplace such as engineering maintenance, without voice commands and the use of the hands [30]. Another is hands free interaction with mobile displays [2, 8]. A significant use case is as an assistive technique for motor impaired users. This could be either with mobile devices that have limited eye tracking capability, or in gaze control of applications where dwell is problematic, e.g. games [15]. Gestures may be less suitable however when interacting with, or being seen by, other people if the reasons for the eye movements are misinterpreted [1].

Making gaze gestures is quite different from other visual tasks, such as reading or visual search. Gestures involve making deliberate eye movements, and generally extracting little or no information from the component fixations. By contrast in reading, eye movements are directed by characteristics of the task (top-down processes) and of the visual stimulus (bottom-up processes) [24].

Normally the visual system requires a target for the eyes to fixate upon. There may be suitable fixation targets within the displayed data or there may not be. The question then arises of whether specific fixation targets should be provided in order for someone to be able to make these patterns of eye movements efficiently and reliably. If fixation targets are to be superimposed on the display surface, then they should have minimal impact on the information displayed upon it.

The research question addressed in this paper is what the effect on gaze gesture performance will be of different amounts of visual information specifically aimed at supporting making fixations. We aim to help interaction designers to understand how to support making gaze gestures while viewing an information display.

We present a detailed study of how specific support in making fixations impacts gesture speed and error rates. The work is novel in that it investigates gaze gesture performance using a high sample rate tracker. Facilitated by the sample rate, this is the first study to offer explanations of differences in gesture performance in terms of number and durations of fixations.

Background

During normal visual work, the eyes are constantly moving. Within this stream of normal eye movements, a pattern of deliberate eye movements that constitutes the gaze gesture has to be detected. Different types of gestures can be categorized then according to (1) how the start and end of the pattern is recognized (gesture segmentation), (2) how the pattern of eye movements is detected, and (3) how complex the pattern is.

(1) Recognizing the start and end of the pattern

Gesture segmentation refers to recognizing the start and end of a gesture pattern. This may use a starting fixation in a particular location and possibly a terminating fixation in the same location or zone. Here all gestures start and end in the same location, and the gesture consists of the sequence of locations visited in between. Another approach to segmentation is to use a dwell in a particular location to signal the start of a gesture. Alternatively, there is no explicit segmentation and the stream of zones or directions arising from normal eye movements is continuously parsed. A gesture is identified as soon as a valid sequence is detected.

(2) Gesture detection schemes

The pattern of eye movements that make up the gesture can be detected in several ways. These are boundary crossing, active zones, changes in saccade direction, shape-tracing, eye-based head gestures and smooth-pursuit. Each scheme has different properties that may be appropriate for different use scenarios and applications.

Boundary Crossing [9, 12, 14]. A gesture is registered by a fixation on one side of a boundary followed by another fixation on the other side of it. In order to prevent unintentional registrations of gestures, a gesture may require multiple crossings (over and back) to be completed in sequence. The boundary may be soft, i.e. that of an on-screen object, or hard such as the edge of the screen.

Active Zones [4, 15, 20, 26, 29]. Instead of simply crossing a boundary, a gesture is registered by hit testing whether fixations occur in specific designated areas of the screen or zones and in a particular sequence. Changing the number of zones, or the sequence in which zones are visited, produces a different gesture. An example of such a scheme in context of gaze control of games is shown in Figure 1.

Figure 1: Active zones used for detecting gaze gestures while playing World of Warcraft located around the player character. The white lines indicate a 3-stroke gesture and not were visible during use [15].

Changes in Saccade Direction [7]. A gesture is a change in the direction of the gaze path without reference to any external features (such as a boundaries or zones). The gesture can be made anywhere and the pattern consists of a sequence of directions. A scheme may define a number of patterns, and the normal gaze path is monitored by a classifier to determine if any of the patterns have been generated. The patterns may be of varying levels of complexity, although the simpler the pattern the greater the risk of the classifier producing false positives.

Shape tracing [9, 26]. A gesture results from an attempt to trace the outline of a shape with the gaze path, for example two lines at right angles, a square or a circle. This may use the edges of an on-screen object as a visual guide, or not.

Eye-based head gestures [19, 22]. A head mounted eye tracker will detect a characteristic pattern of eye movements if the head is moved, with say a nod, while the viewer continues to look at an object. The rationale is that controlled, deliberate head movements are easier to make than deliberate eye movements.

Smooth pursuit gestures [17, 6]. Smooth pursuit gestures result from tracking the eyes while a person looks at a moving object in the world or on a display surface. Normal saccadic eye movement is suspended during smooth pursuits. The gestures would be characterized by the direction, velocity and possibly shape of the motion path.

(3) Pattern Complexity
The complexity of the pattern of movements is described by the number of deliberate eye movements or 'strokes'. In the literature, this complexity ranges from single stroke gestures [21] up to 6 stroke gestures [8]. High numbers of strokes are typically used to reduce the risk of false positives where no explicit segmentation event is used. However, higher numbers of strokes carry an overhead of both time to make the gesture, and effort. In a study [15] of eye movements made during game playing, there were between 3 to 5 times as many normal eye movements that would have been interpreted as 2-stroke horizontal and vertical gestures compared with 2-stroke diagonal gestures. Significantly there were no patterns of eye movements that would have been interpreted as 3-stroke gestures.

Gestures investigated in the current study
We chose to investigate an active zones scheme with explicit segmentation. The sequence of zones began with a fixation in the center zone followed by one or more fixations outside the center zone and continued until the next fixation back in the center. This was motivated by the prevalence of this approach in the literature and alignment with the previous investigation of gestures in games. As no naturally occurring patterns of eye movements that could be interpreted as 3-stroke gestures had previously been found, we considered it unnecessary to study any greater complexity. Thus, the current study considered only 2-stroke and 3-stroke gestures.

EXPERIMENT
The effect on gaze gesture performance of providing different amounts of visual information to aid making fixations was investigated in an experiment. Four zones were arranged around the center of the display. The zones extended to the edges of the display in each direction. The distance from the edge of the zone to the center of the display was chosen as a compromise between reducing the risk of unintended gestures and the effort required to make deliberate eye movements.

The information added to the display to enable the viewer to fixate within the zone was split into two types. One was the visualization of the size and location of the zone, and the other was the provision of small fixation targets within the zones.

In all conditions, the center zone was visible as a circular blue-grey semi-transparent overlay, shown in Figure 2a.

The visualization of the outer zones was one variable and was represented by 3 levels:

- no visualization of the outer zone (Figure 2a)
- showing only the *leading border* of the zone closest to the center zone (Figure 2b), and
- showing the size and location of the *zone area* by means of a blue semi-transparent overlay and a black border (Figure 2c).

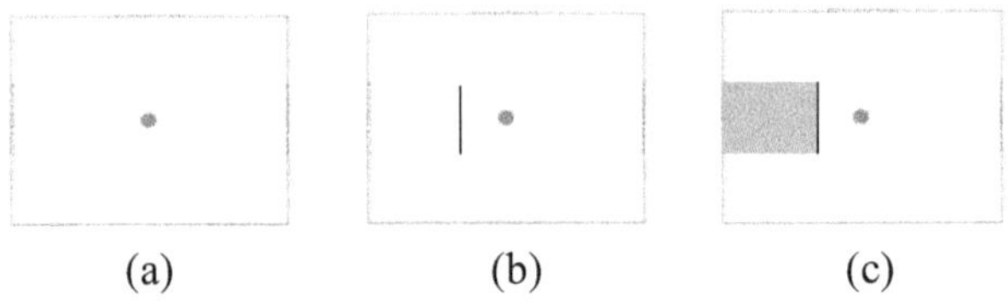

Figure 2: Three levels of visualizing an outer zone: (a) no visualization, center zone only is visible (b) leading border (c) zone area

The provision of fixation targets was a second variable and was represented by 2 levels:

- no dot, and
- small circular black dot in the center of zone.

These conditions are summarized in Figure 3.

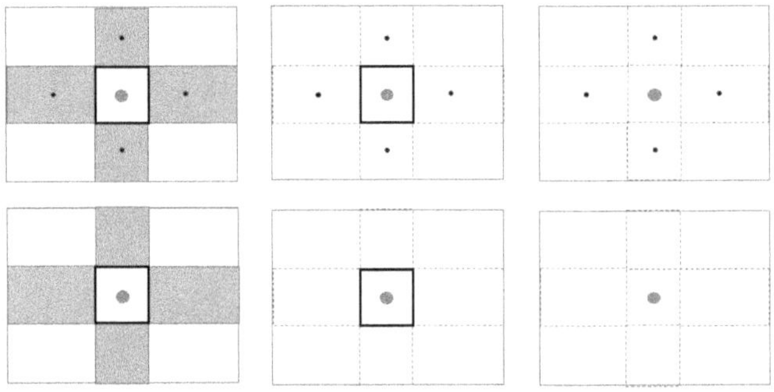

Figure 3. Six conditions arising from 3 levels of the visualization variable and 2 levels of the fixation target variable. The dotted lines show the extents of the active zones and were not visible on the display.

Previous work [15] had shown that 2-stroke gestures consisting of horizontal and vertical eye movements were completed more quickly than ones with diagonal movements, although the difference was small. In the case of 3-stroke gestures the difference was not significant. Other studies of gaze gesture performance have also reported different speeds of gesture completion depending on whether the gesture consisted of horizontal/vertical eye movements or diagonal movements [10]. The peak velocities for diagonal movements is less than those on the horizontal/vertical meridians [3], which may indicate that diagonal deliberate eye movements are more difficult to control.

We expected that the impact of adding information to the display to aid making fixations would be influenced by the difficulty of making the gesture. We considered the difficulty of making the gesture to be determined by the predominant direction of eye movement and by gesture complexity. We compared gestures consisting primarily of horizontal/vertical eye movements with those consisting primarily of diagonal eye movements. Gesture complexity was represented by 2 levels, 2-stroke and 3-stroke gestures. These variables are illustrated in Figure 4 below.

In summary, there are four independent variables in the study

- Zone visualization: 3 levels (no visualization, leading border only visible, zone area visible)
- Fixation targets: 2 levels (absent, present)
- Predominant direction of eye movement during gesture: 2 levels (horizontal/vertical, diagonal)
- Gesture complexity: 2 levels (2 strokes, 3 strokes)

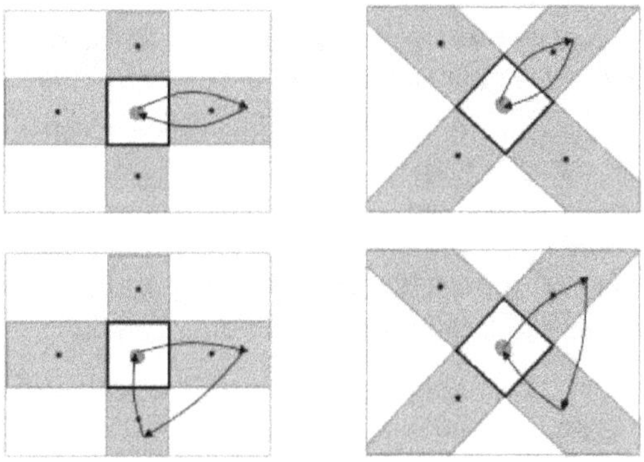

Figure 4: Two stroke gestures shown above and three stroke gestures shown below. Gestures consisting predominantly of horizontal/vertical eye movements are shown on the left and of diagonal eye movements are shown on the right.

Dependent Variables

The indicators of performance that were studied were speed and accuracy.

Speed is the time to complete an error-free gesture. The duration of the gesture was defined as being from the onset of the saccade that left the center zone, to include fixations and intermediate saccades in the zones that made up the gesture, and terminating with the end of the first saccade to land back in the center zone. The fixation prior to the gesture commencing and the first fixation on terminating are each specifically excluded from the duration of the gesture. This is important as the duration of either (or both) of these is large in comparison with the total duration of the gesture, particularly in the case of the 2-stroke gesture.

An *error* is defined as one of the following cases

- a pattern of eye movements where a fixation in the zone or zones that comprise the gesture is omitted,
- a pattern which includes fixations in zones that are not part of the gesture,
- a pattern in the case of 3 stroke gesture where the zones are visited in the wrong order, and
- trials where the gesture has not been completed within 3 seconds.

Fixations made outside any of the zones did not constitute an error, as long as fixations were made in the zones in the order prescribed by a particular pattern.

Experimental Design and Procedure

Three-stroke gestures clearly take longer to complete than 2-stroke gestures as they entail at least one extra saccade and one extra fixation. Consequently, we analyzed the data for each separately to reduce the complexity of the data model in the analysis of variance. The data for both 2- and 3-stroke gestures were collected in the same sessions.

A 3x2x2 repeated measures factorial design was used for each number of strokes. With 3 levels of visualization (none, leading borders, zone area) * 2 levels of targets (no targets, targets) * 2 levels of direction (horizontal/vertical, diagonal) this gives 12 combinations. For each combination, there were 4 initial directions of eye movement (either up, right, down, left, or upper left, upper right, lower right, lower left). Thus 48 trials are needed to provide all possible combinations. The initial direction was not considered as an independent variable but the trials were balanced with respect to this. The 48 trials were randomized into 2 sets of 24 trials for each participant. This gave a total of 4 sets of 24 trials, 2 for 2 stroke gestures and 2 for 3 stroke gestures. These 96 trials constituted one block. For each participant, this block was repeated in the same order once following a rest break. This was to give the opportunity of comparing individual gesture completion times between blocks knowing that each repetition would be separated by the same number of trials.

Participants

Twenty-four participants were recruited from staff and students at the University of Tampere. However, data for one participant was lost, leaving 23 complete data sets.

Fifteen of the participants were male, nine were female. Their ages varied from 19 to 57, with an average of 29. Fifteen had uncorrected vision.

In accordance with university ethics procedures, participants were each given and signed a written description of the purpose of the experiment. They were told that they could withdraw at any time without any negative consequence. The written description stated that all data collected during their trial would be scored securely and used anonymously.

Data collection

All data for each participant was collected in a single session. Each session lasted approximately 1 hour and 10 minutes. The session had 3 parts, practice, first block of trials, and second block of trials. The eye tracker was re-calibrated at the beginning of the first and second block with a procedure involving looking at a matrix of 9 dots on the screen. There was no re-calibration within blocks, but a drift check was made at the beginning of each trial.

The first part lasted 20 minutes and consisted of a spoken introduction to the experiment and to the eye tracking equipment, and the administration of the written consent. It included a demonstration of the different gestures and the different amounts of visual information provided. It included

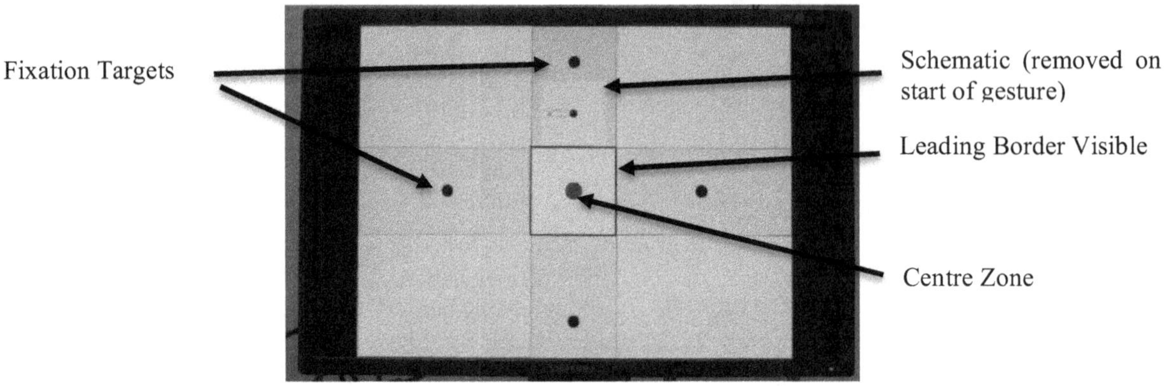

Figure 5: Appearance of screen at the start of a trial where both zone area and fixation targets are visible. A schematic of the gesture to be performed, here a 2-stroke horizontal gesture to the left, is overlaid on the upper part of the screen

a training session where the participant could practice making the gestures.

Following a break of a few minutes, the second part commenced. The first block of 96 trials was conducted as 4 sets of 24 trials. After each set the participant could rest and move. Each trial commenced with a mouse click under participant control.

At the start of a trial, the screen appeared with the particular combination of zone visualization, fixation targets and orientation (see Figure 5). The actual gesture to be performed was shown in a small schematic in the upper central part of the screen. All trials in a set were either 2 stroke or 3 stroke gestures. The participant memorized the action required and then looked at the center zone, which caused the schematic to be removed. After a 2 second delay, the color of the circular center zone changed to green, which together with a simultaneous beep signal informed the participant that they could make the gesture when they were ready. On completing the gesture, the center zone returned to the default blue-grey color. If an error occurred, feedback was given by an audio signal and the center zone turning red briefly after the terminating fixation before reverting to the default color. The next trial commenced when the participant clicked the mouse button. After the 96 trials were completed, the participant was asked to leave the lab and take a 20-minute break.

On their return, the third part commenced. The 96 trials were repeated in the same order as in the second session.

Equipment Used

An EyeLink 1000 eye tracker from SR Research was used together with a headrest, which provided a sample rate of 1000Hz. The tracker reports saccades made by the eyes. A fixation then is defined as any gap between the end of one saccade and the start of the next. Low sample rate trackers, of say 30Hz, are not able to do this accurately. A full discussion of fixation definition is given in Holmqvist [11]. The eye tracker was located on a desk and participants viewed the display seated at a distance of 985 mm.

The eye tracking systems that will be used for actual gesture detection in the situations described in the introduction will be far less accurate and have a far lower sample rate than the tracker we have used. The use of an accurate high sample rate tracker provided detailed information about eye movements and fixations made within a gesture.

The size of the components and the distances between these from Figure 5 are shown in Table 1.

Distance	Visual Angle
Center Zone diameter	1.0
Fixation target diameter	0.6
Center zone edge to leading border	1.9
Center zone edge to inside edge of nearest fixation target	6.5

Table 1: distances between on-screen objects in degrees of visual angle, viewing distance 985 mm

Hypotheses and expected results

We hypothesized that the more information provided, the better the gesture performance would be. We also hypothesized that the impact of providing visual support would have a more positive effect on performance as gestures became more difficult to make. In accordance with our previous work [15], we expected a learning effect and that the times and errors made during the second block of trials would be less than the first block of trials. We expected that 2-stroke horizontal/vertical gestures would be made more quickly than 2-stroke diagonal ones.

RESULTS

Presence of a learning effect between blocks of trials

There were 4 repeated trials within each combination of experimental conditions, balanced across the initial direction of eye movement. The average of the error-free gesture durations of these 4 trials was taken as the score for each participant. Error trials were excluded from the average. There were no combinations of conditions for any participant where all 4 trials were in error and using the average duration avoids the problem of missing data. The means and standard deviations of all participant scores is shown in Table 2.

		Block 1	Block 2
2 stroke	mean (ms)	704.8	617.4
	(std dev)	(174.6)	(176.7)
3 stroke	mean (ms)	1163.0	1058.4
	(std dev)	(293.8)	(249.0)

Table 2: Means and standard deviations of average gesture durations for error free trials for each participant, n =23

A 2x2 factorial analysis of variance (blocks and strokes) was conducted on the data summarized in Table 2. This showed that there was a significant main effect for blocks ($F(1,22) = 10.4$, $p = 0.004$) and a significant main effect for strokes ($F(1,22) = 205.0$, $p < 0.001$), but no significant interaction blocks x strokes interaction effect ($F(1,22) = 0.308$, $p = 0.58$). On the basis of this, we are justified in analyzing the data for the blocks and for the strokes separately.

The total numbers of trials in the study was 4416 (96 trials/block * 2 blocks * 23 participants). Of these 225 were error trials (5.1%). These were distributed across Blocks and Number of Strokes as shown in Table 3.

	Block 1	Block 2	Total
2 stroke	45	14	**59**
3 stroke	101	65	**166**
Total	**146**	**79**	**225**

Table 3: Distribution of 225 error trials between Blocks for 2 and 3 stroke gestures

Blocks and the number of strokes a gesture has are not independent in terms of the numbers of errors made (using Chi-Square(1), $p = 0.033$). Performance when making 2 stroke gestures improves more than 3 stroke gestures between the two blocks in terms of numbers of errors.

Two stroke gestures

Data from the second block of trials only was analyzed in order to study the impact of the independent variables on practiced performance. The means and standard deviations of the average completion times of the error-free gestures for each participant made in each treatment condition is shown in Table 4.

	Diagonal			Horizontal/Vertical		
	None	Leading Border	Zone Area	None	Leading Border	Zone Area
no targets	665.7 (227.9)	652.7 (189.8)	662.3 (217.9)	633.2 (223.4)	620.7 (144.0)	594.6 (182.3)
targets	617.7 (243.8)	650.1 (265.5)	569.3 (175.6)	616.6 (229.4)	575.3 (201.2)	560.0 (178.2

Table 4: Means and standard deviations of participant score (in milliseconds) for error free trials 2-stroke gestures, n = 23, Block 2 data only

The means, together with 95% within-participant confidence intervals, are shown in Figure 6. Here data from the individual trials is used and the between-participant variability is removed. This is done by normalizing the data between participants such that each has the same average [5]. This is only for visualization of the data and not for statistical comparisons.

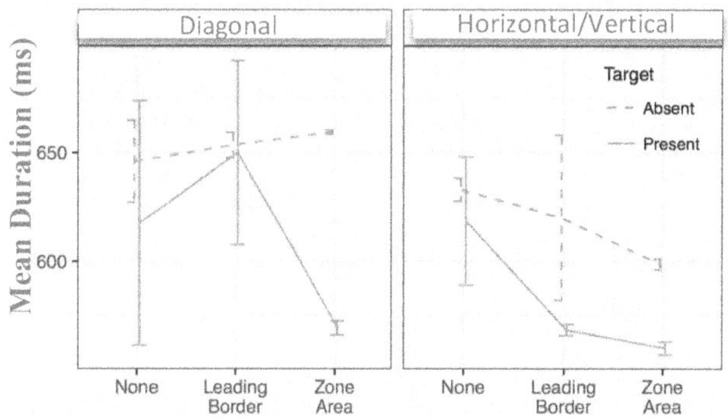

Figure 6: Mean values with 95% within-subject confidence intervals

An analysis of variance used a 3 factor within-participants repeated measures design with direction of eye movement (diagonal, horizontal/vertical), visualization of active zone (none, leading borders, zones), and presence of fixation targets (no targets, targets) as the factors.

Mauchly's Test indicated that the assumption of sphericity had been violated (Chi-Square (2) = 17.9, $p < 0.001$) therefore degrees of freedom were corrected using Greenhouse-Geisser estimates of sphericity ($\eta = 0.635$).

There were significant main effects of the direction of eye movement ($F(1,22) = 12.4$, $p = 0.002$), and the presence of fixation targets ($F(1,22) = 5.9$, $p = 0.024$), but not of visualization of zones ($F(1.27,27.9) = 2.48$, $p = 0.12$). There were no significant 2-way or 3-way interaction effects. The directions of these main effects were as predicted.

Gestures consisting of diagonal eye movements took significantly longer to make than those consisting of only horizontal/vertical eye movements.

Providing fixation targets enabled gestures to be made more quickly than when these were not provided.

There is no overall main effect for visualization of zones. As there is a main effect for direction of eye movement, we analyzed the data for horizontal/vertical gestures separately. We can assume sphericity (Mauchly's Test, Chi-Square (2) = 0.75, $p = 0.69$) within this data. A 2 (no targets, targets) x 3 (no visualization, leading borders, zones) factorial analysis of variance showed that there is a main effect for visualization ($F(2,22) = 4.2$, $p = 0.021$) as well as for targets ($F(1,22) = 4.77$, $p = 0.04$). There was no significant interaction effect ($F(2,44) = 0.24$, $p = 0.8$). Examination of the significant effect of visualization by pairwise post-hoc comparisons, with the Bonferoni adjustment applied shows that only the *no visualization* and *zone area* conditions are significantly different from each other (p = 0.022).

So only in the case of horizontal/vertical 2-stroke gestures did visualization of the zone improve performance.

The total numbers of errors made summed across participants when attempting 2 stroke gestures is shown in Table 5.

Practiced 2-stroke gestures

	Diagonal		Horizontal/Vertical	
	no targets	targets	no targets	targets
None	4	0	1	1
Leading Border	1	0	1	1
Zone Area	2	0	3	0

Table 5: Absolute frequencies of errors, Block 2 data only, 23 participants made 4 gestures per condition = 92 trials per cell, a total of 14 errors in 1104 trials

While it should be remembered that the data refers to well-practiced behavior (Block 2 data only), the numbers of errors are very low. In the fixation target conditions, there are nearly no errors for either diagonal or horizontal/vertical eye movements.

Three stroke gestures

The corresponding data for the 3 stroke gestures is shown in Table 6, again from Block 2 trials only. The scores are the averages of the repeated error-free trials in each condition.

	Diagonal			Horizontal/Vertical		
	None	Leading Border	Zone Area	None	Leading Border	Zone Area
no targets	1122.8 (294.8)	1191.6 (299.7)	1195.6 (531.7)	1123.6 (292.4)	1123.6 (292.4)	1049.2 (277.6)
targets	958.2 (238.5)	942.0 (249.5)	1036.3 (329.3)	996.7 (302.5	1023.2 (330.3)	996.5 (260.5)

Table 6: Mean and standard deviations of participant scores (in milliseconds) for 3–stroke gestures per participant, Block 2 data only, n = 23

A similar visualization of the averages and 95% within-participant confidence intervals is shown in Figure 7.

Mauchly's Test indicated that the assumption of sphericity had been violated (Chi-Square (2) = 10.9, p = 0.004) therefore degrees of freedom were corrected using Greenhouse-Geisser estimates of sphericity (η = 0.711).

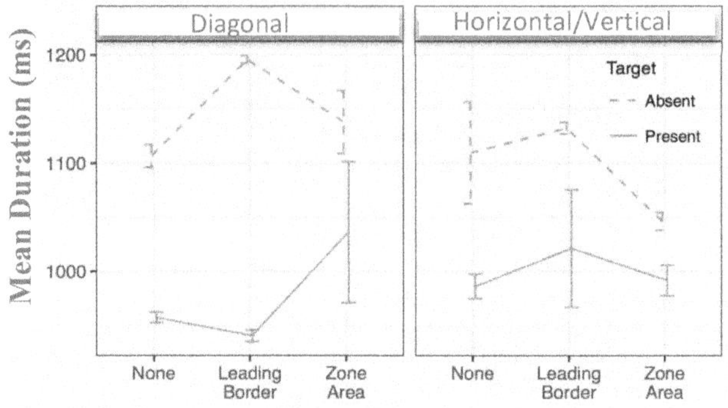

Figure 7: Mean values with 95% within-subject confidence intervals

There was a significant main effect of the presence of fixation targets (F(1,22) = 30.5, p < 0.001), but not of visualization (F (1.42,31.5) = 0.32, p = 0.65), nor of the predominant direction of eye movement (F(1,22) = 0.63, p = 0.44), and there were no significant 2-way or 3-way interaction effects. However, the interaction between direction of eye movement and fixation targets approaches, although does not reach, significance (F(1,22) = 3.94, p = 0.06).

The corresponding error data (Table 7) shows considerably more errors for 3 stroke gestures where there are no fixation targets in comparison with 2 stroke gestures. Most of these errors result from missing either the first or the second zone. These 'miss' errors are reduced by the extent of visualizing the zones. In the fixation target conditions, however, the error rate is almost zero, regardless of the direction of eye movement and the visualization of the zone.

Investigating causes of performance differences

We can examine the composition of gestures in terms of saccades and fixations to try to explain some of the observed differences in times to complete gestures. Why should gestures get faster with practice or with the presence of fixation targets? Are there fewer fixations, or shorter fixations, or both? The data provided by the eye tracker enables reliable segmentation of the time to complete a gesture into its component saccades and fixations. Saccades are ballistic and are generally very short in duration compared with fixations. We can examine possible reasons for the improvement in speed for 2 stroke gestures in terms of the fixations made during the gesture.

To recap, the gesture duration is from the start of the saccade leaving the center zone to the end of the saccade arriving back in the center zone. The minimum number of fixations is 1, so a *minimal gesture* consists a single saccade from the center zone followed by a single fixation in the outer zone and then a saccade back to the center zone.

	Practiced 3-stroke gestures			
	Predominantly diagonal eye movements		Predominantly horizontal/vertical eye movements	
	no targets	targets	no targets	targets
None	17 *(5+4 [a]+8[b])*	1	12 *(4+3 [a]+5[b])*	2
Leading Border	13 *(6+5 [a]+2[b])*	1	5 *(1+2 [a]+2[b])*	2
Zone Area	6 *(3+2 [a]+1[b])*	0	4 *(2+0 [a]+2[b])*	2

Table 7: Absolute frequencies of errors, Block 2 data only, 23 participants made 4 gestures per condition = 92 trials per cell, a total of 65 errors in 1104 trials, [a] missed 1st zone, [b] missed 2nd zone

Two findings involving improvement in speed of completion of 2 stroke gestures are examined here.

(i) 2 stroke gestures in Block 2 are made more quickly than those in Block 1

Table 8 shows the absolute numbers of 2 stroke gestures completed with 1, 2 and more than 2 fixations respectively. The duration values shown are the means of the single fixation durations or the means of the sum of the 2 fixations. The standard deviations of these distributions are shown in brackets. In Block 2, 87% of all gestures were completed at most 2 fixations. The difference between the distribution of frequencies between Block 1 and Block 2 is significant (Chi-Square (2), $p < 0.001$).

nr of fixations	Block 1 n	cum %	duration (ms)	Block 2 n	cum %	duration (ms)
1	384	36.3	436.9 (195.7)	544	49.9	413.3 (178.1)
2	487	82.2	563.5 (224.8)	404	87	481.1 (181.2)
3+	188	100		142	100	
total	1059			1090		

Table 8: Comparison of the numbers of fixations made in error-free 2 stroke gestures between Block 1 and Block 2, together with means and standard deviations

One reason then for the performance improvement with practice is that the proportion of minimal gestures increases from Block 1 (36.3%) to Block 2 (49.9%). It can be seen that the sum of the 2 fixations is far less than 2 x the duration of the single fixation. Breaking down the combined durations in row 2 of Table 8, Table 9 shows the mean durations of the first and second fixations respectively. This suggests that a *corrective saccade* is being made between the 2 fixations [28].

	n	1st fixation mean (ms)	2nd fixation mean (ms)
Block 1	487	200.7	362.7
Block 2	404	177.4	303.3

Table 9: For gestures completed with 2 fixations only, means of the first and second fixation durations respectively for Block 1 and for Block 2

If this is the case, then the effect of practice is to reduce the number of corrective saccades being made while making the gesture. Fully practiced performance could be tentatively assumed to be the case where all gestures are minimal gestures and made with 1 fixation only.

(ii) Gestures made with horizontal or vertical eye movements were made more quickly than those made with diagonal eye movements.

Table 10 offers a similar explanation for the difference found between the times to complete gestures with horizontal and vertical eye movements and diagonal eye movements respectively. The differences in the frequencies of gestures completed with 1 fixation, with 2 fixations and more than 2 fixations are significant (Chi-Square (2), $p = 0.013$). The probability of completing a horizontal-vertical gesture with one fixation is 0.538, while it is 0.461 for diagonal movement gestures. There is no apparent difference in the durations of the component fixations. The higher probability of making diagonal gestures with 2 or more fixations means that sample means of whole durations are higher.

nr of fixations	Horizontal /Vertical n	cum %	duration	Diagonal n	cum %	duration
1	293	53.8%	411 (165.8)	251	46.1%	416 (191.8)
2	194	89.4%	479 (185.4)	210	84.6%	483 (177.6)
3+	58	100%		84	100%	
total	545			545		

Table 10: Comparison between the numbers of fixations made while making error-free horizontal/vertical gestures and diagonal 2 stroke gestures respectively, Block 2 data only

DISCUSSION

The study shows that for practiced performance there is a clear relationship between the difficulty of making a gaze gesture and the amount of visual support provided on the display surface. This may be seen as self-evident. However, the results show the impact of different types of visual support, which in turn impacts upon how much information needs to be overlaid on the display with the attendant risk of interfering with the information being presented or viewed.

Two stroke gestures

The study shows that for 2-stroke gestures consisting of horizontal/vertical eye movements that almost error-free performance can be obtained without any additional visual support. These gestures can however be made more quickly with the addition of fixation targets, or by the visualization of the zones. There was no significant interaction effect between these 2 variables. Completion times of diagonal 2-stroke gestures are significantly longer. Here only the provision of fixation targets had a significant effect on completion time. Showing the area or the leading border outer zones around the center zone had no effect on completion time of diagonal gestures.

Considering practiced performance, the average completion time for horizontal/vertical gestures without fixation targets was 633.2ms, which dropped to 616.2ms when targets were provided. The corresponding times for diagonal gestures were 665.2ms and 617.2ms respectively.

Error rates for 2-stroke gestures with fixation targets were always low (<1%), and for horizontal/vertical gestures low even without targets.

Performance in terms of fixations

Measuring eye position with a very high sample rate eye tracker has enabled the compositions of gestures in terms of saccades and fixations to be studied. This enables us to offer explanations of why overall gesture completion time should be reduced under particular conditions. The notion of a *minimal gesture* is introduced to describe a gesture that is completed with a single fixation in a zone. The effect of practice was to increase the proportion of minimal gestures in relation to the proportion of gestures that were completed with 2 or more fixations. The average duration of a single fixation (in the region of 415ms) is much longer than those normally observed during other tasks. The average duration in silent reading is in the range 225 – 250ms, or for visual search in the range of 180 – 275ms [25]. As a 2-stroke gesture contains a reversal of direction of eye movement, then inhibition of return may contribute to the increased duration [23]. The combined durations of 2 fixations within a zone is much less than 2 times the duration of a single fixation, which suggests that gestures made with 2 fixations include a corrective saccade between these.

The difference between the times to complete horizontal/vertical gestures and diagonal gestures can also be explained in terms of the different proportions of minimal gestures. More horizontal/vertical gestures are completed with a single fixation than are diagonal gestures. The durations of the fixations are similar in each case.

Three stroke gestures

With 3-stroke gestures, very low error rates are obtained simply by adding fixation targets. This produces significantly faster completion times as well. Just by providing fixation targets with no other visualization, at least a 98% accuracy rate for 3 stroke gestures (2 or fewer errors in 92 trials) can be achieved, regardless of the predominant direction of eye movement. However, high error rates arise for 3 stroke gestures if fixation targets are not provided, as shown in Table 7. The majority of these arise from missing either the first zone or the second zone, particularly in the absence of any visual guidance about the location of the zone. While this might seem fairly obvious, it underlines the need for the designer to ensure that appropriate targets are always available when reliable gesture performance is expected.

Average completion times for 3-stroke gestures where only fixation targets are provided are below 1 second (958.2 ms where 2 of the strokes are diagonal and 996.7ms where 2 of the strokes are horizontal or vertical). This difference was not significant.

Comparison with other work

The results can usefully be compared with those reported by Rozado et al [26]. They reported a mean gesture completion time for a 3-stroke gesture of 1620 ms, and 2590 ms for the same gesture with a 500 ms dwell to signal the start of the gesture and a 500 ms dwell to stop it. Our 3-stroke gesture durations are shorter by a factor of a third. Also in that study, they reported error rates of 94% accuracy after practice when not using an explicit start and stop signal. They reported obtaining a 98% accuracy rate when gestures were made with the total extra time overhead of 1000 ms to start and stop the gesture. Rozado's study demonstrated that high accuracy and gesture durations of a comparable magnitude to those obtained in our study can be obtained using low-cost eye tracking equipment. As noted in the introduction, one of the main benefits of gaze gestures over other gaze interaction techniques is their robustness to less accurate eye position measurements and lower sample rates.

Implications for the design of a gesture scheme

Although simple horizontal/vertical 2-stroke gestures can be made quickly and reliably without any additional visual support, these can be expected to occur normally in the course of looking at the display. These would give rise to false positives (eye movements wrongly interpreted as gestures) if no explicit segmentation is used.

There are several ways to reduce the risk of false positives. One is to use more complex gestures. Different visual tasks will invoke different patterns of normal eye movements. We noted earlier that when using gaze gestures to interact with a computer game there were no unintentional 3-stroke gestures made during extended periods of normal game play [15]. Alternatively, a 'gesture' mode could be temporarily activated, say using a 3-stroke gesture or other device, where the center zone and fixation targets are made visible. Gestures would only be recognized in this mode. Two stroke gestures could be used in this mode as the user would know that their eye movements would be interpreted as gestures. This option carries an overhead of an action to enter and to leave the gesture mode. This is analogous to a pop-up menu appearing over an object in response to an activation event such as a right mouse button click.

Further work is needed to study how far the size of the fixation targets and the distance between the center zone and the targets can be scaled down without compromising the reliability and efficiency of making gestures to any significant extent. If the center zone was to be located over objects on the display, then context sensitive commands could be associated with gestures. However, the footprint of the gesture pattern would need to be reduced. The data from this study provides a baseline to study the size / performance trade-off.

Limitations of the current study and future work

The study described in the paper has not verified whether the results obtained hold true while performing the gestures over a variety of different information on a display. It can be argued that there will often be some feature on the display that could act as a fixation target. However, these will change as the displayed information changes and may be of inconsistent quality in terms of the ability to make reliable and efficient gesture patterns.

Another acknowledged limitation of the experiment reported here is that all of the data has been collected using a conventional desktop display. The results have not been verified using a near-eye display equipped with eye tracking capability. This remains as future work.

There is much further work in examining the saccades and fixations made within a gesture in order to understand more what affects performance while making them. This study has shown how improvements in completion time with practice and differences between diagonal and horizontal gestures can be attributed to the numbers of fixations made during gesture completion. The length of the fixations can be studied and in particular whether the inhibition of return mechanism [23] plays a significant role in this. If linear models of saccade duration in relation to the amplitude of eye movements made during gestures give sufficiently stable estimates, then modelling expert performance while making gaze gestures is possible. This could take the form of adding together estimates of the durations of saccades and fixations, and include the probability of a corrective saccade being made.

CONCLUSIONS

The study has investigated and shown how the speed and accuracy of making gaze gestures is related to the amount of information provided on the display surface to aid the user in making the fixations that form part of the gesture. The results show that in their simplest form, 2-stroke gestures using horizontal/vertical eye movements can be made reliably without additional support. Two stroke gestures made with diagonal eye movements and 3-stroke gestures only require the provision of small conspicuous fixation targets to be made reliably. The study has shown how differences in the speed of completing gestures due to practice and to the direction of eye movements can be explained on the basis of the number and duration of fixations made during the gesture. Understanding the composition of gaze gestures in terms of saccades and fixation may well provide a robust basis for modelling expert performance.

ACKNOWLEDGEMENTS

We would like to thank the participants for their time. Our thanks go also to Kari Räihä, Harri Siirtola, Jani Lylykangas, Jari Kangas and Oleg Spakov, all from the University of Tampere, for their input to this paper. Also, we wish to thank Sam Hutton of SR Research for his input. The work was supported by the Academy of Finland.

REFERENCES

1. Deepak Akkil, Andreas Lucero, Jari Kangas, Tero Jokela, Marja Salmimaa, and Roope Raisamo R. 2016. User Expectations of Everyday Gaze Interaction on Smartglasses. In Proceedings of the 9th Nordic Conference on Human-Computer Interaction (NordiCHI '16). ACM, New York, NY, USA, Article 24, 10 pages. DOI: https://doi.org/10.1145/2971485.2971496
2. Mihai Bâce, Teemu Leppänen, David Gil de Gomez, and Argenis Ramirez Gomez. 2016. ubiGaze: ubiquitous augmented reality messaging using gaze gestures. In SIGGRAPH ASIA 2016 Mobile Graphics and Interactive Applications (SA '16). ACM, New York, NY, USA, , Article 11 , 5 pages. DOI: https://doi.org/10.1145/2999508.2999530
3. Wolfgang Becker. 1991. Saccades. In R. Carpenter, Vision and Visual Dysfunction, vol. 8: Eye Movements. Eye movements (pp. 95–137). London: Macmillan.
4. Nikolaus Bee, and Elisabeth Andre. 2008. Writing with Your Eye: A Dwell Time Free Writing System Adapted to the Nature of Human Eye Gaze. In E. André, L. Dybkjaer, W. Minker, H. Neumann, R. Pieraccini, & M. Weber, *Lecture Notes in Computer* Science (Vol. 5078, pp. 111-122). Berlin: Springer
5. Denis Cousineau. 2005. Confidence intervals in within-subject designs: A simpler solution to Loftus and Masson's method. *Tutorial in Quantitative Methods for Psychology,* 1(1), 4–45. http://www.tqmp.org/Content/vol01-1/p042/p042.pdf
6. Murtaza Dhuliawala, Juyong Lee, Junichi Shimizu, Andreas Bulling, Kai Kunze, Thad Starner, and Woontack Woo. 2016. Smooth eye movement interaction using EOG glasses. In *Proceedings of the 18th ACM International Conference on Multimodal Interaction* (ICMI 2016). ACM, New York, NY, USA, 307-311. DOI: https://doi.org/10.1145/2993148.2993181
7. Heiko Drewes, and Albrecht Schmidt. (2007) Interacting with the Computer Using Gaze Gestures. In: Baranauskas C., Palanque P., Abascal J., Barbosa S.D.J. (eds) Human-Computer Interaction – INTERACT 2007. INTERACT 2007. *Lecture Notes in Computer Science*, vol 4663. Springer, Berlin, Heidelberg
8. Heiko Drewes, Alexander De Luca, and Albrecht Schmidt. 2007. Eye-gaze interaction for mobile phones. In *Proceedings of the 4th international conference on*

mobile technology, applications, and systems and the 1st international symposium on Computer human interaction in mobile technology (Mobility '07). ACM, New York, NY, USA, 364-371. DOI=http://dx.doi.org/10.1145/1378063.1378122

9. Henna Heikkilä, and Kari-Jouko Räihä. 2009. Speed and accuracy of gaze gestures. *Journal of Eye Movement Research,* 3(2), pp. 1-14. DOI: http://dx.doi.org/10.16910/jemr.3.2.1

10. Henna Heikkilä and Kari-Jouko Räihä. 2012. Simple gaze gestures and the closure of the eyes as an interaction technique. In *Proceedings of the Symposium on Eye Tracking Research and Applications* (ETRA '12), Stephen N. Spencer (Ed.). ACM, New York, NY, USA, 147-154. DOI=http://dx.doi.org/10.1145/2168556.2168579

11. Kenneth Holmqvist, Marcus Nyström, Richard Andersson, Richard Dewhurst, Halszka Jarodzka, and Joost van de Weijer. (2011). *Eye tracking: a comprehensive guide to methods and measures.* Oxford: Oxford University Press

12. Anke Huckauf and Mario H. Urbina. 2008. Gazing with pEYEs: towards a universal input for various applications. In *Proceedings of the 2008 symposium on Eye tracking research & applications* (ETRA '08). ACM, New York, NY, USA, 51-54. DOI: https://doi.org/10.1145/1344471.1344483

13. Aulikki Hyrskykari, Howell Istance, and Stephen Vickers. 2012. Gaze gestures or dwell-based interaction? *In Proceedings of the Symposium on Eye Tracking Research and Applications* (ETRA '12), Stephen N. Spencer (Ed.). ACM, New York, NY, USA, 229-232. DOI=http://dx.doi.org/10.1145/2168556.2168602

14. Howell Istance, Richard Bates, Aulikki Hyrskykari, and Stephen Vickers. 2008. Snap clutch, a moded approach to solving the Midas touch problem. In *Proceedings of the 2008 symposium on Eye tracking research & applications* (ETRA '08). ACM, New York, NY, USA, 221-228. DOI: https://doi.org/10.1145/1344471.1344523

15. Howell Istance, Aulikki Hyrskykari, Lauri Immonen, Santtu Mansikkamaa, and Stephen Vickers. 2010. Designing gaze gestures for gaming: an investigation of performance. In *Proceedings of the 2010 Symposium on Eye-Tracking Research & Applications* (ETRA '10). ACM, New York, NY, USA, 323-330. DOI=http://dx.doi.org/10.1145/1743666.1743740

16. Jari Kangas, Deepak Akkil, Jussi Rantala, Poika Isokoski, Päivi Majaranta, and Roope Raisamo. 2014. Gaze gestures and haptic feedback in mobile devices. In *Proceedings of the SIGCHI Conference on Human Factors in Computing Systems* (CHI '14). ACM, New York, NY, USA, 435-438. DOI: http://dx.doi.org/10.1145/2556288.2557040

17. Jari Kangas, Oleg Spakov, Poika Isokoski, Deepak Akkil, Jussi Rantala, and Roope Raisamo. 2016. Feedback for Smooth Pursuit Gaze Tracking Based Control. In *Proceedings of the 7th Augmented Human International Conference 2016* (AH '16). ACM, New York, NY, USA, Article 6, 8 pages. DOI: http://dx.doi.org/10.1145/2875194.2875209

18. Päivi Majaranta, & Andreas Bulling. 2014. Eye Tracking and Eye-Based Human–Computer Interaction. *Advances in Phys. Comp.,* 39-65. Springer, London.

19. Diako Mardanbegi, Dan Witzner Hansen, and Thomas Pederson. 2012. Eye-based head gestures. In *Proceedings of the Symposium on Eye Tracking Research and Applications* (ETRA '12), Stephen N. Spencer (Ed.). ACM, New York, NY, USA, 139-146. DOI=http://dx.doi.org/10.1145/2168556.2168578

20. Emilie Mollenbach, John Paulin Hansen, and Martin Lillholm. 2013. Eye Movements in Gaze Interaction. *Journal of Eye Movement Research*, 6(2), 1-15.

21. Emilie Mollenbach, John Paulin Hansen, Martin Lillholm, and Alastair G. Gale. 2009. Single stroke gaze gestures. In *CHI '09 Extended Abstracts on Human Factors in Computing Systems* (CHI EA '09). ACM, New York, NY, USA, 4555-4560. DOI: https://doi.org/10.1145/1520340.1520699

22. Tomi Nukarinen, Jari Kangas, Oleg Špakov, Poika Isokoski, Deepak Akkil, Jussi Rantala, and Roope Raisamo. 2016. Evaluation of HeadTurn: An Interaction Technique Using the Gaze and Head Turns. In *Proceedings of the 9th Nordic Conference on Human-Computer Interaction* (NordiCHI '16). ACM, New York, NY, USA, , Article 43 , 8 pages. DOI: https://doi.org/10.1145/2971485.2971490

23. Michael Posner, and Yoav Cohen. 1984. Components of visual orienting. *Attention and Performance X: Control of Language Processes.* H. Bouma and D. Bonwhuis. Hillsdale, N. J., Erlbaum: 551-556

24. Keith Rayner. 1998. Eye movements in reading and information processing: 20 years of research. *Psychological Bulletin*, 85, 618-660.

25. Keith Rayner. 1995. Eye movements and cognitive processes in reading, visual search, and scene perception. In J. M. Findlay, R. Walker, & R.W. Kentridge (Eds.), *Eye movement research: Mechanisms, processes and applications* (pp. 3-22). Amsterdam: North Holland.

26. David Rozado, Javier S. Agustin, Francisco B. Rodriguez, and Pablo Varona. 2012. Gliding and saccadic gaze gesture recognition in real time. *ACM Trans. Interact. Intell. Syst.* 1, 2, Article 10 (January

2012), 27 pages. DOI=http://dx.doi.org/10.1145/2070719.2070723

27. SensoMotoric Instruments. SMI High Performance eye tracking hmd based on HTC Vive. http://www.smivision.com/en/gaze-and-eye-tracking-systems/products/eye-tracking-htc-vive.html?gclid=CMC9g-zcndECFQcbaQoduK4Caw&cHash=bd18fc124ce9088b07a26a494fd2bed7

28. Jing Tian, Howard Ying, and David Zee. 2013. Revisiting corrective saccades: role of visual feedback. *Vision Research.* August 30; 89: pp. 54–64

29. Jacob O. Wobbrock, James Rubinstein, Michael W. Sawyer, and Andrew T. Duchowski. 2008. Longitudinal evaluation of discrete consecutive gaze gestures for text entry. In *Proceedings of the 2008 symposium on Eye tracking research & applications* (ETRA '08). ACM, New York, NY, USA, 11-18. DOI: https://doi.org/10.1145/1344471.1344475

30. Xianjun Sam Zheng, Cedric Foucault, Patrik Matos da Silva, Siddharth Dasari, Tao Yang, and Stuart Goose. 2015. Eye-Wearable Technology for Machine Maintenance: Effects of Display Position and Hands-free Operation. In *Proceedings of the 33rd Annual ACM Conference on Human Factors in Computing Systems* (CHI '15). ACM, New York, NY, USA, 2125-2134. DOI: http://dx.doi.org/10.1145/2702123.2702305

GazeEverywhere: Enabling Gaze-only User Interaction on an Unmodified Desktop PC in Everyday Scenarios

Simon Schenk, Marc Dreiser, Gerhard Rigoll, Michael Dorr
Technical University Munich
Munich, Germany
{simon.schenk, marc.dreiser, rigoll, michael.dorr}@tum.de

ABSTRACT
Eye tracking is becoming more and more affordable, and thus gaze has the potential to become a viable input modality for human-computer interaction. We present the GazeEverywhere solution that can replace the mouse with gaze control by adding a transparent layer on top of the system GUI. It comprises three parts: i) the SPOCK interaction method that is based on smooth pursuit eye movements and does not suffer from the Midas touch problem; ii) an online recalibration algorithm that continuously improves gaze-tracking accuracy using the SPOCK target projections as reference points; and iii) an optional hardware setup utilizing head-up display technology to project superimposed dynamic stimuli onto the PC screen where a software modification of the system is not feasible. In validation experiments, we show that GazeEverywhere's throughput according to ISO 9241-9 was improved over dwell time based interaction methods and nearly reached trackpad level. Online recalibration reduced interaction target ('button') size by about 25%. Finally, a case study showed that users were able to browse the internet and successfully run Wikirace using gaze only, without any plug-ins or other modifications.

Author Keywords
Eye tracking; Gaze-based interaction; Mouse replacement; Smooth pursuit

INTRODUCTION
Eye tracking has become increasingly popular in the field of human computer interaction, especially in light of the recent introduction of affordable, yet relatively precise eye trackers. Besides the analysis of the user's gaze behaviour for usability measurements, using gaze as input modality has been a field of research for many years. Although gaze has proven to be a fast and reliable input modality for typing [29], and pointing at target positions with gaze is faster than using a mouse [6], using only gaze as an input modality is still not practical. This is because gaze-only interaction poses two major challenges: the Midas touch problem [12], and the "region of uncertainty" problem [15].

Permission to make digital or hard copies of all or part of this work for personal or classroom use is granted without fee provided that copies are not made or distributed for profit or commercial advantage and that copies bear this notice and the full citation on the first page. Copyrights for components of this work owned by others than ACM must be honored. Abstracting with credit is permitted. To copy otherwise, or republish, to post on servers or to redistribute to lists, requires prior specific permission and/or a fee. Request permissions from permissions@acm.org.
CHI 2017, May 6-11, 2017, Denver, CO, USA.
Copyright © 2017 ACM ISBN 978-1-4503-4655-9/17/05 ...$15.00.
http://dx.doi.org/10.1145/3025453.3025455

The Midas touch problem is named after the mythical king who turned everything he touched into gold, and who eventually starved to death because this also applied to his food. In gaze-based interaction, it describes the problem that the gaze patterns required to decide where to interact may already be misclassified as interaction gestures.

The "region of uncertainty" describes the roughly circular area around the measured gaze position in which the actual gaze position can lie. Its size highly depends on three factors: i) The precision of the used eye tracker; ii) the quality of the tracker calibration; and iii) the angle of foveal vision, i.e. the precision of the human fixation itself. Obviously, only the first two factors can be improved using better hard- and software.

Every system providing gaze-based input has to cope with both the Midas touch and the "region of uncertainty", and most systems do so by developing a unique graphical user interface (GUI) for the software in use. This, however, limits the use of gaze as an input modality to those applications, and hence, a different approach for gaze-only interaction is a modification of the GUI at a system level.

We propose GazeEverywhere, a solution that enables gaze-only mouse replacement on any computer without any system level modification. This is done by following a layered interface approach and adding a transparent layer on top of the computer's GUI. This layer is used to show all visual stimuli needed for the gaze interaction and interacts with the operating system only by sending mouse events. It can either be implemented in software by a transparent, always-on-top application, or using an additional hardware, which is also described in this paper.

In particular, our contribution consists of three parts:

1. A combination of dwell time and the state-of-the-art smooth pursuit-based activation method SPOCK [25] that has been shown to be robust against Midas touches, even in conditions with high mental workload (Figure 1, right).

2. An online offset compensation algorithm that uses the smooth pursuit gestures during interaction to detect any tracker offset on-the-fly and that compensates this offset for a better local tracking precision (Figure 6).

3. An optional hardware setup that is able to project superimposed visual information on top of a computer monitor using the same mechanism as in a head-up display and to send mouse events to the controlled computer via a standard USB HID mouse interface (Figure 2).

In a series of three experiments described in the following, we demonstrate that i) SPOCK outperforms a traditional, dwell time-based activation method; ii) online offset compensation improves tracking accuracy; and iii) the interaction technique can be used on off-the-shelf software. All these experiments are done using the optional hardware to demonstrate that gaze interaction is possible even without any software modification.

RELATED WORK

Since gaze-based interaction has been a research field for many years, different solutions exist of how gaze can successfully be applied as an input modality. In particular, these solutions try either to solve the Midas touch problem, or the "region of uncertainty" problem, or both. This is mostly done in separate applications; however, some effort has been put into enabling complete systems for gaze-based interaction.

Reducing the Midas Touch Problem

When using user interfaces with static buttons, the most common gaze-based activation method is dwell time: To activate a button, the user has to look at it for a specific duration. This method is easy to learn and ergonomic [12], but it is also very prone to the Midas touch problem. As a consequence, many studies have tried to determine the optimal dwell time. For example, Majaranta et al. proposed an adjustable dwell time for their gaze typing task [17]. They found out that the required dwell time shortens over time and that the optimal dwell time highly depends on the user. After ten repetitions the optimal dwell time ranged between 180 ms and 380 ms. Other researchers used dwell times between 150 ms and 1000 ms [10, 12, 16]. Penkar et al. pointed out that dwell time can be shortened if active areas are distinct from informative areas, e.g. the content of the button is presented below the dwell area [22].

Since no final conclusion can be drawn for an optimal dwell time, a more promising approach is to prevent Midas touches by using a different gesture for target activation [11, 14, 21, 25].

Huckauf and Urbina used a saccade for activation [11]: When glancing at a target, a visual stimulus appears on one side of the target. To activate the target, an anti-saccade, i.e. a saccade towards the other side of the target, has to be performed. Although this prevents Midas touches in theory, anti-saccades are difficult to perform in practice because of attentional capture and thus the user experience may become unpleasant. Lutteroth et al. [14] followed the design guidelines of Penkar et al. and developed a user interface where additional dwell targets are used for activation: When a user gazes close to clickable targets, these targets are highlighted with different colours. A palette of the used colours is presented next to the monitor and by dwelling at one of these colours, the corresponding target is activated. Since the targets do not have to be fixated precisely, this approach also successfully deals with the "region of uncertainty" problem. Schenk et al. utilized smooth pursuit gestures in their SPOCK activation method [25]: When a target is fixated, two moving disks appear above and below the target, and by following one of these disks the user's eye performs a smooth pursuit which leads to the target activation. The symmetric design of moving targets cancels out the attentional capture and hence Midas touches are rare. In contrast to anti-saccades, smooth pursuits are natural eye movements and thus easy to perform.

Dealing with the "Region of Uncertainty"

The most common solution to circumvent the "region of uncertainty" problem is not to use a selection-activation approach, where a target first has to be selected before it can be activated, but to use a gesture-based approach where different gestures cause different actions directly. These gestures can be either based on saccades [3, 4, 8, 20], or on smooth pursuits [5, 9, 28]. In both cases, gaze episodes, i.e. the gaze position in a certain time frame, are analysed, and the gaze path in those episodes can be compared to predefined patterns. Since only relative eye movements are taken into account, the absolute gaze position is less important and the tracker does not need to be calibrated properly.

Drewes and Schmidt [8] and Møllenbach et al. [20] presented saccade-based interaction methods that did not need any visual stimuli. Where Møllenbach et al. only used single gaze strokes, Drewes and Schmidt connected multiple strokes into one gesture. Bee et al. presented a gaze-based keyboard that was based on multi-stroke gestures [3] and Møllenbach et al. modified this solution and presented it together with other multi-stroke gestures [19]. A different solution for a stroke-based keyboard has been published recently by Best et al. [4].

For smooth pursuit-based interaction, Vidal et al. introduced visual targets that are moving with a constant speed on circular trajectories [28]. When following one of these targets, the user's gaze trajectory is compared to the target trajectories using Pearson's product-moment correlation coefficient [28] and the corresponding target is activated if a matching pair is found. While an initial implementation of this technique enabled gaze-based interaction on a public display [28], Esteves et al. recently used this technique successfully on a smartwatch, demonstrating that even very small circular movements are measurable with an uncalibrated tracker [9].

Although all these gesture-based approaches may be used with low tracker accuracy and big tracker offsets, they require knowledge of the exact positions of the clickable items. Thus, applying them to arbitrary, button-based user interfaces without customizations and deep system integration is difficult.

Skovsgaard et al. investigated a different approach that is applicable to existing, button-based GUIs using a zooming option [27]: When dwelling on a target, the area around the dwell position is magnified and consequently even small targets become clickable. Nevertheless, this approach still requires some form of system integration, i.e. access to the framebuffer, in order to re-render the magnified area.

Integrating Gaze Control in Existing GUIs

Besides trying to solve the two major challenges in gaze-based interaction on an application level, some effort has been made to incorporate gaze into existing systems and hence make these systems controllable via gaze. Salvucci and Anderson [24] developed a specialized WIMP-category (Windows, Icons, Menus, Pointer) GUI that enables partial gaze control. To cope with the "region of uncertainty", they used a probabilistic model to find the most likely click target around the user's gaze position. At the expense of truly hands-free operation, their system did not suffer from the Midas touch problem because the authors used a "gaze button", i.e. a key on the keyboard, to activate targets.

Lankford [13] integrated gaze input into the Windows operating system. As activation method, dwell time was used and different dwell times performed different actions: A short dwell time enabled dragging and dropping the selected item, a longer dwell time clicked the element, and an even longer dwell time performed a double click. The current state of the dwell time was visualized with different colours and markers at the dwell position. To make even small targets clickable, a "zooming methodology" was implemented that shows a magnification of the fixation's surrounding at the centre of the screen.

A similar approach is used in the commercially available system from Tobii Dynavox called Windows Control[1]. This system has two different operation modes: mouse emulation and direct interaction. In the mouse emulation mode, the mouse pointer is fixed to the gaze position and consequently moved with the eye. In order to click, a dwell time is used and the different click modes can be selected via a button bar. In the direct interaction mode, a two stage approach is used for interaction: first, the action to be performed (click, double click, drag-and-drop) is selected from a button bar. Then, an additional dwell time determines where the action is to be applied.

A more recent solution was presented by Ahn et al. [1] in which they augmented a smartphone with gaze-based interaction. Because a smartphone GUI is designed for finger control, the buttons are rather large and the "region of uncertainty" is less of an issue. In this system, a panel displays a set of possible touch gestures, and gaze is used to select one of these gestures to be triggered. The usability of this approach has been tested successfully in an experiment with physically impaired participants.

All these systems have in common that they are deeply integrated into the operating system. Porting them to a different system therefore requires additional effort or may not even be possible.

THE GAZEEVERYWHERE SOLUTION

All the solutions presented above that can successfully apply gaze-based interaction on traditional button-based GUIs needed visual feedback such as additional targets to solve the Midas touch problem [18]. This is either done at the application level, i.e. to enable gaze control for a specific application, or at the system level, i.e. to enable gaze control for all applications by integrating it deeply into the system.

Our solution aims to enable a system-wide gaze interaction, but without any deep system integration. We therefore use a layered interface approach, where a transparent GUI layer is placed on top of the system's GUI. This layer is responsible for drawing the visual stimuli and communicates with the operating system only by sending mouse events. A software implementation of this approach could be an application with a transparent always-on-top window. As a consequence, the application does not occlude any other application windows, whereas the visuals drawn on this layer are always visible. If a software solution is not possible (e.g. because the used operating system does not support any eye-tracking devices, or no applications can be installed on the system), an external hardware can be used to implement the transparent layer.

Software

The main contribution of the GazeEverywhere system is the software component, i.e. the selecting and activating UI elements with gaze only.

Gaze Gestures

Since the chosen gestures have to be applicable to any button-based GUI, gaze gestures as presented in [20] and [28] cannot be used. Instead we chose a mouse emulation where the mouse interaction is performed in two stages: pointing and clicking. To prevent Midas touches, the gestures used for pointing and for clicking are different. For pointing (target selection) we chose a dwell time, since it can be performed easily and quickly. So far, three possible solutions for the clicking method (target activation) have been put forward: anti-saccades [11], fixations [1], or smooth pursuits [25]. Since anti-saccades are rather unergonomic, we only investigate the latter gestures. Hence, we implemented the two interaction gestures SPOCK and multi-stage dwell time (MSDT) as presented in Figure 1; we evaluate their relative performance in Experiment 1. Both gestures use a dwell time for selection, i.e. dwelling at a position moves the mouse pointer on the desktop PC to that position. At the same time, two targets appear above and below the dwell position. The MSDT targets are static and the SPOCK targets are moving up- and downwards with a constant speed of 5 deg/s. Following (SPOCK) or dwelling at (MSDT) one of these targets triggers a mouse click event on the desktop PC.

Gaze Classification

Despite great advances in eye-tracking quality, low-cost eye trackers still provide noisy measurements only. We therefore smoothed the incoming gaze data using an exponential decay filter with an alpha value of 0.2:

$$\text{pos}_t = 0.8 \cdot \text{pos}_{t-1} + 0.2 \cdot \text{gaze\_sample}_t. \qquad (1)$$

For interaction, the performed gaze gestures have to be classified, i.e. the three possible gestures saccade, fixation, and smooth pursuit have to be detected. To do so, we used a sliding window with a window size of 15 samples ($\hat{=}$ 240 ms) and computed the sample-to-sample speed within this window. In a first step, the speed for each of the 15 samples was computed,

[1] http://www.tobiidynavox.com/windows-control/

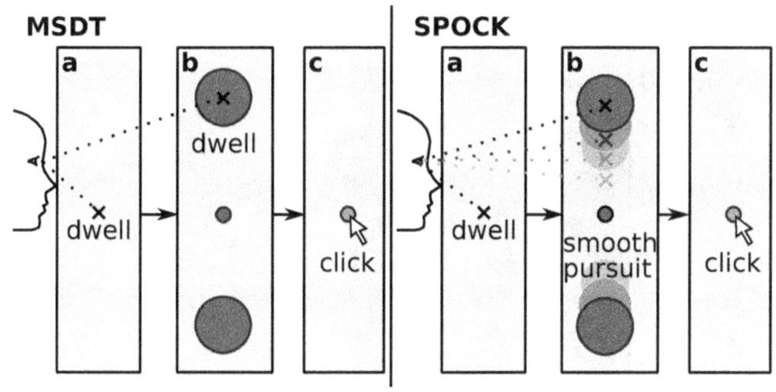

Figure 1. Left (MSDT): after dwelling at a position (a), two static stimuli appear above and below the fixated point; dwelling at one of these (b) performs a mouse click (c). Right (SPOCK): after dwelling at a position (a), two moving stimuli appear above and below the fixated point; following one of these performing a smooth pursuit (b) performs the mouse click (c).

and if the maximum velocity of any sample pair was above 80 deg/s the window was discarded as containing a saccade. If no saccades were detected, the mean speed of the entire window was computed and three different cases were distinguished: If the mean speed was below 4 deg/s, the gesture was classified as fixation; otherwise, if it was above 16 deg/s, the gesture was classified as "fast movement", i.e. a small saccade or a fast smooth pursuit. If the mean speed was between 4 deg/s and 16 deg/s, and all the samples were moving in the same vertical direction (the direction of the smooth pursuit stimuli), the gesture was classified as smooth pursuit.

Hardware Setup

The hardware setup is optional and only needed if a software-only implementation is not applicable. In this case, an additional hardware is used to superimpose all additional visuals on top of the target monitor, and to emulate a USB mouse that is connected to the target PC (Figure 2). Currently, low-cost eye-tracking devices still lack wide-spread operating system support, so that an additional PC may be needed to provide eye tracking for non-Windows computers.

Providing a Transparent Layer

In order to create a transparent layer in hardware, we use a technique similar to the ones of head-up displays known from cars or fighter jets [23]: The content of a secondary image source is reflected directly into the user's line of sight using a transparent reflection surface. Our secondary image source was a LCD monitor that was mounted and carefully aligned horizontally between the user and the target monitor. Similar to the work in [2], a glass pane was mounted at a 45° angle and served as the reflection surface. A Tobii EyeX tracker was used as input device.

Generating Mouse Events

To generate mouse events on the target PC without any additional software, the USB HID device class is used: The gaze computer is connected to the target computer via an Arduino Leonardo board. The microcontroller on this Arduino board contains an USB host controller that appears on the target PC as a standard HID mouse/keyboard device. The gaze computer sends messages to the Arduino via Ethernet and the Arduino

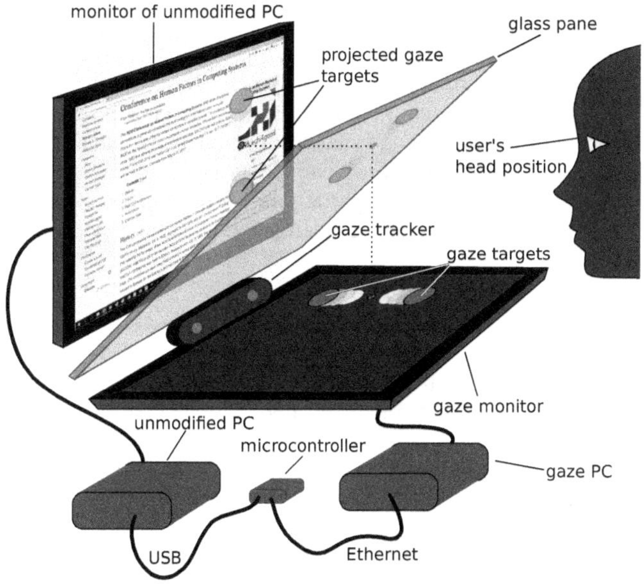

Figure 2. The optional hardware setup superimposing visual targets for the SPOCK activation method onto a computer monitor: targets displayed on the bottom monitor are reflected into the user's line of sight and superimposed on the PC monitor by the glass pane. Mouse events are generated using a microcontroller and sent via USB.

translates these into USB messages that are treated as mouse and keyboard events by all HID-supporting operating systems.

EXPERIMENT 1: ACTIVATION METHOD

We conducted a user study following the ISO 9241-9 standard to address two questions: which of the two presented activation methods performs better, and how well these methods perform compared to existing input devices.

In the standard, pointing devices are tested by activating circular targets. These targets are placed in a circular fashion and have to be activated by successively clicking on them. The order in which they have to be activated is predefined such that the distance between two clicks is maximized. Changing the target size and the target distance changes the difficulty (ID) of the scenario. If a click has been performed outside a target, the corresponding target is counted as an error trial and skipped. The target sizes should be chosen large enough to maintain an error rate of less than 4%. For each trial the mean activation time, i.e. the time between two activations, is measured and a throughput (in bits/s) can be computed. Gaze has been tested before using this standard and showed valid results [30, 31].

In this first experiment the main focus lies only on the activation performance rather than on the pointing performance. Hence, and to assure a fail rate below 4%, we kept the target size constant and varied the target distance to generate a range of difficulties (IDs).

Besides the objective measurements of activation time and throughput we used the NASA TLX and the SUS questionnaire to receive subjective ratings. Furthermore, the gaze coordinates were recorded for a post-hoc analysis of the gaze behaviour.

Participants

Twelve participants (9 male, 3 female) aged between 21 and 27 years (mean: 24.17, SD: 1.4) were recruited for this experiment. All were undergraduate or graduate students at the local lab and none of the students had any experience with eye tracking before. All participants had normal or corrected-to-normal vision and four participants wore optical correction during the experiments (2 glasses, 2 contact lenses).

Experimental Setup and Design

The experiment took place in a quiet lab room with darkened windows and additional artificial light. We used the configuration with the optional hardware setup to make sure that our solution works even under these conditions. This heads-up-display setup produced a small parallax error of about 3 mm and sending the mouse events via USB introduced a delay of 18 ms. The two monitors in use were identical iiyama PROLITE 24" LCD monitors with the dimensions of 521 mm × 293 mm (W × H) and a resolution of 1920 × 1080 pixels; users were seated approximately 700 mm in front of the target PC monitor. The transparent reflection surface was a plastic glass pane with a thickness of about 4 mm. A Tobii EyeX tracker with a sample rate of 60 Hz was used to record the subject's gaze. The software running on the gaze computer was written in C# using the WPF framework[2] and ran with a constant 60 frames per second. The software running on the target PC was the *FittsStudy* tool[3] provided by Wobbrock et al. [30].

The pointing gesture for both activation methods was a 300 ms dwell time. The targets of the second dwell time in the MSDT scenario appeared 120 pixels (3.4°) above and below the original dwell position and had a diameter of 80 pixels (2.3°). The targets for the SPOCK scenario had a diameter of 30 pixels (0.9°) and were moving with a constant speed of 5 deg/s up to a maximum eccentricity of 200 pixels (5.7°), after which they were reset to the original dwell position and started moving outwards again. The dwell time for the second dwell in the MSDT scenario was 300 ms, and the minimum pursuit time in the SPOCK scenario was 250 ms.

The study itself was designed in a two-factorial within-subject design with the main factors being the *Activation method* and the *Target distance*. The target size was constant with 100 pixels (2.9°) and three different target distances were used: 900 pixels (25.7°), 560 pixels (16.0°), and 350 pixels (10.0°), resulting in the IDs of 2.20, 2.75, and 3.35, respectively, which lies within the typical range of IDs in the literature [30].

Procedure

Upon arriving, participants had to fill out an informed consent form. Then the system was introduced and the two different interaction methods were explained to them.

The experiment consisted of two blocks, one for testing the MSDT method, and one for testing SPOCK. In each block, the tracker was first calibrated using a nine-point calibration and

[2]https://msdn.microsoft.com/de-de/library/ms754130(v=vs.110).aspx

[3]https://depts.washington.edu/aimgroup/proj/fittsstudy/

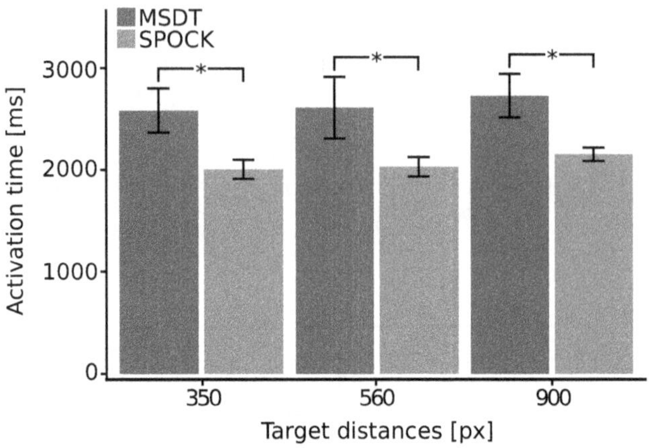

Figure 3. Activation time for the three different target distances and the two different activation methods: activation time was significantly faster for SPOCK.

then the different target sizes were presented in a random order. Each target distance was tested with 13 targets, where the first two targets were for training and discarded in the evaluation. By repeating each distance, each participant had to select 26 targets per distance with each activation method. At the end of each block, the participants had to fill out the NASA TLX and the SUS questionnaire.

Half of the participants started with SPOCK as activation method followed by MSDT and the other half vice versa, to counterbalance any potential learning effects. The experiment took about 30 minutes in total.

Results

Three participants had to be discarded from the evaluation due to tracking difficulties such as excessive offsets that led to high error rates above 40%.

Activation time was roughly similar between the different target distances, but clearly differed with activation method (Figure 3). A paired t-test showed statistical significance between activation methods for all three target distances ($p = 0.012$ for 350 pixels, $p = 0.030$ for 540 pixels, and $p = 0.01$ for 900 pixels). The mean activation time over all target distances was 2639 ms for MSDT and 2061 ms for SPOCK. This results in a throughput of 1.08 bits/s for MSDT and 1.23 bits/s for SPOCK.

Both SUS and NASA did not show any significant differences and the SUS score averaged at 76 points for SPOCK and 80 points for MSDT (SD: 14 and 12, respectively).

Discussion

This first experiment showed that the SPOCK activation method was about 580 ms faster than MSDT. To determine whether this time difference was only based on the time spent on the final activation and not on time spent for the initial selection, we analysed the recorded gaze traces. Figures 4 and 5 show one typical trace for each activation method. For MSDT (Figure 4) four individual parts are clearly distinguishable: Acquiring the selection target, dwelling at the selection target,

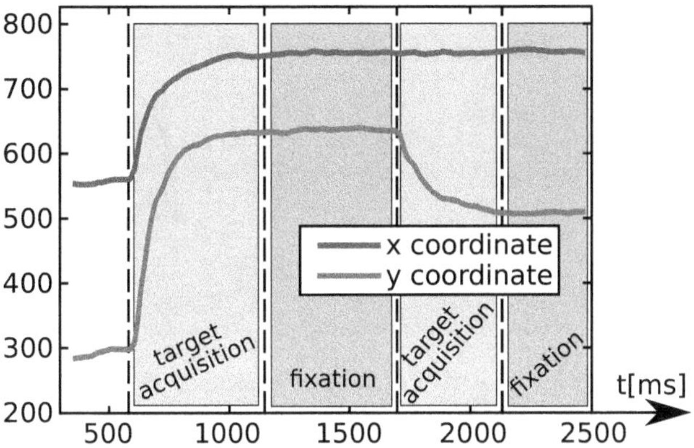

Figure 4. Gaze plot for the MSDT activation method: The 1 s acquiring the second target for fixation slows down the activation.

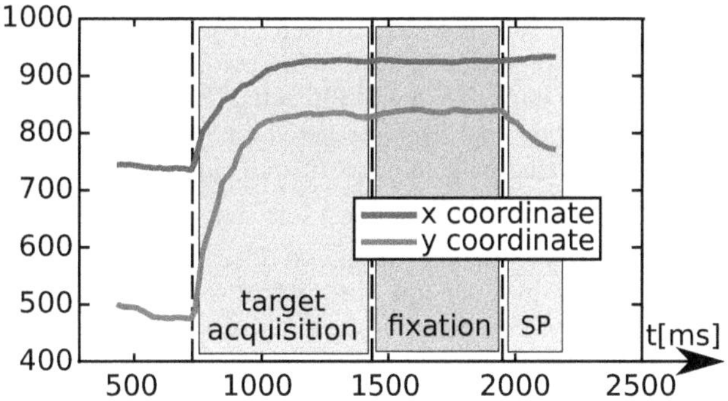

Figure 5. Gaze plot for the SPOCK activation method: No second target acquisition needed. Detecting the smooth pursuit takes only 250 ms.

acquiring the second dwell target, and dwelling at the second dwell target. In contrast, the SPOCK method (Figure 5) comprises only three parts: Acquiring the selection target, dwelling at the selection target, and following the smooth pursuit target. The first two parts of both methods represent the pointing gesture, with the remainder representing the activation. The traces show that in fact a similar amount is spent for the selection gesture for both methods; however, acquiring the second dwell target and dwelling at it for the MSDT activation method takes much longer than performing a smooth pursuit for the SPOCK method.

One could argue that a less aggressive smoothing algorithm could potentially lower the target acquisition time, however, Helmert et al. state that smoothing is a required step when using any dwell-based interaction technique [10].

Compared to other input devices, SPOCK (1.23 bits/s) comes close to the performance of a trackpad (1.7 bits/s), but is still outperformed by joystick (2.1 bits/s) and mouse (4.9 bits/s) [7, 30]. Following the results of this first experiment, SPOCK was used as activation method for the following studies.

INCREASING LOCAL TRACKER ACCURACY

The first experiment showed that a Midas touch free activation method can be implemented with our hardware setup and that this method can achieve a competitive throughput similar to the one of a trackpad. However, to reach an acceptable error rate, a relatively large target size of 100 pixels (as determined in pilot testing) had to be used. In order to make the gaze-based interaction applicable to existing software, this minimum target size had to be further decreased, though, which means to reduce the "region of uncertainty".

However, none of the approaches presented in the related work section could be used, since they all rely on a deep integration in the used GUI. Instead, we aimed to reduce the "region of uncertainty" by increasing the local tracking accuracy. In general, the tracking error of an eye tracker is based on the tracker noise, and the tracker offset. The tracker offset depends on the quality of the used eye model and on the quality of calibration. Typical tracker calibration schemes use 1, 3, 5, or 9 calibration points to optimize the eye model on a global level, but local errors can still be high. However, SPOCK

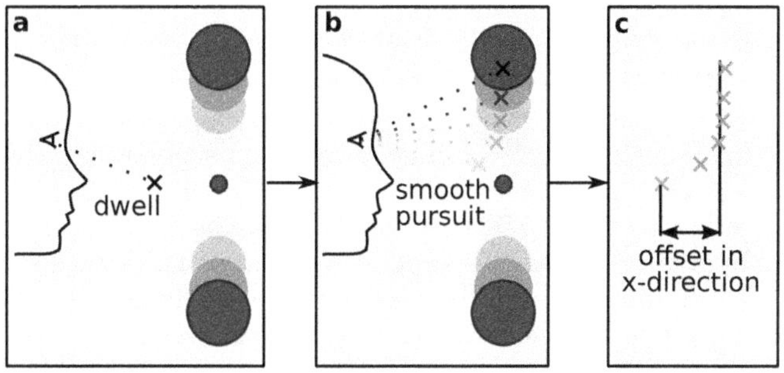

Figure 6. The fixations and smooth pursuit during the interaction can be used to detect the local tracker offset: If an offset exists, the smooth pursuit targets do not appear at the true dwell position, but with this offset (a); when following one of the targets, this offset has to be overcome (b). By comparing the mean x position of the fixation with the mean x position of the SP, the offset can be computed.

allows to continuously reduce these local errors using pursuit targets as implicit calibration points.

Offset Detection

In order to compensate for local tracking offset, it has to be detected first. One way to do so is using the eye movements of the user during the interaction: if an offset exists, the measured fixation point is not the actual fixated point. Hence, the visual targets for activation do not appear directly at the (actual) fixation point, but with an offset. When following one of these targets, this offset is compensated by an eye movement, which can be detected.

Figure 6 shows how this detection works in particular: While dwelling at a position, the x coordinate of the gaze position is stored. When the visual target appears and a smooth pursuit gesture (in y direction) is detected, the average x coordinate of the gaze positions during this smooth pursuit is measured and compared to the stored x coordinate of the dwell. The difference between these two coordinates is the offset of the eye tracker in the x direction.

Since only the offset in one direction can be detected at once, the moving direction of the smooth pursuit targets has to alternate between horizontal and vertical.

Offset Compensation

To compensate for the tracker offset, the detected offset has to be stored and used afterwards. To do so, the active screen area is divided into a 5×5 grid (25 cells). Each cell holds the tracker's offset that has been measured for this cell before. All cells are initialized with an offset of zero, and the stored offset is updated afer each activation.

For each new gaze sample, the stored offset of the nine closest cells are taken into account for compensation. The weight of each offset is computed using the inverse distance weight algorithm [26]:

$$\text{pos}_{\text{comp}}(t) = \text{pos}_{\text{raw}}(t) + \sum_{i=1}^{9} d_i^3 \cdot \sum_{i=1}^{9} \left(\frac{1}{d_i^3} \cdot \text{offset}_i(t)\right), \quad (2)$$

where d_i is the distance from the measured gaze coordinate to the midpoint of the ith cell.

EXPERIMENT 2: RECALIBRATION

To test the performance of our offset compensation and its influence on the interaction accuracy, a second user study was conducted in which we used the same *FittsStudy* tool following the ISO 9241-9 standard as in the first experiment. In contrast to the first experiment, we did not want to test which interaction method has higher throughput, but which one produces better error rates. Therefore, we used a constant target distance of 350 pixels (10°) and five log-spaced target sizes: 100 pixels (2.9°), 64 pixels (1.8°), 41 pixels (1.2°), 26 pixels (0.7°), and 17 pixels (0.5°). The question to answer was if and by what amount the offset compensation decreases the error rate at the different target sizes. Moreover, we were interested for which target size an error rate of 50%, which was the subjective threshold for a still usable system, was achieved. Again, the gaze coordinates were logged as well for a detailed analysis.

Participants

For this experiment, 8 participants (6 male, 2 female) were recruited with an age between 23 and 35 years (mean: 27.37, SD: 3.96). All participants gave written informed consent to take part in the study. They were either researchers or graduate students at the local lab and none had any experience with eye tracking, or gaze-based interaction. Two participants had normal, six corrected-to-normal vision (three wearing contact lenses, three glasses).

Experimental Setup and Design

The hard- and software setup in this experiment was the same as in the first experiment. As activation methods, we used the same parameters as in the first experiment. For the offset compensating method, the moving direction of the smooth pursuit targets alternated between horizontal and vertical for each individual cell; i.e. if the previous offset had been measured in x direction, targets moving in x direction were presented in order to measure the offset in y direction, and vice versa. Hence, the user did not have a direct influence on the target's moving direction. The movement speed and the maximal eccentricity was the same for both directions and the same as for the non-compensating method (5 deg/s; 5.7°).

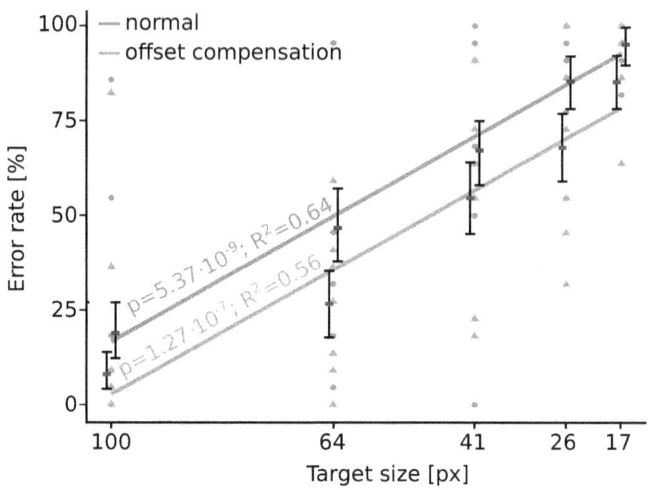

Figure 7. Error rates with and without recalibration. The marked values show the mean error rate for each method and each target size; the whiskers show bootstrapped 99% confidence intervals.

The experiment was designed in a two-factorial within-subject design, with *Target size* and *Input type* as main factors.

Procedure

The experiment itself was divided into two blocks, each one testing one interaction method. At the beginning of each block, the tracker was calibrated with the manufacturer-provided software and validated with a custom routine. Since the calibration quality is crucial for the outcome of this experiment, only calibrations with a maximum validation error of 1.5° were accepted. The validation errors ranged from 0.7° to 1.4° for the non-compensating method, and from 0.5° to 1.5° for the compensating one. In each block, the different target sizes were tested sequentially starting with the largest target and this sequence was repeated once. Each target size was tested with 13 targets and the first two targets of each size were practice targets. This resulted in a total of $2 \times 11 = 22$ measured targets per target size and participant.

To counterbalance any learning effects, half of the participants started with the non-compensating method and the other half with the compensating one.

Results

One participant had to be discarded from analysis due to a technical defect. For the remaining participants we counted the correct clicks and misclicks per target size (in total $7 \times 2 \times 11 = 154$ targets) and then computed the mean error rates as shown in Figure 7. The error rate for the non-compensating method was about 18% higher on average, and the remarkably similar regression slopes indicate that this difference was independent of target size. Error bars in Figure 7 denote the 99% confidence intervals of a 100,000-fold bootstrapping procedure and show that the error rates are significantly different for each interaction method and each target size.

Furthermore, we used the linear regression to check at which target size the error rate is 50%. For the non-compensating condition, this was the case at 64 pixels (1.8°) and for the

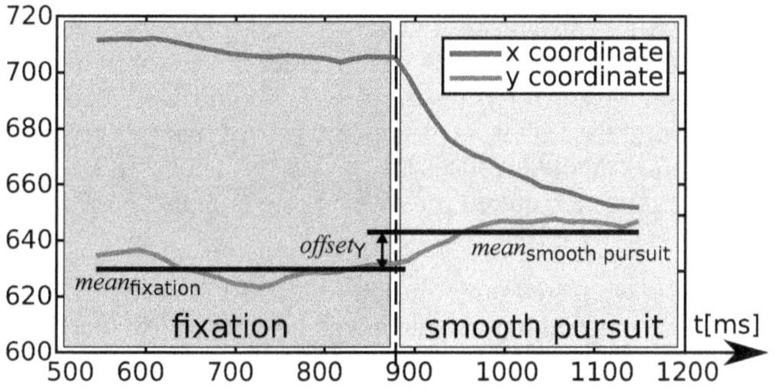

Figure 8. A gaze trace of a smooth pursuit activation: the tracker offset can be computed by comparing the mean y value during the fixation and during the smooth pursuit in x direction.

compensating condition, it was 48 pixels (1.4°), which results in a reduction of 25%.

Discussion

The experiment shows that measuring the local tracker offset is possible and that compensating for it significantly improves the pointing accuracy. It also showed that with the offset calibration in place, targets with a size down to 1.4° become reliably clickable.

To further investigate how well the offset detection actually worked, we analysed the recorded gaze traces, one of which is shown in Figure 8. The smooth pursuit in the x direction starting at about 900 ms is clearly distinguishable from the fixation before. The offset compensating movement in y direction, however, is not easily detectable and by itself might be misclassified as tracker noise or a smooth pursuit. However, when computing the mean y coordinate during fixation period and the mean y coordinate during the smooth pursuit period, the offset in y direction becomes measurable.

EXPERIMENT 3: REAL-LIFE SCENARIO

Inspired by the results of the first two experiments, our goal was to test the usability of our interaction technique in a practical scenario. We therefore created an experiment where an unmodified version of a web browser has to be controlled by gaze only. In this experiment, the participants had to play Wikirace[4].

In Wikirace, each player starts at the same Wikipedia webpage and the goal is to reach a target Wikipedia page with as few clicks as possible. To navigate to the target page, only clicking on Wikipedia links in the current page is allowed. The benefit of this game is that it naturally limits the input modality to mouse only, without putting artificial restrictions on it and hence reflects the everyday scenario of browsing the web. Furthermore, the game character of the experiment forces the participants to read the presented webpage and to select the link they want to click carefully. Thus, any occurring Midas touches would be recognizable.

Participants

Seven participants (6 male, 1 female), all either graduate students, or researchers at the local lab with ages between 23 and

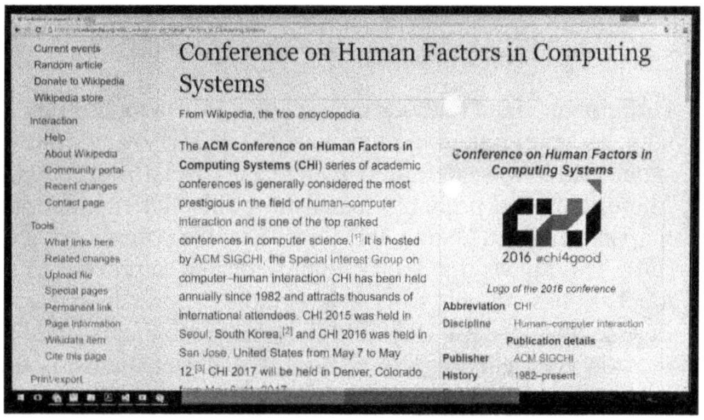

Figure 9. An image of the screen during the Wikirace. The two scroll buttons (red for up, green for down) are placed at the bottom of the screen not to cover any crucial content.

29 years (mean: 26.3, SD: 2.1) took part in this case study. All had normal or corrected-to-normal vision; two already had minor experience with eye tracking, the rest had no experience. Two participants wore glasses during the experiment, and two wore contact lenses.

Experimental Setup and Design

The hardware setup was the same as in the first two experiments and the game was played using an unmodified version of the Google Chrome web browser. To ensure that the links on the website had a clickable height of at least 47 pixels, the built-in scale factor of the browser was set to 125%. In order to provide full browsing capabilities without the need of a keyboard, some scrolling functionality had to be implemented. To do so, two dwell time buttons were used, which were placed over the task bar. These buttons were part of the transparent layer, and were projected onto the target monitor using the additional hardware setup. Dwelling on the left button triggered a "page down" button press and dwelling on the right triggered "page up" button press. The placement of these buttons was carefully chosen not to cover any crucial information on the target monitor.

Participants were asked to think aloud during the experiment, and a short interview was held afterwards. The questions asked in that interview were what they liked/disliked about the input method, whether they noticed the offset compensation, how easy the technique was to learn, and how demanding it was to use for a longer time. During the experiment, each participant's voice was recorded and analysed post-hoc.

Procedure

After filling out an informed consent form, the tracker was calibrated using a nine-point calibration. Then the participants had to play three rounds of Wikirace, where the quickest path contained 6, 5, and 4 pages, respectively. The users were asked to think aloud while playing. There was no recalibration between the rounds and completing all three rounds took between 15 and 35 minutes.

Results and Discussion

The setup did work well in this scenario, and all participants managed to reach the target webpage. The taken paths from

[4]https://en.wikipedia.org/wiki/Wikipedia:Wikirace

the starting page to the target page varied for all participants and had between 7 and 30 nodes.

Participants liked that our method was Midas touch free. P1, who had previous experience with gaze-based interaction, stated that is was "definitely better than dwell time", and that "there, they had probably many more misclicks". Also, participants enjoyed "being able to rest the eye without clicking" (P4). This shows that the symmetric design to prevent Midas touches does not only work in laboratory experiments, but also in practical scenarios. Although some participants rated the method as exhausting, for some it was "less exhausting than expected" (P4). Participants who did find it exhausting did not like looking at a bright monitor for so long and for them, resting the eye helped.

Most of the participants wished that the pointing would be more precise and they stated that they would prefer using the mouse. However, all agreed that this method was good enough for basic interaction and that if "the hand cannot be used, it is a good alternative" (P6). Four participants noticed that "offset compensation did offer more precision" (P2), and some developed a technique where they specifically clicked next to a link for the system to increase local tracking precision. This shows that for the majority of participants, the offset compensation did bring a noticeable benefit.

None of the participants had any trouble learning the method and they stated that "the method worked surprisingly well" (P3). However, they did not like the scroll buttons and had a hard time dwelling at them, because the low position at the edge of the tracking range often caused a loss of tracking, but "except the scroll buttons, everything worked very well" (P5).

In summary, the interaction method worked very well in this experiment and the overall feedback of the participants was very positive, except for the scroll button implementation, which has to be improved further.

CONCLUSION

Gaze can be a intuitive and reliable input modality, especially for people with manual motor impairments or in scenarios where hands-free operation is mandatory. With cheap, yet relatively precise eye trackers entering the end-user market, this input technique appeals even more. Although gaze-based user interaction has been a field of research for many years, no solution exists so far that is able to apply gaze interaction to off-the-shelf software. This is partly because additional visual targets are required for advanced interaction methods, and thus the used software has to be modified in order to provide them.

We showed that it is possible to implement a system-wide gaze-only interaction technique which is usable in everyday scenarios and does not need a deep system integration. We achieved this by following a layered interface approach and putting a transparent GUI layer on top of the system's GUI. In a user study following the ISO 9241-9, we could successfully demonstrate that this approach enabled us to implement state-of-the art interaction techniques (MSDT and SPOCK) and that the SPOCK activation method can achieve a throughput close to that of a touchpad (1.23 bits/s and 1.7 bits/s, respectively).

We further introduced a novel method of how to detect the tracker offset using only the interaction gestures and how to compensate for it on-the-fly. A second user study, also following the ISO 9241-9 standard proved that this error compensation method reduces the click error rate by 18% and that the target size required for an error rate of at most 50% can be decreased by 25%.

Finally, we tested our solution in a real-life scenario, where participants had to navigate a web browser. Particularly, they had to play three rounds of Wikirace, where the goal is to navigate to a target Wikipedia page by only clicking on the hyperlinks. The system technically worked in this practical application and the subjective statements of the participants indicate that the solution is usable in such scenarios.

Limitations and Future Work

There are still some limitations to the system: currently, we are only able to trigger left mouse clicks. Other mouse actions, such as right clicks or mouse wheel events, are not implemented yet. One potential way to implement these actions would be to add a button bar, similar to our scroll buttons, to the transparent layer that lets the user choose between the different mouse events. However, how to implement gaze-based drag-and-drop operations is still an open research question.

The hardware setup in its current state is expensive and bulky. For non-Windows systems, a powerful computer is still required to run the eye-tracking software, but hardware-only eye-tracking modules that do all signal processing on chip are currently under development and thus hardware costs might go down in the future. The size of the hardware setup could be reduced by transparent displays.

ACKNOWLEDGMENTS

We would like to thank the reviewers for their helpful feedback. Our research was supported by the Elite Network Bavaria.

REFERENCES

1. Hyunjin Ahn, Jaeseok Yoon, Gulji Chung, Kibum Kim, Jiyeon Ma, Hyunbin Choi, Donguk Jung, and Joongseek Lee. 2015. DOWELL: Dwell-time Based Smartphone Control Solution for People with Upper Limb Disabilities. In *Proc. of the SIGCHI Conf. Ext. Abst. on Human Factors in Computing Systems (CHI EA '15)*. ACM, New York, NY, USA, 887–892. DOI: http://dx.doi.org/10.1145/2702613.2732862
2. Patrick Bader, Niels Henze, Nora Broy, and Katrin Wolf. 2016. The Effect of Focus Cues on Separation of Information Layers. In *Proc. of the SIGCHI Conf. on Human Factors in Computing Systems (CHI '16)*. ACM, New York, NY, USA, 509–514. DOI: http://dx.doi.org/10.1145/2858036.2858312
3. Nikolaus Bee and Elisabeth André. 2008. Writing with Your Eye: A Dwell Time Free Writing System Adapted to the Nature of Human Eye Gaze. In *Proc. of the 4th IEEE tutorial and research workshop on Perception and Interactive Technologies for Speech-Based Systems: Perception in Multimodal Dialogue Systems (PIT '08)*. Springer, 111–122.

4. Darrell S. Best and Andrew T. Duchowski. 2016. A rotary dial for gaze-based PIN entry. In *Proc. of the 9th Biennial ACM Symp. on Eye Tracking Research & Applications (ETRA '16)*. ACM, 69–76. DOI: http://dx.doi.org/10.1145/2857491.2857527
5. Dietlind Helene Cymek, Antje Christine Venjakob, Stefan Ruff, Otto Hans-Martin Lutz, Simon Hofmann, and Matthias Roetting. 2014. Entering PIN codes by smooth pursuit eye movements. *Journal of Eye Movement Research* 7, 4 (2014), 1–11.
6. Michael Dorr, Martin Böhme, Thomas Martinetz, and Erhardt Barth. 2007. Gaze beats mouse: A case study. In *Proc. of the 3rd Conf. on Communication by Gaze Interaction (COGAIN '07)*. 16–19.
7. Sarah A. Douglas, Arthur E. Kirkpatrick, and I. Scott MacKenzie. 1999. Testing pointing device performance and user assessment with the ISO 9241, Part 9 standard. In *Proc. of the SIGCHI Conf. on Human Factors in Computing Systems (CHI '99)*. ACM, New York, NY, USA, 215–222. DOI: http://dx.doi.org/10.1145/302979.303042
8. Heiko Drewes and Albrecht Schmidt. 2007. Interacting with the Computer Using Gaze Gestures. In *Proc. of the 11th IFIP Int. Conf. on Human-Computer Interaction*. INTERACT '07, Vol. 4663. Springer, Berlin, 475–488. DOI:http://dx.doi.org/10.1007/978-3-540-74800-7{_}43
9. Augusto Esteves, Eduardo Velloso, Andreas Bulling, and Hans Gellersen. 2015. Orbits: Gaze Interaction for Smart Watches using Smooth Pursuit Eye Movements. In *Proc. of the 28th Annual ACM Symp. on User Interface Software and Technology (UIST '15)*. ACM, New York, NY, USA, 457–466. DOI: http://dx.doi.org/10.1145/2807442.2807499
10. Jens R. Helmert, Sebastian Pannasch, and Boris M. Velichkovsky. 2008. Influences of dwell time and cursor control on the performance in gaze driven typing. *Journal of Eye Movement Research* 2, 4 (2008), 1–8.
11. Anke Huckauf and Mario H. Urbina. 2011. Object Selection in Gaze Controlled Systems: What You Don't Look at is What You Get. *ACM Transactions on Applied Perception* 8, 2 (2011), 13:1–13:14. DOI: http://dx.doi.org/10.1145/1870076.1870081
12. Robert J. K. Jacob. 1990. What you look at is what you get: eye movement-based interaction techniques. In *Proc. of the SIGCHI Conf. on Human Factors in Computing Systems (CHI '90)*. ACM, New York, NY, USA, 11–18. DOI:http://dx.doi.org/10.1145/97243.97246
13. Chris Lankford. 2000. Effective Eye-gaze Input into Windows. In *Proc. of the 1st Biennial Symp. on Eye Tracking Research & Applications (ETRA '00)*. ACM, New York, NY, USA, 23–27. DOI: http://dx.doi.org/10.1145/355017.355021
14. Christof Lutteroth, Moiz Penkar, and Gerald Weber. 2015. Gaze vs. Mouse: A Fast and Accurate Gaze-Only Click Alternative. In *Proc. of the 28th Annual ACM Symp. on User Interface Software and Technology (UIST '15)*. ACM, New York, NY, USA, 385–394. DOI: http://dx.doi.org/10.1145/2807442.2807461
15. I. Scott MacKenzie. 2010. An eye on input. In *Proc. of the 6th Biennial ACM Symp. on Eye Tracking Research & Applications (ETRA '10)*. ACM, 11–12. DOI: http://dx.doi.org/10.1145/1743666.1743668
16. John Magee, Torsten Felzer, and I. Scott MacKenzie. 2015. Camera Mouse + ClickerAID: Dwell vs. Single-Muscle Click Actuation in Mouse-Replacement Interfaces. In *Proc. of the 16th Int. Conf. on Human-Computer Interaction (LNCS)*, Vol. 9170. 74–84.
17. Päivi Majaranta, Ulla-Kaija Ahola, and Oleg Špakov. 2009. Fast Gaze Typing with an Adjustable Dwell Time. In *Proc. of the SIGCHI Conf. on Human Factors in Computing Systems (CHI '09)*. ACM, New York, NY, USA, 357–360. DOI: http://dx.doi.org/10.1145/1518701.1518758
18. Päivi Majaranta, Anne Aula, and Kari-Jouko Räihä. 2004. Effects of Feedback on Eye Typing with a Short Dwell Time. In *Proc. of the 3rd Biennial ACM Symp. on Eye Tracking Research & Applications (ETRA '04)*. ACM, 139–146. DOI:http://dx.doi.org/10.1145/968363.968390
19. Emilie Møllenbach, John Paulin Hansen, and Martin Lillholm. 2013. Eye Movements in Gaze Interaction. *Journal of Eye Movement Research* 6, 1 (2013), 1–15.
20. Emilie Møllenbach, John Paulin Hansen, Martin Lillholm, and Alastair G. Gale. 2009. Single Stroke Gaze Gestures. In *Proc. of the SIGCHI Conf. on Human Factors in Computing Systems (CHI EA '09)*. ACM, New York, NY, USA, 4555–4560. DOI: http://dx.doi.org/10.1145/1520340.1520699
21. Diogo Pedrosa, Maria da Graça Pimentel, and Khai N. Truong. 2015. Filteryedping: A Dwell-Free Eye Typing Technique. In *Proc. of the SIGCHI Conf. Ext. Abst. on Human Factors in Computing Systems (CHI EA '15)*. ACM, New York, NY, USA, 303–306. DOI: http://dx.doi.org/10.1145/2702613.2725458
22. Abdul Moiz Penkar, Christof Lutteroth, and Gerald Weber. 2012. Designing for the Eye: Design Parameters for Dwell in Gaze Interaction. In *Proc. of the 24th Australian Computer-Human Interaction Conf. (OzCHI '12)*. ACM, New York, NY, USA, 479–488. DOI: http://dx.doi.org/10.1145/2414536.2414609
23. D. A. Ray. 1969. Head-Up Display. *The Aeronautical Journal* 73, 703 (1969), 622–624. DOI: http://dx.doi.org/10.1017/S0001924000052295
24. Dario D. Salvucci and John R. Anderson. 2000. Intelligent Gaze-added Interfaces. In *Proc. of the SIGCHI Conf. on Human Factors in Computing Systems (CHI '00)*. ACM, New York, NY, USA, 273–280. DOI: http://dx.doi.org/10.1145/332040.332444

25. Simon Schenk, Philipp Tiefenbacher, Gerhard Rigoll, and Michael Dorr. 2016. SPOCK: A Smooth Pursuit Oculomotor Control Kit. In *Proc. of the SIGCHI Conf. Ext. Abst. on Human Factors in Computing Systems (CHI EA '16)*. ACM, New York, NY, USA, 2681–2687. DOI: http://dx.doi.org/10.1145/2851581.2892291

26. Donald Shepard. 1968. A Two-dimensional Interpolation Function for Irregularly-spaced Data. In *Proc. of the 1968 23rd ACM Nat. Conf. (ACM '68)*. ACM, New York, NY, USA, 517–524. DOI: http://dx.doi.org/10.1145/800186.810616

27. Henrik Skovsgaard, Julio C. Mateo, John M. Flach, and John Paulin Hansen. 2010. Small-target Selection with Gaze Alone. In *Proc. of the 6th Biennial ACM Symp. on Eye Tracking Research & Applications (ETRA '10)*. ACM, 145–148. DOI: http://dx.doi.org/10.1145/1743666.1743702

28. Mélodie Vidal, Andreas Bulling, and Hans Gellersen. 2013. Pursuits: spontaneous interaction with displays based on smooth pursuit eye movement and moving targets. In *Proc. of the 2013 ACM Joint Conf. on Pervasive and Ubiquitous Computing (UbiComp '13)*. ACM, New York, NY, USA, 439–448. DOI: http://dx.doi.org/10.1145/2493432.2493477

29. David J. Ward and David J. C. MacKay. 2002. Fast Hands-free Writing by Gaze Direction. *Nature* 418 (2002), 838. DOI:http://dx.doi.org/10.1038/418838a

30. Jacob O. Wobbrock, Kristen Shinohara, and Alex Jansen. 2011. The effects of task dimensionality, endpoint deviation, throughput calculation, and experiment design on pointing measures and models. In *Proc. of the SIGCHI Conf. on Human Factors in Computing Systems (CHI '11)*. ACM, New York, NY, USA, 1639–1648. DOI: http://dx.doi.org/10.1145/1978942.1979181

31. Xuan Zhang and I. Scott MacKenzie. 2007. Evaluating eye tracking with ISO 9241-part 9. In *Proc. of the 12th Int. Conf. of HCI Intelligent Multimodal Interaction Environments, Part III (HCII '07)*. 779–788.

Trajectories of Engagement and Disengagement with a Story-Based Smoking Cessation App

Wally Smith[1], Bernd Ploderer[2], Greg Wadley[1], Sarah Webber[1] and Ron Borland[3]

[1]School of Computing & Information Systems, University of Melbourne, Australia
{wsmith, greg.wadley, s.webber}@unimelb.edu.au

[2]Queensland University of Technology, Brisbane, Australia
b.ploderer@qut.edu.au

[3]Cancer Council Victoria, Melbourne, Australia
Ron.Borland@cancervic.org.au

ABSTRACT

Strong user engagement with digital technologies for behaviour change is often taken as a precursor to their longer-term efficacy. We critically examine this assumption through a qualitative study of a smoking cessation app, called NewLeaf, which allows quitters to swap personal stories. The study examined what influenced people to engage or disengage with NewLeaf, and how the app was deployed in quit attempts during a four week trial. Several properties of swapped stories were reported to promote engagement, including: authenticity, currency, contextualization of advice, and evoking a sense of community. But while the resulting engagement was sometimes productive in supporting quitting, other trajectories of use were observed involving counterproductive engagement, and a surprising pattern of productive disengagement especially among stronger quitters. We discuss how this analysis of different trajectories problematizes any simple interpretation of user engagement as an early indicator of success for behaviour change technologies.

Author Keywords

smoking cessation; health behavior change; engagement; qualitative research

ACM Classification Keywords

H.5.3 Group and Organization Interfaces: Web-based interaction.

INTRODUCTION

Persuasive technology has been a prominent area of HCI research with more than 100 papers at CHI over the last 10 years focused on behaviour change in health and other domains [15]. While the key idea of designing for behaviour change has been popular, the original notion of persuasive technology [11] has been critiqued on a number of fronts [5]. One is its prescriptive stance on what behaviours are deemed desirable, often with a lack of consideration for personal needs and desires [2], and for individual circumstances [9]. There has been debate about whether 'one size fits all', or whether more sensitive design is needed for varying motivations of individuals at different stages of change [14].

In the area of health behaviour change, research into new technologies also faces significant methodological challenges [17,30]. It is typically beyond the scope of HCI research to measure final health outcomes for a population, or even for a sample of study participants. Reasons include, as Klasnja et al. [17] have cogently argued, that the timeframe of health interventions can be several months or years, and that generalizable outcomes are best established through randomized control trials (RCT) as favoured by medical research. Although possible in principle, a longitudinal RCT can lead to a different research focus that takes emphasis away from HCI design. Instead, Klasnja et al. argue in favour of HCI researchers using intermediate indicators of success.

To contribute to the understanding of this burgeoning class of digital technology, our aim here is not to measure the effectiveness of a particular technology or technique, but rather to provide a qualitative account of *How and why people engage with digital tools in their attempt to undertake behaviour change*. Rather than seeking a normative account, we are concerned with the variety and even idiosyncrasies of users and uses. Implicit in much health app design, and related HCI research (including that of the authors), is what can be called the *engagement-efficacy perspective*: the belief that greater engagement with a health technology is a precursor to its longer-term efficacy in addressing the targeted health condition. Taking this perspective does not assume that engagement is sufficient to achieve efficacy, nor even that it is a causal antecedent, but simply that greater engagement is a positive early indicator, in the sense described by Klasnja et al [17], and therefore a good outcome for HCI design.

Some researchers report counter-findings to the engagement-efficacy perspective, identifying cases where people disengage from a technology as part of the positive

Permission to make digital or hard copies of all or part of this work for personal or classroom use is granted without fee provided that copies are not made or distributed for profit or commercial advantage and that copies bear this notice and the full citation on the first page. Copyrights for components of this work owned by others than ACM must be honored. Abstracting with credit is permitted. To copy otherwise, or republish, to post on servers or to redistribute to lists, requires prior specific permission and/or a fee. Request permissions from Permissions@acm.org.
CHI 2017, May 06-11, 2017, Denver, CO, USA
© 2017 ACM.
ISBN 978-1-4503-4655-9/17/05…$15.00
DOI: http://dx.doi.org/10.1145/3025453.3026054

continuation of their behaviour change, including the 'gateway effect' [29], 'happy abandonment' [7]' for various reasons [10]. We aim to build on these accounts and to further critically examine the nature and significance of engagement with behaviour change applications.

The study we report here focuses on smoking cessation. We designed a mobile app, called NewLeaf, and evaluated it with 23 people who were attempting to quit smoking. Despite many developments in recent decades to restrict and curtail the smoking of cigarettes in several countries, almost 6 million people are estimated to die each year from smoking-related disease worldwide, with forecasts of 8 million deaths per year by 2030 [35]. Smoking cessation has therefore been one of the targets of HCI researchers interested in persuasive technology [21, 23, 24, 26].

Underlying our study is a shift away from the persuasive technology paradigm which puts emphasis on whether a tool can 'persuade' people to change. Instead, our premise is that digital tools are better seen as *resources*. Whether users of NewLeaf would successfully embark on a quit attempt is the result of many external factors relating to personal motivation and circumstances. Our concern is not whether NewLeaf acts as the driver of success, but rather with how people might engage with its suite of resources, and how they might deploy them positively, or otherwise, in their quit attempts. And within this, we ask whether engagement with the app is associated with positive experiences of attempting to quit.

NewLeaf was designed with three potential quitting resources. Chief among these was an online forum for people to exchange their personal stories of attempting to quit, widely believed to be a powerful and engaging health resource [18]. For comparison, NewLeaf also provided expert health tips, and online distractions to combat cravings. The app thereby provided multiple options for engagement, thus serving the aims of our study.

BACKGROUND & RELATED LITERATURE

Engagement and behaviour change technology

Engagement is a vital but notoriously hard to define concept in HCI. For Sutcliffe, it is what makes a technology 'attractive' and 'fun' to use [32], while for O'Brien and Toms it is the much broader 'quality of user experience characterized by attributes of challenge, positive affect, endurability, aesthetic and sensory appeal, attention, feedback, variety/novelty, interactivity, and perceived user control.' [20]. Turner has emphasised the centrality of the 'affective' dimension of engagement 'consistent with both our contingent identities and our wider purposes' [33]

Although our study was designed to examine the affective experiences of users of NewLeaf, we use the term 'engagement' here to mean the degree to which people use a digital aid in a way that relates to the purpose of behaviour change. Thus engagement refers to the extent and manner in which people actively used the resources of NewLeaf to help them quit smoking. Conversely, the term 'disengagement' is used to mean withdrawing from active use of the tool.

In the case of smoking cessation, much research shows that smokers are highly reluctant to engage with online social support tools because of concerns about self-presentation, and embarrassment of failure [19]. It is not surprising, then, that designers and researchers set user engagement as a desirable goal. Hence, the engagement-efficacy perspective is implicit in much research and development.

As an illustration, studies in this area are often premised on the reasonable assumption of making apps, or other technologies, more engaging to increase the likelihood of behaviour change down the track. For example, Paay et al [21], through a design workshop with smokers, report that they desire advice that is personalized for their needs, that they can relate to and which is tailored to their stage of quitting (e.g., intending to quit, or currently making a quit attempt). Similarly, Agapie et al [1] designed a system to help people create behaviour change plans with strangers and friends. Interviews showed that participants responded to plans more positively when they were tailored to their goals, routines and preferences. Reno and Poole [26] examined whether and how people would respond to a request for social support to quit smoking on Facebook, and found that people are 10 times more likely to offer support to friends and family members compared to strangers.

Disengagement and behaviour change technology

However, there is also a growing number of counterpoints to the engagement-efficacy perspective. Rooksby et al. [27] used an interview study to uncover a variety of motivations for engaging with personal health apps and devices. Alongside productive uses, were non-productive forms of engagement, e.g., a desire to document one's lifestyle, collect rewards, or simply a fetish for gadgets and technology. A recurring finding of studies of wearable health and activity monitors is that they are typically abandoned after a few months because motivation drops, needs are not met, or because people change to a different system [7,12]. Schwanda et al. [29] have termed this latter outcome the 'gateway effect', showing that persuasive technology can work as a conduit to new activities, and thus reduced engagement with a tool is not always a sign of failure.

In the context of personal energy use, He et al. [14] argue that the design of new technologies aiming to support behaviour change should consider differences among users. In particular, they draw on the transtheoretical model [25], to argue that technologies should engage adaptively to people at different stages of behaviour change, from pre-contemplation, contemplation, preparation, action and finally maintenance of the change. He et al. conclude that 'if technologies are adaptive, a dynamic component should be present (e.g., social networks), as technologies cannot be expected to keep up with complex human motivations'.

The value of personal narratives in behaviour change

An important element of our study was the use of personal stories as a powerful form of content to engage users in behaviour change [13]. By focusing specifically on how personal stories might engage quitters, we are drawing on a long history of research into the benefits of health advice in narrative form [22]. For example, Mamykina et al. [18] designed a story-based mobile health application for people with diabetes, and demonstrated its value for users to maintain a positive self-image, to reassert their competence and to maintain continuity in their self-image over time.

More generally, many researchers report that role models and norms conveyed through narratives can influence behaviour change [16]. Borland [3] argues that habitual behaviours like smoking can be effectively influenced through stories, because they influence our actions on an unconscious level. However, there is also a line of evidence that shared stories may work to protect people's connection to social situations in which the adverse behaviour is prevalent, as in DeSantis' [8] account of cigar smokers.

STUDY METHOD

The NewLeaf smoking cessation app

To explore our questions, we designed and built a smartphone app, called NewLeaf (see Figure 1), which allows smokers to share personal quit stories. Unlike many of the studies reviewed above, which used interviews, design workshops, and hypothetical responses, our aim was to study the role of NewLeaf in real-life quit attempts that took place over the first four weeks following a decision to quit.

Ploderer et al. [24] studied a quit app that presented expert tips about quitting and distractions to cope with cravings for cigarettes. We included these two kinds of content in NewLeaf to serve as comparisons with the personal stories. Most prior work on the power of narratives for health behaviour change has focused on the use of professionally-authored content [16]. In contrast, we were interested in the kinds of engagement achieved by community-generated stories written and shared by smokers and quitters.

To ensure that we had a thriving community from the outset, we drew content from the forum 'StopSmoking' hosted on the Reddit website. This forum receives about 30 posts a day from smokers and ex-smokers and is moderated by long-term quitters. Reddit has a publicly available API that makes it possible to pass content to and from the Reddit server. StopSmoking is pseudonymous and authors are not required to identify themselves. It is known that the anonymity of Reddit contributes to increased self-disclosure in online discussions about sensitive issues such as mental health problems [6].

Our NewLeaf app presented quitter stories from the StopSmoking forum and allowed users to read and post content. We removed many of the features of the full Reddit site, and reduced the rapid turnover of posts so that some stories remained visible for longer. For consistency, both expert tips and distractions were presented in the same way as stories, with comment trails following each item. The expert tips were sourced from counsellors at Quit Victoria, a smoking cessation agency at which one of the authors is based. To source distractions, we allowed users to choose a Reddit forum of non-smoking content relevant to their interests; examples chosen included jokes, world news, science, contemporary art.

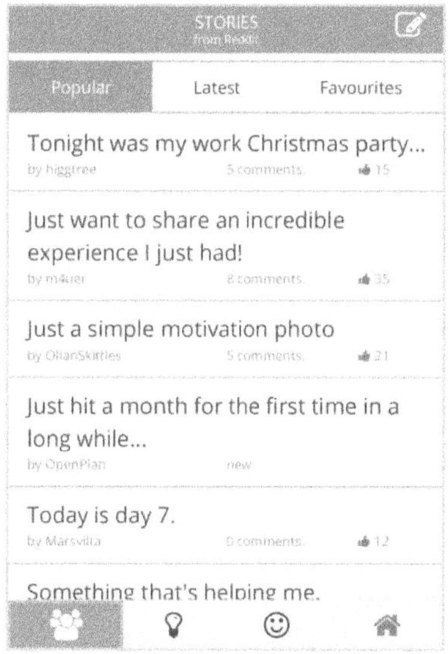

Figure 1. Screen-shot from the NewLeaf app showing a listing of stories, and buttons along the bottom to reach expert tips, distractions and home

Participants and the study procedure

Thirty participants were recruited into the study via an advertisement. Seven did not return for a second interview, leaving 23 participants aged between 23-50, split 11/12 between males and females. They were recruited on the basis of two criteria: being adult smokers who were considering a quit attempt, and being smartphone users.

A first interview was held with each participant to find out their smoking history and quit intentions, and to introduce the app and configure the distractions page to a forum of their choice. Participants were then left to use the app as they wished over the following four weeks. A second in-depth interview was held towards the end of the fourth week to probe experiences of quitting and the nature of engagement with the stories, tips and distractions. Participants were compensated $25 per interview for their time and travel costs. We took strong steps to reduce the potential bias of participants believing they needed to be positive about the app. They were encouraged to be critical, and emphasis was placed on comparing their experience of stories, tips and distractions.

A thematic analysis drawing on the techniques of Braun and Clarke [4] was carried out, using transcribed audio-recordings of the in-depth second interviews, to identify the nature and forms of engagement and disengagement with

NewLeaf. We also tracked usage patterns by recording every 'click' in NewLeaf made during the 4 week trial.

FINDINGS

A common criterion for successful quitting is to be smoke-free for 6 months [34]. It was not possible therefore to examine participants' success of smoking cessation, but rather we focussed on how their quit attempt was proceeding and their engagement with the app.

Based on the second interviews at week 4 of the trial, participants were classified according to the reported success of their quit attempt so far. We first distinguished between those who presented as 'Succeeding' so far (S) from those who presented as 'Not-Succeeding' (N). Among those Succeeding, we further distinguished between those who had totally abstained from smoking throughout the trial (S1-S8) from those with a qualified report (S9-S16) in which they had either cut-down and were on track to quit, or were quitting but had experienced minor relapses. Among those who were Not-Succeeding, we distinguished those who had not managed to make any quit attempt (N1-N4) from those who had tried but relapsed (N5-N7).

Light smokers, who smoke 5 or less cigarettes per day [28], are likely to find quitting less challenging than heavier smokers. Given our intention to explore the variety of experiences we included them in our study, but to provide greater context we label them with the letter L, e.g., S6L.

Participants were asked directly in interviews if they had an overall positive, negative or neutral experience of using each of the three resources in NewLeaf: stories, tips and distractions. These affective responses are summarized in the top rows of Figure 2 (heavy smokers) and Figure 3 (light smokers). Positive experience (shown as +) implies that participants spoke of valuing the resource and believing it to be useful for quitting. Negative reactions (shown as x) implies that participants reported that the resource was annoying, off-putting, pointless, or similar. Figures 2 and 3 show that there was a variety of reactions to the three forms of content. Figure 2 indicates that, among the heavier smokers, stories were more likely to have produced positive affect (shown as + in Figure 2) by participants who reported that they were Succeeding in their quit attempt than by those who were Not-Succeeding. This pattern was not evident among the light smokers (Figure 3).

The lower panels of Figures 2 and 3 show the intensity of usage of NewLeaf over the first 3 weeks of the trial, measured by the number of significant interactions with the app. We do not include the fourth week where there was often a spike of usage during and around the second interview. A significant interaction was defined as one of the following: the opening of a specific content item (story, tip or distraction); posting of an item of content; favouriting or unfavouriting of an item; upvoting or downvoting an item; a login. A score of 1 in Figures 2 and 3 thus represents a simple login to the app, and might involve the undetected browsing of content lists, but did not involve opening of specific items or responding to them. Scores above 1 indicate the inclusion of some of these more significant interactions, up to the highest daily score of 405 which implies a prolonged session of many significant interactions.

Most striking in Figures 2 and 3 is that there is no apparent association between the intensity of using NewLeaf and either the status of participants as being Succeeding or Not-Succeeding, or the affective responses of participants to stories, tips and distractions. Succeeding participants S2 and S12, for example, show high intensity usage over the 3 weeks, but Not-Succeeding N4L, N5, N6 also show moderately high usage. Conversely, the lowest usage is shown by 3 Succeeding participants, S7L, S3 and S11, with the Not-Succeeding N3 and N7L also being relatively low intensity users. This qualitative dissociation between intensity of use and the status of quit attempts is a significant observation which informs our discussion of engagement patterns below.

Trajectories of engagement and disengagement

Thematic analysis of the second interviews revealed a rich variety of experiences in using NewLeaf, including both positive and negative reactions to the app and its value in supporting a quit attempt. Figure 4 shows a conceptual model that was developed through our analysis to classify patterns of engagement and disengagement. We will overview this model first, before describing the evidence that underpins it.

The model in Figure 4 depicts attempts to undergo digitally-mediated behaviour change as a journey, or trajectory, from a current to a desired behaviour state; in this case, from being a smoker to being a non-smoker. In between are various intermediate states defined by different forms of engagement or disengagement with the digital tool. Alternative trajectories of attempted behaviour change are shown in the form of paths that people might follow through these various states. Each person's trajectory may contain a mixture of 'steps forward' towards the desired state, or 'steps backward' towards the current state. The trajectories in Figure 4 are not meant to be exhaustive, but rather they reflect prominent observed patterns in our study participants.

The model thus shows how attempts at digitally-mediated behaviour change might progress along very different trajectories. From the current state as a smoker, each person undertakes *exploratory engagement* with the app, a step which was induced by the procedure of the first interview of our study. Once into the trial, a participant may then shift to a state that we describe as *productive engagement* meaning that they are actively consulting and applying the resources of the app to quitting. However, as our model shows we observed other states that allow for alternative trajectories: *counterproductive engagement*, *non-productive disengagement*, and *productive disengagement*. In the

		Succeeding									Not-Succeeding				
Participant		S2	S12	S5	S1	S9	S4	S10	S3	S11	N5	N6	N1	N2	N3
Base rate cig/day		20	10	8	30	20	10	20	12	10	20	6	10	10	7
		Affective response to NewLeaf resources: + positive x negative (blank indicating neither)													
Stories		+	+	+	+	+	+	+	+		x	+	x	x	x
Tips		x	+	x					x	+		+	x	+	x
Distractions		x	+		x			x				x	x		
		Intensity of Use: Counts of significant interactions with NewLeaf													
Week 1	**1**	405	70	34	108	12	15	44	25	26	30	20	11	13	22
	2	224	18	47	26	24	59	1			36	15		12	2
	3	175	16	15		57	25				14	10	6		
	4	111	3			26	9						3		
	5	134	14			1					28				
	6	109	3	16							6		19		
	7	75	6	34							5	18		4	
Week 2	**8**	46										9			2
	9	73	4								15				
	10	67	2								16				
	11	55	21								5	12		6	
	12	24	3			6								1	
	13	97	4						4			16			2
	14	58										1			
Week 3	**15**	32	13												
	16	27									4				
	17	30	11												
	18	55	2										3		
	19	48	11										1		
	20	21	1							3			1		1
	21	34	4									13			

Figure 2. Data for heavy smokers: Base rates of smoking (top panel); Participants' affective response to stories, tips and distractions in the NewLeaf app (middle panel); and tracking data of the total number of significant interactions with the NewLeaf app by each participant during the study (lower panel) (See Findings section for the definition of significant interactions.)

following sections we explain and describe these states, the evidence for them, and the resulting trajectories.

Productive engagement

Productive engagement is a state envisaged, and hoped for, under the engagement-efficacy perspective. While we argue here is that there are other significant states and trajectories that arise, productive engagement is nevertheless a very important state. This section now considers the shape that productive engagement took in our study by identifying the characteristics of stories, and sometimes expert health tips, that were reported as eliciting meaningful and positive engagement with NewLeaf.

Authenticity, currency and contextualized advice

Participants who were positive about posted stories spoke of them as being more *authentic* than the expert health tips. Curiously, although the stories were themselves simply textual posts, they were experienced as somehow more 'real' and alive than expert health advice: *'it's perspective from real people, real time rather than you're reading a blog post on the internet'* (S2); *'I mean the tips are just tips, like expert tips but the things people post they are real and this actually happened to them'* (S12). Just four Succeeding quitters and two Not-Succeeding quitters, reported that expert tips were valuable because of the credibility of the source (S11, S12, N2, N6). But there was less need to engage with tips frequently as a Not-Succeeding participant pointed out: *'the first few days I saw all the tips that were there ... so it's not like I'm going to be using that feature every day'* (N2).

Related to the sense of the authenticity around stories, participants were positive about their *currency*; that is, they recognised that the stories were recently created, a result of the high turnover of posts and growing comment trails. In contrast, the expert tips were more static: *'if I jumped back in it's like 'oh, I've seen that one already. Why is that still*

		Succeeding							Not-Succeeding	
Participant		S15L	S13L	S6L	S16L	S8L	S14L	S7L	N4L	N7L
Base rate cig/day		3	5	3	0.5	1	3	2	2	4
		Affective response to NewLeaf resources: + positive x negative (blank indicating neither)								
Stories		+		+	x	+	x		x	+
Tips			x				+	+		
Distractions		+	+		+	x	+		+	x
		Intensity of Use: Counts of significant interactions with NewLeaf								
Week 1	**1**	51	54	36	19	30	5	16	21	13
	2	1	27		8	2	8		12	
	3			31					20	21
	4	1			12	1			14	2
	5	8							4	
	6				9	1				
	7	48	6		3		19		13	
Week 2	**8**	6		13					16	
	9	14								6
	10		37							
	11		18						2	
	12								2	
	13								31	
	14	14				4			34	
Week 3	**15**	1	6			2			4	
	16		2			9			14	
	17	10				3				
	18		2							
	19									
	20	4			15				3	
	21									

Figure 3. Data for light smokers: Base rates of smoking (top panel); Participants' affective response to stories, tips and distractions in the NewLeaf app (middle panel); and tracking data of the total number of significant interactions with the NewLeaf app by each participant during the study (lower panel) (See Findings section for the definition of significant interactions.)

sitting there?' It was mainly to hear what other people were saying' (N6).

The greater attraction to stories over expert tips was not because participants were avoiding practical support. On the contrary, and consistent with the notion of productive engagement, most participants strongly preferred stories that contained specific advice that was *contextualized* within the personal narrative: *'I'd prefer that someone who is say on the same page as I am gives me that information rather than a doctor ... '* (S5). As suggested by one participant, the attraction of authenticity, currency and contextualized advice was that they created a sense of agency in the quitter; a feeling that the decision to quit comes from the quitter themself, and not through obedience to a health expert: *'there's still a lot of people out there that are trying to quit, not because we're forced to quit but because it's our own decision to do it'* (S9).

Identifying with the story poster

A further critical aspect underpinning productive engagement was whether participants could identify with the poster's situation and experience: *'Oh, some of them are textbook cases of me, it's like I could have written it'* (S3). For most participants, identifying with others at the same stage of quitting was powerful: *'it's like relating your experience to theirs and trying to find what you can do about it.'* (S12). Some participants noted specifically how similar experiences elicited a particular kind of empathetic engagement: *'for me it was helpful because I started going*

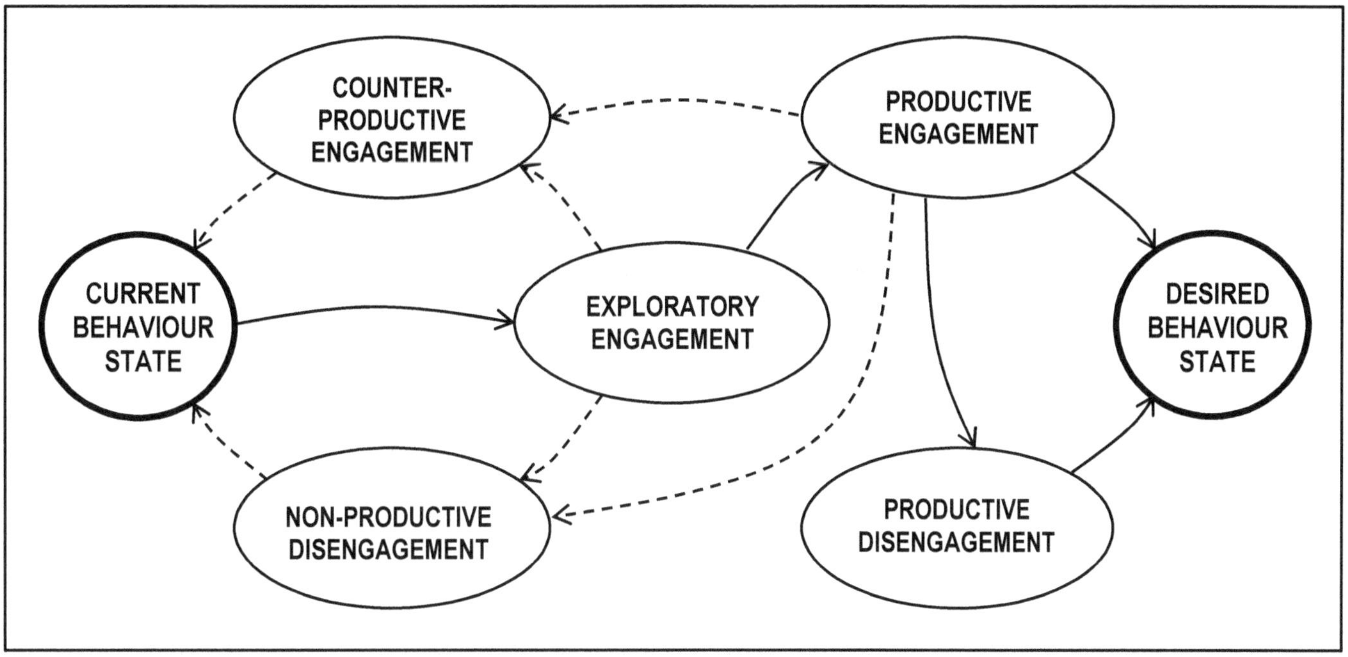

Figure 4. A conceptual model of alternative trajectories of digitally-mediated behaviour change. Solid arrows indicate progress towards the desired behaviour state (of being a non-smoker), while dotted arrows show regression back to the current behaviour state (of being a smoker)

through a lot of, like, the panic stuff and the anxiety stuff and all of that came up for me that's never been there. So it was good to read.' (S2).

Limits of productive engagement

Nearly all participants valued the fact that the online community of quitters presented by NewLeaf was separate from their everyday world of family, friends and colleagues. They valued their anonymity, with many commenting that they would not want to conduct this activity in Facebook. But although they felt secure in the anonymity of NewLeaf, there was extreme reluctance to post content, even among the Succeeding quitters who were productively engaged: *'I know its anonymous but I'm hiding from myself.'* (S3); *'I guess because there is always that chance that you might not succeed and you don't want to put it out there in the public domain.'* (S13L). Others posted with trepidation: *'At first I was like one of those shy people "Should I say something? Should I not say something? What are they going to think of what I've said?" ... and so I ummed and ahhed for a while before I hit the button'* (S9). One clear exception to this was the intensely productive engager S2 who did post and interact successfully: *'... it was quite good and it was when I started ... and it was really rough and they kept checking in, "How are you doing now?"'* (S2).

Non-productive disengagement and counterproductive engagement

As captured in our model in Figure 4, however, not all participants achieved anything resembling productive engagement. For some, lack of interest in the stories, tips and distractions meant that the app simply failed to provide any support for a quit attempt, a state we describe as *non-productive disengagement*. For example, the Not-Succeeding N2 reported how initial exploratory engagement led to non-productive disengagement: *'it really was really informative and it reminds you of how difficult it is, at the end of the day, to quit ... I'm not the sort of person who engages that much with initiatives like that'* (N2)

More interestingly, we also observed *counterproductive engagement* with NewLeaf which involved more sustained use of its quit resources, but with the opposite of the intended effect. This was often expressed as antipathy towards success stories posted by ex-smokers, that grew into a stance against the spirit of NewLeaf and against quitting generally. N6, for example, was a relatively frequent user of the app and a keen reader of stories. But while liking some stories, she experienced ex-smoker stories negatively: *'they're doing it to help and give you encouragement, but I didn't see it that way. I saw it as "I can't believe you have time that you can be bothered doing this" and it didn't make me feel "oh, one day I'll feel like that"'.* (N6) Unusually, N6 went from smoking 6 cigarettes per day to 20 by the second interview, reporting this as being related to other circumstances; again confirming the importance of external factors in participant outcomes.

Also illustrating counterproductive engagement, the light smoker N4L was a relatively steady engager with stories. But for him the experience was overall very negative: *'reading some of the guys' successful experience is... you know, it's like torture to me, because I'm a failure, I didn't make it happen'* (N4L). Further, N4L was adamantly opposed to the potential for social interaction through NewLeaf: *'... I really don't want you guys to make this ...*

like a social app, like Facebook or Twitter ... I don't want two-way. Yeah, one-way is enough...' (N4L). Such negative experiences were high among the Not-Succeeding participants. N1 found it too difficult to engage with any story: *'I just couldn't really relate to myself ... It's like I don't know, ... I don't even know who they are'*. And the idea of posting was repugnant: *'I don't want to expose myself in that sense to others, or strangers, and saying like oh I can't do this or whatever'* (N1). For N5, who had successfully quit in previous years but since relapsed, this sentiment was even stronger: *'... to read people's stories who'd been really successful and gotten a year of not smoking and had really progressed ... I remember what that was like but it was a little bittersweet to read them because I don't know that I had a great deal of faith in myself to be able to get to that point again.'* (N5). N5 did post a story, but the limited response led to more discouragement: *'The responses I got from the big long post were fine but it was all kind of short'* (N5).

Productive disengagement

We now come to the identification of a fourth significant state in the trajectories of some participants, that of *productive disengagement*. This describes situations where participants, who were productively engaging with the app and embarked on a succeeding quit attempt, then actively decided to disengage with the app because it was reminding them of smoking. This was the most striking and surprising observation of our study in which reduced engagement with NewLeaf was associated with a strong quit attempt. Productive disengagement is related to phenomena like the gateway effect [29] in which a tool outlives its usefulness or where people progress from one behaviour change resource to another. But it significantly different. Productive disengagement was not simply NewLeaf reaching the end of its relevance, but involved the active decision to suppress all reminders of the behaviour state of smoking, including quit resources.

Productive disengagement was evidenced primarily in interview reports, but it is also supported by the usage logs, particularly for heavier smokers (Figure 2). It can be seen that while S2 and S12 maintained productive engagement across the 3 weeks of the trial, the other 7 Succeeding quitters stopped almost abruptly during the first week. As one put it: *'I think an app like this has to be something you can use and stop using .. there are some people who clearly come back to this forum years after they've quit but I think most people would rather get that over with'* (S9). The problem of giving up smoking was transferred to, or at least combined with the problem of giving up the app. For some, productive disengagement was not just with the app, S1 reported the same for nicotine chewing gum: *'I just didn't want to have to be to a schedule like smoking cos I'd just be thinking about smoking every time I was doing something.'* (S1).

The state of productive disengagement was noted as being different from the earlier attraction to the app during productive engagement when the aim was *'just keeping the idea of quitting alive in your brain ... like it'd just keep reminding you'* (S10). For participant S9, the realisation that she would need to productively disengage with NewLeaf appeared to occur relatively early on at the outset of the quit attempt. It co-existed with the initial desire to productively engage, and this set up a conflicting initial experience: *'... it was just conscious sitting on my mind that I want a cigarette but I should use the app. Then using the app is actually reminding me of a cigarette'* (S9). This conflict underlay caution about posting her own stories, because it could seem to lock in a form of engagement: *'I have to remember to go back and read what I wrote and did I have replies and that's more of "You're thinking of cigarettes" sort of a thing.'* (S9). Many participants spoke of a desire to go back to the app in the distant but not immediate future: *'you don't want to be reminded. However, I would still... like to check stories of people who have quit for as long as I have or even longer, so I can ... I can look beyond, you know, and aim for like a bigger goal.'* (S5)

The active maintenance of productive engagement and productive disengagement

What characterized the Succeeding quitters in our study from those Not-Succeeding was the way they were able to actively follow a trajectory of productive engagement, often followed closely by productive disengagement. They appeared to use adaptive strategies to stick to this trajectory and to avoid counterproductive engagement or non-productive disengagement. This was despite the Succeeding quitters suffering many of the same negative reactions to stories in NewLeaf as the Not-Succeeding participants.

For example, even among the Succeeding quitters, there was discomfort with the perceived triumphalism of ex-smokers, particularly if they did not express the struggle to reach success: *the stories ... helps you in understanding or helping you through your quit process ... well yeah everything except the ones that say "a hundred days" (S12).* The health tips in NewLeaf could also provoke negative reactions: *'We all know how lung cancer looks like ... It's not like we're back in the 40s and the doctor would open the consulting room with a cigarette in his mouth and tell you smoking is good for you. We know that it's not good for you.'* (S5)

But Succeeding quitters typically avoided moving into a sustained form of counterproductive engagement, by selecting stories that fitted their stage of quitting and which they could relate to and use productively: *'... there's a lot that "I've had a cigarette and I've relapsed" I don't read those ... I do not need verification that you could go backwards.'* (S2); *'So on the first days I would click on stories going my first week as non-smoker, and these days I would go more for like one month'* (S5). Only two of the Succeeding quitters (S3, S10) broke with this pattern and were keen on reading the fully variety of stories: *'it's human and it's good to see the fails as well as the successes because the fails reminds you that even though a person can fail they know what they want to do, they know what's right'* (S3).

It was through the Succeeding quitters' disposition to engage productively with NewLeaf that some experienced through the app a world of people who did not smoke: *'And you see that there are certain people that are very, very prominent already that people mention and go back to and they comment on nearly everything, they're quite active. So it's nice to know that they're there, I guess.'* (S2). This sense of another world appeared to grow from the engaging characteristics of stories, especially their authenticity and currency. Succeeding quitters spoke of this world as one they might soon join. S9 put it: *'Not a quitting club but part of a nice, big group'*. As these quitters productively disengaged with the app, there were signs that they were not rejecting that online world, but rather attempting to transplant it on to their real lives. S5 spoke of going to music festivals, a major trigger for smoking, and how she would in future, as a non-smoker, have an altered engagement with people, and how the stories on the app helped her to see that more positively: *'So when you feel like you're going to lose that, so it's good to feel that you're gaining, you're part of another community that you just didn't know about it or you didn't think about it basically.'* (S5) Conversely, for the Not-Succeeding quitters, who did not enjoy the story forum, it was a counterproductive rejection of any future scenario of being a non-smoker that often underlay their reaction. Participant N5, who made a serious attempt to engage and quit before relapsing, reported: *'maybe it felt a little bit too distant for me like... I don't think I was willing to engage in some sort of solidarity with other people in it.'* (N5).

DISCUSSION

From our study of 23 people's real-life attempts to quit smoking, we have presented a picture of the rich variety of their responses to using an app for behaviour change. The model in Figure 4 offers a way to interpret this variety by conceptualizing alternative trajectories that people might take, passing through different states of engagement and disengagement with the digital aid. The trajectories shown in Figure 4 depict the key paths observed in our study.

Importantly, our model expresses a dissociation between the intensity of using a digital tool and progress towards a desired behaviour state. Four states of the model express this dissociation. Productive engagement entails positive progress in behaviour change coupled with high app use, while non-productive disengagement entails negative progress with low use. Together these are the expected outcomes under the engagement-efficacy perspective that we argued is implicit in much design and research. However, two other states captured in our model are inconsistent with it. Counterproductive engagement entails negative progress in behaviour change coupled with high app use, and productive disengagement entails positive progress with low use.

Our account is supported by the lack of a qualitative association between the intensity of people's interactions with the NewLeaf app and the reported success of their ongoing quit attempts during the first 3 weeks. For the heavier smokers (Figure 2), 2 of the Succeeding participants (S2 and S12) used the app intensively for the whole trial and continued for several days after. But the other 7 Succeeding participants used the app intensively only on the first few days of the trial but then used it very little if at all. Our interpretation, as expressed in the model of Figure 4, is that while S2 and S12 engaged productively with NewLeaf throughout the trial, many of the other Succeeding quitters moved along a trajectory from exploratory to productive engagement, then after a few days on to productive disengagement.

Among the Not-Succeeding participants there was also great variation in the intensity of interaction with the app, but more intermittent use of it across the trial. Some of the Not-Succeeding participants exhibited quite high levels of use but this was often in a state of counterproductive engagement, particularly N5, N6 and N4L. These participants were consumed by an antagonistic reception of other peoples' quitting stories, especially, but not only, those of triumphant ex-smokers. This was distinct from the other Not-Succeeding participants who were not antagonistic but merely failed to engage, a reaction which we describe as non-productive disengagement in Figure 4.

Productive disengagement is a surprising and striking observation of our study. It is related to, but nevertheless distinct from, other reported forms of reduced engagement during behaviour change, such as the 'gateway effect' [29] and 'happy abandonment' [7]. These effects imply situations where people have succeeded with their change, or switch to upgraded or different technologies. Productive disengagement as observed here, in contrast, involved the active attempt to banish thoughts about smoking, and this required not thinking about quitting too. The timing of transitions from productive engagement to disengagement were variable but could happen after as little as one or two days; time for a quitter to gain enough motivation, through the app or elsewhere, and then proceed to a state of not thinking about smoking or quitting.

This interpretation, of a form of active and productive disengagement, as opposed to losing interest, is confirmed by the fact that 8 of the 9 Succeeding quitters in the heavier smoking group (Figure 2) were very positive about the value of stories. They valued them as authentic and current, and preferred them as a source of advice over the expert health tips. Conversely, 4 out of 5 Not-Succeeding heavier smokers had a negative reaction to stories which led some on a trajectory from exploratory to counterproductive engagement, and others from exploration to simply disengaging non-productively as they gave up the tool and their quit attempt. All returned to the current state of being a smoker and not attempting to change, at least for now. While we do not claim any causal connection between the use of stories and quitting, interview testaments, at least for the heavier smokers, were consistent with the idea that engaging productively with stories in NewLeaf was a likely characteristic of people embarked on a Succeeding quit attempt, and not engaging productively with stories more often characterized those who were Not-Succeeding.

These finding can be considered in terms of the trans-theoretical or stages model of quitting. Consistent with He et al's [14] argument that behaviour change apps should tailor their content to people's stage of change, most participants in our study preferred to engage with stories from people in a similar situation to themselves. Moreover, their preferences changed as they moved from being 'just quit' to maintaining an ongoing quit attempt. It was also evident that the Succeeding quitters were able to adaptively select stories to match their situation, suggesting that a story forum can provide 'one size to fit all' in some circumstances. To do this, it must support ready identification of the poster's stage of quitting. It was notable that may Not-Succeeding participants were not able to find suitable stories, and many were fixated on stories that they found off-putting.

Implications of the trajectories model

As noted earlier, Klasnja et al [17] argue that HCI researchers working on health technologies cannot easily measure their success by final health outcomes, so instead they should use intermediate indicators, such as the uptake of behaviours believed to have a positive influence. Engagement with the technology may appear at first to be one such intermediate indicator, in terms of the strength of affective response or in terms of intensity of use. While engagement is of course important, our study points to the dangers of relying on strong user engagement with a behaviour change app as an indicator of success.

The model of alternative trajectories, developed here (Figure 4), offers a set of potentially valuable sensitizing concepts for designers of behaviour change technologies, especially for addiction support. The notion of productive disengagement, in particular, suggests that users need the utmost control over when and how they use these devices, and points to the dangers of conventional prompts like notifications that seek to remind or otherwise draw users back into direct engagement. Rather, the user should be free to disengage and stay disengaged and this should not be treated as a failure of either user or technology. Equally, users should be free to lurk and observe without even gentle coercion to post content or comments. Again such interactions can be perceived as locking in a form of engagement that was not attractive to participants in our study, including those who were Succeeding so far in their quit attempts.

These implications of productive disengagement are mostly applicable to technologies that help people combat addictions like smoking, gambling, alcohol and drug use. In these situations, it is desirable to reach a state of not thinking about the objects of addiction. Other kinds of behaviour change, such as energy conservation, are less relevant perhaps and involve valid goals to make the need for change an ongoing awareness. Yet even in these situations, the notion of productive disengagement has relevance, in that users should preferably internalize new ways of thinking and new habits, so that they become independent of tools. Recent research supports this approach for assistive technology; for example, Stawarz et al [31], working on medication reminder tools, argue for designs that achieve technology-independent habit formation as opposed to ongoing technology-dependence.

CONCLUSION

Our study offers new evidence about the variety of forms of engagement and disengagement with digital tools for behaviour change. It reveals how strong user engagement can sometimes be a positive sign, but only if the user is productively engaged with the tool. However, engagement may be counterproductive, as with antagonistic reactions to content that push users away from their original goal. Equally, users may undertake a counter-intuitive form of productive disengagement in which they actively decide to discontinue using a digital tool. This is not a rejection of the value of the tool, but rather a strategy to banish thinking about adverse behaviours in a positive continuation of the attempt to change.

Our resulting model of alternative trajectories of engagement and disengagement (Figure 4) therefore suggests caution against any simplistic interpretation of usage tracking data as an indicator of success for HCI design of tools for behaviour change. People's trajectories in this domain are typically too complex and subtle to be captured in a numerical log of usage frequency or intensity. At least in the context of addiction support, our model suggests that behaviour change apps should be designed to give users maximum control over their level of engagement and disengagement and avoid features such as notifications that seek to trigger or even lock in particular patterns of use.

Finally, our study illustrates a different perspective to that of persuasive technology. Whether people embark on behaviour change is a result of many external factors, of personal motivation and circumstances. Rather than our NewLeaf tool being seen to persuade people, it is better understood as a resource that allowed Succeeding quitters to channel their various sources of motivation to embark on an attempted behaviour change.

ACKNOWLEDGEMENTS

This research was funded by Cancer Council Victoria and the Australian Research Council (ARC) grant LP110100046. We are also grateful for input from smoking cessation counsellors from Quit Victoria.

REFERENCES

1. Elena Agapie, Lucas Colusso, Sean A. Munson, and Gary Hsieh. 2016. PlanSourcing: Generating Behavior Change Plans with Friends and Crowds. In *Proceedings of the 19th ACM Conference on Computer-Supported Cooperative Work & Social Computing (CSCW '16).* ACM, New York, NY, USA, 119-133. DOI: http://dx.doi.org.ezp.lib.unimelb.edu.au/10.1145/2818048.2819943
2. Eric P.S. Baumer, Sherri Jean Katz, Jill E. Freeman, et al. 2012. Prescriptive Persuasion and Open-ended Social Awareness: Expanding the Design Space of Mobile Health. In *Proceedings of the ACM 2012 Conference on Computer Supported Cooperative Work*, ACM, 475–484. http://doi.org/10.1145/2145204.2145279
3. Ron Borland. 2013. *Understanding Hard to Maintain Behaviour Change: A Dual Process Approach.* John Wiley & Sons, Somerset, UK.
4. Braun, V. and Clarke, V. 2006. Using thematic analysis in psychology. *Qualitative Research in Psychology* 3, 2, 77-101.
5. Hronn Brynjarsdottir, Maria Håkansson, James Pierce, Eric Baumer, Carl DiSalvo, and Phoebe Sengers. 2012. Sustainably Unpersuaded: How Persuasion Narrows Our Vision of Sustainability. In *Proceedings of the SIGCHI Conference on Human Factors in Computing Systems,* ACM, 947–956. http://doi.org/10.1145/2207676.2208539
6. Munmun De Choudhury and Sushovan De. 2014. Mental Health Discourse on reddit: Self-Disclosure, Social Support, and Anonymity.In *Proceedings of 8th International AAAI Conference on Weblogs and Social Media.* Retrieved September 22, 2015 from http://www.aaai.org/ocs/index.php/ICWSM/ICWSM14/paper/view/8075
7. James Clawson, Jessica A. Pater, Andrew D. Miller, Elizabeth D. Mynatt, and Lena Mamykina. 2015. No Longer Wearing: Investigating the Abandonment of Personal Health-tracking Technologies on Craigslist. In *Proceedings of the 2015 ACM International Joint Conference on Pervasive and Ubiquitous Computing*, ACM, 647–658. http://doi.org/10.1145/2750858.2807554
8. Alan D. DeSantis. 2002. Smoke screen: an ethnographic study of a cigar shop's collective rationalization. *Health Communication* 14, 2: 167–198. http://doi.org/10.1207/S15327027HC1402_2
9. Paul Dourish. 2010. HCI and Environmental Sustainability: The Politics of Design and the Design of Politics. In *Proceedings of the 8th ACM Conference on Designing Interactive Systems*, ACM, 1–10. http://doi.org/10.1145/1858171.1858173
10. Epstein, D. A., Caraway, M., Johnston, C., Ping, A., Fogarty, J., and Munson, S. A. 2016. Beyond Abandonment to Next Steps: Understanding and Designing for Life after Personal Informatics Tool Use. In *Proceedings of the 2016 CHI Conference on Human Factors in Computing Systems* (pp. 1109-1113). ACM.
11. B. J. Fogg. 2003. *Persuasive Technology: Using Computers to Change What We Think and Do.* Morgan Kaufmann, Boston.
12. Thomas Fritz, Elaine M. Huang, Gail C. Murphy, and Thomas Zimmermann. 2014. Persuasive Technology in the Real World: A Study of Long-term Use of Activity Sensing Devices for Fitness. In *Proceedings of SIGCHI Conference on Human Factors in Computing Systems, ACM*, 487–496. http://doi.org/10.1145/2556288.2557383
13. Melanie C. Green. 2008. Research challenges in narrative persuasion. *Information Design Journal* 16, 1: 47–52. http://doi.org/10.1075/idj.16.1.07gre
14. Helen Ai He, Saul Greenberg, and Elaine M. Huang. 2010. One Size Does Not Fit All: Applying the Transtheoretical Model to Energy Feedback Technology Design. In *Proceedings of the SIGCHI Conference on Human Factors in Computing Systems*, ACM, 927–936. http://doi.org/10.1145/1753326.1753464
15. Eric B. Hekler, Predrag Klasnja, Jon E. Froehlich, and Matthew P. Buman. 2013. Mind the Theoretical Gap: Interpreting, Using, and Developing Behavioral Theory in HCI Research. In *Proceedings of the SIGCHI Conference on Human Factors in Computing Systems*, ACM, 3307–3316. http://doi.org/10.1145/2470654.2466452
16. Leslie J. Hinyard and Matthew W. Kreuter. 2007. Using Narrative Communication as a Tool for Health Behavior Change: A Conceptual, Theoretical, and Empirical Overview. *Health Education & Behavior* 34, 5: 777–792. http://doi.org/10.1177/1090198106291963
17. Predrag Klasnja, Sunny Consolvo, and Wanda Pratt. 2011. How to evaluate technologies for health behavior change in HCI research. In *Proceedings of the SIGCHI Conference on Human Factors in Computing Systems*, ACM, 3063–3072. http://doi.org/10.1145/1978942.1979396
18. Lena Mamykina, Andrew D. Miller, Elizabeth D. Mynatt, and Daniel Greenblatt. 2010. Constructing identities through storytelling in diabetes management. In *Proceedings of the SIGCHI Conference on Human Factors in Computing Systems*, ACM, 1203–1212. Retrieved September 22, 2015 from http://dl.acm.org/citation.cfm?id=1753507
19. Mark W. Newman, Debra Lauterbach, Sean A. Munson, Paul Resnick, and Margaret E. Morris. 2011. It's not that I don't have problems, I'm just not putting

them on Facebook: challenges and opportunities in using online social networks for health. In *Proceedings of the ACM 2011 conference on Computer supported cooperative work*, ACM, 341–350. http://doi.org/10.1145/1958824.1958876

20. O'Brien HL, Toms EG. 2008. What is user engagement? A conceptual framework for defining user engagement with technology. *Journal of the American Society for Information Science and Technology*, 59(6), 938-55.
21. Jeni Paay, Jesper Kjeldskov, Mikael B. Skov, Lars Lichon, and Stephan Rasmussen. 2015. Understanding Individual Differences for Tailored Smoking Cessation Apps. In *Proceedings of the 33rd Annual ACM Conference on Human Factors in Computing Systems*, ACM, 1699–1708. http://doi.org/10.1145/2702123.2702321
22. James W. Pennebaker and Janel D. Seagal. 1999. Forming a story: The health benefits of narrative. *Journal of clinical psychology* 55, 10, 1243–1254.
23. Bernd Ploderer, Wally Smith, Jon Pearce, and Ron Borland. 2014. A mobile app offering distractions and tips to cope with cigarette craving: A qualitative study. *JMIR mHealth and uHealth* 2, 2, 1-23. http://doi.org/10.2196/mhealth.3209
24. Bernd Ploderer, Wally Smith, Jon Pearce, and Ron Borland. 2015. An Object-Centred Approach to Encourage Online Participation in the Context of Behaviour Change. *Computer Supported Cooperative Work (CSCW)* 24, 1, 39-6433.
25. J. O. Prochaska and W. F. Velicer. 1997. The transtheoretical model of health behavior change. *American journal of health promotion*: AJHP 12, 1: 38–48.
26. Corbin Reno and Erika S. Poole. 2016. It Matters If My Friends Stop Smoking: Social Support for Behavior Change in Social Media. In *Proceedings of the 2016 CHI Conference on Human Factors in Computing Systems*, ACM, New York, NY, USA, 5548-5552. http://dx.doi.org.ezp.lib.unimelb.edu.au/10.1145/2858036.2858203
27. John Rooksby, Mattias Rost, Alistair Morrison, and Matthew Chalmers. 2014. Personal Tracking As Lived Informatics. In *Proceedings of the 32nd Annual ACM Conference on Human Factors in Computing Systems*, ACM, 1163–1172. http://doi.org/10.1145/2556288.2557039
28. Schane, R. E., Ling, P. M. and Glantz, S. A. Health. 2010. Effects of Light and Intermittent Smoking: A Review. *Circulation*, 121, 13, 1518-1522.
29. Victoria Schwanda, Steven Ibara, Lindsay Reynolds, and Dan Cosley. 2011. Side Effects and "Gateway" Tools: Advocating a Broader Look at Evaluating Persuasive Systems. In *Proceedings of the SIGCHI Conference on Human Factors in Computing Systems*, ACM, 345–348. http://doi.org/10.1145/1978942.1978991
30. Katie A. Siek, Gillian R. Hayes, Mark W. Newman, and John C. Tang. 2014. Field Deployments: Knowing from Using in Context. In *Ways of Knowing in HCI*. Springer, New York, 119–142.
31. Katarzyna Stawarz, Anna L. Cox, and Ann Blandford. 2015. Beyond Self-Tracking and Reminders: Designing Smartphone Apps That Support Habit Formation. In *Proceedings of the 33rd Annual ACM Conference on Human Factors in Computing Systems*, ACM, 2653–2662. http://doi.org/10.1145/2702123.2702230
32. Sutcliffe, A. 2009. Designing for User Engagement: Aesthetic and Attractive User Interfaces. Synthesis *Lectures on Human-Centered Informatics*, 2, 1, 1-55.
33. Phil Turner. 2010. The anatomy of engagement. In *Proceedings of the 28th Annual European Conference on Cognitive Ergonomics (ECCE '10)*. ACM, New York, NY, USA, 59-66. DOI=http://dx.doi.org/10.1145/1962300.1962315
34. West, R., Hajek, P., Stead, L., and Stapleton, J. 2005. Outcome criteria in smoking cessation trials: proposal for a common standard. *Addiction* 100, 3, 299–303.
35. World Health Organisation. 2011. *WHO report on the global tobacco epidemic*. WHO. Retrieved September 24, 2015 from http://www.who.int/tobacco/global_report/2011/en/

Lessons from Practice: Designing Tools to Facilitate Individualized Support for Quitting Smoking

Arpita Bhattacharya[1], Roger Vilardaga[2], Julie A. Kientz[1], Sean A. Munson[1]
[1]Human Centered Design and Engineering, DUB Group, University of Washington, Seattle, USA
[2]Psychiatry and Behavioral Sciences, Duke University, Durham, USA
{arpitab; jkientz; smunson}@uw.edu, roger.vilardaga@duke.edu

ABSTRACT
Many health care providers, with a variety of trainings, counsel clients on quitting smoking on a day-to-day basis. In their clinical practice, they draw from and adapt guidelines and research-based strategies to fit individual client situations and challenges. Designers of technologies to support quitting smoking can learn from these real world practices to create tools that better adapt to individual differences. We present findings from interviews with 28 providers with diverse experiences in smoking cessation counselling. Through analysis of their individualization strategies, challenges, and perceptions of technology, we find that providers: (1) individualize context appropriate coping strategies by involving clients in brainstorming, (2) emphasize the need to support nicotine withdrawal in clients, (3) mitigate social triggers and mediate social support for clients, and (4) need to navigate dependencies with other providers for managing medications and comorbid health conditions of clients. With this empirical understanding, we extend the discussion on the design of technology to support quitting smoking, highlight current barriers to individualization, and suggest future opportunities to address these barriers.

Author keywords
Smoking; health; individualization; counseling practice; behavior change; smoking cessation; personalization

ACM Classification Keywords
H.5.m. Information interfaces and presentation (e.g., HCI): Miscellaneous

INTRODUCTION
Approximately 40 million people in the United States smoke cigarettes [32,59]. Smoking is both a behavioral challenge and requires medical support [59]. Needs and challenges of people who want to quit smoking vary at the individual level [42,49]. Although, some people succeed in quitting cold turkey or in a single attempt, most others relapse multiple times [10,11,59]. Individualized external support for treatment and guidance on self-management of smoking behavior from providers, peers, or technology can help individuals cope with challenges in quitting effectively.

Over 70% of people who smoke are in frequent contact with physicians, nurse practitioners, counselors, therapists, and other clinicians [59]. We henceforth use the term *providers* to refer to this collection of practitioners. Strategies have been recommended for in-person smoking cessation counseling to tailor to specific needs of individuals [43,59]. However, primary care physicians and residents are known to face common barriers such as lack of training, time, and resources to support smoking cessation and conflicts in priorities while managing other health conditions [15,39]. Physicians are thus recommended to redirect clients to dedicated tobacco cessation counsellors and/or telephone based quitline counselors for specialized counseling on quitting smoking [39].

Technology has also emerged as an effective medium for the delivery and tailoring of interventions to support quitting smoking, due to its low cost, increasing availability, and computing power, [2,29,58]. Recent research has involved people who have quit or want to quit smoking in design activities to better understand their individual needs [42,49]. Design recommendations from these studies primarily emphasize the need for further individualization based on age, willingness to quit, quitting stage, smoking frequency, and personal goals and preferences such as optional social features [29,42,49]. Most current apps do not address these tailoring needs [1,29].

While previous studies describe client preferences from technology, it is also important to incorporate provider perspectives in design of technology for treatment of nicotine addiction [27,42]. Providers have a wealth of experiential knowledge in how to individualize counseling for people working to quit smoking. Related work using close-ended surveys with providers convey their perception of the importance of various features in technology [42,67]. Less is known about open-ended perspectives of providers on technology, such as why they consider certain features important, needs not met by technology, and how to design for these needs. An empirical understanding of practices and perceptions of providers on technology can help further efforts to understand needs and challenges of individualizing support for smoking cessation in real world contexts.

Permission to make digital or hard copies of all or part of this work for personal or classroom use is granted without fee provided that copies are not made or distributed for profit or commercial advantage and that copies bear this notice and the full citation on the first page. Copyrights for components of this work owned by others than the author(s) must be honored. Abstracting with credit is permitted. To copy otherwise, or republish, to post on servers or to redistribute to lists, requires prior specific permission and/or a fee. Request permissions from Permissions@acm.org.
CHI 2017, May 06 - 11, 2017, Denver, CO, USA
Copyright is held by the owner/author(s). Publication rights licensed to ACM.
ACM 978-1-4503-4655-9/17/05…$15.00
DOI: http://dx.doi.org/10.1145/3025453.3025725

In this study, we took an empirical approach of interviewing 28 providers in the United States with diverse experiences in counseling clients to quit smoking: primary care physicians, mental health care providers, and dedicated tobacco cessation and addiction counselors. In the process of counselling for smoking cessation, providers individualize and adapt to behavioral, medication, and social needs that vary from client to client. In addition, providers face major challenges in managing clients' comorbid health concerns and conflicting priorities of other providers. Our primary contribution is the empirical understanding of provider strategies and perspectives on needs from client-facing technology for smoking cessation. In our discussion, we draw our findings and on prior work's description of client needs to suggest design opportunities and to draw the attention of the HCI community to underexplored challenges in quitting smoking that might be addressed by technology.

RELATED WORK

Tobacco smoking continues to be the leading cause of preventable diseases and death in the United States, and is attributed as cause of over 480,000 deaths a year [32]. In 2014, the annual cost of medical care and loss of productivity due to premature death attributed to smoking-related health consequences was between $289 billion and $333 billion [32]. While smoking is a public health challenge, quitting smoking can be an intensely personal struggle [49].

Individualized nature of quitting smoking

Individuals report different triggers for smoking and relapsing, experience different levels of difficulty with nicotine withdrawal, or may use smoking as a coping strategy for comorbid mental health conditions such as anxiety and depression [16,49]. Comorbid addiction to illicit drugs and alcohol also contribute to relapses or switching to smoking as a drug of choice [54]. Unemployment, homelessness, lack of insurance, and lack of access to healthcare are some socio-economic barriers individuals face in accessing resources to quit smoking [28]. In their quit attempts, some individuals seek expert or peer support, avoid triggering activities and locations, or engage in activities to distract from thoughts of smoking [52]. Interestingly, these activities might function as successful coping strategies for some but act as triggers for others, which reinforces the need for individualized support for behavioral and medical interventions. We discuss "individualized" support or intervention consistent with Lauver et al.'s definition for patient-centered interventions: *"an intervention that is highly customized to a particular individual and that person's situation"* [37].

Evidence-based interventions for quitting smoking

Quitting cold-turkey is occasionally successful, but not medically advisable. The US Clinical guidelines recommends both behavioral (5As: Ask, Advise, Assess, Assist, Arrange) and pharmacotherapy (7 FDA approved medications) [59] as the best practice for smoking cessation counseling. Theory-driven behavioral interventions for smoking cessation [41] include Cognitive Behavioral Therapy (CBT) [14], Acceptance and Commitment Therapy (ACT) [13,24], Contingency Management (CM) [17], and Motivational Interviewing (MI) [66]. The Behavior Change Taxonomy provides a summary of behavior change techniques (BCTs) [44]. The Behavior Change Wheel [45], which is also validated against the English Tobacco cessation guidelines, defines nine categories of interventions—modelling, environmental restructuring, education, persuasion, incentivization, coercion, training, restricting, and enablement. Clinical guidelines for smoking cessation counselling also recommend addressing social triggers, facilitating development of social support, and directing clients to quitline and local support networks [43].

When preparing a quit plan, US clinical guidelines [59] recommend that providers tailor behavioral strategies and medications based on the client's demographics, tobacco use, socio-economic costs of smoking, impact of smoking on others, motivation level, reasons clients want to quit, impact on comorbid health symptoms, concerns about quitting, withdrawal symptoms, and success and difficulties in past attempts at quitting. Interventions may be also tailored based on the individual's willingness to change (MI), Experiential Avoidance (ACT), or stages of change in Transtheoretical model [53]. Tailored interventions are proven to be more effective to support quitting than non-tailored interventions, and technology offers many accessible platforms for tailoring intervention delivery and feedback [58].

Designing individualized technology to quit smoking

Means of delivering technology-based interventions for smoking cessation include telephone conversations, text messaging, web-based applications (such as websites, online communities, social media), and smartphone applications [2,29]. Types of interventions include educational or motivational messages, communicating with counselors and peers [50,52], networking with social media [31,65], automated interventions, self-tracking, and game-based or gamified interventions. Over the years, the number of smoking cessation smartphone applications available for free or low cost has increased to 546 [1,12,29]. Some technology-based applications facilitate tracking cigarettes, monetary, and health benefits, motivational messages, provide a suite of interventions for individuals to choose from, others tailor based on questionnaires on stages of quitting, before assigning interventions [41,58]. However, from a recent content analysis, smartphone applications do not tailor interventions beyond providing trackers, calendars and calculators and rarely follow recommended tailoring guidelines of clinical practice [29].

Design studies recommend individualizing support through technology based on user's quitting stage, age, family situation, and socio-economic situations [49]. Individuals who want to quit also perceived benefits in self-tracking smoking behavior, novelty of information, immediate and meaningful rewards, and achievable coping tips. Clients also differ in preference for social support or consider quitting to be a solo struggle. Some clients also prefer being connected to smoking cessation experts. A study of the QuittyLink app [50,51] showed potential for higher user engagement and increased motivation to quit when intervention messages were personalized by a quit-smoking helpline counselor who remotely reviewed the data users tracked data their mobile device and provided weekly messages.

Needs and perspectives of providers, who are also important stakeholders in the treatment of nicotine addiction, are relatively less studied to inform design of technology. Recent independent survey studies in the US [42] and Australia [67] showed providers have primarily positive attitudes towards potential use of technology for smoking cessation support. Both providers and clients preferred features in applications that allow users to track their progress, personalize, match, and adapt to changing interests and needs of clients, and help manage withdrawal symptoms and medication needs for nicotine addiction [27,42]. However, majority of providers did not consider current apps to be effective for smoking cessation [42]. Research is needed to further incorporate perspectives and expertise of providers on how these needs can be addressed through designing technology for individualized support. Understanding strategies and barriers to in-person counseling can provide insights into opportunities for technology to build upon these strategies and address challenges in practice. To develop an in-depth empirical understanding of provider practices and inform design for individualized needs, we investigated the following research questions:

1. *What are current individualization strategies and tools used by providers in smoking cessation counseling practice?*
2. *What are the challenges perceived by providers in individualizing smoking cessation counseling practice?*
3. *What are the opportunities for technology to facilitate individualized support for quitting smoking?*

METHODS

To answer these research questions, we interviewed 28 health care providers and smoking cessation counselors with diverse experiences across 12 states in the US. Our recruitment email stated that we aimed to interview "health-care providers and counselors assisting clients who want to quit smoking." We stated the purpose of our study to "understand providers' strategies and challenges to inform the design of mobile phone applications for quitting smoking." This may have biased our sample population toward providers who were already using technology or are willing to incorporate technology into their practice. However, we also received responses and interviewed providers who did not have any experience with client-facing technology. We sent our recruitment email to public contacts on websites of state-based helplines for quitting smoking in the US, country-wide mailing lists of tobacco cessation counselors and behavioral health counselors, and snowball sampling of researchers' contacts among health care providers and counselors affiliated with a large university health system. Interviews were conducted from November 2015 to January 2016. Our project was approved by the University's Institutional Review Board. Each participant was compensated $30 in appreciation of their time.

Participants

We interviewed 28 providers who reached out to us from twelve states in the US [WA (11), CO (4), NY (3), CA (2), ID (1), IL (1), KS (1), MA (1), NC (1), NH (1), OK (1), and TX (1)]. The professional background of our participants broadly fell into categories of dedicated counselors and nurses with tobacco cessation and/or addiction counselling training (C#, N=19), mental health care providers (M#, N=5), and primary health care physicians (P#, N=4). Table 1 provides a summary of professional experiences of our participants (detailed participant table in auxiliary materials, Appendix A). Participants reported having between 1 and 30 years of experience in counseling individuals (henceforth referred to as clients). Nine participants self-reported being ex-smokers and had quit smoking between 4-15 years before the interview. All 28 participants reported counseling clients with one or more mental health conditions (e.g., depression, anxiety), physical health conditions (e.g., respiratory and heart diseases), substance abuse (e.g., alcohol, illicit drugs), and also from vulnerable population groups among whom the smoking rates are high [32,59]. Eleven participants had counseled inpatients on quitting smoking in general wards, Intensive Care Units (ICUs), psychiatry (M5, M9), cancer (C26), and thoracic surgery (C14). This diverse range of counselling experiences in participants ensures triangulation of perspectives from multiple stakeholders in our data.

Gender	Female (N=18), Male (N=10)
Example Professional titles	Nurse practitioners, primary care physician, tobacco cessation counselor, addiction counselor, mental health practioner
Type of sessions	Group (N=1, C02), one on one (N=27), both group and one on one (N=6) Face to face (N=26), state based quitline via telephone (N=2, C17, C28), face to face and telephone counseling (N=5)

Table 1: Summary of professional experiences of participants

Study procedures

We conducted one-on-one semi-structured interviews with each participant to understand current individualization strategies and challenges in smoking cessation counseling. The average length of our interviews was 52 minutes (range: 30-84 min). Topics included (1) how participants began the process of counseling someone who wants to quit smoking, (2) modifications they make in their counseling strategies from one client to another, (3) relapse handling, (4) follow up strategies, (5) incorporating informal social support into counseling (friends, family, peers), (6) challenges they face in counseling, (7) current use of tools and technology to assist in counseling, and (8) perceptions of client use of tools and technology for smoking cessation.

We showed participants low-fidelity design sketches (storyboards and wireframes) of a wizard based design of a self-management mobile app illustrating prompts to guide clients to individualize interventions based on their reason to quit, concerns with quitting, interests, example interventions (e.g., mindfulness, yoga), and ways to log and visualize behavior related to smoking (auxiliary materials, Appendix B). These sketches helped elicit responses from the providers on their perceived needs for clients and technology to support quitting smoking. Twenty seven interviews were conducted over phone and one interview was conducted in-person. For phone interviews, we emailed a PDF of our design sketches to each participant. All interviews were audio-recorded with consent and transcribed.

Analysis

First, the first author (AB) randomly selected five interview transcripts and coded them inductively [56]. Next, she conducted affinity diagramming to develop higher level clusters and categories of the codes using both inductive and deductive approach informed by our research questions [30]. AB, the second author (RV) (who read 4 transcripts), and an independent researcher not familiar with the data, were involved in discussions and refinement of affinity clusters. AB used this set of codes to analyze the remaining transcripts while constantly comparing among interviews to understand patterns of similarities and differences across participant perspectives. AB wrote memos on codes and data and shared them with all authors after completing analysis of all interviews. To ensure validity, discussions on findings were conducted with the research team at all stages. We describe our findings that contribute to an in-depth understanding of provider perspectives to inform design of applications for quitting smoking.

FINDINGS

All participants recognized the diverse needs of their clients while quitting smoking and emphasized providing unique and individualized support for each client. While a majority of the participants said they set quit dates with their clients, they added that only a few of their clients succeeded in quitting "cold turkey", i.e. attempting to quit all their cigarettes simultaneously on a set quit date. Majority of their clients required individualized support to reduce smoking over a longer term with multiple setbacks. P10 describes the variation as, *"This [counseling approach] is actually very individualized. Some people find it easier to cut down slowly, but other people feel like if they do that then they will never quit. I have a lot of patients—probably more patients, that cut down slowly than they do quit cold [turkey]."*

Four primary themes in which individualization is key emerged from our analysis: (1) providers brainstorm context appropriate behavioral strategies with clients, (2) providers emphasize support for nicotine withdrawal, (3) providers need to mediate social support for clients, and (4) providers need to navigate dependencies with other providers. Across each theme, we summarize tailoring strategies providers use that are consistent with literature and then expand on perceptions of providers on how they further individualize from what is recommended, barriers they face, tools they use, and their insights on our design prototypes. We then summarize the perceptions of providers and their use of technology based applications for quitting smoking and their perceived barriers to adoption of smartphone applications.

Providers involve clients in brainstorming context-appropriate strategies

For behavioral counseling, strategies mentioned by providers can be roughly summarized by the intervention categories defined by Michie et al. [45]. Providers mentioned using specific sets of strategies for behavioral support based on their expertise or training: CBT (5), MI (8), ACT (1), 5 Ds [5] – Delay, Distract yourself, Deep breathing, Drink water, Discuss your feelings – (4), and clinical guidelines (5As) [59]. Providers said they primarily take on the role of educators and facilitators, emphasize informing clients about options available for support, and support client autonomy. No participant reported using coercion or scare tactics if clients were not ready to quit.

In addition to asking clients initial assessment questions such as their smoking behavior and health condition [59], all providers emphasized assessing the context that each client associated with smoking before setting a quit plan and also after relapses. This assessment helped providers to recommend example strategies to break the association of specific contexts with client's smoking behavior, such as by restructuring the environment. Context was explained by providers as the time of the day, environmental cues, social factors, and the activity that a client engaged in before, during, and after smoking. Providers said they ask clients if they had already identified challenges or factors that triggered their craving in specific contexts, such as if their most difficult cigarette to quit is the morning cigarette or the one at work. C02 also explained context in terms of time of the year and events significant to the client: *"In my experience, people need that one year of birthdays, holidays, anniversaries, season changes et cetera, where they get support around staying tobacco free or nicotine free."*

Recommending intervention strategies after assessing context was a collaborative process between the client and the provider. Providers described this as a process of "*brainstorming.*" To facilitate brainstorming, providers suggested examples from evidence based practices or by modelling, and provided prompts for clients to think about strategies or to come up with their own ideas based on their interests, abilities, likes, and dislikes. As a result of this process, the strategies were highly individualized to fit into the context of the client's daily life and to give clients concrete and actionable strategies to work with. For example; C21 explained, *"Our strategy is to include the patient in brainstorming or developing coping skills to manage some of their biggest challenges, rather than giving them more of a cookie cutter or scripted strategy to help them to deal with their biggest challenges. That varies from individual to individual."*

As tools to assess client smoking behavior and context, most providers rely on verbal recall from clients, but some encourage clients to use paper-based tools between sessions to note these factors such as worksheets, journaling, or index cards with header cues (e.g., "*note your most difficult cigarette to quit*" (M01)). Few providers mentioned maintaining paper based records for themselves, which they referred to during follow-ups. Physicians (N=5) and quitline counselors (N=2) had access to their internal online system for note taking. Quitline counselors share a database linked to the unique id of the caller. However, for some providers, especially in inpatient units (N=11), follow up was not possible to iterate on or determine effectiveness of strategies.

In our design prototype, we anticipated that the user could follow a specific intervention each day (Appendix B, page 16 to 11). Providers however highlighted the need to design a tool that can help clients understand different contexts of smoking within the day and then list strategies for that context. For example, M01 conceptualized, *"[Prompt clients to] 'make a comprehensive list of all the different contexts and all the different situations you're smoking'. Example, in a car, after a meal—because certain coping mechanisms might be more useful in certain contexts than others. So, could be that in a car it's really easy to listen to very loud music but at work, going out on a break, that's really hard [...] You might also wanna have that when the app takes a log of the context that you're smoking—which means you might wanna tie the app notifications to the pertinent event."*

To facilitate brainstorming like process, providers envisioned an app that would prompt suggestions based on what was feasible and actionable for clients, and guided them through complex tasks such as yoga. For example, C11 suggested that the tool should prompt, "'*What can you do if you have an urge to smoke? —some people wanna call the crisis line, some people wanna call a friend, go outside, open a window, eat a vegetable, you know that kind of thing— chew on some gum.' Things that they do already, things they can afford, things they like to do."* Participants particularly liked intervention designs that let the clients create and save their own list of activities to do during quitting (Appendix B, page 23). They suggested it let them enter their own *"specific personal goals"* based on interests and benefits that clients perceived from quitting, such as quitting for a surgery or "*be a transplant candidate*" (C03).

Providers emphasize support for nicotine withdrawal

As per guidelines, medications need to be tailored based on the number of cigarettes, prior successful use of medication, tolerance or ease-of-use, out-of-pocket patient cost, likelihood of adherence, dentures (chewing gum), dermatitis (patch), and comorbid conditions like depression [59]. Twenty six participants reported they recommend the 7 FDA approved quit smoking medications to clients. A common concern expressed by providers was that some clients have misinformation and are fearful of medication side-effects leading to issues of non-adherence and inadequate dosage, which increased clients' struggles with withdrawal symptoms. To alleviate such fears and misconceptions, providers said they first need to educate clients about the physiological components of nicotine addiction and emphasize that addiction is not merely a behavioral or moral issue. Many providers shared paper based tools with clients, such as brochures, handouts, or booklets [3,46,47,61] containing information on addiction and medication. One provider (P08) who did not have brochures in her clinic, printed out information about side-effects of prescribed medication, *"If someone's thinking about starting a medication to quit smoking, I'll print off usually the patient information form of the side-effects and what to expect because I think patients are little bit less scared if they know what to expect out of a medication."*

Even after working with clients on side-effects, preference, and cost of medication, providers mentioned that adherence to right dosage for smoking cessation medications was a major challenge. Specifically, two providers (C02 and C20) said that they have had clients who were not able to taper off of nicotine replacement products as recommended and continued to stay addicted to nicotine in over the counter products for longer periods of time (over 5 years in case of C02's client). According to providers, medication usage required guidance for self-management on clients' side.

In our design prototypes, we did not provide any option to track medications. Some providers highlighted that technology should support the client in managing their medication. For example, C02 explained the need to incorporate support for information and self-management of medication dosage in our design prototype, *"I'd put something in there [design probe]...about exploring the idea of using medication—and they may or may not want to use products. But if they are using [nicotine replacement] products, that will need support and benefits for they will usually use them wrong. And [clinic_name] has studied this and they say that most people, when they are using an over the counter nicotine product, they under dose and they don't dose long enough."*

Some providers, especially those who had experience quitting smoking themselves (N=9), brought to our attention that outcomes for behavioral tracking features shown in our design sketches – such as mood, alertness, cravings, and appetite (Appendix B, page 19)– will vary dynamically due to variations in withdrawal from nicotine and how clients supplement it with pharmacotherapy. For example, C25 who quit smoking herself, explained, *"Depending on how they're quitting it, if they're not using any pharmacotherapy, they could have some of these things be really high and then work down to low. If they're using good pharmacotherapy, these may stay low, but that would also reinforce that, "Hey, the pharmacotherapy is working for me. I'm not having to deal with withdrawal symptoms!"* Providers emphasized the need for appropriate feedback, and guidance to clients to be self-aware, not feel discouraged, and understand trends in their outcomes, especially, in their initial days of quitting. They also suggested that type of behavioral intervention, timing and frequency of reminders and logging prompts be individualized to the dynamic needs of nicotine craving to not remind clients about smoking when they are not craving: depending on the number of cigarettes clients smoke and their medication intake.

Thus, providers emphasized that tools individualize educational interventions for different information needs of a client about medications, encourage adequate dosage, and enable dynamic tracking and feedback based on individual differences in clients' behavioral and physiological responses to withdrawal.

Providers mediate social support for clients

As all clients did not have similar social situations, providers needed to individualize treatment by mediating offline social factors for clients both in terms of negative social triggers and positive social support. Providers perceived that a key barrier to quitting for clients is having a family member or someone with whom they live who also smokes. According to providers, these people prompt clients to smoke and often also contribute to misinformation about smoking, which can make the clients less receptive to treatment and counseling. Some providers believe that even negative pressure from family members who did not smoke can make some clients resistant to counseling, such as nagging the client and/or inflicting emotions of hurt, anger, guilt, or blaming the client for exposure to passive smoking.

To manage social triggers, providers advise clients to not smoke with friends and family who smoke. However, they encourage clients to maintain relations with them outside of smoking activities, as providers also did not want the client to feel socially isolated. All providers emphasized the need and benefits of having social support for quitting smoking from family, friends, a buddy, and/or peers. Their strategies include educating the client and the family together, encourage friends and family members to quit together, and some even arrange for cost-free support for the client and the person who lives with them. C13 explained, *"In fact, our program that we offer for free—for our orientations, I told my boss, 'We need to offer that for anybody living in the household. I don't care if it's a roommate or if it's a family member. If they live with the patient, they can come for free to our program.'"*

For clients who do not have support from close social ties, providers help them identify people in their extended social circle could be their "buddy" – someone they could talk to or call when they have a craving, and can remind them to not smoke. Providers encourage clients to reach out to this person through different means, for example; someone at work, local recreational communities such as the YMCA, or local peer support groups. Interestingly, many providers explained that even people who smoke and do not want to quit with the client could be of support or be a buddy, provided they "promise" to not smoke in presence of the client and not cue the client to smoke.

Few providers said they hand paper-based resources to clients and their social circle on how to ask someone for support (e.g., worksheets, writing letters in workshop) or how to support someone on quitting smoking, respectively. Providers urged clients to call the quitline as a form of expert social support during cravings. For example, M05 explained, *"The reason that [quitline] is probably real good is because the impulse or the urge to use after quitting can last just a few minutes. And so a phone call could make the difference."* Participants perceived that calling, texting, or sharing and connecting with peers online for social support is an effective strategy to counter real time cravings. For example; C28 shared her client's narrative of getting instantaneous conversational support on an online post on their craving: *"One of my clients said to me, 'I had a craving, I went to the app and I put on the app...' I think it was some Facebook app. And he said, 'I am having a craving right now' and right away somebody answers the app and helped him ...you know, support system. 'Don't do it, why do you want to smoke right now?' and they went back and forth on a little chat and then that helped him not to have that one cigarette."* Providers also envisioned that technology could benefit clients by locating and connecting them with offline social support, such as local support groups, and by encouraging clients with appropriate prompts to proactively identify "buddies" in their social circle similar to their counselling process.

Providers need to navigate dependencies

Preferences for medication and struggles with comorbid health conditions vary from one client to another and these are major factors in individualizing smoking cessation counseling. However, a single provider is not equipped with resources to cater to all these needs. Therefore, providers have to individualize treatment for nicotine addiction not only based on client needs but also depending on their own care context, training, resources they have available, and client access to other providers. We found that providers need to redirect clients to other providers for three main activities: (1) specialized counseling and follow up for smoking cessation, (2) prescribing smoking cessation medications, and (3) adjusting treatment for smoking alongside comorbid health conditions. Unresolved conflicts surfaced in this redirection process.

Physicians (N=4) have the ability to prescribe medications, but consistent with prior work [15,39], they are constrained for time. Physicians direct clients to nurses or support staff with tobacco cessation training and/or quitline who are able to dedicate time and are skilled in counseling on quitting smoking. However, nurses and dedicated cessation counselors (N=19) explained that they cannot prescribe medications and need to redirect clients to consult a primary care physician if the client prefers prescription drugs, such as Chantix or Wellbutrin. It was a common perception among providers that each state's quitline gives out nicotine replacement products free of cost, and so they recommend clients call the quitline. Quitline counselors, however, reported that the availability of free nicotine replacement products is timely (e.g., once a year (C17)), depends on their funding program, and eligibility of the client depending on a medical assessment and insurance coverage. C28, a quitline counselor, summarized: *"Sometimes we have programs in which they [clients] could get free patches, but they will still have to go through protocol before they can get the patches...Some insurance would rather pay for the Chantix instead of the patches... We never really give Chantix because that has to be prescribed by their physician."* Thus, quitline counselors also need to relay the client back to their physician for prescribed medications.

While working with clients who have comorbid physical and/or mental illnesses, providers prioritized treatment for smoking differently. For physical illnesses (cancer, respiratory and heart diseases), providers said they prioritize and catalyze client motivation to first quit smoking by educating them on how their smoking habits can aggravate these symptoms. Even though, quitting smoking improves people's mental health, due to differences in receptiveness and abilities of clients with mental illness, 4 out of 5 mental health providers and all others perceived the need to stabilize clients' mental health symptoms before proceeding with counseling a client for smoking. They acknowledged that clients used smoking as a coping strategy for mental health symptoms and struggled to educate clients on misinformation of impact of smoking on mental health. P10, a primary care physician, explained, *"A lot of them are not really listening to you when you're talking to them about health consequences of smoking. So if you're trying to help them stop smoking— if they are very depressed— it's just not gonna work. So you really have to treat the depression before you can focus on the cigarettes."*

Counselors who do not have assessment tools for mental health, relevant background, or appointments with mental health facilities, relied on their subjective discernment of severity of mental health symptoms. These providers said they redirect clients to consult with their primary care physician or mental health care physician to get a diagnosis and readjust treatment. For clients with unstable symptoms, providers emphasized the need to be careful with possible side-effects of medication supplements for nicotine withdrawal (such as irritability, insomnia, and even possible concerns of suicidal and homicidal ideations for drugs such as Chantix [62,63]), and monitor clients closely. C14 explained her concerns in recommending Chantix to her clients with depression due to perceived concerns of inducing suicidal and/or homicidal ideations.

Perceived priorities differed in treating clients with comorbid addiction in two ways: (1) treating clients for quitting smoking together with other drugs and alcohol and (2) treating clients for quitting other drugs first, and then treat them for quitting smoking. Providers who assigned equal priority to quitting smoking perceived alcohol as a common trigger and said that clients also need support to quit alcohol and drugs that impair senses and self-control, at the same time as quitting smoking. C14 explained, "*What's going to happen is you will have quit, maybe it's for a few days, a few weeks, a few months, and you go out drinking, and you look down, the next thing you know, you've got a half a pack of cigarettes and you smoked half a pack... you've clouded your ability to make that decision about what you really wanted.*" They expressed discontent with lack of support for quitting smoking while quitting other substances. The second group of participants considered quitting smoking to be of lower priority than quitting other substances they perceived to be more harmful (harm reduction model [54]) or encouraged client choice in which substance they wanted to quit first. For example, C26 described: *"We had somebody recently who came in and smoking was very low priority because she was drinking very heavily and was wanting to quit drinking, and our psychiatrist wanted her to actually check into an inpatient facility before we would even treat her [for smoking]."* There is evidence that quitting smoking at the same time does not negatively impact drug abuse outcomes and on-going efforts are integrating of substance abuse treatment with smoking cessation [36].

Due to these differences in expertise and priorities, the need to re-direct clients to other providers for medication or mismanaging comorbidities hinder treatment for nicotine addiction. Current technological solutions do not support ways for either providers or clients to manage comorbidities while quitting smoking.

PROVIDER PERCEPTIONS ON USE OF TECHNOLOGY

Consistent with related work [42,67], providers perceived technology to have many benefits to support quitting smoking. Table 2 summarizes current technology-based tools that participants recommend to their clients, and their perceived functions. Providers primarily use technology to share information, follow up with clients over email, phone, or text messages, and/or to broadcast information to clients over longer term on mailing lists. Participants expressed the need to understand the application's source, cost, agenda, whether they are based on evidence based practices, and preferred recommending federal or state affiliated sources and websites. For example, M04 said, *"I do worry, when someone tells me they found a new app, I worry initially like who created it, where they get their funding? Kinda what's their motivation? I like it when they're created by reputable sources...I really worry— is there any hidden agenda or is the science sound."* They also reported that clients perceive benefits from features on smartphone apps such as tracking and viewing "cigarette free time", number of cigarettes, personal health benefits, and money saved. Providers acknowledged that some people are more likely to prefer technology for support over provider visits due to reasons such as perceived stigma, not wanting to appear vulnerable or seek help, and personal choice and privacy.

Type	Tool examples	Functions of tool in counselling as perceived by providers
Websites or Online tools	SmokeFree.gov, NYSmokeFree, tobaccofreeco.org, the EX plan: becomeanex.org, state quitline websites, online communities and anonymous forum boards for peer support, provider's personal website, Facebook, Google docs, question answer forum (Quora)	▪ Access information on quitting smoking resources and coping strategies ▪ Refer to interactive online tools to help clients create quit plan (Ex Plan) ▪ Refer to mobile apps that clients could download ▪ Providers answer questions on forums (Quora) ▪ Clients maintain records of their smoking behavior (Google docs) ▪ Clients look up medications and side-effects before asking providers ▪ Clients connect with peers online to get support and share experiences
Mobile phone applications	*Smoking:* QuitSTART (teens), QuitNow, Tobacco Quit And Save, This is Quitting *Others:* Mood management, mindfulness, diabetes tracking, weight management apps, sleep, pedometer, medication list, Fit Bit, learning CBT techniques	▪ Self-management in absence of provider support ▪ Tracking cigarettes, health, money, mood, physical activity ▪ Counting down time not smoked ▪ Learning coping skills for triggers of smoking ▪ Connecting with peers ▪ Games to keep their hands and mind busy

Table 2: Functions of technology-based tools recommended by providers or perceived used by their clients

C16 explains: *"I think the challenge with the younger people—at least in my experience, has been they don't think they need help. Whereas if they've got an app on their phone, they may have more tendency to use it because no one else will know they're using it...I've done cessation groups at military bases. Often times, they don't want to appear weak."* The younger population makes up the majority of users of smartphone apps for quitting smoking (median age 31 years, range 18-67 years) [9] and quitline services (mean age 39.4 years) [25]. Stigma is also a major barrier to accessing in-person health care treatment for those with concerns of addiction [40] and mental health challenges [7].

When asked who would not benefit from technology, participants attributed client preferences for in-person social support as a potential reason for non-use of technology. For example, C02 who was a peer support group facilitator, perceived that "*people who turn to coming to the support group aren't real mobile app kinda people*." She reported that she also regularly communicated with her clients between sessions on smoking related concerns via phone calls, text messages, and emails, but she preferred technology to initiate contact and for follow-ups or checking with clients, *after* in-person connection was established. P06 perceived that lack of self-motivation in his clients was a key reason his clients seek provider help over use of mobile phone applications to quit smoking: *"The problem most of my patients have is internal motivation—self-drive. And to have a phone saying, ok now go do your yoga when they are homeless on the street or—cigarettes are one of the least of their addictions— it really relies on patient's internal self-motivation. Many of my patients, if they have that [self-motivation], they wouldn't be in my clinic."*

While giving feedback on our design prototypes, providers also explained that while most clients have smart phones, some of their clients either did not own smartphones or will not be able to use smartphone applications for quitting smoking. The specific population groups that providers mentioned include older population (55 years and above), rural population, low income groups, people facing homelessness, people with learning disabilities and symptoms of comorbid health conditions that prevent them from using smartphones, and people with comorbid addiction. Few providers observed that clients mainly use their smartphones for calling features and had difficulty using apps or text messaging features. For example, C21 explained a range of difficulties that could act as barriers to using smartphones for her clients, *"The population I serve, really has challenges with technology. Sometimes, especially if they have a mental health challenge or a learning disability, or if they're a little bit older... [or] don't have as many resources or don't have as many learning experiences. The applications and more advanced technologies – sometimes, not all the time— is outside of the scope of their abilities."* Providers explained this with the caveat that there are exceptions to individuals in these population groups who own smartphones and will be able to use them. Though the rate of use of technology for health care needs is low in older adults [38] and population with challenges of mental health [8,21] and homelessness [33], it is increasing.

DISCUSSION

To summarize, providers work to individualize smoking cessation treatment to specific contexts that clients associate with smoking behavior, differences in client access to and usage of medications for withdrawal symptoms, different social situations that act as trigger or support for clients, and differences in treatment of their comorbid health conditions. We discuss opportunities on how to integrate lessons learned from these findings with needs identified from prior work to better adapt the design of technology for quitting smoking. Our design prototypes were specific to smartphone applications, but we believe these opportunities are applicable across various platforms and tools that providers and clients are comfortable using.

Contextualizing Interventions

We identify three main steps for technology to support interventions that adapt to an individual's context: (1) help the client identify their specific context of smoking, (2) help the client plan for actionable steps to take in those specific contexts, and (3) enable clients to execute the intervention at the time of craving. Current efforts in the design of smoking cessation technology support Step 1 and some in Step 3. There has been less exploration on efforts to support client choice and input through technology while planning interventions in Step 2.

Enabling users to record and visualize situation (similar to activities in context), time, and location of smoking has potential to increase client's self-awareness about their smoking behavior and motivation to quit [50,51]. This design can be extended to allow logging and integration with other elements of context during smoking: people, environmental cues, and special events. Allowing users to label the contexts (such as, in which it is most difficult to quit) could facilitate prioritizing the context to tackle, first. The Ubicomp community continues advance automated sensing technology [55], and we urge for this to continue to be a priority as it can better facilitate tracking contexts than user-initiated logging, which may be difficult and/or socially stigmatizing . Systems may also not need to achieve very high accuracy: they could potential record smoking or craving contexts in the moment. Later, at an opportune moment, they could ask users to verify each and, if an actual craving, to rate its difficulty. Reviewing the captured data plus any data later entered by the user could also support the process of planning interventions to try the next time they are in a similar context.

Just in Time Adaptive Interventions (JITAI) aim to detect specific triggering contexts and "push" micro-randomized interventions to clients [35]. Clients, however, prefer "pull" over "push" messages due to the perception that poorly timed interventions run the risk of reminding them about smoking or they tend to dismiss them [27]. Clients also prefer interventions that are of interest to them, tips that are achievable and relatable to them [48], and rewards that are meaningful to them. Given the rapidly changing physiological and behavioral needs while quitting smoking, there is a need that technology should leverage the knowledge of clients about their varying context and enable clients with skills to respond effectively in vulnerable contexts, such as during cravings.

We found that providers currently individualize to these needs by guiding client input in brainstorming through prompts and examples. To design for a similar process, coping strategies could be grouped into clusters of pertinent contexts tagged by crowdsourcing, expert, or peer feedback similar to how many card sorting programs work. Clients and providers can then work together to make matched suggestions to contexts that trigger smoking in clients. When combined with user feedback or tracked behavior, the crowdsourced clusters can be further matched to an individual's context using machine learning techniques [55] or after a self-experimentation process [34]. Clients can then select, modify, and save lists of strategies per context and revisit them, or the system can remind them of these strategies when similar contexts are detected.

Another way to facilitate such brainstorming might be to scaffold the development of decision rules for which interventions clients will use in which situations. This could even take the form of supporting end user programming [60], such as in If This Then That (IFTTT) [68] and in some other contexts of health [6,22,23]. For example, client can be shown a list of their triggering contexts and a list of coping strategies, which they can match; software could then then help them implement these rules. Opportunities for such client initiated planning could be before anticipated trigger or reflecting after lapsing [52].

It may also be possible to combine this approach with self-experimentation [34], to guide the end-user to generate and test hypotheses on effectiveness of an intervention in a particular context. This has the potential to improve client knowledge firsthand about the effectiveness of different coping strategies. Designs that help clients internalize this knowledge may reduce their dependence on the system for support and help them make decisions next time they face a similar context.

There are many possible approaches to gathering client input about potential interventions, and it is important that research continue to develop them and designers implement them. Gathering client input is an important element of both current provider practices and the *Shared Decision Making* (SDM) model [20] in patient-centered care which encourages clinicians to inform clients, provide them with choices, and help clients make their own decisions in treatment. While such a process can increase the cognitive load on the client, SDM has been shown to be an effective model to help improve patient engagement and outcomes in clinical care [20]. Design research should explore the feasibility and trade-offs of facilitating client input in deciding interventions.

Opportunities to mitigate barriers to individualization

Addressing some barriers to individualization—such as conflicting treatment priorities and medication access—will require public health reforms and policy changes. We hope awareness of these barriers can help designers consider the limitations of technological solutions, and help them identify niches to which they can contribute. Some crucial opportunities for technology to reduce barriers to individualizing care include: catalyzing social support, supporting withdrawal management, and inclusion of individuals who are at high risk and/or facing comorbidities, to also benefit from technology for quitting smoking.

Catalyzing social support

Providers highlight the difficulty a client faces in quitting when their offline social circle is not supportive. Education programs for a client's social circle are not feasible in every clinical setting due to cost, time, and willingness to engage. An area of future research might be to design a closed social networking platform for a selected group of people in offline or online networks of the client, where the provider or client could broadcast tips and recommended strategies that are helpful to support someone to quit [4]. More importantly, these efforts can help reduce stigma and isolation in a client's immediate network, adding to social incentives to quit. However, prior research suggests that not every client may prefer social support [27,49]. For facilitating nuanced preferences, clients may make visible to the network what kind of support they are seeking or not seeking during quitting smoking [57] (if they wish to disclose). Such a design could enable clients to set type and time of support needed, (such as, "need someone to walk with during most difficult morning cigarette"), and social reminders for the buddy. Letting clients nominate more than one "buddy" in the network, and can help share responsibilities, wherein different people can intervene at different times or contexts.

Supporting withdrawal management

Both providers and clients consider features to support nicotine management medications important [27,42], but commercial apps for smoking cessation do not support medication [1,29]. For prescribed medications, close monitoring and dosage adherence can be encouraged through networked apps between provider and client, where the provider enters dosage information and client logs medication intake [19]. Technology should encourage the user to seek assistance on medication support from experts in situations such as undesirable side-effects and emergency support (such as a phone call button) when a facing crisis situation. To facilitate information needs and autonomy, smoking cessation applications should integrate medication information (e.g., instructions on adequate dosage and side-effects when clients or providers enter names of over-the-counter products) and tracking functionalities such as those in the app *Drugs.com* [69].

Clients need apps to adapt to their changing needs during nicotine withdrawal [27]. Insights from providers help us envision a system that can model and predict withdrawal from client logs of smoking intensity and medication intake. For example; in the initial days of quitting, if the client's physiological measures (e.g., mood, alertness) degrade due to withdrawal, the client's motivation may benefit if shown examples—either system generated or from a peer—for how response patterns are expected to vary during quitting. Such feedback can help the client normalize and manage their expectations during quitting. Predicting and projecting expected improvements in behavioral outcomes in far future can encourage clients to continue logging and not smoke. Also, crisis situations can be detected and averted by setting thresholds – such as, if mood levels persistently drop below a threshold level indicating increase of depressive symptoms, the client can be alerted to contact their buddy or care team.

Comorbidities in high-risk population

In addition to supporting or recommending different treatment options for a specific health challenge, there is also a need for tools that can help people better prioritize and coordinate treatment for comorbid health conditions. For example; data-soloing may lead to people receiving conflicting advice from different health applications they use to work on different health goals. Similarly, if someone uses different applications to address comorbid challenges, such as depression, nutrition, and smoking, each application might currently ask them to separately and redundantly track mood, increasing user burden unnecessarily. For those who struggle with comorbid substance addiction, tools should also integrate contextualizing interventions based on specific contexts and patterns of cravings for substance use.

To support quitting needs for people who have comorbid health challenges and socio-economic challenges, for whom smoking rates are also prevalent [32], designers should consider how low cost support can be facilitated—for example; designing for compatibility with low cost devices, minimizing or avoiding cost of data access, and utilizing shared resources such as systems in community based shelters [18]. Designers should also incorporate diverse usability and accessibility needs for aging population and for those with psychiatric symptoms and cognitive and motor difficulties [26,64]. While applications that are universally accessible and support integrated features to manage comorbidities and are ideal, feasibility of how to design such applications by optimizing user-burden needs to be explored.

CONCLUSION

In this study, we examined everyday counseling practices and challenges of providers, and incorporated their insights to inform design of technology that can better assist the complex process of quitting smoking. Future research should explore client perspectives on context-appropriate interventions, the feasibility of technology to facilitate client input for planning context appropriate interventions, and opportunities to support clinical interactions. We suggest several promising research and design opportunities, such as enhancing positive social support, supporting medication management to temper nicotine withdrawal, and including needs of high risk population in design of quitting tools. More effective and individualized tools for smoking cessation can potentially enable more individuals to quit smoking, ultimately reducing risks of serious diseases, while improving their health and quality of life.

ACKNOWLEDGEMENTS

We are thankful to the participants of our study for sharing their expertise and experiences. We thank Beatriz Carlini and Jasmine Zia for their support with recruitment. We thank Chia-Fang Chung, Eric Hekler, Predrag Klasnja, Jordan Eschler, members of Personal Informatics group and iMed group at University of Washington, and our reviewers for their thoughtful feedback. This research was funded in part by the University of Washington Innovation Research Award, National Science Foundation #1553167, National Institute on Drug abuse #K99DA037276, and the Intel Science & Technology Center on Pervasive Computing.

REFERENCES

1. Lorien C. Abroms, J. Lee Westmaas, Jeuneviette Bontemps-Jones, Rathna Ramani, and Jenelle Mellerson. 2013. A content analysis of popular smartphone apps for smoking cessation. *American Journal of Preventive Medicine* 45, 6: 732–736. https://doi.org/10.1016/j.amepre.2013.07.008
2. Lorien C. Abroms, Nalini Padmanabhan, Lalida Thaweethai, and Todd Phillips. 2011. iPhone apps for smoking cessation: A content analysis. *American Journal of Preventive Medicine* 40, 3: 279–285. https://doi.org/10.1016/j.amepre.2010.10.032
3. American Cancer Society. Deciding how to quit: A smoker's guide. Retrieved September 20, 2016 from http://www.cancer.org/downloads/gahc/hp_set_yourself_free.pdf
4. American Cancer Society. 2016. Helping a Smoker Quit: Do's and Don'ts General hints for friends and family. Retrieved September 20, 2016 from http://www.cancer.org/healthy/stayawayfromtobacco/helping-a-smoker-quit
5. American Thoracic Society. 2013. Withdrawal and Relapse from Tobacco Use. *ATS Patient Education Series*. Retrieved September 20, 2016 from http://www.thoracic.org/patients/patient-resources/resources/withdrawal-and-relapse.pdf
6. Madeline Balaam, Stefan Rennick Egglestone, Geraldine Fitzpatrick, Tom Rodden, Ann-Marie Hughes, Anna Wilkinson, Thomas Nind, Lesley Axelrod, Eric Harris, Ian Ricketts, Susan Mawson, and Jane Burridge. 2011. Motivating mobility: designing for lived motivation in stroke rehabilitation. In *Proceedings of the SIGCHI Conference on Human Factors in Computing Systems* (CHI '11). ACM, New York, NY, USA, 3073-3082. https://doi.org/10.1145/1978942.1979397
7. Lisa J. Barney, Kathleen M. Griffiths, Anthony F. Jorm, and Helen Christensen. 2006. Stigma about depression and its impact on help-seeking intentions. *Australian and New Zealand Journal of Psychiatry* 40, 1: 51–54. https://doi.org/10.1111/j.1440-1614.2006.01741.x
8. Dror Ben-Zeev, Kristin E. Davis, Susan Kaiser, Izabela Krzsos, and Robert E. Drake. 2013. Mobile technologies among people with serious mental illness: opportunities for future services. *Administration and Policy in Mental Health and Mental health Services Research* 40, 4: 340–343. https://doi.org/10.1007/s10488-012-0424-x
9. Nasser F. BinDhim, Kevin McGeechan, and Lyndal Trevena. 2014. Who uses smoking cessation apps? A feasibility study across three countries via smartphones. *Journal of Medical Internet Research mHeath and uHealth* 2, 1. https://doi.org/10.2196/mhealth.2841
10. Krysten W. Bold, Abdullah S. Rasheed, Danielle E. McCarthy, Thomas C. Jackson, Michael C. Fiore, and Timothy B. Baker. 2015. Rates and Predictors of Renewed Quitting After Relapse During a One-Year Follow-Up Among Primary Care Patients. *Annals of Behavioral Medicine* 49, 1: 128–140. https://doi.org/10.1007/s12160-014-9627-6
11. Ron Borland, Timea R. Partos, Hua-Hie Yong, K. Michael Cummings, and Andrew Hyland. 2012. How much unsuccessful quitting activity is going on among adult smokers? Data from the International Tobacco Control Four Country cohort survey. *Addiction* 107, 3: 673–682. https://doi.org/10.1111/j.1360-0443.2011.03685.x
12. Jonathan B. Bricker, Wade Copeland, Kristin E. Mull, Emily Y. Zeng, Noreen L. Watson, Katrina J. Akioka, and Jaimee L. Heffner. 2017. Single-arm trial of the second version of an acceptance & commitment therapy smartphone application for smoking cessation. *Drug and Alcohol Dependence* 170: 37–42. https://doi.org/10.1016/j.drugalcdep.2016.10.029
13. Jonathan B. Bricker, Christopher Wyszynski, Bryan Comstock, and Jaimee L Heffner. 2013. Pilot randomized controlled trial of web-based acceptance and commitment therapy for smoking cessation. *Nicotine & Tobacco Research* 15, 10: 1756–1764. https://doi.org/10.1093/ntr/ntt056
14. Richard A. Brown, Christopher W. Kahler, Raymond Niaura, David B. Abrams, Suzanne D. Sales, Susan E. Ramsey, Michael G. Goldstein, Ellen S. Burgess, and Ivan W. Miller. 2001. Cognitive-behavioral treatment for depression in smoking cessation. *Journal of consulting and clinical psychology* 69, 3: 471–80. https://doi.org/10.1037//0022-006X.69.3.471
15. Sofie L. Champassak, Kathy Goggin, Sarah Finocchario-Kessler, Maghen Farris, Maniza Ehtesham, Rachel Schoor, and Delwyn Catley. 2014. A qualitative assessment of provider perspectives on smoking cessation counselling. *Journal of Evaluation in Clinical Practice* 20, 3: 281–287. https://doi.org/10.1111/jep.12124
16. Benjamin Lê Cook, Geoff Ferris Wayne, Nilay E. Kafali, Zimin Liu, Chang Shu, and Michael Flores. 2014. Trends in smoking among adults with mental illness and association between mental health treatment and smoking cessation. *JAMA* 311, 2: 172–182. https://doi.org/10.1001/jama.2013.284985
17. Jesse Dallery and Bethany R. Raiff. 2011. Contingency management in the 21st century: technological innovations to promote smoking cessation. *Substance Use and Misuse* 46, 1: 10–22. https://doi.org/10.3109/10826084.2011.521067
18. Christopher A. Le Dantec, Robert G. Farrell, Jim E. Christensen, Mark Bailey, Jason B. Ellis, Wendy A. Kellogg, and W. Keith Edwards. 2011. Publics in

practice: ubiquitous computing at a shelter for homeless mothers. In *Proceedings of the SIGCHI Conference on Human factors in Computing Systems* (CHI '11). ACM, New York, NY, USA, 1687–1696. https://doi.org/10.1145/1978942.1979189

19. Lindsey Dayer, Seth Heldenbrand, Paul Anderson, Paul O. Gubbins, and Bradley C. Martin. 2013. Smartphone medication adherence apps: Potential benefits to patients and providers. *Journal of the American Pharmacists Association* 53, 2: 172–181. https://doi.org/10.1331/JAPhA.2013.12202

20. Glyn Elwyn, Dominick Frosch, Richard Thomson, Natalie Joseph-Williams, Amy Lloyd, Paul Kinnersley, Emma Cording, Dave Tomson, Carole Dodd, Stephen Rollnick, Adrian Edwards, and Michael Barry. 2012. Shared decision making: A model for clinical practice. *Journal of General Internal Medicine 27*, 1361–1367. https://doi.org/10.1007/s11606-012-2077-6

21. Katrina Gay, John Torous, Adam Joseph, Anand Pandya, and Ken Duckworth. 2016. Digital Technology Use Among Individuals with Schizophrenia: Results of an Online Survey. *JMIR Mental Health* 3, 2: e15. https://doi.org/10.2196/mental.5379

22. Giuseppe Ghiani, Marco Manca, and Fabio Paternò. 2015. Authoring Context-Dependent Cross-Device User Interfaces Based on Trigger/Action Rules. In *Proceedings of the 14th International Conference on Mobile and Ubiquitous Multimedia* (MUM '15). ACM, New York, NY, USA, 313–322. https://doi.org/10.1145/2836041.2836073

23. Giuseppe Ghiani, Marco Manca, Fabio Paternò, and Carmen Santoro. 2016. End-user personalization of context-dependent applications in AAL scenarios. In *Proceedings of the 18th International Conference on Human-Computer Interaction with Mobile Devices and Services Adjunct* (MobileHCI '16). ACM, New York, NY, USA, 1081–1084. https://doi.org/10.1145/2957265.2965005

24. Elizabeth V. Gifford, Barbara S. Kohlenberg, Steven C. Hayes, David O. Antonuccio, Melissa M Piasecki, Mandra L. Rasmussen-Hall, and Kathleen M. Palm. 2004. Acceptance-based treatment for smoking cessation. *Behavior Therapy* 35, 4: 689–705. https://doi.org/10.1016/S0005-7894(04)80015-7

25. Hazel Gilbert, Stephen Sutton, and Gay Sutherland. 2005. Who Calls QUIT®? The characteristics of smokers seeking advice via a telephone helpline compared with smokers attending a clinic and those in the general population. *Public Health* 119, 10: 933–939. https://doi.org/10.1016/j.puhe.2005.03.005

26. Peter Gregor, Alan F. Newell, and Mary Zajicek. 2002. Designing for dynamic diversity: interfaces for older people. In *Proceedings of the fifth international ACM conference on Assistive technologies (Assets '02).* ACM, New York, NY, USA, 151–156. https://doi.org/10.1145/638249.638277

27. Andrea Lisabeth Hartzler, June Bluespruce, Sheryl L. Catz, and Jennifer B. Mcclure. 2016. Prioritizing the mHealth Design Space : A Mixed-Methods Analysis of Smokers ' Perspectives. *JMIR mHealth and uHealth* 4, 3. https://doi.org/10.2196/mhealth.5742

28. Rosemary Hiscock, Linda Bauld, Amanda Amos, Jennifer A. Fidler, and Marcus Munafò. 2012. Socioeconomic status and smoking: A review. *Annals of the New York Academy of Sciences 1248*, 1: 107–123. https://doi.org/10.1111/j.1749-6632.2011.06202.x

29. Bettina B. Hoeppner, Susanne S. Hoeppner, Lourah Seaboyer, Melissa R. Schick, Gwyneth W. Y. Wu, Brandon G. Bergman, and John F. Kelly. 2016. How Smart are Smartphone Apps for Smoking Cessation? A Content Analysis. *Nicotine and Tobacco Research* 18, 5: 1025–1031. https://doi.org/10.1093/ntr/ntv117

30. Karen Holtzblatt, Jessamyn Burns Wendell, and Shelley Wood. 2004. *Rapid contextual design: a how-to guide to key techniques for user-centered design*. Elsevier.

31. Megan A. Jacobs, Caroline O. Cobb, Lorien Abroms, and Amanda L. Graham. 2014. Facebook apps for smoking cessation: A review of content and adherence to evidence-based guidelines. *Journal of Medical Internet Research 16*, 9: e205. https://doi.org/10.2196/jmir.3491

32. Ahmed Jamal, David M. Homa, Erin O'Connor, Stephen D. Babb, Ralph S. Caraballo, Tushar Singh, S. Sean Hu, and Brian A. King. 2015. Current Cigarette Smoking Among Adults - United States, 2005-2014. *MMWR. Morbidity and mortality weekly report* 64, 44: 1233–40. https://doi.org/10.15585/mmwr.mm6444a2

33. Larissa Jennings, Nicole Lee, Deborah Shore, Nancy Strohminger, Burgundi Allison, Donaldson F. Conserve, and Lawrence J. Cheskin. 2016. U.S. Minority Homeless Youth's Access to and Use of Mobile Phones: Implications for mHealth Intervention Design. *Journal of health communication* 21, 7: 725–733. https://doi.org/10.1080/10810730.2015.1103331

34. Ravi Karkar, Jasmine Zia, Roger Vilardaga, Sonali R. Mishra, James Fogarty, Sean A. Munson, and Julie A. Kientz. 2016. A framework for self-experimentation in personalized health. *Journal of the American Medical Informatics Association* 23, 3: 440–448. https://doi.org/10.1093/jamia/ocv150

35. Predrag Klasnja, Eric B. Hekler, Saul Shiffman, Audrey Boruvka, Daniel Almirall, Ambuj Tewari, and Susan A. Murphy. 2015. Micro-randomized trials: An experimental design for developing just-in-time adaptive interventions. *Health Psychology* 34, S: 1220–1228. https://doi.org/10.1037/hea0000305

36. Hannah K. Knudsen, Jessica Muilenburg, and Lillian T.

Eby. 2013. Sustainment of smoking cessation programs in substance use disorder treatment organizations. *Nicotine and Tobacco Research* 15, 6: 1060–1068. https://doi.org/10.1093/ntr/nts242

37. Diane R. Lauver, Sandra E. Ward, Susan M. Heidrich, Mary L. Keller, Barbara J. Bowers, Patricia Flatley Brennan, Karin T. Kirchhoff, and Thelma J. Wells. 2002. Patient-centered interventions. *Research in Nursing & Health* 25, 4: 246–255. https://doi.org/10.1002/nur.10044
38. David M. Levine, Stuart R. Lipsitz, and Jeffrey A. Linde. 2016. Trends in Seniors' Use of Digital Health Technology in the United States , 2011-2014. *JAMA* 316, 5: 538–540. https://doi.org/10.1001/jama.2016.9124
39. Stasi Lubansky, Corrine Y. Jurgens, and Carla Boutin-Foster. 2015. Factors influencing smoking cessation counselling: A qualitative study of medical residents. *Journal of Smoking Cessation 10*, 1: 29–34. https://doi.org/10.1017/jsc.2013.33
40. Jason B. Luoma. 2010. Substance use stigma as a barrier to treatment and recovery. *Addiction Medicine,* 1195–1215. Springer New York. https://doi.org/10.1007/978-1-4419-0338-9_59
41. Lisa A. Marsch, Sarah E. Lord, and Jesse Dallery (Eds.). 2014. *Behavioral Healthcare and Technology: Using Science-based Innovations to Transform Practice*. Oxford University Press.
42. Jennifer B. Mcclure, Andrea L. Hartzler, and Sheryl L. Catz. 2016. Design Considerations for Smoking Cessation Apps: Feedback From Nicotine Dependence Treatment Providers and Smokers. *JMIR mHealth and uHealth* 4, 1: 199–208. https://doi.org/10.2196/mhealth.5181
43. Susan Michie, Natasha Hyder, Asha Walia, and Robert West. 2011. Development of a taxonomy of behaviour change techniques used in individual behavioural support for smoking cessation. *Addictive Behaviors* 36, 4: 315–319. https://doi.org/10.1016/j.addbeh.2010.11.016
44. Susan Michie, Michelle Rchardson, Marie Johnston, Charles Abraham, Jill Francis, Wendy Hardeman, Martin P. Eccles, James Cane, and Caroline E. Wood. 2013. The behavior change technique taxonomy (v1) of 93 hierarchically clustered techniques: building an international consensus for the reporting of behavior change interventions. *Annals of behavioral medicine* 46, 1: 81–95. https://doi.org/10.1007/s12160-013-9486-6
45. Susan Michie, Maartje M. van Stralen, and Rober West. 2011. The behaviour change wheel: A new method for characterising and designing behaviour change interventions. *Implementation Science* 6, 1: 42. https://doi.org/10.1186/1748-5908-6-42
46. National Cancer Institute. Clearing the Air. Retrieved September 20, 2016 from https://smokefree.gov/sites/default/files/pdf/clearing-the-air-accessible.pdf
47. National Cancer Institute. Clear Horizons: A Quit-Smoking Guide for People 50 and Older. Retrieved September 20, 2016 from https://smokefree.gov/sites/default/files/pdf/clear-horizons-accessible.pdf
48. Jeni Paay, Jesper Kjeldskov, Umachanger Brinthaparan, Lars Lichon, Stephan Rasmussen, Nirojan Srikandaraja, Wally Smith, Greg Wadley, and Bernd Ploderer. 2014. *Quitty* : Using Technology to Persuade Smokers to Quit. In *Proceedings of the 8th Nordic Conference on Human-Computer Interaction: Fun, Fast, Foundational* (NordiCHI '14). ACM, New York, NY, USA, 551-560. https://doi.org/10.1145/2639189.2639195
49. Jeni Paay, Jesper Kjeldskov, Mikael B. Skov, Lars Lichon, and Stephan Rasmussen. 2015. Understanding Individual Differences for Tailored Smoking Cessation Apps. In *Proceedings of the 33rd Annual ACM Conference on Human Factors in Computing Systems* (CHI '15). ACM, New York, NY, USA, 1699–1708. https://doi.org/10.1145/2702123.2702321
50. Jeni Paay, Jesper Kjeldskov, Mikael B. Skov, Nirojan Srikandarajah, and Umachanger Brinthaparan. 2015. QuittyLink : Using Smartphones for Personal Counseling to Help People Quit Smoking. In *Proceedings of the 17th International Conference on Human-Computer Interaction with Mobile Devices and Services* (MobileHCI '15). ACM, New York, NY, USA, 98-104. https://doi.org/10.1145/2785830.2785877
51. Jeni Paay, Jesper Kjeldskov, Mikael Skov, Umachanger Brinthaparan, Nirojan Srikandarajah, and Dimitrios Raptis. 2015. QuittyLink : A Mobile Application that helps people Quit Smoking. In *Proceedings of the 17th International Conference on Human-Computer Interaction with Mobile Devices and Services Adjunct* (MobileHCI '15). ACM, New York, NY, USA, 599-606. https://doi.org/10.1145/2786567.2792897
52. Bernd Ploderer, Wally Smith, Jon Pearce, and Ron Borland. 2014. A Mobile app offering distractions and tips to cope with cigarette craving: a qualitative study. *JMIR mHealth and uHealth* 2, 2: e23. https://doi.org/10.2196/mhealth.3209
53. James O. Prochaska and Wayne F. Velicer. 1997. The transtheoretical model of health behavior change. *American Journal of Health Promotion* 12, 1: 38–48. https://doi.org/10.4278/0890-1171-12.1.38
54. Judith J. Prochaska. 2010. Failure to treat tobacco use in mental health and addiction treatment settings: A form of harm reduction? *Drug and Alcohol Dependence 110*, 3: 177–182. https://doi.org/10.1016/j.drugalcdep.2010.03.002

55. Nazir Saleheen, Amin Ahsan Ali, Syed Monowar Hossain, Hillol Sarker, Soujanya Chatterjee, Benjamin Marlin, Emre Ertin, Mustafa Absi, Mustafa al'Absi, and Santosh Kumar. 2015. puffMarker: A Multi-Sensor Approach for Pinpointing the Timing of First Lapse in Smoking Cessation. In *Proceedings of the 2015 ACM International Joint Conference on Pervasive and Ubiquitous Computing* (UbiComp '15). ACM, New York, NY, USA, 999–1010. https://doi.org/10.1145/2750858.2806897
56. Irving Seidman. 2013. *Interviewing as qualitative research: A guide for researchers in education and the social sciences*. Teachers college press.
57. Meredith M. Skeels, Kenton T. Unruh, Christopher Powell, and Wanda Pratt. 2010. Catalyzing Social Support for Breast Cancer Patients. In *Proceedings of the SIGCHI Conference on Human Factors in Computing Systems* (CHI '10). ACM, New York, NY, USA, 173–182. https://doi.org/10.1145/1753326.1753353
58. Victor J. Strecher. 1999. Computer-tailored smoking cessation materials: a review and discussion. *Patient education and counseling* 36, 2: 107–117. https://doi.org/10.1016/S0738-3991(98)00128-1
59. The Clinical Practice Guideline Treating, Tobacco. 2008. A Clinical Practice Guideline for Treating Tobacco Use and Dependence: 2008 Update. *American Journal of Preventive Medicine* 35, 2: 158–176. https://doi.org/10.1016/j.amepre.2008.04.009
60. Khai N. Truong, Elaine M. Huang, and Gregory D. Abowd. 2004. CAMP: A Magnetic Poetry Interface for End-User Programming of Capture Applications for the Home. In *International Conference on Ubiquitous Computing*, 143–160. https://doi.org/10.1007/978-3-540-30119-6_9
61. U. S. Department of Health and Human Services. Smokeless Tobacco: A guide for quitting Tobacco. Retrieved September 20, 2016 from http://www.nidcr.nih.gov/oralhealth/Topics/SmokelessTobacco/Documents/SmokelessTobacco.pdf
62. U.S. Food & Drug Administration. 2011. FDA Drug Safety Communication: Safety review update of Chantix (varenicline) and risk of neuropsychiatric adverse events. Retrieved September 20, 2016 from http://www.fda.gov/Drugs/DrugSafety/ucm276737.htm
63. U.S. Food & Drug Administration. 2015. FDA Drug Safety Communication: FDA updates label for stop smoking drug Chantix (varenicline) to include potential alcohol interaction, rare risk of seizures, and studies of side effects on mood, behavior, or thinking. Retrieved September 20, 2016 from http://www.fda.gov/Drugs/DrugSafety/ucm436494.htm
64. Roger Vilardaga, Javier Rizo, Julie A. Kientz, Michael G. McDonell, Richard K. Ries, and Kiley Sobel. 2016. User Experience Evaluation of a Smoking Cessation App in People With Serious Mental Illness. *Nicotine & Tobacco Research* 18, 5: 1032–1038. https://doi.org/10.1093/ntr/ntv256
65. Greg Wadley, Wally Smith, Bernd Ploderer, Jon Pearce, Sarah Webber, Mark Whooley, and Ron Borland. 2014. What people talk about when they talk about quitting. In *Proceedings of the 26th Australian Computer-Human Interaction Conference on Designing Futures: the Future of Design.* (OzCHI '14). ACM, New York, NY, USA, 388–391. http://dx.doi.org/10.1145/2686612.2686671
66. Miller William R. and Stephen Rollnick. 2012. *Motivational interviewing: Helping people change*. Guilford press.
67. Jane M. Young and Jeanette E. Ward. 2001. Implementing guidelines for smoking cessation advice in Australian general practice : opinions, current practices, readiness to change and perceived barriers. *Family Practice,* 18, 1: 14–20. https://doi.org/10.1093/fampra/18.1.14
68. Web application for planning actions with decision rules: If This Then That (IFFT). Retrieved from https://ifttt.com/
69. Smartphone application and website for medication support: Drugs.com. Retrieved from https://www.drugs.com/apps/

Toward Usable Evidence: Optimizing Knowledge Accumulation in HCI Research on Health Behavior Change

Predrag Klasnja[1], Eric B. Hekler[2], Elizabeth V. Korinek[2], John Harlow[2], Sonali R. Mishra[3]

[1] Group Health Research Insttute
Seattle, WA, USA
klasnja.p@ghc.org

[2] Arizona State University
Phoenix, AZ, USA
{ehekler, evkorine, jharlow}@asu.edu

[3] University of Washington
Seattle, WA, USA
smishra@uw.edu

ABSTRACT

Over the last ten years, HCI researchers have introduced a range of novel ways to support health behavior change, from glanceable displays to sophisticated game dynamics. Yet, this research has not had as much impact as its originality warrants. A key reason for this is that common forms of evaluation used in HCI make it difficult to effectively accumulate—and use—knowledge across research projects. This paper proposes a strategy for HCI research on behavior change that retains the field's focus on novel technical contributions while enabling accumulation of evidence that can increase impact of individual research projects both in HCI and the broader behavior-change science. The core of this strategy is an emphasis on the discovery of causal effects of individual components of behavior-change technologies and the precise ways in which those effects vary with individual differences, design choices, and contexts in which those technologies are used.

Author Keywords

Evaluation methods; behavior change; health informatics; user studies.

ACM Classification Keywords

H.5.2. Information interfaces and presentation (e.g., HCI): User interfaces (Theory and methods); J.3. Computer applications: Life and medical sciences (Health).

INTRODUCTION

Imagine that you are designing a mobile application for stress management. During literature review, you came across UbiFit [9,10], MILES [24], UbiGreen [15], and BeWell [29,32], and inspired by the idea of a glanceable display you decide to incorporate it into your application. But you face a problem: you are developing for iOS, which gives you neither the control of the lock screen nor a mostly empty home screen on which to put your display. You have some ideas—you can create the display as a widget on the iPhone's Today screen, for instance—but before you put in the time and resources to build and test the display, you'd like to use prior research to gauge if it's worth it to use a glanceable display for your target users.

Specifically, you'd like to know the following: (1) How well did the overall UbiFit, MILES, UbiGreen, and BeWell systems do at influencing physical activity, eco-friendly behavior, and social wellbeing? (2) How impactful was the glanceable display component in particular for producing these outcomes? (3) What design differences between the glanceable displays of UbiFit, MILES, UbiGreen, and BeWell were meaningful, and would those design differences matter for your target user? (4) What are the essential features that make an interface a useful and usable glanceable display? For example, does a glanceable display require a passive sensor for the target variable of interest, such as stress, to work effectively? What other design options fit with the concept of a glanceable display (e.g., would a Today widget on iOS count)? (5) What are the characteristics of the users and the contexts of use in UbiFit, MILES, UbiGreen, and BeWell that may have influenced the value (or lack thereof) of their glanceable displays? (6) How likely is it that the glanceable display concept is useful for a target like stress? For example, will frequent reminders of stress end up being more aversive compared to physical activity and thus undermine the usefulness of the glanceable display? (7) How might the design of a glanceable display need to be adjusted for it to be useful for stress management? And, (8) can those adjustments feasibly be implemented on iOS (e.g., the Today screen would be seen a few times a day, but not as often as the lock screen or the home screen. Is this likely to be enough, or should you explore other options, such as an expensive smartwatch)? You reread the papers and gain some insights on the first question, but have only limited guidance related to the other questions, beyond the plausible design suggestions made by the authors with varying degrees of confidence.

The above scenario highlights an important issue related to accumulation and translation of evidence in HCI research on behavior change. While HCI researchers use sophisticated design methods to create innovative technologies for supporting behavior change, how those technologies are evaluated limits the ability to accumulate knowledge needed to make evidence-based decisions during the development of new interventions. In particular, details are missing to understand, with precision, how and why our technolo-

Permission to make digital or hard copies of all or part of this work for personal or classroom use is granted without fee provided that copies are not made or distributed for profit or commercial advantage and that copies bear this notice and the full citation on the first page. Copyrights for components of this work owned by others than the author(s) must be honored. Abstracting with credit is permitted. To copy otherwise, or republish, to post on servers or to redistribute to lists, requires prior specific permission and/or a fee. Request permissions from Permissions@acm.org.
CHI 2017, May 06 - 11, 2017, Denver, CO, USA
Copyright is held by the owner/author(s). Publication rights licensed to ACM.
ACM 978-1-4503-4655-9/17/05...$15.00
DOI: http://dx.doi.org/10.1145/3025453.3026013

gies influence human behavior. One core issue is that commonly used study methods, such as simple pre-post designs and between-person randomized controlled trials, can usually not answer the types of subtle questions (like those above) that could sufficiently inform the design of new systems. Another issue is that our empirical findings and design guidelines are rarely specified at a granular enough level to support effective accumulation of evidence across projects about what kinds of interventions work for whom and under what circumstances. And finally, those findings often do not withstand plausible challenges to causal inference and generalizability that come up when researchers from other disciplines try to take up our work or when HCI grant proposals are evaluated for funding.

The purpose of this paper is to articulate the concept of "usable evidence" that aims to address those limitations of the current HCI evidence base and to propose a research process that can be used to generate such evidence. Key contributions of this paper include: 1) delineation of the concept of usable evidence as a desirable target for HCI research that can facilitate more robust knowledge accumulation in HCI and knowledge transfer to other disciplines; 2) specification of a research process for generating usable evidence that fits with the incentives and constraints of HCI research and that melds lessons from HCI with the new evaluation methodologies being developed in behavioral science; (3) the description of an on-going case-study of this approach to ground the discussion in a pragmatic use-case; and (4) an epistemological discussion about the purposes of scientific evidence in HCI research and the ways that our concept of usable evidence addresses those needs.

RELATED WORK

In its aims and approach, the current paper builds on a growing literature in behavioral science and HCI that calls for better evaluations of behavior-change interventions. In HCI, Klasnja et al. [25] and Hekler et al. [18] have argued for the value of interview data for understanding whether behavior-change technologies (BCTs) are working as intended and how user experience and context of use affect the ability of a technology to effectively support the behavior-change process. More recently, Kay et al. [22] have argued for the use of Bayesian statistics as a way to improve the level of quantitative evidence obtained from deployments of technologies, as many field studies that HCI researchers conduct are underpowered to provide high-quality evidence using frequentist methods. The current paper adds to these suggestions by arguing that the use of proximal outcomes in evaluations of BCTs enables HCI researchers to conduct rigorous efficacy evaluations of their systems within resource constraints of HCI field studies.

In behavioral science, the call for better evidence is rooted in the realization that randomized controlled trials provide evidence of limited utility for translating experimental findings into practice [23] and for informing design of more effective interventions [38], especially digital interventions that leverage mobile technology [28,37]. A key response to this challenge has come from "optimization" methods inspired by Linda Collins's multiphase optimization strategy (MOST) [5,6]. MOST emphasizes evaluations that aim to understand functioning of individual intervention components within a complex intervention, in order to enable creation of streamlined interventions that only include components that have been shown effective. While MOST still sees a randomized controlled trial (RCT) of an optimized intervention as the final step in this evaluation pipeline, its biggest impact in behavioral science has been to affirm the notion that researchers should be focusing on opening the "black box" of intervention effectiveness to better understand how interventions work for particular individuals in context. Our paper embraces the emphasis on the evaluation of individual intervention components, and we argue that this emphasis fits well both with the research questions that HCI researchers working on behavior change care about and the resource constraints of HCI research.

MOST studies can be conducted using a range of experimental designs, including factorial and fractional factorial experiments [4,7], SMART trials [30,35], micro-randomized trials [26,31], system ID experiments [17], and single-case experimental designs [11,12,27]. Many of these designs are useful for testing BCTs, and, as we argue later in the paper, some of them (factorial designs, single-case experiments) are very well suited for HCI BCT evaluations.

Another response to the call for better evidence has been the emphasis on understanding the dynamics of behavior change in order to develop more precise behavioral theories [37,39]. Insofar as BCTs embody theoretical constructs hypothesized to activate specific mechanisms of change, the types of studies we are proposing in this paper advance this goal very directly. In fact, our emphasis on articulation of causal pathways is intended to help researchers generate evidence that can be directly used for theory development.

Finally, our paper builds directly on our work on Agile Science [19], which synthesizes a range of these ideas into a framework for effective knowledge generation and sharing. As we argue below, agile science can be of great utility to HCI researchers by providing a process for clearly articulating how technologies that HCI researchers are developing are supposed to function, enabling rigorous evaluation of the ideas underlying these technologies.

TERMINOLOGY

In this section, we introduce key terms that we will be using in this paper, in order to create a shared vocabulary for the discussion of different types of evidence and their uses.

Usable evidence

We define *usable evidence* as empirical findings about the causal effects of BCTs and how those effects vary with individual differences, context of use, and system design. Such findings are "usable" in that they enable designers, researchers, and even end-users to make evidence-based decisions about what design elements to include in new systems for specific user groups and how exactly individual features of a technology should work to maximize its potential to be effective for those users. The applicability of usable evidence is achieved via an explicit focus on discovering how causal effects of individual components of a technology vary with time, in different contexts, and for different people—differences that are usually washed out in studies that aim for "on average" evidence across groups, such as classical randomized controlled trials. As such, usable evidence can be seen as a BCT equivalent of the evidence sought in precision medicine [2] in order to develop treatments finely tailored to individual genotypes.

Intervention idea

An *intervention idea* is an account of how a technology can bring about behavior change. It describes something a technology can do to help people change behavior. Intervention ideas can come at various levels of specificity. They can be based on hunches—rough ideas about what might work to produce desired outcomes—that come from formative work with target users or anecdotal experience (e.g., helping people remember they feel good when they exercise might make them want to exercise more), or they can be formalized hypotheses with a great deal of empirical support (e.g., self-monitoring daily step count can help people walk more). The process we describe later in the paper is intended, in part, to help researchers better specify their intervention ideas and develop them from hunches to hypotheses that can be formally tested in empirical studies.

Intervention components

By *intervention component* we mean a concrete piece of functionality of a technology that enacts a specific intervention idea for supporting behavior change. Many intervention components implement well-supported intervention ideas (e.g., goal-setting, planning, feedback on progress), such as the behavior-change techniques taxonomized by Susan Michie and colleagues [1,33] through an expert-consensus-based review of components used in complex behavior-change interventions. Other components, like some developed by HCI researchers, implement novel intervention ideas. Either way, as concrete pieces of code, intervention components include the many design decisions that have to be made to translate abstract ideas into a working system. For instance, a goal-setting component of a physical-activity intervention incorporates decisions about units used to set goals (e.g., step count vs. minutes of activity), time frame (daily vs. weekly), a choice of default goals, and various design details of the user interaction of setting a goal (where in the application goal-setting is done, how it is presented, etc.). It is such intervention components, as implemented, that are directly evaluated in individual studies of BCTs.

Distal and proximal outcomes

Every BCT is intended to help individuals attain some long-term goal: lose weight, increase physical activity, manage stress, improve medication adherence, or improve outcomes such as reduced cardiovascular disease, diabetes, or cancer risk. Such outcomes are *distal outcomes*, and they are the kinds of things that are evaluated in RCTs to determine if an intervention is effective. Yet, insofar as they happen, such changes in behavior come about gradually and over time, and they are often due both to the effects of the intervention and other factors, such as, for instance, exogenous shocks (e.g., seeing a friend have a heart attack).

An intervention contributes to the behavior-change process via specific intervention components, each of which is designed to support behavior change through a particular mechanism of action. The direct outcomes of the provision of an intervention component—effects that link the component delivery to the intervention's distal outcomes—are the component's *proximal outcomes*. They represent elements in the causal pathway that the intervention uses to facilitate a desired change in the distal outcomes.

Sometimes, proximal outcomes are just small-scale versions of the intervention's distal outcomes. For example, a proximal outcome for a planning component in a physical activity intervention that helps users plan when and where they will be active the next day might be a single bout of physical activity—a micro component of a habit of being active. Other times, proximal outcomes are different than distal outcomes. For instance, there is a fair bit of literature showing that social support can help individuals struggling with substance use remain sober [16]. An intervention targeting substance use might have a component that encourages communication with sobriety-supporting family and friends. A proximal outcome for such a component might be the number of daily interactions with sobriety-supporting social network.

What's important to note is that the proximal outcome is a desired outcome of a single provision of an intervention component—of a single session of planning, single delivery of a suggestion to be active, single reminder, and so on. Proximal outcomes are the most direct changes that an intervention component is intended to create, changes which, over time, should create the more global changes in behavior and health as defined by distal outcomes. As such, proximal outcomes are key to understanding if an intervention is working as intended because they allow researchers to test individual branches of the causal pathway through which the intervention is hypothesized to change behavior and distal health outcomes. We will return to this point.

Finally, although the distinction is not clear-cut, there are two types of proximal outcomes: behavioral and mechanistic. *Behavioral proximal outcomes* are the types of proximal outcomes we have been discussing—bouts of activity, reaching out to a friend, engaging in craving-surfing, etc.—concrete behaviors that intervention components encourage users to do, which, in turn, move them toward the desired outcome(s). *Mechanistic proximal outcomes* refer to the physiological and psychological changes that intervention components aim to induce, which mediate the behavior-change process. For instance, a reminder to engage in a breathing exercise might be intended to reduce stress, which, in turn, might help a smoker resist lighting a cigarette. A stress sensor, such as cStress [21], can allow researchers to check if sending the reminder affects the user's stress level and, thus, to test the assumption that stress reduction mediates smoking cessation.

Causal pathway

A causal pathway refers to a diagram of the sequence of changes—causes and effects—that are hypothesized to link provision of an intervention to its desired distal outcomes. More simply, a causal pathway is a way to visualize how the intervention is intended to work. In behavioral science, causal pathways are often represented as directed graphs—boxes and arrows showing what is changing what. They represent various effects that each intervention component is hypothesized to have and how those effects influence other downstream outcomes, and, ultimately, desired distal outcomes. Drawing a causal pathway forces one to clearly articulate effects of and relationships among different parts of an intervention, making it possible to check whether the intervention, as conceived, has a hope of working. Causal pathways also enable researchers to design studies that can assess postulated effects and relationships, improving the evidence that results from system evaluations.

Causal pathway diagrams can—and should—include both effects on behaviors and the psychosocial and physiological mechanisms postulated to mediate them, as well as the effects that different parts of the interventions might have on user engagement with the intervention. In addition, causal pathways can help specify factors such as context (e.g., weather), traits (e.g., novelty-seeker), and states of the individual (e.g., being stressed) that might moderate the influence of the intervention on proximal and distal outcomes. Thus, causal pathways are key for developing hypotheses that can be tested in system deployments to determine to what extent the effectiveness of intervention components and systems generalizes [20].

FROM A HUNCH TO A TESTABLE INTERVENTION

As we alluded above, the kind of evidence we are advocating is based on careful experimental tests of intervention components that embody clearly articulated intervention ideas and that have clearly articulated outcomes. But we often start with intervention ideas that are far vaguer, ideas that are based on designer intuitions, hints from formative work with target users, or ideas that emerged from reading the literature. How do we go from such hunches about what we think might work to intervention ideas that are fleshed out enough to be implemented and tested with real users?

To answer this question, we draw on our work on Agile Science [19], a set of methodologies and principles intended to improve knowledge generation and sharing in behavior-change sciences. In particular, a part of the process is called the *Generate Phase*, which is a set of iterative activities that researchers can do to develop their early intervention ideas into testable intervention components with well-specified mechanisms and outcomes. In this section, we provide an outline of the part of that process that targets specification of intervention ideas and outcomes (see [19] for other activities in the generate phase, including user-centered design and simulations studies). In the next section, we illustrate this process with a case study of the development of a walking intervention.

Hunch articulation

The generate phase prototyping work begins with a "hunch," articulated by completing the phrase: "Based on theory and/or understanding potential users, I'm not sure, but I think that (fill in intervention idea) will influence (fill in behavioral outcome of interest)." "I'm not sure" is an important modifier on confidence. If one is sure that the intervention idea will work (or that it won't), then there is no need to test it. Notions about the intervention idea will often come from preparatory work reviewing theory and empirical evidence in the scientific literature, or engaging with users through observation or interviews. With preparatory work complete, researchers can begin to link the intervention idea to behavioral and mechanistic outcomes that the intervention idea is hypothesized to affect.

Niche specification

The initial hunch articulation will usually involve a variety of unstated "niche" specifics. To explore the niche of an intervention idea, researchers should clarify for whom they are designing (e.g. smartphone users, heart attack survivors, Phoenix residents, etc.). Similarly important is whom the intervention idea is not targeting (e.g. highly physically active people, people in a specific climate, people whose culture is mismatched with the intervention, etc.). Beyond specifying the expected users of an intervention, the setting—both in terms of the anticipated context of use and planned temporal patterns of intervention delivery—can help to make an intervention's niche explicit. Two important reasons for specifying the niche in this way is (1) to begin generating information about individual- and contextual-level variables that might affect intervention use and effectiveness, and (2) to generate a list of feasibility checks for potential implementations/prototypes of the intervention idea that is being developed.

Causal pathway mapping

After expressing a hunch and defining its niche, the specific relationship between an intervention idea and its behavioral and mechanistic outcomes can be explored through causal pathway mapping. As we discussed, a causal pathway is a visual representation of the cause and effect chain(s) that link an intervention with its outcomes. This exercise helps clarify exactly *how* an intervention idea is presumed to impact its proximal outcome(s) and, through them, its intended distal outcome(s). Causal pathway mapping begins by listing various outcomes that the intervention idea might affect, as well as drawing on prior literature and niche specification, factors that might influence the impact of the intervention of these outcomes. Outcomes and moderators are then arranged in a directed graph that describes how they relate to one another. For instance, the graph can show that sending someone a suggestion to take a walk has steps over the next 30 minutes as a proximal behavioral outcome, but that this outcome might be dependent on the person's busyness level and weather. The graph could also show that user annoyance (from being pinged) is another potential, albeit undesired, outcome of the walking suggestions. At this stage, researchers should try to be as comprehensive in specifying the causal pathway as their knowledge allows. This allows the causal pathway to become a visual representation of the beliefs about exactly how the intervention is supposed to work (or might not work), which enables generation of hypotheses about the intervention's operation that can be formally tested in empirical studies.

Hunch revision

Mapping the causal pathway will likely evolve the intervention idea, which should be updated in the hunch statement. This is also an opportunity to decide on the primary proximal outcome. When the hunch is first written down, it is usually in terms of a distal (or vague) behavioral outcome. Causal pathway mapping helps identify relevant proximal outcomes that would be more directly influenced by the intervention idea. The revised hunch should reflect these updates in the understanding of the intervention idea and the main outcomes that the idea is intended to impact.

Variation generation

Once the hunch is reasonably well specified, researchers proceed to variation generation—the activity of generating various ways that the intervention idea can affect its proximal outcome. We have found that this works well in the form of group brainstorming, where team members rapidly write on post-it notes, individually first and then collectively, all ideas that come to mind for different forms that the intervention idea can take. Once these ideas are generated, they need to be categorized. Many of the ideas will have the same theme or mechanism, and they can be grouped together. Our preliminary experience with this method has generally produced three to five distinct categories of ideas. The groupings are contender intervention-idea variations, and researchers can then decide to focus on just one of them (thus narrowing how they understand their intervention idea), or they can decide to compare different variations—maybe because they are interested in their relative effectiveness. Either way, the ideas generated in this activity begin to concretize the intervention idea by articulating it in forms that are potentially implementable.

Prototype specification

Building on prior work on parallel development and prototyping [14], there is great value in testing multiple variations of an intervention idea, particularly in an early stage of the process when the goal is to discover which intervention ideas might be potentially useful. To test these variations, they need to be implemented. By a *prototype* we refer to an implementation of an intervention idea that can be tested with real users. Typically, a variation of an intervention idea can be implemented in a number of ways, and resource constraints, feasibility, and interest in particular design aspects will guide how a researcher decides to implement the ideas he/she wants to test. On one end of the spectrum, a prototype can be minimal—a bare-bones implementation that is purely designed to assess whether there is any value at all to the intervention idea that the researcher is considering. For new intervention ideas for which there is little prior literature on which a researcher can draw, testing of such bare-bones prototypes can provide an efficient way to assess whether it is worth investing any more time and resources on the idea (see [13] for advertising probes that are at this level). On the other end of the spectrum, an idea can be implemented as a refined component within a complex system. In either case, once prototypes are created, they enable the researcher to test whether, for whom, and in what contexts these implementations of the idea that the researcher is investigating have their intended effects. As we will shortly see, these kinds of tests are at the core of the concept of usable evidence.

Specification of the experimental design

The final step of the process is a clear delineation of the experimental design that can be used to efficiently test aspects of the causal pathway via the prototypes. There are several options available for this, which we discuss in the Towards Usable Evidence section. For more information on various experimental designs, see [8].

STEP GOAL VARIABILITY: A CASE STUDY OF THE GENERATE-PHASE PROTOTPYING PROCESS

The process we described in the previous section is likely to be too abstract on first reading. To make the process easier to understand, in this section we provide a case study of how the Generate Phase prototyping process was used to develop an intervention idea of using goal variability to help individuals increase their physical activity.

The idea behind this case study emerged in the course of testing of an Android mHealth application, which encouraged regular walking via an adaptive daily step goal and financial incentives for meeting this goal. During exit interviews in the study, participants indicated that they enjoyed that their step goals changed each day, raising the possibility that introduction of variation might be a meaningful way to increase walking behavior. We developed this hunch of an intervention idea using the process described in the last section. The process proceeded as follows:

Initial hunch: "Based on theory and understanding potential users, I'm not sure, but I think that step-goal variability (intervention idea) will help people walk more (behavioral outcome of interest)."

Niche specification: The research team was specifically targeting higher SES, overweight, sedentary, middle-aged adults who used smartphones. The team was not designing for adults with high current activity levels, children, or those with a health condition that might interfere with their ability to walk for exercise. Recruitment was planned to occur through a medium-sized consulting firm and would include employees working remotely. Employees were described as holding a mostly sedentary job, with some employees having access to a sit-to-stand desk.

Causal pathway: The direct relationship between step goal variability and walking behavior was specified visually as:

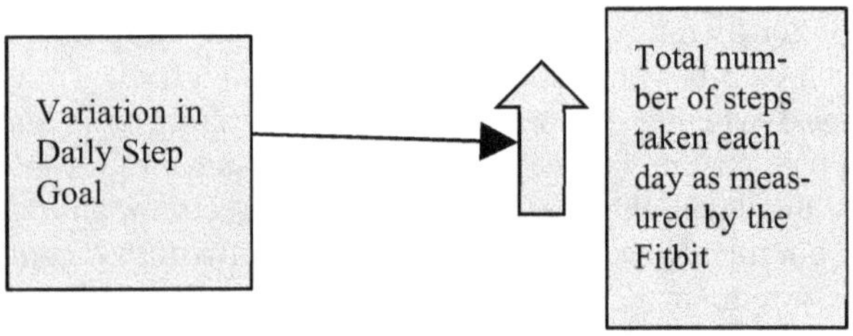

This pathway was hypothesized to be mediated by the following factors:

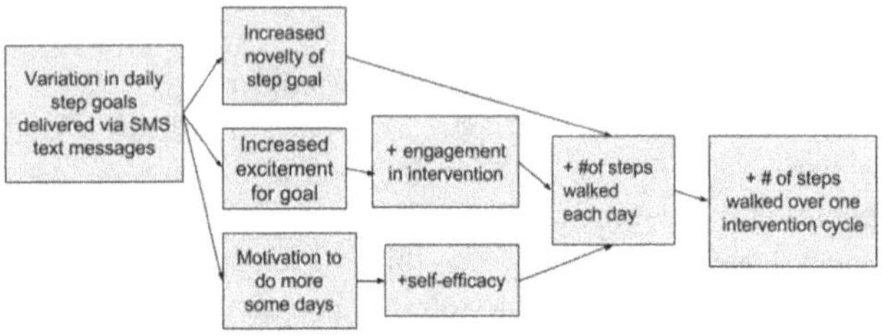

Proximal outcomes: From this model the proximal outcomes were identified as: (1) an increase in the number of steps walked each day, as measured by Fitbit; (2) satisfaction with and enjoyment in the intervention component, as measured by a weekly Qualtrics survey; and (3) an increase in the total number of steps walked over one intervention cycle (one week).

Variations: In this exercise the research team focused on different ways they could vary a step goal to help the population of interest walk more and achieve the target proximal outcomes identified above. Initial brainstorming yielded over 20 different ideas for varying a daily step goal. For example, "graded increasing goals," "surprise days of rest," "one day per week of an extreme goal," "contextually tailored goal," etc. From this list, the research team organized the ideas into three contender groups that represented distinct ways to vary a daily step goal: (1) epic goals; (2) user choice goal; and (3) high amplitude goals.

Prototypes: Due to resource constraints, the research team decided to implement the idea of goal variability via text messages sent to participants each day of the study. Furthermore, the team decided to test all three variations on the variable-goal idea, and it further defined how each variation would function. Intervention variations were defined as follows: *Epic goals*: let user plan for an "epic" goal—defined as more steps than they have ever walked on a single day in the previous month. *User choice goal*: let user choose their own step goal on one weekday and one weekend day. *High amplitude goals:* user receives some atypically high goals and some atypically low goals.

At the end of this process, the research team ended up with prototypes of three versions of the variable-goal idea that could be tested in the field to (1) validate the idea that goal variability could be useful for encouraging walking; (2) compare whether one version/design of this idea works better than others; and (3) assess how this intervention idea impacts different types of outcomes both on average and over time. From this, we developed an experiment (a variant of a single-case design called a Latin Square), which allowed us to study the concept of goal variability. As we'll see next, studies that can answer such questions are central to the concept of usable evidence.

WHAT IS EVIDENCE FOR?

Research is, ultimately, a form of communication. We build our work on the work of others and hope that others, in turn, will benefit from what we have done. As such, to maximize the impact of our work, the evidence we should aim to create through our research should be in the form that makes it maximally useful to others, both in our own field and in related disciplines that would be interested in building on or using our work. In other words, we should aim to create *usable evidence*, evidence that most readily helps other researchers pursue their research goals. In this section, we outline the chief forms that these goals take, and their implications for the forms of evidence we should be striving to generate to support those goals.

Adapting intervention ideas from prior research

An important form of work is adapting intervention ideas previously deployed for new interventions. The scenario that we started this paper with, on using a glanceable display for stress management, is an example of this research goal. In HCI research, adoption of intervention ideas from prior work usually involves introducing some form of novelty (design, technical underpinnings, etc.), but the question a researcher is asking is more general: can I use intervention idea A, potentially with modifications, for context X, where context X might differ from the context in which A was originally used in terms of the behavior, population, circumstances of use, and/or technological constraints?

To answer this question with reasonable confidence, a researcher needs to know several pieces of information: (1) What mechanism of change does A embody, and is that mechanism applicable for the context in which the new intervention would be used? (2) Did the intervention component that implemented intervention idea A have an effect, and if so, for what outcomes did it work? (3) If the intervention component produced an effect, what were the dynamics of the effect, and are those dynamics acceptable for the new context for the intervention? (for instance, reminders that work for a couple of weeks but then slowly stop working might be perfectly fine for increasing adherence to antibiotics, but would not be suitable for adherence to birth control pills); (4) Did idea A work particularly well/poorly for particular types of people or in particular contexts, and how does that translate to the population and circumstances where the new intervention needs to be used? And (5) were there evaluations of different versions or designs of intervention idea A? If so, what does the evidence suggest about how the new intervention may need to be designed to maximize its effectiveness? For instance, do reminders presented as coming from the clinic work differently than reminders that appear to come from a consumer application?

Developing new intervention ideas

Although adoption of intervention ideas from prior work is a common research strategy in behavior-change science, within HCI an arguably even more important research task is creation of new intervention ideas—invention of new ways in which technology can support behavior change. As we saw, new intervention ideas often start as hunches, obtained from formative work or anecdotal evidence, that something might work. Such new intervention ideas do not build on prior literature as directly as adaptations of existing intervention ideas do, but prior evidence is still useful. Most new intervention ideas implement some known mechanism of change, which has been previously tested. Understanding this evidence can help to better define—and design—the new intervention idea. A researcher wants to understand the kinds of effects this mechanism of change is likely to produce, their temporal dynamics, and differences in effects previously found for interventions that implemented this mechanism differently. Have there been implementations that have worked particularly well or particularly poorly? If so, what was distinctive about those implementations, and what does that mean about the intervention idea that the researcher is developing? The clearer the evidence from prior work related to these questions, the easier it is for the researcher to develop the new idea from the start in a way that increases the likelihood of success.

Optimizing interventions for efficacy evaluations

Although HCI researchers usually focus on early-stage evaluations, for intervention ideas to have maximum impact (such as uptake in healthcare), they need to be incorporated into systems that can be tested for efficacy for distal health outcomes, and, if found efficacious, made available more broadly. As Collins et al. have argued [3,6], the time and cost of randomized controlled trials used to robustly establish intervention efficacy only make sense for interventions that have been optimized to only include components that have shown preliminary evidence of efficacy in early-stage studies. To make decisions about which components to include and how to combine them in a complex intervention, researchers need good prior evidence about how each component they are considering works. Results from studies that assessed various versions of the components they are considering enable intervention scientists to incorporate in an intervention they plan to deploy in a large trial the most promising versions of only those intervention components for which they have strong preliminary evidence.

Finding limits of generalization for change mechanisms

For behavioral scientists, questions of generalizability are often just as important as development of effective interventions. They are interested in understanding the change process at a more general level, which means that they are interested in understanding mechanisms that facilitate behavior change and the conditions in which those mechanisms work. But mechanisms cannot be studied in the abstract. They can only be studied via interventions that embody them. As such, robust evidence about the effects of individual intervention components with clearly articulated underlying mechanisms is paramount for furthering our understanding of the process of behavior change and its drivers; and the more granular the evidence, the better. Knowing that a planning component of a physical-activity intervention had an effect on increasing activity is good, but knowing how this effect changed over time, whether the effect was greater for certain types of people (e.g., for people high in conscientiousness), and whether the effect was limited to certain contexts (e.g., when planning was done when the participants were not tired) is better. When such evidence is available for different interventions that implement the same hypothesized mechanism of change, researchers can systematically synthesize the literature to uncover conditions under which each mechanism operates [20]. Such knowledge not only increases our understanding of how the behavior change process works, but also provides a guide for the development of new interventions, as components that leverage a particular mechanism can be designed to be provided only to people and in contexts in which they are most likely to be effective.

TOWARD USABLE EVIDENCE

The research goals we outlined in the last section have much in common in terms of the nature of the evidence that these research activities require. This evidence shares the following characteristics: (1) it focuses on individual intervention components rather than whole systems; (2) it focuses on showing component-specific effects—namely, effects that are directly linked to the provision of each intervention component; and (3) it requires granularity in terms of temporal dynamics and effect moderation. All three of these requirements, we want to suggest, can be achieved by focusing on assessment of proximal outcomes.

In this section, we describe how the focus on proximal outcomes can allow HCI researchers to create robust evidence about causal effects of technologies they are developing, evidence that is well suited to support the full range of research goals outlined in the last section. Just as importantly, we suggest that HCI researchers can do this within the time and resource constraints of typical HCI projects, without the need to recruit hundreds or thousands of individuals or run studies that last many months or years.

Proximal outcomes as chief evaluation targets

As we described in the section on terminology, proximal outcomes are direct behavioral or mechanistic outcomes that an intervention component is designed to have. Importantly, they are outcomes that, if present, could be observable for a single intervention provision, such as a single session of planning or an interaction with a support group.[1] Proximal outcomes are inherently *short-term*—they unfold over minutes, hours, or days, rather than months or years. The accumulation of such outcomes over time creates desired patterns of long-term behavior and health outcomes. Proximal outcomes themselves, however, are those patterns' behavioral, psychological, and physiological building blocks that can be observed at much shorter time-scales.

The short-term nature of proximal outcomes provides three key advantages for HCI evaluations. First, proximal outcomes can be assessed in relatively short studies lasting weeks or months. Since they can be assessed longitudinally, even a short 6-week study can produce 40+ data points per person for a proximal outcome that is assessed daily, such as daily step count or caloric intake. For proximal outcomes of intervention components that can be delivered several times a day, such as reminders to measure blood pressure, this number will be much higher. This means that HCI researchers can assess effects of their interventions on proximal outcomes with good power within the time and resource constraints of typical HCI projects, something that is rarely possible for more distal behavior-change outcomes.

Second, the short-term nature of the outcomes and their repeated measurement means that evaluations can assess not only whether a component has an effect at all, but how that effect changes over time. The dynamics of effects of different types of intervention components and their designs is a key type of data that HCI researchers can contribute to the broader behavior-change science, as the data can be interpreted in the light of rich qualitative evidence that HCI researchers are used to collecting in their studies.

Third, since many BCTs are used in different environments, proximal outcomes will reflect any differences in the impact that those technologies have in these different contexts. Interventions that record contextual information at times when individual components are provided or used enable modeling of the influence that the environment and the person's state have on intervention effectiveness, and how that influence changes over time. Proximal outcomes and context-aware technology thus enable a genuinely new form of evidence about conditions under which individual intervention components work, providing a deeper level of understanding of behavior change processes than was possible.

In summary, focus on proximal outcomes would provide HCI researchers a way to conduct rigorous quantitative evaluations of their novel interventions, contributing both to HCI and broader behavior-change science, all within the resource constraints of typical HCI research.

Looking for causes: Study designs for causal inference

Ultimately, a key question that all developers of BCTs care about is whether their intervention produced the desired effect. This is fundamentally a *causal* question [36], as it asks whether any observed changes in behavior are actually due to the intervention rather than to some other factor. Insofar as behavior change happens, it almost always comes about from a confluence of factors that might include changes in social relationships (a smoker starts dating a non-smoker), exogenous shocks (having a baby or a friend having a heart attack), changes in the physical environment (moving to a more walkable part of town) and so on. In traditional randomized controlled trials, researchers use between-subject random assignment to "balance out" such factors and thus increase confidence that any differences in outcome between the control arm and intervention arm was in fact due to the intervention, and not some other confounder that researchers didn't measure. Use of proximal outcomes, paired with appropriate study designs, enables HCI researchers to apply similarly rigorous casual inference to early-stage evaluations of novel technologies as well. Although a detailed review of experimental designs is beyond the scope of this paper, we briefly review two types of design, factorial experiments and single-case designs, that fit within the constraints of HCI research and can be used to generate evidence of the kind that we argue the field needs.

Factorial designs [4,7] are extensions of the RCT paradigm where intervention provision is randomized to support causal inference. Traditional factorial designs use between-subject randomization to allocate each participant to receive a version of the intervention that contains only certain "levels" of each component. Level might be the presence or absence of a component, different intensity or type of the component and so on. For instance, some participants would get reminders to plan their activity and others would not; some participants would get a daily step goal and others would not. In a factorial design, multiple components can be tested simultaneously, and participants are randomized into cells representing combinations of component levels (e.g., 2x2 cell design for a goals on/off and planning on/off study). Comparing participants in all cells that received one level of a particular component with participants in all cells that received another level of that component provides a way to assess causal effects for that component. In a balanced design (like our 2x2 example), this means that the same number of participants is used to assess effects of each component. The use of proximal outcomes makes traditional factorial designs more efficient, since repeated measurement of these outcomes increases power.

Micro-randomized trials (MRTs) [26,31] are a form of sequential factorial design in which components that can be repeatedly administered (e.g., medication reminders) are

[1] Note that this requirement means that proximal outcomes and intervention components might need to be defined in tandem. If, say, motivational text messages are intended to increase self-efficacy, but changes in self-efficacy can only be seen weekly, the intervention component might be several text messages over a week rather than a single text.

randomized, for each participant, each time that they can be provided. For example, every morning each participant in a walking study could be randomized to receive or not receive a daily step goal. Insofar as the component that is being micro-randomized has a proximal outcome that can be observed both when the component is provided and when it's not provided (e.g., daily step count), the difference in the proximal outcome between all times when the component was provided and all times when the component was not provided gives an estimate of the causal effect of that intervention component. Since in micro-randomized trials this contrast can pool across both between-person and within-person differences in outcome, MRTs require far fewer participants than trials that rely on between-person randomization alone [31]. Studies that last two to three months can often be done with as few as 30 to 40 people. A sample size calculator for MRTs is available at: https://jisun.shinyapps.io/SampleSizeCalculator/

What makes factorial designs particularly powerful for HCI research, is that between-subject and within-subject randomization can be combined in the same study to estimate effects of several components. Some components, like glanceable displays, are either part of a system or they are not; they cannot be given and taken away repeatedly over time. Other "pull components" that individuals access at will, such as educational resources, have the same property. Such components, if they need to be tested, can be randomized at baseline. Other components, such as reminders, messages of encouragement, etc. are inherently designed to be delivered repeatedly over time. Such components can be sequentially randomized. By using such a factorial design, HCI researchers can assess causal effects of their technologies far more rigorously than is possible with observational methods typically used in HCI field studies.

Single-case experimental designs [11,12] provide a different methodology for causal inference by systematically varying when participants have access to an intervention. For instance, after a week of baseline, participants in a walking study might be sent step goals for a week, after which the goals would be withdrawn for another week (often called an A/B/A or reversal design). A researcher would then look to see if the participants' daily steps are different for the week when they received the goals than the weeks when they were not given goals. Such designs provide an efficient way of initially assessing whether an intervention has an effect, often with just a handful of participants (as "control" occurs within an individual, not between). While single-case studies have traditionally evaluated whole interventions, and not individual intervention components, their efficiency makes them a great candidate for doing exploratory studies of simple systems that only include one component that the researcher is developing (such as our goal variability example). Such quick-and-dirty evaluations can provide initial evidence for "is anything here?" questions—providing researchers with a check on whether the intervention idea they are considering is worth exploring further.

Types of evidence

Factorial experiments (and, when thoughtfully used, single case designs), combined with measurement of proximal outcomes, can help generate evidence that is an excellent fit for the research goals we outlined above. They allow researchers to understand functioning of individual intervention components in their systems at a very granular level, allowing them to answer four types of questions:

Is the component having an effect at all?

The most basic type of evidence is gathered by assessing whether, on average, there is a difference in the proximal outcome when the component is present vs. when it's absent, averaging over the duration of the study and other factors. The result, a marginal main effect, tells us if there is any impact of the component on its proximal outcome. In the case of our example of daily step goals, the main effect would tell us whether individuals walk more, on average, when they have a step goal vs. not. Contrasts between multiple versions or designs of a component can also be assessed. Insofar as a component has multiple relevant proximal outcomes, an effect on each can be estimated.

Does the effect of the component change over time?

Since proximal effects are repeatedly measured, factorial studies can also assess if the effect of a component is changing over time. It might be that step goals have a large effect initially, but that this effect slowly dissipates as participants internalize the step goal. Or it might be that participants become habituated to reminders to measure their blood pressure and they stop paying attention to them. This kind of change in the effect over time can be modeled due to the short-term nature of proximal outcomes.

For whom is the intervention working?

A common theme in behavioral science literature is that there is a great deal of heterogeneity of intervention effects, and that they don't work equally well for everyone [20]. Assessing how component effects are moderated by age, gender, or other baseline characteristics thought to be important can create an evidence base that can help researchers tailor interventions to individuals by providing them only with the components or specific designs of those components that are most likely to work for them. For instance, occasionally giving someone a very high activity goal might work well for high novelty seekers (people who are adventurous), but it might turn off low novelty seekers who might do worse if an intervention tries to overly challenge them. Like contextual moderation, which we describe next, moderation by baseline characteristics is a key component of understanding the range of conditions under which an intervention is effective. A thoughtfully selected set of baseline measures could help HCI researchers contribute to this evidence base even in very early-stage evaluations of novel technologies.

In what contexts does the intervention work?

Finally, focus on proximal effects provides an opportunity to assess how the effect of an intervention component is influenced by the context in which the component is used or provided, both in terms of the environment (location, time of day, etc.) and the person's own state (e.g., stress level). It might be that having a step goal is mostly effective when participants have not walked much on the previous day, or when they are in a new location and they are not able to follow regular routines. Or, as we found in a recent study of one of our own systems, it might be that planning of physical activity for the next day works, for sedentary adults, only on weekdays and not on weekends. For individuals who perceive physical activity as an obligation, weekends are, apparently, a time when they want to get a break both from their jobs and from needing to be active. This level of evidence makes it possible to deeply tailor interventions not only to person-level characteristics but also to contexts, providing interventions only when they are most likely to be effective [34]. Across all components of an intervention, such contextual tailoring allows us to both increase effectiveness of our technologies and to reduce user burden that can result from having to engage with an intervention at times and places when its support is not needed or wanted.

These four types of evidence can greatly enrich the granularity with which HCI researchers understand the technologies they are developing and can help to flesh out the types of questions raised in the introduction. When triangulated with qualitative data, such quantitative assessments of intervention effects can go a long way toward helping us understand how and why BCTs function to help individuals make desired changes in their behavior.

Finally, it is important to note that these four types of evidence provide insights about functioning of intervention components *as they were designed and implemented.* In other words, these evaluations directly assess concrete intervention components contained in concrete systems, not the abstract mechanisms of change that are supposed to underlie them. There are two implications of this: first, this means that different designs of an intervention idea can be directly compared by including them as levels of a component in a factorial experiment. For instance, if a researcher wants to compare two designs of a medication reminder (e.g., how it's presented on the screen or framing of the language), these different designs can be assessed by sequentially randomizing them in a micro-randomized trial. If variants are chosen to reflect important points in the design space for a particular intervention idea, such studies can greatly advance our knowledge about which design elements matter, when they matter, and for whom they matter.

Second, as the evidence of the kind we described here accumulates, it becomes possible to synthesize across studies to assess functioning of more general intervention ideas, such as glanceable displays, as the literature would contain results for various forms of such displays. Similarly, results from studies of systems that include different intervention components that rely on the same underlying mechanisms of change (e.g., priming) could be synthesized to gain deeper insights about the functioning of those mechanisms. Both types of synthesis can greatly increase our understanding of the behavior-change process and how to effectively bring about change through technology.

DISCUSSION AND CONCLUSIONS

In this paper we have argued that HCI researchers who develop and evaluate BCTs should adopt an evaluation strategy that focuses on assessment of proximal outcomes of individual intervention components. This strategy has three key advantages: (1) it provides a rigorous way to evaluate efficacy of individual components of a BCT using the types of studies that HCI researchers are accustomed to running; (2) It connects HCI to other behavior-change sciences by helping HCI researchers clearly articulate intervention ideas and mechanisms of action that their technologies embody, making it easier to interpret their findings and to synthesize them with other evidence to better understand the functioning of the constructs and mechanisms on which behavior-change interventions are based; and (3) it provides a way of rigorously assessing comparative effectiveness of different designs of the same intervention idea, creating a much stronger evidence base for design guidelines.

By enabling rigorous evaluations during early-stage technology development, the approach we outlined allows HCI researchers to focus on inventing novel intervention ideas and novel ways to design intervention components, while at the same time creating robust evidence about whether these new ideas and designs are having their intended effects. As the evidence accumulates across studies, the field will be enriched with new intervention strategies that have been found to be effective, as well as with robust knowledge about which design aspects matter when particular intervention strategies, such as self-monitoring of food, are implemented. Insofar as novel intervention components are found to be effective in preliminary studies, HCI researchers could release reusable versions of those components as intervention modules that other researchers can use in their projects [19]. For behavioral scientists who have little design expertise, gaining access to well-designed intervention modules would be a huge win; for HCI researchers, the use of their modules by others would provide broader impact for their work and enable their designs to be further studied to understand more deeply for whom and in what contexts those designs are effective. Finally, as the approach we advocated relies on the ability to measure proximal outcomes, HCI researchers could contribute by creating innovative ways of capturing, in passive or low-burden ways, a range of behavioral and mechanistic outcomes, thus advancing the ability of behavioral-change scientists to more deeply study and understand the processes that make human beings tick.

ACKNOWLEDGEMENTS

This work was supported by funding from the Robert Wood Johnson Foundation (PI: Hekler, 71995) and from the National Heart Lung, and Blood Institute (PI: Klasnja, 1R01HL125440).

REFERENCES

1. Abraham, Charles and Michie, Susan.. 2008. A taxonomy of behavior change techniques used in interventions. *Health Psychol* 27, 3: 379-87. http://doi.org/10.1037/0278-6133.27.3.379

2. Collins, Francis S and Varmus, Harold.. 2015. A new initiative on precision medicine. *New England Journal of Medicine* 372, 9: 793-795.

3. Collins, Linda M, Chakraborty, Bibhas, Murphy, Susan A and Strecher, Victor.. 2009. Comparison of a phased experimental approach and a single randomized clinical trial for developing multicomponent behavioral interventions. *Clinical Trials* 6, 1: 5-15.

4. Collins, Linda M, Dziak, John J and Li, Runze.. 2009. Design of experiments with multiple independent variables: A resource management perspective on complete and reduced factorial designs. *Psychological Methods* 14, 3: 202-224. http://doi.org/10.1037/a0015826

5. Collins, Linda M, Murphy, Susan A, Nair, Vijay N and Strecher, Victor J.. 2005. A strategy for optimizing and evaluating behavioral interventions. *Annals of Behavioral Medicine* 30, 1: 65-73.

6. Collins, Linda M, Murphy, Susan A and Strecher, Victor.. 2007. The multiphase optimization strategy (MOST) and the sequential multiple assignment randomized trial (SMART): new methods for more potent eHealth interventions. *Am J Prev Med* 32, 5 Suppl: S112-8. http://doi.org/10.1016/j.amepre.2007.01.022

7. Collins, Linda M., Dziak, John J., Kugler, Kari C. and Trail, Jessica B.. 2014. Factorial Experiments: Efficient Tools for Evaluation of Intervention Components. *American Journal of Preventive Medicine* 47, 4: 498-504. http://doi.org/10.1016/j.amepre.2014.06.021

8. Consolvo, Sunny, Bentley, Frank and Hekler, Eric B.. 2017. *Mobile User Research: A Practical Guide.* Morgan & Claypool Publisher, Williston, VT .

9. Consolvo, Sunny, Klasnja, Predrag, McDonald, David W, Avrahami, Daniel, Froehlich, Jon, LeGrand, Louis, Libby, Ryan, Mosher, Keith and Landay, James A.. 2008. Flowers or a robot army?: encouraging awareness & activity with personal, mobile displays. In *Proceedings of the 10th international conference on Ubiquitous computing*, 54-63.

10. Consolvo, Sunny, McDonald, David W, Toscos, Tammy, Chen, Mike Y, Froehlich, Jon, Harrison, Beverly, Klasnja, Predrag, LaMarca, Anthony, LeGrand, Louis, Libby, Ryan, Smith, Ian and Landay, James A.. 2008. Activity sensing in the wild: a field trial of UbiFit garden. In *Proceeding of the twenty-sixth annual SIGCHI conference on Human factors in computing systems*, 1797-1806.

11. Dallery, Jesse, Cassidy, Rachel N and Raiff, Bethany R.. 2013. Single-Case Experimental Designs to Evaluate Novel Technology-Based Health Interventions. *Journal of Medical Internet Research* 15, 2: e22. http://doi.org/10.2196/jmir.2227

12. Dallery, Jesse and Raiff, Bethany R.. 2014. Optimizing behavioral health interventions with single-case designs: from development to dissemination. *Transl Behav Med* 4, 3: 290-303. http://doi.org/10.1007/s13142-014-0258-z

13. Dow, Steven.. 2016. Probe to Learn, Probe to Design. *interactions* 23, 4: 22-23. http://doi.org/10.1145/2931079

14. Dow, Steven P, Glassco, Alana, Kass, Jonathan, Schwarz, Melissa, Schwartz, Daniel L and Klemmer, Scott R.. 2010. Parallel Prototyping Leads to Better Design Results, More Divergence, and Increased Self-efficacy. *ACM Trans. Comput.-Hum. Interact* 17, 4: 18:1-18:24. http://doi.org/10.1145/1879831.1879836

15. Froehlich, Jon, Dillahunt, Tawanna, Klasnja, Predrag, Mankoff, Jennifer, Consolvo, Sunny, Harrison, Beverly and Landay, James A.. 2009. UbiGreen: investigating a mobile tool for tracking and supporting green transportation habits. In *Proceedings of the 27th international conference on Human factors in computing systems*, 1043-1052.

16. Havassy, B E, Hall, S M and Wasserman, D A.. 1991. Social support and relapse: commonalities among alcoholics, opiate users, and cigarette smokers. *Addict Behav* 16, 5: 235-46.

17. Hekler, E B, Buman, M P, Poothakandiyil, N, Rivera, D E, Dzierzewski, J M, Aiken Morgan, A, McCrae, C S, Roberts, B L, Marsiske, M and Giacobbi, P R.. 2013. Exploring Behavioral Markers of Long-Term Physical Activity Maintenance: A Case Study of System Identification Modeling Within a Behavioral Intervention. *Health Education & Behavior* 40, 1 Suppl: 51S-62S. http://doi.org/10.1177/1090198113496787

18. Hekler, Eric B, Klasnja, Predrag, Froehlich, Jon E and Buman, Matthew P.. 2013. Mind the theoretical gap: interpreting, using, and developing behavioral theory in HCI research. In *Proceedings of the 2013 ACM annual conference on Human factors in computing systems* (CHI '13), 3307-3316. http://doi.org/10.1145/2466416.2466452

19. Hekler, Eric B, Klasnja, Predrag, Riley, William T, Buman, Matthew P, Huberty, Jennifer, Rivera, Daniel E and Martin, Cesar A.. 2016. Agile science: creating useful products for behavior change in the real world. *Transl Behav Med* 6, 2: 317-28. http://doi.org/10.1007/s13142-016-0395-7

20. Hekler, Eric B, Michie, Susan, Pavel, Misha, Rivera, Daniel E, Collins, Linda M, Jimison, Holly B, Garnett, C, Parral, S and Spruijt-Metz, Donna.. Advancing models and theories for digital behavior change. *American Journal of Preventive Medicine.*

21. Hovsepian, Karen, al'Absi, Mustafa, Ertin, Emre, Kamarck, Thomas, Nakajima, Motohiro and Kumar, Santosh..

2015. cStress: towards a gold standard for continuous stress assessment in the mobile environment. In *Proceedings of the 2015 ACM International Joint Conference on Pervasive and Ubiquitous Computing*, 493-504.

22. Kay, Matthew, Nelson, Gregory and Hekler, Eric.. 2016. Researcher-centered design of statistics: Why Bayesian statistics better fit the culture and incentives of HCI. In *Proceedings of SIGCHI Conference on Human Factors in Computing Systems (CHI '16).*

23. Kessler, Rodger and Glasgow, Russell E.. 2011. A proposal to speed translation of healthcare research into practice: dramatic change is needed. *American journal of preventive medicine* 40, 6: 637-644.

24. King, Abby C, Hekler, Eric B, Grieco, Lauren A, Winter, Sandra J, Sheats, Jylana L, Buman, Matthew P, Banerjee, Banny, Robinson, Thomas N and Cirimele, Jesse.. 2013. Harnessing Different Motivational Frames via Mobile Phones to Promote Daily Physical Activity and Reduce Sedentary Behavior in Aging Adults. *PLoS ONE* 8, 4: e62613. http://doi.org/10.1371/journal.pone.0062613

25. Klasnja, Predrag, Consolvo, Sunny and Pratt, Wanda.. 2011. How to evaluate technologies for health behavior change in HCI research. In *CHI '11: Proceedings of the 2011 annual conference on Human factors in computing systems*, 3063-3072. http://doi.org/10.1145/1978942.1979396

26. Klasnja, Predrag, Hekler, Eric B, Shiffman, Saul, Boruvka, Audrey, Almirall, Daniel, Tewari, Ambuj and Murphy, Susan A.. 2015. Microrandomized trials: An experimental design for developing just-in-time adaptive interventions. *Health Psychol* 34 Suppl: 1220-8. http://doi.org/10.1037/hea0000305

27. Kravitz, R L and Duan, N.. 2014. *Design and Implementation of N-of-1 Trials: a users guide.* Agency for Healthcare Research and Quality, Rockville, MD. from www.effectivehealthcare.ahrq.gov/N-1-Trials.cfm

28. Kumar, Santosh, Nilsen, Wendy J, Abernethy, Amy, Atienza, Audie, Patrick, Kevin, Pavel, Misha, Riley, William T, Shar, Albert, Spring, Bonnie, Spruijt-Metz, Donna, Hedeker, Donald, Honavar, Vasant, Kravitz, Richard, Craig Lefebvre, R, Mohr, David C, Murphy, Susan A, Quinn, Charlene, Shusterman, Vladimir and Swendeman, Dallas.. 2013. Mobile Health Technology Evaluation: The mHealth Evidence Workshop. *Am J Prev Med* 45, 2: 228-36. http://doi.org/10.1016/j.amepre.2013.03.017

29. Lane, Nicholas D, Mohammod, Mashfiqui, Lin, Mu, Yang, Xiaochao, Lu, Hong, Ali, Shahid, Doryab, Afsaneh, Berke, Ethan, Choudhury, Tanzeem and Campbell, Andrew.. 2011. BeWell: A smartphone application to monitor, model and promote wellbeing. In *5th International Conference on Pervasive Computing Technologies for Healthcare (PervasiveHealth2011).*

30. Lei, H, Nahum-Shani, I, Lynch, K, Oslin, D and Murphy, S A.. 2012. A SMART design for building individualized treatment sequences. *Annual Review of Clinical Psychology* 8: 21-48.

31. Liao, Peng, Klasnja, Predrag, Tewari, Ambuj and Murphy, Susan A.. 2016. Sample size calculations for microrandomized trials in mHealth. *Stat Med* 35, 12: 1944-71. http://doi.org/10.1002/sim.6847

32. Lin, Mu, Lane, Nicholas D, Mohammod, Mashfiqui, Yang, Xiaochao, Lu, Hong, Cardone, Giuseppe, Ali, Shahid, Doryab, Afsaneh, Berke, Ethan and Campbell, Andrew T.. 2012. BeWell+: multi-dimensional wellbeing monitoring with community-guided user feedback and energy optimization. In *Proceedings of the conference on Wireless Health*, 10.

33. Michie, Susan, Ashford, Stefanie, Sniehotta, Falko F, Dombrowski, Stephan U, Bishop, Alex and French, David P.. 2011. A refined taxonomy of behaviour change techniques to help people change their physical activity and healthy eating behaviours: the CALO-RE taxonomy. *Psychol Health* 26, 11: 1479-98. http://doi.org/10.1080/08870446.2010.540664

34. Nahum-Shani, Inbal, Hekler, Eric B. and Spruijt-Metz, Donna.. 2015. Building health behavior models to guide the development of just-in-time adaptive interventions: A pragmatic framework. *Health Psychology* 34, Suppl: 1209-1219.

35. Nahum-Shani, Inbal, Qian, Min, Almirall, Daniel, Pelham, William E, Gnagy, Beth, Fabiano, Gregory A, Waxmonsky, James G, Yu, Jihnhee and Murphy, Susan A.. 2012. Experimental design and primary data analysis methods for comparing adaptive interventions. *Psychological methods* 17, 4: 457.

36. Pearl, Judea.. 2009. *Causality.* Cambridge university press.

37. Riley, William T, Rivera, Daniel E, Atienza, Audie A, Nilsen, Wendy, Allison, Susannah M and Mermelstein, Robin.. 2011. Health behavior models in the age of mobile interventions: are our theories up to the task? *Transl Behav Med* 1, 1: 53-71. http://doi.org/10.1007/s13142-011-0021-7

38. Riley, William T and Rivera, Daniel E.. 2014. Methodologies for optimizing behavioral interventions: introduction to special section. *Translational behavioral medicine* 4, 3: 234.

39. Spruijt-Metz, Donna and Nilsen, Wendy.. 2014. Dynamic Models of Behavior for Just-in-Time Adaptive Interventions. *IEEE Pervasive Computing*, 3: 13-17.

Investigating Haptic Perception of and Physiological Responses to Air Vortex Rings on a User's Cheek

Yuka Sato
Graduate School of Design, Kyushu University
Fukuoka, Japan
sato.y.715@s.kyushu-u.ac.jp

Ryoko Ueoka
Faculty of Design, Kyushu University
Fukuoka, Japan
r-ueoka@design.kyushu-u.ac.jp

ABSTRACT
Haptic perception is one of the primary means of interaction with the world. Recent research on affective haptics suggests that it can affect emotional and behavioral responses. In this study, we evaluate user perceptions of haptic stimuli generated by air vortex rings on the cheek and investigate the effects on their physiological responses. To develop a cheek haptic display, we investigated and found that the cheek had enough resolution to perceive the differences in haptic stimuli in a two-point discrimination threshold test of the face. Additionally, the intensities of the haptic stimuli for experiments were determined by investigating the subjective impressions of different stimuli pairs. Finally, we conducted experiments to evaluate quantitatively the effects of four different combinations of haptic stimuli on the physiological responses in terms of stress modification, brainwave activities, task performance, and subjective assessment. The results suggest that different stimuli affect physiological responses and task performance.

Author Keywords
cheek haptic interface; haptic perception; air vortex rings; physiological responses; subjective impression.

ACM Classification Keywords
H.5.2 Information interfaces and presentation (e.g., HCI): User Interfaces – Haptic I/O;

INTRODUCTION
Haptic perception is one of the primary means of interaction with the world and is developed in the early stages of childhood [6]. People learn about the world by physical contact through haptic stimulation. They will have experienced, especially in childhood, carrying and touching a charm, stuffed toy, or blanket to provide ourselves relief from stress. A trustworthy object that gives a sense of security when they touch is known as a security blanket [29]. They agree that some kinds of haptic stimuli relieve their own tension. In contrast, some kinds of haptic stimuli, such as that caused by touching a sharp tip, increases their own tension. In this way, various haptic perceptions give a variety of emotional and behavioral experiences. In fact, the existence of connections between interpersonal haptic feedback and human emotional responses are supported by both physiological and behavioral data in various research studies detailed in [6].

In addition, recent human-computer interaction studies suggest that haptic stimuli affect emotional as well as behavioral responses [7] [22]. These studies suggest that specific patterns of haptic stimulus induce different emotional states or different response times. This research topic is called affective haptics, and it focuses on the design of devices and systems that can detect, process, or display the emotional state of a human by means of the sense of touch. Further, it studies how haptics affects the emotional reactions of humans [4]. Emotional reactions are often quantitatively observed through physiological responses such as heart rate and galvanic skin response (GSR) [7]. Many interface devices have been proposed for sending emotional information by sense of touch. However, systems that characterize the emotional status of a user by haptic stimuli are still an understudied topic [4].

In most conventional HCI studies, haptic stimuli are given to the fingers or hands to investigate their effect on physiological or behavioral responses. This procedure is consistent because these body parts have a high haptic resolution and they are always exposed. However, the face could be another candidate for the locus of the interaction of haptic stimuli because it is always exposed; hence, it is possible to present the tactile stimulus directly on the skin. Indeed, people usually perceive haptic sensation of the wind while driving a car by opening a window, or of the softness of a towel on their faces.

In particular, we noticed that the cheek is where people feel the haptic sensation on a larger area than the nose or the mouth, though the nose and mouth have a higher haptic resolution than the cheek. Other facial areas, such as the forehead that has a larger area among the different facial areas, are susceptible to changes in sensitivity depending on the presence or absence of hair. The cheek is indeed the locus of communication through haptic stimulation such as pecking on someone's cheek for greeting them, which is similar to the form of haptic communication such as a handshake. Therefore, the cheek is an appropriate locus of interaction for a haptic display on the facial area.

Permission to make digital or hard copies of all or part of this work for personal or classroom use is granted without fee provided that copies are not made or distributed for profit or commercial advantage and that copies bear this notice and the full citation on the first page. Copyrights for components of this work owned by others than ACM must be honored. Abstracting with credit is permitted. To copy otherwise, or republish, to post on servers or to redistribute to lists, requires prior specific permission and/or a fee. Request permissions from permissions@acm.org.
CHI'17, May 6-11, 2017, Denver, CO, USA
Copyright © 2017 ACM ISBN 978-1-4503-4655-9/17/05?...$15.00.
DOI: http://dx.doi.org/10.1145/3025453.3025501

Since there are no investigations on haptic perception on a user's cheek yet, we developed a prototype cheek haptic display to evaluate how people perceive haptic stimuli on their cheeks. In order to present haptic stimulus on the cheek, preferably contactless to prevent obtrusiveness, we chose air vortex rings as haptic stimuli for our prototype cheek haptic display. The vortex ring from an air cannon differs from the jet-type wind; it does not diffuse and it travels a long distance with unchanged strength, so it can present a tactile stimulus without contact. Additionally, it generates various haptic intensities by changing the air pressure; hence, it is possible to investigate the difference in impressions depending on the intensities being applied on the cheek.

To develop an interactive cheek haptic display, we first conducted a two-point discrimination (TPD) threshold test of the face to evaluate whether the cheek was sensitive enough to perceive the different haptic stimuli generated by air vortex rings, as a benchmark test for the sensitivity of the air vortex ring haptic stimuli. Second, we developed a prototype interactive cheek haptic display that generated strong and weak air vortex ring intensities by controlling the air pressure in either two or five-second intervals. The intensity of the haptic stimulus was determined by the subjective impression test of the haptic stimuli of different stimuli pairs. Finally, using our prototype system, we also conducted experiments to evaluate quantitatively whether the cheek haptic display, with four different combinations of haptic stimulus intensities and time intervals, affected physiological responses in terms of stress modification. This was accomplished by using changes in the low frequency/high frequency (LF/HF), brainwave activities measured with a portable brainwave sensor (EMOTIV EPOC+) as a pilot test, task performance by analyzing the task performance scores, and a subjective assessment of three feelings: fatigue, conscious drowsiness, and carelessness.

The results suggest that some combinations of haptic stimuli from the air vortex rings induce significantly different physiological responses, although subjective assessment is not affected. In addition, the specific responses or changes observed for the air vortex ring haptic stimuli were not seen for the simple vibration haptic stimulus.

RELATED WORK

Interfaces Using an Air Vortex Ring for Haptic Feedback

As a haptic interface for an unobtrusive interactive media system, air pressure has been suggested [24] [10].

Air vortex rings have also been applied as a non-contact haptic feedback system for gaming [23] [9] or three-dimensional (3D) theater [11]. An air vortex ring has the characteristic of travelling a long distance without decreasing its intensity or velocity. Therefore, it is considered to be a good stimulus for a non-contact haptic displays. These previous approaches mainly used air or vortex rings to add multi-modal sensations to audio-visual media for increasing the sense of immersion of conventional media. Hence, although they applied air vortex ring as a haptic feedback, the purpose of this research is different. Another noticeable difference from previous work except for [11] is that they presented haptic feedback at a single intensity. Because our research goal is to develop a haptic display with various haptic feedback types to control physiological responses of a user, our system has the ability to generate air vortex rings of various intensities. Furthermore, these haptic displays were hand-dominant, and there is not yet a device that presents haptic feedback to the cheek. In [11], the authors presented haptic feedback at two intensities on the face to increase the sense of immersion for 3D theater. The presenting area and function of the display are similar with our research, however the research purpose is different.

Affective Change by Haptic Feedback Systems

Different patterns of brain activities that address the neural aspects of interpersonal touch [19] [20] were scientifically observed by Rolls et al. Different intensities of touch significantly affect brain activities, which is evidence that physiological responses are generated by haptic stimulus. Although in [4], EID described how physiological reactions such as heart rate, facial expressions, electrodermal activity, gesture expressions, or brain activities are possible methods for measuring the quality of experience to observe how a user emotionally reacts to haptic stimuli, there are few studies that use these methods to measure affective haptics quantitatively.

In [7], Gatti et al. measured physiological responses that are related to the responses to emotional stimuli. Although they did not find significant correlations between emotional state with and without friction-based haptic feedback rated by self-assessment and physiological responses, they noted that further investigation might find evidence for relations between haptic interactions and emotional states.

Nishimura et al. proposed a cushion-type tactile feedback device that simulates a false heartbeat for a user to influence his/her evaluation of the attractiveness of female/male images [14]. Although it was a pilot study, they reported that false heartbeats generated by vibrotactile feedback could alter physiological or emotional states.

Alonso et al. proposed Wigo, which is a tangible hand grabbing interface prototype that detects stress by using the trembling motion of a user's hand and provides haptic feedback to support stress reduction [1]. Although a specific result was not obtained, in a small pilot study, the participants said that they appreciated the haptic feedback provided, which helped them relax.

Behavioral Change by Haptic Feedback Systems

Currently, few studies have investigated behavioral change using a haptic interface.

A previous study used a friction-based horizontally rotating fingertip haptic stimulator to investigate behavioral change in terms of response time by varying burst length, continuity, and direction [21]. Of 528 stimulus pairs, they concluded that stimuli with discontinuous forward rotation in a long bursts (100 ms) and continuous forward-backward rotation in short bursts (20 ms) caused the fastest and most accurate reactions. This outcome suggests that even for simple haptic feedback on a fingertip, participants distinguished the stimulus and unconsciously reacted with different behavioral patterns to specific stimulus pairs. This result encourages the hypothesis that different pairs of intensity and interval times generated by our cheek haptic display has the potential to change responses.

FatBelt is an interactive haptic feedback system for motivating dietary control. It gives physical feedback using an inflatable pack worn around the stomach [18]. The authors conducted a two-day experiment and found out that the haptic feedback impacted participants' physical self-concepts. When eating excessive calories, the participants felt like they had actually grown fat. This proof-of-concept work has the potential to actively change a user's dietary behavior by haptic feedback.

TWO-POINT DISCRIMINATION THRESHOLD OF FACE

In order to evaluate whether the cheek is an appropriate body area for tactile stimulation, we evaluated the tactile discrimination ability of 14 areas of the face using the TPD threshold test.

The TPD test measures basic touch acuity by evaluating how far apart two separate points need to be before they are perceived as two points rather than one. We agree that tactile stimulus response is related to the reactions of various mechanoreceptors, so it is not appropriate to conclude that there is a relationship between the accuracy of the tactile stimulus of the TPD test and that of the vortex ring. However, as there are no previous studies on tactile presentation on the cheek, we thought that quantifying the check tactile precision by TPD test could become a useful benchmark. The facial surface is known to be a very sensitive part of the body for perceiving tactile stimulation. According to the Weinstein's TPD test results, the two-point threshold is the second smallest on the face compared to all other body parts [25]. In Weinstein's TPD test, the detailed spatial acuity of the facial surface was not evaluated.

Thus, to verify this previous finding, we conducted a TPD test on 14 areas of left and right side of the face twice to observe the detailed spatial acuity of the facial surface. The minimum distance of the two-point stimulus was 1 mm and the maximum distance was 14 mm. We used an adjustable two-point caliper with a tip radius of 0.5 mm as the TPD stimuli. Applying the method of limits [17] with a gap size of 1 mm randomly tested on each participant, we investigated how far apart two separate points need to be in order to be perceived as two points by poking the cheek surface applying the caliper at right angle for making a hollow of skin about 2 to 4 mm. Examiners did sufficient practice for giving equal pressure of stimulus in each facial area before conducting the experiment. Ten participants (6 males, 4 females, mean age 21.3 years) participated the experiment.

Figure 1 shows the mean TPD results of the 14 facial surface areas. The bottom parts of the face have higher spatial acuity than the upper parts, and the lip areas (areas 10 and 11) have the highest spatial acuity. However, the cheek area (area 9) also has a high spatial acuity (5.8 mm), and is the fifth-highest spatial acuity of the 14 areas.

In conclusion, cheeks have a high spatial acuity, which is sufficient to be able to perceive the difference of various air vortex ring pressures. In addition, as we are able to induce tactile sensations directly on the skin over a comparatively wide and flat area, we concluded that the cheeks are the best area for presenting haptic stimuli.

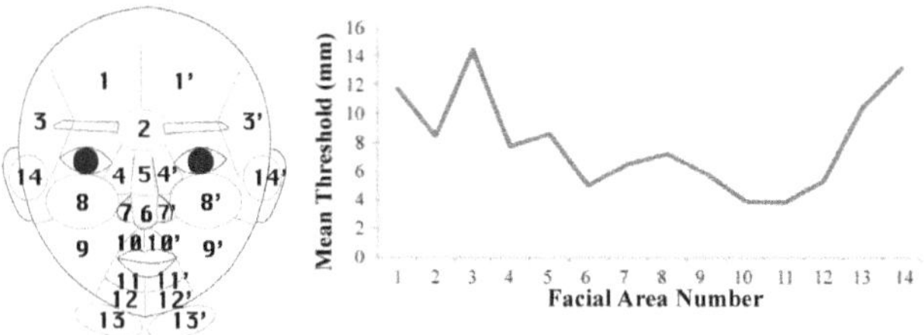

Figure 1. Areas of the face (left) and mean two-point discrimination threshold for each facial area (right)

DEVELOPMENT OF INTERACTIVE CHEEK HAPTIC DISPLAY SYSTEM

Principle of an Air Vortex Ring

We developed an interactive cheek haptic display using a diaphragm valve-type air cannon. When stress is detected, air vortex rings are presented on the cheek for one minute. When the valve is opened by an electrical switch, compressed air is pushed from the tank and it travels towards the surface of the air cannon, as in a microburst, poloidal spinning is generated by viscous friction between the layer of fast outward flow near the surface of the air cannon and the slower-moving fluid above it, and an air vortex ring is generated, as Figure 2 shows. The diameter of an air vortex ring D was set to about 100 mm, based on the average surface cheek area of Asian adults [16].

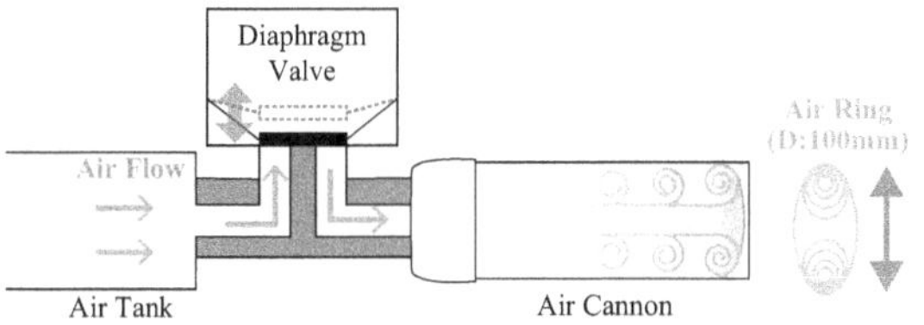

Figure 2. Generation of an air vortex ring

When the tank of the system is filled with air that is relatively higher in pressure than the atmospheric pressure (0.1013 MPa), it generates an air vortex ring with a faster speed, which gives the impression of a strong haptic sensation when it is presented. In contrast, relatively lower pressure air in the tank generates an air vortex ring with slower speed, which gives an impression of a weak and soft haptic sensation when it is presented.

Figure 3 shows a system diagram of the cheek haptic display. Given the radius of the vortex ring we wanted to generate, we chose the aperture D′ of the air cannon to be 50 mm. The principle of air vortex rings states that $D'/L \leq 4$, where L is the length of the cylindrical slug of air pushed out of the nozzle [28]. This ratio is the theoretical threshold value needed to generate the optimum air vortex ring; however, in practice, it usually differs for various vortex systems [23]. We empirically found the optimum ratio to be six in our experimental setup, meaning that the best value for L was 300 mm. Thus, the volume of the air tank is 392.5 cm^3. From this air tank, air at variable pressures is transferred to the air cannon, which creates a stable vortex ring that travels to the surface of the cheek. A silent air compressor and a 20-l air tank containing 0.3 MPa compressed air are connected to the air pressure regulator (SMC ITV2030-212S) that controls the pressure of the compressed air that flows to the air tank. A silent air compressor fills the tank with 0.3 MPa compressed air for about 1.5 min. Figure 4 shows the prototype system. It is portable, can be disassembled easily, and can be installed at any indoor location. The control signals of the diaphragm valves and the air pressure regulator are sent via an Arduino UNO from the device control PC.

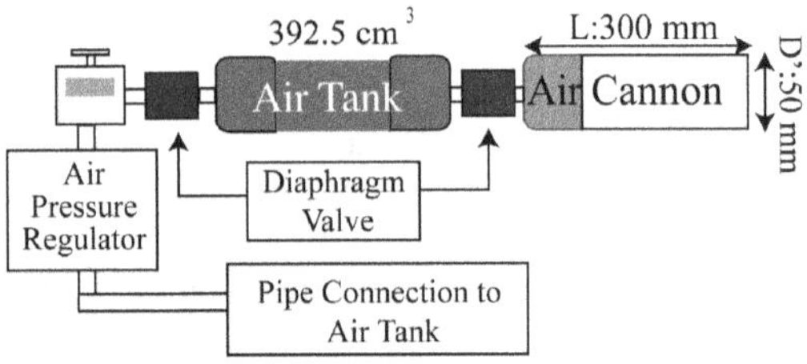

Figure 3. Vortex ring generation system

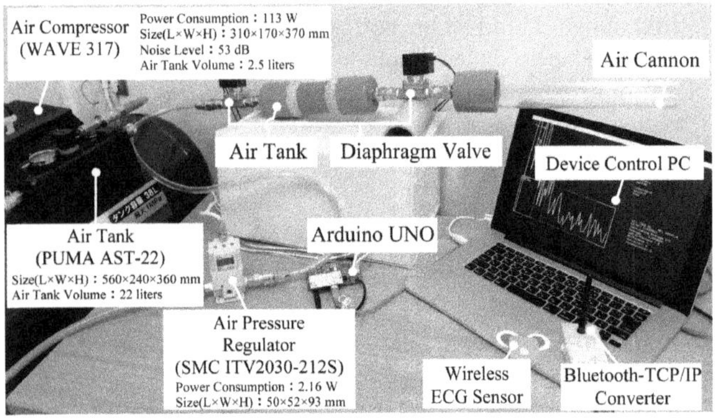

Figure 4. Prototype system

Determining Distance from an Air Cannon to Cheek

Experiment Procedure

Although vortex rings were generated immediately after they were expelled from the air cannon, a certain distance was required to form stable vortex rings. In order to determine the best distance from the nozzle of the air cannon to the cheek for displaying stable vortex rings, we conducted an experiment on all pneumatic pressures used in the experiments in this study and performed an experiment to determine the optimum distance for a vortex ring stabilization by measuring the point of generation and disappearance of a vortex ring. We then calculated the acceleration speed for every 5 cm interval. The minimum value of air pressure (0.06 MPa) was the weakest value of air pressure that would generate an air vortex ring. The maximum value of air pressure (0.20 MPa) was limited by the air pressure of the system's regulator. We conducted 100 trial experiments on eight air pressure values (0.06 - 0.20 MPa in steps of 0.02 MPa) and recorded the generation process using a 240 fps high speed camera (iPad Pro). When setting the experimental environment, we used a black textile as a background to increase the visibility of the vortex ring and used a 100 cm stainless ruler as an objective index. Using the reference lines at every 5 cm interval overlaid on the video, we calculated the speed of a vortex ring in steps of 5 cm by referring to the video frame (4.16 ms/frame) and calculating the acceleration speed in each interval. We also measured the generation and disappearance point of the vortex ring from the video.

Result

Figure 5 shows the mean acceleration speed for each 5 cm interval. In every condition, acceleration speed instantly increases right after the generation of the vortex ring and then decelerates until the acceleration speed reaches zero. The mean distance of the zero acceleration point is 35.0 cm. The generation points of the vortex rings for all conditions range from 15.1 to 25.0 cm. Furthermore, the disappearance points range from 40.1 to 100.0 cm depending on the value of the air pressure. Within the range 30.1 to 40.0 cm, no vortex rings are generated or disappear. Using these results, we set the optimum distance from the tip of the cannon and the cheek to be from 35.0 to 40.0 cm. The acceleration speed is zero and the air vortex ring is stable. As it could cause a subtle difference during an experiment, we set the distance of the system to 40.0 cm so that it intrudes on the desk as little as possible.

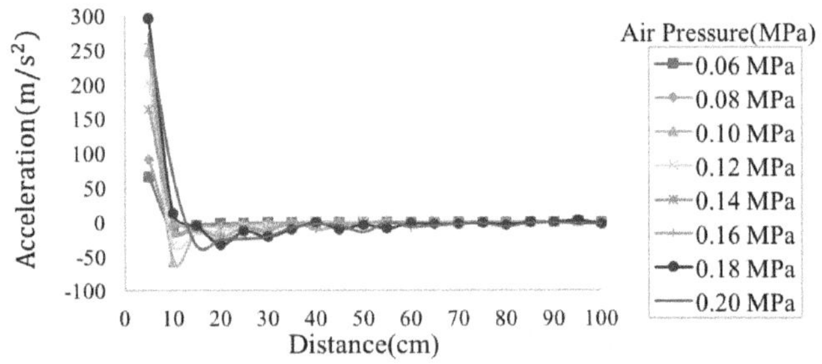

Figure 5. Acceleration speed of eight air pressure values

Subjective Impression Evaluation of Different Air Pressures of Air Vortex Rings

Experiment Procedure

In order to determine the value of air pressure needed to generate air vortex rings with different haptic perceptions on the cheek, we investigated whether the different intensities lead to different impressions of the haptic stimulus to determine the parameters for strong and weak haptic stimuli. Eight air pressure values (0.06 – 0.20 MPa in steps of 0.02 MPa) and two time intervals (2 and 5 s) were used for determining these parameters. In order to eliminate the order effect, we presented the sixteen conditions randomly to each participant. After each condition, participants answered questions using a seven-point bipolar semantic differential scale varying from +3 to -3 that had opposite adjectives at each end. As Table 1 and 2 show, ten types of adjectives pairs depicting intensity and six types of adjectives pairs depicting emotion were chosen from a previous experiment conducted by Hashiguchi et al. [12]. Ten participants (3 males, 7 females, mean age 21.3 years) participated in the experiment. The distance between a participant's cheek and the tip of the air cannon was fixed at 40.0 cm. In order to eliminate the effect of the sound generated when compressed air was expelled from the air cannon, a clamshell noise cancelling headset (SONY MDR-NC600D) playing a white noise sound was worn during the experiment. In addition, in order to avoid visual effects, we asked participant to close his/her eyes during the experiment. Air vortex rings for each condition were presented for 30 s.

	+3	0	-3
(1)	smooth	-	bouncing
(2)	tender	-	painful
(3)	protective	-	piercing
(4)	normal	-	shocking
(5)	patted	-	tapped
(6)	light	-	heavy
(7)	calm	-	furious
(8)	weak	-	strong
(9)	soft	-	solid
(10)	gentle	-	sharp

Table 1. Adjectives pairs for determining the impressions of intensity of the haptic stimuli generated by air flow (from Hashiguchi et al. [12])

	+3	0	-3
(a)	easy	-	uneasy
(b)	comfortable	-	uncomfortable
(c)	safe	-	scary
(d)	relaxed	-	tensed
(e)	calm	-	surprised
(f)	natural	-	artifical

Table 2. Adjectives pairs for determining the impressions of the haptic stimuli generated by air flow (from Hashiguchi et al. [12])

Results

Figure 6 shows the results of the mean impression of intensity of each of the ten types of adjective pairs for 16 conditions. We applied a two-way (2 interval times × 8 air pressures) ANOVA to all ten pairs, which showed a statistically significant difference between each air pressure ($p < .0001$). There was no significant difference between the interval time and no significant difference among the interactive effects between time and air pressure. The results showed that increasing the value of air pressure changed the impression from positive to negative gradually, independently of time interval. In order to determine the values for weak and strong haptic stimulus impressions for use in the experiments, Pearson's correlation coefficient for each adjective pair was applied and showed a statistically significant correlation between all pairs of two variables ($p < .001$). We then applied a two-way (2 interval times × 8 air pressures) ANOVA to the mean impression of the all ten types of pairs, which showed a statistically significant difference between the impression of each air pressure ($F(7, 8) = 129.9$, $p < .001$). There was no significant difference between the interval time and no significant difference among the interactive effects (interval time × air pressure). The results show that the air vortex ring generated by the air at 0.06 MPa generated the weakest impression and the air at 0.18 MPa generated the strongest impression on the cheek.

Figure 7 shows the results of the mean impression of all six types of adjective pairs for 16 conditions. A two-way ANOVA showed a statistically significant difference between the impression of each air pressure ($p < .0001$). There was no significant difference among the interactive effects.
The two adjective pairs (safe–scary, calm–surprised) showed a statistically significant difference between the impression for each time interval ($p < .01$). These results show that the difference of intensity or interval time of the haptic feedback generated by the air vortex ring could give the affective impression of a heartbeat experience. For the easy–uneasy and comfortable–uncomfortable pairs, there was not much difference among the 16 conditions. This indicates that the air vortex ring haptic stimulus is not good at expressing impressions along these axes, however, this could also imply the haptic stimulus was not very annoying under any condition.
Given the significant differences among the air vortex ring haptic stimuli for six impression adjective pairs, we reconfirmed that the air at 0.06 MPa and 0.18 MPa could deliver haptic feedback of different impression of intensities as well as emotions to the participants.

EXPERIMENT 1: PERCEPTION OF AIR VORTEX RINGS

We conducted an experiment to evaluate whether haptic stimuli generated by the air vortex rings could affect physiological responses. We also analyzed whether different stimulus parameters (intensity and time interval) led to different responses.

When the compressed air is pushed out of the nozzle and generates an air vortex ring, a discharge sound is also generated. Even though the participants used noise canceling earphones playing a white noise sound to eliminate surrounding noise, the discharge sound was not completely eliminated. Therefore as a control condition stimulus in this experiment, we used the prerecorded discharge sound of the 0.06 MPa/5 s condition. By comparing the effect of the control condition with the other conditions, we are able to evaluate whether any change of physiological responses are caused by the effect of pure haptic stimulus. When the control condition was executed, the speaker (Gateway Edison 2.0) was set at a distance of 40.0 cm from the cheek.

We intentionally created a stressful situation by asking the participants to perform 30-min SPI and TOEIC exercises on the PC. Five exercise sets of four 30-min tasks were created by combining SPI and TOEIC exercises chosen from textbooks. The time limit of an exercise was taken from the textbook. The exercises with longer time limits were more difficult and those with shorter time limits were easier. When

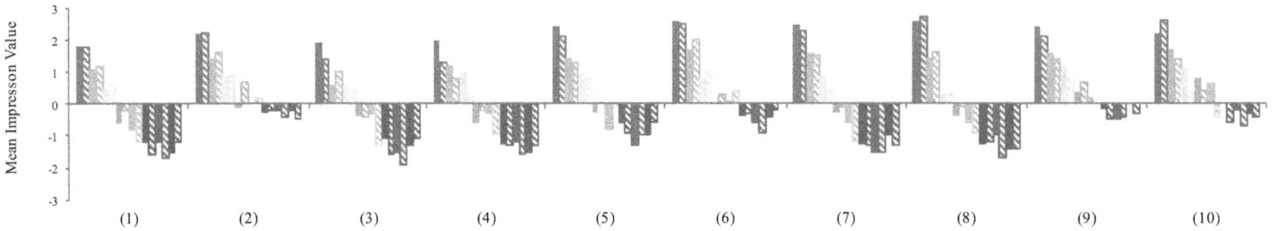

Figure 6. Impression of intensity of sixteen conditions. Solid (2-s interval) and strip (5-s interval) colors represent eight air pressure values (0.06 – 0.20 MPa in steps of 0.02 MPa) respectively. The numeric letters of x axis are equivalent to the numeric letters of Table 1.

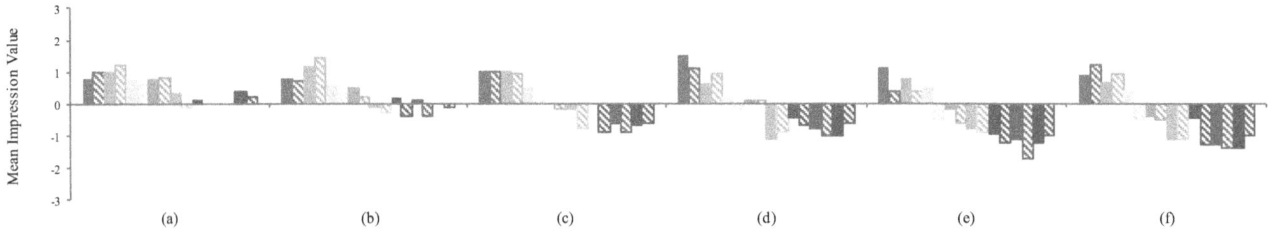

Figure 7. Impression of sixteen conditions. Solid (2-s interval) and strip (5-s interval) colors represent eight air pressure values (0.06 – 0.20 MPa in steps of 0.02 MPa) respectively. The alphabetical letters of x axis are equivalent to the alphabetical letters of Table 2.

the system detected that the participant was in a stressed state, haptic stimuli or audio stimuli were presented. Four set of tasks were conducted for each experiment. The flow of the experiment is illustrated in Figure 8.

Duration	5 min	30 min	30 min	30 min	30 min
Task	Pre-rest	Task 1	Task 2	Task 3	Task 4
Validation of VAS	Yes	Yes	Yes	Yes	Yes
ECG measurement					
EEG measurement					
Cheek haptic display		Baseline Stress level	When the stress level exceeded the baseline, 60 s of air vortex rings were applied to the cheek.		

Figure 8. Experiment flow for experiment 1

In order to detect a participant's stress state, we monitored the increase in the LF/HF of an ECG over its baseline. The ECG was measured by a wireless sensor at 204 Hz (RF-ECG2 GM3) and a customized Bluetooth-TCP/IP signal converter that received the signal and converted it to inter-beat (R-R) intervals to calculate the power spectrum using a fast Fourier transform. We extracted and accumulated both the LF (0.04 to 0.15 Hz) and HF (0.15 to 0.5 Hz) to calculate the LF/HF for the stress state analysis. The baseline of the stress state of each participant was determined by the mean LF/HF of the first task. An increased stress state was then identified when the LF/HF was higher than the baseline for more than 20 of the latest 30 samples. In this case, a haptic stimulus was applied to the cheek for 60 s. The ECG not only interactively monitored a participant's stress state, it also recorded this state during the experiment in a stress state log.

In order to monitor physiological response, we also used a commercial brainwave sensor (EMOTIV EPOC+), which is a wireless 14 channel EEG sensor [5]. Four emotional labels, short-term excitement, meditation, frustration, and engagement, were calculated by the sensor at 256 Hz, and we recorded the value of four affective parameters scaled from 0 to 100 for further analysis using a program we developed in the Xcode environment of OS X using the EMOTIV SDK.

Eleven participants (6 males, 5 females, mean age 21.8 years) participated in the experiment. We combined weak or strong air pressure (0.06 or 0.18 MPa) with short or long intervals (2 or 5 s) to form the haptic stimulus pairs. All participants performed each combination on different days. The experiment was conducted in a partitioned laboratory room with a black curtain to prevent the entry of surrounding visual noise. We set up the experiment in a room with closed windows and controlled temperature set to 25 °C without blowing the air conditioner on the participants. During the experiment, the participant wore an in-ear canal noise canceling headset (SONY MDR-NC300D) playing a white noise sound to standardize the noise environment among the participants. They were asked to have sufficient sleep on the eve of the experiment and finish their lunch at least one hour prior to its start. An example of a participant performing the experiment is shown in Figure 9.

RESULTS

We evaluated the stress state using the LF/HF change as well as observed the absent/focused state using brainwave activities. We also evaluated overall task performance and self-reported assessments of three feelings.

LF/HF Change

We evaluated the mean LF/HF ratio to analyze the effect of each condition on participant stress. The difference in LF/HF from tasks 2 to 4 on the basis of the mean LF/HF ratio of a

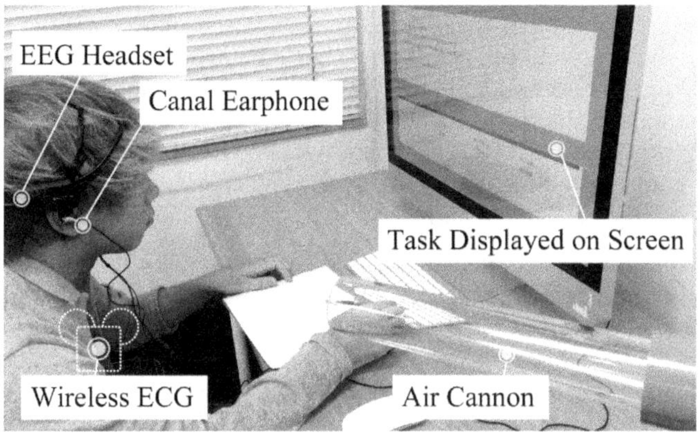

Figure 9. Experimental setup (experiment 1)

5-min pre-test was calculated. The results are shown in Figure 10. As we found no homogeneity of variance, we used a non-parametric one-way ANOVA (the Kruskal-Wallis test) to analyze the results. There was a significant difference (X^2 = 82.329, df = 4, $p < .0001$) among them. A non-parametric multiple comparison using the Steel-Dwass test was used for pairwise analysis. Three conditions of the cheek haptic stimuli (0.06 MPa/5 s: M = 1.025, SD = 0.312; 0.18 MPa/2 s: M = 0.984, SD = 0.364; 0.18 MPa/5 s: M = 1.026, SD = 0.362) were significantly different from the control condition (M = 1.144, SD = 0.362, $p < .01$). The 0.06 MPa/2 s condition was not significant compared to the control condition ($p = .053$).
Among the four haptic stimuli conditions, the 0.18 MPa/2 s condition modified the increase in stress significantly with respect to the other three conditions (0.06 MPa/2 s, 0.06 MPa/5 s ($p < .01$), 0.18 MPa/5 s ($p < .05$)). On the other hand, the 0.06 MPa/2 s condition significantly increased the stress state (0.06 MPa/5 s, 0.18 MPa/5 s ($p < .05$), 0.18 MPa/2 s ($p < .01$)). The reason for this result is discussed in the discussion section.

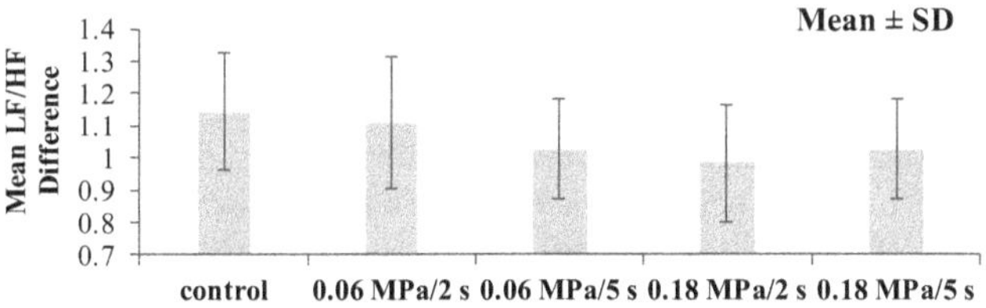

Figure 10. LF/HF change (experiment 1)

Brainwave Activities

In order to observe brainwave activities, we analyzed the ratio of meditation/short-term excitement as the "absent" index and engagement/frustration as the "focused" index using the scores of the four emotional labels that were provided by EMOTIV. Figure 11 shows the results for the absent and focused indices of each condition. For the absent index, as we found no homogeneity of variances, we used a non-parametric one-way ANOVA (Kruskal-Wallis test) for the analysis. There was a significant difference (X^2 = 50.108, df = 4, $p < .0001$) among the five conditions. A non-parametric multiple comparison using the Steel-Dwass test was used for pairwise analysis. Two conditions of the haptic stimuli (0.06 MPa/5 s: M = 0.765, SD = 0.819, $p < .01$; 0.18 MPa/2 s: M = 0.735, SD = 0.471, $p < .05$) were significant with respect to the control condition. Other two conditions of the haptic stimuli (0.06 MPa/2 s and 0.18 MPa/5 s) were not significant compared to the control condition.
As for the focused index, as we found no homogeneity of variances, we used a non-parametric one-way ANOVA (Kruskal-Wallis test) for the analysis. There was a significant difference (X^2 = 110.06, df = 4, $p < .0001$) among the five conditions. A non-parametric multiple comparison using the Steel-Dwass test was used for pairwise analysis. We found that the two 0.06 MPa conditions led to a significantly less focused state than the control condition (0.06 MPa/2 s: M = 1.205, SD = 0.864; 0.06 MPa/5 s: M = 1.436, SD = 0.765, $p < .0001$), whereas the 0.18 MPa/5 s condition led to a significantly highly focused state compared to the 0.06 MPa/5 s condition ($p < .01$).

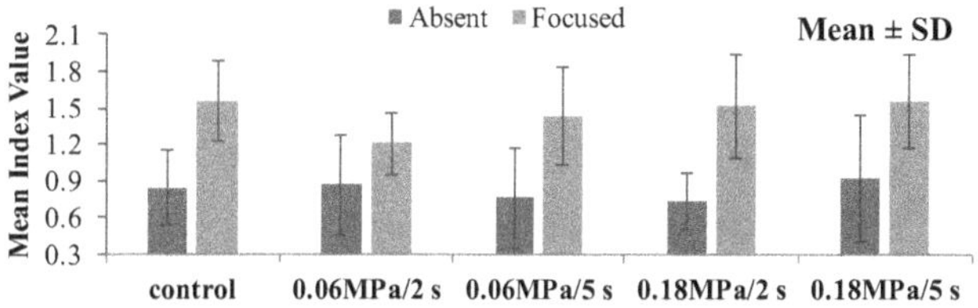

Figure 11. Absent/Focused index (experiment 1)

Task Performance

Because the difficulty of each task was different and the ability of each participant was variable, we did not count the correct/incorrect answers out of the total questions but instead calculated the score based on the difficulty of each task and normalized it. The score for each exercise was determined by its time limit. To normalize the scores, the difference of the mean scores of tasks 2 to 4 with respect to the mean score of the first task was calculated. Figure 12 shows the results.
After confirming the homogeneity of variances by Bartlett's test, a one-way ANOVA was used to compare the task performance under the five conditions. There was a significant difference ($F(4,160) = 3.519$, $p < .01$) among them. A multiple comparison using the Holm method was used for pairwise analysis. The result shows that there are significant differences between two pairs: the 0.18 MPa/2 s (M = 3.389, SD = 7.671) and control conditions (M = -3.654, SD = 10.290, $p < .05$) and the 0.18 MPa/2 s and 0.06 MPa/2 s conditions (M = -1.943, SD = 8.944, $p < .05$).

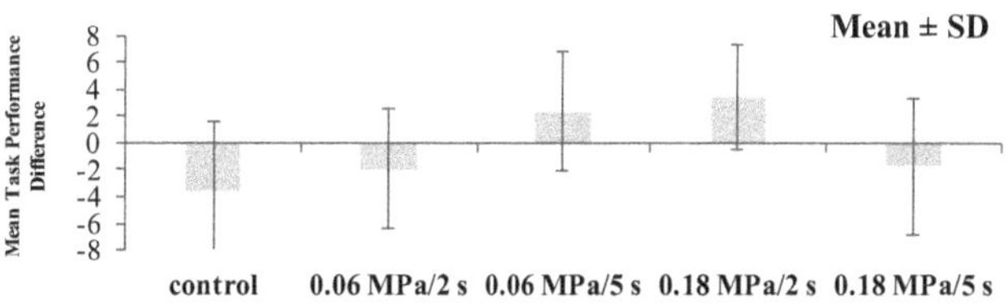

Figure 12. Task performance (experiment 1)

Subjective Assessment

We used a visual analog scale (VAS) of the self-reported ratings of three feelings: fatigue, conscious drowsiness, and carelessness. VAS is a measurement instrument that tries to measure a characteristic or attitude that is believed to range across a continuum of values and cannot easily be directly measured [8]. VAS is operationally a horizontal line and we set the scores of the line in this experiment to range from 0 to 100. A participant marks the line at the point that they feel represents his/her perception of his/her current state.
Figure 13 shows the difference of the mean VAS of tasks 2 to 4 with respect to the mean VAS of the first task. We found no significance among the differences of the five conditions for the three subjective feelings.

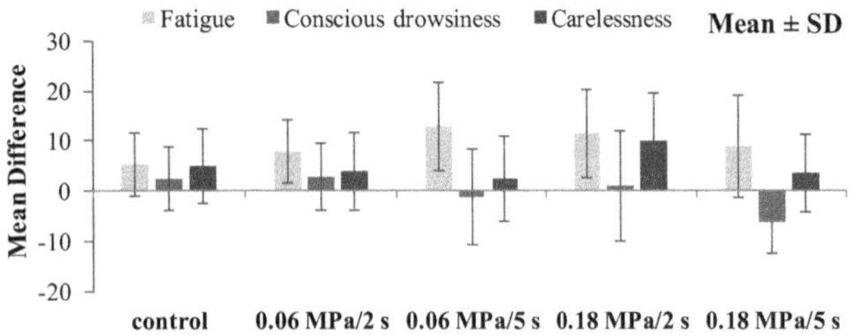

Figure 13. Subjective assessment (experiment 1)

DISCUSSION

All the haptic stimulus conditions, except the 0.06 MPa/2 s condition, successfully inhibited the increase in stress during the experiment. In particular, the 0.18 MPa/2 s condition inhibited the increase in stress significantly, as compared to all other conditions. The results of the absent/focused index analysis showed that the focused index increased while the absent index decreased. These results suggest that the strong haptic stimulus of an air vortex ring with short interval affects the stress state and modifies concentration. For the 0.06 MPa/2 s condition, we observed no modification in the stress. Further, the level of the stressed state was the highest for the cheek haptic stimuli conditions.

These results suggest that the weak haptic stimulus of an air vortex ring with a short interval had little effect on the stress modification. A feedback from participants implied that the 0.18-MPa intensity felt strong and the 0.06-MPa intensity felt gentle or very weak as a haptic sensation, suggesting that they perceived two intensities as different stimuli. In addition, they commented that 2-s interval stimuli were more rhythmic than 5-s interval stimuli. We assumed that the 0.06 MPa/2 s condition–the rhythmic patting of weak intensity haptic stimuli on the cheek–induced an absentminded state, and the participants tried to stay awake during the experiment so that the level of the stressed state was kept high.

In addition, both the 0.06 and 0.18 MPa at 5 s intervals inhibited the increase in stress compared to the control and the 0.06 MPa at 2 s interval. However, the differences in effects between the two conditions were not significant, which suggests that these haptic stimuli affect the stress modification, but a longer time interval may reduce the effect of the difference in haptic intensities. The absent/focused index analysis indicated that both conditions showed a synchronous decrease or increase in both indices compared to the control condition. As the algorithm for the calculation of the emotional labels provided by EMOTIV is not openly available [3], we could not conclude whether the synchronous state of both indices suggested any meaningful result.

As for the task performance, the 0.18 MPa/2 s condition improved the score significantly compared to the control condition as well as the 0.06 MPa/2 s condition. This suggests that the 0.18 MPa/2 s condition caused an increase in the scores whereas the 0.06 MPa/2 s condition caused a decrease in the scores. Both the 0.06 and 0.18 MPa at 5 s intervals had no significance among any of the conditions, which suggests that these cheek haptic-stimuli conditions hardly affected the task performance.

With regard to the subjective assessment, we found no significant difference among all the conditions for the three subjective feelings. One of the reasons for this may be that the series of two-hour problem solving tasks would increase the feelings in these three questions under any condition, so the difference caused by each condition was unclear.
To summarize the results of this experiment, we found that the 0.18 and 0.06 MPa at 2 s intervals had significant differences in the LF/HF change, absent/focused index, and task performance.

EXPERIMENT 2: COMPARISON AGAINST VIBROTACTILE FEEDBACK

In the previous experiment, we found that certain haptic stimuli generated by air vortex rings affect physiological responses. As a comparative experiment, we evaluated whether a haptic stimulus generated by a vibration motor affects them. The procedure of the experiment was the same as that of experiment 1.

The vibration motor was chosen as a comparative stimulus because it is able to present haptic stimulus locally on the cheek area. An air fan was another candidate for the comparative stimulus. However, the air is diffused by the time it reaches the cheek. Hence, this stimulus does not present local stimulus on the cheek like an air vortex ring does. The results of this experiment are limited because we compared only one type of simple vibration stimulus, and a comparison with vibration stimulus does not generalize to all cases. For instance, Obrist et al. [15] presented the design potential of mid-air haptic stimuli for non-arbitrary emotion communication by modulating the frequency, intensity, and duration of ultrasonic haptic feedback.
We intend to evaluate the results in this experiment as a baseline test to compare the results of experiment 1.

As the vibration stimuli, a coin type vibration motor (TPC Motor FM34F: standard voltage 3.0 V, standard speed 13,000 rpm, standard current 100 mA, vibration quantity 17.6 m/s^2 (1.8 G)) was used. The intensity of the stimulus was determined by specifications of the motor, which vibrated at 216 Hz. It was wrapped in a soft cloth and placed on a cheek of the participant using surgical tape. The vibration pattern imitated the standard vibration pattern of a smart phone: a 0.5 Hz 50 % duty signal was presented for 60 s when the system detected that the participant experienced stress. The vibration was controlled by software using an Arduino UNO. Eleven participants (6 males, 5 females, mean age 21.3 years) participated the experiment.

RESULTS

We compared the results obtained under the two haptic stimulus conditions, 0.06 MPa/2 s and 0.18 MPa/2 s, which were found to affect the physiological responses significantly in experiment 1.

LF/HF Change

The result of LF/HF change is shown in Figure 14. As we found no homogeneity of variances, we used a non-parametric one-way ANOVA (Kruskal-Wallis test) for the analysis. There was a significant difference ($X^2 = 30.661$, df = 2, $p < .0001$) among the three conditions. A non-parametric multiple comparison using the Steel-Dwass test was used for pairwise analysis. The result showed that the change in LF/HF for the vibration condition (M = 1.062, SD = 0.44) was significantly low compared to that of the 0.06 MPa/2 s condition and significantly high compared to that of the 0.18 MPa/5 s condition ($p < .05$).

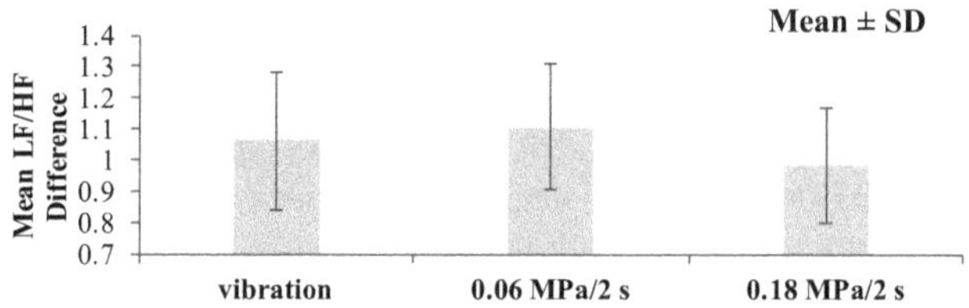

Figure 14. LF/HF change (vibration vs. air vortex ring)

Brainwave Activities

Figure 15 shows the results of the mean absent/focused state. For the absent state, as we found no homogeneity of variances, we used a non-parametric one-way ANOVA (Kruskal-Wallis test) for the analysis. There was a significant difference ($X^2 = 29.194$, df = 2, $p < .0001$) among three conditions. A non-parametric multiple comparison using the Steel-Dwass test was used for pairwise analysis. The results show that the vibration condition (M = 1.045, SD = 1.419) induced a significantly higher absent state than the 0.18 MPa/2 s condition ($p < .0001$). For the focused state, as we found no homogeneity of variances, we used a non-parametric one-way ANOVA (Kruskal-Wallis test) for the analysis. There was a significant difference ($X^2 = 57.852$, df = 2, $p < .0001$) among the three conditions. A non-parametric multiple comparison using the Steel-Dwass test was used for pairwise analysis. The results show that the vibration condition (M = 1.386, SD = 0.558) generated a significantly higher focused state than the 0.06 MPa/2 s condition ($p < .0001$).

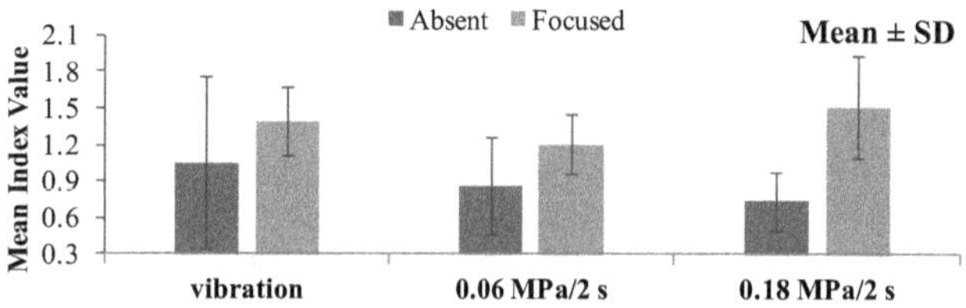

Figure 15. Absent/Focused index (vibration vs. air vortex ring)

Task Performance

The results of the task performance are shown in Figure 16. After confirming the homogeneity of variances by Bartlett's test, a one-way ANOVA was used to compare the task performance obtained under the three conditions. There was a significant difference ($F(2,96) = 3.686$, $p < .05$) among them. However, a multiple comparison using the Tukey HSD test revealed that there was no significant difference between each of the two air vortex ring haptic stimulus conditions and the vibration condition (M = -0.00001, SD = 7.529).

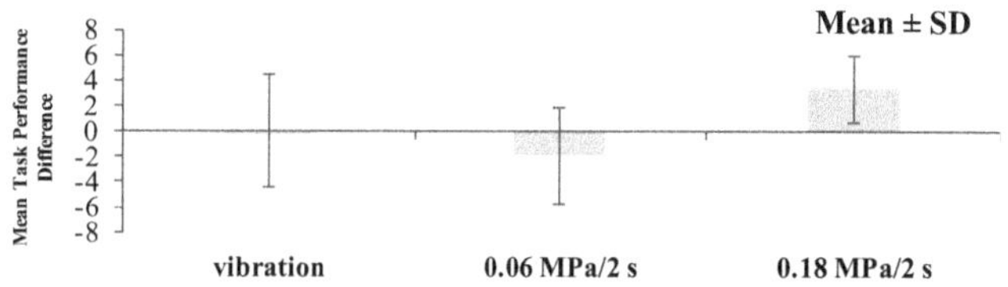

Figure 16. Task performance (vibration vs. air vortex ring)

Subjective Assessment

Figure 17 shows the results of the mean ratings of the three subjective feelings. There were no significant difference in fatigue and conscious drowsiness. However, for carelessness, after confirming the homogeneity of variances by Bartlett's test, a one-way ANOVA was used to compare the task performance obtained under the three conditions. There was a significant difference ($F(2,96) = 8.086$, $p < .0001$) among them. A multiple comparison using the Tukey HSD test confirmed that the vibration condition (M = 23.120, SD = 24.086) induced significantly higher carelessness ratings than both the 0.06 MPa/2 s condition ($p < .0001$) and 0.18 MPa/2 s condition ($p < .05$).

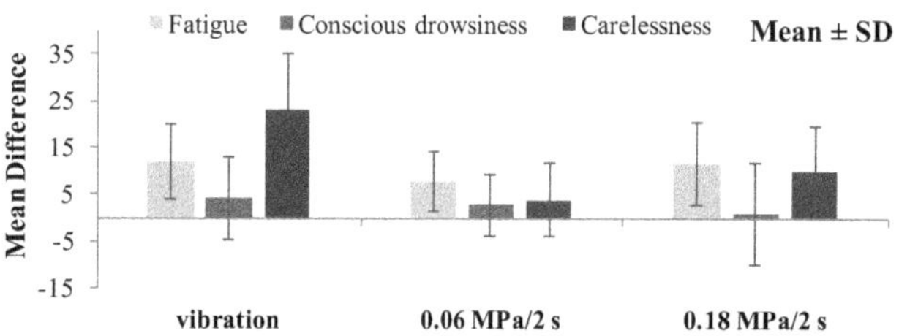

Figure 17. Subjective assessment (vibration vs. air vortex ring)

DISCUSSION

As a comparative experiment, we evaluated whether the haptic stimulus generated by a vibration motor affects physiological responses in a user similarly to the haptic stimulus generated by air vortex rings. With respect to the LF/HF change, we found that the increase in stress was less inhibited by the vibration stimulus compared to the 0.18 MPa/2 s condition. In addition, a decrease in stress was observed compared to the 0.06 MPa/2 s condition, which increased the stress the most. This implies the vibration stimulus neither decreases nor increases stress. With respect to the brainwave activities, we observed a synchronous increase in both absent and focused indices. However, we note that the results of experiment 1 do not suggest any meaningful results with respect to the synchronous state of both indices. With respect to the task performance, we found no significant difference between the results of the vibration and air vortex ring stimuli. This implies that the vibration stimulus neither increase nor decrease the task performance. With respect to the subjective feelings, we found that significantly high ratings of carelessness were observed in the vibration condition. Comments from the participant clarified that the haptic feedback of the vibration prevented concentration during the experiment and the stimuli were annoying.

LIMITATIONS

It is important to mention the limitations that arose in this experiment. To be precise, we do not know the details of the algorithm used to measure the four emotional labels determined by the EMOTIV's proprietary algorithm. Although EMOTIV is widely used in HCI research to measure emotional state objectively in an non-invasive way [2] [13] [27] [26], the raw data of spectral bands recorded as the alpha, beta, and theta states should be computed to get valid results. Although the emotional labels are not fully trustworthy, we observed different tendencies among different conditions in the experiments. Therefore, although we do not know the exact formulae used to derive the labels, we discuss the results of the EEG as an example of the observed tendencies. However, we do not generalize the conclusion in this study.

We also admit the limitation of the number of participants in this experiment being small, and because it was a short-term experiment, we cannot reach definite conclusions yet. However, as an initial experiment, it is meaningful in that we could observe a few physiological responses induced by the air vortex ring haptic stimuli.

In the subjective assessment in experiment 1, we could not find any difference among all stimuli conditions. One of the reasons is that the question topics (fatigue, conscious drowsiness, and carelessness) were inadequate for observing the difference in subjective feelings for this experiment because the series of two-hour problem solving tasks would increase the feelings in the questions in any situation. In addition, because subjective feelings are considered explicit responses, whereas physiological responses or cognitive responses indicated by task performance are implicit, haptic stimuli using air vortex rings may not be effective in affecting explicit feelings yet. We need to conduct the experiments with a greater number of participants, with long-term tasks to evaluate these questions. One function that we have to implement for lengthy experiments is a tracking system that deals with a participant's movements. In this study, because there was only one task in the experiment, which was a short-time computer operation in a sitting position for 30 min, we could present the tactile stimulation on the cheek without having the participant' move much.

CONCLUSION

To develop a haptic display that would present haptic stimulation directly on anyone's skin, we adopted the cheek as a display area after investigating quantitatively that it had enough resolution to perceive the difference in air vortex ring stimuli generated by the system. In addition, we developed an interactive cheek haptic display that presented either a strong or weak intensity stimulus at two- or five-second intervals when a participant experienced stress. The intensities of the display were determined by the experiment, where the subjective impression of sixteen different stimuli pairs were investigated (8 different intensities × 2 time intervals). In this study, we used the strong (0.18 MPa) and weak (0.06 MPa) intensities that the participants felt the most from among the stimuli pairs. These intensities also presented different impressions for six adjective pairs depicting emotion.

Further we conducted an experiment to evaluate how participants perceive haptic stimuli generated by air vortex rings and observed the effect of the air vortex rings on the physiological responses. We found that the 0.06 MPa/2 s condition did not inhibit the increase in stress and led to a low task performance. We also observed a relative increase in the absent state of the brainwave activities. In contrast, the 0.18 MPa/2 s condition effectively inhibited the increase in stress. Furthermore, it led to a high task performance and we observed a relative increase in the focused state of the brainwave activities. In the additional experiment, we compared the effect of stimuli generated by the air vortex rings with that generated by a vibration motor. The simple vibrotactile feedback on the cheek had no effect, but created a subjective feeling that concentration was lost.

Given these results, we will revise the interactive air-vortex-ring haptic display for long-term experiments. By conducting a long-term experiment, we want to find out the varieties of haptic stimuli combinations that induce attention or relaxation depending on the user's situation.

REFERENCES

1. Miguel Bruns Alonso and Caroline C. M. Hummels David V. Keyson. 2008. Squeeze, rock, and roll; can tangible interaction with affective products support stress reduction?. In *Proceedings of the 2nd international conference on Tangible and embedded interaction (TEI '08)*. 105–108. DOI: http://dx.doi.org/10.1145/1347390.1347413

2. Marvin Andujar and Juan E. Gilbert. 2013. Let's learn!: enhancing user's engagement levels through passive brain-computer interfaces. In *CHI '13 Extended Abstracts on Human Factors in Computing Systems*

(CHI EA '13). 703–708. DOI: http://dx.doi.org/10.1145/2468356.2468480

3. Marvin Andujar and Patricia Morreale Juan I. Ekandem, Juan E. Gilbert. 2013. Evaluating Engagement Physiologically and Knowledge Retention Subjectively through Two Different Learning Techniques. In *Proceedings, Part II, Vol. 8005 of Lecture Notes in Computer Science (HCII 2013)*. 335–342. DOI: http://dx.doi.org/10.1007/978-3-642-39262-7_38
4. Mohamad A. Eid and Hussein A. Osman. 2015. Affective Haptics: Current Research and Future Directions. *IEEE Access* 4 (2015). DOI: http://dx.doi.org/10.1109/ACCESS.2015.2497316
5. EMOTIV. 2011. Epoc+ Mobile EEG. (2011). https://www.emotiv.com/product/emotiv-epoc-14-channel-mobile-eeg/.
6. C. S. Alberto Gallace. 2010. The science of interpersonal touch: An overview. *Neuroscience and Biobehavioral Reviews* 34 (2010). DOI: http://dx.doi.org/10.1016/j.neubiorev.2008.10.004
7. Elia Gatti, Giandomenico Caruso, Monica Bordegoni, and Charles Spence. 2013. Can the feel of the haptic interaction modify a user's emotional state?. In *Proc. World Haptics Conference*. IEEE, 247–252.
8. D. Gould, D. Kelly, L. Goldstone, and J. Gammon. 2001. Examining the validity of pressure ulcer risk assessment scales: developing and using illustrated patient simulations to collect the data. *Journal of Clinical Nursing* 10, 5 (2001), 697–706.
9. Sidhant Gupta, Dan Morris, Shwetak Patel, and Desney Tan. 2013. AirWave: Non-Contact Haptic Feedback Using Air Vortex Rings. In *Proc. UbiComp 2013*. ACM, 1–10.
10. Taku Hachisu and Masaaki Fukumoto. 2014. VacuumTouch: Attractive Force Feedback Interface for Haptic Interactive Surface using Air Suction. In *Proc. CHI 2014*. ACM Press, 411–420.
11. S. Hashiguchi, N. Omori, S. Yamamoto, R. Ueoka, and T. Takeda. 2012a. Application to 3D Theater using a Air Pressured Facial Tactile Display. In *Proc. of Asia Digital Art and Design*.
12. S. Hashiguchi, F. Takamori, R. Ueoka, and T. Takeda. 2012b. Evaluation of subjective impression of air pressured facial tactile display by vortex air cannon. *The Journal of Human Interface Symposium* 14, 4 (2012), 73–80.
13. Jin Huang, Yuntao Wang Chun Yu, Siqi Liu Yuhang Zhao, Jie Liu Chou Mo, and Yuanchun Shi Lie Zhang. 2014. FOCUS: enhancing children's engagement in reading by using contextual BCI training sessions. In *Proceedings of the SIGCHI Conference on Human Factors in Computing Systems (CHI '14)*. 1905–1908. DOI: http://dx.doi.org/10.1145/2556288.2557339
14. N. Nishimura, A. Ishi, M.Sato, S. Fukushima, and H. Kajimoto. 2012. Facilitation of Affection by Tactile Feedback of False Heartbeat. In *Proc. CHI 2012*. ACM Press, 2321–2326.
15. Marianna Obrist, Elia Gatti Sriram Subramanian, and Thomas Carter Benjamin Long. 2015. Emotions Mediated Through Mid-Air Haptics. In *Proceedings of the 33rd Annual ACM Conference on Human Factors in Computing Systems (CHI '15)*. 2053 – 2062. DOI: http://dx.doi.org/10.1145/2702123.2702361
16. National Institute of Advanced Industrial Science and Technology. 2001. AIST Japanese head size database 2001. Web. (1 Dec 2001). https://www.dh.aist.go.jp/database/head/index.html.
17. NCSP Pam MS. 2012. What is Method of Limits? (2012). https://www.emotiv.com/product/emotiv-epoc-14-channel-mobile-eeg/.
18. Trevor Pels and Saguna Goel Christina Kao. 2014. FatBelt: motivating behavior change through isomorphic feedback. In *Proceedings of the adjunct publication of the 27th annual ACM symposium on User interface software and technology (UIST'14 Adjunct)*. 123–124. DOI: http://dx.doi.org/10.1145/2658779.2658807
19. E. T. Rolls. 2010. The affective and cognitive processing of touch, oral texture, and temperature in the brain. *Neuroscience and Biobehavioral Reviews* 34 (2010). DOI: http://dx.doi.org/10.1016/j.neubiorev.2008.03.010
20. J. O. D. E.T. Rolls, M.L. Kringelbach, S. Francis, R. Bowtell, and F. McGlone. 2003. Representations of Pleasant and Painful Touch in the Human Orbitofrontal and Cingulate Cortices. *Cerebral Corte* 13, 3 (2003), 308–317. DOI: http://dx.doi.org/10.1093/cercor/13.3.308
21. Katri Salminen, Veikko Surakka, Jani Kylykangas, Jukka Raisamo, Rami Saarinen, Roope Raisamo, Jussi Rantala, and Grigori Evreinov. 2008. Emotional and Behavioral Responses to Haptic Stimulation. In *Proc. CHI 2008*. ACM Press, 1555–1562.
22. Katri Salminen, Veikko Surakka, Jani Lylykangas, Jussi rantala, Pauli Laitinen, and Roope Raisamo. 2011. Evaluations of Piezo Actuated Haptic Stimulations. In *Proc. Affective computing and intelligent interaction(ACII) 2011*. Springer-Verlag, 296–305.
23. Rajinder Sodhi, Ivan Poupyrev, Matthew Glisson, and Ali Israr. 2013. AIREAL: interactive tactile experiences in free air. *ACM Trans. Graph.* 32, 4 (2013), 1–10. DOI: http://dx.doi.org/10.1145/2185520.2185585
24. Yuriko Suzuki, Minoru Kobayashi, and Satoshi Ishibashi. 2002. Design of Force Feedback Utilizing Air Pressure toward Untethered Human Interface. In *Ext. Abstracts CHI 2002*. ACM Press, 808–809.

25. S.Weinstein. 1968. Intensive and extensive aspects of tactile sensitivity as a function of body part, sex and laterality. In *Proc. 1st Int'l Symp. on the Skin Senses*. Springfield, IL,USA, 196–222.
26. Daniel Szafir and Bilge Mutlu. 2012. Pay attention!: designing adaptive agents that monitor and improve user engagement. In *Proceedings of the SIGCHI Conference on Human Factors in Computing Systems (CHI '12)*. 11–20. DOI: http://dx.doi.org/10.1145/2207676.2207679
27. Daniel Szafir and Bilge Mutlu. 2013. ARTFul: adaptive review technology for flipped learning. In *Proceedings of the SIGCHI Conference on Human Factors in Computing Systems (CHI '13)*. 1001–1010. DOI: http://dx.doi.org/10.1145/2470654.2466128
28. A. Weigand and M. Gharib. 1997. On the evolution of laminar vortex rings. *Experiments in Fluids* 22 (1997). DOI: http://dx.doi.org/10.1007/s003480050071
29. Paul Weisberg and James E. Russell. 1971. Proximity and Interactional Behavior of Young Children to Their "Security" Blankets. *Child Development* 42, 5 (1971), 1575–1971.

SkinMarks: Enabling Interactions on Body Landmarks Using Conformal Skin Electronics

Martin Weigel[1] Aditya Shekhar Nittala[1] Alex Olwal[2] Jürgen Steimle[1]
[1] Saarland University, Saarland Informatics Campus, Germany
[2] Google Inc., Mountain View, California, United States
{weigel, nittala, steimle}@cs.uni-saarland.de, olwal@google.com

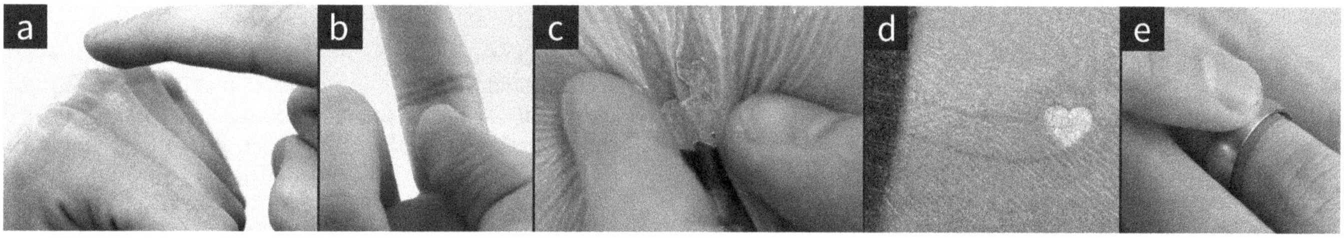

Figure 1: SkinMarks are conformal on-skin sensors and displays. They enable interaction on five types of body landmarks: (a) skeletal landmarks, (b) skin microstructures, (c) elastic landmarks, (d) visual skin landmarks, and (e) accessories.

ABSTRACT
The body provides many recognizable landmarks due to the underlying skeletal structure and variations in skin texture, elasticity, and color. The visual and spatial cues of such body landmarks can help in localizing on-body interfaces, guide input on the body, and allow for easy recall of mappings. Our main contribution are SkinMarks, *novel skin-worn I/O devices* for precisely localized input and output on fine body landmarks. SkinMarks comprise skin electronics on temporary rub-on tattoos. They conform to fine wrinkles and are compatible with strongly curved and elastic body locations. We identify *five types of body landmarks* and demonstrate novel interaction techniques that leverage SkinMarks' unique touch, squeeze and bend sensing with integrated visual output. Finally, we detail on the conformality and evaluate sub-millimeter electrodes for touch sensing. Taken together, SkinMarks expands the on-body interaction space to more detailed, highly curved and challenging areas on the body.

Author Keywords
On-body interaction; on-skin sensing; on-skin display; epidermal electronics; electronic tattoos; fabrication; flexible display.

ACM Classification Keywords
H.5.2. User Interfaces: Input devices and strategies, Interaction Styles, Haptic I/O

This work is licensed under a Creative Commons Attribution International 4.0 License.

Copyright is held by the owner/author(s).
CHI 2017, May 06-11, 2017, Denver, CO, USA
ACM 978-1-4503-4655-9/17/05.
http://dx.doi.org/10.1145/3025453.3025704

INTRODUCTION
The body is recognized as a promising input surface for mobile computing, as it offers a large and quickly accessible area for interaction. Prior research contributed input [11, 12, 14, 16, 17, 26, 27, 29, 41, 45] and output devices [11, 43] for on-body interactions. However, they mostly assume interactive elements to be rather large and only slightly curved.

The human body has various types of landmarks which are distinct from their surroundings. It offers unique possibilities for interaction due to their tactile properties and visual appearance. For example, protruding skeletal landmarks, like the knuckles, provide physical affordances for touching and circling around them. Prior work in human-computer interaction has briefly explored the potential of such unique landmarks. Gustafson et al. [8, 9], for example, suggested using the segments of the finger as distinct input buttons. However, thus far, the majority of potentially beneficial landmarks remain unexplored and unsupported. These include landmarks with highly curved geometries, tactile microstructures, or strong deformability.

This paper presents *SkinMarks*, an enabling technology for interaction on body landmarks. SkinMarks are highly conformal interactive tattoos, which enable precisely localized input and output on five types of body landmarks.

SkinMarks are inspired by recent research on slim, skin-worn sensors and displays [41, 17, 27, 43]. We extend beyond prior work by contributing highly conformal skin electronics with co-located input and output, which are compatible with strongly curved, elastic, and tiny body landmarks. These make it possible to use the plethora of tactile and visual cues on body landmarks for direct, eyes-free, and expressive interaction.

The contributions of this paper are:

- We introduce SkinMarks, novel skin-worn I/O devices with co-located input and output, which are enabled through highly conformal and precisely localized skin electronics.
- We describe a SkinMarks implementation based on temporary rub-on tattoos. It allows for custom-shaped, slim, and stretchable devices that conform to fine body landmarks.
- We identify five types of body landmarks for on-body interaction. They are informed by anatomy, skin properties, and body-worn accessories.
- We demonstrate interaction techniques on body landmarks that leverage SkinMarks' unique touch, squeeze and bend sensing with integrated visual output.
- We present results from technical evaluations and user studies that validate conformity (4 µm to 46 µm thin), precise localization, and touch input on sub-millimeter electrodes.

In summary, SkinMarks is an enabling technology for interactions on body landmarks. The highly conformal skin-worn electronics support precisely localized interactions. They expand the on-body interaction space to more detailed, highly curved, and challenging areas of the body. These advances enable novel interactions on body landmarks, which we will demonstrate in this paper.

RELATED WORK

On-body interaction uses the body as an input surface for always-available input and output in mobile computing. It has been investigated for many body parts, such as, the palm [5, 8, 9, 38, 39], fingers [2, 8, 14, 44], nails [16], arms [12, 24], back of the hand [23], and ears [26].

On-body interaction can involve various aspects of input sensing (such as touch, shear and bend sensing) as well as visual output on the body. Various approaches for input sensing have been investigated. Camera-based sensing, with RGB cameras [28, 37] or depth cameras [5, 11], allows direct input on large areas of the body, but requires line-of-sight to the camera and is susceptible to lighting conditions. Sensors injecting a signal into the body, e.g. bio-acoustic sensors [12] and electromagnetic waves [45] allow for touch and gesture sensing, work on many body locations and do not require a skin overlay. They, however, suffer from low spatial resolution and are limited to single-touch. Magnetic sensing [2, 14] employs magnets and Hall effect sensor grids, which allow for high resolution sensing on small parts of the body. They require augmenting the finger with a magnet and can only sense its position, but not robustly determine surface contact. Photo-reflective sensing [29] recognizes deformations of the skin, e.g. shear, pressure and squeeze. This recognizes the many input modalities beyond touch that can be performed on the skin [42]. Radar-based sensing [22] enables motion, range, and velocity sensing, but makes tracking of spatial configurations difficult. Another approach are on-skin electronics, which form the foundation of SkinMarks. These electronics are placed directly on the skin, thereby enabling direct input and output on the skin.

Landmarks on the body have a long tradition of use in various disciplines, including medical sciences, anthropology, and fine arts. In these contexts, a landmarks mainly act as unique and unambiguous references on or inside the body, e.g., to locate points and areas of interest, to compare biological shapes, or to measure anatomy. In visual arts, for example, body landmarks help artists find forms and assess body proportions. In contrast, in anatomical sciences, landmarks are defined as *structurally consistent loci which can have evolutionary, ontogenic, and/or functional significance, and must be consistently present on all forms under consideration in order to be useful in analysis* [21].

Prior HCI research has shown initial empirical validation that skeletal landmarks can improve interaction. Gustafson et al. show that the tactile features and natural divisions of finger and their segments allow for localization of UI elements in four-column layouts [8] and that palm-based interfaces remain usable when operated eyes-free, due to the tactile cues of the palm [9]. Dezfuli et al. [5] distinguish nine coarse landmarks on palm and fingers. Wang et al. [38] proposed using the joints between the finger segments to distinguish between five discreet buttons per finger. Also the fingertip can be used as a well-distinguishable landmark [30]. In this work, we enable landmark interactions on a considerably wider range of landmark types, by supporting input and output on highly curved geometries (e.g. knuckles), tactile skin microstructures, and landmarks with strong deformability.

We base our SkinMark implementation on the emerging stream of skin electronics and epidermal electronics [18, 10, 15, 40, 19]. These enable skin to become an interactive surface for human-computer interaction [36]. iSkin [41] introduced thin and stretchable skin overlays that capture touch and pressure input for mobile computing. These sensors are made of bio-compatible and stretchable PDMS. Using digital fabrication, they can be customized in size, shape and visual appearance. Stretchis [43] added output with stretchable electroluminescent displays by extending the PrintScreen approach [31]. Skintillates [27] achieved considerably slimmer on-skin touch and bend sensors by screen printing conductive traces on temporary rub-on tattoos. Output was realized with conventional LEDs. DuoSkin [17] uses gold leaf as a conductor and includes touch interaction, NFC communication and thermochromic visual output. Compared with interactive textiles [33], these interfaces conform more closely to skin.

This paper extends beyond this prior work in two ways, to enable interactions on body landmarks: First, we contribute sensors and displays that are compatible with strong curvature, deformation, and strain, which all are inherent to landmarks. Second, we enable sensing on fine and narrow areas of landmarks (e.g. flexure lines). Compared to PDMS-based electronics which are more than ≥200 µm thick [41, 43]), our fabricated touch sensors (4 µm) and EL displays (31 µm to 46 µm) are considerably thinner and hence allow for higher conformality to the body. In contrast to Skintillates and DuoSkin, which investigated geometries of lower curvature at the wrist (≈26 mm), our sensors support non-developable surfaces with small radii, such as the knuckles (≈8 mm). Furthermore, compared to all prior technologies, SkinMarks support touch electrodes that are a magnitude smaller ($\leq$1 mm) than those of prior work ($\geq$8 mm) [17, 27, 41]. This enables interaction on five types of body landmarks, which we introduce in the following section.

LANDMARKS FOR ON-BODY INTERACTION

In the context of HCI, body landmarks have *interactional significance*. Their main purpose is to support and ease on-body interaction. We define body landmarks as follows:

Body landmarks are locations on the body, which are *tactually or visually distinct* from the surroundings.

Body landmarks can be *generic* for all users and *permanent*, similar to landmark definitions in anatomy. However, they can also be *personal* or *temporary*.

Benefits for On-body Interaction

Localization. They help users localize interactive elements on the body by leveraging human sensory and motor capabilities: (1) Proprioception allows for coarse, eyes-free landmark localization. (2) Visual feedback allows for precise adjustments while reaching the body. (3) During the touch, tactile feedback allows for eyes-free adjustments, through the tactile sensation of the touched and of the touching surface.

Guidance. They provide affordances that inform how to interact, and also guide user input. For instance, a flexure line affords linear sliding while the soft webbing in-between fingers affords continuous pressure or stretch input.

Recall. If appropriately chosen, they can help users memorize mappings between body locations and interactive functionality. A landmark can act as a simple visual or haptic cue that reminds the user about the presence of an input widget on her body. Landmarks can also draw upon semantic associations with specific loci on the body.

Types of Body Landmarks

Based on the aforementioned definition of body landmarks, we identified five main types of landmarks that are derived from human anatomy [6] and body adornments [4]:

Skeletal Landmarks. Skeletal landmarks are created by bones and joints in the body, resulting in curved surface geometries. These can be felt by the interacting finger and guide or constrain tactile input on the body, even during eyes-free input. Pioneering research has investigated how finger segments, fingertips and segments of the palm can guide on-skin interaction [5, 8, 9, 30, 38]. Yet, the body offers a much wider variety of skeletal landmarks. For example, the highly curved geometry of a protruding knuckle affords touch contact, while a straight finger affords linear sliding movements. Moving beyond static landmarks, some skeletal landmarks allow for *dynamic* poses. For example, a straight hand has a relatively flat and even surface along the knuckles, which affords linear sliding motions. It can be dynamically transformed to a highly curved area when forming a fist, with four knuckles clearly protruding; this affords interaction on discrete areas.

In addition to skeletal anatomy, the properties of skin allow for additional, previously unexplored, types of landmarks:

Skin Microstructure Landmarks. The fine tactile texture of skin can largely vary, e.g., due to flexure lines, wrinkles, and hair follicles. These tactile cues can be felt by the interacting fingertip. This can generate tiny and fine landmarks that allow for highly localized on-skin interactions.

Elastic Landmarks. The elasticity of skin varies across body locations, depending on the amount of elastin in the dermis layer [20]. For example, a webbing has a considerably higher elasticity than its surrounding. These soft landmarks afford localized skin deformations, such as shearing, stretching, and squeezing, for continuous and expressive on-body input.

Visual Skin Landmarks. Skin varies in its pigmentation and therefore offers landmarks that stand out by their visual properties. For example, birthmarks can form clearly articulated visual entities. These landmarks are highly personal and differ in their occurrence and location across users. Their visual cues support spatial mappings, provide cues for localization, and their shapes afford different touch interactions.

Landmarks of these four types can occur naturally on the body. However, such landmarks could also be actively added or modified by the user, e.g., through make-up, tattoos, or even implants. In addition to these body-intrinsic landmarks, external objects that are worn on the body can create temporary and removable landmarks:

Accessory Landmarks. Body-worn accessories, such as rings, bracelets, earrings, or wristwatches, provide tactile and visual cues on the body. As such, they can function as a temporary, user-generated body landmark. They can be easily located on the body and can offer distinct physical affordances for interaction; e.g., a ring can be touched and rotated [1].

IMPLEMENTATION OF SKINMARKS

Body landmarks create a demanding set of challenges for the implementation of input and output surfaces: First, on-skin electronics must be *conformal* on landmarks, despite their highly curved geometries and extensive skin deformation. Second, interaction with on-skin electronics must be *precisely localized* to allow for interaction on body landmarks that can be small and of irregular geometry.

This section presents the implementation of SkinMarks interactive tattoos, which enable interaction on body landmarks. We start by providing an overview of our fabrication approach. Then we detail on our technical contributions to make SkinMarks conformal on challenging geometries. Finally, we describe the implementation of precisely localized, co-located input and output surfaces for sensing of touch, bend and squeeze input and for visual display.

Fabrication: Multi-layer Functional Inks on Tattoo Paper

Body landmarks can vary greatly for an individual user and between users. We base our implementation of SkinMarks on screen-printed electronics, because it is a flexible method to create small volumes of thin-film sensors and displays that feature a custom shape and a high print resolution [31].

To fabricate an interactive tattoo, we use commercially available temporary tattoo paper (Tattoo Decal Paper) as the substrate, as proposed in recent work [17, 27]. We screen print one or multiple layers of functional inks onto it. After printing each layer, the ink is heat cured with a heat gun (130°C, 3 minutes). After adding a thin adhesive layer, the tattoo is ready to be transferred onto skin.

SkinMarks are powered and controlled using an Arduino microcontroller. We recommend to place the microcontroller at a body location which offers enough space and undergoes little mechanical strain, for instance the wrist. For connecting the tattoo with this location, we extend the tattoo by printed conductive traces that each end with a printed connector surface in close proximity to the microcontroller. We solder a conventional wire onto copper tape and adhere the tape to the isolation layer, under the printed connector.

Conformal Interactive Tattoos: Slim and Stretchable

To ensure that an interactive tattoo is conformal on challenging landmark geometries and robust to stretching, we set out to minimize the thickness of printed functional layers (as suggested in [15]) and to use intrinsically stretchable materials.

Layer thickness is mainly influenced by two factors: screen density and ink viscosity. We minimized the layer thickness by printing with a dense screen (140TT). We further reduced the thickness of conductive structures by printing a conducting polymer (PEDOT:PSS translucent conductor, Gwent C2100629D1, 500-700 Ω/sq). Compared to silver ink, which was used in prior work [27], the ink is less viscous and results in considerably thinner layers. The thickness of a screen-printed layer of PEDOT:PSS conductor is approximately 1 µm, a magnitude slimmer than screen-printed silver in prior work (≈16 µm [27]). A tattoo with a touch sensor measures approximately 4 µm. A tattoo with visual output measures 31 µm to 46 µm, including the tattoo paper. This allows us to introduce temporary tattoos for tactile user input and visual output on highly challenging locations, such as the knuckles.

PEDOT:PSS conducting polymer has an additional important advantage over conductors made of metal, such as silver ink [17] or gold leaf [27]: it is intrinsically stretchable [25]. This does not only make the conductor conform better to challenging geometries; it also makes it considerably more robust to mechanical strain [25]. To further improve the robustness, we recommend laying out conductors in a horse-shoe pattern [13] in locations that are subject to extensive strain (e.g., knuckles, webbing, or wrist) or route traces around such areas, if possible.

Based on these principles, we show conformal touch, bend and squeeze sensors and conformal EL displays that allow for interaction on body landmarks (see Figure 2).

Touch Sensing

Touch has been identified as an important input modality for on-skin electronics [41, 27, 17]. Solutions from prior work used fingertip-sized electrodes [41, 27, 17]. Body landmarks require smaller electrodes for precisely localized interaction on the landmark, e.g. flexure lines.

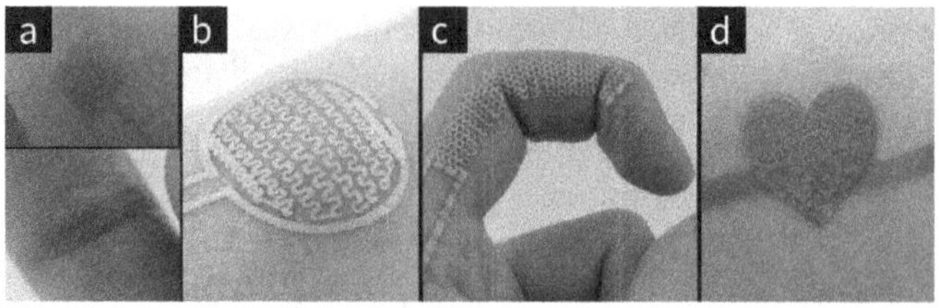

Figure 2: SkinMarks supports: (a) capacitive touch buttons and sliders, (b) squeeze sensors, (c) bend sensors, and (d) electroluminescent displays.

We use capacitive loading mode sensing (single capacitance) to measure touch contact and sliding (Figure 2a). The touch-sensitive electrodes are printed with one conductive layer of PEDOT:PSS and are connected to a commercial capacitive touch controller (Adafruit MPR121). Each tattoo can contain one or multiple custom-shaped electrodes, which can be printed in close proximity to each other. They support interpolation and allow for slider sensor designs [3].

Our evaluation of touch sensors shows that SkinMarks allows for electrodes with a width of 0.25 mm and hence supports small landmarks. This is by an order of magnitude smaller than prior on-skin touch sensors [17, 27, 41].

Squeeze and Bend Sensing

Skin allows for deformation input as a a further modality for tactile on-body interactions, as recommended in [42]. Deformation interaction can be used on various landmarks, but is especially interesting for elastic landmarks to leverage their intrinsic deformability.

We present an embedded sensor for capturing *squeeze input* on skin, based on a printed strain gauge. Squeezing deforms the skin and results in compressive strain on the strain gauge. We found that the intrinsic stretchability of PEDOT:PSS prevents the strain gauge from giving precise readings. Therefore, we use silver ink (Flexible Silver Ink, Gwent C2131014D3). However, our initial tests showed that the brittle silver tends to break easily. To increase the robustness for high-stress areas on the body, we cover the silver pattern with a second layer of PEDOT:PSS containing the exact same pattern. This allows the strain gauge to remain functional, even when the silver connection breaks at a few locations, because the second layer bridges the breaks.

We implemented two squeeze sensor designs. They have a trace width of 0.75 mm. The larger one, designed for the forearm, has a dimension of 60×21 mm with 13 parallel lines laid out in a horse-shoe pattern. The smaller one (Figure 2b) was designed for the head of the ulna, is dimensioned 21×21 mm and features 9 parallel lines.

We evaluated the robustness of squeeze input by measuring the signal to noise ratio [3]. For a sample with a dimension of 60x21 mm, we calculated the average SNR of six squeeze sensors. They were deployed on six locations on the upper limb of five participants, chosen to cover a wide range of skinfolds

(2–23mm; measured with an EagleFit Slim Guide Caliper). Each sensor was squeezed 20 times. The squeeze sensors achieved an average SNR of 17.0 (SD=7.97).

Furthermore, SkinMarks supports *bend sensing*, similar to prior work [27]. We use this principle to detect dynamic pose-changes of skeletal landmarks to allow for dynamic interface elements. The bend sensor on the finger measures 72x8 mm and features 6 parallel lines with the horseshoe pattern. Again, the additional layer of PEDOT:PSS prevents the strain gauge from breaking in case of tiny cracks in the silver layer. We show this principle on the finger (see Figure 2c).

Conformal Touch-sensitive Displays

We contribute tattoo-embedded active displays to allow for custom-shaped, co-located input and visual output on SkinMarks. Our displays have a faster response time than thermochromic displays [17] and are considerably slimmer than prior body-worn LEDs [27] and EL displays [43]. They are thin and robust enough to conform to challenging geometric landmarks, such as knuckles or the flexure lines of the palm. The overall thickness of the display is between 31 μm to 46 μm. It is deformable and captures touch input (see Figure 1c, 2d, and 4).

We base our implementation on electroluminescent (EL) displays, which feature high update rates and energy-efficiency. The implementation follows the basic principle introduced by PrintScreen [31]. In contrast, our displays use two electrodes made of PEDOT-based translucent conductor. As discussed earlier, this allows for thinner and more robust layers. Between the electrodes is one layer of phosphor paste that determines the color of the display. We further reduce the thickness of the display by replacing the dielectric paste used in prior work by a transparent resin binder (Gwent R2070613P2). The resin binder is used as a dielectric and allows for printing thinner layers. Furthermore, it is completely transparent to avoid visible margins, as presented in prior work [31]. The EL display is driven with a Rogers D355B Electroluminescent Lamp Driver IC (145 V; max. 1 mA). It allows for integrated touch sensing by time-multiplexing a display cycle and a capacitive sensing cycle, as introduced in previous work [31].

INTERACTION ON BODY LANDMARKS

SkinMarks enable new forms of on-body interaction. We present novel interaction techniques for the five types of body landmarks: skeletal, skin microstructure, elastic, visual skin, and accessory landmarks.

Tactile Cues on Skeletal Landmarks

The high curvature of skeletal landmarks creates distinct tactile and visual cues, which support on-body interaction in various ways. For one, cues can help the user to memorize mappings; for instance, the user can associate an input element with a specific knuckle. Second, cues can also help localize the input element while looking at it or feeling the geometry through the touching finger. In addition, different geometries afford for different interactions. Last but not least, unique geometries can also be formed by a group of multiple adjacent landmarks, such as the four knuckles of a hand.

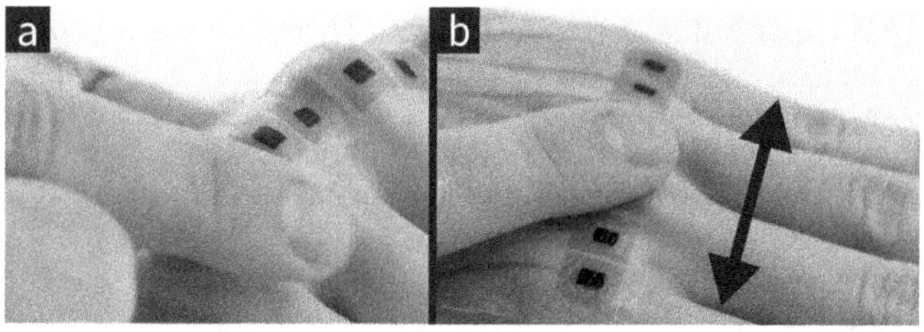

Figure 3: Interaction on challenging, highly curved skeletal landmarks: (a) tapping the peaks and valleys for discrete input; (b) sliding along the knuckles for continuous input.

We demonstrate these benefits for on-body interaction by deploying a touch-sensitive SkinMark sensor on the knuckles (Figure 3). SkinMarks allow for input on the knuckles (knuckle peaks) and around the knuckles (knuckle valleys), both areas with a high curvature. These can be used to distinguish multiple different input elements that are associated with either a valley or a peak. We demonstrate that the knuckles can be used as discreet touch elements (fist) or as a slider that provide small tactile ticks (flat hand).

Dynamic Interface Elements using Pose-based Input

Body movement allows for dynamic interface elements using pose-based input on skeletal body landmarks. The ability to change the pose on demand enables various novel interactions. For instance, when the user is making a fist the knuckles have a high curvature, clearly exposing the knuckle peaks. This allows for precisely locating discrete touch buttons. In contrast, while doing a flat hand, the knuckles form a relatively flat surface, which allows for continuous sliding (see Figure 3).

SkinMarks can capture the current body pose and change the interface dynamically. To illustrate this, we implemented a music player control, which is worn on the side of the index finger (Figure 4). It contains a printed bend sensor overlaid with touch-sensitive display elements. Those elements change their functionality based on the pose of the finger. When the index finger is straight, it affords continuous and linear movement along the finger (Figure 4a). It then acts as a volume slider. When it is bent, the flexure lines at the joints become more prominent; they visually and tactually split the input area into three distinct areas (Figure 4b).

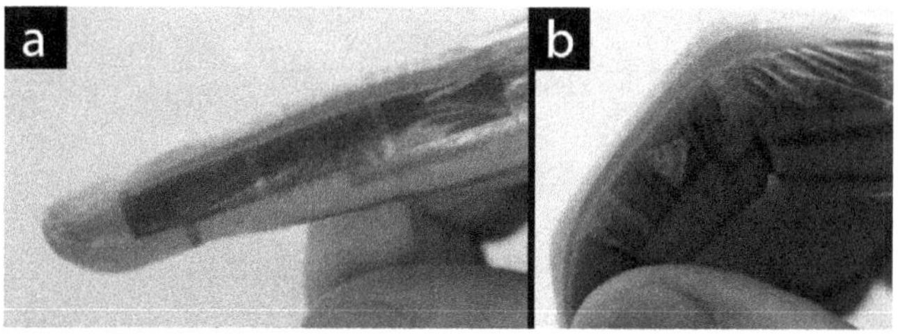

Figure 4: Using body posture to dynamically change functionality: (a) Straight finger for linear movements, e.g. to control volume, (b) bent finger for discrete touch areas.

These afford discrete touch input. Therefore, when bent, the interface switches to three discrete buttons for play/pause, next song and previous song. The integrated displays show which mode is active, either by illuminating the buttons or the slider. Switching between these modes is fast, easy and discreet to perform.

Precise Touch Input on Skin Microstructure Landmarks

Body landmarks can be small and still very beneficial for on-body interaction. Our temporary tattoos allow for precise application on the landmark and for precise touch elements. This allows for sensing touch input exactly on the location of a tiny landmark to use its tactile properties.

We demonstrate this with a new interaction technique that makes use of tactile skin surface-structure: The Wrinkle Slide interaction technique. A touch sensor augments one or multiple flexure lines (the larger wrinkles) on a finger. By *sliding along* the flexure line, the user can continuously adjust a value. A selection can be made by tapping. The precise tactile cues of the flexure line allow for tactile localization and guide the user during sliding, without requiring visual attention. The technique also allows for one-handed input using the thumb of the same hand (thumb-to-finger input). Therefore, it can support interactions in busy mobile scenarios, e.g., while running. We demonstrate its use as a one-handed remote to control the volume of a mobile music player.

The wrinkle slider contains two triangular printed electrodes, which together measure 30×4.5 mm (Figure 5a). They are used for capacitive touch sensing. Interpolation allows to capture the touch location on the slider. SkinMarks are thin enough to closely conform to flexure lines and allow feeling of the wrinkle through the sensor tattoo.

A similar sensor design allows for toggle input (Figure 5b). The user switches the toggle on or off by *sliding across* a flexure line. The tactile feedback provides interactional awareness to the user. The input is sensed with two parallel slim electrodes. The temporal signature in their touch response determines the direction of the slide. The input can be mapped to opposed commands, e.g. to accept or decline calls.

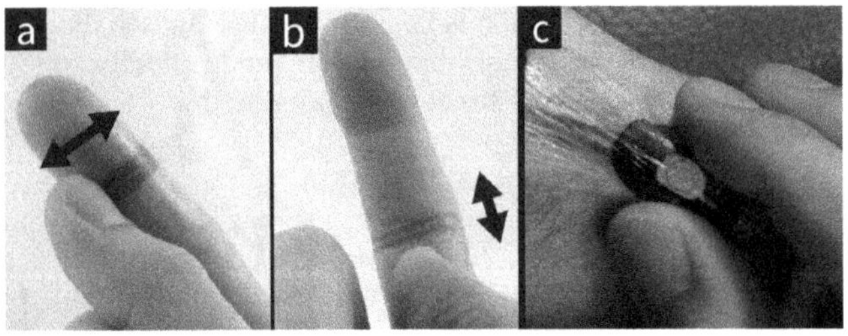

Figure 5: SkinMarks allow for precise touch input on skin microstructures: (a) wrinkle slider and (b) wrinkle toggle. (c) Interacting on an elastic landmark.

Expressive Deformation Input on Elastic Landmarks

Localized deformation input enriches the input vocabulary of landmarks. For example, an interface can distinguish between touch input and squeeze input to trigger different commands.

We demonstrate deformation input on the circular protrusion on the wrist created by the head of the ulna bone. This location is easily localizable through its visual and tactile cues. We implemented a *CaptureMark* (Figure 5c). The CaptureMark is a circular ball for capturing virtual objects in augmented reality games, e.g. treasures or Pokémon. The user is notified about virtual objects with an audio feedback. The user can attempt catching it by squeezing the tattoo. Afterwards, the CaptureMark blinks and finally lights up for a few seconds to notify the user that the virtual object is caught.

Dynamic Visual Cues on Visual Skin Landmarks

Visual landmarks on the skin can be leveraged to provide personalized and dynamic visual cues for on-body interaction. To illustrate this type of landmark interaction, we have implement a *HeartMark* (Figure 6b), a touch-sensitive heart-shaped display to augment a birthmark. The HeartMark notifies the user about the availability of a loved one. Touching it starts a call with that person.

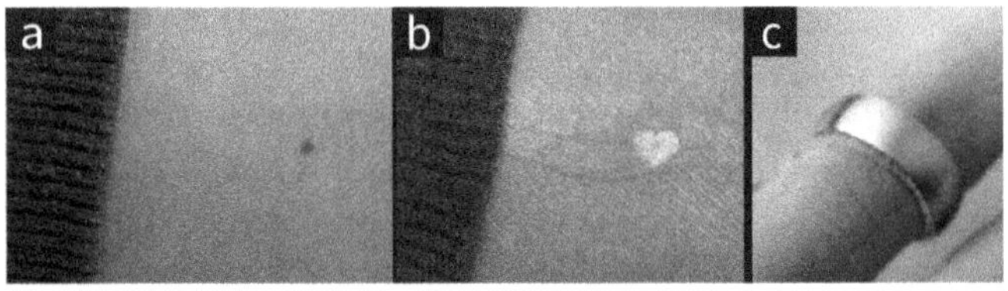

Figure 6: SkinMarks can augment visual skin landmarks, e.g. birthmarks (a–b), and passive accessories, e.g. a ring (c).

Interaction on Passive Accessories

Body-worn passive accessories can function as a landmark for interaction, given that they provide unique tactile and visual cues. Although accessories are widely used, they have not been integrated with on-body electronics. SkinMarks enable interaction with passive objects in two ways: First, it enables skin illumination under and around the object using on-body displays, similar to ScatterWatch [32]. Second, it can make accessories touch-sensitive, through capacitance tags [34]. Touch sensing requires the accessory to be conductive; this holds true for a wide variety of jewelry and other accessories. Neither interaction require modification of the passive accessory.

We implemented an augmentation for a wedding ring (Figure 6c), to allow for subtle communication between both partners. Touching the ring creates a glow around the partner's ring. This is made possible by affixing an interactive tattoo at the finger segment where the ring is worn. The tattoo contains a non-exposed conductor which lies under the ring and capacitively couples with it for touch sensing. Moreover, it contains a visual display that slightly extends beyond the ring, for on-demand illumination.

TECHNICAL EVALUATION

This section presents results from technical experiments that investigate the two key technical contributions of SkinMarks: First, do SkinMarks support interaction on challenging landmarks by *conforming to skin* despite high curvatures and strong elasticity? Second, do SkinMarks allow for *precisely localized interaction* on fine landmarks?

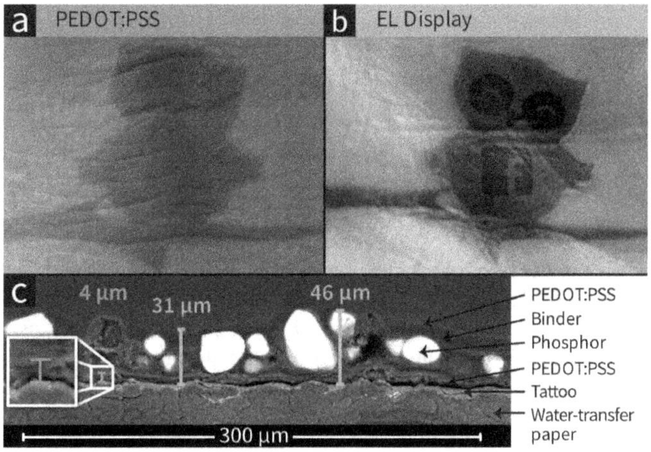

Figure 7: SkinMarks conform to wrinkles: (a) a tattoo with PEDOT:PSS conductor; (b) tattoo with EL display. (c) Cross-section of a tattoo with printed EL display, taken with a scanning electron microscope (SEM).

Conformal Form Factor

We investigated the two main factors for conformal electronics: thickness and stretchability.

To investigate the layer thickness of printed inks on a SkinMark, we analyzed cross-sections of printed SkinMark tattoos on the water-transfer paper with a Scanning Electron Microscope (SEM). Figure 7 shows the various layers of inks. A layer of PEDOT:PSS layers is approximately 1 µm thick (≈4 µm with tattoo paper). A full TFEL display is between 31 µm to 46 µm thick (Figure 7c). These numbers demonstrate the vastly reduced display thickness compared to prior interactive tattoos [17, 27] and TFEL displays [31, 43]. Figure 7 a&b illustrate how SkinMark tattoos closely conform to wrinkles. Our results confirm prior research of Jeong et al. [15], which show that elastomer membranes of 5 µm have excellent conformality even to small wrinkles, while membranes of 36 µm have good conformality on larger wrinkles (e.g. flexure lines).

Our experiments showed that the stretchability of the tattoo substrate ranges between 25–30%. PEDOT:PSS retains conductivity up to 188% strain and is reversibly stretchable up to 30% strain [25]. For comparison, the stretchability of the human epidermis is around 20% [35]. The combination of both makes SkinMarks intrinsically stretchable and more robust against strain than metals (e.g. [17, 27]).

Precise Localization: Touch Input and Tattoo Application

We validate the two necessary conditions for precisely localized input. First, can touch input be accurately sensed on sub-millimeter electrodes? Second, are users able to apply tattoos with a high spatial accuracy on the landmarks?

Touch Input on Sub-Millimeter Electrodes

Methodology. We recruited 12 voluntary participants (2 female, 22–32 years, mean 26.8 years). Electrodes of different widths (1.0, 0.75, 0.5, and 0.25mm) were screen printed with PEDOT:PSS on tattoo paper and applied to the flexure line of the index finger of the non-dominant hand. The participants were asked to touch each line 30 times for 2 seconds to collect enough data points in the touched and non-touched state. Participants could freely choose how they touch the tattoo. The electrodes were connected to a commercial capacitive touch controller (Adafruit MPR121). This interfaced with an Arduino, which was using a serial connection to a PC for data logging. Each session took approximately 25 minutes, including 5 minutes of training.

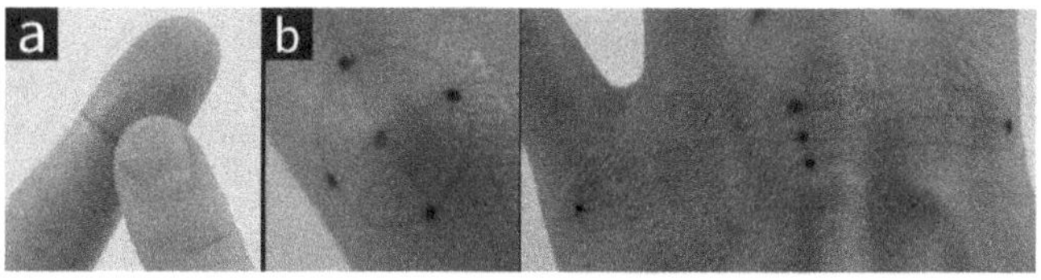

Figure 8: Study setup: (a) evaluation of touch on sub-millimeter electrodes and (b) of precise tattoo application.

Results. We measured the signal to noise ratio (SNR) of capacitive sensing for each line width. For 1 mm, the average SNR was 56.3 (SD=20.9). It was 41.2 (SD=16.4) for 0.75 mm width and 20.1 (SD=9.5) for 0.5 mm width. For the smallest electrode of 0.25 mm, the average SNR was 13.1 (SD=5.5). For each single data point, the SNR was above 7.0, which is the required SNR for robust touch sensing [3].

Precise Application of SkinMarks Tattoos

Applying temporary rub-on tattoos on planar areas is a straightforward task, but precise alignment on curved landmarks can be more challenging. Hence, the second key requirement for precise and accurate interaction on body landmarks is that the user can apply the interactive rub-on tattoo on skin with a high degree of spatial accuracy.

Methodology. We recruited six voluntary participants (1 female, 25–28 years, mean age 26.3 years). Each participant had to precisely apply four substrates of tattoo paper at four challenging locations: knuckles (skeletal landmark), head of ulna (skeletal landmark), flexure lines on the finger (skin microstructure landmark), and birthmark (visual skin landmark). The order of presentation of tattoos was counter-balanced. The tattoos had fine target points (see Figure 8). The participants had to align these target lines precisely with the target points that the experimenter had marked on the participant's skin. For the birthmark, the participants were free to choose any location on the forearm. We instructed the participants how to apply a temporary rub-on tattoo, before letting them apply all four tattoos on their own. We took visual surface scans to measure the error offset for each of the tattoo locations. Each session took approximately 30 minutes.

Results. The results show an inherent ability of users to apply tattoos with a millimeter or even sub-millimeter accuracy at challenging landmarks. The mean error of placement was below 1.0 mm for all locations. Most precise were birthmark (mean=0.16 mm, max=1.0 mm) and flexure line (mean=0.26 mm, max=0.7 mm), followed by knuckles (mean=0.84 mm, max=1.8 mm) and the head of ulna (mean=0.74 mm, max=2.2 mm).

DISCUSSION, LIMITATIONS, AND FUTURE WORK

This section discusses practical insights, limitations, and lessons we have learned during the nine-month-long design and implementation of several iterations of prototypes.

Printing and Fabrication. Each tattoo is personalized and individually fabricated. In our experiments, fabrication of a functional tattoo required between 3–3.5 hours. Preparing the screen printing mask took the longest time ($\approx$ 2.5 h). One mask can, however, contain designs for multiple tattoo prints. The actual printing and curing is fast for touch sensor tattoos ($\approx$ 5 min) and takes between 30–60 minutes for fabricating all layers of a display tattoo. These manual steps can be largely automated using high-end industrial screen printing tools. We envision that in the near-term future a personalized interactive tattoo can be printed in less than a minute on a desktop printer.

Connector and Power. During prototyping, we found that the connector is the weakest element in the chain. This is because the connection between printed conductors, which are slim and flexible, and external conductors, which tend to be much thicker and more rigid, is subject to strong mechanical forces. Our final solution connects each connection pad on the tattoo with a slim connector made of flexible copper tape ($\approx$30 μm). Applying the adhesive layer to the entire tattoo, except the connectors, helps to ensure proper connection. Aligning the tattoo on the connector can be eased by visually marking the connector areas on the backside of water-transfer tattoo paper. Future prototypes would benefit from further miniaturizing of the technology to enable a complete system within the tattoo layers. As a first step, miniaturized rigid microcontrollers (e.g., Intel Curie) could be combined with flexible batteries to enable capable, yet less flexible, areas, with on-skin advanced computation and control. Alternatively, the use of RFID/NFC [19, 17] could enable remote powering of basic sensors and allow communication through modulated backscatter. Other approaches include power harvesting of thermal energy or motion using piezoelectronics, where the limited efficiency and bandwidth might still be sufficient for certain types of sensing and transmission.

Safety. Electroluminescent displays are driven using high-voltage, but low-current AC [31]. We recommend using a current-limiter circuit. We found that the adhesion layer does not guarantee sufficient insulation of the current of electroluminescent (EL) displays from the skin. We recommend two additional layers of rub-on tattoo under SkinMarks to ensure proper electrical isolation (each layer is $\approx$3 μm). This approach also ensures that ink does not contact the user's skin. According to prior work [7], PEDOT:PSS does not cause skin irritations and has no long-term toxicity under direct contact.

Tattoo Application. For close conformality on body landmarks that allow for dynamic pose-changes, e.g. knuckles, we recommend to apply the temporary tattoo in the flat pose. Otherwise the tattoo application requires more attention to avoid gaps at retracted locations, where the tattoo might not touch the skin. We also found that tattoos covering larger area (>5 cm in one dimension) are challenging to apply on landmarks with high curvatures, because the water-transfer paper is relatively stiff before application. If possible, we recommend having multiple smaller tattoos covering the same area. For example, the electrodes and wires can be divided into individual tattoos for each knuckle and aligned separately.

Unintentional input is one of the open issues in on-body interaction. From our experience we noticed that protruding landmarks and the inner areas of the palm are more susceptible to unintentional input when compared to other locations. Landmarks located at locations that retract, such as the area in-between the knuckles, seem promising to reduce the likelihood of unintentional input. Another approach consists of using more expressive gestures that are more robust by design, such as the presented directional toggle gesture or squeeze-based input.

Additional Landmarks. While the five types of landmarks introduced in this paper cover a wide range of scenarios and interactions, there remain more landmarks to be investigated. This includes even finer skin microstructures (like hair), artificial visual skin texture (like permanent tattoos, tan lines, and henna art), and a wider range of accessories (including earrings and piercings). Other skin properties, e.g., the distribution of cutaneous receptors, could also be beneficial for on-body interaction and should be investigated in future work.

Empirical Investigations. This work contributed toward enabling interaction on body landmarks. Additionally, we plan to explore and quantify the benefits of body landmarks for on-skin interactions through empirical investigations. Future work should also study SkinMarks in longitudinal user experiments to see how SkinMarks can fit in users' everyday routines.

CONCLUSIONS

We have introduced *SkinMarks*, a technical enabler for interaction on small, highly curved, and deformable body landmarks. It expands the on-body interaction space toward more detailed interaction on challenging body areas. SkinMarks are temporary interactive tattoos. They sense touch on sub-millimeter electrodes, capture squeeze and bend input, and support active visual output. Through a vastly reduced tattoo thickness and increased stretchability, a SkinMark is sufficiently thin and flexible to conform to irregular geometry, like flexure lines and protruding bones, while still allowing the user to reference those landmarks tactually or visually. We introduced five types of body landmarks that are supported by our technology. We demonstrated novel interactions on each of these landmarks to advance on-body interaction towards more detailed, highly curved and challenging body locations.

ACKNOWLEDGMENTS

This project received funding from the Cluster of Excellence on Multimodal Computing and Interaction, from the European Research Council (ERC) under the European Union's Horizon 2020 research and innovation programme (grant agreement No 714797), and from a Google Faculty Research Award. We thank Chaithin Anil Kumar for his help with the fabrication and Lena Hegemann (both Saarland University) for her help with the video editing. We thank Steven Nagels and Wim Deferme (University of Hasselt) for their support on characterizing the prints.

REFERENCES

1. Daniel Ashbrook, Patrick Baudisch, and Sean White. 2011. Nenya: Subtle and Eyes-free Mobile Input with a Magnetically-tracked Finger Ring. In *Proceedings of the SIGCHI Conference on Human Factors in Computing Systems (CHI '11)*. ACM, New York, NY, USA, 2043–2046. DOI: http://dx.doi.org/10.1145/1978942.1979238
2. Liwei Chan, Rong-Hao Liang, Ming-Chang Tsai, Kai-Yin Cheng, Chao-Huai Su, Mike Y. Chen, Wen-Huang Cheng, and Bing-Yu Chen. 2013. FingerPad: Private and Subtle Interaction Using Fingertips. In *Proceedings of the 26th Annual ACM Symposium on User Interface Software and Technology (UIST '13)*. ACM, New York, NY, USA, 255–260. DOI: http://dx.doi.org/10.1145/2501988.2502016
3. Burke Davison. 2010. Techniques for robust touch sensing design. *AN1334 Microchip Technology Inc* (2010).
4. Margo DeMello. 2007. *Encyclopedia of body adornment*. Greenwood Press.
5. Niloofar Dezfuli, Mohammadreza Khalilbeigi, Jochen Huber, Florian Müller, and Max Mühlhäuser. 2012. PalmRC: Imaginary Palm-based Remote Control for Eyes-free Television Interaction. In *Proceedings of the 10th European Conference on Interactive Tv and Video (EuroiTV '12)*. ACM, New York, NY, USA, 27–34. DOI: http://dx.doi.org/10.1145/2325616.2325623
6. R. Drake, R.L. Drake, W. Vogl, and A.W.M. Mitchell. 2012. *Gray's Basic Anatomy*. Elsevier - Health Sciences Division. https://books.google.de/books?id=Qchc5WZ7IPkC
7. Yang Guo, Michael T. Otley, Mengfang Li, Xiaozheng Zhang, Sneh K. Sinha, Gregory M. Treich, and Gregory A. Sotzing. 2016. PEDOT:PSS Wires Printed on Textile for Wearable Electronics. *ACS Applied Materials & Interfaces* 8, 40 (2016), 26998–27005. DOI: http://dx.doi.org/10.1021/acsami.6b08036 PMID: 27632390.
8. Sean Gustafson, Christian Holz, and Patrick Baudisch. 2011. Imaginary Phone: Learning Imaginary Interfaces by Transferring Spatial Memory from a Familiar Device. In *Proceedings of the 24th Annual ACM Symposium on User Interface Software and Technology (UIST '11)*. ACM, New York, NY, USA, 283–292. DOI: http://dx.doi.org/10.1145/2047196.2047233
9. Sean G. Gustafson, Bernhard Rabe, and Patrick M. Baudisch. 2013. Understanding Palm-based Imaginary Interfaces: The Role of Visual and Tactile Cues when Browsing. In *Proceedings of the SIGCHI Conference on Human Factors in Computing Systems (CHI '13)*. ACM, New York, NY, USA, 889–898. DOI: http://dx.doi.org/10.1145/2470654.2466114
10. Mallory L. Hammock, Alex Chortos, Benjamin C.-K. Tee, Jeffrey B.-H. Tok, and Zhenan Bao. 2013. 25th Anniversary Article: The Evolution of Electronic Skin (E-Skin): A Brief History, Design Considerations, and Recent Progress. *Advanced Materials* 25, 42 (2013), 5997–6038. DOI: http://dx.doi.org/10.1002/adma.201302240
11. Chris Harrison, Hrvoje Benko, and Andrew D. Wilson. 2011. OmniTouch: Wearable Multitouch Interaction Everywhere. In *Proceedings of the 24th Annual ACM Symposium on User Interface Software and Technology (UIST '11)*. ACM, New York, NY, USA, 441–450. DOI: http://dx.doi.org/10.1145/2047196.2047255
12. Chris Harrison, Desney Tan, and Dan Morris. 2010. Skinput: Appropriating the Body As an Input Surface. In *Proceedings of the SIGCHI Conference on Human Factors in Computing Systems (CHI '10)*. ACM, New York, NY, USA, 453–462. DOI: http://dx.doi.org/10.1145/1753326.1753394
13. Hong Hocheng and Chao-Ming Chen. 2014. Design, Fabrication and Failure Analysis of Stretchable Electrical Routings. *Sensors* 14, 7 (2014), 11855. DOI: http://dx.doi.org/10.3390/s140711855
14. Da-Yuan Huang, Liwei Chan, Shuo Yang, Fan Wang, Rong-Hao Liang, De-Nian Yang, Yi-Ping Hung, and Bing-Yu Chen. 2016. DigitSpace: Designing Thumb-to-Fingers Touch Interfaces for One-Handed and Eyes-Free Interactions. In *Proceedings of the 2016 CHI Conference on Human Factors in Computing Systems (CHI '16)*. ACM, New York, NY, USA, 1526–1537. DOI:http://dx.doi.org/10.1145/2858036.2858483
15. Jae-Woong Jeong, Woon-Hong Yeo, Aadeel Akhtar, James J. S. Norton, Young-Jin Kwack, Shuo Li, Sung-Young Jung, Yewang Su, Woosik Lee, Jing Xia, Huanyu Cheng, Yonggang Huang, Woon-Seop Choi, Timothy Bretl, and John A. Rogers. 2013. Materials and Optimized Designs for Human-Machine Interfaces Via Epidermal Electronics. *Advanced Materials* 25, 47 (2013), 6839–6846. DOI: http://dx.doi.org/10.1002/adma.201301921
16. Hsin-Liu (Cindy) Kao, Artem Dementyev, Joseph A. Paradiso, and Chris Schmandt. 2015. NailO: Fingernails As an Input Surface. In *Proceedings of the 33rd Annual ACM Conference on Human Factors in Computing Systems (CHI '15)*. ACM, New York, NY, USA, 3015–3018. DOI: http://dx.doi.org/10.1145/2702123.2702572
17. Hsin-Liu (Cindy) Kao, Christian Holz, Asta Roseway, Andres Calvo, and Chris Schmandt. 2016. DuoSkin: Rapidly Prototyping On-skin User Interfaces Using Skin-friendly Materials. In *Proceedings of the 2016 ACM International Symposium on Wearable Computers (ISWC '16)*. ACM, New York, NY, USA, 16–23. DOI: http://dx.doi.org/10.1145/2971763.2971777
18. Dae-Hyeong Kim, Nanshu Lu, Rui Ma, Yun-Soung Kim, Rak-Hwan Kim, Shuodao Wang, Jian Wu, Sang Min Won, Hu Tao, Ahmad Islam, Ki Jun Yu, Tae-il Kim, Raeed Chowdhury, Ming Ying, Lizhi Xu, Ming Li,

Hyun-Joong Chung, Hohyun Keum, Martin McCormick, Ping Liu, Yong-Wei Zhang, Fiorenzo G. Omenetto, Yonggang Huang, Todd Coleman, and John A. Rogers. 2011. Epidermal Electronics. *Science* 333, 6044 (2011), 838–843. DOI: http://dx.doi.org/10.1126/science.1206157

19. Jeonghyun Kim, Anthony Banks, Huanyu Cheng, Zhaoqian Xie, Sheng Xu, Kyung-In Jang, Jung Woo Lee, Zhuangjian Liu, Philipp Gutruf, Xian Huang, Pinghung Wei, Fei Liu, Kan Li, Mitul Dalal, Roozbeh Ghaffari, Xue Feng, Yonggang Huang, Sanjay Gupta, Ungyu Paik, and John A. Rogers. 2015. Epidermal Electronics with Advanced Capabilities in Near-Field Communication. *Small* 11, 8 (2015), 906–912. DOI: http://dx.doi.org/10.1002/smll.201402495

20. Paul A. J. Kolarsick, Maria Ann Kolarsick, and Carolyn Goodwin. 2011. Anatomy and Physiology of the Skin. *Journal of the Dermatology Nurses' Association* 3, 4 (2011). http://journals.lww.com/jdnaonline/Fulltext/2011/07000/Anatomy_and_Physiology_of_the_Skin.3.aspx

21. Subhash Lele and Joan T. Richtsmeier. 1991. Euclidean distance matrix analysis: A coordinate-free approach for comparing biological shapes using landmark data. *American Journal of Physical Anthropology* 86, 3 (1991), 415–427. DOI: http://dx.doi.org/10.1002/ajpa.1330860307

22. Jaime Lien, Nicholas Gillian, M. Emre Karagozler, Patrick Amihood, Carsten Schwesig, Erik Olson, Hakim Raja, and Ivan Poupyrev. 2016. Soli: Ubiquitous Gesture Sensing with Millimeter Wave Radar. *ACM Trans. Graph.* 35, 4, Article 142 (July 2016), 19 pages. DOI: http://dx.doi.org/10.1145/2897824.2925953

23. Jhe-Wei Lin, Chiuan Wang, Yi Yao Huang, Kuan-Ting Chou, Hsuan-Yu Chen, Wei-Luan Tseng, and Mike Y. Chen. 2015. BackHand: Sensing Hand Gestures via Back of the Hand. In *Proceedings of the 28th Annual ACM Symposium on User Interface Software & Technology (UIST '15)*. ACM, New York, NY, USA, 557–564. DOI: http://dx.doi.org/10.1145/2807442.2807462

24. Shu-Yang Lin, Chao-Huai Su, Kai-Yin Cheng, Rong-Hao Liang, Tzu-Hao Kuo, and Bing-Yu Chen. 2011. Pub - Point Upon Body: Exploring Eyes-free Interaction and Methods on an Arm. In *Proceedings of the 24th Annual ACM Symposium on User Interface Software and Technology (UIST '11)*. ACM, New York, NY, USA, 481–488. DOI: http://dx.doi.org/10.1145/2047196.2047259

25. Darren J. Lipomi, Jennifer A. Lee, Michael Vosgueritchian, Benjamin C.-K. Tee, John A. Bolander, and Zhenan Bao. 2012. Electronic Properties of Transparent Conductive Films of PEDOT:PSS on Stretchable Substrates. *Chemistry of Materials* 24, 2 (2012), 373–382. DOI: http://dx.doi.org/10.1021/cm203216m

26. Roman Lissermann, Jochen Huber, Aristotelis Hadjakos, and Max Mühlhäuser. 2013. EarPut: Augmenting Behind-the-ear Devices for Ear-based Interaction. In *CHI '13 Extended Abstracts on Human Factors in Computing Systems (CHI EA '13)*. ACM, New York, NY, USA, 1323–1328. DOI: http://dx.doi.org/10.1145/2468356.2468592

27. Joanne Lo, Doris Jung Lin Lee, Nathan Wong, David Bui, and Eric Paulos. 2016. Skintillates: Designing and Creating Epidermal Interactions. In *Proceedings of the 2016 ACM Conference on Designing Interactive Systems (DIS '16)*. ACM, New York, NY, USA, 853–864. DOI: http://dx.doi.org/10.1145/2901790.2901885

28. Pranav Mistry, Pattie Maes, and Liyan Chang. 2009. WUW - Wear Ur World: A Wearable Gestural Interface. In *CHI '09 Extended Abstracts on Human Factors in Computing Systems (CHI EA '09)*. ACM, New York, NY, USA, 4111–4116. DOI: http://dx.doi.org/10.1145/1520340.1520626

29. Masa Ogata, Yuta Sugiura, Yasutoshi Makino, Masahiko Inami, and Michita Imai. 2013. SenSkin: Adapting Skin As a Soft Interface. In *Proceedings of the 26th Annual ACM Symposium on User Interface Software and Technology (UIST '13)*. ACM, New York, NY, USA, 539–544. DOI: http://dx.doi.org/10.1145/2501988.2502039

30. Uran Oh and Leah Findlater. 2014. Design of and Subjective Response to On-body Input for People with Visual Impairments. In *Proceedings of the 16th International ACM SIGACCESS Conference on Computers & Accessibility (ASSETS '14)*. ACM, New York, NY, USA, 115–122. DOI: http://dx.doi.org/10.1145/2661334.2661376

31. Simon Olberding, Michael Wessely, and Jürgen Steimle. 2014. PrintScreen: Fabricating Highly Customizable Thin-film Touch-displays. In *Proceedings of the 27th Annual ACM Symposium on User Interface Software and Technology (UIST '14)*. ACM, New York, NY, USA, 281–290. DOI: http://dx.doi.org/10.1145/2642918.2647413

32. Henning Pohl, Justyna Medrek, and Michael Rohs. 2016. ScatterWatch: Subtle Notifications via Indirect Illumination Scattered in the Skin. In *Proceedings of the 18th International Conference on Human-Computer Interaction with Mobile Devices and Services (MobileHCI '16)*. ACM, New York, NY, USA, 7–16. DOI: http://dx.doi.org/10.1145/2935334.2935351

33. Ivan Poupyrev, Nan-Wei Gong, Shiho Fukuhara, Mustafa Emre Karagozler, Carsten Schwesig, and Karen E. Robinson. 2016. Project Jacquard: Interactive Digital Textiles at Scale. In *Proceedings of the 2016 CHI Conference on Human Factors in Computing Systems (CHI '16)*. ACM, New York, NY, USA, 4216–4227. DOI: http://dx.doi.org/10.1145/2858036.2858176

34. Jun Rekimoto. 2002. SmartSkin: An Infrastructure for Freehand Manipulation on Interactive Surfaces. In *Proceedings of the SIGCHI Conference on Human Factors in Computing Systems (CHI '02)*. ACM, New York, NY, USA, 113–120. DOI: http://dx.doi.org/10.1145/503376.503397

35. Tsuyoshi Sekitani, Martin Kaltenbrunner, Tomoyuki Yokota, and Takao Someya. 2014. Imperceptible Electronic Skin. *SID Information Display* 30, 1 (2014), 20–25. http://informationdisplay.org/IDArchive/2014/JanuaryFebruary/FrontlineTechnologyImperceptibleElectronic.aspx

36. Jürgen Steimle. 2016. Skin–The Next User Interface. *Computer* 49, 4 (Apr 2016), 83–87. DOI: http://dx.doi.org/10.1109/MC.2016.93

37. Emi Tamaki, Takashi Miyak, and Jun Rekimoto. 2010. BrainyHand: A Wearable Computing Device Without HMD and It's Interaction Techniques. In *Proceedings of the International Conference on Advanced Visual Interfaces (AVI '10)*. ACM, New York, NY, USA, 387–388. DOI: http://dx.doi.org/10.1145/1842993.1843070

38. Cheng-Yao Wang, Wei-Chen Chu, Po-Tsung Chiu, Min-Chieh Hsiu, Yih-Harn Chiang, and Mike Y. Chen. 2015a. PalmType: Using Palms As Keyboards for Smart Glasses. In *Proceedings of the 17th International Conference on Human-Computer Interaction with Mobile Devices and Services (MobileHCI '15)*. ACM, New York, NY, USA, 153–160. DOI: http://dx.doi.org/10.1145/2785830.2785886

39. Cheng-Yao Wang, Min-Chieh Hsiu, Po-Tsung Chiu, Chiao-Hui Chang, Liwei Chan, Bing-Yu Chen, and Mike Y. Chen. 2015b. PalmGesture: Using Palms As Gesture Interfaces for Eyes-free Input. In *Proceedings of the 17th International Conference on Human-Computer Interaction with Mobile Devices and Services (MobileHCI '15)*. ACM, New York, NY, USA, 217–226. DOI: http://dx.doi.org/10.1145/2785830.2785885

40. R. Chad Webb, Andrew P. Bonifas, Alex Behnaz, Yihui Zhang, Ki Jun Yu, Huanyu Cheng, Mingxing Shi, Zuguang Bian, Zhuangjian Liu, Yun-Soung Kim, Woon-Hong Yeo, Jae Suk Park, Jizhou Song, Yuhang Li, Yonggang Huang, Alexander M. Gorbach, and John A. Rogers. 2013. Ultrathin conformal devices for precise and continuous thermal characterization of human skin. *Nature Materials* 12, 10 (Oct 2013), 938–944. http://dx.doi.org/10.1038/nmat3755 Article.

41. Martin Weigel, Tong Lu, Gilles Bailly, Antti Oulasvirta, Carmel Majidi, and Jürgen Steimle. 2015. iSkin: Flexible, Stretchable and Visually Customizable On-Body Touch Sensors for Mobile Computing. In *Proceedings of the 33rd Annual ACM Conference on Human Factors in Computing Systems (CHI '15)*. ACM, New York, NY, USA, 2991–3000. DOI: http://dx.doi.org/10.1145/2702123.2702391

42. Martin Weigel, Vikram Mehta, and Jürgen Steimle. 2014. More Than Touch: Understanding How People Use Skin As an Input Surface for Mobile Computing. In *Proceedings of the SIGCHI Conference on Human Factors in Computing Systems (CHI '14)*. ACM, New York, NY, USA, 179–188. DOI: http://dx.doi.org/10.1145/2556288.2557239

43. Michael Wessely, Theophanis Tsandilas, and Wendy E. Mackay. 2016. Stretchis: Fabricating Highly Stretchable User Interfaces. In *Proceedings of the 29th Annual Symposium on User Interface Software and Technology (UIST '16)*. ACM, New York, NY, USA, 697–704. DOI: http://dx.doi.org/10.1145/2984511.2984521

44. Sang Ho Yoon, Ke Huo, Vinh P. Nguyen, and Karthik Ramani. 2015. TIMMi: Finger-worn Textile Input Device with Multimodal Sensing in Mobile Interaction. In *Proceedings of the Ninth International Conference on Tangible, Embedded, and Embodied Interaction (TEI '15)*. ACM, New York, NY, USA, 269–272. DOI: http://dx.doi.org/10.1145/2677199.2680560

45. Yang Zhang, Junhan Zhou, Gierad Laput, and Chris Harrison. 2016. SkinTrack: Using the Body As an Electrical Waveguide for Continuous Finger Tracking on the Skin. In *Proceedings of the 2016 CHI Conference on Human Factors in Computing Systems (CHI '16)*. ACM, New York, NY, USA, 1491–1503. DOI: http://dx.doi.org/10.1145/2858036.2858082

tactoRing: A Skin-Drag Discrete Display

Seungwoo Je[1] Brendan Rooney[2] Liwei Chan[3] Andrea Bianchi[1]

[1]Department of Industrial Design, KAIST, Daejeon, Korea {Seungwoo_je, andrea}@kaist.ac.kr

[2]Department of Mathematical Sciences, KAIST, Daejeon, Korea brooney@kaist.ac.kr

[3]Computer Science, National Chiao Tung University, Hsinchu, Taiwan liweichan @cs.nctu.edu.tw

ABSTRACT

Smart rings are an emerging wearable technology particularly suitable for discrete notifications based on haptic cues. Previous work mostly focused on tactile actuators that stimulate only specific skin receptors on the finger, resulting in limited information expressiveness. We propose *tactoRing*, a novel tactile display that, by dragging a small tactor on the skin around the finger, excites multiple skin areas resulting in more accurate cue recognition. In this paper we present the hardware and a perception study to understand the ability of users to recognize eight distinct points around the finger. Moreover, we show two different techniques to encode information through skin-dragging motion with accuracy up to 94%. We finally showcase a set of applications that, by combining sequences of tactile stimuli, achieve higher expressiveness than prior methods.

AUTHOR KEYWORDS

Haptics; wearable; ring; eyes-free; skin-drag.

ACM Classification Keywords

H.5.2. [Information interfaces and presentation]: User Interfaces – Haptic I/O

INTRODUCTION

Smart rings are becoming more popular, receiving both commercial endorsement and attention from researchers [29]. Like other wearable devices, they benefit from the social acceptability of traditional jewelry [22], but also from direct contact with the finger skin. These properties make them particularly suitable for always-available input interactions [1, 5, 18, 24, 35], and rich but subtle notifications [21, 28]. It is therefore unsurprising that researchers have explored a variety of notification modalities for smart rings and similar finger augmentation devices, including: light [16]; small displays [30]; sound [28]; and, in particular, tactile feedback. Several types of tactile feedback have been considered, including: vibration patterns [3, 12, 21]; pressure and shear [36]; force [15, 19, 26]; and, poke and thermal [28].

Permission to make digital or hard copies of all or part of this work for personal or classroom use is granted without fee provided that copies are not made or distributed for profit or commercial advantage and that copies bear this notice and the full citation on the first page. Copyrights for components of this work owned by others than ACM must be honored. Abstracting with credit is permitted. To copy otherwise, or republish, to post on servers or to redistribute to lists, requires prior specific permission and/or a fee. Request permissions from Permissions@acm.org.
CHI 2017, May 06-11, 2017, Denver, CO, USA
© 2017 ACM. ISBN 978-1-4503-4655-9/17/05...$15.00
DOI: http://dx.doi.org/10.1145/3025453.3025703

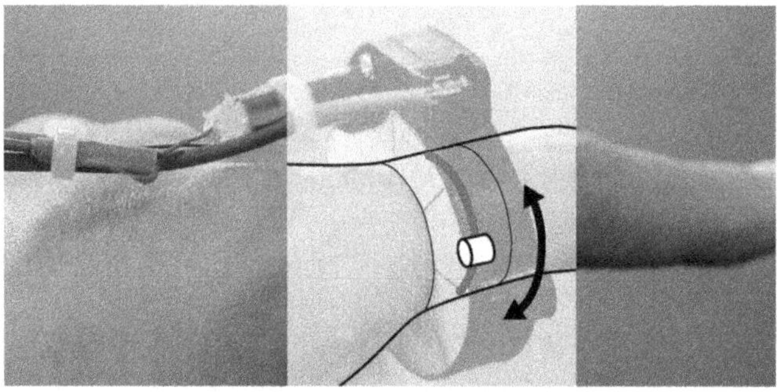

Figure 1. *tactoRing* contains a small movable skin-drag tactor that can rotate around the finger. Motion is indicated by the black arrow, and the dragging surface area in red.

However, while tactile notifications have the benefit of not requiring constant attention from users, and support eyes-free interactions, the expressiveness and the amount of information that can be clearly communicated to users through the haptic channel using currently available finger wearable devices is quite limited. In fact, most of these devices operate by exciting only a small set of tactile skin receptors [13, 36]. They fail to exploit the spatial resolution of the finger skin, which is capable of disambiguating points as close as 2-5mm [14, 33].

In this paper we present *tactoRing*, a novel haptic ring that excites the user's skin by dragging a small movable tactor (i.e., a small tactile actuator, such as a pin) around the finger. By simultaneously stimulating the Merkel cells on the epidermis (SA1) through pressure, and the Meissner corpuscles (RA1) and the Ruffini's endings (SA2) in the dermis through stretching the skin and low frequency vibrations (e.g., rubbing) [14], we are able to achieve higher discrete spatial resolution on the finger and convey richer and more expressive messages to users than traditional methods.

This paper describes the *tactoRing* prototype in detail, and demonstrates its accuracy with a series of user studies. Specifically, we investigated the capability of users to perceive the movable tactor and discern its dragging motion to different locations around the finger. To overcome low spatial resolution, we present two different interaction techniques based on skin dragging (*DoublePoint* and *VirtualPoint*) and demonstrate, with a study, that they are suitable for accurate identification of eight unique targets around the finger. Finally, we instantiate concrete examples of usage for the presented techniques in four applications, and indicate possible future research directions.

RELATED WORK

Haptic output through finger augmentation has been explored for applications such as: manipulating virtual objects [7, 19, 36]; pointing devices [6, 18]; delivering eyes-free notifications [21, 28]; intimate communications [25]; accessibility [10]; and, guiding fingers [11]. While multi-finger augmentation with several degrees of freedom is possible, and is much studied [e.g., 9, 15], this approach is infeasible for wearable devices. Therefore, this paper focuses on a single-point actuation method. The rest of the related work covers only techniques that provide temporal and spatial haptic output through finger augmentation.

Temporal and Spatial Haptic Output on the Finger

Early examples of temporal encoding of tactile feedback adopted "Morse-like" vibration patterns using a single actuator [31]. This model was later generalized in the concept of *Tactons* [3], an identifiable set of tactile icons that can be created with different vibration parameters such as frequency, amplitude, duration, and rhythm. However, temporal signals are more difficult to interpret and memorize than spatial ones. Utilizing the spatial resolution of the finger's skin, Khurelbaatar et al. [17] presented an electrode-tactile grid placed on the back of a touchscreen that can display different tactile shapes on a single fingertip. *NailTactors* [12] instruments a nail with an array of vibration motors, allowing the finger to perceive directional and numerical cues through spatial encoding of vibrations.

Haptic Cues that Poke, Stretch, Pull and Drag the Skin

Beyond temporal and spatial encoding of tactile feedback, recent research explored novel haptic modalities by applying tangential forces on the skin to expand haptic expressiveness while improving the capability of skin recognition. Tapping and rubbing skin as intimate haptic cues were first proposed by Li et al. [20]. *NotiRing* [28] presented a user study comparing taps against other types of haptic notifications (vibration and thermal). The result echoed Li's finding that tapping feels natural and simulates an affective human touch. Skin stretching and pulling (i.e., rubbing) were also explored. Prior work [2, 4] demonstrated that stretching and pulling provide more accurate directions than vibrotatctile stimuli because they excite a wider range of skin receptors.

Highly relevant work about lateral skin stretching on the fingerpad was proposed by Provancher et al. [26]. Results show that even small amounts of tangential skin stretching (0.25-0.75 mm) can greatly increase the perception of friction, and that this technique is suitable for communicating directional cues in four directions [8]. This work was further extended leading to the development of complex non-wearable devices for 5-degree-of-freedom directional cue communication [9] and a graspable 3-degree-of-freedom device capable of rendering both normal and tangential skin deformation [27]. Finally, Ion et al. [13] combined the idea of skin stretching with that of skin dragging, and proposed a wearable skin-drag display that draws spatial cues on the wrist using a dragging tactor.

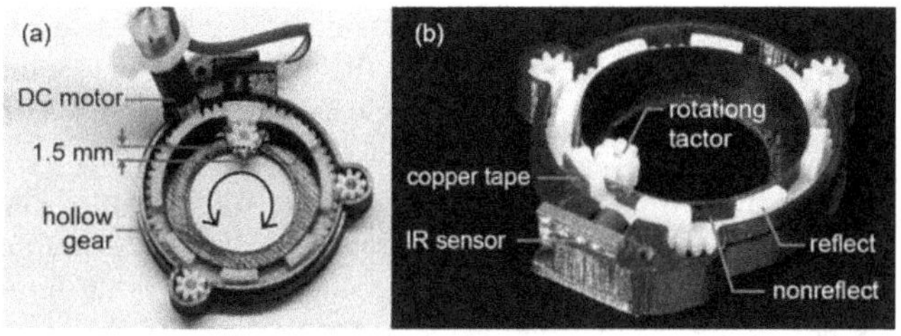

Figure 2. Working principles and detail description of the components of *tactoRing*.

Our work differs from the work on skin stretching by Provancher [26] and the work on wrist-wearable dragging display by Ion [13], because of the wearable form factor of the proposed skin-dragging display (specifically, a ring), and because of the type of haptic stimulus generated. In fact, we mainly focus on dragging on a continuous non-flat contact surface. Though skin dragging shares common elements with stretching, as explained in [13], these interactions are different for both the number and the type of mechanoreceptors involved, and the size and geometry of the area. We are not aware of any prior work that presented high-resolution spatial haptic encoding of discrete information on the finger. In this work, we introduce a haptic ring based on the one-dimensional (1-D) skin-drag movement of a small tactor, and present evidence of its high accuracy in discerning distinct spatial dragging locations around the finger.

SKIN-DRAGGING RING

tactoRing is a novel haptic ring which works by mechanically dragging a small tactor in a 1-D path around the user's finger (Figure 1). Like previous skin-dragging interfaces designed for different body parts [4, 13], *tactoRing* stimulates both slow- and fast-adapting mechanoreceptors on the epidermis and the dermis (SA1, SA2, RA1). As a consequence, the user can clearly perceive a small localized pressure applied to the skin when the tactor is dragged, and therefore determine its locations.

Prototype

tactoRing (Figure 2) is based on a system of spur gears (0.5 module) and a small DC motor (LCP06-A03V-0136 with torque 120gf-cm, 25 mA at 3V) capable of spinning a tactor along the inner face of the ring. An infrared (IR) sensor (SG-2BC) mounted on the bridge of the ring is used to track and encode the relative motion of the gears, and to infer the tactor location around the finger. All components are housed in an external case which was 3-D printed using PolyLactic Acid (PLA). The case has a diameter of 35mm, and the finger hole has a diameter customizable up to 20.68mm (US size 11). Inside the ring, three spur gears (8 teeth, 5mm face width) are positioned 120° apart and surround a larger hollow gear (60 teeth, 2.5mm face width) which was custom designed and 3-D printed with *VeroWhite* material. The hollow gear profile has eight reflective and non-reflective regions used by the IR sensor to distinguish eight locations 45° apart.

The tactor is placed on the inner side of the hollow gear, mounted on a flat extrusion. When the gear moves, the tactor also moves. The tactor is also shaped as a gear that can rotate on itself, and it is placed in such way that it protrudes only 1.5mm from the case toward the inside of the ring. The rationale for the choice of a gear-shaped rotating tactor is that the finger is not perfectly cylindrical and the distribution of tissues is uneven, so the tactor needs to adapt to different surfaces. Empirically we found that a small fixed tactor (<3mm) is not equally perceived around the finger, and a longer tactor can be entangled in the skin generating a stalling torque. Therefore, we adopted the design of a rotating gear where each tooth of the gear acts as a pin when in contact with the skin, and the rotation of the gear minimizes friction caused during dragging. Since the spatial resolution on the proximal phalanx (the part of the fingers closest to the metacarpus) is 5mm, the adjacent teeth of the tactors are perceived as a single entity [14, 33].

The ring is wired to an external electronic board used for driving the motor, and an Arduino UNO, connected to a PC, for reading the sensor data and controlling the tactor location. Analog readings from the IR sensor are sampled on the Arduino controller at 10 KHz, then filtered using a low-pass filter with 15 Hz cutoff frequency (Hamming window, order 100). By physically applying reflective copper on the region of the hollow that corresponds to the tactor location, we are able to identify when the tactor is placed in front of the IR sensor (this region corresponds to 0° and we refer to it as *home*). The remaining reflective and non-reflective regions of the gear are identified using adaptive thresholds that are dynamically adjusted at run-time using a moving average with a window of 800 samples.

The PC software is written in Java and consists of a graphical interface containing several controllers for changing the ring behavior. Using this software, it is possible to change the motor speed (160 rpm, 180 rpm, and 200 rpm) and direction (left, right). It is also possible to choose a target dragging location (or sequences of locations) among the eight designated regions, and to recalibrate the ring by moving the tactor to *home*. Finally, the PC software enables external devices, such as tablets and mobile devices, to wirelessly connect and issue commands to the ring using the Open Sound Control (OSC) protocol.

Prototype Validation

Since *tactoRing* works by mechanically stimulating the skin around the finger with a movable part, it is necessary that the tactor is permanently in contact with the user's skin. An oversized ring would result in imprecise perception, while an undersized ring could obstruct the motion of the tactor. Accordingly, the ring size should be appropriate for the user who wears it. We therefore built two rings with different sizes. Because we could not find suitable data in the ergonomic database for the size of the proximal phalanx of the index finger, we collected finger sizes for 48 participants (22 female) from our institution and chose the two most common sizes. We then built a large ring (covering US size 10-11) and small one (US size 7-8), respectively suitable for the 35% and 31% of the population that we sampled.

We then recruited 20 participants (10 for each ring size, 10 females, mean age 25.4, SD 2.6) for a pilot study aimed to test whether the tactor movement was accurate and reliable across finger sizes. In the pilot, no user input was required. Instead, users simply wore the ring of their size while our software instructed the tactor to follow 10 randomized motion sequences. Each sequence consisted of movements to 40 locations (5 for each of the 8 target locations, every 45°) with the motor spinning at maximum speed (200 rpm). At the end of every sequence we manually inspected the actual tactor location and checked whether it matched with the location reported by the software. This is a simple way to verify whether any obstruction altered the tactor motion. The pilot took about 15 minutes per participant and in total we collected data for 200 sequences of motions (100 for each ring size). The rings performed with overall accuracy of 97.5% (small: 97%, large: 98%) with a total of 5 errors (each distance one from the expected target). We concluded that the ring performance was sufficient for further user studies and, to avoid errors propagating through an entire experimental session, we modified the controlling software to perform an implicit recalibration anytime the tactor was moved to *home*.

EVALUATION OF TARGET RECOGNITION

We conducted a user study to investigate the ability of users to distinguish among different tactor dragging locations. In this experiment, the term *location* is used to identify not a single-point stimulation around the finger, but a dragging motion pattern, which ends in a specific target point. We tested three configurations, *complete*, *square* and *diamond* (Figure 3). The *complete* configuration has eight target locations spaced 45° apart, starting from 0°; the *square* and *diamond* configurations each have four target locations spaced 90° apart, starting respectively from 45° and 0°. Clearly, the *square* and *diamond* configurations together form the *complete* configuration. Considering the high spatial resolution of the skin on the proximal phalanx (5 mm), the size of the tactor (5mm), and the diameter of our rings (57.2mm and 64.9mm), we formed the hypothesis that all three configurations result to similar recognition performance with comparable error rates, input time, and cognitive workload.

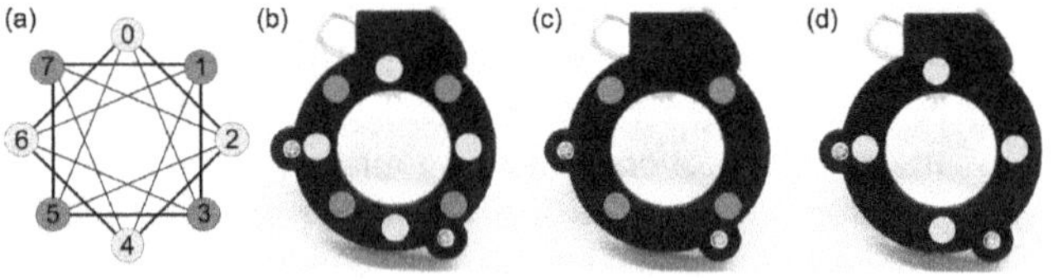

Figure 3. The targets modeled as a graph (a); the *complete* (b), *square* (c), and *diamond* (d) configurations of targets.

We recruited 12 volunteers (5 female) from our institution, aged 22-30 (M: 24.2, SD: 2.3) with finger size 8 or 11. Four participants reported familiarity with haptic interfaces and wearable devices, and two regularly wear a ring. None had prior experience with smart rings. Participants were compensated with 10 USD in local currency.

Following a repeated measures design, participants tested each configuration in a fully balanced Latin square order. In each configuration users wore a ring on the index of the left hand (Figure 4.a), and completed a series of selection trials with randomized target locations (see next section for details) using their right hand. In each trial, the tactor moved in a specific target location, using the shortest path, and stopped. After two seconds, users could select the perceived location on a graphical interface with the available options for the current configuration. This visual interface was displayed on a tablet (Figure 4.b) and wirelessly synchronized with the ring software. The tablet also provided auditory feedback during an initial training phase, using beeps to indicate hits and buzzes to indicate misses.

In total, each participant entered 240 trials for the *complete* 8-target configuration (30 repetitions per target); of which the first 80 trials (10 repetitions) were considered as training and discarded from the analysis. Similarly, for each of the two 4-targets configurations, users entered 120 trials; 40 of which discarded as training (10 repetitions). In total we collected 1920 valid trials (8 targets x 20 repetitions x 12 participants) for the *complete* configuration, and 960 trials (4 targets x 20 repetitions x 12 participants) for each of the *square* and *diamond* configurations. Finally, for each configuration users completed a NASA TLX questionnaire to measure cognitive workload.

Trials Randomization

In this section we describe the trial randomization method for the *complete* configuration; the other two configurations were handled analogously. The objective is to generate a sequence of randomized trials with eight target locations, each repeated exactly 30 times, that are not easy to guess (in other words, the information leakage from the skin-dragging motion of the tactor should be minimized). Therefore, we required consecutive trials of the experiments to be always at a fixed distance of either 2 or 3 target locations. That is because repeated positions in consecutive trials would be trivial to identify, and positions adjacent, or antipodal, to the

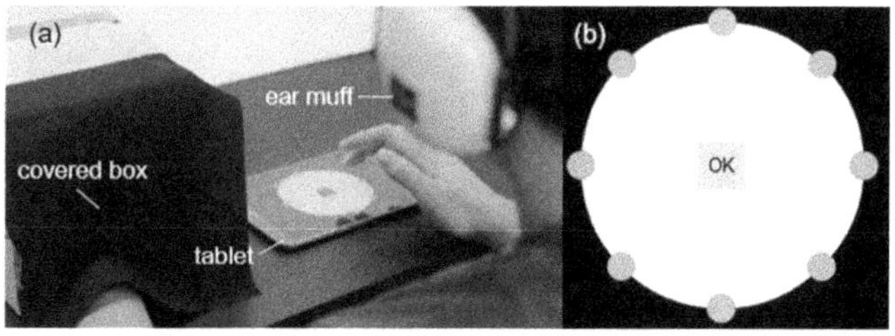

Figure 4. The experimental setup (a) and an example of GUI used by the participants for the target selection task.

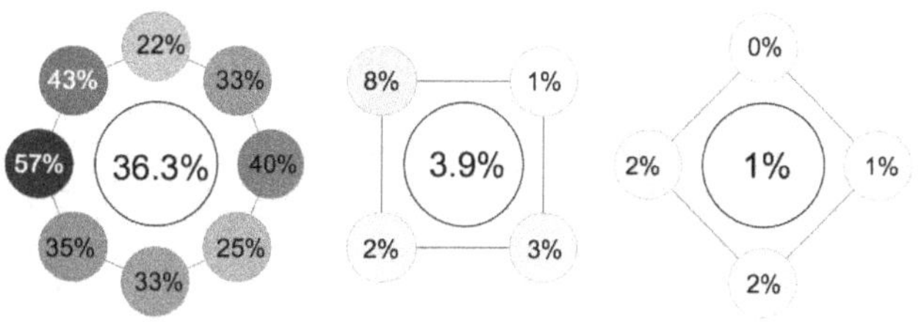

Figure 5. Target error rates for each configuration. The average error rate is displayed in the center of each figure.

current tactor location could be easily inferred from the duration of the dragging motion.

Although it is easy to generate a random sequence of target positions that satisfy either the distance constraint, or the frequency constraint, doing both simultaneously is a difficult task. Specifically, this problem is equivalent to finding a Hamilton path (a path that visits every vertex exactly once [34]) in a graph with 240 vertices and 14,400 edges. Finding a Hamilton path is known to be a NP-complete problem [32], and our input graph is too large to generate valid random sequences in a reasonable time. Therefore, we used an alternative method that generates sequences of targets by combining subsequences obtained from the Hamilton cycles of the small graph in Figure 3.a. First, we enumerated the Hamilton cycles in that graph using brute force. From these we obtained 56 sequences of length 8 starting at the *home* location. We then concatenated 30 of these, chosen uniformly at random, and cyclically permuted the resulting sequences to randomize their starting positions (the first trial of the experiment). The resulting sequence satisfies our restrictions.

Results and Findings

Results were analyzed using one-way ANOVA tests followed by Bonferroni correction post-hoc analysis with α=0.05. Sphericity was assessed with Mauchley's test, and, if violated, Greenhouse-Geisser corrections were employed. Error rates in the *complete*, *square* and *diamond* configurations were respectively 36.3%, 3.9% and 1% (Figure 5). Specifically, in the *complete* configuration participants made on average 58 errors (SD: 28), of which 92% consisted of *1-errors* (i.e., selections one location away from the target). The *square* configuration resulted with an average of 3.1 errors (SD: 4.9), 97% of which were *1-errors*, and the *diamond* configuration resulted in an average of 0.8 errors (SD: 2.3), 80% of which were *1-errors*. Error rates

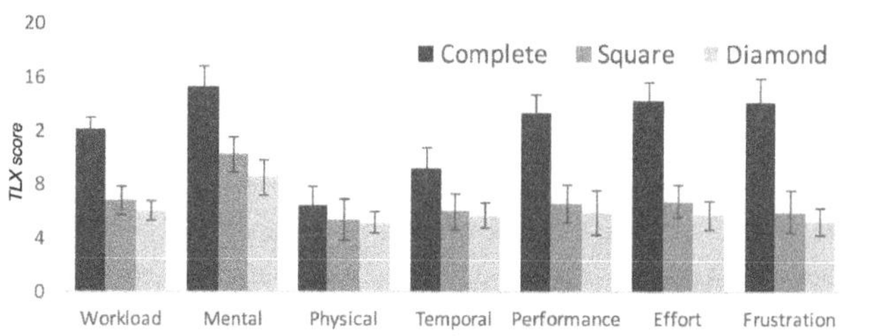

Figure 6. The results for the cognitive load based on the NASA TLX questionnaire. The vertical axis indicates the TLX score.

were tested statistically significant across interfaces ($F_{(1.13,12.4)}$=38.2, $p<0.01$, η^2_p=0.39) with the *complete* configuration performing worse than the others ($p<0.01$). Also the cognitive workload measures from the TLX (Figure 6) were statistically different ($F_{(2,22)}$=37.6, $p<0.01$, η^2_p=0.77) with the *complete* configuration performing worse than the others ($p<0.01$). The average input time for the *complete*, *square* and *diamond* configurations were respectively 1.2s (SD: 0.3), 1s (SD: 0.2), and 1s (SD: 0.3). We found statistical differences ($F_{(2,22)}$=7.18, $p<0.01$, η^2_p=0.39), but only the *complete* and *diamond* comparison was significant ($p<0.01$).

Our main hypothesis was that the three interfaces would perform similarly, regardless the number and location of the targets, simply because the spatial resolution of the skin on the finger is higher than the size of tactor utilized. We reject such hypothesis, as we observed that the *complete* configuration performed significantly worse than the other two. In fact, both *square* and *diamond* configurations had an accuracy of over 96%, but the *complete* configuration achieved only 63%, demonstrating that selecting a correct location out of eight targets was challenging. This result is corroborated by the TLX data about the cognitive workload, and by the post-hoc informal interviews we had with the participants (all participants agreed that the *complete* configuration was the most difficult). By comparing the differences between configurations we can also conclude that the overall accuracy did not depend on the target locations, but rather on their density. If specific parts of the fingers had lower sensitivity, we should have reported low performance for specific targets across configurations, but that did not happen. Finally, the fact that the majority of errors (80%-97%) were *1-errors*, further demonstrates that accuracy depended on the density rather than the location of the target locations around the finger.

NEW TECHNIQUES FOR TARGET SELECTION

From the previous study we concluded that identifying eight dragging locations around the finger is a difficult and error-prone task. In this section, we present two different interaction techniques that, by utilizing skin-dragging motion, allow users to correctly identify the same eight target locations from the previous study with better performance. These techniques use a pair of motions to represent a single target location. This introduces a second point that acts as a reference for the desired target. Our hypothesis is that users will be able to better identify the same targets that led to poor recognition rate in the previous study. The two techniques we present are named *DoublePoint* and *VirtualPoint* (Figure 7).

With *DoublePoint*, a target is represented by a motion pattern with a sequence of dragging motions starting from 0° and with the second motion spanning exactly 45°. The two motions are separated by a 200ms pause and can be either to the left or the right. For example, the target number 3 (135°) is encoded as the motion 0° ➔ 90° pause 90° ➔ 135°, while the target 1 (45°) is encoded as 0° ➔ 90° pause 90° 🡐 45° (➔ and 🡐 meaning right and left movements). Figure 7-left shows the motion encodings for each target using the *DoublePoint* encoding scheme.

With *VirtualPoint* (Figure 7-right), a target is still identified by two distinct drag motions starting from 0° and separated by a 200ms pause, but a target is described as the middle point between the locations of the first and second stops. For example, target 3 is encoded as the motion 0° ➔ 90° pause 90° ➔ 180°, because the middle point between 90° and 180° is 135°. Similarly, target 1 can be described with the motion 0° ➔ 90° pause 90° 🡐 0°, resulting in 45°. *VirtualPoint*, differently from *DoublePoint*, encodes any target only using the four cardinal points (0°, 90°, 180°, 270°). In the previous study, these proved to be well recognized by all the users.

EVALUATION OF DOUBLEPOINT AND VIRTUALPOINT

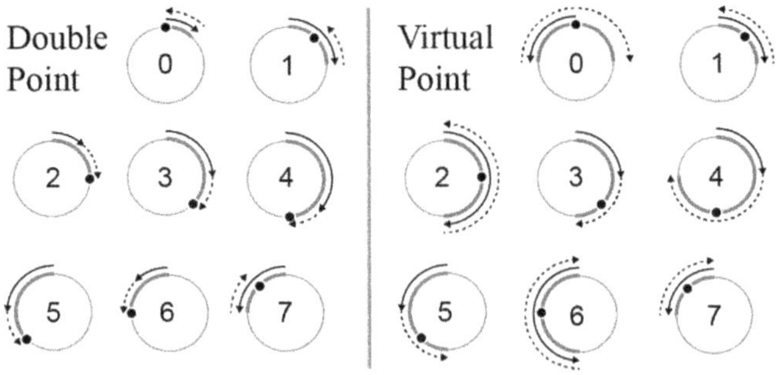

Figure 7. Selections using *DoublePoint* (a) and *VirtualPoint* (b). Destination targets are indicated with a black dot, motions with arrows (the second motion is dotted). The skin area stimulated by the dragging motion is highlighted in red.

To validate our design, we conducted a second user study similar to the previous one. We recruited again from our institution 12 participants (5 female), aged 22 to 26 (M: 23.5, SD: 1.1) with ring size 8 or 11. Following a repeated measure design, every participant tested the *DoublePoint* and *VirtualPoint* interfaces in balanced order, then completed a NASA TLX questionnaire. Each interface was tested for 240 trials (30 repetitions x 8 targets), of which the first 80 (10 repetitions) were discarded as training. During the training phase participants received an auditory feedback and could consult a drawing of the motions as in Figure 7. Finally, unlike the previous experiment, all motion sequences started from 0°. So after each input trial, the system automatically

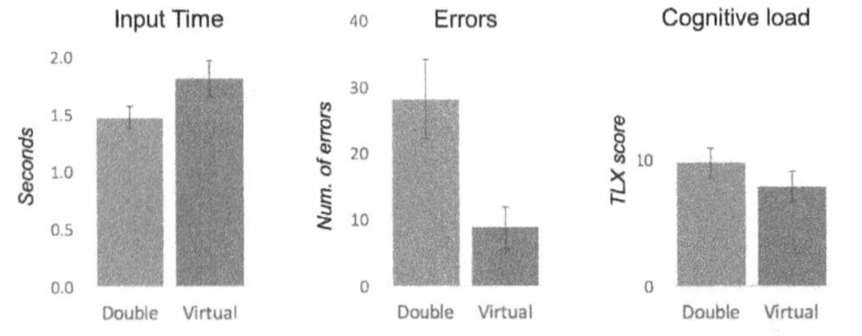

Figure 8. *DoublePoint* and *VirtualPoint* performance for input time, error rate, and cognitive workload measured with a TLX.

placed the tactor at *home*. Participants were compensated 10 USD in local currency.

Results and Findings

Results were analyzed using a paired t-test with α=0.05. Average input times, number of errors, and cognitive workload are reported in Figure 8, and all revealed statistical differences. Input with *DoublePoint* was significantly faster ($t_{(11)}$=2.22, p<0.05) than with *VirtualPoint*, but was also more error prone ($t_{(11)}$=4.5, p<0.01) and cognitively difficult ($t_{(11)}$=2.3 p<0.05). Specifically, the *DoublePoint* error rate (18%) is about three times larger than that of *VirtualPoint* (5%). Confusion matrices and error rates for each motion sequence are indicated in Figure 9. For *DoublePoint*, clearly the targets 2-3-4 and 5-6, were confused with each other because of the similarities in the motion sequences. Finally, the error rate for *1-errors* was 68% for *DoublePoint* and only 48% for *VirtualPoint*.

DISCUSSION AND EXAMPLE APPLICATIONS

The *DoublePoint* and *VirtualPoint* selection techniques presented in the previous section achieve, in two different ways, the same objective: they allow users to disambiguate eight distinct point around the finger using the skin-dragging motion of a tactor. Despite the differences in performance, it is clear that both techniques resulted in more accurate selections than absolute targeting of eight locations, as in the first experiment (error rates of 18% and 5% vs. 36% of the complete configuration). Specifically, identifying a single point though a pair of motions was perceived as easier to distinguish than static spatial recognition, because the dragging motion offered a clearly distinguishable reference point for comparison. This result is also aligned with past findings [23] which indicated that cutaneous spatial acuity is better for dynamic rather than static stimuli. Also, as an immediate result, the number of *1-errors* was greatly reduced from the previous experiment. Overall, the accuracy of 94% found in *VirtualPoint* demonstrates the feasibility of our approach as an alternative to vibrotactile encodings [3, 12] for the communication of distinguishable haptic cues.

	0	1	2	3	4	5	6	7
0	91.2%	11.3%	4.2%	0.7%		0.8%	2.1%	5.4%
1	2.0%	84.6	0.4%	6.7%	3.8%			0.4%
2	1.7%	1.7%	93.3%	11.7%	0.8%		0.4%	
3		1.7%	0.8%	79.6%	30.8%	0.4%		0.8%
4				1.3%	64.2%	1.7%	0.4%	
5					0.4%	87.5%	19.6%	6.3%
6	3.8%		1.3%			7.9%	77.1%	5.4%
7	1.3%	0.7%				1.7%	0.4%	81.7%
Err	8.8%	15.4%	6.7%	20.4%	35.8%	12.5%	22.9%	18.3%

	0	1	2	3	4	5	6	7
0	93.5%	0.4%	1.7%	0.4%		0.4%	3.3%	3.3%
1		99.6%	3.8%	2.1%				3.3%
2	0.8%		93.3%		0.4%		1.7%	
3	0.8%		0.4%	97.1%	4.2%	1.7%	0.4%	0.8%
4	0.4%				95.0%	1.7%	0.4%	
5	0.4%			0.4%	0.4%	95.8%		0.4%
6	2.1%		0.8%			0.4%	93.8%	3.0%
7	3.0%						0.4%	89.2%
Err	7.5%	0.4%	6.7%	2.9%	5.0%	4.2%	6.2%	10.8%

Figure 9. Confusion matrices for the *DoublePoint* (left) and *VirtualPoint* (right) techniques. Columns represent challenges and rows the participants' input.

In terms of differences between the two approaches, *VirtualPoint* is arguably cognitively more demanding (e.g., it requires more training) than *DoublePoint*, but interestingly it is easier at the physiological perception level. In fact, with *VirtualPoint* users only needed to distinguish among four cardinal points, instead of the eight distinct dragging locations necessary for the *DoublePoint*. The trade-off between cognitive load and perception clearly emerged in this experiment, showing that for simple tasks such as recognizing pairs of motions as in the *VirtualPoint* technique, higher accuracy can be achieved by simplifying the perception task at the expense of slightly higher cognitive load.

Finally, we argue that *DoublePoint* could perform better if the motion sequences were redesigned to be less ambiguous. For example, both targets 3 and 4 consist of two long motions on the right, followed by a short motion in the same direction. We believe that by changing some of these encodings, we could achieve better performance (for example, motion 3 could be encoded as 0° ➔ 180° pause 180° 🡐 135°). Future work will investigate possible different motion encodings and their accuracy.

Applications

We present four possible practical applications for *tactoRing* and the targeting techniques described in this paper. In these examples, the haptic feedback can be composed of single motions, dragging selections using the *VirtualPoint* and *DoublePoint* techniques, or even sequences of these motions for more expressiveness.

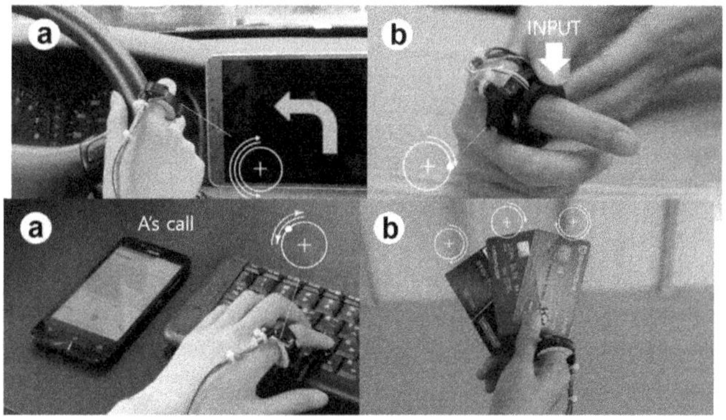

Figure 10. Two applications demonstrating *tactoRing* use for eyes-free delivery of qualitative and quantitative information.

We developed four proof-of-concept applications using the existing platform. The first two applications are examples of how different motion targets on the ring can be associated with different meaning. As in Figure 10.a, we developed an Android application that simulates phone calls, incoming messages and calendar events. When any of these events happen, a notification is initiated by moving the *tactoRing* to a pre-specified targets. The user can then disambiguate, eyes-free, among different callers or notifications without interrupting their primary activities. In Figure 10.b dragging motions on the ring are mapped to quantities. We developed an application that simulate a card payment system: when a debit card (with an RFID) is placed on a reader, the user is notified of how much money is left on the card. For example, the tactor movement to the target location at 45° means that 25% of the initial budget is still available on the card, while the movement to location 180° signifies that 50% of the money available was spent. Also, in this application the information is mapped to locations on the ring and the users can understand them through eyes-free interaction.

Another possible class of applications works by conveying exact directions on the ring through tactile feedback. For example, Figure 11.a is a prototype of a car navigation interface, where street directions (left, right, forward, turn back) can be signaled on the hand, without the need for additional visual information. Finally, Figure 11.b presents an input-output ring: using a set of four capacitive electrodes placed around the *tactoRing* we are able to discern touch input in the four cardinal locations and transmit those locations to a remote user, who is also wearing the *tactoRing*. This application is open-ended and leads to a variety of scenarios. For example, the *tactoRing* platform could form an implicit and effective tele-communications tool for remote users to communicate through touch input and receive messages as tactile stimuli on the ring.

CONCLUSIONS

In this paper we presented *tactoRing*, the first example of a wearable skin-drag display capable of encoding discrete locations around the finger. We presented the description of a smart ring prototype with a movable tactor which rotates around the finger, and presented evidence of accuracy with users engaged in targeting task with up to eight different locations. Based on the performance in the first study, we then designed two interaction techniques (*DoublePoint* and *VirtualPoint*) that exploit the ability of humans to distinguish dragging motion on the skin (motion excites more skin receptors than static contact). With a second study we demonstrated that both techniques achieve higher results than absolute targeting of static locations. Finally, we presented a set of applications to showcase how skin-dragging cues, single or sequential, can be used to encode complex information without the need of additional visual feedback.

This work also has several limitations and possible areas of improvement. The current hardware is wearable but bulky and power-hungry due to the motor. We reckon that smaller and more efficient motors could be employed. In addition, we acknowledge that the material choice for both the ring body and the tactor (e.g., rigid PLA and plastic vs. elastic material or rubber) could impact performance and perception thresholds for dragging. So further investigation is necessary to determine the effects of materials. We also acknowledge that our results are strongly linked with the stimulated surface area of the finger's proximal phalanx, and different perception thresholds may be expected on other body parts, with their unique density of skin receptors. Therefore, we feel it is important to investigate tactile dragging perception on other continuous non-planar surfaces, such as the wrist, forearms [23], legs and the neck by modifying the form-factor of the interfaces (e.g., bracelets, necklaces).

Possible future directions include: developing smaller hardware capable of adapting to different surface areas; testing tactors of different shapes, size and materials; and, further studies to gauge perception performance. Following Ion [13], we are interested in comparing directional and compound dragging cues for encoding with one-dimensional motions, with the performance of *DoublePoint* and *VirtualPoint* techniques with revised distinctive drag-motion sets. Moreover, similarly to Roument et al. [28], we are interested in differences of perception for dragging motions in static vs dynamic positions (e.g., walking). Also, following the prominent work on tactons [3], we are interested in exploring more complex dragging-pattern encoding using temporal elements, direction and speed of motion, and even sequences of motions.

ACKNOLEDGEMENTS

This paper was supported by the MSIP, Korea, under the G-ITRC support program (IITP-2016-R6812-16-0001) supervised by the IITP.

REFERENCES

1. Daniel Ashbrook, Patrick Baudisch, and Sean White. 2011. Nenya: subtle and eyes-free mobile input with a magnetically-tracked finger ring. In Proceedings of the SIGCHI Conference on Human Factors in Computing Systems (CHI '11). ACM, New York, NY, USA, 2043-2046.
2. Karlin Bark, Jason W. Wheeler, Sunthar Premakumar, Mark R. Cutkosky. (2008). Comparison of skin stretch and vibrotactile stimulation for feedback of proprioceptive information. In Proc. HAPTICS'08, 71–78.
3. Stephen Brewster and Lorna M. Brown. 2004. Tactons: structured tactile messages for non-visual information display. In Proceedings of the fifth conference on Australasian user interface - Volume 28 (AUIC '04).
4. Nathaniel A. Caswell, Ryan T. Yardley, Markus N. Montandon, William R. Provancher. 2012. Design of a forearm-mounted directional skin stretch device. In Proc. HAPTICS'12, 365–370.
5. Liwei Chan, Rong-Hao Liang, Ming-Chang Tsai, Kai-Yin Cheng, Chao-Huai Su, Mike Y. Chen, Wen-Huang Cheng, and Bing-Yu Chen. 2013. FingerPad: private and subtle interaction using fingertips. In Proceedings of the 26th annual ACM symposium on User interface software and technology (UIST '13). ACM, New York, NY, USA, 255-260.
6. Ke-Yu Chen, Kent Lyons, Sean White, and Shwetak Patel. 2013. uTrack: 3D input using two magnetic sensors. In Proceedings of the 26th annual ACM symposium on User interface software and technology (UIST '13). ACM, New York, NY, USA, 237-244.
7. Francesco Chinello, Monica Malvezz, Claudio Pacchierotti, and Domenico Prattichizzo. A three DoFs wearable tactile display for exploration and manipulation of virtual objects. 2012. In

Proceedings 2012 IEEE Haptics Symposium (HAPTICS). IEEE. p. 71-76.

8. Brian T. Gleeson, Scott K. Horschel, and William R. Provancher. Communication of direction through lateral skin stretch at the fingertip. In Proceedings of EuroHaptics conference, 2009 and Symposium on Haptic Interfaces for Virtual Environment and Teleoperator Systems. World Haptics 2009. Third Joint. IEEE, 2009. p. 172-177.
9. Ashley L. Guinan, Nicholas C. Hornbaker, Markus N. Montandon, Andrew J. Doxon, and William R. Provancher. Back-to-back skin stretch feedback for communicating five degree-of-freedom direction cues. In Proceedings of World Haptics Conference (WHC), 2013. IEEE, 2013. p. 13-18.
10. Michitaka Hirose, and Tomohiro Amemiya. Wearable finger-braille interface for navigation of deaf-blind in ubiquitous barrier-free space. Proceedings of the HCI International. Vol. 4. 2003.
11. Chih-Pin Hsiao, Richard Li, Xinyan Yan, and Ellen Yi-Luen Do. 2015. Tactile Teacher: Sensing Finger Tapping in Piano Playing. In Proceedings of the Ninth International Conference on Tangible, Embedded, and Embodied Interaction (TEI '15). ACM, New York, NY, USA, 257-260.
12. Meng-Ju Hsieh, Rong-Hao Liang, and Bing-Yu Chen. 2016. NailTactors: eyes-free spatial output using a nail-mounted tactor array. In Proceedings of the 18th International Conference on Human-Computer Interaction with Mobile Devices and Services (MobileHCI '16). ACM, New York, NY, USA, 29-34.
13. Alexandra Ion, Edward Jay Wang, and Patrick Baudisch. 2015. Skin Drag Displays: Dragging a Physical Tactor across the User's Skin Produces a Stronger Tactile Stimulus than Vibrotactile. In Proceedings of the 33rd Annual ACM Conference on Human Factors in Computing Systems (CHI '15). ACM, New York, NY, USA, 2501-2504.
14. Lynette A. Jones and Susan j. Lederman. 2006. Human Hand Function. Oxford University Press.
15. Haruhisa Kawasaki, Yasuhiko Doi, Shinya Koide, Takahiro Endo, and Tetsuya Mouri. Hand haptic interface incorporating 1D finger pad and 3D fingertip force display devices. 2010. In Proceedings 2010 IEEE International Symposium on Industrial Electronics. IEEE. p. 1869-1874.
16. Hamed Ketabdar, Peyman Moghadam, and Mehran Roshandel. 2012. Pingu: A new miniature wearable device for ubiquitous computing environments. InProceedings Complex, Intelligent and Software Intensive Systems (CISIS).
17. Sugarragchaa Khurelbaatar, Yuriko Nakai, Ryuta Okazaki, Vibol Yem, and Hiroyuki Kajimoto. 2016. Tactile Presentation to the Back of a Smartphone with Simultaneous Screen Operation. In Proceedings of the 2016 CHI Conference on Human Factors in Computing Systems (CHI '16).
18. Wolf Kienzle and Ken Hinckley. 2014. LightRing: always-available 2D input on any surface. In Proceedings of the 27th annual ACM symposium on User interface software and technology (UIST '14). ACM, New York, NY, USA, 157-160.
19. Hwan Kim, Minhwan Kim, and Woohun Lee. 2016. HapThimble: A Wearable Haptic Device towards Usable Virtual Touch Screen. In Proceedings of the 2016 CHI Conference on Human Factors in Computing Systems (CHI '16). ACM, New York, NY, USA, 3694-3705.
20. Kevin A. Li, Patrick Baudisch, William G. Griswold, and James D. Hollan. 2008. Tapping and rubbing: exploring new dimensions of tactile feedback with voice coil motors. In Proceedings of the 21st annual ACM symposium on User interface software and technology (UIST '08).
21. Stefan Marti and Chris Schmandt. 2005. Giving the caller the finger: collaborative responsibility for cellphone interruptions. In CHI '05 Extended Abstracts on Human Factors in Computing Systems (CHI EA '05). ACM, New York, NY, USA, 1633-1636.
22. Cameron S. Miner, Denise M. Chan, and Christopher Campbell. 2001. Digital jewelry: wearable technology for everyday life. In CHI '01 Extended Abstracts on Human Factors in Computing Systems (CHI EA '01). ACM, New York, NY, USA, 45-46.
23. Ulf Norrsell, Hakan Olausson. 1994. Spatial cues serving the tactile directional sensibility of the human forearm. Journal of Physiology, 478 (3), 533-540.
24. Masa Ogata, Yuta Sugiura, Hirotaka Osawa, and Michita Imai. 2012. iRing: intelligent ring using infrared reflection. In Proceedings of the 25th annual ACM symposium on User interface software and technology (UIST '12). ACM, New York, NY, USA, 131-136.
25. Gilang Andi Pradana, Adrian David Cheok, Masahiko Inami, Jordan Tewell, and Yongsoon Choi. 2014. Emotional priming of mobile text messages with ring-shaped wearable device using color lighting and tactile expressions. In Proceedings of the 5th Augmented Human International Conference (AH '14). ACM, New York, NY, USA, Article 14 , 8 pages.
26. William R. Provancher, and Nicholas D. Sylvester. Fingerpad skin stretch increases the perception of virtual friction. In Proceedings of IEEE Transactions on Haptics, 2009, 2.4: 212-223.

27. Zhan Fan Quek, Samuel B. Schorr, Ilana Nisky, William R. Provancher, and Allison M. Okamura. Sensory substitution using 3-degree-of-freedom tangential and normal skin deformation feedback. In Proceedings of 2014 IEEE Haptics Symposium (HAPTICS). IEEE, 2014. p. 27-33.
28. Thijs Roumen, Simon T. Perrault, and Shengdong Zhao. 2015. NotiRing: A Comparative Study of Notification Channels for Wearable Interactive Rings. In Proceedings of the 33rd Annual ACM Conference on Human Factors in Computing Systems (CHI '15). ACM, New York, NY, USA, 2497-2500.
29. Roy Shilkrot, Jochen Huber, Jürgen Steimle, Suranga Nanayakkara, and Pattie Maes. 2015. Digital Digits: A Comprehensive Survey of Finger Augmentation Devices. ACM Comput. Surv. 48, 2, Article 30 (November 2015), 29 pages.
30. Chao-Huai Su, Liwei Chan, Chien-Ting Weng, Rong-Hao Liang, Kai-Yin Cheng, and Bing-Yu Chen. 2013. NailDisplay: bringing an always available visual display to fingertips. In Proceedings of the SIGCHI Conference on Human Factors in Computing Systems (CHI '13). ACM, New York, NY, USA, 1461-1464.
31. Hong Z. Tan, Nathaniel I. Durlach, William M. Rabinowitz, Charlotte M. Reed. 1997. Reception of morse code through motional, vibrotactile and auditory stimulation. Perception & Psychophysics 59, 7.
32. Leslie G. Valiant. 1979. The complexity of enumeration and reliability problems. SIAM Journal on Computing, 8 (3), 410-421.
33. Åke B. Vallbo, and Roland S. Johansson. Properties of cutaneous mechanoreceptors in the human hand related to touch sensation. Hum Neurobiol 3.1 (1984): 3-14.
34. Douglas B. West. 1996. Introduction to graph theory. Prentice Hall.
35. Xing-Dong Yang, Tovi Grossman, Daniel Wigdor, and George Fitzmaurice. 2012. Magic finger: always-available input through finger instrumentation. In Proceedings of the 25th annual ACM symposium on User interface software and technology (UIST '12). ACM, New York, NY, USA, 147-156.
36. Vibol Yem, Ryuta Okazaki, and Hiroyuki Kajimoto. 2016. FinGAR: combination of electrical and mechanical stimulation for high-fidelity tactile presentation. In ACM SIGGRAPH 2016 Emerging Technologies (SIGGRAPH '16). ACM, New York, NY, USA, Article 7, 2 pages.

Fingertip Tactile Devices for Virtual Object Manipulation and Exploration

Samuel B. Schorr and Allison M. Okamura
Stanford University
Department of Mechanical Engineering
sschorr@stanford.edu, aokamura@stanford.edu

ABSTRACT
One of the main barriers to immersivity during object manipulation in virtual reality is the lack of realistic haptic feedback. Our goal is to convey compelling interactions with virtual objects, such as grasping, squeezing, pressing, lifting, and stroking, without requiring a bulky, world-grounded kinesthetic feedback device (traditional haptics) or the use of predetermined passive objects (haptic retargeting). To achieve this, we use a pair of finger-mounted haptic feedback devices that deform the skin on the fingertips to convey cutaneous force information from object manipulation. We show that users can perceive differences in virtual object weight and that they apply increasing grasp forces when lifting virtual objects as rendered mass is increased. Moreover, we show how naive users perceive changes of a virtual object's physical properties when we use skin deformation to render objects with varying mass, friction, and stiffness. These studies demonstrate that fingertip skin deformation devices can provide a compelling haptic experience appropriate for virtual reality scenarios involving object manipulation.

Author Keywords
Haptics; Virtual Reality; Mass Perception

ACM Classification Keywords
H.5.1 Multimedia Information Systems: Artificial, augmented, and virtual realities; H.5.2 User Interfaces: Haptic I/O

INTRODUCTION
Recent developments in head mounted virtual reality displays have led to dramatic improvement in the quality and accessibility of virtual experiences. These displays enable impressive visual experiences, but advancements in haptic interaction are needed to create a truly immersive experience. Kinesthetic haptic devices (robotic manipulators that generate an external force on the user) enable compelling haptic interaction with virtual worlds, but these devices are restricted to small tabletop workspaces, and require users to interact with the virtual world through a physical tool rather than with their bare hands.

Permission to make digital or hard copies of all or part of this work for personal or classroom use is granted without fee provided that copies are not made or distributed for profit or commercial advantage and that copies bear this notice and the full citation on the first page. Copyrights for components of this work owned by others than ACM must be honored. Abstracting with credit is permitted. To copy otherwise, or republish, to post on servers or to redistribute to lists, requires prior specific permission and/or a fee. Request permissions from permissions@acm.org.
CHI 2017, May 6-11, 2017, Denver, CO, USA.
Copyright is held by the owner/author(s). Publication rights licensed to ACM.
ACM ISBN 978-1-4503-4655-9/17/05 ...$15.00.
http://dx.doi.org/10.1145/3025453.3025744

There is a need for haptic devices that render compelling force information while allowing direct haptic interaction with virtual environments.

When we manipulate objects in the real world, local forces at the fingertips cause deformation of the skin on the fingerpads, providing information about the objects' physical properties. Mechanorecepters in the skin are capable of sensing both low and high frequency information about force magnitude, direction, and texture [1], [11]. We developed two 3-degree-of-freedom (DoF) fingertip tactile devices to deform the skin on the fingerpads in a manner similar to direct object manipulation. The devices use a novel tether and bias-spring actuation method, along with the well characterized delta mechanism, to allow high fidelity motors and encoders to be mounted longitudinally on the back of the finger, with small size and weight. During a grasp and lift maneuver, the high friction element touching the skin, called the tactor, can move both normally against the fingerpad (as when grasping) and laterally (as when lifting). The ability to render both normal and lateral tactile feedback makes these devices particularly well suited for conveying forces during object manipulation.

Traditionally, researchers have focused on vibration feedback as a tactile solution for conveying force and contact information [12], [14], [23]. While vibration is suitable to convey contact events and texture, it does not directly convey direction and magnitude information, preventing its use as a force substitute. More recently, researchers have investigated tactile devices that apply forces to the fingerpad. When appended to the end of traditional kinesthetic devices, these tactile devices have been shown to increase the perception of virtual stiffness and friction [20], [21], [22], aid in the discrimination of textures during environment exploration [5], and in some cases replace force feedback entirely while preserving performance in teleoperated tasks [17], [24].

The evidence of effective tactile feedback has led researchers to develop haptic devices that allow direct touch with virtual environments. An example of a wearable kinesthetic device is Dexmo [7], which is grounded to the back of the hand and provides force to resist grasping motions. Carter et al. developed a system that uses focused ultrasound to project points of haptic feedback on user hands [2]. Others have developed tactile devices worn on the finger, recreating interaction forces at the fingerpad. Minamizawa et al. used a fingertip moving belt design in conjunction with an Omega.3 haptic device to render virtual mass [15]. Prattichizzo et al. [19] and Perez et al.

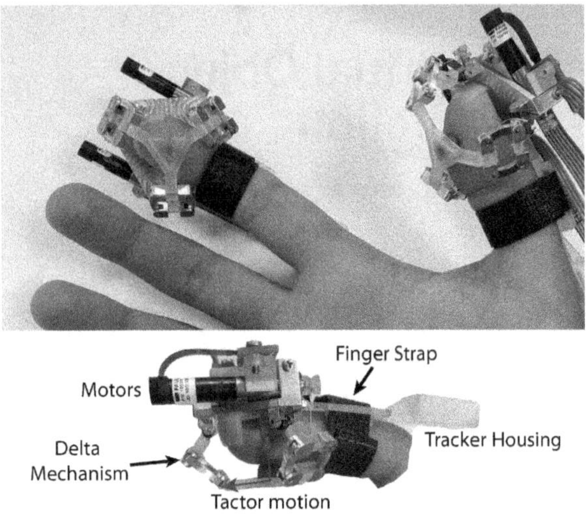

Figure 1. Fingertip devices on the index finger and thumb. Each device tactor can move in 3-DoF against the fingerpad (normally and laterally), with minimal encumberance.

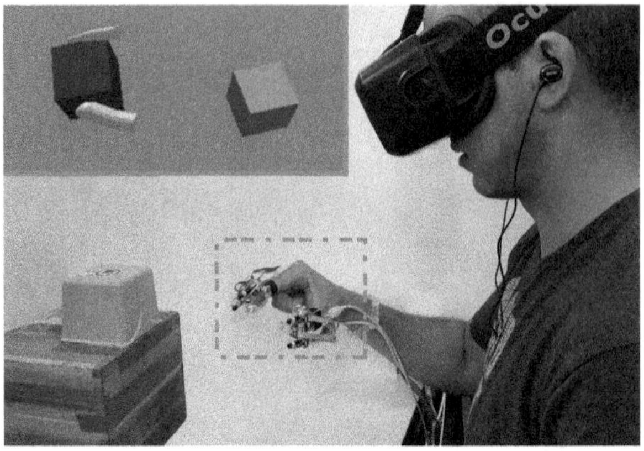

Figure 2. Example of the experimental setup during both experiments. Devices were worn on the index finger and thumb and used to render virtual environment forces while the scene was rendered on an Oculus DK2 display.

[18] developed wearable devices that compress a platform normal to the fingerpad and also change the platform orientation. Leonardis et al. [13] developed a wearable device capable of moving in 3 degrees of freedom that reduced grip forces during virtual lifting when compared to no haptic feedback.

While many tactile devices have been shown to improve performance during specific isolated tasks, the effect of tactile feedback on naive perception of mass, a percept that normally includes a kinesthetic component, needs further investigation. The role of tactile feedback in mass perception is especially important since it has been suggested that humans integrate visual and haptic information in an optimal fashion, minimizing the variance in a final estimate by combining the two senses [4]. While some parameters can be estimated solely through visual feedback, mass requires haptic sensation because vision cannot be used to determine the density of objects. Though tactile feedback for perception of mass has been investigated with the aid of traditional kinesthetic devices or object props [26], [15], [6], to the authors' knowledge, this work is the first direct investigation of virtual mass perception and other object physical properties when using only a finger grounded skin deformation device.

Our new devices have 3 purely translational degrees of freedom, making them particularly well suited for rendering forces that act in multiple directions during object manipulation, such as weight, friction, and stiffness. We performed two user studies to investigate how virtual objects are perceived with fingertip skin deformation feedback. The results show that users can distinguish between virtual objects with different mass, and also how naive user perception of virtual object properties is affected when the mass, stiffness, or friction of the virtual objects is modified.

SYSTEM DESIGN

The fingertip tactile devices (Fig. 1) have two separate components. The first is a finger grounding interface that straps to the medial phalanx. Several sizes of this interface were created to enable use with participants of varying finger size. Grounding to the medial phalanx helps distribute forces from the tactor and results in a stimulus that feels like it originates from an external source. The interface holds a magnetic tracking sensor from an Ascension 3D Guidance trakSTAR system, which provides tracking information about the position and orientation of the fingers in free space at 200 Hz.

The second component of the devices is the delta mechanism, which attaches to the finger grounding interface via a dovetail feature. The delta mechanism moves in 3 DoF with a $10\times10\times5$ mm workspace and has the ability to make and break contact with the fingerpad. It weighs approximately 32 g and is bounded by a box of size $21.5\times48.8\times40.2$ mm. The position of the delta mechanism was controlled using a Sensoray 826 I/O board to output desired motor torques to linear current amplifiers. The bias springs in the base revolute joints provide mechanism torques in one direction, while the Faulhaber 0615 DC motors with 06/1K 64:1 gearboxes spool the tethers attached to the base links to provide torques in the other direction. The delta mechanism is capable of up to 7.5 N of normal force and 2 N of lateral force. CAD models of the entire assembly can be found on https://github.com/sschorr/WearableDevice.

Virtual environments were created using CHAI3D [3], which uses the god-object algorithm [9] for determining dynamic object interaction forces. This algorithm uses a proxy point that is attached to the haptic interaction point (HIP) by a virtual spring (surface stiffness). When the HIP moves within a virtual object, the proxy point is constrained to the object surface, stretching the spring and determining a virtual interaction force. The neutral position of each device tactor was set for each participant by moving the tactor into the fingerpad by approximately 0.5 mm. This initial offset normal to the fingerpad prevents the tactor from slipping laterally across the finger during use. During haptic rendering, the orientation of the devices in free space was used to transform the force vector of the virtual interaction force into the reference frame of the delta mechanism. The device tactors were then com-

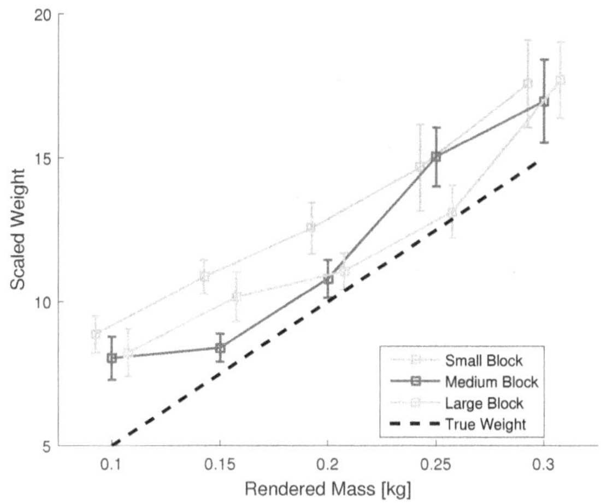

Figure 3. Mean participant response weight for each block mass and size. The true scaled weight is based on the "standard" block with mass 0.2 kg and weight "10". Error bars indicate standard error.

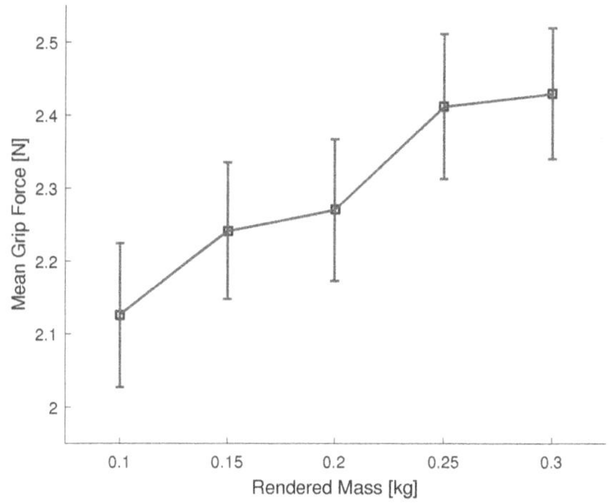

Figure 4. Mean grip force for each rendered mass. Error bars indicate standard error.

manded to move 2.1 mm/N from the neutral position in the vector direction of the virtual environment interaction forces, based on the mean lateral stiffness of the fingerpad [16]. The virtual environment and resulting interaction forces were updated at approximately 3 kHz with overall system latency of approximately 20-30 ms from user input motion to visuohaptic rendering, the majority from tracker delay. An Oculus DK2 was used to display the virtual environment to users. Participants wore noise canceling headphones playing white noise during the experiments. The system setup is shown in Fig. 2.

MASS PERCEPTION STUDY

The objective of this experiment was to determine how virtual object mass and size affected weight perception of device users. Six participants, five with engineering backgrounds, completed the experiment after giving informed consent. The experimental procedure was approved by Stanford University's Institutional Review Board.

Methods

Participants evaluated the weight of virtual blocks with heights of 50, 100, or 150 mm and masses of 100, 150, 200, 250, or 300 g. Blocks were presented in pairs where the first was always the "standard" block (100 mm tall and 200 g). Participants were asked to grasp the block between the index finger and thumb and lift it approximately 15 cm. They were then told that the standard block has a weight of "10" and were presented with one of the alternative blocks. Participants were asked to evaluate its weight with a number relative to the 10 of the standard block, using a magnitude estimation scale. Each combination of block size and weight was presented 5 times for a total of 75 trials per participant.

Results

Mean participant response weight for each mass and block size is indicated in Fig. 3. Participant perceived weight increased with increasing block mass for all block sizes. Fig. 4 shows the mean grip force per rendered mass. Participants used increased grip force to lift the blocks as the rendered mass was increased.

We fit a linear mixed-effects model via maximum-likelihood to the response variables of evaluated weight and grip force. Block mass and size were included as fixed-effects terms and differences in participant performance were included as a random-effect term. An ANOVA test to determine if coefficients representing the fixed-effects terms were equal to 0 indicated that block mass had a significant effect on perceived weight and mean grip force ($F_{1,447} = 156.3, p < 0.001$ and $F_{1,447} = 13.56, p < 0.001$, respectively). The effect of block size on perceived weight and grip force was not statistically significant.

Discussion

The statistically significant effect of rendered mass on participant perceived weight indicates that participants were able to use the tactile devices to discriminate between virtual objects of varying mass. While participants perceived the masses as having a narrower weight range than previous real world experiments [10], the weight range reported with the devices actually more closely matches the true scaled weight. When lifting an object, the resulting force vector on the finger is determined both by the normal force associated with the grasping of the object, and the gravity force during the lift. Participants were able to parse the force vector rendered by tactile feedback and interpret the component representing the object weight.

We did not see a strong effect of the size-weight illusion [25] that has previously been shown with objects of varying size. This phenomenon has been shown to work in virtual reality with both real objects [10] and kinesthetic haptic devices [8]. In our experiment, the smallest block had the highest mean reported weight across all masses, but there was no statistically significant effect of block size on perceived weight. It could be that the lack of kinesthetic resistance during the lifting motion, which would result in different lifting accelerations for each mass given a specific lift force, prevented the manifestation of the illusion. Further research is needed to determine whether the effect can occur with purely tactile feedback.

Cutaneous sensory information is known to be critical for skilled grasping [27], and the increase in mean grip force with increasing rendered mass shows that participants were modifying their grip based on the real-time estimation of the object mass. When lifting objects in the real world, grip force is typically regulated to prevent object slipping. The devices' ability to provide information about normal grasping force and object mass allowed users to modulate grip force based on the mass of the object being lifted.

PHYSICAL PROPERTIES STUDY

The previous study required that users consider the haptic stimulus they received as mass. We now investigate how the manipulation of various virtual object properties affects perception when naive users are free to manipulate objects in an unprompted manner. Six participants, different from those in the previous study and with no previous experience using skin deformation devices, completed the experiment after giving informed consent. Five of the six participants had engineering backgrounds. The experimental procedure was approved by Stanford University's Institutional Review Board.

Experiment Procedure

In this experiment, participants were presented with a virtual environment consisting of two small blocks on a table. Both blocks had the same size and shape, but were different colors to make them easily distinguishable. Each pair of blocks presented to the participants had matching physical properties with the exception of one varying property: mass (50 g vs. 250 g), stiffness (60 N/m vs. 180 N/m), or friction coefficient between the user's virtual finger and object ($\mu = 0.5$ vs. $\mu = 4$). The experiment participants had no prior knowledge of the virtual parameters being investigated and were only told to freely manipulate the two blocks on the table and describe any noticeable differences between their physical properties. Participants were not time restricted and were allowed to continue until they felt they had adequately described the differences, usually 5-10 minutes. Each participant explored all 3 varying properties in a Balanced Latin Squares order.

Results

Fig. 5 describes the relationship between the physical parameter that was changed and the perceived parameter changes reported by the participants. When the virtually rendered mass was changed, 5 of the 6 participants reported a difference in perceived mass, 3 reported a difference in stiffness, and 1 reported a difference in friction. When the rendered stiffness was changed, 4 participants reported a change in mass, 3 reported a change in stiffness, and 3 reported a change in friction. Finally, when the rendered friction was changed, 2 participants reported a change in mass and 6 reported a change in friction. Importantly, when participants correctly identified the parameter being changed, they always correctly identified which block had the higher and lower values.

Discussion

While many participants perceived a change in the direct physical parameter being modified in the study, many of them also perceived changes in other physical parameters that were not modified. Knowledge of these crossovers in object property perception helps developers avoid unintentionally undermining the intended rendering effects.

		Perceived Change		
		mass	stiffness	friction
Virtual Rendered Change	mass	5/6	3/6	1/6
	stiffness	4/6	3/6	3/6
	friction	2/6	0/6	6/6

Figure 5. Fraction of participants that responded with a perceived parameter change based on the virtually rendered parameter changes. Participants' responses were unprompted, and some responded with multiple perceived changes for the single rendered change.

Most notably, 4 of the 6 participants responded that increasing the object stiffness made the object feel heavier. When questioned further about this observation, some said that they thought the stiffer block was heavier due to the increased forces they felt while holding it. Without an underlying kinesthetic force on the fingerpads, the additional feedback of the resulting from the object's higher stiffness was perceived to be increased force from weight. The dual of this effect was also observed, as 3 of the 6 participants perceived a change in stiffness when the mass of the virtual block was altered. Again, it is likely that participants exhibiting this crossover perceived increased or decreased intensity on the fingerpads rather than directly evaluating the vector directions of the stimulus they felt – normal to the fingerpads for stiffness, and downwards with gravity for mass.

All of the participants recognized altered friction properties of the surface, many specifically using words like "slippery" or "sticky". The effective rendering and perception of frictional forces is critical for modulating interaction forces during manipulation. This likely contributed to the significant effect of object mass on grip force in the previous study.

CONCLUSIONS

We developed fingertip tactile devices to investigate how cutaneous skin deformation could contribute to a compelling, immersive haptics experience for virtual reality without the bulk of traditional kinesthetic haptic devices. We showed that participants are not only able to perceive variations in the weight of virtual objects, but also to modulate their grip force commensurate with the mass of the object being manipulated. Furthermore, we show how changing various physical properties of virtual objects affects completely naive user perception during device use. While users often directly perceive the altered virtual property, there are also frequent situations in which users perceive a different altered characteristic. With the knowledge obtained from these studies, we can create haptically interactive virtual environments with a better understanding of the relationship between rendered and perceived virtual object properties.

REFERENCES

1. I. Birznieks, P. Jenmalm, A. W. Goodwin, and R. S. Johansson. 2001. Encoding of Direction of Fingertip Forces by Human Tactile Afferents. *The Journal of Neuroscience* 21, 20 (2001), 8222–8237.
2. T. Carter, S. A. Seah, B. Long, B. Drinkwater, and S. Subramanian. 2013. UltraHaptics: multi-point mid-air haptic feedback for touch surfaces. In *ACM Symposium on User Interface Software and Technology*. 505–514.
3. F. Conti, F. Barbagli, D. Morris, and C. Sewell. 2005. CHAI3D: An open-source library for the rapid development of haptic scenes. In *IEEE World Haptics Conference*. 21–29.
4. M. O. Ernst and M. S. Banks. 2002. Humans integrate visual and haptic information in a statistically optimal fashion. *Nature* 415, 6870 (2002), 429–433.
5. M. Gabardi, M. Solazzi, D. Leonardis, and A. Frisoli. 2016. A new wearable fingertip haptic interface for the rendering of virtual shapes and surface features. In *IEEE Haptics Symposium*. 140–146.
6. A. Girard, M. Marchal, F. Gosselin, A. Chabrier, F. Louveau, and A. LÃl'cuyer. 2016. HapTip: Displaying Haptic Shear Forces at the Fingertips for Multi-Finger Interaction in Virtual Environments. *Frontiers in ICT* 3 (2016), 6.
7. X. Gu, Y. Zhang, W. Sun, Y. Bian, D. Zhou, and P. O. Kristensson. 2016. Dexmo: An Inexpensive and Lightweight Mechanical Exoskeleton for Motion Capture and Force Feedback in VR. In *Conference on Human Factors in Computing Systems*. 1991–1995.
8. M. Hara, C. Asada, T. Higuchi, and T. Yabuta. 2004. Perceptual illusion in virtual reality using haptic interface. In *IEEE/RSJ International Conference on Intelligent Robots and Systems*. 3901–3906.
9. W. S. Harwin and N. Melder. 2002. Improved haptic rendering for multi-finger manipulation using friction cone based god-objects. In *Eurohaptics Conference*.
10. E. Heineken and F. P. Schulte. 2007. Seeing size and feeling weight: The size-weight illusion in natural and virtual reality. *Human Factors: The Journal of the Human Factors and Ergonomics Society* 49, 1 (2007), 136–144.
11. K. O. Johnson. 2001. The roles and functions of cutaneous mechanoreceptors. *Current Opinion in Neurobiology* 11, 4 (2001), 455 – 461.
12. K.J. Kuchenbecker, J. Fiene, and G. Niemeyer. 2006. Improving contact realism through event-based haptic feedback. *IEEE Transactions on Visualization and Computer Graphics* 12, 2 (2006), 219–230.
13. D. Leonardis, M. Solazzi, I. Bortone, and A. Frisoli. 2015. A wearable fingertip haptic device with 3 DoF asymmetric 3-RSR kinematics. In *IEEE World Haptics Conference*. 388–393.
14. W. McMahan, J. Gewirtz, D. Standish, P. Martin, J.A. Kunkel, M. Lilavois, A. Wedmid, D. I. Lee, and K. J. Kuchenbecker. 2011. Tool contact acceleration feedback for telerobotic surgery. *IEEE Transactions on Haptics* 4, 3 (2011), 210 –220.
15. Kouta Minamizawa, Domenico Prattichizzo, and Susumu Tachi. 2010. Simplified design of haptic display by extending one-point kinesthetic feedback to multipoint tactile feedback. In *IEEE Haptics Symposium*. 257–260.
16. N. Nakazawa, R. Ikeura, and H. Inooka. 2000. Characteristics of human fingertips in the shearing direction. *Biological Cybernetics* 82, 3 (2000), 207–214.
17. C. Pacchierotti, D. Prattichizzo, and K. J. Kuchenbecker. 2016. Cutaneous feedback of fingertip deformation and vibration for palpation in robotic surgery. *IEEE Transactions on Biomedical Engineering* 63, 2 (2016), 278–287.
18. A. G. Perez, D. Lobo, F. Chinello, G. Cirio, M. Malvezzi, J. S. Martín, D. Prattichizzo, and M. A. Otaduy. 2015. Soft finger tactile rendering for wearable haptics. In *IEEE World Haptics Conference*. 327–332.
19. D. Prattichizzo, F. Chinello, C. Pacchierotti, and M. Malvezzi. 2013. Towards wearability in fingertip haptics: A 3-DoF wearable device for cutaneous force feedback. *IEEE Transactions on Haptics* 6, 4 (2013), 506–516.
20. W. R. Provancher and N. D. Sylvester. 2009. Fingerpad skin stretch increases the perception of virtual friction. *IEEE Transactions on Haptics* 2, 4 (2009), 212–223.
21. Z. F. Quek, S. B. Schorr, I. Nisky, A. M. Okamura, and W. R. Provancher. 2014. Sensory substitution using 3-degree-of-freedom tangential and normal skin deformation feedback. In *IEEE Haptics Symposium*. 27–33.
22. Z. F. Quek, S. B. Schorr, I. Nisky, W. R. Provancher, and A. M. Okamura. 2015. Sensory substitution and augmentation using 3-degree-of-freedom skin deformation feedback. *IEEE Transactions on Haptics* 8, 2 (2015), 209–221.
23. R. E. Schoonmaker and C. G. L. Cao. 2006. Vibrotactile force feedback system for minimally invasive surgical procedures. In *IEEE International Conference on Systems, Man and Cybernetics*. 2464 –2469.
24. S. B. Schorr, Z. F. Quek, I. Nisky, W. R. Provancher, and A. M. Okamura. 2015. Tactor-induced skin stretch as a sensory substitution method in teleoperated palpation. *IEEE Transactions on Human-Machine Systems* 45, 6 (2015), 714–726.
25. L. Sjöberg. 1969. Sensation scales in the size weight illusion. *Scandinavian Journal of Psychology* 10, 1 (1969), 109–112.
26. J. M. Suchoski, A. Barron, C. Wu, Z. F. Quek, S. Keller, and A. M. Okamura. 2016. Comparison of kinesthetic and skin deformation feedback for mass rendering. In *IEEE International Conference on Robotics and Automation*. 4030–4035.
27. A. G. Witney, A. Wing, J.L. Thonnard, and A. M. Smith. 2004. The cutaneous contribution to adaptive precision grip. *Trends in Neurosciences* 27, 10 (2004), 637–643.

BrushTouch: Exploring an Alternative Tactile Method for Wearable Haptics

Evan Strasnick[1] estrasni@stanford.edu
Jessica R. Cauchard[1,2] jcauchard@acm.org
James A. Landay[1] landay@cs.stanford.edu

[1]Stanford University, Stanford, CA, USA [2]IDC Herzliya, Herzliya, Israel

Figure 1. Left to right: A user wearing a novel haptic wearable prototype, comparing the recognizability of haptic cues with different forms of tactile stimulation, following navigational instructions through haptic cues.

ABSTRACT

Haptic interfaces are ideal in situations where visual/auditory attention is impossible, unsafe, or socially unacceptable. However, conventional (vibrotactile) wearable interfaces often possess a limited bandwidth for expressing information. We explore a novel form of tactile stimulation through brushing, and demonstrate BrushTouch, a wearable prototype for brushing haptics. We also present schemes for conveying information such as time and direction through multi-tactor wrist-worn haptic interfaces. To evaluate BrushTouch, two user studies were run, comparing it to a conventional vibrotactile wristband across a number of tasks in both lab and mobile conditions. We show that for certain cues brushing can be more accurately recognized than vibration, enabling more effective spatial schemes for presenting information through haptic means. We then show that BrushTouch is capable of greater information transfer using such cues. We believe that brushing, as with other non-vibrotactile haptic techniques, merits further investigation as potential vehicles for richer haptic feedback.

ACM Classification Keywords

H.5.2. Information Interfaces and Presentation: Haptic I/O

Author Keywords

haptics; tactile; wearables; vibrotactile; wayfinding; brush; brushtouch;

INTRODUCTION AND RELATED WORK

Numerous scenarios exist where visual attention is either unavailable (e.g., one is driving), undesirable (e.g., it is socially unacceptable), or impossible (e.g., for the visually impaired). Similarly, audio can be difficult to hear in many environments, and wearing headphones may even be dangerous. Thus, we require systems that are discreet, can be used without sacrificing visual or auditory attention, and are usable for individuals with sensory impairments.

Permission to make digital or hard copies of all or part of this work for personal or classroom use is granted without fee provided that copies are not made or distributed for profit or commercial advantage and that copies bear this notice and the full citation on the first page. Copyrights for components of this work owned by others than ACM must be honored. Abstracting with credit is permitted. To copy otherwise, or republish, to post on servers or to redistribute to lists, requires prior specific permission and/or a fee. Request permissions from Permissions@acm.org.
CHI 2017, May 06-11, 2017, Denver, CO, USA
©2017 ACM. ISBN 978-1-4503-4655-9/17/05...$15.00
DOI: http://dx.doi.org/10.1145/3025453.3025759

Wearable haptic solutions have taken a variety of form factors including watches [4], belts [20, 23], vests [7], gloves [26], and shoes [25]. Typical use cases include wayfinding [23, 25, 26], guidance of physical motion [13], and driving [10].

Such systems require an informational bandwidth large enough to be both expressive and efficient. Though vibrotactile (VT) techniques have a number of advantages making them ideal for many devices, a single VT element is in fact a low-bandwidth channel for information transfer [22]. Prior work investigated "tactons", structured units of VT stimulus, to encode messages [2]. They present a limited recognition rate under variations of parameters, such as 80% recognition for roughness (amplitude) [3] and frequency [11]. These rates decline considerably outside of a controlled laboratory setting for Duration, Interval, and Intensity [17].

Vibrotactile Stimulations

Thus, to reliably express even simple messages, it becomes necessary to build complex cues consisting of multiple stimuli across the temporal domain (encoding "patterns"). Patterns are consistently the most recognizable of features [3], with ActiVibe [4] reaching 96% recognition rate in the lab and 89% *in-situ*. Yet, such patterns quickly grow towards unusable lengths for messages beyond the most basic, and conveying real world information can require substantial learning.

An alternate approach is to extend across the spatial domain. For example, a wrist-worn device could utilize the space around the wrist, signaling different cues by activating tactors at different locations. We note several advantages to varying signals across space instead of time. Firstly, signals can be sent in a shorter duration of time, reducing draws on the user's attention. Moreover, there are numerous types of real-world information that already utilize a radial metaphor (e.g., time).

We expect that prior familiarity with the representation will result in a reduced learning phase.

Previous studies have demonstrated that properly distributing multiple tactors improves informational bandwidth. A 41.6% increase in bitrate is found for a 4-motor system arranged around the wrist as opposed to on the top of it [16]. Yet, there are limits to the number of tactors we can utilize in an area, primarily dictated by the spatial resolution of human perception. Thus, we reason that by improving the resolution with which haptic stimuli can be localized, we can increase the informational bandwidth of a wrist-worn haptic device.

The literature shows relatively low spatial acuity for VT stimuli on the wrist and forearm. Chen et al. were able to obtain ~50% recognition on the wrist using a 3x3 VT array with sites spaced 25 mm apart [5]. Cholewiak and Collins found that increasing the distance between stimulus sites on the wrist from 25 to 50 mm improved recognition by nearly 15% [6]. Jones et al. characterized the effects of surface waves that propagate across the skin as a result of vibration, finding that at least 6 cm of separation was necessary between tactors on the forearm to prevent mislocalizations [14].

Non-Vibrational Haptic Stimulation

Diverse non-VT haptic wearable devices have emerged, often claiming increased recognition rates over VT analogues. Feedback mechanisms include shape change [9], skin stretch/drag [8, 12], tapping [13], squeezing [1], and tickling [15]. As each modality is likely to evoke a different response across the range of mechanoreceptors in human skin [24], it to our advantage to explore their properties and uses in haptic devices. For example, tapping, dragging, squeezing, and twisting methods all differed qualitatively and quantitatively from VT output on a wrist rotation guidance task [21]. To the best of our knowledge, light brushing against the surface of the skin - perhaps less impacted by the surface waves characteristic of vibration - remains unexplored in this way.

BRUSHTOUCH PROTOTYPE

To explore the possibility of brush-based tactile stimulation, we created BrushTouch, a haptic wearable prototype (Figure 1). It consists of six individually-controllable cylindrical DC rotational motors equally spaced about a stretchable wristband (Figure 2). The number of tactors is based on prior findings that six (VT) motors on the wrist is an ideal compromise between spatial acuity and informational bandwidth [18]. We designed BrushTouch to allow for a valid comparison to an equivalent VT band.

A piece of soft foam is attached to the shaft of each motor via removable Gorilla Tape. As the motors rotate (~100 Hz), the foam brushes against the skin, resulting in a unique tactile sensation. Different lengths of brush are used to accommodate the wrist size of the user (width = 10 mm, thickness = 1 mm). Each device was worn with the tactors arranged as shown in Figure 4, as in [19]. We used PKN12 3V DC motors (NMB technologies), driven by an Arduino controller. The Arduino receives commands via Bluetooth from an Android smartphone and triggers the appropriate motor response. The entire system is portable and powered by a USB 5V supply.

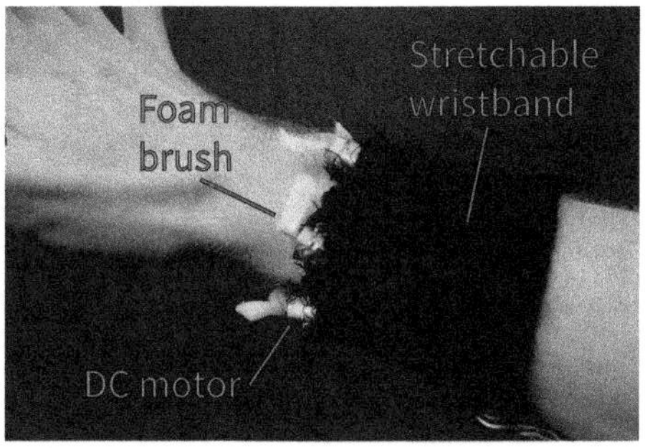

Figure 2. The BrushTouch prototype, composed of a stretchable wristband and 6 DC motors with foam brushes.

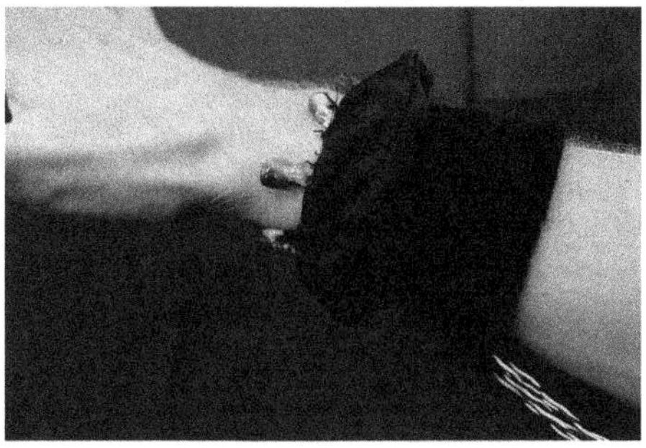

Figure 3. The vibration-style device.

VALIDATION

BrushTouch was evaluated with two user studies: first to gauge its performance relative to a conventional VT device across a variety of tasks in the lab, and then to compare these devices in a real-world mobile setting. We designed a VT wristband analogous to those found in prior work [18, 19]. The band (Figure 3) consists of six cylindrical vibration motors, arranged around the wrist in the same configuration as BrushTouch. The motors are 2000 RPM, 3V DC motors, run at the same current as the BrushTouch prototype.

Experiment 1

The first study compared BrushTouch to an equivalent VT device in terms of participants' ability to 1) recognize the activation of a specific motor or combination of motors, and 2) extract semantic information from that haptic cue.

Setup

We recruited 14 volunteers (9 m) from our institution, aged 18-30, all right-handed. The study lasted one hour, and participants were compensated $20 for their time. Each participant carried out a total of five tasks in each of the two device conditions (Brush vs. Vibration). The tasks were presented in the same order on each device, and the ordering of the two device conditions was counterbalanced between participants.

Training

Users performed the study while seated at a computer. For each device condition, participants were fit with the device on their right wrists, then underwent a calibration to make sure that they could perceive each motor at equal amplitude and in the correct location. For each trial, to avoid any differences in sensation caused by varying the arm or hand position, the participant would lift their hand from the mouse to an outstretched neutral position in midair to receive a haptic pulse, then return

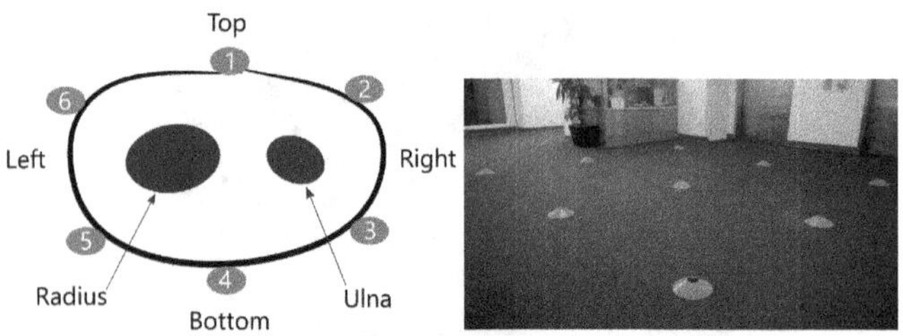

Figure 4. Left: Tactor layout on the wrist for both devices. Right: Setup for the walking study (Experiment 2).

to the mouse to select their response. Participants positioned their right hand behind a screen to prevent seeing the device during the trials, and listened to music through headphones to ensure that auditory cues from the motors could not be heard.

After each task was explained, the participant completed six training trials prior to beginning the experimental trials. At the conclusion of the study, the participant filled out a qualitative evaluation of the two devices.

Pilot Study

The design of our tasks was informed by a pilot study (N = 6) conducted to explore how to optimally design multi-motor schemes for encoding information. Notably, for the simultaneous activation of multiple motors, participants were able to far more accurately identify motor combinations that were adjacent as opposed to non-adjacent ($p < .005$). Thus, our semantic schemes were designed to utilize adjacent motor pairs when simultaneous stimuli were required.

Tasks

Participants completed the following tasks, in order, on each device. Responses were indicated by clicking the corresponding label on a diagram displayed on a screen in front of them:

- *Single Motor Identification (SINGLE)*
  Each trial consisted of the activation (2 s) of a single motor. Participants indicated the perceived motor on a diagram similar to Figure 4. (24 trials)
- *Multiple Motor Identification (MULTI)*
  Each trial consisted of the simultaneous activation (2 s) of two nonidentical motors. Participants indicated the perceived motors on a diagram similar to Figure 4. (30 trials)
- *Single/Adjacent Motor Identification (MIXED-ADJ)*
  Each trial consisted of the activation (2 s) of either a single motor or two adjacent motors (each with 50% probability). Participants indicated the perceived motor(s) on a diagram similar to Figure 4. This task was designed to dissociate the discrimination of the stimuli used in the TIME and DIRECTION tasks from the additional cognitive load of translating these cues into semantic meanings. (20 trials)
- *Determining Time (TIME)*
  Participants were asked to determine the time (to 5-minute resolution) from haptic cues. Each trial consisted of an hour cue and a minute cue (1s each) being sent with a 500 ms pause in between. Hour and minute cues were represented either by the activation of a single motor (indicating one of the six even digits on a clock located directly on the position of a motor) or by the simultaneous activation of two adjacent motors (indicating the odd digit on a clock located in between the two positions matching those two motors). Participants indicated the time that they perceived by clicking first the hour then the minute position on an interactive clock face. (20 trials)
- *Determining Direction (DIRECTION)*
  Participants were asked to determine a cardinal direction from haptic cues. Each trial consisted of the activation of either a single motor (indicating one of the cardinal directions aligned with the motors with the top motor is designated as North [N, NE, NW, S, SE, SW]), the two adjacent motors on the right side of the wrist (indicating East), or the two adjacent motors on the left side of the wrist (indicating West). Participants indicated the direction that they perceived by clicking the corresponding position on an interactive compass rose. (20 trials)

Task	*Vibration %accuracy*	*Brush %accuracy*	*p Value*
SINGLE	89.0	93.5	**.036**
MULTI	64.8	75.0	**.001**
MIXED-ADJ	73.6	75.7	.544
TIME	55.7	58.2	.513
DIRECTION	87.1	86.1	.699

Table 1. Averaged accuracy for each task across the two devices in Experiment 1, and p-value resulting from repeated-measures ANOVA.

Experiment 2

A follow-up study was carried out to compare the performance of the devices under close to real world conditions. Ten new participants (6 m), aged 18-26, were recruited from our institution. Participants were first trained to identify directional cues as in Experiment 1, and then used these cues in a turn-by-turn navigation task (20 trials). The experiment took place in an open indoor space with a grid of 8 possible locations marked by a perimeter of cones (Figure 4). Each participant performed the task with both devices in a counterbalanced order.

For each trial, participants would walk towards the central cone in a natural manner with their arm down by their side. They would then receive a haptic signal and change their course to end up at the indicated target cone along the perimeter. When the participant had finished at their destination, their choice of direction was recorded. All eight directions were possible in each trial. Participants wore a light backpack while walking to hold the power supply and circuitry.

EXPERIMENTAL RESULTS

For each task, a repeated-measures ANOVA was performed to compare participants' accuracy rates across each of the two device conditions (Table 1). Significant differences between the device conditions are observed in both the SINGLE and MULTI tasks. No significant differences in time to completion between the two devices were observed in any task ($p = .05$).

To further investigate these differences and why they do not persist into the remaining three tasks, we analyzed separately the adjacent and non-adjacent stimulus combinations in the

Task: MULTI	*Vibration*	*BrushTouch*
IT_{est}	2.5085	2.8705
2^{ITest}	5.69	7.31
Number of discriminable signals	> 5	> 7
Task: SINGLE	*Vibration*	*BrushTouch*
IT_{est}	1.9980	2.2439
2^{ITest}	3.99	4.74
Number of discriminable signals	<= 4	> 4

Table 2. Information Transfer for the SINGLE and MULTI tasks.

Qualitative Measure	*Vibration*	*Brush*	*p Value (2-tail)*
Effort on Time Task	5.92	5.67	.571
Confidence on Time Task	3.42	3.67	.586
Effort on Direction Task	4.50	4.17	.457
Confidence on Direction Task	4.75	5.00	.429
Comfort	5.58	4.33	.003

Table 3. Mean values from a 7-point Likert qualitative evaluation of the two devices.

MULTI task. For activations of adjacent motors, the accuracy was 79.8% for the VT device and 82.7% for the brush device (not significant). However, for non-adjacent combinations, the accuracy was only 54.8% for the VT device and 69.8% for the brush device ($p < .05$).

To assess the differences in capability for expressing information between the two devices in this task, we use the Information Transfer measure described by Chen et al. [5]:

$$IT_{est} = \sum_{j=1}^{k}\sum_{i=1}^{k}(\frac{n_{ij}}{n}\log_2(\frac{n_{ij}\cdot n}{n_i\cdot n_j}))$$

where k is the number of distinct stimuli, n is the total number of trials, n_i is the number of trials where stimulus i appeared, n_j is the number of trials where response j was given, and n_{ij} is the number of trials where stimulus i was responded to by response j.

This formula estimates the amount of information, in bits, transmitted from each stimuli to the response. The integer part of $2^{IT_{est}}$ is interpreted as the number of distinct cues which can be reliably distinguished using the device. Table 2 compares the information transfer of the two devices, as well as the number of distinct cues that can be identified by each.

The qualitative survey compared effort required to complete each task, confidence in cues received on each task, and general comfort of the devices. Participants were asked to agree with sentiments on a 7-point Likert scale. Means were lower for effort and higher for confidence on the brush device, but failed to reach statistical significance (Table 3). Comfort was rated as significantly lower ($p < .01$) on the brush device.

Experiment 2

The mean accuracy was 84.5% for the VT device and 83.5% for the brush device (not significant). These results show no significant decrease in performance from the lab study in either condition. Participants were able to quickly learn the directional scheme with little training, despite not having been first trained on simpler tasks as in Experiment 1.

DISCUSSION

BrushTouch demonstrated a significant improvement in recognition over the VT device for both single and 2-tactor stimuli. This difference corresponded to a $5 \rightarrow 7$ increase in number of identifiable cues for a 2-tactor scheme, suggesting that it is indeed possible to convey information more efficiently using brushing. However, the significant differences are exhibited only in *non-adjacent* stimuli pairs, and thus the two devices performed similarly on the DIRECTION and TIME tasks.

Interestingly, these results imply a difference between adjacent and non-adjacent cues which may prove useful in designing multi-stimulus schemes on haptic wearables. When stimuli were adjacent, both devices showed significantly better performance, and the disparity in accuracy between the two shrunk considerably. We suspect that users may apply different cognitive heuristics in determining the source of a stimuli in the adjacent and non-adjacent cases. When users feel two activated tactors in adjacent proximity, they can choose with confidence the two neighboring tactors in the rough area where the stimuli was felt. This reduces ambiguity as compared to feeling two distinct stimuli in different locations, which must each be resolved to a single motor among neighbors. Whether or not such heuristics generalize to more complicated tasks than raw identification requires additional investigation.

In general, both devices were able to convey direction relatively successfully in both a controlled and mobile setting, whereas the TIME task proved too difficult, even in the lab setting. The mean accuracies for single tactor identification are consistent with prior results in the literature [18].

LIMITATIONS AND FUTURE WORK

The prototype does present limitations in comparison to its VT counterpart. It requires a greater degree of calibration to each user's wrist, as the various brushes need to be sized properly to make contact with the skin without dragging or stalling. In addition, the mechanism does not actuate if covered by clothing or pressed against a surface. Comfort was also rated as lower, though familiarity may play a role in this rating.

While our prototype was used as a proof-of-concept to explore brushing sensations, the next iteration will focus on engineering a more robust, comfortable brushing wearable. A full design process is needed to explore the various shapes, sizes, and materials of brushes, as well as the motors, band, and drive parameters to optimize the sensation. More generally, in addition to exploring other new modes of haptic stimulation, future work should examine how more complex stimuli (e.g. dynamic actuation patterns from prior work) compare across these alternative output modalities.

CONCLUSION

We created BrushTouch, a wearable prototype that uses brushing as an alternative to VT sensation to more effectively convey haptic cues. The results of our evaluation show that haptic interfaces using spatially distributed tactors can be made more effective using non-VT forms of tactile stimulation. We hope that this work will inspire others to continue to explore alternatives to VT haptics, enabling richer and more usable haptic interfaces.

REFERENCES

1. Matthew A. Baumann, Karon E. MacLean, Thomas W. Hazelton, and Ashley McKay. 2010. Emulating human attention-getting practices with wearable haptics. In *Haptics Symposium, 2010 IEEE*. IEEE, 149–156.
2. Stephen a. Brewster and Lorna M. Brown. 2004. Non-visual information display using tactons. *CHI'04 extended abstracts on Human factors in Computing Systems* 28 (2004), 787–788. DOI: http://dx.doi.org/10.1145/985921.985936
3. Lorna M Brown, Stephen a Brewster, and Helen C Purchase. 2005. A first investigation into the effectiveness of Tactons. *Eurohaptics Conference* March (2005), 167–176. DOI: http://dx.doi.org/10.1109/WHC.2005.6
4. Jessica R Cauchard, Janette L Cheng, Thomas Pietrzak, and James A Landay. 2016. ActiVibe: Design and Evaluation of Vibrations for Progress Monitoring. *CHI '16 Proceedings of the 2016 ACM Conference on Human Factors in Computing Systems* (2016), 1–11.
5. Hsiang Yu Chen, Joseph Santos, Matthew Graves, Kwangtaek Kim, and Hong Z. Tan. 2008. Tactor localization at the wrist. *Lecture Notes in Computer Science (including subseries Lecture Notes in Artificial Intelligence and Lecture Notes in Bioinformatics)* 5024 LNCS (2008), 209–218. DOI: http://dx.doi.org/10.1007/978-3-540-69057-3{_}25
6. Roger W. Cholewiak and Amy A. Collins. 2003. Vibrotactile localization on the arm: Effects of place, space, and age. *Perception & Psychophysics* 65, 7 (2003), 1058–1077. DOI: http://dx.doi.org/10.3758/BF03194834
7. S. Ertan, C. Lee, A. Willets, H. Tan, and A. Pentland. 1998. A wearable haptic navigation guidance system. *Digest of Papers. Second International Symposium on Wearable Computers (Cat. No.98EX215)* (1998), 164–165. DOI: http://dx.doi.org/10.1109/ISWC.1998.729547
8. Brian T. Gleeson, Scott K. Horschel, and William R. Provancher. 2010. Design of a fingertip-mounted tactile display with tangential skin displacement feedback. *Haptics, IEEE Transactions on* 3, 4 (2010), 297–301.
9. Liang He, Cheng Xu, Ding Xu, and Ryan Brill. 2015. PneuHaptic: delivering haptic cues with a pneumatic armband. In *Proceedings of the 2015 ACM International Symposium on Wearable Computers*. ACM, 47–48.
10. Cristy Ho, Hong Tan, and Charles Spence. 2005. Using spatial vibrotactile cues to direct visual attention in driving scenes. *Transportation Research Part F: Traffic Psychology and Behaviour* 8, 6 (2005), 397–412.
11. Eve Hoggan and Stephen Brewster. 2007. New Parameters for Tacton Design. *CHI '07 Extended Abstracts on Human Factors in Computing Systems* (2007), 2417–2422. DOI: http://dx.doi.org/10.1145/1240866.1241017
12. Alexandra Ion, Edward Jay Wang, and Patrick Baudisch. 2015. Skin Drag Displays: Dragging a Physical Tactor across the User's Skin Produces a Stronger Tactile Stimulus than Vibrotactile. In *Proceedings of the 33rd Annual ACM Conference on Human Factors in Computing Systems*. ACM, 2501–2504.
13. Yeon Sub Jin, Han Yong Chun, Eun Tai Kim, and Sungchul Kang. 2014. Vt-ware: A wearable tactile device for upper extremity motion guidance. In *Robot and Human Interactive Communication, 2014 RO-MAN: The 23rd IEEE International Symposium on*. IEEE, 335–340.
14. L. A. Jones, D. Held, and I. Hunter. 2010. Surface waves and spatial localization in vibrotactile displays. In *2010 IEEE Haptics Symposium*. 91–94. DOI: http://dx.doi.org/10.1109/HAPTIC.2010.5444673
15. Espen Knoop and Jonathan Rossiter. 2015. The Tickler: A Compliant Wearable Tactile Display for Stroking and Tickling. In *Proceedings of the 33rd Annual ACM Conference Extended Abstracts on Human Factors in Computing Systems*. ACM, 1133–1138.
16. Michael Matscheko, Alois Ferscha, Andreas Riener, and Manuel Lehner. 2010. Tactor Placement in Wrist Worn Wearables. *Proceedings of the International Symposium on Wearable Computers - ISWC '10* (2010), 1–8. DOI: http://dx.doi.org/10.1109/ISWC.2010.5665867
17. Huimin Qian, Ravi Kuber, Andrew Sears, and Elizabeth Stanwyck. 2014. Determining the efficacy of multi-parameter tactons in the presence of real-world and simulated audio distractors. *Interacting with Computers* 26, 6 (2014), 572–594. DOI: http://dx.doi.org/10.1093/iwc/iwt054
18. S. Schaetzle, T. Hulin, C. Preusche, and G. Hirziner. 2006. Evaluation of Vibrotactile Feedback to the Human Arm. *EuroHaptics 2006* (2006), 557–560.
19. Simon Schätzle and Bernhard Weber. 2015. Towards Vibrotactile Direction and Distance Information for Virtual Reality and Workstations for Blind People. In *International Conference on Universal Access in Human-Computer Interaction*. Springer, 148–160.
20. Mayuree Srikulwong and Eamonn O'Neill. 2011. A comparative study of tactile representation techniques for landmarks on a wearable device. *Proceedings of the 2011 annual conference on Human factors in computing systems* (2011), 2029–2038. DOI: http://dx.doi.org/10.1145/1978942.1979236
21. Andrew A Stanley and Katherine J Kuchenbecker. 2012. Evaluation of tactile feedback methods for wrist rotation guidance. *Haptics, IEEE Transactions on* 5, 3 (2012), 240–251.
22. Ian R. Summers. 2000. Single Channel Information Transfer Through The Skin : Limitations and Possibilities. *Les Cahiers de l'Audition* 13, January (2000), 34–37.
23. K Tsukada and M Yasumura. 2004. ActiveBelt: Belt-Type Wearable Tactile Display for Directional Navigation. *Ubiquitous Computing* 3205 (2004), 384–399. DOI: http://dx.doi.org/10.1007/b99948

24. Å B Vallbo, Roland S Johansson, and others. 1984. Properties of cutaneous mechanoreceptors in the human hand related to touch sensation. *Human Neurobiology* 3, 1 (1984), 3–14.
25. Ramiro Velãzquez, Omar Bazán, and Marco Magaña. 2009. A shoe-integrated tactile display for directional navigation. In *Intelligent Robots and Systems, 2009. IROS 2009. IEEE/RSJ International Conference on*. IEEE, 1235–1240.
26. John S Zelek, Sam Bromley, Daniel Asmar, and David Thompson. 2003. A haptic glove as a tactile-vision sensory substitution for wayfinding. *Journal of Visual Impairment and Blindness* 97, 10 (2003), 621–632.

HCI, Solidarity Movements and the Solidarity Economy

Vasilis Vlachokyriakos[1], Clara Crivellaro[1], Pete Wright[1], Evika Karamagioli[6], Eleni-Revekka Staiou[6], Dimitris Gouscos[6], Rowan Thorpe[7], Antonio Krüger[2], Johannes Schöning[3], Matt Jones[4], Shaun Lawson[5], Patrick Olivier[1]

[1]Open Lab Newcastle University UK first.last1@ncl.ac.uk

[2]Saarland University Saarbrücken Germany last@dfki.de

[3]Uni. of Bremen Bremen, Germany last@uni-bremen.de

[4]Swansea University UK always@acm.org

[5]Northumbria University Newcastle, UK first.last@northumbria.ac.uk

[6]Univ. of Athens, Greece last@media.uoa.gr

[7]Open Lab: Athens Greece rowan@olathens.com

ABSTRACT

The financial crisis and austerity politics in Europe has had a devastating impact on public services, social security and vulnerable populations. Greek civil society responded quickly by establishing solidarity structures aimed at helping vulnerable citizens to meet their basic needs and empower them to co-create an anti-austerity movement. While digital technology and social media played an important role in the initiation of the movement, it has a negligible role in the movement's on-going practices. Through embedded work with several solidarity structures in Greece, we have begun to understand the 'solidarity economy' (SE) as an experiment in direct democracy and self-organization. Working with a range of solidarity structures we are developing a vision for a 'Solidarity HCI' committed to designing to support personal, social and institutional transformation through processes of agonistic pluralism and contestation, where the aims and objectives of the SE are continuously re-formulated and put into practice.

Author Keywords

Solidarity economy; social movements; digital civics;

ACM Classification Keywords

H.5.m. Information interfaces and presentation (e.g., HCI): Miscellaneous;

INTRODUCTION

The financial crisis that has unfolded in Europe since 2008 has had a profound impact on national economies and local communities alike. This impact has been especially pronounced in states of Southern Europe, which have proved to be acutely vulnerable to global financial fluctuations. The resultant austerity imposed in the majority of EU member states has in turn transformed a financial crisis into a cultural and socio-political one. Moreover, this transformation has had the most severe impact on vulnerable communities and populations. The subsequent deterioration of living conditions and deep distrust of political institutions has meant that citizens have taken *"the matter in their hands"* [10] and formed new social and solidarity movements (SMs). These movements, while struggling to mitigate the effects of austerity, have begun addressing everyday basic needs for food, clothing, education and health services by building voluntary-based solidarity structures. In doing so, these groups have developed and implemented innovative forms of "doing" social and solidarity economies based on social participation and self-organization and thus exemplifying an alternative to austerity [42].

In this paper we report on findings from nine months of engagements with the Solidarity Economy (SE) in Greece. With the establishment of a local lab in Athens, we sought to gain a deep understanding of Athens-based solidarity movements and develop a collaborative relationship with the intention of assisting the development of technologies that would support them in their day-to-day activities. Drawing on our participation in events and popular assemblies, interviews and informal discussions with key people in the sector, and field diaries we contribute to HCI concerned with the role of technology and digital tools in supporting progressive forms of social activism. We do this by providing insights that capture SMs' sociopolitical innovation through building an alternative economy based on solidarity; and by reporting the complexities at play in these groups' internal self-organization processes, as well as external collaborations with other movements and institutions. Our design implications provide a roadmap to embed values of solidarity, democratic participation and citizen empowerment in the systems that we design and build.

HCI, COMMUNITY ACTIVISM AND SOCIAL MOVEMENTS

The HCI research community has increasingly shown interest in exploring and understanding the role of communication technologies in both social movements [17,29,59,60] and community action [2,12,35,40,57]. Studies have focused on the way digital technologies have supported social movements' mobilization [11,59],

Permission to make digital or hard copies of part or all of this work for personal or classroom use is granted without fee provided that copies are not made or distributed for profit or commercial advantage and that copies bear this notice and the full citation on the first page. Copyrights for third-party components of this work must be honored. For all other uses, contact the Owner/Author.
Copyright is held by the owner/author(s).
CHI 2017, May 06-11, 2017, Denver, CO, USA
ACM 978-1-4503-4655-9/17/05.
http://dx.doi.org/10.1145/3025453.3025490

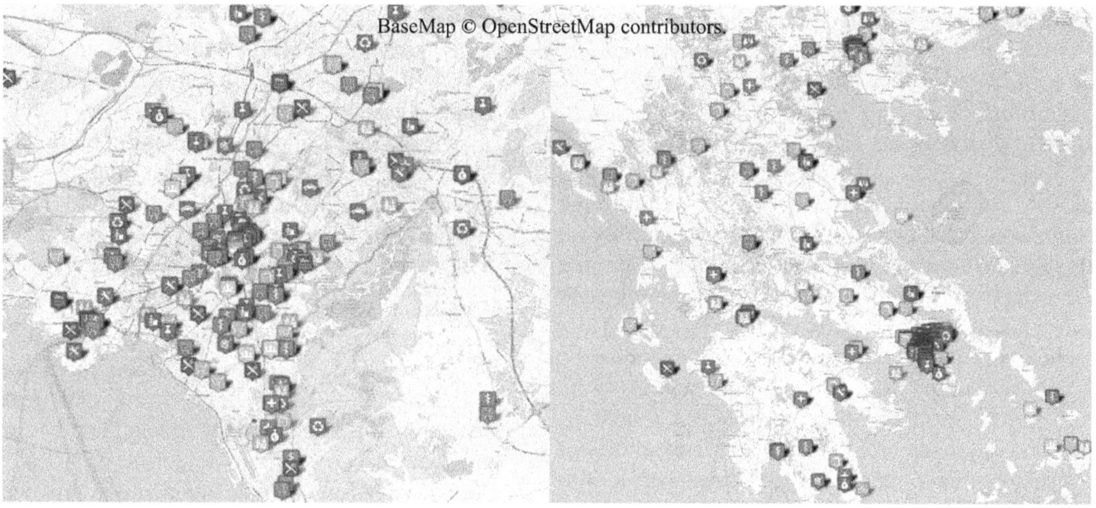

Figure 1: Indicative maps of SMs in Greece (right) and in Attica, Athens (left). Pins represent various types of SMs: social clinics, pharmacies, schools, time banks, no-middlemen goods distribution networks, soup kitchens, work cooperatives, alternative currencies etc. For an interactive version of the map see [52].

community organization [13,57] and crowdfunding [16]. Research has also explored the role of multimodal discursive spaces and political processes that underpin social movement formation, their values and activities in small [12] and large scale political action [17,26].

Studies have also examined the particular role of social media in large scale social movements, the Egyptian and Tunisian revolution [10,59,60], the EU social forum [46], the Occupy movement [11] and the Umbrella Movement in China [29]. Authors here have argued for examining and paying more attention to the often 'invisible' micro-dynamics, divergences, practices, tasks and actions, which underpin movements' activities and that are often omitted from the literature [29]. In this respect, authors have argued for the necessity of doing "on the ground studies" in order to gain a thorough understanding of the practices and the potential role of ICT in these political processes [29,59].

Other authors have poured considerable efforts into the way interaction design and HCI might support community action in everyday life [13,28,38,49,54], as well as in environmental [2] and health activism [40]. Like social movement studies, this work also requires a very thorough understanding of the context in order to develop systems that can support meaningful community practices and action [40]. In this regard, Aoki et al. have explored the role of ICT in respect to the decision making processes and strategy alignments across activists' groups concerned with environmental issues [2]. Yet, other authors have advocated for an agonistic approach when designing for everyday social movements and community action—suggesting that fostering spaces of conflicting multi-vocal collectives have significant potential to engender alternative forms of social innovation [7,38].

With this paper, we build on and extend this work by providing an in-depth analysis on the work and processes of SMs' self-organizing practices and the impact of their work in everyday life within a SE. From our insights, we provide guidelines for the design of systems for the solidarity economy, while also drawing deeper implications for HCI concerned with its role in social movements and more broadly in forms of community activism and social innovation.

CONTEXT

The economic crisis precipitated a drastic change in the stratification of Greek society, intensifying social inequality, exacerbating the threat of poverty and creating a new underclass of outcasts in large urban centers. The cumulative shrinkage of GDP by 25% from 2008 to the end of 2013 led to a dramatic spike in unemployment [51], which resulted in national demonstrations. The protests of 2008 in response to the imminent global financial crisis and to the privatisation of public spaces in Greece, were one of the first events that gave rise to the Greek solidarity movement in its current form. Indeed, it was around that period that a civic drive towards self-organisation, self-management and self-empowerment began to emerge with the (informal) establishment of several self-managed spaces, social centres and local citizen initiatives [31]. These events also formed the ground for what became the occupation of the Syntagma square in the summer of 2011 and the initiation of grassroots collectives whose goal was to address basic needs while raising issues of democracy and social justice [31,43]. Syntagma square events, aligned with the Spanish 'indignados' and as well as a host of other 'occupy' movements around the globe, were an experiment of horizontal democracy and empowerment through participation and self-organisation [31].

Following the summer of 2011, these practices, self-managed spaces and self-organising collectives—what we refer to as *solidarity movements (SMs)*—began to spread across Athens as a broad spectrum of state and non-state actors mobilized to provide social support to those most affected by the economic crisis. Thus, "*the movement spread out into the social fabric, with neighborhood assemblies [...] spreading alternative economic practices such as consumer co-operatives, ethical banking, exchange networks and many other such forms of living differently*" [9]. The role and position of SMs in society is twofold [3,42]: firstly, through collective organization, they cover every day basic needs for food, clothing, education and health services, thus operating as a buffer mechanism in the face of a collapsing welfare and public service; and secondly, they exemplify physical spaces where practical alternatives to austerity can emerge, be contested and re-worked through experimentations with alternative forms of economy through solidarity, participation and organization [3,5]. Indicative examples of solidarity structures in Greece include: time banks, no-middlemen goods distribution networks, soup kitchens, work cooperatives, social clinics and pharmacies, solidarity schools, alternative currencies, self-managed factories and artist collectives. At this time, various sources suggest the existence of around 400 SMs (see Figure 1). To give an indication of the scale of these movements and their operations, according to [1], in Attica there are: 40 solidarity clinics in Greece, with an average of 46 volunteers per clinic, and receiving regularly around 2000 visits per clinic per month; 47 food solidarity structures and 21 solidarity kitchens with around 56 volunteers per group, which for example, in 2014 distributed 4318 parcels of food fortnightly; 45 without middlemen goods distribution groups with more than 5000 tons of distributed products for the years 2012-2014.

METHODOLOGY

Already familiar with the sociopolitical context in Greece, we have been engaging with solidarity movements since November 2015. Adopting an Action Research approach [25], the first author (a Greek national) moved back to Greece and established a local digital civics lab (Open Lab: Athens) in order to engage and develop long-term partnerships with SMs, towards the co-creation of processes, novel technologies and tools that might benefit their day-to-day activities.

Over the course of the last nine months, the first author engaged with over 13 solidarity structures, including: three solidarity clinics and pharmacies; one soup kitchen network; two 'without middlemen' grocery cooperatives; two self-managed factories; two self-organised refugee camps; one time-bank network; one solidarity school; and one collective—Solidarity for All—serving as a communication hub for the SE. Engagements with each of the movements typically entailed: initial meetings; targeted follow-up discussions; participation in assemblies; IT support meetings; and participating in the groups' events. In this paper, we report on and draw from data gathered across all of these engagements including over 500 minutes of recorded meetings and semi-structured interviews, our experiences participating in SM assemblies, events and volunteering sessions, notes from participatory observations, semi-structured interviews and informal discussions. In the next section, by following a thematic analysis approach [8] on this dataset, we report insights where we consider how the SE is practiced as a form of human economy, its internal self-organising mechanisms through popular assemblies and coordination committees and its relation with other economic actors such as the public and third sectors. Names of structures and people have been anonymised.

MAKING THE 'SOLIDARITY ECONOMY'

Solidarity as a counter-austerity practice strives to empower the disempowered through the forging of new social relations and bonds between people within and across solidarity structures. It is about understanding the other in order to give and receive support, and to form reciprocal relations and alternative horizontal self-organization practices. According to Jean-Louis Laville, solidarity when seen as an alternative economy can be defined as having two dimensions: the socio-political and the socioeconomic [23:225–235]. The socio-political dimension is an alternative form of participatory democracy while the socioeconomic—a hybrid between non-monetary and no middlemen economies—operates between reciprocity, redistribution and the market [23,27:25–41]. Below, we report our experiences on how these two dimensions are enacted in solidarity practice in Greece. The names of SM members have been anonymised.

Solidarity economy as a 'human economy'

The solidarity economy is understood in a number of ways by the extremely diverse actors in this sector. They operate as informal social networks and self-help groups, which have neither a formal organisational structure nor are registered with any official authority. Due to the multiple and diverse political orientations and actual practices of these schemes, no definitive classification can be created. Nonetheless, SMs share a set of values that distinguish them from the practices of the dominant economy: they build communities based on cooperation and collaboration rather than competition; they are based on mutuality and reciprocity in bold contrast with isolation and atomization; they exemplify an alternative model of self-organization based on direct democracy and horizontal participation rather than centralised control; and they encourage pluralism and diversity as opposed to imposing a global monoculture. SMs do not reject the state and the markets; they do not try to break away from capitalism; rather, they disagree with its current configuration [44]. Attempts to form a SE are attempts to shed light upon "this blind spot in order to look for new frontiers between the economy and politics" [23].

Ultimately, SE attempts to reconfigure relations, both material and social [4]. This is reflected for example through the attempt of many goods distribution networks and no-middlemen cooperatives to change the relations between production and consumption [42]. Example actions include the assessment of farmers' practices against SMs' standards and values (e.g. fair trade practices, labour rights etc.) and the circumvention of intermediaries and the establishment of personal relations between producers to consumers. As a member of a time bank network tells us, the SE aspire: *"an economy of needs not markets, to better social relations, towards an everyday struggle, with our own conditions"* [member of time bank network].

Most groups try to cover their needs through mainly non-monetary donations (e.g. equipment and tools) and skill sharing practices. Deprivation of financial, political and human resources undermines efforts by these structures to scale up their activities. However, close co-operation among solidarity networks and collectives facilitates resourcing their activities. For instance, in some cases local solidarity networks engage in economic transactions acting in co-operation with non-profit organizations; in the social clinics sector, doctors prescribe medication for uninsured individuals by adding it to medication prescribed for insured individuals; municipal authorities tolerate occupations of public buildings and the creation of new autonomous political/economic spaces; and others. The exchange of resources and know-how between groups contributes to the formation and reproduction of the SE.

A fundamental part of SE is its pedagogic and political awakening (i.e. raising political awareness) character. For example, being part of a time bank network that allows skill sharing between members provides a practical experience of an alternative organisational practice and economic relation: *"When you give things to apolitical people they see it with scepticism […] you need to change this mentality of equivalency* [between market economy and SE] *so that we will equate your work with someone else's* […] *and stop people from thinking 'how much would what I do cost outside* [i.e. when done professionally in the market economy]*"* [member of solidarity school]. So being part of such a network enables members to reflect on a different economic relation in society, one that puts solidarity and collective well-being first. Key to this pedagogy of participation in the SE is enabling people through awaking political consciousness. A key member of a soup kitchen network explains: *"it is not just a matter of feeding people; we are cooking with people, we cook, we live and we eat together; it's a lunch with our fellowman on the street.* […] *This is about awaking consciousness. The giving is more important than the taking"* [member of soup kitchen network]. Here an iconic figure, a key person within one of the biggest food distribution networks in Greece, explains how enabling someone to give to a fellow man is more important than someone receiving help, as it puts the SE in practice by awaking political consciousness for the effects of austerity politics and neoliberal economics and as a result has a proliferative effect.

SE is continuously under reconfiguration through these movements' internal self-reflection processes and creative tensions. This involves the pursuit and formulation of the movement's identity, moulded by internal decision-making processes, political beliefs and party affiliations, and partnership with organisations from various sectors that define the scale of collaborations. In this regard, every 'transaction' that takes place in the SE (e.g. a collaboration with a research lab or accepting resources from a foundation) supports, extends but also reshapes and reinvents the SE. Such transactions aim at satisfying temporal human needs. For example, the current manifestation of a solidarity movement as a school, clinic, time bank etc. is only a solidarity movement's temporary response to the current needs of the people and local community. As human needs change, these movements adjust their practices and reassess the ways with which they address everyday problems: "[…] *we didn't get together to create a voluntary school; the school was the outcome of an alternative political action and this movement might create something different in the future and that's how a solidarity group should work"* [member of solidarity school]. Here a member of a solidarity school explains how the volunteer-run school is not a means to an end but it's a manifestation of a political action that might change form based on the human and societal needs that will have to be addressed.

Time bank networks are good examples of how the SE attempts to reconfigure social and material relations. New members of a time bank register by completing a skills form. This allows them to help according to their capacity to do so. When a 'service' is being fulfilled, for example a teacher delivering a class, or a lawyer helping with bookkeeping, these services are being written down, which allows the group to see how active each sector is and try to balance services among people. This has to be done carefully in order to avoid transferring 'market logic' to solidarity spaces while giving stimuli for people to participate:

"An impersonal time bank for me is the worse. Its transferring the market logic to non-monetary economy. If we build our non-monetary interactions with market references and rules, it's like we burn an opportunity" [member of time bank network].

This response was triggered by a discussion about an '*unsuccessful*' centralised time bank for all municipalities in Athens. This time bank was based on an online platform that didn't require solidarity structures to be formed in physical spaces, and as a result making the exchange of services impersonal while creating a more 'formal' environment which strictly equated how much someone gives to how much someone takes. This 'transferred market logic to non-monetary interactions' which fails to advance the SE as an alternative to market economy. As a member of a time bank network explains, the imbalances between the give-and-take in this local time bank (for instance a teacher volunteering more hours than a lawyer) are being at least partially liaised through the members' participation in popular assemblies and the governance of the collective:

"So in order to balance these things, how much someone gets with how much someone gives, we decided to have

assembly meetings when they can decide reciprocal actions of socio-political nature, not for us but for people outside. This adds another motivation of reciprocity" [member of time bank network].

Assemblies and Self-organization

A fundamental part of the SE is self-organisation through horizontal participation. For most movements self-organisation is achieved through regular thematic or general popular assemblies which take place in a group's 'house'—a physical space where these groups meet regularly and operate, which can be a public space leased free by the local council, squats and abandoned buildings, or private spaces rented through a group's solidarity fund. Some solidarity structures arrange various subgroups that meet in separate assemblies and others have one tactical general assembly per week. Example subgroups include groups specializing in: communication, logistics, volunteer coordination and others depending on the SM (e.g. a clinic may have a doctors' and a pharmacists' assembly). The choice of approach primarily depends on the number of people involved in them or political, cultural and ideological justifications for such configurations. For example, popular assemblies for a solidarity school include meetings about the schedule for the next few months, discussions about meeting the needs of the schools (e.g. whiteboards), discussions about actions to support the local community (e.g. running festivals, organizing seminars), self-reflections of how the structure operates and the level of satisfaction of the students and parents etc.

These assemblies are in general open to the public, except for the ones that have a good reason to be closed – for example the meeting of doctors of a clinic to discuss a particular case (even though there are groups that are very introvert and as a result not as open to the public). In the majority of the schemes, recipients of social support participate in the popular assemblies and take an active part in their running. Indeed, this is a key characteristic of the SE in Greece: people might start movements for self-help purposes (e.g. unemployment) and members that receive support (e.g. visitors of social clinics) become more and more involved in their running by participating in assemblies, cultural events, etc. In addition to helping vulnerable populations, this contributes to the spreading of SE values and practices.

Decision-making in these meetings is achieved through horizontal participation, either through voting or unanimously, depending on the values of the group (e.g. ideological and cultural trajectories) but also depending on practical limitations such as the size of the assemblies. Key members of each group that had a central role in initiating a structure, typically play the role of coordinators in order to facilitate discussions. Other mundane jobs include creating preliminary agendas and taking minutes, which are typically done by people who have the will and skills to do them. Some of these groups operate by using a system of rotating roles in which training and skill sharing is pivotal.

Even though the impact of these groups' activities on society and on vulnerable populations (e.g. 2000 people visiting social clinics per month) prove their success, this experiment in self-organisation, fueled by the idiosyncrasies of the financial and sociopolitical crisis in Greece, is not easy to realize. For example, one of the coordinators of a solidarity school describes us the internal conflicts of such structures: *"It's a struggle of internal associations, it's a power struggle, there is a space being claimed here"* [coordinator of solidarity school]. Considering that some of these SMs have operated for the last 5-10 years without fixed hierarchies, these difficulties act as barriers for the further reproduction of solidarity in other physical spaces or for their long-term sustainability.

Many of the people that we engaged with cited the lack of more complex processes for facilitating horizontal participation in popular assemblies as wearying the movement. For example, in a discussion about the processes that are followed in popular assemblies, a key member of the solidarity school talks about these difficulties: *"Direct democracy and horizontal participation is not an easy task, and also it is not something that we have to "sanctify"* [...]. *You appreciate the role of an institution* [referring to a more structured organisation] *when you find yourself in these situations and you* need *to make decisions through these meetings* [i.e. popular assemblies]*"*. Here a member of the time bank network refers to the lack of regulations for various roles and the lack of more explicit methods to allow decision-making to be achieved. This lack of regulations or of a 'statute' for the group allows the formation of obscure hierarchies: "*when you are in an association, a partnership, a political party, a construct that has members, you operate with what the statutes provide you with as a member. Which you can cite, it is a tool, it is in some cases a mandate of justice. A more libertarian group like ours is more susceptible to manipulation* [...]*"* [member of time bank network]. 'Manipulation' here refers to the possibility of someone to guide the group towards specific decisions due to the absence of a statute for members' participation.

However, the dynamic and fluid character of self-organisation that results in the creation of temporary and obscured hierarchies is also a driver for members' engagement, as members constantly reassess their roles while reconfiguring the movement itself. As a result, participation in a popular assembly is understood and experienced as "*taking something back*" or as a more complex reciprocal give-and-take relation. In a conversation about this complex reciprocal relation, one member of a solidarity school explains how these assemblies should also allow the further refinement of the decided actions outside of these meetings as "*not to exhaust the assembly*". For example, the details of events such as festivals, or the availabilities of people for scheduled activities.

A key process in the organisation of popular assemblies, and one that also signifies the group's internal power structure, is the setting of the assembly's agenda. The agenda determines the issues to be contested at these meetings, but also the ideological, political and societal framework in which these issues are to be discussed. For example, as a key figure in a social clinic explained: *"The public assembly takes all the decisions, you won't tell a doctor how to do their job but you will tell them who to accept, so the assembly decided that we welcome uninsured, impoverished, and unemployed; this was later changed to add the low-paid pensioners with specific characteristics"*. Here, a member of a social clinic, describes how the values of the solidarity clinic define a framework within which the clinic operates and all subsequent decisions are being made. Similarly, a key member of a solidarity school describes how assembly attendees are given *"a well specified frame in which we can decide, through the documents we give them, which coordinates the meetings towards specific actions"*. Here '*the well specified frame*' refers to the preparation that a core group of people must do in order to prioritise the needs of the group. By doing so, as in the clinic above, they make sure that the core values of the group are reflected in the operations that they prioritise and put for discussion (e.g. how the scarce funding should be spent, proposing reciprocal actions for the local community etc.). Nonetheless, through participating in many of these assemblies, we observed how the agenda is created dynamically by participants during these assemblies.

Finally, as key tool of the SE, popular assemblies are considered an important vehicle for the members' political education (as also discussed in [43]). Political education through engagement, both within and outside the assembly was a recurrent theme in discussions. For example, here a member of a time bank explains how through popular assemblies, "*you upgrade the political role of citizens with everyday references. You try to get people to understand that the assembly is a tool, not a political theory.*" [member of time bank]. In contrast to political theories and far-reaching ideological discussions, an assembly is a practical manifestation of a citizen's role in the SE.

All in all, the common space in which these meetings are held and its configuration; the mutuality and reciprocity between the members of the group; the lack of explicit hierarchies which allows for a continuous reconfiguration of power relations; the uncertainty of the size of the assemblies and the people that join them; and the dynamic alteration of the agenda during the meetings; create an 'arena' which, even though disagreements are manifest, allow for the productive confrontation between divergent viewpoints.

Coordination and Synergies

Solidarity structures were initiated after the occupation of the Syntagma square the summer of 2011, and as a result they were the products of a social mobilization. As such, the facilitation of synergies between solidarity structures is fundamental for the perpetuation of its social movement character and for the spreading of the SE values in society. These synergies are being mainly achieved through: social networks, with geographically neighboring structures collaborating for covering their needs and exchanging know-how and resources; coordination committees, which are meetings organized between various solidarity structures of the same sector (e.g. all the social clinics meeting once per month to discuss the sharing of medicine etc.); and through the 'Solidarity for all' network, a communication node among solidarity structures for the sharing of expertise and resources.

The 'Solidarity for all' (S4A) network plays a key role in facilitating this communication between structures of the SE. S4A was initiated in 2012 (funded by Syriza political party, currently in government) as a communication node among solidarity structures for the sharing of practical expertise and resources. As one member of S4A describes the network's goal as "*to create a node of communication of all these collectives without us being 'the networking' because we were created later than these collectives* [...]. *We were trying to make spaces, we don't have a coordination role, we couldn't anyway our position is very sensitive, but we create spaces and meetings that the solidarity movements can come together and coordinate by themselves*" [member of S4A]. S4A's contribution to the SE is significant in creating the connections between solidarity structures that share the same values and practices.

For example, one of the people we met in the solidarity school describes how in trying to work together with another school: "[...] *communication is hard, they don't want to, because they want to keep their independent character, they want a political party/organisation with a solidary face. That's one example. There are other schools that are just a façade, so essentially they don't exist*" [member of solidarity school]. This diversity between the groups originates from diverse political cultures and social movements in Greece that are distinct from SMs (e.g. parliamentary left, anarchist movements, autonomous movements etc.). These differences in turn impact the ways in which solidarity structures interact with the state and other institutions (such as S4A), as well as the agencies from which they seek resources. As a result, in some cases solidarity-making becomes a site of internal contestation itself which creates impediments for synergies.

S4A is trying to facilitate communication while also maintaining the solidarity structure's independent and decentralised character. However, it faces difficulties that originate in tensions created when social movements interact with such state (or pseudo-state) institutions. One coordinator of a social clinic described this as *"an overgeneralisation of the possibilities of synergy and cooperation,* [...], *that if we work together we can move this thing forward. What I learned is that this is an oxymoron for the autonomy that we want to exist in these structures*" [social clinic coordinator]. Here our contact talks from experience about the difficulties of cooperating with significantly diverse groups within the SE, and how these synergies can in some cases come in direct contrast with the autonomy of these groups.

Digital technology is seen as a possible mediator. Indeed, one of S4A's first actions was to make an online platform that allows various groups to create their own pages and maintain an online blog, while also geographically mapping these structures. Even though this platform serves as a useful database for the solidarity sector in Greece, it is rarely used by solidarity groups themselves, which choose to maintain their own Facebook pages or WordPress sites. One of the members of a solidarity school talks about the role of technology for collaborations:

"What I am trying to explain is that it is not about making a big network or a big umbrella and it will just work, there are so many political issues and you don't know to whom to talk to, you move on with the ones that are willing to. It [technology] *is good for massive things to happen* [e.g. better coordination between the movements]. *For example, with the work that we do, coordinating the self-organised schools in Greece, we now understand which ones are solidarity schools (with a political thinking), who has an understanding of volunteering which is a bit, my hobby or something to talk about with my friends etc.* [...] *The technical part* [technology] *is necessary to get evolved, but it needs to evolve in parallel with the other. We need to advance our political communication the very basic communication; what we are, where are we aiming at, why, how do we want this to work; dynamically but also in a propellant way."* [member of solidarity school]

This member here talks in the context of creating such platforms to enable synergies between SMs, taking S4A's online geographical mapping of these groups (similar to the one in Figure 1) as an example. He describes how such systems are problematic as they don't dig deeper into the real issues that prevent various solidarity structures from collaborating, such as the diversity of values, internal decision-making practices and motivations. In the end, it is about identifying the groups that work for the spreading of the SE while finding ways to work together in a decentralised and independent character. This becomes particularly challenging as the identity of these structures and the understanding of the SE change dynamically.

Solidarity movement and institutions

The relation of solidarity structures with the state, the local councils and other third sector organizations depends on a structure's ideological and cultural trajectory and values. The groups and people that we engaged with were generally encouraging collaborations with local councils. In some cases, and when there is political will from both sides (solidarity structures and councils), the council supports these groups through allowing them to be based in public buildings, paying utility bills such as the electricity or internet, donating resources, raising visibility of these structures' work etc. In general, however, the relation between local institutions, the state and solidarity structures is very complex and it changes dynamically. For example, one of the solidarity schools is based in a low rise building that was given to the group to use by the local council after local citizens' struggles. Since then and after the elections, the local council has changed and its support is not as strong: *"Unfortunately for the local council they don't want to be linked with the group because they cannot understand this kind of social politics that is produced here and this cannot be produced by the council"* [member of solidarity school].

The relation with the state is complex because of these groups' reformist character: in addition to helping fellow people through various actions, they target the reform of local governance models and the public sector and this creates tensions: *Structures are reformist; they are not the tools of the revolution, not trade unions, not substitutes of the state, or of the lack of* [economic] *liquidity"*. A member of a solidarity school talks about the relation of the movement with the local councils: *"The coexistence of an institution, the council, with the people's assembly is necessary. That's why I believe that the local councils need to change how they work, it needs to be a mixture of the institutional with people's participation. The councils need to drive these movements but also allow a percentage to be decided by people's assemblies"* [member of solidarity school]. As a result, a solidarity structure's role in society is transformative rather than substitutive:

"The dynamic of a solidarity structure can be greatly multipliable. I mean, the reflection of the social ties and relations, not for profit, but for creating points of reference and a social transformation; not as a substitute [of the public sector]*"* [member of social clinic]. It is about covering the holes that the lack of public sector funding and austerity politics has created while transforming the public sector to match these structures values: *"These are systemic holes that we are engaged with, trying to re-signify things but really what we do is covering insufficiencies which, however, we want to cover them in all levels, political and ideological; this is what we want"* [member of solidarity school].

It is not only the transformative function of SMs, but also the tension between substitution and transformation of the public sector, that can be seen more clearly in the health sector. Social solidarity clinics and pharmacies accept patients with no insurance that can't get access to the National Health System (NHS) and as a result these structures can seem to be replacing the public sector. In this case, campaigning for access of everyone to the NHS and raising visibility about cases of patients excluded from the NHS becomes fundamental for such transformation to take place. For example, one of the people we met from one of the biggest social clinics in Greece explains how at least the rhetoric of the government about access for everyone to the NHS changed after the social clinics' activities:

"[...] *due to the political pressure that this and other social clinics put* [to the state] *from January 2014 onwards* [...] *also because we had a patient that died while we had already called the ministry of health* [...] *and from that point the government started to talk about access of everyone to the NHS* [...] *there is a huge underfunding of the NHS so whatever the legal framework there is a complete destruction of the NHS. These days even the insured ones cannot get their medicines, they go to the hospitals and they don't afford to give them their medicine, so the result is more or less the same* [...]*"* [member of social clinic]

Indeed, this dual character of the SM, as both a buffer for immediate needs and as a form of resistance to the imposed austerity politics, is one of its key characteristics: *"The work that we do here is dual, 50% is what you see here, the other 50% is about the struggle for the rights of our patients which is the only way that there can be an important change* [...] *the appropriate funding of the national health service, the employment of staff etc."* [member of social clinic]

Also interesting is the distinction of this 'fourth sector' of economy from what is typically understood as the third sector; a distinction that influences the extent of possible collaborations. Our experiences align with work such as Rakopoulos [44] and Arampatzi [3] which suggests that the third sector and the NGOs are seen by SMs as "welfare middlemen" [32] and as a result serving aggressive markets against the state. Without disregarding the critical work of the many organisations of the third sector in Greece, the third sector is regarded in these solidarity structures as "a benign form of capitalism" [44,45] that masks the politico-economic causes of the crisis and as a result pursues contradictory goals. However, in a number of cases solidarity groups become formal organisations (e.g. NGOs or cooperatives): *"Many solidarity groups do that* [establish NGOs] *in order to exist because unfortunately there is a huge legal gap in cases like ours, so you become something that you are not, take a form of something that doesn't represent what you do and what you believe in, we can't work here with a management board, with a president, it can't happen, it is against everything"* [member of time bank network]

DESIGNING FOR THE SOLIDARITY ECONOMY

The work of SMs exemplifies an alternative form of economy, an economy driven by human rather than market needs; an economy based on relations that recognize the interdependency of our lives, while transforming them to embody care and mutual respect rather than exploitation. In our findings, we show how this new way of thinking about and enacting social and material relations has implications for decision-making practices, coordination between different structures operating in the SE and in collaboration with formal public and third sector institutions.

Below we discuss how HCI is positioned in such complex, lively and diverse hubs of social innovation. We discuss how we might support solidarity economies through designing for transformation; how HCI design and technology might accommodate and harness the productive, dynamic and conflictual dimensions of movements' self-organization practices; and more broadly, we ask what a Solidarity HCI might look like.

Designing for transformation

At the center of SE is the belief that people are capable of developing their own solutions to economic problems through the collective production and distribution of resources and services. Fundamental to this is the collective debating and (re)envisioning of how this production and distribution should be actualized. In this sense, SE is not a "blue-print" for how an alternative economy should operate, but "a collective process of imagination and creation that continually seeks connections and possibilities while holding on to its transformative commitment" [27:28].

Our research has highlighted the transformative nature of SMs through: the cultivation of political awareness and political education through participation; the transformation of economic relations to prioritise solidarity and collective well-being; and the transformation of the public and third sector institutions to reflect SE values. For us, SE practices for us point to greater questions for Digital Civics and HCI researchers concerned with how to effectively support and sustain social movements [17] and community action [20,39,50,58]; questions around whether and how should HCI be supporting the sustainability of existing SEs and their spreading in other contexts; and questions on whether technology can play a role in facilitating public institutions to scaffold and sustain SMs' formation.

Previous work has shown the lack of institutional and social infrastructures to support activist groups advocating and organizing for change [12,41,53]. At the same time, social media technologies (e.g. Facebook) provide some organizational spaces for these groups to discuss and organize for action [12,29,46], even if this is limited to information dissemination and forum-like discussion pages. Beyond this however, digital technology has not yet responded to the challenges of dealing with the complexity of the transformational character of SE.

Yet research in HCI and elsewhere has begun to explore the potential for digital platforms to be transformed into a fully cooperative relational model [48]. In addition, HCI researchers are developing digital commissioning platforms that aim to re-configure relations between citizens and institutions by providing ways in which citizens can self-organize to identify their community needs and eventually co-design services to meet them (e.g. [6,22]). While these are noteworthy projects that begin to tackle ways in which HCI can play a role in scaffolding the formation of citizen movements, they arguably still operate on assumptions that do not fully contribute to the co-creation of human economies. Indeed, as we have seen in the example of the time-bank system, the transfer of a market logic into non-monetary interactions retains market rules that misconstrue the values of the SE aiming instead at developing radical alternatives to neoliberal economies. Beyond platform cooperativism, designing for SE processes requires HCI to begin envisioning, debating and actually contributing to the building of alternative economies through the systems and tools that we create. Such systems should support cooperation and reciprocity of various actors while allowing the constant co-creation of collective identities through direct democracy and horizontal participation. We call on HCI to move away from a market logic to a logic of *human relations and ongoing transformation.*

The fundamental goal of SE is the transformation, rather than elimination, of the public sector. In Greece, this is achieved through creating a 'point of reference' through SMs' everyday practices and ongoing struggle. This has implications for the design of systems that enable relational models of service provision [22,39,47], as even though existing models enable the creation and delivery of services, they might also run against SE values by replacing rather than reforming the public sector. For example, technology to support social clinics should, in addition to facilitating mundane operations, also raise political awareness and advocate through visibility and transparency about the consequences of the lack of open access to the NHS and struggle to reform it. As a result, any form of technology for relational infrastructures if it is to serve the SE must take into account the SE's transformative goals.

Designing for contestation

Our experiences of SMs' internal processes of self-organisation (i.e. popular assemblies) point to the lively and productive dimension of contestations where collectives with divergent ideologies, visions and cultures, united by common values, continuously (re)formulate their collective identity. This however, does not come without disagreements. Dissensus is prevalent, especially when divergent (micro)political projects come into play. From our participation in these spaces, we contend that it is how these disagreements are contested that exemplifies an alternative model of democracy and self-organization. At its core, it is a model of 'radical democracy' [30] which allows movements to enact solidarity while also dynamically reformulating the groups collective identities. Drawing from Chantel Mouffe [36,37], these assemblies can be understood as spaces of *agonistic pluralism* in which different political projects can be contested, discarded or formed; spaces where 'radical democracy' is being experimented with. Consensus is of course fundamental for the enactment of solidarity practices; nevertheless, it takes the form of a 'conflictual consensus'—a consensus based on the temporal and dynamic power relations within groups, through shared core values.

In line with previous work [7,19], we also highlight the necessity of designing for agonistic spaces, while also pointing to the challenges involved in the context of SMs in Greece. Our insights show how the lack of explicit hierarchies, a 'statute of participation' and the constant reconfiguration of roles and agendas present significant challenges for developing design processes and systems that can accommodate and sustain such horizontal practices. We might imagine not only ways in which technologies make visible the pluralism of perspectives and practices [7,14,38], but also to document them in ways that can be utilised dynamically across times and assemblies. Also, we might come up with online or situated systems that favour temporariness, informality and fluidity as opposed to permanence. Yet whatever technology and intervention we might design, we must also be mindful and resist attempts to normalise and regulate activities and relations in the SE.

Even though collaboration across solidarity groups is fundamental for sustaining and reproducing the SE, coordination across groups has been so far challenging. Despite S4A's attempt to enable synergies, tensions emerge from the desire of the groups to both be part of a bigger collective movement and to maintain autonomy. In some cases, these divergent and dynamic political identities, all struggling to formulate a collective identity for the SE lead to the creation of potentially 'antagonistic relations' [37]. Any technology to support such synergies should acknowledge the possibility of antagonisms to emerge[1] and facilitate the creation of spaces in which such antagonisms can be transformed to agonistic ones based on the common values of the SE. Technology was positioned critically by participants, not only as failing to accommodate the variety of identities of solidarity groups and their decentralised nature, but also as failing to foster opportunities for proactive and dynamic relations across different groups.

Previous research suggested an approach to social networking sites as technologies of affiliation, alignment, and identification [20], and how mapping tools could support different advocacy groups connecting to one another through their values and political actions [2]. What our experiences and insights show though, is that even if groups might be affiliated through the same values and political actions, SMs have significantly different identities, which are always in the process of becoming. Systems (like the S4A website) can be seen as technology that tends to "brand" or in some way "fix" an identity *for* groups, thereby negating the always becoming nature of SM identities. More broadly, what emerged from our insights is that designing for contestation and agonism necessitates the recognition of SMs' identity formation as an ongoing endeavor constantly shaped in dynamic terms. Technologies and systems should thus support and sustain the SMs' micro and macro dynamics within and between SMs and between movements and other institutions.

Solidarity HCI

SMs' commitment, passion and drive in their endeavour of re-distributing the "seeds of solidarity" through action (e.g.

[1] Also discussed in [15] as counter-publics digital democracy

"doing" solidarity in practice) show the extent to which social movements can be bearers of values of communal living and goals around which institutional values can be transformed [10]. Our experience of working with SMs—beyond our concern for how technology might support their actions—also led us to reflect more broadly on what a Solidarity HCI might look like. That is, how HCI practice might embed the values of SE in systems that it develops.

Authors have developed ways for thinking and talking about the politics embedded in any systems' design [18,20,33] and begun to search for ways in which to examine the unintentional consequences of our work. Feenberg [21] talked of the need to look beyond technologies' intended primary functionality—technology also entails secondary effects, which are not necessarily designed for. Yet, these secondary effects are actually how technologies have their greatest impacts [21,56]. Arguably, many HCI systems promote and sustain a logic that is adverse to principles of solidarity—fostering individualism, the simplification of human relations [55] and a market logic with significant negative effects on social welfare and justice [48].

Authors engaged in HCI work and elsewhere strongly advocate for intervening in the injustices and economic exploitation effected by neo-liberal technologies [24,34,48]. We argue that this should be HCI's first step towards adopting SE's ethos in design and towards the search for radically different directions, not just metaphors, for the research and for the technologies we build. Here, we hope HCI researchers can be inspired as much as we are by the work of solidarity movements. We invite HCI researchers and institutions to begin to imagine what would it mean to embed the logic and values of solidarity both socially and economically in the systems we build. We ask, what would HCI design and technology build to "spread the seeds of solidarity" as both primary and secondary effects.

Besides such critical questions around the values embedded in the systems that HCI builds—we also need to reflect on our role as researchers, and the methods, timescales and processes we employ when working with social movements and communities of action. Here, HCI researchers have begun to critically reflect on what it means to work in socio-political and economic contexts [17,29,59]. Kow et al. have pointed to the dangers inherent in working with social movements and Dimond et al. have described the emotional and political commitment that working in such contexts demands [17], and yet other researchers have depicted the hardship experienced in working in context with high level risks [59].

Researchers in these contexts who, like us have taken an action-oriented approach towards the co-creation of knowledge and technological responses to needs, have reflected on the way collaborating with social movements requires them to take a "political stance and become aligned with those who we are conducting research with" [17]. It is undeniable that through our intellectual, practical, and emotional investment in working with solidarity structures and with the establishment of our presence in Greece, we sought to begin exploring one way in which we can commit to working with movements beyond the limited timescales of conventional projects. Our approach however, should not be considered as a panacea for any context of civic significance, but on the contrary, a call for an increased awareness of the political and economic power relations of the contexts that we engage in. We invite HCI researchers working in these contexts to begin to engage in deeper reflections on what it may mean to work in this way, in order to begin envisioning, debating and actually building alternative sustainable economies for an HCI committed to solidarity as a way of life.

CONCLUSION

In this paper, we have presented insights from our ongoing on-the-ground engagements with SMs in Greece. We have provided an in-depth examination of their sociopolitical practices as well as how alternative socioeconomic models are shaped in practice. Based on our insights, we have contributed guidelines for the design of systems that support SMs' practices and reflect their values. Such systems should mirror and accommodate the movements' commitment to personal, social and institutional transformation, as well as spaces of agonistic pluralism, where aims and objectives for the solidarity economy are continuously re-formulated and put in practice.

Finally, we highlighted the significant potential for HCI to meaningfully engage with these spaces of social innovation and design technologies that support civic action effectively and responsibly. That is, how HCI practice and HCI researchers might be bearers of values of solidarity and radical democratic participation through the systems that we conceive and build.

ACKNOWLEDGEMENTS

This research was funded by the EPSRC Digital Economy Research Center (EP/M023001/1), and would not be possible without the contribution of various actors of the Solidarity Economy in Greece. Special thanks must go to the Citizen Movement of Moschato (Mesopotamia), to the Metropolitan Community Clinic at Helliniko and The Other Human. The Volkswagen foundation has also contributed in making this research paper open access.

REFERENCES

1. Solidarity for All. 2014. *Building hope against fear and devastation*. Retrieved from https://goo.gl/Vd68uT
2. Paul M Aoki, R J Honicky, Alan Mainwaring, et al. 2009. A Vehicle for Research: Using Street Sweepers to Explore the Landscape of Environmental Community Action. *ACM Transactions on Computer-Human Interaction*: 10. http://doi.org/10.1145/1518701.1518762
3. Athina Arampatzi. 2014. Resisting austerity: the spatial politics of solidarity and struggle in Athens, Greece.

4. Athina Arampatzi. 2016. The spatiality of counter-austerity politics in Athens, Greece: Emergent "urban solidarity spaces." *Urban Studies*: 4209801662931l.
5. Athina Arampatzi and Walter J. Nicholls. 2012. The urban roots of anti-neoliberal social movements: The case of Athens, Greece. *Environment and Planning A* 44, 11: 2591–2610. http://doi.org/10.1068/a44416
6. Madeline Balaam, Rob Comber, Ed Jenkins, Selina Sutton, and Andrew Garbett. 2015. FeedFinder: A location-mapping mobile application for breastfeeding women. In *Proceedings of the 33rd Annual ACM Conference on Human Factors in Computing Systems*, 1709–1718.
7. Erling Björgvinsson, Pelle Ehn, and Per-Anders Hillgren. 2012. Agonistic participatory design: working with marginalised social movements. *CoDesign* 8, 2–3: 127–144.
8. Virginia Braun and Victoria Clarke. 2006. Using thematic analysis in psychology. *Qualitative Research in Psychology* 3, 2: 77–101. http://doi.org/10.1191/1478088706qp063oa
9. Manuel Castells. 2012. Where are the "indignados" going? *La Vanguardia*. Retrieved September 21, 2016 from https://goo.gl/7wL06M
10. Manuel Castells. 2015. *Networks of outrage and hope: Social movements in the Internet age*. John Wiley & Sons.
11. Sasha Costanza-Chock. 2012. Mic check! Media cultures and the Occupy movement. *Social movement studies* 11, 3–4: 375–385.
12. Clara Crivellaro, Rob Comber, John Bowers, Peter C Wright, and Patrick Olivier. 2014. A pool of dreams: facebook, politics and the emergence of a social movement. In *Proceedings of the SIGCHI Conference on Human Factors in Computing Systems*, 3573–3582.
13. Clara Crivellaro, Rob Comber, Martyn Dade-Robertson, Simon Bowen, Peter Wright, and Patrick Olivier. 2015. Contesting the City: Enacting the Political Through Digitally Supported Urban Walks. In *Proceedings of the SIGCHI Conference on Human Factors in Computing Systems*, 2853–2862.
14. Clara Crivellaro, Alex Taylor, Vasilis Vlachokyriakos, Rob Comber, Bettina Nissen, and Pete Wright. 2016. Re-making places: HCI, "Community Building" and Change. In *Proceedings of the SIGCHI Conference on Human Factors in Computing Systems*.
15. Lincoln Dahlberg. 2011. Re-constructing digital democracy: An outline of four "positions." *new media & society*: 1461444810389569.
16. Javier Ramos Diaz and Bruno González Cacheda. 2016. Financing Social Activism: Crowdfunding and Advocatory Social Movement in Spain in Times of Crisis. In *Proceedings of the 9th International Conference on Theory and Practice of Electronic Governance*, 139–148.
17. Jill P Dimond, Michaelanne Dye, Daphne LaRose, and Amy S Bruckman. 2013. Hollaback!: the role of storytelling online in a social movement organization. In *Proceedings of the 2013 conference on Computer supported cooperative work*, 477–490.
18. Carl DiSalvo. 2010. Design, Democracy and Agonistic Pluralism. *Proceedings of the design research society conference*.
19. Carl DiSalvo. 2012. *Adversarial design*. The MIT Press.
20. Paul Dourish. 2010. HCI and environmental sustainability: the politics of design and the design of politics. In *Proceedings of the Designing Interactive Systems Conference*, 1–10. http://doi.org/10.1145/1858171.1858173
21. Andrew Feenberg and Alastair Hannay. 1995. Technology and the Politics of Knowledge.
22. Andy Garbett, Rob Comber, Edd Jenkins, and Patrick Olivier. 2016. App Movement: A Platform for Community Commissioning of Mobile Applications. In *Proceedings of the SIGCHI Conference on Human Factors in Computing Systems*.
23. Keith Hart, Jean-Louis Laville, and Antonio David Cattani. 2010. *The human economy*.
24. David Harvey. 2000. *Spaces of hope*. University of California Press.
25. Gillian R Hayes. 2011. The relationship of action research to human-computer interaction. *ACM Transactions on Computer-Human Interaction (TOCHI)* 18, 3: 15.
26. Philip N Howard, Aiden Duffy, Deen Freelon, Muzammil Hussain, Will Mari, and Marwa Mazaid. 2011. Opening closed regimes: what was the role of social media during the Arab Spring? In *Project on Information Technology and Political Islam*, 1–30.
27. Emily Kawano, Thomas Neal Masterson, and Jonathan Teller-Elsberg. 2009. Solidarity economy I: Building alternatives for people and planet. *Center for Popular Economics, Amherst, MA, USA*.
28. Bran Knowles, Mark Lochrie, Paul Coulton, and Jon Whittle. 2014. BARTER: promoting local spending behavior. In *CHI'14 Extended Abstracts on Human Factors in Computing Systems*, 1933–1938.
29. Yong Ming Kow, Yubo Kou, Bryan Semaan, and Waikuen Cheng. 2016. Mediating the Undercurrents: Using Social Media to Sustain a Social Movement. In *Proceedings of the 2016 CHI Conference on Human Factors in Computing Systems*, 3883–3894. http://doi.org/10.1145/2858036.2858186
30. Ernesto Laclau and Chantal Mouffe. 2001. *Hegemony and socialist strategy: Towards a radical democratic politics*. Verso.
31. Lila Leontidou. 2010. Urban social movements in "weak"civil societies: The right to the city and cosmopolitan activism in Southern Europe. *Urban Studies* 47, 6: 1179–1203.
32. David Lewis and Nazneen Kanji. 2009. *Non-governmental organizations and development*. Routledge.
33. Ann Light. 2011. The politics of representing cultures in ubiquitous media: challenging national cultural norms by studying a map with Indian and British users. *Personal and Ubiquitous Computing* 15, 6: 585–596.
34. Chris J Martin. 2016. The sharing economy: A pathway to sustainability or a nightmarish form of neoliberal capitalism? *Ecological Economics* 121: 149–159.
35. Andrés Monroy-Hernández, Shelly Farnham, Emre Kiciman, Scott Counts, and Munmun De Choudhury. 2013. Smart societies: from citizens as sensors to collective action. *interactions* 20, 4: 16–19.
36. Chantal Mouffe. 2000. *The democratic paradox*. Verso.

37. Chantal Mouffe. 2005. *On the political.* Psychology Press.
38. Sissel Olander, Tau Ulv Lenskjold, Signe Louise Yndigegn, and Maria Foverskov. 2011. Mobilizing for community building and everyday innovation. *interactions* 18, 4: 28–32.
39. Patrick Olivier and Peter Wright. 2015. Digital civics: taking a local turn. *interactions* 22, 4: 61–63.
40. Andrea Parker, Vasudhara Kantroo, Hee Rin Lee, Miguel Osornio, Mansi Sharma, and Rebecca E Grinter. 2012. Health promotion as activism: building community capacity to effect social change. In *Proceedings of the SIGCHI Conference on Human Factors in Computing Systems*, 99–108.
41. Pamela Pietrucci. 2011. "Poetic" publics: Agency and rhetorics of "netroots" activism in post-earthquake L'Aquila. *The Journal of Community Informatics* 6, 3.
42. Theodoros Rakopoulos. 2014. The crisis seen from below, within, and against: from solidarity economy to food distribution cooperatives in Greece. *Dialectical Anthropology* 38, 2: 189–207.
43. Theodoros Rakopoulos. 2014. Resonance of solidarity: meanings of a local concept in anti-austerity Greece. *Journal of Modern Greek Studies* 32, 2: 313–337.
44. Theodoros Rakopoulos. 2015. "Movementality", Economic Democracy and Social Reproduction during Crisis. *Economy for and Against Democracy* 2: 161.
45. Joan Roelofs. 1995. The third sector as a protective layer for capitalism. *Monthly Review* 47, 4: 16.
46. Saqib Saeed, Markus Rohde, and Volker Wulf. 2011. Analyzing political activists' organization practices: findings from a long term case study of the european social forum. *Computer Supported Cooperative Work (CSCW)* 20, 4–5: 265–304.
47. Guy Schofield, Tom Bartindale, and Peter Wright. 2015. Bootlegger: Turning Fans into Film Crew. In *Proceedings of the 33rd Annual ACM Conference on Human Factors in Computing Systems*, 767–776.
48. Trebor Scholz. 2014. Platform Cooperativism vs. the Sharing Economy. *Medium*. Retrieved January 8, 2016 from https://goo.gl/EowzuJ
49. Patrick C Shih, Victoria Bellotti, Kyungsik Han, and John M Carroll. 2015. Unequal time for unequal value: Implications of differing motivations for participation in timebanking. In *Proceedings of the 33rd Annual ACM Conference on Human Factors in Computing Systems*, 1075–1084.
50. M Silberman, Lisa Nathan, Bran Knowles, et al. 2014. Next steps for sustainable HCI. *interactions* 21, 5: 66–69.
51. Dimitris A Sotiropoulos and Dimitris Bourikos. 2014. Economic crisis, social solidarity and the voluntary sector in Greece. *Journal of Power, Politics & Governance* 2, 2: 33–53.
52. EleniRevekka Staiou. 2016. Organosi20.gr. Retrieved September 21, 2016 from https://goo.gl/Nl9PNJ
53. Ali ayebi. 2013. Planning activism: using social media to claim marginalized citizens' right to the city. *Cities* 32: 88–93.
54. AlexS Taylor, Siân Lindley, Tim Regan, et al. 2015. Data-in-Place: Thinking through the Relations Between Data and Community. In *Proceedings of the SIGCHI Conference on Human Factors in Computing Systems*, 2863–2872.
55. Sherry Turkle. 2012. *Alone together: Why we expect more from technology and less from each other*. Basic books.
56. Tyler Veak. 2000. Whose technology? Whose modernity? Questioning Feenberg's questioning technology. *Science, technology, & human values* 25, 2: 226–237.
57. Vasilis Vlachokyriakos, Rob Comber, Karim Ladha, et al. 2014. PosterVote: Expanding the Action Repertoire for Local Political Activism. In *Proceedings of the Designing Interactive Systems Conference.*
58. Vasillis Vlachokyriakos, Clara Crivellaro, Christopher A Le Dantec, Eric Gordon, Pete Wright, and Patrick Olivier. 2016. Digital Civics: Citizen Empowerment With and Through Technology. In *Proceedings of the 2016 CHI Conference Extended Abstracts on Human Factors in Computing Systems*, 1096–1099.
59. Volker Wulf, Konstantin Aal, Ibrahim Abu Kteish, et al. 2013. Fighting against the wall: social media use by political activists in a Palestinian village. In *Proceedings of the SIGCHI Conference on Human Factors in Computing Systems*, 1979–1988.
60. Volker Wulf, Kaoru Misaki, Meryem Atam, David Randall, and Markus Rohde. 2013. "On the ground"in Sidi Bouzid: investigating social media use during the tunisian revolution. In *Proceedings of the 2013 conference on Computer supported cooperative work*, 1409–1418.

Environmental Protection and Agency: Motivations, Capacity, and Goals in Participatory Sensing

Paul Aoki
aoki@acm.org

Allison Woodruff*
woodruff@acm.org

Baladitya Yellapragada
University of California, Berkeley
baladityay23@berkeley.edu

Wesley Willett
University of Calgary
wj@wjwillett.net

ABSTRACT

In this paper we consider various genres of citizen science from the perspective of citizen participants. As a mode of scientific inquiry, citizen science has the potential to "scale up" scientific data collection efforts and increase lay engagement with science. However, current technological directions risk losing sight of the ways in which citizen science is actually practiced. As citizen science is increasingly used to describe a wide range of activities, we begin by presenting a framework of citizen science genres. We then present findings from four interlocking qualitative studies and technological interventions of community air quality monitoring efforts, examining the motivations and capacities of citizen participants and characterizing their alignment with different types of citizen science. Based on these studies, we suggest that data acquisition involves complex multi-dimensional tradeoffs, and the commonly held view that citizen science systems are a win-win for citizens and science may be overstated.

Author Keywords

Citizen Science; Environmental Sensing.

ACM Classification Keywords

H.5.m. Information interfaces and presentation (e.g., HCI): Miscellaneous.

INTRODUCTION

In environmental research, *citizen science* [29] is frequently touted as a means for both "scaling up" academic research and increasing lay engagement with scientific issues and practice. Involvement of non-professionals in scientific inquiry is seen as a way to refocus research productively on issues of societal concern [13,39]; educate citizens about science [6,51]; and benefit scientific practice through the use of citizens to collect measurement data and local knowledge [10,12,42].

Two particular approaches to citizen science have received the bulk of attention in computing research: supporting *expert amateurs* (including institutions like the Audubon Christmas Bird Count [47]) and facilitating *community action* (e.g., *street science* [13]). The Christmas Bird Count is a coordinated wildlife survey conducted by bird hobbyists around the world, whereas community action campaigns involve non-expert community residents in the process of characterizing local environmental conditions. The expert amateur approach resonates with many long-standing themes in HCI/CSCW research and has led to work on tools for open knowledge communities, collaborative visualization, and structured discussion. This work has also spawned a variety of general-purpose platforms like Sensr [31], Ohmage [48], and ODK [26]) intended to support a wide range of data collection activities by expert amateurs. Similarly, the community action approach resonates with recent themes in sensor network research [2] and has led to work on infrastructure for participatory mobile sensing (e.g., [39,44]).

However, an early focus on generalizable research – notably, on infrastructure for collaboration and data collection, things that computing research does well – risks losing sight of some of the particulars of citizen science as it is actually practiced. Such efforts often overlook: (1) the behavioral **motivations** of citizens to contribute to particular environmental causes, (2) the **capacity** of citizens to participate in activities necessary to a meaningful scientific campaign, and (3) the **alignment** of technologies with the ultimate goals of the collective scientific effort.

These issues become particularly salient when we consider that the design of infrastructure for related domains such as crowdsourcing is typically predicated on narrowing and simplifying participants' roles to reduce the impact of human variability on the data "product." This attitude is mirrored in the literature on citizen science, which is filled with comments to the effect of "scientists who design research projects have to write study protocols that take citizen scientists into account...protocols should limit what citizen scientists are asked to do" [10] and "the public doesn't know how to handle complex equipment" [5]. Do such design goals, as practically justified as they might be, match what "the public" wants to achieve?

In this paper, we consider the experience of citizen science from the perspective of the citizen participants. Our goal is to inform the design of participatory sensing systems. The analysis here draws on qualitative design fieldwork comprised of an interlocking series of citizen science

* Woodruff is currently at Google Inc.

Permission to make digital or hard copies of all or part of this work for personal or classroom use is granted without fee provided that copies are not made or distributed for profit or commercial advantage and that copies bear this notice and the full citation on the first page. Copyrights for components of this work owned by others than the author(s) must be honored. Abstracting with credit is permitted. To copy otherwise, or republish, to post on servers or to redistribute to lists, requires prior specific permission and/or a fee. Request permissions from Permissions@acm.org.
CHI 2017, May 06 - 11, 2017, Denver, CO, USA Copyright is held by the owner/author(s). Publication rights licensed to ACM.
ACM 978-1-4503-4655-9/17/05...$15.00 DOI: http://dx.doi.org/10.1145/3025453.3025667

projects conducted over the course of the past eight years. This involved three years of concentrated engagement, including four user studies and technological interventions, followed by intermittent observation over the following five years. Based on this extended engagement, we seek to unravel the assumptions resulting from uncritical adoption of *expert amateur* and *community action* viewpoints as well as the straightforward application of tropes from social media and sensor networks.

We begin with a background on citizen science and provide a framework for citizen science genres. Next, we describe the goals and methods of our studies. Drawing on our fieldwork, we present findings on participants' motivations in environmental action and participants' individual and collective capacities for citizen science. We then discuss how these align with different types of citizen science. We conclude with a discussion of the practical tensions among various goals in the design of participatory sensing systems.

BACKGROUND

In the computing literature, critiques of citizen science have tended to highlight the very limited involvement of citizens in science practice – especially in the popular areas of participatory sensing [17,19] and crowdsourcing [40]. However, the term is being actively applied to an even wider range of environmental science and natural history activities[1]. One documentary study [54] divided projects into primarily scientific (physical or virtual) or systemic (action/monitoring or education), but follow-on survey research [55] showed that ¾ of projects examined basically gave equal weight to science, action/monitoring and education. In this section, we describe archetypal work that has been classified as citizen science, noting variation in the degree of agency afforded to citizen-participants.

For the purposes of our discussion, we divide observational scientific practice using a linearized model of scientific method [24], a model in which a set of goals, ideas and hypotheses drive a study design (*preparation*); a set of study protocols are executed (*data collection*); and the resulting data set is analyzed and related back to the original ideas (*post-collection*). This is a caricature, as science practice typically proceeds in a more ad hoc, iterative manner [9,12,24]. Our main motivation is to separate data collection from the steps before and after it.

Citizen Science: Origins and Genres of Practice

There are many genres of citizen science, and the ideas underlying them have a long history [20,47]. For example, Shirk et al. [45] categorize five genres of participation in citizen science research ranging from purely "contractual" research in which communities contract professional scientists, to "collegial" in which citizens conduct research independently with varying degrees of outside affirmation or recognition. These distinct genres can be seen as arising from two main historical threads – one with the primary goal of using citizens to facilitate science, and the other subordinating science to citizens' political goals.

Citizen Science – Facilitating Scientific Agendas

The now-widespread use of non-professionals for data collection [10,20,42] is the best-known form of what we might call the *expert collectors* genre. The pre- and post-collection work of study design and data analysis remain in the control of professional scientists, and the role of citizens is carefully defined and constrained to maximize the scientific utility of their labor. The Christmas Bird Count is an oft-cited example of this, yet it also highlights the fact that such work can require considerable domain expertise (recognizing birds) even if that expertise is not that of professional science (analyzing data) [51]. To encourage participation, web-based tools for data submission now commonly include online community tools (e.g., [1,32]).

Inspired by the popularity of projects like the Christmas Bird Count, computing researchers are creating crowdsourcing-style projects for environmental research. The availability of wirelessly connected mobile computing devices and inexpensive sensors has driven a great deal of recent research in mobile participatory sensing – the organized collection of sensor data using personal mobile devices [2]. A typical *sensing citizens* vision assumes a scale trade-off – i.e., high spatiotemporal data coverage will result from the mass participation enabled by cheap platforms and sensors, and that coverage can make up for limitations imposed by an ad hoc, de-skilled data collection process as well as those resulting from the use of cheap sensors [28]. A sensing citizens perspective is often applied when participant tasks can be usefully constrained, for example an effort in which participants execute clearly defined tasks to track chlorine usage [30].

Citizen Science – Enabling Collective Agendas

A different thread of work has been inspired by action research in the social sciences. The primary objective here is to effect changes in local conditions as opposed to the construction of (academic) scientific knowledge.[2]

[1] Notable online citizen science projects appear in a number of disciplines, such as molecular biology (e.g., FoldIt, http://fold.it). However, environmental observations are still predominant—for examples, see project registries at http://citizenscience.org and http://scistarter.com. While platforms like Zooniverse (http://zooniverse.org) run crowdsourced image labeling and transcription projects in a variety of scientific domains, environmental observations also make up the majority of their efforts. To keep the domain-specific content of this paper manageable, and because the main focus of this paper is on participatory sensing, we limit our discussion to the environmental sciences and focus on on-the-ground activities rather than online participation.

[2] Other common forms of citizen participation in change processes include participation in the representative electoral processes, formal policy-setting processes, or informal agenda-setting processes [49]. In the latter two forms, activities may be epistemically scientific (requiring access to scientific resources and expertise), but they may also focus on identity politics or even be explicitly subversive [8].

What we will call *community research* takes many closely related forms [56], such as participatory research in the social and health sciences [34] and street science in the environmental sciences [13]. The scientific resources and professional scientific training available to community activists is generally limited, so data often takes the form of qualitative local knowledge instead of quantitative measurements. One path to address this limit involves local youth as *student scientists* who learn about conventional science practice and become aware of environmental issues (e.g., [25]). Another path is to enroll community members as *citizen scientists* with the specific aim of creating new knowledge, data products that are good enough to use in policy/regulatory arenas (e.g., [37,39]). Obviously, these paths increase the involvement of participants in conventional science practice.

Technologists, artists, and activists are hybridizing community research with the same crowdsourcing ideas that inspired participatory sensing. What we call *community reporting* resembles community research in that it uses participatory sensing data in a qualitative way to raise environmental or political awareness within communities (e.g., [17,35,44]). However, the intensity, duration, and capture of local knowledge tend to be reduced.

Similar ideas and language (e.g., participation, science) are used in all of these genres. However, the disparate sources and influences of these ideas – including the recent ability to scale them using crowdsourcing and sensing technology – result in quite different emphases in terms of the data collected, and also impact how the data can be applied.

Ideal Types of Data-Centric Practice

Detaching these various genres of citizen science from their specific origins and goals for a moment, it is helpful to arrange them into an ideal type [53] system (Figure 1) based on their goals and approaches to data collection. (These ideal types are meant to be analytically useful, as opposed to thoroughly descriptive or precisely definitional.)

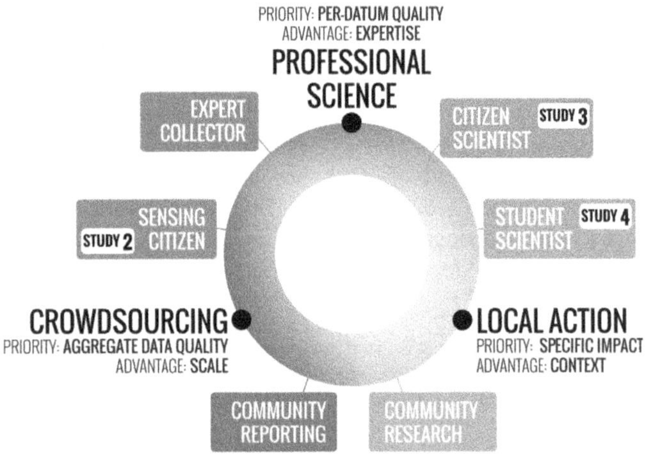

Figure 1. Different types of data-centric community and science practice. Studies 2-4 show the focus of our fieldwork.

When all portions of a study are handled by professionals, we might simply call this first ideal type *professional science*. The primary goal of data collection in professional science is quality – not just maximizing the accuracy and minimizing the uncertainty of measurements, but characterizing their limitations, reproducibility and traceability. Strategies for achieving such goals include developing detailed technical knowledge of the measurement apparatus, careful construction of study protocols, and thorough documentation.

Economic realities and geographic constraints have long incentivized professional scientists to try to use amateur labor, which shares with *crowdsourcing* the key goal of maximizing the usable labor captured from participants. Crowdsourcing also shares the strategies of extreme division of labor and task standardization. Participant agency tends to be limited to the willingness to participate and work for the benefit of science practice. In particular, because of the difficulties of involving non-professionals in pre- and post-study practices, participation is often limited to data collection (whereas the goals and potential uses of the data are typically driven by study design).

A third ideal type of science-oriented activity might be called *local action*. The primary goal here is to effect change in local conditions. Participant agency is an explicit part of the activity – community goals, not those of scientific practice, drive what the project aims to achieve.

Overlaying our citizen science genres into this ideal type system (Figure 1) allows us to both consider the seemingly disparate goals of the projects and participants, and illustrate common tensions between them.

STUDIES

Our analysis draws upon post-hoc reflection on a series of four studies with interlocking goals and timelines. All four engagements centered on local air quality monitoring in a dense urban community in northern California. We chose to focus on air quality specifically because it represents a situated, locally relevant environmental problem with the potential to engage and impact a diverse set of contributors. At the same time, accurate and comprehensive air quality monitoring still presents a number of scientific, technical, and coordination challenges [50].

We began with background research on individual motivations for engaging in environmental action. We then collaborated with a local environmental justice NGO on a series of focused interventions. After these engagements concluded, we continued to informally track the progress of the NGO's efforts over the following five-year period.

Research Questions for HCI

In considering the design space of technology to support variations on "citizen science" (and in particular mobile participatory sensing), we explore two research questions.

The first question is, *What drives people to engage with participatory efforts, and what actions and outcomes are meaningful to them?* Engagement in environmental action of any kind is a process [58]. As one survey [18] notes, HCI sustainability research frequently considers the role of persuasive interfaces, social influence, and individual motivations for personal sustainability choices. Further, work has been done on motivations for online participation in citizen science [36]. However, exactly what kinds of meaningful outcomes motivate participants to pursue collective activities like citizen science (and how these interact with their abilities) is not yet well understood.

The second question is, *What are productive ways for citizens to participate?* As suggested in the previous section, different citizen science genres involve varying degrees of effort, formal scientific knowledge, attention to detail, etc. Understanding the realistic limits of citizen participation informs the requirements for technology intended to facilitate citizen science. Many different technologies for participatory sensing and collaborative analysis have been proposed. Some are highly appropriate when the goal is primarily to collect data to facilitate scientific purposes, whereas others are more appropriate when the goal is primarily to serve local residents.

Field Studies

Our field research can be grouped into four studies according to primary research focus and methods. The participants, tasks, and situations differed across studies, allowing us to observe variations in citizens' motivation to participate, their role in data collection and other aspects of science practice, and the types of sensing technology involved. In the three studies involving scientific practice, we participated in planning, execution and surveyor debriefs as well as providing enabling resources (e.g., equipment, technical assistance, funds for surveyor compensation). However, the goals and specific questions of the work itself were driven by our partners' agendas.

All phases of the fieldwork were qualitative. We took detailed field notes during interviews and other interactions. We recorded all formal interviews, meetings and workshops, transcribing relevant segments. At various points over the course of the projects, we performed affinity clustering on the text corpus and iteratively identified and refined emergent themes [7]. The analysis procedure reported here extends the detailed process described in several of the individual field studies [22,57].

Study 1 – Concerned Citizens

To investigate the motivations of individuals who were engaged in environmental action, we conducted exploratory fieldwork in the San Francisco Bay Area over a period of 7 months in 2008. This exploratory study did not involve a technical intervention and, unlike the other three studies, was not tied to a particular genre of citizen science. We conducted formal in-person interviews with 14 participants and informal phone and in-person interviews with approximately 30 additional stakeholders. Participants were selected for interest or involvement in environmental action around air quality. Almost all participants were adults, at a variety of life stages, with a balanced number of male and female participants. Interviews were semi-structured and lasted between 1.5 and 3 hours. The informal interactions followed an open-ended format and varied greatly in length.

Study 2 – Sensing Citizens

To understand more about citizens grappling directly with technical questions, we then engaged with a local environmental justice NGO, the Environmental Indicators Project (EIP). Founded by grassroots activists, EIP has conducted community-based participatory research (CBPR) [34] for many years [14]. EIP is perhaps most widely known for a series of campaigns in which it collected observational ("survey") data on particulate matter emitted by diesel trailer-trucks operating in local residential neighborhoods [38], resulting in a health risk assessment and emissions inventory at the state level [16] and increased monitoring at the air district level [21].

The Sensing Citizens study focused on the collection of air quality data by community surveyors using chemical sensing technology. This pilot study (conducted by approximately 10 surveyors over a 4-month period in 2009) employed wireless sensor platforms developed by the Common Sense project [22] (Figure 2-left) that geolocate and record measured levels of three EPA criteria pollutant gases (CO, NO_2, O_3) using two different off-the-shelf chemical sensor technologies. These devices require no user intervention and, indeed, participants were not required to do anything specific except recharge the devices at night. As such, this was an example of the sensing citizens genre described in the previous section. In both this study and the Citizen Scientists study below, we followed EIP's existing practices for surveyor recruiting (using snowball sampling complemented with local advertising) and incentives.

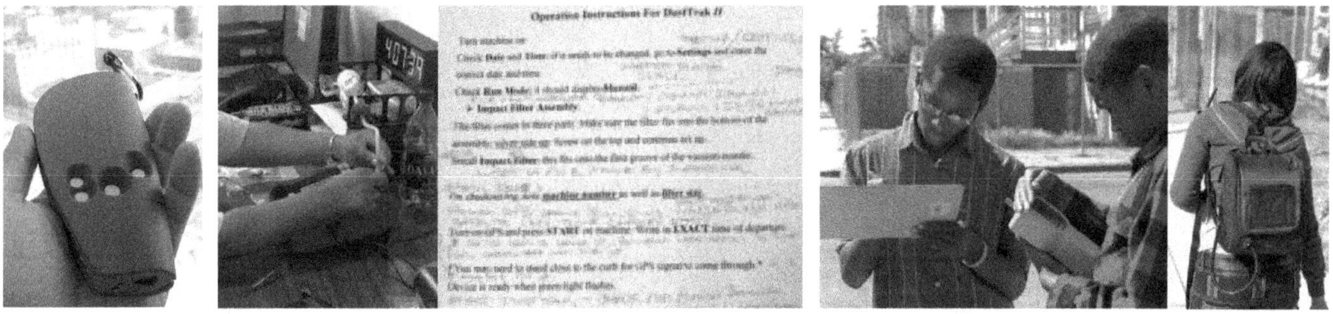

Figure 2. ***Left*–The gas sensor developed for the Sensing Citizens study. *Center*–Calibration and evolving documentation during the Citizen Scientists study. *Right*–Sensing activities conducted during the Student Scientists study.**

Study 3 – Citizen Scientists

While the Sensing Citizens study with chemical sensing devices provided valuable usage data, engaging EIP's staff and community surveyors in deeper scientific investigation required that we shift to EIP's main pollutant of interest, particulate matter (PM). As a result, subsequent campaigns involved off-the-shelf portable aerosol monitors (DustTrak II, Model 8530; TSI Inc.) that log continuous particulate matter readings in the same units as EPA NAAQS (i.e., mg/m^3). Unlike the Common Sense devices, these monitors require considerable operational and administrative attention including maintenance, calibration, manual data management, and record-keeping (Figure 2-center).

In this engagement, data was collected by approximately 20 community surveyors over a period of two years from mid-2009 through mid-2011. Data collection was somewhat intermittent, with the exception of a focused round of approximately 100 shifts during two weeks in February 2010. Surveyors typically carried the monitors for hour-long shifts, walking one of six routes designed by EIP staff. Surveyors and EIP staff frequently reviewed the data in a visualization tool developed by the researchers. In addition to participating in initial orientation and training, some surveyors participated in an EIP capstone workshop and visualization focus groups [57]. The greater involvement of EIP staff and surveyors in the technical aspects of this process makes this an example of the citizen scientist genre.

Study 4 – Student Scientists

To study a third common citizen science genre, we collaborated with an NSF-funded high school science enrichment program, the East Bay Academy for Young Scientists (EBAYS). From a technical perspective, this was fairly similar to the Citizen Scientists study (EIP's request, photo and SMS annotation capabilities were added), but the surveyor population was radically different in terms of their demographics (high school students as opposed to immediate community members) and motivations (curriculum enrichment as opposed to community interest).

In this final engagement, two dozen student surveyors and six instructors collected data using PM sensors over a period of six months during 2010 (Figure 2-right). This initiative including a concentrated summer program in which EIP was actively involved (for example, training the students and instructors in the use of the equipment). The data collection was contextualized with lectures on environmental science and environmental justice as well as data analysis sessions. The students participated in individual interviews, and researchers acted as participant-observers during data collection and analysis. All student surveyors gave final presentations, and some presented their results in a poster session at a national scientific conference.

As the studies progressed, EIP leveraged its extended network to proselytize the work, garnering attention from regulatory agencies and high-ranking government officials, significant press, and numerous requests from other communities who want to conduct similar work. When our research team transitioned to other activities in mid-2011, EIP and EBAYS continued the Citizen Scientists and Student Scientists work, and EIP also began conducting training sessions for other community groups across the country. As of 2016, both groups were still actively engaged in these activities.

WHAT DRIVES PARTICIPATION?

In this section, we discuss participants' motivations for conducting various types of citizen science.

Drive for Personally Relevant Information

The predominant driver of interest for concerned citizens was clearly the desire to gather personally relevant information. Personal health issues (or threats of potential future health issues) triggered concern about air quality.

> "People who have children who have asthma and get more concerned about it, or they're sick themselves and they're concerned about it, that interest makes them want to join a group or find out more about the issue." – *David*[3], *Concerned Citizen*

> "I used to go walking. There were some days I thought I wasn't going to make it home. I'd just get so short of breath." – *Linda, Concerned Citizen*

Participants were eager to get information about how to minimize their exposure. For example, they wanted to receive recommendations for walking routes or driving routes with the lowest potential exposure. Accordingly, while participants had some willingness to collect or view data for more abstract scientific purposes, they were more compelled to gather and view data that was immediately relevant to their own lives. They wanted data about the specific locations in which they personally spent time and about the pollutants with the greatest relevance to their health. For example, they had greater interest in collecting data about particulate matter than in collecting data about ozone or carbon dioxide.

> "For me, I would just be interested in my own local [air quality]." – *Ethan, Concerned Citizen*

Therefore, while concerned citizens were highly motivated to carry devices to collect data about their own exposure, they were not necessarily motivated to collect data that was most strategic from a scientific perspective. Further, their needs may not be met by technical approaches that collate data from a large number of low-accuracy sensors; because people spend the bulk of their time in a few locations where multiple sensors may not be available, conventional instruments that take highly accurate individual samples may be most appropriate for health-focused data.

Although they shared the concerned citizens' interest in personally relevant information, community and educational organizations were more flexible about location and type of data than the individual citizens. As discussed further below, EIP wanted to gather a fairly broad data set

[3] All participant names are pseudonyms.

for exploratory purposes, and funding opportunities played a significant role in guiding their focus. EBAYS' predominant interest was educational, so they were somewhat agnostic to the type and location of data.

Interest in the Environment, not Environmental Science

The community and educational organizations had a desire for citizens to gain an understanding of scientific process and principles, for example so that they could meaningfully participate in community meetings with scientific agencies. However, individual citizens made it clear that their interest in the environment was not necessarily the same as a desire to develop competence in environmental science. Some people may become engaged in the scientific process, but many do not. Participants were typically satisfied by learning about fairly general information and by gaining "awareness," and they tended to be largely uninterested in conducting scientific activities beyond simply collecting data. For example, participants wanted to learn what pollutants they might be exposed to.

> "I don't know what's in the air. That's why I wanted to do this. So that I could learn." – *Jake, Surveyor*

> "All three of my children have asthma, so from that perspective, I wanted to know what was in the air. Not only that—I'm allergic to something out there in the air… So I really would like to know what's hit me..." – *Loretta, Survey Team Leader*

However, participants were less engaged in analyzing or interpreting data. Many did not know, and were not particularly interested in learning, what the numbers meant.

> "What's 2.1? … See, those numbers wouldn't mean a thing to me." – *Abigail, Concerned Citizen*

> "From sensor to sensor, pollutant to pollutant, this one's bad at a hundred and fifty parts per billion, this one's bad at eighty parts per billion, this one's at nine parts per million (laughs) … they could care less." – *Ethan, Concerned Citizen*

Participants such as the surveyors seemed happy to assume that someone else (an expert) would take the data and do something meaningful with it. They were satisfied by "playing their part" by collecting the data, and were not generally inclined to engage with it.

> "Once they receive the data that we give to them, they test it. They know what it is." – *Desiree, Surveyor*

> "[Collecting data] made me feel like I was doing something for Oakland… I think I'm making a difference, and I feel better about myself." – *Darius, Surveyor*

Rather than seeking to explore the data, participants were more interested in being provided with higher-level interpretations that explained their exposure in terms of health effects or "normal" conditions, contextualizing their experience without requiring them to have specific technical knowledge. Overall, participants tended to seek narrowly defined roles as data collectors and assume that (anonymous) experts would fill all other functions.

Awareness, Education, and Advocacy

Citizen science rhetoric often suggests that citizens will leverage the data they collect to take effective political action. However, while participants were convinced that collecting data was useful, they were often vague as to how it would be used. Participants' immediate inclination was to use data to raise awareness among community members, a goal that was also shared by EIP.

> "The most important thing is get it out to the community and the residents who live in these areas who might not be aware." – *Desiree, Surveyor*

> "It's really hard to educate people about environmental issues because they just immediately want to get defensive... But if you provide them with something like this that's engaging, it's graphic, it's factual… then they start to sort of care and they start to sort of understand..." – *Claire, Concerned Citizen*

In practice, this awareness raising was fairly successful in both the Citizen Scientists and Student Scientists studies.

> "I've learned, since I started participating and doing the air study… how small the particulates are that can go through your lungs… pollutants there in the air that I would never have thought about that are entering my body and my children's body." – *Desiree, Surveyor*

> "I talk a lot about it when I'm out and about [collecting data]. People are always asking us what we're doing… and you go into a whole scenario about explaining what you're doing it for and why. It's another way to draw people into what we do, by letting them see us doing it." – *Loretta, Survey Team Leader*

However, participants were somewhat hazy about how this community awareness would be helpful. We attended one community action workshop in which the moderator specifically led a session to educate participants about using data for advocacy, because it did not generally occur to participants to interact with policy makers, and they did not know how to approach this process. Even though the community and educational organizations had a deeper understanding of the political advocacy process, using data in advocacy was not necessarily an immediate goal for them either. The initially desired impact of citizen science was in many ways educational rather than environmental.

> "Another mission of ours is to have students develop problem-solving skills as well as critical thinking skills… They can then utilize those same skills to try and solve problems in their own lives or in their own communities." – *Ben, Science Teacher*

WHAT IS PRODUCTIVE?

As we saw in the previous section, a key motivation for citizens is to answer questions about environmental conditions and the potential effects on community, family and personal health. However, when moving from general information to professional science or community advocacy, additional goals become relevant, and the procedures by which data is collected and managed become critical for its potential use. In this section, we discuss our experiences with citizens and consider their capacity to productively gather and use data in various conditions.

Relevance of "Scientific" Conduct for Non-Scientists

One of the touted benefits of citizen science is that citizens can effectively donate their time and effort, amplifying the efforts of professionally trained scientists. But is it always possible to execute "science" without professional training?

Professional science assumes that "data" is far more than the raw measurements. For reproducibility, data collection procedures and equipment must be recorded, as well as measurement conditions. For analysis and presentation, these factors become part of uncertainty estimates. In professional science practice, all of this is considered as part of study design – it would not make sense, for example, to use equipment and procedures that would be unable to measure the phenomena of interest.

In spite of its non-scientific origins, community advocacy turns out to involve similar concerns. Because advocacy generally occurs in a governmental setting of one kind or another, data-backed arguments are typically presented in terms of standards set by existing laws, which are in turn framed in terms of relatively conservative scientific standards [37]. A key rhetorical strategy is to present citizen data as the product of "good science" [5], meaning that its methodological credibility must be high enough that results cannot be *immediately* dismissed by technical experts.

Hence, while data intended for personal use might be collected using arbitrary methods, data intended for use in scientific or advocacy settings is far more valuable if it is collected and managed according to conventional protocols. To give an example of such a protocol, the technical procedures for our student-scientist study might be summarized in a scientific journal publication as follows:

> Surveyors carried photometric aerosol monitors (DustTrak II Model 8530; TSI Inc., Shoreview, MN) with a 1Hz sampling rate and air flow calibrated each day to 3.0L/min (Model 4146; TSI Inc., Shoreview, MN). Monitors were fitted with TSI impactors (size-selective inlets) with designed 50% cut-points at 2.5μm ($PM_{2.5}$) at 3L/min. The monitors' internal clocks (used to timestamp logged readings and which required manual setting) were re-set at every shift using an NTP-based wall clock. Surveyors walked one of three routes specified by EIP, with positions logged by GPS at 1Hz (AGL-3080; Amod Ltd., Taipei, Taiwan). Monitors were carried using custom backpack cases, with air sampled from the surveyor's breathing zone using 1m conductive silicone rubber hoses (TSI p/n 810688, TSI Inc., Shoreview, MN) attached to the inlet. All monitors were within annual factory calibration against ISO 12103-1:1997 A1 test dust. Local PM characteristics were obtained using the monitor's built-in sampling port and 2-piece, 37mm cassettes loaded with 2μm PTFE filters (SKC p/n 225-308 and 225-27-07; SKC Inc., Eighty Four, PA) at an effective internal flow rate of 2.0L/min. Gravimetric analysis (ALS DataChem Labs, Salt Lake City, UT) applied NIOSH 0500 procedures including field blanks. Readings were manually downloaded from the DustTraks and submitted (with GPS logs) to a system that performed basic quality checks and automatically uploaded data into a database. At pre-selected street intersections, particle count readings were taken at 0.3, 0.5, 1, 2, 5 and 10μm using a multi-channel optical particle counter (Model 983, Fluke Corp., Everett, WA).

Executing these procedures is not simply mechanical and requires considerable technical and administrative attention to detail.

Operations and Maintenance

In our experience, citizens found it highly challenging to develop procedures and documentation for their activities. In the Citizen Scientists study, researchers wrote initial procedures, a customized user manual, and checklists, and trained EIP staff in the use of these. The researchers then encouraged EIP to adapt the procedures and documentation to reflect their specific needs and practices as the work unfolded. This task was delegated to EIP's survey team leader, who had a strong preference for the oral tradition. (As is common in environmental justice communities, many EIP staff and volunteers had had limited opportunities for formal education.) She quickly appropriated the technical procedures and made minor modifications, such as reordering maintenance steps for increased productivity. However, months passed with little progress on the documentation, and necessary information about data provenance was not being recorded. Some EIP staff understood the significance of this (for example, in order to receive funding from the EPA or even provide data as input for EPA decision-making processes, an organization must demonstrate that they have followed extensive EPA quality assurance requirements [23]). EIP staff appealed to the researchers to verbally interview the survey team leader and update the documentation (daily log sheets, etc.) to reflect the new practices that had emerged (Figure 2-center).

> "I didn't do my reading. I just learned the system... It's not really hard to use... I'm trying to figure out which ways to do it faster." – *Loretta, Survey Team Leader*

> "This is a really big problem in a culture where there isn't better than a sixth-grade education and people don't have any technical knowledge or understanding... It's great if [she] learns how to do this, but there's no documentation. She memorized it because she made you tell her 55 times. Tell me every day until I learn it. Well, that's great, but what about the next person?" – *Alex, Community Organization Leader*

In many ways, the citizens and students were highly capable of executing day-to-day procedures. Initial mastery of the technical procedures was rarely a problem when the procedures were codified in advance. For example, EIP staff was competent at charging and calibrating equipment, changing filters, and modifying device settings.

> "It's just a really great experience for the young people and as well for policymakers in the government to see that young people are capable of doing this kind of work and that anyone can really do this work." – *Ben, Science Teacher*

> "The mechanics of data collection... they [the students] were competent at that... But they didn't always understand why they were doing what they were doing." – *Connor, Science Teacher*

However, as is common in tedious work, sticking rigidly to protocols is difficult – especially with an intermittent volunteer population. We saw considerable "practical drift" ([46], p. 194) between the written procedure and collection practice. In some instances, critical metadata was not recorded, GPS data was not collected in conjunction with the air quality data, etc. Volunteers did not always reliably handle mundane tasks such as charging devices nightly.

> "Badge #10 was not charged... (surveyor took some antihistamins [sic] and fell asleep early)." – *Survey log, Sensing Citizens study*

> "Now we have to worry about quality control... we have to keep correcting them on their process and procedure, and that's just going to be a reality of working with volunteers who are doing this one hour a week." – *Alex, Community Organization Leader*

Additionally, some administrative aspects were difficult. For example, many of the EIP staff were not experienced in using computers, so tasks such as saving data with agreed-upon filenames (specified to contain necessary metadata) were challenging and error-prone. As a result of various procedural errors, approximately half of the first 100 shifts were unusable. EIP responded by paying greater attention to learning and enforcing the procedures, and later data collection was more successful.

Monitoring and maintaining complex equipment over the longer-term was challenging for the citizens, as it required a certain level of understanding of its principles of operation. While the researchers encouraged them to become more involved and grow their competence in this area, and the survey team lead was alert and did occasionally notice potential problems, overall they had little interest in deepening their understanding of the equipment. In the end they relied almost entirely on the researchers to ensure the equipment was in good operating condition.

In summary, participants executed day-to-day operations well (when they made it a priority to follow the protocols). However, they relied heavily on the researchers for procedures and documentation, as well as longer-term maintenance and troubleshooting – sometimes because these were not organizational priorities, and sometimes because participants did not yet have the requisite skills. In practical terms, this means that without expert intervention the data being collected might not be considered credible. In fact, according to EIP, the Citizen Scientists study would probably not have been conducted without heavy participation from outside researchers.

Sensitive to these concerns, EIP articulated that the work was more complicated than they had anticipated, often expressing a strong desire for the type of equipment in the Sensing Citizens study (equipment that required minimal operation and maintenance, and no interaction with data files), which they came to call "passive" equipment. Such equipment was unfortunately not an option, as consumer-grade particulate matter sensors (like AirBeam [3] or the Air Quality Egg [4]) had not yet come to market, and the need to measure PM dominated other concerns. However, on other occasions, the same EIP staff also expressed concerns about such passive equipment – noting that it might compromise engagement and undermine their educational goals. They were eager to participate fully and did not want the researchers to "dumb things down". Ultimately it became clear that the ideal technology would involve active participation and learning, but not too much. Ideally, new opportunities for participant involvement would lie in the zone of proximal development [52] and build on participants' existing knowledge and capabilities.

> "This citizen data gathering has to be completely passive or it's never gonna work!" – *Alex, Community Organization Leader*

> "It can be done much more easily than the way we do it, but we choose not to simply treat a volunteer or a student as a pack mule… We want them to learn something…" – *Alex*

> "In a sense, I don't want it to be fully automated. I want it to be an accessible process that doesn't take me a month and a half to teach someone… walking that line between automation and engagement is an important one, because you know we could have dogs carrying the thing around the neighborhood if all we want to do is collect data." – *Alex*

Aligning Study Design, Execution, and Goals

Approaches like CBPR or street science [13] posit that the community has latent questions – that local knowledge can be elicited and converted into both questions with a scientific formulation as well as influencing the reformulation of scientific questions in non-scientific form when appropriate. However, it may be hard to get people to articulate local knowledge. For example, the environment and residents of our target community are both over-studied. Some have posited that urban sensing may cause people to lose hope [15]. But, in fact, even without such sensing, members of the community have had so many people tell them things are wrong that it becomes difficult to elicit specific formulations.

> "Polluted, everything is polluted. Soil is polluted, water is polluted… The air is polluted. Everybody has asthma. It's all sooty. Starting from that, what would we need to know for them to ask a more specific question?" – *Alex, Community Organization Leader*

Hence, one must not only offer data but must also offer a specific course of action [5]. This can elicit more focused concerns – for example, particulate matter as opposed to environment or even air quality.

Even after hypotheses were posed, participants found it difficult to design a study plan that would yield data relevant to the hypotheses. Sometimes this was due to practical considerations such as the limits of volunteer schedules. For example, community members, the Air District, and a local atmospheric chemistry professor all provided EIP guidance about the times at which it would be most productive to collect data (e.g., the times of day the particulate matter levels were highest). However, volunteers were not readily available at those times, so EIP routinely collected data at times that were less valuable from both the scientific and community perspectives. Further, individual concerns can overtake organizational priorities. For example, one of the EIP staff had a personal interest in illegal dumping. She was attracted to this issue because it was concrete (unlike air quality) – one could easily identify misbehavior, report an offender to the city, etc. Accordingly, she significantly modified the data collection plan in the Student Scientists study such that the students refocused much of their effort on taking pictures of trash in the neighborhood, rather than gathering air quality data.

Participants also found it difficult to align their expectations of the data with the nature of the data being collected. For example, when EIP was designing a study plan, they articulated goals such as showing spatial variation in particulate matter levels or generally exploring the data to see what phenomena emerged. However, the study plan resulted in data that was geographically and temporally sparse (limited locations, inconsistent times of day, etc.), and from a scientific perspective this data was ill-suited to answer their questions. Despite receiving expert input expressing grave reservations about this approach, they were highly optimistic that if they just pushed forward collecting data, eventually they would have "enough".

> "I think the great value here is creating a tool which over time can either in an organized way or a random way accumulate tons and tons of data... it doesn't matter in a sense where [volunteers] go, how long they stayed there, what they did, the data is coming together. And eventually we have a picture that represents the cumulative experience of the community."
> – *Alex, Community Organization Leader*

The reality on the ground was that these campaigns were often "data first, questions later", personal interests and availability of volunteers often trumped focused agendas, and the data collection method was often poorly suited to the data collection goals. Accordingly, the resulting data was of limited use from all perspectives, being poorly suited to answer either scientific *or* community questions.

Leveraging the Data

Many citizen science projects expect citizens to not only gather data, but to explore and use it as well. However, such activities may be more difficult and less common than traditionally assumed. In all of our studies that involved data collection, citizen groups made relatively little progress in leveraging the data. Previous research has often proposed collaborative visualization [27] and its associated discussion tools are as means to focus and direct citizen activity [33,57]. Our research team provided the participants with user-friendly, custom tools, but the limitations of the tools and the limitations of the computer and analytic skills of the participants were both challenges.

Participants in the Citizen Scientists and Student Scientists studies gradually converged on the following types of analysis: (1) noticing the "baseline" level for a given day (e.g., "today was mostly 17s but yesterday was mostly 6s"); and (2) noticing where "spikes" (i.e., high PM values) occurred and inferring that locations with repeated spikes might be hotspots. Much focus in citizen science environmental monitoring is on hotspots, and it is indeed recognized that research is needed because the health effects of hotspot exposure are not well understood [11]. Searching for hotspots was fun and engaging – for example, one participant reported that PM levels were elevated near a taco truck. However, while participants had a number of theories about possible explanations for elevated levels and captured contextual information about potential sources during surveys, little progress was made on reproducing data or modifying study design to further investigate problem areas or provide credible evidence of causes.

In addition to their own analyses, EIP and EBAYS drew on a member of the research team to assist with analysis. Ultimately, participants presented preliminary data in some venues, but usually framed it as an example of what might be possible with these methods rather than an actual result.

ALIGNING SCIENCE WITH PARTICIPANT MOTIVATIONS

We now consider the alignment of participant motivations and capabilities with the ideal types of citizen science. Framing narratives from these ideal types suggest that: (1) citizens will play a role in the scientific process – designing studies and analyzing data (*professional science*), (2) citizens will collect the types of data that are needed, in the locations where data is needed (*crowdsourcing*), and (3) citizens will take action and use the data that is collected for advocacy (*local action*). We argue that while our participants had some natural interest in performing these duties, their predominant interests lay elsewhere (at least initially). However, participants' interests were often sufficiently aligned with the desired science outcomes that carefully designed interventions could still leverage them.

Professional science. As described in our findings above, participants had moderate motivation to participate in data collection and limited motivation and capacity to participate in pre- and post- data collection tasks such as study design and data analysis. Individuals may appear disinterested in specific processes and analyses ("low incidence of public engagement in research tasks outside of data collection, management, and analysis" [55]), but their individual and collective motivations are generally still rooted in the (anticipated) relevance of the findings. Capacity for data collection was mixed, but our experience has been that complexity of the equipment itself is perhaps the least of problems. Although individuals may have limited ability to do infrequent complex tasks (as when regulatory workers observe that "citizens can't use complex equipment" [5]), with training they can successfully execute detailed processes [37]. While volunteers often have limited time, attention, and skills, most did in fact execute well when correct procedures and attention to detail were clearly established and reinforced.

The most serious capacity issues related to complex problems and "big picture" thinking – identifying and troubleshooting issues with complicated equipment, designing effective procedures and study plans, ensuring that data aligns with goals, analyzing data, etc. Individuals may not be very good at formulating questions or understanding how to answer them, but that does not mean they do not have their own interests. These interests tended not to be abstract intellectual curiosity or emotional engagement with the environment (as posited by prior research [39]), but were instead concrete and personal.

Crowdsourcing. Citizen participants were capable of performing the extensive data collection envisioned in this narrative, but were not always motivated to do so. Participants were primarily interested in collecting personally relevant data, and had limited incentives to gather data for aggregation or general scientific purposes.

Local action. As noted earlier, participants were not generally motivated to take action (although the organizations were more interested in doing so). Moreover, both the participants and the organizations had fairly limited capacity to leverage the data for advocacy. However, while individuals may not understand precisely how data can be used in science or policy, they were also not entirely comfortable delegating to the scientists which outcomes the data should serve.

As hybrids of the ideal types, most of citizen science genres presume that citizens will readily embrace tasks that are more complex than those our participants tolerated. Designers may want to carefully target a very narrow band of activity (with just the right amount of participation and learning) so that citizens' can "do" science and advocacy with relatively low investment and barriers.

IMPLICATIONS FOR DESIGN

Past research has suggested that the main opportunities for design for citizen science are tools for data-sharing (e.g., [41]) and collaborative sensemaking (e.g., [33]). Given the discussion above, we believe that more basic systems-level questions inevitably play a large role in the viability of participatory sensing systems. From a technical perspective, an ideal sensing system would involve no user intervention (ideal ease-of-use) and would provide individual readings that would be perfectly accurate, precise and repeatable. Yet, in practice, sensing technologies are imperfect, which creates tensions between the goals of the various data-centric practices. As a result, organizers, designers, and scientists must be cognizant of participant motivations and tailor systems and processes accordingly–sometimes in ways that look different from stereotypical formulations of citizen science.

Designing for Professional Science

High per-measurement (datum) quality typically requires higher-cost equipment and/or higher skill on the part of data collectors. As we saw our Citizen Scientists study, both requirements tend to result in fewer measurements. As we have seen, this can lead to reduced spatial and temporal coverage, which can make analysis difficult and reduce participant motivation. As a result, where research must rely on distributed data collection to deliver high-quality data, systems should be designed explicitly to guide and incentivize consistent collection procedures. Tracking provenance and process, supporting in-situ validation, and encouraging participant awareness of analyses can all help ensure data quality remains high [43].

Designing for Crowdsourcing

In theory, a massive data collection campaign can achieve all goals, since large numbers of lower-quality measurements could approximate a more accurate sensing system. However, using this approach, failing to reach a critical data density will also result in a failure to meet all other goals. As we have seen, citizens who spend time and effort to take physical measurements tend to be concerned with the environment around them – their families, their immediate neighborhood, etc. If the measurements taken around the surveyors' areas of interest are very sparse, they may have little value. Even with denser coverage, aggregated measurements may not produce good estimates if sufficient spatial coverage is not achieved. In either case, local action goals will not be met, and meeting science goals will be challenging. This suggests that networks of low-accuracy sensors carried by volunteers (like those deployed in the Sensing Citizens study) may not be an ideal solution for large-scale collection. Instead, resources might be better spent developing low-cost, high-accuracy, fixed sensors, and building dense sensing networks that can meet the needs of both individuals and scientists.

Designing for Local Action

Because environmental problems usually arise from proximity to industrial activity, the citizens involved in action campaigns typically have lower average income and education levels than stereotypical "expert amateurs". As a result, action organizations often value science activities as opportunities for education and community engagement. Given the challenges associated with obtaining high-quality and high-coverage data via citizen collection, citizen action campaigns may benefit from alternative models that reduce the dependency between data collection and engagement. Rather than relying on citizen participants to gather essential baseline data, these organizations may be better off collecting data via other means, and creating opportunities for public participation on top of that data.

CONCLUSION

In this paper, we have examined the citizen science experience from the perspective of citizen participants. Drawing on four interlocking qualitative studies and technological interventions, we have identified a number of ways in which citizen motivations, capacity, and goals are poorly aligned with scientific agendas. The reality on the ground was far from the commonly held view that citizen science systems are a win-win for citizens and science. Rather, data acquisition involves complex multi-dimensional tradeoffs, and efforts that fail to consider these tradeoffs can result in data that is not useful to either citizens or science. We illustrated these tradeoffs with a framework of citizen science genres, which can inform priorities for intervention and invention. In light of these findings, technologies and participatory methods that can bridge the gap between citizen and scientific stakeholders represent a promising goal for citizen science research.

ACKNOWLEDGMENTS

We gratefully acknowledge the support of Brian Beveridge, Margaret Gordon, Cassandra Martin, and all of our other collaborators at the West Oakland Environmental Indicators Project (WOEIP), as well as Tony Marks-Block and the staff and students at the East Bay Academy for Young Scientists (EBAYS). We also thank our Common Sense collaborators Neil Kumar, Alan Mainwaring, Chris Myers, Steven Rousso-Schindler, and Sushmita Subramanian for their contributions to the technological interventions. We are grateful to Intel for its generous support for this work.

REFERENCES

1. John C. Abbott and Damon Broglie. 2005. OdonataCentral. com: a model for the web-based delivery of natural history information and citizen science. *American Entomologist* 51, 4: 240–243.
2. Tarek Abdelzaher, Yaw Anokwa, Péter Boda, Jeff Burke, Deborah Estrin, Leonidas Guibas, Aman Kansal, Samuel Madden, and Jim Reich. 2007. Mobiscopes for human spaces. *IEEE Pervasive Computing* 6, 2: 20–29. https://doi.org/10.1109/MPRV.2007.38
3. AirCasting.org. *The AirCasting Platform*. Retrieved July 22, 2016 from http://aircasting.org/
4. AirQualityEgg.com. *Air Quality Egg: Community-led Sensing Network*. Retrieved July 22, 2016 from http://airqualityegg.com/
5. Paul M. Aoki, R.J. Honicky, Alan Mainwaring, Chris Myers, Eric Paulos, Sushmita Subramanian, and Allison Woodruff. 2009. A Vehicle for Research: Using Street Sweepers to Explore the Landscape of Environmental Community Action. *Proceedings of the SIGCHI Conference on Human Factors in Computing Systems (CHI '09)*: 375–384. https://doi.org/10.1145/1518701.1518762
6. Philip Bell, Bruce Lewenstein, Andrew W. Shouse, and Michael A. Feder (eds.). 2009. *Learning Science in Informal Environments*. Committee on Learning Science in Informal Environments; Board on Science Education; Center for Education; Division of Behavioral and Social Sciences and Education. National Academies Press, Washington, D.C. Retrieved July 15, 2016 from http://www.nap.edu/catalog/12190
7. Hugh Beyer and Karen Holtzblatt. 1997. *Contextual Design: Defining Customer-Centered Systems*. Morgan Kaufmann, San Francisco, CA, USA.
8. Benjamin Bratton and Natalie Jeremijenko. 2008. *Suspicious Images, Latent Interfaces*. Architectural League of New York, New York.
9. Karin Knorr Cetina. 1999. *Epistemic Cultures: How the Sciences Make Knowledge*. Harvard University Press, Cambridge, MA.
10. Jeffrey P. Cohn. 2008. Citizen Science: Can Volunteers Do Real Research? *BioScience* 58, 3: 192. https://doi.org/10.1641/B580303
11. Committee on Air Quality Management in the United States; Board on Environmental Studies and Toxicology; Board on Atmospheric Sciences and Climate; Division on Earth and Life Studies; National Research Council. 2004. *Air Quality Management in the United States*. National Academies Press, Washington, D.C. Retrieved July 15, 2016 from http://www.nap.edu/catalog/10728
12. Caren B. Cooper, Janis Dickinson, Tinas Phillips, and Rick Bonney. 2007. Citizen science as a tool for conservation in residential ecosystems. *Ecology and Society* 12, 2.
13. Jason Corburn. 2005. *Street science: community knowledge and environmental health justice*. MIT Press, Cambridge, MA.
14. Steve Costa, Meena Palaniappan, Arlene K. Wong, Jeremy Hays, Clara Landeiro, and Jane Rongerude. 2002. Neighborhood knowledge for change: The West Oakland environmental indicators project.
15. Dana Cuff, Mark Hansen, and Jerry Kang. 2008. Urban sensing: Out of the Woods. *Communications of the ACM* 51, 3: 24–33. https://doi.org/10.1145/1325555.1325562
16. Pingkuan Di, Carolyn Suer, Greg Harris, Bonnie Soriano, Michele Houghton, Nicole Dolney, Andy Alexis, Chengfeng Wang, Shuming Du, and Alvaro Alvarado. 2008. Diesel Particulate Matter Health Risk Assessment for the West Oakland Community. Retrieved July 15, 2016 from http://www.arb.ca.gov/ch/communities/ra/westoakland/westoakland.htm
17. Carl DiSalvo, Marti Louw, Julina Coupland, and MaryAnn Steiner. 2009. Local issues, local uses. In *Proceeding of the ACM Conference on Creativity and Cognition (C&C '09)*, 245–254. https://doi.org/10.1145/1640233.1640271
18. Carl DiSalvo, Phoebe Sengers, and Hrönn Brynjarsdóttir. 2010. Mapping the landscape of sustainable HCI. In *Proceedings of the SIGCHI Conference on Human Factors in Computing Systems (CHI '10)* (CHI '10), 1975–1984. https://doi.org/10.1145/1753326.1753625
19. Paul Dourish. 2010. HCI and environmental sustainability. In *Proceedings of the ACM Conference on Designing Interactive Systems (DIS '10)* (DIS '10), 1–10. https://doi.org/10.1145/1858171.1858173
20. Sam Droege. 2007. Just because you paid them doesn't mean their data are better. In *Citizen Science Toolkit Conference*, 13–26.
21. Dick Duker, Michael Basso, Kurt Malone, Ken Crysler, and Mark Stoelting. 2010. 2009 Air Monitoring Network Report.
22. Prabal Dutta, Paul M. Aoki, Neil Kumar, Alan Mainwaring, Chris Myers, Wesley Willett, and Allison Woodruff. 2009. Common Sense: participatory urban sensing using a network of handheld air quality monitors. In *Proceedings of the ACM Conference on*

Embedded Networked Sensor Systems (SenSys '09), 349–350. https://doi.org/10.1145/1644038.1644095

23. EPA. 2012. Volunteer Monitor's Guide to Quality Assurance Project Plans. *Environmental Protection*, 841: 1–2.
24. Fred N. Finley and M. Cecilia Pocoví. 2000. Considering the scientific method of inquiry. *Inquiring into Inquiry Learning and Teaching in Science*: 47–62.
25. Danaë Stanton Fraser, Hilary Smith, Ella Tallyn, Dave Kirk, Steve Benford, Duncan Rowland, Mark Paxton, Sara Price, and Geraldine Fitzpatrick. 2005. The SENSE Project: A Context-inclusive Approach to Studying Environmental Science Within and Across Schools. In *Proceedings of the Conference on Computer Support for Collaborative Learning (CSCL '05)* (CSCL '05), 155–159.
26. Carl Hartung, Adam Lerer, Yaw Anokwa, Clint Tseng, Waylon Brunette, and Gaetano Borriello. 2010. Open Data Kit: Tools to Build Information Services for Developing Regions. In *Proceedings of the ACM/IEEE Conference on Information and Communication Technologies and Development (ICTD '10)* (ICTD '10). https://doi.org/10.1145/2369220.2369236
27. Jeffrey Heer, Fernanda B Viégas, and Martin Wattenberg. 2007. Voyagers and Voyeurs: Supporting Asynchronous Collaborative Information Visualization. In *Proceedings of the SIGCHI Conference on Human Factors in Computing Systems (CHI '07)* (CHI '07), 1029–1038. https://doi.org/10.1145/1240624.1240781
28. R.J. Honicky, Eric A. Brewer, Eric Paulos, and Richard White. 2008. N-SMARTS: Networked Suite of Mobile Atmospheric Real-time Sensors. In *Proceedings of the SIGCOMM workshop on Networked Systems for Developing Regions (NSDR '08)*, 25–30. https://doi.org/10.1145/1397705.1397713
29. Alan Irwin. 1995. *Citizen Science: A Study of People, Expertise and Sustainable Development.* Routledge, London.
30. Joseph "Jofish" Kaye, David Holstius, Edmund Seto, Brittany Eddy, and Michael Ritter. 2012. Using NFC phones to track water purification in Haiti. In *Extended Abstracts of the SIGCHI Conference on Human Factors in Computing Systems* (CHI '12 Extended Abstracts), 677–690. https://doi.org/10.1145/2212776.2212839
31. Sunyoung Kim, Jennifer Mankoff, and Eric Paulos. 2013. Sensr. In *Proceedings of the ACM Conference on Computer Supported Cooperative Work (CSCW '13)* (CSCW '13), 1453–1462. https://doi.org/10.1145/2441776.2441940
32. Tracy Lee, Michael S. Quinn, and Danah Duke. 2006. Citizen, science, highways, and wildlife: Using a web-based GIS to engage citizens in collecting wildlife information. *Ecology and Society* 11, 1.
33. Kurt Luther, Scott Counts, Kristin B. Stecher, Aaron Hoff, and Paul Johns. 2009. Pathfinder: An Online Collaboration Environment for Citizen Scientists. In *Proceedings of the SIGCHI Conference on Human Factors in Computing Systems (CHI '09)* (CHI '09), 239–248. https://doi.org/10.1145/1518701.1518741
34. Meredith Minkler and Nina Wallerstein (eds.). 2011. *Community-Based Participatory Research for Health: From Process to Outcomes*. Jossey-Bass.
35. Greg Niemeyer, Antero Garcia, and Reza Naima. 2009. Black cloud: patterns towards da future. *Proceedings of the ACM International Conference on Multimedia*: 1073–1082. https://doi.org/10.1145/1631272.1631514
36. Oded Nov, Ofer Arazy, and David Anderson. 2014. Scientists@Home: What Drives the Quantity and Quality of Online Citizen Science Participation? *PLoS ONE* 9, 4: e90375. https://doi.org/10.1371/journal.pone.0090375
37. Gwen Ottinger. 2010. Buckets of resistance: Standards and the effectiveness of citizen science. *Science, Technology & Human Values* 35, 2: 244–270.
38. Meena Palaniappan, Diana Wu, and Jacki Kohleriter. 2003. *Clearing the Air: Reducing Diesel Pollution in West Oakland.* Pacific Institute, Oakland, CA. Retrieved July 26, 2016 from http://pacinst.org/publication/clearing-the-air/
39. Eric Paulos, R.J. Honicky, and Ben Hooker (eds.). 2009. Citizen Science: Enabling Participatory Urbanism. *IGI Global.* https://doi.org/10.4018/978-1-60566-152-0.ch028
40. Danial Qaurooni, Ali Ghazinejad, Inna Kouper, and Hamid Ekbia. 2016. Citizens for Science and Science for Citizens: The View from Participatory Design. In *Proceedings of the 2016 CHI Conference on Human Factors in Computing Systems* (CHI '16), 1822–1826. https://doi.org/10.1145/2858036.2858575
41. Sasank Reddy, Gong Chen, Brian Fulkerson, Sung Jin Kim, Unkyu Park, Nathan Yau, Junghoo Cho, Mark Hansen, and John Heidemann. 2007. Sensor-Internet Share and Search — Enabling Collaboration of Citizen Scientists. *ACM Workshop on Data Sharing and Interoperability on the World-wide Sensor Web*, Section 3: 11–16.
42. Dirk S. Schmeller, Pierre Yves Henry, Romain Julliard, Bernd Gruber, Jean Clobert, Frank Dziock, Szabolcs Lengyel, Piotr Nowicki, Eszter D??ri, Eduardas Budrys, Tiiu Kull, Kadri Tali, Bianca Bauch,

Josef Settele, Chris Van Swaay, Andrej Kobler, Valerija Babij, Eva Papastergiadou, and Klaus Henle. 2009. Advantages of Volunteer-Based Biodiversity Monitoring in Europe. *Conservation Biology* 23, 2: 307–316. https://doi.org/10.1111/j.1523-1739.2008.01125.x

43. S Andrew Sheppard and Loren Terveen. 2011. Quality is a Verb : The operationalization of data quality in a citizen science community. *Proceedings of the International Symposium on Wikis and Open Collaboration (WikiSym '11)*: 29–38. https://doi.org/10.1145/2038558.2038565
44. K Shilton, N Ramanathan, S Reddy, V Samanta, J Burke, D Estrin, M Hansen, and M Srivastava. 2008. Participatory Design of Sensing Networks: Strengths and Challenges. In *Proceedings of the Conference on Participatory Design* (PDC '08), 282–285.
45. Jennifer L. Shirk, Heidi L. Ballard, Candie C. Wilderman, Tina Phillips, Andrea Wiggins, Rebecca Jordan, Ellen McCallie, Mathew Minarchek, bruce C. Lewenstein, Marianne E. Krasny, and Rick Bonney. 2012. Public participation in scientific research: a framework for intentional design. *Ecology and Society* 17, 2: 29. https://doi.org/10.5751/ES-04705-170229
46. Scott A. Snook. 2002. *Friendly Fire*. Princeton University Press, Princeton, NJ.
47. Susan Leigh Star and James R. Griesemer. 1989. Institutional Ecology, `Translations' and Boundary Objects: Amateurs and Professionals in Berkeley's Museum of Vertebrate Zoology, 1907-39. *Social Studies of Science* 19, 3: 387–420. https://doi.org/10.1177/030631289019003001
48. H. Tangmunarunkit, J. Kang, Z. Khalapyan, J. Ooms, N. Ramanathan, D. Estrin, C. K. Hsieh, B. Longstaff, S. Nolen, J. Jenkins, C. Ketcham, J. Selsky, F. Alquaddoomi, and D. George. 2015. Ohmage: A General and Extensible End-to-End Participatory Sensing Platform. *ACM Transactions on Intelligent Systems and Technology* 6, 3: 1–21. https://doi.org/10.1145/2717318
49. Sylvia Noble Tesh. 2000. *Uncertain Hazards: Environmental Activists and Scientific Proof.* Cornell University Press.
50. Jonathan E. Thompson. 2016. Crowd-sourced air quality studies: A review of the literature & portable sensors. *Trends in Environmental Analytical Chemistry* 11: 23–34. https://doi.org/10.1016/j.teac.2016.06.001
51. Deborah J. Trumbull, Rick Bonney, Derek Bascom, and Anna Cabral. 2000. Thinking scientifically during participation in a citizen-science project. *Science Education* 84, 2: 265–275. https://doi.org/10.1002/(SICI)1098-237X(200003)84:2<265::AID-SCE7>3.0.CO;2-5
52. L.S. Vygotsky. 1980. *Mind in Society: The Development of Higher Psychological Processes*. Harvard University Press. Retrieved from https://books.google.fr/books?id=Irq913lEZ1QC
53. Max Weber. 1949. "Objectivity" in social science and social policy. *The methodology of the social sciences* 78: 50–112.
54. Andrea Wiggins and Kevin Crowston. 2011. From Conservation to Crowdsourcing: A Typology of Citizen Science. In *Hawaii International Conference on System Sciences*, 1–10. https://doi.org/10.1109/HICSS.2011.207
55. Andrea Wiggins and Kevin Crowston. 2012. Goals and Tasks: Two Typologies of Citizen Science Projects. In *Hawaii International Conference on System Sciences*, 3426–3435. https://doi.org/10.1109/HICSS.2012.295
56. Candie C. Wilderman. 2007. Models of Community Science: Design Lessons From the Field. In *Citizen Science Toolkit Conference*.
57. Wesley Willett, Paul Aoki, Neil Kumar, Sushmita Subramanian, and Allison Woodruff. 2010. Common sense community: Scaffolding mobile sensing and analysis for novice users. In *International Conference on Pervasive Computing*, 301–318. https://doi.org/10.1007/978-3-642-12654-3_18
58. Allison Woodruff, Jay Hasbrouck, and Sally Augustin. 2008. A Bright Green Perspective on Sustainable Choices. In *Proceedings of the SIGCHI Conference on Human Factors in Computing Systems (CHI '08)*, 313–322. https://doi.org/10.1145/1357054.1357109

Providing Online Crisis Information: An Analysis of Official Sources during the 2014 Carlton Complex Wildfire

Apoorva Chauhan
Department of Computer Science
Utah State University
apoorva.chauhan@aggiemail.usu.edu

Amanda Lee Hughes
Department of Computer Science
Utah State University
amanda.hughes@usu.edu

ABSTRACT
Using the 2014 Carlton Complex Wildfire as a case study, we examine who contributes official information online during a crisis event, and the timeliness and relevance of the information provided. We identify and describe the communication behaviors of four types of official information sources (Event Based Resources, Local Responders, Local News Media, and Cooperating Agencies), and collect message data from each source's website, public Facebook page, and/or Twitter account. The data show that the Local News Media provided the highest quantity of relevant information and the timeliest information. Event Based Resources shared the highest percentage of relevant information, however, it was often unclear who managed these resources and the credibility of the information. Based on these findings, we offer suggestions for how providers of official crisis information might better manage their online communications and ways that the public can find more timely and relevant online crisis information from official sources.

Author Keywords
Social computing; social media; crisis informatics; wildfire; risk communication.

ACM Classification Keywords
H.5.3 Groups & Organization Interfaces—collaborative computing, computer-supported cooperative work, organizational design

INTRODUCTION
Timely and accurate communication of official information is a vital component of managing any emergency or crisis event [17,19,29,44]. We define "official information" as that information whose source is perceived by the public as more authoritative and/or trustworthy. Effective official information can provide members of the public with lifesaving protective measures, facilitate relief and recovery efforts, and reduce anxiety and fears [32,38,49]. This information may be distributed by emergency response agencies (e.g., fire and police departments, emergency management organizations, non-profit disaster relief groups), public officials (e.g., city mayors, governors), public works organizations (e.g., transportation authorities, utility companies), or the broadcast news media [10].

Permission to make digital or hard copies of all or part of this work for personal or classroom use is granted without fee provided that copies are not made or distributed for profit or commercial advantage and that copies bear this notice and the full citation on the first page. Copyrights for components of this work owned by others than the author(s) must be honored. Abstracting with credit is permitted. To copy otherwise, or republish, to post on servers or to redistribute to lists, requires prior specific permission and/or a fee. Request permissions from Permissions@acm.org.
CHI 2017, May 06 - 11, 2017, Denver, CO, USA
Copyright is held by the owner/author(s). Publication rights licensed to ACM.
ACM 978-1-4503-4655-9/17/05...$15.00
DOI: http://dx.doi.org/10.1145/3025453.3025627

A variety of traditional mechanisms exist for distributing official information during a crisis event, including broadcast media (television, radio, and newspaper), sirens, phone messages, face-to-face interactions, and community meetings [16]. In addition, online media (websites, blogs, email, and various forms of social media) have introduced communication mechanisms that support more timely and wide-spread interaction with the public [6,11,15,21]. However, as online communication options continue to proliferate, decisions around how to best communicate official information to the online public have become increasingly difficult. Decisions require knowledge about the capabilities and limitations of each online media type, the affected audience, and the circumstances of the crisis event. Providers of official information must also consider their ability to use and maintain each online communication channel. Similarly, it can be challenging for members of the public to know where to look for official online information and to understand what information can be trusted amidst a flood of socially-generated data [2].

To better understand and address these challenges, we examine how providers of official information used multiple online media during the 2014 Carlton Complex Wildfire. We identify and categorize the types of sources that provided official information in this context and describe their features and communication behaviors. We also examine the relevance and timeliness of the information these sources provide. We conclude with suggestions for how providers of official crisis information might better manage their online communications and ways that the public can find more timely and relevant online crisis information from official sources.

BACKGROUND

Online Media Use in Crisis
This research engages in a *crisis informatics* [8,23] line of inquiry that turns a critical eye to the complex socio-

technical information environment that surrounds a crisis event. In this context, scholars have examined the role online media (and in particular social media) play around many crisis events, including both natural (e.g., 2004 Indian Ocean Tsunami [20], 2005 Hurricane Katrina [4,30], 2012 Hurricane Sandy [13,27], and 2013 Colorado floods [5]) and man-made (e.g., 2007 Virginia Tech shooting [23], 2010 Deepwater Horizon Oil Spill [41], and 2013 Boston Marathon Bombing [9,43]) disasters. Through online media, those affected by a crisis event converge online to seek and share information and assist in response efforts [12] regardless of location and more quickly than what was previously possible [22]. Official emergency responders and other providers of official information increasingly use online media to communicate and interact with the public that they serve and to gather information that can be used in their efforts [6,11,13,15,42]. In turn, members of the public can find, generate, and distribute online crisis information as they seek to engage with others and understand how a crisis event affects them [21,25,28,36].

Official Information through Online Media

A growing body of research examines how providers of official information use online media to convey their messages [1,6,13,15,26,43]. Social media, in particular, have made emergency responders reconsider the traditional one-way communication model—where they only push information to the public—in favor of a more interactive two-way communication model [11,24]. Through online media, providers of official information can engage in communication with the public, which can help distribute information more quickly and directly [6]. Researchers hypothesize that this two-way communication may result in the exchange of higher quality information and reduced reliance on broadcast media to distribute official crisis communications [11]. Consequently, in this research, we seek to understand whether emergency responders provided better information (in terms of relevance, quantity, and timeliness) around the Carlton Complex Wildfire than broadcast media sources.

Providing timely official information online is important because people affected by a crisis will seek information elsewhere if they cannot find it from official sources [31]. In seeking information from non-official sources, people may act on information that is incomplete or inaccurate. In offering timely, accurate information, providers of official information can also play an important role in mitigating the spread of rumor during crisis events [1]. However, the adoption of tools like social media into emergency responder practice pose many socio-technical challenges such as issues of credibility and trust, lack of support from management, organizational conflicts, poor tools, and a shortage of resources and training [3,11,15,26,33,39].

Despite much empirical work, we still know little about how online media fit into official crisis communication strategies [11,13]. Further, prior research is limited in that it tends to focus on how a single emergency responder or type of responder uses online media (typically a single platform) to communicate official information. In this paper, we seek to better understand the different types of official information providers and how they use multiple online platforms (i.e., websites, Facebook, and Twitter) to communicate crisis information. We also evaluate the relevance and timeliness of official online crisis information, to determine what online platforms and official sources provide the most relevant and timely information.

Event of Study – Carlton Complex Wildfire

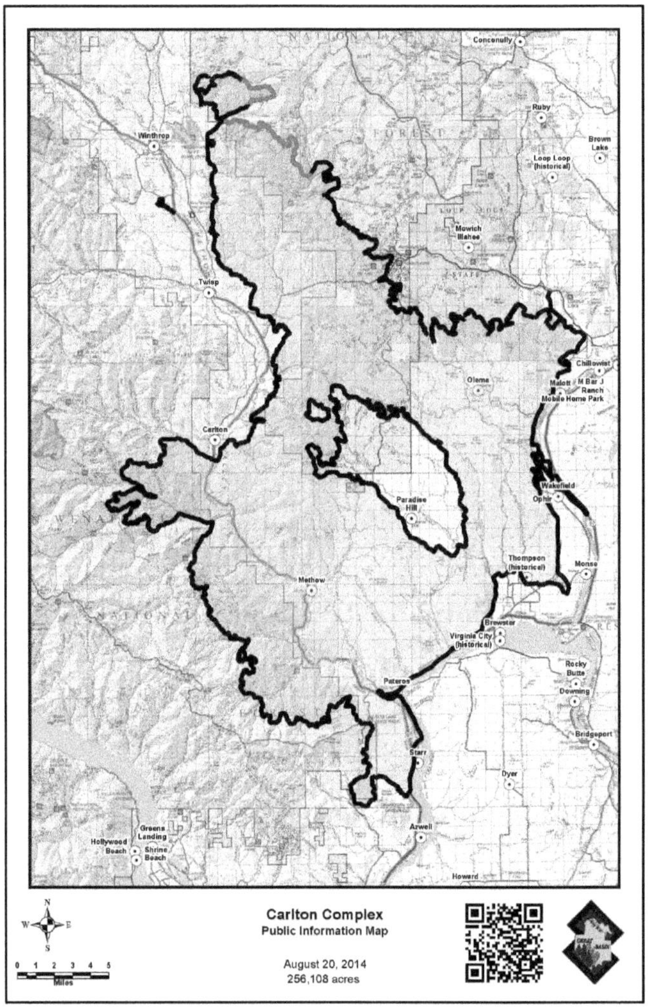

Figure 1. Carlton Complex Wildfire Perimeter Map for August 20, 2014 [46]

On July 14, 2014, lightning in the Methow River Valley started four wildfires: the Cougar Flat, French Creek, Gold Hike, and Stokes fires. These fires later merged (by July 20) to form the Carlton Complex Wildfire.

The Carlton Complex Wildfire burned 256,108 acres to become the largest wildfire in the history of the US state of Washington [18,34], affecting the cities and communities of Okanogan and Chelan counties (see Figure 1). The wildfire caused several closures, evacuations and power outages in and around the cities of Pateros, Malott, Brewster, Carlton, Methow, Twisp and Winthrop. The wildfire consumed more than 322 homes as well as 149 other structures and cost at least $60 million in damages [18]. On July 23, 2014, US President Barack Obama declared the Carlton Complex Wildfire a federal emergency disaster. The fire slowed due to rain on July 24, allowing 60% containment by July 26 [34]. Finally, the fire was 100% contained by August 24, 2014 [48].

METHOD

Identifying Official Information Sources

We began this research by investigating the Carlton Complex Wildfire and the circumstances surrounding the event. Primary sources included media coverage found through Google searches and InciWeb (an interagency all-risk incident web information management system that is run by the United States Forest Service). Through this investigation, we identified the geographic regions affected by the wildfire and many of the official information sources associated with the event (i.e., emergency responders and news media from the affected regions, cities, communities, and counties). Our purpose was to identify sources that those who were directly affected by the Wildfire would have turned to for official information. Names of many of the agencies who participated in the event response were obtained from the Carlton Complex Wildfire's InciWeb page [47]. We also found information sources by searching on "Carlton Complex Wildfire" using the Google, Facebook, and Twitter search engines. Finally, we uncovered additional official sources as we analyzed information sent from our initial list of sources. Using iterative sorting and clustering, we divided these official sources into four categories based on their purpose: 1) Event Based Resources, 2) Local Responders, 3) Local News Media, and 4) Cooperating Agencies. In total, we identified 8 Event Based Resources, 25 Local Responders, 7 Local News Media, and 5 Cooperating Agencies.

Event Based Resources

Event based resources were named after the Carlton Complex Wildfire and were dedicated to reporting information about it. An example of this resource type is the public *Carlton Complex Wildfire* Facebook page, which describes itself as a provider of "official fire information." These resources are of particular interest because while they appear to be sources of official information about the Wildfire, it was often unclear who actually maintained and posted the information found there. Event Based Resources have been mentioned in prior research [37], but not beyond noting that they exist and provide information specific to the crisis event they are associated with.

Local Responders

Local responders are the agencies of the affected cities and communities who were most directly involved in the Carlton Complex Wildfire response. Examples of Local Responders include the police, fire and emergency medical services of the affected region, and the emergency management agencies of the affected counties.

Local News Media (LNM)

Local news media include the broadcast media agencies of all the affected cities, communities, and counties. The area did not have a local television station, but they did have several newspapers and radio stations that maintained an online presence. We did not include media sources outside the immediately affected region in our dataset, though the Wildfire did receive national attention; non-local media sources tend to repeat information already conveyed by the local media but with less detail and frequency [40].

Cooperating Agencies

Cooperating agencies are those agencies that assisted in the response to the Carlton Complex Wildfire, yet their assistance was usually on the periphery and not as central as Local Responders. This category includes non-profit service organizations (e.g., American Red Cross), federal agencies (e.g., Bureau of Indian Affairs, Bureau of Land Management, and Fish and Wildlife service), and state agencies (e.g., Washington State Department of Natural Resources, and Washington State Department of Transportation).

Data Collection

Next, we determined the websites, public Facebook pages, and Twitter accounts that belonged to each of the official information sources identified above—if they existed. We assumed that if a webpage or social media page or account could not be reasonably found via a basic web search (or a couple of basic web searches) using the Google, Facebook, and Twitter search engines, it was unlikely to have served as a useful source of official information around the event. Table 1 shows the number of websites, Facebook pages, and Twitter accounts found for each official information source type.

Official Sources	# Websites	# FB Pages	# Twitter Accounts	Total
Event Based Resources	1	5	2	8
Local Responders	20	15	7	42
Local News Media	4	7	7	18
Cooperating Agencies	5	4	5	14

Table 1: Number of Websites, Facebook (FB) Pages, and Twitter Accounts that belong to Official Information Sources

We then collected all the Facebook posts and tweets of these official information sources using the Facebook Graph API and the Twitter Search API respectively. The relevant pages (those concerning the Carlton Complex Wildfire) from the identified websites were downloaded and stored as pdf documents for coding and analysis. The data collection timeframe was July 14 – Aug 24, 2014. We chose these dates because the Carlton Complex Wildfire began on July 14, 2014 and was reported 100% contained on August 24, 2014. Table 2 lists the number of websites, pages, or accounts found, and the number of pages, posts, or tweets collected for all three online media.

Online Media	# Websites, Pages or Accounts	# Pages, Posts or Tweets	# On-Topic Pages, Posts or Tweets
Websites	30	83	83
Facebook	31	2,232	1,576
Twitter	21	3,416	2,466

Table 2. Number of Websites, Facebook Pages, & Twitter Accounts and the Related Pages, Posts, & Tweets Analyzed

Data Analysis

We began data analysis by reading all the collected pages, posts, and tweets to determine which were about the Carlton Complex Wildfire. All coding schemes were iteratively developed between the two authors (both experienced coders). Each author labeled the posts separately, after which the results were compared. Any conflicts were collaboratively discussed until consensus could be reached. Messages relevant to this event, such as size of the wildfire, wildfire containment, wildfire progression, evacuation related information, weather and smoke conditions, donations, fundraisers, etc., were marked as on-topic. Messages that were irrelevant to this event, such as updates about other wildfires (that were burning at the same time as the Carlton Complex Wildfire but did not directly impact the same area), construction closures, and other local news, such as information about thefts, road accidents, etc., were marked as off-topic. Table 2 lists the total numbers of on-topic pages, posts, and tweets analyzed.

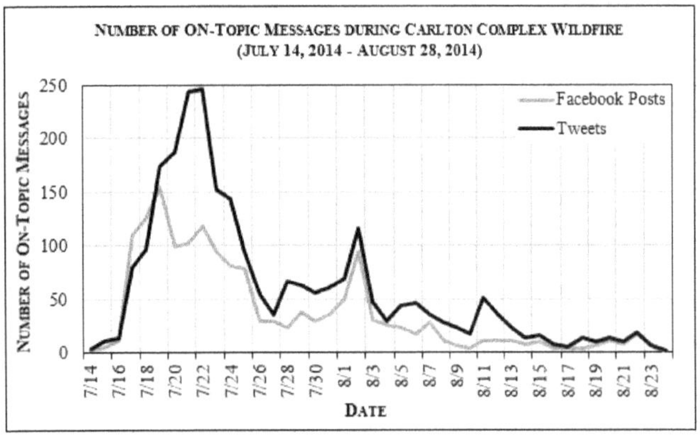

Figure 2: Number of On-Topic Messages during the Carlton Complex Wildfire (July 14, 2014 – August 24, 2014)

Figure 2 shows the number of on-topic Facebook posts, and tweets during each day of the collection timeframe. The significant increase in on-topic posts around July 22 related to the growing size of the wildfire, which resulted in mass evacuations and property damage. The spike on August 2 was caused by another fire—the Rising Eagle Road Fire—that started on August 1 [50]. Due to its proximity, this fire was later included in the Carlton Complex Wildfire [51].

To better trace when information was available and who was providing it across the online media in our datasets, we identified two important pieces of public information typically conveyed during a wildfire event: 1) the number of homes destroyed by the fire and 2) the current fire evacuation level for the affected communities. Information regarding the number of houses consumed by a wildfire indicates the effect of the fire on the community and the severity of the wildfire when compared to other (or previously experienced) fires. Information regarding evacuation levels can inform protective measures and save lives [45]. In addition to their importance, we used these two pieces of information because they were easier to track compared to other more variable types of information such as the location of evacuation centers, donation drop-off areas, roads/forest closures, etc. We read and coded every tweet, post, and webpage to determine if they contained information about the number of houses consumed by the wildfire and/or fire evacuation levels.

Next, we plotted this data by time for the reports of homes burned and evacuation levels (reported later in this paper). These plots allowed us to cluster the data around particular pieces of information within the larger information stream, such as a report of a level 3 evacuation or a report that 100 homes had burned. These clusters were then used to determine what information source first reported each piece of information in our data set. Finally, we also determined who posted the most relevant (on-topic) information as well as the highest percentage of relevant information.

FINDINGS

We report our findings in two sections. The first section describes the characteristics and information sharing behaviors of the four types of official information sources identified in this study. The second section traces official reports of the number of houses burned and evacuation levels during the Carlton Complex Wildfire.

Official Information Sources

Event Based Resources

Event Based Resources refer to online media that were specifically dedicated to the Carlton Complex Wildfire. The name of each of these resources typically made them easier to find and helped people know that they offered information about the Carlton Complex Wildfire. Some resources were named directly after the Wildfire (e.g., *@CarltonComplex*), while some were named after the Wildfire's location (e.g., *Methow Valley Fire Information*). Other resources had names that described their purpose. For example, the *Carlton Complex, WA Wildfire Lost and Found Pets-NDARRT* Facebook page was dedicated to helping pets displaced by the Wildfire. In another case, we discovered that the administrator of the *@CarltonComplex* Twitter account had stopped updates once the fire had subsided and started channeling communications through the *@upperfallsfire* Twitter account:

> **@CarltonComplex via Twitter** (08/11/2014 04:23pm): In an effort to consolidate fire information sources, @CarltonComplex will no longer be updated. Follow @upperfallsfire for updates.

The Upper Falls Fire was another prominent fire in the area at the time. Because of the message above, we suspected that the *@upperfallsfire* Twitter account might also be a source for information about the Carlton Complex Wildfire. Indeed, we found that 37.8% (see Table 3) of the messages posted by *@upperfallsfire* were relevant to the Carlton Complex Wildfire, and so we included it in our dataset as an Event Based Resource.

Name	First Post	Last Post	# On-Topic
Website			
Carlton Complex Assistance Network	07/27/14	03/26/15	4
Facebook Pages			
Carlton Complex Wildfire	07/17/14	08/11/14	172 (89.1%)
Carlton Complex (Camp)	07/20/14	09/16/15	2 (100%)
Carlton Complex Fire Relief & Assistance Network	07/23/14	10/15/16	47 (52.2%)
Methow Valley Fire Information	07/17/14	08/25/16	88 (97.8%)
Carlton Complex, WA Wildfire Lost and Found Pets-NDARRT	07/18/14	10/14/16	96 (88.1%)
Twitter Accounts			
@CarltonComplex	07/19/14	08/11/14	406 (95.3%)
@upperfallsfire	08/06/14	08/23/14	17 (37.8%)

Table 3: Event Based Resources and On-Topic Posts

Most (5 of 8) of the Event Based Resources did not provide information about who or what organization managed these websites and social media accounts. Thus, it was not always clear whether the information provided was accurate or who was accountable for the information. One resource (the *@CarltonComplex* Twitter account) was described as a source of "official information" but no further evidence was offered around who was running the account. In another case, we discovered that the US Forest Service managed one of the Event Based Resources (the *Carlton Complex Wildfire* Facebook page). However, this information was only discovered indirectly through a Facebook post by a Local News Media agency. Because these Event Based Resources were so tied to the Carlton Complex Wildfire (unlike the other resources in our dataset), we tracked how long these resources remained active following the event (see Table 3). We defined event based resources as 'active' if they had some kind of recent activity on their pages or accounts within the past year (2016). This is interesting because event based resources, in most cases, were created to provide information about a particular event. If they remain active today (after 2+ years), it is evident that their purpose has changed over time. Findings show that some (3 of 8) resources became inactive within two months after 100% containment of Wildfire. A few (2 of 8) resources were still active up to a year following the event, while the last three resources remain active today (having most recently posted in August and October 2016). These three active Event Based Resources have since broadened their scope of concern beyond the Carlton Complex Wildfire to include wildfire events at the county and/or state level.

Online Media Type	# On-Topic Messages
Facebook	405 (83.7%)
Twitter	423 (89.8%)

Table 4: Average Number of On-Topic Posts by Event Based Resources on Facebook and Twitter

Event Based Resources averaged the most on-topic Facebook (83.7%) and Twitter (89.8%) posts of any official information type. Even though none of these Event Based Resources existed prior to the Wildfire, they attracted much interest in a short amount of time. The most popular Facebook Page—*Carlton Complex Wildfire*—collected over 10,500 likes. The *Carlton Complex Wildfire* Facebook Page (172 on-topic posts) and *@CarltonComplex* Twitter account (406 on-topic tweets) were the most active Event Based Resources.

Local Responders

The dataset of Local Responders includes the official websites, Facebook pages, and Twitter accounts of the public officials, fire and police departments, and emergency management agencies of the affected area.

Different Local Responders have different jurisdictions. For example, a county agency has responsibilities around the entire county, whereas a city agency is responsible only for city activities. This difference is reflected in the online messages of these agencies:

> **Okanogan County Sheriff Office via Facebook** (07/19/2014 10:11am): Currently the information available to us is that there have been NO STATUS

CHANGES. Omak is still at Level 0 Okanogan is at Level 1 and Malott is at Level 3.

Winthrop Washington via Facebook (07/21/2014 12:37pm): The latest update is that Winthrop expects to have power restored by the weekend!

In the first post, the Okanogan County Sheriff Office offers information about three different cities that fall within their county. In the second post, Winthrop city officials provide information for the city of Winthrop only.

More than half of the online messages (72% Facebook posts and 56% tweets) posted by the Local Responders were wildfire-related (see Table 5). The *Okanogan County Sheriff Office* Facebook Page (189 on-topic posts) and *Chelan County Emergency Management* Twitter account (700 on-topic tweets) were the most active.

Online Media Type	# On-Topic Messages
Facebook	224 (72.0%)
Twitter	757 (56.0%)

Table 5: Average Number of On-Topic Posts by Local Responders on Facebook and Twitter

Local News Media

Our Local News Media dataset consists of the official websites, Facebook pages, and Twitter accounts of the online local news media (e.g., Okanogan Valley Gazette-Tribune, Quad City Herald, and Methow Valley News) and the online local radio stations (e.g., Okanogan County Amateur Radio Club W7ORC and KTRT 97.5 The Root). The Local News Media have a broader scope of concern compared to the Local Responders who were primarily dedicated to a specific aspect of the response effort. Thus, their websites, Facebook pages, and Twitter accounts posted a wide variety of information around the wildfires, including messages about the number of houses burned by wildfire, fire evacuation levels, local events, business closures, power outages/restoration, and road closures.

The Local News Media averaged the second highest number of on-topic messages, following the Event Based Resources. Table 6 shows that 79.5% Facebook posts and 80.3% tweets by Local News Media were on-topic. The *Methow Valley News* Facebook Page (479 On-Topic posts) and the *@MethowNews* Twitter account (442 On-Topic tweets) were the most active Local News Media.

Online Media Type	# On-Topic Messages
Facebook	910 (79.5%)
Twitter	937 (80.3%)

Table 6: Average Number of On-Topic Posts by Local News Media on Facebook and Twitter

Cooperating Agencies

Our dataset of Cooperating Agencies comprises the websites, Facebook pages, and Twitter accounts of service organizations, and federal and state agencies that supported the Wildfire response. Every agency in this category had a narrowly defined role and set of responsibilities with regard to the Carlton Complex Wildfire. For example, the Washington Department of Fish and Wildlife (WDFW) mostly posted about the effects of wildfire on natural habitats, whereas the Washington State Department of Transportation (WSDOT) posted about the effects of wildfire on transportation (e.g., road closures and detours).

Cooperating Agencies averaged the least on-topic Facebook (12.6%) and Twitter (38.9%) posts of any official information type (see Table 7). This low level of relevant content was likely because these agencies were less involved in the Carlton Complex Wildfire response efforts. The *Washington State Department of Natural Resources* Facebook page (32 on-topic posts) and *@waDNR_fire* Twitter account (221 on-topic tweets) were the most active Cooperating Agencies.

Online Media Type	# On-Topic Messages
Facebook	37 (12.6%)
Twitter	349 (38.9%)

Table 7: Average Number of On-Topic Posts by Cooperating Agencies on Facebook and Twitter

Relevance of Official Information Sources

Event Based Resources averaged the highest percentage of on-topic messages within their own message streams, followed by the Local News Media, Local Responders, and finally, Cooperating Agencies. This order reflects the role that each of these official information sources played in the response. The purpose of the Event Based Resources was to report information around the Wildfire. The Local News Media were heavily involved in distributing important crisis information to the public. Local Responders were responsible for much of the local response effort, but their reporting of the event was less significant, and once the Wildfire lessened in severity, many responders moved on to reporting other, unrelated types of information. Cooperating Agencies had the least relevant information, which is not surprising considering they were more peripherally involved with the Wildfire response efforts.

ANALYSIS OF ONLINE MEDIA CONTENT

Houses Consumed by Wildfire

First, we analyzed the number of houses consumed by the Carlton Complex Wildfire. This information can help city and government officials to estimate the damage caused by a fire. It is also useful for determining if a disaster qualifies for a federal emergency declaration and federal aid [7]. This information can also help affected citizens understand the severity of the fire, which in turn might affect their decision to take protective action or to evacuate.

We plotted the collected data (see Figure 3) to determine 1) how the information regarding houses consumed by wildfire was conveyed over time, and 2) the first reporters of the information. The graph depicts how the Wildfire temporally progressed, showing how reports of the number of houses burned changed from only a few houses on July 17 to around 300 houses on July 25—a span of only 8 days.

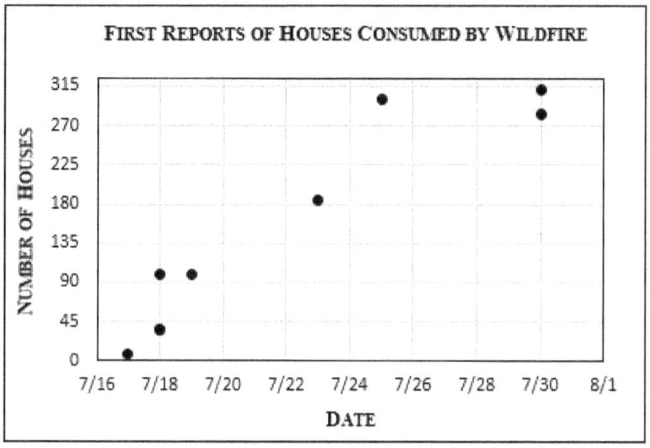

Figure 3. First Reports of the Number of Houses Consumed by the Carlton Complex Wildfire

Information around the number of houses burned was sometimes difficult to graph. In a few instances, agencies did not report the exact number of houses burned, but rather gave a range (e.g., 80-100 homes burned) or they described it using non-specific, approximate language (e.g., several homes burned). Such data is not represented in Figure 3.

Official Sources	# Web Pages	# FB Posts	# Tweets	Total
Event Based Resources	0	29	7	36
Local Responders	0	3	25	28
Local News Media	13	76	54	143
Cooperating Agencies	2	1	3	6

Table 8. Number of Official Web Pages, Facebook (FB) Posts, and Tweets that Reported the Number of Houses Consumed by the Carlton Complex Wildfire

Official Sources	# Web Posts	# FB Posts	# Tweets	Total
Event Based Resources	0	0	0	0
Local Responders	0	1	1	2
Local News Media	2	2	4	8
Cooperating Agencies	2	0	0	2

Table 9. First Reports of Houses Consumed by the Wildfire

Local News Media (143 posts) were the most active reporters for houses consumed by the wildfire (see Table 8). Most first reports of the number of houses consumed by fire came from the Local News Media (66.7%), and in most cases, the Local News Media reported this information via Twitter (see Table 9). This finding suggests that the official Twitter accounts of Local News Media sent information earlier than the other information resources in our dataset. However, care should be taken when applying this finding because the sample rate is low (N=12).

Fire Evacuation Levels

Next, we analyzed reports of fire evacuation levels during the Carlton Complex Wildfire. The evacuation level for a community is a critical (possibly lifesaving) piece of information. Here we analyze the messages regarding evacuation levels, the way these levels changed during the fire, and when they were reported to the public through the online media examined in this study. The evacuation levels for this wildfire ranged in severity from 0 to 3. Level 0 indicates no evacuations, while level 3 indicates immediate emergency evacuations.

To simplify our analysis, we considered fire evacuation level messages only for cities. We did not consider levels given for forests and roads because they were difficult to map to a particular geographic location for comparison. No fire evacuation levels were issued at the county level.

City	Number of Evacuation Level Messages
Winthrop	48
Carlton	38
Twisp	38
Pateros	33
Pleasant Valley	32
Brewster	23
Chiliwist	16
Omak	12
Okanogan City	11
Chelan	6
Malott	6
Manson	6
Tonasket	3
Union Valley	1

Table 10. Number of Evacuation Level Messages per City

We grouped our data based on geographic regions, creating a different group of data for each city affected by the Carlton Complex Wildfire. Table 10 shows the number of evacuation level messages for each of the 15 cities found in the data. The more severely a city was affected by the wildfire, the more evacuation level messages were issued.

Fire evacuation levels were always reported with respect to a specific geographic region. Unlike reports of the number of homes burned, evacuation level reports were always expressed in integer values (in the range 0-4), and were never reported in a range or in a descriptive way:

> **@CarltonComplex via Twitter** (07/21/2014 03:48pm): #CarltonComplex Urgent Update: Pleasant Valley area now under LEVEL 3 IMMEDIATE EVACUATION. Highway 20 closed between Twisp & Okanogan

The Local News Media were the most active reporters of fire evacuation levels (see Table 11).

Official Sources	# Web Pages	# FB Posts	# Tweets	Total
Event Based Resources	0	101	100	201
Local Responders	0	52	98	150
Local News Media	47	204	202	453
Cooperating Agencies	15	2	16	33

Table 11. Number of Official Web Pages, Facebook Posts, and Tweets that Contain Evacuation Level Information

Next, we mapped the data for each cities and identified the first reporters of each change in evacuation level. The Local News Media were the first to report 57.3% of the fire evacuation levels (see Table 12). The Local News Media reported most of this information (all but 3 messages) equally across Facebook and Twitter. Upon further investigation, we discovered that some of the Local News Media had linked their Facebook and Twitter accounts and many identical messages were pushed out over the two platforms at the same time. In this case, the official Twitter accounts and Facebook pages of Local News Media sent information earlier than the Local News Media's websites.

Official Sources	# Web Pages	# FB Posts	# Tweets	Total
Event Based Resources	0	7	4	11
Local Responders	0	9	1	10
Local News Media	3	18	18	39
Cooperating Agencies	8	0	0	8

Table 12. First Reports of Evacuation Levels for the 15 Cities Affected by the Carlton Complex Wildfire

Relevance of Provided Information

Using the data collected around the number of houses consumed by fire and the evacuation levels, the Local News Media provided the most relevant information in terms of quantity, followed by Event Based Resources, Local Responders, and lastly, Cooperating Agencies. Local News Media sources provided more than double the number of messages that the Event Based Resources provided. This finding demonstrates how much more involved the Local News Media were in sharing information, and as a result they may be a richer source of crisis information for the affected public.

DISCUSSION

In this paper, we identified four types of official information sources and analyzed the timeliness and relevance of the information these sources provided during the 2014 Carlton Complex Wildfire. This categorization better articulates the roles, interests, and responsibilities of different official information sources and helps explain what type of information emergency responders, members of the public, and researchers might expect from these sources. We now discuss broader implication of this research and offer recommendations for how to improve the effectiveness of official online crisis communications.

Timeliness of Official Information Sources

For both the number of houses consumed by fire and the evacuation levels, the Local News Media had the most first reports of this information. Earlier, we hypothesized that local responders would provide the most timely information because they now have more ability through online media to share information directly with the public through social media [11]. The data, however, disproves this hypothesis because it demonstrates that the Local News Media are still heavily relied upon to distribute timely information to the public in an online setting (at least for the Carlton Complex Wildfire).

Event Based Resources

We included Event Based Resources as sources of official information because we found that in many cases these resources either claimed to be a source of official information or they were managed by an official emergency response agency. In other cases, where "official" status was not so clear, the name of the online account tied it to the Carlton Complex Wildfire. So, at least in name, the account appeared to be official. Recent research has shown that official accounts can shape social media conversation and mitigate misinformation and false rumor around a crisis event [1]. Thus, understanding who manages these Event Based accounts, their purpose in creating these accounts, and the current intentions of account owners is important and would reveal much about the lifecycle of these accounts and their usefulness for crisis information seekers. To this end, we plan to study Event Based Resources more deeply in future crisis events.

Three of the Event Based Resources in this study continue to remain active long after the Wildfire for which they were originally created. These resources clearly filled an outstanding need in the community and continue to do so. Thus, Event Based Resources can serve another purpose in bringing community needs and challenges around a crisis event to the attention of a broader audience. As such, these resources may be a good place for emergency responders, humanitarian organizations, and volunteers to look for unmet crisis needs that they can help address. From a Human Computer Interaction (HCI) perspective, we might consider how we can better support the shifting purpose and role of a social media group or community over time. For instance, how can we design a platform that makes the history of an online community more transparent?

Toward More Effective Official Online Crisis Information

We suggest several ways that providers of official information can improve their communication efforts. First, information providers should clearly identify themselves and their purpose when using online media. Doing so lends credibility to the information source and gives the affected public someone to hold accountable for the quality of information [10]. Many of the Event Based Resources were managed by reputable emergency response agencies, but they never clearly identified themselves. Similarly, we could not identify the source for several Event Based Resources that made claims that they were official sources of information, whether through the name of the resource or through its description. We recommend that official emergency responders monitor these accounts to ensure that the information they provide is accurate, especially if the public sees them as a source of official information. Monitoring these accounts will allow emergency responders to adjust their own communications to correct misinformation or respond to requests for information. Responders may even point the public to these sources if the information they provide is credible and meets a particular need that cannot be met by the official response (e.g., helping reunite pets with their owners).

We also offer insight into how members of the public might choose information sources from the many available options to obtain better official information during a crisis event. Based on our findings, the Local News Media provided the timeliest information and the highest number of relevant messages around the event, which suggests that the Local News Media were the best source of general information about the Wildfire. While the Event Based Resources provided the highest percentage of relevant information, it was not always clear how trustworthy the information was. If members of the public are looking for a specific type of information (i.e., road closures), the best source of information is likely to be an official source more directly affiliated with that information (i.e., a transportation authority). Lastly, most social media platforms are open and anyone can create an account/page around a particular event or topic. One solution for helping the public understand which Event Based Resources are more authoritative is to verify the resource's account. On some social media platforms, accounts can be verified so that people know that the account is run by the entity that claims to own the account. However, this verification process can take considerable time to complete. The problem is that Event Based Resources are created in response to a specific event (usually unforeseen), which leaves no time to complete such a verification process before the account would need to be used. Streamlining the verification process, or perhaps allowing a new account to be directly linked to a previously verified account may be a possible technical solution to this problem.

Broader Implications

Though this research only looks at data from the Carlton Complex Wildfire, findings can also inform future research of crisis information more broadly. Specifically, this research unpacks who is providing official information during a crisis and identifies the different types of information each provides. This analysis lays the foundation for richer and more nuanced study of official crisis information sources, beyond assuming they all share similar motivations, behaviors, challenges, and scopes of concern—a simplifying assumption that much research in the domain makes. Better understanding of the types of official information available around a crisis and their features can also inform machine learning algorithms and text classifiers that seek to extract important crisis information from social media streams [14]. For example, a tool that automatically detects new Event Based Resources around an emerging crisis event could benefit both emergency responders and members of the public as they try to quickly assess the impact of the event.

Beyond the crisis context, this research also applies to other HCI domains where it is important to understand what online information is available and what online sources are credible. For example, the design considerations shared above around how to provide a more robust verification process for social media accounts and how to support the shifting purpose and role of a social media group over time are broadly applicable to more general use of any social media platform. As another example, social media accounts are created and used every day around different types of non-crisis events (e.g., political rallies, sporting events, celebrations, etc.), and Event Based Resources regularly appear during these events (i.e., a Twitter account created to report on a particular political election). Study of the characteristics and content of these event specific social media accounts (as was done in this study) can help researchers and the public better understand how to interpret and filter the information these accounts provide.

Limitations & Future Work

Our focus on online media limits what can be said about all the official information available to those affected by the Carlton Complex Wildfire. Further, we used trace online data in our analyses, which does not allow us to account for the intentions of those who provided the information. Future work could take a more comprehensive approach to mapping the public information space around a crisis event by including additional sources of official information such as briefings and public meetings, TV news media content, and physical information booths and boards. This information could be supplemented with interviews of official information providers. Together these data would allow researchers to create a more complete picture of how official information is created and shared around a crisis event and across both online and offline media platforms. Next, when designing this research, we considered conducting interviews with the public affected by this Wildfire to understand how the public used and perceived online official information, but too much time had passed. The challenge of collecting ephemeral data is a well-known problem in the disaster research domain [35]. Thus, our ongoing research will seek to develop interview protocols for obtaining timely feedback from populations affected by disaster events. Finally, we may also look at the information dissemination patterns for other types of events (such as terrorist attacks, hurricanes, etc.) in the future to see if findings from this research apply in different contexts.

CONCLUSION

By analyzing the online media posts of official information providers during the Carlton Complex Wildfire, we offer new empirical insight into who provides this information, how the information is provided, and the timeliness and relevance of the information. In particular, we note that the Local News Media continue to play a primary role in distributing official crisis information online despite new possibilities for emergency responders to share information directly with the public through social media. As online communications continue to proliferate, it becomes increasingly difficult for the public to sort through the deluge of available data to find credible crisis information that is relevant and helpful. This research is an important first step toward understanding what types of official online information is provided and how members of the public might find it.

REFERENCES

1. Cynthia Andrews, Elodie Fichet, Yuwei Ding, Emma S. Spiro, and Kate Starbird. 2016. Keeping Up with the Tweet-dashians: The Impact of "Official" Accounts on Online Rumoring. In *Proceedings of the 19th ACM Conference on Computer-Supported Cooperative Work & Social Computing* (CSCW '16), 452–465.
2. Lucinda Austin, Brooke Fisher Liu, and Yan Jin. 2012. How Audiences Seek Out Crisis Information: Exploring the Social-Mediated Crisis Communication Model. *Journal of Applied Communication Research* 40, 2: 188–207.
3. Rowena L. Briones, Beth Kuch, Brooke Fisher Liu, and Yan Yin. 2011. Keeping Up with the Digital Age: How the American Red Cross uses Social Media to Build Relationships. *Public Relations Review* 37, 1: 37–43.
4. Michael Crutcher and Matthew Zook. 2009. Placemarks and Waterlines: Racialized Cyberscapes in Post-Katrina Google Earth. *Geoforum* 40: 523–534.
5. Shideh Dashti, Leysia Palen, Mehdi P Heris, Kenneth M Anderson, Scott Anderson, and Jennings Anderson. 2014. Supporting Disaster Reconnaissance with Social Media Data: A Design-Oriented Case Study of the 2013 Colorado Floods. In *Proceedings of the Information Systems for Crisis Response and Management Conference (ISCRAM 20014).*
6. Sebastian Denef, Petra S. Bayerl, and Nico Kaptein. 2013. Social Media and the Police-Tweeting Practices of British Police Forces during the August 2011 Riots. In *Proceedings of the 2013 Conference on Human Factors in Computing Systems (CHI 2013)*, 3471–3480.
7. Gazette-Tribune. 2014. State Federal Delegation Backs Inslee's Request for Major Disaster Declaration. *Okanogan Valley Gazette-Tribune*. Retrieved April 27, 2016 from http://www.gazette-tribune.com/news/state-federal-delegation-backs-inslees-request-for-major-disaster-declaration/68353/
8. Chris Hagar and Caroline Haythornthwaite. 2005. Crisis, Farming & Community. *The Journal of Community Informatics* 1, 3: 41–52.
9. Y. Linlin Huang, Kate Starbird, Mania Orand, Stephanie A. Stanek, and Heather T. Pedersen. 2015. Connected Through Crisis: Emotional Proximity and the Spread of Misinformation Online. In *Proceedings of the 18th ACM Conference on Computer Supported Cooperative Work & Social Computing* (CSCW '15), 969–980.
10. Amanda L. Hughes and Apoorva Chauhan. 2015. Online Media as a Means to Affect Public Trust in Emergency Responders. In *Proceedings of the 2015 Information Systems for Crisis Response and Management Conference (ISCRAM 2015).*
11. Amanda L. Hughes and Leysia Palen. 2012. The Evolving Role of the Public Information Officer: An Examination of Social Media in Emergency Management. *Journal of Homeland Security and Emergency Management* 9, 1.
12. Amanda L. Hughes, Leysia Palen, Jeannette Sutton, Sophia B. Liu, and Sarah Vieweg. 2008. "Site-Seeing" in Disaster: An Examination of On-Line Social Convergence. In *Proceedings of the Information Systems for Crisis Response and Management Conference (ISCRAM 2008).*
13. Amanda L. Hughes, Lise Ann St. Denis, Leysia Palen, and Kenneth M. Anderson. 2014. Online Public

Communications by Police & Fire Services during the 2012 Hurricane Sandy. In *Proceedings of the 2014 International Conference on Human Factors in Computing Systems (CHI 2014)*, 1505–1514.

14. Muhammad Imran, Carlos Castillo, Fernando Diaz, and Sarah Vieweg. 2015. Processing Social Media Messages in Mass Emergency: A Survey. *ACM Comput. Surv.* 47, 4: 67:1–67:38.
15. Mark Latonero and Irina Shklovski. 2011. Emergency Management, Twitter, and Social Media Evangelism. *International Journal of Information Systems for Crisis Response and Management* 3, 4: 1–16.
16. Michael K. Lindell and Ronald W. Perry. 1987. Warning Mechanisms in Emergency Response Systems. *Iternational Journal of Mass Emergencies and Disasters* 5, 2: 137–153.
17. Michael K. Lindell and Ronald W. Perry. 2004. *Communicating Environmental Risk in Multiethnic Communities*. SAGE Publications, Thousand Oaks, CA.
18. Michelle McNiel. 2014. Cost of Fighting Carlton Complex Hits $60 million; 322 Homes Destroyed. Retrieved May 27, 2016 from http://www.wenatcheeworld.com/news/2014/aug/07/carlton-complex-now-cost-60-million-and-destroyed-nearly-500-structures/
19. Dennis S. Mileti and Colleen Fitzpatrick. 1992. The Causal Sequence of Risk Communication in the Parkfield Earthquake Prediction Experiment. *Risk Analysis* 12, 3: 393–400.
20. Dhiraj Murthy. 2013. New Media and Natural Disasters: Blogs and the 2004 Indian Ocean Tsunami. *Information, Communication & Society* 16, 7: 1176–1192.
21. Leysia Palen and Sophia B. Liu. 2007. Citizen Communications in Crisis: Anticipating a Future of ICT-supported Public Participation. In *Proceedings of the 2007 Conference on Human Factors in Computing Systems (CHI 2007)*, 727–736.
22. Leysia Palen and Sarah Vieweg. 2008. The Emergence of Online Widescale Interaction in Unexpected Events. In *2008 ACM Proceedings of Computer Supported Cooperative Work Conference*, 117–126.
23. Leysia Palen, Sarah Vieweg, Sophia B. Liu, and Amanda L. Hughes. 2009. Crisis in a Networked World. *Social Science Computing Review* 27, 4: 467–480.
24. Laura E. Pechta, Dale C. Brandenburg, and Matthew W. Seeger. 2010. Understanding the Dynamics of Emergency Communication: Propositions for a Four-Channel Model. *Journal of Homeland Security and Emergency Management* 7, 1.
25. Sung-Yueh Perng, Monika Büscher, Ragnhild Halvorsrud, Lisa Wood, Michael Stiso, Leonardo Ramirez, and Amro Al-Akkad. 2012. Peripheral Response: Microblogging During the 22/7/2011 Norway Attacks. In *Proceedings of the Information Systems for Crisis Response and Management Conference (ISCRAM 2012).*
26. Linda Plotnick, Starr Roxanne Hiltz, Jane A. Kushma, and Andrea H. Tapia. 2015. Red Tape: Attitudes and Issues Related to Use of Social Media by U.S. County-Level Emergency Managers. In *Proceedings of the Information Systems for Crisis Response and Management Conference (ISCRAM 20015).*
27. Tobias Preis, Helen Susannah Moat, Steven R. Bishop, Philip Treleaven, and H. Eugene Stanley. 2013. Quantifying the Digital Traces of Hurricane Sandy on Flickr. *Scientific Reports* 3.
28. Yan Qu, Philip Fei Wu, and Xiaoqing Wang. 2009. Online Community Response to Major Disaster: A Study of Tianya Forum in the 2008 Sichuan Earthquake. In *Proceedings of the 2009 Hawaii International Conference on System Sciences (HICSS 2009)*, 1–11.
29. Barbara Reynolds and Matthew W. Seeger. 2005. Crisis and Emergency Risk Communication as an Integrative Model. *Journal of Health Communication* 10, 1: 43–55.
30. Irina Shklovski, Moira Burke, Sara Kiesler, and Robert Kraut. 2010. Technology Adoption and Use in the Aftermath of Hurricane Katrina in New Orleans. *American Behavioral Scientist* 53, 8: 1228–1246.
31. Irina Shklovski, Leysia Palen, and Jeannette Sutton. 2008. Finding Community through Information and Communication Technology in Disaster Response. In *Proceedings of the 2008 Conference on Computer Supported Cooperative Work (CSCW 2008)*, 127–136.
32. John H. Sorensen and Barbara V. Sorensen. 2007. Community Processes: Warning and Evacuation. In *Handbook of Disaster Research*, Havidan Rodriguez, Enrico L. Quarantelli and Russell R. Dynes (eds.). Springer New York, New York, NY, 183–199.
33. Lise Ann St. Denis, Amanda L. Hughes, and Leysia Palen. 2012. Trial by Fire: The Deployment of Trusted Digital Volunteers in the 2011 Shadow Lake Fire. In *Proceedings of the Information Systems for Crisis Response and Management Conference (ISCRAM 2012).*
34. Seattle Times Staff. 2014. Crews Plan Controlled Burn Near Carlton Complex Wildfire. *The Seattle Times*. Retrieved April 19, 2016 from http://www.seattletimes.com/seattle-news/crews-plan-controlled-burn-near-carlton-complex-wildfire/

35. Robert A. Stallings. 2007. Methodological Issues. In *Handbook of Disaster Research*, Havidán Rodríguez, Enrico L. Quarantelli and Russell R. Dynes (eds.). Springer New York, New York, NY, 55–82.

36. Kate Starbird and Leysia Palen. 2011. "Voluntweeters:" Self-Organizing by Digital Volunteers in Times of Crisis. In *Proceedings of the 2011 Conference on Human Factors in Computing Systems (CHI 2011)*, 1071–1080.

37. Kate Starbird, Leysia Palen, Amanda L. Hughes, and Sarah Vieweg. 2010. Chatter on the Red: What Hazards Threat Reveals about the Social Life of Microblogged Information. In *Proceedings of the ACM 2010 Conference on Computer Supported Cooperative Work (CSCW 2010)*, 241–250.

38. Geoffrey Stockdale and Rahul Sood. 1989. *Emergency Public Information: A Quick Response Study of Coalinga*. Natural Hazards Research and Applications Information Center, Institute of Behavioral Science, University of Colorado at Boulder.

39. Jeannette N. Sutton. 2009. Social Media Monitoring and the Democratic National Convention: New Tasks and Emergent Processes. *Journal of Homeland Security and Emergency Management* 6, 1.

40. Jeannette N. Sutton, Leysia Palen, and Irina Shklovski. 2008. Backchannels on the Front Lines: Emergent Use of Social Media in the 2007 Southern California Fires. In *Proceedings of the Information Systems for Crisis Response and Management Conference (ISCRAM 2008)*.

41. Jeannette N. Sutton, Emma Spiro, Carter Butts, Sean Fitzhugh, Britta Johnson, and Matt Greczek. 2013. Tweeting the Spill: Online Informal Communications, Social Networks, and Conversational Microstructures during the Deepwater Horizon Oilspill. *International Journal of Information Systems for Crisis Response and Management* 5, 1: 58–76.

42. Jeannette N. Sutton, Emma Spiro, Sean Fitzhugh, Britta Johnson, Ben Gibson, and Carter T. Butts. 2014. Online Message Amplification in the Boston Bombing Response. In *Proceedings of the Information Systems for Crisis Response and Management Conference (ISCRAM 20014)*.

43. Jeannette N. Sutton, Emma S. Spiro, Sean Fitzhugh, Britta Johnson, Ben Gibson, and Carter T. Butts. 2014. Terse Message Amplification in the Boston Bombing Response. In *Proceedings of the Information Systems for Crisis Response and Management Conference (ISCRAM 2014)*.

44. Kathleen J. Tierney, Michael K. Lindell, and Ronald W. Perry. 2001. *Facing the Unexpected: Disaster Preparedness and Response in the United States*. John Henry Press, Washington D.C.

45. United Nations Secretariat of the International Strategy for Disaster Reduction (UNISDR). 2010. *Early Warning Practices can Save Many Lives: Good Practices and Lessons Learned*. Bonn, Germany. Retrieved from http://www.unisdr.org/files/15254_EWSBBLLfinalwe b.pdf

46. US Forest Service. 2014. Carlton Complex Fire Perimeter Map August 20, 2014. Retrieved from http://inciweb.nwcg.gov/incident/map/3967/1/39520/

47. US Forest Service. 2014. Carlton Complex Wildfire: Incident Overview. Retrieved from http://inciweb.nwcg.gov/incident/3967/

48. US Forest Service. 2014. Carlton Complex Wildfire: Fire Update 8-24-14. Retrieved from http://inciweb.nwcg.gov/incident/article/3967/24094/

49. Ricardo J. Wray, Jennifer Rivers, Amanda Whitworth, and Keri Jupka. 2006. Public Perceptions About Trust in Emergency Risk Communication: Qualitative Research Findings. *International Journal of Mass Emergencies and Disasters* 24, 1: 45–75.

50. InciWeb: 8/1/14 Evacuation Update 8pm. Retrieved August 18, 2016 from http://inciweb.nwcg.gov/incident/article/3967/22887/

51. InciWeb: 8/3/14 Carlton Complex 9am Update. Retrieved August 18, 2016 from http://inciweb.nwcg.gov/incident/article/3967/22956/

"Algorithms ruin everything": #RIPTwitter, Folk Theories, and Resistance to Algorithmic Change in Social Media

Michael A. DeVito
Northwestern University
Evanston, IL, USA
devitom@u.northwestern.edu

Darren Gergle
Northwestern University
Evanston, IL, USA
dgergle@northwestern.edu

Jeremy Birnholtz
Northwestern University
Evanston, IL, USA
jeremyb@northwestern.edu

ABSTRACT
As algorithmically-driven content curation has become an increasingly common feature of social media platforms, user resistance to algorithmic change has become more frequent and visible. These incidents of user backlash point to larger issues such as inaccurate understandings of how algorithmic systems work as well as mismatches between designer and user intent. Using a content analysis of 102,827 tweets from #RIPTwitter, a recent hashtag-based backlash to rumors about introducing algorithmic curation to Twitter's timeline, this study addresses the nature of user resistance in the form of the complaints being expressed, folk theories of the algorithmic system espoused by users, and how these folk theories potentially frame user reactions. We find that resistance to algorithmic change largely revolves around expectation violation, with folk theories acting as frames for reactions such that more detailed folk theories are expressed through more specific reactions to algorithmic change.

Author Keywords
Algorithms; algorithm awareness; folk theories; technology continuance; user resistance; social media; algorithmic curation; expectation violation; machine classification

ACM Classification Keywords
H.5.m. Information interfaces and presentation (e.g., HCI):

INTRODUCTION
Algorithmically-driven content curation systems such as the Facebook Newsfeed or Instagram Feed are an increasingly common feature of social media platforms [3, 11, 13]. These systems often change more frequently than traditional technological systems [13], and that change has sometimes been met with public resistance from users. Prominent examples include early backlash when Facebook's Newsfeed was introduced [15] (and expanded [1]) as well as more recent negative reactions to changes in Twitter's Timeline [26] and Instagram's feed [22]. These negative user reactions to algorithmic change may indicate larger problems extending beyond these commercial platforms such as inaccurate user understandings of how the systems work, both before and after potential changes (e.g., [5, 10, 11]), as well as designer misunderstandings of what users see as important aspects of platforms (e.g. [25]).

Permission to make digital or hard copies of all or part of this work for personal or classroom use is granted without fee provided that copies are not made or distributed for profit or commercial advantage and that copies bear this notice and the full citation on the first page. Copyrights for components of this work owned by others than ACM must be honored. Abstracting with credit is permitted. To copy otherwise, or republish, to post on servers or to redistribute to lists, requires prior specific permission and/or a fee. Request permissions from Permissions@acm.org.
CHI 2017, May 06-11, 2017, Denver, CO, USA
© 2017 ACM. ISBN 978-1-4503-4655-9/17/05…$15.00
DOI: http://dx.doi.org/10.1145/3025453.3025659

User misunderstanding of algorithmically-driven curation systems has been documented [5, 10, 11, 29], with the implication that more accurate understandings might lead to increased user agency and success in achieving goals, as well as increased user trust in these systems [10, 21]. This could also help address emerging skill and literacy gaps around algorithms (e.g., [10, 13]). Moreover, increased sensitivity to how users (mis)understand systems may help designers avoid negative reactions to platform change.

As it stands, however, we know little about why users resist algorithmic changes or the extent to which users understand the systems they are resisting. Existing theories that aim to understand acceptance and rejection of new technologies and changes focus primarily on relatively slow-changing organizational settings where user agency is limited by a lack of outside choice (e.g., [2, 8, 24]). These theories could be valuable in understanding reactions to algorithmic change, but are difficult to apply directly to the unique situation of constantly-updated, algorithmically-driven social media feeds, where users are not employees, have numerous other platform options, and often have a central and strong voice in establishing popular sentiment with respect to the system.

Recent research suggests that folk theories, which capture a user's working understanding of system operation [12, 28] and can act as a high-level frame for shaping user expectations [7, 27], may be a useful window into understanding user resistance to algorithmic change [5, 10, 12]. User expectations are a key element of this problem, as reactions are likely driven by the degree to which a change fulfills or violates their expectations of the system [2, 24]. Moreover, user reactions themselves are a potentially valuable source of data in that they can reveal both latent folk theories and system expectations.

If we are to make progress in this area, it is important to understand the nature of user reactions to changes in algorithmically-driven systems (and especially their complaints), what folk theories users articulate in the face of algorithmic change, and how these folk theories are expressed through and potentially frame user reactions.

In this paper, we address these questions by examining an "in the wild" corpus of tweets in response to a 2016 BuzzFeed News article (falsely) claiming that Twitter would change the organization of its timeline from simple reverse chronological order to one based on algorithmically-determined relevance to each user [18]. This article prompted an outpouring of sentiment on Twitter using the #RIPTwitter hashtag [26], even though the described changes were not made to the platform's feed algorithm.

We examine the entire English-language #RIPTwitter corpus via human and machine content classification. Our results suggest that: 1) user resistance to algorithmic change is primarily based on the potential violation of specific prior expectations set up by the user; 2) implicitly-expressed user folk theories regarding these offending algorithms are mostly nonspecific, in that they consider algorithms as external agents of change, but do in some cases rise to the level of theories about how the algorithms actually work; and 3) user folk theories regarding algorithms seem to be related to user reactions, such that more specific folk theories tend to be linked to more specifically-expressed reactions.

BACKGROUND

The #RIPTwitter tweets feature direct discussion of and reaction to algorithms, in which users likely draw on their folk theories of algorithmic operation. In this section of the paper, we review theories of technology acceptance and rejection with a focus on understanding the nature of resistance to new technology and on how users develop and articulate folk theories of how these systems operate.

Resistance to Algorithmic Change

The #RIPTwitter tweets can be seen as an immediate outpouring of possible reasons for accepting or rejecting changes to Twitter's core content delivery mechanism. One useful theoretical model for considering these reasons to reject or accept is the expectation-confirmation model (ECM)[1]. This model holds that continued use of information technology is determined by continually-confirmed user satisfaction, a product of the interplay between user expectations and the technology's performance relative to those expectations [2]. ECM has been extended to take perceived ease of use and user enjoyment into account [31], as well as task/technology fit [25]. In all versions, expectations are key: continued use requires that users' initial and, more importantly, continually-reevaluated expectations of a technology are met. In considering rumored Twitter changes, continued use of Twitter would depend on whether it continued to fulfill users' expectations of it.

Expectation violation is also at the heart of resistance to technology change. As a baseline, a technology's status quo serves as the basis for an expectation, which can potentially be violated by change. The violation's negative impact can be exacerbated by high switching costs and a user-perceived lack of agency in the decision [20].

Expectation violations directly threaten the user's understood status quo, which Lapointe and Rivard [24] have identified as a key driver of resistance to new technologies. In their model of resistance to technology implementation, they posit a process in which users assess the match between the features of a new technology and the place that technology would occupy in their lives. If that assessment of the consequences of the new technology threatens the status quo, resistance begins.

As an example of how the ECM and related theories play out, we can briefly look at an example of user backlash against Facebook's News Feed. The backlash centered around changes to both visibility and curation of content alongside the introduction of the News Feed feature, which regularly displayed content from other users, as a "home" page instead of the user's own profile [15]. Users had prior experience and an established expectation that content would only be displayed to certain people on certain pages. The rumored change to a feed where any content was potentially displayed to all of a user's contacts represented an abrupt overturning of the status quo for both information flow and privacy, and therefore was likely a significant expectation violation for many users. As such, the rumored change was resisted, to the extent that Facebook had to temporarily backtrack, publically apologize, reengineer the feed, and re-launch after taking user complaints into account.

In this prior case, and potentially in the case of #RIPTwitter, the new, algorithmically-driven system appears to threaten a status quo. However, the Facebook example took place before the word "algorithm" had entered common public lexicon, and #RIPTwitter allows us to look at a response predicated directly on responding not just to an algorithm's effects, but to the introduction of the algorithm itself. In turn, this allows us to examine if the documented focus on expectation violations in the Facebook case was also present for #RIPTwitter's instance of resistance to algorithmic change. Accordingly, we asked:

RQ1: *What reasons for resistance to the idea of algorithmic change did participants in #RIPTwitter express?*

Understanding the Changing Algorithm

As noted above, user expectations of technology may be shaped by perceived use cases [25], but they are also potentially shaped at a higher level by user understanding of the system's inner workings [27].

Prior work has shown that users of algorithmically-driven platforms may not be aware of their algorithmic nature. Those that do have some idea of what is going on often understand through folk theories which are, in general,

[1] We also considered longstanding theories such as the technology acceptance model [8]. However, though algorithmic curation could be considered a new technology, it was introduced to users within the framework of the core Twitter technology; as such, continuance is a more appropriate lens with which to examine #RIPTwitter.

oversimplifications and often inaccurate [10, 11, 29]. However, this lack of technical knowledge is not necessarily a barrier to acceptance or resistance.

Several related lines of work have established that user folk theories can function in the place of specific knowledge of what an algorithm does [12], allowing the individual to respond to an algorithm's perceived behavior, an arrangement that Bucher has labeled the "algorithmic imaginary" [5]. In this manner, folk theories, acting in place of actual technical knowledge, can affect how users respond to a system. Similarly, Orlikowski and Gash have established that users respond to change in technology based off of their own assumptions, expectations, and knowledge of how a system works [7, 27]. In this case, user folk theories constitute those assumptions, expectations, and knowledge, and essentially act as the contextual frames through which users interact with a system. As such, examining these folk theories can give us insight into how users' working understandings of algorithmic systems might affect the expression of user resistance.

In considering what constitutes a "folk theory," we started with Gelman & Legare's [12] concept of "intuitive causal explanatory theories that people construct to explain, interpret, and intervene in the world around them." We found this definition too restrictive, as it assumes strict causal reasoning. According to Orlikowski & Gash, the technological frames that individuals use to understand and react to technology are based not just on knowledge, but assumptions and expectations as well, especially those concerning consequences, and constitute an exercise in sensemaking [27]. In acting as a type of sensemaking frame, we argue that a folk theory can call on relevant, yet informal, abstract, or partial ideas, as noted by Keil [19], and need not be mechanistic to express an assumption about the consequences of a technology. As such, we adopt an expanded definition of "folk theories" as *intuitive, informal theories that individuals develop to explain the outcomes, effects, or consequences of technological systems, which guide reactions to and behavior towards said systems*. This includes causal models of how an algorithm might work, as well as opinions and attitudes about possible consequences of how it operates.

Prior work by Eslami et al. on directly eliciting folk theories regarding the Facebook Newsfeed found that users had a variety of highly specific folk theories, ranging from curation on the basis of personal engagement with other accounts, content, or types of content, to attempts by the platform to balance out types of friends or content [10]. These can be considered specifically causal speculations on what algorithms do, with an additional theory that attributes curation to "randomness." Similarly, Rader and Gray found evidence of folk theories that pointed specifically to causal mechanisms, such as a platform's attempt to provide "relevant" or popular content [29]. In both cases, the folk theories elicited were usually developed to the point of the user making specific, mechanism-level causal claims.

#RIPTwitter is a somewhat different situation. In contrast to the above studies, expressed folk theories are based on speculation as to how a system will work rather than how a system does work. However, this type of implicit folk theory can still be a window into how users believe a system operates (or will operate) and how that belief guides behavior and understanding [12]. In fact, it may actually bring us closer to an understanding of how these systems are operationally understood "in the wild" [16]. In turn, this may allow us to determine the extent to which reactions to change in algorithmically-driven systems are framed by and subsequently expressed in user folk theories [5, 12, 27]. Accordingly, we asked:

RQ2A: *What folk theories of algorithmic influence over Twitter were displayed by #RIPTwitter participants?*

RQ2B: *Do certain types of reactions to algorithmic change reflect the expression of different folk theories?*

METHODS

To explore these questions, we used a content analysis of the entire English-language corpus of #RIPTwitter tweets. As this corpus represents a single event or case, an extensive, in-depth look at the whole phenomenon is essential, per [33]. As such, we used human content coding to classify a subset of the corpus for both quantitative [32] and thematic [34] analysis, and then used supervised machine classification to broaden our analysis to the whole corpus, per [30].

Data Collection

Our data set consisted of 102,827 unique English-language tweets that used the #RIPTwitter hashtag. These were collected via the Twitter REST API during the five-day period when the hashtag was active after the inciting article ([18]) was posted, February 5 - 10, 2016. This collection resulted in an initial corpus of 250,482 tweets. The initial corpus was then filtered in R, using an API-provided flag to remove retweets and the *textcat* package to identify and remove non-English tweets. Though this data was exclusively pulled from public Twitter accounts, we have treated it as if it were private throughout the coding and analysis process, and only reproduce tweets in this article that are still posted and public as of submission.

As it was not possible for human coders to review all 102,827 tweets, we randomly selected a subset of 10,050 tweets to act as a first point of analysis as well as the ground truth training data for the subsequent supervised machine learning model.

Data Set Characteristics

As our data come entirely from one platform during one incident, we suggest caution in interpreting our results. Twitter's users include about 23% of all online adults, and demographically trends younger, more urban, educated, and non-white than other social media platforms [9]. We were focused on studying the reactions of individual Twitter users, not the reactions of groups, and as such we examined our dataset to check that it was appropriate for this individual focus. We found no single individuals who dominated the #RIPTwitter discussion, suggesting that our data represent all #RIPTwitter participants, and not just a few loud individuals. In the hand-coded set, 9,063 individual accounts are represented, with none comprising more than 0.004% of the set; in the full corpus, there are 71,171 accounts, with none comprising more than 0.003%. We also checked to see if the corpus contained back-and-forth dialog between users or long threads from individuals, both of which would threaten the validity of our claims. Only 10% of tweets contain an @mention, and less than 0.01% of the tweets are from recurring users, suggesting very few conversations or threads. Thus, we believe the data is appropriate for our goal.

Coding Procedure

We iteratively and inductively developed a three-level (valence, reaction, algorithm theory) coding scheme through discussion between the lead author and three undergraduate research assistants acting as coders, per [32]. The entire scheme was also reviewed by the authors during the process.

The three coders applied the coding scheme, starting with a 4,572-tweet training phase in which tweets were coded in small blocks, compared and reconciled by all coders. Once agreement was consistently above 70% for all categories, an additional 5,478 tweets were coded by a single coder, with 20% of this second group subsequently cross-coded by an additional coder, which resulted in acceptable Cohen's kappa reliability scores (per [23]) for all levels of the scheme (valence: 0.85, reaction: 0.79, algorithm theory: 0.78).

Classification Procedure

To better capture the entire English-language #RIPTwitter phenomenon, we then applied machine learning to classify the remaining 92,777 tweets with the same coding scheme. This was executed in Python using NLTK and scikit-learn. We used the hand-coded set as ground truth to train a series of support vector machine (SVM) classifiers, a common classifier for text-based problems [30].

For each classifier, each tweet was processed through a pipeline that first normalized the text. Normalization included standard steps such as removing whitespace and punctuation; however, to preserve as much data as possible from the short tweets, and to account for frequent use of casual language, we preserved word lengthening (e.g., "noooooooo" as more emotive than "no") per [4, 17], and added a flag to indicate that a tweet was "shouting" if it was more than 50% uppercase letters. We also normalized URLs and direct @mentions. URLs were resolved to their endpoint to counter link shortening, and the top 30% of URLs were given unique flags, with the rest receiving a generic URL flag. Similarly, the top 5% of @mentions, plus a list of news organization handles, were given unique @name flags, while the rest received a generic @mention flag. Both of these cutoffs represent the point at which their respective distributions, both of which were long-tailed, flatten out. After cleaning, the tweets were run through NLTK's Twitter-specific tokenizer, which preserves emoji and emoticons, and then a tf-idf vectorizer to extract unigrams and bigrams. Finally, we used a chi-square test to select the top 30% of features for use in the final classifiers.

Three SVM classifiers were trained on this ground truth set with kernel parameters optimized via grid search. The classifier for valence used a linear kernel and, to combat class imbalance, had synthetic minority-class data added to the training set via SMOTE [6]. The classifiers for reaction and algorithm theory used a radial basis function kernel. All classifiers were evaluated using 10-fold cross validation to produce mean F1 scores (valence: 0.83, reaction: 0.67, algorithm theory: 0.76).

RESULTS

In this section, we first establish the nature of the #RIPTwitter resistance by reviewing the reasons participants expressed for their resistance to Twitter's change. We then explore the nature of users' expressed understanding of algorithmically-driven systems by examining the folk theories gleaned from participants' expressions. Finally, we show a relationship between user reaction and user folk theories. Note that we present results from our hand-coded dataset side-by-side with the machine-classified set. Results for both sets are similar, though not identical.

Reacting to an Algorithmic Rumor

First, we asked what reasons #RIPTwitter participants expressed for resisting change to Twitter (RQ1). Before answering this question, however, we checked the overall emotional valence of the tweets to validate the implicit assumption that #RIPTwitter was an instance of resistance.

A Negative Reaction

To check the actual valence of #RIPTwitter, we classified the emotional valence of each tweet's overall expressed feeling towards the rumored changes. Tweets were classified as "positive" if they expressed positive emotional reactions, such as pleasure, excitement, or gratitude, e.g.:

```
3/ In short, I think any algo-timeline (as a
new choice to surface great Tweets) is a great
move. The best is yet to be. #RIPTwitter
```

Tweets were classified as "negative" if they expressed implicit or explicit negative emotional reactions towards the rumored change, such as frustration, sadness, or anger, e.g.:

```
#RIPTwitter I hate Facebook because of this.
Why are you doing this to me. You got rid of
the star and now the timeline.
```

Tweets were classified as "neutral" if the overall sentiment of the tweet committed to neither of these emotional reactions, and remained even-keeled, e.g.:

```
Change is usually good. But change can also
suck. We'll see which one this ends up being.
#RIPTwitter
```

Supporting the assumption of a predominantly negative reaction, we found that 68% of the tweets (6,826) in the

Reaction	Definition	Example	Percentage (N)
Generalized Anger / Frustration	The user is expressing a simple disapproval, admonishment, accusation, or other expression of anger or frustration, without specifics.	*Fuck your algorithms @twitter #Riptwitter*	31.2% (2,587) 27.1% (23,484)
Metacommentary	The user is discussing #RIPTwitter itself as a phenomenon.	*Ironically, we're live-tweeting the death of Twitter's live feed. Do it now, while you still can! #RIPTwitter*	14.5% (1,206) 16.3% (14,132)
Explicit Expectation Violation	The user has identified some key worth or utility regarding Twitter that is now potentially being removed, replaced, or otherwise violated.	*Just don't, @twitter. We like chronological tweets. And live tweeting. And TWITTER BEING TWITTER. Leave it alone. #RIPTwitter*	12.8% (1,062) 15.3% (13,207)
Platform Duplication	The user is primarily commenting on Twitter attempting to copy another platform.	*Hey @twitter, If we liked Facebook, we'd be on Facebook. @jack #RIPTwitter*	11.9% (996) 14.7% (12,698)
Resignation	The user accepts that the rumored changes will inevitably happen, and may be searching for a new platform of choice.	*Looks like Twitter is going to turn into garbage. Was only a matter of time before the last good social media was ruined... #riptwitter*	8.9% (745) 11% (9,552)
Confusion	The user expresses genuine confusion over what #RIPTwitter is about.	*#RIPTwitter Wait what's happening?! Can someone explain?!?*	6.2% (512) 5.9% (5,160)
Platform Attachment	The user is primarily expressing general attachment or loyalty to Twitter as the user understands it (in actual or idealized form).	*Twitter you're perfect just the way or are. You don't have to change for anyone. Stay beautiful Twitter, please stay beautiful #RIPTwitter*	4.7% (394) 3.7% (3,217)
Ignoring Feature Requests	The user has called out Twitter for even considering the rumored changes when other critical requests (e.g., spam, abuse controls, edit button) have not been met.	*people: we want an edit button* *twitter: a what?* *people: an ed-* *twitter: algorithmic timeline. got it! :)* *#RIPTwitter"*	4.2% (348) 3.9% (3,343)
Wait and See	The user is inconclusive and either holding off judgement or posing conditional terms for acceptance or rejection of the rumored changes.	*Not willing to say #RIPTwitter until after the roll-out. If I have an option to go back to chronological, then no harm done.*	3.4% (281) 1.6% (1,394)
Economic Motivation	The user has identified the rumored changes as explicitly economically motivated, a "cash grab."	*Relevance=What is "relevant" to Twitter making $. It's ALL $ making. #SadButTrue #RIPTwitter*	1.5% (126) 0.3% (294)
Fixing the Problems	The user has identified the rumored changes as a potential fix for existing problems.	*What's with #RIPTwitter? Timelines are full of garbage. Surfacing the interesting bits would be a welcomed change.*	0.6% (48) 0.1% (53)

Note: Top percentages indicate results for hand coding; bottom percentages indicate results for machine classification. Tweets classified as off-topic/spam or purely informational (15.9% of the full corpus) are excluded, as they express no actual reaction.

Table 1: Classification categories for user reactions to the rumored algorithmic changes to Twitter.

hand-coded set had a negative valence, while 31% (3,146) were neutral. Only 77 tweets (0.77%) in the hand-coded set were coded as positive. The results from the SVM-classified entire corpus follow a similar pattern: 74.2% negative (76,327), 24.4% neutral (26,254), and 0.2% positive (245).

To ensure #RIPTwitter was not a negatively-valenced fringe conversation in a broader response to this rumor, we also looked for more positive responses by examining tweets from this period with hashtags often used to praise Twitter: "#goodjobtwitter" and "#thankstwitter." However, we found little evidence: "#thankstwitter" was not used during this time, and "#goodjobtwitter" was used rarely and often sarcastically. We are thus confident that #RIPTwitter and the overall reaction to rumored Twitter changes were negative.

Violating the Status Quo

After verifying the negative overall valence of #RIPTwitter, we sought to better understand what reasons users might have for resisting by examining how participants expressed their resistance (RQ1). Overall, user reactions paint a clear picture of resistance prompted by perceived violations of their expected status quo, expressed in a variety of ways.

Our inductive coding scheme resulted in 11 distinct types of reaction messages (see Table 1). As we examined the tweets in each category, we realized that the categories seemed to differ from each other in the level of detail with which participants described their expectations, perceptions of the status quo and potential violations of those expectations.

Based on this observation, we created a rough ordering of categories by the level of detail that typified tweets in that category. This ranges from the explicit mention of both a status quo expectation and how it is violated (*explicit expectation violation*) to the implicit assumption of the entire platform as currently constituted as the status quo and any change as a violation (*generalized anger/frustration*). In between these extremes lie categories that vary in the extent to which detailed descriptions are needed to express that type of reaction. We draw on this rough ordering in our analyses, but note that – apart from the clear endpoints – we cannot make fine-grained distinctions between categories. Note that two reaction types (*metacommentary* and *confusion*) did not fit this description pattern, so were not part of this exercise.

The clearest illustrations of perceived threats to user expectations around the status quo were found in the *explicit expectation violation* tweets. As Table 1 shows, these tweets mention the rumored changes as endangering specific features or the core functionality or "twitter-ness" that makes Twitter, Twitter:

```
I love Twitter because it's Twitter. Reordering
the timeline would be well... NOT Twitter.
#RIPTwitter
```

Explicit expectation violations were coded only when an expectation could be gleaned from the tweet, suggesting that the user had a specific use case for the technology, and/or a distinct place for that technology in their lives. In some cases, these expectations could be about what makes Twitter unique in a larger sense. For example, users may have come to expect that Twitter would provide them with certain types of social utility and functionality, e.g.:

```
I like twitter for a reason. It's a great
platform to share views and opinions. Please
don't take that reason away from me.
#RIPTwitter
```

In other cases, this was a very specific use case, where Twitter has an inherent value in fulfilling or completing some key task for which the user relies on the platform. Live-tweeting, in particular, was frequently mentioned:

```
Just don't, @twitter. We like chronological
tweets. And live tweeting. And TWITTER BEING
TWITTER. Leave it alone. #RIPTwitter
```

Similarly, Twitter's functionality as a key source for breaking information was called out as a valued part of the current status quo, for both civic and personal reasons:

```
Twitter - "We'll get to the earthquake in a
second. But first, here are some cat pictures
we think you might like." #RIPTwitter
```

```
I use Twitter for live updates on things -
sports. That's why Twitter is amazing. What's
the point of a fucking algorithm????
#RIPTwitter
```

In all these cases, participants articulated an already-formed expectation of how Twitter "should" perform relative to their use case. There is a sense in which this can be seen essentially as an ad-hoc assessment of task/technology fit. This direct expression of an expectation that might be violated shows a clear sense of a (perceived) status quo among participants. To them, Twitter *is* or *is for* a distinct part of their online lives.

This understanding of an imperiled status quo (and, therefore, imperiled platform value) can also be found in many of the less frequently observed categories, such as platform duplication, resignation, platform attachment, economic motivation, and fixing the problems, totaling slightly over a third of the entire corpus (33.6% hand coded / 37.9% machine classified). Definitions and examples of these categories are in Table 1, but ultimately, despite ostensibly centering on other complaints about the system (e.g., an unseemly level of monetization in the case of *economic motivation*), they all also express that there is an implicitly or explicitly recognized status quo on Twitter that users see as threatened by the coming change. The more explicit cases, such as *platform duplication*, specifically call out Twitter as a distinct platform, and express an expectation that it will remain unique, e.g.:

```
Why can't Twitter just be fucking unique
instead of copying Facebook #RIPTwitter
```

The more implicit coding categories, such as *platform attachment*, recognize that there is something special about Twitter, sometimes in a very personal way, without necessarily being specific, e.g.:

```
I'm sorry it took something like this for me to
say it, but @twitter has been one of the only
joys in my life. #RIPTwitter
```

In these implicit cases, we still see evidence of expectations around Twitter's nature that are seen to be threatened. These may not be expectations in the sense discussed in the literature reviewed above, but it is clear that these concerns are important and influencing the user's reactions in similar ways. We will return to this point in the discussion.

Even tweets classified as *generalized anger/frustration*, which are by their nature less focused on specific platform features than many of the other categories, have an implicit concern for a status quo. As noted in the first line of Table 1, they are often about venting and admonishment, or dark, disparaging humor. They also turn to outright insult to Twitter as a company and its CEO in particular, sometimes rising to the level of threats. Individuals such as this one seem to seek an outlet for their frustration:

```
Just found out about the Twitter algorithm
thing. Here's my letter to Twitter, in which I
voice my full opinion:
FUCK YOU
#RIPTwitter
```

These tweets may not express specific reasons for being upset, but it seems clear that these individuals believe the

Code	User Folk Theory	Example	Percentage (N)
Abstract Theories			
Generic	Algorithm will affect the timeline in some nonspecific way; algorithm is largely defined as an external force.	*Algorithms ruin everything #RIPTwitter*	33.5% (778) 39.5% (8,769)
Opposition	Algorithm will oppose the current status quo of a chronological timeline; algorithm is largely defined by what it is not.	*it's called TIMEline not ALGORITHMICline #RIPTwitter*	20.7% (713) 32.6% (7, 237)
Comparison	Algorithm will operate exactly as another platform does; algorithm is defined exclusively as another platform's whole way of operating.	*These proposed twitter changes sound awful. I don't need another facebook-like feed. #RIPTwitter*	4.9% (113) 1.8% (401)
Operational Theories			
Popularity	Algorithm will display content based on overall popularity of content or specific accounts (e.g., celebrities), either across the platform or a smaller network (e.g., geographic area).	*Showing tweets in order by most popular, LOL some tweets will never be seen. #RIPTwitter*	11.6% (270) 10.3% (2,277)
Platform Directed	Algorithm will display what Twitter as an entity wants users to see.	*Only huge accounts will be in timelines. And advertisers. Just like Facebook. You'll see only what Twitter says you'll see. #RIPTwitter*	11.5% (266) 8.8% (1,954)
Relevance	Algorithm will use some user-based metric (e.g., clicks, page views, strength of ties, etc.) to select content that it believes the user wants to see.	*Let me decide what I want to see not what you think I want to see. #RIPTwitter*	7.8% (181) 6.9% (1,539)

Note: For percentage, top numbers indicate results for hand coding; bottom numbers indicate results for machine classification.

Table 2: Classification categories for user folk theories about the rumored Twitter timeline algorithm

likely impact of the rumored change would be negative. In many cases, these participants are essentially objecting to change of any type. This can be read as a very general violation of an ill-defined expectation that things will remain as they are now. This is another illustration of how people's attachment to the nature or features of a system cause concern that changes to those features might threaten the value they derive from the system. Where the source of this value is unclear, people seem to see any change as a possible threat to that value.

Theorizing the Rumored Algorithm

To better understand what might be framing or influencing user resistance, we also investigated the folk theories expressed by #RIPTwitter participants about the rumored algorithm (RQ2A). In particular, we wondered if specific types of folk theories would influence the way people discussed the rumored changes, and if this could help us understand people's perceptions of how the system works and why/how they derive value from it.

We found six distinct types of user folk theories (see Table 2). Overall, it appears that the folk theories expressed via #RIPTwitter do not show detailed, causal theories of how algorithmic curation might work. However, we did find a diversity of more general, high-level theories which seem to indicate differing levels of user understanding. That difference allows us to group the theories into two broad categories: *operational theories* and *abstract theories*.

Operational theories demonstrate a specific understanding that there are some criteria by which an algorithm must make curation decisions, and comprised a minority of all expressed theories (30.9% hand coded / 26% machine classified). As shown in Table 2, operational theories included: content popularity, Twitter's internal priorities, and some formulation of what is deemed relevant for the user. For example, these users implicitly point to popularity/platform priorities and relevance as decision criteria, respectively:

```
Your TL will be filled with only popular
tweets, ads and promoted accounts :(
#RIPTwitter
```

```
Appears Twitter will be using an algorithm to
place tweets IT feels you'd wish to see before
others. Seems very wrong. #Uneasy #RIPTwitter
```

Though most operational theories lack detail on how an algorithm works, they do express a baseline understanding of algorithmic curation.

In direct contrast, abstract theories, which include the generic, opposition, and comparison classifications, account for most of the theories expressed. They do not include specific attempts to theorize how an algorithm might actually operate. Instead, they rely on a more general sense that an algorithm is something that will, in turn, cause something to happen to the Twitter timeline: just generically "something" in the case of *generic*, something different than the status quo in the case of *opposition*, and something similar to another platform in the case of *comparison*. For example, these users

User Reaction	Abstract Folk Theories Generic	Opposition	Comparison	Operational Folk Theories Relevance	Platform Directed	Popularity
Generalized Anger / Frustration	438.48*	307.62*	39.99*	80.16*	1.79	0.76
Metacommentary	219.31*	52.34*	14.92*	85.27*	9.97	15.06*
Explicit Expectation Violation	967.27*	384.35*	54.89*	450.82*	28.60*	41.60*
Platform Duplication	5.22	13.48*	1385.19*	27.88*	12.07*	34.11*
Confusion	62.60*	14.60*	2.68	13.48*	5.52	7.53
Resignation	1.04	0.01	21.15*	62.45*	3.75	69.00*
Platform Attachment	6.22	79.93*	0.35	14.26*	7.39	26.72*
Ignoring Feature Requests	123.88*	14.03*	2.47	8.64	40.04*	37.01*
Wait and See	11.43	4.55	1.78	14.98*	11.38	12.39*
Economic Motivation	0.64	15.01*	0.37	5.21	151.47*	0.66
Fix the Problems	0.07	0.00	0.38	0.14	0.40	0.30

*Note: * = statistically significant after Bonferroni correction, α = 0.00075; red/dark cells indicate combinations occurring less than expected by chance, green/light cells indicate combinations occurring more than expected by chance; white cells not significant.*

Table 3: Chi-Square tests of significant differences between expected and observed cell counts across user reactions to algorithmic change and user folk theories; based on machine classification of the #RIPTwitter English-language corpus.

are aware of the algorithm primarily as a generic "other" and as a force that will disturb the status quo, respectively:

```
Twitters bout to be ran by an algorithm
#RIPTwitter
```

```
Twitter don't change your algorithm, we like it
just like this..... #riptwitter
```

Ultimately, only a minority of the total corpus expressed any level of algorithmic theory, as is to be expected based on previous work. In the hand coded set, 23.1% of tweets (2,321) expressed a folk theory; in the machine classified set, 21.61% of tweets (22,239) expressed a theory. Overall, these results suggest that where responses expressed a theory, they were diverse and reflected diverse levels of understanding.

Matching Theory to Reaction

Finally, we investigated whether certain types of reactions to algorithmic change expressed different types of user folk theories (RQ2B) in order to better understand how these theories might frame or influence reactions to change.

At a high level, there does appear to be a relationship between specific type of algorithm theory expressed and reaction to algorithmic change, as chi-square tests indicate the two variables are not independent (hand coding χ^2 = 788.39, df = 50, p < .0001, N = 2,297; machine classified χ^2 = 4901.07, df = 50, p < .0001, N = 21,506).

To answer the question in more detail, we used a contingency analysis via post-hoc single degree-of-freedom chi-square tests with a Bonferroni correction applied (corrected α = 0.00075). This analysis suggests that the different levels we found in the first two sections of results are linked, such that more specifically focused types of reactions are more likely to express more specific folk theories, and less specifically focused types of reactions are more likely to express less specific folk theories. This suggests in turn that more detailed levels of algorithmic knowledge, as expressed through folk theories, may allow or prompt more detailed, and therefore actionable, expressions of resistance. This may seem intuitive or obvious at first, but this isn't the case. It would theoretically be quite reasonable to react with a specific feature in mind, but describe it with an abstract theory (such as the hypothetical "The timeline makes Twitter what it is. Algorithms will destroy it") and vice versa.

The more specific, or operational, folk theories (popularity, platform directed, and relevance) we found in RQ2A, are expressed through more specific reactions to algorithmic change more frequently than would be expected by chance. As noted in Table 3, explicit expectation violations, arguably the most specific user reaction type as it requires a specific use or property of the platform to be violated, more frequently express all three types of operational theory than would be expected by chance. Additionally, economic motivation reactions appear to frequently express a platform directed algorithm theory (68.52% hand coded; 45.1% machine classified), as users are specifically theorizing a causal mechanism that primarily benefits the platform in economic terms. Similarly, resigned reactions appear to express a popularity algorithm theory significantly more frequently than would be expected by chance (30.17% hand coded; 17.62% machine classified), which coincides with a common exasperated attitude seen in these tweets, e.g.:

```
Bro, I'm done. It's all just gonna be a big
popularity contest. #RIPTwitter
```

In direct contrast to this, the abstract algorithm theories (generic, opposition, and comparison), were expressed more frequently through less specific reactions than would be expected by chance. For example, platform duplication reactions appear to frequently express a comparison algorithm theory (35.8% hand coded; 13% machine classified), as users are reacting in relation to another platform. Similarly, reactions classified as ignoring feature requests also frequently express a generic algorithm theory (62.79% hand coded; 63.27% machine classified), which coincides with a frequent view of the rumored algorithm as an ill-defined solution to a problem that Twitter doesn't actually have, e.g.:

```
MASSES: "We want more than 140 & edits"
TWITTER: "Ok great, well just fuck up
everything including your timeline, instead
#RIPTwitter
```

Importantly, the plurality of users that reacted with generalized anger/frustration appear to be expressing a generic algorithm theory (46.7% hand coded; 56.42% machine classified), significantly more than expected by chance. This suggests that the most abstract theories are often expressed through the least explicit responses to change.

In an interesting contrast to the generalized anger/frustration case, the plurality of users who reacted with explicit expectation violations appeared to be expressing an opposition-based algorithm theory, where the algorithm opposes the status quo (47.54% hand coded; 45% machine classified). As noted above, while opposition is not one of the operational algorithm theories, it does require a solid knowledge of the status quo. This suggests that, even in the absence of operational theories, more specific folk theories are expressed through more specific reactions to change.

DISCUSSION

By examining the English-language #RIPTwitter corpus, we have gained insight into the ways users express both their reasons for reacting negatively to algorithmic change and the folk theories with which they conceptualize the system itself. We found that user resistance is centered on violations of the user's expectations of a platform's status quo, and that this core concern is expressed in a variety of ways with varying levels of detail. We also found evidence of both operational and abstract user folk theories that vary in their level of detail or expressed user knowledge. Finally, we have shown a relationship between type of user reaction to change and level of detail in the accompanying algorithm theory, such that more detailed folk theories occur with more detailed negative reactions. All of this has implications for understanding what users value in social media platforms, how users conceptualize algorithmically-driven content curation systems, and how understanding one may be a potential window into understanding the other.

Expanded Expectations: A Personal Threat

Our findings regarding users' reactions to change present an opportunity to reevaluate and extend long-standing theories for the new realities of social media platforms. As noted in our results, the primary component of negative participant reactions was the possibility of a changed status quo that might violate expectations. At its core, this is consistent with both the ECM [2, 31] and Lapointe and Rivard's resistance framework [24], as they center around continued confirmation of expectation satisfaction to keep users using a system. There is continued utility to understanding rejection (and acceptance) of systems using these theories, but to do so we must expand them to include new elements, including the additional expectations being violated.

Overall, we found expectations were focused on each user's value for the system, essentially an ad-hoc form of task/technology fit [25], but our results show that value is derived from other sources as well. Where value from systems described by these theories in the past stemmed from functionality such as the ability to complete work tasks or communicate effectively within organizations, #RIPTwitter participants showed that they derived value from work, personal, and community tasks, as well as much more abstract community dynamics. As we noted in our results, these community dynamics can include a simple sense of belonging, or of Twitter being a safe space for self-expression or emotional support. Task/technology fit here is less directly about supporting a task, but rather about whether changes to information delivery mechanisms within a community would impact how that community functions.

Compared with sources of system value in these theories, the more abstract sources of value, or system expectations that we saw do not require a discrete violation episode to seem potentially threatening to users. As we saw in our generalized anger/frustration results, even the very prospect of any change at all provoked intense, vulgar, and sometimes personal backlash for users that were valuing a perceived characterization of the system as a whole instead of an individual component. We saw users value, and therefore set expectations of, the system whether or not they understood their actual reasons for using a system. They were willing to draw their proverbial lines in the sand over what may seem like small changes to designers or researchers.

As such, future work on expectation violations and user resistance can still derive value from models like the ECM as a starting point, but should be cognizant of the expanded set of circumstances that might trigger "expectation violations" for users.

User Folk Theories: Few Specifics, Yet Deep Diversity

Our findings regarding users' folk algorithm theories present an interesting look into not just how users are conceptualizing the rumored timeline curation algorithm, but how they might be defining "algorithm" to begin with. As noted in our results, we found both abstract and operational folk theories reflecting two notions of algorithms: as an other or interloper, and the algorithm as a process requiring decision criteria, respectively.

This is a different gradation of algorithmic awareness than has been previously considered in empirical work, as prior studies (e.g., [5, 10, 11, 29]) have focused on operational theories, defining algorithmic awareness as starting at what we call operational folk theories. Our findings indicate that a finer-grained definition of algorithmic awareness, which includes the abstract folk theories we have found, may be necessary to capture the full scope of what people understand about algorithms. This allows algorithmic understanding, as a concept, as well as future studies that deal with algorithmic understanding, to consider the perspectives of users who are newly or vaguely aware of algorithms as a concept, but have not progressed to theorizing how the algorithms operate. This expanded concept of algorithmic awareness would also lend empirical support to theoretical work (e.g., [14]) which argues that "algorithm" is defined in a multi-faceted way that goes beyond the technical meaning to account for social science and colloquial use of the term.

One type of folk theory we did not find were the complex, mechanism-level theories found by Eslami et. al. [10] as well as in prior folk theory work (e.g. [5, 11, 29]); even the theories we labeled "operational" were less detailed than many of the theories they elicited. This points to an important methodological implication, as our studies use two different methods of folk theory identification with diverging results. These prior studies used direct elicitation methods from lab-based and interview scenarios, while our study used indirect, inferential analysis of text "in the wild." This suggests that future research should take into account (and, potentially, directly compare) the potential differences between directly elicited and indirectly identified theories noted by [16] as the two methods may be revealing different sides of a user's folk theory: a causal theory stemming from active cognition of the algorithm at time of elicitation for the former, and a more implicit, always-extant "theory in use" for the latter.

Contextual Frames: An Open Question

Finally, our findings regarding how user folk theories frame or influence reactions to change point to an important open question. We saw a relationship between these two concepts, such that more explicit folk theories are expressed through more explicit reactions. This suggests that the context of a person's reaction to and sense of personal expectation regarding a system should be considered when investigating folk theories, and vice versa, but further points to the need for discussing the relationship between a folk theory, reaction to change, and a system's value for the user.

We have reason to believe, as we have explained in the literature review and noted in our results, that folk theories act as a frame for user reactions. Orlikowski and Gash's work [7, 27] indicates that, for technology in general, prior assumptions about how a system works (here, user folk theories) act as a contextual frame for how a user reacts to that technology (here, their reason for resisting algorithmic change), and our results, viewed through this lens, could be an indicator that this paradigm applies even outside of its original business IT adoption context. As it appears that folk theories set the frame in which algorithmic change is processed and either accepted or rejected, it may be essential to take the context of an individual's algorithmic folk knowledge into account when studying reactions to algorithmically-driven systems.

However, we do not show a causal relationship, and it is also possible that the inverse is true. In that case, expressed folk theories could be highlighting a post-hoc attempt by users to rationalize their expectations of system value by forming an appropriate folk theory of how the system works on a technical level. For example, an individual who explicitly values and expresses the fact that their use case/value proposition for Twitter is being able to see exactly what is going on, right at this moment, could rationalize a folk theory of an upcoming algorithmic change which directly threatens that, such as a relevance theory which would completely upend the value proposition. The implication of this possibility would be a new opportunity to understand how folk theories are formed, and would somewhat mirror the expectations of direct elicitation methods (e.g. [12, 16]).

Limitations

As with any study, certain limitations merit caution when interpreting these findings. First, as #RIPTwitter was an event that individuals had to self-select into, we cannot be sure how the participants map to Twitter's whole user base; however, we have, at the very least, provided a window into the folk theories and expectations of some of the platform's most vocal power-users. Second, as noted in our methods section, this data is based on a single case on a single platform, and therefore is tied to the circumstances of that platform and case. Future work should look at similar incidents on other platforms, as well as seek out implicit user reactions and folk theories that are not in response to an isolated incident. Third, as this case is based around early resistance to a rumor of algorithmic change, future work should also examine user reactions and folk algorithm theories during later steps of the change process. These include during and after implementation, in situations where algorithmic change is noticed incrementally by users, and in situations with constant A/B testing. Finally, as the corpus used was exclusively English-language, future work should examine potential cross-cultural differences in these areas.

CONCLUSION

#RIPTwitter was prompted by a rumor from a BuzzFeed article. In the end, some small-scale features to promote relevant tweets were added to the Twitter Timeline, but the non-chronological algorithmic apocalypse prophesied by the community did not come to pass. However, examining this outpouring of sentiment has proven a useful exercise regardless, and provided a better understanding of both reasons why users resist algorithmic change and how their folk theory-based understandings of algorithmically-driven systems may relate to those reactions. This points a way forward towards understanding, assessing, and improving user knowledge of algorithmic systems.

ACKNOWLEDGEMENTS

We acknowledge partial support from the US National Science Foundation (IIS-1217143/003), valuable research assistance from Bennett Hensey, Minkyong Kim, and Justine Yucesan, and valuable insights from the anonymous reviewers and the associate chair.

REFERENCES

1. Daniel Bates and Rob Waugh. 2011. Facebook blog is inundated with thousands of protests as users start Facebook group 'We Hate the New News Feed'. Retrieved from http://www.dailymail.co.uk/sciencetech/article-2039726/Facebook-changes-Thousands-protests-We-hate-new-news-feed-group.html
2. Anol Bhattacherjee. 2001. Understanding Information Systems Continuance: An Expectation-Confirmation Model. *MIS Quarterly*, 25, 3: 351-370.
3. Engin Bozdag. 2013. Bias in algorithmic filtering and personalization. *Ethics and Information Technology*, 15, 3: 209-227.
4. Samuel Brody and Nicholas Diakopoulos. 2011. Cooooooooooooooollllllllllllll!!!!!!!!!!!!!!: using word lengthening to detect sentiment in microblogs. In *Proceedings of the Conference on Empirical Methods in Natural Language Processing*, 562-570.
5. Taina Bucher. 2016. The algorithmic imaginary: exploring the ordinary affects of Facebook algorithms. *Information, Communication & Society*, 1-15.
6. Nitesh V. Chawla, Kevin W. Bowyer, Lawrence O. Hall, and W. Philip Kegelmeyer. 2002. SMOTE: Synthetic Minority Over-sampling Technique. *Journal of Artificial Intelligence Research*, 16, 1: 321-357.
7. Elizabeth Davidson. 2006. A technological frames perspective on information technology and organizational change. *The Journal of Applied Behavioral Science*, 42, 1: 23-39.
8. Fred D Davis. 1989. Perceived usefulness, perceived ease of use, and user acceptance of information technology. *MIS Quarterly*, 13, 3: 319-340.
9. Maeve Duggan. 2015. *Mobile Messaging and Social Media 2015*. Pew Research Center, Washington, DC.
10. Motahhare Eslami, Karrie Karahalios, Christian Sandvig, Kristen Vaccaro, Aimee Rickman, Kevin Hamilton, and Alex Kirlik. 2016. First I “like” it, then I hide it: Folk Theories of Social Feeds. In *Proceedings of the 34rd Annual SIGCHI Conference on Human Factors in Computing Systems*, 2371-2382.
11. Motahhare Eslami, Aimee Rickman, Kristen Vaccaro, Amirhossein Aleyasen, Andy Vuong, Karrie Karahalios, Kevin Hamilton, and Christian Sandvig. 2015. "I always assumed that I wasn’t really that close to [her]": Reasoning about invisible algorithms in the news feed. In *Proceedings of the 33rd Annual SIGCHI Conference on Human Factors in Computing Systems*, 153-162.
12. Susan A Gelman and Cristine H Legare. 2011. Concepts and folk theories. *Annual Review of Anthropology*, 40, 1: 379-398.
13. Tarleton Gillespie. 2014. The Relevance of Algorithms. In *Media technologies: Essays on communication, materiality, and society*, Tarleton Gillespie, Pablo Boczkowski and Kirsten Foot (ed.). MIT Press, Cambridge, MA, 167-193.
14. Tarleton Gillespie. 2016. Algorithm. In *Digital Keywords*, Benjamin Peters (ed.). Princeton University Press, Princeton, NJ, 18-30.
15. Christopher M Hoadley, Heng Xu, Joey J Lee, and Mary Beth Rosson. 2010. Privacy as information access and illusory control: The case of the Facebook News Feed privacy outcry. *Electronic commerce research and applications*, 9, 1: 50-60.
16. Natalie Jones, Helen Ross, Timothy Lynam, Pascal Perez, and Anne Leitch. 2011. Mental Models: An Interdisciplinary Synthesis of Theory and Methods. *Ecology and Society*, 16, 1.
17. Yoram M Kalman and Darren Gergle. 2014. Letter repetitions in computer-mediated communication: A unique link between spoken and online language. *Computers in Human Behavior*, 34, 2014: 187-193.
18. Alex Kantrowitz. 2016. Twitter To Introduce Algorithmic Timeline As Soon As Next Week. Retrieved from http://www.buzzfeed.com/alexkantrowitz/twitter-to-introduce-algorithmic-timeline-as-soon-as-next-we
19. Frank C Keil. 2010. The feasibility of folk science. *Cognitive science*, 34, 5: 826-862.
20. Hee-Woong Kim and Atreyi Kankanhalli. 2009. Investigating User Resistance to Information Systems Implementation: A Status Quo Bias Perspective. *MIS Quarterly*, 33, 3: 567-582.
21. René F Kizilcec. 2016. How Much Information?: Effects of Transparency on Trust in an Algorithmic Interface. In *Proceedings of the 2016 CHI Conference on Human Factors in Computing Systems*, 2390-2395.
22. Amy Kraft. 2016. Backlash continues over Instagram's new algorithm. Retrieved from http://www.cbsnews.com/news/backlash-continues-over-instagrams-new-algorithm/
23. J Richard Landis and Gary G Koch. 1977. The Measurement of Observer Agreement for Categorical Data. *Biometrics*, 33, 1: 159-174.
24. Liette Lapointe and Suzanne Rivard. 2005. A Multilevel Model of Resistance to Information Technology Implementation. *MIS Quarterly*, 29, 3: 461-491.
25. Tor J Larsen, Anne M Sørebø, and Øystein Sørebø. 2009. The role of task-technology fit as users’ motivation to continue information system use. *Computers in Human Behavior*, 25, 3: 778-784.

26. Brett Molina. 2016. CEO Dorsey responds to Twitter timeline outrage. Retrieved from http://www.usatoday.com/story/tech/news/2016/02/06/twitter-may-change-timelines-and-no-one-happy/79925572/

27. Wanda J Orlikowski and Debra C Gash. 1994. Technological frames: making sense of information technology in organizations. *ACM Transactions on Information Systems (TOIS)*, 12, 2: 174-207.

28. Stephen J Payne. 2003. Users' mental models: The very ideas. In *HCI Models, Theories, and Frameworks: Toward a Multidisciplinary Science*, John M Carroll (ed.). Morgan Kaufmann, Burlington, MA, 135-156.

29. Emilee Rader and Rebecca Gray. 2015. Understanding User Beliefs About Algorithmic Curation in the Facebook News Feed. In *Proceedings of the 33rd Annual ACM Conference on Human Factors in Computing Systems*, 173-182.

30. H Andrew Schwartz and Lyle H Ungar. 2015. Data-Driven Content Analysis of Social Media A Systematic Overview of Automated Methods. *The ANNALS of the American Academy of Political and Social Science*, 659, 1: 78-94.

31. James YL Thong, Se-Joon Hong, and Kar Yan Tam. 2006. The effects of post-adoption beliefs on the expectation-confirmation model for information technology continuance. *International Journal of Human-Computer Studies*, 64, 9: 799-810.

32. Robert Philip Weber. 1990. *Basic Content Analysis*. Sage, Thousand Oaks, CA.

33. Robert K Yin. 2003. *Case Study Research: Design and Methods*. Sage Publications, Thousand Oaks, CA.

34. Yan Zhang and Barbara M. Wildemuth. 2009. Qualitative analysis of content. In *Applications of Social Research Methods to Questions in Information and Library Science*, Barbara M. Wildemuth (ed.). Libraries Unlimited., Westport, CT, 308-319.

The Bag of Communities: Identifying Abusive Behavior Online with Preexisting Internet Data

Eshwar Chandrasekharan[1], Mattia Samory[2], Anirudh Srinivasan[1], Eric Gilbert[1]
[1]Georgia Institute of Technology, [2]University of Padua
[1]Atlanta GA 30332 USA, [2]35122 Padua Italy
eshwar3@gatech.edu, samoryma@dei.unipd.it, asrinivasan45@gatech.edu, gilbert@cc.gatech.edu

ABSTRACT
Since its earliest days, harassment and abuse have plagued the Internet. Recent research has focused on in-domain methods to detect abusive content and faces several challenges, most notably the need to obtain large training corpora. In this paper, we introduce a novel computational approach to address this problem called *Bag of Communities* (BoC)—a technique that leverages large-scale, preexisting data from other Internet communities. We then apply BoC toward identifying abusive behavior within a major Internet community. Specifically, we compute a post's similarity to 9 other communities from 4chan, Reddit, Voat and MetaFilter. We show that a BoC model can be used on communities "off the shelf" with roughly 75% accuracy—no training examples are needed from the target community. A dynamic BoC model achieves 91.18% accuracy after seeing 100,000 human-moderated posts, and uniformly outperforms in-domain methods. Using this conceptual and empirical work, we argue that the BoC approach may allow communities to deal with a range of common problems, like abusive behavior, faster and with fewer engineering resources.

Author Keywords
social computing; online communities; abusive behavior; moderation; machine learning

ACM Classification Keywords
H.4.m. Information Systems Applications: Miscellaneous

INTRODUCTION
A key challenge for online communities is moderation. For example, the founders of the social media startup Yik Yak spent months of their early time removing hate speech [6]. Twitter has stated publicly that dealing with abusive behavior remains its most pressing challenge [63]. Many sites have disabled the ability to comment at all because of problems moderating those spaces [15], and empirical work has shown

Permission to make digital or hard copies of all or part of this work for personal or classroom use is granted without fee provided that copies are not made or distributed for profit or commercial advantage and that copies bear this notice and the full citation on the first page. Copyrights for components of this work owned by others than the author(s) must be honored. Abstracting with credit is permitted. To copy otherwise, or republish, to post on servers or to redistribute to lists, requires prior specific permission and/or a fee. Request permissions from Permissions@acm.org.
CHI 2017, May 06 - 11, 2017, Denver, CO, USA
Copyright is held by the owner/author(s). Publication rights licensed to ACM.
ACM 978-1-4503-4655-9/17/05$15.00
DOI: http://dx.doi.org/10.1145/3025453.3026018

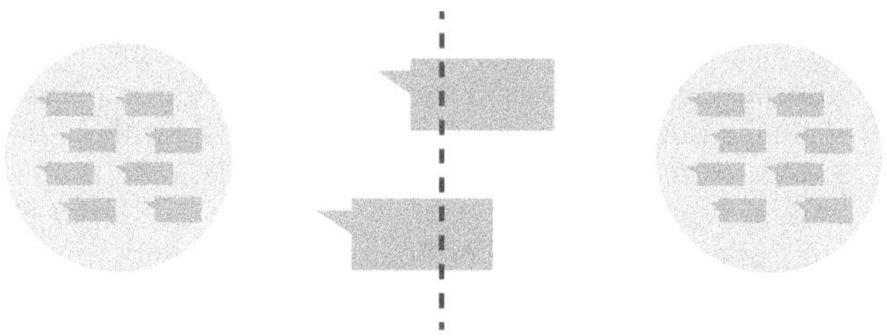

Figure 1. A conceptual illustration of Bag of Communities approach, here with two source communities employed. When new and unlabeled posts are generated in a community, similarity scores can be assigned by comparing them to preexisting posts from other communities (*blue* and *pink*, in this example). A downstream classifier uses similarity scores to make predictions, in our case about abusive behavior.

that people leave platforms after being the victims of online abuse [27]. Moreover, recent Pew surveys indicate that abuse happens online much more frequently than often suspected: approximately 40% of Internet users report being the subject of online abuse at some point, with underrepresented users most often targeted [18, 19, 25].

On most sites today, moderation takes two primary forms: distributed social moderation [20, 30, 49, 50] and machine learning-based approaches [6, 10]. In the former, a site's users triage submissions via voting or reporting mechanisms—after which the site can take action. In the latter, online communities compile large datasets of example posts that have been moderated off-site, and thereafter train machine learning algorithms. The distributed social moderation approach is appealing because it can be deployed quickly and easily, and offloads the work of moderation to a large human workforce; yet, it requires vast amounts of human labor from the very people you would rather not see abusive posts (i.e., your users). Machine learning-based approaches can help by algorithmically triaging comments for a much smaller number of (perhaps paid) human moderators; yet, they typically require vast amounts of labeled training data.

This paper bridges this data gap by introducing a new analytic concept for studying and building online communities: the *Bag of Communities* (BoC) approach. In brief, BoC aims to sidestep site-specific models (and their data) by computing similarity scores between one community's data and preexisting data from other online communities. In this paper, we introduce the concept of BoC and use it in an "existence proof:" identifying abusive posts from a major online community. Relying on 10M posts collected from 9 different online communities from 4chan, Reddit, Voat and MetaFilter, we show that a BoC-based linguistic classifier outperforms an in-domain classifier with access to over 4 years of site-specific data. We demonstrate that a BoC classifier can be used on a target community[1] off the shelf with roughly 75% accuracy—no training examples are needed from the target community. That is, an algorithm with access to only *out-of-domain* data can predict abusive posts in another community—without access to data from that community. In addition to this static model, we also explore a dynamic BoC model mimicking scenarios where newly moderated data arrives in batches. It outperforms a solely in-domain model at every batch size, achieving 91.18% accuracy (95% precision) after seeing 100,000 human-moderated posts. This is notable since it implies that while the BoC approach will help communities without moderators to generate training data (static model), the BoC will continue to boost systems that predict abusive behavior after years of professional moderation (dynamic model).

For CMC and HCI theory, BoC provides a new analytic lens through which existing online phenomena may be examined. For example, a researcher might use BoC to empirically derive a taxonomy of online communities based on their similarity to one another. From a systems perspective, BoC may allow sites to address a variety of common problems. In addition to identifying abusive behavior (the focus of the present work), sites need to sort content based on its likelihood to be interacted with, identify spam, and decide whether a post requires intervention by professionals (e.g., suicidal ideation). In the latter case, for example, one could imagine deploying BoC using r/suicidewatch, a Reddit suicide support forum, as a companion data source. In essence, BoC could allow communities (especially new ones with limited resources) to spend their time on what *differentiates* them from other places on the Internet, and less time on common problems shared across sites.

Next, we review existing work, and then formally define BoC. Then, we present our empirical investigation into identifying abusive posts from a major online community using data gathered from 4chan, Reddit, Voat and MetaFilter. Finally, we reflect on some of the opportunities presented by BoC, as well as some of the limitations and opportunities introduced by our empirical work.

RELATED WORK

In this section, we discuss related work on online antisocial behavior, and how it often focuses on in-domain methods. We conclude by laying out the challenges faced by current methods, and discuss how our work helps address these problems.

Commonly deployed moderation approaches

Having plagued online communities for years, technical, design and moderation approaches have been invented to cope with abusive posts (e.g., [28, 31, 34]). A simple existing approach is to designate a separate place where members can "take it outside," places sometimes communicated through FAQs (such as on Usenet) [56]. Reprimands for violations might include private emails, or even public censure [56]. To take one example, many sports-centric forums have designated trash-talk threads, suggesting to members that the behavior is acceptable here but not elsewhere. More sophisticated approaches exist as well. In widespread use today is distributed social moderation, on sites such as Reddit, Hacker News, Yahoo! Answers, Facebook, Yik Yak and Slashdot [20, 30, 49, 50]. In this model, other users vote up or vote down content as they see fit, perhaps even reporting highly objectionable content through special reporting mechanisms (i.e., Facebook's bullying report mechanism, or Reddit's reporting mechanisms). Also in widespread use are centralized moderation mechanisms, embodied in technical designs on sites like Reddit and other forums, where a small number of power users maintain order over the community by removing abusive posts manually. Several popular sites, like YouTube and Facebook, have teams of human moderators, who manually go through posts, and scrub the site of offensive or malicious content [7]. Finally, a handful of slightly more technical approaches are reported to exist within certain communities: word-ban lists and source-ban lists take action when users try to post something objectionable, or from somewhere objectionable. For example, sites like Yik Yak employ manually assembled word-ban lists (i.e., specific terms that flag a user's post) [6], and sites like Hacker News and Yelp employ source-ban lists where users may not post from IP addresses originating from known proxies and Tor. Some communities take the approach of promoting quality content, rather than demoting abuse, which might have the desired effect of improving online discourse. Studies have investigated the extent to which a subset of the criteria at play in the selection of high quality comments by the New York Times as "NYT Picks," can be operationalized computationally [14, 42].

Drawbacks of deployed approaches

While partially effective and used at scale, all the existing approaches described above suffer from drawbacks. First, the "take it outside" approach assumes that the objectionable behavior will remain locked away in the specially-designated area; however, we know from press accounts [41] as well as academic research (e.g., [40]) that norms often bleed over into neighboring communities. Second, both the distributed and centralized moderation approaches require a great deal of human labor [29, 44, 64]. In the centralized approach, the labor falls on a small number of volunteers who must work tirelessly to maintain the community; in the distributed approach, sites ask their users to deal with exactly the type of content they wish their users did not have to see. Moreover, we know from empirical work that these voting mechanisms are susceptible to herding effects [36], underprovision [21], and potential collusion as flagging can be used to indicate disagreement or dislike of a post that is not otherwise inappropriate or profane [32], casting doubt on their reliability. Third, the more technical word-ban lists and source-ban lists are crude by modern standards, and have been observed to perform poorly [57]. For word-ban lists, you need only consider in how many different ways swear words are used (i.e.,

[1] Anonymized for reasons explained later.

exclamation, disbelief, exasperation, insult, etc.) to see the difficulty in applying blanket word-bans. Systems that only consider the source (i.e., banning or shadow-banning users coming from Tor [17]) inadvertently censor users who, for example, try to hide from repressive governments.

In-domain approaches to moderate antisocial behavior

Prior research has looked at technical approaches to moderating online antisocial behavior. All of them tend to focus on in-domain methods to study different kinds of antisocial behavior and develop strategies to counter them. Studies have shown that antisocial behavior like undesirable posting [9, 10, 59], and textual cyberbullying [16, 65] can be identified based on the presence of insults, user behavior and topic models. In recent years, politeness has been studied in online settings, to help keep online interactions more civil. Researchers have built a *politeness* classifier using a computational framework for identifying linguistic aspects of politeness [11]. While these methods are effective within-domain, learning *across domains or communities* remains an open question.

Challenges faced by current work

Current moderation techniques employed by researchers and community moderators face key challenges. Supervised detection techniques require labeled ground truth data for building and evaluating a model. These data are difficult to obtain, and manual annotation is a common approach to address this challenge. But this task requires a large amount of manual labor to hand-annotate (or label) the data. This method is also inherently subject to biases in the annotator's judgment, which could affect the quality of the analysis results [8].

A constant struggle is to identify good data sets that researchers can study. Communities do not publicly share data containing moderated content due to privacy and public relations concerns. This restricts data access, and makes it difficult to model the types of abuse present in a community. In addition, new and emerging online communities lack enough data from their respective users. A new community has by definition few contributions, and therefore even fewer labeled examples; this does not allow them to build robust automated detection systems for identifying abusive content. As a result, building cross-domain moderation systems remains a challenge. Yet, studies have shown that it is important to define community tolerance for abusive behavior as early as possible [61].

BoC aims to address many, but not all, of these challenges. In particular, cross-community similarity allows online communities to piggyback on the data of others, requiring far fewer (and perhaps no) labeled training examples. BoC may form the backbone of cross-domain classifiers built on the data of many Internet communities.

BAG OF COMMUNITIES (BOC)

In this section, we define a new approach to identify certain kinds of online behavior by leveraging large-scale, preexisting data from other Internet communities. The intuition behind our approach is to use the similarity of a post to a known, existing community as a feature in later classification. For example, a post that seems at home within a corpus of 4chan posts may likely be inappropriate for npr.org.

First, we define a method to compute cross-community similarity (CCS), a building block of our approach. We then introduce a new model where a variety of CCS data points act in concert to aid predictions in a new community. Analogous to the well-known Bag of Words representation, we call this the *Bag of Communities* approach.

Cross-Community Similarity (CCS)

Let S be a source community, with whose data we will compare a community of interest—or target community T. While one could approach representing S and T in a variety of ways, it seems natural to model S and T via their posts: let $p \in \mathbb{R}^n$ be a vector-space representation of a post in n dimensions. S and T then comprise all vectors corresponding to their constituent posts. One dimension might represent whether the post was created on a weekday, another might represent whether it contains the word "happy," another might represent whether the post contains an image, etc.

S and T could represent posts along a variety of (possibly infinite) dimensions: temporal characteristics (burstiness vs. spread-out), posting medium (textual vs. image-centric), network structure (connected vs. disconnected), identity (anonymous vs. identifiable), community norms (supportive vs. judgmental). In this paper, we focus on a linguistic representation: the words and phrases used in S and T serve to define S and T. That is to say, a post is represented as a vector with 1's connoting a word or phrase's presence, and 0's otherwise.

There are as many ways to compute $CCS(S,T)$ as there are to compute similarity between vector spaces [1, 24, 33]. Its application may drive the particular method. For example, a straightforward approach might involve computing the centroids s and t of S and T, respectively, and next computing $cos(\theta)$ for the angle θ between them. However, we adopt an approach in this paper inspired by Granger causality [23]. Let M_S be a statistical model that predicts (real-valued) membership in S. $CCS(S,T)$ is then the information provided by $M_S(p)$ in predicting membership in T, for some post p. In other words, we let a model predicting membership in S to predict membership in T. This is analogous to the Granger-causal idea of letting one time series at time t predict the value in another time series at time $t+k$. By "information provided by $M_S(p)$," we mean that M_S may not be used directly, but as the raw material of some encapsulating function. The range of $CCS(S,T)$ is $[0,1]$, with $CCS(S,T) = 0$ for entirely dissimilar communities and $CCS(S,T) = 1$ for entirely similar communities.

Bag of Communities definition

In a Bag of Communities representation, a post $p \in T$ generates CCS scores $CCS(S_1,T)$, $CCS(S_2,T)$, $CCS(S_3,T)$, ... for a variety of source communities S_1, S_2, S_3, ... A Bag of Communities model develops a function $f(CCS(S_1,T), CCS(S_2,T), CCS(S_3,T), ..., T)$ that maps these CCS scores and local, site-specific information to a prediction in $[0,1]$.

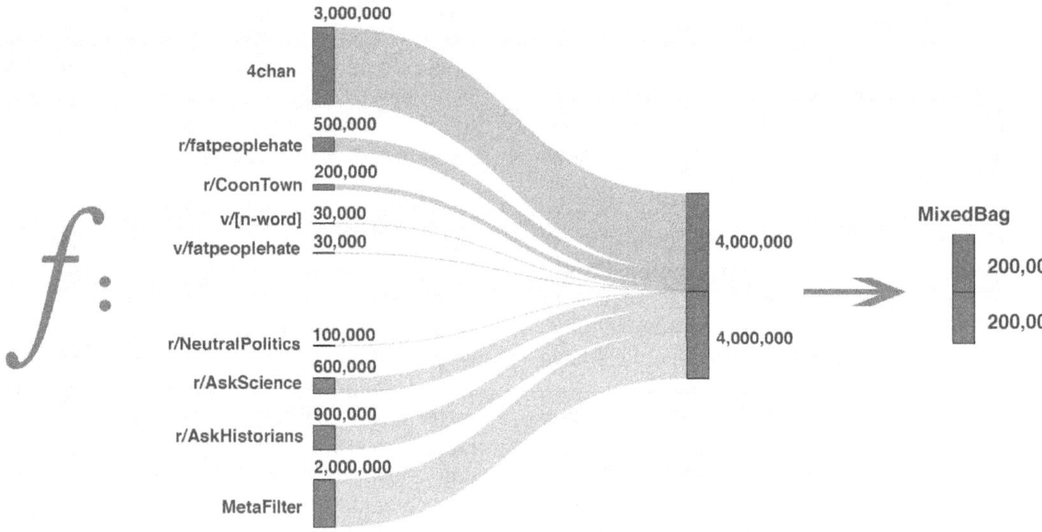

Figure 2. An illustration of the overarching Bag of Communities concept, along with the approximate number of posts collected from each source community in our empirical work. Cross-community similarity values are obtained by comparing target community posts to preexisting posts from source communities ($CCS(S_i, T)$). Communities in *red* were selected because we hypothesized they contained abusive content and those in *green* because they are well-moderated. The goal is to learn a function that maps the source communities to the target community.

In other words, as illustrated in Figure 1, a post might be compared against 4chan, MetaFilter, hateful subreddits, etc. These scores are then fed to another, higher-level classifier that also takes site-specific information into account. In other words, an ensemble classifier might use site-specific information (e.g., the words and phrases used in *that* community) along with CCS scores representing similarity to 4chan, MetaFilter, etc. to make a prediction. Figure 2 illustrates the overall process in function notation, mapping the domain of source communities to the range of the target community.

SOURCE AND TARGET COMMUNITIES

Next, we explore using the BoC approach in predicting abusive behavior in a new online community. We draw data from 9 communities from 4chan, Reddit, MetaFilter and Voat—with MixedBag[2] as our *target* community. Our BoC models will aim to learn from content on source communities, and make predictions about a post's likelihood of being labeled as abusive on MixedBag.

Next, we look at our source and target communities in more detail, and explain the motivation behind using each community to build our BoC models.

Source: 4chan's /b/ and /pol/

4chan is made up of themed online discussion boards, where users generally post anonymously. 4chan is popularly known as the "Internet hate machine" [53], and "the rude, raunchy, underbelly of the Internet" [39]. The use of racist, sexist and homophobic language is common on 4chan. Groups are often referred to using a "fag" suffix (e.g., new members are "newfags", British users are "britfags"), and a common response to any self-shot picture by a woman is "tits or GTFO" [3].

/pol/ is 4chan's *politically incorrect* board. As per 4chan's rules page, /pol/ is a board where debate and discussion related to politics and current events is welcome. /b/ is 4chan's "random" board, and is 4chan's first and most active board, representing 30% of all 4chan traffic. In the words of its creator, /b/ is the "life force of the website," and a place for "rowdiness and lawlessness" [60]. These boards are infamous for exhibiting a range of explicit content. Despite being a funny, open and creative board that is credited for the creation and promotion of numerous memes, the content on /b/ is frequently intentionally offensive, with little held sacred.

Source: Reddit's r/fatpeoplehate and r/CoonTown

In the wake of Reddit's new anti-harassment policy, the website banned several hate communities that it found in violation of the site's rules [4, 52]. According to Reddit's announcement, "We will ban subreddits that allow their communities to use the subreddit as a platform to harass individuals when moderators don't take action." [48]

We collected posts from two of Reddit's most controversial communities which routinely engaged in hate speech,

[2]Pseudonym for the actual target website/community, as per research agreement.

namely *r/fatpeoplehate* and *r/CoonTown*. r/fatpeoplehate is a fat shaming community devoted to posting (among other things) pictures of overweight people for ridicule [52]. It was one of the most prominent removals from Reddit, and had 151,404 subscribers at the time of its banning, as reported by Reddit Metrics.[3]

r/CoonTown is a racist subreddit dedicated to violent hate speech against black people. It contained "a buffet of crude jokes and racial slurs, complaints about the liberal media, links to news stories that highlight black-on-white crime or Confederate pride, and discussions of black people appropriating white culture." [35] It had 21,168 subscribers at the time of banning, as reported by Reddit Metrics.[4]

Source: Voat's v/fatpeoplehate and v/[n-word]

Voat is a media aggregator website which claims to emphasize free speech above all other values. Following Reddit's banning of subreddits for violating its harassment policy, users from those banned communities migrated to Voat, creating hate subverses to take the place of their banned subreddit counterparts [26, 37]. In particular, we collected posts from v/[n-word] and v/fatpeoplehate, which are the Voat equivalents of r/CoonTown and r/fatpeoplehate on Reddit.

Source: MetaFilter

In addition to sites like 4chan and Voat, we also try to use well-moderated sites, like MetaFilter, as distractors or counterexamples of abusive content. MetaFilter requires $5 to establish an account, and is one of the most strictly moderated communities on the Internet. Moderators hide inappropriate material quickly, and reinforce positive norms by making good behavior far more visible than bad [55]. Whenever needed, moderators step in and temporarily suspend an offending user's account.

Source: r/AskHistorians, r/AskScience & r/NeutralPolitics

r/AskHistorians and r/AskScience are communities that are actively moderated, and have well-defined rules regarding user behavior and interactions on the subreddit. These rules are regularly enforced by moderators and exist to ensure that debates on the subreddit do not devolve into personal insults or ad hominem attacks.

r/AskScience urges its users to "Be civil: Remember the human and follow Reddiquette", in its guidelines [45, 46]. r/AskHistorians has a strict "Civility" rule which says, "All users are expected to behave with courtesy and politeness at all times. We will not tolerate racism, sexism, or any other forms of bigotry. This includes Holocaust denialism. Nor will we accept personal insults of any kind." [47]

r/NeutralPolitics is a well-moderated community "dedicated to evenhanded, empirical discussion of political issues." The community urges its users to be courteous in its comment rules,[5] which states that "Name calling, sarcasm, demeaning language, or otherwise being rude or hostile to another user will get your comment removed."

[3] http://redditmetrics.com/r/fatpeoplehate
[4] http://redditmetrics.com/r/CoonTown
[5] https://www.reddit.com/r/NeutralPolitics/wiki/guidelines

Target: MixedBag

We have a research partnership with a large online community who provided data moderated off-site for violating abuse policies. Getting data such as these is typically a major hurdle, as companies fear the blowback that may occur after its release. As per our partnership agreement, we will refer to this target community using a pseudonym: *MixedBag*. The community has on the order of 100M users, and is typical of user-generated content sites: the site has profiles, posts, comments, friends, etc. We obtained comments that were deleted by the site's moderators as abusive, and flagged by users, as part of this partnership.

A notable challenge is that *a priori*, the target and source sites share little in common. For example, MixedBag is a pseudonymous community where conversation is structured into threads of comments, in response to a piece of shared content; 4chan is an image board where anonymous people often post short and unrelated phrases in response.

DATA

We collected data from each of our source communities, as well as data from MixedBag as target data. In our static model, we use the source and target datasets as classic train and test datasets. In the dynamic model, we iteratively allow a model trained on source data to update itself as it sees new batches of target data.

Source data

We collected varying amounts of data from each source community, as it was available:

- **3M posts** from 4chan /b/ and /pol/ boards, spanning 14 months in 2015 and 2016
- **700K posts** from r/fatpeoplehate and r/CoonTown, spanning January to July 2015
- **70K posts** from v/fatpeoplehate and v/[n-word], spanning August 2015 to February 2016
- **2M posts** from MetaFilter, which contains all posts archived on the site, spanning July 1999 to July 2015
- **1.5M posts** from r/AskScience and r/AskHistorians, spanning 2007 to 2015
- **130K posts** from r/NeutralPolitics, spanning 2007 to 2015

We also obtained **3.5M** random comments from MixedBag, which were publicly available at the time of data collection. The comments serve as distractors for building a BoC model: they represent a random sample of the site's publicly visible comments. In total, we collected over **10M** posts to serve as training data using a variety of archives and crawlers. *Note:* our training phase does not give static models access to comments moderated from MixedBag.

Target data

To evaluate our model, we obtained the text in **200,000** *moderated comments* from MixedBag. The dataset contains over 4 years of human-curated data—comments moderated off-site

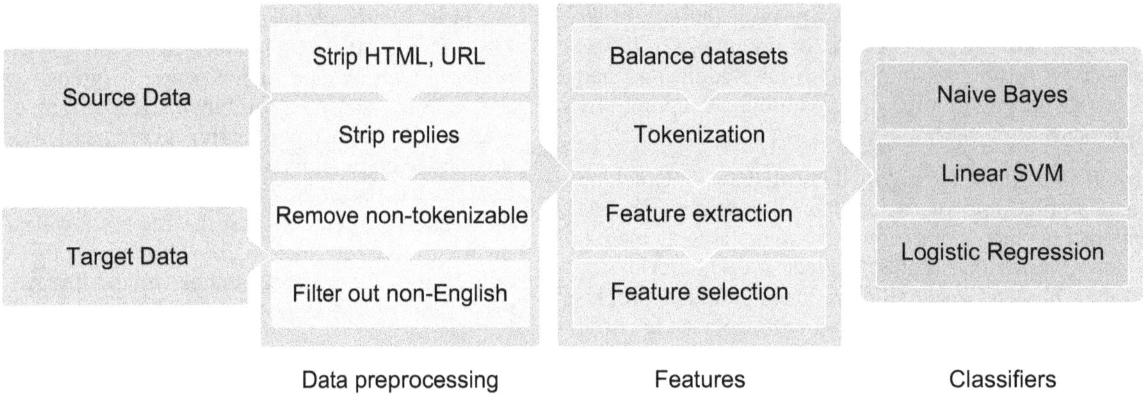

Figure 3. Flowchart depicting the overall *CCS* model-building pipeline. After collecting Bag of Communities and MixedBag data, text undergoes a number of preprocessing steps before acting as input for three different classifiers. Each *CCS* classifier tries to distinguish a source community's posts from a random background cohort of distrators.

by moderators and users for violating abuse policies. As mentioned before, these data were given to us by MixedBag as part of a research partnership. We also obtained the textual content of **200,000** random MixedBag comments, which were still present online during the time of data collection, using the same procedure as in the section above. Note that there is no overlap between (on-site) MixedBag comments used for training and testing.

To provide readers a sense of the types of comments moderated off-site, the following randomly-sampled ones represent typical instances. Readers are forewarned that most are offensive and "not safe for work" (NSFW):

> SO I WILL LOOK YOU'RE FAMILY UP ON WHITEPAGES AND MURDER YOU!!
>
> Lol, go kill yourself
>
> go fuk yourself ugly
>
> YOUR GRANDFATHER IS BURING IN HELL KIKE!!
>
> hehehe! we're gonna have a lot of fun with this! now, lie on your back.
>
> This is full of fail and AIDS!
>
> awwwww what a cute [n-word]

APPLYING BOC TO ABUSIVE BEHAVIOR ONLINE

We used the data collected from our *Bag of Communities* and MixedBag to build and evaluate multiple machine-learning models. In this section, we will discuss the components of our BoC model and steps in the model's pipeline. For reference and overview, Figure 3 visualizes the pipeline for training every internal *CCS* estimator.

Data preprocessing

We began preprocessing the data sets by stripping replies, HTML elements and URLs in the collected comments. Next, we discarded posts that were not tokenizable. These were comments that were either not in Unicode or did not contain any text/tokens. Finally, we performed language detection and discarded comments that were not in English. We used *langdetect* [54], an open-source Java library, for language identification.

Balancing datasets

After the preprocessing steps, we shuffle the datasets and balance them to ensure an equal number of posts from each class. Note that balancing the number of samples from each class likely does not mimic real-world situations. In general, abusive posts are relatively rare. However, balancing across all conditions ensures that we can easily interpret model fits relative to one another. In other words, since the in-domain model will also act on the balanced datasets, balancing will not privilege either approach.

Tokenization & feature extraction

We tokenize comments, and break the text contained in each comment into words. Using these words, we go on to build the vocabulary for all comments in the sample. Each comment is represented as a feature vector of all words and phrases present in the vocabulary (i.e., a *Bag of Words* (BoW) model). The feature values are either the binary-occurrence values (present or not) or the frequency of occurrence. We extract n-grams ($n \in [1, 2, 3]$) from the text and perform vectorization using a Hashing Vectorizer. Hashing Vectorizers create a mapping between tokens and their corresponding feature value (TF-IDF) [43].

Feature selection

We compute the ANOVA F-values for the provided sample, and select the most distinguishing features using the F-value between features and labels. We perform feature selection on features in the *top k* in $[100, 10^3, 10^4, all]$. For example, when *top* $k = 10^3$, only the top $1,000$ BoW features are selected based on their ANOVA F-values.

Classifiers

To build internal *CCS* estimators, we ran classifications tests using three different classifiers: *Multinomial Naive Bayes* (NB), *Linear Support Vector Classification* (LinearSVC), and

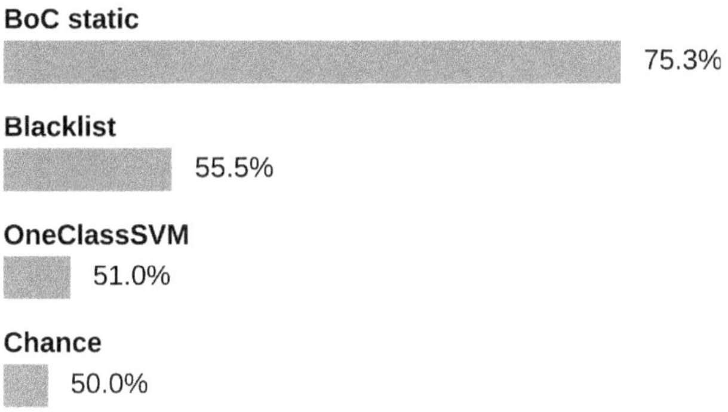

Figure 4. Accuracy values for baselines and the BoC static model. *Chance* refers to a random classifier.

Logistic Regression (Logit). Our BoC models use the output likelihoods from these classifiers as internal estimators.

Parameter search

We ran classification tests on the datasets using different settings to identify the best configuration for our BoC model. We performed a grid search on a held out 5% sample of our data, provided by *GridSearchCV* [43]; it exhaustively generates candidates from a grid of parameter values specified in the grid shown in Table 1. For example, *n-gram range* refers to the range of n-grams extracted, and with *n-gram range* = (1, 3), we extracted uni-grams, bi-grams and tri-grams. These parameter values were used to find the best configuration for our models, and are used in all subsequent phases.

BoC static model

We explore two models in this paper. The first we call the "BoC static model," a model that sees no data from the MixedBag target data at all. This BoC static model trains the underlying *CCS* estimators, but gets no access to test data; therefore, it resembles a pre-trained model that could be deployed "off the shelf," similar to how blacklists are often used in practice today.

Parameter	Values	Best Value
n-gram range	[(1,1), (1,2), (1,3)]	(1,3)
binary	[on, off]	off
lowercase	[on, off]	on
max features	$[2^{22}, 2^{26}]$	2^{26}
tf-idf	[on, off]	on
alpha	[0.1, 0.01]	0.01
feature selection	[on, off]	on
top k	$[100, 10^3, 10^4, all]$	10^4
classifier	NB, LinearSVC, Logit	NB

Table 1. Grid of parameter values used when running classification tests to find the best combination of parameter values for our model. The best values shown for all the parameters, found with a grid search, were used in all classifiers. *max features* refers to the upper limit placed upon the hashing vectorizer.

Model	Precision	Recall	Accuracy
BoC static	77.49%	71.24%	75.27%
In-domain	88.20%	91.66%	89.77%
Only abuse BoC dynamic	95.04%	85.85%	**91.18**%
All BoC dynamic	91.09%	87.93%	90.20%

Table 2. Precision, recall and accuracy for different models. The dynamic (online learning) models were trained on 100,000 test samples.

We built two different baselines to compare with our BoC static model, and arrive at performance (lower) bounds.

BoC static baseline: Blacklist

We first trained a model to classify an input comment as abusive or not based on the presence of blacklisted words. We obtained a list of profane terms used in previous work [58]. Such list-based detection mechanisms are commonly deployed in the wild. This model essentially checks for the presence of at least *threshold* number of blacklisted term(s) in the comment. We tested the model for all values of $threshold \in [1, 2, 3, \ldots]$.

BoC static baseline: OneClassSVM

In the absence of labeled, rare and supposedly different data points, one known approach is treating such points as outliers of a known distribution. In our case, we trained a OneClassSVM [43] to learn the distribution of n-grams for naturally-occurring MixedBag posts, in the hope that abusive posts will deviate from this distribution. The OneClassSVM was trained on just 3.5 million random MixedBag posts, and tested on the target data from MixedBag. The parameter configurations used are shown in Table 1.

BoC dynamic model

In addition to the static model, we also explore a "dynamic" (or online learning) model that iteratively sees more and more target community data to aid prediction. This mimics what an upstart community might face when building its own abuse detection models as new moderator labels come in. The BoC dynamic model uses these data in conjunction with internal *CCS* estimators to make final predictions. That is, it has access to the cross-community similarity scores, $CCS(S_i, T)$, described earlier, which gives the likelihood of a (target) post belonging to a (source) community S_i.

In particular, the dynamic BoC model is provided with similarities to each source community, $CCS(S_i, T)$, which is the *predict_proba*() returned by an internal estimator (NB) trained on source community data. These probability scores are used as features, in addition to textual features learned from the target community data by the final estimator (also NB), which predicts whether a given post is abusive or not. We compare it against a purely in-domain linguistic model with the same parameter setting. Both models—the online, in-domain model and the dynamic BoC model—are trained the same way, on a fractional batch of the target data, and then evaluated on the remaining (unseen) target data.

More formally, at a given iteration where the model sees a fractional batch of size f of the target data, the models are

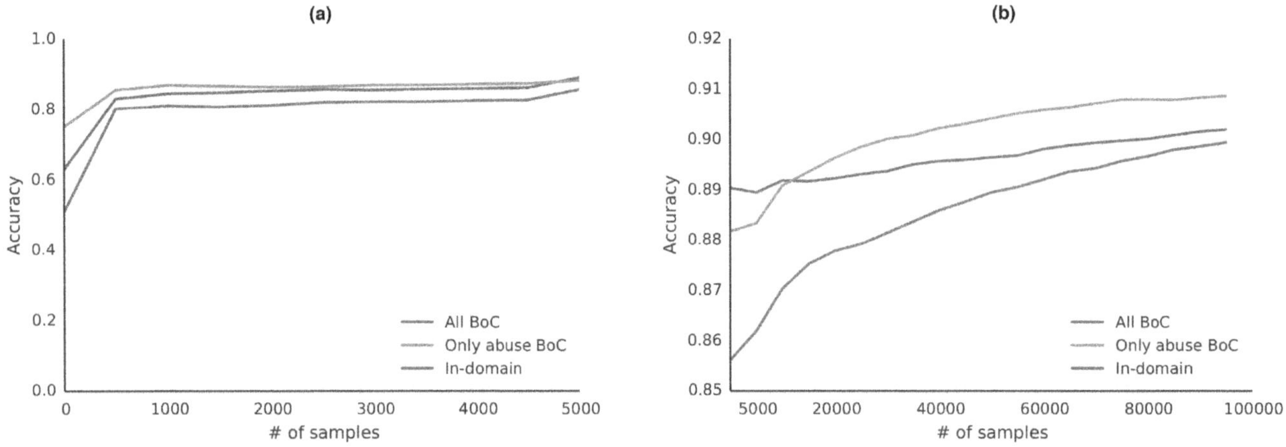

Figure 5. Dynamic model performance when trained only on target community (MB) data and including CCS, BoC features. *In-domain* denotes the plain partial fit model that uses only MB data, *Only abuse BoC* denotes the dynamic model only using communities that are hypothesized abusive, and *All BoC* denotes the dynamic model using all communities in our dataset. Performance of the models when iteratively trained on up to 5,000 target community samples are shown in (a), and the remaining batch sizes in (b). The plots are separated for better resolution, and (b) is scaled up for clarity.

constructed as follows:

$$M_{in} \sim BoW(f \cdot MB)$$

$$M_{dyn} \sim BoW(f \cdot MB) + CCS(S_i, T), \forall S_i \in BoC(all)$$

$$M_{dynabuse} \sim BoW(f \cdot MB) + CCS(S_i, T), \forall S_i \in BoC(abuse)$$

All models build BoW linguistic models of the data to which they have access so far. The *in-domain* model (M_{in} above) is trained only on posts from the target community, and does not see any of the BoC data. The *all BoC dynamic* model (M_{dyn} above), is trained on posts from the target community, in addition to CCS (internal) estimations from all 9 source communities. Whereas the *only abuse BoC dynamic* model ($M_{dynabuse}$ above) uses CCS estimations from only the abusive communities (i.e., 4chan, r/fatpeoplehate, r/CoonTown, v/[n-word], v/fatpeoplehate).

We aimed to observe the growth in accuracy of predictions over time (as more and more moderated posts from the community are available for training the model) and understand when the performance values saturate.

RESULTS

While we ran trials with three different classifiers (see above), Multinomial Naive Bayes (NB) performed best in all conditions. The simplest model, its performance may reflect its limited ability to overfit the training data. Hereafter, we report results for the NB model across conditions. The parameter values used for the best model are available in Table 1.

BoC static model performance

We compared the performance of our best BoC static model with two different baselines. Figure 4 displays the accuracies across models. We observed that the Blacklist gave a best performance of 55% (with threshold 1), while the OneClassSVM achieved an accuracy of 51%. Our BoC static model performed at 75.3% accuracy.

BoC dynamic model performance

The *BoC dynamic* online learning models performed uniformly better than a purely *in-domain* model built only using moderated posts from the target community. The differences in performance of the *in-domain*, *all BoC dynamic*, and *only abuse BoC dynamic* models at various stages of data access are shown in Figure 5. At 0 test samples seen, the in-domain model performed at 51% accuracy (it is equivalent to a single-class classifier used to detect outliers, without any access to moderated posts). The BoC dynamic models outperformed the purely in-domain model even after 100,000 (moderated) test samples were seen. The best performing BoC dynamic model achieved 91.18% accuracy, after seeing 100,000 (moderated) test samples. At all batch sizes measured, the differences are statistically significant.

DISCUSSION

We find that the Granger-causal, CCS-based, *Bag of Communities* models perform well in both static and dynamic settings. The static model likely performs well enough right now that it could be deployed as is with human oversight on a new community; the dynamic model uniformly outperforms purely in-domain classifiers with access to years of curated data. This means that models operating entirely on out-of-domain (4chan, Reddit, Voat and MetaFilter) data can learn significant cross-domain knowledge applicable to a community the model has never seen before. Given that we performed no domain adaptation [2, 12, 13], this result signals deep overlap between, for instance, large-scale preexisting Internet data and comments on another site.

We do not intend to intimate with these results that sites should substitute a BoC model for their existing moderation systems. Rather, this paper presents a promising empirical result about the utility of using preexisting community data to inform abuse detection. It suggests that gathering data from other communities could be extremely useful. Next, we reflect on our models, discuss some of their error patterns, strategize about selecting source communities, and conclude with reflection on how designers and researchers could use BoC models.

Reflection on models

In post-hoc inspection we observed that our BoC-based model identified a significantly larger variety of *abusive* content than the other models. This is in accordance with the high precision values achieved by the BoC classifiers when classifying abusive content (see Table 2). This derives from the source communities. For instance, the BoC data provides background information not available to the in-domain model, ranging from popular Internet phrases (e.g., "full of fail", "FOR THE LULZ") and terms (e.g., "desu", "nips") to variants of commonly used terms (e.g., "fuk"). Most of these comments were not identified by the in-domain model, as it sees only a handful of such terms in MixedBag posts.

As seen in Table 2, the BoC exhibit better precision-to-recall trade-offs than purely in-domain models. That is, they naturally seem to trade recall for precision more than the in-domain models. In discussions with site operators, this seems to be the way they would prefer the model's error patterns to behave. As many social media companies are owned and operated in the United States, concerns about censorship understandably pervade discussions around moderation [62]. High precision models (i.e., if the model declares it "abusive," then it very likely is, even at the cost of missing more abusive posts on average) would fit well in this context.

Error analysis

Both the in-domain and the BoC models missed a significant fraction of abusive posts. In an error analysis, many of them used character-level substitutions to evade automatic filters (e.g., "f**king", "f**k"), but were identified by human moderators on MixedBag. You could imagine normalization filters that help to uncover substitutions like these [5], a fruitful area for future work improving these models and data pipelines. Run of the mill spam also seemed to evade all models, suggesting that a future enhancement would be to add existing spam filters to data pipeline in Figure 3.

Some moderated posts were sarcastic in nature, and automatic detection of sarcasm is an open research problem [22, 51]. While neither the in-domain models nor the BoC could catch these instances, they were identified by human moderators on MixedBag:

> if i had a dollar for every pixel in this picture, i'd have 50
>
> Oh mai gowd I have never been so enlightened in mai hole laif.
>
> aww your going blind ???

Reflecting the noise of the real world, we also observed the presence of non-abusive posts in our test samples, which were (perhaps wrongly) removed by site moderators. Sometimes, moderators delete entire threads of comments, posted in response to inflammatory or offensive (parent) posts. Examples of likely mislabeled data:

> This is really cool! Superb job < 3
>
> Wonderful job
>
> Its WOW!
>
> Aww! You should nominate him for [award]! See [link] for details, okay?

Best performing model: Only abuse BoC

r/NeutralPolitics, r/AskScience, r/AskHistorians and MetaFilter are all well-moderated communities. We observed that training the *All BoC* model including data from these communities, in addition to the hypothesized abusive communities, increased the number of false positives (i.e., non-abusive posts being misclassified as being abusive). This can be attributed to the fact that typical (onsite) content found in MixedBag is more similar to 4chan, v/[n-word], v/fatpeoplehate, r/fatpeoplehate and r/CoonTown, than the former. In other words, the content found on the former communities are too polite (or well-moderated), and observed to not be representative of the normative behavior in the target community. As a result, the *Only abuse BoC* model achieved the best accuracy in our tests.

Choosing source communities

The choice of 4chan boards, hate-filled subreddits and subverses as source communities required some community-level insight. The intuition that many of these communities perform "bad behavior" motivated our data collection. We have also looked at a variety of well-moderated communities like MetaFilter, r/AskHistorians and r/AskScience, and r/NeutralPolitics as counterexamples.

How do you choose the community data required for BoC? At present, there is some "black magic" involved in collecting the right communities so as to be useful for a given context—not unlike the infrequently discussed black magic surrounding feature engineering in many applied machine learning contexts. For the moment, we believe this will be driven by the problem at hand. Intuition and domain knowledge will likely drive BoC data collection, and more work should be done to explore how to reduce search and collection costs. While community data such as this only needs to be collected once, it does require some investment of time and energy to write crawlers, debug them, etc.

However, it is possible to envision scenarios where many of the Internet's most important and popular communities have been crawled, stored, and used in training *CCS* classifiers. For example, given the encouraging results in the present work, we have recently explored simply building a *CCS* classifier for every subreddit, for all contributions ever posted to that subreddit. Even with a strict threshold on activity level (i.e., only include subreddits above a certain subscriber level, or post level), this would number in the thousands. You can imagine doing something similar among many well-connected communities (in the social network sense [38]) on Twitter. An API could live between an implementing application and all these data sources, essentially generating thousands of *CCS* feature vectors for applications. Scaling up in this manner seems very promising.

Design Implications

We have released our models under an LGPL license. We host the pre-trained internal *CCS* estimators used for both the static and dynamic models we presented here.[6] Even at this early stage in the research, we believe the present BoC models can be used to address the challenge of moderating new, emerging and established communities. As demonstrated in this conceptual and empirical work, the BoC approach may allow communities to deal with a range of common problems, like abusive behavior, faster and with fewer engineering resources.

Communities themselves may choose to operationalize the models we provide in a number of ways. A site might choose to wrap them in a human-in-the-loop system, where moderators review comments triaged by BoC score. Another community with fewer resources may automatically hold comments that score above a certain threshold, requiring users to petition to have them looked at by a human moderator. We hope that the open source models provide the kind of flexibility necessary for site operators to build these and other moderation approaches.

Theoretical Implications

As alluded to in the *Introduction*, the BoC approach may enable new kinds of theoretical advances. Returning to our example of a maximal BoC classifier that returns thousands of similarity features for all of Reddit, these scores place communities in a metric space: they are embedded in a high-dimensional space either closer or farther away from other communities. In this way, this approach might allow a more theoretically-inclined researcher to extract latent clusters of online communities into a taxonomy. An advantage of using semi-automated clustering techniques such as this one is that it would update as the Internet changes, without requiring another full round of researcher effort. We hope to see theoretical work exploring approaches along these lines.

LIMITATIONS & FUTURE WORK

While we find these results encouraging, they raise a number of questions, challenges and issues. Here, we reflect on some of the limitations present in our work, with an eye toward how we and others might build upon it.

Focus on linguistic information. The empirical part of this paper only examines the similarity between words and phrases in two communities. We have left out many pieces of data including temporality, other media such as images, etc. Work exploring and including these data would paint a richer picture of communities, and very possibly aid in prediction tasks. For example, it seems very reasonable to assume that reply chain dynamics (i.e., fast-arriving replies vs. slow-arriving replies) might interact with a post's likelihood of exhibiting abusive properties.

Focus on one target community. Here, we only look at the transference of information between 4chan, Reddit, Voat, MetaFilter, and one community, MixedBag. While we find the results encouraging and surprising, whether BoC-based techniques will work with other communities remains open. While we see it as a positive to have obtained MixedBag data at all, given the challenges facing companies who would release it, we encourage other researchers to explore extending the BoC approach to other target communities. For example, we are currently aware of another research lab looking to extend this work to moderated comments from various subreddits (observable through the open Reddit API).

Human-in-the-loop systems. In real situations, human moderators will still need to supervise any automated triage system, including ones built on BoC. It remains open exactly how well BoC would fare in situations like these, and how best to design it to do so. We see this as very profitable future line of work for human-centered computing researchers, as it will certainly involve talking with and understanding the work of professional and amateur community moderators.

CONCLUSION

We presented a new method for transferring one community's data to another—the *Bag of Communities* approach—and apply it to a key challenge faced by communities and moderators. To the best of our knowledge, the BoC representation is novel within social computing and applied machine learning more generally. Further, we presented an existence proof of Bag of Communities: building a classifier for identifying abusive content using data from 4chan, Reddit, Voat and MetaFilter. We hope that other designers find BoC useful in predicting a variety of important online phenomena; we hope researchers can make use of it to examine other communities with the Bag of Communities representation.

ACKNOWLEDGMENTS

We thank the social computing group at Georgia Tech, the Coral Project, Nate Matias and the Media Lab workshop for their valuable inputs that improved this work. This work is supported by NSF grant IIS-1553376.

REFERENCES

1. Ricardo Baeza-Yates, Berthier Ribeiro-Neto, and others. 1999. *Modern information retrieval*. Vol. 463. ACM press New York.
2. Shai Ben-David, John Blitzer, Koby Crammer, Alex Kulesza, Fernando Pereira, and Jennifer Wortman Vaughan. 2010. A theory of learning from different domains. *Machine learning* 79, 1-2 (2010), 151–175.
3. Michael S Bernstein, Andrés Monroy-Hernández, Drew Harry, Paul André, Katrina Panovich, and Gregory G Vargas. 2011. 4chan and/b: An Analysis of Anonymity and Ephemerality in a Large Online Community.. In *ICWSM*. 50–57.
4. Sam Biddle. August, 5, 2015. Reddit (Finally) Bans CoonTown. http://gawker.com/reddit-finally-bans-coontown-1722332877, *Gawker* (August, 5, 2015).
5. Samuel Brody and Nicholas Diakopoulos. 2011. Cooooooooooooooollllllllllllll!!!!!!!!!!!!!!: using word lengthening to detect sentiment in microblogs. In

[6]https://bitbucket.org/ceshwar/bag-of-communities.git

Proceedings of the conference on empirical methods in natural language processing. Association for Computational Linguistics, 562–570.

6. Brooks Buffington. April 4, 2015. Personal communication. (April 4, 2015).
7. Catherine Buni and Soraya Chemaly. 2016. The Secret Rules of the Internet, Apr. 2016. *http://www.theverge.com/2016/4/13/11387934/internet-moderator-history-youtube-facebook-reddit-censorship-free-speech* (2016).
8. Nan Cao, Conglei Shi, Sabrina Lin, Jie Lu, Yu-Ru Lin, and Ching-Yung Lin. 2016. TargetVue: Visual Analysis of Anomalous User Behaviors in Online Communication Systems. *Visualization and Computer Graphics, IEEE Transactions on* 22, 1 (2016), 280–289.
9. Stevie Chancellor, Zhiyuan Jerry Lin, and Munmun De Choudhury. 2016. This Post Will Just Get Taken Down: Characterizing Removed Pro-Eating Disorder Social Media Content. In *Proceedings of the 2016 CHI Conference on Human Factors in Computing Systems*. ACM, 1157–1162.
10. Justin Cheng, Cristian Danescu-Niculescu-Mizil, and Jure Leskovec. 2015. Antisocial Behavior in Online Discussion Communities. In *Ninth International AAAI Conference on Web and Social Media*.
11. Cristian Danescu-Niculescu-Mizil, Moritz Sudhof, Dan Jurafsky, Jure Leskovec, and Christopher Potts. 2013. A computational approach to politeness with application to social factors. In *Proc. ACL'13*.
12. Hal Daumé III. 2009. Frustratingly easy domain adaptation. *arXiv preprint arXiv:0907.1815* (2009).
13. Hal Daume III and Daniel Marcu. 2006. Domain adaptation for statistical classifiers. *Journal of Artificial Intelligence Research* (2006), 101–126.
14. Nicholas Diakopoulos. Apr. 2015a. Picking the NYT Picks: Editorial criteria and automation. (Apr. 2015).
15. Nicholas A Diakopoulos. 2015b. The Editor's Eye: Curation and Comment Relevance on the New York Times. In *Proceedings of the 18th ACM Conference on Computer Supported Cooperative Work & Social Computing*. ACM, 1153–1157.
16. Karthik Dinakar, Roi Reichart, and Henry Lieberman. 2011. Modeling the detection of Textual Cyberbullying.. In *The Social Mobile Web*. 11–17.
17. Roger Dingledine, Nick Mathewson, and Paul Syverson. 2004. *Tor: The second-generation onion router*. Technical Report. DTIC Document.
18. Bruce Drake. 2014. The darkest side of online harassment: Menacing behavior. *Pew Research Center, http://www.pewresearch.org/fact-tank/2015/06/01/the-darkest-side-of-online-harassment-menacing-behavior/* (2014).
19. Maeve Duggan. 2014. Online harassment: Summary of findings. *Pew Research Center, http://www. pewinternet. org/2014/10/22/online-harassment/(accessed 02 June 2015)* (2014).
20. Randy Farmer and Bryce Glass. 2010. *Building web reputation systems*. " O'Reilly Media, Inc.". 243–276 pages.
21. Eric Gilbert. 2013. Widespread underprovision on reddit. In *Proceedings of the 2013 conference on Computer supported cooperative work*. ACM, 803–808.
22. Roberto González-Ibánez, Smaranda Muresan, and Nina Wacholder. 2011. Identifying sarcasm in Twitter: a closer look. In *Proceedings of the 49th Annual Meeting of the Association for Computational Linguistics: Human Language Technologies: short papers-Volume 2*. Association for Computational Linguistics, 581–586.
23. Clive WJ Granger. 1969. Investigating causal relations by econometric models and cross-spectral methods. *Econometrica: Journal of the Econometric Society* (1969), 424–438.
24. Jiawei Han, Micheline Kamber, and Jian Pei. 2011. *Data mining: concepts and techniques*. Elsevier.
25. Susan Herring, Kirk Job-Sluder, Rebecca Scheckler, and Sasha Barab. 2002. Searching for safety online: Managing "trolling" in a feminist forum. *The Information Society* 18, 5 (2002), 371–384.
26. Lauren Hockenson. July, 9, 2015. What is Voat, the site Reddit users are flocking to? http://thenextweb.com/insider/2015/07/09/what-is-voat-the-site-reddit-users-are-flocking-to/, (July, 9, 2015).
27. Ruogu Kang, Laura Dabbish, and Katherine Sutton. 2016. Strangers on Your Phone: Why People Use Anonymous Communication Applications. In *Proceedings of the 19th ACM Conference on Computer-Supported Cooperative Work & Social Computing*. ACM, 359–370.
28. Sara Kiesler, Robert Kraut, Paul Resnick, and Aniket Kittur. 2012. Regulating behavior in online communities. *Building Successful Online Communities: Evidence-Based Social Design. MIT Press, Cambridge, MA* (2012), 125–178.
29. Amy Jo Kim. 2000. *Community building on the web: Secret strategies for successful online communities*. Addison-Wesley Longman Publishing Co., Inc.
30. Cliff Lampe and Paul Resnick. 2004. Slash (dot) and burn: distributed moderation in a large online conversation space. In *Proceedings of the SIGCHI conference on Human factors in computing systems*. ACM, 543–550.
31. Lawrence Lessig. 1999. *Code and other laws of cyberspace*. Vol. 3. Basic books New York.

32. Jing-Kai Lou, Kuan-Ta Chen, and Chin-Laung Lei. 2009. A collusion-resistant automation scheme for social moderation systems. In *Consumer Communications and Networking Conference, 2009. CCNC 2009. 6th IEEE*. IEEE, 1–5.

33. Christopher D Manning, Prabhakar Raghavan, Hinrich Schütze, and others. 2008. *Introduction to information retrieval*. Vol. 1. Cambridge university press Cambridge.

34. Bamshad Mobasher, Robin Burke, Runa Bhaumik, and Chad Williams. 2007. Toward trustworthy recommender systems: An analysis of attack models and algorithm robustness. *ACM Transactions on Internet Technology (TOIT)* 7, 4 (2007), 23.

35. Justin Wm. Moyer. July, 17, 2015. Coontown': A noxious, racist corner of Reddit survives recent purge. https://www.washingtonpost.com/news/morning-mix/wp/2015/07/17/coontown-a-noxious-racist-corner-of-reddit-survives-recent-purge/, *The Washington Post* (July, 17, 2015).

36. Lev Muchnik, Sinan Aral, and Sean J Taylor. 2013. Social influence bias: A randomized experiment. *Science* 341, 6146 (2013), 647–651.

37. Edward Newell, David Jurgens, Haji Mohammad Saleem, Hardik Vala, Jad Sassine, Caitrin Armstrong, and Derek Ruths. 2016. User Migration in Online Social Networks: A Case Study on Reddit During a Period of Community Unrest. In *Tenth International AAAI Conference on Web and Social Media.*

38. Mark EJ Newman. 2006. Modularity and community structure in networks. *Proceedings of the national academy of sciences* 103, 23 (2006), 8577–8582.

39. Fox News. Apr. 2009. 4Chan: The Rude, Raunchy Underbelly of the Internet. http://www.foxnews.com/story/2009/04/08/4chan-rude-raunchy-underbelly-internet.html. (Apr. 2009).

40. Elinor Ostrom. 2015. *Governing the commons.* Cambridge university press.

41. Ellen Pao. July 16, 2015. Former Reddit CEO Ellen Pao: The trolls are winning the battle for the Internet. http://wapo.st/1HJM82l, (July 16, 2015).

42. Deokgun Park, Simranjit Sachar, Nicholas Diakopoulos, and Niklas Elmqvist. 2016. Supporting comment moderators in identifying high quality online news comments. In *Proc. Conference on Human Factors in Computing Systems (CHI).*

43. Fabian Pedregosa, Gaël Varoquaux, Alexandre Gramfort, Vincent Michel, Bertrand Thirion, Olivier Grisel, Mathieu Blondel, Peter Prettenhofer, Ron Weiss, Vincent Dubourg, and others. 2011. Scikit-learn: Machine learning in Python. *The Journal of Machine Learning Research* 12 (2011), 2825–2830.

44. Jenny Preece and Diane Maloney-Krichmar. 2003. Online communities: focusing on sociability and usability. *Handbook of human-computer interaction* (2003), 596–620.

45. Reddit. 2014. Remember the human. https://www.reddit.com/r/blog/comments/1ytp7q/remember_the_human/. (2014).

46. Reddit. 2015a. Reddiquette. https://www.reddit.com/wiki/reddiquette. (2015).

47. Reddit. 2015c. Subreddit rules. https://www.reddit.com/r/AskHistorians/wiki/rules. (2015).

48. Reddit. June, 10, 2015b. Removing harassing subreddits (self announcement). https://www.reddit.com/r/announcements/comments/39bpam removing_harassing_subreddits/, (June, 10, 2015).

49. Paul Resnick, Ko Kuwabara, Richard Zeckhauser, and Eric Friedman. 2000. Reputation systems. *Commun. ACM* 43, 12 (2000), 45–48.

50. Paul Resnick and Richard Zeckhauser. 2002. Trust among strangers in internet transactions: Empirical analysis of ebays reputation system. *The Economics of the Internet and E-commerce* 11, 2 (2002), 23–25.

51. Ellen Riloff, Ashequl Qadir, Prafulla Surve, Lalindra De Silva, Nathan Gilbert, and Ruihong Huang. 2013. Sarcasm as Contrast between a Positive Sentiment and Negative Situation.. In *EMNLP*, Vol. 13. 704–714.

52. Adi Robertson. June, 10, 2015. Reddit bans 'Fat People Hat' and other subreddits under new harassment rules. http://www.theverge.com/2015/6/10/8761763/reddit-harassment-ban-fat-people-hate-subreddit, *The Verge* (June, 10, 2015).

53. P. Shuman. Jul 2007. Fox 11 investigates: anonymous. https://www.youtube.com/watch?v=DNO6G4ApJQY. (Jul 2007).

54. N. Shuyo. 2010. Language detection library for java. (2010).

55. Leiser Silva, Lakshmi Goel, and Elham Mousavidin. 2009. Exploring the dynamics of blog communities: the case of MetaFilter. *Information Systems Journal* 19, 1 (2009), 55–81.

56. Christine B Smith, Margaret L McLaughlin, and Kerry K Osborne. 1997. Conduct control on Usenet. *Journal of Computer-Mediated Communication* 2, 4 (1997), 0–0.

57. Sara Sood, Judd Antin, and Elizabeth Churchill. 2012a. Profanity use in online communities. In *Proceedings of the SIGCHI Conference on Human Factors in Computing Systems*. ACM, 1481–1490.

58. Sara Owsley Sood, Judd Antin, and Elizabeth F Churchill. 2012b. Using Crowdsourcing to Improve Profanity Detection.. In *AAAI Spring Symposium: Wisdom of the Crowd.*

59. Sara Owsley Sood, Elizabeth F Churchill, and Judd Antin. 2012c. Automatic identification of personal insults on social news sites. *Journal of the American Society for Information Science and Technology* 63, 2 (2012), 270–285.

60. R. Sorgatz. 2009. Macroanonymous is the new microfamous. http://fimoculous.com/archive/post-5738.cfm. (2009).

61. Abhay Sukumaran, Stephanie Vezich, Melanie McHugh, and Clifford Nass. 2011. Normative influences on thoughtful online participation. In *Proceedings of the SIGCHI Conference on Human Factors in Computing Systems*. ACM, 3401–3410.

62. Nabiha Syed and Ben Smith. Jun. 2015. A First Amendment For Social Platforms. https://medium.com/@BuzzFeed/a-first-amendment-for-social-platforms-202c0eab7054. (Jun. 2015).

63. Nitasha Tiku and Casey Newton. February 4, 2015. Twitter CEO:We suck at dealing with abuse.. http://www.theverge.com/2015/2/4/7982099/twitter-ceo-sent-memo-taking-personal-responsibility-for-the, *The Verge* (February 4, 2015).

64. Ruth L Williams and Joseph Cothrel. 2000. Four smart ways to run online communities. *MIT Sloan Management Review* 41, 4 (2000), 81.

65. Jun-Ming Xu, Benjamin Burchfiel, Xiaojin Zhu, and Amy Bellmore. 2013. An Examination of Regret in Bullying Tweets.. In *HLT-NAACL*. 697–702.

PersaLog: Personalization of News Article Content

Eytan Adar[1], Carolyn Gearig[1], Ayshwarya Balasubramanian[2], Jessica Hullman[3]

[1]University of Michigan, Ann Arbor, MI {eadar,ccgearig}@umich.edu

[2]Deloitte Arlington, VA ayshwaryabalasubramanian@gmail.edu

[3]University of Washington Seattle, WA jhullman@uw.edu

ABSTRACT
Content personalization—automatically modifying text and multimedia features *within* articles based on the reader's individual features—is evolving as a new form of journalism. Informed by constraints articulated through a survey of journalists, we have implemented PersaLog, a novel system for creating personalized content (e.g., text and interactive visualizations). Because crafting, and validating, personalized content can be challenging to scale across articles (unlike feed personalization), we offer a simple Domain Specific Language (DSL), and editing environment, to support this task. PersaLog is particularly designed to support the personalization of existing text and visualizations. Our work provides guidelines for personalization as well as a system that allows for both subtle and dramatic personalization-driven content changes. We validate PersaLog using case and lab studies.

ACM Classification Keywords
H.5.1 Information Interfaces and Presentation (e.g. HCI): Multimedia Information Systems

Author Keywords
Personalized Content, News Personalization, Guidelines

INTRODUCTION
Personalization and customization in journalism has a long history. Print and news broadcasters have long crafted localized editions in "native formats" (printed papers or TV shows). Providers like the *The New York Times* have offered printed editions based on a reader's location and, more recently, personalized homepages on the web. Aggregators, such as Google News, allow readers to customize their news feeds in a number of ways. Content producers benefit from this type of *feed personalization* as it allows them to leverage archival content and create local or hyper-local editions. Readers benefit from lessened information overload and increased engagement.

Content personalization—automated changes to the facts presented in a single news article according to inferable properties of the reader–has only begun to emerge as a viable feature. Through content personalization, a news site automatically customizes *text* and *multi-media* (e.g., visualizations) for a specific article. Automated content personalization allows a journalist to write one article that automatically customizes itself for many readers. As with *feed* personalization, *content* personalization, can increase engagement and learning (e.g., [13]); and supports behavioral change (e.g., [17]). Organizations with access to talented journalists, designers, and engineers, such as *The New York Times*, have begun to provide custom (one-off) personalized experiences. In May 2015 [2] and April 2016 [1], *The Times* published stories that personalized maps and text for each reader based on reader location (see Figure 1). Visualizations, including maps, charts, and tables were dynamically altered to focus on the reader's location (e.g., automated zooming on the map, local comparable counties in the table, etc.). Text modifications, similarly, personalize information (e.g., *local* poverty numbers, probability of overcoming poverty, etc.). Unfortunately, the rarity of such stories signals the difficulty in creating this kind of material.

Feed personalization has been much easier to adopt, in part, because a single algorithm can be applied across an entire site. The algorithm can combine inferences about the reader as well as prior behavior to make personalized article *suggestions*–a more traditional ranking problem. In contrast, content personalization requires significant, article-specific work. Multiple individuals in a news organization (e.g., authors, editors, copyeditors, fact-checkers, programmers, graphic designers) must contribute to build inference engines, personalization rules, and visualizations that can be modified to present personalized views. The effort is further complicated by the lack of design guidelines and tools that can be applied easily to new content.

In this paper we present PersaLog, a Domain Specific Language (DSL) and system for creating personalized news article content[1]. PersaLog supports personalization of both new content and existing, unpersonalized, information. In addition to allowing a journalist to personalize *generic* text content, PersaLog provides similar support for existing interactive visualizations. While direct-manipulation interaction (e.g., brush, filter, etc.) are common features, the event model they use is difficult to script–a key requirement for automatically putting them into a personalized state. PersaLog wraps existing visualizations, such as those built with D3, so that they can become part of the personalized content experience.

We define content personalization for news as: *"an automated change to the* ***set of facts*** *that appear in an* ***article's content*** *based on* ***properties of the reader****."* PersaLog's support for *user modelling* allows the journalist to identify *properties*

[1]We use different fonts when we want to distinguish between the system (PersaLog) and language (PERSALOG).

Permission to make digital or hard copies of all or part of this work for personal or classroom use is granted without fee provided that copies are not made or distributed for profit or commercial advantage and that copies bear this notice and the full citation on the first page. Copyrights for components of this work owned by others than ACM must be honored. Abstracting with credit is permitted. To copy otherwise, or republish, to post on servers or to redistribute to lists, requires prior specific permission and/or a fee. Request permissions from permissions@acm.org.

CHI 2017, May 06-11, 2017, Denver, CO, USA

© 2017 ACM. ISBN 978-1-4503-4655-9/17/05...$15.00

DOI: **http://dx.doi.org/10.1145/3025453.3025631**

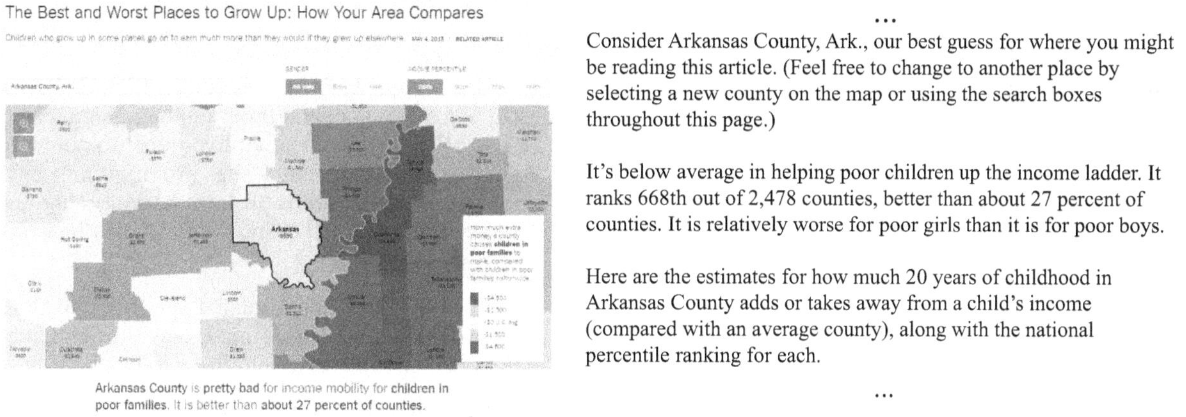

Figure 1. Sample personalization of image and graphic in The Times' article "The Best and Worst Places to Grow Up: How Your Area Compares" (Simulated view generated from a computer in Dewitt, Arkansas which is in Arkansas County.)

of the reader: features and preferences of the reader/viewer from intrinsic (e.g., personality traits) to extrinsic (e.g., age), and from explicit (e.g., the name I provided when signing up) to inferred (e.g., movie interests inferred from from past search behaviors. PersaLog currently supports two common properties: geolocation and demographic inference.

Authors can personalize content–which includes text and multimedia features (e.g., charts, static or interactive, photographs, videos, etc.)–through PERSALOG or higher-level GUI tools. PersaLog supports modifying any web page element that can be programmatically changed, thus reconfiguring the *set* of facts in the article. *Facts* are the information-carrying 'atomic units' by which the journalist can personalize content (adding, removing, or emphasizing key facts). For example, "unemployment in county Y is $x\%$" may only be an interesting fact to residents of Y or nearby locations, and could be replaced by more *locally* relevant information. In another article, "*Sobotka* is the prime minister of the Czech Republic" is a contextualizing fact valuable to readers outside the Czech Republic.

To determine the best design for PersaLog, we surveyed 22 media professionals and interviewed creators of personalized content from *The New York Times* and *Washington Post*, with the goal of understanding definitions, possibilities, and limitations of personalized content. Our work contributes a distillation of this information into a broader set of guidelines and design criteria for content personalization in news, which we utilize explicitly in architecting and building PersaLog. PersaLog is designed to serve the needs of journalists in *creating* personalized content to increase engagement and educational value. Conversely, the system simplifies deployment to *consumers*. We describe a number of innovations designed to support a broad set of personalization pipelines and demonstrate their applicability through a set of case studies and a controlled lab study to validate the usability of the DSL.

RELATED WORK

News Personalization

Feed personalization, or automated curation of articles based on information about an individual, was originally implemented to help people deal with information overload (e.g., [11]). Research has since expanded to support presentation of archival content, increasing engagement, and the creation of 'sub-properties' (e.g., local news through hyper-localization) [59]. Collaborative filtering approaches have been broadly studied as mechanisms for filtering, sorting, or organizing a stream of news articles [11, 22]. Subsequent research has found that feed personalization can also increase engagement (e.g., [10]). News services including the *BBC*, *The New York Times*, *The Huffington Post* and *NPR* and aggregators (e.g., Google News) have integrated feed personalization.

Content personalization[2] is much less evident in journalism research and practice. A recent article by *The New York Times* (see Figure 1) is one highly visible example [2]. The article dynamically adjusts visualizations (e.g., a thematic map) and article text based on geolocation (inferred by IP address). In the context of broadcast news, the *BBC* has used *object-based broadcasting*–content 'chunking'–to shorten or otherwise personalize broadcasts while still retaining coherence [34]. Creating interactive features is time and resource consuming. Smaller publishers, without the resources of *The Times*, would be particularly constrained in their ability to produced personalized content given current technology.

Abstractly, any article with interactive content may appear to support personalization (i.e., is *adaptable* [49]). Take the example of an article that contains a map that users can modify based on ZIP code. Contrast this to the article that *automatically* infers (i.e., is *adaptive*) the ZIP code from the reader's IP address to adjust the visualization. In developing PersaLog, we focus on the latter definition of personalization. That is, if the *only* way an article's content is changed is in reaction to the reader's *direct manipulation*, we do not consider this personalization (though we acknowledge that such actions produce personally-relevant views).

Personalization in other domains

Personalization is often used outside of the news domain. For example, personalized advertising is fundamental to advertis-

[2]We note that *feed personalization* is sometimes also called *content personalization* in the media. We use the more specific meaning here.

ing practice and Internet-based ads (e.g., [51, 42]). Advertisers on Facebook can customize ads based on properties of location (e.g., whether a user lives there, is currently at a location or has been there recently) and other demographic data (e.g., age, gender, educational level and interests inferred from trends in a user's profile) [19]. Google supports locally-targeted results (e.g., a query for "pizza" will return different ads depending on location) [27]. In contrast to advertising, *news-driven* content personalization brings new challenges based on journalistic values such as transparency [55].

Content personalization is often effective in *learning environments* (e.g., [13]). Specific instances include environments that: tailor content based on learning-style [37, 50]; use fictional text to achieve learning objectives, such as by replacing generic terms with personally-relevant ones (e.g., favorite foods in word problems) [13, 16]; and support self-regulated learning [15, 43]. In medical applications, patient education (e.g., personalized pamphlets for behavioral change [56]) has also benefited from personalization (e.g., see [17, 26]). To make complex information more relatable, recent visualization tools automatically generate maps that show a user a personalized spatial analogy for a distance, area, or other spatial reference that she encounters in an article [36]. While the specific objectives and values of content creators in these domains are often different from news, they inspire our design.

Work in *adaptive hypermedia* and *education* ([18, 39]) led to sophisticated ways to modify hypertext-like structures or text by 'bundling' hypermedia objects based on higher-level design goals (e.g., education). These systems leverage a user model for personalization but often build experiences from the ground-up, rather than augmenting existing content. Hypertext DSLs (e.g., [6, 47]) inspire our design, but are generally too complex for end-users to learn or use (and tend to be evaluated for expressiveness rather than usability). *Natural Language Generation*, focuses on automatically generating unstructured text (e.g., [54]) from structured content (e.g., a database of animal characteristics). Like adaptive hypermedia, NLG can be personalized through a user model [46]. While our goal is not to fully automate the generation of personalized text, we can apply these ideas to improve PersaLog. For example, personalization may generate a large set of article variants [38] which may be difficult to copy-edit. Automated 'repair' features of NLG [31] can test and correct personalized text.

Adaptive interfaces that customize GUI layouts based on prior use or end-user properties are a form of personalization (e.g., [20, 23, 24, 60]). These are often built to improve productivity and usability by streamlining direct manipulation. Though they are different in intent from content personalization, some of the guidelines that emerge from our survey of journalists align with best practices in adaptive interface research at a high level. For example, a lack of user control is noted in the broader interface personalization literature [20, 32].

Research and applied work in End-User Programming (EUP) also provides some guidance in our development of PersaLog (see [40] for a survey). Various solutions provide DSLs to enable control over applications, devices, and–most closely to our domain–Web environments [14, 61]. While EUP often targets individual (i.e., 'code for one's self' [40]), rather than large-scale deployment, there are notable exceptions (e.g., CoScripter [41]). With PERSALOG we have adopted a 'little-language' approach [3]. In contrast to many DSLs, PERSALOG is neither a general programming language nor a library (e.g., [4]). As with the adaptive-hypertext environments [7, 21], we do not believe visual programming environments (e.g. [63]) will naturally fit into the journalist habitats (i.e., CMS systems [57, 62]). However, this may be worth pursuing in future research.

Superficially, PersaLog is related to web-templating languages such as PHP, Mustache, Jinja2, etc. While elements of PersaLog can be integrated into these tools, the PERSALOG language was (a) developed to support personalization tasks, and (b) designed to more easily modify *existing* unpersonalized content (including visualizations) to enable personalization.

CURRENT EXAMPLES

We have identified three recent examples of content personalization from *The New York Times* [1, 2, 53] and one from the *Washington Post* [45]. We summarize key implementation details and our interviews with their authors (Kevin Quealy, Graphics Editor at *The Times* [52] and Darla Cameron and Denise Lu, Graphics Editors at *The Washington Post* [9]).

The focus of all four articles was geography and we found four mechanisms for personalization in text: *"You are here" (YaH)* which declare where the article thinks the reader is (e.g., "... rethink what they know about health costs in **Arlington, VA** ..."); *comparative with data (CD)* where local places are related to others with numerical data (e.g., "It ranks **175th** out of 2,478 counties"); *relative comparison (RC)* (e.g., "If you're poor and live in the **New York** area, it's better to be in **Putnam county** ..."); and *local statistics (LS)* (e.g., "... researchers examined prices at **7** hospitals in **Arlington, VA** ... founds surgery can cost ... **$22,800** ..."). Personalized visualizations consisted of maps, bar charts, scatter plots and tables.

We identified the following in the articles: [1] personalized 7 of 14 paragraphs (3 YaH, 2 CD, 1 RC, 1 LS), 1 map and 2 tables; [2] personalized 9 of 18 (3 YaH, 3 CD, 1 RC, 2 LS), 1 map, 1 chart, and 3 tables, this article also allowed interaction to focus on different genders or income percentile which further changed the text; [53] personalized 4 of 38 paragraphs (2 YaH, 1 RC, 2 LS), and 3 of 6 visualizations (a dot plot, scatter plot, and bar chart); [45] personalized 1 of 20 paragraphs (LS), 1 of 9 maps and 1 of 2 charts.

In terms of implementing geolocation, *The Times* leverages an existing server-based solution within *The Times* organization. Mr. Quealy indicated that this greatly simplified his work. It is notable that a smaller organization may not have this capability. The *Post* utilized the HTML5 Geolocation service–an opt-in, browser based solution. This makes the the personalization obvious (a feature recognized by the *Post* reporters). However, it is disruptive (a pop-up requests location access) and will not work on all browsers. Our interviews all emphasized resource constraints (time and developer access) as major reasons why new personalized pages are difficult to create. Specifically, that a great deal of care was necessary to ensure that the content "made sense" and worked consistently (e.g., failure modes if there was no data). Grammatical correctness was critical. For example, correct pluralization, comparative language, and in the case of the wealth article [2], gender and income (e.g., "richest girls" vs. "poorest boys").

FORMATIVE SURVEY OF JOURNALISTS

To inform our development of PersaLog, we conducted a survey of journalism professionals. We were interested in how journalistic values, such as transparent reporting, impact personalization. We also wanted to understand the specific workflows (editorial decision-making, deadlines, etc.), resources (data and personnel), constraints, and possible barriers to adoption. Our survey broadly targeted: 1) how journalists currently understand personalization, 2) the perceived benefits and risks of content personalization, 3) possible dimensions (e.g., location, age, political orientation, etc.) for content personalization, and 4) attitudes towards adoption in a news organization. The survey captured basic information such as the journalist's specific role and content responsibilities in the news organization. We circulated the survey by sending it to our contacts in journalism, including professionals at national and local publications, through Facebook groups for journalists, and through Twitter. We did not target data journalists or those expected to have strong programming backgrounds.

Twenty-two journalists completed our survey, including: 6 reporters, 3 graphic developers/designers, and 6 with other editorial roles (e.g., visual editor for a large national newspaper, editor for experimental mobile projects at a national newspaper). Seven other respondents held unique positions including: digital product analyst (national paper), audience development editor (national magazine), and a videographer (university newspaper). Fifty percent of respondents worked in journalism for 1-3 years, 27% for 4-6 years, and 14% worked over 6 years. Six work directly with graphic production and editing, and another 14 with graphics in some fashion (e.g., content editors who manage overall story presentation, text and visuals). Eleven participants answered a "programming inventory." Of these, most (10) reported experience with Excel, Google Spreadsheets, and all (11) with HTML/CSS. Four (of 11) considered themselves highly competent at JavaScript[3].

Responses

When asked "What does content personalization mean to you?" (before being provided with a definition) the majority of journalists we surveyed (16 out of 22) described feed or homepage personalization. Only 6 described content personalization as content adapted to reader properties. As one graphics developer (P20) put it, content personalization is "[M]aking a national story mean something specific and (hopefully) different for every reader based on their background." Others mentioned specific reader properties in their definitions: "Targeting of content based on either imputed (IP or other geographic coding) or provided (registration-related) information" (P3). After we defined content personalization and provided examples, our respondents identified features on which they could imagine personalizing. Location was the most frequently mentioned property for personalizing content (16 respondents), followed by age (12), prior internet behavior (9), gender (5), political preferences (4), and race (3).

Our respondents described various high-level goals for personalization, including increasing relevancy of the content (5), making the news more relatable or engaging (5), increasing memorability (3), prompting users to read the article in the first place (3), gradually introducing complex data (1), more effective communication (1), improving news comprehension (1), and increasing length of visit, recirculation, and brand loyalty (1). Several respondents expressed the importance of considering how the specific personalized content adds to the article. As one respondent (P3) described, content personalization is "an editorial decision like any other. Sometimes, the national context is important and the local data is meaningless noise. Sometimes, the opposite is true . . . [Y]ou have to decide all of this on a case-by-case basis." Privacy and bias issues, as we describe below, were noted by respondents and influence our design. At the high level, some of the guidelines we identify below are common to all systems with personalization (e.g., bias). However, the relative weight of each is unique to content personalization in the news domain.

Guideline 1: Anticipate potential bias—Content personalization is likely to occur per-article, rather than uniformly applied to an entire site. This lessens the possibility of algorithmic curation introduced biases known as "filter bubbles" or "echo chambers" (e.g., [5]). However, 8 respondents were concerned that bias may emerge, for example through the continuous use of the *same* personalization features in the *same* way (e.g., only providing local unemployment information in every article about unemployment). One journalist (P16) noted that, "if something ... isn't as 'bad' in a certain reader's area, they may disregard an issue, like income inequality." Another (P15) likened personalization to "hiding information from [readers] because your algorithm thinks it is irrelevant . . . , then they might leave . . . with an unintended conclusion."

Guideline 2: Provide reader control—Multiple journalists expressed interest in using content personalization provided that readers were given some control. This notion is related to *scrutability* (the ability to inspect the model) in personalized learning systems [35]. If, "the personalization gave readers the option to view others' personalizations, I would use it," one said (P8), and ". . . personalization is terrific in speaking directly to readers as long as there is still broader context for the information being presented or the option for the reader to see the general text/graphics," said another (P10). Journalists described how the ability to disable personalization may satisfy (some) privacy concerns, allow for a common view for discussion, and provide additional context to reduce bias.

Guideline 3: Signal personalization—To support reader control, a personalized interface should convey to the reader that content has been altered. The need to ensure that a reader knows *how and where* an article's text and images has been personalized may lead to the development of consistent visual cues (e.g., we utilize double underlines).

Guideline 4: Consider inference quality–Several journalists expressed concern with, what they perceived, as the low

[3]these numbers may be biased as journalists without programming experience may have ignored this aspect of the survey.

precision of automated inference. Journalists are well aware of the 'horror stories' of geolocation and data mining gone awry [30]. These respondents seemed to distrust implicitly inferred information. One journalist (P6) stated, "I would be hesitant to make a claim about a city based on raw data and not actually reporting from the ground or talking to sources." Ideally, a personalization system could incorporate inference confidence into display decision. For example, if the precision of an inferred property like socioeconomic status is expected to be low for certain regions, the system would not personalize.

Guideline 5: Sensitivity to reader privacy—Seven of our respondents remarked on the potential of personalization to inspire concerns about privacy. "Requesting personal information can be a big turn off for users and many will choose not to interact with your application at all," said an interaction designer (national paper) about graphics that request reader information (P19). She described her organization's existing attitude on personal information: "It's important to make users feel like their information is protected." This range of responses was also evident in reader reactions to *The Times'* personalized articles [58]. Additional research is necessary to determine *reader attitudes* around privacy for personalized content, but we suspect that an emphasis on sourcing materials and provenance may partially assuage concerns (e.g., by providing transparency on inference mechanisms and the availability of the data outside of the interface).

Guideline 6: Minimize application complexity for creators—A frequent theme in journalists' responses was that content personalization was desirable but would require more resources than their organization could easily provide. The limited technological capabilities of some journalists were one concern. Journalism workflows for a single article can involve many stakeholders with varying levels of technical expertise, content personalization tools should be accessible to users with limited programming background. From our interviews (with Quealy, Cameron and Lu), this was by far the most salient concern. All three described the difficulty in ensuring that language of the article worked (e.g., comparative language, unit pluralization, capitalization, etc.) and that an overall high-quality user-experience was maintained. An explicit design decision for PersaLog is not to provide complete automation in the *construction* of personalized content. Total automation is not required, or desired, as producing accurate, readable, grammatical content is placed at a premium.

Guideline 7: Design for scale—Respondents voiced concerns over manual effort for personalization: "The more you personalize (the stricter) the more data you have to present, more content you have to write" (P10). To scale personalization without requiring significant effort on a per-story basis, PersaLog should be designed with 'reuse' in mind. Mr. Quealy, for example, reflected on *The Times'* advantage in being able to leverage existing geolocation infrastructure. Our goal is to provide those with less resources with similar capabilities by creating a robust and reusable codebase.

PERSALOG ARCHITECTURE

We have created PersaLog, a JavaScript-based infrastructure and DSL, to facilitate content personalization. PersaLog is comprised of a simple set of tools that can be applied to existing content and which adhere to the guidelines outlined by our survey (Figure 2 summarizes the architecture). End-users create web pages with embedded PERSALOG code, either directly in HTML, or by using one of our editing tools (Fig. 2a). Visualizations and other graphical elements can also be integrated. Because most existing visualizations do not offer personalization features, PersaLog programmatically 'wraps' these to allow the journalist to automate direct manipulation interactions that were available in the original visualization (e.g., brushing, clicking, form filling). The *unpersonalized* content is transformed by PersaLog by translating PERSALOG code directly into JavaScript (i.e., transpiling). The standardization of the architecture enables experienced developers to add, or integrate, new personalization features into PersaLog. We describe each feature at a high-level below but point to `http://persalog.news` for more details and live examples.

User-modelling (e) occurs when a reader accesses a PersaLog-enabled page. Leveraging various implemented classifiers (f), PersaLog automatically attempts to build a user model (g). Services can be both internal and external to the PersaLog infrastructure. In the simplest case, the end-user's IP address is used to geolocate the individual. Other classifiers can predict demographics based on location, past use patterns or database values (for 'registered' end-users). Consistent with Guideline 2, any inference can be overriden by the reader. The generated user model, together with the compiled page, are passed to a *display reconfiguration* engine that re-renders the page. Automatically generated widgets allow the reader to disable personalization or change 'perspective.' Guidelines 1 and 2, anticipating bias and providing reader control, strongly informed the design of our reader-driven reconfigurability.

To test PERSALOG code, we have constructed a number of test harnesses (i) that can simulate different browsers and inputs (e.g., testing access from all unique zip codes). Depending on application, pieces of the architecture can be shifted easily from the client to server (e.g., Node.js). For example, pages can be personalized *on the server* before being passed to the client (this may have computational advantages). Alternatively, execution of the PersaLog can be done entirely in the browser. This off-loads work and supports privacy policies where high end-user control is preferred (Guideline 5). Our default instantiation of PersaLog is for compilation to happen at the browser, but user modelling to be handled on the server.

PersaLog Constructs: If-Segment-Then-Do

PERSALOG has two main constructs: *segment* and *do*. We use the term 'segment' based on its common usage in advertising. Both the user modelling components and rendering infrastructure utilize a pipeline of JavaScript functions. Each function accept a *person* object as input and an optional target (for rendering). When called, the functions assign one or more segment labels to the person and execute some action based on the value (e.g., gender, age; add sentences about that gender and age profile to text) and then pass the 'person' to the next function (PersaLog maintains a sequence of these functions and executes them serially). An analogous dataflow architec-

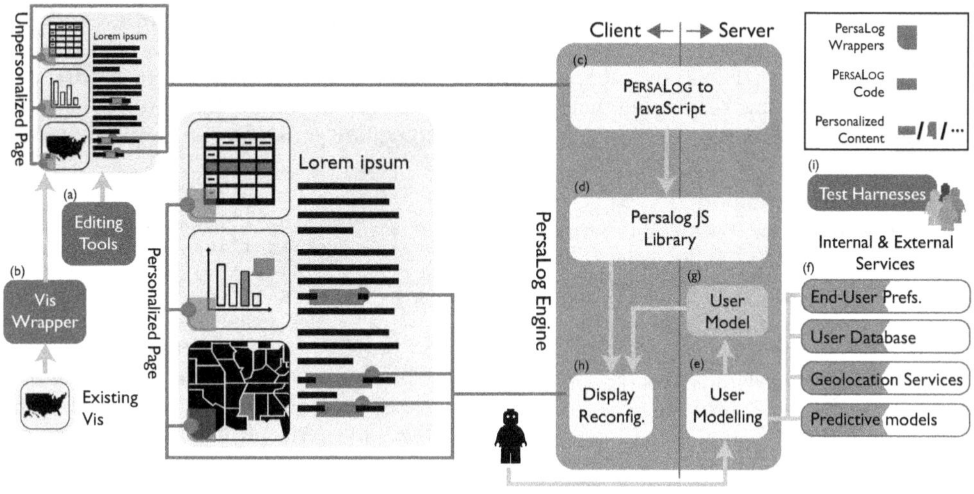

Figure 2. PersaLog Architecture

ture is the 'if-this-then-that' (IFTTT) style of programming: *if the person belongs to some segment, do something.*

Segmenting maps the person to a "type." This may be based on inference (i.e., given your surfing behavior I would put you in the 'teenager' segment or given the IP address, the reader would be 'segmented' by city, state and country), or based on explicit groupings or knowledge (e.g., based on the age provided by the user on sign-up, I place them into standard categories: 15-24, 25-44, 45-64, 65+, etc.). At the extreme is segmenting by unique visitor, which essentially creates a unique page for every individual. Regardless of the mechanism, the act of segmenting is equivalent to mapping a domain (i.e., all readers) into a range (i.e., segments). In PersaLog this is achieved either by using built-in code or by defining the functions using the PERSALOG language.

Using PersaLog to Create Personalized Content

PERSALOG *Code Blocks*

The rendering infrastructure for PersaLog works by: (1) identifying PERSALOG code blocks in a document; (2) generating "placeholder" HTML span in the text; and (3) interpreting the PERSALOG to determine what to place inside these dividers.

PERSALOG code blocks are hidden in HTML comment tags. This ensures that if PersaLog fails to execute, valid, readable content will still be generated. For example:

```
<div> Hello viewer. <!-- PersaLog
   ... PersaLog code here...
--></div>
```

During a document setup phase, PersaLog will add a new *span* inside of the *div* element, initially set to empty but with a unique id that is linked to the PERSALOG code in that block:

```
<div> Hello viewer. <span id="personal-1"/>
<!-- PersaLog  ...  --> </div>
```

If the PERSALOG code generates a string referring to the end-user's county, upon execution, the new HTML would be:

```
<div> Hello viewer. <span id="personal-1">
You seem to live in Livingston County</span>
<!-- PersaLog  ...  --> </div>
```

A PERSALOG code block can also refer to an existing HTML element (uniquely identified). In this case, output will be rendered into the matching DOM element rather than a newly created one. The original PERSALOG code remains embedded in the HTML and allowing the reader to inspect the personalization logic if they are interested (Guideline 3).

Personalizing Visualizations

Interactivity in visualizations is often driven by user actions (e.g., *mouseover* or *clicks*). Our goal for PersaLog is to ensure that these actions *can* be executed through code for two reasons. First, an interactive visualization, even one not intended for personalization, can often be personalized based on direct interactions. For example, a thematic map showing unemployment in the US may bring up key statistics by mousing over a particular state. If our goal is to personalize based on this action, we must simulate this mouse event. Second, we want to ensure that personalization doesn't create bias by limiting access (Guideline 1). A viewer that has disabled personalization should be able to use the standard interactive features to arrive at personalized content (manually). Thus, we should not execute actions that are impossible for a human to reproduce.

A special JavaScript file (*wrapper.js*) can be added to any existing page with interactive content or visualizations. The code operates on the content in two ways. First, all interactive HTML content (e.g., form elements) are identified and 'named.' Second, visualization content (currently only D3) is analyzed. We use a technique similar to that of the D3 Deconstructor [29] to 'parse' a visualization back into tabular representations. Roughly, each graphical 'mark' (e.g., rectangles, ellipses, or any other SVG shape) are isolated and connected back to the original data source. The unique identifiers in the data become the "names" (this allows us to say things like "click, California" instead of "click, 4th rectangle"). Specific mouse actions can be applied to visual elements that map to specific data rows. Internally, when invoking 'mouseover, California,' PersaLog will find the correct row, find the matching SVG element, and trigger the specific event. While this technique requires that columns with unique names (preferably, human readable ones) in the original data tables, we have found this to be a reasonable assumption. Wrapped content can be reused in different contexts. PersaLog supports this by extracting the visual elements and displaying them in an embedded iframe (thus supporting reuse).

PERSALOG Syntax and Implementation

Below we describe key elements of PERSALOG syntax and execution. A sample block of PERSALOG code is:

```
if {{age}} <= 18 ::: print a
if {{age}} <= 65 ::: print b
default ::: print c
```

Variables are enclosed in double curly brackets (i.e., *{{foo}}*). Bracketing of this type, including double curly braces, was selected as it is common in HTML templating systems (e.g., AngularJS). All variables are bound to the *person* (a 'dictionary' object defined globally that holds all user model keys). Thus, *{{age}}* translates to *person['age']*. Evaluation of a PERSALOG code block proceeds from top to bottom. If all the conditions for a line are met, the person is placed in a virtual segment and the 'do' portion of the code is executed (in this case printing a single character) and the block is considered finished. If conditions on any line fail, the next line is executed. The PersaLog parser transforms this code into the following JavaScript block[4]:

```
function persalogBlock1_3(p,t) {
    if (p['age'] <= 18) {
        setSegment(p,'1_3','0');
        t.innerHTML = 'a';
    } else if (p['age'] <= 65) { ...
        t.innerHTML = 'b';
    } else { ...
        t.innerHTML = 'c';
    }
}
```

Each PERSALOG code block is transformed into a single JavaScript function, and each function is executed in turn during personalization (the person model and 'print target' are passed as arguments). The *setSegment* function assigns the person to a segment (in this case a 'virtual' one that PersaLog automatically created). *If* functions in PERSALOG can have a boolean form (e.g., *({{age}} > 10) && ({{age}} <= 20)* or *{{city}} endsWith 's'*–which is useful for generating grammatical correct pluralization when printing).

In some situations it is preferable to segment using a "fuzzy" match: that is, the closest match given a set of segments. PERSALOG supports a segmentation operator (*segmentby*) that is equivalent to a SQL JOIN but with more sophisticated criteria. The construction assumes the existence of a table (loaded with the *loadsegment* operator, one of the few exceptions to the segment-do language):

```
file: bigcities.csv

    big_city,    geoloc,           population
    New York,    "40.7,-74.0",     8.4M
    Chicago,     "41.8,-87.6",     2.7M
    Los Angeles, "34.0,-118.2",    10M
```

[4]This is a modified listing, additional code is added to bullet-proof the execution with try/catch statements. Also note that each block is uniquely identified

This comma-separated file is loaded and a new *segment database* called *bigcities* is loaded into the PersaLog namespace. Column names can be arbitrary but columns that start with *geoloc* are treated as locations and parsed into latitude/-longitude pairs. We can then create code such as:

```
loadsegment bigcities.csv

segmentby {{location}} nearestGeo
    {{bigcities.city}} setas
    {{closest}} ::: print you're
    closest to {{closest}} which
    has {{population}} residents.
default ::: donothing
```

Abstractly, one can think of *segmentby* as a large if/else that finds an optimal matching segment based on (potentially fuzzy) criteria. Rather than returning a boolean, as in the case of the *if* style construction, *segmentby* will return the best match. In the case above, the *nearestGeo* command cycles through each segment, finding the segment that best matches–which, in this case, is geographically nearest to our reader. The matching segment name is put into a *closest* variable (an optional criteria). The table columns for the matching segment (i.e., row) become part of that person's profile (e.g., *population*). This allows the PersaLog user to specify actions like *print {{population}}*. Other segmentation rules include: exact matches (e.g., *{{city}} matches {{bigcities.big_city}}*)–only people who live in one of the three cities will match); and nearest numerically. New JavaScript functions can be added to the core library and called in the same way. Such functions must simply produce one of the rows (or -1) and a 'distance' score. 'Distance' is semantically meaningful. In the geographical case it represents miles and can be used for further filtering (e.g., *{{closest_distance}}* <= 50 to require that reader be less than 50 miles away from some point).

Do-style operations include *print* (any HTML content can be produced here), *set* (set variables in the person's profile), *donothing* (a "null op"), and *vis*. Vis operations take as argument a function name and information to pass. For example, a PersaLog-enabled map might feature a *centerOn(location)* function which we could invoke as *'vis centerOn location'*. Visualizations 'wrapped' by PersaLog automatically have a set of functions they expose in this way (e.g., *mouseover*, *submit*, *click*, and other standard direct-manipulation events).

Any number of *segmenting* and *do* operations can be placed on a line: $c_0 ::: c_1 ::: \ldots ::: c_n$. When translating statements like this, PersaLog will find all *segmenting* functions (*do* or *segmentby*) and create a conjunctive query. For example, if c_1 and c_4 create segments, the translation would be: *if* $(c_1 \wedge c_4)$ *{ do* $c_0, c_2, c_3, c_5, \ldots$*}*.

User Modelling

Like segmenting functions, user modelling functions accept a 'person' profile object as input and will *enhance* the profile through annotation. User modelling can take place within the browser or by using a remote server. The decision of where these services are housed can be based on the privacy policy (Guideline 5) as well as computational and memory constraints. For example, PersaLog currently offers geocoding services (IP address → geographical location). The database

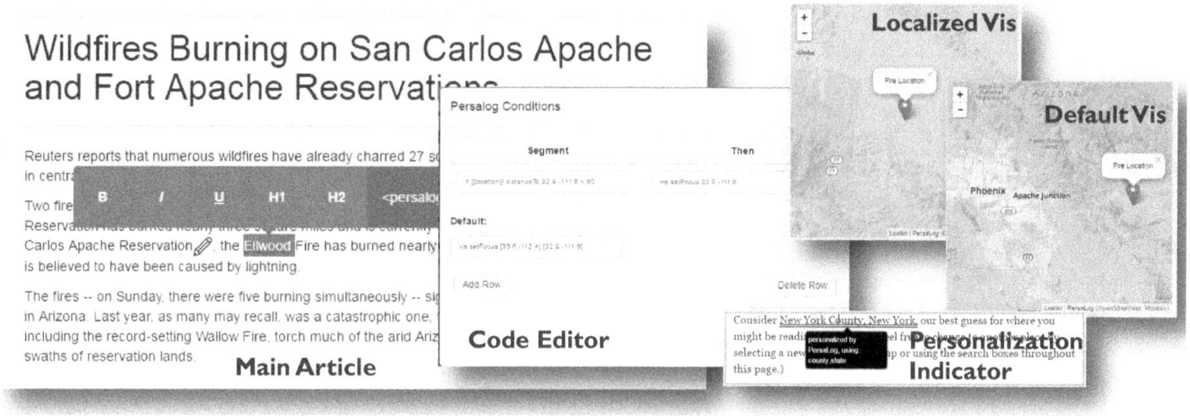

Figure 3. Examples of the editor view for the article and code. Personalized maps (upper right) are shown for this article. One for nearby residents (localized) and one for remote readers who see a map relating the fire to a known location (Phoenix, AZ). The bottom right figure is an example of a personalization indicator.

housing this information is fairly large and can not reasonably be transmitted to every requesting client.

Currently, we support geolocation, an imperfect but widely used form of inference [33], through data offered by the MaxMind GeoIP service (**www.maxmind.com**). This produces latitude/longitude information based on IP address (from which zip codes, city, county, and state identification can be extracted). Once a location has been inferred, other location-specific features (e.g., *time zone*) are added. We have also built a simplified demographic inference engine based census data (specifically the American Community Survey) to support inference of demographic properties such as gender, age, and occupation based on physical location. This type of "weak" inference provides a maximum likelihood estimate based on the prevailing category. For example, we might infer that a person is more likely female because the particular city is 51% female. In keeping with Guideline 4–consider inference quality–PersaLog can report both a confidence in a particular inference as well as probability distributions over possible segments. Distributions are represented as probability density functions (PDFs) over the possible classes (e.g., probability of male versus female versus unknown, or probability of $age = 1, 2, 3, \ldots, 100$. End users can use this information in deciding whether, and how, to use the inference. PERSALOG offers a special notation for this: $\{\{variable|PDF_{filter}\}\}$, where PDF_{filter} is area under the curve (AUC) of the PDF for a particular variable, v, given the filter. The filter may include ranges (e.g., $14 - -18$ or > 21) and categorical filters (e.g., 'Engineer,Doctor'). A special *mostlikely* keyword can be combined with the *segmentby*:

```
segmentby mostlikely {{age|<18}} {{age|18-45}}
   {{age|>45}} setas {{agebin}}
```

This will segment based on *age* into one of three categories (based on which is mostly likely given the max AUC). For example, if distribution shows the biggest 'mass' under the range of 18–45, the *agebin* variable will be set to *18-45*. We do not anticipate this feature to be used by novice end-users, but provide the functions for more sophisticated applications where inference is highly noisy.

Additional user modelling engines (and more sophisticated user-models, e.g., [8]) can be added depending on the application. For services with 'ground-truth' classification, classifiers can be trained to infer properties as distinct as age, gender, political affiliation, and reading level from browsing or search behavior [12, 25, 48]. We emphasize that it is not the goal of the current prototype to innovate in inference algorithms but rather to support their integration. PersaLog also supports the use of non-inferred (i.e., explicit) user information. For example, if the site supports client registration with demographic information, PersaLog can obtain and use this information. Finally, PersaLog supports an override of user models (an end-user can change their model) and disabling of personalization, aligning with Guideline 2. Both inferred and explicit user attributes can persist beyond a specific page through cookies or as URL arguments (both are currently supported). Note that inferences can build upon each other: IP address can lead to location which can lead to demographic properties. The "inference pathway" (a directed acyclic graph) is maintained by PersaLog so that an override earlier in the pathway (e.g., to location) will optionally (but by default) "invalidate" the subsequent inferences, which are then recalculated.

UIs for Editing & Viewing

Creators of PersaLog-aware code can use the editor of their choice. We believe that using pseudo-code or markup languages while editing an article is familiar to journalists and many CMS's support this kind of writing (e.g., [62] and the New York Times' ArchieML [57]). Furthermore, our respondents indicated a broad knowledge of tools such as Excel and Google Spreadsheets, which have DSLs for manipulating data. For journalists comfortable with this level of programming, we have constructed a large sample database of PersaLog code (Guideline 7). That said, we recognize that that not all journalists will want to modify this code directly. Thus we have constructed additional interfaces including a "spreadsheet" style interface and a "wizard" to generate PersaLog code at a much higher level (Guideline 6).

Content creators can edit content in a modified version of the open-source Medium blogging system's editor [44]. A

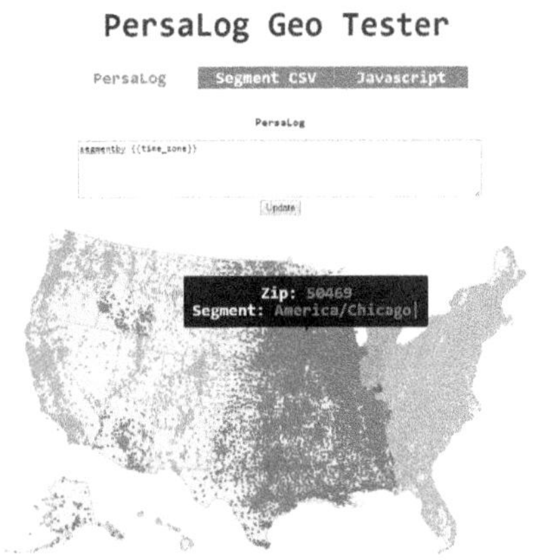

Figure 4. Visual test system–each point on the map is a simulated user, segmented by the PERSALOG code (and automatically colored)

menu for inserting images or formatting headings has been extended to insert PERSALOG code (see Figure 3, at left). A dialog box containing a two-column table is opened (Figure 3, middle). Each row in the table is inserted as a PERSALOG string (i.e., *A ::: B*–roughly the if/then structure, though the second column is optional to support *segmentby* and other constructs). A pencil icon (✐) indicates where this code is embedded; clicking brings up the editing dialog. The editor can export the page, with PERSALOG code, once finished.

By default we provide a number of features to: (a) indicate that personalization is happening (a fixed page footer), (b) that it can be changed (a dialog box is opened, allowing the reader to change their 'model'), and (c) that it can be disabled. Additionally, when mousing-over personalized content, a tooltip displays which "features" (e.g., age, location, etc.) were used to generate the content. This is done automatically by mining the code blocks. These feature are built to support Guidelines 2 and 3 concerning transparency and control.

Test Harnesses

We have created multiple test systems to allow writers to experiment and test PERSALOG code (Guideline 6), and which also support viewing how different readers will see the rendered page to gain awareness of potential biases (Guideline 1). These tools create simulated end-users (e.g., 30k with unique IP addresses corresponding to zip codes) that can be 'pushed' through a PersaLog personalization pipeline. Figure 4, a *map test harness*, is a visualization of these individuals plotted on a map. Different PERSALOG code will result in different colors based on segmentation. A similar page allows for testing of text and visualization 'blocks' by iterating over the simulated user sets. The generated JavaScript code is displayed and the 'object' corresponding to different people can be modified and sent through the pipeline. A third harness generates the text output for a simulated user base, identifies errors, and groups results (useful, for example, for validating pluralization).

EVALUATION

In addition to our survey guidelines, PersaLog and its specific features have been informed by feedback we received from journalists and through our interviews. To validate that PersaLog provides coverage of desired features we have constructed a number of case studies and a lab study.

PersaLog Understanding, Modification, and Construction

To evaluate the PERSALOG language among potential users we ran a study with 11 upper-level undergraduates working at a large university's newspaper. All had created news content but few had coding experience and none programmed regularly (four had taken introductory Python or C++ courses which are broadly required by many majors). Participants were given a printed tutorial explaining PERSALOG followed by a paper-based test consisting of 11 questions (see supplementary material) with three question types. Eight *interpretation* questions focused on describing the output of PERSALOG code (presented with the profile of the viewer, and using both complex and simple forms of segmentation), one *code modification* task asked the participant to extend code, and two *creation* problems had participant create code from scratch using different segmentation rules (traditional if/else as well as "segementby"). The tutorial provided sample code but no sample specifically answered the questions. Participants received $20. Median quiz time was 18 minutes (max: 23).

The median correct score was 8 (of 11). We labeled each incorrect answer as either a syntax error (e.g., used a single curly brace instead of doubles) or a more significant error (the mistake would not produce the correct result even if the syntax error were corrected). The median syntax errors was 1 (mean 1.45) and other errors was 2 (mean 2.27). While most questions were answered correctly by most participants, two were often incorrect. One was a piece of "buggy" code where the order of 'if' operations on a range were reversed (*if* $x < 22 \ldots$ *; if* $x < 18 \ldots$ what happens when $x = 17$?). The second required creating a complicated segmentation followed by a second code if/else codeblock (none of the examples in the tutorial used this structure). Of the remaining questions, four were answered correctly by 8-9 students, and five were answered correctly by 10-11.

We designed this evaluation to focus on the PERSALOG language rather than the tools we created. This represents a 'worst-case:' students were largely untrained with PERSALOG aside from the tutorial, completed the task on paper (no explicit 'debugging support' or 'test-and-check' style programming), and were provided only a limited set of examples. Our goal was to determine language usability rather than identifying strengths and weaknesses in the "development environment."

Case Studies

We describe a set of case studies for stress testing PersaLog components using a diverse visualizations that show broad coverage of 'wrapping' and demonstrate expressiveness.

'How Your Area Compares'

We reverse engineered the code *The Times'* article [2], "The Best and Worst Places to Grow Up: How Your Area Compares," (Figure 1) to identify those places where personalization happened. While many personalized elements are straightforward (e.g., imputing user location and presenting relevant data), a few specific outliers exist (e.g., specific code around New

York and Washington DC). Once we identified these, we wrote PERSALOG code to generate this content. For all textual and visual elements, we were able to generate analogous content using PERSALOG code. This exercise also allowed us to test critical features. For example, we used string tests to ensure that pluralizations were grammatically correct. As part of this exercise we built our own generic visualizations (e.g., count-level thematic maps) which we 'wrapped.'

It is difficult to compare the PERSALOG-based version directly to *The Times* based on line-count. On the one hand, PersaLog does not require any complex operations to select DOM elements and offers a consistent inference library and has a simplified language for choosing what to display. However, the code we studied from *The Times* was obfuscated, compressed, and clearly made to be efficient (e.g., using shorthand: *if ? then : else*). We believe PERSALOG balances conciseness and readability for a broader population. The code for visualizations would largely be equivalent between the PersaLog and original versions. However, because PersaLog can wrap existing visualizations, we can leverage existing interactive assets and make them 'personalization compatible.' A final interesting difference is that the news publications' JavaScript often incorporated data-processing (e.g., transforming .234 to 23%). PersaLog does not remove the burden of generating or cleaning data. For example, the original article has a database of neighboring counties that are richer or poorer than your own. Currently, PersaLog treats this as a pre-processing step.

Visualization Tests

In addition to many simple D3 visualizations, we have also tested PersaLog within the context of more complex interactive visualizations. For example:

- Jim Vallandingham's "How Much Money do the Movies We Love Make?" (**http://vallandingham.me/vis/movie/**), an interactive visualization that allows the viewer to find movies by genre and plot them on a *rating* versus *profit* scatter plot. The visualization contained a number of brushing and search interactions, none of which were 'scriptable' originally. The PersaLog wrapper bound names to different interface and visual objects allowing us to perform actions like "select genre Action" and "mouseover film Iron Man." We have demonstrated personalization of this page based on reader age, setting the initial genre based on this inference.
- The Guardian's "Is Barack Obama the President?" (**http://www.isbarackobamathepresident.com/**), a whimsical visualization using balloons to represent states in the Obama–Romney election (2012). Hovering over a balloon provides more election information. We automatically invoke a hover over the viewer's home state. Again, the visualization was not originally designed to be controlled in this way and there were no "hooks" to the Texas object, for example.

Additional Examples

We have also created personalized articles that respond to age (indicating a reading level), by changing images and text to explain ion channels to an K-8 reader versus someone more advanced. Mr. Quealy [52] indicated that often this varying detail was important with technical material, with existing solutions largely composed of having 'expert explanations' pulled out as additional material (e.g., around topics like credit default swaps). We also built a hyperlocal personalization that changes maps based on location. An article about a forest fire shows either a broader map (if the reader is remote) or a focused one (if the visitor is a local). Journalists who work in local papers describe hyperlocalization as a way to take content that is broad (i.e., syndicated from a national/regional sources) and modifying it to boost local relevance.

DISCUSSION AND FUTURE WORK

Content personalization offers significant opportunities for content producers and readers alike. While PersaLog's implementation is designed to support the guidelines derived from our survey when possible, conventions and guidelines must be developed outside of the technical infrastructure. For example, content providers can hide the fact that personalization is happening by simply disabling our "PersaLog" buttons. Future work may include developing best-practices that can be more broadly applied (e.g., not inferring personalization features or accessing data that will not be used). Other unintended consequences of personalization (e.g., the diminishing value of comments when everyone sees different content) may lead to technical innovations that provide balanced personal–global spaces. These implications require serious consideration about the underlying values a site would like to engender.

In designing and experimenting with PersaLog, we identified specific and general personalization mechanisms. For example, some textual annotations are useful for drawing attention in a visualization. These could be packaged as visualization libraries to make them more viable for personalization. We have also begun to identify general design patterns for content personalization (e.g., personalized content should include "facts" that are a superset of the non-personalized). Deploying PersaLog in the wild, among practicing journalists, would allow us to test the ecological validity of our approach, iterate on the language and system design. With broader use and experimentation, re-usable design patterns will also likely emerge. Additional evaluations of the language (e.g., [28]) may also provide insights for future versions.

CONCLUSIONS

We introduced the PersaLog system and PERSALOG DSL. Like feed personalization, content personalization can enhance learning and behavioral changes in readers and increase engagement. In designing tools that support these features we have identified a number of unique properties and requirements that emerge in the context of news personalization. We report on a survey of journalism professionals that helped us define a set of guidelines for content personalization. Using this feedback, we have created a novel system that supports a broad set of personalizations that can be applied to existing and new (non-personalized) text and graphical content.

ACKNOWLEDGEMENTS

This was supported by the NSF under grant IIS-1421438. We are gratefully to our many respondents for their input.

REFERENCES

1. Gregor Aisch, Quoctrung Bui, Amanda Cox, and Kevin Quealy. 2016. Where the Poor Live Longer: How Your

Area Compares. *The New York Times*, April 11, Available: *http://nyti.ms/1SryMtT*. (2016).

2. Gregor Aisch, Eric Buth, Matthew Block, Amanda Cox, and Kevin Quealy. 2015. The Best and Worst Places to Grow Up: How Your Area Compares. *The New York Times*, May 4, 2015, Available: *http://nyti.ms/1KGrkJM*. (2015).
3. Jon Bentley. 1986. Programming Pearls: Little Languages. *Commun. ACM* 29, 8 (Aug. 1986), 711–721. DOI:http://dx.doi.org/10.1145/6424.315691
4. Michael Bolin, Matthew Webber, Philip Rha, Tom Wilson, and Robert C. Miller. 2005. Automation and Customization of Rendered Web Pages. In *Proceedings of the 18th Annual ACM Symposium on User Interface Software and Technology (UIST '05)*. ACM, New York, NY, USA, 163–172. DOI: http://dx.doi.org/10.1145/1095034.1095062
5. Engin Bozdag. 2013. Bias in algorithmic filtering and personalization. *Ethics and Information Technology* 15, 3 (2013), 209–227.
6. Paul De Bra, Evgeny Knutov, David Smits, Natalia Stash, and Vinicius F. C. Ramos. 2013. GALE: a generic open source extensible adaptation engine. *New Review of Hypermedia and Multimedia* 19, 2 (2013), 182–212. DOI: http://dx.doi.org/10.1080/13614568.2013.806961
7. Paul De Bra, Natalia Stash, David Smits, Cristóbal Romero, and Sebastián Ventura. 2007. *Authoring and Management Tools for Adaptive Educational Hypermedia Systems: The AHA! Case Study*. Springer Berlin Heidelberg, Berlin, Heidelberg, 285–308. DOI: http://dx.doi.org/10.1007/978-3-540-71974-8_11
8. Peter Brusilovsky and Eva Millán. 2007. *User Models for Adaptive Hypermedia and Adaptive Educational Systems*. Springer Berlin Heidelberg, Berlin, Heidelberg, 3–53. DOI:http://dx.doi.org/10.1007/978-3-540-72079-9_1
9. Darla Cameron and Denise Lu. 2016. Personal interview, July 12. (2016).
10. Gina Masullo Chen, T Makana Chock, Hillary Gozigian, Ryan Rogers, Arushi Sen, Valarie N Schweisberger, Joseph Steinhardt, and Yi Wang. 2011. Personalizing news websites attracts young readers. *Newspaper Research J.* 32, 4 (2011), 22–38.
11. Pascal R Chesnais, Matthew J Mucklo, Jonathan Sheena, and others. 1995. The Fishwrap personalized news system. In *2nd International Workshop Community Networking, 1995*. IEEE, New York, NY, 275–282.
12. Kevyn Collins-Thompson, Paul N. Bennett, Ryen W. White, Sebastian de la Chica, and David Sontag. 2011. Personalizing Web Search Results by Reading Level. In *Proceedings of the 20th ACM International Conference on Information and Knowledge Management (CIKM '11)*. ACM, New York, NY, USA, 403–412. DOI: http://dx.doi.org/10.1145/2063576.2063639
13. Diana I Cordova and Mark R Lepper. 1996. Intrinsic motivation and the process of learning: Beneficial effects of contextualization, personalization, and choice. *J. of Educational Psychology* 88, 4 (1996), 715.
14. Allen Cypher, Mira Dontcheva, Tessa Lau, and Jeffrey Nichols. 2010. *No Code Required: Giving Users Tools to Transform the Web*. Morgan Kaufmann Publishers Inc., San Francisco, CA, USA.
15. Nada Dabbagh and Anastasia Kitsantas. 2012. Personal Learning Environments, social media, and self-regulated learning: A natural formula for connecting formal and informal learning. *The Internet and higher education* 15, 1 (2012), 3–8.
16. Judy Davis-Dorsey, Steven M Ross, and Gary R Morrison. 1991. The role of rewording and context personalization in the solving of mathematical word problems. *J. of Educational Psychology* 83, 1 (1991), 61.
17. Chrysanne Di Marco, Peter Bray, H Dominic Covvey, Donald D Cowan, Vic Di Ciccio, Eduard Hovy, Joan Lipa, and Cathy Yang. 2006. Authoring and generation of individualized patient education materials. In *AMIA Annual Symposium Proceedings*, Vol. 2006. American Medical Informatics Association, Bethesda, MD, 195.
18. Paula J Durlach and Alan M Lesgold. 2012. *Adaptive technologies for training and education*. Cambridge University Press, New York, NY.
19. Facebook. 2017. Ads Guide. *https://www.facebook.com/business/ads-guide/*. (2017).
20. Leah Findlater and Joanna McGrenere. 2008. Impact of Screen Size on Performance, Awareness, and User Satisfaction with Adaptive Graphical User Interfaces. In *Proceedings of the SIGCHI Conference on Human Factors in Computing Systems (CHI '08)*. ACM, New York, NY, USA, 1247–1256. DOI: http://dx.doi.org/10.1145/1357054.1357249
21. Jonathan G.K. Foss and Alexandra I. Cristea. 2010. The Next Generation Authoring Adaptive Hypermedia: Using and Evaluating the MOT3.0 and PEAL Tools. In *Proceedings of the 21st ACM Conference on Hypertext and Hypermedia (HT '10)*. ACM, New York, NY, USA, 83–92. DOI:http://dx.doi.org/10.1145/1810617.1810633
22. Evgeniy Gabrilovich, Susan Dumais, and Eric Horvitz. 2004. Newsjunkie: Providing Personalized Newsfeeds via Analysis of Information Novelty. In *Proceedings of the 13th International Conference on World Wide Web (WWW '04)*. ACM, New York, NY, USA, 482–490. DOI: http://dx.doi.org/10.1145/988672.988738
23. Krzysztof Z. Gajos, Mary Czerwinski, Desney S. Tan, and Daniel S. Weld. 2006. Exploring the Design Space for Adaptive Graphical User Interfaces. In *Proceedings of the Working Conference on Advanced Visual Interfaces (AVI '06)*. ACM, New York, NY, USA, 201–208. DOI: http://dx.doi.org/10.1145/1133265.1133306

24. Krzysztof Z. Gajos, Katherine Everitt, Desney S. Tan, Mary Czerwinski, and Daniel S. Weld. 2008. Predictability and Accuracy in Adaptive User Interfaces. In *Proceedings of the SIGCHI Conference on Human Factors in Computing Systems (CHI '08)*. ACM, New York, NY, USA, 1271–1274. DOI: http://dx.doi.org/10.1145/1357054.1357252

25. Arline T Geronimus, John Bound, and Lisa J Neidert. 1996. On the validity of using census geocode characteristics to proxy individual socioeconomic characteristics. *J. Amer. Statist. Assoc.* 91, 434 (1996), 529–537.

26. Stefan Göbel, Sandro Hardy, Viktor Wendel, Florian Mehm, and Ralf Steinmetz. 2010. Serious Games for Health: Personalized Exergames. In *Proceedings of the 18th ACM International Conference on Multimedia (MM '10)*. ACM, New York, NY, USA, 1663–1666. DOI: http://dx.doi.org/10.1145/1873951.1874316

27. Google. 2017. Google Ads. *https://www.google.com/ads/*. (2017).

28. T.R.G. Green and M. Petre. 1996. Usability Analysis of Visual Programming Environments: A 'Cognitive Dimensions' Framework. *Journal of Visual Languages & Computing* 7, 2 (1996), 131 – 174. DOI: http://dx.doi.org/10.1006/jvlc.1996.0009

29. Jonathan Harper and Maneesh Agrawala. 2014. Deconstructing and Restyling D3 Visualizations. In *Proceedings of the 27th Annual ACM Symposium on User Interface Software and Technology (UIST '14)*. ACM, New York, NY, USA, 253–262. DOI: http://dx.doi.org/10.1145/2642918.2647411

30. Kashmir Hill. 2016. How an internet mapping glitch turned a random Kansas farm into a digital hell. *Fusion*, April 10, Available: *http://fusion.net/story/287592/internet-mapping-glitch-kansas-farm/*. (2016).

31. Graeme Hirst, Chrysanne DiMarco, Eduard Hovy, and Kimberley Parsons. 1997. *Authoring and Generating Health-Education Documents That Are Tailored to the Needs of the Individual Patient*. Springer Vienna, Vienna, 107–118. DOI: http://dx.doi.org/10.1007/978-3-7091-2670-7_14

32. Kristina Höök. 2000. Steps to take before intelligent user interfaces become real. *Interacting with computers* 12, 4 (2000), 409–426.

33. B. Huffaker, M. Fomenkov, and k. claffy. 2011. *Geocompare: a comparison of public and commercial geolocation databases - Technical Report* . Technical Report. Cooperative Association for Internet Data Analysis (CAIDA).

34. Chris J. Hughes, Mike Armstrong, Rhianne Jones, and Michael Crabb. 2015. Responsive Design for Personalised Subtitles. In *Proceedings of the 12th Web for All Conference (W4A '15)*. ACM, New York, NY, USA, Article 8, 4 pages. DOI: http://dx.doi.org/10.1145/2745555.2746650

35. Judy Kay. 2000. Stereotypes, Student Models and Scrutability. In *Proceedings of the 5th International Conference on Intelligent Tutoring Systems (ITS '00)*. Springer-Verlag, London, UK, UK, 19–30. http://dl.acm.org/citation.cfm?id=648030.745813

36. Yea-Seul Kim, Jessica Hullman, and Maneesh Agrawala. 2016. Generating Personalized Spatial Analogies for Distances and Areas. In *Proceedings of the 2016 CHI Conference on Human Factors in Computing Systems*. ACM, New York, NY, USA, 38–48. DOI: http://dx.doi.org/10.1145/2858036.2858440

37. Aleksandra Klašnja-Milićević, Boban Vesin, Mirjana Ivanović, and Zoran Budimac. 2011. E-Learning personalization based on hybrid recommendation strategy and learning style identification. *Computers & Education* 56, 3 (2011), 885–899.

38. Scott Klein. 2013. How To Edit 52,000 Stories at Once. *ProPublica Nerd Blog*, Jan. 24, 2013, Available: *https://goo.gl/5QipBA*. (2013).

39. Evgeny Knutov, Paul De Bra, and Mykola Pechenizkiy. 2009. AH 12 years later: a comprehensive survey of adaptive hypermedia methods and techniques. *New Review of Hypermedia and Multimedia* 15, 1 (2009), 5–38.

40. Andrew J. Ko, Robin Abraham, Laura Beckwith, Alan Blackwell, Margaret Burnett, Martin Erwig, Chris Scaffidi, Joseph Lawrance, Henry Lieberman, Brad Myers, Mary Beth Rosson, Gregg Rothermel, Mary Shaw, and Susan Wiedenbeck. 2011. The State of the Art in End-user Software Engineering. *ACM Comput. Surv.* 43, 3, Article 21 (April 2011), 44 pages. DOI: http://dx.doi.org/10.1145/1922649.1922658

41. Gilly Leshed, Eben M. Haber, Tara Matthews, and Tessa Lau. 2008. CoScripter: Automating & Sharing How-to Knowledge in the Enterprise. In *Proceedings of the SIGCHI Conference on Human Factors in Computing Systems (CHI '08)*. ACM, New York, NY, USA, 1719–1728. DOI: http://dx.doi.org/10.1145/1357054.1357323

42. Yuping Liu and LJ Shrum. 2002. What is interactivity and is it always such a good thing? Implications of definition, person, and situation for the influence of interactivity on advertising effectiveness. *J. of Advertising* 31, 4 (2002), 53–64.

43. Catherine McLoughlin and Mark JW Lee. 2010. Personalised and self regulated learning in the Web 2.0 era: International exemplars of innovative pedagogy using social software. *Australasian Journal of Educational Technology* 26, 1 (2010), 28–43.

44. MediumEditor Open Source Team. 2016. MediumEditor. *https://yabwe.github.io/medium-editor/*. (2016).

45. Ted Mellnik, Darla Cameron, Denise Lu, Emily Badger, and Kat Downs. 2016. America's great housing divide: Are you a winner or loser? *Washington Post*, April 28, 2016, Available: *http://wapo.st/housing*. (2016).

46. Maria Milosavljevic. 1997. *Augmenting the User's Knowledge via Comparison*. Springer Vienna, Vienna, 119–130. DOI: http://dx.doi.org/10.1007/978-3-7091-2670-7_15

47. Alejandro Montes García, Paul De Bra, George H.L. Fletcher, and Mykola Pechenizkiy. 2014. A DSL Based on CSS for Hypertext Adaptation. In *Proceedings of the 25th ACM Conference on Hypertext and Social Media (HT '14)*. ACM, New York, NY, USA, 313–315. DOI: http://dx.doi.org/10.1145/2631775.2631782

48. Dan Murray and Kevan Durrell. 2000. *Inferring Demographic Attributes of Anonymous Internet Users*. Springer Berlin Heidelberg, Berlin, Heidelberg, 7–20. DOI: http://dx.doi.org/10.1007/3-540-44934-5_1

49. Reinhard Oppermann and R Rasher. 1997. Adaptability and adaptivity in learning systems. *Knowledge transfer* 2 (1997), 173–179.

50. Shahida M. Parvez and Glenn D. Blank. 2008. *Individualizing Tutoring with Learning Style Based Feedback*. Springer Berlin Heidelberg, Berlin, Heidelberg, 291–301. DOI: http://dx.doi.org/10.1007/978-3-540-69132-7_33

51. Paul A Pavlou and David W Stewart. 2000. Measuring the effects and effectiveness of interactive advertising: A research agenda. *J. of Interactive Advertising* 1, 1 (2000), 61–77.

52. Kevin Quealy. 2016. Personal interview, July 1. (2016).

53. Kevin Quealy and Margot Sanger-Katz. 2015. The Experts Were Wrong About the Best Places for Better and Cheaper Health Care. *The New York Times*, December 15, 2016, Available: *http://nyti.ms/1IRnP6J*. (2015).

54. Ehud Reiter, Robert Dale, and Zhiwei Feng. 2000. *Building natural language generation systems*. MIT Press, Cambridge, MA.

55. Mark Christopher Roberts. 2007. *Measuring the relationship between journalistic transparency and credibility*. Ph.D. Dissertation. University of South Carolina.

56. Celette Sugg Skinner, Victor J Strecher, and Harm Hospers. 1994. Physicians' recommendations for mammography: do tailored messages make a difference? *American Journal of Public Health* 84, 1 (1994), 43–49.

57. Michael Strickland, Archie Tse, Matthew Ericson, and Tom Giratikanon. 2016. ArchieML. *http://archieml.org/*. (2016).

58. Margaret Sullivan. 2015. When News Gets (Too?) Personal. *The New York Times*, Public Editor's Journal, Dec. 17, *http://nyti.ms/1T3H9hs*. (2015).

59. The New York Times. 2015. Innovation. May 24, 2015. (2015).

60. Theophanis Tsandilas and m. c. schraefel. 2005. An Empirical Assessment of Adaptation Techniques. In *CHI '05 Extended Abstracts on Human Factors in Computing Systems (CHI EA '05)*. ACM, New York, NY, USA, 2009–2012. DOI: http://dx.doi.org/10.1145/1056808.1057079

61. Blase Ur, Melwyn Pak Yong Ho, Stephen Brawner, Jiyun Lee, Sarah Mennicken, Noah Picard, Diane Schulze, and Michael L. Littman. 2016. Trigger-Action Programming in the Wild: An Analysis of 200,000 IFTTT Recipes. In *Proceedings of the 2016 CHI Conference on Human Factors in Computing Systems (CHI '16)*. ACM, New York, NY, USA, 3227–3231. DOI: http://dx.doi.org/10.1145/2858036.2858556

62. Shan Wang. 2016. The Los Angeles Times built its own journalist-friendly story editor, and it's now rolling out to all of Tronc. *Nieman Lab*, August 10, 2016, Available: *goo.gl/c7wFVm*. (2016).

63. Jeffrey Wong and Jason I. Hong. 2007. Making Mashups with Marmite: Towards End-user Programming for the Web. In *Proceedings of the SIGCHI Conference on Human Factors in Computing Systems (CHI '07)*. ACM, New York, NY, USA, 1435–1444. DOI: http://dx.doi.org/10.1145/1240624.1240842

You Want Me to Work with *Who*? Stakeholder Perceptions of Automated Team Formation in Project-based Courses

Farnaz Jahanbakhsh, Wai-Tat Fu, Karrie Karahalios, Darko Marinov, Brian Bailey
University of Illinois at Urbana
{fjahan4, wfu, kkarahal, marinov, bpbailey}@illinois.edu

ABSTRACT
Instructors are increasingly using algorithmic tools for team formation, yet little is known about how these tools are applied or how students and instructors perceive their use. We studied a representative team formation tool (CATME) in eight project-based courses. An instructor uses the tool to form teams by surveying students' working styles, skills, and demographics–then configuring the criteria as input into an algorithm that assigns teams. We surveyed students (N=277) in the courses to gauge their perceptions of the strengths and weaknesses of the tool and ideas for improving it. We also interviewed instructors (N=13) different from those who taught the eight courses to learn about their criteria selections and perceptions of the tool. Students valued the rational basis for forming teams but desired a stronger voice in criteria selection and explanations as to why they were assigned to a particular team. Instructors appreciated the efficiency of team formation but wanted to view exemplars of criteria used in similar courses. This work contributes recommendations for deploying team formation tools in educational settings and for better satisfying the goals of all stakeholders.

Author Keywords
Algorithms; CATME; Education; Team formation.

ACM Classification Keywords
H.5.3 [Information Interface and Presentation]: Group and Organization Interfaces--Collaborative computing.

INTRODUCTION
Teamwork can provide the multiple perspectives and diverse skills needed for solving complex problems [4, 18]. Industry rates the ability to work in teams as one of the most desirable soft skills in prospective employees [33]. The Accreditation Board for Engineering and Technology requires graduates to demonstrate "an ability to function effectively on teams to accomplish a common goal" [2]. Given its importance, more instructors are emphasizing teamwork in their courses.

Permission to make digital or hard copies of all or part of this work for personal or classroom use is granted without fee provided that copies are not made or distributed for profit or commercial advantage and that copies bear this notice and the full citation on the first page. Copyrights for components of this work owned by others than ACM must be honored. Abstracting with credit is permitted. To copy otherwise, or republish, to post on servers or to redistribute to lists, requires prior specific permission and/or a fee. Request permissions from Permissions@acm.org.
CHI 2017, May 06-11, 2017, Denver, CO, USA
© 2017 ACM. ISBN 978-1-4503-4655-9/17/05…$15.00
DOI: http://dx.doi.org/10.1145/3025453.3026011

A challenge faced by instructors who want to incorporate teamwork into their courses is how to form student teams, especially in courses with diverse student makeup. To meet this challenge, instructors can now use tools that automate the team formation workflow [27]. An advantage is that these tools make it easier for instructors to compose student teams, and ideally "good" teams by applying findings from studies relating attributes of team composition to team performance and satisfaction [3, 6-8, 15, 17-21, 28, 30, 31, 34, 39].

However, despite knowing much about how teams *should* be formed, there is little knowledge of how instructors apply team formation tools in practice, or how students perceive their use. For example, what criteria do instructors apply and why? How do students and instructors perceive the tradeoffs of an automated approach for team formation? How could the approach be improved? Answering these questions is important because team assignments can affect students' project outcomes, learning, and course grades [35]. It is also important for instructors because by adopting these tools they are assuming the responsibility for team formation.

We report on a field study of a representative team formation tool (CATME [1]) deployed in eight project-based courses over two semesters. An instructor uses the tool to form teams by first surveying students' working styles, skills, and demographics, among other criteria; then configuring these criteria as input to an algorithm that optimizes the team assignments. We surveyed students (N=277) in the courses to gauge their perceptions of the strengths and weaknesses of the tool and ideas for improving it. In addition to collecting the criteria used in these courses, we interviewed instructors (N=13) outside of these eight courses to gain further insight into the criteria selections and experiences of using the tool.

We found that students appreciated the rational basis for grouping them, but they wanted a stronger voice in the criteria selection phase because the assignments would affect them and wanted explanations as to why they were assigned to a given team. Despite these suggestions, students reported being reasonably satisfied with the teams assigned by the tool (μ=4.0 on a 5-point scale). Instructors valued the increased efficiency of team formation and the ability to blame the tool in cases where students were dissatisfied with their team assignment. However, instructors also reported wanting to browse exemplars of successful criteria applied in similar courses and ways to explore how various criteria configurations in the tool would affect the team assignments.

The contributions of this work are: 1) recommendations for deploying team formation tools in educational settings and for better satisfying the goals of students and instructors; and 2) results creating better awareness of how students and instructors perceive the tradeoffs of this type of tool.

RELATED WORK

We situate our work in the context of prior studies of team formation tools, how the use of team formation tools can support effective team composition, and how a tool-based approach compares to other approaches for team formation.

Studies of Team Formation Tools

Despite the increased use of team formation tools, only a few studies of such tools have been performed in course settings. One study showed that the use of a team formation tool can optimize team assignments with respect to instructor-defined criteria better than the instructor [27]. Redmond deployed a team formation tool that emphasized schedule compatibility and reported that students perceived the team assignments as fair [32]. However, this finding was based on the instructor having received few complaints from students rather than an explicit measure of their perceptions. Tafliovich et al. used a team formation tool to assign students to teams and studied how students wanted their teams to be evaluated [38].

Our work shares the goal of studying a team formation tool in academic courses. However, our work is novel because we are studying perceptions of the team formation experience, including ratings of student satisfaction with the assignments and open-ended responses to interpret those ratings. We also analyze the criteria applied by instructors and how the automated team formation workflow can be improved.

Achieving Effective Team Composition

Team composition is known to affect team performance and satisfaction [35]. For example, research shows that teams with a balance of personality types perform better and have higher satisfaction than teams with a surplus of leader-type personalities [28]. Bear and Woolley found that the percent of women on a team correlates with higher collective intelligence [7] while Jehn et al. reported that gender balanced teams have higher satisfaction with their team experiences [24]. Team performance is also improved when the team has diverse skills relevant to their chosen project and a team size commensurate with the project scope [19].

The benefit of a criteria-based team formation tool is that an instructor can potentially use it to create teams by applying findings from the corpus of prior studies. The benefit is especially desired in courses where students have diverse demographics, prior performance, and skills. However, the number of possible configurations in a team formation tool leaves many gaps relative to the configurations that were tested in the prior studies. Also, the instructors using these tools may not be experts on the topic of team formation. It is therefore unclear how instructors would approach selecting the criteria in practice. Our study addresses this gap by examining the criteria selected by instructors in fourteen courses using one representative tool and by sharing how instructors feel these decisions can be better supported.

Approaches to Team Formation

Three common approaches to team formation in courses include self-selection, random, and criteria-based. Self-selection requires students to form their own teams. The key advantage of this approach is that the teams can experience increased initial cohesiveness [37], and the approach is often preferred by those who have potential teammates in mind [30]. The disadvantage is that students typically select teammates similar to themselves [22]. Homogenous teams typically lack the skill diversity needed for the work [6] and can be susceptible to groupthink [23]. This approach is also problematic in courses where students are less familiar with one another (e.g., inter-disciplinary courses) and are unable to join a team. The instructor must then develop a strategy for how to assign the remaining students to teams. Random assignment ensures that all students are placed on a team, but like self-selection, this approach is unlikely to provide teams with the necessary resources for performing the work [10].

To overcome the limitations of random assignment and self-selection, instructors are increasingly applying criteria-based approaches. The literature favors this decision. For example, empirical studies have shown that teams formed using a criteria-based approach outperform self-selected teams [8] and randomly assigned teams [41], assuming the criteria are grounded in team composition theory (e.g., see [19, 35]). However, teams formed with criteria-based approaches can still experience teamwork issues such as social loafing, lack of trust, and decision conflicts [9], but these issues should be no different than in teams formed with other approaches.

In these prior studies of criteria-based team formation, the criteria were selected and controlled for experimentation. In practice, less is known as to how instructors choose the criteria or why, what criteria they choose, and how students perceive an algorithmic intervention into the team formation workflow. Our study contributes to filling this gap.

THE TEAM FORMATION TOOL

We studied the Comprehensive Assessment for Team-Member Effectiveness (CATME) tool that automates the team formation workflow [1]. CATME is representative of the class of criteria-based team formation tools. We chose CATME because it is grounded in team formation theory [27], is an online tool and freely available to instructors upon request, and is used in courses at many universities.

To begin team formation, the instructor selects from a set of criteria available in the tool, based on what s/he believes is most appropriate for her/his course. The tool defines 27 criteria, including schedules, skills, academic performance, working styles, and demographics. The instructor can revise and extend the criteria and how the associated questions are phrased in the survey. Once finalized, the tool generates an online survey with questions relating to the selected criteria and distributes it by email to the students in the course.

After students respond to the survey, the instructor reviews the aggregated data, specifies the desired team size, and assigns a weight to each criterion in the range [-5, +5]. Selecting a negative weight for a criterion prioritizes groups with differing responses to the associated survey question, whereas a positive weight prioritizes groups with similar responses. For example, assigning -5 for a criterion related to skills (e.g., are you best at visual design, programming, or writing?) prefers skill diversity in groups. The magnitude of the weight for a criterion indicates its impact relative to the other criteria. A weight of 0 instructs the algorithm to ignore the criterion. The tool defaults some of the criteria to non-zero weights, but without explanation, and the instructors in our study almost always changed them.

The instructor can review the team assignments, adjust the criteria configuration, and re-run the algorithm. Given its use of a randomized greedy algorithm to satisfy the constraints, the tool may produce different team compositions for each run. Instructors have the option to accept the initial team assignments or generate alternatives and select the one that they believe to be most satisfactory. An instructor may also specify which students should (not) be placed on the same team in the tool. Once finalized, the system notifies students of the team assignments and shares their contact information.

RESEARCH QUESTIONS

Our study aspires to understand automated team formation from the perspectives of its key stakeholders: students and instructors. We focus on two sets of questions:

SQ1: Having been assigned to a team via an automated method, how satisfied are students with their assignments?

SQ2: What strengths and weaknesses do students perceive in an automated approach to team formation?

SQ3: What do students suggest for improving the approach?

IQ1: What strengths and weaknesses do instructors perceive of this approach to team formation?

IQ2: What are the implications of the instructor and student perceptions for improving automated team formation?

Answering these questions contributes to the base of knowledge for team composition from perspectives beyond team performance. It also highlights some of the unexpected consequences of algorithmic intervention in team formation.

METHOD

To answer these questions, we conducted a mixed methods study. It consisted of a survey with both structured and open-ended questions distributed to students and semi-structured interviews with instructors who had used the tool (CATME). The study was approved by our Institutional Review Board.

Courses Deploying CATME

The team formation tool was deployed for the first time in eight computer science courses at the University of Illinois. The deployment was part of an internal educational initiative to improve the consistency, efficiency, and effectiveness of team formation in engineering courses. The instructors of the eight courses agreed to deploy the tool, as each was grappling with the challenges of forming student teams in a large course. Prior to this deployment, the most common method of team formation in these courses was self-formation. The research team assisted with the tool in these courses, but the choice of the criteria was left to the instructors. The eight courses listed in the left-hand half of Table 1 display the instructor's selected criteria for that course.

Three courses (Software Engineering I, UI Design, and HCI) were offered in Fall 2015 and the remaining five (Software Engineering II, Social Visualization, The Art and Science of Web Programming, Mobile Design, and User Interface Design – a second time) were offered in Spring 2016.

The total enrollment in these courses was 869 students. The majority came from Computer Science and Electrical and Computer Engineering (80%). Most were upper-level undergraduates or first-year graduate students (96%). For the design-oriented courses, a fraction of the students came from non-engineering majors such as Psychology, Information Science, and Art and Design. All of the courses required the students to complete between one and five group projects during the semester. Some projects lasted a few weeks; others lasted the majority of the semester. Team size was course dependent, and varied from 3 to 8 students.

In all courses, there was a very high response rate to the team formation surveys, ranging from 83% to 97%, indicating that students were vested in the team formation process.

Student Survey

To gauge the students' perspectives on the use of a team formation tool, we developed an online survey. The survey contained two structured questions (5-point scale): 1) How satisfied were you with your team members? (1=Not satisfied, 5=Very satisfied) 2) Do you recommend using CATME for team formation in future courses? (1=Don't recommend, 5=Strongly recommend), followed by three open-ended questions: 3) If you prefer another method of team formation, please describe; 4) What do you see as the strengths of using CATME to form teams?; and 5) What do you see as the weaknesses of using CATME to form teams?

This survey was announced in the courses during final exam week or just prior to it. It was made clear that the students' participation in the survey would have no impact on their grades and that the course staff would not know who chose to participate until after the grades were finalized. There was no compensation for filling out the survey. The survey was completed online and the responses were anonymized. The students also filled out consent forms to allow us to use their data for research. A total of 277 students provided responses to the study survey and gave consent. Of those who reported gender on the survey, there were 35 females and 200 males.

Some respondents were enrolled in two or more of these courses. However, given the size of the dataset and the focus of our research questions, we believe this issue is inconsequential to the findings of the work.

Interviews with Instructors

We conducted semi-structured interviews with 13 instructors who were using CATME on their own initiative. Instructors involved in the initial deployment were not interviewed since our planning interactions may have biased their attitudes. Seven interviewees had used the tool in one course and the others had used it more than once. Interviewees were offered \$10 for participation. Of these instructors, nine reported reading team formation literature prior to using CATME.

The interview focused on the instructors' motivations for using the team formation tool in their courses, the criteria they used, and the perceived strengths and weaknesses of the tool. The interview questions are shown in Table 2. Each interview lasted 30 minutes and was audio recorded. The recordings were transcribed and the originals destroyed.

Interviewees had deployed the tool in five lower- and seven upper-level undergraduate courses in engineering. Eight interviewees shared the criteria configurations used in their courses; listed in the rightmost six columns of Table 1. Two pairs of the interviewees had taught two courses jointly and had decided on the criteria together.

Qualitative Data Analysis

To analyze the free-form responses from the student surveys, we partitioned the responses into idea units. An idea unit is a coherent unit of thought [36]. The partitioning resulted in a total of 824 units from 258 students who had provided a response to at least one of the open-ended survey questions.

To develop the coding taxonomy, a member of the research team conducted a first pass over the idea units and assigned preliminary categories. Subsequent passes were performed to revise the categories such that they were reasonably exclusive and relevant to our research focus. Each category was given a label, definition, and example idea unit.

Using the taxonomy, the same member of the research team categorized all of the idea units. To test inter-rater reliability, another coder was trained on the categories. A sample of the idea units (about 11%) were labeled by the coder. Both the training and test samples were selected such that they covered all of the categories with the same distribution as the full dataset. Cohen's Kappa was 0.75 and exceeded the recommended threshold for accepting the results [26].

The interview data was similarly partitioned into idea units. We focused on units related to the instructors' motivation for adopting the tool, perceived advantages and disadvantages, and thoughts for improvement. This data set contained 114 idea units. Given the similarity of questions and responses, we were able to label the instructor idea units using the taxonomy derived from the student data with only minimal revision. Table 3 shows the full taxonomy. Each category includes the number of students and instructors whose responses had at least one idea unit referencing that category. Following the prior procedure, Cohen's Kappa for inter-rater reliability for labeling the instructor idea units was 0.82.

Criteria	Topics in HCI	Software Engr. I	Software Engr. II	UI Design (first)	UI Design (second)	Web Develop.	Social Viz.	Mobile Design	Project Mgmt (I1)	Thermal Behavr (I2)	Comp. Eng. I (I4, I5)	Hydraulics (I3)	Mech. Design II (I7)	Conservation (I10, I12)
Schedule		5	5	5	5		5	5	5		5		5	4
Big-Picture vs Detail-Oriented		-4		-5			-3	-2	-3	-2	-1		-2	-2
Gender	5	4		5			-1	5	-3	-5	5		2	
GPA	-4	-4		-5				-5	-3	-5	0		-2	4
Leadership Role		-4		-5			-4	-2	-3	0	-1			-2
Race		4		-3			0		-3	-5	5		-3	
Writing Skills				-1			-3	-3	-3		-1	-3		-3
Weekend Meetings		5	2				4				2	2		5
Leadership Preference		-4		-2			3	-2	-3	-2				
Commitment Level		-4		3		0	3		-3					2
English Skills		-3					-2	-2			-1			
Previous Course Grade										-5	-4	-1		5
Software Skills		-4							-3			-1		-3
Class Year				-3			3					-4		
Course skills (programming, graphic design, communication, etc.)				-5	-5		-2							
Possession of Mturk Account	-5													
Potential Roles in Web Dev						-5								
Coding Experience								-5						

Table 1. A sample of the most selected default and custom criteria in the courses in our deployment and taught by the instructors interviewed who shared their data. For each criterion, a negative weight groups students with differing responses; positive weights group by similar responses. A weight of 0 ignores the criterion. A criterion is left blank if the instructor did not collect the data on the CATME survey. Criteria available in the tool are shown above the heavy border; a sample of the custom criteria is below it.

RESULTS

Table 1 shows the criteria configurations for the courses involved in the deployment and the courses taught by the instructors interviewed who shared their data. The criteria were not uniform between courses. Our study revealed that many factors affect the selections, including the instructor's goals for the team work and for the course, prior experiences with team formation, and preference. For example, one novel use of the tool by an instructor was to form learning groups:

> *"Our goals were not only the projects but also there were learning teams. So learning teams meet weekly. They help each other with homework. That's basically the idea. They're like study groups."* (I4)

The table shows interesting patterns in the selections. First, the most frequently selected criterion and with the most common weight was *schedule*, indicating that instructors felt finding common free time was important for team formation. The next most frequent criterion was *big-picture / detailed-oriented*; instructors agreed that teams should have a mix of these working styles, as signified by the consistent use of a negative weight. A third pattern was related to *gender* as the weights spanned the full range of values. A positive weight favors teams with at least as many females as males, and is recommended for courses where women are the minority [31]. Reasons for the negative weights could range from uninformed choices to usability flaws; yet these differences highlight how the decisions could have a large impact on student experiences and need better support in the interface.

Differences in the criteria also reflect different perspectives on how teams should be created. For example, some instructors felt that teams should mix academic performance (where self-reported *GPA* serves as a proxy), as this would allow the weaker students to learn from the stronger ones:

> "*If you group students with similar academic ability... the people who may not be strong academically, don't have as much opportunity to be brought up and the people who are very strong academically never have to work with anyone who's not strong academically. If the goal is a learning experience which mimics what they will find when they get a job... they're gonna have to work with people of all different backgrounds and abilities.*" (I7, set GPA to '-2')

Other instructors disagreed, believing that teams with only weaker students need to elevate their project performance:

> "*...people with similar grades were mixed together,... The students [with lower GPAs who are grouped together] are used to maybe not working as hard. So they're still relying on someone else to pull the weight. But there's a transition that happens in every single one of those groups. At some point in the semester they each start becoming more self-reliant. They start pulling each other. That group almost always finishes at the very top in terms of their final project and in terms of their overall semester grades.*" (I10, set GPA to '4')

1. Can you characterize the course(s) in which you have used CATME?
2. Can you characterize the students in those courses?
3. What motivated you to use CATME for team formation in the course? What methods did you use prior to CATME and why did you switch?
4. Can you describe the criteria configuration you typically select?
5. What policies do you have for team formation? Can students switch teams once assigned? Can students give input for team members?
6. What are the advantages of using CATME for team formation?
7. What are the disadvantages of using CATME for team formation?
8. How could the use of CATME for team formation be improved?

Table 2. Questions for the instructor interviews.

SQ1: Student Perspectives

Students were mostly satisfied with the team assignments (μ=4.0, s=1.0) with 75.1% rating their satisfaction a 4 or 5. Only 9.4% of the students rated it unsatisfactory (rating of 1 or 2). The degree to which all students recommended the tool was lower (μ=3.58, s=1.52). Just over half (54.7%) would recommend or strongly recommend the approach in future courses. A smaller fraction (15.0%) would not recommend it, and 30.3% were unsure (rating of 3). Gender did not affect ratings of team satisfaction (t(235)=1.00, p=0.32) or recommendations (t(232)=-0.68, p=0.50). The patterns were generally consistent across the courses, despite the use of different criteria. However, students were less certain whether the positive team experience could be replicated:

> *"Maybe this time we got lucky that we had a great team, since I heard other team[s] did not do well."* (S427020);

> *"...CATME does not always work 100% of the time. Most of the time it seemed to match by schedule, but whether or not you will end up in a good team is still based on luck..."* (S427123).

Note that students are anonymously identified with the string "S" + course number + three-digit student identifier. The notation "S=n" for a category indicates that n number of students have cited that category in their responses. Each category was counted at most once per student so as not to skew the counts toward the response of any one student. Table 3 summarizes the categories of perceived strengths and weaknesses and ideas for improvement reported by students.

SQ2: Perceived Strengths by Students

We elaborate on some of the strengths based on how often they were cited and our interpretation of their importance.

Appreciate the use of rational criteria (S=177). The team formation tool organizes students into teams using specified criteria. Students valued the fact that there was rationale for the assignments, but only if the rationale matched their own interpretation of the "right" criteria: *"...CATME asked important questions when forming teams..."* (S427015). One implication is that instructors may want to show students how the criteria are set and how teams are formed.

Of the specific criteria cited in students' responses, the two most desired criteria were schedule compatibility (S=78) and diversity within teams (S=83). By grouping students who have similar schedules, teams should find it easier to meet: *"I believe matching the time availability is the biggest strength. This way, even with a big group, we can most likely meet at our desirable time"* (S427083). This issue was highlighted primarily by students in courses where teams consisted of at least five members. Students also believe their team could tackle difficult projects if comprised of diverse demographics, disciplinary skills, and leadership roles:

> *"Tries to match strengths and weaknesses of a group so that groups have all the resources they need"* (S467015).

> *"as our four team members come from three different discipline[s] (HCI, Software Engineering, Systems and Networking), in the brainstorming sessions, each of us attack the problem from our own domain. Thus the brainstorming sessions were full of interesting discussions"* (S565020)

Since prior work has shown that perceived diversity can reduce ratings of group satisfaction [34], the fact that many students reported diversity as a strength was surprising.

Learn to work with unfamiliar people (S=43). The tool's team formation algorithm considers criteria such as working styles and demographics, but not prior interaction or social relations between students. As a result, teams will likely be comprised of students who are unfamiliar with one another. The majority of students who referenced this issue saw this as a strength, though some perceived it as a weakness (S=20).

By being grouped with individuals they did not know, students reported having to learn team management and collaboration skills: *"This method also requires students to learn team management skills more similar to what is done in industry."* (S498rk014). They also view the situation as an opportunity to meet and befriend new people and become better prepared for industry jobs: *"Because people have to be used to working in different teams. It is very rare that they can choose their teammates."* (S427061).

Reduce stress and burden (S=37). With self-formation, the most common prior approach to team formation in the courses studied, the requirement to find teammates can be stressful. The team formation tool reduces this stress and simplifies the process. Three representative statements were:

> *"It's extremely beneficial for students from departments other than the dominants (CS, ECE) of this source who have few acquaintances."* (S565007)

> *"If you do not have friends in the class, CATME assures everyone has a group without feeling left out."* (S498bb009).

> *"No effort is required. You don't need to meet other people in the class or search for good partners, it is automatic."* (S498bb013).

SQ2: Perceived Weaknesses by Students

We elaborate on two of the common weaknesses cited by students. The full range of cited weaknesses are in Table 3.

Mismatch between student and instructor preferred criteria (S=108). A frequently cited weakness was when students' interpretation of what criteria should have been selected did not match the instructor selections: *"Some questions should not have been in the form [survey]"* (S465002). Fifty-five students wanted the instructor to consider personality traits, motivation, and personal work habits for team formation. As some of these criteria are already in the tool, the instructor could partially address this issue by adapting their selections.

Other issues would be difficult to capture in the tool because they only surface after teams begin working together: *"It does not talk about the characters of the teammates - if someone gets really frustrated when work is not done according to their style, or their deadline etc."* (S467002). One way to reduce such conflicts is to incorporate team building activities soon after teams are formed (e.g., [11]).

There was also disagreement around some criteria, such as schedules. While many students valued schedule matching when forming teams, others did not (S=15). These students reasoned that their schedules change as they add or drop courses or get involved in activities and this criterion should be given less weight: *"Scheduling is hardly a good metric of assigning teammates. Student schedules are far too volatile for them to stick with the given schedule"* (S467014).

Students sometimes agreed on the inclusion or exclusion of certain criteria, but disagreed on the weights. An example centers on language proficiency. Some students favored a mixture of proficient and not-so-proficient English speakers in a team. Their rationale is that the presence of a proficient speaker helps with essays and presentations: *"All of our teammates are non-native speakers..., so compared to others team with at least [one] native-speaker..., it is a little bit unfair"* (S565009). Others considered this to be a hindrance to effective communication within the group: *"If you are put into a group with random people, there could be a huge language barrier that prevents work from being done efficiently. For example, there are a lot of international students from China that don't speak English that well. I am not Chinese and don't understand it, so it would be difficult to communicate ideas with them..."* (S465001)

One way to resolve the issue of criteria mismatch is for the instructor to involve the students in choosing the criteria. For example, an approach taken by one of the instructors in our study was to show the tool live on the lecture screen and work through the criteria configuration with the entire class.

Lack of transparency (S=54). Students reported lack of transparency as another weakness of the tool. When notified of their assignment, teams do not receive any explanation as to why they were selected to work together. Without such explanations, for example, teams may fail to recognize the presence of a particular skill or role in their group know who

	Category	Definition	Example
Strengths	Based on rational criteria (S=177; I=3)	Criteria perceived to be important for forming teams.	*"I do like the idea of matching people with similar schedules especially for large teams."* (S427118)
Strengths	Reduce stress and burden (S=37; I=13)	Reduces anxiety / burden / discomfort for having to find teammates, or the convenience of its use.	*"It's extremely beneficial for students from departments other than the dominants (CS, ECE) of this course who have few acquaintances."* (S565007); *"And why did I switch?... Well, I didn't wanna do it by hand anymore. And I wanted to try an online system, [and to see] if it's easy, if it's gonna be good for the students and these kind of things. And maybe regarding using it in the future in a bigger class where doing it by hand would be a huge pain."* (I13)
Strengths	Learn to work with unfamiliar people (S=43; I=2)	Meeting new people as in a real world job, or developing authentic team skills.	*"it's very like the real-life scenarios, that we can't choose who to work with sometimes, and we have to deal with these situations very often."* (S565001); *"I think that our program is really designed to prepare the students for industry jobs and graduate schools where they have to work in teams so it's tough sometimes dealing with human aspects of engineering courses. So, I would like to systematize it. This is nice."* (I7)
Strengths	Level the playing field (S=12; I=5)	Giving a fair chance of being assigned to a good group.	*"The biggest advantage I see from using CATME is the fair environment it creates for a class. It prevents students who know each other and work well together from being able to form super groups."* (S427012); *"And it's nothing the students are gonna discuss with me a lot. Because they feel that since I outsourced it to something that is considered to be some programmed platform, there's less of a personal bias in it. I think that's an advantage. If I would do it on my own, they would probably say you did this and you did that, this can be done differently."* (I2)
Strengths	Free of relationship biases (S=6; I=0)	Teams do not consist of friends. Members cannot rely on friendship to refrain from doing work.	*"Working with friends can be awkward especially if one of them doesn't do their part."* (S498rk014)
Strengths	Positive comparison or view (S=64; I=1)	Strengths that did not fit in other categories.	*"CATME is great!"* (S428009)
Strengths / Weaknesses	Lack of transparency (S=54; I=3 as strength, I=6 as weakness)	Not knowing how the teams are formed, having little clue as to what the strengths and weaknesses of one's team members are.	*"I have no idea if the survey we filled is actually useful. I don't know what kind of algorithm the CATME is using to form a team so it's seems to be just random I guess."* (S427008); *"They [the students] always say "We don't have anybody that knows this topic in our group. I think we're at a disadvantage.". It's not true. They just don't know. They don't know that this person had this prerequisite. They just assume that we don't have anybody who knows this topic."* (I3, citing as a weakness); *"I like that the students think it's not us, we're not trying to manipulate them in any way although we are. "* (I6, citing it as a strength)
Weaknesses	Mismatch between student and instructor preferred criteria (S=108; I=0)	Students do not agree with the criteria selections made by the instructor.	*"In creating a schedule, CATME's schedule is not particularly useful due to changes in people's lives and events that may only happen during a given week that can throw meeting times awry."* (S427109)
Weaknesses	Burdensome to learn and use (S=29; I=8)	Problems with the tool's user interface or documentation); or the perceived burden of having to learn / use it.	*"The user interface is very unintuitive, causing multiple members of the team to incorrectly fill out the time they were available."* (S427121); *"The disadvantage is that it's another piece of time and the students are very busy, we're very busy. You'd definitely want to use all the tools available but you don't want to have it become a burden on the students."* (I10)
Weaknesses	No validation of responses (S=20; I=2)	Team assignments could be influenced by inaccurate responses since they cannot be verified. Susceptible to gaming the system.	*"Ranking your abilities on a spectrum is also very relative. One student's 'somewhat proficient' may be another student's 'very proficient'."* (S467015); *"[it] allows people to game system. Because when people realize they're in the same lab together,... they say I wanna be on the team with you so then we'll both select midnight to 4am on Wednesdays and lo and behold they're always together. Because nobody else is gonna select [that time]. So it's kind of dubious in that regard but that's ok."* (I11)
Weaknesses	Lack of consideration for team preferences (S=20; I=0)	Requests to be (not) grouped with others were not considered.	*"inability to add strong preferences for people that you would like to work with, although this may just be intentional, it would be nice if the course allowed for more control on how people choose to work with."*(S428013)
Weaknesses	Team chemistry and communication (S=13; I=0)	Team struggles to communicate, or lacks team chemistry.	*"It's also hard sometimes to communicate with new people whom you've never worked with before because you don't know the best way to get a hold of them is."* (S498bb019)
Weaknesses	Cold start (S=8; I=0)	Need to break the ice with the assigned team.	*"team synergy can be slow to build."* (S498bb003)
Weaknesses	Immeasurability of criteria (S=0; I=1)	There are criteria that surveys cannot measure.	*"you're not measuring certain features that are important like management and the ability to meet the deadlines."* (I3)
Weaknesses	Negative comparison or view (S=54; I=0)	Weakness that cannot fit in the other categories.	*"Only rating it low because of negative experience with it. Not sure if self-formed teams would work better, but I don't see any advantage of using this system."* (S427101)

Ideas for Improvement	Integrate students' team preferences (S=21; I=1)	Mixing teams created via the tool and self-assembled teams	*"Random assignment teams with self-formed suggestions would be nice, that way teams wouldn't be so disparate."* (S465016); *"...making sure they can do preferred and unpreferred"* (I9)
	Expand criteria and aid criteria decisions (S=4; I=10)	Ranged from having better defaults, expanded criteria, and other UI improvements.	*"It would be nice to add metrics for matching students based on how likely they are to attend class and keep up with the work."* (S465015); *"...getting more feedback from others that have used team formation about what would be good criteria and good weights to use, when they've been successful at using it.* (I9)
	Support iteration (S=2; I=0)	Iterating until a good team is formed	*"It would be interesting to see what the result would be if the steps are: filling survey in CATME -> assigning groups ->group meet and know each other -> confirm or decline assignment -> reassign groups."* (S565010)
	Add a help wanted forum (S=5; I=0)	Create place for students to exchange skills and strengths for recruitment.	*"Perhaps we could get people to shout out ideas and get people to join their idea and form a team instead. That's what CS 198 does."* (S427009)
	Other ideas (S=3; I=2)	Ideas not fitting in any of the other categories.	*"Instead of self rank, they should be an individual project at the start of the semester. The individual would then submit their work to highlight their strengths, weaknesses, and work ethic. Their peers will then decide who they want to work with and would create a balanced team."* (S467021)

Table 3. The full taxonomy used to categorize idea units from the student surveys and instructor interviews. It contains strengths, weaknesses, and ideas for improvement as top-level categories, and a set of lower-level categories within each of them. In the lower level categories, 'S=' and 'I=' are the numbers of students and instructors whose responses contained that category.

possesses it: *"I don't know any of my partners['] skills and backgrounds, so it's hard to assess what they can be capable of when dividing up tasks"* (S427127).

Unaware of how the tool's algorithm forms teams or why, some students formed their own hypotheses: *"[CATME is] discriminating (why does it need to know my ethnicity, GPA, etc.)"* (S465011); This phenomenon is similar to how users hypothesize how the invisible Facebook curation algorithm chooses content for their News Feed [13, 14].

To address the issue, an instructor could share the team members' survey responses or have the team work through a self-assessment of their skills and working styles. The tool could also be enhanced to report how the team scores on the various criteria and highlight their strengths as a team. Future research is needed to test how increasing transparency of the team formation process would affect team effectiveness.

SQ3: Ideas for Improvement from Students

We elaborate on two suggestions for improvement from students. All of the themes for improvement are in Table 3.

Integrate student preferences with the tool (S=21). One idea for improvement was to let students select part of their team: *"Might want to have an option where you can specify one teammate you want and if the other person reciprocates then there's a good chance they get teamed up?"* (S498rk010); *"The win-win situation would be to let students choose between [a] self-formed team or CATME. So those who knows [sic] whom to team up with can choose their own teammates. And the other students who do not know anyone (or do not want to form their own teams) can sign up to be matched through CATME."* (S465004).

Use help wanted forums (S=5). A few students felt that different projects required different skills and working styles. They suggested to use a forum in which students could post what attributes they are looking for in team members, or what they could bring to a team. This way, they can recruit team members, or be recruited by others: *"I tend to prefer picking teammates through something of a posting board. It allows individuals to match themselves based on what they value personally to find best fits for themselves"* (S498rk001).

IQ1 and IQ2: Instructor Perspectives

We describe strengths and weaknesses of the team formation tool from the perspective of instructors. In most cases, the instructors' opinions matched with students'. We elaborate on issues that we believe are insightful and unique relative to what has been discussed from the student perspectives.

Strengths. Instructors identified reducing their burden and student stress (I=13), leveling the playing field to give all teams an equal chance of success (I=5), criteria-based matching (I=3), students' needing to learn to work with unfamiliar people (I=2), and the lack of transparency of the algorithm (I=3) as strengths of the tool. All but the last were also cited by students. Table 3 describes all these strengths.

All of the instructors interviewed cited increased efficiency of the team formation process as a key strength of the tool (I=13). The tool allows for quickly revising the criteria and reviewing the resulting teams, which would not be feasible if the teams were assigned manually: *"The efficiency of distributing students with respect to various criteria is very attractive to me because all I've to do is click a button. I don't have to sit there and do it for hours and hours."* (I7). The instructors also viewed the use of the tool as an anxiety reducer for students: "*I often tell the students at the beginning of 201 when they're graduating from U of I, they're leaving with a professional degree. So their experience in that first year is similar to the experience of a first-year law student or first year medical students, which tends to be incredibly stressful. So I feel like this CATME approach, basically having teams, is a great way to reduce the stress and make all a little bit more manageable*" (I10).

Some instructors (I=3) felt the lack of transparency of the process was desirable for at least two reasons. First, they believed students should not be conscious of how criteria such as race or gender were used: *"We certainly wanted to do what we could based on some literature that we should for example group under-represented minorities for example women together and we just wanted to make sure that some of those things were artificially emplaced and not that the students sort of feel that we were targeting them in any way. So CATME provides a little bit of anonymity in that sense because we just tell them it's an algorithm and based on what you fill in it'll optimize your group preferences but we don't tell them what the algorithm behind the scenes did"* (I6).

Second, instructors felt the tool allows them to deflect blame to the software if some students are dissatisfied with their team: *"Theoretically you can blame the software if things don't go right. If the students aren't allowed to self-assemble and if the faculty members were going to assemble it just randomly, there's always some who are disgruntled"* (I9).

Weaknesses. Instructors also perceived weaknesses of the tool: it was burdensome to learn and use (I=8), there are no means to validate student responses to the survey (I=2), and certain criteria are not measurable (I=1). Some instructors also viewed the lack of transparency as a weakness, whereas others saw it as a strength. All except the immeasurability of criteria were also identified as weaknesses by the students.

Instructors (I=6) who considered lack of transparency as a weakness deemed it important for students to know why they are placed on a given team. They believed such knowledge would eliminate many doubts about one's team assignment and would spare instructors the need for explanation: *"One comment I was getting from some students is that they don't understand why they're put together with certain students in a team; because we don't wanna release the other students' information to them for privacy reasons. But CATME could generate an anonymized summary for me. So a lot of people keep asking "why am I with this person in a team"* (I3).

Instructors believed that effective team formation requires matching along certain criteria, but that some criteria have no means of proper self-measurement (I=1). One example is commitment, which is part of the built-in criteria in the tool and often selected by instructors (see Table 1): *"I don't know if you can measure that. I don't think anybody would ever say I have a low level of commitment. At the first deliverable people put in their hours. Second one other courses started to take their time and some people just stopped doing anything. So everybody can commit at a high level if they have nothing to do. When you have a lot of stuff to do, that's when the question of how committed you are comes in"* (I3).

Ideas for Improvement. A unique suggestion from the instructors was to include better guidelines for configuring the criteria (I=3). This would make the user interface more usable and the process more effective since instructors are not always well versed on the latest literature for team formation. In particular, they expressed wanting the tool to offer in-situ explanations for the available criteria: *"I know that there's been a lot of research on some of these approaches to team formation. It would be nice if as you're choosing which things you would use for team formation you could just kinda click and see why [it] is important to group things similarly or these things dissimilarly. That way you just have all the information available to you"* (I10).

DISCUSSION AND FUTURE WORK

In this study, we gauged perceived strengths and weaknesses of a team formation tool from the perspectives of students and instructors. For students, the strengths of the tool were: it is based on rational criteria, removes the stress of finding teammates, and promotes learning to work with new people. Instructors identified similar strengths, but also noted the efficiency of forming teams and the ability to deflect blame when students were dissatisfied with their team assignment.

For key weaknesses, students identified mismatches between their preferred criteria and the instructor's selections, not knowing why they were assigned to a team, the inability to specify preferred team members, and a cold start phase due to team members' typically not knowing one another prior to the course. Instructors also identified the inability to properly measure some of the criteria as a weakness.

From our results, we identified several recommendations for instructors to address these weaknesses and improve the deployment of a team formation tool. One recommendation is to engage students in selecting which criteria are selected as input to the tool's algorithm. As mentioned in our study, instructors could poll students live during lecture and use the results to make selections in the tool or focus student input on a narrower set of criteria while explaining the rationale for the criteria already selected. Instructors could also allow students to rank the criteria as part of the survey procedure performed at the onset of team formation. Instructors could use the rankings to assign the criteria weights in the tool. The rankings could be collected separately, or tool designers could implement this feature in the team formation survey.

Another recommendation is to provide each team with an explanation for its formation and why it is "good." This could take the form of an anonymized summary of the team members' responses to the survey, how the team scored on the criteria, or how the team' scores relate to other teams as a way to highlight their strengths and weaknesses. As stated by one instructor: *"If CATME could give us an anonymized report for the team that these are the strengths; these are the weaknesses of your team. That lets the teams think the system is fair to them" (I3).* Instructors could also create and give teams a rubric based on the selected criteria to self-assess their qualities. This could also serve as an activity to address the cold start phase experienced when teams first meet.

A final recommendation for instructors is to give students more agency in the selection of their teammates. To support preferences, instructors could allow students to form partial teams and use the tool to complete the teams. This approach echoes prior work advocating for constrained self-formation [5], while also achieving the benefits of a criteria-based approach (e.g., skill diversity in the teams). Instructors could also use the tool to generate multiple team assignments, have the teams meet and rank their preferences, and include this data as a criterion in the tool [29]. These approaches could yield higher team satisfaction, but knowing the effects on team performance would require future work.

An interesting aspect of the criteria configurations reported in Table 1 is that no two courses were the same. This can be explained in part by the courses having different learning goals and student makeup. Some instructors targeted the experience of learning; others the importance of project outcomes and grades. These differences highlight the need for team formation tools to better support instructors. One implication for tool designers is to provide more effective defaults and in-situ explanations in the user interface for criteria selection. A second implication is to offer a dynamic visualization that shows how modifying the criteria affects the assignments. Last, tool designers should create an online catalogue of exemplars of configurations used by instructors that could be browsed by course topic and student makeup.

Some criteria configurations could also be due to irrational or uninformed choices. Despite instructors having good intentions, the operationalizations of the intent may be flawed. For example, eight of the instructors discussed their rationale for the gender criteria weight, but also expressed uncertainty whether it was "correct." These sentiments echo the instructors' need for guidance within the interface. While some instructors were aware of the tool's algorithm, with the number of possible criteria, predicting the team assignments is a challenge. We see this challenge only growing, as this genre of tool will continue to consider more criteria (e.g., imagine scanning students' social media profiles to infer personality traits) and apply more sophisticated modeling. How does one assign weights to an expansive set of criteria and when the relations between the criteria are difficult to grasp? Similarly, some students were briefed on the rationale for the team formation tool during lecture. Might they have been swayed by the framing of systems like CATME, believing in the promise of the tool [25]?

We used Spearman's ρ to test how student ratings of team satisfaction (scale was 1-5) related to their project scores (normalized to 0-100). This was tested in five of our courses. The others were not included due to limitations of our data set. The correlations were small to modest, and inconsistent in direction. The values were positive for three courses (ρ=0.21, p=0.45; ρ=0.38, p=0.09; ρ=0.19, p=0.02), and negative for the others (ρ=-0.57, $p<0.01$; ρ=-0.11, p=0.60). We interpret this pattern to mean that one's satisfaction with his or her team assignment is only loosely related to the project grade. Additional work is needed to better understand what factors influence students' ratings of team assignments.

We see several additional directions for future work. First, team composition is important, but it is only one factor affecting team outcomes. Future work should compare how team composition affects performance relative to enhancing team dynamics such as psychological safety [12, 40]. The outcome would help instructors know whether to allocate more attention to team formation or to creating activities that strengthen team member relations. Second, future work could study the inclusion of additional criteria such as social intelligence [16] as inputs to the matching algorithm, which would enable balancing teams along additional axes. Third, this work examined the use of a team formation tool in the context of courses. Future work should study such tools in other teamwork settings such as in hackathons and design competitions. Finally, future work is needed to test the generalizability of our findings in courses with different student makeup, criteria selections and matching algorithms.

LIMITATIONS

One limitation is that the student perceptions reported in this study were largely based on students enrolled in computer science courses. Since these students are knowledgeable of algorithms, their perspectives may not be representative of students in other disciplines. A second limitation of our study is that student perceptions of the team formation process could be affected by how instructors configured the tool. Given the scale of all possible combinations of the criteria available in the tool, it was not possible to analyze this relationship. Third, our study was conducted in courses taught in a single academic unit at the same institution, and may not be representative of different teaching cultures.

CONCLUSION

Instructors are increasingly leveraging algorithmic tools to organize students into teams in educational settings. We reported on student and instructor experiences with team formation as defined by one tool (CATME) that is widely used in university courses. Students reported being satisfied (μ=4.0 on 5-point scale) with the teams assigned by the tool, but were less certain about its use in the future. To improve student satisfaction, instructors can give students a stronger voice in the criteria configuration process and make them aware as to *why* they were assigned to a particular team (e.g., give anonymized summaries showing how the teams scored on the criteria). Instructors appreciated increased efficiency of team formation but also wanted the tool to offer aids such as exemplars and in-situ explanations for selecting the most appropriate criteria for their course and the ability to explore how various configurations affect team assignments.

ACKNOWLEDGMENTS

This work was partially funded by the Strategic Instructional Innovations Program at the University of Illinois and by NSF award CCF-1439957. We thank professors Tao Xie, Ranjitha Kumar, and Alex Kirlik for helping with data collection. We also thank Helen Wauck and Sanorita Dey for helping with data analysis, and Yiwen Xu and Yi-Chieh Lee for assisting with the initial deployment of the team formation tool.

REFERENCES

1. CATME Smarter Teamwork. Available from: http://info.catme.org/.
2. ABET. Criteria for Accrediting Computing Programs: Effective for Reviews During the 2014-2015 Accreditation Cycle. Available from: http://www.abet.org/wp-content/uploads/2015/04/E001-14-15-EAC-Criteria.pdf.
3. Anthony Lising Antonio, Mitchell J Chang, Kenji Hakuta, David A Kenny, Shana Levin and Jeffrey F Milem. 2004. Effects of racial diversity on complex thinking in college students. *Psychological Science*, 15 (8): 507-510. http://dx.doi.org/10.1111/j.0956-7976.2004.00710.x
4. Ernesto Arias, Hal Eden, Gerhard Fischer, Andrew Gorman and Eric Scharff. 2000. Transcending the individual human mind - creating shared understanding through collaborative design. *ACM Transactions on Computer-Human Interaction*, 7 (1): 84-113. http://dx.doi.org/10.1145/344949.345015
5. Donald R Bacon, Kim A Stewart and William S Silver. 1999. Lessons from the best and worst student team experiences: How a teacher can make the difference. *Journal of Management Education*, 23 (5): 467-488. http://dx.doi.org/10.1177/105256299902300503
6. Donald R Bacon, Kim A Stewart and Sue Stewart-Belle. 1998. Exploring predictors of student team project performance. *Journal of Marketing Education*, 20 (1): 63-71. http://dx.doi.org/10.1177/027347539802000108
7. Julia B Bear and Anita Williams Woolley. 2011. The role of gender in team collaboration and performance. *Interdisciplinary Science Reviews*, 36 (2): 146-153. http://dx.doi.org/10.1179/030801811X13013181961473
8. James L Brickell, David B Porter, Michael F Reynolds and Richard D Cosgrove. 1994. Assigning students to groups for engineering design projects: A comparison of five methods. *Journal of Engineering Education*, 83 (3): 259-262. http://dx.doi.org/10.1002/j.2168-9830.1994.tb01113.x
9. Rupert Brown. 2000. *Group Processes: Dynamics Within and Between Groups*. Blackwell Publishing.
10. Kenneth J Chapman, Matthew Meuter, Dan Toy and Lauren Wright. 2006. Can't we pick our own groups? The influence of group selection method on group dynamics and outcomes. *Journal of Management Education*, 30 (4): 557-569. http://dx.doi.org/10.1177/1052562905284872
11. Dawn R Deeter-Schmelz, Karen Norman Kennedy and Rosemary P Ramsey. 2002. Enriching our understanding of student team effectiveness. *Journal of Marketing Education*, 24 (2): 114-124. http://dx.doi.org/10.1177/0273475302242004
12. Amy Edmondson. 1999. Psychological Safety and Learning Behavior in Work Teams. *Administrative Science Quarterly*, 44 (2): 350-383. http://dx.doi.org/10.2307/2666999
13. Motahhare Eslami, Karrie Karahalios, Christian Sandvig, Kristen Vaccaro, Aimee Rickman, Kevin Hamilton and Alex Kirlik. 2016. First I "like" it, then I hide it: Folk Theories of Social Feeds. *Proceedings of the ACM Conference on Human Factors in Computing Systems*, ACM, 2371-2382. http://dx.doi.org/10.1145/2858036.2858494
14. Motahhare Eslami, Aimee Rickman, Kristen Vaccaro, Amirhossein Aleyasen, Andy Vuong, Karrie Karahalios, Kevin Hamilton and Christian Sandvig. 2015. I always assumed that I wasn't really that close to [her]: Reasoning about Invisible Algorithms in News Feeds. *Proceedings of the ACM Conference on Human Factors in Computing Systems*, ACM, 153-162. http://dx.doi.org/10.1145/2702123.2702556
15. Graham D Fenwick and Derrick J Neal. 2001. Effect of gender composition on group performance. *Gender, Work & Organization*, 8 (2): 205-225. http://dx.doi.org/10.1111/1468-0432.00129
16. Daniel Goleman. 1998. *Working with emotional intelligence*. Bantam.
17. Narasimhaiah Gorla and Yan Wah Lam. 2004. Who should work with whom?: building effective software project teams. *Communications of the ACM*, 47 (6): 79-82. http://dx.doi.org/10.1145/990680.990684
18. J. Richard Hackman (ed.). 1990. *Groups That Work (and Those That Don't): Creating Conditions for Effective Teamwork*. Jossey-Bass Publishers, San Francisco.
19. Sujin K Horwitz and Irwin B Horwitz. 2007. The effects of team diversity on team outcomes: A meta-analytic review of team demography. *Journal of Management*, 33 (6): 987-1015. http://dx.doi.org/10.1177/0149206307308587
20. Roland Hübscher. 2010. Assigning students to groups using general and context-specific criteria. *IEEE Transactions on Learning Technologies*, 3 (3): 178-189. http://dx.doi.org/10.1109/TLT.2010.17
21. David Hunkeler and Julie E Sharp. 1997. Assigning functional groups: The influence of group size, academic record, practical experience, and learning style. *Journal of Engineering Education*, 86 (4): 321-332. http://dx.doi.org/10.1002/j.2168-9830.1997.tb00305.x

22. David S Jalajas and Robert I Sutton. 1984. Feuds in student groups: Coping with whiners, martyrs, saboteurs, bullies, and deadbeats. *Journal of Management Education*, 9 (4): 94-102. http://dx.doi.org/10.1177/105256298400900413

23. Irving Lester Janis. 1982. *Groupthink: Psychological studies of policy decisions and fiascoes*. Houghton Mifflin Boston.

24. Karen A Jehn, Gregory B Northcraft and Margaret A Neale. 1999. Why differences make a difference: A field study of diversity, conflict and performance in workgroups. *Administrative Science Quarterly*, 44 (4): 741-763. http://dx.doi.org/10.2307/2667054

25. George Lakoff and Mark Johnson. 2008. *Metaphors we live by*. University of Chicago press.

26. J. Richard Landis and Gary G. Koch. 1977. The Measurement of Observer Agreement for Categorical Data. *Biometrics*, 33 (1): 159-174. http://dx.doi.org/10.1145/2675133.267516610.2307/2529310

27. Richard A Layton, Misty L Loughry, Matthew W Ohland and George D Ricco. 2010. Design and validation of a web-based system for assigning members to teams using instructor-specified criteria. *Advances in Engineering Education*, 2 (1): 1-28.

28. Ioanna Lykourentzou, Angeliki Antoniou, Yannick Naudet and Steven P Dow. 2016. Personality Matters: Balancing for Personality Types Leads to Better Outcomes for Crowd Teams. *Proceedings of the ACM Conference on Computer-Supported Cooperative Work & Social Computing*, ACM, 260-273. http://dx.doi.org/10.1145/2818048.2819979

29. Ioanna Lykourentzou, Robert Kraut and Steven P. Dow. 2017. Team Dating Leads to Better Online Ad Hoc Collaborations. *Proceedings of the ACM Conference on Computer Supported Cooperative Work & Social Computing*, to appear.

30. Sakthi Mahenthiran and Pamela J Rouse. 2000. The impact of group selection on student performance and satisfaction. *International Journal of Educational Management*, 14 (6): 255-265. http://dx.doi.org/10.1108/09513540010348043

31. Barbara Oakley, Richard M Felder, Rebecca Brent and Imad Elhajj. 2004. Turning student groups into effective teams. *Journal of Student Centered Learning*, 2 (1): 9-34.

32. Michael A Redmond. 2001. A computer program to aid assignment of student project groups. *ACM SIGCSE Bulletin*, 134-138. http://dx.doi.org/10.1145/366413.364562

33. Marcel M Robles. 2012. Executive perceptions of the top 10 soft skills needed in today's workplace. *Business Communication Quarterly*, 75 (4): 453-465. http://dx.doi.org/10.1177/1080569912460400

34. Timothy S Schoenecker, Kathryn D Martell and Joseph F Michlitsch. 1997. Diversity, performance, and satisfaction in student group projects: An empirical study. *Research in Higher Education*, 38 (4): 479-495. http://dx.doi.org/10.1023/A:1024966627400

35. Greg L Stewart. 2006. A meta-analytic review of relationships between team design features and team performance. *Journal of Management*, 32 (1): 29-55. http://dx.doi.org/10.1177/0149206305277792

36. A.L. Strauss. 1987. *Qualitative Analysis for Social Scientists*. Cambridge University Press.

37. James T Strong and Rolph E Anderson. 1990. Free-riding in group projects: Control mechanisms and preliminary data. *Journal of Marketing Education*, 12 (2): 61-67. http://dx.doi.org/10.1177/027347539001200208

38. Anya Tafliovich, Andrew Petersen and Jennifer Campbell. 2016. Evaluating Student Teams: Do Educators Know What Students Think? *Proceedings of the ACM Technical Symposium on Computing Science Education*, ACM, 181-186. http://dx.doi.org/10.1145/2839509.2844647

39. Martin Wessner and Hans-Rüdiger Pfister. 2001. Group formation in computer-supported collaborative learning. *Proceedings of the ACM Conference on Supporting Group Work*, ACM, 24-31. http://dx.doi.org/10.1145/500286.500293

40. Anita Williams Woolley, I. Aggarwal and Thomas W. Malone. 2015. Collective intelligence in teams and organizations. Malone, T.W. and Bernstein, M.S. eds. *The handbook of collective intelligence*, MIT Press, Cambridge, MA, in press.

41. Anita Williams Woolley, Christopher F. Chabris, Alex Pentland, Nada Hashmi and Thomas W. Malone. 2010. Evidence for a Collective Intelligence Factor in the Performance of Human Groups. *Science*, 330 (6004): 686-688. http://dx.doi.org/10.1126/science.1193147

Multimodal Classification of Moderated Online Pro-Eating Disorder Content

Stevie Chancellor*
Georgia Tech
Atlanta, GA USA
schancellor3@gatech.edu

Yannis Kalantidis
Yahoo Research
San Francisco, CA USA
ykalant@image.ntua.gr

Jessica A. Pater
Georgia Tech
Atlanta, GA USA
pater@gatech.edu

Munmun De Choudhury
Georgia Tech
Atlanta, GA USA
munmund@gatech.edu

David A. Shamma
Centrum Wiskunde &
Informatica (CWI)
Amsterdam, Netherlands
aymans@acm.org

ABSTRACT
Social media sites are challenged by both the scale and variety of deviant behavior online. While algorithms can detect spam and obscenity, behaviors that break community guidelines on some sites are difficult because they have multimodal subtleties (images and/or text). Identifying these posts is often regulated to a few moderators. In this paper, we develop a deep learning classifier that jointly models textual and visual characteristics of pro-eating disorder content that violates community guidelines. Using a million Tumblr photo posts, our classifier discovers deviant content efficiently while also maintaining high recall (85%). Our approach uses human sensitivity throughout to guide the creation, curation, and understanding of this approach to challenging, deviant content. We discuss how automation might impact community moderation, and the ethical and social obligations of this area.

ACM Classification Keywords
H.5.m. Information Interfaces and Presentation (e.g. HCI): Miscellaneous

Author Keywords
content moderation; social media; pro-eating disorder; deep learning; computer vision; deviant behavior; Tumblr

INTRODUCTION
With an increasing volume of data, online social platforms like Facebook and Tumblr face an increasing task of identifying content that violates policies and guidelines. Potential violations include accidentally posting copyrighted material [34], deceptive online reviews [64], and online harassment [61], among others. In this paper, we refer to violations of explicit rules and community guidelines as *deviant* content. When managing deviant content, platforms trade-off scalability and contextualization. To handle data volume, platforms have adopted some automated measures, most famously to identify spam [31]. Research has classified complex deviant behaviors as well, like trolling and abusive language [1, 21]. Yet, detecting these kinds of subtleties at scale has been elusive—most platforms rely on human moderators to review content.

Our area of interest is the Tumblr pro-eating disorder (pro-ED) community. Tumblr is a microblogging social network founded in 2007 focusing on short-form content sharing. Tumblr's community guidelines prohibit the glorification of self-harm, including promoting eating disorders and their accompanying lifestyles. This includes "content that urges or encourages others to…cut or injure themselves; [or to] embrace anorexia, bulimia, or other eating disorders" [85]. Posts in pro-ED communities can break these guidelines by encouraging eating disorders as a healthy lifestyle alternative, glorifying low weight and thinness [25]. They share extremely low calorie diets, pictures of underweight individuals, and stories of dangerous behaviors like dramatic weight control measures.

The Tumblr pro-ED community is a case study in detecting complex deviant content. Pro-ED communities have challenged social media platforms because of their pervasiveness despite explicit moderation against the community [17]. Not all content in pro-ED communities is dangerous [14] nor do all images qualify for removal—the same photo of a model could be used for a pro-ED blog or a fitness blog for motivation. However, for the content that is dangerous, psychological research shows that there are unique social contagion-like effects on those who are exposed to this content [10]. These posts might also encourage self-harm in users by letting them "live through" others' self-harm experiences [56].

In spite of these risks to the broader Tumblr community, deviant pro-ED content is rarely reported to moderators. This is because pro-ED communities are often "hidden in plain

*This work was conducted while author was at Yahoo.

Permission to make digital or hard copies of all or part of this work for personal or classroom use is granted without fee provided that copies are not made or distributed for profit or commercial advantage and that copies bear this notice and the full citation on the first page. Copyrights for components of this work owned by others than ACM must be honored. Abstracting with credit is permitted. To copy otherwise, or republish, to post on servers or to redistribute to lists, requires prior specific permission and/or a fee. Request permissions from Permissions@acm.org.
CHI 2017, *May 06-11, 2017, Denver, CO, USA*
©2017 ACM. ISBN 978-1-4503-4655-9/17/05 ...$15.00
DOI: http://dx.doi.org/10.1145/3025453.3025985

sight", adopting the use of atypical language or tags [17]. This reduces the chance that outsiders to these communities will encounter and report them. Further, individuals within these communities, looking for support in maintaining disordered behaviors, are unlikely to recognize dangerous pro-ED content as violations of community guidelines. Compounding these concerns about deviant behavior are the use of images in pro-ED communities. These images show explicit negative emotions and graphic content of thinness, motivation for starvation, and even pictures of self-injury [66]. This presents two unique challenges for existing moderation strategies. First, state-of-the-art approaches in automated detection of deviant content primarily rely on textual signals [20, 21]. When these methods are applied in the context of pro-ED, they are likely to miss the rich signals that are distinctively conveyed through images [39]. Second, for human moderators who must interact with this emotionally challenging and sensitive content, it may require domain-specific knowledge as well as an "emotional shield" [4, 19].

Prior work in HCI, mental wellness, and prediction has focused on the identification of specific mental wellness challenges like depression[26] or assessing more general wellness states of those who have posted to pro-ED communities[14]. This work is distinct from these works in three major ways. First, the prediction task in our work is identifying deviant content, not a post or a user who engages with this content. Second, we offer a novel methods contribution by bringing deep learning to social computing to understand more than just text content. Third, this paper actively scaffolds another methods contribution in HCI to building context-sensitive deep learning approaches to identifying deviant content.

In this paper, we address these challenges in detection and moderation of sensitive deviant content like pro-ED. We propose, develop, and evaluate a supervised learning model that distinguishes between deviant pro-ED content and acceptable content. Our proposed model is *multimodal*—it uses both textual and visual characteristics of pro-ED content. For this, we leverage recent advances in computer vision [72] and large-scale text mining [63]. Our model directly incorporates *human assessments* and works to support moderation pipelines with domain knowledge and reduced emotional stress.

To build this multimodal human-machine hybrid classifier, we first curate a dataset of nearly a million pro-ED posts on Tumblr. We then bring in human sensitivity by deploying an iterative expert rating task that identifies thousands of pro-ED posts as potential community guideline violations. Using this annotated data for training, we then evaluate a state-of-the-art Deep Neural Network classifier [54]. This classifier has high performance in detecting deviant pro-ED content—accuracy: 89% and F1: 65%. Importantly, we show that this model performs comparably well in classifying our expert rated posts and the posts actually removed by moderators for breaking community guidelines. We finally discuss the design, ethical, and social implications of our approach for both existing and next generation content moderation systems.

Our project considered ethics at all steps, and we looked to prior work in how to handle sensitive, removed content [5, 15]. All data, including posts that were later removed, were publicly available when we obtained the dataset. The authors had no research interactions with users, nor did they interact with Tumblr by reporting posts. Researchers contacted several users to obtain passive consent to use their photos in the paper (ref. Supplemental Materials). This means that our research did not qualify for ethics board review. To preserve the security and privacy of our data, all photos were stored and accessed from secured, firewalled servers. We do not report any results with personally identifying information, including identifying pictures, tags, or usernames. Some images are graphic.

RELATED WORK

Our work builds on research in HCI and social computing, including online deviance and content moderation and sensitive domains like pro-eating disorder.

Defining Deviant Behavior

We define *deviant behavior* as actions that are socially outside the norms for a community or group of people [3]. Behaviors can be violations of explicit rules and laws or social standards and norms. Deviant behaviors are contextual—whether a behavior is considered "bad" is dependent on the circumstances, the community, and the timing of that particular activity.

Many stakeholders develop and negotiate what is deviant on a particular website. These norms may be contained in explicit Terms of Service agreements, community guidelines, site-wide usage policies, and even unwritten expectations of a community; what becomes deviant is negotiated and constantly iterated on by these stakeholders. This can include the platform owners of the site, the moderators and administrators, and the individual users themselves [51]. Many studies have explored why deviant behavior exists in online communities, using psychological explanations of deviant behavior [35, 78, 79] as well as perspectives on the community itself [30, 41].

We study deviant behavior in a sensitive community: the pro-ED community. These behaviors are deviant as they break Tumblr's Community Guidelines, but there are unique concerns with this kind of content. Pro-ED behaviors have actual contagion effects; that is, when others see content promoting an eating disorder, these negative emotions can spread to others [60]. This is amplified by the fact that looking at self-harm lets users "live through" others' self-harm experiences [56].

Quantitative Studies of Online Deviant Behaviors

The HCI community has investigated deviant behaviors in online communities for over two decades [11, 77], and recently this topic has gained renewed attention. In this section, we focus on quantitative and machine learning methods to detect and predict online deviant behaviors.

Classification tasks on deviant behaviors fall into a few specific areas. One is predicting when someone may be engaging in cyberbullying or online harassment [42, 68]. Other work focuses on identifying trolling and antisocial behaviors. This uses the unique linguistic features of trolling news comments [20, 21], finding anti-social behavior in online games [9], or using psychological cues to understand the habits of trolls [12]. Research on identifying Wikipedia vandals incorporates user analysis [1, 44] and meta data like revision history [84] into their prediction task. Finally, there is work that uses the act of deletion as the response variable in the prediction [22, 74]. Close to our work is Chancellor et al. [15] that built a classifier to predict whether Instagram posts would be removed from the platform; however, the work did not detect deviance from the perspective of moderators.

These works offers empirical evidence that social platforms provide signals of deviant behaviors using primarily text analysis. In pro-ED communities, images are a strong visual signal used for self-disclosure [66]. Images are a powerful means of expression that can covey feelings and emotions too complex for written communication [39]. They can also be a tool for identity management and communication techniques [75]. Therefore, we believe images are an important signal in the pro-ED community. Our work examines how the integration of both images and text can predict deviant pro-ED content, improving on the capacities of either separately.

Pro-ED Communities

Pro-eating disorder (or pro-ED) communities are groups that promote eating disorders as an alternative lifestyle choice rather than the dangerous mental disorder that they are. Users in these communities share diet advice, inspirational images of thin bodies, and general support to maintain low body weight and thinness. In this section, we discuss the unique appearances of pro-ED communities online and why they have challenged social networking platforms.

Pro-ED communities are a subset of and blend easily into eating disorder communities at large [17]. Importantly, not all posts about eating disorders are dangerous. For example, someone can post about their struggles with an eating disorder without encouraging others to adopt their behaviors. Because of this, the content around eating disorder communities online is contextually complex. On Instagram, users can move between promoting eating disorders and struggling to stop their behaviors on the same user account [14]. These nuances have led platforms like Tumblr to establish community guidelines that distinguish between these kinds of content [85].

Despite these guidelines, these communities persist on social platforms [57]. Qualitative research on three social networks show users appropriate pro-ED channels for negative health outcomes [66]. On Instagram, pro-ED communities adopt more linguistically variant tags after platform-enforced moderation, and these new communities are more likely to discuss suicidal and self-harm ideas [17]. Additionally, there is often collision between the pro-recovery community (that sites often want to support) and the pro-ED community [16, 25] that occasionally play out on the site [88]. Given the efforts of platforms to curb pro-ED, we believe an algorithmic approach boosted by knowledge of community moderation practices complements current approaches to handling pro-ED content.

Moderation Strategies in Online Communities

Since the emergence of online communities, moderation strategies have been a critical area of research [11, 24, 50, 77]. One moderation style allows users to moderate their own content. On one extreme, 4chan content is unmoderated, and the community has informal moderation of good content by "bumping" desirable threads and using the "sage" command to comment without bumping [8]. Many sites build explicit social moderation systems, where users can publicly vote for or against content on the site. This is used on sites like Reddit, MetaFilter, Yik Yak, Stack Exchange, and Slashdot. The effectiveness of these social moderation strategies are mixed and are often dependent on user engagement with these systems [38, 55].

Another style of moderation uses outright banning strategies. In this case, platforms either ban keywords about deviant behaviors, ban users, or delete entire communities. In many cases, outright banning of keywords limits the dissemination of certain kinds of content, like spam or pornography. However, these kind of moderation strategies can have unintended consequences. On Instagram, researchers studied behavior patterns following banning of tags in pro-ED communities and found that users developed new lexical variants to avoid these keyword bans [17]. On Reddit, the site banned several hateful subreddits, r/fatpeoplehate and r/coontown (a subreddit dedicated to degrading black people), and the community reacted strongly both for and against the banning [13].

Finally, another strategy uses human moderators to evaluate content. Almost all sites have volunteer or paid moderators to police content. Not all moderator actions are negative—some approaches help editors find beautiful weather photos [73], where others help find good social media content [2] and high-quality news comments [29, 65]. Between these three approaches, human decision-making is the common thread; these examples motivate us to use human judgments in our multimodal classification method.

DATA

In this section we present our data collection method in three steps: (1) building a master dataset of photo posts associated with eating disorders; (2) identifying content removed by Tumblr moderators for guideline violations; and (3) building a dataset of Tumblr posts semantically close but unrelated to eating disorders. Figure 1 shows our data-gathering strategy.

Overview of Tumblr

Tumblr is a microblogging and social networking site founded in 2007. Users post multimedia content to short-form personal blogs. The site has social components, like following and messaging other blogs and reblogging content. As of September 2016, Tumblr had over 300 million blogs and 45 million daily posts, making it one of the most popular social network sites[1].

Posts on Tumblr can be placed into 9 post types: `text`, `photo`, `video`, `audio`, `quote`, `question`, `link`, `caption`, or `GIF`[2]. About 75% of Tumblr posts are photo posts [18]. Tumblr does not have explicit community structures, like dedicated forums, where users would specifically post content about eating disorders. Instead, communities on Tumblr form around hashtags [43].

Building the Master Pro-ED Dataset

Our master dataset contains about 877,000 public photo posts from the Tumblr pro-ED community between November 2015

[1] http://www.tumblr.com/press

[2] https://www.tumblr.com/docs/en/api/v2

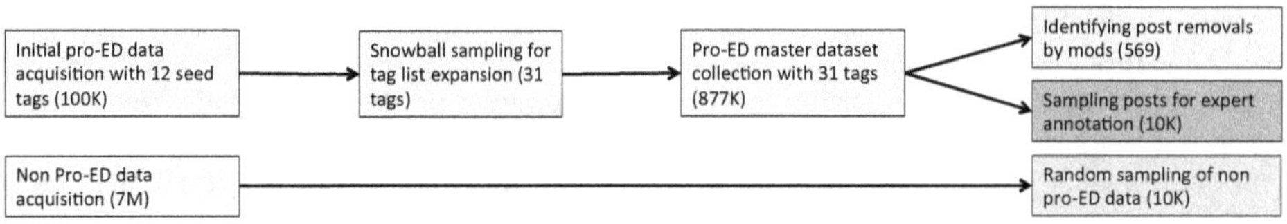

Figure 1: Schematic flowchart of our data collection strategy.

and August 2016. To assemble this dataset, we used the following approach:

Seed Data Collection. First, we crawled one month of public Tumblr posts to create a set of eating disorder and pro-ED tags. We referred to the list of tag suggestions made in the works of Chancellor et al [17] and De Choudhury [25]; both developed a lexicon of pro-ED related tags for Instagram and Tumblr, respectively. Compiling the two studies, we developed a short list of 12 known eating disorder and pro-ED tags[3] including #anorexia, #eating disorder, #pro ana, and #thighgap. Because Tumblr allows for whitespaces in their tags, we also included spaces that naturally separate words or phrases. For example, we included both #eating disorder and #eatingdisorder in our data crawl. This initial crawl with 12 seed tags returned about 100,000 seed posts from May 2016.

eating disorder	thinspo	thynspo	bonespo
eatingdisorder	proana	pro ana	thighgap
mia	ednos	anorexia	pro anorexia

Table 1: Examples of our tags used to crawl pro-ED posts.

Snowball Sampling. Using our seed tags, we used the methods in [17] to snowball and select additional eating disorder and pro-ED tags in our 100,000 photo posts from May 2016. From this list, we filtered for all tags that co-occurred with our initial set of 12 seed tags above a certain probability threshold (2%). We excluded tags related to recovery (*e.g.*, #ed recovery) or that were too general (*e.g.*, #ugly, #fat or #sad teen). This produced 31 unique tags for our final data collection. Some example tags are given in Table 1.

Final Data Collection. Next, we used the 31 tags to get a sample of pro-ED photo posts shared between November 2015 and August 2016. We ran a list-based filter on these posts to exclude posts with salacious tags (*e.g.*, #boobs) or recovery-related tags—recovery tags are known to promote healthy behaviors [16], and therefore unlikely to break Tumblr's guidelines. This master dataset contains about 877,000 photo posts from November 2015 to August 2016. For each post, we gathered its metadata and image. Summary statistics and graphs are provided in Table 2 and in Figure 2. We indicate the 25 most frequent tags in Table 3.

Compiling Posts Removed By Tumblr Moderators

The second step of our data collection is finding photo posts removed by Tumblr moderators for violating Tumblr's community guidelines. Recall that Tumblr community guidelines prohibit the glorification of self-harm and eating disorders like anorexia or bulimia [85]. When Tumblr staff removes a post for breaking community guidelines, they overwrite the original image with a new image that says that Tumblr removed the original for violating community guidelines seen in Figure 3. This action indicates if a post was removed by a moderator.

[3] The 12 seed tags were #anorexia, #anoreixa, #eating disorder, #eatingdisorder, #ednos, #proana, #pro ana, #thinspo, #thynspo, #thighgap, #thigh gap.

Unique Blogs	118106	Unique Tags	297,597
Average Posts/Blogs	7.43	Average Tags/Post	8.85
Median Posts/Blogs	1	Median Tags/Post	6
Standard Deviation	84.47	Standard Deviation	7.56

Table 2: Summary statistics of the master dataset of 877,998 Tumblr posts. This includes how many posts Tumblr blogs generate as well as the use of tags per post.

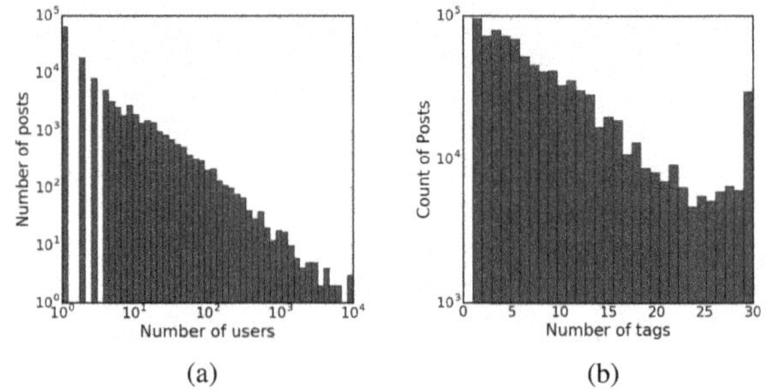

Figure 2: (a) Distribution of posts over users, and (b) distribution of tags over posts in the master dataset.

Figure 3: Default image used by Tumblr to substitute images in posts that violate community guidelines.

To gather moderator-removed posts, we first downloaded all images in our master dataset. This download happened in June and August 2016 (to get July and August's photo data). Using a strategy similar to [15], we re-downloaded the same set of images in September 2016. To detect images that were taken down for violating community guidelines, we tracked images with changes in file size and used a fast visual similarity approach [47] to find images identical to the default image in Figure 3. We found 569 posts removed by Tumblr moderators between June and September 2016.

thinspo	skinny	ana	thin	anorexia
thinspiration	mia	ed	bulimia	eating disorder
depression	fitspo	thigh gap	anorexic	depressed
suicide	proana	sad	anxiety	suicidal
self harm	motivation	pro ana	goals	tw

Table 3: Top 25 tags in our master dataset.

We found that the proportion of photo posts removed due to breaking the guidelines is low. We have several hypotheses that might explain this phenomenon. Even with the most aggressive moderator removal, social media platforms cannot examine all content that should be removed from their platforms. Most platforms rely on reported data from users to drive their curation and content moderation efforts [19]. Second, in communities like pro-ED, posts glorifying self-harm behaviors like purging or extreme food restriction are less likely to be flagged by community members who are deliberately seeking this content. These communities are often "hidden in plain sight" where anyone can find them, but their tags prevent most outside parties from discovering the community [17].

Collecting Non Pro-ED Data

Finally, we collected a sample of Tumblr photo posts that are semantically close to pro-ED images but are topically unrelated. We first manually inspected a sample of 200 posts in the master dataset that were not removed due to community guideline violations. We obtained tags in these posts unrelated to deviant pro-ED behaviors [15]. Examples of these tags include: #outfit, #fashion, #selfie, #fitness, and #fitchicks. Using these tags, we gathered a large set of over seven million posts from August 2016 and excluded posts with any of the 31 pro-ED tags from the master dataset. From this, we randomly sampled about 10,000 public photo posts.

METHODS

In this section, we describe how the data was used to detect deviant pro-ED content on Tumblr as well as the details of our deep learning classification framework.

Methodological Challenges in Detecting Deviant Content

In sensitive communities like pro-ED, it is not surprising that there are only a few examples of deviant content that were *actually moderated*. This slows down getting sufficient gold standard labels (or ground truth) to train a robust classifier.

There is also additional complexity in this classification task. As shown in prior work [14], humans are good at identifying the obvious extremes of what abides by community guidelines (*e.g.*, fitness posts versus pro-ED diet advice). However, certain pro-ED posts are challenging for humans and moderators alike (*e.g.*, thinspiration versus pro-ED diet advice). With access to only the posts that moderators removed, there is no way to identify the posts that moderators found challenging but eventually allowed to stay on the platform.

At first glance, these challenges might be addressed by crowdsourcing the ground truth labels, a technique used in many supervised learning problems [53, 76]. However, due to the inherent subtleties in pro-ED posts, there is a major resource cost as well as an emotional cost to identifying sensitive material [66]. It may also be challenging to find crowdworkers with significant skill to accurately assess these posts [14].

To tackle these challenges, our classification framework learns from ground truth assessments of deviant pro-ED content from domain experts. They have knowledge of both Tumblr's community practices, guidelines, and the pro-ED community. Our experts labeled content into three categories: (1) posts that clearly do not violate the guidelines; (2) those that do conform to guidelines, but are difficult to assess; and (3) deviant pro-ED content or potential violations. This solution addresses both the need for skill and the human sensitivity we want to bring into our method. Training and testing on challenging examples also provides insights into our classifier's performance over a range of deviant or non-deviant posts. This approach more closely replicates how we expect our human-machine moderation system to be developed by others.

Iterative Expert Rating Task for Ground Truth

In this section, we describe our rating task to use human judgment to develop a ground truth dataset.

Rater Credibility and Expertise. Our 3 raters are authors on this paper and are social computing researchers who have considerable research experience in quantitative and qualitative studies of mental health, specifically pro-ED. One rater was employed at Yahoo, the parent company of Tumblr.

Developing a Rationale for Assessing Guideline Violations. We wanted to objectively capture what might constitute removal from Tumblr's platform for "promoting or glorifying eating disorders or self harm." [85] Defining this involves context around the post as well as the community itself—recall that posting to a pro-ED tag is not necessarily grounds for removal on Tumblr. As the guidelines specify, this kind of content must, "urge or encourage others to: cut or injure themselves; embrace anorexia, bulimia, or other eating disorders; or commit suicide." [85] Therefore, we holistically evaluated a post to decide if it might be deviant content. We interpreted promotion either as encouraging the maintenance of an eating disorder or promoting related actions. The researchers used the posts' tags, image, the caption, and the author's username.

In the first iteration, the three raters independently rated 250 public Tumblr posts randomly sampled from the master dataset (ref. Data section). Ratings were based on a three-point scale: photo posts that would potentially be removed due to guideline violation (rating 3); posts that might be a challenging case of moderation but are actually not guideline violations (rating 2); and posts that should continue to remain on Tumblr (rating 1).

Then, the raters resolved rating differences and designed a shared rulebook that included their rationale to assess posts:

- *Rating 3:* This category contained posts where the whole post promoted negative behaviors or actions. This included: pro-eating disorder diet advice, extreme calorie restriction posts, or starvation; posts promoting beauty or transformation through thinness or starvation; glorification of thin body parts associated with eating disorders (collar bones, hip bones, disproportionately slender legs or arms, visibly prominent rib cages, etc.); and body checks.

Acronym	Description	#Posts
GV	*Guideline Violations:* Posts that have been removed from Tumblr by moderators	569
PGV	*Potential Guideline Violations:* Posts that were annotated to be potentially violating community guidelines	1,207
GCS	*Guideline Conforming—Simple:* Posts that were annotated to conform to community guidelines. Also includes the posts acquired by filtering for fitness and appearance related tags	11,545
GCH	*Guideline Conforming—Hard:* Posts annotated to be challenging in their assessment of adherence to community guidelines	2,087

Table 4: Description and statistics of different datasets used in classification.

	Training	Validation	Testing
Positives	80% PGV (966)	20% PGV (241)	GV (569)
Negatives	56% GCS (6465), 56% GCH (1169)	14% GCS (1616), 14% GCH (292)	30% GCS (3464), 30% GCH (626)

Table 5: Composition of training, validation, and test data. Numbers in brackets indicate the number of posts.

- *Rating 2:* This category contained posts with a mismatch between tags/captions and the images. This also included discussion about mental illness and eating disorders without actively promoting them. This included: general discussion about mental health or eating disorders; pro-ED tags with a safe photograph; mental illness discussion; and comments about potential relapsing to pro-ED lifestyles.
- *Rating 1:* These were posts that did not show pro-ED sentiments at all. This included general "thinspiration" or fitness motivation; fitness posts; photos of models; posts encouraging recovery or support; posts unrelated to eating disorders.

With this rulebook, the researchers rated an additional set of 50 posts to test the convergence of their rating system. Using Fleiss' interrater reliability metric κ, we found high agreement ($\kappa = 0.7$) between the three raters. Additionally, we measured how well our ratings identified posts that should be removed (rating 3) and the posts with clear signals of guideline conformity (rating 1) and found that interrater reliability was higher ($\kappa = .8$). In our initial sample of 50 posts following rater calibration, 15/50 of posts received at least one 3, 13 had two 3s, and 8 had three 3s. Greater agreement for distinctive post categories further bolsters the rigor of our rating task.

For the final step in our rating task, another 5000 posts were randomly selected from our master dataset (without replacement from the previous rating samples), and two raters assigned a single score to every post. Prior work shows that the most dangerous content in these communities is relatively uncommon [14] and we predicted it would be our smallest category. To boost the size of this category for the classification task, we identified the top 25 tags on other posts labeled as a 3 in the initial set of 5000. Using these tags to filter, we identified a final sample of 960 photo posts from our master dataset—this narrowed our search space of finding posts most likely to be a 3 so we could quickly bulk up our set of posts with a rating of 3. The same raters rated these additional posts. In total, 5960 posts were rated.

In Figure 4 we provide examples of rated content. These pictures are publicly available, but to respect the users, we obtained passive online consent to use their photos. Image A was rated 1 and had fitness and wellness tags. Image B shows a drawing and had mental illness tags. Image C is a very slim person and had tags that encouraged starvation.

(a) Rating: 1 (b) Rating 2 (c) Rating 3

Figure 4: Example images rated 1, 2, 3 for their likelihood of violating community guidelines. Passive online consent was sought from the account owners (see Supplementary Materials for verbiage of the consent we sought).

Constructing Training, Validation, and Test Datasets

Bringing our data collection and rated posts together, we discuss the construction of the training, validation, and test sets.

Positive Examples/Class 1: Our positive examples (deviant content) for *training* and *validation* included posts that rated as a 3—posts that potentially violate the community guidelines (referred to as PGV or Potential Guideline Violations now on). We split this dataset 80% for *training* and 20% for *validation*. Our positive examples for *testing* included posts that were taken down from Tumblr by the moderators (referred to as GV, or Guideline Violations). Using this approach, we can judge the performance of our classifier against existing moderation.

Negative Examples/Class 0: Our negative examples contained three sets of data: (1) photo posts gathered in the Data section unrelated to eating disorders; (2) the annotated posts that were rated a 1; (3) the annotated posts rated a 2. Because the first two sets of negative posts are likely to have distinctive visual and textual markers in contrast to pro-ED posts, we refer to them as GCS (or Guideline Conforming—Simple). The third set of posts are challenging or contextually complex, so we refer to them as GCH (or Guideline Conforming—Hard). We randomly split this combined set of negative examples into 70% for *training* and *validation* and 30% for *testing*. In Table 4 we summarize the data in our classification tasks and their corresponding counts. In Table 5, we outline the dataset compositions used in training, validation, and testing.

Classification Framework

We present a state-of-the-art multimodal classifier to identify deviant pro-ED content. We discuss our method for obtaining visual features from the images, how we represent their tags, and finally a supervised deep learning framework that incorporated these features in a jointly trained classifier.

Representing Visual Content of Image Posts

Image content representation has evolved greatly with a shift from local features and bag-of-words representations to aggregated features and global image representations [27, 40, 45, 58, 67, 81]. With the recent advances in GPUs and the amount of training data available, the computer vision community has revisited Deep Convolutional Neural Networks (CNNs), *i.e.*, neural networks with many hidden layers and millions of parameters. When trained on big image databases like ImageNet [72], CNNs have been shown to "effortlessly" improve previous state-of-the-art results in many computer vision applications, *e.g.*, image classification [54] and visual search [6, 48, 82]. The aggregated approaches as well as the CNN-based ones all produce a *global* image signature, *i.e.*, a high-dimensional feature vector in Euclidean space.

We extracted visual features of our image posts by starting with the publicly available pre-trained AlexNet model from the Caffe deep learning framework [46]. We experimented with two types of features from this CNN. The $4k$-dimensional $fc7$ features, *i.e.*, the features after the second fully connected layer (we refer the reader to [54] for more details). Limited by the amount of available annotated data for our problem and in pursuit of a more compact representation, we use dimensionality reduction to get the features down to $d = 128$ dimensions. To reduce dimensionality, we use principle component analysis, learned using $fc7$ features from a public 100 Million YFCC100M image set [37, 80]. We define the visual features for an image i as $\mathscr{V}_i \in \mathbb{R}^D$, where $D = \{128, 4096\}$.

Text Embeddings and Aggregation

To extract text features, we used the *skip-gram* model [62] and *word2vec* [63] training. Recent work has used word2vec for tag prediction [28, 87]. The principal force behind the skip-gram model is the use of *context as supervision.* As a learning objective in a generic text representation scenario, skip-gram tries to maximize classification of a word based on another word in the same sentence. Here, we do not target tag or word prediction but choose to *aggregate* the individual learned tag representations of posts given by word2vec into a single compact post representation.

We create our tag contexts through *tag co-occurrencs* and form our supervision signal from all possible pairs of tags that appear in a post. Given a set $T_i = \{t_1, \dots, t_T\}$ of T_i tags for post i we construct the set of co-occurring tag pairs $\mathscr{P}_i$: $\{(t_j, t_k) \forall j, k \in T_i\}$ with the objective to maximize the average log probability spanning all tag pairs in i [62, 63]. We form our tag dictionary $\mathscr{D}$ using the most common (top-40K) tags from our training dataset. After learning the embeddings, each tag in our dictionary is now represented by a dense compact vector, that lies in a space $\mathscr{E} \in \mathbb{R}^E$ of dimensionality $E = 128$, where tags that often co-occur are *close*. Examples of nearest neighbors in the embedded space are shown in Table 6. The word2vec model produces semantically relevant tags in our dataset for ED-related terms: for example, #anorexic co-occurs most strongly with #starving and #anamia, two tags related to pro-ED actions and ideations.

More formally, the model maps every tag $t_j \in \mathscr{D}$ to an embedding vector $e_j \in \mathscr{E}$ and now an image. Photo post i is represented by the set $\mathscr{T}_i = \{e_1, \dots, e_{T_d}\}$ where now only a subset T_d of all post tags that are present in the dictionary are kept. In order to have one compact tag representation per post,

Tag	Closest tags in embedded space
anorexic	starving, thinspriation, overweight, anamia, thinspi
thigh	gap, gab, highs, thighspo, hips
anorexia	bulima, okay, bulimia, anorexyc, skynnny
harm	self, self-harm, injury, tw:, disappointment
ana	collarbones, eddies, anarexic, skinnygirl, anotexia
ed	manorexia, Ed, relapse, warriors, disorder
love	couple, passion, life, followers, kiss
thinspo	thinspire, anabuddy, pretty, thin, thinspiration
bulimic	bulimia, depressed, starve, bulimix, purge

Table 6: Top 5 nearest neighbors in the embedded space.

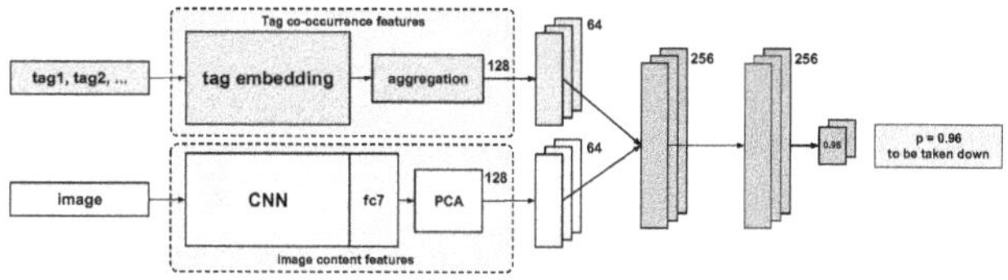

Figure 5: Our multimodal deep neural network architecture.

we aggregated the tag embeddings using average pooling, *i.e.* by averaging all vectors per image.

Learning a Deep Multimodal Neural Network (DNN)

Given a post i with visual features $\mathscr{V}_i$ and textual features $\mathscr{T}_i$, we want to use both to learn whether or not this is deviant pro-ED content. Formulating this as a classification problem, we jointly learn from both modalities. Our joint model outputs a function $f(\mathscr{V}_i, \mathscr{T}_i)$ that models the probability $p(y|i)$ of whether a post is deviant.

Multimodal models have been used for tag prediction [28, 87], image captioning [52] and categorization [36, 70]. Our model follows the same basic structure of [36], where two streams, one per modality, are first independent and then concatenated to learn a joint embedding before the final classifier. However, we divert from the architecture of [36] by adding a fully connected layer on top of the tag embeddings as well as adding multiple layers after concatenation. An overview of the model is shown in Figure 5. Layers in the CNN block follow the AlexNet model [54] while all added layers are fully connected. Although our model can be trained end-to-end, we chose to only learn the last layers of each modality jointly with all subsequent multimodal layers. We trained the model using the Adagrad [32] optimizer and the softmax cross entropy as our loss function. Although the depth and width choices for our model are limited due to limited ground truth data, we experimented with deep architectures with up to 3 joint layers.

RESULTS

Evaluation Protocol and Methods Compared

We compare the Deep Neural Network (DNN) to text-only, image-only, and multimodal Support Vector Machines (SVMs) [23]. In all cases, we use the training, validation and testing datasets presented in Table 5 and the features presented in the previous section, *i.e.* CNN-based visual features $\mathscr{V}_i$ and textual features $\mathscr{T}_i$ from word2vec embeddings. For the multimodal SVM, the two are first concatenated. We experimented with both linear and Radial Basis Function (RBF)

Method	Tags	Vis	Metrics				
			Acc	*P*	*R*	*AUC*	*F1*
SVM	✓		0.89	0.72	0.41	0.61	0.53
SVM		✓	0.85	0.53	0.36	0.49	0.43
SVM	✓	✓	**0.86**	**0.54**	**0.81**	**0.69**	**0.65**
SVM-4k	✓	✓	0.86	0.56	0.50	0.57	0.53
DNN-l1-256	✓	✓	0.90	0.67	0.74	0.72	0.70
DNN-l2-128	✓	✓	0.88	0.57	0.82	0.71	0.67
DNN l2-256	✓	✓	**0.90**	**0.62**	**0.85**	**0.75**	**0.72**
DNN-l2-512	✓	✓	0.90	0.66	0.75	0.73	0.70
DNN l3-256	✓	✓	0.90	0.65	0.75	0.72	0.69

Table 7: Results for the validation dataset. Our best performing SVM and DNN are bolded.

Method	Tags	Vis	Metrics				
			Acc	*P*	*R*	*AUC*	*F1*
SVM	✓		0.88	0.50	0.25	0.42	0.33
SVM		✓	0.73	0.30	0.90	0.60	0.45
SVM	✓	✓	**0.86**	**0.46**	**0.85**	**0.66**	**0.59**
SVM-4k	✓	✓	0.88	0.50	0.46	0.51	0.48
DNN-l1-256	✓	✓	0.90	0.57	0.70	0.65	0.62
DNN-l2-128	✓	✓	0.87	0.49	0.82	0.67	0.61
DNN-l2-256	✓	✓	**0.89**	**0.52**	**0.85**	**0.70**	**0.65**
DNN-l2-512	✓	✓	0.88	0.52	0.60	0.58	0.56
DNN l3-256	✓	✓	0.89	0.54	0.71	0.64	0.61

Table 8: Results for the test dataset. Our best performing SVM and DNN are bolded.

kernels and found performance to be similar. We report results on the classifier trained with the Radial Basis Function (RBF) kernel (C=100, g=0.01). We also report results using the 4K-dimensional visual features for the SVM.

We experimented with different configurations for the DNN, varying the trainable parameters both through the depth (*i.e.* the number of layers added) and width (*i.e.* the size of each layer) of our model. For brevity, we will only present results for the top performing configurations at each depth in Tables 7 and 8. We refer to different configurations of our model as *DNN-lX-Y*, where X stands for the number of joint layers and Y for their size. During training we used a batch size of 64 and a learning rate of 0.01 in most cases. We set the probability threshold of the classifier to $p = 0.5$. We report accuracy (A), precision (P), recall (R), F1-measure and area under the curve (AUC), also known as average precision [7].

Classifier Performance on Validation and Test Data

In Tables 7 and 8, we present results for the SVMs and the DNN over the validation and test sets. We varied model parameters for all methods in the validation set and applied the best performing models at the test set. In this discussion, we report our best-performing models for the multimodal SVM and the DNN-l2-256 models measured by AUC.

In our validation step, the multimodal SVM outperforms both unimodal ones by 8–20%, and the deep models outperform the multimodal SVM by 2–6%. Interestingly, higher dimensionality features (the 4K SVM) did not result in higher performance for the SVM—we hypothesize that this model might be overfitting on the training data with the large feature space. However,

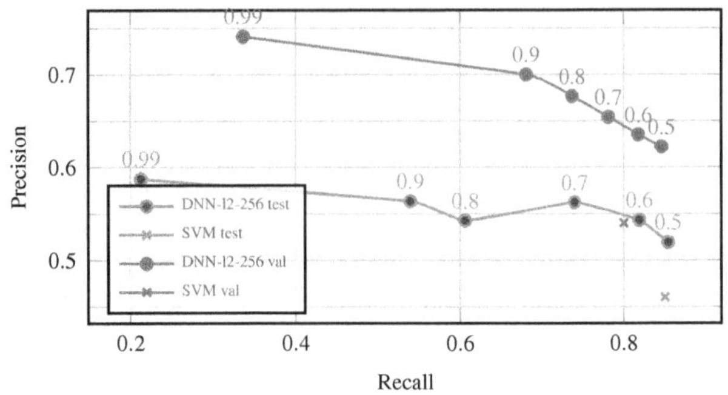

Figure 6: Precision-Recall curve for our classification with the best performing deep (DNN-l2-256) and SVM models.

increasing the deep model's parameter set size makes the model perform better on both the validation and the test sets (3–12% improvement over all other deep models). In Figure 6, we show precision versus recall curves when changing the probability threshold to identify deviant pro-ED content.

We report results on the test set. From Table 8, our DNN outperforms our state-of-the-art SVM. Our DNN l2–256 model achieves an accuracy of 0.89, a precision of 0.52, a recall of 0.85, and an AUC of 0.7. This is a 3% improvement in accuracy over the best SVM (0.86) and a 4% increase in AUC (SVM at 0.66). Our recall is particularly high, indicating that our method is robust against false negatives. What is contributing to the improvement of AUC is a 6% increase in our precision, a significant step in precision. That is, our DNN is able to capture fewer false positives while maintaining recall.

Finally, between the validation and test sets, we see one interesting result: for almost all of the SVM and the deep models, relative performance is preserved between the validation and testing phases. For the best performing SVM, the validation AUC is 0.69 ($F1 = 0.65$) and testing AUC is 0.66 ($F1 = 0.59$). For our DNN, the validation AUC is 0.75 ($F1 = 0.72$) and testing AUC is 0.70 ($F1 = 0.65$). This emphasizes the power of our human-machine method—our hand-curated, expertly rated dataset of pro-ED posts and the posts removed by moderators capture similar visual and textual cues.

Accuracy and Error Analysis

We present a qualitative analysis of example posts and their classification outcomes. Specifically, we identify posts with visual similarity but distinctive contexts and meanings with different classification outcomes. Since we conduct these analyses on images removed from the Tumblr platform, the actual images are not included; however we provide descriptions of their visual and textual content to assist in interpretation.

We begin with a *true positive* ($P(\text{Class}_1) = 0.67$), or example A. In the post, there is a black and white photograph of person laying down that emphasizes the midsection. The midsection of the person is particularly emaciated, and their hip bones and rib cage are very visible. In general, there is a strong emphasis on their bone structure. The image also emphasizes their thinness because the person is wearing a very baggy sweater. The face is not visible. The post has a few tags, like #thinspo. Our classifier correctly marked this post.

Example B is a post in a similar pose that is an example of a *false positive*. This was not taken down from Tumblr, but the classifier felt strongly that it should be removed ($P(\text{Class}_1) = 0.99$). This post is a black and white photo of an individual's midsection laying down. The person is slim but appears at a healthy body weight. The post is tagged with about seven tags, with #pro ana and #thinspo as the most concerning. One reason why the classifier might have been confused is that the pose and coloring is suggestive of common poses seen in the dataset—emphasis on a body part like the hips or ribs. We also noticed that black and white photos were often the most likely candidates for removal, perhaps because they are seen as more somber and sad [69]. However, the person in the image is at what appears to be a healthy bodyfat level, which is why it was likely not removed. The tags are not necessarily motivation for taking actions that promote an eating disorder.

Our next example C is a *true negative* ($P(\text{Class}_1) = 0.04$). This post was not removed from Tumblr, and our classifier agreed with this. This post is a black and white photograph of an individual seated outside smoking a cigarette. The whole body is visible, including the face. The person is slim and the pose highlights their slender legs. The post has several tags, including #fashion and #model. Although this person is slim and seems to be emphasizing her legs, the photo appears to be of a model relaxing. Because the tags confirm this contextualization, we believe that the classifier picked up on this context and was able to correctly identify this image.

The final example D is a *false negative* ($P(\text{Class}_1) = 0.29$). The classifier labeled this post as safe, however this was removed from the platform for violating guidelines. The image contains a color photo of an individual laying on a bed wearing a bra and jeans. The whole body is visible in the photo, including the face. It does not appear that the person has low body fat. At the bottom of the photo, the words "stay strong. starve on" are included. The photo has five tags including #thinspoo and #skinny. There are some elements of the post that the classifier may be misinterpreting. The vast majority of our positive examples were black and white photographs, and it is unusual to have a color photo in this dataset. Further, the photo shows a full body with a face. Most positive examples do not show a person's face. In this case, however, the text overlaid on the image indicates that this image promotes starvation. The deep learning model we built does not incorporate optical character recognition—we found so few images in our rated dataset had text that we did not implement it as a layer in our CNN. This might be why the classifier misclassified this post—it was not able to "read" the text on the photograph to discern that it was promoting starvation.

DISCUSSION

In this paper, we introduced a multimodal classification approach to detect deviant pro-ED Tumblr content. We built a dataset with a combination of human and machine curated examples. We found images are a powerful signal that work with text to characterizing subtle cues of posts in sensitive, complex domains like pro-ED. Importantly, we showed that a deep-learning, convolutional neural network is a powerful method to distinguish deviant content from other content; CNNs outperforms state-of-the art supervised machine learning techniques like SVMs. We demonstrate a novel methodological advancement in machine learning on a problem of broad and profound importance to HCI research and practice.

Our work showed that humans can carefully curate a dataset with similar classification performance to posts removed by Tumblr moderators. This is a powerful discovery for research in deviant behavior communities like pro-ED that suffer from small, challenging, or difficult-to-find datasets. Expert-created datasets can be used in these cases, and algorithms can be developed to detect this kind of content. We are optimistic that researchers of deviant behavior and practitioners may borrow from our method and can tackle problems in these spaces.

Designing Intelligent Moderation Systems

Our multimodal approach tempered with human sensitivity can be a flexible, yet powerful mechanism to address moderation challenges on social media. We developed this method with Tumblr in mind, where there are active human moderators that review user-reported content for community guidelines violations. In practice, we believe our method could be used in human-machine moderation systems, where it could improve moderation *scale*, *efficiency*, and *skill development*:

(1) Our method could be a broad "first pass" for human moderators to scale up their tasks. By surfacing posts that likely break the guidelines, our method could prune the search space of posts that need intervention. Moderators could also focus on violations that are not reported by the platform's users, e.g., due to the clandestine nature of the pro-ED community [17], or are reported once they reach many users.

(2) Building on the above design direction, our method could also be used in an online learning-based moderation system [59]. Moderators could set the decision threshold of the classifier per context and need. They could also adjust the desired balance between false positives and false negatives. This is an important consideration for moderation of sensitive content like pro-ED—moderators of different platforms may want more or less stringency to reflect what their community guidelines consider harmful behaviors. The moderators could provide feedback to our method so it can learn from images that it misclassifies (*i.e.*, re-tune the CNN). These systems have been extremely successful in online text classification and image retrieval [83]. We think this kind of moderation system would improve efficiency and also help the system 'evolve' over time by learning from misclassifications.

(3) Moderation of sensitive content like pro-ED needs a unique set of skills to assess community harm or guideline violations compared to other kinds of content (*e.g.*, salacious content). This skill set is often gained over time, potentially making new moderator training a time-consuming and emotionally intensive process [5]. We believe our method could design novel moderation training systems to help new moderators recognize objectively codified rules from prior deviant content.

Managing Impacts to Current Moderation Practices

Our proposed intelligent moderation systems could increase the posts drawn to the attention of moderators—this has both benefits and drawbacks. For communities that actively use human moderators, these systems inevitably increase the posts that a moderator will need to check. This will likely place strain on existing moderation practices, might change labor expectations, hiring needs, or other human or capital consequences. There might also be unintended consequences on what were once manually moderated communities. Rampant automated moderation of content perceived to be deviant by a human-machine system could additionally discourage user participation on a platform. It also presents difficult, unique challenges in contexts where content incorrectly marked as deviant is accidentally taken down.

One way to manage these tensions is with the trade-off of precision and recall in the design of an algorithm. Our results had higher recall and were therefore more robust against false negatives. Said another way, our method would pull more potentially deviant content to the attention of moderators. This feature is valuable where our method works alongside the moderators; high recall will expose moderators to more content than they may normally find. However, in an automated context, designers might favor higher precision. This would prevent safe content from being removed from the platform and negatively affecting genuine user participation. Summarily, we believe developing these moderation systems need careful and considerate execution and implementation.

Ethical and Social Challenges

Our work underscores an important ethical and social question—do social networks have an obligation to curate this content on their platforms? Social networks, and communities more broadly, are inherently defined both by the content they permit on the platform as well as the content they remove.

One might argue that social networks should allow as much speech as possible. For issues like copyright infringement, social networks have a legal obligation to remove that content. However, for socially contentious subjects like pro-ED, social networks might not necessarily choose to ban them. In some cases, the community may feel that it is better for these people to identify and express themselves. Other work has also shown that, after banning certain tags on Instagram, the pro-ED community became more insular and focused on more dangerous ideas [17]. There is also promising research that suggests discussing dangerous ideas might help people disinhibit themselves from self-harm [33].

On the other hand, there are those that value moderation of deviant content for its ability to constrain sentiments that might harm individuals or communities. In particular, pro-ED behaviors show contagion-like effects [60], and research has shown that this discourse can encourage others to maintain or continue their dangerous behaviors [71]. Some might argue that, because the social network can shape discourse, this kind of content should be taken down because it is "toxic" to the community [49]. This argument could be extended to other kinds of content. Another argument for moderation is for user engagement—if the negative content causes people to leave or stop participating, the content should be removed.

This is by no means an exhaustive analysis of the benefits and drawbacks to content moderation, nor do we decide whether these platforms have these social obligations. In fact, this only scratches the surface of a complicated set of issues around content moderation, social networks, and deviant behavior like pro-ED. It will take collaborations from industry professionals, researchers, designers, psychologists, and other stakeholders to make decisions in this area.

Limitations and Future Work

One limitation is that we only used public data in this paper and our method did not learn from any private pro-ED content. Because there are few posts identified as actual moderator removals, we could not use them in training our classifiers. While our approach performed equally well on validation and test data, misclassifications may be attributed to the classifier's inability to learn from decisions that drive moderator removals. We could not identify posts that received the attention of a moderator but are still public.

These concerns could be solved in future work with mixed methods working with a social media platform. We could gather information of true positives (removals) and true negatives (posts that were flagged but stay public) to train our models. Researchers could also interview moderators to better understand removal procedures. This was successful in other algorithmic approaches that assist human editors in finding photos [73], and we see this as a promising next step.

Another limitation of our deep learning approach relates to interpretability of the results of the deep learning models. These deep learning models are significantly more powerful; however, they do not produce interpretable results about what features are most important. We recognize that this could present challenges to non-expert end users, like moderators, who could integrate the outputs of this method into their workflow. We believe ongoing research in machine learning interpretability [86] can help resolve these issues in the future.

Finally, despite satisfactory performance, we acknowledge the gap that exists between being able to identify potential guideline violations versus being able to cross-check those assessments with an actual moderator. A future extension could solicit feedback from moderators as an additional way to assess the effectiveness of our proposed method.

CONCLUSION

In this paper, we described a semi-automated method to identify pro-ED posts on Tumblr that violate their community guidelines. Our method jointly incorporated visual and text cues from photo posts to build a deep neural network based classifier to handle this task. Employing a hand-curated dataset of nearly a million pro-ED Tumblr posts, this classifier incorporated human sensitivity by consulting expert ratings on a sample of posts. Our results showed that this deep-learning model performed comparably to ground truth that included actually moderated Tumblr data. Through this work, we demonstrate the power that humans and machines can have when they are used together on a contextually-rich and complicated classification task as identifying deviant pro-ED content.

ACKNOWLEDGMENTS

This work was partly supported through a Yahoo Faculty Engagement Award to De Choudhury.

REFERENCES

1. B Thomas Adler, Luca De Alfaro, Santiago M Mola-Velasco, Paolo Rosso, and Andrew G West. 2011.

Wikipedia vandalism detection: Combining natural language, metadata, and reputation features. In *Computational linguistics and intelligent text processing*. Springer, 277–288.

2. Eugene Agichtein, Carlos Castillo, Debora Donato, Aristides Gionis, and Gilad Mishne. 2008. Finding high-quality content in social media. In *Proceedings of the 2008 international conference on web search and data mining*. ACM, 183–194.
3. Ronald L Akers. 1977. Deviant behavior: A social learning approach. (1977).
4. Nazanin Andalibi and Andrea Forte. 2016. Social Computing Researchers, Vulnerability, and Peer Support. In *Ethical Encounters in HCI: Research in Sensitive and Complex Settings Workshop at the Conference on Human Factors in Computing Systems*.
5. Nazanin Andalibi, Pinar Ozturk, and Andrea Forte. 2017. Sensitive Self-disclosures, Responses, and Social Support on Instagram: the case of #depression. In *Proceedings of the ACM Conference on Computer Supported Cooperative Work & Social Computing*. Forthcoming.
6. Artem Babenko, Anton Slesarev, Alexandr Chigorin, and Victor Lempitsky. 2014. Neural Codes for Image Retrieval. In *ECCV*.
7. Ricardo A. Baeza-Yates and Berthier A. Ribeiro-Neto. 2011. *Modern Information Retrieval - the concepts and technology behind search, Second edition*. Pearson Education Ltd., Harlow, England.
8. Michael S Bernstein, Andrés Monroy-Hernández, Drew Harry, Paul André, Katrina Panovich, and Gregory G Vargas. 2011. 4chan and/b: An Analysis of Anonymity and Ephemerality in a Large Online Community.. In *ICWSM*.
9. Jeremy Blackburn and Haewoon Kwak. 2014. Stfu noob!: predicting crowdsourced decisions on toxic behavior in online games. In *Proceedings of the 23rd international conference on World wide web*. ACM, 877–888.
10. Dina LG Borzekowski, Summer Schenk, Jenny L Wilson, and Rebecka Peebles. 2010. e-Ana and e-Mia: A Content Analysis of Pro–Eating Disorder Web Sites. *American journal of public health* 100, 8 (2010), 1526.
11. Amy Bruckman, Pavel Curtis, Cliff Figallo, and Brenda Laurel. 1994. Approaches to managing deviant behavior in virtual communities. In *Conference Companion on Human Factors in Computing Systems*. ACM, 183–184.
12. Erin E Buckels, Paul D Trapnell, and Delroy L Paulhus. 2014. Trolls just want to have fun. *Personality and individual Differences* 67 (2014), 97–102.
13. Alissa Centivany and Bobby Glushko. 2016. 'Popcorn Tastes Good': Participatory Policymaking and Reddit's 'Amageddon". In *Proceedings of the SIGCHI Conference on Human Factors in Computing Systems*.
14. Stevie Chancellor, Zhiyuan Lin, Erica L Goodman, Stephanie Zerwas, and Munmun De Choudhury. 2016b. Quantifying and Predicting Mental Illness Severity in Online Pro-Eating Disorder Communities. In *Proceedings of the 19th ACM Conference on Computer-Supported Cooperative Work & Social Computing*. ACM, 1171–1184.
15. Stevie Chancellor, Zhiyuan Jerry Lin, and Munmun De Choudhury. 2016a. "This Post Will Just Get Taken Down": Characterizing Removed Pro-Eating Disorder Social Media Content. In *Proceedings of the 2016 CHI Conference on Human Factors in Computing Systems*. 1157–1162.
16. Stevie Chancellor, Tanushree Mitra, and Munmun De Choudhury. 2016c. Recovery Amid Pro-Anorexia: Analysis of Recovery in Social Media. In *Proceedings of the 2016 CHI Conference on Human Factors in Computing Systems*. ACM, 2111–2123.
17. Stevie Chancellor, Jessica Pater, Trustin Clear, Eric Gilbert, and Munmun De Choudhury. 2016d. #thyghgapp: Instagram Content Moderation and Lexical Variation in Pro-Eating Disorder Communities. In *Proceedings of the 2016 Conference on Computer Supported Cooperative Work & Social Computing(CSCW)*. ACM.
18. Yi Chang, Lei Tang, Yoshiyuki Inagaki, and Yan Liu. 2014. What is tumblr: A statistical overview and comparison. *ACM SIGKDD Explorations Newsletter* 16, 1 (2014), 21–29.
19. Adrien Chen. 2014. The Laborers Who Keep Dick Pics and Beheadings Out of Your Facebook Feed. (2014). `https://www.wired.com/2014/10/content-moderation/`
20. Justin Cheng, Michael Bernstein, Cristian Danescu-Niculescu-Mizel, and Jure Leskovic. 2017. Anyone Can Become a Troll: Causes of Trolling Behavior in Online Discussions. In *Proceedings of the ACM Conference on Computer Supported Cooperative Work & Social Computing*. Forthcoming.
21. Justin Cheng, Cristian Danescu-Niculescu-Mizil, and Jure Leskovec. 2015. Antisocial Behavior in Online Discussion Communities. In *International Conference on Weblogs and Social Media (ICWSM)*. AAAI.
22. Denzil Correa and Ashish Sureka. 2014. Chaff from the wheat: characterization and modeling of deleted questions on stack overflow. In *Proceedings of the 23rd international conference on World wide web*. ACM, 631–642.
23. Corinna Cortes and Vladimir Vapnik. 1995. Support-vector networks. *Machine learning* 20, 3 (1995), 273–297.
24. John P Davis, Shelly Farnham, and Carlos Jensen. 2002. Decreasing online 'bad' behavior. In *CHI'02 Extended Abstracts on Human Factors in Computing Systems*. ACM, 718–719.
25. Munmun De Choudhury. 2015. Anorexia on Tumblr: A Characterization Study. In *Proc. Digital Health*.

26. Munmun De Choudhury, Michael Gamon, Scott Counts, and Eric Horvitz. 2013. Predicting depression via social media. In *AAAI Conference on Weblogs and Social Media*.

27. J. Delhumeau, PH. Gosselin, H. Jegou, and P. Perez. 2013. Revisiting the VLAD Image representation. In *ACM Multimedia*.

28. Emily Denton, Jason Weston, Manohar Paluri, Lubomir Bourdev, and Rob Fergus. 2015. User conditional hashtag prediction for images. In *Proceedings of the 21th ACM SIGKDD International Conference on Knowledge Discovery and Data Mining*. ACM, 1731–1740.

29. Nicholas A Diakopoulos. 2015. The Editor's Eye: Curation and Comment Relevance on the New York Times. In *Proceedings of the 18th ACM Conference on Computer Supported Cooperative Work & Social Computing*. ACM, 1153–1157.

30. Judith S Donath and others. 1999. Identity and deception in the virtual community. *Communities in cyberspace* 1996 (1999), 29–59.

31. Harris Drucker, Donghui Wu, and Vladimir N Vapnik. 1999. Support vector machines for spam categorization. *IEEE Transactions on Neural networks* 10, 5 (1999), 1048–1054.

32. John Duchi, Elad Hazan, and Yoram Singer. 2011. Adaptive subgradient methods for online learning and stochastic optimization. *Journal of Machine Learning Research* 12, Jul (2011), 2121–2159.

33. T Emmens and A Phippen. 2010. Evaluating Online Safety Programs. *Harvard Berkman Center for Internet and Society.[23 July 2011]* (2010).

34. Casey Fiesler, Cliff Lampe, and Amy S Bruckman. 2016. Reality and perception of copyright terms of service for online content creation. In *Proceedings of the 19th ACM Conference on Computer-Supported Cooperative Work & Social Computing*. ACM, 1450–1461.

35. Jesse Fox and Margaret C Rooney. 2015. The Dark Triad and trait self-objectification as predictors of men's use and self-presentation behaviors on social networking sites. *Personality and Individual Differences* 76 (2015), 161–165.

36. Andrea Frome, Greg S Corrado, Jon Shlens, Samy Bengio, Jeff Dean, Tomas Mikolov, and others. 2013. Devise: A deep visual-semantic embedding model. In *Advances in neural information processing systems*. 2121–2129.

37. Pierre Garrigues, Sachin Farfade, Hamid Izadinia, Kofi Boakye, and Yannis Kalantidis. 2016. Tag Prediction at Flickr: a View from the Darkroom. *arXiv preprint arXiv:1612.01922* (2016).

38. Eric Gilbert. 2013. Widespread underprovision on reddit. In *Proceedings of the 2013 conference on Computer supported cooperative work*. ACM, 803–808.

39. Val Gillies, Angela Harden, Katherine Johnson, Paula Reavey, Vicky Strange, and Carla Willig. 2005. Painting pictures of embodied experience: The use of nonverbal data production for the study of embodiment. *Qualitative research in psychology* 2, 3 (2005), 199–212.

40. Philippe-Henri Gosselin, Naila Murray, Hervé Jégou, and Florent Perronnin. 2014. Revisiting the Fisher vector for fine-grained classification. *Pattern Recognition Letters* 49 (2014), 92–98.

41. Lynne Hall and Carlisle E George. 1999. Law and Punishment in Virtual Communities. *Proceedings of Cybersociety* (1999).

42. Sameer Hinduja and Justin W Patchin. 2014. *Bullying beyond the schoolyard: Preventing and responding to cyberbullying*. Corwin Press.

43. Yuheng Hu, Lydia Manikonda, Subbarao Kambhampati, and others. 2014. What We Instagram: A First Analysis of Instagram Photo Content and User Types.. In *ICWSM*.

44. Sara Javanmardi, David W McDonald, and Cristina V Lopes. 2011. Vandalism detection in Wikipedia: a high-performing, feature-rich model and its reduction through Lasso. In *Proceedings of the 7th International Symposium on Wikis and Open Collaboration*. ACM, 82–90.

45. H. Jégou, M. Douze, C. Schmid, and P. Perez. 2010. Aggregating Local Descriptors into a Compact Image Representation. In *CVPR*.

46. Yangqing Jia, Evan Shelhamer, Jeff Donahue, Sergey Karayev, Jonathan Long, Ross Girshick, Sergio Guadarrama, and Trevor Darrell. 2014. Caffe: Convolutional Architecture for Fast Feature Embedding. In *Proceedings of the 22Nd ACM International Conference on Multimedia (MM '14)*. ACM, New York, NY, USA, 675–678. DOI: http://dx.doi.org/10.1145/2647868.2654889

47. Yannis Kalantidis, Lyndon Kennedy, Huy Nguyen, Clayton Mellina, and David A Shamma. 2016a. LOH and behold: Web-scale visual search, recommendation and clustering using Locally Optimized Hashing. *ECCV VSM Workshop* (2016).

48. Yannis Kalantidis, Clayton Mellina, Flickr Vision, and Simon Osindero. 2016b. Cross-dimensional Weighting for Aggregated Deep Convolutional Features. In *VSM Workshop, ECCV*.

49. Ruogu Kang, Laura Dabbish, and Katherine Sutton. 2016. Strangers on Your Phone: Why People Use Anonymous Communication Applications. In *Proceedings of the 19th ACM Conference on Computer-Supported Cooperative Work & Social Computing*. ACM, 359–370.

50. Sara Kiesler, Robert Kraut, Paul Resnick, and Aniket Kittur. 2012. Regulating behavior in online communities. *Building Successful Online Communities: Evidence-Based Social Design. MIT Press, Cambridge, MA* (2012).

51. Amy Jo Kim. 2000. *Community building on the web: Secret strategies for successful online communities.* Addison-Wesley Longman Publishing Co., Inc.

52. Ryan Kiros, Ruslan Salakhutdinov, and Richard S Zemel. 2014. Unifying visual-semantic embeddings with multimodal neural language models. *arXiv preprint arXiv:1411.2539* (2014).

53. Aniket Kittur, Boris Smus, Susheel Khamkar, and Robert E Kraut. 2011. Crowdforge: Crowdsourcing complex work. In *Proceedings of the 24th annual ACM symposium on User interface software and technology.* ACM, 43–52.

54. Alex Krizhevsky, Ilya Sutskever, and Geoffrey E Hinton. 2012. Imagenet classification with deep convolutional neural networks. In *NIPS.*

55. Cliff Lampe and Paul Resnick. 2004. Slash (dot) and burn: distributed moderation in a large online conversation space. In *Proceedings of the SIGCHI conference on Human factors in computing systems.* ACM, 543–550.

56. A Laye-Gindhu and KA Schonert-Reichl. 2005. Nonsuicidal self-harm among community adolescents: Understanding the "whats" and "whys" of self-harm. *Journal of Youth & Adolescence* 34, 5 (2005), 447–457.

57. Stephanie M. Lee. 2016. Why Eating Disorders Are So Hard For Instagram And Tumblr To Combat. (2016). https://www.buzzfeed.com/stephaniemlee/why-eating-disorders-are-so-hard-for-instagram-and//-tumblr-to

58. D.G. Lowe. 2004. Distinctive Image Features from Scale-Invariant Keypoints. *IJCV* 60, 2 (2004), 91–110.

59. Justin Ma, Lawrence K Saul, Stefan Savage, and Geoffrey M Voelker. 2009. Identifying suspicious URLs: an application of large-scale online learning. In *Proceedings of the 26th annual international conference on machine learning.* ACM, 681–688.

60. Jeanne B Martin. 2010. The development of ideal body image perceptions in the United States. *Nutrition Today* 45, 3 (2010), 98–110.

61. J. Nathan Matias, Amy Johnson, Whitney Erin Boesel, Brian Keegan, Jaclyn Friedman, and Charlie DeTar. 2015. Reporting, Reviewing, and Responding to Harassment on Twitter. *CoRR* abs/1505.03359 (2015). http://arxiv.org/abs/1505.03359

62. Tomas Mikolov, Kai Chen, Greg Corrado, and Jeffrey Dean. 2013. Efficient estimation of word representations in vector space. *arXiv preprint arXiv:1301.3781* (2013).

63. T Mikolov and J Dean. 2013. Distributed representations of words and phrases and their compositionality. *Advances in neural information processing systems* (2013).

64. Arjun Mukherjee, Vivek Venkataraman, Bing Liu, and Natalie S Glance. 2013. What yelp fake review filter might be doing?. In *ICWSM.*

65. Deokgun Park, Simranjit Sachar, Nicholas Diakopoulos, and Niklas Elmqvist. 2016. Supporting comment moderators in identifying high quality online news comments. In *Proc. Conference on Human Factors in Computing Systems (CHI).*

66. Jessica A Pater, Oliver L Haimston, Nazanin Andalibi, and Elizabeth D Mynatt. 2016. "Hunger Hurts but Starving Works": Characterizing the Presentation of Eating Disorders Online. In *Proceedings of the 19th ACM conference on Computer Supported Cooperative Work & Social Computing (CSCW).*

67. F. Perronnin, Y. Liu, J. Sanchez, and H. Poirier. 2010. Large-Scale Image Retrieval with Compressed Fisher Vectors. In *CVPR.*

68. Rebecca Rafferty and Thomas Vander Ven. 2014. "I Hate Everything About You": A Qualitative Examination of Cyberbullying and On-Line Aggression in a College Sample. *Deviant behavior* 35, 5 (2014), 364–377.

69. Andrew G Reece and Christopher M Danforth. 2016. Instagram photos reveal predictive markers of depression. *arXiv preprint arXiv:1608.03282* (2016).

70. Zhou Ren, Hailin Jin, Zhe Lin, Chen Fang, and Alan Yuille. 2016. Joint Image-Text Representation by Gaussian Visual-Semantic Embedding. In *ACM Multimedia*, Vol. 4.

71. Denise Restauri. 2012. "Tumblr to Pinterest to Instagram – The Self-Harm 'Thinspo' Community Is House-Hunting". (2012). http://www.forbes.com/sites/deniserestauri/2012/04/16/tumblr-to-pinterest-to-instagram-self-harm-thinspo//-community-is-house-hunting

72. Olga Russakovsky, Jia Deng, Hao Su, Jonathan Krause, Sanjeev Satheesh, Sean Ma, Zhiheng Huang, Andrej Karpathy, Aditya Khosla, Michael Bernstein, and others. 2014. Imagenet large scale visual recognition challenge. *arXiv preprint arXiv:1409.0575* (2014).

73. David A Shamma, Lyndon Kennedy, Jia Li, Bart Thomee, Haojian Jin, and Jeff Yuan. 2016. Finding Weather Photos: Community-Supervised Methods for Editorial Curation of Online Sources. In *Proceedings of the 19th ACM Conference on Computer-Supported Cooperative Work & Social Computing.* ACM, 86–96.

74. Manya Sleeper, Justin Cranshaw, Patrick Gage Kelley, Blase Ur, Alessandro Acquisti, Lorrie Faith Cranor, and Norman Sadeh. 2013. I read my Twitter the next morning and was astonished: A conversational perspective on Twitter regrets. In *Proceedings of the SIGCHI Conference on Human Factors in Computing Systems.* ACM, 3277–3286.

75. Brian K Smith, Jeana Frost, Meltem Albayrak, and Rajneesh Sudhakar. 2006. Facilitating narrative medical discussions of type 1 diabetes with computer visualizations and photography. *Patient Education and Counseling* 64, 1 (2006), 313–321.

76. Rion Snow, Brendan O'Connor, Daniel Jurafsky, and Andrew Y Ng. 2008. Cheap and fast—but is it good?: evaluating non-expert annotations for natural language tasks. In *Proceedings of the conference on empirical methods in natural language processing*. Association for Computational Linguistics, 254–263.

77. Janet Sternberg. 2012. *Misbehavior in cyber places: The regulation of online conduct in virtual communities on the Internet*. Rowman & Littlefield.

78. John Suler. 2004. The online disinhibition effect. *Cyberpsychology & behavior* 7, 3 (2004), 321–326.

79. John R Suler and Wende L Phillips. 1998. The bad boys of cyberspace: Deviant behavior in a multimedia chat community. *CyberPsychology & Behavior* 1, 3 (1998), 275–294.

80. Bart Thomee, Benjamin Elizalde, David A Shamma, Karl Ni, Gerald Friedland, Douglas Poland, Damian Borth, and Li-Jia Li. 2016. YFCC100M: The new data in multimedia research. *Commun. ACM* 59, 2 (2016), 64–73.

81. Giorgos Tolias, Yannis Avrithis, and Hervé Jégou. 2015. Image Search with Selective Match Kernels: Aggregation Across Single and Multiple Images. *International Journal of Computer Vision* (2015), 1–15.

82. Giorgos Tolias, Ronan Sicre, and Hervé Jégou. 2016. Particular object retrieval with integral max-pooling of CNN activations. In *ICLR*.

83. Simon Tong and Edward Chang. 2001. Support vector machine active learning for image retrieval. In *Proceedings of the ninth ACM international conference on Multimedia*. ACM, 107–118.

84. Khoi-Nguyen Tran and Peter Christen. 2015. Cross-language learning from bots and users to detect vandalism on wikipedia. *IEEE Transactions on Knowledge and Data Engineering* 27, 3 (2015), 673–685.

85. Tumblr. 2016. "Tumblr Community Guidelines". (2016). `https://www.tumblr.com/policy/en/community`

86. Alfredo Vellido, José David Martín-Guerrero, and Paulo JG Lisboa. 2012. Making machine learning models interpretable.. In *ESANN*, Vol. 12. Citeseer, 163–172.

87. Jason Weston, Sumit Chopra, and Keith Adams. 2014. # TagSpace: Semantic embeddings from hashtags. (2014).

88. Elad Yom-Tov, Luis Fernandez-Luque, Ingmar Weber, and P Steven Crain. 2012. Pro-Anorexia and Pro-Recovery Photo Sharing: A Tale of Two Warring Tribes. *J Med Internet Res* (2012).

WritLarge: Ink Unleashed by Unified Scope, Action, & Zoom

Haijun Xia[1,2], Ken Hinckley[1], Michel Pahud[1], Xiao Tu[1], and Bill Buxton[1]
[1]Microsoft Research, Redmond, WA, United States, {kenh, mpahud, xiaotu, bibuxton:}@microsoft.com
[2]Dynamic Graphics Project Lab, University of Toronto, Canada, haijunxia@dgp.toronto.edu

ABSTRACT
WritLarge is a freeform canvas for early-stage design on electronic whiteboards with pen+touch input. The system aims to support a higher-level flow of interaction by 'chunking' the traditionally disjoint steps of *selection* and *action* into unified *selection-action phrases*. This holistic goal led us to address two complementary aspects:

- SELECTION, for which we devise a new technique known as the *Zoom-Catcher* that integrates pinch-to-zoom and selection in a single gesture for fluidly selecting and acting on content;

plus:

- ACTION, where we demonstrate how this addresses the combined issues of navigating, selecting, and manipulating content. In particular, the designer can transform select ink strokes in flexible and easily-reversible representations via *semantic*, *structural*, and *temporal* axes of movement that are defined as conceptual 'moves' relative to the specified content.

This approach dovetails zooming with lightweight specification of scope as well as the evocation of context-appropriate commands, at-hand, in a location-independent manner. This establishes powerful new primitives that can help to scaffold higher-level tasks, thereby unleashing the expressive power of ink in a compelling manner.

Author Keywords
electronic whiteboard; pen+touch; bimanual input; toolglass.

ACM Classification Keywords
H.5.2 [Information Interfaces and Presentation]: Input

INTRODUCTION
Electronic whiteboards remain surprisingly difficult to use in the context of creativity support and design. A key problem is that once a designer places strokes and reference images on a canvas, actually doing anything useful *with a subset of that content* involves numerous steps. Hence, ***scope***—that is, SELECTION of content—is a central concern, yet current techniques often require switching modes and encircling ink with a lengthy lasso, if not round-trips to the edge of the display [18,51]. Only then can the user take ACTION, such as to copy, refine, or re-interpret content.

Permission to make digital or hard copies of all or part of this work for personal or classroom use is granted without fee provided that copies are not made or distributed for profit or commercial advantage and that copies bear this notice and the full citation on the first page. Copyrights for components of this work owned by others than the author(s) must be honored. Abstracting with credit is permitted. To copy otherwise, or republish, to post on servers or to redistribute to lists, requires prior specific permission and/or a fee. Request permissions from Permissions@acm.org.
CHI 2017, May 06 - 11, 2017, Denver, CO, USA
Copyright is held by the owner/author(s). Publication rights licensed to ACM.
ACM 978-1-4503-4655-9/17/05…$15.00
DOI: http://dx.doi.org/10.1145/3025453.3025664.

Figure 1. *WritLarge* uses bimanual input to integrate *selection* by a multi-touch framing gesture with *action* via the pen.

Such is the stilted nature of selection and action in the digital world. But it need not be so. By contrast, consider an everyday manual task such as sandpapering a piece of woodwork to hew off its rough edges. Here, we use our hands to grasp and bring to the fore—that is, *select*—the portion of the work-object—the wood—that we want to refine. And because we are working with a tool—the sandpaper—the hand employed for this 'selection' sub-task is typically the non-preferred one, which skillfully manipulates the frame-of-reference [22] for the subsequent 'action' of sanding, a complementary sub-task articulated by the preferred hand.

Therefore, in contrast to the disjoint subtasks foisted on us by most interactions with computers, the above example shows how complementary manual activities lend a sense of flow that "chunks" [11] selection and action into a continuous *selection-action phrase* [27]. By manipulating the workspace, the off-hand shifts the context of the actions to be applied, while the preferred hand brings different tools to bear—such as sandpaper, file, or chisel—as necessary.

The main goal of *WritLarge*, then, is to demonstrate similar continuity of action for electronic whiteboards. This motivated free-flowing, close-at-hand techniques to afford unification of selection and action via bimanual pen+touch interaction. To address SELECTION, we designed a lightweight, integrated, and fast way for users to indicate scope, called the *Zoom-Catcher* (Fig. 1), as follows:

> *With the thumb and forefinger of the non-preferred hand, the user just **frames** a portion of the canvas.*

This sounds straightforward, and it is—from the user's perspective. But this simple reframing of pinch-to-zoom affords a transparent, toolglass-like palette—the Zoom-Catcher, manipulated by the nonpreferred hand—which floats above the canvas, and the ink strokes and reference images thereupon. The Zoom-Catcher elegantly integrates numerous steps: it dovetails with pinch-to-zoom, affording multi-scale interaction; serves as mode switch, input filter, and an illumination of a portion of the canvas—thereby doubling as a lightweight specification of scope; and once latched-in, it sets the stage for ACTION by evoking commands at-hand, revealing context-appropriate functions in a location-independent manner, where the user can then act on them with the stylus (or a finger).

Building from this key insight, our work contributes unified SELECTION and ACTION by bringing together the following:

- Lightweight specification of scope via the Zoom-Catcher.
- In a way that continuously dovetails with pinch-to-zoom.
- Thus affording unified, multi-scale selection and action with pen+touch, and both hands, in complementary roles.
- These primitives support flexible, interpretation-rich, and easily-reversible representations of content, with a clear mental model of **levels** spatially organized along ***semantic*, *structural*, and *temporal* axes of movement**.
- Our approach thereby unleashes many natural attributes of ink, such as the position, size, orientation, textual content, and implicit structure of handwriting.
- And in a way that leaves the user in complete control of *what* gets recognized—as well as *when* recognition occurs—so as not to break the flow of creative work [14].
- A preliminary evaluation of the system with users suggests the combination of zooming and selection in this manner works extremely well, and is self-revealing for most users.

The structure of the paper that follows is somewhat unusual because our goals are holistic, seeking to establish a new approach to unified selection and action through higher-level selection-action phrases, rather than (for example) following the formula of a classic technique paper focusing on just the selection step. At first, we focus on the Zoom-Catcher, unpacking its properties and detailing its design evolution in depth. In the latter half of the paper, we then switch gears and show how this foundation evokes a rich set of in-context commands close at-hand, particularly by transforming select ink strokes in easily-reversible representations along our semantic, structural, and temporal axes of movement. Collectively these contributions aim to reduce the impedance mismatch of human and technology, thus enhancing the interactional fluency between a creator's ink strokes and the resulting representations at their command.

AN EXAMPLE OF INK UNLEASHED—HOLY COW!

Figure 2 shows how our approach unleashes latent attributes of ink. The user just frames the desired handwriting with thumb and forefinger, and uses one of the radial menus thus revealed to move one step up our 'semantic' representational axis. The recognized text *with the location, point size, and baseline orientation intact* then appears on the canvas.

The user can just as easily back out of this representation, by stroking the radial menu in the reverse direction to move one level down the semantic axis—that is, to 'unrecognize' the text and revert to the original hand-drawn strokes. This is just one example of the flexibility of representation [23,54,71] and re-interpretation [58] afforded by *WritLarge*.

Note how the style of interaction afforded by this example—particularly the simplicity of expressing all of these attributes simultaneously through the ink itself—contrasts with much of current practice. Presentation software, for example, requires many steps: create a text box, place it approximately in the right place, size it, type in the text string, orient it, select the text, adjust the point size, and then re-position the rotated text box to its final desired location.

But *WritLarge* achieves this in fewer steps, and in a direct-at-hand manner. The Zoom-Catcher indicates what to recognize, and when to recognize it—all in a single unified selection-action phrase. The remarkable economy and continuity of gesture thus achieved harkens back to the dovetailing, and sense of flow, in our early motivating example of sandpapering rough edges off a piece of wood.

Figure 2. The *Zoom-Catcher* indicates an area of the canvas via the nonpreferred hand (Top). The user can then act on it with the preferred hand, such as to recognize handwriting (Bottom)—including position, point size, and orientation.

Next, we unpack the Zoom-Catcher in more depth, which will allow us to contrast its properties with Related Work.

ZOOM-CATCHER: UNIFIED SCOPE, ACTION & ZOOM

The Zoom-Catcher offers a new way to select multiple objects with the nonpreferred hand through multitouch, using a *framing gesture* that indicates the area to select by the relative orientation of thumb and forefinger. 'Framing' content in this manner is a naturally-occurring human behavior to focus attention and reference annotations to a portion of a page [30]. Yet to our knowledge, leveraging both the position and orientation of the off-hand to specify the scope of a selection on a large electronic whiteboard is novel.

While framing is a natural behavior, it posed an interesting design challenge because at the outset it seemed likely to conflict with pinch-to-zoom, which of course is also a two-finger gesture. But as we ultimately discovered, reconciling framing with pinch-to-zoom affords a novel unification, such that the Zoom-Catcher co-exists—and indeed is continuous with—pinch-to-zoom. The twist is that both *zoom* and *select* interpretations of the gesture exist simultaneously as the interaction gets underway. At any subtle hesitation while zooming, selection feedback starts to fade in. Users encounter this while navigating, and quickly grasp that it affords selection, thus leading them to discover this capability without further explanation. Or they can ignore it, and continue to zoom without difficulty.

That is the high-level view. But the Zoom-Catcher is the result of careful iterative design that puts several desirable properties into play all at once, in a way not fully realized before. We can unpack these properties (P0–P12) as follows:

P0. ***Grounded in Inking as the neutral state.*** By default, the pen lays ink on the canvas, making writing and sketching the foundation of the creative experience.

Yet, when user brings *the nonpreferred hand* to task, our system unifies selection, action, and zoom in a way that:

P1. ***Leverages a natural human gesture***, two-finger framing, to focus attention on an area [30]; which in turn

P2. ***Dovetails with pinch-to-zoom***, its electronic heir-apparent, such that framing and zooming interpretations of the gesture are *simultaneously* active; and

P3. ***Self-reveals by piggybacking on a familiar gesture,*** which leads users to discover the Zoom-Catcher while navigating the canvas; and by this unification also

P4. ***Affords multi-scale interaction,*** which allows users to access large, small, or out-of-reach areas alike.

These approachable transactions get users started without explanation. The Zoom-Catcher then reveals its presence and affords interaction with select content via:

P5. ***Fading in a semi-transparent palette***, which resembles a shadowy projection of the cleft between thumb and forefinger, and floats above the canvas; and thus

P6. ***Illuminates objects in an* orientable *canvas region***, making them 'pop' from the surround, and resulting in

P7. ***A lightweight scoping tool*** with clear feedback of the objects selected.

These attributes put the scaffolding in place for the higher-level actions we set out to support. The Zoom-Catcher then:

P8. ***Evokes commands close at-hand***, yielding location-independent interaction [51], such that the interface

P9. ***Reveals only context-appropriate functions***, with multiple radial menus that support further interesting functionalities (as discussed later in this paper); and also

P10. ***Provides a nonpreferred-hand, spatial mode switch*** that is spring-loaded by muscular tension; wherein

P11. ***An input filter acts on strokes from the stylus***, or subsequent preferred-hand touches, in a 'gesturing through the looking glass' manner [7]; and finally

P12. ***Always returns to the neutral state on release of the nonpreferred hand,*** such that the entire spring-loaded transaction—despite its richness—comes full circle, and the user is back to the primary task of design-sketching.

Some aspects of these properties (P0-P12) do appear in previous systems. However, the Zoom-Catcher is the first technique to articulate and bring together all of these benefits for fluid pen+touch interaction on electronic whiteboards.

RELATED WORK

WritLarge is a creativity support tool that draws from interaction techniques for ink, and large displays. Framing as a gesture to indicate scope—as well as integrated commands, modes, selection, and action—are all important ingredients.

Creativity Support Tools for Design

A key challenge for design and creativity support tools lies in balancing the rapid capture of ideas at the speed of thought, versus the ability to explore and refine those ideas once captured [10,26,61,63]. The former is well-suited to analog, freeform techniques such as writing and sketching with a stylus. The latter often involves adding structure, or semantics, as reinterpretations of the underlying freeform ink strokes and reference images [26,58,61]. What is needed are multiple interpretation-rich representations that allow one to back up, reinterpret moves, and shift directions [23,54,71]. Yet added structure (i.e. spatial rearrangement, recognition) can be harmful [39,62] unless "smart but silent" [34]—that is, applied selectively, and fully under the user's control.

Interaction Techniques for Ink and Large Displays

Electronic whiteboards often transform digital ink, such as to group, list, or tabulate. Avoiding fixed locations for interface elements is a critical issue often tied up with mode switching, gestures, and the interface metaphor itself [4,48,51].

Tivoli [46] organizes ink via lasso selection, long a go-to method for ink [12]. Yet drawing lassos [21,45] is tedious for large or hard-to-reach areas. Harpoon's velocity-sensitive area cursors offer one strategy to address this [41]. Automatic clustering of strokes, as in Suggero [43] and cLuster [49], offer another. But all of these approaches still rely on the pen, and thus the preferred hand, to select objects. This reliance on the pen serializes SELECTION: it adds an extra step that can't overlap with ACTION. By contrast, our approach of *framing with the non-preferred hand* unifies selection and action into the same continuous workflow.

However, we must also point out that the Zoom-Catcher is not intended for complex selections with low target cohesiveness; this is an intentional trade-off that optimizes for the common case of straightforward selections in our whiteboard scenarios. The Zoom-Catcher thus affords an intermediate level of control between lassoing—which is slow—and tapping on objects—which relies on the system to properly group ink marks. Our way of indicating general areas via multi-touch thus complements other approaches.

Musink [65] is an ink-based tool for music composers that has many synergies with our work, particularly in the way it lets users specify multiple levels of interpretation, and how it uses multiple representations (to move interaction between digital-paper and computer). Another strategy is *translucent patches* [35] that define persistent areas, via lasso selection, that can layer recognition behaviors. Flatland [47] similarly uses 'segments' that expand as the user writes, but this requires users to be constantly aware of (and potentially distracted by) how their strokes are being segmented. NotePals [15] supports sharing notes to a group, while TEAM STORM [23] affords working with multiple ideas in parallel across whiteboard and tablet. *WritLarge* supports similar capabilities but shows how selecting and working with portions of an electronic canvas might be made more fluent by combining pen and touch, with both right hand and left.

The Spotlight [32] illuminates large areas (P6) from a distance, but does *not* select, nor integrate subsequent actions; it focuses the attention of others on an area. Drag-and-pop highlights a distant target [3], but it is an indirect way of pointing—not a selection method. The Vacuum explores selection and manipulation of remote objects [5], but does not combine multiple-object selection with action. And while various refinements of zooming have been suggested (e.g. [2,18,50]), none dovetail with selection. Indeed, the Zoom-Catcher sidesteps many issues of action at-a-distance, or indication of large areas, through integration of pan and zoom continuously within selection itself.

Uses of Multi-Touch, and Framing, to Indicate Scope

People manipulate paper with the nonpreferred hand while writing [22]. Framing the work-area between thumb and index finger is a natural "behavior to focus attention" [30] on part of the page. VIDEOPLACE [36] and ActiveDesk [9,13] offered early examples of grasping an object in this manner.

In Hands-on-Math [72], users frame part of a page to fold it; the nonpreferred hand indicates scope for *one* at-hand action, *fold*. GatherReader [28] also uses framing to select part of a page—partly echoing some of our design properties (P5,P6 and P10-12), but critically not the ability to indicate scope in an *orientable* manner (P7) to allow coming at a desired selection from different suitable angles, nor evocation of commands (P8-9). The eTab [6] acts as an at-hand input filter that reveals context-appropriate commands (P8-11), but requires use of an additional tangible device on top of a tablet. Our approach extends and generalizes such benefits through a novel unification with pinch-to-zoom (P2-P4).

Pen+touch [22] uses a framing gesture with the nonpreferred hand to hold down a *single object*, such as a photo. To include multiple objects, the user must tap-select them in sequence or resort to lasso selection. By contrast *WritLarge* is consistent with *pen+touch = new tools* but shows a much richer way of indicating a scope containing multiple objects.

Integration of Commands, Modes, Selection, and Action

ToolGlass [7] provides a mobile palette, manipulated via trackball and nonpreferred hand. The preferred hand then 'clicks through' a tool to apply it to the object below. This integrates the two actions. However, the 'scope' is limited to a click—a single point—rather than area-selection via multi-touch. And the inputs are indirect—with trackball and mouse—as opposed to direct—with pen and touch on the display itself. T3 extends the toolglass paradigm to pen input, with a puck for the nonpreferred hand, and even a thumb-wheel for interleaving zoom with other interactions [38]; indeed, T3's use of bimanual input and its holistic approach to designing interactions are foundational to our work. However, it remains unclear how to achieve this kind of fluidity with direct touch (and pen), as opposed to T3's indirect setting using desktop digitizers without touch.

A single pen gesture can combine multiple actions, including selection, action, and direct manipulation [1,37]. Gestures convey an additional benefit when they select an object *and* evoke an action (P8) close at-hand [7,37,51]. However, overburdening a pen stroke complicates gestures and may require a *delimiter* [27] as an extra step. Furthermore, because a single modality (the pen) provides all of these functions, mode-switching also becomes necessary [42,60].

Holding a spring-loaded mode with the non-preferred hand [55,60,64] is a fast way to switch modes [40,42]. While this approach can scale to more than one mode [29,57], and to multi-touch [24,67,68], the literature offers few examples of techniques that combine modes with selection, action, manipulation—and now zoom. This consideration hints at a deeper concern, namely that 'selection' is oft-treated as a fundamental operation, with its own mode. For example, Foley et al. [19] list *Select* as one of six elemental tasks. But selection is a sub-task: it comprises only part of the user's task-flow, a prelude to *action* on the indicated scope. The higher-level task is a compound one of *selection-action*.

Our objective is to obviate 'selection' as a separate mode, and extra step, by integrating this sub-task into nonpreferred-hand mode switching *and* the performance of the action itself. The result is a continuous motor-sensory act that takes place at this higher conceptual level via the Zoom-Catcher.

This resonates with chunking [11], and phrasing of selection-action [7,27,38], for pen+touch in particular [8,24,28,30,44]. We show how this can foster a new approach to creativity support on electronic whiteboards, and in particular our analysis articulates numerous desirable properties (P0-P12) that we then proceed to integrate under a common umbrella.

WRITLARGE: FREEFORM CREATIVITY SUPPORT

To explore the potential of these directions we implemented a creativity support tool that runs on a large electronic whiteboard, the 84" Microsoft Surface Hub, which supports both pen and multi-touch. The same application runs on the Surface Pro 4 tablet, which also has pen+touch.

Overall UI Architecture and Metaphor

In accordance with our desire to provide a freeform creativity support tool for early-stage design, ideation, and informal discussions, inking is the center of the experience. By default *WritLarge* simply acts as a whiteboard, where bringing the pen to the screen leaves ink. The user is free to sketch, mark-up, and handwrite however desired without worrying about accidentally triggering pen gestures or recognition features.

The basic unit of work in *WritLarge* is a drawing canvas. The user can pan and zoom the canvas, but canvases are delineated into individual screens. The metaphor is thus similar to a large paper flip-chart, with subsequent sheets (canvases) arranged horizontally. If the user zooms out far enough, the series becomes visible, in a slide-sorter type of view. This allows the user to quickly grab a clean whiteboard and storyboard a sequence of ideas. Canvases themselves are selectable with the Zoom-Catcher and may thereby be duplicated or rearranged through direct-manipulation. A horizontal swipe flips through the sequence of 'charts.'

The application has no permanently visible UI. The entire screen is devoted to the user's content on the canvas. The canvas supports ink strokes as well as freeform layout of reference images. All actions arise from the canvas itself, through the framing gesture and evocation of the Zoom-Catcher. We do not use any barrel-buttons on the pen. To act on ink strokes and other objects, the user brings the Zoom-Catcher over them with the nonpreferred hand, and gestures through the semi-transparent palette or its associated radial menus. Because *WritLarge* achieves this solely using pinch-to-zoom, rather than relying on an out-of-band gesture or button press, our approach has potential utility for many other applications. Also, as a proof-of-concept for small-group design sessions, a single tablet (also running *WritLarge)* can pair and share selected content with the Hub.

Implementation

WritLarge is a Universal Windows App (UWA) built on Windows 10 with (simultaneous) pen and multi-touch reported through standard system events. We use the built-in Windows handwriting recognition components since such algorithms are not our focus. As such, our recognition results of course aren't perfect—but the user may easily back out of them by reverting to ink strokes. Graphics effects and feedback are rendered using the Win2D SDK. The Surface Hub and Surface Pro 4 communicate over wireless TCP.

DESIGN OF THE ZOOM-CATCHER

So far we've discussed a number of properties exhibited by the Zoom-Catcher, but we have not yet detailed its design. Of particular importance is the simultaneity of selection and zooming, and some of the considerations and alternatives we iteratively worked through to arrive at this design.

As a starting point, we envisioned transactions such as the *Holy cow!* of Fig. 2. But this raised two key design questions:

1. *What is the scope* of strokes to recognize, or re-structure?
2. *When is recognition triggered*—and how can the user indicated other desired shifts between representations?

To bring good answers to these questions and make the resulting transactions fast and fluent for users, we started exploring ways to use the non-preferred hand to select areas in a lightweight way, and particularly via two-finger framing [30]. We realized immediately this would collide with pinch-to-zoom, but our objective was to first see how the interaction felt (through informal pilot tests and expert opinion), and determine whether it was even worth pursuing.

Dwell Time to Distinguish Selection?

One of the first things we experimented with was triggering selection based on dwell time. Touching down and holding the framing gesture in place for a fixed timeout triggered selection. But, after trying several different time-outs ranging from 1500, 1000, 750, 350, or even 150ms we arrived at the conclusion that any choice of time-out interval would raise problems. The very short time-outs tended to trigger by accident while the user was thinking, or fine-tuning a pinch-to-zoom—and yet even then, they slowed down interaction when selection was desired. But longer time-outs were annoying because they slowed selection to a crawl—echoing previous results showing that dwell time is an inefficient mode-switching technique [42]. Not satisfied, we kept searching for other approaches.

Two Fingers to Zoom, Three Fingers to Select?

We also tried making pinch-to-zoom vs. selection a predictable and learnable manual skill, based on the number of fingers brought to the canvas. We reserved two fingers for zoom, and instead used three fingers to switch to area-based selection. This avoided the ambiguity of a time-out, but switching between two- and three-finger postures stifled the interaction in other ways. It still wasn't very fast. It didn't feel comfortable. And it lost much of the natural appeal of framing with thumb and forefinger. After a pilot test with four users, one participant summed it up as follows: "*I don't like [three finger framing], because I have to always remember three finger is framing, and sometimes I do use three fingers to drag the canvas or zoom it. I also don't like that I always have to keep all the fingers down to control the region. It felt pretty stiff to rotate with three fingers.*"

Speculative Execution of both Zooming and Selection

Eventually we realized that pinch-to-zoom and selection aren't necessarily mutually incompatible, so we asked: *Why not perform both?* This is reminiscent of *speculative execution* in pipelined microprocessor design, as well as handling multiple inputs with uncertainty [59]. This insight led us to consider a design where the interface proceeds with *both* selection *and* zooming interpretations of a two-finger gesture, simultaneously.

At first, the pinch-to-zoom interpretation of two-finger gestures dominates selection: panning and zooming responds immediately, and initially no selection feedback is shown. That is, the "semi-transparent palette" of the Zoom-Catcher, per property (P5), is still fully faded out, and invisible. But if the user hesitates while zooming, we start to fade in *only the illumination of the selected objects (P6)*—the highlighting feedback—for all objects contained fully within the selection region, in a nuanced and understated way. And if pinch-zoom motion resumes, all selection feedback fades out fully.

But not until the user holds the framing gesture stationary—defined as less than 10mm of finger movement over a 500ms window—does the selection feedback (and radial menus) fade in fully. At this point the Zoom-Catcher "latches in" and the semi-transparent palette of (P5) appears as in Figure 2.

However, critically, the user does *not* have to wait 500ms to act on the highlighted objects. Since the radial menus start fading in with the object highlighting, the user can short-circuit the fade-in transition by touching down on a menu immediately—or by grabbing the objects, such as to drag them (as a unit) to a new position. Indeed, from the instant two fingers touch down on the canvas, the invisible 'selection area' is active, and can be acted upon by the user. As users acquire skill with the technique, they can learn to anticipate this, and interact without waiting for the timeout.

Once the Zoom-Catcher latches in, the pan/zoom interpretation is no longer active and the user can move, reorient, and adjust the angle subtended by the Zoom-Catcher without disturbing the canvas. To return to pan/zoom, the user must lift their nonpreferred hand—which dismisses the Zoom-Catcher—and then reengage.

This approach allows zooming to be freely combined with selection highlighting (P2,P4) until the Zoom-Catcher latches in. The user can zoom in close to select a single ink stroke (Figure 3a), or zoom far away to select large areas or objects that would otherwise be out-of-reach (Figure 3b).

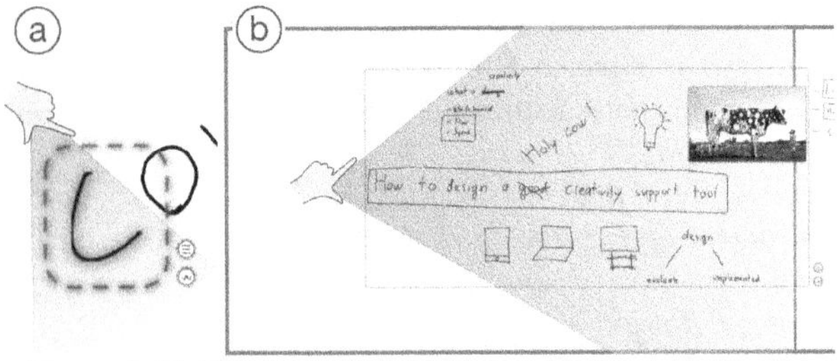

Figure 3. Unification of multi-scale selection with the Zoom-Catcher allows the user to access (a) small objects by zooming in, and (b) large or out-of-reach areas by zooming out.

Nuances of the Selection Feedback

We carefully designed the visualization of the semi-transparent palette to foster its perception as a natural extension of the hand. Rather than a sharp-angled cone for the selection area (e.g. as used by the ActiveDesk [9,13]), we give it a soft shape that echoes the cleft between thumb and forefinger (P5)—thereby fitting into the hand, so that it feels like a projection of one's reach. We also use this rounded area at the apex of the palette as a place where the user can tuck away objects and carry them 'in the fold' of the thumb-forefinger cleft. This serves as a temporary clipboard known as *The Fold*, discussed in more detail later.

The palette is rendered with a semi-transparent gradient that trails off with the distance from the apex, much as the light cast by a flashlight beam fades away. This fits the "illumination" metaphor (P6) were trying to establish and also lends the selection area a soft-edged feel, in keeping with the informal, relaxed use-cases of the application itself.

To highlight objects in the selection, we render them with a bright-red outer glow. We also show a dashed-line roundtangle around all the selected objects, with two radial menus at the lower right. We render all these objects *on top of* the semi-transparent palette so that they visually pop (in contrast to other objects on the canvas that may be nearby, but not included in the selection).

State Machine for the Zoom-Catcher

We implement the Zoom-Catcher as a simple state machine (Figure 4). The interaction starts in the *Neutral* state, with zero or one finger on the display, and transitions to *Speculating*—with both pinch-to-zoom and selection active—as soon as a second finger touches down. When selection feedback starts to fade in during the *Speculating* state, it does so proportional to the system's confidence in the degree of movement vs. hesitation. Once the user holds the framing posture stable for long enough—or the user short-circuits the fade-in animation by engaging directly with the selected area, or the radial menus—the *Framing* interpretation latches in.

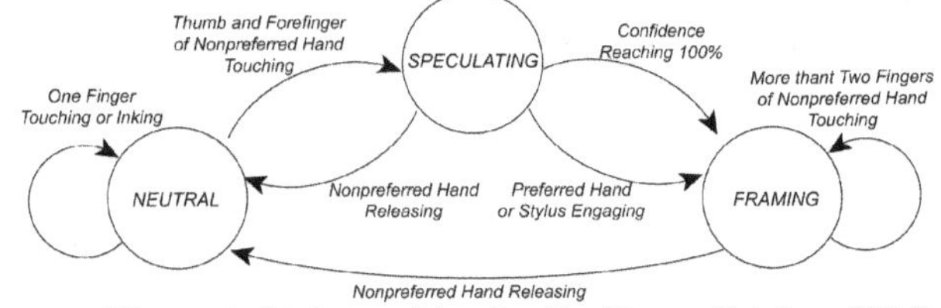

Figure 4. State machine for the Zoom-Catcher. While 'speculating,' both pinch-to-zoom and the proportional fading of selection feedback are simultaneously active.

Flexibility of Posture and Adjustment of the Framing Gesture

Note that in the *Speculating* and *Framing* states, more than two fingers can rest on the canvas if desired. This relaxes the posture required, and makes the gesture more flexible, forgiving, and natural because it doesn't depend on a specific number of fingers [70]. In our own use we find this helps to reduce arm fatigue because the whole hand can rest comfortably on the screen. This flexibility applies to zooming, selection, and the Zoom-Catcher itself.

Adjusting the Selection Area

By re-orienting thumb and forefinger the user can steer the Zoom-Catcher around, such as to come at a cluttered area from another angle where it is easier to select only the objects desired (e.g. Figure 3a). The distance between fingers also controls the angle subtended by the Zoom-Catcher, making it easy to cast it wide, or focus it into a narrow beam, depending on the surround of other objects nearby. Currently, we only support right-handers, so the Zoom-Catcher initially projects its selection region to the right. We plan to add a setting for left-handed users in the near future.

By default the Zoom-Catcher extends 1/5 of the way across the canvas. If it is necessary to adjust this, the user can simply swipe the Zoom-Catcher with the preferred hand to directly adjust its extent. The user just touches down and drags the semi-transparent palette to modify it (Figure 5).

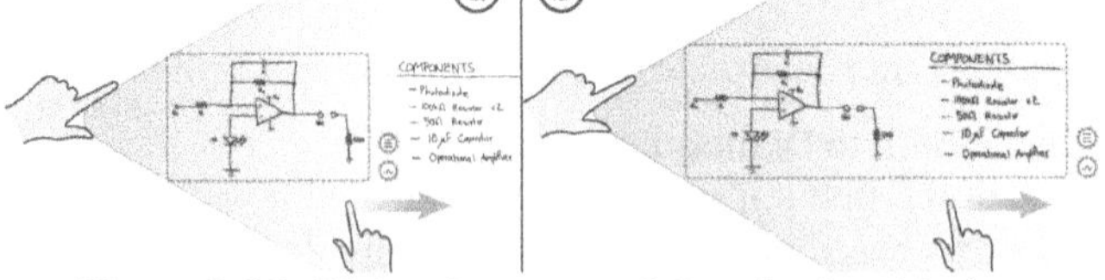

Figure 5. Modifying the extent of the selection (a) via a bimanual swipe with the preferred hand (b).

Framing Region as Mode Switch and Input Filter
The framing region also serves as a nonpreferred-hand mode switch (P10) that allows the user to gesture-through the semi-transparent palette, thus integrating a further interesting capability into this simple hand posture. Pen strokes within the palette are interpreted as a gesture, rather than leaving ink. For example, the user can lasso specific ink strokes as a fallback for refining the selection in tricky cases (e.g. for dense areas of the canvas). Likewise, touches within this region are treated differently. For example, the user can drag the selected ink strokes to a new position on the canvas, or dab a finger on an image to blend its colors. Hence, the framing region doubles as an input filter (P11) that modifies the interpretation of pen or touch gestures in this area.

Evoking Context-Appropriate Commands Close At-Hand
To support transition to ACTION, the Zoom-Catcher evokes commands at-hand (P8). In addition to gesturing-through the palette (such as lasso selection with the pen), two radial menus that reveal only context-appropriate functions (P9) fade in with the selection, and appear at its lower right. These are the *Actions Menu* (Fig. 6, top) and the *Representations Menu* (Fig. 6, bottom). Note the user need not wait for these menus to fully fade-in before accessing their functions.

The *Actions Menu* includes four commands: *Duplicate*, *Share*, *Search*, and *The Fold*. *Duplicate* allows a downward swipe on the menu to copy the selection and place it in a single uninterrupted movement [27,37,53]. *Search* performs a web image search from the selected phrase, while *Share* allows passing select content to a collaborator via a paired (co-located) tablet. We'll further detail *The Fold* shortly.

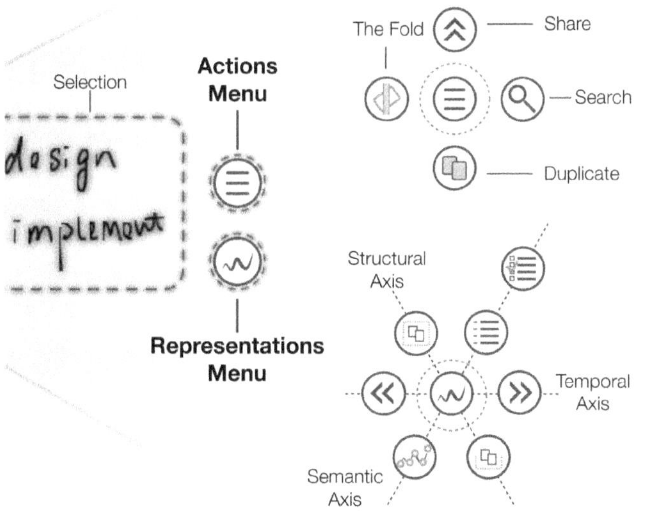

Figure 6. Exploded view of radial menus on selection. (a) The *Actions Menu* (top) always contains generic *Share, Search, Duplicate,* and *Fold* commands. (b) the *Representations Menu* (bottom) provides spatial, temporal, and semantic axes of movement defined as conceptual moves relative to the content.

The *Representations Menu* is also radial. It encapsulates three conceptual axes of movement: *semantic*, *structural*, and *temporal*. These conceptual axes offer a key contribution because they afford facile re-interpretation of the selected objects in a variety of ways, including 'un-interpreting' moves in a manner analogous to a local undo operation. As we will show, this richness of expression complements the at-hand and in-context nature of the Zoom-Catcher, and thereby demonstrates some benefits of more holistically phrasing together *selection* and *action* in *WritLarge*.

The Fold: An At-Hand Place to Tuck Things Away
"The Fold" is a special area at the apex of the Zoom-Catcher's semi-transparent palette where the user can tuck objects for later use. This serves as a lightweight clipboard for multiple objects. But unlike Fix-and-Float [56], the Attic [16], Toolspaces [52], or Pocket [28]—all of which require stashing objects at a particular area of the screen, such as the bottom edge—the Fold is always at hand, and therefore supports this capability in a location-independent manner.

From the Actions Menu, Selecting *The Fold* animates the selection into the curved apex of the Zoom-Catcher. When the user later makes the framing gesture again, any items in the Fold are visible and can be dragged out one-by-one. This is convenient for transporting objects long distances, or across canvases. And by zooming out, entire canvases (even multiple canvases) can be selected and pulled into the Fold, which makes it easy to storyboard alternative sequences.

Summary of the Zoom-Catcher
As we have seen, the Zoom-Catcher integrates quite a few capabilities, but it is important not to lose sight that from the user's perspective, it is astonishingly simple. One simply brings thumb and forefinger to screen and nearby objects light up. Its design carefully integrates numerous desirable properties (P0-P12). Yet by tight integration and continuity of action, they all essentially collapse into a single step that follows from the familiar gesture of pinch-to-zoom.

With this foundation firmly in place, we now show some interesting ways that *WritLarge* leverages this powerful scoping tool. In particular, it affords a user experience with an unusually flexible notion of moves between multiple representations, arranged along three conceptual axes of movement: semantic, structural, and temporal.

REPRESENTATIONAL AXES OF MOVEMENT
We argued earlier that creativity support tools can benefit from flexible moves among multiple interpretation-rich representations. This affords the back-and-forth re-interpretation typical of many design, creation, and collaborative ideation scenarios [26,58,61,63] where one wishes to nimbly explore a variety of alternatives—or multiple ideas in parallel [23,54,71].

WritLarge achieves this through *three conceptual axes of movement* that are organized into *levels*. These axes include:

- **Semantic**: the *meaning* that the system ascribes to the selected objects. The default semantic, of course, is that of the ink stroke. But the semantics can be elevated to recognize text, or to identify list structure—as well as drop down a level, to the individual points of the stroke.

- **Structural**: the spatial arrangement of the objects, which can be freeform (i.e. no structure), grouped, or arranged in a grid. Objects in a structure revert to their original arrangement if the user drops down to the freeform level.
- **Temporal**: the time-ordering of the objects, which allows scrubbing back and forth in time to see (for example) the selected ink strokes in a previous state of completion.

Each of these axes may offer multiple gradations of representation. The user can progressively add formality and structure to a representation by moving ***up a level***, or revert to a less-structured representation by moving ***down a level*** in the opposite direction. Hence, adding different types of structure takes on a spatial metaphor that is well-suited to "the intelligent use of space" [33], and it furthermore makes the notion of reversing course intuitive by expressing this as a simple movement in the opposite direction.

While one can envision a very wide range of functionalities along these three axes, as a technology probe [31] and proof of concept, *WritLarge* at present explores a small number of levels for each axis. However, exercising restraint on the number of operations possible also helps to afford our simple spatial arrangement of these features into linear axes that offer just a few levels. While this approach might not scale to a much larger number of representations, going too far in terms of adding features and complexity would move *WritLarge* away from being the freeform creativity support tool that it is, and closer to a full-blown "computer program" and the burdens of formality [62] that tend to come along with that. As such, we chose to favor keeping things simple.

Representations as 'Patches'

The user can gradually instill or remove representations from content on the canvas. Moving up a representational level creates a new type of object, which is inserted on the canvas in place of the lower-level objects. These behave much like *patches* [35,47]: they filter input events, allowing objects to interpret pen and touch inputs in a way that suits the data type involved. This adds to the richness of techniques available.

The Semantic Axis

The semantic axis of movement is arranged diagonally on the Representations Menu from lower left, to upper right. It supports semantics at the level of points, ink strokes, recognized text, lists, checkboxes, diagram nodes, and tables.

Note that the levels available depend on the selection. Reference images, for example, currently only support two levels: the image itself, or dropping down a semantic level to the pixels, which allows a small set of image-editing operations. And for ink strokes, the *list* semantic is only available if the standard Windows handwriting recognizer can extract a list structure from the selected strokes. Likewise, the *diagram node* semantic only applies to handwriting that is circled or surrounded by a hand-drawn box. As stated earlier, our focus is not on the recognition technology itself; that is not our contribution here. Rather, it is the fluid and simple way in which we can surface this variety of capabilities on the scope indicated by the user.

From Strokes to Recognized Text

Zoom-catching a short handwritten phrase and moving up one semantic level leads to our early motivating *Holy cow!* example (Fig. 2) that recognizes not only the text itself, but also preserves the position, point size, and orientation of handwritten strokes. But by selecting the recognized text and dropping down a semantic level, the user can revert to the original ink strokes to make corrections or add a few words. This reversal of representations—essentially, a localized undo function [25] that operates only on the selection—is extremely simple to express in *WritLarge*, yet demonstrates a capability rarely encountered in inking applications.

From List to Diagram

If the recognizer detects a list structure in the zoom-caught strokes, the list representation becomes available on the semantic axis. The system provides feedback that this semantic is available by changing the icon at the center of the Representations Menu. Moving up a semantic level then recognizes the text and formats it as a bulleted list. The user can drag individual list items around with a finger to re-order them, which shows an example of how the 'patch' can filter input events. Similarly, if the user moves up one more level to the checkbox representation, a pen stroke can check off items as the user completes them, for example.

From Hand-drawn Grids, to Tables, and Back Again

WritLarge also includes a simple heuristic for recognizing a hand-drawn grid of rows and columns as a formatted table. If the selection includes such a grid, the table representation becomes available along the semantic axis and the user can move up a level to recognize it. Strokes drawn across the formatted table add new rows or columns. But rather than offering a complex UI for merging cells, for example, the user can instead drop down to the semantic level of the points making up the ink strokes, use the pen's eraser to remove divisions, and then move back up to the table level to re-recognize it (Fig. 7). Handwriting on top of a table cell is automatically recognized as text.

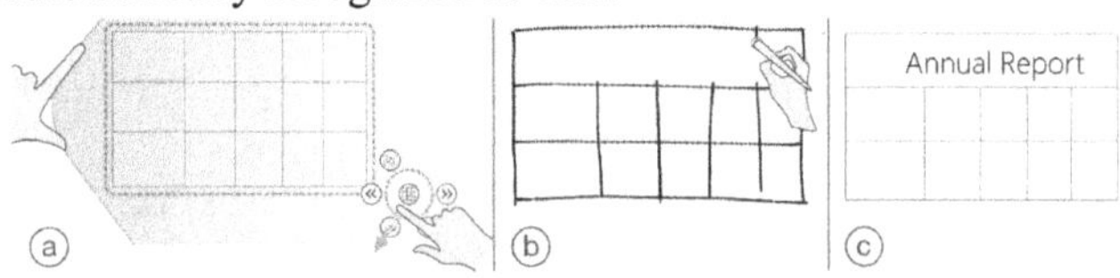

Figure 7. (a) Moving a recognized table down to the points level (b) allows editing the strokes, such as to merge cells. (c) Handwriting on tables is immediately recognized as text.

The Structural Axis

By default, objects such as ink strokes or reference images are treated at the *freeform* level—that is, without any inherent structure. Moving up the structural axis affords a number of spatial rearrangements of the selected objects.

Grouping Objects and Arranging in Grids

Moving up one structural level groups the selected objects. This does not change their visual appearance, but allows them to subsequently be directly manipulated as a unit. Swiping one further level up from the group representation rearranges the objects in a fixed grid (Fig 8). Once arranged in the grid, the user can drag items between grid positions to re-order them. Pen strokes drawn on the grid snap to the grid positions as well. Dropping back down to the freeform level reverts the objects to their original spatial arrangement. And of course, the user can intermingle semantic and structural shifts of representation to achieve various effects (see video).

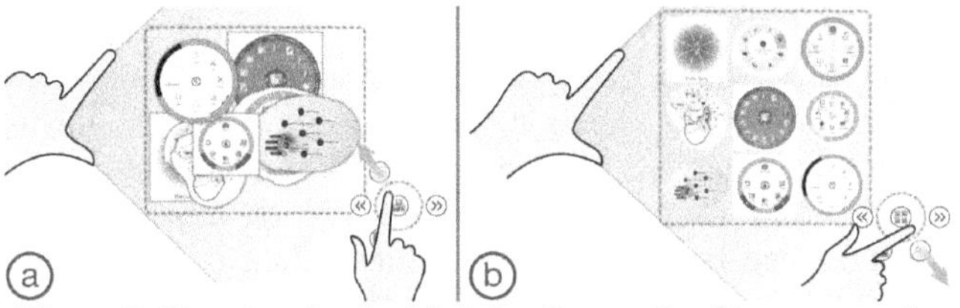

Figure 8. Structural axis. (a) A freeform pile of images can be reorganized into a grid layout by moving up the structural axis. (b) Dropping back down one level of structure reverts to the original freeform layout.

The Temporal Axis

The temporal axis is easy to explain but rich in capability. It provides an easily expressed notion of pulling a particular area of the canvas back in time, essentially serving as a local undo function, scoped to a region readily indicated by the Zoom-Catcher. The user simply scrubs forward and back—left and right from the Representations Menu—to roll back their ideas in time (Fig. 9). Note that this is articulated through continuous sliding, and does not require repetitive swiping motions to move further along the temporal axis.

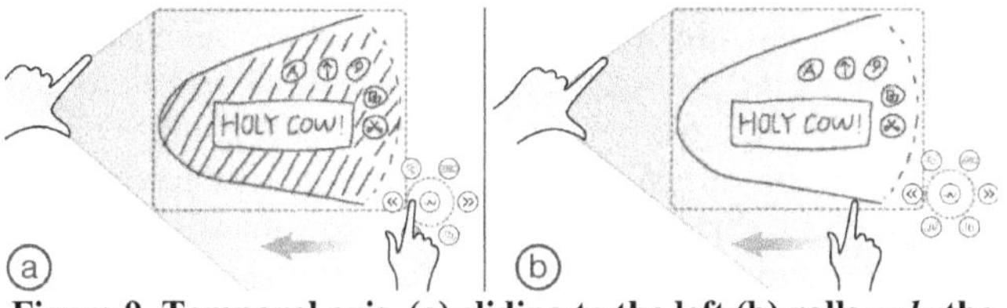

Figure 9. Temporal axis. (a) sliding to the left (b) rolls *only* the content in scope back to a previous state.

PRELIMINARY EVALUATION WITH TEST USERS

We conducted an informal evaluation to gain feedback from participants about our interaction techniques. We were particularly interested in how users would discover and use the Zoom-Catcher, their reactions to the four conceptual axes of movement, and whether users would feel that *WritLarge* affords a continuous and fluid flow of ink-based creation.

Participants and Procedure

We recruited 8 participants (4 female) aged between 24-32 years. All had used touch devices for at least 3 years. Before being introduced to the interaction techniques, participants were asked to briefly explain their ongoing work to the experimenter by inking using *WritLarge* on an 84" Microsoft Surface Hub. This allowed us to introduce the interaction techniques with participant-created content. The study focused on the use of the Zoom-Catcher, as well as the *semantic* and *structural* axes, as we felt those were the most provocative—and in need of user feedback. After trying each technique, participants filled out a questionnaire, and responded to a 10-15 minute interview. The study took ~1hr.

Results

Results are reported in a 7-point Likert scale with 1 labelled "strongly disagree" and 7 labelled "strongly agree".

Discoverability of Zoom-Catcher

As the Zoom-Catcher layers a new interpretation onto pinch-to-zoom, we sought to explore whether participants would discover this. Once participants finished inking on the canvas, they were asked to manipulate the canvas with their hands. All participants were able to activate and discover the Zoom-Catcher, as visual feedback starts to fade in when more than one finger touches the screen. All participants were able to immediately associate the interaction's purpose with selection because of the visual feedback.

At this point, participant behavior diverged. Five participants continued moving their fingers to manipulate the scope, as our design intended. The other three released their fingers, thinking this would lock in the selection, and then tried to touch the screen again. This suggests that adding a way to pin the selection in place—perhaps by pressing harder [20]—would be interesting to try. Furthermore, 6/8 participants discovered that they could directly manipulate the selected content with their preferred hand, such as to drag ink strokes to a new location on the canvas. Overall, this validates that piggybacking the Zoom-Catcher on "framing" and the familiar pinch-to-zoom gesture (as in properties P1-P3) afforded self-revelation of its core capabilities.

Scope-to-Select with Zoom-Catcher

Participants responded very positively to using the framing gesture to select content. They found the technique easy to learn (four 7/7 ratings, the rest 6/7). Participants responded to "I could use this technique (framing to select content) to quickly select the content I wanted" with four 7/7, three 6/7, and one 5/7. Participants acknowledged that "*most of the time you don't need the granularity of a lasso to select objects* and *forcing people to go around and do the lasso is just painful.*" With Zoom-Catcher, they only had to "*put the two fingers there and just get it.*" The advantages of zoom-catching over lasso selection was most salient when selecting a large area: "*I just kind of shrink it, zoom it out, and then select it.*" This further validates that our design successfully allowed the participants to dovetail pinch-to-zoom with selection as intended; users perceived no conflict.

Participants also reported the *"arc-radius model"* allowed "*an intuitive feel how it's gonna appear, even without explicitly knowing beforehand and seeing it on the screen.*" This shows that users could successfully anticipate the selection region, and plan their actions accordingly, even before the selection feedback fully faded in. Participants also felt that, despite its simplicity, the Zoom-Catcher covered most of their selection needs well. They also appreciated our inclusion of lasso selection as a fallback for difficult cases.

Semantic and Structural Axes

Participants found changing representations by moving along the conceptual axes easy to learn. They rated both the semantic axis (one 7/7, six 6/7, and one 5/7) and the structural axis (four 7/7, three 6/7, and one 5/7) fairly highly. Participants liked the ability to easily reinterpret the content they created: "*I like that you can easily convert analog things to digital, and that the objects can have different levels of abstraction.*" They immediate saw the benefits of using the axes to "*prepare presentation, brainstorm, and help my design.*" As one participant described, "*sometimes when things are digitized, I would like to keep a copy of physical one, so that I can go back to the raw sketches and add more things to it. Your tool really has the potential to just let me to going back and forth from analog and digital.*"

The movement and feedback of the axes was also easy to understand; as one participant noted "*It's very intuitive. You don't even need to explain them to me. Are they standard?*" Participants who had used similar features in other applications found spatially organizing these capabilities in the axes "*makes much more sense than listing the commands out, as the axis movement matches what I have in mind.*"

Participants found the concept of axes was "*extensible and universal.*" As one participant noted, "*any idea, essentially, will start from something scratch and simple, and then you refine it and build upon it.*" Several participants felt that these capabilities held great promise, and encouraged further development of the concept, as they believed one "*can go very very far with it.*" But several participants did suggested showing *all* the levels available on each of the axes to make it easier to move directly to the level they wanted, especially "*if there are many levels associated with the selected content.*" Since the radial menu currently only shows adjacent levels, not all of them, the design could clearly benefit from enhancing the visibility of any additional levels.

Fluid Workflow and Maintenance of User Control

The overall workflow of the *WritLarge* application was well-received. Participants found framing with one hand, and executing actions with the other, "*played together very well*" and allowed working "*in a really fast way*; *it feels very natural and fast that I can use both of my hands; you don't even need to think about it.*" Participants also appreciated that the interface allowed them to "*always focus on sketching stuff*" by giving them full control of when and how the content should shift representations—if at all—making users feel "*more productive*" in the flow of creativity.

DISCUSSION

We have argued that to elevate the fluidity of whiteboard interaction, SELECTION should *not* be considered as an elemental task [19] that is a separate step (or mode, or tool), but rather should be regarded as part of a continuous "chunking" of manual activity that specifies a higher-level command—the ACTION. And, while we believe *WritLarge* provides a convincing demonstration this possibility, that is not to say that techniques cannot go further still in the quest for full unification as SELECTION-ACTION phrases.

One key issue is the manner in which the Zoom-Catcher emerges from the canvas, via speculative execution of both *select* and *zoom* interpretations of two-fingered gestures. Earlier, we motivated and justified this design in detail, and all evidence from our preliminary evaluation suggests it works extremely well. However, we have not yet established quantitatively how (or even *if*) this differs from a simple tap-and-hold gesture. We designed our fade-in such that expert users can short-circuit the animation, by immediately manipulating the selection, or targeting the radial menus even before they've fully faded in. But it is not yet clear to what extent users can take advantage of this to realize performance faster than a dwell time. Future work should probe this by subjecting variations of our technique to a "true cost" analysis of the mode-switching time [17,42].

A second issue is the way the Zoom-Catcher dovetails with zoom. Early on, one can adjust the zoom to afford multi-scale selection, but once the Zoom-Catcher latches in, zooming is no longer possible. It may be possible to enhance the fluidity of these transitions—in both directions—such as by using pressure, or perhaps other nuances of multi-touch.

Third, ideally the Zoom-Catcher should scale to a larger set of commands. We support a few gestures directly on the selection, but not as many as Pen+Touch [30], for example. And for most of our contextual actions, we resort to radial menus, which can only comfortably handle 8 commands. At present we have two such menus, and of course more could be added, but are there other approaches, such as those explored by the Hotbox [37] or HandMark [66]? And for that matter, although we believe having a small number of rich representations is a sweet spot in the design, we have not yet explored how far one might push this: how many more levels could be handled along these conceptually simple axes?

Fourth, and finally, it remains unclear how to adapt the Zoom-Catcher to multiple, collaborating users. Indeed, there may be opportunities to extend the representations we make available with a collaborative "social axis" as well, since social interaction plays such a key role in support of creativity [63]. Another key technical issue is identifying which user is touching the whiteboard, and with what hand, where wearable sensing (for example) may be helpful [69]. Also, zooming is a global mode that affects the entire canvas, so some way to handle zoom (such as a fisheye lens) that does not disrupt the other user's work is needed.

CONCLUSION AND FUTURE WORK

Taken as a whole, the design of *WritLarge* sought to open new vistas for freeform content on electronic whiteboards. The system achieves this in a unique way, using carefully crafted input techniques that afford unified scope, action, and zoom, with pen-plus-touch—and both hands—in natural and complementary roles. While much yet remains to be done to extend and prove out this approach, the results so far appear quite promising. Our hope is that these contributions can help to reduce the impedance mismatch between the creator and their strokes on the canvas, thus bringing the rich, actionable, and flexible representations of *ink unleashed* readily to hand.

RIGHTS FOR FIGURES

Figures 1-9 © Haijun Xia, 2016.

REFERENCES

1. Anand Agarawala and Ravin Balakrishnan. 2006. Keepin' it real: pushing the desktop metaphor with physics, piles and the pen. In *Proceedings of the SIGCHI conference on Human Factors in computing systems*, 1283-1292. http://doi.acm.org/10.1145/1124772.1124965.
2. Jeff Avery, Mark Choi, Daniel Vogel, Edward Lank. 2014. Pinch-to-zoom-plus: an enhanced pinch-to-zoom that reduces clutching and panning. In *Proceedings of the 27th annual ACM symposium on User interface software and technology (UIST '14)*, 595-604. http://dx.doi.org/10.1145/2642918.2647352
3. P. Baudisch, E. Cutrell, D. Robbins, M. Czerwinski, P. Tandler, B. Bederson, A. Zierlinger. 2003. Drag-and-Pop and Drag-and-Pick: Techniques for Accessing Remote Screen Content on Touch- and Pen-operated Systems. In *Interact 2003*, 57-64.
4. Benjamin B. Bederson, James D. Hollan, Allison Druin, Jason Stewart, David Rogers, David Proft. 1996. Local tools: an alternative to tool palettes. In *Proceedings of the 9th annual ACM symposium on User interface software and technology (UIST '96)*, 169-170. http://dx.doi.org/10.1145/237091.237116.
5. Anastasia Bezerianos and Ravin Balakrishnan. 2005. The vacuum: facilitating the manipulation of distant objects. In *Proceedings of the SIGCHI Conference on Human Factors in Computing Systems (CHI '05)*, 361-370. http://dx.doi.org/10.1145/1054972.1055023.
6. Andrea Bianchi, So-Ryang Ban, Ian Oakley. 2015. Designing a Physical Aid to Support Active Reading on Tablets. In *Proceedings of the 33rd Annual ACM Conference on Human Factors in Computing Systems (CHI '15)*, 699-708. http://dx.doi.org/10.1145/2702123.2702303.
7. Eric A. Bier, Maureen C. Stone, Ken Pier, William Buxton, Tony D. DeRose. 1993. Toolglass and Magic Lenses: The see-through interface. In *Proceedings of the 20th annual conference on Computer graphics and interactive techniques (SIGGRAPH '93)*, 73-80. http://dx.doi.org/10.1145/166117.166126
8. Peter Brandl, Clifton Forlines, Daniel Wigdor, Michael Haller, Chia Shen. 2008. Combining and measuring the benefits of bimanual pen and direct-touch interaction on horizontal interfaces. In *Proceedings of the working conference on Advanced visual interfaces (AVI '08)*, 154-61. http://dx.doi.org/10.1145/1385569.1385595.
9. B. Buxton. *The Active Desk*. Retrieved from: http://www.billbuxton.com/ActiveDesk.html.
10. Bill Buxton. 2007. Sketching User Experiences: Getting the Design Right and the Right Design. Morgan Kaufmann.
11. W. Buxton. 1986. Chunking and Phrasing and the Design of Human-Computer Dialogues. In *Proceedings of the IFIP World Computer Congress*, 475-480.
12. W. Buxton, E. Fiume, R. Hill, A. Lee, C. Woo. 1983. Continuous hand-gesture driven input. In *Proceedings of Graphics Interface '83*, 191-195.
13. William Buxton. 1997. Living in augmented reality: Ubiquitous Media and Reactive Environments, in *Video Mediated Communication*, K. Finn, Sellen, A., Wilber, S., Editor. Erlbaum, Hillsdale, NJ, 363-384.
14. M. Csikszentmihalyi. 1991. Flow: The Psychology of Optimal Experience. HarperCollins.
15. Richard C. Davis, James A. Landay, Victor Chen, Jonathan Huang, Rebecca B. Lee, Frances C. Li, James Lin, III Charles B. Morrey, Ben Schleimer, Morgan N. Price, Bill N. Schilit. 1999. NotePals: lightweight note sharing by the group, for the group. In *Proceedings of the SIGCHI conference on Human Factors in Computing Systems (CHI '99)*, 338-345. http://dx.doi.org/10.1145/302979.303107.
16. Steven J. DeRose and A. van Dam. 1999. Document structure and markup in the FRESS hypertext system. *Markup Languages* 1, 1 (January): 7-32.
17. R. F. Dillon, Jeff D. Edey, Jo W. Tombaugh. 1990. Measuring the true cost of command selection: techniques and results. In *Proceedings of the SIGCHI Conference on Human Factors in Computing Systems (CHI '90)*, 19-26. http://dx.doi.org/10.1145/97243.97247
18. George Fitzmaurice, Azam Khan, Robert Piek\, \#233, Bill Buxton, Gordon Kurtenbach. 2003. Tracking menus. In *Proceedings of the 16th annual ACM symposium on User interface software and technology*, 71-79. http://doi.acm.org/10.1145/964696.964704.
19. J. D. Foley, V. L. Wallace, P. Chan. 1984. The human factors of computer graphics interaction techniques. *IEEE Computer Graphics and Applications* 4, 11: 13-48.
20. Clifton Forlines, Chia Shen, Bill Buxton. 2005. Glimpse: a novel input model for multi-level devices. In *CHI '05 Extended Abstracts on Human Factors in Computing Systems (CHI EA '05)*, 1375-1378. http://dx.doi.org/10.1145/1056808.1056920.
21. Tovi Grossman, Ken Hinckley, Patrick Baudisch, Maneesh Agrawala, Ravin Balakrishnan. 2006. Hover widgets: using the tracking state to extend the capabilities of pen-operated devices. In *Proceedings of the SIGCHI Conference on Human Factors in Computing Systems (CHI'06)*, 861-870. http://doi.acm.org/10.1145/1124772.1124898.
22. Yves Guiard. 1987. Asymmetric division of labor in human skilled bimanual action: The kinematic chain as a model. *Journal of Motor Behavior* 19, 4: 486-517.

23. Joshua Hailpern, Erik Hinterbichler, Caryn Leppert, Damon Cook, Brian P. Bailey. 2007. TEAM STORM: demonstrating an interaction model for working with multiple ideas during creative group work. In *Proceedings of the 6th ACM SIGCHI conference on Creativity & cognition (C&C '07)*, 193-202. http://dx.doi.org/10.1145/1254960.1254987
24. William Hamilton, Andruid Kerne, Tom Robbins. 2012. High-performance pen + touch modality interactions: a real-time strategy game eSports context. In *Proceedings of the 25th annual ACM symposium on User interface software and technology (UIST '12)*, 309-318. http://dx.doi.org/10.1145/2380116.2380156.
25. Gary Hardock, Gordon Kurtenbach, William Buxton. 1993. A marking based interface for collaborative writing. In *Proceedings of the 6th annual ACM symposium on User interface software and technology (UIST '93)*, 259-266. https://doi.org/10.1145/168642.168669.
26. Thomas T. Hewett. 2005. Informing the design of computer-based environments to support creativity. *Int. J. Hum.-Comput. Stud.* 63, 4-5 (October 2005): 383-409. http://dx.doi.org/10.1016/j.ijhcs.2005.04.004.
27. Ken Hinckley, Patrick Baudisch, Gonzalo Ramos, Francois Guimbretiere. 2005. Design and analysis of delimiters for selection-action pen gesture phrases in scriboli. In *Proceedings of the SIGCHI conference on Human factors in computing systems*, 451-460. http://doi.acm.org/10.1145/1054972.1055035.
28. Ken Hinckley, Xiaojun Bi, Michel Pahud, Bill Buxton. 2012. Informal Information Gathering Techniques for Active Reading. In *Proceedings of the SIGCHI Conference on Human Factors in Computing Systems (CHI '12)*, 1893-1896. http://dx.doi.org/10.1145/2207676.2208327.
29. Ken Hinckley, Francois Guimbretiere, Patrick Baudisch, Raman Sarin, Maneesh Agrawala, Ed Cutrell. 2006. The springboard: multiple modes in one spring-loaded control. In *Proceedings of the SIGCHI conference on Human Factors in computing systems*, 181-190. http://doi.acm.org/10.1145/1124772.1124801.
30. Ken Hinckley, Koji Yatani, Michel Pahud, Nicole Coddington, Jenny Rodenhouse, Andy Wilson, Hrvoje Benko, Bill Buxton. 2010. Pen + Touch = New Tools. In *Proceedings of the 23nd annual ACM symposium on User interface software and technology*, 27-36. http://doi.acm.org/10.1145/1866029.1866036.
31. Hilary Hutchinson, Wendy Mackay, Bo Westerlund, Benjamin B. Bederson, Allison Druin, Catherine Plaisant, Michel Beaudouin-Lafon, Stéphane Conversy, Helen Evans, Heiko Hansen, Nicolas Roussel, Björn Eiderbäck. 2003. Technology probes: inspiring design for and with families. In *Proceedings of the SIGCHI Conference on Human Factors in Computing Systems (CHI '03)*, 17-24. http://dx.doi.org/10.1145/642611.642616.
32. Azam Khan, Justin Matejka, George Fitzmaurice, Gordon Kurtenbach. 2005. Spotlight: directing users' attention on large displays. In *Proceedings of the SIGCHI Conference on Human Factors in Computing Systems (CHI '05)*, 791-798. http://dx.doi.org/10.1145/1054972.1055082.
33. David Kirsh. 1995. The intelligent use of space. *Artificial Intelligence* 73: p. 31-68.
34. Scott R. Klemmer, Mark W. Newman, Ryan Farrell, Mark Bilezikjian, James A. Landay. 2001. The designers' outpost: a tangible interface for collaborative web site. In *Proceedings of the 14th annual ACM symposium on User interface software and technology*, 1-10. http://doi.acm.org/10.1145/502348.502350.
35. Axel Kramer. 1994. Translucent patches-dissolving windows. In *Proceedings of the 7th annual ACM symposium on User interface software and technology (UIST '94)*, 121-130. http://dx.doi.org/10.1145/192426.192474.
36. Myron W. Krueger, Thomas Gionfriddo, Katrin Hinrichsen. 1985. VIDEOPLACE-an artificial reality. In *Proceedings of the SIGCHI Conference on Human Factors in Computing Systems (CHI '85)*, 35-40. http://dx.doi.org/10.1145/317456.317463.
37. Gordon Kurtenbach and William Buxton. 1991. Issues in combining marking and direct manipulation techniques. In *Proceedings of the 4th annual ACM symposium on User interface software and technology*, 137-144. http://doi.acm.org/10.1145/120782.120797.
38. Gordon Kurtenbach, George Fitzmaurice, Thomas Baudel, Bill Buxton. 1997. The design of a GUI paradigm based on tablets, two-hands, and transparency. In *Proceedings of the SIGCHI conference on Human factors in computing systems*, 35-42. http://doi.acm.org/10.1145/258549.258574.
39. James A. Landay and Brad A. Myers. 2001. Sketching Interfaces: Toward More Human Interface Design. *Computer* 34, 3 (March 2001): 56-64. http://dx.doi.org/10.1109/2.910894.
40. Edward Lank, Jaime Ruiz, William Cowan. 2006. Concurrent bimanual stylus interaction: a study of non-preferred hand mode manipulation. In *Proceedings of Graphics Interface 2006 (GI '06)*, 17-24.
41. Jakob Leitner and Michael Haller. 2011. Harpoon selection: efficient selections for ungrouped content on large pen-based surfaces. In *Proceedings of the 24th annual ACM symposium on User interface software and technology (UIST '11)*, 593-602. http://dx.doi.org/10.1145/2047196.2047275.
42. Yang Li, Ken Hinckley, Zhiwei Guan, James A. Landay. 2005. Experimental analysis of mode switching techniques in pen-based user interfaces. In *Proceedings of the SIGCHI Conference on Human Factors in Computing Systems (CHI '05)*, 461-470. http://doi.acm.org/10.1145/1054972.1055036.

43. David Lindlbauer, Michael Haller, Mark Hancock, Stacey D. Scott, Wolfgang Stuerzlinger. 2013. Perceptual grouping: selection assistance for digital sketching. In *Proceedings of the 2013 ACM international conference on Interactive tabletops and surfaces (ITS '13)*, 51-60. http://dx.doi.org/10.1145/2512349.2512801.
44. Fabrice Matulic and Moira C. Norrie. 2013. Pen and touch gestural environment for document editing on interactive tabletops. In *Proceedings of the 2013 ACM international conference on Interactive tabletops and surfaces (ITS '13)*, 41-50. http://dx.doi.org/10.1145/2512349.2512802.
45. Sachi Mizobuchi and Michiaki Yasumura. 2004. Tapping vs. circling selections on pen-based devices: evidence for different performance-shaping factors. In *Proceedings of the SIGCHI Conference on Human Factors in Computing Systems (CHI '04)*, 607-614. http://dx.doi.org/10.1145/985692.985769.
46. Thomas P. Moran, Patrick Chiu, William van Melle. 1997. Pen-based interaction techniques for organizing material on an electronic whiteboard. In *Proceedings of the 10th annual ACM symposium on User interface software and technology*, 45-54. http://doi.acm.org/10.1145/263407.263508.
47. Elizabeth D. Mynatt, Takeo Igarashi, W. Keith Edwards, Anthony LaMarca. 1999. Flatland: new dimensions in office whiteboards. In *Proceedings of the SIGCHI conference on Human Factors in Computing Systems (CHI '99)*, 346-353. http://dx.doi.org/10.1145/302979.303108
48. Ken Perlin and David Fox. 1993. Pad: an alternative approach to the computer interface. In *Proceedings of the 20th annual conference on Computer graphics and interactive techniques (SIGGRAPH '93)*, 57-64. http://dx.doi.org/10.1145/166117.166125.
49. Florian Perteneder, Martin Bresler, Eva-Maria Grossauer, Joanne Leong, Michael Haller. 2015. cLuster: Smart Clustering of Free-Hand Sketches on Large Interactive Surfaces. In *Proceedings of the 28th Annual ACM Symposium on User Interface Software & Technology (UIST '15)*, 37-46. http://dx.doi.org/10.1145/2807442.2807455.
50. Ken Pfeuffer, Jason Alexander, Hans Gellersen. 2016. Partially-indirect Bimanual Input with Gaze, Pen, and Touch for Pan, Zoom, and Ink Interaction. In *Proceedings of the 2016 CHI Conference on Human Factors in Computing Systems (CHI '16)*, 2845-2856. http://dx.doi.org/10.1145/2858036.2858201.
51. Ken Pier and James A. Landay, *Issues for Location-Independent Interfaces*. 1992: Technical Report ISTL92-4, Xerox Palo Alto Research Center.
52. Jeffrey S. Pierce, Matthew Conway, Maarten van Dantzich, George Robertson. 1999. Toolspaces and glances: storing, accessing, and retrieving objects in 3D desktop applications. In *Proceedings of the 1999 symposium on Interactive 3D graphics (I3D '99)*, 163-168. http://dx.doi.org/10.1145/300523.300545.
53. Stuart Pook, Eric Lecolinet, Guy Vaysseix, Emmanuel Barillot. 2000. Control menus: excecution and control in a single interactor. In *CHI '00 Extended Abstracts on Human Factors in Computing Systems (CHI EA '00)*, 263-264. http://dx.doi.org/10.1145/633292.633446.
54. A. T. Purcell and J. S. Gero. 1998. Drawings and the design process. *Design Studies* 19, 4: 389-430.
55. J. Raskin. 2000. The Humane Interface: New Directions for Designing Interactive Systems. ACM Press.
56. George G. Robertson and Stuart K. Card. 1997. Fix and float: object movement by egocentric navigation. In *Proceedings of the 10th annual ACM symposium on User interface software and technology (UIST '97)*, 149-150. http://dx.doi.org/10.1145/263407.263535.
57. Jaime Ruiz and Edward Lank. 2007. A study on the scalability of non-preferred hand mode manipulation. In *Proceedings of the 9th international conference on Multimodal interfaces (ICMI '07)*, 170-177. http://dx.doi.org/10.1145/1322192.1322223.
58. Donald A. Schön. 1992. Designing as reflective conversation with the materials of a design situation. *Research in Engineering Design* 3, 3: 131-147. http://dx.doi.org/10.1007/BF01580516.
59. Julia Schwarz, Scott Hudson, Jennifer Mankoff, Andrew D. Wilson. 2010. A framework for robust and flexible handling of inputs with uncertainty. In *Proceedings of the 23nd annual ACM symposium on User interface software and technology*, 47-56. http://doi.acm.org/10.1145/1866029.1866039.
60. A. Sellen, G. Kurtenbach, W. Buxton. 1992. The prevention of mode errors through sensory feedback. *Human Computer Interaction* 7, 2: 141-164.
61. Jami J. Shah, Noe Vargas-Hernandez, Joshua D. Summers, Santosh Kulkarni. 2001. Collaborative Sketching (C-Sketch)--An Idea Generation Technique for Engineering Design. *Journal of Creative Behavior* 35, 3 (3rd Qtr 2001): 168-198
62. F. Shipman and C. Marshall. 1999. Formality Considered Harmful: Experiences, Emerging Themes, and Directions on the Use of Formal Representations in Interactive Systems. *Computer Supported Cooperative Work (CSCW)* 8, 4: 333-352.
63. Ben Shneiderman. 2007. Creativity support tools: accelerating discovery and innovation. *Commun. ACM* 50, 12 (December 2007): 20-32. http://dx.doi.org/10.1145/1323688.1323689.
64. L. Tesler. 1981. The smalltalk environment. *Byte* 6, 8: 90-147.
65. Theophanis Tsandilas, Catherine Letondal, Wendy E. Mackay. 2009. Musink: composing music through augmented drawing. In *Proceedings of the SIGCHI Conference on Human Factors in Computing Systems*

(CHI '09), 819-828. http://dx.doi.org/10.1145/1518701.1518827

66. Md. Sami Uddin, Carl Gutwin, Benjamin Lafreniere. 2016. HandMark Menus: Rapid Command Selection and Large Command Sets on Multi-Touch Displays. In *Proceedings of the 2016 CHI Conference on Human Factors in Computing Systems (CHI '16)*, 5836-5848. http://dx.doi.org/10.1145/2858036.2858211.
67. Julie Wagner, Stéphane Huot, Wendy Mackay. 2012. BiTouch and BiPad: designing bimanual interaction for hand-held tablets. In *Proceedings of the SIGCHI Conference on Human Factors in Computing Systems (CHI '12)*, 2317-2326. http://dx.doi.org/10.1145/2207676.2208391.
68. Julie Wagner, Eric Lecolinet, Ted Selker. 2014. Multi-finger chords for hand-held tablets: recognizable and memorable. In *Proceedings of the SIGCHI Conference on Human Factors in Computing Systems (CHI '14)*, 2883-2892. http://doi.acm.org/10.1145/2556288.2556958.
69. Andrew M. Webb, Michel Pahud, Ken Hinckley, Bill Buxton. 2016. Wearables as Context for Guiard-abiding Bimanual Touch. In *Proceedings of the 29th Annual Symposium on User Interface Software and Technology (UIST '16)*, 287-300. https://doi.org/10.1145/2984511.2984564.
70. Jacob O. Wobbrock, Meredith Ringel Morris, Andrew D. Wilson. 2009. User-defined gestures for surface computing. In *Proceedings of the 27th international conference on Human factors in computing systems*, 1083-1092. http://doi.acm.org/10.1145/1518701.1518866.
71. Yasuhiro Yamamoto and Kumiyo Nakakoji. 2005. Interaction design of tools for fostering creativity in the early stages of information design. *Int. J. Hum.-Comput. Stud.* 63, 4-5 (October 2005): 513-535. http://dx.doi.org/10.1016/j.ijhcs.2005.04.023.
72. Robert Zeleznik, Andrew Bragdon, Ferdi Adeputra, Hsu-Sheng Ko. 2010. Hands-on math: a page-based multi-touch and pen desktop for technical work and problem solving. In *Proceedings of the 23nd annual ACM symposium on User interface software and technology*, 17-26. http://doi.acm.org/10.1145/1866029.1866035.

As We May Ink? Learning from Everyday Analog Pen Use to Improve Digital Ink Experiences

Yann Riche
paper@ynr.ch
Riche Design, USA

Nathalie Henry Riche, Ken Hinckley, Sheri Panabaker
{nath, kenh, sheril}@microsoft.com
Microsoft, USA

Sarah Fuelling
sarah@percipient research.com
P. Research, USA

Sarah Williams
sarahgwilliams@ comcast.net
A. K. Design, USA

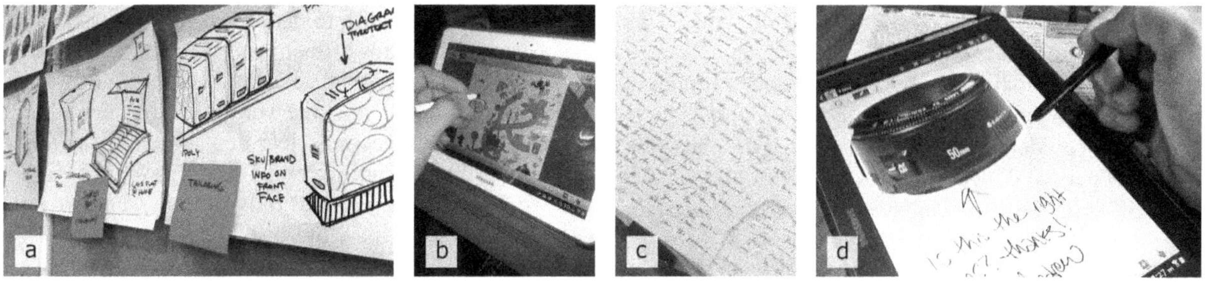

Figure 1. Diary entries from analog and digital pen usage © Microsoft

ABSTRACT
This paper sheds light on gaps and discrepancies between the experiences afforded by analog pens and their digital counterparts. Despite the long history (and recent renaissance) of digital pens, the literature still lacks a comprehensive survey of what types of marks people make and what motivates them to use ink—both analog and digital—in daily life. To capture the diversity of inking behaviors and tease out the unique affordances of pen-and-ink, we conducted a diary study with 26 participants from diverse backgrounds. From analysis of 493 diary entries we identified 8 analog pen-and-ink activities, and 9 affordances of pens. We contextualized and contrasted these findings using a survey with 1,633 respondents and a follow-up diary study with 30 participants, observing digital pens. Our analysis reveals gaps and research opportunities based on pen affordances not yet fully explored in the literature.

Author Keywords
Ink, notes, sketching, writing, annotation, pen input, tablets

ACM Classification Keywords
H.5.2 Information interfaces and Presentation: Input

INTRODUCTION
Although the idea of writing on a computer screen goes back at least to Ivan Sutherland's *Sketchpad* [51], if not the classic 1945 Vannevar Bush essay *As We May Think* [11], the pen has long lingered on the fringes of mainstream computing. The rise of tablets that support multi-touch and high-quality pen input has reinvigorated pen computing. Yet, even for basic mark-up scenarios, they do not seem as natural as analog pen and paper: their *affordances*—defined as perceived and actual properties of objects suggesting activities people do and think they can do with them—differ in many ways.

The body of literature on analog and digital pen experiences is extensive. The research community has generated informative, inventive and inspiring research for many scenarios such as annotations [16,33,34,41,50,61] and note-taking [4,10,37,47,58,60]. While exploring compelling scenarios in-depth drives innovation forward, it is also important to gain an overview of the breadth of activities and understand which ones matter most to people. With this work, we embark on a complementary perspective looking at the breath of pen use, including frequency and the identification of key pen affordances. Our goal is to illuminate disparities and disconnects between digital *vs.* analog pen experiences. Our work thus contributes an observational foundation for "how we may ink" that allows reflection on existing products as well as future innovations.

We tackle this problem first by gathering a large diversity of everyday analog and digital pen activities via two diary studies, and second by quantifying the frequency and importance of these activities in a large survey. In our analyses, we tease out the affordances specific to the pen. This angle allows us to uncover several fundamental differences in activities people do (or think they can do) with an analog pen versus a digital pen. For instance, we found

Permission to make digital or hard copies of all or part of this work for personal or classroom use is granted without fee provided that copies are not made or distributed for profit or commercial advantage and that copies bear this notice and the full citation on the first page. Copyrights for components of this work owned by others than the author(s) must be honored. Abstracting with credit is permitted. To copy otherwise, or republish, to post on servers or to redistribute to lists, requires prior specific permission and/or a fee. Request permissions from Permissions@acm.org.
CHI 2017, May 06 - 11, 2017, Denver, CO, USA
Copyright is held by the owner/author(s). Publication rights licensed to ACM.
ACM 978-1-4503-4655-9/17/05...$15.00
DOI: http://dx.doi.org/10.1145/3025453.3025716

that people tend to associate the analog pen with a *drafting* tool to ideate and think (Figure 1a); whereas they associate the digital pen with a *crafting* tool to refine and share work-products (Figure 1b). Our analysis also reveals that many scenarios addressed by an ecosystem of individual apps in the digital world, are, in fact, tightly and fluidly interwoven in the analog world such as tearing out piece of a journal entry to use as an in-place reminder (Figure 1c). We also identified which unique affordances of digital pens are particularly compelling to people, such as annotating digital content, or sharing instantly across large distances (Fig. 1d).

In summary, then, this paper contributes the following:

- A first attempt at presenting the breadth of pen activities people perform in daily life; as well as their frequency, popularity and people's perception of their importance;
- A first attempt at identifying *9* affordances of the pen (plus 3 for digital pen) and their impact on activities;
- A study of digital pen-and-tablet activities and an analysis of gaps, limitations, and advantages compared to analog;
- Reflections on research opportunities for digital pens;
- A data corpus of ~600 anonymized diary entries and codes available at https://aka.ms/aswemayink.

RELATED WORK

The literature on pen and ink is incredibly rich and the body of knowledge on mark-up for specific scenarios is certainly deepening every year. For instance, research efforts have investigated active reading [8,13,18,20,40,54,55,62], note-taking [4,9,43,53,62,65], the use of pen for creativity and design [5,9,17,25,27] and collaborating with others [15,29,31]. Research also probes the types of marks people make on walls [41], whiteboards [60], and as annotations [16,33,34,41,50,61]. Most of these previous studies of mark-up focus on specific activities or task domains. However, mark-up pervades a diversity of tasks and workflows, a rich ecology that only partially overlaps that of 'office work' and 'documents.' Our work provides a glimpse of this diversity, while further updating and contextualizing our understanding of these pen tasks in the smartphone era.

Affordances of the Pen

To uncover the fundamental differences between the analog and digital pen experiences, we focus on the unique affordances of pens. We use the term *affordances* in the spirit of Sellen and Harper's seminal work [43], as *a set of perceived and actual properties of objects suggesting activities people do and think they can do with them.* Our goal is to identify affordances specific to pens, so as to compare the analog *vs.* digital experiences, and identify gaps.

The Myth of the Paperless Office [43] enumerated key affordances of paper in knowledge work and compared these to the affordances of digital technologies, pointing out gaps and opportunities for future research. Note that several of these affordances of paper—such as 'Marking up a document while reading' or 'Interweaving reading and writing'—are intimately tied to the pen. And, although comprehensive, the nature of the studies still leaves some questions unanswered. Do further affordances emerge if we focus primarily on the pen? What if we extend our view beyond office work, to mark-up in everyday life? How is the pen interwoven with other tasks, or modalities of expression? Has the role of paper evolved with the popularization of smartphones, tablets, and e-paper devices?

In general, it is difficult to disentangle the affordances of pen from those of paper in the literature. At times this is warranted; Kidd [22], for example, points out the significance of ink lies not in the marks upon the paper, but rather the lasting impressions left on the knowledge workers themselves. Yet, still, to deeply process information it often seems necessary for office workers to set pen to paper, or for designers to sketch out ideas on a whiteboard [14,57], and when we venture into the would-be digital equivalents of these media, it becomes clear that some affordances of pens are not wholly unified with the (no longer co-present) affordances of paper. Not only is paper interwoven with a great many activities, but also for many of these—such as work-related reading [1]—the pen plays a critical role that only partially overlaps that of paper itself. For these reasons, we believe that taking a closer look at the affordances specific to the pen is essential.

Affordances of Pen & Ink vs. Digital Media

With our studies, we seek to contrast analog and digital behaviors. Previous research reports similar efforts. For instance, some subtle nuances of affordance for analog vs. digital touch have been noted even for the simple physical act of turning pages while reading [32,46], in part because incidental contact is a key negative affordance of touch-enabled displays, a problem exacerbated when people rest their palm on a screen while writing [2,3]. As such, on digital devices the perceived affordances of 'pen' may be influenced by those of 'touch.' In early work O'Hara et al. contrasted use of paper vs. on-line documents [38]. Terrenghi et al. [56] contrast physical versus digital media on tabletops, but did not include stylus interactions in their analysis. However, like our work, they find insidious and at times non-obvious nuances of affordance between analog and digital actions that *seem* identical (but perhaps not nearly enough so).

Morris et al. [36] compared active reading on paper to a vertical desktop, horizontal tabletop, and multiple tablets. While some differences emerged, many classic observations (such as reading interleaved with writing [43]) still held in the digital settings. Yet, the study focused only on active reading in a laboratory task—not a wide diversity of tasks—and the work's focus was not on the affordances of the pen. Our approach differs from these efforts as we draw our observations from participants with diverse backgrounds using pen and ink for their own purposes, and in their natural environments—home, office, or the many places in-between.

APPROACH

Building a perspective on the wide range of pen activities and scenarios as well as their frequency and importance to people and comparing them to their digital counterparts is an ambitious and challenging task. As a first step, we opted for a mixed method approach, combining qualitative diary studies with a small set of individuals, and quantitative answers to a survey with a large audience.

In the first diary study, we selected heavy analog pen users with a diverse set of backgrounds and occupations. We wanted to elicit insights about a variety of activities and tease out the role of analog pens from people who use them frequently. The goal was not to quantify or generalize findings but to gather new, rich and diverse entries. We then contrasted insights from analog pen use with insights gained from a complementary diary study with digital pen users. The participants in this second study had a unique perspective since they already owned (and used) a digital pen. This allowed us to elicit affordances specific to the digital pen. Finally, to contextualize insights from both studies with a broader population, we conducted a survey to quantify the frequency and popularity of the pen activities we had identified. The survey also served to tease out the relative importance of pen affordances to a larger population.

STUDY 1: ANALOG PEN

To develop a holistic view of how and why people use a pen in their daily life, we conducted a diary study with a small yet diverse set of participants. We simply asked them to share with us a photograph of an activity they carried out with a pen, pencil or marker, commenting on their reasons for doing so. Our goal was to unpack the diversity of day-to-day activities that people engage in with a pen, and their motivations to do so, to tease out unique affordances of the analog pen. Thus, we asked participants to vary the intent and context of these entries as much as possible. The resulting 493 photos and comments revealed a diversity of activities.

Participants and Data Collection

We used an online diary research service called *dscout* to recruit participants and collect data. We used a survey to screen for frequent use of analog pen and paper (daily or more). A few open-ended questions helped us assess the motivation of the participants and their ability to articulate their thoughts well. We carefully selected 26 participants, for their diversity of background and occupations which we hypothesized would lead to a diversity of activities. We recruited students, teachers, engineers, designers, writers, architects, physicians and home-makers, 12 male and 14 female. The mean age was 31 (sd=8) and all lived in the US. Each owned a smartphone and a computer. Participants used their phone to take a photo and enter comments to capture what is in the photo and why they chose analog vs digital. We asked them to provide at least 20 snippets.

Data Analysis

Our participants provided between 4 and 24 snippets each, with a majority providing 20, for a total of 493 snippets. Out of the 493 entries in the original dataset, we could classify 466 (94.5%), the rest being too blurry or including comments too vague to be coded.

A complete, anonymized view of the diary entries, along with supplemental study material is available at:

http://aka.ms/aswemayink

AF1: Externalizing thoughts and memorizing
AF2: Producing high-fidelity marks
AF3: Tacit and automatic use
AF4: Capturing non-committal information
AF5: Interweaving symbolic and figurative content
AF6: Integrating information in context
AF7: Rich personal expression
AF8: Reliability and dependability
AF9: Immediacy of capture

Figure 2. List of the pen affordances

PA1: Ideation
PA2: Collaboration and coordination
PA3: Information scraps
PA4: Personal communication
PA5: Annotations
PA6: Recordings
PA7: Crafts
PA8: Doodles and Games

Figure 3. List of the pen activities

Using a grounded theory approach [49], we initially coded the data along many axes: the type of activities conducted with a pen, the types of marks and pens, writing support used, and motivations and possible intent for each activity. Via iterations and discussions, three researchers developed in parallel a final code set for pen activities and pen affordances, finalized after an inter-coder agreement of 95% on 10% of the data. Our code set included low-level codes which we then aggregated into the set of categories presented below. While the lower-level codes are perhaps more exhaustive and indicate subtle nuances in types of affordances and activities, they are difficult to convey efficiently in a conference paper. We chose to report a higher level of abstraction while making the full code-set available. Figure 2 provides an overview of the analog pen affordances, and Figure 3 of the high-level analog pen activities we coded.

Nine Affordances of Pen

To analyze how pens are particularly suitable devices for information capture, we first describe nine key affordances of pen, which we also seek to contrast with prior art.

The affordances (denoted hereafter as AF1-9) are distinct from those associated with the paper itself [43]. We also separately categorized the entries into eight core pen activities (PA1-8) that draw upon and relate back to the affordances in a variety of ways—and thereby provide another layer of depth and motivation to the affordances themselves. For each affordance and pen activity we draw out specific examples, usually with a direct quotation from the user's diary entry, and identify the entry in our online corpus with a notation such as '[#12345].' Also, to authentically capture the 'voice' of user remarks, we report all of their comments verbatim (including typos).

AF1. Externalizing thoughts and memorizing: Many participants surfaced the cognitive benefits of using a pen: *"I find that I take in a lot more information when I write it down as opposed to type it."* [#12564]. Externalizing thinking by writing and sketching when solving problems offloads working memory and enhances cognition by creating persistent referents [24,53]. Evidence also suggests that hand-writing notes promotes deeper processing and recall of information [6,21,37].

AF2. Producing high-fidelity marks: Most adults have invested a tremendous amount of day-to-day experience in the skilled production of marks, if not design-sketching and artistic expression. As a lever-arm controlled by a tripod of opposing muscle groups [30], the pen becomes an extension of the hand—if not an extension of thought itself [24]—offering high precision and fluidity of expression.

AF3. Tacit and automatic use: With experience the pen becomes so familiar that its use is completely tacit, and automatic, to the extent that the tool itself seems to disappear [42]. *"It feels like more "work" if I start out taking notes on a computer"* [#12414]. As such, the pen consumes minimal attention and cognitive resources, keeping the writer "in the flow" of creative work [5]—or free to multi-task and interleave other real-world activities such as listening to a teleconference call, attending socially to colleagues at a meeting, or reading a book.

AF4. Capturing non-committal information: Hand-written artifacts communicate an implicit 'draft', 'working', 'incomplete' or 'uncertain' nature. Indeed, ambiguity, sketchiness, and incompleteness can spark new associations and re-interpretations of design sketches [15,47]. Ink allows capture of information in non-committal form, which can feel safer than typing something into a report or spreadsheet when one is uncertain of the quality or provenance of the data. Yet, the notation might gain value with the mere passage of time, or upon revision—or it can simply can be disregarded if later deemed incorrect or unimportant: *"Jotting down my to do list in my note pad..will be discarded once i've checked things of...would never use my phone or computer because this list is constantly changing"* [#12433].

AF5. Interweaving symbolic and figurative content: Pen affords a versatile input, allowing users to capture and style text while interweaving it with non-alphanumeric content and illustrations. Pen naturally integrates multiple textual attributes (e.g. location, size of the print, weight, orientation) that would require adjusting many settings in document editing software. Many thoughts do not have a pure written form, but can take the shape of, or benefit from, other visual additions such as diagrams, or symbols and equations, which often require effort to create on digital devices. *"there tend to be a lot of mathematical symbols that are in the text and it is a pain to type them out."* [#12755].

AF6. Integrating information in context: We observed that

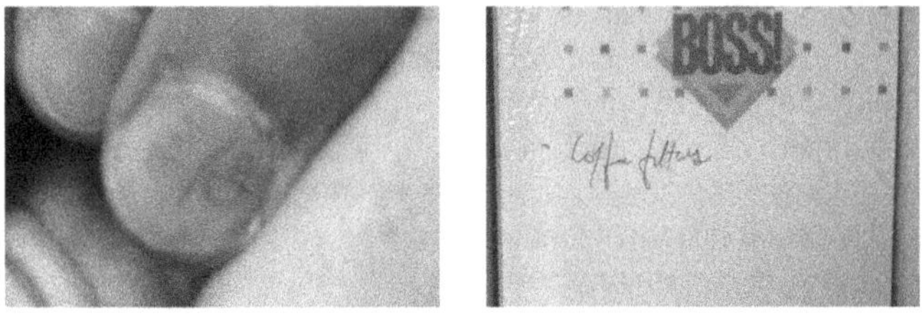

Figure 4. Writing on fingernails and on the fridge © Microsoft

inking is frequently driven by context. Examples include leaving a personal note in a loved one's lunch bag, or jotting a reminder on a post-it and leaving it on the boss' computer. Here, the ink has double value: it first indicates some action to take, or attribute, through the textual content; and second it modifies or 'selects' the object of concern by the very act of marking it up. This can also be used as a form of layering of information on top of another context, sometimes referred to as a 'palimpsest' [57]. This context might be a typeset document, a whiteboard with a collaborator's mark-up already on it that one now partially over-writes, or perhaps even a calendar page with appointments penciled in at an earlier time. These uses point to the pen as a cross-surface implement: it enables people to lay marks upon various physical media, often placed strategically at the location that a particular task or activity occurs. For instance, one participant wrote crib-notes on his fingernail for an exam [#12805]; another left a reminder on her fridge regarding meal preparation [#12724] (Figure 4). These examples show how the location of the content—as well as the identity of the marked-up object—both serve the information need.

AF7. Rich personal expression: Handwriting is easily identifiable as a human-made artefact, unique to one person. In pedestrian form this makes it clear who contributed a particular idea to a whiteboard session, for example; but in more profound examples a hand-printed note serves as a form of symbolic gift-giving that can help to deepen social ties or tighten the bonds of intimate relationships. The organic, freeform, and artisanal nature of handwritten artefacts affords such expressiveness: *"Typing a personal note feels like it would defeat the purpose. That would take the personality and sincerity out of the gesture."* [#12642].

AF8. Reliability and dependability: Pens are cheap and ubiquitous in most home and office environments. The availability (or ready replacement) of a writing implement is therefore far more dependable than digital capture devices with screens that shatter if dropped, innards that short-out if drenched during field-work, batteries that drain after a few hours of use, and when (not if) the user loses the special pen. As a result, the reliability of handwritten notes as an information capture method is hard to beat: *"you never know* *when the computer might freeze, crash, the note-taking program might rainbow wheel and you have to force quit [...] I can always rely on my hand to be working properly"* [#12588].

AF9. Immediacy of capture: Defaulting to note-taking with a pen often results from time urgency to capture fleeting thoughts [17] as well as during rapid ideation [45]. *"When I come up with an idea, I need to capture it quickly."* [#12431]. The pen, often tucked between the fingers or behind the ear, is quick to access and one can start writing immediately. By contrast, getting out a device, turning it on, and signing in—not to mention finding the right area of the right application in the right mode of use—can effectively kneecap the quick capture of information. *"We didn't need to wait for something to load or click through a program, we had it all right there in front of us."* [#12874]

Eight Pen Activities

To complement our analysis of pen affordances, we also sought to provide a holistic view of the types of activities people use analog pens for. We describe here eight meta-activities (See Figure 3) extracted from the diary entries, and provide a discussion of how they relate to pen affordances. While these pen activities (PA1-8) provide general categories for what the participants produced, it was not uncommon for some to overlap. For instance, a collaborative brainstorming session generated artifacts that we classified as either ideations, collaboration, or both.

PA1. Ideations correspond to artifacts produced when participants brainstorm ideas or think through problems either by themselves or with others (Figure 1b). As outlined by our participants, this activity is tightly coupled with the supportive nature of the pen for ideation and problem solving (AF1): *"I'm sure I was working on this on the train or waiting for an appt or something. I find it much easier to sketch and work out ideas on paper."* [#12766]. Another theme is the non-committal capture of ideas (AF4): *"It helps me to organize my thoughts and determine if my swirling ideas and concepts even make sense before committing the show to a digital treatment format."* [#12414]. Participants also emphasized the pen's ability to help focus on the task at hand (AF3): *"I can't follow what I'm doing as easily as when I handwrite things."* [#12414].

Additionally, several affordances of pens are tightly coupled with those of paper, making pen and paper a particularly compelling combination for ideation. Paper enables people to capture information without any constraint of format or layout, and the pen's flexible input nature (AF5) enables concentration on the content rather than the means of capture (AF3). Not only can pens write on many substrates in the physical world, paper also allows people to (re)organize artefacts they mark in space, and to layer ideas on top of each other (AF6): *"We're constantly rearranging, grouping, and drawing on top of our ideas."* [#12774].

PA2. Collaboration and coordination correspond to artifacts produced when communicating or performing collaborative activities with others. The artifacts were produced to articulate difficult models or concepts as a live

"Here I just had a discussion with my director about a concept we were working on. Basically, I started sketching my understanding of the idea and then he grabbed the pen and started sketching over and next to my sketch."[#12874]

"Whenever something pops into my head I have to write it down before I forget. As you can see from the photo, I'll grab whatever piece of paper is around ... My goal is to write down my idea, and as much of it as I can, before I forget it." [#12431]

Figure 5. Examples of collaboration and information scraps © Microsoft

communication aid, to externalize information by creating a shared workspace, and to create common ground for a shared understanding and coordinating efforts. This activity is tightly coupled with versatility of the pen to convey visual concepts (AF5)—many of the entries here included sketches or diagrams. The ease of layering information using ink (AF6) also seems to be a factor in choosing the pen for such activities (Figure 5, top). Collaboration and coordination activities also benefit the ability to ink in many locations and contexts (AF6). For instance, placing the content in a shared workspace enables group members to notice it, read it, and act on it. The availability (AF8) of pens also makes it easy for collaborators to contribute at moment's notice (AF9).

PA3. Information scraps are 'micro-notes' that are often created in the moment to fit a short-term goal [7,28]. At times information scraps are derived from other contexts because there is no 'good' location to file or note the information. This category includes todo, packing, and grocery lists; reminders to oneself or others; driving directions and other brief instructions; and short-term memory aids, and logs. In these activities, participants often mentioned immediacy (AF9) and the contextual role (AF6) of pen and ink. Immediacy is critical for information scraps (Figure 5, bottom): in a task that might take only two seconds to complete, a 30-second context switch to an electronic tablet is a non-starter. Contextualization, in turn, allows tying the content to the proximity of where it is needed—such as an asterisk in a document margin or a '*dirty*' post-it on a dishwasher. "*Children respond better to visual notes so they can constantly be reminded, especially younger children.*" [#12606].

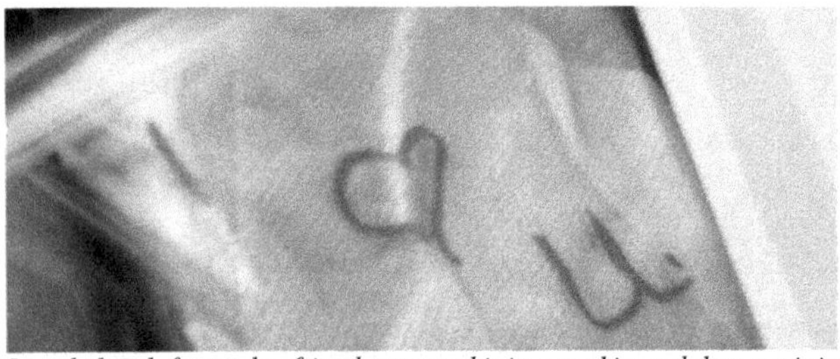

I made lunch for my boyfriend, wrapped it in a napkin and then put it in a plastic sandwich bag... I know that his job is difficult and stressful and I try and take any opportunity I can to make him smile throughout the day." [#12642]

Figure 6. Example of personal communication © Microsoft

PA4. Personal communication corresponds to artifacts created specifically to contribute to a personal relationship. They included hand-written letters, postcards, or messages embedded in context. The personal (AF7) and unique (AF2) nature of handwriting and drawing plays an essential role in these activities. In an environment where emails and texts become the norm, using the pen to communicate with others can strengthen social bonds and reflect the uniqueness of the relationship. *"Handwritten thank-yous are a must; typing one would just seem lazy & rude. Too impersonal if done digitally."* [#12533]. The additional effort required by hand-crafted communication signifies the value of the relationship: *"On special occasions I will write cards for friends. People know more effort is put in with real stuff."* [#12730]. The contextual placement of the content (AF6) may be key, emphasizing the intimacy of the relationship. For instance, one participant was thoughtful of when and where the recipient would see her message (Figure 6).

PA5. Annotations refer to handwritten content on top of reference material, in a clear figure-ground relationship. With annotations, the handwritten content would lose its meaning if removed from this context. Activities included writing on a printed calendar or engaging in active reading to enhance understanding and recall (AF1). Non-alphanumeric marks (AF5) such as underlines, arrows, and highlights are often prevalent in annotation scenarios [41]. We also coded tasks such as filling forms or signing checks and documents as a form of annotation. The mark-up is layered on top of such forms, and the location (context) is what gives the marks their meaning (AF6), both of which fit our definition for annotation. This category also includes labeling documents or objects (Figure 7 top left) to communicate information to others, such as a description of the contents of a box, or a list of required actions for a co-worker. Because pen and paper combine the content being captured (the label) with a specific context in the physical world, people leverage this unity of context and content as terse, complementary, and information-rich modalities.

PA6. Recordings are artifacts of pen activity concurrent and related to another ongoing activity. Recordings occur in both work and personal contexts, and are often created for oneself to afford reference and recall (AF1). For students, writing is

Figure 7. Examples of annotations, crafts, doodles, and recordings © Microsoft

motivated by the need to understand and retain the information. "*I don't know exactly why, but I think the tactile feeling of actually writing something engrains it in my brain much more than just pressing keys.*" [#12564]. The ability to flexibly intermingle notes, figures, sketches, and diagrams (AF5) is also a recurring motivation. "*Writing out note is quicker and I can draw arrows and do math more easily.*" [#12560]. Other recordings, such as lab or field notes, capture details for later use in reports, emails, or other documents. In such situations, an individual's attention is often primarily occupied by a real-world task for long periods of time (1 hour or more), so capturing information without distraction is critical (AF3). The faith that the content would be reliably recorded (AF8) was also a common motivator: (Figure 7 bottom right): *"When talking with a client, I like all my notes to be on a hard copy because of the chance a digital file may be deleted or lost."* [#12654].

PA7. Crafts correspond to artifacts carefully crafted with pen and paper for oneself or for others. In these entries, the product of the writing or drawing is an artifact that has a purpose and a value of its own, akin to an art piece (Figure 7 top right). These artifacts often end up being shared, and/or kept as mementos. The long standing relationship of people with pen makes this input mechanism a natural extension of their body (AF2) and often enables them to feel an emotional connection to the material they produce. "*I do find writing long hand to be relaxing and I have a closer relationship to the material then if I was writing on my computer.*" [#12749]

PA8. Doodles and games. In contrast to crafts, doodles are short-lived artifacts that may never be looked at again. Examples include squiggles drawn on the corner of a page during phone calls, or playing games such as Sudoku while waiting for an appointment. The most common motivation for using pen for doodles is the serendipitous access and the spontaneous and inconspicuous nature of the activity (AF8,

Figure 8. Digital pen devices in the diary study

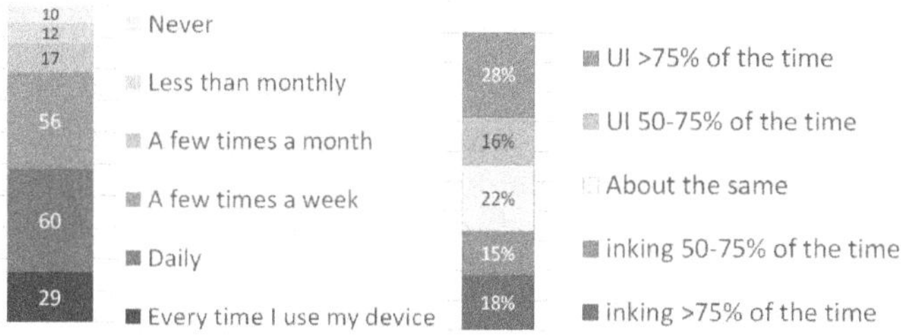

Figure 9. Quantifying the use of digital pens

AF9). *"I doodle on the agenda cause it keeps me occupied during the boring meeting! No computers allowed."* [#12545] (Figure 7 bottom left). Due to its tacit use (AF3), immediate readiness (AF9) and the uniqueness of the output (AF7), freeform mark-up with a pen offers a more expressive medium than a computer screen. *"I drew this guy to capture my feeling about the subject. I wouldn't want to have to open a program to be able to express my thoughts"* [#12716]

STUDY2: DIGITAL PEN

In this section, we contrast the affordances for analog pens derived from our observations against those of digital pens. To achieve this, we first performed a follow-up diary study with *digital* pen users to tease out activities and affordances of digital pen technologies and identify any discrepancies with their analog counterparts. Second, we conducted an online survey to understand the prevalence and frequency of scenarios in both analog and digital pen use. This allowed us to identify popular and frequent activities related to pens, with an eye towards identifying any that appeared absent or degraded in digital pen-based experiences—and vice-versa.

Methodology for Diary Study of Digital Pen Use

We again used *dscout*, with a similar methodology as for the first diary study, but with a focus on digital pens, which include active digital pens as well as passive capacitive pens for touch devices such as iPads. While we consider hybrid augmented-paper technologies (such as Anoto) to be 'digital' pens, none of our participants reported owning such a device. We recruited 30 participants (13 female, 17 male) who used digital pens (Figure 8). None participated in Study 1 and all participants used their digital pen at least weekly. Mean age was 36 (sd=9) and occupations included student, homemaker and graphic artist.

Each diary entry consisted of a photo, plus comments on the activity. Participants also provided their motivations for using a digital pen, and on the importance and quality of the experience. Because they had to answer more questions for each entry than Study 1, we requested only five entries. They provided between 1 and 10 entries, for a total of 178 entries. We coded the data with categories from Study 1.

Survey Methodology

We recruited 1633 participants (excluding partially filled surveys or participants failing to answer captcha questions) via Amazon Mechanical Turk, compensating them $2 for their participation. Most respondents (71.8%) were between 18 and 39 years of age and 59% reported using a computing device more than 4 hours a day. They reported a variety of occupations in IT (15%), education (15%), healthcare (12%), retail (11%) and 35% were students. The survey contained 60 questions to gather demographics (8), type and use of analog pen (20), electronic devices (15) and digital pen (14). Note that only 185 out of 1633 owned a digital pen (11%) and answered the latter questions, including Galaxy Note, Surface Pro, and iPad combined with a capacitive stylus.

In the rest of this section, we report the results from both our diary study and the survey to contrast the use of analog pens vs digital pens. We use the quantitative results from the survey to provide frequency and prevalence of activities and motivations for using analog or digital pens; and the qualitative results from our diary study to illustrate some of these activities and identify reasons for differences in usage or expectations.

New Digital Pen Affordances and Activities

The entries from our diary study confirmed that most analog pen activities (PA1-8) have a digital counterpart, although not many entries dealt with collaboration and coordination (PA2) or personal communication (PA4). Our coding of these entries also led to one additional activity:

PA9. UI interactions and non-ink traces. This activity includes tapping, scrolling and pointing to interface elements (somewhat analogous to gesturing and pointing with a pen) as well as interactions with the app content such as lasso selection. These entries showcased a variety of context for interacting with the pen: from inputting text on a keyboard to navigating a map or playing a game. This activity reveals the digital pen as a substitute for touch, mouse or trackpad.

In addition, our analysis of the entries revealed three affordances specific to the pen:

AF10. Accuracy for pointing and dragging. Participants felt that the pen was more precise than touch. This affordance is related to (AF2, high-fidelity marks), where users leverage fine-motor skill with a tool. *"I prefer with my digital pen because it feels better when touching the screen and it's more accurate"* [#98951]. *"I just have got used to using a pen--using a mouse just feels clumsy to me."* [#98057].

AF11. Versatility in the style of traces, where a single pen produces strokes of various colors or shape: *"I'm an artist*

[...] while I typically like to use a more variable material like ebony pencil or charcoal, it's nice to use a digital pen and iPad while laying on the couch." [#99148]

AF12. Dynamic editing and history, where the digital trace can be easily deleted or edited: *"I love that i can record our sketching while we play and we then edit it to playback and sometimes the top best we edit and make our own home movies ..."* [#99178].

Contrasting Analog and Digital Pen Usage

Results from our survey confirmed that analog pen and paper plays a significant role in people's lives: 72% of respondents reported using pen and paper 1 hour or more per day, 32% at 3 hours or more. Yet, for those who owned a digital pen—11% of the survey respondents—its use was rather limited (Figure 9). Over 50% used their digital pen less than daily. Note also that digital pen owners did not report using analog pens less than the rest of the respondents. To gain insight into what people do with digital *vs.* analog pens, we asked respondents what their frequent pen activities were, and if they used digital pens *more* or *less* than expected for each.

Most popular and frequent analog pen activities reported by our respondents are information scraps (PA3, 79%) and annotations (PA5, 73%). However, over 40% of digital pen users reported that using their digital pen less than expected for these activities. To understand why, we analyzed the reasons respondents gave for using analog pens, identifying affordances of the pen that may not hold for digital pens. In particular, the contextualization of information (AF6)—a motivation for using analog pens over computers for 76% of survey respondents—is critical for annotations. Yet in-place annotation experiences are vastly inconsistent for digital pen users, making it difficult to support this activity. Digital artefacts are siloed in different file types, often unreadable or uneditable by other apps, and the UI for pen annotation differs widely across apps as well—if supported at all.

Regarding information scraps, any immediacy of the pen (AF9) is often lost as it takes far longer to find and launch an app than to grab a piece of paper and click a pen.

We also looked at what activities people performed most often with digital pens. Using the digital pen to interact with the UI (PA9) represents a substantial part of today's digital pen experiences. Many digital pen owners (67%, see Figure 9) reported using their pen as much or even more for interacting with the interface than for actual inking. While device manufacturers might tout this new use as a putative benefit of digital pens, one could equally well argue that it poses a fundamental shortcoming if it compromises the natural affordances of analog pen-and-ink. But either way this finding underscores the shift in expected use that participants experienced for digital pens: over 50% reported using the digital pen for inking far less than anticipated when making the purchase in the first place.

Digital Pen Falls Short of Expectations

To reflect on compelling scenarios for the digital pen, we need to consider not only the frequency and popularity of activities, but what matters to people. The top 5 reasons cited by digital pen owners for purchasing a device revolved around ink's ability to engage cognitive processes more deeply with better recall (AF1). Yet few respondents reported using their devices for daily ideation (15%), or recording (39%), and overall 37% reported using their digital pen less than expected for these activities.

To contrast with the survey findings, we looked for instances in the digital pen diary study where participants surfaced benefits from externalizing thinking and deeper processing of information with digital ink (AF1): *"I feel more creative and mind flows better vs typing."* [#97663], or "*This activity is best done with a pen because of muscle memory already associated with taking notes."* [#97662]. While this suggests that several affordances of the analog pen at least partially hold for its digital counterpart, comments also indicated compromised dependability in the digital realm (AF8): "*Sometimes The pen wouldn't pick up my marks which was kind of frustrating."* [#99310]. Participants also noted technological barriers to the fidelity of their marks (AF2): *"A better feeling pen, and more accuracy with handwriting digitally would be preferred.*" [#97027]. Or, regarding the feel of digital inking, "*The only thing that is missing is a bit of tactile feedback"* [#98961].

Compelling Scenarios for the Digital Pen

The personal expression afforded by a pen (AF7) is the top reported advantage of the analog pen over computing devices in our survey (77%), followed by uniqueness of what is created (74%). Several activities for which this affordance matters most may even be enhanced by a digital pen. For example, our survey indicates that crafts (PA7) were among the most compelling for digital-pen users. Over 20% of digital pen users reported using their pen more than they had anticipated for these activities. Several diary study entries point to the versatility of the digital pen offering a virtually unlimited set of stroke styles (AF11), and the dynamic editing of the output (AF12) contributing to make the digital experience more compelling than analog. Yet, other activities for which AF7 matters, such as keeping a diary or handwriting correspondence, are not supported much by today's software. Investigating these scenarios further could showcase the unique affordances that digital pen offers.

Another example of a potential asset of digital technologies is the ability to archive and retrieve handwritten notes. The survey revealed that 66% of respondents are confident that the computer keeps their content safe, and 58% that it makes retrieval easier. However, even if ink is archived, ease of retrieval does not yet seem to be fully realized: *"Wish I could search through it, I.e. handwriting recognition."* [#97748]. Even if we make the dubious assumption that handwriting recognition is always available, and accurate, it still lacks consistent integration across applications and platforms.

STUDY LIMITATIONS

Our approach combines two diary studies with a limited number of participants, to provide a rich corpus of examples, and a survey with a larger population, to assess the prevalence of activities and scenarios for analog and digital pen. As with all studies, they have a number of limitations.

The participants of our diary studies are certainly biased towards more heavy users of ink and, while we selected for a diverse set of people, it remains probable that the set of activities we collected is not exhaustive nor representative of the general public, and could certainly be augmented with additional studies. There are also several limitations pertaining to the survey. In particular, many questions asked participants to self-report their most frequent activities or rank them by importance. As with all self-reported measures, these responses may not be representative of reality.

Note that we also focused primarily on pen as a mark-up tool. Yet pen is often used in the analog world in conjunction with meaningful, non-mark-up gestures [52]. Hence, when considering the affordances of the pen we must remember they are intimately interwoven with those of the hand [59]—that is, the many forms of 'touch' observable on modern touchscreen devices [19] that we did not capture in our studies. Issues only become more complicated and nuanced when one considers hybrid analog-digital inking solutions (e.g. [27,48,58]), or when one inks with an ordinary pen on post-its that are tracked by a sensing system [25], to name a few examples that weren't included in our studies.

DISCUSSION AND RESEARCH OPPORTUNITIES

Our ambitious goal is to bring a new, wider perspective on the types of activities people perform with analog and digital pen, teasing out the specific affordances of pen. We discuss research opportunities resulting from our studies below.

Affordances of Pen vs. Affordances of Paper

Our work takes an orthogonal and complementary perspective from Sellen and Harper's affordances of paper, focusing on the input mechanism rather than the capture medium. This angle enabled us to collect data that revealed intersections between pen and paper affordances, sometimes expanding them; and also outlined some of the unique affordances of the pen, independently of the capture medium, hinting at a different set of research opportunities.

Several affordances of pen and of paper are tightly coupled: AF6 (integrating information in context), for example, is partially covered by *marking up documents*. When focusing on the pen, this affordance also includes the marking up of physical objects and spaces, pointing to a different set of research directions in augmented reality for example. Other affordances are unique to the pen and the quality of marks produced, such as AF7 (the personal expression inherent in an individual's handwritten artefacts).

The data we collected also suggest the possibility of further affordances of paper. For instance, participants mentioned how paper can be easily transformed (cut, torn, folded) to fit in different contexts (ripped out of a notebook, placed in one's pocket, or passed to someone else), illustrating how paper artefacts can easily be repurposed in new contexts after-the-fact (pinned, taped, inserted). And even though paper is cheap and easily disposable, it can also serve as a reliable medium for storage, in contrast to the "dark ages" of digital photography, for example. These examples hint that a broad re-analysis of the affordances of paper (either from our data, or future studies focused on this aspect) may very well extend the affordances identified by Sellen and Harper.

(Re)focusing on Scenarios and Affordances that Matter

Insights from our studies indicate that most frequent analog scenarios performed by a large portion of our participants (information scraps and annotations) are poorly supported by digital pens today. Scenarios perhaps less frequent but that matter to people, often motivating them to own a digital pen in the first place, (ideations and recordings) do not transfer well to digital either. Tacit use (AF3), contextualization (AF6), reliability (AF8) and immediacy (AF9) play an important role in making these scenarios compelling with a digital pen. We encourage the community to search for solutions to better transfer these to the digital world. Clearly the solutions in existing commercial practice fall short of the potential here. For instance, one could design a digital pen scenario that avoids distraction by limiting system notifications during inking activities. Our studies also showcase scenarios (e.g. personal communications) and unique affordances of digital pens (AF10-12) that could perhaps motivate greater adoption of digital ink, if done well.

Flexible Data: Fluid Interweaving of Varied Ink Scenarios

The data we collected suggests that different analog pen activities are often intertwined. Our survey indicates that 41% of people report conducting three or more analog pen activities daily, and diary entries at times reveal complex interstitial activities afforded by analog pens. For instance, a notebook meant to be used for class notes might also contain a 'contact'—the phone number of a peer—with whom a student needs to coordinate on a project.

In the analog world, flexible data leads to seamless and opportunistic transitions. But in the digital world, ink loses its flexibility—and, if recognized, may even lose its underlying ink-stroke representation—as it becomes siloed in applications that support specific scenarios (taking notes vs. managing contacts vs. reading and annotating documents). The user is thus forced into a premature choice of which app to use, even though at the time of making the note, the user doesn't know its future use (or uses)—if any. Designing for fluid transitions between activities may avoid the traps of such premature commitment, or perhaps more deeply mapping the interdependence of activities may be instrumental to enable "flexible data" scenarios with appeal to a wider audience.

Conflicting Affordances of Digital and Analog Ink

A fundamental issue for digital ink is whether pen input always leaves behind ink strokes, in a manner faithful to marking with an analog pen, or whether it is sometimes takes on a special digital interpretation, such as a scratch-out or lasso gesture [12,35,39], or even mouse cursor control. Perhaps surprisingly, our observations of both digital and analog pen use suggest that there is not yet any clear-cut answer to this design dilemma.

Should our guidepost to digital ink be the analog pen? Analog pens, by sheer virtue of laying down ink no matter the context, shed these technology-laden expectations. One could design a digital pen that only ever lays down ink. Yet, current digital pen owners seem to purchase these devices with the expectation that an expensive digital pen can do more than just lay ink on the screen.

The alternative is to accept that digital pens will shift in function depending on the current device, application, and mode. Although good mode-switching techniques [26,44] can mitigate such shifts, a designer with a critical eye would be correct to point out that presence of one interpretation competes with and undermines the affordances of the other. If a pen only inks, it cannot serve as a precise pointing device for interacting with UI elements. Yet a device where the pen is primarily a pointing device and secondarily an inking device seems equally unpalatable. Such a dual-purpose approach, where the pen can serve as an inking device *and* a pointing device, would seem to place a burden on the user to remember (or predict) what effect the pen will produce when they bring it to the screen. Thus either design decision seems detrimental to the analog (and digital) affordances of ink.

Resolving this conflict in a satisfactory manner may be one the greatest challenges facing the design of future digital-pen devices. We suspect the solution lies in extreme attention to detail in design. Achieving predictable, consistent, and habit-forming behaviors requires the app ecosystem to provide consistent experiences as opposed to heterogeneous interface components with numerous interactions for switching modes, or for features such as changing the ink color. Much research and design is needed to fully unlock the the nimble representations afforded by the 'flexible data' inherent in ink strokes, which may ultimately manifest as cross-application (and cross-device) paradigms for laying down and interacting with ink. In the meantime, understanding the tradeoffs of inking-only vs. mixed-use devices may offer a more practical avenue.

Beyond the heterogeneity of digital pen apps, our observations suggest that ink recognition itself may be at odds with the value (and affordances) of ink that remains *ink*. The pen affords an infinite vocabulary of shapes, lines, and symbols that cannot be recognized perfectly in a context-independent manner. By enticing people with the value of easy and exhaustive retrieval enabled by ink recognition, one risks turning an organic and artisanal modality which serves an imprecise, ambiguous, and pervasively flexible mode of expression into one that is a well-ordered but sterile set of pre-defined symbols so that it conforms to the structure and formality demanded by most experiences with computers.

Draft vs Craft

One recurring theme in our data is the idea that while digital pen experiences might be well-suited for *crafting* and polishing artefacts, they currently lack critical affordances for *drafting*—ideating to decide what needs to be crafted. In other words, people associate analog pen with creativity and ideation, and digital technologies to producing a finished product. So how do we reconcile the two? How do we make make the leap from *freeflow* to *workflow*, such that a digital pen compelling for ideation can transition to the creation of a more polished and shareable end-product as well?

While this question remains open, we propose several considerations. Earlier, we noted how analog pen affordances are well-aligned with some of the processes at play in ideation. Analog pens are tacit (AF3), allowing the tool to disappear from attention such that only creation of the idea itself remains. Analog affordances such as immediacy (AF8) and jotting down ideas in non-committal form (AF4) are key to creativity, areas which remain barriers to use of the pen for "craft" in digital contexts due even to mundane issues such as start-up time and the accuracy and feel of the pen digitizer. Indeed, some advantages of digital experiences—such as archiving and multi-tasking—seem to fundamentally conflict with the "drafting" experience. Reconsidering automatic archiving of ink, or the role (or even appropriateness) of recognition features, may provide people with a place more akin to paper, where information can either mature and become valuable for archiving and sharing; or be discarded without any traces as time demonstrates its lack of usefulness (e.g. [23]). While intentionally leaving out such "must-have" features of digital ink might seem an extreme design stance, such a shift in perspective may ultimately prove necessary to change how people perceive digital ink.

CONCLUSION

This work attempts to build a comprehensive view of analog and digital pen experiences. We contributed insights on the breadth of activities conducted with a pen today. And, to compare and contrast the two, we teased out affordances of the pen, distinguishing them from the affordances of paper versus those of digital technologies. We believe these affordances will lay a foundation for reflecting on *"how we may ink,"* raising key implications for the design of a rich and sustainable set of digital pen experiences. Our approach revealed several critical affordances that are either lacking or poorly supported in current digital experiences—insights that can and perhaps should encourage closer scrutiny of the assumptions underlying digital pens so as to better inform future generations of electronic paper and digital screens.

ACKNOWLEDGEMENTS

We would like to thank all the study participants as well as the user experience team at Microsoft Surface.

REFERENCES

1. Annette Adler, Anuj Gujar, Beverly L. Harrison, Kenton O'Hara, Abigail Sellen. 1998. A diary study of

work-related reading design implications for digital reading devices. In *CHI'98*, 241 - 248.

2. Michelle Annett, Fraser Anderson, Walter F. Bischof, Anoop Gupta. 2014. The pen is mightier: understanding stylus behaviour while inking on tablets. In *Proceedings of Graphics Interface 2014 (GI '14)*, 193-200.
3. Michelle Annett, Anoop Gupta, Walter F. Bischof. 2014. Exploring and Understanding Unintended Touch during Direct Pen Interaction. *ACM Trans. Comput.-Hum. Interact.* 21, 5: Article 28 (39pp). http://doi.acm.org/10.1145/2674915
4. Aaron Bauer and Kenneth R. Koedinger. 2007. Selection-based note-taking applications. In *Proceedings of CHI 2007*, 981-990.
5. B. Bederson. 2004. Interfaces for Staying in the Flow. *Ubiquity* 5, 27 (Sept. 1-7).
6. Mohammed Belatar and François Coldefy. 2010. Sketched menus and iconic gestures, techniques designed in the context of shareable interfaces. In *ACM International Conference on Interactive Tabletops and Surfaces (ITS '10)*, 143-146. http://doi.acm.org/10.1145/1936652.1936681.
7. Michael Bernstein, Max Van Kleek, David Karger, mc schraefel. 2008. Information scraps: How and why information eludes our personal information management tools. *ACM Transactions on Information Systems (TOIS)*.
8. Andrea Bianchi, So-Ryang Ban, Ian Oakley. 2015. Designing a Physical Aid to Support Active Reading on Tablets. In *Proceedings of the 33rd Annual ACM Conference on Human Factors in Computing Systems (CHI '15)*, 699-708. http://dx.doi.org/10.1145/2702123.2702303.
9. Richard Boardman and M. Angela Sasse. 2004. "Stuff goes into the computer and doesn't come out": a cross-tool study of personal information management. In *Proceedings of the SIGCHI Conference on Human Factors in Computing Systems (CHI '04)*, 583-590. http://dx.doi.org/10.1145/985692.985766.
10. Peter Brandl, Christoph Richter, Michael Haller. 2010. NiCEBook: supporting natural note taking. In *CHI '10*, 599-608.
11. V. Bush. 1945. As we may think. *Atlantic Monthly* 176: 101-108.
12. W. Buxton, E. Fiume, R. Hill, A. Lee, C. Woo. 1983. Continuous hand-gesture driven input. In *Proceedings of Graphics Interface '83*, 191-195.
13. N. Chen, F. Guimbretiere, A. Sellen. 2012. Designing a Multi-Slate Reading Environment to Support Active Reading Activities. *TOCHI* 19, 3: Article 18 (35 pp.). http://doi.acm.org/10.1145/2362364.2362366
14. Mauro Cherubini, Gina Venolia, Rob DeLine, Andrew J. Ko. 2007. Let's go to the whiteboard: how and why software developers use drawings. In *Proceedings of the SIGCHI Conference on Human Factors in Computing Systems (CHI '07)*, 557-566. http://dx.doi.org/10.1145/1240624.1240714.
15. Richard C. Davis, James A. Landay, Victor Chen, Jonathan Huang, Rebecca B. Lee, Frances C. Li, James Lin, III Charles B. Morrey, Ben Schleimer, Morgan N. Price, Bill N. Schilit. 1999. NotePals: lightweight note sharing by the group, for the group. In *Proceedings of the SIGCHI conference on Human Factors in Computing Systems (CHI '99)*, 338-345. http://dx.doi.org/10.1145/302979.303107.
16. G. Golovchinsky, M. N. Price, B. Schilit. 1999. From Reading to Retrieval: Freeform Ink Annotations as Queries. In *SIGIR'99*, 19-25.
17. Thomas T. Hewett. 2005. Informing the design of computer-based environments to support creativity. *Int. J. Hum.-Comput. Stud.* 63, 4-5 (October 2005): 383-409. http://dx.doi.org/10.1016/j.ijhcs.2005.04.004.
18. Ken Hinckley, Xiaojun Bi, Michel Pahud, Bill Buxton. 2012. Informal Information Gathering Techniques for Active Reading. In *Proceedings of the SIGCHI Conference on Human Factors in Computing Systems (CHI '12)*, 1893-1896. http://dx.doi.org/10.1145/2207676.2208327.
19. Ken Hinckley and Bill Buxton. 2016. Inking Outside the Box: How Context Sensing Affords More Natural Pen (and Touch) Computing, in *Revolutionizing Education with Digital Ink*, T. Hammond, Editor. Springer International Publishing Switzerland.
20. M. Hong, A. M. Piper, N. Weibel, S. Olberding, J. Hollan. 2012. Microanalysis of active reading behavior to inform design of interactive desktop workspaces. In *Proceedings of ITS '12*.
21. Dominik P. Käser, Maneesh Agrawala, Mark Pauly. 2011. FingerGlass: efficient multiscale interaction on multitouch screens. In *Proceedings of the SIGCHI Conference on Human Factors in Computing Systems (CHI '11)*, 1601-1610. http://dx.doi.org/10.1145/1978942.1979175.
22. A. Kidd. 1994. The marks are on the knowledge worker. In *Proceedings of CHI'94*.
23. Kenrick Kin, Maneesh Agrawala, Tony DeRose. 2009. Determining the benefits of direct-touch, bimanual, and multifinger input on a multitouch workstation. In *Proceedings of Graphics Interface 2009*, 119-124.
24. D. Kirsh. 1995. Complementary strategies: why we use our hands when we think. In *Proceedings of 7th Annual Conference of the Cognitive Science Society.*, 212-217.
25. Scott R. Klemmer, Mark W. Newman, Ryan Farrell, Mark Bilezikjian, James A. Landay. 2001. The designers' outpost: a tangible interface for collaborative web site. In *Proceedings of the 14th annual ACM symposium on User interface software and technology*, 1-10. http://doi.acm.org/10.1145/502348.502350.
26. Yang Li, Ken Hinckley, Zhiwei Guan, James A. Landay. 2005. Experimental analysis of mode switching

techniques in pen-based user interfaces. In *Proceedings of the SIGCHI Conference on Human Factors in Computing Systems (CHI '05)*, 461-470. http://doi.acm.org/10.1145/1054972.1055036.

27. Chunyuan Liao, Francois Guimbretiere, Ken Hinckley, Jim Hollan. 2008. Papiercraft: A gesture-based command system for interactive paper. *ACM Trans. Comput.-Hum. Interact* 14, 4 (Article 18 (Jan. 2008)).
28. Min Lin, Wayne G. Lutters, Tina S. Kim. 2004. Understanding the micronote lifecycle: improving mobile support for informal note taking. In *Proceedings of the SIGCHI Conference on Human Factors in Computing Systems (CHI '04)*, 687-694. http://dx.doi.org/10.1145/985692.985779.
29. P. Luff and C. Heath. 1998. Mobility in collaboration. In *Proc. CSCW '98 Conf. on Computer Supported Cooperative Work*, 305-314.
30. Christine Mackenzie and Thea Iberall. 1994. The Grasping Hand. Advances in Psychology 104, ed. G. Stelmach and P. Vroon. North Holland.
31. N. Marquardt, K. Hinckley, S. Greenberg. 2012. Cross-Device Interaction via Micro-mobility and F-formations. In *UIST '12.*
32. C. Marshall. 2005. Turning the Page on Page Navigation. In *Proceedings of the 5th ACM/IEEE-CS Joint Conference on Digital Libraries (JCDL '05)*, 225-234.
33. Catherine C. Marshall. 1997. Annotation: from paper books to the digital library. In *ACM International Conference on Digital Libraries*, 131-140.
34. Catherine C. Marshall and A. J. Bernheim Brush. 2004. Exploring the relationship between personal and public annotations. In *Proceedings of the 4th ACM/IEEE-CS joint conference on Digital libraries (JCDL '04)*, 349-357. http://dx.doi.org/10.1145/996350.996432.
35. Thomas P. Moran, Patrick Chiu, William van Melle. 1997. Pen-based interaction techniques for organizing material on an electronic whiteboard. In *Proceedings of the 10th ACM symposium on User interface software and technology (UIST'97)*, 45-54. http://doi.acm.org/10.1145/263407.263508.
36. M. R. Morris, A.J.B. Brush, B.R. Meyers. 2007. Reading Revisited: Evaluating the Usability of Digital Display Surfaces for Active Reading Tasks. In *Proc. Tabletop'07*, 79-86.
37. Pam A. Mueller and Daniel M. Oppenheimer. 2014. The Pen Is Mightier Than the Keyboard: Advantages of Longhand Over Laptop Note Taking. *Psychological Science* 25, 6 (June 1, 2014): 1159-1168. 10.1177/0956797614524581.
38. Kenton O'Hara and Abigail Sellen. 1997. A comparison of reading paper and on-line documents. In *Proceedings of the ACM SIGCHI Conference on Human factors in computing systems (CHI '97)*, 335-342. http://dx.doi.org/10.1145/258549.258787.
39. Ken Pier and James A. Landay, *Issues for Location-Independent Interfaces*. 1992: Technical Report ISTL92-4, Xerox Palo Alto Research Center.
40. M. N. Price, B. Schilit, G. Golovchinsky. 1998. XLibris: The Active Reading Machine. In *CHI'98 Extended Abstracts*, 2 pp.
41. Bill N. Schilit, Gene Golovchinsky, Morgan N. Price. 1998. Beyond paper: supporting active reading with free form digital ink annotations. In *ACM CHI Conference on Human Factors in Computing Systems*, 249-256.
42. Donald Schön and John Bennett. 1996. Reflective conversation with materials, in *Bringing Design to Software*, T. Winograd, Editor. ACM, New York, NY, USA, 171-189.
43. A. J. Sellen and H. R. Harper. 2002. The myth of the paperless office. MIT Press.
44. A. Sellen, G. Kurtenbach, W. Buxton. 1992. The prevention of mode errors through sensory feedback. *Human Computer Interaction* 7, 2: 141-164.
45. Jami J. Shah, Noe Vargas-Hernandez, Joshua D. Summers, Santosh Kulkarni. 2001. Collaborative Sketching (C-Sketch)--An Idea Generation Technique for Engineering Design. *Journal of Creative Behavior* 35, 3 (3rd Qtr 2001): 168-198
46. Hirohito Shibata and Kengo Omura. 2011. Effects of paper on page turning: comparison of paper and electronic media in reading documents with endnotes. In *Proceedings of the 9th international conference on Engineering psychology and cognitive ergonomics (EPCE'11)*, 92-101.
47. M. Shilman, Zile Wei, S. Raghupathy, P. Simard, D. Jones. 2003. Discerning structure from freeform handwritten notes. In *Document Analysis and Recognition*, 60-65.
48. L. Stifelman, B. Arons, C. Schmandt. 2001. The audio notebook: paper and pen interaction with structured speech. In *CHI '01*, 182-189.
49. Anselm Strauss and Juliet Corbin. 1998. Basics of Qualitative Research: Grounded Theory Procedures and Techniques. 2nd edition ed. SAGE Publications, Inc.
50. Craig J. Sutherland, Andrew Luxton-Reilly, Beryl Plimmer. 2016. Freeform digital ink annotations in electronic documents: A systematic mapping study. *Comput. Graph.* 55, C (April 2016): 1-20. http://dx.doi.org/10.1016/j.cag.2015.10.014.
51. Ivan E. Sutherland. 1963. Sketchpad: a man-machine graphical communication system. In *Proceedings of the May 21-23, 1963, spring joint computer conference (AFIPS '63 (Spring))*, 329-346. http://dx.doi.org/10.1145/1461551.1461591.
52. Kentaro Takano, Hirohito Shibata, Junko Ichino, Hashiyama Tomonori, Shun'ichi Tano. 2014. Microscopic analysis of document handling while reading paper documents to improve digital reading device. In *Proceedings of the 26th Australian*

Computer-Human Interaction Conference on Designing Futures: the Future of Design (OzCHI '14), 559-567. http://dx.doi.org/10.1145/2686612.2686701.

53. Yoshiki Takeoka, Takashi Miyaki, Jun Rekimoto. 2010. Z-touch: an infrastructure for 3d gesture interaction in the proximity of tabletop surfaces. In *ACM International Conference on Interactive Tabletops and Surfaces (ITS '10)*, 91-94. http://dx.doi.org/10.1145/1936652.1936668.
54. C. Tashman and W. K. Edwards. 2011. Active Reading and Its Discontents: The Situations, Problems and Ideas of Readers. In *CHI'11*.
55. C. Tashman and W. K. Edwards. 2011. LiquidText: A Flexible, Multitouch Environment to Support Active Reading. In *CHI'11*.
56. L. Terrenghi, D. Kirk, A. Sellen, S. Izadi. 2007. Affordances for manipulation of physical versus digital media on interactive surfaces. In *CHI '07*, 1157-66.
57. Jagoda Walny, Sheelagh Carpendale, Nathalie Henry Riche, Gina Venolia, Philip Fawcett. 2011. Visual Thinking In Action: Visualizations As Used On Whiteboards. *IEEE Transactions on Visualization and Computer Graphics* 17, 12 (December 2011): 2508-2517. http://dx.doi.org/10.1109/TVCG.2011.251.
58. Nadir Weibel, Adam Fouse, Colleen Emmenegger, Whitney Friedman, Edwin Hutchins, James Hollan. 2012. Digital pen and paper practices in observational research. In *CHI '12*, 1331-1340.
59. F. R. Wilson. 1998. The Hand: How its use shapes the brain, language, and human culture. Pantheon Books.
60. Ming Ye, P. Viola, S. Raghupathy, H. Sutanto, Chengyang Li. 2007. Learning to Group Text Lines and Regions in Freeform Handwritten Notes. In *Document Analysis and Recognition (ICDAR 2007)*, 28-32.
61. Dongwook Yoon, Nicholas Chen, François Guimbretière. 2013. TextTearing: opening white space for digital ink annotation. In *UIST '13*, 107-112.
62. Dongwook Yoon, Ken Hinckley, Hrvoje Benko, François Guimbretière, Pourang Irani, Michel Pahud, Marcel Gavriliu. 2015. Sensing Tablet Grasp + Micro-mobility for Active Reading. In *Proceedings of the 28th Annual ACM Symposium on User Interface Software & Technology (UIST '15)*, 477-487. http://dx.doi.org/10.1145/2807442.2807510.

Thumb + Pen Interaction on Tablets

Ken Pfeuffer[1,2], Ken Hinckley[1], Michel Pahud[1], Bill Buxton[1]
[1]Microsoft Research, Redmond, WA, USA, {kenh, mpahud, bibuxton}@microsoft.com
[2]Interactive Systems, Lancaster University, UK, k.pfeuffer@lancaster.ac.uk

ABSTRACT
Modern tablets support simultaneous pen and touch input, but it remains unclear how to best leverage this capability for bimanual input when the nonpreferred hand holds the tablet. We explore Thumb + Pen interactions that support simultaneous pen and touch interaction, with both hands, in such situations. Our approach engages the thumb of the device-holding hand, such that the thumb interacts with the touch screen in an *indirect* manner, thereby complementing the *direct* input provided by the preferred hand. For instance, the thumb can determine how pen actions (articulated with the opposite hand) are interpreted. Alternatively, the pen can point at an object, while the thumb manipulates one or more of its parameters through indirect touch. Our techniques integrate concepts in a novel way that derive from marking menus, spring-loaded modes, indirect input, and multi-touch conventions. Our overall approach takes the form of a set of probes, each representing a meaningfully distinct class of application. They serve as an initial exploration of the design space at a level which will help determine the feasibility of supporting bimanual interaction in such contexts, and the viability of the Thumb + Pen techniques in so doing.

Author Keywords
pen+touch; thumb; tablet; bimanual input; postures of use.

ACM Classification Keywords
H.5.2. Information interfaces and presentation: Input

INTRODUCTION
Modern tablet devices support simultaneous pen and touch technology, opening a range of new bimanual input capabilities that complement the now-common multi-touch paradigm [7,18]. Up to now, research in this space has mainly focused on stationary systems, such as desk-supported or wall-mounted systems, which leave both hands free to interact with the device.

However, the mobility of tablets results in their use in a broader set of postures and physical contexts. These can include situations where there is no supporting surface: for example, consider a user seated on a train, reclined on the couch, or enjoying a garden bench at the park. And even when supported—such as by a kickstand—the device might be gripped for stability, or simply out of comfort. Such scenarios give rise to our interest in providing the benefits of fluid pen and touch input *with both hands*, despite one of the hands (typically the nonpreferred) being partially encumbered by holding or otherwise supporting the tablet.

Permission to make digital or hard copies of all or part of this work for personal or classroom use is granted without fee provided that copies are not made or distributed for profit or commercial advantage and that copies bear this notice and the full citation on the first page. Copyrights for components of this work owned by others than the author(s) must be honored. Abstracting with credit is permitted. To copy otherwise, or republish, to post on servers or to redistribute to lists, requires prior specific permission and/or a fee. Request permissions from Permissions@acm.org.
CHI 2017, May 06 - 11, 2017, Denver, CO, USA
Copyright is held by the owner/author(s). Publication rights licensed to ACM.
ACM 978-1-4503-4655-9/17/05…$15.00
DOI: http://dx.doi.org/10.1145/3025453.3025567

Figure 1: Thumb + Pen interaction enables simultaneous bimanual pen+touch while holding a tablet with the off-hand.

We explore *Thumb + Pen* techniques as a way to still reap many benefits of simultaneous pen and touch interaction in such situations. In our approach, the thumb of the nonpreferred, device-holding hand interacts with the touch screen, augmenting and complementing actions articulated using the preferred hand with the pen (Figure 1). Relative to *direct* interactions articulated by the preferred hand—which might involve pen or touch—those of the thumb of the nonpreferred hand are primarily *indirect,* and use only touch.

To go one level deeper, Figure 2 introduces a few examples of what underlies such interactions. For instance, the thumb can independently support the pen by taking over secondary menu interactions (a), but can also thereby hold spring-loaded modes [16] while the pen interacts with the main canvas (b). Alternatively, users can manipulate both modalities at the same time, e.g. by using the pen to indicate an object through pointing, while the thumb indirectly controls one or more of the indicated object's parameters through touch (c). We will delve into this design space (and resulting interaction techniques) in more detail shortly, to shed light on the diverse, yet largely unexplored, possibilities of Thumb + Pen interaction.

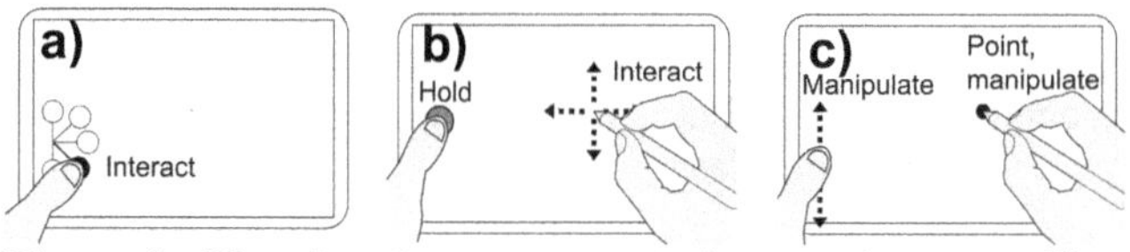

Figure 2: The thumb can support the pen by controlling secondary menu interactions (a), holding spring-loaded modes (b), or performing manipulations simultaneous to the pen (c).

By way of technology probes [19], we then explore the applicability of such techniques to three (intentionally) divergent applications:

Spreadsheet (Figure 3a): Here we see how productive work can nevertheless be performed in the informal ad-hoc posture of a hand-held tablet. This is accomplished through *thumb widgets*, button-like elements that users can hold with their thumb to enable various functionality with the pen. The widgets integrate radial menus that determine the pen's mode while the user's thumb continues to hold down the widget.

Browser (Figure 3b): The consumption-oriented browser application demonstrates context-aware Thumb + Pen interaction, such as triggering a radial menu at the pen's location, or offering navigation shortcuts (e.g. forward, back, or tab switching), depending on what actions the user is currently performing with the pen.

Shape Manipulation (Figure 3c): This prototype provides an interface where both Thumb + Pen can be used, simultaneously, to manipulate shapes. The thumb enables pen input to map to different functions, such as inking, dragging, or shape creation. The thumb can also be used to adjust parameters such as size, transparency, or the layer level of the object that is currently indicated by the pen.

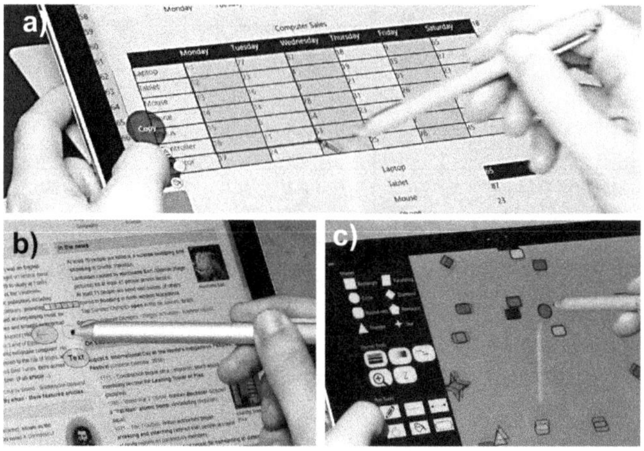

Figure 3: Thumb + Pen allow hand-held tablets to support tasks such as editing and formatting spreadsheets (a), web navigation (b), or manipulating properties of objects indicated via pen (c).

In sum, our research contributes the following:

- Introduction of pen and thumb interaction that makes bimanual pen + touch possible from physically relaxed postures or when the nonpreferred hand is otherwise occupied with supporting the device.
- Key techniques necessary for effective Pen + Thumb UIs:
  - Spring-loaded mode buttons that are configured through an integrated marking menu.
  - Indirect input menus to extend the thumb's reach.
  - Thumb indirection to the pen target for simultaneous thumb and pen input on one object.
- Design of spreadsheet, browser, and shape manipulation applications that put the techniques in context, and provide new application areas for pen and touch such as fluid pen based zoom, copy & paste, tab-switching, context-aware ink, search by ink, and 3D object control.
- A preliminary evaluation of the applications with users.

Our work constitutes an early-stage probe which suggests: (1) that many of the benefits of simultaneous pen and touch can be achieved, despite one hand being simultaneously occupied holding the tablet, and (2) that the Thumb + Pen techniques presented represent an approach that has the potential to deliver these benefits across a range of applications. In addition, it illuminates new aspects and considerations for pen+touch input in common tablet scenarios, where most device use would otherwise be constrained by the conflicting need to hold the tablet.

RELATED WORK

As is always the case, our work builds upon that of others. Key influences include work on pen and touch, (indirect) thumb interaction, and bimanual interaction on tablets.

Pen and Touch Interaction

Pen and touch interaction has been extensively explored on stationary computers in a variety of applications, such as reading [15], design [7,18,28,40], document work [31,44], games [14], or education [45]. These works are influenced by Guiard's observations on bimanual asymmetry in manual activities: the nonpreferred hand sets the frame of input for the preferred hand [12].

Nonpreferred hand input is effective for mode switching of the pen in the preferred hand [26], and research shows various ways to accomplish this. Brandl et al. explored different hand gestures combined with pen input, where each gesture leads to different pen tools [7]. Hinckley et al. advocate a holistic *pen writes, touch manipulates* division of labor between the modalities: by default, the pen writes, but e.g. when touching an object before pen input, the pen acquires different tools such as scissors or copying the object. Other techniques include dynamic touch-menus [45], finger chording, or menu areas [14] that users can trigger before or during pen input to change mode. Indeed, bimanual pen and touch yields diverse possibilities, including the Thumb + Pen interactions explored here.

Thumb Interaction on Tablets and Indirect Touch

On tablets, bimanual interaction is different as users often hold the device with the nonpreferred hand [39]. When gripping the device, the user's thumb is free for input but its limited reach raises different design challenges. Analysis of the thumb's spatial and gestural input capabilities have led to designs where the UI adapts better to the thumb's comfortable reaching area [5,22,23,33,34,38].

Indirect touch input can virtually extend the thumb's reach, i.e. inverse cursors [23], virtual thumbs [25] or back-of-device inputs [41,42] that provide users indirect handles to remote targets on tablets. Benefits of indirection include interaction over distance [10], occlusion-free manipulation [27], or enhanced precision of touch [2,4,36]. Potential conflicts between the two modes are avoided by spatially separating direct and indirect input (i.e. *spatial moding* [8,41]), or employing widgets that enable indirect control within a direct touch interface [1,6].

Bimanual Interaction on Tablets

Wagner et al.'s BiPad work investigated how the thumb of the holding hand provides an opportunity for bimanual combinations with the preferred hand's touch input [39]. For example, with the nonpreferred *vs.* preferred hand touches spatially distinguished in the UI, users can hold spring-loaded modes to change the preferred hand's touch mode. SPad [11] extends this approach with a nonpreferred-hand menu offering multiple options for modes of the preferred hand's touch input. Our work makes similar use of bimanual tablet input, with spatial moding and spring-loaded modes, but differs as follows: 1) we focus on touch *and pen*, which provides distinct capabilities such as hover, inking, drawing, and writing; 2) we apply mode-switches to the preferred hand pen, *but not preferred-hand touch*, for consistency with the established tablet multi-touch paradigm; 3) we integrate bimanual thumb and pen input with marking menus.

The potential for pen and touch on tablets has been indicated in early prototypes [30,43] and spreadsheet tasks [46]. With pen and touch increasingly available on modern tablets, we take a deeper look at Thumb + Pen design possibilities.

DESIGNING THUMB + PEN INTERACTION

By *Thumb + Pen*, we mean interaction techniques where the preferred hand's pen actions are supported by the nonpreferred hand's thumb. The techniques vary in how each thumb and/or pen input is employed. Underlying each thumb/pen input are two interaction considerations:

Direct *vs.* Indirect: This relates to the degree of indirection as per Beaudouin-Lafon's Instrumental Interaction [3], and denotes the spatial offset that *"is the distance on the screen between the logical part of the instrument and the object it operates on."* In this context, 'direct' means no spatial offset.

Explicit *vs.* Implicit: How much of the user's attention is primarily focused on an input, per Buxton's *foreground / background* framework [9]. We apply this to Thumb + Pen by considering a user's touch or pen input as *implicit* when it primarily resides in the background of a user's attention—such as the thumb simply holding a mode—or *explicit* when the input is the foreground task focus. Note that implicit *vs.* explicit is a matter of degree, not a strict dichotomy [21].

Figure 4 illustrates how various interactive techniques can be characterized relative to these two considerations. For instance, writing with a pen is direct+explicit, as users explicitly employ the pen for direct ink. Notably, interaction techniques that combine both Thumb + Pen modalities can map to both of the classes.

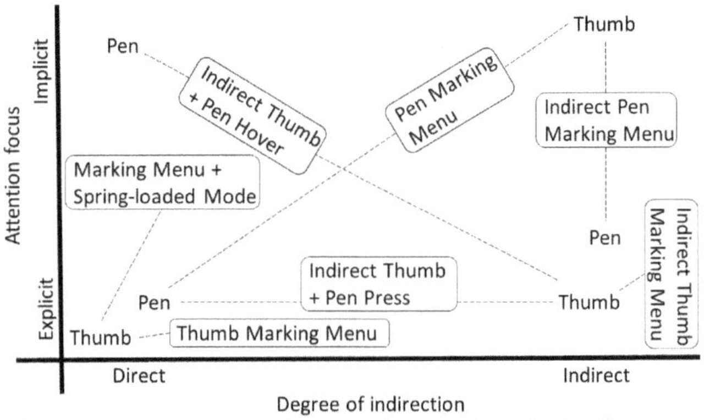

Figure 4: Thumb + Pen design space, including our example interaction techniques.

Interaction Techniques

We now delve into some representative examples from this framework for bimanual Thumb + Pen interaction on tablets. The techniques and their properties are summarized in Table 1. Our discussion emphasizes flexibility of interaction with respect to various *task strategies* [29].

Technique	Thumb	Pen
Thumb Marking Menu	Direct+explicit	
Marking Menu + Spring-loaded Mode	Direct+explicit	
Indirect Thumb Marking Menu	Indirect+explicit	
Pen Marking Menu	Indirect+implicit	Direct+explicit
Indirect Pen Marking Menu	Indirect+implicit	Indirect+explicit
Indirect Thumb + Pen Hover	Indirect+explicit	Direct+implicit
Indirect Thumb + Pen Press	Indirect+explicit	Direct+explicit

Table 1: Interaction techniques, and how they afford different interaction properties for the thumb/pen modalities.

Thumb Marking Menu (Figure 5): We started with a basic marking menu [24] operated by the thumb. This enables users to quickly access options, even though the hand holds the device. This interaction is explicit, via direct touch input.

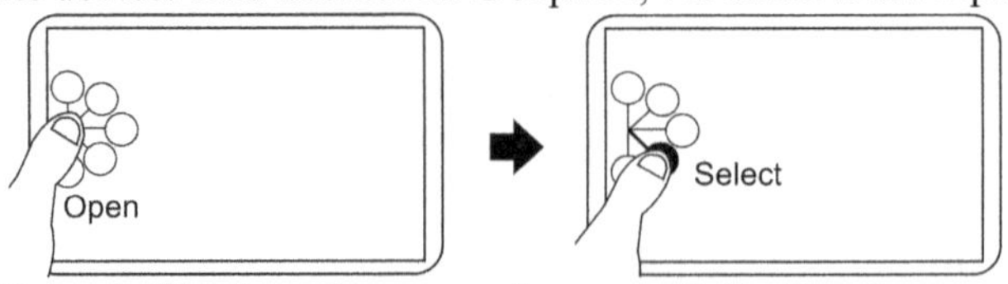

Figure 5: Fixed marking menu for use with the thumb.

Marking Menu + Spring-loaded Mode (Figure 6): In certain cases, thumb operated marking menus are augmented by spring-loaded modes. That is, the item – typically a mode – is sustained only as long as the thumb remains in physical contact with it. As soon as the thumb "releases" the button, the system "springs back" to the default condition. Effectively, this makes the selection a *non-latching switch* and the muscular tension required to maintain the temporary state helps prevent mode errors [37]. With this technique, touch actions of the nonpreferred hand can easily change the mode in which actions of the pen, controlled by the preferred hand, are interpreted by the system. This builds on the work by Wagner et al. [39], the main difference being our use of marking menus and stylus.

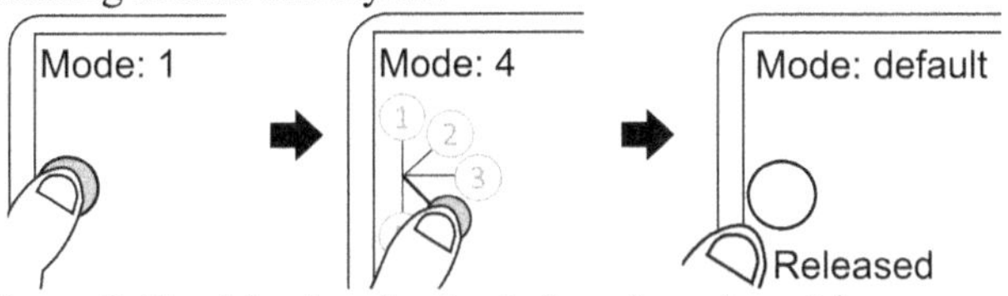

Figure 6: Combined spring-loaded mode and marking menu.

Indirect Thumb Marking Menu (Figure 7): The thumb's reach is limited to the area close to where the user grasped the tablet—thus affording only a few elements in the marking menu. To ameliorate this, we integrate indirect touch input to extend the user's physical reach with virtual handles [25,41]. To avoid interference with the direct touch usage of the marking menu itself, indirect input only activates when the user triggers specific menu items: as users slide their thumb over such an item, a handle appears that stretches from the thumb's direct position to a remote position in a pop-up slider. While in this state, dragging the thumb indirectly moves the handle, allowing control of a parameter at a higher control-display gain. Lifting the thumb sets the parameter and exits the menu. This transaction affords rapid access to many modes with manipulation of continuous values (similar to FaST Sliders [32]).

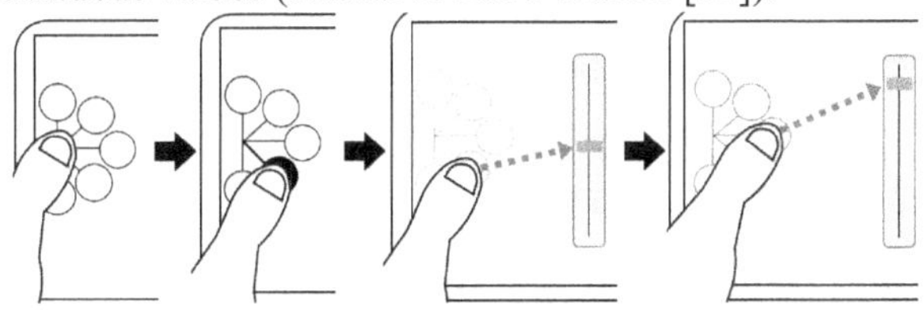

Figure 7: Extending a marking menu item with indirect input.

However, users are not confined to a thumb-only task strategy. For instance, when the thumb has opened the slider as in Figure 7 (3rd subfigure), users can also employ their pen to directly select the slider's cursor position.

Pen Marking Menu (Figure 8): Alternatively, the marking menu can pop up under the pen tip, even if triggered by the thumb; this maintains visual focus on the workspace near the preferred hand (rather than the controls under the thumb of the non-preferred hand). Pen input, by itself, always writes [18]—the default pen semantic—but when the user presses down the thumb while the pen is in-range, a marking menu appears at the pen tip. Then, pen strokes select menu items.

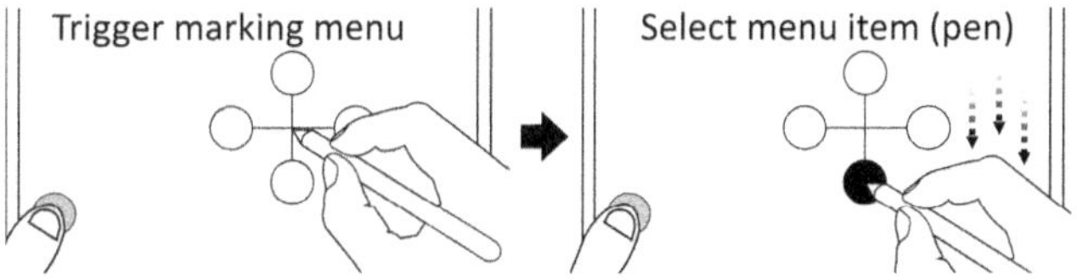

Figure 8 : The thumb triggers a marking menu at the pen location, and the pen then operates the menu.

Thumb-Operated Pen Marking Menu (Figure 9): In this variant of the Pen Marking Menu, the thumb (rather than the pen) slides to select a menu item. For instance, if the user doesn't want to disturb the position of the pen tip (perhaps because the pen-hover location indicates an object) he or she can still control the menu via an indirect, directional flick with their thumb.

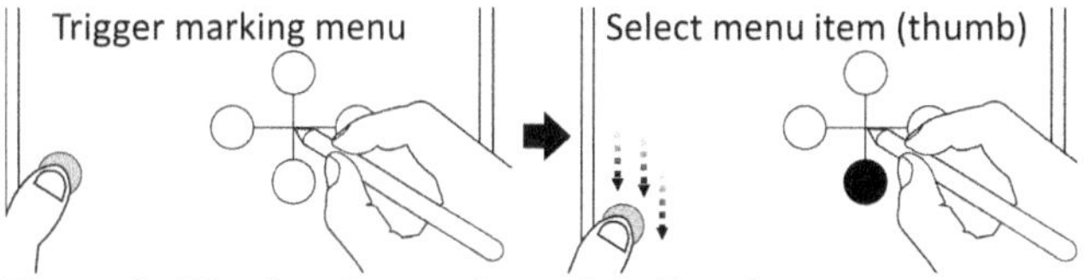

Figure 9: The thumb can trigger & indirectly operate menus.

Indirect Pen Marking Menu (Figure 10): Similar to the Thumb Marking Menu, indirect input can extend *the pen's* reach to control a distant UI element. When the pen slides over such a menu item, an indirect handle appears that allows indirect manipulation, shifting the pen from direct to indirect input. This allows the pen to manipulate parameters of fixed, distant UI elements such as web browser tabs (Figure 21), thereby avoiding cumbersome and distracting round trips.

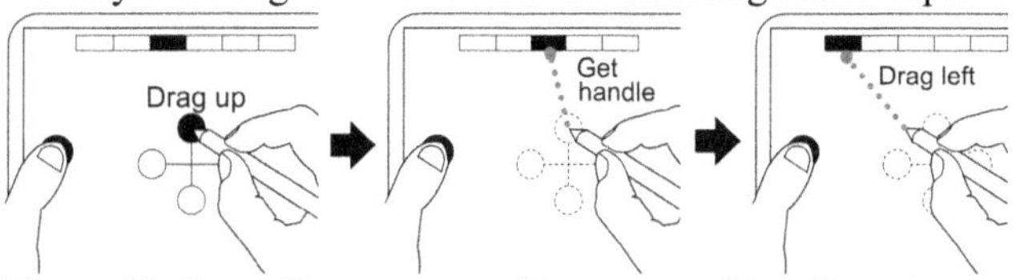

Figure 10: Extending a pen marking menu with indirect input.

Concurrent Input with Indirect Thumb + Direct Pen

The above techniques focused on control of a single modality at a time: either the thumb, with touch—or the preferred hand, operating the pen. Yet, concurrent input from both hands, and both modalities, is also possible within our Thumb + Pen framework. Even though the thumb is partially occupied by holding the device, small-scale manipulation remains possible, even as the preferred hand articulates pen strokes. The resulting degrees-of-freedom of the (indirect) thumb movement and the (direct) on-object pen movement afford hybrid direct/indirect interactions [17,35]. We considered two variations for such hybrid techniques:

Indirect Thumb + Direct Pen Hover (Figure 11): Users can indicate an object by pen-hover, while the thumb manipulates certain attributes of the selected object. For example, a user can scale an object that is too small for a two-finger pinch-to-zoom gesture by hovering over the object with the pen, and then sliding the thumb to (indirectly) control the 1D scaling factor as shown below.

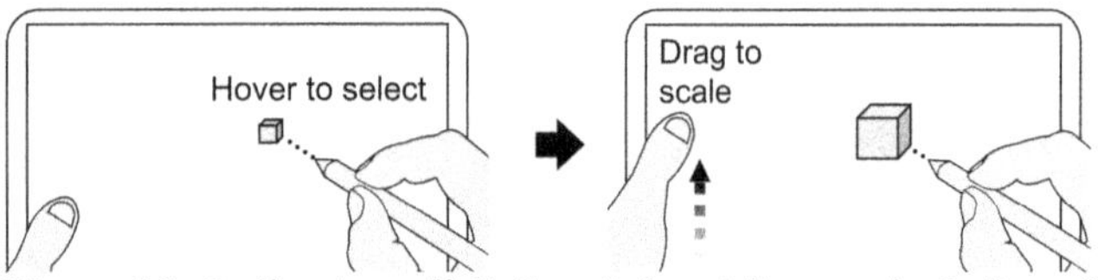

Figure 11: Indirect, explicit thumb input for manipulation of the target that is implicitly indicated by pen hover.

Indirect Thumb + Direct Pen Drag (Figure 12): Together, the thumb and pen can provide multiple degrees-of-freedom for concurrent manipulation. This may suit tasks such as selecting an object with integral control of both 2D position and 1D depth (layering) [20]. What is interesting here is that object selection (directly, with the pen) transitions without interruption to a compound 2D+1D manipulation (with the pen positioning the selected object, and indirect thumb movement controlling the depth layer). Hence, this illustrates a novel class of multi-modal (pen + touch), bimanual (thumb + pen), and mixed-mode (indirect + direct) mappings.

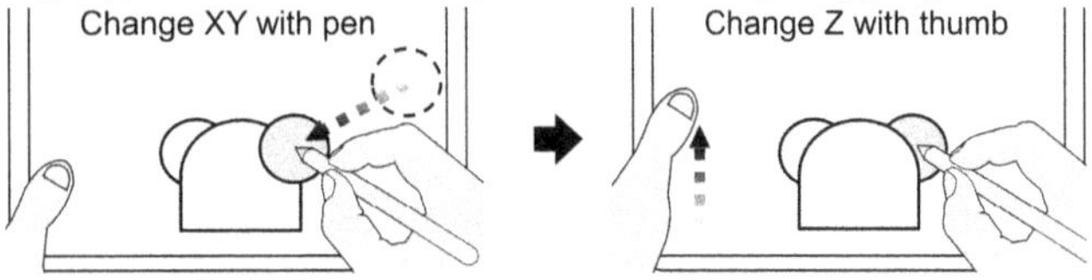

Figure 12: Using thumb and pen to control more than two dimensions simultaneously, such as the 2D position of an object with the pen, and the depth position with the thumb.

APPLICATION PROBES

To explore how the interaction techniques apply to realistic environments, we built three technology probes: spreadsheet, browser, and shape manipulation. The probes provide specific, practical examples for Thumb + Pen techniques, but also go beyond individual techniques by illustrating the integration and workflow of multiple techniques that complement one another within the same application context. The probes were built on a Microsoft Surface Pro 4 in C#. Spreadsheet and Shapes use the Universal Windows Platform; the Browser uses Awesomium and Windows Forms, with Windows Raw Input for pen+touch.

SPREADSHEETS

Bringing spreadsheets to tablets provides users with the possibility to enter, manipulate, and analyze cell data in more informal situations. In Spreadsheet, touch performs pan and zoom navigation, but rather than interactions showcasing the pen's ability to ink [46], we focus on common spreadsheet-cell actions such as copy-paste, formatting, or data editing.

Indeed, in this context, cell selection is the most common activity, and thus in contrast to the rule-of-thumb that "the pen writes" [18], we found *the pen selects* to be a better choice for the default role of the pen in our Spreadsheet. Yet, through Thumb + Pen input, we can also support facile interleaving of inking—as well as many other modes and operations—with the selection of cells, via three Marking Menu + Spring-loaded Mode controls (c.f. Figure 6):

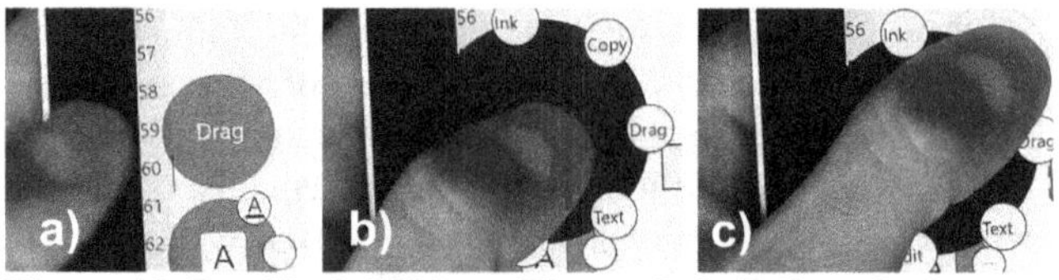

Figure 13: Pen Tools Widget: The mode is indicated when not in use (a). The marking menu appears on thumbpress (b), and changes mode when the thumb slides to a new tool (c).

Pen Tools Widget

The first widget supports tools that users configure using a marking-menu with spring-loaded control (Figure 13).

Copy-paste and drag mode: Copy and paste (or drag and drop) helps to create, combine, and manage cell data. Our implemented technique supports two task strategies.

- Single-stroke (Figure 14): Copy-paste can be chunked into a single stroke. Dragging the pen selects cells (a), and tapping the thumb on the Pen Tools Widget copies them (b). But using the pen, the user can continue dragging the selected cells to the desired position (c), until lifting the pen pastes the content (d). Integrating this entire sequence into a continuous transaction affords a succession of quick copy-paste operations.
- Two-stroke: If the target of a paste operation is far away, the user must navigate between the *copy* and *paste* steps. Hence the two-stroke variant of our technique supports interleaving multi-touch gestures between the first pen stroke, which selects a range of cells, and the second pen stroke, which moves and pastes the cells at their final location—all while the thumb continues holding the Pen Tools Widget to maintain the *Copy* mode.

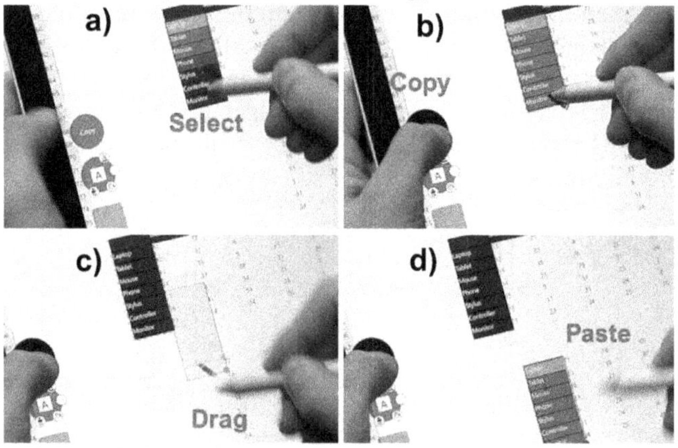

Figure 14: Select & copy cells, to then drag and paste them.

Inking (Figure 15): Freeform inking provides a fresh contrast to the highly structured cells of spreadsheets. Persistent mark-up, however, could be distracting and interfere with typical spreadsheet work. We therefore tie ink annotations to the currently-selected range of cells. Clearing the selection hides the ink. Selecting a different range of cells reveals only the annotations associated with that selection. This keeps the spreadsheet clean, while allowing the user to make a plurality of annotations tied to different ranges. This design allows the pen experience to remain authentic to spreadsheets—where the core transaction of selecting cells is the default mode—

while still allowing fluid transitions to free-form inking, in a manner tailored to the long-established expectations of spreadsheet users.

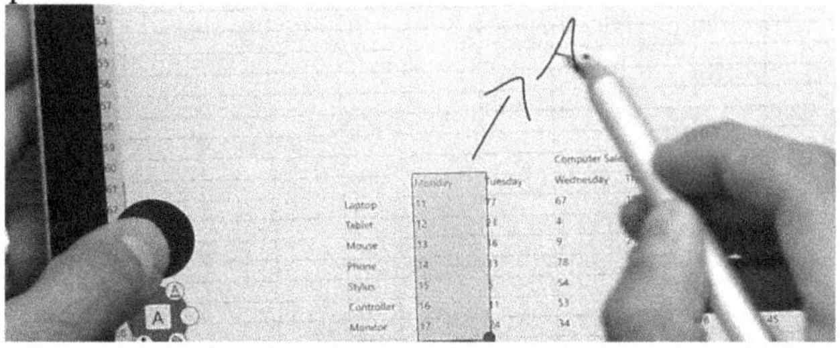

Figure 15: Inking, that is context-aware to the selected cells.

Cell editing (Figure 16): We added a mode where users can utilize their pen for manipulation of numeric data. Sliding the pen up and down acts as a valuator that adjusts the numeric value of the selected cells, with a Vernier effect proportional to the horizontal movement of the pen: when close by, the cells adjust precisely, in small steps. But when the pen is far away, the values change rapidly, at a higher gain. Thus, the technique affords exploring the relationships encoded in spreadsheet formulas, through direct spatial manipulation of a range of values, which is not possible when entering numeric values one-by-one. And using the pen as an indirect valuator, with dynamically controlled fine vs. coarse manipulation, serves rapid exploration of 'what if' scenarios.

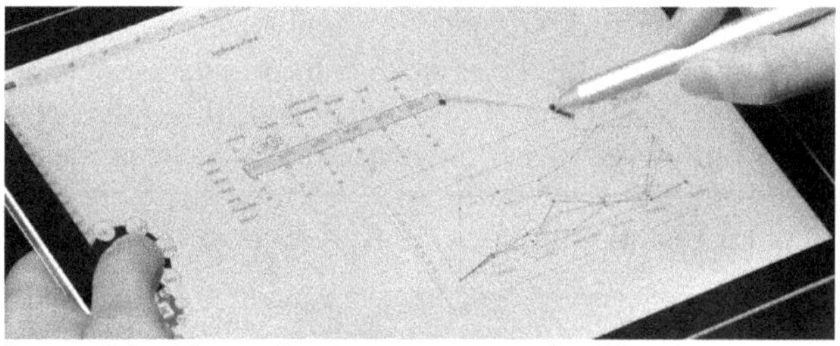

Figure 16: After selecting a range of cells, the user can continuously adjust the values by relative movement of the pen.

Format Widget (Figure 17)

Cell formatting allows adding visual structure to ease viewing and sense-making of data. Here users select cells, and then apply the style by tapping on this widget. Users can configure text color, cell color, and border width through the *Indirect Thumb Marking Menu* (Figure 7). The indirect menu is controlled by a cursor with a basic snapping mechanism for switching colors. A higher control-display gain (300%) is applied to afford the limited range of thumb movement: little motion is required to steer the cursor. For example, users can rapidly navigate through our color palette that has 5x4=20 choices, while the high-gain, indirect mapping accommodates the thumb's limited reach.

Navigation Widget (Figure 18)

While using the pen, the user can only pan and zoom with the preferred hand by interleaving pen and multi-touch input (e.g. by tucking the pen between the fingers). Yet, because the non-preferred hand must hold the device, pinch-to-zoom is not a viable option for the nonpreferred hand, either.

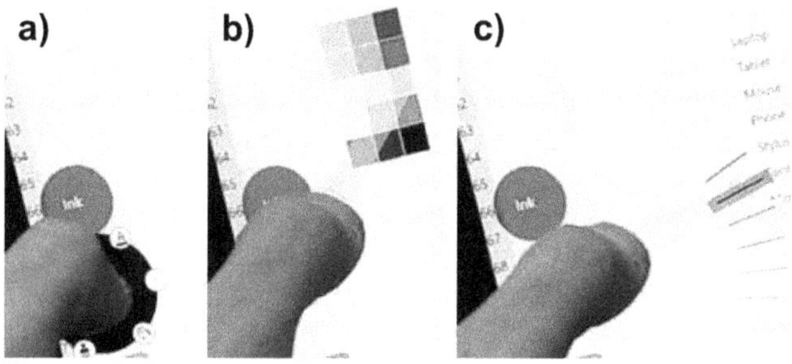

Figure 17: The Format Widget (a) provides rapid configuration of colors (b) or stroke width (c) with thumb only input.

We therefore designed a thumb widget that allows users to pan and zoom while the pen remains in use based on *Indirect Thumb + Pen Hover / Press* (Figure 11). By sliding the thumb on the Navigation Widget, this triggers a zoom with the center-of-expansion at the pen tip. The pen can be in contact with the screen, or indicate the center-of-expansion by hovering. Panning is also supported as a spring-loaded mode: when users hold the Navigation Widget, dragging the pen pans the canvas, allowing concurrent pan and zoom. This is especially useful when using the pen to copy-paste cells to a region beyond the current view. This allows users to work in a fluid manner without constantly shifting their pen grip.

Figure 18: With the Navigation Widget, users pan with the pen, and zoom at the pen's position with thumb scroll gestures.

Summary

Our Spreadsheet probe illustrated diverse uses of Thumb + Pen interaction in productivity scenarios. Combining marking menus with spring-loaded modes enables users to access a variety of tools for the pen, while simply lifting the thumb always returns to the default cell-selection mode.

While this may be at odds with the rule-of-thumb that the *"the pen writes"* [18], more importantly it remains consistent with and illustrative of what may be a higher-level principle, namely that (1) *a digital pen affords a plurality of functions*, and can do so in a fluid manner so long as (2) *the pen reverts to **the application's neutral state** upon relaxation of the nonpreferred-hand.* Indeed, our experience with this probe convinces us that "the pen writes" would be the wrong choice for Spreadsheet: our design decision that ***the pen selects*** was borne out by the workflow and combinations with other modes thus afforded, where ink, formatting, and data editing all take place in the context of the cells indicated by the pen.

BROWSER

Browsing on a tablet is comfortable but comes with issues, such as the need to toggle the virtual keyboard, to invoke 'long-press' context menus, or to reach remote menus, that we aim to approach with Thumb + Pen input. The UI follows the *pen writes, touch manipulates* principle [18]: the pen can annotate websites and write in the address bar, while touch allows tap, scroll, and pinch-to-zoom. We extend this functionality with the following Thumb + Pen techniques, for easy access to navigation and browser functions.

Background Tab Activation (Figure 19): Browsers support multiple browsing instances, to allow for parallel loading and viewing of websites. On tablet UIs, tabs are loaded by a long-touch that opens a context menu with the corresponding option. In contrast, desktop browsers provide efficient *control + click* options without the delay of a long-touch. We therefore added a *thumb + click* method: hold the thumb and tap with the pen on a link to open it in a background tab, making tab opening easier. This takes advantage of the ease of pressing the thumb down, to enable a long-established functionality of desktop browsers.

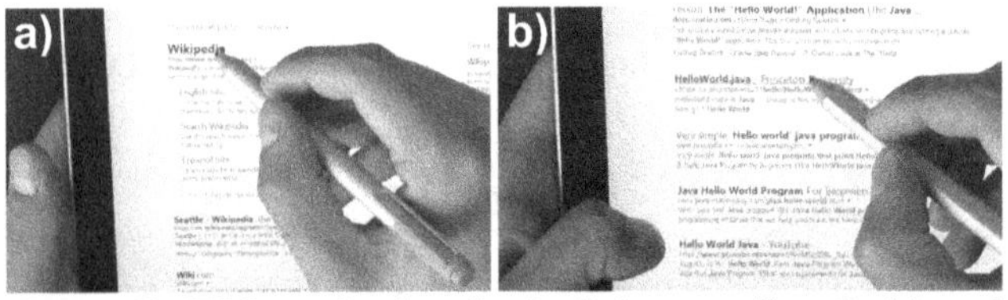

Figure 19: Without the thumb, the link opens directly (a), and with the thumb, it opens in a background tab for later use (b).

Marking Menu (Figure 20): Secondary browser tasks, such as back/forward or the tabmenu, are often placed in persistent menus, requiring physical reach-out to the top of the UI. We instance a *Pen Marking Menu* (Figure 8) to cover these secondary features, while effectively eliminating tedious round-trips to fixed-location menus. The menu supports the following options:

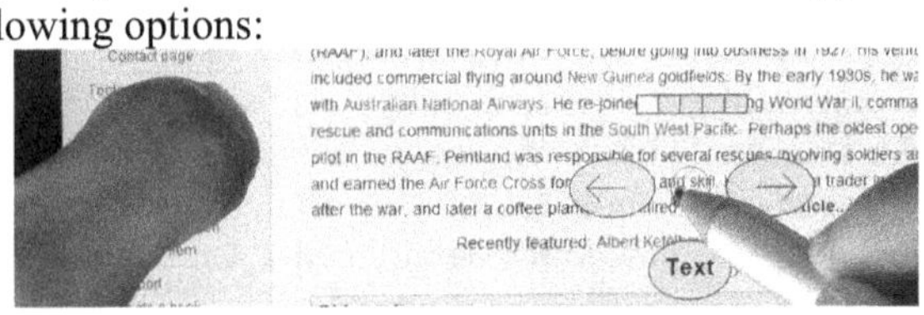

Figure 20: The pen marking menu opens with thumb press.

- Back/forward Navigation: A flick left/right will go back/forward in the page history.
- Switch between pen ink vs. text selection: The pen writes and annotates by default – but selecting text precisely with the pen can be equally important, e.g. to search for information or copy text. Stroking down on this menu affords rapid toggling between *ink* vs. *text selection* mode.
- *Indirect Pen Marking Menu*, as a tabmenu shortcut (Figure 21). Users acquire an indirect handle that stretches to the current tab, and pen left/right movement moves the handle. Thus, the user can, in a way, rapidly riffle through the list of tabs available. The control-display gain is increased for easier movement through the tab list; fine pen movement leads to rapid switching (300% gain). Although this technique is less intuitive, as the pen that affords direct manipulation is used indirectly, users gain a method to efficiently riffle through tabs without having to physically reach for each tab.

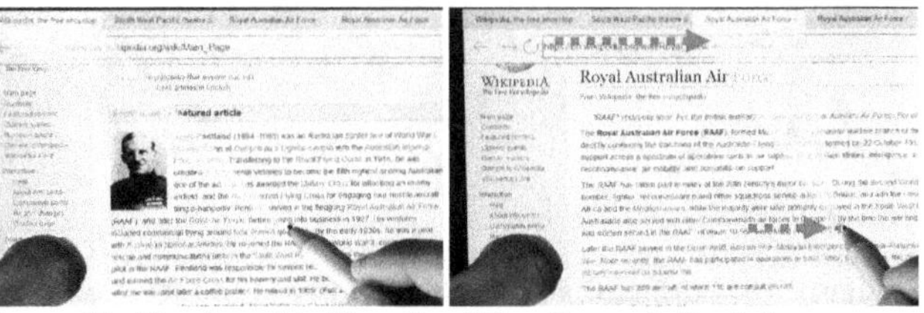

Figure 21: Pen input indirectly riffles through the tabmenu.

Text Context Menu: Users frequently mark text in browsers, often followed by actions e.g. copy or print. In current UIs, long-touch opens context menus that we aim to avoid because of its delay. In our prototype, after users selected text with the pen, an icon is placed at the last pen's position that indicates a marking menu for copy, print, search, and search in tab. Three strategies are possible to interact with it:

- Pen: Press the pen on the icon, and use a flick to select an option. This technique affords easy, one-handed use.
- Thumb+Pen: Press the thumb down to open and hold the menu – use an explicit pen tap to select an item. Compared to the first technique, this method makes consecutive tasks easier as pen-flick gestures are eliminated.
- Thumb (Figure 22): Press the thumb down to open and hold the menu – use thumb-flicks to indirectly select the option. This further improves consecutive actions: the pen selects texts one after each other, and each time the thumb issues a quick flick to trigger the contextual command.

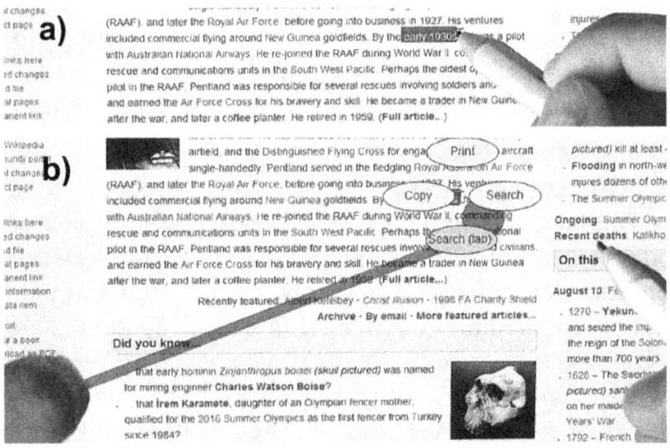

Figure 22: After selecting text with the pen (a), thumb input indirectly controls a context marking menu (b).

Address Bar Thumb Support (Figure 23): Writing with the pen can become difficult, e.g. when there is no writing space, or when the ink is recognized incorrectly. We added two thumb support techniques to use while inking on the address bar, based on the *Indirect Thumb + Pen Hover* technique. Horizontal thumb input scrolls the address bar, for more space when writing long lines. Vertical thumb input allows users to select alternative ink suggestions. This works on a word-per-word basis; users hover the pen over a word, and drag the thumb vertically to scroll the ink suggestion list. By simply hovering over a few words, and each time scrolling with the thumb, users can rapidly correct whole sentences.

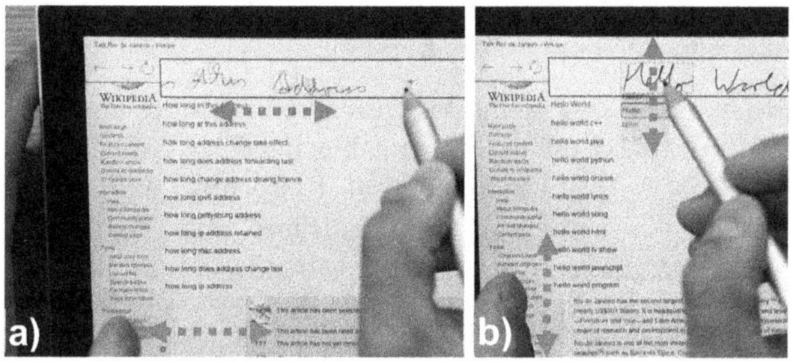

Figure 23: Horizontal thumb input scrolls the address bar (a), vertical input scrolls ink suggestions of hovering words (b).

Summary

Taken together, the addition of Thumb + Pen can render browsers more functional on tablets. The pen adds link clicking, text selection, and writing capabilities, and the user's thumb indirectly supports these tasks. Notably, Thumb + Pen allows similar combinations as mouse and keyboard, e.g. opening tabs in the background (*control + click*), or switching between tabs (*control + tab*), bringing tablet browsers closer to their efficient desktop counterparts.

SHAPE MANIPULATION TOOL

Design programs like Adobe Illustrator or PowerPoint allow users to manipulate objects and shapes with a diverse range of tools. We extend this functionality with bimanual, concurrent manipulation of one object by two tools, i.e. instancing the *Simultaneous Thumb + Pen* techniques.

The pen manipulates as usual, but we designed a specific UI element for the thumb manipulation. A slider-like area located along the left border of the screen is allocated for this purpose. Otherwise, users can access a standard tool palette menu (c.f. Figure 25, left) to change drawing modes for each modality, respectively. Pen modes include free ink, straight line, shape insert, hand (drag) tool, fill color, and marquee selection. Thumb modes include adjustment of size, alpha level, width/height, canvas zoom, and layer level of objects. We now describe exemplary Thumb + Pen combinations:

Zoom and Ink (Figure 24): Similar to the Spreadsheet probe, we apply zooming with the *Indirect Thumb + Pen Hover* technique. Here users can navigate to small regions for detailed manipulation and get back to an overview of the whole, by zooming into the pen's position through thumb scrolling. The advantage here is that right after the zoom, users can immediately start inking, with the pen already located at the area of interest. Further, occlusion is reduced: as users only hover over the area of interest, users can clearly see the details appearing when zooming in.

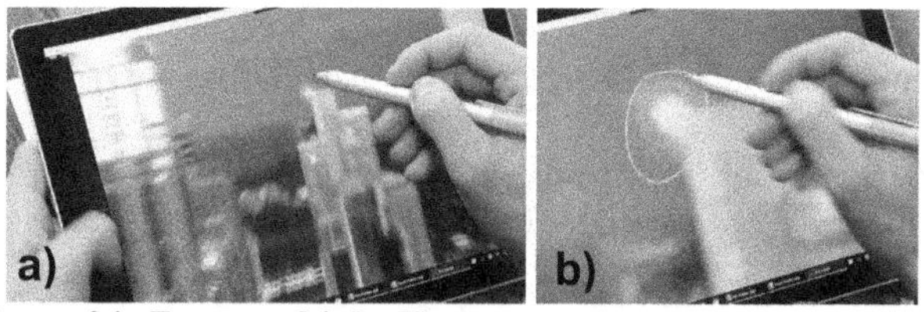

Figure 24: Zoom and ink: Users can zoom at the pen position by scrolling with the thumb (a), and then immediately ink (b).

Object Location and Layer Control (Figure 25): Layers allow users to move shapes to the fore and back, often through a separate layer menu. We designed a complementary method where the user's thumb controls the layer level of the object selected by the pen, instancing the *Indirect Thumb + Pen Drag* technique (Figure 12). This works particularly well with the pen moving the object across the canvas, while the thumb indirectly controls the third dimension (the layers). This results in a compound technique integrating pen and thumb that makes this 2D+1D task feel more like a single action.

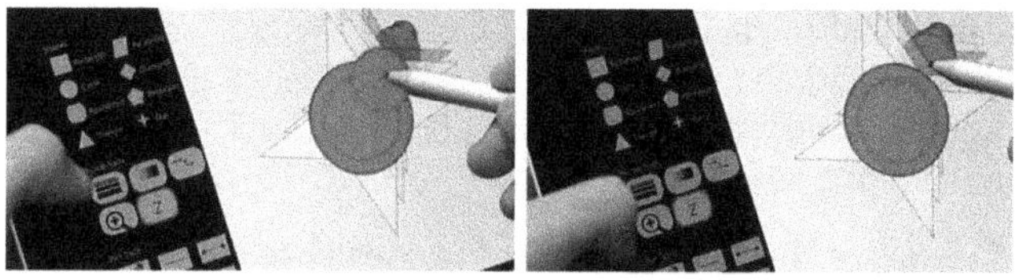

Figure 25: While the pen controls the 2D position, thumb dragging moves the selected object between the layers.

Two-point Control (Figure 26): Symmetric bimanual two-point input [12] is effective for spatial manipulations such as 'rubber-banding' a line or stretching opposite corners of a rectangle [45]. In the tablet case, one hand holds the device, making direct two-point control difficult. We explored a technique where the thumb indirectly controls the object at the exact point indicated. In this mode, users press the pen down to an object, and then the pen controls the selected point on the object. If the user chooses to press down their thumb, it controls the top-left corner. Thumb input then behaves like a touchpad: multiple dragging gestures ratchet the corner, and thereby adjust the shape's size. Rather than using two free hands and consequently losing the tablet grip, users gain a method to control two points concurrently while keeping a comfortable grip.

Figure 26: Two-point control of a rectangle.

Summary

Three examples in this application show the diversity of simultaneous Thumb + Pen interactions when users can configure any mode to each modality – and use them in concert. Each example affords a subtly different use of tasks: *Zoom and Ink* makes the transition between two tasks seamless, the *Position and Layer* technique joins two subtasks into a unitary whole in one object, and *Two-Point Control* maps thumb and pen to symmetric bimanual tasks.

INFORMAL USER EVALUATION

We conducted an informal evaluation to get insights about Thumb + Pen interaction techniques. Note that an in-depth study of each technique is needed, e.g. to identify performance benefits – but considering the scope of this work, our focus is to 1) get user feedback about the usability of individual techniques, and 2) get general insights about Thumb + Pen interaction across techniques.

Setup: Users conducted the study sitting on a couch in an empty office. The tablet was a 12.3" Surface Pro 4, with no cables attached. Users were free to choose a comfortable posture with the tablet, with the goal to use the thumb of the holding hand with ease. Most users leaned back on the couch and put the tablet on their lap.

Procedure: In each 1-hour session, users began with a tryout session to get familiar with the application. Then they were instructed to perform specific artificial tasks. The tasks are detailed in the results section. Users were free to continue with the task if desired. There were 2 tasks per application, to which they gave written feedback after the trials. We asked to point out at least one positive and negative aspect per task.

Participants: 11 right handed users from 25 to 44 years (M=29.4, SD=5.3, 5 female) volunteered. All users were IT students/employees and experienced with the three application types. On a scale from 1 (rarely) to 5 (daily), users rated their experience with phones as 5 (SD=0), tablets as 2.2 (SD=1.3), and tablet+stylus as 1.5 (SD=1).

Spreadsheet

Users first experienced mode-switching with the three thumb widgets. After initial training, users commented that they are *"easy to use, easy to find options and quick action"* (P6), and liked that it's a *"fun and new way to use Excel. Makes it easier to use on a tablet without a mouse"* (P7). Afterwards, users began with the tasks:

Formatting cells task: In this task, users were presented with a table that was pre-filled with data. The task was to format the table with colors using the indirect menus. This included two color styles (for the table head, and content, respectively) to configure and apply, see Figure 25 for a sample result. Most users stated it is fast and easy to use, e.g. P4 stated it is *"fast, doesn't need to go into a menu, all the buttons are where your hand is"*, or P7 found *"it doesn't seem like any additional effort is required to use these features than it does on a laptop or desktop with a mouse versus pen"*. However, 5 users stated it was *"confusing about [the] current status, and also the order of clicks"* (P6), or it is *"not intuitive when selecting a cell style vs changing the cell style"* (P1). Currently, we separate these tasks (set style, then tap to apply style), but in principle these tasks could be merged in a future iteration.

Copy & Paste task: This task involved multiple copy and paste operations on the same table data used in the task above. Users were instructed to first copy single, then multiple cells in the current spreadsheet area. Then, users copied multiple cells to remote spreadsheet areas using pan/zoom operations between copy/paste. Overall, users felt it compared to desktop use, explaining that it is a *"similar experience with copy and paste with a keyboard, just replaced with hand control"* (P6), or even faster (P1: *"[it is] much more exciting than ctrl-copy or clicking copy, faster in my opinion"*). Beyond efficiency, P11 commented: *"[it is] easier than using Excel on a PC. It's fun even"*). Yet, errors were noted (e.g. P8: *"I made some mistakes initially but got used to it"*), particularly for pasting (P1: *"not sure when to click copy/paste"*, P3: *"[the] paste state [is] not clear, [and] multi paste [is] not possible"*), which could be improved with clearer visual design and further pasting refinements.

Browser

First, users got familiar with the pen marking menu of the browser (as enabled by Thumb + Pen) for e.g. back/forward navigation. 5 users pointed out ease of use (e.g. U1: *"Easy to access, intuitive, and useful options"*). Two users commented that the radial menu *"appeared pretty late"* (P1). We designed a delay for expert use without a visual menu, but in future the system might include an adaptive delay based on user experience. Next, users performed two tasks:

Tab-switching task: In this task, users were instructed to perform tab-switching using the indirect pen marking menu. The task involved multiple tab-switches where the experimenter pointed out each tab to target. Between the switches, users performed brief web interactions. The indirect control was initially surprising to users and needed brief introduction, but then users liked the *"fluidity of interaction once learned"* (P2), that it is *"much faster than clicking tabs one by one"* (P1), and that they *"don't move the hand to the top to switch tab"* (P5). In a hypothetical case of a lot of tabs, two users worried that *"multiple tabs might take effort scrolling through. I normally have 30-40 tabs open"* (P10) – cursor acceleration could potentially improve this.

Address-bar-inking task: In this task, users first searched a short phrase (1-2 words), then a longer question, using ink in the address bar. Users were instructed to select one of the written words and change the recognized word for each trial. Users found using the pen *"easy for writing down, I don't need to type"* (P5), and that it *"eliminates the need for an onscreen keyboard which takes up a lot of screen space"* (P9). Other users didn't like inking as *"handwriting is too messy, plus writing by hand is not that fun"* (P11), and as *"search is a little bit hard, because of recognition accuracy"* (P6). A few users found our thumb based correction method difficult (P9: *"hard to fix all the spelling, needed more manual effort then just typing"*). But when the recognition worked, users were positive: *"it understood my writing! The 'scroll across the writing' feature is super useful"* (P10).

Shape Manipulation Tool

Users began by getting acquainted with the grid menu, and found it *"easy to access, quick and intuitive"* (P11) as it is *"like current drawing apps I am accustomed to"* (P9). Improvement of the thumb slider's design was suggested, to make it *"more intuitive, as some actions were discrete and some were continuous"* (P4). Then, users performed tasks:

Object location + layer control task: We designed a scenario that displays an array of overlapping star shapes, and another with a pile of circles in the screen's corner. The task was to layer the circles between the stars (c.f. Figure 25). Here, users stated that *"3d layering becomes easy"* (P10) and it is *"easy to use and learn"* (P6). 5 users had issues with the absolute depth-change we used, that needs *"a lot of scrolling to get to rear layers"* (P7), which can be improved by only changing layers between visually-overlapping shapes.

Draw + zoom task: Here users were first presented with many small shapes (c.f. Figure 3c). Users were instructed to zoom into 5 of the shapes, and draw a letter in each of them – by using the pen based zooming approach. Users found the zooming *"easy, intuitive to use"* (P2), as it is *"similar to the mouse wheel, user adaptability will be easy"* (P10). But users also stated an issue of *"unintended zooming into wrong region when not hovering"* (P3). A higher pen-hover range than available on current tablets might improve the technique.

Discussion

The user feedback and our observations suggested the following insights regarding user reactions to Thumb + Pen:

Learning effort vs. utility: In most cases, little instruction from the experimenter was necessary for user to quickly grasp the techniques, suggesting the techniques had utility which suited the application contexts for which they were designed. Learning was made easier as the techniques were based on well-studied UI concepts such as marking menus. However, seeing an immediate benefit within a familiar application (e.g. Browser) was captivating to the user, and led to a satisfactory result after training.

Direct vs. indirect techniques: While direct input techniques were mostly intuitive, indirect input needed more instruction as it was unexpected on tablets. Techniques based on direct marking menus and spring-loaded modes were quickly learned, whereas indirect techniques such as tab switching or zooming were initially less intuitive on a tablet. Notably, when learned, users were positive about the indirect techniques for the benefit gained. For example, tab switching was positively received across users, particularly for its utility in everyday browser interactions.

Integral vs. separable bimanual tasks: Simultaneous Thumb + Pen input as explored in the shape manipulations needed instruction too, but with the right task users naturally employed bimanual input even though one hand was occupied with holding the device. Our observations aligned with prior findings that applying simultaneous input is easier when tasks are integrated [20]. Rather than applying two distinct tasks (zoom *vs.* draw), two integral actions in one task felt easier (layer + position control of one object).

CONCLUSION

We explored bimanual pen+touch possibilities designed for combined use of thumb (nonpreferred hand) and pen (preferred hand) that affords comfortable laid-back tablet use. Thumb touches considered as direct input enables mode switching of the pen. As indirect input, users can employ their thumb to manipulate the pen's target. The combination with the pen affords a design space that extends tablet interfaces beyond the existing direct manipulation paradigm.

By exploring interaction techniques across three distinct applications, we highlight new interface elements and combinations designed for tablets. In Spreadsheet, the thumb widgets allow changing the mode of the pen, as well as changing the mode that applies to the pen. Integration of marking menus enhances the thumb's reach. In the browser, we provided context aware menus triggered by Thumb + Pen, offering users additional navigation functionality to reduce the amount of reaching and tapping on menu elements. Pen-specific tasks (e.g. annotation, search, or text selection) can be enhanced with indirect thumb input to rapidly interact with context menus, or to correct written ink.

Our future work involves further pursuing the specific technique *per se*, and testing how our approach works in other conditions such as when standing, for left-handers, or for long-term use. Further we aim for the development of a better understanding of how such techniques can work in concert with the more general set of pen + touch techniques. For example, in situations where one might move from using one to the other, how can the design of each be tailored to maximize skill transfer, and the fluidity of interaction?

RIGHTS FOR FIGURES

Figures 1-26 © Ken Pfeuffer, 2017.

REFERENCES

1. Martha Abednego, Joong-Ho Lee, Won Moon, and Ji-Hyung Park. 2009. I-Grabber: Expanding Physical Reach in a Large-display Tabletop Environment Through the Use of a Virtual Grabber. In *Proceedings of the ACM International Conference on Interactive Tabletops and Surfaces* (ITS '09), 61–64. http://doi.org/10.1145/1731903.1731917

2. Pär-Anders Albinsson and Shumin Zhai. 2003. High precision touch screen interaction. In *Proceedings of the SIGCHI Conference on Human Factors in Computing Systems (CHI'03)*, 105–112.

3. Michel Beaudouin-Lafon. 2000. Instrumental Interaction: An Interaction Model for Designing post-WIMP User Interfaces. In *Proceedings of the SIGCHI Conference on Human Factors in Computing Systems* (CHI '00), 446–453. http://doi.org/10.1145/332040.332473
4. Hrvoje Benko, Andrew D Wilson, and Patrick Baudisch. 2006. Precise selection techniques for multi-touch screens. In *Proceedings of the SIGCHI Conference on Human Factors in Computing Systems (CHI'06)*, 1263–1272. http://doi.org/http://dx.doi.org/10.1145/1124772.1124963
5. Joanna Bergstrom-Lehtovirta and Antti Oulasvirta. 2014. Modeling the Functional Area of the Thumb on Mobile Touchscreen Surfaces. *Proceedings of the ACM SIGCHI Conference on Human Factors in Computing Systems (CHI'14)*: 1991–2000. http://doi.org/10.1145/2556288.2557354
6. Anastasia Bezerianos and Ravin Balakrishnan. 2005. The vacuum: facilitating the manipulation distant objects. In *Proceedings of the SIGCHI Conference on Human Factors in Computing Systems (CHI '05)*, 361–370.
7. Peter Brandl, Clifton Forlines, Daniel Wigdor, Michael Haller, and Chia Shen. 2008. Combining and measuring the benefits of bimanual pen and direct-touch interaction on horizontal interfaces. In *Proceedings of the Working Conference on Advanced Visual Interfaces (AVI'08)*, 154–161. http://doi.org/10.1145/1385569.1385595
8. Ed Brown, William Buxton, and Kevin Murtagh. 1990. Windows on Tablets As a Means of Achieving Virtual Input Devices. In *Proceedings of the IFIP TC13 Third Interational Conference on Human-Computer Interaction* (INTERACT '90), 675–681.
9. William Buxton. 1995. Integrating the periphery and context: A new taxonomy of telematics. In *Proceedings of graphics interface 1995 (GI'95)*, 239–246.
10. Clifton Forlines, Daniel Vogel, and Ravin Balakrishnan. 2006. HybridPointing: Fluid Switching Between Absolute and Relative Pointing with a Direct Input Device. In *Proceedings of the 19th Annual ACM Symposium on User Interface Software and Technology* (UIST '06), 211–220. http://doi.org/10.1145/1166253.1166286
11. Cédric Foucault, Manfred Micaux, David Bonnet, and Michel Beaudouin-Lafon. 2014. SPad: A Bimanual Interaction Technique for Productivity Applications on Multi-touch Tablets. In *Proceedings of the Extended Abstracts of the Annual ACM Conference on Human Factors in Computing Systems* (CHI EA '14), 1879–1884. http://doi.org/10.1145/2559206.2581277
12. Yves Guiard. 1987. Asymmetric Division of Labor in Human Skilled Bimanual Action: The Kinematic Chain as a Model. In *Journal of Motor Behavior*, 486–517.
13. Yves Guiard, Renaud Blanch, and Michel Beaudouin-Lafon. 2004. Object Pointing: A Complement to Bitmap Pointing in GUIs. In *Proceedings of Graphics Interface 2004* (GI '04), 9–16.
14. William Hamilton, Andruid Kerne, and Tom Robbins. 2012. High-performance Pen + Touch Modality Interactions: A Real-time Strategy Game eSports Context. In *Proceedings of the 25th Annual ACM Symposium on User Interface Software and Technology* (UIST '12), 309–318. http://doi.org/10.1145/2380116.2380156
15. Ken Hinckley, Xiaojun Bi, Michel Pahud, and Bill Buxton. 2012. Informal Information Gathering Techniques for Active Reading. *Proceedings of the SIGCHI Conference on Human Factors in Computing Systems (CHI'12)*: 1893–1896. http://doi.org/10.1145/2207676.2208327
16. Ken Hinckley, Francois Guimbretiere, Patrick Baudisch, Raman Sarin, Maneesh Agrawala, and Ed Cutrell. 2006. The Springboard: Multiple Modes in One Spring-loaded Control. In *Proceedings of the SIGCHI Conference on Human Factors in Computing Systems* (CHI '06), 181–190. http://doi.org/10.1145/1124772.1124801
17. Ken Hinckley and Daniel Wigdor. 2012. The Human-computer Interaction Handbook. In (3rd ed.), Julie A Jacko (ed.). Taylor & Francis, 151–168.
18. Ken Hinckley, Koji Yatani, Michel Pahud, et al. 2010. Pen + touch = new tools. *Proceedings of the 23nd annual ACM symposium on User interface software and technology (UIST '10)*: 27. http://doi.org/10.1145/1866029.1866036
19. Hilary Hutchinson, Wendy Mackay, Bo Westerlund, et al. 2003. Technology Probes: Inspiring Design for and with Families. In *Proceedings of the SIGCHI Conference on Human Factors in Computing Systems* (CHI '03), 17–24. http://doi.org/10.1145/642611.642616
20. Robert J K Jacob, Linda E Sibert, Daniel C McFarlane, and M Preston Mullen Jr. 1994. Integrality and Separability of Input Devices. *ACM Trans. Comput.-Hum. Interact.* 1, 1: 3–26. http://doi.org/10.1145/174630.174631
21. Wendy Ju. 2015. The design of implicit interactions. *Synthesis Lectures on Human-Centered Informatics* 8, 2: 1–93.
22. Amy; Karlson. 2008. Understanding One-Handed Use of Mobile Devices. *Handbook of Research on User Interface Design and Evaluation for Mobile Technology Volume I*: 86–101. http://doi.org/10.4018/978-1-59904-

871-0

23. Amy K. Karlson and Benjamin B. Bederson. 2007. ThumbSpace: Generalized One-Handed Input for Touchscreen-Based Mobile Devices. *Proceedings of the Conference on Human-Computer Interaction (INTERACT'07)* 4662, Part I: 324–338. http://doi.org/10.1007/978-3-540-74796-3_30
24. Gordon Kurtenbach and William Buxton. 1994. User Learning and Performance with Marking Menus. In *Proceedings of the SIGCHI Conference on Human Factors in Computing Systems* (CHI '94), 258–264. http://doi.org/10.1145/191666.191759
25. Jianwei Lai and Dongsong Zhang. 2014. ExtendedThumb: A Motion-based Virtual Thumb for Improving One-handed Target Acquisition on Touch-screen Mobile Devices. In *Proceedings of the Extended Abstracts of the 32Nd Annual ACM Conference on Human Factors in Computing Systems* (CHI EA '14), 1825–1830. http://doi.org/10.1145/2559206.2581158
26. Edward Lank, Jaime Ruiz, and William Cowan. 2006. Concurrent Bimanual Stylus Interaction: A Study of Non-preferred Hand Mode Manipulation. In *Proceedings of Graphics Interface 2006* (GI '06), 17–24.
27. David Lee, KyoungHee Son, Joon Hyub Lee, and Seok-Hyung Bae. 2012. PhantomPen: Virtualization of Pen Head for Digital Drawing Free from Pen Occlusion & Visual Parallax. In *Proceedings of the 25th Annual ACM Symposium on User Interface Software and Technology* (UIST '12), 331–340. http://doi.org/10.1145/2380116.2380159
28. Pedro Lopes, Daniel Mendes, Bruno Araújo, and Joaquim a. Jorge. 2011. Combining bimanual manipulation and pen-based input for 3D modelling. *Proceedings of the Eighth Eurographics Symposium on Sketch-Based Interfaces and Modeling (SBIM '11)* 1: 15. http://doi.org/10.1145/2021164.2021168
29. Wendy E Mackay. 2002. Which Interaction Technique Works when?: Floating Palettes, Marking Menus and Toolglasses Support Different Task Strategies. In *Proceedings of the Working Conference on Advanced Visual Interfaces* (AVI '02), 203–208. http://doi.org/10.1145/1556262.1556294
30. Nobuyuki Matsushita, Yuji Ayatsuka, and Jun Rekimoto. 2000. Dual Touch: A Two-handed Interface for Pen-based PDAs. In *Proceedings of the 13th Annual ACM Symposium on User Interface Software and Technology* (UIST '00), 211–212. http://doi.org/10.1145/354401.354774
31. Fabrice Matulic and Moira C. Norrie. 2013. Pen and touch gestural environment for document editing on interactive tabletops. *Proceedings of the 2013 ACM international conference on Interactive tabletops and surfaces (ITS '13)*: 41–50. http://doi.org/10.1145/2512349.2512802
32. Michael McGuffin, Nicolas Burtnyk, and Gordon Kurtenbach. 2002. FaST Sliders: Integrating Marking Menus and the Adjustment of Continuous Values. In *Proceedings of the Graphics Interface 2002 Conference (GI'02)*, 35--42.
33. D. Odell and V. Chandrasekaran. 2012. Enabling comfortable thumb interaction in tablet computers: a Windows 8 case study. *Proceedings of the Human Factors and Ergonomics Society Annual Meeting* 56: 1907–1911. http://doi.org/10.1177/1071181312561278
34. Antti Oulasvirta, Anna Reichel, Wenbin Li, et al. 2013. Improving Two-Thumb Text Entry on Touchscreen Devices. *Proceedings of the Conference on Human Factors in Computing Systems (CHI'13)*: 2765–2774. http://doi.org/10.1145/2470654.2481383
35. Ken Pfeuffer, Jason Alexander, and Hans Gellersen. 2016. Partially-indirect Bimanual Input with Gaze, Pen, and Touch for Pan, Zoom, and Ink Interaction. In *Proceedings of the SIGCHI Conference on Human Factors in Computing Systems* (CHI '16), 2845–2856. http://doi.org/10.1145/2858036.2858201
36. R L Potter, L J Weldon, and B Shneiderman. 1988. Improving the Accuracy of Touch Screens: An Experimental Evaluation of Three Strategies. In *Proceedings of the SIGCHI Conference on Human Factors in Computing Systems (CHI '88)*, 27–32. http://doi.org/http://doi.acm.org/10.1145/57167.57171
37. Abigail J Sellen, Gordon P Kurtenbach, and William A S Buxton. 1992. The Prevention of Mode Errors Through Sensory Feedback. *Hum.-Comput. Interact.* 7, 2: 141–164. http://doi.org/10.1207/s15327051hci0702_1
38. Matthieu B Trudeau, Paul J Catalano, Devin L Jindrich, and Jack T Dennerlein. 2013. Tablet Keyboard Configuration Affects Performance, Discomfort and Task Difficulty for Thumb Typing in a Two-Handed Grip. *PloS one* 8, 6: e67525. http://doi.org/10.1371/journal.pone.0067525
39. Julie Wagner, Stéphane Huot, and Wendy Mackay. 2012. BiTouch and BiPad: Designing Bimanual Interaction for Hand-held Tablets. In *Proceedings of the SIGCHI Conference on Human Factors in Computing Systems* (CHI '12), 2317–2326. http://doi.org/10.1145/2207676.2208391
40. Jagoda Walny, Bongshin Lee, Paul Johns, Nathalie Henry Riche, and Sheelagh Carpendale. 2012. Understanding pen and touch interaction for data exploration on interactive whiteboards. *IEEE Transactions on Visualization and Computer Graphics* 18, 12: 2779–2788.

http://doi.org/10.1109/TVCG.2012.275

41. Katrin Wolf and Niels Henze. 2014. Comparing pointing techniques for grasping hands on tablets. *Proceedings of the 16th international conference on Human-computer interaction with mobile devices & services (MobileHCI '14)*: 53–62. http://doi.org/10.1145/2628363.2628371
42. Katrin Wolf, Robert Schleicher, and Michael Rohs. 2014. Ergonomic characteristics of gestures for front- and back-of-tablets interaction with grasping hands. *Proceedings of the 16th international conference on Human-computer interaction with mobile devices & services (MobileHCI'14)*: 453–458. http://doi.org/10.1145/2628363.2634214
43. Ka-Ping Yee. 2004. Two-handed Interaction on a Tablet Display. In *Extended Abstracts on Human Factors in Computing Systems* (CHI EA '04), 1493–1496. http://doi.org/10.1145/985921.986098
44. Dongwook Yoon, Nicholas Chen, François Guimbretière, and Abigail Sellen. 2014. RichReview: Blending Ink, Speech, and Gesture to Support Collaborative Document Review. In *Proceedings of the 27th Annual ACM Symposium on User Interface Software and Technology* (UIST '14), 481–490. http://doi.org/10.1145/2642918.2647390
45. Robert Zeleznik, Andrew Bragdon, Ferdi Adeputra, and Hsu-Sheng Ko. 2010. Hands-on Math: A Page-based Multi-touch and Pen Desktop for Technical Work and Problem Solving. In *Proceedings of the 23Nd Annual ACM Symposium on User Interface Software and Technology* (UIST '10), 17–26. http://doi.org/10.1145/1866029.1866035
46. Emanuel Zgraggen, Robert Zeleznik, and Philipp Eichmann. 2016. Tableur : Handwritten Spreadsheets. *CHI Extended Abstracts on Human Factors in Computing Systems (CHI EA'16)*: 2362–2368.

Experimental Analysis of Mode Switching Techniques in Touch-based User Interfaces

Hemant Bhaskar Surale, Fabrice Matulic, Daniel Vogel
Cheriton School of Computer Science, University of Waterloo
hsurale, fabrice.matulic, dvogel@uwaterloo.ca

ABSTRACT

This paper presents the results of a 36 participant empirical comparison of touch mode-switching. Six techniques are evaluated, spanning current and future techniques: long press, non-dominant hand, two-fingers, hard press, knuckle, and thumb-on-finger. Two poses are controlled for: seated with the tablet on a desk and standing with the tablet held on the forearm. Findings indicate pose has no effect on mode switching time and little effect on error rate; using two-fingers is fastest while long press is much slower; non-preferred hand and thumb-on-finger also rate highly in subjective scores. The experiment protocol is based on Li et al.'s pen mode-switching study, enabling a comparison of touch and pen mode switching. Among the common techniques, the non-dominant hand is faster than pressure with touch, whereas no significant difference had been found for pen. Our work addresses the lack of empirical evidence comparing touch mode-switching techniques and provides guidance to practitioners when choosing techniques and to researchers when designing new mode-switching methods.

ACM Classification Keywords

H.5.2. : User Interfaces- *Interaction Techniques*

Author Keywords

multi-touch; touch input; mode switching;

INTRODUCTION

Most interfaces have multiple modes in which input is mapped to different actions. In a touch interface, the current mode can change how a single touch is interpreted: for example, it could draw a line, pan the canvas, select a shape, or enter a command. Switching between modes can be frequent, so finding optimum *mode-switching* methods is important. There have been numerous experimental investigations comparing mode-switching techniques for pucks, mice, and pens [32, 13, 36, 54, 28], but there has been no comprehensive analysis of mode-switching techniques for touch input.

This is surprising considering that a number of touch mode-switching techniques have been developed. Some are unique to touch since they rely on features such as multiple contacts [10, 46], using knuckles or other parts of the hand [23, 39], or characteristics of finger contact [6, 47]. Some touch mode-switching techniques are similar to those evaluated with pens, such as using pressure [42, 25] or using the non-dominant hand [15, 57]. However, generalizing pen-based empirical results to touch is highly speculative, considering distinct touch characteristics like reduced precision from "fat fingers" [3, 14, 50] and greater friction [9]. This lack of formal comparisons of touch mode-switching techniques may be one reason why current mode-switching methods for touch seem limited compared to other input methods.

In this paper, we compare the performance of six mode-switching techniques for touch input on a tablet: the standard long press, pressing a button with the non-dominant hand, two-finger multi-touch, pressing hard, using the knuckle, and touching the thumb to the side of the finger. The investigated techniques include current methods, new methods recently made available in commercial devices, and techniques likely possible in the near future. Given the tablet mobility, we also control for two poses: seated with the tablet on a desk and standing while holding the tablet. Our evaluation protocol is based on Li et al.'s widely cited comparison of pen mode-switching [36]. This increases the replicability and validity of our work, and enables a discussion of touch versus pen mode-switching. Direct comparisons are possible for pressure, long press, and non-preferred hand, and to some extent thumb-on-finger and knuckle if considered analogues to Li et al.'s pen barrel button and eraser.

Our results contribute the following results and insights:

- Techniques ordered from fastest to slowest are: two-fingers, non-preferred hand button, finger-on-thumb, knuckle or hard press, and much slower long-press.
- A sitting or standing pose has no effect on speed and little or no effect on errors (only hard press and non-preferred hand error rates showed some interaction with pose).
- Pressing hard was perceived to be the least accurate, one of the most fatiguing, and hardest to learn technique.
- Compared to Li et al.'s results for pen, our touch mode-switching timings and error rates are higher (except for knuckle compared to eraser).
- Our results can inform design, returning to the opening example: one finger could draw, two fingers pan, thumb-on-finger to select, and knuckle for a command menu.

Permission to make digital or hard copies of all or part of this work for personal or classroom use is granted without fee provided that copies are not made or distributed for profit or commercial advantage and that copies bear this notice and the full citation on the first page. Copyrights for components of this work owned by others than ACM must be honored. Abstracting with credit is permitted. To copy otherwise, or republish, to post on servers or to redistribute to lists, requires prior specific permission and/or a fee. Request permissions from Permissions@acm.org.
CHI 2017, May 06–11, 2017, Denver, CO, USA
© 2017 ACM. ISBN 978-1-4503-4655-9/17/05...$15.00.
DOI: http://dx.doi.org/10.1145/3025453.3025865

BACKGROUND AND RELATED WORK

We build on, and extend research developing new mode-switching techniques and formal experiments to analyse them.

Mode Switching Techniques

Early mode-switching techniques focused on pucks, mice, and especially pens (styli). We provide a brief overview of pen techniques first since they have been arguably the most thoroughly studied and are the topic of Li et al.. We subsequently focus on multi-touch input, the most relevant to our work.

Pen Input

With pens, there is a common need to switch between an inking mode and a command input mode, but many techniques can be combined to support multiple modes. Perhaps the most straightforward method to switch the pen mode, other than the classic "long press" with the nib, is to press a button. This can be single-handed, using the barrel button on the pen [36], a touch sensor below the palm of the writing hand [51], or more commonly with the other (non-dominant) hand [40, 1, 33, 28]. Using two hands exploits the benefits of bimanual interaction [32, 27]. Li et al. [36] found a physical button activated by the non-dominant hand was both faster and more accurate. A later study by Tu et al. led to similar results [54].

Having a well-positioned button on a device is not always a practical solution and there is often a need to trigger multiple mode switches. Additional techniques have been proposed to overcome those limitations. On pen and touch tabletop systems, there is a large body of work examining different postures performed with the non-dominant hand on the surface to activate command modes for the pen held by the dominant hand [7, 31, 41]. Other techniques include short stroke gestures [26, 34, 20], pressing firmly or lightly [36, 54, 45], stylus rolling [5], contacting with different parts of a multi-faceted crayon [56], and pen-holding postures [52, 30].

Touch Input

Many mode-switching techniques designed for pens or other devices have been applied to direct touch input. For instance, typing capital letters by holding the shift key with the other hand is a simple form of non-preferred hand mode activation. Even the shape of the non-dominant hand [58, 61, 24] or the number of fingers used [60] can trigger a mode change. BiPad [57] and SPad [15] explore the possibility of using the hand holding a tablet to activate different modes by pressing soft buttons. Pressure [42, 25, 46] and grip-based [17] controls have also received much attention. Some of the latest mobile devices integrate pressure-based technology and functionality (3D Touch, Force Touch, Press Touch etc.) [53]. The number, shape and mobility of fingers afford further interaction possibilities. Multiple fingers performing similar path movement (two- three-finger swipes etc.) can be used to trigger different actions [35, 60] and if individual fingers can be identified, interactions can be made finger-specific [10]. Further properties of finger input such as contact size [6], slight rolling movements [47] and which part of a finger touches the display [23] can also be recognized to support mode-switching or general interactions.

Mode Switching Analysis

With many possible mode-switching techniques, it is no wonder researchers have attempted to develop models and evaluation protocols to rigorously assess their performance under different settings. Using the non-dominant hand for pen mode switching has been studied in detail by Ruiz et al. who developed a temporal model [48], Lank et al. [33] who show concurrent mode-switching is fastest, and Ruiz and Lank [49] who explore these aspects with multiple modes.

To compare performance of mode-switching techniques, a common methodology is Dillon et al's "subtraction technique" [11]. It determines the precise cost of mode-switching by subtracting the time to perform the same series of tasks using a single mode and when alternating between two modes. It is the approach for comparing pen mode switching techniques in Hinckley et al. [28], Song et al. [52], and Li et al.'s[36] highly cited comparison on which we model our work.

We are unaware of a comprehensive study systematically examining and comparing mode-changing techniques for direct touch input. The touch techniques explicitly or implicitly used to trigger mode changes that have been proposed have mostly been superficially or individually evaluated for non-frequent mode-switches. Therefore, it is not clear how well they fare compared to each other and in a context, where state changes are very frequent. Furthermore, the results for pen-based mode-switching may not transfer to touch input, not to mention that touch input enables other techniques such as multiple touches not applicable to pens.

MODE SWITCHING TECHNIQUES

We chose six mode switching techniques among those in current use, described in previous research, or soon plausible given emerging sensor capabilities. Some are analogous to the pen mode switching techniques tested by Li et al. [36]. All techniques were designed for a tablet when placed on a desk, or when supported with the non-dominant arm.

Long Press

Performing a long press (also called "press-and-hold" or "dwelling") is a common method to trigger command modes in current touch interfaces. For example, Android and IOS use a long press to organize app launch icons. We use a long press duration of 500ms , the default Android setting. Li et al. also included a pen long press, but used a 1000ms duration.

Long press detection begins after touch down with a "hold detection phase": as long as finger movement remains within a 3mm radius bounding circle centred on the initial touch point, the finger is considered held still. A circle 25mm in diameter is displayed around the touch point showing the progression towards the 500ms duration. If the finger remains in the box for 500ms, the mode is activated. If the finger exits the box before that time, the hold detection phase restarts with a new bounding circle centred on the new finger position. Our 3mm radius bound is twice that used by Li et al. to account for touch sensor noise. Once detected, the mode remains engaged until touch up regardless of subsequent finger movement. We did not implement a second "hold through" phase to cancel the mode switch like Li et al. because, to our knowledge, this is not used on touch input devices or needed for the experiment.

Two-Finger Multi-touch

One of the simplest distinctions for touch input is whether one or two fingers contact the display at the same time. This is common in Android and IOS, and researchers have used two fingers to activate marking menus [35] and distinguish between dragging and hovering in the DTMouse technique [12]. There is no equivalent technique with pen input.

A two-finger touch is detected when two correlated touches occur soon after initial touch down. For our experiment, two touches must be detected before crossing into the first rectangle (typically less than 80ms). To remain comparable with other single touch techniques, a single input position is defined using the midpoint between touch points. We selected the midpoint based on pilot tests examining the perceived input point for two touches. This positioning is also used for DTMouse in hover mode. Once detected, the mode remains engaged until touch up regardless of the number of touches.

Non-Preferred Hand

Touch interfaces can support using the non-preferred hand to activate a mode with soft buttons, a simple example is holding the SHIFT key while typing. Li et al. found that pressing a physical button was one of the fastest ways to activate a mode with pen input. Our equivalent technique uses a rendered touch button since it is more practical with current tablets.

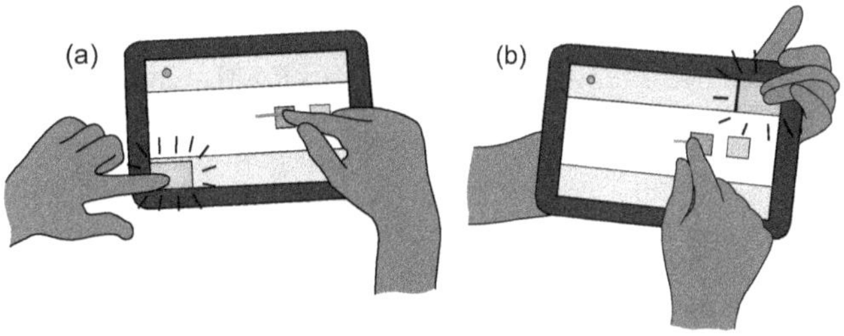

Figure 1: Position of the mode-switch button (in green) activated by the non-preferred hand when (a) sitting; and (b) standing.

To engage the mode, the non-dominant hand presses and holds a 45 × 25mm button before the dominant hand touches down. Once the touch down event occurs, the mode remains engaged until both the dominant-hand touch up event occurs *and* the mode switch button is released. We require the button to be pressed before the dominant hand touch down to be consistent with Li et al.. The mode button location is dependent on the participant's handedness and whether the tablet is supported by a surface (e.g. sitting at a desk) or supported by the non-dominant forearm (e.g. when standing). When supported by a surface, the button is displayed at the bottom-left (or bottom-right) corner (Fig. 1-left). When supported by the non-dominant arm, the button is displayed at the top-right (or top-left) corner (Fig. 1-right). This enables the user to reach and tap the mode switch button comfortably with the fingers of the hand holding the device, a common posture reported by Wagner et al. [57] We fixed button locations and sizes for our experiment, but techniques exist to automatically detect how a mobile device is held so such mode-switch button could be positioned accordingly [17].

Hard Press

Pressure-based touch interaction has been described in previous work [2, 4, 25, 46] and recent technology developments suggest pressure sensing will be supported on commercial touch devices in the near future [53]. Using pressure-based mode-selection for pens has been well studied (e.g. [45]) and it was a method evaluated in Li et al.'s experiments.

Most current touch devices report a simulated pressure reading based on the size of the touch contact. On vision-based tabletops the actual contact size is captured by a camera [4], but capacitive devices estimate it from the signal strength. We found simulated pressure with capacitive tablets is unreliable due to factors like skin moisture, relative humidity, and body hydration. To get a true measure of pressure, we initially experimented with placing multiple external force-sensitive resistors under the tablet and training a classifier to recognize touch events with normal and hard pressure. This worked reasonably well on a desk, but designing a housing for accurate sensing when standing proved difficult. Instead we detect hard presses indirectly, based on muscle tension sensed using a MYO electromyographic (EMG) armband. Benko et al. used the same technique with a similar EMG sensor [2]. Note that our objective is to simulate a future pressure sensing technique in our experiment; we are not proposing that people wear a MYO armband when using a tablet.

A simple threshold-based classifier is trained for each participant (Li et al. used a global threshold for pressure across all participants, but found it unreliable). To train, the participant crosses through five rectangles, alternating between a normal touch and a hard press touch according to rectangle colour. This is repeated 4 times. The data from the 8 armband EMG sensors are smoothed using the one-euro filter [8] and synchronized with the touch events and expected type of touch. The median and standard deviation of each sensor signal for normal touches and hard presses is calculated using events logged from touch down until the rectangle is entered. All sensors where the hard press median minus two standard deviations is greater than the normal touch median plus two standard deviations are considered *differentiating* sensors. If less than two differentiating sensors are found, the armband is adjusted and the training repeated. Otherwise, each sensor is assigned a threshold equal to the hard press median minus two standard deviations (EMG signals for hard press are always greater than normal press). Once trained, a touch is considered a hard press if two or more of the differentiating electrodes exceed the thresholds determined in training. A 5-person pilot found the method was almost 99% accurate.

To use hard press for mode-switching, sufficient pressure must be applied to the tablet screen to cross the threshold. During the experiment, a hard press must be identified before crossing into the rectangle. The mode is disengaged upon touch up.

Thumb-on-Finger

Pressing a "barrel button" is a classic way to change the mode using a pen, and this technique was included in Li et al's study.

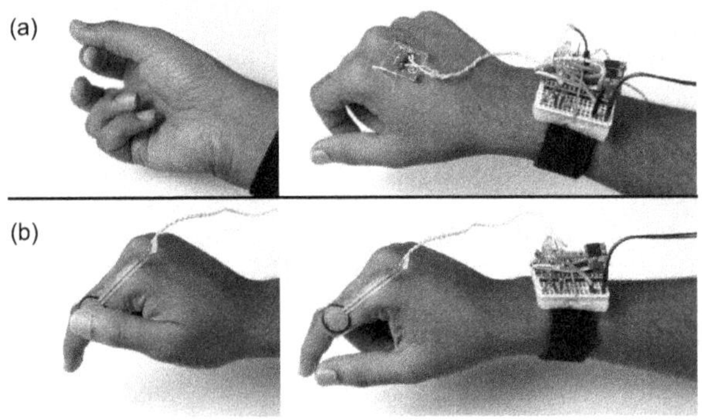

Figure 2: Hardware to robustly detect future input actions for the purpose of the experiment: (a) knuckle touches using accelerometer; and (b) thumb-on-finger using pressure sensor attached to index finger.

We approximate barrel button mode-engagement for touch input with a thumb press on the index finger, similar to techniques used for mid-air clicking [21, 55] and NanoStylus [62]. We anticipate that with technologies such as Project Soli [19], these types of gestures will be able to be sensed.

In our experiment, we use a wearable device with a force-sensitive resistor (FSR) taped to the proximal phalanges of the index finger (Fig. 2 b). We ensured this apparatus did not impede natural touch interaction with the tablet. The FSR is 12.7 mm in diameter and 0.47 mm thick. The sensing range is 0 to 175 psi and we used a global threshold of 51 psi to detect when the thumb lightly contacts the finger. The FSR is connected to an ATmega328 Arduino strapped to the wrist. The Arduino sends pressure readings to the tablet over Bluetooth. To reduce weight, an external battery is connected to the wearable device with a lightweight wire.

The mode is activated by pressing the thumb to the side of the index finger before touching down. Once the touch down event occurs, the mode remains active until both the touch up event occurs *and* the thumb is released from the finger.

Knuckle

Using the knuckle for touch input has been described in Marquardt et al. [39] and Tapsense [23]. Knuckle-sensing is already offered on some smartphones [16]. Turning the hand over to engage the knuckle also bears some similarity to using the eraser end of a pen, a mode-switching technique included in Li et al.'s study.

Our tablet does not sense knuckles natively, so we simulate a future knuckle sensor. An ADXL335 3-axis accelerometer mounted on the back of the hand with tape detects wrist rotation. Specifically, the mode is switched when the z axis of the accelerometer exceeds a 90 degree angle (it is 0 degree when the sensor is horizontal). This simple threshold is sufficient to differentiate between knuckle and normal finger pad touches. The accelerometer is connected to the same wrist-mounted apparatus used for thumb-on-finger sensing. In our experiment, all but one participant used their middle finger knuckle to perform this technique. Given the mechanics of the movement, the mode must be engaged before the first touch. The mode remains active until both the touch up event occurs *and* the wrist rotates back to the finger pad touch orientation.

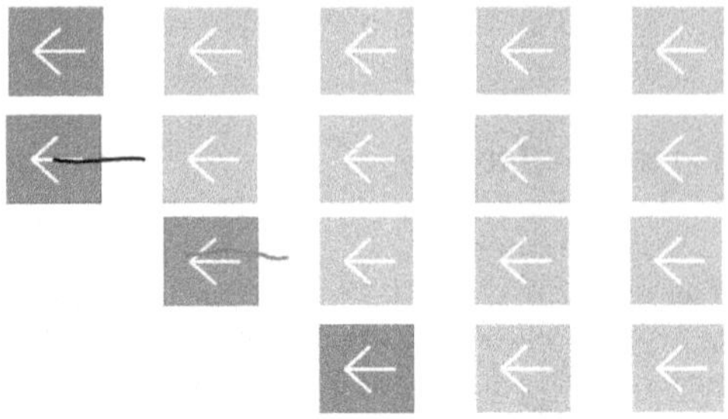

Figure 3: Compound task: five oriented rectangles (180° shown) are crossed while alternating between default and command modes. Each row above is a screen capture of the task (top to bottom): about to cross first baseline target; crossing first target; crossing second "moded" target; about to cross third baseline target. The baseline task looks identical except all rectangles are grey and only the default mode is used.

EXPERIMENT

The goal of this experiment is to compare mode-switching time, error rates, and subjective ratings for the six techniques described above. Given the mobile nature of tablets, both seated and standing poses are tested. The experiment task and design is a near-replication of Li et al.'s [36] pen mode-switching study.

Participants

We recruited 36 participants (mean age 24.1 SD = 2.4, 8 women, all right-handed). 24 participants had experience using multi-touch tablets. A $10 remuneration was provided.

Apparatus

The experiment was performed on a Google Nexus 10 tablet (1.7 GHz Cortex A15 CPU with 1 GB RAM) running Android OS 5.1.1. The tablet's 264 × 178 mm display has a resolution of 2560 × 1600 px, a density of 11.8 px/mm (300 PPI). The device weighs approximately 603 grams. The experiment task code was written in Processing using the Android export library. Using Ng. et al.'s method [44] and a 240 fps camera, end-to-end latency was 100 ms, comparable to current apps.

Tasks

Our experimental tasks are closely based on Li et al. [36]. Five 20 × 22 mm rectangles are crossed in succession where the 20 mm ends form two parallel crossing targets (Fig. 3). Note that 20 mm crossing targets are 63% larger than the minimum size recommend by Luo and Vogel to achieve a 4% error rate [37]. The rectangle is a simplification of the pie section used by Li et al.. All five rectangles are displayed in a horizontal row, all oriented in the same direction with the required crossing direction indicated by a white arrow.

There are two task variations. In the *baseline* task, five grey rectangles are shown and the participant crosses them using standard touch input. In the *compound* task, the five rectangles alternate between grey and red, with the first rectangle grey. The participant must cross each grey rectangle using standard touch input and each red rectangle using the specified mode-switching technique. All touches leave a trail for feedback, black for standard touches and red when the mode is engaged. Note that the red or black trails function only as an abstract representation of two different modes. A small circle in the top-left corner of the display also turns red when the mode is engaged. If there is any crossing or mode error, a beep sounds and the rectangle must be crossed again to continue. Error detection and classification are described below.

Design and Procedure

The experiment is a repeated measures mixed design. The participant POSE while using the tablet is a between-subjects factor (SIT or STAND). Half of the participants completed all tasks while seated with the tablet placed flat on a table and the other half completed all tasks while standing with the tablet held on their non-dominant forearm. The mode-switching TECHNIQUE is a within-subjects factor with levels corresponding to the six mode-switching techniques (LONGPRESS, TWOFINGER, NONPREF, HARDPRESS, THUMB, KNUCKLE).

Participants were randomly assigned to a POSE condition and TECHNIQUE order was counter-balanced using a 6 × 6 Latin square. For each TECHNIQUE, there was a 1 to 3 min training period (after wearable hardware was attached and calibrated for HARDPRESS, THUMB, and KNUCKLE). Once training was over, the participant completed 9 BLOCKS of tasks. Odd numbered blocks were entirely baseline tasks and even numbered blocks entirely compound tasks. Before each block, the participant had to press a start button. Each block presented the task using 4 crossing directions (N, E, S, W) in random order. Note that Li et al.'s design had 8 directions, but they report no significant differences. Our four cardinal directions are representative of common actions like swiping, and a reduced number of directions enabled all six techniques to be tested in less than 1 hour with minimal fatigue. Participants were allowed to take breaks between blocks.

In sum there were: 6 TECHNIQUES × 9 BLOCKS (5 baseline, 4 compound) × 4 directions × 5 rectangle crossing = 1,080 rectangle crossings per participant.

Quantitative Measures

Three measures are calculated from experiment event logs.

Errors and Error Rates

Like Li et al., we identify three types of errors. A *crossing error* occurs if the touch stroke did not cross both ends of the rectangle in the correct order and direction. This captures errors related to crossing accuracy. An *out-of-target error* occurs if the touch stroke did not intersect with any part of the rectangle. This most often captures a case when the participant intentionally aborted a rectangle crossing. These errors are only possible on the current rectangle, strokes intersecting with other rectangles are ignored. A *mode error* occurs when the wrong mode is used to cross a rectangle. In other words, stroking a grey rectangle with red or vice versa. Mode errors are only possible in compound tasks.

We further distinguish between mode-in and mode-out errors. A *mode-in error* occurs when the participant fails to transition from standard touch input to the specified mode-switching technique. This is detected during the second or fourth rectangle crossing. A *mode-out error* is when the participant fails to transition from the specified mode-switching technique to standard touch input. This is detected during the third or fifth rectangle crossing. Finally, a *combined error* occurs if any of the errors above happen. Each of these error types are recorded as an indicator variable: 1 if the error occurred and 0 otherwise. The mean value of one type of indicator variable across trials produces the corresponding error rate.

Crossing Time

The crossing time is the duration between the touch up event after the previous rectangle was crossed until the touch up event after the current rectangle is crossed. There are four measurable rectangle crossings per task.

Mode-switching Time

Naively, one might directly compare crossing times in the baseline task with crossing times in the compound task (where a mode switch was required). However, both crossings share a common overhead of moving from the end of the previous rectangle to the start of the current rectangle. Therefore, we use the "subtraction method" used by Li et al. (adopted from Dillon et al. [11]) to isolate mode-switching time.

The method defines three cycles during a task. The first cycle is from the moment the start button is pressed until the touch up event after crossing the first rectangle. The second cycle begins immediately after, ending when all fingers are lifted after crossing the third rectangle. The third cycle begins immediately after, ending when all fingers are lifted after crossing the fifth rectangle. The second and third cycles are *full cycles*. During the compound task, each full cycle captures a complete mode-switch operation: the participant switches into a mode using the specified technique, crosses a rectangle, switches out of the mode, crosses another rectangle, and lifts their finger(s). The purpose of the first cycle is to ensure standard touch input is used before the second cycle. In each block, there are 8 full cycles (two cycles per direction). For each technique, each participant completes 32 full cycles with mode switching (in the 4 compound task blocks) and 40 full cycles with standard touch input only (in the 5 baseline task blocks).

The subtraction method isolates mode switching time using mean times from second and third cycles. For each block, the mean time for second and third cycle is calculated using error-free cycles (recall there are four task directions per block, so each full cycle is repeated four times). The mode-switch time is calculated by subtracting the mean full cycle time of two adjacent baseline blocks from the mean full cycle time from a compound block. In total, this provides 8 mode-switch time measurements per-participant, per-technique (2 per block).

RESULTS

All results, including subjective ratings, are continuous, so the same analysis procedure was used for all data. Specifically, we performed repeated measures ANOVA and pairwise t-tests with Bonferonni corrections when main or interaction effects were found. For interaction effects, we restricted pairwise tests to comparing means across factor dimensions independently. When the assumption of sphericity was violated, degrees of freedom were adjusted using Greenhouse-Geisser ($\epsilon < 0.75$) or Huynh-Feldt ($\epsilon \geq 0.75$). Non-normal skewed distributions, were corrected using a log transform or Aligned Rank Transform [59] depending on the severity and direction of skewness.

Data Pre-Processing

We examined error-free *crossing times* to identify outliers more than 3 standard deviations from the mean for each TASK divided by POSE. This removed 4.6% of the rectangle crossing trials (3.8% to 6.7% per technique), comparable to similar touch experiments [37].

Using the remaining error-free full cycles, we used the subtraction method described above to calculate *mode-switch times*. Visual inspection of the mode-switch times distribution suggested non-normality, confirmed by a Shapiro-Wilk and Anderson–Darling tests. To compensate, we log-transformed all data points for mode-switch time. There were 33 data points with slightly negative mode-switch times. This only appeared for TWOFINGER, the fastest technique. To compensate, we first added 306ms to all times to guarantee positive values required by the log function. Note that this log transformed data is used for statistical tests involving mode-switch time. All times presented in the paper are actual measured values. Error rate distributions did not suggest non-normality.

Learning Effects

To determine if performance changed during the four compound blocks, we tested for effects of POSE × TECHNIQUE × BLOCK on *mode-switch time* and *combined error rate*. We found no statistically significant interaction involving block indicating no learning effect across blocks. This matches the performance stability noted by Li et al. All blocks are used in subsequent analyses.

Mode-Switching Time

We expected POSE would alter how the techniques were performed, but there was no significant main effect of POSE, or POSE × TECHNIQUE interaction effect on MODE-SWITCH TIME. There was a significant main effect of TECHNIQUE ($F_{5,170}$ = 109.52, p < .0001, η_p^2 = .76). Post hoc tests found all TECHNIQUES significantly different p < .0001, except HARD PRESS and KNUCKLE. Ranking TECHNIQUES from fastest to slowest mode-switch time: TWOFINGER (222ms); NONPREF (311ms); THUMB (408ms); KNUCKLE and HARDPRESS (500ms and 568ms respectively, not significantly different); and LONGPRESS (1244ms). LONGPRESS is more than twice as slow as the next fastest techniques and more than five times slower than the fastest technique.

Comparing the switching times of techniques used in Li et al., we notice that our values are systematically higher. For NONPREF and HARDPRESS, the authors report mean times of 139ms and 284ms respectively, which are roughly half of our values. Tu et al. [54] also evaluated those techniques and while the pressure-based technique is reportedly even faster (mean time 228ms), the timing for their version of NONPREF, 304ms, is very similar to ours.

Although there was no effect of POSE, we examine TECHNIQUE by POSE given our a priori control. For each POSE, we ran a one-way ANOVA for TECHNIQUE on *mode-switch time*. Main effects were found for SIT ($F_{5,85}$ = 69.60, p < .0001, η_p^2 = .80) and STAND ($F_{5,85}$ = 44.42, p < .0001, η_p^2 = .72). The pattern of post hoc differences was very similar to the TECHNIQUE main effect (all p < .0001). The only difference is for STAND: there

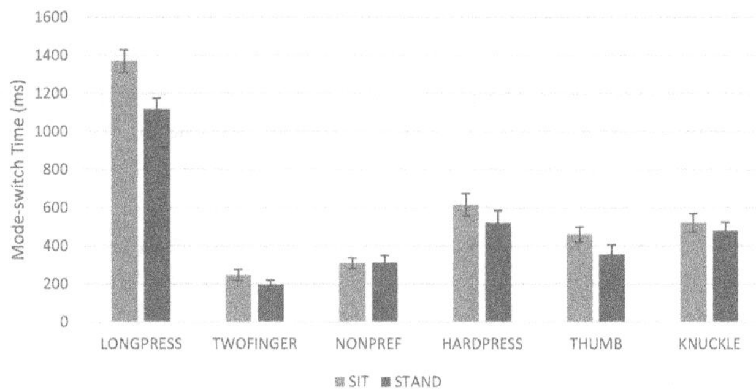

Figure 4: Mean mode-switch times by POSE and TECHNIQUE with 95% CI.

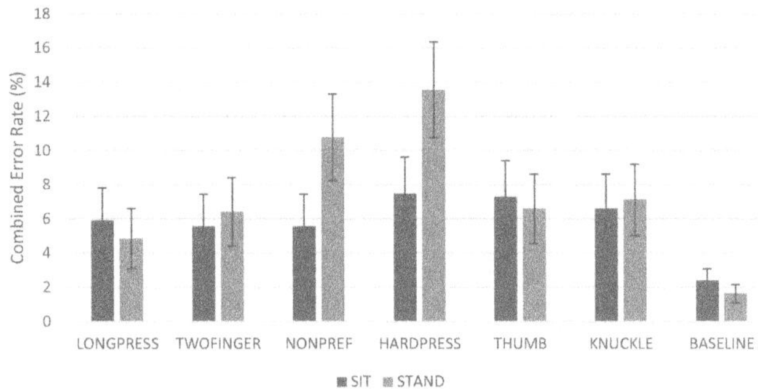

Figure 5: *Combined error rate* for TECHNIQUES by POSE

was one other non-significant difference between THUMB and NONPREF. Without that one exception, the order of TECHNIQUES from fastest to slowest is consistent between POSES and with combined poses (see Fig. 4).

Error Analysis

Before examining specific error rates for techniques and poses, we note that the *overall error rate* for baseline crossing cycles is a 4.1% with no detectable differences between POSE. This rate suggests participants were balancing speed and accuracy [63] and is low enough to suggest using the subtraction method is valid. Li et al. do not report baseline rates.

Unlike mode-switch time, we did find a significant interaction for POSE × TECHNIQUE on *combined error rate* ($F_{3.40,115.66}$ = 3.02, p = .012, η_p^2 = .081). There was a significant main effect for TECHNIQUE as well, but the interaction with pose is most relevant. To determine if the technique combined error rate was significantly different between poses, we performed six pairwise tests. With Bonferonni correction, only a borderline difference in HARDPRESS p = .06 exists. Like mode-switch time, it appears that POSE has little or no effect on overall error rate.

Continuing to explore the significant interaction, we examine if the technique *combined error rates* were significantly different using pairwise tests between techniques when considering SIT and STAND separately. For SIT, we found no significantly different techniques. The measured rates ranged between 4.8% and 7.5%. Again, we observe a contrast with Li et al.'s reported error rates, which are systematically lower. Their hold technique led to the most errors (due to a slippery screen) and NonPrefHand to the lowest rates. Tu et al. once more show different results (Holding being the least error-causing

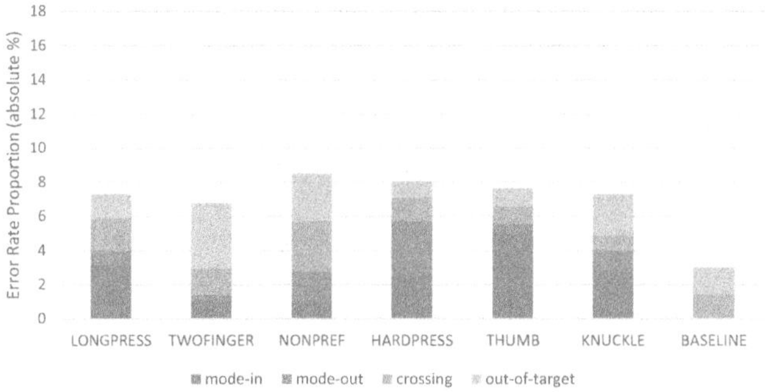

Figure 6: Proportion of specific error rates for TECHNIQUES for SIT. Note more than one type of specific error can occur during a cycle.

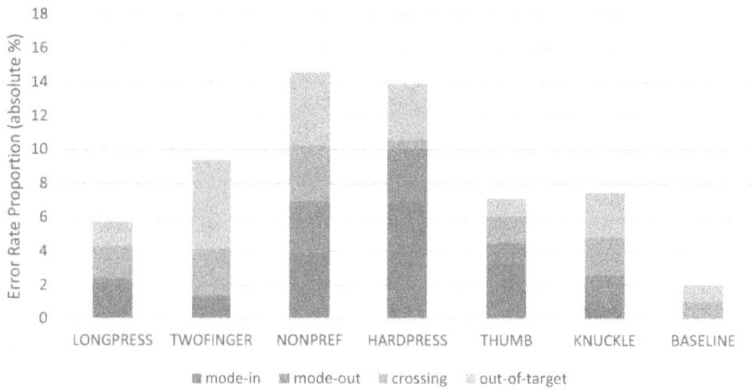

Figure 7: Proportion of specific error rates for TECHNIQUES for STAND. Note more than one type of specific error can occur during a cycle.

technique in their experiment) and error rate ranges that are partially closer to ours.

For STAND, we found significant differences between TWOFINGER and HARDPRESS, LONGPRESS and HARDPRESS (both $p < .05$), and a borderline difference between NONPREF and LONGPRESS ($p = .05$). The measured rate for HARDPRESS is 13.5% and NONPREF is 10.8%, with the remaining techniques ranging between 3.3% and 7.1%. This provides more evidence that, relative to the other techniques, HARDPRESS and NONPREF are harder to perform when standing.

We also investigate the effect of POSE and TECHNIQUE on specific types of errors (illustrated by POSE in Fig. 6 & 7).

For *crossing error rate*, we found a main effect for TECHNIQUE ($F_{5,170} = 3.97, p < .001, \eta_p^2 = .104$). Post hoc tests showed NONPREF had a higher rate (3.9%) than HARDPRESS (1.2%) and THUMB (1.5%). Measured rates were between 1.2% and 3.9%.

For *out-of-target error rate*, we also found a main effect for TECHNIQUE ($F_{5,170} = 5.41$, $p < .0001$, $\eta_p^2 = .14$). Post hoc tests showed the rate for THUMB (1.0%) was lower than KNUCKLE (2.6%), NONPREF (5.0%), and TWOFINGER (5.9%). Also HARDPRESS (2.5%) was lower than TWOFINGER. Measured rates were between 1.0% and 6.3%. Note that Li et al. had almost no out-of-target errors.

For *mode-in error rate*, TECHNIQUE had a main effect but we focus on the more relevant significant POSE × TECHNIQUE interaction ($F_{5,170} = 2.44$, $p = .036$, $\eta_p^2 = .066$). For SIT, post hoc tests showed TWOFINGER (1.0%) was lower than LONGPRESS (3.1%). For STAND, KNUCKLE (0.7%) was lower than HARDPRESS (6.9%) (all $p < .05$). Measured rates were between 1.0% and 5.0% for SIT and between .07% and 6.9% for STAND.

For *mode-out error rate*, TECHNIQUE had a main effect ($F_{3.56,121.07} = 6.28$, $p < .001$, $\eta_p^2 = .16$). Post hoc tests showed TWOFINGER (0.3%) was lower than NONPREF (2.4%) and HARDPRESS (3.1%) HARDPRESS was higher than THUMB (0.9%) and LONGPRESS (0.6%) (all $p < .05$). Measured rates were between 0.3% and 3.1%. There is some evidence that NONPREF and HARDPRESS both are more difficult to disengage.

Subjective Ratings

After completing trials for all techniques, participants provided subjective ratings of the techniques with respect to six aspects: ease-of-learning, ease-of-use, accuracy, speed, eye fatigue, and hand fatigue. All ratings were on a continuous numeric scale from 1 to 5, with 1 being the worst score (e.g. low accuracy, hard to learn, very fatiguing) and 5 the best (e.g. high accuracy, easy to learn, not fatiguing).

Table 1 summarizes subjective ratings by POSE. The distributions for ratings was non-normal due to high negative skewness, so the values were transformed using the Aligned Rank Transform method [59]. ANOVAs performed on this transformed data did not reveal any significant main effects or interactions involving POSE on any any of the ratings. However, there are significant main effects for TECHNIQUE regardless of POSE. We report the main results of pairwise comparisons between TECHNIQUE for each rating.

- For *hand fatigue* and *ease-of-use*, HARDPRESS and KNUCKLE were reported respectively more tiring and less easy to use compared to the other techniques (all $p < .032$). This is understandable, given the pressure and wrist efforts required. Participant feedback confirmed the difficulty and physical demand of HARDPRESS (seven people) with one participant commenting that it almost felt like breaking the tablet. As for KNUCKLE, two participants reported it was tiring and two pointed out that it resulted in increased occlusion; however, two people also said it was "fun". For NONPREF, four participants remarked that the technique required well-timed coordination and thus getting used to to be efficient. For the standing position, we also observed that participants with small hands (two in particular) sometimes had trouble reaching the button with the fingers of the non-preferred hand across the bezel of the tablet.
- In terms of *ease-of-learning*, HARDPRESS was rated significantly harder to master than LONGPRESS and TWOFINGER ($p = .0043$ and $p = .0102$ respectively). We believe this is because participants had to learn to adjust touch pressure levels to be able to activate the two different modes reliably as well as because of the extra training required for the EMG classifier.
- With respect to *accuracy*, HARDPRESS was consistently perceived as having the lowest precision ($p < .007$ compared to all other techniques). Note that HARDPRESS and NONPREF have the highest overall error rates, yet HARDPRESS was rated more accurate. Hence, there appears to be an increased perception of poor accuracy with HARDPRESS. For TWOFINGER, we observed that, during training, participants needed a

SIT	LONG PRESS	TWO FINGER	NON PREF	HARD PRESS	THUMB	KNUCKLE
Learning	4.4±.21	4.4±.20	4.7±.13	3.7±.32	4.6±.14	4.1±.23
Ease-of-Use	3.9±.24	4.2±.22	4.0±.28	3.0±.31	4.3±.24	2.7±.26
Accuracy	4.3±.20	4.1±.26	4.5±.16	3.2±.26	4.3±.20	4.2±.18
Speed	2.6±.23	4.3±.22	4.2±.17	3.4±.30	4.2±.20	3.4±.33
Eye Fatigue	4.7±.15	4.8±.10	4.8±.12	4.4±.25	4.7±.17	4.5±.21
Hand Fatigue	3.7±.27	4.1±.27	4.4±.22	3.0±.32	4.0±.26	3.0±.31
Combined	3.9±.1	4.3±.1	4.4±.1	3.5±.1	4.4±.1	3.6±.1
STAND	LONG PRESS	TWO FINGER	NON PREF	HARD PRESS	THUMB	KNUCKLE
Learning	4.6±.22	4.7±.16	3.9±.32	3.8±.26	4.3±.24	4.0±.27
Ease-of-Use	3.9±.22	4.2±.24	3.2±.36	3.0±.31	3.9±.29	3.2±.33
Accuracy	4.5±.18	4.2±.19	3.9±.33	3.1±.28	4.1±.23	3.8±.26
Speed	2.8±.30	4.6±.20	3.4±.30	3.3±.27	4.1±.26	3.4±.25
Eye Fatigue	5.0±.0	5.0±.0	4.9±.05	4.9±.05	5.0±.0	4.7±.17
Hand Fatigue	4.3±.30	4.5±.18	3.6±.32	2.9±.34	4.3±.26	3.6±.30
Combined	4.2±.1	4.5±.1	3.8±.1	3.5±.1	4.3±.1	3.8±.1

Table 1: Mean subjective ratings: SIT (top) and STAND (bottom).

short adaptation time to position their two fingers for the ink to appear at the desired spot.

- Finally, regarding *speed*, TWOFINGER was rated significantly faster than all other techniques except THUMB ($p < .01$), THUMB was judged faster than HARDPRESS, KNUCKLE and LONGPRESS ($p < .013$) and LONGPRESS considered significantly slower than all techniques except HARDPRESS ($p < .03$). All those results are consistent with the time measurements.

DISCUSSION

Our results provide evidence that regardless of whether a tablet is used flat on a desk, or held by the non-dominant arm while standing, the performance characteristics and subjective impressions of these techniques are comparable. This may bolster the validity of other non-mode-switching touch input studies evaluated only when a tablet is laid flat on a desk (e.g. [38, 18, 43]). However, more styles of touch input need to be tested in sitting and standing poses to verify any general claims.

Regarding mode-switching techniques, our results show long press is the worst and two-finger multi-touch the best, unless target accuracy is critical. When accuracy is needed, thumb-on-finger is the best option with lower out-of-target errors than two-finger (and others) and lower crossing errors than non-preferred hand. Subjective ratings for thumb-on-finger do not indicate a pattern of any strong preference or dislike. One caveat is that, although there were no significant differences for thumb-on-finger in mode-in errors, the measured values are high (Figs. 6 and 7). Given the high variance preventing statistical difference, individual mastery of thumb-on-finger mode-switching varies.

When considering mode-switching time only, non-preferred hand, knuckle, and hard press are all within 100ms from the mean time for thumb-on-finger. At first this may suggest they are all comparable, but high rates of mode-switching errors and a pattern of lower subjective ratings cast doubt on using pressure for touch mode-switching. Although there is subjective support for the non-preferred hand, it has a higher mode-out error rate than other techniques and a surprising pattern of frequent crossing and out-of-target errors.

Given the novelty of using a knuckle for touch input, we were surprised to see it perform as well as it did. It has an overall error rate comparable to the best techniques with one of the lowest mode-in error rates. Although out-of-target errors are higher than some, there is no statistical evidence of a higher crossing error rate. This is encouraging considering we expected the increased occlusion to make knuckle crossing wildly inaccurate. However, subjective ratings and comments show a pattern of mild dislike due to higher fatigue and perceived slower speed. Note that only two-finger and knuckle *instantly* combine the mode-switch with the initial touch position. This "merging of command selection and direct manipulation" has been shown to be beneficial [22].

Subtraction Method Validity

Like Li et al., we confirm that we can apply the subtraction method in our experimental protocol since drawing and positioning movements are not strictly fixed as in Dillon et al.'s point-connecting task [11]. We accomplish this by comparing the *total movement distance* in a full cycle between baseline and compound tasks. A sufficiently small difference indicates that movements required for the two types of tasks were similar. Due to how we logged multiple simultaneous touches, automatic calculation of movement time for non-preferred hand and multi-touch proved error-prone. We chose to not include them in this analysis. Among techniques, non-preferred hand and multi-touch are arguably the most similar to non-mode touching crossing movements.

For the remaining four techniques, we found a mean movement distance for a full cycle to be 55.2mm (690px). This is 1.4mm greater than the baseline condition, in which mean movement distance was 53.8mm (672px). This difference of only 2.7%, compares favourably with Li et al.'s difference of 4.7mm (20px)[1], or 3.4%. Li et al. also report a similar single full cycle mean movement distance of 66 mm (290px). This demonstrates using the subtraction method was valid.

Temporal Pattern Analysis

We analyse the temporal submovements pattern to understand different techniques, and use this to classify them into different temporal models. This is directly based on the "keystroke level analysis" performed by Li et al.. We use the same models and compare our results with their findings.

A full cycle can be decomposed into four submovements with corresponding times:

$$T_{cycle} = T_{P1} + T_{C1} + T_{P2} + T_{C2}$$

where T_{Pi} is the time taken to position the finger in the air before crossing the ith rectangle and T_{Ci} is the time taken to drag the finger on the display and cross the ith rectangle. T_{Pi} begins on touch up of the previous rectangle and ends on touch down of the ith rectangle. T_{Ci} begins on touch down and ends on touch up after crossing through the ith rectangle.

Each two-rectangle full cycle during a compound task requires crossing rectangle 1 (the 'red' one) with the mode engaged and crossing rectangle 2 (the 'grey' one) with the mode disengaged.

[1] Li et al. used a 12.1" diagonal, 1024 × 768px TabletPC.

	BASELINE	LONG PRESS	TWO FINGER	NON PREF	HARD PRESS	THUMB	KNUCKLE
T_{P1}	323	392	375	486	415	502	546
T_{C1}	196	1239	210	189	420	276	267
T_{P2}	317	415	435	419	514	433	510
T_{C2}	195	220	200	208	234	218	218
T_{ENG}	N/A	1130	401	318	459	536	544
T_{DIS}	N/A	51	100	421	91	61	531
T_{GES}	N/A	552	284	779	466	303	799

Table 2: Cycle decomposition times (ms).

Therefore, the mode is engaged either during T_{P1}, or near the beginning of T_{C1}. The time to engage a mode T_{ENG} is the duration from the start of a cycle until the mode is engaged. Note that T_{ENG} equals T_{P1} if the mode is engaged precisely at touch down (e.g. knuckle); T_{ENG} may be less than T_{P1} if the mode can be engaged before touch down (e.g. non-preferred hand); and T_{ENG} may be greater than T_{P1} if the mode is engaged after touch down (e.g. hard press). T_{GES} is the time spent gesturing, defined from the later of mode engagement and touch down until touch up. Beyond these durations defined by Li et al., we define a mode disengage time T_{DIS} as the duration from disengagement until touch up.

Table 2 provides mean times for these submovements for all techniques. A further verification that the task and subtraction method worked as it should is that the T_{C2} times are the same for the baseline task and all techniques. As in Li et al., our absolute timings for T_{C2} all appear close to the baseline. To verify this, we conducted a one-way ANOVA for the effect of technique (including baseline) on T_{C2}. There was a main effect ($F_{4.07,138.27} = 9.5754$, $p < .001$) and post hoc tests reveal that all but two-finger multi-touch are significantly different. However, the differences between all techniques and the baseline is less than 40 ms.

Temporal models

All techniques follow the temporal models described in Li et al.'s keystroke level analysis. Although the authors did not perform statistical tests on timing decompositions, we provide this extra level of validation when applicable.

Using Non-Preferred Hand and Thumb-on-Finger

The two techniques obey the same temporal model, as they require the mode to be engaged before touch down, with release possible during, or after completion of the gesture. As in Li et al., we calculate an estimate of the gesture engagement time by subtracting T_{P1} of the baseline task from T_{P1} of the compound task. We obtain 164ms for NONPREF and 179ms for THUMB, with no significant difference between them. This contrasts with Li et al., where the mode engagement time for NonPrefHand and BarrelButton were 65ms and 144ms respectively, a greater difference.

Disregarding the absolute timings which are systematically lower for Li et al., we believe there may be two reasons for this greater difference. First, it may be easier and faster to hit the index finger with one's thumb than to reach and press a barrel button on a stylus. Second, although our participants held their finger poised above the touchscreen button before each non-dominant hand trial, Li et al.'s NonPrefHand participants could exploit the physical button by resting their finger on it to minimize activation and eliminate targeting. The physical button may have been the primary reason for the very strong performance of NonPrefHand in Li et al.. Perhaps the full potential of non-preferred hand mode-switching cannot be realized on a touchscreen.

Using Long Press (Hold)

Li et al. note that there is a difference between the T_{P1} timings of Hold and the baseline even though gesture mode engagement is started upon touch down and thus, at first glance, the two T_{P1} should be close. They attribute this difference to an additional preparation time needed when slowing down the pen movement to hold it in a steady position. We also observe this phenomenon with a statistically significant difference of 69.5ms between the T_{P1} timings ($p < .0001$), albeit a much lower one.

Li et al. also calculate the time participants took to respond to the feedback showing that the mode had been engaged (a full circle) using the formula:

$$T_{response} = T_{ENG} + T_{P1} - Holdtime$$

Their response time is 137ms. Ours is: $1130 - 392 - 500 = 238$ms.

Using Hard Press (Pressure) and Two-Finger Multi-touch

In Li et al., Pressure is the technique with the lowest T_{P1}, but again, without statistical analyses we do not know if timings are significantly different from other techniques. Even though HARDPRESS appears to be third best only from the mean values, ANOVAs and post hoc tests do not reveal any significant differences between the T_{P1} values for HARDPRESS, TWOFINGER and LONGPRESS and hence we are not able to conclude which of the three techniques has the shortest positioning time.

Similar to Li et et al., we calculate the time to increase touch pressure to the required level in order to activate the gesture mode: $T_{ENG} - T_{P1} = 45$ms. This value is much lower than their 176ms. We attribute that to the possibility that it might be easier to sense and apply the required pressure level using direct input than with an instrument such as a stylus. The fact that we used an EMG armband with a high data rate and adapted pressure thresholds for each participant might also have been factors.

Like Li et al, we observe that drawing with HARDPRESS takes more time than without (the difference between the two T_{C1} values is 223ms, which is significant). The difference is likely even more pronounced with a finger than with a stylus due to the increased friction of dragging (Li et al. report a drawing time of 176ms, but, once more, we cannot determine if the differences are significant).

The model for TWOFINGER is similar, as the mode is engaged after touch down and has to be maintained throughout the moded action. However, we expect the time to engage the mode after touch down to be very short, as the two fingers are usually put down almost simultaneously. Similar to hard press, we calculate the engagement time after touch down, which is $T_{ENG} - T_{P1} = 26$ms. A t-test confirms that the difference with HARDPRESS is significant ($p < .0001$).

Using Knuckle
Our knuckle technique follows the temporal model of the Eraser in Li et al.. The authors notice very similar T_{C1} timings for the Eraser and the baseline task, meaning that drawing with the eraser end of the stylus requires no extra effort. This was not the case with KNUCKLE. Drawing with the knuckle took an extra 71ms, statistically significant compared to the baseline ($p < .0001$). Li et al. further calculate times to turn and revert the pen in order to use the eraser by subtracting the T_{P1} and T_{P2} timings. They report values of 661ms and 555ms. A stylus being typically longer and the rotation required to use its eraser larger, our wrist-rotation times for KNUCKLE are predictably lower: 223ms and 193ms respectively.

Improvements to Mode-Switching Techniques

None of the techniques we tested were perfect in all aspects. Even two-finger multi-touch suffers from accuracy problems when the demands for targeting and tracing precision are high. To improve that, a cursor could appear between fingers when approaching the screen (assuming pre-touch sensing is available [29]). For hard press, it would be interesting to see if a device with built-in touch pressure sensors and a smart adaptive thresholding algorithm could improve the measured and perceived accuracy as well as reduce fatigue.

For KNUCKLE, our realisation of the technique is based on the rotation of the wrist, which causes both strain and occlusion problems. Those issues might be alleviated if knuckle interaction could be performed without turning the hand (i.e. by bending the finger and using the distal interphalangeal joint).

Regarding techniques which require the mode switch to be engaged before touch down, mode-in errors would presumably be reduced if that condition is relaxed so the mode change could occur after touching the device. This has been shown in pen mode-switching for direct manipulation contexts that permit late mode activation [33, 48]. The extended period allowed for the switch could be chosen depending on the application context and which functions the moded and non-moded actions are mapped to: a long period if late mode engagement has minimal disturbance (e.g. changing stroke style) and a short period when late mode engagement would be disruptive (e.g. switching between panning and inking).

Hybrid techniques are an interesting avenue for exploration. For example, pressure-based activation could be combined with non-preferred-hand to simulate behaviour of a physical button: the fingers of the non-preferred hand could rest on the screen to minimize activation time and eliminate targeting. This might be especially helpful when supporting the tablet with that non-preferred hand, as the holding posture is maintained at all times and therefore stability is likely increased. It would be particularly interesting to see how techniques can be combined to support several mode changes, such as combining two-finger or knuckle with non-preferred hand.

LIMITATIONS

While our experiments provide insightful results, we acknowledge their scope of validity and the limitations within which they can be interpreted. First, since our study design followed Li et al., we operate with the same constraints regarding a single mode switch applied with a relatively high and regular frequency in a synthetic linear task. This design allowed us to perform fine-grained analyses, but further studies could validate our results in more realistic and less controlled tasks. Furthermore, applications often include more than two modes, so techniques could also be evaluated with multiple modes to assess scalability.

Although we strived to design optimized and representative techniques, there are possible limitations in the way they were implemented. Knuckle, hard press, and pressure required participants to wear extra sensors. Although none reported any particular impediment or discomfort, results for those techniques might change if alternate sensing was used. For non-preferred hand, the size and position of the trigger button was fixed for all participants. Prior work and several pilot tests informed our final design, but size and position could be personalized to individual people, especially when used in a standing position. Finally, the dwell time used to activate a long-press naturally influences the performance and accuracy of the switch. Our choice of 500ms is used in popular operating systems, but this could be further optimized.

CONCLUSION

We presented a detailed analysis of touch input mode-switching techniques. Our results can be used as guidelines for selecting mode-switching techniques. When restricted to current device capabilities, two-finger multi-touch should be selected if accuracy is not critical and a non-preferred hand button otherwise. As more advanced sensors are available, touching the thumb to the side of the finger will also be a good choice. Using the knuckle works surprisingly well, though many people perceive it as being inaccurate and uncomfortable. In most cases, long press should be avoided. In contrast to reasonable performance for pen pressure mode-switching reported by Li et al. [36], using pressure for touch mode-switching appears problematic. It is possible that hard press performance and perceived inaccuracy may improve on a device with built-in pressure sensors, but we suspect this has more to do with touch friction and fatigue.

Though numerous experimental investigations have compared mode-switching techniques for pucks, mice, and pens, we believe we are the first to do so for touch input. This work fills an important knowledge gap, especially when considering how fundamental mode-switching is to touch interaction.

ACKNOWLEDGMENTS

This work was made possible by funding from NSERC Discovery Grant (#402467) and a Google Focused Award project on context-aware mobile computing.

REFERENCES

1. Dzmitry Aliakseyeu, Miguel A. Nacenta, Sriram Subramanian, and Carl Gutwin. 2006. Bubble Radar: Efficient Pen-based Interaction. In *Proceedings of the Working Conference on Advanced Visual Interfaces (AVI '06)*. ACM, New York, NY, USA, 19–26. DOI: http://dx.doi.org/10.1145/1133265.1133271

2. Hrvoje Benko, T. Scott Saponas, Dan Morris, and Desney Tan. 2009. Enhancing Input on and Above the Interactive Surface with Muscle Sensing. In *Proceedings of the ACM International Conference on Interactive Tabletops and Surfaces (ITS '09)*. ACM, New York, NY, USA, 93–100. DOI:http://dx.doi.org/10.1145/1731903.1731924

3. Hrvoje Benko and Daniel Wigdor. 2010. *Imprecision, Inaccuracy, and Frustration: The Tale of Touch Input*. Springer London, London, 249–275. DOI: http://dx.doi.org/10.1007/978-1-84996-113-4_11

4. Hrvoje Benko, Andrew D. Wilson, and Patrick Baudisch. 2006. Precise selection techniques for multi-touch screens. In *Proceedings of the SIGCHI conference on Human Factors in computing systems*. ACM, Montréal, Québec, Canada, 1263–1272. DOI: http://dx.doi.org/10.1145/1124772.1124963

5. Xiaojun Bi, Tomer Moscovich, Gonzalo Ramos, Ravin Balakrishnan, and Ken Hinckley. 2008. An Exploration of Pen Rolling for Pen-based Interaction. In *Proceedings of the 21st Annual ACM Symposium on User Interface Software and Technology (UIST '08)*. ACM, New York, NY, USA, 191–200. DOI: http://dx.doi.org/10.1145/1449715.1449745

6. Sebastian Boring, David Ledo, Xiang 'Anthony' Chen, Nicolai Marquardt, Anthony Tang, and Saul Greenberg. 2012. The Fat Thumb: Using the Thumb's Contact Size for Single-handed Mobile Interaction. In *Proceedings of the 14th International Conference on Human-computer Interaction with Mobile Devices and Services (MobileHCI '12)*. ACM, New York, NY, USA, 39–48. DOI:http://dx.doi.org/10.1145/2371574.2371582

7. Peter Brandl, Clifton Forlines, Daniel Wigdor, Michael Haller, and Chia Shen. 2008. Combining and Measuring the Benefits of Bimanual Pen and Direct-touch Interaction on Horizontal Interfaces. In *Proceedings of the Working Conference on Advanced Visual Interfaces (AVI '08)*. ACM, New York, NY, USA, 154–161. DOI: http://dx.doi.org/10.1145/1385569.1385595

8. Géry Casiez, Nicolas Roussel, and Daniel Vogel. 2012. 1 € Filter: A Simple Speed-based Low-pass Filter for Noisy Input in Interactive Systems. In *Proceedings of the SIGCHI Conference on Human Factors in Computing Systems (CHI '12)*. ACM, New York, NY, USA, 2527–2530. DOI: http://dx.doi.org/10.1145/2207676.2208639

9. A. Cockburn, D. Ahlström, and C. Gutwin. 2012. Understanding Performance in Touch Selections: Tap, Drag and Radial Pointing Drag with Finger, Stylus and Mouse. *Int. J. Hum.-Comput. Stud.* 70, 3 (March 2012), 218–233. DOI: http://dx.doi.org/10.1016/j.ijhcs.2011.11.002

10. Ashley Colley and Jonna Häkkilä. 2014. Exploring Finger Specific Touch Screen Interaction for Mobile Phone User Interfaces. In *Proceedings of the 26th Australian Computer-Human Interaction Conference on Designing Futures: The Future of Design (OzCHI '14)*. ACM, New York, NY, USA, 539–548. DOI: http://dx.doi.org/10.1145/2686612.2686699

11. R. F. Dillon, Jeff D. Edey, and Jo W. Tombaugh. 1990. Measuring the true cost of command selection: techniques and results. *Proceedings of the SIGCHI conference on Human factors in computing systems Empowering people - CHI '90* April (1990), 19–26. DOI: http://dx.doi.org/10.1145/97243.97247

12. Alan Esenther and Kathy Ryall. 2006. Fluid DTMouse: Better Mouse Support for Touch-based Interactions. In *Proceedings of the Working Conference on Advanced Visual Interfaces (AVI '06)*. ACM, New York, NY, USA, 112–115. DOI: http://dx.doi.org/10.1145/1133265.1133289

13. George W. Fitzmaurice and William Buxton. 1997. An Empirical Evaluation of Graspable User Interfaces: Towards Specialized, Space-multiplexed Input. In *Proceedings of the ACM SIGCHI Conference on Human Factors in Computing Systems (CHI '97)*. ACM, New York, NY, USA, 43–50. DOI: http://dx.doi.org/10.1145/258549.258578

14. Clifton Forlines, Daniel Wigdor, Chia Shen, and Ravin Balakrishnan. 2007. Direct-touch vs. Mouse Input for Tabletop Displays. In *Proceedings of the SIGCHI Conference on Human Factors in Computing Systems (CHI '07)*. ACM, New York, NY, USA, 647–656. DOI: http://dx.doi.org/10.1145/1240624.1240726

15. Cédric Foucault, Manfred Micaux, David Bonnet, and Michel Beaudouin-Lafon. 2014. SPad: A Bimanual Interaction Technique for Productivity Applications on Multi-touch Tablets. In *CHI '14 Extended Abstracts on Human Factors in Computing Systems (CHI EA '14)*. ACM, New York, NY, USA, 1879–1884. DOI: http://dx.doi.org/10.1145/2559206.2581277

16. Ina Fried. 2016. This new technology lets you control your phone with more than just your fingertips. (Aug. 2016). http://www.recode.net/2016/8/30/12639718/qeexo-phone-gestures-knuckles

17. Mayank Goel, Jacob Wobbrock, and Shwetak Patel. 2012. GripSense: Using Built-in Sensors to Detect Hand Posture and Pressure on Commodity Mobile Phones. In *Proceedings of the 25th Annual ACM Symposium on User Interface Software and Technology (UIST '12)*. ACM, New York, NY, USA, 545–554. DOI: http://dx.doi.org/10.1145/2380116.2380184

18. Alix Goguey, Mathieu Nancel, Géry Casiez, and Daniel Vogel. 2016. The Performance and Preference of Different Fingers and Chords for Pointing, Dragging, and Object Transformation. In *Proceedings of the 2016 CHI Conference on Human Factors in Computing Systems (CHI '16)*. ACM, New York, NY, USA, 4250–4261. DOI: http://dx.doi.org/10.1145/2858036.2858194

19. Google. 2016. Project Soli. (2016). https://atap.google.com/soli/ Accessed: 2016-08-23.

20. Tovi Grossman, Ken Hinckley, Patrick Baudisch, Maneesh Agrawala, and Ravin Balakrishnan. 2006. Hover Widgets: Using the Tracking State to Extend the Capabilities of Pen-operated Devices. In *Proceedings of the SIGCHI Conference on Human Factors in Computing Systems (CHI '06)*. ACM, New York, NY, USA, 861–870. DOI:http://dx.doi.org/10.1145/1124772.1124898

21. Tovi Grossman, Daniel Wigdor, and Ravin Balakrishnan. 2004. Multi-finger Gestural Interaction with 3D Volumetric Displays. In *Proceedings of the 17th Annual ACM Symposium on User Interface Software and Technology (UIST '04)*. ACM, New York, NY, USA, 61–70. DOI:http://dx.doi.org/10.1145/1029632.1029644

22. François Guimbretière, Andrew Martin, and Terry Winograd. 2005. Benefits of Merging Command Selection and Direct Manipulation. *ACM Trans. Comput.-Hum. Interact.* 12, 3 (Sept. 2005), 460–476. DOI:http://dx.doi.org/10.1145/1096737.1096742

23. Chris Harrison, Julia Schwarz, and Scott E. Hudson. 2011. TapSense: Enhancing Finger Interaction on Touch Surfaces. In *Proceedings of the 24th Annual ACM Symposium on User Interface Software and Technology (UIST '11)*. ACM, New York, NY, USA, 627–636. DOI: http://dx.doi.org/10.1145/2047196.2047279

24. Chris Harrison, Robert Xiao, Julia Schwarz, and Scott E. Hudson. 2014. TouchTools: Leveraging Familiarity and Skill with Physical Tools to Augment Touch Interaction. In *Proceedings of the SIGCHI Conference on Human Factors in Computing Systems (CHI '14)*. ACM, New York, NY, USA, 2913–2916. DOI: http://dx.doi.org/10.1145/2556288.2557012

25. Seongkook Heo and Geehyuk Lee. 2012. ForceDrag: Using Pressure As a Touch Input Modifier. In *Proceedings of the 24th Australian Computer-Human Interaction Conference (OzCHI '12)*. ACM, New York, NY, USA, 204–207. DOI: http://dx.doi.org/10.1145/2414536.2414572

26. Ken Hinckley, Patrick Baudisch, Gonzalo Ramos, and Francois Guimbretiere. 2005. Design and Analysis of Delimiters for Selection-action Pen Gesture Phrases in Scriboli. In *Proceedings of the SIGCHI Conference on Human Factors in Computing Systems (CHI '05)*. ACM, New York, NY, USA, 451–460. DOI: http://dx.doi.org/10.1145/1054972.1055035

27. Ken Hinckley, Mary Czerwinski, and Mike Sinclair. 1998. Interaction and Modeling Techniques for Desktop Two-handed Input. In *Proceedings of the 11th Annual ACM Symposium on User Interface Software and Technology (UIST '98)*. ACM, New York, NY, USA, 49–58. DOI:http://dx.doi.org/10.1145/288392.288572

28. Ken Hinckley, Francois Guimbretiere, Patrick Baudisch, Raman Sarin, Maneesh Agrawala, and Ed Cutrell. 2006. The springboard: multiple modes in one spring-loaded control. In *Proceedings of the SIGCHI conference on Human Factors in computing systems - CHI '06*. ACM Press, New York, New York, USA, 181. DOI: http://dx.doi.org/10.1145/1124772.1124801

29. Ken Hinckley, Seongkook Heo, Michel Pahud, Christian Holz, Hrvoje Benko, Abigail Sellen, Richard Banks, Kenton O'Hara, Gavin Smyth, and William Buxton. 2016. Pre-Touch Sensing for Mobile Interaction. In *Proceedings of the 2016 CHI Conference on Human Factors in Computing Systems (CHI '16)*. ACM, New York, NY, USA, 2869–2881. DOI: http://dx.doi.org/10.1145/2858036.2858095

30. Ken Hinckley, Michel Pahud, Hrvoje Benko, Pourang Irani, François Guimbretière, Marcel Gavriliu, Xiang 'Anthony' Chen, Fabrice Matulic, William Buxton, and Andrew Wilson. 2014. Sensing Techniques for Tablet+Stylus Interaction. In *Proceedings of the 27th Annual ACM Symposium on User Interface Software and Technology (UIST '14)*. ACM, New York, NY, USA, 605–614. DOI: http://dx.doi.org/10.1145/2642918.2647379

31. Ken Hinckley, Koji Yatani, Michel Pahud, Nicole Coddington, Jenny Rodenhouse, Andy Wilson, Hrvoje Benko, and Bill Buxton. 2010. Pen + Touch = New Tools. In *Proceedings of the 23Nd Annual ACM Symposium on User Interface Software and Technology (UIST '10)*. ACM, New York, NY, USA, 27–36. DOI: http://dx.doi.org/10.1145/1866029.1866036

32. Paul Kabbash, William Buxton, and Abigail Sellen. 1994. Two-handed Input in a Compound Task. In *Proceedings of the SIGCHI Conference on Human Factors in Computing Systems (CHI '94)*. ACM, New York, NY, USA, 417–423. DOI: http://dx.doi.org/10.1145/191666.191808

33. Edward Lank, Jaime Ruiz, and William Cowan. 2006. Concurrent Bimanual Stylus Interaction: A Study of Non-preferred Hand Mode Manipulation. In *Proceedings of Graphics Interface 2006 (GI '06)*. Canadian Information Processing Society, Toronto, Ont., Canada, Canada, 17–24. http://dl.acm.org/citation.cfm?id=1143079.1143083

34. Jakob F. Leitner, Florian Perteneder, Can Liu, Christian Rendl, and Michael Haller. 2013. Kolibri: Tiny and Fast Gestures for Large Pen-based Surfaces. In *Proceedings of the SIGCHI Conference on Human Factors in Computing Systems (CHI '13)*. ACM, New York, NY, USA, 1789–1798. DOI: http://dx.doi.org/10.1145/2470654.2466236

35. G. Julian Lepinski, Tovi Grossman, and George Fitzmaurice. 2010. The Design and Evaluation of Multitouch Marking Menus. In *Proceedings of the SIGCHI Conference on Human Factors in Computing Systems (CHI '10)*. ACM, New York, NY, USA, 2233–2242. DOI: http://dx.doi.org/10.1145/1753326.1753663

36. Yang Li, Ken Hinckley, Zhiwei Guan, and James A. Landay. 2005. Experimental analysis of mode switching techniques in pen-based user interfaces. In *Proceedings of the SIGCHI conference on Human factors in computing systems - CHI '05*. ACM Press, New York, New York, USA, 461. DOI: http://dx.doi.org/10.1145/1054972.1055036

37. Yuexing Luo and Daniel Vogel. 2014. Crossing-based Selection with Direct Touch Input. In *Proceedings of the SIGCHI Conference on Human Factors in Computing Systems (CHI '14)*. ACM, New York, NY, USA, 2627–2636. DOI: http://dx.doi.org/10.1145/2556288.2557397

38. Yuexing Luo and Daniel Vogel. 2015. Pin-and-Cross: A Unimanual Multitouch Technique Combining Static Touches with Crossing Selection. In *Proceedings of the 28th Annual ACM Symposium on User Interface Software & Technology (UIST '15)*. ACM, New York, NY, USA, 323–332. DOI: http://dx.doi.org/10.1145/2807442.2807444

39. Nicolai Marquardt, Johannes Kiemer, David Ledo, Sebastian Boring, and Saul Greenberg. 2011. Designing user-, hand-, and handpart-aware tabletop interactions with the TouchID toolkit. In *Proc. ITS*. 21–30. http://doi.acm.org/10.1145/2076354.2076358

40. Nobuyuki Matsushita, Yuji Ayatsuka, and Jun Rekimoto. 2000. Dual Touch: A Two-handed Interface for Pen-based PDAs. In *Proceedings of the 13th Annual ACM Symposium on User Interface Software and Technology (UIST '00)*. ACM, New York, NY, USA, 211–212. DOI:http://dx.doi.org/10.1145/354401.354774

41. Fabrice Matulic and Moira C. Norrie. 2013. Pen and Touch Gestural Environment for Document Editing on Interactive Tabletops. In *Proceedings of the 2013 ACM International Conference on Interactive Tabletops and Surfaces (ITS '13)*. ACM, New York, NY, USA, 41–50. DOI:http://dx.doi.org/10.1145/2512349.2512802

42. Takashi Miyaki and Jun Rekimoto. 2009. GraspZoom: Zooming and Scrolling Control Model for Single-handed Mobile Interaction. In *Proceedings of the 11th International Conference on Human-Computer Interaction with Mobile Devices and Services (MobileHCI '09)*. ACM, New York, NY, USA, Article 11, 4 pages. DOI: http://dx.doi.org/10.1145/1613858.1613872

43. Mathieu Nancel, Daniel Vogel, Bruno De Araujo, Ricardo Jota, and Géry Casiez. 2016. Next-Point Prediction Metrics for Perceived Spatial Errors. In *Proceedings of the 29th Annual Symposium on User Interface Software and Technology (UIST '16)*. ACM, New York, NY, USA, 271–285. DOI: http://dx.doi.org/10.1145/2984511.2984590

44. Albert Ng, Julian Lepinski, Daniel Wigdor, Steven Sanders, and Paul Dietz. 2012. Designing for Low-latency Direct-touch Input. In *Proc. UIST*. 453–464. http://doi.acm.org/10.1145/2380116.2380174

45. Gonzalo Ramos and Ravin Balakrishnan. 2003. Fluid interaction techniques for the control and annotation of digital video. In *Proceedings of the 16th annual ACM symposium on User interface software and technology*. ACM, Vancouver, Canada, 105–114.

46. Christian Rendl, Patrick Greindl, Kathrin Probst, Martin Behrens, and Michael Haller. 2014. Presstures: Exploring Pressure-sensitive Multi-touch Gestures on Trackpads. In *Proceedings of the SIGCHI Conference on Human Factors in Computing Systems (CHI '14)*. ACM, New York, NY, USA, 431–434. DOI: http://dx.doi.org/10.1145/2556288.2557146

47. Anne Roudaut, Eric Lecolinet, and Yves Guiard. 2009. MicroRolls: Expanding Touch-screen Input Vocabulary by Distinguishing Rolls vs. Slides of the Thumb. In *Proceedings of the SIGCHI Conference on Human Factors in Computing Systems (CHI '09)*. ACM, New York, NY, USA, 927–936. DOI: http://dx.doi.org/10.1145/1518701.1518843

48. Jaime Ruiz, Andrea Bunt, and Edward Lank. 2008. A Model of Non-preferred Hand Mode Switching. In *Proceedings of Graphics Interface 2008 (GI '08)*. Canadian Information Processing Society, Toronto, Ont., Canada, Canada, 49–56. http://dl.acm.org/citation.cfm?id=1375714.1375724

49. Jaime Ruiz and Edward Lank. 2007. A study on the scalability of non-preferred hand mode manipulation. In *Proceedings of the 9th international conference on Multimodal interfaces*. ACM, 170–177.

50. Farzan Sasangohar, I Scott MacKenzie, and Stacey D Scott. 2009. Evaluation of mouse and touch input for a tabletop display using Fitts' reciprocal tapping task. In *Proceedings of the Human Factors and Ergonomics Society Annual Meeting*, Vol. 53. SAGE Publications, 839–843.

51. Itiro Siio and Hitomi Tsujita. 2006. Mobile Interaction Using Paperweight Metaphor. In *CHI '06 Extended Abstracts on Human Factors in Computing Systems (CHI EA '06)*. ACM, New York, NY, USA, 1325–1330. DOI: http://dx.doi.org/10.1145/1125451.1125697

52. Hyunyoung Song, Hrvoje Benko, Francois Guimbretiere, Shahram Izadi, Xiang Cao, and Ken Hinckley. 2011. Grips and Gestures on a Multi-touch Pen. In *Proceedings of the SIGCHI Conference on Human Factors in Computing Systems (CHI '11)*. ACM, New York, NY, USA, 1323–1332. DOI: http://dx.doi.org/10.1145/1978942.1979138

53. Alex Todd. 2016. Apple 3D Touch vs Huawei Press Touch vs ZTE Force Touch. (Feb. 2016). https://recombu.com/mobile/article/apple-3d-touch-vs-huawei-press-touch-vs-zte-force-touch

54. Huawei Tu, Xing-Dong Yang, Feng Wang, Feng Tian, and Xiangshi Ren. 2012. Mode switching techniques through pen and device profiles. In *Proceedings of the 10th asia pacific conference on Computer human interaction - APCHI '12*. ACM Press, New York, New York, USA, 169. DOI: http://dx.doi.org/10.1145/2350046.2350081

55. Daniel Vogel and Ravin Balakrishnan. 2005. Distant Freehand Pointing and Clicking on Very Large, High Resolution Displays. In *Proceedings of the 18th Annual ACM Symposium on User Interface Software and Technology (UIST '05)*. ACM, New York, NY, USA, 33–42. DOI: http://dx.doi.org/10.1145/1095034.1095041

56. Daniel Vogel and Géry Casiez. 2011. Conté: Multimodal Input Inspired by an Artist's Crayon. In *Proceedings of the 24th Annual ACM Symposium on User Interface Software and Technology (UIST '11)*. ACM, New York, NY, USA, 357–366. DOI: http://dx.doi.org/10.1145/2047196.2047242

57. Julie Wagner, Stéphane Huot, and Wendy Mackay. 2012. BiTouch and BiPad: designing bimanual interaction for hand-held tablets.. In *Proceedings of the 2012 ACM annual conference on Human Factors in Computing Systems - CHI '12*. ACM Press, New York, New York, USA, 2317. DOI: http://dx.doi.org/10.1145/2207676.2208391

58. Daniel Wigdor, Hrvoje Benko, John Pella, Jarrod Lombardo, and Sarah Williams. 2011. Rock & rails: extending multi-touch interactions with shape gestures to enable precise spatial manipulations. In *UIST (CHI '11)*. 1581–1590. DOI: http://dx.doi.org/10.1145/1978942.1979173 ACM ID: 1979173.

59. Jacob O. Wobbrock, Leah Findlater, Darren Gergle, and James J. Higgins. 2011. The Aligned Rank Transform for Nonparametric Factorial Analyses Using Only Anova Procedures. In *Proceedings of the SIGCHI Conference on Human Factors in Computing Systems (CHI '11)*. 143–146.

60. Mike Wu and Ravin Balakrishnan. 2003. Multi-finger and whole hand gestural interaction techniques for multi-user tabletop displays. In *Proceedings of the 16th annual ACM symposium on User interface software and technology*. ACM, Vancouver, Canada, 193–202. DOI: http://dx.doi.org/10.1145/964696.964718

61. Mike Wu, Chia Shen, Kathy Ryall, Clifton Forlines, and Ravin Balakrishnan. 2006. Gesture Registration, Relaxation, and Reuse for Multi-Point Direct-Touch Surfaces. In *Proceedings of the First IEEE International Workshop on Horizontal Interactive Human-Computer Systems*. IEEE Computer Society, Washington, DC, USA, 185–192. DOI: http://dx.doi.org/10.1109/TABLETOP.2006.19 ACM ID: 1110635.

62. Haijun Xia, Tovi Grossman, and George Fitzmaurice. 2015. NanoStylus: Enhancing Input on Ultra-Small Displays with a Finger-Mounted Stylus. In *Proceedings of the 28th Annual ACM Symposium on User Interface Software & Technology (UIST '15)*. ACM, New York, NY, USA, 447–456. DOI: http://dx.doi.org/10.1145/2807442.2807500

63. Shumin Zhai, Jing Kong, and Xiangshi Ren. 2004. Speed–accuracy tradeoff in Fitts' law tasks—on the equivalency of actual and nominal pointing precision. *International Journal of Human-Computer Studies* 61, 6 (Dec. 2004), 823–856. DOI: http://dx.doi.org/10.1016/j.ijhcs.2004.09.007

ForceEdge: Controlling Autoscroll on Both Desktop and Mobile Computers Using the Force

Axel Antoine[1,2], **Sylvain Malacria**[1] **and Géry Casiez**[2]
[1]Inria, France [2]Université de Lille, France
axel.antoine@etudiant.univ-lille1.fr, sylvain.malacria@inria.fr, gery.casiez@univ-lille1.fr

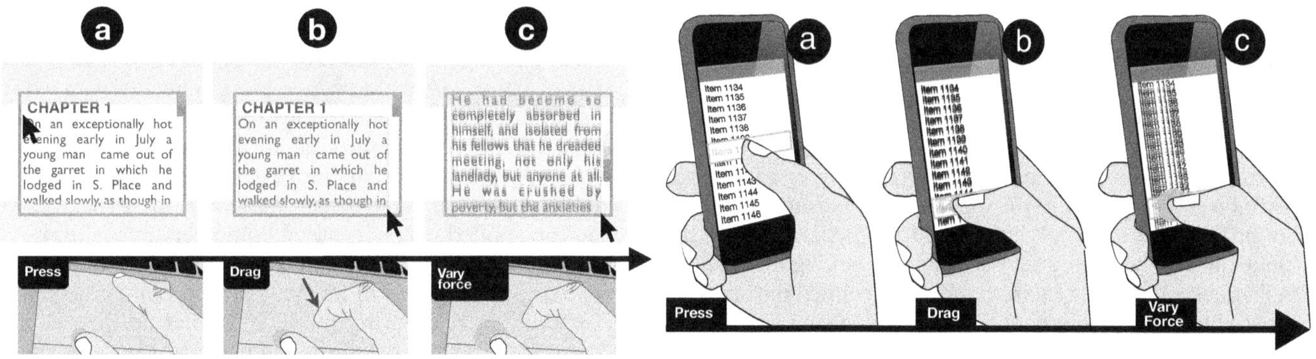

Figure 1: A user interacting with ForceEdge on a laptop computer (left) and on a smartphone (right). Left: She wants to select a large portion of text. In that purpose, (a) she presses the physical button of the trackpad and then (b) moves her finger on the trackpad to move the pointer in the control area. (c) She controls scrolling rate by varying the force applied to the trackpad. Right: she wants to move an object. (a) she starts moving the object, then (b) moves her finger in the control area and (c) controls scrolling rate by varying the force applied to the touchscreen.

ABSTRACT

Operating systems support autoscroll to allow users to scroll a view while in dragging mode: the user moves the pointer near the window's edge to trigger an "automatic" scrolling whose rate is typically proportional to the distance between the pointer and the window's edge. This approach suffers from several problems, especially when the window is maximized, resulting in a very limited space around it. Another problem is that for some operations, such as object drag-and-drop, the source and destination might be located in different windows, making it complicated for the computer to understand user's intention. In this paper, we present ForceEdge, a novel autoscroll technique relying on touch surfaces with force-sensing capabilities to alleviate the problems related to autoscroll. We report on the results of three controlled experiments showing that it improves over macOS and iOS systems baselines for top-to-bottom select and move tasks.

Author Keywords

Autoscroll; trackpad; touchscreen; scrolling; force control.

ACM Classification Keywords

H.5.2 Information interfaces (e.g. HCI): User interfaces

Permission to make digital or hard copies of all or part of this work for personal or classroom use is granted without fee provided that copies are not made or distributed for profit or commercial advantage and that copies bear this notice and the full citation on the first page. Copyrights for components of this work owned by others than ACM must be honored. Abstracting with credit is permitted. To copy otherwise, or republish, to post on servers or to redistribute to lists, requires prior specific permission and/or a fee. Request permissions from Permissions@acm.org.
CHI'17, May 06–11, 2017, Denver, CO, USA
© 2017 ACM. 978-1-4503-4655-9/17/05...$15.00.
DOI: http://dx.doi.org/10.1145/3025453.3025605

INTRODUCTION

Autoscroll, also known as edge-scrolling, is an interaction technique that allows users to scroll a viewport while in dragging mode: the user drags the pointer in a dedicated control area near the viewport's edge to trigger an "automatic" scrolling whose rate is usually proportional to the distance between the pointer and the viewport's edge. Autoscroll typically allows to scroll while *selecting* objects (e.g. a long portion of text) or while *moving* them (e.g. for drag-and-drop operations), both on desktop and mobile computers. And while alternative methods exist, previous work suggests that autoscroll remains used for selecting long portions of texts [1].

In spite of its wide availability, autoscroll still suffers from several limitations [1]. First, most autoscroll methods over-rely on the size of the control area, that is, the larger it is, the faster scrolling rate can be. Therefore, the level of control depends on the available distance between the viewport and the edge of the display, which can be limited. This is for example the case with small displays or when the view is maximized. This is also the case on touch-based devices such as smartphones that combine both limited screen real estate and maximized views. Second, depending on the task, the users' intention can be ambiguous. For *select* tasks (*e.g.* selecting a portion of text), there is no ambiguity about the viewport that contains the user's intended target: it has to reside within the viewport that contained the starting point (*e.g.* position where the user started selecting text). However, *move* tasks (*e.g.* dragging and dropping a file) are ambiguous as the user's target may be located within the initial viewport or in a different one on the same display (*e.g.* during drag-and-drop between windows). To reduce this ambiguity, the size of the control area is drastically smaller for move than for select tasks [1], which consequently 1) also affects scrolling rate control as the user has a limited input area to control the scrolling speed and 2) create inconsistency for similar operations operated in different contexts as the transfer functions to control the scrolling rate is different from one task to the other.

Several state-of-the-art input devices now offer *normal force-sensing* capabilities (typically, Force Touch trackpads on Apple Macbook [2], the Apple Magic Trackpad 2 [4], or the touchscreens of most recent iPhones [3]). In this paper, we explore how these force-sensing capabilities can be used to overcome the above-mentioned limitations of autoscroll, on both conventional desktop and mobile computers. Indeed, force-sensing is an interesting candidate for overcoming autoscroll limitations, especially when scrolling rate increases with the force applied to the input device, because: 1) users are usually already applying a (relatively soft) force on the input device when using autoscroll and 2) varying force on the input device does not require to move the pointer, thus making it possible to offer control to the user while using a small and consistent control area regardless of the task and the device.

In the following sections, after reviewing the use of force in Human-Computer Interaction, we present the design and evaluation of ForceEdge, an autoscroll technique that exploits force sensing capabilities for autoscrolling on both desktop and mobile computers. We first describe the theoretical foundations and the design of ForceEdge, as well as the transfer function used to convert the force applied to the input device in scrolling displacements. We then report on the results of two controlled experiments that compared ForceEdge to the macOS system baselines on a desktop computer, including for select tasks when the viewport edge is close from the border of the display. Finally, we report the results of an experiment that compared ForceEdge to the autoscroll techniques included on iOS for both *move* and *select* tasks.

THE DESIGN AND LIMITATIONS OF AUTOSCROLL

Various autoscroll techniques exist in commercial systems and applications. Aceituno et al. [1] recently reverse-engineered and compared 19 desktop autoscroll techniques from various operating systems and software applications in both select and move tasks. Their study confirmed that the control area usually expands to the edge of the display for select tasks (all reverse-engineered techniques), but is much more constrained for move tasks (all reverse-engineered techniques but one). It also confirmed that the vast majority of autoscroll techniques rely on rate-control based on the distance between the pointer and the viewport edge. This approach suffers from several problems. First, the available space around the viewport might be limited in some configurations, for instance with maximized windows, making it harder to control scrolling rate. Second, previous research suggest that rate-control is not adapted to isotonic devices such as trackpads and mouse controllers [36, 12]. Third, for *move* operations, the system cannot anticipate whether or not the target is located in the same viewport as the source. As a result, the system does not know which view should be scrolled, requiring alternative methods to raise this ambiguity, typically a smaller control area combined with a delay, which as a side-effect tends to limit user control. Finally, the system poorly suggests that autoscroll is available and what the size and location of the control areas are [1].

Novel autoscroll techniques have been proposed in the literature [25] or as inventions [7, 23]. Bardon et al. [7] proposed a relative position-based technique that scrolls the view of a given magnitude for every pointer movement outside and away from the viewport. This method remains restricted by the screen real estate as the pointer cannot endlessly move away from the viewport. Malacria et al. [25] proposed PushEdge and SlideEdge, two autoscroll techniques also using position-based control, but that *block* the pointer as it reaches the edge of the viewport and transform subsequent pointing device movements into scrolling displacements. These methods showed promising results for select tasks, but their application to move tasks remain unclear. Moreover, these methods could not be applied to touch-based computers as it is impossible to *block* the finger at the display edge. Finally, Kwatinetz et al. [23] proposed in a patent to map pointer acceleration to scrolling rate during move tasks, but no theoretical nor empirical evidence demonstrated the benefits of this approach.

Other works investigated specifically (and exclusively) the disambiguation problem during move tasks [8, 9, 24]. Indeed, the most common approach in current systems is to constrain the size of the control area, and sometimes to activate autoscroll after a short delay [1]. Berry et al. proposed as an alternative to use a dedicated physical button on the pointing device to specify which view the user wants to autoscroll [9]. Li et al. proposed a similar approach relying on a specific key of the keyboard [24]. Finally, Belfiore et al. proposed to trigger autoscroll only if the velocity of the mouse pointer is above a certain threshold when it enters the control area [8].

NORMAL FORCE FOR AUTOSCROLL

The psychophysics of normal force through fingers

The psychophysics of applying force (and by extension, pressure) through fingers have been extensively studied [16, 18, 19, 21, 27, 31], with Wilson's PhD thesis [34] providing an extensive review.

Overall, applying force on a surface through fingers relies on muscles located predominantly outside the hand, the sensory receptors of these muscles providing an instant feedback to the user on how much force is applied [22]. The maximum force that one can perform with a finger is around 17 N for a woman, and 45 N for a man, with a resolution of 0.3 N, regardless of the applied force [33]. It is usually accepted that the precision with which one can apply force when only inherent haptic feedback is available is relative to the magnitude of the pressure compared to one Maximum Voluntary Contraction (MVC), which corresponds to the maximum force one can apply. The relationship is approximately U-shaped, as precision decreases when applying low and high levels of pressure (relative to MVC) [19]. Also, additional visual feedback can significantly influence the precision of applied force with the index finger [20].

Detecting variation in applied force in touch-based HCI
From a hardware perspective, different methods can be used to estimate the normal force applied to a touch-sensitive surface. The most direct method is to use *force-sensing resistors* (FSR) [35], sensors whose resistance change when force is applied and that can be used to directly estimate a normal force in Newtons (N). It is possible to position FSRs between a smartphone and its case to estimate the normal and tangential force applied on its touchscreen [17, 26]. Strain gauges are also commonly used to measure force, typically by the Apple Magic Trackpad 2 [2] that can estimate a force up to 10 N.

Another method is to combine capacitive sensing with accelerometers values to estimate force when it bends a touch-surface, which is how the most recent Apple iPhone smartphones proceed [5]. From an input perspective, increasing the force applied to the touchscreen indeed increases the force estimated by the system. However, the actual value measured is not a force in Newtons. As a result, the returned value for a given force (in N) can vary depending on the user, the impedance of the finger, etc.

Touch-sensitive surfaces also provide a *pseudo-pressure* value that depends on the size of the contact area. While the size of the contact area generally increases with force [30], pseudo-pressure cannot be used to accurately measure normal force since different contacts with same area size can be performed with different forces, especially depending on the finger.

Finally, Goel et al. [13] proposed to combine orientation, contact area size and vibrations of a smartphone to infer the amount of pressure applied on a touchscreen, but managed to discriminate between three discrete levels of force only.

Use of force for autoscrolling
To the best of our knowledge normal force sensing has never been used or studied as an input canal for improving autoscroll techniques. Commercial products currently use force sensing for a limited number of very specific interaction scenarios, few of them in relation with autoscroll. The closest usage to autoscroll in commercial products is probably the use of force in Apple Quicktime where varying the pressure on fast-forward and rewind buttons will accelerate the rate at which a video file is browsed.

However, several interaction techniques using the force for improving document navigation have been proposed in the literature. Ramos et al. proposed to control the scroller of a scrollbar using a force-sensitive stylus, by mapping scrolling accuracy on the applied force [28]. Miyaki et al. used force for designing GraspZoom, an interaction technique combining force and tiny circular gestures for scrolling and zooming on a smartphone [26]. Heo and Lee [17] used tangential forces applied on a touchscreen as a method for quickly scrolling to the top or bottom of a document. In this case, the tangential force is used as a shortcut mechanism. Spelmezan et al. positioned additional FSRs on the outer edge of a smartphone to support rate-based scrolling [32]. Finally, pseudo-pressure was also used, either to decrease inertial scrolling speed [6] or changing the zoom level of a document [10].

Conceptually speaking, the most related work is probably Push-Push [14, 15] that proposes to use a threshold on force in order to discriminate when a touchscreen is *touched* or *pressed* (strongly touched). The user can perform *press* actions, for instance to define the start- and end- points of a text selection, and *touch* actions (as well as hovering over the touchscreen) to navigate in the document. While Push-Push can be used to perform similar tasks as autoscroll, it is a different interaction mechanism (yet compatible) that can be seen as using shift+click actions on a desktop computer. Moreover, Aceituno et al. [1] showed that autoscroll remains used, even when alternative methods are available, which motivates to improve autoscroll methods rather than designing novel interaction techniques that might ultimately remain unused.

FORCEEDGE

Concept
ForceEdge (illustrated Figure 1) has been designed to overcome the limitations of current autoscroll methods, by not relying on the distance between the pointer and the window edge. Instead, autoscroll velocity increases with the force applied to the input device.

Three conditions are required to trigger ForceEdge. First, the user has to enter and maintain *dragging* mode (figure 1-a), typically for text selection or a drag-and-drop operation. Second, the user has to move the pointer in a dedicated control area located in the vicinity of the viewport's edge. Third, the force applied on the pointing device has to be above a certain threshold (figure 1-b). Once ForceEdge is activated, the user controls scrolling velocity by applying more or less force on the input device (figure 1-c). ForceEdge scrolls as long as the pointer remains in the control area and the force remains above another threshold.

ForceEdge has several theoretical advantages over existing autoscroll techniques.

First, because ForceEdge does not rely on the distance between the pointer and the window edge, the size of the control area does not have to be as large as with existing techniques for text selection (that is, expanding from the viewport to the edge of the display). As a result, the control area can be the exact same size for selection and drag-and-drop operations, making interacting with ForceEdge consistent regardless of the task.

Then, ForceEdge does not require significant hand movement compared to current text selection or drag-and-drop operations. Since these operations imply that the button of the input device (*e.g.* trackpad) is already pressed, users can control scrolling velocity by adjusting the force applied to the device.

Finally, ForceEdge can be easily adapted to both desktop and touch-based interfaces, as long as the input device is force sensitive, which is the case for some commercially available trackpads and touchscreens [2, 3, 4, 5].

ForceEdge transfer function
The transfer function defines the mapping between the force applied on the touch surface in Newtons and the scrolling speed in millimeters per second. Using physical units allows to

design a transfer function that is replicable as it is independent of the device input and output resolutions and frequencies [11]. We first determined the relationship between the raw force input from an Apple Magic Trackpad 2 and the force applied in Newtons using brasses of known weights and we simulated a touch by wiring the hand to the weight. We obtained the following linear relationship between the raw input measures raw_{input} and the force F in Newtons: $F = 9.8\,10^{-3} \times raw_{input} + 1.3\,10^{-3}; (R^2 = 0.99)$.

We first experimented a simple linear function but it did not yield a good control of the scrolling rate. Inspired by the transfer function designed for the TrackPoint [29], we used a sigmoid parabolic shape function (Figure 2). First the function requires a dead band near zero force to avoid accidental activations. In addition, as the user is already applying some force on the surface during dragging, we defined an hysteresis where the user has to apply more than 3.4 N to activate ForceEdge (trigger curve on Figure 2) and then switch to the control curve above 3.8 N. The beginning of the control curve is designed to get an accurate control at low scrolling rate without introducing too much strain in fine motor control. For long distances reaching, high speed is required. We defined a plateau at 800 mm/s, reached at 8 N (which is less than half the the max force females can apply [33]) to get a speed high enough and keep the content on screen perceivable, if not readable. The transition between low and high speeds follows a parabolic shape to keep best control at moderate speeds.

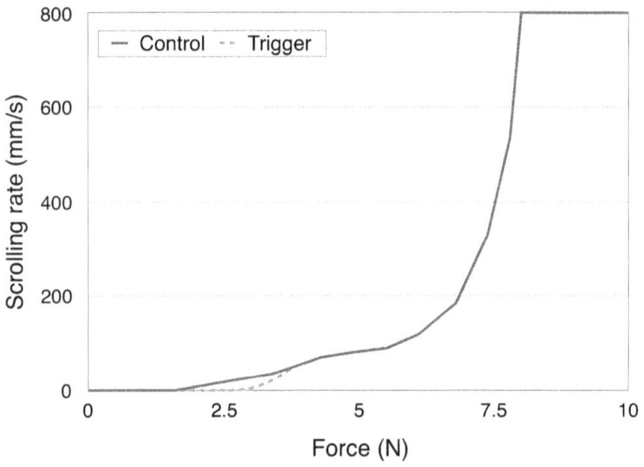

Figure 2: ForceEdge transfer function mapping the normal force applied on the surface in Newtons to the scrolling rate in millimetres per second. The function relies on an hysteresis to avoid accidental activations and keep a good control over the scrolling speed: the *trigger* curve is used upon invocation of autoscroll and switches to the *control* curve once the force applied reaches 3.8 N.

The activation threshold of 3.4 N was defined after running a pilot experiment to determine how much force users apply during dragging operations. We asked 12 participants to perform sequences of 45 *select* and *move* tasks using an Apple Magic Trackpad 2 connected to a 15" Macbook pro laptop. We implemented in Objective-C/Cocoa a dedicated software that displayed in blue various lines of text (10, 70, 210 lines) that the participants had to select or move using the default macOS autoscroll method, giving a total of 1080 trials. The average force applied to the trackpad was 2.8 N (σ =0.2 N). The average force applied was relatively similar for *select* (2.7 N) and *move* (3.0 N) operations. The average maximum force applied was 4 N (σ =0.2 N). For operations that did not require autoscroll, the average (2.6 N) and maximum (3.5 N) forces applied were slightly less than for the others (3.0 N and 4.2 N respectively). The activation threshold of 3.4 N was chosen as a value in-between the average force and maximum force, as a good trade-off to minimize accidental activations of ForceEdge while keeping a good range of force to control the scrolling speed.

To fine tune the transfer function, we designed an application to interactively manipulate control points and perform autoscroll tasks. The application also highlighted the current force being applied on the transfer function curve: the curve from zero force to current force was thicker. This information was then used to adjust the scrolling speed for a given force if necessary. Based on trial and error, the transfer function designers (the co-authors of this work) tuned the different parts of the curve until getting what was considered as a correct control of the scrolling rate for each part of the curve.

When several fingers are in contact with the trackpad, the total force is used to control ForceEdge. We also considered using only the force from the first or last finger in contact but informal tests revealed this mapping was more difficult to discover and did not appear to offer more control. For mobile devices, we decided to use the same transfer function by simply replacing the force applied in Newtons (value between 0 and 10 N for the trackpad) by the force estimated by the touchscreen (value between 0 and 6.67 for an iPhone6S, not in Newtons). As a result, the activation threshold on the smartphone is 2.3 units and the control curve is reached for 2.5 units.

STUDY 1: FORCEEDGE ON DESKTOP

We conducted a first experiment to compare the performance and perceived workload between *ForceEdge* and the macOS *System-Based* autoscroll methods in top-to-bottom *select* and *move* tasks on a desktop computer.

Method and apparatus

Our experimental method was strongly inspired by Malacria et al. [25] and Aceituno et al. [1] experimental procedures. The experiment was conducted on a 15" Apple Macbook Pro running macOS 10.11.5, with display resolution set to 1440×900 pixels, 110 ppi. Input was provided through an Apple Magic Trackpad 2 with force-sensing capabilities. The overall force value applied on the trackpad was used for ForceEdge. Experimental software was written in Objective-C with the Cocoa API. Contact point locations and force values were monitored using Apple's private multitouch API. The software implemented ForceEdge, and it used Apple NSTextViews' default rate-based autoscroll methods for the baseline conditions, whose behaviours are described in [1].

Procedure, task and design

Participants were instructed to perform a sequence of top-to-bottom autoscroll operations (*select* and *move*) as quickly and accurately as possible. The window was displayed at the centre of the screen, was 104 mm tall and contained 5496 lines of text typeset with *Helvetica Neue* 13px (figure 3). For each trial of the *select* condition, participants had to select a section of text framed and coloured blue – starting ten lines from the bottom of the viewport, and varying in size (in the following, we will refer to size as *distance*, since it is the distance the user had to scroll). For each trial of the *move* condition, participants had to drag a line highlighted in blue, located ten lines from the bottom of the viewport, and drop it on a target located at varying distance. Supposing that autoscroll is mainly target-directed, we overlaid a gradient on the scrollbar as a hint of the number of lines participants had to autoscroll. As the task was one-dimensional, selecting anywhere on a line selected the entire line. Each selection required concurrently dragging and scrolling using the requested autoscroll technique. Other scrolling methods were disabled. Once in dragging mode, the control area was emphasized as a semi-opaque blue area (see figure 3) regardless of the task or technique used. We decided to emphasize the control areas because the lack of visibility of the control areas has been highlighted as a potential issue for autoscroll techniques [1], especially for move tasks where it can result in accidental start and stop of the autoscroll, for both the ForceEdge and Baseline conditions.

To complete a trial, participants had to move the pointer to the top of the starting target (blue text), press the pointing device to start the selection (and enter in dragging mode), and autoscroll downwards until they reached the destination. Once the pointer was positioned over the target line, they could leave dragging mode to complete the operation by releasing the trackpad button. If the entire required text was not correctly selected or the line was not dropped at the right position, an error was recorded, and the trial was repeated until successfully completed. Participants were free to rest anytime between trials, as long as they were not operating the pointing device.

The experiment used a $2 \times 2 \times 3 \times 3$ within-subjects design for the factors: *task* (Select or Move), *technique* (ForceEdge or Baseline), *block* (1-3, with the first block serving as opportunity for learning the new method), and *distance* (short: 15; long: 135; longest: 250 lines). The order of *task* and *technique* was counterbalanced across participants. Distances were presented in ascending order, one for each *block*, with 5 consecutive repetitions for a given distance within a block – for a total of $2 \times 2 \times 3 \times 3 \times 5 = 180$ correct trials per participant. Participants completed NASA-TLX worksheets after each technique. The experiment lasted ~30 minutes.

Participants

Sixteen university staff and students (one female) participated in the experiment (mean age 25.7, SD=4.4). Ten used a mouse as main pointing device, but all were familiar with trackpads.

Hypothesis and dependant measures

The primary hypothesis were **H1:** selection time would be lower for ForceEdge than for system-based functions; and **H2:** ForceEdge would offer better control and result in less overshoots in long-selections. Therefore, the primary dependant measures were the total time to complete the trial and the overshoot distance.

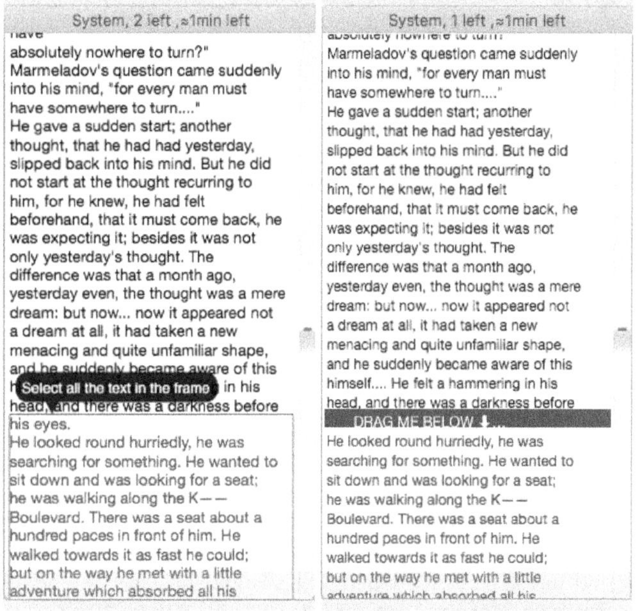

Figure 3: The interface used for our experiments. For select tasks (left), participants had to select the entire text framed in blue. For move tasks (right), participants had to drag the top line and drop it on the last blue line. For both tasks, a gradient was overlaid on the scrollbar as a hint of the number of lines participants had to autoscroll. For each technique, the control area was highlighted in blue (here for ForceEdge)

Results

Trial time

Trial time is the main dependent measure and is defined as the total selection/move time, from the first pointer movement after the trackpad button was pressed, to the button release. Trials marked as errors were removed from the timing analysis.

Repeated-measures ANOVA[1] revealed significant effect of *block* on trial time ($F_{2,30} = 62.1$, $p < 0.0001$, $\eta_p^2 = 0.80$; block 1: 6.6s, 2: 5.5s, 3:5.2s). Pairwise comparisons showed a significant decrease ($p < 0.0001$) in the trial time between the first block and the two remaining, due to a familiarization with the experimental procedure. As we are concerned with user performance after familiarization, the first block was removed from subsequent analysis.

The overall trial time was 6.4s for *select* tasks, and 4.4s for *move* tasks. It was 4.3s with *ForceEdge* and 6.4s with *Baseline*. Repeated measures ANOVA showed a significant main effect of *task* ($F_{1,15} = 61.4$, $p < 0.0001$, $\eta_p^2 = 0.80$), *technique* ($F_{1,15} = 121.6$, $p < 0.0001$, $\eta_p^2 = 0.89$), *distance* ($F_{1.1,17.3} = 108.6$, $p < 0.0001$, $\eta_p^2 = 0.88$) and significant *task* × *technique* ($F_{1,15} = 42.7$, $p < 0.0001$, $\eta_p^2 = 0.74$), *task* × *distance* ($F_{2,30} = 34.2$, $p < 0.0001$, $\eta_p^2 = 0.69$), *technique* × *distance* ($F_{2,30} = 78.2$, $p < 0.0001$, $\eta_p^2 = 0.84$) and *task* × *technique* × *distance* ($F_{2,30} = 19.8$, $p < 0.0001$, $\eta_p^2 = 0.57$) interactions on trial time. For each *task*, post-hoc analysis showed significant differences ($p < 0.003$) between ForceEdge and Baseline. For *select* tasks, the average trial time was 4.1s with

[1]Greenhouse-Geisser corrections to the degrees of freedom were applied when sphericity was violated. Pairwise comparisons used Bonferroni correction.

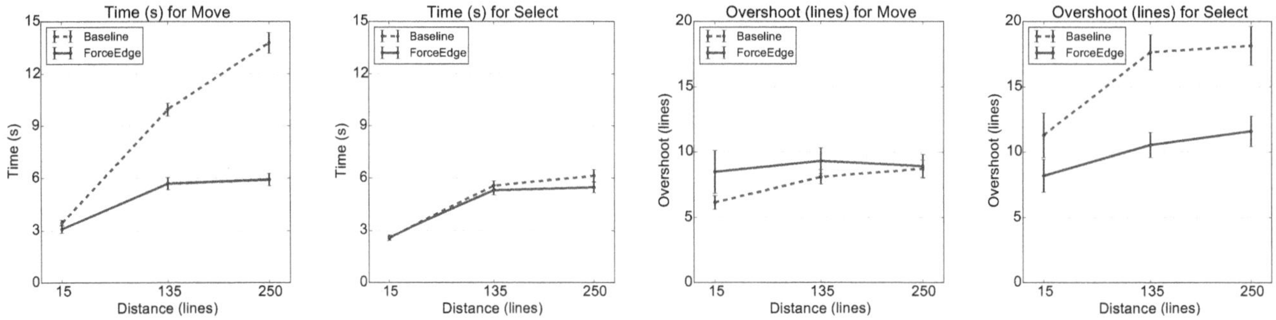

Figure 4: Results of Study 1, from left to right: trial time (s) for move, time (s) for select, overshoot (lines) for move, overshoot (lines) for select.

ForceEdge and 4.6s with Baseline. For *move* tasks, average trial time was 4.5s with ForceEdge and 8.2s with Baseline. As a result **H1** is confirmed. Pairwise comparisons showed significant differences ($p < 0.01$) between the two techniques for each distance of the two tasks, except for the shortest distance and the Select task where ForceEdge and Baseline showed similar performance (Figure 4).

Overshoot distance

Overshoot distance was measured as the maximum scroll distance beyond the target bounds that was reached during the trial. Trials marked as error were removed from the analysis.

Repeated-measures ANOVA revealed a significant main effect of *block* ($F_{2,30} = 4.2$, $p < 0.03$, $\eta_p^2 = 0.22$) and significant *block* × *distance* interaction ($F_{4,60} = 3.5$, $p < 0.02$, $\eta_p^2 = 0.19$) on overshoot distance. Pairwise comparisons showed a significant increase ($p < 0.03$) in the overshoot distance between the first block and the two other ones, only for the shortest distance (Block 1: 7.0 lines, 2: 9.5 lines, 3: 9.1 lines). There was also a significant ($p < 0.03$) increase in the overshooting distance between blocks 1 and 3 (Block 1: 9.8 lines, 2:11.0 lines, 3:10.8 lines). As these results do not clearly suggest a learning or fatigue effect, we kept all blocks for subsequent analysis.

Repeated-measures ANOVA revealed a significant main effect of *task* ($F_{1,15} = 44.7$, $p < 0.0001$, $\eta_p^2 = 0.75$), *technique* ($F_{1,15} = 15.3$, $p < 0.001$, $\eta_p^2 = 0.50$), *distance* ($F_{2,30} = 17.3$, $p < 0.0001$, $\eta_p^2 = 0.54$) and significant *task* × *technique* ($F_{1,15} = 54.0$, $p < 0.0001$, $\eta_p^2 = 0.78$) and *technique* × *distance* ($F_{2,30} = 5.9$, $p < 0.007$, $\eta_p^2 = 0.28$) interactions on overshoot distance. Post-hoc analysis reveal that for the Move task the overshooting distance is significantly ($p < 0.0001$) lower for ForceEdge (10.1 lines) compared to Baseline (15.7 lines) (Figure 4). As a result **H2** is partially validated: the better results obtained with ForceEdge for the Move task cannot be simply explained by lower overshooting distances, but because of a limited control of scrolling velocity. There is also a significant ($p < 0.002$) difference between the shortest distance (8.5 lines) and the two other ones (medium: 11.4 lines, long: 11.8 lines).

Error rate

Error rate is measured as the percentage of trials not successfully completed. Repeated-measures ANOVA revealed significant effect of *block* on error rate ($F_{2,30} = 11.8$, $p < 0.0001$, $\eta_p^2 = 0.44$; Block 1: 8.4%, 2: 4.6%, 3: 5.1%). Pairwise comparisons showed a significant decrease ($p < 0.037$) in the error rate between the first block and the two remaining. No other effect was found.

NASA-TLX Subjective preferences

A Friedman analysis on the NASA-TLX responses found significant effects for *performance* ($\chi^2(3) = 14.1, p < 0.005$) and *frustration* ($\chi^2(3) = 21.9, p < 0.0001$). Wilcoxon post-hoc analysis revealed participants found themselves significantly ($p < 0.002$) more successful using ForceEdge compared to Baseline, in both tasks. They also had higher frustration ($p < 0.007$) using Baseline compared to ForceEdge in both tasks. Finally, out of the 16 participants, 14 participants preferred ForceEdge over the baseline for move tasks, and 12 preferred it for select tasks.

STUDY 2: FORCEEDGE WHEN CLOSE-TO-EDGE

The results of the previous experiment highlighted the benefits of ForceEdge compared to the system baseline for both tasks, with a smaller effect size for select tasks. It is likely that the actual performance of the system baseline for this task is actually overrated as the experimental procedure used a relatively small window centred on screen, which is a 'best case' scenario for the baseline because of the large control area outside the window.

In this follow-up experiment, we compared the performance, amount of control and perceived workload between ForceEdge and the System-Based autoscroll for select tasks, with different amount of space between the window and the display edge. The main hypothesis was that selection time would be lower for ForceEdge than for the system baseline when the window is close from the display edge.

Method

Our experimental method was based on Study 1, with modifications described below.

Procedure, task and design

Participants were instructed to perform a sequence of top-to-bottom text selections using the given autoscroll as quickly and accurately as possible. We decided to investigate select tasks only as the system-based function for move tasks is theoretically not influenced by the distance between the window and display edge because the size of the control area is consistant regardless of the window configuration. The window was displayed with its bottom edge either 5.2 (*center*), 2.6

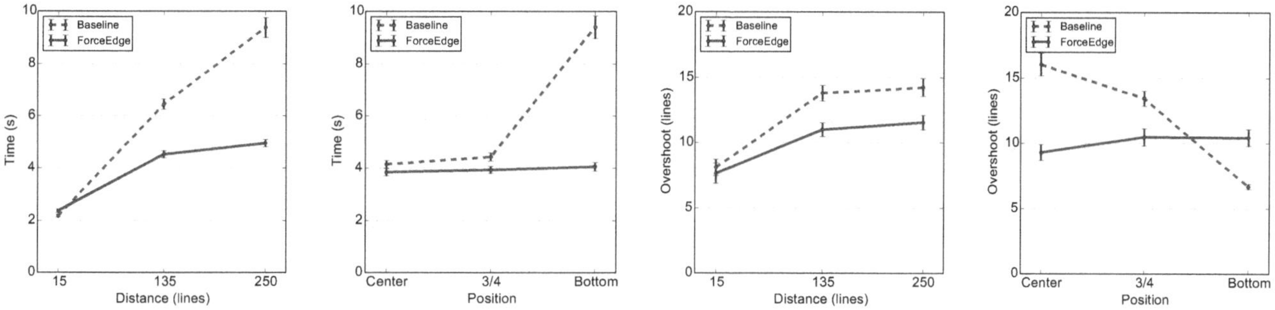

Figure 5: Results of study 2, from left to right: trial time (s) per distance, per position; overshoot (lines) per distance, per position

(3/4) or 0.4 (*bottom*) cm away from the bottom edge of the display. Center is the same condition as in study 1. Bottom corresponds approximately to the height of a status bar, which is usually the only space available for performing autoscroll when a window is maximized. All other characteristics of the experiment were the same as in Study 1.

The experiment used a $2 \times 3 \times 3 \times 3$ within-subjects design for the factors: *technique* (ForceEdge or Baseline), *position* (Center, 3/4 or Bottom), *block* (1-3), and *distance* (short: 15; long: 135; longest: 250 lines). The order of *technique* and *position* was counterbalanced across participants. *Distance* were still presented in ascending order, one for each *block*, with 5 consecutive repetitions for a given distance within a block – for a total of $2 \times 3 \times 3 \times 3 \times 5 = 270$ correct trials per participant. Primary dependent measures were the same as in Study 1. Participants completed NASA-TLX worksheets after each technique. The experiment lasted ~40 minutes.

Participants

The same sixteen university staff and students participated in the experiment right after Study 1.

Hypothesis and dependant measures

Primary hypothesis were **H1:** selection time with baseline would increase when the window is close from the display edge; and **H2:** Baseline would result in less overshoots when the window is close from the display edge because of a capped scrolling rate. Therefore, primary dependant measures were the total time to complete the trial and the overshoot distance.

Results

Trial time

Trials marked as errors were removed from the timing analysis. Repeated-measures ANOVA revealed significant effect of *block* on trial time ($F_{2,30} = 5.4$, $p < 0.01$, $\eta_p^2 = 0.27$; block 1: 5.0s, 2: 4.9s, 3: 4.9s). Pairwise comparisons showed a significant decrease ($p < 0.006$) in the trial time between the first and last blocks. Considering the mean absolute difference between the first and last block is very small, we kept all blocks for subsequent analysis. Repeated-measures ANOVA revealed a significant main effect of *technique* ($F_{1,15} = 356.0$, $p < 0.0001$, $\eta_p^2 = 0.96$), *position* ($F_{2,30} = 623.9$, $p < 0.0001$, $\eta_p^2 = 0.98$), *distance* ($F_{1.1,17.4} = 418.3$, $p < 0.0001$, $\eta_p^2 = 0.96$) and significant *technique* $\times$ *position* ($F_{1.3,19.1} = 384.7$, $p < 0.0001$, $\eta_p^2 = 0.97$), *technique* $\times$ *distance* ($F_{2,30} = 376.2$, $p < 0.0001$, $\eta_p^2 = 0.96$), *position* $\times$ *distance* ($F_{4,60} = 565.8$, $p < 0.0001$, $\eta_p^2 = 0.97$) and *technique* $\times$ *position* $\times$ *distance* ($F_{4,60} = 293.9$, $p < 0.0001$, $\eta_p^2 = 0.95$) interactions on trial time. Post-hoc analysis reveal that for Baseline the bottom position is significantly ($p < 0.0001$) slower compared to the two other positions (bottom: 9.4s, 3/4: 4.4s, center: 4.1s), when ForceEdge remains on average at 3.9s. No significant differences between *position* was found for ForceEdge. As a result **H1** is confirmed. Significant differences ($p < 0.03$) were found between ForceEdge and Baseline for each *position* $\times$ *distance*, except for the center position and short distance and also for the 3/4 position and the medium distance (Figure 5). ForceEdge is significantly faster than Baseline for all *position* $\times$ *distance*, except for the shortest distance ($p < 0.03$) where it is significantly slower (ForceEdge: 2.4s, Baseline: 2.2s).

Overshoot distance

Trials marked as errors were removed from the overshoot distance analysis. Repeated-measures ANOVA revealed no significant main effect of *block* thus all blocks were kept for the analysis. Significant main effects were found for *technique* ($F_{1,15} = 13.6$, $p < 0.002$, $\eta_p^2 = 0.50$), *position* ($F_{2,30} = 57.3$, $p < 0.0001$, $\eta_p^2 = 0.80$), *distance* ($F_{1.1,17.1} = 21.2$, $p < 0.0001$, $\eta_p^2 = 0.64$) and significant *technique* $\times$ *position* ($F_{2,30} = 86.7$, $p < 0.0001$, $\eta_p^2 = 0.84$), *technique* $\times$ *distance* ($F_{2,30} = 11.9$, $p < 0.0001$, $\eta_p^2 = 0.30$) and *technique* $\times$ *position* $\times$ *distance* ($F_{2.5,37.9} = 4.4$, $p < 0.02$, $\eta_p^2 = 0.26$) interactions on overshooting distance. Post-hoc analysis revealed significant ($p < 0.001$) differences between the two techniques for each *position*. ForceEdge shows significantly less overshooting than Baseline for the center (ForceEdge: 9.3 lines, Baseline: 16.0 lines) and 3/4 (ForceEdge: 10.4 lines, Baseline: 13.4 lines) positions while it is the opposite (ForceEdge: 10.4 lines, Baseline: 6.6 lines) for the bottom position (Figure 5). Thus **H2** is confirmed. For the bottom position, ForceEdge has significantly ($p < 0.0001$) higher overshooting distance compared to Baseline for all distances. For the center and 3/4 positions, it is the opposite ($p < 0.01$) for all distances, except for the short distance and the 3/4 positions where there is no significant difference.

Error rate

Repeated-measures ANOVA revealed a significant main effect of *technique* ($F_{1,15} = 7.9$, $p < 0.02$, $\eta_p^2 = 0.35$) on error rate. Pairwise comparison reveal that ForceEdge has a significantly higher ($p < 0.02$) error rate compared to Baseline (ForceEdge: 6.6%, Baseline 4.3%). No other effect or interaction was found.

NASA-TLX and subjective preferences
A Friedman analysis on the NASA-TLX responses found significant effects for *performance* ($\chi^2(1) = 6.2, p < 0.01$) and *frustration* ($\chi^2(1) = 5.4, p < 0.02$). Wilcoxon post-hoc analysis revealed participants found themselves significantly ($p < 0.003$) more successful using ForceEdge compared to Baseline. They also had higher frustration ($p < 0.001$) using Baseline compared to ForceEdge. In this condition, 14 participants out of 16 preferred using ForceEdge than the system baseline.

STUDY 3: FORCEEDGE ON SMARTPHONES

Autoscroll is an interaction technique available on various platforms, including touch-based computers such as tablets or smartphones. In the context of autoscroll, touch-based interaction has several significant differences with conventional desktop interactions, mostly because it does not follow the WIMP (Window Icon Menus Pointer) paradigm. First, a touch-contact is usually less accurate than a system pointer. Second, mobile operating systems tend to rely on fullscreen views rather than windows, thus removing available space between the window and display edge. Third, dragging mode is activated via various methods, for instance a time delay or by moving the finger from a specific location on screen. Finally, the finger is not constrained within the bounds of the display, which can result in leaving the dragging mode by moving the finger out of the tracking area of the display, even though it is still in contact with the surface. For these reasons, we decided to conduct a third experiment to compare the performance and perceived workload between *ForceEdge* and the *System-Based* autoscroll methods in top-to-bottom *select* and *move* tasks on a smartphone.

Method and apparatus

Our experimental method was based on Study 1 and conducted on an iPhone 6S running iOS 10 beta. Input was provided through the touch-screen with force-estimating capabilities of the smartphone. Experimental software was written in Objective-C using the CocoaTouch API.

Techniques
We decided to compare ForceEdge to the autoscroll methods used in Apple iOS for moving objects and selecting text.

ForceEdge. ForceEdge adopted the same behaviour as in the desktop experiment, therefore the same interaction technique was used regardless of the task (move or select). The only difference with the desktop was in the mapping between the force applied to the touchscreen and the scrolling rate, as detailed at the end of the *ForceEdge transfer function* section.

Baseline for move. The size of the control area for autoscrolling while moving an object on iOS starts from the edge of the display and expands off-screen. Conceptually, the control of the autoscrolling-rate remains distance-based, except that it depends on the proportion of the moved object that is intersecting the control area. Autoscrolling rate starts from 15 mm/s as soon as the moved object intersects the control area, and linearly increase up to 70 mm/s.

Baseline for select. The view autoscrolls when the finger is positioned in a 3 mm high control area, located near the edges of the display. Unlike conventional autoscrolls, the transfer is time-based rather than distance-based, that is scrolling rate starts at 4.6 mm/s and increases over time for eventually reaching 1560 mm/s after 3.5 seconds. As a result, autoscrolling rate can only increase and users must move their finger out of the control area (or lift it off the screen) in order to stop autoscrolling and reset scrolling rate.

Procedure, task and design

Participants were instructed to perform a sequence of top-to-bottom autoscroll operations (*select* and *move*) as quickly and accurately as possible. The view was displayed as a full screen view with the exact same physical properties as the view of study 1 and 2, that is 104mm tall, containing 5496 lines of text typeset with *Helvetica Neue*. To complete each trial, participants had to select a section of text or drag a line to a specific target, as in previous studies. A gradient was still overlaid on the right side of the view as a hint of the number of lines participants had to autoscroll. Every selection required to use the requested autoscroll technique. Other scrolling methods were disabled. Participants were free to hold and operate the smartphone with the finger/hand(s) they wanted.

To complete a trial, participants had to position their finger on the starting target, move their finger in the control area and autoscroll downwards until they reached the destination. Once the finger was positioned over the target line, they could lift their finger off to complete the operation. If the trial was not correct, an error was recorded, and the trial was repeated. Since the core of the experiment was to investigate performance with autoscroll techniques, and not mode switchers to perform select and move operations on touch-based devices the conventional touch scrolling techniques were disabled. As a result, any touch event selected/moved the object located underneath it. Moreover, in order to minimize errors because of the low accuracy of the finger, the software corrected touch events that were exactly one line above or below the starting target so the selection actually started from the target line. Participants were not informed of this correction mechanism.

The experiment used the exact same $2 \times 2 \times 3 \times 3$ within-subjects design than study 1 for the factors: *task* (Select or Move), *technique* (ForceEdge or Baseline), *block* (1-3, with the first block serving as opportunity for learning the new method), and *distance* (short: 15; long: 135; longest: 250 lines). Primary dependant measures were the same as in study 1 and 2. Participants completed NASA-TLX worksheets after each technique. The experiment lasted ~30 minutes.

Participants

Sixteen university staff and students (eight of which took part in the previous experiments) participated in the experiment (two female, mean age 27.5, SD=5.6). All owned a touch-based device such as a tablet or a smartphone.

Hypothesis and dependant measures

The primary hypothesis were **H1:** that selection time would be lower for ForceEdge than for system-based functions, and **H2:** that ForceEdge would result in less error; Therefore, the primary dependant measures were the total time to complete the trial and the overshoot distance and the error rate.

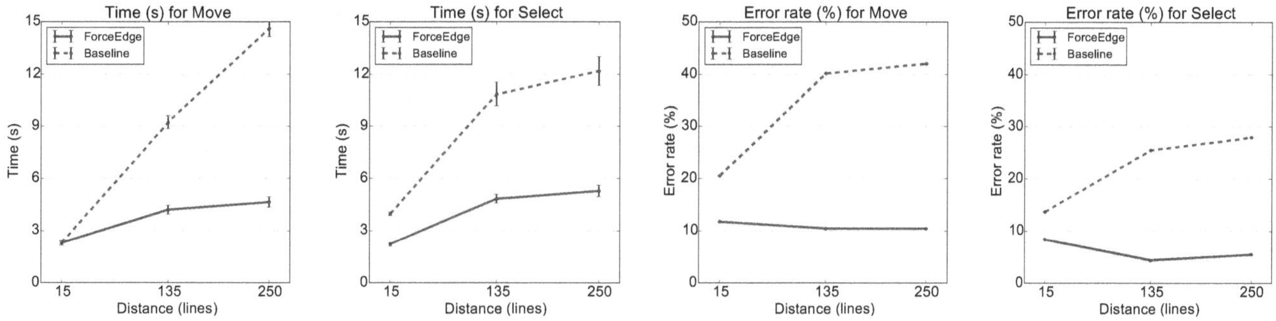

Figure 6: Results of Study 3, from left to right: trial time (s) for move, time (s) for select, error rate (%) for move, error rate (%) for select.

Results

Trial time

Trial time is the main dependent measure and is defined as the total selection/move time, from the first finger movement after the touchscreen was touched, to the finger release. Trials marked as errors were removed from the timing analysis. Repeated-measures ANOVA revealed significant effect of *block* on trial time ($F_{2,30} = 29.9$, $p < 0.0001$, $\eta_p^2 = 0.66$; block 1: 6.9s, 2: 6.2s, 3: 6.0s). Pairwise comparisons showed a significant decrease ($p < 0.0001$) between the first and the two remaining. The first block was thus removed from subsequent analysis. Repeated measures ANOVA showed a significant main effect of *technique* ($F_{1,15} = 453.9$, $p < 0.0001$, $\eta_p^2 = 0.97$), *distance* ($F_{1.2,18.3} = 175.3$, $p < 0.0001$, $\eta_p^2 = 0.92$) and significant *task* × *distance* ($F_{2,30} = 8.3$, $p < 0.001$, $\eta_p^2 = 0.36$), *technique* × *distance* ($F_{2,30} = 203.8$, $p < 0.0001$, $\eta_p^2 = 0.93$) and *task* × *technique* × *distance* ($F_{2,30} = 19.1$, $p < 0.0001$, $\eta_p^2 = 0.56$) interactions on trial time. For each *task* and *distance* post-hoc analysis showed significant lower trial times ($p < 0.0001$) for ForceEdge compared to Baseline, except for the Move task and the shortest distance where there was no significant difference (Figure 6, left). Overall the trial time was 3.6s using ForceEdge and 8.6s for baselines (Select: 3.9s ForceEdge, 8.7s baseline; Move: 3.4s ForceEdge, 8.5s baseline). As a result **H1** is confirmed.

Overshoot distance

No significant effect of *block* was found on overshooting distance. Repeated-measures ANOVA revealed a significant main effect of *task* ($F_{1,15} = 15.2$, $p < 0.001$, $\eta_p^2 = 0.50$), *distance* ($F_{2,30} = 7.4$, $p < 0.002$, $\eta_p^2 = 0.33$) and significant *task* × *technique* ($F_{1,15} = 11.0$, $p < 0.005$, $\eta_p^2 = 0.42$), *technique* × *distance* ($F_{2,30} = 7.9$, $p < 0.002$, $\eta_p^2 = 0.34$) and *task* × *technique* × *distance* ($F_{2,30} = 7.5$, $p < 0.002$, $\eta_p^2 = 0.33$) interactions on overshoot distance. Post-hoc analysis reveal that for the Move task and for each *distance* the overshooting distance is significantly ($p < 0.006$) larger for ForceEdge compared to Baseline. However for the Select task and the medium and long distances, it is significantly ($p < 0.04$) lower for ForceEdge compared to Baseline, except for the shortest distance where no significant difference was found. Overall overshooting distance was 16.9 lines for ForceEdge and 15.7 lines for Baselines.

Error rate

No significant effect of *block* was found on error rate. Repeated measures ANOVA showed a significant main effect of *task* ($F_{1,15} = 42.6$, $p < 0.0001$, $\eta_p^2 = 0.74$), *technique* ($F_{1,15} = 116.4$, $p < 0.0001$, $\eta_p^2 = 0.89$), *distance* ($F_{2,30} = 10.2$, $p < 0.0001$, $\eta_p^2 = 0.40$) and a significant *task* × *technique* ($F_{1,15} = 5.3$, $p < 0.035$, $\eta_p^2 = 0.26$) interaction on error rate. For both tasks pairwise comparisons showed significant ($p < 0.0001$) lower error rates for ForceEdge compared to Baseline (Select, ForceEdge: 4.4%, Baseline: 16.1%; Move, ForceEdge: 8.3%, Baseline: 28.5%) as illustrated figure 6 (right). In addition there is a significant ($p < 0.004$) difference between the error rate for the short distance (10.5%) and the two other ones (16.2%). As a result **H2** is validated.

NASA-TLX and subjective preferences

A Friedman analysis on the NASA-TLX responses found significant effects for *mental* ($\chi^2(3) = 24.3, p < 0.0001$), *physical* ($\chi^2(3) = 13.2, p < 0.004$), *temporal* ($\chi^2(3) = 32.0, p < 0.0001$), *performance* ($\chi^2(3) = 34.2, p < 0.0001$), *effort* ($\chi^2(3) = 31.3, p < 0.0001$) and *frustration* ($\chi^2(3) = 43.9, p < 0.0001$). Post-hoc analysis reveal significant negative answers for Baseline compared to ForceEdge in both tasks for all criteria, except for mental demand where there is no significant differences for the Select task. Finally, all participants preferred ForceEdge over the system baselines for both select and move tasks.

Performance compared to the desktop

To know if participants were more efficient using ForceEdge on desktop or mobile we kept ForceEdge data from experiments 1 and 3. Considering all conditions except the device were the same in the two experiments, the *device* was a between-subject factor while *task*, *block* and *distance* remained within-subject factors. The ANOVA showed a significant effect for the *device* × *task* interaction ($F_{1,30} = 8.1$, $p < 0.008$, $\eta_p^2 = 0.21$). Post-hoc comparisons showed a significant ($p < 0.02$) difference between mobile and desktop, only for the Move task (desktop: 4.5s, mobile: 3.4s).

DISCUSSION

Studies 1 and 2 compared ForceEdge to the the current macOS autoscroll baselines. Study 1 showed that ForceEdge improves over these baselines for top-to-bottom select and move tasks. While the benefits are significant for Move tasks, resulting in a trial time 45% shorter with ForceEdge, the benefits remain limited for *select* tasks (11% faster). One possible explanation is because the experiment was conducted with a window centred on screen, which corresponds to the best case scenario for the pointer-to-edge distance based baselines. Therefore, study 2 compared ForceEdge to the macOS baseline for select tasks with various configurations of windows. The results confirmed that unlike ForceEdge, the baseline is strongly influenced by the space available around the window, with trial time being as much as 141% longer with the baseline than with ForceEdge when the space around the window is limited. Finally, study 3 compared ForceEdge to the current iOS autoscroll baselines. The results showed that it improves on performance (58% faster) and resulted in less error (16% absolute difference), among others because users tend to move their finger out of the tracking zone of the touchscreen with the pointer-to-viewport distance based method. These studies confirmed the potential of ForceEdge when operated on a trackpad (desktop) or touchscreen (mobile), and that it is neither affected by the task or the location of the window.

Why did ForceEdge work for both tasks/platforms?

Our experiments showed that ForceEdge improved on macOS and iOS baselines for top-to-bottom autoscrolling operations.

This performance advantage can be explained through the fact that ForceEdge relies on the specific input canal of force-sensing, which is unlikely to be affected by the specific issues of autoscroll identified by Aceituno et al. [1]. Indeed, unlike conventional methods, varying force does not require pointer operations. Moreover, the user is most of the time already applying force to the input device when in need for autoscroll (because in dragging mode). In the end, interacting with ForceEdge required to 1) enter dragging mode, 2) position the pointer (or finger) in the control area and 3) control autoscrolling rate by varying force. These 3 steps are performed the exact same way for both tasks. This explains why the performance was similar with ForceEdge for both tasks, unlike with the system baselines.

ForceEdge outperformed the system baselines on the smartphone for similar reasons. The results are emphasized by the fact that the available space for controlling autoscroll on mobile devices is very limited because the views are almost systematically in full screen mode, which is probably the reason why iOS designers decided to implement a time-based method rather than a distance-based one. That being said, our experiment highlights the limitations of that approach as ForceEdge outperformed this time-based baseline by 58%. In addition, the comparison of the results of Study 1 and Study 3 suggests that ForceEdge is as efficient on desktop computers than on smartphones. The small difference in term of performance is likely to be the result of various factors (different participants, different force sensing technology) but the overall performance is very satisfying. This result suggests that ForceEdge could possibly be as efficient with other input devices, for instance a force-sensing mouse controller.

Limitations of our studies

Our experimental design had a limited number of baseline, distance and direction conditions in order to ensure that our experiments would be of bearable durations.

On the mobile platform, we used the default iOS behaviors as we are not aware of any better alternative that we could have used. On the desktop platform, we compared ForceEdge to the macOS system baselines in a concern of replicating the experiment from [25] and because for the distances we tested, it did not significantly differ from other rate-based methods in previous studies [1]. And while methods from the literature such as Slide-Edge [25] were shown promising for select operations on desktop, it is unclear how to apply them to move operations. That being said, comparing ForceEdge to other system-baselines remains interesting but is left as future work.

Finally, our experimental procedure focused on top-to-bottom autoscrolling operations because current GUIs still heavily rely on 1D vertical layouts (e.g, webpages, word processing, file browsers). However, motor performance can differ according to the direction and testing ForceEdge under these conditions is another interesting perspective for future work.

Compatibility with existing systems and techniques

ForceEdge relies on force-sensing input devices, that become more and more available on the market [4, 3]. This input canal however remains barely used in the current operating systems. Typically, the force sensing capabilities of the state-of-the-art input devices remain unexploited during the autoscroll operations, on both desktop and mobile computers, leaving room for including ForceEdge in current operating systems without interfering with the other interaction techniques.

Moreover, ForceEdge remains compatible with the alternatives that can be used for performing two-points operations, such as using Shift+click on desktop computers, or Push-Push [14, 15] on smartphones, so that the user can freely choose the most appropriate technique for the task at hand.

Accidental activation

One theoretical benefit of ForceEdge that we did not evaluate is its robustness toward accidental activations of autoscroll. A proper evaluation of this would have required a dedicated experiment, possibly asking participants to move an object between overlapping windows. We decided to focus our evaluations on the overall performance of ForceEdge and leave the evaluation to this specific aspect to future work. Moreover, when scrolling rate increases with the force applied on the device, an accidental activation of autoscroll is likely to be at one of the lowest possible rate, resulting in a limited accidental scrolling which is of relatively low cost to the user. Finally, participants in the experiments did not mention any specific problem regarding the accidental activation.

CONCLUSION

We have presented ForceEdge, a novel autoscroll technique which exploits the force-sensing capabilities of state-of-the-art input devices. ForceEdge does not suffer from the limitations of conventional autoscroll techniques and can be applied to both desktop and mobile computers. We compared ForceEdge to the current system baselines on the macOS and iOS platforms, and our results show that ForceEdge improves over these baselines for top-to-bottom select and move tasks.

ACKNOWLEDGMENTS

This work was partially supported by ANR (TurboTouch, ANR-14- CE24-0009).

REFERENCES

1. J. Aceituno, S. Malacria, P. Quinn, N. Roussel, A. Cockburn, and G. Casiez. 2017. The design, use, and performance of edge-scrolling techniques. *International Journal of Human-Computer Studies* 97 (2017), 58 – 76. DOI:http://dx.doi.org/10.1016/j.ijhcs.2016.08.001
2. Apple. 2014. ForceTouch Trackpad. (9 September 2014). http://ns.inria.fr/mjolnir/forceedge/forcetouch.pdf, retrieved December 21st, 2016 from https://support.apple.com/en-us/HT204352.
3. Apple. 2015a. iPhone6S. (25 September 2015). http://ns.inria.fr/mjolnir/forceedge/iphones.pdf, retrieved December 21st, 2016 from http://www.apple.com/iphone/compare/.
4. Apple. 2015b. Magic Trackpad 2. (13 October 2015). http://ns.inria.fr/mjolnir/forceedge/magictrackpad.pdf, retrieved December 21st, 2016 from http://www.apple.com/magic-accessories/.
5. Apple. 2015c. Video explaining 3D Touch on iPhones. (25 September 2015). http://ns.inria.fr/mjolnir/forceedge/3dtouch.mp4, Retrieved December 21st, 2016 from http://www.apple.com/.
6. Mathias Baglioni, Sylvain Malacria, Eric Lecolinet, and Yves Guiard. 2011. Flick-and-brake: Finger Control over Inertial/Sustained Scroll Motion. In *CHI '11 Extended Abstracts on Human Factors in Computing Systems (CHI EA '11)*. ACM, New York, NY, USA, 2281–2286. DOI: http://dx.doi.org/10.1145/1979742.1979853
7. Didier D. Bardon, Richard E. Berry, Shirley L. Martin, S. A. Morgan, John M. Mullay, and Craig A. Swearingen. 1997. Method for Auto-Scroll with Greater User Control. *IBM Technical Disclosure Bulletin* 40, 6 (June 1997), 181–182. http://ip.com/IPCOM/000118763
8. Joseph D. Belfiore, Christopher J. Guzak, Christopher E. Graham, Stepehn M. Madigan, Tandy W. Trower, II, Randall L. Kerr, and Adrian M. Wyard. 1998. Auto-scrolling during a drag and drop operation. (1998). http://www.google.com/patents/US5726687
9. Richard E. Berry, Stephen S. Fleming, and A. C. Temple. 1991. Auto-Scroll During Direct Manipulation. *IBM Technical Disclosure Bulletin* 33, 11 (April 1991), 312.
10. Sebastian Boring, David Ledo, Xiang 'Anthony' Chen, Nicolai Marquardt, Anthony Tang, and Saul Greenberg. 2012. The Fat Thumb: Using the Thumb's Contact Size for Single-handed Mobile Interaction. In *Proceedings of the 14th International Conference on Human-computer Interaction with Mobile Devices and Services (MobileHCI '12)*. ACM, New York, NY, USA, 39–48. DOI:http://dx.doi.org/10.1145/2371574.2371582
11. Géry Casiez and Daniel Vogel. 2008. The Effect of Spring Stiffness and Control Gain with an Elastic Rate Control Pointing Device. In *Proceedings of the SIGCHI Conference on Human Factors in Computing Systems (CHI '08)*. ACM, New York, NY, USA, 1709–1718. DOI: http://dx.doi.org/10.1145/1357054.1357321
12. Géry Casiez, Daniel Vogel, Qing Pan, and Christophe Chaillou. 2007. RubberEdge: Reducing Clutching by Combining Position and Rate Control with Elastic Feedback. In *Proceedings of the 20th Annual ACM Symposium on User Interface Software and Technology (UIST '07)*. ACM, New York, NY, USA, 129–138. DOI: http://dx.doi.org/10.1145/1294211.1294234
13. Mayank Goel, Jacob Wobbrock, and Shwetak Patel. 2012. GripSense: using built-in sensors to detect hand posture and pressure on commodity mobile phones. In *Proceedings of the 25th annual ACM symposium on User interface software and technology*. ACM, 545–554.
14. Jaehyun Han, Sunggeun Ahn, and Geehyuk Lee. 2014. Push-push: A Two-point Touchscreen Operation Utilizing the Pressed State and the Hover State. In *Proceedings of the Adjunct Publication of the 27th Annual ACM Symposium on User Interface Software and Technology (UIST'14 Adjunct)*. ACM, New York, NY, USA, 103–104. DOI:http://dx.doi.org/10.1145/2658779.2658797
15. Jaehyun Han and Geehyuk Lee. 2015. Push-Push: A Drag-like Operation Overlapped with a Page Transition Operation on Touch Interfaces. In *Proceedings of the 28th Annual ACM Symposium on User Interface Software & Technology (UIST '15)*. ACM, New York, NY, USA, 313–322. DOI: http://dx.doi.org/10.1145/2807442.2807457
16. Henning Henningsen, Bettina Ende-Henningsen, and Andrew M Gordon. 1995. Contribution of tactile afferent information to the control of isometric finger forces. *Experimental brain research* 105, 2 (1995), 312–317.
17. Seongkook Heo and Geehyuk Lee. 2011. Force gestures: augmenting touch screen gestures with normal and tangential forces. In *Proceedings of the 24th annual ACM symposium on User interface software and technology*. ACM, 621–626.
18. Elizabeth Househam, John McAuley, Thompson Charles, Timothy Lightfoot, and Michael Swash. 2004. Analysis of force profile during a maximum voluntary isometric contraction task. *Muscle & nerve* 29, 3 (2004), 401–408.
19. Lynette A Jones. 1989. Matching forces: constant errors and differential thresholds. *Perception* 18, 5 (1989), 681–687.
20. Lynette A Jones. 2000. Visual and haptic feedback in the control of force. *Experimental brain research* 130, 2 (2000), 269–272.
21. Lynette A Jones and Ian W Hunter. 1983. Perceived force in fatiguing isometric contractions. *Perception & Psychophysics* 33, 4 (1983), 369–374.
22. Lynette A Jones and Susan J Lederman. 2006. *Human hand function*. Oxford University Press.
23. Andrew Kwatinetz. 1996. Scrolling contents of a window. (1996). http://www.google.com/patents/US5495566

24. Shih-Gong Li and Theodore Jack London Shrader. 1998. Scrolling a target window during a drag and drop operation. (1998). http://www.google.com/patents/US5740389

25. Sylvain Malacria, Jonathan Aceituno, Philip Quinn, Géry Casiez, Andy Cockburn, and Nicolas Roussel. 2015. Push-Edge and Slide-Edge: Scrolling by Pushing Against the Viewport Edge. In *Proceedings of the 33rd Annual ACM Conference on Human Factors in Computing Systems (CHI '15)*. ACM, New York, NY, USA, 2773–2776. DOI: http://dx.doi.org/10.1145/2702123.2702132

26. Takashi Miyaki and Jun Rekimoto. 2009. GraspZoom: Zooming and Scrolling Control Model for Single-handed Mobile Interaction. In *Proceedings of the 11th International Conference on Human-Computer Interaction with Mobile Devices and Services (MobileHCI '09)*. ACM, New York, NY, USA, Article 11, 4 pages. DOI: http://dx.doi.org/10.1145/1613858.1613872

27. Xiao-Dong Pang, Hong Z Tan, and Nathaniel I Durlach. 1991. Manual discrimination of force using active finger motion. *Perception & psychophysics* 49, 6 (1991), 531–540.

28. Gonzalo Ramos and Ravin Balakrishnan. 2005. Zliding: Fluid Zooming and Sliding for High Precision Parameter Manipulation. In *Proceedings of the 18th Annual ACM Symposium on User Interface Software and Technology (UIST '05)*. ACM, New York, NY, USA, 143–152. DOI: http://dx.doi.org/10.1145/1095034.1095059

29. Joseph D. Rutledge and Ted Selker. 1990. Force-to-motion Functions for Pointing. In *Proceedings of the IFIP TC13 Third Interational Conference on Human-Computer Interaction (INTERACT '90)*. North-Holland Publishing Co., Amsterdam, The Netherlands, The Netherlands, 701–706. http://dl.acm.org/citation.cfm?id=647402.725310

30. Elaine R Serina, Eric Mockensturm, CD Mote, and David Rempel. 1998. A structural model of the forced compression of the fingertip pulp. *Journal of biomechanics* 31, 7 (1998), 639–646.

31. Jacob J Sosnoff and Karl M Newell. 2005. Intermittent visual information and the multiple time scales of visual motor control of continuous isometric force production. *Perception & psychophysics* 67, 2 (2005), 335–344.

32. Daniel Spelmezan, Caroline Appert, Olivier Chapuis, and Emmanuel Pietriga. 2013. Side Pressure for Bidirectional Navigation on Small Devices. In *Proceedings of the 15th International Conference on Human-computer Interaction with Mobile Devices and Services (MobileHCI '13)*. ACM, New York, NY, USA, 11–20. DOI:http://dx.doi.org/10.1145/2493190.2493199

33. Hong Z Tan, Mandayam A Srinivasan, Brian Eberman, and Belinda Cheng. 1994. Human factors for the design of force-reflecting haptic interfaces. *Dynamic Systems and Control* 55, 1 (1994), 353–359.

34. Graham Alasdair Wilson. 2013. *Using pressure input and thermal feedback to broaden haptic interaction with mobile devices*. Ph.D. Dissertation. University of Glasgow.

35. S. I. Yaniger. 1991. Force Sensing Resistors: A Review Of The Technology. In *Electro International, 1991*. 666–668. DOI: http://dx.doi.org/10.1109/ELECTR.1991.718294

36. Shumin Zhai. 1995. *Human performance in six degree of freedom input control*. Ph.D. Dissertation. University of Toronto.

Finding Common Ground: A Survey of Capacitive Sensing in Human-Computer Interaction

Tobias Grosse-Puppendahl[1], Christian Holz[1], Gabe Cohn[1], Raphael Wimmer[2], Oskar Bechtold[3], Steve Hodges[1], Matthew S. Reynolds[4], Joshua R. Smith[4]
[1]Microsoft Research, Cambridge, UK / Redmond, WA, USA; {tgp, cholz, gabe, shodges}@microsoft.com
[2]University of Regensburg, Regensburg, Germany; raphael.wimmer@ur.de
[3]Technische Universität Darmstadt, Darmstadt, Germany; oskar.bechtold@stud.tu-darmstadt.de
[4]University of Washington, Seattle, WA, USA; jrs@cs.washington.edu, matt.reynolds@ee.washington.edu

ABSTRACT
For more than two decades, capacitive sensing has played a prominent role in human-computer interaction research. Capacitive sensing has become ubiquitous on mobile, wearable, and stationary devices—enabling fundamentally new interaction techniques on, above, and around them. The research community has also enabled human position estimation and whole-body gestural interaction in instrumented environments. However, the broad field of capacitive sensing research has become fragmented by different approaches and terminology used across the various domains. This paper strives to unify the field by advocating consistent terminology and proposing a new taxonomy to classify capacitive sensing approaches. Our extensive survey provides an analysis and review of past research and identifies challenges for future work. We aim to create a common understanding within the field of human-computer interaction, for researchers and practitioners alike, and to stimulate and facilitate future research in capacitive sensing.

Author Keywords
survey; capacitive sensing; electric field sensing

ACM Classification Keywords
H.5.2. Information Interfaces and Presentation: User Interfaces - Graphical user interfaces; Input devices & strategies

INTRODUCTION
Capacitive sensing has become so ubiquitous that it is hard to imagine the world without it. We are surrounded by capacitive sensors—from the touchscreens and touchpads on our phones, tablets, and laptops, to the capacitive "buttons" frequently used on consumer electronics devices and commercial equipment. In addition to widespread adoption in products, the use of capacitive sensing is common in human-computer interaction research, with examples ranging from grasp detection to the estimation of human positioning.

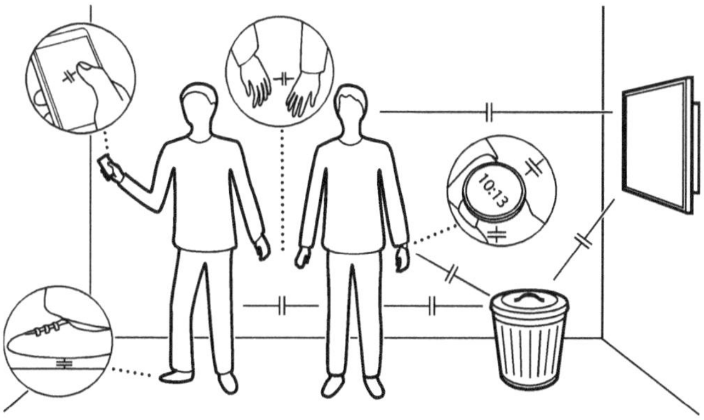

Figure 1. Capacitance (⫲) naturally exists between people, their devices, and conductive objects in the environment. By measuring it, capacitive sensors can infer the position and proximity of users and other objects, supporting a range of different applications. However, this inherent capacitive coupling between objects also increases ambiguity of sensor readings and adds noise.

As shown in Figure 1, a plethora of natural capacitances exist between the people, devices and objects in the environment. It is important to realize that the capacitances shown in the figure are not capacitor components purchased from an electronics supplier. Instead, they represent the natural *capacitive coupling* between various objects. By measuring these ever-changing values it is possible to infer relative position, motion and more—supporting a multitude of interaction techniques and applications. The small size, low cost, and low power aspects of capacitive sensing make it an appealing technology for both products and research prototypes. Furthermore, its ability to support curved, flexible, and stretchable surfaces has enabled interaction designers to work with non-rigid objects and surfaces. The human-computer interaction community has developed numerous interaction modalities using capacitive sensing to operate devices from a distance, including gesture recognition and whole-body interaction.

With such a long history and so many different applications and instantiations of the technology, it is not surprising that the field has spawned research across many different domains, and with it a variety of different terminologies. For example, the terms *capacitive sensing* and *electric field sensing*

Permission to make digital or hard copies of all or part of this work for personal or classroom use is granted without fee provided that copies are not made or distributed for profit or commercial advantage and that copies bear this notice and the full citation on the first page. Copyrights for components of this work owned by others than ACM must be honored. Abstracting with credit is permitted. To copy otherwise, or republish, to post on servers or to redistribute to lists, requires prior specific permission and/or a fee. Request permissions from Permissions@acm.org.
CHI 2017, May 06 - 11, 2017, Denver, CO, USA
Copyright is held by the owner/author(s). Publication rights licensed to ACM.
ACM 978-1-4503-4655-9/17/05$15.00
DOI: http://dx.doi.org/10.1145/3025453.3025808

refer to the same basic technique. In this paper, we will exclusively use the former. Similarly, various terms are used to describe the different types of capacitive sensing systems, such as self-capacitance and mutual-capacitance, both of which in conjunction with x/y grids are commonly referred to as projected-capacitive sensing. Other common terms include capacitive loading, shunt, and transmit modes; passive and active sensing; and static electric field sensing. This varied terminology can make it difficult to recognize the similarities and differences between established capacitive sensing systems, or to understand the contributions of new techniques.

In this paper we summarize and reflect on past work in the field with the aim of providing a resource for others working in the area of capacitive sensing. The contributions of this paper include: (1) a unified taxonomy to describe and classify capacitive sensing technologies, (2) a discussion of guidelines for reproducibility and challenges for future research, and (3) a thorough review and analysis of past work.

BACKGROUND ON CAPACITIVE SENSING

History

While some animal species including electric fish and sharks have evolved organs capable of natural capacitive sensing [84], human exploitation only dates back about a century. In 1907, Cremer reported using a string electrometer—a sensitive current measuring device—to measure the physical motion of a beating frog heart [39]. The heart was placed between the plates of a capacitor, and as it moved with each beat a change in capacitance was observed. Later, in 1920, Léon Theremin demonstrated a gesture-controlled electronic musical instrument known as the the *Theremin*, consisting of two capactively tuned resonant circuits controlling pitch and volume [56]. While capacitive sensing grew to be an important tool for many engineering applications, such as sensing distance, acceleration, force, pressure, *etc.*, its use in HCI was limited at first. In 1973, engineers at CERN implemented a capacitive touch screen [11], and further work on touch surfaces grew rapidly in the 1980s and 1990s, including the introduction of the multi-touch capacitive tablet in 1985 [121]. In 1995, Zimmerman *et al.* [236] introduced new capacitive sensing approaches for HCI that went far beyond touch sensing on surfaces. With the widespread use of capacitive touch pads, displays, and other interactive devices on desktop, mobile, and wearable computers, the impact of capacitive sensing has exploded over the past 20 years.

Physical Principles of Capacitive Sensing

Capacitive sensing can be used to estimate physical properties such as touch, proximity, or deformation by measuring the capacitance (*i.e.*, the ability to store charge in an electric field) between two or more conductors. These conductors, often called *electrodes*, are commonly solid metal parts, but they can also be made from other conductive materials including foils, transparent films (*e.g.*, indium tin oxide, ITO), plastics, rubbers, textiles, inks, and paints. In other cases, electrodes include the human body or objects in the environment.

Figure 2 depicts a *lumped circuit* model consisting of a transmit electrode, a receive electrode, part of a human body (to be sensed), and a simplified view of the natural capacitances between them—each usually no more than several 100 pFs [64, 190]. Most capacitive sensing systems work by measuring changes in capacitive coupling between the human body and these transmit and receive electrodes. The role of *ground* is also important—it simply refers to a common potential to which all of the objects relevant to the system are electrically coupled. Without this common ground, capacitive sensing systems do not have a shared reference, which is critical to operation in many cases. Ground may refer to the electric potential of the floor, as depicted in Figure 1, or to the Earth itself. However, it is important to realize that in some cases, the ground potential is not the floor or the Earth, but simply a local common reference such as the human body itself, or the ground plane of a circuit board.

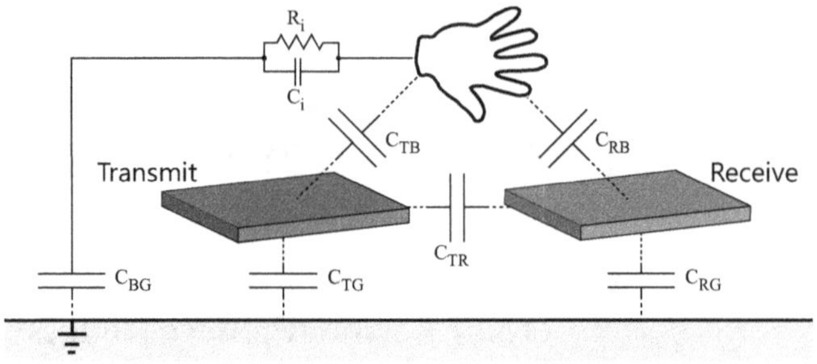

Figure 2. Lumped circuit model of capacitive sensing as introduced by Smith *et al.* [186]. Depending on the sensing mode, different capacitances are controlled or measured.

A capacitance exists whenever two electrodes are separated by some distance. When the conductors are at different electric potentials, an electric field exists between them. Capacitance C is the measure of the charge Q (*i.e.*, number of electrons) that a capacitor holds when a certain electric potential V is applied: $C = Q/V$. The SI unit of capacitance is the farad (F). Typical capacitances in HCI applications are on the order of picofarads (pF or 10^{-12} F) and primarily depend on three properties: the size and shape of the electrodes [133], the distance between them, and the dielectric properties of any material which lies between them. Furthermore, when the electric potentials on the conductors are time-varying, a current known as the *displacement current* flows through the capacitor. We refer to related work for simple [225] and detailed [10] explanations of this general principle.

Capacitance is often measured by observing the displacement current that flows when the electrodes are driven by time-varying voltages with frequencies below 1 MHz [40]. However, some capacitive sensing approaches leverage higher frequencies, *e.g.*, by detuning an RFID antenna [108, 124], measuring phase differences of signals capacitively coupled to the human body [231], or measuring reflections caused by capacitive changes along a transmission line [81, 105, 222].

Advantages and Limitations

Capacitive sensors can be used for a wide variety of applications because the electrodes—where the interaction occurs—can be physically decoupled from the location of the sensing circuitry. This enables extremely large (*e.g.*, room sized) or extremely small (*e.g.*, microscopic) electrodes which can be fabricated from a variety of materials, including curved, flexible, and stretchable substrates. They can often be prototyped quickly using everyday materials, then subsequently mass-produced at low-cost. They typically have a minimal height profile and can be hidden under opaque, non-conductive materials, and can be arranged in large, high-resolution scanned arrays. Capacitive sensing is purely electrical, low power, and requires only cheap driving electronics with no moving parts or mechanical intermediaries [87]. A major advantage over other sensing modalities is the ability to sense a wide field of view at very close distances without a lens.

Although this "lens-less" property is a great advantage, it also serves as a limitation since capacitive sensors cannot "focus" their sensing on a specific area, which can reduce range [73, 190, 225] and introduce ambiguous readings [188, 66]. Additional limitations include electromagnetic noise [67, 38, 37] in the face of insufficient grounding, particularly on wearable devices [36]. Furthermore, touch interaction using capacitive sensing lacks inherent tactile feedback and can therefore result in inadvertent activation [87].

A TAXONOMY FOR CAPACITIVE SENSING

In the 1995 landmark paper, Zimmerman *et al.* proposed a taxonomy to describe types of capacitive sensing by introducing three *active* operating modes [236]. Over the following two decades, there has been a significant body of work in the field of capacitive sensing, including new methods of sensing that do not fit into the taxonomy originally outlined.

Having provided a background on capacitive sensing in the previous section, we now define consistent terminology and describe a new taxonomy which extends the classification proposed by Zimmerman *et al.* This new taxonomy defines a method for clearly grouping and classifying capacitive sensing approaches using two independent dimensions, as shown in Figure 3. Sensing techniques can be described as either *active* or *passive*. They can also be grouped into four different operating modes: *loading*, *shunt*, *transmit*, and *receive*.

Active vs. Passive Sensing

Zimmerman *et al.* conducted their initial research in the field of *active* capacitive sensing. In active capacitive sensing, a known signal is generated on the transmit electrode(s), capacitively coupled onto the body part, and then coupled into the receive electrode(s). The presence and movement of the body part can be sensed by measuring the strength of the signal coupled onto the receive electrode(s). Most of the past work in capacitive sensing has focused on active sensing, including capacitive touch buttons, touchpanels, and touchscreens.

In addition to active sensing, there is a growing body of work using *passive* capacitive sensing. While active sensing systems must *actively* generate an electric field, passive sensing systems rely on existing—external or ambient—electric fields which are *passively* sensed. The active vs. passive terminology is used analogously for other sensor types (*e.g.*, passive infrared sensors, which receive infrared energy radiated by warm objects). Passive capacitive sensing is sometimes referred to as ambient or opportunistic electric field sensing. Some examples of ambient electric field sources include

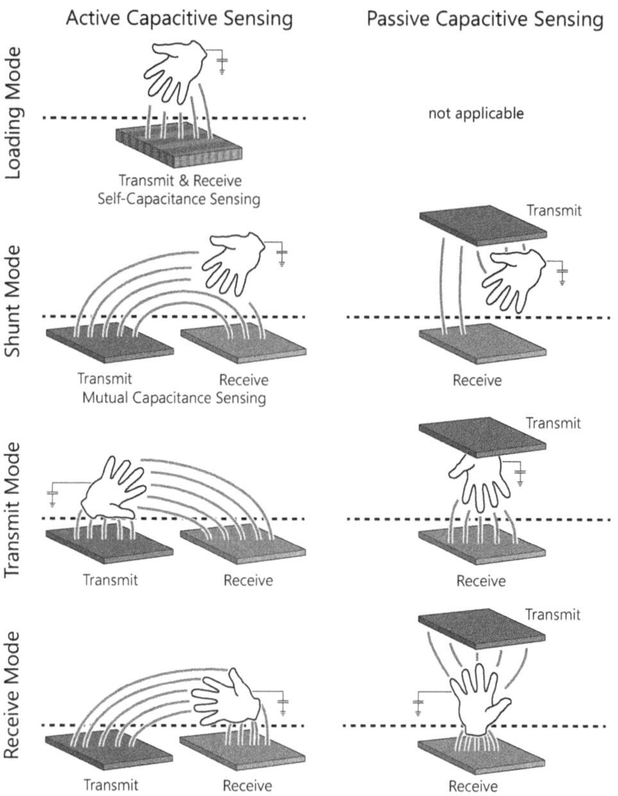

Figure 3. Capacitive sensing techniques can be divided into four operating modes: loading, shunt, transmit and receive. Except for loading mode, each mode may be implemented using active or passive sensing. The dashed line represents the boundary between the sensing system (bottom) and the environment (top).

power lines and appliances, and the low frequency electrostatic fields produced by the triboelectric effect when a user moves. Since the sensing system does not control the transmit signal, passive systems tend to be less precise and more susceptible to changes in their environment. Despite these limitations, passive capacitive sensing has shown promise in its ability to sense human activities with minimal power and infrastructure [36, 37, 38, 67, 156].

Operating Modes

The operating mode of a capacitive sensing system depends on the relative position between the human body and the transmit and receive electrodes, which in turn defines the relative magnitudes of the capacitances shown in Figure 2. This is independent of the system being either active or passive. In all cases an electric field is generated between the transmit electrode and ground, and a field is sensed between the receive electrode and ground. Although Figure 3 depicts only a single transmit and receive electrode, many capacitive sensing systems have multiple transmit and/or receive electrodes.

Loading Mode

Loading mode is the simplest and most common type of capacitive sensing. Here, the same electrode is used for both transmit and receive. The body capacitively loads the electrode and causes a displacement current to flow through the body to ground. As the body gets closer to the electrode, the capacitive coupling (C_{TB}) increases and so does the displacement current, which allows the system to sense the proximity of the body. Since the transmit and receive electrodes are the same, and are both part of the sensing system, there is no passive variant of loading mode. Due to its simplicity, loading mode is widely used for touch sensing, including capacitive buttons and touch panels. Commercial touch panels that use loading mode are often labeled as *self-capacitance* sensors. Electrodes are easy to shield [165, 213, 220], which makes for large detection ranges, *e.g.*, in 3D gesture recognition [63] or noise-resilient touchscreens [11].

Shunt Mode

In shunt mode, the transmit and receive electrodes are distinct, and thus there is some capacitive coupling between them (C_{TR}). When the human body is in proximity to the electrodes, it will capacitively couple to both the transmit and receive electrodes with about the same order of magnitude as the coupling between the electrodes (*i.e.*, $C_{TR} \approx C_{TB} \approx C_{RB}$). This will cause a displacement current to flow through the body to ground (i_{BG}), and will thus reduce the displacement current flowing from the transmit to the receive electrode (i_{TR}). By measuring the decrease in displacement current at the receive electrode, the body's proximity can be determined. In active capacitive sensing, shunt mode is often used for grid-based touch sensors [9] and interactive surfaces [161]. This is because all combinations of the grid electrodes can be exploited to yield high resolution sensing [73, 236]. As a result, shunt mode is often used for commercial touch panels, which are commonly labeled as *mutual-capacitance* sensors. In passive sensing, it is possible to detect when the human body shunts an electric field emitted by the infrastructure (*e.g.*, power lines and appliances). This enables indoor localization and gesture recognition [38, 156].

Transmit Mode

Transmit mode is similar to shunt mode, except that the body is very close to the transmitter. This proximity means that the coupling between the body and the transmitter is much greater than the coupling between the body and the receiver or between the transmitter and the receiver (*i.e.*, $C_{TB} \gg C_{RB}$, $C_{TB} \gg C_{TR}$). In this mode, the body essentially becomes an extension of the transmit electrode. When the body gets closer to the receive electrode, the displacement current into the receive electrode (i_{RB}) increases. In active capacitive sensing, transmit mode allows for a human-mediated detection of an electric field, *e.g.*, to identify the floor tiles being occupied with remote sensors on the ceiling [207]. In passive capacitive sensing, transmit mode corresponds to the class of off-body sensors, *e.g.*, detecting a change in body potential when a person takes a step using remote sensors [4, 197].

Receive Mode

Receive mode is the inverse of transmit mode—the body is very closely coupled to the receive rather than the transmit electrode (*i.e.*, $C_{RB} \gg C_{TB}$, $C_{RB} \gg C_{TR}$). In this case, the body acts as an extension of the receive electrode and can pick up nearby electric fields, using the same operating principle as transmit mode. In active capacitive sensing, receive mode is mostly used when multiple transmit electrodes emit different fields [40]. In passive sensing, on-body sensors use receive mode, to enable gesture recognition [37], touch sensing [38, 58], and object identification [117].

Transmit + Receive Mode (Intrabody Coupling)

A combination of transmit and receive mode occurs when the body has similar coupling to both the transmit and receive electrodes, yet the direct coupling between the electrodes is much less (*i.e.*, $C_{TB} \approx C_{RB} \gg C_{TR}$). In this case, the human body acts as a conductor between both electrodes [49], and since this hybrid-mode is common, we refer to it as *intrabody coupling*. Past work used many terms to describe this hybrid-mode, including active intrabody communication, body channel communication [235, 7], passive bioelectrical measurements [157], and active bioimpedance sensing [97].

RESEARCH CHALLENGES

Having provided a common context for work in the domain of capacitive sensing via the taxonomy in the previous section, we now describe a number of ongoing research challenges. We first discuss challenges that generally relate to methodology and then move on to specific topics.

Towards Better Reproducibility

Throughout our literature review, we regularly observed that reconstructing a particular sensing approach would prove difficult due to missing details (*e.g.*, the number of sensors or the type of grounding). Only 68 of the surveyed papers report sensing range (27× touch, 29× <50 cm, 12× 100 - 300 cm). The employed metrics vary widely. Of course, the necessary level of detail depends on the type of contribution—fewer details are needed for new applications of well-known capacitive sensing principles, but new approaches to capacitive sensing demand more detailed descriptions.

To enable reproducibility, we suggest that papers describing *applications* of capacitive sensing include: (1) whether active or passive sensing is used, (2) the operating mode, (3) the number of transmit and receive electrodes, as well as their material and shape, and (4) the hardware and software being used to conduct the measurement (*e.g.*, Arduino using CapLib). We suggest that *new approaches* in capacitive sensing additionally include: (5) how the sensor, the human body, and related objects in the environment are grounded, (6) a detailed description of hardware, including a schematic, (7) the sensor operating frequency, (8) the sample or scan rate, sample bit-depth, and any other relevant details that will enable others to understand the physical setup. If proximity is being measured, we suggest that the reported *range* corresponds to the state in which the detection accuracy for a human body part is expected to be greater than 95% (derived from [102]).

Sensitivity to Grounding

As mentioned earlier, the grounding of the sensor(s) and user(s) is a critical aspect of capacitive sensor behavior. This is especially important in battery-powered applications, which often rely on a very weakly coupled ground reference, *e.g.*, to measure external electric fields [36, 37, 38, 68, 235]. When battery-powered devices are connected to grounded measurement equipment or long test leads, the performance is artificially improved by the enhanced ground coupling, as a small grounded sensor tends to work better than a large ungrounded sensor [6]. Some wearable prototypes in the literature make use of external ground connections while prototyping, but would not work as standalone wearables.

To realize applications that suffer from insufficient grounding, two options exist. One is to enlarge the size of the ground plane [68, 235], but that can be a problem for some wearable applications. The other option is using a sensor with very high input impedance to detect small displacement currents [50, 79]. We refer the reader to additional literature on the various aspects of grounding [68, 100, 176, 202].

Implications for Real-World Deployments

Today's widely available machine learning models have enabled researchers to make inferences on potentially high-dimensional capacitive sensor data relatively easily. However, much of this research—particularly N-fold cross-validation applied to data collected in relatively static laboratory settings—has treated these learning models as a black box. It is often hard to judge whether these classifiers would generalize effectively in a more realistic setting than in the specific experimental conditions reported. The concern is that these models are fragile, and therefore will likely break if any environmental changes occur [179]. Unfortunately, such changes are inherent in capacitive sensing through varying ground-coupling [119], changing user behavior over time [180], or environmental noise [38, 37, 225]. Although real-world deployments are very challenging, especially in terms of collecting ground-truth data, they are essential to demonstrate feasibility beyond a controlled lab setting.

As a complement to machine learning, we see a challenge of future research in models that are motivated by the underlying physics of capacitive sensing, the physical structure of the human body, and the sensing environment. For example, spatial models [66, 67, 168] help recognize the underdetermination of a problem [168], and produce inferences that are less dependent on users [198, 138] and environments. Using these models, a spatial representation of the surroundings can be obtained much like a 3D camera [53, 186]. This area of research is often called free space electric field tomography and was extensively researched in the 1990s [190, 186, 188]. Since then, little work has followed on developing spatial models that leverage electric field imaging [66]. A renewed effort around physically-motivated spatial models could enable capacitive sensing to truly 'see' the world, as such models provide an intermediary layer between raw sensor readings and machine learning by reconstructing human body parts in full 3D to provide an even richer context.

Support for End-to-End Prototyping

Over the last several years, researchers have made capacitive sensing—particularly electrode design—more accessible by developing systems that support rapid prototyping and evaluation. A study by Unander *et al.* showed good performance using electrodes printed with both silver- and carbon-based ink [203]. New silver nanoparticle [105] and microparticle [170] ink technologies now allow electrode shapes and configurations to be prototyped rapidly. We are also beginning to see the emergence of stretchable electrodes [217], which is ideal for wearable applications. Software systems, such as Midas [175] support the integration of electrode patterns with sensing electronics. Several works incorporate electrodes into 3D printed structures, enabling fast prototyping [20, 149, 177] and easy personalization [61].

While the integration of electrodes is much easier now than a few years ago, compact integrated end-to-end capacitive systems remain difficult to prototype. For example, CupidMZ [27] and NailO [103] required custom PCB circuitry to achieve wearable form factors. Other researchers have applied off-the-shelf electronic hardware for wearable systems (particularly Arduino [126, 208]), but this comes at the expense of form factor. In the future, we envision electronics prototyping tools (*e.g.*, CircuitStickers [91]) to support the integration of capacitive sensing electronics and electrodes into 2D and 3D printed structures. This would enable better miniaturization and robustness, and thus facilitate real-world deployments and longitudinal studies in realistic settings.

Reducing Form Factor & Instrumentation

Due to the emergence of wearable interactive devices, such as augmented tattoos [98] and finger rings [215], the physical size of batteries is becoming a limiting factor for many capacitive systems [103]. To move beyond batteries as the determining factor for device size, researchers have been optimizing power consumption, for example by using low-power passive sensors for motion [36] and touch [45, 58]. However, for many applications, passive sensing does not offer sufficient fidelity in the sensor readings. Hence, the opportunity to combine active and passive sensing systems exists, in which the passive sensor runs in a low-power state and enables the higher-power active sensor only when it detects a signal of interest [36]. Gong *et al.* used a similar approach to implement power-efficient indoor localization [57]. Exploring sensible combinations of both sensing types can enhance battery life, enable harvested energy sources, extend perceptive capabilities, and allow for smaller form factors in the future.

Besides reducing the form factor of the electronics, it is often hard to achieve the same with electrodes. For example, in many capacitive indoor localization systems, a significant amount of instrumentation is needed underneath the floor [15, 194, 205]. Reusing parts of the environmental infrastructure for active sensing seems promising. For example, by injecting a signal into the power line of a house [148, 195], it can act as a transmit electrode for an indoor localization system. Other unused conductive structures include door knobs [173] or even floating water [41].

Enabling Flexible and Stretchable Applications

The ability to use capacitive sensors on non-rigid substrates has enabled touch sensing in a number of new application domains, including wearables. Flexible and stretchable interfaces enable new types of interaction [60, 77] and support ubiquitous deployments, *e.g.*, in fabric and clothing [8, 30, 152, 185] or directly on the human body [98, 103, 217].

An inherent challenge arises when flexible interfaces are worn in close proximity to the body, as human motion causes substantial capacitance changes between the electrodes and the body [76, 152]. To prevent false activation, it becomes necessary to sense the deformation or motion of the electrode to compensate for artifacts in the signal. This can be achieved by using multiple types of capacitive sensing [58], biphasic electrode configurations [191], or other sensor types (*e.g.*, resistive pressure and bend sensors [58, 164]). While the use of electro-optic crystals is largely unexplored in HCI, their sensitivity to electric field changes appears promising, especially on or around the human body [50, 183].

Another significant challenge is the fabrication of conductive materials that are durable while still remaining flexible and stretchable. Recent advances in material science and chemical engineering have resulted in conductive polymers for the creation of flexible and stretchable electronics [128], conductive yarns [152], foils [137], liquid metals [44, 128, 125], and non-rigid micro and nano-structures [83, 193]. These new materials are well suited for interfacing with the organic and dynamic contours of the human body. As such techniques become more available, the HCI community should leverage them for creating novel applications in on-body capacitive sensing using flexible and stretchable electrodes.

Unifying Approaches to Interpret Electric Fields

Within buildings, power lines and appliances emit an almost omnipresent ambient electric field [37, 38, 156]. Similarly, electric fields generated by mobile devices, such as smartphones [99] and household electronics [117] have been leveraged in passive capacitive sensing systems. An extension of this approach can be used to detect touches and gestures around uninstrumented appliances by leveraging unique properties of their operation, *e.g.*, through compact fluorescent lamps [72] or liquid crystal displays [28].

Electric fields are also produced due to human motion—the result of static charging, explained by the triboelectric effect [23], and by very low frequency changes in the capacitive coupling between the body and the environment during motion [36, 47, 67, 116, 197]. Furthermore, extremely weak electric fields are produced by the human body itself, including those generated by the human heart and other muscles. Although challenging to detect, heart activity has been sensed capacitively at distances of 40–100 cm [79, 157].

The electric field in our environment results from a superposition of fields produced by all the sources listed above and more. To date, most research has drawn from just one of these for specific applications [37, 38, 67, 117, 157, 156]. A challenge arises when analyzing multiple electric field sources with the same technical system. Ultimately, we envision miniaturized devices that detect indoor locations, user identities, user actions, and physiological signals — all at the same time. We also expect future wearables to distinguish between indoor and outdoor activities and to reliably count footsteps.

Enriching Sensing with Communications

In the early 2000s, Rekimoto *et al.* introduced combining sensing *and* communications using touch-sensitive surfaces, clothing, and wearable devices [159, 161]. More recent work has used wearables to communicate with touchscreens for token-based [214, 215] and biometric [97] authentication. However, the data rate of these approaches is limited by the slow update rates of commercial touchscreen controllers.

While through-body transmissions between surfaces and devices been demonstrated using other modalities [160, 219], enabling them using capacitive sensing requires rethinking mobile devices as a medium for both sensing touches and emitting signals for *two-way* communication. A recent project prototyped this by switching the touchscreen scanning on and off, achieving up to 50 bits per second [85]. If touchscreens were to be intentionally designed for the purpose of communication, much higher data rates could result.

On larger interactive surfaces, messages could be encoded and decoded locally in certain areas to exploit spatial correspondences in interaction design [161]. Applications range from transferring data from displays to smartwatches or using sensor-augmented tangible objects in proximity to touchscreens for gaming applications. Even when a screen is off, embedded electrodes can act as a hub for intrabody communications of data to other users [235] or touched devices [146].

LITERATURE REVIEW

In this section, we describe the literature review which informed our taxonomy and discussion of outstanding research challenges. In the review we focus on novel research on capacitive sensing techniques and applications in human-computer interaction. Thus, we exclude technologies that measure the intrinsic properties of a material (*e.g.*, capacitive pressure sensors), as well as uses of commercial sensing systems, such as common touch screens.

In our experience, most HCI-related capacitive-sensing research is indexed by ACM and IEEE digital libraries. Therefore, we conducted an initial full-text search in these databases in June 2016. To avoid overlooking relevant publications, we searched for occurrences of *electric field* or *capacitive* together with search terms indicating human-computer interaction (activity, gesture, interaction, movement, touch). This search resulted in over 5,900 papers, which we loaded into a custom-developed paper management system. In the next stage, each paper was examined by at least one reviewer. Most papers were dismissed as off-topic as they did not fit the aforementioned criteria. By scanning the referenced literature of the papers matching our criteria, we added another 26 papers. The resulting 255 papers were then reviewed by at least two authors and tagged in various dimensions to allow us to identify trends among all papers.

Overall, our literature review comprises the 193 papers that we identified through our filtering process. Tagging all papers has allowed us to identify trends across this large body of work. Unsurprisingly, the majority of papers (125/193) present novel applications of capacitive sensing, while 100 papers include a hardware contribution. About one quarter of all papers present a quantitative study (54) or an algorithm contribution (45). About 32 papers include a model of the electrical properties, while 12 present simulation results. Interestingly, 22 papers present toolkits for capacitive sensing, but only 3 of them are open-source [64, 175, 225].

As we noted before, a multitude of terms has been applied to different types of capacitive sensing; however, the existing HCI literature shows significantly less variance. While many surveyed papers do not explicitly mention the sensing principle used, 75 papers use the generic term "capacitive sensing," while 11 of them use the term "electric field sensing." Besides these terms, a long but thin tail of alternative terms exist, such as "skin potential level," "projected capacitance," "electrostatic induction," and "human body electric potential."

Earlier in the paper, we presented a taxonomy for describing and classifying the different types of capacitive sensing. We have grouped much of the past literature using our taxonomy and distinguishing by application domain to present an overview of the research space, organized as in Table 1. As shown in the table and detailed throughout this section, capacitive sensing has been used to enable a wide variety of HCI applications using a variety of sensing techniques.

Active Capacitive Sensing	Passive Capacitive Sensing
Loading mode	
Augmenting clothes & fabric [8, 43, 76, 152, 158, 159, 185]	Not applicable
Augmenting the human body [75, 98, 103, 126, 208, 218, 232]	
Gesture recognition [1, 2, 16, 46, 64, 63, 120, 103, 126, 152, 185, 209, 224, 226]	
Grip & grasp recognition [25, 33, 32, 41, 86, 87, 138, 139, 162, 107, 112, 129, 168, 223]	
Indoor localization & whole-body movements [3, 15, 42, 69, 75, 112, 194, 220]	
Prototyping user interfaces [20, 91, 108, 120, 105, 140, 149, 175, 184, 177, 201, 203]	
Ubiquitous touch interfaces [12, 18, 16, 64, 127, 112, 126, 153, 173, 208, 226]	
Shape sensing [40, 95]	
Shunt mode	
Augmenting clothes and fabric [92, 172, 159, 169]	Gesture recognition [37, 38, 136]
Augmenting the human body [30, 96, 217, 234]	Indoor localization [156, 37, 57, 38, 136]
Touch and gesture recognition [66, 93, 119, 120, 122, 189, 190, 187]	
Grip & grasp recognition [78, 131, 210, 229]	
Prototyping user interfaces [57, 58, 64, 142]	
Whole-body motions [54, 55, 162, 183, 194]	
Transmit mode	
Indoor localization [111, 205, 204]	Indoor localization [67, 136]
Whole-body movements [207]	Step detection [67, 116, 115, 155, 197, 233]
User distinction [150]	User identification [67]
	Input controller [45]
	Prototyping user interfaces [58]
Transmit + receive mode (intrabdoy coupling)	
Activity/physiological sensing [31, 216]	Identifying objects & users [85, 97, 117]
Intrabody communication (HCI) [68, 85, 97, 132, 146, 196, 235]	Step detection [163]
Indoor localization [57]	Whole-body movements [36, 109]
User identification and biometrics [95, 97, 215, 132, 214]	
Receive mode	
Touch and gesture recognition [40]	Gestures [36, 37, 109]
User distinction [40]	Identifying touched objects [117]
	Indoor localization [37, 38, 57]
	Whole-body movements [36]

Table 1. Past work on capacitive sensing grouped using our taxonomy. Most works apply active loading mode, whereas we found few papers that use active receive mode.

Sensing Goal

Touch Sensing

The most ubiquitous form of capacitive sensing is the touch-sensitive surface and the touchscreen [9], which emerged from early prototypes in the 1970s [11]. Through the 1980s, the HCI community made significant advancements by developing custom hardware to enable multi-touch screens [121]. Later projects, including SmartSkin [161] and DiamondTouch [40] have highlighted the interaction potential of this emerging technology. More information on the large space of capacitive touch sensing can be found in surveys by Buxton [21], Barrett and Omote [9], and Schoening *et al.* [178]. Due to the broad availability of commercial touchscreen devices today, HCI research on fundamentally new touchscreen hardware is rare. Some exceptions exist, such as interactions based on a combination of capacitive sensing techniques in a novel device (*e.g.*, Pretouch [86] on a Fogale display) or new low-latency touch screens [122].

Touch sensing on surfaces other than displays has been investigated to create more expressive computing devices and peripherals, including mice [210], keyboards [13, 45], tablet PCs [88], pens [192], and tangibles [52, 68, 118]. Sensors distributed around the screen can help to avoid visual occlusion [139] or to enable interaction on near-eye displays [130].

As high-resolution touch input has become ubiquitous for desktop and mobile computing, lower resolution capacitive touch solutions have also been widely used in wearable technologies. Some wearable applications include touch surfaces on belts [43], finger rings [26, 218], devices worn near the ear [126], on fingernails [103], or even implanted underneath skin [96]. Following the emergence of flexible conductive materials, such as conductive paint and yarn, wearable interfaces have made hair extensions touch-sensitive [208] and enabled touch sensing on clothing [76, 92, 152]. Sensing touch input directly on the human body has recently been explored through augmenting skin with tattoos [98, 217].

Capacitive sensing has also been used to detect user interaction with the environment. Active sensing approaches instrument objects in the environment to sense user input, including plants [153] and household objects, such as door knobs [173]. Other work has passively sensed electric fields that are generated by the power lines and appliances in the environment, and monitored changes to observe touch events on instrumented objects [45, 58], walls [38], or appliances [117].

User Grip & Grasp

Beyond sensing mere touch locations, capacitive sensors yield a rich enough signal to determine the shape of grasps on instrumented objects and devices [221]. Since capacitive sensors can adapt to arbitrary surfaces, researchers have sensing for grasp detection on mice for gesture input to desktop computers [87, 210] and interactive balls [78, 199].

In recent years, research has focused on mobile devices that detect the user's grasp to support interaction [32, 33, 107, 198, 223]. To distinguish between commonly-used grasps, a relatively large number of sensors is often needed. Either high-resolution active shunt mode grids [88, 131, 192, 199, 210, 229] or a multitude of loading mode sensors [33, 107] deliver enough information to determine grasp. Some specific applications have used fewer sensors, for example to adapt the screen rotation depending on the user's grip [32], to start an application [118], or to sense a small number of different grasps through only a few sensors [223]. While the sensor data is often fed into a machine-learning classifier to estimate the grasp, specialized spatial sensors deliver the actual shape of grasps from estimated finger and hand proximities [86].

Sensing Tangibles on the Touchscreen Surface

Recognizing tangible objects on the surface of touchscreens has been shown to enrich the interactive experience by providing physicality [24]. These tangible interfaces are often realized by adding passive components to the bottom of the tangible. Fake touch points that spread across the bottom surface of the object allow the touchscreen to detect the object's position, orientation and identity it much like a 2D barcode [24, 101, 113, 161]. However, this approach only works while a user is touching an object and thus a capacitance to ground is present through the body. Voelker *et al.* demonstrated a modified approach that bridges multiple touch points to enable ungrounded detection of tangibles [211, 212].

To communicate dynamic information between devices, touch events have been triggered on the screen using nearby voltage sources, *e.g.*, to perform biometric [97] or token-based [215] authentication. While the former sends a signal through the user's body, the latter is part of the class of direct capacitive communication. Similarly, Yu *et al.* uses active tags to encode information with high-voltage signals, which touchscreens receive when tags are placed on the surface [230]. Today's commercial styli are similar in their implementation, such as the Atmel maxStylus [5] or the Microsoft Surface Pen [135]—both use the capacitive sensor of the touch device for detecting and distinguishing touch from pen input. These devices are effectively grounded through the user when touched, and they transmit a signal through an electrode that couples to the screen.

3D Gesture Sensing

Capacitive sensing can be extended beyond surface interactions to enable proximity-based recognition of objects, which has been explored for 3D gesture interaction since the mid-1990s [236]. Early gesture recognition systems include the the compact Field Mice [187] and Lazy Fish [190] platforms, which evolved into the modular School-Of-Fish [188] platform. The latter detects gestures at distances up to 1 m [190]. This early work focused on gestural interactions for manipulating 3D objects [187], new forms of musical expression [144], and enabling tangible interactions [190].

More recent work has investigated generic proximity-sensing surfaces that sense 3D input to control computers [1, 2, 14, 16, 48, 66, 78, 120] and home automation systems [62]. More specialized deployments recognize proximity-based gestures in cars [17, 46] or on clothing [185]. Proximity-sensing surfaces deployed on or near displays [86, 119, 167, 168, 190] enable smartphones to show context-dependent menus before the touch contact [86], launch apps based on grasp [25], or detect 3D gestures above the surface [119]. Systems that operate near displays are particularly challenging due to noise and nearby-conductive structures [224].

Indoor Localization

Active sensing approaches for indoor localization commonly involve embedding large loading mode electrodes underneath floor tiles to determine on which tile the user is standing [15, 57, 194]. Alternatively, the entire floor can act as a single transmit electrode using transmit mode. In such a constellation, the signal from several receive electrodes around the environment has been shown to determine the user's location [206, 207]. To reduce the required instrumentation, signals can be injecting directly into existing powerlines in place of dedicated transmit electrodes [19].

Similarly, some passive sensing systems leverage the ambient electric fields generated by the power lines and appliances to estimate the user's location [38, 57, 136, 156]. As these systems rely on ambient fields, they require prior training and are sensitive to changes in the environment. By detecting changes in the characteristic body electric potential during walking motions [47], passive capacitive sensors can detect indoor locations [67, 136], recognize gait patterns [36, 115, 116, 197, 233], or identify users [67].

Posture & Whole-Body Tracking

Capacitive systems that infer a user's pose often operate on the same principles as the indoor localization systems mentioned above. In an instrumented space, researchers have implemented body-pose tracking using active transmit mode [204, 207] and loading mode [220] sensing. Dance and athletics have been captured by transmitting signals among multiple sensor nodes [6]. Wearable systems usually offer a more specialized way of determining postures or motion. Using signal fingerprinting, ambient electric fields generated from the power lines have been used to passively recognize postures [38] and whole-body movements [37]. Passively perceiving changes in body electric potential through movement has been used to recognize steps [36, 67, 155, 163] and arm movements [36, 155]. By observing changes in body impedance, researchers have detected different poses [85].

User Identification and Biometric Sensing

Beyond detecting locations, it is often desirable to identify which user caused a touch. Systems have thus reused touch as a channel to transmit the identity of a wrist token to the touch device for authentication and personalization [132, 159].

Other systems *distinguish* simultaneous users without the need of a wearable token. Grosse-Puppendahl *et al.* 's ceiling sensors reconstruct users' electric potentials and distinguishes them from the characteristic changes while walking [67]. DiamondTouch configures the seats around the table as receive electrodes and determines the user that caused a touch through a receiver in each seat that observes the table's signal upon touch [40]. Similarly, measuring the user's impedance to ground upon touch has been shown to enable distinguishing two simultaneous users [80]. The same approach can determine if two wearable devices are on the same body through intrabody communication [149].

To *identify* and authenticate users from a touch using the user's fingerprint, a capacitive sensor requires an extremely high density sensor array [182]. Such capacitive fingerprint scanners are typically dedicated components using swipe and area sensors for authentication on and across [94] devices. Although in wide use, such scanners cannot currently be made from transparent materials for integration into a screen. To prototype interactions with touch devices that identify each user upon touch, Holz and Knaust demonstrated a wristband that measures biometric features and transmits them to the touchscreen using intrabody communication [97].

Physiological Sensing

In addition to sensing biometrics for user identification and authentication on touchscreens, capacitive sensors have been used to create wearable devices that sense physiological signals during wear. Capacitive sensors have been embedded into clothing for detecting breathing [31], swallowing [30], and drinking [31]. Passive sensors can detect gait patterns including limping [36, 67, 115, 116]. Capacitive sensors have also been used to detect arm [232] and facial [158] muscle activity as an alternative to electromyography. These systems work by sensing changes in the proximity of the skin to a wearable during muscle flexion. Capacitive textile arrays have also been embedded into clothing to sense gestures and movement detection in patients with limited mobility [185] and other health-related applications [200].

Instrumenting Everyday Objects

Clothing. The integration of capacitive touch sensors into clothing was first explored in 1998 [143]. Researchers have since used this approach to implement health applications [8, 30, 185] and ubiquitous touch interfaces [43, 76, 92, 143, 152]. Sensors have thereby been placed on pants [172, 185], belts [43, 196], shoes [145], gloves [104, 209], and jackets [152]. However, manufacturing techniques and long-term deployments (*i.e.*, surviving wash cycles) remain open research areas for such systems [152].

Furniture. Due to its simplicity and ease of shielding [69, 226], active loading mode is dominantly used for posture and touch recognition on furniture. Researchers have thereby augmented couches [69, 110], bath tubs [89], beds [42], chairs [112, 236], lamps [72], and tables [16, 90, 226] with capacitive sensing. Less conventional applications include fabric-based sensors inside bed sheets to enable low-power communication with wearable devices [68] or to recognize sleep postures [169].

Rooms. Room-size deployments of capacitive systems are often used for indoor localization, but have also been used for interactive art installations [18, 151] and gait recognition [115, 116]. To ease with the deployment of large form factors, electrodes can be printed on flexible rolls [57].

Cars. Detecting the presence of adult passengers to ensure the safe deployment of airbags is a common application of capacitive sensing [54, 55, 202]. Other applications have focused on user distinction [150] and gesture recognition using sensors in the steering wheel [46, 166] and armrests [17].

Musical Instruments. The thin profile of capacitive electrodes allows them to be unobtrusively integrated with existing musical instruments. Paradiso *et al.* first explored this with a cello bow and an augmented baton [144], and subsequent work has been applied to guitars [59, 70] and pianos [134].

Sensor Design and Fabrication

Electrode design is a fundamental aspect of prototyping capacitive sensing applications. Besides traditional materials, such as copper or other metal plates, a growing variety of electrode designs have been made from conductive inks and paints as shown in Table 2. Through the use of inkjet printing, electrodes on both, flexible and cuttable substrates can be prototyped [57, 58, 105, 108, 141, 142]. As an alternative to inkjet printing, vinyl cutters can create customized adhesive electrodes [175] or cut a substrate for composite electrode materials, *e.g.*, conductive tattoos [98]. To build larger sensing systems, conductive paint can be used to apply electrodes on wall surfaces [18, 174]. To bridge the resulting gap between electrodes and electronics, CircuitStickers use pre-fabricated adhesive electronic components [91].

With the emergence of 3D printing, researchers have started to explore prototyping objects with integrated capacitive electrodes. For example, capacitive sensing can be enabled on printed objects by filling tubes inside the objects with conductive inks [174], interrupting the print process to integrate electronics [181] or combining conductive and non-conductive print materials [20, 123, 177]. Conductive yarns and fabrics open new possibilities for flexible electrode design, *e.g.*, the integration into clothing [8, 30, 92, 152, 185]. Conductive paint has also been applied to retrofit existing clothing with sensing capabilities [76, 200]. The durability of textile-based electrodes remains a challenge (*e.g.*, to support multiple washing cycles) [152].

Sensing electronics

The choice of electronics depends primarily on the operating mode as shown in Table 3. Hardware for the shunt, transmit, and receive modes is similar and usually consists of an oscillator connected to the transmit electrode to generate an electric field, and an amplifier and analog-to-digital converter (ADC) connected to the receive electrode. In loading mode,

Copper - highly conductive, flexible	**Silver** - non-corrosive, flexible
→Wire[15, 45, 161, 169, 197]	→Ink [76, 87, 105, 108, 203]+
→Foil [32, 117, 146, 171, 78, 236]+	→Thread/Yarn [185]
→Vinyl [175]	→Plate [67]
→Plate [64, 66, 120, 226, 224]+	**Carbon** - enabling electrical conductivity
→PCB	→Ink [203]
→Rigid [16, 35, 40, 158, 229]+	→Carbon-filled PDMS (cPDMS) [217]
→Flex [25, 107, 138, 192, 210]+	→Filament [20, 123, 177]
→Tape [42, 64, 132, 162]	**ITO** - transparent electrodes [64, 119, 199]
→Ink [59, 57, 58]	**Anisotropic materials** - directing e-fields
→Paint [18]	→Anisotropic 'Zebra' tape [91]
→Metalization [208]	→Anisotropic 'Zebra' rubber [24]
Gold - non-corrosive, skin-friendly	**Other materials**
→Gold leaf [98]	→Water [41, 173] & Plants [153]
→Gold coating [11]	→Ionized gas [72]
Aluminum - flexible, high availability	→Metal objects [43, 68, 173, 207, 226]+
→Foil [70, 147, 196, 202]	→Electro-optic crystal [50, 183]
→Mylar [190]	→PEDOT:PSS [64, 142]

Table 2. Materials used for capacitive electrodes: Copper and silver are the most prominent materials for realizing capacitive electrodes.

Shunt / Transmit / Receive Mode	Loading Mode
3D gesture controllers:	**Touch and proximity sensors:**
→MGC3130 [119]	→555 timer [19, 225, 64, 224]
Electric-field receiving amplifiers:	→AD7142 [92]
→MCP6041 [36]	→AD7147 [138, 73]
→OPA2322 [68]	→Arduino + CapTouch [201, 105, 175, 208]+
→OPA2350 [64]	→AT42QT1070 [118]
Electric-field sensors:	→CY8C2x [27, 59]
→Plessey PS25451 [67]	→Microcontroller [12, 29, 162]
Capacitance-to-digital converters:	→MPR121 [33, 43, 91, 139, 177]+
→AD7746 [96, 206]	→QT110x [92, 13, 175]
→AD7747 [76]	**Touch matrix sensors:**
Touch matrix sensors:	→MTCH6102 [103, 152]
→QT60248 [198, 199]	**Shield driver:**
→CY8CTMA463 [88, 229]	→THS4281 [64]
Development kits:	**Development kits:**
→Fogale display [86]	→SK7-ExtCS1 sensor pack [168, 167]
→RTL2832U SDR [85, 117]	→Fogale display [86]
	→Touché [80, 153, 173]

Table 3. Electronics hardware used in capacitive sensing literature.

MCU-based implementations (*e.g.*, Arduino CapLib) and 555 timers are commonly used. As shown in Table 3, specialized commercial hardware is also available specifically for capacitive sensing, with the MPR121 touch sensor being the most popular device. While most of the work mentioned above uses a single operating frequency, other recent work (*e.g.*, Touché [173]) has used a multiple frequency approach [154]. In some scenarios, the use of multiple frequencies can provide additional sensing information, though the effect on the signal is often similar across the frequencies being sensed [22, 100], and thus there is often little information gain.

Signal Modeling and Processing

Modeling & Physical Understanding

The first step to understanding a sensing problem is typically to develop a representative physical model. Researchers have traditionally used equivalent or lumped circuit models, such as the one shown in Figure 2 [190, 235, 236]. Particularly for loading mode, simple plate-capacitor models are dominantly used to model the distance between the body and the electrodes [30, 158, 168, 225]. In transmit mode, equivalent circuit models describe the coupling between the transmit and receive electrodes and the body [40, 67, 205]. Equivalent circuit models exist for shunt mode [55], which often use point charge estimations [66, 187] to model distance relationships. To compensate for physical inaccuracies, experimentally determined correction factors [66, 67, 187] or customized fit functions [156, 206] are applied.

When a field is measured passively, it is important to understand the electric field source. For example, a human body accumulates charge via the triboelectric effect [23], and thus varying electric fields are produced when the capacitive coupling between the user and environment changes, *e.g.*, through steps or other movements [36, 47, 67, 115, 116, 197].

Extensive research has been conducted in modeling the electric properties of the human body—most fundamentally gaining an understanding of the impedance of different types of tissues [49, 51]. Modeling such properties is important for intrabody communications [74, 228, 235], and for exploiting the transmit and receive modes. Equivalent circuit models can quickly become more complex when environmental effects, such as grounding [34] or wet skin [227] are considered. Several papers have shown that the human body reacts similarly to different frequencies [7, 22, 100], though Schenk *et al.* point out that it is hard to obtain such data with statistical significance [176]. There are no indications that the electric fields typically used in capacitive sensing systems have adverse effects on users' health [71, 235].

Classification & Continuous Object Tracking

Capacitive sensing inherently involves inferring information from signal data, either discrete (*e.g.*, for touch recognition) or continuous (*e.g.*, for estimating user positions). Thresholding is ubiquitously applied to realize discrete classifiers, *e.g.*, to passively sense user foot steps [163, 197], touches [12], or presence [42, 226]. If more than one state is being detected (*e.g.*, multiple postures on a couch), classifiers, such as support vector machines [78, 80, 107, 117] or decision trees [69, 109, 185, 208] are frequently used. In contrast to classification, models that determine continuous properties are often physically motivated. Such models can be based on pseudo-probability distributions that estimate the most probable system state, for example 3D hand positions [66, 167, 168, 187]. Researchers have used particle filters to enable real-time operation when multiple degrees-of-freedom are being calculated [66, 167, 168]. Le Goc *et al.* take a different approach by applying random decision forests directly to the highly non-linear sensing problem of measuring thumb positions in proximity to a touchscreen [119].

Sensor Fusion

Inertial measurement units (IMU) are often paired with capacitive systems in order to reveal more contextual information [65, 88], or to provide an additional dimension for user input [114, 130, 209]. IMUs have also been used to correlate whole-body movements to capacitive sensing data [109, 194] and avoid accidental interactions [107]. Other work has combined acoustic sensors [16], cameras [48] and resistive sensors [112, 140, 145] with capacitive approaches.

CONCLUSION

Capacitive sensing has been a key enabler for research in HCI for more than two decades. It provides a sensing modality that is cheap, easy to integrate, and enables rich interactions. For the same reasons, capacitive sensing has become an integral part of many wearable, mobile, and stationary devices. As such, we expect capacitive sensing to continue to have a prominent role in the coming decades.

In this paper, we have presented an analysis and review of the past literature as a reference for others working in this field. As we plan future research around novel sensing technologies and interaction techniques, we think it is important to understand the existing work, learn from its benefits and limitations, and build upon it. The taxonomy we have proposed describes and classifies the various types of capacitive sensing found in the literature. We hope it provides a useful baseline for the community and helps others set their work in the context of previous research. We also hope that our discussion of research challenges will inform and inspire others in the community to continue developing innovately capacitive sensing or may in the future.

REFERENCES

1. Fatemeh Aezinia, YiFan Wang, and Behraad Bahreyni. 2011. Touchless capacitive sensor for hand gesture detection. In *IEEE SENSORS Proceedings*. IEEE. DOI: http://dx.doi.org/10.1109/icsens.2011.6127321
2. Fatemeh Aezinia, Yifan Wang, and Behraad Bahreyni. 2012. Three dimensional touchless tracking of objects using integrated capacitive sensors. *IEEE Transactions on Consumer Electronics* 58, 3 (2012), 886–890. DOI: http://dx.doi.org/10.1109/tce.2012.6311332
3. Alireza Ramezani Akhmareh, Mihai Teodor Lazarescu, Osama Bin Tariq, and Luciano Lavagno. 2016. A Tagless Indoor Localization System Based on Capacitive Sensing Technology. *Sensors* 16(9) (2016).
4. Alan D. Aronoff. 1965. *Electrostatic Means for Intrusion Detection and Ranging*. Technical Report. National Technical Information System.
5. Atmel. 2016. mXTS220 maXStylus multiSense: One sensor to implement both a stylus and touch simultaneously. http://www.atmel.com/products/touchsolutions/touchscreens/active_stylus.aspx. (2016). Accessed 2016-09-18.
6. Ryan Aylward and Joseph A. Paradiso. 2007. A Compact, High-Speed, Wearable Sensor Network for Biomotion Capture and Interactive Media. In *2007 6th International Symposium on Information Processing in Sensor Networks*. IEEE. DOI: http://dx.doi.org/10.1109/ipsn.2007.4379698
7. Heribert Baldus, Steven Corroy, Alberto Fazzi, Karin Klabunde, and Tim Schenk. 2009. Human-centric connectivity enabled by body-coupled communications. *IEEE Commun. Mag.* 47, 6 (jun 2009), 172–178. DOI: http://dx.doi.org/10.1109/mcom.2009.5116816
8. Rebecca Baldwin, Stan Bobovych, Ryan Robucci, Chintan Patel, and Nilanjan Banerjee. 2015. Gait analysis for fall prediction using hierarchical textile-based capacitive sensor arrays. In *2015 Design, Automation Test in Europe Conference Exhibition (DATE)*. 1293–1298. DOI: http://dx.doi.org/10.7873/DATE.2015.0943
9. Gary Barrett and Ryomei Omote. 2010. Projected-capacitive touch technology. *Information Display* 26, 3 (2010), 16–21.
10. Larry K. Baxter. 1997. *Capacitive Sensors: Design and Applications*. IEEE Press.
11. Frank Beck and Bent Stumpe. 1973. *Two devices for operator interaction in the central control of the new CERN accelerator*. Technical Report. CERN.
12. Ray Bittner and Mike Sinclair. 2009. VersaPatch: A Low Cost 2.5D Capacitive Touch Sensor. In *Human-Computer Interaction. Novel Interaction Methods and Techniques*. Springer Science + Business Media, 407–416. DOI: http://dx.doi.org/10.1007/978-3-642-02577-8_44
13. Florian Block, Hans Gellersen, and Nicolas Villar. 2010. Touch-display keyboards: transforming keyboards into interactive surfaces. In *Proceedings of the 28th international conference on Human factors in computing systems - CHI '10*. ACM. DOI: http://dx.doi.org/10.1145/1753326.1753498
14. Andreas Braun and Pascal Hamisu. 2011. Designing a multi-purpose capacitive proximity sensing input device. In *Proceedings of the 4th International Conference on PErvasive Technologies Related to Assistive Environments - PETRA '11*. ACM. DOI: http://dx.doi.org/10.1145/2141622.2141641
15. Andreas Braun, Henning Heggen, and Reiner Wichert. 2012. CapFloor – A Flexible Capacitive Indoor Localization System. In *Evaluating AAL Systems Through Competitive Benchmarking. Indoor Localization and Tracking*. Springer Science + Business Media, 26–35. DOI: http://dx.doi.org/10.1007/978-3-642-33533-4_3
16. Andreas Braun, Stefan Krepp, and Arjan Kuijper. 2015. Acoustic Tracking of Hand Activities on Surfaces. In *Proceedings of the 2Nd International Workshop on Sensor-based Activity Recognition and Interaction (WOAR '15)*. ACM, Article 9, 5 pages. DOI: http://dx.doi.org/10.1145/2790044.2790052
17. Andreas Braun, Stephan Neumann, Sönke Schmidt, Reiner Wichert, and Arjan Kuijper. 2014. Towards interactive car interiors. In *Proceedings of the 8th Nordic Conference on Human-Computer Interaction Fun, Fast, Foundational - NordiCHI '14*. ACM. DOI: http://dx.doi.org/10.1145/2639189.2670191
18. Leah Buechley, David Mellis, Hannah Perner-Wilson, Emily Lovell, and Bonifaz Kaufmann. 2010. Living wall: programmable wallpaper for interactive spaces. In *Proceedings of the international conference on Multimedia - MM '10*. ACM. DOI: http://dx.doi.org/10.1145/1873951.1874226
19. William Buller and Brian Wilson. 2006. Measuring the Capacitance of Electrical Wiring and Humans for Proximity Sensing with Existing Electrical Infrastructure. In *2006 IEEE International Conference on Electro/Information Technology*. IEEE. DOI: http://dx.doi.org/10.1109/eit.2006.252172
20. Jesse Burstyn, Nicholas Fellion, Paul Strohmeier, and Roel Vertegaal. 2015. *PrintPut: Resistive and Capacitive Input Widgets for Interactive 3D Prints*. Springer International Publishing, Cham, 332–339. DOI: http://dx.doi.org/10.1007/978-3-319-22701-6_25
21. Bill Buxton. 2016. Multi-Touch Systems that I Have Known and Loved. (2016). http://www.billbuxton.com/multitouchOverview.html [Online; accessed 21-September-2016].

22. Maria Amparo Callejon, David Naranjo-Hernandez, Javier Reina-Tosina, and Laura M Roa. 2013. A comprehensive study into intrabody communication measurements. *IEEE Transactions on Instrumentation and Measurement* 62, 9 (2013), 2446–2455. DOI: http://dx.doi.org/10.1109/TIM.2013.2258766

23. G.S.P. Castle. 1997. Contact charging between insulators. *Journal of Electrostatics* 40/41 (1997), 13–20.

24. Liwei Chan, Stefanie Müller, Anne Roudaut, and Patrick Baudisch. 2012. CapStones and ZebraWidgets: sensing stacks of building blocks, dials and sliders on capacitive touch screens. In *Proceedings of the 2012 ACM annual conference on Human Factors in Computing Systems - CHI '12*. ACM. DOI: http://dx.doi.org/10.1145/2207676.2208371

25. Wook Chang, Kee Kim, Hyunjeong Lee, Joon Cho, Byung Soh, Jung Shim, Gyunghye Yang, Sung jung Cho, and Joonah Park. 2006. Recognition of Grip-Patterns by Using Capacitive Touch Sensors. In *2006 IEEE International Symposium on Industrial Electronics*. IEEE. DOI: http://dx.doi.org/10.1109/isie.2006.296083

26. Ranajit Chatterjee and Fumtoshi Matsuno. 2006. Design of A Touch Sensor Based Single Finger Operated Wearable User-Interface Terminal. In *2006 SICE-ICASE International Joint Conference*. IEEE. DOI: http://dx.doi.org/10.1109/sice.2006.314614

27. Ranajit Chatterjee and Fumtoshi Matsuno. 2008. Capacitive touch sensor based user-interface : Generic design considerations and development of an wearable input device. In *SICE Annual Conference, 2008*. 2299–2303. DOI: http://dx.doi.org/10.1109/SICE.2008.4655048

28. Ke-Yu Chen, Gabe A. Cohn, Sidhant Gupta, and Shwetak N. Patel. 2013. uTouch: sensing touch gestures on unmodified LCDs. In *Proceedings of the SIGCHI Conference on Human Factors in Computing Systems - CHI '13*. ACM. DOI: http://dx.doi.org/10.1145/2470654.2481356

29. Bernard Cheng, Antonio Gomes, Paul Strohmeier, and Roel Vertegaal. 2014. Mood fern: exploring shape transformations in reactive environments. In *Proceedings of the 11th Conference on Advances in Computer Entertainment Technology - ACE '14*. ACM. DOI: http://dx.doi.org/10.1145/2663806.2663818

30. Jingyuan Cheng, Oliver Amft, and Paul Lukowicz. 2010. Active Capacitive Sensing: Exploring a New Wearable Sensing Modality for Activity Recognition. In *Lecture Notes in Computer Science*. Springer Science + Business Media, 319–336. DOI: http://dx.doi.org/10.1007/978-3-642-12654-3_19

31. Jingyuan Cheng and Paul Lukowicz. 2008. Towards wearable capacitive sensing of physiological parameters. In *2008 Second International Conference on Pervasive Computing Technologies for Healthcare*. IEEE. DOI: http://dx.doi.org/10.1109/pcthealth.2008.4571087

32. Lung-Pan Cheng, Meng Han Lee, Che-Yang Wu, Fang-I Hsiao, Yen-Ting Liu, Hsiang-Sheng Liang, Yi-Ching Chiu, Ming-Sui Lee, and Mike Y. Chen. 2013a. IrotateGrasp: automatic screen rotation based on grasp of mobile devices. In *Proceedings of the SIGCHI Conference on Human Factors in Computing Systems - CHI '13*. ACM. DOI: http://dx.doi.org/10.1145/2470654.2481424

33. Lung-Pan Cheng, Hsiang-Sheng Liang, Che-Yang Wu, and Mike Y. Chen. 2013b. iGrasp: grasp-based adaptive keyboard for mobile devices. In *Proceedings of the SIGCHI Conference on Human Factors in Computing Systems - CHI '13*. ACM. DOI: http://dx.doi.org/10.1145/2470654.2481422

34. Namjun Cho, Jerald Yoo, Seong-Jun Song, Jeabin Lee, Seonghyun Jeon, and Hoi-Jun Yoo. 2007. The human body characteristics as a signal transmission medium for intrabody communication. *IEEE transactions on microwave theory and techniques* 55, 5 (2007), 1080–1086. DOI: http://dx.doi.org/10.1109/TMTT.2007.895640

35. Tanay Choudhary, Saurabh Kulkarni, and Pradyumna Reddy. 2015. A Braille-based mobile communication and translation glove for deaf-blind people. In *2015 International Conference on Pervasive Computing (ICPC)*. IEEE. DOI: http://dx.doi.org/10.1109/pervasive.2015.7087033

36. Gabe Cohn, Sidhant Gupta, Tien-Jui Lee, Dan Morris, Joshua R. Smith, Matthew S. Reynolds, Desney S. Tan, and Shwetak N. Patel. 2012. An ultra-low-power human body motion sensor using static electric field sensing. In *Proceedings of the 2012 ACM Conference on Ubiquitous Computing - UbiComp '12*. ACM. DOI: http://dx.doi.org/10.1145/2370216.2370233

37. Gabe Cohn, Daniel Morris, Shwetak Patel, and Desney Tan. 2012. Humantenna: using the body as an antenna for real-time whole-body interaction. In *Proceedings of the 2012 ACM annual conference on Human Factors in Computing Systems - CHI '12*. ACM. DOI: http://dx.doi.org/10.1145/2207676.2208330

38. Gabe Cohn, Daniel Morris, Shwetak N. Patel, and Desney S. Tan. 2011. Your noise is my command: sensing gestures using the body as an antenna. In *Proceedings of the 2011 annual conference on Human factors in computing systems - CHI '11*. ACM. DOI: http://dx.doi.org/10.1145/1978942.1979058

39. Max Cremer. 1907. Ueber die Registrierung mechanischer Vorgänge auf electrischem Wege, speziell mit Hilfe des Saitengalvanometers und Saitenelectrometers. *Münchner Medizinische Wochenschrift* 54 (August 1907), 1629–1630.

40. Paul Dietz and Darren Leigh. 2001. DiamondTouch: a multi-user touch technology. In *Proceedings of the 14th annual ACM symposium on User interface software and technology - UIST '01*. ACM. DOI: http://dx.doi.org/10.1145/502348.502389

41. Paul Dietz, Jonathan Westhues, John Barnwell, Jefferson Y. Han, and William Yerazunis. 2006. Submerging technologies. In *ACM SIGGRAPH 2006 Emerging technologies on - SIGGRAPH '06*. ACM. DOI: http://dx.doi.org/10.1145/1179133.1179164

42. Maxim Djakow, Andreas Braun, and Alexander Marinc. 2014. *MoviBed - Sleep Analysis Using Capacitive Sensors*. Springer International Publishing, Cham, 171–181. DOI: http://dx.doi.org/10.1007/978-3-319-07509-9_17

43. David Dobbelstein, Philipp Hock, and Enrico Rukzio. 2015. Belt: An Unobtrusive Touch Input Device for Head-worn Displays. In *Proceedings of the 33rd Annual ACM Conference on Human Factors in Computing Systems - CHI '15*. ACM. DOI: http://dx.doi.org/10.1145/2702123.2702450

44. Collin B. Eaker and Michael D. Dickey. 2015. Liquid metals as ultra-stretchable, soft, and shape reconfigurable conductors. In *SPIE Defense+ Security*. International Society for Optics and Photonics, 946708–946708.

45. H. M. Elfekey and H. A. Bastawrous. 2013. Design and implementation of a new thin cost effective AC hum based touch sensing keyboard. In *2013 IEEE International Conference on Consumer Electronics (ICCE)*. IEEE. DOI: http://dx.doi.org/10.1109/icce.2013.6487036

46. Christoph Endres, Tim Schwartz, and Christian A. Müller. 2011. Geremin": 2D microgestures for drivers based on electric field sensing. In *Proceedings of the 15th international conference on Intelligent user interfaces - IUI '11*. ACM. DOI: http://dx.doi.org/10.1145/1943403.1943457

47. T. Ficker. 2006. Electrification of human body by walking. *Journal of Electrostatics* 64 (2006), 10–16.

48. Sean Follmer, Micah Johnson, Edward Adelson, and Hiroshi Ishii. 2011. deForm: an interactive malleable surface for capturing 2.5D arbitrary objects, tools and touch. In *Proceedings of the 24th annual ACM symposium on User interface software and technology - UIST '11*. ACM. DOI: http://dx.doi.org/10.1145/2047196.2047265

49. Kenneth R Foster and Henry C Lukaski. 1996. Whole-body impedance–what does it measure? *The American journal of clinical nutrition* 64, 3 (1996), 388S–396S.

50. Masaaki Fukumoto and Mitsuru Shinagawa. 2005. CarpetLAN: A Novel Indoor Wireless(-like) Networking and Positioning System. In *Lecture Notes in Computer Science*. Springer Science + Business Media, 1–18. DOI: http://dx.doi.org/10.1007/11551201_1

51. S. Gabriel, R.W. Lau, and C. Gabriel. 1996. The dielectric properties of biological tissues: II. Measurements in the frequency range 10 Hz to 20 GHz. *Physics in Medicine and Biology* 41, 11 (1996), 2251–2269.

52. Steven Gelineck, Dan Overholt, Morten Büchert, and Jesper Andersen. 2013. Towards an Interface for Music Mixing based on Smart Tangibles and Multitouch. In *New Interfaces for Musical Expression*. Association for Computing Machinery.

53. E.R. Generazio. 2015. Electric Potential and Electric Field Imaging with Applications. *Materials Evaluation* 73, 11 (Nov. 2015).

54. Boby George, Hubert Zangl, and Thomas Bretterklieber. 2009. Seat Occupancy Detection Based on Capacitive Sensing. *IEEE Trans. Instrum. Meas.* 58, 5 (may 2009), 1487–1494. DOI: http://dx.doi.org/10.1109/tim.2009.2009411

55. Boby George, Hubert Zangl, Thomas Bretterklieber, and Georg Brasseur. 2010. A Combined Inductive & Capacitive Proximity Sensor for Seat Occupancy Detection. *IEEE Trans. Instrum. Meas.* 59, 5 (may 2010), 1463–1470. DOI: http://dx.doi.org/10.1109/tim.2010.2040910

56. Albert Glinsky. 2000. *Theremin: Ether Music and Espionage*. University of Illinois Press. http://books.google.de/books?id=6DHlQJcMpBQC

57. Nan-Wei Gong, Steve Hodges, and Joseph A. Paradiso. 2011. Leveraging conductive inkjet technology to build a scalable and versatile surface for ubiquitous sensing. In *Proceedings of the 13th international conference on Ubiquitous computing - UbiComp '11*. ACM. DOI: http://dx.doi.org/10.1145/2030112.2030120

58. Nan-Wei Gong, Jürgen Steimle, Simon Olberding, Steve Hodges, Nicholas Edward Gillian, Yoshihiro Kawahara, and Joseph A. Paradiso. 2014. PrintSense: a versatile sensing technique to support multimodal flexible surface interaction. In *Proceedings of the 32nd annual ACM conference on Human factors in computing systems - CHI '14*. ACM. DOI: http://dx.doi.org/10.1145/2556288.2557173

59. Nan-Wei Gong, Nan Zhao, and Joseph A. Paradiso. 2011. A Customizable Sensate Surface for Music Control. In *Proceedings NIME'11 (NIME'11)*.

60. Daniel Gotsch, Xujing Zhang, Jesse Burstyn, and Roel Vertegaal. 2016. HoloFlex: A Flexible Holographic Smartphone with Bend Input. In *Proceedings of the 2016 CHI Conference Extended Abstracts on Human Factors in Computing Systems (CHI EA '16)*. ACM, 3675–3678. DOI: http://dx.doi.org/10.1145/2851581.2890258

61. Daniel Groeger, Elena Chong Loo, and Jürgen Steimle. 2016. HotFlex: Post-print Customization of 3D Prints Using Embedded State Change. In *Proceedings of the 2016 CHI Conference on Human Factors in Computing Systems (CHI '16)*. ACM, New York, NY, USA, 420–432. DOI: http://dx.doi.org/10.1145/2858036.2858191

62. Tobias Grosse-Puppendahl, Sebastian Beck, and Daniel Wilbers. 2014a. Rainbowfish: visual feedback on gesture-recognizing surfaces. In *Proceedings of the extended abstracts of the 32nd annual ACM conference on Human factors in computing systems - CHI EA '14*. ACM. DOI: http://dx.doi.org/10.1145/2559206.2574787

63. Tobias Grosse-Puppendahl, Sebastian Beck, Daniel Wilbers, Steeven Zeiß, Julian von Wilmsdorff, and Arjan Kuijper. 2014b. Ambient Gesture-Recognizing Surfaces with Visual Feedback. In *Distributed, Ambient, and Pervasive Interactions*. Springer Science + Business Media, 97–108. DOI: http://dx.doi.org/10.1007/978-3-319-07788-8_10

64. Tobias Grosse-Puppendahl, Yannick Berghoefer, Andreas Braun, Raphael Wimmer, and Arjan Kuijper. 2013. OpenCapSense: A rapid prototyping toolkit for pervasive interaction using capacitive sensing. In *2013 IEEE International Conference on Pervasive Computing and Communications (PerCom)*. IEEE. DOI: http://dx.doi.org/10.1109/percom.2013.6526726

65. Tobias Grosse-Puppendahl, Eugen Berlin, and Marko Borazio. 2012. Enhancing Accelerometer-Based Activity Recognition with Capacitive Proximity Sensing. In *Ambient Intelligence*. Lecture Notes in Computer Science, Vol. 7683. Springer Berlin Heidelberg, 17–32. DOI: http://dx.doi.org/10.1007/978-3-642-34898-3_2

66. Tobias Grosse-Puppendahl, Andreas Braun, Felix Kamieth, and Arjan Kuijper. 2013. Swiss-cheese extended: an object recognition method for ubiquitous interfaces based on capacitive proximity sensing. In *Proceedings of the SIGCHI Conference on Human Factors in Computing Systems - CHI '13*. ACM. DOI: http://dx.doi.org/10.1145/2470654.2466186

67. Tobias Grosse-Puppendahl, Xavier Dellangnol, Christian Hatzfeld, Biying Fu, Mario Kupnik, Arjan Kuijper, Matthias R. Hastall, James Scott, and Marco Gruteser. 2016. Platypus: Indoor Localization and Identification Through Sensing of Electric Potential Changes in Human Bodies. In *Proceedings of the 14th Annual International Conference on Mobile Systems, Applications, and Services (MobiSys '16)*. ACM, 17–30. DOI: http://dx.doi.org/10.1145/2906388.2906402

68. Tobias Grosse-Puppendahl, Sebastian Herber, Raphael Wimmer, Frank Englert, Sebastian Beck, Julian von Wilmsdorff, Reiner Wichert, and Arjan Kuijper. 2014. Capacitive near-field communication for ubiquitous interaction and perception. In *Proceedings of the 2014 ACM International Joint Conference on Pervasive and Ubiquitous Computing - UbiComp '14 Adjunct*. ACM. DOI: http://dx.doi.org/10.1145/2632048.2632053

69. Tobias Grosse-Puppendahl, Alexander Marinc, and Andreas Braun. 2011. Classification of User Postures with Capacitive Proximity Sensors in AAL-Environments. In *Lecture Notes in Computer Science*. Springer Science + Business Media, 314–323. DOI: http://dx.doi.org/10.1007/978-3-642-25167-2_43

70. Enric Guaus, Tan Hakan Ozaslan, Eric Palacios, and Josep Lluis Arcos. 2010. A Left Hand Gesture Caption System for Guitar Based on Capacitive Sensors. In *International Conference on New Interfaces for Musical Expression (NIME)*. 238–243.

71. ICNIRP Guideline. 1998. Guidelines for limiting exposure to time-varying electric, magnetic, and electromagnetic fields (up to 300 GHz). *Health Phys* 74, 4 (1998), 494–522.

72. Sidhant Gupta, Ke-Yu Chen, Matthew S. Reynolds, and Shwetak N. Patel. 2011. LightWave: using compact fluorescent lights as sensors. In *Proceedings of the 13th international conference on Ubiquitous computing - UbiComp '11*. ACM. DOI: http://dx.doi.org/10.1145/2030112.2030122

73. Iman Habib, Niklas Berggren, Erik Rehn, Gustav Josefsson, Andreas Kunz, and Morten Fjeld. 2009. DGTS: Integrated Typing and Pointing. In *Human-Computer Interaction – INTERACT 2009*. Springer Science + Business Media, 232–235. DOI: http://dx.doi.org/10.1007/978-3-642-03658-3_30

74. Keisuke Hachisuka, Yusuke Terauchi, Yoshinori Kishi, Ken Sasaki, Terunao Hirota, Hiroshi Hosaka, Katsuyuki Fujii, Masaharu Takahashi, and Koichi Ito. 2006. Simplified circuit modeling and fabrication of intrabody communication devices. *Sensors and Actuators A: Physical* 130-131 (aug 2006), 322–330. DOI: http://dx.doi.org/10.1016/j.sna.2006.04.044

75. Marian Haescher, Denys J. C. Matthies, Gerald Bieber, and Bodo Urban. 2015. CapWalk: A Capacitive Recognition of Walking-based Activities As a Wearable Assistive Technology. In *Proceedings of the 8th ACM International Conference on PErvasive Technologies Related to Assistive Environments (PETRA '15)*. ACM, Article 35, 8 pages. DOI: http://dx.doi.org/10.1145/2769493.2769500

76. Marius Hagan and Horia-Nicolai Teodorescu. 2013. Intelligent clothes with a network of painted sensors. In *2013 E-Health and Bioengineering Conference (EHB)*. IEEE. DOI: http://dx.doi.org/10.1109/ehb.2013.6707390

77. Jaehyun Han, Jiseong Gu, and Geehyuk Lee. 2014. Trampoline: A Double-sided Elastic Touch Device for Creating Reliefs. In *Proceedings of the 27th Annual ACM Symposium on User Interface Software and Technology (UIST '14)*. ACM, 383–388. DOI: **http://dx.doi.org/10.1145/2642918.2647381**

78. Seungju Han and Joonah Park. 2013. Grip-Ball: A spherical multi-touch interface for interacting with virtual worlds. In *2013 IEEE International Conference on Consumer Electronics (ICCE)*. IEEE. DOI: **http://dx.doi.org/10.1109/icce.2013.6487035**

79. C. J. Harland, T. D. Clark, and R. J. Prance. 2002. Electric potential probes - new directions in the remote sensing of the human body. *Measurement Science and Technology* 13, 2 (2002), 163. **http://stacks.iop.org/0957-0233/13/i=2/a=304**

80. Chris Harrison, Munehiko Sato, and Ivan Poupyrev. 2012. Capacitive fingerprinting: exploring user differentiation by sensing electrical properties of the human body. In *Proceedings of the 25th annual ACM symposium on User interface software and technology - UIST '12*. ACM. DOI: **http://dx.doi.org/10.1145/2380116.2380183**

81. Takahiro Hashizume, Takuya Sasatani, Koya Narumi, Yoshiaki Narusue, Yoshihiro Kawahara, and Tohru Asami. 2016. Passive and Contactless Epidermal Pressure Sensor Printed with Silver Nano-particle Ink. In *Proceedings of the 2016 ACM International Joint Conference on Pervasive and Ubiquitous Computing (UbiComp '16)*. ACM, 190–195. DOI: **http://dx.doi.org/10.1145/2971648.2971705**

82. Yuki Hayashida, Ryo Sugiyama, Yusuke Ido, Akito Suzuki, Yasuaki Takizawa, Mitsuru Shinagawa, Yuichi Kado, and Nozomi Haga. 2014. Capacitance Model of Embedded Transciever for Intra-body Communication. In *Proceedings of the 9th International Conference on Body Area Networks*. Institute for Computer Sciences, Social Informatics and Telecommunications Engineering (ICST). DOI: **http://dx.doi.org/10.4108/icst.bodynets.2014.258238**

83. Junwen He, Ralph G Nuzzo, and John A Rogers. 2015. Inorganic materials and assembly techniques for flexible and stretchable electronics. *Proc. IEEE* 103, 4 (2015), 619–632. DOI: **http://dx.doi.org/10.1109/JPROC.2015.2396991**

84. W. Heiligenberg. 1977. *Principles of electrolocation and jamming avoidance in electric fish: a neuroethological approach*. Springer-Verlag. **http://books.google.de/books?id=cKpqAAAAMAAJ**

85. Mehrdad Hessar, Vikram Iyer, and Shyamnath Gollakota. 2016. Enabling On-body Transmissions with Commodity Devices. In *Proceedings of the 2016 ACM International Joint Conference on Pervasive and Ubiquitous Computing (UbiComp '16)*. ACM, 1100–1111. DOI: **http://dx.doi.org/10.1145/2971648.2971682**

86. Ken Hinckley, William Buxton, Seongkook Heo, Michel Pahud, Christian Holz, Hrvoje Benko, Abigail Sellen, Richard Banks, Kenton O'Hara, and Gavin Smyth. 2016. Pre-Touch Sensing for Mobile Interaction. In *Proceedings of the 2016 CHI Conference on Human Factors in Computing Systems - CHI '16*. ACM. DOI: **http://dx.doi.org/10.1145/2858036.2858095**

87. Ken Hinckley and Mike Sinclair. 1999. Touch-sensing input devices. In *Proceedings of the SIGCHI conference on Human factors in computing systems the CHI is the limit - CHI '99*. ACM. DOI: **http://dx.doi.org/10.1145/302979.303045**

88. Ken Hinckley, Andrew Wilson, Michel Pahud, Hrvoje Benko, Pourang Irani, François Guimbretière, Marcel Gavriliu, Xiang 'Anthony' Chen, Fabrice Matulic, and William Buxton. 2014. Sensing techniques for tablet+stylus interaction. In *Proceedings of the 27th annual ACM symposium on User interface software and technology - UIST '14*. ACM. DOI: **http://dx.doi.org/10.1145/2642918.2647379**

89. Shigeyuki Hirai, Yoshinobu Sakakibara, and Hironori Hayashi. 2013. Enabling Interactive Bathroom Entertainment Using Embedded Touch Sensors in the Bathtub. In *Lecture Notes in Computer Science*. Springer Science + Business Media, 544–547. DOI: **http://dx.doi.org/10.1007/978-3-319-03161-3_49**

90. Nguyen Huy Hoang Huy, Gihan Hettiarachchi, Youngki Lee, and Rajesh Krishna Balan. 2016. Small Scale Deployment of Seat Occupancy Detectors. In *Proceedings of the 3rd International on Workshop on Physical Analytics (WPA '16)*. ACM, 25–30. DOI: **http://dx.doi.org/10.1145/2935651.2935660**

91. Steve Hodges, Nicolas Villar, Nicholas Chen, Tushar Chugh, Jie Qi, Diana Nowacka, and Yoshihiro Kawahara. 2014. Circuit stickers: peel-and-stick construction of interactive electronic prototypes. In *Proceedings of the 32nd annual ACM conference on Human factors in computing systems - CHI '14*. ACM. DOI: **http://dx.doi.org/10.1145/2556288.2557150**

92. Paul Holleis, Albrecht Schmidt, Susanna Paasovaara, Arto Puikkonen, and Jonna Häkkilä. 2008. Evaluating capacitive touch input on clothes. In *Proceedings of the 10th international conference on Human computer interaction with mobile devices and services - MobileHCI '08*. ACM. DOI: **http://dx.doi.org/10.1145/1409240.1409250**

93. Christian Holz and Patrick Baudisch. 2010. The Generalized Perceived Input Point Model and How to Double Touch Accuracy by Extracting Fingerprints. In *Proceedings of the SIGCHI Conference on Human Factors in Computing Systems (CHI '10)*. ACM, 581–590. DOI: **http://dx.doi.org/10.1145/1753326.1753413**

94. Christian Holz and Frank R. Bentley. 2016. On-Demand Biometrics: Fast Cross-Device Authentication. In *Proceedings of the 2016 CHI Conference on Human Factors in Computing Systems (CHI '16)*. ACM, New York, NY, USA, 3761–3766. DOI: http://dx.doi.org/10.1145/2858036.2858139

95. Christian Holz, Senaka Buthpitiya, and Marius Knaust. 2015. Bodyprint: Biometric User Identification on Mobile Devices Using the Capacitive Touchscreen to Scan Body Parts. In *Proceedings of the 33rd Annual ACM Conference on Human Factors in Computing Systems (CHI '15)*. ACM, New York, NY, USA, 3011–3014. DOI: http://dx.doi.org/10.1145/2702123.2702518

96. Christian Holz, Tovi Grossman, George Fitzmaurice, and Anne Agur. 2012. Implanted User Interfaces. In *Proceedings of the SIGCHI Conference on Human Factors in Computing Systems (CHI '12)*. ACM, 503–512. DOI: http://dx.doi.org/10.1145/2207676.2207745

97. Christian Holz and Marius Knaust. 2015. Biometric Touch Sensing: Seamlessly Augmenting Each Touch with Continuous Authentication. In *Proceedings of the 28th Annual ACM Symposium on User Interface Software & Technology (UIST '15)*. ACM, New York, NY, USA, 303–312. DOI: http://dx.doi.org/10.1145/2807442.2807458

98. Cindy Hsin-Liu Kao, Christian Holz, Asta Roseway, Andres Calvo, and Chris Schmandt. 2016. DuoSkin: Rapidly Prototyping On-Skin User Interfaces Using Skin-Friendly Materials. In *Proceedings of the International Symposium on Wearable Computers 2016 (ISWC'16) (ISWC'16)*. ACM. DOI: http://dx.doi.org/10.1145/2971763.2971777

99. Manh Huynh, Phuc Nguyen, Marco Gruteser, and Tam Vu. 2015. POSTER: Mobile Device Identification by Leveraging Built-in Capacitive Signature. In *Proceedings of the 22Nd ACM SIGSAC Conference on Computer and Communications Security (CCS '15)*. ACM, 1635–1637. DOI: http://dx.doi.org/10.1145/2810103.2810118

100. J. H. Hwang, T. W. Kang, and S. W. Kang. 2011. Measurement results of human body's signal loss with multiple subjects for human body communication. In *2011 IEEE International Symposium on Antennas and Propagation (APSURSI)*. IEEE. DOI: http://dx.doi.org/10.1109/aps.2011.5996624

101. Kohei Ikeda and Koji Tsukada. 2015. CapacitiveMarker: novel interaction method using visual marker integrated with conductive pattern. In *Proceedings of the 6th Augmented Human International Conference on - AH '15*. ACM. DOI: http://dx.doi.org/10.1145/2735711.2735783

102. ISO 10012-1:1992-01 1992. ISO/TC 176/SC 3. Quality assurance requirements for measuring equipment - Part 1: Metrological confirmation system for measuring equipment (ISO 10012-1:1992-01, *withdrawn*). (1992).

103. Hsin-Liu (Cindy) Kao, Artem Dementyev, Joseph A. Paradiso, and Chris Schmandt. 2015. NailO: Fingernails as an Input Surface. In *Proceedings of the 33rd Annual ACM Conference on Human Factors in Computing Systems - CHI '15*. ACM. DOI: http://dx.doi.org/10.1145/2702123.2702572

104. N. Karlsson, B. Karlsson, and P. Wide. A glove equipped with finger flexion sensors as a command generator used in a fuzzy control system. In *IMTC/98 Conference Proceedings. IEEE Instrumentation and Measurement Technology Conference (Cat. No.98CH36222)*. IEEE. DOI: http://dx.doi.org/10.1109/imtc.1998.679825

105. Yoshihiro Kawahara, Steve Hodges, Benjamin S. Cook, Cheng Zhang, and Gregory D. Abowd. 2013. Instant inkjet circuits: lab-based inkjet printing to support rapid prototyping of UbiComp devices. In *Proceedings of the 2013 ACM international joint conference on Pervasive and ubiquitous computing - UbiComp '13*. ACM. DOI: http://dx.doi.org/10.1145/2493432.2493486

106. Behailu Kibret, MirHojjat Seyedi, Daniel T. H. Lai, and Micheal Faulkner. 2014. Investigation of Galvanic-Coupled Intrabody Communication Using the Human Body Circuit Model. *IEEE Journal of Biomedical and Health Informatics* 18, 4 (jul 2014), 1196–1206. DOI: http://dx.doi.org/10.1109/jbhi.2014.2301165

107. Kee-Eung Kim, Wook Chang, Sung-Jung Cho, Junghyun Shim, Hyunjeong Lee, Joonah Park, Youngbeom Lee, and Sangryong Kim. 2006. Hand Grip Pattern Recognition for Mobile User Interfaces. In *Proceedings of the 18th Conference on Innovative Applications of Artificial Intelligence - Volume 2 (IAAI'06)*. AAAI Press, 1789–1794. http://dl.acm.org/citation.cfm?id=1597122.1597138

108. Sangkil Kim, Yoshihiro Kawahara, Apostolos Georgiadis, Ana Collado, and Manos M. Tentzeris. 2013. Low-cost inkjet-printed fully passive RFID tags using metamaterial-inspired antennas for capacitive sensing applications. In *2013 IEEE MTT-S International Microwave Symposium Digest (MTT)*. IEEE. DOI: http://dx.doi.org/10.1109/mwsym.2013.6697644

109. Yuhwan Kim, Seungchul Lee, Inseok Hwang, Hyunho Ro, Youngki Lee, Miri Moon, and Junehwa Song. 2014. High5: promoting interpersonal hand-to-hand touch for vibrant workplace with electrodermal sensor watches. In *Proceedings of the 2014 ACM International Joint Conference on Pervasive and Ubiquitous Computing - UbiComp '14 Adjunct*. ACM. DOI: http://dx.doi.org/10.1145/2632048.2632072

110. Sauli Kivikunnas, Esko Strommer, Marko Korkalainen, Tapio Heikkila, and Mikko Haverinen. 2010. Sensing sofa and its ubiquitous use. In *2010 International Conference on Information and Communication Technology Convergence (ICTC)*. IEEE. DOI: http://dx.doi.org/10.1109/ictc.2010.5674767

111. Tero Kivimaki, Timo Vuorela, Miika Valtonen, and Jukka Vanhala. 2013. Reliability of the TileTrack capacitive user tracking system in smart home environment. In *ICT 2013*. IEEE. DOI: http://dx.doi.org/10.1109/ictel.2013.6632162

112. Heather Knight, Jae-Kyu Lee, and Hongshen Ma. 2008. Chair Alarm for patient fall prevention based on Gesture Recognition and Interactivity. In *2008 30th Annual International Conference of the IEEE Engineering in Medicine and Biology Society*. IEEE. DOI: http://dx.doi.org/10.1109/iembs.2008.4650012

113. Sven Kratz, Tilo Westermann, Michael Rohs, and Georg Essl. 2011. CapWidgets: Tangible Widgets Versus Multi-touch Controls on Mobile Devices. In *CHI '11 Extended Abstracts on Human Factors in Computing Systems (CHI EA '11)*. ACM, 1351–1356. DOI: http://dx.doi.org/10.1145/1979742.1979773

114. Paul G. Kry and D. K. Pai. 2006. Grasp recognition and manipulation with the tango. In *International Symposium on Experimental Robotics*, Vol. 10. Springer.

115. K. Kurita. 2010. New Approach to Touch Sensing Technique Based on Measurement of Current Generated by Electrostatic Induction. In *iSAIRAS*.

116. K. Kurita, R. Takizawa, and H. Kumon. 2009. Detection of human walking motion based on measurement system of current generated by electrostatic induction. In *ICCAS-SICE, 2009*. 5485–5488.

117. Gierad Laput, Chouchang Yang, Robert Xiao, Alanson Sample, and Chris Harrison. 2015. EM-Sense: Touch Recognition of Uninstrumented, Electrical and Electromechanical Objects. In *Proceedings of the 28th Annual ACM Symposium on User Interface Software & Technology (UIST '15)*. ACM, 157–166. DOI: http://dx.doi.org/10.1145/2807442.2807481

118. Mathieu Le Goc, Pierre Dragicevic, Samuel Huron, Jeremy Boy, and Jean-Daniel Fekete. 2015. SmartTokens: Embedding Motion and Grip Sensing in Small Tangible Objects. In *Proceedings of the 28th Annual ACM Symposium on User Interface Software & Technology (UIST '15)*. ACM, 357–362. DOI: http://dx.doi.org/10.1145/2807442.2807488

119. Mathieu Le Goc, Stuart Taylor, Shahram Izadi, and Cem Keskin. 2014. A low-cost transparent electric field sensor for 3d interaction on mobile devices. In *Proceedings of the 32nd annual ACM conference on Human factors in computing systems - CHI '14*. ACM. DOI: http://dx.doi.org/10.1145/2556288.2557331

120. Chia-Hsun Lee and Ted Selker. 2004. iSphere: A Proximity-based 3D Input Device. In *ACM SIGGRAPH 2004 Posters (SIGGRAPH '04)*. ACM, 72–. DOI: http://dx.doi.org/10.1145/1186415.1186499

121. S. K. Lee, W. Buxton, and K. C. Smith. 1985. A Multi-touch Three Dimensional Touch-sensitive Tablet. In *Proceedings of the SIGCHI Conference on Human Factors in Computing Systems (CHI '85)*. ACM, 21–25. DOI: http://dx.doi.org/10.1145/317456.317461

122. Darren Leigh, Clifton Forlines, Ricardo Jota, Steven Sanders, and Daniel Wigdor. 2014. High Rate, Low-latency Multi-touch Sensing with Simultaneous Orthogonal Multiplexing. In *Proceedings of the 27th Annual ACM Symposium on User Interface Software and Technology (UIST '14)*. ACM, 355–364. DOI: http://dx.doi.org/10.1145/2642918.2647353

123. Simon J. Leigh, Robert J. Bradley, Christopher P. Purssell, Duncan R. Billson, and David A. Hutchins. 2012. A Simple, Low-Cost Conductive Composite Material for 3D Printing of Electronic Sensors. *PLoS ONE* 7, 11 (11 2012), 1–6. DOI: http://dx.doi.org/10.1371/journal.pone.0049365

124. Hanchuan Li, Eric Brockmeyer, Elizabeth J. Carter, Josh Fromm, Scott E. Hudson, Shwetak N. Patel, and Alanson Sample. 2016. PaperID: A Technique for Drawing Functional Battery-Free Wireless Interfaces on Paper. In *Proceedings of the 2016 CHI Conference on Human Factors in Computing Systems (CHI '16)*. ACM, 5885–5896. DOI: http://dx.doi.org/10.1145/2858036.2858249

125. Yiliang Lin, Christopher Cooper, Meng Wang, Jacob J Adams, Jan Genzer, and Michael D Dickey. 2015. Handwritten, soft circuit boards and antennas using liquid metal nanoparticles. *Small* 11, 48 (2015), 6397–6403. DOI: http://dx.doi.org/10.1002/smll.201502692

126. Roman Lissermann, Jochen Huber, Aristotelis Hadjakos, Suranga Nanayakkara, and Max Mühlhäuser. 2014. EarPut: augmenting ear-worn devices for ear-based interaction. In *Proceedings of the 26th Australian Computer-Human Interaction Conference on Designing Futures the Future of Design - OzCHI '14*. ACM. DOI: http://dx.doi.org/10.1145/2686612.2686655

127. Wei Liu, Bing Qiang Ng, Terrence Lim, Liu Bin, Boon Hee Soong, Adnan Nasir, and Merrill Chia. 2012. A novel RFID and capacitive sensing based smart bookshelf. In *2012 18th IEEE International Conference on Networks (ICON)*. IEEE. DOI: http://dx.doi.org/10.1109/icon.2012.6506540

128. Tong Lu, Lauren Finkenauer, James Wissman, and Carmel Majidi. 2014. Rapid Prototyping for Soft-Matter Electronics. *Advanced Functional Materials* 24, 22 (2014), 3351–3356. DOI: http://dx.doi.org/10.1002/adfm.201303732

129. Chenchi Luo, Milind A. Borkar, Arthur J. Redfern, and James H. McClellan. 2012. Compressive Sensing for Sparse Touch Detection on Capacitive Touch Screens. *IEEE Journal on Emerging and Selected Topics in Circuits and Systems* 2, 3 (sep 2012), 639–648. DOI: http://dx.doi.org/10.1109/jetcas.2012.2217033

130. Kent Lyons, Seung Wook Kim, Shigeyuki Seko, David Nguyen, Audrey Desjardins, Mélodie Vidal, David Dobbelstein, and Jeremy Rubin. 2014. Loupe: a handheld near-eye display. In *Proceedings of the 27th annual ACM symposium on User interface software and technology - UIST '14*. ACM. DOI: http://dx.doi.org/10.1145/2642918.2647361

131. Jani Mäntyjärvi, Kjell Nybergh, Johan Himberg, and Kari Hjelt. 2004. *Touch Detection System for Mobile Terminals*. Springer Berlin Heidelberg, Berlin, Heidelberg, 331–336. DOI: http://dx.doi.org/10.1007/978-3-540-28637-0_32

132. N. Matsushita, S. Tajima, Y. Ayatsuka, and J. Rekimoto. 2000. Wearable key: device for personalizing nearby environment. In *Wearable Computers, The Fourth International Symposium on.* 119–126. DOI: http://dx.doi.org/10.1109/ISWC.2000.888473

133. Brian Mayton, Louis LeGrand, and Joshua R Smith. 2010. An electric field pretouch system for grasping and co-manipulation. In *Robotics and Automation (ICRA), 2010 IEEE International Conference on.* IEEE, 831–838. DOI: http://dx.doi.org/10.1109/ROBOT.2010.5509658

134. Andrew P. McPherson, Adrian Gierakowski, and Adam M. Stark. 2013. The space between the notes: adding expressive pitch control to the piano keyboard. In *Proceedings of the SIGCHI Conference on Human Factors in Computing Systems - CHI '13*. ACM. DOI: http://dx.doi.org/10.1145/2470654.2481302

135. Microsoft. 2016. Surface Pen and Touch Digitizer. https://www.microsoft.com/surface/en-us/support/hardware-and-drivers/surface-pen-pro-4. (2016). Accessed 2016-09-18.

136. Adiyan Mujibiya and Jun Rekimoto. 2013, *revised 2015*. Mirage: exploring interaction modalities using off-body static electric field sensing. In *Proceedings of the 26th annual ACM symposium on User interface software and technology - UIST '13*. ACM. DOI: http://dx.doi.org/10.1145/2501988.2502031

137. Anh Nguyen, Raghda Alqurashi, Zohreh Raghebi, Farnoush Banaei-kashani, Ann C. Halbower, Thang Dinh, and Tam Vu. 2016. In-ear Biosignal Recording System: A Wearable For Automatic Whole-night Sleep Staging. In *Proceedings of the 2016 Workshop on Wearable Systems and Applications (WearSys '16)*. ACM, 19–24. DOI: http://dx.doi.org/10.1145/2935643.2935649

138. Mohammad Faizuddin Mohd Noor, Andrew Ramsay, Stephen Hughes, Simon Rogers, John Williamson, and Roderick Murray-Smith. 2014. 28 frames later: predicting screen touches from back-of-device grip changes. In *Proceedings of the 32nd annual ACM conference on Human factors in computing systems - CHI '14*. ACM. DOI: http://dx.doi.org/10.1145/2556288.2557148

139. Ian Oakley and Doyoung Lee. 2014. Interaction on the edge: offset sensing for small devices. In *Proceedings of the 32nd annual ACM conference on Human factors in computing systems - CHI '14*. ACM. DOI: http://dx.doi.org/10.1145/2556288.2557138

140. Simon Olberding, Nan-Wei Gong, John Tiab, Joseph A. Paradiso, and Jürgen Steimle. 2013. A cuttable multi-touch sensor. In *Proceedings of the 26th annual ACM symposium on User interface software and technology - UIST '13*. ACM. DOI: http://dx.doi.org/10.1145/2501988.2502048

141. Simon Olberding, Sergio Soto Ortega, Klaus Hildebrandt, and Jürgen Steimle. 2015. Foldio: Digital Fabrication of Interactive and Shape-Changing Objects With Foldable Printed Electronics. In *Proceedings of the 28th Annual ACM Symposium on User Interface Software & Technology (UIST '15)*. ACM, 223–232. DOI: http://dx.doi.org/10.1145/2807442.2807494

142. Simon Olberding, Michael Wessely, and Jürgen Steimle. 2014. PrintScreen: fabricating highly customizable thin-film touch-displays. In *Proceedings of the 27th annual ACM symposium on User interface software and technology - UIST '14*. ACM. DOI: http://dx.doi.org/10.1145/2642918.2647413

143. Maggie Orth, Rehmi Post, and Emily Cooper. 1998. Fabric Computing Interfaces. In *CHI 98 Conference Summary on Human Factors in Computing Systems (CHI '98)*. ACM, 331–332. DOI: http://dx.doi.org/10.1145/286498.286800

144. Joseph A. Paradiso and Neil Gershenfeld. 1997. Musical Applications of Electric Field Sensing. *Computer Music Journal* 21 (1997), 69–89.

145. Joseph A. Paradiso, Stacy J. Morris, Ari Y. Benbasat, and Erik Asmussen. 2004. Interactive therapy with instrumented footwear. In *Extended abstracts of the 2004 conference on Human factors and computing systems - CHI '04*. ACM. DOI: http://dx.doi.org/10.1145/985921.986059

146. Duck Gun Park, Jin Kyung Kim, Jin Bong Sung, Jung Hwan Hwang, Chang Hee Hyung, and Sung Weon Kang. 2006. TAP: Touch-and-play. In *Proceedings of the SIGCHI Conference on Human Factors in Computing Systems (CHI '06)*. ACM, 677–680. DOI: http://dx.doi.org/10.1145/1124772.1124873

147. Kurt Partridge, Bradley Dahlquist, Alireza Veiseh, Annie Cain, Ann Foreman, Joseph Goldberg, and Gaetano Borriello. 2001. Empirical measurements of intrabody communication performance under varied physical configurations. In *Proceedings of the 14th annual ACM symposium on User interface software and technology - UIST '01*. ACM. DOI: http://dx.doi.org/10.1145/502348.502381

148. Shwetak N. Patel, Khai N. Truong, and Gregory D. Abowd. 2006. *PowerLine Positioning: A Practical Sub-Room-Level Indoor Location System for Domestic Use*. Springer Berlin Heidelberg, Berlin, Heidelberg, 441–458. DOI: http://dx.doi.org/10.1007/11853565_26

149. Huaishu Peng, Jennifer Mankoff, Scott E. Hudson, and James McCann. 2015. A Layered Fabric 3D Printer for Soft Interactive Objects. In *Proceedings of the 33rd Annual ACM Conference on Human Factors in Computing Systems (CHI '15)*. ACM, 1789–1798. DOI: http://dx.doi.org/10.1145/2702123.2702327

150. Carl A. Pickering. 2008. *Human Vehicle Interaction Based On Electric Field Sensing*. Springer Berlin Heidelberg, Berlin, Heidelberg, 141–154. DOI: http://dx.doi.org/10.1007/978-3-540-77980-3_11

151. Ingrid Maria Pohl. 2013. Folded sensitive surface. In *Proceedings of the 9th ACM Conference on Creativity & Cognition - C&C '13*. ACM. DOI: http://dx.doi.org/10.1145/2466627.2481212

152. Ivan Poupyrev, Nan-Wei Gong, Shiho Fukuhara, Mustafa Emre Karagozler, Carsten Schwesig, and Karen E. Robinson. 2016. Project Jacquard: Interactive Digital Textiles at Scale. In *Proceedings of the 2016 CHI Conference on Human Factors in Computing Systems (CHI '16)*. ACM, 4216–4227. DOI: http://dx.doi.org/10.1145/2858036.2858176

153. Ivan Poupyrev, Philipp Schoessler, Jonas Loh, and Munehiko Sato. 2012. Botanicus Interacticus: Interactive Plants Technology. In *ACM SIGGRAPH 2012 Emerging Technologies (SIGGRAPH '12)*. ACM, Article 4, 1 pages. DOI: http://dx.doi.org/10.1145/2343456.2343460

154. Ivan Poupyrev, Zhiquan Yeo, Joshua D. Griffin, and Scott Hudson. 2010. Sensing Human Activities with Resonant Tuning. In *CHI '10 Extended Abstracts on Human Factors in Computing Systems (CHI EA '10)*. ACM, 4135–4140. DOI: http://dx.doi.org/10.1145/1753846.1754115

155. A. Pouryazdan, R. J. Prance, H. Prance, and D. Roggen. 2016. Wearable Electric Potential Sensing: A New Modality Sensing Hair Touch and Restless Leg Movement. In *Proceedings of the 2016 ACM International Joint Conference on Pervasive and Ubiquitous Computing: Adjunct (UbiComp '16)*. ACM, 846–850. DOI: http://dx.doi.org/10.1145/2968219.2968286

156. H. Prance, P. Watson, R. J. Prance, and S. T. Beardsmore-Rust. 2012. Position and movement sensing at metre standoff distances using ambient electric field. *Measurement Science and Technology* 23, 11 (2012), 115101. http://stacks.iop.org/0957-0233/23/i=11/a=115101

157. R. J. Prance, S. T. Beardsmore-Rust, P. Watson, C. J. Harland, and H. Prance. 2008. Remote detection of human electrophysiological signals using electric potential sensors. *Applied Physics Letters* 93, 3 (2008).

158. Ville Rantanen, Hanna Venesvirta, Oleg Spakov, Jarmo Verho, Akos Vetek, Veikko Surakka, and Jukka Lekkala. 2013. Capacitive Measurement of Facial Activity Intensity. *IEEE Sensors J.* 13, 11 (nov 2013), 4329–4338. DOI: http://dx.doi.org/10.1109/jsen.2013.2269864

159. Jun Rekimoto. GestureWrist and GesturePad: unobtrusive wearable interaction devices. In *Proceedings Fifth International Symposium on Wearable Computers*. IEEE. DOI: http://dx.doi.org/10.1109/iswc.2001.962092

160. Jun Rekimoto. 1997. Pick-and-drop: A Direct Manipulation Technique for Multiple Computer Environments. In *Proceedings of the 10th Annual ACM Symposium on User Interface Software and Technology (UIST '97)*. ACM, 31–39. DOI: http://dx.doi.org/10.1145/263407.263505

161. Jun Rekimoto. 2002. SmartSkin: an infrastructure for freehand manipulation on interactive surfaces. In *Proceedings of the SIGCHI conference on Human factors in computing systems Changing our world, changing ourselves - CHI '02*. ACM. DOI: http://dx.doi.org/10.1145/503376.503397

162. Jun Rekimoto, Takaaki Ishizawa, Carsten Schwesig, and Haruo Oba. 2003. PreSense: interaction techniques for finger sensing input devices. In *Proceedings of the 16th annual ACM symposium on User interface software and technology - UIST '03*. ACM. DOI: http://dx.doi.org/10.1145/964696.964719

163. Jun Rekimoto and Hua Wang. 2004. Sensing GamePad: electrostatic potential sensing for enhancing entertainment oriented interactions. In *Extended abstracts of the 2004 conference on Human factors and computing systems - CHI '04*. ACM. DOI: http://dx.doi.org/10.1145/985921.986089

164. Christian Rendl, David Kim, Sean Fanello, Patrick Parzer, Christoph Rhemann, Jonathan Taylor, Martin Zirkl, Gregor Scheipl, Thomas Rothländer, Michael Haller, and Shahram Izadi. 2014. FlexSense: A Transparent Self-sensing Deformable Surface. In *Proceedings of the 27th Annual ACM Symposium on User Interface Software and Technology (UIST '14)*. ACM, 129–138. DOI: http://dx.doi.org/10.1145/2642918.2647405

165. Ferran Reverter, Xiujun Li, and Gerard C M Meijer. 2006. Stability and accuracy of active shielding for grounded capacitive sensors. *Measurement Science and Technology* 17, 11 (2006), 2884. http://stacks.iop.org/0957-0233/17/i=11/a=004

166. Wintersberger Riener. 2011. 3D Theremin: A Novel Approach for Convenient Point and Click-Interactions in Vehicles. In *3rd International Conference on Automotive User Interfaces and Interactive Vehicular Applications (AutomotiveUI'11)*. Adjunct proceedings.

167. Simon Rogers, John Williamson, Craig Stewart, and Roderick Murray-Smith. 2010. FingerCloud: uncertainty and autonomy handover incapacitive sensing. In *Proceedings of the 28th international conference on Human factors in computing systems - CHI '10*. ACM. DOI: http://dx.doi.org/10.1145/1753326.1753412

168. Simon Rogers, John Williamson, Craig Stewart, and Roderick Murray-Smith. 2011. AnglePose: robust, precise capacitive touch tracking via 3d orientation estimation. In *Proceedings of the 2011 annual conference on Human factors in computing systems - CHI '11*. ACM. DOI: http://dx.doi.org/10.1145/1978942.1979318

169. Silvia Rus, Tobias Grosse-Puppendahl, and Arjan Kuijper. 2014. *Recognition of Bed Postures Using Mutual Capacitance Sensing*. Springer International Publishing, Cham, 51–66. DOI: http://dx.doi.org/10.1007/978-3-319-14112-1_5

170. Analisa Russo, Bok Yeop Ahn, Jacob J. Adams, Eric B. Duoss, Jennifer T. Bernhard, and Jennifer A. Lewis. 2011. Pen-on-Paper Flexible Electronics. *Advanced Materials* 23, 1 (2011), 3426–3430. DOI: http://dx.doi.org/10.1002/adma.201101328

171. A. P. Sample, D. J. Yeager, and J. R. Smith. 2009. A capacitive touch interface for passive RFID tags. In *2009 IEEE International Conference on RFID*. IEEE. DOI: http://dx.doi.org/10.1109/rfid.2009.4911212

172. T. Scott Saponas, Chris Harrison, and Hrvoje Benko. 2011. PocketTouch: through-fabric capacitive touch input. In *Proceedings of the 24th annual ACM symposium on User interface software and technology - UIST '11*. ACM. DOI: http://dx.doi.org/10.1145/2047196.2047235

173. Munehiko Sato, Ivan Poupyrev, and Chris Harrison. 2012. Touché: enhancing touch interaction on humans, screens, liquids, and everyday objects. In *Proceedings of the 2012 ACM annual conference on Human Factors in Computing Systems - CHI '12*. ACM. DOI: http://dx.doi.org/10.1145/2207676.2207743

174. Valkyrie Savage, Ryan Schmidt, Tovi Grossman, George Fitzmaurice, and Björn Hartmann. 2014. A Series of Tubes: Adding Interactivity to 3D Prints Using Internal Pipes. In *Proceedings of the 27th annual ACM symposium on User interface software and technology - UIST '14*. ACM. DOI: http://dx.doi.org/10.1145/2642918.2647374

175. Valkyrie Savage, Xiaohan Zhang, and Björn Hartmann. 2012. Midas: fabricating custom capacitive touch sensors to prototype interactive objects. In *Proceedings of the 25th annual ACM symposium on User interface software and technology - UIST '12*. ACM. DOI: http://dx.doi.org/10.1145/2380116.2380189

176. Tim C. W. Schenk, Nafiseh Seyed Mazloum, Luc Tan, and Peter Rutten. 2008. Experimental characterization of the body-coupled communications channel. In *2008 IEEE International Symposium on Wireless Communication Systems*. IEEE. DOI: http://dx.doi.org/10.1109/iswcs.2008.4726053

177. Martin Schmitz, Mohammadreza Khalilbeigi, Matthias Balwierz, Roman Lissermann, Max Mühlhäuser, and Jürgen Steimle. 2015. Capricate: A Fabrication Pipeline to Design and 3D Print Capacitive Touch Sensors for Interactive Objects. In *Proceedings of the 28th Annual ACM Symposium on User Interface Software & Technology (UIST '15)*. ACM, 253–258. DOI: http://dx.doi.org/10.1145/2807442.2807503

178. Johannes Schöning, Peter Brandl, Florian Daiber, Florian Echtler, Otmar Hilliges, Jonathan Hook, Markus Löchtefeld, Nima Motamedi, Laurence Muller, Patrick Olivier, Tim Roth, and Ulrich von Zadow. 2008. *Multi-Touch Surfaces: A Technical Guide*. techreport. http://drehscheibe.in.tum.de/forschung/pub/reports/2008/TUM-I0833.pdf.gz

179. D. Sculley, Gary Holt, Daniel Golovin, Eugene Davydov, Todd Phillips, Dietmar Ebner, Vinay Chaudhary, and Michael Young. 2014. Machine Learning: The High Interest Credit Card of Technical Debt. In *SE4ML: Software Engineering for Machine Learning (NIPS 2014 Workshop)*.

180. X. Shang, R.N.J. Veldhuis, A.M. Bazen, and W.P.T. Ganzevoort. 2005. Algorithm design for grip-pattern verification in smart gun. In *Proceedings of ProRISC 2005, 16th Annual Workshop on Circuits, Systems and Signal Processing*. STW Technology Foundation, Utrecht, The Netherlands, 674–678. http://doc.utwente.nl/53692/

181. C. Shemelya, F. Cedillos, E. Aguilera, E. Maestas, J. Ramos, D. Espalin, D. Muse, R. Wicker, and E. MacDonald. 2013. 3D printed capacitive sensors. In *SENSORS, 2013 IEEE*. 1–4. DOI: http://dx.doi.org/10.1109/ICSENS.2013.6688247

182. S. Shigematsu, H. Morimura, Y. Tanabe, T. Adachi, and K. Machida. 1999. A single-chip fingerprint sensor and identifier. *IEEE Journal of Solid-State Circuits* 34, 12 (Dec 1999), 1852–1859. DOI: http://dx.doi.org/10.1109/4.808910

183. M. Shinagawa, M. Fukumoto, K. Ochiai, and H. Kyuragi. 2004. A Near-Field-Sensing Transceiver for Intrabody Communication Based on the Electrooptic Effect. *IEEE Trans. Instrum. Meas.* 53, 6 (dec 2004), 1533–1538. DOI: http://dx.doi.org/10.1109/tim.2004.834064

184. Michael Shorter, Jon Rogers, and John McGhee. 2014. Enhancing Everyday Paper Interactions with Paper Circuits. In *Proceedings of the 2014 Conference on Designing Interactive Systems (DIS '14)*. ACM, 39–42. DOI: http://dx.doi.org/10.1145/2598510.2598584

185. Gurashish Singh, Alexander Nelson, Ryan Robucci, Chintan Patel, and Nilanjan Banerjee. 2015. Inviz: Low-power personalized gesture recognition using wearable textile capacitive sensor arrays. In *2015 IEEE International Conference on Pervasive Computing and Communications (PerCom)*. IEEE. DOI: http://dx.doi.org/10.1109/percom.2015.7146529

186. J. R. Smith. 1995. *Toward Electric Field Tomography*. Master's thesis. MIT.

187. J. R. Smith. 1996. Field mice: Extracting hand geometry from electric field measurements. *IBM Syst. J.* 35, 3.4 (1996), 587–608. DOI: http://dx.doi.org/10.1147/sj.353.0587

188. J. R. Smith. 1999. *Electric Field Imaging*. Ph.D. Dissertation. MIT.

189. J. R. Smith, C. Salthouse, and N. Gershenfeld. 1999. Code-division multiplexing of a sensor channel: a software implementation. *IEEE J. Select. Areas Commun.* 17, 4 (apr 1999), 725–731. DOI: http://dx.doi.org/10.1109/49.761048

190. J. R. Smith, T. White, C. Dodge, J. Paradiso, N. Gershenfeld, and D. Allport. 1998. Electric field sensing for graphical interfaces. *IEEE Comput. Grap. Appl.* 18, 3 (1998), 54–60. DOI: http://dx.doi.org/10.1109/38.674972

191. James R Solberg, Kevin M Lynch, and Malcolm A MacIver. 2008. Active electrolocation for underwater target localization. *The International Journal of Robotics Research* 27, 5 (2008), 529–548.

192. Hyunyoung Song, Hrvoje Benko, Francois Guimbretiere, Shahram Izadi, Xiang Cao, and Ken Hinckley. 2011. Grips and Gestures on a Multi-touch Pen. In *Proceedings of the SIGCHI Conference on Human Factors in Computing Systems (CHI '11)*. ACM, 1323–1332. DOI: http://dx.doi.org/10.1145/1978942.1979138

193. Lingnan Song, Amanda C Myers, Jacob J Adams, and Yong Zhu. 2014. Stretchable and reversibly deformable radio frequency antennas based on silver nanowires. *ACS applied materials & interfaces* 6, 6 (2014), 4248–4253. DOI: http://dx.doi.org/10.1021/am405972e

194. M. Sousa, A. Techmer, A. Steinhage, C. Lauterbach, and P. Lukowicz. 2013. Human tracking and identification using a sensitive floor and wearable accelerometers. In *2013 IEEE International Conference on Pervasive Computing and Communications (PerCom)*. IEEE. DOI: http://dx.doi.org/10.1109/percom.2013.6526728

195. Erich P. Stuntebeck, Shwetak N. Patel, Thomas Robertson, Matthew S. Reynolds, and Gregory D. Abowd. 2008. Wideband Powerline Positioning for Indoor Localization. In *Proceedings of the 10th International Conference on Ubiquitous Computing (UbiComp '08)*. ACM, 94–103. DOI: http://dx.doi.org/10.1145/1409635.1409649

196. Masato Takahashi, Charith Lasantha Fernando, Yuto Kumon, Shuhey Takeda, Hideaki Nii, Takuji Tokiwa, Maki Sugimoto, and Masahiko Inami. 2011. Earthlings Attack!: a ball game using human body communication. In *Proceedings of the 2nd Augmented Human International Conference on - AH '11*. ACM. DOI: http://dx.doi.org/10.1145/1959826.1959843

197. Kiyoaki Takiguchi, Takayuki Wada, and Shigeki Toyama. 2007. Human Body Detection that Uses Electric Field by Walking. *Journal of Advanced Mechanical Design, Systems, and Manufacturing* 1, 3 (2007), 294–305. DOI: http://dx.doi.org/10.1299/jamdsm.1.294

198. Brandon T. Taylor and V Michael Bove. 2008. The bar of soap: a grasp recognition system implemented in a multi-functional handheld device. In *Proceeding of the twenty-sixth annual CHI conference extended abstracts on Human factors in computing systems - CHI '08*. ACM. DOI: http://dx.doi.org/10.1145/1358628.1358874

199. Brandon T. Taylor and V. Michael Bove. 2009. Graspables: grasp-recognition as a user interface. In *Proceedings of the 27th international conference on Human factors in computing systems - CHI 09*. ACM. DOI: http://dx.doi.org/10.1145/1518701.1518842

200. H. N. Teodorescu. 2013. Textile-, conductive paint-based wearable devices for physical activity monitoring. In *E-Health and Bioengineering Conference (EHB), 2013*. 1–4. DOI: http://dx.doi.org/10.1109/EHB.2013.6707241

201. Takahiro Tsujii, Naoya Koizumi, and Takeshi Naemura. 2014. Inkantatory paper: dynamically color-changing prints with multiple functional inks. In *Proceedings of the adjunct publication of the 27th annual ACM symposium on User interface software and technology - UIST'14 Adjunct*. ACM. DOI: http://dx.doi.org/10.1145/2658779.2659103

202. David Tumpold and Armin Satz. 2009. Contactless seat occupation detection system based on electric field sensing. In *2009 35th Annual Conference of IEEE Industrial Electronics*. IEEE. DOI: http://dx.doi.org/10.1109/iecon.2009.5414836

203. Tomas Unander, Hans-Erik Nilsson, and Bengt Oelmann. 2007. Printed touch sensor for interactive packaging and display. In *Polytronic 2007 - 6th International Conference on Polymers and Adhesives in Microelectronics and Photonics*. IEEE. DOI: http://dx.doi.org/10.1109/polytr.2007.4339128

204. Miika Valtonen, Lasse Kaila, Jaakko Mäentausta, and Jukka Vanhala. 2011. Unobtrusive Human Height and Posture Recognition with a Capacitive Sensor. *J. Ambient Intell. Smart Environ.* 3, 4 (Dec. 2011), 305–332. DOI: http://dx.doi.org/10.3233/AIS-2011-0120

205. Miika Valtonen, Jaakko Maentausta, and Jukka Vanhala. 2009. TileTrack: Capacitive human tracking using floor tiles. In *2009 IEEE International Conference on Pervasive Computing and Communications*. IEEE. DOI: http://dx.doi.org/10.1109/percom.2009.4912749

206. Miika Valtonen, Henrik Raula, and Jukka Vanhala. 2010. Human body tracking with electric field ranging. In *Proceedings of the 14th International Academic MindTrek Conference on Envisioning Future Media Environments - MindTrek '10*. ACM. DOI: http://dx.doi.org/10.1145/1930488.1930527

207. Miika Valtonen and Jukka Vanhala. 2009. Human tracking using electric fields. In *2009 IEEE International Conference on Pervasive Computing and Communications*. IEEE. DOI: http://dx.doi.org/10.1109/percom.2009.4912795

208. Katia Vega, Marcio Cunha, and Hugo Fuks. 2015. Hairware: The Conscious Use of Unconscious Auto-contact Behaviors. In *Proceedings of the 20th International Conference on Intelligent User Interfaces - IUI '15*. ACM. DOI: http://dx.doi.org/10.1145/2678025.2701404

209. Ansh Verma, Gabriel Culbertson, and Karthik Ramani. 2014. Chiron: interpreting signals from capacitive patterns and inertial sensors for intuitive shape modeling. In *Proceedings of the extended abstracts of the 32nd annual ACM conference on Human factors in computing systems - CHI EA '14*. ACM. DOI: http://dx.doi.org/10.1145/2559206.2581161

210. Nicolas Villar, Xiang Cao, Billy Chen, Shahram Izadi, Dan Rosenfeld, Hrvoje Benko, John Helmes, Jonathan Westhues, Steve Hodges, Eyal Ofek, and Alex Butler. 2009. Mouse 2.0: multi-touch meets the mouse. In *Proceedings of the 22nd annual ACM symposium on User interface software and technology - UIST '09*. ACM. DOI: http://dx.doi.org/10.1145/1622176.1622184

211. Simon Voelker, Christian Cherek, Jan Thar, Thorsten Karrer, Christian Thoresen, Kjell Ivar Øvergård, and Jan Borchers. 2015. PERCs: Persistently Trackable Tangibles on Capacitive Multi-Touch Displays. In *UIST '15: Proceedings of the 28th Annual ACM Symposium on User Interface Software and Technology (UIST '15)*. ACM, New York, NY, USA, 351–356. DOI: http://dx.doi.org/10.1145/2807442.2807466

212. Simon Voelker, Kosuke Nakajima, Christian Thoresen, Yuichi Itoh, Kjell Ivar Øvergård, and Jan Borchers. 2013. PUCs: detecting transparent, passive untouched capacitive widgets on unmodified multi-touch displays. In *Proceedings of the 2013 ACM international conference on Interactive tabletops and surfaces - ITS '13*. ACM. DOI: http://dx.doi.org/10.1145/2512349.2512791

213. J.M. Vranish and R.L. McConnell. 1992. Driven shielding capacitive proximity sensor. (Nov. 24 1992). US Patent 5,166,679.

214. Tam Vu, Akash Baid, Simon Gao, Marco Gruteser, Richard Howard, Janne Lindqvist, Predrag Spasojevic, and Jeffrey Walling. 2012. Distinguishing users with capacitive touch communication. In *Proceedings of the 18th annual international conference on Mobile computing and networking - Mobicom '12*. ACM. DOI: http://dx.doi.org/10.1145/2348543.2348569

215. Tam Vu and Marco Gruteser. 2013. Personal Touch-Identification Tokens. *IEEE Pervasive Comput.* 12, 2 (apr 2013), 10–13. DOI: http://dx.doi.org/10.1109/mprv.2013.33

216. Y. Wang, C. Yu, L. Du, J. Huang, and Y. Shi. 2014. BodyRC: Exploring Interaction Modalities Using Human Body as Lossy Signal Transmission Medium. In *Ubiquitous Intelligence and Computing (UTC-ATC-ScalCom)*. 260–267. DOI: http://dx.doi.org/10.1109/UIC-ATC-ScalCom.2014.73

217. Martin Weigel, Tong Lu, Gilles Bailly, Antti Oulasvirta, Carmel Majidi, and Jürgen Steimle. 2015. iSkin: Flexible, Stretchable and Visually Customizable On-Body Touch Sensors for Mobile Computing. In *Proceedings of the 33rd Annual ACM Conference on Human Factors in Computing Systems - CHI '15*. ACM. DOI: http://dx.doi.org/10.1145/2702123.2702391

218. Mathias Wilhelm, Daniel Krakowczyk, Frank Trollmann, and Sahin Albayrak. 2015. eRing: multiple finger gesture recognition with one ring using an electric field. In *Proceedings of the 2nd international Workshop on Sensor-based Activity Recognition and Interaction - WOAR '15*. ACM. DOI: http://dx.doi.org/10.1145/2790044.2790047

219. Andrew D. Wilson and Hrvoje Benko. 2010. Combining Multiple Depth Cameras and Projectors for Interactions on, Above and Between Surfaces. In *Proceedings of the 23Nd Annual ACM Symposium on User Interface Software and Technology (UIST '10)*. ACM, 273–282. DOI: http://dx.doi.org/10.1145/1866029.1866073

220. Raphael Wimmer. 2011. *Capacitive Sensors for Whole Body Interaction*. Springer London, London, 121–133. DOI: http://dx.doi.org/10.1007/978-0-85729-433-3_10

221. Raphael Wimmer. 2015. *Grasp-sensitive surfaces: utilizing grasp information for human-computer interaction*. Ph.D. Dissertation. University of Munich. https://edoc.ub.uni-muenchen.de/18095/

222. Raphael Wimmer and Patrick Baudisch. 2011. Modular and Deformable Touch-sensitive Surfaces Based on Time Domain Reflectometry. In *Proceedings of the 24th Annual ACM Symposium on User Interface Software and Technology (UIST '11)*. ACM, 517–526. DOI: http://dx.doi.org/10.1145/2047196.2047264

223. Raphael Wimmer and Sebastian Boring. 2009. HandSense: discriminating different ways of grasping and holding a tangible user interface. In *Proceedings of the 3rd International Conference on Tangible and Embedded Interaction - TEI '09*. ACM. DOI: http://dx.doi.org/10.1145/1517664.1517736

224. Raphael Wimmer, Paul Holleis, Matthias Kranz, and Albrecht Schmidt. 2006. Thracker - Using Capacitive Sensing for Gesture Recognition. In *26th IEEE International Conference on Distributed Computing Systems Workshops (ICDCSW'06)*. IEEE. DOI: http://dx.doi.org/10.1109/icdcsw.2006.109

225. Raphael Wimmer, Matthias Kranz, Sebastian Boring, and Albrecht Schmidt. 2007a. A Capacitive Sensing Toolkit for Pervasive Activity Detection and Recognition. In *Fifth Annual IEEE International Conference on Pervasive Computing and Communications (PerCom'07)*. IEEE. DOI: http://dx.doi.org/10.1109/percom.2007.1

226. Raphael Wimmer, Matthias Kranz, Sebastian Boring, and Albrecht Schmidt. 2007b. CapTable and CapShelf - Unobtrusive Activity Recognition Using Networked Capacitive Sensors. In *2007 Fourth International Conference on Networked Sensing Systems*. IEEE. DOI: http://dx.doi.org/10.1109/inss.2007.4297395

227. Yu Xie, Yinlin Li, Zhonghua Huang, and Zhanzhong Cui. 2009. Preliminary study of rain effect on channel gain of body area communication. In *2009 Joint Conferences on Pervasive Computing (JCPC)*. IEEE. DOI: http://dx.doi.org/10.1109/jcpc.2009.5420102

228. Ruoyu Xu, Wai Chiu Ng, Hongjie Zhu, Hengying Shan, and Jie Yuan. 2012. Equation Environment Coupling and Interference on the Electric-Field Intrabody Communication Channel. *IEEE Transactions on Biomedical Engineering* 59, 7 (jul 2012), 2051–2059. DOI: http://dx.doi.org/10.1109/tbme.2012.2197212

229. Dongwook Yoon, Ken Hinckley, Hrvoje Benko, François Guimbretière, Pourang Irani, Michel Pahud, and Marcel Gavriliu. 2015. Sensing Tablet Grasp + Micro-mobility for Active Reading. In *Proceedings of the 28th Annual ACM Symposium on User Interface Software & Technology - UIST '15*. ACM. DOI: http://dx.doi.org/10.1145/2807442.2807510

230. Neng-Hao Yu, Li-Wei Chan, Lung-Pan Cheng, Mike Y. Chen, and Yi-Ping Hung. 2010. Enabling tangible interaction on capacitive touch panels. In *Adjunct proceedings of the 23nd annual ACM symposium on User interface software and technology - UIST '10*. ACM. DOI: http://dx.doi.org/10.1145/1866218.1866269

231. Yang Zhang, Junhan Zhou, Gierad Laput, and Chris Harrison. 2016. SkinTrack: Using the Body As an Electrical Waveguide for Continuous Finger Tracking on the Skin. In *Proceedings of the 2016 CHI Conference on Human Factors in Computing Systems (CHI '16)*. ACM, 1491–1503. DOI: http://dx.doi.org/10.1145/2858036.2858082

232. Enhao Zheng, Baojun Chen, Qining Wang, Kunlin Wei, and Long Wang. 2012. A wearable capacitive sensing system with phase-dependent classifier for locomotion mode recognition. In *2012 4th IEEE RAS & EMBS International Conference on Biomedical Robotics and Biomechatronics (BioRob)*. IEEE. DOI: http://dx.doi.org/10.1109/biorob.2012.6290721

233. W. Zheng and Z. Cui. 2011. Determination of velocity and direction of human body motion based on electrostatic measurement. In *Consumer Electronics, Communications and Networks (CECNet), 2011 International Conference on*. 4035–4039. DOI: http://dx.doi.org/10.1109/CECNET.2011.5769004

234. Junhan Zhou, Yang Zhang, Gierad Laput, and Chris Harrison. 2016. AuraSense: Enabling Expressive Around-Smartwatch Interactions with Electric Field Sensing. In *Proceedings of the 29th Annual ACM Symposium on User Interface Software & Technology (UIST '16)*. ACM. DOI: http://dx.doi.org/10.1145/2984511.2984568

235. Thomas G. Zimmerman. 1996. Personal Area Networks: Near-field intrabody communication. *IBM Syst. J.* 35, 3.4 (1996), 609–617. DOI: http://dx.doi.org/10.1147/sj.353.0609

236. Thomas G. Zimmerman, Joshua R. Smith, Joseph A. Paradiso, David Allport, and Neil Gershenfeld. 1995. Applying Electric Field Sensing to Human-computer Interfaces. In *Proceedings of the SIGCHI Conference on Human Factors in Computing Systems (CHI '95)*. ACM Press/Addison-Wesley Publishing Co., 280–287. DOI: http://dx.doi.org/10.1145/223904.223940

bioSync: A Paired Wearable Device for Blending Kinesthetic Experience

Jun Nishida
Artificial Intelligence Laboratory
University of Tsukuba, Japan/JSPS
jun.nishida@acm.org

Kenji Suzuki
Artificial Intelligence Laboratory
University of Tsukuba, Japan/JST
kenji@ieee.org

ABSTRACT
We present a novel, paired, wearable system for combining the kinesthetic experiences of two persons. These devices allow users to sense and combine muscle contraction and joint rigidity bi-directionally. This is achieved through kinesthetic channels based on electromyogram (EMG) measurement and electrical muscle stimulation (EMS). We developed a pair of wearable kinesthetic input-output (I/O) devices called bioSync that uses specially designed electrodes to perform biosignal measurement and stimulation simultaneously on the same electrodes.

In a user study, participants successfully evaluated the strength of their partners' muscle contractions while exerting their own muscles. We confirmed that the pair of devices could help participants synchronize their hand movements through tapping, without visual and auditory feedback. The proposed interpersonal kinesthetic communication system can be used to enhance interactions such as clinical gait rehabilitation and sports training, and facilitate sharing of physical experiences with Parkinson's patients, thereby enhancing understanding of the physical challenges they face in daily life.

ACM Classification Keywords
H.5.2 User Interfaces: Haptic I/O, Interaction Styles

Author Keywords
Blending Kinesthetic Experience; Electrical Muscle Stimulation; Electromyogram Signals; Rehabilitation

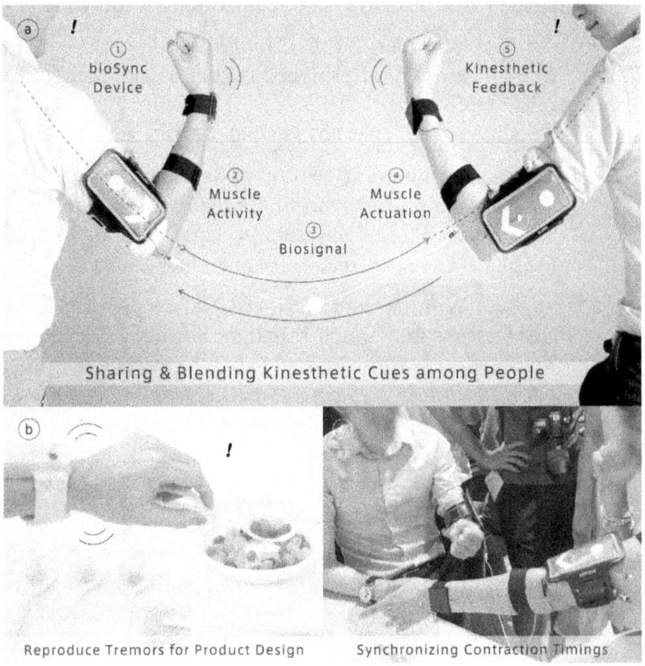

Figure 1. (a) Synchronizing and combining muscle activities among people (b) Reproducing kinesthetic experience of Parkinson's impairment for use in supporting product design (c) Participants express surprise when the muscle activity is jacked in by the demonstrator

INTRODUCTION
Perceiving one's own muscle activity is important to understanding one's physical actions. There are several situations in which it would be beneficial to be able to perceive another person's muscle activity and share their kinesthetic experience. Examples of such situations are interactions between sports players and coaches during physical training and interactions between physical therapists and patients with neuromuscular disorders, such as Parkinson's disease during their rehabilitation. However, it is difficult for one person to perceive another person's muscle activity, and a suitable interface for perceiving and transmitting kinesthetic experience accurately in real time has not been developed yet.

In this paper, we propose a system for blended kinesthetic interaction between two persons using wearable kinesthetic input-output (I/O) devices. The system, called bioSync, is illustrated in Fig. 1(a). In developing this system, we attempted to achieve both perception and expression of bodily motions and muscle activity. Using this system, which consists primarily of a pair of devices worn by the two users, muscle contractions of one user are detected by means of electromyogram (EMG) measurement and are reproduced, by means of electrical muscle stimulation (EMS), as muscle contractions of the other user, and vice versa. We have explored the possibilities of kinesthetic synchronization and implemented very early prototypes that used five independent electrodes for the

Permission to make digital or hard copies of all or part of this work for personal or classroom use is granted without fee provided that copies are not made or distributed for profit or commercial advantage and that copies bear this notice and the full citation on the first page. Copyrights for components of this work owned by others than ACM must be honored. Abstracting with credit is permitted. To copy otherwise, or republish, to post on servers or to redistribute to lists, requires prior specific permission and/or a fee. Request permissions from permissions@acm.org.
CHI 2017, May 6-11, 2017, Denver, CO, USA.
Copyright © 2017 ACM ISBN 978-1-4503-4655-9/17/05 ...$15.00.
http://dx.doi.org/10.1145/3025453.3025829

measurement and stimulation [1, 2, 3]. We hypothesized that combining the muscle activities between users in real time with the spatial consistency of muscle exertion and output presentation and with the consistency of sensation modality would provide an intuitive and easy-to-learn means of understanding both muscle activities and bodily motion.

Contribution

- Modeling of the blending of kinesthetic interaction between two persons based on EMG measurement and EMS
- Implementation of bioSync devices with the same electrodes used for EMG measurement and EMS to achieve kinesthetic I/O at 100 Hz via wireless communication
- Development of a method for muscular stimulation with dynamic adjustment over a wide frequency range
- Assessment of the interaction and the system by means of a user study in which kinesthetic I/O with low communication latency (approx. 20 ms) allowed synchronization of rhythmic muscle contraction without visual and auditory feedback

The main contribution of this paper is the presentation of a novel style of interpersonal kinesthetic communication called blended kinesthetic interaction. A key property of the blended kinesthetic interaction is that the kinesthetic feedback can be both shared and merged in that the wearers are able to simultaneously perceive the strength of voluntary contractions produced by the wearers and involuntary contractions produced by stimulation. The bioSync devices developed in this study are kinesthetic I/O devices that can estimate and interrupt a wearer's muscle activity at the same time. The devices are wearable and easy to attach to a wearer's body. We validate this concept by conducting a rhythmic synchronization experiment and demonstrating the reproduction of disease experience using bioSync devices.

RELATED WORK

Many studies on the transmission and sharing of users' sensations or skills have been conducted in field of computer-supported cooperative work.

Perspective Sharing

One effective way to convey a person's physical interactions and presence in an immersive manner is by transferring, exchanging, or blending their first-person views (FPVs) while presenting them on a head-mounted display (HMD). For instance, a wearable vision system that transfers a 360° FPV to a remote viewer has been developed to assist in remote collaboration between two people [4]. Another study reported that showing multiple FPVs in parallel on a HMD allowed people to complement and enhance each other's memories and decisions in executing a drawing task [5]. Such techniques have also been used to transfer motor performance between a teacher and a learner [6, 7]. In an user study on motion synchronization between an expert and a beginner performing juggling actions, the mixing ratio of their FPVs was found to indicate the type of motion skill to be transmitted. For example, exchanging views was found to be useful for synchronizing motion velocity, whereas blending views was useful for synchronizing the positions of limbs.

These studies have shown that perspective sharing enables the transmission of a person's bodily motions and skills to another in an immersive manner. However, it is difficult to share muscle activity since it is hard to observe it visually. We incorporate the findings on the importance of blending ratio in our kinesthetic interaction model by using a blended perceptual function f and blended stimulus function p, which are illustrated in Fig. 2.

Haptic and Kinetic Sharing

A number of devices have been developed that convey one's haptic or kinetic performance to another person for enriching mediated communication by amplifying another person's social presence. inTouch [8] allows separated users to feel virtual sensations of a shared object through somatosensory interactions by using connected mechanical rollers. Similarly, a paired shape-shifting stick [9] was proposed that allows users to feel the movements and presence of a performer by mimicking the remote user's stick movements. Another study demonstrated the ability of haptic devices to convey several emotions, including anger, disgust, fear, and joy, using handshaking actions [10]. Sharing video and haptic, or video and physical interaction with a remote user also enhances the feelings of being close to another person [11, 12]. As previous research shows, interpersonal haptic communication makes it possible to enhance not only task performance but also remote users' sensations of presence, reality of existence, and users' ratings of trust and togetherness [13]. In this study, we propose a novel style of interpersonal kinesthetic communication that permits people to perceive other people's muscle activities. We consider these the social and psychological aspects of the haptic feedback provided by this system by means of user studies and demonstrations.

Kinesthetic Representation

Some wearable devices have been developed for identifying and representing muscle activity in medical applications. Conventional desktop-type electromyography is capable of displaying muscle activity in the form of waveforms on a monitor. This provides accurate and quantitative kinesthetic information but requires frequent sight-line movement between the monitor and the measurement point. To resolve mismatches in the spatial consistency between the presentation point and the measurement point, a wearable, light-emitting suit for sensing contraction strength using light fibers [14], and a wearable audio device that converts contraction strength into acoustic waves [15, 16] have been proposed. Research with these devices has shown that identifying and sharing kinesthetic experience with therapists assists in medical rehabilitation and sports training. However, in these visual and acoustic systems, the presentation area is limited to the user's field of vision, and the amount of information provided is limited to that from a single muscle tissue when the feedback is acoustic in nature. Furthermore, the substitution among different types of sensation modalities requires adequate prior learning procedures.

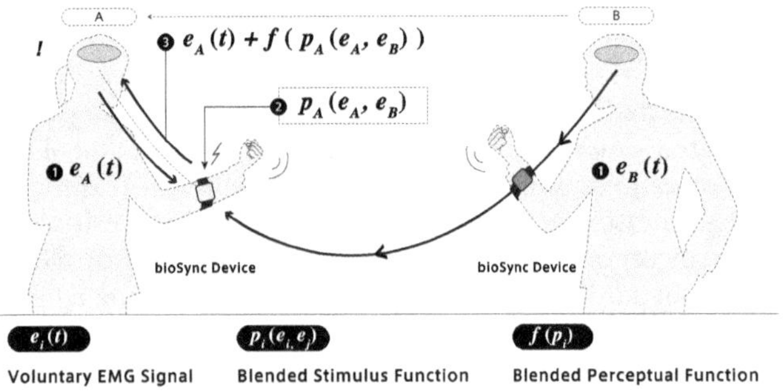

Figure 2. Model of Blended Kinesthetic Interaction

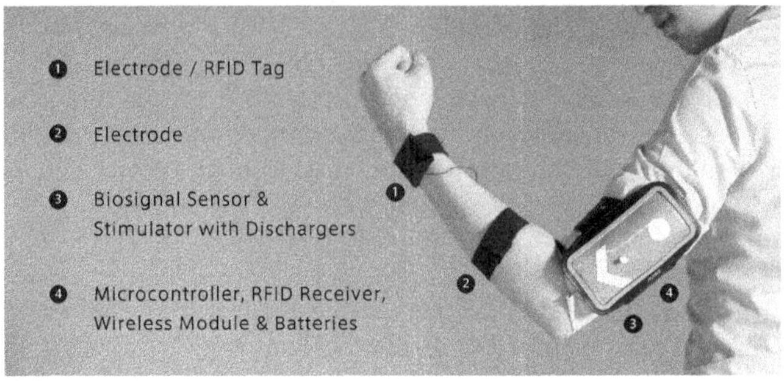

Figure 3. Overview of the developed device, bioSync

EMS Interfaces

The direct approach to presenting kinesthetic information to a body is through EMS in which muscles are actuated involuntarily through electrodes on the skin. This technique was developed for use in bio-feedback therapy [17], and has recently been used in the HCI field such as Pose-IO [18] by Lopes et al. and PossessedHand by Tamaki et al. [19]. The Pose-IO system makes use of the fact that users are able to estimate the wrist angle posed by EMS without visual feedback. They demonstrated that users could perceive the playback time of a movie through their wrist angles, and control it using hand gestures. EMS systems have the unique characteristic of being able to induce and trigger bodily motions that involve strong motion memories after stimulus, without using any actuators. This allows body actuation systems to be configured in wearable dimensions. This concept has also been used in perceiving affordance for manipulating tools and objects [20]. Wearable EMS systems are also used to generate haptic feedback from virtual reality environments to users for enriching visual feedback [21, 22]. In this manner, EMS techniques have been used for achieving communication between a user and objects or a virtual world.

BLENDING KINESTHETIC EXPERIENCE

In this study, we aim to assist mutual understanding of one's bodily activity with multiple persons, such as muscle contraction and joint rigidity, which are difficult to observe visually. To achieve this, we propose a blended kinesthetic interaction that allows the following operations: 1) Sharing (=): Synchronizes two persons' muscle activities including not only contraction strengths but also the contraction timings, 2) Subtraction (-): Perceives their difference in persons' muscle contraction strengths, and 3) Addition (+): Assists in adjusting a person's contractions by adding the other person's contraction strength. These blending operations are accomplished using a muscle I/O technique. In contrast to previously developed approaches to sharing haptic sensation [8, 9], the system developed in this study focuses not on an individual user's specific interactions with a physical interface but rather with the kinesthetic activities associated with a wide variety of interactions between two people in several situations. In previous EMS studies [18, 20], accelerators or motion capture systems were used to acquire wearer's hand gestures. The device developed in this study measures biosignals related to muscle activity, making it possible to estimate bodily activities even though the user does not move any limbs but just contracts muscles. These advantages allow physical therapists or sports instructors to understand a patient's or learner's invisible but voluntary intentions concerning bodily motions in an easy and intuitive manner through a somatosensory channel. In this paper, we discuss the validity of the interaction and feasibility of possible scenarios through its modeling, implementation, performance evaluation, and user studies.

Interaction Modeling

Figure 2 illustrates the proposed model for an interaction involving users A and B. A situation in which user A receives kinesthetic information from user B (one-way communication) is illustrated. $e_i(t), p_i(e_i, e_j)$, and $f(p_i)$ represent the wearer i's voluntary EMG signal at time t, the stimulation pulse based on the EMG signals of wearer i and the partner j, and the kinesthetic blending function, respectively. Each user's muscle contractions are detected by an EMG sensor and conveyed to the bioSync device worn by the other user via a wireless module. Each user's voluntary contractions are reproduced as the other user's muscle exertions by means of EMS. Since the stimulation and measurement are achieved at the same position, modality, and time, users are able to understand each other's activities without depending on visual observation. The interaction sequence is as follows:

1) Voluntary actions: Both users A and B perform their voluntary muscle activities. These activities $e_A(t), e_B(t)$ are estimated from measurement of surface EMG signals by the bioSync devices worn by the two users. **2) Muscle actuation**: The users' muscles are stimulated based on the blending pulse function $p_i(e_A, e_B)$, which is described by using stimulus frequency (1/T)[Hz] and pulse width $D(t)$[us] at time t as shown in Eq.(1). The stimulus frequency (1/T [Hz]) ranges from 1Hz to 100Hz while measuring e_i (Eq.(2)), and the pulse width $D(t)$ is defined by using the weighting factor $a_{i,j}$, contraction strength $e_{i,j}$, time constant $\tau_{i,j}$ of the wearer i and j, and activation function g (Eq.(3)). We used a simple step function as the activation function g with threshold θ when we conducted rhythmic action synchronization experiment. For the demonstration, we adapted another function that presents the subtraction between two users' contraction strengths.

$$p_i(e_i, e_j) = u(T, D(t)) \quad (1)$$

$$T : 1Hz < 1/T < 100Hz \quad (2)$$

$$D(t) = g(a_i e_i(t - \tau_i) + a_j e_j(t - \tau_j))[us] \quad (3)$$

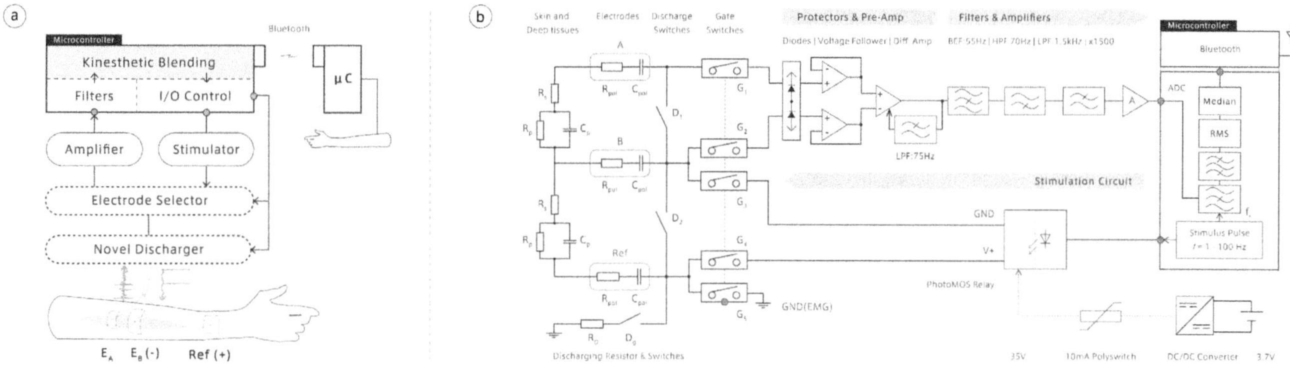

Figure 4. (a) System Architecture (b) Process Diagram

and **3) Blended feedback**: The perceived kinesthetic feedback is represented as $e_A(t) + f(p_i(e_A, e_B))$. The function f is a perceptual function that represents the blended kinesthetic feedback of a user's voluntary and involuntary movement. We investigated the behavior of the perceived function f experimentally and verified that it is a linear function.

Interaction Properties and Benefits

The proposed interaction has the following characteristics and benefits: 1) **Spatial consistency**; In the bioSync device, the stimulus circuit and biosignal measurement circuit share specially designed electrodes. The electrode matches the spatial relations of the input and output. In addition to this, the electrode positions of the two users are the same. We assume spatial consistency to simplify user interaction learning. 2) **Sensory consistency**; As the user's muscle actuation and the device's EMS presentation are performed in the same modality, kinesthesia provides a more intuitive understanding and easier perception of motion sensation, compared to sensory substitution methods, in that minimal prior learning is required. The reason for adopting EMS is that it induces strong motion memories, which assist in self-learning after training. and 3) **Temporal consistency with interactivity**; The musculoskeletal systems of the users are synchronized while they share the same time and space. This allows the device to be used to teach and be taught the contraction timings between users.

bioSync: A Paired Kinesthetic I/O Device

To achieve the proposed interpersonal kinesthetic communication in an actual environment, we developed a pair of wearable kinesthetic I/O devices, called bioSync (Fig. 3). Each bioSync device is equipped with a custom designed electrode system that performs EMG measurement and EMS simultaneously. Each bioSync is also equipped with a wireless communication module and a radio-frequency identification (RFID) tag, which is used to detect and pair with other bioSync devices by touching the wearer's wrist to the partner's bioSync device.

METHODOLOGY AND CONFIGURATION

Figure 4(a) shows the system architecture for the proposed system. It consists of electrodes, a stimulation circuit, an EMG measuring circuit, a microprocessor, and a Bluetooth module to communicate with other bioSync devices.

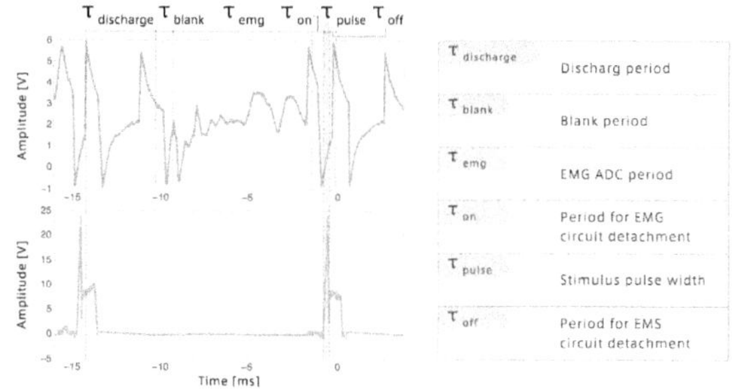

Figure 5. Timing Chart of Measurement, Stimulation and Discharge

EMG Measurement During Stimulation

Figure 4(b) illustrates the processing diagram of the developed device. In order to achieve fast and simultaneous measurement and stimulation operations using common electrodes, a gate switching mechanism and a mechanism for discharging residual potential (the body retains a net charge following the stimulus) are required. The former is designed for protecting the measurement circuit from the stimulus voltage, and the latter is used for modifying the connection path of the electrodes. Hence, the system includes three electrodes (A, B, Ref), discharge switches (D_i), and gate switches (G_i) along with an EMG measurement circuit and a stimulation circuit. Each switch is activated based on an operation timings as shown in Fig. 5. The period of discharging, blank, EMG acquisition, EMG circuit detachment, stimulus pulse width, and EMS circuit attachment are defined as $\tau_{discharge}$, τ_{blank}, τ_{emg}, τ_{on}, τ_{pulse}, and τ_{off}, respectively. The stimulation cycle can be adjusted from 1 to 100Hz, and stimulus pulse width can be adjusted from 0 to 800us. The process sequence is as follows: 1) the electrodes are connected to the input ports of the measurement circuit by the gate switches $(G_{1,2,5})$. The measurement starts after τ_{blank}[ms] which is required for stabilizing the waveform; 2) after the measurement (τ_{emg}[ms]), the electrodes are detached from the measurement circuit and connected to the stimulation circuit by the gate switches $(G_{3,4})$ after τ_{on}[ms]; 3) when the stimulus (τ_{pulse}[us]) ends, the electrodes are detached again and wait for τ_{off}[ms]. Finally, the discharging switches $(D_{1,2,g})$ are activated for $\tau_{discharge}$[ms]. This type of simultaneous operation, using a fewer number of electrodes, allows to reduce the size of the device and facilitates the configuration of the electrodes array. The timings τ_i

and resistor R_D values for a stimulus frequency of 40Hz are; $\tau_{discharge} = 7ms, \tau_{blank} = 3ms, \tau_{emg} = 10ms, \tau_{on} = 2ms, \tau_{off} = 2ms, \tau_{pulse} = 0us - 800us, R_D = 180k\Omega$.

A conventional discharging method is to short each electrode after stimulus in order to discharge the naturally existing capacitors of the body (C_p, C_{pol}) [17]. In the proposed method, a ground (0V) voltage connection following the electrode shorts is established using the discharge switch, D_g. In addition to this, a discharging register R_D is inserted between the electrodes and the ground for consuming the residual voltage, resulting in a reduction in the overshoot noise in the EMG signal. This mechanism helps in discharging of the residual potential, and stabilizing the measurements after the stimulus. We also propose a method that permits dynamic adjustment of the stimulus frequency. The stimulation cycle can be adjusted from 1Hz to 100Hz, thereby enabling dynamic adaption to various skin conditions and purposes, compared to related devices [23].

EMG Measurement

A diagram of the EMG measurement system is also shown in Fig. 4(b). The system consists of two electrodes, one reference electrode, single-pole-dual-throw analog switches (AQV252, Panasonic, Inc.) that function as a protection gate to protect the measuring circuit from stimulation pulses, a voltage follower for impedance adjustment, a differential amplifier, a Twin-T-type RC notch filter (f_c = 55Hz) to cut out AC noise, a second-order RC low pass filter (f_c = 1kHz) to remove high-frequency noise, an inverting amplifier, and a voltage limiter to protect the microprocessor (Atmel, Inc., ATmega 32U4). While the system is acquiring EMG signals, the input ports of the voltage follower are connected to the electrodes. During the period of stimulation, the input ports are grounded in order to stabilize the signal wave. Fig. 7 shows the implementation of the device.

High-order digital filters are used to cut out AC noise and pulse noise which comes from the EMS. We use bi-quad filter systems that are computationally inexpensive and easy to implement on a microcontroller. A third-order notch filter is used for reducing pulse noise from EMS. The cut-out frequency(f_c) is dynamically set to the stimulation frequency. A second-order low-pass filter is used for eliminating frequencies other than the EMG frequencies (60Hz to 1kHz). The root mean square (RMS) of 20 measured samples is calculated to estimate the muscular tension. Finally, to screen out pulse noise caused by artifacts or outliers, the median of five RMS samples is calculated and sent to the other bioSync device.

Electrode Configuration

Figure 8 illustrates the electrode placement and configuration. We used three electrode pads, A, B, and Ref of sizes 30mm × 40mm, 20mm × 40mm, and 40mm × 40mm, respectively. We set the distance between electrodes A and B to 20mm to avoid a strong effect on the measurement electrode A from the stimulus electrode B. PMMA gel pads (HV-DOUSI-310, OMRON, Inc.) were used. A pulse amplitude of 35V is generated by a DC/DC converter (INA226, Texas Instruments, Inc.) using a 3.7V Li-Po battery.

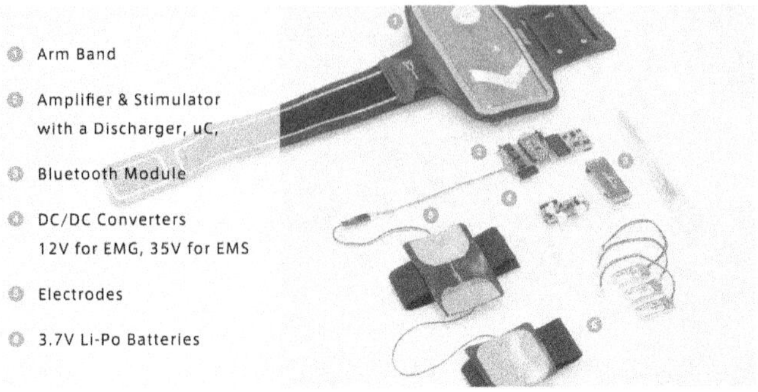

Figure 6. System Configuration

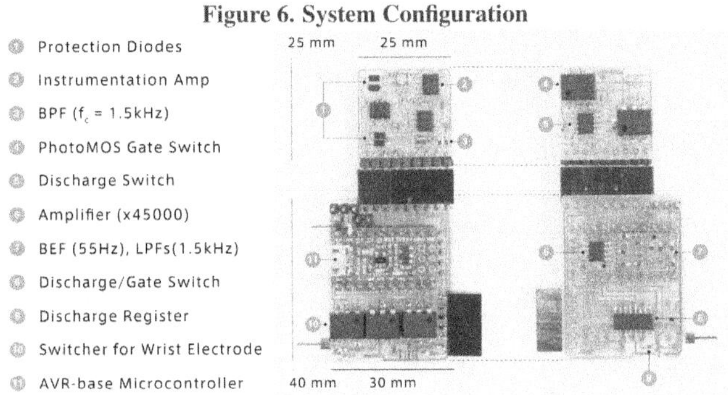

Figure 7. Device Implementation

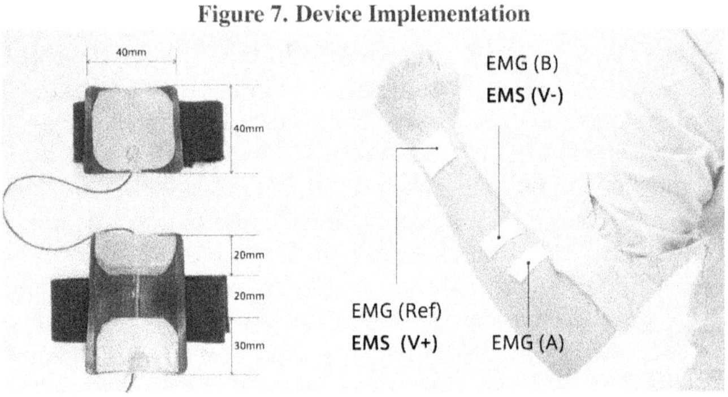

Figure 8. Electrodes Placement

RFID-based Connection

To enable users of the bioSync devices to interact intuitively with each other, an RFID tag (ISO 14443A standard tag) is embedded in the wrist electrode of each device, and an RFID receiver (NXP Semiconductors, Inc., MFRC552) is encased in the arm band. The bioSync devices can be paired by one user touching a user's wrist to the other user's arm band.

PERFORMANCE EVALUATION

1. System Latency

We evaluated the communication latency of the devices using a wireless configuration for verifying that the devices were suitable for use for bi-directional haptic communication.

Task and Apparatus

Signal triggers are generated when a bioSync measures a biosignal and the other bioSync device produces a stimulus signal. We measured the triggers from both devices by using an oscilloscope (Agilent Technologies, Inc., MSO-X3034A) and defined the temporal difference between them as the latency.

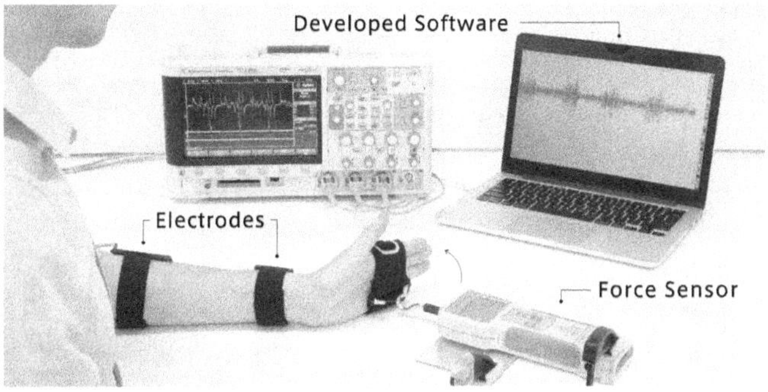

Figure 9. Experiment Setup: Performance Measurement

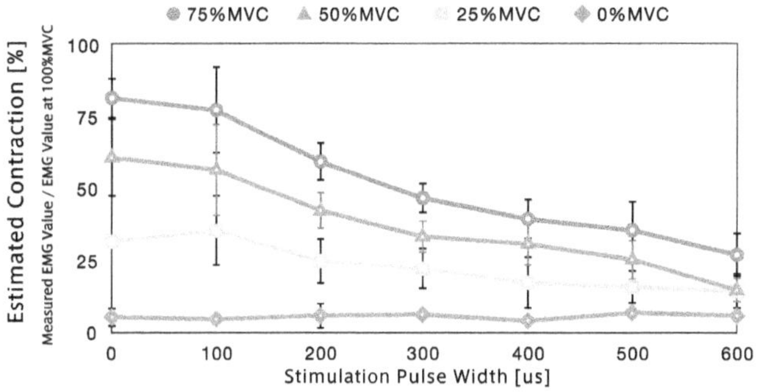

Figure 10. Experiment Result: Performance Measurement

The Bluetooth modules were paired before the start of the experiment and were placed 40cm apart, with no obstacle in their communication path. The switching (stimulus) frequency f_s was set to 40Hz in order to achieve the most intense muscle contraction in this particular subject (25-year-old male). We conducted 25 trials in this evaluation.

Results

The average latency was 20.9ms (SD=5.6ms). The device performed a loop program consists of the measurement with discharging, a filtering process, UART output and reading via the Bluetooth module, and stimulation. Thus, the maximum latency depends on the stimulation frequency. In this experiment, the frequency was 40Hz, and the theoretical maximum latency was 25ms. This is almost the same as the average measured latency. In the bioSync device, the stimulus frequency can be adjusted from 1Hz to 100Hz. Muscle actuation is usually achieved when the stimulus frequency is higher than 20Hz. We therefore set 20Hz as the minimum stimulus frequency.

2. Performance Measurement

We next evaluated the biosignal measurement performance under various stimulus conditions for understanding the electrical characteristics of the I/O circuit. EMG signals can be affected by the stimulus signals even if the discharging time $\tau_{discharge}$ is fixed. By investigating the relation between the applied pulse strength and the measured contraction strength, we were able to identify the appropriate software compensation for the electrical characteristics.

Task and Apparatus

Figure 9 illustrates the experimental setup. Each participant wears a bioSync device, and pulls the tip of the digital force sensor (IMADA, Inc., ZP-1000N) using the cuff, by extending the wrist. Before the experiment is started, each participant's 100% maximum voluntary contraction (MVC) is measured using the force sensor and the developed EMG recording software. Then each participant is asked to reproduce his 75%MVC[N], 50%MVC[N], 25%MVC[N] and 0%MVC[N], while stimulus with durations in the range of 0 to 600 us (in increments of 100 us) were applied. The measured EMG signals were converted to percentages of the EMG value at 100%MVC. The participants were able to see a display of the force sensor to check the accuracy of each percentage of the MVC. The electrodes were placed on the extensor digitorum muscle.

Participants

Five healthy subjects from our local organization participated in a total of 420 trials (5 participants × 7 stimulus strengths × 4 levels of %MVC strengths × 3 repetitions). The trials required approximately 20 minutes per participant.

Results

Figure 10 illustrates the measured contraction percentage and applied stimulus width results. As the stimulus pulse width increased, the measured contraction decreased almost linearly.

USER STUDY

3. Subjective Perceptual Experiment

In this experiment, we investigated how bioSync users recognized their partners' contraction strength, as reproduced by the stimulation, while the users were contracting their own muscles simultaneously. The results were used to identify the blended perceptual function f illustrated in Fig. 2.

Task and Apparatus

The participants evaluated and reported the applied stimulus level on a five-point scale while they contracted their own muscles at 50%MVC, 25%MVC, and 0%MVC. The bioSync device, the force sensor, and the cuff were used in the same manner as the previous experiment, but this time the participants were only able to look at the display of the force sensor only before the start of each session. In addition, to eliminate the influence of visual feedback, they were not allowed to look at their arms during the session. The 100%MVC was measured before the start of the experiment, in the same manner as in the previous performance experiment.

Participants

Five healthy participants from our local organization participated in a total of 375 trials (5 participants × 5 stimulus strengths × 3 type of %MVC strength × 5 repetitions; 2 female, mean age = 24.6 years, SD=1.85 years). Two out of five participants had experienced EMS before. The trials require approximately 20 minutes per participant.

Results

Figure 11(a) illustrates the results for the perceived strength. The results confirm that the users were able to recognize both their voluntary contractions and reproduced muscle contractions at the same time on a five-point scale. The perceived

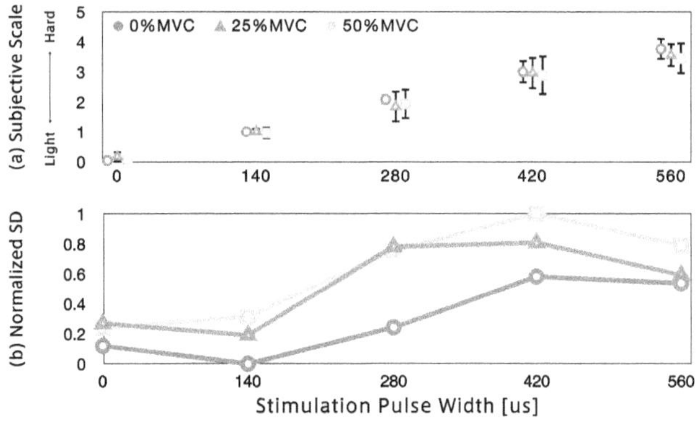

Figure 11. Experiment Result: Subjective Perceptual Evaluation

strength can be approximated linearly. Fig. 11(b) illustrates the normalized standard deviation of each pulse width. As the stimulus strength increased, the standard deviation increased.

4. Rhythmic Activity Synchronization

We also conducted a series of tests to verify that the interpersonal communication via the kinesthetic channel could support the synchronization of two persons' rhythmic muscle contraction timing. The results were used to assess whether the bioSync device could be employed in practical scenarios, such as clinical gait rehabilitation and sports training, in which the synchronization of timing plays an important role.

Task and Apparatus

Figure 12 illustrates the experimental setup. Each participant and the experimenter participated in a follower-experimenter and experimenter-follower session twice. The experimenter was a colleague (25 years old), who participated in the entire experiment (24 trials).

Initially, both the experimenter and the participant performed rhythmic wrist actions according to their own frequencies. After 3-4 seconds, the bioSync devices were activated, and then kinesthetic cues were exchanged between these two persons. Once the participant recognized that the rhythmic action was synchronized with the master side, time measurement was commenced using a stopwatch to record the sync time reported by the participant.

A partition was placed between the demonstrator and the participant so that the participant and the demonstrator could not recognize the partner's contraction timings. The wrist angles and periods of the rhythmic action were calculated from the measured marker positions (OptiTrack Inc., V100:R2). The thresholds were adjusted before the experiments were started. In this experiment, to simplify the exchanging signals, we configured weighting factors a as $a_i = 0$, $a_j = 1$. Hence, the wearer i's stimulus function p_i was a stepping function using threshold θ as shown in Eq.(4).

$$D(t) = \begin{cases} 600us & (e_j(t) > \theta) \\ 0us & (otherwise) \end{cases} \quad (4)$$

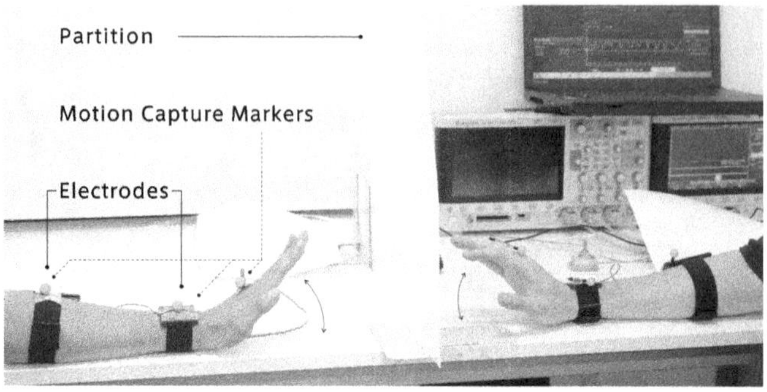

Figure 12. Experiment Setup: Rhythmic Activity Synchronization

Participants

Six healthy participants from our local organization participated in a total of 24 trials (6 participants × 2 follower-experimenter sessions × 2 experimenter-follower sessions). The trials required approximately 35 minutes per participant.

Results

Figure 13 presents the measured sync time and sync time reported by the participant (the participants followed the experimenter's timing). The average measured sync time was 8.1s (SD=3.91s), and the average reported sync time was 13.8s (SD=3.94s). In all cases, the measured sync time was shorter than the reported sync time. Note that Subject 1 required more time to synchronize with the experimenter than the other subjects did. After the experiment, Subject 1 stated that the contractions reproduced by the stimulus were strong and that his voluntary contractions were interrupted excessively, resulting in his having difficulty in controlling his voluntary movements. Figure 14 shows the time-series graph of the rhythmic action period for Subject 2 and the experimenter. After the sync started, the follower immediately changed his rhythm to that of the experimenter and tried to maintain the same period.

5. Embodied Impairment Experience

Using the bioSync devices, it is possible to not only blend users' kinesthetic experiences but also simulate Parkinson's motor impairments by providing stimulus in the frequency range of 8Hz to 15Hz. We employed this capability to gain insight into the bodily movements of Parkinson's sufferers during the activities in daily life (ADL). As described in the applications section, simulating and/or transferring physiological tremors from patients to healthy people, including designers and caregivers, could assist in product design procedures and their understanding of the disease. In this pilot study, we simulated Parkinson's tremors in participants to investigate the similarity of the simulated tremors with actual tremors and the feasibility of using the bioSync device to observe users' tremor behaviors.

Task and Apparatus

Figure 15(a) illustrates the experimental setup for the tremor evaluation. One participant wore a bioSync while holding a spoon. A three-axis accelerometer was placed on the tip of the index finger, as shown in Fig. 15(b). In the observation

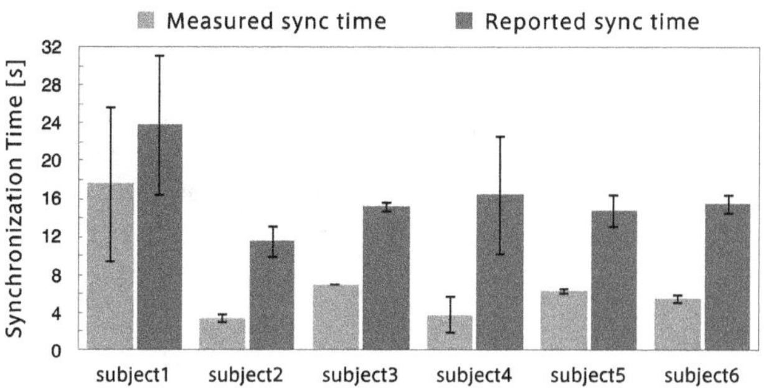

Figure 13. Experiment Result: Rhythmic Activity Synchronization

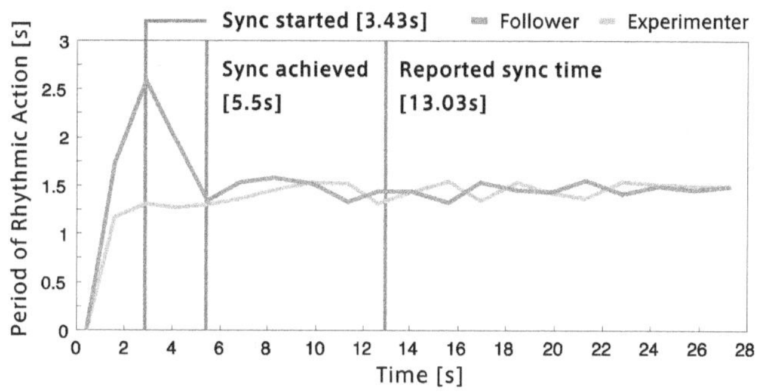

Figure 14. Experiment Result: Rhythmic Activity Synchronization. Subject 2 successfully followed the experimenter's rhythm.

experiment, demo visitors tried to scoop up gummy candies by using various types of spoons, as shown in Fig. 16(b), while undergoing the reproduced action of physiological hand tremors. We then asked the visitors to choose the spoon type best suited to the task, and collected feedback comment about the experience. The spoon types used in the experiment are described next. The (b-1) sample is a spoon that is available in the market. The dimensions are 33mm × 50mm × 8mm (depth). The (b-2) spoon has an additional 5 mm of depth. The (b-3) spoon has a bend added to the b-1 form to make it easier to keep food inside. The (b-4) spoon has a curved handle added to the b-3 spoon to make it easier to pick up.

Participants

One healthy participant (25 years old) participated in the preliminary evaluation. The other participants consisted of more than 100 visitors whose age ranged from 20 to 60 years.

Results

Figure 15(b) illustrates the measured fingertip accelerations. Frequencies in the range of 3Hz to 20 Hz were measured. This frequency range is almost the same as that of actual Parkinson's tremors, as described in related study [27].

All of the visitors agreed that the b-4 spoon shown in Fig. 16, which had a handle and a bend, was the most useful spoon and the easiest to maintain in a stable grasp. Most of the visitors reported that it was somewhat difficult to hold the candies inside the b-1 spoon because the depth was not sufficient to keep the candies inside with shaking hands. In addition, some participants dropped the b-1 spoon as shown in Fig. 16(a)-1,2. Some visitors reported that the b-2 spoon was easy to use to hold candies while subjected to tremors because of its greater depth; however, they found it slightly difficult to place all of the scooped candies into their mouths because of the depth. The b-3 spoon was described by some as being a usable spoon; however, the visitors commented on not only the ease of using the spoon to scoop up candies but also the ease of picking up the spoon itself. The b-4 spoon was identified as the most usable spoon and the easiest spoon to pick up by hand when experiencing tremors (Fig. 16(a)-3). We also obtained several feedback comments from the visitors that indicate their surprise at the new experiences and difficulties in manipulating their fingers and objects such as: "I never imagined tremors would be like this!", "Now I understand what the disease is like and the difficulties patients face in daily life", "It's very

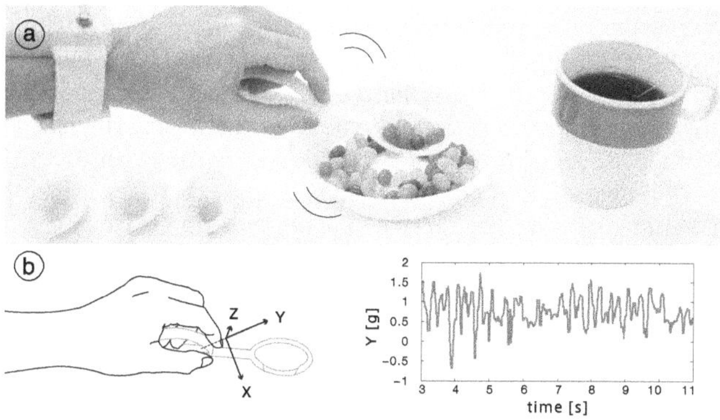

Figure 15. Experiment Setup and Result: Impairment Experience

hard to control my smartphone using my fingers", "It's scary! stop!", "Now I feel relieved..." (after the device was turned off). We also acquired comments after we demonstrated the synchronization interaction "I feel very weird because it is like someone is inside my arm and manipulating muscles..".

DISCUSSIONS

System Evaluation, Latency, and Performance

From the performance experiment, we observed that the measured contractions decreased when the applied pulse increased. This linear trend can be attributed to the electrical characteristics of the I/O circuit. The changes could be fitted linearly, hence it is possible to compensate by a linear function. In the future, we plan to conduct another perceptual experiment to investigate the reduction in a bioSync device wearer's voluntary contractions with reproduced contractions, and assess the effects of both the electrical and perceptual characteristics.

Subjective Perceptual Experiment

In the perceptual experiment, the participants could recognize reproduced muscle contractions and rate them on a five-point scale accurately, while they were contracting their own muscles. A similar result was obtained in [18], where the participants could recognize their wrist angle accurately using EMS based on their kinesthetic feedback. Hence, we confirm that the kinesthetic feedback mechanism in our setup also works correctly. We also observe that the standard deviation increased when the pulse width increased. This might be the effect of the wearer's voluntary contractions on the perception of the reproduced contractions. Another perceptual experiment would be required to study this phenomenon in detail and to assess the relevance of the signal-dependency noise theory [24]. According to this, neural control signals are corrupted by noise that increases in variance as with the size of the motor control signal increases.

Rhythmic Activity Synchronization

In the user study of the synchronization of rhythmic action, subject 1 reported that excessive involuntary contractions affected the performance of the synchronization. This could have been caused by the electrode positioning and personal muscular characteristics. This indicates that a prior adjustment is required for each subject to normalize the perceptual and kinesthetic experience among users. We discuss the positional optimization issue in the limitations section. In future work, we plan to investigate the relationship between kinesthetic communication latency and synchronization performance. Another aspect we would like to address is the learning effect, which we could not verify in the current experiment since the number of trials for each participant was small. However, we found that synchronization time is always shorter when the experimenter who had longer prior training and participated in the entire experiment, follows the participant's rhythmic action. Some participants also stated that, at the beginning of the experiment, they did not have enough confidence to recognize and report the time when sync was accomplished. These results suggest that several trials are required to understand new interpersonal kinesthetic communication. Another preliminary experiment showed that the rhythmic actions of two persons could be synchronized even if they are not assigned as an experimenter or a follower, and are treated equally.

Embodied Impairment Experience

In the pilot study on the simulated embodied Parkinson's experience, we received considerable feedback comments that indicated the existence of kinesthetic memory after the experiment. This suggests that reproduced kinesthetic impairment experience may be more effective in learning the neurological characteristics of the impairment than learning through some other modality. We would like to verify the practicality of this approach in a future study. Some visitors also reported experiencing the existence of a remote user's presence through the kinesthetic channel, while synchronizing muscle activity between two persons. Thus, interpersonal kinesthetic communication is capable of enhancing the feeling of togetherness and reality of existence, in a manner similar to that of interpersonal haptic communication [8, 12, 13].

LIMITATIONS

Electrode Placement

In the bioSync device proposed in this study, one set of electrodes is used for both stimulation and measurement. This limits the bandwidth of the kinesthetic information exchanged. By placing more electrodes encircling the forearm, it would be possible to transmit expressive cues through kinesthetic channels in a manner similar to that of haptic manipulators [10]. Placing more electrodes on muscles would require positional optimization. This is a common issue in EMS research

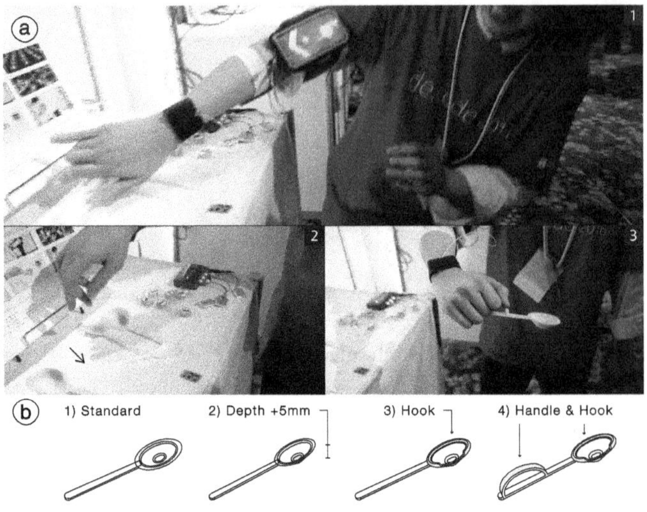

Figure 16. Demonstration at Exhibition: Impairment Experience

field because the perceived strength and involuntary contraction level depend on the stimulated muscle. In the proposed system, the electrode position is established empirically based on several trials. Hence, the positional optimization of the common electrodes is required in our system as well. There have been several studies on placement optimization for EMG or EMS using array electrodes and machine learning systems [19, 25]. These techniques can be applied to the bioSync system. The discharging effect in a multi-electrode environment should be investigated as well.

Blending of Contraction Strength

In this study, we focused mainly on the implementation of bidirectional communication and the temporal characteristics of blended kinesthetic interaction rather than on contraction strength. Although we have reported the results of a perceptual study involving the blended muscle activity and contraction strength of two users, the further qualitative evaluation of the proposed interaction is required. The difference between muscle activity and the perception of it will also be investigated in a future study.

POSSIBLE APPLICATIONS

(a) Shared Embodied Experience

It is very difficult for people to understand the characteristics of a patient's experience of physical impairment. For instance, product and architectural designers should fully understand how the symptoms affect physical interactions in a daily life, in order to be able to apply this knowledge in improving tools and residential buildings. Checklists and guidelines such as housing enabler models [26] or field evaluations involving patients have typically been used as tools in design. In addition to these, we propose a virtualized Parkinson's embodiment using the bioSync devices so that people who do not have Parkinson's, including caregivers, can easily experience and understand the tremors and challenges that Parkinson's sufferers face in the daily life (Fig. 17(a)). This can provide empirical and embodied knowledge of the impairments, which are usually difficult to explain using words. The amplitude, frequency

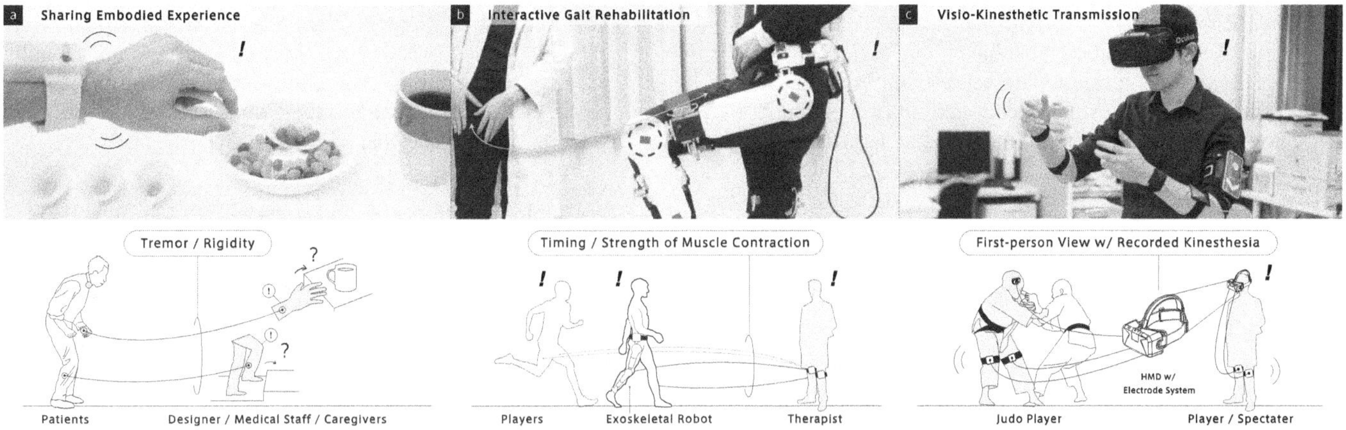

Figure 17. Concrete Scenarios: (a) Neuromuscular symptoms such as those of Parkinson's impairment can be recorded and reproduced for evaluating product and spatial design. (b) Interactive gait training with a power-assist exoskeletal robot accomplished by sharing the timing of the backward kick-out, and sports training by sharing muscle tensions with trainers. (c) Reviewing physical body motions by experiencing recorded kinesthetic feedback with a first-person view through a HMD system.

and target body are variable; as a consequence, designers can perform a number of different experimental trials and evaluate the usability of products and spaces under various conditions. Compared with a conventional tremor desktop-type simulator [27], transforming the wearer's embodiment into that of another would provide more realistic and persuasive experience, likewise transforming visual and haptic sensation [28].

(b) Interactive Rehabilitation and Sports Training

Gait training with a power-assist exoskeletal robot is increasingly becoming popular. The Hybrid Assistive Limb (HAL) developed by Sankai et al. [29], which consists of EMG sensors and lower-limb exoskeletons, was developed for intention-based walking support for paraplegia patients. It is important to learn the timing of each gate phase, such as backward kick-out, during gait training. However, the motors in the exoskeletons are limited in that they can not produce instantaneous actions to the user. bioSync can enable a patient and a therapist to share and learn the timings for such quick exertions, thereby creating the possibility for enhanced monitoring and interactive teaching. In sports training, it is important for coaches to perceive not only players' form and motions but also player's muscle activities. The timing of muscle exertion is important in running and swimming training, for instance, and the flow of muscle exertion is important in pitching and gymnastics motion training, for instance. Interactive kinesthetic feedback between players and coaches would allow players to perceive the correct forms and motions.

(c) Visio-kinesthetic Transmission

To achieve an effective training procedure with immersive and realistic feedback for sports spectating and skill transmission, we propose the use of a visio-kinesthetic experience transmission system using the bioSync device with a HMD system. The user can record and replay not only physical bodily movements but also muscle activities simultaneously. Combining these modalities would help in gaining body ownership and togetherness for a remote user, in the similar manner to the related work [30] that shares visual and tactile sensation to be another.

CONCLUSION

In this paper, we proposed and modeled a novel style of interpersonal kinesthetic communication, called the blended kinesthetic interaction that allows people to mutually perceive and interrupt each other's muscle activity. To achieve this interaction, we developed paired wearable kinesthetic I/O devices that are equipped with a specially designed electrodes system for simultaneous EMG measurement and stimulation at 100Hz via low-latency wireless communication (approx. 20ms). We also proposed dynamically adjustable frequency stimulation over a wide range of frequencies (1-100Hz), which allows the bioSync device to be adapted to various skin conditions and purposes. Through the perceptual experiment, it was verified that the bioSync users were able to recognize reproduced muscle contractions and rate them on a five-point scale while they were contracting their own muscles. It was also verified that the kinesthetic interpersonal communication allows people to synchronize the rhythmic action without visual and audio feedback. We also conducted a pilot study on providing a simulated embodied impairment experience. The results suggested that reproducing the neurological action of Parkinson's tremors could enhance the understanding of the disease. These findings would provide design ideas for the kinesthetic interaction, and contribute to potential applications such as education, design, and medical activities, that reveals new aspects of human behaviors for embodied and social experiences.

APPENDIX

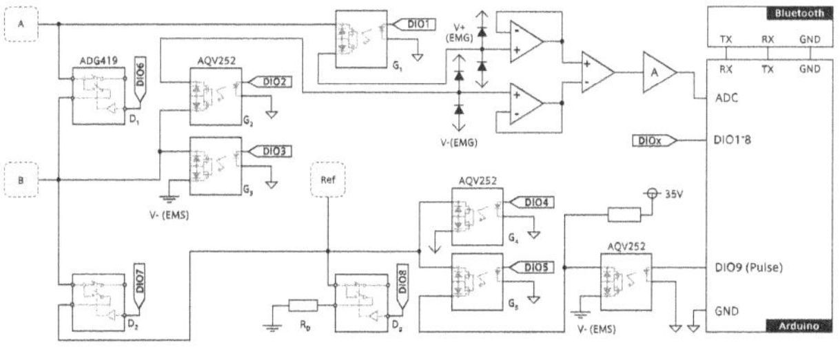

Figure 18. Schematic of bioSync's Circuitry

REFERENCES

1. Jun Nishida, Kanako Takahashi, and Kenji Suzuki. 2015. A wearable stimulation device for sharing and augmenting kinesthetic feedback. In Proceedings of the 6th Augmented Human International Conference (AH '15). ACM, New York, NY, USA, 211-212. DOI: http://dx.doi.org/10.1145/2735711.2735775
2. Jun Nishida, Kenji Suzuki. 2016. bioSync: Wearable haptic I/O device for synchronous kinesthetic interaction. In Proceedings of IEEE Virtual Reality (VR), pp.243-244. DOI: http://dx.doi.org/10.1109/VR.2016.7504744
3. Jun Nishida and Kenji Suzuki. 2016. bioSync: Synchronous Kinesthetic Experience among People. In Proceedings of the 2016 CHI Conference Extended Abstracts on Human Factors in Computing Systems (CHI EA '16). ACM, New York, NY, USA, 3742-3745. DOI: http://dx.doi.org/10.1145/2851581.2890244
4. Shunichi Kasahara and Jun Rekimoto. 2014. JackIn: integrating first-person view with out-of-body vision generation for human-human augmentation. In Proceedings of the 5th Augmented Human International Conference (AH '14). ACM, New York, NY, USA, , Article 46 , 8 pages. DOI: http://dx.doi.org/10.1145/2582051.2582097
5. Shunichi Kasahara, Mitsuhito Ando, Kiyoshi Suganuma, and Jun Rekimoto. 2016. Parallel Eyes: Exploring Human Capability and Behaviors with Paralleled First Person View Sharing. In Proceedings of the 2016 CHI Conference on Human Factors in Computing Systems (CHI '16). ACM, New York, NY, USA, 1561-1572. DOI: http://dx.doi.org/10.1145/2858036.2858495
6. Hiroyuki Iizuka, Daisuke Kondo, Hiroki Kawasaki, Hideyuki Ando, and Taro Maeda. 2011. Coordinated behavior between visually coupled dyads. In Proceedings of the 2nd Augmented Human International Conference (AH '11). ACM, New York, NY, USA, , Article 23 , 4 pages. DOI: http://dx.doi.org/10.1145/1959826.1959849
7. H. Kawasaki, H. Iizuka, S. Okamoto, H. Ando and T. Maeda. 2010. Collaboration and skill transmission by first-person perspective view sharing system, 19th International Symposium in Robot and Human Interactive Communication, Viareggio, pp. 125-131. DOI: http://dx.doi.org/10.1109/ROMAN.2010.5598668
8. Scott Brave and Andrew Dahley. 1997. inTouch: a medium for haptic interpersonal communication. In CHI '97 Extended Abstracts on Human Factors in Computing Systems (CHI EA '97). ACM, New York, NY, USA, 363-364. DOI: http://dx.doi.org/10.1145/1120212.1120435
9. Ken Nakagaki, Chikara Inamura, Pasquale Totaro, Thariq Shihipar, Chantine Akikyama, Yin Shuang, and Hiroshi Ishii. 2015. Linked-Stick: Conveying a Physical Experience using a Shape-Shifting Stick. In Proceedings of the 33rd Annual ACM Conference Extended Abstracts on Human Factors in Computing Systems (CHI EA '15). ACM, New York, NY, USA, 1609-1614. DOI: http://dx.doi.org/10.1145/2702613.2732712
10. Jeremy N. Bailenson, Nick Yee, Scott Brave, Dan Merget and David Koslow. 2007. Virtual Interpersonal Touch: Expressing and Recognizing Emotions Through Haptic Devices. Journal of Human Computer Interaction. vol.22, No.3, 325-353. DOI: http://dx.doi.org/10.1080/07370020701493509
11. Daniel Leithinger, Sean Follmer, Alex Olwal, and Hiroshi Ishii. 2014. Physical telepresence: shape capture and display for embodied, computer-mediated remote collaboration. In Proceedings of the 27th annual ACM symposium on User interface software and technology (UIST '14). ACM, New York, NY, USA, 461-470. DOI: http://dx.doi.org/10.1145/2642918.2647377
12. Hideyuki Nakanishi, Kazuaki Tanaka, and Yuya Wada. 2014. Remote handshaking: touch enhances video-mediated social telepresence. In Proceedings of the SIGCHI Conference on Human Factors in Computing Systems (CHI '14). ACM, New York, NY, USA, 2143-2152. DOI: http://dx.doi.org/10.1145/2556288.2557169
13. Scott Brave, Clifford Nass and Erenee Sirinian. 2001. Force-Feedback in computer-mediated communication. Proceedings of HCI International '2001 (the 9th International Conference on Human-Computer Interaction), New Orleans, USA, Volume 3, 145-149.
14. N. Igarashi, K. Suzuki, H. Kawamoto and Y. Sankai. 2010. bioLights: Light emitting wear for visualizing lower-limb muscle activity, 2010 Annual International Conference of the IEEE Engineering in Medicine and Biology, 6393-6396. DOI: http://dx.doi.org/10.1109/IEMBS.2010.5627306
15. Y. Tsubouchi and K. Suzuki. 2010. BioTones: A wearable device for EMG auditory biofeedback. In Proc of Annual International Conference of the IEEE Engineering in Medicine and Biology, Buenos Aires, 6543-6546. DOI: http://dx.doi.org/10.1109/IEMBS.2010.5627097
16. Dozza, M., Horak, F.B. and Chiari, L. 2007. Auditory biofeedback substitutes for loss of sensory information in maintaining stance. Experimental Brain Research, Vol.178, No.1, 37-48. DOI: http://dx.doi.org/10.1007/s00221-006-0709-y
17. Raafat Shalaby, Thomas Schauer, Wolfgang Liedecke and Jorg Raisch. 2010. Amplifier design for EMG recording from stimulation electrodes during functional electrical stimulation leg cycling ergometry, Biomedizinische Technik/Biomedical Engineering. Vol. 56, Issue 1, 23-33, DOI: https://doi.org/10.1515/bmt.2010.055
18. Pedro Lopes, Alexandra Ion, Willi Mueller, Daniel Hoffmann, Patrik Jonell, and Patrick Baudisch. 2015. Proprioceptive Interaction. In Proceedings of the 33rd Annual ACM Conference on Human Factors in Computing Systems (CHI '15). ACM, New York, NY, USA, 939-948. DOI: http://dx.doi.org/10.1145/2702123.2702461

19. Emi Tamaki, Takashi Miyaki, and Jun Rekimoto. 2011. PossessedHand: techniques for controlling human hands using electrical muscles stimuli. In Proceedings of the SIGCHI Conference on Human Factors in Computing Systems (CHI '11). ACM, New York, NY, USA, 543-552. DOI: http://dx.doi.org/10.1145/1978942.1979018

20. Pedro Lopes, Patrik Jonell, and Patrick Baudisch. 2015. Affordance++: Allowing Objects to Communicate Dynamic Use. In Proceedings of the 33rd Annual ACM Conference on Human Factors in Computing Systems (CHI '15). ACM, New York, NY, USA, 2515-2524. DOI: http://dx.doi.org/10.1145/2702123.2702128

21. Pedro Lopes and Patrick Baudisch. 2013. Muscle-propelled force feedback: bringing force feedback to mobile devices. In Proceedings of the SIGCHI Conference on Human Factors in Computing Systems (CHI '13). ACM, New York, NY, USA, 2577-2580. DOI: http://dx.doi.org/10.1145/2470654.2481355

22. Pedro Lopes, Alexandra Ion, and Patrick Baudisch. 2015. Impacto: Simulating Physical Impact by Combining Tactile Stimulation with Electrical Muscle Stimulation. In Proceedings of the 28th Annual ACM Symposium on User Interface Software & Technology (UIST '15). ACM, New York, NY, USA, 11-19. DOI: http://dx.doi.org/10.1145/2807442.2807443

23. Y. Muraoka. 2001. Development of an emg recording device from stimulation electrodes for functional electrical stimulation. Frontiers of Medical and Biological Engineering: The International Journal of the Japan Society of Medical Electronics and Biological Engineering, vol.11, No.4, 323-333. DOI: http://dx.doi.org/10.1163/156855701321138969

24. C. M. Harris and D. M. Wolpert. 1998. Signal-dependent noise determines motor planning. Nature, 394, pp.780–784

25. Manami Katoh, Narihiro Nishimura, Maki Yokoyama, Taku Hachisu, Michi Sato, Shogo Fukushima, and Hiroyuki Kajimoto. 2013. Optimal selection of electrodes for muscle electrical stimulation using twitching motion measurement. In Proceedings of the 4th Augmented Human International Conference (AH '13). ACM, New York, NY, USA, 237-238. DOI: http://dx.doi.org/10.1145/2459236.2459279

26. S. Iwarsson. 1999. The housing enabler: An objective tool for assessing accessibility, The British Journal of Occupational Therapy, vol.62, No.11, pp.491-497.

27. G. P. Rosati Papini, M. Fontana and M. Bergamasco. 2016. Desktop Haptic Interface for Simulation of Hand-Tremor. IEEE Transactions on Haptics, vol. 9, no. 1, 33-42, Jan.-March 1. DOI: http://dx.doi.org/10.1109/TOH.2015.2504971

28. Jun Nishida, Hikaru Takatori, Kosuke Sato, and Kenji Suzuki. 2015. CHILDHOOD: wearable suit for augmented child experience. In ACM SIGGRAPH 2015 Emerging Technologies (SIGGRAPH '15). ACM, New York, NY, USA, Article 7, DOI: http://dx.doi.org/10.1145/2782782.2792501

29. Suzuki, K., Mito, G., Kawamoto, H., Hasegawa, Y. and Sankai, Y. 2007. Intention-based walking support for paraplegia patients with Robot Suit HAL, Advanced Robotics, Vol.21, pp.1441–1469. DOI: http://dx.doi.org/10.1163/156855307781746061

30. Bertrand Philippe, Daniel Gonzalez-Franco, Arthur Pointeau, and Christian Cherene. 2014. The Machine to be Another - Embodied Telepresence using human performers. Prix Ars Electronica (2014).

Modeling Cumulative Arm Fatigue in Mid-Air Interaction based on Perceived Exertion and Kinetics of Arm Motion

[1]Sujin Jang, [2]Wolfgang Stuerzlinger, [3]Satyajit Ambike, [1]Karthik Ramani*

[1]School of Mechanical Engineering and
[3]Department of Health and Kinesiology
Purdue University, West Lafayatte, IN, USA
{jang64, ramani, sambike}@purdue.edu

[2]School of Interactive Arts + Technology
Simon Fraser University
Vancouver, CA
w.s@sfu.ca

ABSTRACT

Quantifying cumulative arm muscle fatigue is a critical factor in understanding, evaluating, and optimizing user experience during prolonged mid-air interaction. A reasonably accurate estimation of fatigue requires an estimate of an individual's strength. However, there is no easy-to-access method to measure individual strength to accommodate inter-individual differences. Furthermore, fatigue is influenced by both psychological and physiological factors, but no current HCI model provides good estimates of cumulative subjective fatigue. We present a new, simple method to estimate the maximum shoulder torque through a mid-air pointing task, which agrees with direct strength measurements. We then introduce a cumulative fatigue model informed by subjective and biomechanical measures. We evaluate the performance of the model in estimating cumulative subjective fatigue in mid-air interaction by performing multiple cross-validations and a comparison with an existing fatigue metric. Finally, we discuss the potential of our approach for real-time evaluation of subjective fatigue as well as future challenges.

Author Keywords

Mid-air interaction; perceived exertion; cumulative fatigue model; maximum arm strength; biomechanical arm model.

ACM Classification Keywords

H.5.2. Information Interfaces and Presentation (e.g. HCI): User Interfaces

INTRODUCTION

Recent advances in sensing technologies have produced low-cost human motion tracking methods (e.g., MS Kinect, Leap Motion), and these methods are being leveraged to study and adopt natural human motion for the design of mid-air interactions in various environments (e.g., AR/VR [37, 40], medical operations [36], gaming [33], and virtual design [54]). Physical ergonomics is an important design factor for mid-air interaction [8, 26, 30]. In particular, arm fatigue – the so-called "Gorilla arm" effect [2] – is known to negatively impact user experience and hamper prolonged use of mid-air interfaces. Fatigue is a complex phenomenon defined as the decline in maximal force or power capacity of muscle due to sustained activation [20]. This means that sub-maximal forces, such as those encountered in most mid-air interactions, can be sustained for extended periods even as fatigue accumulates. However, users will typically perceive the accumulation of fatigue (i.e., feel the arm getting heavier), and this may negatively impact their experience. Furthermore, subjective fatigue and its perceived intensity are influenced not only by the task demands and the individual's current physiological state, but also by the history of the individual's movement choices. Consequently, models estimating the current fatigue of a user must be based on continuous measurement of the ongoing interaction. Although the term "Arm fatigue" appears in more than 300 publications in HCI over the last decade, we do not have good predictive models of cumulative fatigue that account for variable and intermittent periods of interaction.

Another practical issue in quantifying muscle fatigue is the measurement of an individual's maximal strength. The fatigue rate for a given task depends on the proportion of muscular strength that the task consumes. Naturally, fatigue estimation requires the quantification of an individual's maximal ability [19], and biomechanists typically achieve this by recording the maximal forces (or joint torques) that the subject can produce under isometric conditions [34, 41, 44]. However, these measurements require expensive force sensors and specialized test rigs, making sensor-based strength measurements impractical for HCI research.

Lastly, physiological and psychological human factors both influence fatigue [20], and thus, user experience as well [28]. To better evaluate and understand the effect of fatigue on user experience, we need congruent models that account for both influences [28, 32]. Current models to quantify fatigue are mostly informed by direct measurements of forces or physiological signals (e.g., movement dynamics, muscle forces), and rarely account for the perceived effect of fatigue accumulation. These direct measurements are invasive, require specialized equipment, and therefore, are not practical for implementation in HCI. Subjective fatigue evaluation (e.g., Borg scales [11]) requires no set-up and provides useful information of the user experience. However, direct verbalization and reporting is necessary, which, again interferes with the user's interactive experience. Thus, existing objective and subjective methods for evaluating fatigue can be cumbersome and invasive as multiple recordings are required during tasks.

*School of Electrical and Computer Engineering (by courtesy)

Permission to make digital or hard copies of all or part of this work for personal or classroom use is granted without fee provided that copies are not made or distributed for profit or commercial advantage and that copies bear this notice and the full citation on the first page. Copyrights for components of this work owned by others than ACM must be honored. Abstracting with credit is permitted. To copy otherwise, or republish, to post on servers or to redistribute to lists, requires prior specific permission and/or a fee. Request permissions from permissions@acm.org.
CHI 2017, May 6-11, 2017, Denver, CO, USA.
Copyright © 2017 ACM ISBN 978-1-4503-4655-9/17/05 ...$15.00.
http://dx.doi.org/10.1145/3025453.3025523

In HCI, researchers recently investigated the role of muscle fatigue [7, 8, 30]. However, previous work mostly considers instantaneous muscle contractions, and thus cannot quantify cumulative muscle fatigue. Also, previous work is informed by physical measures (e.g., muscle forces and torques), and does not quantify fatigue perception, which is necessary for the accurate evaluation of user experience during interaction.

This paper addresses the above-mentioned issues in evaluating cumulative arm fatigue during mid-air interaction. First, we propose a simple and effective method to estimate an individual's maximal shoulder torque using a mid-air pointing task. We use a camera-based skeleton tracking system to capture arm movements, and then compute the shoulder-joint forces and torques during the pointing task, which subjects perform till volitional failure. Then, we use the *Intensity–Endurance Time* curve [41] to estimate the maximum shoulder torque without a direct force or torque measurement. *Intensity* is the ratio between the maximum and current torque exerted at the shoulder. *Endurance time* (ET) is the duration of muscular exertion before the volitional failure. We validate our indirect maximum torque estimation method via comparisons with direct measurements obtained with a force sensor.

Second, we introduce a method to quantify cumulative arm fatigue based on the three-compartment muscle model (TCM) [56]. The model allows muscle units to be in either an active (M_A), fatigue (M_F), or rest (M_R) state and defines state-transition rules. This enables quantification of cumulative fatigue when both task and rest periods appear during interaction. By optimizing the free model parameters to minimize the difference between the model and user-reported estimates of perceived fatigue, we account for both physical and psychological processes that influence perceived fatigue. We investigate the performance of the model in predicting subjective fatigue in mid-air pointing tasks through cross-validations and a comparison with an existing metric.

Our contributions include: (1) a simple and effective method to estimate the maximum shoulder torque through a mid-air pointing task; (2) a cumulative fatigue model that estimates subjective fatigue using movement kinetics measured during ongoing mid-air interaction; (3) experimental validation of the cumulative fatigue model for estimating subjective arm fatigue; and (4) a procedure for modeling the cumulative fatigue that accounts for subject specificity of muscle fatigue. Below, we describe related work, techniques, experimental methods, and the analysis of experimental results. Our findings show the potential of the model in predicting subjective fatigue in mid-air interactions. We discuss the challenges for further developing the model to quantify arm muscle fatigue derived from subjective and biomechanical factors.

RELATED WORK

Here we review prior work related to objective and subjective evaluation of muscle fatigue, cumulative fatigue models, and muscle fatigue evaluation for mid-air interactions.

Objective Fatigue Evaluation

Muscle fatigue is quantified based on changes in various physiological quantities such as muscle activation (measured using electromyography (EMG) [14]), intra cellular acidosis [55], arterial oxygen [3], blood pressure [49], and heart rate [48]. Such invasive methods are impractical for HCI.

Another method uses a measurement of maximum muscular strength. The maximum capacity of muscular exertion is defined as the "*maximum voluntary contraction* (MVC)", and it is commonly expressed as a force (N) or a torque ($N \cdot m$). Reduction in MVC during a continuous task is considered as a reliable assessment of muscle fatigue. Biomechanists commonly measure MVC using force sensors in specialized test rigs (e.g., [1, 29, 47]). However, such set-ups are invasive, not easily accessible, and impractical for evaluating muscle fatigue during HCI tasks.

Ratings of Perceived Exertion

There are several psychometric scales commonly used for evaluating subjective fatigue such as Likert scale [13], NASA-TLX [27], VAS (visual analog signal) [9], and ratings of perceived exertion (RPE) [12]. Such subjective evaluation based on the muscular sensation is also a result of physiological changes [4], and it should be carefully considered in evaluating muscle fatigue. The Borg RPE scales, given their reproducibility and sensitivity [12], have been extensively used in psychological evaluation of muscle fatigue as a complement to physiological measures in various field of research (e.g., sports [21], medicine [43], ergonomics [10]). Borg CR10 [12] is a categorical rating with ratio properties (0$\sim$10 points), and it has been used to assess perceived exertions in body parts such as the hand and the arm [22, 39, 51]. The Borg CR10 scale uses verbal anchors and numbers to map the magnitude of exertion to a scalar invariance scale.

Several studies have shown that the Borg CR10 scale is strongly correlated with objective measures, such as EMG [17, 53], and that it is reliable at lower levels of force exertion (e.g., holding a weight less than 2$\sim$3 kg [44]). This makes the Borg CR10 scale particularly suitable for evaluating fatigue in mid-air interaction, where relatively little or no external load is exerted on the arms (bare-hand interactions).

Cumulative Muscle Fatigue Model

Due to the analytic complexity of describing fatigue, few models are available to properly quantify muscle fatigue. The Endurance Time (ET)–Intensity curve (e.g., Rohmert's curve [46]) has been extensively used to empirically model the effect of fatigue on the task endurance time in static exertion tasks. Although this approach is useful in estimating fatigue-induced ET, it cannot be used for more complex tasks involving dynamic load conditions or recovery during rest periods. Liu et al. [38] proposed a dynamic muscle model based on three muscle states: rest (M_R), active (M_A), and fatigue (M_F). However, this model has only been validated under constant, maximum effort, and thus it is not generalizable to dynamic load conditions such as arm movements interspersed with rest periods. Xia et al. [56] proposed a three-compartment muscle (TCM) model by introducing a feedback controller term between the active (M_A) and rest (M_R) muscle states. More recently, Frey-Law et al. [24] validated the TCM model in estimating ET under static load conditions, and obtained a set of joint-specific model parameters. This enables the model to predict the muscle activation states under various task conditions (i.e., static and dynamic load conditions). However, their validation was still limited to static load conditions. Sonne et al. [50] further experimentally validated the performance of the TCM model in predicting fatigue during grasping and thumb contraction tasks by providing a task-specific, optimized fatigue model.

Similarly, we optimize the TCM model for estimating shoulder joint fatigue. Also, we optimize the model using both subjective fatigue ratings and movement kinematics. Once optimized, our model estimates previously unseen subjective fatigue levels based only on kinematic measurements. We are not aware of any prior work that achieves this.

Quantifying Muscle Fatigue in Mid-Air Interactions

In HCI, there are two closely related studies on quantifying arm fatigue during mid-air interaction. Consumed Endurance (CE) [30] is an easy-to-implement metric for estimating ET in mid-air selection tasks. The authors showed a strong correlation between CE and the Borg scale. Yet, CE is based on Rohmert's ET curve [46], which is only valid for static load conditions, and thus CE does not consider rest and its effect on cumulative fatigue [56]. Also, CE is assumed to be zero at exertion levels below 15%. This controversial assumption [23, 41] limits use of CE for evaluating mid-air interaction with low exertion levels. CE also uses generic maximum shoulder torque values, even though shoulder strength is subject-specific [41]. In contrast, we propose a novel method to measure an individual's maximum shoulder torque that does not require expensive sensors, and which shows strong agreement with traditional, contact-based measurements.

Bachynsky et al. [7, 8] introduced a biomechnical simulation to evaluate muscle activation. This work showed the potential of simulation-based approaches to quantify the effect of fatigue on the design of touch-based and mid-air interactions. However, the simulation only considers muscle contractions in a static optimization, and thus cannot quantify cumulative muscle fatigue. Also, Bachynsky et al. [6] observed that their simulation output does not correlate well with subjective fatigue measures. This makes their simulation results less comparable with our model estimates.

Unlike existing approaches, we consider cumulative arm fatigue involving both interaction and rest periods without limiting the range of exertion. Furthermore, our model quantifies the user's perception of fatigue, which is likely more directly related to the user experience during mid-air interaction.

ESTIMATING ARM MUSCLE FATIGUE

Here we describe our method for quantifying arm fatigue by introducing three-compartment muscle model, biomechanical arm model, and maximum shoulder torque estimation.

Three-Compartment Fatigue Model

We introduce the three-compartment muscle (TCM) model for estimating active, rest, and fatigue muscle states (see [24, 56] for more details). The TCM model assumes that the motor units involved in a task can be in one of three possible states: *active* (motor units receiving neural activation and contributing to the current task), *fatigued*, (fatigued motor units without activation), or *resting* (inactive motor units that are not required for the current task). Figure 1 shows the three muscle unit states, and the relations between them. $M_F(\%)$ is the proportion, or 'compartment' of motor units that are currently in fatigued state, $M_A(\%)$ is the compartment of active motor units, and $M_R(\%)$ is the proportion of motor units at rest. Each compartment of motor states is expressed as a percentage of the *maximum voluntary contraction* (%MVC). Since motor-unit recruitment is binary (they are either contracted or not), $M_A = 100\%$ indicates that all motor units are recruited for a MVC task. A sub-maximal task implies $M_A < 100\%$. The three motor unit states are related as:

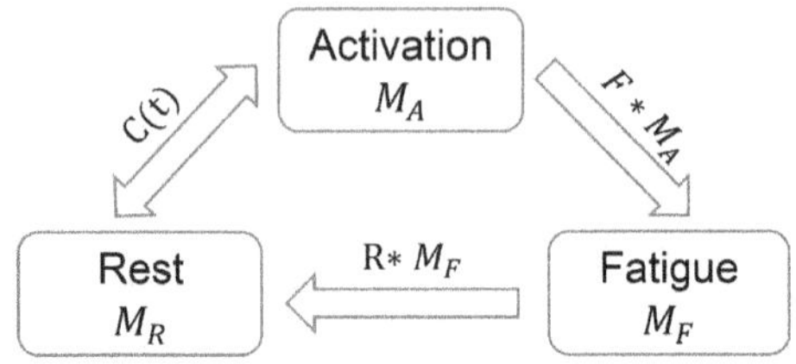

Figure 1. Three-compartment muscle (TCM) model

$$\frac{dM_R}{dt} = -C(t) + R * M_F,$$
$$\frac{dM_A}{dt} = C(t) - F * M_A,$$
$$\frac{dM_F}{dt} = F * M_A - R * M_F,$$

where F and R, are the model parameters defining the rate at which active motor units are fatiguing, and the rate at which fatigued motor units recover and enter the rest state, respectively, and $C(t)$ is motor unit activation function defined as:

$$C(t) = \begin{cases} L_D(TL - M_A) & \text{if } M_A < TL, M_R > TL - M_A \\ L_D M_R & \text{if } M_A < TL, M_R \leq TL - M_A \\ L_R(TL - M_A) & \text{if } M_A \geq TL \end{cases}$$

where TL is the target load defined as a torque ratio $[T_{current}/T_{max}] * 100(\%)$, L_D is the muscle force development factor, and L_R is the relaxation factor. The last two parameters are set to 10 based on the sensitivity analysis by Frey-Law et al. [24].

Model Fitting

We used the optimization toolbox in MATLAB to optimize the TCM and to identify the model parameters (F and R) for mid-air interaction. The pattern search method [5] was used to minimize the root mean squared errors (RMSE) between the perceived exertion (Borg scale ratings) and the size of the fatigued motor unit compartment (M_F):

$$\underset{F,R}{\text{minimize}} \quad \sqrt{\frac{1}{n}\sum_{i=1}^{n}[\phi(M_F(i)) - B(i)]^2}$$
$$\text{subject to} \quad F \in [F_{lb}, F_{ub}], R \in [R_{lb}, R_{ub}]$$

where n is the number of fitting data, $M_F(i)$ is the fatigue level estimation, $B(i)$ is the Borg scale rating, and the upper and lower bounds of the parameters are defined as $F_{lb} =$

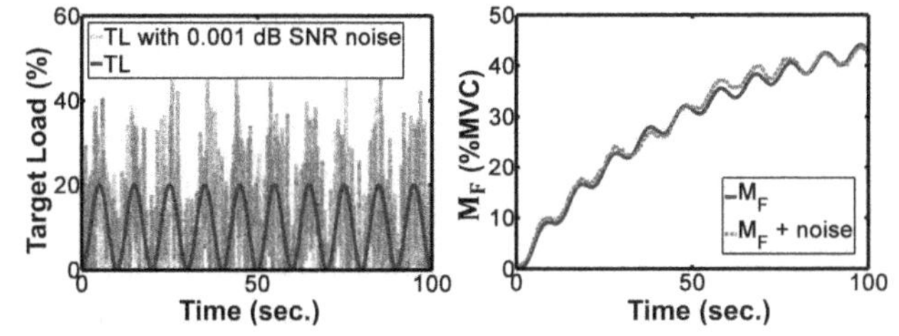

Figure 2. Simulated fatigue estimates (M_F) using the TCM model with 0.001 dB noise. Left: Input (TL) to the model w/ and w/o noise. Right: comparison of estimation results w/ and w/o noise.

$R_{lb} = 0.001, F_{ub} = 0.0182*100$, and $R_{ub} = 0.00168*100$. The upper bounds are defined by multiplying the constant parameters recommended by Frey-Law et al. [24] with 100. We assume a linear relationship between the Borg scale and %MVC (proportion of current and maximum torque) based on a review of their relationship [42]. $\phi(\cdot)$ is a linear function mapping the fatigue estimation $M_F(i)$ to the Borg scale. We define the linear mapping as $\phi(x) = 0.0875*x$. This means a value of '8' in Borg CR10 scale is equivalent to 90% of M_F.

Sensitivity Analysis of Fatigue Estimation

Since we target the use of off-the-shelf vision-based skeleton tracking systems (e.g., Kinect), we need to deal with the fact that such tracking is more susceptible to noise and jitters compared to marker-based tracking systems (e.g., Vicon, OptiTrack). Therefore, we tested the sensitivity of the TCM model to the presence of severe noise. Simulation results (see Figure 2) showed that the model is relatively insensitive to jitters and errors in torque estimation (mean absolute error, M= 1.00, SD=0.98 in %MVC).

Biomechanical Upper Limb Model

Fatigue development rate is joint specific, and the shoulder fatigues much faster than the elbow or wrist during arm movements [23]. Therefore, we assume that arm fatigue is mostly attributable to shoulder-joint fatigue, and the shoulder-joint strength is the most relevant design-related parameter for mid-air interaction.

Estimating shoulder fatigue using the TCM model requires two inputs: the maximum joint torque (T_{max}) and the time-course of torque exerted at the joint ($T(t)$). Our new method to estimate T_{max} will be discussed in the next section. Here we briefly introduce a standard procedure to measure the shoulder joint torque $T(t)$ based on a biomechanical arm model [15]. We model the upper limb as rigid bodies (*links*) connected in series by *joints* [45]. Figure 3 shows the model defined by a 4 degree-of-freedom (DOF) serial chain (shoulder:3, elbow:1). The biomechanical arm model equations and the Newton-Euler inverse dynamics procedure [15] to compute the shoulder torque (T) are provided in the Appendix.

Estimating Maximum Shoulder Torque

To estimate the muscle strength of users, we propose a procedure where users perform a fatiguing exercise by holding a weight in the air. This procedure eliminates the need of a force sensor and dynamic measurements for estimating the maximal shoulder torque. In this isometric exercise, users are asked to flex the shoulder and maintain the arm in the horizontal position while holding a weight (e.g., 1.36 kg for female and 2.27 kg for male subjects). To guide subjects in maintaining this posture, a simple pointing task is designed. A circular target is fixed at the same height as the shoulder, and placed in front of the body at maximum arm extension (see Figure 4(b)). The target is displayed on screen, and can only be "touched" when the user holds the correct posture.

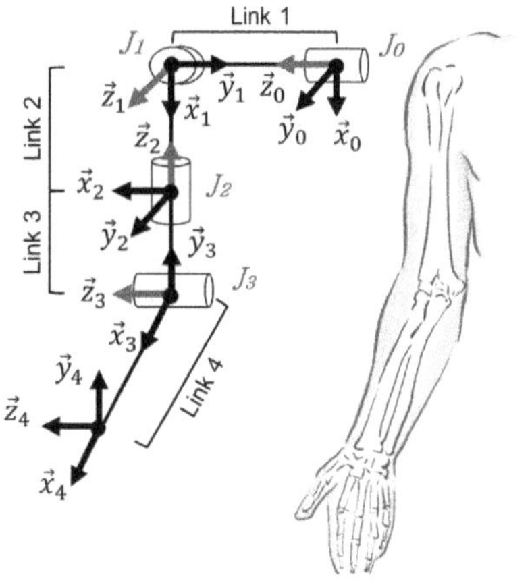

Figure 3. Biomechanic model of the upper limb.

We compute the time course of the shoulder torque $T(t)$ using the upper limb biomechanics model and measure the endurance time while subjects perform the isometric exercise. The subjects are assumed to exert constant shoulder torque for this isometric test, and we compute the average shoulder torque exerted during the exercise (T_{avg}). We use the equation of maximal shoulder capacity (%MVC) and endurance time (ET) experimentally derived by Mathiassen et al. [41]: $ET = a * \exp(-b * \%MVC)$, where %MVC is the ratio of current and maximum shoulder torque ($T_{current}/T_{max} * 100\%$), and a and b are experimentally defined constants (40.609 and 0.097). To find the maximum torque T_{max}, we invert Mathiassen's equation as:

$$T_{max} = \frac{-b * T_{avg}}{\log(ET/a)} \times 100 \tag{1}$$

This yields an estimate of the the maximum shoulder torque (involving the anterior deltoid, coracobrachialis, biceps, and pectoralis major muscles). We compare this indirect measurement with traditional sensor-based ones in our experiments.

EXPERIMENTAL METHODS

With the two experiments described below, we validate (1) a method to estimate maximal shoulder-joint torque using kinematic measurements with the Kinect camera and (2) the three-compartment muscle (TCM) model for estimating cumulative shoulder fatigue during mid-air interaction. We focus on a "virtual hand" mid-air pointing task, a fundamental mode of interaction in 3D user interfaces.

General Setup

We used a Microsoft Kinect sensor and the corresponding SDK to track arm movements. Data were sampled at 50

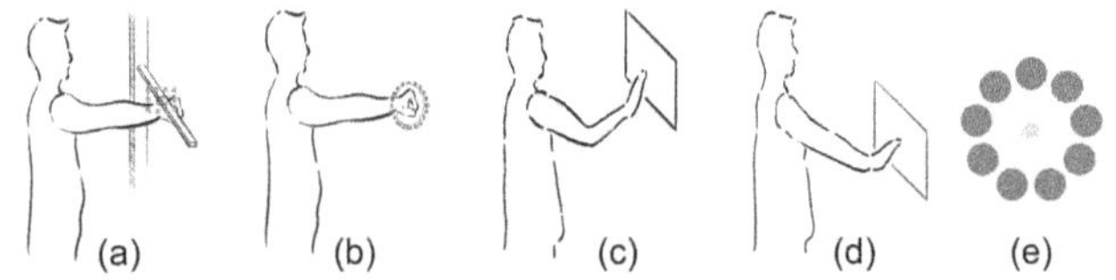

Figure 4. (a): sketch of the dynamometer setup, (b): posture for isometric exercise, (c) and (d): different interaction zones for pointing task, and (e): target circles arranged on a 2D plane. Target width is 10 cm and distance is 30 cm (red: target to select, green: pointer).

frames/second using a laptop with a Core i7 2.90GHz CPU and 16 GB RAM. The computer was connected to a short-throw projector to display the task interface. The physical size of projected screen on the wall was 1.6×0.95 meter, and the Kinect camera was located 1 meter in front of the screen and 1 meter above the floor. Participants stood 3 meters in front of the screen. The setup was identical for both experiments. Joint torques were obtained from the camera data using the inverse dynamics computations described in the Appendix. A moving-average filter (15th order) was used to smooth the joint-torque trajectories.

Mid-Air Pointing Tasks

To systematically collect arm movements and analyze resultant arm fatigue, we designed a mid-air pointing experiment based on the ISO 9241-9 standard [35, 52], to minimize the impact of confounding factors on the subjective fatigue measurement during the pointing tasks. This task has participants point at a circle of targets with a given width in a sequence that matches the movement distance to the circle diameter (see Figure 4(e)). Haga et al. [25] noted that task difficulty significantly affects subjects' perceived fatigue. In our experiments, we aim to measure perceived fatigue level only affected by muscular effort, not by task difficulty. We observed during pilot studies that learning affects the perceived fatigue. Consequently, it is important to provide enough training time and ensure that the pointing task was not too challenging. Thus, we decided to fix the task difficulty by using a single index of difficulty (ID). We also noticed that the tracking performance of the Kinect can affect the ID of pointing tasks as it may interfere with movement time and error rate. In our pilot studies, we tested a range of target widths (5.0 to 15.0 cm) with a fixed distance (30 cm) to identify those that show no degradation of pointing performance in terms of throughput. In the end, we decided to use a target width of 10 cm width at 30 cm distance, corresponding to an ID of 2.18.

Participants

We recruited 24, right-handed volunteers (20 male, 4 female) from the local university campus. The age ranged from 20 to 34 years (M = 25.5 yrs); height ranged from 154 to 185 cm (M = 174.1 cm); weight from 48.1 to 112 kg (M=73.6 kg); upper arm length from 25.5 to 38 cm (M=33.5 cm); lower arm length from 22.5 to 29.5 cm (M=26.8 cm); and hand length ranged from 17.5 to 22 cm (M=20 cm). No subject had a musculoskeletal disorder or neurological disease. The average duration of experience with mid-air interfaces ranged from 0 to 5 years (M=0.6 yrs).

Score	Definition	Note
0	Nothing At All	No arm fatigue
0.5	Very, Very Weak	Just noticeable
1	Very Weak	As taking a short walk
2	Weak	Light
3	Moderate	Somewhat but Not Hard to Go on
4	Somewhat Heavy	
5	Heavy	Tiring, Not Terribly Hard to Go on
6		
7	Very Strong	Strenuous. Really Push Hard to Go on
8		
9		
10	Extremely Strong	Extremely strenuous. Worst ever experienced

Table 1. Borg CR10 scales with verbal anchoring.

Design

Each subject first performed a training session. Subsequently, he/she performed two experimental tasks: (1) maximum shoulder torque generation and (2) mid-air pointing.

Training

Pilot testing confirmed that subjects learned the pointing tasks within a few (< 5) minutes, and that learning affected subjective fatigue ratings. Therefore, to minimize any potential impact of learning on the perceived exertion, we provided at least 5 minutes of training where subjects practiced the experimental pointing task (Exp. 2). After the training session, we provided at least 5 minutes of rest time to minimize any fatigue effects from the training.

Borg [11] observed that by providing appropriate verbal anchors and instructions with corresponding muscular sensation, the fatigue ratings can be used to compare inter-individual differences. We adopted Borg's technique and provided detailed instructions on using the Borg CR10 scale with verbal anchoring (see Table 1). The Borg CR10 scale and Table 1 were displayed on screen throughout the experiments.

Exp. 1: Maximum Shoulder Torque Measurements

In this session, we measured the maximum shoulder torque of each subject using two methods: (1) direct measurement using a force sensor and (2) indirect measurement based on an isometric fatiguing exercise.

To directly measure the maximum shoulder torque, we used a dynamometer (MicroFET2, Hoggan Scientific LLC) fixed on a test rig. Figure 4(a) shows an overview of the set-up where the dynamometer (green box) is fixed to a test rig at the same height as the shoulder. Subjects were encouraged to exert maximal upward force with their right arm against the dynamometer. Following the direct maximum torque measurement procedure described by Mathiassen et al. [41], we recorded the best of three trials, each lasting 3 seconds, with a 2 minute interval between repetitions as the maximum force F_{max}. We calculated the maximum shoulder torque as:

$$T_{max,D} = (m_{UA} + m_{LA} + m_H) * G * C + F_{max} * (L_{UA} + L_{LA}),$$

where $T_{max,D}$ is the maximum shoulder torque obtained from the direct force measurement; L_{UA} and L_{LA} are, respectively, the upper and lower arm length; m_{UA} and m_{LA} are, respectively, the mass of the upper and lower arm; m_H

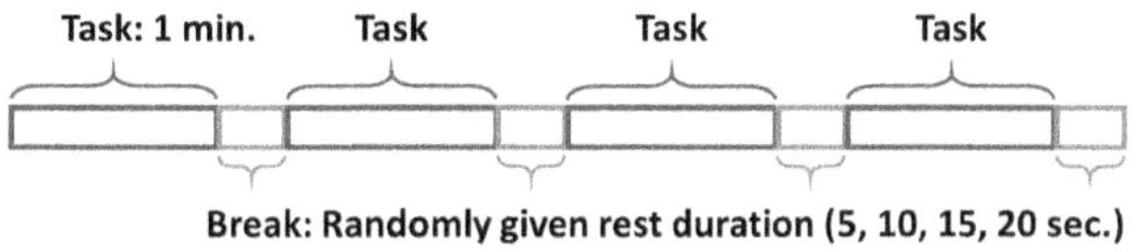

Figure 5. Experimental protocol of pointing task. An experiment block consists of 1 minute of pointing task and either one of 5/10/15/20 seconds of rest, and each pointing task conditions consists of four blocks.

is the mass of the hand; G is 9.81 m/s^2; and C is the distance between the shoulder joint and the center of mass of the arm.

In the isometric exercise, we followed the procedure of indirectly estimating maximum shoulder torque described in the previous section. Subjects were asked to hold a weight (2.27 kg for males and 1.36 kg for females, to account for expected gender-based strength differences) in their dominant hand, flex the shoulder till the arm was horizontal and maintain this posture till failure. Subjects saw feedback of their pointing position on screen. We measured the endurance time as the duration between the start of the trial and when subjects indicated volitional failure to maintain the arm posture, or when the hand position was below the target for over 2 seconds. The average torque T_{avg} exerted by their shoulder was computed using inverse dynamics (see the Appendix). Then we obtain the indirectly measured maximum shoulder torque $T_{max,I}$ using Equation 1. During this trial, subjects were required to report their current Borg rating every 20 seconds. These ratings were not utilized for further analysis, but the exercise provided the subjects with Borg rating experience before the next experimental task.

Exp. 2: Mid-Air Pointing Experiments

The main goal of this experiment is to collect subjective fatigue ratings and corresponding biomechanics measures. Then, we aim to generate a cumulative fatigue model that accurately describes the relationship between the two variables. To study this relationship in a principled way, we first need to identify what factors in the interaction design decisively affect cumulative fatigue.

In prior work [30, 31] the authors observed that users get more rapidly fatigued when their arm moves higher from its resting position and extended further away from the body. We chose to investigate the height of the interaction zone as an experimental condition with a fixed range of arm extension, specifically a posture at approximately half of maximum arm stretch. Rest periods are also a decisive factor contributing to cumulative fatigue: the less rest we take, the more we get fatigued. We chose to control these two variables in our study design directly (2$\times$2 experiment conditions). Then we further investigate the applicability of the model for estimating subjective fatigue in different interaction conditions. Figure 4(e) shows the targets arranged on a 2D plane at two different locations (see Figure 4(c),(d)), one at shoulder level and the other midway between the shoulder and waist.

Pilot tests revealed that if subjects perform mid-air tasks in all four conditions (i.e., at least four mid-air pointing tasks in a series), subjects had a higher chance to experience learning and pre-fatigue effects. Thus, we designed our experiment with rest period conditions as a between-subject factor and interaction space conditions as a within-subject one. Each group had 12 participants (2 females), and subjects were given two randomly ordered interaction space conditions. Each group experienced a different order of rest periods – [20s-5s-15s-10s] for group 1 and [5s-10s-20s-15s] for group 2 – during approximately 5 minutes of pointing tasks.

Procedure

We first introduced the entire experimental procedure to the subjects, and surveyed their current physical state and mood along with background information. Then an experimenter measured the body segment parameters of subjects including total weight, height, upper arm length (shoulder to elbow), lower arm length (elbow to wrist), and hand length (wrist to the third finger tip). Based on these measurements, we computed the inertial properties of each upper limb segment based on De Leva's estimation method [16], and used those for the inverse dynamics computations (see Appendix for details).

Next, subjects started the training session for the mid-air pointing tasks. They performed all interaction space conditions in the main experiments with the guidance that they should "hit as many targets as possible while keeping good pointing accuracy". This is a typical instruction given for Fitts' Law studies, and used to spur the subject's motivation and effort in performing the tasks. We used the same instruction in the second sub-experiment (Exp. 2) to induce and maintain non-trivial arm fatigue during the tasks. After the training session, subjects had at least 5 minutes of rest.

Subsequently, subjects performed the direct maximum shoulder torque measurement. There were three blocks in this measurement consisting of 3 seconds of maximal force exertion and 2 minutes of rest. After the direct force measurement, we provided at least 15 minutes of mandatory rest to ensure no after-task interference, as done in traditional procedures [41]. Then subjects performed the isometric load exercise till they experienced task failure. This was followed by another 30 minutes of mandatory rest.

After this break, we started the mid-air pointing section (Exp. 2). There were two experimental conditions in this session. Each sub-task consists of four task blocks, and each block includes 1 minute of a pointing task and either one of 5, 10, 15, and 20 seconds of rest period (see Fig 5). Subjects took 30 minutes of mandatory rest in between sub-tasks to ensure that there is no interference from prior sub-task. Subjects provided Borg ratings every 20 second during the pointing tasks, and at the start and end of the rest period.

RESULTS

Here we first compare the indirect maximal shoulder torque estimates with the sensor-based direct measurements. Second, we show the effect of rest periods on the Borg ratings. Lastly, we investigate the performance of the TCM model in estimating the subjective fatigue level during mid-air interaction. Table 2 shows the all experiment conditions presented in the mid-air pointing experiments (Exp. 2). In the rest of this section, we denote group 1 and 2 as G1 and G2, and the

	Group 1	Group 2
Interaction zones	G1-H:shoulder level	G2-H:shoulder level
	G1-L:waist level	G2-L:waist level
Rest order	[20s, 5s, 15s, 10s]	[5s, 10s, 20s, 15s]

Table 2. Experimental conditions in the mid-air pointing tasks (Exp. 2).

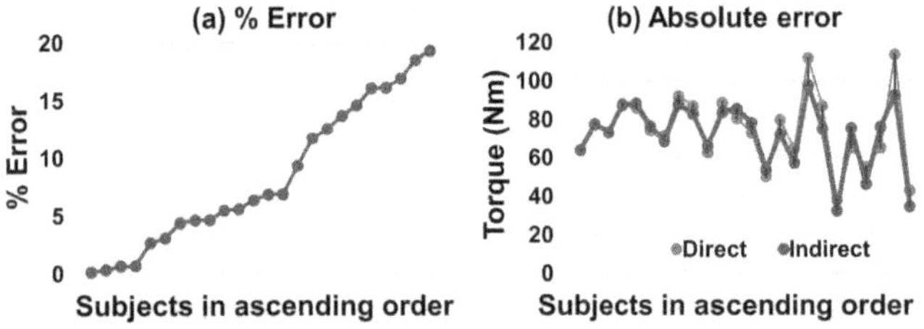

Figure 6. Results of indirect maximum shoulder torque measurement using an isometric fatiguing exercise, sorted by %error across subjects (x-axis). The results are compared with sensor-based direct measures.

high and low interaction zones as H and L. Then, we further analyze the factors on the estimation performance.

Validating Indirect Maximum Muscular Strength Measure

In the isometric load exercise (Exp. 1), we recorded the endurance time and the averaged shoulder torque (T_{avg}). By using these measures in Equation 1, we computed the indirect maximum shoulder torque ($T_{max,I}$). We also recorded the maximum shoulder force exerted toward a dynamometer and computed the direct maximum shoulder torque ($T_{max,D}$) from the force measures. We compared these two measures by evaluating *%error*= $\frac{|T_{max,I}-T_{max,D}|}{T_{max,D}} * 100\%$ and *absolute error* = $|T_{max,I} - T_{max,D}|$. Figure 6 shows the errors between $T_{max,I}$ and $T_{max,D}$. Results show only 6.1 Nm (SD=5.0) absolute error and 8.4% (SD=6.21%) relative error. A paired-samples t-Test showed no significant difference between $T_{max,I}$ and $T_{max,D}$ (t(23)=1.576, p=0.129).

Borg CR10 Scale Ratings across Subjects

Figure 7 shows the averaged Borg ratings for each experimental conditions. In Figure 7(a), G1-H shows a slow development of fatigue relative to G2-H. This is expected, as G1-H has 20 seconds rest in the first task block while G2-H has only 5 seconds rest. Thus, G2-H is a more fatiguing task condition compared to G1-H. A similar trend is visible in Figure 7(b), where G1-L and G2-L are compared. Both rest period conditions ultimately lead to arm muscle fatigue as the average Borg ratings reach their maximum towards the end of the last task block. The introduction of shorter rest periods at the beginning of the tasks seems to affect the overall fatigue level as the highest averaged Borg rating was 6.54 and 3.79 in G1-H and G1-L respectively, while G2-H and G2-L were 6.13 and 3.50. Figure 7 also shows the range of Borg ratings across all subjects. There are large variations across subjects in Borg ratings (average variation range=3.2, min=1, max=6).

Model Performance in Estimating Perceived Exertion

To evaluate the performance of the model in estimating subjective fatigue, we performed multiple cross-validations on interaction conditions and subjects. We also drew a comparison with an existing fatigue metric (CE [30]).

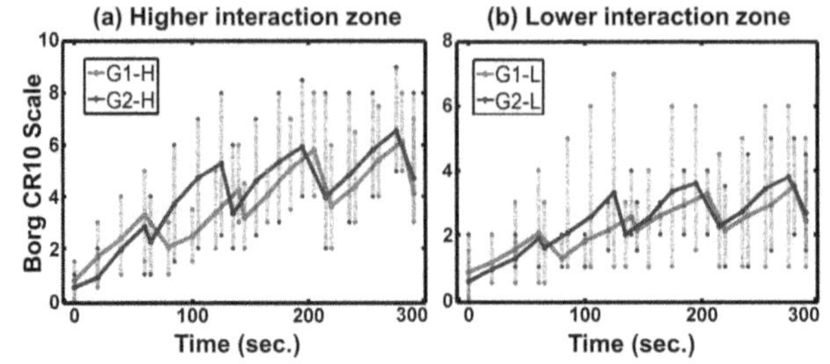

Figure 7. Borg CR10 ratings by 24 subjects during the mid-air pointing tasks. (a) shows the ratings in the high interaction zone in G1-H and G2-H. (b) shows the ratings in the low interaction zone in G1-L and G2-L.

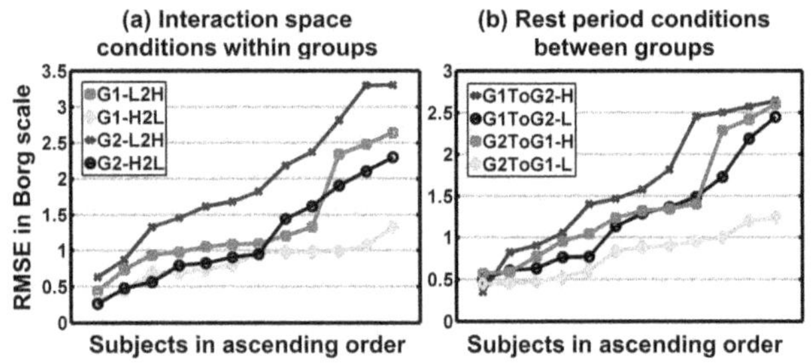

Figure 8. Results of cross-validation across (a): interaction space conditions within groups and (b): rest period conditions between groups. The subjects are sorted by the ascending order of RMSE.

Cross-Validating Interaction Space Conditions

To investigate the applicability of the cumulative fatigue model to different interaction space conditions–higher or lower interaction space–we designed a cross validation test where the model is optimized only with either one of interaction zone conditions. Then we tested it on the data set of the other condition. The cross-validations are performed in each group separately to see the performance in isolation without the potentially confounding effects of rest periods. In total, there were four cross-validations in this experiment, G1-H $\leftrightarrow$ G1-L (2) and G2-H $\leftrightarrow$ G2-L (2). Figure 8(a) depicts the RMSE of each subject data in ascending order. The averaged RMSEs of each cross validation are: G1-L2H = 1.36 (SD=0.72), G1-H2L = 0.83 (SD=0.28), G2-L2H = 1.95 (SD=0.87), and G1-H2L = 1.18 (SD=0.68) on the Borg scale. The overall RMSE is 1.33 (SD=0.77).

Between Subject Groups in Different Conditions

To demonstrate the applicability of the model to different conditions, such as the order of rest period and subjects, we designed a cross validation where the model is optimized using either one of two group's data. Then the model is tested with the other group's data. In this validation, we can evaluate how well the model can be used in different situations. There were total four cross-validations: G2$\rightarrow$G1-H/L (2) and G1$\rightarrow$G2-H/L (2). Figure 8(b) shows the between-group cross-validation results. The averaged RMSEs of each cross validation are: 'G2ToG1-H' = 1.38 (SD=0.70), 'G2ToG1-L' = 0.79 (SD=0.29), 'G1ToG2-H' = 1.63 (SD=0.78), and 'G2ToG1-L' = 1.24 (SD=0.64) on the Borg scale. The overall RMSE is 1.26 (SD=0.35), which is slightly lower than the cross-validation between interaction space conditions (1.33). To further investigate the statistical difference between the

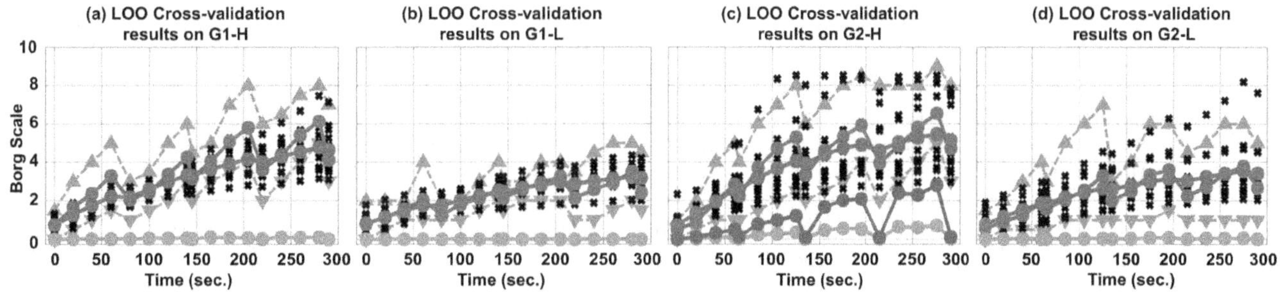

Figure 9. Results of the leave-one-out cross-validation of the model across all subject data. Green-upward/downward triangles: upper/lower bound of ground truth, blue circles: averaged ground truth, black crosses: TCM estimates, red circles: averaged TCM estimates, orange circles: averaged CE [30] estimates, purple circles: averaged CE estimates on the subject data with average %MVC above 15% (only observed in G2-H condition).

cross validation results between groups, we performed a paired t-test. Results showed no significant difference in the averaged RMSE (t(47)=-0.713, p=0.479). Thus, we conclude that the between group conditions did not affect the estimation performance of the model.

Effect of Interaction Conditions on Fatigue Estimation

To investigate the effect of task conditions–interaction zones and rest period order–on the estimation performance measured in RMSE, we performed a mixed factors ANOVA test with *rest period order* as between-subject factor and *interactions zones* as within-subject factor. We optimized the model using all data collected from the experiments (24 subjects × 2 interaction tasks), and obtained the model parameters as $F = 0.0146$ and $R = 0.0022$. The ANOVA results showed that there is no significant interaction effect between rest order and interaction zone ($F_{1,22} = 0.026$, $p = 0.874$); no significant difference between rest order conditions ($F_{1,22} = 2.361$, $p = 0.390$); but also that the interaction zone conditions are significantly different ($F_{1,22} = 26.812$, $p < 0.001$). Overall, the upper interaction zone (RMSE-M=1.52, SD=0.76) showed higher fatigue estimation errors compared to the lower condition (RMSE-M=0.98, SD=0.54).

The parameter optimization discussed above is ecologically less sound since it was performed using all subject data. To illustrate the robustness of our results, we decided to perform a leave-one-out (LOO) cross-validation for the fatigue models generated for each subject. For example, the first subject's data is excluded from optimizing the model, so that we can also test the model toward unseen subject's data. We assume that the RMSE measured using each model is independent from each other (i.e., only one data is eliminated in the optimization, and it does not affect the model parameters). We performed the same mixed factors ANOVA test, but with the models generated from the LOO cross-validations. With this, we obtained similar results in that there is no significant interaction effect between rest order and interaction zone ($F_{1,22} = 0.109$, $p = 0.745$); no significant effect of the two rest order conditions ($F_{1,22} = 3.589$, $p = 0.071$); and a significant effect of interaction zone conditions ($F_{1,22} = 17.350$, $p < 0.001$). Similar to the previous ANOVA test, the upper interaction zone (mean RMSE=1.50, SD=0.74) showed higher fatigue estimation errors compared to the lower condition (mean RMSE=1.03, SD=0.56). Based on these two congruent ANOVA test results, we conclude that the estimation performance of the TCM model is less affected by changes of rest duration compared to interaction space conditions.

Comparison with Consumed Endurance Metric

To compare the estimation performance of our model with an existing fatigue metric, *Comsumed Endurance* (CE [30]), we computed CE on all subject data used in the LOO cross-validation test. For CE, we used each subject's maximum shoulder torque and the torque profile measured during the pointing tasks. The averaged %MVC ($= T/T_{max} * 100\%$) for each subject observed during the pointing tasks was 11.79% (Range=[8.11,17.43]). We converted CE estimates to the Borg scale with $CE * 0.1 = Borg$, as identified by Hincapié-Ramos et al. [30]. The *total interaction time* for CE included both active and rest periods. As CE only quantifies instantaneous fatigue, we used averaged CE values of each period in between Borg ratings to estimate cumulative fatigue.

Figure 9 shows an overview of the results for the TCM model (ours) and CE across all subject data. The averaged TCM estimates (red circles) mostly follow the trend of averaged Borg ratings (blue circles). Also, individual Borg estimates (black crosses) are well within the min-max bounds (green triangles) of the Borg ratings. As CE automatically yields a fatigue level of zero for behaviors that induce exertion below 15%MVC, CE fails to properly quantify the fatigue level in all conditions. As our tasks mostly involved exertion below this threshold (avg.=11.79%MVC), this causes CE to underestimate fatigue. This fundamental limitation of CE yields larger overall errors compared to TCM in all task conditions (TCM: overall-RMSE=1.46, Range=[0.83,1.90], CE: overall-RMSE=3.45, Range=[2.42,4.25]).

We also compared our model with CE specifically for the data with averaged %MVC higher than 15% (N=4, avg. %MVC-Mean=15.93%, Range=[15.01,17.43]). Our TCM model (overall-RMSE=0.93, Range=[0.67,1.19]) still showed lower error than CE (overall-RMSE=2.96, Range=[2.12,3.60]). As shown in Figure 9(c) (purple circles), CE tends to almost monotonously increase while underestimating fatigue levels. Also, CE estimates drop suddenly close to zero during rest periods, failing to capture the continuity of fatigue.

In contrast to CE, our TCM model does not limit the range of exertion when estimating cumulative fatigue. Also, our model considers both rest and active periods, and correctly predicts cumulative fatigue for intermittent task periods.

Inter-individual Factors on Model Performance

We examined the potential effect of (1) subject's background (e.g., age, overall tiredness, experience with mid-air interfaces), (2) physical measurements (weight, height, limb length), and (3) variables collected during the maximum torque estimation (errors in the estimation, endurance time, maximum torque) on the errors in estimating subjective fatigue. We performed a Pearson's product-moment test with these individual variables, and none of them showed a significant correlation with the estimation errors. We further examined the relationship between Borg ratings and shoulder joint torque. These two parameters are directly used in both optimizing and evaluating the fatigue model, so it is worth investigating their effects on the estimation performance. In particular, we examined the ratio ($r_{B/T}$) between Borg ratings and shoulder joint torque during the mid-air pointing tasks: $r_{B/T} = \frac{Borg_{avg}}{T_{avg}}$, where $Borg_{avg}$ is the average of Borg ratings and T_{avg} is the average of shoulder torques collected from a subject performing a mid-air pointing task. We performed a linear regression analysis between $r_{B/T}$ and RMSE measured in the leave-one-out cross validation with all data. Results showed that there was a strong correlation between the estimation error and $r_{B/T}$ ($F_{1,46} = 109.148$, $p < 0.001$) with an R^2 of 0.704. A multiple linear regression was further calculated to predict the RMSE based on both factors $Borg_{avg}$ and T_{avg}. Results showed that the two factors explained 70.4% of the variance ($R^2 = 0.704$, $F_{2,45} = 53.401$, $p < 0.001$). However, only $Borg_{avg}$ was a significant predictor ($\beta = 0.687, p < 0.001$). This can be explained by (1) a significant correlation between subject's internal variability of Borg ratings and estimation errors and (2) limitations of the linear function ($\phi(\cdot)$) mapping Borg ratings to the estimate fatigue level M_F.

DISCUSSION

Our results validated the value of our approach for estimating subjective fatigue only using a camera-based skeleton tracking system instead of expensive and hard-to-access methods that are impractical for HCI.

Simple and Effective Shoulder Torque Measures

A comparison between our indirect maximum shoulder torque measurement through a simple mid-air pointing task showed no significant difference compared to traditional methods. To our knowledge, this is the first method to estimate an individual's maximum shoulder torque with only vision-based skeleton tracking sensors. We envision that our simple but effective method can be used in various HCI scenarios. For example, personalized training programs for Kinect-based at-home therapy applications [57] could be adapted to each individual's strength using our method.

Reliable Performance in Estimating Subjective Fatigue

Our results showed good estimation of subjective fatigue (maximum-mean-RMSE=1.95 (SD=0.87) observed in G2-L2H, minimum-mean-RMSE=0.79 (SD=0.29) observed in G2ToG1-L). Given the variability in subjective evaluations of fatigue, we believe that our model did well in generating such low errors. This approach is a significant stepping-stone to investigate the relation between subjective and objective fatigue. The computational complexity for implementing our algorithm is low, and it is implementable in real-time (50Hz).

Limitations and Future Work

While our model showed overall good estimation performance (overall-RMSE=1.46 in the LOO cross-validation), we identified some limitations that should be addressed in future work. First, our proposal is based on an assumption that through properly transforming biomechanical information we can estimate the perceived exertion level. However, as subjective fatigue is influenced by both physiological and psychological changes, there are several potential factors that could not be modeled with our two parameters. In the experiments, we observed that some subjects indicated much higher Borg ratings than what one might expect. For example, subject 19 reported about 8 to 10 %MVC while performing the pointing tasks, but indicated the highest Borg ratings–expressed in his native language–among all participants. This suggests that this subject may experience fatigue and rest differently compared to others (i.e., beyond the normal range for F and R parameters). Such inter-individual difference should be further studied to reduce estimation errors.

Second, our current assumption of a linear mapping between the perceived exertion and the maximum joint force should be revisited. Some psychophysical relations between muscular intensity and perceived exertion ratings can be described by power functions [12]. In the future, we will focus on identifying such a mapping function for a focus group of subjects.

We also plan to extend our approach to broader and complex interaction scenarios. For example, we can apply the TCM model to other mid-air interaction tasks (e.g., rotation, docking) by fitting the model parameters, as long as the corresponding data (joint torque, Borg ratings) is available. In general, fatigue is task-dependent [19, 20], and different model parameters might be needed for different tasks.

We are also looking at testing the model on tasks that involve highly-trained movements during interaction with varying rest periods, such as playing gesture-based games. Our model already quantifies the effect of rest on cumulative fatigue well, but it might be possible to improve estimation accuracy for varying rest periods via weighted optimization.

CONCLUSION

We presented a framework for evaluating subjective fatigue using only a vision-based skeleton tracking system. First, we proposed an indirect method to estimate the maximum shoulder torque through a simple mid-air pointing task. Comparison with traditional sensor-based direct measures showed no significant difference between the two methods. Second, we applied the three-compartment muscle model for estimating subjective arm fatigue. To our best knowledge, this is the first attempt to quantify cumulative subjective arm fatigue in a continuous task involving rest periods using only biomechanical information generated by a vision system. Overall, our model showed good estimation performance in multiple cross-validations. Statistical analysis revealed that the model's performance was robust to changes in the duration

Link	θ_i	α_i	m_i	${}^i\vec{S}_i$	${}^i\bar{I}_i$
1	θ_1	$-\frac{\pi}{2}$	0	$\vec{0}$	$0_{3\times3}$
2	$\theta_2-\frac{\pi}{2}$	$\frac{\pi}{2}$	0	$\vec{0}$	$0_{3\times3}$
3	$\theta_3+\frac{\pi}{2}$	$\frac{\pi}{2}$	m_{UA}	$[0,d_{UA},0]^{\mathrm{T}}$	$diag(I_{UAx},I_{UAz},I_{UAy})$
4	θ_4	0	$m_{LA}+m_H$	$[d_4,0,0]^{\mathrm{T}}*$	$diag(I_{4z},I_{4x},I_{4y})*$

Table 3. D-H and body segment parameters for 4-DOF arm model (*: find detailed definition in the paragraph below).

of rest, but relatively less robust to changes of the interaction zone. Moreover, our model outperformed an existing fatigue metric (CE [30]) as ours has no limits on the range of exertion considered and takes rest correctly into account.

ACKNOWLEDGEMENTS
We thank the reviewers for their valuable feedback. This work was partly supported by the National Science Foundation (Award # 1538868 CMMI). Any opinions, findings, and conclusions or recommendations expressed in this material are those of the author(s) and do not necessarily reflect the views of NSF.

Source Code Availability
The fatigue model implementation and the biomechanical upper limb analysis will be released on the project website: `http://www.tinyurl.com/cumulative-arm-fatigue`

APPENDIX: BIOMECHANICAL ARM MODEL
In Figure 3, four cylinders represent 1-DOF revolute joints ($J_0\sim J_3$), and vectors $\vec{z}_0\sim\vec{z}_3$ indicate their respective rotation axis. The first three joints ($J_0\sim J_2$) share the same position at the shoulder joint, and J_3 is attached at the elbow joint. Thus, the arm is a 4-DOF serial chain (shoulder:3, elbow:1). J_i connects i^{th} and $(i+1)^{\text{th}}$ link, and the link 0 is fixed to the ground body. The coordinate frame 0:$(\vec{x}_0,\vec{y}_0,\vec{z}_0)$ is the base, and its origin is at J_0. The frame i:$(\vec{x}_i,\vec{y}_i,\vec{z}_i)$ is attached to link i, and its origin is at J_i ($i\in[1,2,3]$). Lastly, the frame 4:$(\vec{x}_4,\vec{y}_4,\vec{z}_4)$ is fixed at the end of the lower arm (wrist joint).

Kinematic Analysis
We use De Leva's standard approach [16] to estimate the body segment parameters (BSPs) of the upper arm (UA), lower arm (LA), and hand (H), including the mass (m_{UA}, m_{LA}, m_H), the center of mass (COM) distance (d_{UA}, d_{LA}, d_H), and the moment of inertia matrix ($\in\mathbb{R}^{3\times3}$) of the arm segments ($\bar{I}_{UA}=diag(I_{UAx},I_{UAy},I_{UAz})$, $\bar{I}_{LA}=diag(I_{LAx},I_{LAy},I_{LAz})$, $\bar{I}_H=diag(I_{Hx},I_{Hy},I_{Hz})$) based on each individual's upper-arm (L_{UA}), forearm (L_{LA}), and hand (L_H) lengths, and total mass of body (m_{Tot}). We compute the COM distances by $d_{UA}=L_{UA}(100-\bar{L}_{UA})$, $d_{LA}=-L_{LA}(100-\bar{L}_{LA})$, $d_H=L_H*\bar{L}_H$; and body part masses by $m_{UA}=m_{Tot}*\bar{m}_{UA}$, $m_{LA}=m_{Tot}*\bar{m}_{LA}$, $m_H=m_{Tot}*\bar{m}_H$, where $\bar{L}_i$s and $\bar{m}_i$s are, respectively, gender dependent %length and %mass parameters [16].

The orientation of each joint axis is specified using the Denavit-Hartenberg (D-H) notation [18]. Table 3 defines the D-H parameters for the 4-DOF arm model, where θ_i is the rotation angle of ith link about $\vec{z}_{i-1}$ axis, and α_i is the angle between $\vec{z}_{i-1}$ and $\vec{z}_i$ about $\vec{x}_{i-1}$ axis. Based on the D-H parameters, the rotational matrices among the coordinate frames are constructed as:

$$^{i-1}R_i=\begin{bmatrix}cos(\theta_i) & -cos(\alpha_i)sin(\theta_i) & sin(\alpha_i)sin(\theta_i)) \\ sin(\theta_i) & cos(\alpha_i)cos(\theta_i) & -sin(\alpha_i)cos(\theta_i) \\ 0 & sin(\alpha_i) & cos(\alpha_i)\end{bmatrix}$$

where ${}^{i-1}R_i\in\mathbb{R}^{3\times3}$ is a rotation matrix transforming any vector in the ith frame into the (i-1)th frame [1].

Newton-Euler Inverse Dynamics
To compute joint torques from a given arm motions represented by the biomechanics model, we use a recursive Newton-Euler dynamics formulation (RNE) [15]. It first computes velocities and accelerations of each link from the 1st to 4th link, and then computes joint forces and torques in reverse order. Thus, the effects of forces and torques are propagated from the last (distal) to the first (proximal) link: Outward recursion ($1\rightarrow4$):

$$\begin{aligned}
{}^i\vec{\omega}_i &= {}^iR_{i-1}[{}^{i-1}\vec{\omega}_{i-1}+\hat{z}\dot{\theta}_i],\\
{}^i\dot{\vec{\omega}}_i &= {}^iR_{i-1}[{}^{i-1}\dot{\vec{\omega}}_{i-1}+\hat{z}_0\ddot{\theta}_i+{}^{i-1}\vec{\omega}_{i-1}\times\hat{z}_0\dot{\theta}_i],\\
{}^i\dot{\vec{v}}_i &= {}^i\dot{\vec{\omega}}_i\times{}^i\vec{P}_i^*+{}^i\vec{\omega}_i\times[{}^i\vec{\omega}_i\times{}^i\vec{P}_i^*]+{}^iR_{i-1}{}^{i-1}\dot{\vec{v}}_{i-1},\\
{}^i\vec{a}_i &= {}^i\dot{\vec{\omega}}_i\times{}^i\vec{S}_i+{}^i\vec{\omega}_i\times[{}^i\vec{\omega}_i\times{}^i\vec{S}_i]+{}^i\dot{\vec{v}}_i
\end{aligned}$$

Inward recursion ($4\rightarrow1$):

$$\begin{aligned}
{}^i\vec{f}_i &= {}^iR_{i+1}{}^{i+1}\vec{f}_{i+1}+m_i{}^i\vec{a}_i,\\
{}^i\vec{n}_i &= {}^iR_{i+1}[{}^{i+1}\vec{n}_{i+1}+{}^{i+1}R_i{}^i\vec{P}_i^*\times{}^{i+1}\vec{f}_{i+1}]\\
&\quad+[{}^i\vec{P}_i^*+{}^i\vec{S}_i]\times(m_i{}^i\vec{a}_i)+{}^i\bar{I}_i{}^i\dot{\vec{\omega}}_i+{}^i\vec{\omega}_i\times({}^i\bar{I}_i{}^i\vec{\omega}_i)
\end{aligned}$$

where $\hat{z}=[0,0,1]^{\mathrm{T}}$; ${}^i\vec{\omega}_i$ and ${}^i\dot{\vec{\omega}}_i$ are, respectively, the angular velocity and acceleration vectors of the ith link [2]; ${}^i\dot{\vec{v}}_i$ and ${}^i\vec{a}_i$ are, respectively, the linear acceleration vectors of the origin of the ith frame and COM for the ith link; ${}^i\vec{f}_i$ and ${}^i\vec{n}_i$ are, respectively, the force and moment exerted on the ith link by the (i-1)th link; ${}^i\vec{P}_i^*$ is a vector linking the origin of the (i-1)th and ith frame; ${}^i\vec{S}_i$ is a vector linking the origin of the ith frame and COM of the ith link; m_i is the mass of the ith link; and ${}^i\bar{I}_i\in\mathbb{R}^{3\times3}$ is a diagonal inertia matrix. The last three variables are constant BSPs and defined in Table 3. We calculate BSPs of link 4 by combining forearm and hand as one rigid body: $m_4=m_{LA}+m_H$, $d_4=\frac{d_{LA}*m_{LA}+d_H*m_H}{m_{LA}+m_H}$, $I_{4x}=I_{LAx}+I_{Hx}$, $I_{4y}=I_{LAy}+m_{LA}(d_4-d_{LA})^2+I_{Hy}+m_H(d_4-d_H)^2$, $I_{4z}=I_{LAz}+m_{LA}(d_4-d_{LA})^2+I_{Hz}+m_H(d_4-d_H)^2$. We set the initial values as ${}^0\vec{\omega}_0={}^0\dot{\vec{\omega}}_0={}^5\vec{f}_5={}^5\vec{n}_5=\vec{0}$ and ${}^0\dot{\vec{v}}_0=[-9.81,0,0]^T$ m/s^2. Finally, we compute the shoulder torque as:

$$T=\sqrt{\tau_0+\tau_1+\tau_2},$$

where $\tau_i=[({}^{i+1}\vec{n}_{i+1})^{\mathrm{T}}({}^{i+1}R_i\hat{z})]^2$ and $\hat{z}=[0,0,1]^{\mathrm{T}}$.

[1] $[{}^{i-1}R_i]^{-1}=[{}^{i-1}R_i]^{\mathrm{T}}={}^iR_{i-1}$

[2] A leading superscript F of a vector ${}^F\vec{x}\in\mathbb{R}^3$ indicates that the vector is referenced to the coordinate frame F.

REFERENCES

1. Biodex dynamometer. http://www.biodex.com/physical-medicine/products/dynamometers.
2. Gorilla arm. http://www.computer-dictionary-online.org/?q=gorilla%20arm.
3. Amann, M., Romer, L. M., Pegelow, D. F., Jacques, A. J., Hess, C. J., and Dempsey, J. A. Effects of arterial oxygen content on peripheral locomotor muscle fatigue. *Journal of Applied Physiology 101*, 1 (2006), 119–127.
4. Åstrand, P.-O. *Textbook of work physiology: physiological bases of exercise*. Human Kinetics, 2003.
5. Audet, C., and Dennis Jr, J. E. Analysis of generalized pattern searches. *SIAM Journal on Optimization 13*, 3 (2002), 889–903.
6. Bachynskyi, M., Oulasvirta, A., Palmas, G., and Weinkauf, T. Is motion capture-based biomechanical simulation valid for hci studies?: study and implications. In *Proceedings of the 32nd annual conference on Human factors in computing systems*, ACM (2014), 3215–3224.
7. Bachynskyi, M., Palmas, G., Oulasvirta, A., Steimle, J., and Weinkauf, T. Performance and ergonomics of touch surfaces: A comparative study using biomechanical simulation. In *Proceedings of the 33rd Annual Conference on Human Factors in Computing Systems*, ACM (2015), 1817–1826.
8. Bachynskyi, M., Palmas, G., Oulasvirta, A., and Weinkauf, T. Informing the design of novel input methods with muscle coactivation clustering. *ACM Trans. Comput.-Hum. Interact. 21*, 6 (Jan. 2015), 30:1–30:25.
9. Bijur, P. E., Silver, W., and Gallagher, E. J. Reliability of the visual analog scale for measurement of acute pain. *Academic emergency medicine 8*, 12 (2001), 1153–1157.
10. Borg, G. Psychophysical scaling with applications in physical work and the perception of exertion. *Scandinavian journal of work, environment & health* (1990), 55–58.
11. Borg, G. *Borg's perceived exertion and pain scales.* Human kinetics, 1998.
12. Borg, G. A. Psychophysical bases of perceived exertion. *Med sci sports exerc 14*, 5 (1982), 377–381.
13. Carifio, J., and Perla, R. J. Ten common misunderstandings, misconceptions, persistent myths and urban legends about likert scales and likert response formats and their antidotes. *Journal of Social Sciences 3*, 3 (2007), 106–116.
14. Cifrek, M., Medved, V., Tonković, S., and Ostojić, S. Surface emg based muscle fatigue evaluation in biomechanics. *Clinical Biomechanics 24*, 4 (2009), 327–340.
15. Craig, J. J. *Introduction to robotics: mechanics and control*, vol. 3. Pearson Prentice Hall Upper Saddle River, 2005.
16. De Leva, P. Adjustments to zatsiorsky-seluyanov's segment inertia parameters. *Journal of biomechanics 29*, 9 (1996), 1223–1230.
17. Dedering, Å., Németh, G., and Harms-Ringdahl, K. Correlation between electromyographic spectral changes and subjective assessment of lumbar muscle fatigue in subjects without pain from the lower back. *Clinical Biomechanics 14*, 2 (1999), 103–111.
18. Denavit, J., and Hartenberg, R. S. A kinematic notation for lower-pair mechanisms based on matrices. *Trans. ASME, J. Appl. Mech. 22*, 2 (1965), 215 – 221.
19. Enoka, R. M., and Duchateau, J. Muscle fatigue: what, why and how it influences muscle function. *The Journal of physiology 586*, 1 (2008), 11–23.
20. Enoka, R. M., and Stuart, D. G. Neurobiology of muscle fatigue. *Journal of applied physiology 72*, 5 (1992), 1631–1648.
21. Eston, R. Use of ratings of perceived exertion in sports. *International journal of sports physiology and performance 7*, 2 (2012), 175–182.
22. Freivalds, A. *Biomechanics of the upper limbs: mechanics, modeling and musculoskeletal injuries*. CRC press, 2011.
23. Frey-Law, L. A., and Avin, K. G. Endurance time is joint-specific: a modelling and meta-analysis investigation. *Ergonomics 53*, 1 (2010), 109–129.
24. Frey-Law, L. A., Looft, J. M., and Heitsman, J. A three-compartment muscle fatigue model accurately predicts joint-specific maximum endurance times for sustained isometric tasks. *Journal of biomechanics 45*, 10 (2012), 1803–1808.
25. Haga, S., Shinoda, H., and Kokubun, M. Effects of task difficulty and time-on-task on mental workload. *Japanese Psychological Research 44*, 3 (2002), 134–143.
26. Harrison, C., Ramamurthy, S., and Hudson, S. E. On-body interaction: armed and dangerous. In *Proceedings of the Sixth International Conference on Tangible, Embedded and Embodied Interaction*, ACM (2012), 69–76.
27. Hart, S. G., and Staveland, L. E. Development of nasa-tlx (task load index): Results of empirical and theoretical research. *Advances in psychology 52* (1988), 139–183.
28. Hassenzahl, M., and Tractinsky, N. User experience-a research agenda. *Behaviour & information technology 25*, 2 (2006), 91–97.
29. Hayes, K., Walton, J. R., Szomor, Z. L., and Murrell, G. A. Reliability of 3 methods for assessing shoulder strength. *Journal of Shoulder and Elbow surgery 11*, 1 (2002), 33–39.

30. Hincapié-Ramos, J. D., Guo, X., Moghadasian, P., and Irani, P. Consumed endurance: A metric to quantify arm fatigue of mid-air interactions. In *Proceedings of the 32nd annual conference on Human factors in computing systems*, ACM (2014), 1063–1072.

31. Hofmann, M., Brger, R., Frost, N., Karremann, J., Keller-Bacher, J., Kraft, S., Bruder, G., and Steinicke, F. Comparing 3d interaction performance in comfortable and uncomfortable regions. In *Proceedings of the GI-Workshop VR/AR* (2013), 3–14.

32. Hornbæk, K., and Law, E. L.-C. Meta-analysis of correlations among usability measures. In *Proceedings of the SIGCHI conference on Human factors in computing systems*, ACM (2007), 617–626.

33. Höysniemi, J., Hämäläinen, P., and Turkki, L. Wizard of oz prototyping of computer vision based action games for children. In *Proceedings of the 2004 conference on Interaction design and children: building a community*, ACM (2004), 27–34.

34. Hunter, S. K., Duchateau, J., and Enoka, R. M. Muscle fatigue and the mechanisms of task failure. *Exercise and sport sciences reviews 32*, 2 (2004), 44–49.

35. ISO, I. 9241-9 ergonomic requirements for office work with visual display terminals (vdts)-part 9: Requirements for non-keyboard input devices (fdis-final draft international standard), 2000. *International Organization for Standardization.*

36. Jacob, M. G., and Wachs, J. P. Context-based hand gesture recognition for the operating room. *Pattern Recognition Letters 36* (2014), 196–203.

37. Kaiser, E., Olwal, A., McGee, D., Benko, H., Corradini, A., Li, X., Cohen, P., and Feiner, S. Mutual disambiguation of 3d multimodal interaction in augmented and virtual reality. In *Proceedings of the 5th international conference on Multimodal interfaces*, ACM (2003), 12–19.

38. Liu, J. Z., Brown, R. W., and Yue, G. H. A dynamical model of muscle activation, fatigue, and recovery. *Biophysical journal 82*, 5 (2002), 2344–2359.

39. Lloyd, A., Gandevia, S., and Hales, J. Muscle performance, voluntary activation, twitch properties and perceived effort in normal subjects and patients with the chronic fatigue syndrome. *Brain 114*, 1 (1991), 85–98.

40. Malik, S., McDonald, C., and Roth, G. Hand tracking for interactive pattern-based augmented reality. In *Proceedings of the 1st International Symposium on Mixed and Augmented Reality*, IEEE (2002), 117–126.

41. Mathiassen, S. E., and Åhsberg, E. Prediction of shoulder flexion endurance from personal factors. *International Journal of Industrial Ergonomics 24*, 3 (1999), 315–329.

42. Morishita, S., Yamauchi, S., Fujisawa, C., and Domen, K. Rating of perceived exertion for quantification of the intensity of resistance exercise. *International Journal of Physical Medicine & Rehabilitation 2013* (2014).

43. Noble, B. J. Clinical applications of perceived exertion. *Medicine and science in sports and exercise 14*, 5 (1981), 406–411.

44. Öberg, T., Sandjö, L., and Kadefors, R. Subjective and objective evaluation of shoulder muscle fatigue. *Ergonomics 37*, 8 (1994), 1323–1333.

45. Raikova, R. A general approach for modelling and mathematical investigation of the human upper limb. *Journal of biomechanics 25*, 8 (1992), 857–867.

46. Rohmert, W. Ermittlung von erholungspausen für statische arbeit des menschen. *European Journal of Applied Physiology and Occupational Physiology 18*, 2 (1960), 123–164.

47. Roy, J.-S., Ma, B., MacDermid, J. C., and Woodhouse, L. J. Shoulder muscle endurance: the development of a standardized and reliable protocol. *BMC Sports Science, Medicine and Rehabilitation 3*, 1 (2011), 1.

48. Segerstrom, S. C., and Nes, L. S. Heart rate variability reflects self-regulatory strength, effort, and fatigue. *Psychological science 18*, 3 (2007), 275–281.

49. Sjøgaard, G., Savard, G., and Juel, C. Muscle blood flow during isometric activity and its relation to muscle fatigue. *European journal of applied physiology and occupational physiology 57*, 3 (1988), 327–335.

50. Sonne, M. W., and Potvin, J. R. A modified version of the three-compartment model to predict fatigue during submaximal tasks with complex force-time histories. *Ergonomics 59*, 1 (2016), 85–98.

51. Spielholz, P. Calibrating borg scale ratings of hand force exertion. *Applied Ergonomics 37*, 5 (2006), 615–618.

52. Teather, R., and Stuerzlinger, W. Pointing at 3D targets in a stereo head-tracked virtual environment. In *Proceedings of the Symposium on 3D User Interfaces*, IEEE (2011), 87–94.

53. Troiano, A., Naddeo, F., Sosso, E., Camarota, G., Merletti, R., and Mesin, L. Assessment of force and fatigue in isometric contractions of the upper trapezius muscle by surface emg signal and perceived exertion scale. *Gait & posture 28*, 2 (2008), 179–186.

54. Vinayak, Murugappan, S., Liu, H., Ramani, K., et al. Shape-it-up: Hand gesture based creative expression of 3d shapes using intelligent generalized cylinders. *Computer-Aided Design 45*, 2 (2013), 277–287.

55. Westerblad, H., Allen, D. G., and Lännergren, J. Muscle fatigue: lactic acid or inorganic phosphate the major cause? *Physiology 17*, 1 (2002), 17–21.

56. Xia, T., and Law, L. A. F. A theoretical approach for modeling peripheral muscle fatigue and recovery. *Journal of biomechanics 41*, 14 (2008), 3046–3052.

57. Zhao, W., Feng, H., Lun, R., Espy, D. D., and Reinthal, M. A. A kinect-based rehabilitation exercise monitoring and guidance system. In *Software Engineering and Service Science (ICSESS), 2014 5th IEEE International Conference on*, IEEE (2014), 762–765.

Women's Safety in Public Spaces: Examining the Efficacy of Panic Buttons in New Delhi

Naveena Karusala & Neha Kumar
Georgia Institute of Technology
Atlanta, Georgia, USA
{nkarusala3, neha.kumar}@gatech.edu

ABSTRACT

We present a qualitative inquiry through the lens of feminist Human-Computer Interaction (HCI) into women's perceptions of personal safety in New Delhi, India. Since a brutal gang-rape incident took place in Delhi in December 2012 and received global attention, women's safety has been the focus of much attention India-wide. In April 2016, the Indian government issued a mandate that all mobile phones sold in India 2017 onwards must include a panic button for women's safety. We draw on interview and survey data to examine women's responses to the mandate, also investigating what factors influence their perceptions of safety, positively and negatively. Our findings indicate that women's sense of safety may be deconstructed into a multitude of factors–personal, public, social, technological–that must align for this sense of safety to be preserved. We then discuss the implications these factors have for the success and (re-)design of the panic button and similar interventions.

Author Keywords

Safety; Gender; India; HCI4D; Feminist HCI

ACM Classification Keywords

H.5.m. Information Interfaces and Presentation (e.g. HCI): Miscellaneous

INTRODUCTION

Concerns regarding violations of women's safety have been foregrounded in India ever since the December 2012 brutal gang rape of a 23-year-old woman in the capital city of New Delhi. There was widespread public outcry of unprecedented magnitude, with protests occurring not only in the capital, but also in other cities and nations [20]. Media attention spread globally "within a matter of days" [27] and media reports on rape increased overall [12]. The event also resulted in a reassessment of criminal law regarding sexual assault and women's safety, though not all recommendations have been implemented [32]. In 2014, 2,069 rape cases were reported in New Delhi, compared to 1,571 cases in 2013 [26]. The number of reported cases of molestation rose by nearly 25% to 4,179 in the same period [26].

Permission to make digital or hard copies of all or part of this work for personal or classroom use is granted without fee provided that copies are not made or distributed for profit or commercial advantage and that copies bear this notice and the full citation on the first page. Copyrights for components of this work owned by others than ACM must be honored. Abstracting with credit is permitted. To copy otherwise, or republish, to post on servers or to redistribute to lists, requires prior specific permission and/or a fee. Request permissions from permissions@acm.org.
CHI 2017, May 6-11, 2017, Denver, CO, USA.
Copyright © 2017 ACM ISBN 978-1-4503-4655-9/17/05 ...$15.00.
http://dx.doi.org/10.1145/3025453.3025532

In an effort to improve women's safety, the central government of India issued a mandate in April 2016. Phone manufacturers nationwide are now required to implement a panic button for women's safety on every new mobile phone [38]. In order to make the panic button effective, India's various contact numbers for emergency services have been consolidated into one, which is currently functioning and accepting calls [38]. To learn more about the public response to this mandate, we conducted an interpretive study of women's safety in New Delhi, drawing on interview and survey data. We began the conversation with participants' views regarding the new panic button, before engaging in a focused discussion of women's experiences and conceptualizations regarding personal safety in public spaces. Our research assesses the appropriateness of this panic button as a technology intervention for women's safety, as seen through the eyes of women in New Delhi.

Questions around gender and technology design are not new to the field of human computer interaction (HCI). Gender-focused HCI work in the past has included meta-analyses of how gender is represented in technologies [13, 14, 7], the role of gender in online communities [28, 37, 23, 15], and designing technology for women [34, 4, 19]. In recent years, the scope of HCI research has expanded to explore the design of technology for women's personal safety in public spaces in both developed and developing countries [30, 1].

Our study looks at a large-scale intervention of safety technology in India. We use the lens of feminist HCI in the process of analyzing and discussing our findings. The feminist HCI framework as described by Bardzell suggests a commitment to feminist as well as scientific objectives [5], providing room to reflect on how exactly our findings are situated among the power imbalances perpetuated by the patriarchal value system. To pursue such an analysis, we begin with providing a definition of safety based on our empirical findings. We view personal safety as a state in which one is protected from or need not feel compelled to think of ways in which to protect oneself from immediate threats to the individual person, such as people who seem to or actually have the intent to harm one's physical or mental well-being. We also recognize that terms referring to women's safety issues, such as street harassment, sexual assault, and sexual violence, overlap with each other. We study all forms of violence women face in public spaces, but focus on real or anticipated situations that might bring to test the efficacy of the panic button.

In the next section, we present works related to technology and women's safety that we have considered in our effort to determine the successes and pitfalls of prior interventions. We then describe our methodological approach, before presenting our findings and their implications for the success of the panic button in New Delhi. There are two key takeaways that we discuss. First, we use our findings to explain what India's current implementation of the panic button likely could and could not accomplish with regards to improving women's safety. Second, we use a feminist HCI framework to make recommendations for designing a system in which the panic button might play a successful role in addressing women's safety concerns.

RELATED WORK

The basis of our study is the literature on women's safety practices in public spaces and safety technology. Our research extends prior work by offering a more nuanced assessment of women's safety in New Delhi as it focuses on an ongoing large scale implementation of interventionist safety technology using the lens of feminist HCI.

Existing research has shown that there are common situations in which people tend to feel unsafe, such as places that are unfamiliar, not well-lit, far from a safe or familiar place, or notorious for being unsafe [6]. People tend to feel safe in places that are more familiar, where their social network is present, or when the perception of having their social network present is apparent [6, 10, 30]. Women, in particular, tend to be concerned when walking alone in unsafe areas, using public transit, in the presence of unfamiliar men, or in very crowded places such as concerts or markets [1, 6]. Especially in India, women are concerned when using public transit (possibly as a result of public transit being more widely used) [6]. A study of public spaces in New Delhi found male-dominated areas like cigarette shops, car parks, dilapidated buildings, and parks without good lighting to be most unsafe, while residential areas, crowded night markets and parks, and patrolled areas were safest [36]. We extend these findings by examining how public spaces, along with other autonomous actors, contribute to women's sense of safety in New Delhi.

In light of gender differences in navigation of public spaces, research has highlighted the impact of constantly dealing with threats to personal safety. Women may feel helpless, faced with the lack of public discourse on women's safety and the limits on their mobility [1]. Simultaneously, bringing attention to street harassment can itself be a source of shame and embarrassment [1]. Women also tend to avoid reporting to the police, as police may be viewed as unhelpful or partake in harassment themselves [17]. Reporting sexual crimes can result in the woman being shamed, being blamed for supposedly provocative behavior, or being made light of [17]. We examine the diverse actors and norms that contribute to these situations, through the case of India's panic button.

Drawing on the above understanding of women's safety practices, multiple studies have taken place with the purpose of seeing if information and communication technology (ICT) might play a role towards women's safety. In studying the safety practices of people navigating an urban setting at night, Satchell and Foth [30] found that women, men, and sex workers acted very differently. Women pretended to talk or text on their phones in order to give the perception that they are close to a social network that can aid them in case of an emergency [30]. Men tended to see their phone as a tool to call for help after an incident started to occur [30]. Meanwhile, sex workers would talk on the phone with their managers or co-workers, constantly updating them regarding their location so that in case of an emergency, the police could be sent to their exact location [30]. Blom et al. showed that women also called to notify loved ones on arrival to their destination [6]. Dimond et al. addressed ICT use in the more private context of domestic violence, recommending a redesign of ICTs to respect women's need for privacy and control over communication when escaping the abuser [11].

To expand the function of ICTs in women's safety in public spaces, multiple projects such as Protibadi [1], Safestreet [2], Harassmap [39], ComfortZones [6], CityWatch [18], and Hollaback! [10] have designed similar features: alarms to draw attention of passers-by, quick and silent methods of contacting friends or police, maps displaying locations of frequent harassment (often created with crowd-sourced data), and methods of describing and sharing experiences of street harassment with others. There were multiple social and technical issues that came up with these designs. Alarms, though effective in scenarios where there are many bystanders, could also be a source of embarrassment and unwanted attention [1]. The desire to contact police also differed by culture. In one study, women in the U.S. preferred contacting the police, while women in India preferred contacting their social circle [6]. Maps such as Harassmap and ComfortZones, which indicated locations with a high frequency of sexual harassment incidents, sometimes allowed women to avoid those areas and broke through literacy barriers using visuals [39, 6]. However, these types of maps are also perceived as another form of unfair adjustment that women have to make to be safe [39]. ComfortZones, which used a tagging feature to label a location as comfortable or uncomfortable, was also deemed to provide too little information to be useful for navigation decisions [6]. Finally, sharing experiences of sexual harassment, either immediately with the touch of a button or more descriptively in a website posting, gave women space to relate to or become more aware of street harassment, while also challenging misconceptions and normalization of street harassment [9, 10]. Variations on these core features were special assurances of anonymity of information to reduce social stigma and real time notifications of entering high risk areas as women traveled [2]. We extend this work by viewing a current large scale implementation of interventionist safety technology through the lens of feminist HCI and analyzing its efficacy in correcting power imbalances.

To evaluate the panic button with feminist HCI principles, we draw on Bardzell's framework [5], focusing on the values of **participation**, **pluralism**, **ecology**, and **advocacy**. Pluralism is the idea that a universal design does not exist [5]. Pluralism and participation work together to inform a design process that purposefully asks for and recognizes differing needs within a user base [5]. The quality of ecology encourages us to think about how a technology reflexively designs the environment in which it is being used [5]. Advocacy focuses on ensuring technology is progressive and attempts to bring about political emancipation [5]. To apply these concepts to our study, we think about the "who questions" as suggested by Muller [25]. We ask *who* speaks for women regarding their safety and *who* is allowed to design how women ensure safety. In doing so, we also draw inspiration from Dimond's application of feminist HCI to Hollaback!, a social movement organization and forum to discuss street harassment [9, 10].

METHODOLOGY

We conducted our study (post institutional review board approval) in New Delhi from June to August 2016. The methods we used included 17 semi-structured interviews and an in-depth survey with 30 responses (through viral distribution). Both instruments asked the same questions with the goal of understanding women's opinions on the panic button mandate and experiences with personal safety in public spaces. The questions covered participants' demographics, commute practices, views on the panic button, conceptualizations of and experiences with safety, and technology use for personal safety. Examples included "Are you aware of the new nationwide mandate on having a panic button on every phone? How do you feel about it?", "What are your thoughts on personal safety? Is it a concern?", "Is it more of a concern here in Delhi than in, say, other parts of the country or the world?", and "Have you ever been in a situation wherein you or anybody you know felt that your personal safety was threatened?"

Our survey targeted men and women at or above the age of 18 living in New Delhi currently or up until recently. The authors, other researchers in New Delhi, and study participants shared the survey link on various social media channels. We note that because the survey was distributed so widely, people who did not live in New Delhi also responded to it. Rather than discounting these responses, we used them to compare ideas of safety between New Delhi and other Indian cities. Although we did not initially plan to include men in our sample, some did respond to our survey, and we analyzed this data as well to see how it compared against women's responses. Overall, the interviews allowed us to delve deeper into participants' thoughts and experiences, while the survey provided a bird's eye view of trends across different demographics.

We conducted our interviews in English with women between the ages of 21 and 33, all residing (and working/studying) in New Delhi. We began by recruiting five women in their late 20s and asked them to refer any women in New Delhi between the ages of 18 and 40 who would be interested in participating in a study regarding women's safety. As a result of utilizing snowball sampling, we were generally referred to participants who were in a similar age range and comparable socioeconomic status [16].

Responses to closed-ended questions in the interview and survey were analyzed by calculating percentages and cross-tabulated (as fitting) to view percentages for a certain gender or income bracket. Responses to open-ended questions in the interview and survey were coded using interpretive qualitative analysis [24]. We conducted "open coding" by going through each response to questions and selecting concepts. Examples included "I talk to my parents while riding in autos" and "I avoid walking alone in dark places". Further iterations of coding resulted in the formation of categories such as "social contact: calling or messaging family" or "locations: avoiding isolated areas". These categories were consolidated into six factors that shape women's sense of safety, which we describe in our findings.

Participants

The majority of interview participants were single women from middle-income households. Ten of 17 participants interviewed came from families who made more than INR 10 lakhs (approx. USD 15K) annually. Two of 17 participants came from families who made between INR 2.5 lakhs (approx. USD 3.7K) and INR 10 lakhs. Three of 17 participants indicated that they made less than INR 2.5 lakhs, but this number includes two participants who were referring to their own income, as opposed to their family's income as a whole. Family income was more representative of a person's socioeconomic status as the majority of participants lived with their family; three lived in a paying guest apartment and two lived in a hostel. Every participant traveled for work or university at least once a week, with many traveling for work or university three to four times or more per week.

Survey respondents were from 18 to 64 years old, with an average age of 30. Among them, 18 of 25 respondents were women and seven were men. Nineteen of 25 respondents' families had an income of above INR 10 lakhs annually. Respondents resided in the Indian cities of New Delhi, Gurgaon, Faridabad, Bikaner, Calcutta, Rohtak, Bangalore, Kanpur, Mumbai, Zirakpur, and Hyderabad, with a plurality residing in New Delhi. Twenty-two of 24 respondents traveled alone to work or university three to four times or more per week.

We note that our findings are focused on women of middle and high socioeconomic status (SES) who are educated and lead lives of relative privilege. These women's transportation choices, access to technology, and familial support likely differ from those of women from lower SES. As a result of these differences, the women in our sample are, broadly speaking, at lower risk of safety concerns that come with the inability to afford private transportation, not having a smartphone with mobile data, living in places that lack security, and respectability politics. Nevertheless, our participants are still target users of the panic button–women with mobile phones. By interviewing these women, we wished to examine what the panic button could change for women who had abundant access to resources because, despite this access, they still face pervasive and serious safety concerns. Understanding personal safety in a high-resource context is illuminating because it sets a standard of what safety technology can and cannot accomplish even in 'best-case scenarios'.

Reflexivity

Our interpretation of the data we collected is undoubtedly shaped by our background and experiences with safety. We are both women of Indian origin and were in New Delhi during the time of the study. We have both also experienced personal safety concerns in New Delhi, and on a regular basis.

As a result, we had an experiential understanding of participants' responses and chose to view the findings and make design recommendations via the lens of feminist HCI so as to draw out the way power imbalances make safety an ongoing concern for the women we studied.

FINDINGS

We now present the findings from our study, highlighting six factors that we found most influence women's safety. We use a feminist HCI framework to asses how each factor exerts control over women's safety, or in asking "the who questions" [25], how each factor speaks for women and designs the process of ensuring safety.

Safety in Public Spaces

Every participant talked about safety in terms of the various public spaces they encountered in their daily lives. Public spaces that exhibited certain characteristics that we will describe below were deemed safe or unsafe, to roam freely in or to avoid altogether.

Intensity of Crowds

Locations could always be categorized as isolated or crowded, with isolated areas judged to be unsafe. Crowded areas tended to be main streets that had the most shops or vehicles, public transportation during the day, markets, and malls. Participants preferred such areas because crowds could be a deterrent to street harassment or sexual assault due to the fact that there was an increased likelihood of someone intervening in the case of an emergency or supporting a woman in rebuking a harasser. When asked why she considered malls to be safe places, P2 said the following:

> *"In malls, there are so many people... You can't eve-tease in front of people, you might get beaten up... In Delhi, 70% percent of the time, people will come and help you."*

Women preferred crowds whether it was day or night, with some participants disliking isolated areas even during the daytime, which was considered the safest time to be in public spaces by every participant. In fact, isolation was the most cited reason New Delhi was considered unsafe past 9 pm, after which the number of people in public spaces dropped considerably. Notably, the presence of crowds only made it more likely that there would be helpful bystanders. Some participants still felt that there was a chance no one would care enough to intervene in an emergency and that they had to be aware of their surroundings even in non-isolated areas.

On the other end of the spectrum, participants thought extremely large crowds were unsafe as well. While isolation meant there may not be anyone nearby to help, high-density areas provided a cloak of anonymity to perpetrators of street harassment. P1 described a situation in which crowds helped facilitate an instance of street harassment:

> *"So in India the carnivals or exhibitions are very, very crowded... even in metros, it is so crowded that people try to purposely stick to you or come closer to you as an excuse because the place is very crowded."*

At the same time, sheer numbers did not explain how comfortable a woman felt in a public space. Women did not always have to be on the lookout for danger in areas with "filtered" populations, regardless of how crowded it was. For example, participants who traveled on the metro alone preferred riding in the women's compartment because they wanted to avoid the increased likelihood of staring or groping in the general compartments crowded by men. Participants felt the safest public spaces were malls or upscale neighborhoods because one could wear revealing clothing without being harassed. Mall security would limit what a person could bring with them into the building and malls generally only attracted people of higher socioeconomic status, which many participants felt was an indicator, albeit an unreliable one, of a more tolerant mindset towards women's freedom of choice. Finally, women generally felt safest in their homes because their surroundings were limited to their family and people purposefully allowed in the house. In all these areas, there are limits to the type of people who women could potentially come in contact with, filtering out people who seemed more likely to threaten women's safety.

These scenarios represent Rosenfeld and Noterman's argument that power determines whether a space is safe, as opposed to a space being objectively safe or unsafe [29]. Large crowds could be a negative factor because they allowed groping, but crowds of women in the women's compartment of the metro were acceptable because women do not exert power over one another in the same way men exert power over women with the threat of harassment or assault.

Cities and Cultural Norms

The attention New Delhi has received for women's safety, being dubbed the "rape capital," prompted us to question whether or not women felt New Delhi as a whole is unsafe compared to other cities in India.

For some survey respondents and interview participants, New Delhi was not any more unsafe than other cities. For these participants, lack of safety stemmed more from being in an unfamiliar area, hearing about unsafe situations in any foreign cities, or not having family residing in the area, rather than New Delhi's reputation as an unsafe city. Many interview participants with this mindset felt that there is no place that is truly safe and one must always be cautious of their surroundings. Often, they could also cite unsafe experiences in other cities. P5 explained the following:

> *"For example, when we went on vacation last year... We were in London... It's relative. They think that it's safer, because of the media hype that is created, but there's stabbings and other things you don't get to know unless you read the papers. In terms of women going out, there's more women that you can see on the tube, but I wouldn't say it's safe because I've seen women being harassed on the tube as well and people are more openly harassing them because the culture is such that you can greet people... you wouldn't talk to strangers, but over there, it's rude not to."*

For others, New Delhi was especially unsafe in comparison to other places they had visited, lived, or heard stories about. Sixty percent of survey respondents felt that personal safety is more of a concern in New Delhi than in other parts of the world. Fewer than half of them resided in New Delhi. These respondents generally cited a perception of more frequent reports of sexual assault in New Delhi. Twenty-seven percent of those who responded felt that personal safety may be more of a concern in New Delhi than in other parts of the world. Once again, fewer than half of these respondents resided in New Delhi. Of the respondents who resided in New Delhi, all but one respondent said personal safety is more of a concern in New Delhi than in other parts of the world. The city most commonly cited as being safer than New Delhi was Mumbai. Mumbai was considered a safer city by many participants because women were not as restricted–they could travel on the streets at night without fear of harm, wear more revealing clothing, and were not often approached by strangers. As a result, there were indeed more women on the streets, even late at night, reinforcing the feeling of safety. While Mumbai provided a sense of safety that was largely cultural, specific regulations in other cities afforded women a sense of safety. P12 described Chandigarh as a highly regulated city:

> *"Everything shuts off by 12... so there is no late night clubbing... In Delhi... they know that if somebody drops [trash] over there, you let it be over there. Nobody else is going to pick it up. Chandigarh is considered one of the cleanest cities because they know you don't have to drop it on the road. They follow all the traffic rules because there are regulations... Over here, there is no rule of dropping a girl back after 6 pm Over there, if any girl has a problem, or anything, if she wants to be dropped after 6 pm, there are police vehicles doing that."*

Regulations played a role in women's perceptions of other cities as well. Ahmedabad, for example, is in Gujurat, a dry state, which one participant felt made it safer due to a lower likelihood of encountering drunkards loitering at night who might harass women passing by.

Once again, participants displayed a preference for places where they are able to exercise power. Regulated places use law and order to ensure power imbalances between men and women do not have to be confronted. Places culturally different from New Delhi, like Mumbai, actually level the imbalances through a self-reinforcing cycle–people do not feel the need to control women's freedom of choice, so women continue to exercise freedom of choice.

Role of Technology

ICTs were naturally integrated into participants' daily safety routines. As we describe, women used smartphones to hold strangers accountable for their actions and to simulate their social network even when alone. We also describe the caveats that participants felt technology has in the realm of safety.

Holding Strangers Accountable

In the event that one entered a situation in which someone could *potentially* harm them, participants used their phones to create accountability. Participants felt that if a potential perpetrator knows he can be held accountable for any crime he might commit, he would be less likely to commit one. Using phones for accountability primarily applied when traveling. When using a hired car or auto rickshaw, participants would save and send photos of the driver and license plate to family members before getting into the vehicle. P17 explained how accountability made her feel more safe:

> *"One thing that I've learned from my elders or my brothers is that even if the cab driver doesn't do anything to you, just be safe, just do it in front of him–click a picture of him, click a picture of the cab, and say that I'm sending it to my brother or wherever I'm going, so that they have a track of it. He'll at least be sure everybody at least knows who he is, so he better not do anything."*

Participants also used their phones to send their location to family or friends when riding in a hired car or auto rickshaw. This practice was very common and Uber and Ola, ride-sharing services commonly used in New Delhi, implement this feature directly in their mobile apps. The idea behind sending one's location was that if the driver were to go somewhere other than the intended destination, loved ones would know where to find the participant and track down the driver. Here, women use phones to hold strangers accountable in situations where there is no accountability.

Accessing One's Social Network

Accessing one's social network via phone was another method of maintaining a sense of safety in potentially dangerous situations. When in isolated areas or riding in cars or auto rickshaws, participants would talk on their phone or pretend to talk on their phone to a family member or friend, giving potential perpetrators the perception that they have someone to notify in case of an emergency. This finding corroborates previous studies conducted in western countries that show that mobile phones signal a connection to others when in unsafe areas [22, 30]. We found in addition that many participants made a ritual out of it, always calling a parent, sibling, or friend on their commute from work or when traveling at nighttime. One participant described a time when she was traveling via a hired car alone at 3 am, and her family planned ahead to be on the phone with her for the entire ride. In these scenarios, women use ICTs to simulate their social network, though this does imply that perpetrators view a lone woman as powerless.

Notably, finding oneself in the situations described above with regards to transportation was greatly related to income level. According to the survey, not having one's own personal transportation was more prevalent among those with lower family incomes. Sixty-two percent of those who responded used a personal car to travel to and from work or university, while the rest of the respondents used methods such as public transportation, auto rickshaws, hired cars, or walking. Personal car was the most popular mode of transportation for both men and women. However, personal cars were overwhelmingly more popular among those whose families earn more than INR 10 lakhs (approx. USD 15K) annually.

Caveats to Technology Use

Despite the usefulness of mobile phones in the above scenarios, there were still issues that could arise when relying on phones for safety. Participants noted that phones were the first thing perpetrators would try to take away from a woman to ensure they cannot call for help or send their location to anyone, highlighting the amount of power ICTs provide women in ensuring their safety. Even if the perpetrator did not take their phones, some participants mentioned that their phone was not always an accessible form of aid in an emergency because it could be lost in their handbag or requires multiple button presses to unlock and then contact someone.

The panic button was mostly talked about in the context of its effectiveness as well. Many participants felt that the panic button would not be useful because perpetrators of a crime will not be deterred by anything. P10 described how a perpetrator's desire to commit crimes against women is stronger than any deterrent:

> *"What is the button eventually going to do? ... If someone wants to do something, I mean ... the chances of being caught are anyway there. I'm not sure it's going to make a difference in terms of how the person committing the crime looks at it."*

Participants also had little faith that there was enough workforce and technological infrastructure to respond to all the incoming calls to a national emergency number. As a result, many participants said they were very skeptical about the national emergency number, but would use it in a true emergency in the off chance that it actually results in the police arriving. However, with the qualification that these measures do work, some participants felt that the panic button could be useful because it would be a deterrent, as described by P9:

> *"A person who would be thinking about trying to do something ... he'll also know that this person has a device with a panic button, and it can be tracked back to him, so it is a deterrent. There would be some problem or there would be investigations and things like that and can act as a deterrent."*

Like-minded participants felt that if the perpetrator of a crime knew there could be consequences or at least complications in the process of committing a crime, they would be less likely to attempt to do so.

Social Presence and Influence

Intersecting with location and technology use to affect participants' sense of safety were their interactions with people in public spaces and the influence of their social network.

Strangers and Friends

Participants felt the most unsafe in the presence of strangers that seemed likely to sexually harass or assault women, especially when alone in public spaces. Participants generally had a set of descriptors that they felt were characteristic of this type of stranger, including being inebriated, poorly dressed, or having a leer. However, some participants also explained that it is impossible to actually tell who has bad intentions and who does not–perpetrators of street harassment or sexual assault could be the complete opposite of the description above. Though these participants had a heuristic of what a dangerous person looked like, they still felt they could not rely on it entirely.

Participants also felt unsafe when they were required to rely on strangers to accomplish something, such as when taking a hired car or auto rickshaw. Because participants' mobility was temporarily controlled by an unfamiliar person, the potential for a dangerous situation increased. Such a situation would be made even more dangerous if there was no possibility of external help, as described by P9:

> *"There was this guy, and he felt sleepy, and I had to go to Greater Noida. He left me in the middle of the road saying 'I'm sleepy, I cannot drive you.' So I had to get out of the car... I asked him to go back to a very crowded sort of a market place that I had seen... which he did, and then I stood in a place where there are shops, you know, public place kind of a thing and booked another cab... Being on the road alone, where there is no other human being walking on the road other than me, cars moving past me, it was very far from my house, I didn't know anybody there."*

Having family or friends, particularly male friends, accompanying participants made them feel safer. When asked if there are situations in which she feels completely safe, P12 said the following:

> *"When I'm with someone... it's a very sexist statement but I would feel more safe if I'm with a guy. I don't know any martial arts or something like that, so physical strength... "*

A man was seen to offer not only physical strength, but also the perception that the woman was protected and not to be approached. Similarly, participants assumed they were protected when accompanied by family. P5 described the extent to which she expected family to be a protective measure:

> *"We were in CP, the poshest of all places... This creepy guy was stalking my sister, fully aware that we are with my family... That's one of the weirdest things I've ever seen. He had the abandon to do that when I was with my family."*

Here, a woman's companions have power over her safety. It is easy to imagine scenarios in which women's mobility is limited by the availability of her friends or family. Some participants' preference for male companions also points to how perpetrators might view women as only having power by virtue of the man who is with her.

The Concern of a Loved One

In expanding our lens outside of occurrences in public spaces, we learned how women's social networks affected their sense of safety. For some participants, having their parents worry about their safety made them *feel the need* to feel unsafe and avoid certain areas. P1 described how her parents' concern made her concerned as well:

> *"...my parents, who are staying out of Delhi have started feeling that Delhi is very unsafe although it is equally safe or unsafe. So that is a concern. They have become more conscious. Because they are over concerned about me, that disturbs me."*

As a result, the concern of family, if perceived as exaggerated, could cause women to worry excessively about safety or take more precautions than they would otherwise. The power exercised upon women's safety here stems from parents' concern imposed upon women's perception of their own safety.

However, social influence was not always perceived negatively. Many participants, when asked which areas they felt were most unsafe, would list particular roads around their homes or college campuses that they avoided. When asked why they felt those areas were unsafe, it was often because they had heard of incidents happening there from family and friends. Based on these accounts, the space developed a reputation for being unsafe and was therefore avoided.

Pervasive Sexist Attitudes
Beyond personal social networks, many participants felt that New Delhi harbored a large proportion of people that still held onto sexist attitudes. When asked why New Delhi might be particularly unsafe for women, participants mentioned the large influx of rural migrants from the states of Haryana and Uttar Pradesh. Participants felt these migrants held tightly onto traditional gender roles, relegating women to the domestic sphere and viewing them as sexual objects, especially when they deviate from their specified roles. P6 described the phenomenon as such:

> *"If somebody is coming from a village to the city, they see that women are working everyday, they travel late at night, they're unaccompanied also, they wear whatever they want, and they can even talk back to you, so they can't handle it. It's more of a power assertion... When they're adjusting to globalization or urbanization, then such changes happen and it takes generations to fix it."*

However, patriarchal values did not always manifest so blatantly. Some participants felt that the very structures in place to keep women safe perpetuated the idea that it is the woman's responsibility to protect herself from men. P6 also mentioned the following issues:

> *"If there are girls who go to the metro in a miniskirt, they're laughed at... A lot of families don't let their girls go anywhere unaccompanied... You also have to deal with the opposite sex very carefully... do not give the wrong idea, or do not seem provocative... There are stigmas around women who may have casual relationships. People might call them sluts or whores."*

In such a culture, the burden is placed on women to protect themselves from unsafe situations, instead of expecting men to respect women's choices and bodies.

Perceptions of Law Enforcement
As Blom et al. [6] and Ahmed et al. [1] describe, women's perceptions of police tend to be mixed. We describe the perception women in New Delhi have of the police and the situations in which they are helpful or unhelpful.

Police and General Safety
When police were in charge of general regulation of the population, participants felt they were effective in maintaining law and order and deterring crimes against women. Participants who saw the New Delhi metro as a very safe mode of transportation said that it is highly regulated, with security screenings, guards, and train stops every few minutes, all of which ensure that someone committing a crime will eventually be noticed and punished. For the same reason, participants felt safer in areas where there was more security. P8 described the difference security regulations make in a private neighborhood compared to a government-owned complex:

> *"I stay in a normal development made by government authorities. When you're part of a private development, your whole locality is owned by an organization and they charge you to keep you safe. So there'll be guards, there'll be security systems always that'll be monitoring who enters... which car is coming. So the chances of someone breaking into your house–very less."*

Women feel they can trust the police with more general public safety duties, such as monitoring and screening. In these scenarios, police act as a deterrent that prevents crimes from happening in the first place.

Police and Women's Safety
By contrast, police were considered highly untrustworthy not only in responding to calls for help in the event of an emergency, but also when it came to dealing specifically with street harassment or sexual assault. Participants felt that initiatives like the panic button and national emergency number would only work if there was an efficient and reliable police system in the back-end (which they agreed was absent). They were unsure of whether or not there would be a response if someone pressed the button or called the number. If there was a response, it was not certain if police would arrive on time or if they would further harass the person in need of help.

Participants said that police officers could themselves be the source of harassment, with officers being complicit in staring or teasing. One participant recounted an experience that greatly influenced her perception of police, where she was walking down a busy street and it was a police officer who stared her up and down as she walked by. P5 summarized her experience as follows:

> *"On governmental measures, I'm very skeptical... I don't find things working. The political system is a mess. Especially in Delhi, you don't have the police in your control. It's luck if you get to meet good people."*

The kind of power police have is very different when it comes to public safety as opposed to women's personal safety. With regards to personal safety, the fear is not only that police cannot use their power in a constructive way, but that they will abuse their power, manifesting in victim-blaming and harassment.

Mass Media Coverage of Safety Concerns

The media was another entity that we found to shape women's sense of safety. Through coverage of street harassment and sexual assault in public spaces, the media increased awareness of possible unsafe situations. As a result, women changed their safety practices to avoid such situations. A significant example would be the greatly reduced use of private buses after the Nirbhaya rape case (mentioned earlier) was publicized in 2012 [21]. P12 described a similar instance of media coverage changing her behavior:

> *"You know more things... I remember this one time–the whole dressing room situation. I think they said that you should check once before you change in a dressing room because... it's like a mirror and behind it, it's actually a window, so there were some ways of how you check that. So I think that's how you build up precautions and during that time, I actually did that. Yeah, they do inform you about a lot of things. It's a good thing."*

Particularly for participants who lived with their parents, parents would doubly warn their daughters to avoid such situations and take precautions based on what the media suggested. P12 described why her mother is more concerned about traveling in cabs at night than she is:

> *"Sometimes it's just annoying... I'm not in a very restricted house but yeah, I would definitely get a call from my mom if I'm not home by 10:00, 10:30... I'm OK with it, but my mother is not OK with it. She's like, 'I don't want you to travel in a cab at night.'... I know what to do. I can send the status. But still, again, those stories, the bad things, they stay in her head for a long time."*

The media and social networks clearly exercise power over women's safety–the media provides knowledge that social influences use to speak *for* women. The media provides an image of women's safety which women can either agree or disagree with, as seen in P12's contrasting descriptions of media's influence. However, even when a woman is not particularly concerned with safety, social influence is more guided by the media than the woman, resulting in her taking a precaution because of someone else's imperative.

Personal Choices Regarding Safety

In navigating the factors mentioned above, participants designed their daily habits to take back as much control of their safety as they could. Participants avoided traveling alone, particularly after 9 pm. They planned their routines such that they were home by 9. They also planned their attire according to what they would be doing that day. Staying indoors or in upscale areas and using personal cars instead of walking or taking public transportation and auto rickshaws meant one could wear more revealing clothing. If they knew they had to walk or take an auto rickshaw that day, they would have to carry a cover up or wear more conservative clothing. P3 also explained the significant toll such precaution-taking had on her:

> *"As a woman, it becomes my duty to protect myself... I cannot trust the people around me... So I just trust myself and my senses or very close friends of mine or my family, because you hear about so many instances... that you really feel uncomfortable."*.

Participants greatly preferred acting in a precautionary way rather than in a reactionary way, because of the serious impacts an unsafe situation could have. P1 shared the following thoughts on using the panic button in case of an emergency:

> *"If something happens to me, I will call. It is very reactive. It is not [about] doing anything to protect safety. If something happens, we will call. If something doesn't happen... "*

The extent to which participants would make any attempt to ensure safety even if it might not be effective is highlighted by men's survey responses when asked if they would use the panic button. Twenty percent of men who responded said they would not use the panic button. Meanwhile, no women responded saying they would not use the panic button, despite the respondents being made up of 28% men and 72% women.

In the actual event of an emergency, reactions to threats to personal safety were very different based on the intensity of the threat. When asked how they respond to street harassment, participants' reactions varied widely. When confronted with staring, many participants said they ignore it, while others glare back or escalate to verbally telling the person to stop staring. In response to inappropriate touching, many participants said they berate the person publicly. In fact, one participant said she felt it was her duty to do so in the hopes of preventing that person from doing something similar in the future. Such experiences with day-to-day street harassment were commonplace and participants described their reactions in terms of what they have done in the past. When asked what they would do in an emergency situation, where there was an imminent high intensity threat, many participants had to speculate as they had not experienced such situations before. Participants said they would first try to attract attention in order to get immediate help. They would also try to escape in any way possible, including trying to run away or fight back with something on hand, like a pen, heavy object, or stones. Some participants mentioned that if possible, they would try to call someone for help on their phone. Participants who had experience with serious imminent threats described the same patterns of reaction–they tried to escape in any way possible and fight back while drawing attention from anyone that happened to be nearby.

DISCUSSION

Our findings highlight that women's sense of safety is incredibly complex. There are multiple factors that exert power over women, affecting their sense of safety and behavior accordingly. Hypothetically, a panic button should be able to utilize law and order to prevent instances of sexual assault in public spaces. However, the mandate will likely be ineffective in doing so because it does little to interact with and even misunderstands the power that the factors we mentioned above have on women's safety. In the following sections, we describe the gaps in how a panic button interfaces with these factors, recommendations for closing the gaps, and an explanation of why these recommendations would be effective situated in the feminist HCI framework.

Limits of the Panic Button

The panic button in its current form does not address the realities of emergency situations, women's perceptions of technology and safety, and structural aspects of women's safety.

Flaws in Form

Integrating the panic button into mobile phones may seem intuitive since these devices are pervasive and heavily used across the country [33]. However, focusing on **participation** as per the feminist HCI framework, we have found that using phones as a container for this technology subjects the panic button to the same limits phones have in emergency situations. Participants explained that a phone is not always easily accessible in an emergency because it could be hidden in their handbag or out of their reach. Perpetrators are also aware of the fact that phones are useful devices for calling for help and would likely take it away from a woman as soon as possible. Though a panic button might make calling for help more accessible by requiring fewer button presses, the physical device itself may not be accessible.

Misalignment with Women's Values

The current design of the panic button is not very compatible with the principle of **pluralism**, discounting the diverse ways women view safety. Thinking of threats to personal safety in two stages, where a women starts to feel unsafe and is then confronted with an actual threat, the panic button intervenes too late in the timeline, making it little more than a reactionary tool. Some participants felt that the impacts of sexual assault were too significant to risk and valued proactively reaching out for help much more than reaction. However, other participants were more concerned that using the panic button any earlier in the stages of escalation would be problematic because the situation might not escalate, resulting in embarrassment if the police were to arrive for no reason. As a result, being able to walk the fine line between the two stages is highly preferred.

Additionally, all women do not always want to contact the police in an emergency, which the panic button automatically does. Because of a common perception of the police as not only unresponsive, but also complicit in indifference to safety issues experienced by women, victim-blaming, and even harassment, they are not always seen as trustworthy. Such a universal design could actually result in some women avoiding using the panic button.

Lack of Infrastructural Support

The panic button has little infrastructural backing. The panic button's success depends on assumptions that may not hold true according to women's conceptualizations of safety. Namely, implementation of the panic button assumes that police will respond quickly every time the button is pressed. The Indian government has made an attempt to make this a reality by consolidating India's emergency numbers. However, due to the sheer number of people the police system must support and the existing culture of non-response as perceived and experienced by women, the panic button may not result in any useful help. Even worse, the deterrent value that some participants felt the panic button could have could deteriorate if perpetrators realize a police response is uncertain or unlikely. Currently, the button also has no supporting campaign or targeted media coverage that provides awareness of its implementation. The question remains as to whether awareness is expected to arise naturally out of media coverage, is the responsibility of the companies marketing their phones, or is the responsibility of the Indian government. Based on our findings, mass media can prompt behavior change, but this characteristic can be more purposefully leveraged to make safety technology like the panic button more effective.

Finally, the button does not interact with social influence on women's safety. Parents' worry about their daughters' safety stemming from stories they hear from the media and their social network will not likely abate due to phones having panic buttons. Our findings showed that some participants sent parents their location or called them while traveling alone because their parents wanted them to. A panic button alone does not address the parents' worry and the resulting burden placed on women to take precautions for their parents' sake. From a standpoint of **ecology** from the feminist HCI framework, there is much room to observe how the implementation of the panic button needs to address multiple stakeholders and be backed up by key institutions.

Expanding the Limits of the Panic Button

To bridge these gaps between the panic button and other factors that influence women's safety, we offer recommendations for redesigning the panic button and addressing systemic issues that are likely to impact its effectiveness. Such a focus is particularly important for safety technology to be implemented by a national government on a large scale. A top-down mandate from an authoritative actor presents itself as an opportunity to ask for specific requirements as needed and to make widespread systemic changes that would be in alignment with the mandate.

Designing for Values First

As mentioned above, mobile phones, though they have a wide reach, are not the best form to ensure accessibility. A standalone wearable device, a device that connects to one's phone like a smart watch, or an add-on to an accessory could be methods of ensuring the panic button is almost always reachable. The button itself could be made easy to press but also to require enough presses to avoid accidental activation, perhaps utilizing a series of multiple quick presses or a single long press. Such a design could make it unlikely that someone would activate emergency functions by accident on a device they wear all the time, avoiding embarrassment and needless pressure on emergency services.

Additionally, some women may want the safety of notifying their social network as they start to feel unsafe or simply need to placate worried parents. While phones best provide the perception of access to a social network because women can audibly talk on the phone about where they are, where they are going, or who is around them, the panic button could be programmed so that women can effortlessly update their social network with their location if necessary. The function should also fit women's conceptualizations of safety. Because women may not always want to contact police in emergencies, the panic button could have configurable contacts to easily reach family, friends, or co-workers based on where one is traveling [1].

Designing to match these values is key to fulfilling the participatory and pluralistic aspects of feminist HCI. Our design recommendations are informed by a nuanced understanding of women's perceptions of personal safety, ensuring women are the ones speaking and designing for themselves. Though women unanimously faced safety issues, they did not all perceive them in the same way. Therefore, we design the panic button to address as many needs as possible. For example, there were indeed some participants who were okay with calling the police in an emergency, but there were many who were not, creating a limiting factor that we must design for. As a result, we make design recommendations keeping customizability in mind.

Integrating Infrastructure

Different functionalities and form factor, however, are not sufficient to make a panic button effective in the sociocultural context of New Delhi. First, it is imperative that the government increase the accountability of police in terms of responsiveness to emergencies. There could be a system that evaluates how frequently and why stations do not respond to emergencies in order to evaluate the cause of non-responsiveness in police stations and penalize them if necessary. There could also be measures to address slow response time. One possible solution to this issue proposed by researchers in Fiji is a system in which the police force is tracked by RFID chips so that officers closest to an emergency can quickly be assigned to respond to it [3]. The system could also be used specifically in New Delhi to prompt the assigned officers to respond to the emergency if they are not making an attempt to do so. Another ICT-oriented solution that places the responsibility of safety on physical spaces is to implement components of a smart city [8], such as emergency call buttons located along sidewalks. Both these examples of ICT use could reestablish reliability and predictability in women's navigation of public spaces, forming a stable "context of trust" [31] in New Delhi that women do not have to constantly create by themselves.

The government could work with mass media to accurately promote the panic button (and hopefully still will). Carefully guiding the information disseminated by media about the panic button and national emergency number could make more people aware of how the technologies work together to make it easier to get help in an emergency. A purposeful media campaign would follow the principle of self-disclosure by avoiding any misinformation about what the button can and cannot do so as to prevent false senses of safety.

At this point, we note the challenges in designing for the quality of **advocacy**, i.e. transformative change. Sterling explains that interventions like the panic button are designed for something that should not be happening in the first place and that they rely on certain assumptions of how sexual assault "typically happens" [35]. Certainly this means that a singular intervention cannot be a panacea for violence against women. Therefore, we ask how we can make the panic button more than a technology that expects women to protect themselves against sexual assault. Additionally, though many participants valued precaution over reaction, precaution encourages women to restrict their movement and continuously worry about their safety. As a result, we define progress as women being free of the cognitive burden of ensuring their personal safety. We emphasize the importance of addressing infrastructural issues so that reactivity may be a legitimate option for women. This is especially pressing when less tangible sociocultural values are deeply entrenched in patriarchy.

Furthermore, advocating for infrastructural reform enables participatory and pluralistic technology to begin reflexively designing the ecosystem it is in. For example, if issues with the police system in New Delhi are properly addressed, a panic button could better pose a legitimate threat to perpetrators of sexual assault. Without addressing the law enforcement system, the panic button would be ineffective in the first place, no matter how well it might address women's safety needs. Without addressing or utilizing the external factors that have power on women's safety, safety technology may not be effective on a large scale.

Limitations

Though these recommendations could have a positive impact on women's safety, they are based on a relatively homogeneous sample that does not include women who face the safety risks that come from lack of economic privilege. Findings and recommendations related to having a smartphone or wearables are not wholly applicable to women with feature phones or no phones because their technology practices differ. Interaction with the media and one's social network regarding safety may also differ because of cultural and lifestyle differences. A deeper examination of how safety practices differ among socioeconomic strata would strengthen recommendations for large (or small) scale safety interventions.

CONCLUSION

In the process of studying women's reactions to the recent mandate issued by the Indian government to implement panic buttons on every phone by 2017, we produce a nuanced assessment of how women view personal safety in public spaces in New Delhi. We describe the power exercised by physical characteristics of spaces, ICTs, social networks, media, police, and women themselves on women's safety and discuss how these interactions might adversely impact the effectiveness of the current implementation of panic buttons. We then provide technological and infrastructural design recommendations based on Bardzell's feminist HCI framework [5] to improve the likely effectiveness of the intervention. As these recommendations are a starting point, future work might *(1)* pursue a thorough understanding of safety issues of women from more diverse economic backgrounds and *(2)* examine the realities and challenges of infrastructural change in New Delhi, drawing from research on large-scale collaboration and information systems.

ACKNOWLEDGMENTS

We are grateful to Michael Muller and our anonymous reviewers for their constructive and invaluable feedback.

REFERENCES

1. Syed Ishtiaque Ahmed, Steven J Jackson, Nova Ahmed, Hasan Shahid Ferdous, Md Rashidujjaman Rifat, ASM Rizvi, Shamir Ahmed, and Rifat Sabbir Mansur. 2014. Protibadi: a platform for fighting sexual harassment in urban bangladesh. In *Proceedings of the 32nd annual ACM conference on Human factors in computing systems*. ACM, 2695–2704.
2. Mohammed Eunus Ali, Shabnam Basera Rishta, Lazima Ansari, Tanzima Hashem, and Ahamad Imtiaz Khan. 2015. SafeStreet: empowering women against street harassment using a privacy-aware location based application. In *Proceedings of the Seventh International Conference on Information and Communication Technologies and Development*. ACM, 24.
3. John Ayoade, Preetika Anand, and Varunesh Rao. 2007. RFID Location Tracking System for Enhancing Police Services. In *ASME 2007 International Design Engineering Technical Conferences and Computers and Information in Engineering Conference*. American Society of Mechanical Engineers, 19–28.
4. Madeline Balaam, Rob Comber, Ed Jenkins, Selina Sutton, and Andrew Garbett. 2015. FeedFinder: A Location-Mapping Mobile Application for Breastfeeding Women. In *Proceedings of the 33rd Annual ACM Conference on Human Factors in Computing Systems (CHI '15)*. ACM, New York, NY, USA, 1709–1718. DOI: http://dx.doi.org/10.1145/2702123.2702328
5. Shaowen Bardzell. 2010. Feminist HCI: taking stock and outlining an agenda for design. In *Proceedings of the SIGCHI Conference on Human Factors in Computing Systems*. ACM, 1301–1310.
6. Jan Blom, Divya Viswanathan, Mirjana Spasojevic, Janet Go, Karthik Acharya, and Robert Ahonius. 2010. Fear and the city: role of mobile services in harnessing safety and security in urban use contexts. In *Proceedings of the SIGCHI Conference on Human Factors in Computing Systems*. ACM, 1841–1850.
7. Margaret Burnett, Anicia Peters, Charles Hill, and Noha Elarief. 2016. Finding Gender-Inclusiveness Software Issues with GenderMag: A Field Investigation. In *Proceedings of the 2016 CHI Conference on Human Factors in Computing Systems (CHI '16)*. ACM, New York, NY, USA, 2586–2598. DOI: http://dx.doi.org/10.1145/2858036.2858274
8. Hafedh Chourabi, Taewoo Nam, Shawn Walker, J Ramon Gil-Garcia, Sehl Mellouli, Karine Nahon, Theresa A Pardo, and Hans Jochen Scholl. 2012. Understanding smart cities: An integrative framework. In *System Science (HICSS), 2012 45th Hawaii International Conference on*. IEEE, 2289–2297.
9. Jill P Dimond. 2012. *Feminist HCI for real: Designing technology in support of a social movement*. Ph.D. Dissertation. Georgia Institute of Technology.
10. Jill P Dimond, Michaelanne Dye, Daphne LaRose, and Amy S Bruckman. 2013. Hollaback!: the role of storytelling online in a social movement organization. In *Proceedings of the 2013 conference on Computer supported cooperative work*. ACM, 477–490.
11. Jill P Dimond, Casey Fiesler, and Amy S Bruckman. 2011. Domestic violence and information communication technologies. *Interacting with Computers* 23, 5 (2011), 413–421.
12. Daniel Drache and Jennifer Velagic. 2013. A report on sexual violence journalism in four leading Indian English language publications before and after the Delhi bus rape. *Available at SSRN 2277310* (2013).
13. Susan M. Dray, Daniela K. Busse, Anke Marei Brock, Anicia N. Peters, Shaowen Bardzell, Allison Druin, Margaret M. Burnett, Elizabeth F. Churchill, Gayna Williams, Karen Holtzblatt, and Diane Murray. 2014. Perspectives on Gender and Product Design. In *CHI '14 Extended Abstracts on Human Factors in Computing Systems (CHI EA '14)*. ACM, New York, NY, USA, 53–56. DOI: http://dx.doi.org/10.1145/2559206.2559218
14. Susan M. Dray, Andrea Peer, Anke M. Brock, Anicia Peters, Shaowen Bardzell, Margaret Burnett, Elizabeth Churchill, Erika Poole, and Daniela K. Busse. 2013. Exploring the Representation of Women Perspectives in Technologies. In *CHI '13 Extended Abstracts on Human Factors in Computing Systems (CHI EA '13)*. ACM, New York, NY, USA, 2447–2454. DOI: http://dx.doi.org/10.1145/2468356.2468799
15. Casey Fiesler, Shannon Morrison, and Amy S. Bruckman. 2016. An Archive of Their Own: A Case Study of Feminist HCI and Values in Design. In *Proceedings of the 2016 CHI Conference on Human Factors in Computing Systems (CHI '16)*. ACM, New York, NY, USA, 2574–2585. DOI: http://dx.doi.org/10.1145/2858036.2858409
16. Leo A Goodman. 1961. Snowball sampling. *The annals of mathematical statistics* (1961), 148–170.
17. Nadia Ilahi. 2009. Gendered contestations: An analysis of street harassment in Cairo and its implications for womens access to public spaces. *Surfacing: An Interdisciplinary Journal for Gender in the Global South* 2 (2009), 56–69.
18. Cristina Kadar and Irena Pletikosa Cvijikj. 2014. CityWatch: the personalized crime prevention assistant. In *Proceedings of the 13th International Conference on Mobile and Ubiquitous Multimedia*. ACM, 260–261.
19. Tzu-I Lee, Yih-Harn Chiang, Jiayi Guo, Mu-Tsz Chen, and Yue Chen. 2016. Dot-it: Managing Nausea and Vomiting for A Peaceful Pregnancy with Personal Pattern Exploration. In *Proceedings of the 2016 CHI Conference Extended Abstracts on Human Factors in Computing Systems (CHI EA '16)*. ACM, New York, NY, USA, 20–25. DOI: http://dx.doi.org/10.1145/2851581.2890631

20. Sharmila Lodhia. 2015. From living corpse to India's daughter: Exploring the social, political and legal landscape of the 2012 Delhi gang rape. In *Women's Studies International Forum*, Vol. 50. Elsevier, 89–101.
21. Niharika Mandhana and Anjani Trivedi. 2012. Indians Outraged Over Rape on Moving Bus in New Delhi. (2012).
22. Wendy March, Dawn Nafus, Laurel Swan, and Alex S Taylor. 2008. Night and darkness: interaction after dark. In *CHI'08 Extended Abstracts on Human Factors in Computing Systems*. ACM, 3985–3988.
23. Amanda Menking and Ingrid Erickson. 2015. The Heart Work of Wikipedia: Gendered, Emotional Labor in the World's Largest Online Encyclopedia. In *Proceedings of the 33rd Annual ACM Conference on Human Factors in Computing Systems (CHI '15)*. ACM, New York, NY, USA, 207–210. DOI: http://dx.doi.org/10.1145/2702123.2702514
24. Sharan B Merriam. 2002. *Qualitative research in practice: Examples for discussion and analysis*. Jossey-Bass Inc Pub.
25. Michael Muller. 2011. Feminism asks the Who questions in HCI. *Interacting with Computers* 23, 5 (2011), 447–449.
26. OSAC. 2015. India 2015 Crime and Safety Report: New Delhi. (2015).
27. Mark Phillips, Fargol Mostofian, Rajeev Jetly, Nazar Puthukudy, Kim Madden, and Mohit Bhandari. 2015. Media coverage of violence against women in India: a systematic study of a high profile rape case. *BMC women's health* 15, 1 (2015), 1.
28. Gabriela T. Richard and Yasmin B. Kafai. 2016. Blind Spots in Youth DIY Programming: Examining Diversity in Creators, Content, and Comments Within the Scratch Online Community. In *Proceedings of the 2016 CHI Conference on Human Factors in Computing Systems (CHI '16)*. ACM, New York, NY, USA, 1473–1485. DOI:http://dx.doi.org/10.1145/2858036.2858590
29. Heather Rosenfeld and Elsa Noterman. 2014. Safe space: Towards a reconceptualization. *Antipode* 46, 5 (2014), 1346–1365.
30. Christine Satchell and Marcus Foth. 2011. Welcome to the jungle: HCI after dark. In *CHI'11 Extended Abstracts on Human Factors in Computing Systems*. ACM, 753–762.
31. Bryan Semaan and Gloria Mark. 2011. Creating a context of trust with ICTs: restoring a sense of normalcy in the environment. In *Proceedings of the ACM 2011 conference on Computer supported cooperative work*. ACM, 255–264.
32. Prachi Sharma, MK Unnikrishnan, and Abhishek Sharma. 2014. Sexual violence in India: addressing gaps between policy and implementation. *Health policy and planning* (2014), czu015.
33. Sanjay Kumar Singh. 2008. The diffusion of mobile phones in India. *Telecommunications Policy* 32, 9 (2008), 642–651.
34. Carmen Stavrositu and S. Shyam Sundar. 2008. Can Blogs Empower Women?: Designing Agency-enhancing and Community-building Interfaces. In *CHI '08 Extended Abstracts on Human Factors in Computing Systems (CHI EA '08)*. ACM, New York, NY, USA, 2781–2786. DOI: http://dx.doi.org/10.1145/1358628.1358761
35. S Sterling. 2013. Designing for trauma: the roles of ICTD in combating violence against women (VAW). In *Proceedings of the Sixth International Conference on Information and Communications Technologies and Development: Notes-Volume 2*. ACM, 159–162.
36. Kalpana Viswanath and Surabhi Tandon Mehrotra. 2007. 'Shall We Go out?'Women's Safety in Public Spaces in Delhi. *Economic and political weekly* (2007), 1542–1548.
37. Yi-Chia Wang, Moira Burke, and Robert E. Kraut. 2013. Gender, Topic, and Audience Response: An Analysis of User-generated Content on Facebook. In *Proceedings of the SIGCHI Conference on Human Factors in Computing Systems (CHI '13)*. ACM, New York, NY, USA, 31–34. DOI: http://dx.doi.org/10.1145/2470654.2470659
38. Huizhong Wu. 2016. India says every phone must have a panic button by 2017. (2016).
39. Chelsea Young. 2014. HarassMap: using crowdsourced data to map sexual harassment in Egypt. *Technology Innovation Management Review* 4, 3 (2014), 7.

Technologies and Social Justice Outcomes in Sex Work Charities: Fighting Stigma, Saving Lives

Angelika Strohmayer
Open Lab,
Newcastle University
Newcastle upon Tyne, UK
a.strohmayer@newcastle.ac.uk

Mary Laing
Social Sciences,
Northumbria University
Newcastle upon Tyne, UK
mary.laing@northumbria.ac.uk

Rob Comber
Open Lab,
Newcastle University
Newcastle upon Tyne, UK
robert.comber@newcastle.ac.uk

ABSTRACT
Sex workers' rights are human rights, and as such are an issue inherently based in social, criminal, and political justice debates. As HCI continues to move towards feminist and social justice oriented research and design approaches, we argue that we need to take into consideration the difficulties faced by sex workers; and explore how technology can and does mediate social justice outcomes for them. We contribute directly to this challenge by providing an empirical account of a charity whose work is built on the underlying move towards social and criminal justice for sex workers in the UK. Through ethnographic fieldwork, meetings, interviews, surveys, and creative workshops we describe the different points of view associated with the charity from a variety of stakeholders. We discuss their service provision and the ways in which HCI is uniquely positioned to be able respond to the needs of and to support sex work support services.

Author Keywords
Social justice; activism; sex work; ethnography; charities; feminist HCI.

ACM Classification Keywords
K.4.1 Public Policy Issues (Human safety)

INTRODUCTION
"If you care about gender equality or poverty or migration or public health, then sex worker rights matter to you" – Toni Mac, member of the Sex Worker Open University, the English Collective of Prostitutes, and a sex worker [36].

Within HCI there has been a shift towards more socially complex topics [14,17,51,52,59] and a subsequent adoption of methodologies [8,21,29,58] that begin to take this complexity into consideration. This move has been shown through innovations in building technologies that address social justice issues, but also in thinking more theoretically around topics such as postcolonial computing [28,29], feminist HCI [7,47], social justice-oriented interaction design [21], the move towards seeing participants as citizens and agents within the research [43] and the importance of including various stakeholders in studies [18]. With this paper we extend this work and address marginalisation and social injustice as they relate to sex workers, and how institutional and individual use of digital technology can enable collaborative and cumulative social justice outcomes. We explore the technological reality and needs of a national charity working to reduce stigma attached to, and violence experienced by sex workers called National Ugly Mugs (NUM). Through the involvement of various stakeholders (charity staff, charity board, their members and their social media followings) we introduce an argument for HCI, and particularly social justice-oriented HCI [21], to engage and work with a variety of sex workers and sex work related groups, organisations, and charities.

Our contributions to HCI are threefold: (1) we bring to the forefront the importance of addressing sex work and sex worker rights as part of HCI's move towards social justice, feminist, activist and digital civics approaches; (2) we provide an empirical study of the ways in which a support service utilises mundane technologies in innovative ways; and (3) we discuss the digital mediation of social justice outcomes. With this paper we argue for the continuation of the socially-oriented trend in HCI by extending conversations in civic engagement to the realm of sex worker rights and the underlying social and criminal justice advocacy within this, particularly understanding how technology mediates directed and diffuse social justice outcomes and where tensions arise among the material forms of social justice. We embrace the complex interplay of these approaches when working in a politically, socially and culturally complex space. In doing so, we explore the unique and important challenges faced in this space and elaborate on opportunities that these challenges present for future research.

BACKGROUND AND RELATED WORK
We situate our work predominantly as it relates to sex work in the UK. We provide an overview of the current legal, political and policing standing of sex work in the UK, before demonstrating HCI's existing work on social justice, sex work and related industries.

This work is licensed under a Creative Commons Attribution International 4.0 License.

Copyright is held by the owner/author(s).
CHI 2017, May 06-11, 2017, Denver, CO, USA
ACM 978-1-4503-4655-9/17/05.
http://dx.doi.org/10.1145/3025453.3025615

Sex Work in the UK

Sex work is typically understood to be the exchange of a sexual service for pay. This might include services which involve bodily contact (for example, penetrative or oral sex), massage or other types of body work or the provision of particular intimate encounters (e.g. the girlfriend experience, wherein the hours paid for by the client may involve activities other than sex or bodily contact). Non-contact sexual services (e.g. virtual services like web-cam sex, phone sex, or sex chat) can be considered sex work, although this is sometimes contested – for example, some exotic dancers reject the term sex worker.

People of all genders buy and sell sex; legal frameworks relating to sex work in England and Wales (prostitution law in Scotland and Northern Ireland is devolved) are gender neutral, following a regulationist system where it is legal for individual consenting adults to engage in sex for pay in a private space [27]. Having said this, there is a range of provisions in place to make the industry invisible: soliciting for the purposes of prostitution, loitering and working off-street with others all violate the law. Evidence suggests that this regulatory system is harmful to sex workers, forcing them to choose between arguably safer modalities of work (inside, together) and breaking the law [45].

In January 2015 the Home Affairs Select Committee (HASC) launched an inquiry in England and Wales on prostitution law. The interim report published in July 2016 recommend that individuals should be able to work together off-street for safety, that soliciting should be decriminalised and that previous cautions and convictions should be deleted from the records of sex workers [31]. The report has been welcomed by sex workers and allies; calls for the full decriminalisation of the sex industry (as recommended by Amnesty International [5]) have been made. Radical feminist groups, who argue that sex work is intrinsically exploitative and that the sex industry should be abolished, have responded that the committee should reconsider a prohibitionist mode of regulation wherein the purchase of sex is criminalised (otherwise known as the 'Swedish Model').

In terms of on-the-ground regulation, the relationship between sex workers and police is geographically varied. However, historically relationships have been strained; the quasi-criminalised status of sex work, the stigma experienced by sex workers, previous poor experience, police services positioning them as 'undeserving victims' and concerns about being 'outed' as a sex worker are all barriers to reporting crimes [57]. Both individually and collectively, however, sex workers have developed methods of working to enhance safety and wellbeing: for example through peer-to-peer reporting systems, screening processes and sharing information about potentially dangerous clients. Specialist services have also worked hard to develop relationships with local agencies to provide case management and integrated care for this *"marginalised and dynamic"* [24] group, despite recent funding cuts, changes in policing, and a political shift towards 'exiting' (or supporting sex workers to stop sex working) rather than support for evidence based public health approaches [24].

Sex, Sex Work, and HCI

The sex industry, and practices of buying and selling sex have evolved alongside societal developments, perhaps most importantly technology. Cunningham [16] raises important legal and regulatory questions in 'Prostitution 2.0' where online activity incentivises reputation-building and screening of the sex worker to reduce risks and social stigma of sex work, although this was only found to be the case in some age groups. According to Cunningham, sex workers who solicit online engage in less risky behaviour, although street based workers who are displaced to this space carry on their existing, risky, behaviours. Peppet [44] builds on these by outlining his imagined 'Prostitution 3.0' where a third-party internet provider mediates an exchange between client and sex worker that determines whether the client or sex worker has a history of violence or crime, their health status at their last sexual health testing, and cross-references any reported misbehavior from other sex workers and shares this information anonymously. Upon meeting both parties undergo an iris scan to ensure they are the *"safe, healthy, and uncoerced counterpart"* they were expecting. Through this, Peppet believes the intermediary is legally obligated to maintain confidentiality of both identities, but also that intelligence will be shared with law enforcement if the interaction results in violence, fraud, or disease transmission. While he addresses the need for laws and policy to change, he does not take into consideration in the imagined scenario the societal change that would need to occur to make this kind of transaction safer for both parties; it also removes any possibility of independent sex working.

In HCI there is little work that addresses the sex industry directly; some studies aim to demystify porn [53], and explore how users interact with the popular 'porn 2.0' site: YouPorn, others describe user taxonomies of free internet pornography on Reddit [50], or classify pornographic image detection as a one-class classification task [35]. While all of these papers address an element of sex work (pornography), they all conducted their work with pornography that is freely available on the internet rather than addressing it as a sex working issue.

Furthermore, HCI has begun to discuss sex from a sex-positive feminist perspective through workshops and publications (eg. workshops such as "Why we should talk about sex" [11] and papers on pleasure [6] and sex toys for sexual wellbeing [22]). Playful and creative interactions are being used to develop discourses around sex and sexuality [60], and women's sexual health [3,4]. Contrastingly, when exploring the world of (*voluntary* [2]) sex work and (*forced* [2]) sex labour, HCI seems to have focused on more traditional views and methodologies, looking at the role of data sources in human trafficking [49,56] and sex tourism [19].

Although sex workers are often seen as being marginalised in society and hard-to-reach, in regards to technology they *"represent a unique demographic for high technology penetration, multiple devices per person, and intensive usage in their everyday practices."* [48] Sambasivan et al., for example, have designed a phone broadcasting system for urban sex workers in India [48] in collaboration with a charity and have improved reach and informed sex workers about health issues. Wall et al. [55] have taken a health-focus on sex work in Zambia, where it was found that fingerprint-linked patient tracking and data collection was a feasible option in resource restrained areas (although the sex workers often refused to give their fingerprints due to a perceived lack of privacy).

The contrast between feminist HCI literature, [7,8] with its link to pleasure in sex [6,22], and sex work within HCI [19,48,55] is striking. While the feminist side explores the positives of sex, putting the woman and her pleasure at the centre, the sex work and labour literature sees sex workers as women who need to be tracked and informed about health issues in a top-down model. This opens up a space that takes into consideration the self-efficacy of sex workers, political concerns of the sex worker rights movement, relational models and approaches and the potential to open up space for sex workers of all genders.

With this paper we hope to move the conversation of social justice-oriented HCI towards a space that has traditionally not been explored: sex work. We do this through a case study of a charity working with digital technologies as facilitators for their work. They do this with sex workers, other organisations, police and policy development to fulfil their aim of 'fighting stigma, saving lives'. Through our case study we make light of the views stakeholders have of the charity and the work they do.

CASE STUDY: NATIONAL UGLY MUGS

The role of NUM is to reduce and tackle violence against sex workers, fight stigma, campaign for the rights of sex workers and to fight for criminal and social justice outcomes. Their approach to this is underlined by principles of social justice, as the CEO points out, recognising their political role: *"The work we do makes us an authority on the issue and with that comes a responsibility to advocate for change. If our mission is to improve the safety of sex workers how can we remain silent when policies are introduced that will harm them?"* [23]

They are a membership charity, meaning that their services are only available to those who have signed up through their website. It is only after a background check that people will be accepted as members; only sex workers, escort sites, establishments and organisations who directly support sex workers are able to join. Once a member, all the direct services provided by NUM are available: the ability to file a report, receiving alerts and the possibility to cross-check whether a client's phone number has previously been reported through the number checker. In addition to these direct services to members, NUM play an advocacy role alongside other sex worker rights advocates on social media, in blogs and other online publications. They also provide training for police and front-line service providers, function as a point of contact for good practice guidance and signpost to other support services that cater to sex workers.

Much of the work NUM do is conducted by or through the use of traditional technologies in innovative ways. NUM has taken the bottom-up approach of 'ugly mugs' schemes (the process of sharing information about dangerous clients and situations among sex workers to warn others of potential harms) and utilise digital technologies to share information on a national scale. The technology enables them to be more efficient in how they share the information and gives them the unique possibility of recording acts of violence committed against sex workers. The front-line services and advocacy work NUM do creates a space where they are utilising bottom-up approaches to support top-down dissemination of the information they collect.

METHODOLOGY

This study is based in a socially, politically, culturally and technologically complex design space, We take a feminist research approach that incorporates the importance of complexity [10,18,54], relationships [20] and values of culture, locality and language as part of the context we are working within [9,28–30,37]. As part of this, we see our collaboration with NUM as a mutually beneficial partnership where the work we do supports their service provision while also leading towards the design, development, and evaluation of novel technologies. As such, we respond to Law's wish to see researchers work *"as happily, creatively and generously as possible"* [33].

Researcher Self-Disclosure

The first author is an ally to the sex worker rights movement, favouring the decriminalization of the industry. The authors have collaborated with NUM for a year on this project; one author is on the board of the charity, and another of the authors has supported NUM through social media and at events. Each author relates differently to sex work and the sex worker rights movement, but are all in favour of the decriminalization of the industry, and are in support of putting including sex worker voices in research and policy development.

METHODS AND PARTICIPANTS

As described above, this paper addresses an inherently political topic with varying viewpoints. Following our feminist methodology, we engaged in multiple methods to address concerns from different groups, individuals and perspectives. While we strove for inclusivity, recruiting participants who are sex workers is difficult. Because of this, we engaged in recruitment through the large NUM membership base, as well as their social media following, and engaged with one other charity who is a member of NUM that works directly with sex workers working primarily on the streets. This recruitment strategy brought about a tension between the attempt at diversity and recruiting through channels that already engage with NUM. Because of this, most respondents were NUM members at the time of the study, which means that the views represented in this paper are only the views of those who know about NUM and have felt the charity has enough value to go through the membership sign-up process.

To reach as many different voices as possible, and to utilise existing research and service delivery practices of NUM and our other partners, we employed five data collection methods: two surveys, interviews, workshops, and ethnographic fieldwork. In order to give the entire membership of NUM (sex workers, organisations, charities, and projects working with sex workers or in spaces where service users are likely to be sex working, as well as establishments where sex workers work) a chance to take part, we developed a survey for sex workers, and a survey for members of staff working in organisations, charities or projects that are members. From these surveys we recruited individuals to take part in (phone) interviews or have meetings with us. This approach allowed us to reach rural and mobile workers. In order to engage sex workers working from the street (who were underrepresented in our surveys and interviews) we developed workshops for participants during regular drop-in sessions at a specific health and wellbeing charity. In order to obtain a more in-depth understanding of NUM staff opinions we conducted ethnographic fieldwork that was supported by formal and informal interviews with staff and an analysis of NUM's social media networks and online presence through their website and publications.

In total, 78 participants directly responded to the surveys (50 sex workers and 28 project staff), 10 took part in interviews (4 staff and 6 sex workers – 3 cis women, 1 cis man, 2 trans women) and 12 in design workshops (although more women were present during the drop-in times). In total, NUM employs seven staff, who comprised the immediate network of participants in the ethnographic fieldwork.

FINDINGS: UNDERSTANDING NUM

Here we collate and intersperse the findings from surveys, interviews, workshops and personal field notes to provide details around the expectations NUM members have of the organisation, the reporting and alerting process and the different understandings of what NUM is from different stakeholders by providing vignettes alongside other sources of data we collected.

Members' expectations of NUM

When asked why members signed up to the NUM scheme, 72.6% of respondents replied that they had wanted to receive alerts of dangerous people and situations. The majority of these people (41.8%) wanted to receive these alerts via e-mail, 17.6% wanted to receive them via SMS and 13.2% wanted to look up alerts by logging in to the NUM website and going through the archive of alerts. 18.7% of respondents said they wanted to join the scheme to use the number checker. The number checker is a piece of software where members can enter any phone number to check whether a report has been made including that phone number. If a report had been made, this is flagged up by the system and the sex worker is then able to make a more informed decision as to whether or not to see the client. Despite the large number of people wanting to receive alerts, only 6.6% of members initially signed up to make a report themselves.

Both sex workers and staff from other charities reported a high level of satisfaction with the NUM scheme: 87% of sex workers and 95.7% of staff from other charities said their expectations had been met. One participant said: *"I receive relevant updates, they give me all the information I need to know and I can keep track for future reference".* Many of the responses however were pragmatic, but also very emotional: *"This is the first time since working in the business that I've ever been warned properly about potential abusers."* While statements like this draw immediate attention to the positive outcomes of engaging with NUM, they also allude to the political nature of sex work and the charity sector within this space: despite a large number of charities across the UK supporting and offering services for sex workers, not all services are supportive in the ways in which sex workers want to be supported. Despite local ugly mugs schemes created by charities, some respondents did not feel informed well enough about the dangers of their work. One respondent made this clear in their statement: *"It gives me an extra peace of mind about the client".*

Social Justice Outcomes

Some of the complexities of the social justice outcomes associated with sex workers and NUM can be found in a rap written collaboratively by sex workers, volunteers, centre staff, NUM staff and the first author at the centre the creative workshops were held at:

There once was a ugly mug
Who behaved just like a thug
He thought he was clever and would be free forever
Alas he was wrong, for the women were strong and all stuck together
Reporting his dong
The women rejoiced at the time
For he was punished for his crime

The collaboration brought out conversations around the purpose of reporting as well as more nuanced conversations on how the women would react to an 'ugly mug' being sentenced for the crime they committed. In light of the particular experiences of one sex worker (who had been assaulted, reported that crime through NUM, shared information with police and whose perpetrator was sentenced to over 15 years in prison for his crimes) the ending was changed to reflect the following: the women were pleased that the perpetrator had been punished, but since the feelings associated with such a crime, from the survivors' perspective, would not disappear with the verdict, they would still not feel safe in their work. While achieving a desired criminal justice outcome, the rap highlights some of the varied social justice outcomes that are related to crime, such as continued feeling of vulnerability, injustice and emotional distress.

Volunteers and sex workers alike took the workshop to stand in solidarity with sex workers who had experienced violent crimes, and as a chance to spread positive messages around staying safe, the positive emotions that come out of reporting a crime and the support that is available if someone were to report a crime committed against them. The outcomes are now hung up in the drop-in space to continue to allow for the women to share their stories, to showcase the work they have done and to open conversations around violence committed against sex workers, and to reduce the stigma.

Reports and Alerts

One of the main foci of the pilot evaluation [32] that was carried out as part of the initial NUM scheme and one of the main reasons for sex workers to join the scheme (72.6%) is the alerting process. Since *"the system only works if people make reports"*, however, we will also address the reporting aspect of the charity as these two services are inherently intertwined. As mentioned before, sex workers are able to report crimes committed against them to NUM who will then turn this report into alerts for other sex workers.

There are several ways in which sex workers can report crimes committed against them to NUM:

(1) They can become members themselves and access services including alerts, the number checker, and completing an online report form directly.

(2) They can engage with an organisationthat is a member: be able to access the front-line services provided by them as well as those provided by NUM. Organisational members are guided to share all alerts relevant to their area, and according to good practice guidance of NUM, should be supporting the reporting process.

In order to explore the reporting practices in more detail, we used website analytics, surveys, interviews and the ethnographic fieldwork. Once logged in on the website 12% of the members head directly to the 'Report' tab from the homepage. On average they spend only 13 seconds deciding which kind of report they would like to make: (1) a full report, (2) a mini report, or (3) download the form. 52% of the people on this page then decide to make a full report. Each full report form is auto-filled with basic information provided by the members' profile and is given a unique number. On average they spend 13:42 minutes writing this report. Once on the 'Full Report' page there is a 0% bounce rate, meaning that a member who clicks this page interacts with the page in some way before leaving it; it does not, however, mean that everyone who accesses the page fills out and makes a report. 27% of members exit the website from this page and 13% go back to the homepage.

Despite most people interacting with the form in some way, not everyone who starts to fill out the form finishes it. Some sex workers have said that filling out the form is *"cathartic"*, but for many the form is too long and complex to fill out for incidents that are not seen as 'violent enough'. This idea is also supported by missing identifying unique numbers of report forms that reach the organisation: each time a report form is opened on the website it is given a unique number, so when NUM staff receive report 122 and 124, it becomes clear that whoever opened the form to start a report between those two (123) did not finish the report.

Depending on the level of consent given by the person filing the report, NUM process the information to be shared with police either anonymously or with contact information from the reportee. If the reporting member chooses to take the next step and report to the police, NUM will support them in doing so with the view of achieving a criminal justice outcome where possible. So far NUM have assisted in the conviction of 22 serial offenders [40]. Below, we provide an example of one way in which sex workers report to NUM and how this process affects them.

Those who have reported an incident did this mainly to *"warn other sex workers in the area"* but also to feel strong or safe: *"There is a sense of emotional security knowing that there is an organisation that is on the side of sex workers and our lives, safety, physical and emotional welfare is of importance"* and another respondent said that *"NUM emails help to remind me not to be complacent"*.

Even those who have not reported an incident, or those who do not engage in *"vanilla"* sex work (work that is culturally seen as standard or conventional sex work – the respondent who used this term was a dominatrix) and as such feel like they have very different experiences of the work they are doing, see the scheme as a chance to fight back against social and criminal injustices against sex workers: *"it's a great idea as for years working girls have been abused and said nothing now they can"*. In a way, the act of reporting (and even simply receiving alerts) becomes a type of activism that empowers sex workers to speak up for their human and labour rights. On top of this, monitoring data that has been collected by NUM over the years has been used in campaigns and reports organised and written by, with and for sex worker rights activists.

Having said all of this, it became increasingly clear through the survey, but particularly when talking to sex workers about the scheme in interviews and informal chats, that a certain threshold needs to be crossed for a sex worker to report to NUM: *"It wasn't a big incident, just a jerk so gave an informal heads up"*. This informal 'heads up' was given on a specific alerting thread on an online forum for sex workers not associated with NUM. Despite NUM making it clear in their training and on their website that any incident can be reported through their systems, the length of the form, and the time and effort it takes to communicate the incident makes some people think twice about putting in a report if *"It was not a violent offence, simply harassment or persistent time wasting"*. Many members use other informal alerting forums, sites and networks for incidents that they feel are not significant enough to write a NUM report for. Consequently, the organisation comes to represent specific forms of violence and abuse (ones meriting criminal prosecution), and the modes of reporting and interaction support this focus. More informal and peer-to-peer modes of sharing reports, and therefore possibly achieving preventative (i.e. avoidance) outcomes, end up not being fully integrated into the service or the collectivising work NUM undertakes.

Reporting Practices

According to the sex workers we communicated with, the entirety of NUM can only function if *"reports are being made"*, but what role does NUM reporting play in the fabric that is an age old practice of ugly mugs reports among sex workers? Historically, this is a peer-to-peer practice that has been adapted and changed by several local projects developing paper-based area specific ugly mugs schemes, and later a national technology-supported ugly mugs scheme to widen reach, increase efficiency and increase social and criminal justice outcomes for the sex worker rights movement as a whole. Digital technology has mediated the possible expansion of such schemes to the national (and potentially global) scale. The social justice outcomes reported by sex workers in this study demonstrate social, affective and political complexities at the individual scale, though the broader picture is a positive one – NUM moves support workers closer to positive outcomes and supports continued restorative work beyond victimisation. As such, the reporting and alerting practices no longer (only) serve to increase safety among sex workers, but also to record these incidents and as such be able to argue for policy change.

We have shown that different people have different expectations of and feelings towards the social and criminal justice process and outcomes of a report, as well as the writing of the report in itself. Simply, reporting mechanisms need to allow people with diverse backgrounds, needs, experience of use and access to technologies to be able to make reports. Although underreporting of crimes committed against sex workers has improved by NUM practice [40], there are still certain crimes committed against sex workers that are not necessarily seen as crimes, but rather as 'hazards of the job' (e.g. verbal abuse). These crimes need to be reported, and should be reported, so any future developments of the reporting mechanisms at NUM should take this into consideration – perhaps this could be done by creating a part of the form or even a new form for those incidents where punters are *'"just a jerk"* that do not necessarily require criminal justice action but are useful intelligence for monitoring social justice improvements among sex workers in longitudinal studies. Sex workers are already engaging in these practices in peer-to-peer alerting forums and providing mechanisms which record such acts can make visible the multiple forms of violence against sex workers and the social (as well as criminal) injustice associated with it.

Alerting Practices

NUM members file reports as an act of solidarity among sex workers and to warn others, which in turn makes all those involved in the alerting (the person writing the report to form the alert, and the person reading the alert) feel safer.

When talking to women who engage with NUM through a third party it has become evident that there is no clear distinction between that organisation and NUM when it comes to reporting and alerting practices. Taking into account that members who engage with NUM through third parties tend to be sex workers with more chaotic lives than those who directly engage with the NUM form, the overwhelming majority of people who interact directly with NUM did this to receive alerts. Regardless of how sex workers receive alerts they help to give them a sense of emotional and perceived security as well as a direct change in practice (it has been calculated that 1,600 crimes have been prevented and due to a NUM alert [40]). Having said this, depending on the different groups of people that receive alerts, NUM's brand identity and trustworthiness fluctuates in importance. If, for example, we take a woman who engaged with a charity, NUM's name is arguably not too important: they trust that the support service is providing them with reliable information. For a sex worker going directly to NUM, however, the trust that the charity has built up over the years, and the emotional security they provide as described above, become a driving force in whether they are going to report (and as such create an alert of) a crime committed against them. As such, the alerts (regardless of whether they received this from an online forum, a booklet or wall in a third party office space, or directly from NUM via e-mail, SMS, or their website) are invaluable to sex workers and are an example of information and communication practices and experiences [21] and a means of addressing social justice concerns.

DISCUSSION: A DIFFERENT SIDE OF NUM

The seemingly straightforward reporting and alerting processes to feel safer and more knowledgeably about 'ugly mugs' becomes more complicated when also addressing the ways in which NUM staff see the work they do. For the staff the reason for this entire process is to improve the underpinning criminal and social justice outcomes for sex workers: *"If we didn't speak out to change these laws or challenge unacceptable policing wouldn't we be neglecting our duty?"* [23]. Their duty is to have a political standpoint on sex work, policy and laws, to not only provide this work as an act of charity but to genuinely care about the outcomes of the work they do, and to find ways in which the charity can advocate for these political and socio-cultural outcomes while simultaneously being allies to sex workers. As such, they were also involved in the designing of this study, particularly the surveys. This shows the investment of NUM staff in the project as a whole. Since the design of the survey was a collaboration between all of these stakeholders, the outcomes were also possible to utilise in a number of ways: for training purposes (some of the findings from the surveys were used in police training for a specific local force), for annual reports, grant applications (some of the quantitative and qualitative data we collected will be used to support their claims), publications and implications for future design work that may be carried out with the organisation.

NUM as a charity and NUM as individual members of staff are continuously involved in different aspects related to sex work rights activism. They engage with sex workers, policy changes, academics, journalists and others about their thoughts on topics and discuss these in the office. They often incorporate arguments that come out of research they have read, and engage in conversation with sex workers around these topics. They are politically active on social media, particularly Twitter, and regularly engage in activist activities to assist their members' causes.

NUM are engaged in politics; they provide charity, advocacy, and allyship while also thoroughly caring for sex worker wellbeing. This is exemplified in their involvement to remove a map that was released in May 2016 and contained sex workers' names, addresses and phone numbers; in some cases these were personal and non-public pieces of information that also included sex workers' non-working names. The map was allegedly crowdsourced and shared by an anti-sex work campaign group in Germany, and media outlets and sex workers have called the creation of it 'The German Whore Hunt 2.0'. After being informed about this by sex workers on Twitter, NUM staff joined in in the activism that took part overnight to file as many reports against this map as possible, to force Google to remove it. While this wouldn't stop the information being on the internet, as anyone could have downloaded or saved all the information while it was online, it was a deed of activism to attempt to protect the identities of sex workers. Although sex work is legalised in Germany, there is still a lot of stigma attached to the profession, and many workers keep their job secret from friends, relatives or other employers.

This is an example of the work that is carried out by NUM members of staff that is often hidden. While they utilise social media to mobilise their members, this kind of work is seen as separate from the 'actual' work, both geographically and practically, that NUM does: the national reporting and alerting system. As was shown above, members of the organisation see NUM as an organisation that alerts sex workers of ugly mugs; they do not see them as political leaders in sex work debates despite seeing them on social media and at events. In this sense, NUM's digital activities are themselves fragmented, though not to their detriment. Rather, the ability to act in multiple arenas and across spaces allows NUM to actively create social justice outcomes for sex workers.

Mobilisation Practices

NUM's mission statement is itself a call for mobilisation: it is possible to end violence against sex workers only by addressing the problem through multiple channels. NUM sees the alerting and reporting practices as means to an end in social and criminal justice, rather than the end in themselves. NUM chooses to do this through safeguarding, protecting and advocating for and with sex workers. Here we outline three ways in which NUM mobilises their members. Through this they challenge existing power structures [39] (moving power towards sex workers and away from police and charities) to create the type of participatory structure that can lead to empowerment.

For many of the NUM members, the reporting and alerting processes are the main purpose of the charity. At the same time, however, NUM utilises social media, policy documents [41,42] and publications [12,23] to mobilise their members. As such, social media in itself becomes a mobilisation tool through which NUM is able to find, disseminate and interact with overtly and covertly political campaigns (for example their involvement in the 'German Whore Hunt 2.0). More research is needed to fully understand their use of social media as a tool for political mobilisation in the sex worker rights movement, but staying within the scope of this paper, social media is one means in which they mobilise.

Another means of mobilising members is the reporting process in itself. By providing members with the possibility of sharing information with police, NUM is creating a mobilisation platform that gives those using it full autonomy in how to (or even whether) to use it. By telling their story and alerting others, they are creating a movement to remove the taboo of addressing crimes committed against sex workers (which can be seen as a social justice outcome of NUM). At the same time, the chance to share intelligence with police also allows direct empowerment through the criminal justice process. On a collective level the accumulation of this data is creating a space for NUM to advocate for policy change [41,42], as they have done successfully in the most recent Home Affairs Select Committee that urges a change in law to decriminalise sex workers operating together [26].

A third way in which NUM services are a means of mobilising activists in the sex worker rights movement for social justice outcomes is through research. Over the years NUM have conducted their own research projects [32] and have been involved in numerous projects with universities [12,15]. As was shown through their involvement with this study, results from the various research methods were used in a number of different scenarios. The outcomes of the creative workshop were used to empower other women who come to the drop-in centre to make reports, quotes from the survey were used in trainings provided by NUM, statistics are being used in grant applications, and the findings overall are being used to continue to develop and improve services. As such, NUM involvement in research helps further their social and criminal justice outcomes by disseminating results through a number of channels.

IMPLICATIONS FOR DESIGN

Taking the lead from Dombrowski et al.'s [21] definition of social justice as a *"constantly evolving mechanism for thinking through power, privilege, and access"* and how these affect social structures, our paper is an attempt to portray such a process. We have provided an example of a study where both the researcher's and partner organisation's intensions as well as the underlying premise of the methodology employed within the study are based in ideas of social justice. On the one hand, we demonstrate the nuance of how social justice outcomes can be orchestrated and designed in digitally mediated interactions. On the other hand, however, the study has pragmatic and direct links to improving existing practice and services within the partner organisation, ensuring not only a theoretical (or methodological) dedication to social justice, but also a tangible, generative [7] one.

A Note on Ethical Considerations

Throughout the paper we have provided findings from surveys, interviews and creative workshops. We now discuss these in more detail, focusing on (1) technologies for harm reduction, (2) the value of mundane technologies, and (3) technologies to fight the stigma attached to sex work. Despite providing implications for future work in technology development and methodology for HCI, we believe that as researchers working in this space we have a requirement that, particularly when engaging in feminist or social justice-oriented research, we must dedicate our research to be political and (in one way or another) further social justice outcomes for our participants and research partners. Particularly when working with sex workers and their mechanisms for furthering social and criminal justice outcomes, we need to keep this inherent need in mind. We question whether it is necessary for academia to fully understand practices of sex workers and whether a technology developed by non-sex working researchers or designers, although potentially increasing reach and efficiency, would be an ethical contribution or only an interesting space of study based in technological solutionism and cultural appropriation. Below, we highlight implications for working and designing with and for sex workers, but ask of researchers to keep these ethical questions in mind when developing technologies in this space.

Generalizability and Impact

NUM is a unique charity that provides an 'ugly mugs' scheme on a national level, but across the world there are many different types of sex work support projects that provide this type of scheme on a local or regional level. As such, the findings presented in this paper are unique to NUM. The impact the work has had thus far (findings have been used in trainings for a British police force and a categorical change has been made to the alert titles which influences the way they are shared) is specific to NUM. Having said this, the strategies for technology development below can be used by similar sex work support projects that deliver similar services worldwide, for example through membership of the Global Network of Sex Work Projects (NSWP). Furthermore, they will be utilized in projects that are part of an interconnected web of collaborations with sex work support services at local, national, and international levels.

Technologies for Harm Reduction

When designing technologies for sex workers and sex worker support charitites we need to ensure that they are designed in such a way that they give agency to sex workers and must ensure they are in accordance with evidence-based public health approaches [24]. Rekart [46], for example, argues that through this kind of approach risky environments, harm, diminished quality of life, and vulnerability are turned into supportive environments with reduced harm, to lead to improved life quality and subsequently empowerment for sex workers. In their model this leads to a space where sex workers are enabled and they argue sex workers are able to leave prostitution. 11 years later, and taking a sex positive feminist and social justice approach that incorporates ideals portrayed by the sex worker rights movement [13,38], we would argue that by developing technologies that enable the types of changes in harm reduction as outlined by Rekart would enable sex workers to continue doing the work they do in a safer and more supportive environment.

At the beginning of this paper we described what prostitution 2.0 [16] and 3.0 [44] (would) look like. While Peppet's description of prostutition 3.0 would allow for more security for both the sex worker and their client, it does little to promote independent working; in his fiction, there will always be a third party intermediary to scaffold the interaction, resulting in a loss of agency which can be seen as a form of increased harm; they must be trusted by both sides, and as such would provide reliable information. Taking into consideration Grenfell et al.'s [24] argument for the collaboration and combination of policy environment, community interventions and tailored individual responses, as well as the reputation and trust that NUM have developed, it is unclear who the third party intermediary would most likely be. Arguably, even without being at the technological or political level of prostitution 3.0, technology already plays the role of a third party: sex workers advertise online, and it is often the first point of contact between sex worker and client. Those soliciting online generally engage in less risky behaviour [16]. As was shown in our paper sex workers share information about clients online either through peer-networks, online forums or more formally through NUM.

With the kind of work we described above it becomes less important to have an intermediary between sex worker and client, as independence and peer-sharing are encouraged. As such, the ideas of prostitution 3.0 are, at least in some ways, at odds with the work that is being carried out by NUM and other sex worker rights activists as a technological intermediary may create different forms of 'harm'. Perhaps the most obvious form of harm may be associated with violence or health, but other forms of harm also need to be considered. For example, the significant challenge of the 'German Whore Hunt 2.0' resonates further with the issues of centralised and 'trusted' intermediaries. While HCI has begun to address pornography [50,53], they have not addressed it as a sex working issue. As HCI researchers, we should publically address the topics we are talking about head on through our methodologies and the dissemination of our work [1,18,54], but also as a strategy with which we design and develop technologies [7], leading towards social justice outcomes [21]. We continue the discussion on harm-reduction by exploring the types of technologies that could be useful for this development by looking back at the data we have provided and arguing for the power in the mundane, before tackling an issue that technologies associated with Rekart's model of harm reduction would not necessarily address: stigma.

Mundane Technologies

Many sex workers use NUM services because they want to receive alerts via SMS, e-mail or from the website. They use the intelligence they receive from these sources to keep track of potentially life-saving information for future reference. In turn, this makes them feel safer by improving both their physical and emotional welfare; one respondent even went as far as saying that the e-mails help them remember not to be complacent and to take care of themselves. This personal and felt security and safety itself is a social justice outcome since it is part of how marginalisation (sex workers are stigmatised by society [38]) and oppression (sex workers have been systematically left out of LGBT rights history [13], as well as debates on the legality of their work [34], or even feminist debates on the 'morality' of the work they do [2]) impact *"experiences of and practices with technology"* [21]. In this case, sex workers are utilising these mundane technologies to reduce their marginalisation and oppression by working together with NUM to create spaces where they are 'enabled' [46] to do the work they do in a supportive, harm reduced, improved quality of life and empowered way. For many, the reporting/alerting process is the first time that sex workers who have been abused can say something about this abuse in an anonymous, respected and non-judgmental way.

At the same time the alerts are in themselves agents of social justice that empower sex workers to experience supportive environments and reduced harm [46]. For those who have experienced (violent) crimes committed against them, the filling out of the report form has been found to be *"cathartic"* and a way of addressing the issue for themselves. People who themselves have never had to use the report form however may also be empowered by its existence. The women in the drop-in centre in particular had very positive messages to share about the reporting process; they encouraged others to share their stories and several of them took the opportunity of decorating a puzzle piece to share this message. Coming back to our argument for designing technologies for harm reduction, simply the provision of the reporting and alerting process gives people a felt emotional security in knowing that there is a well-respected, wide-reaching charity that is on the side of sex workers. It is this respectability that is important, and perhaps it is a step towards prostitution 3.0 [44], without the more intrusive information sharing (such as the sharing of health records).

Although it may seem like something incredibly simple, making changes to the report form to make it shorter or more user friendly could have a huge effect on increasing reporting, as many do not finish the current form. As was shown above the reporting process in itself, as well as the alert created from the report are important elements of fighting for the rights of sex workers, of allowing sex workers to share their stories in a non-judgmental environment, and to be part of a larger movement. At the same time, it is also an incredibly personal act which could result in feelings of empowerment. In turn the combination of these personal (by reporting), community-wide (by sharing alerts) and national conversations (for example through sharing intelligence with police or data with the HASC [41]) would allow the conversation of violence committed against sex workers on a number of levels. As such, small changes to the materiality of mundane technologies (such as the alerts shared through e-mail, SMS or the website or the report form in itself) would be supported by recorded evidence and in some cases could lead not only to social justice, but also criminal justice (a perpetrator being tried for their crimes) and policy [26] outcomes. In instances such as these examples, it becomes the role of the HCI research to be a 'critical friend' in the process of the interpretation of the data, commenting on current technology use, and developing implications of both of these to further social and criminal justice goals of sex workers and NUM in an introspective and ethical manner. For instance, through the work undertaken in this project this has been tangibly manifested, for example in changes to the format of alert-titles that are sent out.

Fighting Stigma, Saving Lives

While mundane technologies and technologies for harm reduction have the potential to have direct social justice impacts, one area of sex working and service provision of charities that have not yet been addressed is the topic of stigma. NUM's aim is to end violence against sex workers, and they argue they do this, at least in part, through the reduction of stigma. Looking more specifically at the ways in which they approach their activism, it becomes clear that they engage in both fragmented and centralised practices.

Stigma is a socially constructed phenomenon that cannot be attributed to individuals. Those who are affected by it, however, are part of a network of agents in the stigma-reduction process [25]. Heijnders and Van Der Meij [25] have conducted a literature review of stigma-reduction strategies in HIV/AIDS, mental illness, leprosy, TB and epilepsy, and have identified five levels at which interventions should take place: intrapersonal, interpersonal, organisational and institutional, community level, and governmental and structural. We utilise their findings as a framework for exploring the ways in which technologies could be utilised (and have been utilised by NUM) to reduce stigma attached to crimes committed against sex workers, but since interventions should cater to changes at a number of these levels, we choose to discuss and explore the means in which technologies are used to affect change [21] to stigma through political, socio-cultural and individual means.

On a political level NUM utilises mundane technologies to communicate with other organisations, police and policy makers to develop good practice guidance for service provision [24], and for effects in policy development (such as the HASC inquiry into prostitution [26,41,42]). NUM utilises mundane technologies such as social media to mobilise not only their members but also the wider community, as well as online articles written by the CEO (eg. [23]). Through the alerting process (either through fragmented online forums, partially centralised through charities who are members of NUM, or in a completely centralised process through NUM directly) and the reporting process (where the act of reporting, but also the possibility of creating a report in itself) NUM utilise mundane technologies to affect immediate change in individuals' perceptions.

Above, we have described the ways in which NUM utilise technologies, and we argue that these are a *just* sustainability, or a sustainable change to an ecosystem that improves the quality of life within it [21], that demands ways of *"accounting for difference and inequality"* at not only a societal [21] but also individual scale. Heijinders and Van Der Meij [25] make it explicitly clear that interventions must work across all of their five levels to be able to reduce stigma rather than working only on a societal scale as a cornerstone to sustainability [21]. As such any technologies we develop for harm reduction, or indeed any mundane technologies we improve, should be adaptable and effective in several of these levels; in the long run these technologies would hopefully work towards saving lives (as is shown in the number of potential violent crimes that have been prevented through NUM service provision [40]). We imagine these technologies to be simple to use, single-purpose and highly adaptable applications of the existing processes, and encourage designers to develop technologies for mundane, unconventional and potentially deviant activities [51]. As such, the technologies should aim to fight stigma while also aiding the movement towards a more socially just world; creating a space designers should strive to innovate within.

CONCLUSIONS

While the alerting and reporting practices of ugly mug schemes can be (and to some degree are) facilitated through bottom-up approaches through forums, there is value in institutionalising these through trusted charities to address underlying social and criminal justice goals. Implying the fight for social and criminal justice requires more than simply alerting others as it requires the passing-on of information to police; we argue it also needs public education through activism, advocacy and training.

Every opportunity that is afforded by technology is a double-edged sword. We must engage in conversations and reflections surrounding the risks and affordances of technology development, and should result in designs that follow '*just* sustainabilities' [21] for wholesome improvements in the ecology that sex workers, sex work support charities, activists and researchers work within. In turn this leads us to problematise how we approach social justice as a representation of technologies, in technologies and through technologies, meaning that social justice is not an outcome of design in itself, but also that there isn't a single 'orientation' of social justice that all design and research processes will adhere to. In a way, the issues of centralisation and fragmentation become an issue, or mechanism, to move towards (and ultimately reach) a space of social justice of a multi-dimensional nature, where multiple, contiguous accounts and stakeholders are contextualised in aspects of justice [21]. This means that when various stakeholders work together to make systematic changes the outcomes can lead towards a more socially just environment.

ACKNOWLEDGEMENTS

We would like to thank all interview and survey respondents, as well as the women who engaged in our creative workshops. A particularly large thank you goes out to NUM and all the staff for the work they do in supporting and advocating for sex workers, the support they have shown for this ongoing project, and for commenting on this paper before the review and publication process. This research was funded through the EPSRC Centre for Doctoral Training in Digital Civics (EP/L016176/1). Some data may be accessible under appropriate agreement or here: http://dx.doi.org/10.17634/154300-39.

BIBLIOGRAPHY

1. Yoko Akama and Ann Light. 2012. A candor in reporting. *Proceedings of the 2012 ACM annual conference extended abstracts on Human Factors in Computing Systems Extended Abstracts - CHI EA '12*, ACM Press, 281. http://doi.org/10.1145/2212776.2212806
2. Priscilla Alexander. 2010. Feminism, Sex Workers, and Human Rights. In *Whores and other Feminists*, Jill Nagle (ed.). Routledge, Oxon, 83–97.
3. Teresa Almeida. 2015. Designing intimate wearables to promote preventative health care practices. *Proceedings of the 2015 ACM International Joint Conference on Pervasive and Ubiquitous Computing and Proceedings of the 2015 ACM International Symposium on Wearable Computers - UbiComp '15*, ACM Press, 659–662. http://doi.org/10.1145/2800835.2809440
4. Teresa Almeida, Gavin Wood, Dean Saraf, and Madeline Balaam. 2015. Labella. *Proceedings of the 2015 British HCI Conference on - British HCI '15*, ACM Press, 310–311. http://doi.org/10.1145/2783446.2783626
5. Amnesty International. 2016. AMNESTY INTERNATIONAL POLICY ON STATE OBLIGATIONS TO RESPECT, PROTECT AND FULFIL THE HUMAN RIGHTS OF SEX WORKERS. *Amnesty International*. Retrieved September 16, 2016 from https://www.amnesty.org/en/documents/pol30/4062/2016/en/
6. Jeffrey Bardzell and Shaowen Bardzell. 2011. Pleasure is your birthright. *Proceedings of the 2011 annual conference on Human factors in computing systems - CHI '11*, ACM Press, 257. http://doi.org/10.1145/1978942.1978979
7. Shaowen Bardzell. 2010. Feminist HCI. *Proceedings of the 28th international conference on Human factors in computing systems - CHI '10*, ACM Press, 1301. http://doi.org/10.1145/1753326.1753521
8. Shaowen Bardzell and Jeffrey Bardzell. 2011. Towards a feminist HCI methodology. *Proceedings of the 2011 annual conference on Human factors in computing systems - CHI '11*, ACM Press, 675. http://doi.org/10.1145/1978942.1979041
9. Eli Blevis, Susanne Bødker, John Flach, et al. 2015. Ecological Perspectives in HCI. *Proceedings of the 33rd Annual ACM Conference Extended Abstracts on Human Factors in Computing Systems - CHI EA '15*, ACM Press, 2401–2404. http://doi.org/10.1145/2702613.2702634
10. Susanne Bødker. 2015. Third-wave HCI, 10 years later---participation and sharing. *interactions* 22, 5, 24–31. http://doi.org/10.1145/2804405
11. Johanna Brewer, Joseph "Jofish" Kaye, Amanda Williams, and Susan Wyche. 2006. Sexual interactions. *CHI '06 extended abstracts on Human factors in computing systems - CHI EA '06*, ACM Press, 1695. http://doi.org/10.1145/1125451.1125765
12. Alex Bryce, Rosie Campbell, Jane Pitcher, et al. 2015. Male escorting, safety and National Ugly Mugs. In *Queer Sex Work*, Mary Laing, Katy Pilcher and Nicola Smith (eds.). Routledge, Oxon. Retrieved from https://books.google.co.uk/books?hl=en&lr=&id=XGDABgAAQBAJ&oi=fnd&pg=PT289&dq=violence+against+escorts&ots=EixdCSZ7Vo&sig=Qhbf91ON82Z6rdQqR4Ml_iPc8zw#v=onepage&q=violence against escorts&f=false
13. Melinda Chateauvert. 2013. *Sex Workers Unite: A History of the Movement from Stonewall to SlutWalk*. Beacon Press, Boston, MA.
14. Rachel Clarke, Peter Wright, Madeline Balaam, and John McCarthy. 2013. Digital portraits. *Proceedings of the SIGCHI Conference on Human Factors in Computing Systems - CHI '13*, ACM Press, 2517. http://doi.org/10.1145/2470654.2481348
15. Laura Connelly. 2014. Working Conditions and Job Satisfaction in Sex Work Pilot.
16. Scott Cunningham and Todd D. Kendall. 2011. Prostitution 2.0: The changing face of sex work. *Journal of Urban Economics* 69, 3, 273–287. http://doi.org/10.1016/j.jue.2010.12.001
17. Christopher A. Le Dantec and W. Keith Edwards. 2008. The view from the trenches. *Proceedings of the ACM 2008 conference on Computer supported cooperative work - CSCW '08*, ACM Press, 589. http://doi.org/10.1145/1460563.1460656
18. Christopher A. Le Dantec and Sarah Fox. 2015. Strangers at the Gate. *Proceedings of the 18th ACM Conference on Computer Supported Cooperative Work & Social Computing - CSCW '15*, ACM Press, 1348–1358. http://doi.org/10.1145/2675133.2675147
19. Christina DeCurtis. 2003. Prostitution, Sex Tourism on the Internet. *ACM SIGCAS Computers and Society* 33, 1, 3. http://doi.org/10.1145/966498.966502
20. Christian Dindler and Ole Sejer Iversen. 2014. Relational expertise in participatory design. *Proceedings of the 13th Participatory Design Conference on Research Papers - PDC '14*, ACM Press, 41–50. http://doi.org/10.1145/2661435.2661452

21. Lynn Dombrowski, Ellie Harmon, and Sarah Fox. 2016. Social Justice-Oriented Interaction Design: Outlining Key Design Strategies and Commitments. *Proceedings of the 2016 ACM Conference on Designing Interactive Systems*, 656–671. http://doi.org/10.1145/2901790.2901861

22. Anna Eaglin and Shaowen Bardzell. 2011. Sex toys and designing for sexual wellness. *Proceedings of the 2011 annual conference extended abstracts on Human factors in computing systems - CHI EA '11*, ACM Press, 1837. http://doi.org/10.1145/1979742.1979879

23. Alex Feis-Bryce. 2015. Why the Third Sector Must Be Political. *The Huffington Post*. Retrieved July 5, 2016 from http://www.huffingtonpost.co.uk/alex-feisbryce/third-sector-politics_b_7783312.html

24. Pippa Grenfell, Janet Eastham, Georgina Perry, and Lucy Platt. 2016. Decriminalising sex work in the UK. *BMJ (Clinical research ed.)* 354, 9, i4459. http://doi.org/10.1136/bmj.i4459

25. Miriam Heijnders and Suzanne Van Der Meij. 2006. The fight against stigma: An overview of stigma-reduction strategies and interventions. *Psychology, Health & Medicine* 11, 3, 353–363. http://doi.org/10.1080/13548500600595327

26. Home Affairs Committee. 2016. *Prostitution*. London. Retrieved September 15, 2016 from http://www.publications.parliament.uk/pa/cm201617/cmselect/cmhaff/26/26.pdf

27. Phil. Hubbard. 2011. *Cities and sexualities*. Routledge.

28. Lilly C. Irani and Paul Dourish. 2009. Postcolonial interculturality. *Proceeding of the 2009 international workshop on Intercultural collaboration - IWIC '09*, ACM Press, 249. http://doi.org/10.1145/1499224.1499268

29. Lilly Irani, Janet Vertesi, Paul Dourish, Kavita Philip, and Rebecca E. Grinter. 2010. Postcolonial computing. *Proceedings of the 28th international conference on Human factors in computing systems - CHI '10*, ACM Press, 1311. http://doi.org/10.1145/1753326.1753522

30. Robert R. Johnson. 2000. Nardi and O'Day's information ecologies. *ACM Journal of Computer Documentation* 24, 2, 78. http://doi.org/10.1145/337271.337286

31. Mary Laing. 2016. After Keith Vaz: why the Home Affairs Select Committee's prostitution inquiry must continue. *The Conversation*.

32. Mary Laing, Jane Pitcher, and With Adele Irving. 2013. National Ugly Mugs Pilot Scheme Evaluation Report.

33. John Law. 2004. *After Method: Mess in Social Science Research*. Routledge, Oxon.

34. Carol Leigh. 2010. Inventing Sex Work. In *Whores and other Feminists*, Jill Nagle (ed.). Routledge, New York, 225–231.

35. Yi Liu, Chuangbai Xiao, Zhe Wang, and Chunxiao Bian. 2012. An one-class classification approach to detecting porn image. *Proceedings of the 27th Conference on Image and Vision Computing New Zealand - IVCNZ '12*, ACM Press, 284–289. http://doi.org/10.1145/2425836.2425893

36. Toni Mac. 2016. *The laws that sex workers really want*. TED. Retrieved from https://www.ted.com/talks/toni_mac_the_laws_that_sex_workers_really_want

37. David Martin and Ian Sommerville. 2004. Patterns of cooperative interaction. *ACM Transactions on Computer-Human Interaction* 11, 1, 59–89. http://doi.org/10.1145/972648.972651

38. Jill Nagle. 2010. Introduction. In *Whores and other Feminists*, Jill Nagle (ed.). Routledge, Oxon.

39. Pradeep Narayanan. 2003. Empowerment through Participation: How Effective Is This Approach? on JSTOR. *Economic and Political Weekly* 38, 25, 2484–2486. Retrieved from http://www.jstor.org/stable/4413702?seq=1#page_scan_tab_contents

40. National Ugly Mugs. 2015. *Impact Report*. Retrieved September 13, 2016 from https://uknswp.org/um/uploads/UglyMugsA6Brochurev4.pdf

41. National Ugly Mugs. 2016. *Written evidence submitted by National Ugly Mugs*. London. Retrieved September 15, 2016 from http://data.parliament.uk/writtenevidence/committeeevidence.svc/evidencedocument/home-affairs-committee/prostitution/written/29064.pdf

42. National Ugly Mugs. 2016. *Supplementary written evidence submitted by National Ugly Mugs*. London. Retrieved September 15, 2016 from http://data.parliament.uk/writtenevidence/committeeevidence.svc/evidencedocument/home-affairs-committee/prostitution/written/30848.pdf

43. Patrick Olivier and Peter Wright. 2015. Digital civics. *interactions* 22, 4, 61–63. http://doi.org/10.1145/2776885

44. Scott R. Peppet. 2012. Prostitution 3.0. *Iowa Law Review* 98. Retrieved September 6, 2016 from http://heinonline.org/HOL/Page?handle=hein.journals/ilr98&id=2061&div=56&collection=journals

45. J. Pitcher and M. Wijers. 2014. The impact of different regulatory models on the labour conditions, safety and welfare of indoor-based sex workers. *Criminology and*

Criminal Justice 14, 5, 549–564. http://doi.org/10.1177/1748895814531967

46. Michael L Rekart. 2005. Sex-work harm reduction. *The Lancet* 366, 9503, 2123–2134. http://doi.org/10.1016/S0140-6736(05)67732-X
47. Jennifer A. Rode. 2011. A theoretical agenda for feminist HCI. *Interacting with Computers* 23, 5, 393–400. http://doi.org/10.1016/j.intcom.2011.04.005
48. Nithya Sambasivan, Julie Weber, and Edward Cutrell. 2011. Designing a phone broadcasting system for urban sex workers in India. *Proceedings of the 2011 annual conference on Human factors in computing systems - CHI '11*, ACM Press, 267. http://doi.org/10.1145/1978942.1978980
49. Daniel Ribeiro Silva, Andrew Philpot, Abhishek Sundararajan, Nicole Marie Bryan, and Eduard Hovy. 2014. Data integration from open internet sources and network detection to combat underage sex trafficking. *Proceedings of the 15th Annual International Conference on Digital Government Research - dg.o '14*, ACM Press, 86–90. http://doi.org/10.1145/2612733.2612746
50. Allegra W. Smith. 2015. Porn architecture. *Communication Design Quarterly Review* 3, 1, 17–23. http://doi.org/10.1145/2721882.2721885
51. Angelika Strohmayer, Rob Comber, and Madeline Balaam. 2015. Exploring Learning Ecologies among People Experiencing Homelessness. *Proceedings of the 33rd Annual ACM Conference on Human Factors in Computing Systems - CHI '15*, ACM Press, 2275–2284. http://doi.org/10.1145/2702123.2702157
52. Anja Thieme, Jayne Wallace, Paula Johnson, et al. 2013. Design to promote mindfulness practice and sense of self for vulnerable women in secure hospital services. *Proceedings of the SIGCHI Conference on Human Factors in Computing Systems - CHI '13*, ACM Press, 2647. http://doi.org/10.1145/2470654.2481366
53. Gareth Tyson, Yehia Elkhatib, Nishanth Sastry, and Steve Uhlig. 2013. Demystifying porn 2.0. *Proceedings of the 2013 conference on Internet measurement conference - IMC '13*, ACM Press, 417–426. http://doi.org/10.1145/2504730.2504739
54. John Vines, Rachel Clarke, Peter Wright, John McCarthy, and Patrick Olivier. 2013. Configuring participation. *Proceedings of the SIGCHI Conference on Human Factors in Computing Systems - CHI '13*, ACM Press, 429. http://doi.org/10.1145/2470654.2470716
55. Kristin M Wall, William Kilembe, Mubiana Inambao, et al. 2015. Implementation of an electronic fingerprint-linked data collection system: a feasibility and acceptability study among Zambian female sex workers. *Globalization and health* 11, 1, 27. http://doi.org/10.1186/s12992-015-0114-z
56. Hao Wang, Congxing Cai, Andrew Philpot, Mark Latonero, Eduard H. Hovy, and Donald Metzler. 2012. Data integration from open internet sources to combat sex trafficking of minors. *Proceedings of the 13th Annual International Conference on Digital Government Research - dg.o '12*, ACM Press, 246. http://doi.org/10.1145/2307729.2307769
57. Westminster Sex Worker Task Group. 2013. *Violence Faced By Sex Workers In Westminster: Recommendations Report*. Retrieved from http://transact.westminster.gov.uk/docstores/publications_store/policy-scrutiny/sex-worker-report-2013.pdf
58. Amanda M. Williams and Lilly Irani. 2010. There's methodology in the madness. *Proceedings of the 28th of the international conference extended abstracts on Human factors in computing systems - CHI EA '10*, ACM Press, 2725. http://doi.org/10.1145/1753846.1753857
59. Jill Palzkill Woelfer, Amy Iverson, David G. Hendry, Batya Friedman, and Brian T. Gill. 2011. Improving the safety of homeless young people with mobile phones. *Proceedings of the 2011 annual conference on Human factors in computing systems - CHI '11*, ACM Press, 1707. http://doi.org/10.1145/1978942.1979191
60. Matthew Wood, Gavin Wood, and Madeline Balaam. 2015. Talk About Sex. *Proceedings of the 2015 Annual Symposium on Computer-Human Interaction in Play - CHI PLAY '15*, ACM Press, 795–798. http://doi.org/10.1145/2793107.2810270

A Human-Centered Approach to Algorithmic Services: Considerations for Fair and Motivating Smart Community Service Management that Allocates Donations to Non-Profit Organizations

Min Kyung Lee
Center for Machine Learning & Health, Machine Learning Dept.
Carnegie Mellon University
Pittsburgh, PA USA
mklee@cs.cmu.edu

Ji Tae Kim
School of Design
Carnegie Mellon University
Pittsburgh, PA USA
jitaekim@andrew.cmu.edu

Leah Lizarondo
412 Food Rescue
Pittsburgh, PA USA
leah@412foodrescue.org

ABSTRACT
Algorithms are increasingly being incorporated into diverse services that orchestrate multiple stakeholders' needs and interests. How can we design these algorithmic services to make decisions that are not only efficient, but also fair and motivating? We take a human-centered approach to identify and address challenges in building human-centered algorithmic services. We are in the process of building an allocation algorithm for 412 Food Rescue, an organization that matches food donations with non-profit organizations. As part of this ongoing project, we conducted interviews with multiple stakeholders in the service—organization staff, donors, volunteers, recipient non-profits and their clients, and everyday citizens—in order to understand how the allocation algorithm, interfaces, and surrounding work practices should be designed. The findings suggest that we need to understand and account for varying fairness notions held by stakeholders; consider people, contexts, and interfaces for algorithms to work fairly in the real world; and preserve meaningfulness and social interaction in automation in order to build fair and motivating algorithmic services.

Author Keywords
Algorithmic services, fairness, allocation, motivation, community service, donation, service design, automation.

ACM Classification Keywords
H.5.m. Information interfaces and presentation (e.g., HCI): Miscellaneous.

Permission to make digital or hard copies of all or part of this work for personal or classroom use is granted without fee provided that copies are not made or distributed for profit or commercial advantage and that copies bear this notice and the full citation on the first page. Copyrights for components of this work owned by others than the author(s) must be honored. Abstracting with credit is permitted. To copy otherwise, or republish, to post on servers or to redistribute to lists, requires prior specific permission and/or a fee. Request permissions from Permissions@acm.org.
CHI 2017, May 06 - 11, 2017, Denver, CO, USA
Copyright is held by the owner/author(s). Publication rights licensed to ACM.
ACM 978-1-4503-4655-9/17/05…$15.00
DOI: http://dx.doi.org/10.1145/3025453.3025884

INTRODUCTION
Algorithms are increasingly being incorporated into services in diverse industries. They connect supply and demand in real time, matching drivers with riders and independent workers with clients [19, 35, 37, 38, 39]. They also optimize how resources are allocated in public services and urban planning, determining the locations of shared bicycle racks and electronic car charging stations or the routes of self-driving vehicles [2, 4, 23]. In these services, algorithms take on the role of managing multiple stakeholders' needs and participation. How can we build an algorithmic service that is not only efficient but also fair and motivating to participants? In these services, algorithms are often invisible; how do we ensure certain stakeholders are not overlooked, intentionally or unintentionally?

Understanding human considerations and requirements for these algorithmic services is a critical first step in addressing these questions. In response to the expanding applications of algorithms and emerging evidence that they can be unfair or unethical [15, 29, 34], scholars have increasingly sought ways to make these systems more beneficial to society; this line of research highlights the importance of defining what is desirable and ethical in the first place to inform the design of the technology [24, 27]. For example, even though "fair" algorithms have been developed in mathematics and economics, such algorithms may not be perceived as fair in social contexts, because "fairness" in society has diverse ontological roots [20].

When algorithms are integrated into services, further complications arise. Services involve multiple stakeholders [30], who may have conflicting expectations about fairness. Successful service delivery requires all these stakeholders' participation. In addition, previous studies suggest that choosing the "right" interface design and algorithmic assumptions about human behaviors and incentives is important for motivating participation [19, 37].

In this paper, we take a human-centered approach in order to identify considerations for building fair and motivating algorithmic services. We work with 412 Food Rescue, a local organization that takes food donations, matches them with non-profits, and coordinates volunteers to pick up and deliver the donations to the recipient organizations. A human manager currently makes the allocation decisions, but as the organization is struggling to meet increasing demand, we are building an algorithmic service system to take on this role. Most algorithmic services exist in the commercial sector, in which both the design process and inner workings of the algorithms are hidden from the public; this project therefore offers an important and rare opportunity to explore the process and challenges of designing human-centered algorithmic services.

The algorithmic service in this case will improve the efficiency of the food rescue organization's work with limited resources. It also necessitates formalizing the heuristics and practices that the community manager uses to allocate donations and coordinate multiple stakeholders. Our research questions are: What does it mean for an allocation algorithm to be "fair" in this context? How can we design the automated aspects so that the service motivates people and works as well as or even better than the existing service? To address these questions, we interviewed multiple stakeholders in the service—the food rescue organization, donors, volunteers, recipient non-profits and their clients, and everyday citizens. Drawing from these interviews, we argue algorithmic service designers should understand and accommodate stakeholders' multiple fairness notions; consider people, contexts, and interfaces for algorithms to work fairly in the field; and carefully decide what and how to automate to preserve meaningfulness and social interaction.

Our work makes contributions to the field of human-computer interaction and emerging academic scholarship in the social and ethical implications of algorithms and artificial intelligence. It offers an example of a human-centered approach to algorithmic services, and identifies challenges and considerations for designing fair and motivating algorithmic service systems.

RELATED WORK

Our work is situated in the literature on algorithmic technologies, fairness, value-sensitive design and service design, and technologies for underserved populations and non-profit organizations.

Social implications of algorithmic technologies

As the use of algorithms is becoming more prevalent in many sectors of society, both scholarly and industry efforts are increasingly being made to understand the social implications of algorithmic technologies [11, 17, 19, 31] and how these algorithmic technologies can be designed to make ethical and moral decisions that benefit people and societies [22, 24, 27]. Our work contributes to this growing body of work by focusing on fairness.

Recent research has shown that machine learning algorithms can make unfair decisions due to the unintended consequences of choices made in the development process or biases in the training data set [15, 34]. Even in the case of artificial intelligence, a recent study suggests that mathematically-proven fair division algorithms may not be perceived as fair because they do not match social concepts of fairness [20]. In response, interdisciplinary scholars have begun to investigate methods to achieve fairness in algorithmic systems [44]; Crawford and Calo recently pointed out a gap in current research on artificial intelligence, arguing for the importance of conducting social-systems analysis at every stage of development [5]. Our work fills this gap by presenting a human-centered approach to understanding fairness in algorithmic services in context at the conception and design stages.

Fairness

The key value that our work examines is fairness. In the Cambridge Dictionary, fairness is defined as "the quality of treating people equally or in a way that is right or reasonable." Fairness forms the basis of human society, and has multiple ontological bases. We review two main operationalizations of fairness.

Equality

An equality model ignores differences in recipient's circumstances and distributes resources or rewards equally [21]. Theories of equality are usually characterized by a concern for the welfare of those in society who are the least advantaged. By equally satisfying basic human needs, they form a principle of justice. Some social psychologists propose that equality is the fundamental principle of a multi-criterion system favored in cooperative, as opposed to competitive, relationships [18]. Studies on the effects of different allocation methods also support the idea that equally distributing rewards produces a high level of satisfaction and harmony among group members [1]. Equal allocation reduces negative socio-emotional behaviors, such as dissatisfaction and antagonism [21]. From the standpoint of the allocator, the task of choosing a recipient can become harder to make in some contexts, which is why some authors argue that an equality model might be the only just way to resolve indeterminacies in decision-making [32].

Equity

An equity model embraces individual differences and distributes resources in accordance with each recipient's need or performance. Walster et al. [41] posit the existence of one simple justice principle to which all notions of fairness can be reduced—namely, equity. Their view is that individuals consider an allocation fair if the outcome-input ratio of all group members is equal [26]. How an allocator defines and weighs need or performance is, however, context-dependent. In a blood donor matching system, patients' information, such as blood type, tissue type, size of the organ, medical urgency of the patient, time on the waiting list, and distance, are weighted and ranked in order of degree of need. In healthcare, a person's need depends on some combination of the degree of gravity, urgency, and entrenchment [16]. The assessment of an individual's need or performance can also vary significantly depending on the allocator's ethnic background, age, and gender. In a study examining the effects of culture on equitable allocation, Indian respondents favored need alone much more than the Americans who favored equality or merit. Given the differences in the general level of available resources between India and the U.S., the results support the idea that culture impacts allocation decision-making [26].

Service design and value-sensitive design

Our approach draws on service design [30] and value-sensitive design [12]. Service design considers multiple stakeholders' needs and work processes in the design process. Value-sensitive design shows how design choices, intentional or unintentional, can lead to biases in decision-making or compromises in important user values. For example, Batya and Nissenbaum [14] explain how the order of items in a list can promote the selection of top items. Miller et al. [25] surveyed "value tensions" surrounding groupware in a company and design choices that can balance stakeholders' values. This orientation toward multiple stakeholders' values inspires our work. We focus on fairness in allocation, which has not been explicitly investigated through value-sensitive design methods.

Technologies for underserved populations and non-profit organizations

Many human-computer interaction researchers have explored the use and design of technologies for underserved populations [3, 6, 7]. Topically, the thread of research that addresses "food insecurity" is most relevant to our work. Dombrowski et al. [9] explored opportunities for designing location-based systems to address local food needs, and found that the role of outreach workers is critical in expanding food assistance programs [10]. She also highlighted the values of food justice, expanding food options, utilizing local resources, and localizing control [8], which we observe in our work. Previous research has highlighted the use of technology in non-profits and discussed how existing media and other technologies might not fit their purposes [40]. On the other hand, the food rescue organization that we work with is a new, non-profit start-up which embraces social media and mobile phone technologies to coordinate and execute its work.

BACKGROUND: SMART COMMUNITY SERVICE MANAGEMENT

We have been working with 412 Food Rescue, a local food rescue organization in Pittsburgh, since January 2016 as part of an ongoing project on improving services for food-insecure and homeless populations.

Food rescue organization

412 Food Rescue is a non-profit food recovery service established in March 2015. The organization works with restaurants, caterers, food retailers, wholesalers, and universities in Pittsburgh, Pennsylvania in the United States and "saves" food that is nearing its expiration date, is leftover from events, or is damaged, bruised, or partially moldy. Since its launch, the organization has redistributed about one million pounds of food that otherwise would have been wasted to about two hundred forty community organizations, including food pantries, housing authorities, refugee camps, retirement homes, homeless shelters, and soup kitchens, to alleviate food insecurity and reduce food waste around Pittsburgh with the help of their volunteers. The organization prides itself on helping every donation reach a community organization in need. The organization's ability to quickly match donations with recipient organizations and coordinate volunteers for on-demand deliveries has been highly praised, and played a big role in their fast growth as an organization.

The core function of the food rescue organization is to connect donors, volunteers, and recipient organizations. When a donating organization calls the food rescue organization to notify them of leftovers to be picked up from their location, the manager asks about the size and contents of the food donation, and evaluates how many households or individuals the food can serve. The manager then calls community organizations that may be in need of the donation item. Once the food is matched to a recipient, the volunteer opportunity is posted on the food rescue organization's social media page, emailed to previous volunteers, or occasionally circulated by calling volunteers who have taken similar delivery routes in the past. The food retailer hands the donated food to the volunteers once they arrive on site and the volunteers deliver the food to the community organization the operation manager chose.

Decision to introduce an algorithmic service system

The food rescue organization has been experiencing growing pains, being a small team. Currently one community manager and an intern are responsible for matching donations with an appropriate recipient organization, as well as recruiting and coordinating volunteer efforts simultaneously. The task of orchestrating multiple stakeholders and coordinating volunteer efforts can become overwhelming for such a small team to do. It is particularly difficult when the coordinator has to find recipient organizations with available staff members to take donations and volunteers who can transport these items all within a very short time window. Donations come at random times throughout the day and occasionally multiple donations arrive at the same time. No matter the coordinator's skill level, it is simply not feasible for an individual to handle multiple requests simultaneously at scale. The organization also acknowledges that because of the demands for fast execution, many matching decisions are made for convenience, i.e., food is sent to organizations that the coordinator happens to remember at the time or that are known to pick up their phone. There is therefore room to improve the matching process, to distribute donations across diverse recipient organizations and make the distribution more "fair." For these reasons, the organization strategically decided to build an algorithmic system that could take on some of these roles. This system will have a database of donating organizations, recipient organizations, and volunteers; when there is a donation request, an algorithm will recommend recipient organizations and once the manager selects one or confirms, it will send out a call to volunteers through a smart phone app.

RESEARCH QUESTIONS

In this context, we explore the following research questions: 1) The human manager uses her discretion and heuristics to make fair allocation decisions. An algorithm will require more formalized rules. To that end, what is "fair" allocation from the perspectives of multiple stakeholders? 2) Using this system will automate some of the decision-making tasks and human-human interactions in the service workflow. How can these automated aspects be designed so that the service motivates people and works as well as or even better than the existing service?

METHOD

To address the research questions, we conducted semi-structured interviews with thirty-one participants who represented multiple stakeholders in the service (Table 1).

Community Manager
Community Manager at Food Rescue Organization
Donors
D1 Fresh Produce Distributor | **D2** Farm Alliance Manager | **D3** Director of Purchasing at Dining Service Provider | **D4** Supermarket Chain Marketing Team
Recipient Organizations
R1 Food Pantry Director | **R2** Homeless Medical Outreach Specialist | **R3** Food Pantry Public Relations Coordinator | **R4** Food Pantry Operation Coordinator | **R5** Food Pantry Manager
Volunteers
V1 African American Female 60s | **V2** Caucasian Female 30s | **V3** Caucasian Female 40s | **V4** Caucasian Male 30s | **V5** Caucasian Female 60s
Clients
C1 African American Male 30s | **C2** Caucasian Male 30s | **C3** African American Female 40s | **C4** African American Female 50s | **C5** African American Female 20s
Everyday Citizens
E1 Taiwanese American Male 20s | **E2** Chinese American Male 20s | **E3** Caucasian Male 20s | **E4** Middle Eastern Male 20s | **E5** Indian Female 20s | **E6** Caucasian Female 20s

Table 1. List of Interviewees and Affiliations

Participants

We were introduced to the food rescue organization's community manager as we built our relationship with the organization. Other stakeholders, such as the donors, volunteers, and recipient organizations, were recruited through an email list compiled by the food rescue organization. Food pantry clients were solicited for interviews at the food pantry with the permission of the director. Everyday citizens were recruited for interviews in public places, such as cafés.

Interview procedure

The first half of the interview was open-ended and began with questions on participants' current practices and their general thoughts on what would be a fair way of distributing donations. Our algorithm concepts (described below) were used as a probe during the second half of the interview. The concepts helped participants further articulate and compare their notion of fairness to ones with which they disagreed.

Algorithm concept probes

Drawing from the fairness literature review, we created handouts with informational illustrations of three allocation models: efficiency-, equality-, and equity-centric allocations. All models assumed that an allocation algorithm would first filter the organizations that were open and in need of the items, and then make the allocation decision among them. The efficient allocation picked the recipient organization closest to the donation location; the equal allocation gave all the recipient organizations an equal chance and picked one randomly; and the equity allocation gave a higher probability of being chosen to the recipient organizations with greater needs before picking one randomly. These handouts were meant to initiate the conversation; participants could pick one, mix the ideas, or come up with their own. In order to probe what they thought a fair equity model would look like, we also prepared different factors that the equity model could use; the list included organizational (e.g., budget and size), client (e.g., belonging to a minority), and geographical (e.g., food desert, average income) characteristics. We asked them to rank the factors in importance in assessing degrees of need. This was again to promote the participants' own thinking, rather than to make a statistical claim.

Interview questions

We interviewed the community manager twice for a total of three hours. We first asked her to describe her latest allocation decisions, her typical decision process, and what "fair" meant to her in this context. We then asked her opinions on the three allocation models, what she thought was the fairest, and how she felt about automation and its potential impact on work practices and relationships with multiple stakeholders. For donors, volunteers, and recipient organizations, each interview took about thirty minutes. We adopted and used the questions used for the community manager to include their activities with the food rescue organization. For food pantry clients, each interview took about fifteen minutes, as we tried to fit the interview within the time they spent waiting for their turn at the pantry. For everyday citizens, each interview took about thirty minutes. For the pantry clients and everyday citizens, the same set of questions was used, except for the question on the organization's work practices and relationships.

Analysis

One of the two interviewers took notes during the interviews. Interviews were audio recorded if permission was granted from the participants. We did not record the pantry client interviews as they were conducted in a sensitive location. We qualitatively analyzed our interview notes and transcripts [28, 33]. The interviewers met regularly as a group and went over the data to organize commonalities and differences into concepts of fairness and derive themes regarding the reactions to automation in each stakeholder group. We then compared different stakeholder groups in order to find challenges and opportunities in the interactions between the stakeholders, and to devise design principles that could address them.

FINDINGS

We report our findings from the interviews for each of the stakeholders.

Community manager

The community manager is responsible for matching donations with an appropriate non-profit and coordinating volunteer efforts simultaneously. She is dedicated to the organization's mission to reduce food waste and end hunger. She worked in non-profit organizations for seven years prior to joining the food rescue organization.

Combination of efficiency and equity as fair allocation

The community manager believes that a mix of the efficiency and equity models is the fairest, and has herself been mixing the two to make fair allocations: *"First [...] I think about what the proximity is. [...] I have [...] a general radius in my head [...] about all the organizations that are within a given geographic area. Those are [...] the first choice for a donation. Unless I happen to know that there's an organization with a dire need [...] that's outside of that radius, then they might jump ahead. Then the equity allocation [...] comes in [...] as I try to make sure that I'm distributing equitably throughout the whole universe."* As partly described in the quote, when the manager receives a call about a donation, she first looks at the size and content of the donation, thinks about potential recipients who could use that donation, who would require less than thirty minutes of travel, and who would be open to taking the donation. For example, perishable donations are sent to organizations that can keep the food refrigerated. She then narrows down this list using several heuristics to decide which organization needs the donation most. The heuristics combine food type and quantity, the organization's size, the last time that they received donations, etc. For example, she sent a donation of twenty sandwiches to an organization with a small set of clients, so that all of the clients could enjoy the food. When she remembers a particular organization that expressed their preference, she tries to match it to that organization. She also tries to keep small donations within the county for efficiency.

With 238 recipient organizations that the food rescue organization donates to, the community manager admitted some limitations of her current approach to being fair. "*[The information that] I feel my brain doesn't automatically boot up is an assessment of who haven't I donated to in a while, especially because sometimes they tend to fall off my radar, like it's easy for me to donate to the same place twice. I would like to make sure that geographically we are diverse in our distribution.*" She also mentioned other factors that play a role in decisions: *"[I might be over-donating to this place] because they're easy to get ahold of on the phone or maybe because I really like the staff member or maybe because a kid smiled at me the last time I was there.*" She felt that an algorithmic system would help her make decisions more objectively, by reminding her of organizations that had not received donations in a while or had been receiving too much.

Algorithms' inability to empathize with recipients' needs

The manager worried that an algorithmic allocation would lack intuition and empathy in decision-making: *"My concerns are that a computer will never have that sort of the intimate human understanding of the recipients and their needs."* The manager on multiple occasions referred to a neighborhood which she cared for that was located in a food desert. She worried that the neighborhood might be further put at a disadvantage: *"I have trouble getting stuff to [the neighborhood] and I have this very non-logical passionate desire to take care of those people. A computer won't have that. If I have trouble making it happen and I ache for the people down in [the neighborhood] how is a computer ever going to prioritize that?"*

Social relationships and automated interaction

According to the manager, personally interacting with the volunteers and donors plays a big role in motivating volunteers and maintaining relationships with donors. She was concerned about the recent push by the food rescue organization for automated volunteer coordination to handle the greater demand they were facing: *"We're going in that direction where it's sort of like the Uber where you accept and you're just not going to have the same relationships with them. Maybe at that point you don't need them because the volunteer's [...] like, 'Who cares who does it?' It's [...] less important about who takes the volunteer opportunity."* Personally interacting with donors secures a strong partnership which seems to be in the best interest of the organization, which relies on donations. As the community organizer said, *"You develop [...] that interpersonal relationship with the donors which makes them feel better about donating and it makes them feel better about donating to us as opposed to anybody else. So just from an organizational survival standpoint. [...] I'd be really hesitant to [automate that interaction]."*

Volunteers

Volunteers transport donations to recipient organizations using their own vehicles. On average, completing one delivery takes an hour or longer when making multiple stops for larger donations. Our participants had various occupations, including two stay-at-home parents, one full-time worker, one business owner, and one retired individual. Participants with flexible schedules volunteered ad hoc, with some fitting regular, long-term opportunities into their schedules. All supported the organization's mission of reducing food waste and ending hunger.

Varying fairness concepts dependent on resources & beliefs
Volunteers had the most varying perspectives on what they perceived as the fairest allocation model. Three participants viewed the equality model as the fairest, one chose the equity model, and the other chose the efficiency model. Their concepts of fairness were closely related to their personal beliefs and resources. For example, proximity-based, efficient allocation was considered fair because it uses less fuel and time, allowing volunteers to fit the deliveries into their busy schedules. V3, who delivered to a nearby community organization on a weekly basis, preferred this model for its local impact: *"I want something that is close because of the amount of time I spend doing it [...] but also because then it feels like it has a greater impact for my immediate community and it's making a difference with the people who live closer to me."* On the other hand, other volunteers did not think efficient allocation was fair. Participant V1, who regularly delivered donations to neighborhoods that are not centrally located, was particularly concerned that the recipients farthest from the donation site would by underserved by efficient allocation: *"But how is that fair? Say this is where the black community is, so again we are pushed out because we don't live close to the donation area."*

Three participants (V2, V4, V5) found equal allocation to be fair, and mentioned that it eliminates any discrimination in decision-making. They found the equity model to be unfair and expressed their concerns about ranking one organization over another. Two participants wondered how anyone could adequately rank the needs of the recipient organizations. Participant V5 said, *"I don't know how they measure the need. That is difficult to measure; in a food pantry, at any given day, [many] are in need. As far as ranking I don't know how to rank that."* Participant V2 who previously worked in a grocery store said, *"If an organization is actually accepting this food [that's about to expire] and taking the time to cut out the rotten parts [...] you won't see privilege in these organizations. Degree of need might not even exist. Anyone who is taking this food is high in need."* Through their up-close interactions with and observations of recipient organizations, these volunteers might have gained more concrete, experiential knowledge about recipient organizations, which may have made them feel less favorably toward supposedly equitable decisions that were based on abstract factors.

One other participant found equitable allocation to be fair. Participant V1 said, *"When you are looking at the greatest need, that's really fulfilling the mission of the organization because [...] it shouldn't be about what's easy for me to get around, it's about who needs it the most"*

Reluctance to travel farther or go to certain locations
While most volunteers found the equality or equity model fairer than an efficiency model, they were also worried that these models would make food rescue require more energy and resources. Participant V2 expressed, *"I probably mostly would keep the same radius. It's not often that I go any further than around here."* Another concern was the perceived safety of the area. V2, who volunteers often with her son, was wary of certain areas: *"There are parts of the city I don't feel like taking him to because I have to leave him in the car to help bring food out and stuff."* Even when the travel time was minimal, she was hesitant to volunteer for particular neighborhoods. These concerns highlight the need for an algorithm that is fair to all stakeholders, including the volunteers themselves, not just the clients.

However, some volunteers mentioned a few factors that might encourage them to take more distant trips. For example, for participant V5, the quantity of rescued food mattered most: *"Saving a lot of food matters if I am going far. [...] It's somebody who needs food, I don't care who gets it."* For participant V1, helping her own underserved communities mattered most: *"They weren't delivering into the black community and what they needed was drivers [...] who had no problem going into the community [...] making sure that the people got a fair distribution of the food. So the food rescue organization asked me, because I'm so involved in the community."*

Efficiency and reduced biases in algorithmic allocation
Most interviewed volunteers welcomed an allocation algorithm. An advantage that participants repeatedly mentioned was that an algorithm would make the decision-making process easier and quicker, allowing the food rescue coordinator more time to recruit new donors and recipients (V2, V3, V4). Participant V3 believed that the algorithm could eliminate potential bias when having to decide between choosing one recipient over the other.

Automation as an opportunity for information exchange
Most of the interviewed volunteers were not regularly socially interacting with the community manager, and a proposal to automate existing modes of communication did not seem to impact social dynamics. An exception was participant V1, who showed a preference for social interaction with the food rescue organization. She regularly communicated with the manager about recipient organizations' preferences, to improve allocation and better meet the needs of her recipient communities. On the other hand, other volunteers also gained valuable information about the preferences of certain recipient organizations through their personal interactions during deliveries, but did not communicate this information to the manager. For example, participant V2 said, *"I'm getting to know the types of organizations and like who they serve and what they need,"* but when asked if she shared any of this knowledge with the manager, she said, *"I just kind of do what they say they need, I [...] figured they are short staffed and really busy so I keep it short and sweet with them. [...] Usually I'll send them a picture and tell them how many pounds of food [...] and they can post it on their page, but that's*

usually all the communication that we have." A centralized communication channel in a mobile app could help volunteers share such information with the manager.

Donors

Donors are the suppliers of the food rescue organization. They donate extra food resulting from failed predictions of demand or products that fail to meet quality standards. Donors were glad to work with a food rescue organization that would take food on demand, rather than having to donate to food banks or throw it away. The quantities varied, ranging from a large pallet to a few boxes of food. The types of donated food included dented cans, fruits with moldy spots, unsold bread, and fresh produce that was leftover or had defects.

Efficiency- and equity-based fairness concepts

Overall, most donors emphasized the importance of proximity-based, efficient allocation. Participant D4 also mentioned that the efficient model was well-aligned with her organization's philosophy: *"For us as a company that focuses on being hyper-local, the more of a local impact the better."* On the other hand, Participant D3, who donated in large quantities, raised a concern that continuously donating to the closest recipient could overwhelm them with donations they could not handle.

In contrast to volunteers, who mostly favored an equality model, none of the interviewed donors preferred the equality model. They did not find it to be efficient nor necessarily considerate of the organizations' needs, despite the cost of travelling further for food rescues. Instead, all wished to maximize the impact of their donations, and the equity model fit this motive. Participant D4 said, *"We like to have a local impact [...], but I do recognize that there are [...] communities [...] that are further out who have a higher need. [...] I want to give where I know our company money is going to have the greatest impact."*

Reduced bias but lost intuition in algorithmic allocations

The majority of the donors preferred automating allocation decisions for its efficiency and to streamline the process. Like other stakeholders, some donors said that an algorithm would be more objective in decision-making; others were worried that automating the process would lose the human aspects involved in the decision-making process of the food rescue organization. Participants D2 and D3 wished for the automated algorithm to have a manual override, hoping that it could be used as a tool for guidance for the community manager rather than as a final decision-maker. Most donors, thought highly of what the food rescue organization was doing and trusted the organization to have a good overview of need across all the recipients.

Managing relationships with the food rescue organization

Overall, donors did not mind an automated system replacing the social interactions they had with the food rescue manager. When determining allocations of food, the social relationship seemed less of a concern to them. As participant D2 said, *"I can see the emotion gets lost, less personal, but I don't know if that is a bad thing. [...] Human connection would be nice but [the service] won't lose anything."* However, donors seemed to value personal relationships when negotiating partnerships, and showed preferences for organizations they got along well with. As participant D4 expressed, *"If someone is difficult to work with I cut off the relationship [...] I won't put in the effort, because there are 100 more organizations in line. You want to work with people you would like to work with."*

Recipient organizations

Most recipient organizations were serving communities near their locations. They all received government funding to stock food for their clients, and most were buying inexpensive items with a longer shelf life to maximize their limited budget. The organizations did not rely solely on food rescue donations, but enjoyed receiving donations that were rare to have in stock, such as fresh fruit and vegetables, milk, artisan bread, personal care products, and household items. However, while the food rescue donations were helpful, some also mentioned the considerable effort and labor required to coordinate pick-ups. Recipients especially felt this way for donations that were unfit for their clients' needs or received in excessive quantities.

Equity in theory, equality in practice

Many organizations worried that an efficiency-based model would allocate donations only to the closest recipients, which would be unfair to those who were not centrally located. Two recipients acknowledged their pantries were located near major grocery chains and that they were receiving frequent donations from these stores; yet they said that they would be okay with an equality- or equity-based model even if it might give them less of an advantage.

Most recipients initially thought the equity model to be the fairest; they agreed that organizations had varying degrees of need. However, when asked to rank factors that could be used to assess the needs of different organizations, three participants opted out of the activity entirely. They expressed concerns about the difficulty of ranking organizations who are all equally in need. One participant said it would be tricky to prioritize factors; for example, organizations that primarily serve minors already receive more funding. The participant also thought factors like the general income level of a neighborhood would not accurately portray the needs of the people who are forced to move to different neighborhoods due to gentrification. Another said it would be difficult to judge different levels of their clients' needs: "I don't know *whose hunger is more important to address—whether they were hungry for 10 years or 10 weeks."* Rather than thinking about the varying needs of organizations, R3 suggested adding a measure of efficiency to the model, which accounted for how quickly a recipient could distribute donations.

Regularity as important as fairness

Many participants who thought the equality or equity model to be fair were cautious of randomly assigning donations to recipients because of the unpredictability of when and what donation to expect. Participant R5 said, *"These are extras and add-ons, what comes from food rescue are organic and fresh, the stuff that I usually don't have access to, it is kind of a cool bonus, stuff that people don't normally get to try. [The equality model] is fair [...] but then [there are always] the other ones [that] don't get any of it. If [the allocation cycle] is once a month [...] there is a whole another month they don't get a shot at the food [if they were not picked]."*

Reduced bias but lost intuition in algorithmic allocations

Like other stakeholders, more than half of the recipients explicitly said an algorithm would be less biased than a human making allocation decisions (R1, R4, R5). R5 said, *"It helps if they know who you are [...] That can work well but that can work against people because [...] whoever is giving it out might not like that organization [...] and skip over that organization so the algorithm takes that out of the mix."* Many also mentioned efficiency as an upside of an algorithmic allocation: *"Trying to get matched up for these donations can involve a lot of phone calls, [...] having a computer making these decisions would be a more efficient process overall."* (R4) However, R4 worried an algorithm would lack human intuition: *"Recently the [manager] knew that there were a lot of mangoes available, and asked if we would want them because we worked with a lot of refugee families from Southeast Asia [...] that was a neat kind of a donation that wouldn't have been made in this model [...] but overall for efficiency it makes a lot of sense."*

Clients of the recipient organizations

Clients get donated foods from the recipient organizations, such as food pantries and housing authorities, to get through the month or stretch their fixed income. Our interviewees were clients of one food pantry. Items donated by the food rescue organization added to their monthly food quota from the food pantry and were often items rarely seen in the pantry, like fresh produce, milk, and healthy alternatives. The food pantry clients did not know where a particular donation came from unless the item was labeled with the donor's organization. This particular pantry offered a supermarket-style experience to give clients their choice of food, and ran on a first-come-first-serve model.

Equity-based fairness concept

All client participants found the equity model to be the fairest and acknowledged that factors like living in a food desert or working low-income jobs should increase a population's chances of receiving donations. Participant C1 mentioned that the allocation model could benefit from collective votes from people about which factors they thought should be used in determining need.

Reduced biases in algorithmic allocation

Pantry clients approved of an algorithm making allocation decisions instead of a human manager. Participants C3 and C4 regarded computers to be blind to ethnicity and human discrimination, unless the computer algorithm itself portrayed bias. Participant C4 also commented, *"Computers are taking human jobs anyways."*

Everyday citizens

Everyday citizens found the equity model to be the fairest. Participant E1 explained, *"As of the principle, I lean more toward whoever needs it more gets it, so ideals are good."* Everyday citizens, who were not direct stakeholders, rarely mentioned efficiency and had varying but strong opinions on how to assess degree of need. The equity allocation model was thought by all everyday citizen participants to be a better version of equality, except for participant E1. Participant E1 referred to equity as simply a "more intense" version of equality due to the random selection of recipients: *"An organization in high need with a 50 percent chance of receiving a donation might still lose to an organization of lower need. And for rare donations, the organization in high need can be left with a sour taste in their mouth."* This concern also resonates with the recipient organizations' emphasis on the importance of regularity. One participant proposed a model in which recipient organizations could connect and coordinate with each other in real time to decide who was in the most need.

DISCUSSIONS AND IMPLICATIONS

Our research suggests that taking a human-centered approach to understand multiple stakeholders' perspectives is an important first step in designing an algorithm. It allows designers to balance multiple stakeholders' needs and interests without overlooking anyone. Participants also appreciated having a transparent process that aimed to incorporate their interests and feedback into the design of the allocation and coordination process. In the following section, we discus challenges and considerations for designing fair and motivating algorithmic services.

Fair algorithms: What is fair and how to decide

Many services that currently rely on human workers or experts' allocation decisions are beginning to use algorithmic tools to replace or assist the decision-makers. Embedding algorithms in service management necessitates formalized rules of fairness, in line with the recent attention on the case of triage [43]. Our research reveals the importance of and challenges in defining fairness rules for algorithms that appeal to multiple stakeholders.

Plural fairness concepts within and across stakeholders

Literature on fairness has shown that the concept of fairness is context-dependent, varying by cultures and tasks. Consistent with the literature, our findings show multiple concepts of fairness within and across stakeholders in the context of allocation. Within stakeholders, personal beliefs and organizational philosophies all influenced individuals' fairness concepts. Some people believed *efficient* allocation to be fair, because it enabled them to directly impact their surrounding communities. Some believed *equal* allocation to be fair, as they felt that areas further away from donor organizations should have the same chance of receiving donations as closer ones; these participants generally had difficulty judging the degree of recipient organizations' needs, as they felt that all the organizations deserved help equally regardless of size, budget, or the characteristics of the populations served. Others believed *equitable* allocation to be fair, such that organizations that needed donations most should get them first; however, participants' methods for discerning degree of need varied.

Differences across stakeholders also emerged depending on their roles and whether they directly interacted with the clients of recipient organizations, whom the allocation decisions immediately impacted. The community manager and most of the donors, pantry clients, and everyday citizens deemed the equity-centric allocation model to be fair. They valued maximizing the utility of donations. On the other hand, most of volunteers and recipient organizations, who directly interacted with recipient organizations and their clients, thought the equality-centric allocation model to be fair. They expressed difficulties in judging the degree of needs or importance of different causes. This difference might be explained by psychological distance from donation recipients. As front-line workers, volunteers and staff in recipient organizations have visceral experiences with donation recipients; in-person observation of the facilities and donated goods and interpersonal interactions might enable them to see nuances and contexts that are difficult to capture in the abstract factors that are used to prioritize needs in the equity model. This tension in stakeholders' fairness concepts is similar to the difficulties that hospital workers experienced when they operationalized triage rules to decide which patients need to be treated first in a disaster situation [43].

Designing fair algorithms

The plurality of fairness concepts held by multiple stakeholders poses challenges in defining which fairness principles algorithms should embody. Drawing from our findings, we propose two potential ways to design algorithmic services—collectively defining one global fairness rule, or enabling local operations of fairness principles by stakeholders. A democratic, open process can be used to collectively build fair allocation algorithms. Many participants suggested a poll, or at least wanted to know the rules and weightings of different factors in an algorithm, so that they could tailor their input to the allocation algorithm. Our findings also show the importance of creating close feedback loops between stakeholders who make allocation decisions and front-line stakeholders who execute decisions and are directly impacted by algorithmic decisions. Decision-makers can propose a fair rule based on holistic information about recipients, whereas volunteers and recipients can provide hands-on feedback on recipients' preferences and how the decisions actually fare in the field.

Alternatively, instead of determining one global concept of fairness, designers can embrace the plurality of fairness. Algorithms can process massive amounts of data, which means they can store and respond to each person's individual input. Instead of imposing an external model of fairness on users, what if we could enable different stakeholders to act according to what they individually believe fair? For example, different donors might specify the ways in which they prefer their donations be distributed per donation, such that community organizations could emphasize local impact while organizations targeting food deserts could specify as such. The algorithmic donation matching system could also transparently display the reasoning behind each assignment, motivating volunteers by giving them more say in the kinds of donations they deliver and the organizations they help. Further research needs to be done on the processes of determining fair algorithms and to understand the pros and cons of different operationalizations of fairness in the long run.

Beyond fair algorithms: Considering people, contexts, and interfaces in algorithmic services in the real world

Our findings suggest that to design fair algorithmic services, we need to go beyond asking what is conceptually fair. We need to also think about how to make the algorithmic service system work fairly when implemented in the real world. Even if the algorithms themselves make "fair" decisions, the systems may still deliver unfair results if the people participating in the service are not motivated to follow the decisions.

Transparency of algorithmic decisions for trust and adoption

A previous ethnographic study on emergency dispatchers' adoption patterns of a new automated dispatch decision-making system is relevant to our work [42]. The study showed that even though the error rates in automated dispatching were as low as they had been prior to automation, the dispatchers did not trust the results and wanted to verify everything themselves using pens and paper, even six months after its introduction. In our case, similar reservations were displayed by the community manager, who makes the final allocation decisions. She has been using her own heuristics and logic to make allocation decisions for 1.5 years. If the algorithmic suggestions do not seem to make sense, she may start to override the system's recommendations on a regular basis, reintroducing her preferences and implicit biases to the process. Thus to maintain the fairness of the system, it is important that the interface explain the algorithm's recommendations and help the decision-maker make sense of them.

Accounting for unintentional biases and motivations

Our findings also suggest that we need to understand stakeholders' unintentional biases that might make algorithmic systems function unfairly, and design strategies to account for them. Interviews with the volunteers suggested that even when an algorithmic service makes a decision to allocate donations to lower-income areas or food deserts, volunteers may not sign up if the areas are perceived as dangerous or require longer trips. These attitudes are consistent with on-demand workers' behaviors, such as when TaskRabbit workers require higher pay-offs to go to the suburbs [37] and Uber and Lyft drivers turn off "driver-mode" in areas perceived as dangerous [19]. In such cases, it is important for volunteers to understand why the decision was made. For example, one volunteer said she did not mind driving longer distances if she knew she was rescuing high-quality or larger quantities of food, or if it was for a cause that she cared about, such as feeding hungry children. Highlighting this information and explicitly saying why the donation matters may motivate volunteers to take the longer trips to food deserts, or go to areas that are not on their usual routes. The food rescue organization specifically recruited a volunteer from an underserved community to facilitate transportation to the area. Actively recruiting volunteers from distant or low-income areas could help the allocation service function more fairly.

Preserving meanings and social interactions in automation of algorithmic services

Initially we were concerned that people might have negative attitudes toward an algorithmic service taking on some of the roles of a human community manager. On the contrary, all participants positively responded to the algorithm's efficiency and lack of bias. However, they also pointed out important aspects of human interactions that need to be preserved in algorithmic interactions.

Respecting empowerment in automation

Our interviews also suggested that we should consider the importance of emotion and meaningfulness when deciding how much of the workflow to automate. Zuboff's ethnographic observations of newly-automated workplaces suggest that different types of automated tasks can make workers feel powerless or lose expertise on the one hand, or, on the other hand, feel empowered and free from meaningless work [45]. In our interviews with the community manager, we observed that the very act of making the allocation decisions gives her an opportunity to find meaning in her work—she thinks about the "dire needs" of the recipient organizations, remembers their unique preferences, and finds joy when she successfully satisfies those preferences. Automating this process—by making the decision and only asking for her final confirmation, or even by suggesting the top three options—may make this task too simple and less meaningful. Further research would be needed to find the balance between increasing efficiency and fairness on the one hand and making the task meaningful on the other.

Automating social interactions

Donors, volunteers, and recipient organizations are the stakeholders with whom the community manager directly interacts, through phone calls, text messages, or face-to-face meetings. Our findings suggest that we should not automate all these interactions equally. While they were okay with communicating through an app or texts, donors still wanted to have opportunities to socially interact with the manager for smoother coordination or to get to know her; this interpersonal relationship seemed to contribute to their trust of the food rescue organization. It will therefore be important to preserve opportunities for the manager to interact personally and directly with these stakeholders. On the other hand, recipient organizations and volunteers were more open to automating their interactions with the community manager, except for a subset of volunteers who already interact regularly with the manager. Automation may also "expand" the positive potential of social interactions between the community manager and volunteers and recipient organizations by facilitating communication. Volunteers who more frequently interacted with the community manager mentioned discussing recipient organizations' needs and logistics. However, the manager did not seem to keep up this same level of interaction with the majority of volunteers or recipient organizations, at least based on their phone calls, social media, and text messages. It would therefore be extremely useful for the manager to have a central, automatic method of communicating with the larger set of volunteers at the same time and collecting what they learn about each donor or organization, including information about recipients' particular preferences and constraints.

LIMITATIONS AND FUTURE WORK

Our work has limitations. We explored what people think is fair based on the principles and logic of allocation in a non-profit domain in the United States, but people's opinions on fairness and reactions to algorithms may differ depending on their cultures and work contexts. Our interviews allowed us to thoroughly understand multiple stakeholders' rich, nuanced thoughts and feelings about fairness and algorithmic automation, but the sample size was small. In addition, people's thoughts and behaviors might change once they have actually interacted with an algorithm. Our future research will draw from the findings reported in the paper to create algorithms, simulations, prototypes, and systems, and investigate people's experiences and behaviors with a larger sample.

CONCLUSION

Many services in our society are using algorithms to improve their functionality. We know that algorithms can make services more efficient, but how can we make these algorithmic services fair and motivating for multiple stakeholders as well? We conducted interviews with stakeholders involved in a food rescue organization that plans to introduce an algorithmic allocation and coordination service. Our findings suggest that we need to understand and account for varying fairness notions held by different stakeholders; consider people, contexts, and interfaces for algorithms to work fairly in the real world; and preserve meaningfulness and social interaction in automation to build fair and motivating algorithmic services. Our work offers an example of a social-systems analysis of an algorithmic system at both the conception and design stages, which we hope will inspire the design of emerging algorithmic systems.

ACKNOWLEDGEMENTS

This work was supported by NSF1651566. We thank our participants who shared valuable insights with us.

REFERENCES

1. Robert F. Bales, "A set of categories for the analysis of small group interaction." *American Sociological Review* 15, no. 2 (1950): 257-263.
2. John E. Bell, and Patrick R. McMullen. "Ant colony optimization techniques for the vehicle routing problem." *Advanced Engineering Informatics* 18, no. 1 (2004): 41-48.
3. Deana Brown and Rebecca E. Grinter. "Designing for Transient Use: A Human-in-the-loop Translation Platform for Refugees." In *Proceedings of the 2016 CHI Conference on Human Factors in Computing Systems*, pp. 321-330. ACM, 2016.
4. Donna Chen, Kara M. Kockelman, and Moby Khan. "The electric vehicle charging station location problem: a parking-based assignment method for Seattle." In *Transportation Research Board 92nd Annual Meeting*, vol. 340, pp. 13-1254. 2013.
5. Kate Crawford and Ryan Calo. "There is a blind spot in AI research." *Nature 538, no. 7625* (2016): 311.
6. Christopher A. Le Dantec, Robert G. Farrell, Jim E. Christensen, Mark Bailey, Jason B. Ellis, Wendy A. Kellogg, and W. Keith Edwards. "Publics in practice: Ubiquitous computing at a shelter for homeless mothers." In *Proceedings of the SIGCHI Conference on Human Factors in Computing Systems*, pp. 1687-1696. ACM, 2011.
7. Tawanna R. Dillahunt, and Amelia R. Malone. "The promise of the sharing economy among disadvantaged communities." In *Proceedings of the 33rd Annual ACM Conference on Human Factors in Computing Systems*, pp. 2285-2294. ACM, 2015.
8. Lynn Dombrowski. "Designing SocioTechnical Food Justice." *iConference 2015 Proceedings* (2015).
9. Lynn Dombrowski, Jed R. Brubaker, Sen H. Hirano, Melissa Mazmanian, and Gillian R. Hayes. "It takes a network to get dinner: designing location-based systems to address local food needs." In *Proceedings of the 2013 ACM international joint conference on Pervasive and ubiquitous computing*, pp. 519-528. ACM, 2013.
10. Lynn Dombrowski, Amy Voida, Gillian R. Hayes, and Melissa Mazmanian. "The labor practices of service mediation: a study of the work practices of food assistance outreach." In *Proceedings of the SIGCHI Conference on Human Factors in Computing Systems*, pp. 1977-1986. ACM, 2012.
11. Motahhare Eslami, Aimee Rickman, Kristen Vaccaro, Amirhossein Aleyasen, Andy Vuong, Karrie Karahalios, Kevin Hamilton, and Christian Sandvig. 2015. I always assumed that I wasn't really that close to [her]: Reasoning about invisible algorithms in the news feed. In *Proceedings of the 33rd Annual SIGCHI Conference on Human Factors in Computing Systems*. 153-162.
12. Batya Friedman. *Human values and the design of computer technology*. No. 72. Cambridge University Press, 1997.
13. Batya Friedman, Alan Borning, Janet L. Davis, Brian T. Gill, Peter H. Kahn Jr, Travis Kriplean, and Peyina Lin. "Laying the foundations for public participation and value advocacy: Interaction design for a large scale urban simulation." In *Proceedings of the 2008 international conference on Digital government research*, pp. 305-314. Digital Government Society of North America, 2008.
14. Batya Friedman and Helen Nissenbaum. "Bias in computer systems." *ACM Transactions on Information Systems (TOIS)* 14, no. 3 (1996): 330-347.
15. Aniko Hannak, Gary Soeller, David Lazer, Alan Mislove, and Christo Wilson. "Measuring price discrimination and steering on e-commerce web sites." In Proceedings of the 2014 conference on internet measurement conference, pp. 305-318. ACM, 2014.
16. Tony Hope, Lars Peter Østerdal, and Andreas Hasman. "An inquiry into the principles of needs-based allocation of health care." *Bioethics* 24, no. 9 (2010): 470-480.
17. Lucas D. Introna, and Helen Nissenbaum. "Shaping the Web: Why the politics of search engines matters." The information society 16, no. 3 (2000): 169-185.
18. James Konow. 2003. "Which is the fairest one of all? A positive analysis of justice theories." *Journal of economic literature 41*, no. 4, 1188-1239.
19. Min Kyung Lee, Daniel Kusbit, Evan Metsky, and Laura Dabbish. "Working with machines: The impact of algorithmic and data-driven management on human workers." In *Proceedings of the 33rd Annual ACM Conference on Human Factors in Computing Systems*, pp. 1603-1612. ACM, 2015.
20. Min Kyung Lee and Su Baykal. Algorithmic mediation in group decisions: Fairness perceptions of algorithmically mediated vs discussion based social division. To appear in CSCW 2017.
21. Gerald S. Leventhal, "The distribution of rewards and resources in groups and organizations." *Advances in experimental social psychology* 9 (1976): 91-131.
22. Jamy Li, Xuan Zhao, Mu-Jung Cho, Wendy Ju, and Bertram F. Malle. *From Trolley to Autonomous Vehicle: Perceptions of Responsibility and Moral Norms in Traffic Accidents with Self-Driving Cars*. No. 2016-01-0164. SAE Technical Paper, 2016.
23. Jenn-Rong Lin and Ta-Hui Yang. "Strategic design of public bicycle sharing systems with service level constraints." *Transportation research part E: logistics and transportation review* 47, no. 2 (2011): 284-294.

24. Bertram F. Malle, Matthias Scheutz, Thomas Arnold, John Voiklis, and Corey Cusimano. "Sacrifice One For the Good of Many?: People Apply Different Moral Norms to Human and Robot Agents." In *Proceedings of the tenth annual ACM/IEEE international conference on human-robot interaction*, pp. 117-124. ACM, 2015.
25. Jessica K. Miller, Batya Friedman, Gavin Jancke, and Brian Gill. "Value tensions in design: the value sensitive design, development, and appropriation of a corporation's groupware system." In *Proceedings of the 2007 international ACM conference on Supporting group work*, pp. 281-290. ACM, 2007.
26. Viginia Murphy-Berman, John J. Berman, Purnima Singh, Anju Pachauri, and Pramod Kumar. "Factors affecting allocation to needy and meritorious recipients: A cross-cultural comparison." *Journal of Personality and Social Psychology* 46, no. 6 (1984): 1267.
27. One hundred year study on artificial intelligence (AI100) https://ai100.stanford.edu
28. Michael Quinn Patton. *Qualitative evaluation and research methods*. SAGE Publications, inc, 1990.
29. Eli Pariser. *The filter bubble: How the new personalized web is changing what we read and how we think*. Penguin, 2011.
30. Andy L Polaine. Løvlie, and Ben Reason. "Service design." *From Implementation to Practice. New York: Reosenfeld Media* (2013).
31. Christian Sandvig, Kevin Hamilton, Karrie Karahalios, and Cedric Langbort. "Auditing algorithms: Research methods for detecting discrimination on internet platforms." *Data and Discrimination: Converting Critical Concerns into Productive Inquiry* (2014).
32. Peter Stone. "Why lotteries are just." *Journal of Political Philosophy* 15, no. 3 (2007): 276-295.
33. Anselm Strauss and Juliet Corbin. *Basics of qualitative research: Techniques and procedures for developing grounded theory* . Sage Publications, Inc, 1998.
34. Latanya Sweeney. "Discrimination in online ad delivery." *Queue* 11, no. 3 (2013): 10.
35. TaskRabbit. www.taskrabbit.com
36. Alex S. Taylor, Siân Lindley, Tim Regan, David Sweeney, Vasillis Vlachokyriakos, Lillie Grainger, and Jessica Lingel. "Data-in-place: Thinking through the relations between data and community." In *Proceedings of the 33rd Annual ACM Conference on Human Factors in Computing Systems*, pp. 2863-2872. ACM, 2015.
37. Jacob Thebault-Spieker, Loren G. Terveen, and Brent Hecht. "Avoiding the south side and the suburbs: The geography of mobile crowdsourcing markets." In *Proceedings of the 18th ACM Conference on Computer Supported Cooperative Work & Social Computing*, pp. 265-275. ACM, 2015.
38. Uber. www.uber.com
39. Upwork. www.upwork.com
40. Amy Voida, Ellie Harmon, and Ban Al-Ani. "Bridging between organizations and the public: volunteer coordinators' uneasy relationship with social computing." In *Proceedings of the SIGCHI Conference on Human Factors in Computing Systems*, pp. 1967-1976. ACM, 2012.
41. Elaine Walster, Ellen Berscheid, and G. William Walster. "NEW DIRECTIONS IN EQUITY RESEARCH" 2." Advances in experimental social psychology 9 (1976): 1.Harvard
42. Jack Whalen. "Expert systems versus systems for experts: Computer-aided dispatch as a support system in real-world environments." *Cambridge Series on Human Computer Interaction* (1995): 161-183.
43. Whose Lives Should Be Saved? Researchers Ask the Public. New York Times, 2016. http://www.nytimes.com/triage
44. Workshop on Fairness, Accountability, and Transparency in Machine Learning. http://www.fatml.org
45. Shoshana Zuboff. *In the age of the smart machine: The future of work and power*. Basic books, 1988.

Class Confessions: Restorative Properties in Online Experiences of Socioeconomic Stigma

Eugenia Ha Rim Rho[1], Oliver L. Haimson[1], Nazanin Andalibi[2], Melissa Mazmanian[1], Gillian R. Hayes[1]
[1] Department of Informatics, University of California, Irvine, Irvine, CA, USA
[2] College of Computing & Informatics, Drexel University, Philadelphia, PA, USA
{hrrho, ohaimson, m.mazmanian, hayesg}@uci.edu, naz@drexel.edu

ABSTRACT
In this paper, we examine stigma related to class identity online through an empirical examination of Elite University Class Confessions (EUCC). EUCC is an online space that includes a Facebook page and a surrounding sociotechnical ecosystem. It is a community of, for, and about low-income and first generation students at an elite university. By bringing in a community that learns and engages with users' socioeconomic struggles, EUCC engenders unique restorative properties for students experiencing class stigma. EUCC's restorative properties foster new ways of understanding one's stigmatized identity through meaning-making interactions in a networked sociotechnical system. We discuss how EUCC's design shapes the nature of user interactions around class stigma, and explore in depth how people experience stigma differently through the restorative properties of EUCC.

Author Keywords
Stigma; low-SES; low-income; identity; networked publics; social networking sites; restorative properties.

ACM Classification Keywords
H.5.3. Group and Organization Interfaces: Web-based interaction

INTRODUCTION
On March 22, 2015, First Generation and Low Income Association (FGLIA[1]), a student organization from an elite U.S. University, launched a Facebook page that is part of a sociotechnical system we refer to as "Elite University Class Confessions" (EUCC[1]). In addition to its Facebook page, EUCC is comprised of multiple social technologies such as Tumblr, Twitter, Google Docs, email, etc. through which Elite University students engage in issues surrounding class stigma on campus. EUCC's most active and widely used platform is their Facebook page, on which students who self-identify as first generation (e.g., the first in their family to attend college) or low socioeconomic status (SES) share deidentified personal confessions around poverty-induced challenges. According to its posted mission statement, EUCC's purpose is to highlight different experiences people on campus have related to class, first generation status, and other intersectional identities.

Permission to make digital or hard copies of all or part of this work for personal or classroom use is granted without fee provided that copies are not made or distributed for profit or commercial advantage and that copies bear this notice and the full citation on the first page. Copyrights for components of this work owned by others than the author(s) must be honored. Abstracting with credit is permitted. To copy otherwise, or republish, to post on servers or to redistribute to lists, requires prior specific permission and/or a fee. Request permissions from Permissions@acm.org.
CHI 2017, May 06 - 11, 2017, Denver, CO, USA
Copyright is held by the owner/author(s). Publication rights licensed to ACM.
ACM 978-1-4503-4655-9/17/05...$15.00
DOI: http://dx.doi.org/10.1145/3025453.3025921

EUCC allows users who feel stigmatized to engage in difficult conversations without personally identifying themselves. Confessions on EUCC often contain sensitive information that identifies the posters as part of a stigmatized group. These "stigma symbols" can lead to social judgment in traditional identifiable communication [29]. To post confessions on EUCC, posters submit private messages to the administrators either through EUCC's Tumblr or Facebook page. Administrators then filter and moderate the content to ensure it meets community rules, primarily around privacy and anonymity for all posters. Posts are then published in their original and unedited forms with an attached auto-incremented number indicating the order in which the message was received (see Figure 1).

There is little HCI work investigating online experiences of socioeconomic stigma. Through this paper, we contribute to HCI by highlighting the combination of design, human-interaction, technology practices, and norms that offer restorative properties for users who feel marginalized in their social community. We introduce the concept of *restorative properties,* or semi-stable sociotechnical arrangements that enable specific opportunities for action, reflection, and communication in relation to stigmatized identities. Together, we find that restorative properties influence the experiences of posters, commenters, and readers around class stigma, ultimately fostering a new experience and understanding around stigmatized issues for users.

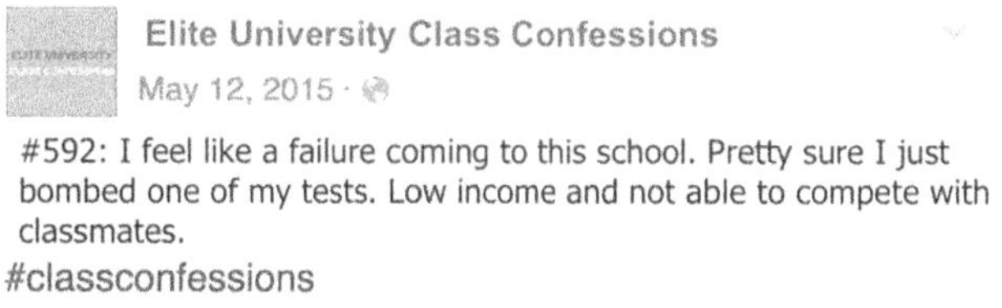

Figure 1. An example class confession post on the Elite University Class Confessions (EUCC) Facebook page.

[1] We use alternate names for the student group and university to avoid inadvertent identification. Similarly, we altered all screen shots and quotes in small ways to reduce potential for backtracing these data through online search.

BACKGROUND AND RELATED WORK

Being Low-SES at Elite Institutions

Low-income students face a multitude of class-based challenges as they start college [30,49]. At Ivy Leagues like Elite, lower SES students enter an environment dominated by a peer group endowed with relatively greater social, cultural, and economic capital [42,58]. Some low-income students must keep up with classes while struggling to afford the next meal, juggle several work-study positions, and financially support families back home [4,19].

Given the taboo nature of income-related hardships in the context of an elite institution, low-SES individuals often feel unable to disclose, share, or seek advice around such issues [4,30,37]. These students who are unable to discuss their life experiences report more loneliness and anxiety because of it [4,16,30,37,47–49]. Confronted with such feelings of isolation and fear of exposure [29,30], students are often cut off from others from whom they could seek support in either on or offline formats.

To "fit in", many lower income students at elite institutions attempt to socially and culturally adapt to people and institutions [42,58] different from those they encountered in the past. Yet, such process of identity assimilation can trigger feelings of shame, alienation, ambiguity, and displacement [30,47,49]. In fact, research has shown that low-income boys living in more affluent neighborhoods exhibit greater behavioral problems than those growing up in poorer communities [46]. In another study, low-income students experienced more psychosocial problems as the percentage of peers with middle- or high-income or college-educated parents increased [17]. Simply put, these studies suggest "kids living in poverty see themselves—and their prospects—differently when they're surrounded by other children who have more than them" [5]. In this paper, we bring into relief how an online community that arose around low-income students at an Ivy League institution offers alterative views to these prospects around class stigma.

Experiences of Stigmatized Identities

Goffman defines stigma as an attribute that differentiates and classifies a person negatively within a particular identity category. This difference can "socially discredit" a person by separating the individual from what is "felt to be ordinary and natural", rendering the different person as a "less desirable kind" [29]. This classification does not reside in a person [15,29,37], but rather in the conditions of interactions [7] through which that attribute is perceived and experienced [4,28,29,43] in a social group. Similarly, Mead's seminal work on the nature of self demonstrates that one's understanding of self arises from interacting with others [43]. According to Mead, people derive their identity from the relationship developed with those within their social space [43]. Identity formation is a process of responding to the "organized attitudes of the others" in relation to the "I", ultimately forming the expected "Me" in the community to which the individual belongs. [43]

Identity is thus not an inherent trait possessed by a person, but instead is routinely and reflexively understood by that person depending on their history, activities, and social context [26,27]. Unsurprisingly, the variety of social contexts that people inhabit cause tensions between different selves that emerge in each [26], requiring management of conflicting identities that is often difficult in modern sociotechnical systems [41]. While online spaces were once seen as platforms for identity experimentation [55,59], such behavior is no longer the norm online. Current social media platforms often rely on single user identifiers, making it difficult for people who wish to express stigmatized parts of their identities to fully engage in mainstream SNS (social networking site) [2,6].

In this study, we examine how a stigmatized identity (low-income) co-exists in tandem with a seemingly incongruent identity (Elite University student), particularly as experienced in an online sociotechnical space. We outline the restorative properties of this space that influence this experience.

Outsiders Finding Support on SNS Communities

HCI researchers have explored safe SNS communities for stigmatized individuals in various contexts. Prior research demonstrates that SNS interactions can help first generation and low-income students in their process of identity work when transitioning to college [45]. Others have shown how anonymous college confession boards function as an avenue of interaction and support for socially stigmatized students on campus [6].

While online support groups for stigmatized individuals take on various forms and shapes, molded to fit the needs of the users and their struggles, many of them share similar characteristics. First, membership barriers can be high. Interaction and disclosure within marginalized groups can enhance trust bonds among members, while legitimizing and strengthening group membership and identity [39,50]. Yet, these online spaces are sometimes designed to be exclusive for members who feel separation from those who do not share, or are not familiar with, their stigmatized identities. For example, Autcraft is an online community for children with autism and their families, built around a semi-private Minecraft server and SNSs such as Facebook. To join, a user must first complete an application declaring having autism or being a friend or family member of someone who is already a member [53]. Another example is Vive Les Roses!, an online pregnancy and mothering support group whose organizers deliberately keep the group small, private, and unknown to the general public [40].

Second, safe online spaces for stigmatized individuals often enable a separation of identities: one that is revealed to the support group where the user's stigma is known and discussed in exchange for help, and one outside of the support community where the person tries to conceal their stigma in everyday life. For example, sexual abuse survivors use temporary technical identities called "throwaway" accounts instead of their primary Reddit accounts to seek support and engage in first-time disclosures of their experiences [2]. Moreover, some Instagrammers use "separate" or "secret" accounts to find one another through hashtags related to stigmatized topics (e.g., #depression), forming ad-hoc support groups [3].

Such qualities of SNS support groups may be necessary to ensure protection from unwanted exposure. In fact, without them, it can be difficult for stigmatized persons to participate or receive online support in networked publics [8,9], like Facebook. A networked public is a space constructed through networked technologies and "the imagined collective that emerges as a result of the intersection of people, technology, and practice" [8,9]. Because managing public and private boundaries in collapsed contexts is complicated on networked publics [8], SNSs can be difficult spaces for users to share experiences related to their stigmatized identities. For example, transgender individuals who wish to receive support from friends through a networked public such as Facebook experience great distress synching their complex stigmatized identities with their Facebook accounts [31].

However, while rare, it is also possible for SNS support groups to enable congruence between one's stigmatized identity (e.g., low-income) and one's larger social context (e.g., Elite University student), and to do so with relatively low barriers of entry. In this paper, we analyze one such community to examine the restorative properties of a safe online space for outsiders that challenges prior notions of typical online support groups. EUCC is a unique online space that provides a safe community for posters while at the same time pushes the stigmatized community into a highly open and networked public on the SNS.

METHODS

There are 37 university-based Class Confession pages on Facebook in the US, including the one at Elite University, which had 77,682 people "talking about this" (a real-time statistic count for keywords entered in the Facebook search bar) at the time of our data collection. As an Elite University alumnus, the first author was able to gain access to EUCC's founders, organizers, posters, and readers. In this section, we describe the research site, data collection and analysis methods used in this work.

EUCC and its Sociotechnical Ecosystem

Elite University's First Generation and Low Income Association (FGLIA) created EUCC in 2015. FGLIA is an approximately 500-member student organization with a board consisting of 10 students. "FGLIA" is used interchangeably on EUCC by posters and commenters to denote "first generation and low-income", or to refer to the student organization that founded EUCC. Although EUCC was first launched as a Tumblr page, FGLIA realized the greater population of Elite University did not use Tumblr regularly. In March 2015, this prompted FGLIA to transition the confession board to Facebook, where more Elite students were socially active online. In its first year the EUCC Facebook page had 969 posts and 6705 Facebook likes. While EUCC is not solely restricted to the school's student population (e.g., alumni, parents, professors, and prospective students have also posted anonymously), the majority of posts are authored by current students who self-identify as low-SES.

In sum, EUCC includes several social technologies, people, processes, and policies forming a sociotechnical ecosystem [54]. Posters and commenters communicate using email, private instant messages, Google Docs, and other technologies in combination with Facebook, Tumblr, and Twitter. Thus, while our data primarily originate from EUCC's Facebook page, we consider the full sociotechnical ecosystem, when discussing the experience of stigma in this online space.

EUCC's sociotechnical system also includes substantial human involvement in the process of publishing anonymized posts. Posters who wish to make confessions on EUCC send their confessions in the form of a private Facebook message to one of two student moderators. These two moderators, who are often first generation and low-income students themselves, are elected every semester by vote from the organization's members and board. Moderators oversee the Facebook page by collectively managing the publication, aggregation, and interaction of the anonymized posts.

Data Collection

Using Facepager, a Facebook-approved third party app for generic data retrieval through Facebook's API, we extracted all posts and comments (all publicly viewable) from EUCC's first year period (March 2015 – March 2016) on Facebook (969 posts). Our data include both anonymized confessions submitted by posters and announcements made by EUCC administrators. Of the 969 posts, 633 posts had comments, with the longest thread including 20 comments. Each confessional post was published by the Facebook page administrator and only identifiable by its publication number. However, commenters are identifiable by their Facebook account name. Hence, during the data extraction process, we gathered comments without collecting the commenter's Facebook account name.

Additionally, the first author conducted four semi-structured interviews with FGLIA members, including three who helped create EUCC. In this paper, we refer to all interviewees using pseudonyms. The first and second interviewees graduated the year prior to data collection, but were an important part of EUCC's early founding process. The third interviewee served as one of the two Facebook page moderators, managing the publication process of incoming confessions at the time of this writing. The last interviewee was an active user of EUCC who also helped coordinate on/offline activities through the Facebook page.

All four interviewees self-identified as either first generation or low-income and were between the ages of 21-25.

Interview questions focused on understanding the motives and processes for using, creating, and managing EUCC. Interviews were conducted between January and May 2016 using video-chat and phone calls, lasting from 45 to 70 minutes. We recognize the limitation of our interviews, which consist primarily of EUCC organizers. However, our main analysis is based on the large corpus of posts and comments, and it is not possible to contact the posters without revealing their identity through the moderators. Hence, we find this tradeoff to be reasonable for the purpose and scope of our analysis.

Data Analysis

We approached our primary data through a grounded inductive coding process [56]. The first author used memoing and mapping techniques to identify emergent themes and patterns. One such pattern indicated changes in the way posters personally perceived or experienced class stigma on EUCC. To further understand the nature of these changes, we used axial coding to delve into the text with more depth [56]. We then performed discourse analysis [25] on a subset of selected texts to analyze the languages that serve as evidence for EUCC's influence on the posters' experience of being low-SES. Discourse analysis is a form of textual analysis that involves identifying patterns, relationships, and values in textual data [25]. Then, we identified, grouped, and analyzed EUCC's sociotechnical designs that shape people's interactions on the platform. The authors met regularly throughout to collaboratively analyze data and to generate and organize themes.

RESULTS

We first describe the sociotechnical configurations that shape the nature of interactions on EUCC. Then we identify EUCC's restorative properties through which posters' experiences of stigma change.

Sociotechnical Features Shaping Interactions

In this section, we present the sociotechnical configurations of EUCC that shape the interactional relationships among posters, commenters, readers, and FGLIA organizers.

1. Moderated Anonymity

On EUCC, anonymity prevents connecting low-income identities with Elite University student identities. Such anonymity fosters openness and honesty when discussing stigmatized identities. For example, one poster confesses how the same disclosure in an identified context led to social ostracism among friends:

#110: I have had sex for money to pay for food and housing over winter breaks. Rather than working 15hrs in work study, I can work for 2 and make twice the money. I told one of my friends about it and she ended up telling my entire group of friends. They did not understand and stopped talking to me after almost 2 years of friendship.

EUCC allows posters like #110 to share such sensitive content while shielding themselves from the potential risks they may face without anonymity. Such sharing in turn can open the minds of other users in a manner that facilitates new forms of support. Readers who encounter this post on EUCC may not realize beforehand that fellow campus students sometimes engage in sex work to make ends meet, thus experiencing stigma both for being low-SES and a sex worker. Furthermore, while the poster was met with negative responses from friends when confessing in person, the anonymous post itself gained 42 Facebook "Likes", which are often experienced as gestures of support [11] on EUCC.

Anonymity also allows posters to discuss the background assumptions behind stigmatized aspects of their identities. Providing an avenue to discuss how individuals personally experience social attributes as stigma enables users to detail the specific ways in which these attributes shape daily interactions with others. For Tyler in #589, the anonymity afforded by EUCC gives him the space to talk about his identity and vent about the background contexts through which others see him:

#589: I hate telling people about my struggles. I would not even be using EUCC if it was not anonymous. People look at you differently when they know you're poor. You suddenly go from "damn Tyler is smart and cool" to "damn Tyler is smart for a poor kid", "fuckin Tyler out here gettin that social mobility", "big homie Tyler finna be the first to graduate in his family", "Tyler out here facing adversity". Stop it. Treat me normally. I'm still Tyler. Just Tyler. Not poor Tyler. Not rich Tyler. Just Tyler. (real name not Tyler)

The anonymity afforded by EUCC gives the poster the ability to continue to be *"Just Tyler"* among his friends and acquaintances in identified settings, while enabling him to engage explicitly with his low-SES identity in a safer space. On EUCC, he can be recognized as being low-SES, yet *"still Tyler"*. Here we see how EUCC users can strategically make visible certain identities, or portions thereof, while protecting others through the anonymity enabled by the platform and surrounding policies.

2. Anonymous Requests & Identifiable Responses

On EUCC, posters are anonymous while commenters are identifiable through Facebook accounts. This configuration allows exchange of multiple forms of social support.

In certain social settings, a request for information can leave the asker vulnerable. For example, requests may carry information that associates the person requesting help with their stigmatized identities (e.g., mental health, financial advice, etc.). Asking for help can be especially difficult for low-SES students due to lack of knowledge, connections, resources, and shame [10,23,36]. However, EUCC's anonymity allows posters to make broad requests from a wide variety of people while disclosing their potential ignorance and stigmatized identities to only a small group of moderators. For example, one poster anonymously seeks information on mental health support groups, identifying as multiple intersectional stigmatized identities—a transfer student, someone struggling to keep up with the workload, and a person with mental health challenges:

#MentalHealth #837 Being a recent transfer student has been a challenge. It's even harder when you feel like a freshman getting used to college life in the city. It is tough finishing the semester knowing I am under credits and suffering from depression and anxiety. Can anyone recommend any support groups on campus I can join? Or just any advice? I want next semester to be better.

Posters can receive informational support directly through EUCC. However, other types of support also emerge. For example, multiple types of support are evidenced in the responses to post #837, including private messages:

Comment 1: I am also a transfer student to this school as well. Please private message me if you feel comfortable doing so. It's tough here and my first year was the worst, but it can get so much better.

This response demonstrates both network support (demonstration that the person receiving the support is a part of a group who face similar challenges) and emotional support (empathy and caring) [18]. Two anonymous posters chatting back and forth online are also likely to exchange esteem support, such as compliments [18]. However, tangible support requires further identification, often only possible after the building of trust through deidentified interpersonal communication [18]. In this scenario, the poster can act upon the offered help or not, enabling him/her to decide whether to receive support without the risk of being exposed to the whole EUCC audience or to the commenter in an interpersonal interaction. This approach privileges the original poster's agency and anonymity, made possible by the assemblage of human and technological actors at play.

On the other hand, commenters' identification exposes them to a degree of vulnerability. We have no way of knowing how many people would offer help—even just in the form of commiseration—in the face of a different sociotechnical system that offers anonymity for commenters as well as posters. We speculate that some may not comment directly on EUCC's Facebook page due to their own concerns about being visible by their Facebook account name.

Another response to the post above (#837), however, gives insight into how multiple types of support can converge in a comment from someone willing to be made vulnerable:

Comment 2: Your school health plan should cover on-campus counseling sessions for free. I went to the counseling center every week and it has helped me manage similar issues you are dealing with – depression, anxiety, moving here from another country. I had to give it some time until I clicked with my counselor, but it definitely helped me. It could be helpful for you too. Good luck!

Commenter 2 offers informational, emotional, and network support from personal experience. The commenter also discloses sensitive identity information that echoes mutual understanding and background similar to the poster. In offering advice, the commenter reveals a variety of stigma identifiers all in the service of supporting the poster who remains anonymous. These self-disclosures further contribute to perceived network support and a sense of belonging that may help change the nature of interaction through which posters experience social stigma.

3. Enforcement of Accountability

Prior research links anonymity to less accountability, more disinhibition [57], and more support seeking [2] in online spaces. However, anonymity and accountability in tandem enable protection and an atmosphere of safety on EUCC. In the context of EUCC, a safe atmosphere implies a space where a poster's personally identifiable information is not traceable to the disclosure's content. It also means that in this space, posters can reasonably engage in frank discussions on difficult topics with moderators preventing harassment from the audience. Hence, EUCC moderators work to ensure safety and accountability by explicitly and manually deidentifying posts. At the same time, they know who the posters are and can hold them accountable for deviations from the norms and policies of the community. The administrative policies as posted highlight the delicate balance the people who run the system must strike. They seek to maintain anonymity, enable free expression, and protect against unintended disclosure by others:

POSTED BY ADMIN: Hi there! EUCC was created to give people a platform to share experiences relating to their socioeconomic status. We strive to have anonymity in all aspects of this page. We hope that you will do the same as well. That being said: we will NOT tolerate people posting other people's names on posts or outing people. If you comment something like "Oh, this person is actually named...." we will automatically DELETE the comment and BAN you. Anonymity is paramount to us and we will not tolerate people who try to violate that.

This message demonstrates that anonymity is actively realized in this sociotechnical space. This kind of work could not be supported through human organization nor technological design alone. To achieve the appropriate balance between anonymity and accountability, EUCC makes use of a variety of platforms, procedures, and policies. For example, Tumblr is known to explicitly support multiple pseudonymous identities [52], while Facebook frequently extolls the virtues of the accountability of "real names" [32]. Somewhere in between these extremes sit a variety of other platforms and services used by EUCC, such as email, Google docs, and so on. It is this ecology of approaches and tools that enables EUCC to employ moderated anonymity as a powerful workaround to overly restrictive or overly open approaches of any one of these systems.

For example, nine months after EUCC launched, posters submitted multiple requests for help regarding housing over winter break. In response, EUCC organizers connected students who needed housing with those willing to provide it. However, Eddie, a former FGLIA board member notes, *"this was especially tricky"*, because *"there were a lot of people here and there who needed help, offering help"*, but *"no systemized way of matching them together"*. Furthermore, this matching required identification and risk of exposure. To manage these risks, organizers created a Google Docs survey to recruit student helpers, asking them to provide contact information (including university ID), what kind of space was offered, for how long, and why the helper was offering the space:

Can you share a little about yourself? Why are you offering space? It often makes people feel more comfortable reaching out if they know a little about the person they're contacting for help.

Volunteers were made visible to posters through a Google Spreadsheet that organizers shared directly with those in need after receiving an email requesting housing assistance. This mechanism allowed posters to contact individuals while remaining anonymous to the rest of the community.

FGLIA board members then leveraged these same data alongside a Change.org petition to convince the school housing administration to change winter housing policy. Eddie describes how FGLIA used multiple platforms to show how existing housing policies were affecting students:

A big aspect of this was that people saw online how many people were in danger over winter break...I do think that there is something wrong with the way we [the school and campus community] are handling lower income students. EUCC and FGLIA have brought attention to that.

Using a variety of platforms to organize and match collective help with those who need it increases volunteers' accountability while minimizing risk for requesters who prefer to be anonymous. Similarly, EUCC's location within Elite provides an additional layer of accountability, as does the location of other class confession sites within their universities. System administrators reassure posters that their content is by and for the community with policies and procedures surrounding who can post, from where they can post, and so on. For example, in response to one such line of inquiry, EUCC responds:

... using a tracking tool to see where our visitors are coming from (Statcounter), 19/20 of the last people to visit EUCC were on Elite University wifi or visited our page while in [city]. Thus, we are not very worried. Edit: You're still submitting anonymously! We are only able to see what wifi you're using/the city you're in.

In practice, these rules are hard to enforce and narrow the scope of the anonymity afforded by EUCC. However, they do provide some level of assurance regarding who might reasonably post and read the content. FGLIA ensures that the platform, through the work of those who maintain it, is accountable to the needs of those who use it.

4. Unique Identifiers and Moderator Involvement

Posts are displayed using numeric unique identifiers through which the community creates threads of response of both identifiable comments and anonymous posts. However, different opinions can spark backlash and direct attacks in these threads. To manage these risks, moderators sometimes interject as one of the commenters and refer to specific post numbers to mediate different perspectives. In some cases, moderators also express their personal opinion by directly participating in the conversation:

Comment 19: As one of the EUCC moderators, I am excited at the rightful push-back and perspective provided to #679. However, as #681 explains, #679 relates to class inequality, which is why it was posted...we promote respectful discussion on this page, but respectful does not equate with filtering or not posting posts which are not the most supportive of disadvantaged students/what we want to hear.

In this comment, the moderator participates in the conversation thread by taking a specific side by noting the "rightful push-back" against post #679. Instead of appearing in the thread as "Elite University Class Confessions", the moderator chose to write the comment through her Facebook account name. Revealing and leveraging both her identity as a fellow student and role as a moderator, the moderator does not seem to shy away from editorializing in the process of intervening among commenters.

In another example of active moderation, poster #506 defends her own personal choices as a low-income person:

#506: just because I'm low-income doesn't mean I can't own nice things. I wear Michael Kors, Calvin Klein, and other designer brands, because I'm really good at finding deals for $20 and less. However, I'm ashamed to wear nice clothes because I'm afraid that it will add to this image of welfare queen that people seem to have of me.

Another poster responds to this post with criticism by choosing to make him/herself anonymous by posting a new post rather than a comment that would reveal the user's account name. Furthermore, the response post is published only after a moderator inserts an addendum in parentheses to clarify the intentions of allowing a potentially negative and conflicting response:

[Posting to help illuminate stereotypical attitudes and misconceptions people have towards lower income people]

#511: @506 I mean you're not a welfare queen, good for you for finding deals, but honestly maybe if you saved some of that money and spent less on designer clothing, you could add to your savings to get out of the lower class.

Posters can also use their unique identifier to refer back to themselves from a previous post yet still remain anonymous. Unique identifiers on EUCC work to facilitate interaction between posters, or between past and present versions of the same poster. Further, they offer a single-use yet persistent identity that allows meaningful dialogue to occur without identification, thus enabling them to fully engage in the context in which their stigma is conversed:

#531: @511 this is the person who posted 506. I shop once a year to replace old items not appropriate to wear anymore, spending $100-150 max. Even if I saved $150 a year, it's not enough for tuition, rent, health insurance, or anything that would help me "get out of the lower class".

At times, disagreements on EUCC also engender perspective-taking, in which the thread of comments exposes both the poster, commenters, and readers to new and diverse viewpoints. The original #506 confession produces two comments while 14 commenters respond to response post #511. Among them, several provide counter-perspectives to the follow-up poster #511's stance:

Comment 3: Why do the poor constantly have to justify their wants and desires? Because I'm poor I can't have anything nice? I "always" have to be in saving mode? Do you realize how that can break a person? Do I sacrifice my spirit simply b/c I was born in a different class than you? Some might say I'm being too hard about $20 of clothing but it's not just clothing. People judge because I dare keep nice things I have earned in better times. I had a sweet job for one year and bought myself a Coach wallet from the outlet as a gift to myself. I still have that wallet. I carried it with me while I was homeless. I remove my food stamp card from it with pride. Other people judge me for it; why am I on food stamps if I can afford Coach? They don't know the whole story and quite frankly, they may still judge me even if they did. But that wallet is a sign of better times and I'm not going to stop using it just because it makes others uncomfortable about class lines.

Comment 14: Spending money on "designer clothing" (which I'm sure here refers to something from banana republic, not Versace) IS a way of lifting yourself out of poverty. Being well dressed and well groomed changes the way people perceive and interact with you. Being poor is not just the suffering of hunger, it's also the pain of being a second class citizen.

According to Vince who helped found EUCC, *"[people] sometimes have no idea what the reality of low-income means"*. Publishing incoming posts that seem to directly attack original posters can serve as a way to highlight such ignorance as well as a diversity of perspectives. In fact, our findings indicate that rich dialogue on conflicting perspectives can potentially raise awareness towards the different facets of class stigma.

Moderator involvement in filtering comment threads is reported to increase the quality of discussion as evidenced in news organizations sites [20], which may be impactful here. However, we leave it to future research to determine whether findings from broad audience news sites with anonymous moderators might apply to a tightknit community with known moderators. Unique identifiers and thoughtful moderation allow interaction among users in this community that engenders diverse perspective-taking. This can challenge existing attitudes and encourage dialogue around stigmatized identities that was not possible before.

Restorative Properties of EUCC

In this section, we bring attention to EUCC's restorative properties. Restorative properties offer users alternate understanding and experiences of their stigmatized identities by interacting with others on EUCC. In our data, low-income students attribute alternative and more positive interactions around their stigmatized identities to EUCC. Using their "confessions", we analyze EUCC's restorative properties and how the sociotechnical space fosters positive experiences around socioeconomic stigma on campus.

Creating a Community of Outsiders in a Networked Public

Poster #265 confesses to have *"gotten to a point where I just walk into class and hate everyone at Elite"* when he/she is *"surrounded by others who constantly talk about the vacations they've been on, how great their birthday was, or how they ate out for every meal last week"*.

The persistence and scalability of online networked publics [8] can push the experience of other people's "vacations" and "birthdays" into the poster's SNS spaces in the form of photos and check-ins from their social ties on Facebook. For Michelle, a low-income student at Elite, Facebook updates from peers sharing pictures of Spring Break trips and check-ins to expensive restaurants once made her feel isolated and disconnected as an Elite student. Scrolling through her Facebook newsfeed made her believe most Elite students were *"richer than me for sure"*, and *"probably have nothing in common with me"*, or *"don't get my issues"*.

Facebook, where low-income students are connected to other Elite students, can amplify feelings of being an outsider. However, EUCC deliberately carves out a space in a highly networked SNS page, allowing stigmatized individuals to find people with mutual experiences through social ties as an Elite student:

#665: EUCC is the best thing to ever happen at Elite. Before, I was absolutely overwhelmed by students' wealth and immediately felt ashamed of my mediocre background. This forum gives me so much hope. Where are you all? Let's hang out. Immediately. #classconfessions

Prior to EUCC, many students felt alone in their struggles, assuming they were one of the very few dealing with class stigma on campus:

#286: I am an older non-traditional student and before reading everyone's confessions I felt so disconnected from the campus. I had no idea there were so many other people struggling like me. I don't feel so alone in my journey now.

Being able to look at confessions from other students echoing familiar experiences helps some like poster #286 to realize that fellow Elite students might identify with his/her difficulties. Knowing there are "so many other people" by simply reading through EUCC posts mitigates the poster's sense of isolation and disconnect as an Elite student. Another poster echoes how a similar assumption changed through EUCC:

#189: I attend meetings for FGLIA but there's only maybe 20-30 people per meeting. It made me think that there were honestly only 20-30 other people on campus dealing with the same problems as I am. Thanks Class Confessions, because now I see there is a whole entire silent group of people in my shoes who are just invisible <3 thanks for bringing a voice to the community that can't/don't want to/are too tired to attend the meetings.

Many posters confess how social risks make it "difficult" and "shameful" to engage in face-to-face and identifiable offline interactions. Prior to EUCC, this made finding a community of like-minded students challenging. However, we show in this work how EUCC's online presence helps provide visibility and voice to an otherwise invisible community of people with a stigmatized identity.

Expressing Separate Incongruent Identities in Tandem

At a place where posters are under constant pressure of not fitting into the socio-cultural prestige that comes with wealth and education, the opportunity to talk about being an Elite student, but one that is also "low-income", "homeless", or "international" is rare [30,37]. However, on EUCC, posters who experience class struggles while attending Elite routinely express separate, incongruent, and intersectional identities not typical for an average Elite student:

#578: I send my social worker from the homeless shelter updates on my grades after every semester. It's a good way to keep in touch and to let him know I am still living my dream. I am not sure that's a common thing to do at Elite.

Posters like #578 may be unable to discuss on-going life experiences incongruent with his/her Elite student identity on identifiable social media platforms used by other Elite students. On Facebook, people tend to share primarily positive content [12,35,44] rather than information related to their stigmatized identities. This "positivity bias" [51] can make it harder to share experiences that might be perceived poorly by their connections who seem to *"[have] it all figured out"*:

#799 Before discussions on Class Confessions, I thought every other student on campus had it all figured out and I was the only one struggling with talking to professors and finding food. Now I know I'm not the only one with issues of not fitting and being low income.

As a first generation or low-income student, issues such as "struggling to talk to professors" or "finding food" may be kept silent, especially because one is also an Elite student. With EUCC, these students can talk about such incongruent identities and experiences without feeling like an outsider to the campus community.

Overcoming Limitations of Exchanging Physical Help

Finding a physical venue of interaction is difficult for low-SES students at Elite, in part because *"people experience a lot of shame with [being low-income on campus]"*, according to Ari. Ari, who serves as one of the two current moderators and is an active member of the FGLIA board, describes how shame became salient at a campus coat drive:

A lot of people were embarrassed to get coats even if they needed it. They asked us to meet elsewhere. There is that shame at [Elite] that is elevated at an unhealthy degree, especially when you are surrounded by so much privilege.

This particular event required people to pick up donated coats at a public space on campus, thereby identifying themselves as people in need of such support. At a place like Elite, spaces where students can be identified by others as low-income can be daunting, especially for those who do not wish to disclose their SES status. EUCC, on the other hand, functions as an avenue where users can minimize their identity exposure to a few people and still receive tangible help if they choose to act on it. Responding to posters who express specific needs, commenters offer posters material support, ranging from feminine products, textbooks, and food to monetary donations and housing. One commenter who wished to help posters who could not afford to eat during finals week is also mindful of their identities as low-income students:

In case people are worried about their identity being revealed, I'm totally happy to handover money or food to one of the FGLIA crew and you guys just handle it, or I'm also happy to handle the logistics and you can let them know that I'm a hermit grad student so I won't know anyone from their social circle anyways.

Such correspondence between posters, commenters, and organizers work together to enable stigmatized students to receive help from a wider audience of people at Elite who may otherwise be difficult to reach. In return, posters can find tangible support and connect with *"people who get it"*:

#WhatHasChanged #798 Since last year, I have found people who get it (thanks, FGLIA!). I have also found tangible support I didn't know existed. Meals and emergency housing! I had no idea this support existed.

Individual and collective help from networked ties also makes posters feel more positive about themselves in relation to their class identity on campus. The "organized attitude" [43] felt through FGLIA and EUCC allows one poster to embrace his/her identity as a first generation student:

#796 The gratitude I have for FGLIA. I am inspired by FGLIA members making these resources available for students here at Elite through EUCC. Because of FGLIA, I have embraced being a first generation student. Thank you

EUCC provides an alternative space and setting through which exchange of support can take place. Not only does this hybrid on/offline exchange help provide material and tangible assistance that are often desperately needed by first generation and low-income peers on campus, but also assist students in embracing their stigmatized identities.

Opening Perspectives

On EUCC, dialogue around class issues and stigmatized identities routinely takes place. Such discussions can raise awareness as well as challenge biases against socioeconomic stereotypes. Together, these conversations provide new perspectives through which people understand stigmatized attributes:

#405: Reading the Confessions has unsettled me: both b/c I realize how much the 1-5% can learn from the lower-income people, but also b/c I realize how much the lower-income people have to learn about the 1-5%. I was born "lower-income", but not anymore. Life isn't easier up here, life is life, and life's hard. We must work to keep it. But ppl up here do need to realize what runs their "easy" lives. Who are the ppl who made ur clothes & built ur house?

Here, the poster brings authority to the post by speaking as someone who has been both poor and rich. Discussion around socioeconomic issues is diverse and often conflicting. Further, by raising awareness about the struggles faced by low-income students, EUCC pushes the exposure of low-SES and first generation issues beyond its immediate population, enabling new forms of perspective-taking from those with privileged backgrounds:

#380: I was talking to a wealthy student on campus that reads the Confessions page. They were shocked at the number of low-income students on this campus and called the EUCC page 'enlightening.' (They also told me that they've talked with their friends about ways to help their classmates.) Here's to the empathy we are helping others realize. I'm proud of everyone that reads/posts on this page.

As shown in this example, EUCC may potentially educate and influence how some non-low-SES people (e.g., EUCC commenters and audience members) view low-income stigma and their own privilege in relation to it.

Engagement with the broad EUCC and FGLIA communities may also inform how people think about addressing class issues. The community provides a variety of new mechanisms to connect with those who need support. Interactions between people of different classes also enable students to learn from and empathize with each other:

#539: I swiped in [meals for] a couple of people today, because I always have plenty of swipes I never use. They messaged me a few minutes later thanking me for giving them what will be their only meal for the day. I don't think I've ever felt so many things at once in my entire life. I take so many things for granted, like extra spending money and extra meal swipes. But if I can offer help and make anyone's life a little easier, that's all I really need.

Offering meal swipes at campus dining halls is one of the most common responses to EUCC posts that confess to hunger on campus. This poster shares what it is like to have engaged in such exchange with another poster. In essence, EUCC pushes the difficult experiences of stigmatized individuals into a highly networked and public SNS space involving and exposing personal struggles of socioeconomic stigma to social ties who may not have similar experiences or challenges like poster #539.

DISCUSSION

In this work, we show how EUCC's combination of sociotechnical features (moderated anonymity; anonymous requests and identifiable responses; enforcement of accountability; and unique identifiers and moderator involvement) shapes user interactions around stigma. We also introduce the concept of *restorative properties*, which we define as semi-stable sociotechnical arrangements that provide users specific opportunities for action, reflection, and communication in relation to their stigmatized identities. We present restorative properties both as a new analytical construct for HCI and social computing researchers, and as a strategy for online support groups whose members may benefit from experiencing stigma in different ways. By using this approach, communities can provide an interactive space for both those who share a stigmatized identity and their broader peer group.

Integration of Disparate Social Memberships

Marginality refers to "human membership in more than one community of practice" [1]. Alluding to Robert Park's "marginal man", Bowker and Star describe a stigmatized person as someone who has "double vision by virtue of having more than one identity to negotiate" [7], like the posters on EUCC. Similarly, Stone refers to those who inhabit multiple disparate identity categories as "boundary creatures" with a heightened sense of vision [55]. Through these lenses, we see how stigmatization occurs through multiple memberships in disparate communities where an individual must frequently switch between the norms of each community [7,33].

Throughout our data, posters express that they do not belong on campus with their fellow Elite students whom they assume to be different from themselves. Membership in one group is described in these posts as mutually exclusive to the other. EUCC, in effect, challenges this perception. EUCC grounds the locus of discussion and expression of marginalized statuses *within* a common membership identity as Elite students. We see this in the way posters discuss incongruent identities in tandem, implying rightful belonging in both seemingly separate groups.

Here, there is a sense of integration in identity memberships for posters who are able to discuss and express a stigmatized identity (low-income) in relation to a non-stigmatized identity (Elite student). This is a significant departure from existing online support groups that partition those with stigmatized identities away from others to discuss issues related to their stigma privately [21]. While membership exclusivity in these safe online spaces may be necessary for protection of personal identity [53] or strengthening of group identity [39,50], it can also foster separation rather than bridging of those who are in the marginalized circle and those who are not.

Past HCI literature on online support groups has shown that admitting to a negative identity online within a shared identity group increases trust, reduces stigma, and acts as a membership card for that group [24]. EUCC, conversely, expands the group membership boundary to include not only marginalized individuals, but the larger campus community of Elite students. This is critical, because true membership in the context of EUCC does not mean just being part of a low-income community or just being an Elite student. It means being both.

Tangible Help & Belonging Through (In)visibility

Prior studies have demonstrated that exchange of emotional or informational support is more frequent than tangible assistance [13,14,22] in computer-mediated support groups. Other ways of soliciting tangible support online require revealing personal hardship using real names. However, our findings indicate that the sociotechnical configuration of anonymous requests combined with identifiable responses helps users overcome constraints in asking for and providing tangible help through EUCC. Commenters' names are visible, increasing these volunteers' accountability (as well as vulnerability), but also the ease of coordinating help with a specific poster. For some, this changes how they view their ability to help those within the EUCC community. In addition, these interpersonal exchanges help some posters view peers whom they previously considered outsiders to their struggles, as empathetic students willing to provide help through EUCC.

Furthermore, EUCC's scalability [8] as a networked public helps provide visibility and voice to an otherwise invisible community of people with a stigmatized identity. Outsiders are, by definition, spread out across a population and do not feel a part of the larger community. Due to shame and persistence of identities in a real-name SNS or face-to-face interaction, it is difficult to foster community around stigmatized identities. Thus, discussions about class issues at Elite are either highly visible in public contexts or largely invisible in personal interactions between close friends. However, EUCC emerges as a hybrid on/offline community allowing stigmatized people to come together and identify as part of a group without having to come out personally as part of that group.

Opening Perspectives as A Source of Learning

Poverty is often distant from and irrelevant to people who do not experience it first-hand, particularly in increasingly stratified and homogenous social media feeds [60]. As shown in our findings, there is a lack of knowledge and understanding towards what it means to come from a different socioeconomic status.

On EUCC, posts are given unique identifiers that foster multiple threads of response, exposing the posters, commenters, and readers to new and diverse viewpoints. This fosters education and engagement that can potentially alter the contextual understanding of stigmatized identities on campus. This increases awareness of the underlying assumptions that perpetuate class stigma on campus.

In contrast, learning about stigmatized experiences of those within a user's immediate community is limited on SNS support groups formed through Reddit [2] or Instagram[3], because these groups do not engage external audiences who are unfamiliar with the stigma. On Yik Yak, stigmatized users are exclusively grouped by location proximity or topic [6,34] rather than focused on a specific stigmatized identity. Grouping people geographically can allow a local group identity to emerge [34]. However, such a broad grouping limits the opportunity for interaction and discussion of particular stigma-related issues across different social groups, which helps disparate identities become congruent for marginalized users.

Bringing an outsider into a larger circle of people who may not necessarily identify with the same stigmatized statuses is risky. Yet, the restorative properties that characterize EUCC provide an artful integration between different social worlds to form an ongoing and stable relationship that transcends existing boundaries. Thus, EUCC serves as an opportunity for learning and education across different social groups [38] without placing the burden of education on the marginalized students. EUCC is an example of a sociotechnical system that leverages this difficult balance well.

CONCLUSION

EUCC is a sociotechnical system that includes the people, policies, and practices of Elite University and the FGLIA organization as well as the infrastructure of a variety of technological platforms. This unique combination of human and technical actors provides a venue and structure for producing, experiencing, and learning about stigma. The aggregation of practices we encounter on EUCC, therefore, informs our scholarly thinking about stigma in light of ever evolving sociotechnical systems. By creating the conditions under which stigmatized disclosures and exchange of support could take place in a sociotechnical system, EUCC offers restorative properties that give posters a sense of belonging and affinity. While motivating sociotechnical designs that take users' stigmatized identities into consideration is no easy task, we argue through this work that restorative properties can affect change in the social context through which people experience stigma.

ACKNOWLEDGEMENTS

We would like to thank the participants for sharing their personal experiences during the interview. We also thank the people whose posts and comments we analyzed in this study. We also thank our colleague Kate Ringland, the anonymous reviewers, and our shepherd who provided numerous advice and feedback for this paper.

REFERENCES

1. Vibe Aarkrog and Christian Helms Jørgensen. 2008. *Divergence and Convergence in Education and Work.* Peter Lang.
2. Nazanin Andalibi, Oliver L. Haimson, Munmun De Choudhury, and Andrea Forte. 2016. Understanding Social Media Disclosures of Sexual Abuse Through the Lenses of Support Seeking and Anonymity. In *Proceedings of the 2016 CHI Conference on Human Factors in Computing Systems* (CHI '16), 3906–3918. https://doi.org/10.1145/2858036.2858096
3. Nazanin Andalibi, Pinar Ozturk, and Andrea Forte. 2017. Sensitive Self- disclosures, Responses, and Social Support on Instagram: the Case of #Depression. In *Proceedings of the 20th ACM Conference on Computer Supported Cooperative Work & Social Computing* (CSCW '17). https://doi.org/http://dx.doi.org/10.1145/2998181.2998243
4. Elizabeth Aries and Maynard Seider. The Interactive Relationship Between Class Identity and the College Experience: The Case of Lower Income Students. Retrieved August 1, 2016 from http://itp.wceruw.org/documents/Aries_Seider_2005_TheInteractiveRelationshipBetweenClassIdentityandtheCollegeExperience.pdf
5. Emily Badger. 2015. The Surprising Cost of Growing Up Poor In the Shadow of Wealth. *Washington Post.* Retrieved September 15, 2016 from https://www.washingtonpost.com/news/wonk/wp/2015/01/23/the-surprising-cost-of-growing-up-poor-in-the-shadow-of-wealth/
6. Jeremy Birnholtz, Nicholas Aaron Ross Merola, and Arindam Paul. 2015. "Is It Weird to Still Be a Virgin": Anonymous, Locally Targeted Questions on Facebook Confession Boards. In *Proceedings of the 33rd Annual ACM Conference on Human Factors in Computing Systems* (CHI '15), 2613–2622. https://doi.org/10.1145/2702123.2702410
7. Geoffrey C. Bowker and Susan Leigh Star. 2000. *Sorting things out: Classification and its consequences.* MIT press.
8. Danah Boyd. 2008. Taken Out of Context: American Teen Sociality in Networked Publics. University of California, Berkeley. Retrieved December 17, 2016 from http://www.danah.org/papers/TakenOutOfContext.html
9. Danah Boyd. 2010. Social Network Sites as Networked Publics: Affordances, Dynamics, and Implications. *ResearchGate.* Retrieved December 30, 2016 from https://www.researchgate.net/publication/265035948_Social_Network_Sites_as_Networked_Publics_Affordances_Dynamics_and_Implications
10. Alberto F. Cabrera and Steven M. La Nasa. 2001. On the Path to College: Three Critical Tasks Facing America's Disadvantaged. *Research in Higher Education* 42, 2: 119–149. https://doi.org/10.1023/A:1026520002362
11. Caleb T. Carr, D. Yvette Wohn, and Rebecca A. Hayes. 2016. as social support: Relational closeness, automaticity, and interpreting social support from paralinguistic digital affordances in social media. *Computers in Human Behavior* 62: 385–393. https://doi.org/10.1016/j.chb.2016.03.087
12. Hui-Tzu Grace Chou and Nicholas Edge. 2011. "They Are Happier and Having Better Lives than I Am": The Impact of Using Facebook on Perceptions of Others' Lives. *Cyberpsychology, Behavior, and Social Networking* 15, 2: 117–121. https://doi.org/10.1089/cyber.2011.0324
13. Neil S. Coulson, Heather Buchanan, and Aimee Aubeeluck. 2007. Social support in cyberspace: A content analysis of communication within a Huntington's disease online support group. *Patient Education and Counseling* 68, 2: 173–178. https://doi.org/10.1016/j.pec.2007.06.002
14. Constantinos K. Coursaris and Ming Liu. 2009. An analysis of social support exchanges in online HIV/AIDS self-help groups. *Computers in Human Behavior* 25, 4: 911–918. https://doi.org/10.1016/j.chb.2009.03.006
15. Jennifer Crocker and Brenda Major. 1989. Social stigma and self-esteem: The self-protective properties of stigma. *Psychological Review* 96, 4: 608–630. https://doi.org/10.1037/0033-295X.96.4.608
16. Jean-Claude Croizet and Theresa Claire. 1998. Extending the Concept of Stereotype Threat to Social Class: The Intellectual Underperformance of Students from Low Socioeconomic Backgrounds. *Personality and Social Psychology Bulletin* 24, 6: 588–594. https://doi.org/10.1177/0146167298246003
17. Robert Crosnoe. 2009. Low-Income Students and the Socioeconomic Composition of Public High Schools. *American Sociological Review* 74, 5: 709–730. https://doi.org/10.1177/000312240907400502
18. Carolyn E. Cutrona and Julie A. Suhr. 1992. Controllability of Stressful Events and Satisfaction With Spouse Support Behaviors. *Communication Research* 19, 2: 154–174. https://doi.org/10.1177/009365092019002002
19. Alexa Davis. Food Insecurity On Campus: Is Your Ivy Leaguer Starving? *Forbes.* Retrieved August 1, 2016 from http://www.forbes.com/sites/alexadavis/2015/12/17/food-insecurity-on-campus-is-your-ivy-leaguer-starving/
20. Nicholas Diakopoulos and Mor Naaman. 2011. Towards Quality Discourse in Online News Comments. In *Proceedings of the ACM 2011 Conference on Computer Supported Cooperative Work* (CSCW '11), 133–142. https://doi.org/10.1145/1958824.1958844
21. Judith Donath. 1999. Identity and deception in the virtual community. In *Communities in Cyberspace.* Psychology Press.

22. Kristen Campbell Eichhorn. 2008. Soliciting and Providing Social Support Over the Internet: An Investigation of Online Eating Disorder Support Groups. *Journal of Computer-Mediated Communication* 14, 1: 67–78. https://doi.org/10.1111/j.1083-6101.2008.01431.x
23. Nicole B. Ellison, D. Yvette Wohn, and Michael G. Brown. 2014. Social Media and College Access. *interactions* 21, 4: 62–65. https://doi.org/10.1145/2630008
24. Jolene Galegher, Lee Sproull, and Sara Kiesler. 1998. Legitimacy, Authority, and Community in Electronic Support Groups. *Written Communication* 15, 4: 493–530. https://doi.org/10.1177/0741088398015004003
25. James Paul Gee. 2014. *An Introduction to Discourse Analysis: Theory and Method*. Routledge.
26. Kenneth Gergen. 1992. *The Saturated Self: Dilemmas of Identity in Contemporary Life*. Basic Books.
27. Anthony Giddens. 1991. *Modernity and Self-identity: Self and Society in the Late Modern Age*. Stanford University Press.
28. Erving Goffman. 1956. *The presentation of self in everyday life*. University of Edinburgh, Edinburgh.
29. Erving Goffman. 2009. *Stigma: Notes on the Management of Spoiled Identity*. Simon and Schuster.
30. Robert Granfield. 1991. MAKING IT BY FAKING IT Working-Class Students in an Elite Academic Environment. *Journal of Contemporary Ethnography* 20, 3: 331–351. https://doi.org/10.1177/089124191020003005
31. Oliver L. Haimson, Jed R. Brubaker, Lynn Dombrowski, and Gillian R. Hayes. 2015. Disclosure, Stress, and Support During Gender Transition on Facebook. In *Proceedings of the 18th ACM Conference on Computer Supported Cooperative Work & Social Computing* (CSCW '15), 1176–1190. https://doi.org/10.1145/2675133.2675152
32. Oliver L. Haimson and Anna Lauren Hoffmann. 2016. Constructing and enforcing "authentic" identity online: Facebook, real names, and non-normative identities. *First Monday* 21, 6. Retrieved August 29, 2016 from http://firstmonday.org/ojs/index.php/fm/article/view/6791
33. D. Fox Harrell. 2009. Computational and Cognitive Infrastructures of Stigma: Empowering Identity in Social Computing and Gaming. In *Proceedings of the Seventh ACM Conference on Creativity and Cognition* (C&C '09), 49–58. https://doi.org/10.1145/1640233.1640244
34. Matthew Heston and Jeremy Birnholtz. 2016. (In)visible cities: an exploration of social identity, anonymity and location-based filtering on yik yak. https://doi.org/10.9776/16152
35. B. Hogan. 2010. The Presentation of Self in the Age of Social Media: Distinguishing Performances and Exhibitions Online. *Bulletin of Science, Technology & Society* 30, 6: 377–386. https://doi.org/10.1177/0270467610385893
36. Grace YoungJoo Jeon, Nicole B. Ellison, Bernie Hogan, and Christine Greenhow. 2016. First-Generation Students and College: The Role of Facebook Networks As Information Sources. In *Proceedings of the 19th ACM Conference on Computer-Supported Cooperative Work & Social Computing* (CSCW '16), 887–899. https://doi.org/10.1145/2818048.2820074
37. Sarah E. Johnson, Jennifer A. Richeson, and Eli J. Finkel. 2011. Middle class and marginal? Socioeconomic status, stigma, and self-regulation at an elite university. *Journal of Personality and Social Psychology* 100, 5: 838–852. https://doi.org/10.1037/a0021956
38. Alexandra Juhasz. 2012. An Idea Whose Time is Here: FemTechNet – A Distributed Online Collaborative Course (DOCC). *Ada: A Journal of Gender, New Media, and Technology*. Retrieved December 28, 2016 from http://adanewmedia.org/2012/11/issue1-juhasz/
39. Martin Lea, Russell Spears, and Daphne de Groot. 2001. Knowing Me, Knowing You: Anonymity Effects on Social Identity Processes within Groups. *Personality and Social Psychology Bulletin* 27, 5: 526–537. https://doi.org/10.1177/0146167201275002
40. Barbara L. Ley. 2007. Vive Les Roses!: The Architecture of Commitment in an Online Pregnancy and Mothering Group. *Journal of Computer-Mediated Communication* 12, 4: 1388–1408. https://doi.org/10.1111/j.1083-6101.2007.00378.x
41. Noëmi Manders-Huits. 2010. Practical versus moral identities in identity management. *Ethics and Information Technology* 12, 1: 43–55. https://doi.org/10.1007/s10676-010-9216-8
42. Heidi Mattson. 2013. *Ivy League Stripper: A Memoir*. Skyhorse Publishing, Inc.
43. George Herbert Mead. 2009. *Mind, Self, and Society: From the Standpoint of a Social Behaviorist*. University of Chicago Press.
44. Soraya Mehdizadeh. 2010. Self-Presentation 2.0: Narcissism and Self-Esteem on Facebook. *Cyberpsychology, Behavior, and Social Networking* 13, 4: 357–364. https://doi.org/10.1089/cyber.2009.0257
45. Tsubasa Morioka, Nicole B. Ellison, and Michael Brown. 2016. Identity Work on Social Media Sites: Disadvantaged Students' College Transition Processes. In *Proceedings of the 19th ACM Conference on Computer-Supported Cooperative Work & Social Computing* (CSCW '16), 848–859. https://doi.org/10.1145/2818048.2819959
46. Candice L. Odgers, Sachiko Donley, Avshalom Caspi, Christopher J. Bates, and Terrie E. Moffitt. 2015. Living alongside more affluent neighbors predicts greater involvement in antisocial behavior among low-income boys. *Journal of Child Psychology and Psychiatry* 56, 10: 1055–1064. https://doi.org/10.1111/jcpp.12380

47. Joan M. Ostrove. 2003. Belonging and Wanting: Meanings of Social Class Background for Women's Constructions of their College Experiences. *Journal of Social Issues* 59, 4: 771–784. https://doi.org/10.1046/j.0022-4537.2003.00089.x
48. Joan M. Ostrove and Susan M. Long. 2001. White Women's Social Class Identity and the College Experience. Retrieved August 1, 2016 from http://eric.ed.gov/?id=ED457510
49. Joan M Ostrove and Susan M Long. 2007. Social Class and Belonging: Implications for College Adjustment. *The Review of Higher Education* 30, 4: 363–389. https://doi.org/10.1353/rhe.2007.0028
50. S. D. Reicher, R. Spears, and T. Postmes. 1995. A Social Identity Model of Deindividuation Phenomena. *European Review of Social Psychology* 6, 1: 161–198. https://doi.org/10.1080/14792779443000049
51. Leonard Reinecke and Sabine Trepte. 2014. Authenticity and Well-being on Social Network Sites: A Two-wave Longitudinal Study on the Effects of Online Authenticity and the Positivity Bias in SNS Communication. *Comput. Hum. Behav.* 30: 95–102. https://doi.org/10.1016/j.chb.2013.07.030
52. Bryce J. Renninger. 2014. "Where I can be myself … where I can speak my mind" : Networked counterpublics in a polymedia environment. *New Media & Society*: 1461444814530095. https://doi.org/10.1177/1461444814530095
53. Kathryn E. Ringland, Christine T. Wolf, LouAnne E. Boyd, Mark S. Baldwin, and Gillian R. Hayes. 2016. Would You Be Mine: Appropriating Minecraft As an Assistive Technology for Youth with Autism. In *Proceedings of the 18th International ACM SIGACCESS Conference on Computers and Accessibility* (ASSETS '16), 33–41. https://doi.org/10.1145/2982142.2982172
54. Kathryn E. Ringland, Christine T. Wolf, Heather Faucett, Lynn Dombrowski, and Gillian R. Hayes. 2016. "Will I always be not social?": Re-Conceptualizing Sociality in the Context of a Minecraft Community for Autism. In *Proceedings of ACM CHI Conference on Human Factors in Computing Systems 2016.*, 1256–1269. https://doi.org/10.1145/2858036.2858038
55. Allucquère Rosanne Stone. 1996. *The War of Desire and Technology at the Close of the Mechanical Age.* MIT Press.
56. Anselm Strauss and Juliet M. Corbin. 1998. *Basics of Qualitative Research: Techniques and Procedures for Developing Grounded Theory.* SAGE Publications.
57. John Suler. 2004. The Online Disinhibition Effect. *CyberPsychology & Behavior* 7, 3: 321–326. https://doi.org/10.1089/1094931041291295
58. Ron Suskind. 2010. *A Hope in the Unseen: An American Odyssey from the Inner City to the Ivy League.* Crown/Archetype.
59. Sherry Turkle. 1999. Cyberspace and Identity. *ResearchGate* 28, 6: 643–648. https://doi.org/10.2307/2655534
60. 2014. What does poverty look like on social media? *Global Social Media Impact Study*. Retrieved August 1, 2016 from http://blogs.ucl.ac.uk/global-social-media/2014/08/02/how-does-poverty-looks-like-on-social-media/

Activity as the Ultimate Particular of Interaction Design

Annika Waern
Uppsala University
Uppsala, Sweden
annika.waern@im.uu.se

Jon Back
Uppsala University
Uppsala, Sweden
jon.back@im.uu.se

ABSTRACT
In the turn towards practice-oriented research in interaction design, one of the most important proposals has been the emphasis on the 'ultimate particulars' produced by design, as embodiments of design knowledge. In current HCI research, those particulars are almost always taken to be 'things' – artefacts or singular systems. We argue that this emphasis may have come at a cost that can be described as a loss of identity; interaction design research was never primarily concerned with the design of artefacts, but with how humans act and interact with each other with and through artefacts.

We propose a complementary perspective by looking at design projects and traditions where the 'ultimate particulars' can be considered to be *activities* rather than things. The article is concerned with how knowledge needs to be articulated in the scholarly engagement with such design practices. We argue that engagement with activity-centric design gets design research one step closer towards understanding salient contemporary design practices and what Buchanan calls 'environmental design'.

Author Keywords
Research through design; third wave HCI; ultimate particular; activity-centric design; second order design; environmental design

ACM Classification Keywords
H.5.m. Information interfaces and presentation (e.g., HCI): Miscellaneous

INTRODUCTION
The pragmatic approach to design theory in HCI has contributed with a necessary and fruitful shift from a positivistic perspective on design as science, towards a focus on design conceptualisations that are particular and generative [55,64]. Storni [56] summarises this perspective as "RtD [Research through Design] is rigorous when it is modest, accountable, and generative." One of the central realisations has been the role of actual designs, the "ultimate particulars", as embodiment of design knowledge.

Permission to make digital or hard copies of all or part of this work for personal or classroom use is granted without fee provided that copies are not made or distributed for profit or commercial advantage and that copies bear this notice and the full citation on the first page. Copyrights for components of this work owned by others than ACM must be honored. Abstracting with credit is permitted. To copy otherwise, or republish, to post on servers or to redistribute to lists, requires prior specific permission and/or a fee. Request permissions from Permissions@acm.org.
CHI 2017, May 06-11, 2017, Denver, CO, USA
© 2017 ACM. ISBN 978-1-4503-4655-9/17/05...$15.00
DOI: http://dx.doi.org/10.1145/3025453.3025990

This has led to an increased focus on *things*, in the form of singular systems, interfaces, and artefacts. They are designed in research projects, studied in field studies, and brought forth at conferences as demonstrations. In this article, we argue that this may have come at a non-negligible cost, the risk of losing focus on *what it is that interaction designers design*. Buchanan described interaction design as fundamentally concerned with "how human beings relate to other human beings through the mediating influence of products" [15]. But this relationship is varying as well as ephemeral, it emerges in changing practices as well as in the momentary activity, and it is not necessarily circumscribed by a singular "thing". We argue that a strongly artefact-centric approach to design imbues a level of technology-determinism in third wave HCI.

Three trends in society makes this an important thing to address. Firstly, interactive systems are getting increasingly integrated within all aspects of everyday life [14]and hence, designing and evaluating them in isolation is not sufficient. Secondly, less and less are systems designed as stable products: they are continuously updated and maintained as online services in dialogue with use [33], making it a problematic idea that a design project ends with a product being produced. Thirdly, information technology is becoming an essential part of both local and broader societal infrastructures [2] and it becomes essential to understand how such structures are being designed. Buchanan calls the latter 'environmental design', the design of such complex and pervasive systems that increasingly influence our everyday life.

In this article, we explore an alternative design paradigm in which the ultimate particular is not a thing, but an *activity*. There exist design traditions that strive to directly design what people do, using multiple resources to influence people's activity. We propose that by focussing on the performed activity, activity-centric design is able to take on design tasks that span multiple design resources and levels. We investigate how activity-centric design knowledge can be articulated and communicated within a designer community and in a scholarly context, and draw upon work within HCI and adjacent fields to develop an understanding of knowledge articulations for activity-centric design.

BACKGROUND

The ultimate particular

While research through design (RtD) has a long history within HCI, it is only during the last decade that we have seen an ontological debate concerning what knowledge is meaningfully produced by it [16,23,40,49,55,64]. This ontological problem arises from the observation lucidly expressed already by Simon [52]: that design is not about what is, but about what *could, or ought to, be*.

The concept of the 'ultimate particular' was first articulated Stolterman [68], as a way to highlight the role of concrete design solutions as articulations of design knowledge. Stolterman argued that design is different from science in that while science is concerned with general truths, design is concerned with creating specific solutions to particular problems - *the ultimate particulars*. Gaver [23] further argued that theory always will underspecify design, in that "practitioners will be faced by innumerable decisions whatever theory they use", while many of the aspects of a successful design will not be captured by any specific theory. In relation to the Popperian ideals of science, Gaver [23] argues that design knowledge is unlikely to be falsifiable (as it builds on the fact that something was constructed), but rather is inspirational and generative of new designs. Furthermore, the strife of design is to constantly look for new opportunities and expansions to what is considered 'possible', making also convergence an unlikely and to some extent undesirable development. Stolteman's identification of the ultimate particular as well as Gaver's critique of attempts to scientize design, raise intricate questions about what knowledge is meaningfully produced in RtD.

In a meta-level analysis of the research production from the field, Löwgren [40] proposed the concept of *intermediate level knowledge* as an all-encompassing term for articulations of design knowledge that go beyond the singular artifact, but is less universal than a grand theory. Intermediate level knowledge is characterized by its practical usefulness in design, but it is underspecified in the sense that it will not always hold, and the conditions under which it will hold are not easily articulated. Löwgren included a wide range of knowledge contributions (such as methods and evaluation frameworks, design concepts and patterns, and design critique) as forms of intermediary knowledge. Later work has focused more specifically on concepts that abstract on particular design solutions. Examples include *strong concepts* as "design elements abstracted beyond particular instances which have the potential to be appropriated by designers and researchers to extend their repertoires and enable new particulars instantiations" [30], *bridging concepts* as theoretically founded articulations supported by multiple design exemplars [16], and *experiential qualities* as characterizations of interaction experiences that emerge from the use of a range of designs [53]. In a meta-analysis of these contributions, Pierce identifies them as *concept-things*, combining a collection of artifacts with a description that articulate their common features [22].

The concept of annotated portfolios as suggested by Gaver and Bowers [21], is particularly radical. These comprise a collection of designed artefacts, with annotations done by the designer to highlight what they consider to be particularly interesting properties and design choices. In contrast to the previously mentioned forms of intermediate level knowledge, the annotated portfolios need not be framed by an overarching concept. Rather, it is the designers' choice to present them together that shapes their connection and establishes the lens through which they can be attributed with a commonality. The result is a nuanced communication of an aesthetic approach, rather than an articulation of an abstract concept.

Bardzell et al [7] have highlighted that the production on knowledge as concept-things prioritizes the designers' intentions and interpretations over those of a user or a critical reader. While this certainly is a valid critique, it can also be seen as a defining feature on the articulation of knowledge that is generative of design: the pragmatic approach to RtD in third way HCI privileges the designer's perspective over that of users.

The debate summarized above has served to shape a foundational and pragmatic perspective on RtD that is not questioned in this article. But here, we wish to highlight that in all of this work the 'ultimate particulars' that are being annotated, that work as exemplars of concepts, or even read by critics, are almost always assumed to be *things*.

Activity-Centric HCI research

A focus on activity was brought forwards early in HCI, as an alternative to the at the time dominant paradigm of approaches based on human factors such as theories of cognition [44]. This "second wave HCI" [14] is represented both by situational approaches [58,57] and by the development and use of activity theory as a tool in interaction design [44,35]. The focus lies on "understanding technology as part of the larger scope of human activities" [35:5]. This body of work has largely been holistic and analytical in nature, looking at the social practices with and around technology. A central argument is that activity manifests within a complex meshwork of practices, material properties, and human actors, and that the use and effect of an interactive system cannot be understood in isolation without taking this meshwork into account.

There are strong methodological contributions from this field. Originating in the recognition of interaction as a situated and complex activity, researchers emphasized the need for iterative design and for involving users throughout the design process [6], and advocated a shift towards considering users less as novices, and more as skilled experts in their own work practice [20]. Recently, theories of materiality have been brought into this perspective, questioning in particular the very notion of design processes as something separate from use [13]: an artefact in use is not shaped just by its design but also by its use and its users.

Second Wave Critique of Third Wave

In her scrutiny of third wave HCI [14], Bødker frames the third wave as a counter-movement, "the focus of the third wave, to some extent, seems to be defined in terms of what the second wave is not". Based on this observation, she argues that some important perspectives from second wave may have been lost. To illustrate what has been missed, Bødker brings forward first the "multiplicity of interaction", and the work that "humans do to make multiple objects work together". Bødker brings forward the plethora of work situation studies from the second wave, that highlight the complexity of any concrete work situation. While the overarching ambitions of the third paradigm (at least as expressed by Harrison et al [27]) certainly take this into account, it persists as an adequate critique of the artefact-centred approach to articulating design knowledge.

Bødker acknowledges that third wave HCI has been apt to adopt new forms of interaction, in particular physical and tangible interaction but also bringing about a material perspective even on "immaterials", the kinds of technologies which typically are not rendered visible and controllable to user [2]. However, she argues, this comes at the cost of focussing primarily on the interactions with a designed system or artefact. The everyday work of '"making-do", creating bricolage solutions to everyday or work challenges, is not easily accommodated by this approach [62].

A related critique has recently been articulated by Taylor [61]. In a study of an urban bike rental system, Taylor developed a deep understanding of what features of the system design contribute to shape its use. His conclusion is that the instances of human computer interaction, such as in what way the user identifies herself to the bike, has a very marginal effect on the use patterns. Instead, the patterns of use emerge from the rules and regulations implemented in the system infrastructure (in particular how one pays for the service), together with the location of bike stations in the city. Taylor argues that if we are to understand anything about the design of such complex and pervasive systems, we cannot restrict ourselves to looking at the design of interactions.

Indeed, much of the technologies that pervade through life do so through infrastructuring; they provide frameworks for activity that are rendered meaningful through the uses, changes and additions that users develop within and around the technology. As pointed out by Bjögvinsson et al. [13], the design project for such technology is only part of the lifecycle of a product, and "both the beginning and end of a designed device is open and hardly ever constrained to the limits of the project". Bjögvinsson et al. argue that interaction design must shift focus from the design of things to the "kinds of socio-material assemblies that Bruno Latour so strikingly has characterized as collectives of humans and nonhumans" [13], and from this perspective advocate a more embedded perspective on design. In particular, they argue that participation in design can take place both during the design project (as advocated by classical participatory design) but also in use, what the authors call *design after design*.

While Bjögvinsson et al. bring forward this argument to highlight the users' role in shaping infrastructures over time, the emergence of online connectivity also has had the effect that *designers need not leave products over to users*. The Internet has made production of the ultimate particular a perpetually on-going process, in constant dialogue with end user practices. Today, few interactive products are stable: instead, they (at least in part) have become services that are maintained online, and where functionalities and interaction models are continuously updated. Examples are legion in the area of online games and social media as illustrated by the concept of "Perpetual Beta" [33], and include online software updates of consumer devices including phones and portable computers. In Ehn's words, project-time extends over most of use-time [13] creating an ongoing interaction between designers and users that is ripe with possibility but also with tension. With online services, the designers (or at least their companies) tend to never let go of their products: they continuously monitor and react to emerging uses, and often retain the final say in what uses will be encouraged or prohibited [48].

To summarise, the focus on artefacts as the ultimate particulars produced by RtD can be criticised from multiple perspectives: that it takes focus from the complexity of a use situation and the work humans do in creating bricolage solutions, that artefacts may not adequately represent design solutions integrating multiple resources and levels of design, and that the view of artefacts as the end product of design does not capture the potentially complex interplay between designers and users in design after design.

CONSEQUENCES OF ARTIFACT FOCUSSED DESIGN RESEARCH

As previously discussed, the pragmatic approach to design research in HCI has developed a focus on research that is particular and generative. Here, we retain that perspective, looking for ways to articulate design knowledge that are directly generative of design.

Buchanan described interaction design as fundamentally concerned with "how human beings relate to other human beings through the mediating influence of products" [15]. This is a relationship that is variable and fundamentally ephemeral, manifest in in-the-moment actions and social activities, and emerging as persistent practices only over time.

This is acknowledged also in artefact-centric approaches to RtD, in how context, use and subjective experience is foregrounded in empirical work. However, anchoring such discussions in the design of specific artefacts opens up for a form of technology determinism. In studies, the observations will typically be focussed, filtered or limited to concern the technology on trial. Very often they will primarily concern interactions with the technology in use (rather than, say, the work related to carrying, installing, or configuring the technology [47]). Secondly, trials typically focus on identifying re-occurring behaviours that reasonably can be attributed to the artefact. It is taken for granted that the only interesting effects are those that reoccur, and therefore can be argued to be semi-generic effects of introducing the artefact. Taken together, these perspectives create a view of design knowledge that is technology-deterministic, in the way it expects the technology to shape its use.

It should be emphasised that many of the prioritised design qualities in third wave HCI, including e.g. design for ambiguity [24], design for appropriation [18,29] and design for interactional empowerment [31,53], strive to circumvent technology determinism through opening up for uses that were not preconceived by the designer. In a brief meta-reflection on such design strategies, Höök [28] argues that what these design concepts do, is to propose a balance between the role of the designer and the user, leaving a carefully crafted room for meaning-making in interpretation and use. This does not mean that these approaches negate the very idea of technology determinism, but they present strategies to open up for appropriation by deliberately underspecifying use.

ACTIVITY-CENTRIC DESIGN

The key feature of activity-centric design is that it aims to influence (and sometimes control) what people *do*. But since the activities are performed by the people participating in them, this influence is indirect, through the creation of *something* (combinations of objects, spaces, instructions, interactive systems, etcetera [42]) that contribute to shaping the activity at hand. Activity-centric design considers these as secondary and mutable, meaning that they may change over time if the design-project time overlaps with use time.

Since activities are performed by the participants, they are not under full control by designers. In this sense, activity-centric design is always *second order* design: while the design goal is related to the activity, designed artefacts constitute the only possible means to achieve it.

Activity-centric design knowledge thus comes across as both more indirect and more designer-centric than artefact-centric design. A way to understand the difference is through Redström's distinction between defining use "through design" or "through use"[49]. In artefact-centric design these are alternative and complementary perspectives, where the role of participatory design is to put them in dialogue with each other in other ways than through a final, designed, artefact. The activity-centric perspective privileges the designer's intention (the definition of use through design), but sees it only as a way of *influencing* the definition of use through use. (Also, the very concept of 'use' becomes problematic in activity-centric design, as the designed activity is not necessarily directed towards a designed artefact.)

The perspective on activity-centric design as second order has been developed primarily within game design studies, and origins in how games typically allow for a wide variability in play. Salen and Zimmerman [50] express this as

"The goal of successful design is meaningful play, but play is something that emerges from the functioning of the rules. As a game designer, you can never directly design play."

This perspective guides our framing of activity-centric design. However, the game analytical take on second order design lacks one important consideration that must be taken into account in interaction design research. In game design, it is commonly understood that a design fully frames the space of possible play activities. Early game studies would sometimes consider games to be closed formal systems, but also informal methodologies such as the MDA ('Mechanics Dynamics Aesthetics') framework [32] will typically consider the play (dynamics) of a game to be a property of the *system* and as such completely specified by its rules (mechanics). Game design studies basically considers the definition of use through use to be *caused*, rather than influenced, by definition of use through design. This again gives rise to a form of artefact determinism: while game design studies will appreciate, and study the full range of possible behaviors offered in play, this space is still typically seen as completely circumscribed by the composite, designed artefact that is the game.

This simplification arises from how playing a game can be characterized by the voluntary submission to a set of rules [59]. It has been criticized for prioritizing a mode of analysis that leaves out the work done by players in collectively establishing and maintaining such rules [11]. In most interaction design research, we cannot assume that the participant activities are fully determined by any given design [4].

Delimiting the concept of activity

The proposed perspective is inspired by more holistic approaches towards understanding and designing for activity including situated and activity theory approaches [12,26,35]. In particular, we subscribe to the usefulness of the concept of (collective) activity as an intermediate level of analysis above the level of singular actions. Just as in activity theory [35], we consider an activity to be made up of multiple in-the-moment actions by individual participants – a collection of things that *people and things do*. Actions of this kind are to some extent observable allowing for a third person perspective [38], even if mere observation will not capture the reasons for, or the experiences in, doing them.

But where activity theorists defines an activity as "a form of doing directed to an object" (or objective) [36], we instead look upon activities as framed by a conscious design effort. In the following, we will talk about (designed) activity as collections of actions united by the fact that they are influenced by one and the same design solution and as such can be considered an effect of deliberate design.

The reason for this scope is the aim to approach the articulation of design knowledge. While activity theory is well suited to capture the everyday bricolage solutions that shape much human activity, it primarily presents an analytical perspective. Design research in this tradition has primarily contributed with process and method knowledge (see e.g. [17,62]). By framing activity instead through the lens of deliberate design, we maintain the RtD aim to privilege the designer perspective, and to express knowledge in relation to design aims. However, it should be noted that in activity design, one must never lose track of that design only influences and does not determine the activity. Within the scope of actions influenced by a design solution, some are actions that are not interactions with design itself. For example, the decision to *not* engage with a design is also influenced by its existence.

In the same line, we do not see activities as collections of interactions with technology. In this, we follow Buchanan [15] who argues that interaction design should not be taken as always including information technology, but instead is fundamentally concerned with action as such. Buchanan argues that the products that interaction designers design are "experiences or activities or services".

Our core motivation for moving away from interaction design as interaction with and through technology originates in observations such as Taylor's [61]. We are moving into a society where information technology is increasingly becoming part of the infrastructure of life, integrated into our every movement and activity. The use of technology is increasingly being influenced by a range of phenomena and factors that lie outside its reach. Factors that influence our everyday engagement with technology include such diverse aspects as physical space, rules and regulations, cultural habits, and physical information sources. Activity-centric design opens up for considering all of them materials available for design. This is one important way in which looking at activities as the ultimate particular of interaction design may take us one step closer towards what Buchanan discusses as environmental design [15]; the design of such complex and pervasive systems that increasingly influence our everyday life.

Activities are Unique and Emphemeral

If we are to consider activities as the ultimate particulars of interaction design, we must embrace their uniqueness and ephemerality [52]. Whereas artifacts can be copied and the copies can for all intent and purposes be identical to the original, an activity is always unique. Activities cannot be packaged and shipped. Even when activities are tightly scripted to be repeatable, the same actors under the exact same conditions cannot perform the exact same activity twice – it is different in the very least in that it is performed a second time and that the experiences from already having performed it influence how it is performed.

DESIGN KNOWLEDGE AS CONCEPT—ACTIVITIES

In this section, we look into existing design practices and previous work in HCI to develop an understanding of how activity-centric design knowledge can be articulated. In this, we are not looking for process knowledge– ways of designing – but for how intermediate level knowledge about design solutions can be articulated and communicated. We retain a pragmatic RtD perspective in that we are looking for ways to articulate design knowledge that are, in Storni's words, modest, accountable and generative [56].

While activity-centric design practices exist in a variety of fields, we have in this article chosen to highlight practices within the fields of game and performance design. The main reason for this lies in that such designs are relatively well contained – their purpose is to influence a coherent experience that takes place over a set time interval and often in a particular setting or location. The level of control that designers have over the staging of such activities present ample design opportunities and as such, they form a useful resource in understanding the design opportunities also in less constrained settings. Finally, relevant theory has been developed in these fields. It also matters to the authors that they are predominantly voluntary activities: players and audiences (and to some extent also performers) are free to engage and disengage from such activities.

In the quest for activity-centric design knowledge, Pierce's [46] characterization of design knowledge as concept-things is less appropriate. A pragmatic perspective on activity-centric design will instead need to package and communicate knowledge as *concept-activities*. This change of perspective affects both what concepts are put in focus, and how the design examples are constructed and made available. Here, we first discuss how activity-centric design is documented, to then look into activity-centric design concepts and finally how activities can be made available, as ultimate particulars.

Scripting Activity

As discussed above, activity-centric design is done indirectly, through the design of other things. In many forms of activity-centric design and in particular in performance arts that thing is a *script*: a designed artefact that instructs the participants to do certain actions, and by this serves to guide the execution of an activity so that it can be seen as an instance of it. Scripts can be considered artefacts generated by artefact-centric design: they are persistent, and their completion ends (a distinctive part of) the design process. A script will often also delimit the designer's control over the resulting activity, by leaving its execution to somebody else. Scripts are not the sole way in which activity-centric design manifests, but they are common.

Scripts are legion in art: theatre scripts and music scores are just two examples. They also feature in live performance art, such as when Loke et al [37] reflect on how "the scripting of the entire process is an important aspect, with care being given to timing, cues and transitions". Through the development of technology supported live art and pervasive games, scripts have featured in design studies within third wave HCI as well as game studies [10,34,37,54].

However, scripts do not function in the way we typically think of artefacts in artefact-centric design. Scripts are in one way or another instructions; they are not acted on or through, but serve as guidance for action. Furthermore, scripts do not "generate" activities or experiences; they always underspecify the activity and there is a level of creativity involved in interpreting a script. In many scripted art forms, there are specific roles in this process including directors, conductors, performance artists, performers, and documenters (e.g. photographers). The circumstances and variations of interpreting a script are always unique.

Scripts can also specify activity more or less precisely. For example, the classic western music score specify the activity in great detail and in a uniform manner that is understandable by the suitably trained performer while still giving room for creative interpretation [41]. By contrast, table-top role-playing is supported by loosely constructed diegetic world construction and rule systems [24], that require a facilitator in the form of a game-master who creates specific challenges, determines conflict outcome, and creates interesting narratives to control the dramatic curve. Within the Nordic larp community, recent attempts to create 'scenarios' present even more open ways to script activity [23]. Even board games, with their rules and goals and intended forms of engagement, can be interpreted as a form of scripting.

Human facilitation, as in the example of the theatre director or the game-master, opens up for approaches to scripting that leave ample room for participants to influence the activity as it develops [44]. Some scripting techniques have been developed with this in mind, such as the concept of "story beats" that was developed for the alternate reality game *Conspiracy for good* [66]. These were pre-scripted scenes that were not designed to play out at a particular point in time or space. Instead, the game-masters (who in this case also were the designers) would select a suitable occasion for triggering a beat depending on what the participants were doing. Using scripting methods such as beats can enable designs where different participants can experience very different storylines; all beats may not even play out during a singular event.

Finally, while scripting often works as a way to commodify and communicate activity-centric design, scripts are not always created for this purpose. The "careful scripting" that Loke et al discuss [48] was most likely never communicated outside the designer team. Its primary role was to synchronize the performing team and fine-tune the experience for participants. Such scripts can be under constant refinement over multiple instances, and might not ever manifest in a stable form of documentation. These forms of scripting are typical when artists or designers stay in control over the activity, and never leave their art over to performers, conductors, or participants.

To conclude, scripts function as way to develop, document and communicate activity-centric design and could be appropriated also as a way to articulate activity-centric design knowledge produced by RtD. However, the form of scripting and the intended functions and roles involved in interpreting a script, will greatly influence the type of control that designers exert over the actual activity. In light of this, investigating and developing *forms* of scripting emerges as an interesting research topic within activity-centric design research.

Activity-centric concepts in HCI

Notable examples of activity-centric design concepts have been brought forward within HCI. The examples below have been selected as they represent ways to conceptualize activity-centric design knowledge at a more abstract level: they focus on what participants do, rather than on specific aspects of the designed artefacts. The selection is intended to be illuminative rather than exhaustive, as the approaches present rather different perspectives on activity.

Affordances

The concept of affordances [33–35,56] represents one of the earliest and still most influential approaches to activity-centric design. While affordances are properties of the world they are relational; they speak of how objects can be acted upon by specific actors. Broadly speaking, the set of affordances offered for a particular actor in a particular context delimits the set of activities possible in that context. Gibson [33] emphasizes how our learned understanding of physical affordances is functional – we learn how to act on an affordance directly, not how to recognize it through passive perception.

In HCI, the concept has been used in design research as properties of interfaces. HCI distinguishes between perceived and functional affordances [31,56]. The related design ideal states that users should be able to perceive what they can do in an interface. This means that the concept has been reinterpreted as a property of interface itself, rather than a relation between interface and user.

From the activity-centric design perspective, affordance is still a first-order construct. It describes a design as actions enabled by the designed artefact. The concept of affordances may serve to anchor a second-order activity-centric design in some of the artefacts supporting it, but it is not sufficient to express all aspects of second order design. For example, it is not particularly meaningful to analyze scripts in terms of affordances.

Trajectories

The trajectories framework [9,10] presents a way to analyze and describe various paths through a designed experience, with a focus on trans-medial experiences involving multiple resources. The framework highlights in particular the transitions between different forms of engagement or interaction (e.g. moving from physical to online participation). It is particularly interesting in that it takes into account how all participants may not experience the designed trajectory, or the even same trajectory as any other participant. The participant's individual trajectory is acknowledged to be potentially unique.

Loke et al [48] articulate a similar but more abstract perspective, in their approach to scripted participatory experiences. Based in ritual theory [8], they describe the overarching path through such experiences as an initial entry, the journey through the experience, and a post-event debrief which functions to reconnect to the outer world. This perspective is much more high-level and generic, and presents less support for acknowledging or documenting the uniqueness of an individual experience.

Verbs

Trajectories are primarily temporally organized, and function less well to articulate design concepts and features where controlling the temporal sequence is not a central aspect of the design. We have already discussed a variant of scripting that is less temporally oriented, the story beats approach from Conspiracy for Good [54]. The story beats were however tightly connected to the type of experience designed (a pervasive game-mastered roleplaying experience) and are less suitable as a generic approach to expressing activity-centric design knowledge.

A framework that shows potential for a less temporally oriented approach to expressing activity-centric design knowledge has been suggested by Paulos and Pierce [45]. Their design domain is sustainable energy consumption, and the authors do not develop their approach into a generic method of expressing design knowledge. What Paulos and Pierce do is to create a vocabulary of actions, expressed as *verbs*, that reflect what people can do with micro-amounts of energy. Their precise vocabulary includes the verbs 'collect/harvest', 'store/keep', 'share/distribute' and 'activate/express'. This collection of verbs has a number of properties that makes it very different from other articulations of activity-centric design knowledge.

Firstly, these verbs could be seen as a form of affordances: they express a relation between human actors and energy in terms of how humans can act on energy, that is made visible/tangible through the design of interactive artefacts that have modes of sensing and visualizing the energy flow. The strategy of making the invisible visible or tangible has also been explored in participatory design investigations of infrastructuring [17], but Paulos and Pierce go further in how they suggest a particular set of verbs, with a clear goal of guiding activity in a particular direction.

Note that energy is present in everything that humans do and every object that humans use. It is possible to conceive using the same verbs to describe interactions that do not manifest at all in interactive technology or designed artefacts. A large stone will work to store energy independently of if this capacity is measured or recorded in any way. A person can share micro-amounts of energy with another by holding their hands to warm them. Even if these are not measured by built-in technology, they could be made accessible to a system through human facilitation.

The verb collection that Paulos and Peirce proposes is transitive – it consists of verbs that express that something is *acted upon*. This is what makes it possible to talk about them as affordances (in relation to something intangible) and why they can be designed as interactions of interactive technology. In general, a verb collection may express anything that people are supposed to do as part of an activity. Some forms of scripting, such as the training schema that a trainer uses for an aerobics class (Bend! Jump!), consist primarily of sequences of verbs.

It is also interesting to notice how Paulos and Peirce conceive their space of verbs as implementable in a range of devices, where a singular device would only implement a few. It is only taken together, merging the interactions over all of these devices, that the actions create the activity of sustainable energy management.

The collection of verbs is in itself important. It is very clear that it realizes a coherent design intent; it is at the same time constraining and liberating. While it is clearly possible to conceive other things that could be done to energy (such as the wider verb 'consume'), the authors deliberately limit their verbs to things that make practical sense in the context of very small amounts of energy. At the same time, the concept of 'sharing' energy is novel, and different from what we typically think of something we do with energy. The set of verbs shape a space of activity that is different than what we are used to do with energy today, and by that, has the potential to change our relation to energy.

In this sense, the verbs are similar to what in game design theory is called *core mechanics*, the central modes of action that a player can use to influence the game state. Zimmerman [63] argues that the structures that delimit play work at the same time to restrict and enable the play activity. Constraints work to inspire participants to activities they may not think of on their own, and engaging within given constraints can foster experiences and insights that otherwise would be inaccessible. The collection of verbs that Paulos and Peirce present share these properties.

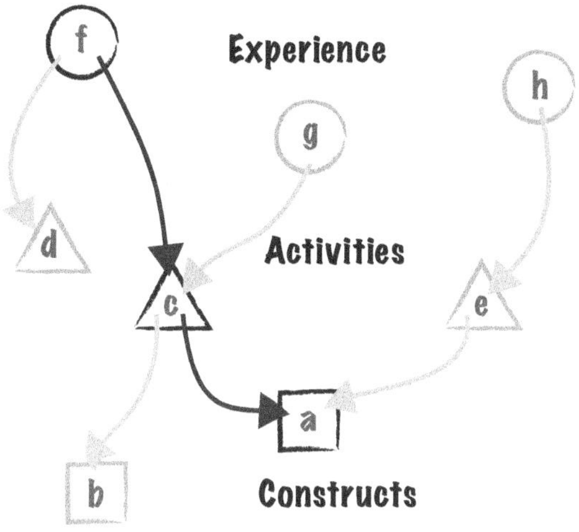

Figure 1. A FaTE representation of a designed activity. An activity (c) is supported by two different constructs (a and b) of which only a is part of the design. The sought participant experience (f), related to multiple activities (c and d), and the designed activity (c) may contribute also to an unintended experience (g). Adapted from [4], reprinted with permission.

But the verb collection by Paulos and Pierce go one step further, as the emerging activity of energy consumption is one that the singular user would never fully experience. It would be a phenomenon emerging at the level of a community of users. In this sense, Paulos and Peirce take an important step towards what Buchanan calls 'environmental design' [15], addressing design of the world we live in rather than the individual's experience of a specific product.

FaTE

One of the pitfalls with artefact-centered design concepts lies in 'design determinism' - a tendency to assume that it is the design that generate an activity. As discussed above, this has sometimes been done in game design theory.

The FaTE framework [4] was proposed in direct dialogue with the MDA framework [32] as a way to address design determinism. FaTE proposes a way to look upon participant activity as supported, but not generated or constrained by, by the design at hand. The activity is influenced by the design, but also by a large range of factors that designers have no control over and may not even be aware of (see figure 1, and notice in particular how the arrows are directed in line with the actors' intent of use).

The FaTE framework assumes that a design can be divided into small units, constructs, representing the collection of designed elements that are created to support a specific designed activity. These are appropriated by actors in their activities, and the latter contribute to their experiences[1].

[1] FaTE is based on a holistic perspective on experience. For example, the expectations that participants bring with them into the activity is considered part of the experience, in that they affect how participants chose to engage.

Back [4] argues that design knowledge is usefully articulated as relationships between adjacent layers of constructs. Design knowledge can for example articulate how participants with certain types of former experience will act, or how a particular activity can be encouraged or discouraged by a design construct.

Conceptualizing activity, a summary

The selected conceptualizations represent ways that activity-centric design knowledge has been articulated in interaction design research. All have been used to express what actors do, or can do. With the exception of affordances, they also represent collections of actions at a more abstract level, which makes it possible to talk about them as articulations of activity-centric design.

In order to represent design knowledge, this is however not quite sufficient. There must also be some kind of reason for advocating that some activity should follow this pattern, such as when Paulos and Peirce develop their particular set of verbs as a step towards more sustainable energy consumption [45]. In their work, the desirable effect (energy saving) is itself a high-level activity concept, but the effects could just as well be related to e.g. actor experiences.

Documenting Activity

If activities are the ultimate particulars of activity-centric design, they too should be made available as means of communicating design. There must be a way to *show* the activity itself, as part of the communication within the design and research communities, in a way that can carry the same weight as the artefact does in artefact-centric design.

The uniqueness of activity

The most obvious way that activities can be shown is by offering ways to engage in the activity first-hand. Just as playing a game is an essential part of play research [1], activity-centric design scholars need to be given ways to engage with other people's activity designs.

However, this is not quite enough, as relying on the subjective experience does not take into account that activities are ephemeral and unique. In the context of event design, it is not uncommon to spend considerable resources on the design of events that only happen once (see e.g. [34,54]). But even when activity-centric design is directed towards activities that can be considered repeatable (e.g. through scripting), every instance is still a unique activity, both in more or less subtle differences in how it plays out, and in what the participants experience. Furthermore, if there is a particular intended audience for a design, there is no guarantee that a participating scholar or designer behaves in any way similar to that audience, and this will affect the experience for the scholar and potentially also for other participants.

For these reasons, the articulation of activity design knowledge must rely on offering ways to participate in the activity, but also on documentation of activity design *as it plays out*. Documentation is not just a needed as part of the evaluation process, but constitutes a central way to *show* the activity to other designers and scholars.

In the actual performance of an activity, it is no longer the designer but the participants that have the final say in how the activity plays out. This means that it becomes important to embrace the *uniqueness* of activity. For example, it can be important to document how a particular group of participants manages to re-invent an activity, especially if this represents a significant co-design event with lasting effects on later activities. (There are historic chess matches have done [51].) It may be equally important to bring out large-scale but unique patterns of change, especially for large-scale persistent services. An example of the latter is when game scholars study how the meta-game changes over time in online games [19].

In embracing uniqueness, it is for the same reason also important to embrace *subjectivity*. The documentation of activities will often require that something of the participant's attitudes and experiences towards the activity are captured, as they are effectively co-designers of their own activity. Sundström et al [60] report on an interesting way of encouraging participants themselves record video of their in-situ activities. While this group used the method to document use of a designed artefact, the method is alo suitable for documenting designed activities [5], as long as these are reasonably contained in time and space.

Showing time and temporal flow

While activity design need not be focused on sequencing actions, the activity itself takes place over time. In showing an activity it thus is always important to also document the flow of time. The most obvious way to do this is through recording it, e.g. by filming from multiple perspectives and/or logging data from as many sources as possible.

This approach is however problematic. The most obvious problem is that such a data set will be unwieldy and for all practical purposes un-shareable. Where a designed artefact typically can be picked up and manipulated and interacted with immediately, navigating raw data set will often require hours and hours of investigation for it to even begin to make sense. Recordings fall short of *showing* the activity in the same immediate way as a designed artefact.

While this obstacle can potentially be overcome through adequate navigation tools, the data set will still not adequately represent time as experienced by the participants [10]. Again, we meet with issues related to representing not only an outsider perspective of 'what happened', but also the subjective perspective of what the participants felt that they were doing, what they were engaged with, and what they experienced [41]. In the personal experience, some events will be considered more significant, whereas others will be entirely disregarded as unimportant. Some events will be perceived as related to each other; through design or coincidence. The experience of time will vary, so that the same 'objective' amount can sometimes be experienced as long and sometimes as short.

Hence, more curated forms of documentation may not only be more easily digested, but also provide more insight into the activity. Carefully cut and annotated video presents one such opportunity [39,41]. An interesting alternative is to represent time using layout and narration techniques from comics [43]. This format was used by Back [3,4] in documenting street performers shows to uncover some of their design strategies and tools. The comic layout allows for complex ways to represent time and space. In particular, the space between individual images (the gutter) typically represents flow of time, but in an indeterminate and vague way that allows for representing subjective time experiences [43].

Back uses the format to present an outsider perspective of the observed activity. The presentation is based on a careful transcription of video data and subsequent interaction analysis, placing emphasis on spatial movement and non-verbal interactions. The comic book layout is based on images captured from the original video, using original quotes as speech bubbles. The gutter between images is used to illustrate central transitions in the configuration of the show and the participants. This is just one possible use of comics as a format for representing activity; the same form could be used to capture the designer's intent and salient design decisions.

Such curated forms of documentation will by necessity include a level of analysis. They will highlight specific aspects of the activity and hide others. They reflect both the activity as a designed particular, and a subjective interpretation of it. It is possible to combine multiple forms of documentation to highlight multiple perspectives on a design: one could be created by the participants to represent their subjective experience of the activity, other by journalists and critics. If curated by designers, they fulfil a very similar purpose to annotated portfolios [21].

DISCUSSION

The articulation of design knowledge at an activity level liberates interaction design research from considering interactive technology design as its ultimate outcome. Though most of the projects discussed above include some technological aspect, they draw upon a wide range of design resources and lead to the design of a wide range of systems, environments, rules and scripts. This way, the articulations of activity-centric design knowledge can serve to address domains in which multiple levels of design interact, and avoid the technology-determinism that often feature in artefact-centric design studies. Activity-centric design is also inherently open to the option to *not* designing any technology intervention [8].

Furthermore, our case examples show that the articulation of design knowledge at the activity level is well suited for capturing knowledge in domains where the design project time extends over use time. The 'story beats' approach to scripting, the trajectories framework [9,10] and the more abstract liminal path design described by Loke et al [37] have been developed as tools to capture the design of activities that are, while ongoing, orchestrated by artists.

Finally, activity-centric design presents some tools towards what Buchanan calls 'environmental design' [15]. In this article, this is represented by the work by Paulos and Peirce [45] on energy consumption, indicating that activity-centric design could be a viable way to, or at least an element of, articulating environmental design. However, as this article limits its discussion to examples of activity-centric design that are reasonably contained, none of our examples address the complex bricolage practices that Bødker emphasize in her criticism of third wave HCI.

There is however a risk involved with activity-centric design, related to the role of the designer. In striving for predictability and repeatability, designers and theorists alike may gravitate towards modes of articulation that exert high levels of control.

That this does happen (and also that it sometimes is a perfectly viable approach) can be seen in many forms of scripting in performative art practices, such as in music scores. Most formats for scripting exert much more detailed control over the designed activity than what is done by notable examples from third wave HCI (such as ludic or inquisitive design [16,22,25]). Compared to music scores, the trajectories framework is more open for variation, but it is still based on the assumption that there is *some* kind of designed trajectory through the experience. From this perspective, the concepts of story beats from Conspiracy for Good [54] and the verbs from Citizen energy [45] represent design articulations that are more open for participants to shape their own activity. To some extent, activity-centric design *must* impose constraints on activity in order to design anything at all. Consider how Suits as well as Zimmerman [59,63] talk about the constraints of a game as simultaneously "liberating and constraining" the activity.

In light of this, the authors would like to emphasize the importance of participatory design. Ehn [13] has discussed strategies for bringing participatory design principles forth into the domain of infrastructuring and most of these can be adopted in activity design. The goal should be to maintain a dialogue between the designer and audience communities, where the latter are seen as legitimate participants in the design community and vice versa.

The authors wish to again emphasize the importance of designing, documenting and analyzing activities as *unique*. If a design that is done to be repeatable plays out very differently in every instance, this is not necessarily a sign of bad design. Instead, it may be a sign of a design that is open for appropriation and adaptation by the participants. We consider it an important challenge for RtD in third wave HCI, to find articulations of activity-centric design knowledge that present rich opportunities for co-design and appropriation.

CONCLUSION

This article argues that it is possible to consider activities as the ultimate particulars produced by interaction design. While the proposal to consider activities as ultimate particulars is inspired by previous activity-centric approaches to HCI, it is different in that it specifically targets the articulation of design knowledge within the designer community of practice. This motivates our perspective on activity as circumscribed by a specific design intervention.

Grounded in an analysis of multiple examples of activity-centric design knowledge, we argue that this is a viable approach. It opens up ways to discuss design practices and objectives that do not manifest in products, but in singular events as well as in more persistent activities or recurring practices. Articulating design knowledge at the activity level opens up opportunities for addressing domains where design uses a multitude of resources, and where design and use are aligned and intermixed in a joint creative process.

Much remains to be done. Research challenges arise from understanding forms of scripting, and how these relate to other design resources as well as to the designed activity. We have further highlighted the importance of finding ways to document and analyze activities as ephemeral and unique, and to develop forms of representation that are accepted within the designer and scholarly community as reflective of the phenomenon at hand. We have emphasized the need to find articulations of activity-centric design knowledge that present rich opportunities for co-design and appropriation.

Finally, we wish to bring attention to how we have scoped the concept of activity as circumscribed by design. As with all design-related knowledge, this scope is limited and may not always be well-defined. Many of our examples are taken from the domains of play and experience design; domains that have the advantage of being reasonably contained. When we move towards infrastructuring and environmental design, it becomes much more difficult to draw this line. The challenge in addressing such domains arise from delimiting activity in a way still allows for the articulation of generative design knowledge.

ACKNOWLEDGMENTS

The authors are in debt to Mareike Glöss and the anonymous reviewers for insightful comments and reading recommendations.

REFERENCES

1. Espen Aarseth. 2003. Playing Research: Methodological approaches to game analysis. In *Proceedings of the digital arts and culture conference*, 28–29.

2. Timo Arnall. 2014. Exploring "Immaterials": Mediating design's invisible materials. *International Journal of Design* 8, 2: 101–117.
3. Jon Back. 2015. The Embarrassing act of becoming a street performance audience. In *CHI"15 Embarrassing Interactions Workshop, CHI"15.*
4. Jon Back. 2016. Designing Public Play: Playful engagement, constructed activity, and player experience. Ph.D. thesis, Uppsala University, Uppsala.
5. J. Back and A. Waern. 2013. We are two strong women: Designing Empowerment in a Pervasive Game. *Proceedings of DiGRA* 2013.
6. Liam Bannon. 1991. From human factors to human actors: The role of psychology and human-computer interaction studies in system design. *Design at work: Cooperative design of computer systems* 25: 44.
7. Jeffrey Bardzell, Shaowen Bardzell, and Lone Koefoed Hansen. 2015. Immodest Proposals: Research Through Design and Knowledge. In *Proceedings of the 33rd Annual ACM Conference on Human Factors in Computing Systems*, 2093–2102.
8. Eric PS Baumer and M. Silberman. 2011. When the implication is not to design (technology). In *Proceedings of the SIGCHI Conference on Human Factors in Computing Systems*, 2271–2274.
9. Steve Benford and Gabriella Giannachi. 2008. Temporal trajectories in shared interactive narratives. In *Proceedings of the SIGCHI Conference on Human Factors in Computing Systems*, 73–82.
10. Steve Benford, Gabriella Giannachi, Boriana Koleva, and Tom Rodden. 2009. From Interaction to Trajectories: designing coherent journeys through user experiences. 709–718.
11. Karl Bergström. 2010. The implicit rules of board games: On the particulars of the lusory agreement. In *Proceedings of the 14th International Academic MindTrek Conference: Envisioning Future Media Environments*, 86–93.
12. Olav W. Bertelsen and Susanne Bødker. 2003. Activity theory. *HCI models, theories, and frameworks: Toward a multidisciplinary science*: 291–324.
13. Erling Bjögvinsson, Pelle Ehn, and Per-Anders Hillgren. 2012. Design Things and Design Thinking: Contemporary participatory design challenges. *Design Issues* 28, 3: 101–116.
14. Susanne Bødker. 2006. When second wave HCI meets third wave challenges. In *Proceedings of the 4th Nordic conference on Human-computer interaction: changing roles*, 1–8.
15. Richard Buchanan. 2001. Design research and the new learning. *Design issues* 17, 4: 3–23.
16. Peter Dalsgaard and Christian Dindler. 2014. Between theory and practice: bridging concepts in HCI research. In *Proceedings of the 32nd annual ACM conference on human factors in computing systems*, 1635–1644.
17. Lorenzo Davoli and Johan Redström. 2014. Materializing infrastructures for participatory hacking. In *Proceedings of the 2014 conference on Designing interactive systems*, 121–130.
18. Alan Dix. 2007. Designing for appropriation. In *Proceedings of the 21st British HCI Group Annual Conference on People and Computers: HCI... but not as we know it-Volume 2*, 27–30.
19. Scott Donaldson. 2016. Towards a typology of metagames. In *Proceedings of the Australasian Computer Science Week Multiconference*, 73.
20. Pelle Ehn. 1993. Scandinavian design: On participation and skill. *Participatory design: Principles and practices*: 41–77.
21. Bill Gaver and John Bowers. 2012. Annotated portfolios. *interactions* 19, 4: 40–49.
22. William Gaver. 2009. Designing for homo ludens, still. In *(Re)Searching The Digital Bauhaus*. Springer, 163–178. Retrieved January 4, 2017 from http://link.springer.com/chapter/10.1007%2F978-1-84800-350-7_9
23. William Gaver. 2012. What should we expect from research through design? In *Proceedings of the SIGCHI conference on human factors in computing systems*, 937–946.
24. William Gaver, Jacob Beaver, and Steve Benford. 2003. Ambiguity as a resource for design. In *Proceedings of the SIGCHI conference on Human factors in computing systems*, 233–240.
25. William Gaver, John Bowers, Andrew Boucher, Hans Gellerson, Sarah Pennington, Albrecht Schmidt, Anthony Steed, Nicholas Villars, and Brendan Walker. 2004. The drift table: designing for ludic engagement. In *CHI'04 extended abstracts on Human factors in computing systems*, 885–900.
26. Geraldine Gay and Helene Hembrooke. 2004. *Activity-Centered Design: An ecological approach to designing smart tools and usable systems*. MIT Press.
27. Steve Harrison, Deborah Tatar, and Phoebe Sengers. 2007. The three paradigms of HCI. In *Alt. Chi. Session at the SIGCHI Conference on Human Factors in Computing Systems San Jose, California, USA*, 1–18.
28. Kristina Höök. 2004. Active co-construction of meaningful experiences: but what is the designer's role?

In *Proceedings of the third Nordic conference on Human-computer interaction*, 1–2.

29. Kristina Höök. 2006. Designing familiar open surfaces. In *Proceedings of the 4th Nordic conference on Human-computer interaction: changing roles*, 242–251.

30. Kristina Höök and Jonas Löwgren. 2012. Strong concepts: Intermediate-level knowledge in interaction design research. *ACM Transactions on Computer-Human Interaction (TOCHI)* 19, 3: 23.

31. Kristina Höök, Anna Ståhl, Petra Sundström, and Jarmo Laaksolaahti. 2008. Interactional empowerment. In *Proceedings of the SIGCHI Conference on Human Factors in Computing Systems*, 647–656.

32. Robin Hunicke, Marc LeBlanc, and Robert Zubek. 2004. MDA: A formal approach to game design and game research. In *Proceedings of the AAAI Workshop on Challenges in Game AI.*

33. Melinda Jacobs and Tanja Sihvonen. 2011. In Perpetual Beta? On the participatory design of Facebook games. In *Think Design Play: The Fifth International Conference of the Digital Research Association (DIGRA).*

34. Staffan Jonsson, Annika Waern, Markus Montola, and Jaakko Stenros. 2007. Game mastering a pervasive larp. Experiences from momentum. In *PerGames 2007: Proceedings of the 4th International Symposium on Pervasive Gaming Applications.*

35. Victor Kaptelinin and Bonnie Nardi. 2012. Activity theory in HCI: Fundamentals and Reflections. *Synthesis Lectures Human-Centered Informatics* 5, 1: 1–105.

36. Kari Kuutti. 1996. Activity theory as a potential framework for human-computer interaction research. *Context and consciousness: Activity theory and human-computer interaction*: 17–44.

37. Lian Loke and George Poonkhin Khut. 2014. Intimate aesthetics and facilitated interaction. In *Interactive Experience in the Digital Age*. Springer, 91–108.

38. Lian Loke and Toni Robertson. 2013. Moving and making strange: An embodied approach to movement-based interaction design. *ACM Transactions on Computer-Human Interaction (TOCHI)* 20, 1: 7.

39. Jonas Löwgren. 2011. The need for video in scientific communication. *ACM Interactions* 18, 1: 22.

40. Jonas Löwgren. 2013. Annotated portfolios and other forms of intermediate-level knowledge. *ACM Interactions* 20, 1: 30–34.

41. Elena Márquez Segura and Laia Turmo. Submitted manuscript. Sketching the ephemeral.

42. Elena Márquez Segura, Annika Waern, Jin Moen, and Carolina Johansson. 2013. The design space of body games: technological, physical, and social design. In *Proceedings of the SIGCHI conference on Human Factors in computing systems*, 3365–3374.

43. Scott McCloud. 1993. Understanding comics: The invisible art. *Northampton, Mass.*

44. Bonnie A. Nardi. 1996. *Context and consciousness: activity theory and human-computer interaction*. MIT Press.

45. Eric Paulos and James Pierce. 2011. Citizen Energy: Towards Populist Interactive Micro-Energy Production. In *System Sciences (HICSS), 2011 44th Hawaii International Conference on*, 1–10.

46. James Pierce. 2014. On the presentation and production of design research artifacts in HCI. In *Proceedings of the 2014 conference on Designing interactive systems*, 735–744.

47. James Pierce and Eric Paulos. 2015. Making Multiple Uses of the Obscura 1C Digital Camera: Reflecting on the Design, Production, Packaging and Distribution of a Counterfunctional Device. In *Proceedings of the 33rd Annual ACM Conference on Human Factors in Computing Systems*, 2103–2112.

48. Patrick Prax. 2012. Co-creative interface development in MMORPGs–the case of World of Warcraft add-ons. *Journal of Gaming & Virtual Worlds* 4, 1: 3–24.

49. Johan Redström. 2008. RE: Definitions of use. *Design studies* 29, 4: 410–423.

50. Katie Salen and Eric Zimmerman. 2004. *Rules of play: Game design fundamentals*. MIT press.

51. David Shenk. 2011. *The immortal game*. Souvenir Press.

52. Herbert A. Simon. 1996. *The sciences of the artificial.* MIT press.

53. Anna Ståhl, Jonas Löwgren, and Kristina Höök. 2014. Evocative balance: Designing for interactional empowerment.

54. Jaakko Stenros, Jussi Holopainen, Annika Waern, Markus Montola, and Elina Ollila. 2011. Narrative friction in alternate reality games: Design insights from conspiracy for good. In *Proceedings of DiGRA 2011 Conference: Think Design Play, Utrecht, The Netherlands. DiGRA.*

55. Erik Stolterman. 2008. The nature of design practice and implications for interaction design research. *International Journal of Design* 2, 1: 55–65.

56. Cristiano Storni. 2015. A personal perspective on research through design. *interactions* 22, 4: 74–76.

57. Lucy Suchman. 2007. *Human-machine reconfigurations: Plans and situated actions*. Cambridge University Press.

58. Lucy A. Suchman. 1987. *Plans and situated actions: The problem of human-machine communication*. Cambridge university press.

59. Bernard Suits. 1978. *Grasshopper: Games, Life and Utopia*. Toronto, ON: University of Toronto Press.

60. Petra Sundström, Anna Ståhl, and Kristina Höök. 2007. In situ informants exploring an emotional mobile messaging system in their everyday practice. *International Journal of Human-Computer Studies* 65, 4: 388–403.

61. Alex Taylor. 2015. After interaction. *ACM Interactions* 22, 5: 48–53.

62. Anna Vallgårda and Ylva Fernaeus. 2015. Interaction Design as a Bricolage Practice. In *Proceedings of the Ninth International Conference on Tangible, Embedded, and Embodied Interaction*, 173–180.

63. Eric Zimmerman. 2004. *Narrative, interactivity, play, and games: Four naughty concepts in need of discipline*. MIT Press, Cambridge, MA.

64. John Zimmerman, Jodi Forlizzi, and Shelley Evenson. 2007. Research through design as a method for interaction design research in HCI. In *Proceedings of the SIGCHI conference on Human factors in computing systems*, 493–502.

Intuition in Design: Reflections on the Iterative Aesthetics of Form

Haakon Faste
Interaction Design Program
California College of the Arts
1111 Eighth Street
San Francisco, CA 94107

ABSTRACT
Curious to reflect on the factors contributing to the internal decision-making processes of intuitive design, a reflective study was established to systematically examine and document the practice of intuition while performing an iterative aesthetic task. Autoethnographic techniques were used to document the reflective practices that occurred over numerous iterations spanning several weeks of activity. Our analysis concludes with a summary of reflections on how intuition informs judgment in design cognition. We examine four dimensions of intuition in design—efficiency, inspiration, curiosity, and insight—and the reflective and sensory inputs that drive intuitive speculation and impulse.

Author Keywords
Design; Intuition; Iteration; Self-Reflection; Decision-Making

ACM Classification Keywords
H5.m. Information interfaces and presentation (e.g., HCI): Miscellaneous.

INTRODUCTION
Design activity requires constant decision-making and seldom follows a predetermined plan. As the use of Human-Computer Interaction (HCI) technologies becomes increasingly widespread, systemic, and highly contextualized, the designers of interactive systems must increasingly be able to fluently and flexibly react to the shifting terrain of complex, ambiguous, and even unknown demands on their work. This requires that they have a keenly developed sense of their internal, intuitive skills [10, 22]. Indeed, perhaps one of the most important characteristics of expert designers is their ability to approach challenging and ambiguous projects with optimism and confidence, adapting to changing constraints with the ability to make real-time aesthetic (i.e. feeling-based) judgments.

Numerous authors have emphasized the importance of intuition in the processes of design, including perspectives drawn from industrial design [45], engineering [12], mathematics [4], etc. In a systematic analysis of interviews with Nobel laureates in physics, chemistry, and medicine, for example, Marton et al. describe scientific intuition as "characterized as having a certitude based on a feeling or a perception of almost aesthetic or quasi-sensory nature… [it] seems to develop through extended and varied experiences of the object of research and is apparently based on an initially vague, global, not fully conscious, anticipatory perception of the solution searched for" [24]. In generative design activities where envisioning possible alternative futures is the goal of the research process, intuition plays an essential role as it allows "a simultaneous grasp of the whole, well in advances of knowing its parts in detail" [ibid], and elucidates possible future states in the mind of the envisioning designer to guide the "right" action. Suri observes that the ultimate intent of all design research is "to expose patterns underlying the rich reality of people's behaviors and experiences, to explore reactions to probes and prototypes, and to shed light on the unknown through iterative hypothesis and experiment." [42] Indeed, the intuitive nature of design activity involves constant reflection on the process of making throughout the design research activity [18, 46]. In this regard intuitive design is a process of intentional self-leadership that both inspires imagination and informs how individuals interact in the world [40].

This paper describes the results of an investigation specifically performed to reflect on the intuitive nature of decision-making when developing design concepts. We were curious to investigate what happens in the designer's mind as he or she internally reflects on the actions performed while designing, especially when unconstrained by external requirements. Not only does a designer's sense of intuition have a tremendous influence on project outcomes, one of the explicit goals of most interaction design projects is also to design intuitive experiences for those who use them. A deeper understanding of intuition is therefore central to the improvement of HCI design practice in two ways: it is among the primary mechanisms designers use to evaluate their decisions, and it informs their ability to relate with their eventual users. For the purposes of this study we begin with an examination of the literature on intuition in HCI and design, followed by a description and insights from a qualitative investigation of intuitive aesthetic judgment in an iterative design project.

INTUITION IN DESIGN PRACTICE
Intuition is a reflexive and innate kind of knowing, a form of inner guidance responsive to insights arising from the synthesis of inward and outward focus [13]. Intuitive thought emerges through a subconscious "scanning" of the

Permission to make digital or hard copies of all or part of this work for personal or classroom use is granted without fee provided that copies are not made or distributed for profit or commercial advantage and that copies bear this notice and the full citation on the first page. Copyrights for components of this work owned by others than ACM must be honored. Abstracting with credit is permitted. To copy otherwise, or republish, to post on servers or to redistribute to lists, requires prior specific permission and/or a fee. Request permissions from Permissions@acm.org.
CHI 2017, May 06 - 11, 2017, Denver, CO, USA
Copyright is held by the owner/author. Publication rights licensed to ACM.
ACM 978-1-4503-4655-9/17/05…$15.00
DOI: http://dx.doi.org/10.1145/3025453.3025534

senses: externally through our embodied perceptions, and internally as a kind of pre-cognitive experience beyond rational or verbal awareness. Yet while intuition may be defined in this way as subconscious and "unaware" experience, it can also be understood as a conscious and reflective act of assessing the results of an action performed. In this second sense, intuition is understood as a rational and highly cognitive activity. For the purposes of this paper our concept of intuition shall be kept somewhat flexible to include both the constructive and evaluative processes of subconscious intuition as well as its reflective nuances as a conscious act.

Philosophers have dealt directly with intuition for centuries (e.g. Spinoza's *Ethics* [42], Kant's *The Critique of Pure Reason* [21]), but the pre-cognitive aspect of intuition has made it difficult to empirically study. This is in part because cognitive scientists have struggled with a lack of vocabulary to describe intuitive experiences [34], combined with a marked decline in contemplative approaches considering introspection as a valid method of investigation [41]. As a result, the majority of empirical research on intuitive knowing has been relegated to qualitative techniques including in-depth interviews [23], journal content analysis [27], and reflections on intuitive processes through self-exploration [13]. While some researchers have pursued hybrid approaches combining all of the above [34], others have proposed integrated models of analytical and intuitive decision-making where both approaches are used in a complementary and iterative fashion [41, 43]. In the spirit of advancing these discussions in the context of contemporary interaction design practice, our investigation centers explicitly on the role of intuition over time as an iterative practice combining spontaneous judgment and the more deliberate evolution of goals.

While little work has been done tying intuitive practices to the design of interactive systems in particular, the traits of intuition in creative practice are well studied. Most researchers agree that intuitive events originate beyond consciousness, process information holistically, and involve perceptions that are frequently accompanied by emotion (e.g. feeling uplifted, or anxious). People who score high on intuition in psychological tests also tend to score high on creativity and divergent thinking [44], critical attributes for design practice and creativity training [36, 39]. Dane and Pratt identify three kinds of intuition that may explain its importance to human evolution: problem solving intuition, moral intuition, and creative intuition [9]. We feel that a finely tuned sense of intuition underlies the best design practices in each case, in part because designers both learn and innately experience what others have not yet experienced through the act of creating and sensing the results of a given design. In doing so they hone the conscious ability to engage in intuitive insight, affective cognition, and the openness to extra-rational modes of thinking and bodily awareness that are necessary for aesthetic judgment and the perception of quality [12, 34]. Intuition is also central to creative motivation, since, as Thomson writes, the creative individual's "psychoneurobiological capacity to flexibly and dynamically shift states enables heightened intuitive processing that directly informs the inspiration process." [44] In this regard intuition provides a certain kind of dynamic charge to all creative activity—what Maritain refers to as "intuitive pulsion"—that is both intellectual and emotional, evokes nearly unconscious and imperceptible images driving pre-conscious associations, and channels impulses from the sensed environment into speculative, creative action [24].

The power of intuition is magnified in practice through constant cycles of expression and testing that validate or contradict our intuitive knowing and facilitate learning [26]. Schön has identified two primary ways in which designers reflect on these intentional processes of making: reflection *in action* (insight gained through the action of performing design activity), and reflection *on action* (insight gained by stepping away and assessing the results of that activity) [34]. By combining these two approaches, designers draw on their internal, intuitive, best guess judgments about how and what course of action to pursue. In this regard sketching is both a mechanism for *seeing* and *imagining* previously unrealized solutions [26]. Learning to become aware of and trust in these inner motivations is central to the reflective mindset necessary in the performance of a task that best accomplishes the designer's goals [28]. In other words, a designer's aptitudes are shaped by their reflective and iterative application of intuitive methods.

To know that they are making the right decisions, designers must be confident trusting their intuitive knowledge and have fluency when performing the necessary subjective judgments enabling creative discovery and evaluation [29]. Among the primary ways that designers accomplish this is by creating tentative "sketches" of possible designs to evaluate their potential as useful and usable eventual outcomes. Buxton [6] identifies two primary aims of sketching behavior in design: generating as many different ideas as possible to make sure that the designer is "making the right thing," and iterative cycles of prototyping development to increase the fidelity of a design such that the designer can be sure that they are "making it right." Both types of behavior can be considered cognitive mechanisms used by the designers to insure that a landscape of possibilities has been explored and the "best" option(s) pursued. Through iterative processes of expressing and developing numerous such designs, possible solutions can be experienced first-hand by the designer and key stakeholders, and the most important perceived features (and failures) of the design can be identified and addressed.

The intuitive act relies on more than simply generating numerous alternatives, it necessarily requires choosing between them. Internal judgments are made by the designer performing the task as to which of the alternatives is preferable based on a variety of criteria, both internal and sensed. Honed over time, the ability to make these sorts of qualitative decisions can be considered the designer's systemic ("intuitive") method, through which insight and technical mastery are developed [29, 8]. In support of these aims, common design approaches often entail strategies for participant-involvement in the evaluation of artifacts—through "talk aloud" sessions or more carefully structured user-experience prototype testing, and so on [20, 1]. In time, such practices lead to a highly trained sense of generative intuition regarding the aesthetics of form, as well as a heightened and critical attunement to empathy—the synthetic intuition of others' feelings [18, 32].

To summarize, intuition is a critical aspect of design expertise. While intuition in design is generally described as an innate and automatic skill, we believe it is more appropriately framed as an ability that may be learned through experiential practice. This is true in both generative and evaluative aspects of the design process. The framework presented in Figure 1 highlights the role intuition plays as an internal aid in both divergent and convergent design activities.

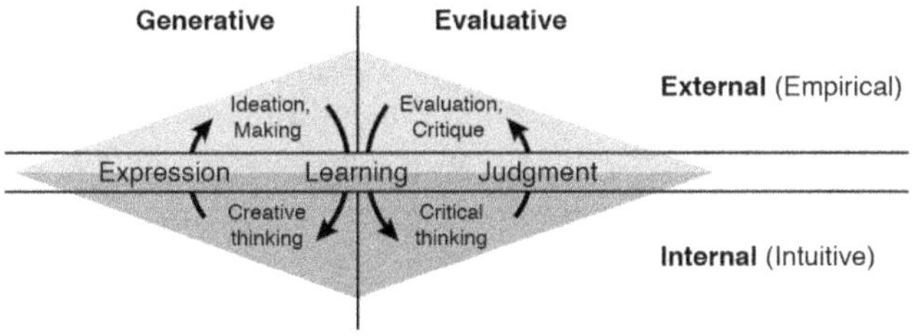

Figure 1. Experienced designers leverage intuition to guide both expressive and judgmental acts. Over time, intuition is learned.

Finally, it should also be noted that a highly attuned sense of intuition in design does not necessarily lead to intuitive design outcomes. Intuitive judgment is tightly bound to the designer's intent, and intentionality is highly subjective and dependent on context [40]. When employing speculative design methods [13, 9], for example, the designers' intent often derives from an unconventional kind of personal and cultural intuition: the heightened perception of anticipated aesthetic discomfort necessary to anticipate the provocation of reactions from people in situations of interest. In such cases the design may be intentionally (or unintentionally) counter-intuitive, and reactions may vary regardless of the designer's intent. Stated differently, not only are the internal motivations guiding a designer's work an essential element of the psychology of design [7], the intentional nature of intuition makes it difficult if not impossible to empirically measure. We therefore resort to reflective methods for the purposes of our study, the details of which are described in the following section.

METHODOLOGY AND OBSERVATIONS

Although the direct study of intuition presents unique challenges, HCI researchers routinely employ a host of social science methodologies that are appropriate for the task. As mentioned previously, popular methods include observational ethnographic approaches such as experience sampling, participant interviews and think aloud protocols. Rode [36] has observed that ethnography is essentially a *reflexive* science in that it satisfies four criteria defined by Burawoy [4]: it intervenes in the world to gather data; it seeks to understand and contextualize what the data means by reflecting on how it was gathered; it finds structural patterns in what was observed; and, in doing so, it extends theory. The HCI community has embraced ethnographic methods because it allows researchers to understand the behaviors and feelings of users in an objective an empirical way, and develop them into insights that enable the evaluation and construction of knowledge. Yet the community has also tended to prefer "realist ethnography"—a strain of ethnography which prioritizes just some of these aspects as a means of defamiliarisation by allowing researchers to obtain critical distance from their own culture—over confessional and impressionistic ethnographic approaches that allow readers to more fully understand the process of data gathering and the ethnographer's place within it [36]. Patton describes these more introspective approaches broadly as *autoethnography*: the qualitative means for "studying one's own culture and oneself as part of that culture" [33].

We employed an autoethnographic approach for this study for three main reasons. First, while it limits our observations to individual and subjective experience, we feel that such methods are necessary for the study of intuition in particular given its internal, reflective nature. As a research method autoethnography provides great value because it allows for deeply personal and internally consistent narratives to be captured and learned from. While this can also be true of other qualitative methods, none of them so directly address the *performative* aspects of intuitive design. Binder et al. note that design action is performative in that involves expressive and experiential processes of awareness; they write "Ways of gaining knowledge that some might refer to as techniques need to be invented anew every time: they do not exist as entities independent from the individuals and groups of people who perform them." [2]. Kuutti et al. have emphasized that there is a difference between what can be known by an external observer and one involved in an activity, for example, and that acting in concrete situations is a valid form of producing new knowledge [22].

Second, building on the previous point, we believe that quality design practice is essential for quality design outcomes, and intuition is a well-established mechanism for successful design practice and scientific discovery. Dourish emphasizes that tacit design knowledge applies generally to situations in which we understand "what to do" without being able to express "how to do it." [10] Zimmerman et al. observe that design research is essentially practice-based action as it is realized through the practice of doing design [47]. Given this, it seems reasonable that research on intuition can and should directly incorporate intuitive methods. Our aim was to structure the performance of an iterative design task in such a way as to capture and document the internal and intuitive decision-making processes confronted by the designer in practice. We believe it is essential for designers to practice and learn directly from in their work, and HCI researchers are no exception.

Third, not only are there intrinsic benefits to demonstrating new reflexive/autoethnographic practices within the HCI community, it is also important to extend relevant knowledge *through* practice. We believe the quality of the methods we use has the potential to influence the results we achieve (i.e., "the medium is the message). Intuitive design methods are likely to be increasingly important in HCI with the rise of ubiquitous AI systems capable of making their own intuitive decisions.

Study Overview

Our study took place in the Human-Computer Interaction Institute in the School of Computer Science at Carnegie Mellon University, where the author was a member of the design research faculty. The author has a PhD in virtual experience design, and over 15 years of experience as a professional design consultant in industry. The ultimate goal of the study was to identify and define a cultural "vocabulary of design intuitions" that can be used to enhance a practitioner's awareness of their reflective process [13].

For our purposes we limited our study to the iterative design of a physical form. Our intent was to examine intuition in the context of a focused and personal act of design, as opposed to a broader set of users, systems, or application domains. With this goal, the author performed a series of iterative three-dimensional prototype construction projects and carefully documented their creation. Personal journal entries were used to catalogue the various internal hypotheses, desires, blocks, new ideas, and so forth that occurred during the process of creating the prototypes. The project concluded by writing up these notes clearly in narrative form and then coding and synthesizing the results into an insights framework using an iterative grounded theory approach [7]. The self-report writeup was printed and analyzed in numerous passes involving different colored highlighter pens. On the first pass an open coding scheme was assigned to each different color of highlighter. This identified high-level codes based on the phrasing of the narrative and nature of the intuitive act described. Photographs were also taken of the evolving design at each stage. Given the highly personal nature of this project I will use the first person tense when describing these activities in detail for the remainder of the paper. Likewise, given the intuitive nature of the methods involved I will describe the study's methodology entirely in the context of the intuitive process of applying the method.

Given that my primary focus of research interest was the intuitive process, the investigation was explicitly designed to be simple and spontaneous with few external constraints beyond basic tools (a laser cutter), materials (cardboard), and my own prior knowledge and experiences as a designer. While the focus of the design activity was not on an interactive (i.e. digital) product, my feeling was that whether conscious or not—introspective discourse is central to design intuition and this intuitive process is inherently interactive. Significant design research has studied human-human interaction and human-computer interaction. Less work has focused explicitly on human-self interaction.

Framing the Prototype Exercise and Getting Started

I began the project with the knowledge that designers actively build things as a way of thinking (i.e., think to build and build to think [2]), and so chose a research domain that involved the physical prototyping of a three-dimensional object. My department had a prototyping laboratory equipped with a laser-cutter that I was eager to use, since I had never experimented with one at length. The decision was made to use the laser-cutter exclusively as my prototyping tool. Regarding the nature of the project to be built, my plan was specifically to not have a plan. Rather, the intention was for the nature of the project to emerge in an intuitive way through the act of designing. Consequently, the observations reported here not only focus on the intuitive functional and aesthetic decisions made in the iterative prototype construction process, but also involve the learning and exploration introduced by the constraint of being required to use an unfamiliar tool as my primary means of expression. The project continued until I felt it had satisfied the intuitive aesthetic goals of being elegant, rigorous, and "feeling done." This took eight iterations.

Iteration 1: The Tower

My first prototype had no clearly defined vision in mind other than to use the laser cutter to construct some kind of three-dimensional model. Near the laser cutter were lots of boxes, so I decided to use cardboard as a material given its high availability, low cost, and structural qualities. The available boxes were white on the exterior and brown on the interior, and needed to be cut down with an X-Acto knife to fit in the bed of the laser cutter. This required unexpected measuring and material preparation. Also, the power settings on the laser required adjustment, in a software print dialogue box, so that the material would be cut all of the way through without catching fire. Having never used the machine before, this involved some experimentation on scrap material.

The decision was made to cut numerous triangles from a single sheet of cardboard, with a notch removed from each of the corners. My intuition was that these notches, cut to precisely the same thickness as the cardboard material, would allow two triangles to slide together forming a simple joint at 90-degrees that would be both structurally interesting and lead to unexpected geometric possibilities when assembled. This also allowed me to cut a full sheet of identical triangles from a sheet of cardboard, efficiently preventing material waste.

Despite my prior planning and testing, two unexpected errors occurred on my first attempt to cut a full sheet of material. First, despite my prior testing the laser didn't quite cut all the way through the cardboard on the majority of the sheet. I took note of the power setting so that I could increase it on the next pass. Second, the laser began cutting two inches lower than I had anticipated, running off the bottom of the cutting bed and over the same lower edge of cardboard several times with the laser and starting a small fire. Regardless, a substantial number of the triangles I desired were produced and could be used for assembly.

Figure 2. The first laser-cut cardboard construction.

The form I ended up constructing is shown in figure 2. To arrive at this form, I simply began connecting triangles together and soon realized that eventually the geometry of the space could be made to produce spherically-connected "structural units" that could then be assembled to create much larger structures. Careful attention was paid to the "internal" or "external" positioning of the white face of the cardboard, with the intent of creating a "symmetrical" three-dimensional pattern. This in turn influenced my positioning of future pieces during the assembly process. At one point I also ran out of triangles and had to cut more, which I used to create "feet" for the tower to stand on. Given my unhappiness with the seemingly "unfinished" corner-notches that stuck out at the periphery, I also designed and cut some small circular pieces (with notches) to "plug" these gaps, as shown in the picture.

Iteration 2: Rigid Internal Support for Exterior Sphere

I was pleased with my first iteration, and immediately knew what I wanted to do next. During the process of assembling the first model, I had become particularly intrigued with how the central structural units of the tower formed a robust spherical geometry. Deconstructing the tower to just one of these single spherical units, it occurred to me, as I held it, that this structure could be used to provide the internal rigidity necessary for the construction of a truly spherical architecture of some kind. My plan was to use the pre-existing triangle pieces as a starting point and extend them spherically outwards with the aim of forming something round.

Figure 3. The second iteration: a spherical structure with rigid internal support. Note the 4-way junctions that join the curves.

For the next iteration I therefore did some measurements of the geometry at play and sketched up the additional parts, in Adobe Illustrator (the software driving the laser cutter), for an additional assembly consisting of 3 great circles intersecting at 90 degrees. Since the internal structure was already assembled, cutting these additional pieces was reasonably quick. The assembled result, shown in Figure 3, proved to be extremely robust, but not nearly as spherical as I had originally imagined. Indeed, as I held it in my hand it felt extremely rectilinear: in the absence of a well-defined "outer shell" structure it felt more like a cube than a sphere.

Iteration 3: A Spherical Shell

The second iteration raised numerous new considerations. My intended desire to create a spherical form, and its subsequent lack of roundness, had made me curious to explore a new strategy of construction. In the first two iterations, my main consideration had been efficiently using pre-existing material (in the first case) and a pre-existing structure (in the second). While aesthetic considerations had been present when making key decisions, the practical desire had been one of speed and convenience.

Now holding the second iteration in my hand I became aware that it would be possible to construct a spherical shell requiring no internal support. This structure could be built out of intersecting great circles using tabs at each node to hold the sphere together. Doing so would require abandoning the majority of my existing geometry, apart from the three primary great circles that intersect at right angles, and the introduction of secondary curved "trusses" to fill in the gaps of the spherical shell.

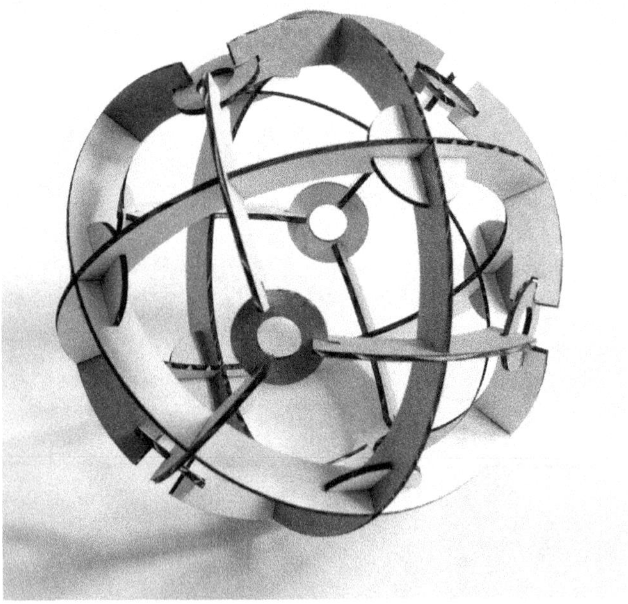

Figure 4. The first spherical shell, with ring-nodes to fix a mistake.

The challenge now became one of envisioning the eventual three-dimensional form in a program that was cutting out flat two-dimensional pieces. Given the geometry of the primary curves, I decided to cut a notch halfway between the nodes along the arc of each primary truss, and T a secondary truss into the structure at this point. My first attempt cutting new pieces was a geometric failure, however: I over and under shot the connection points given the strangeness of spherical geometry. To address this problem, I ended up cutting special "ring"-shaped pieces for these nodes to fill the gaps in the sphere precisely where the secondary trusses didn't quite meet. The result (Figure 4) is aesthetically quite nice, in large part because there are two sets of differing nodes: 4-way primaries, and 3-way secondaries filled with a ring. Careful attention had to be paid to keep the white and brown sides of the cardboard aligned such that the great arcs continued consistently depending on their rotation around the sphere.

Despite my setbacks I was quite pleased with the spherical shell. It is an interesting shape to ponder, to roll on the floor, and to toss in the air. The sphere was just trusses without a skin, however, so I imagined the "shell" of the sphere being wrapped in elastic or spandex to effectively cover its surface. Alternatively I imagined a mechanical solution: a significant number of more densely packed trusses. This would require a totally fresh re-design of the laser-cut parts.

Iteration 4: Prototype Segment of a Spherical Shell

My next starting point was to look up geodesic domes on Wikipedia, where I discovered a link to the Platonic solids. While interesting, polygons are not spheres and none of their topologies aligned with my cardboard geometry—these were not what I wanted. Further searching led me to the Johnson solids, which intuitively felt much better for some reason. I was particularly drawn to the "deltoidal icositetrahedron," which has kite-shaped sides measuring a ratio of 1:1.292893. "These I can use," I imagined, "to generate a new set of great circles… they will intersect each other at sixteen 8-pointed vertices and eight 6-pointed vertices… (I think)!"

Careful trigonometry was involved to reduce the perceived problem to a clear mathematical model. Not only was I suddenly inspired to learn about spherical geometry—not something that I would ever have imagined at the project's outset—numerous details of the design, such as how the thickness of the cut material affects the design of each two-dimensional object where junctions occur, needed to be considered. Not having done much math since high-school, this version took much longer to mock up in Illustrator.

Compositionally I decided to emphasize the next iteration's shell-like nature by decreasing the relative size of the node junctures to make them less prominent. A clear assembly pattern was also emerging, including the addition of tertiary bars that slid into the spaces between the trapezoids formed by the intersecting primary and secondary struts. Figure 5 shows a screenshot of one of the numerous virtual "jigs" I constructed to envision the intersection of trusses at each of the differing nodes, since a much more rigorous underlying model needed to be constructed off of which to design each of the truss elements needed to cut the design.

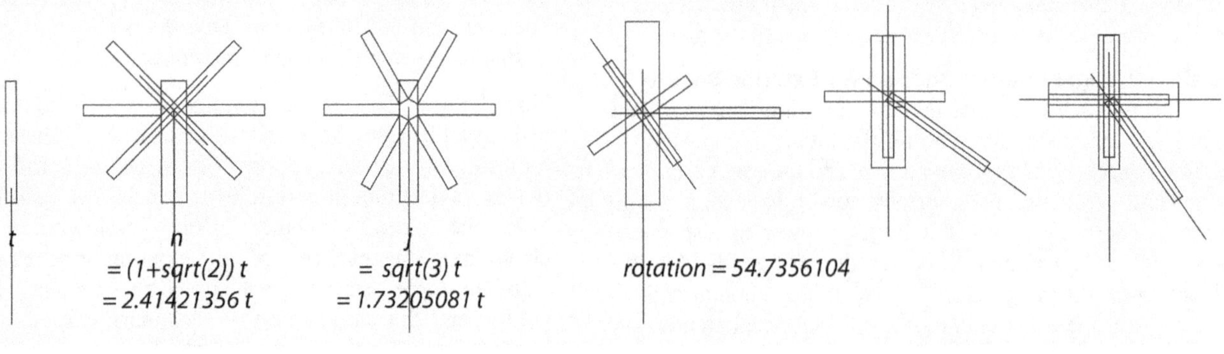

Figure 5. A screenshot from Illustrator showing the virtual "jigs" I constructed to model the notched joints of the various nodes.

A single sheet of cardboard was cut with the laser to test the geometry of a section of a larger sphere. Everything fit together nicely, although the reduction in node size did indicate a potential future problem: the thinner the shell, and the shallower the notches, the less structural strength in each joint. Since only a piece of the shell was being constructed it was difficult to imagine the strength of a completely assembled sphere.

Iteration 5: A Complete Sphere

A significant amount of material is required to go from a 2 dimensional pattern to a 3 dimensional shape. With no more cardboard left at the original thickness, more cardboard was located and the next iteration was cut at 80% size to compensate for a reduction in material thickness at joints. This had two effects. First, less material was required, so additional parts could be added to each printed page. It also reduced the size (and robustness) of the final sphere—which even at 80% size was significantly larger than the previous iteration.

With this version numerous structural factors became clear. The forces acting on a spherical shell are quite powerful, and the long and thin design of the new cardboard trusses could not consistently handle the torque of assembly without crushing. Tensions were also powerful enough to overcome the friction holding together each node, so the completed sphere had a tendency to pull itself apart. At first it was not clear if the mathematical model was slightly off or if the node junctions were too weak, but for the time being, I reasoned, glue and pins might suffice to hold the spherical shell together.

After trying to glue the model together by force (figure 6), I ultimately determined the sphere's mathematical model was off, since the secondary segments still seemed too short. This was frustrating, as I already thought I had fixed this once before. I returned to the computer file to check the template, and yes, indeed, something was wrong because (secondary + tertiary + secondary + tertiary + secondary + tertiary) trusses did not equal 360°. In short, my spherical geometry was off and needed to be re-calculated.

Figure 6. The first complete spherical shell, requiring glue to compensate for weak joints and mathematical error.

The mathematical problem consumed my attention for much of an afternoon. Several web pages were visited describing the basics of spherical geometry: great circles, lunes, the spherical triangle rule (angles always add up to more than 180°), conversion of degrees to radians (i.e.: *What is a radian*? This is very important!), and finally, the Pythagorean theorem for spheres (not easily located in the first several pages I found, and critical to what I was attempting to solve). Curiosity at this point was driving my continued motivation, with the end goal vision of designing a sphere that was "perfect." Aesthetic concerns with this iteration also came to mind: while the thin shell was nice, it also had a lot less personality than the previous version, and the surface was still not smoothly "filled." Adding quaternary segments on the next revision seemed like it would help resolve this issue.

Figure 7. On the sixth iteration, everything fit together as planned.

Iteration 6: Complete Sphere to "Three Degrees"

With the mathematical modeling of the sphere complete in my illustrator files, I laser cut a complete new sphere using six sheets of cardboard. The result was a complete sphere that, when assembled, fit perfectly together (figure 7). The resulting sphere was quite satisfactory, and I was amazed with the beauty and elegance of thoughtful mathematics. Aesthetically this new sphere was graceful, with the diversity of truss thicknesses (quaternary segments were thinner) adding a nice, almost baroque element to the shell. Returning to my office after a few hours away, I had a near-transcendent moment as the sun shone through the window and onto the sphere, casting a shadow on the wall. I could feel the Earth turning as the shadow slowly slid down the wall, and meditated on it quietly for a few minutes before returning to work. Perhaps 20 minutes later I looked up: the shadow had completely changed, and a red hue burned through the window. It was a far more dynamic, different light, with dramatically different shadows. At this moment I also noticed numerous different ways in which the fundamental shape of a sphere can be subdivided, based on this particular topological map, to create numerous alternate designs that would be interesting to explore.

Iteration 7: Matte Board Sphere – Colors and Combinations

I went to the art store to get some matte board, knowing that its thin stiffness would allow the ability to cut far more parts from one sheet of material and result in a smaller product with a denser construction. It also occurred to me that I would like to experiment with combining different colors of material board together in one sphere to evidence different shapes. I ended up selecting a black board and a white board that were both the same thickness.

Relative to the previous iterations, laying out the lasercut parts was a dream! One and a half full spheres fit perfectly on a page. To ensure that no glue would be required, I printed some demo parts on scrap board at various dimensions to scale the notches to the anticipated thickness range (40%, 35%, and 30%) and tested how snuggly they fit together. 30% was best, but it was a little too tight. I therefore created a page layout at 31%, not wanting to risk the assembly being too loose, and laser cut one black sheet and one white sheet of parts. This resulted in enough pieces to assemble a total of three spheres with different combinations of colors.

Assembly took far longer than expected, but relative to the cardboard the matte board was wonderful (figure 8). As a material it's much stiffer and more dense than cardboard, so

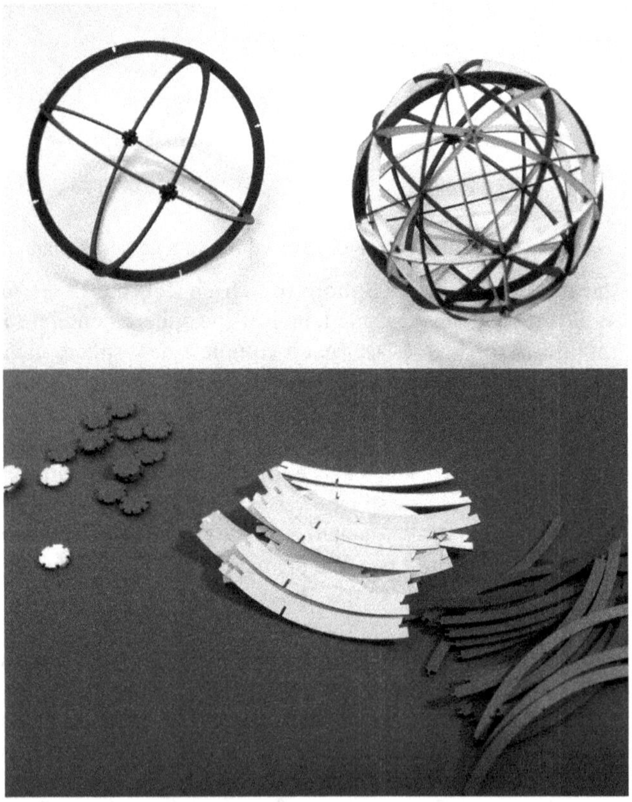

Figure 8. Assembly and parts for the final (matte board) iteration.

the resulting spheres felt much more solid. I began by assembling some black pieces, since they were cut first. I made one semi-complete sphere, and one partial sphere using only the primary struts. This latter construction was beautiful in itself, and I was struck by the simple elegance of the sphere's great circles. While assembling the parts, sometimes I had to use force to jam the pieces together, and the joints got slightly crushed or the pieces deformed. I often had to use the X-Acto knife to poke everything into place, as a dentist would, pushing the tip of each truss into its corresponding gap. Nuances of these small assembly tasks could have been improved with iteration on the architecture of each joint, but the tertiary segments fit perfectly and the sphere held together with no glue at all. Although the quaternary segments were extremely fragile, especially the endpoints that were designed to fit tightly into targeted grooves, once the sphere was assembled I was able to perform a "quality check" to insure that all of the node junctions were re-centered and tight.

Aesthetically this sphere met with my stamp of approval. It was satisfying to look at and I placed it on my desk to photograph and admire. When I tossed it in the air and caught it the structure withstood pressure from all directions. It had a very firm shape and felt complete.

Iteration 8: Assemblies and Reflection on Future Action

Pride in the success of the seventh iteration inspired me to create a series of additional spheres that fully demonstrated the robustness of the design and provided an opportunity for further reflection. I began by cleaning-up minor details in the sphere's Illustrator file and printing two additional sheets of black and white parts. It occurred to me that, using just these two colors, there were numerous possible modes of assembly given all of the permutations and combinations of colors across 5 sets of pieces (two different node types and three different kinds of great circle). I could create white spheres or black spheres with white or black nodes, or I could swap some sets of great circles with the alternate color to highlight different topological structures. This made me curious about the mathematics of topology and further possibilities of assembly. It also struck me that, although this study had begun with little specific direction, each iteration had progressively refined the course of future action towards the perfection of an emerging idea. I had become more inclined to pay attention to nuanced details of the design, and attained a heightened awareness of their consequences with each subsequent action. And now, through this act of refinement, a complexity of seemingly infinite patterns was attaining clarity as each permutation lead to countless additional possibilities.

Put another way, with each successive spherical construction a more advanced system of thought had emerged. The project had begun as an intuitive exploration and ended in a systematic process for the assembly and refinement of spherical objects. I had constructed routines to support my evolving intuition of their structure, and in doing so had enhanced my perceptions and ability to shape their design. Not only had the nature of the sphere as a "designable" form become increasingly evident, each subsequent move had become systemized, practiced and refined. Furthermore, motivation and inspiration had emerged through intuitive learning—the weighing of possible outcomes against what felt most aesthetically and insightfully "right." Best of all, the open-ended freedom and motivation associated with the initial intuitive action remained: I could choose at this point whether to dig deeper on the technical aspects of studying the sphere or the formative aesthetics of refining its shape. Having arrived at the intersection of speculative possibility and sensory reflection, I had created a personal system of knowledge capable of motivating continued iterations in a highly complex design space.

DISCUSSION

Self-reflection is an essential aspect of creative design. Yet while it is routinely acknowledged and studied in HCI design research (e.g. [15, 17]), intuition itself is seldom addressed in HCI literature independent from the influence of external reflection and feedback. Indeed, most discussions of reflectivity in design center on user testing or other forms of social engagement, such as participatory design or cultural probes [16]. Design students and educators are quite familiar with the role of "critique" as an educational practice that is used to enhance reflection on design practice and teach critical thinking, for example. Clearly such reflective practices are critical to enhancing the *use* of successful designs, allowing technology to shape and to scale "external" or distributed cognition, as with crowdsourcing systems for instance. The challenge addressed by this paper is to take a different focus by emphasizing the internal act of intuition as performed by the designer during the act of design. By focusing on the self-perceptions and reflections on intuition through an intuitive design activity, my hope is to shine additional light on the role of intuition in the act of designing.

It is important to acknowledge that the self-reflective methodology employed in this paper is not without limitations, nor is it an easy or conventional approach to HCI research. The fundamental limitation arises from the need to translate inner felt experience (specifically the feeling of having "intuited" something) into an externalized and generalizable form. In this case we feel that the auto-ethnographic approach we have employed is appropriate because it allows for the immediate experience of an intuition to be captured first hand—as well as the subsequent reflection on what was intuited. In the self-report narrative on the previous pages, for example, I regularly included statements that were intuited as part of the firsthand experience but which appear (when presented as narrative transcriptions) to be an after-reflection on the design process instead of a firsthand intuition. Discussing the first prototyping iteration, for example, I wrote "My intuition was that these notches, cut to precisely the same thickness as the cardboard material, would allow two triangles to slide together forming a simple joint at 90-degrees that would be both structurally interesting and lead to unexpected geometric possibilities when assembled." This is problematic, as it can give rise to the perception that our understanding of intuition lacks clarity. On one hand intuition has been defined as "reflexive knowing" (a kind of pre-cognitive experience beyond rational and verbal awareness), and on the other it involves what could be understood in a Schönean sense as the combining of "reflection in action" and "reflection on action," a reflexive stepping away and assessing the results of design activity. In practice we believe it is very difficult to separate these two intuitive modes, since what we do is informed by our guiding "inner voice," which itself is an intuitive response to the perceptual/cognitive situation presented. As the diagram presented in Figure 1 represented, what we learn from the world affects our intuitive actions or "inner" response. Moreover, we have used the notion of intuition interchangeably to refer to both generative activities and evaluative activities, which could be perceived as two rather different acts of consciousness. Or are they? We believe suggesting that they are different acts of consciousness is an after-reflection on the nature of intuition, but that in actuality firsthand intuitive experience is both generative *and* evaluative: it is the generation of an intent based on an (internal) evaluation about what to intend. We acknowledge our framing of these issues has involved substantial methodological prescriptions, but in practical terms, for the designer making an intuitive impulse, reflective action and perception are tightly coupled in performance.

A grounded-theory synthesis of the observations from the previous section revealed how numerous dimensions of intuitive knowing affect the choices designers make when pursuing their craft. For example many of the self-reflections captured in the narrative included pragmatic motivations towards a clear course of subsequent action (e.g. the desire to create something using the available triangular parts following the first attempt to use the laser cutter). Another code captured moments of "insight" during the creative process, such as learnings that prepared me to avoid future mistakes. After the first pass through the data, identified "codes" were synthesized to identify four main "clusters" reflective of the more granular details. I then attempted to make sense of these clusters by placing them into a 2x2 framework to understand the basic dimensions that made them unique from one another. Through this exercise it became clear that each area represented an underlying "motivation" for the intuitive action. Specifically, four key motivators that characterized the experienced intuitions were identified: curiosity, efficiency, inspiration, and insight, described in greater detail below.

Figure 9 presents the identified framework for the analysis of design intuition that will guide the remainder of our discussion. The model defines a 2x2 matrix along two axes drawn from the experiential data gathered on intuitive cognition in design: impulsive vs. reflective action and speculative vs. sensory stimuli/intent. This framework is not intended to encapsulate the complex field of theory surrounding intuition research, nor is it advanced as a model summarizing the behavior of intuition in design. Rather, it is referred to simply as a visual guide to our discussion. As described above, the model itself was derived from a grounded theory analysis of the autoethnographic narrative in the previous section that resulted in the open coding scheme that was used in the analysis of the data.

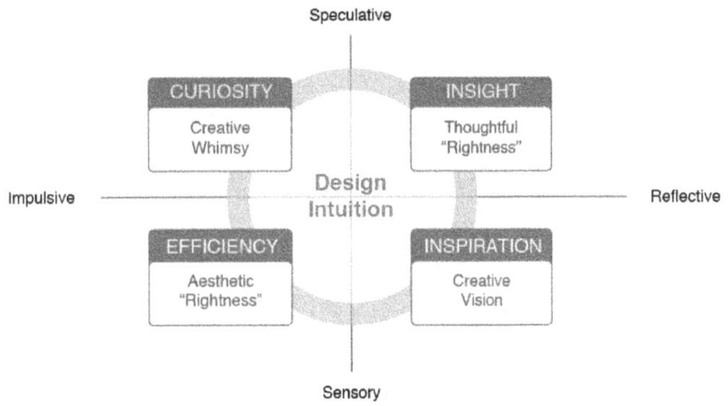

Figure 9. A summary of insights on intuition in design, drawn from grounded-theory synthesis of autoethnographic data.

First, the findings revealed numerous intuitions that were driven by *curiosity*, or creative whimsy. Curiosity is essential to design intuition as a prompt for speculative and impulsive creative action. This is essential for advancing the design action in the absence of concrete insights or external guidance. Indeed, not only did curiosity drive me to perform this study, it led me to experiment with and re-arrange cardboard pieces, see if it was possible to construct spherical shells, and explore their mathematical complexities. In this regard, the designer's curious impulse to ask "what if?" is a critical motivating factor in the quest for knowledge. Creative whimsy also allows the navigation of functional constraints, such as a lack of materials or technical setback. When undeterred by a commitment to unknown outcomes, designers are empowered to learn by doing and gain new insights and confidence through design intuition.

Second, intuition is critical for the *efficiency* of design because it allows for "feeling based" aesthetic judgments to be made that allow for immediate action. Such decisions tend to value elegant, holistic solutions that resolve ambiguity and refresh the cognitive stage. In my first and third iterations, for example, the simple introduction of a "finishing detail" cleared the canvas for the next phase of action. The desire for aesthetic "rightness" also streamlines the process of design: cutting a full sheet of identical triangles maximizes the pieces while eliminating waste; holding a finished model that "feels right" in the hand is an indication that the mathematical model is good. Although it sometimes leads to failure on deeper reflection, designers must learn to trust their intuitive aesthetic judgments to maintain creative momentum—the synthesis of alternative courses of action. These insights are supported by recent design theory; in an examination of the role and development of expertise in design, Cross notes that often design process follows a pattern of 'opportunistic solution development' which has been hypothesized to reduce the cognitive cost of efficient design behavior [8].

Third, beautifully crafted objects also attract attention and playful interaction, leading to the *inspiration* necessary to drive creative vision. The intuitive reflection upon sensory stimuli is what motivates the desire to achieve aesthetic rightness. When we are pleased with our accomplishments we are driven to achieve more. At many steps in my process of self-reflection, pleasure was derived from a reflective sensation of what else might be be possible. For example: how the sun's drifting shadow, projecting across the cosmos, illuminates the geometry of spherical cardboard and inspires countless possibilities that were previously unsensed; how the shell of the structure could be wrapped in elastic or spandex; how it ought to be possible to create something equivalent to a Hoberman sphere [30] that transforms each face of a cube into a sphere; how scaling this up to an architectural structure would allow the Pompidou to turn into into Epcot center, etc.

Finally, it is only by drawing on the intuitive knowledge of what has worked in the past that *insight* can be realized and actualized. Insight requires an intuitive struggle to achieve an understanding capable of grasping the "rightness" of the knowing involved. Such intuition provides designers with a means to frame their practice more intelligently through speculative hypothetical questioning and the learning that results. At many points in the sphere project I advanced blindly into areas with little prior knowledge (e.g. a deep immersion into spherical geometry) and came away with new insights on ways to achieve my goals—whether through the pursuit of new learning or the development of new tools, like improved software features for cutting cardboard that dynamically adjust for material thickness in response to an envisioned 3D form. These intuitions not only enabled the anticipation of future errors, they guided the deeper courses of action necessary for complex design.

Intuition is the ability to acquire knowledge without the explicit use of reason or inference, and it is "in this immediate, pre-representational and pre-discursive experience of the world that all our cognitive activity seems to be rooted." [34] In this framing, the design of HCI systems extends beyond computers or systems of people to all intuitive interactions we have with the world—not just with digital tools or with cardboard spheres, but to the differentials of self that we pass to the world we inhabit. Applied to design activity, intuition provides a means for intelligently framing and acting upon immediate options to guide the possibility of their eventual outcome. My hope is that this discussion has provided a useful framework for understanding the complex nature of intuition in design.

REFERENCES

1. Battarbee, K., "Co-Experience: Product Experience as Social Interaction," *Product Experience*, 2008.
2. Binder, T., De Michelis, G., Ehn, P., Jacucci, G., Linde, P., and Wagner, I., *Design Things*, MIT press, 2011
3. Brown, T., *Change by Design: How Design Thinking Transforms Organizations and Inspires Innovation*, Harper Business, 2009.
4. Burawoy, M., "The Extended Case Method," *Sociological Theory*, **16**(1), 1998, p4-33.

5. Burton, L., "Why is Intuition so Important to Math-ematicians but Missing from Mathematics Education?" *For the Learning of Mathematics*, **19**(2), 1999.
6. Buxton, B., *Sketching User Experiences: Getting the Design Right and the Right Design*, Morgan Kaufmann, 2007.
7. Corbin, J. & Strauss, A., "Grounded theory research: Procedures, canons, and evaluative criteria," *Qualitative Sociology,* **13**(1), 1990, pp. 3-21.
8. Cross, N., "Expertise in Design: An Overview," *Design Studies*, **25**(5), September 2004.
9. Dane, E., and Pratt, M. G., "Conceptualizing and Measuring Intuition: A Review of Recent Trends," *Int. Review of Industrial and Organizational Psych.*, **24**, 2009.
10. Dourish, P., *Where the Action Is: The Foundations of Embodied Interaction*, MIT Press, 2001
11. Dunne, T., and Raby, F. *Speculative Everything*, MIT Press, 2013.
12. Faste, R., "The Role of Aesthetics in Engineering," *Japan Society of Mech. Eng. (JSME) Journal*, Winter 1995.
13. Ferguson, G., *Cracking the intuition code*, Chicago, IL: NTC/Contemporary Books, 1999.
14. Fisher, J. (ed.), *Technologies of Intuition*, YYZBooks, Toronto, 2006.
15. Fleck, R., and Fitzpatrick, G., "Reflecting on Reflection: Framing a Design Landscape," *Proc. OZCHI*, 2010
16. Gaver, B., Dunne, T., Pacenti, E., "Cultural Probes", in *Interactions*, **6**(1), 1998, pp. 21-29.
17. Gerritsen, D., Olsen, J., Tasse, D., Vlahovic, T., Gulotta, R., Odom, W., Wiese, J., and Zimmerman, J., "Mailing Archived Emails as Products: Probing the Value of Virtual Collections," *Proc. CHI*, 2016
18. Glegg, G., *The Design of Design*, Cambridge University Press, 1969.
19. Goodyear, R. K. "Inference and Intuition as Components of Empathy," *Counselor Education and Supervision*, **18**, 1979, pp. 214-222.
20. Holtzblatt, K., and Beyer, H. *Contextual Design*, Morgan Kaufmann, 1998.
21. Kant, I., *The Critique of Pure Reason*, 1787.
22. Kuutti, K., Iacucci, G., and Iacucci, C., "Acting to know: improving creativity in the design of mobile services by using performances," *Proc. Creativity & Cognition*, 2002
23. Landry, L. "A study of the experience, use, and develop-ment of intuition," *Electronic Doctoral Dissertations for UMass Amherst,* Paper AAI9120905, 1991.
24. Maritain, J. *Creative Intuition in Art and Poetry*, Pantheon Books, 1953
25. Marton, F., Fensham, P., and Chaiklin, S., "A Nobel's eye view of scientific intuition," *International Journal of Science Education*, **16**(4), 1994.
26. McKim, R., *Experiences in Visual Thinking*, Brooks/Cole, 1972.
27. Morris, L. E. "Strategies and tactics to access intuition: A look at the moment of solution," unpublished Ph.D. dissertation, Virginia Polytechnic/State University, 1990.
28. Noë, A., *Action in Perception: Representation and Mind*, MIT Press, 2005.
29. Osborn, A.F., *Applied Imagination*, Scribner, 1953.
30. O'Reilly, O. M. and Varadi, P. C. "Hoberman's Sphere, Euler Parameters and Lagrange's Equations," *Journal of Elasticity*, **56**, 1999, pp. 171-180.
31. Pahl, G., W. Beitz, J. Feldhusen, and K.-H. Grote, *Eng. Design: A Systematic Approach*, Springer 2007.
32. Patnaik, D. *Wired to Care: How Companies Prosper When They Create Widespread Empathy*, FT Press, 2009.
33. Patton, M.Q., *Qualitative Research & Evaluation Methods*, Sage Publications 3rd edition, 2003.
34. Petitmengin-Peugeot, C., "The intuitive experience," *Journal of Consciousness* **6**(2-3), 1999, 43-77.
35. Piha, H., "Intuition: A Bridge to the Coenesthetic World of Experience," *Journal of the Americal Psychoanalytic Association*, **53**(1), 2005, pp. 29-31.
36. Rode, J., "Reflexivity in Digital Anthropology," *Proc. CHI*, 2011
37. Rode, J., Blythe, M., and Nardi, B., "Qualitative Research in HCI," *Extended abstracts of CHI*, 2012
38. Schön, D., *The Reflective Practitioner: How Professionals Think in Action*, Ashgate, 1995.
39. Scott, G., Leritz, L. E., and Mumford, M. D., "The Effectiveness of Creativity Training: A Quantitative Review," *Creativity Research*, **16**(4), 2004, pp. 361–388.
40. Searle, J., *Intentionality: An Essay in the Philosophy of Mind*, Cambridge University Press, 1983.
41. Sinclair, M., and Ashkanasy, N. M., "Intuition: Myth or Decision Making Tool?", *Mgt. Learning*, **36**(3), 2005
42. Spinoza, B., *Ethics*, 1677.
43. Suri, J.F., "Informing Our Intuition: Design Research for Radical Innovation," *Rotman Magazine*, November 2008.
44. Thomson, P., "Are the Muses Real? Intuitive Inspiration, Possession and Dissociation," in Fisher, J. (ed.), *Technologies of Intuition*, YYZBooks, Toronto, 2006.
45. Tovey, M., "Styling and design: intuition and analysis in industrial design," *Design Studies*, **18**(1), 1997.
46. Zimmerman, J., Forlizzi, J. and Evenson, S., "Research Through Design as a Method for Interaction Desgin Research in HCI," *Proc. CHI*, 2007
47. Zimmerman, J., Stolterman, E., Forlizzi, J., "An Analysis and Critique of Research through Design," *Proc. Designing Interactive Systems*, 2010

Understanding Public Evaluation: Quantifying Experimenter Intervention

Julie R. Williamson and John Williamson
University of Glasgow
Glasgow, Scotland, United Kingdom
{Julie.Williamson, JohnH.Williamson}@glasgow.ac.uk

Figure 1. Public evaluations are difficult and messy. The real world experience captured in public spaces is both integral to authentic experience and challenging for researchers. Tedious hours can be spent waiting for potential users to approach a public display (left), the activities of others in public space can be disruptive (centre), and serious hardware failures can mean failed data capture (right).

ABSTRACT
Public evaluations are popular because some research questions can only be answered by turning "to the wild." Different approaches place experimenters in different roles during deployment, which has implications for the kinds of data that can be collected and the potential bias introduced by the experimenter. This paper expands our understanding of how experimenter roles impact public evaluations and provides an empirical basis to consider different evaluation approaches. We completed an evaluation of a playful gesture-controlled display – not to understand interaction at the display but to compare different evaluation approaches. The conditions placed the experimenter in three roles, steward observer, overt observer, and covert observer, to measure the effect of experimenter presence and analyse the strengths and weaknesses of each approach.

Author Keywords
Public Evaluation; Public Displays; In the Wild Methods.

ACM Classification Keywords
H.5.2. User Interfaces: Evaluation/Methodology.

INTRODUCTION
In meteorology, the butterfly effect refers to small changes - metaphorically the fluttering of a butterfly's wings - having a large knock-on effect on the weather. For interactive public technology, the equivalent might be the very literal distraction of a passing butterfly suddenly drawing away users' attention from an installation. The delicate and unpredictable relationship between public technology, the environment in which it is situated, and potential users calls for careful "in the wild" study to authentically capture experiences. Such evaluations are difficult to control, as shown in Figure 1, and experimenter intervention is often required. Experimenter interventions can also reveal valuable insights into behaviour and motivation, but represent a very large butterfly indeed.

Some research questions can only be answered through real world evaluation [20]. Results found in lab studies alone may not be a good predictor of usage in real world contexts [14]. Investigations of *user experience*, as opposed to usability, need "in the wild" methods to understand complex social and physical contexts, explore how experiences develop over time, and uncover new and unexpected uses [15]. There are diverse approaches to such evaluations, and even the meaning of "in the wild" is not widely agreed [18]. It is often used interchangeably with field trials [1,4], deployments [1], and intervention-based studies [34]. In this paper, we restrict our scope to "in the wild" studies of stationary technology in public and semi-public places, for example public displays and interactive installations. Crucially, this involves *intervening* (through the installation of technology) within a *real world place* (not a lab simulation). We refer to studies of these interventions as *public evaluations* throughout this paper.

Popular approaches to *public evaluations* include controlled on-the-street studies [6,25], observational studies [23,33], and steward observation [29]. However, there is limited work reflecting on the bias implications of these

Permission to make digital or hard copies of all or part of this work for personal or classroom use is granted without fee provided that copies are not made or distributed for profit or commercial advantage and that copies bear this notice and the full citation on the first page. Copyrights for components of this work owned by others than ACM must be honored. Abstracting with credit is permitted. To copy otherwise, or republish, to post on servers or to redistribute to lists, requires prior specific permission and/or a fee. Request permissions from Permissions@acm.org.
CHI 2017, May 06-11, 2017, Denver, CO, USA
© 2017 ACM. ISBN 978-1-4503-4655-9/17/05...$15.00
DOI: http://dx.doi.org/10.1145/3025453.3025598

approaches. Many investigators decide on approach based on personal experience, preference, and perceptions of reviewer acceptability. Foundational work reflecting on "in the wild" methods [for example 3,11,20] provides valuable insights, but the field lacks systematic empirical work that investigates the implications of *experimenter roles* on data collection. Debates about approach focus on how much the experimenter should intervene during evaluation, ranging from overtly creating a controlled experience (for example [6]) to completely unstewarded experience (for example [35]). The key question for public evaluation is: how does experimenter intervention distort results?

This is a foundational problem throughout science, but *public evaluations* are particularly fragile with respect to intervention bias.

Demand characteristics In public evaluations users' behaviours are significantly influenced by *demand characteristics* [4], a bias introduced when participants act to satisfy perceived desires of the experimenter. A lonely looking researcher in front of a display can attract pity interactions that do not represent genuine desires to interact.

Unfamiliarity Public evaluations often introduce new concepts that lack existing practice [8] where investigator presence and instruction will significantly influence how participants react. The pose and subtle reactions of an experimenter might be the only cues a potential user can quickly grasp at an unfamiliar, experimental art installation.

Shyness Finally, public evaluations often explore voluntary interactions, which users may quickly abandon in the face of difficulty, discomfort, or external pressure. A passer-by's fleeting curiosity about a new street installation might easily be diverted by the gaze of a watching observer.

Anecdotal evidence indicates presence of an experimenter introduces bias, but the magnitude and attributes of these effects have not been quantified for public evaluations. This is exacerbated by pressure to present public evaluation studies as predictable, replicable, and comparable [4], which diminishes or ignores sources of bias.

This paper provides an empirical basis to consider the effect of experimenter roles in different evaluation approaches. To do this, we evaluated a playful gesture-controlled display, controlling not the interaction techniques but the experimenter roles. The conditions had experimenters take on three roles: steward observer; overt observer; and covert observer. We combined this with high-density quantitative measurements to precisely quantify the impact of experimenter presence. For this first time, this captures how experimenter presence introduces bias and documents anomalies arising from observation.

This paper:

- Identifies the core methodological challenges of public evaluations
- Details an empirical evaluation of the impact of three common public evaluation approaches in practice
- Shows that experimenter role has a dramatic and clearly measurable effect on how people use public installations
- Lays out a systematic experimental framework for investigating observation roles in public evaluation.

CHALLENGES FOR PUBLIC EVALUATIONS

Although there are clear benefits to evaluating "in the wild", real world deployments are hard [4]. Public evaluations are logistically complex and resource intensive, especially compared to traditional lab evaluations [17]. Researchers need to work with project partners and external organisations to negotiate site access, install equipment, and agree on issues such as security, visual identity, electricity, and ethics. Researchers face significant engineering challenges to create quality prototypes that users will take seriously, and robust enough prototypes that users won't break them. Wild users respond in unusual and expected ways, resulting in obscure errors, data collection failures, and even deliberate vandalism. This is compounded by the fact the studies often run over long periods of time – days or weeks rather than hours or minutes.

Solving these practical issues is essential. But, more importantly, the *experimental design* must be capable of capturing aspects of authentic behaviour. This needs to be solved before trials start: there are often no second chances. The event that supported the evaluation may have passed, the deployment site may no longer be available, and resources may simply be spent, or word may spread that an installation is broken or buggy. Despite this, public evaluations are "worth the hassle" [27] because of the rich and otherwise inaccessible results they offer. However, there is little empirical work that informs researchers on the impact of different approaches. There is a lack of theory to guide "in the wild" evaluations [26], and evaluating new interactions can be difficult when users have no idea what to expect [8,9]. The biases introduced can be severe and unpredictable [4], making it difficult to produce robust and replicable results.

We organise the *methodological* challenges in public evaluation into three themes; *experience control*, *authenticity,* and *ethics.*

Experience Control

Public evaluations require researchers to give up direct control of interactions. It is this shift of control from experimenter to participant during "in the wild studies" [26] that makes experimental design so much more challenging than traditional lab studies. For example, participants cannot be treated as equivalent and interchangeable units, conditions may be unbalanced, and difficult to identify confounding factors pollute results.

Experimental design means balancing control with ecological validity [16]. Increased intervention increases control but also increases bias. For example, *demand characteristics* [4] will be amplified where participants have more contact with the experimenter. The verbal framing of on-the-street studies like [6,25] can significantly influence results [4]. *Anomalies*, or unplanned interruptions during public evaluations, are an essential part of the experience of public technologies but introduce unpredictability into data collection. For example, in our study, we encountered a truck that blocked views from recording equipment, a procession that drew attention from the display, friends of the experimenter approaching and engaging in poorly-timed conversations, and the distracting activity of nearby animals.

When discussing experimental control, our evaluation addresses the following questions:

- Does asserting control during an evaluation change users' behaviours?
- Can desired behaviours be elicited without experimenter intervention?

Authenticity

We do "in the wild" evaluation to collect ecologically valid data [5,7]. But defining what "valid" or "authentic" data constitutes in public evaluations is hard and the research community lacks a shared ideal of validity [1]. There are strong but conflicting arguments for covert methods [34], mixed methods [33], and participant observations [15,29].

Questions about authenticity often focus on qualitative versus quantitative data and there are strong opinions on both sides. While quantitative comparisons may not capture important aspects of "in the wild" experiences [27], qualitative results are hard to generalise and may be difficult to reproduce. The push for design recommendations and other "generalizable" results from qualitative work also over simplifies such methods in a harmful way, failing to capture the strengths of in depth qualitative inquiry [10]. Rejecting pressure to make "in the wild" studies objective and reproducible [4] with neatly packaged results [10] leads to a mixed methods approach that embraces the variability of public evaluations.

Researchers have a wide spectrum of tools to collect data from experiments. These include usage logs, video and audio recordings, participant observation, on-the-street interviews, and overt or covert observation. There are a range of techniques for analysing these data streams, for example pedestrian tracking [36], f-formations [19], and the audience funnel framework [22].

Understanding non-use and avoidance is essential in situated technologies [2], and requires data collection methods that support this. This helps to mitigate the bias of *lead participants* [4], participants whom actively help the trial and/or perform exemplary interactions, by putting the rarity of their interactions into context.

This paper explores the authenticity of data when results differ for different evaluation styles. Our discussion revolves around the following questions:

- What should be the considered the "ground truth" for real world interactions?
- Are results biased when analysis favours interacting users, ignoring or downplaying the role of non-interacting users?

Ethics

There are significant practical and theoretical ethical challenges in public evaluations [32,34]. The core ethical issue is that capturing authentic experience may demand that participants not be aware they are involved in an evaluation [32][34].

Public evaluations often blur the boundaries between public events and research [12], placing investigators in a complex ethical situation. Practical challenges such as gaining appropriate ethical approval, choosing whether to gather explicit informed consent from participants, and ensuring participant safety have been discussed thoroughly in previous work [12,32,34]. Methodological challenges around recruitment, motivation, and intervention are harder to address. Reilly et al. [24] discuss the ethics of using public events to access participants who may otherwise be uninterested in participating in research evaluations. Waern [32] discusses the importance of recognizing that public evaluations are interventions that inevitably alter public spaces that people are actively using, perhaps for the worse.

We analyse the specific ethical issues that arise when experimenters take on different roles during evaluation, addressing the following questions:

- What are the ethical issues of intervening with face-to-face encounters in public spaces?
- To what extent does unwitting participation undermine a passer-by's right to refuse participation?

PUBLIC EVALUATION APPROACHES

Approaches to public evaluations are incredibly varied, and of the key decisions is the role of the investigator. Investigator roles fall into three main categories; *steward observer*, *overt observer*, and *covert observer*. This has implications for the types of data that can be collected (covert observation precludes interviews, for example) and the behavioural bias induced. Figure 2, organises the prominent display-based and tangible interface examples from the literature according to the type of data collected (qualitative and quantitative) and the level of experimental control (controlled and uncontrolled).

Steward Observer

As a *steward observer*, the investigator takes an active role in managing, curating, and controlling the experience of the participant. Unlike ethnographic *participant observation,* steward observers take on a different role from users, actively presenting themselves as stewards, owners, or performers.

Researchers took an immersive role in *humanaquarium* [17], an interactive performance where the audience could participate through a touch sensitive enclosure around the performers. Touch input during the performance changed the audio output of the performers' instruments and the visual projections behind the performers. The *humanaquarium* researchers used their experiences from performing to inform the design of the installation.

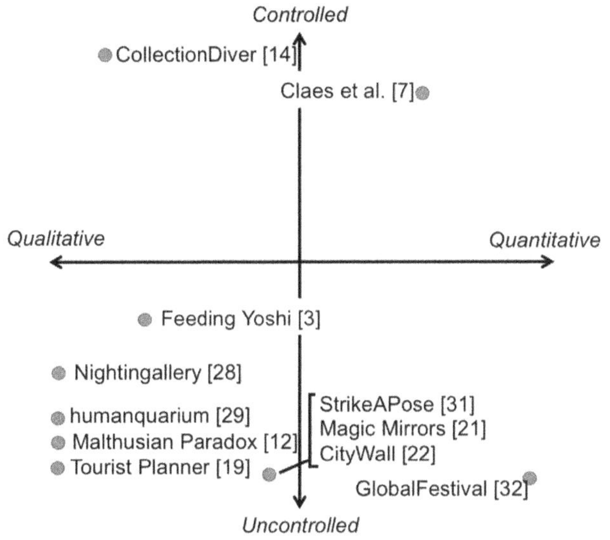

Figure 2. The evaluation studies discussed in this paper are organised based on experimental control (controlled to uncontrolled) and the primary data collected (qualitative to quantitative).

Nightingallery [30] positioned researchers as circus barkers, attracting and guiding users to interact with an animatronic bird. In both *humanaquariam* and *Nightingallery* the researchers provided guidance in an open-ended interaction.

In contrast, Claes et al. [6] used steward observers to recruit passers-by in a public space to complete a series of tasks with the public tangible display. Hinrichs et al. [13] completed an *in situ* study of a tangible library search interface called *CollectionDiver*, but rather than passers-by, explicitly recruited participants. Participants completed a series of tasks with the interface and were then interviewed.

Steward observation allows researchers to produce in depth, qualitative results, where researchers can probe specific questions and elicit specific behaviours.

Overt Observer

An *overt observer* observes without actively intervening during interaction, although survey or interview data may be gathered after interaction. Overt observation is often used to add qualitative results to interaction logs and video analysis, but the impact of the overt observation on this data has not previously been evaluated. For example, passers-by may be deterred by overt observers or feel uncomfortable when approached after interaction.

In *City Wall* researchers observed users at a multi-touch display [23] and used on-the-street interviews to complement observation notes and video analysis. A similar approach was used to evaluate the *StrikeAPose* gesture controlled display [33] and *Magic Mirrors* [22]. In each case, on-the-street interviews were gathered by approaching users after they had interacted with the display.

However, the selection bias effects (diverting shy users) of overt observation on interaction is not currently known. The ethics of approaching users in this way is also unclear, where they may regret interactions when they realise they are involved in a study.

Covert Observer

As a *covert observer*, the investigator does not maintain any visible presence or intervene in any way during evaluation. This approach relies on quantitative and qualitative analysis based on video or audio recordings and interaction logs.

The *GlobalFestival* [35] information display was evaluated completely through video analysis, combining automatic pedestrian tracking [36] with detailed manual analysis of interactive segments. *The Tourist Planner* [21] table top display was evaluated using a combination of overt observation (first phase of study) and covert observation (second phase of study) through video data. Covert observation is similar to evaluations of pervasive mobile technologies, for example *The Malthusian Paradox* [11] and *Feeding Yoshi* [3]. These both recruited participants in advance and asked them to use pervasive applications in everyday life without the experimenter present. However, pervasive games grant different agency to users than public evaluations. In pervasive games, users are explicitly recruited and knowingly participate, choosing when and where they want to interact.

Although covert observation removes the possibility of gathering on-the-street responses from users, advocates argue that this represents the most ecologically valid experience [34]. Because public displays have such a delicate balance between interaction and non-interaction, overt and stewarded observation may seriously distort the self-selection of interacting users.

UNDERSTANDING PUBLIC EVALUATION

We set out to quantitatively capture the effects of experiment roles on the interaction/non-interaction bias and distorting effects on the interaction experience. We developed *Silly Hats Only*, a playful gesture controlled display. We performed multiple evaluations of this display, with the experimenter role as the controlled independent variable.

Silly Hats Only

Silly Hats Only is a playful installation where users can see their silhouettes as captured by a depth camera, as shown in

Figure 3. Physically, it consists of a large freestanding display in a busy public walkway. When they make a teapot gesture (putting your hand on your hip), similar to the interactions used in *StrikeAPose* [33], a silly hat is drawn upon their head while they maintain the teapot pose. When users approach the display, their silhouette appears alongside an animation demonstrating the teapot gesture.

Figure 3. When a user performs the teapot gesture, their silhouette will get a silly hat. An animation in the bottom left of the screen demonstrates the gesture.

The goal was *not* to analyse the interaction, but to create a study scenario that captured the essence of public evaluation. We used this to evaluate the impact of the experiment role directly.

Our core question is: **How do experimenter roles influence the data collected during a public evaluation?**

To answer this, we contextualised this question in terms measurable variables relevant to our installation:

Q1: What are users' preferred interaction distances when playing with a gesture-enabled display?

Q2: How do higher rates of pedestrian traffic on the walkway influence interaction distance?

Experimental Design

Three conditions placed the experimenter in different roles; steward observer, overt observer, and covert observer.

Steward observer

The steward observer condition was based on the approach developed by Claes et al. [6]. The steward observer stood close to the display and recruited participants from passers-by. Participants were recruited if they 1) approached the experimenter or 2) walked close enough to be captured by the depth camera and showed an interest in the display. Each participant was then asked to perform a series of tasks and answer questions about their experiences.

In this condition, the following data was captured:

- Structured Usage Data (task timelines)
- Quantitative Responses (interaction logs)
- Qualitative Responses (interview questions)
- Overhead Video (tracking pedestrian motion)

Overt Observer

The overt observer condition had the experimenter seated roughly five meters from the display (within the overhead video frame). The experimenter kept an open notebook visible and sat oriented towards the display. The experimenter did not intervene, but would answer questions if approached. Although many overt observer studies include follow-up questions with passers-by who have engaged, we chose to exclude this to minimise disruption.

This condition gathered the following data:

- Quantitative Responses (interaction logs)
- Observation Notes (in person)
- Overhead Video (pedestrian motion tracking)

Covert Observer

The covert observer condition had no visible experimenter. The experimenter gathered observation notes from a live video stream from indoors.

This condition gathered the following data:

- Quantitative Responses (interaction logs)
- Observation Notes (from video, same perspective as pedestrian tracking)
- Overhead Video (pedestrian motion tracking)

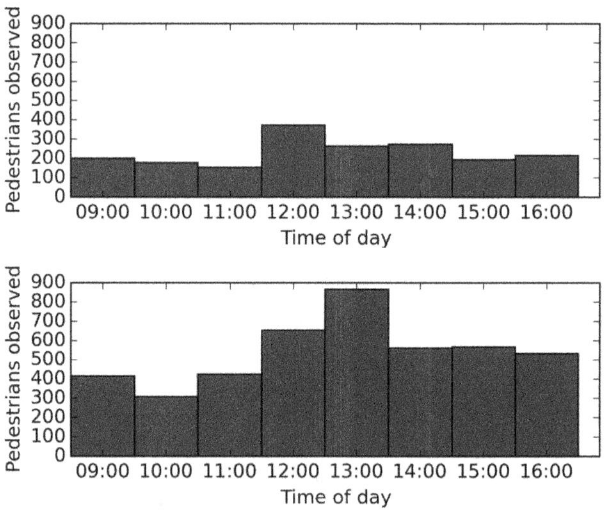

Figure 4. Passers-by per hour on low-traffic day (top) and high traffic day (bottom) during a special event. Units are minutes from 9am.

Hardware and Setting

The evaluation used a 42" high definition screen in a waterproof grey "monolith" enclosure, as shown in Figure 3. Depth images were captured using a Kinect 2.0 device[1]

[1] Kinect 2.0

https://developer.microsoft.com/en-us/windows/kinect/develop

placed below the display and processed using the OpenNI libraries[2]. The experimental software logged all interaction events and position data for all user silhouettes captured by the depth camera. Overhead video, from a camera positioned 15m above and 15m behind the installation, was captured for qualitative and quantitative analysis. The display was positioned in an outdoor semi-pedestrianised walkway that had regular foot traffic throughout the day, as shown in Table 1.

Table 1. Total numbers for passers-by and users observed during each condition. Users are counted as all silhouettes captured by the depth camera. Users are broken down into more refined categories in Figure 10.

	Total Hours	Total Passers-by	Total Users
Baseline	20	6810	N/A
Steward Observer	4	1634	401 (25%)
Overt Observer	4	1769	378 (21%)
Covert Observer	4	2000	570 (29%)

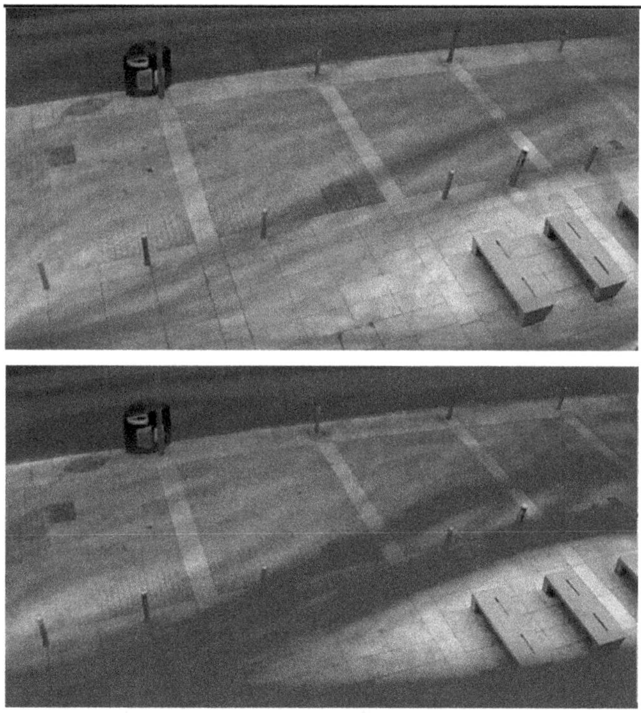

Figure 5. Baseline pedestrian motion in the space used for evaluation. Each blue line represents the motion of one pedestrian through the space [extracted automatically from video]. Top: Low traffic baseline, N=1993, Bottom: High traffic baseline, N=4817. Pedestrian routes are similar in both high and low traffic days.

[2] OpenNI - http://structure.io/openni

RESULTS

Data was collected in two separate weeks to capture "high" and "low" pedestrian traffic levels, as shown in Figure 4. Six hours of interaction data (two one-hour blocks per condition) and ten hours of baseline data were collected during a "low traffic" period (typical footfall) and six hours of interaction and ten hours of baseline data during a "high traffic" (a special event). The order of the condition (experimenter role) blocks was randomised, with the display installed during daytime hours between 10:00 and 18:00.

These results are based on a total twelve hours of interaction data (four one-hour blocks for each of the three conditions) and twenty hours of baseline pedestrian motion data (two ten hour blocks) gathered in the walkway. The baseline data was captured without any installation present.

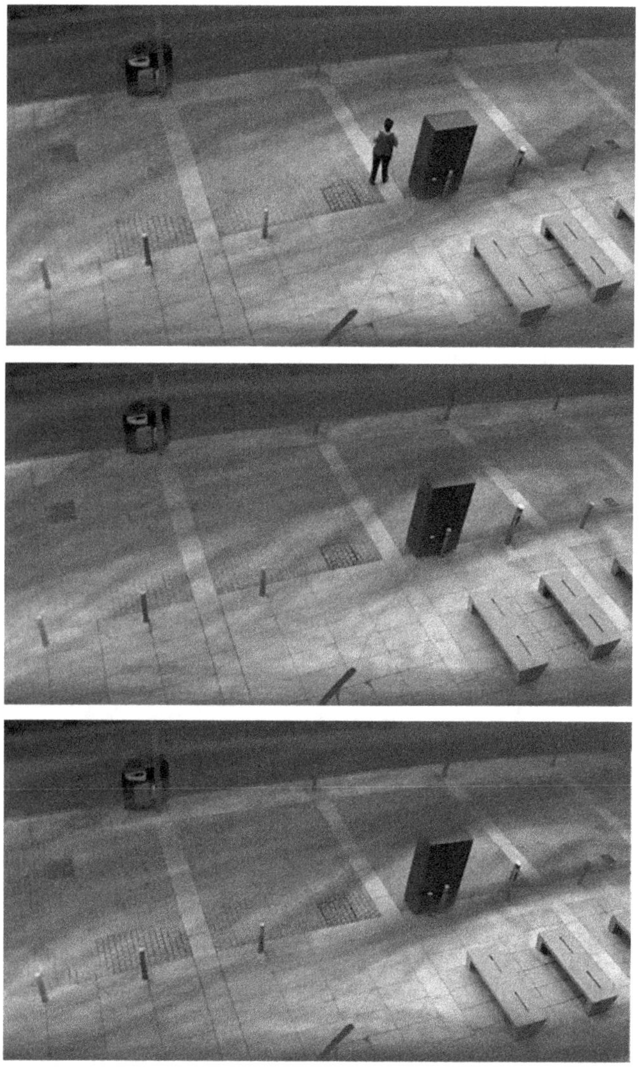

Figure 6. Pedestrian traffic for three evaluation conditions. Each blue line represents the motion of one pedestrian through the space [extracted automatically from video]. Top: Steward Observer, N= 1634, Middle: Overt Observer, N=1769, Bottom: Covert Observer, N=2000.

Figure 4 shows the footfall per hour during the baseline datasets and Figure 6 shows visualisations of the pedestrian traffic on the baseline days. Although footfall is roughly doubled during the high traffic period, patterns of routes between low and high traffic days are similar. Table 1 gives an overview of the raw data.

Pedestrian Traffic

The pedestrian data was generated using open source pedestrian tracking software [36]. Figure 6 visualises how the display disrupts the pedestrian traffic in the walkway, with many passers-by walking behind the display or giving a wider berth in front. In the baseline data in Figure 5, a common route runs through the walkway near the third bollard on the left, but this is dramatically reduced when the installation is present as passers-by swerve to avoid the display.

The area directly in front of the display where interaction can occur is still a busy thoroughfare. At peak times, interacting users would likely be "in the way" of others moving through the walkway. Many passers-by walked close enough to be captured by the depth camera but did not stop to interact and were unlikely to be aware they had even passed through the interactive zone. We further explore different "interaction styles" based on interaction duration and engagement with the activation gesture in the "Interaction Profiles" section of this paper.

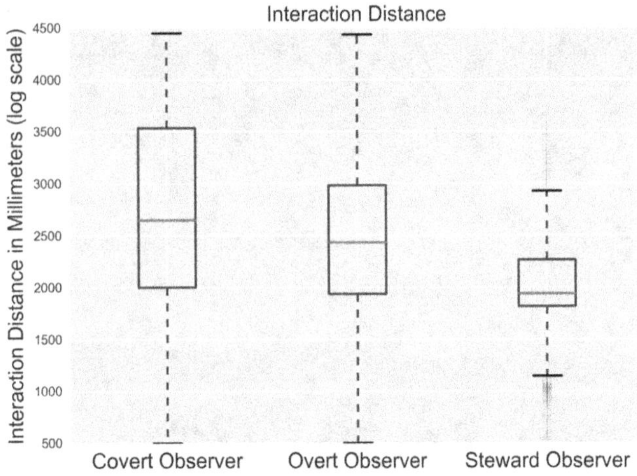

Figure 7: Average standing distance from the display for each condition in millimetres.

Pedestrian traffic was most disrupted in the steward observer condition, where passers-by clearly avoided the entire area around the experimenter. This disruption has ethical implications, as the intervention potentially made passers-by uncomfortable in the walkway. Such disruption also influenced non-interaction and participant self selection, potentially changing the kind of participants that would be attracted to the display.

Answering Q1 and Q2

For Q1, each condition resulted in different standing distances. Users' average standing distance was 2642 mm for covert, 2360 mm for overt, and 1966 mm for steward, as shown in Figure 7. Using a two-tailed t-test for this normally distributed data and Cohen's d for effect size, pairwise comparisons show that each condition is significantly different.

- covert-overt, $p<0.001$ and $d=0.3$
- covert-steward, $p<0.001$ and $d=0.8$
- overt-steward, $p<0.001$ and $d=0.5$

The different between covert and overt conditions has a medium effect size (>0.2), indicating these differences would be difficult to observe without statistical analysis. However, the differences between covert-steward and overt-steward conditions have a large effect size (>0.4), indicating these differences could be easily observed with the naked eye. The average difference spans over 650mm between covert and steward conditions, which covers a substantial different in a busy walkway.

These results demonstrate a significantly skewed result. For example, if the steward observer condition alone was used to determine how closely a gesture controlled display could safely be placed near a bicycle path, users would likely stand in the bicycle path during interaction based on the typical overt or covert interaction distances. In this case, the steward observer fails to provide results that reflect users' realistic behaviour.

Users in the steward condition were also much more uniform in their standing positions and interacted in a much smaller range of areas. The presence of the experimenter stabilised interaction and removed randomness in the data (for example from passers-by walking around interacting users during overt and covert observations). This stabilising effect removes some of the realism of that data and fails to capture the noise and bustle of the walkway.

For Q2, qualitative data indicated that users were worried about "blocking the walkway" which explains their closer standing distance to the display. This, however, did not reflect what people did in practice. Observation notes gathered during the covert and overt conditions indicate that user did not seem to worry about blocking others in the walkway, often positioning themselves in the centre of the thoroughfare. Figure 8 shows some examples of how people positioned themselves while interacting. Figure 9, top, shows a large group blocking a large section of the walkway while playing with the display. Figure 9, middle, shows a user making shadow puppets before calling over another user to show him the display. Figure 9 bottom, shows one user who repeatedly looked back at friends seated behind her while she interacted with the display.

Interview Data

One advantage to steward observation is the opportunity to gather qualitative feedback during on-the-street interviews. Although some users' feedback could have been derived from qualitative analysis of the overt or covert video logs, some insights could clearly only have been gathered through direct questioning.

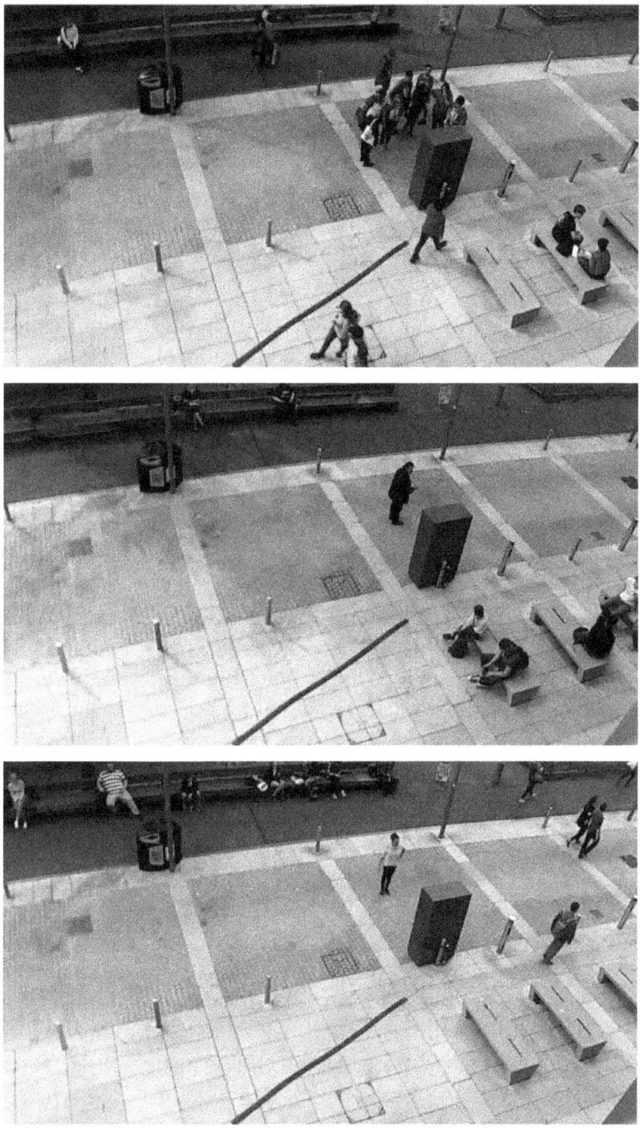

Figure 8. Users often interacted with the display in the centre of the walkway. Top: A large group blocks the majority of the walkway. Middle: Shadow puppets amuse a passer-by. Bottom: A user performs the gesture with an audience watching.

Participants discussed elements of the display's functionality, for example that it was possible to interact while encumbered and that multiple users could interact simultaneously. Participants also frequently mentioned that they would stand as close to the display as possible to prevent blocking the walkway (although as we have seen, they did not do this in practice). One passer-by mentioned that she was returning to the display after seeing it previously to show her daughter because it reminded her of something from her home city. Understanding how her previous experiences led her to interact with *Silly Hats Only* in multiple sessions could not have been understood from video analysis alone. Overall, participants stated that although the interactions were silly, they had no reservations about using the display in the crowded walkway. These themes are comparable to results from similar displays, such as *StrikeAPose* [33].

There were some practical issues with running the steward observer condition. This was the most laborious of the three conditions, requiring the experimenter to actively recruit participants and remain energetic for long periods of time while standing at the display. Three passers-by declined to participate after speaking to the experimenter. Of those who did agree to participate, several participants expressed some discomfort during the evaluation. For example, one participant said that "I don't know where we are going with this. I don't know what is the purpose of this." Recruiting people on-the-street has the potential to make user uncomfortable, either by refusing to participate or by participating when they really would rather not.

Interaction Profiles

Users of *Silly Hats Only* can be broken down into different "profiles" of use based on interaction duration and engagement with the activation gesture. Inspired by the Audience Funnel Framework [22] and proxemic interaction [31], we divided all users captured by the Kinect into four categories: *unaware, accidental, curious*, and *engaged*. Our categories are defined such that they can be automatically based on duration of visibility and number of interactions. The Audience Funnel Framework requires data about whether a user glances at the display, or returns after previous interaction. This could be possible in the near future, for example using more advanced skeleton tracking [28], but is not currently reliable using the OpenNI libraries that *Silly Hats Only* was dependent on.

Unaware users were visible for less than five seconds and did not perform the activation gesture. This represents users walking in front of the display without slowing. *Accidental* users were visible for less than five seconds but performed the activation gesture at least once. These users did not stop or slow to view the display and so the activation was likely accidental. *Curious* users were visible for five seconds or more but did not perform the activation gesture. Such users may have slowed to view the display or stopped completely, but failed to understand or notice the activation gesture. Finally, *engaged* users spent five seconds for more at the display and performed the activation gesture at least once.

Figure 9 shows users for each condition grouped in these four categories. By looking at the number of passers-by that convert to active users, the *conversion rate*, we can see significant differences. Using the N-1 Chi-Square test to compare *conversion rates*, there is a significant difference between the conversions rates for all three conditions.

- Overt-covert: $p<0.001$, 100% chance Covert has a higher conversion rate

- Steward-overt: $p<0.02$, 98% chance Steward has a higher conversion rate
- Steward-covert: $p<0.007$, 99% chance Covert has a higher conversion rate

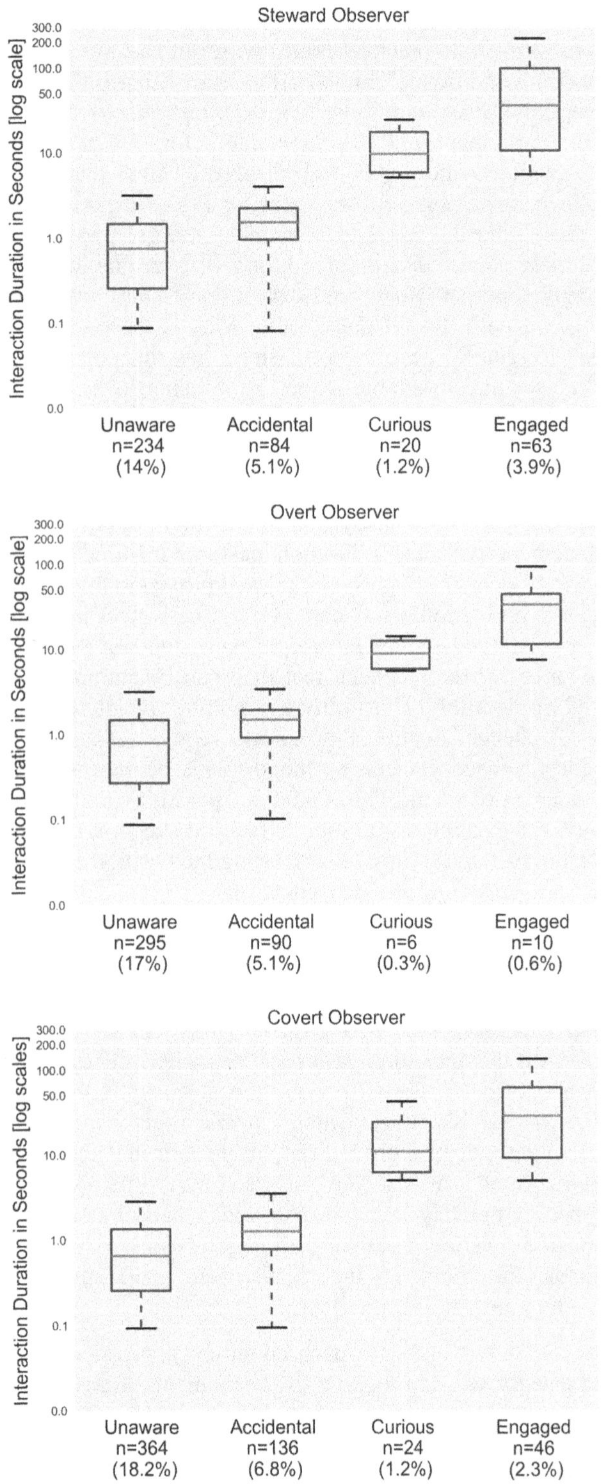

Figure 9. All users have been organised into four categories based on duration of visibility and number of interactions. Percentages show proportion of users out of total observed passers-by.

The most interesting results contrast the behaviour of *engaged* users between the overt and covert observer. The presence of the overt observer significantly influenced *conversation rate,* or the proportion of users that actively engaged with the display. In the Covert condition, 3.5% of passers-by engaged with or were curious of the display. In the Overt condition, this dropped dramatically to 0.9%. Overt observation also disturbed the actions of *curious* users. Users were less likely to explore the display for more than ten seconds if they could not discover how to interact, when they felt they were being observed.

DISCUSSION

Perhaps the most important result is the significantly lowered conversion rates (the proportion of all passers-by that end up spending five seconds or more at the display) when an overt observer is present. In this case, conversion rates dropped to below 1%, from 3.5% in the covert observer condition.

This raises the key question of which users are being driven away? Are they drawn from the same population as users who interacted, or does the observation systematically exclude certain kinds of users? In our experiment, overt observers were unable to effectively "camouflage" themselves, especially during the low traffic conditions when they especially stood out. Future investigation might consider these questions across a finer-grained spectrum of camouflage, with levels between fully overt and covert.

In the steward observer condition, we observed strong "stabilising" effects, leading to much more uniform interactions than when users were left to their own devices. For our case, these stabilising effects were severe enough that the experiment could no longer authentically capture real world usage. Although direct responses captured interesting anecdotes, it arguably did not add significantly to the results. Other experiments, which involve more nuanced interactions or depend more heavily on personal experience, may derive more value from this type of qualitative data.

Our approach lays the foundation for a systematic framework for evaluation observer roles and evaluation methods in public spaces by measuring pedestrian traffic. These results provide an empirical baseline that captures the most common approaches, but further conditions could expand this framework. For example, our study did not include a non-interactive display condition. Additionally, our system was relatively simplistic in its interaction and capabilities. Further research exploring non-interactive displays, non-functioning displays, and more complex displays would significantly expand our understanding of observer effects in a wider range of scenarios.

The significance and magnitude of the observer effects seen even in this simple and playful installation suggest that observation must be very carefully considered in public evaluation. However, in some cases unstewarded installation may not be practical or meaningful. For example, researchers may be integrated within the installation itself like in *humanaquarium* [29]. In this case, we would be interested in understanding if bias is introduced depending upon the experimenter's mindset; whether they view the installation as evaluation or a performance.

Public evaluations involve complicated and subtle ethical questions, which come to the forefront when there is direct contact between experimenter and (possibly unwitting) participant. In our stewarded condition, the refusal of consent by passers-by and potential discomfort of apparently consenting participants raises ethical questions. Does recruiting people from the street create negative experiences of the public space for some passers-by? Is this counterbalanced by the potential positive effect of an improved installation? Do researchers have a heavier responsibility in safeguarding the public from discomfort than other users of the space (street performers, work men, protesters)? The literature does not address users' reactions to being approached after interaction, but our steward condition suggests that this could potentially be a negative interaction, where an otherwise positive experience may be tinged with regret upon discovering they are part of an evaluation. How can that regret be addressed? Does mere deletion of an individual users' data really address the negative experience of a realisation of unwitting participation?

CONCLUSION

We completed an evaluation of a gesture controlled public display to quantify how experimenter roles distorted results. We used a playful gesture controlled display as a test-bed for different experimenter roles. Our evaluation cast the experimenter as a covert observer, overt observer, and steward observer. We treated the covert observation condition as the ground truth -- the closest approximation of an authentic experience -- capturing users' undisturbed behaviours and willing interactions. The results demonstrate that overt observation significantly reduced interaction rates and discouraged users from exploring the interaction if they initially failed to activate the display. While the active recruitment in the steward observer case maintained interaction rates, it influenced pedestrian movement and significantly altered user behaviour, resulting in artificially uniform interactions at an unnaturally close distance to the display. We propose that systematic control of experimenter roles in public evaluations, and the use of high-density, high-quality measurements like pedestrian tracking are essential in quantifying the observer effect in the fragile and unstable domain of public evaluations. This protocol gives qualitative researchers a way to bracket the authenticity of their results with quantitative, replicable metrics.

REFERENCES

1. Florian Alt, Stefan Schneegass, Albrecht Schmidt, Jörg Müller, and Nemanja Memarovic. 2012. How to evaluate public displays. *2012 International Symposium on Pervasive Displays (PerDis'12)*: #17.
2. Eric P. S. Baumer, Jenna Burrell, Morgan G. Ames, Jed R. Brubaker, and Paul Dourish. 2015. On the importance and implications of studying technology non-use. *Interactions* 22, 2: 52–56.
3. Marek Bell, Matthew Chalmers, Louise Barkhuus, Malcolm Hall, Scott Sherwood, Paul Tennent, Barry Brown, Duncan Rowland, and Steve Benford. 2006. Interweaving Mobile Games With Everyday Life. *Proceedings of the SIGCHI Conference on Human Factors in Computing Systems (CHI'06)*: 417–426.
4. Barry Brown, Stuart Reeves, and Scott Sherwood. 2011. Into the wild: Challenges and opportunities for field trial methods. *SIGCHI Conference on Human Factors in Computing Systems (CHI'11)*, May: 1657–1666.
5. Scott Carter, Jennifer Mankoff, Scott R. Klemmer, and Tara Matthews. 2008. Exiting the Cleanroom: On Ecological Validity and Ubiquitous Computing. *Human–Computer Interaction* 23, 1: 47–99.
6. Sandy Claes, Niels Wouters, Karin Slegers, and Andrew Vande Moere. 2015. Controlling In-the-Wild Evaluation Studies of Public Displays. In *Proceedings of the ACM CHI'15 Conference on Human Factors in Computing Systems*, 81–84.
7. A Crabtree and A Chamberlain. 2013. Introduction to the special issue of "The Turn to The Wild." *ACM Transactions on ...* 20, 3: 0–3.
8. Andy Crabtree. 2004. Design in the absence of practice: breaching experiments. *Proceedings of the 5th conference on Designing interactive systems: processes, practices, methods, and techniques*: 59–68.
9. Andy Crabtree. 2004. Taking technomethodology seriously: hybrid change in the ethnomethodology–design relationship. *European Journal of Information Systems* 13, October 2003: 195–209.
10. Paul Dourish. 2006. Implications for Design. *SIGCHI conference on Human Factors in computing systems.\n*: 541–550.
11. Elizabeth Evans, Martin Flintham, and Sarah Martindale. 2014. The Malthusian Paradox: performance in an alternate reality game. *Personal and Ubiquitous Computing* 18, 7: 1567–1582.

12. Dustin Freeman, Nathan LaPierre, Fanny Chevalier, and Derek Reilly. 2013. Tweetris. *Proceedings of the 9th ACM Conference on Creativity & Cognition - C&C '13*: 224.

13. Uta Hinrichs, Simon Butscher, Jens Müller, and Harald Reiterer. 2016. Diving in at the Deep End: The Value of Alternative In-Situ Approaches for Systematic Library Search. *Proceedings of the 2016 CHI Conference on Human Factors in Computing Systems*: 4634–4646.

14. Eva Hornecker and Emma Nicol. What Do Lab-based User Studies Tell Us About In-the-Wild Behavior ? Insights from a Study of Museum Interactives.

15. Rose Johnson, Yvonne Rogers, Janet van der Linden, and Nadia Bianchi-Berthouze. 2012. Being in the Thick of In-the-wild Studies: The Challenges and Insights of Researcher Participation. *Proceedings of the SIGCHI Conference on Human Factors in Computing Systems*: 1135–1144.

16. Jesper Kjeldskov and Mikael B Skov. 2014. Was it Worth the Hassle ? Ten Years of Mobile HCI Research Discussions on Lab and Field Evaluations. *Acm*: 43–52.

17. Jesper Kjeldskov, Mikael B Skov, Benedikte S Als, and Rune T Høegh. 2004. Is It Worth the Hassle ? Exploring the Added Value of Evaluating the Usability of Context-Aware Mobile Systems in the Field. *Mobile Human-Computer Interaction Proceedings of the 6th International Symposium*: 61–73.

18. Jean Lave, Lucy Suchman, and Ed Hutchins. 2013. Introduction to the Special Issue of " The Turn to The Wild ." 20, 3: 0–3.

19. P Marshall, Y Rogers, and N Pantidi. 2011. Using F-formations to analyse spatial patterns of interaction in physical environments. *Cscw 2011*, Cscw: 3033–3042.

20. Paul Marshall, Richard Morris, Yvonne Rogers, Stefan Kreitmayer, Matt Davies, and Milton Keynes. 2011. Rethinking " Multi-user ": An In-the-Wild Study of How Groups Approach a Walk-Up-and-Use Tabletop Interface. 3033–3042.

21. Paul Marshall, Richard Morris, Yvonne Rogers, Stefan Kreitmayer, and Matthew Davies. 2011. Rethinking "Multi-User" - An In-The-Wild Study of How Groups Approach a Walk-Up-and-Use Tabletop Interface. *Proceedings of the International Conference on Human Factors in Computing Systems (CHI'11)*: 3033–3042.

22. Daniel Michelis and Jörg Müller. 2011. The Audience Funnel: Observations of Gesture Based Interaction With Multiple Large Displays in a City Center. *International Journal of Human-Computer Interaction* 27, 6: 562–579.

23. Peter Peltonen, Esko Kurvinen, Antti Salovaara, Giulio Jacucci, Tommi Ilmonen, John Evans, Antti Oulasvirta, and Petri Saarikko. 2008. ``It's Mine, Don't Touch!'': Interactions at a Large Multi-Touch Display in a City Centre. *Proceeding of the twenty-sixth annual CHI conference on Human factors in computing systems - CHI '08*: 1285.

24. Derek Reilly, Fanny Chevalier, and Dustin Freeman. 2014. Blending Arts Event and HCI Research. In *Interactive Experience in the Digital Age: Evaluating New Art Practice*. 22–23.

25. Julie Rico and Stephen A. Brewster. 2010. Usable Gestures for Mobile Interfaces: Evaluating Social Acceptability. *Proceedings of the SIGCHI Conference on Human Factors in Computing Systems (CHI'10)*: 887–896.

26. Y Rogers. 2011. Interaction design gone wild: striving for wild theory. *Interactions* 18, 4: 58–62.

27. Yvonne Rogers, Kay Connelly, Lenore Tedesco, William Hazlewood, Andrew Kurtz, Robert E. Hall, Josh Hursey, and Tammy Toscos. 2007. Why It's Worth the Hassle - The Value of In-Situ Studies When Designing Ubicomp. *UbiComp'07* 4717: 336–353.

28. Jiamin Shi and Florian Alt. 2016. The Anonymous Audience Analyzer – Visualizing Audience Behavior in Public Space. *CHI Extended Abstracts on Human Factors in Computing Systems*: 3766–3769.

29. Robyn Taylor, Guy Schofield, John Shearer, Jayne Wallace, Peter Wright, Pierre Boulanger, and Patrick Olivier. 2011. Designing from within: humanaquarium. *Proceedings of CHI 2011*: 1855–1864.

30. Robyn Taylor, Guy Schofield, John Shearer, Peter Wright, Pierre Boulanger, and Patrick Olivier. 2014. Nightingallery: theatrical framing and orchestration in participatory performance. *Personal and Ubiquitous Computing* 18, 7: 1583–1600.

31. Daniel Vogel and Ravin Balakrishnan. 2004. Interactive Public Ambient Displays: Transitioning from Implicit to Explicit, Public to Personal, Interaction with Multiple Users. *UIST '04: Proceedings of the 17th annual ACM symposium on User interface software and technology* 6, 2: 137–146.

32. Annika Waern. 2016. The Ethics of Unaware Participation in Public Interventions. *Proceedings of the 2016 CHI Conference on Human Factors in Computing Systems*: 803–814.

33. Robert Walter, Gilles Bailly, and Jörg Müller. 2013. StrikeAPose: revealing mid-air gestures on public displays. In *SIGCHI Conference on Human Factors in Computing Systems (CHI'13)*, 841–850.

34. Julie R. Williamson and Daniel Sundén. 2015. Deep Cover HCI. *Proceedings of the 33rd Annual ACM Conference Extended Abstracts on Human Factors in Computing Systems - CHI EA '15*: 543–554.

35. Julie R. Williamson, Daniel Sundén, and Jay Bradley. 2015. GlobalFestival: Evaluating Real World Interaction on a Spherical Display. *Proceedings of the Joint International Conference on Pervasive and Ubiquitous Computing and the International Symposium on Wearable Computers (Ubicomp/ISWC'15)*: 1251–1261.

36. Julie R. Williamson and John Williamson. 2014. Analysing Pedestrian Traffic Around Public Displays. In *Proceedings of The International Symposium on Pervasive Displays - PerDis '14*, 13–18.

Challenges in Public Display Deployments: A Taxonomy of External Factors

Ville Mäkelä[1], Sumita Sharma[1], Jaakko Hakulinen[1], Tomi Heimonen[2], Markku Turunen[1]
[1]University of Tampere, Tampere, Finland
[2]University of Wisconsin - Stevens Point, Wisconsin, USA
{ville.mi.makela, sumita.s.sharma, jaakko.hakulinen, markku.turunen}@sis.uta.fi,
tomi.heimonen@uwsp.edu

ABSTRACT
Public display deployments are often subjected to various surprising and unwanted effects. These effects are frequently due to *external factors* – properties and phenomena that are unrelated to the deployment. Therefore, we conducted a literature review within the public display domain to investigate the causes behind the reported issues. This work presents a taxonomy of external factors affecting deployments, consisting of six categories: *weather*, *events*, *surroundings*, *space*, *inhabitants*, and *vandalism*. Apart from a few positive examples, we predominantly found negative effects arising from these factors. We then identified four ways of addressing the effects: *ignoring*, *adapting, solving*, and *embracing*. Of these, ignoring and adapting are substantially more frequent responses than solving and embracing – emphasizing the need for researchers to adapt. We present real-world examples and insights on how researchers and practitioners can address the effects to better manage their deployments.

Author Keywords
Public displays; pervasive displays; challenges; taxonomy; external factors; deployments; literature review.

ACM Classification Keywords
H.5.m. Information interfaces and presentation (e.g., HCI): Miscellaneous.

INTRODUCTION
Public displays are actively deployed and studied in various contexts, from shopping and transportation to entertainment. Much of the current focus in public display research is on understanding user behavior and interaction, and on models describing the dynamics of users [10,23,47, 49,69] and the components of the deployment [46]. Although public display applications presented in prior research generally appear to be successful, researchers often experience various surprising challenges.

Permission to make digital or hard copies of all or part of this work for personal or classroom use is granted without fee provided that copies are not made or distributed for profit or commercial advantage and that copies bear this notice and the full citation on the first page. Copyrights for components of this work owned by others than ACM must be honored. Abstracting with credit is permitted. To copy otherwise, or republish, to post on servers or to redistribute to lists, requires prior specific permission and/or a fee. Request permissions from Permissions@acm.org.
CHI 2017, May 06-11, 2017, Denver, CO, USA
© 2017 ACM. ISBN 978-1-4503-4655-9/17/05…$15.00
DOI: http://dx.doi.org/10.1145/3025453.3025798

Some past works provide retrospective guidelines based on subjective experiences with various challenges in public deployments [19,31,62]. However, a large segment of articles describing public deployments are less explicit in their reporting of these challenges. This is in part because the challenges faced are not necessarily vital to the research questions - or the "take-away message" - of their studies. Any experienced challenges are typically mentioned very briefly, for example, to explain why certain research approaches were not possible, or to provide rationale for sub-optimal design decisions that had to be made.

The work presented in this paper is based on the realization that many of these challenges (or *effects*) are due to *external factors*, i.e., they are caused by properties and phenomena that are unrelated to the deployment. The motivation for this work stems from our own experiences with various public display deployments in which we have encountered surprising issues due to external factors that have been difficult to identify and control. We believe there is now enough collective experience within the pervasive display community to shed light on the extent and type of challenges caused by external factors. This led us to conduct a literature review of reported issues to better understand their role in public display deployments. To our knowledge, we are the first to approach challenges with public display deployments from this perspective. This work addresses the following research questions:

- **RQ1:** Which types of external factors affect public deployments?
- **RQ2:** How do researchers react to the effects of external factors?

We identified and collected a set of 61 issues with public deployments caused by external factors (10 issues from our own experiences, and 51 from the literature). Then, using affinity diagramming, we categorized both the causes for the issues as well as the researchers' reactions to the issues. In addressing RQ1, we identified six categories of external factors: *weather, events, surroundings, place, inhabitants*, and *vandalism*. In addressing RQ2, we identified that researchers' reaction to these issues can be categorized as: *embracing*, *solving*, *ignoring*, and *adapting*. We found that ignoring (39%) and adapting to (39%.) issues are much more prominent than solving (13%) and embracing (8%).

The experienced issues are rarely fully solved during deployments, which we believe is because external factors are difficult or impossible to control, and their effects are often surprising. Hence, researchers must instead be prepared to adapt to such situations by adjusting the properties of the deployment. The infrequency of embracing, on the other hand, shows that such effects are most often negative, and are difficult to take advantage of. Both conclusions show the importance of recognizing external factors, and being prepared to address them.

By building on the collective experiences of the HCI community working within the public deployments domain, we provide a taxonomy of external factors. We highlight examples of each type of external factors, and provide guidelines for identifying potential factors that could affect their deployments, and describe common approaches for tackling these issues.

The paper is organized as follows. We first discuss the methodology, in which we describe the deployments from which we draw our real-world experiences, and the literature review, and the process of creating the taxonomy of external factors. Following, we present each category of external factors in detail and discuss approaches for addressing each of them. Finally, we discuss the significance of our findings.

METHODOLOGY

To systematically investigate external factors with public deployments, we gathered issues caused by external factors from our own experiences as well as from existing literature, and categorized the found issues using the affinity diagramming approach.

We only included issues wherein a clear external cause could be identified. Therefore, we did not account for internal issues, that is, issues arising from the deployment itself, due to e.g., poor design solutions.

Case Deployments

We first gathered issues from two of our own deployments. Since our focus in this paper is on external factors, and not on interaction with the installations, we present the deployments only briefly, primarily describing the deployment locations.

The *Information Wall* is a gesture-controlled public information display. We implemented two different versions, however in both versions, users navigate location-relevant content, such as local events and lunch menus of nearby cafeterias, by using mid-air gestures in front of the display (Figure 1 – B and C). The first Information Wall was deployed at a university campus for one year, from April 2013 to April 2014. The next version was deployed in the same location with identical equipment from October 2014 to April 2015. The deployment setting (Figure 1A) is a large, open space with a high volume of pedestrian traffic. It contains two major landmarks: a cafeteria that students, staff and visitors regularly use, and a large auditorium with several hundred seats. Information Wall was conveniently projected on a wall roughly between these two landmarks with a ceiling-mounted full HD projector.

The second deployment, *EnergyLand*, is a gesture-based system for initiating conversations on novel energy-efficient solutions for smart homes. Users interact with virtual objects in game-like tasks to understand ways to incorporate green energy practices inside their homes (Figure 1D). EnergyLand was a part of a Smart House installation at an annual Finnish housing fair in summer

Figure 1. Public displays and their locations. A) Panorama of the deployment location for Information Wall from the installation's perspective. Cafeteria on the far left, auditorium on the far right. B) Information Wall. C) Information Wall 2. D) EnergyLand. E) The deployment location for EnergyLand at a housing fair. The installation is at the far back of the room.

2012 (Figure 1E). EnergyLand was installed in a 7 by 5 meter rectangular area inside a large 400 square meter Smart House tent. EnergyLand consisted of three large interactive screens arranged along the length of a wall and three poles on the opposite wall held a projector each, one for each screen. Microsoft Kinect sensors were used for gesture recognition, and a computer/laptop was placed under each screen. Two sets of speaker arrays were placed above the left and right screens, and a 5.1 channel speaker system under the center screen and under the projectors.

From these two deployments, we gathered a total of 10 issues that were caused by external factors. We will describe these issues later in the paper, when we present the taxonomy of external factors.

Literature Review

For the literature review, we gathered a collection of papers using snowball sampling. First, we included papers that we were already familiar with due to our work on the field, such as those by Ojala et al. [54], Alt et al. [6], and Müller et al. [49,52]. Then, we reviewed the references in these papers, and added cited papers to the collection based on their title, or what was said about them in the citing paper. Following, we used Google Scholar to look for additional papers citing the papers already in the collection, and added papers based on the title and abstract. With this method, we gathered a collection of 132 papers. Of these, we further identified those that presented an in-the-wild public display deployment, or challenges or lessons learned regarding such, or discussed user behavior around public displays. This resulted in the final collection of 71 publications that were used in the literature review.

Two researchers carefully reviewed the 71 publications and noted down every issue, challenge, or observation that was attributable to an external factor. We found a total of 51 issues from 22 publications (several papers reported more than one issue). The 71 reviewed publications are listed in the references of this paper, with the 22 papers that were part of the taxonomy marked with an asterisk.

The fact that most reviewed papers did not report any issues suggests that a large segment of experienced issues within the HCI community may go unreported. Furthermore, as noted earlier, such issues are rarely the focus of research papers. Rather, we specifically had to look for them within the fine details of the papers – for example, issues were often only briefly mentioned to explain why certain study decisions were made.

Outcome

The final data set consisted of 61 issues, including 10 issues from our own deployments and 51 issues from the literature. Issues from both sources were treated equally during the process, i.e., no special emphasis was put on our own experiences. Therefore, our own experiences formed a ~16% contribution to RQ1 and RQ2.

To address RQ1, we utilized affinity diagramming to categorize the findings. The process was conducted by three researchers – the two researchers who conducted the literature review, and a third researcher for a fresh perspective. We considered that the process was complete when a *consensus* was reached, that is, when all three researchers agreed with every issue and the category they were assigned to. This resulted in six categories: *weather*, *events*, *surroundings*, *space*, *inhabitants*, and *vandalism*, which will be discussed in detail in the next chapter.

As a second layer of analysis (RQ2), we considered the strategies researchers used to deal with the observed issues, and identified four categories of responses. *Ignoring* means doing nothing to address or control the observed effect. *Adapting* means either changing some property of the deployment that introduces a trade-off (a suboptimal solution), or addressing the effect once while not ensuring that the same effect will not happen again. *Solving* refers to a permanent solution that either eliminates the original cause, or changes some property of the deployment to eliminate the effect, without introducing a trade-off. Finally, *embracing* means taking advantage of the observed effect, to turn the negative into positive.

EXTERNAL FACTORS IN PUBLIC DEPLOYMENTS

Our taxonomy of external factors consists of *weather*, *events*, *surroundings*, *space*, *inhabitants*, and *vandalism*. In this chapter, we present each category in detail, and discuss how to recognize and deal with these factors All sources that contributed towards this taxonomy are presented in Table 1.

The distribution of issues per cause and reaction are presented in Figure 2. Of the 61 issues, 39% were *ignored*, while 39% were *adapted* to. Only 13% of the issues were *solved*, and 8% were *embraced*. In this section, we will also provide examples of how researchers dealt with the experienced issues with respect to these reaction types.

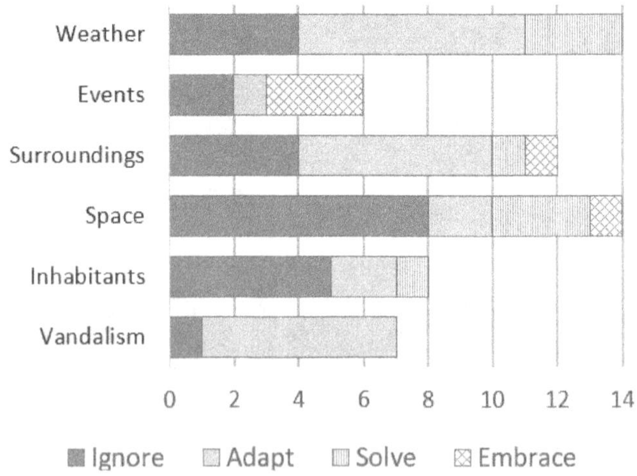

Figure 2. Distribution of issues per cause and reaction.

	Ignored	Adapted	Solved	Embraced
Weather	**EnergyLand** Ojala et al. [54] x 2 Valkanova et al. [68]	**EnergyLand** Ackad et al. [2] x 2 Ackad et al. [3] Harris et al. [31] x 2 Fischer & Hornecker [25]	**EnergyLand** Dalsgaard & Halskov [19] Harris et al. [31]	
Events	**Information Wall** O'Hara et al. [53]	O'Hara et al. [53]		Schroeter et al. [60] Akpan et al. [4] Finke et al. [23]
Surroundings	Ackad et al. [2], Storz et al. [62] Dalsgaard & Halskov [19] Fischer et al. [24]	Harris et al. [31] x 4 Storz et al. [62] Memarovic et al. [46]	Harris et al. [31]	Tomitsch et al. [67]
Space	Schroeter et al. [60] x 2 Fischer et al. [24] Churchill et al. [17], Kukka et al. [44] Peltonen et al. [57], Müller et al. [51] Fischer & Hornecker [25]	**EnergyLand** Fischer & Hornecker [25]	Müller et al. [52] Fischer et al. [24] Fischer & Hornecker [25]	Cao et al. [13]
Inhabitants	**Information Wall** x 2 Storz et al. [62] Dalsgaard & Halskov [19] x 2	**Information Wall** x 2	**Information Wall**	
Vandalism	Taylor et al. [65]	Dalsgaard & Halskov [19] x 4 Heikkinen et al. [33] Müller et al. [51]		

Table 1. Summary of reported challenges that contributed to the taxonomy, divided by cause and reaction.

Weather

Weather is a diverse, unstable and unpredictable phenomenon, and can affect both indoor and outdoor public deployments in various ways. We found that the primary causes for issues in the *weather* category are sunlight, rain, temperature, and humidity.

Reported Causes

Sunlight has caused issues especially with display visibility and sensor performance. In our Energyland installation, even though the installation was located inside a large, completely covered tent, the sunlight was bright enough to penetrate the tent's fabric and interfere with the Kinect sensors, which rendered the system unusable. We solved the problem by hanging thick, dark black curtains above our installation (Figure 3) to improve the gesture recognition.

Ackad et al. [2] also reported two issues with sunlight with their outdoor gesture-controlled display. Sunlight interfered with the sensors, as well as hindered the visibility of screen content. They adapted to the issues by only running the system from 6 pm until midnight, when sunlight no longer hit the deployment space. Similarly, Fischer and Hornecker [25] only ran their media façade system after dusk, since the projections were not visible enough in daylight. Harris et al. [31] reported varying visibility with their screen in an outdoor setting, and added hoods to the screens to minimize the effect from external lighting. Likewise, Ojala et al. [54] report low visibility with their UBI-hotspots in direct sunlight, however this issue was ignored.

Figure 3. Curtains hung above the EnergyLand installation to prevent issues with sunlight.

Rain resulted in serious issues with our EnergyLand installation near the end of the fair when a rain storm soaked parts of the floor and destroyed the computer running the system and one of the speakers. While the computer was quickly replaced with another unit, we were unable to replace the speakers within the available time frame. Hence, visitors had to experience the system without a soundscape for the remainder of the fair.

Harris et al. [31] had issues with rain and other harmful weather conditions with their deployment that was setup in the woods. They needed to keep an eye on the weather forecast at all times. To offer some protection for the equipment, polythene bags were used. A back-up procedure was to simply not run the setup on very rainy days. Dalsgaard and Halskov [19] reported an interesting effect from rain on their motion-tracking media façade installation. Reflections from puddles after rainfall were incorrectly identified as people by the sensor. This was eventually solved when colorful carpets were installed to more clearly mark the interaction areas.

More general-purpose weather effects were reported in several papers. A pilot study of a public voting installation by Valkanova et al. [68] suffered from unpleasant weather conditions (rain, wind, cold) that resulted in fewer users (and interviewees), as most passersby were not motivated to stay outdoors. Ackad et al. [3] studied user behavior on an outdoor installation, and had to schedule their studies based on weather conditions. Ojala et al. [54] noticed that winter months affected the UBI-hotspot usage as their capacitive touch screen foils did not respond to gloves. During the deployment of their setup in the woods, Harris et al. [25] noticed that high levels of humidity will attenuate radio waves, which they needed to tune on the spot.

Recommendations

The effects of *weather* can range from screen visibility issues to destruction of equipment. Since weather cannot be controlled, researchers must be aware of its potential effects and be ready to adapt. Representative examples of such adaptations are those by Ackad et al. [2] and Fischer and Hornecker [25], wherein the deployment was run only during evenings to avoid sunlight issues. However, while they could work around the issue by decreasing the deployment time, this workaround is far from optimal.

Weather can also have positive effects. Ojala et al. [55] found that sunny and warm days result in more users as well as increased interaction times, and interestingly, this phenomenon was also observed in indoor locations. This is likely because even for indoor activities, people still need to go out and move to the location – and they may be encouraged to do so by the nice weather.

We present the following considerations:

- Consider the effects of sunlight on the deployment: sunlight affects screen visibility as well as the performance of many motion tracking sensors.
- Cover sensitive hardware. Rain and humidity can cause surprising issues even in seemingly well covered environments.
- Consider how weather conditions affect people. Warm and sunny weather can result in more interactions and increased interaction times, even for indoor locations [55]. Inclement weather, such as cold and wind, decreases the number of people outside and their willingness to interact [68].

Events

As one category, we consider *events*, such as festivals, that temporarily (but significantly) alter the characteristics of the deployment space or its surroundings, hence affecting the installation.

Reported Causes

With our Information Wall installation, we observed issues caused by an event for the elderly that was held in the nearby auditorium and the adjacent lecture rooms. Despite the large, open deployment space, it became unusually full when hundreds of people poured out of the rooms. Some noticed the display and came to investigate, and some tried interacting with it. However, other people constantly disrupted the interaction (and observation) by moving past the display between the users and the sensor, effectively blocking both the sensor and the screen. We also observed some discomfort from the users, as they ultimately felt they were in the way of others when interacting. These observations did not lead to any action on our part, as there were no easy solutions available.

O'Hara et al. [53] reported that a temporary outdoor urban beach was installed in front of the large BBC screen in Birmingham. Because the BBC screen required users to execute large physical movements, and because the beach installation expected crowds, this was a safety hazard. To overcome this, barriers were erected around the active gameplay area to keep the crowds safely separated, and a professional speaker was also introduced to help manage the crowd and gameplay, which increased financial costs.

Some positive effects due to events have also been reported. A deployment by Finke et al. [23] was surrounded by tables, chairs and a coffee bar. At the end of the student semester, more chairs and tables were brought into the deployment space to offer students sufficient room to prepare for their final exams. This resulted in a larger audience and more interactions with the system. In addition, Akpan et al. [4] reported that a party held at the premises in which their interactive Shadow Wall was installed resulted in a much higher amount of interactions as well as longer durations of interactions, as the party transformed the configuration of the space to a more relaxed one. O'Hara et al. [53] also mention that the above-mentioned temporary beach somewhat changed the nature of the space, as people who were interviewed mentioned that they came to the place to rest, take a break, wait, sit or socialize.

A general observation of the effects of events was made by Schroeter et al. [60] who noted that events change the demographic in the area. For instance, they state that on normal days, people around public displays can be "broad and diverse in terms of their interests". However, during events, usually a more specific crowd is present. Thus, the effect of events can be embraced, for example by focusing the content of the display towards this specific group.

Recommendations
Events typically have two effects. First, they alter the social setting of the space. For instance, O'Hara et al. [53] and Akpan et al. [4] experienced a positive effect, as an event resulted in a more favorable, relaxed setting. Second, events affect crowds and people flow. Events often equal to higher amounts of people, which can lead to security risks and interference with interaction, but can also lead to positive effects, such as an increased number of users. We derive three practical considerations from the reported issues:

- Stay aware of the magnitude and nature of upcoming events in the area. Events affect the social setting, demographics, and the amount of people.
- The deployment should be robust enough to handle interference caused by crowds, even if such crowds are not normally present. For instance, people in the background should not prevent others from interacting.
- It is possible to turn events to one's advantage, by tailoring the content of the deployment to serve the participants of the event. Events tend to bring in more users and foster interaction in general.

Surroundings
As the third category, we consider *surroundings*, which refers to areas and their persistent characteristics surrounding the deployment space. This includes nearby buildings, their functions, and traffic. Research on public deployments has focused extensively on the effects of immediate surroundings near a display, such as people flow and its subsequent interaction effects. However, several issues reported in literature point towards the effects of buildings and artifacts surrounding the area of deployment, from which the display or installation is likely not visible.

Reported Causes
Tomitsch et al. [67] report a higher flow of people before and after a show in the theater, adjacent to their installation, and how the nature of each show would affect the demographic of people in the area. For Fischer et al. [24], the day-time pedestrian traffic near their installations was dominated by students from a nearby university and at night by visitors to a nearby theater. Ackad et al. [2] further note that due to an adjacent theater near their installation, passersby often had limited time to interact, as they were on their way to see a show. Yet contrary to *events*, the functions of the surroundings are perennial. Therefore, public displays should be designed to account for the effects of surroundings, for example by designing content that serves the theater visitors [1,2].

Surroundings can also impact the deployment's hardware. Storz et al. [62] had an installation that was in a tunnel under a heavily trafficked street. Diesel exhaust continuously interfered with their equipment, for example by clogging the projector filters used in the installation, despite custom-built cases, housings, and other prior preparations. Furthermore, maintaining the hardware required closing the road, which was especially difficult during high traffic periods such as university semesters. For Harris et al. [31], their setup in the woods needed to be disassembled on a daily basis to prevent moisture deposits from accumulating on electrical boards. Dalsgaard and Halskov [19] reported windows across the street from their installation causing reflections, which were incorrectly interpreted as people by their motion-controlled system.

Moreover, surroundings can create adverse deployment conditions, including lack of electricity or unreliable network connectivity. Harris et al. [31] had no access to electricity for their deployment that was set up in the woods. Generators were not an option due to noise and running cables to each device would have been impractical. They adapted to the issue by using batteries and low-power devices where possible. Further, trees blocked GPS signals and radio frequencies. This was solved by adding three booster antennas for their own network. Due to the dynamic and unstable nature of woods and similar areas, the ground can change from hard to soft and shift unexpectedly. Solutions included placing network access points to trees and adding base plates to the ground where required. Issues with network connectivity within the deployment location were solved by Memarovic et al. [46] by connecting wireless receivers from the rooftops of local houses to the installation. It was also important to make at least a part of the content available offline in case of network issues.

Recommendations
Understanding the functions of surroundings, for example nearby buildings, traffic conditions and vegetation, provides a better understanding of the potential user demographics and technical limitations. We present three considerations:

- Identify key locations in the surrounding areas, such as theaters and malls, as they provide further insight for times of day with large crowds and specific demographics.
- Consider the possibility of designing for these locations. Ackad et al. [1,2] tailored the content of their public display to serve the visitors to a nearby theater. Ideally one should take this into account a priori in the fundamental design decisions of the deployment.
- Technical limitations need to be studied before the deployment to accommodate network failures, power issues, and other potential factors that may interfere with the equipment.

Factors in *surroundings* may have similar effects as those in the *events* category, such as increased people flow; however, the differentiation is based on the prevalence of cause. Properties of the *surroundings* are permanent, and cannot be made to go away without architectural interventions.

Space
We consider *space* as the physical attributes of the deployment area, whereas with the previously discussed *surroundings* category we refer to areas outside of the

deployment area. With *space*, we follow the definition of Harrison and Dourish [32]: space is the actual physical structure of a "three-dimensional environment in which objects and events occur". A space is made a place by its inhabitants [32]; therefore, place is the social and cultural construct within a physical space. Issues arising due to inhabitants of a space are discussed later in the *inhabitants* category. Here, we report issues that were caused by properties of the deployment space.

Reported Causes

In EnergyLand, we had access to the floorplan of the tent and used it to define the installation layout. However, a few days before the deployment, the location managers informed us that details provided of the space were incorrect – there was a double wall structure inside the tent and the thickness of the wall was not provided. We had to adapt by setting the first and third display at an angle (Figure 3), when originally all displays were supposed to be parallel to the wall. Although such a small change may seem trivial, studies have shown that display orientation can have a significant effect on the dynamics of the installation [41]. Moreover, the angles made the interaction spaces for each display somewhat overlap. Fischer and Hornecker [25] also report discrepancies between their initial plan for a media façade installation and the actual physical properties of the façade, and they had to adjust accordingly.

Schroeter et al. [60] note that due to their installation's size and positioning amongst other booths at their deployment location, the visibility of their display was limited. For Fischer et al. [24], a railway track ran across their installation space, with the media façade being on one side of the tracks and the interactive controller device on the other. This prevented them from connecting their system with a network cable, and regular Wi-Fi was not an option due to electrical interference from the trams. A solution was found in the form of a GSM USB adapter. In another case, Fischer and Hornecker [25] had to cover the illumination of an entrance to an underground parking space, as it interfered with their media façade. Müller et al. [52] reported that after moving the installation to a different space, patches on the floor would be recognized by system as users while actual far away users were not. Both issues were solved by moving the camera to floor level.

For Müller et al. [51], nearby elevators influenced the use of their public display installation as people would often interact with the system while they waited but abruptly stop when the elevator arrived. In CityWall [57], people waited out the rain under the sun shade on the installation window without even realizing that it is interactive. Furthermore, Fischer et al. [24] state that their installation was jammed when around 70 people suddenly came out of a bus from a stop nearby. Churchill et al. [17] noted that by installing a display in a foyer with a T-junction, people moving in the space were colliding with those interacting with the display. Kukka et al. [44] noted that one of their displays was sandwiched between two bulletin boards, located in a busy walkway opening to a cafeteria. Instead of making the display more noticeable, this instigated display avoidance.

However, not all space dynamics are perceived as being negative by researchers. An installation by Cao et al. [13] was located at a public university atrium, which had open seating, a café nearby, and access to classrooms. This resulted in increased traffic, especially when classes were ending or starting. This was desirable for the researchers as it promoted the usage of their installation. Moreover, Fischer and Hornecker [25] found that the built environment, such as pillars and trees, can create "comfort spaces" wherein people can comfortably observe the installation. While Fischer and Hornecker [25] also note that these comfort spaces might "interfere with designers' intentions of achieving a certain situation in a given setting", we note that they also encourage people to engage with the installation, as people can first observe how it works without being "out in the open".

Recommendations

Researchers must study and understand the functions of the space, comparable to the previously presented *surroundings* category. A somewhat similar approach was utilized by Müller et al. [50] when designing interactive displays for shop windows, as they observed the deployment space with regards to people flow and passersby attention, to identify the most suitable windows for the displays. However, we emphasize the focus on identifying *external factors*. We present the following considerations:

- Observe the physical characteristics of the space, including the layout, placement of doorways, pillars, elevators, machinery, and other displays and installations. Further, identify how said characteristics affect people flow and the use of the space.
- Identify permanent structures, such as pillars and other objects, within the layout that can potentially create "comfort spaces" for the users. Fischer and Hornecker [25] found that these spaces allow people to comfortably observe the installation.

By knowing the physical characteristics of the space, one can predict some of the effects on the deployment. Once there is a clear understanding of the space, researchers can begin to map out the use of the space by its *inhabitants*.

Inhabitants

Deployment spaces, as well as the surrounding areas, are usually filled with a multitude of people, each with varying roles. While current pervasive display research largely investigates people as passersby, i.e., potential users, with the term *inhabitants* we consider their usual, day-to-day roles within the space, such as students, janitorial staff, security guards, and store owners.

For clarification, stakeholders are not part of the *inhabitants* category, as stakeholders are an internal part of the deployment project, and are therefore not an external factor.

It is notable, however, that the same person can be both - the key is the *role* the person is acting on. For instance, location managers can be stakeholders, and the actions they undertake *as stakeholders* would not be considered an external factor, however they would still be inhabitants in their usual roles as location managers. For further reading on stakeholders, we refer to Elhart et al. [22] and Hosio et al. [34].

Reported Causes

With our Information Wall installation at a university campus, security guards kept turning off the projector at night. We were unaware of this for a long time, but eventually found out when we asked the local managers to investigate if the projector was faulty. One of the managers contacted the security guards to ask if they, by any chance, are turning the screen off during their nightly rounds. Indeed, the guards were turning off the projector because they assumed that it should not be on during the night. The real cause was surprising, as we were at no point in contact with the guards. In fact, we never even *saw* the guards.

We also experienced various other surprises regarding local inhabitants. The large, open deployment space is occasionally used to set up temporary stands. For instance, members of student organizations occasionally set up stands to sell tickets to parties, and members of various clubs set up stands to promote their club and recruit new members. We experienced several occurrences wherein the stands had been set up so that they obstructed the use of our installation, or at the very least made interacting uncomfortable, even though there was plenty of room in the space for the stands to be positioned elsewhere.

Sometimes we found furniture or other equipment temporarily positioned so that they obstructed or hindered the use of Information Wall. Some of these were presumably left behind from the above-mentioned stands when they were taken down. Each time, we simply moved the furniture slightly to ease the situation, but left the furniture to be cleaned up by the people responsible for them. Additionally, we observed two occasions where a janitor's cart was positioned partly in front of the installation – but the janitor was nowhere in sight. We took no action to address the issue, however we would have sought out the janitors if the issue had been more frequent.

Another interesting occurrence happened with local students. As part of the Information Wall, a cupboard (which contained the PC running the system) was placed underneath the screen, and the Kinect sensor was placed on top of the cupboard. Once, we found that the nearby coat hanger was (almost) full, so a group of people had left their jackets on top of the cupboard, completely covering the Kinect, which prevented the system from being used.

Dalsgaard and Halskov [19] installed a webcam-enabled public display behind the windows in the grocery section of a local department store. A local manager lowered sun-blinds in some of the windows, preventing the webcam from seeing passersby. Storz et al. [62] discuss that in one of their deployment locations, local managers tested the fire alarms weekly, during which time the power was cut off from the deployment space.

Recommendations

An important insight arises from the *inhabitants* category. Inhabitants are unrelated to the deployment - none of the reported issues involved intentional interference with the deployment (perhaps apart from the guards, however it was not their *intention* to disrupt the deployment). Rather, issues arising from this category are primarily due to inhabitants conducting their usual, everyday routines, and the deployment is simply in the way. From the inhabitants' perspective, it could be argued that it is the deployment that is invading *their* space.

To further enable communication with the inhabitants, a practical suggestion is to add background and contact information near the installation in case the inhabitants have issues or questions. With our Information Wall installation, we received a request by staff from another school to add temporary content about an upcoming event to our installation. In the absence of contact information near the display, these people had to go through multiple channels to finally ascertain who to contact about the display.

For *inhabitants*, we present the following considerations:

- Observe and identify different groups of inhabitants, and further aim to identify their routines and tasks in the space. Then, analyze how these routines and tasks could interfere with the deployment, and adjust the design accordingly.
- Consider engaging in a discussion with the inhabitants, and informing them of the deployment and its purpose, particularly if the deployment is likely to interfere with their normal routines.
- Consider adding contact details near the deployment.

Vandalism

With *vandalism*, we primarily refer to intentional interference with the deployment as well as the destruction of equipment. Public deployments are sometimes at the mercy of people who may not be regular inhabitants. Most notably, it is not realistic to consider vandalism to be a person's primary activity as an inhabitant, which is why vandalism should be considered a separate category.

Reported Causes

Heikkinen et al. [33] (also mentioned in Ojala et al., [54]) report that the safety glass of one of their outdoor installations was purposefully broken – the system was down for two weeks, and the expenses for repairs were significant. Similarly, Dalsgaard and Halskov [19] report that their information stand displaying videos on a bus shelter was destroyed. Dalsgaard and Halskov [19] further report that in one of their outdoor media façade installations, someone tried to remove a colorful carpet from the ground, possibly with the assumption that the carpet was enabling the interactions. In reality, the carpet was there to merely mark the interaction area more clearly.

In addition to physical harm, vandalism can stem from rude or unacceptable behavior. Dalsgaard and Halskov [19] reported a few instances wherein users would upload erotic content to one of their public systems which allowed uploading low-resolution animations. They also reported a user recording obscene gestures in an installation that allowed users to record short clips to be shown in displays around the city. The recorded clips had to be checked and edited before showing them to the public.

We also found an interesting link between misuse of an installation and playful behavior. Taylor et al. [65] installed a display aimed at gathering opinions on issues relevant to the local community. Users could give their opinion on polls by pressing corresponding buttons below the display. However, it was discovered that some people were interacting merely to play around with the system (to experience it) and pressing the buttons uncontrollably. Therefore, the results of the polls, which otherwise could have been useful to the community, were skewed.

Müller et al. [51] observed users engaging in (unintended) harmful activities through playful behavior, when studying transitioning between mid-air gestures and touch in their MirrorTouch installation. They reported two occasions where users first interacted with increasingly expressive mid-air gestures, and when transitioning to touch, they interacted with the screen so roughly that researchers needed to intervene to prevent damage to the installation.

Many more authors have observed playful behavior where they have not expected it, even though no actual issues have been encountered due to it. Examples of such are presented in [19,52,57,67].

Recommendations

The effects of *vandalism* range from destruction of equipment to unintentional interference with the deployment. There may also be a link between playful behavior and misuse. While playful behavior has many benefits, such as enticing interaction [67,70], researchers should be aware of the possible negative consequences as well. We found a case where playful behavior turned too extreme and was about to lead to damaged hardware [51], and a case where playful interaction interfered with the serious purpose of an installation [65].

It is difficult to predict vandalism or misuse; however, to address some of them, we offer the following considerations:

- Go into the "mindset" of a vandal. What are the easy targets for vandalism? Consider attaching all parts of the deployment to something sturdy, and hiding components, such as wires, from plain sight.
- Consider moderating user-generated content. Dalsgaard and Halskov [19] experienced several occurrences wherein improper content was uploaded. Fortunately, such instances seem to be rare. For instance, Elhart et al. [22] had to go to great lengths to prepare for improper content due to requirements from stakeholders; however, they experienced no issues.

DISCUSSION AND CONCLUSION

In this work, we investigated *external factors* that cause many surprising and unwanted effects on public display deployments. We conducted a literature review and, using affinity diagramming, identified a taxonomy of external factors: *weather*, *events*, *surroundings*, *space*, *inhabitants*, and *vandalism*. We found that our experience about the primarily negative effects of these factors hold true within the larger HCI community as well.

Our work differentiates itself from past research in two ways. First, we draw upon the *collective experiences* within the HCI community. Some past work has discussed challenges with public deployments, and while they offer valuable insights, the challenges have only been individual research groups' experiences [19,31,62]. However, many of the issues we collected have come from publications in which these issues were not the focus. This, in part, underlines the need to bring these experiences together. Second, we are the first to approach these challenges from the perspective of *cause*. This is important in offering a practical approach towards identifying and adapting to potential issues. From our viewpoint, researchers should be encouraged to look beyond the observed challenges, as identifying the cause may help in addressing the issue.

In addition to the taxonomy of external factors, we investigated how researchers deal with issues arising from these factors, and identified four types of reactions: *ignoring*, *adapting*, *solving*, and *embracing*. Ignoring and adapting to issues were much more common responses, which suggests that the issues are often surprising, and are difficult to solve completely.

We note that in this work, we quantified how researchers *eventually* reacted to the issues. Based on our experiences and some examples found in the literature, for many issues that were ignored or adapted to, researchers initially reviewed their options and, in the absence of good and easy solutions, had to resort to sub-optimal solutions (adapting), or had to ignore the issue. In deciding the action to take, researchers must evaluate how severe the issue is, and consider available options and how much effort they require as opposed to the resources available.

When evaluating the severity of an issue, the purpose of the deployment is worth considering, as many public deployments are conducted to study a specific phenomenon. For instance, for a public deployment investigating display blindness in some form, an interaction-related issue might not be as severe as it would in many other scenarios. In

Weather	• Consider the effects of sunlight on the deployment as it affects screen visibility and the performance of sensors. • Cover sensitive hardware, as rain and humidity can cause surprising issues. • Consider how weather affects people. Good weather may increase the number of interactions, and bad weather may have the opposite effect – even for indoor deployments.
Events	• Stay aware of the magnitude and nature of upcoming events in the area - events may alter the social setting, demographics, and the amount of people. • Design the deployment to handle large crowds, even if such crowds are not normally present. • Consider turning events to the deployment's advantage, for instance, by tailoring the content to serve the participants of the event. Events tend to bring in more users and foster interaction.
Surroundings	• Identify key locations in the surrounding areas, such as theaters and malls, and consider how they affect the demographics in the area at different times of day. • Consider designing content for the deployment that is specific to these locations. • Identify technical limitations to accommodate network failures, power issues, and other potential factors that may interfere with the equipment.
Space	• Observe the physical characteristics of the space, e.g., the layout, doorways, pillars, elevators, and machinery. Identify how these characteristics affect people flow and the use of the space. • Identify pillars and other objects within the layout that can potentially create "comfort spaces" for the users, which may encourage people to observe and subsequently interact.
Inhabitants	• Observe and identify different groups of inhabitants, and their routines and tasks in the space. Analyze how their routines and tasks could interfere with the deployment. • Consider informing and engaging the inhabitants, particularly if the deployment is likely to interfere with inhabitants' normal routines. • Add contact details near the deployment.
Vandalism	• Go into the "mindset" of a vandal, and identify easy and obvious targets for vandalism. Attach all parts of the deployment to something sturdy, and hide easy targets, such as wires. • Consider moderating user-generated content, as people may upload improper material.

Table 2. Considerations for external factors in public deployments.

addition, many research-oriented deployments are short-term in nature, due to which some issues might receive less attention than they would in long-term deployments.

In defining the available options in each situation, an important factor is the level of control one has over the deployment and the surrounding area. Researchers rarely own the deployment space, which significantly limits the amount and extent of available options. This brings us back to the importance of *adapting* to issues. Solving issues completely is difficult and, as we observed in this work, not always possible.

In conclusion, with this work, we hope to bring attention to external factors and help researchers reflect on and report issues experienced in public deployments. The prevailing approach in reporting deployments is to focus on *successes*; experienced issues are often considered threats to the integrity of the studies. In fact, experienced challenges can often be more informative than the successes, and can aid researchers and practitioners in carrying out more successful deployments. Moreover, there are now good venues to publish such experiences (e.g., CHI Stories).

We provide a go-to summary of the taxonomy of external factors with practical considerations in Table 2. The main contribution of our work is to help researchers and practitioners design *for* external factors, and be more prepared to address the effects. This is achieved in three ways. First, by using the taxonomy of the external factors, one can more easily identify such factors within the deployment. Second, we provide practical insights for each category, and report several examples on how past work has addressed the encountered issues. Third, we show that one must be prepared to adapt – many observed negative effects usually require changes in the deployment. Overall, we wish to provide a useful framework for understanding external factors and hope that it is built upon by the community, by sharing how the issues were reacted to in future deployments.

REFERENCES

1. Christopher Ackad, Rainer Wasinger, Richard Gluga, Judy Kay, and Martin Tomitsch. 2013. Measuring interactivity at an interactive public information display. In *Proceedings of the 25th Australian Computer-Human Interaction Conference: Augmentation, Application, Innovation, Collaboration* (OzCHI '13), Haifeng Shen, Ross Smith, Jeni Paay, Paul Calder, and Theodor Wyeld (Eds.). ACM, New York, NY, USA, 329-332. DOI: http://dx.doi.org/10.1145/2541016.2541091
2. Christopher Ackad, Andrew Clayphan, Martin Tomitsch, and Judy Kay. 2015. An in-the-wild study of learning mid-air gestures to browse hierarchical information at a large interactive public display. In *Proceedings of the 2015 ACM International Joint Conference on Pervasive and Ubiquitous Computing* (UbiComp '15). ACM, New York, NY, USA, 1227-1238. DOI: http://dx.doi.org/10.1145/2750858.2807532 *
3. Christopher Ackad, Martin Tomitsch, and Judy Kay. 2016. Skeletons and Silhouettes: Comparing User Representations at a Gesture-based Large Display. In *Proceedings of the 2016 CHI Conference on Human Factors in Computing Systems* (CHI '16). ACM, New York, NY, USA, 2343-2347. DOI: http://dx.doi.org/10.1145/2858036.2858427 *
4. Imeh Akpan, Paul Marshall, Jon Bird, and Daniel Harrison. 2013. Exploring the effects of space and place on engagement with an interactive installation. In *Proceedings of the SIGCHI Conference on Human Factors in Computing Systems* (CHI '13). ACM, New York, NY, USA, 2213-2222. DOI: http://dx.doi.org/10.1145/2470654.2481306 *
5. Florian Alt, Albrecht Schmidt, and Jörg Müller . 2012. Advertising on Public Display Networks. *IEEE Computer* 45, 5 (May 2012), 50-56. DOI= https://doi.org/10.1109/MC.2012.150
6. Florian Alt, Stefan Schneegaß, Albrecht Schmidt, Jörg Müller, and Nemanja Memarovic. 2012. How to evaluate public displays. In *Proceedings of the 2012 International Symposium on Pervasive Displays* (PerDis '12). ACM, New York, NY, USA, , Article 17 , 6 pages. DOI=http://dx.doi.org/10.1145/2307798.2307815
7. Moritz Behrens, Ava Fatah gen. Schieck, Efsathia Kostopoulou, Steve North, Wallis Motta, Lei Ye, and Holger Schnadelbach. 2013. Exploring the effect of spatial layout on mediated urban interactions. In *Proceedings of the 2nd ACM International Symposium on Pervasive Displays* (PerDis '13). ACM, New York, NY, USA, 79-84. DOI=http://dx.doi.org/10.1145/2491568.2491586
8. Gisele Bennett, Gitte Lindgaard, Bruce Tsuji, Kay H. Connelly, and Katie A. Siek. 2006. Reality testing: HCI challenges in non-traditional environments. In *CHI '06 Extended Abstracts on Human Factors in Computing Systems* (CHI EA '06). ACM, New York, NY, USA, 1679-1682. DOI=http://dx.doi.org/10.1145/1125451.1125761
9. Gilbert Beyer, Florian Alt, Jörg Müller, Albrecht Schmidt, Karsten Isakovic, Stefan Klose, Manuel Schiewe, and Ivo Haulsen. 2011. Audience behavior around large interactive cylindrical screens. In *Proceedings of the SIGCHI Conference on Human Factors in Computing Systems* (CHI '11). ACM, New York, NY, USA, 1021-1030. DOI=http://dx.doi.org/10.1145/1978942.1979095
10. Harry Brignull and Yvonne Rogers. 2003. Enticing people to interact with large public displays in public spaces. In *Proceedings of INTERACT*, 3, 17-24.
11. Barry Brown, Stuart Reeves, and Scott Sherwood. 2011. Into the wild: challenges and opportunities for field trial methods. In *Proceedings of the SIGCHI Conference on Human Factors in Computing Systems* (CHI '11). ACM, New York, NY, USA, 1657-1666. DOI=http://dx.doi.org/10.1145/1978942.1979185
12. Susanne Bødker. 2006. When second wave HCI meets third wave challenges. In *Proceedings of the 4th Nordic conference on Human-computer interaction: changing roles* (NordiCHI '06), Anders Mørch, Konrad Morgan, Tone Bratteteig, Gautam Ghosh, and Dag Svanaes (Eds.). ACM, New York, NY, USA, 1-8. DOI=http://dx.doi.org/10.1145/1182475.1182476
13. Xiang Cao, Michael Massimi, and Ravin Balakrishnan. 2008. Flashlight jigsaw: an exploratory study of an ad-hoc multi-player game on public displays. In *Proceedings of the 2008 ACM conference on Computer supported cooperative work* (CSCW '08). ACM, New York, NY, USA, 77-86. DOI=http://dx.doi.org/10.1145/1460563.1460577 *
14. John M. Carroll. 2003. The Blacksburg Electronic Village: A Study in Community Computing. *Lecture Notes in Computer Science* 3081 (September 2003), 43-65. DOI= http://dx.doi.org/10.1007/11407546_3
15. Scott Carter and Jennifer Mankoff. 2005. Prototypes in the Wild: Lessons from Three Ubicomp Systems. *IEEE Pervasive Computing* 4, 4 (October 2005), 51-57. DOI=http://dx.doi.org/10.1109/MPRV.2005.84
16. Chien-Hsu Chen, Hsiao-Mei Hung, I-Jui Lee, Yu-Wen Chen, and Fong-Gong Wu. 2011. Observe the user interactive behavior with a large multi-touch display in public space. In *Proceedings of the 6th international conference on Universal access in human-computer interaction: context diversity - Volume Part III* (UAHCI'11), Constantine Stephanidis (Ed.), Vol. Part III. Springer-Verlag, Berlin, Heidelberg, 141-144.

17. Elizabeth F. Churchill, Les Nelson, Laurent Denoue, Jonathan Helfman, and Paul Murphy. 2004. Sharing multimedia content with interactive public displays: a case study. In *Proceedings of the 5th conference on Designing interactive systems: processes, practices, methods, and techniques* (DIS '04). ACM, New York, NY, USA, 7-16. DOI=http://dx.doi.org/10.1145/1013115.1013119 *
18. Céline Coutrix, Kai Kuikkaniemi, Esko Kurvinen, Giulio Jacucci, Ivan Avdouevski, and Riikka Mäkelä. 2011. FizzyVis: designing for playful information browsing on a multitouch public display. In *Proceedings of the 2011 Conference on Designing Pleasurable Products and Interfaces* (DPPI '11). ACM, New York, NY, USA, , Article 27 , 8 pages. DOI=http://dx.doi.org/10.1145/2347504.2347534
19. Peter Dalsgaard and Kim Halskov. 2010. Designing urban media façades: cases and challenges. In *Proceedings of the SIGCHI Conference on Human Factors in Computing Systems* (CHI '10). ACM, New York, NY, USA, 2277-2286. DOI=http://dx.doi.org/10.1145/1753326.1753670 *
20. Peter Dalsgaard, Christian Dindler, and Kim Halskov. 2011. Understanding the dynamics of engaging interaction in public spaces. In *Proceedings of the 13th IFIP TC 13 international conference on Human-computer interaction - Volume Part II* (INTERACT'11), Pedro Campos, Nuno Nunes, Nicholas Graham, Joaquim Jorge, and Philippe Palanque (Eds.), Vol. Part II. Springer-Verlag, Berlin, Heidelberg, 212-229.
21. Paul Dourish. 2006. Re-space-ing place: "place" and "space" ten years on. In *Proceedings of the 2006 20th anniversary conference on Computer supported cooperative work* (CSCW '06). ACM, New York, NY, USA, 299-308. DOI=http://dx.doi.org/10.1145/1180875.1180921
22. Ivan Elhart, Marc Langheinrich, Nemanja Memarovic, and Elisa Rubegni. 2016. A good balance of costs and benefits: convincing a university administration to support the installation of an interactive multi-application display system on campus. In *Proceedings of the 5th ACM International Symposium on Pervasive Displays* (PerDis '16). ACM, New York, NY, USA, 197-203. DOI: http://dx.doi.org/10.1145/2914920.2915029
23. Matthias Finke, Anthony Tang, Rock Leung, and Michael Blackstock. 2008. Lessons learned: game design for large public displays. In *Proceedings of the 3rd international conference on Digital Interactive Media in Entertainment and Arts* (DIMEA '08). ACM, New York, NY, USA, 26-33. DOI=http://dx.doi.org/10.1145/1413634.1413644 *
24. Patrick Tobias Fischer, Christian Zöllner, and Eva Hornecker. 2010. VR/Urban: Spread.gun - design process and challenges in developing a shared encounter for media façades. In *Proceedings of the 24th BCS Interaction Specialist Group Conference* (BCS '10). British Computer Society, Swinton, UK, UK, 289-298. *
25. Patrick Tobias Fischer and Eva Hornecker. 2012. Urban HCI: spatial aspects in the design of shared encounters for media facades. In *Proceedings of the SIGCHI Conference on Human Factors in Computing Systems* (CHI '12). ACM, New York, NY, USA, 307-316. DOI=http://dx.doi.org/10.1145/2207676.2207719 *
26. Adrian Friday, Nigel Davies, and Christos Efstratiou. 2012. Reflections on Long-Term Experiments with Public Displays. IEEE Computer 45, 5 (May 2012), 42-49. DOI= https://doi.org/10.1109/MC.2012.155
27. Kazjon Grace, Rainer Wasinger, Christopher Ackad, Anthony Collins, Oliver Dawson, Richard Gluga, Judy Kay, and Martin Tomitsch. 2013. Conveying interactivity at an interactive public information display. In *Proceedings of the 2nd ACM International Symposium on Pervasive Displays* (PerDis '13). ACM, New York, NY, USA, 19-24. DOI=http://dx.doi.org/10.1145/2491568.2491573
28. Sukeshini A. Grandhi, Gina Joue, and Irene Mittelberg. 2011. Understanding naturalness and intuitiveness in gesture production: insights for touchless gestural interfaces. In *Proceedings of the SIGCHI Conference on Human Factors in Computing Systems* (CHI '11). ACM, New York, NY, USA, 821-824. DOI=http://dx.doi.org/10.1145/1978942.1979061
29. Saul Greenberg and Michael Rounding. 2001. The notification collage: posting information to public and personal displays. In *Proceedings of the SIGCHI Conference on Human Factors in Computing Systems* (CHI '01). ACM, New York, NY, USA, 514-521. DOI=http://dx.doi.org/10.1145/365024.365339
30. Jonna Häkkilä, Olli Koskenranta, Maaret Posti, Leena Ventä-Olkkonen, and Ashley Colley. 2013. Clearing the virtual window: connecting two locations with interactive public displays. In *Proceedings of the 2nd ACM International Symposium on Pervasive Displays* (PerDis '13). ACM, New York, NY, USA, 85-90. DOI=http://dx.doi.org/10.1145/2491568.2491587
31. Eric Harris, Geraldine Fitzpatrick, Yvonne Rogers, Sara Price, Ted Phelps, and Cliff Randell. 2004. From Snark to Park: Lessons learnt moving pervasive experiences from indoors to outdoors. In *Proceedings of the fifth conference on Australasian user interface* (AUIC '04), Australian Computer Society, Inc., 39-48. *

32. Steve Harrison and Paul Dourish. 1996. Re-place-ing space: the roles of place and space in collaborative systems. In *Proceedings of the 1996 ACM conference on Computer supported cooperative work* (CSCW '96), Mark S. Ackerman (Ed.). ACM, New York, NY, USA, 67-76. DOI=http://dx.doi.org/10.1145/240080.240193
33. Tommi Heikkinen, Tomas Lindén, Timo Ojala, Hannu Kukka, Marko Jurmu, and Simo Hosio. 2010. Lessons learned from the deployment and maintenance of ubi-hotspots. In *Proceedings of the Fourth International Conference on Multimedia and Ubiquitous Engineering* (MUE '10), 1-6. http://dx.doi.org/10.1109/MUE.2010.5575054 *
34. Simo Hosio, Jorge Goncalves, Hannu Kukka, Alan Chamberlain, and Alessio Malizia. 2014. What's in it for me: Exploring the Real-World Value Proposition of Pervasive Displays. In *Proceedings of The International Symposium on Pervasive Displays* (PerDis '14), Sven Gehring (Ed.). ACM, New York, NY, USA, , Pages 174 , 6 pages. DOI=http://dx.doi.org/10.1145/2611009.2611012
35. Simo Hosio, Hannu Kukka, Jorge Goncalves, Vassilis Kostakos, and Timo Ojala. 2016. Toward Meaningful Engagement with Pervasive Displays. *IEEE Pervasive Computing* 15, 3 (July 2016), 24-31. DOI= https://doi.org/10.1109/MPRV.2016.58
36. Elaine M. Huang and Elizabeth D. Mynatt. 2003. Semi-public displays for small, co-located groups. In *Proceedings of the SIGCHI Conference on Human Factors in Computing Systems* (CHI '03). ACM, New York, NY, USA, 49-56. DOI=http://dx.doi.org/10.1145/642611.642622
37. Elaine M. Huang, Anna Koster, and Jan Borchers. 2009. Overcoming Assumptions and Uncovering Practices: When Does the Public Really Look at Public Displays?. In *Proceedings of the 6th International Conference on Pervasive Computing* (Pervasive '08), Jadwiga Indulska, Donald J. Patterson, Tom Rodden, and Max Ott (Eds.). Springer-Verlag, Berlin, Heidelberg, 228-243. DOI=10.1007/978-3-540-79576-6_14 http://dx.doi.org/10.1007/978-3-540-79576-6_14
38. Giulio Jacucci, Ann Morrison, Gabriela T. Richard, Jari Kleimola, Peter Peltonen, Lorenza Parisi, and Toni Laitinen. 2010. Worlds of information: designing for engagement at a public multi-touch display. *In Proceedings of the SIGCHI Conference on Human Factors in Computing Systems* (CHI '10). ACM, New York, NY, USA, 2267-2276. DOI=http://dx.doi.org/10.1145/1753326.1753669
39. Wendy Ju and David Sirkin. 2010. Animate objects: how physical motion encourages public interaction. In *Proceedings of the 5th international conference on Persuasive Technology* (PERSUASIVE'10), Thomas Ploug, Per Hasle, and Harri Oinas-Kukkonen (Eds.). Springer-Verlag, Berlin, Heidelberg, 40-51. DOI=http://dx.doi.org/10.1007/978-3-642-13226-1_6
40. Marko Jurmu, Masaki Ogawa, Sebastian Boring, Jukka Riekki, and Hideyuki Tokuda. 2013. Waving to a touch interface: descriptive field study of a multipurpose multimodal public display. In *Proceedings of the 2nd ACM International Symposium on Pervasive Displays* (PerDis '13). ACM, New York, NY, USA, 7-12. DOI=http://dx.doi.org/10.1145/2491568.2491571
41. Maurice Ten Koppel, Gilles Bailly, Jörg Müller, and Robert Walter. 2012. Chained displays: configurations of public displays can be used to influence actor-, audience-, and passer-by behavior. In *Proceedings of the SIGCHI Conference on Human Factors in Computing Systems* (CHI '12). ACM, New York, NY, USA, 317-326. DOI=http://dx.doi.org/10.1145/2207676.2207720
42. Matthias Korn and Susanne Bødker. 2012. Looking ahead: how field trials can work in iterative and exploratory design of ubicomp systems. In *Proceedings of the 2012 ACM Conference on Ubiquitous Computing* (UbiComp '12). ACM, New York, NY, USA, 21-30. DOI=http://dx.doi.org/10.1145/2370216.2370221
43. Kai Kuikkaniemi, Giulio Jacucci, Marko Turpeinen, Eve Hoggan, and Jörg Müller. 2011. From Space to Stage: How Interactive Screens Will Change Urban Life. *IEEE Computer* 6, 44 (June 2011), 40-47. DOI=http://dx.doi.org/ 10.1109/MC.2011.135
44. Hannu Kukka, Heidi Oja, Vassilis Kostakos, Jorge Gonçalves, and Timo Ojala. 2013. What makes you click: exploring visual signals to entice interaction on public displays. In *Proceedings of the SIGCHI Conference on Human Factors in Computing Systems* (CHI '13). ACM, New York, NY, USA, 1699-1708. DOI: http://dx.doi.org/10.1145/2470654.2466225 *
45. Scott Mcquire. 2010. Rethinking media events: Large screens, public space broadcasting and beyond. *New Media & Society* 12, 4 (June 2010), 567-582. DOI= http://dx.doi.org/10.1177/1461444809342764
46. Nemanja Memarovic, Marc Langheinrich, Keith Cheverst, Nick Taylor, and Florian Alt. 2013. P-LAYERS -- A Layered Framework Addressing the Multifaceted Issues Facing Community-Supporting Public Display Deployments. ACM *Transactions in Computer-Human Interaction* 20, 3, Article 17 (July 2013), 34 pages. DOI=http://dx.doi.org/10.1145/2491500.2491505 *
47. Daniel Michelis and Jörg Müller. 2011. The Audience Funnel: Observations of Gesture Based Interaction with Multiple Large Displays in a City Center. In *International Journal of Human–Computer Interaction* 27,6, 562-579. http://dx.doi.org/10.1080/10447318.2011.555299

48. Jörg Müller, Dennis Wilmsmann, Juliane Exeler, Markus Buzeck, Albrecht Schmidt, Tim Jay, and Antonio Krüger. 2009. Display Blindness: The Effect of Expectations on Attention towards Digital Signage. In *Proceedings of the 7th International Conference on Pervasive Computing* (Pervasive '09), Hideyuki Tokuda, Michael Beigl, Adrian Friday, A. J. Brush, and Yoshito Tobe (Eds.). Springer-Verlag, Berlin, Heidelberg, 1-8. DOI=http://dx.doi.org/10.1007/978-3-642-01516-8_1

49. Jörg Müller, Florian Alt, Daniel Michelis, and Albrecht Schmidt. 2010. Requirements and design space for interactive public displays. In *Proceedings of the 18th ACM international conference on Multimedia* (MM '10). ACM, New York, NY, USA, 1285-1294. DOI=http://dx.doi.org/10.1145/1873951.1874203

50. Jörg Müller, Robert Walter, Gilles Bailly, Michael Nischt, and Florian Alt. 2012. Looking glass: a field study on noticing interactivity of a shop window. In *Proceedings of the SIGCHI Conference on Human Factors in Computing Systems* (CHI '12). ACM, New York, NY, USA, 297-306. DOI=http://dx.doi.org/10.1145/2207676.2207718

51. Jörg Müller, Gilles Bailly, Thor Bossuyt, and Niklas Hillgren. 2014. MirrorTouch: combining touch and mid-air gestures for public displays. In *Proceedings of the 16th international conference on Human-computer interaction with mobile devices & services* (MobileHCI '14). ACM, New York, NY, USA, 319-328. DOI=http://dx.doi.org/10.1145/2628363.2628379

52. Jörg Müller, Dieter Eberle, and Konrad Tollmar. 2014. Communiplay: a field study of a public display mediaspace. In *Proceedings of the SIGCHI Conference on Human Factors in Computing Systems* (CHI '14). ACM, New York, NY, USA, 1415-1424. DOI=http://dx.doi.org/10.1145/2556288.2557001 *

53. Kenton O'Hara, Maxine Glancy, and Simon Robertshaw. 2008. Understanding collective play in an urban screen game. In *Proceedings of the 2008 ACM conference on Computer supported cooperative work* (CSCW '08). ACM, New York, NY, USA, 67-76. DOI=http://dx.doi.org/10.1145/1460563.1460576 *

54. Timo Ojala, Hannu Kukka, Tomas Lindén, Tommi Heikkinen, Marko Jurmu, Simo Hosio, and Fabio Kruger. 2010. UBI-hotspot 1.0: Large-scale long-term deployment of interactive public displays in a city center. In *Fifth International Conference on Internet and Web Applications and Services* (ICIW), IEEE, 285-294. IEEE. *

55. Timo Ojala, Vassilis Kostakos, Hannu Kukka, Tommi Heikkinen, Tomas Lindén, Marko Jurmu, Simo Hosio, Fabio Kruger, and Daniele Zanni. 2012. Multipurpose Interactive Public Displays in the Wild: Three Years Later. *IEEE Computer* 45, 5 (May 2012), 42-49. DOI=http://dx.doi.org/10.1109/MC.2012.115

56. Gonzalo Parra, Joris Klerkx, and Erik Duval. 2014. Understanding Engagement with Interactive Public Displays: an Awareness Campaign in the Wild. In *Proceedings of The International Symposium on Pervasive Displays* (PerDis '14), Sven Gehring (Ed.). ACM, New York, NY, USA, , Pages 180 , 6 pages. DOI=http://dx.doi.org/10.1145/2611009.2611020

57. Peter Peltonen, Esko Kurvinen, Antti Salovaara, Giulio Jacucci, Tommi Ilmonen, John Evans, Antti Oulasvirta, and Petri Saarikko. 2008. It's Mine, Don't Touch!: interactions at a large multi-touch display in a city centre. In *Proceedings of the SIGCHI Conference on Human Factors in Computing Systems* (CHI '08). ACM, New York, NY, USA, 1285-1294. DOI=http://dx.doi.org/10.1145/1357054.1357255 *

58. Mark Perry, Steve Beckett, Kenton O'Hara, and Sriram Subramanian. 2010. WaveWindow: public, performative gestural interaction. In *ACM International Conference on Interactive Tabletops and Surfaces* (ITS '10). ACM, New York, NY, USA, 109-112. DOI=http://dx.doi.org/10.1145/1936652.1936672

59. Constantin Schmidt, Jörg Müller, and Gilles Bailly. 2013. Screenfinity: extending the perception area of content on very large public displays. In *Proceedings of the SIGCHI Conference on Human Factors in Computing Systems* (CHI '13). ACM, New York, NY, USA, 1719-1728. DOI: http://dx.doi.org/10.1145/2470654.2466227

60. Ronald Schroeter, Marcus Foth, and Christine Satchell. 2012. People, content, location: sweet spotting urban screens for situated engagement. In *Proceedings of the Designing Interactive Systems Conference* (DIS '12). ACM, New York, NY, USA, 146-155. DOI=http://dx.doi.org/10.1145/2317956.2317980 *

61. Fabius Steinberger, Marcus Foth, and Florian Alt. 2014. Vote With Your Feet: Local Community Polling on Urban Screens. In *Proceedings of The International Symposium on Pervasive Displays* (PerDis '14), Sven Gehring (Ed.). ACM, New York, NY, USA, , Pages 44 , 6 pages. DOI=http://dx.doi.org/10.1145/2611009.2611015

62. Oliver Storz, Adrian Friday, Nigel Davies, Joe Finney, Corina Sas, and Jennifer Sheridan. 2006. Public Ubiquitous Computing Systems: Lessons from the e-Campus Display Deployments. *IEEE Pervasive Computing* 5, 3 (July 2006), 40-47. DOI=http://dx.doi.org/10.1109/MPRV.2006.56 *

63. Mirjam Struppek. 2006. Urban Screens – The Urbane Potential of Public Screens for Interaction. *Intelligent Agent* 6, 2.

64. Nick Taylor and Keith Cheverst. 2012. Supporting Community Awareness with Interactive Displays.

IEEE Computer 45, 5 (May 2012), 26–32. DOI=http://dx.doi.org/10.1109/MC.2012.113

65. Nick Taylor, Justin Marshall, Alicia Blum-Ross, John Mills, Jon Rogers, Paul Egglestone, David M. Frohlich, Peter Wright, and Patrick Olivier. 2012. Viewpoint: empowering communities with situated voting devices. In *Proceedings of the SIGCHI Conference on Human Factors in Computing Systems* (CHI '12). ACM, New York, NY, USA, 1361-1370. DOI=http://dx.doi.org/10.1145/2207676.2208594 *
66. Nick Taylor, Keith Cheverst, Peter Wright, and Patrick Olivier. 2013. Leaving the wild: lessons from community technology handovers. In *Proceedings of the SIGCHI Conference on Human Factors in Computing Systems* (CHI '13). ACM, New York, NY, USA, 1549-1558. DOI: http://dx.doi.org/10.1145/2470654.2466206
67. Martin Tomitsch, Christopher Ackad, Oliver Dawson, Luke Hespanhol, and Judy Kay. 2014. Who cares about the Content? An Analysis of Playful Behaviour at a Public Display. In *Proceedings of The International Symposium on Pervasive Displays* (PerDis '14), Sven Gehring (Ed.). ACM, New York, NY, USA, , Pages 160 , 6 pages. DOI=http://dx.doi.org/10.1145/2611009.2611016 *
68. Nina Valkanova, Robert Walter, Andrew Vande Moere, and Jörg Müller. 2014. MyPosition: sparking civic discourse by a public interactive poll visualization. In *Proceedings of the 17th ACM conference on Computer supported cooperative work & social computing* (CSCW '14). ACM, New York, NY, USA, 1323-1332. DOI=http://dx.doi.org/10.1145/2531602.2531639 *
69. Daniel Vogel and Ravin Balakrishnan. 2004. Interactive public ambient displays: transitioning from implicit to explicit, public to personal, interaction with multiple users. In *Proceedings of the 17th annual ACM symposium on User interface software and technology* (UIST '04). ACM, New York, NY, USA, 137-146. DOI=http://dx.doi.org/10.1145/1029632.1029656
70. Robert Walter, Gilles Bailly, and Jörg Müller. 2013. StrikeAPose: revealing mid-air gestures on public displays. In *Proceedings of the SIGCHI Conference on Human Factors in Computing Systems* (CHI '13). ACM, New York, NY, USA, 841-850. DOI: http://dx.doi.org/10.1145/2470654.2470774
71. Robert Walter, Gilles Bailly, Nina Valkanova, and Jörg Müller. 2014. Cuenesics: using mid-air gestures to select items on interactive public displays. In *Proceedings of the 16th international conference on Human-computer interaction with mobile devices & services* (MobileHCI '14). ACM, New York, NY, USA, 299-308. DOI: http://dx.doi.org/10.1145/2628363.2628368

* Part of the taxonomy of external factors.

All referenced papers were part of the literature review.

Author Index

NOTES

NOTES

NOTES

NOTES

NOTES

NOTES

NOTES

NOTES

NOTES

NOTES

NOTES

NOTES

NOTES

NOTES

NOTES

NOTES

NOTES

NOTES

NOTES

NOTES

www.ingramcontent.com/pod-product-compliance
Lightning Source LLC
LaVergne TN
LVHW082344011026
849160LV00024B/1050